Compact Oxford English Dictionary

for University and College Students

Edited by
Catherine Soanes
with Sara Hawker

OXFORD
UNIVERSITY PRESS

OXFORD

UNIVERSITY PRESS

Great Clarendon Street, Oxford OX2 6DP

Oxford University Press is a department of the University of Oxford.
It furthers the University's objective of excellence in research, scholarship,
and education by publishing worldwide in

Oxford New York

Auckland Cape Town Dar es Salaam Hong Kong Karachi
Kuala Lumpur Madrid Melbourne Mexico City Nairobi
New Delhi Shanghai Taipei Toronto

With offices in

Argentina Austria Brazil Chile Czech Republic France Greece
Guatemala Hungary Italy Japan Poland Portugal Singapore
South Korea Switzerland Thailand Turkey Ukraine Vietnam

Oxford is a registered trade mark of Oxford University Press
in the UK and in certain other countries

© Oxford University Press 2006

Dictionary text based on the *Compact Oxford English Dictionary of Current
English*, third edition, 2005

Database right Oxford University Press (maker)

British Library Cataloguing in Publication Data

Data available

Library of Congress Cataloging in Publication Data

Data available

Typeset in Frutiger and Parable
by Interactive Sciences Ltd, Gloucester
Printed in Italy
by L.E.G.O. S.p.A., Lavis (TN)

ISBN 978-0-19-929625-5

5

Contents

■ Preface   iv
■ Note on trademarks and proprietary status   v
■ Guide to the use of the dictionary   vi

Compact Oxford English Dictionary
for University and College Students   1

EFFECTIVE WRITING FOR COLLEGE AND CAREER   *centre section*

Preface

The *Compact Oxford English Dictionary for University and College Students* is a new dictionary that has been tailored to meet students' requirements. The main part of the dictionary aims to provide up-to-date and accessible information on the vocabulary of contemporary English, including a wide selection of terms from specialist areas such as computing. There is also a centre section which has been specially written for students, which gives practical advice on essentials such as essays, referencing, and job applications, as well as help with English spelling, grammar, and punctuation. Both this section and the dictionary were compiled after close consultation with college and university students to ensure that their particular needs were addressed.

The dictionary is based on the *Compact Oxford English Dictionary* (3rd edition, 2005). It is directly informed by the evidence of how the language is actually used today, drawing on the analysis of hundreds of millions of words of real English (taken from books, newspapers, specialist journals, and the Internet) contained in the Oxford English Corpus. This information is presented in a clear, concise, and accessible way; definitions focus on the typical meanings of words and are written so as to enable you to understand the meaning of a word quickly and easily, without having to look up technical terms elsewhere in the dictionary.

The dictionary covers a broad range of vocabulary: while the focus is on the core language of contemporary English, there is also a wide selection of technical terms from specialist areas such as medicine, computing, and biology (for example, *endorphin*, *echinacea*, and *bitmap*). Extra language help is given in boxed notes, which offer clear guidance on points of grammar and the use of good English and highlight words which are often confused, such as *affect* and *effect*. There are also thousands of example sentences showing how words are really used. Pronunciations are given using a simple respelling system which is easy to understand.

The centre section of the dictionary, *Effective Writing for College and Career*, has been specially written to help students to do better in their studies and get on in life. It includes practical guidance on writing essays and dissertations, taking notes, referencing and bibliographies, and preparing CVs/résumés. There is also a section containing detailed advice on spelling, grammar, and punctuation, giving you the essential tools to write good, clear English in any situation. You can also access more

information, including extra samples of good writing and self-assessment
tests, at the Online Resource Centre (www.oup.com/uk/dictionaries/coedfs).

The dictionary's attractive two-colour design and an open layout, with
each new section of an entry (phrases, derivatives, usage notes, and
etymologies) on a new line, ensure that you can quickly look up individual
sections, senses, and entries.

The editor would like to thank the New Words team of the *Oxford English
Dictionary* for their help in identifying and drafting new words. Phyllis
Creme and Anne McGee of the Centre for the Advancement of Learning
and Teaching at University College London provided valuable advice on
the centre section of the dictionary.

Note on trademarks and proprietary status

This dictionary includes some words which have, or are asserted to have, proprietary
status as trademarks or otherwise. Their inclusion does not imply that they have acquired
for legal purposes a non-proprietary or general significance, nor any other judgement
concerning their legal status. In cases where the editorial staff have some evidence that a
word has proprietary status this is indicated in the entry for that word by the label
trademark, but no judgement concerning the legal status of such words is made or implied
thereby.

Guide to the use of the dictionary

The *Compact Oxford English Dictionary for University and College Students* is designed to be as straightforward and easy to use as possible. This section provides details on how dictionary entries are structured, the policy on alternative spellings, the pronunciation system, the treatment of different categories of English, and the abbreviations used.

You will find detailed information and advice on such matters as spelling, grammar, and punctuation in the *Brush up your English* section in the centre of the dictionary.

▶ STRUCTURE OF ENTRIES

Here is an explanation of the main types of information in the dictionary.

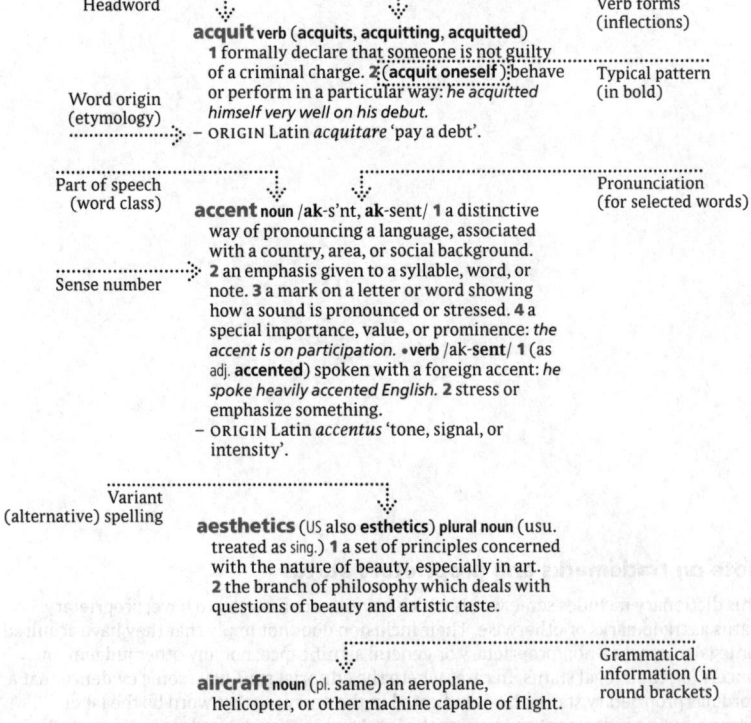

Headword

acquit verb (**acquits, acquitting, acquitted**)
1 formally declare that someone is not guilty of a criminal charge. 2 (**acquit oneself**): behave or perform in a particular way: *he acquitted himself very well on his debut.*
– ORIGIN Latin *acquitare* 'pay a debt'.

Verb forms (inflections)

Typical pattern (in bold)

Word origin (etymology)

Part of speech (word class)

accent noun /ak-s'nt, ak-sent/ 1 a distinctive way of pronouncing a language, associated with a country, area, or social background. 2 an emphasis given to a syllable, word, or note. 3 a mark on a letter or word showing how a sound is pronounced or stressed. 4 a special importance, value, or prominence: *the accent is on participation.* ●verb /ak-sent/ 1 (as adj. **accented**) spoken with a foreign accent: *he spoke heavily accented English.* 2 stress or emphasize something.
– ORIGIN Latin *accentus* 'tone, signal, or intensity'.

Pronunciation (for selected words)

Sense number

Variant (alternative) spelling

aesthetics (US also **esthetics**) plural noun (usu. treated as sing.) 1 a set of principles concerned with the nature of beauty, especially in art. 2 the branch of philosophy which deals with questions of beauty and artistic taste.

aircraft noun (pl. same) an aeroplane, helicopter, or other machine capable of flight.

Grammatical information (in round brackets)

Regional label
(showing where word
is used)

airplane noun N. Amer. an aeroplane.

aitch noun the letter H.
– PHRASES **drop one's aitches** fail to pronounce
the letter *h* at the beginning of words.
– ORIGIN Old French *ache*.

Phrases and
expressions

Homonym number
(shows different
word with the same
spelling)

alight[1] verb 1 (**alight on**) (of a bird) land or
settle on something. 2 formal get off a train or
bus. 3 (**alight on**) happen to notice something.
– ORIGIN Old English.
alight[2] adverb & adjective 1 on fire. 2 shining
brightly.

alternate verb /**awl**-ter-nayt/ 1 occur or do in
turn repeatedly: *the narrative alternates
personal observation with historical fact.*
2 change repeatedly between two contrasting
states: *his mood alternated between aggression
and morose despair.* • adjective /**awl**-ter-nuht/
1 every other: *the service runs on alternate days.*
2 (of two things) each following and
succeeded by the other in a regular pattern:
*put alternate layers of potatoes and fish in the
casserole dish.* 3 chiefly N. Amer. another term for
ALTERNATIVE.

Cross reference to
another word in the
dictionary
(in small capitals)

– DERIVATIVES **alternately** adverb **alternation**
noun.
– ORIGIN Latin *alternare* 'do by turns'.

Derivatives
(in alphabetical
order)

Usage note

USAGE: The use of **alternate** to mean
alternative (as in *we will need to find alternate
sources of fuel*) is common in North American
English, though it is still regarded as incorrect
by many people in Britain.

Plural form

amigo /uh-**mee**-goh/ noun (pl. **amigos**) informal,
chiefly N. Amer. a friend.
– ORIGIN Spanish.

Usage label
(showing how word
is used)

appeal verb 1 make a serious or earnest
request. 2 be attractive or interesting: *activities
that appeal to all.* 3 ask a higher court of law to
reverse the decision of a lower court. 4 Cricket
(of the bowler or fielders) call on the umpire
to declare a batsman out. • noun 1 an act of
appealing. 2 the quality of being attractive or
interesting: *the popular appeal of football.*
– ORIGIN Latin *appellare* 'to address'.

Subject label

Example of use
(taken from real
evidence)

aught /awt/ (also **ought**) pronoun old use
anything at all.
– ORIGIN Old English.

Label
(showing whether
word is still used)

▶ SPELLING

The main form of each word given in the dictionary is the accepted British spelling. Although there is only one way that most words can be spelled, sometimes other spellings (called *variants*) are also acceptable. Such spellings are given after the headword, e.g. **adaptor** (also **adapter**), or before a particular sense if the alternative spelling only applies to that sense. In all such cases the spelling given as the headword is the one that most people use. The label US shows spellings that are used in American English, e.g. **colour** (US **color**).

Where verbs can be spelled with either an **-ize** or **-ise** ending, the two spellings are given in the following way: **apologize** (or **apologise**), to show that either spelling can be used. The spelling **-ise** is far more common in British English, while **-ize** is usually found in American writing and in English in other parts of the world, although it is used in British English as well. Whichever spelling you choose, you should aim to be consistent: do not spell *organize* with a 'z' in one part of a piece of work and with an 's' on the next page.

There is a detailed guide to spelling, including common errors, in the *Brush up your English* section in the centre of the dictionary.

▶ PRONUNCIATIONS

The *Compact Oxford English Dictionary for University and College Students* uses a respelling system for pronunciations which is easy to understand. The dictionary gives a pronunciation for any word which might cause difficulty to native English speakers; it does not provide pronunciations for everyday words that are familiar to everyone, such as *table* or *large*. Foreign pronunciations are always shown in the way an English speaker would say them, e.g. /kor-don **bler**/ (cordon bleu). Pronunciations are divided into syllables by means of hyphens. The stress is shown in thick dark type, e.g. /**ab**-duh-muhn/ (abdomen).

List of Respelling Symbols

Vowels	Examples	Vowels	Examples	Vowels	Examples	Vowels	Examples
a	as in **cat**	ee	as in **meet**	oh	as in **most**	u	as in **cup**
ah	as in **calm**	eer	as in **beer**	oi	as in **join**	uh	as in **along**
air	as in **hair**	er	as in **her**	oo	as in **soon**	uu	as in **book**
ar	as in **bar**	ew	as in **few**	oor	as in **poor**	y	as in **cry**
aw	as in **law**	i	as in **pin**	or	as in **corn**	yoo	as in **unit**
ay	as in **say**	I	as in **eye**	ow	as in **cow**	yoor	as in **Europe**
e	as in **bed**	o	as in **top**	oy	as in **boy**		

Consonants	Examples	Consonants	Examples	Consonants	Examples	Consonants	Examples
b	as in **bat**	kh	as in **loch**	p	as in **pen**	w	as in **will**
ch	as in **chin**	l	as in **leg**	r	as in **red**	y	as in **yes**
d	as in **day**	m	as in **man**	s	as in **sit**	z	as in
f	as in **fat**	n	as in **not**	sh	as in **shop**		**zebra**
g	as in **get**	ng	as in **sing**,	t	as in **top**	zh	as in
h	as in **hat**		**finger**	th	as in **thin**		**vision**
j	as in **jam**	nk	as in	*th*	as in **this**		
k	as in **king**		**thank**	v	as in **van**		

▶ TYPES OF ENGLISH

The majority of the words and senses in this dictionary are all part of standard English, which means that they are the kinds of words we use in every type of situation, from chatting with friends to a formal report. Some words, however, are suitable only for certain contexts or are found only in certain types of writing, and where this is the case a descriptive marker called a *label* is used to indicate what type of English the word belongs to.

This dictionary uses three different types of descriptive label:

- **register** labels refer to the particular level of use in the language, indicating whether a term is informal, historical, and so on. The labels used in this dictionary are listed below. You will find more information and advice on choosing the right word for different contexts in the section called *Striking the right note: appropriate language* in the centre of the dictionary.

- **geographical** labels mark a word as belonging to a variety of English used in a particular part of the world. While most of the words used in standard British English will be the same as those used in other regional varieties, there are some words which are only found in one type of English. The regional types of English labelled in the dictionary are British, US and North American (i.e. both Canada and the US), Australian and New Zealand, South African, Indian, and West Indian.

- **subject** labels are used to show that a word or sense is associated with a particular subject field or specialist activity, such as Music, Chemistry, or Football.

Register labels

- **formal:** normally used only in writing, such as in official documents (e.g. **abode**)
- **informal:** normally used only in speaking, writing, or email to people we know well (e.g. **telly**)

- **dated:** no longer used by most English speakers, but still used by older people (e.g. **rotter**)
- **old use:** old-fashioned language, not in ordinary use today, though sometimes used to give an old-fashioned effect and also found in the literature of the past (e.g. **begone**)
- **historical:** only used today to refer to something that is no longer part of modern life (e.g. **blunderbuss**)
- **literary:** found only or mainly in literature (e.g. **foe**)
- **technical:** normally used only in technical language, though not restricted to a particular subject field (e.g. **dorsal**)
- **humorous:** used to sound funny or playful (e.g. **rocket science**)
- **euphemistic:** used instead of a more direct or rude term (e.g. **powder room** instead of 'women's toilet')
- **dialect:** only used in certain local regions of the UK (e.g. **bide**)
- **derogatory:** deliberately intended to express a low opinion or insult someone else (e.g. **bimbo**)
- **offensive:** likely to cause offence, especially racial offence, whether the person using it means to or not
- **vulgar slang:** very informal language, usually relating to sexual activity or bodily functions, which most people regard as taboo and may cause offence

Geographical labels

English is spoken throughout the world, and, while most of the words used in British English will be the same as those used in American or Australian English, there are some words which are only found in one regional variety of English. For example, the normal word in American English for a pavement is **sidewalk**, while the normal word in Australian English for a large sheep or cattle farm is **station**. These kinds of words are given a geographical marker.

The label Brit. means that the word is found typically in British English but is not found in American English, though it may be found in other varieties such as Australian English. The labels US and N. Amer., on the other hand, mean that the word or phrase is typically American and is not standard in British English, though it may be found elsewhere.

▶ ABBREVIATIONS USED IN THE DICTIONARY

adj.	adjective	NZ	New Zealand	S. African	South African
fem.	feminine	part.	participle	sing.	singular
N. Amer.	North American	pl.	plural	usu.	usually
N. English	Northern English	pronunc.	pronunciation		

Aa

A¹ (also **a**) noun (pl. **As** or **A's**) **1** the first letter of the alphabet. **2** indicating the first, best, or most important in a set. **3** Music the sixth note of the scale of C major.
– PHRASES **from A to B** from one place to another. **from A to Z** covering or including the entire range or scope of something.

A² abbreviation **1** ampere(s). **2** (**Å**) angstrom(s). **3** answer.

a¹ (**an** before a vowel sound) determiner **1** used when mentioning someone or something for the first time; the indefinite article. **2** one single: *a hundred.* **3** per: *typing 60 words a minute.* **4** someone like (the name specified): *you're no better than a Hitler.*
– ORIGIN Old English.

a² abbreviation **1** (in travel timetables) arrives. **2** (used before a date) before. [Latin *ante.*]

a- (often **an-** before a vowel) prefix not; without: *atheistic.*
– ORIGIN from Greek.

@ symbol 'at', used: **1** to indicate cost or rate per unit. **2** in Internet addresses between the user's name and the domain name: *john.smith@oup.com.*

A1 adjective informal excellent.

A3 noun a standard European size of paper, 420 × 297 mm.

A4 noun a standard European size of paper, 297 × 210 mm.

A5 noun a standard European size of paper, 210 × 148 mm.

AA abbreviation **1** Alcoholics Anonymous. **2** Automobile Association. **3** anti-aircraft.

aardvark /ard-vark/ noun an African mammal with a tubular snout and a long tongue, feeding on ants and termites.
– ORIGIN South African Dutch, 'earth pig'.

AB abbreviation **1** able seaman. **2** Alberta.

ab noun (usu. **abs**) informal an abdominal muscle.

aback adverb (in phrase **take someone aback**) shock or surprise someone: *I was taken aback by the question.*
– ORIGIN Old English.

abacus /ab-uh-kuhss/ noun (pl. **abacuses**) a frame with rows of wires along which beads are slid, used for counting.
– ORIGIN Greek *abax* 'slab, drawing board'.

abaft /uh-**bahft**/ adverb & preposition Nautical in or behind the stern of a ship.
– ORIGIN from the old word *baft* 'in the rear'.

abalone /a-buh-**loh**-ni/ noun an edible sea creature which has a shell lined with mother-of-pearl.

– ORIGIN from an American Indian language.

abandon verb **1** desert or leave permanently: *he abandoned his family and moved to London.* **2** give up a course of action completely. **3** (**abandon oneself to**) make no attempt to resist something: *she abandoned herself to his kiss.* • noun complete lack of self-control or self-consciousness: *dancers swung their bodies with wild abandon.*
– DERIVATIVES **abandonment** noun.
– ORIGIN Old French *abandoner.*

abandoned adjective wild and uninhibited.

abase /uh-**bayss**/ verb (**abase oneself**) behave in a way that is demeaning or degrading.
– DERIVATIVES **abasement** noun.
– ORIGIN Old French *abaissier* 'to lower'.

abashed adjective embarrassed or ashamed.
– ORIGIN from Old French *esbair* 'utterly astound'.

abate /uh-**bayt**/ verb (of something bad) become less severe or widespread: *the epidemic showed no sign of abating.*
– DERIVATIVES **abatement** noun.
– ORIGIN Old French *abatre* 'to fell'.

abattoir /**ab**-uh-twar/ noun Brit. a slaughterhouse.
– ORIGIN French, from *abattre* 'to fell'.

abbé /a-bay/ noun (in France) an abbot or other clergyman.

abbess /**ab**-biss/ noun a woman who is the head of an abbey of nuns.

abbey noun (pl. **abbeys**) a building occupied by a community of monks or nuns.
– ORIGIN Old French *abbeie.*

abbot noun a man who is the head of an abbey of monks.
– ORIGIN Greek *abbas* 'father'.

abbreviate /uh-**bree**-vi-ayt/ verb shorten a word, phrase, or text.
– ORIGIN Latin *abbreviare*, from *brevis* 'short'.

abbreviation noun a shortened form of a word or phrase.

ABC noun **1** the alphabet. **2** an alphabetical guide to something. **3** the basic facts of a subject.

abdicate /**ab**-di-kayt/ verb **1** (of a king or queen) give up the throne. **2** fail to fulfil or carry out a duty or responsibility.
– DERIVATIVES **abdication** noun.
– ORIGIN Latin *abdicare.*

abdomen /**ab**-duh-muhn/ noun **1** the part of the body which contains the stomach, intestines, and reproductive organs. **2** the rear

a

part of the body of an insect, spider, or crustacean.
- DERIVATIVES **abdominal** /ab-dom-in'l/ adjective **abdominally** adverb.
- ORIGIN Latin.

abduct verb take someone away, typically using force to do so.
- DERIVATIVES **abductee** noun **abduction** noun **abductor** noun.
- ORIGIN Latin *abducere*.

abeam adverb at right angles to a ship's or an aircraft's length.

abed adverb old use in bed.

Aberdeen Angus noun a Scottish breed of black beef cattle.

Aberdonian /a-ber-doh-ni-uhn/ adjective relating to Aberdeen. • noun a person from Aberdeen.
- ORIGIN Latin *Aberdonia*.

aberrant /uh-berr-uhnt/ adjective not normal or acceptable: *his aberrant behaviour*.

aberration /a-buh-ray-sh'n/ noun 1 an action, event, or way of behaving that is not normal or acceptable. 2 a temporary failure of judgement or concentration: *a mental aberration*.
- ORIGIN Latin, from *aberrare* 'to stray'.

abet /uh-bet/ verb (**abets, abetting, abetted**) (usu. in phrase **aid and abet**) encourage or assist someone to do something wrong, in particular to commit a crime.
- DERIVATIVES **abetment** noun **abettor** (also **abetter**) noun.
- ORIGIN from Old French *beter* 'hound, urge on'.

abeyance /uh-bay-uhnss/ noun (in phrase **in/into abeyance**) temporarily suspended or not in use.
- ORIGIN Old French *abeer* 'aspire after'.

ABH abbreviation Brit. actual bodily harm.

abhor /uhb-hor/ verb (**abhors, abhorring, abhorred**) hate or detest: *he abhorred sexism*.
- ORIGIN from Latin *horrere* 'to shudder'.

abhorrent adjective disgusting or hateful.
- DERIVATIVES **abhorrence** noun.

abide verb 1 (**abide by**) accept or obey a rule or decision. 2 (**cannot abide**) dislike very much: *I can't abide lies*. 3 (of a feeling or memory) last for a long time. 4 old use live in a place.
- ORIGIN Old English, 'wait'.

abiding adjective lasting a long time; enduring: *an abiding love of the countryside*.
- DERIVATIVES **abidingly** adverb.

ability noun (pl. **abilities**) 1 the power or capacity to do something. 2 skill or talent.
- ORIGIN Latin *habilitas*.

abject /ab-jekt/ adjective 1 very unpleasant and degrading: *families living in abject poverty*. 2 completely without pride or dignity: *an abject apology*.
- DERIVATIVES **abjectly** adverb.
- ORIGIN Latin *abjectus* 'rejected'.

abjure /uhb-joor/ verb formal swear to give up a belief or claim.
- ORIGIN Latin *abjurare*.

ablation /uh-blay-sh'n/ noun 1 the surgical removal of body tissue. 2 the loss of solid material such as ice or rock by melting, evaporation, or erosion.

- ORIGIN Latin.

ablative /ab-luh-tiv/ adjective Grammar (of a case) indicating an agent, instrument, or source, expressed by 'by', 'with', or 'from' in English.

ablaze adjective burning fiercely.

able adjective (**abler, ablest**) 1 having the power, skill, or means to do something. 2 skilful and competent: *a very able public speaker*.
- DERIVATIVES **ably** adverb.
- ORIGIN Latin *habilis* 'handy'.

able-bodied adjective physically fit and healthy.

able seaman noun a rank of sailor in the Royal Navy above ordinary seaman and below leading seaman.

ablutions /uh-bloo-shuhnz/ plural noun formal or humorous the process of washing oneself.
- ORIGIN Latin, from *abluere* 'wash away'.

ABM abbreviation anti-ballistic-missile.

abnegation /ab-ni-gay-sh'n/ verb formal the giving up of something which is valuable or desired.
- DERIVATIVES **abnegate** verb.
- ORIGIN from Latin *negare* 'deny'.

abnormal adjective differing from what is normal or typical.
- DERIVATIVES **abnormally** adverb.
- ORIGIN Greek *anōmalos* 'uneven'.

abnormality noun (pl. **abnormalities**) 1 a feature or event which is not normal: *babies with congenital abnormalities*. 2 the state of being abnormal.

Abo /ab-oh/ noun (pl. **Abos**) Austral. informal, offensive an Aboriginal.

aboard adverb & preposition on or into a ship, train, or other vehicle.

abode noun formal or literary a person's house or home.
- ORIGIN from **ABIDE**.

abolish verb officially put an end to a system, law, or practice.
- ORIGIN Latin *abolere* 'destroy'.

abolition noun the official ending of a system, law, or practice: *the abolition of the death penalty*.

abolitionist noun a person who supports the abolition of something, especially capital punishment or (in the past) slavery.
- DERIVATIVES **abolitionism** noun.

A-bomb noun an atom bomb.

abominable adjective 1 very unpleasant and causing disgust: *an abominable crime*. 2 informal very bad; terrible.
- DERIVATIVES **abominably** adverb.
- ORIGIN Latin *abominabilis*.

Abominable Snowman noun the yeti.

abominate /uh-bom-i-nayt/ verb formal detest something or someone.

abomination noun 1 a thing that causes disgust or hatred. 2 a feeling of hatred.

aboriginal adjective 1 inhabiting or existing in a land from the earliest times or from before the arrival of colonists. 2 (**Aboriginal**) relating to the Australian Aboriginals. • noun 1 a person who has inhabited a land from the earliest times. 2 (**Aboriginal**) a member of one of the original peoples of Australia.

aborigine /ab-uh-ri-ji-nee/ noun an original

inhabitant of a land, especially (**Aborigine**) an Australian Aboriginal.
– ORIGIN from Latin *ab origine* 'from the beginning'.

abort verb **1** carry out the abortion of a fetus. **2** (of a pregnant woman or female animal) have a miscarriage. **3** bring to a premature end because of a problem or fault: *the helicopter was forced to abort its mission due to a blizzard.*
– ORIGIN Latin *aboriri* 'miscarry'.

abortifacient /uh-bor-ti-**fay**-shuhnt/ Medicine adjective (of a drug) causing an abortion. • **noun** a drug that causes an abortion.

abortion noun **1** a surgical operation in which a human pregnancy is deliberately brought to an end. **2** the natural ending of a pregnancy before the fetus is able to survive on its own.

abortionist noun derogatory a person who carries out abortions.

abortive adjective (of an action) failing to achieve the intended result; unsuccessful: *an abortive military coup.*

abound verb **1** exist in large numbers or amounts. **2** (**abound in/with**) have in large numbers or amounts: *woodlands abounding with spring flowers.*
– ORIGIN Latin *abundare* 'overflow'.

about preposition & adverb **1** on the subject of; concerning. **2** used to indicate movement within an area or location in a place: *she looked about the room.* **3** approximately.
– PHRASES **be about to** be on the point of.
– ORIGIN Old English.

about-turn (also chiefly N. Amer. **about-face**) noun Brit. **1** Military a turn made so as to face the opposite direction. **2** a complete change of opinion or policy.

above preposition & adverb **1** at a higher level than. **2** rather or more than: *he valued safety above comfort.* **3** (in printed text) mentioned earlier.
– PHRASES **above board** legitimate and honest. **above oneself** having too high an opinion of oneself. **not be above** be capable of doing something dishonest or dishonourable.
– ORIGIN Old English.

abracadabra exclamation a word said by conjurors when performing a trick.
– ORIGIN Latin.

abrade /uh-**brayd**/ verb scrape or wear away the surface of something.
– ORIGIN Latin *abradere*.

abrasion /uh-**bray**-zh'n/ noun **1** a patch of skin which has been damaged by being scraped. **2** the scraping or wearing away of the surface of something.

abrasive /uh-**bray**-siv/ adjective **1** able to polish or clean a hard surface by rubbing or grinding. **2** showing little concern for the feelings of other people; harsh or unkind: *a politician renowned for his abrasive manner.* • **noun** a substance used for cleaning or polishing hard surfaces.
– DERIVATIVES **abrasively** adverb **abrasiveness** noun.

abreast adverb **1** side by side and facing the same way. **2** (**abreast of**) up to date with: *I shall keep you abreast of any developments.*

abridge verb shorten a text or film.

– DERIVATIVES **abridgement** (also **abridgment**) noun.
– ORIGIN Old French *abregier*.

abroad adverb **1** in or to a foreign country or countries. **2** felt or talked about by many people: *there was a new mood abroad.* **3** over a wide area: *millions of seed are scattered abroad.* **4** old use out of doors.

abrogate /**ab**-ruh-gayt/ verb formal cancel or end a law or agreement.
– DERIVATIVES **abrogation** noun
– ORIGIN Latin *abrogare*.

abrupt adjective **1** sudden and unexpected: *the car came to an abrupt halt.* **2** brief to the point of rudeness: *an unnecessarily abrupt response.*
– DERIVATIVES **abruptly** adverb **abruptness** noun.
– ORIGIN Latin *abruptus* 'broken off, steep'.

ABS abbreviation anti-lock braking system.

abscess /**ab**-sess/ noun a swelling on the skin or in the body, containing pus.
– ORIGIN Latin *abscessus*.

abscissa /ab-**siss**-uh/ noun (pl. **abscissae** /ab-**siss**-ee/ or **abscissas**) Mathematics the distance from a point on a graph to the vertical or y-axis; the x-coordinate.
– ORIGIN from Latin *abscissa linea* 'cut-off line'.

abscond /uhb-**skond**/ verb leave a place hurriedly and secretly to escape from custody or avoid arrest.
– DERIVATIVES **absconder** noun.
– ORIGIN Latin *abscondere* 'hide'.

abseil /**ab**-sayl/ verb Brit. climb down a steep rock face using a rope coiled round the body and fixed at a higher point.
– DERIVATIVES **abseiler** noun **abseiling** noun.
– ORIGIN German *abseilen*.

absence noun **1** the state of being away from a place or person. **2** (**absence of**) the non-existence or lack of: *the absence of reliable information.*

absent adjective /**ab**-s'nt/ **1** not present: *the number of pupils absent from school.* **2** showing that someone is not paying attention: *an absent expression.* • verb /uhb-**sent**/ (**absent oneself**) leave or stay away from somewhere.
– DERIVATIVES **absently** adverb.
– ORIGIN from Latin *abesse* 'to be away'.

absentee noun a person who is absent.

absenteeism noun frequent absences from work or school without good reason.

absent-minded adjective forgetful or tending not to pay attention.
– DERIVATIVES **absent-mindedly** adverb **absent-mindedness** noun.

absinthe /**ab**-sinth/ noun a green aniseed-flavoured liqueur, formerly made with wormwood.
– ORIGIN French.

absolute adjective **1** not qualified or reduced in any way; total: *absolute silence.* **2** having unlimited power: *an absolute ruler.* **3** not related or compared to anything else: *absolute moral principles.* **4** Law (of a decree) final. • **noun** Philosophy a value or principle which is universally valid or which can be viewed without relation to other things.
– ORIGIN Latin *absolutus* 'freed, unrestricted'.

absolutely adverb **1** completely; entirely: *she*

a

trusted him absolutely. **2** used for emphasis or to express agreement.

absolute majority noun a majority over all rivals or opposition considered as a group; more than half.

absolute pitch noun Music **1** perfect pitch. **2** pitch according to a fixed standard defined by the frequency of the sound vibration.

absolute temperature noun a temperature measured from absolute zero in kelvins.

absolute zero noun the lowest temperature theoretically possible (zero kelvins, −273.15 °C).

absolution noun formal forgiveness of a person's sins.
– ORIGIN Latin.

absolutism noun the political principle that a ruler or government should have unlimited power.
– DERIVATIVES **absolutist** noun & adjective.

absolve /uhb-**zolv**/ verb declare someone to be free from guilt, responsibility, or sin.
– ORIGIN Latin *absolvere* 'set free, acquit'.

absorb /uhb-**zorb**/ verb **1** take in or soak up liquid or another substance. **2** understand information fully. **3** incorporate something smaller or less powerful: *the family firm was absorbed into a larger group.* **4** use up time or resources. **5** reduce the effect or strength of sound or an impact. **6** interest someone and hold their attention completely: *she was absorbed in her work.*
– DERIVATIVES **absorbable** adjective **absorber** noun.
– ORIGIN Latin *absorbere* 'suck in'.

absorbent adjective able to soak up liquid easily.
– DERIVATIVES **absorbency** noun.

absorbing adjective holding someone's interest completely; very interesting.

absorption noun **1** the process by which one thing absorbs or is absorbed by another. **2** the state of being engrossed in something.
– DERIVATIVES **absorptive** adjective.

abstain verb **1** restrain oneself from doing or enjoying the pleasure of something: *they abstained from alcohol for two months.* **2** formally choose not to vote.
– DERIVATIVES **abstainer** noun.
– ORIGIN Latin *abstinere* 'hold from'.

abstemious /uhb-**stee**-mi-uhss/ adjective deliberately limiting one's consumption of food or alcohol.
– DERIVATIVES **abstemiously** adverb **abstemiousness** noun.
– ORIGIN Latin *abstemius*.

abstention /uhb-**sten**-sh'n/ noun **1** a deliberate decision not to vote. **2** abstinence.

abstinence /**ab**-sti-nuhnss/ noun the avoidance of something enjoyable, such as food or alcohol.
– DERIVATIVES **abstinent** adjective.
– ORIGIN Latin *abstinentia*.

abstract adjective /**ab**-strakt/ **1** relating to ideas or qualities rather than physical things. **2** (of art) using colour and shapes to create an effect rather than attempting to represent reality accurately. • verb /uhb-**strakt**/ take out or remove something. • noun /**ab**-strakt/ **1** a

summary of a book or article. **2** an abstract work of art.
– DERIVATIVES **abstractly** adverb
– ORIGIN from Latin *abstrahere* 'draw away'.

abstracted adjective not concentrating on what is happening; preoccupied.
– DERIVATIVES **abstractedly** adverb.

abstraction noun **1** the quality of being abstract. **2** something which exists only as an idea. **3** a preoccupied state of mind. **4** the action of removing something.

abstruse /uhb-**strooss**/ adjective difficult to understand: *an abstruse philosophical controversy.*
– ORIGIN Latin *abstrusus* 'concealed'.

absurd adjective completely unreasonable or illogical; ridiculous.
– DERIVATIVES **absurdity** noun **absurdly** adverb.
– ORIGIN Latin *absurdus* 'out of tune'.

abundance /uh-**bun**-duhnss/ noun **1** a very large quantity of something. **2** the state of having a very large quantity of something: *vines grew in abundance.*
– ORIGIN from Latin *abundare* 'to overflow'.

abundant adjective **1** existing or available in large quantities; plentiful. **2** (**abundant in**) having plenty of: *riverbanks abundant in beautiful wild plants.*

abundantly adverb **1** in large quantities; plentifully. **2** extremely: *he made it abundantly clear that he would not tolerate racism.*

abuse verb /uh-**byooz**/ **1** use badly or wrongly: *he had abused his position as a doctor.* **2** treat a person or animal with cruelty or violence. **3** speak to someone in an insulting and offensive way. • noun /uh-**byooss**/ **1** the wrong use of something: *an abuse of public funds.* **2** cruel and violent treatment of a person or animal. **3** insulting and offensive language.
– DERIVATIVES **abuser** noun.
– ORIGIN Latin *abuti* 'misuse'.

abusive adjective **1** very offensive and insulting. **2** involving cruelty and violence: *an abusive relationship.*
– DERIVATIVES **abusively** adverb.

abut /uh-**but**/ verb (**abuts**, **abutting**, **abutted**) be next to or touching: *the US states which abut the Great Lakes.*
– ORIGIN Old French *abouter.*

abutilon /uh-**byoo**-ti-lon/ noun a herbaceous plant or shrub with showy yellow, red, or mauve flowers.
– ORIGIN Latin.

abutment noun a structure supporting the side of an arch, especially at the end of a bridge.

abysmal /uh-**biz**-m'l/ adjective **1** extremely bad. **2** literary very deep.
– DERIVATIVES **abysmally** adverb.

abyss /uh-**biss**/ noun a very deep chasm or hole.
– ORIGIN from Greek *abussos* 'bottomless'.

abyssal adjective relating to the depths of the ocean.

Abyssinian /ab-i-**sin**-i-uhn/ historical adjective relating to Abyssinia (the former name of Ethiopia). • noun a person from Abyssinia.

AC abbreviation **1** alternating current. **2** appellation contrôlée. **3** athletic club.

Ac symbol the chemical element actinium.

a/c abbreviation **1** account. **2** (also **A/C**) air conditioning.

acacia /uh-**kay**-shuh/ noun a tree or shrub with yellow or white flowers, found in warm climates.
– ORIGIN Greek *akakia.*

academe /**ak**-uh-deem/ noun (often in phrase **the groves of academe**) literary academia.

academia /a-kuh-**dee**-mi-uh/ noun the world of teaching and research conducted at universities and colleges or the people involved in it.

academic adjective **1** relating to education and scholarship. **2** not connected to a real situation; of theoretical interest only. • noun a teacher or scholar in a university or college.
– DERIVATIVES **academically** adverb.

academician /uh-ka-duh-**mish**-uhn/ noun **1** a member of an academy. **2** N. Amer. an academic.

academicism /a-kuh-**dem**-i-siz'm/ noun the practice of keeping to formal or conventional rules and traditions in art or literature.

academy noun (pl. **academies**) **1** a place of study or training in a special field. **2** a society or institution of distinguished scholars, artists, or scientists. **3** US & Scottish a secondary school.
– ORIGIN Greek, from *Akadēmos*, the name of the garden where Plato taught.

Academy award noun an award given by the Academy of Motion Picture Arts and Sciences for achievement in the film industry; an Oscar.

acanthus /uh-**kan**-thuss/ noun a plant or shrub with spiny decorative leaves.
– ORIGIN Greek, from *akantha* 'thorn'.

a cappella /a kuh-**pel**-luh/ adjective & adverb (of music) sung without instrumental accompaniment.
– ORIGIN Italian, 'in chapel style'.

ACAS /**ay**-kas/ abbreviation (in the UK) Advisory, Conciliation, and Arbitration Service.

accede /uhk-**seed**/ verb (usu. **accede to**) formal **1** agree to a demand or request. **2** take up an office or position: *he acceded to the throne in 1972.*
– ORIGIN Latin *accedere* 'come to'.

accelerando /uhk-sel-uh-**ran**-doh, uh-chel-/ adverb & adjective Music with a gradual increase of speed.
– ORIGIN Italian.

accelerant noun a substance used to help fire spread.

accelerate /uhk-**sel**-uh-rayt/ verb **1** begin to move more quickly. **2** increase in rate, amount, or extent: *inflation started to accelerate.*
– ORIGIN Latin *accelerare*, from *celer* 'swift'.

acceleration noun **1** the rate at which a vehicle increases speed. **2** an increase in the rate, amount, or extent of something: *the acceleration of economic reform.*

accelerator noun **1** a foot pedal which controls the speed of a vehicle. **2** Physics a piece of equipment which causes charged particles to move at high speeds.

accelerometer /uhk-sel-uh-**ro**-mi-ter/ noun an instrument for measuring the acceleration of a moving vehicle.

accent noun /**ak**-s'nt, **ak**-sent/ **1** a distinctive way of pronouncing a language, associated with a country, area, or social background. **2** an emphasis given to a syllable, word, or note. **3** a mark on a letter or word showing how a sound is pronounced or stressed. **4** a special importance, value, or prominence: *the accent is on participation.* • verb /ak-**sent**/ **1** (as adj. **accented**) spoken with a foreign accent: *he spoke heavily accented English.* **2** stress or emphasize something.
– ORIGIN Latin *accentus* 'tone, signal, or intensity'.

accentuate /uhk-**sen**-tyuu-ayt/ verb make more noticeable or prominent: *a deep tan which accentuated his blue eyes.*
– DERIVATIVES **accentuation** noun.

accept verb **1** agree to receive or do something offered. **2** believe to be valid or correct: *the committee accepted his explanation.* **3** admit responsibility or blame for something. **4** make someone welcome. **5** come to terms with an unwelcome situation: *she had to accept the fact that he might not return.*
– DERIVATIVES **acceptance** noun **acceptor** noun.
– ORIGIN Latin *acceptare.*

> USAGE: Do not confuse **accept** with **except.** **Accept** means 'agree to receive or do something' (*she accepted the job*), whereas **except** means 'not including; apart from' (*I work every day except Sunday*).

acceptable adjective **1** able to be accepted. **2** good enough; adequate: *the food was just about acceptable.*
– DERIVATIVES **acceptability** noun **acceptably** adverb.

access noun **1** the means or opportunity to approach or enter a place. **2** the right or opportunity to use something or see someone: *do you have access to a computer?* **3** the process of obtaining information stored in a computer's memory. **4** literary an attack or outburst of an emotion: *an access of rage.* • verb **1** enter a place. **2** obtain data stored in a computer.
– ORIGIN from Latin *accedere* 'come to'.

accessible adjective **1** able to be reached or used. **2** friendly and easy to talk to. **3** easily understood or enjoyed: *her writing is straightforward and very accessible.*
– DERIVATIVES **accessibility** noun **accessibly** adverb.

accession noun **1** the gaining of an important position or rank: *her accession to the throne.* **2** the process of formally joining a group or organization. **3** a new item added to a library or museum collection.

accessorize (or **accessorise**) verb add a fashion accessory to a garment.

accessory noun (pl. **accessories**) **1** a thing which can be added to something else to make it more useful or attractive. **2** a small article carried or worn to improve the look of a garment. **3** Law a person who helps someone commit a crime without taking part in it.
– ORIGIN Latin *accessorius* 'additional thing'.

accident noun **1** an unexpected and unpleasant event. **2** an event that is unforeseen or has no apparent cause.

a

- PHRASES **by accident** in a way that is not planned or organized.
- ORIGIN from Latin *accidere* 'to fall or happen'.

accidental adjective happening by accident: *a verdict of accidental death.* •noun a sign attached to a musical note indicating a momentary departure from the key signature.
- DERIVATIVES **accidentally** adverb.

accidie /ak-si-di/ noun literary depression, apathy, or listlessness.
- ORIGIN Greek *akēdia.*

acclaim verb praise enthusiastically and publicly: *the car was acclaimed as the best in its class.* •noun enthusiastic public praise.
- ORIGIN Latin *acclamare.*

acclamation noun loud and enthusiastic approval or praise.

acclimatize (or **acclimatise**) verb adapt to a new climate or new conditions.
- DERIVATIVES **acclimatization** noun.
- ORIGIN French *acclimater.*

accolade /ak-kuh-layd/ noun something given as a special honour or as a reward for excellence.
- ORIGIN first meaning 'a touch on a person's shoulders with a sword when knighting them': from Provençal *acolada* 'embrace around the neck'.

accommodate verb **1** provide lodging or space for: *the boat accommodates 40 passengers.* **2** adapt to or fit in with: *they tried hard to accommodate the children's needs.*
- ORIGIN Latin *accommodare.*

accommodating adjective willing to help or fit in with someone's wishes.

accommodation noun **1** a place where someone may live or stay. **2** a settlement or compromise.

accommodation address noun Brit. an address used by a person unable or unwilling to give a permanent address.

accompaniment noun **1** a musical part played to support a voice, group, or other instrument. **2** something that adds to or improves something else: *the sauce is a perfect accompaniment to all fish dishes.*

accompanist noun a person who plays a musical accompaniment.

accompany verb (**accompanies, accompanying, accompanied**) **1** go somewhere with someone. **2** be present or occur at the same time as: *violent winds accompanied by rain, hail, or snow.* **3** play musical support or backing for a voice, group, or other instrument.
- ORIGIN Old French *accompagner.*

accomplice /uh-**kum**-pliss/ noun a person who helps another commit a crime.
- ORIGIN from Latin *complex* 'allied'.

accomplish verb achieve or complete something successfully.
- ORIGIN Old French *acomplir.*

accomplished adjective highly skilled: *an accomplished musician.*

accomplishment noun **1** something that has been achieved successfully: *his military accomplishments.* **2** a skill or special ability. **3** the successful achievement of a task.

accord verb **1** give power or status to someone.

2 (**accord with**) be in agreement or consistent with: *his views accorded with those of Merivale.*
•noun **1** an official agreement or treaty. **2** agreement in opinion or feeling: *we are in accord on all points.*
- PHRASES **of one's own accord** willingly. **with one accord** in a united way.
- ORIGIN Old French *acorder* 'reconcile, be of one mind'.

accordance noun (in phrase **in accordance with**) in a way conforming with: *a ballot held in accordance with trade union rules.*

according adverb (**according to**) **1** as stated by someone. **2** following or agreeing with: *the event did not go according to plan.*

accordingly adverb **1** in a way that is appropriate. **2** therefore.

accordion /uh-kor-di-uhn/ noun a musical instrument played by stretching and squeezing with the hands to work a bellows, the notes being sounded by buttons or keys.
- DERIVATIVES **accordionist** noun.
- ORIGIN from Italian *accordare* 'to tune'.

accost verb approach someone and speak to them, especially in a rude or aggressive way.
- ORIGIN French *accoster.*

account noun **1** a description of an event or experience. **2** a record of money spent and received. **3** a service through a bank or firm by which funds are held on behalf of a customer or goods or services are supplied on credit. **4** importance: *money was of no account to her.*
•verb regard in a particular way: *her visit could not be accounted a complete success.*
- PHRASES **account for 1** supply or form a particular amount or part of: *the industry accounts for 11 per cent of the US economy.* **2** give a satisfactory explanation of. **call someone to account** ask someone to explain a mistake or bad performance. **on someone's account** for someone's benefit: *don't trouble yourself on my account.* **on account of** because of. **on no account** under no circumstances. **take account of** take something into consideration. **turn something to** (**good**) **account** turn something to one's advantage.
- ORIGIN Old French *acont*, from *conter* 'to count'.

accountable adjective responsible for one's actions and expected to explain them.
- DERIVATIVES **accountability** noun.

accountant noun a person who keeps or checks financial accounts.
- DERIVATIVES **accountancy** noun.

accounting noun the keeping of financial accounts.

accoutred /uh-koo-tuhd/ (US **accoutered**) adjective clothed or equipped.
- ORIGIN from French *accoutrer.*

accoutrement /uh-koo-truh-muhnt, uh-koo-ter-muhnt/ (US **accouterment**) noun an item of clothing or equipment required for a particular activity.

accredit verb (**accredits, accrediting, accredited**) **1** (**accredit something to**) attribute something to someone. **2** give official authorization to someone or something. **3** send a diplomat or journalist to a particular place or post.
- DERIVATIVES **accreditation** noun.

– ORIGIN French *accréditer*.

accrete /uh-**kreet**/ verb grow or be formed by a gradual build-up of new layers.
– ORIGIN Latin *accrescere* 'grow'.

accretion /uh-**kree**-sh'n/ noun 1 the process of growing or increasing in size as the result of a gradual build-up of new layers of something. 2 a thing formed or added in this way.

accrue /uh-**kroo**/ verb (accrues, accruing, accrued) 1 (of money) be received in regular or increasing amounts. 2 collect or receive payments or benefits.
– DERIVATIVES accrual noun.
– ORIGIN Old French *acreistre* 'increase'.

acculturate /uh-**kul**-chuh-rayt/ verb successfully absorb someone or something into a different culture or social group.
– DERIVATIVES acculturation noun.

accumulate /uh-**kyoo**-myuu-layt/ verb 1 gather together a number or quantity of something. 2 increase in number or quantity: *very large debts accumulated*.
– DERIVATIVES accumulation noun accumulative adjective.
– ORIGIN Latin *accumulare* 'heap up'.

accumulator noun Brit. 1 a large rechargeable electric cell. 2 a bet placed on a series of events, the winnings and stake from each being placed on the next.

accurate /ak-kyuu-ruht/ adjective 1 correct in all details: *an accurate description*. 2 reaching an intended target: *an accurate shot*.
– DERIVATIVES accuracy noun accurately adverb.
– ORIGIN from Latin *accurare* 'do with care'.

USAGE: On the distinction between **accurate** and **precise**, see the note at **PRECISE**.

accursed /uh-**ker**-sid, uh-**kerst**/ adjective 1 literary under a curse. 2 informal horrible.

accusation noun a claim that someone has done something illegal or wrong.

accusative /uh-**kyoo**-zuh-tiv/ noun a grammatical case used for the object of a verb.
– ORIGIN from Latin *casus accusativus* 'the case showing cause'.

accusatory /uh-**kyoo**-zuh-tuh-ri/ adjective suggesting that one believes a person has done something wrong: *an accusatory stare*.

accuse verb claim that someone has committed a crime or done something wrong: *he was accused of attempted murder*.
– DERIVATIVES accuser noun.
– ORIGIN Latin *accusare* 'call to account'.

accustom verb 1 (accustom someone/thing to) make someone or something used to. 2 (be accustomed to) be used to.
– ORIGIN Old French *acostumer*.

accustomed adjective customary; usual: *his accustomed route*.

AC/DC adjective 1 alternating current/direct current. 2 informal bisexual.

ace noun 1 a playing card with a single spot on it, the highest card in its suit in most games. 2 informal a person who is very good at a particular activity: *a snooker ace*. 3 Tennis a service that an opponent is unable to return. •adjective informal very good.
– PHRASES **ace up one's sleeve** a plan or piece of information kept secret until needed. **within**

an ace of very close to.
– ORIGIN Latin *as* 'unity, a unit'.

acellular /ay-**sel**-yuu-ler/ adjective Biology 1 not divided into or containing cells. 2 consisting of one cell only.

acer /**ay**-suh/ noun a maple or related tree, having leaves with five lobes.
– ORIGIN Latin.

acerbic /uh-**ser**-bik/ adjective (of a person or their remarks) sharply critical and forthright.
– DERIVATIVES acerbically adverb acerbity noun.
– ORIGIN Latin *acerbus* 'sour-tasting'.

acetaminophen /uh-see-tuh-**min**-uh-fen, uh-set-uh-/ noun North American term for PARACETAMOL.

acetate /**a**-si-tayt/ noun 1 Chemistry a salt or ester of acetic acid. 2 fibre or plastic made of a substance produced from cellulose.

acetic acid /uh-**see**-tik/ noun the acid that gives vinegar its characteristic taste.
– ORIGIN Latin *acetum* 'vinegar'.

acetone /**a**-si-tohn/ noun a colourless liquid used as a solvent.
– ORIGIN from **ACETIC ACID**.

acetylene /uh-**set**-i-leen/ noun a gas which burns with a bright flame, used in welding.
– ORIGIN from **ACETIC ACID**.

ache noun a continuous or long-lasting dull pain. •verb 1 suffer from an ache. 2 (ache for/ to do) feel great desire for or to do: *he ached to see her again*.
– DERIVATIVES aching adjective.
– ORIGIN Old English.

achieve verb succeed in doing something by effort, skill, or courage.
– DERIVATIVES achievable adjective achiever noun.
– ORIGIN Old French *achever* 'come or bring to a head'.

achievement noun 1 a thing that is done successfully: *the government's greatest economic achievement*. 2 the process of achieving something.

Achilles heel /uh-**kil**-leez/ noun a weak or vulnerable point.
– ORIGIN from *Achilles*, a hero in Greek myth whose mother plunged him into the River Styx when he was a baby to make his body safe from harm or injury; only the heel by which she held him was untouched by the water.

Achilles tendon noun the tendon which connects the calf muscles to the heel.

achondroplasia /uh-kon-druh-**play**-zi-uh, ay-kon-druh-**play**-zi-uh/ noun a hereditary condition in which the bones of the arms and legs fail to grow to the normal size.
– ORIGIN from **A-** + Greek *khondros* 'cartilage' + *plasis* 'moulding'.

achromatic /a-kroh-**mat**-ik/ adjective 1 transmitting light without separating it into its constituent colours. 2 without colour.

achy (also **achey**) adjective (achier, achiest) suffering from an ache or aches.

acid noun 1 a substance with chemical properties which include turning litmus red, neutralizing alkalis, and dissolving some metals. 2 informal the drug LSD. •adjective 1 having the properties of an acid; having a pH of less than 7. 2 sharp-tasting or sour. 3 (of a remark) bitter or cutting.

a

– DERIVATIVES **acidly** adverb **acidy** adjective.
– ORIGIN Latin *acidus*.

acid drop noun Brit. a boiled sweet with a sharp taste.

acid house noun a kind of fast, repetitive synthesized dance music.

acidic /uh-sid-ic/ adjective 1 containing acid. 2 having a sour taste.

acidify verb (**acidifies, acidifying, acidified**) make or become acid.
– DERIVATIVES **acidification** noun.

acidity noun 1 the level of acid in something. 2 bitterness or sharpness in a person's remarks or tone.

acid jazz noun a kind of dance music incorporating elements of jazz, funk, soul, and hip hop.

acidophilus /a-si-dof-i-luss/ noun a bacterium used to make yogurt.
– ORIGIN Latin.

acid rain noun rainfall made acidic by atmospheric pollution resulting from the burning of coal or oil in factories.

acid test noun a conclusive test of the success, truth, or value of something.
– ORIGIN from the use of nitric acid to test whether or not a metal is gold.

acidulate /uh-sid-yoo-layt/ verb make something slightly acidic.

acidulous /uh-sid-yoo-luhss/ adjective sharp-tasting; sour.

ack-ack noun Military, informal anti-aircraft gunfire or guns.
– ORIGIN signallers' former name for the letters AA.

ackee /a-ki/ noun the fruit of a West African tree, eaten as a vegetable.
– ORIGIN from Kru (a West African language).

acknowledge verb 1 accept or admit that something exists or is true: *he acknowledged that he had made mistakes.* 2 confirm that one has received or is grateful for: *please acknowledge receipt of this letter.* 3 show that one has noticed someone by making a gesture of greeting.
– ORIGIN from the former verb *knowledge* (in the same sense).

acknowledgement (also **acknowledgment**) noun 1 the action of acknowledging something or someone. 2 something done or given to express gratitude.

acme /ak-mi/ noun the point at which something is at its best or most highly developed.
– ORIGIN Greek *akmē* 'highest point'.

acne noun a skin condition causing many red pimples on the face.
– ORIGIN Greek *aknas*.

acolyte /ak-uh-lyt/ noun 1 an assistant or follower. 2 a person helping a priest in a religious service.
– ORIGIN Latin *acolytus*.

aconite /ak-uh-nyt/ noun 1 a poisonous plant with pink or purple flowers. 2 (also **winter aconite**) a small spring-flowering plant with yellow flowers.
– ORIGIN Greek *akoniton*.

acorn noun the fruit of the oak tree, a smooth oval nut in a cup-like base.

– ORIGIN Old English.

acoustic /uh-koo-stik/ adjective 1 relating to sound or hearing. 2 not having electrical amplification: *an acoustic guitar.* ● noun (**acoustics**) 1 the features of a room or building that affect how it transmits sound. 2 the branch of physics concerned with the properties of sound.
– DERIVATIVES **acoustical** adjective **acoustically** adverb.
– ORIGIN Greek *akoustikos*.

acquaint verb 1 (**acquaint someone with**) make someone aware of or familiar with: *take time to acquaint yourself with your new surroundings.* 2 (**be acquainted**) know someone personally.
– ORIGIN Latin *accognitare*.

acquaintance noun 1 a person one knows slightly. 2 familiarity with or knowledge of someone or something.

acquiesce /ak-wi-ess/ verb accept something without protest.
– ORIGIN Latin *acquiescere*.

acquiescent adjective ready to accept or do something without protest.
– DERIVATIVES **acquiescence** noun.

acquire verb 1 come to have; obtain: *I managed to acquire a copy of the tape.* 2 learn or develop a quality or skill: *he acquired a taste for whisky.*
– DERIVATIVES **acquirement** noun **acquirer** noun.
– ORIGIN Latin *acquirere* 'get in addition'.

acquired taste noun a thing that one at first dislikes but comes to like over time.

acquisition /ak-wi-zi-sh'n/ noun 1 an object that has recently been obtained. 2 the action of acquiring or obtaining something.

acquisitive adjective too interested in obtaining money or possessions.
– DERIVATIVES **acquisitively** adverb **acquisitiveness** noun.

acquit verb (**acquits, acquitting, acquitted**) 1 formally declare that someone is not guilty of a criminal charge. 2 (**acquit oneself**) behave or perform in a particular way: *he acquitted himself very well on his debut.*
– ORIGIN Latin *acquitare* 'pay a debt'.

acquittal noun an official judgement that a person is not guilty of the crime with which they have been charged.

acre /ay-ker/ noun a unit of land area equal to 4,840 square yards (0.405 hectare).
– DERIVATIVES **acreage** noun.
– ORIGIN Old English, originally referring to the amount of land a pair of oxen could plough in a day.

acrid /ak-rid/ adjective having an unpleasantly strong and bitter smell or taste.
– ORIGIN from Latin *acer.*

acrimonious /ak-ri-moh-ni-uhss/ adjective angry and bitter: *a long and acrimonious debate.*

acrimony /ak-ri-muh-ni/ noun feelings of anger and bitterness.
– ORIGIN Latin *acrimonia.*

acrobat noun an entertainer who performs spectacular gymnastic feats.
– ORIGIN from Greek *akrobatos* 'walking on tiptoe'.

acrobatic adjective involving or performing

spectacular gymnastic feats. •noun (**acrobatics**) spectacular gymnastic feats. •

– DERIVATIVES **acrobatically** adverb.

acronym /**ak**-ruh-nim/ noun a word formed from the initial letters of other words (e.g. *laser*).

– ORIGIN from Greek *akron* 'end' + *onoma* 'name'.

acrophobia /ak-ruh-**foh**-biuh/ noun extreme fear of heights.

– DERIVATIVES **acrophobic** adjective.

– ORIGIN Greek *akron* 'summit'.

acropolis /uh-**krop**-uh-liss/ noun the citadel of an ancient Greek city, built on high ground.

– ORIGIN Greek, from *akron* 'summit' + *polis* 'city'.

across preposition & adverb from one side to the other of something.

– PHRASES **across the board** affecting or applying to everyone or everything.

– ORIGIN from Old French *a croix, en croix* 'in or on a cross'.

acrostic /uh-**kross**-tik/ noun a poem or puzzle in which certain letters in each line form a word or words.

– ORIGIN from Greek *akron* 'end' + *stikhos* 'row, line of verse'.

acrylic adjective (of a synthetic fabric, plastic, or paint) made from acrylic acid.

– ORIGIN from Latin *acer* 'pungent' + *oleum* 'oil'.

acrylic acid noun Chemistry a strong-smelling organic acid.

act verb **1** take action; do something. **2** take effect or have a particular effect: *a substance that acts on nerves in the digestive system.* **3** behave in a particular way: *he acts as if he owns the place.* **4** (**act as**) fulfil the function of: *she often acted as an interpreter.* **5** (**act for/on behalf of**) represent the interests of someone. **6** (as adj. **acting**) temporarily doing the duties of another person: *the acting president.* **7** perform a role in a play or film. •noun **1** a thing done. **2** a law passed formally by a parliament. **3** a way of behaving that is not genuine or sincere: *she's putting on an act.* **4** a main division of a play, ballet, or opera. **5** a short piece of entertainment in a show: *a comedy act.* **6** a performer or performing group.

– PHRASES **act of God** an event caused by natural forces beyond human control. **act up** informal behave badly. **get in on the act** informal become involved in an activity to share its benefits.

– ORIGIN Latin *actus* 'event, thing done'.

actinide /**ak**-ti-nyd/ noun any of the series of fifteen radioactive metallic elements from actinium to lawrencium in the periodic table.

actinium /ak-**tin**-i-uhm/ noun a rare radioactive metallic chemical element found in uranium ores.

– ORIGIN Greek *aktis* 'ray'.

action noun **1** the process of doing something to achieve an aim. **2** a thing done. **3** the effect or influence of something such as a chemical. **4** a lawsuit. **5** armed conflict: *servicemen missing in action.* **6** the way in which something works or moves. **7** informal exciting activity: *a preview of the weekend's sporting action.* •verb deal with something: *your request will be actioned.*

– PHRASES **in action** performing an activity; in operation. **out of action** not working.

actionable adjective Law giving someone grounds to take legal action.

action painting noun a technique and style of painting in which paint is thrown or poured on to the canvas.

action replay noun Brit. a playback of part of a television broadcast.

action stations plural noun chiefly Brit. the positions taken up by military personnel in preparation for action.

activate verb make something act or start working: *the security alarms had been activated.*

– DERIVATIVES **activation** noun **activator** noun.

activated carbon (also **activated charcoal**) noun charcoal that has been treated to increase its ability to absorb gases and dissolved substances.

active adjective **1** moving or tending to move about often or energetically. **2** (of a person's mind) alert and lively. **3** doing something regularly: *sexually active adults.* **4** functioning: *the watermill was active until 1960.* **5** (of a volcano) erupting or having erupted in the past. **6** having a chemical or biological effect: *salicylic acid is the active ingredient in aspirin.* **7** Grammar referring to verbs in which the subject is the person or thing performing the action and which can take a direct object (e.g. *she loved him* as opposed to the passive form *he was loved*).

– DERIVATIVES **actively** adverb.

– ORIGIN Latin *activus.*

active service noun direct involvement in military operations as a member of the armed forces.

activist noun a person who campaigns for political or social change.

– DERIVATIVES **activism** noun.

activity noun (pl. **activities**) **1** a situation in which things are happening or being done. **2** busy or energetic action or movement. **3** a thing that a person or group does or has done: *sporting and social activities.*

actor noun a person whose profession is acting.

– DERIVATIVES **actorish** adjective.

actress noun a female actor.

– DERIVATIVES **actressy** adjective.

actual adjective **1** existing in fact: *those were his actual words.* **2** existing now; current: *actual income.*

– ORIGIN Latin *actualis.*

actual bodily harm noun Law, Brit. minor injury inflicted on a person by the deliberate action of another, considered less serious than grievous bodily harm.

actuality noun (pl. **actualities**) **1** the state of existing in fact; reality: *the £100 mentioned was in actuality £100,000.* **2** (**actualities**) existing conditions or facts.

actualize (or **actualise**) verb make something real.

– DERIVATIVES **actualization** noun.

actually adverb **1** in reality. **2** used to emphasize or contradict something: *he actually expected me to be pleased!*

actuary /**ak**-choo-uh-ri/ noun (pl. **actuaries**) a

a

person who compiles and analyses statistics in order to calculate insurance risks and premiums.
– DERIVATIVES **actuarial** adjective.
– ORIGIN Latin *actuarius* 'bookkeeper'.

actuate /ak-choo-ayt/ verb **1** cause a machine to operate. **2** motivate someone to act: *they were actuated by malice.*
– DERIVATIVES **actuation** noun **actuator** noun.

acuity /uh-**kyoo**-i-ti/ noun keenness of thought, vision, or hearing.
– ORIGIN Latin *acuitas.*

acumen /ak-yoo-muhn/ noun the ability to make good judgements and take quick decisions.
– ORIGIN Latin, 'sharpness, point'.

acupoint /ak-yoo-poynt/ noun any of the supposed energy points on the body where acupuncture needles are inserted or manual pressure is applied during acupressure.

acupressure /ak-yoo-pre-sher/ noun a form of alternative therapy related to acupuncture in which specific points of the body are pressed to stimulate the flow of energy.

acupuncture /ak-yoo-pungk-cher/ noun a system of complementary medicine in which fine needles are inserted in the skin at specific points along supposed lines of energy.
– DERIVATIVES **acupuncturist** noun.
– ORIGIN from Latin *acu* 'with a needle' + PUNCTURE.

acute adjective **1** (of something bad) serious or severe: *an acute housing shortage.* **2** (of an illness) coming sharply to a crisis. Often contrasted with **CHRONIC**. **3** showing or having insight; perceptive. **4** (of a sense) highly developed: *an acute sense of smell.* **5** (of an angle) less than 90°.
– DERIVATIVES **acutely** adverb **acuteness** noun.
– ORIGIN Latin *acutus* 'sharpened'.

acute accent noun a mark (´) placed over certain letters in some languages to indicate pronunciation (e.g. in *fiancée*).

AD abbreviation Anno Domini (used to show that a date comes the specified number of years after the traditional date of Jesus's birth).
– ORIGIN Latin, 'in the year of the Lord'.

> USAGE: **AD** is normally written in small capitals and should be placed **before** the numerals, as in *AD 375*. However, when the date is spelled out, you should write *the third century AD*.

ad noun informal an advertisement.

adage /ad-ij/ noun a popular saying expressing a widely accepted truth.
– ORIGIN Latin *adagium.*

adagio /uh-**dah**-ji-oh/ Music adverb & adjective in slow time. • noun (pl. **adagios**) a passage in slow time.
– ORIGIN from Italian *ad agio* 'at ease'.

adamant adjective refusing to be persuaded or to change one's mind: *he is adamant that he is not going to resign.*
– DERIVATIVES **adamantly** adverb.
– ORIGIN Greek *adamas* 'invincible'.

adamantine /a-duh-**man**-tyn/ adjective literary unable to be broken.

Adam's apple noun a projection at the front of the neck formed by the thyroid cartilage.

– ORIGIN from the belief that a piece of the forbidden fruit became lodged in Adam's throat.

adapt verb **1** make something suitable for a new use or purpose. **2** become adjusted to new conditions: *older workers are struggling to adapt to change.*
– DERIVATIVES **adaptive** adjective.
– ORIGIN Latin *adaptare.*

adaptable adjective able to adjust to or be altered for new conditions or uses.
– DERIVATIVES **adaptability** noun.

adaptation (also **adaption**) noun **1** the action of adapting. **2** a film or play adapted from a written work.

adaptogen /a-**dap**-tuh-juhn/ noun (in herbal medicine) a natural substance believed to help the body adapt to stress.
– DERIVATIVES **adaptogenic** adjective.

adaptor (also **adapter**) noun **1** a device for connecting pieces of equipment. **2** Brit. a device for connecting several electric plugs to one socket.

ADC abbreviation **1** aide-de-camp. **2** analogue to digital converter.

add verb **1** join to or put with something else: *a new wing was added to the building.* **2** put together two or more numbers or amounts to calculate their total value. **3** (**add up**) increase in amount, number, or degree: *watch those air miles add up!* **4** say something as a further remark. **5** (**add up**) informal make sense.
– ORIGIN Latin *addere.*

addendum /uh-**den**-duhm/ noun (pl. **addenda** /uh-**den**-duh/) an extra item added at the end of a book or other publication.
– ORIGIN Latin, 'that which is to be added'.

adder noun a poisonous snake with a dark zigzag pattern on its back.
– ORIGIN Old English *nædre* 'serpent, adder'.

addict noun a person who is addicted to something.

addicted adjective **1** physically dependent on a particular substance. **2** devoted to a particular interest or activity: *I'm addicted to crime novels.*
– ORIGIN from Latin *addicere* 'assign'.

addiction noun the fact or condition of being addicted to something.

addictive adjective **1** (of a substance or activity) causing someone to become addicted to it. **2** relating or prone to addiction.
– DERIVATIVES **addictively** adverb.

addition noun **1** the action of adding. **2** a person or thing that is added: *the mirror would make a handsome addition to a bathroom.*

additional adjective extra to what is already present or available: *we need additional information.*
– DERIVATIVES **additionally** adverb.

additive noun a substance added to something to improve or preserve it.

addle verb **1** confuse someone. **2** (as adj. **addled**) (of an egg) rotten. • adjective (in combination) not clear; muddled: *an addle-brained adolescent.*
– ORIGIN from Old English, 'liquid filth'.

address noun **1** the details of the place where someone lives or an organization is situated. **2** a formal speech. **3** a number identifying a location in a data storage system or computer memory. **4** a string of characters which identifies a destination for email messages. • **verb 1** write a name and address on an envelope or parcel. **2** formal speak to someone. **3** think about and begin to deal with: *the industry has started to address the problem.* – DERIVATIVES **addressable** adjective **addresser** noun. – ORIGIN from Latin *ad-* 'towards' + *directus* 'direct'.

addressee /ad-re-see/ noun the person to whom something is addressed.

adduce /uh-**dyooss**/ verb refer to something as evidence. – ORIGIN Latin *adducere*.

adenoids /ad-uh-noydz/ plural noun a mass of tissue between the back of the nose and the throat, sometimes hindering speaking or breathing in children. – DERIVATIVES **adenoidal** adjective. – ORIGIN from Greek *adēn* 'gland'.

adept adjective /ad-ept, uh-**dept**/ very good at doing something; skilled: *I became adept at inventing excuses.* • noun /**ad**-ept/ a person who is skilled at doing something. – DERIVATIVES **adeptly** adverb **adeptness** noun. – ORIGIN from Latin *adipisci* 'obtain, attain'.

adequate adjective satisfactory or acceptable in quality or quantity: *an adequate supply of fuel.* – DERIVATIVES **adequacy** noun **adequately** adverb. – ORIGIN from Latin *adaequare* 'make equal to'.

à deux /ah **der**/ adverb for or involving two people: *dinner à deux.* – ORIGIN French.

adhere /uhd-**heer**/ verb (**adhere to**) **1** stick firmly to something. **2** follow, observe, or support: *members must adhere to a code of practice.* **3** represent something truthfully. – DERIVATIVES **adherence** noun. – ORIGIN Latin *adhaerere*.

adherent /uhd-**heer**-uhnt/ noun a person who supports a particular party, person, or set of ideas. • adjective sticking firmly to something.

adhesion /uhd-**hee**-*zh*'n/ noun **1** the action of adhering to something. **2** Medicine an abnormal joining of surfaces in the body as a result of inflammation or injury.

adhesive /uhd-**hee**-siv/ noun a substance used for sticking things together. • adjective able to stick to something; sticky. – DERIVATIVES **adhesively** adverb **adhesiveness** noun.

ad hoc /ad hok/ adjective & adverb formed or done for a particular purpose only: *an ad hoc committee.* – ORIGIN Latin, 'to this'.

ad hominem /ad hom-i-nem/ adverb & adjective (of an argument) personal rather than objective. – ORIGIN Latin, 'to the person'.

adieu /uhd-**dyoo**/ exclamation chiefly literary goodbye. – ORIGIN Old French.

Adi Granth /ah-di-**grunt**/ noun another term for **GURU GRANTH SAHIB**. – ORIGIN Sanskrit, 'first book'.

ad infinitum /ad in-fi-**ny**-tuhm/ adverb forever in the same way: *I could quote Dylan lyrics ad infinitum.* – ORIGIN Latin, 'to infinity'.

adios /addi-**oss**/ exclamation (in Spanish-speaking countries) goodbye. – ORIGIN Spanish.

adipose /ad-i-pohss/ adjective technical (of body tissue) used for storing fat. – ORIGIN from Latin *adeps* 'fat'.

adit /ad-it/ noun a horizontal access or drainage passage in a mine. – ORIGIN Latin *aditus* 'approach, entrance'.

adjacent /uh-**jay**-s'nt/ adjective next to or adjoining something else. – DERIVATIVES **adjacency** noun. – ORIGIN from Latin *adjacere* 'lie near to'.

adjective noun a word used to describe a noun, such as *sweet*, *red*, or *technical.* – DERIVATIVES **adjectival** adjective. – ORIGIN Old French *adjectif.*

adjoin verb be next to and joined with: *the dining room adjoins a conservatory.* – ORIGIN from Latin *adjungere* 'join to'.

adjourn /uh-**jern**/ verb **1** break off a meeting or legal case with the intention of resuming it later. **2** postpone a judicial sentence. **3** (of a group) go to another room or place, especially to relax: *they adjourned to a local pub.* – DERIVATIVES **adjournment** noun. – ORIGIN Old French *ajorner*, from *a jorn nome* 'to an appointed day'.

adjudge verb (especially of an authority) make a decision about someone or something: *she was adjudged guilty.* – ORIGIN Latin *adjudicare.*

adjudicate /uh-**joo**-di-kayt/ verb **1** make a formal judgement on a disputed matter. **2** judge a competition. – DERIVATIVES **adjudication** noun **adjudicator** noun. – ORIGIN Latin *adjudicare* 'adjudge'.

adjunct /a-jungkt/ noun an additional and supplementary part: *computer technology is an adjunct to learning.* – DERIVATIVES **adjunctive** adjective. – ORIGIN from Latin *adjungere* 'adjoin'.

adjure /uh-**joor**/ verb formal solemnly urge someone to do something. – ORIGIN Latin *adjurare.*

adjust verb **1** alter something slightly so as to achieve a desired result: *he adjusted his tie.* **2** become used to a new situation. **3** assess loss or damages when settling an insurance claim. – DERIVATIVES **adjustability** noun **adjustable** adjective **adjuster** noun. – ORIGIN Old French *ajoster* 'to approximate'.

adjustment noun **1** a minor change made so as to correct or improve something: *the company will make adjustments to its packaging.* **2** the action of adjusting.

adjutant /a-juu-tuhnt/ noun a military officer acting as an administrative assistant to a senior officer. – ORIGIN from Latin *adjutare* 'be of service to'.

adjuvant /aj-uu-vuhnt/ adjective (of medical treatment) applied after initial treatment for cancer to prevent secondary tumours. • noun a substance which improves the body's immune response to an infection or foreign body. – ORIGIN from Latin *adjuvare* 'help towards'.

ad-lib verb (**ad-libs, ad-libbing, ad-libbed**)

a

speak or perform in public without preparing beforehand. •adverb & adjective **1** spoken without previous preparation. **2** as much and as often as required: *the price includes meals and drinks ad lib.* •noun an unprepared remark or speech.
– ORIGIN abbreviation of Latin *ad libitum* 'according to pleasure'.

ad litem /ad **ly**-tem/ adjective Law acting in a lawsuit on behalf of people who cannot represent themselves.
– ORIGIN Latin, 'for the lawsuit'.

admin noun informal, chiefly Brit. administration.

administer verb **1** manage or put into effect: *the hospital is administered by the local NHS trust.* **2** give out a drug or remedy.
– ORIGIN Latin *administrare*.

administrate verb manage an organization.
– DERIVATIVES **administrator** noun.

administration noun **1** the organization and running of a business or system. **2** the action of giving out or applying something. **3** the government in power.

administrative adjective relating to the running of a business, organization, etc.
– DERIVATIVES **administratively** adverb.

admirable /ad-mi-ruh-b'l/ adjective deserving respect and approval.
– DERIVATIVES **admirably** adverb.

admiral noun **1** the most senior commander of a fleet or navy. **2** (**Admiral**) a naval officer of the second most senior rank.
– ORIGIN from an Arabic word meaning 'commander'.

Admiral of the Fleet noun the highest rank of admiral in the Royal Navy.

Admiralty noun (pl. **Admiralties**) (in the UK) the government department formerly in charge of the Royal Navy (now part of the Ministry of Defence).

admire verb **1** regard with respect or approval: *I admire your courage.* **2** look at something with pleasure.
– DERIVATIVES **admiration** /ad-muh-**ray**-sh'n/ noun **admirer** noun **admiring** adjective.
– ORIGIN Latin *admirari* 'wonder at'.

admissible adjective **1** acceptable or valid. **2** having the right to be admitted to a place.
– DERIVATIVES **admissibility** noun.

admission noun **1** entry to or permission to enter a place or organization: *the team were refused admission to the League.* **2** a confession. **3** a person admitted to hospital for treatment.

admit verb (**admits**, **admitting**, **admitted**) **1** confess to be true or to be the case: *I admit that I was relieved when he went.* **2** allow someone into a place or organization. **3** accept someone into a hospital for treatment. **4** accept something as valid. **5** (**admit of**) allow the possibility of: *the new skirts admit of easy free walking.*
– ORIGIN Latin *admittere* 'let into'.

admittance noun the process of entering or the fact of being allowed to enter: *we were unable to gain admittance to the hall.*

admixture noun technical a mixture.
– DERIVATIVES **admix** verb.

admonish verb **1** reprimand someone firmly. **2** earnestly urge or warn someone.

– DERIVATIVES **admonishment** noun **admonition** noun
– ORIGIN Latin *admonere*.

admonitory /uhd-**mon**-it-tuh-ri/ adjective giving or expressing a warning or reprimand: *she lifted an admonitory finger.*

ad nauseam /ad **naw**-zi-am/ adverb to an annoyingly excessive extent: *they recycle one idea ad nauseam.*
– ORIGIN Latin, 'to sickness'.

ado noun trouble; fuss: *I left without further ado.*
– ORIGIN from northern dialect *at do* 'to do'.

adobe /uh-**doh**-bi/ noun a kind of clay used to make sun-dried bricks.
– ORIGIN from Spanish *adobar* 'to plaster'.

adolescent /ad-uh-**le**-s'nt/ adjective in the process of developing from a child into an adult. •noun an adolescent boy or girl.
– DERIVATIVES **adolescence** noun.
– ORIGIN from Latin *adolescere* 'to mature'.

Adonis /uh-**doh**-niss/ noun a very handsome young man.
– ORIGIN the name of a beautiful youth in Greek mythology.

adopt verb **1** legally take another person's child and bring it up as one's own. **2** choose an option or course of action. **3** take on an attitude or position: *he adopted a patronizing tone.* **4** formally approve or accept someone or something.
– DERIVATIVES **adoptable** adjective **adoptee** noun **adopter** noun **adoption** noun.
– ORIGIN Latin *adoptare*.

adoptive adjective **1** (of a child or parent) in that relationship by adoption. **2** (of a place) chosen by a person as their permanent place of residence.

adorable adjective very lovable or charming.
– DERIVATIVES **adorably** adverb.

adore verb **1** love and respect someone greatly. **2** informal like very much: *she adores Mexican cuisine.*
– DERIVATIVES **adoration** noun **adorer** noun **adoring** adjective.
– ORIGIN Latin *adorare* 'to worship'.

adorn verb make something more attractive or beautiful.
– DERIVATIVES **adornment** noun.
– ORIGIN Latin *adornare*.

adrenal /uh-**dree**-n'l/ adjective relating to a pair of glands above the kidneys which produce adrenalin and other hormones.

adrenalin /uh-**dre**-nuh-lin/ (also **adrenaline**) noun a hormone produced by the adrenal glands that increases rates of blood circulation, breathing, and carbohydrate metabolism.

adrenalized /uh-**drenn**-uh-lyzd/ (or **adrenalised**) adjective excited, tense, or highly charged.

Adriatic /ay-dri-**at**-ik/ adjective relating to the region of the **Adriatic Sea**, between Italy and the Balkans.

adrift adjective & adverb **1** (of a boat) drifting without control. **2** no longer fixed in position. **3** Brit. informal failing to reach a target or winning position: *the team are two points adrift of the leaders.*

adroit /uh-**droyt**/ adjective clever or skilful: *an*

adroit administrator.
- ORIGIN from French *à droit* 'according to right, properly'.

ADSL abbreviation asymmetric digital subscriber line, a technology for transmitting digital information over standard telephone lines.

adsorb /uhd-**zorb**/ verb (of a solid) hold molecules of a gas, liquid, or dissolved substance in a layer on its surface.
- DERIVATIVES **adsorbent** adjective & noun **adsorption** noun.

adulation /ad-yuu-**lay**-sh'n/ noun excessive admiration.
- DERIVATIVES **adulate** verb **adulatory** adjective.
- ORIGIN from Latin *adulari* 'fawn on'.

adult /**ad**-ult, uh-**dult**/ noun 1 a person who is fully grown and developed. 2 Law a person who has reached the age of majority. • adjective 1 fully grown and developed. 2 for or typical of adults: *adult education.*
- DERIVATIVES **adulthood** noun.
- ORIGIN Latin *adultus.*

adulterate /uh-**dul**-tuh-rayt/ verb make something poorer in quality by adding another substance.
- DERIVATIVES **adulterant** adjective **adulteration** noun.
- ORIGIN Latin *adulterare* 'to corrupt'.

adulterer noun (fem. **adulteress**) a person who has committed adultery.
- ORIGIN from Latin *adulterare* 'to corrupt'.

adultery noun sexual intercourse between a married person and a person who is not their husband or wife.
- DERIVATIVES **adulterous** adjective.

adumbrate /**ad**-um-brayt/ verb formal 1 give a general idea of; outline: *his essay developed the arguments adumbrated in his earlier message.* 2 be a warning of a future event.
- DERIVATIVES **adumbration** noun.
- ORIGIN Latin *adumbrare* 'shade, overshadow'.

advance verb 1 move forwards. 2 make progress. 3 put forward a theory or suggestion. 4 hand over payment to someone as a loan or before it is due: *he advanced me a month's salary.* • noun 1 a forward movement. 2 a development or improvement. 3 an amount of money advanced to someone. 4 (**advances**) approaches made to someone with the aim of starting a sexual or romantic relationship. • adjective done, sent, or supplied beforehand.
- ORIGIN Old French *avancer.*

advanced adjective 1 far on in development or progress: *an advanced computer network.* 2 complex; not basic.

advanced level noun fuller form of **A LEVEL**.

advanced subsidiary level noun (in the UK except Scotland) a GCE exam at a level between GCSE and advanced level.

advancement noun 1 the promotion of a cause or plan: *the advancement of science.* 2 the promotion of a person in rank or status. 3 a development or improvement.

advantage noun 1 a condition or factor that puts one in a more favourable position: *our technology will help you build a competitive advantage.* 2 Tennis a score marking a point between deuce and winning the game.
- PHRASES **take advantage of 1** make unfair use

of something for one's own benefit. 2 make good use of the opportunities offered by something.
- ORIGIN Old French *avantage.*

advantageous /ad-vuhn-**tay**-juhss/ adjective good or useful in a particular situation.
- DERIVATIVES **advantageously** adverb.

advent /**ad**-vent/ noun 1 the arrival of an important person or thing: *the days before the advent of air conditioning.* 2 (**Advent**) (in Christian belief) the coming or second coming of Jesus. 3 (**Advent**) the first season of the Church year, leading up to Christmas.
- ORIGIN Latin *adventus* 'arrival'.

Adventist noun a member of a Christian sect which believes that the second coming of Jesus is about to happen.
- DERIVATIVES **Adventism** noun.

adventitious /ad-vuhn-ti-**shuhss**/ adjective 1 happening by chance. 2 (of roots) growing directly from the stem or other upper part of a plant.
- ORIGIN Latin *adventicius* 'coming to us from abroad'.

adventure noun 1 an unusual, exciting, and daring experience. 2 excitement arising from danger or risk: *she travelled the world in search of adventure.*
- DERIVATIVES **adventuresome** adjective.
- ORIGIN from Latin *adventurus* 'about to happen'.

adventurer noun (fem. **adventuress**) 1 a person willing to take risks or use dishonest methods to gain wealth or power: *a political adventurer.* 2 a person who enjoys or looks for adventure.

adventurism noun willingness to take risks in business or politics.
- DERIVATIVES **adventurist** noun & adjective.

adventurous adjective open to or involving new or daring methods or experiences: *an adventurous cook.*
- DERIVATIVES **adventurously** adverb **adventurousness** noun.

adverb noun a word or phrase that gives more information about an adjective, verb, other adverb, or a sentence (e.g. *gently, very, fortunately*).
- DERIVATIVES **adverbial** adjective & noun.
- ORIGIN Latin *adverbium.*

adversarial /ad-ver-**sair**-i-uhl/ adjective involving conflict or opposition: *the media's adversarial attitude toward the military.*

adversary /**ad**-ver-suh-ri/ noun (pl. **adversaries**) an opponent in a contest, dispute, or conflict.
- ORIGIN Latin *adversarius* 'opposed, opponent'.

adverse /**ad**-verss/ adjective preventing success or progress; harmful or unfavourable.
- DERIVATIVES **adversely** adverb.
- ORIGIN Latin *adversus* 'against, opposite'.

USAGE: Do not confuse **adverse** with **averse**. **Adverse** means 'harmful' or 'unfavourable' (*adverse publicity*), whereas **averse** means 'strongly disliking' or 'opposed' (*I am not averse to helping out*).

adversity noun (pl. **adversities**) a difficult or unpleasant situation.

advert[1] /**ad**-vert/ noun Brit. informal an advertisement.

a

advert² /uhd-**vert**/ verb (**advert to**) formal refer to something.
– ORIGIN Latin *advertere* 'turn to'.

advertise verb **1** present or describe a product, service, or event in the media so as to promote sales. **2** publicize information about a job vacancy. **3** make a quality or fact known: *she coughed to advertise her presence.*
– DERIVATIVES **advertiser** noun **advertising** noun.
– ORIGIN from Latin *advertere* 'turn to'.

advertisement noun a notice or display advertising something.

advertorial /ad-ver-**tor**-i-uhl/ noun an advertisement in the style of an editorial or objective journalistic article.

advice noun **1** guidance or recommendations about what someone should do. **2** a formal notice of a financial transaction.
– ORIGIN Old French *avis*.

> **USAGE:** Do not confuse **advice** with **advise**. **Advice** means 'recommendations about what someone should do' (*your doctor can give you advice on diet*), whereas **advise** means 'recommend that someone should do something' (*I advised him to leave*).

advisable adjective to be recommended; sensible: *it's advisable to book in advance.*
– DERIVATIVES **advisability** noun.

advise verb **1** recommend that someone should do something; offer advice: *I advised him to go home.* **2** inform someone formally about a fact or situation.
– DERIVATIVES **adviser** (also **advisor**) noun.
– ORIGIN Old French *aviser*.

> **USAGE:** On the confusion of **advise** and **advice**, see the note at **ADVICE**.

advised adjective behaving as someone would recommend; sensible.
– DERIVATIVES **advisedly** adverb.

advisory adjective having the power to make recommendations but not to ensure that they are carried out.

advocaat /ad-vuh-**kah**/ noun a liqueur made with eggs, sugar, and brandy.
– ORIGIN Dutch, 'advocate'.

advocate noun /ad-vuh-**kuht**/ **1** a person who publicly supports or recommends a particular cause or policy: *he was an untiring advocate of reform.* **2** a person who pleads a case on someone else's behalf. **3** Scottish term for **BARRISTER**. •verb /ad-vuh-**kayt**/ publicly recommend or support something.
– DERIVATIVES **advocacy** noun.
– ORIGIN Latin *advocare* 'call (to one's aid)'.

adze (US **adz**) noun a tool similar to an axe, with an arched blade at right angles to the handle.
– ORIGIN Old English.

Aegean /i-**jee**-uhn/ adjective relating to the region of the **Aegean Sea**, between Greece and Turkey.

aegis /**ee**-jiss/ noun the protection, backing, or support of someone: *the negotiations were conducted under the aegis of the UN.*
– ORIGIN Greek *aigis* 'shield of Zeus'.

aeolian harp /ee-**oh**-li-uhn/ noun a stringed instrument that produces musical sounds when a current of air passes through it.
– ORIGIN from *Aeolus*, the Greek god of the winds.

aeon /**ee**-on/ (US or technical also **eon**) noun **1** an indefinite and very long period of time: *they'd left aeons ago.* **2** a major division of geological time, subdivided into eras.
– ORIGIN Greek *aiōn* 'age'.

aerate /**air**-ayt/ verb introduce air into something.
– DERIVATIVES **aeration** noun **aerator** noun.
– ORIGIN from Latin *aer* 'air'.

aerated adjective **1** (of a liquid) made fizzy by being charged with carbon dioxide. **2** Brit. informal agitated, angry, or overexcited.

aerial noun a structure that sends or receives radio or television signals. •adjective **1** existing or taking place in the air. **2** involving the use of aircraft.
– ORIGIN from Greek *aēr* 'air'.

aerialist noun a person who performs acrobatics on a tightrope or trapezes.

aerie noun US spelling of **EYRIE**.

aero- /**air**-oh/ combining form **1** relating to air: *aerobic.* **2** relating to aircraft: *aerodrome.*
– ORIGIN from Greek *aēr* 'air'.

aerobatics plural noun (treated as sing. or pl.) skilful and exciting movements performed in an aircraft for entertainment.
– DERIVATIVES **aerobatic** adjective.

aerobic /air-**oh**-bik/ adjective **1** relating to physical exercise intended to improve the intake of oxygen and its movement around the body. **2** Biology using oxygen from the air: *aerobic bacteria.*
– DERIVATIVES **aerobically** adverb.
– ORIGIN from **AERO-** + Greek *bios* 'life'.

aerobics plural noun (treated as sing. or pl.) aerobic exercises.

aerodrome noun Brit. a small airport or airfield.

aerodynamic adjective **1** relating to aerodynamics. **2** (of an object) having a shape which reduces the drag from air moving past.
– DERIVATIVES **aerodynamically** adverb.

aerodynamics plural noun **1** (treated as sing.) the branch of science concerned with the movement of solid bodies through the air. **2** (treated as pl.) the aspects of an object which make it aerodynamic.
– DERIVATIVES **aerodynamicist** noun.

aerofoil noun Brit. a curved structure, such as a wing, designed to give an aircraft lift in flight.

aerogramme (US **aerogram**) noun another term for **AIR LETTER**.

aeronautics plural noun (usu. treated as sing.) the study or practice of travel through the air.
– DERIVATIVES **aeronautic** adjective **aeronautical** adjective.
– ORIGIN from Greek *aēr* 'air' + *nautēs* 'sailor'.

aeroplane noun Brit. a fixed-wing powered flying vehicle that is heavier than the air.
– ORIGIN from French *aéro-* 'air' + Greek *-planos* 'wandering'.

aerosol noun a substance sealed in a container under pressure and released as a fine spray.
– ORIGIN from **AERO-** + **SOL²**.

aerospace noun the branch of technology and industry concerned with aviation and space flight.

aesthete /**eess**-theet/ (US also **esthete**) noun a person who is appreciative of art and beauty.

aesthetic /eess-**thet**-ik/ (US also **esthetic**) adjective **1** concerned with beauty or the appreciation of beauty. **2** having a pleasant appearance. •**noun** a set of principles underlying the work of a particular artist or artistic movement.
– DERIVATIVES **aesthetically** adverb **aestheticism** noun.
– ORIGIN from Greek *aisthesthai* 'perceive'.

aesthetics (US also **esthetics**) plural noun (usu. treated as sing.) **1** a set of principles concerned with the nature of beauty, especially in art. **2** the branch of philosophy which deals with questions of beauty and artistic taste.

aether noun variant spelling of ETHER (in senses 3 and 4).

aetiology /ee-ti-**ol**-uh-ji/ (US **etiology**) noun **1** Medicine the cause of a disease or condition. **2** the investigation of a cause or a reason.
– DERIVATIVES **aetiological** adjective.
– ORIGIN from Greek *aitia* 'a cause'.

afar adverb literary at or to a distance.

AFC abbreviation Association Football Club.

affable adjective good-natured and sociable.
– DERIVATIVES **affability** noun **affably** adverb.
– ORIGIN Latin *affabilis*.

affair noun **1** an event of a specified kind or that has previously been referred to: *I want the wedding to be a family affair.* **2** a matter that a person is responsible for. **3** a love affair. **4** (**affairs**) matters of public interest. **5** (**affairs**) business and financial dealings.
– ORIGIN from Old French *à faire* 'to do'.

affect¹ verb **1** make a difference to: *the damp has affected my health.* **2** move someone emotionally.
– DERIVATIVES **affecting** adjective.
– ORIGIN Latin *afficere*.

> USAGE: Affect and effect are often confused. Affect is a verb meaning 'make a difference to' (*the damp has affected my health*). Effect is used both as a noun meaning 'a result' (*the substance has a painkilling effect*) and as a verb meaning 'bring about a result' (*I effected a cost-cutting exercise*).

affect² verb **1** pretend to have or feel something. **2** use or wear in an artificial way or so as to impress: *he'd affected a British accent.*
– ORIGIN Latin *affectare* 'aim at'.

affectation /af-fek-**tay**-sh'n/ noun behaviour, speech, or writing that is artificial and designed to impress.

affected adjective artificial and designed to impress.
– DERIVATIVES **affectedly** adverb.

affection noun a feeling of fondness or liking.

affectionate adjective readily showing affection.
– DERIVATIVES **affectionately** adverb.

affective adjective Psychology relating to moods, feelings, and attitudes.

affiance /uh-**fy**-uhnss/ verb (**be affianced**) literary be engaged to marry.
– ORIGIN Old French *afiancer*.

affidavit /af-fi-**day**-vit/ noun Law a written statement for use as evidence in court, sworn on oath to be true.

– ORIGIN Latin, 'he has stated on oath'.

affiliate verb /uh-**fil**-i-ayt/ officially link a person or group to an organization. •**noun** /uh-**fil**-i-uht/ a person or group linked to a larger organization.
– DERIVATIVES **affiliation** noun.
– ORIGIN Latin *affiliare* 'adopt as a son'.

affinity noun (pl. **affinities**) **1** a natural liking or sympathy for someone or something. **2** close similarity in structure, qualities, or origin: *there is a stylistic affinity between the mosaics.* **3** the tendency of a substance to combine with another.
– ORIGIN from Latin *affinis* 'related'.

affirm verb state something firmly or publicly.
– DERIVATIVES **affirmation** noun.
– ORIGIN Latin *affirmare*.

affirmative adjective agreeing with a statement or to a request: *an affirmative answer.* •**noun** a statement or word indicating agreement. •**exclamation** chiefly N. Amer. yes.
– DERIVATIVES **affirmatively** adverb.

affirmative action noun chiefly N. Amer. action favouring those people who are often discriminated against.

affix verb /uh-**fiks**/ attach or fasten something to something else. •**noun** /**af**-fiks/ Grammar a letter or letters added to a word in order to alter its meaning or create a new word.
– DERIVATIVES **affixation** noun.
– ORIGIN Latin *affixare*.

afflict verb cause pain or trouble to: *the problems that afflict inner-city communities.*
– DERIVATIVES **affliction** noun.
– ORIGIN from Latin *affligere* 'knock down, weaken'.

affluent adjective having a great deal of money; wealthy.
– DERIVATIVES **affluence** noun.
– ORIGIN from Latin *affluere* 'flow freely'.

afford verb **1** (**can/could afford**) have enough money, time, or other resources for something. **2** provide or supply: *the rooftop terrace affords beautiful views.*
– ORIGIN Old English, 'promote, perform'.

affordable adjective reasonably priced; not expensive.
– DERIVATIVES **affordability** noun **affordably** adverb.

afforestation /uh-for-ris-**tay**-sh'n/ noun the process of planting trees on an area of land in order to form a forest.

affray noun Law, dated a breach of the peace by fighting in a public place.
– ORIGIN from Old French *afrayer* 'disturb, startle'.

affront noun an action or remark that causes offence. •**verb** offend or insult: *she was affronted by his familiarity.*
– ORIGIN from Old French *afronter* 'to slap in the face, insult'.

Afghan /**af**-gan/ noun a person from Afghanistan. •**adjective** relating to Afghanistan.
– ORIGIN Pashto.

Afghan coat noun Brit. a kind of sheepskin coat with the skin outside.

Afghan hound noun a silky-haired breed of dog used for hunting.

a

afghani /af-**gah**-ni/ noun (pl. **afghanis**) the basic monetary unit of Afghanistan.
– ORIGIN Pashto.

aficionado /uh-fi-shuh-**nah**-doh/ noun (pl. **aficionados**) a person who is very knowledgeable and enthusiastic about an activity or subject.
– ORIGIN Spanish, 'amateur'.

afield adverb to or at a distance.

aflame adjective in flames.

afloat adjective & adverb **1** floating in water. **2** on board a ship or boat. **3** out of debt or difficulty: *he takes odd jobs to keep afloat.*

aflutter adjective in a state of agitated excitement.

afoot adverb & adjective **1** happening or in preparation: *plans are afoot for a festival.* **2** chiefly N. Amer. on foot.

afore preposition old use or dialect before.

afore- prefix before; previously: *aforementioned.*

aforementioned adjective referring to a thing or person previously mentioned.

a fortiori /ay for-ti-**or**-ry/ adverb for an even stronger reason.
– ORIGIN from Latin *a fortiori argumento* 'from stronger argument'.

afoul adverb (in phrase **run/fall afoul of**) N. Amer. come into conflict or difficulty with: *he ran afoul of the boss and resigned.*

afraid adjective feeling fear or anxiety.
– PHRASES **I'm afraid** expressing polite regret.
– ORIGIN from Old French *afrayer* 'disturb, startle'.

afresh adverb in a new or different way.

African noun **1** a person from Africa, especially a black person. **2** a person descended from black African people. ● adjective relating to Africa or Africans.
– DERIVATIVES **Africanize** (or **Africanise**) verb.

African American chiefly US noun an American of African origin. ● adjective relating to African Americans.

African violet noun a small East African plant with velvety leaves and violet, pink, or white flowers.

Afrikaans /af-ri-**kahns**/ noun a language derived from Dutch, one of the official languages of South Africa.
– ORIGIN Dutch, 'African'.

Afrikaner /af-ri-**kah**-ner/ noun an Afrikaans-speaking white person in South Africa.
– DERIVATIVES **Afrikanerdom** noun.

Afro noun (pl. **Afros**) a hairstyle consisting of a mass of very tight curls all round the head.

Afro- combining form African: *Afro-American.*

Afro-American adjective & noun chiefly US another term for AFRICAN AMERICAN.

Afro-Caribbean noun a person descended from African people who lives in or comes from the Caribbean. ● adjective relating to Afro-Caribbeans.

aft /ahft/ adverb & adjective at, near, or towards the stern of a ship or tail of an aircraft.
– ORIGIN probably related to ABAFT.

after preposition **1** in the time following an event or another period of time. **2** next to and following something in order or importance. **3** behind someone. **4** so as to have, get, or find:

most of them are after money. **5** in reference to: *he was named after his grandfather.* ● **conjunction & adverb** in the time following an event. ● adjective nearer the stern of a ship.
– PHRASES **after all** in spite of any suggestion otherwise. **after hours** after normal working or opening hours.
– ORIGIN Old English.

afterbirth noun the placenta and other material that is discharged from the womb after a birth.

afterburner noun an auxiliary burner in the exhaust of a jet engine.

aftercare noun care of a person after a stay in hospital or on release from prison.

after-effect noun an effect that follows some time after its cause.

afterglow noun **1** light remaining in the sky after the sun has set. **2** good feelings remaining after a pleasant experience: *basking in the afterglow of victory.*

afterlife noun (in some religions) life after death.

aftermath noun the results of an unpleasant or important event: *prices soared in the aftermath of the drought.*
– ORIGIN from AFTER + dialect *math* 'mowing'.

afternoon noun the time from noon or lunchtime to evening.

afters plural noun Brit. informal the dessert course of a meal.

aftershave noun a scented lotion for putting on a man's face after shaving.

aftershock noun a smaller earthquake following the main shock of a large earthquake.

aftersun adjective (of a lotion) put on the skin after sunbathing.

aftertaste noun a strong or unpleasant taste lingering in the mouth after eating or drinking.

afterthought noun something thought of or added later.

afterwards (US also **afterward**) adverb at a later or future time.

afterword noun a section at the end of a book.

afterworld noun a world that a person enters after death.

Ag symbol the chemical element silver.
– ORIGIN from Latin *argentum.*

again /uh-**gen**, uh-**gayn**/ adverb **1** once more. **2** returning to a previous position or condition: *he closed the locker and sat down again.* **3** in addition to what has already been mentioned.
– ORIGIN Old English.

against preposition **1** opposing or disagreeing with. **2** close to or touching. **3** so as to anticipate and prepare for a difficulty. **4** as protection from: *I turned up my collar against the wind.* **5** in contrast to: *the benefits must be weighed against the costs.* **6** so as to reduce, cancel, or secure money owed, due, or lent. **7** (in betting) in anticipation of the failure of: *the odds were 5–1 against England.*
– PHRASES **have something against someone** dislike or bear a grudge against someone.

agape adjective (of a person's mouth) wide open.

agar /ay-gar/ (also **agar-agar** /ay-gar-ay-gar/) noun a jelly-like substance obtained from seaweed, used as a thickener in foods and in biological cultures.
– ORIGIN Malay.

agaric /ag-uh-rik/ noun a fungus with gills on the underside of the cap, e.g. a mushroom.
– ORIGIN Greek *agarikon* 'tree fungus'.

agate /ag-uht/ noun a semi-precious variety of quartz with a striped appearance.
– ORIGIN Greek *akhatēs*.

agave /uh-gay-vi, uh-gah-vi/ noun an American plant with narrow spiny leaves and tall flower stems.
– ORIGIN from Greek *Agauē*, one of the daughters of Cadmus in Greek mythology.

age noun **1** the length of time that a person or thing has existed. **2** a particular stage in someone's life: *children of primary school age.* **3** old age. **4** a distinct period of history: *the Elizabethan age.* •verb (**ages**, **ageing** or **aging**, **aged**) **1** grow or cause to appear old or older: *some foods may protect your eyes as you age.* **2** (of an alcoholic drink, cheese, etc.) mature.
– PHRASES **come of age** be legally recognized as an adult (in UK law at 18).
– DERIVATIVES **ageing** noun & adjective.
– ORIGIN from Latin *aevum*.

aged adjective **1** /ayjd/ of a specified age: *he died aged 60.* **2** /ay-jid/ having lived or existed for a long time; old.

ageism noun prejudice or discrimination on the grounds of a person's age.
– DERIVATIVES **ageist** adjective & noun.

ageless adjective not ageing or appearing to age.

agency noun **1** an organization or government department providing a particular service: *an advertising agency.* **2** action or intervention producing a result: *channels carved by the agency of running water.*

agenda noun **1** a list of items to be discussed at a meeting. **2** a list of matters to be dealt with.
– ORIGIN Latin, 'things to be done'.

agent noun **1** a person who provides a service, typically by organizing dealings between two other parties: *a travel agent.* **2** a spy. **3** a person or thing that takes an active role or produces a particular effect: *bleaching agents.*
– ORIGIN from Latin *agere* 'to do'.

agent noun noun a noun which refers to a person or thing that performs the action of a verb, usually ending in *-er* or *-or*, e.g. *worker, accelerator.*

agent provocateur /a-zhon pruh-vo-kuh-ter/ noun (pl. **agents provocateurs** pronunc. same) a person employed to tempt others to break the law and therefore be convicted.
– ORIGIN French, 'provocative agent'.

age of consent noun the age at which a person's consent to sexual intercourse is legally valid.

age-old adjective very old.

agglomerate verb /uh-glom-uh-rayt/ collect or form into a mass. •noun /uh-glom-uh-ruht/ a mass or collection of things.
– DERIVATIVES **agglomeration** noun.
– ORIGIN Latin *agglomerare* 'add to'.

agglutinate /uh-gloo-ti-nayt/ verb firmly stick together to form a mass.
– DERIVATIVES **agglutination** noun.
– ORIGIN Latin *agglutinare* 'cause to adhere'.

aggrandize (or **aggrandise**) /uh-gran-dyz/ verb increase the power or importance of: *the description 'subediting' aggrandizes the nature of my task.*
– DERIVATIVES **aggrandizement** noun.
– ORIGIN French *agrandir*, from Latin *grandis* 'large'.

aggravate verb **1** make worse: *military action would only aggravate the situation.* **2** informal annoy someone.
– DERIVATIVES **aggravating** adjective **aggravation** noun.
– ORIGIN Latin *aggravare* 'make heavy'.

USAGE: Some people think that it is incorrect to use **aggravate** to mean 'annoy someone'. However, this sense dates back to the 17th century and is widely used in modern English.

aggravated adjective Law (of an offence) made more serious by related circumstances.

aggregate noun /ag-gri-guht/ a whole formed by combining several different elements: *the council is an aggregate of three regional assemblies.* •verb /ag-gri-gayt/ combine into a whole. •adjective /ag-gri-guht/ formed or calculated by combining many separate items.
– DERIVATIVES **aggregation** noun.
– ORIGIN from Latin *aggregare* 'herd together'.

aggression noun hostile or violent behaviour or attitudes: *a link between extensive TV viewing and aggression in children.*
– ORIGIN from Latin *aggredi* 'to attack'.

aggressive adjective **1** very hostile or angry. **2** determined and forceful: *an aggressive campaign to reduce energy use.*
– DERIVATIVES **aggressively** adverb **aggressiveness** noun.

aggressor noun a person or country that attacks without being provoked.

aggrieved adjective resentful because of unfair treatment.
– ORIGIN from Latin *aggravare* (see **AGGRAVATE**).

aggro noun Brit. informal aggressive, violent behaviour.

aghast /uh-gahst/ adjective filled with horror or shock: *he looked aghast at the blood on his blazer.*
– ORIGIN from former *gast* 'frighten'.

agile /a-jyl/ adjective **1** able to move quickly and easily. **2** quick-witted or shrewd.
– DERIVATIVES **agilely** adverb **agility** noun.
– ORIGIN Latin *agilis*.

agitate verb **1** make someone troubled or nervous. **2** campaign to arouse public concern about something: *they have begun to agitate for better living conditions.* **3** stir or disturb a liquid briskly.
– ORIGIN Latin *agitare* 'agitate, drive'.

agitation noun **1** a state of anxiety or nervous excitement. **2** the action of agitating to arouse concern about something.

agitator noun a person who urges others to protest or rebel.

agitprop /aj-it-prop/ noun political propaganda, especially in the arts.

a

– ORIGIN Russian.

aglet /ag-luht/ noun a metal or plastic tube fixed round each end of a shoelace.
– ORIGIN French *aiguillette* 'small needle'.

aglow adjective glowing.

AGM abbreviation Brit. annual general meeting.

agnostic /ag-noss-tik/ noun a person who believes that one cannot know whether or not God exists.
– DERIVATIVES **agnosticism** noun.

ago adverb before the present (used with a measurement of time).
– ORIGIN from the former verb *ago* 'to pass'.

> USAGE: When **ago** is followed by a clause, you should use **that** rather than **since**, e.g. *it was ten years ago that I left home* (not *it was ten years ago since I left home*).

agog adjective very eager to hear or see something: *I was agog with curiosity.*
– ORIGIN from Old French *en* 'in' + *gogue* 'fun'.

agonize (or **agonise**) verb **1** worry greatly: *I didn't agonize over the problem.* **2** (often as adj. **agonizing**) cause great pain to: *an agonizing death.*

agony noun (pl. **agonies**) great pain or distress.
– ORIGIN Greek *agōnia*.

agony aunt (or **agony uncle**) noun Brit. informal a person who offers advice in an agony column.

agony column noun Brit. informal a column in a newspaper or magazine offering advice on readers' personal problems.

agora /ag-uh-rah/ noun (pl. **agorot** or **agoroth** /ag-uh-roht, ag-uh-rohth/) a unit of money of Israel, equal to one hundredth of a shekel.
– ORIGIN Hebrew, 'small coin'.

agoraphobia /ag-uh-ruh-foh-bi-uh/ noun irrational fear of open or public places.
– DERIVATIVES **agoraphobic** adjective & noun.
– ORIGIN from Greek *agora* 'marketplace'.

agrarian /uh-grair-i-uhn/ adjective relating to agriculture.
– ORIGIN from Latin *ager* 'field'.

agree verb (**agrees**, **agreeing**, **agreed**) **1** have the same opinion as another person or people. **2** (**agree to/to do**) be willing to do something suggested by another person. **3** (of two or more people) decide on something. **4** (**agree with**) be consistent with: *your body language doesn't agree with what you're saying.* **5** (**agree with**) be good for: *he ate something which didn't agree with him.*
– ORIGIN Old French *agreer*.

agreeable adjective **1** enjoyable or pleasant. **2** willing to agree to something. **3** able to be agreed on; acceptable: *a compromise which is agreeable to both employers and unions.*
– DERIVATIVES **agreeableness** noun **agreeably** adverb.

agreement noun **1** the act of agreeing or the state of being agreed: *we failed to reach agreement.* **2** an arrangement or contract agreed between people, typically one that is legally binding.

agribusiness noun **1** agriculture run on strictly commercial principles. **2** the group of industries concerned with agricultural produce and services.

agriculture noun the science or practice of farming, including the rearing of crops and animals.
– DERIVATIVES **agricultural** adjective **agriculturalist** noun **agriculturally** adverb **agriculturist** noun.
– ORIGIN from Latin *ager* 'field' + *cultura* 'cultivation'.

agrimony /ag-rim-uh-ni/ noun a plant with slender stalks of yellow flowers.
– ORIGIN Greek *argemōnē* 'poppy'.

agrochemical noun a chemical used in agriculture.

agronomy /uh-gron-uh-mi/ noun the science of soil management and crop production.
– DERIVATIVES **agronomic** adjective **agronomist** noun.
– ORIGIN from Greek *agros* 'field' + *-nomos* 'arranging'.

aground adjective & adverb (with reference to a ship) on or on to the bottom in shallow water.

ague /ay-gyoo/ noun old use malaria or another illness involving fever and shivering.
– ORIGIN from Latin *acuta febris* 'acute fever'.

ahead adverb **1** further forward in space or time: *we should plan ahead.* **2** in the lead.
– PHRASES **ahead of 1** in front of; before. **2** earlier than.

ahistorical /ay-hi-sto-ri-k'l/ adjective lacking historical perspective; not historical.

ahoy exclamation Nautical a call to attract attention.

AI abbreviation artificial intelligence.

aid noun **1** help or support. **2** money or resources given to help a country in need.
• verb help or support: *women, aided by their children, cleaned the fish.*
– PHRASES **in aid of** chiefly Brit. in support of.
– ORIGIN from Latin *juvare* 'help'.

aide /ayd/ noun an assistant to a political leader.

aide-de-camp /ayd-duh-kom/ noun (pl. **aides-de-camp** pronunc. same) a military officer acting as a personal assistant to a senior officer.
– ORIGIN French.

aide-memoire /ayd-mem-wah/ noun (pl. **aides-memoires** or **aides-memoire** pronunc. same) **1** a note or book used to help one remember something. **2** an informal diplomatic message.
– ORIGIN French.

Aids noun a disease, caused by the HIV virus and transmitted in body fluids, in which the sufferer's natural defences against infection are destroyed.
– ORIGIN from the initial letters of *acquired immune deficiency syndrome.*

aikido /I-kee-doh/ noun a Japanese martial art that uses locks, holds, throws, and the opponent's own movements.
– ORIGIN Japanese, 'way of adapting the spirit'.

ail verb old use cause suffering or trouble to someone.
– ORIGIN Old English.

aileron /ayl-uh-ron/ noun a hinged part on the back of an aircraft's wing, used to control the balance of the aircraft.
– ORIGIN French, 'small wing'.

ailing adjective in poor health or condition: *the country's ailing economy.*

ailment noun a minor illness.

aim verb **1** point a weapon or camera at a target. **2** direct something at someone or something: *the programme is aimed at a wide audience.* **3** try to achieve something. • noun **1** a purpose or intention. **2** the aiming of a weapon or missile.
– PHRASES **take aim** point a weapon at a target.
– ORIGIN from Latin *aestimare* 'estimate'.
aimless adjective without purpose or direction: *aimless wandering.*
– DERIVATIVES **aimlessly** adverb **aimlessness** noun.
ain't contraction informal **1** am not; are not; is not. **2** has not; have not.

USAGE: **Ain't** is not good English and should not be used when speaking or writing in a formal situation.

aioli /l-oh-li/ noun mayonnaise seasoned with garlic.
– ORIGIN French.
air noun **1** the invisible mixture of gases surrounding the earth, mainly oxygen and nitrogen. **2** the open space above the earth's surface: *I threw the ball up in the air.* **3** the earth's atmosphere as a medium for transmitting radio waves. **4** (**an air of**) an impression of: *there was an air of sadness about her.* **5** (**airs**) an affected and condescending manner. **6** a tune or short song. • adjective using aircraft: *air travel.* • verb **1** express an opinion or complaint publicly. **2** broadcast a programme on radio or television. **3** expose a room or washed laundry to fresh or warm air.
– PHRASES **airs and graces** Brit. affected behaviour that is intended to impress. **on** (or **off**) **the air** being (or not being) broadcast on radio or television. **up in the air** (of an issue) still to be settled. **walk on air** feel very happy or pleased.
– DERIVATIVES **airless** adjective.
– ORIGIN Greek *aēr.*
airbag noun a safety device that inflates rapidly when there is a sudden impact, so protecting a vehicle's occupants in a collision.
airbase noun a base for military aircraft.
air bed noun Brit. an inflatable mattress.
airborne adjective **1** carried through the air. **2** (of an aircraft) flying.
air brake noun a vehicle brake worked by air pressure.
airbrick noun Brit. a brick perforated with small holes, used to ventilate a building.
airbrush noun an artist's device for spraying paint by means of compressed air. • verb **1** paint a picture or alter a photograph with an airbrush. **2** alter or remove undesirable elements or people to present an improved version of reality: *the failures are airbrushed from history.*
air chief marshal noun a high rank of RAF officer, above air marshal and below Marshal of the RAF.
air commodore noun a rank of RAF officer, above group captain and below air vice-marshal.
air conditioning noun a system for controlling the humidity, ventilation, and temperature in a building or vehicle.
– DERIVATIVES **air-conditioned** adjective **air conditioner** noun.

air corridor noun a route over a foreign country which aircraft must take.
aircraft noun (pl. same) an aeroplane, helicopter, or other machine capable of flight.
aircraft carrier noun a large warship from which aircraft can take off and land.
aircraftman (or **aircraftwoman**) noun (pl. **aircraftmen** or **aircraftwomen**) the lowest rank in the RAF, below leading aircraftman (or leading aircraftwoman).
aircrew noun (pl. **aircrews**) (treated as sing. or pl.) the crew of an aircraft.
air cushion noun the layer of air supporting a hovercraft or similar vehicle.
airdrop noun an act of dropping supplies, troops, or equipment by parachute.
Airedale noun a large rough-coated black-and-tan breed of terrier.
– ORIGIN from *Airedale,* a district in Yorkshire.
airer noun Brit. a frame or stand for airing or drying laundry.
airfare noun the price to be paid by an aircraft passenger for a journey.
airfield noun an area of land set aside for the take-off, landing, and maintenance of aircraft.
air force noun a branch of the armed forces concerned with fighting or defence in the air.
airframe noun the body of an aircraft as distinct from its engine.
airfreight noun the carriage of goods by aircraft.
air freshener noun a scented substance or device for disguising unpleasant smells in a room.
air gun noun **1** a gun which uses compressed air to fire pellets. **2** a tool using very hot air to strip paint.
airhead noun informal a stupid person.
air hostess noun Brit. a stewardess in a passenger aircraft.
airing noun **1** an act of exposing laundry or a place to warm or fresh air. **2** a public expression of an opinion or discussion of a subject.
air kiss noun a kiss close to a person's face, but without making contact.
air letter noun a sheet of light paper folded and sealed to form a letter for sending by airmail.
airlift noun an act of transporting supplies by aircraft, typically in an emergency.
airline noun **1** an organization providing a regular passenger air service. **2** (**air line**) a pipe supplying air.
airliner noun a large passenger aircraft.
airlock noun **1** a stoppage of the flow in a pump or pipe, caused by an air bubble. **2** a compartment with controlled pressure and airtight doors at each end, to allow people to move between areas at different pressures.
airmail noun a system of transporting mail overseas by air.
airman (or **airwoman**) noun (pl. **airmen** or **airwomen**) **1** a pilot or member of the crew of an aircraft in an air force. **2** a member of the RAF below commissioned rank.
air marshal noun a high rank of RAF officer,

a

above air vice-marshal and below air chief marshal.

air mile noun **1** a nautical mile used as a measure of distance flown by aircraft. **2 (Air Miles)** trademark points (equivalent to miles of free air travel) collected by buyers of airline tickets and other products.

air pistol (or **air rifle**) noun a gun which uses compressed air to fire pellets.

airplane noun N. Amer. an aeroplane.

air plant noun a tropical American plant that grows on trees, with long narrow leaves that absorb water and nutrients from the atmosphere.

airplay noun broadcasting time devoted to a particular record, performer, or type of music.

air pocket noun **1** a hollow space containing air. **2** a region of low pressure causing an aircraft to lose height suddenly.

airport noun a complex of runways and buildings for the take-off, landing, and maintenance of civil aircraft, with facilities for passengers.

air pump noun a device for pumping air into or out of an enclosed space.

air quality noun the degree to which the air in a place is pollution-free.

air raid noun an attack in which bombs are dropped from aircraft on to a ground target.

air-sea rescue noun a rescue from the sea using aircraft.

airship noun a power-driven aircraft kept aloft by a body of gas (usually helium) which is lighter than air.

airsick adjective feeling sick due to air travel.

airside noun the area beyond passport and customs control in an airport terminal.

airspace noun the part of the air above and subject to the laws of a particular country.

airspeed noun the speed of an aircraft relative to the air through which it is moving.

airstream noun a current of air.

airstrip noun a strip of ground for the take-off and landing of aircraft.

airtight adjective **1** not allowing air to escape or pass through. **2** having no weaknesses: *an airtight alibi.*

airtime noun **1** the time during which a broadcast is being transmitted. **2** the time during which a mobile phone is in use.

air traffic control noun the ground-based staff and equipment concerned with controlling air traffic within a particular area.
– DERIVATIVES **air traffic controller** noun.

air vice-marshal noun a high rank of RAF officer, above air commodore and below air marshal.

airwaves plural noun the radio frequencies used for broadcasting.

airway noun **1** the passage by which air reaches the lungs. **2** a tube for supplying air to the lungs in an emergency. **3** a recognized route followed by aircraft.

airworthy adjective (of an aircraft) safe to fly.
– DERIVATIVES **airworthiness** noun.

airy adjective (**airier**, **airiest**) **1** (of a room or building) spacious and well ventilated. **2** not treating something as important; casual: *her*

airy unconcern for economy.
– DERIVATIVES **airily** adverb **airiness** noun.

airy-fairy adjective informal, chiefly Brit. vague and unrealistic.

aisle /rhymes with mile/ noun **1** a passage between rows of seats in a public building, aircraft, or train. **2** a passage between sets of shelves in a shop.
– DERIVATIVES **aisled** adjective.
– ORIGIN Latin *ala* 'wing'.

aitch noun the letter H.
– PHRASES **drop one's aitches** fail to pronounce the letter *h* at the beginning of words.
– ORIGIN Old French *ache*.

aitchbone noun **1** the buttock or rump bone of cattle. **2** a cut of beef lying over the rump bone.
– ORIGIN from Latin *natis* 'buttock', + BONE.

ajar adverb & adjective (of a door or window) slightly open.
– ORIGIN from Old English, 'a turn'.

AK abbreviation Alaska.

aka abbreviation also known as.

akee noun variant spelling of ACKEE.

akimbo adverb with hands on the hips and elbows turned outwards.
– ORIGIN probably from Old Norse.

akin adjective similar in nature or type: *a road more akin to an army assault course.*
– ORIGIN from *of kin.*

akvavit /ak-vuh-vit/ noun variant spelling of AQUAVIT.

AL abbreviation Alabama.

Al symbol the chemical element aluminium.

à la /ah lah/ preposition in the style or manner of: *a publicity stunt à la Joan Crawford.*
– ORIGIN French.

alabaster /al-uh-bah-ster, al-uh-bass-ter/ noun a white, semi-transparent form of the mineral gypsum, often carved into ornaments.
● adjective literary smooth and white: *pale, alabaster skin.*
– ORIGIN Greek *alabastos, alabastros.*

à la carte /ah lah kart/ adjective (of a menu) listing dishes that can be ordered as separate items, rather than part of a set meal.
– ORIGIN French, 'according to the card'.

alacrity noun brisk eagerness or enthusiasm: *she accepted the invitation with alacrity.*
– ORIGIN from Latin *alacer* 'brisk'.

Aladdin's cave noun a place filled with a great number of interesting or precious items.
– ORIGIN from the story of *Aladdin* in the *Arabian Nights' Entertainments.*

à la mode /ah lah mohd/ adverb & adjective up to date; fashionable.
– ORIGIN French.

alarm noun **1** anxious or frightened awareness of danger. **2** a warning of danger: *I hammered on the door to raise the alarm.* **3** a warning sound or device. ● verb **1** frighten or disturb someone or something. **2** (**be alarmed**) be fitted or protected with an alarm.
– ORIGIN from Italian *all' arme!* 'to arms!'

alarm clock noun a clock that can be set to sound an alarm at a particular time, used to wake someone up.

alarmist noun a person who exaggerates a danger, so causing needless alarm. ● adjective

creating needless alarm.
– DERIVATIVES **alarmism** noun.

alas exclamation literary or humorous an expression of grief, pity, or regret: *I, alas, am dieting.*
– ORIGIN Old French *a las*, from Latin *lassus* 'weary'.

alb noun a long white robe worn by clergy and servers in some Christian Churches.
– ORIGIN from Latin *tunica alba* 'white garment'.

albacore /al-buh-kor/ noun a tuna of warm seas which is an important food fish.
– ORIGIN Arabic.

Albanian noun 1 a person from Albania. 2 the language of Albania. • adjective relating to Albania.

albatross noun (pl. **albatrosses**) 1 a very large seabird with long narrow wings, found chiefly in the southern oceans. 2 a burden: *the radioactive albatross around the nuclear power industry's neck.* [referring to Coleridge's *The Rime of the Ancient Mariner.*]
– ORIGIN Arabic, 'the diver'.

albeit /awl-**bee**-it/ conjunction though: *I got up, albeit rather groggily.*
– ORIGIN from *all be it.*

albino /al-**bee**-noh/ noun (pl. **albinos**) a person or animal born without pigment in the skin and hair (which are white) and the eyes (which are usually pink).
– DERIVATIVES **albinism** /al-bi-ni-z'm/ noun.
– ORIGIN from Latin *albus* 'white'.

Albion noun literary Britain or England.
– ORIGIN Latin.

album noun 1 a blank book in which photographs, stamps, or other items can be kept. 2 a collection of musical recordings issued as a single item.
– ORIGIN Latin, 'blank tablet'.

albumen /al-byuu-muhn/ noun egg white, or the protein contained in it.
– ORIGIN from Latin *albus* 'white'.

albumin /al-byuu-min/ noun a form of protein that is soluble in water and is found especially in blood serum and egg white.

alchemy /al-kuh-mi/ noun 1 the medieval forerunner of chemistry, concerned particularly with attempts to convert common metals into gold. 2 a seemingly magical or mysterious process: *watching the great chef create culinary alchemy.*
– DERIVATIVES **alchemical** adjective **alchemist** noun.
– ORIGIN from Greek *khēmia, khēmeia* 'art of transmuting metals'.

alcohol noun 1 a colourless volatile liquid which is the intoxicating ingredient in drinks such as wine, beer, and spirits. 2 drink containing alcohol. 3 Chemistry any organic compound containing a hydroxyl group –OH: *propyl alcohol.*
– ORIGIN Arabic, 'the kohl'.

alcoholic adjective 1 relating to alcohol. 2 affected by alcoholism. • noun a person affected by alcoholism.

alcoholism noun addiction to alcoholic drink.

alcopop noun Brit. informal an alcoholic drink similar to a sweet soft drink.

alcove noun a recess in the wall of a room.
– ORIGIN Arabic, 'the vault'.

aldehyde /al-di-hyd/ noun Chemistry an organic compound formed by the oxidation of an alcohol.
– ORIGIN from Latin *alcohol dehydrogenatum* 'alcohol deprived of hydrogen'.

al dente /al den-tay/ adjective & adverb (of food) cooked so as to be still firm when bitten.
– ORIGIN Italian, 'to the tooth'.

alder noun a tree of the birch family, which bears catkins and has toothed leaves.
– ORIGIN Old English.

alderman noun (pl. **aldermen**) 1 historical a member of an English county or borough council, next in status to the Mayor. 2 (or **alderwoman**) N. Amer. & Austral. an elected member of a city council.
– ORIGIN Old English, 'chief, patriarch'.

ale noun chiefly Brit. beer other than lager, stout, or porter.
– ORIGIN Old English.

aleatory /ay-lee-uh-tri/ (also **aleatoric**) adjective depending on the throw of a dice or on chance.
– ORIGIN from Latin *aleator* 'dice player'.

alehouse noun dated an inn or pub.

alembic /uh-**lem**-bik/ noun a container with a long, downward-sloping spout leading from the top, formerly used in distilling.
– ORIGIN from Greek *ambix* 'cup'.

alert adjective 1 quick to notice and respond to danger or possible problems: *be alert to early signs of stress.* 2 quick-thinking; intelligent.
• noun 1 the state of being watchful for danger or possible problems: *we should be on the alert for terrorists.* 2 a warning of danger. • verb warn someone about a danger or problem.
– DERIVATIVES **alertly** adverb **alertness** noun.
– ORIGIN from Italian *all' erta* 'to the watchtower'.

A level noun (in the UK except Scotland) the higher of the two main levels of the GCE exam.
– ORIGIN abbreviation of ADVANCED LEVEL.

Alexander technique noun a system designed to promote well-being through retraining one's habits of posture.
– ORIGIN named after the Australian-born actor Frederick Matthias *Alexander.*

alexandrine /a-lig-**zahn**-dryn/ adjective (of a line of verse) having six iambic feet. • noun an alexandrine line.
– ORIGIN French, from Alexander the Great, the subject of an Old French poem in alexandrines.

alfalfa /al-**fal**-fuh/ noun a plant with clover-like leaves and bluish flowers, grown in warm climates for fodder.
– ORIGIN Arabic, 'green fodder'.

alfresco /al-**fress**-koh/ adverb & adjective in the open air: *an alfresco meal.*
– ORIGIN Italian *al fresco.*

alga /al-guh/ noun (pl. **algae** /al-jee, al-gee/) a simple plant of a large group that contain chlorophyll but lack true stems, roots, and leaves, e.g. seaweed.
– DERIVATIVES **algal** adjective.
– ORIGIN Latin, 'seaweed'.

algebra /al-ji-bruh/ noun the branch of mathematics in which letters and other

a

symbols are used to represent numbers and quantities.

- DERIVATIVES **algebraic** /al-ji-**bray**-ik/ adjective **algebraist** noun.
- ORIGIN Arabic, 'the reunion of broken parts'.

Algerian noun a person from Algeria. •adjective relating to Algeria.

-algia combining form used to form nouns referring to pain in a specified part of the body: *neuralgia.*
- DERIVATIVES **-algic** combining form.
- ORIGIN from Greek *algos* 'pain'.

Algonquian /al-gong-kwi-uhn/ (also **Algonkian** /al-gong-ki-uhn/) noun 1 a large family of North American Indian languages, including Cree, Blackfoot, and Cheyenne. 2 a speaker of Algonquian. •adjective relating to Algonquian.

Algonquin /al-gong-kwin/ (also **Algonkin** /al-gong-kin/ noun 1 a member of an American Indian people living in Canada along and westwards of the Ottawa River. 2 the language of the Algonquins. •adjective relating to the Algonquins.
- ORIGIN Micmac, 'at the place of spearing fish and eels'.

algorithm /al-guh-ri-*th*'m/ noun a process or set of rules used in calculations or other problem-solving operations.
- DERIVATIVES **algorithmic** adjective.
- ORIGIN Arabic, 'the man of Kwārizm' (referring to a 9th-century mathematician).

alias /**ay**-li-uhss/ adverb also known as: *Eric Blair, alias George Orwell.* •noun 1 a false identity. 2 an identifying label used to access a computer file, command, or address.
- ORIGIN Latin, 'at another time, otherwise'.

aliasing noun 1 Physics & Telecommunications the misidentification of a signal frequency, introducing distortion or error. 2 the use of aliases to identify computer files, commands, etc.

alibi /**a**-li-by/ noun (pl. **alibis**) 1 a claim or piece of evidence that one was elsewhere when an alleged act took place. 2 informal an excuse: *there can be no more alibis for failure.* •verb (**alibis, alibiing, alibied**) informal provide an alibi for someone.
- ORIGIN from Latin, 'elsewhere'.

USAGE: **Alibi** means 'a claim by a person that they were elsewhere'. The informal meaning 'an excuse' is regarded as incorrect by some people and should be avoided in careful writing.

Alice band noun a flexible band worn to hold back the hair.
- ORIGIN named after the heroine of *Alice's Adventures in Wonderland* by Lewis Carroll.

alien adjective 1 belonging to a foreign country. 2 unfamiliar or unacceptable: *extravagance is alien to his measured approach to life.* 3 relating to beings from other worlds. •noun 1 a foreigner. 2 a being from another world.
- DERIVATIVES **alienness** noun.
- ORIGIN Latin *alienus.*

alienable adjective Law able to be transferred to new ownership.

alienate verb 1 make someone feel isolated or estranged. 2 lose the support or sympathy of:

I wanted to keep the friends I had and not alienate any of them.
- DERIVATIVES **alienation** noun.
- ORIGIN Latin *alienare.*

alight[1] verb 1 (**alight on**) (of a bird) land or settle on something. 2 formal get off a train or bus. 3 (**alight on**) happen to notice something.
- ORIGIN Old English.

alight[2] adverb & adjective 1 on fire. 2 shining brightly.

align verb 1 put things in a straight line or in the correct position in relation to something else. 2 (**align oneself with**) give support to: *newspapers align themselves with certain political parties.*
- DERIVATIVES **alignment** noun.
- ORIGIN from French *à ligne* 'into line'.

alike adjective similar to each other: *the brothers were very much alike.* •adverb in a similar way.
- ORIGIN Old English.

alimentary adjective relating to food or nutrition.
- ORIGIN from Latin *alimentum* 'nourishment'.

alimentary canal noun the whole passage along which food passes through the body during digestion.

alimony noun chiefly N. Amer. financial support for a husband or wife after separation or divorce.
- ORIGIN from Latin *alimonia* 'nutriment'.

A-line adjective (of a garment) slightly flared from a narrow waist or shoulders.

aliquot /**a**-li-kwot/ noun 1 technical a portion or sample taken for analysis or treatment. 2 (also **aliquot part** or **portion**) Mathematics a quantity which divides into another a whole number of times.
- ORIGIN Latin, 'some, so many'.

A-list (or **B-list**) noun a list of the most (or second most) famous or sought-after people, especially in show business.

alive adjective 1 living; not dead. 2 continuing in existence or use: *keeping hope alive.* 3 alert and active. 4 (**alive to**) aware of and willing to respond to: *I am very alive to the challenges we face.* 5 (**alive with**) teeming with something.

alkali /**al**-kuh-ly/ noun (pl. **alkalis**) a compound, such as lime, with particular chemical properties including turning litmus blue and neutralizing or effervescing with acids.
- ORIGIN first referring to a saline substance obtained from the ashes of plants: from Arabic, 'fry, roast'.

alkaline /al-kuh-lyn/ adjective containing an alkali or having the properties of an alkali; having a pH greater than 7.
- DERIVATIVES **alkalinity** /al-kuh-**lin**-it-i/noun.

alkaloid /**al**-kuh-loyd/ noun Chemistry any of a class of organic compounds containing nitrogen which have significant physiological effects on humans.

alkane /**al**-kayn/ noun Chemistry any of the series of saturated hydrocarbons whose simplest members are methane and ethane.
- ORIGIN from **ALKYL**.

alkene /**al**-keen/ noun Chemistry any of the series of unsaturated hydrocarbons containing a double bond, of which the simplest member is ethylene.
- ORIGIN from **ALKYL**.

alkyl /al-kīl, -kil/ noun Chemistry a hydrocarbon radical derived from an alkane by removal of a hydrogen atom.
– ORIGIN German *Alkohol* 'alcohol'.

all predeterminer & determiner **1** the whole quantity or extent of. **2** any whatever: *he denied all knowledge.* **3** the greatest possible. •pronoun everything or everyone. •adverb **1** completely. **2** used to show an equal score: *one-all.*
– PHRASES **all along** from the beginning. **all and sundry** everyone. **all but** very nearly. **all for** informal strongly in favour of. **all in** informal exhausted. **all in all** on the whole. **all out** using every effort. **all over the place** informal **1** everywhere. **2** in a disordered state. **all round 1** in all respects. **2** for or by each person: *drinks all round.* **all told** in total. **at all** in any way. **in all** in total. **on all fours** on hands and knees. **one's all** one's greatest effort.
– ORIGIN Old English.

Allah /al-luh/ noun the name of God among Muslims (and Arab Christians).
– ORIGIN Arabic.

allay /uh-**lay**/ verb reduce or end fear, concern, or difficulty.
– ORIGIN Old English, 'lay down or aside'.

all-clear noun a signal that danger or difficulty is over.

allegation /a-li-**gay**-sh'n/ noun an unproven claim that someone has done something illegal or wrong.

allege /uh-**lej**/ verb claim that someone has done something illegal or wrong: *he alleged that he'd been assaulted.*
– DERIVATIVES **alleged** adjective **allegedly** adverb.
– ORIGIN Old French *esligier*, from Latin *lis* 'lawsuit'.

allegiance /uh-**lee**-juhnss/ noun loyalty or commitment to a superior person or to a group or cause: *I have no allegiance to any political party.*
– ORIGIN Old French *ligeance.*

allegorize (or **allegorise**) verb interpret or represent something symbolically.

allegory /**al**-li-guh-ri/ noun (pl. **allegories**) a story, poem, or picture which contains a hidden symbolic meaning.
– DERIVATIVES **allegorical** /ali-**gor**-ik-uhl/ adjective **allegorically** adverb **allegorist** noun.
– ORIGIN Greek *allēgoria.*

allegretto /al-li-**gret**-toh/ adverb & adjective Music at a fairly brisk speed.
– ORIGIN Italian.

allegro /uh-**lay**-groh/ Music adverb & adjective at a brisk speed. •noun (pl. **allegros**) a piece of music to be performed at a brisk speed.
– ORIGIN Italian, 'lively'.

allele /al-**eel**/ noun each of two or more alternative forms of a gene that arise by mutation and are found at the same place on a chromosome.
– DERIVATIVES **allelic** adjective.
– ORIGIN from Greek *allēl-* 'one another'.

alleluia /al-li-**loo**-yuh/ exclamation variant spelling of HALLELUJAH.

Allen key noun trademark a spanner designed to fit into and turn an **Allen screw** (one with a hexagonal socket in the head).
– ORIGIN from the *Allen* Manufacturing Company, Connecticut.

allergen /**al**-ler-juhn/ noun a substance that causes an allergic reaction.

allergenic /al-ler-**jen**-ik/ adjective likely to cause an allergic reaction.

allergic adjective **1** caused by or relating to an allergy. **2** having an allergy.

allergy noun (pl. **allergies**) a medical condition in which the body reacts badly when it comes into contact with a particular substance.
– DERIVATIVES **allergist** noun.
– ORIGIN from Greek *allos* 'other'.

alleviate /uh-**lee**-vi-ayt/ verb make pain or a problem less severe: *yoga can help alleviate insomnia.*
– DERIVATIVES **alleviation** noun.
– ORIGIN Latin *alleviare* 'lighten'.

alley noun (pl. **alleys**) **1** a narrow passageway between or behind buildings. **2** a path in a park or garden. **3** a long, narrow area in which skittles and bowling are played.
– ORIGIN Old French *alee* 'walking or passage'.

alleyway noun an alley between or behind buildings.

alliance noun **1** a relationship established between countries or organizations for a joint purpose: *Saudi Arabia's alliance with the United States.* **2** the state of being joined or associated.

allied adjective **1** relating to or part of an alliance. **2** (**Allied**) relating to Britain and its allies in the First and Second World Wars. **3** (**allied to/with**) combined or together with: *skilled craftsmanship allied to technology.*

alligator noun a large reptile similar to a crocodile but with a broader and shorter head.
– ORIGIN from Spanish *el lagarto* 'the lizard'.

alligator pear noun N. Amer. an avocado.

all-in adjective Brit. inclusive of everything: *an all-in fee.*

all-inclusive adjective **1** including everything or everyone. **2** relating to a holiday or resort in which all or most meals, drinks, and activities are included in the overall price.

all-in-one adjective combining two or more items or uses in a single unit.

all-in wrestling noun Brit. wrestling with few or no restrictions.

alliteration noun the occurrence of the same letter or sound at the beginning of words that are close together, as in *sing a song of sixpence.*
– DERIVATIVES **alliterative** adjective.
– ORIGIN from Latin *littera* 'letter'.

allium /**al**-i-uhm/ noun (pl. **alliums**) a plant of a genus that includes onions, leeks, and garlic.
– ORIGIN Latin, 'garlic'.

allocate verb give or distribute something: *all the tickets have been allocated to tour operators.*
– DERIVATIVES **allocable** adjective **allocator** noun.
– ORIGIN Latin *allocare.*

allocation noun **1** the action of allocating something. **2** an amount of a resource given to someone.

allopathy /uh-**lo**-puh-thi/ noun the conventional treatment of disease, using drugs that have effects opposite to the symptoms.
– DERIVATIVES **allopath** noun **allopathic** adjective.

a

allot verb (allots, allotting, allotted) give or share out something: *equal time was allotted to each task.*
– ORIGIN from Latin *loter* 'divide into lots'.

allotment noun 1 Brit. a plot of land rented by a person from a local authority, for growing vegetables or flowers. 2 the action of allotting something. 3 an amount allotted to someone.

allotrope /al-luh-trohp/ noun Chemistry each of two or more different physical forms in which an element can exist (e.g. graphite, charcoal, and diamond as forms of carbon).
– DERIVATIVES allotropic adjective.
– ORIGIN from Greek *allotropos* 'of another form'.

allow verb 1 let someone have or do something. 2 decide that something is legal or acceptable. 3 provide or set aside: *allow an hour or so for driving.* 4 (allow for) take into consideration: *income rose by 11 per cent allowing for inflation.* 5 accept that something is true.
– DERIVATIVES allowable adjective allowedly adverb.
– ORIGIN from Latin *allaudare* 'to praise'.

USAGE: On the confusion of **allowed** and **aloud**, see the note at ALOUD.

allowance noun 1 the amount of something allowed: *the recommended daily allowance of 1,300 mg calcium.* 2 a sum of money paid regularly to a person. 3 Brit. an amount of money that can be earned or received free of tax.
– PHRASES make allowances for 1 take something into consideration. 2 treat someone less harshly because of their difficult circumstances.

alloy noun /al-loy/ 1 a mixture of two or more metals. 2 an inferior metal mixed with a precious one. • verb /uh-loy/ mix metals to make an alloy.
– ORIGIN from Latin *alligare* 'bind'.

all right adjective 1 satisfactory; acceptable. 2 able to be done or to happen; allowable. • adverb fairly well. • exclamation expressing or asking for agreement or acceptance.

all-round (US **all-around**) adjective 1 having a wide range of abilities or uses. 2 in many or all respects: *his all-round excellence.*

all-rounder noun Brit. a person with a wide range of skills.

All Saints' Day noun a Christian festival in honour of all the saints, held on 1 November.

All Souls' Day noun a Catholic festival with prayers for the souls of the dead in purgatory, held on 2 November.

allspice noun the dried fruit of a Caribbean tree, used as a spice in cookery.

all-time adjective not bettered or surpassed: *the all-time record.*

allude verb (allude to) 1 mention briefly: *offering no evidence, he alluded airily to 'scientific findings'.* 2 refer to someone or something in an indirect way.
– ORIGIN Latin *alludere.*

allure noun powerful attractiveness or charm. • verb (often as adj. alluring) strongly attract or charm: *the alluring scent of lemon.*
– DERIVATIVES allurement noun. alluringly adverb.
– ORIGIN from Latin *luere* 'a lure'.

allusion noun an indirect reference to something.
– ORIGIN from Latin *alludere* 'allude'.

allusive adjective using or containing indirect references to something: *elaborate, allusive prose.*
– DERIVATIVES allusively adverb allusiveness noun.

alluvium /uh-loo-vi-uhm/ noun a fertile deposit of clay, silt, and sand left by flood water.
– DERIVATIVES alluvial adjective.
– ORIGIN Latin.

ally /al-ly/ noun (pl. allies) 1 a person, organization, or country that cooperates with another. 2 (the Allies) the countries that fought with Britain in the First and Second World Wars. • verb /uh-ly/ (allies, allying, allied) 1 (ally something to/with) combine a resource or quality with another in a way that benefits both: *he allied his racing experience with his father's business skill.* 2 (ally oneself with) side with or support something.
– ORIGIN from Latin *alligare* 'bind together'.

-ally suffix forming adverbs from adjectives ending in -al (such as *radically* from *radical*).

alma mater /al-muh mah-ter (or may-ter)/ noun the school, college, or university that one once attended.
– ORIGIN Latin, 'bountiful mother'.

almanac /al-muh-nak/ (also **almanack**) noun 1 a calendar giving important dates and information, such as the phases of the moon. 2 an annual handbook containing information of general or specialist interest.
– ORIGIN Greek *almenikhiaka.*

almighty adjective 1 having complete or very great power: *an almighty army.* 2 informal very big; enormous. • noun (the Almighty) a name or title for God.

almond noun the oval edible nut-like seed (kernel) of the almond tree.
– ORIGIN from Greek *amugdalē.*

almond paste noun marzipan.

almoner /ah-muh-nuhr/ noun historical an official who distributed donations of food or money to the poor.
– DERIVATIVES almonry noun (pl. almonries).

almost adverb very nearly.
– ORIGIN Old English.

alms /ahmz/ plural noun old use money or food given to poor people.
– ORIGIN from Greek *eleēmosunē* 'compassion'.

almshouse noun historical a house founded by charity, offering accommodation for poor people.

aloe /a-loh/ noun 1 a succulent tropical plant with thick tapering leaves. 2 (aloes or bitter aloes) a strong laxative obtained from the bitter juice of some kinds of aloe.
– ORIGIN Greek *aloē.*

aloe vera noun a jelly-like substance obtained from a kind of aloe, used to soothe the skin.
– ORIGIN Latin, 'true aloe'.

aloft adjective & adverb up in or into the air.
– ORIGIN Old Norse.

alone adjective & adverb 1 on one's own; by oneself. 2 isolated and lonely. 3 only; exclusively: *it was a smile for him alone.*
– PHRASES leave (or let) someone/thing alone

1 abandon someone or something. **2** stop interfering with someone or something.
– DERIVATIVES **aloneness** noun.
– ORIGIN from **ALL** + **ONE**.

along preposition & adverb **1** moving forward on. **2** extending in a horizontal line on. **3** in or into company with other people: *she'd brought along a friend.*
– PHRASES **along with** together with or at the same time as. **be** (or **come**) **along** arrive.
– ORIGIN Old English.

alongside (N. Amer. also **alongside of**) preposition **1** close to the side of; next to. **2** at the same time as.

aloof adjective cool and distant: *they were polite but faintly aloof.*
– DERIVATIVES **aloofly** adverb **aloofness** noun.
– ORIGIN from **LUFF**; originally meaning 'away and to windward!' (with the ship kept away from a lee shore or other hazard).

alopecia /a-luh-**pee**-shuh/ noun Medicine abnormal loss of hair; baldness.
– ORIGIN Greek *alōpekia* 'fox mange'.

aloud adverb out loud; so as to be heard.

> USAGE: Do not confuse **aloud** with **allowed**. **Aloud** means 'out loud' (*I read the letter aloud*), whereas **allowed** means 'permitted' (*smoking is not allowed in the office*).

alp noun **1** a high mountain. **2** (the **Alps**) a high range of mountains in Switzerland and adjoining countries.
– ORIGIN Greek *Alpeis.*

alpaca /al-**pak**-uh/ noun (pl. same or **alpacas**) **1** a long-haired domesticated South American mammal related to the llama. **2** the wool of the alpaca.
– ORIGIN Spanish.

alpenstock /**al**-puhn-stok/ noun a long iron-tipped stick used by walkers in hilly country.
– ORIGIN German, 'Alp stick'.

alpha /**al**-fuh/ noun **1** the first letter of the Greek alphabet (A, α). **2** Brit. a first-class mark given for a piece of work. •adjective referring to the dominant animal or person in a group: *an alpha male.*
– PHRASES **alpha and omega** the beginning and the end.

alphabet noun an ordered set of letters or symbols used to represent the basic speech sounds of a language.
– ORIGIN from Greek *alpha* and *bēta*, the first two letters of the Greek alphabet.

alphabetical adjective in the order of the letters of the alphabet.
– DERIVATIVES **alphabetic** adjective **alphabetically** adverb.

alphabetize (or **alphabetise**) /**al**-fuh-buh-tyz/ verb arrange words in alphabetical order.

alphanumeric /al-fuh-nyoo-**me**-rik/ adjective made up of or using both letters and numerals.

alpha particle noun Physics a helium nucleus, especially as given out by some radioactive substances.

alpine adjective **1** relating to or found on high mountains. **2** (**Alpine**) relating to the Alps. •noun a plant which grows on high mountains.

alpinist /**al**-pi-nist/ noun a person who climbs high mountains.

already adverb **1** before the time in question. **2** as surprisingly soon or early as this: *you aren't leaving already?*

alright adjective, adverb, & exclamation variant spelling of **ALL RIGHT**.

> USAGE: Many people consider the spelling **alright** (rather than **all right**) to be unacceptable in formal writing, even though other single-word forms such as **altogether** have long been accepted as standard.

Alsatian noun Brit. a German shepherd dog.
– ORIGIN Latin, 'Alsace', a region of NE France.

also adverb in addition.
– ORIGIN Old English.

also-ran noun a person who is unsuccessful in a race or contest.

altar noun **1** the table in a Christian church at which the bread and wine are consecrated in communion services. **2** a table or other structure on which religious offerings are made.
– ORIGIN Latin, from *altus* 'high'.

altar boy noun a boy who assists a priest during a service.

altarpiece noun a painting or other work of art set above and behind an altar.

alter verb make or become different: *she had to alter her holiday plans.*
– ORIGIN from Latin *alter* 'other'.

alteration noun a change or modification.

altercation /awl-ter-**kay**-sh'n/ noun a noisy disagreement.
– ORIGIN Latin.

alter ego /awl-ter **ee**-goh/ noun **1** another side to someone's normal personality. **2** a close friend who is very like oneself.
– ORIGIN Latin, 'other self'.

alternate verb /**awl**-ter-nayt/ **1** occur or do in turn repeatedly: *the narrative alternates personal observation with historical fact.* **2** change repeatedly between two contrasting states: *his mood alternated between aggression and morose despair.* •adjective /awl-**ter**-nuht/ **1** every other: *the service runs on alternate days.* **2** (of two things) each following and succeeded by the other in a regular pattern: *put alternate layers of potatoes and fish in the casserole dish.* **3** chiefly N. Amer. another term for **ALTERNATIVE**.
– DERIVATIVES **alternately** adverb **alternation** noun.
– ORIGIN Latin *alternare* 'do by turns'.

> USAGE: The use of **alternate** to mean **alternative** (as in *we will need to find alternate sources of fuel*) is common in North American English, though it is still regarded as incorrect by many people in Britain.

alternate angles plural noun two equal angles on opposite sides of a line crossing two parallel lines.

alternating current noun an electric current that reverses its direction many times a second. Compare with **DIRECT CURRENT**.

alternative adjective **1** (of one or more things) available as another possibility. **2** differing from the usual or traditional form of

a

something: *people attracted to alternative lifestyles.* • noun one of two or more available possibilities.
– DERIVATIVES **alternatively** adverb.

USAGE: Some people say that you can only have a maximum of two alternatives (because the word **alternative** comes from Latin *alter* 'other of two'). References to more than two alternatives are, however, normal in modern standard English.

alternative energy noun energy produced in ways that do not use up natural resources or harm the environment.

alternative medicine noun medical treatment that does not follow the usual practices of Western medicine, e.g. herbalism.

alternator noun a dynamo that generates an alternating current.

although conjunction **1** in spite of the fact that. **2** however; but.

altimeter /al-ti-mee-ter/ noun an instrument which indicates the altitude reached by something, especially an aircraft.

altiplano /al-ti-plah-noh/ noun (pl. **altiplanos**) a broad, high, level region in central South America.
– ORIGIN Spanish.

altitude noun the height of an object or point above sea level or ground level.
– ORIGIN from Latin *altus* 'high'.

altitude sickness noun illness resulting from a shortage of oxygen in places that are high above sea or ground level.

alto /al-toh/ noun (pl. **altos**) the highest adult male or lowest female singing voice. • adjective referring to the second or third highest of a family of instruments: *an alto sax.*
– ORIGIN from Italian *alto canto* 'high song'.

altogether adverb **1** completely. **2** in total. **3** on the whole.
– PHRASES **in the altogether** informal naked.

USAGE: Note that **altogether** and **all together** do not mean the same thing. **Altogether** means 'in total' (*there are six bedrooms altogether*), whereas **all together** means 'all in one place' (*it was good to have a group of friends all together*) or 'all at once' (*they came in all together*.)

altruism /al-troo-i-z'm/ noun unselfish concern for the needs and well-being of other people.
– DERIVATIVES **altruist** noun **altruistic** adjective **altruistically** adverb.
– ORIGIN from Italian *altrui* 'somebody else'.

alum /al-uhm/ noun a crystalline compound of aluminium and potassium, used in dyeing and tanning animal skin.
– ORIGIN Latin *alumen*.

alumina /uh-loo-mi-nuh/ noun aluminium oxide, a chemical compound found in many types of rock.
– ORIGIN Latin *alumen* 'alum'.

aluminium /al-yoo-min-i-uhm/ (US **aluminum** /uh-loo-mi-nuhm/) noun a lightweight silvery-grey metallic element that is resistant to rust or corrosion.

aluminize (or **aluminise**) /uh-loo-mi-nyz/ verb coat something with aluminium.

alumnus /uh-lum-nuhss/ noun (pl. **alumni** /uh-lum-ny/; fem. **alumna** /uh-lum-nuh/, pl. **alumnae** /uh-lum-ni/) a former student of a particular school, college, or university.
– ORIGIN Latin, 'pupil'.

alveolus /al-vee-oh-luhss/ noun (pl. **alveoli** /al-vee-oh-lee/) **1** any of the many tiny air sacs in the lungs. **2** the bony socket for the root of a tooth.
– DERIVATIVES **alveolar** adjective.
– ORIGIN Latin, 'small cavity'.

always adverb **1** on all occasions; at all times. **2** forever. **3** repeatedly. **4** failing all else.

alyssum /al-iss-uhm/ noun (pl. **alyssums**) a plant with small white or yellow flowers.
– ORIGIN Greek *alusson*.

Alzheimer's disease /alts-hy-merz/ noun a disorder which causes progressive mental deterioration, typically affecting older people.
– ORIGIN named after the German neurologist Alois *Alzheimer.*

AM abbreviation amplitude modulation.

Am symbol the chemical element americium.

am first person singular present of **BE**.

a.m. abbreviation before noon.
– ORIGIN from Latin *ante meridiem.*

amah /ah-muh/ noun (in the Far East or India) a female domestic servant or a woman employed to look after a young child or children.
– ORIGIN Portuguese *ama.*

amalgam /uh-mal-guhm/ noun **1** a mixture or blend. **2** an alloy of mercury with another metal, especially one used for dental fillings.
– ORIGIN Greek *malagma* 'an emollient'.

amalgamate /uh-mal-guh-mayt/ verb **1** combine or unite to form one organization or structure: *the paper later amalgamated with other publications.* **2** mix a metal with mercury to make an alloy.
– DERIVATIVES **amalgamation** noun.

amanuensis /uh-man-yoo-en-siss/ noun (pl. **amanuenses** /uh-man-yoo-en-seez/) a writer's assistant.
– ORIGIN Latin, from *servus a manu* 'slave at handwriting, secretary'.

amaranth /am-uh-ranth/ noun a plant of a family that includes love-lies-bleeding.
– ORIGIN from Greek *amarantos* 'not fading'.

amaretti /am-uh-ret-ti/ plural noun Italian almond-flavoured biscuits.
– ORIGIN Italian, from *amaro* 'bitter'.

amaretto /am-uh-ret-oh/ noun a brown almond-flavoured Italian liqueur.

amaryllis /am-uh-ril-liss/ noun a plant with large trumpet-shaped flowers.
– ORIGIN Greek *Amarullis*, a name for a country girl in pastoral poetry.

amass verb build up over time: *he amassed a fortune of more than $13 million.*
– ORIGIN Latin *amassare.*

amateur noun **1** a person who takes part in a sport or other activity for pleasure, rather than as as a profession or job. **2** a person who is not skilled at a particular activity. • adjective **1** non-professional: *an amateur photographer.* **2** done in an unskilful way.
– DERIVATIVES **amateurism** noun.
– ORIGIN French, 'lover'.

amateurish adjective not done or made skilfully.

amatory /am-uh-tuh-ri/ adjective relating to sexual love or desire.
– ORIGIN from Latin *amare* 'to love'.

amaze verb surprise someone very much.
– DERIVATIVES **amazement** noun.
– ORIGIN Old English.

amazing adjective 1 very surprising: *it's amazing how quickly she adapted.* 2 informal very good or impressive.
– DERIVATIVES **amazingly** adverb.

Amazon /am-uh-zuhn/ noun 1 (in Greek mythology) a member of a race of female warriors. 2 a very tall, strong woman.
– ORIGIN Greek *Amazōn*.

Amazonian /am-uh-**zoh**-ni-uhn/ adjective 1 relating to the River Amazon. 2 (of a woman) very tall and strong.

ambassador noun 1 a diplomat sent by a state as its permanent representative in a foreign country. 2 a person who represents or promotes something: *he is a great ambassador for football.*
– DERIVATIVES **ambassadorial** adjective
– ORIGIN Italian *ambasciator.*

amber noun 1 a hard translucent yellowish substance formed from the fossilized resin of certain ancient trees, used in jewellery. 2 a honey-yellow colour.
– ORIGIN Old French *ambre.*

ambergris /**am**-ber-greess/ noun a waxy substance produced by sperm whales, used in perfume manufacture.
– ORIGIN from Old French *ambre gris* 'grey amber'.

ambidextrous /am-bi-**dek**-struhss/ adjective able to use the right and left hands equally well.
– ORIGIN from Latin *ambi-* 'on both sides' + *dexter* 'right-handed'.

ambience /**am**-bi-uhnss/ (also **ambiance**) noun the character and atmosphere of a place: *the gentle colour scheme creates a relaxing ambience.*

ambient /**am**-bi-uhnt/ adjective 1 relating to the surrounding area: *the ambient temperature.* 2 referring to a style of electronic instrumental music with no persistent beat, used to create a relaxed atmosphere.
– ORIGIN Latin, from *ambire* 'go round'.

ambiguity /am-bi-**gyoo**-i-ti/ noun (pl. **ambiguities**) the quality of having more than one possible meaning or interpretation.

ambiguous /am-**big**-yoo-uhss/ adjective 1 (of language) having more than one possible meaning. 2 not clear or decided: *a European state whose position had long been ambiguous.*
– DERIVATIVES **ambiguously** adverb.
– ORIGIN Latin *ambiguus* 'doubtful'.

ambit noun the scope or extent of something: *the need to bring the activity within the ambit of federal law.*
– ORIGIN Latin *ambitus* 'circuit'.

ambition noun 1 a strong desire to do or achieve something: *her burning ambition was to be world champion.* 2 the desire or determination to become successful or rich.

– ORIGIN from Latin *ambire* 'go around (canvassing for votes)'.

ambitious adjective 1 having or showing a determination to succeed. 2 requiring a great deal of effort, time, or money to succeed: *an ambitious six-year development plan.*
– DERIVATIVES **ambitiously** adverb.

ambivalent /am-**biv**-uh-luhnt/ adjective having mixed feelings about something or someone.
– DERIVATIVES **ambivalence** noun **ambivalently** adverb.
– ORIGIN from Latin *ambi-* 'on both sides' + *valere* 'be worth'.

amble verb walk at a leisurely pace. • noun a leisurely walk.
– ORIGIN Latin *ambulare* 'to walk'.

ambrosia noun 1 Greek & Roman Mythology the food of the gods. 2 something that tastes or smells very pleasant.
– DERIVATIVES **ambrosial** adjective.
– ORIGIN Greek, 'elixir of life'.

ambulance noun a vehicle equipped for taking sick or injured people to and from hospital.
– ORIGIN French, from Latin *ambulare* 'walk'.

ambulance chaser noun derogatory, chiefly N. Amer. a lawyer who encourages accident victims to make claims for damages in a court of law.

ambulant /**am**-byoo-luhnt/ adjective Medicine able to walk about; not confined to bed.

ambulatory /**am**-byoo-luh-tri/ adjective 1 relating to walking or able to walk: *ambulatory patients.* 2 movable; mobile: *an ambulatory data recorder.* • noun (pl. **ambulatories**) an aisle or cloister in a church or monastery.

ambuscade /am-buh-**skayd**/ noun dated an ambush.
– ORIGIN French *embuscade.*

ambush noun a surprise attack made by people lying in wait in a concealed position. • verb attack a person or group of people from a concealed position.
– ORIGIN Old French *embusche*, from a Latin word meaning 'to place in a wood'.

ameba noun (pl. **amebae** or **amebas**) US spelling of **AMOEBA**.

ameliorate /uh-**mee**-li-uh-rayt/ verb formal make something bad or unsatisfactory better.
– DERIVATIVES **amelioration** noun.
– ORIGIN Latin *meliorare.*

amen /ah-men, ay-men/ exclamation said at the end of a prayer or hymn, meaning 'so be it'.
– ORIGIN Greek, from a Hebrew word meaning 'truth, certainty'.

amenable /uh-**meen**-uh-b'l/ adjective 1 willing to cooperate or be persuaded to do something. 2 (**amenable to**) able to be affected by: *conditions that are amenable to medical intervention.*
– DERIVATIVES **amenability** noun.
– ORIGIN Old French *amener* 'bring to'.

amend verb make small changes or improvements to a document, proposal, etc.
– ORIGIN Latin *emendare* 'to correct'.

amendment noun a small change or improvement made to a document, proposal, etc.

amends plural noun (in phrase **make amends**)

a

do something to show that one regrets a wrong or unfair action: *I want to make amends for the way I treated her.*

amenity /uh-**meen**-i-ti/ noun (pl. **amenities**) a useful or desirable feature of a place: *a convenient location, close to all local amenities.*
– ORIGIN from Latin *amoenus* 'pleasant'.

amenorrhoea /uh-men-uh-**ree**-uh/ (US **amenorrhea**) noun the abnormal absence of menstrual periods.
– ORIGIN Latin, from Greek *men* 'month' and *rhein* 'flow'.

Amerasian /a-muh-**ray**-shuhn/ adjective having one American and one Asian parent. • noun an Amerasian person.

American adjective relating to the United States or to the continents of America. • noun a person from the United States or any of the countries of North, South, or Central America.
– DERIVATIVES **Americanize** (or **Americanise**) verb.

Americana /uh-me-ri-**kah**-nuh/ plural noun things associated with the United States.

American dream noun the ideal of equality of opportunity associated with the US.

American football noun a kind of football played in the US with an oval ball on a field marked out as a gridiron.

American Indian noun a member of the native peoples of America.

> USAGE: **American Indian** has been steadily replaced in the US by the term **Native American**, especially in official contexts. However, **American Indian** is still widespread in general use even in the US, and is generally acceptable to American Indians themselves.

Americanism noun a word or phrase used or originating in the US.

americium /am-uh-**riss**-i-uhm/ noun a radioactive metallic chemical element made by high-energy atomic collisions.
– ORIGIN from *America*, where it was first made.

Amerindian /am-uh-**rin**-di-uhn/ (also **Amerind** /am-uh-rind/) noun & adjective another term for **AMERICAN INDIAN**.

amethyst /am-uh-**thist**/ noun a precious stone consisting of a violet or purple variety of quartz.
– ORIGIN Greek *amethustos* 'not drunken' (because the stone was believed to prevent drunkenness).

Amharic /am-**ha**-rik/ noun the Semitic official language of Ethiopia.
– ORIGIN from *Amhara*, a region of Ethiopia.

amiable adjective friendly and pleasant.
– DERIVATIVES **amiability** noun **amiably** adverb.
– ORIGIN Old French.

amicable /am-i-kuh-b'l/ adjective friendly and without disagreement or dispute: *an amicable working relationship.*
– DERIVATIVES **amicably** adverb.
– ORIGIN from Latin *amicus* 'friend'.

amice /a-mis/ noun a white cloth worn on the neck and shoulders by a priest celebrating Holy Communion.
– ORIGIN Latin.

amid (or **amidst**) preposition surrounded by; in

the middle of.

amide /**ay**-myd, a-mid/ noun Chemistry **1** an organic compound containing the group –C(O)NH$_2$. **2** a salt-like compound containing the anion NH$_2^-$.
– ORIGIN from **AMMONIA**.

amidships adverb & adjective in the middle of a ship.

amigo /uh-**mee**-goh/ noun (pl. **amigos**) informal, chiefly N. Amer. a friend.
– ORIGIN Spanish.

amine /**ay**-meen/ noun Chemistry an organic compound obtained from ammonia.

amino acid noun any of about twenty organic compounds which form the basic constituents of proteins.

amir /uh-**meer**/ noun variant spelling of **EMIR**.

Amish /**ah**-mish/ plural noun a strict Protestant sect living mainly in the US states of Pennsylvania and Ohio.
– ORIGIN from the name of the Swiss preacher Jakob *Amman*.

amiss adjective not quite right: *he didn't notice that anything was amiss.* • adverb wrongly or badly: *everything had gone amiss.*
– PHRASES **not go amiss** Brit. be welcome and useful. **take something amiss** be offended by something that is said.
– ORIGIN probably from Old Norse, 'so as to miss'.

amity /am-i-ti/ noun formal friendly relations between people or countries.
– ORIGIN Old French *amitie*, from Latin *amicus* 'friend'.

ammeter /am-mi-ter/ noun an instrument for measuring electric current in amperes.

ammo noun informal ammunition.

ammonia /uh-**moh**-ni-uh/ noun a colourless, strong-smelling gas that forms an alkaline solution in water, which is used as a cleaning fluid.
– ORIGIN from *sal ammoniac*, a substance obtained near the temple of Jupiter *Ammon* in Egypt.

ammonite /am-uh-nyt/ noun an extinct sea creature with a spiral shell, found as a fossil.
– ORIGIN from Latin *cornu Ammonis* 'horn of Ammon', from the fossil's resemblance to the ram's horn associated with the god Jupiter Ammon.

ammonium /uh-**moh**-ni-uhm/ noun Chemistry the ion NH$_4^+$, present in solutions of ammonia and in salts obtained from ammonia.

ammunition noun **1** a supply of bullets and shells. **2** points used to support one's case in an argument or debate: *the analysis provided vital ammunition to anti-nuclear campaigners.*
– ORIGIN from French *la munition* 'the fortification'.

amnesia /am-**nee**-zi-uh/ noun loss of memory.
– DERIVATIVES **amnesiac** noun & adjective.
– ORIGIN Greek, 'forgetfulness'.

amnesty noun (pl. **amnesties**) **1** an official pardon given to people convicted of political offences. **2** a period during which people admitting to particular offences are not punished: *there will be no amnesty for people who have not paid the tax.*
– ORIGIN Greek *amnēstia* 'forgetfulness'.

amniocentesis /am-ni-oh-sen-tee-siss/ **noun** (pl. **amniocenteses** /am-ni-oh-sen-tee-seez/) a medical procedure in which a sample of amniotic fluid is taken from a pregnant woman's womb in order to check for abnormalities in the fetus.
– ORIGIN from **AMNION** + Greek *kentēsis* 'pricking'.

amnion /am-ni-uhn/ **noun** (pl. **amnions** or **amnia**) the innermost membrane surrounding an embryo.
– DERIVATIVES **amniotic** adjective.
– ORIGIN Greek, 'caul'.

amniotic fluid **noun** the fluid surrounding a fetus before birth.

amoeba /uh-mee-buh/ (US also **ameba**) **noun** (pl. **amoebas** or **amoebae** /uh-mee-bee/) a microscopic animal that is made up of a single cell and is able to change its shape.
– DERIVATIVES **amoebic** adjective **amoeboid** adjective.
– ORIGIN Greek *amoibē* 'change'.

amok /uh-mok/ (also **amuck**) **adverb** (in phrase **run amok**) behave in an uncontrolled and disorderly way.
– ORIGIN Malay, 'rushing in a frenzy'.

among (chiefly Brit. also **amongst**) **preposition** 1 surrounded by; in the middle of. 2 included or occurring in. 3 shared by; between.
– ORIGIN Old English.

amontillado /uh-mon-ti-lah-doh/ **noun** (pl. **amontillados**) a medium dry sherry.
– ORIGIN Spanish, from *Montilla*, a town in southern Spain.

amoral /ay-mo-ruhl/ **adjective** without morals; not concerned about right or wrong.
– DERIVATIVES **amorality** noun.

> **USAGE:** Amoral does not mean the same as immoral: while immoral means 'not following accepted standards of morality', amoral means 'without morals'.

amorous **adjective** showing or feeling sexual desire.
– DERIVATIVES **amorously** adverb.
– ORIGIN from Latin *amor* 'love'.

amorphous /uh-mor-fuhss/ **adjective** without a definite shape or form.
– ORIGIN Greek *amorphos*.

amortize (or **amortise**) /uh-mor-tyz/ **verb** Finance gradually pay off a debt.
– DERIVATIVES **amortization** noun.
– ORIGIN Old French *amortir*.

amount **noun** 1 the total number, size, or value of something. 2 a quantity: *add a small amount of water*. • **verb** (**amount to**) 1 add up to a total. 2 be the equivalent of: *a degree of carelessness that amounted to gross negligence*.
– ORIGIN from Old French *amont* 'upward'.

amour /uh-moor/ **noun** a secret love affair.
– ORIGIN from Latin *amor* 'love'.

amour propre /a-moor prop-ruh/ **noun** a feeling of self-respect.
– ORIGIN French.

amp[1] **noun** short for **AMPERE**.

amp[2] **noun** informal short for **AMPLIFIER**.

amperage /am-puh-rij/ **noun** the strength of an electric current, measured in amperes.

ampere /am-pair/ **noun** the base unit of electric current in the SI system.
– ORIGIN named after the French physicist André-Marie *Ampère*.

ampersand /am-per-sand/ **noun** the sign &, standing for *and*.
– ORIGIN from *and per se and*, i.e. '& by itself represents *and*'.

amphetamine /am-fet-uh-meen/ **noun** a drug used illegally as a stimulant.
– ORIGIN from its chemical name.

amphibian **noun** a cold-blooded animal such as a frog or toad which lives in water when young and on land as an adult.
– ORIGIN from Greek *amphi* 'both' + *bios* 'life'.

amphibious /am-fib-i-uhss/ **adjective** 1 living in or suited for both land and water. 2 (of a military operation) involving forces landing at a place from the sea.

amphitheatre (US **amphitheater**) **noun** a round building consisting of tiers of seats surrounding a central space for dramatic or sporting events.
– ORIGIN from Greek *amphi* 'on both sides' + *theatron* 'theatre'.

amphora /am-fuh-ruh/ **noun** (pl. **amphorae** /am-fuh-ree/ or **amphoras**) an ancient Greek or Roman jar with two handles and a narrow neck.
– ORIGIN Latin, from Greek *amphi-* 'on both sides' + *phoreus* 'bearer'.

ample **adjective** 1 enough or more than enough; plentiful: *there was ample room for storage*. 2 large: *her ample bosom*.
– DERIVATIVES **amply** adverb.
– ORIGIN Latin *amplus*.

amplifier **noun** an electronic device for increasing the strength of electrical signals.

amplify **verb** (**amplifies, amplifying, amplified**) 1 increase the strength of sound or electrical signals. 2 add details to a story or statement.
– DERIVATIVES **amplification** noun.
– ORIGIN Latin *amplificare*.

amplitude **noun** 1 Physics the maximum amount by which an alternating current or electromagnetic wave can vary from its average level. 2 great size or extent.

amplitude modulation **noun** the modification of a radio wave by varying its amplitude, used as a method of broadcasting an audio signal.

ampoule /am-pool/ (US also **ampule** /am-pyool/) **noun** a small sealed glass capsule which contains a measured quantity of liquid ready for an injection.
– ORIGIN Latin *ampulla* 'flask'.

ampulla /am-pool-luh/ **noun** (pl. **ampullae** /am-pool-lee/) 1 a roughly spherical ancient Roman flask with two handles. 2 a flask holding the consecrated oil in a church.
– ORIGIN Latin.

amputate /am-pyoo-tayt/ **verb** cut off a limb in a surgical operation.
– DERIVATIVES **amputation** noun.
– ORIGIN Latin *amputare*.

amputee **noun** a person who has had a limb amputated.

amuck /uh-muk/ **adverb** variant spelling of **AMOK**.

amulet /am-yoo-lit/ **noun** an ornament or small

a

piece of jewellery worn as protection against evil, illness, or danger.
– ORIGIN Latin *amuletum*.

amuse verb 1 make someone laugh or smile. 2 provide someone with an enjoyable or interesting activity: *he amused himself by writing poetry*.
– DERIVATIVES **amused** adjective **amusing** adjective.
– ORIGIN Old French *amuser* 'entertain, deceive'.

amusement noun 1 the state or experience of finding something funny. 2 something that causes laughter or provides entertainment.

amusement arcade noun Brit. an indoor area containing coin-operated machines on which games may be played.

amusement park noun a large outdoor area with fairground rides and other entertainments.

amylase /**am**-i-layz/ noun Biochemistry an enzyme found in saliva that converts starch into sugars.

amyl nitrite noun a liquid used in medicine to expand blood vessels and sometimes inhaled for its stimulant effect on the body.

an determiner the form of the indefinite article 'a' used before words beginning with a vowel sound.

USAGE: It is better to use **a** rather than **an** before words beginning with an initial **h** that is sounded, such as *historical* and *hotel*. **An** was common in the 18th and 19th centuries because the initial **h** in such words was then often not pronounced.

an- prefix variant spelling of **a-** before a vowel (as in *anaemia*).

Anabaptist /an-nuh-**bap**-tist/ noun a member of a Protestant religious group believing that only adults should be baptized.
– ORIGIN from Greek *ana-* 'again' + *baptismos* 'baptism'.

anabolic steroid /an-uh-**bol**-ik/ noun a synthetic hormone taken illegally to improve a competitor's performance in a sport.

anabolism /uh-**nab**-uh-li-z'm/ noun a metabolic process in which complex molecules are formed from simpler ones and energy is stored. The opposite of **CATABOLISM**.
– DERIVATIVES **anabolic** adjective.
– ORIGIN Greek *anabolē* 'ascent'.

anachronism /uh-**nak**-ruh-ni-z'm/ noun a thing which belongs or is appropriate to a period of time other than the one in which it exists or is placed: *such lavish houses seemed anachronisms, relics of a long-gone era*.
– DERIVATIVES **anachronistic** adjective **anachronistically** adverb.
– ORIGIN from Greek *ana-* 'backwards' + *khronos* 'time'.

anaconda /an-uh-**kon**-duh/ noun a very large snake of the boa family, found in tropical South America.
– ORIGIN Sinhalese, 'whip snake'.

anaemia /uh-**nee**-mi-uh/ (US **anemia**) noun a shortage of red cells or haemoglobin in the blood, causing paleness and lack of energy.
– ORIGIN from Greek *an-* 'without' + *haima* 'blood'.

anaemic (US **anemic**) adjective 1 suffering from anaemia. 2 not lively or exciting: *an anaemic performance*.

anaerobic /an-air-**oh**-bik/ adjective Biology not using oxygen from the air.
– DERIVATIVES **anaerobically** adverb.

anaesthesia /an-iss-**thee**-ziuh/ (US **anesthesia**) noun inability to feel pain, especially as caused by an anaesthetic.
– ORIGIN from Greek *an-* 'without' + *aisthēsis* 'sensation'.

anaesthetic /an-iss-**thet**-ik/ (US **anesthetic**) noun a drug or gas that makes one unable to feel pain.

anaesthetist /uh-**neess**-thuh-tist/ (US **anesthetist**) noun a medical specialist who gives anaesthetics to patients.

anaesthetize (or **anaesthetise**, US **anesthetize**) /uh-**neess**-thuh-tyz/ verb give an anaesthetic to a patient.
– DERIVATIVES **anaesthetization** noun.

anagram /an-uh-gram/ noun a word or phrase formed by rearranging the letters of another.
– ORIGIN from Greek *ana-* 'back, anew' + *gramma* 'letter'.

anal /**ay**-n'l/ adjective 1 relating to the anus. 2 fussily concerned about minor details and orderliness.
– DERIVATIVES **anally** adverb.

analgesia /an-uhl-**jee**-zi-uh/ noun Medicine the loss of sensitivity to pain.
– ORIGIN from Greek *an-* 'not' + *algein* 'feel pain'.

analgesic /an-uhl-**jee**-zik/ noun a pain-relieving drug. ●adjective having a pain-relieving effect.

analogous /uh-**nal**-uh-guhss/ adjective alike or comparable in certain ways: *an analogous situation*.
– ORIGIN Greek *analogos* 'proportionate'.

analogue /an-uh-log/ (US also **analog**) adjective (also **analog**) relating to electronic information or signals represented by a varying physical effect (e.g. voltage or the position of a pointer) rather than by a digital display. ●noun a person or thing that is like or comparable to another.

analogy /uh-**nal**-uh-ji/ noun (pl. **analogies**) 1 a way of explaining or clarifying something by comparing it to something else: *an analogy between the workings of nature and those of human societies*. 2 a partial similarity.
– DERIVATIVES **analogical** adjective.

anal-retentive adjective Psychoanalysis excessively fussy and concerned with orderliness (supposedly because of problems with toilet-training in infancy).

analysand /uh-**nal**-i-zand/ noun a person who is undergoing psychoanalysis.

analyse (US **analyze**) verb 1 examine something in detail in order to explain it or discover its structure or composition. 2 psychoanalyse someone.

analysis /uh-**nal**-i-siss/ noun (pl. **analyses** /uh-**nal**-i-seez/) 1 a detailed examination of the features or structure of something: *an analysis of the causes of unemployment*. 2 the separation of something into its component parts. 3 psychoanalysis.

– ORIGIN from Greek *analuein* 'unloose'.

analyst noun 1 a person who carries out an analysis. 2 a psychoanalyst.

analytical (also **analytic**) adjective relating to or using analysis.
– DERIVATIVES **analytically** adverb.

analyze verb US spelling of ANALYSE.

anaphora /uh-**naff**-uh-ruh/ noun the repetition of a word or phrase at the beginning of successive statements, used for rhetorical effect.
– ORIGIN Greek, 'repetition'.

anaphylactic shock /a-nuh-**fil**-ak-tik/ noun Medicine a severe allergic reaction to something that the body has become extremely sensitive to.
– ORIGIN from Greek *ana-* 'again' + *phulaxis* 'guarding'.

anarchic /uh-**nar**-kik/ adjective having no controlling rules or principles.

anarchist /a-nuh-kist/ noun a person who believes that all forms of government should be abolished.
– DERIVATIVES **anarchism** noun **anarchistic** adjective.

anarchy /a-nuh-ki/ noun a state of disorder due to the lack of any form of government or control.
– ORIGIN from Greek *an-* 'without' + *arkhos* 'chief, ruler'.

anathema /uh-**na**-thuh-muh/ noun something that one detests: *racism was anathema to her.*
– ORIGIN Greek, 'thing devoted to evil'.

anathematize (or **anathematise**) /uh-**na**-thuh-muh-tyz/ verb curse or condemn: *a church council anathematized those who refused to conform.*

anatomize (or **anatomise**) verb examine and analyse in detail: *successful comedy is notoriously difficult to anatomize.*

anatomy noun (pl. **anatomies**) 1 the scientific study of bodily structure. 2 the bodily structure of a person, animal, or plant. 3 a detailed examination or analysis: *an anatomy of the disaster.*
– DERIVATIVES **anatomical** /an-uh-**tom**-i-k'l/ adjective **anatomically** adverb **anatomist** noun.
– ORIGIN from Greek *ana-* 'up' + *tomia* 'cutting'.

ANC abbreviation African National Congress.

ancestor noun 1 a person from whom one is descended. 2 something from which a later species or version has developed: *an ancestor of the horse.*
– ORIGIN from Latin *antecedere* 'go before'.

ancestral /an-**sess**-truhl/ adjective relating to or inherited from a person's ancestor or ancestors: *his ancestral home.*

ancestry noun (pl. **ancestries**) a person's ancestors or the people from which they are descended: *her Irish ancestry.*

anchor noun a heavy metal object used to moor a ship to the sea bottom. •verb 1 moor a ship with an anchor. 2 fix firmly in position: *the rope was anchored to the rocks.*
– ORIGIN Greek *ankura*.

anchorage noun a place where ships may be anchored safely.

anchorite /ang-kuh-ryt/ noun historical a person who lives in isolation from others for religious reasons.
– ORIGIN from Greek *anakhōrein* 'retire'.

anchorman (or **anchorwoman**) noun (pl. **anchormen** or **anchorwomen**) a person who presents a live television or radio programme and coordinates the contributions of those taking part.

anchovy /an-**choh**-vi/ noun (pl. **anchovies**) a small fish of the herring family, with a strong flavour.
– ORIGIN Spanish and Portuguese *anchova*.

ancien régime /on-si-an ray-**zheem**/ noun (pl. **anciens régimes** pronunc. same) a political or social system that has been replaced by a more modern one.
– ORIGIN French, 'old rule'.

ancient adjective 1 belonging to or dating from the very distant past: *an ancient civilization.* 2 very old: *an ancient pair of jeans.* •noun (**the ancients**) the people of ancient times.
– DERIVATIVES **anciently** adverb.
– ORIGIN Old French *ancien*, from Latin *ante* 'before'.

ancillary /an-**sil**-luh-ri/ adjective 1 providing support to the main activities of an organization: *ancillary staff.* 2 additional; extra: *ancillary accommodation.*
– ORIGIN from Latin *ancilla* 'maidservant'.

and conjunction 1 used to connect words, clauses, or sentences. 2 used to connect two identical words to show gradual change, continuing action, or great extent: *getting better and better.* 3 (connecting two numbers) plus. 4 informal (after a verb) to: *try and do it.*
– ORIGIN Old English.

USAGE: Some verbs, especially **try**, **come**, and **go**, can be followed by **and** rather than **to** in sentences like *we should try and help them.* The use with **and** is very common but in formal writing or speech it is best to say **to**: *we should try to help them.*
  Many people think that **and**, together with other conjunctions such as **but** and **because**, should not be used to start a sentence, the argument being that such a sentence expresses an incomplete thought. However, **and** has long been used in this way in both written and spoken English, and it is quite acceptable to do so.

andante /an-**dan**-tay/ Music adverb & adjective in a moderately slow tempo. •noun a passage to be performed at a moderately slow tempo.
– ORIGIN Italian, 'going'.

Andean /an-**dee**-uhn, an-di-uhn/ adjective relating to the Andes mountains of South America.

andiron /an-dy-uhn/ noun either of a pair of metal stands used to support wood burning in a fireplace.
– ORIGIN Old French *andier*.

Andorran /an-**dor**-uhn/ noun a person from Andorra, a small self-governing principality in the southern Pyrenees. •adjective relating to Andorra.

androgen /an-druh-juhn/ noun a male sex hormone, such as testosterone.
– ORIGIN from Greek *anēr* 'man' + *genēs* '-born, of a specified kind'.

androgynous /an-**dro**-ji-nuhss/ adjective

a

partly male and partly female.
– DERIVATIVES **androgyny** /an-**dro**-ji-ni/ noun.
– ORIGIN from Greek *anēr* 'man' + *gunē* 'woman'.

android /an-droyd/ noun (in science fiction) a robot with a human appearance.
– ORIGIN from Greek *anēr* 'man'.

anecdotal /an-ik-**doh**-t'l/ adjective (of a story) not necessarily true because based on someone's personal account of an event rather than on facts.
– DERIVATIVES **anecdotally** adverb.

anecdote /an-ik-doht/ noun a short entertaining story about a real incident or person.
– ORIGIN from Greek *anekdota* 'things unpublished'.

anemia noun US spelling of ANAEMIA.

anemic adjective US spelling of ANAEMIC.

anemometer /an-i-**mom**-i-ter/ noun an instrument for measuring the speed of the wind.
– ORIGIN Greek *anemos* 'wind'.

anemone /uh-**nem**-uh-ni/ noun a plant having brightly coloured flowers with dark centres.
– ORIGIN Greek, 'windflower'.

aneroid barometer /an-uh-royd/ noun a barometer that measures air pressure by the action of air on the flexible lid of a box containing a vacuum.
– ORIGIN from Greek *a-* 'without' + *nēros* 'water'.

anesthesia etc. noun US spelling of ANAESTHESIA etc.

aneurysm /an-yuu-ri-z'm/ (also **aneurism**) noun Medicine an excessive swelling of the wall of an artery.
– ORIGIN Greek *aneurusma* 'widening'.

anew adverb 1 in a new or different way. 2 once more; again.

angel noun 1 a spiritual being acting as an attendant or messenger of God, represented as being of human form with wings. 2 a very beautiful, kind, or good person. 3 informal a person who gives financial backing to a theatrical production.
– ORIGIN Greek *angelos* 'messenger'.

angel cake (N. Amer. also **angel food cake**) noun a very light, pale sponge cake.

angel dust noun informal the hallucinogenic drug phencyclidine hydrochloride.

angelfish noun (pl. same or **angelfishes**) a tropical fish with large fins, often vividly coloured or patterned.

angel hair noun a type of pasta consisting of very fine long strands.

angelic adjective 1 relating to angels. 2 very beautiful, innocent, or kind: *his small angelic face.*
– DERIVATIVES **angelically** adverb.

angelica /an-**jel**-li-kuh/ noun the stalks of a sweet-smelling plant, preserved in sugar and used in cake decoration.
– ORIGIN from Latin *herba angelica* 'angelic herb' (it was believed to be effective against poisoning and disease).

angelus /**an**-juh-luhss/ noun 1 a Roman Catholic prayer commemorating the Incarnation of Jesus, said at morning, noon,

and sunset. 2 a ringing of bells to signal the times of the angelus.
– ORIGIN from Latin *Angelus domini* 'the angel of the Lord', the opening words of the prayer.

anger noun a strong feeling of extreme displeasure. • verb make someone angry.
– ORIGIN Old Norse, 'grief'.

angina /an-**jy**-nuh/ (also **angina pectoris** /pek-tuh-riss/) noun a condition marked by severe pain in the chest, caused by an inadequate supply of blood to the heart.
– ORIGIN from Greek *ankhonē* 'strangling' + Latin *pectoris* 'of the chest'.

angioplasty /**an**-ji-oh-plas-ti/ noun (pl. **angioplasties**) a surgical operation to repair or unblock a blood vessel, especially an artery in the heart.

angiosperm /**an**-ji-oh-sperm/ noun a plant of a large group that have flowers and produce seeds enclosed in a carpel, including herbaceous plants, shrubs, grasses, and most trees.
– ORIGIN from Greek *angeion* 'container'.

Angle noun a member of an ancient Germanic people who founded kingdoms in the north and east of England in the 5th century AD.
– ORIGIN Latin *Anglus* 'inhabitant of *Angul*' (in northern Germany); related to ENGLISH.

angle¹ noun 1 the space between two intersecting lines or surfaces at or close to the point where they meet. 2 a position from which someone or something is viewed: *the camera angle shifted from side view to a full-face close-up.* 3 a particular way of considering something: *let's look at the issue from a different angle.* • verb 1 move or place something in a slanting position. 2 present information from a particular point of view: *angle your answer so that it is relevant to the job for which you are applying.*
– DERIVATIVES **angled** adjective.
– ORIGIN Latin *angulus* 'corner'.

angle² verb 1 fish with a rod and line. 2 try to get something by indirectly prompting someone to offer it: *she was angling for sympathy.*
– DERIVATIVES **angler** noun **angling** noun.
– ORIGIN Old English.

angle bracket noun either of a pair of marks in the form < >, used to enclose words or figures so as to separate them from their context.

angle grinder noun a device with a rotating abrasive disc, used to grind, polish, or cut metal and other materials.

angle iron noun a building material consisting of pieces of iron or steel with an L-shaped cross section, able to be bolted together.

anglerfish noun (pl. same or **anglerfishes**) a marine fish that lures prey within reach of its mouth with a fleshy filament projecting from its snout.

Anglican adjective relating to the Church of England or any Church associated with it. • noun a member of the Anglican Church.
– DERIVATIVES **Anglicanism** noun.
– ORIGIN Latin *Anglicanus*, from *Anglus* 'Angle'.

Anglicism noun a word or phrase that is peculiar to British English.

anglicize (or **anglicise**) verb make English in

form or character: *he anglicized his name from Gutman to Goodman.*
– DERIVATIVES **anglicization** noun.

Anglo- combining form **1** English: *anglophone.* **2** English or British and ...: *Anglo-Latin.*
– ORIGIN from Latin *Anglus* 'English'.

Anglo-Catholic adjective a member of a section of the Church of England which is close to Catholicism in its beliefs and worship.
– DERIVATIVES **Anglo-Catholicism** noun.

Anglocentric adjective considered in terms of England or Britain; seeing English or British culture as most important.

Anglo-Indian adjective **1** relating to or involving both Britain and India. **2** of mixed British and Indian parentage. **3** chiefly historical of British descent or birth but having lived for a long time in India. •noun an Anglo-Indian person.

Anglo-Irish adjective **1** relating to both Britain and Ireland (or specifically the Republic of Ireland). **2** of mixed English and Irish parentage. **3** of English descent but born or living in Ireland.

Anglophile noun a person who likes or greatly admires England or Britain.
– DERIVATIVES **Anglophilia** noun.

anglophone adjective English-speaking.

Anglo-Saxon noun **1** a Germanic inhabitant of England between the 5th century and the Norman Conquest. **2** an English person. **3** chiefly N. Amer. any white, English-speaking person. **4** the Old English language.

Angolan /ang-goh-luhn/ noun a person from Angola, a country in SW Africa. •adjective relating to Angola.

angora /ang-gor-uh/ noun **1** a cat, goat, or rabbit of a long-haired breed. **2** a fabric made from the hair of the angora goat or rabbit.
– ORIGIN from *Angora* (now Ankara) in Turkey.

angostura /ang-guh-styoor-uh/ noun **1** a bitter bark from a South American tree, used as a flavouring. **2** (also **Angostura bitters** trademark) a kind of tonic.
– ORIGIN from *Angostura* (now Ciudad Bolívar) in Venezuela.

angry adjective (**angrier, angriest**) **1** feeling or showing anger. **2** (of a wound or sore) red and inflamed.
– DERIVATIVES **angrily** adverb.

angst /angst/ noun a strong feeling of anxiety about life in general. •adjective.
– DERIVATIVES **angsty** adjective.
– ORIGIN German, 'fear'.

angstrom /ang-struhm/ noun Physics a unit of length equal to one hundred-millionth of a centimetre, 10^{-10} metre.
– ORIGIN named after the Swedish physicist A. J. *Ångström.*

anguish noun severe pain or distress. •verb be very distressed: *I was anguishing about whether I'd made the right decision.*
– ORIGIN Latin *angustia* 'tightness'.

anguished adjective feeling or expressing severe pain or distress.

angular /ang-gyuu-ler/ adjective **1** having angles or sharp corners. **2** (of a person) lean and bony. **3** Physics measured by means of an angle.

– DERIVATIVES **angularity** noun **angularly** adverb.

anhydrous /an-hy-druhss/ adjective Chemistry containing no water.
– ORIGIN from Greek *an-* 'without' + *hudōr* 'water'.

aniline /an-i-leen/ noun an oily liquid used in making dyes, drugs, and plastics.
– ORIGIN from Arabic, 'indigo' (from which it was originally obtained).

animadvert /an-im-uhd-vert/ verb (**animadvert on/against**) formal speak out against or criticize someone or something.
– DERIVATIVES **animadversion** noun.
– ORIGIN from Latin *animus* 'mind' + *advertere* 'to turn'.

animal noun **1** a living organism that can move about of its own accord and has specialized sense organs and nervous system. **2** a mammal, as opposed to a bird, reptile, fish, or insect. **3** a brutal or uncivilized person. **4** a particular type of person or thing: *she's a political animal.* •adjective physical rather than spiritual or intellectual: *animal lust.*
– ORIGIN from Latin *animalis* 'having breath'.

animalcule /ani-mal-kyool/ noun chiefly literary a microscopic animal.

animalism noun physical and instinctive behaviour; animality.
– DERIVATIVES **animalistic** adjective.

animality noun physical and instinctive human behaviour, like that of animals.

animal magnetism noun a quality of powerful sexual attractiveness.

animate verb /an-i-mayt/ **1** bring life or new vigour to: *Christianity animated a society and reshaped it.* **2** give a film or character the appearance of movement using animation. •adjective /an-i-muht/ alive; having life.
– DERIVATIVES **animator** noun.
– ORIGIN from Latin *anima* 'life, soul'.

animated adjective **1** full of interest or energy; lively: *an animated conversation.* **2** (of a film) made using animation.
– DERIVATIVES **animatedly** adverb.

animation noun **1** the state of being full of life or energy; liveliness. **2** the technique of filming a sequence of drawings or positions of models to create the appearance of movement. **3** (also **computer animation**) the creation of moving images by means of a computer.

animatronics /an-im-uh-tron-iks/ plural noun (treated as sing.) the creation and operation of lifelike robots, especially for use in films.
– DERIVATIVES **animatronic** adjective.

anime /an-i-may/ noun Japanese animated films, typically having a science fiction theme.
– ORIGIN Japanese.

animism /an-i-mi-z'm/ noun the belief that all things in nature, such as plants and hills, have a soul.
– DERIVATIVES **animist** noun **animistic** adjective.
– ORIGIN from Latin *anima* 'life, soul'.

animosity /an-i-moss-i-ti/ noun (pl. **animosities**) strong hostility; hatred.
– ORIGIN Latin *animositas.*

animus /an-i-muhss/ noun hatred or hostility.
– ORIGIN Latin, 'spirit, mind'.

anion /an-I-uhn/ noun Chemistry an ion with a negative charge. The opposite of **CATION**.

a

– DERIVATIVES **anionic** adjective.
– ORIGIN from **ANODE** + **ION**.

anise /an-iss/ noun a plant grown for its aromatic seeds (aniseed).
– ORIGIN Greek *anison* 'anise, dill'.

aniseed noun the seed of the plant anise, used as a flavouring.

ankh /angk/ noun an ancient Egyptian symbol of life in the shape of a cross with a loop instead of the top arm.
– ORIGIN Egyptian, 'life, soul'.

ankle noun 1 the joint connecting the foot with the leg. 2 the narrow part of the leg between the ankle joint and the calf.
– ORIGIN Old English.

anklet noun a chain or band worn round the ankle.

ankylosing spondylitis noun see SPONDYLITIS.

anna noun a former unit of money of India and Pakistan, equal to one sixteenth of a rupee.
– ORIGIN Hindi.

annal /an-nuhl/ noun 1 (annals) a historical record of events year by year. 2 a record of the events of one year.
– DERIVATIVES **annalist** noun.
– ORIGIN from Latin *annales libri* 'yearly books'.

annatto /uh-na-toh/ noun an orange-red dye obtained from a tropical fruit, used for colouring foods.
– ORIGIN Carib.

anneal /uh-neel/ verb heat metal or glass and allow it to cool slowly, to remove internal stresses.
– ORIGIN Old English, 'set on fire'.

annelid /an-ni-lid/ noun a worm with a body made up of segments, such as an earthworm.
– ORIGIN from Latin *anelus* 'small ring'.

annex verb /an-neks/ 1 seize territory and add it to one's own. 2 (usu. as adj. **annexed**) add or attach something: *the annexed document*.
• noun /an-neks/ (chiefly Brit. also **annexe**) (pl. **annexes**) 1 a building attached or near to a main building, used for additional space. 2 an addition to a document.
– DERIVATIVES **annexation** noun.
– ORIGIN Latin *annectere* 'connect'.

annihilate /uh-ny-i-layt/ verb 1 destroy completely: *this bomb could annihilate them all*. 2 defeat someone completely.
– DERIVATIVES **annihilation** noun **annihilator** noun.
– ORIGIN Latin *annihilare* 'reduce to nothing'.

anniversary noun (pl. **anniversaries**) the date on which an event took place in a previous year.
– ORIGIN from Latin *anniversarius* 'returning yearly'.

Anno Domini /an-noh dom-i-ny/ adverb full form of **AD**.

annotate /an-nuh-tayt/ verb add explanatory notes to a piece of writing.
– DERIVATIVES **annotation** noun **annotator** noun.
– ORIGIN Latin *annotare* 'to mark'.

announce verb 1 make a public statement about something. 2 be a sign of: *lilies announce the arrival of summer*.
– DERIVATIVES **announcer** noun.
– ORIGIN from Latin *nuntius* 'messenger'.

announcement noun 1 a public statement. 2 the action of announcing something.

annoy verb make someone slightly angry.
– DERIVATIVES **annoyed** adjective **annoying** adjective.
– ORIGIN from Latin *mihi in odio est* 'it is hateful to me'.

annoyance noun 1 the feeling or state of being annoyed. 2 a thing that annoys someone.

annual adjective 1 happening once a year. 2 calculated over or covering a year: *annual income*. 3 (of a plant) living for a year or less. • noun 1 a book published once a year under the same title but with different contents. 2 an annual plant.
– DERIVATIVES **annually** adverb.
– ORIGIN from Latin *annus* 'year'.

annualized (or **annualised**) adjective (of a rate of interest, inflation, or return on investment) recalculated as an annual rate.

annuity noun (pl. **annuities**) a fixed sum of money paid to someone each year.
– ORIGIN from Latin *annuus* 'yearly'.

annul /uh-nul/ verb (annuls, annulling, annulled) declare a law, marriage, or other legal contract to be invalid.
– DERIVATIVES **annulment** noun.
– ORIGIN from Latin *nullum* 'nothing'.

annular /an-yuu-ler/ adjective technical ring-shaped.
– ORIGIN from Latin *anulus* 'small ring'.

annunciation noun 1 (the Annunciation) the announcement by the angel Gabriel to the Virgin Mary that she was to be the mother of Jesus. 2 a Church festival commemorating the Annunciation, held on 25 March.
– ORIGIN from Latin *annuntiare* 'announce'.

annus horribilis /an-uhss ho-ree-bil-is/ noun a disastrous or unlucky year for someone or something.
– ORIGIN Latin.

annus mirabilis /mi-rah-bil-is/ noun a remarkable or very good year for someone or something.
– ORIGIN Latin, 'wonderful year'.

anode /an-ohd/ noun an electrode with a positive charge. The opposite of CATHODE.
– ORIGIN Greek *anodos* 'way up'.

anodized /an-uh-dyzd/ (or **anodised**) adjective (of metal, especially aluminium) coated with a protective oxide layer by electrolysis.

anodyne /an-uh-dyn/ adjective unlikely to cause offence or disagreement; bland: *anodyne tales of small-town life*. • noun a painkilling drug or medicine.
– ORIGIN Greek *anôdunos* 'painless'.

anoint verb 1 smear or rub someone with oil, especially as part of a religious ceremony. 2 choose someone to replace another in a job or role: *the Social Democrats will anoint their candidate for chancellor in March*.
– ORIGIN from Latin *inungere*.

anomalous /uh-nom-uh-luhss/ adjective differing from what is standard or normal: *anomalous results*.
– DERIVATIVES **anomalously** adverb.
– ORIGIN from Greek *an-* 'not' + *homalos* 'even'.

anomaly /uh-nom-uh-li/ noun (pl. **anomalies**) something that differs from what is standard or normal.

anomie /**an**-uh-mi/ noun lack of the usual standards of expected or good behaviour.
– ORIGIN from Greek *anomos* 'lawless'.

anon adverb old use or informal soon; shortly.
– ORIGIN Old English, 'in or into one'.

anonymous /uh-**non**-i-muhss/ adjective **1** with a name that is not known or made known: *an anonymous letter.* **2** having no outstanding or individual features: *an anonymous building on an anonymous street.*
– DERIVATIVES **anonymity** /an-uh-**nim**-iti/ noun **anonymously** adverb.
– ORIGIN Greek *anōnumos* 'nameless'.

anorak noun **1** a waterproof jacket with a hood. **2** Brit. informal a person with an obsessive interest in something.
– DERIVATIVES **anorakish** adjective **anoraky** adjective.
– ORIGIN Greenland Eskimo.

anorexia /an-uh-**rek**-si-uh/ (also **anorexia nervosa** /ner-**voh**-suh/) noun a psychological disorder in which a person refuses to eat because they are afraid of becoming fat.
– ORIGIN from Greek *an-* 'without' + *orexis* 'appetite'.

anorexic (also **anorectic**) adjective **1** relating to anorexia. **2** informal very thin. • noun a person with anorexia.

another determiner & pronoun **1** one more. **2** different from the one already mentioned.

answer noun **1** something said or written in reaction to a question or statement. **2** a solution to a problem: *the hormone has been touted as the answer to ageing.* • verb **1** give an answer. **2** (**answer back**) give a cheeky reply. **3** satisfy a need. **4** (**answer to**) be responsible to someone. **5** defend oneself against an accusation. **6** (**answer for**) be responsible or to blame for: *Larry has got a lot to answer for.*
– DERIVATIVES **answerer** noun.
– ORIGIN Old English.

answerable adjective **1** (**answerable to**) responsible to someone. **2** (**answerable for**) responsible for something.

answering machine noun a machine which gives a recorded answer to a telephone call and can record a message from the caller.

answerphone noun Brit. an answering machine.

ant noun a small insect, usually wingless, living with many others in a highly organized group.
– ORIGIN Old English.

antacid /an-**tass**-id/ adjective (of a medicine) preventing excess stomach acid.

antagonism /an-**tag**-uh-ni-z'm/ noun open hostility or opposition.

antagonist noun an open opponent or enemy of someone or something.
– DERIVATIVES **antagonistic** adjective.
– ORIGIN from Greek *antagōnizesthai* 'struggle against'.

antagonize (or **antagonise**) verb make hostile: *Louis had no wish to antagonize his parents.*

Antarctic adjective relating to the region surrounding the South Pole.
– ORIGIN Greek *antarktikos* 'opposite to the north'.

ante /**an**-ti/ noun a stake put up by a player in poker or brag before receiving cards.
– PHRASES **up** (or **raise**) **the ante** increase what is at stake or under discussion.
– ORIGIN Latin, 'before'.

ante- prefix before; preceding: *antecedent.*

anteater noun a mammal with a long snout, feeding on ants and termites.

antebellum /an-ti-**be**-luhm/ adjective occurring or existing before a war, especially the US Civil War.
– ORIGIN from Latin *ante* 'before' and *bellum* 'war'.

antecedent /an-ti-**see**-duhnt/ noun **1** a thing that occurs or exists before another: *the antecedents to aggressive actions.* **2** (**antecedents**) a person's ancestors and social background. **3** Grammar an earlier word, phrase, or clause to which a following pronoun refers back. • adjective coming before in time or order.
– ORIGIN from Latin *antecedere* 'go before'.

antechamber noun a small room leading to a main one.

antedate verb **1** come before something in time. **2** indicate that a document or event belongs to an earlier date.

antediluvian /an-ti-di-**loo**-vi-uhn/ adjective **1** belonging to the time before the biblical Flood. **2** ridiculously old-fashioned: *antediluvian video games.*
– ORIGIN from ANTE- + Latin *diluvium* 'deluge'.

antelope noun a swift deer-like animal with upward-pointing horns, native to Africa and Asia.
– ORIGIN Greek *antholops.*

antenatal adjective Brit. during pregnancy; before birth.

antenna /an-**ten**-nuh/ noun (pl. **antennae** /an-**ten**-nee/) **1** each of a pair of long, thin parts on the heads of some insects, shellfish, etc., used for feeling. **2** (pl. also **antennas**) an aerial.
– ORIGIN Latin *antemna* 'yard' (of a ship's mast).

antepenultimate adjective last but two in a series.

ante-post adjective Brit. (of a bet) placed before the runners are known, on a horse thought likely to be entered.

anterior adjective technical at or nearer the front. The opposite of POSTERIOR.
– ORIGIN Latin.

anteroom noun a small room leading to a larger one.

anthem noun **1** an uplifting song associated with a group or cause, especially one chosen by a country to express patriotic feelings. **2** a musical setting of a religious text to be sung by a choir during a church service.
– DERIVATIVES **anthemic** /an-**thee**-mik/ adjective.
– ORIGIN from Latin *antiphona* 'antiphon'.

anther noun the part of a flower's stamen that contains the pollen.
– ORIGIN Greek *anthos* 'flower'.

anthill noun a mound-shaped nest built by ants or termites.

anthology noun (pl. **anthologies**) a collection of poems or other pieces of writing or music.

- DERIVATIVES **anthologist** noun **anthologize** (or **anthologise**) verb.
- ORIGIN from Greek *anthos* 'flower' + *-logia* 'collection'.

anthracite /an-thruh-syt/ noun hard coal that burns with little flame and smoke.
- ORIGIN from Greek *anthrax* 'coal'.

anthrax /an-thraks/ noun a serious disease of sheep and cattle, caused by a bacterium and able to be transmitted to humans.
- ORIGIN Greek *anthrax* 'coal, boil'.

anthropocentric /an-thruh-poh-sen-trik/ adjective regarding humankind as the most important element of existence.
- DERIVATIVES **anthropocentrism** noun.

anthropoid adjective referring to the higher primate mammals, including monkeys, apes, and humans.
- ORIGIN from Greek *anthrōpos* 'human being'.

anthropology /an-thruh-pol-uh-ji/ noun the study of societies, cultures, and human origins.
- DERIVATIVES **anthropological** adjective **anthropologist** noun.
- ORIGIN from Greek *anthrōpos* 'human being'.

anthropomorphic /an-thruh-puh-mor-fik/ adjective (of a god, animal, or object) treated as if having human feelings.
- DERIVATIVES **anthropomorphism** noun.

anthropophagy /an-thruh-pof-uh-ji/ noun the eating of human flesh by other humans; cannibalism.
- ORIGIN from Greek *anthrōpophagos* 'man-eating'.

anti preposition opposed to; against.

anti- prefix **1** opposed to; against: *anti-aircraft.* **2** preventing or relieving: *antibacterial.* **3** the opposite of: *anticlimax.*
- ORIGIN Greek.

antibacterial adjective active against bacteria.

antibiotic noun a medicine that destroys bacteria or slows their growth.
- ORIGIN from Greek *biōtikos* 'fit for life'.

antibody noun (pl. **antibodies**) a protein produced in the blood to destroy an antigen (harmful substance).

Antichrist noun an enemy of Jesus believed by the early Church to appear before the end of the world.

anticipate verb **1** be aware of a future event and prepare for it. **2** regard as probable: *she anticipated scorn on her return to acting.* **3** look forward to something. **4** happen or do something before: *he anticipated Bates's theories on mimicry.*
- DERIVATIVES **anticipator** noun **anticipatory** adjective.
- ORIGIN Latin *anticipare.*

anticipation noun the action of anticipating something.

anticlimax noun a disappointing end to an exciting series of events.
- DERIVATIVES **anticlimactic** adjective.

anticline /an-ti-klyn/ noun a ridge or fold of rock in which the strata slope downwards from the crest. Compare with **SYNCLINE**.
- ORIGIN from **ANTI-** + Greek *klinein* 'lean'.

anticlockwise adverb & adjective Brit. in the opposite direction to the way in which the hands of a clock move round.

anticoagulant noun a substance that prevents the blood from clotting.

anticonvulsant noun a drug that prevents or reduces the severity of epileptic fits or other convulsions.

antics plural noun foolish, outrageous, or amusing behaviour.
- ORIGIN from Italian *antico* 'antique', also 'grotesque'.

anticyclone noun an area of high atmospheric pressure around which air slowly circulates, usually resulting in calm, fine weather.
- DERIVATIVES **anticyclonic** adjective.

antidepressant noun a drug used to relieve depression.

antidote noun **1** a medicine taken to counteract a poison. **2** something that counteracts an unpleasant feeling or situation: *laughter is a good antidote to stress.*
- ORIGIN Greek *antidoton.*

antifreeze noun a liquid added to water to prevent it from freezing, used in the radiator of a motor vehicle.

antigen /an-ti-juhn/ noun a harmful substance which causes the body to produce antibodies.
- DERIVATIVES **antigenic** adjective.

Antiguan /an-tee-gwuhn/ noun a person from Antigua, or the country of Antigua and Barbuda, in the West Indies. • adjective relating to Antigua or Antigua and Barbuda.

anti-hero (or **anti-heroine**) noun a central character in a story, film, or play who lacks typical heroic qualities.

antihistamine noun a drug that counteracts the effects of histamine, used in treating allergies.

anti-inflammatory adjective (of a drug) used to reduce inflammation.

antilogarithm noun Mathematics the number of which a given number is the logarithm.

antimacassar /an-ti-muh-kass-er/ noun a cloth put over the back of a chair to protect it from grease and dirt.
- ORIGIN from **ANTI-** + *Macassar*, a kind of hair oil formerly used by men.

antimalarial adjective used to prevent malaria. • noun an antimalarial drug.

antimatter noun Physics matter consisting of the antiparticles of the particles that make up normal matter.

antimicrobial /an-ti-mi-kroh-bi-uhl/ adjective active against microbes. • noun a substance which acts against microbes.

antimony /an-ti-muh-ni/ noun a brittle silvery-white metallic element.
- ORIGIN Latin *antimonium.*

antinomian /an-ti-noh-mi-uhn/ adjective believing that Christians are released by grace from obeying moral laws. • noun a person with such a belief.
- DERIVATIVES **antinomianism** noun.
- ORIGIN from Greek *anti-* 'against' + *nomos* 'law'.

antinomy /an-tin-uh-mi/ noun (pl. **antinomies**) formal a contradiction between two beliefs or conclusions that are reasonable in themselves; a paradox.
- ORIGIN from Greek *anti* 'against' + *nomos* 'law'.

antioxidant noun a substance that counteracts oxidation.

antiparticle noun Physics a subatomic particle with the same mass as a given particle but an opposite electric charge or magnetic effect.

antipasto /an-ti-**pas**-toh/ noun (pl. **antipasti** /an-ti-**pas**-ti/) an Italian hors d'oeuvre.
– ORIGIN from Italian *anti-* 'before' + *pasto* 'food'.

antipathy /an-**ti**-puh-thi/ noun (pl. **antipathies**) a strong feeling of dislike.
– DERIVATIVES **antipathetic** adjective.
– ORIGIN from Greek *anti-* 'against' + *pathos* 'feeling'.

anti-personnel adjective (of weapons) designed to kill or injure people rather than to damage buildings or equipment.

antiperspirant noun a substance applied to the skin to prevent or reduce sweating.

antiphon /an-ti-fuhn/ noun (in the Christian Church) a short chant sung before or after a psalm or canticle.
– ORIGIN from Greek *antiphōna* 'harmonies'.

antiphonal /an-**tif**-fuh-n'l/ adjective sung or recited alternately between two groups.

Antipodes /an-**ti**-puh-deez/ plural noun (**the Antipodes**) Australia and New Zealand (in relation to the northern hemisphere).
– DERIVATIVES **Antipodean** adjective & noun.
– ORIGIN from Greek *antipodes* 'having the feet opposite'.

antipsychotic noun a drug used to treat psychotic disorders.

antipyretic /an-ti-**py**-ret-ik/ adjective (of a drug) used to prevent or reduce fever.

antiquarian /an-ti-**kwair**-i-uhn/ adjective relating to the collection or study of antiques, rare books, or antiquities. • noun (also **antiquary**) a person who studies or collects antiquarian items.
– DERIVATIVES **antiquarianism** noun.

antiquated adjective old-fashioned or outdated.

antique noun a decorative object or piece of furniture that is valuable because of its age. • adjective 1 (of an object) valuable because of its age. 2 old-fashioned or outdated.
– ORIGIN Latin *antiquus* 'former, ancient'.

antiquity noun (pl. **antiquities**) 1 the distant past, especially before the Middle Ages. 2 an object from the distant past. 3 great age: *a church of great antiquity*.

antirrhinum /an-ti-ry-nuhm/ noun (pl. **antirrhinums**) a snapdragon.
– ORIGIN from Greek *anti-* 'imitating' + *rhis* 'nose' (from the flower's resemblance to an animal's snout).

antiscorbutic adjective preventing or curing scurvy.

anti-Semitism noun hostility to or prejudice against Jews.
– DERIVATIVES **anti-Semite** noun **anti-Semitic** adjective.

antiseptic adjective 1 preventing the growth of microorganisms that cause disease or infection. 2 so clean or pure as to lack character: *the antiseptic modernity of a conference centre*. • noun an antiseptic substance.

antiserum noun (pl. **antisera**) a blood serum containing antibodies against specific antigens (harmful substances).

antisocial adjective 1 (especially of behaviour) conflicting with accepted standards and causing annoyance. 2 not wanting to mix with other people.
– DERIVATIVES **antisocially** adverb.

antithesis /an-**ti**-thuh-siss/ noun (pl. **antitheses** /an-**ti**-thuh-seez/) 1 a person or thing that is the direct opposite of another. 2 the putting together of contrasting ideas or words to produce an effect in speaking or writing.
– ORIGIN from Greek *antitithenai* 'set against'.

antithetical /an-ti-**thet**-i-k'l/ adjective opposed to or incompatible with each other: *those whose religious beliefs are antithetical to mine*.

antitoxin noun an antibody that counteracts a toxin.

antitrust adjective chiefly US (of laws) preventing or controlling monopolies, so assisting fair competition.

antivenin /an-ti-**ven**-in/ noun an antiserum containing antibodies against poisons in the venom of snakes.

antiviral adjective (of a drug or treatment) effective against viruses.

antivivisectionist noun a person who is opposed to the use of live animals for scientific research.

antler noun each of a pair of branched horns on the head of an adult male deer.
– ORIGIN Old French *antoillier*.

antonym /**an**-tuh-nim/ noun a word opposite in meaning to another (e.g. *bad* and *good*).
– ORIGIN from Greek *anti-* 'against' + *onoma* 'a name'.

anus /**ay**-nuhss/ noun the opening at the end of the digestive system through which solid waste leaves the body.
– ORIGIN Latin.

anvil noun a heavy iron block on which metal can be hammered and shaped.
– ORIGIN Old English.

anxiety noun (pl. **anxieties**) 1 a feeling of unease or worry. 2 strong concern or eagerness: *the housekeeper's anxiety to please*.

anxious adjective 1 feeling or causing worry or unease: *she became anxious about his debts*. 2 very eager and concerned to do something.
– DERIVATIVES **anxiously** adverb **anxiousness** noun.
– ORIGIN Latin *anxius*.

any determiner & pronoun 1 one or some of a thing or things, no matter how much or how many. 2 whichever or whatever one chooses. • adverb at all.
– ORIGIN Old English.

USAGE: When used as a pronoun **any** can be used with either a singular or a plural verb, depending on the rest of the sentence: *we needed more sugar but there wasn't any left* (singular verb, to match 'sugar') or *are any of the new videos available?* (plural verb, to match 'videos').

anybody pronoun anyone.

a

anyhow adverb **1** anyway. **2** in a careless or haphazard way.

anyone pronoun any person or people.

anything pronoun a thing of any kind, no matter what.
– PHRASES **anything but** not at all.

anyway adverb **1** used to emphasize something just said or to change the subject. **2** nevertheless.

anywhere adverb in or to any place. • pronoun any place.

Anzac noun a soldier in the Australian and New Zealand Army Corps (1914–18).

AOB abbreviation (at the end of an agenda for a meeting) any other business.

aorta /ay-or-tuh/ noun the main artery supplying blood from the heart to the rest of the body.
– DERIVATIVES **aortic** adjective.
– ORIGIN Greek *aortē*.

apace adverb literary quickly: *sales are growing apace.*
– ORIGIN from Old French *a pas* 'at (a considerable) pace'.

Apache /uh-pa-chi/ noun (pl. same or **Apaches**) a member of an American Indian people living chiefly in New Mexico and Arizona.
– ORIGIN probably from an American Indian word meaning 'enemy'.

apart adverb **1** separated by a distance in time or space. **2** having distinctive qualities: *wrestlers were a breed apart.* **3** into pieces.
– PHRASES **apart from 1** except for. **2** as well as.
– ORIGIN from Latin *a parte* 'at the side'.

apartheid /uh-par-tayt/ noun the official system of segregation or discrimination on racial grounds formerly in force in South Africa.
– ORIGIN Afrikaans, 'separateness'.

apartment noun **1** chiefly N. Amer. a flat. **2** (**apartments**) a private suite of rooms in a very large house.
– ORIGIN from Italian *appartare* 'to separate'.

apathetic /a-puh-the-tik/ adjective not interested or enthusiastic.
– DERIVATIVES **apathetically** adverb.

apathy /ap-uh-thi/ noun lack of interest or enthusiasm: *the task of overcoming voter apathy.*
– ORIGIN from Greek *apathēs* 'without feeling'.

apatosaurus /uh-pa-tuh-sor-uhss/ noun a huge plant-eating dinosaur with a long neck and tail; a brontosaurus.
– ORIGIN from Greek *apatē* 'deceit' + *sauros* 'lizard'.

APC abbreviation armoured personnel carrier.

ape noun **1** an animal similar to a monkey but without a tail, such as a gorilla or chimpanzee. **2** informal a stupid or clumsy person. • verb imitate in an absurd or unthinking way: *his sons aped those who were more westernized.*
– ORIGIN Old English.

aperçu /a-pair-soo/ noun (pl. **aperçus**) a comment which makes a clever or entertaining point.
– ORIGIN French, 'thing perceived'.

aperient /uh-peer-i-uhnt/ adjective (of a drug) used to relieve constipation.
– ORIGIN from Latin *aperire* 'to open'.

aperitif /uh-pe-ri-teef, uh-pe-ri-teef/ noun a drink of alcohol taken before a meal.
– ORIGIN French.

aperture /a-per-cher/ noun **1** an opening, hole, or gap. **2** the variable opening by which light enters a camera.
– ORIGIN from Latin *aperire* 'to open'.

Apex /ay-peks/ noun a system of reduced fares for air or rail journeys booked in advance.
– ORIGIN from Advance Purchase Excursion.

apex /ay-peks/ noun (pl. **apexes** or **apices** /ay-pi-seez/) the top or highest point: *the paper was regarded as the apex of journalism.*
– ORIGIN Latin, 'peak, tip'.

aphasia /uh-fay-ziuh/ noun the inability to understand or produce speech, as a result of brain damage.
– DERIVATIVES **aphasic** adjective & noun.
– ORIGIN from Greek *aphatos* 'speechless'.

aphelion /ap-hee-li-uhn/ noun (pl. **aphelia** /ap-hee-li-uh/) the point in the orbit of a planet, asteroid, or comet at which it is furthest from the sun. The opposite of **PERIHELION**.
– ORIGIN from Greek *aph' hēlion* 'from the sun'.

aphid /ay-fid/ noun a greenfly or similar small insect feeding on the sap of plants.
– ORIGIN Greek *aphis*.

aphorism /af-uh-ri-z'm/ noun a short clever phrase which states something true.
– DERIVATIVES **aphoristic** adjective.
– ORIGIN Greek *aphorismos* 'definition'.

aphrodisiac /af-ruh-diz-i-ak/ noun a food, drink, or other thing that arouses sexual desire.
– DERIVATIVES **aphrodisiacal** adjective.
– ORIGIN from *Aphrodite*, the Greek goddess of love.

apiary /ay-pee-uh-ri/ noun (pl. **apiaries**) a place where bees are kept.
– DERIVATIVES **apiarist** noun.
– ORIGIN from Latin *apis* 'bee'.

apical /ay-pi-k'l/ adjective technical relating to or forming an apex.
– ORIGIN from Latin *apex* 'peak, tip'.

apices plural of **APEX**.

apiculture /ay-pi-kul-cher/ noun technical bee-keeping.
– ORIGIN from Latin *apis* 'bee'.

apiece adverb to, for, or by each one; each.

aplenty adjective in abundance: *he has work aplenty.*

aplomb /uh-plom/ noun calm self-confidence: *he took the penalty with aplomb.*
– ORIGIN from French *à plomb* 'straight as a plumb line'.

apnoea /ap-nee-uh/ (US **apnea**) noun a medical condition in which a person temporarily stops breathing, especially during sleep.
– ORIGIN from Greek *apnous* 'breathless'.

apocalypse /uh-pok-uh-lips/ noun **1** an event involving great and widespread destruction. **2** (**the Apocalypse**) the final destruction of the world, as described in the biblical book of Revelation.
– ORIGIN from Greek *apokaluptein* 'reveal'.

apocalyptic /uh-po-kuh-lip-tik/ adjective relating to or resembling the destruction of the world: *an apocalyptic war.*

Apocrypha /uh-**pok**-ri-fuh/ plural noun (treated as sing. or pl.) those books of the Old Testament not accepted as part of Hebrew scripture and excluded from the Protestant Bible at the Reformation.
– ORIGIN from Latin *apocrypha scripta* 'hidden writings'.

apocryphal /uh-**pok**-ri-f'l/ adjective 1 widely known but unlikely to be true: *an apocryphal story.* 2 relating to the Apocrypha.

apogee /ap-uh-jee/ noun 1 the highest point in the development of something: *they regarded Alexandria as the apogee of civilization.* 2 the point in the orbit of the moon or a satellite at which it is furthest from the earth. The opposite of PERIGEE.
– ORIGIN from Greek *apogaion diastēma*, 'distance away from earth'.

apolitical adjective not interested or involved in politics.

apologetic adjective admitting and showing regret for a wrongdoing.
– DERIVATIVES **apologetically** adverb.

apologetics plural noun (treated as sing. or pl.) reasoned arguments defending a theory or doctrine.

apologia /ap-uh-**loh**-ji-uh/ noun a formal written statement defending one's opinions or behaviour.
– ORIGIN Latin, 'apology'.

apologist noun a person who offers an argument in defence of something controversial: *an apologist for fascism.*

apologize (or **apologise**) verb say sorry for something that one has done wrong: *we apologize for any inaccuracy.*

apology noun (pl. **apologies**) 1 an expression of regret for a wrongdoing. 2 (**an apology for**) a very poor example of: *it's an apology for a bridge, built of leftover stones.*
– ORIGIN Greek *apologia* 'a speech in one's own defence'.

apophthegm /ap-uh-them/ (US **apothegm**) noun a short phrase stating a general truth.
– ORIGIN from Greek *apophthengesthai* 'speak out'.

apoplectic /a-puh-**plek**-tik/ adjective 1 overcome with anger. 2 dated relating to apoplexy (stroke).

apoplexy /a-puh-plek-si/ noun (pl. **apoplexies**) 1 extreme anger. 2 dated unconsciousness or inability to move or feel, caused by a stroke.
– ORIGIN from Greek *apoplēssein* 'disable by a stroke'.

apostasy /uh-**poss**-tuh-si/ noun the abandonment of a belief or principle.
– ORIGIN Greek *apostasis* 'desertion'.

apostate /ap-uh-stayt/ noun a person who abandons a belief or principle.

a posteriori /ay-po-ster-i-or-I/ adjective & adverb involving reasoning based on known facts to deduce causes.
– ORIGIN Latin, 'from what comes after'.

apostle noun 1 (**Apostle**) each of the twelve chief disciples of Jesus. 2 an enthusiastic and pioneering supporter of an idea or cause: *he's an apostle of the single currency.*
– ORIGIN Greek *apostolos* 'messenger'.

apostolate /uh-**pos**-tuh-layt/ noun 1 the position or authority of a religious leader. 2 evangelistic activity.

apostolic /a-puh-**stol**-ik/ adjective 1 relating to the Apostles. 2 relating to the Pope, regarded as the successor to St Peter.

apostrophe /uh-**poss**-truh-fi/ noun 1 a punctuation mark (') used to show either possession or the omission of letters or numbers. 2 a passage in a speech or poem that turns away from the subject to address an absent person or thing.
– ORIGIN from Greek *apostrephein* 'turn away'.

USAGE: The apostrophe should be used to show that a person or thing relates or belongs to someone or something (*Sue's cat, yesterday's weather*) or that letters or numbers have been omitted (*he's gone; the winter of '99*). Do not use an apostrophe to form the plural of ordinary words, as in *apple's*, or in the possessive pronouns **its**, **hers**, **yours**, or **theirs**.

apostrophize (or **apostrophise**) verb 1 punctuate a word with an apostrophe. 2 address a separate passage in a speech or poem to an absent person or thing.

apothecary /uh-**poth**-uh-kuh-ri/ noun (pl. **apothecaries**) old use a person who prepared and sold medicines.
– ORIGIN from Greek *apothēkē* 'storehouse'.

apothegm noun US spelling of APOPHTHEGM.

apotheosis /uh-po-thi-**oh**-siss/ noun (pl. **apotheoses** /uh-po-thi-**oh**-seez/) 1 the highest point: *science is the apotheosis of the intellect.* 2 the raising of someone to the rank of a god.
– DERIVATIVES **apotheosize** (or **apotheosise**) verb.
– ORIGIN from Greek *apotheoun* 'make a god of'.

appal (US **appall**) verb (**appals, appalling, appalled**) 1 cause great shock or dismay to: *I am appalled at his lack of understanding.* 2 (as adj. **appalling**) informal shockingly bad.
– DERIVATIVES **appallingly** adverb.
– ORIGIN Old French *apalir* 'grow pale'.

apparatchik /ap-puh-**rat**-chik/ noun 1 chiefly derogatory an official in a large political organization. 2 chiefly historical a member of the administrative system of a communist party.
– ORIGIN Russian.

apparatus /ap-puh-**ray**-tuhss/ noun (pl. **apparatuses**) 1 the equipment needed for a particular activity or purpose. 2 the complex structure of an organization: *the apparatus of government.*
– ORIGIN Latin.

apparel /uh-**pa**-ruhl/ noun formal clothing. • verb (**apparels, apparelling, apparelled; US apparels, appareling, appareled**) old use clothe someone.
– ORIGIN Old French *apareillier*.

apparent adjective 1 clearly seen or understood; obvious. 2 seeming real, but not necessarily so: *his apparent lack of concern.*
– DERIVATIVES **apparently** adverb.
– ORIGIN from Latin *apparere* 'appear'.

apparition noun a remarkable thing that makes a sudden appearance, especially a ghost.

appeal verb 1 make a serious or earnest request. 2 be attractive or interesting: *activities that appeal to all.* 3 ask a higher court of law to

reverse the decision of a lower court. **4** Cricket (of the bowler or fielders) call on the umpire to declare a batsman out. • **noun 1** an act of appealing. **2** the quality of being attractive or interesting: *the popular appeal of football*.
– ORIGIN Latin *appellare* 'to address'.

appealing adjective attractive or interesting.
– DERIVATIVES **appealingly** adverb.

appear verb **1** come into sight or existence: *Pat appeared at the door.* **2** give a particular impression; seem: *she appeared antisocial.* **3** perform in a film, play, etc. **4** present oneself formally in a law court. **5** be published.
– ORIGIN from Latin *parere* 'come into view'.

appearance noun **1** the way that someone or something looks or seems: *you can improve your appearance with make-up.* **2** an act of appearing.
– PHRASES **keep up appearances** keep up an impression of wealth or well-being.

appease verb make someone calmer or less hostile by agreeing to their demands.
– DERIVATIVES **appeasement** noun **appeaser** noun.
– ORIGIN Old French *apaisier*.

appellant /uh-**pel**-uhnt/ noun Law a person who appeals to a higher court to reverse the decision of a lower court.

appellate /uh-**pel**-uht/ adjective Law (of a court) dealing with appeals.

appellation /ap-puh-**lay**-sh'n/ noun formal a name or title.
– ORIGIN from Latin *appellare* 'to address'.

append verb add something to the end of a document or piece of writing.
– ORIGIN Latin *appendere* 'hang on'.

appendage noun a thing attached to or projecting from something larger or more important.

appendectomy /a-pen-**dek**-tuh-mi/ (Brit. also **appendicectomy** /uh-pen-di-**sek**-tuh-mi/) noun (pl. **appendectomies**) a surgical operation to remove the appendix.

appendicitis /uh-pen-di-**sy**-tiss/ noun inflammation of the appendix.

appendix noun (pl. **appendices** or **appendixes**) **1** a small tube of tissue attached to the lower end of the large intestine. **2** a section of additional information at the end of a book.
– ORIGIN from Latin *appendere* 'hang on'.

appertain /ap-per-**tayn**/ verb (**appertain to**) formal relate to: *the law appertaining to businesses is rather different.*
– ORIGIN Latin *appertinere*.

appetite noun **1** a natural desire to satisfy a bodily need, especially for food. **2** a liking or inclination: *the UK's growing appetite for the Internet.*
– DERIVATIVES **appetitive** adjective.
– ORIGIN Latin *appetitus* 'desire for'.

appetizer (or **appetiser**) noun a small dish of food or a drink taken before a meal to stimulate the appetite.

appetizing (or **appetising**) adjective causing a pleasant feeling of hunger.

applaud verb **1** show approval by clapping. **2** express approval of: *the world applauded his courage.*
– ORIGIN from Latin *plaudere* 'to clap'.

applause noun approval shown by clapping.

apple noun the round fruit of a tree of the rose family, with green or red skin and crisp flesh.
– PHRASES **the apple of one's eye** a person of whom one is extremely fond and proud. [first referring to the pupil of the eye.] **a rotten** (or **bad**) **apple** informal a corrupt person in a group, likely to have a bad influence on the others. **upset the apple cart** spoil a plan.
– DERIVATIVES **appley** adjective.
– ORIGIN Old English.

apple-pie order noun perfect neatness or order.

applet /**ap**-lit/ noun Computing a small application running within a larger program.

appliance noun a device designed to perform a specific task: *a gas appliance.*

applicable adjective relevant or appropriate: *most of the book is applicable to any country.*
– DERIVATIVES **applicability** noun.

applicant noun a person who applies for something.

application noun **1** a formal request to an authority. **2** the action of applying something. **3** practical use or relevance: *this principle has no application to the present case.* **4** sustained effort; hard work. **5** a computer program designed to fulfil a particular purpose.

applicator noun a device for inserting or applying something.

applied adjective practical rather than theoretical: *applied chemistry.*

appliqué /uh-**plee**-kay/ noun decorative needlework in which fabric shapes are sewn or fixed on to a fabric background.
– DERIVATIVES **appliquéd** adjective.
– ORIGIN French, 'applied'.

apply verb (**applies, applying, applied**) **1** make a formal request: *he applied for a job as a plumber.* **2** bring something into operation or use. **3** be relevant: *the regulations apply to all member states.* **4** put a substance on a surface. **5** (**apply oneself**) put all one's efforts into a task.
– ORIGIN Latin *applicare* 'fold, fasten to'.

appoint verb **1** give a job or role to someone. **2** decide on a time or place.
– DERIVATIVES **appointee** noun.
– ORIGIN Old French *apointer.*

appointed adjective **1** (of a time or place) prearranged. **2** equipped or furnished: *a luxuriously appointed lounge.*

appointment noun **1** an arrangement to meet someone. **2** a job or position. **3** the action of appointing someone to a job. **4** (**appointments**) the furniture or fittings in a room.

apportion verb share something out.
– DERIVATIVES **apportionment** noun.
– ORIGIN from Latin *portionare* 'divide into portions'.

apposite /**ap**-puh-zit/ adjective very appropriate; apt.
– ORIGIN from Latin *apponere* 'apply'.

apposition noun **1** chiefly technical the positioning of things next to each other. **2** Grammar a relationship in which a word or phrase is placed next to another in order to qualify or explain it (e.g. *my friend Sue*).

appraisal noun **1** an act of assessing someone

or something. **2** a formal assessment of an employee's performance.

appraise verb **1** assess the quality or nature of: *she appraised the damage and groaned.* **2** give an employee an appraisal. **3** (of an official valuer) set a price on something.
– DERIVATIVES **appraisee** noun **appraiser** noun.
– ORIGIN alteration of **APPRISE**.

USAGE: **Appraise** is often confused with **apprise**. **Appraise** means 'assess someone or something', whereas **apprise** means 'inform someone' (*psychiatrists were apprised of his condition*).

appreciable adjective large or important enough to be noticed.
– DERIVATIVES **appreciably** adverb.

appreciate /uh-**pree**-shi-ayt/ verb **1** recognize the worth of: *that's a son who appreciates his mother.* **2** understand a situation fully. **3** be grateful for something. **4** rise in value or price.
– DERIVATIVES **appreciator** noun.
– ORIGIN Latin *appretiare* 'appraise'.

appreciation noun **1** recognition of the worth of something. **2** gratitude. **3** a favourable written assessment of a person or their work. **4** increase in value.

appreciative adjective feeling or showing gratitude or pleasure.
– DERIVATIVES **appreciatively** adverb **appreciativeness** noun.

apprehend verb **1** seize or arrest someone for a crime. **2** understand something.
– ORIGIN from Latin *prehendere* 'lay hold of'.

apprehension noun **1** worry or fear about what might happen. **2** understanding. **3** the action of arresting someone.

apprehensive adjective worried or afraid about what might happen: *she was apprehensive about attending classes.*
– DERIVATIVES **apprehensively** adverb.

apprentice noun a person learning a skilled practical trade from an employer. • verb employ someone as an apprentice.
– DERIVATIVES **apprenticeship** noun.
– ORIGIN from Old French *apprendre* 'learn'.

apprise verb inform or tell: *I had better apprise you of the situation.*
– ORIGIN French *apprendre* 'learn, teach'.

USAGE: On the confusion of **apprise** and **appraise**, see the note at **APPRAISE**.

approach verb **1** come near to someone or something in distance, time, or standard. **2** go to someone with a proposal or request. **3** start to deal with in a particular way: *one must approach the matter with caution.* • noun **1** a way of dealing with something. **2** an initial proposal or request. **3** the action of approaching. **4** a way leading to a place.
– ORIGIN from Latin *appropiare* 'draw near'.

approachable adjective **1** friendly and easy to talk to. **2** able to be reached from a particular direction or by a particular means: *the peak is approachable via a six-mile hike.*
– DERIVATIVES **approachability** noun.

approbation /ap-ruh-**bay**-sh'n/ noun approval; praise.
– ORIGIN from Latin *approbare* 'approve'.

appropriate adjective /uh-**proh**-pri-uht/ suitable or proper in the circumstances: *there is an appropriate time for training.* • verb /uh-**proh**-pri-ayt/ **1** take something for one's own use without permission. **2** allocate money for a special purpose.
– DERIVATIVES **appropriately** adverb **appropriateness** noun **appropriation** noun **appropriator** noun.
– ORIGIN Latin *appropriare* 'make one's own'.

approval noun **1** the belief that someone or something is good. **2** official acceptance that something is satisfactory.
– PHRASES **on approval** (of goods) able to be returned to a supplier if unsatisfactory.

approve verb **1** believe that someone or something is good or acceptable: *I don't approve of romance.* **2** officially accept something as satisfactory.
– ORIGIN from Latin *approbare*.

approved school noun Brit. historical a residential institution for young offenders.

approximate adjective /uh-**prok**-si-muht/ almost but not completely accurate. • verb /uh-**prok**-si-mayt/ **1** come close in nature or quantity to: *shoppers can create a computer image that approximates their body shape.* **2** estimate something fairly accurately.
– DERIVATIVES **approximately** adverb.
– ORIGIN Latin *approximatus*.

approximation /uh-prok-si-**may**-sh'n/ noun **1** an approximate figure or result. **2** the action of estimating something fairly accurately.

appurtenances /uh-**per**-ti-nuhn-siz/ plural noun formal accessories associated with a particular activity.
– ORIGIN from Latin *appertinere* 'belong to'.

APR abbreviation annual (or annualized) percentage rate.

après-ski /**ap**-ray skee/ noun social activities following a day's skiing.
– ORIGIN French, 'after skiing'.

apricot noun an orange-yellow fruit resembling a small peach.
– ORIGIN from Latin *praecox* 'early-ripe'.

April noun the fourth month of the year.
– ORIGIN Latin *Aprilis*.

April Fool's Day noun 1 April, traditionally an occasion for playing tricks.

a priori /ay pry-**or**-I/ adjective & adverb based on theoretical reasoning rather than actual observation.
– ORIGIN Latin, 'from what is before'.

apron noun **1** a protective garment covering the front of one's clothes and tied at the back. **2** an area on an airfield used for manoeuvring or parking aircraft. **3** (also **apron stage**) a strip of stage projecting in front of the curtain.
– PHRASES **tied to someone's apron strings** dominated or excessively influenced by someone.
– ORIGIN Old French *naperon* 'small tablecloth'.

apropos /a-pruh-**poh**/ preposition with reference to: *she kept smiling down at her plate, apropos of nothing.*
– ORIGIN French *à propos*.

apse /apss/ noun a large recess with a domed or arched roof at the eastern end of a church.
– DERIVATIVES **apsidal** /**ap**-si-d'l/ adjective.
– ORIGIN Greek *apsis* 'arch, vault'.

a

apt adjective **1** appropriate; suitable. **2** having a tendency to: *junior recruits are most apt to have low morale.* **3** quick to learn.
– DERIVATIVES **aptly** adverb **aptness** noun.
– ORIGIN Latin *aptus* 'fitted'.

aptitude noun a natural ability or tendency: *a youth with a remarkable aptitude for maths.*
– ORIGIN from Latin *aptus* 'fitted'.

aqua- /ak-wuh/ combining form relating to water: *aqualung.*
– ORIGIN Latin *aqua* 'water'.

aqualung noun another term for SCUBA.

aquamarine noun **1** a precious stone consisting of a light bluish-green variety of beryl. **2** a light bluish-green colour.
– ORIGIN from Latin *aqua marina* 'seawater'.

aquanaut noun a diver.
– ORIGIN from Latin *aqua* 'water' + Greek *nautēs* 'sailor'.

aquaplane verb **1** (of a vehicle) slide uncontrollably on a wet surface. **2** ride on an aquaplane. • noun a board for riding on water, pulled by a speedboat.
– ORIGIN from Latin *aqua* 'water' + PLANE¹.

aqua regia /ree-juh/ noun a highly corrosive mixture of concentrated nitric and hydrochloric acids.
– ORIGIN Latin, 'royal water' (because it is able to dissolve gold).

aquarelle /ak-wuh-**rel**/ noun the technique of painting with thin, transparent watercolours.
– ORIGIN from Italian *acquarella* 'watercolour'.

aquarist /**ak**-wuh-rist/ noun a person who keeps an aquarium.

aquarium noun (pl. **aquaria** or **aquariums**) a water-filled glass tank for keeping fish and other water creatures and plants.
– ORIGIN Latin.

Aquarius /uh-**kwair**-i-uhss/ noun a constellation (the Water Carrier) and sign of the zodiac, which the sun enters about 21 January.
– DERIVATIVES **Aquarian** noun & adjective.

aquatic /uh-**kwat**-ik/ adjective **1** relating to water. **2** living in or near water. • noun an aquatic plant or animal.

aquatint noun a print resembling a watercolour, made using a copper plate etched with acid.
– ORIGIN from Italian *acqua tinta* 'coloured water'.

aquavit /**ak**-wuh-veet/ (also **akvavit** /**ak**-vuh-veet/) noun an alcoholic spirit made from potatoes.
– ORIGIN from Norwegian, Swedish, and Danish *akvavit* 'water of life'.

aqua vitae /**vee**-ty, **vy**-tee/ noun old use strong alcoholic spirit, especially brandy.
– ORIGIN Latin, 'water of life'.

aqueduct /**ak**-wuh-dukt/ noun a long channel or raised bridge-like structure, used for carrying water across country.
– ORIGIN from Latin *aquae ductus* 'conduit'.

aqueous /**ay**-kwee-uhss/ adjective relating to or containing water.
– ORIGIN from Latin *aqua* 'water'.

aqueous humour noun the clear fluid in the eyeball in front of the lens.

aquifer /**ak**-wi-fer/ noun a body of rock that holds water or through which water flows.
– ORIGIN from Latin *aqua* 'water' and *-fer* 'bearing'.

aquilegia /ak-wi-**lee**-juh/ noun a garden plant bearing showy flowers with backward-pointing spurs.
– ORIGIN probably from Latin *aquilegus* 'water-collecting'.

aquiline /**ak**-wi-lyn/ adjective **1** (of a nose) curved like an eagle's beak. **2** like an eagle.
– ORIGIN from Latin *aquila* 'eagle'.

AR abbreviation US Arkansas.

Ar symbol the chemical element argon.

Arab noun **1** a member of a Semitic people inhabiting much of the Middle East and North Africa. **2** a breed of horse originating in Arabia.
– DERIVATIVES **Arabize** (or **Arabise**) verb.
– ORIGIN Arabic.

arabesque /a-ruh-**besk**/ noun **1** a ballet posture in which one leg is extended horizontally backwards and the arms are outstretched. **2** an ornamental design consisting of intertwined flowing lines. **3** a musical passage with a highly ornamented melody.
– ORIGIN from Italian *arabesco* 'in the Arabic style'.

Arabian adjective relating to Arabia or its people. • noun historical an Arab.

Arabic noun the Semitic language of the Arabs, written from right to left. • adjective relating to the Arabs or Arabic.

arabica /uh-**rab**-ik-uh/ noun a type of coffee bean widely grown in tropical Asia and Africa.
– ORIGIN Latin, 'Arabic'.

Arabic numeral noun any of the numerals 0, 1, 2, 3, 4, 5, 6, 7, 8, and 9.

Arabism noun **1** Arab culture or identity. **2** an Arabic word or phrase.
– DERIVATIVES **Arabist** noun & adjective.

arable adjective **1** (of land) used or suitable for growing crops. **2** (of crops) able to be grown on arable land.
– ORIGIN from Latin *arare* 'to plough'.

arachnid /uh-**rak**-nid/ noun an invertebrate animal of a class including spiders, scorpions, mites, and ticks.
– ORIGIN from Greek *arakhnē* 'spider'.

arachnophobia /uh-rak-nuh-**foh**-bi-uh/ noun extreme fear of spiders.
– DERIVATIVES **arachnophobe** noun.
– ORIGIN from Greek *arakhnē* 'spider'.

arak noun variant spelling of ARRACK.

Aramaic /a-ruh-**may**-ik/ noun an ancient Semitic language still spoken in parts of the Middle East. • adjective relating to Aramaic.
– ORIGIN Greek *Aramaios* 'of Aram' (the biblical name of Syria).

Aran adjective (of knitwear) featuring patterns of cable stitch and diamond designs, as made traditionally in the Aran Islands off the west coast of Ireland.

Arapaho /uh-**rap**-uh-hoh/ noun (pl. same or **Arapahos**) **1** a member of a North American Indian people living on the Great Plains. **2** the language of the Arapaho.
– ORIGIN from an American Indian word meaning 'many tattoo marks'.

Arawak /a-ruh-wak/ noun (pl. same or
Arawaks) **1** a member of a group of native
peoples of the Greater Antilles and northern
and western South America. **2** any of the
languages of the Arawak.
– ORIGIN Carib.

arbiter /ar-bi-ter/ noun **1** a person who settles a
dispute. **2** a person who has influence in a
particular area: *an arbiter of taste.*
– ORIGIN Latin, 'judge, supreme ruler'.

arbitrage /ar-bi-trahzh/ noun the buying and
selling of assets at the same time in different
markets or in derivative forms, taking
advantage of the differing prices.
– DERIVATIVES **arbitrageur** /ar-bi-trah-zher/
noun.
– ORIGIN from French *arbitrer* 'give judgement'.

arbitrary /ar-bi-truh-ri, ar-bi-tri/ adjective
1 not appearing to be based on any reason or
system: *an arbitrary decision.* **2** (of power or
authority) used without restraint.
– DERIVATIVES **arbitrarily** adverb **arbitrariness**
noun.
– ORIGIN from Latin *arbiter* 'judge, supreme
ruler'.

arbitrate verb (of an independent person or
body) officially settle a dispute.
– DERIVATIVES **arbitration** noun.
– ORIGIN from Latin *arbiter* 'judge, supreme
ruler'.

arbitrator noun an independent person or
body officially appointed to settle a dispute.

arbor[1] noun **1** an axle on which something
revolves. **2** a device holding a tool in a lathe.
– ORIGIN French *arbre* 'tree, axis'.

arbor[2] noun US spelling of **ARBOUR**.

arboreal /ar-bor-i-uhl/ adjective **1** living in
trees. **2** relating to trees.
– ORIGIN from Latin *arbor* 'tree'.

arboretum /ar-buh-ree-tuhm/ noun (pl.
arboretums or **arboreta**) a botanical garden
devoted to trees.
– ORIGIN from Latin *arbor* 'tree'.

arboriculture /ah-buh-ri-kul-cher/ noun the
cultivation of trees and shrubs.

arbour (US **arbor**) noun a garden shelter formed
by trees or climbing plants trained over a
framework.
– ORIGIN from Latin *herba* 'grass, herb',
influenced by *arbor* 'tree'.

arc noun **1** a curve forming part of the
circumference of a circle. **2** a curving passage
of something in the air: *he swung his torch in a
wide arc.* **3** a luminous electrical discharge
between two points. • verb (**arcs**, **arcing**, **arced**)
1 move in an arc: *the ball arced over the goal.*
2 (as noun **arcing**) the forming of an electric
arc.
– ORIGIN Latin *arcus* 'bow, curve'.

arcade noun **1** a covered passage with arches
along one or both sides. **2** a covered walk with
shops along one or both sides. **3** Architecture a
series of arches supporting a wall.
– DERIVATIVES **arcading** noun.
– ORIGIN from Latin *arcus* 'bow, curve'.

Arcadian adjective literary rural in an
unrealistically pleasant way.
– ORIGIN from *Arcadia*, a region of southern
Greece.

arcana /ar-kay-nuh, ar-kah-nuh/ plural noun
(sing. **arcanum**) mysteries or secrets.
– ORIGIN Latin.

arcane /ar-kayn/ adjective understood by few
people; mysterious: *arcane arguments about
economics.*
– DERIVATIVES **arcanely** adverb.
– ORIGIN from Latin *arcere* 'shut up'.

arch[1] noun **1** a curved structure spanning an
opening or supporting the weight of a bridge,
roof, or wall. **2** the inner side of the foot. • verb
form or make a curved shape.
– DERIVATIVES **arched** adjective.
– ORIGIN from Latin *arcus* 'bow'.

arch[2] adjective self-consciously playful or
teasing.
– DERIVATIVES **archly** adverb **archness** noun.
– ORIGIN from **ARCH-**, by association with the
sense 'rogue' in words such as *arch-scoundrel.*

arch- combining form **1** chief; main: *archbishop.*
2 foremost: *arch-enemy.*
– ORIGIN from Greek *arkhos* 'chief'.

Archaean /ah-kee-uhn/ (US **Archean**) adjective
Geology relating to the earlier part of the
Precambrian aeon (before about 2,500 million
years ago).
– ORIGIN from Greek *arkhaios* 'ancient'.

archaeology (US also **archeology**) noun the
study of human history and prehistory
through the excavation of sites and the
analysis of objects found in them.
– DERIVATIVES **archaeologic** adjective
archaeological adjective **archaeologist** noun.
– ORIGIN from Greek *arkhaios* 'ancient'.

archaeopteryx /ar-ki-op-tuh-riks/ noun the
oldest known fossil bird, of the late Jurassic
period, which had feathers and wings like a
bird, but teeth and a bony tail like a dinosaur.
– ORIGIN from Greek *arkhaios* 'ancient' + *pterux*
'wing'.

archaic /ar-kay-ik/ adjective **1** very old or old-
fashioned. **2** belonging to former or ancient
times.
– DERIVATIVES **archaically** adverb.
– ORIGIN Greek *arkhaios* 'ancient'.

archaism /ar-kay-is'm/ noun **1** an old or old-
fashioned word or style of art or language.
2 the use of old or old-fashioned features or
styles in language or art.

archangel /ark-ayn-j'l/ noun an angel of a high
rank.

archbishop noun the chief bishop responsible
for a large district.

archdeacon noun a senior Christian priest
ranking immediately below an archbishop.

archduchess noun **1** the wife or widow of an
archduke. **2** historical a daughter of the Emperor
of Austria.

archduke noun **1** a chief duke. **2** historical a son
of the Emperor of Austria.

Archean adjective US spelling of **ARCHAEAN**.

arch-enemy noun a chief enemy.

archeology noun US spelling of **ARCHAEOLOGY**.

archer noun a person who shoots with a bow
and arrows.
– ORIGIN from Latin *arcus* 'bow'.

archery noun the activity or sport of shooting
with a bow and arrows.

archetype /ar-ki-typ/ noun **1** a very typical

a

example: *she's the archetype of the single American female.* **2** an original model from which other forms are developed. **3** a recurrent symbol in literature or art.
– DERIVATIVES **archetypal** adjective **archetypical** adjective **archetypically** adverb.
– ORIGIN from Greek *arkhe-* 'primitive' + *tupos* 'a model'.

archiepiscopal /ah-ki-i-**pis**-kuh-puhl/ adjective relating to an archbishop.

Archimedes' principle noun Physics a law discovered by the Greek mathematician Archimedes (*c.*287–212 BC), stating that a body immersed in a fluid is subject to an upward force equal to the weight of fluid the body displaces.

archipelago /ar-ki-**pel**-uh-goh/ noun (pl. **archipelagos** or **archipelagoes**) a group of many islands.
– ORIGIN from Greek *arkhi-* 'chief' + *pelagos* 'sea'.

architect noun **1** a person who designs buildings and supervises their construction. **2** a person who originates or realizes an idea or project: *the architects of the green revolution.*
– ORIGIN Greek *arkhitektōn* 'chief builder'.

architectonic /ar-ki-tek-**ton**-ik/ adjective **1** relating to architecture or architects. **2** having a clearly defined and artistically pleasing structure: *architectonic cheekbones.*
• noun (**architectonics**) (treated as sing.) the scientific study of architecture.

architecture noun **1** the art or practice of designing and constructing buildings. **2** the style in which a building is designed and constructed: *Gothic architecture.* **3** the complex structure of something.
– DERIVATIVES **architectural** adjective.

architrave /**ar**-ki-trayv/ noun **1** (in classical architecture) a main beam resting across the tops of columns. **2** the frame around a doorway or window.
– ORIGIN from Latin *trabs* 'a beam'.

archive /**ar**-kyv/ noun **1** a collection of historical documents or records. **2** a complete record of the data in a computer system, stored on a less frequently used medium.
• verb place or store something in an archive.
– DERIVATIVES **archival** adjective.
– ORIGIN from Greek *arkheia* 'public records'.

archivist /**ar**-ki-vist/ noun a person who is in charge of archives.

arch-rival noun the chief rival of a person, team, or organization.

archway noun a curved structure forming a passage or entrance.

arc lamp (also **arc light**) noun a light source using an electric arc.

Arctic adjective **1** relating to the regions around the North Pole. **2** living or growing in the regions around the North Pole. **3** (**arctic**) informal (of weather) very cold. • noun (**the Arctic**) the regions around the North Pole.
– ORIGIN from Greek *arktos* 'bear, Ursa Major, pole star'.

arcuate /**ah**-kyoo-uht/ adjective technical curved.
– ORIGIN from Latin *arcus* 'bow, curve'.

ardent adjective **1** very enthusiastic; passionate:

an ardent supporter of organic agriculture. **2** old use burning or glowing.
– DERIVATIVES **ardently** adverb.
– ORIGIN from Latin *ardere* 'to burn'.

ardour (US **ardor**) noun great enthusiasm; passion.
– ORIGIN from Latin *ardere* 'to burn'.

arduous adjective difficult and tiring.
– DERIVATIVES **arduously** adverb **arduousness** noun.
– ORIGIN Latin *arduus* 'steep, difficult'.

are second person singular present and first, second, third person plural present of **BE**.

area noun **1** a part of a place, object, or surface. **2** the extent or measurement of a surface. **3** a space allocated for a specific use: *a picnic area.* **4** a subject or range of activity. **5** a sunken enclosure leading to a basement.
– DERIVATIVES **areal** adjective.
– ORIGIN Latin, 'piece of level ground'.

area code noun a telephone dialling code.

arena noun **1** a level area surrounded by seating, in which sports and other public events are held. **2** an area of activity: *conflicts within the political arena.*
– ORIGIN Latin *harena, arena* 'sand, sand-covered place of combat'.

aren't contraction **1** are not. **2** am not (only used in questions): *I'm right, aren't I?*

areola /uh-**ree**-uh-luh/ noun (pl. **areolae** /uh-**ree**-uh-lee/) Anatomy a small circular area, especially the darker skin surrounding a human nipple.
– ORIGIN Latin, 'small open space'.

arête /uh-**ret**/ noun a sharp mountain ridge.
– ORIGIN French.

argent adjective & noun literary & Heraldry silver.
– ORIGIN Latin *argentum* 'silver'.

Argentine noun & adjective another term for **ARGENTINIAN**.

Argentinian noun a person from Argentina.
• adjective relating to Argentina.

argon noun an inert gaseous chemical element, present in small amounts in the air.
– ORIGIN from Greek *argos* 'idle'.

argosy /**ar**-guh-si/ noun (pl. **argosies**) literary a large merchant ship, originally one from Ragusa (now Dubrovnik) or Venice.
– ORIGIN from Italian *Ragusea nave* 'vessel of *Ragusa*'.

argot /**ar**-goh/ noun the jargon or slang of a particular group or area of activity: *the argot of city planning.*
– ORIGIN French.

arguable adjective **1** able to be argued or asserted: *it is arguable that the company was already experiencing problems.* **2** open to disagreement.
– DERIVATIVES **arguably** adverb.

argue verb (**argues, arguing, argued**) **1** exchange conflicting views heatedly. **2** give reasons or evidence in support of something: *those who argue that terrorism always fails are right.*
– PHRASES **argue the toss** informal, chiefly Brit. dispute a decision already made.
– DERIVATIVES **arguer** noun.
– ORIGIN Latin *arguere* 'prove, accuse'.

argument noun **1** a heated exchange of

conflicting views. **2** a set of reasons given in support of something.

argumentation noun systematic reasoning in support of something.

argumentative adjective apt to argue.

argy-bargy /ah-ji-**bah**-ji/ noun informal, chiefly Brit. noisy quarrelling.
– ORIGIN from **ARGUE**.

argyle /rhymes with mile/ noun a pattern used in knitwear, consisting of coloured diamonds on a plain background.
– ORIGIN from *Argyll*, the Scottish clan on whose tartan the pattern is based.

aria /**ah**-ri-uh/ noun a long accompanied song for a solo voice in an opera or oratorio.
– ORIGIN Italian.

arid adjective **1** very dry because having little or no rain. **2** uninteresting; unsatisfying.
– DERIVATIVES **aridity** noun.
– ORIGIN from Latin *arere* 'be dry or parched'.

Aries /**air**-eez/ noun a constellation (the Ram) and sign of the zodiac, which the sun enters about 20 March.
– DERIVATIVES **Arian** noun & adjective.
– ORIGIN Latin.

aright adverb dialect correctly; properly.
– ORIGIN Old English.

arise verb (past **arose**; past part. **arisen**) **1** come into being or come to notice: *new difficulties had arisen*. **2** (**arise from/out of**) occur as a result of: *back pain can arise from a multitude of problems*. **3** formal get or stand up.
– ORIGIN Old English.

aristocracy /a-ris-**tok**-ruh-si/ noun (pl. **aristocracies**) the highest social class, consisting of people of noble birth with hereditary titles.
– ORIGIN from Greek *aristos* 'best' + *-kratia* 'power'.

aristocrat /**ar**-is-tuh-krat, uh-**ris**-tuh-krat/ noun a member of the aristocracy.

aristocratic adjective relating to or typical of the aristocracy.
– DERIVATIVES **aristocratically** adverb.

Aristotelian /a-ris-tuh-**tee**-li-uhn/ adjective relating to the theories of the Greek philosopher Aristotle (384–322 BC). • noun a student or follower of Aristotle or his philosophy.

arithmetic noun /uh-**rith**-muh-tik/ **1** the branch of mathematics concerned with the properties and manipulation of numbers. **2** the use of numbers in counting and calculation. • adjective /a-rith-**met**-ik/ relating to arithmetic.
– DERIVATIVES **arithmetical** adjective **arithmetically** adverb **arithmetician** noun.
– ORIGIN from Greek *arithmētikē tekhnē* 'art of counting'.

arithmetic progression (also **arithmetic series**) noun a sequence of numbers in which each differs from the preceding one by a constant quantity (e.g. 9, 7, 5, 3, etc.).

ark noun **1** (in the Bible) the ship built by Noah to save his family and two of every kind of animal from the Flood. **2** (also **Holy Ark**) a chest or cupboard housing the Torah scrolls in a synagogue. **3** (**Ark of the Covenant**) the chest which contained the laws of the ancient Israelites.
– PHRASES **out of the ark** Brit. informal very old or old-fashioned.
– ORIGIN Latin *arca* 'chest'.

arm¹ noun **1** each of the two upper limbs of the human body from the shoulder to the hand. **2** a side part of a chair supporting a sitter's arm. **3** a narrow strip of water or land projecting from a larger area. **4** a branch or division of an organization.
– PHRASES **arm in arm** with arms linked. **cost an arm and a leg** informal be very expensive. **keep someone/thing at arm's length** avoid close contact with someone or something. **with open arms** with great affection or enthusiasm.
– DERIVATIVES **armful** noun **armless** adjective **armload** noun.
– ORIGIN Old English.

arm² verb **1** supply someone with weapons. **2** provide with essential equipment or information: *we were armed with all sorts of statistics*. **3** activate the fuse of a bomb or missile so that it is ready to explode.
– ORIGIN from Latin *arma* 'armour, arms'.

armada /ar-**mar**-duh/ noun a fleet of warships.
– ORIGIN Spanish, from Latin *armare* 'to arm'.

armadillo /ar-muh-**dil**-loh/ noun (pl. **armadillos**) an insect-eating mammal of Central and South America, with a body covered in bony plates.
– ORIGIN Spanish, 'little armed man'.

Armageddon /ar-muh-**ged**-duhn/ noun **1** (in the New Testament) the last battle between good and evil before the Day of Judgement. **2** a catastrophic conflict or event: *the threat of nuclear Armageddon*.
– ORIGIN Hebrew, 'hill of Megiddo' (Book of Revelation, chapter 16).

Armagnac /**ah**-muhn-yak/ noun a type of brandy made in Aquitaine in SW France.
– ORIGIN the former name of a district in Aquitaine.

armament /**ar**-muh-muhnt/ noun **1** (also **armaments**) military weapons and equipment. **2** the equipping of military forces for war.
– ORIGIN from Latin *armare* 'to arm'.

armature /**ar**-muh-cher/ noun **1** the rotating coil of a dynamo or electric motor. **2** any moving part of an electrical machine in which a voltage is induced by a magnetic field. **3** a piece of iron placed across the poles of a magnet to preserve its power. **4** the protective covering of an animal or plant.
– ORIGIN Latin *armatura* 'armour'.

armband noun **1** a band worn around the upper arm to indicate something, such as a person's role or identity. **2** an inflatable plastic band worn around the upper arm as a swimming aid.

armchair noun an upholstered chair with side supports for the sitter's arms. • adjective experiencing something through reading, television, etc. rather than doing it: *an armchair traveller*.

armed adjective equipped with or involving a firearm.

armed forces plural noun a country's army, navy, and air force.

Armenian /ah-**meen**-i-uhn/ noun **1** a person from Armenia. **2** the language of Armenia.

• **adjective** relating to Armenia.

armhole noun each of two openings in a garment through which the wearer puts their arms.

armistice /**ar**-miss-tiss/ noun a truce.
– ORIGIN from Latin *arma* 'arms' + *-stitium* 'stoppage'.

armlet noun a bracelet worn round the upper arm.

armlock noun a method of restraining someone by holding their arm bent tightly behind their back.

armoire /ah-**mwah**/ noun a cupboard or wardrobe.
– ORIGIN French.

armor noun US spelling of ARMOUR.

armorer noun US spelling of ARMOURER.

armorial adjective relating to heraldry or coats of arms.

armory noun US spelling of ARMOURY.

armour (US **armor**) noun 1 the metal coverings formerly worn to protect the body in battle. 2 (also **armour plate**) the tough metal layer covering a military vehicle or ship. 3 military vehicles as a whole. 4 the protective layer or shell of some animals and plants.
– DERIVATIVES **armoured** adjective.
– ORIGIN from Latin *arma* 'armour, arms'.

armourer (US **armorer**) noun 1 a maker or supplier of weapons or armour. 2 an official in charge of the arms of a warship or regiment.

armour-plated adjective covered with armour plate.

armoury (US **armory**) noun (pl. **armouries**) 1 a store or supply of arms. 2 a set of resources available for a purpose: *the growing police armoury of speed cameras.*

armpit noun a hollow under the arm at the shoulder.

armrest noun an arm of a chair.

arms plural noun 1 guns and other weapons. 2 the heraldic emblems on a coat of arms.
– PHRASES **a call to arms** a call to prepare for conflict. **up in arms** strongly opposed to and protesting about something.
– ORIGIN Latin *arma*.

arms control noun international agreement to limit the production and accumulation of arms.

arms race noun a situation in which nations compete for superiority in developing and stockpiling weapons.

arm-wrestling noun a contest in which two seated people clasp hands and try to force each other's arm down on to a surface.

army noun (pl. **armies**) 1 an organized military force equipped for fighting on land. 2 a large number of similar people or things: *an army of cleaners.*
– ORIGIN from Latin *armare* 'to arm'.

arnica /**ah**-ni-kuh/ noun a plant with yellow daisy-like flowers, used for the treatment of bruises.
– ORIGIN Latin.

aroha /a-ro-**huh**/ noun NZ 1 love; affection. 2 sympathy.
– ORIGIN Maori.

aroma noun 1 a pleasant and distinctive smell. 2 a particular quality or atmosphere: *the*

aroma of officialdom.
– ORIGIN Greek, 'spice'.

aromatherapy noun the use of aromatic oils obtained from plants for healing or to promote well-being.
– DERIVATIVES **aromatherapeutic** adjective **aromatherapist** noun.

aromatic adjective 1 having a pleasant and distinctive smell. 2 (of an organic compound such as benzene) containing a flat ring of atoms in its molecule. • noun an aromatic plant, substance, or compound.
– DERIVATIVES **aromatically** adverb.

arose past of ARISE.

around adverb 1 on every side. 2 so as to face in the opposite direction. 3 in or to many places throughout an area. 4 without purpose. 5 available or present. 6 approximately.
• **preposition** 1 on every side of. 2 in or to many places throughout. 3 so as to encircle or embrace. 4 following a circular route round.

arouse verb 1 bring about a feeling or response: *the invitation had aroused my curiosity.* 2 excite someone sexually. 3 awaken someone from sleep.
– DERIVATIVES **arousal** noun.
– ORIGIN from ROUSE.

arpeggio /ar-**pej**-ji-oh/ noun (pl. **arpeggios**) the notes of a musical chord played in rapid succession.
– ORIGIN Italian.

arrack /**ar**-uhk/ (also **arak** /uh-**rak**/) noun an alcoholic spirit made in Eastern countries from the sap of the coco palm or from rice.
– ORIGIN Arabic, 'sweat'.

arraign /uh-**rayn**/ verb call someone before a court to answer a criminal charge.
– DERIVATIVES **arraignment** noun.
– ORIGIN Old French *araisnier*.

arrange verb 1 put tidily or in a particular order: *the columns are arranged in rows.* 2 organize or plan for something. 3 adapt a musical composition for performance with instruments or voices other than those originally specified.
– DERIVATIVES **arrangeable** adjective **arranger** noun.
– ORIGIN Old French *arangier*.

arrangement noun 1 a plan for a future event: *I made arrangements to meet him.* 2 an agreement to do something. 3 something made up of items placed in an attractive or ordered way: *a flower arrangement.* 4 an arranged musical composition.

arrant /a-ruhnt/ adjective utter; complete: *what arrant nonsense!*
– ORIGIN variant of ERRANT, originally in phrases such as *arrant thief*, meaning 'outlawed, roving thief'.

arras /**ar**-uhss/ noun a tapestry wall hanging.
– ORIGIN named after the French town of *Arras*.

array noun 1 an impressive display or range: *a bewildering array of choices.* 2 an ordered arrangement of troops. 3 literary elaborate or beautiful clothing. • verb 1 display or arrange in a neat or impressive way: *bottled waters are arrayed on crushed ice.* 2 (**be arrayed in**) be elaborately clothed in something.
– ORIGIN Old French *arei*.

arrears plural noun money owed that should

already have been paid.
- PHRASES **in arrears 1** behind with paying money that is owed. **2** (of wages or rent) paid at the end of each period of work or occupation.
- ORIGIN Old French *arere*.

arrest verb **1** seize someone by legal authority and take them into custody. **2** stop or delay progress or a process: *the spread of the disease can be arrested.* **3** (as adj. **arresting**) attracting attention. •noun **1** an act of arresting someone. **2** a sudden stop.
- DERIVATIVES **arrestingly** adverb.
- ORIGIN Latin *restare* 'remain, stop'.

arrhythmia /uh-**rith**-mi-uh/ noun a medical condition in which the heart beats with an irregular or abnormal rhythm.
- DERIVATIVES **arrhythmic** adjective.
- ORIGIN Greek *arruthmia* 'lack of rhythm'.

arrival noun **1** the action of arriving. **2** a person or thing that has just arrived or appeared.

arrive verb **1** reach a destination. **2** be brought or delivered. **3** (of a moment or event) happen: *spring has finally arrived.* **4** (**arrive at**) reach a conclusion or decision. **5** informal become successful and well known.
- ORIGIN Old French *ariver*, from Latin *ripa* 'shore'.

arrivederci /a-ree-vuh-**der**-chi/ exclamation goodbye until we meet again.
- ORIGIN Italian, 'to the seeing again'.

arriviste /a-ri-**veest**/ noun often derogatory a person who has recently become wealthy or risen in social status or is ambitious to do so.
- ORIGIN French.

arrogant adjective having an exaggerated sense of one's own importance or abilities.
- DERIVATIVES **arrogance** noun **arrogantly** adverb.
- ORIGIN from Latin *arrogare* 'claim for oneself'.

arrogate /a-ruh-gayt/ verb take or claim something for oneself without justification.
- DERIVATIVES **arrogation** noun.
- ORIGIN Latin *arrogare*.

arrondissement /a-ron-dees-mon, a-ron-**dees**-mon/ noun **1** (in France) a subdivision of a local government department. **2** an administrative district of Paris.
- ORIGIN French.

arrow noun **1** a stick with a sharp pointed head, designed to be shot from a bow. **2** a symbol resembling an arrow, used to show direction or position.
- DERIVATIVES **arrowed** adjective.
- ORIGIN Old Norse.

arrowroot noun a plant that yields a fine-grained starch used in cookery and medicine.
- ORIGIN Arawak, 'meal of meals', altered by association with ARROW and ROOT¹, the plant's tubers being used to absorb poison from arrow wounds.

arroyo /uh-**roy**-oh/ noun (pl. **arroyos**) US a deep gully cut by the action of fast-flowing water in an arid area.
- ORIGIN Spanish.

arse noun Brit. vulgar slang a person's bottom.
- ORIGIN Old English.

arsenal noun a store of weapons and ammunition.

- ORIGIN Arabic, 'house of industry'.

arsenic noun a brittle steel-grey chemical element with poisonous compounds.
- DERIVATIVES **arsenical** adjective **arsenide** noun.
- ORIGIN Greek *arsenikon*.

arson noun the criminal act of deliberately setting fire to property.
- DERIVATIVES **arsonist** noun.
- ORIGIN from Latin *ardere* 'to burn'.

art¹ noun **1** the expression of creative skill in a visual form such as painting or sculpture. **2** paintings, drawings, and sculpture as a whole. **3** (**the arts**) the branches of creative activity, such as painting, music, and drama. **4** (**arts**) subjects of study mainly concerned with human culture (as contrasted with scientific or technical subjects). **5** a skill: *the art of conversation.*
- ORIGIN Latin *ars*.

art² old-fashioned or dialect second person singular present of BE.

art deco noun a decorative art style of the 1920s and 1930s, characterized by geometric shapes.
- ORIGIN French *art décoratif* 'decorative art'.

artefact /**ar**-ti-fakt/ (US **artifact**) noun a useful or decorative man-made object.
- ORIGIN from Latin *arte* 'using art' + *factum* 'something made'.

arterial /ar-**teer**-i-uhl/ adjective **1** relating to an artery or arteries. **2** relating to an important transport route.

arteriosclerosis /ar-teer-i-oh-skluh-**roh**-siss/ noun thickening and hardening of the walls of the arteries.

artery noun (pl. **arteries**) **1** any of the tubes through which blood flows from the heart around the body. **2** an important transport route.
- ORIGIN Greek *artēria*.

artesian well /ar-**tee**-*zh*'n/ noun a well bored vertically into a layer of water-bearing rock that is lying at an angle, the water coming to the surface by natural pressure.
- ORIGIN from *Artois*, a region in France.

artful adjective clever, especially in a cunning way.
- DERIVATIVES **artfully** adverb **artfulness** noun.

art house noun a cinema which shows artistic or experimental films.

arthritis /ar-**thry**-tiss/ noun painful inflammation and stiffness of the joints.
- DERIVATIVES **arthritic** /ar-**thri**-tik/ adjective & noun.
- ORIGIN from Greek *arthron* 'joint'.

arthropod /**ar**-thruh-pod/ noun an invertebrate animal with a body divided into segments and an external skeleton, such as an insect, spider, or crab.
- ORIGIN from Greek *arthron* 'joint' + *pous* 'foot'.

Arthurian /ah-**thyoor**-i-uhn/ adjective relating to the reign of the legendary King Arthur of Britain.

artichoke noun (also **globe artichoke**) a vegetable consisting of the unopened flower head of a thistle-like plant.
- ORIGIN from Arabic.

article noun **1** a particular object. **2** a piece of

a

writing in a newspaper or magazine. **3** a separate clause or paragraph of a legal document. **4** (**articles**) a period of professional training as a solicitor, architect, surveyor, or accountant. • verb (**be articled**) (of a solicitor, architect, etc.) be employed under contract as a trainee.
– PHRASES **article of faith** a firmly held belief.
– ORIGIN Latin *articulus* 'small connecting part'.

articled clerk noun a law student employed as a trainee.

articular adjective Anatomy relating to a joint.

articulate adjective /ar-**tik**-yuu-luht/ **1** able to speak fluently and clearly. **2** having joints or jointed segments. • verb /ar-**tik**-yuu-layt/ **1** pronounce words distinctly. **2** clearly express in words: *the president articulated the feelings of the vast majority.* **3** form a joint. **4** (as adj. **articulated**) having sections connected by a flexible joint.
– DERIVATIVES **articulacy** noun **articulately** adverb **articulateness** noun **articulator** noun.
– ORIGIN from Latin *articulus* 'small connecting part'.

articulation noun **1** the expression of an idea or feeling in words. **2** the formation of distinct sounds in speech. **3** the state of being jointed.

artifact noun US spelling of ARTEFACT.

artifice /**ar**-ti-fiss/ noun the use of skill or cunning in order to trick or deceive: *the artifice of 1980s pop culture.*
– ORIGIN from Latin *ars* 'art' + *facere* 'make'.

artificer /ar-**ti**-fi-ser/ noun **1** a person skilled in making or planning things. **2** a skilled mechanic in the armed forces.

artificial adjective **1** made as a copy of something natural: *artificial flowers.* **2** not sincere; affected.
– DERIVATIVES **artificiality** noun **artificially** adverb.
– ORIGIN from Latin *ars* 'art' + *facere* 'make'.

artificial insemination noun the injection of semen into the vagina or womb of a woman or female animal, as a medical method of fertilizing an egg.

artificial intelligence noun the performance by computers of tasks normally requiring human intelligence.

artificial respiration noun the forcing of air into and out of a person's lungs to make them begin breathing again.

artillery noun **1** large-calibre guns used in warfare on land. **2** a branch of the armed forces trained to use artillery.
– ORIGIN from Old French *atillier* 'equip, arm'.

artisan noun a skilled worker who makes things by hand.
– DERIVATIVES **artisanal** adjective.
– ORIGIN from Latin *artire* 'instruct in the arts'.

artist noun **1** a person who paints or draws as a profession or hobby. **2** a person who practises or performs any of the creative arts. **3** informal a person who practises a particular activity: *a con artist.*
– ORIGIN from Latin *ars* 'art'.

artiste /ar-**teest**/ noun a professional singer or dancer.
– ORIGIN French, 'artist'.

artistic adjective **1** having creative skill. **2** relating to or characteristic of art or artists:

an artistic temperament. **3** pleasing to look at: *artistic designs.*
– DERIVATIVES **artistically** adverb.

artistry noun creative skill or ability: *the artistry of the pianist.*

artless adjective **1** sincere, straightforward, or unpretentious: *an artless, naive girl.* **2** without skill; clumsy.
– DERIVATIVES **artlessly** adverb.

art nouveau /ar noo-**voh**, art noo-**voh**/ noun a style of art and architecture of the late 19th and early 20th centuries, having intricate linear designs and flowing curves.
– ORIGIN French, 'new art'.

artwork noun illustrations for inclusion in a publication.

arty (chiefly N. Amer. also **artsy**) adjective (**artier**, **artiest**) informal interested or involved in the arts in an affected way.
– DERIVATIVES **artiness** noun.

arugula /uh-**roog**-yu-luh/ noun N. Amer. the salad vegetable rocket.
– ORIGIN Italian dialect *arucula*.

arum /**air**-uhm/ noun cuckoo pint or a related plant.
– ORIGIN Greek *aron*.

arum lily noun a tall lily-like African plant of the arum family.

Aryan /**air**-i-uhn/ noun **1** a member of a people speaking an Indo-European language who spread into northern India in the 2nd millennium BC. **2** the language of the ancient Aryans. **3** (in Nazi ideology) a non-Jewish person of Caucasian race. • adjective relating to the Aryan people.
– ORIGIN from Sanskrit, 'noble'.

As symbol the chemical element arsenic.

as adverb used in comparisons to refer to the extent or amount of something. • conjunction **1** while. **2** in the way that. **3** because. **4** even though. • preposition **1** in the role of; being: *a job as a cook.* **2** while; when.
– PHRASES **as for** with regard to. **as yet** until now or that time.
– ORIGIN Old English, 'similarly'.

> **USAGE:** Some people think that you should say *he's not as shy as I* (rather than *he's not as shy as me*), but this sounds stilted and is now rarely used in normal speech. For more information, see the note at **PERSONAL PRONOUN**.

asafoetida /a-suh-**feet**-i-duh/ (US **asafetida**) noun an unpleasant-smelling gum obtained from the roots of a plant, used in herbal medicine and Indian cooking.
– ORIGIN from Latin *asa* 'mastic' + *foetida* 'stinking'.

asana /**ah**-suh-nuh/ noun a posture adopted in hatha yoga.
– ORIGIN from Sanskrit *āsana*.

asap abbreviation as soon as possible.

asbestos noun a fibrous silicate mineral used in fire-resistant and insulating materials.
– ORIGIN from Greek, 'unquenchable'.

asbestosis /az-be-**stoh**-sis, as-be-**stoh**-sis/ noun a serious lung disease, often accompanied by cancer, resulting from breathing asbestos dust.

ASBO (also **Asbo**) abbreviation Brit. antisocial

behaviour order.

ascend verb **1** go up; rise or climb: *I ascended the stairs.* **2** move up in rank or status.
– DERIVATIVES **ascender** noun.
– ORIGIN Latin *ascendere*.

ascendant adjective **1** rising in power or influence. **2** Astrology (of a planet or sign of the zodiac) just above the eastern horizon.
– PHRASES **in the ascendant** rising in power or influence.
– DERIVATIVES **ascendancy** noun.

ascension noun **1** the action of rising in status. **2** (**Ascension**) the ascent of Jesus into heaven after the Resurrection.

ascent noun **1** an act of ascending something: *the first ascent of the Matterhorn.* **2** an upward slope.

ascertain /ass-er-**tayn**/ verb find out for certain: *an investigation to ascertain the cause of the accident.*
– DERIVATIVES **ascertainable** adjective **ascertainment** noun.
– ORIGIN Old French *acertener*, from Latin *certus* 'settled, sure'.

ascetic /uh-**set**-ik/ adjective strictly self-disciplined and avoiding any pleasures or luxuries. • noun an ascetic person.
– DERIVATIVES **asceticism** noun.
– ORIGIN from Greek *askētēs* 'monk'.

ASCII /**ass**-ki/ abbreviation Computing American Standard Code for Information Interchange.

ascorbic acid /uh-**skor**-bik/ noun vitamin C.
– ORIGIN from Latin *scorbutus* 'scurvy'.

ascribe verb (**ascribe something to**) **1** consider something to be caused by: *he ascribed his fits of depression to the divorce.* **2** consider that a particular quality belongs to someone or something: *those who ascribe great importance to his theories.*
– DERIVATIVES **ascription** noun.
– ORIGIN from Latin *scribere* 'write'.

asdic noun a form of sonar developed by the British in the First World War to detect submarines.
– ORIGIN from the initial letters of *Anti-Submarine Detection Investigation Committee*.

aseptic /ay-**sep**-tik/ adjective free from harmful bacteria, viruses, and other microorganisms.

asexual adjective **1** not having sexual feelings or associations. **2** (of reproduction) not involving sexual activity. **3** not having sexual organs.
– DERIVATIVES **asexually** adverb.

ash¹ noun **1** the powder remaining after something has been burned. **2** (**ashes**) the remains of a human body after cremation. **3** (**the Ashes**) a cricket trophy awarded for winning a Test match series between England and Australia. [from a mock obituary published in 1882, which referred to the symbolic remains of English cricket after an Australian victory.]
– DERIVATIVES **ashy** adjective.
– ORIGIN Old English.

ash² noun a tree with winged fruits and hard pale wood.
– ORIGIN Old English.

ashamed adjective feeling embarrassed or guilty.

– ORIGIN Old English.

Ashanti /uh-**shan**-ti/ (also **Asante**) noun (pl. same) a member of a people of south central Ghana.
– ORIGIN the name in Akan (an African language).

ash blonde (also **ash blond**) adjective very pale blonde.

ashen adjective very pale as a result of shock, fear, or illness.

Ashkenazi /ash-kuh-**nah**-zi/ noun (pl. **Ashkenazim** /ash-kuh-**nah**-zim/) a Jew of central or eastern European descent. Compare with SEPHARDI.
– ORIGIN from *Ashkenaz*, a grandson of Noah.

ashlar /**ash**-ler/ noun large square-cut stones used as the surface layer of a wall.
– ORIGIN Old French *aisselier*.

ashore adverb to or on the shore or land.

ashram /**ash**-ruhm/ noun a Hindu religious retreat or community.
– ORIGIN Sanskrit, 'hermitage'.

ashtanga /ash-**tang**-uh/ noun a type of yoga based on eight principles and consisting of a series of poses performed in rapid succession, combined with deep, controlled breathing.
– ORIGIN from a Sanskrit word meaning 'eight'.

ashtray noun a small receptacle for tobacco ash and cigarette ends.

Ash Wednesday noun the first day of Lent in the Christian Church.
– ORIGIN from the custom of marking the foreheads of penitents with ashes on that day.

Asian /**ay**-zh'n/ noun a person from Asia or a person of Asian descent. • adjective relating to Asia.

> USAGE: In Britain **Asian** is used to refer to people who come from (or whose parents came from) the Indian subcontinent, while in North America it is used to refer to people from the Far East.

Asiatic /ay-zi-**at**-ik/ adjective relating to Asia.

> USAGE: Altough it is standard in scientific and technical use, **Asiatic** can be offensive when used of individual people: use **Asian** instead.

A-side noun the side of a pop single regarded as the main one.

aside adverb **1** to one side; out of the way. **2** in reserve. • noun **1** an actor's remark spoken to the audience rather than the other characters. **2** a remark that is not directly related to the main subject of discussion.
– PHRASES **aside from** apart from.

asinine /**ass**-i-nyn/ adjective extremely stupid or foolish.
– ORIGIN Latin *asinus* 'ass'.

-asis (also **-iasis**) suffix forming the names of diseases: *psoriasis.*
– ORIGIN Greek.

ask verb **1** say something in order to get an answer or some information. **2** say that one wants someone to do, give, or allow something: *she asked me to help her.* **3** (**ask for**) request to speak to someone. **4** expect or demand something from someone: *you are asking too much of her.* **5** invite someone to a social occasion. **6** (**ask someone out**) invite

a

someone out on a date. **7 (ask after)** Brit. make polite enquiries about someone's health or well-being.
– PHRASES **for the asking** for little or no effort or cost: *the job was his for the asking.*
– ORIGIN Old English.

askance /uh-**skanss**, uh-**skahnss**/ adverb with a suspicious or disapproving look.
– ORIGIN unknown.

askew /uh-**skyoo**/ adverb & adjective not straight or level.

asking price noun the price at which something is offered for sale.

aslant adverb & preposition at or across at a slant.

asleep adjective & adverb in or into a state of sleep.

AS level noun (in the UK except Scotland) an exam or a pass at advanced subsidiary level.

asp noun 1 a small viper with an upturned snout. 2 the Egyptian cobra.
– ORIGIN Greek *aspis.*

asparagus /uh-**spa**-ruh-guhss/ noun a vegetable consisting of the tender young shoots of a tall plant.
– ORIGIN Greek *asparagos.*

aspartame /uh-**spah**-taym/ noun a low-calorie artificial sweetener.
– ORIGIN from *aspartic acid*, a related chemical named after *asparagus.*

aspect noun 1 a particular part or feature of something: *a training course covering all aspects of the business.* 2 a particular appearance or quality: *the black eyepatch gave his face a sinister aspect.* 3 the side of a building facing a particular direction.
– ORIGIN Latin *aspectus*, from *aspicere* 'look at'.

aspect ratio noun the ratio of the width to the height of an image on a television screen.

aspen noun a poplar tree with small rounded leaves.
– ORIGIN dialect.

Asperger's syndrome /as-per-juhz/ noun a mild form of autism.
– ORIGIN named after the Austrian psychiatrist Hans *Asperger.*

asperity /uh-**spe**-ri-ti/ noun harshness of tone or manner.
– ORIGIN from Latin *asper* 'rough'.

aspersions /uh-**sper**-sh'nz/ plural noun in phrase **cast aspersions on**) make critical or unpleasant remarks about: *no one is casting aspersions on you or your officers.*
– ORIGIN from Latin *aspergere* 'sprinkle'.

asphalt /**ass**-falt/ noun a dark tar-like substance used in surfacing roads or waterproofing buildings.
– ORIGIN Greek *asphalton.*

asphodel /**ass**-fuh-del/ noun a plant of the lily family with clusters of yellow or white flowers on a long stem.
– ORIGIN Greek *asphodelos.*

asphyxia /uh-**sfik**-si-uh/ noun a condition arising when the body is deprived of oxygen, causing unconsciousness or death.
– ORIGIN Greek *asphuxia*, from *a-* 'without' + *sphuxis* 'pulse'.

asphyxiate verb 1 kill someone by depriving them of oxygen. 2 die as a result of a lack of oxygen.

– DERIVATIVES **asphyxiation** noun.

aspic noun a savoury jelly made with meat stock.
– ORIGIN French, 'asp', the colours of the jelly being compared with those of the snake.

aspidistra /ass-pi-**diss**-truh/ noun a plant of the lily family with broad tapering leaves.
– ORIGIN Greek *aspis* 'shield'.

aspirant /**ass**-pi-ruhnt/ noun a person with strong ambitions to do or be something.

aspirate verb /**ass**-pi-rayt/ 1 pronounce a word with the sound of the letter *h* at the start. 2 remove fluid from a part of the body using suction. 3 technical inhale. • noun /**ass**-pi-ruht/ the sound of the letter *h.*
– ORIGIN Latin *aspirare.*

aspiration noun a strong desire to do or have something; an ambition: *he never showed any aspirations for political office.*

aspirational adjective 1 having a strong desire to do or have something: *young, aspirational women.* 2 referring or relating to something which people strongly desire to do or have: *an aspirational lifestyle.*

aspirator noun an instrument or device for removing fluid from a part of the body by suction.

aspire verb have strong ambitions to be or do something: *she aspired to study at Cambridge.*
– DERIVATIVES **aspiring** adjective.
– ORIGIN Latin *aspirare.*

aspirin noun (pl. same or **aspirins**) a medicine used in tablet form to relieve pain and reduce fever and inflammation.
– ORIGIN from its chemical name.

ass[1] noun 1 a donkey or related small wild horse. 2 informal a stupid person.
– ORIGIN Latin *asinus.*

ass[2] noun North American form of **ARSE**.

assail verb 1 attack someone or something violently. 2 (of an unpleasant feeling) come upon someone suddenly and strongly: *she was assailed by doubts and regrets.*
– ORIGIN Latin *assalire*, from *salire* 'to leap'.

assailant noun an attacker.

assassin noun a person who assassinates someone.
– ORIGIN Arabic, 'hashish eater' (referring to a fanatical Muslim sect at the time of the Crusades who were said to use hashish before murder missions).

assassinate verb murder an important person for political or religious reasons.
– DERIVATIVES **assassination** noun.

assault noun 1 a violent attack. 2 Law an act that threatens physical harm to a person. 3 a determined attempt to do something difficult: *a winter assault on Mt Everest* • verb attack someone violently.
– ORIGIN Old French *assauter*, from Latin *saltare* 'to leap'.

assault and battery noun Law the action of threatening a person together with making physical contact with them.

assault course noun Brit. a series of demanding physical challenges, used for training soldiers.

assault rifle noun a lightweight rifle which may be set to fire automatically or semi-automatically.

assay /uh-**say**, ass-ay/ noun the process of testing a metal or ore to establish its composition or purity. • verb **1** test a metal or ore to establish its composition or purity. **2** old use attempt.
– ORIGIN Old French *assai*, *essai* 'trial'.

assegai /**ass**-uh-gy/ noun (pl. **assegais**) a slender iron-tipped spear used by southern African peoples.
– ORIGIN Arabic, 'the spear'.

assemblage noun **1** a collection or gathering of things or people: *a rich assemblage of 16th-century paintings.* **2** something made of pieces fitted together.

assemble verb **1** come or bring together: *a crowd assembled outside the gates.* **2** fit together the component parts of: *supplied in flat-pack form, the shed is easily assembled.*
– DERIVATIVES **assembler** noun.
– ORIGIN Old French *asembler*.

assembly noun (pl. **assemblies**) **1** a group of people gathered together. **2** a body of people with powers to make decisions and laws. **3** a regular gathering of teachers and pupils in a school. **4** the action of assembling the component parts of something.

assembly line noun a series of workers and machines in a factory which assemble the component parts of identical products in successive stages.

assent /uh-**sent**/ noun approval or agreement. • verb agree to a request or suggestion: *both parties assented to the terms of the agreement.*
– ORIGIN Latin *assentire*.

assert verb **1** state a fact or belief confidently and firmly: *he asserted that he had no intention of stepping down.* **2** make other people recognize something by behaving confidently and forcefully: *a young woman seeking to assert her independence.* **3** (**assert oneself**) behave in a confident and forceful way.
– ORIGIN Latin *asserere* 'claim, affirm'.

assertion noun **1** a confident and forceful statement. **2** the action of asserting something.

assertive adjective having or showing a confident and forceful personality.
– DERIVATIVES **assertively** adverb **assertiveness** noun.

asses plural of ASS¹, ASS².

assess verb **1** calculate or estimate the value, importance, or quality of: *a survey to assess the damage caused by the oil spill.* **2** set the value of a tax for a person or property.
– DERIVATIVES **assessment** noun **assessor** noun.
– ORIGIN Latin *assidere* 'sit by' (later 'levy tax').

asset noun **1** a useful or valuable thing or person. **2** (**assets**) the property owned by a person or company.
– ORIGIN Old French *asez* 'enough'.

asset-stripping noun the practice of buying of a company which is in financial difficulties at a low price and then selling its assets separately at a profit.

asseveration /uh-sev-uh-**ray**-sh'n/ noun formal a solemn or emphatic declaration or statement.
– DERIVATIVES **asseverate** verb.

– ORIGIN Latin, from *asseverare*.

assiduous /uh-**sid**-yoo-uhss/ adjective showing or done with great care and thoroughness: *he was assiduous in his duties.*
– DERIVATIVES **assiduity** /ass-i-**dyoo**-i-ti/ noun **assiduously** adverb.
– ORIGIN Latin *assiduus*.

assign verb **1** give a task or duty to someone: *work duties were assigned at the beginning of the shift.* **2** give someone a job or task: *she had been assigned to a new post.* **3** regard something as belonging to or being caused by: *a mosaic assigned to the late third century BC.*
– ORIGIN Latin *assignare*.

assignation noun a secret meeting, especially one between lovers.

assignment noun **1** a task allocated to someone as part of a job or course of study. **2** the assigning of a job or task to someone.

assimilate verb **1** take in and understand information or ideas. **2** absorb and integrate people or ideas into a wider society or culture: *they were assimilated into mainstream American society.* **3** absorb and digest food or nutrients.
– DERIVATIVES **assimilable** adjective **assimilation** noun.
– ORIGIN Latin *assimilare*.

assist verb give help or support to someone.
– ORIGIN Latin *assistere* 'stand by'.

assistance noun help or support.

assistant noun **1** a person who ranks below a senior person. **2** a person who provides help in a particular role or type of work: *an administrative assistant.*

assize /uh-**syz**/ (also **assizes**) noun historical a court which sat at intervals in each county of England and Wales.
– ORIGIN Old French *assise*.

associate verb /uh-**soh**-shi-ayt/ **1** connect in one's mind: *I associated wealth with freedom.* **2** frequently meet or have dealings with: *she began associating with Marxists.* **3** (**be associated with** or **associate oneself with**) be involved with. • noun /uh-**soh**-shi-uht/ a work partner or colleague. • adjective /uh-**soh**-shi-uht/ **1** connected with an organization or business. **2** belonging to an organization but not having full membership.
– ORIGIN Latin *associare*.

association noun **1** a group of people organized for a joint purpose. **2** a connection or relationship: *his close association with the university.* **3** an idea, memory, or feeling that is connected to someone or something: *the name had unpleasant associations for him.*

Association Football noun Brit. more formal term for SOCCER.

associative adjective **1** relating to or involving association. **2** Mathematics producing the same result however quantities are grouped, as long as their order remains the same, such that for example $(a \times b) \times c = a \times (b \times c)$.

assonance /**ass**-uh-nuhnss/ noun the rhyming of vowels only (e.g. *hide*, *line*) or of consonants but not vowels (e.g. *cold*, *killed*).
– ORIGIN Latin *assonare* 'respond to'.

assorted adjective of various different sorts put together: *a plate of assorted vegetables.*
– ORIGIN Old French *assorter*.

assortment noun a collection of different things: *an assortment of boots and shoes.*

assuage /uh-**swayj**/ verb 1 make an unpleasant feeling less intense: *his letter assuaged the fears of most members.* 2 satisfy an appetite or desire.
– ORIGIN Old French *assouagier*, from Latin *suavis* 'sweet'.

assume verb 1 accept as true or being the case without having proof: *he assumed she was married.* 2 take responsibility or control. 3 begin to have: *foreign trade has assumed greater importance in recent years.* 4 pretend to have: *he assumed an air of indifference.*
– ORIGIN Latin *assumere.*

assuming conjunction based on the assumption that.

assumption noun 1 a thing that is assumed to be true. 2 the assuming of responsibility or control. 3 (**Assumption**) the taking up of the Virgin Mary into heaven, according to Roman Catholic doctrine.

assurance noun 1 a statement or promise intended to give someone confidence. 2 confidence in one's own abilities. 3 chiefly Brit. life insurance.

> USAGE: **Assurance** is used of insurance policies under whose terms a payment is guaranteed, either after a fixed term or on the death of the insured person; **insurance** is the general term, and is used in particular of policies under whose terms a payment would be made only in certain circumstances (e.g. accident or death within a limited period).

assure verb 1 tell someone that something is definitely true or will be the case: *she assured him that everything was under control.* 2 make something certain to happen: *victory would assure their promotion.* 3 chiefly Brit. insure a person's life.
– ORIGIN Old French *assurer.*

assured adjective 1 having or showing confidence: *her calm, assured voice.* 2 protected against change or ending: *an assured tenancy.*
– DERIVATIVES **assuredly** adverb.

Assyrian /uh-**sirr**-i-uhn/ noun an inhabitant of Assyria, an ancient country in what is now Iraq.

astatine /**ass**-tuh-teen/ noun a very unstable radioactive chemical element belonging to the halogen group.
– ORIGIN Greek *astatos* 'unstable'.

aster noun a garden plant of the daisy family, typically having purple or pink flowers.
– ORIGIN Greek, 'star'.

asterisk noun a symbol (*) used in text as a pointer to a note elsewhere.
– ORIGIN Greek *asteriskos* 'small star'.

astern adverb behind or towards the rear of a ship or aircraft.

asteroid /**ass**-tuh-royd/ noun a small rocky planet orbiting the sun.
– ORIGIN Greek *asteroeidēs* 'starlike'.

asthma /**ass**-muh/ noun a medical condition causing difficulty in breathing.
– DERIVATIVES **asthmatic** adjective & noun.
– ORIGIN Greek, from *azein* 'breathe hard'.

astigmatism /uh-**stig**-muh-tiz'm/ noun a defect in an eye or lens which prevents it from focusing properly.
– DERIVATIVES **astigmatic** /a-stig-**mat**-tik/ adjective.
– ORIGIN Greek *stigma* 'point'.

astilbe /uh-**stil**-bi/ noun a plant with plumes of tiny white, pink, or red flowers.
– ORIGIN Latin.

astir adjective 1 in a state of excited movement. 2 awake and out of bed.

astonish verb surprise or impress someone greatly.
– DERIVATIVES **astonished** adjective **astonishing** adjective **astonishment** noun.
– ORIGIN Old French *estoner* 'stun', from Latin *tonare* 'to thunder'.

astound verb shock or greatly surprise someone.
– DERIVATIVES **astounded** adjective **astounding** adjective.
– ORIGIN related to **ASTONISH**.

astrakhan /ass-truh-**kan**/ noun the dark curly fleece of a type of young lamb from central Asia.
– ORIGIN named after the Russian city of *Astrakhan.*

astral /**ass**-truhl/ adjective relating to the stars.
– ORIGIN Latin *astrum* 'star'.

astray adverb away from the right path or direction.
– ORIGIN from Old French *estraie.*

astride preposition & adverb 1 with a leg on each side of something. 2 (as adverb) (of a person's legs) wide apart.

astringent /uh-**strin**-juhnt/ adjective 1 (of a substance) making body tissue contract. 2 harsh or severe in manner or style: *her astringent comments.* • noun an astringent lotion used medically or as a cosmetic.
– DERIVATIVES **astringency** noun **astringently** adverb.
– ORIGIN Latin *astringere* 'pull tight'.

astro- combining form relating to the stars or to outer space: *astronaut.*
– ORIGIN Greek *astron* 'star'.

astrobiology noun the branch of biology concerned with the discovery or study of life on other planets or in space.
– DERIVATIVES **astrobiologist** noun.

astrolabe /**ass**-truh-layb/ noun an instrument formerly used for measuring the altitudes of stars and calculating latitude in navigation.
– ORIGIN Greek *astrolabos* 'star-taking'.

astrology noun the study of the supposed influence of stars and planets on human affairs.
– DERIVATIVES **astrologer** noun **astrological** adjective **astrologically** adverb.

astronaut noun a person trained to travel in a spacecraft.
– ORIGIN from Greek *astron* 'star' + *nautēs* 'sailor'.

astronautics plural noun (treated as sing.) the science and technology of space travel and exploration.

astronomical adjective 1 relating to astronomy. 2 informal extremely large: *astronomical fees.*
– DERIVATIVES **astronomic** adjective

astronomically adverb.

astronomical unit noun a unit of measurement equal to the mean distance from the earth to the sun, 149.6 million kilometres.

astronomy noun the science of stars, planets, and the universe.
– DERIVATIVES **astronomer** noun.

astrophysics plural noun (treated as sing.) the branch of astronomy concerned with the physical nature of stars and planets.
– DERIVATIVES **astrophysical** adjective **astrophysicist** noun.

astute adjective good at making accurate judgements; shrewd.
– DERIVATIVES **astutely** adverb **astuteness** noun.
– ORIGIN Latin *astutus*.

asunder adverb literary apart.
– ORIGIN Old English.

asylum noun 1 protection from danger, especially for those who leave their own country as a result of suffering persecution for their political beliefs. 2 dated an institution for the care of people who are mentally ill.
– ORIGIN Greek *asulon* 'refuge'.

asymmetrical adjective having sides or parts that do not correspond in size, shape, or arrangement; lacking symmetry.
– DERIVATIVES **asymmetric** adjective **asymmetrically** adverb.

asymmetric bars plural noun a pair of bars of different heights used in gymnastics.

asymmetry /ay-**sim**-mi-tri/ noun (pl. **asymmetries**) lack of symmetry between the sides or parts of something.

asymptomatic /uh-sim-tuh-**mat**-ik/ adjective producing or showing no symptoms of a disease or condition.

asynchronous adjective not existing or occurring at the same time.
– DERIVATIVES **asynchronously** adverb **asynchrony** noun.

At symbol the chemical element astatine.

at preposition used to express: 1 location, arrival, or time. 2 a value, rate, or point on a scale. 3 a state or condition. 4 the object or target of a look, shot, action, or plan.
– PHRASES **at that** in addition; furthermore.
– ORIGIN Old English.

atavistic /at-uh-**viss**-tik/ adjective related or reverting to the feelings or behaviour of the earliest humans: *an atavistic fear of the dark*.
– DERIVATIVES **atavism** noun **atavistically** adverb.
– ORIGIN Latin *atavus* 'forefather'.

ataxia /uh-**tak**-siuh/ noun Medicine the loss of the ability to control or coordinate one's movements.
– ORIGIN Greek, 'disorder'.

ATC abbreviation 1 air traffic control or controller. 2 Air Training Corps.

ate past of EAT.

atelier /uh-**tel**-i-ay/ noun a workshop or studio used by an artist or designer.
– ORIGIN French.

atheism /**ay**-thi-i-z'm/ noun disbelief in the existence of a god or gods.
– DERIVATIVES **atheist** noun **atheistic** adjective,
– ORIGIN from Greek *a-* 'without' + *theos* 'god'.

Athenian /uh-**thee**-ni-uhn/ noun a person from Athens in Greece. • adjective relating to Athens.

atherosclerosis /ath-uh-roh-skluh-**roh**-siss/ noun a disease of the arteries in which fatty material is deposited on their inner walls.
– DERIVATIVES **atherosclerotic** adjective.
– ORIGIN from Greek *athērē* 'groats' + *sklērōsis* 'hardening'.

athlete noun 1 a person who is good at sports. 2 a person who competes in track and field events.
– ORIGIN Greek *athlētēs*, from *athlon* 'prize'.

athlete's foot noun a contagious fungal infection affecting the skin between the toes.

athletic adjective 1 fit and good at sport. 2 Brit. relating to athletics.
– DERIVATIVES **athletically** adverb **athleticism** noun.

athletics plural noun (usu. treated as sing.) chiefly Brit. the sport of competing in track and field events.

athwart /uh-**thwort**/ preposition & adverb from side to side of something; across.
– ORIGIN from an old sense of THWART, meaning 'across'.

Atkins diet noun trademark in the US a high-protein, high-fat diet in which carbohydrates are severely restricted.
– ORIGIN named after the American cardiologist R. C. *Atkins*.

Atlantic adjective relating to the Atlantic Ocean.
– ORIGIN first referring to Mount Atlas in Libya; named after the god *Atlas* (see ATLAS).

atlas noun a book of maps or charts.
– ORIGIN named after the Greek god *Atlas*, shown on early atlases as supporting the pillars of the universe.

ATM abbreviation automated teller machine.

atmosphere noun 1 the gases surrounding the earth or another planet. 2 the quality of the air in a place: *the smoky atmosphere of an industrial town*. 3 an overall tone or mood: *a hotel with a friendly, relaxed atmosphere*. 4 a unit of pressure equal to the pressure of the atmosphere at sea level, 101,325 pascals (roughly 14.7 pounds per square inch).
– ORIGIN from Greek *atmos* 'vapour' + *sphaira* 'globe'.

atmospheric adjective 1 relating to the atmosphere of the earth or another planet. 2 creating a distinctive mood, especially one of romance, nostalgia, or excitement: *a very atmospheric location*.
– DERIVATIVES **atmospherically** adverb.

atmospherics plural noun electrical disturbances in the atmosphere, that interfere with telecommunications.

ATOL /**a**-tol/ abbreviation (in the UK) Air Travel Organizer's Licence.

atoll /**a**-tol/ noun a ring-shaped coral reef or chain of islands.
– ORIGIN Maldivian.

atom noun 1 the smallest particle of a chemical element that can exist. 2 an extremely small amount: *she did not have an atom of strength left.*
– ORIGIN Greek *atomos* 'indivisible'.

atom bomb noun (also **atomic bomb**) a bomb whose explosive power comes from the fission (splitting) of the nuclei of atoms.

a

atomic adjective **1** relating to an atom or atoms. **2** relating to nuclear energy or weapons.

atomic mass unit noun a unit of mass used to express atomic and molecular weights, equal to one twelfth of the mass of an atom of carbon-12.

atomic number noun the number of protons in the nucleus of a chemical element's atom, which determines its place in the periodic table.

atomic theory noun the theory that all matter is made up of tiny indivisible particles (atoms).

atomic weight noun another term for RELATIVE ATOMIC MASS.

atomize (or **atomise**) verb convert a substance into very fine particles or droplets.
– DERIVATIVES **atomization** noun.

atomizer (or **atomiser**) noun a device for sending out water, perfume, or other liquids as a fine spray.

atonal /ay-toh-n'l/ adjective not written in any musical key.
– DERIVATIVES **atonality** noun.

atone verb (**atone for**) make amends for a sin, crime, or other wrongdoing.
– ORIGIN from *at one*.

atonement noun **1** the action of making amends for a sin, crime, or other wrongdoing. **2** (**the Atonement**) the reconciliation of God and humankind brought about through the death of Jesus.

atop preposition on the top of.

ATP abbreviation Brit. automatic train protection.

atrium /ay-tri-uhm/ noun (pl. **atria** /ay-tri-uh/ or **atriums**) **1** a central hall rising through several storeys and having a glazed roof. **2** an open area in the centre of an ancient Roman house. **3** each of the two upper cavities of the heart.
– DERIVATIVES **atrial** adjective.
– ORIGIN Latin.

atrocious /uh-troh-shuss/ adjective **1** horrifyingly cruel or wicked. **2** extremely bad or unpleasant.
– DERIVATIVES **atrociously** adverb.
– ORIGIN Latin *atrox* 'cruel'.

atrocity /uh-tross-i-ti/ noun (pl. **atrocities**) an extremely cruel or wicked act.

atrophy /a-truh-fi/ verb (**atrophies, atrophying, atrophied**) **1** (of body tissue or an organ) waste away. **2** gradually become weaker: *the local shipbuilding industry had atrophied.* • noun the condition or process of atrophying.
– ORIGIN from Greek *atrophia* 'lack of food'.

atropine /at-ruh-peen/ noun a poisonous compound found in deadly nightshade.
– ORIGIN from *Atropos*, one of the Fates in Greek mythology.

attach verb **1** fasten or join one thing to another. **2** include a condition as part of an agreement. **3** attribute importance or value to: *they attached great importance to this research.* **4** appoint someone for special or temporary duties: *I was attached to another working group.*
– DERIVATIVES **attachable** adjective.
– ORIGIN Old French *atachier*.

attaché /uh-tash-ay/ noun a person on an ambassador's staff who has a specific responsibility or works in a particular area of activity: *a military attaché.*
– ORIGIN French, 'attached'.

attaché case noun a small, flat briefcase for carrying documents.

attached adjective very fond of someone: *Mark became increasingly attached to Tara.*

attachment noun **1** an extra part attached to something in order to perform a particular function: *a detachable roof rack with attachments for carrying bikes.* **2** a computer file sent with an email. **3** the action of attaching one thing to another. **4** affection or fondness.

attack verb **1** take violent action against someone or something. **2** (of a disease, chemical, etc.) act harmfully on: *meningitis attacks the brain.* **3** criticize fiercely and publicly: *he attacked the government's defence policy* **4** begin to deal with a problem or task in a determined way. **5** (in sport) attempt to score goals or points. • noun **1** an act of attacking someone or something. **2** a sudden short period of an illness: *a bad attack of flu.* **3** the players in a team whose role is to attack.
– DERIVATIVES **attacker** noun.
– ORIGIN Italian *attaccare* 'join battle'.

attain verb **1** succeed in achieving something one has worked for: *he attained the rank of Brigadier.* **2** reach a particular age, size, or level: *the cheetah can attain speeds of 97 kph.*
– DERIVATIVES **attainable** adjective.
– ORIGIN Latin *attingere*.

attainder /uh-tayn-der/ noun historical the forfeiting of land and civil rights as a result of being sentenced to death.
– ORIGIN Old French *ateindre* 'accomplish, bring to justice'.

attainment noun **1** the achieving of something. **2** something that one has achieved: *his educational attainments.*

attar /at-tar/ noun a sweet-smelling oil made from rose petals.
– ORIGIN Arabic, 'perfume, essence'.

attempt verb make an effort to do something. • noun an effort to do something.
– ORIGIN Latin *attemptare*.

attend verb **1** be present at an event. **2** go regularly to a school, church, etc. **3** (**attend to**) deal with or pay attention to: *he had important business to attend to.* **4** occur at the same time as or as a result of: *the unfortunate events that attended their arrival.* **5** escort and assist an important person.
– DERIVATIVES **attendee** noun **attender** noun.
– ORIGIN Latin *attendere*.

attendance noun **1** the action of attending a place or event: *her infrequent attendance at church.* **2** the number of people present at a particular occasion.

attendant noun **1** a person employed to provide a service to the public: *a museum attendant.* **2** an assistant to an important person. • adjective occurring at the same time or as a result of: *obesity and its attendant health problems.*

attention noun **1** the mental faculty of considering or taking notice of someone or something: *he turned his attention to the* educational system. **2** special care or consideration: *a child in need of medical attention.* **3** (**attentions**) things done to express an interest in or please someone: *she was flattered by his attentions.* **4** an erect position taken by a soldier, with the feet together and the arms straight down the sides of the body.

attention deficit disorder noun a condition found in children, marked by hyperactivity, poor concentration, and learning difficulties.

attentive adjective **1** paying close attention to something: *an attentive audience.* **2** considerate and helpful: *the staff were friendly and attentive.*
– DERIVATIVES **attentively** adverb **attentiveness** noun.

attenuate /uh-**ten**-yoo-ayt/ verb **1** make something weaker or less effective. **2** make someone or something thin or thinner.
– DERIVATIVES **attenuation** noun.
– ORIGIN Latin *attenuare* 'make slender'.

attest /uh-**test**/ verb **1** provide or act as clear evidence of: *the collection attests to his interest in mythology.* **2** declare that something is true or is the case.
– DERIVATIVES **attestation** noun.
– ORIGIN Latin *attestari*.

Attic adjective relating to Attica in Greece, or to ancient Athens.

attic noun a space or room inside the roof of a building.
– ORIGIN Latin *Atticus* 'Attic'.

attire formal or literary noun clothes of a particular kind: *formal evening attire.* • verb (**be attired**) be dressed in clothes of a particular kind: *he was attired in a dark lounge suit.*
– ORIGIN Old French *atirer* 'equip'.

attitude noun **1** a way of thinking or feeling: *his attitude to the job had changed.* **2** a position of the body. **3** informal self-confident or uncooperative behaviour.
– DERIVATIVES **attitudinal** adjective.
– ORIGIN Italian *attitudine* 'suitability'.

attitudinize (or **attitudinise**) /at-ti-**tyoo**-di-nyz/ verb adopt or express an attitude for effect.

attorney /uh-**ter**-ni/ noun (pl. **attorneys**) **1** a person appointed to act for another in legal matters. **2** chiefly US a lawyer.
– ORIGIN Old French *atorner* 'assign'.

Attorney General noun (pl. **Attorneys General**) the most senior legal officer in some countries.

attract verb **1** cause someone to come to a place or event or participate in an attraction. **2** cause a particular reaction: *the decision attracted widespread criticism.* **3** cause someone to have a liking for or interest in: *many men were attracted to her.* **4** draw something closer by exerting a force on it.
– DERIVATIVES **attractor** noun.
– ORIGIN Latin *attrahere* 'draw near'.

attractant noun a substance which attracts something.

attraction noun **1** the action or power of attracting someone or something. **2** an interesting or appealing feature or quality: *the apartment's main attraction is the large pool.*

3 Physics a force under the influence of which objects tend to move towards each other.

attractive adjective **1** pleasing in appearance: *a very attractive man.* **2** having features or qualities that arouse interest: *an attractive investment proposition.* **3** relating to attraction between physical objects.
– DERIVATIVES **attractively** adverb **attractiveness** noun.

attribute verb /uh-**trib**-yoot/ (**attribute something to**) regard something as belonging to, made, or being caused by: *he attributed his success to his parents' unwavering support.* • noun /**at**-tri-byoot/ **1** a characteristic quality or feature: *she has the key attributes of any journalist.* **2** an object that is traditionally associated with a person or thing: *the hourglass is an attribute of Father Time.*
– DERIVATIVES **attributable** /uh-**trib**-yoo-tuh-b'l/ adjective **attribution** noun.
– ORIGIN Latin *attribuere* 'assign to'.

attributive /uh-**trib**-yuu-tiv/ adjective Grammar (of an adjective) coming before the word that it describes, as *old* in *the old dog.* Contrasted with PREDICATIVE.
– DERIVATIVES **attributively** adverb.

attrition /uh-**tri**-sh'n/ noun **1** the gradual reduction of something's strength or effectiveness through prolonged attack or pressure. **2** the wearing away of something by friction.
– DERIVATIVES **attritional** adjective.
– ORIGIN Latin *atterere* 'to rub'.

attune verb (**be attuned**) be receptive to and able to understand someone or something: *a royal family more attuned to the feelings of the public.*

atypical /ay-**tip**-i-k'l/ adjective not representative of a type, group, or class.
– DERIVATIVES **atypically** adverb.

Au symbol the chemical element gold.
– ORIGIN Latin *aurum*.

aubergine /**oh**-ber-zheen/ noun chiefly Brit. a purple egg-shaped vegetable.
– ORIGIN French.

aubretia /aw-**bree**-shuh/ (also **aubrietia**) noun a trailing plant with purple, pink, or white flowers.
– ORIGIN named after the French botanist Claude *Aubriet*.

auburn /**aw**-bern/ noun a reddish-brown colour.
– ORIGIN Old French *auborne*.

au courant /oh kuu-**ron**/ adjective **1** well informed about something. **2** fashionable; up to date.
– ORIGIN French, 'in the (regular) course'.

auction /**awk**-sh'n/ noun a public sale in which goods or property are sold to the highest bidder. • verb sell an item or items at an auction.
– ORIGIN Latin, 'increase, auction'.

auctioneer noun a person who conducts auctions.

audacious /aw-**day**-shuhss/ adjective **1** willing to take daring risks. **2** showing a lack of respect; rude or impudent.
– DERIVATIVES **audaciously** adverb **audaciousness** noun **audacity** noun.
– ORIGIN Latin *audax* 'bold'.

a

audible adjective able to be heard.
– DERIVATIVES **audibility** noun **audibly** adverb.
– ORIGIN Latin *audire* 'hear'.

audience noun **1** the people gathered to see or listen to a play, concert, film, etc. **2** a formal interview with a person in authority.
– ORIGIN Latin *audire* 'hear'.

audio- combining form relating to hearing or sound: *audio-visual*.
– ORIGIN Latin *audire* 'hear'.

audio frequency noun a frequency capable of being perceived by the human ear, generally between 20 and 20,000 hertz.

audiology /or-di-ol-uhji/ noun the branch of science and medicine concerned with the sense of hearing.
– DERIVATIVES **audiological** adjective **audiologist** noun.

audio tape noun magnetic tape on which sound can be recorded.

audio typist noun a typist who types documents from recorded dictation.

audio-visual adjective using both sight and sound.

audit /aw-dit/ noun an official examination of an organization's accounts. • verb (**audits**, **auditing**, **audited**) make an official examination of an organization's accounts.
– ORIGIN from Latin *audire* 'hear' (because an audit was originally presented orally).

audition noun an interview for an actor, singer, etc. in which they give a practical demonstration of their skill. • verb assess or be assessed by means of an audition.

auditor noun **1** a person who carries an audit of an organization's accounts. **2** a listener.

auditorium noun (pl. **auditoriums** or **auditoria**) **1** the part of a theatre or hall in which the audience sits. **2** chiefly N. Amer. a large public hall.
– ORIGIN Latin.

auditory adjective relating to the sense of hearing.

au fait /oh fay/ adjective (**au fait with**) having a good or detailed knowledge of something: *she was au fait with all the latest technology.*
– ORIGIN French, 'to the point'.

auger /aw-ger/ noun a tool resembling a large corkscrew, for boring holes.
– ORIGIN Old English.

> **USAGE:** On the confusion of **auger** and **augur**, see the note at **AUGUR**.

aught /awt/ (also **ought**) pronoun old use anything at all.
– ORIGIN Old English.

augment /awg-**ment**/ verb increase the amount, size, or value of: *many people work overtime to augment their income.*
– DERIVATIVES **augmentation** noun.
– ORIGIN Latin *augmentare*.

au gratin /oh gra-tan/ adjective sprinkled with breadcrumbs or grated cheese and browned: *ratatouille au gratin.*
– ORIGIN French, 'by grating'.

augur /aw-ger/ verb (**augur well/badly**) be a sign of a good or bad outcome: *the announcement does not augur well for the economy.*
– ORIGIN Latin, 'person who interprets omens'.

> **USAGE:** Do not confuse the verb **augur**, meaning 'be a sign of a good or bad outcome', with the noun **auger**, which is a tool for boring holes.

augury /aw-gyuu-ri/ noun (pl. **auguries**) a sign of what will happen in the future; an omen.

August noun the eighth month of the year.
– ORIGIN named after the Roman emperor *Augustus* Caesar.

august /aw-**gust**/ adjective inspiring respect and admiration.
– ORIGIN Latin *augustus* 'venerable'.

Augustan /or-gus-tuhn/ adjective **1** relating to or written during the reign of the Roman emperor Augustus. **2** relating to a classical style of 17th- and 18th-century English literature.

auk /awk/ noun a black and white seabird with short wings.
– ORIGIN Old Norse.

auld lang syne /awld lang **syn**/ noun times long past.
– ORIGIN Scots, 'old long since'.

au naturel /oh nat-uh-rel/ adjective & adverb in the most simple or natural way.
– ORIGIN French.

aunt noun the sister of one's father or mother or the wife of one's uncle.
– ORIGIN Old French *ante*.

auntie (also **aunty**) noun (pl. **aunties**) informal a person's aunt.

Aunt Sally noun (pl. **Aunt Sallies**) **1** a game in which players throw sticks or balls at a wooden dummy. **2** an easy target for criticism.

au pair /oh **pair**/ noun a foreign girl employed to look after children and help with housework in exchange for board and lodging.
– ORIGIN French, 'on equal terms'.

aura /aw-ruh/ noun (pl. **auras**) **1** the distinctive atmosphere or quality associated with someone or something: *the hotel had an aura of glamour and excitement.* **2** a supposed invisible force surrounding a living creature.
– ORIGIN Greek, 'breeze, breath'.

aural /aw-ruhl/ adjective relating to the ears or the sense of hearing.
– DERIVATIVES **aurally** adverb.
– ORIGIN Latin *auris* 'ear'.

> **USAGE:** Do not confuse **aural** with **oral**. **Aural** means 'relating to the ears or sense of hearing' (*her new album provides pure aural pleasure*), whereas **oral** means 'spoken' or 'relating to the mouth' (*oral communication*).

aurar plural of **EYRIR**.

aureate /or-i-uht/ adjective made of or having the colour of gold.
– ORIGIN from Latin *aurum* 'gold'.

aureole /aw-ri-ohl/ noun **1** (in paintings) a bright circle surrounding a person to indicate that they are holy. **2** a circle of light around the sun or moon.
– ORIGIN from Latin *aureola corona* 'golden crown'.

au revoir /aw ruh-**vwar**/ exclamation goodbye.
– ORIGIN French, 'to the seeing again'.

auricle /o-ri-k'l/ noun **1** the external part of the ear. **2** an upper cavity of the heart.

– ORIGIN Latin *auricula* 'little ear'.

aurochs /or-oks/ noun (pl. same) a large extinct wild ox.
– ORIGIN German.

aurora /aw-ror-ruh/ noun a phenomenon characterized by streamers of coloured light in the sky near the earth's magnetic poles, known as the Northern Lights (**aurora borealis** /bo-ri-ay-liss/) near the North Pole and the Southern Lights (**aurora australis** /oss-stray-liss/) near the South Pole.
– ORIGIN Latin, 'dawn, goddess of the dawn'.

auscultation /or-skuhl-tay-shuhn/ noun listening to sounds from the heart, lungs, or other organs with a stethoscope.
– ORIGIN Latin, from *auscultare* 'listen to'.

auspice /awss-piss/ noun (in phrase **under the auspices of**) with the support or protection of: *elections held under the auspices of the United Nations*.
– ORIGIN first meaning 'an omen', from Latin *auspicium*.

auspicious /aw-spi-shuhss/ adjective suggesting that there is a good chance of success: *his new posting has not got off to an auspicious start*.
– DERIVATIVES **auspiciously** adverb.

Aussie (also **Ozzie**) noun (pl. **Aussies**) & adjective informal Australia or Australian.

austere /oss-teer/ adjective 1 severe or strict in appearance or manner. 2 without comforts or luxuries: *their austere living conditions*.
– DERIVATIVES **austerely** adverb.
– ORIGIN Greek *austēros*.

austerity /oss-te-ri-ti/ noun (pl. **austerities**) 1 strictness or severity of appearance or manner. 2 difficult economic conditions resulting from a cut in public spending.

austral /ost-ruhl/ adjective technical of the southern hemisphere.
– ORIGIN Latin *australis*.

Australasian /oss-truh-lay-zh'n, oss-struh-lay-sh'n/ adjective relating to Australasia, a region made up of Australia, New Zealand, and islands of the SW Pacific.

Australian noun a person from Australia. • adjective relating to Australia.
– ORIGIN from Latin *Terra Australis* 'the southern land'.

Australian Rules plural noun (treated as sing.) a form of football played on an oval field with an oval ball by teams of eighteen players.

Austrian noun a person from Austria. • adjective relating to Austria.

Austrian blind noun a ruched blind which extends part of the way down a window.

autarchy noun (pl. **autarchies**) 1 another term for AUTOCRACY. 2 variant spelling of AUTARKY.

autarky /aw-tar-ki/ (also **autarchy**) noun (pl. **autarkies**) 1 economic independence or self-sufficiency. 2 an economically independent state or society.
– DERIVATIVES **autarkic** adjective.
– ORIGIN from Greek *autarkēs*.

auteur /oh-ter/ noun a film director regarded as the author of their films.
– ORIGIN French, 'author'.

authentic adjective 1 of undisputed origin; genuine: *the letter is now accepted as an authentic document*. 2 based on facts; accurate.
– DERIVATIVES **authentically** adverb **authenticity** noun.
– ORIGIN Greek *authentikos*.

authenticate verb prove or show something to be genuine.
– DERIVATIVES **authentication** noun **authenticator** noun.

author /aw-ther/ noun 1 a writer of a book or article. 2 a person who thinks of a plan or idea.
– DERIVATIVES **authoress** noun **authorial** /aw-thor-i-uhl/ adjective **authorship** noun.
– ORIGIN Latin *auctor*.

authoritarian /aw-tho-ri-tair-i-uhn/ adjective in favour of or demanding strict obedience to authority. • noun an authoritarian person.
– DERIVATIVES **authoritarianism** noun.

authoritative /aw-tho-ri-tuh-tiv/ adjective 1 true or accurate and so able to be trusted: *authoritative information*. 2 commanding and self-confident; likely to be respected and obeyed: *his quiet but authoritative voice*. 3 coming from an official source.
– DERIVATIVES **authoritatively** adverb **authoritativeness** noun.

authority noun (pl. **authorities**) 1 the power to give orders to other people and enforce their obedience. 2 a person or organization with official power. 3 official permission to do something: *the money was spent without parliamentary authority*. 4 recognized knowledge about or expertise in something. 5 a person with expert knowledge of a particular subject: *he was an authority on the stock market*.
– ORIGIN Old French *autorite*.

authorize (or **authorise**) verb give official permission for: *the UN Security Council authorized the use of force*.
– DERIVATIVES **authorization** noun.

Authorized Version noun an English translation of the Bible made in 1611.

autism /aw-ti-z'm/ noun a mental condition in which a person has great difficulty in communicating with others.
– DERIVATIVES **autistic** adjective.
– ORIGIN Greek *autos* 'self'.

auto adjective & noun short for AUTOMATIC.

Autobahn /aw-toh-bahn/ noun a German motorway.
– ORIGIN German, from *Auto* 'car' + *Bahn* 'road'.

autobiography noun (pl. **autobiographies**) an account of a person's life written by that person.
– DERIVATIVES **autobiographer** noun **autobiographical** adjective.

autochthonous /or-tok-thuh-nuhss/ adjective inhabiting a place from the earliest times; indigenous.

autoclave /or-toh-klayv/ noun a strong heated container used for processes using high pressures and temperatures, e.g. steam sterilization.
– ORIGIN from Greek *auto-* 'self' + Latin *clavis* 'key' (because it is self-fastening).

autocracy /aw-tok-ruh-si/ noun (pl. **autocracies**) 1 a system of government in which one person has total power. 2 a state governed by a person with total power.

a

– ORIGIN from Greek *autos* 'self' + *kratos* 'power'.

autocrat noun 1 a ruler who has total power. 2 a person who insists on complete obedience from others.

autocratic adjective 1 relating to a ruler who has total power. 2 taking no account of other people's wishes and insisting on complete obedience: *his autocratic management style*.
– DERIVATIVES **autocratically** adverb.

autocue noun Brit. trademark a device used as a television prompt which displays a speaker's script on a screen which is not visible to the audience.

auto-da-fé /aw-toh-da-**fay**/ noun (pl. **autos-da-fé** pronunc. same) the burning of a heretic by the Spanish Inquisition.
– ORIGIN Portuguese, 'act of the faith'.

autodial verb (autodials, autodialling, autodialled; US autodials, autodialing, autodialed) Computing (of a modem) automatically dial a telephone number or establish a connection with a computer.

autodidact /aw-toh-dy-dakt/ noun a self-taught person.
– ORIGIN Greek.

autofocus noun a device focusing a camera or other device automatically.

autogiro (also **autogyro**) noun (pl. **autogiros**) a form of aircraft with unpowered freely rotating horizontal blades and a propeller.
– ORIGIN Spanish, from *auto-* 'self' + *giro* 'gyration'.

autograph noun 1 a celebrity's signature written for a fan or admirer. 2 a manuscript or musical score in an author's or composer's own handwriting. • verb write one's signature on something.
– ORIGIN Greek *autographos* 'written with one's own hand'.

autoimmune adjective (of disease) caused by antibodies or lymphocytes produced by the body to counteract substances naturally present in it.

automate verb convert a process or facility so that it can be operated by automatic equipment.

automated teller machine noun a machine that provides cash and other banking services when a special card is inserted.

automatic adjective 1 operating by itself without human control. 2 (of a firearm) able to load bullets automatically and fire continuously. 3 done or occurring without conscious thought or as a matter of course: *an automatic decision*. 4 enforced without question because of a fixed rule: *murder carries an automatic life sentence*. • noun an automatic machine.
– DERIVATIVES **automatically** adverb **automaticity** noun.
– ORIGIN Greek *automatos* 'acting by itself'.

automatic pilot noun a device for keeping an aircraft on a set course.
– PHRASES **on automatic pilot** doing something out of habit and without thinking.

automation /aw-tuh-**may**-sh'n/ noun the use of automatic equipment in manufacturing or similar processes.

automatism /aw-**tom**-uh-tiz'm/ noun action which does not involve conscious thought or intention.

automaton /aw-**tom**-uh-tuhn/ noun (pl. **automata** /aw-**tom**-uh-tuh/ or **automatons**) 1 a moving mechanical device resembling a human being. 2 a machine which operates according to coded instructions.
– ORIGIN from Greek *automatos* 'acting of itself'.

automobile noun N. Amer. a motor car.

automotive /aw-tuh-**moh**-tiv/ adjective relating to motor vehicles.

autonomic /or-tuh-**nom**-ik/ adjective relating to the part of the nervous system that controls involuntary bodily functions such as digestion.

autonomous adjective self-governing or independent.
– DERIVATIVES **autonomously** adverb.

autonomy /aw-**ton**-uh-mi/ noun 1 the possession or right of self-government. 2 freedom of action: *a structure that gives greater autonomy to employees*.
– ORIGIN from Greek *autonomos* 'having its own laws'.

autopilot noun short for **AUTOMATIC PILOT**.

autopsy /**aw**-top-si/ noun (pl. **autopsies**) an examination of a dead body to discover the cause of death.
– ORIGIN from Greek *autoptēs* 'eyewitness'.

autoroute noun a French motorway.
– ORIGIN French.

autostrada /aw-toh-**strah**-duh/ noun an Italian motorway.
– ORIGIN Italian.

autosuggestion noun the hypnotic or subconscious adoption of an idea which one has originated oneself.

autumn noun chiefly Brit. the season after summer and before winter.
– DERIVATIVES **autumnal** adjective.
– ORIGIN Latin *autumnus*.

auxiliary /awg-**zil**-yuh-ri/ adjective providing extra help and support. • noun (pl. **auxiliaries**) a person or thing that provides extra help or support.
– ORIGIN from Latin *auxilium* 'help'.

auxiliary verb noun a verb used in forming the tenses, moods, and voices of other verbs (e.g. *be*, *do*, and *have*).

avail verb 1 (**avail oneself of**) formal use or take advantage of: *she did not avail herself of my advice*. 2 help or benefit someone. • noun use or benefit: *his protests were to little avail*.
– ORIGIN Latin *valere* 'be strong, be of value'.

available adjective 1 able to be used or obtained. 2 free to do something: *the nurse is only available in the mornings*.
– DERIVATIVES **availability** noun.

avalanche /**av**-uh-lahnsh/ noun 1 a mass of snow and ice falling rapidly down a mountainside. 2 an overwhelming amount: *an avalanche of gifts*.
– ORIGIN French.

avant-garde /a-von **gard**/ adjective (in the arts) new and experimental. • noun (**the avant-garde**) new and experimental ideas or artists.

– DERIVATIVES **avant-gardism** noun **avant-gardist** noun.
– ORIGIN French, 'vanguard'.

avarice noun extreme greed for wealth or material things.
– ORIGIN from Latin *avarus* 'greedy'.

avaricious /av-uh-**ri**-shuhss/ adjective very greedy for wealth or material things.

avast /uh-**vahst**/ exclamation Nautical stop; cease.
– ORIGIN Dutch *hou'vast* 'hold fast!'

avatar /**av**-uh-tar/ noun Hinduism a god or goddess appearing in bodily form on earth.
– ORIGIN Sanskrit, 'descent'.

Ave Maria /ah-vay muh-**ree**-uh/ noun a prayer to the Virgin Mary used in Catholic worship.
– ORIGIN the opening words in Latin, 'hail, Mary!'

avenge verb punish or harm someone in return for a wrong.
– DERIVATIVES **avenger** noun.
– ORIGIN from Latin *vindicare* 'vindicate'.

avenue noun 1 a broad road or path. 2 a way of approaching or achieving something: *the discovery has opened up new avenues of research.*
– ORIGIN from French *avenir* 'arrive, approach'.

aver /uh-**ver**/ verb (**avers, averring, averred**) formal declare something to be the case.
– ORIGIN from Latin *verus* 'true'.

average noun 1 the result obtained by adding several amounts together and then dividing the total by the number of amounts. 2 a usual amount or level. • adjective 1 being an average. 2 usual or ordinary. 3 not very good; mediocre. • verb 1 amount to or achieve as an average: *her website averaged 30,000 hits a day.* 2 calculate the average of something.
– DERIVATIVES **averagely** adverb **averageness** noun.
– ORIGIN French *avarie* 'damage to ship or cargo'; the modern sense came from the sharing of the costs of things lost at sea between the owners of the ship and of the cargo.

averse adjective (**averse to**) strongly disliking or opposed to: *he's not averse to change.*
– ORIGIN from Latin *avertere* (see **AVERT**).

> USAGE: On the confusion of **averse** and **adverse**, see the note at **ADVERSE**.

aversion noun strong opposition or dislike.
– DERIVATIVES **aversive** adjective.

avert verb 1 turn away one's eyes. 2 prevent an undesirable event.
– ORIGIN from Latin *vertere* 'to turn'.

avian /**ay**-vi-uhn/ adjective relating to birds.
– ORIGIN from Latin *avis* 'bird'.

aviary /**ay**-vi-uh-ri/ noun (pl. **aviaries**) a large enclosure for keeping birds in.

aviation noun the activity of operating and flying aircraft.
– ORIGIN from Latin *avis* 'bird'.

aviator noun dated a pilot.

aviculture /**ay**-vi-kul-cher/ noun the breeding of birds.
– DERIVATIVES **avicultural** adjective **aviculturist** noun.

avid adjective keenly interested or enthusiastic: *avid baseball fans.*

– DERIVATIVES **avidity** noun **avidly** adverb.
– ORIGIN from Latin *avere* 'crave'.

avionics plural noun (usu. treated as sing.) electronics used in aviation.

avocado noun (pl. **avocados**) a pear-shaped fruit with a rough skin, pale green flesh, and a large stone.
– ORIGIN Spanish.

avocation /av-uh-**kay**-shuhn/ noun formal a hobby or minor occupation.
– ORIGIN from Latin *avocare* 'call away'.

avocet /**av**-uh-set/ noun a long-legged wading bird with an upturned bill.
– ORIGIN Italian *avosetta*.

avoid verb 1 keep away from or stop oneself from doing something. 2 prevent from happening: *book early to avoid disappointment.*
– DERIVATIVES **avoidable** adjective **avoidably** adverb **avoidance** noun.
– ORIGIN Old French *evuider* 'clear out, get rid of'.

avoirdupois /av-war-dyoo-**pwah**/ noun a system of weights based on a pound of 16 ounces or 7,000 grains. Compare with **TROY**.
– ORIGIN from Old French *aveir de peis* 'goods of weight'.

avow verb declare or confess something openly.
– DERIVATIVES **avowal** noun **avowed** adjective.
– ORIGIN from Latin *advocare* 'summon in defence'.

avuncular /uh-**vung**-kyuu-ler/ adjective friendly and kind towards a younger person.
– ORIGIN from Latin *avunculus* 'maternal uncle'.

AWACS /**ay**-waks/ abbreviation airborne warning and control system.

await verb 1 wait for an event. 2 be in store for: *many dangers await them.*

awake verb (past **awoke**; past part. **awoken**) 1 stop sleeping. 2 make or become active again. • adjective not asleep.

awaken verb 1 stop sleeping; awake. 2 stir up a feeling.
– DERIVATIVES **awakening** noun & adjective.

award verb give something officially as a prize, payment, or reward. • noun 1 a payment, prize, or honour given to someone. 2 the giving of an award.
– ORIGIN Old French *esguarder* 'consider, ordain'.

aware adjective having knowledge of a situation or fact: *everyone is aware of ageing.*
– DERIVATIVES **awareness** noun.
– ORIGIN Old English.

awash adjective covered or flooded with water.

away adverb 1 to or at a distance. 2 into a place for storage. 3 until disappearing: *the sound died away.* 4 continuously or persistently. • adjective (of a sports fixture) played at the opponents' ground.
– ORIGIN Old English.

awe noun a feeling of great respect mixed with fear. • verb fill someone with awe.
– ORIGIN Old English.

aweigh adjective (of a ship's anchor) raised just clear of the seabed.

awesome adjective 1 very impressive or daunting: *the awesome power of the sea.* 2 informal excellent.

awestruck adjective filled with awe.

awful adjective 1 very bad or unpleasant. 2 used for emphasis: *an awful lot.* 3 old use causing awe.
– DERIVATIVES **awfulness** noun.

awfully adverb 1 informal very or very much. 2 very badly or unpleasantly.

awhile adverb for a short time.

awkward adjective 1 hard to do or deal with: *awkward questions.* 2 causing embarrassment or inconvenience. 3 feeling embarrassed. 4 not graceful; clumsy.
– DERIVATIVES **awkwardly** adverb **awkwardness** noun.
– ORIGIN from Old Norse.

awl noun a small pointed tool used for piercing holes.
– ORIGIN Old English.

awn /awn/ noun a stiff bristle growing from the ear or flower of barley, rye, and grasses.
– ORIGIN Old Norse.

awning noun a sheet of canvas stretched on a frame, used for shelter.
– ORIGIN unknown.

awoke past of AWAKE.

awoken past participle of AWAKE.

AWOL /ay-wol/ adjective Military absent but without intent to desert.
– ORIGIN from *absent without (official) leave.*

awry /uh-ry/ adverb & adjective away from the expected course or position.
– ORIGIN from WRY.

axe (US also **ax**) noun 1 a tool with a heavy blade, used for chopping wood. 2 (**the axe**) severe cost-cutting action: *thirty staff are facing the axe.* • verb 1 cancel or reduce something by a large amount. 2 dismiss someone ruthlessly.
– PHRASES **have an axe to grind** have a private reason for doing something.
– ORIGIN Old English.

axes plural of AXIS.

axial /ak-si-uhl/ adjective relating to or forming an axis.
– DERIVATIVES **axially** adverb.

axil /ak-sil/ noun the upper angle where a leaf joins a stem.
– ORIGIN Latin *axilla* 'armpit'.

axiom /ak-si-uhm/ noun a statement regarded as accepted or obviously true.
– DERIVATIVES **axiomatic** adjective.
– ORIGIN Greek *axiōma* 'what is thought fitting'.

axis /ak-siss/ noun (pl. **axes** /ak-seez/) 1 an imaginary line through a body, about which it rotates. 2 an imaginary line about which a regular figure is symmetrically arranged.

3 Mathematics a fixed reference line for the measurement of coordinates.
– ORIGIN Latin, 'axle, pivot'.

axle /ak-s'l/ noun a rod passing through the centre of a wheel or group of wheels.
– ORIGIN Old Norse.

axolotl /ak-suh-lot'l/ noun a Mexican salamander which lives in water and remains a newt-like larva throughout its life.
– ORIGIN Nahuatl, 'water servant'.

axon noun the long thread-like part of a nerve cell.
– ORIGIN Greek, 'axis'.

ayah /rhymes with higher/ noun a nanny employed by Europeans in India or another former British territory.
– ORIGIN Portuguese *aia* 'nurse'.

ayatollah /I-uh-tol-luh/ noun a Shiite religious leader in Iran.
– ORIGIN from Arabic, 'token of God'.

aye[1] /rhymes with my/ (also **ay**) exclamation old use or dialect yes. • noun a vote for a proposal.
– ORIGIN probably from *I*, first person personal pronoun.

aye[2] /rhymes with may/ adverb old use or Scottish always; still.
– ORIGIN Old Norse.

Ayurveda /ah-yoor-vay-duh/ noun the traditional Hindu system of medicine, using diet, herbal treatment, and yogic breathing.
– DERIVATIVES **Ayurvedic** adjective
– ORIGIN from Sanskrit *āyus* 'life' + *veda* '(sacred) knowledge'.

AZ abbreviation Arizona.

azalea /uh-zay-li-uh/ noun a shrub with brightly coloured flowers.
– ORIGIN from Greek *azaleos* 'dry' (because the shrubs flourish in dry soil).

Azerbaijani /a-zuh-by-jah-ni/ noun (pl. **Azerbaijanis**) a person from Azerbaijan. • adjective relating to Azerbaijan or Azerbaijanis.

azimuth /az-i-muhth/ noun Astronomy the horizontal direction of a celestial object, measured from the north or south point of the horizon.
– DERIVATIVES **azimuthal** adjective.
– ORIGIN Arabic, 'the way, direction'.

Aztec /az-tek/ noun a member of the American Indian people dominant in Mexico before the Spanish conquest.
– ORIGIN Nahuatl, 'person of Aztlan', their legendary place of origin.

azure /az-yuur/ noun a bright blue colour.
– ORIGIN from Persian, 'lapis lazuli'.

Bb

B¹ (also **b**) noun (pl. **Bs** or **B's**) **1** the second letter of the alphabet. **2** Music the seventh note of the scale of C major.

B² abbreviation **1** (in chess) bishop. **2** black (used in describing grades of pencil lead). • symbol the chemical element boron.

b abbreviation **1** (**b.**) born. **2** Cricket bowled by. **3** Cricket bye(s).

BA abbreviation **1** Bachelor of Arts. **2** British Airways.

Ba symbol the chemical element barium.

baa verb (**baas, baaing, baaed**) (of a sheep or lamb) bleat. • noun the cry of a sheep or lamb.
– ORIGIN imitating the sound.

babble verb **1** talk rapidly in a foolish or confused way. **2** (of a stream) flow with a continuous murmur. • noun **1** foolish or confused talk. **2** a babbling sound.
– DERIVATIVES **babbler** noun.
– ORIGIN German *babbelen*.

babe noun **1** literary a baby. **2** informal an attractive young woman. **3** informal an affectionate form of address for a lover.

babel /**bay**-b'l/ noun a confused noise made by a number of voices.
– ORIGIN from the Tower of *Babel* in the Bible, where God confused the languages of the builders.

baboon noun a large monkey with a long snout, large teeth, and a pink rump.
– ORIGIN from Old French *babuin* or Latin *babewynus*.

babushka /buh-**boosh**-kuh/ noun (in Russia) an old woman or grandmother.
– ORIGIN Russian, 'grandmother'.

baby noun (pl. **babies**) **1** a child or animal that is newly or recently born. **2** a timid or childish person. **3** informal a person's lover. **4** (**one's baby**) one's particular responsibility or concern. • adjective small or immature in comparison with others of the same kind: *baby carrots.* • verb (**babies, babying, babied**) treat someone too protectively.
– PHRASES **be left holding the baby** informal be left with an unwelcome responsibility.
– DERIVATIVES **babyhood** noun **babyish** adjective.
– ORIGIN probably imitating a child's first attempts at speech.

baby boom noun informal a temporary marked increase in the birth rate, especially the one following the Second World War.
– DERIVATIVES **baby boomer** noun.

baby-doll adjective referring to a style of women's clothing resembling that traditionally worn by a young child.

Babylonian /ba-bi-**loh**-ni-uhn/ noun a person from Babylon or Babylonia, an ancient city and kingdom in Mesopotamia (part of what is now Iraq). • adjective relating to Babylon or Babylonia.

babysit verb (**babysits, babysitting, babysat**) look after a child or children while the parents are out.
– DERIVATIVES **babysitter** noun.

baccalaureate /ba-kuh-**lor**-i-uht/ noun **1** an exam that qualifies candidates for higher education. **2** a university bachelor's degree.
– ORIGIN from Latin *baccalaureus* 'bachelor'.

baccarat /**bak**-kuh-rah/ noun a gambling card game in which players bet against a banker.
– ORIGIN French *baccara*.

bacchanal /ba-kuh-**nuhl**/ noun chiefly literary a wild and drunken party or celebration.
– ORIGIN from *Bacchus*, the Greek or Roman god of wine.

Bacchanalia /ba-kuh-**nay**-li-uh/ plural noun (also treated as sing.) **1** the ancient Roman festival of the god Bacchus. **2** (**bacchanalia**) drunken celebrations.
– DERIVATIVES **bacchanalian** adjective.

bacchant /**bak**-kuhnt/ noun (fem. **bacchante** /buh-**kan**-ti/, pl. **bacchantes** /buh-**kan**-teez/) a priest or follower of the Greek or Roman god Bacchus.

baccy noun Brit. informal tobacco.

bachata /ba-**cha**-tuh/ noun a style of romantic music originating in the Dominican Republic.
– ORIGIN Caribbean Spanish, 'party, good time'.

bachelor noun **1** a man who has never been married. **2** a person who holds a first degree from a university.
– DERIVATIVES **bachelorhood** noun.
– ORIGIN Old French *bacheler* 'a young man wishing to become a knight'.

bachelorette noun N. Amer. a young unmarried woman.

Bach flower remedies /bach/ plural noun preparations of the flowers of various plants used in a system of complementary medicine.
– ORIGIN named after the British physician Edward *Bach*.

bacillus /buh-**sil**-luhss/ noun (pl. **bacilli** /buh-**sil**-lee/) a rod-shaped bacterium.
– DERIVATIVES **bacillary** adjective.
– ORIGIN Latin, 'little stick'.

back noun **1** the rear surface of a person's body from the shoulders to the hips. **2** the upper surface of an animal's body, equivalent to a

b

person's back. **3** the side or part of something that is furthest from the front or that is not normally seen or used. **4** a player in a team game who plays in a defensive position behind the forwards. •**adverb 1** in the opposite direction from that in which one is facing or travelling. **2** so as to return to an earlier or normal position or state. **3** into the past. **4** in return. •**verb 1** give support to: *the scheme is backed by the Education Secretary.* **2** walk or drive backwards. **3** bet money on a person or animal winning a race or contest. **4** (**back on/on to**) (of a building or other structure) have its back facing or adjacent to something. **5** cover the back of an object. **6** provide musical accompaniment to a singer or musician. **7** (of the wind) change direction anticlockwise around the points of the compass. •**adjective 1** of or at the back. **2** in a remote or less important position. **3** relating to the past.

– PHRASES **back and forth** to and fro. **the back of beyond** a very remote place. **back down** admit defeat. **back off** draw back from confrontation. **back out** withdraw from a commitment. **back to front** Brit. with the back at the front and the front at the back. **back something up** Computing make a spare copy of data or a disk. **behind someone's back** without a person's knowledge. **get** (or **put**) **someone's back up** annoy someone. **put one's back into** tackle a task in a determined and energetic way. **turn one's back on** ignore; reject. **with one's back to** (or **up against**) **the wall** in a desperate situation.

– DERIVATIVES **backer** noun **backless** adjective.
– ORIGIN Old English.

backache noun prolonged pain in one's back.

backbeat noun Music a strong accent on one of the normally unaccented beats of the bar.

backbencher noun (in the UK) a member of parliament who does not hold a government or opposition post and who sits behind the front benches in the House of Commons.
– DERIVATIVES **backbench** adjective.

backbiting noun spiteful talk about a person who is not present.

back boiler noun Brit. a boiler supplying hot water, built in behind a fireplace or integral to a gas fire.

backbone noun **1** the spine. **2** the chief support of a system or organization: *small customers are the backbone of a profitable business.* **3** strength of character.

back-breaking adjective (of manual labour) physically demanding.

back burner noun (in phrase **on the back burner**) set aside because low priority.

back catalogue noun all the works previously produced by a recording artist, record company, or film director.

backchat noun Brit. informal rude or cheeky remarks.

backcloth noun Brit. a backdrop.

backcomb verb chiefly Brit. comb the hair towards the scalp to make it look thicker.

backdate verb Brit. **1** make something valid from an earlier date. **2** put an earlier date to a document than the actual one.

back-door adjective underhand or secret.

backdrop noun **1** a painted cloth hung at the back of a theatre stage as part of the scenery. **2** the setting or background for an event.

backfire verb **1** (of a vehicle or its engine) undergo a mistimed explosion in the cylinder or exhaust. **2** produce the opposite effect to what was intended: *his trick backfired on him.*

backgammon noun a board game in which two players move their pieces around triangular points according to the throw of dice.
– ORIGIN from **BACK** + an Old English word meaning 'game'.

background noun **1** part of a picture, scene, or description that forms a setting for the main figures or events. **2** information or circumstances that influence or explain something: *the historical background to the rebellion.* **3** a person's education, experience, and social circumstances. **4** a persistent low level of radioactivity, noise, etc. present in a particular environment. •**verb** form a background to something.

backhand noun (in racket sports) a stroke played with the back of the hand facing in the direction of the stroke. •**verb** strike someone or something with a backhanded blow or stroke.

backhanded adjective **1** made with the back of the hand facing in the direction of movement. **2** expressed in an indirect or ambiguous way: *a backhanded compliment.*

backhander noun **1** a backhand stroke or blow. **2** Brit. informal a bribe.

backhoe (Brit. also **backhoe loader**) noun a mechanical digger with a bucket attached to a hinged boom.

backing noun **1** help or support. **2** a layer of material that forms or strengthens the back of something. **3** (especially in popular music) music or vocals accompanying the main singer.

backing track noun a recorded musical accompaniment.

backlash noun **1** a strong and adverse reaction by a large number of people: *the backlash against GM food.* **2** recoil between parts of a mechanism.

backlist noun a publisher's list of books published before the current season and still in print.

backlog noun a build-up of matters needing to be dealt with.

backlot noun an outdoor area in a film studio where large sets are made and some outside scenes are filmed.

backpack noun a rucksack. •**verb** travel carrying one's belongings in a rucksack.
– DERIVATIVES **backpacker** noun.

back passage noun Brit. euphemistic a person's rectum.

back-pedal verb **1** reverse a previous action or opinion. **2** move the pedals of a bicycle backwards (formerly so as to brake).

backroom adjective relating to secret work or planning.

back-seat driver noun informal a passenger in a car who gives the driver unwanted advice.

b

backside noun informal a person's bottom.

backslapping noun the offering of hearty congratulations or praise.

backslash noun a backward-sloping diagonal line (\).

backslide verb (past and past part. **backslid**) return to bad ways.
– DERIVATIVES **backslider** noun **backsliding** noun.

backspace noun a key on a typewriter or computer keyboard used to move the carriage or cursor backwards. • verb move a typewriter carriage or computer cursor backwards.

backspin noun a backward spin given to a moving ball, causing it to stop more quickly or rebound at a steeper angle.

back-stabbing noun the action of criticizing someone while pretending to be friendly.

backstage adverb & adjective behind the stage in a theatre.

backstairs adjective secret or underhand: *backstairs deals.*

backstitch noun a method of sewing with overlapping stitches.

backstory noun (pl. **backstories**) a history or background created for a fictional character in a film or television programme.

backstreet noun a minor street. • adjective acting or done secretly and typically illegally: *backstreet abortions.*

backstroke noun a swimming stroke in which the swimmer lies on their back and lifts their arms alternately out of the water in a backward circular movement.

back-to-back adjective 1 Brit. (of houses) built in a terrace backing on to another terrace, with a wall or alley between. 2 following one after the other.

backtrack verb 1 retrace one's steps. 2 reverse one's previous opinion or position: *he denied that he was backtracking on his promise.*

backup noun 1 help or support. 2 a person or thing kept ready to be used if necessary.

backward adjective 1 directed towards the back. 2 having made less progress than is normal or expected. • adverb variant of **BACKWARDS.**
– PHRASES **not backward in** not lacking the confidence to do something.
– DERIVATIVES **backwardly** adverb **backwardness** noun.

backwards (also **backward**) adverb 1 towards one's back. 2 back towards the starting point. 3 opposite to the usual direction or order.
– PHRASES **bend over backwards** informal try one's hardest to be fair or helpful. **know something backwards** be completely familiar with something.

backwash noun waves flowing outwards behind a ship.

backwater noun 1 a stretch of stagnant water on a river. 2 a place or state in which no development is happening: *the country remains an economic backwater.*

backwoods plural noun chiefly N. Amer. 1 remote uncleared forest land. 2 a region that is remote or has few inhabitants.
– DERIVATIVES **backwoodsman** noun (pl. **backwoodsmen**).

backyard noun 1 Brit. a yard at the back of a building. 2 N. Amer. a back garden.
– PHRASES **in one's (own) backyard** informal the area close to where one lives.

bacon noun salted or smoked meat from the back or sides of a pig.
– PHRASES **bring home the bacon** informal make money or achieve success.
– ORIGIN Old French.

bacteria plural of **BACTERIUM.**

bacteriological adjective 1 relating to bacteriology or bacteria. 2 relating to germ warfare.

bacteriology /bak-teer-i-ol-uh-ji/ noun the study of bacteria.
– DERIVATIVES **bacteriologist** noun.

bacterium noun (pl. **bacteria**) a member of a large group of microscopic single-celled organisms, many kinds of which can cause disease.
– DERIVATIVES **bacterial** adjective **bacterially** adverb.
– ORIGIN from Greek *baktērion* 'little rod'.

USAGE: **Bacteria** is the plural form of **bacterium** and should always be used with the plural form of the verb: *the bacteria are killed by thorough cooking.*

Bactrian camel /bak-tri-uhn/ noun a camel with two humps, native to central Asia.
– ORIGIN named after the ancient empire of *Bactria* in central Asia.

bad adjective (**worse, worst**) 1 of poor quality or a low standard. 2 unwelcome or unpleasant: *bad news.* 3 severe or serious. 4 wicked or evil. 5 (**bad for**) harmful to: *fatty food is bad for you.* 6 injured, ill, or diseased. 7 (of food) decayed. 8 (**badder, baddest**) informal, chiefly N. Amer. excellent.
– PHRASES **too bad** informal regrettable but unable to be changed.
– DERIVATIVES **badness** noun.
– ORIGIN perhaps from Old English, 'womanish man'.

bad blood noun hostility or hatred between people.

bad debt noun a debt that will not be repaid.

baddy (also **baddie**) noun (pl. **baddies**) informal a wicked or evil person in a book, film, or play.

bade /bayd/ past of **BID**².

bad faith noun intention to deceive: *they were accused of negotiating in bad faith.*

bad form noun an offence against accepted behaviour.

badge noun a small flat object worn by a person to show who they are or what they do.
– ORIGIN unknown.

badger noun a heavily built mammal with a grey and black coat and a white-striped head, which lives underground. • verb pester someone to do something.
– ORIGIN perhaps from **BADGE**, because of the animal's head markings.

bad hair day noun informal a day on which everything goes wrong.

badinage /bad-i-nahzh/ noun witty conversation.
– ORIGIN French.

badlands plural noun poor land with very little soil.

badly adverb (**worse, worst**) **1** in a way that is not acceptable or satisfactory. **2** severely; seriously. **3** very much.
– PHRASES **badly off** not wealthy; poor.

badminton noun a game with rackets in which a shuttlecock is hit back and forth across a net.
– ORIGIN named after *Badminton* in SW England.

bad-mouth verb informal criticize someone.

bad-tempered adjective easily angered or annoyed.

baffle verb make someone feel bewildered or puzzled. • noun a device for controlling or stopping the flow of sound, light, gas, or a fluid.
– DERIVATIVES **bafflement** noun **baffling** adjective.
– ORIGIN perhaps related to French *bafouer* 'ridicule'.

bag noun **1** a flexible container with an opening at the top. **2** (**bags**) loose folds of skin under a person's eyes. **3** (**bags of**) informal, chiefly Brit. plenty of. **4** informal an unpleasant or unattractive woman. • verb (**bags, bagging, bagged**) **1** put something in a bag. **2** succeed in getting: *get there early to bag a seat.* **3** succeed in killing or catching an animal. **4** (of clothes) form loose bulges.
– PHRASES **in the bag** informal sure to be gained.
– DERIVATIVES **bagful** noun **bagger** noun
– ORIGIN perhaps from Old Norse.

bagatelle /ba-guh-**tel**/ noun **1** a game in which small balls are hit into numbered holes on a board. **2** something unimportant.
– ORIGIN Italian *bagatella.*

bagel /**bay**-g'l/ noun a ring-shaped bread roll with a heavy texture.
– ORIGIN Yiddish.

baggage noun **1** luggage packed with belongings for travelling. **2** past experiences or long-held attitudes regarded as having an undesirable influence: *emotional baggage.* **3** dated a cheeky or unpleasant girl or woman.
– ORIGIN Old French *bagage.*

baggy adjective (**baggier, baggiest**) loose and hanging in bulges or folds.
– DERIVATIVES **bagginess** noun.

bag lady noun informal a homeless woman who carries her possessions in shopping bags.

bagman noun (pl. **bagmen**) US & Austral./NZ informal an agent who collects or distributes the proceeds of illicit activities.

bagpipe (also **bagpipes**) noun a musical instrument with pipes that are sounded by wind squeezed from a bag.
– DERIVATIVES **bagpiper** noun.

baguette /ba-**get**/ noun a long, narrow French loaf.
– ORIGIN French.

bah exclamation an expression of contempt.

Baha'i /bah-**hah**-i/ (also **Bahai**) noun (pl. **Baha'is**) **1** a religion founded in Persia, emphasizing that there is one god and that humankind and all religions are essentially one. **2** a follower of the Baha'i faith.
– ORIGIN from Arabic, 'splendour'.

Bahamian /buh-**hay**-mi-uhn/ noun a person from the Bahamas. • adjective relating to the Bahamas.

Bahraini /bah-**ray**-ni/ noun a person from Bahrain. • adjective relating to Bahrain.

baht /baht/ noun (pl. same) the basic unit of money of Thailand.
– ORIGIN Thai.

Bahutu plural of **HUTU**.

bail[1] noun **1** the temporary release of an accused person before they are tried, often on condition that a sum of money is promised to the court to ensure they attend the trial. **2** money paid to a court for this reason. • verb release an accused person on payment of bail.
– PHRASES **go** (or **stand**) **bail** provide bail money for an accused person. **jump bail** informal fail to appear for trial after being released on bail.
– ORIGIN Old French, 'custody, jurisdiction'.

bail[2] noun **1** Cricket either of the two crosspieces resting on the stumps. **2** a bar on a typewriter or computer printer which holds the paper steady. **3** a bar separating horses in an open stable.
– ORIGIN Old French *baile* 'palisade, enclosure'.

bail[3] (Brit. also **bale**) verb **1** scoop water out of a ship or boat. **2** (**bail out**) make an emergency parachute descent from an aircraft. **3** (**bail someone/thing out**) rescue from a difficulty: *the state will not bail out loss-making enterprises.*
– ORIGIN from French *baille* 'bucket'.

bailey noun (pl. **baileys**) the outer wall of a castle.
– ORIGIN probably from Old French *baile* 'palisade, enclosure'.

Bailey bridge noun a prefabricated steel bridge designed for rapid assembly, especially in military operations.
– ORIGIN named after the English engineer Sir Donald *Bailey.*

bailiff noun **1** chiefly Brit. a sheriff's officer who delivers writs, seizes property to clear rent that is owed, and carries out arrests. **2** Brit. the agent of a landlord.
– ORIGIN Old French *baillif.*

bailiwick /**bay**-li-wik/ noun **1** (**one's bailiwick**) one's area of activity or interest: *after the war, the Middle East remained his bailiwick.* **2** Law a district over which a bailiff has authority.
– ORIGIN from **BAILIFF** + Old English *wick* 'dwelling place'.

bain-marie /ban muh-**ree**/ noun (pl. **bains-marie** or **bain-maries** pronunc. same) a pan of hot water in which a cooking container is placed for slow cooking.
– ORIGIN French, 'bath of Maria', said to be the name of an alchemist.

bairn noun chiefly Scottish & N. English a child.
– ORIGIN Old English.

bait noun **1** food put on a hook or in a trap to attract fish or other animals. **2** variant spelling of **BATE**. • verb **1** taunt or tease someone. **2** set dogs on an animal that is trapped or tied up. **3** put bait on a hook or in a trap or net.
– PHRASES **rise to the bait** react to taunting or temptation exactly as someone intended.
– ORIGIN Old Norse, 'pasture, food'.

baize noun a green felt-like material, used for covering billiard and card tables.
– ORIGIN from French *bai* 'chestnut-coloured'.

bake verb **1** cook food by dry heat in an oven. **2** heat something so as to dry or harden it.

3 informal be or become very hot in hot weather. • **noun** a dish consisting of a mixture of ingredients baked in an oven.
– ORIGIN Old English.

baked beans plural noun baked haricot beans, cooked in tomato sauce and tinned.

Bakelite noun trademark an early brittle form of plastic.
– ORIGIN named after the Belgian-born chemist Leo H. *Baekeland*, who invented it.

baker noun a person whose trade is making bread and cakes.
– PHRASES **baker's dozen** a group of thirteen. [from the former bakers' custom of adding an extra loaf to a dozen sold to a retailer, this being the retailer's profit.]
– DERIVATIVES **bakery** noun (pl. **bakeries**).

Bakewell tart noun Brit. a baked open tart consisting of a pastry case lined with jam and filled with almond sponge cake.
– ORIGIN named after the town of *Bakewell* in Derbyshire.

baking powder noun a mixture of sodium bicarbonate and cream of tartar, used in baking to make cakes rise.

baking soda noun sodium bicarbonate.

baklava /**bah**-kluh-vuh/ noun a Middle Eastern dessert made of filo pastry filled with chopped nuts and soaked in honey.
– ORIGIN Turkish.

baksheesh /bak-**sheesh**/ noun (in India and some eastern countries) a small sum of money given as charity, a tip, or a bribe.
– ORIGIN Persian.

balaclava noun a close-fitting woollen hat covering the whole head and neck except for the face.
– ORIGIN first worn by soldiers in the Crimean War and named after *Balaclava*, site of a battle in that war.

balafon /**bal**-uh-fon/ noun a large xylophone with hollow gourds as resonators, used in West African music.
– ORIGIN from a West African language.

balalaika /ba-luh-**ly**-kuh/ noun a Russian musical instrument like a guitar with a triangular body and three strings.
– ORIGIN Russian.

balance noun **1** a state in which weight is distributed evenly, enabling a person or thing to remain steady and upright. **2** a situation in which different elements are equal or in the correct proportions: *elections left the political balance almost unchanged.* **3** mental or emotional stability. **4** a device for weighing. **5** a predominating amount: *the balance of opinion was that work was important.* **6** an amount that is the difference between money received and money spent in an account: *a healthy bank balance.* **7** an amount still owed when part of a debt has been paid. • **verb 1** be or put in a steady position. **2** compare the value of one thing with another. **3** establish a balance of proportions or elements in: *she manages to balance work and family life.* **4** compare sums of money owed and paid to an account to ensure that they are equal.
– PHRASES **balance of payments** the difference in total value between payments into and out of a country over a period. **balance of power**

1 a situation in which states of the world have roughly equal power. **2** the power held by a small group when larger groups are of equal strength. **balance of trade** the difference in value between a country's imports and exports. **be** (or **hang**) **in the balance** be in an uncertain state. **on balance** when everything is considered.
– DERIVATIVES **balancer** noun.
– ORIGIN from Latin *libra bilanx* 'balance having two scale pans'.

balance sheet noun a written statement detailing what a business owns and what it owes at a particular point in time.

balboa /bal-**boh**-uh/ noun the basic unit of money of Panama.
– ORIGIN named after the Spanish explorer Vasco Núñez de *Balboa*.

balcony noun (pl. **balconies**) **1** an enclosed platform projecting from the outside of a building. **2** the highest tier of seats in a theatre or cinema.
– DERIVATIVES **balconied** adjective.
– ORIGIN Italian *balcone*.

bald adjective **1** having very little or no hair on the head. **2** (of an animal) not covered by the usual fur, hair, or feathers. **3** (of a tyre) having the tread worn away. **4** without any extra detail or explanation: *the bald facts.*
– DERIVATIVES **balding** adjective **baldish** adjective **baldly** adverb **baldness** noun.
– ORIGIN probably from a former word meaning 'white patch'.

baldachin /**bawl**-duh-kin/ (also **baldaquin** pronunc. same) noun a ceremonial canopy over an altar, throne, or doorway.
– ORIGIN first referring to a rich brocade from Baghdad: from Italian *Baldacco* 'Baghdad'.

balderdash noun senseless talk or writing; nonsense.
– ORIGIN unknown.

bale¹ noun a large wrapped or bound bundle of paper, hay, or cotton. • **verb** make up paper, hay, or cotton into bales.
– DERIVATIVES **baler** noun.
– ORIGIN probably from Dutch.

bale² verb Brit. variant spelling of **BAIL**³.

baleen /buh-**leen**/ noun whalebone.
– ORIGIN Latin *balaena* 'whale'.

baleen whale noun any of the kinds of whale that have plates of whalebone in the mouth for straining plankton from the water.

baleful adjective causing or threatening to cause harm: *she watched him with baleful eyes.*
– DERIVATIVES **balefully** adverb.
– ORIGIN Old English, 'evil'.

Balinese /bah-li-**neez**/ noun (pl. same) a person from Bali. • **adjective** relating to Bali.

balk verb & noun chiefly US variant spelling of **BAULK**.

Balkan /**bawl**-k'n/ adjective relating to the countries on the peninsula in SE Europe surrounded by the Adriatic, Ionian, Aegean, and the Black seas. • **noun** (**the Balkans**) the Balkan countries.

Balkanize (or **Balkanise**) verb divide a region or organization into smaller states or groups who oppose each other.
– DERIVATIVES **Balkanization** noun.

b

ball¹ noun **1** a rounded object that is kicked, thrown, or hit in a game. **2** a single throw or kick of the ball in a game. **3** a rounded part or thing: *the ball of the foot*. • verb squeeze or form something into a ball.
– PHRASES **the ball is in your court** it is up to you to make the next move. **keep one's eye on** (or **take one's eye off**) **the ball** keep (or fail to keep) one's attention focused on the matter in hand. **on the ball** alert to new ideas or methods. **play ball** informal cooperate. **start** (or **get** or **set**) **the ball rolling** make a start.
– ORIGIN Old Norse.

ball² noun a formal social gathering for dancing.
– PHRASES **have a ball** informal enjoy oneself very much.
– ORIGIN from Latin *ballare* 'to dance'.

ballad noun **1** a poem or song telling a popular story. **2** a slow sentimental or romantic song.
– DERIVATIVES **balladeer** noun **balladry** noun.
– ORIGIN from Latin *ballare* 'to dance'.

ballade /ba-**lahd**/ noun **1** a poem with sets of three verses, each ending with the same line, and a short verse in conclusion. **2** a short, lyrical piece of music, especially one for piano.
– ORIGIN earlier spelling of **BALLAD**.

ball-and-socket joint noun a joint in which a rounded end lies in a socket, allowing movement in all directions.

ballast noun **1** a heavy substance carried by a ship or hot-air balloon to keep it stable. **2** gravel or coarse stone used to form the base of a railway track or road.
– ORIGIN probably German or Scandinavian.

ball bearing noun **1** a bearing in which the parts are separated by a ring of small metal balls which reduce friction. **2** a ball used in such a bearing.

ballboy (or **ballgirl**) noun a boy (or girl) who fetches balls that go out of play during a tennis match or baseball game.

ballcock noun a valve which automatically tops up a cistern when liquid is drawn from it.

ballerina noun a female ballet dancer.
– ORIGIN from Italian *ballerino* 'dancing master'.

ballet noun **1** an artistic form of dancing performed to music, using set steps and gestures. **2** a creative work of this form.
– DERIVATIVES **balletic** adjective.
– ORIGIN Italian *balletto* 'a little dance'.

balletomane /**bal**-it-oh-mayn/ noun a ballet enthusiast.

ball game noun a game played with a ball.
– PHRASES **a different** (or **whole new**) **ball game** informal a situation that is completely different from a previous one.

ballistic /buh-**liss**-tik/ adjective **1** relating to projectiles or their flight through the air. **2** moving under the force of gravity only.
– PHRASES **go ballistic** informal fly into a rage.
– ORIGIN from Greek *ballein* 'to throw'.

ballistic missile noun a missile which is initially powered and guided but falls under gravity on to its target.

ballistics plural noun (treated as sing.) the science of projectiles and firearms.

ballocks plural noun variant spelling of **BOLLOCKS**.

balloon noun **1** a small rubber bag which is inflated and used as a toy or a decoration. **2** (also **hot-air balloon**) a large bag filled with hot air or gas to make it rise in the air, with a basket for passengers hanging from it. **3** a rounded outline containing the words or thoughts of characters in a comic strip. • verb **1** swell outwards. **2** increase rapidly: *the company's debt ballooned in the last five years.* **3** (usu. as noun **ballooning**) travel by hot-air balloon.
– DERIVATIVES **balloonist** noun.
– ORIGIN French *ballon* or Italian *ballone* 'large ball'.

ballot noun **1** a way of voting secretly on something, usually by placing paper slips in a box. **2** (**the ballot**) the total number of votes cast in such a way. • verb (**ballots, balloting, balloted**) **1** obtain a secret vote from members. **2** cast one's vote on an issue.
– ORIGIN Italian *ballotta* 'little ball' (from the former practice of voting by placing a ball in a container).

ballpark noun **1** N. Amer. a baseball ground. **2** informal an area or range within which an estimate is likely to be correct. • adjective informal approximate: *a ballpark figure.*

ballpoint pen noun a pen with a tiny ball as its writing point.

ballroom noun a large room for formal dancing.

ballroom dancing noun formal social dancing in couples.

balls vulgar slang plural noun **1** testicles. **2** courage; nerve. **3** Brit. nonsense. • verb (**balls something up**) bungle something.

balls-up noun Brit. vulgar slang a bungled task or action.

ballsy adjective (**ballsier, ballsiest**) informal bold and confident.

ball valve noun a one-way valve opened and closed by pressure on a ball which fits into a cup-shaped opening.

bally /**ba**-li/ adjective & adverb Brit. old-fashioned euphemism for **BLOODY** (in sense 3).

ballyhoo noun informal excessive publicity or fuss.
– ORIGIN unknown.

balm noun **1** a fragrant ointment used to heal or soothe the skin. **2** something that soothes or heals: *the story was balm to American hearts.*
– ORIGIN from Latin *balsamum* 'balsam'.

balmy adjective (**balmier, balmiest**) (of the weather or a period of time) pleasantly warm.

baloney /buh-**loh**-ni/ noun informal nonsense.
– ORIGIN perhaps from *bologna*, a type of smoked sausage.

balsa /**bawl**-suh/ (also **balsa wood**) noun very lightweight timber from a tropical American tree, used for making models.
– ORIGIN Spanish, 'raft'.

balsam /**bawl**-suhm/ noun **1** a scented resin obtained from certain trees and shrubs, used in perfumes and medicines. **2** a plant grown for its pink or purple flowers.
– DERIVATIVES **balsamic** adjective.
– ORIGIN Greek *balsamon*.

balsamic vinegar noun dark, sweet Italian vinegar that has been matured in wooden barrels.

balti /**bawl**-ti, **bal**-ti/ noun (pl. **baltis**) a spicy Pakistani dish that is cooked in a small two-handled pan.
– ORIGIN Urdu, 'pail'.

Baltic adjective relating to the Baltic Sea or those states on its eastern shores.

baluster /**ba**-luh-ster/ noun a short pillar forming part of a series supporting a rail.
– ORIGIN French *balustre*.

balustrade /ba-luh-**strayd**/ noun a railing supported by balusters.
– DERIVATIVES **balustraded** adjective.

bambino /bam-**bee**-noh/ noun (pl. **bambini** /bam-**bee**-nee/ or **bambinos**) a baby or young child.
– ORIGIN Italian, 'little silly'.

bamboo noun a giant tropical grass with hollow woody stems.
– ORIGIN Malay.

bamboo shoot noun a young shoot of bamboo, eaten as a vegetable.

bamboozle verb informal cheat or deceive someone.
– ORIGIN unknown.

ban¹ verb (**bans, banning, banned**) officially forbid something or prevent someone from doing something. • noun an official order forbidding something.
– ORIGIN Old English, 'summon by a public proclamation'.

ban² /bahn/ noun (pl. **bani** /**bah**-ni/) a unit of money of Romania, equal to one hundredth of a leu.
– ORIGIN Romanian.

banal /buh-**nahl**/ adjective very ordinary and unoriginal: *songs with banal, repeated words.*
– DERIVATIVES **banality** noun (pl. **banalities**) **banally** adverb.
– ORIGIN first meaning 'compulsory': from French *ban* 'summons'.

banana noun a long curved fruit of a tropical or subtropical tree, with yellow skin and soft flesh.
– PHRASES **go** (or **be**) **bananas** informal become (or be) mad or angry.
– ORIGIN from an African language.

banana republic noun derogatory a small country that is politically unstable because its economy is dominated by a single export controlled by foreign businesses.

banana split noun a sweet dish made with bananas cut down the middle and filled with ice cream, sauce, and nuts.

band¹ noun 1 a flat, thin strip or loop of material used as a fastener, for reinforcement, or as decoration. 2 a stripe or strip of a different colour or nature from its surroundings: *a band of cloud.* 3 a range of values within a series: *the lower-rate tax band.* 4 a range of frequencies or wavelengths in a spectrum: *the UHF band.* • verb 1 fit a band on or round something. 2 mark something with a stripe or stripes. 3 put in a range or category: *the train fares are banded according to time of day.*
– DERIVATIVES **banding** noun.
– ORIGIN Old English.

band² noun 1 a small group of musicians and singers who play pop, jazz, or rock music. 2 a group of musicians who play brass, wind, or percussion instruments. 3 a group of people with the same aim or a shared feature. • verb form a group to achieve the same aim: *people banded together to help each other.*
– ORIGIN Old French *bande*.

bandage noun a strip of material used to bind up a wound or to protect an injury. • verb bind a wound of part of the body with a bandage.
– ORIGIN French.

bandanna /ban-**dan**-nuh/ (also **bandana**) noun a square of brightly coloured fabric worn on the head or around the neck.
– ORIGIN Hindi.

B. & B. abbreviation bed and breakfast.

bandbox noun a circular cardboard box for carrying hats.

bandeau /**ban**-doh/ noun (pl. **bandeaux** /**ban**-dohz/) 1 a narrow band worn round the head to hold the hair in position. 2 a woman's strapless top consisting of a band of fabric fitting around the bust.
– ORIGIN Old French *bandel* 'small band'.

bandicoot /**ban**-di-koot/ noun an insect-eating marsupial of Australia and New Guinea.
– ORIGIN from a word in an Indian language meaning 'pig-rat'.

bandit noun a member of a gang of armed robbers.
– DERIVATIVES **banditry** noun.
– ORIGIN from Italian *bandito* 'banned'.

bandleader noun a player at the head of a musical band.

bandolier /ban-duh-**leer**/ (also **bandoleer**) noun a shoulder belt with loops or pockets for cartridges.
– ORIGIN French *bandoulière*.

bandsaw noun a power saw consisting of an endless moving steel belt with a serrated edge.

bandstand noun a covered outdoor platform for a band to play on.

bandwagon noun an activity or cause that has suddenly become fashionable or popular: *the company is jumping on the Green bandwagon.*

bandwidth noun 1 a range of frequencies used in telecommunications. 2 the ability of a computer network or other telecommunication system to transmit signals.

bandy¹ adjective (**bandier, bandiest**) (of a person's legs) curved outwards so that the knees are wide apart.
– ORIGIN perhaps from former *bandy* 'curved hockey stick'.

bandy² verb (**bandies, bandying, bandied**) pass on or discuss an idea, rumour, or name in a casual or uninformed way: *£40,000 is the figure that has been bandied about.*
– PHRASES **bandy words** exchange angry remarks.
– ORIGIN perhaps from French *bander* 'take sides at tennis'.

bane noun a cause of great distress or annoyance: *the phone was the bane of my life.*
– ORIGIN Old English, 'thing causing death, poison'.

bang noun 1 a sudden loud sharp noise. 2 a

b

sudden painful blow. **3** (**bangs**) N. Amer. a fringe of hair cut straight across the forehead. • **verb 1** hit or put down something forcefully and noisily. **2** make or cause to make a bang. **3** vulgar slang (of a man) have sex with someone. • **adverb** informal, chiefly Brit. exactly: *bang on time.*
– PHRASES **bang on** Brit. informal exactly right. **bang on about** Brit. informal talk about something boringly and at length. **bang someone up** Brit. informal imprison someone. **with a bang** suddenly or impressively.
– ORIGIN imitating the sound.

banger noun Brit. informal **1** a sausage. **2** an old car. **3** a loud explosive firework.

Bangladeshi /bang-gluh-**desh**-i/ noun (pl. same or **Bangladeshis**) a person from Bangladesh. • **adjective** relating to Bangladesh.

bangle noun a rigid bracelet worn around the arm.
– ORIGIN Hindi.

bani plural of **BAN²**.

banish verb **1** make someone leave a place as an official punishment. **2** get rid of: *I banished the thought from my mind.*
– DERIVATIVES **banishment** noun.
– ORIGIN Old French *banir.*

banister (also **bannister**) noun **1** (also **banisters**) the uprights and handrail at the side of a staircase. **2** a single upright at the side of a staircase.
– ORIGIN from **BALUSTER**.

banjax /**ban**-jaks/ verb informal ruin or defeat someone or something.
– ORIGIN Anglo-Irish.

banjo noun (pl. **banjos** or **banjoes**) a musical instrument like a guitar, with five strings, a circular body, and a long neck.
– DERIVATIVES **banjoist** noun.
– ORIGIN from *bandore,* a kind of lute.

bank¹ noun **1** the land alongside a river or lake. **2** a long, high slope, mound, or mass: *mud banks.* **3** a set of similar things grouped together in rows. • **verb 1** heap or form a substance into a mass or mound. **2** (of an aircraft or vehicle) tilt sideways in making a turn. **3** build a road, railway, or sports track higher at the outer edge of a bend.
– ORIGIN Old Norse.

bank² noun **1** an organization offering financial services, especially loans and the safekeeping of customers' money. **2** a stock or supply available for use: *a blood bank.* **3** a site or container where something may be left for recycling: *a paper bank.* **4** (**the bank**) the store of money or tokens held by the banker in some gambling or board games. • **verb 1** deposit money or valuables in a bank. **2** have an account at a bank. **3** (**bank on**) rely on confidently: *he can't bank on their support.*
– PHRASES **break the bank** informal cost more than one can afford.
– ORIGIN first meaning a money dealer's table: from Latin *banca* 'bench'.

bankable adjective certain to bring profit and success.
– DERIVATIVES **bankability** noun.

bank card noun a cheque card.

banker¹ noun **1** a person who manages or owns a bank. **2** the person who keeps the bank in some gambling or board games.

banker² noun Austral./NZ informal a river flooded to the top of its banks.

bank holiday noun Brit. a public holiday, when banks are officially closed.

banking noun the business activity of a bank.

banknote noun a piece of paper money issued by a central bank.

bank rate noun another term for **BASE RATE**.

bankroll noun N. Amer. **1** a roll of banknotes. **2** available funds. • **verb** informal support someone or something financially.

bankrupt adjective **1** declared in law as unable to pay one's debts. **2** completely lacking in a particular good quality or value: *their cause is morally bankrupt.* • **noun** a person judged by a court to be bankrupt. • **verb** make a person or organization bankrupt.
– DERIVATIVES **bankruptcy** noun (pl. **bankruptcies**).
– ORIGIN from Italian *banca rotta* 'broken bench'.

banksia /**bangk**-si-uh/ noun an evergreen Australian shrub with flowers resembling cylindrical brushes.
– ORIGIN named after the English botanist Sir Joseph *Banks.*

banner noun **1** a long strip of cloth bearing a slogan or design, hung up or carried on poles. **2** an advertisement on a website in the form of bar, column, or box. • **adjective** N. Amer. excellent; outstanding: *a banner year.*
– ORIGIN Old French *baniere.*

bannister noun variant spelling of **BANISTER**.

bannock /**ban**-uhk/ noun Scottish & N. English a round, flat loaf.
– ORIGIN Old English.

banns plural noun a public announcement of an intended marriage read out in a parish church.
– ORIGIN plural of **BAN¹**.

banoffi pie /buh-**nof**-i/ (also **banoffee pie**) noun a flan filled with bananas, toffee, and cream.
– ORIGIN from **BANANA** + **TOFFEE**.

banquet /**bang**-kwit/ noun an elaborate and formal meal for many people. • **verb** (**banquets**, **banqueting**, **banqueted**) give or take part in a banquet.
– ORIGIN French, 'little bench'.

banquette /bang-**ket**/ noun an upholstered bench along a wall.
– ORIGIN French.

banshee noun (in Irish legend) a female spirit whose wailing warns of a death in a house.
– ORIGIN from Old Irish *ben síde* 'woman of the fairies'.

bantam noun a chicken of a small breed.
– ORIGIN probably named after the province of *Bantam* in Java.

bantamweight noun a weight in boxing and other sports between flyweight and featherweight.

banter noun the good-humoured exchange of teasing remarks. • **verb** exchange remarks in a good-humoured teasing way.
– ORIGIN unknown.

Bantu /ban-**too**/ noun (pl. same or **Bantus**) **1** a member of a large group of peoples of central and southern Africa. **2** the group of languages spoken by the Bantu.

– ORIGIN Bantu, 'people'.

USAGE: **Bantu** is a strongly offensive word in South African English, especially when used to refer to individual black people.

banyan /ban-yan/ (also **banian**) noun an Indian fig tree with spreading branches from which roots grow downwards to the ground and form new trunks.
– ORIGIN from Gujarati, 'trader' (because first used by Europeans to refer to a tree under which traders had built a pagoda).

banzai /ban-**zy**/ exclamation a cry used by the Japanese when going into battle or in greeting their emperor.
– ORIGIN Japanese, 'ten thousand years (of life to you)'.

baobab /**bay**-oh-bab/ noun a short African tree with a very thick trunk and large edible fruit.
– ORIGIN probably from an African language.

bap noun Brit. a soft, round, flattish bread roll.
– ORIGIN unknown.

baptism noun the Christian rite of sprinkling a person with water or dipping them in it, as a sign that they have been cleansed of sin and have entered the Church.
– PHRASES **baptism of fire** a difficult new experience.
– DERIVATIVES **baptismal** adjective.
– ORIGIN from Greek *baptizein* 'immerse, baptize'.

Baptist noun a member of a Protestant group believing that only adults should be baptized and that this should be by total immersion in water.

baptistery (also **baptistry**) noun (pl. **baptisteries**) a building or part of a church used for baptism.

baptize (or **baptise**) verb 1 admit someone to the Christian Church by the rite of baptism. 2 give a name or nickname to: *the media baptized the murderer 'The Babysitter'.*
– ORIGIN Greek *baptizein* 'immerse, baptize'.

bar[1] noun 1 a long rigid piece of wood, metal, etc. 2 a counter, room, or place where alcoholic drinks or refreshments are served. 3 a small shop or counter serving refreshments or providing a service: *a snack bar.* 4 a barrier or obstacle: *her humble beginnings were no bar to becoming head of state.* 5 any of the short units into which a piece of music is divided, shown on a score by vertical lines. 6 (**the bar**) the place in a courtroom where an accused person stands during a trial. 7 (**the Bar**) the profession of barrister. 8 (**the Bar**) barristers or (in America) lawyers as a group. 9 Brit. a metal strip added to a medal as an additional distinction. • verb (**bars, barring, barred**) 1 fasten something with a bar or bars. 2 forbid from doing something or prevent from going somewhere: *they were barred from every pub.* • preposition chiefly Brit. except for.
– PHRASES **be called** (or **go**) **to the Bar** Brit. be allowed to practise as a barrister. **behind bars** in prison.
– DERIVATIVES **barred** adjective.
– ORIGIN Old French *barre*.

bar[2] noun a unit of pressure equivalent to a hundred thousand newtons per square metre.
– ORIGIN Greek *baros* 'weight'.

barathea /ba-ruh-**thi**-uh/ noun a fine woollen cloth.
– ORIGIN unknown.

barb noun 1 a sharp backward-pointing part of the head of an arrow, a fish hook, etc., that makes it difficult to remove from something it has pierced. 2 a spiteful remark. 3 a barbel at the mouth of some fish.
– DERIVATIVES **barbless** adjective.
– ORIGIN from Latin *barba* 'beard'.

Barbadian /bah-**bay**-di-uhn/ noun a person from Barbados. • adjective relating to Barbados.

barbarian /bar-**bair**-i-uhn/ noun 1 (in ancient times) a member of a people not belonging to the Greek, Roman, or Christian civilizations. 2 an uncivilized or cruel person. • adjective uncivilized or cruel.
– ORIGIN from Greek *barbaros* 'foreign'.

barbaric /bar-**ba**-rik/ adjective 1 savagely cruel. 2 lacking sophistication; primitive.
– DERIVATIVES **barbarically** adverb.

barbarism /**bar**-buh-ri-z'm/ noun 1 extreme cruelty. 2 an uncivilized or primitive state. 3 a word or expression which is badly formed according to traditional rules, e.g. the word *television*, which is formed from two different languages.

barbarity /bar-**ba**-ri-ti/ noun (pl. **barbarities**) 1 extreme cruelty. 2 lack of culture and civilization.

barbarous /**bar**-buh-ruhss/ adjective 1 extremely cruel. 2 primitive; uncivilized.
– DERIVATIVES **barbarously** adverb.

barbecue noun 1 an outdoor meal or party at which food is grilled over a charcoal fire. 2 a grill used at a barbecue. • verb (**barbecues, barbecuing, barbecued**) cook food on a barbecue.
– ORIGIN from Spanish *barbacoa* 'wooden frame'.

barbecue sauce noun a spicy sauce made from tomatoes, chillies, etc.

barbed adjective 1 having a barb or barbs. 2 (of a remark) spiteful.

barbed wire noun wire with clusters of short, sharp spikes along it.

barbel /**bar**-b'l/ noun 1 a long, thin growth hanging from the mouth or snout of certain fish. 2 a large freshwater fish with barbels hanging from the mouth.
– ORIGIN Latin *barbellus* 'small barbel'.

barbell /**bar**-bel/ noun a long metal bar to which discs of varying weights are attached at each end, used for weightlifting.

barber noun a person who cuts men's hair and shaves or trims beards as an occupation. • verb cut or trim a man's hair.
– ORIGIN Old French *barbe* 'beard'.

barberry noun (pl. **barberries**) another term for BERBERIS.
– ORIGIN Old French *berberis*.

barbershop noun a style of singing in which four men sing in close harmony without musical backing.

barbican /**bar**-bi-kuhn/ noun a double tower above a gate or drawbridge of a castle or fortified city.
– ORIGIN Old French *barbacane*.

b

bar billiards plural noun (treated as sing.) Brit. a form of billiards in which balls are struck into holes guarded by pegs.

barbiturate /bar-**bit**-yuu-ruht/ noun a kind of sedative drug derived from a synthetic compound (**barbituric acid**).
– ORIGIN from German *Barbitursäure*.

bar chart (also chiefly N. Amer. **bar graph**) noun a diagram in which different quantities are represented by rectangles of varying height.

bar code noun a set of stripes printed on a product, able to be read by a computer to provide information on prices and quantities in stock.

bard¹ noun old use or literary a poet. **2** (**the Bard**) Shakespeare. **3** (**Bard**) the winner of a prize for Welsh verse at an Eisteddfod.
– DERIVATIVES **bardic** adjective.
– ORIGIN Celtic.

bard² verb cover meat or game with rashers of fat bacon before roasting.
– ORIGIN from French *barde*.

bare adjective **1** not clothed or covered. **2** without the appropriate or usual covering or contents: *a big, bare room.* **3** without detail; basic. **4** only just enough: *a bare majority.* • verb uncover or reveal: *the dog bared its teeth.*
– PHRASES **with one's bare hands** without using tools or weapons.
– DERIVATIVES **barely** adverb **bareness** noun.
– ORIGIN Old English.

USAGE: On the confusion of bare and bear, see the note at **BEAR¹**.

bareback adverb & adjective on a horse without a saddle.

bareboat adjective (of a boat or ship) hired without a crew.

barefaced adjective shameless and undisguised: *a barefaced lie.*

barefoot (also **barefooted**) adjective & adverb wearing nothing on one's feet.

bareheaded adjective & adverb without a covering for one's head.

barf verb informal, chiefly N. Amer. vomit.
– ORIGIN unknown.

bargain noun **1** an agreement made between people as to what each will do for the other. **2** a thing offered for sale or bought for a low price. • verb **1** negotiate the terms of an agreement. **2** (**bargain for/on**) expect: *I got more information than I'd bargained for.*
– PHRASES **drive a hard bargain** press hard for a deal in one's favour. **into the bargain** in addition.
– DERIVATIVES **bargainer** noun.
– ORIGIN Old French *bargaine*.

barge noun **1** a long flat-bottomed boat for carrying freight on canals and rivers. **2** a large ornamental boat used for pleasure or on ceremonial occasions. • verb **1** move forcefully or roughly: *she barged into the flat and accosted him.* **2** (**barge in**) intrude or interrupt rudely or awkwardly.
– ORIGIN Old French.

bargee /bar-**jee**/ noun chiefly Brit. a person in charge of or working on a barge.

bargepole noun a long pole used to push a barge along.

– PHRASES **would not touch someone/thing with a bargepole** informal would refuse to have anything to do with someone or something.

bar graph noun chiefly N. Amer. a bar chart.

barista /buh-**ri**-stuh/ noun a person who serves in a coffee bar.
– ORIGIN Italian, 'barman'.

barite noun variant spelling of **BARYTE**.

baritone noun an adult male singing voice between tenor and bass. • adjective referring to an instrument that is second lowest in pitch in its family: *a baritone sax.*
– ORIGIN from Greek *barus* 'heavy' + *tonos* 'tone'.

barium /**bair**-i-uhm/ noun a soft, reactive metallic chemical element.
– ORIGIN from Greek *barus* 'heavy'.

barium meal noun a substance containing barium sulphate, which is swallowed so that the stomach or intestines can be seen on an X-ray.

bark¹ noun the sharp sudden cry of a dog, fox, or seal. • verb **1** give a bark. **2** shout something in a fierce or abrupt way.
– PHRASES **one's bark is worse than one's bite** one is not as fierce as one seems. **be barking up the wrong tree** informal be pursuing a mistaken idea or course of action.
– ORIGIN Old English.

bark² noun the tough protective outer covering of the trunk and branches of a tree. • verb scrape the skin off one's shin by accidentally hitting it.
– ORIGIN Old Norse.

bark³ noun old use or literary a ship or boat.
– ORIGIN variant of **BARQUE**.

barker noun informal a person at a fair who calls out to passers-by to persuade them to visit a sideshow.

barking adjective Brit. informal completely mad.

barley noun a cereal plant with bristly heads, the grains of which are used in brewing and animal feed.
– ORIGIN Old English.

barley sugar noun an amber-coloured sweet made of boiled sugar.

barley water noun Brit. a drink made from water and a boiled barley mixture.

barm noun the froth on fermenting malt liquor.
– ORIGIN Old English.

barmaid noun a woman who serves drinks in a bar or pub.

barman noun (pl. **barmen**) chiefly Brit. a man who serves drinks in a bar or pub.

bar mitzvah /bar **mits**-vuh/ noun a religious ceremony in which a Jewish boy aged 13 takes on adult responsibilities under Jewish law.
– ORIGIN Hebrew, 'son of the commandment'.

barmy adjective (**barmier**, **barmiest**) Brit. informal mad or silly.
– DERIVATIVES **barminess** noun.
– ORIGIN first meaning 'frothy': from **BARM**.

barn noun a large farm building used for storage or for housing livestock.
– ORIGIN Old English, 'barley house'.

barnacle /**bar**-nuh-k'l/ noun a small shellfish which attaches itself permanently to underwater surfaces.
– DERIVATIVES **barnacled** adjective.

– ORIGIN Latin *bernaca*.

barnacle goose noun a goose with a white face and black neck.

– ORIGIN from the former belief that the bird hatched from barnacles.

barn dance noun **1** a party with country dancing. **2** a dance for a number of couples moving round a circle.

barnet /**bar**-nit/ noun Brit. informal a person's hair.

– ORIGIN from rhyming slang *barnet fair* (a horse fair held at *Barnet*, Herts.).

barney noun (pl. **barneys**) Brit. informal a noisy quarrel.

– ORIGIN unknown.

barn owl noun a pale-coloured owl with a heart-shaped face.

barnstorm verb chiefly N. Amer. **1** tour rural districts putting on shows or giving flying displays. **2** make a rapid tour as part of a political campaign.

barnstorming adjective very flamboyant, forceful, and successful: *barnstorming speeches.*

barnyard noun chiefly N. Amer. a farmyard.

barograph /**ba**-ruh-grahf/ noun a barometer that records its readings on a moving chart.

barometer /buh-**rom**-i-ter/ noun **1** an instrument that measures atmospheric pressure, used in forecasting the weather. **2** an indicator of change: *furniture is a barometer of changing tastes.*

– DERIVATIVES **barometric** adjective.

– ORIGIN from Greek *baros* 'weight'.

baron noun **1** a man belonging to the lowest rank of the British nobility. **2** historical a man who held lands or property from the sovereign or an overlord. **3** a powerful person in business or industry: *a press baron.*

– DERIVATIVES **baronial** /buh-**roh**-ni-uhl/ adjective.

– ORIGIN Latin *baro* 'man, warrior'.

baroness noun **1** the wife or widow of a baron. **2** a woman holding the rank of baron.

baronet noun a man who holds a title below that of baron, with the status of a commoner.

– DERIVATIVES **baronetcy** noun.

barony noun (pl. **baronies**) the rank and estates of a baron.

baroque /buh-**rok**/ adjective **1** relating to a highly decorated style of European architecture, art, and music of the 17th and 18th centuries. **2** very elaborate or showy. • noun the baroque style or period.

– ORIGIN from Portuguese *barroco* 'irregularly shaped pearl'.

barouche /buh-**roosh**/ noun historical a four-wheeled horse-drawn carriage with a collapsible hood over the rear half.

– ORIGIN Italian *baroccio* 'two-wheeled carriage'.

barque /bark/ noun **1** a sailing ship with three masts. **2** literary a boat.

– ORIGIN Latin *barca* 'ship's boat'.

barrack[1] verb provide soldiers with accommodation.

barrack[2] verb Brit. jeer loudly at a performer or speaker.

– ORIGIN probably from Northern Irish dialect.

barracks plural noun (often treated as sing.) a large building or group of buildings for housing soldiers.

– ORIGIN Italian *baracca* or Spanish *barraca* 'soldier's tent'.

barracuda /ba-ruh-**koo**-duh/ noun (pl. same or **barracudas**) a large, slender predatory fish of tropical seas.

– ORIGIN unknown.

barrage /ba-**rahzh**/ noun **1** a continuous artillery bombardment over a wide area. **2** an overwhelming number of things coming in rapid succession: *a barrage of questions.* **3** a barrier built across a river to control the water level. • verb bombard someone with questions or complaints.

– ORIGIN from French *barrer* 'to bar'.

barrage balloon noun a large anchored balloon, typically with netting suspended from it, used as an obstacle to low-flying enemy aircraft.

barramundi /ba-ruh-**mun**-di/ noun (pl. same or **barramundis**) a large, chiefly freshwater fish of Australia and SE Asia.

– ORIGIN probably from an Aboriginal language.

barre /bar/ noun a horizontal bar at waist level used by ballet dancers as a support during exercises.

– ORIGIN French.

barrel noun **1** a large cylindrical container bulging out in the middle and with flat ends. **2** a measure of capacity for oil and beer (36 imperial gallons for beer and 35 for oil). **3** a tube forming part of an object such as a gun or a pen. • verb (**barrels**, **barrelling**, **barrelled**; US **barrels**, **barreling**, **barreled**) **1** put something into a barrel or barrels. **2** informal, chiefly N. Amer. drive or move very fast.

– PHRASES **over a barrel** informal at a great disadvantage.

– ORIGIN Latin *barriclus* 'small cask'.

barrel organ noun a small pipe organ that plays a preset tune when a handle is turned.

barrel vault noun a vault in a roof forming a half cylinder.

barren adjective **1** (of land) too poor to produce vegetation. **2** (of a female animal) unable to bear young. **3** bleak and lifeless: *huge barren rooms.* **4** lacking meaning or meaningful achievements: *he scored yesterday to end his barren spell.*

– DERIVATIVES **barrenness** noun.

– ORIGIN Old French *barhaine*.

barrette /ba-**ret**/ noun a hairslide.

– ORIGIN French, 'small bar'.

barricade /ba-ri-**kayd**/ noun a makeshift barrier erected to block a road or entrance. • verb block or defend something with a barricade.

– ORIGIN from Spanish *barrica* 'cask' (barrels often being used to build barricades).

barrier noun **1** an obstacle that prevents movement or access. **2** something that prevents or hinders communication or progress: *a language barrier.*

– ORIGIN Old French *barriere*.

barrier cream noun Brit. a cream used to protect the skin from damage or infection.

barrier method noun contraception using a device or preparation which prevents sperm

b

from reaching an ovum.

barrier reef noun a coral reef close to the shore but separated from it by a channel of deep water.

barring preposition except for; if not for.

barrio /ba-ri-oh/ noun (pl. **barrios**) 1 (in a Spanish-speaking country) a district of a town. 2 (in the US) the Spanish-speaking quarter of a town or city.
– ORIGIN Spanish.

barrister noun chiefly Brit. a lawyer qualified to argue a case in court, especially in the higher courts. Compare with **SOLICITOR**.
– ORIGIN from **BAR**[1].

barrow[1] noun Brit. a two-wheeled handcart used by street traders.
– ORIGIN Old English, 'stretcher, bier'.

barrow[2] noun an ancient burial mound.
– ORIGIN Old English.

Bart abbreviation Baronet.

bartender noun a person serving drinks at a bar.
– DERIVATIVES **bartending** noun.

barter verb exchange goods or services for other goods or services. • noun trading by bartering.
– ORIGIN probably from Old French *barater* 'deceive'.

baryon /ba-ri-on/ noun Physics a subatomic particle with a mass equal to or greater than that of a proton.
– ORIGIN from Greek *barus* 'heavy'.

baryte /ba-ryt/ (also **barytes** /buh-ry-teez/, **barite**) noun a colourless or white mineral consisting of barium sulphate.
– ORIGIN from Greek *barus* 'heavy'.

basal /bay-s'l/ adjective chiefly technical forming or belonging to a base.

basal metabolic rate noun the rate at which the body uses energy while at rest to maintain vital functions such as breathing.

basalt /ba-sawlt/ noun a dark fine-grained volcanic rock.
– DERIVATIVES **basaltic** /buh-**sawl**-tik/ adjective.
– ORIGIN from Greek *basanos* 'touchstone'.

bascule bridge /bas-kyool/ noun a type of bridge with a section which can be raised and lowered using counterweights.
– ORIGIN French *bascule* 'see-saw'.

base[1] noun 1 the lowest or supporting part of something. 2 a foundation, support, or starting point: *the town's economic base collapsed.* 3 the main place where a person works or stays. 4 a centre of operations: *a military base.* 5 a main element or ingredient to which others are added. 6 Chemistry a substance capable of reacting with an acid to form a salt and water. 7 Mathematics the number on which a system of counting is based, e.g. 10 in conventional notation. 8 Baseball each of the four stations that must be reached in turn to score a run. • verb 1 use something as the foundation for: *the film is based on a novel.* 2 situate something at a centre of operations.
– PHRASES **touch base** informal briefly make or renew contact.
– DERIVATIVES **based** adjective.
– ORIGIN Greek *basis* 'base, pedestal'.

base[2] adjective 1 without moral principles: *the baser instincts of greed and selfishness.* 2 old use of low social class.
– DERIVATIVES **baseness** noun.
– ORIGIN Latin *bassus* 'short'.

baseball noun a team game played with a bat and ball on a diamond-shaped circuit of four bases, around all of which a batsman must run to score.

baseball cap noun a cotton cap with a large peak.

base jump noun a parachute jump from a fixed point, e.g. a high building.
– ORIGIN from *building, antenna-tower, span, earth* (referring to the types of structure used).

baseless adjective not based on fact; untrue.

baseline noun 1 a minimum or starting point used for comparisons. 2 (in tennis, volleyball, etc.) the line marking each end of a court.

basement noun a room or floor below ground level.
– ORIGIN probably from former Dutch, 'foundation'.

base metal noun a common non-precious metal such as copper, tin, or zinc.

base rate noun the interest rate set by the Bank of England for lending to other banks, used as the basis for interest rates generally.

bases plural of **BASE**[1] and **BASIS**.

bash informal verb 1 hit someone or something hard. 2 (**bash something out**) produce something rapidly and carelessly. • noun 1 a heavy blow. 2 a party. 3 Brit. an attempt: *she'll have a bash at anything.*
– DERIVATIVES **basher** noun.
– ORIGIN perhaps from **BANG** and **SMASH**.

bashful adjective shy and easily embarrassed.
– DERIVATIVES **bashfully** adverb **bashfulness** noun.
– ORIGIN from **ABASHED**.

BASIC noun a simple high-level computer programming language.
– ORIGIN from *Beginners' All-purpose Symbolic Instruction Code.*

basic adjective 1 forming an essential foundation; fundamental: *certain basic rules must be obeyed.* 2 consisting of the minimum required or offered: *a basic wage.* 3 Chemistry containing or having the properties of a base; alkaline. • noun (**basics**) essential facts or principles of a subject.

basically adverb 1 in the most fundamental respects. 2 used to sum up a more complex situation: *I basically did the same thing every day.*

basil noun a herb of the mint family, used in cookery.
– ORIGIN from Greek *basilikos* 'royal'.

basilica /buh-zil-i-kuh/ noun 1 (in ancient Rome) a large oblong public building with two rows of columns and a domed recess at one end. 2 a Christian church of a similar design.
– ORIGIN from Greek *basilikos* 'royal'.

basilisk /baz-i-lisk/ noun 1 a mythical reptile whose gaze or breath could kill. 2 a long, slender Central American lizard.
– ORIGIN Greek *basiliskos* 'little king, serpent'.

basin noun 1 a large bowl or open container for preparing food or holding liquid. 2 a circular valley or natural depression. 3 an area drained

by a river and its tributaries. **4** an enclosed area of water for mooring boats.
– ORIGIN Latin *bacinus*.

basis noun (pl. **bases** /**bay**-seez/) **1** the underlying support for an idea or process. **2** the principles according to which an activity is carried on: *she needed coaching on a regular basis.*
– ORIGIN Greek, 'step, pedestal'.

bask verb **1** lie in warmth and sunlight for pleasure. **2** (**bask in**) take great pleasure in: *he was basking in the glory of his first book.*
– ORIGIN perhaps related to Old Norse, 'bathe'.

basket noun **1** a container for holding or carrying things, made from interwoven strips of cane or wire. **2** Basketball a net fixed to a hoop, used as the goal. **3** a group or range of currencies or investments.
– ORIGIN Old French.

basketball noun a team game in which goals are scored by throwing a ball through a net fixed on a hoop.

basket case noun informal a useless person or thing.
– ORIGIN first referring to a soldier who had lost all four limbs.

basketry noun **1** the craft of basket-making. **2** baskets as a whole.

basketwork noun material woven in the style of a basket.

basking shark noun a large shark which feeds on plankton and swims slowly close to the surface.

basmati rice /baz-**mah**-ti/ noun a kind of long-grain Indian rice with a delicate aroma.
– ORIGIN Hindi, 'fragrant'.

Basque /bask, bahsk/ noun **1** a member of a people living in the western Pyrenees in France and Spain. **2** the language of the Basques.
– ORIGIN Latin *Vasco* 'inhabitant of Vasconia' (the Latin name also of Gascony in SW France).

basque /bask/ noun a woman's close-fitting bodice, typically with a short continuation below waist level.
– ORIGIN from **Basque**, referring to traditional Basque dress.

bas-relief /**bass**-ri-leef/ noun Art low relief.
– ORIGIN Italian *basso-rilievo*.

bass[1] /bayss/ noun **1** the lowest adult male singing voice. **2** informal a bass guitar or double bass. **3** the low-frequency output of transmitted or reproduced sound. • adjective referring to an instrument that is lowest in pitch in its family: *a bass clarinet.*
– DERIVATIVES **bassist** noun.
– ORIGIN alteration of **BASE**[2].

bass[2] /bass/ noun (pl. same or **basses**) the common freshwater perch (fish).
– ORIGIN Germanic.

bass clef noun Music a clef placing F below middle C on the second-highest line of the stave.

basset (also **basset hound**) noun a breed of hunting dog with a long body, short legs, and long ears.
– ORIGIN from French *bas* 'low'.

bassinet /ba-si-**net**/ noun a child's wicker cradle.
– ORIGIN French, 'little basin'.

basso /**bass**-oh/ noun (pl. **bassos** or **bassi** /**bass**-i/) a bass voice or vocal part.
– ORIGIN Italian, 'low'.

bassoon /buh-**soon**/ noun a large bass woodwind instrument of the oboe family.
– DERIVATIVES **bassoonist** noun.
– ORIGIN from Italian *basso* 'low'.

basso profundo /pruh-**fun**-doh/ noun (pl. **bassos profundos** or **bassi profundi** /pruh-**fun**-di/) a bass singer with an exceptionally low range.

bastard noun **1** old use or derogatory a person born to parents who are not married to each other. **2** informal an unpleasant person. **3** Brit. informal a person of a specified kind: *the poor bastard.* • adjective no longer in a pure or original form: *a bastard language.*
– ORIGIN Latin *bastardus*.

bastardize (or **bastardise**) verb (often as adj. **bastardized**) make something impure by adding new elements: *a bastardized form of French.*
– DERIVATIVES **bastardization** noun.

bastardy noun old use illegitimacy.

baste[1] verb pour fat or juices over meat during cooking.
– DERIVATIVES **baster** noun
– ORIGIN unknown.

baste[2] verb sew something with long, loose stitches in preparation for permanent sewing.
– ORIGIN Old French *bastir* 'sew lightly'.

bastinado /ba-sti-**nah**-doh/ noun chiefly historical a form of punishment or torture that involves caning the soles of someone's feet.
– ORIGIN from Spanish *bastón* 'stick, cudgel'.

bastion /**bass**-ti-uhn/ noun **1** a projecting part of a fortification allowing an increased angle of fire. **2** something that preserves particular principles or activities: *the town was a bastion of Conservatism.*
– ORIGIN Italian *bastione*.

bat[1] noun an implement with a handle and a solid surface, used in sports for hitting the ball. • verb (**bats, batting, batted**) **1** (in sport) take the role of hitting rather than throwing the ball. **2** hit someone or something with the flat of one's hand. **3** (**bat something around/about**) informal casually discuss an idea.
– PHRASES **off one's own bat** Brit. informal of one's own accord.
– ORIGIN Old English, 'club, stick, staff'.

bat[2] noun **1** a flying mammal with wings that extend between the fingers and limbs, active at night. **2** (**old bat**) informal an unattractive and unpleasant woman.
– PHRASES **have bats in the belfry** informal be eccentric or mad.
– ORIGIN Scandinavian; sense 2 is from an old slang term for 'prostitute' or from **BATTLEAXE**.

bat[3] verb (**bats, batting, batted**) flutter one's eyelashes.
– PHRASES **not bat an eyelid** informal show no surprise or concern.
– ORIGIN from Old French *batre* 'to beat'.

batch noun **1** a quantity of goods produced or dispatched at one time. **2** a group of people or things. **3** Computing a group of records processed

b

as a single unit. • verb arrange things in batches.
– ORIGIN first meaning 'quantity baked at one time': from Old English.

bate (also **bait**) noun Brit. informal, dated an angry mood.
– ORIGIN from **BAIT**.

bated adjective (in phrase **with bated breath**) in great suspense.
– ORIGIN from **ABATE**.

> USAGE: The correct spelling is **with bated breath** (not *baited*).

bath noun 1 a large tub that is filled with water for washing one's body. 2 an act of washing in a bath. 3 (also **baths**) Brit. a building containing a public swimming pool or washing facilities. 4 a container holding a liquid in which an object is immersed in chemical processing. • verb Brit. wash someone in a bath.
– ORIGIN Old English.

Bath bun noun Brit. a round currant bun topped with icing or sugar.
– ORIGIN named after the city of *Bath* in SW England.

bath chair noun dated an invalid's wheelchair.
– ORIGIN named after *Bath* in SW England, which attracted invalids because of its hot springs.

bathe /bayth/ verb 1 wash by immersing one's body in water. 2 chiefly Brit. take a swim. 3 soak or wipe something gently with liquid to clean or soothe it. 4 fill with or envelop in something: *my desk is bathed in sunlight*. • noun Brit. a swim.
– DERIVATIVES **bather** noun.
– ORIGIN Old English.

bathing suit (Brit. also **bathing costume**) noun chiefly N. Amer. a swimming costume.

bathos /bay-thoss/ noun (in literature) an unintentional change in mood from the important and serious to the trivial or ridiculous.
– DERIVATIVES **bathetic** /buh-thet-ik/ adjective.
– ORIGIN Greek, 'depth'.

bathrobe noun a towelling dressing gown.

bathroom noun 1 a room containing a bath and usually also a washbasin and toilet. 2 N. Amer. a room containing a toilet.

bath salts plural noun crystals that are dissolved in bathwater to soften or perfume it.

bathtub noun chiefly N. Amer. a bath.

bathysphere /bath-i-sfeer/ noun a manned spherical vessel for deep-sea observation.
– ORIGIN from Greek *bathus* 'deep'.

batik /ba-teek/ noun a method of producing coloured designs on cloth by waxing the parts not to be dyed.
– ORIGIN from Javanese, 'painted'.

batiste /buh-teest/ noun a fine linen or cotton fabric.
– ORIGIN French.

batman noun (pl. **batmen**) dated (in the British armed forces) an officer's personal attendant.
– ORIGIN from Old French *bat* 'packsaddle'; the word originally referred to an orderly in charge of the *bat horse* which carried the officer's baggage.

bat mitzvah /baht mitz-vuh/ noun a religious ceremony in which a Jewish girl aged twelve years and a day takes on adult responsibilities under Jewish law.
– ORIGIN Hebrew, 'daughter of commandment'.

baton noun 1 a thin stick used to conduct an orchestra or choir. 2 a short stick passed from runner to runner in a relay race. 3 a stick carried and twirled by a drum major. 4 a police officer's truncheon.
– ORIGIN from Latin *bastum* 'stick'.

baton round noun Brit. a large rubber or plastic bullet used in riot control.

batsman noun (pl. **batsmen**) a player who bats in cricket.

battalion /buh-tal-i-uhn/ noun a large body of troops, forming part of a brigade.
– ORIGIN French *bataillon*.

batten[1] noun a long wooden or metal strip for strengthening or securing something. • verb strengthen or fasten something with battens.
– PHRASES **batten down the hatches 1** secure a ship's tarpaulins. 2 prepare for a difficult situation.
– ORIGIN Old French *batant*.

batten[2] verb (**batten on**) thrive or prosper at the expense of: *multinational monopolies batten on the working classes*.
– ORIGIN Old Norse, 'get better'.

Battenberg noun chiefly Brit. an oblong marzipan-covered sponge cake in two colours.
– ORIGIN named after the town of *Battenberg* in Germany.

batter[1] verb 1 hit someone or something hard and repeatedly. 2 damage or harm: *the space programme has been battered by bureaucratic wrangling*.
– DERIVATIVES **batterer** noun.
– ORIGIN Old French *batre* 'to beat'.

batter[2] noun a mixture of flour, egg, and milk or water, used for making pancakes or coating food before frying.
– DERIVATIVES **battered** adjective.
– ORIGIN from Old French *batre* 'to beat'.

batter[3] noun a player who bats in baseball.

battering ram noun a heavy object swung or rammed against a door to break it down.

battery noun (pl. **batteries**) 1 a device containing one or more electrical cells, for use as a source of power. 2 an extensive series: *a battery of tests*. 3 Brit. a set of small cages used for keeping poultry in a relatively small space. 4 Law unlawful physical attack on another person. 5 a group of heavy guns.
– ORIGIN first meaning 'metal articles made by hammering': from Latin *battuere* 'to beat'.

battle noun 1 a prolonged fight between organized armed forces. 2 a long and difficult struggle or conflict: *a battle of wits*. • verb fight or struggle with determination: *the city's two tabloids are battling for survival*.
– DERIVATIVES **battler** noun.
– PHRASES **battle royal** a fierce fight or dispute.
– ORIGIN from Latin *battuere* 'to beat'.

battleaxe (US also **battleax**) noun 1 a large axe used in ancient warfare. 2 informal an aggressive older woman.

battlecruiser noun an early 20th-century warship that was faster and more lightly armoured than a battleship.

battledore /ba-tuhl-dor/ noun 1 (also **battledore and shuttlecock**) a game played with a shuttlecock and rackets, a forerunner of badminton. 2 the small racket used in this game.
– ORIGIN perhaps from Provençal *batedor* 'beater'.

battledress noun combat uniform worn by soldiers.

battlefield (also **battleground**) noun the piece of ground on which a battle is fought.

battlement noun a parapet at the top of a wall with gaps for firing from, forming part of a fortification.
– DERIVATIVES **battlemented** adjective.
– ORIGIN from Old French *batailler* 'fortify with movable turrets'.

battleship noun a heavily armoured warship with large-calibre guns.

batty adjective (**battier, battiest**) informal mad.
– DERIVATIVES **battiness** noun.
– ORIGIN from BAT².

batwing adjective (of a sleeve) having a deep armhole and a tight cuff.

bauble /baw-b'l/ noun a small, showy trinket or decoration.
– ORIGIN Old French *baubel* 'child's toy'.

baud /rhymes with code/ noun (pl. same or **bauds**) Computing a unit of transmission speed for electronic signals, corresponding to one information unit or event per second.
– ORIGIN named after the French engineer Jean M. E. *Baudot*.

baulk /bawlk/ (chiefly US also **balk**) verb 1 (**baulk at**) hesitate to accept an idea. 2 thwart or hinder a plan or person. • noun a roughly squared timber beam.
– ORIGIN from Old Norse, 'partition'.

bauxite /bawk-syt/ noun a clay-like rock from which aluminium is obtained.
– ORIGIN from the French village of *Les Baux*, where it was first found.

bavarois /ba-vuh-wah/ (also **bavaroise** /ba-vuh-wahz/) noun a cold creamy dessert set with gelatin.
– ORIGIN French, 'Bavarian'.

bawdy adjective (**bawdier, bawdiest**) dealing with sex in a comical way.
– DERIVATIVES **bawdiness** noun.
– ORIGIN from Old French *baude* 'shameless'.

bawdy house noun old use a brothel.

bawl verb 1 shout out noisily. 2 (**bawl someone out**) reprimand someone angrily. 3 weep noisily. • noun a loud shout.
– ORIGIN imitating the sound.

bay¹ noun a broad curved inlet of the sea.
– ORIGIN Old French *baie*.

bay² (also **bay laurel** or **sweet bay**) noun an evergreen Mediterranean shrub with aromatic leaves that are used in cookery.
– ORIGIN from Latin *baca* 'berry'.

bay³ noun 1 a window area that projects outwards from a wall. 2 an area allocated for a purpose: *a loading bay.* 3 a compartment with a particular function in an aircraft, motor vehicle, or ship: *a bomb bay.*
– ORIGIN from Latin *batare* 'to gape'.

bay⁴ adjective (of a horse) reddish-brown with black points. • noun a bay horse.

– ORIGIN from Latin *badius*.

bay⁵ verb (of a dog) howl loudly. • noun the sound of baying.
– PHRASES **at bay** trapped or cornered. **hold** (or **keep**) **someone/thing at bay** prevent someone or something from approaching or having an effect.
– ORIGIN Old French *abaiier* 'to bark'.

bayberry noun (pl. **bayberries**) a North American shrub with aromatic leathery leaves and waxy berries.

bayonet noun a long blade fixed to the muzzle of a rifle for hand-to-hand fighting. • verb (**bayonets, bayoneting, bayoneted**) stab someone with a bayonet. • adjective referring to a type of fitting for a light bulb which is pushed into a socket and then twisted into place.
– ORIGIN French *baïonnette* 'dagger', named after the French town of *Bayonne*, where the daggers were made.

bayou /by-oo/ noun (pl. **bayous**) (in the southern US) a marshy outlet of a lake or river.
– ORIGIN Louisiana French.

bay rum noun a perfume for the hair, distilled originally from rum and bayberry leaves.

bay window noun a window built to project outwards from a wall.

bazaar /buh-zar/ noun 1 a market in a Middle Eastern country. 2 a sale of goods to raise funds for charity.
– ORIGIN Persian, 'market'.

bazooka noun a short-range rocket launcher used against tanks.
– ORIGIN probably from US slang *bazoo* 'kazoo'.

BBC abbreviation British Broadcasting Corporation.

BBQ abbreviation barbecue.

BC abbreviation 1 before Christ (used to show that a date comes the specified number of years before the traditional date of Jesus's birth). 2 British Columbia.

> USAGE: **BC** is normally written in small capitals and placed **after** the numerals, as in 72 BC.

bcc abbreviation blind carbon copy.

BCE abbreviation before the Common Era (indicating dates before the Christian era).

BCG abbreviation Bacillus Calmette-Guérin, an anti-tuberculosis vaccine.

BD abbreviation Bachelor of Divinity.

BE abbreviation 1 Bachelor of Education. 2 Bachelor of Engineering.

Be symbol the chemical element beryllium.

be verb (sing. present **am; are; is**; pl. present **are**; 1st and 3rd sing. past **was**; 2nd sing. past and pl. past **were**; present subjunctive **be**; past subjunctive **were**; present part. **being**; past part. **been**) 1 (usu. **there is/are**) exist; be present. 2 take place. 3 have the specified state, nature, or role: *the floor was uneven.* 4 come; go; visit. • auxiliary verb 1 used with a present participle to form continuous tenses: *they are coming.* 2 used with a past participle to form the passive voice. 3 used to indicate something that is due to, may, or should happen.
– PHRASES **the be-all and end-all** informal the

b

most important aspect. **-to-be** of the future: *his bride-to-be.*
– ORIGIN Old English.

be- prefix forming verbs: **1** all over; all round: *bespatter.* **2** thoroughly; excessively: *bewilder.* **3** expressing transitive action: *bemoan.* **4** affect with or cause to be: *becalm.* **5** (forming adjectives ending in -*ed*) having; covered with: *bejewelled.*
– ORIGIN Old English.

beach noun a pebbly or sandy shore at the edge of the sea or a lake. • verb bring or come on to a beach from the water.
– ORIGIN perhaps related to Old English, 'brook'.

beachcomber noun a person who searches beaches for articles of value.

beachhead noun a defended position on a beach taken from the enemy by landing forces.

beachwear noun clothing suitable for wearing on the beach.

beacon noun **1** a fire lit on the top of a hill as a signal. **2** a signal light for ships or aircraft. **3** a radio transmitter signalling the position of a ship or aircraft.
– ORIGIN Old English, 'sign, portent, ensign'.

bead noun **1** a small piece of glass, stone, etc., threaded in a string with others to make a necklace or rosary. **2** a drop of a liquid on a surface. **3** a small knob forming the foresight of a gun. **4** the reinforced inner edge of a tyre. • verb (often as adj. **beaded**) decorate or cover with beads: *a beaded bag.*
– ORIGIN Old English, 'prayer' (each bead on a rosary representing a prayer).

beadle noun Brit. **1** a ceremonial officer of a church, college, etc. **2** historical a parish officer dealing with petty offenders.
– ORIGIN Old English, 'a person who makes a proclamation'.

beady adjective (of a person's eyes) small, round, and observing things clearly.
– DERIVATIVES **beadily** adverb.

beagle noun a small, short-legged breed of hound.
– ORIGIN perhaps from Old French *beegueule* 'open-mouthed'.

beagling noun hunting with beagles.

beak noun **1** a bird's horny projecting jaws; a bill. **2** Brit. informal a magistrate or schoolmaster.
– DERIVATIVES **beaked** adjective **beaky** adjective.
– ORIGIN Latin *beccus.*

beaker noun Brit. **1** a tall plastic cup. **2** a cylindrical glass container used in laboratories.
– ORIGIN Old Norse.

beam noun **1** a long piece of timber or metal used as a support in building. **2** a narrow horizontal length of timber for balancing on in gymnastics. **3** a ray or shaft of light or particles. **4** a radiant smile. **5** a ship's breadth at its widest point. • verb **1** transmit a radio signal or broadcast. **2** shine brightly. **3** smile radiantly.
– PHRASES **off beam** informal on the wrong track; mistaken.
– ORIGIN Old English, 'tree, beam'.

bean noun **1** an edible seed growing in long

pods on certain plants. **2** the hard seed of a coffee or cocoa plant. **3** informal a very small amount or nothing at all: *there is not a bean of truth in the report.*
– PHRASES **full of beans** informal lively; in high spirits. **old bean** Brit. informal, dated a friendly form of address to a man.
– ORIGIN Old English.

beanbag noun **1** a small bag filled with dried beans and used in children's games. **2** a large cushion filled with polystyrene beads, used as a seat.

bean counter noun informal an accountant or bureaucrat who is excessively concerned with controlling expenditure.

bean curd noun another term for TOFU.

beanfeast noun Brit. informal a party with plentiful food and drink.
– ORIGIN first referring to an annual dinner given to employees, which always featured beans and bacon.

beanie noun (pl. **beanies**) a small close-fitting hat worn on the back of the head.
– ORIGIN perhaps from BEAN (in the old-fashioned sense 'head').

beano noun (pl. **beanos**) Brit. informal a party.
– ORIGIN from BEANFEAST.

beanpole noun informal a tall, thin person.

bean sprouts plural noun the edible sprouting seeds of certain beans.

bear¹ verb (past **bore**; past part. **borne**) **1** carry someone or something. **2** have something as a quality or visible mark. **3** support a weight. **4** (**bear oneself**) behave in a specified way: *she bore herself with dignity.* **5** manage to tolerate: *the grief was more than he could bear.* **6** (**cannot bear**) strongly dislike someone or something. **7** give birth to a child. **8** (of a tree or plant) produce fruit or flowers. **9** turn and go in a specified direction: *bear left.*
– PHRASES **bear down on** approach in a purposeful or threatening way. **bear fruit** have good results. **bear someone a grudge** feel resentment against someone. **bear something in mind** remember something and take it into account. **bear on** be relevant to. **bear something out** support or confirm something. **bear up** stay cheerful in difficult circumstances. **bear with** be patient or tolerant with. **bear witness** (or **testimony**) **to** provide evidence of.
– ORIGIN Old English.

USAGE: Do not confuse **bear** with **bare**. **Bear** means 'carry' (*he was bearing a tray of food*) or 'tolerate', whereas **bare** is an adjective that means 'naked' or a verb meaning 'uncover or reveal' (*he bared his chest*).

bear² noun **1** a large, heavy mammal with thick fur and a very short tail. **2** Stock Exchange a person who sells shares hoping to buy them back later at a lower price. Often contrasted with BULL¹. [probably from a proverb warning against 'selling the bear's skin before one has caught the bear'.]
– PHRASES **like a bear with a sore head** Brit. informal very irritable.
– ORIGIN Old English.

bearable adjective able to be endured.
– DERIVATIVES **bearably** adverb.

bear-baiting noun historical a form of entertainment which involved setting dogs to attack a captive bear.

beard noun 1 a growth of hair on the chin and lower cheeks of a man's face. 2 a tuft of hairs or bristles on certain animals or plants. • verb boldly confront or challenge someone daunting.
– DERIVATIVES **bearded** adjective **beardless** adjective.
– ORIGIN Old English.

bearer noun 1 a person or thing that carries something. 2 a person who presents a cheque or other order to pay money.

bear hug noun a rough, tight embrace.

bearing noun 1 a person's way of standing, moving, or behaving: *a man of dignified bearing.* 2 the way in which something is related to or influences something else: *past accidents can have a bearing on back problems.* 3 (usu. **bearings**) a part of a machine that allows one part to rotate or move in contact with another. 4 direction or position relative to a fixed point. 5 (**one's bearings**) awareness of one's position in relation to one's surroundings: *I checked my map to get my bearings.* 6 a heraldic emblem.

bearish adjective resembling a bear, especially in being surly or clumsy.

bear market noun Stock Exchange a market in which share prices are falling.

Béarnaise sauce /bay-uh-**nayz**/ noun a rich sauce thickened with egg yolks and flavoured with tarragon.
– ORIGIN named after the French region of *Béarn.*

bearskin noun a tall cap of black fur worn ceremonially by certain troops.

beast noun 1 an animal, especially a large or dangerous mammal. 2 a very cruel or wicked person.
– ORIGIN Latin *bestia.*

beastie noun (pl. **beasties**) Scottish or humorous a small animal or insect.

beastly adjective Brit. informal very unpleasant.
– DERIVATIVES **beastliness** noun.

beast of burden noun an animal used for carrying loads.

beat verb (past **beat**; past part. **beaten**) 1 hit someone repeatedly and violently. 2 hit something repeatedly to flatten it or make a noise. 3 defeat someone or overcome something. 4 do or be better than: *he beat his own world record.* 5 informal baffle someone. 6 (of the heart) throb. 7 (of a bird) move the wings up and down. 8 stir cooking ingredients vigorously. 9 move across land striking at the vegetation to raise game birds for shooting. • noun 1 a main accent in music or poetry. 2 a throb of the heart. 3 a movement of a bird's wings. 4 a brief pause. 5 an area patrolled by a police officer. • adjective informal completely exhausted.
– PHRASES **beat about the bush** discuss a matter without coming to the point. **beat down** shine very brightly. **beat someone down** force someone to reduce the price of something. **beat it** informal leave. **beat someone up** attack someone and hit them repeatedly. **beat a retreat** withdraw quickly to avoid something.

off the beaten track isolated.
– DERIVATIVES **beatable** adjective **beater** noun.
– ORIGIN Old English.

beatbox noun informal 1 a drum machine. 2 a radio or radio cassette player for playing loud pop music.

beat generation noun a movement of young people in the 1950s and early 1960s who rejected conventional society.

beatific /bee-uh-**tif**-ik/ adjective 1 feeling or expressing intense happiness. 2 (in the Christian Church) bestowing spiritual blessedness.
– DERIVATIVES **beatifically** adverb.

beatify /bi-at-i-fy/ verb (**beatifies, beatifying, beatified**) (in the Roman Catholic Church) announce that a dead person is in a state of spiritual bliss, the first step towards making them a saint.
– DERIVATIVES **beatification** noun.
– ORIGIN from Latin *beatus* 'blessed'.

beatitude /bi-at-i-tyood/ noun very great happiness or blessedness.

beatnik noun a young person associated with the beat generation.

beat-up adjective informal worn out by overuse.

beau /boh/ noun (pl. **beaux** or **beaus** /bohz, boh/) dated 1 a boyfriend or male admirer. 2 a dandy.
– ORIGIN French, 'handsome'.

Beaufort scale /**boh**-fert/ noun a scale of wind speed ranging from force 0 to force 12.
– ORIGIN named after the English admiral Sir Francis *Beaufort.*

Beaujolais /**boh**-zhuh-lay/ noun a light red wine produced in the Beaujolais district of SE France.

beau monde /boh **mond**/ noun fashionable society.
– ORIGIN French, 'fine world'.

beauteous adjective literary beautiful.

beautician noun a person whose job is to give beauty treatments.

beautiful adjective 1 very pleasing to the senses or to the mind. 2 of a very high standard; excellent.
– DERIVATIVES **beautifully** adverb.

beautify verb (**beautifies, beautifying, beautified**) make someone or something beautiful.
– DERIVATIVES **beautification** noun.

beauty noun (pl. **beauties**) 1 a combination of qualities that is very pleasing to the senses or to the mind. 2 a beautiful woman. 3 an excellent example of something. 4 an attractive feature or advantage. • adjective intended to make someone more attractive: *beauty treatment.*
– ORIGIN Latin *bellus* 'beautiful, fine'.

beauty contest noun a contest in which the winner is the woman judged the most beautiful.

beauty queen noun the winner of a beauty contest.

beauty salon (also **beauty parlour**) noun an establishment in which hairdressing and beauty treatments are carried out.

beauty sleep noun humorous sleep that helps one remain young and attractive.

b

beauty spot noun **1** Brit. a place with beautiful scenery. **2** a small artificial mole worn by a woman on the face.

beaux plural of BEAU.

beaver noun (pl. same or **beavers**) **1** a large rodent with a broad tail and strong teeth that lives partly in water. **2** a hat made of beaver fur. **3** a very hard-working person. • verb informal work hard: *she beavered away to keep things running smoothly.*
– ORIGIN Old English.

bebop /bee-bop/ noun a type of jazz characterized by complex harmony and rhythms.
– ORIGIN imitating the rhythm.

becalm verb (**be becalmed**) (of a sailing ship) be unable to move through lack of wind.

became past of BECOME.

because conjunction for the reason that; since.
– PHRASES **because of** by reason of.
– ORIGIN from *by cause.*

> USAGE: Confusion can arise when **because** follows a negative such as *not*. For example, the sentence *he didn't go because he was ill* could mean either 'the reason he didn't go was that he was ill' or 'being ill wasn't the reason for him going; there was another reason'. Use a comma when the first meaning is intended (*he didn't go, because he was ill*), or avoid using **because** after a negative altogether.
> On starting a sentence with **because**, see the note at AND.

béchamel /bay-shuh-mel/ noun a rich white sauce flavoured with herbs and other seasonings.
– ORIGIN named after the Marquis Louis de *Béchamel.*

beck[1] noun N. English a stream.
– ORIGIN Old Norse.

beck[2] noun (in phrase **at someone's beck and call**) always having to be ready to obey someone's orders.
– ORIGIN from BECKON.

beckon verb **1** make a gesture to encourage or instruct someone to approach or follow. **2** seem appealing or inviting: *the wide open spaces of Australia beckoned.*
– ORIGIN Old English.

become verb (past **became**; past part. **become**) **1** begin to be. **2** develop into: *the child will become an adult.* **3** (**become of**) happen to: *what would become of her now?* **4** suit or be appropriate to: *celebrity status did not become him.*
– ORIGIN Old English.

becoming adjective **1** (of clothing) looking good on someone. **2** appropriate or suitable.
– DERIVATIVES **becomingly** adverb.

becquerel /bek-kuh-rel/ noun Physics a unit of radioactivity in the SI system.
– ORIGIN named after the French physicist A-H. *Becquerel.*

BEd abbreviation Bachelor of Education.

bed noun **1** a piece of furniture for sleeping on. **2** an area of ground where flowers and plants are grown. **3** a part or layer on which something rests or is supported: *roast chicken on a bed of herbs.* **4** a layer of rock. **5** the bottom of the sea or a lake or river. **6** informal a bed as a place for sexual activity. • verb (**beds, bedding, bedded**) **1** provide someone with or settle into sleeping accommodation. **2** fix something firmly. **3** informal have sex with someone. **4** (**bed something out**) transfer a plant from a pot to the ground.
– PHRASES **a bed of roses** a comfortable or easy situation or activity.
– DERIVATIVES **bedded** adjective.
– ORIGIN Old English.

bed and board noun lodging and food.

bed and breakfast noun **1** sleeping accommodation and breakfast in a guest house or hotel. **2** a guest house.

bedazzle verb greatly impress someone with brilliance or skill.

bed-blocking noun Brit. the long-term occupation of hospital beds, due to a shortage of suitable care elsewhere.

bedbug noun a wingless bug which sucks the blood of sleeping humans.

bedchamber noun old use a bedroom.

bedclothes plural noun coverings for a bed, such as sheets and blankets.

bedding noun **1** bedclothes. **2** straw or similar material for animals to sleep on.

bedding plant noun an annual plant produced for planting in a garden in the spring.

bedeck verb decorate lavishly: *the town was bedecked with flags.*

bedevil verb (**bedevils, bedevilling, bedevilled**; US **bedevils, bedeviling, bedeviled**) cause continual trouble to: *the devices were bedevilled by mechanical failures.*

bedfellow noun **1** a person or thing closely associated with another: *laughter and tragedy are not such strange bedfellows.* **2** a person sharing a bed with another.

bedhead noun Brit. an upright board or panel fixed at the head of a bed.

bedizen /bi-dy-zuhn/ verb literary decorate someone or something gaudily.
– ORIGIN from former *dizen* 'deck out'.

bedjacket noun a soft loose jacket worn when sitting up in bed.

bedlam /bed-luhm/ noun a scene of uproar and confusion.
– ORIGIN from the name of the mental hospital of St Mary of *Bethlehem* in London.

bedlinen noun sheets, pillowcases, and duvet covers.

Bedouin /bed-oo-in/ (also **Beduin**) noun (pl. same) an Arab living as a nomad in the desert.
– ORIGIN Arabic, 'dwellers in the desert'.

bedpan noun a container used as a toilet by a bedridden patient.

bedpost noun any of the four upright supports of a bedstead.

bedraggled adjective untidy or dishevelled.

bedridden adjective having to stay in bed because of sickness or old age.

bedrock noun **1** solid rock underlying loose deposits such as soil. **2** underlying or basic principles: *self-sufficiency was the bedrock of the regime.*

bedroom noun a room for sleeping in.

bedside manner noun a doctor's approach to a patient.

bedsit (also **bedsitter**) noun Brit. a rented room consisting of a combined bedroom and living room.

bedsore noun a sore caused by lying in bed in one position for a long time.

bedspread noun a decorative cloth used to cover a bed.

bedstead noun the framework of a bed.

bedstraw noun a plant with small flowers and slender leaves, formerly used for stuffing mattresses.

bedtime noun the usual time when someone goes to bed.

bed-wetting noun urinating unintentionally while asleep.

bee noun 1 a stinging winged insect which collects nectar and pollen and produces wax and honey. 2 a meeting for communal work or amusement: *a sewing bee.*
– PHRASES **the bee's knees** informal an outstandingly good person or thing. **have a bee in one's bonnet** informal be obsessed with something.
– ORIGIN Old English.

beech noun a large tree with grey bark and hard, pale wood.
– ORIGIN Old English.

bee-eater noun a brightly coloured insect-eating bird with a curved bill and long tail.

beef noun 1 the flesh of a cow, bull, or ox, used as food. 2 informal strength or power: *he was brought in to give the team more beef.* 3 informal flesh with well-developed muscle. 4 (pl. **beefs**) informal a complaint or grievance. • verb informal 1 (**beef something up**) make stronger or more substantial: *rifles were supplied to the police to beef up security.* 2 complain about someone or something.
– ORIGIN Old French *boef.*

beefburger noun a fried or grilled cake of minced beef eaten in a bun.

beefcake noun informal men with well-developed muscles.

beefeater noun a Yeoman Warder or Yeoman of the Guard in the Tower of London.
– ORIGIN formerly a derogatory term for a well-fed servant.

beefsteak noun a thick slice of steak, especially rump steak.

beef tomato (chiefly N. Amer. also **beefsteak tomato**) noun a large, firm variety of tomato.

beefy adjective (**beefier, beefiest**) 1 informal muscular or powerful. 2 tasting like beef.

beehive noun 1 a structure in which bees are kept. 2 a woman's domed and lacquered hairstyle popular in the 1960s.

beekeeping noun the occupation of owning and breeding bees for their honey.
– DERIVATIVES **beekeeper** noun.

beeline noun (in phrase **make a beeline for**) hurry directly to.
– ORIGIN a bee is said to take a straight line instinctively when returning to the hive.

Beelzebub /bi-el-zi-bub/ noun the Devil.
– ORIGIN Hebrew, 'lord of flies'.

been past participle of **BE**.

beep noun a short, high-pitched sound made by electronic equipment or a vehicle horn. • verb produce a beep.
– DERIVATIVES **beeper** noun.
– ORIGIN imitating the sound.

beer noun an alcoholic drink made from fermented malt flavoured with hops.
– ORIGIN from Latin *biber* 'a drink'.

beer belly (also **beer gut**) noun informal a man's fat stomach caused by excessive beer-drinking.

beer garden noun a garden next to a pub, where drinks are served.

beer mat noun Brit. a small cardboard mat for resting glasses on in a pub or bar.

beery adjective informal 1 smelling or tasting of beer. 2 influenced by the drinking of beer: *a burst of beery laughter.*

bee-stung adjective informal (of a woman's lips) full and red.

beeswax noun wax produced by bees to make honeycombs, used for wood polishes and candles.

beet noun a plant with a fleshy root, grown for food and for processing into sugar.
– ORIGIN Latin *beta.*

beetle[1] noun an insect with the forewings modified into a hard case that covers the hindwings and abdomen. • verb informal make one's way hurriedly.
– ORIGIN Old English, 'biter'.

beetle[2] noun a very heavy mallet.
– ORIGIN Old English.

beetle[3] verb (usu. as adj. **beetling**) project or overhang: *his beetling brows.*
– ORIGIN from **BEETLE-BROWED**.

beetle-browed adjective having prominent or bushy eyebrows.
– ORIGIN uncertain.

beetroot noun chiefly Brit. the edible dark-red root of a variety of beet.

beezer adjective Brit. informal, dated excellent.
– ORIGIN unknown.

BEF abbreviation British Expeditionary Force.

befall verb (past **befell**; past part. **befallen**) literary (especially of something bad) happen to: *a terrible tragedy befell him.*

befit verb (**befits, befitting, befitted**) be appropriate for: *as befits a Quaker, he was a humane man.*
– DERIVATIVES **befitting** adjective.

before preposition, conjunction, & adverb 1 during the time preceding. 2 in front of. 3 rather than.
– ORIGIN Old English, from **BY** + **FORE**.

beforehand adverb in advance.

befriend verb become a friend to someone.

befuddle verb (often as adj. **befuddled**) muddle or confuse someone.
– DERIVATIVES **befuddlement** noun.

beg verb (**begs, begging, begged**) 1 ask someone earnestly or humbly for something. 2 ask for food or money as charity. 3 (**beg off**) withdraw from something planned or promised: *they went to see the fireworks—I begged off.*
– PHRASES **beg the question 1** invite an obvious question. **2** assume the truth of something without arguing it. **go begging** be available because unwanted by others.

b

– ORIGIN probably Old English.

began past of **BEGIN**.

begat old-fashioned past of **BEGET**.

beget /bi-get/ verb (**begets, begetting, begot**; past part. **begotten**) literary **1** cause: *vengeance begets vengeance.* **2** produce a child.
– DERIVATIVES **begetter** noun.
– ORIGIN Old English, 'get, obtain by effort'.

beggar noun **1** a person who lives by begging for food or money. **2** informal a person of a particular type: *lucky beggar!* • verb make someone very poor.
– PHRASES **beggar belief** (or **description**) be too extraordinary to be believed or described.

beggarly adjective **1** very small in amount. **2** very poor.

beggary noun a state of extreme poverty.

begin verb (**begins, beginning, began**; past part. **begun**) **1** perform or undergo the first part of an action or activity. **2** come into being. **3** have as its starting point: *the track begins at the village.* **4** (**begin on**) set to work on something. **5** informal have any chance of doing: *I can't begin to describe my confusion.*
– DERIVATIVES **beginner** noun **beginning** noun.
– ORIGIN Old English.

begone exclamation old use go away at once!

begonia /bi-goh-ni-uh/ noun a garden or house plant with brightly coloured flowers.
– ORIGIN named after the French botanist Michel *Bégon.*

begorra /bi-go-ruh/ exclamation used to express surprise (traditionally attributed to the Irish).
– ORIGIN alteration of *by God.*

begot past of **BEGET**.

begotten past participle of **BEGET**.

begrudge verb **1** feel envious that someone possesses or enjoys something: *I've never begrudged my father his achievements.* **2** give something reluctantly or resentfully.

beguile verb **1** charm or trick someone. **2** literary help time pass pleasantly.
– DERIVATIVES **beguiling** adjective.

beguine /bay-geen/ noun a popular dance of Caribbean origin, similar to the foxtrot.
– ORIGIN from French *béguin* 'infatuation'.

begum /bay-guhm/ noun Indian **1** a Muslim woman of high rank. **2** (**Begum**) the title of a married Muslim woman.
– ORIGIN Turkish, 'princess'.

begun past participle of **BEGIN**.

behalf noun (in phrase **on behalf of** or **on someone's behalf**) **1** in the interests of a person, group, or principle. **2** as a representative of someone.
– ORIGIN from former *on his halve* and *bihalve him*, both meaning 'on his side'.

behave verb **1** act or operate in a specified way: *he always behaved like a gentleman.* **2** (also **behave oneself**) act in a polite or proper way.
– ORIGIN from BE- + HAVE in the sense 'bear oneself in a particular way'.

behaved adjective acting in a specified way: *a well-behaved child.*

behaviour (US **behavior**) noun the way in which someone or something behaves: *he was shocked by the behaviour of the fans.*
– DERIVATIVES **behavioural** adjective.

behaviourism (US **behaviorism**) noun the theory that behaviour can be explained in terms of conditioning, and that psychological disorders are best treated by altering behaviour patterns.
– DERIVATIVES **behaviourist** noun & adjective.

behead verb execute someone by cutting off their head.

beheld past and past participle of **BEHOLD**.

behemoth /bi-hee-moth/ noun **1** a huge creature. **2** something very large, especially an organization.
– ORIGIN Hebrew, 'monstrous beast'.

behest /bi-hest/ noun (in phrase **at the behest of**) literary at the request or command of.
– ORIGIN Old English, 'a vow'.

behind preposition & adverb **1** at or to the back or far side of. **2** further back than other members of a group. **3** in support of. **4** responsible for an event or plan. **5** less advanced than. **6** late in achieving or paying something. **7** remaining after the departure or death of. • noun informal a person's bottom.
– ORIGIN Old English.

behindhand adjective late or slow in doing something.

behold verb (past and past part. **beheld**) old use or literary see or observe someone or something.
– DERIVATIVES **beholder** noun.
– ORIGIN Old English.

beholden adjective owing a debt or thanks to someone in return for a favour: *they don't want to be beholden to anyone.*

behove /bi-hohv/ (US **behoove** /bi-hoov/) verb (**it behoves someone to do**) formal it is necessary or appropriate for someone to do something: *if my brother is ill, then it behoves me to see him.*
– ORIGIN Old English.

beige noun a pale whitish-brown colour.
– ORIGIN French.

being noun **1** the state of existing; existence: *the town came into being because there was gold nearby.* **2** the nature of a person. **3** a living creature: *alien beings.*

bejewelled (US **bejeweled**) adjective decorated with jewels.

belabour (US **belabor**) verb **1** attack someone physically or verbally. **2** argue or discuss in excessive detail: *there's no need to belabour the point.*

Belarusian /bel-luh-rush-uhn, bel-luh-ruu-si-uhn/ (also **Belarussian**) noun **1** a person from Belarus in eastern Europe. **2** the Slavic language of Belarus. • adjective relating to Belarus.

belated adjective coming or happening late or too late: *a belated birthday present.*
– DERIVATIVES **belatedly** adverb **belatedness** noun.

belay /bee-lay, bi-lay/ verb **1** fix a rope round a rock, pin, or other object to secure it. **2** nautical slang stop! • noun an act of belaying.

bel canto /bel kan-toh/ noun a style of operatic singing using a full, rich, broad tone.
– ORIGIN Italian, 'fine song'.

belch verb **1** noisily expel wind from the stomach through the mouth. **2** give out smoke or flames with great force. • noun an act of belching.
– ORIGIN Old English.

beldam /bel-duhm/ (also **beldame**) noun old use an old woman.
– ORIGIN from Old French *bel* 'beautiful' + **DAM²**.

beleaguered adjective **1** in difficulties: *the beleaguered telecom industry*. **2** (of a place) under siege.
– ORIGIN from Dutch *belegeren* 'camp round'.

belemnite /bel-uhm-nyt/ noun a type of extinct marine mollusc with a bullet-shaped internal shell, found as a fossil.
– ORIGIN from Greek *belemnon* 'dart'.

belfry noun (pl. **belfries**) the place in a bell tower or steeple in which bells are housed.
– ORIGIN Old French *belfrei*.

Belgian noun a person from Belgium. • adjective relating to Belgium.

Belial /bee-li-uhl/ noun the Devil.
– ORIGIN Hebrew, 'worthlessness'.

belie verb (**belies**, **belying**, **belied**) **1** fail to give a true idea of: *her fast reflexes belied her age*. **2** show something to be untrue or unjustified.
– ORIGIN Old English, 'deceive by lying'.

belief noun **1** a feeling that something exists or is true, especially one without proof. **2** a firmly held opinion. **3** (**belief in**) trust or confidence in: *we must have belief in our own capabilities*. **4** religious faith.
– PHRASES **beyond belief** astonishing; incredible.
– ORIGIN Old English.

believe verb **1** accept that something is true or someone is telling the truth. **2** (**believe in**) feel certain that someone or something exists. **3** think that something is the case: *I believe we've already met*. **4** have religious faith.
– DERIVATIVES **believability** noun **believable** adjective **believably** adverb **believer** noun.

Belisha beacon /buh-lee-shuh/ noun (in the UK) an orange ball containing a flashing light, mounted on a post at each end of a zebra crossing.
– ORIGIN named after Leslie Hore-*Belisha*, British Minister of Transport when the beacons were introduced.

belittle verb dismiss someone or something as unimportant.

Belizean /be-leez-i-uhn/ (also **Belizian**) noun a person from Belize, a country in Central America. • adjective relating to Belize.

bell noun **1** a metal cup-shaped object that sounds a clear musical note when struck. **2** a device that buzzes or rings to give a signal. **3** a bell-shaped thing. **4** (**bells**) a musical instrument consisting of a set of metal tubes, played by being struck. **5** Nautical the time as indicated every half-hour of a watch by the striking of the ship's bell one to eight times. • verb Brit. informal telephone someone.
– PHRASES **bells and whistles** attractive additional features or trimmings. **give someone a bell** Brit. informal telephone someone. **ring a bell** informal sound vaguely familiar.
– ORIGIN Old English.

belladonna /bel-luh-don-nuh/ noun **1** deadly nightshade. **2** a drug made from deadly nightshade.
– ORIGIN from Italian *bella donna* 'beautiful lady'.

bell-bottoms plural noun trousers with a marked flare below the knee.

bellboy (also **bellhop**) noun chiefly N. Amer. a porter in a hotel.

belle /bel/ noun a beautiful girl or woman.
– ORIGIN French.

belle époque /bel ay-pok/ noun the period of settled and comfortable life before the First World War.
– ORIGIN French, 'fine period'.

belles-lettres /bel-let-ruh/ plural noun literary essays written and read for their elegant style.
– ORIGIN French, 'fine letters'.

bellflower noun a plant with blue, purple, or white bell-shaped flowers.

bellicose /bel-li-kohss/ adjective aggressive and ready to fight.
– DERIVATIVES **bellicosity** /bel-li-koss-iti/ noun.
– ORIGIN from Latin *bellum* 'war'.

belligerence /buh-li-juh-ruhnss/ (also **belligerency**) noun aggressive or warlike behaviour.

belligerent adjective **1** hostile and aggressive. **2** engaged in a war or conflict. • noun a nation or person engaged in war or conflict.
– DERIVATIVES **belligerently** adverb.
– ORIGIN from Latin *belligerare* 'wage war'.

Bellini /be-lee-ni/ noun (pl. **Bellinis**) a cocktail consisting of peach juice mixed with champagne.
– ORIGIN named after the Venetian painter Giovanni *Bellini*.

bell jar noun a bell-shaped glass cover used in a laboratory.

bellow verb **1** give a loud, deep roar of pain or anger. **2** shout or sing something very loudly. • noun a loud, deep shout or sound.
– ORIGIN perhaps from Old English.

bellows plural noun **1** a device consisting of a bag with two handles, used for blowing air into a fire. **2** an object or device with folded sides that allow it to expand and contract.
– ORIGIN probably from Old English, 'belly'.

bell-ringing noun the activity or pastime of ringing church bells or handbells.
– DERIVATIVES **bell-ringer** noun.

Bell's palsy noun paralysis of the facial nerve, causing muscular weakness in one side of the face.
– ORIGIN named after the Scottish anatomist Sir Charles *Bell*.

bellwether noun **1** the leading sheep of a flock, with a bell on its neck. **2** a leader or indicator: *university campuses are often the bellwether of change*.

belly noun (pl. **bellies**) **1** the front part of the human body below the ribs, containing the stomach and bowels. **2** a person's stomach. **3** the rounded underside of a ship or aircraft. **4** the top surface of a violin or similar instrument, over which the strings are placed. • verb (**bellies**, **bellying**, **bellied**) swell or bulge: *the sails bellied out in the breeze*.
– PHRASES **go belly up** informal go bankrupt.
– DERIVATIVES **bellied** adjective.
– ORIGIN Old English, 'bag'.

bellyache informal noun a stomach pain. • verb complain noisily or persistently.

belly button noun informal a person's navel.

bellyflop noun informal a dive into water, landing flat on one's front.

bellyful noun a sufficient amount to eat.
- PHRASES **have a bellyful of** informal have more than enough of something.

belly laugh noun a loud unrestrained laugh.

belong verb 1 (**belong to**) be the property of someone. 2 (**belong to**) be a member of a group or organization. 3 be rightly put into a particular position or category: *I put the chair back where it belonged.* 4 feel at ease in a particular place or with a particular group.

belongings plural noun a person's movable possessions.

beloved adjective dearly loved. • noun a much loved person.

below preposition & adverb 1 at a lower level than. 2 mentioned further on in a piece of writing.

belt noun 1 a strip of leather or other material worn round the waist to support or hold in clothes or to carry weapons. 2 a continuous band in machinery that transfers motion from one wheel to another. 3 a strip or encircling area: *the asteroid belt.* 4 informal a heavy blow. • verb 1 fasten or secure something with a belt. 2 hit someone or something very hard. 3 (**belt something out**) informal sing or play something loudly and forcefully. 4 informal rush or dash. 5 (**belt up**) Brit. informal be quiet.
- PHRASES **below the belt** disregarding the rules; unfair. [from the idea of an illegal blow in boxing.] **belt and braces** Brit. providing double security, by using two means to the same end. **tighten one's belt** cut one's spending. **under one's belt** safely or satisfactorily achieved or acquired.
- DERIVATIVES **belted** adjective.
- ORIGIN Latin *balteus* 'girdle'.

belter noun informal 1 an outstanding example: *Owen made the goal with a belter of a pass.* 2 a loud, forceful singer or song.

beltway noun US a ring road.

beluga /buh-loo-guh/ noun (pl. same or **belugas**) 1 a small white toothed whale of Arctic waters. 2 a very large sturgeon from which caviar is obtained.
- ORIGIN from Russian, 'white'.

belvedere /bel-vi-deer/ noun a summer house or open-sided gallery positioned to command a fine view.
- ORIGIN Italian, 'beautiful sight'.

belying present participle of **BELIE**.

BEM abbreviation British Empire Medal.

bemoan verb express discontent or sorrow about something.

bemuse verb confuse or bewilder someone.
- DERIVATIVES **bemused** adjective **bemusement** noun.

ben noun Scottish a high mountain.
- ORIGIN Scottish Gaelic and Irish.

bench noun 1 a long seat for more than one person. 2 a long work table in a workshop or laboratory. 3 (**the bench**) the office of judge or magistrate. 4 (**the bench**) a seat at the side of a sports field for coaches and players not taking part in a game.
- ORIGIN Old English.

benchmark noun 1 a standard against which things may be compared: *champagne will remain the quality benchmark for all sparkling*

wines. 2 a surveyor's mark cut in a wall and used as a reference point in measuring altitudes.

bench press noun an exercise in which one lies on a bench with feet on the floor and raises a weight with both arms.

bench test noun a test carried out on a product before it is released.

bend[1] verb (past and past part. **bent**) 1 give or have a curved or angled shape, form, or course: *the road bends right and then left.* 2 lean or curve the body downwards. 3 force or be forced to give in: *a refusal to bend to mob rule.* 4 interpret or modify a rule to suit someone. 5 direct one's attention or energies to a task. • noun 1 a curved or angled part or course. 2 a kind of knot used to join two ropes together, or one rope to another object. 3 (**the bends**) (treated as sing.) decompression sickness.
- PHRASES **bend someone's ear** informal talk to someone at length or to ask a favour. **round the bend** informal mad.
- DERIVATIVES **bendable** adjective
- ORIGIN Old English, 'put in bonds, tension a bow'.

bend[2] noun Heraldry a broad diagonal stripe from top left to bottom right of a shield.
- ORIGIN Old French *bende* 'flat strip'.

bender noun informal 1 a drinking bout. 2 Brit. a shelter made by covering a framework of bent branches with canvas. 3 Brit. derogatory a male homosexual.

bend sinister noun Heraldry a broad diagonal stripe from top right to bottom left of a shield (a supposed sign of illegitimacy).

bendy adjective (**bendier**, **bendiest**) 1 Brit. capable of bending; flexible. 2 having many bends: *bendy country roads.*

beneath preposition & adverb extending or directly underneath. • preposition of lower status or worth than.
- ORIGIN Old English.

Benedictine /ben-i-dik-teen/ noun 1 a monk or nun of a Christian religious order following the rule of St Benedict. 2 trademark a liqueur based on brandy, originally made by Benedictine monks in France. • adjective relating to St Benedict or the Benedictines.

benediction noun 1 the speaking of a blessing. 2 the state of being blessed.
- ORIGIN from Latin *benedicere* 'bless'.

benefaction /ben-i-fak-sh'n/ noun formal a donation or gift.
- ORIGIN from Latin *bene facere* 'do good (to)'.

benefactor noun a person who gives money or other help.
- DERIVATIVES **benefactress** noun.

benefice /ben-i-fiss/ noun (in the Christian Church) an office whereby a member of the clergy receives accommodation and income in return for their duties.
- ORIGIN Latin *beneficium* 'favour, support'.

beneficent /bi-nef-i-suhnt/ adjective doing or resulting in good: *a beneficent democracy.*
- DERIVATIVES **beneficence** noun.

beneficial adjective having a good effect; favourable.
- DERIVATIVES **beneficially** adverb.

beneficiary noun (pl. **beneficiaries**) a person

who benefits from something, especially a trust or will.

benefit noun 1 advantage or profit gained from something: *the benefits of a private education.* 2 a payment made by the state or an insurance scheme to someone entitled to receive it. 3 a public performance to raise money for a charity. • verb (**benefits, benefiting** or **benefitting, benefited** or **benefitted**) 1 receive an advantage: *areas that would benefit from regeneration.* 2 bring advantage to someone or something.
– PHRASES **the benefit of the doubt** an acceptance that a person is truthful or innocent if the opposite cannot be proved.
– ORIGIN Latin *benefactum* 'good deed'.

benevolent /bi-nev-uh-luhnt/ adjective 1 well meaning and kindly. 2 (of an organization) charitable rather than profit-making.
– DERIVATIVES **benevolence** noun **benevolently** adverb.
– ORIGIN from Latin *bene* 'well' + *velle* 'to wish'.

Bengali /ben-gaw-li/ noun (pl. **Bengalis**) 1 a person from Bengal in the north-east of the Indian subcontinent. 2 the language of Bangladesh and West Bengal. • adjective relating to Bengal.
– ORIGIN Hindi.

benighted adjective 1 lacking understanding of cultural, intellectual, or moral matters: *you're a provincial, benighted fool.* 2 old use unable to travel further because night has fallen.

benign /bi-nyn/ adjective 1 kind and gentle. 2 not harmful or harsh; favourable: *Spain's benign climate.* 3 (of a tumour) not malignant.
– DERIVATIVES **benignity** /bi-nig-ni-ti/ noun **benignly** adverb.
– ORIGIN Latin *benignus*.

benignant /bi-nig-nuhnt/ adjective less common term for BENIGN.

Beninese /ben-i-neez/ noun a person from Benin, a country in West Africa. • adjective relating to Benin.

benison /ben-i-suhn/ noun literary a blessing.
– ORIGIN Old French *beneiçun*.

bent past and past participle of BEND¹. adjective 1 having a curve or sharp curve. 2 Brit. informal dishonest; corrupt. 3 Brit. informal, derogatory homosexual. 4 (**bent on**) determined to do or have something. • noun a natural talent or inclination: *a man of a religious bent.*

bentwood noun wood that is artificially shaped for making furniture.

benumb verb deprive someone of feeling.

benzene /ben-zeen/ noun a volatile liquid hydrocarbon present in coal tar and petroleum.
– ORIGIN from French *benjoin*, referring to a resin obtained from an East Asian tree.

benzine /ben-zeen/ (also **benzin** /ben-zin/) noun a mixture of liquid hydrocarbons obtained from petroleum.

benzodiazepine /ben-zoh-di-ay-zi-peen/ noun any of a class of organic compounds used as tranquillizers, such as Valium.

bequeath /bi-kweeth/ verb 1 leave property to someone by a will. 2 pass on: *he ditched the unpopular policies bequeathed to him.*
– ORIGIN Old English.

bequest noun 1 a legacy bequeathed to someone. 2 the action of bequeathing something.

berate verb scold or criticize someone angrily.

Berber /ber-ber/ noun a member of a people native to North Africa.

berberis /ber-buh-ris/ noun a spiny shrub with yellow flowers and red berries.
– ORIGIN Latin *barbaris*.

bereave verb (**be bereaved**) be deprived of a close relation or friend through their death.
– DERIVATIVES **bereavement** noun.
– ORIGIN Old English.

bereft adjective 1 (**bereft of**) deprived of or lacking: *her room was bereft of colour.* 2 sad and lonely because someone has died or gone away.
– ORIGIN from BEREAVE.

beret /be-ray/ noun a flat round cap of felt or cloth.
– ORIGIN French, 'Basque cap'.

bergamot /ber-guh-mot/ noun 1 an oily substance extracted from Seville oranges, used as flavouring in Earl Grey tea. 2 a herb of the mint family.
– ORIGIN named after *Bergamo* in Italy.

beriberi /be-ri-be-ri/ noun a disease causing inflammation of the nerves and heart failure, due to a deficiency of vitamin B_1.
– ORIGIN Sinhalese.

berk /berk/ noun Brit. informal a stupid person.
– ORIGIN abbreviation of *Berkeley* or *Berkshire Hunt*, rhyming slang for 'cunt'.

berkelium /ber-kee-li-uhm/ noun a radioactive metallic chemical element.
– ORIGIN named after the University of *Berkeley* in California.

berm /berm/ noun a raised bank or flat strip of land on the edge of a river, canal, or road.
– ORIGIN French *berme*.

Bermudan /buh-myoo-duhn/ (also **Bermudian**) noun a person from Bermuda. • adjective relating to Bermuda.

Bermuda shorts plural noun casual knee-length shorts.

berry noun (pl. **berries**) 1 a small round juicy fruit without a stone. 2 Botany a fruit that has its seeds enclosed in a fleshy pulp, e.g. a banana or tomato.
– ORIGIN Old English.

berserk /buh-zerk/ adjective out of control with anger or excitement: *the crowd went berserk.*
– ORIGIN Old Norse.

berth noun 1 a place for a ship to moor at a wharf or harbour. 2 a bunk on a ship or train. • verb moor a ship in a berth.
– PHRASES **give someone/thing a wide berth** stay well away from someone or something.
– ORIGIN probably from a nautical use of BEAR¹.

beryl /be-ril/ noun a transparent pale green, blue, or yellow mineral used as a gemstone.
– ORIGIN Greek *bērullos*.

beryllium /buh-ril-li-uhm/ noun a hard, grey, lightweight metallic chemical element.

beseech verb (past and past part. **besought** or **beseeched**) literary ask someone urgently or pleadingly to do or give something: *they beseeched him to stay.*

b

– ORIGIN Old English.

beset verb (**besetting**; past and past part. **beset**) (of an unwelcome or unpleasant situation) affect or trouble someone or something continuously: *the consortium has been beset by financial difficulties.*
– ORIGIN Old English.

beside preposition **1** at the side of; next to. **2** compared with. **3** in addition to; apart from.
– PHRASES **beside oneself** frantic with worry. **beside the point** irrelevant.

besides preposition in addition to; apart from.
● adverb in addition; as well.

besiege verb **1** surround a place with armed forces in order to force it to surrender. **2** crowd round someone oppressively: *she was besieged by newsmen.* **3** overwhelm with requests or complaints: *the radio station was besieged with calls.*
– DERIVATIVES **besieger** noun.
– ORIGIN Old French *asegier.*

besmirch /bi-**smerch**/ verb damage someone's reputation.

besom /**bee**-zuhm/ noun a broom made of twigs tied round a stick.
– ORIGIN Old English.

besotted /bi-**sot**-tid/ adjective completely infatuated with someone.
– ORIGIN from **sot**.

besought past and past participle of **BESEECH**.

bespatter verb splash something with liquid: *his shoes were bespattered with mud.*

bespeak verb (past **bespoke**; past part. **bespoken**) formal **1** be evidence of: *the attractive tree-lined road bespoke money.* **2** order something in advance.

bespectacled adjective wearing glasses.

bespoke adjective Brit. (of a product or item of clothing) made to a particular customer's requirements: *a bespoke shirt.*

best adjective **1** of the highest quality. **2** most suitable or sensible. ● adverb **1** to the highest degree or standard; most. **2** most suitably or sensibly. ● noun **1** (**the best**) that which is of the highest quality. **2** (**one's best**) the highest standard one can reach. ● verb informal outwit or defeat someone.
– PHRASES **at best** taking the most optimistic view of a situation. **the best of three** (or **five** etc.) victory achieved by winning the majority of a specified odd number of games. **the best part of** most of. **get the best of** overcome: *the disease almost got the best of her.* **had best** find it most sensible to do something: *I'd best be going.* **make the best of** get what limited advantage one can from a situation. **six of the best** Brit. six strokes of the cane as a punishment.
– ORIGIN Old English.

best boy noun the assistant to the chief electrician of a film crew.

bestial /**bess**-ti-uhl/ adjective **1** relating to or like an animal or beast. **2** savagely cruel: *bestial and barbaric acts.*
– DERIVATIVES **bestially** adverb.
– ORIGIN Latin *bestia* 'beast'.

bestiality noun **1** savagely cruel behaviour. **2** sexual intercourse between a person and an animal.

bestiary /**bes**-ti-uhri/ noun (pl. **bestiaries**) a medieval collection of descriptions of various kinds of animals.

bestir verb (**bestirs**, **bestirring**, **bestirred**) (**bestir oneself**) make a physical or mental effort; rouse oneself to activity.

best man noun a man chosen by a bridegroom to assist him at his wedding.

bestow verb award an honour, right, or gift to someone: *he wore the medals bestowed upon him by the President.*
– DERIVATIVES **bestowal** noun.
– ORIGIN Old English.

bestride verb (past **bestrode**; past part. **bestridden**) have a leg on either side of something.

best-seller noun a book or other product that sells in very large numbers.
– DERIVATIVES **best-selling** adjective.

besuited /bi-**soo**-tid/ adjective (of a man) wearing a suit.

bet verb (**bets**, **betting**; past and past part. **bet** or **betted**) **1** risk money or property against someone else's on the outcome of an unpredictable event such as a race. **2** informal feel sure: *I bet she made it all up.* ● noun **1** an act of betting money on something. **2** an amount of money betted: *a £10 bet.* **3** informal an option: *Austria is your best bet for summer skiing.* **4** (**one's bet**) informal one's opinion: *my bet is that she'll stay.*
– PHRASES **you bet** informal of course; certainly.
– DERIVATIVES **bettor** (also **better**) noun.
– ORIGIN perhaps from a former word meaning 'abetting'.

beta /**bee**-tuh/ noun **1** the second letter of the Greek alphabet (Β, β). **2** Brit. a second-class mark given for a piece of work.

beta blocker noun a drug used to treat angina and reduce high blood pressure.

betake verb (past **betook**; past part. **betaken**) (**betake oneself to**) literary go to a place.

beta particle (also **beta ray**) noun Physics a fast-moving electron given off by some radioactive substances.

betel /**bee**-t'l/ noun the leaf of an Asian plant, chewed as a mild stimulant.
– ORIGIN Portuguese.

betel nut noun the seed of a tropical palm tree, often chewed with betel leaves.

bête noire /bet **nwar**/ noun (pl. **bêtes noires** pronunc. same) (**one's bête noire**) a person or thing that one particularly dislikes.
– ORIGIN French, 'black beast'.

bethink verb (past and past part. **bethought**) (**bethink oneself**) formal come to think about something.

betide verb literary happen, or happen to someone.

betimes adverb literary in good time; early.

betoken verb literary be a warning or sign of: *the blue sky betokened a day of good weather.*

betony /**bet**-uh-ni/ noun (pl. **betonies**) a plant of the mint family with purple flowers.
– ORIGIN Latin.

betook past of **BETAKE**.

betray verb **1** endanger one's country, a person, or group of people by treacherously helping an enemy. **2** be disloyal to: *many of the*

unemployed felt betrayed by the government.
3 unintentionally reveal something: *Lou's heightened colour betrayed her embarrassment.*
– DERIVATIVES **betrayal** noun **betrayer** noun.
– ORIGIN from Latin *tradere* 'hand over'.

betrothed formal adjective engaged to be married. • noun (**one's betrothed**) the person to whom one is engaged to be married.
– DERIVATIVES **betrothal** noun.
– ORIGIN from **TRUTH**.

better adjective **1** more satisfactory or effective. **2** partly or fully recovered from an illness or injury. • adverb **1** in a more satisfactory or effective way. **2** to a greater degree; more. • noun **1** something that is better. **2** (**one's betters**) dated or humorous people who are superior to oneself in social status. • verb **1** improve on: *a record bettered by only one other non-league team.* **2** (**better oneself**) improve one's social status.
– PHRASES **better off** in a more favourable position, especially financially. **the better part of** most of. **get the better of** defeat or overcome: *no one had ever got the better of her.* **had better** ought to do something: *I'd better get on with my work.*
– ORIGIN Old English.

USAGE: In the phrase **had better do something** the word **had** is often dropped in informal speech, as in *you better not come tonight*. In writing, the **had** may be shortened to **'d** but it should not be dropped altogether (*you'd better not come tonight*).

better half noun informal a person's husband, wife, or partner.

betterment noun the improvement of someone or something: *the betterment of society.*

between preposition & adverb **1** at, into, or across the space separating two things. **2** in the period separating two points in time. • preposition **1** indicating a connection or relationship. **2** by combining the resources or actions of two or more parties.
– PHRASES **between ourselves** (or **you and me**) in confidence.
– ORIGIN Old English.

USAGE: A preposition such as **between** takes the object case and is correctly followed by object pronouns such as **me** rather than subject pronouns such as **I**. It is therefore correct to say **between you and me** rather than **between you and I**.

betwixt preposition & adverb old use between.
– PHRASES **betwixt and between** informal neither one thing nor the other.
– ORIGIN Old English.

bevel noun **1** (in carpentry) a sloping surface or edge. **2** (also **bevel square**) a tool for marking angles in carpentry and stonework. • verb (**bevels, bevelling, bevelled**; US **bevels, beveling, beveled**) cut a sloping edge on an object.
– ORIGIN Old French, from *baif* 'open-mouthed'.

beverage noun a drink other than water.
– ORIGIN Old French *bevrage*.

bevvy noun (pl. **bevvies**) Brit. informal an alcoholic drink.

– ORIGIN abbreviation of **BEVERAGE**.

bevy /rhymes with heavy/ noun (pl. **bevies**) a large group of people or things: *a bevy of children.*
– ORIGIN unknown.

bewail verb express great regret or sorrow over: *she wept copiously and bewailed her bad luck.*

beware verb be cautious and alert to risks or dangers: *beware of pickpockets at the train and bus stations.*
– ORIGIN from *be ware* 'be aware'.

bewilder verb puzzle or confuse someone.
– DERIVATIVES **bewildering** adjective **bewilderment** noun.
– ORIGIN from the old word *wilder*, meaning 'lead or go astray'.

bewitch verb **1** cast a spell over someone. **2** enchant and delight someone.
– DERIVATIVES **bewitching** adjective **bewitchment** noun.
– ORIGIN from **WITCH**.

bey /bay/ noun (pl. **beys**) historical the governor of a province in the Ottoman Empire.
– ORIGIN Turkish *beg* 'prince, governor'.

beyond preposition & adverb **1** at or to the further side of. **2** outside the range or limits of. **3** to or in a state where something is impossible: *the engine was beyond repair.* **4** happening or continuing after. **5** apart from.
– ORIGIN Old English.

bezel /**bez**-uhl/ noun a groove holding a gemstone or the glass cover of a watch in position.
– ORIGIN Old French.

bezique /bi-**zeek**/ noun a card game for two players, played with a double pack of 64 cards.
– ORIGIN French *bésigue*.

Bh symbol the chemical element bohrium.

bhaji /**bah**-ji/ (also **bhajia** /**bah**-juh/) noun (pl. **bhajis, bhajia**) (in Indian cooking) a small flat cake or ball of vegetables, fried in batter.
– ORIGIN Hindi.

bhang /bang/ (also **bang**) noun (in India) cannabis leaves used as a narcotic.
– ORIGIN Hindi.

bhangra /**bahng**-gruh/ noun a type of popular music combining Punjabi folk traditions with Western pop music.
– ORIGIN Punjabi.

b.h.p. abbreviation brake horsepower.

bhuna /**boo**-nuh/ (also **bhoona**) noun a medium-hot dry curry.
– ORIGIN Urdu.

Bhutanese /boo-tuh-**neez**/ noun a person from Bhutan, a small kingdom in the Himalayas. • adjective relating to Bhutan.

Bi symbol the chemical element bismuth.

bi- /by/ combining form **1** two; having two: *biathlon.* **2** occurring twice in every one or once in every two: *bicentennial.* **3** lasting for two: *biennial.*
– ORIGIN Latin.

biannual adjective occurring twice a year.
– DERIVATIVES **biannually** adverb.

bias noun **1** an inclination or prejudice in favour of or against a particular person or thing: *some people alleged there was a bias towards the Tories.* **2** a slanting direction across the grain of

a fabric. **3** the tendency of a ball in the game of bowls to swerve because of the way it is weighted. **4** Electronics a steady voltage, applied to an electronic device, that can be adjusted to change the way the device operates. • **verb** (**biases, biasing, biased** or **biassing, biassed**) cause someone to have an opinion or prejudice in favour of or against: *he claimed the judge was biased against him.*
– ORIGIN French *biais.*

bias binding noun a narrow strip of fabric cut across the grain, used to bind hems.

biathlon noun a sporting event combining cross-country skiing and rifle shooting.
– ORIGIN from Greek *athlon* 'contest'.

bib noun **1** a piece of cloth or plastic fastened under a child's chin to keep its clothes clean while it is eating. **2** the part of an apron or pair of dungarees that covers the chest.
– PHRASES **one's best bib and tucker** informal one's smartest clothes.
– ORIGIN probably from Latin *bibere* 'to drink'.

bibelot /bib-uh-loh/ noun a small ornament or trinket.
– ORIGIN French.

Bible noun **1** the Christian scriptures, consisting of the Old and New Testaments. **2** the Jewish scriptures. **3** (**bible**) informal a book regarded as giving comprehensive and reliable information about something: *the professional electrician's bible.*
– ORIGIN Greek *biblion* 'book'.

Bible Belt noun the areas of the southern and middle western US and western Canada where many Protestants believe in a literal interpretation of the Bible.

biblical adjective relating to or found in the Bible.
– DERIVATIVES **biblically** adverb.

bibliography /bib-li-og-ruh-fi/ noun (pl. **bibliographies**) **1** a list of the books or articles referred to in a scholarly work. **2** a list of books on a particular subject or by a particular author. **3** the study of books and their production.
– DERIVATIVES **bibliographer** noun **bibliographic** adjective.
– ORIGIN from Greek *biblion* 'book'.

bibliophile /bib-li-oh-fyl/ noun a person who collects or loves books.

bibulous /bib-yuu-luhss/ adjective formal very fond of drinking alcohol.
– ORIGIN from Latin *bibere* 'to drink'.

bicameral /by-kam-uh-ruhl/ adjective (of a parliament or other legislative body) having two chambers.
– ORIGIN from Latin *camera* 'chamber'.

bicarbonate noun **1** Chemistry a compound containing HCO_3 negative ions together with a metallic element. **2** (also **bicarbonate of soda**) sodium bicarbonate.

bicentenary noun (pl. **bicentenaries**) the two-hundredth anniversary of an event.
– DERIVATIVES **bicentennial** noun & adjective.

biceps /by-seps/ noun (pl. same) a large muscle in the upper arm which flexes the arm and forearm.
– ORIGIN Latin, 'two-headed' (because the muscle has two points of attachment).

bichon frise /bee-shuhn freez/ noun a breed of toy dog with a curly white coat.
– ORIGIN from French *barbichon* 'little water spaniel' + *frisé* 'curly-haired'.

bicker verb argue about unimportant things.
– ORIGIN unknown.

bicuspid /by-kus-pid/ noun a tooth with two cusps or points. • **adjective** having two cusps or points.
– ORIGIN from Latin *cuspis* 'sharp point'.

bicycle noun a vehicle with two wheels held in a frame one behind the other, propelled by pedals. • **verb** ride a bicycle.
– DERIVATIVES **bicyclist** noun.
– ORIGIN from Greek *kuklos* 'wheel'.

bid[1] verb (**bids, bidding**; past and past part. **bid**) **1** offer a price for something, especially at an auction. **2** (**bid for**) offer to do work or supply goods for a stated price. **3** try to get or achieve: *the British number one is bidding for his fourth title.* • **noun 1** an offer to buy something. **2** an offer to do work or supply goods at a stated price. **3** an effort to get or achieve something: *a bid for power.*
– DERIVATIVES **bidder** noun **bidding** noun.
– ORIGIN Old English.

bid[2] verb (**bids, bidding**; past **bid** or **bade**; past part. **bid**) **1** utter a greeting or farewell to someone. **2** old use order someone to do something.
– ORIGIN Old English, 'ask'.

biddable adjective meekly ready to obey instructions.

bidden old-fashioned past participle of **BID**[2].

biddy noun (pl. **biddies**) informal an old woman.
– ORIGIN unknown.

bide verb old use or dialect remain or stay in a place.
– PHRASES **bide one's time** wait patiently for a good opportunity to do something.
– ORIGIN Old English.

bidet /bee-day/ noun a low basin used for washing one's genital and anal area.
– ORIGIN French, 'pony'.

biennial /by-en-ni-uhl/ adjective **1** taking place every other year. Compare with **BIANNUAL**. **2** (of a plant) living for two years. • **noun 1** a biennial plant. **2** an event celebrated or taking place every two years.
– DERIVATIVES **biennially** adverb.
– ORIGIN from Latin *annus* 'year'.

bier /beer/ noun a movable platform on which a coffin or dead body is placed before burial.
– ORIGIN Old English.

biff informal verb hit someone or something hard with the fist. • **noun** a sharp blow with the fist.
– ORIGIN probably imitating the sound.

bifid /by-fid/ adjective technical (of a part of a plant or animal) divided into two parts by a deep cleft or notch.
– ORIGIN Latin *bifidus.*

bifocal adjective (of a lens) made in two sections, one with a focus for seeing distant things and one for seeing things that are close. • **noun** (**bifocals**) a pair of glasses with bifocal lenses.

bifurcate /by-fur-kayt/ verb (of a road, river, etc.) divide into two branches or forks.
– DERIVATIVES **bifurcation** noun.
– ORIGIN from Latin *furca* 'a fork'.

big adjective (**bigger, biggest**) **1** of great size,

power, or extent. **2** very important or serious: *a big decision.* **3** older or grown-up: *my big sister.* **4** informal very popular: *fast food isn't big in Iceland.*
– PHRASES **be big with child** old use be in a late stage of pregnancy. **the Big Apple** informal New York City. **the big screen** informal the cinema. **think big** informal be ambitious. **too big for one's boots** informal conceited.
– DERIVATIVES **biggish** adjective **bigness** noun.
– ORIGIN unknown.

bigamy /bi-guh-mi/ noun the crime of marrying someone while already married to another person.
– DERIVATIVES **bigamist** noun **bigamous** adjective.
– ORIGIN from BI- + Greek *-gamos* 'married'.

big band noun a large group of musicians playing jazz or swing music.

Big Bang noun the rapid expansion of extremely dense matter which, according to current cosmological theories, marked the origin of the universe.

Big Brother noun a person or organization exercising total control over people's lives.
– ORIGIN from the name of the fictitious head of state in George Orwell's novel *Nineteen Eighty-Four.*

big dipper noun Brit. a roller coaster.

big end noun the larger end of the connecting rod in a piston engine.

Bigfoot noun (pl. same) a large, hairy ape-like creature, supposedly found in NW America.

big game noun large animals hunted for sport.

big-head noun informal a conceited person.
– DERIVATIVES **big-headed** adjective.

big hitter noun another term for HEAVY HITTER.

bight /rhymes with light/ noun **1** a long inward curve in a coastline. **2** a loop of rope.
– ORIGIN Old English.

big mouth noun informal a person who boasts, or one who cannot keep secrets.

bigot /bi-guht/ noun a person with strong and prejudiced views who will not listen to the opinions of others.
– DERIVATIVES **bigoted** adjective **bigotry** noun.
– ORIGIN French.

big shot (also **big noise**) noun informal an important person.

big top noun the main tent in a circus.

big wheel noun a Ferris wheel.

bigwig noun informal an important person.

bijou /bee-zhoo/ adjective small and elegant: *a bijou apartment.*
– ORIGIN French, 'jewel'.

bike informal noun a bicycle or motorcycle. • verb ride a bicycle or motorcycle.
– DERIVATIVES **biker** noun.

bikini noun (pl. **bikinis**) a women's two-piece swimsuit.
– ORIGIN named after *Bikini* atoll in the western Pacific, where an atom bomb was exploded in 1946 (because of the garment's devastating effect).

bikini line noun the area of skin around the pubic mound as revealed by the high-cut legs of a bikini.

bilateral adjective **1** having two sides. **2** involving two parties: *bilateral discussions.*
– DERIVATIVES **bilaterally** adverb.

bilberry noun (pl. **bilberries**) the small blue edible berry of a shrub found on heathland and high ground.
– ORIGIN probably Scandinavian.

Bildungsroman /bil-dungz-roh-mahn/ noun a novel about one person's formative years or spiritual education.
– ORIGIN German, from *Bildung* 'education' + *Roman* 'a novel'.

bile noun **1** a bitter fluid which helps digestion, produced by the liver and stored in the gall bladder. **2** anger or irritability.
– ORIGIN Latin *bilis.*

bile duct noun the tube which conveys bile from the liver and the gall bladder to the duodenum.

bilge noun **1** the bottom of a ship's hull. **2** (also **bilge water**) dirty water that collects in the bilge. **3** informal nonsense.
– ORIGIN probably from BULGE.

bilharzia /bil-haht-si-uh/ noun a disease caused by infestation of the body with a type of parasitic flatworm.
– ORIGIN named after the German physician T. *Bilharz*, who discovered the parasite.

bilingual adjective **1** speaking two languages fluently. **2** expressed in or using two languages: *a bilingual dictionary.*
– DERIVATIVES **bilingualism** noun **bilingually** adverb.

bilious /bi-lee-uhss/ adjective **1** affected by nausea or vomiting. **2** relating to bile. **3** spiteful or bad-tempered.
– DERIVATIVES **biliously** adverb **biliousness** noun.

bilk verb informal cheat or defraud someone.
– ORIGIN perhaps a variant of BAULK.

Bill noun (**the Bill** or **the Old Bill**) Brit. informal the police.
– ORIGIN familiar form of the man's name *William.*

bill[1] noun **1** a printed or written statement of the money owed for goods or services. **2** a draft of a proposed law presented to parliament for discussion. **3** a programme of entertainment at a theatre or cinema. **4** N. Amer. a banknote. **5** an advertising poster. • verb **1** list a person or event in a programme of entertainment. **2** (**bill someone/thing as**) describe someone or something as: *the vehicle has been billed as the car of the future.* **3** send a statement of charges to a person or organization.
– PHRASES **a clean bill of health** a statement confirming that someone is in good health or that something is in good condition. **fit the bill** be suitable for a particular purpose.
– DERIVATIVES **billing** noun.
– ORIGIN Old French *bille.*

bill[2] noun **1** the beak of a bird. **2** a narrow piece of land projecting into the sea: *Portland Bill.*
– PHRASES **bill and coo** informal behave or talk in a loving and sentimental way.
– ORIGIN Old English.

billabong noun Austral. a branch of a river forming a backwater or stagnant pool.
– ORIGIN from an Aboriginal language.

billboard noun a large board used to display advertisements; a hoarding.

billet[1] /bil-it/ noun a civilian house where soldiers live temporarily. • verb (**billets,**

b

billeting, billeted) provide soldiers with temporary accommodation in a civilian house.
– ORIGIN Old French *billette* 'small document'.

billet² /bi-lit/ noun **1** a thick piece of wood. **2** a small bar of metal.
– ORIGIN Old French *billette* and *billot* 'little tree trunk'.

billet-doux /bil-li-doo/ noun (pl. **billets-doux** /bil-li-**dooz**/) chiefly humorous a love letter.
– ORIGIN French, 'sweet note'.

billfold noun N. Amer. a man's wallet.

billhook noun a tool with a curved blade, used for pruning.

billiards plural noun (treated as sing.) a game for two people, played on a billiard table with three balls.
– ORIGIN French *billard*.

billiard table noun a cloth-covered rectangular table used in billiards, snooker, and some forms of pool, with six pockets at the corners and sides into which balls are struck with cues.

billion cardinal number (pl. **billions** or (with numeral or quantifying word) same) **1** a thousand million; 1,000,000,000 or 10^9. **2** Brit. dated a million million (1,000,000,000,000 or 10^{12}). **3** (**billions**) informal a very large number or amount: *billions of tiny sea creatures*.
– DERIVATIVES **billionth** ordinal number.
– ORIGIN French.

billionaire noun a person owning money and property worth at least a billion pounds or dollars.

bill of exchange noun a document instructing a person to pay a stated sum of money to someone on a particular date.

bill of fare noun dated a menu.

bill of lading noun a document giving full details of a ship's cargo.

bill of rights noun a written statement of the basic rights of a country's citizens.

billow verb **1** (of smoke, cloud, or steam) roll outward: *smoke was billowing from the chimney.* **2** (of fabric or a garment) fill with air and swell out: *her dress billowed out around her.* • noun **1** a large rolling mass of cloud, smoke, or steam. **2** old use a large wave.
– DERIVATIVES **billowy** adjective.
– ORIGIN Old Norse.

billy (also **billycan**) noun (pl. **billies**) Brit. a metal cooking pot with a lid and folding handle, used in camping.
– ORIGIN perhaps from an Aboriginal word meaning 'water'.

billy goat noun a male goat.
– ORIGIN *Billy*, familiar form of the man's name *William*.

bimbo noun (pl. **bimbos**) informal, derogatory an attractive but unintelligent young woman.
– DERIVATIVES **bimbette** noun.
– ORIGIN Italian, 'little child'.

bimetallic adjective made or consisting of two metals.

bimonthly adjective & adverb appearing or taking place twice a month or every two months.

bin Brit. noun **1** a container for rubbish. **2** a large storage container: *a bread bin.* **3** a partitioned stand or case for storing bottles of wine. • verb

(**bins**, **binning**, **binned**) throw something away by putting it in a rubbish bin.
– ORIGIN Old English.

binary /by-nuh-ri/ adjective **1** composed of or involving two things. **2** using or relating to a system of numbers with two as its base, using the digits 0 and 1. • noun (pl. **binaries**) **1** the binary system of notation. **2** Astronomy a system of two stars revolving round their common centre.
– ORIGIN Latin *binarius*.

bind verb (past and past part. **bound**) **1** tie or fasten something tightly together. **2** restrain someone by tying their hands and feet: *he was bound and gagged.* **3** wrap or encircle tightly: *her blonde hair was bound with a scarf.* **4** stick together in a single mass: *mix the flour with the coconut and enough egg white to bind them.* **5** hold together as a united group: *the religious and social rituals which bind people together.* **6** require someone to do something by law or because of a contract. **7** (**bind someone over**) (of a court of law) require someone to do something: *he was bound over to keep the peace.* **8** fix together and enclose the pages of a book in a cover. **9** trim the edge of a piece of material with a fabric strip. • noun informal an annoying or difficult situation.
– ORIGIN Old English.

binder noun **1** a cover for holding magazines or loose papers together. **2** a reaping machine that binds grain into sheaves. **3** a bookbinder.

bindery noun (pl. **binderies**) a workshop or factory in which books are bound.

bindi /bin-dee/ noun (pl. **bindis**) a decorative mark worn in the middle of the forehead by Indian women.
– ORIGIN Hindi.

binding noun **1** a strong covering holding the pages of a book together. **2** fabric cut or woven in a strip, used for binding the edges of a piece of material. • adjective (of an agreement) putting someone under a legal obligation.

bindweed noun a plant with trumpet-shaped flowers that twines itself round things.

bin-end noun Brit. one of the last bottles from a bin of wine.

binge informal noun a short period of uncontrolled indulgence in an activity, especially eating or drinking. • verb (**binges**, **bingeing** or US also **binging**, **binged**) do something, especially eat, without being able to control oneself.
– DERIVATIVES **binger** noun.
– ORIGIN unknown.

bingo noun a game in which players mark off randomly called numbers on printed cards, the winner being the first to mark off all their numbers. • exclamation **1** a call by someone who wins a game of bingo. **2** said to express satisfaction at a sudden good event.
– ORIGIN unknown.

binnacle /bin-ak'l/ noun a casing for holding a ship's compass.
– ORIGIN Spanish *bitácula*, *bitácora* or Portuguese *bitácola*.

binocular /bi-nok-yuu-ler/ adjective adapted for or using both eyes.
– ORIGIN from Latin *bini* 'two together' + *oculus* 'eye'.

binoculars plural noun an instrument with a separate lens for each eye, used for viewing distant objects.

binomial /by-noh-mi-uhl/ noun Mathematics an algebraic expression consisting of two terms linked by a plus or minus sign. • adjective consisting of two terms.
– ORIGIN from Latin *bi-* 'having two' + Greek *nomos* 'part'.

bint noun Brit. informal, derogatory a girl or woman.
– ORIGIN Arabic.

bio- combining form **1** relating to life or living beings: *biosynthesis*. **2** biological; relating to biology: *biohazard*.
– ORIGIN from Greek *bios* 'human life'.

biochemistry noun the branch of science concerned with the chemical processes which occur within living organisms.
– DERIVATIVES **biochemical** adjective **biochemist** noun.

biochip noun a device acting like a silicon chip, with components made from biological molecules or structures.

biocide /by-oh-syd/ noun a substance that is poisonous to living organisms, such as a pesticide.

biodegradable adjective (of a substance or object) capable of being decomposed by bacteria or other living organisms.
– DERIVATIVES **biodegradability** noun **biodegradation** noun **biodegrade** verb.

biodiesel noun a biofuel intended as a substitute for diesel.

biodiversity noun the variety of plant and animal life in the world or in a particular habitat.

bioengineering noun **1** genetic engineering. **2** the use of artificial tissues or organs in the body. **3** the use of organisms or biological processes in industry.
– DERIVATIVES **bioengineer** noun & verb.

biofeedback noun the electronic monitoring of a normally automatic bodily function in order to train someone to control that function of their own accord.

bioflavonoid /by-oh-**flay**-vuh-noyd/ noun any of a group of compounds occurring mainly in citrus fruits and blackcurrants, sometimes regarded as vitamins.

biofuel noun fuel obtained directly from living matter.

biogas noun gaseous fuel, especially methane, produced by the fermentation of organic matter.

biographical adjective relating to or dealing with a particular person's life: *detailed biographical information*.

biography noun (pl. **biographies**) an account of a person's life written by someone else.
– DERIVATIVES **biographer** noun.

biohazard noun a risk to human health or the environment resulting from biological research.

bioinformatics /by-oh-in-for-**mat**-iks/ plural noun (treated as sing.) the science of collecting and analysing complex biological data such as genetic codes.

biological adjective **1** relating to biology or living organisms. **2** (of a parent or child) related by blood. **3** relating to the use of harmful microorganisms as weapons of war. **4** (of a detergent) containing enzymes to help in the removal of stains.
– DERIVATIVES **biologically** adverb.

biological clock noun a natural mechanism that controls certain regularly recurring physical processes in an animal or plant, such as sleeping.

biological control noun the control of a pest by non-chemical means, by bringing a natural enemy or predator of the pest into the environment.

biology noun **1** the scientific study of living organisms. **2** the features of a particular organism or class of organisms: *the biology of marine plants*.
– DERIVATIVES **biologist** noun.

bioluminescence /by-oh-loo-mi-**ness**-uhnss/ noun the production of light by living creatures such as glow-worms and deep-sea fishes.
– DERIVATIVES **bioluminescent** adjective.

biomass noun **1** the total quantity of organisms in a given area. **2** organic matter used as a fuel, especially in the production of electricity.

biome /by-ohm/ noun a large community of plants and animals occupying a major habitat, such as forest or tundra.

biomorph noun a design or decorative form resembling or representing a living organism.
– DERIVATIVES **biomorphic** adjective.

bionic adjective **1** relating to the use of electrically powered artificial body parts. **2** informal having ordinary physical powers increased by the use of such artificial body parts.

biopharmaceutical /by-oh-far-muh-**syoo**-ti-k'l/ noun a pharmaceutical substance, especially a protein or peptide, produced by biotechnology.

biopic /by-oh-pik/ noun informal a film about the the life of a particular person.

biopsy /by--op-si/ noun (pl. **biopsies**) an examination of tissue taken from the body, to discover the presence, cause, or extent of a disease.
– ORIGIN from Greek *bios* 'life' + *opsis* 'sight'.

biorhythm noun a recurring cycle in the physiology or functioning of the body, such as the daily cycle of sleeping and waking.

biosphere noun the parts of the earth's surface and atmosphere which are inhabited by living things.

biosynthesis noun the production of complex molecules within living organisms or cells.
– DERIVATIVES **biosynthetic** adjective.

biota /by-oh-tuh/ noun the animal and plant life of a particular region, habitat, or geological period.
– ORIGIN Greek *biotē* 'life'.

biotechnology noun the use of microorganisms in industry and medicine for the production of antibiotics, hormones, etc.
– DERIVATIVES **biotechnological** adjective **biotechnologist** noun.

bioterrorism noun the use of harmful

biological or biochemical substances as weapons of terrorism.

– DERIVATIVES **bioterrorist** noun.

biotic /by-ot-ik/ adjective relating to living things and the effect they have on each other.

– ORIGIN from Greek *bios* 'life'.

biotin /by-uh-tin/ noun a vitamin of the B complex, found in egg yolk, liver, and yeast.

– ORIGIN from Greek *bios* 'life'.

biowarfare noun biological warfare.

bioweapon noun a harmful organism or biological substance used as a weapon of war.

bipartisan adjective involving the agreement or cooperation of two political parties.

– DERIVATIVES **bipartisanship** noun.

bipartite adjective 1 involving two separate parties: *a bipartite agreement*. 2 technical consisting of two parts.

biped /by-ped/ noun an animal that walks on two feet.

– DERIVATIVES **bipedal** /by-pee-d'l/ adjective.

– ORIGIN from Latin *bi-* 'having two' + *pes* 'foot'.

biplane noun an early type of aircraft with two pairs of wings, one above the other.

bipolar adjective 1 (especially of an electronic device) having two poles. 2 having two opposite extremes: *a bipolar view of the world*.

– DERIVATIVES **bipolarity** noun.

bipolar disorder noun more recent term for MANIC DEPRESSION.

birch noun 1 a slender tree with thin peeling bark and hard fine-grained wood. 2 (**the birch**) historical a punishment in which a person was beaten with a bundle of birch twigs.

– ORIGIN Old English.

bird noun 1 a warm-blooded egg-laying animal which has feathers, wings, and a beak, and typically is able to fly. 2 informal a person of a particular kind: *she's a sharp old bird*. 3 Brit. informal a young woman, or a man's girlfriend.

– PHRASES **the birds and the bees** informal basic facts about sex, as told to a child.

– ORIGIN Old English.

birdbrain noun informal a stupid person.

birdcage noun a cage for pet birds.

birder noun informal a birdwatcher.

– DERIVATIVES **birding** noun.

bird flu noun a severe type of influenza that affects birds, especially poultry, and that can also be fatal to humans.

birdie noun (pl. **birdies**) 1 informal a little bird. 2 Golf a score of one stroke under par at a hole. • verb (**birdies**, **birdying**, **birdied**) Golf play a hole with a score of one stroke under par.

– ORIGIN the golf term is from US slang *bird*, meaning any first-rate thing.

birdlime noun a sticky substance spread on to twigs to trap small birds.

bird of paradise noun (pl. **birds of paradise**) a tropical bird, the male of which has brightly coloured plumage.

bird of passage noun (pl. **birds of passage**) 1 dated a bird that migrates. 2 a person who passes through a place without staying.

bird of prey noun (pl. **birds of prey**) a bird that feeds on animal flesh, such as a hawk.

birdseed noun a blend of seeds for feeding birds.

bird's-eye view noun a general view of something from a high position above it.

bird's nest soup noun (in Chinese cookery) a soup made from the dried gelatinous coating of the nests of swifts and other birds.

birdsong noun the musical sounds made by birds.

bird table noun Brit. a small raised platform in a garden on which food for birds is placed.

birdwatching noun the hobby of observing birds in their natural environment.

– DERIVATIVES **birdwatcher** noun.

biretta /bi-ret-tuh/ noun a square cap with three flat projections on top, worn by Roman Catholic clergymen.

– ORIGIN Italian *berretta* or Spanish *birreta*.

biriani noun variant spelling of BIRYANI.

biro noun (pl. **biros**) Brit. trademark a ballpoint pen.

– ORIGIN named after the Hungarian inventor László József *Biró*.

birr /ber/ noun the basic unit of money of Ethiopia.

– ORIGIN Amharic.

birth noun 1 the emergence of a baby or other young from the body of its mother. 2 the beginning of something: *the birth of modern jazz*. 3 a person's origin or ancestry: *he is of noble birth*.

– DERIVATIVES **birthing** noun.

– PHRASES **give birth** produce a child or young animal.

– ORIGIN Old Norse.

birth certificate noun an official document recording a person's name, their place and date of birth, and the names of their parents.

birth control noun the prevention of unwanted pregnancies, especially through the use of contraception.

birthdate noun the date on which a person is born.

birthday noun the annual anniversary of the day on which a person was born.

birthing pool noun a large circular tub in which a woman is able to give birth to her baby while lying in water.

birthmark noun an unusual, typically permanent, mark on the body which is there from birth.

birth mother noun a woman who has given birth to a child, as opposed to an adoptive mother.

birthplace noun 1 the place where a person was born. 2 the place where something began or originated: *the birthplace of modern art*.

birth rate noun the number of live births per thousand of population per year.

birthright noun 1 a right or privilege that a person has as a result of being born into a particular family, social class, or place. 2 a natural or basic right possessed by all people: *a college education should be regarded as everyone's birthright*.

birthstone noun a gemstone popularly associated with the month or astrological sign of a person's birth.

biryani /bi-ri-ah-ni/ (also **biriani**) noun an Indian dish made with highly seasoned rice and meat, fish, or vegetables.

– ORIGIN Urdu.

biscuit noun 1 Brit. a small, flat cake baked until crisp. 2 a light brown colour. 3 porcelain or other pottery which has been fired but not glazed.

– PHRASES **take the biscuit** (or chiefly N. Amer. **cake**) informal be the most surprising or annoying thing that has happened.

– DERIVATIVES **biscuity** adjective.

– ORIGIN from Latin *bis* 'twice' + *coquere* 'to cook' (because biscuits were originally cooked in a twofold process: first baked and then dried out in a slow oven).

bisect verb divide something into two parts.

– DERIVATIVES **bisection** noun **bisector** noun.

– ORIGIN from Latin *secare* 'to cut'.

bisexual adjective **1** sexually attracted to both men and women. **2** Biology having characteristics of both sexes. • noun a person who is sexually attracted to both men and women.

– DERIVATIVES **bisexuality** noun.

bishop noun **1** a senior member of the Christian clergy, usually in charge of a diocese. **2** a chess piece with a top shaped like a mitre, that can move diagonally in any direction.

– ORIGIN Greek *episkopos* 'overseer'.

bishopric noun the position or diocese of a bishop.

bismuth /biz-muhth/ noun a brittle reddish-grey metallic element resembling lead.

– ORIGIN from German *Wismut*.

bison noun (pl. same) a shaggy-haired wild ox with a humped back.

– ORIGIN Latin.

bisque¹ /bisk, beesk/ noun a rich soup made from lobster or other shellfish.

– ORIGIN French.

bisque² /bisk/ noun another term for BISCUIT (in sense 3).

bistro /bee-stroh/ noun (pl. **bistros**) a small, inexpensive restaurant.

– ORIGIN French.

bit¹ noun **1** a small piece or quantity of something. **2** (a bit) a short time or distance.

– PHRASES **a bit** rather; slightly: *you're a bit late.* **bit by bit** gradually. **bit of stuff** (or **fluff**) informal a girl or young woman. **bit on the side** Brit. informal a person with whom one is unfaithful to one's partner. **do one's bit** informal make a useful contribution to a task or enterprise. **to bits 1** into pieces. **2** informal very much: *he was thrilled to bits.*

– ORIGIN Old English, 'bite, mouthful'.

bit² past of BITE.

bit³ noun **1** a metal mouthpiece attached to a bridle, used to control a horse. **2** a tool or part of a tool for boring or drilling. **3** the part of a key that engages with the lock lever.

– PHRASES **get the bit between one's teeth** begin to tackle a task with determination.

– ORIGIN Old English, 'biting, a bite'.

bit⁴ noun Computing a unit of information expressed as either a 0 or 1 in binary notation.

– ORIGIN from BINARY and DIGIT.

bitch noun **1** a female dog, wolf, fox, or otter. **2** informal a spiteful or unpleasant woman. **3** (a bitch) informal a difficult or unpleasant thing or situation: *working the night shift is a bitch.* • verb informal make spiteful comments.

– ORIGIN Old English.

bitchy adjective (**bitchier**, **bitchiest**) informal spiteful.

– DERIVATIVES **bitchily** adverb **bitchiness** noun.

bite verb (past **bit**; past part. **bitten**) **1** cut into something with the teeth. **2** (of a snake, insect, or spider) wound someone or something with a sting, pincers, or fangs. **3** (of a fish) take the bait or lure on the end of a fishing line into the mouth. **4** (of a tool, tyre, etc.) grip a surface. **5** (of a policy or situation) take effect, with unpleasant consequences: *in hospitals, the strike action was beginning to bite.* **6** (bite something back) stop oneself saying something. • noun **1** an act of biting. **2** a piece of food bitten off. **3** Dentistry the bringing together of the teeth when the jaws are closed. **4** informal a quick snack. **5** a sharpness or strength of flavour: *chicory leaves add colour and bite to a salad.* **6** a feeling of cold in the air.

– PHRASES **bite the bullet** make oneself do something difficult or unpleasant that can no longer be avoided. [from the old custom of giving wounded soldiers a bullet to bite on when undergoing surgery without anaesthetic.] **bite the dust** informal die or be killed. **bite the hand that feeds one** deliberately hurt or offend a person who is trying to help. **bite off more than one can chew** take on a commitment one cannot fulfil. **bite one's tongue** make a desperate effort to avoid saying something.

– DERIVATIVES **biter** noun.

– ORIGIN Old English.

biting adjective **1** (of a wind) very cold and unpleasant. **2** harshly critical: *a biting commentary on contemporary society.*

– DERIVATIVES **bitingly** adverb.

bitmap noun the information used to control an image or display on a computer screen, in which each item corresponds to one or more bits of information.

bit part noun a small acting role in a play or a film.

bitten past participle of BITE.

bitter adjective **1** having a sharp taste or smell; not sweet. **2** causing pain or unhappiness: *the decision came as a bitter blow.* **3** feeling anger, hurt, and resentment. **4** (of a conflict) intense and full of hatred: *a long and bitter dispute.* **5** (of wind or weather) intensely cold. • noun **1** Brit. bitter-tasting beer that is strongly flavoured with hops. **2** (bitters) (treated as sing.) alcohol flavoured with bitter plant extracts, used as an ingredient in cocktails.

– PHRASES **to the bitter end** to the very end, in spite of severe difficulties.

– DERIVATIVES **bitterly** adverb **bitterness** noun.

– ORIGIN Old English.

bitter lemon noun Brit. a fizzy soft drink flavoured with lemons and having a slightly bitter taste.

bittern noun a marshland bird of the heron family, noted for the male's deep booming call.

– ORIGIN Old French *butor*.

bitter orange noun another term for SEVILLE ORANGE.

bittersweet adjective **1** sweet with a bitter aftertaste. **2** bringing pleasure mixed with a touch of sadness.

bitty adjective (**bittier**, **bittiest**) Brit. informal made

b

up of small parts that seem unrelated.

bitumen /bit-yuu-muhn/ noun a black sticky substance obtained naturally or from petroleum, used for road surfacing.
– DERIVATIVES **bituminous** /bi-**tyoo**-mi-nuhss/ adjective.
– ORIGIN Latin.

bituminous coal noun a type of black coal that burns with a characteristically bright smoky flame.

bivalve noun a mollusc that lives in water and has two hinged shells, such as an oyster, mussel, or scallop. • adjective (also **bivalved**) having a hinged double shell.

bivouac /bi-voo-ak/ noun a temporary camp without tents, used especially by soldiers or mountaineers. • verb (**bivouacs, bivouacking, bivouacked**) stay in a bivouac.
– ORIGIN French.

bivvy noun (pl. **bivvies**) informal a small tent or temporary shelter.
– ORIGIN abbreviation of **BIVOUAC**.

biweekly adjective & adverb appearing or taking place every two weeks or twice a week.

biz noun informal business.

bizarre /bi-**zar**/ adjective very strange or unusual.
– DERIVATIVES **bizarrely** adverb **bizarreness** noun.
– ORIGIN from Italian *bizzarro* 'angry'.

Bk symbol the chemical element berkelium.

blab verb (**blabs, blabbing, blabbed**) informal reveal information that should have been kept secret.

blabber verb informal talk at length about foolish or unimportant things.

blabbermouth noun informal a person who reveals secrets or talks too much.

black adjective 1 of the very darkest colour. 2 (of coffee or tea) served without milk. 3 relating to the human group having dark-coloured skin. 4 marked by tragedy, disaster, or despair: *the blackest day of the war.* 5 (of humour) presenting tragic or distressing situations in comic terms. 6 full of anger or hatred: *he threw me a black look.* • noun 1 black colour. 2 a member of a dark-skinned people. • verb 1 make something black, especially by applying black polish or make-up. 2 Brit. dated refuse to deal with a person or thing as a way of taking industrial action.
– PHRASES **black out** lose consciousness; faint. **black something out** make a room or building dark by switching off all the lights and covering the windows. **in the black** not owing any money.
– DERIVATIVES **blackish** adjective **blackly** adverb **blackness** noun.
– ORIGIN Old English.

USAGE: In Britain the word **black** is the most widely used and generally accepted term used to refer to African peoples and their descendants. In the US **African American** is currently the preferred term.

blackamoor /blak-uh-mor/ noun old use a black African or a very dark-skinned person.
– ORIGIN from **BLACK** + **MOOR**.

black and white adjective (of a situation or debate) involving clear-cut opposing opinions

or issues.

black art (also **black arts**) noun black magic.

blackball verb reject a candidate applying to become a member of a private club.
– ORIGIN from the practice of voting against something by placing a black ball in a ballot box.

black bean noun a cultivated variety of soy bean.

black belt noun a black belt worn by an expert in judo, karate, and other martial arts.

blackberry noun (pl. **blackberries**) the purple-black edible fruit of a prickly climbing shrub.

blackberrying noun the activity of picking blackberries.

black bile noun (in medieval science and medicine) one of the four bodily humours, believed to be associated with a melancholy temperament.
– ORIGIN translation of Greek *melankholia* (see **MELANCHOLY**).

blackbird noun a type of thrush, the male of which has black plumage and a yellow bill.

blackboard noun a large board with a dark surface for writing on with chalk.

black box noun a flight recorder in an aircraft.

blackcap noun a type of warbler (bird), the male of which has a black cap.

blackcurrant noun the small round edible black berry of a shrub.

black economy noun the part of a country's economic activity which is not recorded or taxed by its government.

blacken verb 1 become or make black or dark. 2 damage or destroy someone's reputation.

black eye noun an area of bruised skin round the eye caused by a blow.

blackfly noun (pl. **blackflies**) a black or dark green aphid which infests crops.

Blackfoot noun (pl. same or **Blackfeet**) a member of an allied group of North American Indian peoples of the north-western plains.

blackguard /blag-gerd/ noun dated a man who behaves in a dishonourable or dishonest way.
– ORIGIN first referring to a group of kitchen servants.

blackhead noun a lump of oily matter blocking a hair follicle.

black hole noun a region of space which has a gravitational field so intense that no matter or radiation can escape from it.

black ice noun a transparent layer of ice on a road surface.

blacking noun black paste or polish.

blackjack noun 1 chiefly N. Amer. a gambling card game similar to pontoon. 2 N. Amer. a flexible lead-filled truncheon.

blackleg noun Brit. derogatory a person who continues working when their fellow workers are on strike.

blacklist noun a list of people or groups seen as unacceptable or untrustworthy. • verb put the name of a person or group on a blacklist: *the players were blacklisted by the world cricket authorities.*

black magic noun a type of magic which involves the summoning of evil spirits.

blackmail noun 1 the crime of demanding

money from someone in return for not revealing information that could disgrace them. **2** the use of threats or other pressure in an attempt to persuade someone to do something they do not want to do: *she resorted to emotional blackmail.* • verb **1** demand money from someone in return for not revealing information that could disgrace them. **2** force someone to do something by using threats or other pressure: *he blackmailed her into marrying him.*
– DERIVATIVES **blackmailer** noun.
– ORIGIN Old Norse, 'speech, agreement'.

Black Maria /muh-**ry**-uh/ noun informal a police vehicle for transporting prisoners.
– ORIGIN said to be named after *Maria* Lee, a black woman who kept a Boston boarding house and helped police take drunk and disorderly customers to jail.

black mark noun informal a record of the fact that someone has done something that is disapproved of by others.

black market noun the illegal buying and selling of goods that are officially controlled or hard to obtain.
– DERIVATIVES **black marketeer** noun.

black mass noun an imitation of the Roman Catholic Mass, performed in worship of the Devil.

blackout noun **1** a period when all lights must be switched off during an enemy air raid. **2** a sudden failure of an electrical power supply. **3** a temporary loss of consciousness. **4** an official suppression of information: *a total news blackout.*

black pudding noun Brit. a black sausage containing pork, dried pig's blood, and suet.

Black Rod (in full **Gentleman Usher of the Black Rod**) noun the chief usher of the House of Lords and the Lord Chamberlain's department.

black sheep noun informal a member of a family or group who is regarded by the other members as a source of shame or embarrassment.

blackshirt noun a member of a Fascist organization.
– ORIGIN so named because of the black uniforms worn by the Italian Fascists before and during the Second World War.

blacksmith noun **1** a person who makes and repairs things in iron by hand. **2** a person who shoes horses; a farrier.

black spot noun Brit. a place where a particular unwelcome event or situation occurs frequently or is very bad: *an unemployment black spot.*

blackthorn noun a thorny shrub with white flowers and blue-black fruits (sloes).

black tie noun men's formal evening clothes, specifically a black bow tie worn with a dinner jacket.

blackwater fever noun a severe form of malaria in which blood cells are rapidly destroyed, resulting in dark urine.

black widow noun a highly poisonous American spider having a black body with red markings.

bladder noun **1** a sac in the abdomen which receives urine from the kidneys and stores it for excretion. **2** an inflated or hollow flexible bag.
– ORIGIN Old English.

bladderwort noun a water plant with small air-filled sacs which keep it afloat.

bladderwrack noun a type of seaweed with long, flat brown fronds which contain sacs filled with air.

blade noun **1** the flat part of a knife or other tool or weapon that has a sharp edge for cutting. **2** the broad flat part of an oar, leaf, or other object. **3** a long narrow leaf of grass. **4** informal, dated a dashing young man.
– ORIGIN Old English.

blag Brit. informal verb (**blags, blagging, blagged**) **1** obtain something by lying or clever persuasion: *they were trying to blag some free tickets.* **2** steal something. • noun a robbery.
– DERIVATIVES **blagger** noun.
– ORIGIN perhaps from French *blaguer* 'tell lies'.

blame verb feel or state that someone or something is responsible for a bad or unfortunate act, situation, or occurrence: *he blamed Francis for his mother's death.* • noun responsibility for a bad or unfortunate act, situation, or occurrence: *she's trying to put the blame on me.*
– PHRASES **be to blame** be responsible for a bad or unfortunate act, situation, or occurrence.
– DERIVATIVES **blameworthy** adjective.
– ORIGIN Old French *blasmer.*

blameless adjective free from responsibility for any bad or unfortunate act, situation, or occurrence.

blanc /blonk/ adjective (of wine) white.
– ORIGIN Old French.

blanch /blahnch/ verb **1** make or become white or pale. **2** prepare vegetables by plunging them briefly in boiling water. **3** peel almonds by scalding them.
– ORIGIN from Old French *blanc* 'white'.

USAGE: Do not confuse **blanch** with **blench**. **Blanch** means 'make or become white or pale' (*the cold light blanched her face*), while **blench** means 'flinch suddenly through fear or pain' (*I've seen saddle sores that would make you blench.*).

blancmange /bluh-**monzh**/ noun Brit. a sweet jelly-like dessert made with cornflour and milk.
– ORIGIN from Old French *blanc* 'white' + *mangier* 'eat'.

bland adjective **1** lacking strong qualities and therefore uninteresting: *bland, mass-produced pop music.* **2** showing little emotion: *his bland expression.*
– DERIVATIVES **blandly** adverb **blandness** noun.
– ORIGIN Latin *blandus* 'soft, smooth'.

blandishments plural noun flattering remarks intended to persuade someone to do something.

blank adjective **1** not marked or decorated; bare or plain: *a blank piece of paper.* **2** not understanding or reacting: *he gave me a blank look.* **3** complete; absolute: *a blank refusal.* • noun **1** a space left to be filled in a document. **2** a cartridge containing gunpowder but no bullet. **3** an empty space or period of time.

•**verb 1** hide or cover: *the sun had gone, blanked out by the smoke.* **2** Brit. informal deliberately ignore someone.
– PHRASES **draw a blank** get no response or result.
– DERIVATIVES **blankly** adverb **blankness** noun.
– ORIGIN Old French *blanc* 'white'.

blank cheque noun **1** a signed cheque with the amount left for the person cashing it to fill in. **2** complete freedom of action.

blanket noun **1** a large piece of woollen material used as a warm covering. **2** a thick mass or layer of something: *a blanket of cloud.* •**adjective** covering all cases; total: *a blanket ban on tobacco advertising.* •**verb** (**blankets, blanketing, blanketed**) cover completely with a thick layer: *the countryside was blanketed in snow.*
– DERIVATIVES **blanketing** noun.
– ORIGIN Old French *blanc* 'white'.

blanket stitch noun a looped stitch used on the edges of material too thick to be hemmed.

blank verse noun poetry which has a regular rhythm but does not rhyme.

blare verb sound loudly and harshly: *a police car with its siren blaring.* •**noun** a loud, harsh sound.
– ORIGIN Dutch or German *blaren.*

blarney noun talk intended to be charming, flattering, or persuasive.
– ORIGIN named after the *Blarney* Stone in Ireland, said to give the gift of persuasive speech to anyone who kisses it.

blasé /blah-zay/ adjective unimpressed with or indifferent to something because one has seen or experienced it many times before.
– ORIGIN French.

blaspheme /blass-feem/ verb speak disrespectfully about God or sacred things.
– DERIVATIVES **blasphemer** noun.
– ORIGIN from Greek *blasphēmos* 'evil-speaking'.

blasphemous /blass-fuh-muhss/ adjective disrespectful towards God or sacred things.
– DERIVATIVES **blasphemously** adverb.

blasphemy /blass-fuh-mi/ noun (pl. **blasphemies**) disrespectful talk about God or sacred things.

blast noun **1** an explosion, or the destructive wave of air spreading outwards from it. **2** a strong gust of wind or air. **3** a single loud note of a horn or whistle. **4** N. Amer. informal an enjoyable experience. •**verb 1** blow something up with explosives. **2** (**blast off**) (of a rocket or spacecraft) take off. **3** produce loud music or noise. **4** strike a ball hard. **5** informal criticize someone or something fiercely. •**exclamation** Brit. informal expressing annoyance.
– PHRASES (**at**) **full blast** at maximum power or volume.
– DERIVATIVES **blaster** noun.
– ORIGIN Old English.

blasted adjective informal used to express annoyance: *make your own blasted coffee!*

blast furnace noun a smelting furnace using blasts of hot compressed air.

blast-off noun the launch of a rocket or spacecraft.

blatant adjective (of an act considered to be bad) done in an open, obvious, and unashamed way: *a blatant abuse of human rights.*
– DERIVATIVES **blatancy** noun **blatantly** adverb.
– ORIGIN first used by the poet Edmund Spenser; perhaps from Scots *blatand* 'bleating'.

blather /blath-er/ (also **blither**) verb talk at length without making much sense. •**noun** rambling talk.
– ORIGIN Old Norse.

blaze noun **1** a very large or fiercely burning fire. **2** a very bright light or display of colour. **3** a conspicuous display or outburst of something: *a blaze of publicity.* **4** a white stripe down the face of a horse or other animal. **5** (**blazes**) informal a euphemism for 'hell': *go to blazes!* •**verb 1** burn or shine fiercely or brightly. **2** (of guns) be fired repeatedly or wildly. **3** present news or information in a prominent way.
– PHRASES **blaze a trail 1** mark out a path or route. **2** be the first to do something.
– DERIVATIVES **blazing** adjective.
– ORIGIN Old English; sense 3 of the verb is from German or Dutch *blāzen* 'to blow'.

blazer noun **1** a jacket worn by schoolchildren or sports players as part of a uniform. **2** a man's smart jacket which does not form part of a suit.

blazon /blay-zuhn/ verb **1** display or describe prominently or vividly: *his name was blazoned across the theatre's hoardings.* **2** Heraldry depict a coat of arms. •**noun** old use a coat of arms.
– ORIGIN Old French *blason* 'shield'.

bleach verb **1** make something white or lighter by the use of chemicals or by exposing it to sunlight. **2** clean or sterilize a drain, sink, etc. with bleach. •**noun** a chemical used to lighten things and also to sterilize drains, sinks, etc.
– ORIGIN Old English.

bleacher noun N. Amer. a cheap seat in an uncovered part of a sports ground.

bleak adjective **1** bare and exposed to the weather: *the bleak snow-covered hillside.* **2** empty or unwelcoming; without pleasant features: *a bleak room in a grimy hotel.* **3** (of a situation) not hopeful or encouraging: *HIV patients in the town face a bleak future.*
– DERIVATIVES **bleakly** adverb **bleakness** noun.
– ORIGIN Old English or Old Norse, 'white, shining'.

bleary adjective (**blearier, bleariest**) (of a person's eyes) dull and not focusing properly, especially as a result of tiredness.
– DERIVATIVES **blearily** adverb.
– ORIGIN probably from German *blerre* 'blurred vision'.

bleat verb **1** (of a sheep or goat) make a weak, wavering cry. **2** speak or complain in a weak or petulant way. •**noun** a bleating sound.
– ORIGIN Old English.

bleed verb (past and past part. **bled**) **1** lose blood from the body. **2** take blood from someone as a former method of medical treatment. **3** informal deprive of money or resources: *bogus refugees bled the country of £100 million through benefit fraud.* **4** (of dye or colour) seep into an adjoining colour or area. **5** allow fluid or gas to escape from a closed system through a valve. •**noun** an instance of losing blood from a part of the body.

– ORIGIN Old English.

bleeder noun Brit. informal a person regarded with scorn or pity: *the poor bleeder split his head open.*

bleeding adjective Brit. informal used for emphasis or to express annoyance.

bleeding heart noun informal, derogatory a person considered to be too soft-hearted or liberal.

bleep noun a short high-pitched sound made by an electronic device. •verb **1** make a bleep. **2** contact someone by using a bleeper.
– ORIGIN imitating the sound.

bleeper noun Brit. a small portable electronic device which bleeps when someone wants to contact the wearer.

blemish noun **1** a small mark or flaw which spoils the appearance of something. **2** a fault or failing. •verb spoil the appearance of something.
– ORIGIN Old French *blesmir* 'make pale, injure'.

blench verb flinch suddenly through fear or pain.
– ORIGIN Old English, 'deceive'.

> **USAGE:** On the confusion of **blench** and **blanch**, see the note at **BLANCH**.

blend verb **1** mix a substance with another substance so that they combine together. **2** combine with something in an attractive or harmonious way: *costumes, music, and lighting all blend together.* **3** be an unobtrusive or attractive part of something by being similar in appearance or behaviour: *a tourist resort designed to blend in with the natural surroundings.* •noun a mixture of different things or people.
– ORIGIN probably Scandinavian.

blender noun an electric device used for liquidizing or chopping food.

blenny noun (pl. **blennies**) a small sea fish with spiny fins and a scaleless skin.
– ORIGIN from Greek *blennos* 'mucus' (because the fish is covered with mucus).

bless verb **1** ask God to protect someone or something: *may God bless you and keep you.* **2** make holy by performing a religious rite: *the priest had broken the bread and blessed the wine.* **3** praise God. **4** (**be blessed with**) have or be given something that is greatly wished for: *we have been blessed with a baby boy.*
– PHRASES **bless you!** said to a person who has just sneezed.
– ORIGIN Old English.

blessed /bless-id, blest/ adjective **1** made holy. **2** protected by God. **3** bringing welcome pleasure or relief: *blessed sleep.* **4** informal used in mild expressions of exasperation.
– DERIVATIVES **blessedly** adverb **blessedness** noun.

blessing noun **1** God's favour and protection. **2** a prayer asking for this. **3** something for which one is very grateful: *it's a blessing we're alive.* **4** a person's approval or support: *he gave the plan his blessing.*
– PHRASES **a blessing in disguise** something that at first seems unfortunate but eventually has good results.

blew past of **BLOW**[1].

blewit /bloo-it/ noun an edible mushroom with a pale yellowish-beige or lilac cap.
– ORIGIN probably from **BLUE**[1].

blight noun **1** a plant disease, especially one caused by fungi. **2** a thing that spoils or damages something: *an ugly building which is a blight on the landscape.* **3** ugly or neglected urban landscape. •verb **1** infect plants with blight. **2** spoil or destroy: *lives blighted by economic hardship.*
– ORIGIN unknown.

blighter noun Brit. informal a person regarded with scorn or pity.

Blighty noun Brit. informal (used by soldiers serving abroad) Britain or England.
– ORIGIN from Urdu, 'foreign, European'.

blimey exclamation Brit. informal expressing surprise or alarm.
– ORIGIN altered form of *God blind* (or *blame*) *me!*

blimp noun informal **1** (also **Colonel Blimp**) Brit. a pompous person with conservative views. **2** a small airship or barrage balloon.
– DERIVATIVES **blimpish** adjective.
– ORIGIN sense 1 is taken from the name of a cartoon character; sense 2 is of unknown origin.

blind adjective **1** not able to see. **2** done without being able to see or without having certain information: *a blind tasting of eight wines.* **3** not noticing or realizing something: *I am not blind to her shortcomings.* **4** not controlled by reason: *they left in blind panic.* **5** (of a corner or bend in a road) impossible to see round. **6** informal the slightest: *it didn't do a blind bit of good.* •verb **1** make someone or something blind. **2** make someone no longer able to think clearly or sensibly: *they were blinded by hatred.* **3** (**blind someone with**) confuse or overawe someone with something they do not understand: *a manual which does not blind you with computer science.* •noun **1** a screen for a window. **2** something designed to conceal one's real intentions. •adverb without being able to see clearly.
– PHRASES **bake something blind** bake a flan case without a filling. **blind drunk** informal extremely drunk. **turn a blind eye** pretend not to notice.
– DERIVATIVES **blindly** adverb **blindness** noun.
– ORIGIN Old English.

blind alley noun **1** a cul-de-sac. **2** a course of action that does not produce useful results.

blind date noun a meeting with a person one has not met before, with the aim of developing a romantic relationship.

blinder noun Brit. informal an excellent performance in a game or race.

blindfold noun a piece of cloth tied around the head to cover someone's eyes. •verb put a blindfold on someone so that they cannot see. •adverb Brit. with a blindfold covering the eyes: *I could find my way around the place blindfold.*
– ORIGIN Old English.

blinding adjective **1** (of light) very bright. **2** (of pain) very intense: *a blinding headache.* **3** informal very skilful and exciting: *a blinding performance.*
– DERIVATIVES **blindingly** adverb.

blind man's buff (US also **blind man's bluff**) noun a game in which a blindfold player tries to catch others while being pushed about by them.

- ORIGIN from *buff* 'a blow', from Old French.

blind side noun a direction in which a person has a poor view of approaching traffic or danger.

blind spot noun 1 a small area of the retina in the eye that is insensitive to light. 2 an area where a person's view is obstructed. 3 an area or subject about which a person lacks understanding or impartiality: *he has a blind spot where his daughter is concerned.*

blindworm noun another term for SLOW-WORM.

bling-bling (also **bling**) noun & adjective US informal used to refer to expensive, showy clothing and jewellery, or the style or attitudes associated with them.
- ORIGIN perhaps in imitation of light reflecting off jewellery.

blini /blee-ni/ (also **blinis**) plural noun pancakes made from buckwheat flour.
- ORIGIN Russian.

blink verb 1 shut and open the eyes quickly. 2 (of a light) flash on and off. • noun an act of blinking the eyes.
- PHRASES **on the blink** informal out of order.
- ORIGIN Scots variant of BLENCH.

blinker noun (**blinkers**) chiefly Brit. 1 a pair of small pieces of leather attached to a horse's bridle to prevent the horse seeing sideways. 2 a thing that prevents someone from understanding a situation fully: *the party is now freed from its ideological blinkers* • verb put blinkers on a horse.

blinkered adjective 1 (of a horse) wearing blinkers. 2 having or showing a narrow or limited outlook or point of view: *the blinkered attitude of the football establishment.*

blinking adjective Brit. informal used to express annoyance: *a blinking nuisance.*

blip noun 1 a very short high-pitched sound made by an electronic device. 2 a small flashing point of light on a radar screen. 3 an unexpected and usually temporary change in the pattern of a situation or process: *a blip in what has otherwise been a successful career.* • verb (**blips**, **blipping**, **blipped**) (of an electronic device) make a blip.
- ORIGIN imitating the sound.

bliss noun 1 a state or feeling of perfect happiness. 2 a state of spiritual blessedness.
- ORIGIN Old English.

blissful adjective extremely happy.
- DERIVATIVES **blissfully** adverb.

blister noun 1 a small bubble on the skin filled with watery liquid, typically caused when the skin is rubbed against another surface or by burning. 2 a similar swelling, filled with air or fluid, on the surface of painted wood, heated metal, etc. • verb form or cause to form blisters: *his skin was beginning to blister with the heat.*
- ORIGIN perhaps from Old French *blestre* 'swelling, pimple'.

blistering adjective 1 (of heat) intense. 2 (of criticism) very forceful: *a blistering attack on the government.* 3 extremely fast, energetic, or impressive: *he set a blistering pace.*
- DERIVATIVES **blisteringly** adverb.

blithe /blyth/ adjective 1 showing a casual lack of concern about something: *a blithe disregard for the rules of the road* 2 literary happy.

- DERIVATIVES **blithely** adverb **blitheness** noun.
- ORIGIN Old English.

blither /blith-er/ verb & noun variant spelling of BLATHER.

blithering adjective informal complete: *you blithering idiot.*

BLitt abbreviation Bachelor of Letters.
- ORIGIN from Latin *Baccalaureus Litterarum.*

blitz noun 1 an intensive or sudden military attack. 2 (**the Blitz**) the German air raids on Britain in 1940–1. 3 informal a sudden and concentrated effort to deal with something: *the Department launched a blitz on drink-drivers.* • verb attack or seriously damage a place in a blitz.
- ORIGIN abbreviation of BLITZKRIEG.

blitzkrieg /blits-kreeg/ noun an intense military campaign intended to bring about a rapid victory.
- ORIGIN German, 'lightning war'.

blizzard noun a severe snowstorm with high winds.
- ORIGIN unknown.

bloat verb swell or cause to swell with fluid or gas.
- DERIVATIVES **bloated** adjective.
- ORIGIN perhaps from an Old Norse word meaning 'soft'.

bloater noun a herring that has been soaked in salt water and smoked.

blob noun 1 a drop of a thick liquid or sticky substance. 2 a roundish mass or shape.
- DERIVATIVES **blobby** adjective.

bloc noun a group of countries or political parties who have formed an alliance.
- ORIGIN French, 'block'.

block noun 1 a large piece of a solid material with flat surfaces on each side. 2 Brit. a large single building divided into separate flats or offices. 3 a group of buildings with streets on all four sides. 4 a large quantity of things regarded as a unit: *a block of shares.* 5 a thing that makes movement or progress difficult: *a block to career advancement.* 6 a solid area of colour on a surface. 7 (also **cylinder block** or **engine block**) a large metal moulding containing the cylinders of an internal-combustion engine. 8 a pulley or system of pulleys mounted in a case. • verb 1 prevent movement or flow in a road, passage, pipe, etc.: *all three lanes were blocked with traffic.* 2 hinder or prevent: *unions threatened to block the deal.*
- PHRASES **block something out** exclude something unpleasant from one's thoughts or memory. **knock someone's block off** informal hit someone on the head. **put one's head** (or **neck**) **on the block** informal put one's position or reputation at risk by doing or saying something.
- DERIVATIVES **blocker** noun.
- ORIGIN Dutch.

blockade noun an act of sealing off a place to prevent goods or people from entering or leaving. • verb seal off a place to prevent goods or people from entering or leaving.

blockage noun an obstruction which makes movement or flow difficult or impossible.

block and tackle noun a lifting mechanism consisting of ropes, a pulley block, and a hook.

blockbuster noun informal a film or book that is a great commercial success.
– DERIVATIVES **blockbusting** adjective.
block capitals plural noun plain capital letters.
blockhead noun informal a very stupid person.
blockhouse noun a reinforced concrete shelter used as an observation point.
block letters plural noun block capitals.
block vote noun Brit. a vote made by a person who represents a number of other people, the power of their vote being proportional to the number of people they represent.
blog noun a weblog. • verb (**blogs, blogging, blogged**) (usu. as noun **blogging**) regularly update a weblog.
– DERIVATIVES **blogger** noun.
bloke noun Brit. informal a man.
– ORIGIN Shelta.
blokeish (also **blokish** or **blokey**) adjective Brit. informal stereotypically male in behaviour and interests.
blonde adjective (also **blond**) **1** (of hair) fair or pale yellow. **2** having fair hair and a light complexion. • noun a woman with blonde hair.
– ORIGIN French.
blood noun **1** the red liquid that circulates in the arteries and veins, carrying oxygen and carbon dioxide. **2** a person's family background: *she must have Irish blood.* **3** dated a fashionable and dashing young man. • verb initiate someone in an activity: *clubs are too slow in blooding young players.*
– PHRASES **be** (or **run**) **in one's blood** be a natural or fundamental part of one's character and, typically, of the character of other family members: *writing is in her blood.* **blood, sweat, and tears** extremely hard work. **first blood 1** the first shedding of blood in a fight. **2** the first point or advantage gained in a contest. **have blood on one's hands** be responsible for someone's death. **make someone's blood boil** informal make someone extremely angry. **make someone's blood run cold** horrify someone. **new** (or **fresh** or **young**) **blood** new (or younger) members of a group or organization, especially those seen as having new and invigorating ideas or skills. **of the blood** (**royal**) literary royal. **someone's blood is up** someone is angry and in a fighting mood.
– ORIGIN Old English.
bloodbath noun an event in which many people are killed violently.
blood brother noun a man who has sworn to treat another man as a brother.
blood count noun a calculation of the number of corpuscles (red and white blood cells) in a particular quantity of blood.
blood-curdling adjective horrifying; extremely frightening.
blood feud noun a lengthy conflict between families involving a cycle of revenge killings.
blood group noun any of the various types into which human blood is classified for medical purposes.
bloodhound noun a large hound with a very keen sense of smell, used in tracking.
bloodless adjective **1** without violence or killing: *a bloodless coup.* **2** (of the skin) looking very pale; drained of colour. **3** lacking emotion or vitality: *a pedantic, bloodless character.*
– DERIVATIVES **bloodlessly** adverb.
bloodletting noun **1** historical the surgical removal of some of a patient's blood for medical purposes. **2** violence during a war or conflict.
bloodline noun a pedigree, set of ancestors, or line of descent.
blood money noun **1** money paid to compensate the family of a murdered person. **2** money paid to a hired killer.
blood orange noun an orange of a variety with red flesh.
blood poisoning noun a serious illness which occurs when harmful microorganisms have infected the blood.
blood pressure noun the pressure of the blood in the circulatory system, which is closely related to the force and rate of the heartbeat.
blood pudding (also **blood sausage**) noun black pudding.
blood relation (also **blood relative**) noun a person who is related to another by birth.
bloodshed noun the killing or wounding of people.
bloodshot adjective (of the eyes) having the whites tinged with blood.
blood sport noun a sport involving the hunting, wounding, or killing of animals.
bloodstock noun thoroughbred horses.
bloodstream noun the blood circulating through the body.
bloodsucker noun **1** an animal or insect that sucks blood. **2** informal a person who extorts money from other people.
– DERIVATIVES **bloodsucking** adjective.
blood sugar noun the concentration of glucose in the blood.
bloodthirsty adjective taking great pleasure in violence and killing.
blood vessel noun a vein, artery, or capillary carrying blood through the body.
bloody adjective (**bloodier, bloodiest**) **1** covered with or containing blood. **2** involving much violence or cruelty: *a bloody military coup.* **3** informal, chiefly Brit. used to express anger or shock, or for emphasis. • verb (**bloodies, bloodying, bloodied**) cover or stain something with blood.
– DERIVATIVES **bloodily** adverb **bloodiness** noun.
Bloody Mary noun (pl. **Bloody Marys**) a drink consisting of vodka and tomato juice.
bloody-minded adjective Brit. informal deliberately uncooperative.
bloom verb **1** produce flowers; be in flower. **2** be or become very healthy: *she had bloomed during her pregnancy.* • noun **1** a flower. **2** the state or period of blooming: *the apple trees were in bloom.* **3** a youthful or healthy glow in a person's complexion: *the rosy bloom in her cheeks.* **4** a delicate powdery deposit on the surface of fruits.
– ORIGIN Old Norse.
bloomer[1] noun Brit. a large loaf with diagonal slashes on a rounded top.
– ORIGIN unknown.

b

b

bloomer² noun Brit. informal, dated a stupid mistake.
– ORIGIN from **BLOOMING**.

bloomers plural noun **1** women's loose-fitting knee-length knickers. **2** historical women's loose-fitting trousers, gathered at the knee or ankle.
– ORIGIN named after the American social reformer Mrs Amelia J. *Bloomer.*

blooming adjective Brit. informal used to express annoyance or for emphasis: *of all the blooming cheek!*

blooper noun informal, chiefly N. Amer. an embarrassing mistake.
– ORIGIN first referring to an electronic device which made a loud, howling sound.

blossom noun **1** a flower or a mass of flowers on a tree or bush. **2** the state or period of flowering: *the cherry trees are in blossom.* • verb **1** (of a tree or bush) produce flowers. **2** develop in a promising or healthy way: *their friendship blossomed into romance.*
– ORIGIN Old English.

blot noun **1** a mark or stain, especially one made by ink. **2** a thing that spoils something that is otherwise good or attractive: *the only blot in his dazzling career.* • verb (**blots, blotting, blotted**) **1** dry a wet surface or substance with an absorbent material. **2** mark, stain, or spoil: *the eyesores which have blotted our cityscapes.* **3** (**blot something out**) cover or hide something from view. **4** (**blot something out**) try to keep an unpleasant memory or thought from one's mind: *he tried to blot out the image of Helen's sad face.*
– PHRASES **blot one's copybook** Brit. spoil one's good reputation.
– ORIGIN probably Scandinavian.

blotch noun a large irregular mark.
– DERIVATIVES **blotched** adjective **blotchy** adjective.
– ORIGIN from **BLOT** and **BOTCH**.

blotter noun a pad of blotting paper.

blotting paper noun absorbent paper used for soaking up excess ink when writing.

blotto adjective informal extremely drunk.

blouse noun **1** a garment like a shirt, worn by women. **2** a type of jacket worn as part of military uniform. • verb make a garment hang in full, loose folds.
– ORIGIN French.

blouson /bloo-zon/ noun a short loose-fitting jacket.
– ORIGIN French.

blow¹ verb (past **blew**; past part. **blown**) **1** (of wind) move creating a current or air. **2** carry or be carried by the wind: *my tent had blown away.* **3** send out air through pursed lips. **4** force air through the mouth into a musical instrument. **5** sound the horn of a vehicle. **6** (of an explosion) force something out of place: *the blast blew out the windows.* **7** burst or burn out through pressure or overheating: *the fuse in the plug had blown.* **8** shape molten glass by forcing air into it through a tube. **9** informal spend money recklessly. **10** informal waste an opportunity: *they blew their championship chances.* **11** informal reveal or expose something: *one mistake could blow his cover.* • noun **1** an act of blowing something. **2** a strong wind.
– PHRASES **blow a fuse** (or **gasket**) informal lose

one's temper. **blow hot and cold** keep changing one's mind. **blow someone's mind** informal impress or affect someone very strongly. **blow one's nose** clear one's nose of mucus by blowing through it. **blow over** (of trouble) fade away without having any serious effects. **blow one's top** informal lose one's temper. **blow up 1** explode. **2** lose one's temper. **3** develop suddenly and violently: *a crisis blew up between the two countries in 1967.* **blow something up 1** make something explode. **2** inflate something.
– ORIGIN Old English.

blow² noun **1** a powerful stroke with a hand or weapon. **2** a sudden shock or disappointment: *his departure will be a terrible blow to the prime minister.*
– PHRASES **come to blows** start fighting after a disagreement.
– ORIGIN unknown.

blow-by-blow adjective (of a description of an event) giving all the details in the order in which they happened.

blow-dry verb dry the hair with a hand-held dryer, arranging it into a particular style.

blower noun **1** a device that creates a current of air to dry or heat something. **2** Brit. informal a telephone.

blowfish noun (pl. same or **blowfishes**) a fish that is able to inflate its body when it is alarmed.

blowfly noun (pl. **blowflies**) a bluebottle or similar large fly which lays its eggs on meat and carcasses.

blowhard noun N. Amer. informal a boastful or pompous person.

blowhole noun **1** the nostril of a whale or dolphin on the top of its head. **2** a hole in ice for breathing or fishing through. **3** a vent for air or smoke in a tunnel.

blow job noun vulgar slang an act of fellatio.

blowlamp noun Brit. a blowtorch.

blown past participle of **BLOW¹**.

blowout noun **1** an occasion when a vehicle tyre bursts or an electric fuse melts. **2** informal a large meal.

blowpipe noun **1** a weapon consisting of a long tube through which an arrow or dart is blown. **2** a long tube used for blowing glass.

blowsy /rhymes with drowsy/ (also **blowzy**) adjective (of a woman) red-faced and untidy in appearance.
– ORIGIN from an old word meaning 'a beggar's female companion'.

blowtorch noun a portable device producing a very hot flame, used to burn paint off a surface.

blowy adjective (**blowier, blowiest**) windy or windswept.

BLT noun a sandwich filled with bacon, lettuce, and tomato.

blub verb (**blubs, blubbing, blubbed**) informal sob noisily.
– ORIGIN abbreviation of **BLUBBER²**.

blubber¹ noun the fat of sea mammals, especially whales and seals.
– DERIVATIVES **blubbery** adjective.
– ORIGIN first referring to foam on the sea.

blubber² verb informal sob noisily.

– ORIGIN probably imitating the sound.

bludgeon noun a thick stick with a heavy end, used as a weapon. • verb **1** hit someone repeatedly with a bludgeon or other heavy object. **2** bully into doing something: *he bludgeoned Congress into approving the measures.*
– ORIGIN unknown.

bludger noun Austral./NZ informal a scrounger.
– ORIGIN abbreviation of *bludgeoner.*

blue¹ adjective (**bluer, bluest**) **1** of the colour of the sky on a sunny day. **2** informal sad or depressed. **3** informal having sexual or pornographic content: *a blue movie.* **4** Brit. informal politically conservative. • noun **1** blue colour or material. **2** Brit. a person who has represented Cambridge University or Oxford University at a particular sport in a match between the two universities.
– PHRASES **blue on blue** Military referring to an attack made by one's own side that accidentally harms one's own forces. [from the use of blue to indicate friendly forces in military exercises.] **once in a blue moon** informal very rarely. **out of the blue** informal unexpectedly.
– DERIVATIVES **blueness** noun.
– ORIGIN Old French *bleu.*

blue² verb (**blues, bluing** or **blueing, blued**) Brit. informal, dated spend money in a reckless or wasteful way.
– ORIGIN perhaps from **BLOW¹**.

blue baby noun a baby born with bluish skin as the result of a lack of oxygen in the blood.

bluebell noun a woodland plant with clusters of blue bell-shaped flowers.

blueberry noun (pl. **blueberries**) the small blue-black berry of a North American shrub.

bluebird noun an American songbird, the male of which has a blue head, back, and wings.

blue-blooded adjective born into a royal or aristocratic family.

bluebottle noun a large fly with a metallic-blue body.

blue cheese noun cheese containing veins of blue mould, such as Stilton.

blue-chip adjective (of a company or shares) considered to be a reliable investment.
– ORIGIN from the *blue chip* used in gambling games, which usually have a high value.

blue-collar adjective chiefly N. Amer. relating to manual work or workers.

blue-eyed boy noun Brit. informal, chiefly derogatory a person who is held in high regard by someone else and treated with special favour.

bluegrass noun **1** (also **Kentucky bluegrass**) a meadow grass grown for fodder in North America. **2** a kind of traditional American country music played on banjos and guitars.

blue-green algae plural noun cyanobacteria.

blueish adjective variant spelling of **BLUISH**.

Blue Peter noun a blue flag with a white square in the centre, raised by a ship about to leave port.

blueprint noun **1** a design plan or other technical drawing. **2** something which acts as a plan or model: *a blueprint for an integrated transport system.*
– ORIGIN from the original process in which

prints were composed of white lines on a blue ground or of blue lines on a white ground.

blue ribbon noun (also **blue riband**) a blue silk ribbon given to the winner of a competition or as a mark of great distinction.

blues plural noun **1** (treated as sing. or pl.) a type of slow, sad music which originated among black Americans in the southern US. **2** (**the blues**) informal feelings of sadness or depression.
– DERIVATIVES **bluesy** adjective.
– ORIGIN from *blue devils* 'depression'.

blue-sky adjective informal creative or visionary and not yet having a practical use or application: *blue-sky research.*

bluesman noun (pl. **bluesmen**) a male performer of blues music.

bluestocking noun often derogatory an intellectual or literary woman.
– ORIGIN in reference to literary parties held in 18th-century London by three society ladies, where some of the men wore blue worsted stockings (as opposed to the more formal black silk ones).

blue tit noun a small songbird with a blue cap, greenish-blue back, and yellow underparts.

blue whale noun a bluish-grey whale which is the largest living animal.

bluey adjective almost or partly blue.

bluff¹ noun an attempt to deceive someone into believing that one knows or will do something. • verb try to deceive someone about what one knows, or about what one can or is going to do: *she knew him well enough to suspect that he was bluffing.*
– PHRASES **call someone's bluff** challenge someone to do what they are threatening to do, in the belief that they will not in fact be able to.
– DERIVATIVES **bluffer** noun.
– ORIGIN Dutch *bluffen* 'brag'.

bluff² adjective (of a person or their manner) frank and direct but in a good-natured way.
– DERIVATIVES **bluffness** noun.
– ORIGIN from **BLUFF³**.

bluff³ noun a steep cliff or slope.
– ORIGIN unknown.

bluish (also **blueish**) adjective having a blue tinge.

blunder noun a stupid or careless mistake. • verb **1** make a blunder. **2** move clumsily or as if unable to see.
– ORIGIN probably Scandinavian.

blunderbuss noun historical a gun with a short, wide barrel, firing balls or lead bullets.
– ORIGIN Dutch *donderbus* 'thunder gun'.

blunt adjective **1** lacking a sharp edge or point. **2** very frank and direct: *a blunt statement of fact.* • verb **1** make or become blunt. **2** make weaker or less effective: *this coming and going between home and school blunted his alertness.*
– DERIVATIVES **bluntly** adverb **bluntness** noun.
– ORIGIN perhaps Scandinavian.

blur verb (**blurs, blurring, blurred**) make or become unclear or less distinct: *tears blurred her vision.* • noun something that cannot be seen, heard, or recalled clearly.
– DERIVATIVES **blurry** adjective (**blurrier, blurriest**).

b

b

– ORIGIN perhaps from **BLEARY**.

blurb noun informal a short description written to promote a book, film, or other product.
– ORIGIN coined by the American humorist Gelett Burgess.

blurt verb say something suddenly and without careful thought.
– ORIGIN probably imitating the sound.

blush verb become red in the face through shyness or embarrassment. •noun **1** an instance of blushing. **2** literary a pink tinge.
– DERIVATIVES **blushing** adjective.
– ORIGIN Old English.

blusher noun chiefly Brit. a cosmetic used to give a warm colour to the cheeks.

bluster verb **1** talk in a loud or aggressive way with little effect. **2** (of wind or rain) blow or beat fiercely and noisily. •noun loud and empty talk.
– DERIVATIVES **blusterer** noun **blustery** adjective.
– ORIGIN imitating the sound.

BM abbreviation **1** Bachelor of Medicine. **2** British Museum.

BMA abbreviation British Medical Association.

BMI abbreviation body mass index, a measure of whether someone is over- or underweight calculated by dividing their weight in kilograms by the square of their height in metres.

B-movie noun a low-budget film supporting a main film in a cinema programme.

BMX abbreviation bicycle motocross (referring to bicycles designed for cross-country racing).

boa noun **1** a large snake which winds itself round its prey and crushes it to death. **2** a long, thin stole of feathers or fur worn around a woman's neck.
– ORIGIN Latin.

boar noun (pl. same or **boars**) **1** (also **wild boar**) a wild pig with tusks. **2** an uncastrated domestic male pig.
– ORIGIN Old English.

board noun **1** a long, thin, flat piece of wood used in building. **2** a thin, flat, rectangular piece of stiff material used for various purposes. **3** a group of people who control an organization. **4** the provision of regular meals in return for payment: *board and lodging.* •verb **1** get on or into a ship, aircraft, or other vehicle. **2** receive meals and accommodation in return for payment. **3** (of a pupil) live in school during term time. **4** (**board something up/over**) cover or seal something with pieces of wood.
– PHRASES **go by the board** (of a plan or principle) be abandoned or rejected. [from nautical use meaning 'fall overboard'.] **on board** on or in a ship, aircraft, or other vehicle. **take something on board** informal fully consider or accept a new idea or situation. **tread the boards** informal appear on stage as an actor.
– ORIGIN Old English.

boarder noun **1** a pupil who lives in school during term time. **2** a person who forces their way on to a ship in an attack.

board game noun a game that involves the movement of counters or other objects around a board.

boarding house noun a private house providing food and lodging for paying guests.

boarding school noun a school in which the pupils live during term time.

boardroom noun a room in which a board of directors meets regularly.

boardsailing noun another term for **WINDSURFING**.
– DERIVATIVES **boardsailor** noun.

boardwalk noun **1** a wooden walkway across sand or marshy ground. **2** N. Amer. a promenade along a beach or waterfront.

boast verb **1** talk about oneself with excessive pride. **2** possess an impressive or admirable feature: *the resort complex boasts ten pools.* •noun an act of boasting.
– DERIVATIVES **boaster** noun.
– ORIGIN unknown.

boastful adjective showing excessive pride in oneself.
– DERIVATIVES **boastfully** adverb **boastfulness** noun.

boat noun a vessel for travelling on water. •verb travel in a boat for pleasure.
– PHRASES **be in the same boat** informal be in the same difficult situation as others. **push the boat out** Brit. informal spend or celebrate extravagantly. **rock the boat** informal disturb an existing situation.
– DERIVATIVES **boating** noun **boatload** noun.
– ORIGIN Old English.

boatel noun **1** a waterside hotel with facilities for mooring boats. **2** a moored ship used as a hotel.
– ORIGIN blend of **BOAT** and **HOTEL**.

boater noun **1** a flat-topped straw hat with a brim. **2** a person who travels in a boat.

boathook noun a long pole with a hook and a spike at one end, used for moving boats.

boathouse noun a shed at the edge of a river or lake used for housing boats.

boatman noun (pl. **boatmen**) a person who provides transport by boat.

boat people plural noun refugees who have left a country by sea.

boatswain /boh-s'n/ (also **bo'sun** or **bosun**) noun a ship's officer in charge of equipment and the crew.
– ORIGIN from **BOAT** + **SWAIN**.

boat train noun a train scheduled to connect with the arrival or departure of a boat.

boatyard noun a place where boats are built or stored.

Bob noun (in phrase **Bob's your uncle**) Brit. informal said when a person thinks a task will be easy to complete.

bob[1] verb (**bobs**, **bobbing**, **bobbed**) **1** make or cause to make a quick, short movement up and down. **2** curtsy briefly. •noun a quick, short movement up and down.
– ORIGIN unknown.

bob[2] noun **1** a short hairstyle hanging evenly all round. **2** a weight on a pendulum, plumb line, or kite-tail. **3** a bobsleigh. •verb (**bobs**, **bobbing**, **bobbed**) cut hair in a bob.
– ORIGIN unknown.

bob[3] noun (pl. same) Brit. informal a shilling.
– ORIGIN unknown.

bobbin noun a cylinder, cone, or reel holding thread.

– ORIGIN French *bobine*.

bobble[1] **noun** a small ball made of strands of wool.
– DERIVATIVES **bobbly** adjective.
– ORIGIN from **BOB**[2].

bobble[2] **verb** informal move with an irregular bouncing motion.
– ORIGIN from **BOB**[1].

bobby noun (pl. **bobbies**) Brit. informal, dated a police officer.
– ORIGIN after Sir *Robert* Peel, the British Prime Minister who established the Metropolitan Police.

bobby pin noun N. Amer. & Austral./NZ a sprung hairpin or small clip.
– ORIGIN from **BOB**[2].

bobcat noun a small North American lynx with a striped and spotted coat and a short tail.
– ORIGIN from **BOB**[2], with reference to its short tail.

bobsleigh (N. Amer. **bobsled**) **noun** a sledge with brakes and a steering mechanism, used for racing down an ice-covered run.
– DERIVATIVES **bobsleighing** noun.

bobtail noun a docked tail of a horse or dog.

Boche /bosh/ **noun** (**the Boche**) informal, dated Germans, especially German soldiers.
– ORIGIN French soldiers' slang, 'rascal' (applied to Germans in World War I).

bod noun informal **1** a body. **2** chiefly Brit. a person.

bodacious /boh-**day**-shuhss/ **adjective** N. Amer. informal excellent, admirable, or attractive.
– ORIGIN perhaps a blend of **BOLD** and **AUDACIOUS**.

bode verb (**bode well/ill**) be a sign of a good or bad outcome: *sales trends in 2001 bode well for the year.*
– ORIGIN Old English, 'proclaim, foretell'.

bodega /buh-**day**-guh/ **noun** (in Spanish-speaking countries) a cellar or shop selling wine and food.
– ORIGIN Spanish.

bodge verb Brit. informal make or repair something badly or clumsily.
– DERIVATIVES **bodger** noun.
– ORIGIN alteration of **BOTCH**.

bodhi tree noun variant of **BO TREE**.

bodhrán /bow-**rahn**/ **noun** a shallow one-sided Irish drum.
– ORIGIN Irish.

bodice noun 1 the part of a woman's dress which is above the waist. **2** a woman's sleeveless undergarment, often laced at the front.
– ORIGIN formerly *bodies*, plural of **BODY**.

bodice-ripper noun informal, humorous a sexually explicit historical novel or film.

bodily adjective relating to the body. • **adverb** by taking hold of a person's body with force: *the blast lifted me bodily off the floor.*

bodkin noun a thick, blunt needle with a large eye, used for drawing tape or cord through a hem.
– ORIGIN perhaps Celtic.

body noun (pl. **bodies**) **1** the whole physical structure of a person or an animal. **2** the trunk of the body. **3** a corpse. **4** the main or central part: *the body of the plane filled with smoke.* **5** a mass or collection. **6** an organized group of people with a common function: *a regulatory body.* **7** technical an object: *the path taken by the falling body.* **8** a full flavour in wine. **9** fullness of a person's hair. **10** Brit. a woman's close-fitting stretch garment for the upper body. • **verb** (**bodies, bodying, bodied**) (**body something forth**) formal give physical form to something abstract.
– PHRASES **keep body and soul together** stay alive in difficult circumstances.
– DERIVATIVES **bodied** adjective.
– ORIGIN Old English.

body bag noun a bag used for carrying a corpse from a battlefield, accident, or the scene of a crime.

body blow noun 1 a heavy punch to the body. **2** a severe setback.

bodyboard noun a short, light surfboard ridden in a prone position.
– DERIVATIVES **bodyboarder** noun **bodyboarding** noun.

bodybuilder noun a person who strengthens and enlarges their muscles through exercise such as weightlifting.

body clock noun a person's biological clock.

body double noun a stand-in for a film actor during stunt or nude scenes.

bodyguard noun a person employed to protect an important or famous person.

body language noun the communication of one's feelings by the movement or position of one's body.

body politic noun the people of a nation or society considered as an organized group of citizens.

body shop noun chiefly N. Amer. a garage where repairs to the bodywork of vehicles are carried out.

bodysnatcher noun historical a person who illegally dug up corpses for dissection.

body stocking noun a woman's one-piece undergarment covering the torso and legs.

bodysuit noun another term for **BODY** (in sense 10).

bodysurf verb surf without using a board.

body warmer noun a sleeveless padded jacket.

bodywork noun the metal outer shell of a vehicle.

Boer /rhymes with *more* or *mower*/ **noun** an early Dutch and Huguenot settler of southern Africa. • **adjective** relating to the Boers.
– ORIGIN Dutch, 'farmer'.

boff N. Amer. informal **verb 1** hit someone. **2** have sex with someone. • **noun 1** a blow or punch. **2** an act of sexual intercourse.

boffin noun Brit. informal a scientist.
– ORIGIN unknown.

bog noun 1 an area of soft, wet, muddy ground. **2** Brit. informal a toilet. • **verb** (**be/get bogged down**) **1** be or become stuck in mud. **2** be prevented from progressing: *we are hopelessly bogged down in bureaucracy.*
– DERIVATIVES **bogginess** noun **boggy** adjective.
– ORIGIN Irish or Scottish Gaelic *bogach*.

bogey[1] Golf **noun** (pl. **bogeys**) a score of one stroke over par at a hole. • **verb** (**bogeys, bogeying, bogeyed**) play a hole in one stroke over par.
– ORIGIN perhaps from **BOGEY**[2], referring to the

Devil as an imaginary player.

bogey² (also **bogy**) noun (pl. **bogeys**) **1** an evil or mischievous spirit. **2** a cause of fear or alarm: *the bogey of recession.* **3** Brit. informal a piece of mucus in the nose.
– ORIGIN a former name for the Devil.

bogeyman (also **bogyman**) noun (pl. **bogeymen**) an evil spirit.

boggle verb informal **1** be astonished or baffled: *the mind boggles at the spectacle.* **2** (**boggle at**) hesitate to do something.
– ORIGIN probably related to **BOGEY²**.

bogie /boh-gi/ noun (pl. **bogies**) chiefly Brit. a supporting frame with wheels, fitted on a pivot beneath the end of a railway vehicle.
– ORIGIN unknown.

BOGOF /bog-off/ abbreviation buy one, get one free.

bog-standard adjective Brit. informal, derogatory ordinary; basic.

bogus adjective not genuine or true: *a bogus police officer.*
– ORIGIN unknown.

bogy noun (pl. **bogies**) variant spelling of **BOGEY²**.

Bohemian /boh-hee-mi-uhn/ noun **1** a person, especially an artist or writer, who does not follow accepted standards of behaviour. **2** a person from Bohemia, a region of the Czech Republic. •adjective **1** unconventional: *the Bohemian life of Montparnasse.* **2** relating to Bohemia.
– DERIVATIVES **Bohemianism** noun.
– ORIGIN sense 1 is from French *bohémien* 'Gypsy' (because Gypsies were thought to come from Bohemia).

boho /boh-hoh/ noun (pl. **bohos**) & adjective informal term for **BOHEMIAN** (in sense 1).

bohrium /bor-iuhm/ noun a very unstable chemical element made by high-energy atomic collisions.
– ORIGIN named after the Danish physicist Niels *Bohr.*

boil¹ verb **1** (with reference to a liquid) reach or cause to reach the temperature at which it bubbles and turns to vapour. **2** cook or be cooked in boiling water: *boil the potatoes for 20 minutes.* **3** seethe or bubble; be turbulent. **4** (of a person or emotion) be stirred up. **5** (**boil down to**) amount to: *everything boils down to money in the end.* •noun **1** the action of boiling; boiling point. **2** a state of great activity or excitement: *the team have gone off the boil.*
– ORIGIN from Latin *bullire* 'to bubble'.

boil² noun an inflamed pus-filled swelling on the skin.
– ORIGIN Old English.

boiled sweet noun Brit. a hard sweet made of boiled sugar.

boiler noun a fuel-burning device for heating water.

boilerplate noun **1** rolled steel plates for making boilers. **2** standardized pieces of writing for use as clauses in contracts. **3** N. Amer. stereotyped or clichéd writing.

boiler suit noun Brit. a one-piece suit worn as overalls for heavy manual work.

boiling adjective **1** at or near boiling point.

2 informal extremely hot.

boiling point noun the temperature at which a liquid boils.

boisterous adjective **1** noisy, lively, and high-spirited: *boisterous gangs of youths.* **2** literary (of weather or water) wild or stormy.
– DERIVATIVES **boisterously** adverb **boisterousness** noun.
– ORIGIN unknown.

bolas /boh-luhss/ noun (treated as sing. or pl.) (especially in South America) a missile consisting of a number of balls connected by cord, thrown to entangle the limbs of animals.
– ORIGIN Spanish and Portuguese, 'balls'.

bold adjective **1** confident and brave: *the company's bold new approach.* **2** (of a colour or design) strong or vivid. **3** dated lacking respect; impudent. **4** (of type) having thick strokes. •noun a bold typeface.
– PHRASES **as bold as brass** so confident as to be disrespectful.
– DERIVATIVES **boldly** adverb **boldness** noun.
– ORIGIN Old English.

bole noun a tree trunk.
– ORIGIN Old Norse.

bolero noun (pl. **boleros**) /buh-lair-oh/ **1** a Spanish dance in simple triple time. **2** /bol-uh-roh/ a woman's short open jacket.
– ORIGIN Spanish.

boletus /buh-lee-tuhss/ (also **bolete**) noun (pl. **boletuses**) a toadstool with pores rather than gills on the underside of the cap.
– ORIGIN Greek *bōlitēs.*

bolivar /boli-vah, bo-lee-vah/ noun the basic unit of money of Venezuela.
– ORIGIN named after Simon *Bolívar,* who liberated Venezuela from the Spanish.

Bolivian noun a person from Bolivia. •adjective relating to Bolivia.

boliviano /buh-liv-i-ah-noh/ noun (pl. **bolivianos**) the basic unit of money of Bolivia.
– ORIGIN Spanish, 'Bolivian'.

boll /rhymes with hole/ noun the rounded seed capsule of plants such as cotton.
– ORIGIN Dutch *bolle* 'rounded object'.

bollard noun **1** Brit. a short post used to prevent traffic from entering an area. **2** a short post on a ship or quayside for securing a rope.
– ORIGIN perhaps from Old Norse, 'bole'.

bollocking (also **ballocking**) noun Brit. vulgar slang a severe reprimand.
– DERIVATIVES **bollock** verb.

bollocks (also **ballocks**) plural noun Brit. vulgar slang **1** the testicles. **2** (treated as sing.) nonsense; rubbish.
– ORIGIN related to **BALL¹**.

Bollywood noun the Indian popular film industry, based in Bombay (now Mumbai).
– ORIGIN blend of *Bombay* and *Hollywood.*

bolo tie /boh-loh/ noun N. Amer. a tie consisting of a cord around the neck with a large ornamental fastening at the throat.
– ORIGIN alteration of *bola tie,* from its resemblance to the **BOLAS**.

Bolshevik /bol-shi-vik/ noun historical **1** a member of the majority group within the Russian Social Democratic Party, which seized power in the Revolution of 1917. **2** a person with revolutionary or politically radical views.

– DERIVATIVES **Bolshevism** noun **Bolshevist** noun.
– ORIGIN from Russian *bol'she* 'greater'.

bolshie (also **bolshy**) adjective Brit. informal hostile or uncooperative.
– ORIGIN from **BOLSHEVIK**.

bolster noun **1** a long, firm pillow. **2** a part in a tool, vehicle, or structure providing support or reducing friction. •**verb** support or strengthen: *the conservation zones should help to bolster tourism.*
– DERIVATIVES **bolsterer** noun.
– ORIGIN Old English.

bolt¹ noun **1** a long metal pin with a head that screws into a nut, used to fasten things together. **2** a bar that slides into a socket to fasten a door or window. **3** a flash of lightning. **4** a short, heavy arrow shot from a crossbow. **5** the sliding piece of the breech mechanism of a rifle. •**verb 1** fasten something with a bolt. **2** run away suddenly: *they bolted down the stairs.* **3** eat food quickly. **4** (of a plant) grow quickly upwards and stop flowering as seeds develop.
– PHRASES **a bolt from** (or **out of**) **the blue** a sudden and unexpected event. **bolt upright** with the back very straight. **have shot one's bolt** informal have done everything possible but still not succeeded. **make a bolt for** try to escape by running suddenly towards something.
– DERIVATIVES **bolter** noun.
– ORIGIN Old English.

bolt² noun a roll of fabric, originally as a measure.
– ORIGIN from **BOLT¹**.

bolt-hole noun chiefly Brit. a place where a person can escape to and hide.

bolus /boh-luhss/ noun (pl. **boluses**) **1** a small rounded mass of something, especially of food being swallowed. **2** a large pill used in veterinary medicine. **3** a single dose of a medicinal drug given all at once.
– ORIGIN Greek *bōlos* 'clod'.

bomb noun **1** a container of material capable of exploding or causing a fire. **2** (**the bomb**) nuclear weapons as a whole. **3** (**a bomb**) Brit. informal a large sum of money. •**verb 1** attack someone or something with a bomb or bombs. **2** Brit. informal move very quickly. **3** informal fail badly: *the film bombed, losing ten million dollars.*
– PHRASES **go down a bomb** Brit. informal be very successful. **go like a bomb** Brit. informal **1** be very successful. **2** move very fast.
– ORIGIN Italian *bomba*.

bombard verb /bom-bard/ **1** attack someone or something continuously with bombs or other missiles. **2** direct a continuous flow of questions or information at: *they were bombarded with complaints.* **3** Physics direct a stream of high-speed particles at a substance. •**noun** /bom-bard/ an early form of cannon, which fired a stone ball.
– DERIVATIVES **bombardment** noun.
– ORIGIN from Old French *bombarde* 'a cannon' or French *bombarder*.

bombardier /bom-buh-deer/ noun **1** a rank of non-commissioned officer in certain artillery regiments, equivalent to corporal. **2** a member of a bomber crew in the US air force

responsible for aiming and releasing bombs.
– ORIGIN French.

bombast /bom-bast/ noun language that sounds impressive but has little meaning.
– DERIVATIVES **bombastic** /bom-bas-tik/ adjective **bombastically** adverb.
– ORIGIN Old French *bombace* 'cotton used as padding'.

Bombay duck noun dried bummalo (fish) eaten as an accompaniment to curries.
– ORIGIN from *bummalo* (a South Asian fish), by association with the Indian city of *Bombay* (now Mumbai).

Bombay mix noun an Indian spiced snack consisting of lentils, peanuts, and deep-fried strands of gram flour.

bombazine /bom-buh-zeen/ noun a twill dress fabric of worsted and silk or cotton.
– ORIGIN from Latin *bombycinus* 'silken'.

bombe /bomb/ noun a frozen dome-shaped dessert.
– ORIGIN French, 'bomb'.

bombed adjective informal intoxicated by drink or drugs.

bomber noun **1** an aircraft that drops bombs. **2** a person who plants bombs, especially as a terrorist.

bomber jacket noun a short jacket gathered at the waist and cuffs by elasticated bands and having a zip front.

bombinate /bom-bin-ayt/ verb literary buzz; hum.
– ORIGIN Latin *bombinare*.

bombshell noun **1** something that comes as a great surprise or shock. **2** informal a very attractive woman.

bona fide /boh-nuh fy-di/ adjective genuine; real: *she was a bona fide expert.* •**adverb** chiefly Law without intention to deceive.
– ORIGIN Latin, 'with good faith'.

bona fides /boh-nuh fy-deez/ noun (treated as pl.) evidence proving that a person is what they claim to be; credentials.
– ORIGIN Latin, 'good faith'.

bonanza noun **1** a situation creating an increase in wealth, profit, or good luck: *a natural gas bonanza for Britain.* **2** a large amount of something desirable.
– ORIGIN Spanish, 'good weather, prosperity'.

bon appétit /bon a-puh-tee/ exclamation used to wish someone an enjoyable meal.
– ORIGIN French, 'good appetite'.

bonbon noun a sweet.
– ORIGIN from French *bon* 'good'.

bonce noun Brit. informal a person's head.
– ORIGIN unknown.

bond noun **1** a thing used to tie or fasten things together. **2** (**bonds**) ropes or chains used to hold someone prisoner. **3** a force or feeling that unites people: *the bonds between mother and daughter.* **4** an agreement with legal force. **5** a certificate issued by a government or a public company promising to repay borrowed money at a fixed rate of interest and at a specified time. **6** N. Amer. a sum of money paid as bail. **7** (also **chemical bond**) a strong force of attraction holding atoms together in a molecule. •**verb 1** join or be joined securely to something else. **2** form a relationship based on shared feelings or experiences: *you naturally*

bond with people in that sort of situation.
– PHRASES **in bond** (of goods) stored by customs until the importer pays the duty owing.
– ORIGIN variant of **BAND**[1].

bondage noun **1** the state of being a slave. **2** sexual practice that involves the tying up of one partner.
– ORIGIN from Old Norse *bóndi* 'tiller of the soil'; influenced by **BOND**.

bonded adjective **1** joined securely together. **2** bound by a legal agreement.

bond paper noun high-quality writing paper.

bondsman noun (pl. **bondsmen**) **1** a person who takes responsibility for the payment of a bond. **2** old use a slave.

bone noun **1** any of the pieces of hard, whitish tissue making up the skeleton in vertebrates. **2** the hard material of which bones consist. **3** a thing made or formerly made of bone, such as a strip of stiffening for an undergarment.
• verb **1** remove the bones from meat or fish before cooking. **2** (**bone up on**) informal study a subject intensively.
– PHRASES **bone of contention** a subject over which there is continuing disagreement. **close to the bone 1** (of a remark) accurate to the point of causing discomfort. **2** (of a joke or story) near the limit of decency. **have a bone to pick with someone** informal have reason to quarrel or be annoyed with someone. **in one's bones** felt or believed deeply or instinctively. **make no bones about** be straightforward in stating or dealing with something. **work one's fingers to the bone** work very hard.
– DERIVATIVES **boneless** adjective.
– ORIGIN Old English.

bone china noun white porcelain containing the mineral residue of burnt bones.

bone dry adjective very or completely dry.

bonehead noun informal a stupid person.

bone idle adjective very lazy.

bonemeal noun ground bones used as a fertilizer.

boner noun N. Amer. **1** informal a stupid mistake. **2** vulgar slang an erection of the penis.

boneshaker noun Brit. informal an old vehicle with poor suspension.

bonfire noun an open-air fire lit to burn rubbish or as a celebration.
– ORIGIN first referring to a fire on which bones were burnt.

Bonfire Night noun (in the UK) 5 November, on which fireworks are let off, bonfires lit, and figures representing Guy Fawkes burnt, in memory of the Gunpowder Plot of 1605.

bongo noun (pl. **bongos**) each of a pair of small drums, held between the knees and played with the fingers.
– ORIGIN Latin American Spanish *bongó*.

bonhomie /bon-uh-mee/ noun good-natured friendliness.
– DERIVATIVES **bonhomous** adjective.
– ORIGIN French.

bonito /buh-nee-toh/ noun (pl. **bonitos**) a small tuna with dark stripes.
– ORIGIN Spanish.

bonk informal verb **1** hit someone or something. **2** have sex. • noun **1** an act or sound of hitting

someone or something. **2** an act of sexual intercourse.
– ORIGIN imitating the sound of hitting.

bonkers adjective informal mad; crazy.
– ORIGIN unknown.

bon mot /bon moh/ noun (pl. **bons mots** pronunc. same or /bon **mohz**/) a clever or witty remark.
– ORIGIN French, 'good word'.

bonnet noun **1** a woman's or child's hat tied under the chin and with a brim framing the face. **2** a soft hat like a beret, worn by men and boys in Scotland. **3** Brit. the hinged metal canopy covering the engine of a motor vehicle.
– DERIVATIVES **bonneted** adjective.
– ORIGIN Old French *bonet*.

bonny (also **bonnie**) adjective (**bonnier**, **bonniest**) chiefly Scottish & N. English **1** attractive; healthy-looking. **2** sizeable; considerable: *she's worth a hundred thousand pounds, a bonny sum.*
– ORIGIN perhaps related to Old French *bon* 'good'.

bonsai /bon-sy/ noun the art of growing ornamental trees or shrubs in small pots so as to restrict their growth.
– ORIGIN Japanese, 'tray planting'.

bonus noun **1** a sum of money added to a person's wages for good performance. **2** an unexpected and extra benefit: *as an added bonus, prizewinners will have their adventures videoed.* **3** Brit. an extra dividend or issue paid to a company's shareholders.
– ORIGIN Latin, 'good'.

bon vivant /bon vee-von/ noun (pl. **bon vivants** or **bons vivants** pronunc. same) a person who enjoys a sociable and luxurious lifestyle.
– ORIGIN French, 'person living well'.

bon viveur /bon vee-ver/ noun (pl. **bon viveurs** or **bons viveurs** pronunc. same) another term for **BON VIVANT**.
– ORIGIN from French *bon* 'good' and *viveur* 'a living person'.

bon voyage /bon voy-yahzh/ exclamation have a good journey.
– ORIGIN French, 'good journey'.

bony adjective (**bonier**, **boniest**) **1** relating to or containing bones. **2** so thin that the bones can be seen.
– DERIVATIVES **boniness** noun.

bony fish noun a fish with a skeleton of bone rather than cartilage.

bonzer adjective Austral./NZ informal excellent.
– ORIGIN perhaps from **BONANZA**.

boo exclamation **1** said suddenly to surprise someone. **2** said to show disapproval or contempt. • verb (**boos**, **booing**, **booed**) say 'boo' to show disapproval.
– ORIGIN imitating the lowing of oxen.

boob[1] Brit. informal noun an embarrassing mistake. • verb make an embarrassing mistake.
– ORIGIN from **BOOBY**[1].

boob[2] noun informal a woman's breast.
– ORIGIN from **BOOBY**[2].

boo-boo noun informal a mistake.
– ORIGIN from **BOOB**[1].

boob tube noun informal **1** Brit. a woman's tight-fitting strapless top. **2** N. Amer. television; a television set.

booby[1] noun (pl. **boobies**) **1** informal a stupid

person. **2** a large tropical seabird of the gannet family.
– ORIGIN probably from Spanish *bobo*.

booby² noun (pl. **boobies**) informal a woman's breast.
– ORIGIN from dialect *bubby*.

booby prize noun a prize given to the person who comes last in a contest.

booby trap noun an object containing a hidden device that is designed to explode when someone touches it. •verb (**booby-trap**) place a booby trap in or on an object or area.

boodle noun informal money, especially that gained or spent dishonestly.
– ORIGIN from Dutch *boedel, boel* 'possessions, disorderly mass'.

boogie noun (also **boogie-woogie**) (pl. **boogies**) **1** a style of blues played on the piano with a strong, fast beat. **2** informal a dance to pop or rock music. •verb (**boogies, boogieing, boogied**) informal dance to pop or rock music.
– ORIGIN unknown.

boogie board noun a short, light surfboard ridden in a prone position.

book noun **1** a written or printed work consisting of pages fastened together along one side and bound in covers. **2** a main division of a literary work or of the Bible. **3** a bound set of blank sheets for writing in: *an exercise book*. **4** (**books**) a set of records or accounts. **5** a set of tickets, stamps, matches, etc., bound together. **6** a bookmaker's record of bets accepted and money paid out. •verb **1** reserve accommodation, a ticket, etc. **2** (**book in**) register one's arrival at a hotel. **3** engage a performer or guest for an event. **4** (**be booked up**) have all places or dates reserved. **5** make an official note of the details of someone who has broken a law or rule.
– PHRASES **bring someone to book** officially ask someone to explain their behaviour. **by the book** strictly according to the rules. **in someone's bad** (or **good**) **books** in disfavour (or favour) with someone. **on the books** contained in a list of members, employees, or clients. **take a leaf out of someone's book** imitate someone in a particular way. **throw the book at someone** informal charge or punish someone as severely as possible.
– DERIVATIVES **bookable** adjective **booker** noun **booking** noun.
– ORIGIN Old English, 'to grant by charter'.

bookbinder noun a person skilled in the craft of binding books.
– DERIVATIVES **bookbinding** noun.

bookcase noun an open cabinet containing shelves on which to keep books.

book club noun an organization which sells its members selected books at reduced prices.

bookend noun a support placed at the end of a row of books to keep them upright.

bookie noun (pl. **bookies**) informal a bookmaker.

bookish adjective **1** devoted to reading and studying: *he cut a bookish, schoolmasterly figure*. **2** (of language) literary in style.

bookkeeping noun the activity of keeping records of financial dealings.
– DERIVATIVES **bookkeeper** noun.

booklet noun a small, thin book with paper

covers.

bookmaker noun a person whose job is to take bets, calculate odds, and pay out winnings.

bookmark noun **1** a strip of leather or card used to mark a place in a book. **2** a record of the address of a computer file, Internet page, etc., enabling quick access by a user. •verb record the address of a computer file, Internet page, etc. for quick access.

bookshelf noun (pl. **bookshelves**) a shelf on which books can be stored.

bookshop noun a shop that sells books.

bookstall noun a kiosk where books, magazines, etc. are sold.

book value noun the value of a security or asset as entered in a firm's books. Often contrasted with **MARKET VALUE**.

bookworm noun informal a person who greatly enjoys reading.

Boolean /boo-li-uhn/ adjective (of a system of notation) used to represent logical operations by means of the binary digits 0 (false) and 1 (true), especially in computing and electronics.
– ORIGIN named after the English mathematician George *Boole*.

boom¹ noun **1** a loud, deep, resonant sound. **2** a period of great prosperity or rapid economic growth. •verb **1** make a loud, deep, resonant sound. **2** experience a period of rapid economic growth: *business is booming*.
– DERIVATIVES **boomy** adjective.
– ORIGIN imitating the sound.

boom³ noun **1** a pivoted spar to which the foot of a vessel's sail is attached. **2** a movable arm carrying a microphone or film camera. **3** a floating beam used to contain oil spills or to form a barrier across the mouth of a harbour.
– ORIGIN Dutch, 'beam, tree, pole'.

boomerang noun a curved flat piece of wood that can be thrown so as to return to the thrower, used by Australian Aboriginals as a hunting weapon.
– ORIGIN from an Aboriginal language.

boon noun **1** something that is helpful or beneficial: *the detailed information is a boon to researchers*. **2** old use a favour or request.
– ORIGIN Old Norse.

boon companion noun a close friend.
– ORIGIN first meaning 'good fellow': *boon* from Old French *bon* 'good'.

boondocks plural noun (**the boondocks**) N. Amer. informal rough or isolated country.
– ORIGIN Tagalog, 'mountain'.

boondoggle noun N. Amer. informal an unnecessary, wasteful, or fraudulent project.
– ORIGIN unknown.

boonies plural noun short for **BOONDOCKS**.

boor /bor, boor/ noun a rough and bad-mannered person.
– DERIVATIVES **boorish** adjective **boorishly** adverb **boorishness** noun.
– ORIGIN German *bŭr* or Dutch *boer* 'farmer'.

boost verb **1** help or encourage to increase or improve: *praise certainly boosts confidence*. **2** N. Amer. push someone from below. •noun **1** a source of help or encouragement. **2** an increase. **3** N. Amer. a push from below.
– ORIGIN unknown.

b

booster noun **1** a source of help or encouragement: *the rodeo is a morale booster for employees.* **2** a dose of a vaccine that increases or renews the effect of an earlier one. **3** the part of a rocket or spacecraft used to give acceleration after lift-off. **4** a device for increasing electrical voltage or signal strength.

boot[1] noun **1** an item of footwear covering the foot and ankle, and sometimes the lower leg. **2** Brit. a space at the back of a car for carrying luggage. **3** informal a hard kick. ● verb **1** kick something hard. **2** (**boot someone out**) informal force someone to leave. **3** start a computer and put it into a state of readiness for operation. [from **pull oneself up by one's bootstraps** (see **BOOTSTRAP**).]
– PHRASES **the boot is on the other foot** the situation is now reversed. **give someone** (or **get**) **the boot** informal dismiss someone (or be dismissed) from a job. **old boot** informal an ugly or disliked old woman. **put the boot in** Brit. informal attack someone when they are already in a vulnerable position.
– DERIVATIVES **bootable** adjective **booted** adjective.
– ORIGIN Old Norse, or Old French *bote*.

boot[2] noun (in phrase **to boot**) as well.
– ORIGIN Old English, 'advantage, remedy'.

bootblack noun a person who makes a living by polishing boots and shoes.

boot camp noun chiefly N. Amer. **1** a military training camp with very harsh discipline. **2** a military-style prison for young offenders.

boot-cut adjective (of jeans or other trousers) flared very slightly below the knee, so as to be worn over boots.

bootee (also **bootie**) noun **1** a baby's soft shoe. **2** a woman's short boot.

booth noun **1** an enclosed compartment allowing privacy when telephoning, voting, etc. **2** a small temporary structure used for selling goods or staging shows at a market or fair.
– ORIGIN from Old Norse, 'dwell'.

bootlace noun a cord or leather strip for lacing boots.

bootleg adjective (of alcoholic drink or a recording) made or distributed illegally. ● verb (**bootlegs, bootlegging, bootlegged**) make or distribute alcoholic drink or a recording illegally. ● noun an illegal musical recording.
– DERIVATIVES **bootlegger** noun.
– ORIGIN from the smugglers' practice of hiding bottles in their boots.

bootless adjective old use (of an action) not successful or useful.
– ORIGIN Old English, 'not able to be compensated for by payment'.

bootlicker noun informal a person who tries to gain favour by servile behaviour.

bootstrap noun a loop at the back of a boot, used to pull it on.
– PHRASES **pull oneself up by one's bootstraps** improve one's position by one's own efforts.

booty[1] noun valuable stolen goods.
– ORIGIN German *büte, buite* 'exchange, distribution'.

booty[2] noun N. Amer. informal a person's bottom.
– ORIGIN from **BODY** or **BOTTY**.

bootylicious adjective US informal sexually attractive.

booze informal noun alcoholic drink. ● verb drink large quantities of alcohol.
– DERIVATIVES **boozy** (**boozier, booziest**) adjective.
– ORIGIN from Dutch *büsen* 'drink to excess'.

boozer noun informal **1** a person who drinks large quantities of alcohol. **2** Brit. a pub.

booze-up noun Brit. informal a heavy drinking session.

bop[1] informal noun chiefly Brit. **1** a dance to pop music. **2** a social occasion with dancing. ● verb (**bops, bopping, bopped**) dance to pop music.
– DERIVATIVES **bopper** noun.
– ORIGIN shortening of **BEBOP**.

bop[2] informal verb (**bops, bopping, bopped**) hit or punch someone quickly. ● noun a quick blow or punch.
– ORIGIN imitating the sound.

boracic /buh-**rass**-ik/ adjective consisting of or containing boric acid.

borage /bo-rij/ noun a plant with bright blue flowers and hairy leaves.
– ORIGIN Latin *borrago*.

borax /bor-aks/ noun a white mineral that is a compound of boron, used in making glass and as a flux in soldering or smelting.
– ORIGIN Latin.

Bordeaux /bor-**doh**/ noun (pl. same /bor-**dohz**/) a wine from the Bordeaux region of SW France.

bordello /bor-**del**-oh/ noun (pl. **bordellos**) literary a brothel.
– ORIGIN Italian.

border noun **1** a boundary between two countries or other areas. **2** a decorative band around the edge of something. **3** a strip of ground along the edge of a lawn for planting flowers or shrubs. ● verb **1** form a border around or along: *a pool bordered by palm trees.* **2** (of a country or area) be next to another. **3** (**border on**) come close to being: *he fought the war with a ruthlessness that bordered on the maniacal.*
– ORIGIN Old French *bordeure*.

borderline noun a boundary. ● adjective on the boundary between two states or categories: *references may be requested in borderline cases.*

bore[1] verb **1** make a hole in something with a drill or other tool. **2** hollow out a gun barrel or other tube. ● noun **1** the hollow part inside a gun barrel or other tube. **2** the diameter of a bore: *a small-bore rifle.*
– DERIVATIVES **borer** noun.
– ORIGIN Old English.

bore[2] noun a dull and uninteresting person or activity. ● verb make someone feel tired and uninterested by dull talk or behaviour.
– DERIVATIVES **boring** adjective.
– ORIGIN unknown.

bore[3] (also **tidal bore**) noun a steep-fronted wave caused by the meeting of two tides or by a tide rushing up a narrow estuary.
– ORIGIN perhaps from Old Norse.

bore[4] past of **BEAR**[1].

boreal /bor-i-uhl/ adjective chiefly technical of the North or northern regions.
– ORIGIN from Latin *Boreas*, the god of the north wind.

bored adjective feeling tired and impatient because one is doing something dull or one has nothing to do.

USAGE: You should use **bored by** or **bored with** rather than **bored of**. Although **bored of** is often used informally, it is not acceptable in standard written English.

boredom noun the state of being bored.

borehole noun a deep, narrow hole in the ground made to find water or oil.

boric /bor-ik/ adjective Chemistry of boron.

boric acid noun a compound derived from borax, used as a mild antiseptic.

borlotti bean /bor-lot-i/ noun a type of kidney bean with a pink speckled skin that turns brown when cooked.
- ORIGIN Italian *borlotti*, plural of *borlotto* 'kidney bean'.

born adjective 1 existing as a result of birth. 2 (**-born**) having a particular nationality: *a German-born philosopher.* 3 having a natural ability to do a particular job: *a born engineer.* 4 (**born of**) existing as a result of: *a confidence born of success.*
- PHRASES **born and bred** by birth and upbringing. **in all one's born days** throughout one's life (used for emphasis). **I (or she, etc.) wasn't born yesterday** I am (or she, etc. is) not foolish or easily deceived.
- ORIGIN Old English, past participle of BEAR[1].

USAGE: Do not confuse **born**, which means 'existing as a result of birth' (*she was born in Hull*) with **borne**, which is the past participle of bear and means 'carried' (*the coffin was borne by eight soldiers; water-borne bacteria*).

born-again adjective 1 (of a person) newly converted to a personal faith in Jesus. 2 newly converted to and very enthusiastic about a cause: *born-again environmentalists.*

borne past participle of BEAR[1]. adjective (**-borne**) carried by the thing specified: *water-borne bacteria.*

Bornean /bor-ni-uhn/ noun a person from Borneo. • adjective relating to Borneo.

boron /bor-on/ noun a crystalline chemical element used in making alloy steel and in nuclear reactors.
- ORIGIN from BORAX.

borough /rhymes with thorough/ noun 1 Brit. a town (as distinct from a city) with a corporation and privileges granted by a royal charter. 2 an administrative division of London or of New York City. 3 a municipal corporation in certain US states.
- ORIGIN Old English, 'fortress, citadel'.

borrow verb 1 take and use something belonging to someone else with the intention of returning it. 2 have money on loan from a person or bank. 3 take and use a word or idea from another language or person.
- PHRASES **be (living) on borrowed time** be surviving beyond the time that one was expected to do so.
- DERIVATIVES **borrower** noun.
- ORIGIN Old English.

USAGE: On the confusion of **borrow** and **lend**, see the note at LEND.

borscht /borsht/ (also **borsch** /borsh/) noun a Russian or Polish soup made with beetroot.
- ORIGIN Russian *borshch.*

borstal /bor-st'l/ noun Brit. historical a prison for young offenders.
- ORIGIN named after the English village of *Borstal.*

borzoi /bor-zoy/ noun (pl. **borzois**) a breed of large Russian wolfhound with a narrow head and silky coat.
- ORIGIN from Russian *borzyĭ* 'swift'.

bosh noun informal nonsense.
- ORIGIN Turkish *bos* 'empty, worthless'.

bosky /bos-ki/ adjective literary covered by trees or bushes.
- ORIGIN from BUSH[1].

Bosnian /boz-ni-uhn/ noun a person from Bosnia. • adjective relating to Bosnia.

bosom noun 1 a woman's breasts or chest. 2 loving care or protection: *he went home to the bosom of his family.* • adjective (of a friend) very close.
- DERIVATIVES **bosomy** adjective.
- ORIGIN Old English.

boss[1] informal noun a person who is in charge of a worker or organization. • verb give orders in a domineering way: *now you're an adult I can't boss you around.* • adjective N. Amer. excellent.
- ORIGIN Dutch *baas* 'master'.

boss[2] noun 1 a projecting knob or stud, especially on the centre of a shield. 2 an ornamental carving at the point where the ribs in a ceiling cross.
- ORIGIN Old French *boce.*

bossa nova /bos-suh noh-vuh/ noun a Brazilian dance like the samba.
- ORIGIN Portuguese, 'new tendency'.

boss-eyed adjective Brit. informal cross-eyed or squinting.
- ORIGIN unknown.

bossy adjective (**bossier, bossiest**) informal fond of giving orders; domineering.
- DERIVATIVES **bossily** adverb **bossiness** noun.

bosun /boh-suhn/ (also **bo'sun**) noun variant spelling of BOATSWAIN.

bot noun an autonomous program on a computer network which can interact with systems or users.
- ORIGIN from ROBOT.

botanical adjective relating to botany. • noun a substance obtained from a plant and used in cosmetic and medicinal products.
- DERIVATIVES **botanically** adverb.

botanical garden (also **botanic garden**) noun a place where plants are grown for scientific study and display to the public.

botany /bot-uh-ni/ noun the scientific study of plants.
- DERIVATIVES **botanic** adjective **botanist** noun.
- ORIGIN from Greek *botanē* 'plant'.

botch informal verb perform an action or task badly or carelessly. • noun (also **botch-up**) a badly performed action or task.
- DERIVATIVES **botcher** noun.
- ORIGIN unknown.

both predeterminer, determiner, & pronoun two people or things, regarded together. • adverb applying equally to each of two alternatives.
- PHRASES **have it both ways** benefit from two

conflicting ways of thinking or behaving.
– ORIGIN Old Norse.

USAGE: When **both** is used with **and**, the structures following the two words should be symmetrical: *both at home and at work* is better than *both at home and work*.

bother verb **1** take the trouble to do something. **2** worry, disturb, or upset someone. **3** (**bother with/about**) feel concern about or interest in: *she has never bothered about boys before.* •noun **1** trouble or effort. **2** (**a bother**) a cause of trouble or annoyance. •exclamation Brit. used to express mild irritation.
– ORIGIN Anglo-Irish.

bothersome adjective troublesome; annoying.

bothy /bo-thi/ (also **bothie**) noun (pl. **bothies**) (in Scotland) a small hut or cottage for farm labourers or as a mountain refuge.
– ORIGIN related to Gaelic *both*, *bothan*.

Botox /boh-toks/ noun trademark a drug prepared from botulin (the toxin involved in botulism), used cosmetically to remove wrinkles by temporarily paralysing the muscles of the face.
– DERIVATIVES **Botoxed** adjective.
– ORIGIN from *bo(tulinum) tox(in)*.

bo tree /boh/ (also **bodhi tree**) noun a fig tree native to India and SE Asia, regarded as sacred by Buddhists because it was under such a tree that Buddha's enlightenment took place.
– ORIGIN Sinhalese.

Botswanan /bot-swah-nuhn/ noun a person from Botswana, a country of southern Africa. •adjective relating to Botswana.

bottle noun **1** a container with a narrow neck, used for storing liquids. **2** Brit. informal the courage or confidence to do something: *I lost my bottle completely and ran.* •verb **1** put liquid in bottles. **2** (**bottle something up**) repress or hide one's feelings. **3** (**bottle out**) Brit. informal lose one's nerve and decide not to do something. **4** informal hit someone with a glass bottle.
– PHRASES **hit the bottle** informal start to drink alcohol heavily.
– ORIGIN from Latin *butticula* 'small cask'.

bottle bank noun Brit. a place where used glass bottles may be left for recycling.

bottle-feed verb (**bottle-feeds, bottle-feeding, bottle-fed**) feed a baby with milk from a bottle.

bottle green adjective dark green.

bottleneck noun **1** a narrow section of road where traffic flow is restricted. **2** a cause of delay in a process or system.

bottom noun **1** the lowest point or part. **2** the furthest point or part. **3** the lowest position in a competition or ranking: *life at the bottom of society.* **4** chiefly Brit. a person's buttocks. **5** (also **bottoms**) the lower half of a two-piece garment. •adjective in the lowest or furthest position. •verb **1** (**bottom out**) reach the lowest point before stabilizing or improving: *the property market has probably bottomed out.* **2** (of a ship) touch the bottom of the sea.
– PHRASES **at bottom** basically. **be at the bottom of** be the basic cause of something. **the bottom falls** (or **drops**) **out** something suddenly fails or collapses. **bottoms up!** informal said as a toast before drinking. **get to the bottom of** find an explanation for a mystery.
– DERIVATIVES **bottomless** adjective **bottommost** adjective.
– ORIGIN Old English.

bottom drawer noun Brit. dated household linen stored by a woman in preparation for her marriage.

bottom feeder noun **1** any marine creature that lives on the seabed and feeds by scavenging. **2** N. Amer. informal a member of a group of very low social status who survives by any means possible.

bottom line noun informal **1** the final total of an account or balance sheet. **2** the basic and most important factor: *the bottom line is that the economy is recovering.*

botty noun (pl. **botties**) Brit. informal a person's bottom.

botulism /bot-yuu-li-z'm/ noun food poisoning caused by a bacterium growing on preserved foods that have not been properly sterilized.
– ORIGIN German *Botulismus*, originally 'sausage poisoning'.

bouclé /boo-klay/ noun yarn with a looped or curled strand.
– ORIGIN French, 'buckled, curled'.

boudin /boo-dan/ noun (pl. same) a French type of black pudding.
– ORIGIN French.

boudoir /boo-dwar/ noun a woman's bedroom or small private room.
– ORIGIN French, 'sulking place'.

bouffant /boo-fon/ adjective (of hair) styled so as to stand out from the head in a rounded shape. •noun a bouffant hairstyle.
– ORIGIN French, 'swelling'.

bougainvillea /boo-guhn-**vil**-li-uh/ (also **bougainvillaea**) noun a tropical climbing plant with brightly coloured modified leaves (bracts) surrounding the flowers.
– ORIGIN named after the French explorer L. A. de *Bougainville*.

bough noun a main branch of a tree.
– ORIGIN Old English 'bough or shoulder'.

bought past and past participle of **BUY**.

USAGE: On the confusion of **bought** and **brought**, see the note at **BROUGHT**.

bouillabaisse /boo-yuh-bayss/ noun a rich fish stew or soup, as made originally in Provence.
– ORIGIN French.

bouillon /boo-yon/ noun thin soup or stock made by stewing meat, fish, or vegetables.
– ORIGIN from French *bouillir* 'to boil'.

boulder noun a large rock.
– DERIVATIVES **bouldery** adjective.
– ORIGIN Scandinavian.

boulder clay noun clay containing many large stones, formed when melting glaciers deposit such material.

boule /bool/ (also **boules** pronunc. same) noun a French game similar to bowls, played with metal balls.
– ORIGIN French, 'bowl'.

boulevard /boo-luh-vard/ noun a wide street, typically one lined with trees.
– ORIGIN French, 'rampart', later 'a promenade on the site of a rampart'.

b

boulevardier /boo-luh-**vahd**-yay/ noun a wealthy, fashionable person who is fond of social activities.
– ORIGIN French, 'person who frequents boulevards'.

boulle /bool/ (also **buhl**) noun brass, tortoiseshell, or other material used for inlaying furniture.
– ORIGIN from the name of the French cabinetmaker André *Boulle*.

bounce verb **1** move quickly up or away from a surface after hitting it. **2** move or jump up and down repeatedly. **3** (**bounce back**) recover well after a setback. **4** informal (of a cheque) be returned by a bank when there is not enough money in an account for it to be paid. **5** Brit. informal put pressure on someone to do something. • noun **1** an act of bouncing. **2** energy or self-confidence: *the bounce was back in Jane's step.* **3** health and body in a person's hair.
– ORIGIN perhaps from German *bunsen* 'beat' or Dutch *bons* 'a thump'.

bouncer noun a person employed by a nightclub, pub, etc. to prevent troublemakers entering or to remove them from the building.

bouncing adjective (of a baby) lively and healthy.

bouncy adjective (**bouncier**, **bounciest**) **1** able to bounce or making something bounce: *a bouncy ball.* **2** confident and lively.
– DERIVATIVES **bouncily** adverb **bounciness** noun.

bound¹ verb walk or run with leaping strides. • noun a leaping movement towards or over something.
– ORIGIN French *bondir* 'resound', later 'rebound'.

bound² noun a boundary or limit: *her grief knew no bounds.* • verb **1** form the boundary of something. **2** place something within limits.
– PHRASES **out of bounds 1** (in sport) beyond the field of play. **2** beyond permitted limits.
– ORIGIN from Latin *bodina*.

bound³ adjective going towards somewhere: *a train bound for Edinburgh.*
– ORIGIN from Old Norse, 'get ready'.

bound⁴ past and past participle of **BIND**. adjective **1** (**-bound**) restricted to a place or by a situation: *his job kept him city-bound.* **2** certain to be, do, or have: *there's bound to be a pub open somewhere.* **3** obliged to do something.
– PHRASES **I'll be bound** Brit. I am sure.

boundary noun (pl. **boundaries**) **1** a line marking the limits of an area. **2** a limit, especially of a subject or area of activity. **3** Cricket a hit crossing the limits of the field, scoring four or six runs.
– ORIGIN from **BOUND²**.

bounden /**bown**-d'n/ adjective (in phrase **one's bounden duty**) a responsibility that cannot be ignored; something one feels morally obliged to do.
– ORIGIN old-fashioned past participle of **BIND**.

bounder noun Brit. informal, dated a dishonourable man.

boundless adjective unlimited or immense: *a man of boundless enthusiasm.*

bounteous /**bown**-ti-uhss/ adjective old use bountiful.
– ORIGIN from Old French *bontif* 'benevolent'.

bountiful adjective **1** large in quantity; abundant: *bountiful crops.* **2** giving generously.
– DERIVATIVES **bountifully** adverb.

bounty noun (pl. **bounties**) **1** literary something given or occurring in generous amounts. **2** literary generosity: *people along the Nile depend on its bounty.* **3** a reward paid for killing or capturing someone. **4** historical a sum paid by the state to encourage trade.
– ORIGIN Old French *bonte* 'goodness'.

bounty hunter noun a person who pursues a criminal for a reward.

bouquet /boo-**kay**, boh-**kay**/ noun **1** a bunch of flowers. **2** the characteristic scent of a wine or perfume.
– ORIGIN French.

bouquet garni /boo-kay gah-ni/ noun (pl. **bouquets garnis**) a bunch of herbs used for flavouring a stew or soup.
– ORIGIN French, 'garnished bouquet'.

bourbon /**ber**-buhn/ noun an American whisky distilled from maize and rye.
– ORIGIN named after *Bourbon* County, Kentucky.

bourgeois /**boor**-zhwah/ (also **bourgeoise**) /**boor**-zhwahz/ adjective **1** belonging to or characteristic of the middle class, especially in being materialistic or conventional: *they are the epitome of bourgeois complacency.* **2** (in Marxism) capitalist. • noun (pl. same) a bourgeois person.
– ORIGIN French, from Latin *burgus* 'castle, fortified town'.

bourgeoisie /boor-zhwah-**zee**/ noun (treated as sing. or pl.) **1** the middle class. **2** (in Marxism) the capitalist class.
– ORIGIN French.

bourn¹ /born/ noun dialect a small stream.
– ORIGIN southern English variant of **BURN²**.

bourn² /born/ (also **bourne**) noun literary a boundary or limit.
– ORIGIN French *borne*.

bourrée /boo-ray/ noun a lively French dance like a gavotte.
– ORIGIN French, 'faggot of twigs' (the dance being performed around a twig fire).

bourse /rhymes with *course*/ noun a stock market in a non-English-speaking country, especially in France.
– ORIGIN French, 'purse'.

bout /bowt/ noun **1** a short period of illness or intense activity. **2** a wrestling or boxing match.
– ORIGIN from dialect *bought* 'bend, loop'.

boutique /boo-**teek**/ noun a small shop selling fashionable clothes.
– ORIGIN French.

boutique hotel noun a small stylish hotel situated in a fashionable location in a town or city.

bouzouki /bu-**zoo**-ki/ noun (pl. **bouzoukis**) a long-necked Greek form of mandolin.
– ORIGIN modern Greek *mpouzouki*.

bovine /**boh**-vyn/ adjective **1** relating to cattle. **2** sluggish or stupid: *a look of bovine contentment.* • noun an animal of the cattle group, which also includes buffaloes and bison.
– DERIVATIVES **bovinely** adverb.
– ORIGIN Latin *bovinus*.

b

bovine spongiform encephalopathy noun see **BSE**.

bow¹ /rhymes with toe/ noun **1** a knot tied with two loops and two loose ends. **2** a weapon for shooting arrows, made of curved wood joined at both ends by a taut string. **3** a rod with horsehair stretched along its length, used for playing some stringed instruments. •verb play a stringed instrument using a bow.
– PHRASES **have another string to one's bow** Brit. have a further resource available.
– ORIGIN Old English, 'bend, bow, arch'.

bow² /rhymes with cow/ verb **1** bend the head or upper body as a sign of respect, greeting, or shame. **2** bend with age or under a heavy weight. **3** give in to pressure: *the company bowed to public pressure on GM crops.* **4** (**bow out**) withdraw or retire from an activity. •noun an act of bowing.
– PHRASES **bow and scrape** behave in a servile way. **take a bow** acknowledge applause by bowing.
– ORIGIN Old English, 'bend, stoop'.

bow³ /rhymes with cow/ (also **bows**) noun the front end of a ship.
– ORIGIN German *boog* or Dutch *boeg* 'shoulder or ship's bow'.

bowdlerize (or **bowdlerise**) /bowd-luh-ryz/ verb remove indecent or offensive material from a written work.
– ORIGIN from the name of Dr Thomas *Bowdler*, who published a censored edition of Shakespeare.

bowel /rhymes with towel/ noun **1** the intestine. **2** (**bowels**) the deepest inner parts of something.
– ORIGIN Latin *botellus* 'little sausage'.

bowel movement noun an act of defecation.

bower /rhymes with tower/ noun **1** a pleasant shady place under climbing plants or trees. **2** literary a woman's private room.
– ORIGIN Old English.

bowerbird noun an Australasian bird noted for the male's habit of building an elaborate structure to attract the female.

bowie knife /rhymes with snowy/ noun a long knife with a blade double-edged at the point.
– ORIGIN named after the American frontiersman Jim *Bowie*.

bowl¹ noun **1** a round, deep dish or basin. **2** a rounded, hollow part of an object. **3** a hollow or depression in the landscape. **4** chiefly N. Amer. a stadium for sporting or musical events.
– ORIGIN Old English.

bowl² verb **1** roll a round object along the ground. **2** Brit. move rapidly and smoothly: *we bowled along the country roads.* **3** (**bowl someone over**) knock someone down. **4** (**bowl someone over**) informal greatly impress or overwhelm someone. **5** Cricket (of a bowler) throw the ball towards the wicket, or dismiss a batsman by hitting the wicket with a bowled ball. •noun a large heavy ball used in bowls, tenpin bowling, or skittles.
– ORIGIN from Latin *bulla* 'bubble'.

bow-legged adjective having legs that curve outwards at the knee.

bowler¹ noun **1** Cricket a member of the fielding side who bowls. **2** a player at bowls, tenpin bowling, or skittles.

bowler² noun a man's hard felt hat with a round dome-shaped crown.
– ORIGIN named after the English hatter William *Bowler*.

bowline /boh-lin/ noun **1** a simple knot for forming a non-slipping loop at the end of a rope. **2** a rope attaching the windward side of a square sail to a ship's bow.

bowling noun the game of bowls, tenpin bowling, or skittles.

bowling alley noun a long narrow track along which balls are rolled in skittles or tenpin bowling.

bowling green noun an area of closely mown grass on which the game of bowls is played.

bowls /bohlz/ plural noun (treated as sing.) a game played with wooden bowls, the object of which is to roll one's bowl as close as possible to a small white ball (the jack).

bowman noun (pl. **bowmen**) an archer.

bowsprit /boh-sprit/ noun a pole projecting from a ship's bow, to which the ropes supporting the front mast are fastened.

bow tie noun a necktie in the form of a bow.

bow window noun a curved bay window.

box¹ noun **1** a container with a flat base and sides and a lid. **2** an area enclosed within straight lines on a page or computer screen. **3** an enclosed area reserved for a group of people in a theatre or sports ground, or for witnesses or the jury in a law court. **4** (**the box**) informal, chiefly Brit. television. **5** a service at a newspaper office for receiving replies to an advertisement, or at a post office for keeping letters until collected. **6** Brit. a small country house used when shooting or fishing. **7** (**the box**) Football the penalty area. **8** Brit. a shield for protecting a man's genitals in sport. •verb **1** put something in a box. **2** (**box someone in**) restrict or confine someone.
– PHRASES **think outside the box** informal have original or creative ideas.
– ORIGIN Old English.

box² verb fight an opponent with the fists in padded gloves as a sport. •noun a slap on the side of a person's head.
– PHRASES **box clever** Brit. informal outwit someone. **box someone's ears** slap someone on the side of the head.
– DERIVATIVES **boxing** noun.
– ORIGIN unknown.

box³ noun an evergreen shrub with small glossy leaves and hard wood.
– ORIGIN Greek *puxos*.

boxcar noun N. Amer. an enclosed railway freight wagon.

boxer noun **1** a person who boxes as a sport. **2** a medium-sized breed of dog with a smooth brown coat and pug-like face.

boxer shorts (also **boxers**) plural noun men's loose-fitting underpants resembling shorts.

box girder noun a hollow girder that is square or rectangular in cross section.

Boxing Day noun Brit. a public holiday on the first day after Christmas Day.
– ORIGIN from the former custom of giving tradespeople a Christmas box (gift) on this day.

box junction noun Brit. a road area at a junction marked with a yellow grid, which a vehicle should enter only if its exit is clear.

box number noun a number identifying an advertisement in a newspaper, used as an address for replies.

box office noun a place at a theatre, cinema, etc. where tickets are sold.

box pleat noun a pleat consisting of two parallel creases forming a raised band.

box room noun Brit. a very small room.

boxy adjective (**boxier, boxiest**) **1** squarish in shape. **2** (of a room or space) cramped.

boy noun **1** a male child or youth. **2** a man, especially one who comes from a particular place or who does a particular job: *the inspector was a local boy.* **3** (**boys**) informal men who mix socially or belong to a particular group. •**exclamation** used to express admiration, surprise, etc.
– DERIVATIVES **boyhood** noun **boyish** adjective.
– ORIGIN unknown.

boyar /boh-**yah**/ noun a member of the old aristocracy in Russia, next in rank to a prince.
– ORIGIN Russian *boyarin* 'grandee'.

boycott verb refuse to deal with a person, organization, or country as a punishment or protest. •**noun** an act of boycotting.
– ORIGIN from Captain Charles C. *Boycott*, an Irish land agent so treated in 1880 in an attempt to get rents reduced.

boyfriend noun a person's regular male companion in a romantic or sexual relationship.

Boyle's law noun Chemistry a law stating that the pressure of a given mass of an ideal gas is inversely proportional to its volume at a constant temperature.
– ORIGIN named after the English scientist Robert *Boyle*.

Boy Scout noun North American or old-fashioned term for **scout** (in sense 3).

boysenberry /**boy**-z'n-buh-ri, **boy**-z'n-be-ri/ noun (pl. **boysenberries**) a large red edible blackberry-like fruit.
– ORIGIN named after the American horticulturalist Robert *Boysen*.

bozo /**boh**-zoh/ noun (pl. **bozos**) informal, chiefly N. Amer. a stupid or insignificant man.
– ORIGIN unknown.

BP abbreviation **1** before the present (era). **2** blood pressure.

Bq abbreviation becquerel.

Br symbol the chemical element bromine.

Br. abbreviation **1** British. **2** (in religious orders) Brother.

bra noun a woman's undergarment worn to support the breasts.
– DERIVATIVES **braless** adjective.
– ORIGIN short for **BRASSIERE**.

brace noun **1** a strengthening or supporting device or part. **2** (**braces**) Brit. a pair of straps passing over the shoulders and fastening to the top of trousers to hold them up. **3** a wire device fitted in the mouth to straighten the teeth. **4** (pl. same) a pair of things: *a brace of grouse.* **5** either of two connecting marks { and }, used in printing and music. **6** (also **brace and bit**) a drilling tool with a crank handle and a socket to hold a bit. •**verb 1** make something stronger or firmer with a brace. **2** press one's

body firmly against something to stay balanced. **3** prepare for something demanding or unpleasant: *he braced himself for the interview.*
– ORIGIN from Latin *bracchium* 'arm'.

bracelet noun an ornamental band or chain worn on the wrist or arm.
– ORIGIN from Old French *bras* 'arm'.

brachiopod /**bra**-ki-uh-pod/ noun an invertebrate sea creature with two hinged shells and tentacles used for filter-feeding.
– ORIGIN from Greek *brakhiōn* 'arm' + *pous* 'foot'.

brachiosaurus /bra-ki-oh-**sor**-uhss/ noun a huge plant-eating dinosaur with forelegs much longer than the hind legs.
– ORIGIN from Greek *brakhiōn* 'arm' + *sauros* 'lizard'.

bracing adjective refreshing; invigorating: *bracing winds.*
– DERIVATIVES **bracingly** adverb.

bracken noun a tall fern with coarse fronds.
– ORIGIN Scandinavian.

bracket noun **1** each of a pair of marks ( ) [ ] { } < > used to enclose words or figures. **2** a category of similar people or things: *a high income bracket.* **3** a right-angled support projecting from a wall. •**verb** (**brackets, bracketing, bracketed**) **1** enclose words or figures in brackets. **2** place in the same category: *being bracketed with the world's greatest cricketer was thrill enough.* **3** hold or attach something by means of a bracket.
– ORIGIN from Latin *bracae* 'breeches'.

brackish adjective (of water) slightly salty.
– ORIGIN from German, Dutch *brac.*

bract noun a modified leaf with a flower in the angle where it meets the stem.
– ORIGIN Latin *bractea* 'thin metal plate'.

brad noun a nail with a rectangular cross section and a small head.
– ORIGIN Old Norse.

bradawl /**brad**-awl/ noun a tool for boring holes, resembling a screwdriver.

brae /bray/ noun Scottish a steep bank or hillside.
– ORIGIN Old Norse, 'eyelash'.

brag verb (**brags, bragging, bragged**) say something boastfully. •**noun 1** a boastful statement. **2** a simplified form of poker.
– ORIGIN unknown.

braggadocio /brag-uh-**doh**-chi-oh/ noun boastful or arrogant behaviour.
– ORIGIN from *Braggadocchio*, a boastful character in Spenser's *The Faerie Queene.*

braggart /**brag**-gert/ noun a person who boasts about their achievements or possessions.
– ORIGIN from French *braguer* 'to brag'.

Brahman /**brah**-muhn/ noun (pl. **Brahmans**) **1** (also **Brahmin**) /**brah**-min/ a member of the highest Hindu caste, that of the priesthood. **2** (also **Brahma**) (in Hinduism) the ultimate reality underlying all phenomena.
– ORIGIN Sanskrit.

Brahmin /**brah**-min/ noun **1** variant spelling of **Brahman** (in sense 1). **2** US a socially or culturally superior person.
– DERIVATIVES **Brahminical** adjective.

braid noun **1** threads woven into a decorative band for trimming garments. **2** chiefly N. Amer. a

plaited length of hair. • verb 1 plait hair. 2 edge or trim a garment with braid.
– ORIGIN Old English, 'make a sudden movement' or 'interweave'.

Braille /brayl/ noun a written language for the blind, in which characters are represented by patterns of raised dots.
– ORIGIN named after the blind French educationist Louis *Braille*.

brain noun 1 an organ of soft nervous tissue inside the skull, functioning as the coordinating centre of the nervous system. 2 the ability to use one's intelligence: *she's got brains, that child.* 3 (**the brains**) informal a clever person who is the main organizer in a group. • verb informal hit someone hard on the head with an object.
– PHRASES **have something on the brain** informal be obsessed with something.
– DERIVATIVES **brained** adjective.
– ORIGIN Old English.

brainbox noun Brit. informal a very clever person.

brainchild noun (pl. **brainchildren**) informal an idea or invention originated by a particular person.

brain-dead adjective 1 having suffered brain death. 2 informal very stupid.

brain death noun irreversible brain damage causing the end of independent breathing.

brain drain noun informal the emigration of highly skilled or qualified people from a country.

brainless adjective stupid; very foolish.

brainstem noun the central trunk of the brain, consisting of the medulla oblongata, pons, and midbrain.

brainstorm noun 1 Brit. informal a moment in which one is suddenly unable to think clearly. 2 a group discussion to produce ideas. • verb have a group discussion to produce ideas.

brains trust noun Brit. a group of experts who answer questions in front of an audience.

brain-teaser noun informal a problem or puzzle.

brainwash verb force someone to accept an idea or belief by using mental pressure, constant repetition, etc.

brainwave noun 1 an electrical impulse in the brain. 2 informal a sudden clever idea.

brainy adjective (**brainier, brainiest**) informal intelligent; clever.
– DERIVATIVES **braininess** noun.

braise verb fry food lightly and then stew it slowly in a closed container.
– ORIGIN from French *braise* 'live coals'.

brake[1] noun a device for slowing or stopping a moving vehicle. • verb slow or stop a vehicle with a brake.
– ORIGIN unknown.

> USAGE: Do not confuse **brake** with **break**.
> **Brake** means 'a device for slowing or stopping a vehicle' or 'slow or stop a vehicle' (*I had to brake hard*), whereas **break** mainly means 'separate into pieces' or 'a pause or interruption' (*a tea break*).

brake[2] noun historical an open horse-drawn carriage with four wheels.
– ORIGIN unknown.

brake[3] noun a thicket.

– ORIGIN Old English.

brake drum noun a broad, short cylinder attached to a wheel, against which the brake shoes press to cause braking.

brake horsepower noun an imperial unit equal to one horsepower, used in expressing the power available at the shaft of an engine.

brake shoe noun a long curved block which presses on to a brake drum.

bramble noun 1 a prickly shrub of the rose family, especially a blackberry. 2 Brit. the fruit of the blackberry.
– ORIGIN Old English.

brambling noun a finch with a white rump.
– ORIGIN probably related to **BRAMBLE**.

Bramley (also **Bramley's seedling**) noun (pl. **Bramleys**) a variety of large English cooking apple with green skin.
– ORIGIN named after the English butcher Matthew *Bramley*, in whose garden it first grew.

bran noun pieces of grain husk separated from flour after milling.
– ORIGIN Old French.

branch noun 1 a part of a tree which grows out from the trunk or a bough. 2 a river, road, or railway extending out from a main one. 3 a division of a large organization, subject, etc. • verb 1 divide into one or more branches. 2 (**branch out**) extend one's activities in a new direction: *the company is branching out into Europe.*
– ORIGIN from Latin *branca* 'paw'.

brand noun 1 a type of product manufactured by a company under a particular name. 2 a brand name. 3 an identifying mark burned on livestock with a heated iron. 4 a piece of burning wood. • verb 1 mark livestock with a branding iron. 2 mark out as having a particular shameful quality: *she was branded a liar.* 3 give a brand name to a product.
– ORIGIN Old English, 'burning'.

brandish verb wave or flourish something as a threat or in anger or excitement.
– ORIGIN Old French *brandir*.

brand name noun a name given by the maker to a product or range of products.

brand new adjective completely new.
– ORIGIN with the idea of a brand of wood being 'straight from the fire'.

brandy noun (pl. **brandies**) a strong alcoholic spirit distilled from wine or fermented fruit juice.
– ORIGIN from Dutch *branden* 'burn, distil' + *wijn* 'wine'.

brandy butter noun Brit. a stiff mixture of brandy, butter, and sugar, served with hot desserts.

brandy snap noun Brit. a crisp rolled gingerbread wafer.

brash adjective 1 self-assertive in a rude, noisy, or overbearing way. 2 showy or tasteless in appearance: *the cafe was a brash new building.*
– DERIVATIVES **brashly** adverb **brashness** noun.
– ORIGIN perhaps from **RASH**[1].

brass noun 1 a yellow alloy of copper and zinc. 2 (also **horse brass**) Brit. a flat brass ornament for the harness of a draught horse. 3 a brass memorial plaque in the wall or floor of a

church. **4** brass wind instruments forming a band or section of an orchestra. **5** (also **top brass**) informal people in authority. **6** Brit. informal money.
- PHRASES **brassed off** Brit. informal annoyed; exasperated. **get down to brass tacks** informal start to consider the basic facts.
- ORIGIN Old English.

brass band noun a group of musicians playing brass instruments.

brasserie /brass-uh-ri/ noun (pl. **brasseries**) an inexpensive French or French-style restaurant.
- ORIGIN French, 'brewery'.

brass hat noun Brit. informal a high-ranking officer in the armed forces.

brassica /brass-ik-uh/ noun a plant of a family that includes cabbage, swede, and rape.
- ORIGIN Latin, 'cabbage'.

brassiere /braz-i-er/ noun full form of **BRA**.
- ORIGIN French, 'bodice, child's vest'.

brass rubbing noun the copying of the design on an engraved brass by rubbing heelball (a type of wax) or chalk over paper laid on it.

brassy adjective (**brassier**, **brassiest**) **1** bright or harsh yellow. **2** tastelessly showy or loud: *a tawdry, brassy woman*. **3** harsh or blaring like a brass instrument.

brat noun derogatory or humorous a badly behaved child.
- DERIVATIVES **brattish** adjective.
- ORIGIN perhaps from Old French *brachet* 'hound, bitch'.

bratwurst /brat-verst/ noun a type of fine German pork sausage.
- ORIGIN from German *Brat* 'a spit' + *Wurst* 'sausage'.

bravado noun confidence or a show of confidence that is intended to impress.
- ORIGIN from Spanish *bravo* 'brave'.

brave adjective ready to face and endure danger, pain, or difficulty. •noun dated an American Indian warrior. •verb endure or face unpleasant conditions with courage: *more than 1,000 visitors braved a downpour to get in.*
- DERIVATIVES **bravely** adverb **bravery** noun.
- ORIGIN Italian or Spanish *bravo* 'bold, untamed'.

bravo[1] /brah-voh/ exclamation shouted to express approval for a performer.
- ORIGIN Italian, 'bold'.

bravo[2] /brah-voh/ noun (pl. **bravos** or **bravoes**) dated a thug or hired assassin.
- ORIGIN Italian, 'bold (one)'.

bravura /bruh-vyoor-uh/ noun **1** great skill and brilliance, typically shown in a performance. **2** the display of great daring.
- ORIGIN Italian.

braw /bror/ adjective Scottish fine, good, or pleasing.
- ORIGIN variant of **BRAVE**.

brawl noun a rough or noisy fight or quarrel. •verb fight or quarrel in a rough or noisy way.
- DERIVATIVES **brawler** noun.
- ORIGIN perhaps related to **BRAY**.

brawn noun **1** physical strength as opposed to intelligence. **2** Brit. cooked meat from a pig's or calf's head, pressed with jelly.
- DERIVATIVES **brawny** adjective.

- ORIGIN Old French *braon* 'fleshy part of the leg'.

bray verb **1** (of a donkey) make a loud, harsh cry. **2** (of a person) speak or laugh loudly and harshly. •noun a loud, harsh cry of a donkey.
- ORIGIN from Old French *braire* 'to cry'.

braze verb solder something with an alloy of copper and zinc.
- ORIGIN French *braser* 'solder'.

brazen adjective **1** bold and shameless. **2** old use made of brass. •verb (**brazen it out**) endure a difficult situation with apparent confidence and lack of shame.
- DERIVATIVES **brazenly** adverb.
- ORIGIN Old English.

brazier[1] /bray-zi-er/ noun a portable heater holding lighted coals.
- ORIGIN from French *braise* 'hot coals'.

brazier[2] /bray-zi-er/ noun a person who works in brass.

Brazilian noun a person from Brazil. •adjective relating to Brazil.

Brazil nut noun the large three-sided nut of a South American tree.

breach verb **1** make a gap or hole in something. **2** break a law, rule, or agreement. •noun **1** a gap made in a wall or barrier. **2** an act of breaking a rule or agreement. **3** a break in relations: *he healed the breach with the Prime Minister.*
- PHRASES **breach of the peace** public disturbance, or an act considered likely to cause one. **step into the breach** replace someone who is suddenly unable to do a job.
- ORIGIN Old French *breche*.

bread noun **1** food made of flour, water, and yeast mixed together and baked. **2** informal money.
- PHRASES **bread and butter** a person's main source of income. **break bread** celebrate Holy Communion. **know which side one's bread is buttered** informal know where one's advantage lies.
- ORIGIN Old English.

breadcrumb noun a small fragment of bread.

breaded adjective (of food) coated with breadcrumbs and fried.

breadfruit noun a large round starchy fruit of a tropical tree, used as a vegetable.

breadline noun (usu. in phrase **on the breadline**) Brit. the poorest condition in which it is acceptable to live.

breadstick noun a crisp stick of baked dough.

breadth noun **1** the distance or measurement from side to side of something. **2** wide range: *they have talent but no breadth of vision.*
- ORIGIN related to **BROAD**.

breadwinner noun a person who supports their family with the money they earn.

break verb (past **broke**; past part. **broken**)
1 separate into pieces as a result of a blow, shock, or strain. **2** make or become unable to function: *you've broken the video.* **3** interrupt a sequence or course. **4** fail to observe a law, regulation, or agreement. **5** crush the spirit of someone. **6** beat a record. **7** decipher a code. **8** make a rush or dash. **9** lessen the impact of a fall. **10** suddenly make or become public: *once the news broke, emails circulated worldwide.*
11 (of a person's voice) falter and change

b

tone. **12** (of a boy's voice) change in tone and register at puberty. **13** (of the weather) change suddenly, especially after a fine spell. **14** (of a storm, dawn, or a day) begin. **15** use a banknote to pay for something and receive change. • noun **1** an interruption, pause, or gap. **2** a short rest or holiday. **3** an instance of breaking, or the point where something is broken. **4** a sudden rush or dash: *she made a break for the door.* **5** informal an opportunity or chance. **6** (also **break of serve** or **service break**) Tennis the winning of a game against an opponent's serve. **7** Snooker & Billiards a consecutive series of successful shots.

– PHRASES **break away** escape from someone's control or influence. **break the back of** accomplish the main or hardest part of something. **break cover** (of people or animals being hunted) suddenly leave shelter. **break down 1** suddenly fail or stop functioning. **2** lose control of one's emotions when upset. **break even** reach a point in a business when the profits are equal to the costs. **break in 1** force entry into a building. **2** interrupt with a remark. **break something in 1** make a horse used to being ridden. **2** make new shoes comfortable by wearing them. **break into** burst into laughter, song, or faster movement. **break of day** dawn. **break something off** suddenly stop or end something. **break out 1** (of something unwelcome) start suddenly. **2** escape from confinement. **break something out** informal open and start using something. **break out in** be suddenly affected by: *I broke out in spots.* **break someone's serve** win a game in a tennis match against an opponent's service. **break up 1** (of a gathering or relationship) end or part. **2** chiefly Brit. end the school term. **break wind** release gas from the anus. **break with someone/thing 1** quarrel with someone. **2** go against a custom or tradition. **give someone a break** informal stop putting pressure on someone.

– DERIVATIVES **breakable** adjective & noun.
– ORIGIN Old English.

USAGE: On the confusion of **break** and **brake**, see the note at BRAKE.

breakage noun the action of breaking something or the fact of being broken.

breakaway noun **1** a departure from something established or long-standing. **2** (in sport) a sudden attack or forward movement. • adjective having separated from a larger group or country: *a breakaway republic.*

breakbeat noun a sampled electronic drum beat repeated to form a rhythm used as a basis for dance music or hip hop.

break-dancing noun an energetic and acrobatic style of street dancing.

breakdown noun **1** a failure or collapse. **2** an explanatory analysis of figures or costs.

breaker noun **1** a heavy sea wave that breaks on the shore. **2** a person who breaks or breaks up something.

breakfast noun a meal eaten in the morning, the first of the day. • verb eat breakfast.
– ORIGIN from BREAK + FAST².

break-in noun an illegal forced entry in order to steal something.

breakneck adjective dangerously fast.

breakout noun **1** a forcible escape, especially from prison. **2** an outbreak.

breakthrough noun a sudden important development or success.

break-up noun **1** the breaking up of something into several parts. **2** an end to a relationship.

breakwater noun a barrier built out into the sea to protect a coast or harbour from the force of waves.

bream noun (pl. same) a deep-bodied greenish-bronze freshwater fish.
– ORIGIN Old French *bresme.*

breast noun **1** either of the two protruding organs on a woman's chest which produce milk after childbirth. **2** a person's or animal's chest region. • verb **1** face and move forwards against or through: *I watched him breast the wave.* **2** reach the top of a hill.
– DERIVATIVES **breasted** adjective.
– ORIGIN Old English.

breastbone noun a thin, flat bone running down the centre of the chest, to which the ribs are attached; the sternum.

breastfeed verb (**breastfeeds, breastfeeding, breastfed**) feed a baby with milk from the breast.

breastplate noun a piece of armour covering the chest.

breaststroke noun a style of swimming in which the arms are pushed forwards and then swept back while the legs are tucked in and then kicked out.

breastwork noun a low temporary defence or parapet.

breath noun **1** air taken into or sent out of the lungs. **2** an instance of breathing in or out. **3** a slight movement of air. **4** a hint or suggestion: *he avoided the slightest breath of scandal.*
– PHRASES **breath of fresh air** a refreshing change. **hold one's breath** stop breathing temporarily. **out of breath** gasping for air. **take someone's breath away** astonish or inspire someone. **under one's breath** in a very quiet voice.
– ORIGIN Old English, 'smell, scent'.

breathable adjective **1** (of air) fit to breathe. **2** (of clothing or material) allowing air to the skin so that sweat may evaporate.
– DERIVATIVES **breathability** noun.

breathalyser (US trademark **Breathalyzer**) noun a device used by police for measuring the amount of alcohol in a driver's breath.
– DERIVATIVES **breathalyse** (US **breathalyze**) verb.
– ORIGIN from BREATH and ANALYSE.

breathe verb **1** take air into the lungs and send it out again as a regular process. **2** say something quietly. **3** let air or moisture in or out. **4** give an impression of: *the room breathed an air of efficiency.*
– PHRASES **breathe down someone's neck 1** follow closely behind someone. **2** constantly check up on someone.

breather noun informal a brief pause for rest.

breathing space noun an opportunity to pause, relax, or decide what to do next.

breathless adjective **1** gasping for breath. **2** feeling or causing great excitement, fear,

etc.: *breathless enthusiasm.*
– DERIVATIVES **breathlessly** adverb
breathlessness noun.
breathtaking adjective astonishing or awe-inspiring.
– DERIVATIVES **breathtakingly** adverb.
breath test noun a test in which a driver is made to blow into a breathalyser.
breathy adjective (of a voice) having an audible sound of breathing.
– DERIVATIVES **breathily** adverb.
breccia /bre-chi-uh/ noun rock consisting of angular fragments cemented by finer chalky material.
– ORIGIN Italian, 'gravel'.
bred past and past participle of **BREED**.
breech noun the back part of a rifle or gun barrel.
– ORIGIN Old English, 'garment covering the loins and thighs'.
breech birth noun a birth in which the baby's buttocks or feet are delivered first.
breeches plural noun short trousers fastened just below the knee, now worn for riding or as part of ceremonial dress.
breed verb (past and past part. **bred**) **1** (of animals) mate and then produce offspring. **2** keep animals to produce offspring. **3** bring up in a particular way: *Penny had been beautifully bred.* **4** develop a variety of plant. **5** produce or lead to: *success had bred a certain arrogance.* • noun **1** a distinctive type within a species of animals or plants, especially one deliberately developed. **2** a sort or kind: *a new breed of executive.*
– DERIVATIVES **breeder** noun.
– ORIGIN Old English.
breeding noun upper-class good manners regarded as being passed on from one generation to another.
breeze noun **1** a gentle wind. **2** informal a thing that is easy to do. • verb informal **1** come or go in a casual way. **2** (**breeze through**) deal with or accomplish something with ease.
– ORIGIN probably from Old Spanish and Portuguese *briza.*
breeze block noun Brit. a lightweight building brick made from cinders mixed with sand and cement.
– ORIGIN *breeze* from French *braise* 'live coals'.
breezy adjective (**breezier, breeziest**) **1** pleasantly windy. **2** relaxed and cheerily brisk.
– DERIVATIVES **breezily** adverb **breeziness** noun.
Bren gun noun a lightweight quick-firing machine gun used by the Allies in the Second World War.
– ORIGIN from *Brno* in the Czech Republic (where it was originally made) and *Enfield* (where it was later made).
bresaola /bre-sow-luh/ noun an Italian dish of sliced raw beef that has been cured by salting and air-drying.
– ORIGIN Italian, from *brasare* 'braise'.
brethren old-fashioned plural of **BROTHER**.
plural noun fellow Christians or members of a group: *their baseball brethren.*
Breton /bre-tuhn/ noun **1** a person from Brittany. **2** the Celtic language of Brittany.
– ORIGIN Old French, 'Briton'.

breve /rhymes with sleeve/ noun **1** Music a note twice as long as a semibreve. **2** a written or printed mark (˘) indicating a short or unstressed vowel.
– ORIGIN variant of **BRIEF**.
breviary /bree-vi-uh-ri/ noun (pl. **breviaries**) a book containing the service for each day, used in the Roman Catholic Church.
– ORIGIN Latin *breviarium* 'summary'.
brevity /brev-i-ti/ noun **1** concise and exact use of words. **2** shortness of time.
– ORIGIN from Latin *brevis* 'brief'.
brew verb **1** make beer by soaking, boiling, and fermentation. **2** make tea or coffee by mixing it with hot water. **3** begin to develop: *a real crisis is brewing.* • noun **1** a drink that has been brewed. **2** a mixture of different things: *her smell was a powerful brew of cheap scent and mothballs.*
– DERIVATIVES **brewer** noun.
– ORIGIN Old English.
brewery noun (pl. **breweries**) a place where beer is made.
briar[1] (also **brier**) noun a prickly shrub, especially a wild rose.
– ORIGIN Old English.
briar[2] (also **briar pipe, brier**) noun a tobacco pipe made from the woody nodules of a shrub of the heather family.
– ORIGIN French *bruyère* 'heath, heather'.
bribe verb dishonestly persuade someone to act in one's favour, especially by giving them money. • noun something offered or given to bribe someone.
– DERIVATIVES **bribery** noun.
– ORIGIN Old French *briber, brimber* 'to beg'.
bric-a-brac noun various objects and ornaments of little value.
– ORIGIN from former French *à bric et à brac* 'at random'.
brick noun **1** a small rectangular block of fired or sun-dried clay, used in building. **2** Brit. informal, dated a helpful and reliable person. • verb block or enclose something with a wall of bricks.
– PHRASES **bricks and mortar** buildings, especially housing.
– ORIGIN German, Dutch *bricke, brike*.
brickbat noun **1** a critical remark. **2** a piece of brick used as a missile.
bricklayer noun a person whose job is to build structures with bricks.
– DERIVATIVES **bricklaying** noun.
brick red noun a deep brownish red.
brickwork noun the bricks in a wall or building.
bricolage /bri-kuh-**lahzh**/ noun (in art or literature) the creation of something from a diverse range of available things.
– ORIGIN French.
bridal adjective relating to a bride or a newly married couple.
– ORIGIN from Old English, 'wedding feast'.
bride noun a woman on her wedding day or just before and after the event.
– ORIGIN Old English.
bridegroom noun a man on his wedding day or just before and after the event.
– ORIGIN Old English, 'bride man'.

b

bridesmaid noun a girl or woman who accompanies a bride on her wedding day.

bridge[1] noun **1** a structure carrying a route or railway across a river, road, or other obstacle. **2** the platform on a ship from which the captain and officers direct its course. **3** the upper bony part of a person's nose. **4** a false tooth or teeth supported by natural teeth on either side. **5** the part on a stringed instrument over which the strings are stretched. • verb **1** be or make a bridge over or between something. **2** make a difference or gap between two groups or things less significant: *how do we bridge the gap between politicians and people?*
– ORIGIN Old English.

bridge[2] noun a card game related to whist, played by two partnerships of two players.
– ORIGIN unknown.

bridgehead noun a strong position secured by an army inside enemy territory.

bridge roll noun Brit. a small, soft bread roll with a long, thin shape.

bridging loan (N. Amer. **bridge loan**) noun a sum of money lent by a bank to cover the period of time between the buying of one thing and the selling of another.

bridle noun the headgear used to control a horse, consisting of buckled straps to which a bit and reins are attached. • verb **1** put a bridle on a horse. **2** bring something under control. **3** show resentment or anger: *she bridled at being given an order.*
– ORIGIN Old English.

bridleway (also **bridle path**) noun Brit. a path or track along which horse riders have right of way.

Brie /bree/ noun a kind of soft, mild, creamy cheese.
– ORIGIN named after *Brie* in northern France.

brief adjective **1** lasting a short time. **2** using few words; concise. **3** (of clothing) not covering much of the body. • noun **1** Brit. a set of instructions about a task. **2** Brit. a summary of the facts in a case given to a barrister to argue in court. **3** Brit. informal a solicitor or barrister. **4** a letter from the Pope on a matter of discipline. • verb give someone information so as to prepare them to deal with something.
– PHRASES **hold no brief for** Brit. not support something.
– DERIVATIVES **briefly** adverb.
– ORIGIN from Latin *brevis* 'short'.

briefcase noun a flat rectangular case for carrying books and documents.

briefing noun a meeting for giving information or instructions.

briefs plural noun short, close-fitting underpants.

brier[1] noun variant spelling of BRIAR[1].

brier[2] noun variant spelling of BRIAR[2].

brig[1] noun **1** a two-masted square-rigged ship. **2** informal a prison on a warship.
– ORIGIN short for BRIGANTINE.

brig[2] noun Scottish & N. English a bridge.
– ORIGIN Old Norse.

brigade noun **1** a subdivision of an army, typically consisting of a small number of battalions and forming part of a division.

2 informal, often derogatory a particular group of people: *the anti-smoking brigade.*
– ORIGIN from Italian *brigata* 'company'.

brigadier noun a rank of officer in the British army, above colonel and below major general.

brigadier general noun a rank of officer in the US army, air force, and marine corps, above colonel and below major general.

brigand /brig-uhnd/ noun a member of a gang of bandits.
– DERIVATIVES **brigandage** noun.
– ORIGIN Italian *brigante* '(person) contending'.

brigantine /brig-uhn-teen/ noun a two-masted sailing ship.
– ORIGIN Italian *brigantino*.

bright adjective **1** giving out or filled with light. **2** (of colour) vivid and bold. **3** intelligent and quick-witted. **4** cheerful and lively. **5** (of future prospects) good.
– DERIVATIVES **brightly** adverb **brightness** noun.
– ORIGIN Old English.

brighten verb **1** make or become brighter. **2** make or become happier and more cheerful.

bright spark noun informal, often ironic a clever or witty person.

brill noun a flatfish similar to the turbot.
– ORIGIN unknown.

brilliant adjective **1** (of light or colour) very bright or vivid. **2** exceptionally clever or talented. **3** Brit. informal excellent; marvellous.
– DERIVATIVES **brilliance** (also **brilliancy**) noun **brilliantly** adverb.
– ORIGIN from French *briller* 'to shine'.

brilliantine noun dated scented oil used on men's hair to make it look glossy.

brim noun **1** the projecting edge around the bottom of a hat. **2** the lip of a cup, bowl, or other container. • verb (**brims, brimming, brimmed**) fill or be full to the point of overflowing: *he's brimming with ideas.*
– DERIVATIVES **brimful** adjective **brimmed** adjective.
– ORIGIN perhaps related to German *Bräme* 'trimming'.

brimstone noun **1** a large bright yellow or greenish-white butterfly. **2** old use sulphur.
– ORIGIN Old English.

brindle (also **brindled**) adjective (of a domestic animal) brownish or tawny with streaks of other colour.
– ORIGIN probably Scandinavian.

brine noun water containing dissolved salt.
– ORIGIN Old English.

bring verb (past and past part. **brought**) **1** take or go with someone or something to a place. **2** cause to be in a particular position or state: *the agreement brought an end to hostilities.* **3** cause someone to receive money as income or profit. **4** (**bring oneself to do**) force oneself to do something unpleasant. **5** begin legal action.
– PHRASES **bring something about** cause something to happen. **bring something forward 1** move something planned to an earlier time. **2** propose an idea for consideration. **bring the house down** make an audience laugh or applaud very enthusiastically. **bring something off** achieve something successfully. **bring someone/thing on 1** encourage or help someone to develop or

improve. 2 cause something unpleasant to happen. **bring something out 1** produce and launch a new product or publication. 2 emphasize something. **bring someone round 1** cause an unconscious person to become conscious. 2 persuade someone to agree to something. **bring someone to** cause an unconscious person to become conscious. **bring something to bear** use influence or pressure to achieve a result. **bring something to pass** chiefly literary cause something to happen. **bring someone/thing up 1** look after a child until it is an adult. 2 raise a matter for discussion.
– DERIVATIVES **bringer** noun.
– ORIGIN Old English.

bring-and-buy sale noun Brit. a charity sale at which people donate things to sell.

brink noun 1 the extreme edge of land before a steep slope or a body of water. 2 the point at which a new or unwelcome situation is about to begin: *companies on the brink of bankruptcy*.
– ORIGIN Scandinavian.

brinkmanship /bringk-muhn-ship/ (US also **brinksmanship**) noun the pursuit of a dangerous policy to the limits of safety before stopping.

briny /rhymes with tiny/ adjective relating to brine; salty. • noun (**the briny**) Brit. informal the sea.

brio /bree-oh/ noun energy or liveliness.
– ORIGIN Italian.

brioche /bree-osh/ noun a small, round, sweet French roll.
– ORIGIN French.

briquette /bri-ket/ (also **briquet**) noun a block of compressed coal dust or peat used as fuel.
– ORIGIN French, 'small brick'.

brisk adjective 1 quick, active, or lively. 2 practical and efficient: *a brisk, businesslike tone.* 3 (of wind or the weather) cold but refreshing.
– DERIVATIVES **briskly** adverb **briskness** noun.
– ORIGIN probably from French *brusque* 'lively, fierce'.

brisket noun meat from the breast of a cow.
– ORIGIN perhaps from Old Norse, 'cartilage, gristle'.

brisling /briss-ling/ noun (pl. same or **brislings**) a sprat, typically one smoked and canned.
– ORIGIN Norwegian and Danish.

bristle noun 1 a short, stiff hair on an animal's skin or a man's face. 2 a stiff animal or artificial hair, used to make a brush. • verb 1 (of hair or fur) stand upright away from the skin. 2 react angrily or defensively. 3 (**bristle with**) be covered with or full of: *the island bristles with forts.*
– DERIVATIVES **bristly** adjective.
– ORIGIN Old English.

bristols plural noun Brit. informal a woman's breasts.
– ORIGIN from rhyming slang *Bristol Cities* 'titties'.

Brit noun informal a British person.

Britannia /bri-tan-yuh/ noun a woman wearing a helmet and carrying a shield and trident, used to represent Britain.
– ORIGIN the Latin name for Britain.

Britannic /bri-tan-nik/ adjective dated relating to Britain or the British Empire.

British adjective relating to Great Britain or the United Kingdom.
– DERIVATIVES **Britishness** noun.
– ORIGIN Old English.

Britisher noun informal (especially in North America) a British person.

British thermal unit noun a unit of heat equal to the amount of heat needed to raise 1 lb of water at maximum density through one degree Fahrenheit.

Briton noun 1 a British person. 2 a Celtic inhabitant of southern Britain before and during Roman times.
– ORIGIN Old French *Breton*.

brittle adjective 1 hard but likely to break or shatter easily. 2 sharp or artificial and showing signs of nervousness: *a brittle laugh.*
– DERIVATIVES **brittleness** noun.
– ORIGIN related to an Old English word meaning 'break up'.

brittle bone disease noun a disease in which the bones become brittle, especially osteoporosis.

broach verb 1 raise a subject for discussion. 2 pierce or open a cask or container to draw out liquid.
– ORIGIN Old French *brochier*.

broad adjective 1 having a distance larger than usual from side to side; wide. 2 of a particular distance wide. 3 large in area or range: *a broad expanse of water.* 4 without detail; general: *a broad outline.* 5 (of a hint) clear and unmistakable. 6 (of a regional accent) very strong. • noun N. Amer. informal a woman.
– PHRASES **broad daylight** full daylight; day.
– DERIVATIVES **broadly** adverb **broadness** noun.
– ORIGIN Old English.

broadband noun a telecommunications technique which uses a wide range of frequencies, enabling messages to be sent simultaneously.

broad bean noun a large flat green bean.

broad-brush adjective dealing with something in a general way; lacking in detail: *a broad-brush approach to the problem.*

broadcast verb (past **broadcast**; past part. **broadcast** or **broadcasted**) 1 transmit a programme or information by radio or television. 2 tell something to many people. 3 scatter seeds rather than placing them in rows. • noun a radio or television transmission.
– DERIVATIVES **broadcaster** noun.

Broad Church noun 1 a tradition or group within the Anglican Church which supports a liberal interpretation of doctrine. 2 a group or doctrine which allows for a wide range of views or people.

broadcloth noun a fine wool or cotton cloth.

broaden verb make or become broader.

broad gauge noun a railway gauge which is wider than the standard gauge of 4 ft 8½ in (1.435 m).

broadleaved (also **broadleaf**) adjective (of trees or herbaceous plants) having relatively wide flat leaves, as opposed to conifers or grasses.

b

b

broadloom noun carpet woven in wide widths.

broad-minded adjective tolerant of views or behaviour that are different from one's own; not easily offended.

broadsheet noun **1** a newspaper with a large format. **2** a large piece of paper printed with information on one side only.

broadside noun **1** a strongly worded critical attack. **2** historical a firing of all the guns from one side of a warship. **3** the side of a ship above the water between the bow and quarter.
– PHRASES **broadside on** sideways on.

broadsword noun a sword with a wide blade, used for cutting rather than thrusting.

Brobdingnagian /brob-ding-**nag**-i-uhn/ adjective gigantic.
– ORIGIN from *Brobdingnag*, a land in *Gulliver's Travels* where everything is of huge size.

brocade noun a rich fabric woven with a raised pattern, usually with gold or silver thread.
– DERIVATIVES **brocaded** adjective.
– ORIGIN Spanish and Portuguese *brocado*.

broccoli /**brok**-kuh-li/ noun a vegetable with heads of small green or purplish flower buds.
– ORIGIN Italian.

brochette /bro-**shet**/ noun a dish of meat or fish chunks barbecued, grilled, or roasted on a skewer.
– ORIGIN French, 'little skewer'.

brochure /**broh**-sher/ noun a magazine containing pictures and information about a product or service.
– ORIGIN French, 'something stitched'.

broderie anglaise /broh-duh-ri ong-**glayz**/ noun open embroidery on fine white cotton or linen.
– ORIGIN French, 'English embroidery'.

brogue /brohg/ noun **1** a strong outdoor shoe with perforated patterns in the leather. **2** a noticeable accent, especially Irish or Scottish, when speaking English.
– ORIGIN Scottish Gaelic and Irish *bróg*.

broil verb N. Amer. grill meat or fish.
– ORIGIN Old French *bruler* 'to burn'.

broiler noun **1** a young chicken suitable for roasting, grilling, or barbecuing. **2** N. Amer. a frame or device used for grilling meat or fish.

broke past (and old-fashioned past participle) of BREAK. adjective informal having no money.
– PHRASES **go for broke** informal risk everything in one determined effort.

broken past participle of BREAK. adjective (of a language) spoken hesitantly and with many mistakes, as by a foreigner.
– DERIVATIVES **brokenly** adverb **brokenness** noun.

broken-down adjective **1** worn out and in a bad condition. **2** not working.

broken-hearted adjective overwhelmed by grief or disappointment.

broken home noun a family in which the parents are divorced or separated.

broker noun a person who buys and sells goods or assets for other people. •verb arrange or negotiate a deal or plan.
– DERIVATIVES **brokerage** noun.
– ORIGIN Old French *brocour*.

broker-dealer noun (in the UK) a person combining the former functions of a broker

and jobber on the Stock Exchange.

broking noun Brit. the business or service of buying and selling goods or assets for other people.

brolly noun (pl. **brollies**) Brit. informal an umbrella.

bromeliad /bruh-**mee**-li-ad/ noun a member of a family of tropical American plants.
– ORIGIN named after the Swedish botanist Olaf *Bromel*.

bromide noun **1** a compound of bromine with another chemical element or group. **2** dated a preparation containing potassium bromide, used as a sedative. **3** an unoriginal idea or remark.

bromine /**broh**-meen/ noun a dark red liquid chemical element of the halogen group, with a strong, choking smell.
– ORIGIN from Greek *brōmos* 'a stink'.

bronchi plural of BRONCHUS.

bronchial /**brong**-ki-uhl/ adjective relating to the bronchi or bronchioles.

bronchiole /**brongk**-ki-ohl/ noun any of the minute branches into which the bronchi in the lungs divide.
– ORIGIN Latin *bronchiolus*.

bronchitis /brong-**ky**-tiss/ noun inflammation of the mucous membrane in the bronchial tubes.
– DERIVATIVES **bronchitic** adjective & noun.

bronchus /**brong**-kuhss/ noun (pl. **bronchi** /**brong**-kee/) any of the major air passages of the lungs which spread out from the windpipe.
– ORIGIN Greek *bronkhos* 'windpipe'.

bronco noun (pl. **broncos**) a wild or half-tamed horse of the western US.
– ORIGIN from Spanish, 'rough, rude'.

brontosaurus /bron-tuh-**sor**-uhss/ noun former term for APATOSAURUS.
– ORIGIN from Greek *brontē* 'thunder' + *sauros* 'lizard'.

bronze noun **1** a yellowish-brown alloy of copper and tin. **2** a yellowish-brown colour. **3** an object made of bronze. •verb make a person or part of the body suntanned.
– DERIVATIVES **bronzy** adjective.
– ORIGIN Italian *bronzo*.

Bronze Age noun a historical period that followed the Stone Age and preceded the Iron Age, when tools were made of bronze.

bronze medal noun a medal made of or coloured bronze, awarded for third place in a race or competition.

brooch noun an ornament fastened to clothing with a hinged pin and catch.
– ORIGIN Old French *broche* 'spit for roasting'.

brood noun **1** a family of young animals produced at one hatching or birth. **2** informal all the children in a family. •verb **1** think deeply about an unpleasant subject. **2** (as adj. **brooding**) mysterious or menacing: *the dark, brooding atmosphere.* **3** (of a bird) sit on eggs to hatch them. •adjective (of an animal) kept for breeding: *a brood mare.*
– ORIGIN Old English.

broody adjective (**broodier, broodiest**) **1** (of a hen) wanting to lay or sit on eggs. **2** informal (of a woman) wanting very much to have a baby. **3** thoughtful and unhappy.

– DERIVATIVES **broodily** adverb **broodiness** noun.

brook¹ noun a small stream.
– ORIGIN Old English.

brook² verb formal tolerate or allow: *she would brook no criticism.*
– ORIGIN Old English 'use, possess' (later 'digest, stomach').

broom noun **1** a long-handled brush used for sweeping. **2** a shrub with many yellow flowers and small or few leaves.
– ORIGIN Old English.

broomstick noun a brush with twigs at one end and a long handle, on which witches are said to fly.

Bros plural noun brothers (in names of companies).

broth noun soup made from meat or vegetables cooked in stock.
– ORIGIN Old English.

brothel noun a house where men visit prostitutes.
– ORIGIN related to an Old English word meaning 'deteriorate'.

brother noun **1** a man or boy in relation to other children of his parents. **2** a male associate or fellow member of an organization. **3** (pl. also **brethren**) a (male) fellow Christian. **4** a member of a religious order of men: *a Benedictine brother.*
– DERIVATIVES **brotherly** adjective.
– ORIGIN Old English.

brotherhood noun **1** the relationship between brothers. **2** a feeling of fellowship and understanding. **3** a group of people linked by a shared interest or belief: *a religious brotherhood.*

brother-in-law noun (pl. **brothers-in-law**) **1** the brother of one's wife or husband. **2** the husband of one's sister or sister-in-law.

brougham /broo-uhm/ noun historical **1** a horse-drawn carriage with a roof, four wheels, and an open driver's seat in front. **2** a car with an open driver's seat.
– ORIGIN named after Lord *Brougham*, who designed the carriage.

brought past and past participle of **BRING**.

> USAGE: Do not confuse **bought** and **brought**. Bought is the past tense and past participle of **buy** (*she bought a bar of chocolate*), whereas brought is the past tense and past participle of bring (*the article brought a massive response*).

brouhaha /broo-hah-hah/ noun a noisy and overexcited reaction.
– ORIGIN French.

brow noun **1** a person's forehead. **2** an eyebrow. **3** the summit of a hill or pass.
– DERIVATIVES **browed** adjective.
– ORIGIN Old English.

browbeat verb (past **browbeat**; past part. **browbeaten**) bully or intimidate someone by using stern or abusive words.

brown adjective **1** of a colour produced by mixing red, yellow, and blue, as of dark wood or rich soil. **2** dark-skinned or suntanned.
●noun brown colour or material. ●verb **1** make or become brown by cooking. **2** (**be browned off**) Brit. informal be irritated or depressed.
– DERIVATIVES **brownish** adjective **browny** adjective.

– ORIGIN Old English.

brown ale noun Brit. dark, mild beer sold in bottles.

brown bear noun a large bear with a coat colour ranging from cream to black.

brown belt noun a brown belt marking a level of skill below that of a black belt in judo, karate, or other martial arts.

brown coal noun lignite.

brown dwarf noun Astronomy a celestial object midway in size between a large planet and a small star.

brownfield adjective Brit. (of an urban site) having been previously built on. Compare with GREENFIELD.

brown goods plural noun television sets, audio equipment, and similar household appliances. Compare with WHITE GOODS.

Brownian motion noun Physics the erratic movement of microscopic particles in a fluid, as a result of collisions with the surrounding molecules.
– ORIGIN named after the Scottish botanist Robert *Brown*.

Brownie noun (pl. **Brownies**) **1** (Brit. also **Brownie Guide**) a member of the junior branch of the Guides Association. **2** (**brownie**) a small square of rich chocolate cake. **3** (**brownie**) a kind elf that supposedly does housework secretly.
– PHRASES **brownie point** informal an imaginary good mark given for an attempt to please someone.

browning noun Brit. darkened flour for colouring gravy.

brown-nose noun (also **brown-noser**) informal a person who behaves in a very servile or ingratiating way towards someone in an attempt to gain their approval.

brownout noun chiefly N. Amer. a partial blackout.

brown owl noun another term for TAWNY OWL.

brown rice noun unpolished rice with only the husk of the grain removed.

Brownshirt noun a member of a Nazi military force founded by Hitler in 1921 and suppressed in 1934, with brown uniforms.

brownstone noun N. Amer. **1** a kind of reddish-brown sandstone used for building. **2** a building faced with this kind of sandstone.

brown sugar noun unrefined or partially refined sugar.

brown trout noun (pl. same) the common trout of European lakes and rivers, typically with dark spotted skin.

browse verb **1** look at goods or text in a leisurely way. **2** read or look at computer files via a network. **3** (of an animal) feed on leaves, twigs, etc. ●noun an act of browsing.
– DERIVATIVES **browsable** adjective.
– ORIGIN from Old French *brost* 'young shoot'.

browser noun **1** a person or animal that browses. **2** a computer program used to navigate the World Wide Web.

brucellosis /broo-suh-loh-siss/ noun a disease caused by a bacterium, which chiefly affects cattle.
– ORIGIN from *Brucella*, the name of the bacterium responsible.

bruise noun **1** an area of discoloured skin on

the body, caused by a blow or impact which bursts underlying blood vessels. **2** a similar area of damage on a fruit, vegetable, or plant. • **verb 1** inflict a bruise on someone or something. **2** develop a bruise.
– ORIGIN Old English.

bruiser noun informal, derogatory a tough, aggressive person.

bruising adjective conducted in an aggressive way and likely to be stressful: *a bruising cabinet battle over public spending.* • noun bruises on the skin.

bruit /rhymes with fruit/ verb spread a story or rumour widely.
– ORIGIN Old French *bruire* 'to roar'.

brume noun literary mist or fog.
– ORIGIN French, from Latin *bruma* 'winter'.

Brummie (also **Brummy**) Brit. informal noun (pl. **Brummies**) a person from Birmingham. • adjective relating to Birmingham.

brunch noun a late morning meal eaten instead of breakfast and lunch.

Bruneian /broo-ny-uhn/ noun a person from the sultanate of Brunei. • adjective relating to Brunei.

brunette (US also **brunet**) noun a woman or girl with dark brown hair.
– ORIGIN from French *brun* 'brown'.

brunt noun the chief impact of something bad or unwelcome: *the island bore the brunt of the storm.*
– ORIGIN unknown.

bruschetta /broo-sket-uh/ noun toasted Italian bread soaked in olive oil.
– ORIGIN Italian.

brush[1] noun **1** an implement with a handle and a block of bristles, hair, or wire, used especially for cleaning, smoothing, or painting. **2** an act of brushing. **3** a brief encounter with something bad or unwelcome: *a brush with death.* **4** the bushy tail of a fox. **5** a piece of carbon or metal serving as an electrical contact with a moving part in a motor or alternator. • verb **1** clean, smooth, or apply with a brush. **2** touch something lightly. **3** (**brush someone/thing off** (or **aside**)) dismiss someone or something in an abrupt way: *he brushed aside their questions.* **4** (**brush up on** or **brush something up**) work to improve a skill that has not been used for some time.
– ORIGIN Old French *broisse*.

brush[2] noun chiefly N. Amer. & Austral./NZ undergrowth, small trees, and shrubs.
– ORIGIN Old French *broce*.

brushed adjective **1** (of fabric) having a soft raised nap. **2** (of metal) finished with a non-reflective surface.

brush-off noun informal a rejection or dismissal.

brushstroke noun a mark made by a paintbrush drawn across a surface.

brushwood noun undergrowth, twigs, and small branches.

brushwork noun the way in which a painter uses their brush.

brusque /bruusk/ adjective abrupt or offhand in manner or speech.
– DERIVATIVES **brusquely** adverb **brusqueness** noun.

– ORIGIN French, 'lively, fierce', from Italian *brusco* 'sour'.

Brussels sprout (also **Brussel sprout**) noun the bud of a variety of cabbage, eaten as a vegetable.

brut /rhymes with loot/ adjective (of sparkling wine) very dry.
– ORIGIN French, 'raw, rough'.

brutal adjective **1** savagely violent. **2** not attempting to disguise something unpleasant: *he replied with brutal honesty.*
– DERIVATIVES **brutality** noun **brutally** adverb.

brutalism noun **1** cruelty and savagery. **2** a stark style of architecture that makes use of massive blocks of steel and concrete.

brutalize (or **brutalise**) verb **1** make someone cruel, violent, or callous by repeatedly exposing them to violence. **2** treat someone in a violent way.
– DERIVATIVES **brutalization** noun.

brute noun **1** a violent or savage person or animal. **2** informal a cruel or insensitive person. • adjective **1** involving physical strength alone, rather than thought or intelligence: *brute force.* **2** unpleasant and inescapable: *the brute facts of the human condition.*
– DERIVATIVES **brutish** adjective.
– ORIGIN Latin *brutus* 'dull, stupid'.

bryony /bry-uh-ni/ noun (pl. **bryonies**) a climbing hedgerow plant with red berries.
– ORIGIN Greek *bruōnia*.

BS abbreviation **1** Bachelor of Surgery. **2** British Standard(s).

BSc abbreviation Bachelor of Science.

BSE abbreviation bovine spongiform encephalopathy, a fatal disease of cattle which affects the central nervous system and is believed to be related to Creutzfeldt–Jakob disease in humans.

BSI abbreviation British Standards Institution.

B-side noun the side of a pop single regarded as the less important one.

BST abbreviation British Summer Time (time as advanced one hour ahead of Greenwich Mean Time in the UK between March and October).

BT abbreviation British Telecom.

B2B abbreviation business-to-business, referring to trade carried out via the Internet between businesses.

Btu (also **BTU**) abbreviation British thermal unit(s).

btw abbreviation by the way.

bubble noun **1** a thin layer of liquid enclosing air or another gas. **2** an air- or gas-filled spherical cavity in a liquid or a solidified liquid such as glass. **3** a transparent cover or enclosure in the shape of a dome. • verb **1** (of a liquid) contain rising bubbles of air or gas. **2** (**bubble with**) be filled with an irrepressible feeling: *she was bubbling with excitement.*
– ORIGIN imitating the sound of bubbling.

bubble and squeak noun Brit. a dish of cooked cabbage fried with cooked potatoes.

bubble bath noun sweet-smelling liquid added to bathwater to make it foam.

bubblegum noun chewing gum that can be blown into bubbles.

bubble wrap noun (trademark in the US) protective plastic packaging in the form of sheets containing numerous small air pockets.

bubbly adjective (**bubblier, bubbliest**)
1 containing bubbles. **2** cheerful and high-spirited. ●**noun** informal champagne.

bubo /byoo-boh/ noun (pl. **buboes**) a swollen inflamed lymph node in the armpit or groin.
– DERIVATIVES **bubonic** adjective.
– ORIGIN Greek *boubōn*.

bubonic plague noun a form of plague transmitted by rat fleas, causing swellings (buboes) in the groin or armpits.

buccal /buk-uhl/ adjective technical relating to the cheek or mouth.
– ORIGIN from Latin *bucca* 'cheek'.

buccaneer /buk-kuh-neer/ noun **1** historical a pirate, originally one operating in the Caribbean. **2** a recklessly adventurous and unscrupulous person.
– DERIVATIVES **buccaneering** adjective.
– ORIGIN French *boucanier*.

buck¹ noun **1** the male of some animals, e.g. deer and rabbits. **2** a vertical jump performed by a horse, with the back arched and the back legs thrown out behind. **3** old use a fashionable young man. ●**verb 1** (of a horse) perform a buck. **2** resist or go against: *electricity shares bucked the trend and rallied*. **3** (**buck someone up** or **buck up**) informal make or become more cheerful.
– PHRASES **buck up one's ideas** become more serious and hard-working.
– ORIGIN Old English.

buck² noun N. Amer. & Austral./NZ informal a dollar.
– ORIGIN unknown.

buck³ noun an object placed in front of a poker player whose turn it is to deal.
– PHRASES **the buck stops here** informal the responsibility for something cannot be avoided. **pass the buck** informal shift responsibility to someone else.
– ORIGIN unknown.

buckaroo noun N. Amer. dated a cowboy.
– ORIGIN alteration of **VAQUERO**.

buckboard noun N. Amer. an open horse-drawn carriage with four wheels and seating that is attached to a plank between the front and rear axles.
– ORIGIN from *buck* 'body of a cart' + **BOARD**.

bucket noun **1** a cylindrical open container with a handle, used to carry liquids. **2** (**buckets**) informal large quantities of liquid. **3** a scoop on a dredger, or one attached to the front of a digger or tractor. ●**verb** (**buckets, bucketing, bucketed**) (**bucket down**) Brit. informal rain heavily.
– DERIVATIVES **bucketful** noun.
– ORIGIN Old French *buquet*.

bucketload noun informal a large amount or number.

bucket seat noun a vehicle seat with a rounded back to fit one person.

bucket shop noun informal, derogatory **1** Brit. a travel agency that sells cheap air tickets. **2** an unauthorized office that speculates in stocks or currency using funds that have been dishonestly acquired.

buckle noun a flat frame with a hinged pin, used for fastening a belt or strap. ●**verb 1** fasten a belt or strap with a buckle. **2** bend

and give way under pressure. **3** (**buckle down**) tackle a task with determination.
– ORIGIN Latin *buccula* 'cheek strap of a helmet'; sense 2 is from French *boucler* 'to bulge'.

buckler noun historical a small round shield held by a handle or worn on the forearm.
– ORIGIN from Old French *escu bocler*, 'shield with a boss'.

buck naked adjective informal, chiefly N. Amer. completely naked.

buckram noun coarse linen or other cloth stiffened with paste, used in bookbinding.
– ORIGIN Old French *boquerant*.

Bucks. abbreviation Buckinghamshire.

Buck's Fizz noun Brit. champagne or sparkling white wine mixed with orange juice.
– ORIGIN named after *Buck's Club* in London.

buckshee adjective informal, chiefly Brit. free of charge.
– ORIGIN alteration of **BAKSHEESH**.

buckshot noun coarse lead shot used in shotgun shells.

buckskin noun **1** soft leather made from the skin of deer or sheep. **2** (**buckskins**) clothes or shoes made from buckskin. **3** thick smooth cotton or woollen cloth.

buck teeth plural noun upper teeth that project over the lower lip.
– DERIVATIVES **buck-toothed** adjective.

buckthorn noun a thorny shrub or small tree which bears black berries.

buckwheat noun a plant producing starchy seeds used for animal fodder or milled into flour.
– ORIGIN Dutch *boecweite* 'beech wheat', its grains being shaped like the nuts of the beech tree.

bucolic /byoo-kol-ik/ adjective relating to country life.
– ORIGIN from Greek *boukolos* 'herdsman'.

bud noun **1** a growth on a plant which develops into a leaf, flower, or shoot. **2** Biology an outgrowth from an organism that separates to form a new individual without sexual reproduction taking place. ●**verb** (**buds, budding, budded**) form a bud or buds.
– ORIGIN unknown.

Buddhism /buud-di-z'm/ noun a religion or philosophy, founded by Siddartha Gautama (Buddha; *c.*563–*c.*460 BC), which teaches that enlightenment may be reached by the elimination of earthly desires.
– DERIVATIVES **Buddhist** noun & adjective.

budding adjective beginning to develop and showing signs of promise or success: *their budding relationship*.

buddleia /bud-li-uh/ noun a shrub with clusters of lilac, white, or yellow flowers.
– ORIGIN named after the English botanist Adam *Buddle*.

buddy noun (pl. **buddies**) informal, chiefly N. Amer. a close friend.
– ORIGIN perhaps an alteration of **BROTHER**.

budge verb **1** make or cause to make the slightest movement. **2** change or cause to change an opinion.
– ORIGIN French *bouger* 'to stir'.

budgerigar noun a small Australian parakeet

which is green with a yellow head in the wild.
– ORIGIN Aboriginal.

budget noun **1** an estimate of income and expenditure for a set period of time. **2** the amount of money needed or available for a particular purpose: *a £1 million advertising budget.* **3** (**Budget**) a regular estimate of national income and expenditure put forward by a finance minister. • verb (**budgets, budgeting, budgeted**) allow for in a budget: *they budgeted for a pay award in line with inflation.* • adjective inexpensive.
– DERIVATIVES **budgetary** adjective.
– ORIGIN Old French *bougette* 'little leather bag'; the word first referred to a pouch or wallet and in the 18th century the Chancellor of the Exchequer, in presenting his annual statement, was said 'to open the budget'.

budgie noun (pl. **budgies**) informal a budgerigar.

budo /boo-doh/ noun Japanese martial arts, or the code on which they are based.
– ORIGIN Japanese.

buff[1] noun **1** a yellowish-beige colour. **2** a dull yellow leather with a velvety surface. • verb **1** polish something. **2** give a velvety finish to leather.
– PHRASES **in the buff** informal naked.
– ORIGIN probably from French *buffle* 'buffalo'.

buff[2] noun informal a person who is interested in and very knowledgeable about a particular subject: *a movie buff.*
– ORIGIN from **BUFF**[1], first referring to enthusiastic spectators of fires in New York, because of the firemen's buff-coloured uniforms.

buffalo noun (pl. same or **buffaloes**) **1** a heavily built wild ox with backward-curving horns. **2** the North American bison.
– ORIGIN Latin *bufalus*.

buffer[1] noun **1** (**buffers**) Brit. shock-absorbing devices at the end of a railway track or on a railway vehicle. **2** a person or thing that lessens the impact of something harmful or forms a barrier between adversaries: *she often had to act as a buffer between father and son.* **3** (also **buffer solution**) Chemistry a solution which resists changes in pH when acid or alkali is added to it. **4** Computing a temporary memory area or queue used when creating or editing text, or when transferring data.
– ORIGIN probably from the former verb *buff* 'deaden the force of something'.

buffer[2] noun Brit. informal a foolish or incompetent elderly man.
– ORIGIN probably from the former verb *buff* (see **BUFFER**[1]), or from dialect *buff* 'stutter, splutter'.

buffet[1] /boo-fay, buf-fay/ noun **1** a meal consisting of several dishes from which guests serve themselves. **2** a room or counter selling light meals or snacks.
– ORIGIN Old French *bufet* 'stool'.

buffet[2] /buff-it/ verb (**buffets, buffeting, buffeted**) (especially of wind or waves) strike or push someone or something repeatedly and violently. • noun dated a blow.
– ORIGIN Old French *buffeter*.

buffoon noun a ridiculous but amusing person.
– DERIVATIVES **buffoonery** noun **buffoonish** adjective.

– ORIGIN from Latin *buffo* 'clown'.

bug noun **1** informal a harmful microorganism or an illness caused by a microorganism. **2** chiefly N. Amer. a small insect. **3** informal an enthusiasm for something: *they caught the sailing bug.* **4** a microphone used for secret recording. **5** an error in a computer program or system. • verb (**bugs, bugging, bugged**) **1** conceal a microphone in a room or telephone. **2** informal annoy or bother someone.
– ORIGIN unknown.

bugaboo noun chiefly N. Amer. a cause of fear.
– ORIGIN probably Celtic.

bugbear noun a cause of anxiety or irritation.
– ORIGIN probably from the old word *bug* 'evil spirit' + **BEAR**[2].

bug-eyed adjective with bulging eyes.

bugger vulgar slang, chiefly Brit. noun **1** a person regarded with contempt or pity. **2** an annoying or awkward thing. **3** derogatory a person who commits buggery. • verb **1** have anal intercourse with someone. **2** cause serious harm or trouble to someone or something. **3** (**bugger off**) go away. • exclamation used to express annoyance.
– PHRASES **bugger about/around** act stupidly. **bugger all** nothing.
– ORIGIN Old French *bougre* 'heretic'.

buggery noun anal intercourse.

buggy noun (pl. **buggies**) **1** (also **baby buggy**) a light collapsible pushchair. **2** a small motor vehicle with an open top. **3** historical a light horse-drawn vehicle for one or two people.
– ORIGIN unknown.

bugle[1] noun a brass instrument like a small trumpet, traditionally used for military signals.
– DERIVATIVES **bugler** noun.
– ORIGIN Latin *buculus* 'little ox', from *bos* 'ox': the horn of an ox was used to give signals.

bugle[2] noun a creeping plant with blue flowers on upright stems.
– ORIGIN Latin *bugula*.

bugloss /byoo-gloss/ noun a bristly plant with bright blue flowers.
– ORIGIN Greek *bouglōssos* 'ox-tongued'.

buhl /bool/ noun variant spelling of **BOULLE**.

build verb (past and past part. **built**) **1** construct something by putting parts or materials together. **2** (often **build up**) increase in size or intensity over time. **3** (**build on**) use something as a basis for further progress or development. **4** (**build something in/into**) incorporate something as a permanent part of a larger structure. • noun the size and shape of a person's or animal's body: *a man of stocky build.*
– DERIVATIVES **builder** noun.
– ORIGIN Old English.

building noun **1** a structure with a roof and walls. **2** the process or trade of building houses and other structures.

building society noun Brit. a financial organization which pays interest on members' investments and lends money for mortgages.

build-up noun **1** a gradual increase in something over a period of time. **2** a period of excitement and preparation before an event.

built past and past participle of **BUILD**. adjective of a particular physical build: *a slightly built* *woman.*

built-in adjective included as part of a larger structure.

built-up adjective (of an area) covered by many buildings.

bulb noun **1** the rounded underground base of the stem of some plants, from which the roots grow. **2** a light bulb. **3** an expanded or rounded part at the end of something such as a thermometer.
– ORIGIN Greek *bolbos* 'onion'.

bulbous adjective **1** round or bulging in shape. **2** (of a plant) growing from a bulb.

Bulgarian noun **1** a person from Bulgaria. **2** the Slavic language spoken in Bulgaria. • adjective relating to Bulgaria.

bulgar wheat /bul-guh/ noun a cereal food made from whole wheat partially boiled and then dried.
– ORIGIN Turkish *bulgur* 'bruised grain'.

bulge noun **1** a rounded swelling on a flat surface. **2** informal a temporary increase: *a bulge in the birth rate.* • verb **1** swell or stick out. **2** be full of: *a bag bulging with papers and letters.*
– DERIVATIVES **bulgy** adjective.
– ORIGIN Latin *bulga* 'leather bag'.

bulimia /buu-lim-i-uh/ (also **bulimia nervosa** /ner-voh-suh/) noun an emotional disorder which causes bouts of overeating, followed by fasting or self-induced vomiting.
– DERIVATIVES **bulimic** adjective & noun.
– ORIGIN Greek *boulimia* 'ravenous hunger', from *bous* 'ox' + *limos* 'hunger'.

bulk noun **1** the mass or size of something large. **2** the greater part of something: *the bulk of the club's supporters are well behaved.* **3** a large mass or size of something. **4** roughage in food. • adjective large in quantity: *bulk orders.* • verb (**bulk something up/out**) treat a product so that its quantity appears greater than it really is.
– PHRASES **bulk large** be or seem to be very important. **in bulk** (of goods) in large quantities.
– ORIGIN probably from an Old Norse word meaning 'cargo'.

bulkhead noun a barrier between separate compartments inside a ship or aircraft.

bulky adjective (**bulkier**, **bulkiest**) large and awkward to handle.

bull[1] noun **1** an uncastrated male animal of the cattle family. **2** a large male animal, e.g. a whale or elephant. **3** Brit. a bullseye. **4** Stock Exchange a person who buys shares hoping to sell them at a higher price later. Often contrasted with BEAR[2].
– PHRASES **like a bull in a china shop** behaving clumsily in a delicate situation. **take the bull by the horns** deal decisively with a difficult situation.
– ORIGIN Old Norse.

bull[2] noun an order or announcement issued by the Pope.
– ORIGIN Latin *bulla* 'bubble', later 'seal or sealed document'.

bull[3] noun informal nonsense.
– ORIGIN unknown.

bull bar noun a protective metal grille fitted to the front of a motor vehicle.

bulldog noun a breed of dog with a protruding

lower jaw, a flat wrinkled face, and a broad chest.

bulldog clip noun Brit. trademark a metal device with two flat plates held together by a spring, used to hold papers together.

bulldoze verb **1** clear ground or destroy buildings with a bulldozer. **2** informal use force to do something or deal with someone: *he bulldozed his way to his first Formula One victory.*
– ORIGIN from BULL[1] + -*doze*, an alteration of the noun DOSE.

bulldozer noun a tractor with a broad curved blade at the front for clearing ground.

bullet noun **1** a projectile fired from a small firearm. **2** a solid circle printed before each item in a list.
– ORIGIN French *boulet* 'small ball'.

bulletin noun **1** a short official statement or summary of news. **2** a regular newsletter or report.
– ORIGIN Italian *bullettino* 'little passport'.

bulletin board noun **1** a site on a computer system where users can read or download files supplied by others and add their own files. **2** N. Amer. a noticeboard.

bulletproof adjective able to resist the penetration of bullets.

bullfighting noun the sport of baiting and killing a bull for public entertainment.
– DERIVATIVES **bullfight** noun **bullfighter** noun.

bullfinch noun a finch with mainly grey and black plumage, the male having a pink breast.

bullfrog noun a very large frog with a deep croak.

bullheaded adjective determined and obstinate.

bullhorn noun N. Amer. a megaphone.

bullion noun gold or silver in bulk before being made into coins.
– ORIGIN Old French *bouillon*.

bullish adjective **1** aggressively confident and self-assertive. **2** Stock Exchange characterized or influenced by rising share prices.
– DERIVATIVES **bullishly** adverb **bullishness** noun.

bull market noun Stock Exchange a market in which share prices are rising.

bull-necked adjective (of a man) having a thick neck.

bullock noun a castrated male animal of the cattle family, raised for beef.
– ORIGIN Old English.

bullring noun an arena where bullfights are held.

bullrush noun variant spelling of BULRUSH.

bullseye noun **1** the centre of the target in sports such as archery and darts. **2** a hard peppermint-flavoured sweet.

bullshit vulgar slang noun nonsense. • verb (**bullshits**, **bullshitting**, **bullshitted**) talk nonsense in an attempt to deceive someone.
– DERIVATIVES **bullshitter** noun.

bull terrier noun a dog that is a cross-breed of bulldog and terrier.

bully[1] noun (pl. **bullies**) a person who intimidates or persecutes weaker people. • verb (**bullies**, **bullying**, **bullied**) intimidate or persecute someone.
– PHRASES **bully for you!** often ironic an expression

b

of admiration or approval.
– ORIGIN probably from Dutch *boele* 'lover'.

bully² noun (pl. **bullies**) (also **bully off**) the start of play in field hockey, in which two opponents strike each other's sticks three times and then go for the ball.
– ORIGIN unknown.

bully³ (also **bully beef**) noun informal corned beef.
– ORIGIN from French *bouilli* 'boiled'.

bulrush (also **bullrush**) noun a tall waterside plant with a long brown head.
– ORIGIN probably from **BULL¹** in the sense 'large, coarse'.

bulwark /buul-werk/ noun 1 a defensive wall. 2 a person or thing that acts as a defence: *a bulwark against fascism*. 3 an extension of a ship's sides above deck level.
– ORIGIN German and Dutch *bolwerk*.

bum¹ noun Brit. informal a person's bottom.
– ORIGIN unknown.

bum² informal noun N. Amer. 1 a homeless person or beggar. 2 a lazy or worthless person. • verb (**bums, bumming, bummed**) 1 get something by asking or begging for it: *I bummed a cigarette off him.* 2 (**bum around**) chiefly N. Amer. travel or spend one's time with no particular aim or plan. • adjective bad; wrong: *the first bum note she'd played all evening.*
– ORIGIN probably from **BUMMER**.

bumbag noun Brit. informal a small pouch attached a belt, worn round the waist or hips.

bumble verb move or speak in an awkward or confused way.
– ORIGIN from **BOOM¹**.

bumblebee noun a large hairy bee with a loud hum.

bumf (also **bumph**) noun Brit. informal useless or dull printed information.
– ORIGIN abbreviation of slang *bum-fodder*.

bummer noun informal an annoying or disappointing thing.
– ORIGIN perhaps from German *bummeln* 'stroll, loaf about'.

bump noun 1 a light blow or collision. 2 a hump or swelling on a level surface. • verb 1 knock or run into someone or something with a jolt. 2 travel with a jolting movement: *the car bumped along the rutted track.* 3 (**bump into**) meet someone by chance. 4 (**bump someone off**) informal murder someone. 5 (**bump something up**) informal increase or raise something: *the company bumped up the prices.*
– DERIVATIVES **bumpy** adjective (**bumpier, bumpiest**).
– ORIGIN perhaps Scandinavian.

bumper noun a horizontal bar fixed across the front or back of a motor vehicle to reduce damage in a collision. • adjective exceptionally large or successful: *a bumper crop.*

bumper car noun a dodgem.

bumph noun variant spelling of **BUMF**.

bumpkin noun an unsophisticated person from the countryside.
– ORIGIN perhaps from Dutch *boomken* 'little tree' or *bommekijn* 'little barrel'.

bump-start verb another term for **PUSH-START**.

bumptious adjective irritatingly confident or self-important.

– DERIVATIVES **bumptiously** adverb **bumptiousness** noun.
– ORIGIN from **BUMP**.

bun noun 1 a small cake or bread roll. 2 a hairstyle in which the hair is drawn into a tight coil at the back of the head.
– PHRASES **have a bun in the oven** informal be pregnant.
– ORIGIN unknown.

bunce noun Brit. informal money or profit gained by someone.
– ORIGIN unknown.

bunch noun 1 a number of things growing or fastened together. 2 informal a group of people. 3 informal, chiefly N. Amer. a lot. • verb collect or form into a bunch.
– ORIGIN unknown.

bundle noun 1 a collection of things or quantity of material tied or wrapped up together. 2 a set of nerve, muscle, or other fibres which run parallel to each other. 3 informal a large amount of money. • verb 1 tie or roll something up in a bundle. 2 (**be bundled up**) be dressed in many warm clothes. 3 informal push or carry forcibly: *they bundled him into a van.*
– ORIGIN perhaps from Old English.

bunfight noun Brit. humorous a grand or official tea party or other social function.

bung¹ noun a stopper for a hole in a container. • verb 1 close a container with a bung. 2 (**bung something up**) block something up.
– ORIGIN Dutch *bonghe*.

bung² Brit. informal verb put or throw something somewhere carelessly or casually. • noun a bribe.
– ORIGIN uncertain.

bungalow noun a house with only one storey.
– ORIGIN Hindi, 'belonging to Bengal'.

bungee /bun-ji/ (also **bungee cord** or **rope**) noun a long rubber band encased in nylon, used for securing luggage and in bungee jumping.
– ORIGIN unknown.

bungee jumping noun the sport of leaping from a high place, held by a bungee around the ankles.
– DERIVATIVES **bungee jump** noun **bungee jumper** noun.

bungle verb 1 perform a task clumsily or incompetently. 2 (as adj. **bungling**) tending to make many mistakes. • noun a mistake or failure.
– DERIVATIVES **bungler** noun.
– ORIGIN unknown.

bunion noun a painful swelling on the big toe.
– ORIGIN Old French *buignon*.

bunk¹ noun a narrow shelf-like bed.
– ORIGIN unknown.

bunk² verb (**bunk off**) Brit. informal be absent from school or work without permission.
– PHRASES **do a bunk** leave somewhere hurriedly.
– ORIGIN unknown.

bunk³ noun informal, dated nonsense.
– ORIGIN abbreviation of **BUNKUM**.

bunk bed noun a piece of furniture consisting of two beds, one above the other.

bunker noun 1 a large container for storing

fuel. **2** an underground shelter for use in wartime. **3** a hollow filled with sand, forming an obstacle on a golf course.
– ORIGIN Scots, 'seat or bench'.

bunkhouse noun a building with sleeping accommodation for workers.

bunkum noun informal, dated nonsense.
– ORIGIN named after *Buncombe* County in North Carolina, mentioned in a speech made by its congressman with the sole intention of pleasing his constituents (c.1820).

bunny noun (pl. **bunnies**) informal **1** a child's term for a rabbit. **2** (also **bunny girl**) a nightclub hostess or waitress wearing a skimpy costume with ears and a tail.
– ORIGIN dialect *bun* 'squirrel, rabbit'.

Bunsen burner noun a small adjustable gas burner used in laboratories.
– ORIGIN named after the German chemist Robert *Bunsen*.

bunting¹ noun a songbird with brown streaked plumage and a boldly marked head.
– ORIGIN unknown.

bunting² noun flags and streamers used as decorations.
– ORIGIN unknown.

buoy /boy/ noun a floating object anchored to the sea bed that marks safe navigation channels for boats. • verb **1** keep someone or something afloat. **2** make or remain cheerful and confident: *he was buoyed up by his success.*
– ORIGIN probably from Dutch *boye, boeie*; the verb is from Spanish *boyar* 'to float'.

buoyant adjective **1** able to keep afloat. **2** cheerful and optimistic. **3** (of an economy or market) involved in much successful trade or activity.
– DERIVATIVES **buoyancy** noun **buoyantly** adverb.

BUPA /boo-puh/ abbreviation British United Provident Association, a private health insurance organization.

bur noun see BURR.

burble verb **1** make a continuous murmuring noise. **2** speak at length in a way that is difficult to understand. • noun a continuous murmuring noise.
– ORIGIN imitating the sound.

burbot /ber-buht/ noun a fish that is the only freshwater member of the cod family.
– ORIGIN Old French *borbete*.

burden noun **1** a heavy load. **2** a cause of hardship, worry, or grief: *the tax burden on low-income families.* **3** the main responsibility for a task. **4** the main theme of a speech, book, or argument. • verb **1** load someone or something heavily. **2** cause someone worry, hardship, or grief: *I don't want to burden you with my problems.*
– PHRASES **burden of proof** the obligation to prove that something is true.
– ORIGIN Old English.

burdensome adjective causing worry or difficulty.

burdock noun a plant of the daisy family, with large leaves and prickly flowers.
– ORIGIN from BUR + DOCK³.

bureau /byoor-oh/ noun (pl. **bureaux** or **bureaus** /byoor-ohz/) **1** Brit. a writing desk with drawers and a sloping top that opens downwards to

form a writing surface. **2** N. Amer. a chest of drawers. **3** an office that carries out a particular type of business: *a news bureau.* **4** a government department.
– ORIGIN French.

bureaucracy /byuu-rok-ruh-si/ noun (pl. **bureaucracies**) **1** a system of government in which most decisions are taken by state officials rather than by elected representatives. **2** administrative procedures that are too complicated.

bureaucrat /byoor-oh-krat/ noun an official in an organization or government department who is seen as being too concerned with following administrative guidelines.
– DERIVATIVES **bureaucratic** adjective.

bureaucratize (or **bureaucratise**) /byuu-rok-ruh-tyz/ verb run a state or organization by implementing or following administrative procedures that are too complicated.
– DERIVATIVES **bureaucratization** noun.

bureau de change /byoo-roh duh shonzh/ noun (pl. **bureaux de change** pronunc. same) a place where foreign money can be exchanged.
– ORIGIN French, 'office of exchange'.

burette /byuu-ret/ (US also **buret**) noun a glass tube with measurements on it and a tap at one end, for delivering known amounts of a liquid.
– ORIGIN French.

burgeon /ber-juhn/ verb grow or increase rapidly.
– ORIGIN Old French *bourgeonner* 'put out buds'.

burger noun a hamburger.

burgess noun **1** Brit. old use a citizen of a town or borough. **2** Brit. old use a Member of Parliament for a borough, town, or university. **3** (in the US and formerly in the UK) a magistrate or member of the governing body of a town.
– ORIGIN Old French *burgeis*.

burgh /rhymes with thorough/ noun old use or Scottish a borough or chartered town.
– ORIGIN Scots form of BOROUGH.

burgher /ber-ger/ noun old use a citizen of a town or city.

burglar noun a person who commits burglary.
– ORIGIN Old French *burgier* 'pillage'.

burglarize (or **burglarise**) verb North American term for BURGLE.

burglary noun (pl. **burglaries**) the crime of entering a building illegally and stealing its contents.

burgle verb chiefly Brit. enter a building illegally and steal its contents.

burgundy noun (pl. **burgundiies**) **1** a red wine from Burgundy, a region of east central France. **2** a deep red colour.

burial noun the burying of a dead body.
– ORIGIN Old English.

burin /byoor-in/ noun **1** a steel tool used for engraving. **2** Archaeology a flint tool with a chisel point.
– ORIGIN French.

burka /ber-kuh/ (also **burkha** or **burqa**) noun a long, loose garment covering the whole body, worn in public by some Muslim women.
– ORIGIN Urdu and Persian.

b

b

Burkinan /ber-**keen**-uhn/ noun a person from Burkina, a country in western Africa. •**adjective** relating to Burkina or its people.

burlap /**ber**-lap/ noun chiefly N. Amer. coarse canvas woven from jute or hemp, used to make sacks.
– ORIGIN unknown.

burlesque noun 1 a performance or piece of writing which makes fun of something by representing it in a comically exaggerated way 2 N. Amer. a variety show, typically including striptease. •**verb** (**burlesques, burlesquing, burlesqued**) make fun of someone or something by representing them in a comically exaggerated way.
– ORIGIN French.

burly adjective (**burlier, burliest**) (of a person) large and strong.
– DERIVATIVES **burliness** noun.
– ORIGIN probably from an Old English word meaning 'stately'.

Burman noun (pl. **Burmans**) & adjective another term for **Burmese**.

Burmese noun (pl. same) 1 a member of the largest ethnic group of Burma (now Myanmar) in SE Asia. 2 a person from Burma. 3 (also **Burmese cat**) a cat of a short-coated breed which originated in Asia. •**adjective** relating to Burma or the Burmese.

burn[1] verb (past and past part. **burned** or chiefly Brit. **burnt**) 1 (of a fire) flame or glow while using up a fuel. 2 be or cause to be harmed or destroyed by fire. 3 use a fuel as a source of heat or energy. 4 (of the skin) become red and painful as a result of exposure to the sun. 5 (**be burning with**) experience a very strong desire or emotion: *she was burning with curiosity.* 6 (**burn out**) become exhausted through overwork. 7 produce a CD by copying from an original or master copy. •**noun** an injury caused by burning.
– PHRASES **burn one's boats** (or **bridges**) do something which makes it impossible to return to the previous situation. **burn the candle at both ends** go to bed late and get up early. **burn the midnight oil** work late into the night.
– ORIGIN Old English.

burn[2] noun Scottish & N. English a small stream.
– ORIGIN Old English.

burned adjective variant spelling of **burnt**.

burner noun 1 a part of a cooker, lamp, etc. that gives out a flame. 2 a device for burning something.

burning adjective 1 very strong or deeply felt: *her burning ambition to win.* 2 of great interest and importance; requiring immediate action or attention: *the burning issues of the day.*
– DERIVATIVES **burningly** adverb.

burnish verb polish something by rubbing it. •**noun** the shine on a polished surface.
– ORIGIN Old French *brunir* 'make brown'.

burnous /ber-**nooss**/ (US also **burnoose**) noun a long hooded cloak worn by Arabs.
– ORIGIN Arabic.

burnout noun 1 physical or mental collapse. 2 overheating of an electrical device or component.

burnt (also **burned**) past and past participle of **burn**[1].

burp informal verb 1 belch. 2 make a baby belch after feeding. •**noun** a belch.
– ORIGIN imitating the sound.

burqa noun variant spelling of **burka**.

burr noun 1 a whirring sound. 2 a rough pronunciation of the letter *r*, as in some regional accents. 3 (also **bur**) a prickly seed case or flower head that clings to clothing and animal fur. 4 (also **bur**) a rough edge left on a metal object by the action of a tool. •**verb** make a whirring sound.
– ORIGIN probably Scandinavian.

burrito /bu-**ree**-toh/ noun (pl. **burritos**) a Mexican dish consisting of a tortilla rolled round a filling of minced beef or beans.
– ORIGIN Latin American Spanish.

burro /**boo**-roh/ noun (pl. **burros**) chiefly US a small donkey used as a pack animal.
– ORIGIN Spanish.

burrow noun a hole or tunnel dug by a small animal as a home. •**verb** 1 dig a hole or tunnel. 2 hide underneath or nestle into something. 3 search for something: *he was burrowing among his files.*
– DERIVATIVES **burrower** noun.
– ORIGIN variant of **borough**.

bursar noun chiefly Brit. a person who manages the financial affairs of a college or school.
– ORIGIN from Latin *bursa* 'bag, purse'.

bursary noun (pl. **bursaries**) Brit. a grant, especially one awarded to a student.

bursitis /ber-**sy**-tis/ noun inflammation of a bursa (fluid-filled sac), typically in a shoulder joint.
– ORIGIN from Latin *bursa* 'bag, purse'.

burst verb (past and past part. **burst**) 1 break suddenly and violently apart. 2 be very full: *the wardrobe was bursting with clothes.* 3 move or be opened suddenly and forcibly. 4 (**be bursting with**) feel a very strong emotion or impulse. 5 suddenly begin doing or producing something: *she burst into tears.* •**noun** 1 an instance of bursting. 2 a sudden brief outbreak: *a burst of activity.* 3 a period of continuous effort.
– ORIGIN Old English.

burton noun (in phrase **go for a burton**) Brit. informal be ruined, destroyed, or killed.
– ORIGIN perhaps referring to *Burton* ale, from Burton-upon-Trent.

Burundian /bu-**run**-di-uhn/ noun a person from Burundi, a country in central Africa. •**adjective** relating to Burundi.

bury verb (**buries, burying, buried**) 1 put or hide something underground. 2 place a dead body in the earth or a tomb. 3 cover someone or something completely. 4 hide or try to ignore something: *I buried the memories for years.* 5 (**bury oneself**) involve oneself deeply in something.
– PHRASES **bury one's head in the sand** ignore unpleasant realities.
– ORIGIN Old English.

bus noun (pl. **buses**; US also **busses**) 1 a large motor vehicle carrying customers along a fixed route. 2 a distinct set of conductors within a computer system, to which pieces of equipment may be connected in parallel. •**verb** (**buses, busing, bused**; or **busses, bussing, bussed**) 1 transport or travel in a bus. 2 N. Amer.

clear dirty crockery in a restaurant or cafeteria.
– DERIVATIVES **busload** noun.
– ORIGIN shortening of **OMNIBUS**.

busby noun (pl. **busbies**) a tall fur hat worn by certain military regiments.
– ORIGIN unknown.

bush¹ noun **1** a shrub or clump of shrubs with stems of moderate length. **2** (**the bush**) (in Australia and Africa) wild or uncultivated country. **3** a thick growth of hair.
– ORIGIN Old French *bois* 'wood'.

bush² noun Brit. **1** a metal lining for a hole in which something fits or revolves. **2** a sleeve that protects an electric cable.
– ORIGIN Dutch *busse*.

bushbaby noun (pl. **bushbabies**) a small African mammal with very large eyes.

bushed adjective informal very tired; exhausted.

bushel noun **1** Brit. a measure of capacity equal to 8 gallons (36.4 litres). **2** US a measure of capacity equal to 64 US pints (35.2 litres).
– ORIGIN Old French *boissel*.

bushido /boo-shi-doh, buu-**shee**-doh/ noun the code of honour and morals of the Japanese samurai.
– ORIGIN Japanese.

bushing noun another term for **BUSH²**.

Bushman noun (pl. **Bushmen**) **1** a member of any of several aboriginal peoples of southern Africa. **2** (**bushman**) a person who lives or travels in the Australian bush.

bush telegraph noun an informal network by which information is spread quickly.

bushwhack verb **1** N. Amer. & Austral./NZ live or travel in the bush. **2** N. Amer. & Austral./NZ work clearing scrub and felling trees. **3** N. Amer. ambush someone.
– DERIVATIVES **bushwhacker** noun.

bushy adjective (**bushier**, **bushiest**) **1** growing thickly. **2** covered with bush or bushes.
– DERIVATIVES **bushily** adverb **bushiness** noun.

business noun **1** a person's regular occupation or trade. **2** commercial activity. **3** a commercial organization. **4** work to be done or matters to be attended to. **5** a person's concern: *that's none of your business.* **6** informal a difficult matter. **7** (**the business**) Brit. informal an excellent person or thing.
– PHRASES **in business** (of a commercial organization) operating. **mind one's own business** avoid interfering in other people's affairs.
– ORIGIN Old English, 'anxiety' (from **BUSY** + **-NESS**).

business end noun informal the functional part of a tool or device.

businesslike adjective efficient and practical.

businessman (or **businesswoman**) noun (pl. **businessmen** or **businesswomen**) a person who works in commerce, especially at executive level.

busk verb play music in the street in order to be given money by passers-by.
– DERIVATIVES **busker** noun.
– ORIGIN from former French *busquer* 'seek'.

buskin noun historical a calf-high or knee-high boot.
– ORIGIN probably from Old French *bouzequin*.

busman's holiday noun leisure time spent doing the same thing that one does at work.

bust¹ noun **1** a woman's breasts. **2** a sculpture of a person's head, shoulders, and chest.
– ORIGIN from Latin *bustum* 'tomb, tomb monument'.

bust² informal verb (past and past part. **busted** or **bust**) **1** break, split, or burst. **2** chiefly N. Amer. hit someone hard. **3** chiefly N. Amer. (of the police) raid or search a building. **4** chiefly N. Amer. arrest someone. •noun **1** a period of economic difficulty. **2** a police raid. •adjective **1** Brit. damaged; broken. **2** bankrupt.
– ORIGIN variant of **BURST**.

bustard /**buss**-terd/ noun a large swift-running bird of open country.
– ORIGIN perhaps from Old French *bistarde* and *oustarde*, from Latin *avis tarda* 'slow bird'.

buster noun informal **1** chiefly N. Amer. a form of address to a man or boy. **2** a person or thing that stops a specified thing: *a crime-buster.*

bustier /**buss**-ti-ay/ noun a woman's close-fitting strapless top.
– ORIGIN French.

bustle¹ verb **1** move in an energetic and busy way. **2** (often as adj. **bustling**) (of a place) be full of activity. •noun excited activity and movement.
– ORIGIN perhaps from former *busk* 'prepare'.

bustle² noun historical a pad or frame worn under a skirt to puff it out behind.
– ORIGIN unknown.

bust-up noun informal a serious quarrel or fight.

busty adjective (**bustier**, **bustiest**) informal having large breasts.

busy adjective (**busier**, **busiest**) **1** having a great deal to do. **2** currently occupied with an activity. **3** full of activity: *busy streets.* **4** excessively detailed or decorated. •verb (**busies**, **busying**, **busied**) (**busy oneself**) keep oneself occupied.
– DERIVATIVES **busily** adverb **busyness** noun.
– ORIGIN Old English.

busybody noun (pl. **busybodies**) an interfering or nosy person.

busy Lizzie noun Brit. a plant with many red, pink, or white flowers.

but conjunction **1** in spite of that; nevertheless. **2** on the contrary. **3** other than; otherwise than. **4** old use without it being the case that. •preposition except; apart from. •adverb no more than; only. •noun an objection.
– PHRASES **but for 1** except for. **2** if it were not for. **but then** on the other hand.
– ORIGIN Old English, 'outside, without, except'.

USAGE: On starting a sentence with **but**, see the note at **AND**.

butane /**byoo**-tayn/ noun a flammable hydrocarbon gas present in petroleum and natural gas and used as a fuel.
– ORIGIN from Latin *butyrum* 'butter'.

butch adjective informal masculine in a conspicuous or aggressive way.
– ORIGIN perhaps an abbreviation of **BUTCHER**.

butcher noun **1** a person who cuts up and sells meat as a trade. **2** a person who slaughters animals for food. **3** a person who kills brutally.

b

• **verb 1** slaughter or cut up an animal for food. **2** kill someone brutally. **3** spoil something by doing it badly.
– PHRASES **have** (or **take**) **a butcher's** Brit. informal have a look. [*butcher's* from *butcher's hook*, rhyming slang for a 'look'.]
– DERIVATIVES **butchery** noun (pl. **butcheries**).
– ORIGIN Old French *bochier*.

butler noun the chief manservant of a house.
– ORIGIN Old French *bouteillier* 'cup-bearer'.

butt¹ verb **1** hit someone or something with the head or horns. **2** (**butt in**) interrupt a conversation or activity. • noun a rough push with the head.
– ORIGIN Old French *boter*.

butt² noun **1** a person or thing that is the target of criticism or ridicule. **2** a target or range in archery or shooting.
– ORIGIN Old French *but*.

butt³ noun **1** the thicker end of a tool or a weapon. **2** the stub of a cigar or a cigarette. **3** N. Amer. informal a person's bottom. • verb **1** adjoin or meet end to end. **2** join pieces of timber or other building materials with the ends or sides flat against each other.
– PHRASES **butt naked** informal completely naked.
– ORIGIN from Dutch *bot* 'stumpy'.

butt⁴ noun a cask used for wine, ale, or water.
– ORIGIN Latin *buttis*.

butte /byoot/ noun N. Amer. & technical an isolated hill with steep sides and a flat top.
– ORIGIN French, 'mound'.

butter noun a pale yellow fatty substance made by churning cream. • verb **1** spread something with butter. **2** (**butter someone up**) informal flatter someone.
– PHRASES **look as if butter wouldn't melt in one's mouth** informal appear innocent while being the opposite.
– ORIGIN from Greek *bouturon*.

butter bean noun Brit. a large flat white edible bean.

buttercream noun a mixture of butter and icing sugar used as a filling or topping for a cake.

buttercup noun a plant with bright yellow cup-shaped flowers.

butterfat noun the natural fat contained in milk and dairy products.

butterfingers noun informal a person who often drops things.

butterfly noun (pl. **butterflies**) **1** an insect with two pairs of large wings, which feeds on nectar and is active by day. **2** a showy or frivolous person: *a social butterfly.* **3** (**butterflies**) informal a fluttering sensation felt in the stomach when one is nervous. **4** a stroke in swimming in which both arms are raised out of the water and lifted forwards together.
– ORIGIN Old English.

butterfly nut noun another term for WING NUT.

butter icing noun another term for BUTTERCREAM.

buttermilk noun the slightly sour liquid left after butter has been churned.

butternut squash noun a pear-shaped variety of winter squash with light yellowish-brown rind and orange flesh.

butterscotch noun a brittle sweet made with butter and brown sugar.

buttery¹ adjective containing, tasting like, or covered with butter.

buttery² noun (pl. **butteries**) Brit. a room in a college where food is kept and sold to students.
– ORIGIN Old French *boterie* 'cask store'.

buttie noun (pl. **butties**) variant spelling of BUTTY.

buttock noun either of the two round fleshy parts of the human body that form the bottom.
– ORIGIN Old English.

button noun **1** a small disc or knob sewn on to a garment to fasten it by being pushed through a buttonhole. **2** a knob on an electrical or electronic device which is pressed to operate it. **3** chiefly N. Amer. a decorative badge pinned to clothing. • verb **1** fasten or be fastened with buttons. **2** (**button something up**) informal complete something satisfactorily.
– PHRASES **button one's lip** informal stop or refrain from talking. **buttoned-up** informal conservative or inhibited. **on the button** informal, chiefly N. Amer. precisely.
– DERIVATIVES **buttoned** adjective.
– ORIGIN Old French *bouton*.

buttonhole noun **1** a slit made in a garment to receive a button for fastening. **2** Brit. a flower or spray worn in a lapel buttonhole. • verb informal stop someone so as to begin a conversation.

button mushroom noun a young unopened mushroom.

button-through adjective Brit. (of clothing) fastened with buttons from top to bottom.

buttress /but-triss/ noun **1** a projecting support built against a wall. **2** a projecting portion of a hill or mountain. • verb **1** support something with buttresses. **2** support or reinforce: *I was hoping that facts would buttress my point of view.*
– ORIGIN from Old French *ars bouterez* 'thrusting arch'.

butty (also **buttie**) noun (pl. **butties**) informal, chiefly N. English a sandwich.
– ORIGIN from BUTTER.

butyl /byoo-tyl, -til/ noun Chemistry the radical $-C_4H_9$, derived from butane.

buxom /buk-suhm/ adjective (of a woman) attractively plump and large-breasted.
– ORIGIN first meaning 'compliant': from Old English, 'to bend'.

buy verb (**buys**, **buying**, **bought**) **1** obtain something in exchange for payment. **2** get by sacrifice or great effort: *greatness is dearly bought.* **3** informal accept the truth of: *I don't buy the claim that the ends justify the means.* • noun informal something bought; a purchase.
– PHRASES **buy someone out** pay someone to give up an interest or share in something. **buy time** delay an event so as to have longer to improve one's own position. **have bought it** informal be killed.
– ORIGIN Old English.

USAGE: For an explanation of the difference between **brought** and **bought**, see the note at BROUGHT.

buyer noun **1** a person who buys something. **2** a person employed to buy stock for a retail or manufacturing business.

buyer's market noun an economic situation in which goods or shares are plentiful and buyers can keep prices down.

buyout noun the purchase of a controlling share in a company.

buzz noun **1** a low, continuous humming or murmuring sound. **2** the sound of a buzzer or telephone. **3** an atmosphere of excitement and activity. **4** informal a thrill. •verb **1** make a humming sound. **2** call someone with a buzzer. **3** move quickly. **4** (**buzz off**) informal go away. **5** be full of excitement or activity: *the department was buzzing with the news.* **6** informal (of an aircraft) fly very close to something at high speed.
– ORIGIN imitating the sound.

buzzard /buz-zerd/ noun **1** a large bird of prey which soars in wide circles. **2** N. Amer. a vulture.
– ORIGIN Old French *busard*.

buzz cut noun a very short haircut in which the hair is clipped close to the head.

buzzer noun an electrical device that makes a buzzing noise to attract attention.

buzzword noun informal a technical word or phrase that has become fashionable.

buzzy adjective informal (of a place or atmosphere) lively and exciting.

bwana /bwahnuh/ noun (in East Africa) a form of address for a boss or master.
– ORIGIN Swahili.

by preposition **1** indicating the person or thing performing an action or the means of achieving something. **2** indicating a quantity or amount, or the size of a margin. **3** expressing multiplication, especially in dimensions. **4** indicating the end of a time period. **5** near to; beside. **6** past and beyond. **7** during. **8** according to. •adverb so as to go past. •noun (pl. **byes**) variant spelling of **bye**[1].
– PHRASES **by and by** before long. **by the by** (or **bye**) incidentally. **by and large** on the whole. [first describing the handling of a ship both to the wind and off it.]
– ORIGIN Old English.

by- (also **bye-**) prefix less important; secondary: *by-election.*

bye[1] (also **by**) noun **1** the transfer of a competitor directly to the next round of a competition because they have no opponent assigned to them. **2** Cricket a run scored from a ball that passes the batsman without being hit.

– PHRASES **by the bye** variant spelling of **by the by** (see **by**).
– ORIGIN from **by**.

bye[2] (also **bye-bye**) exclamation informal goodbye.

by-election noun Brit. an election held during a government's term of office to fill a vacant seat.

bygone adjective belonging to an earlier time.
– PHRASES **let bygones be bygones** forget past disagreements and be reconciled.

by-law (also **bye-law**) noun **1** Brit. a regulation made by a local authority. **2** a rule made by a company or society.
– ORIGIN probably from Old Norse, 'town'.

byline noun **1** a line in a newspaper naming the writer of an article. **2** (also **byleine**) (in football) the part of the goal line to either side of the goal.

bypass noun **1** a road passing round a town for through traffic. **2** a secondary channel or connection to allow a flow when the main one is closed or blocked. **3** a surgical operation to make an alternative passage to aid the circulation of blood. •verb **1** go past or round something. **2** avoid a problem or obstacle.

byplay noun secondary action in a play or film.

by-product noun **1** an incidental or secondary product made in the manufacture of something else. **2** an unintended but unavoidable secondary result.

byre /rhymes with fire/ noun Brit. a farm building in which cattle are kept.
– ORIGIN Old English.

byroad noun a minor road.

Byronic /by-ron-ik/ adjective **1** characteristic of Lord Byron (1788–1824) or his poetry. **2** (of a man) attractively mysterious and moody.

bystander noun a person who is present at an event but does not take part.

byte /rhymes with white/ noun a unit of information stored in a computer, equal to eight bits.
– ORIGIN from **bit**[4] and **bite**.

byway noun a minor road or path.

byword noun **1** a notable example: *his name became a byword for luxury.* **2** a proverb or saying.

Byzantine /bi-zan-tyn/ adjective **1** relating to Byzantium (now Istanbul), the Byzantine Empire, or the Eastern Orthodox Church. **2** excessively complicated. **3** very crafty or underhand. •noun a citizen of Byzantium or the Byzantine Empire.

Cc

C¹ (also **c**) noun (pl. **Cs** or **C's**) **1** the third letter of the alphabet. **2** indicating the third item in a set. **3** Music the first note of the scale of C major. **4** the Roman numeral for 100. [abbreviation of Latin *centum* 'hundred'.]

C² abbreviation **1** (**C.**) (on maps) Cape. **2** Celsius or centigrade. **3** (in names of sports clubs) City. **4** (©) copyright. **5** (in Britain) Conservative. **6** Physics coulomb(s). • **symbol** the chemical element carbon.

c abbreviation **1** Cricket caught by. **2** cent(s). **3** (preceding a date or amount) circa. **4** (**c.**) century or centuries. • **symbol** Physics the speed of light in a vacuum.

CA abbreviation California.

Ca symbol the chemical element calcium.

ca. abbreviation (preceding a date or amount) circa.

CAB abbreviation Citizens' Advice Bureau.

cab noun **1** (also **taxi cab**) a taxi. **2** the driver's compartment in a lorry, bus, or train. **3** historical a horse-drawn vehicle for public hire.
– ORIGIN abbreviation of **CABRIOLET**.

cabal /kuh-**bal**/ noun a small group of people who plot secretly to gain political power.
– ORIGIN Latin *cabala* 'Kabbalah'.

Cabala noun variant spelling of **KABBALAH**.

cabaret /**kab**-uh-ray/ noun **1** entertainment held in a nightclub or restaurant while the audience sit at tables. **2** a nightclub or restaurant where cabaret is performed.
– ORIGIN Old French, 'wooden structure, inn'.

cabbage noun **1** a vegetable with thick green or purple leaves surrounding a heart or head of young leaves. **2** Brit. offensive a person whose physical or mental activity is impaired or destroyed as a result of injury or illness.
– ORIGIN Old French *caboche* 'head'.

cabbage white noun a white butterfly whose caterpillars are pests of cabbages and related plants.

Cabbala noun variant spelling of **KABBALAH**.

cabbalistic /kab-uh-**lis**-tik/ adjective relating to or associated with the Kabbalah.
– ORIGIN variant of Kabbalistic (see **KABBALAH**).

cabby (also **cabbie**) noun (pl. **cabbies**) informal a taxi driver.

caber /**kay**-ber/ noun a roughly trimmed tree trunk that is thrown in the Scottish Highland sport of tossing the caber.
– ORIGIN Scottish Gaelic *cabar* 'pole'.

Cabernet Sauvignon /**soh**-vin-yon/ noun a variety of black wine grape originally from the Bordeaux area of France.
– ORIGIN French.

cabin noun **1** a private room on a ship. **2** the passenger compartment in an aircraft. **3** a small wooden shelter or house.
– ORIGIN from Latin *capanna*.

cabin boy noun chiefly historical a boy employed to wait on a ship's officers or passengers.

cabin cruiser noun a motorboat with living accommodation.

cabinet noun **1** a cupboard with drawers or shelves for storing or displaying articles. **2** a wooden box or piece of furniture housing a radio, television, or speaker. **3** (also **Cabinet**) a committee of senior ministers responsible for government policy.
– DERIVATIVES **cabinetry** noun.
– ORIGIN from **CABIN**; sense 3 derives from the former sense 'small private room'.

cabinetmaker noun a skilled joiner who makes furniture or similar high-quality woodwork.

cabin fever noun informal, chiefly N. Amer. depression and irritability resulting from long confinement indoors during the winter.

cable noun **1** a thick rope of wire or hemp. **2** an insulated wire or wires for transmitting electricity or telecommunication signals. **3** a cablegram. **4** Nautical a length of 200 yards (182.9 m) or (in the US) 240 yards (219.4 m). • **verb** dated send a cablegram to someone.
– ORIGIN from Latin *capulum* 'halter'.

cable car noun a small carriage suspended on a moving cable and travelling up and down a mountainside.

cablegram noun historical a telegraph message sent by cable.

cable-knit adjective (of an item of clothing) knitted using cable stitch.

cable stitch noun a combination of knitted stitches resembling twisted rope.

cable television noun a system in which television programmes are transmitted to subscribers by cable.

cabochon /**kab**-uh-shon/ noun a gem that is polished but not cut in facets.
– ORIGIN French, 'small head'.

caboodle noun (in phrase **the whole caboodle** or **the whole kit and caboodle**) informal the whole number or quantity of people or things in question.
– ORIGIN uncertain.

caboose /kuh-**boos**/ noun N. Amer. a wagon with accommodation for the crew on a freight

train.
– ORIGIN Dutch *kabuis* 'kitchen on a ship's deck'.

cabriole leg /kab-ri-ohl/ noun a kind of curved leg characteristic of Chippendale and Queen Anne furniture.
– ORIGIN French, 'light leap' (from the resemblance to the front leg of a leaping animal).

cabriolet /kab-ri-oh-lay/ noun **1** a car with a roof that folds down. **2** a light two-wheeled carriage with a hood, drawn by one horse.
– ORIGIN from French *cabriole* 'light leap' (because of the carriage's motion).

cacao /kuh-kah-oh/ noun the bean-like seeds of a tropical American tree, from which cocoa and chocolate are made.
– ORIGIN Nahuatl.

cachaca /kuh-shah-kuh/ noun a Brazilian white rum made from sugar cane.
– ORIGIN Portuguese *cacaça*.

cache /kash/ noun **1** a hidden store of things. **2** Computing an auxiliary memory from which high-speed retrieval is possible. • verb store something in a cache.
– ORIGIN from French *cacher* 'to hide'.

cachet /ka-shay/ noun **1** the state of being respected or admired; prestige: *he would miss the cachet of working at one of the world's best companies.* **2** a distinguishing mark or seal.
– ORIGIN French.

cachexia /kuh-kek-si-uh/ noun Medicine weakness and wasting of the body.
– ORIGIN Greek *kakhexia*.

cacique /kuh-seek/ noun **1** (in Latin America or the Spanish-speaking Caribbean) a native chief. **2** (in Spain or Latin America) a local political boss.
– ORIGIN from Taino (an extinct Caribbean language).

cack noun Brit. informal excrement.
– ORIGIN Old English.

cack-handed adjective Brit. informal **1** clumsy. **2** derogatory left-handed.

cackle verb **1** laugh in a noisy, harsh way. **2** (of a hen or goose) make a noisy clucking cry. • noun a noisy clucking cry or laugh.
– ORIGIN probably from German *käkelen*.

cacophony /kuh-koff-uh-ni/ noun (pl. **cacophonies**) a mixture of loud and unpleasant sounds.
– DERIVATIVES **cacophonous** adjective.
– ORIGIN Greek *kakophōnia*.

cactus noun (pl. **cacti** /kak-tuhss//kak-ty/ or **cactuses**) a succulent plant with a thick fleshy stem bearing spines but no leaves.
– ORIGIN Greek *kaktos* 'cardoon'.

cad noun dated or humorous a man who behaves dishonourably, especially towards a woman.
– DERIVATIVES **caddish** adjective.
– ORIGIN abbreviation of **CADDIE** or **CADET**.

cadaver /kuh-da-ver/ noun Medicine or literary a corpse.
– ORIGIN from Latin *cadere* 'to fall'.

cadaverous adjective very pale, thin, or bony.

caddie (also **caddy**) noun (pl. **caddies**) a person who carries a golfer's clubs and provides other assistance during a match. • verb (**caddies**, **caddying**, **caddied**) work as a caddie.

– ORIGIN French *cadet* (see **CADET**).

caddis /kad-iss/ (also **caddis fly**) noun a small winged insect having larvae that live in water and build cases of sticks, stones, etc.
– ORIGIN unknown.

caddy noun (pl. **caddies**) a small storage container, especially for tea.
– ORIGIN Malay, referring to a unit of weight of 1⅓ lb (0.61 kg).

cadence /kay-duhnss/ noun **1** the rise and fall in pitch of a person's voice. **2** a sequence of notes or chords making up the end of a musical phrase.
– DERIVATIVES **cadenced** adjective.
– ORIGIN Italian *cadenza*.

cadenza /kuh-den-zuh/ noun a difficult solo passage in a concerto or other musical work, typically near the end.
– ORIGIN Italian.

cadet noun **1** a young trainee in the armed services or police. **2** formal or old use a younger son or daughter.
– DERIVATIVES **cadetship** noun.
– ORIGIN French.

cadge verb informal, chiefly Brit. ask for or get something without giving anything in return.
– DERIVATIVES **cadger** noun.
– ORIGIN from northern English and Scots *cadger* 'travelling dealer'.

cadmium /kad-mi-uhm/ noun a silvery-white metallic chemical element resembling zinc.
– ORIGIN from Latin *cadmia* 'calamine' (it is found with calamine in zinc ore).

cadre /kah-der/ noun **1** a small group of people trained for a particular purpose or profession. **2** /also kay-der/ a group of activists in a revolutionary organization.
– ORIGIN French.

caduceus /kuh-dew-si-uhss/ noun (pl. **caducei** /kuh-dew-si-I/) an ancient Greek or Roman herald's wand, typically one with two serpents twined round it, carried by the messenger god Hermes or Mercury.
– ORIGIN Latin.

caecum /see-kuhm/ (US **cecum** /see-kuh/) noun (pl. **caeca** /see-kuh/) a pouch connected to the junction of the small and large intestines.
– DERIVATIVES **caecal** adjective.
– ORIGIN from Latin *intestinum caecum* 'blind gut'.

Caerns. abbreviation Caernarfonshire.

Caerphilly /kair-fil-i, kuh-fil-i/ noun a kind of mild white cheese, originally made in Caerphilly in Wales.

Caesar /see-zer/ noun a title of Roman emperors, especially those from Augustus to Hadrian.
– ORIGIN family name of the Roman statesman Gaius Julius *Caesar*.

Caesarean /si-zair-i-uhn/ (also **Caesarian**) noun a Caesarean section. • adjective relating to Julius Caesar or the Caesars.

Caesarean section noun a surgical operation for delivering a child by cutting through the wall of the mother's abdomen.
– ORIGIN from the story that Julius Caesar was delivered by this method.

Caesar salad noun a salad consisting of cos lettuce and croutons served with a dressing of

olive oil, lemon juice, raw egg, and Worcester sauce.
– ORIGIN named after *Caesar* Cardini, the Mexican restaurateur who invented it.

caesium /**see**-zi-uhm/ (US **cesium**) noun a soft, silvery, extremely reactive metallic chemical element.
– ORIGIN from Latin *caesius* 'greyish-blue'.

caesura /si-**zyoor**-uh/ noun a pause near the middle of a line of verse.
– ORIGIN Latin.

cafard /ka-**fah**/ noun literary deep depression; melancholy.
– ORIGIN French.

cafe /**ka**-fay/ (also **café**) noun a small restaurant selling light meals and drinks.
– ORIGIN French, 'coffee or coffee house'.

cafe society noun people who spend a lot of time in fashionable restaurants and nightclubs.

cafeteria noun a self-service restaurant.
– ORIGIN Latin American Spanish, 'coffee shop'.

cafetière /ka-fuh-**tyair**/ noun a coffee pot containing a plunger with which the grounds are pushed to the bottom before the coffee is poured.
– ORIGIN French.

caffeine /**kaf**-feen/ noun a substance found in tea and coffee plants which stimulates the central nervous system.
– DERIVATIVES **caffeinated** adjective.
– ORIGIN French *caféine*.

caffè latte /ka-fay **lah**-tay, ka-fay **la**-tay/ noun see **LATTE**.

caftan noun variant spelling of **KAFTAN**.

cage noun **1** a structure of bars or wires in which birds or other animals are confined. **2** any similar structure, especially the compartment in a lift. • verb confine someone or something in a cage.
– ORIGIN Old French.

cagey adjective informal cautiously reluctant to give information: *airlines are cagey about their policy on free upgrades to business class.*
– DERIVATIVES **cagily** adverb **caginess** (also **cageyness**) noun.
– ORIGIN unknown.

cagoule /kuh-**gool**/ (also **kagoul**) noun Brit. a light waterproof jacket with a hood.
– ORIGIN French, 'cowl'.

cahoots /kuh-**hoots**/ plural noun (in phrase **in cahoots**) informal secretly working to achieve something dishonest or underhand with others.
– ORIGIN unknown.

caiman /**kay**-muhn/ (also **cayman**) noun a tropical American reptile similar to an alligator.
– ORIGIN Carib.

Cain noun (in phrase **raise Cain**) informal create trouble or a commotion.
– ORIGIN from *Cain*, eldest son of Adam and Eve and murderer of his brother Abel (Genesis 4).

caipirinha /ky-pi-**rin**-yuh/ noun a cocktail made with cachaça, lime or lemon juice, sugar, and crushed ice.
– ORIGIN Brazilian Portuguese.

caique /ky-**eek**/ noun **1** a light rowing boat used on the Bosporus. **2** a small eastern Mediterranean sailing ship.
– ORIGIN Turkish *kayık*.

cairn noun **1** a mound of rough stones built as a memorial or landmark. **2** (also **cairn terrier**) a small breed of terrier with a shaggy coat.
– ORIGIN Scottish Gaelic *carn*.

caisson /**kay**-suhn/ noun **1** a large watertight chamber in which underwater construction work may be carried out. **2** a vessel or structure used as a gate across the entrance of a dry dock or basin.
– ORIGIN French, 'large chest'.

cajole /kuh-**johl**/ verb persuade someone to do something by coaxing or flattery.
– DERIVATIVES **cajolery** noun.
– ORIGIN French *cajoler*.

Cajun /**kay**-juhn/ noun a member of a French-speaking community in areas of southern Louisiana, descended from French Canadians. • adjective relating to the Cajuns.
– ORIGIN alteration of *Acadian* 'relating to Acadia', a former French colony in Canada.

cake noun **1** an item of soft sweet food made from baking a mixture of flour, fat, eggs, and sugar. **2** a flat round item of savoury food that is baked or fried. • verb (of a thick or sticky substance) cover and form a hard layer on something: *my clothes were caked with mud.*
– PHRASES **a piece of cake** informal something easily achieved. **sell like hot cakes** informal be sold quickly and in large quantities. **take the cake** see take the biscuit at **BISCUIT**.
– DERIVATIVES **cakey** adjective (informal).
– ORIGIN Scandinavian.

cakehole noun Brit. informal a person's mouth.

cakewalk noun informal a very easy task.
– ORIGIN first referring to an American black contest in graceful walking which had a cake as a prize.

Cal abbreviation large calorie(s).

cal abbreviation small calorie(s).

calabash /**kal**-uh-bash/ noun a water container, tobacco pipe, or other object made from the dried shell of a gourd.
– ORIGIN Spanish *calabaza*.

calabrese /**kal**-uh-breez/ noun a bright green variety of broccoli.
– ORIGIN Italian, 'Calabrian' (*Calabria* is a region of SW Italy).

calamine /**kal**-uh-myn/ noun a pink powder consisting of zinc carbonate and ferric oxide, used to make a soothing lotion.
– ORIGIN Latin *calamina*.

calamity noun (pl. **calamities**) a sudden event causing great damage or distress.
– DERIVATIVES **calamitous** adjective **calamitously** adverb.
– ORIGIN Latin *calamitas*.

calash noun another term for **CALECHE**.

calcareous /kal-**kair**-i-uhss/ adjective containing calcium carbonate; chalky.
– ORIGIN from Latin *calx* 'lime'.

calciferol /kal-si-fuh-rol/ noun vitamin D_2, essential for the deposition of calcium in bones.

calciferous /kal-si-fuh-ruhss/ adjective containing or producing calcium salts, especially calcium carbonate.

calcify /**kal**-si-fy/ verb (**calcifies, calcifying,**

calcified) harden something by a deposit of calcium salts.
– DERIVATIVES **calcification** noun.

calcine /**kal**-syn/ verb reduce, oxidize, or dry a substance by exposure to strong heat.
– DERIVATIVES **calcination** noun.
– ORIGIN Latin *calcinare*.

calcite /**kal**-syt/ noun a white or colourless mineral consisting of calcium carbonate.
– ORIGIN German *Calcit*.

calcium noun a soft grey reactive metallic chemical element.
– ORIGIN from Latin *calx* 'lime'.

calcium carbonate noun a white insoluble compound occurring naturally as chalk, limestone, marble, and calcite.

calculate verb **1** determine the amount or number of something mathematically. **2** intend an action to have a particular effect: *his words were calculated to hurt her.* **3** (**calculate on**) include something as an essential element in one's plans.
– DERIVATIVES **calculable** adjective.
– ORIGIN Latin *calculare* 'count'.

calculated adjective done with awareness of the likely consequences: *a calculated act of terrorism.*
– DERIVATIVES **calculatedly** adverb.

calculating adjective craftily planning things so as to benefit oneself.

calculation noun **1** an act of calculating the amount or number of something mathematically. **2** an assessment of the effects of a course of action.

calculator noun something used for making mathematical calculations, in particular a small electronic device.

calculus /**kal**-kyuu-luhss/ noun **1** (pl. **calculuses**) the branch of mathematics concerned with problems involving rates of variation. **2** (pl. **calculi** /**kal**-kyuu-ly/) a hard mass formed by minerals in the kidney, gall bladder, or other organ of the body.
– ORIGIN Latin, 'small pebble' (as used on an abacus).

caldera /kol-**dair**-uh/ noun a large volcanic crater, especially one formed by the collapse of the volcano's mouth.
– ORIGIN from Latin *caldaria* 'boiling pot'.

caldron noun chiefly US variant spelling of **CAULDRON**.

caleche /kuh-**lesh**/ (also **calash**) noun historical **1** a light carriage with a removable folding hood. **2** a woman's hooped silk hood.
– ORIGIN French.

Caledonian /ka-li-**doh**-ni-uhn/ adjective relating to Scotland or the Scottish Highlands.
– ORIGIN from *Caledonia*, the Latin name for northern Britain.

calendar /**ka**-lin-der/ noun **1** a chart or series of pages showing the days, weeks, and months of a particular year. **2** a system by which the beginning, length, and subdivisions of the year are fixed. **3** a list of special days, events, or activities.
– DERIVATIVES **calendrical** /ka-**len**-drik'l/ adjective.
– ORIGIN from Latin *kalendae* (see **CALENDS**).

calender /**kal**-in-duhr/ noun a machine in

which cloth or paper is pressed by rollers to glaze or smooth it.
– ORIGIN French *calendre*.

calends /**kal**-indz/ (also **kalends**) plural noun the first day of the month in the ancient Roman calendar.
– ORIGIN Latin *kalendae, calendae*.

calendula /kuh-**len**-dyoo-luh/ noun a plant of a family that includes the common marigold.
– ORIGIN from Latin *calendae* (see **CALENDS**); perhaps because it flowers for most of the year.

calf[1] noun (pl. **calves**) **1** a domestic cow or bull in its first year. **2** the young of some other large mammals, such as elephants.
– ORIGIN Old English.

calf[2] noun (pl. **calves**) the fleshy part at the back of a person's leg below the knee.
– ORIGIN Old Norse.

calfskin noun leather made from the hide or skin of a calf.

calibrate /**ka**-li-brayt/ verb **1** mark a gauge or instrument with a standard scale of readings. **2** compare the readings of an instrument with those of a standard.
– DERIVATIVES **calibration** noun **calibrator** noun.
– ORIGIN from **CALIBRE**.

calibre /**ka**-li-ber/ (US **caliber**) noun **1** the quality of something, especially a person's ability: *scholars of the highest calibre.* **2** the diameter of the inside of a gun barrel, or of a bullet or shell.
– ORIGIN French.

calico /**ka**-li-koh/ noun (pl. **calicoes** or US also **calicos**) **1** Brit. a type of plain white or unbleached cotton cloth. **2** N. Amer. printed cotton fabric.
– ORIGIN from *Calicut*, a seaport in India where the fabric originated.

Californian noun a person from California. • adjective relating to California.

californium /**ka**-li-**for**-ni-uhm/ noun an unstable, artificially made radioactive metallic chemical element.
– ORIGIN named after *California* University (where it was first made).

caliper /**ka**-li-per/ (also **calliper**) noun **1** (also **calipers**) a measuring instrument with two hinged legs and in-turned or out-turned points. **2** a motor-vehicle or bicycle brake consisting of two or more hinged components. **3** a metal support for a person's leg.
– ORIGIN probably from **CALIBRE**.

caliph /**kay**-lif/ noun historical the chief Muslim civil and religious ruler, regarded as the successor of Muhammad.
– DERIVATIVES **caliphate** noun.
– ORIGIN Arabic, 'deputy of God'.

calisthenics plural noun US spelling of **CALLISTHENICS**.

calk noun & verb US spelling of **CAULK**.

call verb **1** cry out to someone so as to summon them or attract their attention. **2** telephone someone. **3** order or ask someone to go or come somewhere. **4** pay a brief visit. **5** give a specified name or description to: *they called their son David.* **6** fix a date or time for a meeting, election, or strike. **7** predict the outcome of a future event. **8** (of a bird or

C

animal) make its typical cry. **9** inspire or urge someone to do something. •**noun 1** an act or instance of calling. **2** the typical cry of a bird or animal. **3** a brief visit. **4** (**call for**) demand or need for: *there is little call for antique furniture.* **5** a vocation: *his call to be a disciple.*

– PHRASES **call for** require; demand. **call something in** require payment of a loan. **call something off** cancel an event or agreement. **call on/upon** turn to someone as a source of help. **call of nature** euphemistic a need to go to the toilet. **call the shots** (or **tune**) take the initiative in deciding how something should be done. **call someone/thing up 1** summon someone to serve in the army or to play in a team. **2** bring something stored into use. **on call** available to provide a professional service if necessary.

– DERIVATIVES **caller** noun.
– ORIGIN Old Norse.

call centre noun an office in which large numbers of telephone calls, especially from customers, are handled for an organization.

call girl noun a female prostitute who accepts appointments by telephone.

calligraphy noun decorative handwriting or handwritten lettering.

– DERIVATIVES **calligrapher** noun **calligraphic** adjective.
– ORIGIN from Greek *kalligraphos* 'person who writes beautifully'.

calling noun **1** a profession or occupation. **2** a vocation.

calling card noun chiefly N. Amer. a visiting card or business card.

calliope /kuh-**ly**--uh-pi/ noun chiefly historical an American keyboard instrument resembling an organ but with the notes produced by steam whistles.

– ORIGIN from *Calliope*, the Greek Muse of epic poetry.

calliper noun variant spelling of CALIPER.

callipygian /ka-li-**pij**-i-uhn/ adjective literary having well-shaped buttocks.

– ORIGIN from Greek *kallos* 'beauty' + *pūgē* 'buttocks'.

callisthenics /kal-liss-**then**-iks/ (US **calisthenics**) plural noun gymnastic exercises to achieve bodily fitness and grace of movement.

– ORIGIN from Greek *kallos* 'beauty' + *sthenos* 'strength'.

callosity /kuh-**los**-it-i/ noun (pl. **callosities**) technical a thickened and hardened part of the skin; a callus.

callous adjective insensitive and cruel.

– DERIVATIVES **callously** adverb **callousness** noun.
– ORIGIN Latin *callosus* 'hard-skinned'.

calloused (also **callused**) adjective having hardened skin.

callow adjective (of a young person) inexperienced and immature.

– ORIGIN Old English, 'bald'.

call sign (also **call signal**) noun a message or tune broadcast on radio to identify the broadcaster or transmitter.

callus /**kal**-luhss/ noun a thickened and hardened part of the skin or soft tissue.

– ORIGIN Latin, 'hardened skin'.

calm adjective **1** not showing or feeling

nervousness, anger, or other emotions. **2** peaceful, quiet, or undisturbed: *the comfortable, calm atmosphere of my home.* **3** (of the weather) without wind. •**noun** a calm state or period. •**verb** make or become tranquil and quiet: *I tried to calm her down.*

– DERIVATIVES **calmly** adverb **calmness** noun.
– ORIGIN from Greek *kauma* 'heat of the day'.

calmative adjective (of a drug) having a sedative effect.

Calor gas /**ka**-ler/ noun Brit. trademark liquefied butane stored under pressure in portable containers, for domestic use.

– ORIGIN from Latin *calor* 'heat'.

caloric /kuh-**lo**-rik/ adjective chiefly N. Amer. technical relating to heat or calories; calorific.

calorie noun (pl. **calories**) **1** (also **large calorie**) a unit of energy equal to the energy needed to raise the temperature of 1 kilogram of water through 1°C (4.1868 kilojoules). **2** (also **small calorie**) a unit of energy equal to one-thousandth of a large calorie.

– ORIGIN from Latin *calor* 'heat'.

calorific adjective **1** relating to the amount of energy contained in food or fuel. **2** (of food or drink) high in calories.

calorimeter /ka-luh-**rim**-i-ter/ noun a device for measuring the amount of heat involved in a chemical reaction or other process.

– DERIVATIVES **calorimetric** adjective **calorimetry** noun.

calumniate /kuh-**lum**-ni-ayt/ verb formal make false and defamatory statements about someone.

– DERIVATIVES **calumniator** noun.

calumny /**ka**-luhm-ni/ noun (pl. **calumnies**) the making of false statements about someone in order to damage their reputation.

– DERIVATIVES **calumnious** /kuh-**lum**-ni-uhss/ adjective.
– ORIGIN Latin *calumnia*.

Calvados /**kal**-vuh-doss/ noun apple brandy, traditionally made in the Calvados region of Normandy.

calve verb give birth to a calf.

– ORIGIN Old English.

calves plural of CALF¹, CALF².

Calvinism noun the form of Protestantism of John Calvin (1509–64), centring on the belief that God has decided everything that happens in advance.

– DERIVATIVES **Calvinist** noun **Calvinistic** adjective.

calypso /kuh-**lip**-soh/ noun (pl. **calypsos**) a kind of West Indian music or song, typically with improvised words on a topical theme.

– ORIGIN unknown.

calyx /**kay**-liks/ noun (pl. **calyces** /**kay**-li-seez/ or **calyxes**) the sepals of a flower, forming a protective layer around a flower in bud.

– ORIGIN Greek *kalux* 'case of a bud, husk'.

calzone /kal-**tsoh**-nay, kal-**tsoh**-ni/ noun (pl. **calzoni** or **calzones**) a type of pizza that is folded in half before cooking to contain a filling.

– ORIGIN Italian dialect, probably a special use of *calzone* 'trouser leg'.

cam noun **1** a projecting part on a wheel or shaft, designed to come into contact with another part while rotating and cause it to move. **2** a camshaft.

– ORIGIN Dutch *kam* 'comb'.

camaraderie /kam-uh-**rah**-duh-ri/ **noun** trust and friendship between people.
– ORIGIN French.

camber /kam-ber/ **noun 1** a slightly convex or arched shape of a road or other horizontal surface. **2** Brit. a tilt built into a road at a bend or curve. **3** the slight sideways inclination of the front wheels of a motor vehicle.
– DERIVATIVES **cambered** adjective.
– ORIGIN from Old French *chambre* 'arched'.

cambium /kam-bi-uhm/ **noun** (pl. **cambia** /kam-bi-uh/ or **cambiums**) a layer of cells in a plant stem, from which new tissue grows by the division of cells.
– ORIGIN Latin, 'change, exchange'.

Cambodian /kam-boh-di-uhn/ **noun 1** a person from Cambodia. **2** the Khmer language. •**adjective** relating to Cambodia.

Cambrian /kam-bri-uhn/ **adjective 1** Welsh. **2** Geology relating to the first period in the Palaeozoic era, about 570 to 510 million years ago.
– ORIGIN from Latin *Cambria*.

cambric /kam-brik/ **noun** a lightweight, closely woven white linen or cotton fabric.
– ORIGIN named after the town of *Cambrai* in northern France.

Cambs. **abbreviation** Cambridgeshire.

camcorder **noun** a portable combined video camera and video recorder.

came past tense of **COME**.

camel **noun** a large mammal of arid country, with a long neck and either one or two humps on the back.
– ORIGIN Greek *kamēlos*.

camel hair **noun 1** a fabric made from the hair of a camel. **2** fine, soft hair from a squirrel's tail, used in artists' brushes.

camellia /kuh-**mee**-li-uh/ **noun** an evergreen shrub with showy flowers and shiny leaves.
– ORIGIN named after the Moravian botanist Joseph *Kamel*.

Camembert /kam-uhm-bair/ **noun** a kind of rich, soft, creamy cheese originally made near Camembert in Normandy.

cameo /kam-i-oh/ **noun** (pl. **cameos**) **1** a piece of jewellery consisting of a carving of a head shown in profile against a background of a different colour. **2** a short descriptive written sketch. **3** a small part in a play or film for a distinguished actor.
– ORIGIN Latin *cammaeus*.

camera **noun** a device for taking photographs or recording moving images.
– PHRASES **in camera** chiefly Law in private, in particular in the private rooms of a judge. [Latin, 'in the chamber'.]
– DERIVATIVES **cameraman** noun (pl. **cameramen**).
– ORIGIN Latin, 'vault, arched chamber'.

camera obscura /ob-**skyoor**-uh/ **noun** a darkened box or building with a lens or opening for projecting the image of an external object on to a screen inside.
– ORIGIN Latin, 'dark chamber'.

camera-ready **adjective** (of material to be printed) in the right form to be reproduced photographically on to a printing plate.

Cameroonian /ka-muh-**roo**-ni-uhn/ **noun** a person from Cameroon, a country on the west coast of Africa. •**adjective** relating to Cameroon.

camiknickers **plural noun** Brit. a woman's one-piece undergarment which combines a camisole and French knickers.

camisole /kam-i-sohl/ **noun** a woman's loose-fitting undergarment for the upper body.
– ORIGIN French.

camomile /kam-uh-myl/ (also **chamomile**) **noun** a plant with white and yellow flowers, used in herbal medicine.
– ORIGIN Greek *khamaimēlon* 'earth-apple' (because of the apple-like smell of its flowers).

camouflage /kam-uh-flahzh/ **noun 1** the disguising of military forces and equipment by painting or covering them to make them blend in with their surroundings. **2** clothing or materials used as camouflage. **3** the natural colouring or form of an animal which enables it to blend in with its surroundings. •**verb** hide or disguise someone or something by means of camouflage.
– ORIGIN French *camoufler* 'to disguise'.

camp[1] **noun 1** a place with temporary accommodation of tents, huts, etc., for soldiers, refugees, or travelling people. **2** a complex of buildings for holiday accommodation. **3** the supporters of a particular party or set of beliefs: *the liberal and conservative camps.* **4** Brit. a fortified prehistoric site, especially an Iron Age hill fort. •**verb** stay in a tent or caravan while on holiday.
– PHRASES **break camp** take down a tent or the tents of an encampment ready to leave.
– ORIGIN Latin *campus* 'level ground'.

camp[2] **informal** **adjective 1** (of a man) effeminate in an exaggerated or flamboyant way. **2** deliberately exaggerated and theatrical in style. •**noun** camp behaviour or style. •**verb** (usu. **camp it up**) behave in a camp way.
– DERIVATIVES **campy** adjective.
– ORIGIN unknown.

campaign **noun 1** a series of military operations intended to achieve an objective in a particular area. **2** an organized course of action to achieve a goal. •**verb** work in an organized way towards a goal: *groups that campaigned for cheaper anti-Aids drugs.*
– DERIVATIVES **campaigner** noun.
– ORIGIN French *campagne* 'open country', from Latin *campus* 'level ground'.

campanile /kam-puh-**nee**-lay/ **noun** a bell tower, especially one that is separate from a church or other building.
– ORIGIN Italian.

campanology /kam-puh-**nol**-uh-ji/ **noun** the art or practice of bell-ringing.
– DERIVATIVES **campanologist** noun.
– ORIGIN from Latin *campana* 'bell'.

campanula /kam-**pan**-yu-luh/ **noun** another term for **BELLFLOWER**.
– ORIGIN from Latin *campana* 'bell'.

camp bed **noun** Brit. a folding portable bed.

camper **noun 1** a person who spends a holiday in a tent or holiday camp. **2** (also **camper van**) a large motor vehicle with living accommodation.

c

campery noun exaggerated or flamboyant behaviour, especially in homosexual men.

campesino /kam-puh-**see**-noh/ noun (pl. **campesinos**) (in Spanish-speaking countries) a peasant farmer.
– ORIGIN Spanish.

campfire noun an open-air fire in a camp.

camp follower noun 1 a civilian working in or attached to a military camp. 2 a person who associates with a group without making a full contribution to its activities.

camphor /**kam**-fer/ noun a white substance with an aromatic smell and bitter taste, used in insect repellents.
– ORIGIN Latin *camphora*.

campion noun a plant of the pink family, typically having pink or white flowers with notched petals.
– ORIGIN uncertain.

campsite noun a place used for camping, especially one equipped for holidaymakers.

campus noun (pl. **campuses**) 1 the grounds and buildings of a university or college. 2 a branch or area of a university away from the main site.
– ORIGIN Latin, 'level ground'.

campylobacter /kam-pi-loh-bak-tuhr/ noun a genus of bacterium which sometimes causes food poisoning in humans and abortion in animals.
– ORIGIN from Greek *kampulos* 'bent' + BACTERIUM.

camshaft /**kam**-shahft/ noun a shaft with one or more cams attached to it, especially one operating the valves in an internal-combustion engine.

can¹ modal verb (3rd sing. present **can**; past **could**) 1 be able to. 2 used to express doubt or surprise: *he can't have finished.* 3 used to indicate that something is typically the case: *he could be very moody.* 4 be permitted to.
– ORIGIN Old English, 'know'.

> USAGE: The verb **can** is chiefly used to mean 'be able to', as in *can he move?* (i.e. is he physically able to move?). Although it is not wrong to use **can** when requesting permission, it is more polite to say **may** (i.e. *may we leave now?* rather than *can we leave now?*).

can² noun 1 a cylindrical metal container, in particular one in which food or drink is sealed for long-term storage. 2 (**the can**) N. Amer. informal prison. 3 (**the can**) N. Amer. informal the toilet. • verb (**cans**, **canning**, **canned**) preserve food in a can.
– PHRASES **a can of worms** a complex matter that is full of possible problems. **in the can** informal on tape or film and ready to be broadcast or released.
– DERIVATIVES **canner** noun.
– ORIGIN Old English.

Canada goose noun a common brownish-grey North American goose, introduced in Britain and elsewhere.

Canadian noun a person from Canada. • adjective relating to Canada.
– DERIVATIVES **Canadianism** noun.

canaille /kuh-**ny**/ noun derogatory the common people; the masses.
– ORIGIN French, from Italian *canaglia* 'pack of dogs'.

canal noun 1 a waterway cut through land for the passage of boats or for conveying water for irrigation. 2 a tubular passage in a plant or animal conveying food, liquid, or air.
– ORIGIN Latin *canalis* 'pipe, channel'.

canalize (or **canalise**) /**kan**-uh-lyz/ verb 1 convert a river into a canal. 2 convey something through a duct or channel.
– DERIVATIVES **canalization** noun.

canapé /**kan**-uh-pay/ noun a small piece of bread or pastry with a savoury topping, often served with drinks.
– ORIGIN French, 'sofa, couch'.

canard /ka-**nard**/ noun an unfounded rumour or story.
– ORIGIN French, 'duck', also 'hoax'.

canary noun (pl. **canaries**) 1 a bright yellow finch with a tuneful song, popular as a cage bird. 2 (also **canary yellow**) a bright yellow colour.
– ORIGIN from the *Canary* Islands, to which one species of the bird is native.

canasta /kuh-**nass**-tuh/ noun a card game resembling rummy, using two packs and usually played by two pairs of partners.
– ORIGIN Spanish, 'basket'.

cancan noun a lively, high-kicking stage dance originating in 19th-century Parisian music halls.
– ORIGIN French.

cancel verb (**cancels**, **cancelling**, **cancelled**; US also **cancels**, **canceling**, **canceled**) 1 decide that a planned event will not take place. 2 withdraw from or end a formal arrangement. 3 (**cancel something out**) have an equal but opposite effect on: *the heat given off by the fan motor probably cancels out any cooling effect.* 4 mark a stamp, ticket, etc. to show that it has been used and is no longer valid.
– DERIVATIVES **cancellation** noun **canceller** noun.
– ORIGIN Latin *cancellare*.

Cancer noun a constellation (the Crab) and sign of the zodiac, which the sun enters about 21 June.
– DERIVATIVES **Cancerian** /kan-**seer**-i-uhn/ noun & adjective.
– ORIGIN Latin, 'crab'.

cancer noun 1 a disease caused by an uncontrolled division of abnormal cells in a part of the body. 2 a malignant growth or tumour resulting from an uncontrolled division of cells. 3 something evil or destructive that is hard to contain or destroy: *the cancer of racism.*
– DERIVATIVES **cancerous** adjective.
– ORIGIN Latin, 'crab, creeping ulcer'.

candela /kan-**dee**-luh/ noun Physics the SI unit of luminous intensity.
– ORIGIN Latin, 'candle'.

candelabrum /kan-di-**lah**-bruhm/ noun (pl. **candelabra** /kan-di-**lah**-bruh/) a large candlestick or other holder for several candles or lights.
– ORIGIN Latin.

candid adjective truthful and straightforward; frank.
– DERIVATIVES **candidly** adverb.
– ORIGIN from Latin *candidus* 'white'.

candida /kan-di-duh/ noun a yeast-like parasitic fungus that sometimes causes thrush.
– ORIGIN from Latin *candidus* 'white'.

candidate /kan-di-duht, kan-di-dayt/ noun **1** a person who applies for a job or is nominated for election. **2** Brit. a person taking an exam. **3** a person or thing regarded as suitable for something or likely to experience a particular fate: *she was the perfect candidate for a biography.*
– DERIVATIVES **candidacy** noun **candidature** noun (Brit.).
– ORIGIN from Latin *candidatus* 'white-robed', also referring to a candidate for office (who wore a white toga).

candied adjective (of fruit) preserved in a sugar syrup.

candle noun a stick or block of wax or tallow with a central wick which is lit to produce light as it burns.
– PHRASES **cannot hold a candle to** informal be not nearly as good as: *the song can't hold a candle to James Taylor's 'Fire and Rain'.* **the game is not worth the candle** the potential advantages to be gained from something do not justify the cost or trouble involved.
– ORIGIN Latin *candela.*

candlelight noun dim light provided by a candle or candles.
– DERIVATIVES **candlelit** adjective.

Candlemas /kan-d'l-mass/ noun a Christian festival held on 2 February to commemorate the purification of the Virgin Mary and the presentation of Jesus in the Temple.

candlepower noun the illuminating power of a light source, expressed in candelas (formerly candles).

candlestick noun a support or holder for a candle.

candlewick noun a thick, soft cotton fabric with a raised, tufted pattern.

candour (US **candor**) noun the quality of being open and honest.
– ORIGIN Latin *candor* 'whiteness, purity'.

candy noun (pl. **candies**) N. Amer. sweets.
– ORIGIN from French *sucre candi* 'crystallized sugar'.

candyfloss noun Brit. a mass of pink or white fluffy spun sugar wrapped round a stick.

candy-striped adjective patterned with alternating stripes of white and another colour, typically pink.

candytuft noun a plant with small heads of white, pink, or purple flowers.
– ORIGIN from *Candia*, the former name of Crete.

cane noun **1** the hollow jointed stem of tall reeds, grasses, etc., especially bamboo. **2** the slender, flexible stem of plants such as rattan. **3** a woody stem of a raspberry or related plant. **4** a length of cane or a stick used as a support for plants, a walking stick, or for hitting someone as a punishment. •verb hit someone with a cane as a punishment.
– DERIVATIVES **caner** noun.
– ORIGIN Greek *kanna, kannē.*

caned adjective **1** (of furniture) made or repaired with cane. **2** Brit. informal intoxicated with drink or drugs.

canine /kay-nyn/ adjective relating to or resembling a dog or dogs. •noun **1** a dog or other animal of the dog family. **2** (also **canine tooth**) a pointed tooth between the incisors and premolars.
– ORIGIN from Latin *canis* 'dog'.

canister noun a round or cylindrical container.
– ORIGIN Greek *kanastron* 'wicker basket'.

canker noun **1** a destructive fungal disease of trees that results in damage to the bark. **2** a condition in animals that causes open sores. **3** an evil or corrupting influence: *you're tainted with the canker of rebellion.* •verb become infected with canker.
– ORIGIN Latin *cancer* 'crab, creeping ulcer'.

canna noun a lily-like tropical American plant with bright flowers and ornamental leaves.
– ORIGIN Latin.

cannabis noun a drug obtained from the hemp plant.
– ORIGIN Greek *kannabis.*

canned adjective **1** preserved in a sealed can. **2** informal, chiefly derogatory (of music, applause, or laughter) pre-recorded.

cannellini bean /kan-uh-lee-ni/ noun a kidney-shaped bean of a creamy-white variety.
– ORIGIN Italian *cannellini*, 'small tubes'.

cannelloni /kan-nuh-loh-ni/ plural noun rolls of pasta stuffed with a meat or vegetable mixture, typically cooked in a cheese sauce.
– ORIGIN Italian, 'large tubes'.

cannery noun (pl. **canneries**) a factory where food is canned.

cannibal noun a person who eats the flesh of other human beings.
– DERIVATIVES **cannibalism** noun **cannibalistic** adjective.
– ORIGIN Spanish *Canibales*, a variant of *Caribes*, a West Indian people said to eat humans.

cannibalize (or **cannibalise**) verb **1** use a machine as a source of spare parts for another machine. **2** (of an animal) eat an animal of its own kind.
– DERIVATIVES **cannibalization** noun.

cannon noun (pl. usu. same) **1** a large, heavy gun formerly used in warfare. **2** a heavy automatic gun that fires shells from an aircraft or tank. •verb chiefly Brit. (**cannon into/off**) collide with forcefully or at an angle: *the couple behind almost cannoned into us.*
– ORIGIN Italian *cannone* 'large tube'.

cannonade /kan-nuh-nayd/ noun a period of continuous heavy gunfire.

cannonball noun a metal or stone ball fired from a cannon.

cannon fodder noun soldiers regarded only as a resource to be used up in war.

cannot contraction can not.

cannula /**kan**-yoo-luh/ noun (pl. **cannulae** /**kan**-yoo-lee/ or **cannulas**) a thin tube put into the body to administer medication, drain off fluid, or insert a surgical instrument.
– ORIGIN Latin, 'small reed'.

canny adjective (**cannier, canniest**) 1 shrewd, especially in financial or business matters. 2 N. English & Scottish pleasant; nice.
– DERIVATIVES **cannily** adverb **canniness** noun.
– ORIGIN from CAN[1], in the former sense 'know'.

canoe noun a narrow shallow boat with pointed ends, propelled with a paddle or paddles. • verb (**canoes, canoeing, canoed**) travel in or paddle a canoe.
– DERIVATIVES **canoer** noun **canoeist** noun.
– ORIGIN Spanish *canoa*.

canon[1] noun 1 a general rule or principle by which something is judged: *his designs break the canons of fashion.* 2 the works of a particular author or artist that are recognized as genuine. 3 a list of literary works considered to be permanently established as being of the highest quality. 4 a Church decree or law. 5 a piece of music in which a theme is taken up by two or more parts that overlap.
– ORIGIN Greek *kanōn* 'rule'.

canon[2] noun 1 a member of the clergy on the staff of a cathedral. 2 (also **canon regular** or **regular canon**) (fem. **canoness**) a member of certain orders of Roman Catholic clergy that live communally like monks or nuns.
– ORIGIN from Latin *canonicus* 'according to rule'.

canonic /kuh-**non**-ik/ adjective 1 in the form of a musical canon. 2 another term for CANONICAL.
– DERIVATIVES **canonicity** noun.

canonical /kuh-**non**-i-k'l/ adjective 1 accepted as being authentic or established as a standard: *the canonical works of science fiction.* 2 according to the laws of the Christian Church.
– DERIVATIVES **canonically** adverb.

canonize (or **canonise**) verb (in the Roman Catholic Church) officially declare a dead person to be a saint.
– DERIVATIVES **canonization** noun.
– ORIGIN Latin *canonizare* 'admit as authoritative'.

canon law noun the laws of the Christian Church.

canonry noun (pl. **canonries**) the office or position of a canon in the Christian Church.

canoodle verb informal kiss and cuddle amorously.
– ORIGIN unknown.

canopy noun (pl. **canopies**) 1 a cloth covering hung or held up over a throne or bed. 2 a roof-like projection or shelter. 3 the part of a parachute that opens. 4 the top branches of the trees in a forest, forming an almost continuous layer of foliage. • verb (**canopies, canopying, canopied**) (usu. as adj. **canopied**) cover something with a canopy.
– ORIGIN Latin *conopeum* 'mosquito net over a bed'.

cant[1] /rhymes with rant/ noun 1 insincere talk about moral or religious matters. 2 derogatory the language specific to a particular group: *thieves' cant.*

– ORIGIN probably from Latin *cantare* 'to sing'.

cant[2] /rhymes with rant/ verb be or cause to be in a slanting position; tilt. • noun a slope or tilt.
– ORIGIN German *kant, kante* or Dutch *cant* 'point, side, edge'.

can't contraction cannot.

Cantab. /**kan**-tab/ abbreviation relating to Cambridge University.
– ORIGIN from Latin *Cantabrigia* 'Cambridge'.

cantabile /kan-**tah**-bi-lay/ adverb & adjective Music in a smooth singing style.
– ORIGIN Italian, 'singable'.

cantaloupe /**kan**-tuh-loop/ noun a small round variety of melon with orange flesh and ribbed skin.
– ORIGIN from the villa of *Cantaluppi* near Rome.

cantankerous adjective bad-tempered, argumentative, and uncooperative.
– DERIVATIVES **cantankerously** adverb **cantankerousness** noun.
– ORIGIN perhaps from Anglo-Irish *cant* 'auction' and *rancorous*.

cantata /kan-**tah**-tuh/ noun a narrative or descriptive piece of music with vocal solos and normally a chorus and orchestra.
– ORIGIN from Italian *cantata aria* 'sung air'.

canteen noun 1 a restaurant in a workplace, school, or college. 2 Brit. a case containing a set of cutlery. 3 a small water bottle, as used by soldiers or campers.
– ORIGIN Italian *cantina* 'cellar'.

canter noun a pace of a horse between a trot and a gallop, with not less than one foot on the ground at any time. • verb move at a canter.
– ORIGIN short for *Canterbury pace*, the easy pace at which medieval pilgrims were said to travel to Canterbury.

Canterbury bell noun a tall cultivated bellflower with large pale blue flowers.
– ORIGIN named after the bells on Canterbury pilgrims' horses.

canticle /**kan**-ti-k'l/ noun a hymn or chant forming a regular part of a church service.
– ORIGIN Latin *canticulum* 'little song'.

cantilever /**kan**-ti-lee-ver/ noun 1 a long projecting beam or girder fixed at only one end, used in bridge construction. 2 a bracket or beam projecting from a wall to support a balcony, cornice, etc. • verb support something by a cantilever or cantilevers.
– ORIGIN unknown.

canto /**kan**-toh/ noun (pl. **cantos**) one of the sections into which some long poems are divided.
– ORIGIN Italian, 'song'.

canton /**kan**-ton/ noun a political or administrative subdivision of a country, especially in Switzerland.
– ORIGIN Old French, 'corner'.

Cantonese /kan-tuh-**neez**/ noun (pl. same) 1 a person from Canton (another name for Guangzhou), a city in China. 2 a form of Chinese spoken mainly in SE China and Hong Kong. • adjective relating to Canton or Cantonese.

cantonment /kan-**ton**-muhnt/ noun (especially in the Indian subcontinent) a military garrison or camp.

– ORIGIN French *cantonnement*.

cantor /**kan**-tor/ noun **1** an official who sings liturgical music and leads prayer in a Jewish synagogue. **2** a person who sings solo verses to which the choir or congregation in a Christian service respond.
– ORIGIN Latin, 'singer'.

Canuck /kuh-**nuk**/ noun informal a Canadian.
– ORIGIN apparently from *Canada*.

canvas noun (pl. **canvases** or **canvasses**) **1** a strong, coarse unbleached cloth used to make sails, tents, etc., and as a surface for oil painting. **2** an oil painting on canvas. **3** (**the canvas**) the floor of a boxing or wrestling ring, having a canvas covering. **4** either of the tapering ends of a rowing boat used in racing.
– PHRASES **under canvas** in a tent or tents.
– ORIGIN Old French *canevas*, from Latin *cannabis* 'hemp'.

canvass verb **1** visit someone to seek their vote in an election. **2** question someone to find out their opinion. **3** Brit. propose an idea for discussion. • noun an act of canvassing.
– DERIVATIVES **canvasser** noun.
– ORIGIN first meaning 'toss someone in a canvas sheet' (as a sport or punishment).

canyon noun a deep gorge, especially one with a river flowing through it.
– ORIGIN Spanish *cañón* 'tube'.

canyoning noun the sport of jumping into a fast-flowing mountain stream and being carried downstream.

CAP abbreviation Common Agricultural Policy.

cap noun **1** a soft, flat hat with a peak. **2** a soft, close-fitting head covering worn for a particular purpose: *a shower cap*. **3** Brit. a cap awarded to members of a national sports team. **4** a lid or cover for a bottle, pen, etc. **5** the broad upper part of a mushroom or toadstool. **6** an upper limit imposed on spending or borrowing. **7** (also **Dutch cap**) Brit. a contraceptive diaphragm. **8** (also **percussion cap**) a small amount of explosive powder in a metal or paper case that explodes when struck. • verb (**caps**, **capping**, **capped**) **1** put or form a cap, lid, or cover on something. **2** provide a fitting climax to: *she capped a phenomenal year with three Oscar nominations*. **3** place a limit on prices or expenditure. **4** (**be capped**) Brit. be chosen as a member of a national sports team.
– PHRASES **cap in hand** humbly asking for a favour. **set one's cap at someone** dated (of a woman) try to attract a man.
– DERIVATIVES **capful** noun **capper** noun.
– ORIGIN Latin *cappa*.

capability noun (pl. **capabilities**) the power or ability to do something.

capable adjective **1** (**capable of**) having the ability or quality necessary to do: *I'm quite capable of taking care of myself*. **2** able to achieve whatever one has to do; competent.
– DERIVATIVES **capably** adverb.
– ORIGIN from Latin *capere* 'take or hold'.

capacious adjective having a lot of space inside; roomy.
– ORIGIN from Latin *capax* 'capable'.

capacitance /kuh-**pass**-i-tuhnss/ noun the ability of a system to store electric charge, equivalent to the ratio of the change in

electric charge to the corresponding change in electric potential.

capacitor noun a device used to store electric charge.

capacity noun (pl. **capacities**) **1** the maximum amount that something can contain or produce: *the room was filled to capacity*. **2** the ability or power to do something. **3** a specified role or position: *I was engaged in a voluntary capacity*. • adjective fully occupying the available space: *a capacity crowd*.
– ORIGIN from Latin *capere* 'take or hold'.

caparison /kuh-**pa**-ri-s'n/ verb (**be caparisoned**) be dressed in rich decorative coverings or clothes.
– ORIGIN Spanish *caparazón* 'saddlecloth'.

cape¹ noun a short cloak.
– DERIVATIVES **caped** adjective.
– ORIGIN from Latin *cappa* 'covering for the head'.

cape² noun a piece of land that projects into the sea; a headland.
– ORIGIN Latin *caput* 'head'.

Cape gooseberry noun the edible yellow berry of a tropical South American plant, enclosed in a lantern-shaped husk.

capelin /**kayp**-lin/ (also **caplin**) noun a small food fish of the smelt family, found in North Atlantic coastal waters.
– ORIGIN French.

capellini /ka-puh-**lee**-nee/ plural noun pasta in the form of very thin strands.
– ORIGIN Italian, 'small hairs'.

caper¹ verb skip or dance about in a lively or playful way. • noun **1** a playful skipping movement. **2** informal a light-hearted or underhand activity, or a film or novel portraying one: *a futuristic crime caper*.
– DERIVATIVES **caperer** noun.
– ORIGIN from Latin *capreolus* 'little goat'.

caper² noun a pickled flower bud of a southern European shrub, used in sauces and as a garnish.
– ORIGIN Greek *kapparis*.

capercaillie /kap-er-**kay**-li/ noun (pl. **capercaillies**) a large turkey-like grouse of pine forests in northern Europe.
– ORIGIN from Scottish Gaelic *capull coille*, 'horse of the wood'.

capillarity /ka-pi-**lar**-i-ti/ noun the tendency of a liquid in a narrow tube or pore to rise or fall as a result of surface tension.

capillary /kuh-**pil**-luh-ri/ noun (pl. **capillaries**) **1** any of the fine branching blood vessels that form a network between the arteries and veins. **2** (also **capillary tube**) a tube with an internal diameter of hair-like thinness.
– ORIGIN from Latin *capillus* 'hair'.

capillary action noun another term for CAPILLARITY.

capital¹ noun **1** the main city or town of a country or region, typically where the government is based. **2** wealth owned by a person or organization or invested, lent, or borrowed. **3** the amount by which a company's assets exceeds its liabilities. **4** a capital letter. • adjective **1** (of an offence) punishable by death. **2** (of a letter of the alphabet) large in size and of the form used to begin sentences

and names. **3** informal, dated excellent.
– PHRASES **make capital out of** use something to one's advantage.
– ORIGIN from Latin *caput* 'head'.

capital² noun the top part of a pillar or column.
– ORIGIN Latin *capitellum* 'little head'.

capital gain noun a profit from the sale of property or an investment.

capital goods plural noun goods that are used in producing other goods, rather than being bought by consumers.

capitalism noun an economic and political system in which a country's trade and industry are controlled by private owners for profit.
– DERIVATIVES **capitalist** noun & adjective **capitalistic** adjective.

capitalize (or **capitalise**) verb **1** (**capitalize on**) take advantage of: *the software lets you capitalize on new customer opportunities.* **2** provide a company with financial capital. **3** convert income into financial capital. **4** write or print a word or letter in capital letters or with an initial capital.
– DERIVATIVES **capitalization** noun.

capital punishment noun the punishment of a crime by death.

capital sum noun a lump sum of money payable to an insured person or paid as an initial fee or investment.

capitation noun the payment of a fee or grant to a doctor, school, etc., the amount being determined by the number of people that are served.
– ORIGIN from Latin *caput* 'head'.

capitol /kap-i-t'l/ noun **1** (in the US) a building housing a legislative assembly. **2** (**the Capitol**) the seat of the US Congress in Washington DC.
– ORIGIN from Latin *caput* 'head'.

capitulate /kuh-pit-yuu-layt/ verb give in to an opponent or an unwelcome demand.
– DERIVATIVES **capitulation** noun **capitulator** noun.
– ORIGIN from Latin *capitulare* 'draw up under headings'.

caplin noun variant spelling of CAPELIN.

capo¹ /ka-poh/ noun (pl. **capos**) a clamp fastened across all the strings of a guitar or similar instrument to raise their tuning.
– ORIGIN from Italian *capo tasto* 'head stop'.

capo² /ka-poh/ noun (pl. **capos**) chiefly N. Amer. the head of a branch of the Mafia.
– ORIGIN Italian.

capoeira /ka-pu-ay-ruh/ noun a martial art and dance form originating among Angolan slaves in Brazil.
– ORIGIN Portuguese.

capon /kay-pon/ noun a domestic cock that has been castrated and fattened for eating.
– ORIGIN Latin *capo.*

cappuccino /kap-puh-chee-noh/ noun (pl. **cappuccinos**) coffee made with milk that has been frothed up with pressurized steam.
– ORIGIN Italian, 'Capuchin' (because the colour resembles that of a Capuchin monk's habit).

caprice /kuh-preess/ noun a sudden change of mood or behaviour.
– ORIGIN Italian *capriccio* 'sudden start'.

capricious /kuh-pri-shuhss/ adjective prone to sudden changes of mood or behaviour.
– DERIVATIVES **capriciously** adverb **capriciousness** noun.

Capricorn /kap-ri-korn/ noun a constellation and sign of the zodiac (the Goat), which the sun enters about 21 December.
– DERIVATIVES **Capricornian** noun & adjective.
– ORIGIN Latin *capricornus.*

caprine /kap-ryn/ adjective relating to or resembling a goat or goats.
– ORIGIN from Latin *caper* 'goat'.

capri pants /kuh-pree/ (also **capris**) plural noun close-fitting tapered trousers for women.
– ORIGIN named after the Italian island of *Capri.*

capsicum /kap-si-kuhm/ noun (pl. **capsicums**) a sweet pepper or chilli pepper.
– ORIGIN Latin.

capsize verb (of a boat) be overturned in the water.
– ORIGIN perhaps from Spanish *capuzar* 'sink a ship by the head'.

cap sleeve noun a sleeve which extends a short distance from the shoulder and tapers to nothing under the arm.

capstan /kap-stuhn/ noun a broad revolving cylinder with a vertical axis, used for winding a rope or cable.
– ORIGIN Provençal *cabestan.*

capstone noun a stone fixed on top of a wall or prehistoric tomb.

capsule noun **1** a small case or container. **2** a small case of gelatin containing a dose of medicine, that dissolves after it is swallowed. **3** Botany a dry fruit that releases its seeds by bursting open when ripe. • adjective brief, condensed, or compact: *a capsule range of women's separates.*
– DERIVATIVES **capsular** adjective.
– ORIGIN Latin *capsula.*

capsulize (or **capsulise**) verb put information in compact form.

captain noun **1** the person in command of a ship or civil aircraft. **2** a rank of naval officer above commander and below commodore. **3** a rank of officer in the army and in the US and Canadian air forces, above lieutenant and below major. **4** the leader of a team, especially in sports. **5** (in the US) a police officer in charge of a precinct. • verb be the captain of a ship, aircraft, or team.
– DERIVATIVES **captaincy** noun.
– ORIGIN Old French *capitain* 'chief'.

caption noun **1** a title or brief explanation accompanying an illustration or cartoon. **2** a piece of text appearing on screen as part of a film or television broadcast. • verb provide an illustration with a title or explanation.
– ORIGIN Latin, 'capture, seizing'.

captious /kap-shuhss/ adjective formal tending to find fault or raise petty objections.
– ORIGIN Old French *captieux.*

captivate verb attract and hold the interest of someone; charm.
– DERIVATIVES **captivating** adjective **captivation** noun.
– ORIGIN Latin *captivare* 'take captive'.

captive noun a person who has been taken

prisoner or held in confinement. • **adjective**
1 imprisoned or confined. **2** not free to choose an alternative: *a captive audience.*
– DERIVATIVES **captivity** noun.
– ORIGIN Latin *captivus.*

captor noun a person who captures or confines another.

capture verb **1** take control of something by force. **2** take someone prisoner. **3** record accurately in words or pictures: *the illustrations capture the dogs' antics.* **4** cause data to be stored in a computer. • **noun** the action of capturing or the state of being captured.
– DERIVATIVES **capturer** noun.
– ORIGIN from Latin *capere* 'seize, take'.

Capuchin /kap-uh-chin/ noun **1** a friar belonging to a strict branch of the Franciscan order. **2** (**capuchin**) a South American monkey with a hood-like cap of hair on the head.
– ORIGIN from Italian *cappuccino* 'small hood'.

capybara /ka-pi-**bah**-ruh/ noun (pl. same or **capybaras**) a large South American rodent resembling a long-legged guinea pig.
– ORIGIN Tupi, 'grass eater'.

car noun **1** a powered road vehicle designed to carry a small number of people. **2** a railway carriage or (N. Amer.) wagon.
– ORIGIN Latin *carrus* 'two-wheeled vehicle'

carabiner noun variant spelling of **KARABINER**.

carabiniere /ka-ruh-bi-**nyair**-i/ noun (pl. **carabinieri** pronunc. same) a member of the Italian paramilitary police.
– ORIGIN Italian, 'soldier armed with a carbine'.

caracal /ka-ruh-kal/ noun a brown lynx-like cat with black tufted ears, native to Africa and western Asia.
– ORIGIN from Turkish *kara* 'black' + *kulak* 'ear'.

caracul noun variant spelling of **KARAKUL**.

carafe /kuh-**raf**/ noun an open-topped glass flask used for serving wine or water in a restaurant.
– ORIGIN French.

carambola /ka-ruhm-**boh**-luh/ noun a golden-yellow fruit with a star-shaped cross section; starfruit.
– ORIGIN Portuguese.

caramel noun **1** a soft toffee made with sugar and butter. **2** sugar or syrup heated until it turns brown, used as a flavouring or colouring for food.
– DERIVATIVES **caramelize** (or **caramelise**) verb.
– ORIGIN Spanish *caramelo.*

carapace /ka-ruh-payss/ noun the hard upper shell of a tortoise, lobster, or related animal.
– ORIGIN Spanish *carapacho.*

carat /ka-ruht/ noun **1** a unit of weight for precious stones and pearls, equivalent to 200 milligrams. **2** (US also **karat**) a measure of the purity of gold, pure gold being 24 carats.
– ORIGIN Greek *keration* 'carob fruit' (also referring to a unit of weight).

caravan noun **1** Brit. a vehicle equipped for living in, designed to be towed by a car or horse. **2** a group of people travelling together.
– DERIVATIVES **caravanner** noun **caravanning** noun.
– ORIGIN Persian.

caravanserai /ka-ruh-**van**-suh-ry/ noun (pl.

caravanserais) **1** a group of people travelling together; a caravan. **2** historical an inn with a central courtyard in the deserts of Asia or North Africa.
– ORIGIN Persian, 'caravan palace'.

caravel /ka-ruh-vel/ (also **carvel**) noun a small, fast Spanish or Portuguese sailing ship of the 15th–17th centuries.
– ORIGIN Portuguese *caravela.*

caraway /ka-ruh-way/ noun the seeds of a plant of the parsley family, used for flavouring.
– ORIGIN Latin *carui.*

carbide noun a compound of carbon with a metal or other element.

carbine noun **1** a light automatic rifle. **2** historical a short rifle or musket used by cavalry.
– ORIGIN French *carabine.*

carbohydrate noun any of a large group of compounds (including sugars, starch, and cellulose) which contain carbon, hydrogen, and oxygen, found in food and used to give energy.

carbolic acid (also **carbolic**) noun phenol, used as a disinfectant.

carbon noun a non-metallic chemical element which has two main forms (diamond and graphite), and is present in all organic compounds.
– ORIGIN Latin *carbo* 'coal, charcoal'.

carbonaceous /kar-buh-**nay**-shuhss/ adjective consisting of or containing carbon or its compounds.

carbonara /kah-buh-**nah**-ruh/ noun a pasta sauce made with bacon or ham, egg, and cream.
– ORIGIN Italian, 'charcoal kiln'.

carbonate /kar-buh-nayt/ noun a compound containing CO_3 negative ions together with a metallic element.
– DERIVATIVES **carbonation** noun.

carbonated adjective (of a drink) containing dissolved carbon dioxide and therefore fizzy.

carbon black noun a fine carbon powder used as a pigment.

carbon copy noun **1** a copy made with carbon paper. **2** a person or thing identical to another.

carbon dating (also **radiocarbon dating**) noun a method of determining the age of an organic object by measuring the amount of radioactive carbon-14 that it contains.

carbon dioxide noun a colourless, odourless gas produced by burning carbon and organic compounds and by breathing, and absorbed by plants in photosynthesis.

carbon fibre noun a material consisting of thin, strong crystalline filaments of carbon.

carbonic /kah-**bon**-ik/ adjective relating to carbon or carbon dioxide.

carbonic acid noun a very weak acid formed when carbon dioxide dissolves in water.

Carboniferous /kar-buh-**nif**-uh-ruhss/ adjective Geology relating to the fifth period of the Palaeozoic era (about 363 to 290 million years ago), when extensive coal-bearing strata were formed.

carbonize (or **carbonise**) verb convert something into carbon, by heating or burning.
– DERIVATIVES **carbonization** noun.

carbon monoxide noun an odourless toxic flammable gas formed by incomplete burning of carbon.

carbon paper noun thin paper coated with carbon, used for making a copy as a document is being written or typed.

carbon sink noun a forest, ocean, or other natural environment viewed in terms of its ability to absorb carbon dioxide from the atmosphere.

carbon steel noun steel in which the main alloying element is carbon.

carbon tax noun a tax on petrol and other fossil fuels.

carbonyl /kah-buh-nyl, kah-buh-nil/ noun Chemistry a radical consisting of a carbon atom linked to an oxygen atom, present in aldehydes and many other organic compounds.

car boot sale noun Brit. a sale at which people sell things from the boots of their cars.

carborundum /kar-buh-**run**-duhm/ noun a very hard black solid consisting of silicon and carbon, used for grinding, smoothing, and polishing.
– ORIGIN blend of **CARBON** and **CORUNDUM**.

carboxyl /kah-**bok**-syl, kah-**bok**-sil/ noun Chemistry a radical consisting of a carbon atom linked to an oxygen atom and a hydroxyl group, present in organic acids.

carboxylic acid /kah-bok-**sil**-ik/ noun an acid containing a carboxyl group, such as formic and acetic acids.

carboy noun a large globular glass bottle with a narrow neck, used for holding acids.
– ORIGIN Persian, 'large glass flagon'.

carbuncle /**kar**-bung-k'l/ noun **1** a severe abscess or multiple boil in the skin. **2** a polished garnet (gem).
– DERIVATIVES **carbuncular** adjective.
– ORIGIN Latin *carbunculus* 'small coal'.

carburettor /kar-buh-**ret**-ter/ (US also **carburetor**) noun a device in an internal-combustion engine for mixing air with a fine spray of liquid fuel.
– DERIVATIVES **carburetted** (US **carbureted**) adjective.
– ORIGIN from former *carburet* 'combine or fill with carbon'.

carcass (Brit. also **carcase**) noun **1** the dead body of an animal, especially one prepared for cutting up as meat. **2** the remains of a cooked bird after all the edible parts have been removed. **3** the structural framework of a building, ship, or piece of furniture.
– ORIGIN Old French *charcois*.

carcinogen /kar-**sin**-uh-juhn/ noun a substance that can cause cancer.
– DERIVATIVES **carcinogenic** /kar-sin-uh-**jen**-ik/ adjective.
– ORIGIN from **CARCINOMA**.

carcinoma /kar-si-**noh**-muh/ noun (pl. **carcinomas** or **carcinomata** /kar-si-**noh**-muh-tuh/) a cancer arising in the tissues of the skin or of the lining of the internal organs.
– ORIGIN from Greek *karkinos* 'crab'.

card[1] noun **1** thick, stiff paper or thin cardboard. **2** a piece of card for writing on or printed with information. **3** a small rectangular piece of plastic containing personal data in a form that can be read by a computer: *a credit card.* **4** a playing card. **5** (**cards**) a game played with playing cards. **6** informal, dated an odd or amusing person.
– PHRASES **a card up one's sleeve** Brit. a plan or asset that is kept secret until needed. **give someone their cards** (or **get one's cards**) Brit. informal dismiss someone (or be dismissed) from employment. **on the cards** informal possible or likely. **play the —— card** exploit a particular issue, especially for political advantage: *he played the race card to win votes.* **play one's cards right** make the best use of one's assets and opportunities. **put** (or **lay**) **one's cards on the table** state one's intentions openly.
– ORIGIN Greek *khartēs* 'papyrus leaf'.

card[2] verb comb and clean raw wool or similar material with a sharp-toothed instrument to disentangle the fibres before spinning. •noun a toothed implement or machine for combing and cleaning wool.
– DERIVATIVES **carder** noun.
– ORIGIN from Latin *carduus* 'thistle'.

cardamom /**kar**-duh-muhm/ noun the seeds of a SE Asian plant, used as a spice.
– ORIGIN from Greek *kardamon* 'cress' + *amōmon*, a kind of spice plant.

cardboard noun thin board made from layers of paper pasted together or from paper pulp. •adjective (of a fictional character) not realistic.

card-carrying adjective registered as a member of a political party or trade union.

cardiac /**kar**-di-ak/ adjective relating to the heart.
– ORIGIN from Greek *kardia* 'heart'.

cardigan noun a knitted jumper fastening with buttons down the front.
– ORIGIN named after the 7th Earl of *Cardigan*, whose troops first wore such garments in the Crimean War.

cardinal noun **1** a leading Roman Catholic clergyman, nominated by and having the power to elect the Pope. **2** a deep scarlet colour like that of a cardinal's robes. •adjective of the greatest importance; fundamental.
– ORIGIN Latin *cardinalis*, from *cardo* 'hinge'.

cardinal humour noun see **HUMOUR**.

cardinal number noun a number expressing quantity (one, two, three, etc.) rather than order (first, second, third, etc.).

cardinal point noun each of the four main points of the compass (north, south, east, and west).

cardinal sin noun **1** (in Christian tradition) any of the seven deadly sins. **2** a serious error of judgement.

cardinal virtue noun each of the chief moral virtues in medieval philosophy: justice, prudence, temperance, and fortitude.

card index noun a catalogue in which each item is entered on a separate card.

cardiogram noun a record of muscle activity within the heart made by a cardiograph.

cardiograph noun an instrument for recording heart muscle activity.

C

– DERIVATIVES **cardiographer** noun **cardiography** noun.
– ORIGIN from Greek *kardia* 'heart'.

cardiology noun the branch of medicine concerned with the heart.
– DERIVATIVES **cardiological** adjective **cardiologist** noun.
– ORIGIN from Greek *kardia* 'heart'.

cardiopulmonary adjective relating to the heart and the lungs.

cardiovascular adjective relating to the heart and blood vessels.

cardoon noun a tall thistle-like plant related to the globe artichoke, with edible leaves and roots.
– ORIGIN Latin *carduus* 'thistle, artichoke'.

card sharp (also **card sharper**) noun a person who cheats at cards.

cardy (also **cardie**) noun (pl. **cardies**) Brit. informal a cardigan.

care noun 1 the provision of welfare and protection. 2 Brit. the responsibility of a local authority to look after children whose parents are unable to do so: *she was taken into care.* 3 serious attention applied to avoid damage, risk, or error: *handle with care.* 4 a feeling of or cause for anxiety. •verb 1 feel concern or interest. 2 feel affection or liking. 3 (**care for/ to do**) like to have or be willing to do: *would you care for some tea?* 4 (**care for**) look after and provide for the needs of someone or something.
– PHRASES **care of** at the address of. **take care 1** be careful. 2 make sure to do something. **take care of someone/thing 1** keep someone or something safe and provided for. 2 deal with something.
– DERIVATIVES **caring** noun & adjective.
– ORIGIN Old English.

careen /kuh-reen/ verb 1 tilt a ship on its side for cleaning or repair. 2 chiefly N. Amer. move quickly and in an uncontrolled way.
– ORIGIN from Latin *carina* 'a keel'.

career noun an occupation undertaken for a significant period of a person's life, usually with opportunities for progress. •adjective 1 (of a woman) choosing to pursue a profession rather than devoting herself to childcare or housekeeping. 2 working with long-term commitment in a particular profession: *a career diplomat.* •verb move swiftly and in an uncontrolled way: *I careered across the desert at 150 mph.*
– ORIGIN French *carrière* 'racecourse'.

careerist noun a person whose main concern is to progress in their profession.
– DERIVATIVES **careerism** noun.

carefree adjective free from anxiety or responsibility.

careful adjective 1 taking care to avoid harm or trouble; cautious. 2 sensible in the use of something: *he'd always been careful with money.* 3 done with or showing thought and attention.
– DERIVATIVES **carefully** adverb **carefulness** noun.

careless adjective 1 not giving sufficient attention or thought to avoiding harm or mistakes. 2 (**careless of/about**) not concerned or worried about: *he was careless of the truth.* 3 showing no interest or effort.

– DERIVATIVES **carelessly** adverb **carelessness** noun.

carer noun Brit. a family member or paid helper who regularly looks after a sick, elderly, or disabled person.

caress verb touch or stroke someone or something lovingly. •noun a gentle or loving touch.
– DERIVATIVES **caressing** adjective **caressingly** adverb.
– ORIGIN French *caresser.*

caret /ka-ruht/ noun a mark (^, ʌ) placed below a line of text to indicate an insertion.
– ORIGIN Latin, 'is lacking'.

caretaker noun a person employed to look after a public building. •adjective holding power temporarily: *a caretaker government.*

care worker noun Brit. a person employed to support and supervise vulnerable, infirm, or disadvantaged people.

careworn adjective tired and unhappy because of prolonged worry.

cargo noun (pl. **cargoes** or **cargos**) goods carried on a ship, aircraft, or motor vehicle.
– ORIGIN Spanish.

cargo pants plural noun loose-fitting casual cotton trousers with large patch pockets halfway down each leg.

Carib /ka-rib/ noun 1 a member of a South American people living mainly in coastal regions of French Guiana, Suriname, Guyana, and Venezuela. 2 the language of the Carib.
– ORIGIN Spanish *caribe.*

Caribbean /ka-rib-bee-uhn/ adjective relating to the region consisting of the Caribbean Sea, its islands, and the surrounding coasts.

caribou /ka-ri-boo/ noun (pl. same) N. Amer. a reindeer.
– ORIGIN Canadian French.

caricature /ka-ri-kuh-tewr, ka-ri-kuh-cher/ noun a picture or description in which a person's distinctive features are exaggerated for comic effect. •verb make a caricature of someone.
– DERIVATIVES **caricatural** adjective **caricaturist** noun.
– ORIGIN Italian *caricatura.*

caries /kair-eez/ noun decay and crumbling of a tooth or bone.
– DERIVATIVES **carious** adjective.
– ORIGIN Latin.

carillon /ka-ril-lyuhn/ noun a set of bells sounded from a keyboard or by an automatic mechanism.
– ORIGIN Old French *quarregnon* 'peal of four bells'.

carjacking noun the action of stealing a car after violently ejecting its driver.

Carmelite /kar-muh-lyt/ noun a friar or nun of an order founded at Mount Carmel in Israel during the Crusades (c.1154). •adjective relating to the Carmelites.

carminative /kah-min-uh-tiv/ noun a drug that relieves flatulence.
– ORIGIN from Latin *carminare* 'heal by incantation'.

carmine /kar-myn/ noun a vivid crimson colour.
– ORIGIN French *carmin.*

carnage /**kar**-nij/ noun the killing of a large number of people.
– ORIGIN from Latin *caro* 'flesh'.

carnal adjective relating to physical, especially sexual, needs and activities.
– DERIVATIVES **carnality** noun **carnally** adverb.
– ORIGIN from Latin *caro* 'flesh'.

carnal knowledge noun dated, chiefly Law sexual intercourse.

carnation noun a cultivated variety of pink, with double pink, white, or red flowers.
– ORIGIN perhaps based on a misreading of an Arabic word.

carnelian /kar-**nee**-li-uhn/ (also **cornelian**) noun a dull red or pink semi-precious variety of chalcedony (a form of quartz).
– ORIGIN Old French *corneline*.

carnival noun **1** an annual public festivity involving processions, music, and dancing. **2** N. Amer. a travelling funfair or circus.
– DERIVATIVES **carnivalesque** adjective.
– ORIGIN Italian *carnevale*, from Latin *carnelevamen* 'Shrovetide', from *caro* 'flesh' + *levare* 'put away'.

carnivore /**kar**-ni-vor/ noun an animal that feeds on meat.

carnivorous /kar-**niv**-uh-ruhss/ adjective (of an animal) feeding on meat.
– ORIGIN from Latin *caro* 'flesh'.

carob /**ka**-ruhb/ noun the edible brownish-purple pod of an Arabian tree, from which a substitute for chocolate is made.
– ORIGIN Old French *carobe*.

carol noun a religious song or popular hymn sung at Christmas. • verb (**carols, carolling, carolled**; US **carols, caroling, caroled**) **1** (go **carolling**) sing carols in the streets. **2** sing or say something happily.
– DERIVATIVES **caroller** (US **caroler**) noun.
– ORIGIN Old French *carole*.

Carolingian /ka-ruh-**lin**-ji-uhn/ adjective relating to the dynasty founded by Charlemagne's father, which ruled in western Europe from 750 to 987.
– ORIGIN alteration of earlier *Carlovingian*.

carotene /**ka**-ruh-teen/ noun an orange or red substance found in carrots and many other plants, important in the formation of vitamin A.
– ORIGIN from Latin *carota* 'carrot'.

carotenoid /kuh-**rot**-in-oyd/ noun any of a group of mainly yellow, orange, or red pigments, including carotene, which give colour to plant parts such as ripe tomatoes and autumn leaves.

carotid /kuh-**rot**-id/ adjective relating to the two main arteries carrying blood to the head and neck.
– ORIGIN from Greek *karōtis* 'drowsiness, stupor' (because compression of these arteries was thought to cause unconsciousness).

carouse /kuh-**rowz**/ verb drink alcohol and enjoy oneself with others in a noisy, lively way.
– DERIVATIVES **carousal** noun **carouser** noun.
– ORIGIN from German *gar aus trinken*.

carousel /ka-ruh-**sel**/ noun **1** a merry-go-round at a fair. **2** a conveyor system at an airport from which arriving passengers collect their luggage.
– ORIGIN Italian *carosello* 'tournament for knights on horseback'.

carp[1] noun (pl. same) a freshwater fish, often kept in ponds and sometimes farmed for food.
– ORIGIN Latin *carpa*.

carp[2] verb complain about something continually.
– DERIVATIVES **carper** noun.
– ORIGIN Old Norse, 'brag'.

carpaccio /kah-**pach**-i-oh/ noun an Italian hors d'oeuvre consisting of thin slices of raw beef or fish served with a sauce.
– ORIGIN named after the Italian painter Vittore *Carpaccio*, from his use of red pigments.

carpal adjective relating to the bones in the wrist. • noun a bone in the wrist.
– ORIGIN from CARPUS.

carpal tunnel syndrome noun a painful condition of the hand and fingers caused by compression of a major nerve where it passes over the bones in the wrist.

car park noun Brit. an area or building where cars or other vehicles may be left temporarily.

carpe diem /kar-pay **dee**-em/ exclamation make the most of the present time.
– ORIGIN Latin, 'seize the day!'

carpel /**kah**-puhl/ noun the female reproductive organ of a flower, consisting of an ovary, a stigma, and usually a style.
– ORIGIN Greek *karpos* 'fruit'.

carpenter noun a person who makes wooden objects and structures.
– DERIVATIVES **carpentry** noun.
– ORIGIN from Latin *carpentarius artifex* 'carriage-maker'.

carpet noun **1** a floor covering made from thick woven fabric. **2** a large rug. **3** a thick or soft expanse or layer of something: *a carpet of snow and ice*. • verb (**carpets, carpeting, carpeted**) **1** cover a floor with a carpet. **2** Brit. informal reprimand someone severely.
– PHRASES **on the carpet** informal being reprimanded by someone in authority. **sweep something under the carpet** conceal or ignore a problem in the hope that it will be forgotten.
– ORIGIN Old French *carpite* or Latin *carpita* 'woollen covering for a table or bed'.

carpet bag noun a travelling bag of a kind originally made of thick carpet-like fabric.

carpetbagger noun informal, derogatory **1** a politician who tries to get elected in an area where they have no local connections. **2** a person who becomes a member of a mutual building society or insurance company in order to gain financially if the organization abandons its mutual status.
– ORIGIN first referring to a person from the northern states of the US who went to the South after the Civil War to make money.

carpet-bomb verb bomb an area intensively.

carpeting noun material for making carpets or carpets in general.

carpet slipper noun a soft slipper with an upper of wool or thick cloth.

carport noun an open-sided shelter for a car, projecting from the side of a house.

carpus /**kar**-puhss/ noun (pl. **carpi** /**kar**-py/) the

group of small bones in the wrist.
– ORIGIN Greek *karpos* 'wrist'.

carrageen /kar-ruh-geen/ noun an edible red seaweed with flattened branching fronds.
– ORIGIN Irish.

carrel /ka-ruhl/ noun **1** a small cubicle with a desk for a reader in a library. **2** historical a small enclosure or study in a cloister.
– ORIGIN apparently related to CAROL in the former sense 'a ring or enclosure'.

carriage noun **1** a four-wheeled passenger vehicle pulled by two or more horses. **2** Brit. any of the separate passenger vehicles of a train. **3** Brit. the conveying of goods from one place to another. **4** a person's way of standing or moving. **5** a moving part of a machine that carries other parts into the required position. **6** a wheeled support for moving a heavy object such as a gun.
– ORIGIN Old French *cariage*.

carriage clock noun Brit. a portable clock in a rectangular case with a handle on top.

carriageway noun Brit. **1** each of the two sides of a dual carriageway or motorway. **2** the part of a road intended for vehicles.

carrier noun **1** a person or thing that carries or holds something. **2** a company that transports goods or people for payment. **3** a person or animal that transmits a disease to others without suffering from it themselves.

carrier bag noun Brit. a plastic or paper bag with handles, for carrying shopping.

carrier pigeon noun a homing pigeon trained to carry messages.

carrion noun the decaying flesh of dead animals.
– ORIGIN Old French *caroine*, *charoigne*

carrion crow noun a common black crow.

carrot noun **1** the tapering orange root of a plant of the parsley family, eaten as a vegetable. **2** something tempting offered to someone as a means of persuasion: *training that relies more on the carrot than on the stick.*
– ORIGIN Greek *karóton*.

carroty adjective (of a person's hair) orange-red.

carry verb (**carries, carrying, carried**) **1** move or take someone or something from one place to another. **2** have on one's person: *he is believed to be carrying a gun.* **3** support the weight of someone or something. **4** take or accept responsibility or blame. **5** have as a feature or result: *a crime which carries a maximum penalty of 20 years.* **6** take or develop an idea or activity to a particular point: *he carried the criticism much further.* **7** approve a proposal by a majority of votes: *the motion was carried by one vote.* **8** publish or broadcast something. **9** (of a sound or voice) travel **10** (**carry oneself**) stand and move in a particular way. **11** be pregnant with: *she was carrying twins.*
– PHRASES **be/get carried away** lose one's self-control. **carry the can** Brit. informal accept the blame or responsibility for a mistake. **carry the day** be victorious or successful. **carry something forward** transfer figures to a new page or account. **carry someone off 1** take someone away by force. **2** (of a disease) kill someone. **carry something off** succeed in doing something. **carry on 1** continue. **2** informal

be engaged in a love affair. **carry something on** take part in something: *it's difficult to carry on a conversation with him.* **carry something out** perform a task. **carry something over 1** keep something to use or deal with in a new context. **2** postpone an event. **carry something through** bring a project to completion. **carry weight** be influential.
– ORIGIN Old French *carier*, from Latin *carrus* 'wheeled vehicle'.

carrycot noun Brit. a small portable baby's cot.

carry-on noun Brit. informal **1** a fuss. **2** (also **carryings-on**) improper behaviour.

carsick adjective feeling sick as a result of travelling in a car.

cart noun **1** an open horse-drawn vehicle with two or four wheels, used for carrying loads or passengers. **2** a shallow open container on wheels, pulled or pushed by hand. ●verb **1** carry something in a cart or similar vehicle. **2** informal carry a large, heavy, or unwieldy object somewhere with difficulty. **3** take someone somewhere roughly: *the demonstrators were carted off by the police.*
– PHRASES **put the cart before the horse** do things in the wrong order.
– ORIGIN Old Norse.

carte blanche /kart blahnsh/ noun complete freedom to do whatever one wants to do.
– ORIGIN French, 'blank paper'.

cartel /kar-tel/ noun an association of manufacturers or suppliers formed to keep prices high and restrict competition.
– ORIGIN German *Kartell*.

Cartesian /kar-tee-zi-uhn/ adjective relating to the French philosopher René Descartes (1596–1650) and his ideas.
– DERIVATIVES **Cartesianism** noun.
– ORIGIN from *Cartesius*, Latin form of *Descartes*.

Cartesian coordinates plural noun a system for locating a point by reference to its distance from axes intersecting at right angles.

Carthaginian /kah-thuh-jin-i-uhn/ noun a person from the ancient city of Carthage on the coast of North Africa. ●adjective relating to Carthage or its people.

carthorse noun Brit. a large, strong horse suitable for heavy work.

Carthusian /kar-thyoo-zi-uhn/ noun a monk or nun of a strict order founded at Chartreuse in France in 1084. ●adjective relating to this order.
– ORIGIN from *Carthusia*, the Latin name for *Chartreuse*.

cartilage /kar-ti-lij/ noun firm, flexible tissue which covers the ends of joints and forms structures such as the larynx and the external ear.
– DERIVATIVES **cartilaginous** /kar-ti-laj-in-uhss/ adjective.
– ORIGIN Latin *cartilago*.

cartilaginous fish noun a fish with a skeleton of cartilage rather than bone, e.g. a shark or ray.

cartography /kar-tog-ruh-fi/ noun the science or practice of drawing maps.
– DERIVATIVES **cartographer** noun **cartographic** adjective.
– ORIGIN French *carte* 'card, map'.

C

c

carton noun a light cardboard box or container.
– ORIGIN French, from Italian *cartone* 'cartoon'.

cartoon noun 1 a humorous or satirical drawing in a newspaper or magazine. 2 (also **cartoon strip**) a comic strip. 3 a film made from a sequence of drawings, using animation techniques to give the appearance of movement. 4 a full-size drawing made as a preliminary design for a painting or other work of art.
– DERIVATIVES **cartoonist** noun.
– ORIGIN Italian *cartone*, from Latin *carta*, *charta* 'card, map'.

cartouche /kar-toosh/ noun 1 a carved decoration or drawing in the form of a scroll with rolled-up ends. 2 an oval or oblong containing Egyptian hieroglyphs which represent the name and title of a monarch.
– ORIGIN French.

cartridge noun 1 a container holding a spool of film, a quantity of ink, or other item or substance, to be inserted into a mechanism. 2 a casing containing a charge and a bullet or shot for a gun.
– ORIGIN variant of CARTOUCHE.

cartridge paper noun thick, rough-textured drawing paper.

cartwheel noun a circular sideways handspring with the arms and legs extended. • verb perform cartwheels.

carve verb 1 cut into or shape a hard material to produce an object or design: *the tools used to carve marble.* 2 produce a design or object by carving: *I carved my initials on the tree.* 3 cut cooked meat into slices for eating. 4 (**carve something out**) develop a career, reputation, etc. through great effort. 5 (**carve something up**) divide something ruthlessly into separate parts or areas.
– ORIGIN Old English.

carvel /kar-v'l/ noun variant spelling of CARAVEL.

carver noun 1 a person or tool that carves. 2 Brit. the principal chair, with arms, in a set of dining chairs, intended for the person carving meat.

carvery noun (pl. **carveries**) a buffet or restaurant where cooked joints of meat are carved as required.

carving noun an object or design carved from wood or stone as a work of art.

car wash noun a structure containing equipment for washing vehicles automatically.

caryatid /ka-ri-at-id/ noun Architecture a supporting pillar in the form of a clothed female figure.
– ORIGIN Greek *karuatides* 'priestesses of Artemis at Caryae', from *Karuai* (Caryae) in Laconia.

Casanova /ka-suh-noh-vuh/ noun a man notorious for seducing women.
– ORIGIN from the name of the Italian adventurer Giovanni Jacopo *Casanova*.

casbah noun variant spelling of KASBAH.

cascade noun 1 a small waterfall, especially one in a series. 2 a mass of something that falls, hangs, or occurs in large quantities: *a cascade of raindrops.* 3 a succession of devices or stages in a process, each of which triggers

the next. • verb pour downwards rapidly and in large quantities.
– ORIGIN from Italian *cascare* 'to fall'.

cascara /kas-kah-ruh/ (also **cascara sagrada** /suh-grah-duh/) noun a laxative made from the dried bark of a North American shrub.
– ORIGIN Spanish, '(sacred) bark'.

case[1] noun 1 an instance of a particular situation: *a case of mistaken identity.* 2 an instance of a disease, injury, or problem: *1,000 new cases of cancer.* 3 an incident being investigated by the police. 4 a legal action that is to be or has been decided in a court of law. 5 a set of facts or arguments supporting one side of a debate or lawsuit. 6 a person or problem requiring or receiving the attention of a doctor, social worker, etc. 7 Grammar a form of a noun, adjective, or pronoun expressing the relationship of the word to other words in the sentence: *the possessive case.*
– PHRASES **be the case** be so. **in case** so as to allow for the possibility of something happening or being true.
– ORIGIN Latin *casus* 'fall, occurrence, chance'.

case[2] noun 1 a container or protective covering. 2 Brit. a suitcase. 3 a box containing twelve bottles of wine or other drink, sold as a unit. • verb 1 enclose something within a case. 2 informal look round a place before carrying out a robbery.
– ORIGIN Latin *capsa* 'box'.

casebook noun Brit. a written record of cases, kept by a doctor, lawyer, etc.

case-hardened adjective made callous or tough by experience: *a case-hardened politician.*

case history noun a record of a person's background or medical history kept by a doctor or social worker.

casein /kay-seen/ noun the main protein present in milk and (in coagulated form) in cheese.
– ORIGIN from Latin *caseus* 'cheese'.

case law noun the law as established by the outcome of former cases rather than by legislation.

caseload noun the number of cases being dealt with by a doctor, lawyer, or social worker at one time.

casement noun a window set on a vertical hinge so that it opens like a door.
– ORIGIN Latin *cassimentum.*

case study noun 1 a detailed study of the development of a particular person, group, or situation over a period of time. 2 a particular instance of something used or analysed to illustrate a theory or principle.

casework noun social work involving the study of a particular person's family history and personal circumstances.

cash noun 1 money in the form of coins or notes. 2 money in any form: *he was always short of cash.* • verb 1 give or get notes or coins for a cheque or money order. 2 (**cash something in**) convert an insurance policy, savings account, etc. into money. 3 (**cash in on**) informal take advantage of a situation. 4 (**cash up**) Brit. count and check takings at the end of a day's trading.
– PHRASES **cash in hand** Brit. payment in cash

rather than by cheque or other means.
- DERIVATIVES **cashless** adjective.
- ORIGIN Old French *casse* 'box for money', from Latin *capsa* 'box, receptacle'.

cash and carry noun a system of wholesale trading in which goods are paid for in full and taken away by the buyer.

cashback noun **1** a service offered by a shop by which a customer may withdraw cash when buying goods with a debit card. **2** a cash refund offered as an incentive to buyers of certain products.

cash book noun a book in which amounts of money paid and received are recorded.

cash card noun Brit. a plastic card issued by a bank or building society which enables the holder to withdraw money from a cash dispenser.

cash cow noun informal a business or investment that provides a steady income or profit.

cash crop noun a crop produced for selling rather than for use by the grower.

cash desk noun Brit. a counter or compartment in a shop or restaurant where payments are made.

cash dispenser noun Brit. an automated teller machine.

cashew /**ka**-shoo/ noun (also **cashew nut**) the edible kidney-shaped nut of a tropical American tree.
- ORIGIN Tupi.

cash flow noun the total amount of money passing into and out of a business.

cashier¹ noun a person whose job is to pay out and receive money in a shop, bank, or business.
- ORIGIN French *caissier*.

cashier² verb dismiss someone from the armed forces because of a serious wrongdoing.
- ORIGIN French *casser* 'revoke, dismiss'.

cashmere noun fine soft wool, originally that obtained from a breed of Himalayan goat.
- ORIGIN an early spelling of *Kashmir*, a region on the border of India and NE Pakistan.

cashpoint noun Brit. trademark an automated teller machine.

cash register noun a machine used in shops for adding up and recording the amount of each sale and storing the money received.

cash-strapped adjective informal very short of money.

casing noun **1** a cover or shell that protects or encloses something. **2** the frame round a door or window.

casino noun (pl. **casinos**) a public building or room for gambling.
- ORIGIN Italian, 'little house'.

cask noun a large barrel for storing alcoholic drinks.
- ORIGIN French *casque* or Spanish *casco* 'helmet'.

cask-conditioned adjective (of beer) undergoing a second fermentation while stored in a cask and not further processed before it is served.

casket noun **1** a small ornamental box or chest for holding valuable objects. **2** chiefly N. Amer. a coffin.
- ORIGIN perhaps a variant of Old French

cassette 'little box'.

Cassandra /kuh-**san**-druh/ noun a person who makes pessimistic predictions.
- ORIGIN from *Cassandra* in Greek mythology, whose prophecies, though true, were not believed.

cassava /kuh-**sah**-vuh/ noun the starchy root of a tropical American tree, used as food.
- ORIGIN from Taino (an extinct Caribbean language).

casserole noun **1** a large dish with a lid, used for cooking food slowly in an oven. **2** a kind of stew cooked slowly in an oven. • verb cook food slowly in a casserole.
- ORIGIN French.

cassette noun a sealed plastic case containing audio tape, videotape, film, etc., to be inserted into a recorder, camera, or other device.
- ORIGIN French, 'little box'.

cassia /**kas**-i-uh/ noun **1** a tree or plant of warm climates from which senna (a mild laxative) is obtained. **2** the bark of an East Asian tree, from which an inferior kind of cinnamon is obtained.
- ORIGIN Latin.

cassis /ka-**sees**/ (also **crème de cassis**) noun a syrupy blackcurrant liqueur.
- ORIGIN French, 'blackcurrant'.

cassock noun a long garment worn by some Christian clergy and members of church choirs.
- ORIGIN Italian *casacca* 'riding coat'.

cassoulet /**kass**-oo-lay/ noun a stew made with meat and beans.
- ORIGIN French, 'small stew pan'.

cassowary /**kass**-uh-wuh-ri/ noun (pl. **cassowaries**) a very large flightless bird related to the emu, native mainly to New Guinea.
- ORIGIN Malay.

cast verb (past and past part. **cast**) **1** throw something forcefully. **2** cause light or shadow to appear on a surface. **3** direct one's eyes or thoughts towards something. **4** express: *journalists cast doubt on this account.* **5** register a vote. **6** give a part to an actor or allocate parts in a play or film. **7** leave aside: *he jumped in, casting caution to the winds.* **8** throw the hooked and baited end of a fishing line out into the water. **9** shape metal or other material by pouring it into a mould while molten. **10** produce an object by casting metal: *a figure cast in bronze.* **11** describe or present in a particular way: *he cast himself as the embodiment of the American dream.* **12** cause a magic spell to take effect. • noun **1** the actors taking part in a play or film. **2** an object made by casting metal or other material. **3** (also **plaster cast**) a bandage stiffened with plaster of Paris, moulded to support and protect a broken limb. **4** the appearance or nature of someone or something: *minds of a philosophical cast.* **5** a slight squint.
- PHRASES **be cast away** be stranded after a shipwreck. **be cast down** feel depressed. **cast about** (or **around** or **round**) search far and wide. **cast off** Knitting take the stitches off the needle by looping each over the next. **cast something off** release a boat or ship from its

moorings. **cast on** Knitting make the first row of loops on the needle.
– ORIGIN Old Norse.

castanets plural noun a pair of small curved pieces of wood, ivory, or plastic, clicked together by the fingers as an accompaniment to Spanish dancing.
– ORIGIN Spanish *castañeta* 'little chestnut'.

castaway noun a person who has been shipwrecked and stranded in an isolated place.

caste noun each of the hereditary classes of Hindu society.
– ORIGIN Spanish and Portuguese *casta* 'lineage, breed'.

castellated /**kass**-tuh-lay-tid/ adjective having battlements.
– DERIVATIVES **castellation** noun.
– ORIGIN from Latin *castellum* 'little fort'.

caster noun 1 a person or machine that casts. 2 variant spelling of CASTOR.

caster sugar (also **castor sugar**) noun Brit. finely ground white sugar.
– ORIGIN so named because it was suitable for sprinkling from a castor.

castigate /**kass**-ti-gayt/ verb reprimand someone severely.
– DERIVATIVES **castigation** noun.
– ORIGIN Latin *castigare*.

Castilian /ka-**stil**-i-uhn/ noun 1 a person from the Spanish region of Castile. 2 the language of Castile, the standard form of both spoken and literary Spanish. ● adjective relating to Castile or Castilian.

casting noun an object made by casting molten metal or other material.

casting vote noun an extra vote used by a chairperson to decide an issue when votes on each side are equal.

cast iron noun a hard alloy of iron and carbon which can be readily cast in a mould. ● adjective firm and unchangeable: *a cast-iron guarantee.*

castle noun 1 a large fortified building or group of buildings constructed during medieval times. 2 Chess, informal old-fashioned term for ROOK².
– PHRASES **castles in the air** (or **in Spain**) plans or dreams which are never likely to be achieved or fulfilled.
– ORIGIN Latin *castellum* 'little fort'.

cast-off adjective no longer wanted; abandoned or discarded. ● noun a garment that is no longer wanted.

castor /**kah**-ster/ (also **caster**) noun 1 each of a set of small swivelling wheels fixed to the legs or base of a piece of furniture. 2 a small container with holes in the top, used for sprinkling salt, sugar, etc.
– ORIGIN variant of CASTER.

castor oil noun an oil obtained from the seeds of an African shrub, used as a laxative.
– ORIGIN Greek *kastōr* 'beaver': perhaps because an oily substance produced by beavers was formerly used as a laxative.

castor sugar noun variant spelling of CASTER SUGAR.

castrate verb 1 remove the testicles of a male animal or person. 2 deprive someone or something of power or vitality.
– DERIVATIVES **castration** noun **castrator** noun.

– ORIGIN Latin *castrare*.

castrato /ka-**strah**-toh/ noun (pl. **castrati** /ka-**strah**-tee/) historical a male singer castrated before puberty so that he kept a soprano or alto voice.
– ORIGIN Italian.

casual adjective 1 relaxed and unconcerned. 2 done or made without much thought: *a casual remark.* 3 not regular or firmly established; occasional or temporary: *casual jobs.* 4 happening by chance; accidental. 5 (of clothes) suitable for informal everyday wear: *a casual short-sleeved shirt.* ● noun 1 Brit. a temporary or occasional worker. 2 (**casuals**) clothes or shoes suitable for informal everyday wear.
– DERIVATIVES **casually** adverb **casualness** noun.
– ORIGIN Latin *casualis*.

casualization (or **casualisation**) noun the replacement of a permanently employed workforce by workers on temporary contracts.

casualty noun (pl. **casualties**) 1 a person killed or injured in a war or accident. 2 (also **casualty department**) the department of a hospital providing immediate treatment for emergency cases. 3 a person or thing badly affected by an event or situation: *the firm was one of the casualties of the recession.*

casuistry /**kazh**-oo-iss-tri/ noun the use of clever but false reasoning.
– DERIVATIVES **casuist** noun **casuistic** adjective **casuistical** adjective.
– ORIGIN from Latin *casus* 'fall, chance'.

CAT abbreviation Medicine computerized axial tomography.

cat noun 1 a small domesticated mammal with soft fur. 2 a wild animal related to or resembling this, e.g. a lion or tiger.
– PHRASES **the cat's whiskers** (or **the cat's pyjamas**) informal an excellent person or thing. **let the cat out of the bag** informal reveal a secret by mistake. **like a cat on a hot tin roof** informal very agitated or anxious. **put** (or **set**) **the cat among the pigeons** Brit. say or do something likely to cause trouble.
– DERIVATIVES **catlike** adjective.
– ORIGIN Old English.

catabolism /kuh-**tab**-uh-li-z'm/ noun a metabolic process in which complex molecules are broken down to form simpler ones and energy is released. The opposite of ANABOLISM.
– DERIVATIVES **catabolic** adjective.
– ORIGIN Greek *katabolē* 'throwing down'.

cataclysm /**kat**-uh-kli-z'm/ noun a violent upheaval or disaster.
– DERIVATIVES **cataclysmic** adjective **cataclysmically** adverb.
– ORIGIN Greek *kataklusmos* 'deluge'.

catacomb /**kat**-uh-koom/ noun an underground cemetery consisting of tunnels with recesses for tombs.
– ORIGIN Latin *catacumbas*, the name of an underground cemetery near Rome.

catafalque /**kat**-uh-falk/ noun a decorated wooden framework used to support a coffin.
– ORIGIN Italian *catafalco*.

Catalan /**kat**-uh-lan/ noun 1 a person from Catalonia in NE Spain. 2 the language of Catalonia. ● adjective relating to Catalonia.
– ORIGIN Spanish.

catalepsy /kat-uh-lep-si/ noun a medical condition in which a person suffers a loss of consciousness and their body becomes rigid.
– DERIVATIVES **cataleptic** adjective & noun.
– ORIGIN from Greek *katalambanein* 'seize upon'.

catalogue (US also **catalog**) noun 1 a complete list of items arranged in alphabetical or another systematic order. 2 a publication containing details of items for sale. 3 a series of bad things: *a catalogue of disasters.* • verb (**catalogues, cataloguing, catalogued**; US also **catalogs, cataloging, cataloged**) list an item or items in a catalogue.
– DERIVATIVES **cataloguer** noun.
– ORIGIN Greek *katalogos*.

Catalonian /kat-uh-loh-ni-uhn/ adjective & noun another term for **CATALAN**.

catalpa /kuh-tal-puh/ noun a tree with heart-shaped leaves, native to North America and east Asia.
– ORIGIN from an American Indian language.

catalyse /kat-uh-lyz/ (US **catalyze**) verb cause or speed up a reaction by acting as a catalyst.
– DERIVATIVES **catalyser** noun.

catalysis /kuh-tal-i-siss/ noun the speeding up of a chemical reaction by a catalyst.
– DERIVATIVES **catalytic** /kat-uh-lit-ik/ adjective.
– ORIGIN Greek *katalusis* 'dissolution'.

catalyst /kat-uh-list/ noun 1 a substance that increases the speed of a chemical reaction without undergoing any permanent chemical change itself. 2 a person or thing that causes something to happen: *his speech had acted as a catalyst for debate.*

catalytic converter noun a device in the exhaust system of a motor vehicle, containing a catalyst for converting pollutant gases into less harmful ones.

catamaran /kat-uh-muh-ran/ noun a yacht or other boat with twin parallel hulls.
– ORIGIN Tamil, 'tied wood'.

catamite /kat-uh-myt/ noun old use a boy kept by an older man as a homosexual partner.
– ORIGIN Latin *catamitus*.

cataplexy /kat-uh-plek-si/ noun a medical condition in which strong emotion or laughter causes a person to experience sudden weakness in the muscles.
– ORIGIN Greek *kataplēxis* 'stupefaction'.

catapult noun 1 chiefly Brit. a forked stick with an elastic band fastened to the two prongs, used for shooting small stones. 2 historical a military machine for hurling large stones or other missiles. 3 a mechanical device for launching a glider or aircraft. • verb 1 throw something forcefully. 2 move suddenly or very fast.
– ORIGIN Latin *catapulta*.

cataract /kat-uh-rakt/ noun 1 a large waterfall. 2 a medical condition in which the lens of the eye becomes opaque, resulting in blurred vision.
– ORIGIN from Greek *kataraktēs* 'down-rushing'.

catarrh /kuh-tar/ noun excessive mucus in the nose or throat.
– DERIVATIVES **catarrhal** adjective.
– ORIGIN from Greek *katarrhein* 'flow down'.

catastrophe /kuh-tass-truh-fi/ noun an event causing great damage or suffering.
– DERIVATIVES **catastrophic** /kat-uh-strof-ik/ adjective. **catastrophically** adverb.
– ORIGIN Greek *katastrophē* 'overturning, sudden turn'.

catatonia /kat-uh-toh-ni-uh/ noun a condition resulting from schizophrenia or another mental disorder, in which a person experiences both periods of unconsciousness and overactivity.
– ORIGIN from Greek *tonos* 'tone or tension'.

catatonic /kat-uh-ton-ik/ adjective 1 suffering from catatonia. 2 informal inert or completely unresponsive.

cat burglar noun a thief who enters a building by climbing to an upper storey.

catcall noun a shrill whistle or shout of mockery or disapproval. • verb make a catcall.

catch verb (past and past part. **caught**) 1 seize and take hold of a moving object. 2 capture a person or animal. 3 be in time to board a train, bus, etc. or to see a person or event. 4 entangle or become entangled: *she caught her foot in the bedspread.* 5 surprise someone in the act of doing something wrong or embarrassing: *she caught him flirting with another woman.* 6 (**be caught in**) unexpectedly find oneself in an unwelcome situation. 7 become infected with an illness. 8 see, hear, or understand: *I couldn't catch what he said.* 9 gain a person's interest or attention. 10 hit someone or something: *she fell and caught her head on the hearth.* 11 start burning. 12 Cricket dismiss a batsman by catching the ball before it touches the ground. • noun 1 an act of catching something. 2 a device for fastening a door, window, etc. 3 a hidden problem. 4 a break in a person's voice caused by emotion. 5 informal a person thought of as being desirable or suitable as a husband or wife. 6 an amount of fish caught.
– PHRASES **catch one's breath 1** breathe in sharply as a result of a strong emotion. **2** recover one's breath after exercise. **catch someone's eye 1** be noticed by someone. **2** attract someone's attention by making eye contact. **catch on** informal **1** become popular. **2** understand what is meant. **catch someone out** Brit. **1** discover that someone has done something wrong. **2** take someone unawares: *you might get caught out by the weather.* **catch the sun 1** be in a sunny position. **2** Brit. become tanned or sunburnt. **catch up 1** do tasks which one should have done earlier. **2** (**be/get caught up in**) become involved in. **catch someone up** succeed in reaching a person ahead.
– DERIVATIVES **catcher** noun.
– ORIGIN from Latin *captare* 'try to catch'.

catch-all noun a term or category intended to cover all possibilities.

catching adjective (of a disease) infectious.

catchment area (also **catchment**) noun 1 the area from which a hospital's patients or a school's pupils are drawn. 2 the area from which rainfall flows into a river, lake, or reservoir.

catchpenny adjective having a superficially attractive appearance so as to sell quickly.

catchphrase noun a well-known sentence or phrase.

catch-22 noun a difficult situation from which there is no escape because it involves

C

situations which conflict with or are dependent on each other.
– ORIGIN title of a novel by Joseph Heller (1961).

catchword noun a frequently used word or phrase that is associated with or encapsulates a particular thing: *perestroika was the catchword of the Gorbachev era.*

catchy adjective (**catchier, catchiest**) (of a tune or phrase) instantly appealing and easy to remember.
– DERIVATIVES **catchiness** noun.

catechesis /kat-i-kee-sis/ noun religious instruction given to prepare someone for Christian baptism or confirmation.
– ORIGIN Greek *katēkhēsis* 'oral instruction'.

catechism /kat-i-ki-z'm/ noun a summary of the principles of the Christian religion in the form of questions and answers, used for teaching.

catechist noun a Christian teacher, especially one using a catechism.

catechize (or **catechise**) /kat-i-kyz/ verb teach someone about the principles of the Christian religion by means of question and answer, especially by using a catechism.
– ORIGIN from Greek *katēkhein* 'teach orally'.

categorical (also **categoric**) adjective completely explicit and direct.
– DERIVATIVES **categorically** adverb.

categorize (or **categorise**) verb place someone or something in a particular category: *the population is categorized according to age, sex, and socio-economic group.*
– DERIVATIVES **categorization** noun.

category noun (pl. **categories**) a class or group of people or things with shared characteristics.
– ORIGIN Greek *katēgoria* 'statement'.

catenary /kuh-teen-uh-ri/ noun (pl. **catenaries**) a curve formed by a wire, chain, etc. hanging freely from two points on the same horizontal level. •adjective involving or referring to a curve of this type.
– ORIGIN Latin *catena* 'chain'.

cater verb 1 (**cater for**) Brit. provide food and drink at a social event. 2 (**cater for/to**) provide with what is needed or required: *the school caters for children with special needs.* 3 (**cater for**) take something into account. 4 (**cater to**) satisfy a need or demand.
– DERIVATIVES **caterer** noun.
– ORIGIN Old French *acater* 'buy', from Latin *captare* 'seize'.

caterpillar noun 1 the larva of a butterfly or moth. 2 (also **caterpillar track** or **tread**) trademark a steel band passing round the wheels of a vehicle for travel on rough ground.
– ORIGIN perhaps from Old French *chatepelose* 'hairy cat'.

caterwaul /kat-er-wawl/ verb make a shrill howling or wailing noise.

catfight noun informal a fight between women.
– DERIVATIVES **catfighting** noun.

catfish noun (pl. same or **catfishes**) a freshwater or sea fish with whisker-like growths round the mouth.

cat flap noun a small hinged flap in an outer door through which a cat may pass in and out.

catgut noun material used for the strings of musical instruments and formerly for surgical sutures, made of the dried intestines of sheep or horses (but not cats).
– ORIGIN the association with **CAT** is uncertain.

catharsis /kuh-thar-siss/ noun the process of releasing strong but repressed emotions so as to be relieved of them.
– ORIGIN from Greek *kathairein* 'cleanse'.

cathartic /kuh-thar-tik/ adjective providing psychological relief through the expression of strong but previously repressed emotions: *writing the book was a very cathartic experience.*

cathedral noun the principal church of a diocese.
– ORIGIN from Greek *kathedra* 'seat'.

Catherine wheel noun Brit. a firework in the form of a spinning coil.
– ORIGIN named after St *Catherine*, who was martyred on a spiked wheel.

catheter /kath-i-ter/ noun a flexible tube inserted into the bladder or another body cavity to remove fluid.
– ORIGIN from Greek *kathienai* 'send or let down'.

cathode /kath-ohd/ noun an electrode with a negative charge. The opposite of **ANODE**.
– ORIGIN Greek *kathodos* 'way down'.

cathode ray noun a beam of electrons sent out from the cathode of a vacuum tube.

cathode ray tube noun a high-vacuum tube in which cathode rays produce a luminous image on a fluorescent screen, used in televisions and visual display units.

catholic adjective 1 including a wide variety of things: *catholic tastes.* 2 (**Catholic**) Roman Catholic. 3 (**Catholic**) of or including all Christians. •noun (**Catholic**) a Roman Catholic.
– DERIVATIVES **Catholicism** /kuh-thol-i-siz'm/ noun **catholicity** noun.
– ORIGIN Greek *katholikos* 'universal'.

cation /kat-I-uhn/ noun Chemistry an ion with a positive charge. The opposite of **ANION**.
– DERIVATIVES **cationic** /kat-I-on-ik/ adjective.
– ORIGIN from **CATHODE** + **ION**.

catkin noun a spike of small soft flowers hanging from trees such as willow and hazel.
– ORIGIN the former Dutch word *katteken* 'kitten'.

catmint noun a plant with a strong smell that is very attractive to cats.

catnap noun a short sleep during the day. •verb (**catnaps, catnapping, catnapped**) have a catnap.

catnip noun another term for **CATMINT**.
– ORIGIN from **CAT** + Latin *nepeta* 'catmint'.

cat-o'-nine-tails noun historical a whip consisting of a rope made from nine knotted cords, used for flogging people.

cat's cradle noun a child's game in which patterns are formed in a loop of string held between the fingers of each hand.

catseye noun Brit. trademark each of a series of reflective studs marking the lanes or edges of a road.

cat's paw noun a person used by someone else to carry out an unpleasant task on their behalf.

catsuit noun chiefly Brit. a woman's close-fitting

one-piece garment with trouser legs.

catsup noun US another term for **ketchup**.

cattery noun (pl. **catteries**) a place where cats are bred, or looked after while their owners are away.

cattle plural noun large domesticated animals with horns and cloven hoofs; cows, bulls, and oxen.
– ORIGIN Old French *chatel* 'chattel'.

cattle grid (N. Amer. **cattle guard**) noun a metal grid covering a trench across a road, allowing vehicles and pedestrians to cross but not animals.

catty adjective (**cattier**, **cattiest**) spiteful.
– DERIVATIVES **cattily** adverb.

CATV abbreviation community antenna television (cable television).

catwalk noun **1** a narrow platform along which models walk to display clothes. **2** a raised narrow walkway or open bridge.

Caucasian /kaw-kay-zh'n/ adjective **1** relating to a division of humankind covering peoples from Europe, western Asia, and parts of India and North Africa. **2** white-skinned; of European origin. •noun a Caucasian person.

caucus /kaw-kuhss/ noun (pl. **caucuses**) **1** a meeting of a policy-making committee of a political party. **2** a group of people with shared concerns within a larger organization.
– ORIGIN perhaps from an American Indian word meaning 'adviser'.

caudal /kaw-duhl/ adjective of, at, or near the tail or the rear part of an animal's body.
– DERIVATIVES **caudally** adverb.
– ORIGIN Latin *cauda* 'tail'.

caught past and past participle of **catch**.

caul /rhymes with ball/ noun the membrane enclosing a fetus, part of which is sometimes found on a baby's head at birth.
– ORIGIN perhaps from Old French *cale* 'head covering'.

cauldron (also **caldron**) noun a large metal pot, used for cooking over an open fire.
– ORIGIN Old French *caudron*, from Latin *caldarium* 'hot bath'.

cauliflower noun a variety of cabbage with a large flower head of small creamy-white flower buds.
– ORIGIN from former French *chou fleuri* 'flowered cabbage'.

cauliflower ear noun a person's ear that has become thickened or deformed as a result of repeated blows.

caulk /kawk/ (US also **calk**) noun a waterproof substance used in building work to fill cracks and seal joins. •verb **1** seal something with caulk. **2** make a boat or its seams watertight.
– ORIGIN Latin *calcare* 'to tread'.

causal adjective relating to or being a cause of something: *a causal connection between smoking and lung cancer.*
– DERIVATIVES **causally** adverb.

causality noun the relationship between something that happens and the effect it produces.

causation noun **1** the action of causing something. **2** another term for **causality**.

causative adjective acting as a cause of something.

cause noun **1** a person or thing that produces an effect. **2** good reason for thinking or doing something: *there is no cause for concern.* **3** a principle, aim, etc. which one is prepared to support or fight for: *the socialist cause.* **4** a lawsuit. •verb make something, especially something bad, happen.
– PHRASES **cause and effect** the relationship between an action or event and the effect it produces.
– ORIGIN Latin *causa*.

cause célèbre /kawz se-leb-ruh/ noun (pl. **causes célèbres** pronunc. same) a controversial issue arousing great public interest.
– ORIGIN French, 'famous case'.

causeway noun a raised road or track across low or wet ground.
– ORIGIN Old French *causee*.

caustic /kaw-stik/ adjective **1** able to burn or corrode living tissue by chemical action. **2** bitterly critical or sarcastic.
– DERIVATIVES **caustically** adverb.
– ORIGIN from Greek *kaustos* 'combustible'.

caustic soda noun sodium hydroxide.

cauterize (or **cauterise**) /kaw-tuh-ryz/ verb burn the skin or flesh of a wound to stop bleeding or prevent infection.
– DERIVATIVES **cauterization** noun.
– ORIGIN from Greek *kautērion* 'branding iron'.

caution noun **1** care taken to avoid danger or mistakes. **2** warning: *advisers sounded a note of caution.* **3** Brit. an official or legal warning given to someone who has committed a minor offence but has not been charged. •verb **1** warn or advise: *economic advisers cautioned against a tax increase.* **2** Brit. give an official or legal caution to someone. **3** Brit. (of a police officer) advise someone of their legal rights when arresting them.
– PHRASES **throw caution to the wind** (or **winds**) act in a reckless way.
– ORIGIN Latin, from *cavere* 'take heed'.

cautionary adjective acting as a warning.

cautious adjective careful to avoid possible problems or dangers.
– DERIVATIVES **cautiously** adverb **cautiousness** noun.

cava /kah-vuh/ noun a Spanish sparkling wine made in the same way as champagne.
– ORIGIN Spanish.

cavalcade /ka-vuhl-kayd/ noun a procession of vehicles or people on horseback.
– ORIGIN Italian *cavalcare* 'to ride'.

cavalier noun (**Cavalier**) historical a supporter of King Charles I in the English Civil War. •adjective showing a lack of proper concern: *the president's cavalier attitude to America's international obligations.*
– DERIVATIVES **cavalierly** adverb.
– ORIGIN Italian *cavaliere* 'knight, gentleman', from Latin *caballus* 'horse'.

cavalry noun (pl. **cavalries**) (usu. treated as pl.) soldiers who formerly fought on horseback, but who now use armoured vehicles.
– DERIVATIVES **cavalryman** noun (pl. **cavalrymen**).
– ORIGIN Italian *cavallo* 'horse'.

cavalry twill noun strong woollen twilled fabric of a khaki or light brown colour.

cave noun a large natural hollow in the side of a

hill or cliff, or underground. • verb (**cave in**)
1 give way or collapse. **2** finally agree to
someone's demands: *the bank caved in to
pressure from local community groups.*
– ORIGIN from Latin *cavus* 'hollow'.

caveat /**ka**-vi-at/ noun a warning that certain
conditions or provisos need to be taken into
account.
– ORIGIN Latin, 'let a person beware'.

caveat emptor /**emp**-tor/ noun the principle
that the buyer is responsible for checking the
quality and suitability of goods before buying
them.
– ORIGIN Latin, 'let the buyer beware'.

caveman (or **cavewoman**) noun (pl. **cavemen**
or **cavewomen**) a prehistoric person who lived
in caves.

cavern noun a large cave, or chamber in a cave.
– ORIGIN Latin *caverna*.

cavernous adjective (of a room or space) like a
cavern in being very large and empty or dark.

caviar /**ka**-vi-ar/ (also **caviare**) noun the pickled
roe of the sturgeon (a large fish), eaten as a
delicacy.
– ORIGIN French.

cavil /**ka**-vuhl/ verb (**cavils, cavilling, cavilled**; US
cavils, caviling, caviled) make trivial
complaints or objections. • noun a trivial
complaint or objection.
– ORIGIN Latin *cavillari*.

caving noun the activity of exploring caves as a
sport.
– DERIVATIVES **caver** noun.

cavitation noun the formation of bubbles in a
liquid.

cavity noun (pl. **cavities**) **1** a hollow space within
a solid object. **2** a decayed part of a tooth.
– ORIGIN Latin *cavitas*, from *cavus* 'hollow'.

cavity wall noun a wall formed from two
layers of bricks with a space between them.

cavort verb jump or dance around excitedly.
– ORIGIN perhaps an alteration of CURVET.

cavy /**kay**-vi/ noun (pl. **cavies**) a guinea pig or
related South American rodent.
– ORIGIN Latin *cavia*.

caw noun the harsh cry of a rook, crow, or
similar bird. • verb (of a rook, crow, or similar
bird) make a harsh cry.
– ORIGIN imitating the sound.

cayenne /kay-**en**/ (also **cayenne pepper**) noun
a hot-tasting red powder prepared from dried
chillies.
– ORIGIN Tupi.

cayman noun variant spelling of CAIMAN.

CB abbreviation **1** Citizens' Band. **2** (in the UK)
Companion of the Order of the Bath.

CBE abbreviation (in the UK) Commander of the
Order of the British Empire.

CBI abbreviation Confederation of British
Industry.

CC abbreviation **1** Brit. City Council. **2** Brit. County
Council. **3** Cricket Club.

cc (also **c.c.**) abbreviation **1** carbon copy (an
indication that a duplicate has been or should
be sent to another person). **2** cubic
centimetre(s).

CCJ abbreviation (in the UK) county court
judgement, issued by a court after a person
has failed to repay a debt and recorded in that

person's credit history.

CCTV abbreviation closed-circuit television.

CD abbreviation compact disc.

Cd symbol the chemical element cadmium.

cd abbreviation candela.

CD-R abbreviation compact disc recordable, a CD
which can be recorded on once only.

CD-ROM noun a compact disc used in a
computer as a read-only device for displaying
data.
– ORIGIN from *compact disc read-only memory*.

CD-RW abbreviation compact disc rewritable, a
CD on which recordings can be made and
erased a number of times.

CE abbreviation Church of England.

Ce symbol the chemical element cerium.

ceanothus /see-uh-**noh**-thuhss/ noun a North
American shrub with dense clusters of small
blue flowers.
– ORIGIN Greek *keanōthos*, a kind of thistle.

cease verb come or bring to an end; stop.
– PHRASES **without cease** without stopping.
– ORIGIN Latin *cessare*.

ceasefire noun a temporary period when
fighting is stopped.

ceaseless adjective constant; never stopping.
– DERIVATIVES **ceaselessly** adverb.

cecum noun (pl. **ceca**) US spelling of CAECUM.

cedar noun a tall coniferous tree with hard,
sweet-smelling wood.
– ORIGIN Greek *kedros*.

cede /seed/ verb give up power or territory.
– ORIGIN Latin *cedere*.

cedi /**see**-di/ noun (pl. same or **cedis**) the basic
unit of money of Ghana.
– ORIGIN Ghanaian.

cedilla /si-**dil**-luh/ noun a mark (¸) written
under the letter c, especially in French, to
show that it is pronounced like an *s* (e.g.
soupçon).
– ORIGIN Spanish *zedilla* 'little z'.

ceilidh /**kay**-li/ noun a social event with
Scottish or Irish folk music and singing,
traditional dancing, and storytelling.
– ORIGIN Old Irish *céilide* 'visit, visiting'.

ceiling noun **1** the upper inside surface of a
room. **2** an upper limit set on prices, wages, or
spending. **3** the maximum altitude to which an
aircraft can climb.
– ORIGIN from former *ceil* 'line or plaster the
roof of a building'.

celandine /**sel**-uhn-dyn/ noun a yellow-
flowered plant of the buttercup family.
– ORIGIN from Greek *khelidōn* 'swallow'
(because the flowering of the plant was
associated with the arrival of migrating
swallows).

celebrant /**sel**-i-bruhnt/ noun **1** a person who
performs a religious ceremony, especially a
priest who leads the service of Holy
Communion. **2** chiefly N. Amer. a person who
celebrates something.

celebrate verb **1** mark an important occasion
with a social gathering or enjoyable activity.
2 honour or praise someone publicly.
3 perform a religious ceremony, in particular
the Christian service of Holy Communion.
– DERIVATIVES **celebration** noun **celebrator** noun
celebratory adjective.

– ORIGIN Latin *celebrare*.

celebrity noun (pl. **celebrities**) **1** a famous person. **2** the state of being famous.

celeriac /suh-**lair**-i-ak/ noun a variety of celery which forms a large edible root.
– ORIGIN from CELERY.

celerity /si-**le**-ri-ti/ noun old use or literary speed of movement.
– ORIGIN from Latin *celer* 'swift'.

celery noun a plant with crisp juicy stalks, eaten in salads or as a vegetable.
– ORIGIN from Greek *selinon* 'parsley'.

celesta /si-**les**-tuh/ (also **celeste** /si-**lest**/) noun a small keyboard instrument in which felt-covered hammers strike a row of steel plates.
– ORIGIN from French *céleste* 'heavenly' (with reference to the instrument's light, delicate sound).

celestial adjective **1** belonging or relating to heaven. **2** positioned in or relating to the sky or outer space.
– DERIVATIVES **celestially** adverb.
– ORIGIN from Latin *caelum* 'heaven'.

celestial equator noun the projection into space of the earth's equator.

celestial pole noun Astronomy the point on the celestial sphere directly above either of the earth's geographic poles, around which the stars appear to rotate.

celestial sphere noun an imaginary sphere of which the observer is the centre and on which all celestial objects are considered to lie.

celiac disease noun US spelling of COELIAC DISEASE.

celibate /**sel**-i-buht/ adjective **1** not marrying or having sex, especially for religious reasons. **2** not having or involving a sexual relationship. ●noun a person who is celibate.
– DERIVATIVES **celibacy** noun.
– ORIGIN Latin *caelibatus* 'unmarried state'.

cell noun **1** a small room for a prisoner, monk, or nun. **2** the smallest unit of a living organism that is able to reproduce and perform other functions. **3** a small compartment in a larger structure such as a honeycomb. **4** a small group of people working as part of a larger political organization, usually in secret: *a terrorist cell.* **5** a device or unit in which electricity is produced using chemical energy or light, or in which electrolysis takes place.
– ORIGIN Latin *cella* 'storeroom or chamber'.

cellar noun **1** a storage space or room below ground level in a building. **2** a stock of wine.
– ORIGIN Latin *cellarium* 'storehouse'.

cellmate noun a person with whom one shares a cell.

cello /**chel**-loh/ noun (pl. **cellos**) a large instrument of the violin family, held upright on the floor between the legs of the seated player.
– DERIVATIVES **cellist** noun.
– ORIGIN shortening of VIOLONCELLO.

cellophane /**sel**-luh-fayn/ noun trademark a thin transparent wrapping material made from viscose.
– ORIGIN from CELLULOSE.

cellphone noun a mobile phone.

cellular /**sel**-yuu-ler/ adjective **1** relating to or made up of living cells. **2** relating to a mobile

telephone system that uses a number of short-range radio stations to cover the area it serves. **3** (of fabric) woven so as to form holes or hollows that trap air and provide extra insulation. **4** consisting of small compartments or rooms.
– ORIGIN Latin *cellularis*.

cellular phone noun chiefly N. Amer. a mobile phone.

cellulite /**sel**-yuu-lyt/ noun fat that accumulates under the skin, causing a dimpled effect.
– ORIGIN French.

celluloid noun **1** a transparent plastic formerly used for cinema film. **2** the cinema considered as a type of art.

cellulose /**sel**-yuu-lohz/ noun a substance found in all plant tissues, used in making paint, plastics, and man-made fibres.
– DERIVATIVES **cellulosic** adjective.
– ORIGIN French.

cellulose acetate noun a non-flammable substance produced from cellulose, used in making artificial fibres and plastic.

Celsius /**sel**-si-uhss/ adjective relating to a scale of temperature on which water freezes at 0° and boils at 100°.
– ORIGIN named after the Swedish astronomer Anders *Celsius*.

USAGE: **Celsius** rather than **centigrade** is the standard accepted term when giving temperatures.

Celt /kelt/ noun **1** a member of a group of peoples inhabiting much of Europe and the western peninsula of Asia in pre-Roman times. **2** a native of a modern region in which a Celtic language is (or was) spoken.
– ORIGIN Greek *Keltoi* 'Celts'.

Celtic /**kel**-tik/ noun a group of languages including Irish, Scottish Gaelic, Welsh, Breton, Manx, and Cornish. ●adjective relating to Celtic or to the Celts.

cement noun **1** a powdery substance made by strongly heating lime and clay, used in making mortar and concrete. **2** a soft glue that hardens on setting. ●verb **1** fix something with cement. **2** establish firmly: *the occasion cemented our friendship.*
– DERIVATIVES **cementation** noun.
– ORIGIN Latin *caementum* 'quarry stone'.

cemetery noun (pl. **cemeteries**) a large burial ground.
– ORIGIN Greek *koimētērion* 'dormitory'.

cenobite (also chiefly Brit. **coenobite**) noun a member of a community of monks or nuns.
– DERIVATIVES **cenobitic** /see-nuh-**bit**-tik/ adjective.
– ORIGIN from Greek *koinobion* 'convent'.

cenotaph /**sen**-uh-tahf/ noun a monument to members of the armed forces killed in a war.
– ORIGIN from Greek *kenos* 'empty' + *taphos* 'tomb'.

Cenozoic /see-nuh-**zoh**-ik/ (also **Cainozoic**) adjective Geology relating to the era following the Mesozoic era (from about 65 million years ago to the present).
– ORIGIN from Greek *kainos* 'new' + *zōion* 'animal'.

censer noun a container in which incense is

burnt during a religious ceremony.
– ORIGIN from Old French *encens* 'incense'.

censor noun an official who examines material that is to be published and suppresses parts considered offensive or a threat to security. • verb officially suppress unacceptable parts of a book, film, etc.
– DERIVATIVES **censorship** noun.
– ORIGIN from Latin *censere* 'assess'.

censorious /sen-sor-i-uhss/ adjective severely critical.

censure /sen-sher/ verb criticize someone or something severely. • noun strong disapproval or criticism.

> USAGE: **Censure** and **censor** are often confused. **Censure** means 'criticize severely' (*the country was censured for human rights abuses*) or 'strong disapproval', while **censor** means 'officially suppress unacceptable parts of a book, film, or similar work' or 'an official who censors books and other material'.

– ORIGIN from Latin *censura* 'judgement'.

census noun (pl. **censuses**) an official count or survey of a population.
– ORIGIN Latin.

cent noun a unit or money equal to one hundredth of a dollar, euro, or other decimal currency unit.
– ORIGIN from Latin *centum* 'hundred'.

centas /sen-tas/ noun (pl. same) a unit of money of Lithuania, equal to one hundredth of a litas.
– ORIGIN Lithuanian.

centaur /sen-tor/ noun Greek Mythology a creature with the head, arms, and torso of a man and the body and legs of a horse.
– ORIGIN Greek *kentauros*, referring to a people of Thessaly who were expert horsemen.

centavo /sen-tah-voh/ noun (pl. **centavos**) a unit of money of Mexico, Brazil, and certain other countries, equal to one hundredth of the basic unit.
– ORIGIN Spanish and Portuguese.

centenarian noun a person who is a hundred or more years old.

centenary /sen-tee-nuh-ri/ noun (pl. **centenaries**) Brit. the hundredth anniversary of an event.
– ORIGIN from Latin *centenarius* 'containing a hundred'.

centennial adjective relating to a hundredth anniversary. • noun a hundredth anniversary.
– ORIGIN from Latin *centum* 'a hundred'.

center etc. noun US spelling of **CENTRE** etc.

centesimal /sen-tes-i-m'l/ adjective relating to division into hundredths.
– ORIGIN from Latin *centesimus* 'hundredth'.

centésimo /sen-te-si-moh/ noun (pl. **centésimos**) a unit of money of Uruguay and Panama, equal to one hundredth of the basic unit.
– ORIGIN Spanish.

centi- combining form **1** one hundredth: *centilitre*. **2** hundred: *centipede*.
– ORIGIN from Latin *centum* 'hundred'.

centigrade adjective relating to the Celsius scale of temperature.
– ORIGIN from Latin *centum* 'a hundred' + *gradus* 'step'.

> USAGE: On using **centigrade** or **Celsius**, see the note at **CELSIUS**.

centigram (also **centigramme**) noun a metric unit of mass equal to one hundredth of a gram.

centilitre (US **centiliter**) noun a metric unit of capacity equal to one hundredth of a litre.

centime /son-teem/ noun a unit of money equal to one hundredth of a franc or some other decimal currency units (used in France, Belgium, and Luxembourg until the introduction of the euro in 2002).
– ORIGIN from Latin *centesimus* 'hundredth'.

centimetre (US **centimeter**) noun a metric unit of length equal to one hundredth of a metre.

centimo /sen-ti-moh/ noun (pl. **centimos**) a unit of money of a number of Latin American countries (and formerly of Spain), equal to one hundredth of the basic unit.
– ORIGIN Spanish.

centipede noun an insect-like creature with a long body composed of many segments, most of which have a pair of legs.
– ORIGIN from Latin *centum* 'a hundred' + *pes* 'foot'.

central adjective **1** in or near the centre. **2** very important; essential.
– DERIVATIVES **centrality** noun **centrally** adverb.

central bank noun a national bank that provides services for its country's government and commercial banking system, and issues currency.

central heating noun a system for warming a building by heating water or air in one place and circulating it through pipes and radiators or vents.

centralize (or **centralise**) verb bring something under the control of a central authority.
– DERIVATIVES **centralism** noun **centralist** noun & adjective **centralization** noun.

central nervous system noun the complex of nerve tissues that controls the activities of the body.

central processing unit (also **central processor**) noun the part of a computer in which operations are controlled and executed.

central reservation noun Brit. the strip of land between the carriageways of a motorway or other major road.

centre (US **center**) noun **1** a point or part in the middle of something. **2** a place devoted to a specified activity: *a conference centre.* **3** a point from which something spreads or to which something is directed: *the city was a centre of discontent.* **4** the middle player in some team games. • verb **1** place something in the centre. **2** (**centre on/around**) have as a major concern or theme: *several questions centre on funding.*
– PHRASES **centre of gravity** the central point in an object, about which its mass is evenly balanced.
– ORIGIN Latin *centrum*.

centre back noun Football a defender who plays in the middle of the field.

centreboard (US **centerboard**) noun a board lowered through the keel of a sailing boat to reduce sideways movement.

centrefold (US **centerfold**) noun the two

middle pages of a magazine, often containing a single illustration or feature.

centre forward noun Football & Hockey an attacker who plays in the middle of the field.

centre half noun Football a centre back.

centrepiece (US **centerpiece**) noun an object or item that is intended to be a focus of attention: *the centrepiece of the project is the construction of a new theatre.*

centre stage noun the most prominent position. • adverb in or towards the most prominent position.

-centric combining form **1** having a specified centre: *geocentric.* **2** originating from a specified viewpoint: *Eurocentric.*
– DERIVATIVES **-centricity** combining form.
– ORIGIN from Greek *kentrikos.*

centrifugal /sen-tri-**fyoo**-g'l/ adjective Physics moving away from a centre.
– DERIVATIVES **centrifugally** adverb.
– ORIGIN from Latin *centrum* 'centre' + *-fugus* 'fleeing'.

centrifugal force noun Physics a force which appears to cause a body travelling round a central point to fly outwards from its circular path.

centrifuge /**sen**-tri-fyooj/ noun a machine with a rapidly rotating container, used to separate liquids from solids.

centripetal /sen-tri-**pee**-t'l/ adjective Physics moving towards a centre.
– DERIVATIVES **centripetally** adverb.
– ORIGIN from Latin *centrum* 'centre' + *-petus* 'seeking'.

centripetal force noun Physics a force which causes a body travelling round a central point to move inwards from its circular path.

centrist noun a person having moderate political views or policies.
– DERIVATIVES **centrism** noun.

centurion noun the commander of a hundred men in the ancient Roman army.
– ORIGIN from Latin *centuria* 'century'.

century noun (pl. **centuries**) **1** a period of one hundred years. **2** a batsman's score of a hundred runs in cricket. **3** a company of a hundred men in the ancient Roman army.
– ORIGIN Latin *centuria.*

> USAGE: Strictly speaking, centuries run from 01 to 100, meaning that the new century begins on the first day of the year 01 (e.g. 1 January 2001). In practice and in popular belief, however, the new century is regarded as beginning when the significant digits in the date change, e.g. on 1 January 2000, when 1999 became 2000.

CEO abbreviation chief executive officer.

cep /sep/ noun an edible mushroom with a smooth brown cap.
– ORIGIN French *cèpe.*

cephalic /si-**fal**-ik/ adjective technical relating to the head.
– ORIGIN from Greek *kephalē* 'head'.

cephalopod /**sef**-uh-luh-pod/ noun a mollusc of a class including octopuses and squids.
– ORIGIN from Greek *kephalē* 'head' + *pous* 'foot'.

ceramic adjective made of clay that is permanently hardened by heat. • noun (**ceramics**) **1** ceramic articles. **2** (usu. treated as sing.) the art of making ceramic articles.
– DERIVATIVES **ceramicist** noun.
– ORIGIN from Greek *keramos* 'pottery'.

cereal noun **1** a grain used for food, for example wheat, maize, or rye. **2** a grass producing a cereal grain. **3** a breakfast food made from a cereal grain or grains.
– ORIGIN from *Ceres*, the Roman goddess of agriculture.

cerebellum /se-ri-**bel**-luhm/ noun (pl. **cerebellums** or **cerebella** /se-ri-**bel**-luh/) the part of the brain at the back of the skull, which coordinates muscular activity.
– DERIVATIVES **cerebellar** adjective.
– ORIGIN Latin, 'little brain'.

cerebral /suh-**ree**-bruhl/ adjective **1** relating to the cerebrum of the brain. **2** intellectual rather than emotional or physical.
– DERIVATIVES **cerebrally** adverb.

cerebral palsy noun a condition in which a person has difficulty in controlling or moving their muscles, caused by brain damage before or at birth.

cerebration /se-ri-**bray**-sh'n/ noun chiefly formal the working of the brain; thinking.

cerebrospinal /suh-ree-broh-**spy**-n'l/ adjective relating to the brain and spine.

cerebrospinal fluid noun the clear watery fluid which fills the space between membranes in the brain and the spinal chord.

cerebrovascular /suh-ree-broh-**vas**-kyoo-ler/ adjective relating to the brain and its blood vessels.

cerebrum /se-ri-**bruhm**/ noun (pl. **cerebra** /se-ri-**bruh**/) the main part of the brain, located in the front of the skull.
– ORIGIN Latin, 'brain'.

ceremonial adjective **1** relating to or used for ceremonies. **2** (of a post or role) in name only; without real authority or power. • noun another term for CEREMONY.
– DERIVATIVES **ceremonially** adverb.

ceremonious adjective relating or appropriate to grand and formal occasions.
– DERIVATIVES **ceremoniously** adverb.

ceremony noun (pl. **ceremonies**) **1** a formal religious or public occasion, typically celebrating a particular event. **2** the set procedures performed at grand and formal occasions: *the new Queen was proclaimed with due ceremony.*
– PHRASES **stand on ceremony** insist on formal behaviour.
– ORIGIN Latin *caerimonia* 'religious worship'.

cerise /suh-**reess**/ noun a light, clear red colour.
– ORIGIN French, 'cherry'.

cerium /**seer**-i-uhm/ noun a silvery-white metallic chemical element.
– ORIGIN named after the asteroid *Ceres.*

cert noun Brit. informal **1** an event that is certain to happen. **2** a competitor regarded as certain to win.

certain adjective **1** able to be relied on to happen or be the case: *it's certain that more changes are in the offing.* **2** completely sure that something is the case. **3** specific but not actually stated: *he raised certain personal*

C

problems. •pronoun (**certain of**) some but not all.
– ORIGIN Latin *certus* 'settled, sure'.

certainly adverb **1** without doubt; definitely. **2** yes; by all means.

certainty noun (pl. **certainties**) **1** the quality or state of being certain or sure. **2** a fact that is true or an event that is definitely going to take place.

certifiable adjective **1** able or needing to be officially recorded. **2** officially recognized as needing treatment for mental disorder.
– DERIVATIVES **certifiably** adverb.

certificate noun **1** an official document recording a particular fact, event, or achievement. **2** an official classification awarded to a cinema film, indicating its suitability for a particular age group.
– DERIVATIVES **certification** noun.

certify verb (**certifies**, **certifying**, **certified**) **1** confirm or state something in a formal document. **2** officially recognize that someone or something meets certain standards. **3** officially declare someone insane.
– DERIVATIVES **certifier** noun.
– ORIGIN Latin *certificare*.

certitude noun a feeling of absolute certainty.
– ORIGIN Latin *certitudo*.

cerulean /si-**roo**-li-uhn/ adjective deep blue in colour.
– ORIGIN from Latin *caelum* 'sky'.

cervical /ser-vi-k'l, ser-**vy**-k'l/ adjective relating to the neck of the womb.
– ORIGIN from Latin *cervix* 'neck'.

cervical smear noun Brit. a specimen of cells from the neck of the womb, spread on a microscope slide for examination for signs of cancer.

cervix /ser-viks/ noun (pl. **cervices** /ser-vi-seez/) the narrow neck-like passage forming the lower end of the womb.
– ORIGIN Latin.

Cesarean (also **Cesarian**) adjective & noun US spelling of **Caesarean**.

cesium noun US spelling of **caesium**.

cessation noun the ending of something.
– ORIGIN from Latin *cessare* 'cease'.

cession noun the formal giving up of rights, power, or territory by a state.
– ORIGIN from Latin *cedere* 'cede'.

cesspool (also **cesspit**) noun an underground tank or covered pit where liquid waste and sewage are stored before disposal.
– ORIGIN probably from Old French *souspirail* 'air hole'.

c'est la vie /say lah vee/ exclamation expressing resigned acceptance of an undesirable situation.
– ORIGIN French, 'that's life'.

cetacean /si-**tay**-sh'n/ noun a sea mammal of an order including whales and dolphins.
– ORIGIN from Greek *kētos* 'whale'.

ceviche /se-**vee**-chay/ (also **seviche**) noun a South American dish of marinaded raw fish or seafood.
– ORIGIN Latin American Spanish.

Cf symbol the chemical element californium.

cf. abbreviation compare with.
– ORIGIN from Latin *confer* 'compare'.

CFA (also **CFA franc**) noun the basic unit of money of Cameroon, Congo, Gabon, and the Central African Republic.
– ORIGIN from French *Communauté Financière Africaine* 'African Financial Community'.

CFC abbreviation chlorofluorocarbon, a gas that is a compound of carbon, hydrogen, chlorine, and fluorine, used in refrigerators and aerosols and harmful to the ozone layer.

CFE abbreviation (in the UK) College of Further Education.

CFS abbreviation chronic fatigue syndrome.

CGT abbreviation capital gains tax.

CH abbreviation (in the UK) Companion of Honour.

ch. abbreviation chapter.

Chablis /**shab**-lee/ noun a dry white burgundy wine from Chablis in France.

cha-cha noun a ballroom dance with swaying hip movements, performed to a Latin American rhythm.
– ORIGIN Latin American Spanish.

chaconne /shuh-**kon**/ noun **1** a musical composition in a series of varying sections in slow triple time. **2** a stately dance performed to a chaconne.
– ORIGIN French.

Chadian /**chad**-i-uhn/ noun a person from Chad in central Africa. •adjective relating to Chad or Chadians.

chador /**chah**-dor/ (also **chaddar** or **chuddar**) noun a piece of dark cloth worn by Muslim women around the head and upper body, so that only part of the face can be seen.
– ORIGIN Persian, 'sheet or veil'.

chafe verb **1** make or become sore or worn by rubbing against something. **2** rub a part of the body to warm it. **3** become impatient because of a restriction or disadvantage: *the women chafed at earning less than the men.*
– ORIGIN Old French *chaufer* 'make hot'.

chafer noun a large flying beetle of a group including the cockchafer.
– ORIGIN Old English.

chaff[1] /chahf/ noun **1** the husks of grain separated from the seed by winnowing or threshing. **2** chopped hay and straw used as cattle fodder.
– PHRASES **separate** (or **sort**) **the wheat from the chaff** distinguish valuable people or things from worthless ones.
– ORIGIN Old English.

chaff[2] /chaff/ noun light-hearted joking. •verb tease someone.
– ORIGIN perhaps from **chafe**.

chaffinch noun a finch, the male of which has a bluish head, pink underparts, and dark wings.
– ORIGIN Old English.

chafing dish noun **1** a cooking pot with an outer pan of hot water, used for keeping food warm. **2** a metal pan with a heating device below it, used for cooking at table.
– ORIGIN from the original sense of **chafe** 'become warm, warm up'.

chagrin /**sha**-grin/ noun annoyance or shame at having failed. •verb (**be chagrined**) feel annoyed or ashamed.
– ORIGIN French, 'rough skin, shagreen'.

chain noun **1** a connected series of metal links

used for fastening or pulling something, or as jewellery. **2** a connected series, set, or sequence: *a chain of restaurants*. **3** a part of a molecule consisting of a number of atoms bonded together in a series. **4** a measure of length equal to 66 ft. • **verb 1** fasten or confine someone or something with a chain. **2** restrict or limit to a situation or place: *the chef was chained to his stove six days a week*.
– ORIGIN Old French *chaine*.

chain gang noun a group of convicts chained together while working outside the prison.

chain letter noun a letter sent to a number of people, all of whom are asked to make copies and send these to other people, who then do the same.

chain mail noun historical armour made of small metal rings linked together.

chain reaction noun **1** a series of events, each caused by the previous one. **2** a chemical reaction in which the products of the reaction cause other changes.

chainsaw noun a power-driven saw with teeth set on a moving chain.

chain-smoke verb smoke cigarettes one after the other.

chain store noun one of a group of shops owned by one firm and selling the same goods.

chair noun **1** a separate seat for one person, with a back and four legs. **2** the person in charge of a meeting or an organization. **3** a professorship. **4** (**the chair**) US the electric chair. • **verb** act as chairperson of a meeting or organization.
– ORIGIN from Greek *kathedra*.

chairlift noun a series of chairs hung from a moving cable, used for carrying passengers up and down a mountain.

chairman (or **chairwoman**) noun (pl. **chairmen** or **chairwomen**) a person in charge of a meeting or organization.

chairperson noun a chairman or chairwoman.

chaise /shayz/ noun chiefly historical a two-wheeled horse-drawn carriage for one or two people.
– ORIGIN French.

chaise longue /shayz long/ (US also **chaise lounge**) noun (pl. **chaises longues** pronunc. same) a sofa with a backrest at only one end.
– ORIGIN French, 'long chair'.

chakra /chuk-ruh/ noun (in Indian thought) each of seven centres of spiritual power in the human body.
– ORIGIN Sanskrit, 'wheel or circle'.

chalcedony /kal-sed-uh-ni/ noun (pl. **chalcedonies**) a type of quartz with very small crystals, such as onyx.
– ORIGIN Greek *khalkēdōn*.

chalet /sha-lay/ noun **1** a wooden house with overhanging eaves, typically in the Swiss Alps. **2** a small cabin used by holidaymakers.
– ORIGIN Old French *chasel* 'farmstead'.

chalice noun **1** historical a goblet. **2** the wine cup used in Holy Communion.
– ORIGIN Latin *calix* 'cup'.

chalk noun **1** a white soft limestone formed from the skeletal remains of sea creatures. **2** a similar substance made into sticks and used for drawing or writing. • **verb 1** draw or write something with chalk. **2** Brit. charge drinks

bought in a pub or bar to a person's account. **3** (**chalk something up**) achieve something noteworthy.
– PHRASES **as different as chalk and cheese** Brit. completely different. **not by a long chalk** Brit. by no means; not at all.
– DERIVATIVES **chalky** adjective.
– ORIGIN Latin *calx* 'lime'.

chalkboard noun North American term for BLACKBOARD.

challah /hah-luh, khah-lah/ noun (pl. **challahs**) a plaited loaf of white bread, traditionally baked to celebrate the Jewish sabbath.
– ORIGIN Hebrew *ḥallah*.

challenge noun **1** a demanding task or situation. **2** a call to someone to participate in a contest. **3** an action or statement that calls something into question: *a legal challenge to the ruling failed in the High Court*. **4** an attempt to win a sporting contest. • **verb 1** raise doubt as to whether something is true or genuine. **2** invite someone to do something demanding or take part in a fight. **3** (of a sentry) call on someone to prove their identity. **4** Law object to a jury member.
– DERIVATIVES **challenger** noun
– ORIGIN Old French *chalenge*.

challenged adjective **1** euphemistic having a particular disability or impairment: *physically challenged*. **2** humorous lacking in a specified respect: *vertically challenged*.

challenging adjective presenting a test of one's abilities: *a challenging job*.

challis /sha-lis/ noun a lightweight soft clothing fabric made from silk and worsted.
– ORIGIN uncertain.

chalybeate /kuh-lib-i-uht/ adjective (of a natural mineral spring) containing iron salts.
– ORIGIN from Greek *khalups* 'steel'.

chamaeleon noun variant spelling of CHAMELEON.

chamber noun **1** a large room used for formal or public events. **2** one of the parts of a law-making body. **3** (**chambers**) Law, Brit. rooms used by a barrister or barristers. **4** old use a private room, especially a bedroom. **5** an enclosed space or cavity. **6** a cavity in the body, an organ, or a plant. **7** the part of a gun bore that contains the charge. • **adjective** relating to or for a small group of musical instruments: *a chamber orchestra*.
– DERIVATIVES **chambered** adjective.
– ORIGIN from Latin *camera* 'vault, arched chamber'.

chamberlain /chaym-ber-lin/ noun historical an officer who managed the household of a monarch or noble.
– ORIGIN Old French.

chambermaid noun a woman who cleans rooms in a hotel.

chamber music noun instrumental music played by a small ensemble, such as a string quartet.

Chamber of Commerce noun a local association to promote the interests of the business community.

chamber pot noun a bowl kept in a bedroom and used as a toilet.

chambray /sham-bray/ noun a cloth with a white weft and a coloured warp.

c

– ORIGIN from *Cambrai* (see **CAMBRIC**).

chameleon /kuh-**mee**-li-uhn/ (also **chamaeleon**) noun a small lizard that can change colour according to its surroundings.
– DERIVATIVES **chameleonic** adjective.
– ORIGIN from Greek *khamai* 'on the ground' + *leōn* 'lion'.

chamfer /**cham**-fer/ verb Carpentry cut away a right-angled edge or corner to make a symmetrical sloping edge.
– ORIGIN French *chamfrain*.

chamois noun 1 /**sham**-wah/ (pl. same, pronounced /**sham**-wahz/) an agile goat-antelope found in mountainous areas of southern Europe. 2 /**sham**-mi/ (pl. same, pronounced /**sham**-miz/) (also **chamois leather**) soft pliable leather made from the skin of sheep, goats, or deer.
– ORIGIN French.

chamomile noun variant spelling of **CAMOMILE**.

champ[1] verb 1 munch noisily. 2 fret impatiently.
– PHRASES **champ at the bit** be very impatient to start doing something.
– ORIGIN probably imitating the sound.

champ[2] noun informal a champion.

champagne /sham-**payn**/ noun a white sparkling wine from the Champagne region of France.

champers noun Brit. informal champagne.

champion noun 1 a person who has won a sporting contest or other competition. 2 a person who actively supports or defends another person or cause. •verb actively support: *priests who championed human rights.* •adjective Brit. informal or dialect excellent.
– ORIGIN Latin *campion* 'fighter'.

championship noun 1 a sporting contest for the position of champion. 2 the active support of a person or cause.

chance noun 1 a possibility of something happening. 2 (**chances**) the probability of something happening: *spelling errors could jeopardize your chances of promotion.* 3 an opportunity. 4 the way in which things happen without any obvious plan or cause: *they met by chance at a youth hostel.* •verb 1 do something by accident. 2 informal do something even though it is risky.
– PHRASES **on the (off) chance** just in case. **stand a chance** have a likelihood of success. **take a chance** (or **chances**) take a risk.
– ORIGIN from Old French *cheoir* 'fall, befall'.

chancel /**chahn**-s'l/ noun the part of a church near the altar, reserved for the clergy and choir.
– ORIGIN from Latin *cancelli* 'crossbars'.

chancellery /**chahn**-suh-luh-ri/ noun (pl. **chancelleries**) the post or department of a chancellor.

chancellor noun 1 a senior state or legal official of various kinds. 2 (**Chancellor**) the head of the government in some European countries. 3 Brit. the honorary head of a university.
– DERIVATIVES **chancellorship** noun.
– ORIGIN Latin *cancellarius* 'porter, secretary'.

Chancellor of the Exchequer noun the chief finance minister of the United Kingdom.

chancer noun Brit. informal a person who makes the most of any opportunity.

Chancery (also **Chancery Division**) noun (pl. **Chanceries**) (in the UK) the Lord Chancellor's court, a division of the High Court of Justice.
– ORIGIN from **CHANCELLERY**.

chancre /**shang**-ker/ noun a painless ulcer, especially one developing on the genitals in syphilis.
– ORIGIN Latin *cancer* 'creeping ulcer'.

chancy adjective (**chancier**, **chanciest**) informal uncertain; risky.

chandelier /shan-duh-**leer**/ noun a large hanging light with branches for several light bulbs or candles.
– ORIGIN French.

chandler /**chahnd**-ler/ (also **ship chandler**) noun a dealer in supplies and equipment for ships.
– DERIVATIVES **chandlery** noun (pl. **chandleries**).
– ORIGIN Old French *chandelier* 'candle-maker, candle-seller'.

change verb 1 make or become different. 2 exchange something for another: *he scarcely knew how to change a plug.* 3 move from one to another: *I had to change trains.* 4 (**change over**) move from one system or situation to another. 5 exchange a sum of money for the same sum in a different currency or denomination. 6 (**change down** or **up**) Brit. engage a lower (or higher) gear in a vehicle or on a bicycle. •noun 1 the action of changing. 2 a different experience: *heated pools make a welcome change from a chilly beach.* 3 money returned to someone as the balance of the sum paid. 4 money given in exchange for the same sum in larger units. 5 coins as opposed to banknotes. 6 a clean set of clothes. 7 an order in which a peal of bells can be rung.
– PHRASES **change hands** pass to a different owner. **change one's tune** express a very different attitude. **ring the changes** vary the ways of doing something.
– DERIVATIVES **changeless** adjective **changer** noun.
– ORIGIN Old French *changer*.

changeable adjective 1 likely to change in an unpredictable way. 2 able to be changed.
– DERIVATIVES **changeability** noun.

changeling noun a child believed to have been secretly substituted by fairies for the parents' real child.

changeover noun a change from one system or situation to another.

channel noun 1 a band of frequencies used in radio and television transmission, or a station using such a band. 2 a means of communication: *apply through the proper channels.* 3 a passage along which liquid or a watercourse may flow. 4 a wide stretch of water joining two seas. 5 a passage that boats can use in a stretch of water that is otherwise unsafe. 6 an electric circuit which acts as a path for a signal. •verb (**channels**, **channelling**, **channelled**; US **channels**, **channeling**, **channeled**) 1 direct towards a particular purpose: *the money has been channelled into the establishment of DNA banks.* 2 pass something along or through a specified route or medium.
– ORIGIN Latin *canalis* 'pipe, channel'.

channel-hop verb informal change frequently from one television channel to another.

chant noun 1 a repeated rhythmic phrase that is shouted or sung together by a group. 2 a tune to which the words of psalms or other works with irregular rhythm are fitted by singing several syllables or words to the same note. •verb say, shout, or sing in a chant.
– ORIGIN Old French *chanter* 'sing'.

chanter noun the pipe of a bagpipe with finger holes, on which the melody is played.

chanterelle /chahn-tuh-rel/ noun an edible woodland mushroom with a yellow funnel-shaped cap.
– ORIGIN Latin *cantharellus*.

chanteuse /shahn-terz/ noun a female singer of popular songs.
– ORIGIN French.

chantry noun (pl. **chantries**) a chapel or other part of a church established by an endowment in order for masses to be said for the donor's soul.
– ORIGIN from Old French *chanter* 'to sing'.

chanty /shan-ti/ noun (pl. **chanties**) variant spelling of **SHANTY**[2].

Chanukkah noun variant spelling of **HANUKKAH**.

chaos /kay-os/ noun 1 complete disorder and confusion. 2 the formless matter supposed to have existed before the creation of the universe.
– ORIGIN Greek *khaos* 'vast chasm, void'.

chaos theory noun the branch of science concerned with the behaviour of complex systems in which tiny changes can have major effects.

chaotic /kay-ot-ik/ adjective in a state of complete confusion and disorder.
– DERIVATIVES **chaotically** adverb.

chap[1] verb (**chaps, chapping, chapped**) 1 (of the skin) crack and become sore through exposure to cold weather. 2 (as adj. **chapped**) (of the skin) cracked and sore through exposure to cold weather.
– ORIGIN unknown.

chap[2] noun Brit. informal a man.
– ORIGIN from former *chapman* 'pedlar'.

chaparral /sha-puh-ral/ noun N. Amer. vegetation consisting of tangled shrubs and thorny bushes.
– ORIGIN Spanish.

chapatti /chuh-pah-ti/ noun (pl. **chapattis**) (in Indian cookery) a flat cake of wholemeal bread cooked on a griddle.
– ORIGIN Hindi.

chapel noun 1 a small building or room for Christian worship in an institution or large private house. 2 a part of a large church with its own altar. 3 Brit. a place of worship for Nonconformist congregations. 4 Brit. the members or branch of a print or newspaper trade union at a particular place of work.
– ORIGIN Old French *chapele*.

chaperone /shap-uh-rohn/ noun 1 a person who accompanies and looks after another person or people. 2 dated an older woman who accompanies and supervises an unmarried girl at social occasions. •verb accompany and supervise someone.
– ORIGIN French.

chaplain noun a member of the clergy attached to a chapel in a private house or an institution, or to a military unit.
– DERIVATIVES **chaplaincy** noun.
– ORIGIN Old French *chapelain*.

chaplet noun a decorative circular band worn on the head.
– ORIGIN Old French *chapelet* 'little hat'.

chaps plural noun N. Amer. leather trousers without a seat, worn by a cowboy over ordinary trousers to protect the legs.
– ORIGIN short for *chaparajos*, from Mexican Spanish *chaparreras*.

chapter noun 1 a main division of a book. 2 a particular period in history or in a person's life. 3 the governing body of a cathedral or other religious community. 4 chiefly N. Amer. a local branch of a society.
– PHRASES **chapter and verse** an exact reference or authority.
– ORIGIN Old French *chapitre*.

char[1] verb (**chars, charring, charred**) partially burn something so as to blacken the surface.
– ORIGIN probably from **CHARCOAL**.

char[2] Brit. informal noun a charwoman. •verb (**chars, charring, charred**) work as a charwoman.

char[3] noun Brit. informal tea.
– ORIGIN Chinese.

char[4] noun variant spelling of **CHARR**.

charabanc /sha-ruh-bang/ noun Brit. an early form of bus.
– ORIGIN French *char-à-bancs* 'carriage with benches'.

character noun 1 the qualities that make a person different from others. 2 the particular nature of something: *the picturesque character of the Windsor parks*. 3 strength and originality in a person's nature. 4 a person's good reputation. 5 a person in a novel, play, or film. 6 informal an eccentric or amusing person. 7 a printed or written letter or symbol.
– DERIVATIVES **characterful** adjective **characterless** adjective.
– ORIGIN from Greek *kharaktēr* 'a stamping tool'.

character actor noun an actor who specializes in playing unusual people rather than leading roles.

characteristic noun a feature or quality typical of a person, place, or thing. •adjective typical of a particular person, place, or thing: *the characteristic tilt of her head*.
– DERIVATIVES **characteristically** adverb.

characterize (or **characterise**) verb 1 describe the character of someone or something. 2 be typical of: *the rugged hills that characterize this part of Wales*.
– DERIVATIVES **characterization** noun.

charade /shuh-rahd/ noun 1 an absurd pretence. 2 (**charades**) a game of guessing a word or phrase from written or acted clues.
– ORIGIN Provençal *charrado* 'conversation'.

charbroil verb N. Amer. grill food, especially meat on a rack over charcoal.

charcoal noun 1 a black form of carbon obtained when wood is heated in the absence of air. 2 a dark grey colour.
– ORIGIN probably related to **COAL**.

charcuterie /shah-koo-tuh-ri/ noun (pl.

charcuteries) **1** cold cooked meats. **2** a shop selling cold cooked meats.
– ORIGIN French.

chard /chard/ (also **Swiss chard**) noun a variety of beet with edible broad white leaf stalks and green blades.
– ORIGIN French *carde*.

Chardonnay /shah-duh-nay/ noun a white wine made from a variety of grape used for making champagne and other wines.
– ORIGIN French.

charentais /**sha**-ruhn-tay/ noun a small variety of melon with a green rind and orange flesh.
– ORIGIN French, 'from the Charentes region'.

charge verb **1** ask an amount of money as a price for goods or a service. **2** formally accuse someone of something. **3** rush forward so as to attack someone or something. **4** rush in a particular direction: *he charged up the stairs.* **5** entrust someone with a task. **6** store electrical energy in a battery. **7** load or fill a container, gun, etc. **8** fill with a quality or emotion: *the air was charged with menace.* • noun **1** a price asked. **2** a formal accusation made against a prisoner brought to trial. **3** responsibility for care or control: *she felt out of touch with the youngsters in her charge.* **4** a person or thing entrusted to someone's care. **5** a headlong rush forward. **6** the property of matter that is responsible for electrical phenomena, existing in a positive or negative form. **7** energy stored chemically in a battery for conversion into electricity. **8** a quantity of explosive to be detonated in order to fire a gun or similar weapon.
– PHRASES **press charges** accuse someone formally of a crime so that they can be brought to trial.
– DERIVATIVES **chargeable** adjective **charged** adjective.
– ORIGIN Old French *charger.*

charge card noun a credit card issued by a chain store or bank.

chargé d'affaires /shar-zhay da-**fair**/ (also **chargé**) noun (pl. **chargés d'affaires** pronunc. same) **1** an ambassador's deputy. **2** a state's diplomatic representative in a country to which an ambassador has not been sent.
– ORIGIN French, 'a person in charge of affairs'.

chargehand noun Brit. a worker with supervisory duties ranking below a foreman.

charge nurse noun Brit. a nurse in charge of a ward in a hospital.

charger¹ noun **1** a device for charging a battery. **2** historical a horse ridden by a knight or cavalryman.

charger² noun old use a large flat dish.
– ORIGIN Old French *chargeour.*

chargrill verb grill food quickly at a very high heat.

chariot noun a two-wheeled vehicle drawn by horses, used in ancient warfare and racing.
– DERIVATIVES **charioteer** noun.
– ORIGIN Old French.

charisma /kuh-**riz**-muh/ noun **1** attractiveness or charm that can inspire admiration or enthusiasm in other people. **2** (pl. **charismata** /kuh-**riz**-muh-tuh/) (in Christian belief) a special gift given by God.
– ORIGIN Greek *kharisma.*

charismatic adjective **1** having a charm that can inspire admiration in other people. **2** relating to a Christian movement that emphasizes special gifts from God, such as the healing of the sick.
– DERIVATIVES **charismatically** adverb.

charitable adjective **1** relating to the assistance of those in need. **2** not judging others too severely; tolerant.
– DERIVATIVES **charitably** adverb.

charity noun (pl. **charities**) **1** an organization set up to help those in need. **2** the voluntary giving of money or other help to those in need. **3** help or money given to those in need. **4** tolerance in judging others.
– ORIGIN Latin *caritas.*

charlatan /**shar**-luh-tuhn/ noun a person who falsely claims to have a particular skill.
– DERIVATIVES **charlatanism** noun **charlatanry** noun.
– ORIGIN from Italian *ciarlare* 'to babble'.

Charles's law noun a law stating that the volume of an ideal gas at constant pressure is directly proportional to the absolute temperature.
– ORIGIN named after the French physicist Jacques A. C. *Charles.*

charleston noun a lively dance of the 1920s which involved turning the knees inwards and kicking out the lower legs.
– ORIGIN named after the city of *Charleston* in South Carolina, US.

charlie noun (pl. **charlies**) informal **1** Brit. a fool. **2** cocaine.
– ORIGIN from the man's name *Charles.*

charlotte noun a pudding made of stewed fruit with a casing or covering of bread, sponge cake, or biscuits.
– ORIGIN French, from the woman's name *Charlotte.*

charm noun **1** the power or quality of delighting or fascinating others. **2** a small ornament worn on a necklace or bracelet. **3** an object, act, or saying believed to have magic power. • verb **1** delight greatly: *she charmed me with her intelligence.* **2** use one's charm in order to influence someone.
– DERIVATIVES **charmer** noun **charmless** adjective.
– ORIGIN from Latin *carmen* 'song, verse'.

charmed adjective (of a person's life) unusually lucky as though protected by magic. • exclamation dated expressing polite pleasure at an introduction.

charming adjective **1** delightful; attractive. **2** very polite, friendly, and likeable. • exclamation used as an ironic expression of displeasure.
– DERIVATIVES **charmingly** adverb.

charm offensive noun a campaign of flattery and friendliness designed to achieve the support of others.

charnel house noun historical a building or vault in which corpses or bones were piled.
– ORIGIN from Latin *carnalis* 'relating to flesh'.

Charolais /**sha**-ruh-lay/ noun (pl. same) an animal of a breed of large white beef cattle.
– ORIGIN named after the *Monts du Charollais*, hills in eastern France.

charpoy /**chah**-poy/ noun Indian a light bedstead.
– ORIGIN Persian.

charr /char/ (also **char**) noun (pl. same) a trout-like northern freshwater or sea fish.
– ORIGIN perhaps Celtic.

chart noun **1** a sheet of information in the form of a table, graph, or diagram. **2** a geographical map, especially one used for navigation by sea or air. **3** (**the charts**) a weekly listing of the current best-selling pop records. •verb **1** make a map of an area. **2** plot or record something on a chart.
– ORIGIN from Greek *khartēs* 'papyrus leaf'.

charter noun **1** a document granted by a ruler or government, by which an institution such as a university is created or its rights are defined. **2** a written constitution or description of an organization's functions. **3** (in the UK) a written statement of the rights of a specified group of people: *the patient's charter.* **4** the hiring of an aircraft, ship, or motor vehicle. •verb **1** hire an aircraft, ship, or motor vehicle. **2** grant a charter to a university or organization.
– DERIVATIVES **charterer** noun.
– ORIGIN Latin *chartula* 'little paper'.

chartered adjective Brit. (of an accountant, engineer, etc.) qualified as a member of a professional body that has a royal charter.

charter flight noun a flight by an aircraft chartered for a specific journey, not part of an airline's regular schedule.

Chartism noun a UK movement (1837–48) for social and parliamentary reform, the principles of which were set out in *The People's Charter.*
– DERIVATIVES **Chartist** noun & adjective.

chartreuse /shah-**trerz**/ noun a pale green or yellow liqueur made from brandy.
– ORIGIN named after *La Grande Chartreuse*, a monastery near Grenoble where the liqueur was first made.

charwoman noun (pl. **charwomen**) Brit. dated a woman employed as a cleaner in a house or office.
– ORIGIN from former *char* or *chare* 'a chore'.

chary /**chair**-i/ adjective cautiously reluctant: *leaders are chary of reform.*
– ORIGIN Old English, 'sorrowful, anxious'.

chase[1] verb **1** pursue someone or something so as to catch them. **2** hurry or cause to hurry somewhere: *she chased him out of the house.* **3** try to obtain something owed or required. •noun **1** an act of chasing. **2** (**the chase**) hunting as a sport.
– PHRASES **give chase** pursue someone or something so as to catch them.
– ORIGIN Old French *chacier.*

chase[2] verb engrave metal or a design on metal.
– ORIGIN probably from Old French *enchasser* 'enclose'.

chaser noun **1** a person or thing that chases someone or something. **2** informal a strong alcoholic drink taken after a weaker one.

Chasid /**khass**-id/ noun variant spelling of HASID.

chasm noun **1** a deep crack or opening in the earth. **2** a marked difference between people, opinions, or feelings: *the chasm between rich and poor.*
– ORIGIN Greek *khasma* 'gaping hollow'.

Chassid /**khass**-id/ noun variant spelling of HASID.

chassis /**shas**-si/ noun (pl. same /**shas**-siz/) the base frame of a car or other wheeled vehicle.
– ORIGIN French, 'frame'.

chaste adjective **1** refraining from all sex, or from sex outside marriage. **2** without unnecessary decoration; simple.
– ORIGIN Latin *castus* 'morally pure'.

chasten verb (often as adj. **chastened**) make someone feel ashamed or sorry: *you walk like a chastened but defiant kid.*
– ORIGIN Old French *chastier.*

chastise verb reprimand someone severely.
– DERIVATIVES **chastisement** noun.

chastity noun the practice of refraining from all sex, or from sex outside marriage.

chastity belt noun historical a garment or device designed to prevent the woman wearing it from having sex.

chasuble /**chaz**-yuu-b'l/ noun a sleeveless outer garment worn by a Christian priest when celebrating Mass.
– ORIGIN from Latin *casula* 'hooded cloak, little cottage'.

chat verb (**chats**, **chatting**, **chatted**) **1** talk in an informal way. **2** (**chat someone up**) informal talk to someone flirtatiously. •noun an informal conversation.
– ORIGIN shortening of CHATTER.

chateau /**sha**-toh/ noun (pl. **chateaux** or **chateaus** pronunc. same /**sha**-tohz/) a large French country house or castle.
– ORIGIN French.

chatelaine /**sha**-tuh-layn/ noun dated a woman in charge of a large house.
– ORIGIN French.

chatline noun a telephone service which allows conversation among a number of separate callers.

chat room noun an area on the Internet or other computer network where users can communicate.

chat show noun Brit. a television or radio programme in which celebrities talk informally to a presenter.

chattel /**chat**-t'l/ noun a personal possession.
– ORIGIN Old French *chatel.*

chatter verb **1** talk informally about minor matters. **2** (of a bird or monkey) make a series of short, quick high-pitched sounds. **3** (of a person's teeth) click repeatedly together from cold or fear. •noun **1** informal talk. **2** a series of short, quick high-pitched sounds.
– PHRASES **the chattering classes** derogatory educated people considered as a social group prone to expressing liberal opinions.
– DERIVATIVES **chatterer** noun.
– ORIGIN imitating the sound.

chatterbox noun informal a person who chatters.

chatty adjective (**chattier**, **chattiest**) **1** fond of chatting. **2** (of a letter) informal and lively.
– DERIVATIVES **chattily** adverb **chattiness** noun.

chauffeur noun a person employed to drive a car. •verb drive a car or a passenger in a car, especially as one's job.
– ORIGIN French, 'stoker' (by association with steam engines).

chauvinism /**shoh**-vin-i-z'm/ noun **1** extreme or aggressive support for one's own country or group. **2** the belief held by some men that men are superior to women.

– DERIVATIVES **chauvinist** noun & adjective **chauvinistic** adjective.

– ORIGIN named after Nicolas *Chauvin*, a French soldier noted for his extreme patriotism.

chav noun Brit. informal, derogatory a young lower-class person who wears designer clothes and typically behaves in a brash or loutish way.

– ORIGIN perhaps from *Chatham*, Kent, or related to Romany *chavi* 'child'.

cheap adjective **1** low in price. **2** charging low prices. **3** low in price and of poor quality. **4** having no value because achieved in a regrettable way: *her moment of cheap triumph*. • adverb at or for a low price.

– DERIVATIVES **cheaply** adverb **cheapness** noun.

– ORIGIN Old English 'bargaining, trade'.

cheapen verb **1** lower the price of something. **2** reduce the worth of someone or something.

cheapjack adjective chiefly N. Amer. of inferior quality.

cheapskate noun informal a mean person.

– ORIGIN from *skate* 'a disreputable or unpleasant person'.

cheat verb **1** act dishonestly or unfairly in order to gain an advantage. **2** deprive someone of something by dishonest or unfair means. **3** manage to avoid something bad or unwelcome: *he cheated death after falling 20 feet on to a railway line*. • noun **1** a person who cheats. **2** an act of cheating.

– ORIGIN shortening of ESCHEAT.

Chechen /che-chen/ noun (pl. same or **Chechens**) a person from Chechnya, a self-governing republic in SW Russia.

– ORIGIN Russian.

check¹ verb **1** examine the accuracy, quality, or condition of something. **2** make sure that something is the case: *I checked that all the doors were secure*. **3** stop or slow the progress of: *measures to check the growth in crime and violence*. **4** Chess move a piece or pawn to a square where it directly attacks the opposing king. • noun **1** an act of checking the accuracy, quality, or condition of something. **2** a means of controlling or restraining something. **3** Chess a position in which a king is directly threatened. **4** N. Amer. the bill in a restaurant.

– PHRASES **check in** register at a hotel or airport. **check out** settle one's hotel bill before leaving. **check something out** investigate or find out about something. **check up on** investigate something. **in check 1** under control. **2** Chess (of a king) directly attacked by an opponent's piece or pawn.

– DERIVATIVES **checker** noun.

– ORIGIN from a Persian word meaning 'king'.

check² noun a pattern of small squares. • adjective (also **checked**) having a pattern of small squares.

– ORIGIN probably from CHEQUER.

check³ noun US spelling of CHEQUE.

checker noun & verb US spelling of CHEQUER.

checkerboard noun US spelling of CHEQUERBOARD.

check-in noun the place at an airport where a passenger registers before departure.

checklist noun a list of items required or things to be done or considered.

checkmate Chess noun a position of check from which a king cannot escape. • verb put a king into checkmate.

– ORIGIN from Persian, 'the king is dead'.

checkout noun a place where goods are paid for in a supermarket or similar large shop.

checkpoint noun a barrier where security checks are carried out on travellers.

check-up noun a thorough medical or dental examination to detect any problems.

Cheddar noun a kind of firm, smooth cheese originally made in Cheddar in SW England.

cheek noun **1** either side of the face below the eye. **2** either of the buttocks. **3** remarks or behaviour seen as rude or disrespectful. • verb informal speak disrespectfully to someone.

– PHRASES **cheek by jowl** close together. **turn the other cheek** choose not to retaliate after one has been attacked or insulted. [from the Gospel of Matthew, chapter 5.]

– ORIGIN Old English.

cheekbone noun the bone below the eye.

cheeky adjective (**cheekier**, **cheekiest**) showing a lack of respect, often in an amusing way.

– DERIVATIVES **cheekily** adverb **cheekiness** noun.

cheep noun a shrill, squeaky cry made by a young bird. • verb make a cheep.

– ORIGIN imitating the sound.

cheer verb **1** shout for joy or in praise or encouragement. **2** praise or encourage a person, team, etc. with shouts. **3** (**cheer up** or **cheer someone up**) become or make less miserable. **4** give comfort or support to someone. • noun **1** a shout of joy, encouragement, or praise. **2** (also **good cheer**) a feeling of happiness or optimism.

– ORIGIN Old French *chiere* 'face' (first meaning 'face, expression, mood').

cheerful adjective **1** noticeably happy and optimistic. **2** bright and pleasant: *cheerful colours*.

– DERIVATIVES **cheerfully** adverb **cheerfulness** noun.

cheerio exclamation Brit. informal goodbye.

cheerleader noun (in North America) a girl belonging to a group that performs organized chanting and dancing in support of a team at sporting events.

cheerless adjective gloomy and depressing.

cheers exclamation informal **1** expressing good wishes before drinking. **2** chiefly Brit. said to express thanks or on parting.

cheery adjective (**cheerier**, **cheeriest**) happy and optimistic.

– DERIVATIVES **cheerily** adverb **cheeriness** noun.

cheese¹ noun a food made from the pressed curds of milk, either firm or soft in texture.

– ORIGIN Latin *caseus*.

cheese² verb (**be cheesed off**) Brit. informal be irritated or bored.

– ORIGIN unknown.

cheeseburger noun a beefburger with a slice of cheese on it, served in a bread roll.

cheesecake noun **1** a rich sweet tart made with cream and soft cheese on a biscuit base. **2** informal pictures of scantily dressed women posing in a sexually attractive way.

cheesecloth noun thin, loosely woven cotton cloth.

cheese-paring adjective extremely careful about spending money; mean.

cheesy adjective (**cheesier**, **cheesiest**) **1** like cheese in taste, smell, or consistency. **2** informal cheap and low in quality. **3** informal unoriginal or sentimental: *an album of cheesy pop hits*.
– DERIVATIVES **cheesily** adverb **cheesiness** noun.

cheetah /chee-tuh/ noun a large fast-running spotted cat found in Africa and parts of Asia.
– ORIGIN Hindi.

chef noun a professional cook, especially the chief cook in a restaurant or hotel.
– ORIGIN French, 'head'.

chef-d'œuvre /shay derv-ruh/ noun (pl. **chefs-d'œuvre** pronunc. same) a masterpiece.
– ORIGIN French, 'chief work'.

Chelsea boot noun an elastic-sided boot with a pointed toe.
– ORIGIN named after *Chelsea* in London.

Chelsea bun noun Brit. a flat, spiral-shaped currant bun sprinkled with sugar.

Chelsea pensioner noun an inmate of the Chelsea Royal Hospital for old or disabled soldiers.

chemical adjective relating to chemistry or chemicals. • noun a compound or substance which has been artificially prepared or purified.
– DERIVATIVES **chemically** adverb.
– ORIGIN French *chimique*.

chemical engineering noun the branch of engineering concerned with the design and operation of industrial chemical plants.

chemin de fer /shuh-man duh fair/ noun a card game which is a variety of baccarat.
– ORIGIN French, 'railway'.

chemise /shuh-meez/ noun **1** a dress hanging straight from the shoulders. **2** a woman's loose-fitting petticoat or nightdress.
– ORIGIN from Latin *camisia* 'shirt or nightgown'.

chemist noun **1** Brit. a person who is authorized to dispense medicinal drugs. **2** Brit. a shop where medicinal drugs are dispensed and toiletries and other medical goods are sold. **3** a person engaged in chemical research.
– ORIGIN Latin *alchimista* 'alchemist'.

chemistry noun (pl. **chemistries**) **1** the branch of science concerned with the nature and properties of substances and how they react with each other. **2** the chemical properties of a particular substance: *the patient's blood chemistry was monitored regularly*. **3** the interaction between two people, especially when experienced as a strong mutual attraction: *sexual chemistry*.

chemotherapy /kee-moh-the-ruh-pi/ noun the treatment of disease, especially cancer, by the use of chemical substances.

chenille /shuh-neel/ noun fabric with a long velvety pile.
– ORIGIN French, 'hairy caterpillar'.

Chenin blanc /shuh-nan blonk/ (also **Chenin**) noun a white wine made from a variety of grape native to the Loire valley in France.
– ORIGIN French.

cheongsam /chi-ong-sam/ noun a straight, close-fitting silk dress with a high neck, worn by Chinese and Indonesian women.
– ORIGIN Chinese.

cheque (US **check**) noun a written order to a bank to pay a stated sum from an account to a particular person.
– ORIGIN variant of **CHECK**[1], in the former sense 'device for checking the amount of an item'.

chequebook noun a book of forms for writing cheques.

cheque card noun Brit. a card issued by a bank to guarantee payment of a customer's cheques.

chequer (US **checker**) noun **1** (**chequers**) a pattern of alternately coloured squares. **2** (**checkers**) (treated as sing.) N. Amer. the game of draughts. • verb **1** (**be chequered**) be divided into or marked with chequers. **2** (as adj. **chequered**) marked by both successful and unsuccessful periods: *a chequered career*.
– ORIGIN from **EXCHEQUER**, first in the sense 'chessboard'.

chequerboard (US **checkerboard**) noun a board for playing checkers and similar games, having a regular chequered pattern in black and white.

chequered flag noun a flag with a black-and-white chequered pattern, shown to racing drivers at the end of a race.

cherish verb **1** protect and care for someone or something lovingly. **2** keep in one's mind: *I cherish the memory of that visit*.
– ORIGIN Old French *cherir*, from *cher* 'dear'.

Cherokee /che-ruh-kee/ noun (pl. same or **Cherokees**) a member of an American Indian people formerly living in much of the southern US.
– ORIGIN the Cherokees' name for themselves.

cheroot /shuh-root/ noun a cigar that has both ends open.
– ORIGIN Tamil, 'roll of tobacco'.

cherry noun (pl. **cherries**) **1** a small, round bright or dark red fruit with a stone. **2** a bright, deep red colour.
– PHRASES **a bite at the cherry** Brit. an opportunity to do something.
– ORIGIN from Greek *kerasos*.

cherry brandy noun a sweet liqueur made with brandy in which cherries have been soaked.

cherry-pick verb selectively choose the best things or people from those available.

cherry tomato noun a miniature tomato.

chert /chert/ noun a hard, dark, very fine-grained rock composed of silica.
– ORIGIN unknown.

cherub noun **1** (pl. **cherubim** or **cherubs**) a type of angel, represented in art as a chubby child with wings. **2** (pl. **cherubs**) a beautiful or innocent-looking child.
– DERIVATIVES **cherubic** /chuh-roo-bik/ adjective **cherubically** adverb.
– ORIGIN Hebrew.

chervil /cher-vil/ noun a herb with an aniseed flavour, used in cooking.
– ORIGIN Greek *khairephullon*.

Ches. abbreviation Cheshire.

Cheshire /che-sher/ noun a kind of firm, crumbly cheese, originally made in Cheshire.

Cheshire cat noun a cat with a broad fixed grin, as described in Lewis Carroll's *Alice's*

Adventures in Wonderland (1865).
– ORIGIN uncertain, but it is said that *Cheshire* cheeses used to be marked with the face of a smiling cat.

chess noun a board game for two players, the object of which is to put the opponent's king under a direct attack, leading to checkmate.
– ORIGIN from a Persian word meaning 'king'.

chessboard noun a square board divided into sixty-four chequered squares, used for playing chess or draughts.

chest noun 1 the front surface of a person's body between the neck and the stomach. 2 a large strong box in which things may be stored or transported.
– PHRASES **get something off one's chest** informal say something that one has wanted to say for a long time. **keep** (or **play**) **one's cards close to one's chest** informal be extremely secretive about one's plans.
– DERIVATIVES **chested** adjective.
– ORIGIN Greek *kistē* 'box'.

chesterfield noun a sofa whose back and outward-curving arms are padded and of the same height.
– ORIGIN named after a 19th-century Earl of *Chesterfield*.

chestnut noun 1 a shiny brown edible nut which develops within a bristly case. 2 (also **sweet chestnut** or **Spanish chestnut**) the large tree that produces chestnuts. 3 a deep reddish-brown colour. 4 a reddish-brown horse. 5 (**old chestnut**) a joke or story that has become uninteresting because it has been repeated too often.
– ORIGIN from Greek *kastanea* + **NUT**.

chest of drawers noun a piece of furniture consisting of an upright frame fitted with a set of drawers.

chesty adjective Brit. informal having a lot of catarrh in the lungs.
– DERIVATIVES **chestiness** noun.

cheval glass /shuh-**val**/ (also **cheval mirror**) noun a tall mirror fitted at its middle to an upright frame so that it can be tilted.
– ORIGIN French *cheval* 'horse, frame'.

chevalier /shev-uh-**leer**/ noun 1 historical a knight. 2 a member of the French Legion of Honour.
– ORIGIN Old French.

Cheviot /**chev**-i-uht/ noun a large sheep of a breed with short thick wool.
– ORIGIN from the *Cheviot* Hills in northern England and Scotland.

chèvre /**shev**-ruh/ noun French cheese made with goat's milk.
– ORIGIN French, 'goat'.

chevron noun 1 a V-shaped line or stripe, especially one on the sleeve of a soldier's or police officer's uniform to show their rank. 2 Heraldry a broad upside-down V-shape.
– ORIGIN Old French.

chew verb 1 bite and work food in the mouth to make it easier to swallow. 2 (**chew something over**) discuss or consider something at length. • noun 1 an act of chewing something. 2 a thing, especially a sweet, meant for chewing.
– PHRASES **chew the fat** (or **rag**) informal chat in a leisurely way.
– DERIVATIVES **chewable** adjective **chewer** noun.

– ORIGIN Old English.

chewing gum noun a flavoured sweet which is chewed but not swallowed.

chewy adjective (**chewier, chewiest**) (of food) needing much chewing before it can be swallowed.
– DERIVATIVES **chewiness** noun.

Cheyenne /shy-**an**/ noun (pl. same or **Cheyennes**) a member of an American Indian people formerly living between the Missouri and Arkansas Rivers.
– ORIGIN from Dakota (an American Indian language), 'speak incoherently'.

chez /shay/ preposition chiefly humorous at the home of.
– ORIGIN French.

chi² /kee/ (also **qi** or **ki**) noun the circulating life force whose existence and properties are the basis of much Chinese philosophy and medicine.
– ORIGIN Chinese, 'air, breath'.

Chianti /ki-**an**-ti/ noun (pl. **Chiantis**) a dry red Italian wine.
– ORIGIN named after the *Chianti* Mountains in Tuscany.

chiaroscuro /ki-ah-ruh-**skoor**-oh/ noun the treatment of light and shade in drawing and painting.
– ORIGIN Italian, from *chiaro* 'clear, bright' + *oscuro* 'dark, obscure'.

chic /sheek/ adjective (**chicer, chicest**) elegant and stylish. • noun elegance and stylishness.
– DERIVATIVES **chicly** adverb.
– ORIGIN French.

chicane /shi-**kayn**/ noun a sharp double bend created to form an obstacle on a motor-racing track.
– ORIGIN French *chicaner* 'quibble'.

chicanery noun trickery or deception.

Chicano /chi-**kah**-noh, shi-**kah**-noh/ noun (pl. **Chicanos**; fem. **Chicana**, pl. **Chicanas**) chiefly US a North American person of Mexican origin or descent.
– ORIGIN Spanish *mejicano* 'Mexican'.

chichi /**shee**-shee/ adjective intended to be stylish or elegant but seeming over-elaborate or artificial.
– ORIGIN French.

chick noun 1 a young bird, especially one newly hatched. 2 informal a young woman.
– ORIGIN abbreviation of **CHICKEN**.

chicken noun 1 a domestic fowl kept for its eggs or meat. 2 informal a coward. • adjective informal cowardly. • verb (**chicken out**) informal be too scared to do something.
– PHRASES **chicken-and-egg** referring to a situation in which each of two things appears to be necessary to the other.
– ORIGIN Old English.

chicken feed noun informal a very small sum of money.

chickenpox noun an infectious disease causing a mild fever and a rash of itchy inflamed pimples.
– ORIGIN probably so named because of its mildness, in comparison with smallpox.

chicken wire noun wire netting with a hexagonal mesh.

chickpea noun a yellowish seed cooked and

eaten as a vegetable.
– ORIGIN Latin *cicer*.

chickweed noun a small white-flowered plant, often growing as a garden weed.

chicle /**chik**-uhl/ noun the milky latex of the sapodilla tree, used to make chewing gum.
– ORIGIN Nahuatl.

chicory /**chi**-kuh-ri/ noun (pl. **chicories**) 1 a blue-flowered plant with edible leaves and a root which can be used as an additive to or substitute for coffee. 2 North American term for **ENDIVE**.
– ORIGIN Greek *kikhorion*.

chide /chyd/ verb (past **chided** or **chid**; past part. **chided**) scold or rebuke someone.
– ORIGIN Old English.

chief noun 1 a leader or ruler of a people. 2 the head of an organization. • adjective 1 having the highest rank or authority. 2 most important: *the chief reason*.
– DERIVATIVES **chiefdom** noun.
– ORIGIN Old French.

chief constable noun Brit. the head of the police force of a county or other region.

chiefly adverb mainly; mostly.

chief of staff noun the senior staff officer of an armed service or command.

chieftain noun the leader of a people or clan.
– DERIVATIVES **chieftaincy** noun (pl. **chieftaincies**) **chieftainship** noun.
– ORIGIN Old French *chevetaine*.

chiffchaff noun a type of warbler (bird) with drab plumage and a repetitive call.
– ORIGIN imitating its call.

chiffon noun a light, transparent silk or nylon fabric.
– ORIGIN French, from *chiffe* 'rag'.

chiffonier /shif-uh-**neer**/ noun 1 Brit. a low cupboard used as a sideboard or having a bookshelf on top. 2 N. Amer. a tall chest of drawers.
– ORIGIN French.

chigger /**chig**-uhr/ (also **jigger**) noun a tropical flea, the female of which lays eggs beneath the host's skin, causing painful sores.
– ORIGIN variant of **CHIGOE**.

chignon /**sheen**-yon/ noun a knot or coil of hair arranged on the back of a woman's head.
– ORIGIN French, 'nape of the neck'.

chigoe /**chig**-oh/ noun another term for **CHIGGER**
– ORIGIN French *chique*.

chihuahua /chi-**wah**-wuh/ noun a very small breed of dog with smooth hair and large eyes.
– ORIGIN named after *Chihuahua* in northern Mexico.

chilblain noun a painful, itching swelling on a hand or foot caused by poor circulation in the skin during exposure to cold weather.
– ORIGIN from **CHILL** + an Old English word meaning 'inflamed swelling or sore'.

child noun (pl. **children**) 1 a young human being below the age of full physical development. 2 a son or daughter of any age. 3 (**children**) old use the descendants of a family or people.
– PHRASES **child's play** an easy task. **with child** old use pregnant.
– DERIVATIVES **childless** adjective.
– ORIGIN Old English.

childbed noun old use childbirth.

child benefit noun (in the UK) regular payment by the state to the parents of a child up to a certain age.

childbirth noun the action of giving birth to a child.

childcare noun the care of children while the parents are working.

childhood noun the state or period of being a child.

childish adjective 1 like or appropriate to a child. 2 silly and immature.
– DERIVATIVES **childishly** adverb **childishness** noun.

childlike adjective (of an adult) having the good qualities associated with a child, such as innocence.

childminder noun Brit. a person who is paid to look after children in his or her own house.

children plural of **CHILD**.

Chilean /**chil**-i-uhn/ noun a person from Chile. • adjective relating to Chile.

chili noun (pl. **chilies**) US spelling of **CHILLI**.

chill noun 1 an unpleasant feeling of coldness. 2 a feverish cold. • verb 1 make someone or something cold. 2 horrify or frighten someone. 3 (usu. **chill out**) informal calm down and relax. • adjective chilly.
– ORIGIN Old English.

chiller noun a cold cabinet or refrigerator for keeping stored food a few degrees above freezing point.

chilli (also US **chile**, **chili**) noun (pl. **chillies** or US **chiles**, **chilies**) 1 (also **chilli pepper**) a small hot-tasting kind of pepper, used in cooking and as a spice. 2 chilli con carne.
– ORIGIN Nahuatl.

chilli con carne /chil-li kon **kar**-ni/ noun a stew of minced beef and beans flavoured with chilli.
– ORIGIN Spanish *chile con carne* 'chilli pepper with meat'.

chilli powder noun a hot-tasting mixture of ground dried red chillies and other spices.

chillum /**chil**-uhm/ noun (pl. **chillums**) 1 a hookah. 2 a pipe used for smoking cannabis.
– ORIGIN Hindi.

chilly adjective (**chillier**, **chilliest**) 1 unpleasantly cold. 2 unfriendly.
– DERIVATIVES **chilliness** noun.

chimaera noun variant spelling of **CHIMERA**.

chime noun 1 a tuneful ringing sound. 2 a bell or a metal bar or tube used in a set to produce chimes when struck. • verb 1 (of a bell or clock) make a tuneful ringing sound. 2 (**chime in**) interrupt a conversation with a remark.
– ORIGIN probably from **CYMBAL** (interpreted as *chime bell*).

chimera /ky-**meer**-uh/ (also **chimaera**) noun 1 an unrealistic hope or idea. 2 Greek Mythology a fire-breathing female monster with a lion's head, a goat's body, and a serpent's tail.
– ORIGIN Greek *khimaira*.

chimerical /ky-**me**-ri-k'l/ adjective impossible to achieve; unrealistic.

chimney noun (pl. **chimneys**) 1 a vertical pipe which takes smoke and gases up from a fire or furnace. 2 a steep, narrow cleft by which a rock face may be climbed.
– ORIGIN Old French *cheminee*, from Greek *kaminos* 'oven'.

C

chimney breast noun a part of an interior wall that projects to surround a chimney, above a fireplace.

chimney piece noun Brit. a mantelpiece.

chimney pot noun an earthenware or metal pipe at the top of a chimney.

chimney stack noun the part of a chimney that sticks up above a roof.

chimney sweep noun a person whose job is cleaning out the soot from chimneys.

chimp noun informal a chimpanzee.

chimpanzee noun an ape native to west and central Africa.
– ORIGIN Kikongo (a language of the Congo and surrounding areas).

chin noun the part of the face below the mouth.
– PHRASES **keep one's chin up** informal remain cheerful in difficult circumstances. **take it on the chin** informal accept a difficult or unpleasant situation without complaining.
– DERIVATIVES **chinned** adjective.
– ORIGIN Old English.

china noun 1 a fine white ceramic material. 2 household objects made from china.
– ORIGIN from Persian, 'relating to China'.

china clay noun another term for **KAOLIN**.

chinagraph pencil noun Brit. a waxy pencil used to write on china, glass, or other hard surfaces.

Chinaman noun (pl. **Chinamen**) chiefly old use or derogatory a native of China.

China syndrome noun a hypothetical chain of events following the meltdown of a nuclear reactor, in which the core melts deep into the earth.
– ORIGIN so named because China is on the opposite side of the earth from a reactor in the US.

China tea noun tea made from a type of tea plant grown in China, often smoked or with flower petals added.

Chinatown noun a district of a non-Chinese town in which the majority of the population is of Chinese origin.

chinchilla /chin-**chil**-luh/ noun 1 a small South American rodent with soft grey fur and a long bushy tail. 2 a breed of cat or rabbit with silver-grey or grey fur.
– ORIGIN Aymara or Quechua (South American Indian languages).

chine[1] /chyn/ noun the backbone of an animal, or a joint of meat containing part of it.
– ORIGIN Old French *eschine*.

chine[2] /chyn/ noun (in the Isle of Wight or Dorset) a deep, narrow ravine.
– ORIGIN Old English, 'cleft, chink'.

chine[3] /chyn/ noun the angle where the planks or plates at the bottom of a boat or ship meet the side.
– ORIGIN Old English.

Chinese noun (pl. same) 1 the language of China. 2 a person from China. •adjective relating to China.

Chinese burn noun informal a burning sensation inflicted on a person by placing both hands on their arm and then twisting it.

Chinese cabbage noun another term for **CHINESE LEAVES**.

Chinese chequers (US **Chinese checkers**) plural noun (treated as sing.) a board game in which players attempt to move marbles or counters from one corner to the opposite one on a star-shaped board.

Chinese lantern noun 1 a collapsible paper lantern. 2 a plant with white flowers and round orange fruits enclosed in a papery orange-red calyx.

Chinese leaves plural noun a variety of cabbage which does not form a firm heart.

Chinese puzzle noun an intricate puzzle consisting of many interlocking pieces.

Chinese wall noun something that prevents information passing from one person or group to another.

Chinese whispers plural noun (treated as sing.) Brit. a game in which a message is changed by being passed from one person to another in a whisper.

chink[1] noun 1 a narrow opening or crack. 2 a beam of light entering through a chink.
– ORIGIN Old English.

chink[2] verb make a light, high-pitched ringing sound, like that of glasses or coins striking each other. •noun a high-pitched ringing sound.
– ORIGIN imitating the sound.

Chinky (also **Chink**) noun (pl. **Chinkies**) informal, offensive a Chinese person.

chinless adjective 1 (of a man) having a very small chin. 2 informal having a weak character.

chino /**chee**-noh/ noun 1 a cotton twill fabric. 2 (**chinos**) casual cotton trousers, originally made from this fabric.
– ORIGIN Latin American Spanish, 'toasted' (referring to the typical colour of the fabric).

chinoiserie /shin-**wah**-zuh-ri/ noun 1 the use of Chinese images and styles in Western art, furniture, and architecture. 2 objects or decorations made in this style.
– ORIGIN French.

Chinook /chi-**nook**/ noun (pl. same or **Chinooks**) a member of an American Indian people originally living in Oregon.
– ORIGIN Salish.

chinook /chi-**nook**/ noun 1 a warm, dry wind which blows down the east side of the Rocky Mountains at the end of winter. 2 a large North Pacific salmon which is an important food fish.

chintz noun multicoloured cotton fabric with a shiny finish, used for curtains and furniture coverings.
– ORIGIN Hindi, 'spattering, stain'.

chintzy adjective (**chintzier**, **chintziest**) 1 decorated with or resembling chintz. 2 decorated in a colourful but fussy or over-elaborate way: *a chintzy little hotel*.

chinwag noun Brit. informal a chat.

chip noun 1 a small, thin piece cut or broken off from a hard material. 2 a mark left by the removal of such a piece. 3 Brit. a long rectangular piece of deep-fried potato. 4 (also **potato chip**) N. Amer. a potato crisp. 5 a microchip. 6 a counter used in certain gambling games to represent money. 7 (in football or golf) a short, high kick or shot. •verb (**chips**, **chipping**, **chipped**) 1 cut or break a small piece from a hard material. 2 break at

the edge or on the surface. **3** (**chip away**) gradually and relentlessly make something smaller or weaker: *rival firms are chipping away at their market share.* **4** (in football or golf) strike the ball to produce a short, high shot or pass. **5** (as adj. **chipped**) Brit. (of potatoes) cut into chips.
– PHRASES **chip in 1** contribute money to a joint fund. **2** informal interrupt a conversation with a remark. **a chip off the old block** informal someone who resembles their mother or father in character. **a chip on one's shoulder** informal a long-held grievance. **when the chips are down** informal when a serious situation occurs.
– ORIGIN from an Old English word meaning 'cut off'.

chip and PIN noun a way of authorizing payment for goods bought with a credit or debit card in which the card is put into an electronic device and the customer enters their personal identification number.

chipboard noun material made from compressed wood chips and resin.

chipmunk noun a burrowing ground squirrel with light and dark stripes running down the body.
– ORIGIN Ojibwa (an American Indian language).

chipolata noun Brit. a small thin sausage.
– ORIGIN Italian *cipollata* 'dish of onions'.

Chippendale /**chip**-uhn-dayl/ adjective (of furniture) designed by or in the style of the English furniture-maker Thomas Chippendale (1718–79).

chipper adjective informal cheerful and lively.
– ORIGIN perhaps from northern English dialect *kipper* 'lively'.

chipping noun Brit. a small fragment of stone, wood, or similar material.

chippy (also **chippie**) noun (pl. **chippies**) Brit. informal **1** a fish-and-chip shop. **2** a carpenter.

chiropody /ki-**rop**-uh-di/ noun the medical treatment of the feet.
– DERIVATIVES **chiropodist** noun.
– ORIGIN from Greek *kheir* 'hand' + *pous* 'foot'.

chiropractic /ky-roh-**prak**-tik/ noun a system of complementary medicine based on the manipulation of the joints, especially those of the spinal column.
– DERIVATIVES **chiropractor** noun.
– ORIGIN from Greek *kheir* 'hand' + *praktikos* 'practical'.

chirp verb **1** (of a small bird) make a short, sharp, high-pitched sound. **2** say something in a lively and cheerful way. •noun a chirping sound.
– ORIGIN imitating the sound.

chirpy adjective (**chirpier**, **chirpiest**) informal cheerful and lively.
– DERIVATIVES **chirpily** adverb **chirpiness** noun.

chirr /cher/ (also **churr**) verb (of a bird or insect) make a low trilling sound. •noun a low trilling sound.
– ORIGIN imitating the sound.

chirrup verb (**chirrups**, **chirruping**, **chirruped**) (of a small bird) make repeated short high-pitched sounds. •noun a chirruping sound.
– ORIGIN alteration of CHIRP.

chisel noun a hand tool with a long blade and a bevelled cutting edge, used to cut or shape

wood, stone, or metal. •verb (**chisels**, **chiselling**, **chiselled**; US **chisels**, **chiseling**, **chiseled**) **1** cut or shape wood, stone, or metal with a chisel. **2** (as adj. **chiselled**) (of a man's facial features) strongly defined.
– ORIGIN Old French.

chit[1] noun Brit. derogatory a rude or cheeky young woman.
– ORIGIN perhaps related to a dialect word meaning 'sprout'.

chit[2] noun a short official note recording a sum of money owed.
– ORIGIN Hindi, 'note, pass'.

chit-chat informal noun conversation about unimportant things. •verb talk about unimportant things.

chitin /**ky**-tin/ noun a tough substance which forms the external covering of the bodies of arthropods.
– DERIVATIVES **chitinous** adjective.
– ORIGIN Greek *khitōn* (see CHITON).

chiton /**ky**-ton/ noun **1** a long woollen tunic worn in ancient Greece. **2** a marine mollusc that has a shell of overlapping plates.
– ORIGIN Greek *khitōn* 'tunic'.

chitter verb make a twittering sound.
– ORIGIN imitating the sound.

chitterlings /**chit**-uh-lingz/ plural noun the smaller intestines of a pig, cooked for food.
– ORIGIN uncertain.

chivalrous adjective (of a man) polite and gallant, especially towards women.
– DERIVATIVES **chivalrously** adverb.

chivalry noun **1** (in medieval times) the religious, moral, and social code of behaviour which a knight was expected to follow. **2** polite behaviour, especially that of a man towards women.
– DERIVATIVES **chivalric** adjective.
– ORIGIN Old French *chevalerie*, from Latin *caballarius* 'horseman'.

chives plural noun a herb with long tubular leaves, used in cooking.
– ORIGIN Old French.

chivvy (also **chivy**) verb (**chivvies**, **chivvying**, **chivvied**) chiefly Brit. tell someone repeatedly to do something.
– ORIGIN first meaning 'a hunting cry': probably from the ballad *Chevy Chase*.

chlamydia /kluh-**mid**-i-uh/ noun (pl. same) a very small parasitic bacterium which can cause various diseases.
– ORIGIN Greek *khlamus* 'cloak'.

chloral /**klor**-uhl/ noun a colourless liquid used as a sedative.
– ORIGIN French.

chlorate noun Chemistry a salt containing ClO_3 negative ions together with a metallic element: *sodium chlorate*.

chloride /**klor**-yd/ noun a compound of chlorine with another element or group.

chlorinate /**klor**-in-ayt/ verb put chlorine in something.
– DERIVATIVES **chlorination** noun.

chlorine /**klor**-een/ noun a poisonous pale green gaseous chemical element which may be added to water as a disinfectant.
– ORIGIN Greek *khlōros* 'green'.

chlorofluorocarbon /klor-oh-floor-oh-**kar**-b'n/ noun see CFC.

c

chloroform noun a sweet-smelling liquid used as a solvent and formerly as a general anaesthetic.
– ORIGIN from **CHLORINE** + **FORMIC ACID**.

chlorophyll /klo-ruh-fil/ noun a green pigment which enables plants to absorb light so as to provide energy for photosynthesis.
– ORIGIN from Greek *khlōros* 'green' + *phullon* 'leaf'.

chloroplast /klo-ruh-plahst/ noun a structure in green plant cells which contains chlorophyll and in which photosynthesis takes place.
– ORIGIN from Greek *khlōros* 'green' + *plastos* 'formed'.

chocaholic noun variant spelling of **CHOCOHOLIC**.

choccy noun (pl. **choccies**) informal chocolate, or a chocolate sweet.

choc ice noun Brit. a small bar of ice cream with a thin coating of chocolate.

chock noun a wedge or block placed against a wheel to prevent it from moving.
– ORIGIN Old French *çoche*.

chock-a-block adjective informal, chiefly Brit. completely full of people or things pressed close together.
– ORIGIN first in nautical use, with reference to tackle having two blocks (pulleys) running close together.

chock-full adjective informal filled to overflowing.
– ORIGIN unknown.

chocoholic (also **chocaholic**) noun informal a person who is very fond of chocolate.

chocolate noun 1 a food made from roasted and ground cacao seeds, eaten as a sweet or mixed with milk and water to make a drink. 2 a sweet made of or covered with chocolate. 3 a deep brown colour.
– DERIVATIVES **chocolatey** (also **chocolaty**) adjective.
– ORIGIN Nahuatl.

chocolate-box adjective Brit. (of a view or picture) pretty in a conventional or idealized way.

chocolatier /chok-uh-lat-i-er/ noun (pl. pronounced same) a person who makes or sells chocolate.
– ORIGIN French.

choice noun 1 an act of choosing. 2 the right or ability to choose. 3 a range from which to choose: *a menu offering a wide choice of dishes*. 4 a person or thing that has or can be chosen: *this disk drive is the perfect choice for your computer*. • adjective 1 of very good quality. 2 (of language) rude and abusive.
– PHRASES **of choice** chosen as one's favourite or the best: *champagne was his drink of choice*.
– ORIGIN Old French *chois*.

choir noun 1 an organized group of singers, especially one that takes part in church services. 2 the part of a large church between the altar and the nave, used by the choir and clergy.
– ORIGIN Old French *quer*, from Latin *chorus*.

choirboy (or **choirgirl**) noun a boy (or girl) who sings in a church or cathedral choir.

choke verb 1 prevent someone from breathing by blocking or blocking their throat or depriving them of air. 2 have trouble

breathing. 3 fill a space so as to make movement difficult or impossible: *the roads were choked with traffic*. 4 (**choke something back**) suppress a strong emotion: *she choked back tears of rage*. 5 (**choke up** or **be choked up**) feel tearful or very upset. • noun a valve in the carburettor of a petrol engine used to reduce the amount of air in the fuel mixture.
– ORIGIN Old English.

choker noun a necklace or band of fabric which fits closely round the neck.

chokey noun Brit. informal, dated prison.
– ORIGIN Hindi, 'customs house, police station'.

choky adjective 1 having or causing difficulty in breathing. 2 having difficulty speaking as a result of strong emotion.

cholecalciferol /ko-li-kal-sif-uh-rol/ noun a form of vitamin D (vitamin D₃), produced naturally in the skin by the action of sunlight.
– ORIGIN from Greek *kholē* 'gall, bile' + **CALCIFEROL**.

choler /kol-uh/ noun 1 (in medieval science and medicine) one of the four bodily humours, believed to be associated with an irritable temperament. 2 old use anger or bad temper.
– ORIGIN from Greek *kholē* 'bile'.

cholera /kol-uh-ruh/ noun an infectious disease of the small intestine which causes severe vomiting and diarrhoea.
– ORIGIN Latin, 'diarrhoea, bile'.

choleric /kol-uh-rik/ adjective bad-tempered or irritable.

cholesterol /kuh-less-tuh-rol/ noun a compound which occurs normally in most body tissues and is believed to lead to disease of the arteries if present in high concentrations in the blood (e.g. as a result of a diet high in animal fat).
– ORIGIN from Greek *kholē* 'bile' + *stereos* 'stiff'.

chomp verb munch or chew food noisily or vigorously.
– ORIGIN imitating the sound.

chook /chuuk/ noun informal, chiefly Austral./NZ a hen or chicken.
– ORIGIN probably from English dialect *chuck* 'chicken'.

choose verb (past **chose**; past part. **chosen**) 1 pick someone or something out as being the best of two or more alternatives. 2 decide on a course of action: *the men chose to ignore his orders*.
– ORIGIN Old English.

choosy adjective (**choosier**, **choosiest**) informal very careful when making a choice and so hard to please.
– DERIVATIVES **choosiness** noun.

chop¹ verb (**chops**, **chopping**, **chopped**) 1 cut something into pieces with repeated sharp, heavy blows of an axe or knife. 2 strike something with a short, heavy blow. 3 get rid of something or reduce it by a large amount: *the share price was chopped from 50p to 21p*. • noun 1 a thick slice of meat, especially pork or lamb, next to and usually including a rib. 2 a downward cutting blow or movement. 3 (**the chop**) Brit. informal dismissal from employment, or the cancellation of a plan or project.
– ORIGIN variant of **CHAP¹**.

chop² verb (**chops**, **chopping**, **chopped**) (in phrase **chop and change**) Brit. informal repeatedly change one's opinions or behaviour.

- ORIGIN perhaps related to **CHEAP**.

chop-chop adverb & exclamation quickly.
- ORIGIN pidgin English.

chopper noun **1** a short axe with a large blade. **2** informal a helicopter. **3** (**choppers**) informal teeth. **4** informal a type of motorcycle with high handlebars.

choppy (**choppier**, **choppiest**) adjective (of the sea) having many small waves.
- DERIVATIVES **choppiness** noun.

chops plural noun informal a person's or animal's mouth, jaws, or cheeks.
- ORIGIN unknown.

chopstick noun each of a pair of thin, tapered sticks held in one hand and used as eating utensils by the Chinese and Japanese.
- ORIGIN pidgin English, from a Chinese dialect word meaning 'nimble ones'.

chop suey /chop **soo**-i/ noun a Chinese-style dish of meat with bean sprouts, bamboo shoots, and onions.
- ORIGIN Chinese, 'mixed bits'.

choral adjective relating to or sung by a choir or chorus.
- DERIVATIVES **chorally** adverb.

chorale noun a simple, stately hymn tune for a choir or chorus.
- ORIGIN from Latin *cantus choralis*.

chord¹ noun a group of three or more musical notes sounded together in harmony.
- DERIVATIVES **chordal** adjective.
- ORIGIN from **ACCORD**.

> **USAGE:** Do not confuse **chord** with **cord**. **Chord** means 'a group of musical notes' (*an E major chord*), whereas **cord** means 'thin string or rope' or 'a part of the body resembling string or rope' (*the spinal cord*).

chord² noun a straight line joining the ends of an arc.
- PHRASES **strike** (or **touch**) **a chord** say or do something that arouses sympathy, enthusiasm, etc. in others.
- ORIGIN a later spelling of **CORD**.

chordate /kor-dayt/ noun an animal of a large group, including all the vertebrates, which have a skeletal rod of cartilage supporting the body.
- ORIGIN from Latin *chorda* 'rope'.

chore noun a routine or boring task, especially a household one.
- ORIGIN from former *char* or *chare* 'an odd job'.

chorea /ko-**ri**-uh/ noun a disorder of the nervous system characterized by uncontrollable jerky movements.
- ORIGIN Greek *khoreia* 'dancing together'.

choreograph /ko-ri-uh-grahf/ verb compose the sequence of steps and moves for a ballet or other dance.

choreographer /ko-ri-og-ruh-fer/ noun a person who designs the steps and movements for a ballet or other dance.

choreography /ko-ri-og-ruh-fi/ noun **1** the sequence of steps and movements in a ballet or other dance. **2** the art of designing such sequences.
- DERIVATIVES **choreographic** adjective.
- ORIGIN from Greek *khoreia* 'dancing together'.

chorine /kor-een/ noun a chorus girl.

chorister noun a member of a church choir.
- ORIGIN Old French *cueriste*.

chorizo /chuh-**ree**-zoh/ noun (pl. **chorizos**) a spicy Spanish pork sausage.
- ORIGIN Spanish.

chortle verb laugh loudly with pleasure or amusement. • noun a loud laugh of pleasure or amusement.
- ORIGIN coined by Lewis Carroll in *Through the Looking-Glass*; probably a blend of **CHUCKLE** and **SNORT**.

chorus noun (pl. **choruses**) **1** a part of a song which is repeated after each verse. **2** a piece of choral music, especially one forming part of an opera or oratorio. **3** a large group of singers performing with an orchestra. **4** a group of singers or dancers in a musical or an opera. **5** (in ancient Greek tragedy) a group of performers who comment on the main action of the play. **6** something said at the same time by many people. • verb (**choruses**, **chorusing**, **chorused**) (of a group of people) say the same thing at the same time.
- ORIGIN Latin, from Greek *khoros*.

chorus girl noun a young woman who sings or dances in the chorus of a musical.

chose past of **CHOOSE**.

chosen past participle of **CHOOSE**.

choucroute /shoo-kroot/ noun sauerkraut.
- ORIGIN French.

chough /chuff/ noun a black bird of the crow family with a red or yellow bill.
- ORIGIN probably imitating its call.

choux pastry /shoo/ noun very light pastry made with egg, used for eclairs and profiteroles.
- ORIGIN from French *chou* 'cabbage, rosette'.

chow /chow/ noun **1** informal food. **2** (also **chow chow**) a Chinese breed of dog with a tail curled over its back, a bluish-black tongue, and a thick coat.
- ORIGIN from pidgin English *chow chow* 'mixed pickle'.

chowder noun a rich soup containing fish, clams, or corn with potatoes and onions.
- ORIGIN perhaps from French *chaudière* 'stew pot'.

chow mein /chow mayn/ noun a Chinese-style dish of fried noodles with shredded meat or seafood and vegetables.
- ORIGIN Chinese, 'stir-fried noodles'.

chrism /kri-z'm/ noun a consecrated oil used for anointing in rites such as baptism in the Catholic, Orthodox, and Anglican Churches.
- ORIGIN Greek *khrisma* 'anointing'.

Christ noun the title given to Jesus. • exclamation used to express irritation, dismay, or surprise.
- DERIVATIVES **Christlike** adjective **Christly** adjective.
- ORIGIN Greek *Khristos* 'anointed one'.

christen verb **1** name a baby at baptism as a sign of admission to a Christian Church. **2** informal use something for the first time.
- DERIVATIVES **christening** noun.
- ORIGIN Old English, 'make Christian'.

Christendom noun literary the worldwide body of Christians.

Christian adjective relating to or believing in Christianity or its teachings. • noun a person

who has received Christian baptism or is a believer in Christianity.
– DERIVATIVES **Christianize** (or **Christianise**) verb.

Christian era noun the era beginning with the traditional date of Jesus's birth.

Christianity noun the religion based on the teachings and works of Jesus.

Christian name noun a first name, especially one given at baptism.

Christian Science noun the beliefs and practices of the Church of Christ Scientist, a Christian sect.
– DERIVATIVES **Christian Scientist** noun.

Christmas noun (pl. **Christmases**) 1 (also **Christmas Day**) the annual Christian festival celebrating Jesus's birth, held on 25 December. 2 the period immediately before and after 25 December.
– ORIGIN Old English, 'Mass of Christ'.

Christmas cactus noun a succulent South American plant with red, pink, or white flowers.
– ORIGIN because it flowers at about the northern midwinter.

Christmas cake noun Brit. a rich fruit cake covered with marzipan and icing, eaten at Christmas.

Christmas pudding noun Brit. a rich pudding eaten at Christmas, made with flour, suet, and dried fruit.

Christmas rose noun a small white-flowered winter-blooming hellebore.

Christmas tree noun an evergreen or artificial tree decorated with lights and ornaments at Christmas.

chromate /kroh-mayt/ noun Chemistry a salt in which the anion contains both chromium and oxygen.

chromatic adjective 1 relating or referring to a musical scale that rises or falls by semitones. 2 relating to or produced by colour.
– ORIGIN from Greek *khrōma* 'colour, chromatic scale'.

chromatin /kroh-muh-tin/ noun Biology the material of which non-bacterial chromosomes are composed, consisting of DNA and protein (and RNA at certain times).

chromatography /kroh-muh-tog-ruh-fi/ noun Chemistry a technique for separating and analysing a mixture by passing it through a medium in which the components move at different rates.
– DERIVATIVES **chromatogram** noun **chromatograph** noun **chromatographic** adjective.
– ORIGIN from Greek *khrōma* 'colour' (early separations being displayed as coloured bands or spots).

chrome noun a hard shiny metal coating made from chromium. • adjective referring to compounds or alloys of chromium: *chrome steel.*
– DERIVATIVES **chromed** adjective.
– ORIGIN Greek *khrōma* 'colour'.

chromite noun the main ore of chromium, a brownish-black oxide of chromium and iron.

chromium noun a hard white metallic chemical element used in stainless steel and other alloys.

chromosome noun a thread-like structure in a cell nucleus, carrying the genes.
– DERIVATIVES **chromosomal** adjective.
– ORIGIN from Greek *khrōma* 'colour' + *sōma* 'body'.

chronic adjective 1 (of an illness or problem) lasting for a long time. 2 having a bad habit: *a chronic liar.* 3 Brit. informal very bad.
– DERIVATIVES **chronically** adverb.
– ORIGIN Greek *khronikos* 'of time'.

chronic fatigue syndrome noun a medical condition of unknown cause, with fever, aching, and prolonged tiredness and depression.

chronicle noun a written account of historical events in the order of their occurrence. • verb record a series of events in a factual way.
– DERIVATIVES **chronicler** noun.
– ORIGIN Greek *khronika* 'annals'.

chronograph noun an instrument for recording time with great accuracy.

chronological adjective 1 (of a record of events) following the order in which they occurred: *the video shows all his goals in chronological order.* 2 relating to the establishment of the dates of past events.
– DERIVATIVES **chronologically** adverb.

chronology /kruh-nol-uh-ji/ noun (pl. **chronologies**) 1 the arrangement of events in the order of their occurrence. 2 the study of records to establish the dates of past events. 3 a list of events or dates in chronological order.
– DERIVATIVES **chronologist** noun.
– ORIGIN from Greek *khronos* 'time'.

chronometer /kruh-nom-i-ter/ noun an instrument for measuring time accurately in spite of motion or varying conditions.

chrysalis /kriss-uh-liss/ noun (pl. **chrysalises**) 1 a dormant insect pupa, especially of a butterfly or moth. 2 the hard outer case enclosing an insect pupa.
– ORIGIN from Greek *khrusos* 'gold' (because of the metallic sheen of some pupae).

chrysanthemum /kri-san-thi-muhm/ noun (pl. **chrysanthemums**) a garden plant with brightly coloured flowers.
– ORIGIN from Greek *khrusos* 'gold' + *anthemon* 'flower'.

chthonic /k-thonn-ik/ (also **chthonian** /k-thoh-ni-uhn/) adjective literary relating to or inhabiting the underworld.
– ORIGIN from Greek *khthōn* 'earth'.

chub noun (pl. same or **chubs**) a thick-bodied river fish with a grey-green back and white underparts.
– ORIGIN unknown.

Chubb noun trademark a lock with a device for fixing the bolt to prevent it from being picked.
– ORIGIN named after the London locksmith Charles *Chubb.*

chubby adjective (**chubbier, chubbiest**) plump and rounded.
– DERIVATIVES **chubbiness** noun.
– ORIGIN from **CHUB**.

chuck[1] verb informal 1 throw something carelessly or casually. 2 (**chuck something away/out**) throw something away. 3 (**chuck someone out**) force someone to leave a building. 4 give up: *he chucked in his history*

course. **5** (**chuck up**) vomit.
– DERIVATIVES **chucker** noun.
– ORIGIN from CHUCK².

chuck² verb touch someone playfully under the chin. • noun a playful touch under the chin.
– ORIGIN probably from Old French *chuquer* 'to knock, bump'.

chuck³ noun **1** a device for holding a workpiece in a lathe or a tool in a drill. **2** (also **chuck steak**) a cut of beef extending from the neck to the ribs.
– ORIGIN variant of CHOCK.

chuck⁴ noun N. English used as a familiar form of address.
– ORIGIN alteration of CHICK.

chuckle verb laugh quietly or inwardly. • noun a quiet laugh.
– ORIGIN from former *chuck* 'to cluck'.

chucklehead noun informal a stupid person.
– ORIGIN from former *chuckle* 'big and clumsy'.

chuddar noun variant spelling of CHADOR.

chuff verb (of a steam engine) move with a regular puffing sound.
– ORIGIN imitating the sound.

chuffed adjective Brit. informal very pleased.
– ORIGIN from dialect *chuff* 'plump or pleased'.

chug verb (**chugs**, **chugging**, **chugged**) move with a series of muffled explosive sounds, as of an engine running slowly.
– ORIGIN imitating the sound.

chukka noun each of a number of periods into which a game of polo is divided.
– ORIGIN Sanskrit, 'circle or wheel'.

chum informal noun a close friend. • verb (**chums**, **chumming**, **chummed**) (**chum up**) form a friendship with someone.
– DERIVATIVES **chummy** adjective.
– ORIGIN Oxford University slang for a room-mate: probably short for *chamber-fellow*.

chump noun **1** informal a foolish person. **2** Brit. the thick end of a loin of lamb or mutton.
– ORIGIN probably a blend of CHUNK¹ and LUMP¹ or STUMP.

chunder verb informal, chiefly Austral./NZ be sick; vomit.
– ORIGIN probably from rhyming slang *Chunder Loo* 'spew', from the name of a cartoon character.

chunk¹ noun **1** a thick, solid piece. **2** a large amount.
– ORIGIN probably from CHUCK³.

chunk² verb make a muffled, metallic sound.
– ORIGIN imitating the sound.

chunky adjective (**chunkier**, **chunkiest**) **1** bulky and thick. **2** containing chunks.
– DERIVATIVES **chunkily** adverb **chunkiness** noun.

chunter verb Brit. informal **1** chatter or grumble monotonously. **2** move along slowly and noisily.
– ORIGIN probably imitating the sound.

church noun **1** a building used for public Christian worship. **2** (**Church**) a particular Christian organization: *the Catholic Church*. **3** the Christian religion as an institution with political or social influence: *the separation of church and state*.
– ORIGIN from Greek *kuriakon dōma* 'Lord's house'.

churchman (or **churchwoman**) noun (pl.

churchmen or churchwomen) a member of the Christian clergy or of a Church.

Church of England noun the English branch of the Western Christian Church, which has the king or queen as its head.

Church of Scotland noun the national (Presbyterian) Christian Church in Scotland.

churchwarden noun either of two people who are elected by an Anglican congregation to take care of church property and keep order.

churchy adjective **1** excessively pious. **2** resembling a church.

churchyard noun an enclosed area surrounding a church, especially as used for burials.

churl noun **1** a rude and surly person. **2** old use a peasant.
– ORIGIN Old English.

churlish adjective rude and surly.
– DERIVATIVES **churlishly** adverb **churlishness** noun.

churn verb **1** (of liquid) move about vigorously: *the water churned and foamed*. **2** (**churn something up**) break up the surface of an area of ground. **3** (**churn something out**) produce something in large quantities and without much thought. **4** (as adj. **churned up**) upset or nervous. **5** shake milk or cream in a churn to produce butter. • noun **1** a machine for making butter by shaking milk or cream. **2** Brit. a large metal milk can.
– ORIGIN Old English.

chute¹ (also **shoot**) noun **1** a sloping channel for conveying things to a lower level. **2** a water slide into a swimming pool.
– ORIGIN French, 'fall' (of water or rocks).

chute² noun informal a parachute.

chutney noun (pl. **chutneys**) a spicy pickle made of fruits or vegetables with vinegar, spices, and sugar.
– ORIGIN Hindi.

chutzpah /khuuts-puh, huuts-puh/ noun informal extreme self-confidence or audacity.
– ORIGIN Yiddish.

chyle /kyl/ noun a milky fluid which drains from the small intestine into the lymphatic system during digestion.
– ORIGIN Greek *khūlos* 'juice'.

chyme /kym/ noun the fluid which passes from the stomach to the small intestine, consisting of gastric juices and partly digested food.
– ORIGIN Greek *khūmos* 'juice'.

Ci abbreviation curie.

CIA abbreviation Central Intelligence Agency.

ciabatta /chuh-**bah**-tuh/ noun a flattish Italian bread made with olive oil.
– ORIGIN Italian, 'slipper' (from its shape).

ciao /chow/ exclamation informal hello or goodbye.
– ORIGIN Italian.

cicada /si-**kah**-duh/ noun a large insect with long wings, which makes a shrill droning noise after dark.
– ORIGIN Latin.

cicatrix /sik-uh-triks/ (also **cicatrice** /sik-uh-triss/) noun (pl. **cicatrices** /sik-uh-**try**-seez/) a scar.
– ORIGIN Latin.

cicatrize (or **cicatrise**) /sik-uh-**tryz**/ verb heal a wound by scar formation.

C

cicely /siss-i-li/ (also **sweet cicely**) noun (pl. **cicelies**) a white-flowered plant with fern-like leaves.
– ORIGIN Greek *seselis*.

cicerone /chi-chuh-**roh**-ni/ noun (pl. **ciceroni** pronunc. same) a guide who gives information to sightseers.
– ORIGIN Italian, from the Roman writer *Cicero*, probably comparing the guides' knowledge to his learning.

cichlid /sik-lid/ noun a perch-like freshwater fish of a large family.
– ORIGIN Greek *kikhlē*.

CID abbreviation (in the UK) Criminal Investigation Department.

-cide combining form **1** referring to a person or substance that kills: *insecticide*. **2** referring to an act of killing: *suicide*.
– ORIGIN from Latin *-cida*, *-cidium*.

cider noun Brit. an alcoholic drink made from fermented apple juice.
– ORIGIN Old French *sidre*.

cigar noun a cylinder of tobacco rolled in tobacco leaves for smoking.
– ORIGIN French *cigare*.

cigarette noun a cylinder of finely cut tobacco rolled in paper for smoking.
– ORIGIN French, 'little cigar'.

cigarillo /sig-uh-**ril**-loh/ noun (pl. **cigarillos**) a small cigar.
– ORIGIN Spanish.

cilium /si-li-uhm/ noun (pl. **cilia** /si-li-uh/) Biology a microscopic hair-like vibrating structure, occurring on the surface of certain cells.
– DERIVATIVES **ciliary** adjective.
– ORIGIN Latin.

cimbalom /sim-buh-luhm/ noun a large Hungarian dulcimer (musical instrument).
– ORIGIN from Latin *cymbalum* 'cymbal'.

C.-in-C. abbreviation Commander-in-Chief.

cinch noun informal **1** a very easy task. **2** chiefly N. Amer. a certainty.
– ORIGIN from Spanish *cincha* 'girth'.

cinchona /sing-**koh**-nuh/ noun a medicinal drug obtained from the bark of a South American tree, containing quinine.
– ORIGIN named after the Countess of *Chinchón*, who brought the drug to Spain.

cinder noun a small piece of partly burnt coal or wood.
– DERIVATIVES **cindery** adjective.
– ORIGIN Old English.

Cinderella /sin-duh-**rel**-uh/ noun a person or thing that is undeservedly neglected.
– ORIGIN from the fairy story of *Cinderella*, whose family treat her as a servant but who eventually marries Prince Charming.

cine /sin-ee/ adjective relating to film-making: *a cine camera*.

cineaste /sin-i-ast/ noun a person who is fond of or knowledgeable about the cinema.
– ORIGIN French.

cinema noun chiefly Brit. **1** a theatre where films are shown. **2** the production of films as an art or industry.
– DERIVATIVES **cinematic** adjective **cinematically** adverb.
– ORIGIN Greek *kinēma* 'movement'.

cinematograph noun historical, chiefly Brit. an early film projector.

cinematography /sin-i-muh-**tog**-ruh-fi/ noun the art of photography and camerawork in film-making.
– DERIVATIVES **cinematographer** noun **cinematographic** adjective.

cinephile noun an enthusiast of the cinema.

cineraria /sin-uh-**rair**-i-uh/ noun a winter-flowering plant of the daisy family.
– ORIGIN from Latin *cinerarius* 'of ashes' (from the ash-coloured down on the leaves).

cinerary urn /sin-uh-ruh-ri/ noun an urn for holding a person's ashes after cremation.
– ORIGIN from Latin *cinerarius* 'of ashes'.

cinnabar /sin-nuh-bar/ noun **1** a bright red mineral consisting of mercury sulphide. **2** (also **cinnabar moth**) a moth with black and red wings.
– ORIGIN Greek *kinnabari*.

cinnamon /sin-uh-muhn/ noun **1** a spice made from the dried bark of an Asian tree. **2** a yellowish-brown colour.
– ORIGIN Greek *kinnamōmon*.

cinquefoil /singk-foyl/ noun **1** a plant with leaves made up of five small leaves and five-petalled yellow flowers. **2** a decorative design of five arcs arranged inside a circle.
– ORIGIN from Latin *quinque* 'five' + *folium* 'leaf'.

cipher (also **cypher**) noun **1** a code, especially one in which a set of letters or symbols is used to represent others. **2** a key to a code. **3** an unimportant person. **4** dated a zero. • verb put a message into code.
– ORIGIN from Arabic, 'zero'.

circa /ser-kuh/ preposition approximately.
– ORIGIN Latin.

circadian /ser-**kay**-di-uhn/ adjective (of biological processes) recurring on a twenty-four-hour cycle.
– ORIGIN from Latin *circa* 'about' + *dies* 'day'.

circle noun **1** a round plane figure whose boundary consists of points at an equal distance from the centre. **2** a thing or group of people or things shaped like a circle. **3** Brit. a curved upper tier of seats in a theatre. **4** a group of people with a shared profession, interests, or friends. • verb **1** move or be situated all the way around: *the cat circled the room twice*. **2** draw a line around something.
– PHRASES **come** (or **turn**) **full circle** return to a previous position or situation.
– ORIGIN Latin *circulus* 'small ring'.

circlet noun an ornamental circular band worn on the head.

circlip noun Brit. a metal ring sprung into a slot to hold something in place.
– ORIGIN blend of CIRCLE or CIRCULAR and CLIP¹.

circuit noun **1** a roughly circular line, route, or movement. **2** Brit. a track used for motor racing. **3** a system of conductors and components forming a complete path for an electric current. **4** an established series of sporting events or entertainments: *the comedy circuit*. **5** a series of physical exercises performed in one training session. **6** a regular journey by a judge around a district to hear court cases. • verb move all the way around something.
– ORIGIN Latin *circuitus*.

circuit-breaker noun an automatic safety device for stopping the flow of current in an electric circuit.

circuitous /ser-**kyoo**-i-tuhss/ adjective (of a route) longer than the most direct way.

circuitry noun (pl. **circuitries**) a system of electric circuits.

circular adjective **1** having the form of a circle. **2** (of an argument) false because it uses as evidence the point which is to be proved. **3** (of a letter or advertisement) for distribution to a large number of people. • noun a circular letter or advertisement.
– DERIVATIVES **circularity** noun **circularly** adverb.

circularize (or **circularise**) verb distribute circulars to a large number of people.

circular saw noun a power saw with a rapidly rotating toothed disc.

circulate verb **1** move continuously through a closed system or area: *antibodies circulate in the bloodstream.* **2** pass from place to place or person to person. **3** move around a social function and talk to many people.
– DERIVATIVES **circulator** noun.

circulation noun **1** movement around something. **2** the continuous motion of blood round the body. **3** the public availability of something: *a large number of counterfeit tickets are in circulation.* **4** the number of copies sold of a newspaper or magazine.
– PHRASES **in** (or **out of**) **circulation** (of a person) seen (or not seen) in public.
– DERIVATIVES **circulatory** adjective.

circum- prefix about; around: *circumambulate.*
– ORIGIN from Latin *circum* 'round'.

circumambient /ser-kuhm-**am**-bi-uhnt/ adjective chiefly literary extending round; surrounding.

circumambulate /ser-kuhm-**am**-byuu-layt/ verb formal walk all the way round something.
– DERIVATIVES **circumambulation** noun.

circumcise verb **1** cut off the foreskin of a young boy or man as a Jewish or Islamic rite. **2** cut off the clitoris, and sometimes the labia, of a girl or young woman.
– DERIVATIVES **circumcision** noun.
– ORIGIN Latin *circumcidere* 'cut around'.

circumference noun **1** the boundary which encloses a circle. **2** the distance around something.
– DERIVATIVES **circumferential** adjective.
– ORIGIN from Latin *circum* 'around' + *ferre* 'carry'.

circumflex noun a mark (ˆ) placed over a vowel in some languages to indicate a change in the way it is pronounced.
– ORIGIN from Latin *circum* 'around' + *flectere* 'to bend'.

circumlocution /ser-kuhm-luh-**kyoo**-sh'n/ noun the use of many words where fewer would do.
– DERIVATIVES **circumlocutory** adjective.
– ORIGIN from Latin *circum* 'around' + *loqui* 'speak'.

circumnavigate verb go right round something, especially by sail.
– DERIVATIVES **circumnavigation** noun.

circumpolar adjective situated or occurring around one of the earth's poles.

circumscribe verb **1** put limits on; restrict: *the joys of country life were circumscribed by foot-and-mouth disease.* **2** Geometry draw a figure round another, touching it at points but not cutting it.
– DERIVATIVES **circumscription** noun.
– ORIGIN from Latin *circum* 'around' + *scribere* 'write'.

circumspect adjective wary and unwilling to take risks; cautious.
– DERIVATIVES **circumspection** noun **circumspectly** adverb.
– ORIGIN from Latin *circumspicere* 'look around'.

circumstance noun **1** a fact or condition connected with an event or action. **2** unforeseen and influential events that are outside one's control: *a victim of circumstance.* **3** (**circumstances**) a person's financial or personal situation. **4** old use ceremony and public display: *pomp and circumstance.*
– ORIGIN from Latin *circumstare* 'encircle'.

circumstantial adjective **1** (of evidence) strongly suggesting something, but not proving it conclusively. **2** related to the particular circumstances of something: *a circumstantial log of our travels.*
– DERIVATIVES **circumstantiality** noun **circumstantially** adverb.

circumvent /ser-kuhm-**vent**/ verb find a way of avoiding a problem, regulation, or obstacle.
– DERIVATIVES **circumvention** noun.
– ORIGIN Latin *circumvenire.*

circus noun (pl. **circuses**) **1** a travelling company of acrobats, trained animals, and clowns. **2** informal a scene of hectic activity: *a media circus.* **3** (in ancient Rome) a circular sporting arena lined with seats.
– ORIGIN Latin, 'ring or circus'.

cirque /serk/ noun a steep-sided hollow at the head of a valley or on a mountainside.
– ORIGIN French.

cirrhosis /si-**roh**-siss/ noun a chronic liver disease typically caused by alcoholism or hepatitis.
– DERIVATIVES **cirrhotic** adjective.
– ORIGIN from Greek *kirrhos* 'tawny' (often the colour of the liver).

cirrocumulus /si-roh-**kyoo**-myuu-luhss/ noun cloud forming a broken layer of small fleecy clouds at high altitude.

cirrostratus /si-roh-**strah**-tuhss/ noun cloud forming a thin, uniform layer at high altitude.

cirrus /si-ruhss/ noun (pl. **cirri** /si-ry/) **1** cloud forming wispy streaks at high altitude. **2** Zoology & Botany a slender tendril or filament.
– ORIGIN Latin, 'a curl'.

CIS abbreviation Commonwealth of Independent States.

cisco /siss-koh/ noun (pl. **ciscoes**) a northern freshwater whitefish, important as a food fish.
– ORIGIN unknown.

cissy noun & adjective Brit. variant spelling of SISSY.

Cistercian /si-**ster**-sh'n/ noun a monk or nun of an order that is a stricter branch of the Benedictines. • adjective relating to the Cistercians.
– ORIGIN from *Cîteaux* in France, where the order was founded.

c

cistern noun a water storage tank, especially as part of a flushing toilet.
– ORIGIN Latin *cisterna*.

cistus /sis-tuhss/ noun a shrub with large white or red flowers.
– ORIGIN Greek *kistos*.

citadel noun a fortress protecting or overlooking a city.
– ORIGIN French *citadelle* or Italian *cittadella*.

citation noun 1 a quotation from or reference to a book or author. 2 a mention of a praiseworthy act in an official report. 3 a note accompanying an award, giving reasons for it.

cite verb 1 quote a book or author as evidence for an argument. 2 praise someone for a courageous act in an official report. 3 summon someone to appear in court.
– ORIGIN Latin *citare*.

citified adjective chiefly derogatory characteristic of a city: *the obligations of citified life*.

citizen noun 1 a person who is legally recognized as a subject or national of a country. 2 an inhabitant of a town or city.
– DERIVATIVES **citizenry** noun **citizenship** noun.
– ORIGIN Old French *citezein*.

Citizens' Band noun a range of radio frequencies which are allocated for local communication by private individuals.

citric adjective related to citrus fruit.
– ORIGIN from Latin *citrus* 'citron tree'.

citric acid noun a sharp-tasting acid present in the juice of lemons and other sour fruits.

citron noun the large, lemon-like fruit of an Asian tree.
– ORIGIN Latin *citrus* 'citron tree'.

citronella noun a fragrant oil obtained from a South Asian grass, used as an insect repellent and in perfume.

citrus (also **citrus fruit**) noun (pl. **citruses**) a fruit of a group that includes lemons, limes, oranges, and grapefruit.
– DERIVATIVES **citrusy** adjective.
– ORIGIN Latin, 'citron tree'.

cittern /sit-uhn/ noun a stringed instrument similar to a lute, used in 16th- and 17th-century Europe.
– ORIGIN Greek *kithara*, referring to a kind of harp.

city noun (pl. **cities**) 1 a large town, in particular (Brit.) a town created a city by charter and usually containing a cathedral. 2 (**the City**) the part of London governed by the Lord Mayor and the Corporation, especially with regard to its financial and commercial institutions.
– ORIGIN Latin *civitas*.

city father noun a person concerned with the administration of a city.

city hall noun N. Amer. municipal offices or officers.

cityscape noun a city landscape.

city slicker noun informal, derogatory a person with the sophisticated tastes or values associated with people who live in cities.

city state noun chiefly historical a city and surrounding territory that forms an independent state.

City Technology College noun (in the UK) a type of secondary school set up to teach technology and science in inner-city areas.

citywide adjective & adverb extending throughout a city.

civet /siv-it/ noun 1 a slender cat native to Africa and Asia. 2 a strong musky perfume obtained from the scent glands of the civet.
– ORIGIN Arabic.

civic adjective relating to a city or town or to the duties or activities of its citizens.
– DERIVATIVES **civically** adverb.
– ORIGIN Latin *civicus*.

civic centre noun Brit. a building containing municipal offices.

civics plural noun (treated as sing.) the study of the rights and duties of citizenship.

civil adjective 1 relating to ordinary citizens, as distinct from military or church matters. 2 Law non-criminal: *a civil court*. 3 courteous and polite.
– DERIVATIVES **civilly** adverb.
– ORIGIN Latin *civilis*.

civil defence noun the organization and training of civilians for their protection during wartime.

civil disobedience noun the refusal to obey certain laws as a political protest.

civil engineer noun an engineer who designs roads, bridges, dams, and similar structures.

civilian noun a person not in the armed services or the police force. •adjective relating to a civilian.
– ORIGIN from Old French *droit civilien* 'civil law'.

civility noun (pl. **civilities**) 1 politeness and courtesy. 2 (**civilities**) polite remarks used in formal conversation.

civilization (or **civilisation**) noun 1 an advanced stage or system of human social development: *the Victorians equated the railways with progress and civilization*. 2 the process of achieving this. 3 the society and culture of an area.

civilize (or **civilise**) verb 1 bring a place or people to an advanced stage of social development. 2 (as adj. **civilized**) polite and good-mannered.
– DERIVATIVES **civilizer** noun.

civil law noun 1 law concerned with ordinary citizens, rather than criminal, military, or religious affairs. 2 the system of law predominant on the European continent, influenced by that of ancient Rome.

civil liberty noun 1 freedom of action and speech subject to laws established for the good of the community. 2 (**civil liberties**) a person's rights to be subject only to laws established for the good of the community.
– DERIVATIVES **civil libertarian** noun.

Civil List noun (in the UK) a fixed annual allowance voted by Parliament to meet the official expenses incurred by the Queen in her role as head of state.

civil marriage noun a marriage solemnized without a religious ceremony.

civil partnership (also **civil union**) noun a legally recognized union of a same-sex couple, with rights similar to those of marriage.

civil rights plural noun the rights of citizens to political and social freedom and equality.

civil servant noun a member of the civil service.

civil service noun the branches of state administration, excluding military and judicial branches and elected politicians.

civil union noun (in some countries) a legally recognized union of a couple of the same sex, with rights similar to those of marriage.

civil war noun a war between citizens of the same country.

civvy noun (pl. **civvies**) informal **1** a civilian. **2** (**civvies**) civilian clothes, as distinct from uniform.
– PHRASES **Civvy Street** Brit. informal civilian life.

CJD abbreviation Creutzfeldt–Jakob disease.

Cl symbol the chemical element chlorine.

cl abbreviation centilitre.

clack verb make a sharp sound as of a hard object striking another. • noun a clacking sound.
– ORIGIN imitating the sound.

clad old-fashioned or literary past participle of **CLOTHE**. adjective **1** clothed: *leather-clad boys.* **2** covered with cladding.

cladding noun a covering or coating on a structure or material.

clade /klayd/ noun a group of organisms comprising all the evolutionary descendants of a common ancestor.
– ORIGIN Greek *klados* 'branch'.

cladistics /kluh-**diss**-tiks/ plural noun (treated as sing.) a method of classifying animals and plants based on only those shared characteristics which can be deduced to have originated in the common ancestor of a group of species during evolution.
– DERIVATIVES **cladistic** adjective.

claim verb **1** state that something is the case, without being able to give proof. **2** ask for something which one has a right to have: *she went to Germany, where she claimed asylum.* **3** cause the loss of someone's life. **4** request money under the terms of an insurance policy. **5** call for someone's attention. • noun **1** a statement that something is the case. **2** a demand for something to which one has a right. **3** a request for compensation under the terms of an insurance policy.
– DERIVATIVES **claimable** adjective **claimant** noun.
– ORIGIN Latin *clamare* 'call out'.

clairvoyance /klair-**voy**-uhnss/ noun the supposed ability of being able to see future events or to communicate with people who are dead or far away.
– ORIGIN from French *clair* 'clear' + *voir* 'to see'.

clairvoyant noun a person claiming to be able to predict the future or communicate with the dead. • adjective able to predict the future.

clam noun a large shellfish with two shells of equal size. • verb (**clams**, **clamming**, **clammed**) (**clam up**) informal stop talking abruptly.
– ORIGIN Old English, 'a bond or bondage'.

clamber verb climb or move in an awkward and laborious way: *Saul clambered into the back of the truck.* • noun an act of clambering.
– ORIGIN probably from **CLIMB**.

clamdiggers plural noun close-fitting calf-length trousers for women.

clammy adjective (**clammier**, **clammiest**) **1** unpleasantly damp and sticky. **2** (of air) cold and damp.

– DERIVATIVES **clammily** adverb **clamminess** noun.
– ORIGIN from dialect *clam* 'be sticky'.

clamour (US **clamor**) noun **1** a loud and confused noise. **2** a strong protest or demand. • verb (of a group) shout or demand loudly: *the surging crowds clamoured for attention.*
– DERIVATIVES **clamorous** adjective.
– ORIGIN from Latin *clamare* 'cry out'.

clamp noun a brace, band, or clasp for strengthening or holding things together. • verb **1** fasten a thing or things in place or together with a clamp. **2** (**clamp down**) take firm or harsh action to prevent something: *a plan to clamp down on smuggling.* **3** fit a wheel clamp to an illegally parked car.
– DERIVATIVES **clamper** noun.
– ORIGIN probably Dutch.

clampdown noun informal a firm or harsh attempt to prevent something.

clan noun **1** a close-knit group of related families, especially in the Scottish Highlands. **2** a group with a shared interest or characteristic: *a clan of born-again Christians.*
– ORIGIN Scottish Gaelic, 'offspring, family'.

clandestine /klan-**dess**-tin/ adjective kept secret or done secretively.
– DERIVATIVES **clandestinely** adverb **clandestinity** noun.
– ORIGIN Latin *clandestinus*.

clang noun a loud metallic sound. • verb make a clang.
– ORIGIN influenced by Latin *clangere* 'resound'.

clanger noun Brit. informal an embarrassing mistake.

clangour /klang-ger/ (US **clangor**) noun a continuous clanging sound.
– DERIVATIVES **clangorous** adjective.
– ORIGIN from Latin *clangere* 'resound'.

clank noun a loud, sharp metallic sound. • verb make a clank.
– ORIGIN imitating the sound.

clannish adjective (of a group) tending to exclude others outside the group.
– DERIVATIVES **clannishness** noun.

clansman (or **clanswoman**) noun (pl. **clansmen** or **clanswomen**) a member of a clan.

clap[1] verb (**claps**, **clapping**, **clapped**) **1** strike the palms of one's hands together repeatedly, especially to applaud. **2** slap someone encouragingly on the back. **3** put someone or something somewhere quickly or suddenly: *he clapped a hand to his forehead.* • noun **1** an act of clapping. **2** a sudden loud noise, especially of thunder.
– PHRASES **clap someone in jail** (or **irons**) put someone in prison (or in chains).
– ORIGIN Old English, 'throb, beat'.

clap[2] noun informal a sexually transmitted disease, especially gonorrhoea.
– ORIGIN Old French *clapoir*.

clapboard /klap-bord, klabb-uhd/ noun chiefly N. Amer. one of a series of planks of wood with edges horizontally overlapping, used to cover the outer walls of buildings.
– ORIGIN German *klappholt* 'barrel stave'.

clapped-out adjective Brit. informal worn out from age or heavy use.

clapper noun the free-swinging metal piece

inside a bell which strikes the bell to produce the sound.
– PHRASES **like the clappers** Brit. informal very fast or hard.

clapperboard noun hinged boards that are struck together at the beginning of filming to ensure that the the picture and sound machinery begin at the same time.

claptrap noun nonsense: *feminist claptrap.*
– ORIGIN first referring to something designed to make people applaud.

claque /klak/ noun **1** a group of people who follow someone in an obsequious way. **2** a group of people hired to applaud or heckle a performer.
– ORIGIN from French *claquer* 'to clap'.

claret /kla-ruht/ noun **1** a red wine, especially from Bordeaux. **2** a deep purplish red colour.
– ORIGIN from Latin *claratum vinum* 'clarified wine'.

clarify verb (**clarifies, clarifying, clarified**) **1** make easier to understand: *the judges' ruling had clarified the law of rape.* **2** melt butter to separate out the impurities.
– DERIVATIVES **clarification** noun **clarifier** noun.
– ORIGIN Old French *clarifier.*

clarinet noun a woodwind instrument with holes stopped by keys and a mouthpiece with a single reed.
– DERIVATIVES **clarinettist** (US **clarinetist**) noun.
– ORIGIN French *clarinette.*

clarion /kla-ri-uhn/ adjective literary loud and clear. • noun historical a shrill war trumpet.
– PHRASES **clarion call** a strongly expressed demand for action.
– ORIGIN Latin.

clarity noun **1** the state or quality of being easy to understand, see, or hear: *she analyses the pros and cons with admirable clarity.* **2** transparency or purity.
– ORIGIN Latin *clarus* 'clear'.

clash noun **1** a conflict or disagreement. **2** an inconvenient occurrence of dates or events at the same time. **3** a loud discordant sound. • verb **1** (of opposing groups) come into conflict. **2** disagree or be at odds: *Shanghai's decadent culture once clashed with Maoist principles.* **3** (of colours) appear discordant when placed together. **4** (of dates or events) occur inconveniently at the same time: *he was invited to a dinner party, but it clashed with one of his seminars.* **5** strike cymbals together, producing a loud discordant sound.
– ORIGIN imitating the sound.

clasp verb **1** grasp something tightly with one's hand. **2** place one's arms tightly around someone or something. **3** fasten something with a clasp. • noun **1** a device with interlocking parts used for fastening. **2** an act of embracing or grasping.
– ORIGIN unknown.

clasp knife noun a knife with a blade that folds into the handle.

class noun **1** a set or category of people or things having a common characteristic: *a new class of antibiotics.* **2** a system that divides members of a society into sets based on social or economic status. **3** a social division based on social or economic status: *the ruling class.* **4** a group of pupils or students who are taught

together. **5** a lesson. **6** informal impressive stylishness. **7** Biology a principal category into which animals and plants are divided, ranking below phylum or division. **8** Brit. a division of candidates according to merit in a university exam system. • verb put someone or something in a particular category. • adjective informal showing stylish excellence: *a class player.*
– PHRASES **class A** (or **B** or **C**) **drug** Brit. an illegal narcotic drug classified as being of the most harmful and addictive (or a less harmful and addictive) kind.
– ORIGIN Latin *classis* 'division of the Roman people, class'.

class action noun Law, N. Amer. a law suit filed or defended by an individual acting on behalf of a group.

classic adjective **1** judged over time to be of the highest quality. **2** typical: *the classic symptoms of flu.* • noun **1** a work of art that is recognized as being of high quality. **2** a thing which is an excellent example of its kind: *tomorrow's game should be a classic.* **3** (**Classics**) the study of ancient Greek and Latin literature, philosophy, and history. **4** (**the classics**) the works of ancient Greek and Latin writers.
– ORIGIN Latin *classicus* 'belonging to a class'.

classical adjective **1** relating to ancient Greek or Latin literature, art, or culture. **2** (of a form of art or a language) representing the highest standard within a long-established form. **3** (of music) of long-established form or style or (more specifically) written in the European tradition between approximately 1750 and 1830. **4** relating to the first significant period of an area of study: *classical Marxism.*
– DERIVATIVES **classically** adverb.

classicism noun the following of ancient Greek or Roman principles and style in art and literature, generally associated with harmony and restraint.

classicist noun **1** a person who studies Classics. **2** a follower of classicism.

classicizing (or **classicising**) adjective imitating a classical style.

classification noun **1** the action of classifying something. **2** a category into which something is put.
– DERIVATIVES **classificatory** adjective.

classified adjective **1** (of newspaper or magazine advertisements) organized in categories. **2** (of information or documents) officially classed as secret. • noun (**classifieds**) classified advertisements.

classify verb (**classifies, classifying, classified**) **1** arrange a group in classes according to shared characteristics. **2** put in a particular class or category: *it's the only French winery classified as a National Monument.* **3** categorize documents or information as officially secret.
– DERIVATIVES **classifiable** adjective **classifier** noun.

classless adjective **1** (of a society) not divided into social classes. **2** not showing characteristics of a particular social class.
– DERIVATIVES **classlessness** noun.

classmate noun a fellow member of one's school class.

classroom noun a room in which a class of pupils or students is taught.

classy adjective (**classier, classiest**) informal stylish

and sophisticated.
– DERIVATIVES **classily** adverb **classiness** noun.

clatter noun a loud rattling sound as of hard objects striking each other. • verb make or move with a clatter.
– ORIGIN Old English.

clause noun 1 a group of words that includes a subject and a verb, forming a sentence or part of a sentence. 2 a particular and separate item of a treaty, bill, or contract.
– DERIVATIVES **clausal** adjective.
– ORIGIN from Latin *claudere* 'close'.

claustrophobia /kloss-truh-**foh**-bi-uh/ noun extreme or irrational fear of being in an enclosed place.
– DERIVATIVES **claustrophobic** adjective.
– ORIGIN from Latin *claustrum* 'lock, bolt'.

clavichord /**klav**-i-kord/ noun a small early keyboard instrument with a soft tone.
– ORIGIN from Latin *clavis* 'key' + *chorda* 'string'.

clavicle noun technical term for COLLARBONE.
– ORIGIN Latin *clavicula* 'small key'.

claw noun 1 a curved pointed nail on each digit of the foot in birds, lizards, and some mammals. 2 the pincer of a crab, scorpion, or similar creature. • verb 1 (usu. **claw at**) scratch or tear something with the claws or fingernails. 2 (**claw something back**) regain or recover money or power with difficulty.
– DERIVATIVES **clawed** adjective.
– ORIGIN Old English.

claw hammer noun a hammer with one side of the head split and curved, used for extracting nails.

clay noun 1 a heavy sticky earth that can be moulded when wet and baked to make bricks and pottery. 2 literary the substance of the human body: *this lifeless clay.*
– DERIVATIVES **clayey** adjective.
– ORIGIN Old English.

claymore noun historical a type of broadsword used in Scotland.
– ORIGIN Scottish Gaelic *claidheamh* 'great sword'.

clay pigeon noun a saucer-shaped piece of baked clay or other material thrown up in the air as a target for shooting.

clean adjective 1 free from dirt, stains, or harmful substances. 2 maintaining good personal hygiene. 3 not immoral or obscene: *good clean fun.* 4 showing or having no record of offences or crimes: *a clean driving licence.* 5 done according to the rules: *a good clean fight.* 6 free from irregularities; smooth. 7 (of an action) smoothly and skilfully done. • verb 1 make someone or something clean. 2 (**clean someone out**) informal use up or take all someone's money. 3 (**clean up**) informal make a substantial gain or profit. • adverb 1 so as to be free from dirt. 2 informal completely: *I clean forgot her birthday.* • noun an act of cleaning.
– PHRASES **clean and jerk** a weightlifting exercise in which a weight is raised above the head following an initial lift to shoulder level. **a clean sheet** (or **slate**) an absence of existing restraints or commitments. **come clean** (or **make a clean breast of it**) informal fully confess something. **keep one's hands clean** remain uninvolved in something immoral or illegal.

make a clean sweep 1 remove all unwanted people or things ready to start afresh. 2 win all of a group of related sporting contests.
– DERIVATIVES **cleanable** adjective **cleanness** noun.
– ORIGIN Old English.

clean-cut adjective 1 (of a person, especially a man) neat and respectable. 2 sharply outlined.

cleaner noun a person or thing that cleans something.
– PHRASES **take someone to the cleaners** informal cheat or defraud someone of all their money or possessions.

cleanly adverb in a clean way.
– DERIVATIVES **cleanliness** /**klen**-li-nuhss/ noun.

cleanse verb 1 make something thoroughly clean. 2 remove something unpleasant or unwanted from: *he wanted to cleanse bullfighting of its violent aspects.* • noun an act of cleansing.
– DERIVATIVES **cleanser** noun.
– ORIGIN Old English.

clean-shaven adjective (of a man) without a beard or moustache.

clean-up noun an act of cleaning a place.

clear adjective 1 easy to see, hear, or understand. 2 leaving or feeling no doubt. 3 transparent: *a stream of clear water.* 4 free of obstructions or unwanted objects. 5 (of a period of time) free of commitments. 6 free from disease or guilt. 7 (**clear of**) not touching; away from. 8 complete: *seven clear days' notice.* 9 (of a sum of money) net: *a clear profit of £1,100.* • adverb 1 so as to be out of the way of or uncluttered by. 2 with clarity. • verb 1 make or become clear. 2 get past or over something safely or without touching it. 3 show or declare someone to be innocent. 4 give official approval to; authorize: *I cleared him to return to his squadron.* 5 cause people to leave a building or place. 6 (of a cheque) pass through a clearing house so that the money enters a person's account. 7 earn an amount of money as a net profit. 8 pay off a debt.
– PHRASES **clear the air** 1 make the air less humid. 2 defuse a tense situation by frank discussion. **clear the decks** prepare for something by dealing with possible obstacles to progress. **clear off** (or **out**) informal go away. **clear something out** informal empty something. **clear up** 1 (of an illness or other medical condition) become cured. 2 (of the weather) become fine and dry. **clear something up** 1 tidy something by removing unwanted items. 2 solve or explain something. **in the clear** no longer in danger or under suspicion.
– DERIVATIVES **clearness** noun.
– ORIGIN Latin *clarus.*

clearance noun 1 the action of clearing. 2 official authorization for something. 3 clear space allowed for a thing to move past or under another.

clear-cut adjective easy to see or understand.

clearing[1] noun an open space in a forest.

clearing[2] noun Brit. a system used by universities to fill the remaining available undergraduate places before the start of the academic year.

clearing bank noun Brit. a bank which is a member of a clearing house.

clearing house noun 1 a bankers'

c

establishment where cheques and bills from member banks are exchanged. **2** an agency which collects and distributes information.

clearly adverb **1** in a clear way. **2** without doubt; obviously.

clear-out noun chiefly Brit. a removal and disposal of unwanted items or people.

clear-sighted adjective thinking clearly.

clearway noun Brit. a main road other than a motorway on which vehicles are not permitted to stop.

cleat noun **1** a T-shaped projection to which a rope may be attached. **2** a projecting piece of metal or rubber on the sole of a shoe, to prevent a person from slipping.
– DERIVATIVES **cleated** adjective.
– ORIGIN Germanic.

cleavage noun **1** the space between a woman's breasts. **2** a marked difference or division between people. **3** cell division, especially of a fertilized egg cell.

cleave¹ verb (**cleaves, cleaving, clove** or **cleft** or **cleaved**; past part. **cloven** or **cleft** or **cleaved**) **1** split something along a natural grain or line. **2** move forcefully through: *they watched a coot cleave the smooth water.*
– ORIGIN Old English.

cleave² verb (**cleave to**) literary **1** stick fast to. **2** become strongly involved with or emotionally attached to: *sport was something he could cleave to.*
– ORIGIN Old English.

cleaver noun a tool with a heavy broad blade, used for chopping meat.

clef noun Music any of several symbols placed on a stave, indicating the pitch of the notes written on the stave.
– ORIGIN French.

cleft past and past participle of **CLEAVE**¹. adjective split, divided, or partially divided into two.
• noun **1** a crack or split in rock or the ground. **2** a narrow vertical indentation in the chin or other part of the body.
– PHRASES **be (or be caught) in a cleft stick** be in a situation in which any action taken will have undesirable results.

cleft lip noun a split in the upper lip on one or both sides of the centre, present from birth.

cleft palate noun a split in the roof of the mouth which is present from birth.

clematis /klem-uh-tiss/ noun a climbing plant with white, pink, or purple flowers.
– ORIGIN Greek *klēmatis*.

clemency noun the quality of being clement or merciful.

clement adjective **1** (of weather) mild. **2** showing mercy.
– ORIGIN Latin *clemens*.

clementine /klem-uhn-tyn/ noun a deep orange-red variety of tangerine.
– ORIGIN French, from the man's name *Clément*.

clench verb **1** close or press one's teeth or fists together tightly, as a reaction to stress or anger. **2** contract a set of muscles sharply. **3** hold something tightly: *he clenched the steering wheel.*
– ORIGIN Old English; related to **CLING**.

clerestory /kleer-stor-i/ (US also **clearstory**) noun (pl. **clerestories**) the upper part of the nave, choir, and transepts of a large church, with a series of windows which allow light into the central parts of the building.
– ORIGIN from **CLEAR** + **STOREY**.

clergy /kler-ji/ noun (pl. **clergies**) (usu. treated as pl.) the people ordained for religious duties considered as a group, especially those in the Christian Church.
– ORIGIN Latin *clericus* 'clergyman'.

clergyman (or **clergywoman**) noun (pl. **clergymen** or **clergywomen**) a Christian priest or minister.

cleric noun a priest or religious leader.
– ORIGIN Latin *clericus*.

clerical adjective **1** relating to the routine work of an office clerk. **2** relating to the clergy.
– DERIVATIVES **clerically** adverb.

clerical collar noun a stiff upright white collar which fastens at the back, worn by the clergy in some Christian churches.

clerical error noun a mistake made in copying or writing out a document.

clerihew /kle-ri-hew/ noun a short comic verse consisting of two rhyming couplets, usually referring to a famous person.
– ORIGIN named after Edmund *Clerihew* Bentley, the English writer who invented it.

clerk /klark/ noun **1** a person employed in an office or bank to keep records or accounts and to carry out other routine administrative duties. **2** a person in charge of the records of a local council or court. **3** a senior official in Parliament. **4** (also **desk clerk**) N. Amer. a receptionist in a hotel. **5** (also **sales clerk**) N. Amer. an assistant in a shop.
– DERIVATIVES **clerkly** adjective.
– ORIGIN Latin *clericus* 'clergyman'.

clever adjective (**cleverer, cleverest**) **1** quick to understand and learn things. **2** skilled at doing something: *he's very clever with his hands.*
– DERIVATIVES **cleverly** adverb **cleverness** noun.
– ORIGIN perhaps from Dutch or German.

clew noun the lower corner of a sail or that nearer to the stern of the ship.
– ORIGIN related to **CLUE**.

cliché /klee-shay/ (also **cliche**) noun a phrase or idea that has been used so often that it is no longer interesting or effective.
– DERIVATIVES **clichéd** adjective.
– ORIGIN French.

click noun **1** a short, sharp sound. **2** Computing an act of pressing one of the buttons on a mouse.
• verb **1** make or cause to make a click: *the cameras started clicking.* **2** Computing press a mouse button. **3** informal become suddenly clear or understandable. **4** informal (of two people) become friends, especially at the first meeting.
– DERIVATIVES **clickable** adjective.
– ORIGIN imitating the sound.

client noun a person using the services of a professional person or organization.
– ORIGIN Latin *cliens*.

clientele /klee-on-tel/ noun all the clients or customers of a particular shop, restaurant, or other business.
– ORIGIN French.

cliff noun a steep rock face, especially at the edge of the sea.

– ORIGIN Old English.

cliffhanger noun **1** a dramatic ending to an episode of a serial, leaving the audience in suspense. **2** an exciting situation in which the outcome is uncertain.

climacteric /kly-**mak**-tuh-rik/ noun **1** the period of life when fertility is in decline; (in women) the menopause. **2** a critical period or event.

– ORIGIN Greek *klimaktēr*.

climactic /kly-**mak**-tik/ adjective forming an exciting climax.

– DERIVATIVES **climactically** adverb.

> **USAGE:** Do not confuse **climactic** with **climatic**. Climactic means 'forming a climax' (*the thrilling climactic scene*), whereas **climatic** means 'relating to climate' (*climatic and environmental change*).

climate noun **1** the general weather conditions in an area over a long period. **2** a general trend, attitude, or situation: *the current economic climate.*

– DERIVATIVES **climatology** noun **climatological** adjective.

– ORIGIN Greek *klima* 'slope, zone'.

climatic /kly-**mat**-ik/ adjective relating to climate.

– DERIVATIVES **climatically** adverb.

climax noun **1** the most intense, exciting, or important point of something. **2** an orgasm. • verb reach a climax.

– ORIGIN Greek *klimax* 'ladder, climax'.

climb verb **1** go or come up to a higher position. **2** go up a hill, rock face, etc. **3** (of a plant) grow up a supporting structure by clinging to or twining round it. **4** move somewhere, especially with effort or difficulty: *he climbed out through the kitchen window.* **5** increase in amount, value, or power: *the shares climbed 17p to 248p.* **6** (**climb down**) withdraw from a position taken up in an argument or negotiation; admit that one was wrong. • noun **1** an act of climbing. **2** a route up a mountain or cliff.

– DERIVATIVES **climbable** adjective.

– ORIGIN Old English.

climber noun a person who climbs rocks or mountains as a sport.

climbing frame noun Brit. a structure of joined bars for children to climb on.

clime noun chiefly literary a region with a particular climate: *people leaving Britain for sunnier climes.*

– ORIGIN Greek *klima* 'slope, zone'.

clinch verb **1** succeed in achieving or winning: *he clinched a £5 million sponsorship deal.* **2** settle an argument or debate. • noun **1** an act of grappling at close quarters in a fight. **2** informal an embrace.

– ORIGIN from **CLENCH**.

clincher noun informal a fact, argument, or event that settles something decisively.

cling verb (past and past part. **clung**) (**cling to/on to**) **1** hold on tightly to. **2** stick to: *her hair clung to her damp skin.* **3** be unwilling to give up a belief or hope: *she clung to her convictions.* **4** be emotionally dependent on someone.

– ORIGIN Old English.

cling film noun Brit. a thin transparent plastic film that sticks to a surface, used to wrap or cover food.

clingy adjective (**clingier, clingiest**) **1** (of a garment) clinging to the body. **2** (of a person) too emotionally dependent on someone else.

– DERIVATIVES **clinginess** noun.

clinic noun **1** a place where or time when specialized medical treatment or advice is given. **2** an occasion at which advice and training in a particular subject or activity is given: *a tennis clinic.*

– ORIGIN from Greek *klinē* 'bed'.

clinical adjective **1** relating to the observation and treatment of patients (rather than theoretical studies). **2** without feeling or sympathy: *she looked at him with clinical detachment.* **3** (of a place) very clean and plain.

– DERIVATIVES **clinically** adverb.

clinical psychology noun the branch of psychology concerned with the assessment and treatment of mental illness and behavioural problems.

clinician noun a doctor having direct contact with and responsibility for treating patients, rather than one involved with theoretical studies.

clink¹ noun a sharp ringing sound, like that made when metal or glass are struck. • verb make or cause to make a clink.

– ORIGIN Dutch *klinken*.

clink² noun informal prison.

– ORIGIN unknown.

clinker noun the stony remains from burnt coal or from a furnace.

– ORIGIN Dutch *klinken* 'to clink'.

clinker-built adjective (of a boat) having a hull built from overlapping planks secured with nails.

– ORIGIN from an old dialect word *clink*, 'fasten together with nails'.

clip¹ noun **1** a flexible or spring-loaded device for holding an object or objects together or in place. **2** a piece of jewellery that can be fastened on to a garment with a clip. **3** a metal holder containing cartridges for an automatic firearm. • verb (**clips, clipping, clipped**) fasten something with a clip or clips.

– ORIGIN Old English.

clip² verb (**clips, clipping, clipped**) **1** cut or trim something, or cut something out with shears or scissors. **2** trim an animal's hair or wool. **3** strike someone or something with a sharp blow. • noun **1** an act of clipping something. **2** a short sequence taken from a film or broadcast. **3** informal a sharp blow. **4** informal a rapid speed: *they went by at a fast clip.*

– ORIGIN Old Norse.

clip art noun digital pictures and symbols provided with word-processing software.

clipboard noun a small board with a spring clip at the top, used for holding papers and providing support for writing.

clip joint noun informal a nightclub or bar that charges extremely high prices.

clipped adjective (of speech) having short, sharp vowel sounds and clear pronunciation.

clipper noun **1** (**clippers**) an instrument for clipping. **2** a fast sailing ship of the 19th-century.

c

clipping noun **1** a small piece trimmed from something: *grass clippings.* **2** an article cut out of a newspaper or magazine.

clique /*rhymes with* seek/ noun a small group of people who spend time together and are unwilling to allow others to join them.
– DERIVATIVES **cliquey** adjective **cliquish** adjective.
– ORIGIN French.

clitoris /**kli**-tuh-riss/ noun a small sensitive organ at the front end of the female external genitals.
– DERIVATIVES **clitoral** adjective.
– ORIGIN Greek *kleitoris.*

cloaca /kloh-**ay**-kuh/ noun (in some animals) a cavity at the end of the digestive tract into which the urinary and reproductive systems also open, leading to a single opening in the body.
– ORIGIN Latin, 'sewer'.

cloak noun **1** an outer garment that hangs loosely from the shoulders over the arms to the knees or ankles. **2** something that hides or covers: *a cloak of secrecy.* • verb **1** hide or cover: *the summit was cloaked in thick mist.* **2** (as adj. **cloaked**) wearing a cloak.
– ORIGIN Old French *cloke.*

cloak-and-dagger adjective involving intrigue and secrecy.

cloakroom noun **1** a room in a public building where outdoor clothes and bags may be left. **2** Brit. a room that contains a toilet or toilets.

clobber informal noun Brit. clothing and personal belongings. • verb **1** hit someone hard. **2** defeat a person or team heavily.
– ORIGIN unknown.

cloche /klosh/ noun **1** a small glass or plastic cover for protecting outdoor plants or making them develop faster than usual. **2** (also **cloche hat**) a woman's close-fitting bell-shaped hat.
– ORIGIN French, 'bell'.

clock noun **1** an instrument that measures and indicates the time by means of a dial or a digital display. **2** informal a measuring device resembling a clock, such as a speedometer. • verb **1** reach or achieve a particular time, distance, or speed. **2** (**clock in/out** or Brit. **on/off**) record the time of one's arrival at or departure from work, especially by inserting a card in a special clock. **3** Brit. informal see or watch someone or something. **4** informal, chiefly Brit. hit someone on the head. **5** Brit. informal illegally wind back the milometer of a car so that its mileage appears less.
– PHRASES **round the clock** all day and all night. **turn** (or **put**) **back the clock** return to the past or to a previous way of doing things.
– ORIGIN Latin *clocca* 'bell'.

clock-watcher noun a person who constantly checks the time to make sure that they do not work longer than they are supposed to.

clockwise adverb & adjective in the direction of the movement of the hands of a clock.

clockwork noun a mechanism with a spring and toothed gearwheels, used to drive a mechanical clock, toy, or other device.
– PHRASES **like clockwork** very smoothly and easily.

clod noun **1** a lump of earth. **2** informal a stupid person.
– ORIGIN variant of **CLOT.**

cloddish adjective foolish, awkward, or clumsy.

clodhopper noun informal **1** a large, heavy shoe. **2** a foolish, awkward, or clumsy person.

clog noun a shoe with a thick wooden sole. • verb (**clogs, clogging, clogged**) block or become blocked: *the gutters were clogged up with leaves.*
– ORIGIN unknown.

cloisonné /klwah-**zon**-ay/ noun enamel work in which the different colours in the design are separated by strips of flattened wire placed on a metal backing.
– ORIGIN French, 'partitioned'.

cloister /**kloy**-ster/ noun **1** a covered passage round an open courtyard in a convent, monastery, college, or cathedral, usually having a row of columns on the inner side. **2** (**the cloister**) the secluded life of a monk or nun.
– ORIGIN Old French *cloistre*, from Latin *claustrum* 'lock, enclosed place'.

cloistered adjective **1** having or enclosed by a cloister: *a cloistered walkway.* **2** protected from the problems of ordinary life.

clomp verb walk heavily.
– ORIGIN imitating the sound.

clompy adjective variant spelling of **CLUMPY** (in sense 1).

clone noun **1** an animal or plant produced from the cells of another, to which it is genetically identical. **2** a person or thing regarded as an exact copy of another. • verb **1** create an animal or plant as a clone. **2** make an identical copy of something.
– ORIGIN Greek *klōn* 'twig'.

clonk noun a loud sound made by heavy things hitting each other. • verb **1** move with or make a clonk. **2** informal hit.
– ORIGIN imitating the sound.

clop noun a sound made by a horse's hooves on a hard surface. • verb (**clops, clopping, clopped**) move with such a sound.

close¹ /*rhymes with* dose/ adjective **1** only a short distance away or apart in space or time. **2** (**close to**) almost doing or being something: *she was close to tears.* **3** (of a connection or resemblance) strong. **4** (of a person) part of someone's immediate family: *a close relative.* **5** (of a relationship or the people in it) very affectionate or intimate. **6** (of observation or examination) done in a careful and thorough way. **7** uncomfortably humid or airless. • adverb so as to be very near. • noun Brit. **1** a residential street from which there is no access to other streets. **2** the grounds surrounding a cathedral.
– PHRASES **at** (or **from**) **close quarters** (or **range**) very near to someone or something. **close-knit** (of a group of people) united by strong relationships and common interests. **close-run** (of a contest) won or lost by a very small amount. **close shave** (also **close call**) informal a narrow escape from danger or disaster.
– DERIVATIVES **closely** adverb **closeness** noun.
– ORIGIN Old French *clos*, from Latin *claudere* 'close, shut'.

close² /*rhymes with* nose/ verb **1** move something so as to cover an opening. **2** bring two parts of something together: *she closed*

the book. **3** (**close on/in on**) gradually get nearer to or surround someone or something. **4** (**close in**) (of bad weather or darkness) gradually surround someone. **5** (**close in**) (of days) get successively shorter with the approach of the winter solstice. **6** (**close around/over**) encircle and hold. **7** bring or come to an end. **8** finish speaking or writing. **9** (often **close down/up**) (with reference to a business or other organization) stop or cause to stop trading or operating. **10** bring to a conclusion: *he closed a deal with one of the supermarkets.* • noun the end of an event or of a period of time or activity.
– ORIGIN Old French *clore*, from Latin *claudere*.

closed adjective **1** not open or allowing access. **2** not communicating with or influenced by others: *a closed society.*
– PHRASES **behind closed doors** in private. **a closed book** a subject or person about which one knows nothing.

closed-circuit television noun a television system in which the signals are transmitted from one or more cameras by cable to a restricted set of monitors.

closed shop noun a place of work where all employees must belong to a particular trade union.

close harmony noun Music harmony in which the notes of the chord are close together, typically in vocal music.

close season (also **closed season**) noun **1** a period when fishing or the killing of particular animals or game birds is officially forbidden. **2** Brit. a part of the year when a particular sport is not played.

closet noun **1** chiefly N. Amer. a tall cupboard or wardrobe. **2** a small room. **3** old use a toilet. • adjective secret: *a closet socialist.* • verb (**closets, closeting, closeted**) **1** shut oneself away in private to talk to someone or to be alone: *he closeted himself in his room.* **2** (as adj. **closeted**) keeping the fact of being homosexual secret.
– PHRASES **in** (or **out of**) **the closet** not admitting (or admitting) that one is homosexual.
– ORIGIN Old French.

close-up noun a photograph or film sequence taken at close range.

closure noun **1** an act or process of closing something. **2** a device that closes or seals something. **3** (in a parliament) a procedure for ending a debate and taking a vote. **4** a feeling that an emotional or upsetting experience has been resolved.
– ORIGIN from Latin *claudere* 'to close'.

clot noun **1** a thick semi-solid mass formed from a liquid substance, especially blood. **2** Brit. informal a foolish or clumsy person. • verb (**clots, clotting, clotted**) form into clots.
– ORIGIN Old English.

cloth noun (pl. **cloths**) **1** fabric made by weaving or knitting a soft fibre such as wool or cotton. **2** a piece of cloth used for a particular purpose. **3** (**the cloth**) Christian priests as a group.
– ORIGIN Old English.

clothe verb (past and past part. **clothed** or old use or literary **clad**) **1** provide someone with clothes. **2** (**be clothed in**) be dressed in.
– ORIGIN Old English.

clothes plural noun things worn to cover the body.

clothes horse noun **1** a frame on which washed clothes are hung to dry. **2** informal a person who models or is over-concerned with wearing fashionable clothes.

clothes line noun a rope or wire on which washed clothes are hung to dry.

clothes moth noun a small brown moth whose larvae can damage fabric, especially wool.

clothes peg (also N. Amer. **clothespin**) noun Brit. a wooden or plastic clip for securing clothes to a clothes line.

clothier /kloh-thi-er/ noun a person who makes or sells clothes or cloth.

clothing noun clothes.

clotted cream noun chiefly Brit. thick cream made by heating milk slowly and then allowing it to cool while the cream rises to the top in lumps.

cloud noun **1** a white or grey mass of condensed watery vapour floating in the atmosphere. **2** a mass of smoke, dust, etc. **3** a large number of insects or birds moving together. **4** a state or cause of gloom or anxiety: *injury worries cast a cloud over the team's preparations.* • verb **1** (**cloud over**) (of the sky) become full of clouds. **2** make or become less clear: *all sorts of doubts clouded my mind.* **3** (of someone's face or eyes) show sadness, anxiety, or anger.
– PHRASES **have one's head in the clouds** be full of idealistic dreams. **on cloud nine** (or **seven**) extremely happy. **under a cloud** under suspicion of having done wrong.
– DERIVATIVES **cloudless** adjective.
– ORIGIN Old English, 'mass of rock or earth'.

cloudburst noun a sudden violent rainstorm.

cloud cuckoo land noun a state of unrealistic or over-optimistic fantasy.
– ORIGIN translation of Greek *Nephelokokkugia*, the name of a city built by the birds in Aristophanes' comedy *Birds*, from *nephelē* 'cloud' + *kokkux* 'cuckoo'.

cloudy adjective **1** covered with clouds; having many clouds. **2** (of a liquid) not clear or transparent.
– DERIVATIVES **cloudiness** noun.

clout informal noun **1** a heavy blow. **2** influence or power. • verb hit someone hard.
– ORIGIN Old English, 'a patch or metal plate'.

clove[1] noun **1** the dried flower bud of a tropical tree, used as a spice. **2** (**oil of cloves**) a strong-smelling oil extracted from these flower buds and used for the relief of toothache.
– ORIGIN from Old French *clou de girofle* 'nail of gillyflower' (from the shape of the flower buds), GILLYFLOWER being originally the name of the spice.

clove[2] noun any of the small bulbs making up a compound bulb of garlic.
– ORIGIN Old English.

clove[3] past of CLEAVE[1].

clove hitch noun a knot used to fasten a rope to a spar or another rope.
– ORIGIN *clove*, past tense of CLEAVE[1] (because the rope appears as separate parallel lines at the back of the knot).

cloven past participle of CLEAVE[1].

cloven hoof (also **cloven foot**) noun the divided hoof or foot of animals such as cattle, sheep, goats, and deer.

clover noun a plant with round white or deep pink flower heads and leaves with three rounded parts.
– PHRASES **be** (or **live**) **in clover** be living a comfortable life with plenty of money.
– ORIGIN Old English.

clown noun 1 a comic entertainer, especially one in a circus, wearing a traditional costume and exaggerated make-up. 2 a playful and amusing person. •verb behave in a silly or playful way.
– DERIVATIVES **clownish** adjective.
– ORIGIN perhaps German.

cloying adjective so sweet or sentimental as to be unpleasant.
– DERIVATIVES **cloyingly** adverb.
– ORIGIN from Old French *encloyer* 'drive a nail into'.

club¹ noun 1 an association of people who meet regularly to take part in a particular activity. 2 an organization where members can meet, eat meals, and stay overnight. 3 a nightclub with dance music. •verb (**clubs, clubbing, clubbed**) 1 (**club together**) combine with others to do something, especially to collect a sum of money. 2 informal go out to nightclubs.
– DERIVATIVES **clubber** noun.
– ORIGIN from CLUB².

club² noun 1 a heavy stick with a thick end, used as a weapon. 2 (also **golf club**) a club used to hit the ball in golf, with a heavy wooden or metal head on a slender shaft. 3 (**clubs**) one of the four suits in a conventional pack of playing cards, represented by a design of three black leaves on a short stem. •verb (**clubs, clubbing, clubbed**) beat someone or something with a club or similar object.
– ORIGIN Old Norse.

clubbable adjective sociable and popular.
– DERIVATIVES **clubbability** noun.

club class noun Brit. the class of seating on an aircraft designed especially for business travellers.

club foot noun a deformed foot which is twisted so that the sole cannot be placed flat on the ground.

clubhouse noun a building having a bar and other facilities for the members of a club.

clubmoss noun a low-growing flowerless plant.

clubroot noun a disease of cabbages, turnips, etc. in which the root becomes swollen and distorted.

club sandwich noun a sandwich consisting typically of chicken and bacon, tomato, and lettuce, layered between three slices of bread.

cluck verb 1 (of a hen) make a short, low sound. 2 (**cluck over/around**) express fussy concern about someone. •noun the short, low sound made by a hen.
– ORIGIN imitating the sound.

clue noun a fact or piece of evidence that helps to clear up a mystery or solve a problem. •verb (**clues, clueing, clued**) (**clue someone in**) informal inform someone about something.
– PHRASES **not have a clue** informal not know about something, or about how to do something.

– ORIGIN first meaning a ball of thread, as used to guide a person out of a maze.

clued-up (also **clued-in**) adjective informal well informed about a particular subject.

clueless adjective informal having no knowledge, understanding, or ability.
– DERIVATIVES **cluelessness** noun.

clump noun 1 a small group of trees or plants growing closely together. 2 a mass or lump of something. 3 the sound of heavy footsteps.
•verb 1 form into a clump or mass. 2 walk or tread heavily.
– ORIGIN from CLUMP².

clumpy adjective (also **clompy**) Brit. (of shoes or boots) heavy and clumsy-looking.

clumsy adjective (**clumsier, clumsiest**) 1 not smooth or graceful in movement or action. 2 difficult to handle or use. 3 tactless.
– DERIVATIVES **clumsily** adverb **clumsiness** noun.
– ORIGIN probably Scandinavian.

clung past and past participle of CLING.

clunk noun a dull, heavy sound like that made by thick pieces of metal striking together.
•verb move with or make a clunk.
– ORIGIN imitating the sound.

clunky adjective (**clunkier, clunkiest**) informal 1 solid, heavy, and old-fashioned. 2 (of shoes) clumpy.

cluster noun a group of similar things positioned or occurring closely together. •verb form a cluster.
– ORIGIN Old English.

cluster bomb noun a bomb which releases a number of smaller bombs when it explodes.

clutch¹ verb grasp something tightly. •noun 1 a tight grasp. 2 (**clutches**) power or control: *he had fallen into her clutches.* 3 a mechanism for connecting and disconnecting the engine and the transmission system in a vehicle.
– ORIGIN Old English.

clutch² noun 1 a group of eggs fertilized at the same time and laid in a single session. 2 a brood of chicks. 3 a small group of people or things.
– ORIGIN Old Norse.

clutch bag noun a slim, flat handbag without handles or a strap.

clutter verb cover or fill something with an untidy collection of things. •noun 1 things lying about untidily. 2 an untidy state.
– ORIGIN variant of dialect *clotter* 'to clot'.

Cm symbol the chemical element curium.

cm abbreviation centimetre or centimetres.

CMG abbreviation (in the UK) Companion of St Michael and St George (or Companion of the Order of St Michael and St George).

CND abbreviation Campaign for Nuclear Disarmament.

CNN abbreviation Cable News Network.

CO abbreviation 1 Colorado. 2 Commanding Officer.

Co symbol the chemical element cobalt.

Co. abbreviation 1 company. 2 county.

c/o abbreviation care of.

co- prefix 1 (forming nouns) joint; mutual; common: *co-driver.* 2 (forming adjectives) jointly; mutually: *coequal.* 3 (forming verbs) together with another or others: *co-produce.*
– ORIGIN Latin.

coach[1] noun 1 Brit. a single-decker bus with comfortable seats, used for longer journeys. 2 a railway carriage. 3 a closed horse-drawn carriage.
– ORIGIN French *coche*, from *Kocs*, a town in Hungary where horse-drawn carriages were made.

coach[2] noun 1 an instructor or trainer in sport. 2 a tutor who gives private or specialized teaching. •verb train or teach someone as a coach.
– ORIGIN from **COACH**[1].

coach-built adjective Brit. (of a vehicle) having bodywork that has been specially made.
– DERIVATIVES **coachbuilder** noun.

coaching inn noun historical an inn along a route followed by horse-drawn coaches, at which horses could be changed.

coachman noun (pl. **coachmen**) a driver of a horse-drawn carriage.

coachwork noun the bodywork of a road or railway vehicle.

coagulant /koh-**ag**-yoo-luhnt/ noun a substance that causes a fluid to coagulate.

coagulate /koh-**ag**-yoo-layt/ verb (of a fluid, especially blood) change to a solid or semi-solid state.
– DERIVATIVES **coagulation** noun.
– ORIGIN Latin *coagulare* 'curdle'.

coal noun 1 a black rock consisting mainly of carbon formed from the remains of ancient trees and other vegetation and used as fuel. 2 Brit. a piece of coal.
– ORIGIN Old English.

coalesce /koh-uh-**less**/ verb come or bring together to form one mass or whole.
– DERIVATIVES **coalescence** noun.
– ORIGIN Latin *coalescere*.

coalface noun an exposed area of coal in a mine.

coalfield noun a large area rich in underground coal.

coal gas noun a mixture of gases obtained by distilling coal, formerly used for lighting and heating.

coalition /koh-uh-**li**-sh'n/ noun a temporary alliance, especially of political parties forming a government.
– DERIVATIVES **coalitionist** noun.
– ORIGIN Latin, from *coalescere* 'coalesce'.

coal tar noun a thick black liquid distilled from coal, containing various organic chemicals.

coal tit (also **cole tit**) noun a small songbird with a grey back, black cap and throat, and white cheeks.

coaming /koh-ming/ (also **coamings**) noun a raised border round the cockpit or hatch of a boat to keep out water.
– ORIGIN unknown.

coarse adjective 1 rough or harsh in texture. 2 consisting of large grains or particles. 3 rude or vulgar in behaviour or speech.
– DERIVATIVES **coarsely** adverb **coarseness** noun.
– ORIGIN perhaps related to **COURSE**.

coarse fish noun (pl. same) Brit. any freshwater fish other than salmon and trout.

coarsen verb make or become coarse.

coast noun land next to or near the sea. •verb 1 move easily without using power. 2 achieve something without making much effort: *United coasted to victory*.
– PHRASES **the coast is clear** there is no danger of being seen or caught.
– DERIVATIVES **coastal** adjective.
– ORIGIN Latin *costa* 'rib, flank, side'.

coaster noun 1 a small mat for a glass. 2 a ship carrying cargo along the coast from port to port.

coastguard noun an organization or person that keeps watch over coastal waters to help people or ships in danger and to prevent smuggling.

coastline noun a stretch of coast: *a rugged coastline*.

coat noun 1 a full-length outer garment with sleeves. 2 an animal's covering of fur or hair. 3 an enclosing or covering layer or structure. 4 a single application of paint or similar substance. •verb provide with or form a layer or covering: *vanilla ice cream coated with chocolate*.
– ORIGIN Old French *cote*.

coati /koh-**ah**-ti/ noun (pl. **coatis**) a raccoon-like animal found in Central and South America, with a long flexible snout and tail with circular stripes.
– ORIGIN Spanish and Portuguese.

coatimundi /koh-**ah**-ti-mun-di/ noun (pl. **coatimundis**) another term for **COATI**.
– ORIGIN Portuguese.

coating noun a thin layer or covering of something.

coat of arms noun the distinctive heraldic design or shield of a person, family, corporation, or country.

coat of mail noun historical a jacket made of metal rings or plates, used as armour.

coat-tail noun each of the flaps formed by the back of a tailcoat.
– PHRASES **on someone's coat-tails** benefiting from someone else's success.

coax /kohks/ verb 1 gradually or gently persuade someone to do something. 2 manipulate something carefully into a particular situation or position.
– ORIGIN from the old word *cokes*, 'simpleton'.

coaxial /koh-**ak**-si-uhl/ adjective 1 having a common axis. 2 (of a cable or line) transmitting by means of two concentric conductors separated by an insulator.

cob noun 1 Brit. a loaf of bread. 2 a corncob. 3 (also **cobnut**) a hazelnut or filbert. 4 a powerfully built, short-legged horse. 5 a male swan.
– ORIGIN unknown.

cobalt /koh-bolt/ noun a hard silvery-white metallic chemical element, used in alloys.
– ORIGIN German *Kobalt* 'goblin, demon' (from the belief that cobalt had been placed in silver mines by goblins to cause the miners problems).

cobalt blue noun a deep blue pigment containing cobalt and aluminium oxides.

cobber noun Austral./NZ informal a companion or friend.
– ORIGIN perhaps related to English dialect *cob* 'take a liking to'.

cobble[1] noun (also **cobblestone**) a small round

c

stone used to cover road surfaces.
– DERIVATIVES **cobbled** adjective.
– ORIGIN from **COB**.

cobble² verb (**cobble something together**)
produce something quickly and without great
care: *the film was cobbled together from two
separate stories.*
– ORIGIN from **COBBLER**.

cobbler noun **1** a person whose job is mending
shoes. **2** chiefly N. Amer. a fruit pie with a rich
crust. **3** (**cobblers**) Brit. informal nonsense. [first
in the sense 'testicles': from rhyming slang
cobbler's awls 'balls'.]
– ORIGIN unknown.

cobra /koh-bruh/ noun a highly poisonous
snake that spreads the skin of its neck into a
hood when disturbed, native to Africa and
Asia.
– ORIGIN from Portuguese *cobra de capello*
'snake with hood'.

cobweb noun a spider's web, especially an old
or dusty one.
– DERIVATIVES **cobwebbed** adjective **cobwebby**
adjective.
– ORIGIN from Old English *coppe* 'spider'.

coca /koh-kuh/ noun a tropical American shrub
grown for its leaves, which are the source of
cocaine.
– ORIGIN Spanish.

Coca-Cola noun trademark a fizzy non-alcoholic
drink.

cocaine /koh-kayn/ noun an addictive drug
obtained from coca or prepared synthetically,
used as an illegal stimulant and sometimes in
medicine as a local anaesthetic.
– ORIGIN from **COCA**.

coccus /kok-kuhss/ noun (pl. **cocci** /kok-ky/)
Biology any rounded bacterium.
– ORIGIN Greek *kokkos* 'berry'.

coccyx /kok-siks/ noun (pl. **coccyges** /kok-
si-jeez/ or **coccyxes**) a small triangular bone at
the base of the spinal column in humans and
some apes.
– DERIVATIVES **coccygeal** /kok-**sij**-i-uhl/ adjective.
– ORIGIN Greek *kokkux* 'cuckoo' (because the
shape of the human bone resembles a cuckoo's
bill).

cochineal /koch-i-neel/ noun a scarlet dye used
for colouring food, made from the crushed
dried bodies of a kind of insect.
– ORIGIN French *cochenille* or Spanish
cochinilla.

cochlea /kok-li-uh/ noun (pl. **cochleae** /kok-
li-ee/) the spiral cavity of the inner ear,
containing an organ which produces nerve
impulses in response to sound vibrations.
– DERIVATIVES **cochlear** adjective.
– ORIGIN Latin, 'snail shell or screw'.

cock noun **1** a male bird, especially of a domestic
fowl. **2** vulgar slang a man's penis. **3** Brit. informal
nonsense. **4** a firing lever in a gun which can
be raised to be released by the trigger. • verb
1 tilt or bend something in a particular
direction. **2** raise the cock of a gun to make it
ready for firing. **3** (**cock something up**) Brit.
informal spoil or ruin something.
– PHRASES **cock one's ear** (of a dog) raise its
ears to an erect position.
– ORIGIN Latin *coccus*.

cockade /kok-ayd/ noun a rosette or knot of

ribbons worn in a hat as a badge of office or as
part of a livery.
– DERIVATIVES **cockaded** adjective.
– ORIGIN French *cocarde*.

cock-a-hoop adjective extremely pleased.
– ORIGIN from the phrase *set cock a hoop*,
apparently referring to the action of turning
on the tap of a cask and allowing alcohol to
flow.

cock-a-leekie noun a soup traditionally made
in Scotland with chicken and leeks.

cock and bull story noun informal an
unbelievable story, especially one used as an
excuse.

cockatiel /kok-uh-teel/ noun a small crested
Australian parrot with a mainly grey body and
a yellow and orange face.
– ORIGIN Dutch *kaketielje*.

cockatoo /kok-uh-too/ noun a crested parrot
found in Australia and Indonesia.
– ORIGIN Dutch *kaketoe*.

cockatrice /kok-uh-tryss, kok-uh-triss/ noun
1 another term for **BASILISK** (in sense 1).
2 Heraldry a mythical animal represented as a
two-legged dragon with a cock's head.
– ORIGIN Old French *cocatris*.

cockchafer /kok-chay-fuhr/ noun a large
brown flying beetle.
– ORIGIN from **COCK** + **CHAFER**.

cockcrow noun literary dawn.

cocked hat noun a triangular hat with no brim,
pointed at the front, back, and top.
– PHRASES **knock someone/thing into a cocked
hat** completely defeat or outdo someone or
something.

cockerel noun a young domestic cock.

cocker spaniel noun a small breed of spaniel
with a silky coat.
– ORIGIN from **COCK**, because the dog was bred
to flush game birds such as woodcock.

cockeyed adjective informal **1** crooked or askew;
not level. **2** absurd; impractical. **3** having a
squint.

cockfighting noun the sport (illegal in the UK
and some other countries) of setting two
cocks to fight each other.
– DERIVATIVES **cockfight** noun.

cockle noun **1** an edible shellfish with a strong
ribbed shell. **2** (also **cockleshell**) literary a small,
shallow boat.
– PHRASES **warm the cockles of one's heart** give
one a feeling of contentment.
– ORIGIN Old French *coquille* 'shell'.

cockney /kok-ni/ noun (pl. **cockneys**) **1** a person
from the East End of London, traditionally
one born within the sound of Bow Bells. **2** the
dialect or accent used in this area.
– ORIGIN uncertain.

cockpit noun **1** a compartment for the pilot and
crew in an aircraft or spacecraft. **2** the driver's
compartment in a racing car. **3** a place where
cockfights are held.
– ORIGIN from **COCK** + **PIT¹**.

cockroach noun a beetle-like insect with long
antennae and legs, some kinds of which are
household pests.
– ORIGIN Spanish *cucaracha*.

cockscomb noun the crest or comb of a
domestic cock.

cocksure adjective arrogantly confident.
– ORIGIN from former *cock* (a euphemism for *God*) + **SURE**.

cocktail noun **1** an alcoholic drink consisting of a spirit mixed with other ingredients, such as fruit juice. **2** a dish consisting of a mixture of small pieces of food: *a prawn cocktail*. **3** a mixture of different substances or factors, especially when dangerous or unpleasant: *a cocktail of drugs*.
– ORIGIN first meaning a horse with a docked tail.

cock-up noun Brit. informal something done badly or inefficiently.

cocky adjective (**cockier, cockiest**) conceited in a bold or cheeky way.
– DERIVATIVES **cockily** adverb **cockiness** noun.
– ORIGIN from **COCK**.

cocoa noun **1** a powder made from roasted and ground cacao seeds. **2** a hot drink made from cocoa powder mixed with milk or water.
– ORIGIN alteration of **CACAO**.

cocoa bean noun a cacao seed.

cocoa butter noun a fatty substance obtained from cocoa beans, used in confectionery and cosmetics.

coconut noun **1** the large brown seed of a tropical palm, consisting of a hard woody husk surrounded by fibre, lined with edible white flesh and containing a clear liquid (**coconut milk**). **2** the edible white flesh of a coconut.
– ORIGIN from Spanish and Portuguese *coco* 'grinning face'.

coconut ice noun Brit. a sweet made from sugar and desiccated coconut.

coconut shy noun Brit. a fairground sideshow where balls are thrown at coconuts in an attempt to knock them off stands.

cocoon /kuh-koon/ noun **1** a protective silky case spun by the larvae of many insects, in which the pupa develops. **2** a covering that prevents the corrosion of metal equipment. **3** something that envelops someone in a protective or comforting way: *a cocoon of bedclothes*. • verb envelop in a protective or comforting way: *we were cocooned in our sleeping bags*.
– ORIGIN French *cocon*.

cocotte /ko-kot/ noun (usu. in phrase **en cocotte**) a small dish in which individual portions of food can be cooked and served.
– ORIGIN French.

COD abbreviation cash on delivery.

cod[1] (also **codfish**) noun (pl. same) a large sea fish which is important as a food fish.
– ORIGIN perhaps from Old English *codd* 'bag'.

cod[2] adjective Brit. informal not authentic; fake: *a cod Irish accent*.
– ORIGIN uncertain.

coda /koh-duh/ noun **1** Music the concluding passage of a piece or movement. **2** a concluding event, remark, or section.
– ORIGIN Italian, from Latin *cauda* 'tail'.

coddle verb **1** treat someone in an indulgent or overprotective way. **2** cook an egg in water below boiling point.
– ORIGIN uncertain.

code noun **1** a system of words, figures, or symbols used to represent others, especially for the purposes of secrecy. **2** a series of numbers or letters used to classify or identify something. **3** (also **dialling code**) a sequence of numbers dialled to connect a telephone line with another exchange. **4** Computing program instructions. **5** a set of moral principles or rules of behaviour: *a strict code of conduct*. **6** a systematic collection of laws or statutes: *the penal code*. • verb **1** convert the words of a message into a code. **2** (usu. as adj. **coded**) express the meaning of something in an indirect way: *his coded criticism of the prime minister*.
– DERIVATIVES **coder** noun.
– ORIGIN Latin *codex* 'block of wood'.

codeine /koh-deen/ noun a painkilling drug obtained from morphine.
– ORIGIN Greek *kōdeia* 'poppy head'.

codependency noun the state of being too emotionally or psychologically dependent on a partner, especially one who has an illness or addiction and needs care or support.
– DERIVATIVES **codependence** noun **codependent** adjective & noun.

codex /koh-deks/ noun (pl. **codices** /koh-di-seez/ or **codexes**) **1** an ancient manuscript in book form. **2** an official list of medicines, chemicals, etc.
– ORIGIN Latin, 'block of wood'.

codfish noun (pl. same or **codfishes**) another term for **COD**[1].

codger noun informal, derogatory an elderly man.
– ORIGIN perhaps from **CADGE**.

codicil /koh-di-sil/ noun an addition or supplement that explains, changes, or cancels a will or part of one.
– ORIGIN from *codex* 'block of wood'.

codify /koh-di-fy/ verb (**codifies, codifying, codified**) organize procedures or rules into a system.
– DERIVATIVES **codification** noun.

codling[1] noun a young cod.

codling[2] noun any of several varieties of cooking apple.
– ORIGIN uncertain.

codling moth noun a small greyish moth whose larvae feed on apples.

cod liver oil noun oil obtained from the fresh liver of cod, which is rich in vitamins D and A.

codpiece noun (in the 15th and 16th centuries) a pouch covering the genitals, attached to a pair of man's breeches.
– ORIGIN from former *cod* 'scrotum'.

codswallop noun Brit. informal nonsense.
– ORIGIN uncertain.

co-education noun the education of pupils of both sexes together.
– DERIVATIVES **co-educational** adjective.

coefficient /koh-i-fi-sh'nt/ noun Mathematics a quantity placed before and multiplying the variable in an algebraic expression (e.g. 4 in $4x^2$). **2** Physics a multiplier or factor that measures a particular property.

coelacanth /seel-uh-kanth/ noun a large bony sea fish with a tail fin in three rounded parts, known only from fossils until one was found alive in 1938.
– ORIGIN from Greek *koilos* 'hollow' + *akantha* 'spine' (because its fins have hollow spines).

coelenterate /see-**len**-tuh-ruht/ noun Zoology a member of a large group of invertebrate sea animals which usually have a tube- or cup-shaped body that has a single opening fringed with tentacles, such as jellyfish, corals, and sea anemones.
– ORIGIN from Greek *koilos* 'hollow' + *enteron* 'intestine'.

coeliac disease /seel-i-ak/ (US **celiac disease**) noun a condition in which the small intestine fails to digest and absorb food, caused by excessive sensitivity to gluten.
– ORIGIN from Greek *koilia* 'belly'.

coenobite noun chiefly Brit. variant spelling of CENOBITE.

coenzyme noun Biochemistry a compound that is essential for the functioning of an enzyme.

coequal adjective (of two or more people or things) having the same rank or importance. • noun a person or thing equal with another.

coerce /koh-**erss**/ verb persuade an unwilling person to do something by using force or threats.
– DERIVATIVES **coercion** noun **coercive** adjective.
– ORIGIN Latin *coercere* 'restrain'.

coeval /koh-ee-vuhl/ adjective having the same age or date of origin; contemporary. • noun a person of roughly the same age as oneself; a contemporary.
– ORIGIN Latin *coaevus*.

coexist verb **1** exist at the same time or in the same place. **2** exist together in a peaceful or harmonious way.
– DERIVATIVES **coexistence** noun **coexistent** adjective.

coextensive adjective formal extending over the same area, extent, or time: *we are not separate from but coextensive with nature.*

C. of E. abbreviation Church of England.

coffee noun **1** a hot drink made from the roasted and ground bean-like seeds of a tropical shrub. **2** the seeds used to make this drink.
– ORIGIN Arabic.

coffee table noun a small, low table.

coffee-table book noun a large book with many pictures or photographs.

coffer noun **1** a small chest for holding valuables. **2** (**coffers**) used to refer to the money that a government or organization has available to spend: *the company's coffers have run dry.* **3** a decorative sunken panel in a ceiling.
– ORIGIN Old French *coffre*.

cofferdam noun a watertight enclosure pumped dry to allow construction work below the waterline, e.g. when building bridges or repairing a ship.

coffered ceiling noun a ceiling decorated with sunken panels.

coffin noun a long, narrow box in which a dead body is buried or cremated.
– ORIGIN Old French *cofin* 'little basket'.

coffret /kof-rit/ noun a small container.
– ORIGIN Old French.

cog noun **1** a wheel or bar with a series of projections on its edge, which transfers motion by engaging with projections on another wheel or bar. **2** any one of these projections.
– ORIGIN probably Scandinavian.

cogent /koh-juhnt/ adjective (of an argument or case) clear, logical, and convincing.
– DERIVATIVES **cogency** noun **cogently** adverb.
– ORIGIN Latin *cogere* 'compel'.

cogitate /koj-i-tayt/ verb formal think deeply.
– DERIVATIVES **cogitation** noun.
– ORIGIN Latin *cogitare* 'to consider'.

cognac /kon-yak/ noun a high-quality brandy made in Cognac in western France.

cognate /kog-nayt/ adjective **1** (of a word) having the same original form as another in a different language (e.g. English *father*, German *Vater*, and Latin *pater*). **2** formal related; connected. • noun a word that has the same original form as another in a different language.
– ORIGIN Latin *cognatus* 'born together'.

cognition /kog-ni-sh'n/ noun the process of obtaining knowledge through thought, experience, and the senses.
– ORIGIN from Latin *cognoscere* 'get to know'.

cognitive /kog-ni-tiv/ adjective relating to the process of obtaining knowledge through thought, experience, and the senses.
– DERIVATIVES **cognitively** adverb.

cognitive therapy noun a type of psychotherapy based on the belief that psychological problems are caused by negative ways of thinking, which can be avoided or changed.

cognizance /kog-ni-zuhnss/ (or **cognisance**) noun formal knowledge or awareness.
– DERIVATIVES **cognizant** adjective.
– ORIGIN from Latin *cognoscere* 'get to know'.

cognomen /kog-noh-muhn/ noun **1** a name or nickname. **2** (in ancient Rome) an extra name given to a citizen, functioning rather like a nickname and often passed down from father to son.
– ORIGIN Latin.

cognoscenti /kog-nuh-**shen**-ti/ plural noun people who are well informed about a particular subject.
– ORIGIN Italian, 'people who know'.

cogwheel noun another term for COG (in sense 1)

cohabit verb (**cohabits, cohabiting, cohabited**) **1** live together and have a sexual relationship without being married. **2** coexist.
– DERIVATIVES **cohabitation** noun **cohabitee** noun.
– ORIGIN Latin *cohabitare*.

cohere /koh-**heer**/ verb form a unified whole; be logically consistent.
– ORIGIN Latin *cohaerere*.

coherent adjective **1** (of an argument or theory) logical and consistent. **2** able to speak clearly and logically.
– DERIVATIVES **coherence** noun **coherently** adverb.

cohesion /koh-hee-zh'n/ noun the action or fact of holding together or forming a unified whole.

cohesive adjective **1** forming a unified whole: *a cohesive group.* **2** causing people or things to form a unified whole: *a cohesive force.*
– DERIVATIVES **cohesiveness** noun.

cohort /koh-hort/ noun **1** an ancient Roman military unit equal to one tenth of a legion. **2** a

group of people with a shared characteristic: *a cohort of students*. **3** a supporter or companion.
– ORIGIN Latin *cohors* 'yard, retinue'.

cohosh /kuh-**hosh**/ noun a North American plant with medicinal properties.
– ORIGIN from Abnaki.

co-host noun a person who hosts an event or broadcast with another or others. • verb be the co-host of an event or broadcast.

coif /koyf/ noun a close-fitting cap worn by nuns under a veil. • verb /kwahf, kwof/ (**coifs, coiffing, coiffed**; US also **coifs, coifing, coifed**) style or arrange someone's hair.
– ORIGIN Old French *coife* 'headdress'.

coiffeur /kwah-**fer**, kwo-**fer**/ noun (fem. **coiffeuse** /kwah-**ferz**, kwo-**ferz**/) a hairdresser.
– ORIGIN French, from *coiffer* 'arrange the hair'.

coiffure /kwah-**fyoor**/ noun a person's hairstyle.
– DERIVATIVES **coiffured** adjective.

coign /koyn/ noun a projecting corner or angle of a wall.
– ORIGIN variant of **COIN**.

coil noun **1** a length of something wound in a joined sequence of loops. **2** a contraceptive device in the form of a coil, placed inside the womb. **3** an electrical device consisting of a coiled wire, for converting the level of a voltage, producing a magnetic field, or adding inductance to a circuit. • verb arrange or form into a coil.
– ORIGIN Old French *coillir*.

coin noun a flat disc or piece of metal with an official stamp, used as money. • verb **1** invent a new word or phrase. **2** make coins by stamping metal. **3** (usu. **coin it in**) Brit. informal earn large amounts of money quickly and easily.
– ORIGIN Old French, 'wedge, corner'.

coinage noun **1** coins as a whole. **2** the process of producing coins. **3** a system or type of coins in use. **4** a newly invented word or phrase.

coincide /koh-in-**syd**/ verb **1** happen at the same time or place. **2** be the same or similar.
– ORIGIN Latin *coincidere*.

coincidence /koh-**in**-si-duhnss/ noun **1** a remarkable occurrence of events or circumstances at the same time but without apparent connection. **2** the fact of two or more things happening at the same time or being the same.

coincident adjective **1** happening at the same time or in the same place. **2** in agreement or harmony.

coincidental /koh-in-si-**den**-t'l/ adjective resulting from a coincidence; not planned or intentional.
– DERIVATIVES **coincidentally** adverb

Cointreau /**kwun**trō/ noun trademark a colourless orange-flavoured liqueur.
– ORIGIN French.

coir /koy-uh/ noun fibre from the outer husk of the coconut, used in potting compost and for making ropes and matting.
– ORIGIN from a Dravidian word.

coitus /**koy**-tuhss/ noun technical sexual intercourse.
– DERIVATIVES **coital** adjective.
– ORIGIN Latin, from *coire* 'go together'.

coitus interruptus /koy-tuhss in-ter-**rup**-

tuhss/ noun sexual intercourse in which the man withdraws his penis before ejaculation.

Coke noun trademark short for **COCA-COLA**.

coke[1] noun **1** a solid fuel made by heating coal in the absence of air. **2** carbon residue left after the incomplete combustion of petrol or other fuels.
– ORIGIN unknown.

coke[2] noun informal cocaine.

Col. abbreviation Colonel.

col noun the lowest point between two peaks of a mountain ridge.
– ORIGIN French, 'neck'.

cola noun **1** a brown fizzy drink flavoured with an extract of cola nuts, or with a similar flavouring. **2** (also **kola**) a small tropical evergreen tree whose seed (the **cola nut**) contains caffeine.
– ORIGIN Temne (an African language).

colander /**kol**-uhn-der/ noun a bowl with holes in it, used for draining food.
– ORIGIN Latin *colare* 'to strain'.

colcannon /kol-**kan**-uhn/ noun an Irish and Scottish dish of cabbage and potatoes boiled and mashed together.
– ORIGIN from **COLE** + perhaps **CANNON** (it is said that cannonballs were once used to pound vegetables such as spinach).

cold adjective **1** of or at a low or relatively low temperature. **2** not feeling or showing emotion or affection. **3** not influenced by personal feeling or emotion: objective: *the cold facts*. **4** (of a colour) containing pale blue or grey and giving no impression of warmth. **5** (of a scent or trail) no longer fresh and easy to follow. **6** without preparation or rehearsal; unawares: *they went into the test cold*. **7** informal unconscious: *she was out cold*. • noun **1** cold weather or surroundings. **2** an infection in which the mucous membrane of the nose and throat becomes inflamed, causing sneezing and a runny nose.
– PHRASES **cold comfort** little or no consolation under the circumstances. **get cold feet** lose one's nerve. **the cold shoulder** deliberate unfriendliness or rejection. **in cold blood** without pity; in a deliberately cruel way.
– DERIVATIVES **coldly** adverb **coldness** noun.
– ORIGIN Old English.

cold-blooded adjective **1** (of animals, e.g. reptiles and fish) having a body whose temperature varies with that of the environment. **2** without emotion or pity.
– DERIVATIVES **cold-bloodedly** adverb.

cold-call verb visit or telephone someone without being asked to do so in an attempt to sell them goods or services.

cold chisel noun a toughened chisel used for cutting metal.

cold cream noun a cream for cleansing and softening the skin.

cold cuts plural noun chiefly N. Amer. slices of cold cooked meats.

cold frame noun a frame with a glass top in which small plants are grown and protected.

cold fusion noun nuclear fusion supposedly occurring at or close to room temperature.

cold-hearted adjective lacking affection or warmth; unfeeling.

cold snap noun a brief spell of cold weather.

cold sore noun an inflamed blister in or near the mouth, caused by a virus.

cold storage noun preservation of something in a refrigerated room.
– PHRASES **in/into cold storage** so as to be postponed temporarily.

cold sweat noun a state of sweating caused by nervousness or illness.

cold turkey noun informal the abrupt withdrawal from a drug to which one is addicted, often accompanied by sweating and nausea.

cold war noun a state of hostility between the countries allied to the former Soviet Union and the Western powers after the Second World War.

cole noun N. Amer. or old use cabbage, kale, or a similar plant.
– ORIGIN Latin *caulis* 'stem, cabbage'.

coleslaw noun a salad dish of shredded raw cabbage and carrots mixed with mayonnaise.
– ORIGIN Dutch *koolsla*.

coleus /**koh**-li-uhss/ noun a tropical plant with brightly coloured variegated leaves.
– ORIGIN Greek *koleos* 'sheath'.

coley /**koh**-li/ noun (pl. same or **coleys**) another term for SAITHE.
– ORIGIN perhaps from *coalfish*, an alternative name for the coley.

colic noun severe pain in the abdomen caused by wind or obstruction in the intestines.
– DERIVATIVES **colicky** adjective.
– ORIGIN Latin *colicus*.

coliseum /ko-li-see-uhm/ (also **colosseum**) noun (in names) a large theatre, cinema, or stadium.
– ORIGIN from the *Colosseum*, a huge amphitheatre in ancient Rome.

colitis /kuh-**ly**-tis/ noun inflammation of the lining of the colon.

collaborate verb 1 work jointly on an activity or project. 2 betray one's country by cooperating with an enemy.
– DERIVATIVES **collaboration** noun **collaborationist** noun & adjective **collaborative** adjective **collaborator** noun.
– ORIGIN Latin *collaborare*.

collage /**kol**-lah*zh*/ noun 1 a form of art in which various materials are arranged and stuck to a backing. 2 a combination of various things: *the collage of cultures within our nation.*
– ORIGIN French, 'gluing'.

collagen /**kol**-luh-juhn/ noun any of a group of proteins that form the main structural component of animal connective tissue.
– ORIGIN from Greek *kolla* 'glue'.

collapse verb 1 suddenly fall down or give way. 2 (of a person) fall down as a result of illness or fatigue. 3 fail suddenly and completely: *when he died the family business collapsed.* • noun 1 an instance of a structure collapsing. 2 a sudden failure or breakdown.
– ORIGIN Latin *collabi*.

collapsible adjective able to be folded into a small space.

collar noun 1 the part around the neck of a garment, either upright or turned over. 2 a band put around the neck of a dog or other domestic animal. 3 a connecting band or pipe in a piece of machinery. 4 Brit. a cut of bacon taken from the neck of a pig. • verb informal stop or arrest someone.
– DERIVATIVES **collarless** adjective.
– ORIGIN Latin *collare* 'band for the neck'.

collarbone noun either of the pair of bones joining the breastbone to the shoulder blades; the clavicle.

collate /kuh-**layt**/ verb 1 collect and combine documents or information. 2 compare and analyse two or more sources of information.
– DERIVATIVES **collator** noun.
– ORIGIN Latin *collatus* 'brought together'.

collateral /kuh-**lat**-uh-ruhl/ noun something that is promised to someone if one is not able to repay a loan. • adjective 1 additional but less important. 2 situated side by side; parallel.
– DERIVATIVES **collaterally** adverb.
– ORIGIN Latin *collateralis*.

collateral damage noun unintentional casualties and destruction in civilian areas caused by military operations.

collation noun 1 the action of collating something. 2 formal a light informal meal.

colleague noun a person with whom one works.
– ORIGIN Latin *collega* 'partner in office'.

collect[1] /kuh-**lekt**/ verb 1 bring or come together: *a crowd collected at the door.* 2 find or buy items of a particular kind as a hobby. 3 call for and take away someone or something. 4 ask for money or receive a prize or award. 5 (**collect oneself**) regain control of oneself. • adverb & adjective N. Amer. (of a telephone call) to be paid for by the person receiving it.
– ORIGIN Latin *colligere*.

collect[2] /**kol**-lekt/ noun (in the Christian Church) a short prayer used on a particular day or during a particular period.
– ORIGIN Latin *collecta* 'a gathering'.

collectable (also **collectible**) adjective 1 worth collecting; of interest to a collector. 2 able to be collected. • noun (usu. **collectibles**) an item valued by collectors.
– DERIVATIVES **collectability** noun.

collected adjective 1 calm and self-controlled. 2 (of works) brought together in one volume or edition.

collection noun 1 the action of collecting. 2 a number of things that have been collected. 3 a new range of clothes produced by a designer. 4 a regular removal of mail or rubbish.

collective adjective 1 done by or involving all the members of a group. 2 taken as a whole: *the collective power of the workforce.* • noun a business or farm owned or run as a cooperative venture.
– DERIVATIVES **collectively** adverb **collectivity** noun.

collective bargaining noun negotiation of wages and other conditions of employment by an organized body of employees.

collective farm noun a farm or group of farms owned by the state and run by a group of people.

collective noun noun a noun that refers to a group of individuals (e.g. *assembly, family*).

USAGE: A **collective noun** can be used with either a singular verb (*my family was always hard-working*) or a plural verb (*his family were disappointed in him*). It is important to remember that, if the verb is singular, any following pronouns (words such as 'he', 'she', or 'they') must be too: *the government is prepared to act, but not until it knows the outcome of the talks* (not *... until they know the outcome...*).

collectivism noun the ownership of land, business, and industry by the people or the state.
– DERIVATIVES **collectivist** adjective & noun **collectivize** (or **collectivise**) verb.

collector noun 1 a person who collects things of a specified type. 2 an official who is responsible for collecting money owed.

colleen /kol-leen/ noun Irish a girl or young woman.
– ORIGIN Irish *cailín* 'country girl'.

college noun 1 an educational establishment providing higher education or specialized training. 2 (in Britain) any of the independent institutions into which some universities are separated. 3 an organized group of professional people: *the Royal College of Physicians*.
– ORIGIN Latin *collegium* 'partnership'.

College of Arms noun (in the UK) a corporation which officially records and grants heraldic coats of arms.

collegial /kuh-lee-ji-uhl/ adjective 1 relating to a college or its students; collegiate. 2 involving shared responsibility.

collegian /kuh-lee-ji-uhn/ noun a member of a college.

collegiate /kuh-lee-ji-uht/ adjective 1 relating to a college or its students. 2 (of a university) composed of different colleges.

collide verb 1 hit by accident when moving. 2 come into conflict: *the culture of the two companies collided*.
– ORIGIN Latin *collidere*.

collie noun (pl. **collies**) a breed of sheepdog with a long, pointed nose and long hair.
– ORIGIN perhaps from COAL (the breed originally being black).

collier /kol-li-er/ noun chiefly Brit. 1 a coal miner. 2 a ship carrying coal.

colliery noun (pl. **collieries**) a coal mine.

collinear /kol-lin-i-er/ adjective Geometry (of points) lying in the same straight line.

collision noun 1 an instance of a person or object colliding with another. 2 a conflict of ideas, qualities, or groups: *a calculated collision of science and humanity*.

collocate verb /koll-uh-kayt/ (of a word) frequently occur with another: *'maiden' collocates with 'voyage'*. • noun /koll-uh-kuht/ a word that frequently occurs with another.

collocation noun 1 the frequent occurrence of a word with another word or words. 2 a word or group of words that frequently occur together (e.g. *heavy drinker*).
– ORIGIN from Latin *collocare* 'place together'.

colloid /kol-loyd/ noun a homogeneous substance consisting of submicroscopic particles of one substance dispersed in another, as in an emulsion or gel.
– DERIVATIVES **colloidal** adjective.
– ORIGIN from Greek *kolla* 'glue'.

collop /kol-uhp/ noun dialect & N. Amer. a slice of meat.
– ORIGIN Scandinavian.

colloquial /kuh-loh-kwi-uhl/ adjective (of language) used in ordinary conversation; not formal or literary.
– DERIVATIVES **colloquially** adverb.
– ORIGIN from Latin *colloquium* 'conversation'.

colloquialism noun an informal word or phrase.

colloquium /kuh-loh-kwi-uhm/ noun (pl. **colloquiums** or **colloquia** /kuh-loh-kwi-uh/) an academic conference or seminar.
– ORIGIN Latin.

colloquy /kol-luh-kwi/ noun (pl. **colloquies**) formal a conference or conversation.
– ORIGIN Latin *colloquium*.

collude /kuh-lood/ verb cooperate secretly for a dishonest or underhand purpose: *the president accused his opponents of colluding with foreigners*.
– ORIGIN Latin *colludere* 'have a secret agreement'.

collusion noun secret cooperation in order to deceive others.
– DERIVATIVES **collusive** adjective.

collywobbles plural noun informal, chiefly humorous 1 stomach pain or queasiness. 2 intense anxiety.
– ORIGIN from COLIC and WOBBLE.

colobus /kol-uh-buhss/ noun (pl. same) a slender African monkey with silky fur.
– ORIGIN from Greek *kolobos* 'curtailed' (with reference to its shortened thumbs).

cologne /kuh-lohn/ noun eau de cologne or other scented toilet water.

Colombian noun a person from Colombia. • adjective relating to Colombia.

colon¹ /koh-luhn, koh-lon/ noun a punctuation mark (:) used before a list, a quotation, or an explanation.
– ORIGIN Greek *kōlon* 'limb, clause'.

colon² /koh-luhn, koh-lon/ noun the main part of the large intestine, which passes from the caecum to the rectum.
– DERIVATIVES **colonic** /kuh-lonn-ik/ adjective.
– ORIGIN Greek *kolon* 'food, meat'.

colón /ko-lon/ noun (pl. **colones**) the basic unit of money of Costa Rica and El Salvador.
– ORIGIN from Cristóbal *Colón*, the Spanish name of Christopher Columbus.

colonel /ker-nuhl/ noun a rank of officer in the army and in the US air force, above a lieutenant colonel and below a brigadier or brigadier general.
– DERIVATIVES **colonelcy** noun (pl. **colonelcies**).
– ORIGIN from Italian *colonnello* 'column of soldiers'.

colonial adjective 1 relating to a colony or colonialism. 2 in a neoclassical style characteristic of the period of the British colonies in America before independence. • noun a person who lives in a colony.
– DERIVATIVES **colonially** adverb.

colonialism noun the practice of acquiring

control over another country, occupying it with settlers, and exploiting it economically.
– DERIVATIVES **colonialist** noun & adjective.

colonic irrigation noun a therapeutic treatment in which water is inserted via the anus to flush out the colon.

colonist noun an inhabitant of a colony.

colonize (or **colonise**) verb 1 establish a colony in a place. 2 take over for one's own use: *his work has colonized the space outside his studio.*
– DERIVATIVES **colonization** noun **colonizer** noun.

colonnade /kol-uh-**nayd**/ noun a row of evenly spaced columns supporting a roof or other structure.
– DERIVATIVES **colonnaded** adjective.
– ORIGIN French.

colonoscopy /koh-luh-**nos**-kuh-pi/ noun (pl. **colonoscopies**) examination of the colon with a fibre-optic instrument inserted through the anus.

colony noun (pl. **colonies**) 1 a country or area under the control of another country and occupied by settlers from that country. 2 a group of people of one nationality or race living in a foreign place. 3 a place where a group of people with the same interest live together: *a nudist colony.* 4 a community of animals or plants of one kind living close together.
– ORIGIN Latin *colonia* 'settlement, farm'.

colophon /kol-uh-fuhn/ noun a publisher's emblem or imprint.
– ORIGIN Greek *kolophōn* 'summit or finishing touch'.

color noun & verb US spelling of **COLOUR**.

Colorado beetle noun a yellow- and black-striped American beetle whose larvae are highly destructive to potato plants.
– ORIGIN named after the US state of *Colorado.*

coloration (also **colouration**) noun 1 the natural colouring of something. 2 character or tone: *he gives each performance its own emotional coloration.*

coloratura /kol-uh-ruh-**tyoor**-uh/ noun 1 elaborate ornamentation of a vocal melody, especially in opera. 2 a soprano skilled in coloratura singing.
– ORIGIN Italian, 'colouring'.

colossal adjective extremely large.
– DERIVATIVES **colossally** adverb.
– ORIGIN from Latin *colossus.*

colosseum noun variant spelling of **COLISEUM**.

colossus /kuh-**loss**-uhss/ noun (pl. **colossi** /kuh-**loss**-I/) 1 a person or thing of great size or importance. 2 a statue that is much bigger than life size.
– ORIGIN Greek *kolossos.*

colostomy /kuh-**loss**-tuh-mi/ noun (pl. **colostomies**) a surgical operation in which the colon is shortened and the cut end diverted to an opening in the abdominal wall.
– ORIGIN from **COLON²** + Greek *stoma* 'mouth'.

colostrum /kuh-**loss**-truhm/ noun the first fluid produced by the mammary glands after giving birth.
– ORIGIN Latin.

colour (US **color**) noun 1 the property possessed by an object of producing different sensations on the eye as a result of the way it reflects or emits light. 2 one, or any mixture, of the constituents into which light can be separated: *a rich brown colour.* 3 the use of all colours, not only black and white, in photography or television. 4 the shade of the skin as an indication of someone's race. 5 redness of the complexion. 6 interest, excitement, and vitality: *a town full of colour and character.* 7 (**colours**) an item or items of a particular colour worn for identification in sport. 8 (**colours**) the flag of a regiment or ship. •verb 1 change the colour of something. 2 show embarrassment by becoming red; blush. 3 influence, especially in a negative way: *the experiences had coloured her whole existence.*
– PHRASES **show one's true colours** reveal one's real character or intentions.
– ORIGIN Latin *color.*

colourant (US **colorant**) noun a dye or pigment used to colour something.

colouration noun variant spelling of **COLORATION**.

colour-blind adjective unable to distinguish certain colours.
– DERIVATIVES **colour blindness** noun.

coloured (US **colored**) adjective 1 having a colour or colours. 2 offensive wholly or partly of non-white descent. 3 S. African historical of mixed ethnic origin. •noun 1 offensive a person who is wholly or partly of non-white descent. 2 S. African a person of mixed descent, usually speaking Afrikaans or English as their mother tongue. 3 (**coloureds**) clothes or household linen that are any colour but white.

colour-fast adjective dyed in colours that will not fade or be washed out.

colourful (US **colorful**) adjective 1 having many or varied colours. 2 lively and exciting; vivid.
– DERIVATIVES **colourfully** adverb.

colouring (US **coloring**) noun 1 the process or art of applying colour. 2 the appearance of something with regard to its colour. 3 the natural colours of a person's skin, hair, and eyes. 4 a substance used to colour something, especially food.

colourist (US **colorist**) noun an artist or designer who uses colour in a special or skilful way.

colouristic (US **coloristic**) adjective 1 showing a special use of colour. 2 having a variety of musical expression.

colourless (US **colorless**) adjective 1 without colour. 2 lacking character or interest; dull.

colour scheme noun an arrangement or combination of colours.

colour sergeant noun a rank of non-commissioned officer in the Army and Royal Marines, above sergeant and below warrant officer.

colour supplement noun Brit. a magazine printed in colour and issued with a newspaper.

colourway (US **colorway**) noun any of a range of combinations of colours in which something is available.

colposcopy /kol-**pos**-kuh-pi/ noun surgical examination of the vagina and the neck of the womb.
– ORIGIN from Greek *kolpos* 'womb'.

colt /kohlt/ noun **1** a young uncastrated male horse. **2** Brit. a member of a junior sports team.
– ORIGIN Old English.

colter noun US spelling of COULTER.

coltish adjective lively but awkward in one's movements or behaviour.

coltsfoot noun a plant with yellow flowers and large heart-shaped leaves.

columbine /kol-uhm-byn/ noun a plant with purplish-blue flowers.
– ORIGIN from Latin *columba* 'dove' (from the flower's resemblance to a cluster of doves).

column noun **1** an upright pillar supporting an arch or other structure or standing alone as a monument. **2** a line of people or vehicles moving in the same direction. **3** a vertical division of a page. **4** a regular section of a newspaper or magazine on a particular subject or by a particular person: *a weekly column in a Sunday newspaper.* **5** an upright shaft used for controlling a machine.
– DERIVATIVES **columnar** adjective **columned** adjective.
– ORIGIN Latin *columna* 'pillar'.

columnist /kol-uhm-ist/ noun a journalist who writes a column in a newspaper or magazine.

com- (also **co-, col-, con-,** or **cor-**) prefix with; together; altogether: *combine.*
– ORIGIN from Latin *cum* 'with'.

coma /koh-muh/ noun a state of prolonged deep unconsciousness.
– ORIGIN Greek *kōma* 'deep sleep'.

Comanche /kuh-**man**-chi/ noun (pl. same or **Comanches**) a member of an American Indian people of the south-western US.
– ORIGIN the Comanches' name for themselves.

comatose /koh-muh-tohss/ adjective **1** relating to or in a state of coma. **2** humorous very tired or lethargic.

comb noun **1** an object with a row of narrow teeth, used for untangling or arranging the hair. **2** a device for separating and dressing textile fibres. **3** the red fleshy crest on the head of a domestic fowl, especially a cock. **4** a honeycomb. •verb **1** untangle or arrange the hair with a comb. **2** search carefully and systematically: *I combed the shops for a leather jacket.* **3** prepare wool, flax, or cotton for manufacture with a comb.
– ORIGIN Old English.

combat noun fighting, especially between armed forces. •verb (**combats, combating, combated;** also **combats, combatting, combatted**) take action to reduce or prevent: *equipping people to combat crime.*
– ORIGIN from Latin *combattere* 'fight with'.

combatant /kom-buh-tuhnt/ noun a person or nation taking part in fighting during a war.

combative /kom-buh-tiv/ adjective ready or eager to fight or argue.
– DERIVATIVES **combatively** adverb **combativeness** noun.

combat trousers plural noun loose trousers with large patch pockets halfway down each leg.

combe /koom/ (also **coomb** or **coombe**) noun Brit. a short valley or hollow on a hillside or coastline.
– ORIGIN Old English.

comber noun a long curling sea wave.

combination noun **1** something made up of distinct elements: *a combination of drama, dance, and music.* **2** the combining of two or more different things. **3** a sequence of numbers or letters used to open a combination lock. **4** (**combinations**) dated a single undergarment covering the body and legs.
– DERIVATIVES **combinational** adjective.

combination lock noun a lock that is opened by using a specific sequence of letters or numbers.

combine verb /kuhm-**byn**/ **1** join or mix to form a whole. **2** join with others for a common purpose. **3** do at the same time: *an ideal place to combine shopping and sightseeing.* **4** Chemistry unite to form a compound. •noun /kom-byn/ a group of people or companies acting together for a commercial purpose.
– DERIVATIVES **combiner** noun.
– ORIGIN Latin *combinare* 'join two by two'.

combine harvester noun a machine that reaps, threshes, and cleans a cereal crop in one operation.

combining form noun a form of a word used in combination with another element to form a word (e.g. *bio-* 'life' in *biology*).

combo noun (pl. **combos**) informal **1** a small jazz, rock, or pop band. **2** a combination.

combust /kuhm-**bust**/ verb burn or be burned by fire.
– DERIVATIVES **combustor** noun.
– ORIGIN Latin *comburere* 'burn up'.

combustible adjective able to catch fire and burn easily. •noun a substance that is able to catch fire and burn easily.

combustion noun **1** the process of burning. **2** rapid chemical combination with oxygen, producing heat and light.

come verb (past **came**; past part. **come**) **1** move or reach towards or into a place. **2** arrive at a place. **3** happen; take place. **4** have or achieve a specified position in order or priority: *she came second.* **5** pass into or reach a specified state, situation, or state of mind: *my shirt came undone.* **6** be sold or available in a specified form: *the tops come in three sizes.* **7** (also **come, come**) said to correct, reassure, or urge on someone. **8** informal have an orgasm. •preposition informal when a specified time is reached or event happens.
– PHRASES **come about 1** take place. **2** (of a ship) change direction. **come across 1** (also chiefly Brit. **come over**) give a specified impression. **2** meet or find someone or something by chance. **come back** respond, especially vigorously. **come by** manage to get something. **come down on** criticize or punish someone harshly. **come down to** be dependent on a factor. **come forward** volunteer for a task or to give evidence. **come from** originate in something. **come in** prove to be: *I'm sure the money will come in handy.* **come in for** receive a negative reaction. **come into** inherit money or property. **come of 1** result from something. **2** be descended from someone. **come off 1** be accomplished. **2** end up in a specified situation: *he always came off worse in a fight.* **come off it** informal said when expressing strong disbelief. **come on 1** (of a state or condition)

C

start to arrive or happen. **2** (also **come upon**) meet or find someone or something by chance. **come on to** informal make sexual advances towards someone. **come out 1** (of a fact) become known. **2** declare oneself as being for or against something. **3** end up in a specified situation. **4** (of a photograph) be produced satisfactorily or in a specified way. **5** (of the result of a calculation or measurement) emerge at a specified figure. **6** informal openly declare that one is homosexual. **7** Brit. dated (of a young upper-class woman) make one's debut in society. **come out with** say something in a sudden or incautious way. **come over 1** (of a feeling) begin to affect someone. **2** Brit. informal suddenly start to feel a specified way. **come round** chiefly Brit. (chiefly US also **come around**) **1** recover consciousness. **2** be converted to another person's opinion. **come to 1** recover consciousness. **2** (of an expense) reach an amount in total. **3** (of a ship) come to a stop. **come to pass** literary happen. **come up 1** (of a situation or problem) occur or arise. **2** (of a time or event) draw near. **come up with** produce something, especially when pressured or challenged. **come upon 1** attack someone by surprise. **2** see **come on** (sense 2). **come what may** no matter what happens. **have it coming** (**to one**) informal be due to face the unpleasant results of one's behaviour.
– ORIGIN Old English.

> **USAGE:** On the use of **come** followed by **and**, see the note at **AND**.

comeback noun **1** a return to fame or fashionability. **2** informal a quick reply to a critical remark.

comedian noun (fem. **comedienne**) **1** an entertainer whose act is intended to make people laugh. **2** a comic actor.

comedown noun informal **1** a loss of status or importance. **2** a feeling of disappointment or depression.

comedy noun (pl. **comedies**) **1** entertainment consisting of jokes and sketches intended to make people laugh. **2** an amusing film, play, or programme. **3** a humorous play in which the characters find happiness after experiencing difficulty.
– DERIVATIVES **comedic** /kuh-**mee**-dik/ adjective.
– ORIGIN Greek *kōmōidia*.

comedy of manners noun a play, novel, or film that satirizes behaviour in a particular social group.

come-hither adjective informal flirtatious: *a come-hither look.*

comely /**kum**-li/ adjective (**comelier**, **comeliest**) old use or humorous pleasant to look at; attractive.
– DERIVATIVES **comeliness** noun.
– ORIGIN probably from *becomely* 'fitting, becoming'.

come-on noun informal a gesture or remark intended to attract someone sexually.

comestible /kuh-**mess**-ti-b'l/ noun formal or humorous an item of food.
– ORIGIN from Latin *comedere* 'eat up'.

comet /**kom**-it/ noun an object that moves around the solar system, consisting of a nucleus of ice and dust and, when near the sun, a long tail.

– DERIVATIVES **cometary** adjective.
– ORIGIN Greek *komētēs* 'long-haired star'.

comeuppance noun informal a punishment or fate that someone deserves.

comfit /**kum**-fit/ noun dated a sweet consisting of a nut or other centre coated in sugar.
– ORIGIN Old French *confit*.

comfort noun **1** a state of being physically relaxed and free from pain. **2** (**comforts**) things that contribute to physical ease and well-being. **3** relief for unhappiness or worry: *a few words of comfort.* • verb make someone feel less unhappy.
– DERIVATIVES **comforting** adjective.
– ORIGIN from Latin *confortare* 'strengthen'.

comfortable adjective **1** providing or enjoying physical comfort. **2** free from financial worry. **3** (of a victory) easily achieved.
– DERIVATIVES **comfortably** adverb.

comforter noun **1** a person or thing that provides relief from grief or worry. **2** Brit. a baby's dummy.

comfrey /**kum**-fri/ noun (pl. **comfreys**) a plant with clusters of purplish or white bell-shaped flowers.
– ORIGIN from Latin *confervere* 'heal'.

comfy adjective (**comfier**, **comfiest**) informal comfortable: *a comfy chair.*
– DERIVATIVES **comfily** adverb **comfiness** noun.

comic adjective **1** causing or meant to cause laughter. **2** relating to or in the style of comedy. • noun **1** a comedian. **2** a children's magazine containing comic strips.
– ORIGIN Greek *kōmikos*.

comical adjective causing laughter, especially through being ridiculous.
– DERIVATIVES **comically** adverb.

comic opera noun an opera that portrays humorous situations and characters, with much spoken dialogue.

comic relief noun humorous content in a play or novel which offsets more serious parts.

comic strip noun a sequence of drawings in boxes that tell an amusing story.

comity /**kom**-i-ti/ noun (pl. **comities**) **1** formal polite and considerate behaviour towards others. **2** (also **comity of nations**) the mutual recognition by nations of the laws and customs of others.
– ORIGIN from Latin *comis* 'courteous'.

comma noun a punctuation mark (,) showing a pause between parts of a sentence or separating items in a list.
– ORIGIN Greek *komma* 'piece cut off, short clause'.

command verb **1** give an order. **2** be in charge of a military unit. **3** be in a position that gives a good view or control of something: *I climbed up a rocky outcrop commanding a view of the valley.* **4** be in a position to have or secure: *emeralds command a high price.* • noun **1** an order. **2** authority, especially over armed forces: *the officer in command.* **3** the ability to use or control something: *her poor command of English.* **4** a group of officers having control over a particular group or operation. **5** an instruction causing a computer to perform one of its basic functions.
– ORIGIN Latin *commandare*.

commandant /kom-muhn-dant/ noun an officer in charge of a force or institution.

command economy noun another term for **PLANNED ECONOMY**.

commandeer /kom-muhn-deer/ verb 1 officially take possession of something for military purposes. 2 seize for one's own purposes: *the men in the family have commandeered my other computer.*
– ORIGIN Dutch *commanderen* 'command'.

commander noun 1 a person in authority, especially in a military situation. 2 a rank of naval officer next below captain. 3 an officer in charge of a Metropolitan Police district in London. 4 a member of a higher class in some orders of knighthood.

commander-in-chief noun (pl. **commanders-in-chief**) an officer in charge of all of the armed forces of a country.

commanding adjective 1 having or expressing authority. 2 possessing or giving superior strength: *a commanding lead.*
– DERIVATIVES **commandingly** adverb.

commandment noun a rule given by God, especially one of the Ten Commandments.

commando noun (pl. **commandos**) 1 a soldier specially trained for carrying out raids. 2 a unit of commandos.
– ORIGIN Portuguese.

command performance noun a presentation of a play, concert, or film at the request of royalty.

commedia dell'arte /ko-med-iuh del-ah-tay/ noun an Italian kind of improvised comedy popular in the 16th–18th centuries, based on stock characters.
– ORIGIN Italian, 'comedy of art'.

comme il faut /kom eel foh/ adjective correct in behaviour or etiquette.
– ORIGIN French, 'as is necessary'.

commemorate verb take action to honour the memory of: *the town held a silent march to commemorate the dead.*
– DERIVATIVES **commemoration** noun
– ORIGIN Latin *commemorare* 'bring to remembrance'.

commemorative /kuh-mem-muh-ruh-tiv/ adjective acting to honour the memory of an event or person.

commence verb start or be started; begin.
– ORIGIN Old French *commencier.*

commencement noun the beginning of something.

commend verb 1 praise someone or something formally. 2 present as suitable or good; recommend: *I commend you to her without reservation.* 3 (**commend someone/thing to**) chiefly old use entrust someone or something to.
– DERIVATIVES **commendation** noun.
– ORIGIN Latin *commendare.*

commendable adjective deserving praise and approval.
– DERIVATIVES **commendably** adverb.

commensal /kuh-men-s'l/ adjective Biology (of two organisms) having an association in which one benefits and the other derives neither benefit nor harm.
– ORIGIN from Latin *com-* 'sharing' + *mensa* 'a table'.

commensurable /kuh-men-shuh-ruh-b'l/ adjective 1 formal measurable by the same standard: *not every chapter is commensurable with every other.* 2 Mathematics (of numbers) in a ratio equal to a ratio of integers.
– ORIGIN Latin *commensurabilis.*

commensurate /kuh-men-shuh-ruht/ adjective corresponding in size or degree; in proportion: *salary will be commensurate with experience.*
– DERIVATIVES **commensurately** adverb.

comment noun 1 a remark expressing an opinion or reaction. 2 discussion of an issue or event. • verb express an opinion or reaction.
– ORIGIN Latin *commentum* 'device, interpretation'.

commentary noun (pl. **commentaries**) 1 a broadcast spoken account of an event as it happens. 2 the expression of opinions or offering of explanations about an event: *a piece marrying fact and commentary from the paper's Paris correspondent.* 3 a set of explanatory or critical notes on a written work.

commentate verb provide a commentary on a sports match or other event.

commentator noun 1 a person who comments on events, especially in the media. 2 a person who provides a commentary on a live event.

commerce noun 1 the activity of buying and selling, especially on a large scale. 2 dated social dealings between people.
– ORIGIN Latin *commercium* 'trade, trading'.

commercial adjective 1 concerned with or engaged in commerce. 2 making or intended to make a profit. 3 (of television or radio) funded by broadcast advertisements. • noun a television or radio advertisement.
– DERIVATIVES **commerciality** noun **commercially** adverb.

commercialism noun emphasis on making maximum profit.

commercialize (or **commercialise**) verb manage or exploit something in a way designed to make a profit.
– DERIVATIVES **commercialization** noun.

commercial traveller noun Brit. dated a travelling sales representative.

Commie noun (pl. **Commies**) informal, derogatory a communist.

commingle /kom-ming-g'l/ verb literary mix; blend.

comminuted /kom-in-yoo-tid/ adjective technical reduced to minute particles or fragments.
– DERIVATIVES **comminution** noun.
– ORIGIN from Latin *comminuere* 'break into pieces'.

commis chef /kom-i/ noun a junior chef.
– ORIGIN French, 'deputy chef'.

commiserate /kuh-miz-uh-rayt/ verb express sympathy or pity; sympathize.
– DERIVATIVES **commiseration** noun.
– ORIGIN Latin *commiserari.*

commissar /kom-mi-sar/ noun a Communist official responsible for political education.
– ORIGIN Russian *komissar.*

commissariat /kom-mi-sair-i-uht/ noun a

C

military department for the supply of food and equipment.

commissary /**kom**-i-suh-ri/ noun (pl. **commissaries**) **1** a deputy or delegate. **2** N. Amer. a restaurant or food store in a military base or other institution.

commission noun **1** an instruction, command, or duty. **2** a formal request for something to be designed or made. **3** a group of people given official authority to do something. **4** a sum paid to an agent for selling something: *foreign banks may charge a commission.* **5** a warrant conferring the rank of military officer. **6** the committing of a crime or offence. • verb **1** order or authorize the production of: *the council commissioned a study of the issue.* **2** bring something newly produced into working order. **3** appoint someone to the rank of military officer.
– PHRASES **in** (or **out of**) **commission** in (or not in) use or working order.
– ORIGIN Latin.

commissionaire /kuh-mi-shuh-**nair**/ noun Brit. a uniformed door attendant at a hotel, theatre, or other building.
– ORIGIN French.

commissioner noun **1** a person appointed by, or as a member of, an official commission. **2** a representative of the highest authority in an area. **3** the head of the Metropolitan Police in London.

commissioner for oaths noun Brit. a solicitor authorized to administer an oath to a person making an affidavit.

commit verb (**commits, committing, committed**) **1** do something wrong, bad, or illegal. **2** dedicate or allocate to a course or use: *the Government should commit more money to training judges.* **3** (**commit oneself**) promise to do something. **4** (**be committed to**) be in a long-term emotional relationship with someone. **5** (**commit something to**) put something somewhere to preserve it: *she committed each detail to memory.* **6** send someone to prison or psychiatric hospital, or for trial in a higher court.
– ORIGIN Latin *committere* 'join, entrust'.

commitment noun **1** dedication to a cause or activity. **2** a promise to do something. **3** an engagement or duty that restricts freedom of action.

committal noun **1** the sending of someone to prison or psychiatric hospital, or for trial. **2** the burial of a corpse.

committed adjective dedicated to a cause, activity, job, etc.: *a committed democrat.*

committee noun (treated as sing. or pl.) a group of people appointed for a specific function by a larger group.

committee stage noun Brit. the third of five stages of a bill's progress through Parliament, when it may be debated and amended.

commode noun **1** a piece of furniture containing a concealed chamber pot. **2** a chest of drawers of a decorative type popular in the 18th century.
– ORIGIN French, 'convenient, suitable'.

commodify /kuh-**mod**-i-fy/ verb (**commodifies, commodifying, commodified**) turn into or treat as a mere commodity: *a culture in which sexuality is commodified.*
– DERIVATIVES **commodification** noun.

commodious /kuh-**moh**-di-uhss/ adjective formal roomy and comfortable.
– ORIGIN Latin *commodus* 'convenient'.

commodity /kuh-**mod**-i-ti/ noun (pl. **commodities**) **1** a raw material or agricultural product that can be bought and sold. **2** something useful or valuable.
– ORIGIN from Latin *commodus* 'convenient'.

commodore /**kom**-muh-dor/ noun **1** a naval rank above captain and below rear admiral. **2** the president of a yacht club.
– ORIGIN probably from Dutch *komandeur* 'commander'.

common adjective (**commoner, commonest**) **1** occurring, found, or done often; not rare: *remedies for common ailments.* **2** without special qualities or position; ordinary. **3** shared by two or more people or things: *working towards our common goal.* **4** belonging to or affecting the whole of a community: *common land.* **5** Brit. showing a lack of taste and refinement supposedly typical of lower-class people; vulgar. • noun a piece of open land for public use.
– PHRASES **common or garden** Brit. informal of the usual or ordinary type. **in common** in joint use or possession; shared. **in common with** in the same way as.
– DERIVATIVES **commonness** noun.
– ORIGIN Latin *communis*.

commonality noun (pl. **commonalities**) the sharing of common features: *the commonality of grief.*

commonalty /**kom**-uhn-uhl-ti/ noun (treated as pl.) (**the commonalty**) chiefly historical people without special rank or position.

common denominator noun **1** Mathematics a common multiple of the denominators of several fractions. **2** a feature shared by all members of a group.

commoner noun one of the ordinary or common people, as opposed to the aristocracy or to royalty.

Common Era noun another term for CHRISTIAN ERA.

common ground noun views shared by each of two or more parties.

common law noun the part of English law that is based on custom and judicial decisions rather than created by Parliament.

common-law husband (or **wife**) noun a man or woman who has lived with a person long enough to be recognized as a husband or wife, but has not been married in a civil or religious ceremony.

commonly adverb very often; frequently.

common market noun **1** a group of countries imposing few or no duties on trade with one another. **2** (**the Common Market**) the European Union.

common noun noun a noun referring to a class of things (e.g. *tree, cat*) as opposed to a particular person or thing. Often contrasted with PROPER NOUN.

commonplace adjective not unusual or original; ordinary. • noun **1** a usual or ordinary thing. **2** an unoriginal remark; a cliché.

common room noun chiefly Brit. a room in a school or college for use of students or staff outside teaching hours.

Commons plural noun (**the Commons**) **1** the House of Commons. **2** historical the common people regarded as a part of a political system.

common sense noun good sense and sound judgement in practical matters.

commonsensical adjective having or showing common sense.

common time noun a rhythmic musical pattern in which there are two or four beats in a bar.

commonweal /kom-uhn-weel/ noun (**the commonweal**) old use the welfare of the public.

commonwealth noun **1** (**the Commonwealth** or in full **the Commonwealth of Nations**) an association consisting of the UK together with states that were previously part of the British Empire, and dependencies. **2** an independent state or community. **3** a grouping of states or other bodies. **4** (**the Commonwealth**) the republican period of government in Britain between the execution of Charles I in 1649 and the Restoration of Charles II in 1660.

commotion noun a state of confused and noisy disturbance.
– ORIGIN from Latin *com-* 'altogether' + *motio* 'motion'.

communal /kom-**myoo**-n'l/ adjective **1** shared or done by all members of a community. **2** (of conflict) between different communities, especially those having different religions or ethnic origins.
– DERIVATIVES **communality** noun **communally** adverb.
– ORIGIN Latin *communalis*.

communard /kom-yuu-nahd/ noun **1** a member of a commune. **2** (**Communard**) historical a supporter of the Paris Commune.

commune[1] /kom-**myoon**/ noun **1** a group of people living together and sharing possessions and responsibilities. **2** (in France) the smallest district for administrative purposes. **3** (**the Paris Commune**) the short-lived government elected in Paris in 1871, advocating communal organization of society.
– ORIGIN Latin *communia*.

commune[2] /kuh-**myoon**/ verb (**commune with**) share one's intimate thoughts or feelings with: *visitors can stroll the fields and commune with nature.*
– ORIGIN Old French *comuner* 'to share'.

communicable adjective (especially of a disease) able to be communicated to others.

communicant noun a person who receives Holy Communion.

communicate verb **1** share or exchange information or ideas. **2** pass on, transmit, or convey an emotion, disease, heat, etc. **3** (as adj. **communicating**) (of two rooms) having a common connecting door. **4** receive Holy Communion.
– DERIVATIVES **communicator** noun.
– ORIGIN Latin *communicare* 'to share'.

communication noun **1** the action of communicating. **2** a letter or other message. **3** (**communications**) the means of sending or receiving information, such as telephone lines or computers. **4** (**communications**) means of travelling or of transporting goods, such as roads or railways.
– DERIVATIVES **communicational** adjective.

communication cord noun Brit. a cord or chain which a train passenger may pull in an emergency, causing the train to brake.

communicative adjective willing or eager to talk or impart information.

communion noun **1** the sharing of intimate thoughts and feelings: *man's mystical communion with the divine.* **2** (also **Holy Communion**) the service of Christian worship at which bread and wine are consecrated and shared; the Eucharist. **3** an allied group of Christian Churches or communities: *the Anglican communion.*

communiqué /kuh-**myoo**-ni-kay/ noun an official announcement or statement, especially one made to the media.
– ORIGIN French, 'communicated'.

communism noun **1** a political and social system whereby all property is owned by the community and each person contributes and receives according to their ability and needs. **2** a system of this kind derived from Marxism, practised in China and formerly in the Soviet Union.
– DERIVATIVES **communist** noun & adjective **communistic** adjective.
– ORIGIN French *communisme.*

communitarianism /kuh-myoo-ni-**tair**-i-uh-niz-uhm/ noun a theory which emphasizes the responsibility of the individual to the community and the importance of the family unit.
– DERIVATIVES **communitarian** adjective & noun.

community noun (pl. **communities**) **1** a group of people living together in one place. **2** (**the community**) the people of an area as a social group; society. **3** a group of people with a common religion, race, or profession: *the scientific community.* **4** the holding of certain attitudes and interests in common: *the sense of community that organized religion can provide.* **5** a group of interdependent plants or animals growing or living in the same place.
– ORIGIN from Latin *communis* 'common'.

community care noun long-term care for mentally ill, elderly, and disabled people within the community rather than in hospitals or other institutions.

community centre noun a place providing educational or recreational activities for a neighbourhood.

community service noun socially useful work that an offender is required to do instead of going to prison.

commutate /kom-yuu-tayt/ verb regulate or reverse the direction of an alternating electric current, especially to make it a direct current.
– DERIVATIVES **commutation** noun.

commutative /kuh-**myoo**-tuh-tiv/ adjective Mathematics unchanged in result by interchanging the order of quantities, such that for example $a \times b = b \times a$.

commutator /kom-yuu-tay-ter/ noun an attachment connected with the armature of a

C

motor or dynamo, which ensures the current flows as direct current.

commute verb **1** travel some distance between one's home and place of work on a regular basis. **2** reduce a judicial sentence, especially a death sentence, to a less severe one. **3** change one kind of payment or obligation for another.
– DERIVATIVES **commutable** adjective **commuter** noun.
– ORIGIN Latin *commutare*; sense 1 is from *commutation ticket*, the US term for a season ticket.

compact[1] adjective /kuhm-**pakt**/ **1** closely and neatly packed together; dense. **2** having all the necessary parts or features fitted into a small space. • verb /kuhm-**pakt**/ press firmly together; compress: *the waste is compacted and buried*. • noun /**kom**-pakt/ a small flat case containing face powder, a mirror, and a powder puff.
– DERIVATIVES **compaction** noun **compactly** adverb **compactness** noun **compactor** noun.
– ORIGIN from Latin *compingere* 'fasten together'.

compact[2] /**kom**-pakt/ noun a formal agreement or contract.
– ORIGIN from Latin *compacisci* 'make a covenant with'.

compact disc noun a small plastic disc on which music or other digital information is stored in a form that can be read by a laser.

compadre /kom-**pah**-dray/ noun (pl. **compadres**) informal a friend or companion.
– ORIGIN Spanish, 'godfather'.

companion noun **1** a person with whom one spends time or travels. **2** each of a pair of things intended to complement or match each other. **3** (**Companion**) a member of the lowest grade of certain orders of knighthood.
– DERIVATIVES **companionship** noun.
– ORIGIN Old French *compaignon* 'person who breaks bread with another'.

companionable adjective friendly and sociable.
– DERIVATIVES **companionably** adverb.

companionway noun a set of steps leading from a ship's deck down to a cabin or lower deck.
– ORIGIN from former Dutch *kompanje* 'quarterdeck'.

company noun (pl. **companies**) **1** a commercial business. **2** the fact of being with another person or other people: *she is excellent company*. **3** a guest or guests: *we're expecting company*. **4** a gathering of people. **5** a body of soldiers, especially the smallest subdivision of an infantry battalion. **6** a group of actors, singers, or dancers who perform together.
– PHRASES **in company with** together with. **keep someone company** spend time with someone to prevent them feeling lonely or bored.
– ORIGIN Old French *compainie*.

comparable /**kom**-puh-ruh-b'l/ adjective able to be compared with someone or something because having similar aspects: *shoppers can buy groceries online, at prices comparable to their supermarket*.
– DERIVATIVES **comparability** noun **comparably** adverb.

comparative /kuhm-**pa**-ruh-tiv/ adjective **1** measured or judged by comparing one thing with another; relative: *I returned to the comparative comfort of my own home*. **2** involving comparison between two or more subjects or branches of science. **3** (of an adjective or adverb) expressing a higher degree of a quality, but not the highest possible (e.g. *braver; more fiercely*). Contrasted with POSITIVE, SUPERLATIVE.

comparatively adverb to a moderate degree as compared to something else; relatively.

comparator /kuhm-pa-ruh-ter/ noun a device for comparing something measurable with a reference or standard.

compare verb **1** estimate, measure, or note the similarity or difference between: *revenues will amount to £138 million this year, compared to £147 million last year*. **2** (**compare something to**) describe the resemblances of something with something else. **3** be similar to or have a specified relationship with another thing or person: *salaries compare favourably with those of other professions*.
– PHRASES **beyond** (or **without**) **compare** better than all others of the same kind. **compare notes** exchange ideas or information.
– ORIGIN from Latin *compar* 'like, equal'.

comparison noun **1** an instance of comparing things or people. **2** the quality of being similar or equivalent: *there is no comparison between the two offences*.

compartment noun **1** a separate section of a structure or container. **2** a division of a railway carriage marked by partitions.
– DERIVATIVES **compartmental** adjective.
– ORIGIN French *compartiment*.

compartmentalize (or **compartmentalise**) verb divide something into categories or sections.
– DERIVATIVES **compartmentalization** noun.

compass noun **1** an instrument containing a magnetized pointer which shows the direction of magnetic north. **2** (also **compasses**) an instrument for drawing circles and arcs and measuring distances between points, consisting of two arms linked by a movable joint. **3** range or scope: *it would be impossible to bring all the subjects within the compass of a single volume*.
– ORIGIN Old French *compas*.

compassion noun sympathetic pity and concern for the sufferings or misfortunes of others.
– ORIGIN from Latin *compati* 'suffer with'.

compassionate adjective feeling or showing sympathy and concern for others.
– DERIVATIVES **compassionately** adverb.

compassionate leave noun leave from work granted to someone as a result of personal circumstances, especially the death of a close relative.

compatible adjective **1** able to exist or be used together without problems or conflict: *a contemporary design theme that's compatible with any decor*. **2** (of two people) able to have a good relationship; well suited. **3** consistent or in keeping: *the symptoms were compatible with a peptic ulcer*.

- DERIVATIVES **compatibility** noun **compatibly** adverb.
- ORIGIN Latin *compatibilis*.

compatriot /kuhm-**pat**-ri-uht/ noun a fellow citizen or national of a country.
- ORIGIN French *compatriote*.

compel verb (**compels, compelling, compelled**) 1 force or oblige someone to do something. 2 cause by force or pressure: *ground troops would be necessary to compel capitulation*.
- ORIGIN Latin *compellere*.

compelling adjective 1 strongly arousing attention or admiration. 2 not able to be resisted or doubted: *a compelling argument*.
- DERIVATIVES **compellingly** adverb.

compendious adjective formal presenting the essential facts in a detailed but concise way.
- DERIVATIVES **compendiously** adverb.
- ORIGIN Latin *compendiosus* 'advantageous, brief'.

compendium /kuhm-**pen**-di-uhm/ noun (pl. **compendiums** or **compendia** /kuhm-**pen**-di-uh/) 1 a collection of concise but detailed information about a subject. 2 a collection of similar items.
- ORIGIN Latin, 'profit, saving'.

compensate verb 1 give someone something in recognition of loss, suffering, or injury. 2 (**compensate for**) reduce or counteract something undesirable by having an opposite force or effect.
- DERIVATIVES **compensator** noun **compensatory** adjective.
- ORIGIN Latin *compensare* 'weigh against'.

compensation noun 1 something given to someone to compensate for loss, suffering, or injury. 2 something that makes up for an undesirable situation: *getting older has some compensations*. 3 the action of compensating.

compère /**kom**-pair/ Brit. noun a person who introduces the acts in a variety show. • verb act as a compère for a variety show.
- ORIGIN French, 'godfather'.

compete verb 1 try to gain or win something by defeating or being better than others. 2 be able to rival another or others: *in this sort of form no one can compete with Schumacher*.
- ORIGIN Latin *competere*.

competence (also **competency**) noun 1 the ability to do something well. 2 the authority of a court or other body to deal with a particular matter.

competent adjective 1 having the necessary skill or knowledge to do something successfully. 2 acceptable and satisfactory: *she spoke quite competent French*. 3 having legal authority to deal with a particular matter.
- DERIVATIVES **competently** adverb.
- ORIGIN from Latin *competere* in the sense 'be fit or proper'.

competition noun 1 the activity of competing against others. 2 an event or contest in which people compete. 3 the person or people with whom one is competing.

competitive adjective 1 relating to competition. 2 strongly desiring to be more successful than others. 3 as good as or better than others of a similar nature: *we offer*

prompt service at *competitive rates*.
- DERIVATIVES **competitively** adverb **competitiveness** noun.

competitor noun 1 a person who takes part in a sporting contest. 2 an organization or country that competes with others in business or trade.

compilation noun 1 the action of compiling something. 2 a thing, especially a book or record, compiled from different sources.

compile verb 1 produce a book, report, etc. by assembling material from other sources. 2 gather material to produce a book, report, etc.
- ORIGIN Latin *compilare* 'plunder or plagiarize'.

compiler noun 1 a person who compiles information. 2 a computer program that translates instructions from a high-level language into a form which can be executed by the computer.

complacent /kuhm-**play**-s'nt/ adjective satisfied with oneself in a smug or uncritical way.
- DERIVATIVES **complacency** (also **complacence**) noun **complacently** adverb.
- ORIGIN Latin *complacere* 'to please'.

USAGE: Do not confuse **complacent** with **complaisant**. **Complacent** means 'smugly self-satisfied' (*don't be complacent about security*), whereas **complaisant** means 'willing to please' (*the local people were complaisant and cordial*).

complain verb 1 express dissatisfaction or annoyance about something. 2 (**complain of**) state that one is suffering from a symptom of illness.
- DERIVATIVES **complainer** noun.
- ORIGIN Latin *complangere* 'bewail'.

complainant noun Law a person who brings a case against another in certain lawsuits.

complaint noun 1 an act of complaining. 2 a reason for being dissatisfied with something. 3 the expression of dissatisfaction: *a letter of complaint*. 4 an illness or medical condition, especially a minor one.

complaisant /kuhm-**play**-z'nt/ adjective willing to please others or to accept their behaviour without protest.
- DERIVATIVES **complaisance** noun.
- ORIGIN Latin *complacere* 'to please'.

USAGE: On the difference between **complaisant** and **complacent**, see the note at **COMPLACENT**.

complement noun /**kom**-pli-muhnt/ 1 a thing that contributes extra features to something else so as to improve it. 2 the number or quantity that makes something complete: *we have a full complement of staff*. 3 a word or words used with a verb to complete the meaning of the subject (e.g. *happy* in the sentence *we are happy*). 4 Geometry the amount by which a given angle is less than 90°. • verb /**kom**-pli-ment/ add extra features to someone or something in a way that improves.
- DERIVATIVES **complementation** noun.
- ORIGIN from Latin *complere* 'fill up'.

C

USAGE: The words **complement** and **compliment** are often confused. As a verb, **complement** means 'add extra features to someone or something in a way that improves' (*a classic blazer complements a look that's smart or casual*), while **compliment** means 'politely congratulate or praise someone or something' (*he complimented Kate on her appearance*).

complementarity noun (pl. **complementarities**) a situation in which two or more different things improve each other or form a balanced whole.

complementary adjective **1** combining so as to form a whole or to improve each other: *they have different but complementary skills.* **2** relating to complementary medicine.

USAGE: On the confusion of **complementary** and **complimentary**, see the note at **COMPLIMENTARY**.

complementary angle noun either of two angles whose sum is 90°.

complementary colour noun a colour that combined with a given colour makes white or black.

complementary medicine noun medical therapy that is not part of scientific medicine but may be used alongside it, e.g. acupuncture.

complete adjective **1** having all the necessary or appropriate parts; entire. **2** having run its full course; finished. **3** to the greatest extent or degree; total: *a complete ban on smoking.* **4** skilled at every aspect of an activity: *the complete footballer.* **5** (**complete with**) having something as an additional part or feature. •verb **1** finish making or doing something. **2** provide with the items necessary to make entire or complete: *quarry tiles complete the look.* **3** write the required information on a form. **4** Brit. conclude the sale of a property.
– DERIVATIVES **completeness** noun.
– ORIGIN from Latin *complere* 'fill up, finish'.
completely adverb totally; utterly.
completion noun **1** the action of completing something or the state of being completed. **2** Brit. the final stage in the sale of a property, at which point it legally changes ownership.
completist noun an obsessive, typically indiscriminate, collector or fan.
complex adjective **1** consisting of many different and connected parts. **2** difficult to understand; complicated. •noun **1** a group of similar buildings or facilities on the same site. **2** an interlinked system; a network. **3** a group of repressed feelings which lead to abnormal mental states or behaviour. **4** informal a strong concern or anxiety about something.
– DERIVATIVES **complexity** noun (pl. **complexities**) **complexly** adverb.
– ORIGIN Latin *complexus*.
complexion noun **1** the natural colour and texture of the skin of a person's face. **2** the general character of something: *he can single-handedly change the complexion of a game.*
– DERIVATIVES **-complexioned** adjective.
– ORIGIN Latin, 'combination'.
complex number noun Mathematics a number

containing both a real and an imaginary part.
compliance /kuhm-ply-uhnss/ noun the action of obeying an order, rule or request.
compliant adjective **1** tending to be excessively obedient or ready to accept something. **2** in accordance with rules or standards.
– DERIVATIVES **compliantly** adverb.
complicate verb make something more intricate or confusing.
– ORIGIN Latin *complicare* 'fold together'.
complicated adjective **1** consisting of many interconnecting elements; intricate. **2** involving many confusing aspects.
complication noun **1** a thing that complicates something; a difficulty. **2** an involved or confused state: *companies offering a variety of solutions with a minimum of complication.* **3** a secondary disease or condition that makes an already existing one worse.
complicit /kuhm-**pliss**-it/ adjective involved with others in an unlawful activity: *the militant group may be complicit in ten violent incidents.*
complicity noun involvement with others in an unlawful activity.
– ORIGIN from Old French *complice* 'an associate'.
compliment noun /kom-pli-muhnt/ **1** a polite expression of praise or admiration. **2** (**compliments**) formal greetings. •verb /kom-pli-ment/ politely congratulate or praise: *he complimented Kate on her appearance.*
– PHRASES **return the compliment** retaliate or respond in a similar way. **with one's compliments** provided free of charge.
– ORIGIN Italian *complimento* 'fulfilment of the requirements of courtesy'.

USAGE: On the confusion of **compliment** and **complement**, see the note at **COMPLEMENT**.

complimentary adjective **1** praising or approving: *a complimentary remark.* **2** given free of charge.

USAGE: Do not confuse the words **complimentary** and **complementary**. **Complimentary** means 'praising' or 'given free of charge' (*a complimentary breakfast*), whereas **complementary** means 'combining to form a whole or to improve each other' (*they have different but complementary skills*).

compline /kom-plin, kom-plyn/ noun (in the Roman Catholic and High Anglican Church) an evening service traditionally said before retiring for the night.
– ORIGIN from Old French *complie* 'completed'.
comply /kuhm-ply/ verb (**complies, complying, complied**) (often **comply with**) **1** act in accordance with a request or order. **2** meet specified standards: *engines designed to comply with all EU emissions standards.*
– ORIGIN Latin *complere* 'fulfil, fill up'.
component /kuhm-**poh**-nuhnt/ noun a part or element of a larger whole. •adjective being part of a larger whole.
– ORIGIN from Latin *componere* 'put together'.
comport /kuhm-port/ verb (**comport oneself**) formal behave in a particular way: *students who comported themselves well in television interviews.*
– ORIGIN Latin *comportare*.

comportment noun formal a person's behaviour or bearing.

compose verb 1 make up a whole: *the National Congress is composed of ten senators.* 2 create a work of art, especially music or poetry. 3 form a whole by arranging parts in an orderly or artistic way. 4 phrase a letter or other piece of writing with care and thought. 5 (often as adj. **composed**) settle one's features or thoughts. 6 prepare a written work for printing by setting up the characters to be printed.
– ORIGIN Latin *componere* 'put together'.

composer noun a person who writes music.

composite /kom-puh-zit/ adjective 1 made up of various parts. 2 (**Composite**) relating to a classical style of architecture consisting of elements of the Ionic and Corinthian orders. 3 /kom-puh-zyt/ (of a plant) having flower heads consisting of numerous florets, such as a daisy. •noun 1 a thing made up of several parts. 2 /kom-puh-zyt/ a motion for debate composed of two or more related resolutions.
– ORIGIN from Latin *componere* 'put together'.

composition noun 1 the way in which something is made up from different elements: *the molecular composition of cells.* 2 a work of music, literature, or art. 3 a thing made up of various elements. 4 the composing of something. 5 the artistic arrangement of the parts of a picture.
– DERIVATIVES **compositional** adjective.

compositor /kuhm-poz-i-ter/ noun a person who arranges type for printing or who keys text into a composing machine.

compos mentis /kom-poss men-tiss/ adjective having full control of one's mind.
– ORIGIN Latin.

compost noun 1 decayed organic material used as a fertilizer for plants. 2 a mixture of compost with soil used for growing plants. •verb make organic matter into compost.
– DERIVATIVES **composter** noun.
– ORIGIN Latin *composita* 'something put together'.

composure noun the state of being calm and self-controlled.

compote /kom-poht, kom-pot/ noun fruit preserved or cooked in syrup.
– ORIGIN French.

compound¹ noun /kom-pownd/ 1 a thing composed of two or more separate elements. 2 a substance formed from two or more elements chemically united in fixed proportions. 3 a word made up of two or more existing words. •adjective /kom-pownd/ 1 made up or consisting of several elements. 2 (of interest) payable on both capital and the accumulated interest. Compare with SIMPLE. 3 (of a leaf, flower, or eye) consisting of two or more simple parts or individuals in combination. •verb /kuhm-pownd/ 1 make up a composite whole. 2 mix ingredients to form a whole. 3 make something bad worse.
– DERIVATIVES **compounder** noun.
– ORIGIN from Latin *componere* 'put together'.

compound² /kom-pownd/ noun a large open area enclosed by a fence, for example within a prison.
– ORIGIN Malay, 'enclosure, hamlet'.

compound fracture noun an injury in which a broken bone pierces the skin.

compound time noun musical rhythm or metre in which each beat in a bar is subdivided into three smaller units, so having the value of a dotted note.

comprehend /kom-pri-hend/ verb 1 fully understand something. 2 formal include or encompass: *a divine order comprehending all men.*
– ORIGIN Latin *comprehendere*.

comprehensible adjective able to be understood; intelligible.
– DERIVATIVES **comprehensibility** noun.

comprehension noun 1 the ability to understand something. 2 Brit. the school exercise of answering questions on a set passage to test understanding.

comprehensive adjective 1 including or dealing with all or nearly all aspects of something: *a comprehensive guidebook.* 2 Brit. (of a system of secondary education) in which children of all abilities are educated in one school. 3 (of motor-vehicle insurance) providing cover for most risks. 4 (of a victory or defeat) by a large margin. •noun Brit. a comprehensive school.
– DERIVATIVES **comprehensively** adverb **comprehensiveness** noun.

compress verb /kuhm-press/ 1 squeeze or press so as to occupy less space: *the skirt can be compressed into a small bag.* 2 squeeze or press two things together. •noun /kom-press/ a pad of absorbent material pressed on to part of the body to relieve inflammation or stop bleeding.
– DERIVATIVES **compressibility** noun **compressible** adjective **compressive** adjective.
– ORIGIN from Latin *comprimere* 'press together'.

compressed air noun air that is at more than atmospheric pressure.

compression noun 1 the action of compressing something. 2 the reduction in volume (causing an increase in pressure) of the fuel mixture in an internal-combustion engine before ignition.
– DERIVATIVES **compressional** adjective.

compressor noun 1 an instrument or device for compressing something. 2 a machine used to supply air or other gas at increased pressure.

comprise verb 1 be made up of; consist of: *the country comprises twenty states.* 2 (also **be comprised of**) make up a whole: *this breed comprises 50 per cent of the Swiss cattle population.*
– ORIGIN from French *comprendre* 'comprehend'.

USAGE: Traditionally, **comprise** means 'consist of' and should not be used to mean 'make up a whole'. However, a passive use of **comprise** (as in *the country is comprised of twenty states*) is now becoming part of standard English: this has broadly the same meaning as the traditional active sense (*the country comprises twenty states*).

compromise noun 1 an agreement reached by each side making concessions. 2 something that is halfway between conflicting elements: *a compromise between greed and caution.* •verb

1 settle a dispute by each side making concessions. **2** accept standards that are lower than is desirable for practical reasons: *we weren't prepared to compromise on safety.* **3** bring someone into disrepute or danger by reckless behaviour.
– DERIVATIVES **compromiser** noun.
– ORIGIN from Latin *compromittere*.

compromising adjective revealing an embarrassing or incriminating secret.

comptroller /kuhn-**troh**-ler, komp-**troh**-ler/ noun a controller (used in the title of some financial officers).
– ORIGIN variant of **CONTROLLER**.

compulsion noun **1** the compelling of someone to do something. **2** an irresistible urge to do something.

compulsive adjective **1** resulting from or acting on an irresistible urge: *compulsive eating.* **2** powerfully interesting or exciting.
– DERIVATIVES **compulsively** adverb **compulsiveness** noun.

compulsory adjective required by law or a rule; obligatory.
– DERIVATIVES **compulsorily** adverb.

compulsory purchase noun Brit. the buying of privately owned land or property by an official body such as a government department, regardless of whether the owner wants to sell it.

compunction noun a feeling of guilt that prevents or follows wrongdoing: *he felt no compunction about deceiving them.*
– ORIGIN Latin, from *compungere* 'prick sharply'.

computation noun **1** mathematical calculation. **2** the use of computers, especially as a subject of research or study.
– DERIVATIVES **computational** adjective.

compute verb calculate a figure or amount.
– ORIGIN Latin *computare*.

computer noun an electronic device capable of storing and processing information according to a predetermined set of instructions.

computerize (or **computerise**) verb convert something to a system or form which is controlled, stored, or processed by computer.
– DERIVATIVES **computerization** noun.

computer-literate adjective having enough knowledge and skill to be able to use computers.

computing noun the use or operation of computers.

comrade noun **1** (among men) a colleague or a fellow member of an organization. **2** (also **comrade-in-arms**) a fellow soldier.
– DERIVATIVES **comradely** adjective **comradeship** noun.
– ORIGIN Spanish *camarada* 'room-mate'.

con¹ informal verb (**cons, conning, conned**) persuade someone to do or believe something by lying to them. • noun an act of deceiving or tricking someone.
– ORIGIN abbreviation of **CONFIDENCE**, as in *confidence trick.*

con² noun (usu. in phrase **pros and cons**) a disadvantage of or argument against something.
– ORIGIN from Latin *contra* 'against'.

con³ noun informal a convict.

con⁴ (US also **conn**) verb (**cons, conning, conned**) direct the steering of a ship.
– ORIGIN apparently from the old word *cond* 'conduct, guide', from Old French *conduire*.

concatenate /kuhn-**kat**-i-nayt/ verb formal or technical link things together in a chain or series.
– ORIGIN Latin *concatenare* 'link together'.

concatenation /kon-ka-ti-**nay**-sh'n/ noun a series of interconnected things: *a concatenation of events which had led to the murder.*

concave /kon-**kayv**/ adjective having an outline or surface that curves inwards like the inside of a ball. Compare with **CONVEX**.
– DERIVATIVES **concavity** noun.
– ORIGIN Latin *concavus*, from *cavus* 'hollow'.

conceal verb **1** prevent someone or something from being seen. **2** keep something secret.
– DERIVATIVES **concealer** noun **concealment** noun.
– ORIGIN Latin *concelare*, from *celare* 'hide'.

concede verb **1** finally admit or agree that something is true. **2** give up a possession, advantage, or right. **3** admit defeat in a match or contest. **4** fail to prevent an opponent scoring a goal or point.
– ORIGIN Latin *concedere*.

conceit noun **1** excessive pride in oneself. **2** an artistic effect or device. **3** a complicated metaphor.
– ORIGIN from **CONCEIVE**.

conceited adjective excessively proud of oneself.

conceivable adjective capable of being imagined or understood.
– DERIVATIVES **conceivably** adverb.

conceive verb **1** become pregnant with a child. **2** form a plan or idea in the mind: *the project was conceived by a Dutch businessman.*
– ORIGIN Latin *concipere*.

concentrate verb **1** focus all one's attention on a particular object or activity: *she couldn't concentrate on the film.* **2** gather together in large numbers or a mass at one point: *resources should be concentrated in areas where unemployment is highest.* **3** increase the strength of a substance or solution. • noun a concentrated substance or solution.
– DERIVATIVES **concentrator** noun.
– ORIGIN from Latin *con-* 'together' + *centrum* 'centre'.

concentration noun **1** the action or power of concentrating. **2** a close gathering of people or things. **3** the relative amount of a particular substance within a solution or mixture.

concentration camp noun a camp for holding political prisoners, especially in Nazi Germany.

concentric adjective (of circles or arcs) sharing the same centre.
– ORIGIN Latin *concentricus*.

concept noun an abstract idea: *the concept of justice.*
– ORIGIN Latin *conceptum* 'something conceived'.

conception noun **1** the process of conceiving a child. **2** the forming of a plan or idea. **3** the way in which something is viewed or

regarded: *our conception of democracy.*
4 ability to imagine or understand something: *the administration had no conception of women's problems.*

conceptual adjective relating to ideas or concepts.
– DERIVATIVES **conceptually** adverb.

conceptualize (or **conceptualise**) verb form an idea or concept of something in the mind.
– DERIVATIVES **conceptualization** noun.

concern verb **1** relate to; be about. **2** affect or involve: *stop interfering in matters that don't concern you.* **3** make someone anxious or worried. • noun **1** worry or anxiety. **2** a matter of interest or importance: *the court's primary concern is her welfare.* **3** a business or company.
– ORIGIN Latin *concernere.*

concerned adjective worried or anxious.

concerning preposition about.

concert noun a musical performance given in public.
– PHRASES **in concert 1** acting together. **2** giving a live public performance.
– ORIGIN from Italian *concertare* 'harmonize'.

concerted adjective **1** jointly arranged or carried out: *a concerted campaign.* **2** done with great effort or determination.

concertina /kon-ser-tee-nuh/ noun a small musical instrument played by stretching and squeezing a central bellows, each note being sounded by a button. • verb (**concertinas, concertinaing, concertinaed** or **concertina'd**) compress something into folds like those of a concertina.

concerto /kuhn-**cher**-toh/ noun (pl. **concertos** or **concerti** /kuhn-**cher**-ti/) a musical composition for an orchestra and one or more solo instruments.
– ORIGIN Italian.

concert performance noun Brit. a performance of a piece of music written for an opera or ballet without the accompanying dramatic action.

concert pitch noun **1** an international standard for the tuning of musical instruments. **2** a state of readiness and keenness.

concession noun **1** a thing given up or allowed to settle a dispute: *the union was reluctant to make any concessions.* **2** a reduction in price for a certain kind of person. **3** a commercial operation set up within the premises of a larger business. **4** the right to use land or other property for a particular purpose, granted by a government or other controlling body.
– DERIVATIVES **concessionary** adjective.
– ORIGIN Latin.

concessionaire /kuhn-sesh-uh-**nair**/ noun someone who holds a concession.

conch /konch/ noun (pl. **conchs** /kongks/ or **conches** /**kon**-chiz/) a mollusc of tropical seas, with a spiral shell.
– ORIGIN Greek *konkhē* 'mussel, cockle'.

concierge /kon-si-**airzh**/ noun **1** (especially in France) a resident caretaker of a block of flats or small hotel. **2** a hotel employee who assists guests by booking tours, making theatre and restaurant reservations, etc.

– ORIGIN French.

conciliate /kuhn-**sil**-i-ayt/ verb **1** make someone calmer or less angry. **2** act as a mediator in a dispute.
– DERIVATIVES **conciliation** noun **conciliator** noun.
– ORIGIN Latin *conciliare* 'combine'.

conciliatory /kuhn-**sil**-i-uh-tri/ adjective intended to make someone calmer or less angry: *a conciliatory tone of voice.*

concise adjective giving information clearly and in few words.
– DERIVATIVES **concisely** adverb **conciseness** noun **concision** noun.
– ORIGIN Latin *concisus* 'cut up, cut down'.

conclave /**kong**-klayv/ noun **1** a private meeting. **2** (in the Roman Catholic Church) a meeting of cardinals in order to elect a pope.
– ORIGIN Latin, 'lockable room', from *clavis* 'key'.

conclude verb **1** bring or come to an end. **2** arrive at a judgement or opinion by reasoning: *doctors concluded that she had suffered a stroke.* **3** formally settle or arrange a treaty or agreement.
– ORIGIN Latin *concludere.*

conclusion noun **1** an end or finish. **2** the summing-up of an argument or text. **3** a judgement or decision reached by reasoning: *she came to the conclusion that her husband was right.* **4** the settling of a treaty or agreement.

conclusive adjective decisive or convincing: *conclusive evidence.*
– DERIVATIVES **conclusively** adverb.

concoct /kuhn-**kokt**/ verb **1** make a dish or meal by combining different ingredients. **2** invent a story or plan.
– DERIVATIVES **concoction** noun.
– ORIGIN Latin *concoquere* 'cook together'.

concomitant /kuhn-**kom**-i-tuhnt/ formal adjective occurring or naturally connected with something else: *the Gulf crisis and the concomitant rise in oil prices.* • noun a phenomenon that occurs or is naturally connected with something else.
– DERIVATIVES **concomitantly** adverb.
– ORIGIN Latin *concomitari* 'accompany'.

concord noun **1** literary agreement; harmony. **2** a treaty.
– ORIGIN Latin *concordia.*

concordance /kuhn-**kor**-duhnss/ noun **1** an alphabetical list of the important words in a text, usually with quotations from or references to the passages concerned. **2** formal agreement.
– ORIGIN Latin *concordare* 'agree on'.

concordant adjective in agreement; consistent.

concordat /kuhn-**kor**-dat/ noun an agreement or treaty, especially one between the Vatican and a government.

concourse noun **1** a large open area inside or in front of a public building. **2** formal a crowd of people.
– ORIGIN Latin *concursus.*

concrete adjective **1** existing in a physical form; not abstract. **2** specific; definite: *concrete proof.* • noun a building material made from gravel, sand, cement, and water, forming a stone-like mass when dry. • verb cover a surface with concrete.

- DERIVATIVES **concretely** adverb **concreteness** noun.
- ORIGIN Latin *concretus* 'grown together'.

concrete jungle noun an urban area with many large, unattractive, modern buildings.

concretion noun a hard solid mass.

concubine /kong-kyuu-byn/ noun 1 chiefly historical (in societies in which a man may have more than one wife) a woman who lives with a man but has lower status than his wife or wives. 2 old use a man's mistress.
- ORIGIN Latin *concubina*.

concupiscence /kuhn-kyoo-pi-suhnss/ noun formal lust.
- DERIVATIVES **concupiscent** adjective.
- ORIGIN Latin *concupiscere* 'begin to desire'.

concur /kuhn-ker/ verb (**concurs, concurring, concurred**) 1 agree: *the Council concurred with this decision.* 2 happen at the same time.
- ORIGIN Latin *concurrere* 'run together'.

concurrent adjective 1 existing or happening at the same time. 2 Mathematics (of three or more lines) meeting at or approaching one point.
- DERIVATIVES **concurrence** noun **concurrently** adverb.

concuss /kuhn-kuhss/ verb hit someone on the head, making them temporarily unconscious or confused.

concussion noun 1 temporary unconsciousness or confusion caused by a blow on the head. 2 a violent shock as from a heavy blow.
- ORIGIN Latin.

condemn verb 1 express complete disapproval of someone or something. 2 sentence someone to a punishment: *the rebels had been condemned to death.* 3 force someone to endure something unpleasant: *he was condemned to a lifelong struggle with depression.* 4 officially declare something to be unfit for use.
- DERIVATIVES **condemnation** noun **condemnatory** adjective.
- ORIGIN Latin *condemnare*.

condensation noun 1 water from humid air collecting as droplets on a cold surface. 2 the conversion of a vapour or gas to a liquid.

condense verb 1 change from a gas or vapour to a liquid. 2 make something denser or more concentrated. 3 express a piece of writing or speech in fewer words.
- ORIGIN Latin *condensare*.

condensed milk noun milk that has been thickened by evaporation and sweetened.

condenser noun 1 a piece of equipment for condensing vapour. 2 a lens or system of lenses for collecting and directing light. 3 another term for **CAPACITOR**.

condescend verb 1 behave as if one is better than other people. 2 do something that one believes to be below one's dignity or level of importance: *he condescended to see me at my hotel.*
- DERIVATIVES **condescension** noun.
- ORIGIN Latin *condescendere*.

condescending adjective feeling or showing that one thinks one is better than other people.
- DERIVATIVES **condescendingly** adverb.

condign /kuhn-dyn/ adjective formal (of punishment) fitting and deserved.
- ORIGIN Latin *condignus*.

condiment noun a substance such as salt, mustard, or pickle, used to flavour food.
- ORIGIN Latin *condimentum*.

condition noun 1 the state of something or someone, with regard to appearance, fitness, or working order. 2 (**conditions**) the circumstances affecting something: *the health risks associated with poor living conditions.* 3 a state of affairs that must exist before something else is possible: *for a country to borrow money, three conditions must be met.* 4 an illness or medical problem. • verb 1 train or accustom to behave in a certain way: *some students may have been conditioned to respond to authority figures.* 2 have a significant influence on or determine something. 3 bring something into a good or desired state or condition. 4 apply conditioner to the hair.
- PHRASES **on condition that** as long as certain requirements are fulfilled.
- ORIGIN Latin *condicion* 'agreement'.

conditional adjective 1 subject to one or more conditions or requirements being fulfilled; depending on other factors: *a conditional offer.* 2 (of a clause, phrase, conjunction, or verb form) expressing a condition. • noun the conditional form of a verb, for example *should* in *if I should die.*
- DERIVATIVES **conditionally** adverb.

conditioner noun a thing used to improve the condition of something, especially a liquid applied to the hair after shampooing.

condo noun (pl. **condos**) N. Amer. informal short for **CONDOMINIUM** (in sense 1).

condole /kuhn-dohl/ verb (**condole with**) express sympathy for someone.
- ORIGIN Latin *condolere* 'grieve or suffer with'.

condolence noun an expression of sympathy for someone, especially when a relative or close friend has died.

condom noun a thin rubber sheath worn on the penis during sex as a contraceptive or to protect against infection.
- ORIGIN unknown.

condominium /kon-duh-min-i-uhm/ noun (pl. **condominiums**) 1 N. Amer. a building or complex containing a number of individually owned flats or houses. 2 N. Amer. a flat or house in a condominium. 3 the joint control of a state's affairs by other states.
- ORIGIN Latin

condone /kuhn-dohn/ verb overlook or forgive an offence or wrongdoing.
- ORIGIN Latin *condonare* 'refrain from punishing'.

condor noun a very large South American vulture with a bare head and mainly black plumage.
- ORIGIN Spanish.

conduce verb (**conduce to**) formal help to bring something about.
- ORIGIN Latin *conducere* 'bring together'.

conducive adjective (**conducive to**) contributing to or helping to bring something about: *an environment which is conducive to learning.*

conduct noun /kon-dukt/ **1** the way in which a person behaves. **2** management or direction: *the conduct of foreign affairs.* • verb /kuhn-dukt/ **1** organize and carry something out. **2** direct the performance of a piece of music or an orchestra or choir. **3** guide someone to or around a place. **4** (**conduct oneself**) behave in a particular way. **5** transmit heat, electricity, etc. by conduction.
– ORIGIN Latin *conducere* 'bring together'.

conductance noun the degree to which a material conducts electricity.

conduction noun the transmission of heat or electricity directly through a substance.
– DERIVATIVES **conductive** adjective.

conductivity noun the degree to which a particular material conducts electricity or heat.

conductor noun **1** a person who conducts an orchestra or choir. **2** a material or device that conducts heat or electricity. **3** a person who collects fares on a bus. **4** N. Amer. a guard on a train.
– DERIVATIVES **conductress** noun.

conduit /kon-dwit, kon-dyuu-it/ noun **1** a channel for carrying water or other fluid from one place to another. **2** a tube or trough protecting electric wiring.
– ORIGIN Old French.

cone noun **1** an object which tapers from a circular base to a point. **2** (also **traffic cone**) a plastic cone used to separate off sections of a road. **3** the cone-shaped dry fruit of a conifer. **4** one of two types of light-sensitive cell in the retina of the eye, responsible for sharpness of vision and colour perception. Compare with **ROD**.
– ORIGIN Greek *kōnos.*

coney /koh-ni/ (also **cony**) noun (pl. **coneys**) Brit. a rabbit.
– ORIGIN Old French *conin,* from Latin *cuniculus.*

confab noun informal an informal conversation or discussion.

confabulate /kuhn-fab-yuu-layt/ verb formal have a conversation.
– DERIVATIVES **confabulation** noun.
– ORIGIN Latin *confabulari.*

confect /kuhn-fekt/ verb formal make something elaborate or dainty.
– ORIGIN Latin *conficere* 'put together'.

confection noun **1** an elaborate sweet dish. **2** an elaborately constructed thing: *an extravagant confection of marble and gilt.*

confectioner noun a person who makes or sells confectionery.

confectionery noun sweets and chocolates.

confederacy noun (pl. **confederacies**) **1** a league or alliance, especially of confederate states. **2** (**the Confederacy**) the Confederate states of the US.

confederate adjective /kuhn-fed-uh-ruht/ **1** joined by an agreement or treaty. **2** (**Confederate**) referring to the southern states which separated from the US in 1860–1. • noun /kuhn-fed-uh-ruht/ an accomplice or fellow worker. • verb /kuhn-fed-uh-rayt/ (usu. as adj. **confederated**) bring states or groups of people into an alliance.
– ORIGIN Latin *confoederatus.*

confederation noun **1** an alliance of a number of parties or groups. **2** a union of states with some political power belonging to a central authority.

confer /kuhn-fer/ verb (**confers, conferring, conferred**) **1** grant a title, award, benefit, or right to someone: *an honorary degree was conferred on her.* **2** have discussions.
– DERIVATIVES **conferment** noun **conferral** noun.
– ORIGIN Latin *conferre* 'bring together'.

conferee noun a person who attends a conference.

conference noun a formal meeting for discussion or debate.

confess verb **1** admit to a crime or wrongdoing. **2** acknowledge something reluctantly. **3** declare one's sins formally to a priest.
– ORIGIN Old French *confesser.*

confession noun **1** an act of confessing, especially a formal statement admitting to a crime. **2** an account of one's sins given privately to a priest. **3** (also **confession of faith**) a statement setting out essential religious beliefs.

confessional noun **1** an enclosed stall in a church, in which a priest sits to hear confessions. **2** a confession. • adjective **1** referring to speech or writing in which a person admits to private thoughts or incidents in their past. **2** relating to religious confession.

confessor noun **1** a priest who hears confessions. **2** a person who makes a confession.

confetti noun small pieces of coloured paper traditionally thrown over a bride and groom after a marriage ceremony.
– ORIGIN Italian, 'sweets' (from the Italian custom of throwing sweets during carnivals).

confidant /kon-fi-dant/ noun (fem. **confidante** pronunc. same) a person in whom one confides.

confide /kuhn-fyd/ verb **1** tell someone about a secret or private matter in confidence: *he decided to confide in Elizabeth.* **2** (**confide something to**) dated entrust something to the care of someone.
– ORIGIN Latin *confidere* 'have full trust'.

confidence noun **1** the belief that one can have faith in or rely on someone or something. **2** self-assurance resulting from a belief in one's own ability to achieve things. **3** a feeling of trust that someone will not reveal private information to others: *things I had told her in confidence.* **4** a private matter told to someone under the understanding that they will keep it secret.
– PHRASES **in someone's confidence** in a position of trust with someone.

confidence trick noun an act of cheating someone by gaining their trust.

confident adjective **1** feeling confidence in oneself. **2** feeling certainty about something.
– DERIVATIVES **confidently** adverb.

confidential adjective **1** intended to be kept secret: *confidential information.* **2** entrusted with private information: *a confidential secretary.*

– DERIVATIVES **confidentiality** noun **confidentially** adverb.

configuration /kuhn-fi-guh-**ray**-sh'n/ noun an arrangement of the parts of something in a particular way.

configure verb 1 arrange something in a particular way. 2 arrange a computer system so that it is able to perform a particular task.
– DERIVATIVES **configurable** adjective.
– ORIGIN Latin *configurare*.

confine verb /kuhn-**fyn**/ 1 (confine someone/ thing to) keep someone or something within certain limits of space, scope, or time. 2 (be confined to) be unable to leave one's bed, home, etc. due to illness or disability. 3 (be confined) dated (of a woman) remain in bed for a period before, during, and after giving birth.
• noun (confines) /**kon**-fynz/ limits or boundaries.
– ORIGIN from Latin *confinis* 'bordering'.

confined adjective (of a space) small and enclosed.

confinement noun 1 the state of being confined. 2 dated the time at which a woman gives birth.

confirm verb 1 state or show that something is true or correct: *the Stock Exchange confirmed that it was investigating the rumours*. 2 make something definite or formally valid: *hotels usually require a deposit to confirm a booking*. 3 (confirm someone in) make someone feel or believe something more strongly: *the experience confirmed her in her decision not to employ a nanny*. 4 administer the religious ceremony of confirmation to someone.
– DERIVATIVES **confirmatory** adjective.
– ORIGIN Latin *confirmare*.

confirmation noun 1 the action of confirming something. 2 the religious rite at which a baptized person is admitted as a full member of the Christian Church. 3 the Jewish ceremony of bar mitzvah.

confirmed adjective firmly established in a habit, belief, or way of life: *a confirmed bachelor*.

confiscate /**kon**-fi-skayt/ verb take or seize property with authority.
– DERIVATIVES **confiscation** noun.
– ORIGIN Latin *confiscare* 'put away in a chest'.

confit /**kon**-fi/ noun duck or other meat cooked very slowly in its own fat.
– ORIGIN French, 'conserved'.

conflagration /kon-fluh-**gray**-sh'n/ noun a large and destructive fire.
– ORIGIN Latin, from *flagrare* 'to blaze'.

conflate verb combine two or more things into one.
– DERIVATIVES **conflation** noun.
– ORIGIN Latin *conflare* 'kindle, fuse'.

conflict noun /**kon**-flikt/ 1 a serious disagreement or argument. 2 a long-lasting armed struggle. 3 a lack of agreement between opinions, principles, etc.: *a conflict of interests*.
• verb /kuhn-**flikt**/ be different or in opposition: *his theory conflicted with those generally accepted at the time*.
– ORIGIN Latin *conflictus*.

confluence /**kon**-floo-uhnss/ noun 1 a place where two rivers join. 2 an act or the process of two or more things merging.

– ORIGIN from Latin *confluere*.

conform verb 1 obey or follow rules, standards, or conventions: *the kitchen does not conform to hygiene regulations*. 2 be similar in form or type: *families which do not conform to the conventional stereotype*.
– ORIGIN Latin *conformare*.

conformance noun another term for CONFORMITY.

conformation noun the shape or structure of something.

conformist noun a person who behaves or thinks in the same way as most other people, rather than in an original or unconventional way. • adjective conventional.
– DERIVATIVES **conformism** noun.

conformity noun 1 the fact of following or obeying conventions, rules, or laws. 2 similarity in form or type.

confound verb 1 surprise or confuse someone. 2 prove a theory or expectation wrong. 3 defeat a plan, aim, or hope.
– ORIGIN Latin *confundere* 'pour together, mix up'.

confounded adjective informal, dated used to express annoyance.
– DERIVATIVES **confoundedly** adverb.

confraternity noun (pl. **confraternities**) a brotherhood, especially with a religious or charitable purpose.
– ORIGIN Latin *confraternitas*.

confrère /**kon**-frair/ noun a fellow member of a profession.
– ORIGIN French, from Latin *frater* 'brother'.

confront verb 1 come face to face with someone in a hostile or defiant way: *he was confronted by a police officer*. 2 (of a problem) present itself to someone: *the government was confronted with many difficulties*. 3 face up to and deal with a problem. 4 force someone to face or consider something: *she confronted him with her suspicions*.
– ORIGIN Latin *confrontare*.

confrontation noun a situation of angry disagreement or opposition.
– DERIVATIVES **confrontational** adjective.

Confucian /kuhn-**fyoo**-sh'n/ adjective relating to the Chinese philosopher Confucius (551–479 BC) or his philosophy. • noun a follower of Confucius or his philosophy.
– DERIVATIVES **Confucianism** noun **Confucianist** noun & adjective.

confuse verb 1 make someone unable to think clearly or understand something. 2 make something less easy to understand. 3 mistake one person or thing for another.
– DERIVATIVES **confusable** adjective.
– ORIGIN from Latin *confusus*.

confused adjective 1 unable to think clearly or understand something. 2 lacking order and so difficult to understand or make sense of.
– DERIVATIVES **confusedly** adverb.

confusion noun 1 the state of being confused; uncertainty or lack of understanding. 2 a situation or state of panic or disorder. 3 the mistaking of one person or thing for another.

confute verb formal prove a person or an accusation or assertion to be wrong.
– DERIVATIVES **confutation** noun.

– ORIGIN Latin *confutare* 'restrain, answer conclusively'.

conga /kong-guh/ noun **1** a Latin American dance performed by people in single file and consisting of three steps forward followed by a kick. **2** (also **conga drum**) a tall, narrow drum beaten with the hands.
– ORIGIN Spanish, from *congo* 'Congolese'.

congeal /kuhn-**jeel**/ verb (of a liquid substance) become semi-solid, especially on cooling.
– ORIGIN Latin *congelare*, from *gelare* 'freeze'.

congener /kuhn-**jeen**-er/ noun a chemical constituent, especially one which gives a distinctive character to a wine or spirit or is responsible for some of its effects on the body.
– ORIGIN Latin.

congenial /kuhn-**jee**-ni-uhl/ adjective **1** (of a person) pleasant to be with because their qualities or interests are similar to one's own: *congenial company.* **2** pleasant because suited to one's taste or character: *congenial working conditions.*
– DERIVATIVES **congeniality** noun **congenially** adverb.

congenital /kuhn-**jen**-i-t'l/ adjective **1** (of a disease or abnormality) present from birth. **2** having a particular trait as an apparently permanent part of one's character: *a congenital liar.*
– DERIVATIVES **congenitally** adverb.
– ORIGIN from Latin *congenitus* 'born together'.

conger /**kong**-ger/ (also **conger eel**) noun a large eel of coastal waters.
– ORIGIN Greek *gongros*.

congeries /kon-juh-reez/ noun (pl. same) a disorderly collection.
– ORIGIN Latin, 'heap, pile'.

congested adjective **1** so crowded as to make movement difficult or impossible. **2** abnormally full of blood. **3** blocked with mucus.
– ORIGIN Latin *congerere* 'heap up'.

congestion noun the state of being congested, especially by traffic: *the new bridge should ease congestion in the area.*

congestion charge noun Brit. a charge made to drive into an area, typically a city centre, that suffers heavy traffic.

congestive adjective Medicine involving or occurring as a result of a part of the body becoming abnormally full of blood.

conglomerate noun /kuhn-**glom**-muh-ruht/ **1** something consisting of a number of different and distinct things. **2** a large corporation formed by the merging of separate firms. **3** a type of sedimentary rock consisting of rounded fragments cemented together. • verb /kuhn-**glom**-muh-rayt/ gather into or form a conglomerate.
– DERIVATIVES **conglomeration** noun.
– ORIGIN Latin *conglomerare* 'roll or heap together'.

Congolese /kongg-uh-**leez**/ noun (pl. same) **1** a person from the Congo or the Democratic Republic of Congo (formerly Zaire). **2** any of the languages spoken in the Congo region. • adjective relating to the Congo or the Democratic Republic of Congo.

congratulate verb **1** express good wishes or

praise at the happiness or success of someone. **2** (**congratulate oneself**) think oneself lucky or clever.
– DERIVATIVES **congratulatory** adjective.
– ORIGIN Latin *congratulari*.

congratulation noun **1** (**congratulations**) praise or good wishes on a special occasion. **2** the action of congratulating someone.

congregant /**kongg**-rig-uhnt/ noun a member of a congregation.

congregate verb gather into a crowd or mass.
– ORIGIN Latin *congregare*.

congregation noun **1** a group of people gathered together for religious worship. **2** a gathering of people or things.
– DERIVATIVES **congregational** adjective.

Congregationalism noun a system of organization among Christian churches in which individual churches are largely self-governing.
– DERIVATIVES **Congregational** adjective **Congregationalist** noun & adjective.

congress noun **1** a formal meeting or series of meetings between delegates. **2** (**Congress**) a national law-making body, especially that of the US. **3** formal the action of coming together.
– DERIVATIVES **congressional** adjective.
– ORIGIN Latin *congressus*.

congressman (or **congresswoman**) noun (pl. **congressmen** or **congresswomen**) a member of the US Congress.

congruent /**kong**-groo-uhnt/ adjective **1** in agreement or harmony. **2** Geometry (of figures) identical in form.
– DERIVATIVES **congruence** noun.
– ORIGIN from Latin *congruere* 'agree'.

congruous /**kong**-groo-uhss/ adjective in agreement or harmony.
– DERIVATIVES **congruity** /kong-**groo**-it-i/ noun.

conical adjective shaped like a cone.

conic section noun the figure of a circle, ellipse, parabola, or hyperbola formed by the intersection of a plane and a circular cone.

conifer /**kon**-i-fer/ noun a tree bearing cones and evergreen needle-like or scale-like leaves, e.g. a pine or cypress.
– DERIVATIVES **coniferous** adjective.
– ORIGIN Latin, 'cone-bearing'.

conjecture /kuhn-**jek**-cher/ noun an opinion or conclusion based on incomplete information; a guess. • verb form a conjecture; guess.
– DERIVATIVES **conjectural** adjective.
– ORIGIN Latin *conjectura*.

conjoin verb formal join; combine.

conjoined twins plural noun technical term for SIAMESE TWINS.

conjoint adjective formal combined or united.

conjugal /**kon**-juu-g'l/ adjective relating to marriage or the relationship between husband and wife.
– ORIGIN Latin *conjugalis*.

conjugate /**kon**-juu-gayt/ verb give the different forms of a verb.
– DERIVATIVES **conjugation** noun.
– ORIGIN Latin *conjugare* 'yoke together'.

conjunction noun **1** a word used to connect words or clauses (e.g. *and*, *if*). **2** an instance of two or more events occurring at the same point in time or space. **3** Astronomy & Astrology an

C

alignment of two planets so that they appear to be in the same place in the sky.
– PHRASES **in conjunction** together.
– ORIGIN Latin.

conjunctiva /kon-jungk-**ty**-vuh/ noun (pl. **conjunctivae** /kon-jungk-**ty**-vi/) the mucous membrane that covers the front of the eye and lines the inside of the eyelids.
– ORIGIN from Latin *membrana conjunctiva* 'conjunctive membrane'.

conjunctive adjective relating to or forming a conjunction.

conjunctivitis /kuhn-jungk-ti-**vy**-tiss/ noun inflammation of the conjunctiva.

conjuncture noun **1** a combination of events. **2** a state of affairs.

conjure /**kun**-jer/ verb (usu. **conjure something up**) **1** cause a spirit or ghost to appear by magic. **2** cause something to appear as if by magic. **3** create an image of something in the mind: *the books conjure up nostalgic memories of Christmases past*.
– ORIGIN Latin *conjurare* 'conspire'.

conjuring noun a form of entertainment involving apparently magical tricks, typically ones which seem to make objects appear or disappear.

conjuror (also **conjurer**) noun a person who performs conjuring tricks.

conk¹ verb (**conk out**) informal **1** (of a machine) break down. **2** faint or go to sleep. **3** die.
– ORIGIN unknown.

conk² noun Brit. informal a person's nose.
– ORIGIN perhaps from CONCH.

conker noun Brit. **1** the hard, shiny dark brown nut of a horse chestnut tree. **2** (**conkers**) (treated as sing.) a children's game in which each player has a conker on a string and tries to break another player's conker with it.
– ORIGIN dialect, 'snail shell' (with which the game was originally played).

con man noun informal a man who cheats people by using confidence tricks.

conn verb US spelling of CON⁴.

connect verb **1** bring together so as to establish a link. **2** join together so as to provide access and communication: *the buildings were connected by underground passages.* **3** (**be connected**) be related in some way: *bonuses are connected to the firm's performance.* **4** (of a train, bus, etc.) arrive at its destination just before another leaves so that passengers can transfer.
– DERIVATIVES **connector** noun.
– ORIGIN Latin *connectere*.

connecting rod noun the rod connecting the piston and the crankpin in an engine.

connection (Brit. also **connexion**) noun **1** a link or relationship. **2** (**connections**) influential people with whom one has contact or to whom one is related. **3** an opportunity for catching a connecting train, bus, etc.
– PHRASES **in connection with** concerning.

connective adjective connecting one thing to another.

connective tissue noun body tissue that connects, supports, binds, or separates other tissues or organs.

connectivity noun **1** the state or extent of being connected. **2** Computing capacity for the interconnection of systems, applications, etc.

connexion noun variant spelling of CONNECTION.

conning tower noun a raised structure on a submarine, containing the periscope.

connive /kuh-**nyv**/ verb **1** (**connive at/in**) secretly allow a wrongdoing. **2** (often **connive with**) conspire.
– DERIVATIVES **connivance** noun.
– ORIGIN Latin *connivere* 'shut the eyes (to)'.

connoisseur /kon-nuh-**ser**/ noun an expert in matters involving the judgement of beauty, quality or skill: *a connoisseur of Renaissance art.*
– ORIGIN French, from *connaître* 'know'.

connotation /kon-nuh-**tay**-sh'n/ noun an idea or feeling suggested by a word in addition to its main or literal meaning.

connote /kuh-**noht**/ verb (of a word or phrase) imply or suggest something in addition to its main or literal meaning (e.g. the word *mother* connotes qualities such as protection and affection).
– ORIGIN Latin *connotare* 'mark in addition'.

connubial /kuh-**nyoo**-bi-uhl/ adjective literary relating to marriage; conjugal.
– ORIGIN Latin *connubialis*.

conquer verb **1** overcome and take control of a territory or its people by military force. **2** successfully overcome a problem or climb a mountain.
– DERIVATIVES **conqueror** noun.
– ORIGIN Latin *conquirere* 'gain, win'.

conquest noun **1** the action of conquering a territory or its people. **2** a conquered territory. **3** a person whose affection or favour has been won.

conquistador /kon-**kwiss**-tuh-dor/ noun (pl. **conquistadores** /kon-kwiss-tuh-**dor**-ayz/ or **conquistadors**) a Spanish conqueror of Mexico or Peru in the 16th century.
– ORIGIN Spanish.

consanguinity /kon-sang-**gwin**-it-i/ noun formal descent from the same ancestor.
– DERIVATIVES **consanguineous** adjective.
– ORIGIN Latin *consanguineus* 'of the same blood'.

conscience noun a person's moral sense of right and wrong, chiefly as it affects their own behaviour.
– PHRASES **in (all) conscience** in fairness.
– ORIGIN Latin *conscientia* 'knowledge within oneself', from *scire* 'to know'.

conscientious /kon-shi-**en**-shuhss/ adjective **1** diligent and thorough in carrying out one's work or duty. **2** relating to a person's conscience.
– DERIVATIVES **conscientiously** adverb **conscientiousness** noun.

conscientious objector noun a person who refuses to serve in the armed forces for moral reasons.

conscious adjective **1** aware of and responding to one's surroundings. **2** (usu. **conscious of**) aware of something: *I was very conscious of his disappointment.* **3** deliberate: *a conscious effort.*
– DERIVATIVES **consciously** adverb.
– ORIGIN Latin *conscius* 'knowing with others or

in oneself'.

consciousness noun **1** the state of being conscious. **2** one's awareness or perception of something.

conscript verb /kuhn-**skript**/ call someone up for compulsory military service. •noun /**kon**-skript/ a conscripted person.
– DERIVATIVES **conscription** noun.
– ORIGIN from Latin *conscriptus*.

consecrate /**kon**-si-krayt/ verb **1** make or declare something to be holy or sacred. **2** ordain someone to a sacred office, typically that of bishop. **3** (in Christian belief) declare that bread or wine represents or is the body and blood of Jesus.
– DERIVATIVES **consecration** noun.
– ORIGIN Latin *consecrare*.

consecutive /kuhn-**sek**-yuu-tiv/ adjective following in unbroken sequence.
– ORIGIN Latin *consecutivus*.

consensual /kuhn-**sen**-syoo-uhl/ adjective relating to or involving consent or consensus.

consensus /kuhn-**sen**-suhss/ noun general agreement about something.
– ORIGIN Latin.

consent noun permission or agreement. •verb **1** give permission for something. **2** agree to do something.
– ORIGIN from Latin *consentire* 'agree'.

consenting adult noun an adult who willingly agrees to engage in a sexual act.

consequence noun **1** a result or effect, especially one that is unpleasant. **2** importance or relevance: *the past is of no consequence.* **3** dated social distinction.
– ORIGIN Latin *consequentia*.

consequent adjective following as a result or effect of something.
– DERIVATIVES **consequential** adjective **consequently** adverb.

conservancy /kuhn-**ser**-vuhn-si/ noun (pl. **conservancies**) **1** an organization concerned with the preservation of natural resources. **2** a commission controlling a port, river, or catchment area. **3** the conservation of wildlife and the environment.

conservation noun **1** preservation or restoration of the natural environment and wildlife. **2** preservation and repair of archaeological, historical, and cultural sites and objects. **3** careful use of a resource: *energy conservation.* **4** Physics the principle by which the total value of a quantity (e.g. mass or energy) remains constant in a closed system.
– DERIVATIVES **conservationist** noun.

conservative adjective **1** opposed to change and holding traditional values. **2** (in politics) favouring free enterprise and private ownership. **3** (**Conservative**) relating to the Conservative Party. **4** (of an estimate) deliberately low for the sake of caution. •noun **1** a conservative person. **2** (**Conservative**) a supporter or member of the Conservative Party.
– DERIVATIVES **conservatism** noun **conservatively** adverb.

Conservative Party noun a major British right-wing political party which favours free enterprise and private ownership.

conservatoire /kuhn-**ser**-vuh-twar/ noun a college for the study of classical music.
– ORIGIN French.

conservator /kuhn-**serv**-uh-ter, **kon**-suh-vay-ter/ noun a person involved in conservation.

conservatory noun (pl. **conservatories**) **1** Brit. a room with a glass roof and walls, attached to a house and used as a sun lounge or a greenhouse. **2** N. Amer. a conservatoire.

conserve /kuhn-**serv**/ verb **1** protect something from harm or waste. **2** Physics maintain a quantity at a constant overall total. •noun /also kon-serv/ jam or marmalade.
– ORIGIN Latin *conservare*.

consider verb **1** think carefully about something. **2** believe or think: *people considered to be at risk of contracting the disease.* **3** take something into account when making a judgement: *his record is even more remarkable when you consider his age.* **4** look attentively at someone or something.
– ORIGIN Latin *considerare*.

considerable adjective great in size, amount, or importance.
– DERIVATIVES **considerably** adverb.

considerate adjective careful not to harm or inconvenience others.
– DERIVATIVES **considerately** adverb.

consideration noun **1** careful thought. **2** a fact taken into account when making a decision. **3** thoughtfulness towards others. **4** a payment or reward.
– PHRASES **take something into consideration** think about something when making a decision or forming an opinion.

considering preposition & conjunction taking something into consideration. •adverb informal taking everything into account.

consign /kuhn-**syn**/ verb **1** deliver someone or something to someone's possession or care. **2** send goods by a public carrier. **3** (**consign someone/thing to**) put someone or something in a place so as to be rid of them.
– ORIGIN Latin *consignare* 'mark with a seal'.

consignment noun a batch of goods delivered or sent somewhere.

consist verb **1** (**consist of**) be composed of. **2** (**consist in**) have as an essential feature: *poetry consists in the use of emotive language.*
– ORIGIN Latin *consistere* 'stand firm'.

consistency (also **consistence**) noun (pl. **consistencies**) **1** the state of being consistent. **2** the degree of thickness of a substance.

consistent adjective **1** always acting or done in the same way **2** unchanging over a period of time: *consistent growth in the manufacturing sector of the economy.* **3** in agreement with something: *the results are consistent with other research.*
– DERIVATIVES **consistently** adverb.

consistory /kuhn-**siss**-tuh-ri/ noun (pl. **consistories**) **1** (in the Roman Catholic Church) the council of cardinals, with or without the Pope. **2** (also **consistory court**) (in the Church of England) a court presided over by a bishop, for the administration of ecclesiastical law in a diocese.
– ORIGIN Latin *consistorium*.

consolation /kon-suh-**lay**-sh'n/ noun

1 comfort received after a loss or disappointment. 2 a person or thing providing such comfort.
– DERIVATIVES **consolatory** /kuhn-**sol**-uh-tri/ adjective.

consolation prize noun a prize given to a competitor who just fails to win.

console[1] /kuhn-**sohl**/ verb comfort someone in a time of grief of disappointment.
– ORIGIN Latin *consolari*.

console[2] /**kon**-sohl/ noun 1 a panel or unit containing a set of controls. 2 (also **games console**) a small machine for playing computerized video games. 3 the cabinet containing the keyboards, stops, etc. of an organ. 4 an ornamental bracket used to support a structure or fixture on a wall.
– ORIGIN French.

consolidate /kuhn-**sol**-i-dayt/ verb 1 make something stronger or more stable: *the company consolidated its position in the market.* 2 combine two or more things into a single unit: *arrangements can be made to consolidate your debts.*
– DERIVATIVES **consolidation** noun **consolidator** noun.
– ORIGIN Latin *consolidare*, from *solidus* 'solid'.

consommé /kuhn-**som**-may/ noun a clear soup made with concentrated stock.
– ORIGIN French.

consonance /**kon**-suh-nuhnss/ noun agreement or compatibility.

consonant /**kon**-suh-nuhnt/ noun 1 a speech sound in which the breath is at least partly obstructed and which forms a syllable when combined with a vowel. 2 a letter representing such a sound (e.g. *c*, *t*). • adjective (**consonant with**) in agreement or harmony with: *the findings are consonant with recent research.*
– DERIVATIVES **consonantal** adjective.
– ORIGIN Latin *consonare*.

consort[1] noun /**kon**-sort/ a wife or husband, especially of a reigning monarch. • verb /kuhn-**sort**/ (**consort with**) regularly associate with someone.
– ORIGIN Latin *consors* 'sharing, partner'.

consort[2] /**kon**-sort/ noun a small group of musicians performing together, typically playing Renaissance music.
– ORIGIN earlier form of **CONCERT**.

consortium /kuhn-**sor**-ti-uhm/ noun (pl. **consortia** /kuhn-**sor**-ti-uh, kuhn-**sor**-shuh/ or **consortiums**) an association of several companies.
– ORIGIN Latin, 'partnership'.

conspectus /kuhn-**spek**-tuhss/ noun a summary or overview of a subject.
– ORIGIN Latin, 'a view or survey'.

conspicuous /kuhn-**spik**-yoo-uhss/ adjective 1 clearly visible. 2 attracting notice; notable: *his conspicuous bravery.*
– DERIVATIVES **conspicuously** adverb.
– ORIGIN from Latin *conspicere* 'look at attentively'.

conspiracist noun a supporter of a conspiracy theory.

conspiracy noun (pl. **conspiracies**) 1 a secret plan by a group to do something unlawful or harmful. 2 the action of conspiring to do something.

conspiracy theory noun a belief that some secret but influential organization is responsible for an unexplained event.

conspire verb 1 jointly make secret plans to commit a wrongful act. 2 (of circumstances) seem to be acting together to bring about an unfortunate result: *the illness and her failing marriage conspired to make her life intolerable.*
– DERIVATIVES **conspirator** noun **conspiratorial** adjective **conspiratorially** adverb.
– ORIGIN Latin *conspirare* 'agree, plot'.

constable noun Brit. a police officer of the lowest rank.
– ORIGIN from Old French *conestable*, from Latin *comes stabuli* 'head officer of the stable'.

constabulary /kuhn-**stab**-yuu-luh-ri/ noun (pl. **constabularies**) Brit. a police force.

constant adjective 1 occurring continuously: *a constant stream of visitors.* 2 remaining the same: *a constant speed.* 3 faithful and dependable. • noun 1 an unchanging situation. 2 Mathematics & Physics a number or quantity that does not change its value.
– DERIVATIVES **constancy** noun **constantly** adverb.
– ORIGIN Old French, from Latin *constare* 'stand firm'.

constellation noun a group of stars forming a recognized pattern and typically named after a mythological or other figure.
– ORIGIN Latin, from *stella* 'star'.

consternation noun a feeling of anxiety or dismay.
– ORIGIN Latin.

constipated adjective suffering from constipation.
– ORIGIN Latin *constipare* 'crowd or press together'.

constipation noun the condition of having difficulty in emptying the bowels.

constituency /kuhn-**stit**-yoo-uhn-si/ noun (pl. **constituencies**) 1 the group of voters in a particular area who elect a representative to a law-making body. 2 chiefly Brit. the area represented in this way.

constituent adjective 1 being a part of a whole: *the constituent republics of the USSR.* 2 having the power to appoint or elect a representative. 3 able to make or change a political constitution. • noun 1 a voter in a constituency. 2 a component part of something: *the essential constituents of the human diet.*
– ORIGIN Latin, from *constituere* 'establish, appoint'.

constitute /**kon**-sti-tyoot/ verb 1 be a part of a whole: *women constitute over half of the workforce.* 2 be or be equivalent to: *his failure to act constituted a breach of duty.* 3 (**be constituted**) be established by law.
– ORIGIN Latin *constituere* 'establish, appoint'.

constitution noun 1 a body of principles according to which a state or organization is governed. 2 the composition or formation of something. 3 a person's physical or mental state.

constitutional adjective 1 relating to or according to the principles of a constitution. 2 relating to a person's physical or mental state. • noun dated a walk taken regularly to maintain good health.
– DERIVATIVES **constitutionality** noun

constitutionally adverb.

constitutive adjective **1** having the power to establish something. **2** forming a constituent of something.

constrain verb **1** force someone to do something: *he felt constrained to explain.* **2** (as adj. **constrained**) appearing forced or unnatural. **3** severely restrict the scope, extent, or activity of: *most developing countries are constrained by limited resources.*
– ORIGIN Old French *constraindre*.

constraint noun **1** a limitation or restriction: *tight financial constraints.* **2** strict control of one's behaviour or repression of one's feelings.

constrict verb **1** make or become narrower or tighter: *a drug that constricts the blood vessels.* **2** limit or restrict: *political parties constricted by the need to appeal to public opinion.*
– DERIVATIVES **constriction** noun.
– ORIGIN Latin *constringere* 'bind tightly together'.

constrictor noun **1** a snake that kills by squeezing and choking its prey, such as a boa or python. **2** a muscle whose contraction narrows a vessel or passage in the body.

construct verb /kuhn-**strukt**/ **1** build or make something. **2** form something from different elements: *he constructed his own theory of the universe.* •noun /**kon**-strukt/ **1** an idea or theory containing various elements. **2** a thing that has been built or made.
– DERIVATIVES **constructor** noun.
– ORIGIN Latin *construere*.

construction noun **1** the action or process of constructing something. **2** a building or other structure. **3** the industry of erecting buildings or other structures. **4** an interpretation or explanation of something.
– DERIVATIVES **constructional** adjective.

constructive adjective useful and helpful: *constructive suggestions.*
– DERIVATIVES **constructively** adverb.

constructive dismissal noun the changing of an employee's job with the aim of forcing them to resign.

construe verb (**construes, construing, construed**) interpret something in a particular way: *his silence could be construed as an admission of guilt.*
– DERIVATIVES **construal** noun.
– ORIGIN Latin *construere* 'heap together, build'.

consul /**kon**-s'l/ noun **1** a state official living in a foreign city and protecting the state's citizens and interests there. **2** (in ancient Rome) one of two elected chief magistrates who ruled the republic jointly for a year.
– DERIVATIVES **consular** /**kon**-syuu-ler/ adjective.
– ORIGIN Latin.

consulate noun **1** the place where a consul works. **2** (in ancient Rome) the period of office of a consul or the system of government by consuls.

consult verb **1** ask someone for information or advice. **2** discuss something with someone, especially in order to get their approval or permission: *patients are entitled to be consulted about their treatment.* **3** (as adj. **consulting**) acting as a professional adviser to others in the same field.
– DERIVATIVES **consultative** adjective.
– ORIGIN Latin *consultare*.

consultancy noun (pl. **consultancies**) a company giving expert advice in a particular field.

consultant noun **1** a person who provides expert advice professionally. **2** Brit. a senior hospital doctor.

consultation noun **1** the process of consulting someone or discussing something. **2** a meeting to discuss something or to get advice or treatment.

consume verb **1** eat or drink something. **2** use up a resource: *a smaller vehicle which consumes less fuel.* **3** (especially of a fire) completely destroy something. **4** (of a feeling) completely fill the mind of someone: *she was consumed with guilt.*
– DERIVATIVES **consumable** adjective **consuming** adjective.
– ORIGIN Latin *consumere*.

consumer noun a person who buys a product or service for personal use.

consumer durables plural noun Brit. manufactured items that are expected to have a long useful life after they have been purchased.

consumerism noun **1** the preoccupation of society with acquiring goods. **2** the protection of the interests of consumers.
– DERIVATIVES **consumerist** adjective & noun.

consummate verb /**kon**-syuu-mayt/ **1** make a marriage or relationship complete by having sex. **2** complete a transaction. •adjective /kuhn-**sum**-muht/ showing great skill and flair.
– DERIVATIVES **consummately** adverb **consummation** noun.
– ORIGIN Latin *consummare*.

consumption noun **1** the action or process of consuming something. **2** an amount of something that is consumed: *she had managed to reduce her alcohol consumption.* **3** dated a wasting disease, especially tuberculosis.
– DERIVATIVES **consumptive** adjective & noun (dated).

contact noun /**kon**-takt/ **1** the state of touching something. **2** the state of communicating or meeting: *she had lost contact with her son.* **3** a relationship or communication established with someone: *we have good contacts with the local community.* **4** a person who may be asked for information or help. **5** a person who has associated with a patient suffering from a contagious disease. **6** a connection for the passage of an electric current from one thing to another. •verb /**kon**-takt, kuhn-**takt**/ get in touch or communication with someone.
•adjective caused by or operating through physical touch: *contact dermatitis.*
– DERIVATIVES **contactable** adjective.
– ORIGIN Latin *contactus*, from *contingere* 'touch, border on'.

contact lens noun a thin plastic lens placed directly on the surface of the eye to correct visual defects.

contact print noun a photographic print made by placing a negative directly on to sensitized paper, glass, or film and illuminating it.

contact sport noun a sport in which bodily contact between the participants is a necessary feature.

contagion /kuhn-**tay**-juhn/ noun the passing of disease from one person to another by close contact.
– ORIGIN Latin.

contagious adjective 1 (of a disease) spread by direct or indirect contact between people or organisms. 2 having a contagious disease. 3 (of an emotion, attitude, etc.) likely to spread to and affect others: *her enthusiasm is contagious.*

contain verb 1 have or hold within: *a wallet containing cash and credit cards.* 2 control or restrain oneself or a feeling. 3 prevent a problem from becoming worse.
– DERIVATIVES **containable** adjective.
– ORIGIN Latin *continere.*

container noun 1 a box, cylinder, or similar object for holding something. 2 a large metal box for the transport of goods by road, rail, sea, or air.

containerize (or **containerise**) verb pack cargo into containers or transport it in containers.
– DERIVATIVES **containerization** noun.

containment noun the action of keeping something harmful under control.

contaminate verb pollute something by exposing it to or adding a substance that is poisonous or carries disease.
– DERIVATIVES **contaminant** noun **contamination** noun.
– ORIGIN Latin *contaminare.*

contemplate /**kon**-tuhm-playt/ verb 1 look at someone or something thoughtfully. 2 think about: *the idea was too awful to contemplate.* 3 think deeply and at length.
– ORIGIN Latin *contemplari.*

contemplation noun 1 the process of contemplating something. 2 religious meditation.

contemplative /kuhn-**tem**-pluh-tiv/ adjective showing or involving contemplation: *a contemplative mood.* • noun a person whose life is devoted to prayer, especially in a monastery or convent.

contemporaneous /kuhn-tem-puh-**ray**-ni-uhss/ adjective existing at or occurring in the same period of time.
– DERIVATIVES **contemporaneity** /kuhn-tem-puh-ruh-**nay**-i-ti/ noun.
– ORIGIN Latin.

contemporary /kuhn-**tem**-puh-ruh-ri, kuhn-**tem**-puh-ri/ adjective 1 living, occurring, or originating at the same time: *Greek literature contemporary with the New Testament.* 2 belonging to or occurring in the present. 3 modern in style or design. • noun (pl. **contemporaries**) 1 a person or thing existing at the same time as another. 2 a person of roughly the same age as another.
– ORIGIN Latin *contemporarius*, from *tempus* 'time'.

contempt noun 1 the feeling that a person or a thing is worthless or deserves no respect at all. 2 (also **contempt of court**) the offence of being disobedient to or disrespectful of a court of law.
– PHRASES **beneath contempt** utterly worthless. **hold someone/thing in contempt** despise

someone or something.
– ORIGIN Latin *contemptus.*

contemptible adjective deserving to be hated or despised: *a display of contemptible cowardice.*
– DERIVATIVES **contemptibly** adverb.

contemptuous adjective showing or feeling a lack of respect for someone or something.
– DERIVATIVES **contemptuously** adverb.

contend verb 1 (**contend with/against**) struggle to deal with a difficulty: *they may have to contend with racism and discrimination.* 2 (**contend for**) struggle or campaign to achieve something. 3 put forward a position in an argument: *he contends that the judge was wrong.*
– DERIVATIVES **contender** noun.
– ORIGIN Latin *contendere.*

content[1] /kuhn-**tent**/ adjective happy and satisfied. • verb 1 satisfy or please someone. 2 (**content oneself with**) accept something as adequate despite wanting something more or better. • noun a state of happiness or satisfaction.
– PHRASES **to one's heart's content** as much as one wants.
– DERIVATIVES **contentment** noun.
– ORIGIN Latin *contentus.*

content[2] /**kon**-tent/ noun 1 (**contents**) the things that are contained in something. 2 the amount of a particular thing occurring in a substance: *soya milk has a low fat content.* 3 (**contents** or **table of contents**) a list of chapters or sections at the front of a book or periodical. 4 the material dealt with in a speech or text as distinct from its form or style.
– ORIGIN Latin *contentum.*

contented adjective happy and satisfied.
– DERIVATIVES **contentedly** adverb.

contention noun 1 heated disagreement between people. 2 a point of view expressed or asserted.
– PHRASES **in** (or **out of**) **contention** having (or not having) a good chance of success in a contest.
– ORIGIN Latin.

contentious adjective 1 causing or likely to cause disagreement or controversy. 2 tending to provoke arguments.

contest noun /**kon**-test/ 1 an event in which people compete to try to win something. 2 a struggle to win power or control: *the Tory leadership contest.* • verb /kuhn-**test**/ 1 take part in a competition, election, or struggle for a position of power: *one of the first women to contest a parliamentary seat.* 2 challenge or dispute: *he intended to contest his father's will.*
– DERIVATIVES **contestable** adjective.
– ORIGIN Latin *contestari* 'call upon to witness'.

contestant noun a person who takes part in a contest.

context noun 1 the circumstances that form the setting for an event, statement, or idea. 2 the parts that immediately precede and follow a word or passage and make its meaning clear.
– DERIVATIVES **contextual** adjective **contextually** adverb.
– ORIGIN Latin *contextus.*

contextualize (or **contextualise**) verb consider something together with the surrounding words or circumstances.

contiguous /kuhn-**tig**-yoo-uhss/ adjective **1** sharing a border. **2** next or together in sequence.
– DERIVATIVES **contiguity** noun.
– ORIGIN Latin *contiguus* 'touching'.

continent[1] noun **1** any of the world's main continuous expanses of land (Europe, Asia, Africa, North and South America, Australia, Antarctica). **2** (also **the Continent**) the mainland of Europe as distinct from the British Isles.
– ORIGIN from Latin *terra continens* 'continuous land'.

continent[2] adjective **1** able to control the bowels and bladder. **2** self-restrained, especially sexually.
– DERIVATIVES **continence** noun.
– ORIGIN from Latin *continere*, from *tenere* 'to hold'.

continental adjective **1** forming or belonging to a continent. **2** (also **Continental**) coming from or typical of mainland Europe. • noun (also **Continental**) a person from mainland Europe.

continental breakfast noun a light breakfast of coffee and bread rolls.

continental climate noun a relatively dry climate with very hot summers and very cold winters, characteristic of the central parts of Asia and North America.

continental drift noun the gradual movement of the continents across the earth's surface through geological time.

continental quilt noun Brit. a duvet.

continental shelf noun an area of seabed around a large land mass where the sea is relatively shallow.

contingency /kuhn-**tin**-juhn-si/ noun (pl. **contingencies**) **1** a future event or circumstance which is possible but cannot be predicted with certainty. **2** something done in case of a possible event or circumstance occurring: *stores were kept as a contingency against a blockade*.

contingent /kuhn-**tin**-juhnt/ noun **1** a group of people with a common feature, forming part of a larger group. **2** a body of troops or police sent to join a larger force. • adjective **1** (**contingent on**) dependent on something: *the merger is contingent on government approval*. **2** subject to or happening by chance.
– ORIGIN Latin *contingere* 'befall'.

continual adjective **1** constantly or frequently occurring. **2** having no interruptions: *a continual process of growth*.
– DERIVATIVES **continually** adverb.

USAGE: On the distinction between **continual** and **continuous**, see the note at **CONTINUOUS**.

continuance noun formal **1** the state of continuing. **2** the time for which a situation or action lasts.

continuation noun **1** the action or state of continuing. **2** a part that is attached to and is an extension of something else.

continue verb (**continues**, **continuing**, **continued**) **1** keep existing or happening

without stopping: *the rain continued to pour down*. **2** carry on with: *he returned to Britain to continue his work*. **3** carry on travelling in the same direction. **4** start again: *the trial continues tomorrow*.
– ORIGIN Latin *continuare*.

continuity /kon-ti-**nyoo**-i-ti/ noun (pl. **continuities**) **1** the uninterrupted and unchanged existence or operation of something. **2** a logical connection or smooth line of development between things. **3** the maintaining of continuous action and consistent details in the scenes of a film or broadcast. **4** the linking of broadcast items by a spoken commentary.

continuo /kuhn-**tin**-yoo-oh/ noun (pl. **continuos**) (in baroque music) an accompanying part which includes a bass line and harmonies, typically played on a keyboard instrument.
– ORIGIN Italian *basso continuo* 'continuous bass'.

continuous adjective forming an unbroken whole or sequence without interruptions or exceptions.
– DERIVATIVES **continuously** adverb.

USAGE: **Continuous** and **continual** can both mean 'without interruption' (*years of continuous/continual warfare*), but only **continual** can be used to mean 'happening frequently' (*the continual arguments*).

continuous assessment noun Brit. the evaluation of a pupil's progress throughout a course of study, rather than by exams.

continuum /kuhn-**tin**-yoo-uhm/ noun (pl. **continua** /kuhn-**tin**-yoo-uh/) a continuous sequence in which the elements next to each other are very similar, but the last and the first are very different.
– ORIGIN Latin.

contort verb twist or bend something out of its normal shape.
– DERIVATIVES **contortion** noun.
– ORIGIN Latin *contorquere*.

contortionist noun an entertainer who twists and bends their body into strange and unnatural positions.

contour noun **1** an outline of the shape or form of something. **2** (also **contour line**) a line on a map joining points of equal height. • verb mould something into a particular shape.
– ORIGIN French.

contra- prefix against; opposite: *contraception*.
– ORIGIN Latin *contra*.

contraband /**kon**-truh-band/ noun **1** goods that have been imported or exported illegally. **2** trade in smuggled goods.
– ORIGIN Italian *contrabando*.

contraception noun the use of contraceptives to prevent pregnancy.

contraceptive noun a device or drug used to prevent a woman becoming pregnant. • adjective **1** preventing pregnancy. **2** relating to contraception.

contract noun /**kon**-trakt/ **1** a written or spoken agreement intended to be enforceable by law. **2** informal an arrangement for someone to be killed by a hired assassin. • verb /kuhn-**trakt**/ **1** decrease in size, number, or

range. **2** (of a muscle) become shorter and tighter in order to move part of the body. **3** catch or develop a disease. **4** enter into a legally binding agreement with someone. **5** (**contract in/out**) Brit. choose to be or not to be involved in something: *people who have contracted out of the state pension scheme.* **6** (**contract something out**) arrange for work to be done by another organization. **7** become liable to pay a debt.
– DERIVATIVES **contractual** adjective **contractually** adverb.
– ORIGIN Latin *contractus.*

contract bridge noun the standard form of the card game bridge, in which only tricks bid and won count towards the game.

contractible adjective able to be shrunk or capable of contracting.

contractile /kuhn-**trak**-tyl/ adjective technical able to contract or produce contraction.

contraction noun **1** the process of contracting. **2** a shortening of the muscles of the womb occurring at intervals during childbirth. **3** a shortened form of a word or group of words.

contractor noun a person who undertakes a contract to provide materials or labour for a job.

contradict verb deny the truth of a statement made by someone by saying the opposite.
– ORIGIN Latin *contradicere* 'speak against'.

contradiction noun **1** an opposition or lack of agreement between statements, ideas, or features. **2** the action of saying the opposite to something that has already been said.
– PHRASES **contradiction in terms** a statement containing words or ideas that are incompatible in meaning.

contradictory adjective **1** opposed or inconsistent. **2** containing opposing or inconsistent elements.

contradistinction noun distinction made by contrasting the different qualities of two things.

contraflow noun Brit. a temporary arrangement by which the lanes of a dual carriageway or motorway normally carrying traffic in one direction become two-directional.

contraindicate verb Medicine (of a condition or circumstance) suggest or indicate that a particular technique or drug should not be used.
– DERIVATIVES **contraindication** noun.

contralto /kuhn-**tral**-toh/ noun (pl. **contraltos**) the lowest female singing voice.
– ORIGIN Italian.

contraption noun a machine or device that appears strange or unnecessarily complicated.
– ORIGIN perhaps from **CONTRIVE**, by association with **TRAP**.

contrapuntal /kon-truh-**pun**-t'l/ adjective Music relating to or in counterpoint.
– DERIVATIVES **contrapuntally** adverb.
– ORIGIN from Italian *contrapunto* 'counterpoint'.

contrarian /kuhn-**trair**-i-uhn/ noun a person who opposes or rejects popular opinion.

contrariety /kon-truh-**ry**-uh-ti/ noun opposition or inconsistency between two things.

contrariwise /kuhn-**trair**-i-wyz/ adverb **1** in the opposite way. **2** on the other hand.

contrary /**kon**-truh-ri/ adjective **1** opposite in nature, direction, or meaning. **2** (of two or more statements, beliefs, etc.) opposed to one another. **3** /kuhn-**trair**-i/ deliberately inclined to do the opposite of what is expected or desired. • noun (**the contrary**) the opposite.
– PHRASES **to the contrary** with the opposite meaning or implication.
– DERIVATIVES **contrarily** adverb **contrariness** noun.
– ORIGIN Latin *contrarius.*

contrast noun /**kon**-trahst/ **1** the state of being noticeably different from something else when put or considered together: *in contrast to karate, tae kwon do is characterized by its high kicks.* **2** a thing or person noticeably different from another. **3** the degree of difference between tones in a television picture, photograph, or other image. • verb /kuhn-**trahst**/ **1** differ noticeably. **2** compare people or things so as to emphasize differences.
– DERIVATIVES **contrastive** adjective.
– ORIGIN Latin *contrastare.*

contravene /kon-truh-**veen**/ verb **1** commit an act that is not allowed by a law, rule, treaty, etc. **2** conflict with a right or principle.
– DERIVATIVES **contravener** noun **contravention** noun.
– ORIGIN Latin *contravenire.*

contretemps /**kon**-truh-ton/ noun (pl. same or /**kon**-truh-tonz/) a minor disagreement.
– ORIGIN French, originally meaning 'motion out of time'.

contribute /kuhn-**trib**-yoot/ verb **1** give something in order to help achieve or provide something. **2** (**contribute to**) help to cause: *all of these factors can contribute to depression.* **3** give one's views in a discussion.
– DERIVATIVES **contributive** /kuhn-**trib**-yuu-tiv/ adjective **contributor** noun.
– ORIGIN Latin *contribuere* 'bring together, add'.

contribution noun **1** a gift or payment to a common fund or collection. **2** the part played by a person or thing in causing or advancing something: *his contribution to 20th-century music cannot be overstated.* **3** an item that forms part of a journal, book, broadcast, or discussion.

contributory /kuhn-**trib**-yuu-tuh-ri/ adjective **1** playing a part in bringing something about. **2** (of a pension or insurance scheme) operated by means of a fund into which people pay.

con trick noun informal a confidence trick.

contrite /kuhn-**tryt**, **kon**-tryt/ adjective very sorry or regretful for having done wrong.
– DERIVATIVES **contritely** adverb **contrition** noun.
– ORIGIN from Latin *conterere* 'grind down, wear away'.

contrivance noun **1** a clever or inventive device or scheme. **2** the use of skill to create or achieve something.

contrive /kuhn-**tryv**/ verb **1** plan or achieve something in a clever or skilful way. **2** manage to do something foolish.
– DERIVATIVES **contriver** noun.
– ORIGIN Old French *controver* 'imagine,

invent'.

contrived adjective deliberately created rather than arising naturally, and typically seeming artificial.

control noun **1** the power to influence people's behaviour or the course of events. **2** the restriction of something: *crime control.* **3** a means of limiting or regulating something: *exchange controls.* **4** a device by which a machine is regulated. **5** the place where something is checked or from which an activity is directed: *passport control.* **6** a person or thing used as a standard of comparison for checking the results of a survey or experiment. • verb (**controls, controlling, controlled**) **1** have control of; direct or supervise: *she was appointed to control the firm's marketing strategy.* **2** limit or regulate something.
– PHRASES **in control** able to direct a situation, person, or activity. **out of control** no longer manageable. **under control** (of a danger or emergency) being dealt with or contained successfully.
– DERIVATIVES **controllability** noun **controllable** adjective **controllably** adverb **controller** noun.
– ORIGIN Old French *contreroller* 'keep a copy of a roll of accounts'.

controlling interest noun the holding by one person or group of a majority of the stock of a business.

control tower noun a tall building from which the movements of air traffic are controlled.

controversial adjective causing or likely to cause much debate and conflicting opinions.
– DERIVATIVES **controversialist** noun **controversially** adverb.

controversy /kon-truh-ver-si, kuhn-**trov**-er-si/ noun (pl. **controversies**) debate about a matter which arouses conflicting opinions.
– ORIGIN from Latin *controversus* 'turned against, disputed'.

> USAGE: The second pronunciation, with the stress on **-trov-**, is regarded by some people as incorrect.

controvert verb deny the truth of something.
– ORIGIN from Latin *controversus* 'turned against, disputed'.

contumacious /kon-tyuu-**may**-shuhss/ adjective old use or Law wilfully disobedient to authority.
– DERIVATIVES **contumacy** noun.
– ORIGIN from Latin *contumax.*

contumely /kon-**tyoom**-li/ noun (pl. **contumelies**) old use insolent or insulting language or treatment.
– ORIGIN Latin *contumelia.*

contusion /kuhn-**tyoo**-zh'n/ noun Medicine a bruise.
– DERIVATIVES **contuse** verb.
– ORIGIN from Latin *contundere* 'to bruise, crush'.

conundrum /kuh-**nun**-druhm/ noun (pl. **conundrums**) **1** a confusing and difficult problem or question. **2** a riddle.
– ORIGIN unknown.

conurbation /kon-er-**bay**-sh'n/ noun an extended urban area consisting of several

towns merging with the suburbs of a central city.
– ORIGIN from Latin *urbs* 'city'.

convalesce /kon-vuh-**less**/ verb gradually recover one's health after an illness or medical treatment.
– ORIGIN Latin *convalescere.*

convalescent adjective recovering from an illness or medical treatment. • noun a person who is recovering from an illness or medical treatment.
– DERIVATIVES **convalescence** noun.

convection noun transference of mass or heat within a fluid caused by the tendency of warmer and less dense material to rise.
– DERIVATIVES **convect** verb **convective** adjective.
– ORIGIN from Latin *convehere.*

convector noun a heating appliance that circulates warm air by convection.

convene /kuhn-**veen**/ verb come or bring together for a meeting or activity.
– ORIGIN Latin *convenire* 'assemble, agree, fit'.

convener (also **convenor**) noun **1** a person who arranges the meetings of a committee. **2** Brit. a senior trade union official at a workplace.

convenience noun **1** freedom from effort or difficulty: *food today is more about convenience than nourishment.* **2** a useful or helpful thing. **3** Brit. a public toilet.
– PHRASES **at one's convenience** when or where it suits one. **at one's earliest convenience** as soon as one can without difficulty.
– ORIGIN Latin *convenientia.*

convenience food noun a food that has been pre-prepared commercially and so requires little preparation by the consumer.

convenient adjective **1** fitting in well with a person's needs, activities, and plans. **2** involving little trouble or effort.
– DERIVATIVES **conveniently** adverb.

convenor noun variant spelling of **CONVENER**.

convent noun **1** a Christian community of nuns living under monastic vows. **2** (also **convent school**) a school attached to and run by a convent.
– ORIGIN Latin *conventus* 'assembly, company'.

conventicle /kuhn-**ven**-tik'l/ noun historical a secret or unlawful religious meeting, especially of nonconformists.
– ORIGIN Latin *conventiculum* 'place of assembly'.

convention noun **1** a way in which something is usually done: *he is at his best working within the established conventions.* **2** socially acceptable behaviour. **3** an agreement between countries. **4** a large meeting or conference. **5** N. Amer. an assembly of the delegates of a political party to select candidates for office. **6** a body set up by agreement to deal with a particular issue.
– ORIGIN Latin, 'meeting, covenant'.

conventional adjective **1** based on or in accordance with what is generally done or believed. **2** following social conventions; not individual or adventurous. **3** (of weapons or power) non-nuclear.
– DERIVATIVES **conventionality** noun **conventionalize** (or **conventionalise**) verb **conventionally** adverb.

C

converge /kuhn-**verj**/ verb **1** come together from different directions so as eventually to meet. **2 (converge on)** come from different directions and meet at a place.
– DERIVATIVES **convergent** adjective.
– ORIGIN Latin *convergere*.

conversant adjective **(conversant with)** familiar with or knowledgeable about something.

conversation noun an informal spoken exchange of news and ideas between people.
– DERIVATIVES **conversational** adjective.

conversationalist noun a person who is good at or fond of engaging in conversation.

converse¹ /kuhn-**verss**/ verb hold a conversation.
– ORIGIN Latin *conversari* 'keep company with'.

converse² /**kon**-verss/ noun the opposite of a situation, fact, or statement. •adjective opposite.
– DERIVATIVES **conversely** adverb.
– ORIGIN Latin *conversus* 'turned about'.

conversion noun **1** the action of converting someone or something. **2** Brit. a building that has been converted to a new purpose. **3** Rugby a successful kick at goal after a try.

convert verb /kuhn-**vert**/ **1** change in form, character, or function: *grazing lands are being converted to farming*. **2** change money, stocks, or units into others of a different kind. **3** adapt a building for a new purpose. **4** change one's religious faith or other beliefs. **5** Rugby score extra points after a try by a successful kick at goal. •noun /**kon**-vert/ a person who has changed their religious faith or other beliefs.
– DERIVATIVES **converter** (also **convertor**) noun.
– ORIGIN Latin *convertere* 'turn about'.

convertible adjective **1** able to be changed in form, character, or function. **2** (of a car) having a folding or detachable roof. •noun a car with a folding or detachable roof.
– DERIVATIVES **convertibility** noun.

convex /kon-**veks**/ adjective having an outline or surface that curves outwards. Compare with **CONCAVE**.
– DERIVATIVES **convexity** noun.
– ORIGIN Latin *convexus* 'vaulted, arched'.

convey /kuhn-**vay**/ verb **1** transport or carry something to a place. **2** communicate an idea, quality, or feeling. **3** Law transfer the title to property.
– DERIVATIVES **conveyor** (also **conveyer**) noun.
– ORIGIN Latin *conviare* 'escort'.

conveyance noun **1** the action of conveying something. **2** formal a means of transport. **3** the legal process of transferring property from one owner to another.
– DERIVATIVES **conveyancer** noun **conveyancing** noun.

conveyor belt noun a continuous moving belt for transporting objects within a building.

convict verb /kuhn-**vikt**/ declare someone to be guilty of a criminal offence by the verdict of a jury or the decision of a judge in a court of law. •noun /**kon**-vikt/ a person found guilty of a criminal offence and serving a sentence of imprisonment.
– ORIGIN from Latin *convictus* 'demonstrated, convicted'.

conviction noun **1** an instance of formally being found guilty of a criminal offence in a court of law. **2** a firmly held belief or opinion. **3** the feeling or appearance of being sure in one's belief: *his voice lacked conviction*.

convince verb **1** cause someone to believe firmly in the truth of something: *he tried to convince her that everything would be all right*. **2** persuade someone to do something.
– DERIVATIVES **convincer** noun.
– ORIGIN Latin *convincere* 'overcome, demonstrate'.

convincing adjective **1** able to convince. **2** (of a victory or a winner) leaving no margin of doubt.
– DERIVATIVES **convincingly** adverb.

convivial /kuhn-**viv**-i-uhl/ adjective **1** (of an atmosphere or event) friendly and lively. **2** cheerful and sociable.
– DERIVATIVES **conviviality** noun **convivially** adverb.
– ORIGIN from Latin *convivium* 'a feast'.

convocation /kon-vuh-**kay**-sh'n/ noun a large formal assembly of people.
– ORIGIN Latin.

convoke /kuhn-**vohk**/ verb formal call together an assembly or meeting.
– ORIGIN Latin *convocare*.

convoluted /kon-vuh-**loo**-tid/ adjective **1** (of an argument, statement, or story) very complex. **2** twisted or coiled in a complex way.

convolution noun **1** a coil or twist. **2** the state of being coiled or twisted. **3** a complex argument, statement, etc.
– DERIVATIVES **convolutional** adjective.
– ORIGIN from Latin *convolvere* 'roll together'.

convolvulus /kuhn-**volv**-yuu-luhss/ noun (pl. **convolvuluses**) a twining plant with trumpet-shaped flowers.
– ORIGIN Latin, 'bindweed'.

convoy /**kon**-voy/ noun a group of ships or vehicles travelling together under armed protection. •verb (of a warship or armed troops) accompany a group of ships or vehicles for protection.
– PHRASES **in convoy** travelling as a group.
– ORIGIN from Latin *conviare* 'convey'.

convulse /kuhn-**vulss**/ verb **1** suffer convulsions. **2 (be convulsed)** make sudden uncontrollable movements because of emotion, laughter, etc.
– DERIVATIVES **convulsive** adjective **convulsively** adverb.
– ORIGIN Latin *convellere* 'pull violently'.

convulsion noun **1** a sudden irregular movement of the body, caused by the muscles contracting involuntarily. **2 (convulsions)** uncontrollable laughter. **3** a violent social or natural upheaval.

cony noun (pl. **conies**) variant spelling of **CONEY**.

coo verb (**coos**, **cooing**, **cooed**) **1** (of a pigeon or dove) make a soft murmuring sound. **2** speak in a soft gentle voice. •noun a cooing sound.
– ORIGIN imitating the sound.

cooee exclamation informal used to attract attention.
– ORIGIN a signal used by Australian Aboriginals and copied by settlers.

cook verb **1** prepare food or a meal by mixing and heating the ingredients. **2** (of food) be

heated so as to reach an edible state. **3** informal alter something dishonestly. **4** (**cook something up**) informal invent a story, excuse, or plan. •**noun** a person who cooks food.
– PHRASES **cook someone's goose** informal spoil someone's plans.
– ORIGIN from Latin *coquus* 'a cook'.

cookbook noun a recipe book.

cooker noun Brit. **1** an appliance for cooking food. **2** informal an apple that is more suitable for cooking than for eating raw.

cookery noun the practice or skill of preparing and cooking food.

cookhouse noun a building used for cooking, especially on a ranch or military camp.

cookie noun (pl. **cookies**) **1** N. Amer. a sweet biscuit. **2** informal a person of a specified kind: *she's a tough cookie.*
– PHRASES **that's the way the cookie crumbles** informal, chiefly N. Amer. that's the situation, and it must be accepted, however undesirable.
– ORIGIN Dutch *koekje* 'little cake'.

Cook's tour noun informal a rapid tour of many places.
– ORIGIN named after the English travel agent Thomas *Cook.*

cookware noun pots, pans, or dishes in which food can be cooked.

cool adjective **1** fairly cold. **2** keeping one from becoming too hot. **3** not excited, angry, or emotional: *he kept a cool head.* **4** not friendly or enthusiastic. **5** informal fashionably attractive or impressive. **6** informal excellent. **7** informal used to express acceptance or agreement. **8** (**a cool ——**) informal used to emphasize a specified large amount of money: *they pocketed a cool $1 million each.* •**noun** (**the cool**) a fairly low temperature, or a fairly cold place or time: *the cool of the day.* •**verb 1** make or become cool. **2** make or become less excited or angry.
– PHRASES **keep** (or **lose**) **one's cool** informal stay (or fail to stay) calm and controlled.
– DERIVATIVES **coolish** adjective **coolly** adverb **coolness** noun.
– ORIGIN Old English.

coolant noun a fluid used to cool an engine or other device.

cooler noun **1** a device or container for keeping things cool. **2** (**the cooler**) informal prison.

coolibah /koo-li-bah/ noun a North Australian gum tree with very strong, hard wood.
– ORIGIN from an Aboriginal language.

coolie /koo-li/ noun (pl. **coolies**) dated an unskilled native labourer in some Asian countries.
– ORIGIN Hindi, 'day-labourer'.

cooling-off period noun **1** a period after a sale contract is agreed during which the buyer can decide to cancel without losing any money. **2** a period during which the people in a dispute can try to settle their differences before taking further action.

cooling tower noun an open-topped, cylindrical concrete tower, used for cooling water or condensing steam from an industrial process.

coolth /koolth/ noun **1** pleasantly low temperature. **2** informal the quality of being fashionable.

coombe (also **coomb**) noun variant spelling of COMBE.

coon noun **1** N. Amer. short for RACCOON. **2** informal, offensive a black person.

coop /koop/ noun a cage or pen for poultry. •**verb** confine in a small space: *I'm sick of being cooped up at home.*
– ORIGIN Latin *cupa* 'cask, tub'.

co-op /koh-op/ noun informal a cooperative organization.

cooper noun a person who makes or repairs casks and barrels.
– DERIVATIVES **cooperage** noun.
– ORIGIN from Latin *cupa* 'cask, tub'.

cooperate /koh-op-uh-rayt/ (also **co-operate**) verb **1** work together to achieve something. **2** do what is requested.
– DERIVATIVES **cooperation** noun **cooperator** noun.
– ORIGIN Latin *cooperari.*

cooperative (also **co-operative**) adjective **1** involving cooperation. **2** willing to help. **3** (of a farm or business) owned and run jointly by its members, with profits or benefits shared among them. •**noun** an organization owned and run jointly by its members.
– DERIVATIVES **cooperatively** adverb.

co-opt verb **1** make someone a member of a committee or other body by invitation of the existing members. **2** divert to a role different from the usual one: *can a government co-opt private industry to promote its policies?* **3** adopt an idea or policy for one's own use.
– DERIVATIVES **co-optation** noun **co-option** noun.
– ORIGIN Latin *cooptare.*

coordinate (also **co-ordinate**) verb /koh-or-di-nayt/ **1** bring the different elements of a complex activity or organization into an efficient relationship. **2** (**coordinate with**) negotiate with others in order to work together effectively. **3** match or harmonize attractively. •**noun** /koh-or-di-nuht/ **1** Mathematics each of a group of numbers used to indicate the position of a point, line, or plane. **2** (**coordinates**) matching items of clothing. •**adjective** /koh-or-di-nuht/ equal in rank or importance.
– DERIVATIVES **coordinator** noun.
– ORIGIN from Latin *ordinare* 'put in order'.

coordination (also **co-ordination**) noun **1** the organization of things so as to work together effectively. **2** the ability to move different parts of the body smoothly and at the same time.

coot noun **1** (pl. same) a black waterbird with a white bill. **2** (usu. **old coot**) informal a foolish person.
– ORIGIN probably Dutch or German.

cop informal noun a police officer. •**verb** (**cops, copping, copped**) **1** arrest an offender. **2** experience or receive something unwelcome. **3** (**cop off**) Brit. have a sexual encounter. **4** (**cop out**) avoid doing something that one ought to do.
– PHRASES **cop hold of** Brit. take hold of. **cop it** Brit. **1** get into trouble. **2** be killed. **not much cop** Brit. not very good.
– ORIGIN perhaps from Old French *caper* 'seize'.

copal /koh-puhl/ noun resin from certain tropical trees, used to make varnish.

c

– ORIGIN Spanish.

co-parent verb (especially of a separated or unmarried couple) share the duties of bringing up a child. • noun a person who co-parents a child.

cope[1] verb deal effectively with something difficult.
– DERIVATIVES **coper** noun.
– ORIGIN Old French *coper* 'to strike'.

cope[2] noun a long cloak worn by a priest or bishop on ceremonial occasions. • verb (in building) cover a joint or structure with a coping.
– ORIGIN Latin *cappa* 'covering for the head'.

copeck noun variant spelling of **KOPEK**.

Copernican system /kuh-**per**-ni-kuhn/ (also **Copernican theory**) noun the theory proposed by the Polish astronomer Nicolaus Copernicus that the sun is the centre of the solar system, with the planets orbiting round it. Compare with **PTOLEMAIC SYSTEM**.

copier noun a machine that makes exact copies of something.

co-pilot noun a second pilot in an aircraft.

coping noun the curved or sloping top course of a brick or stone wall.
– ORIGIN from **COPE**[2].

copious adjective abundant in supply or quantity: *drinking copious amounts of beer.*
– DERIVATIVES **copiously** adverb **copiousness** noun.
– ORIGIN from Latin *copia* 'plenty'.

copolymer /koh-**po**-li-muhr/ noun Chemistry a polymer made by reaction of two different monomers, with units of more than one kind.

cop-out noun informal an instance of avoiding a commitment or responsibility.

copper[1] noun **1** a red-brown metallic chemical element which is used for electrical wiring and as a component of brass and bronze. **2** (**coppers**) Brit. coins of low value made of copper or bronze. **3** a reddish-brown colour. • verb cover or coat something with copper.
– DERIVATIVES **coppery** adjective.
– ORIGIN from Latin *cyprium aes* 'Cyprus metal'.

copper[2] noun Brit. informal a police officer.
– ORIGIN from **COP**.

copper beech noun a variety of beech tree with purplish-brown leaves.

copper-bottomed adjective Brit. thoroughly reliable.
– ORIGIN first referring to copper sheathing applied to the bottom of a ship.

copperplate noun **1** a polished copper plate with a design engraved or etched into it. **2** a neat, looped style of handwriting. [the copybooks for this were originally printed from copperplates.]

copper sulphate noun a blue crystalline solid used in electroplating and as a fungicide.

coppice noun an area of woodland in which the trees or shrubs are periodically cut back to ground level to stimulate growth. • verb cut back a tree or shrub to ground level.
– ORIGIN Old French *copeiz*.

copra /**kop**-ruh/ noun dried coconut kernels, from which oil is obtained.
– ORIGIN Portuguese and Spanish.

coprocessor noun Computing a microprocessor designed to supplement the capabilities of the primary processor.

copse noun a small group of trees.
– ORIGIN from **COPPICE**.

Copt /kopt/ noun **1** a member of the Coptic Church, the native Christian Church in Egypt. **2** a native Egyptian in the periods of Greek and Roman rule.
– ORIGIN Latin *Coptus*.

Coptic noun the language of the ancient Copts, which survives only in the Coptic Church. • adjective relating to the Copts or their language.

copula /**kop**-yuu-luh/ noun a verb, especially the verb *be*, that links a subject and complement (e.g. *was* in the sentence *I was happy*).
– ORIGIN Latin, 'connection, linking of words'.

copulate /**kop**-yuu-layt/ verb have sexual intercourse.
– DERIVATIVES **copulation** noun **copulatory** adjective.
– ORIGIN Latin *copulare* 'fasten together'.

copy noun (pl. **copies**) **1** a thing made to be similar or identical to another. **2** a single specimen of a particular book, record, etc. **3** material to be printed in a book, newspaper, or magazine. **4** the written part of an advertisement. • verb (**copies**, **copying**, **copied**) **1** make a copy of something. **2** imitate the behaviour or style of: *this view of leadership is copied from business.*
– ORIGIN Latin *copia* 'abundance', later 'transcript'.

copybook noun a book containing models of handwriting for learners to imitate. • adjective exactly in accordance with established standards: *a copybook landing.*

copycat noun informal a person who copies another. • adjective (of an action, especially a crime) done in imitation of another: *copycat attacks.*

copy-edit verb edit written material by checking its consistency and accuracy.
– DERIVATIVES **copy editor** noun.

copyist noun **1** a person who makes copies. **2** a person who imitates the styles of others, especially in art.

copyright noun the exclusive legal right, given to the originator for a fixed number of years, to print, publish, perform, film, or record literary, artistic, or musical material.

copy typist noun a person whose job is to type copies of written drafts.

copywriter noun a person who writes advertisements or publicity material.

coq au vin /kok oh **van**/ noun a casserole of chicken pieces cooked in red wine.
– ORIGIN French, 'cock in wine'.

coquette /ko-**ket**/ noun a woman who flirts.
– DERIVATIVES **coquetry** noun **coquettish** adjective **coquettishly** adverb.
– ORIGIN French, 'wanton female'.

coracle /**ko**-ruh-k'l/ noun a small, round boat made of wickerwork covered with a watertight material, propelled with a paddle.
– ORIGIN Welsh *corwgl*.

coral noun **1** a hard stony substance produced

by certain sea creatures as an external skeleton, typically forming large reefs. **2** precious red coral, used in jewellery. **3** a pinkish-red colour.
– ORIGIN Greek *korallion, kouralion*.

cor anglais /kor ong-glay/ noun (pl. **cors anglais** pronunc. same) a woodwind instrument of the oboe family, sounding a fifth lower than the oboe.
– ORIGIN French, 'English horn'.

corbel /kor-b'l/ noun a projection jutting out from a wall to support a structure above it.
– DERIVATIVES **corbelled** (US **corbeled**) adjective **corbelling** (US **corbeling**) noun.
– ORIGIN Old French, 'little crow'.

cord noun **1** thin string or rope made from several twisted strands. **2** a length of cord. **3** a structure in the body resembling a cord (e.g. the spinal cord). **4** an electric flex. **5** corduroy. **6** (**cords**) corduroy trousers. **7** a measure of cut wood (usually 128 cu. ft, 3.62 cubic metres).
– DERIVATIVES **cording** noun.
– ORIGIN Greek *khordē* 'gut, string'.

> USAGE: On the confusion of **cord** and **chord**, see the note at **CHORD**¹.

cordate /kor-dayt/ adjective Botany & Zoology heart-shaped.
– ORIGIN Latin *cordatus* 'wise', later 'heart-shaped'.

cordial adjective **1** warm and friendly. **2** strongly felt: *I earned his cordial loathing.* •noun **1** Brit. a sweet fruit-flavoured drink. **2** a pleasant-tasting medicine.
– DERIVATIVES **cordiality** noun **cordially** adverb.
– ORIGIN Latin *cordialis*, from *cor* 'heart'.

cordite noun a smokeless explosive used in ammunition.
– ORIGIN from **CORD**, because of its appearance.

cordless adjective (of an electrical appliance) working without connection to a mains supply or central unit.

cordoba /kor-duh-buh/ noun the basic unit of money of Nicaragua.
– ORIGIN named after F. Fernández de *Córdoba*, a former Spanish governor of Nicaragua.

cordon /kor-d'n/ noun **1** a line or circle of police, soldiers, or guards forming a barrier. **2** a fruit tree trained to grow as a single stem. •verb (**cordon something off**) close somewhere off by surrounding it with police or other guards.
– ORIGIN Italian *cordone* and French *cordon*.

cordon bleu /kor-don bler/ adjective (of a cook or cooking) of the highest class.
– ORIGIN French, 'blue ribbon' (once signifying the highest order of French chivalry).

cordon sanitaire /kor-don sa-ni-tair/ noun (pl. **cordons sanitaires** pronunc. same) **1** a line of guards positioned around an area infected by disease, preventing anyone from leaving. **2** a measure designed to prevent communication or the spread of undesirable influences.
– ORIGIN French, 'sanitary line'.

corduroy /kor-duh-roy/ noun a thick cotton fabric with velvety ribs.
– ORIGIN probably from **CORD** + *duroy*, a former kind of lightweight cloth.

core noun **1** the tough central part of various fruits, containing the seeds. **2** the central or most important part: *mysticism was the core of his faith.* **3** the dense metallic or rocky central region of a planet. **4** the central part of a nuclear reactor, which contains the fissile material. •verb remove the core from a fruit.
– DERIVATIVES **corer** noun.
– ORIGIN unknown.

co-respondent noun a person named in a divorce case as having committed adultery with the husband or wife of the person who wants a divorce.

corgi (also **Welsh corgi**) noun (pl. **corgis**) a breed of dog with short legs and a foxlike head.
– ORIGIN from Welsh *cor* 'dwarf' + *ci* 'dog'.

coriander /ko-ri-an-der/ noun a Mediterranean plant of the parsley family, used as a herb in cookery.
– ORIGIN Greek *koriannon*.

Corinthian /kuh-rinth-i-uhn/ adjective **1** relating to Corinth, a city in southern Greece and a city state in ancient Greece. **2** relating to an ornate classical style of architecture having flared capitals with rows of acanthus leaves. •noun a person from Corinth.

cork noun **1** a buoyant, light brown substance obtained from the bark of a kind of Mediterranean oak tree. **2** a bottle stopper made of cork. •verb **1** close or seal a bottle with a cork. **2** (as adj. **corked**) (of wine) spoilt by tannin from the cork.
– ORIGIN ultimately from Latin *quercus* 'oak, cork oak'.

corkage noun a charge made by a restaurant for serving wine that has been brought in by a customer.

corker noun informal an excellent person or thing.
– DERIVATIVES **corking** adjective.

corkscrew noun a device with a spiral metal rod, used for pulling corks from bottles. •verb move or twist in a spiral.

corm noun the underground storage organ of plants such as crocuses, consisting of a swollen stem base covered with scale leaves.
– ORIGIN Greek *kormos* 'trunk stripped of its boughs'.

cormorant /kor-muh-ruhnt/ noun a large diving seabird with a long neck, long hooked bill, and mainly black plumage.
– ORIGIN Old French *cormaran*.

corn¹ noun **1** Brit. the chief cereal crop of a district, especially (in England) wheat or (in Scotland) oats. **2** N. Amer. & Austral./NZ maize. **3** informal something unoriginal or sentimental: *the film is pure corn.*
– PHRASES **corn on the cob** maize when cooked and eaten straight from the cob.
– ORIGIN Old English.

corn² noun a small, painful area of thickened skin on the foot, caused by pressure.
– ORIGIN Latin *cornu* 'horn'.

corncob noun the central woody part of an ear of maize, to which the grains are attached.

corncrake noun a crake (bird) of coarse grasslands, with a distinctive rasping call.

corn dolly noun Brit. a symbolic or decorative model of a human figure, made of plaited straw.

cornea /kor-ni-uh/ noun the transparent layer forming the front of the eye.

- DERIVATIVES **corneal** adjective.
- ORIGIN from Latin *cornea tela* 'horny tissue'.

corned beef noun 1 Brit. beef preserved in brine, chopped and pressed and sold in tins. 2 N. Amer. beef brisket cured in brine and boiled, typically served cold.

cornelian /kor-**nee**-li-uhn/ noun variant spelling of **CARNELIAN**.

corner noun 1 a place or angle where two or more sides or edges meet. 2 a place where two streets meet. 3 a remote area. 4 a difficult or awkward position: *Mick thought it was a crazy idea, but he was in a corner.* 5 (also **corner kick**) Football a free kick taken by the attacking side from a corner of the field. 6 Boxing & Wrestling each of the diagonally opposite ends of the ring, where a contestant rests between rounds. • verb 1 force into a place or situation from which it is hard to escape: *my landlord cornered me as I was going upstairs.* 2 go round a bend in a road. 3 control a market by dominating the supply of a particular commodity.
- ORIGIN Latin *cornu* 'horn, tip, corner'.

corner shop noun Brit. a small shop selling groceries and general goods in a residential area.

cornerstone noun 1 a vital part or basis: *sugar was the cornerstone of the economy.* 2 a stone that forms the base of a corner of a building, joining two walls.

cornet /kor-nit/ noun 1 a brass instrument resembling a trumpet but shorter and wider. 2 Brit. a cone-shaped wafer for holding ice cream.
- DERIVATIVES **cornetist** /kor**nett**ist/ (also **cornettist**) noun.
- ORIGIN Old French, 'little horn'.

cornflakes plural noun a breakfast cereal consisting of toasted flakes made from maize flour.

cornflour noun Brit. finely ground maize flour, used for thickening sauces.

cornflower noun a plant of the daisy family with deep blue flowers.

cornice /kor-niss/ noun 1 an ornamental moulding round the wall of a room just below the ceiling. 2 a horizontal moulded projection crowning a building or structure.
- DERIVATIVES **corniced** adjective **cornicing** noun.
- ORIGIN Italian.

corniche /kor-nish, kor-**neesh**/ noun a road cut into the edge of a cliff and running along a coastline.
- ORIGIN French, 'cornice'.

Cornish adjective relating to Cornwall. • noun the ancient Celtic language of Cornwall.

Cornish pasty noun Brit. a pasty containing seasoned meat and vegetables, especially potato.

cornmeal noun meal made from corn, especially (in the US) maize flour or (in Scotland) oatmeal.

cornrows plural noun (especially among black people) a style of braiding and plaiting the hair in narrow strips to form geometric patterns on the scalp.

cornucopia /kor-nyuu-**koh**-pi-uh/ noun 1 an abundant supply of good things. 2 a symbol of

plenty consisting of a goat's horn overflowing with flowers, fruit, and corn.
- DERIVATIVES **cornucopian** adjective.
- ORIGIN from Latin *cornu copiae* 'horn of plenty'.

corny adjective (**cornier, corniest**) informal unoriginal or very sentimental: *corny jokes.*
- DERIVATIVES **corniness** noun.
- ORIGIN first meaning 'rustic, appealing to country folk'.

corolla /kuh-**rol**-luh/ noun the petals of a flower, typically forming a whorl within the sepals.
- ORIGIN Latin, 'little crown'.

corollary /kuh-**rol**-luh-ri/ noun (pl. **corollaries**) 1 a direct consequence or result. 2 a logical proposition that follows from one already proved. • adjective associated; supplementary.
- ORIGIN Latin *corollarium* 'money paid for a garland or chaplet' (later 'a deduction').

corona /kuh-**roh**-nuh/ noun (pl. **coronae** /kuh-**roh**-nee/) 1 the envelope of gas around the sun or another star. 2 a small circle of light seen round the sun or moon. 3 (also **corona discharge**) Physics the glow around a conductor at high potential. 4 a long, straight-sided cigar.
- DERIVATIVES **coronal** adjective.
- ORIGIN Latin, 'wreath, crown'; sense 4 comes from a proprietary name of a cigar.

coronary adjective relating to the arteries which surround and supply the heart. • noun (pl. **coronaries**) (also **coronary thrombosis**) a blockage of the flow of blood to the heart, caused by a clot in a coronary artery.
- ORIGIN Latin *coronarius* 'resembling or forming a crown'.

coronation noun the ceremony of crowning a sovereign or a sovereign's consort.
- ORIGIN from Latin *coronare* 'to crown'.

coroner /ko-ruh-ner/ noun an official who holds inquests into violent, sudden, or suspicious deaths.
- ORIGIN Old French *coruner*.

coronet /ko-ruh-net/ noun 1 a small or simple crown. 2 a circular decorative band worn on the head.
- ORIGIN Old French *coronete* 'little crown'.

corpora plural of **CORPUS**.

corporal[1] noun a rank of non-commissioned officer in the army, above lance corporal or private first class and below sergeant.
- ORIGIN Italian *caporale*.

corporal[2] adjective relating to the human body.
- ORIGIN Latin *corporalis*.

corporal punishment noun physical punishment, such as caning.

corporate adjective 1 relating to a business corporation. 2 relating to or shared by all members of a group: *corporate responsibility.*
- DERIVATIVES **corporately** adverb.
- ORIGIN from Latin *corporare* 'form into a body'.

corporation noun 1 a large company or group of companies recognized by law as a single unit. 2 Brit. a group of people elected to govern a city, town, or borough.

corporation tax noun Brit. tax paid by companies on their profits.

corporatism noun the control of a state or

organization by large interest groups.
- DERIVATIVES **corporatist** adjective & noun.

corporeal /kor-**por**-i-uhl/ adjective relating to a person's body; physical rather than spiritual.
- DERIVATIVES **corporeality** /kor-por-i-**al**-it-i/ noun.
- ORIGIN Latin *corporealis*.

corps /kor/ noun (pl. **corps** /korz/) **1** a main subdivision of an army in the field, consisting of two or more divisions. **2** a branch of an army assigned to a particular kind of work. **3** a group of people engaged in a particular activity: *the press corps.*
- ORIGIN French.

corps de ballet /kor duh **bal**-lay/ noun (treated as sing. or pl.) **1** the members of a ballet company who dance together as a group. **2** the lowest rank of dancers in a ballet company.

corpse noun a dead body, especially of a person.
• **verb** theatrical slang spoil a piece of acting by forgetting one's lines or laughing uncontrollably.
- ORIGIN Latin *corpus*.

corpulent /kor-pyuu-luhnt/ adjective (of a person) fat.
- DERIVATIVES **corpulence** noun.
- ORIGIN Latin *corpulentus*.

corpus /kor-puhss/ noun (pl. **corpora** /kor-puh-ruh/ or **corpuses**) **1** a collection of written works. **2** a collection of written or spoken material in a form that is readable by a computer.
- ORIGIN Latin, 'body'.

Corpus Christi /kor-puhss **kris**-ti/ noun a Christian feast commemorating the institution of Holy Communion, observed on the Thursday after Trinity Sunday.
- ORIGIN Latin, 'body of Christ'.

corpuscle /kor-pus-s'l/ noun a red or white blood cell.
- DERIVATIVES **corpuscular** adjective.
- ORIGIN Latin *corpusculum* 'small body'.

corral /kuh-**rahl**/ noun N. Amer. a pen for livestock on a farm or ranch. • **verb** (**corrals, corralling, corralled**) **1** N. Amer. put or keep livestock in a corral. **2** gather a group together.
- ORIGIN Spanish and Portuguese.

correct adjective **1** free from error; true; right: *they came up with the correct answer.* **2** meeting accepted social standards. • **verb 1** put right an error or fault. **2** mark the errors in written work. **3** tell someone that they are mistaken. **4** adjust a result or reading to allow for departure from standard conditions.
- DERIVATIVES **correctable** adjective **correctly** adverb **correctness** noun **corrector** noun.
- ORIGIN from Latin *corrigere* 'make straight, amend'.

correction noun **1** the action of correcting something. **2** a change that puts right an error or inaccuracy.
- DERIVATIVES **correctional** adjective (chiefly N. Amer.).

corrective adjective designed to put right something undesirable.

correlate /ko-ruh-layt/ verb have or bring into a relationship in which one thing depends on another and vice versa: *success in the educational system correlates highly with class.*
• **noun** each of two or more related or

complementary things.

correlation noun **1** a relationship in which one thing depends on another and vice versa. **2** the process of correlating two or more things.

correlative /kuh-**rel**-uh-tiv/ adjective **1** having a relationship in which one thing affects or depends on another. **2** (of words such as *neither* and *nor*) corresponding to each other and regularly used together.
- ORIGIN Latin *correlativus*.

correspond verb **1** match or agree almost exactly. **2** be comparable or equivalent in character or form: *many companies assign employees numbers that correspond to their date of hire.* **3** communicate by exchanging letters.
- ORIGIN Latin *correspondere*.

correspondence noun **1** a close similarity, link, or equivalence. **2** letters sent or received.

correspondence course noun a course of study in which student and tutors communicate by post.

correspondent noun **1** a journalist reporting on a particular subject or from a particular country: *a cricket correspondent.* **2** a person who writes letters on a regular basis.

corrida /ko-**ree**-duh/ noun a bullfight.
- ORIGIN from Spanish *corrida de toros* 'running of bulls'.

corridor noun **1** a passage in a building or train, with doors leading into rooms or compartments. **2** a strip of land linking two other areas or following a road or river.
- PHRASES **the corridors of power** the senior levels of government or administration.
- ORIGIN Italian *corridore*, from *corridoio* 'running-place'.

corrie /ko-ri/ noun (pl. **corries**) a steep-sided hollow at the head of a valley or on a mountainside, especially in Scotland.
- ORIGIN Scottish Gaelic and Irish *coire* 'cauldron, hollow'.

corroborate /kuh-**rob**-uh-rayt/ verb confirm or give support to a statement or theory.
- DERIVATIVES **corroboration** noun **corroborative** adjective.
- ORIGIN Latin *corroborare* 'strengthen'.

corroboree /kuh-**rob**-uh-ri/ noun an Australian Aboriginal dance ceremony in the form of a sacred ritual or informal gathering.
- ORIGIN from an Aboriginal word.

corrode /kuh-**rohd**/ verb **1** (with reference to metal or other hard material) wear or be worn away slowly by chemical action. **2** gradually weaken or destroy: *the criticism corroded his reputation.*
- ORIGIN Latin *corrodere*.

corrosion /kuh-**roh**-zh'n/ noun **1** the process of wearing away something. **2** damage caused by this process.

corrosive adjective causing corrosion. • **noun** a corrosive substance.

corrugate /ko-ruh-gayt/ verb **1** contract into wrinkles or folds: *his brown corrugated in a frown.* **2** (as adj. **corrugated**) shaped into alternate ridges and grooves: *corrugated iron.*
- DERIVATIVES **corrugation** noun.
- ORIGIN Latin *corrugare* 'to wrinkle'.

corrupt adjective **1** willing to act dishonestly in

return for money or personal gain. **2** evil or very immoral. **3** (of a written work or computer data) made unreliable by errors or alterations. • verb **1** make dishonest or depraved: *he was corrupted by power.* **2** introduce errors into a written work or computer data.
– DERIVATIVES **corrupter** noun **corruptible** adjective **corruptive** adjective **corruptly** adverb.
– ORIGIN from Latin *corrumpere* 'mar, bribe, destroy'.

corruption noun **1** dishonest or illegal behaviour. **2** the action of corrupting someone or something.

corsage /kor-**sahz**h/ noun a spray of flowers worn pinned to a woman's clothes.
– ORIGIN French.

corsair /kor-**sair**/ noun **1** old use a pirate. **2** historical a privateer, especially one operating in the Mediterranean in the 17th century.
– ORIGIN French *corsaire*.

corselette /kor-suh-**let**, kors-uh-let/ (also **corselet**) noun a woman's undergarment combining corset and bra.

corset noun **1** a woman's tight-fitting undergarment extending from below the chest to the hips, worn to shape the figure. **2** a similar garment worn to support a weak or injured back.
– DERIVATIVES **corseted** adjective **corsetry** noun.
– ORIGIN Old French, 'little body'.

Corsican noun **1** a person from Corsica. **2** the language of Corsica. • adjective relating to Corsica.

cortège /kor-**tezh**/ noun a solemn funeral procession.
– ORIGIN Italian *corteggio* 'entourage or retinue'.

cortex /kor-**teks**/ noun (pl. **cortices** /kor-ti-seez/) the outer layer of a bodily organ or structure, especially the outer, folded layer of the brain (**cerebral cortex**).
– DERIVATIVES **cortical** adjective.
– ORIGIN Latin, 'bark'.

corticosteroid /kor-ti-koh-**ste**-royd, kor-ti-koh-**steer**-oyd/ noun any of a group of steroid hormones produced by the cortex of the adrenal glands.

cortisone /kor-ti-zohn/ noun a steroid hormone used to treat inflammation and allergies.
– ORIGIN from its chemical name.

corundum /kuh-**run**-duhm/ noun extremely hard form of aluminium oxide, used as an abrasive.
– ORIGIN Tamil.

coruscate /ko-ruh-skayt/ verb literary (usu. as adj. **coruscating**) **1** flash; sparkle. **2** be brilliant or exciting: *a coruscating attack on the rock tradition.*
– DERIVATIVES **coruscation** noun.
– ORIGIN Latin *coruscare* 'glitter'.

corvette /kor-**vet**/ noun a small warship designed for convoy escort duty.
– ORIGIN French.

corvine /kor-vyn/ adjective relating to or like a raven or crow.
– ORIGIN from Latin *corvus* 'raven'.

corybantic /kor-i-**ban**-tik/ adjective literary wild; frenzied.
– ORIGIN from Greek *Korubantes*, referring to the priests of the Phrygian goddess Cybele.

corymb /kor-imb/ noun Botany a flower cluster whose lower stalks are proportionally longer so that the flowers form a fairly flat head.
– ORIGIN Greek *korumbos* 'cluster'.

cos[1] /koss/ noun Brit. a variety of lettuce with crisp narrow leaves.
– ORIGIN named after the Greek island of *Cos*.

cos[2] /koz/ abbreviation cosine.

cos[3] /kos, kuhz/ (also '**cos** or **coz**) conjunction Brit. informal short for BECAUSE.

cosec /koh-sek/ abbreviation cosecant.

cosecant /koh-see-kuhnt, koh-**sek**-uhnt/ noun (in a right-angled triangle) the ratio of the hypotenuse to the side opposite an acute angle.

cosh Brit. noun a thick heavy stick or bar used as a weapon. • verb hit someone with a cosh.
– ORIGIN unknown.

co-signatory noun a person or state signing a treaty or other document jointly with others.

cosine /koh-syn/ noun (in a right-angled triangle) the ratio of the side adjacent to a particular acute angle to the hypotenuse.

cosmetic adjective **1** relating to treatment intended to improve a person's appearance. **2** improving only the appearance of something: *the reforms were merely a cosmetic exercise.* • noun (**cosmetics**) substances used to improve the appearance of the face and body.
– DERIVATIVES **cosmetically** adverb.
– ORIGIN Greek *kosmein* 'arrange or decorate'.

cosmic adjective relating to the universe or cosmos.
– DERIVATIVES **cosmical** adjective **cosmically** adverb.

cosmic rays plural noun highly energetic atomic nuclei or other particles travelling through space at a speed approaching that of light.

cosmogony /koz-**mog**-uh-ni/ noun (pl. **cosmogonies**) the branch of science concerned with the origin of the universe, especially the solar system.
– DERIVATIVES **cosmogonic** /koz-muh-**gon**-ik/ adjective **cosmogonist** noun.
– ORIGIN from Greek *kosmos* 'order or world' + *-gonia* '-creating'.

cosmography noun (pl. **cosmographies**) **1** the branch of science which deals with the general features of the universe, including the earth. **2** a description or representation of the universe or the earth.
– DERIVATIVES **cosmographer** noun **cosmographical** adjective.

cosmology noun (pl. **cosmologies**) **1** the science of the origin and development of the universe. **2** a theory of the origin of the universe.
– DERIVATIVES **cosmological** adjective **cosmologist** noun.

cosmonaut noun a Russian astronaut.
– ORIGIN from **cosmos**, on the pattern of *astronaut* and Russian *kosmonavt*.

cosmopolitan /koz-muh-**pol**-i-tuhn/ adjective **1** consisting of people from many different countries and cultures: *Barcelona is a cosmopolitan city.* **2** familiar with and at ease in

different countries and cultures. • **noun 1** a person who is familiar with different countries and cultures. **2** a cocktail made with Cointreau, lemon vodka, cranberry juice, and lime juice.
– DERIVATIVES **cosmopolitanism** noun.
– ORIGIN from Greek *kosmos* 'world' + *politēs* 'citizen'.

cosmos noun the universe seen as a well-ordered whole.
– ORIGIN Greek *kosmos* 'order or world'.

Cossack /koss-ak/ noun a member of a people of southern Russia, Ukraine, and Siberia, noted for their horsemanship and military skill.
– ORIGIN Turkic, 'vagabond, nomad'.

cosset verb (**cossets, cosseting, cosseted**) care for and protect someone in an overindulgent way.
– ORIGIN first meaning a lamb brought up by hand: probably from Old English, 'cottar'.

cost verb (past and past part. **cost**) **1** be able to be bought or done for a specific price: *tickets cost £15*. **2** involve the loss of: *his heroism cost him his life*. **3** (past and past part. **costed**) estimate the cost of something. • noun **1** an amount given or required as payment. **2** the effort or loss necessary to achieve something. **3** (**costs**) legal expenses.
– PHRASES **at all costs** (or **at any cost**) regardless of the price or the effort needed. **to someone's cost** with loss or disadvantage to someone.
– ORIGIN Old French *couster*.

cost accounting noun the recording of all the costs arising in a business in a way that can be used to improve its management.
– DERIVATIVES **cost accountant** noun

co-star noun a cinema or stage star appearing with another or others of equal importance. • verb **1** appear in a film or play as a co-star. **2** (of a film or play) include someone as a co-star.

Costa Rican /kos-tuh ree-kuhn/ noun a person from Costa Rica, a republic in Central America. • adjective relating to Costa Rica.

cost-effective (also **cost-efficient**) adjective effective or productive in relation to its cost.

costermonger /koss-ter-mung-ger/ noun Brit. dated a person who sells fruit and vegetables from a handcart in the street.
– ORIGIN from *Costard* (a type of apple) + -MONGER.

costing noun the estimated cost of producing or undertaking something.

costly adjective (**costlier, costliest**) **1** expensive; not cheap. **2** causing suffering, loss, or disadvantage: *her most costly mistake*.
– DERIVATIVES **costliness** noun.

cost of living noun the level of prices relating to a range of everyday items.

cost price noun the price at which goods are bought by a retailer.

costume noun **1** a set of clothes in a style typical of a particular country or historical period: *authentic Elizabethan costumes*. **2** a set of clothes worn by an actor or performer for a role. **3** Brit. dated a woman's matching jacket and skirt. • verb dress someone in a set of clothes.
– ORIGIN Italian, 'custom, fashion, habit'.

costume drama noun a television or cinema production set in a historical period.

costume jewellery noun jewellery made with inexpensive materials or imitation gems.

costumier /koss-tyoo-mi-er/ (US also **costumer**) noun a maker or supplier of theatrical or fancy-dress costumes.
– ORIGIN French.

cosy (US **cozy**) adjective (**cosier, cosiest**) **1** comfortable, warm, and secure. **2** not seeking or offering challenge or difficulty: *the cosy belief that man is master*. • noun (pl. **cosies**) a cover to keep a teapot or a boiled egg hot. • verb (**cosies, cosying, cosied**) informal (**cosy up to**) try to gain the favour of someone.
– DERIVATIVES **cosily** adverb **cosiness** noun.
– ORIGIN unknown.

cot[1] noun Brit. a small bed with high barred sides for a baby or very young child.
– ORIGIN Hindi, 'bedstead, hammock'.

cot[2] noun **1** a small shelter for livestock. **2** old use a small, simple cottage.
– ORIGIN Old English.

cot[3] abbreviation Mathematics cotangent.

cotangent /koh-tan-juhnt/ noun (in a right-angled triangle) the ratio of the side (other than the hypotenuse) adjacent to a particular acute angle to the side opposite the angle.

cot death noun Brit. the unexplained death of a baby in its sleep.

cote noun a shelter for mammals or birds, especially pigeons.
– ORIGIN Old English.

coterie /koh-tuh-ri/ noun (pl. **coteries**) a small exclusive group of people with shared interests or tastes.
– ORIGIN French.

coterminous /koh-ter-min-uhss/ adjective having the same boundaries or extent: *on the east the area is coterminous with Sweden*
– ORIGIN from Latin *terminus* 'boundary'.

cotoneaster /kuh-toh-ni-as-tuh/ noun a shrub with bright red berries, often grown as a hedge.
– ORIGIN from Latin *cotoneum* 'quince'.

cottage noun a small house, typically one in the country.
– DERIVATIVES **cottagey** adjective.
– ORIGIN Latin *cotagium*.

cottage cheese noun soft, lumpy white cheese made from the curds of skimmed milk.

cottage hospital noun Brit. a small hospital in a country area.

cottage industry noun a business or manufacturing activity carried on in people's homes.

cottage loaf noun Brit. a loaf made from two round pieces of dough, the smaller on top of the larger.

cottage pie noun Brit. a dish of minced meat topped with browned mashed potato.

cottager noun a person living in a cottage.

cottar /ko-ter/ (also **cotter**) noun historical (in Scotland and Ireland) a farm labourer or tenant occupying a cottage in return for labour.
– ORIGIN Old English.

cotter pin noun **1** a metal pin used to fasten two parts of a mechanism together. **2** a split

C

pin that is opened out after being passed through a hole.
– ORIGIN unknown.

cotton noun the soft white fibres which surround the seeds of a tropical and subtropical plant, used to make cloth or thread for sewing. • verb informal (**cotton on**) begin to understand or realize: *I cottoned on to what Bill was saying.*
– DERIVATIVES **cottony** adjective.
– ORIGIN Arabic.

cotton bud noun Brit. a small wad of cotton wool on a short thin stick, used for cosmetic purposes or cleaning the ears.

cotton wool noun Brit. fluffy soft material used for applying or removing cosmetics or bathing wounds.

cotyledon /ko-ti-lee-duhn/ noun the first leaf to grow from a germinating seed.
– ORIGIN Greek *kotulēdōn* 'cup-shaped cavity'.

couch[1] /kowch/ noun 1 a long upholstered piece of furniture for several people to sit on. 2 a long seat with a headrest at one end on which a psychoanalyst's subject or doctor's patient lies during treatment. • verb 1 express in language of a specified type: *the announcement was couched in technical language.* 2 literary lie down.
– ORIGIN Old French *couche*.

couch[2] /kowch, kooch/ (also **couch grass**) noun a coarse grass with long creeping roots.
– ORIGIN Old English.

couchette /koo-shet/ noun 1 a railway carriage with seats convertible into sleeping berths. 2 a berth in a couchette carriage.
– ORIGIN French, 'small couch'.

couch potato noun informal a person who spends a great deal of time watching television.

cougar /koo-ger/ noun North American term for PUMA.
– ORIGIN French *couguar*.

cough verb 1 expel air from the lungs with a sudden sharp sound. 2 (of an engine) make a sudden harsh noise. 3 (**cough something up**) informal give something, especially money, reluctantly. 4 Brit. informal reveal information; confess. • noun 1 an act of coughing. 2 a condition of the throat or lungs causing coughing.
– DERIVATIVES **cougher** noun.
– ORIGIN imitating the sound.

could modal verb past of CAN[1].

USAGE: For advice on **could have** versus **could of**, see the note at HAVE.

couldn't contraction could not.

coulis /koo-li/ noun (pl. same) a thin fruit or vegetable purée, used as a sauce.
– ORIGIN French.

coulomb /koo-lom/ noun the SI unit of electric charge, equal to the quantity of electricity conveyed in one second by a current of one ampere.
– ORIGIN named after the French military engineer Charles-Augustin de *Coulomb*.

coulter /kohltuh/ (US **colter**) noun a vertical cutting blade fixed in front of a ploughshare.
– ORIGIN Latin *culter* 'knife or ploughshare'.

council noun 1 an assembly of people that meets regularly to discuss, advise on, or administer something. 2 a group of people elected to manage a city, county, or district. • adjective Brit. (of housing) provided by a local council.
– ORIGIN Latin *concilium* 'assembly'.

USAGE: Do not confuse **council** with **counsel**. Council means 'a group of people who manage an area or advise on something' (*the city council*), whereas counsel means 'advice' or 'advise someone' (*we counselled him on estate planning*).

councillor (US also **councilor**) noun a member of a council.

council tax noun (in Britain) a tax charged on households by local authorities, based on the estimated value of a property.

counsel noun 1 advice given to someone. 2 (pl. same) a barrister or other legal adviser conducting a case. • verb (**counsels, counselling, counselled**; US **counsels, counseling, counseled**) 1 give advice to: *we counselled him on estate planning.* 2 give professional help and advice to someone with personal or psychological problems. 3 recommend a course of action.
– PHRASES **keep one's own counsel** not reveal one's plans or opinions.
– ORIGIN Latin *consilium* 'consultation, advice'.

counsellor (US **counselor**) noun 1 a person trained to give advice on personal or psychological problems. 2 a senior officer in the diplomatic service. 3 (also **counselor-at-law**) US & Irish a barrister.

count[1] verb 1 calculate the total number of a collection of people or things. 2 say numbers in ascending order. 3 include someone or something when calculating a total. 4 regard or be regarded as being: *people she had counted as her friends.* 5 be important; matter: *it's the thought that counts.* 6 (**count on**) rely on someone or something. 7 (**count someone in** or **out**) include (or exclude) someone in a planned activity. • noun 1 an act of counting. 2 the total found by counting. 3 a point for discussion or consideration: *she is unsuitable on every count.* 4 Law each of the charges against an accused person.
– PHRASES **count the days** (or **hours**) be impatient for time to pass. **keep** (or **lose**) **count** take note of (or forget) the number or amount when counting. **out for the count** 1 Boxing defeated by being knocked to the ground and unable to rise within ten seconds. 2 unconscious or sound asleep.
– DERIVATIVES **countable** adjective.
– ORIGIN Latin *computare* 'calculate'.

count[2] noun a foreign nobleman whose rank corresponds to that of an earl.
– ORIGIN Old French *conte*.

countdown noun 1 an act of counting in reverse order to zero, especially before the launch of a rocket. 2 the final moments before a significant event.

countenance /kown-tuh-nuhnss/ noun a person's face or facial expression. • verb tolerate or agree to: *his mother would never countenance such a marriage.*

– ORIGIN Old French *contenance* 'bearing, behaviour'.

counter[1] noun **1** a long flat fitment over which goods are sold or served or across which business is conducted with customers. **2** a small disc used in board games for keeping the score or as a place marker. **3** a person or thing that counts something. **4** a token representing a coin.

– PHRASES **over the counter** by ordinary sale in a shop, with no need for a prescription or licence. **under the counter** (or **table**) bought or sold secretly and illegally.

– ORIGIN Old French *conteor*.

counter[2] verb **1** speak or act in opposition or response to: *they will bolster the resources devoted to counter terrorism.* **2** Boxing give a return blow while parrying. •adverb (**counter to**) in the opposite direction or in opposition to. •adjective responding to something of the same kind, especially in opposition: *argument and counter argument.* •noun an act which opposes or prevents something else.

– ORIGIN from Latin *contra* 'against'.

counter- prefix **1** opposing or done in return: *counter-attack.* **2** in the opposite direction: *counterpoise.* **3** corresponding: *counterpart.*

– ORIGIN from Latin *contra* 'against'.

counteract verb act against something so as to reduce its force or cancel it out.

– DERIVATIVES **counteraction** noun **counteractive** adjective.

counter-attack noun an attack made in response to one by an opponent. •verb attack someone in response to an attack.

counterbalance noun /kown-ter-bal-uhnss/ **1** a weight that balances another. **2** a factor that has the opposite effect to that of another and so balances it out. •verb /kown-ter-**bal**-uhnss/ have an opposing and balancing effect on: *his steadiness would counterbalance the kid's nervous manner.*

counterblast noun a strongly worded reply to someone else's views.

counterclaim noun a claim made in response to and opposing a previous claim.

counterclockwise adverb & adjective North American term for ANTICLOCKWISE.

counterculture noun a way of life and set of attitudes that are at variance with those accepted by most of society.

counter-espionage noun activities designed to prevent or thwart spying by an enemy.

counterfeit /kown-ter-fit/ adjective made in exact imitation of something valuable with the intention to deceive or defraud others. •noun a forgery. •verb **1** imitate something fraudulently. **2** pretend to feel or possess an emotion or quality.

– DERIVATIVES **counterfeiter** noun.

– ORIGIN Old French *contrefait* 'made in opposition'.

counterfoil noun Brit. the part of a cheque, ticket, or receipt that is kept as a record by the person issuing it.

counter-intuitive adjective at variance with intuition or common-sense expectation.

countermand /kown-ter-**mahnd**/ verb cancel an order.

– ORIGIN Latin *contramandare.*

countermeasure noun an action taken to counteract a danger or threat.

counterpane noun a bedspread.

– ORIGIN from Latin *culcitra puncta* 'quilted mattress'.

counterpart noun a person or thing that corresponds to another: *the minister held talks with his French counterpart.*

counterpoint noun **1** the technique of writing or playing a melody or melodies together with another, according to fixed rules. **2** a melody played together with another. **3** a pleasing or notable contrast to something: *dill crème fraiche was a nice counterpoint to the fish.* •verb **1** add counterpoint to a melody. **2** contrast with something.

– ORIGIN Latin *contrapunctum* '(song) marked over against (the original melody)'.

counterpoise noun & verb another term for COUNTERBALANCE.

counterproductive adjective having the opposite of the desired effect.

Counter-Reformation noun the reform of the Church of Rome in the 16th and 17th centuries which was stimulated by the Protestant Reformation.

counter-revolution noun a revolution opposing a former one or reversing its results.

– DERIVATIVES **counter-revolutionary** adjective & noun.

countersign verb sign a document already signed by another person.

countersink verb (past and past part. **countersunk**) **1** enlarge the rim of a drilled hole so that a screw or bolt can be inserted level with the surface. **2** drive a screw or bolt into such a hole.

countertenor noun the highest male adult singing voice.

counterterrorism noun political or military activities designed to prevent or thwart terrorism.

– DERIVATIVES **counterterrorist** noun.

countervail /kown-ter-**vayl**/ verb (usu. as adj. **countervailing**) counteract something with something of equal force: *a profusion of countervailing opinions.*

– ORIGIN from Latin *contra valere* 'be of worth against'.

counterweight noun a weight that counterbalances another.

countess noun **1** the wife or widow of a count or earl. **2** a woman holding the rank of count or earl.

counting preposition taking account of; including.

countless adjective too many to be counted; very many.

count noun noun a noun that can form a plural and, in the singular, can be used with *a* (the indefinite article), e.g. *books, a book.* Contrasted with MASS NOUN.

countrified (also **countryfied**) adjective characteristic of the country or country life.

country noun (pl. **countries**) **1** a nation with its own government, occupying a particular territory. **2** districts outside large urban areas.

c

3 an area with regard to its physical features: *hill country.*
– PHRASES **across country** not keeping to roads. **go to the country** Brit. test public opinion by dissolving Parliament and holding a general election.
– ORIGIN from Latin *contrata terra* 'land lying opposite'.

country and western noun country music.

country club noun a club with sporting and social facilities, set in a rural area.

country cousin noun an unsophisticated and provincial person.

country dance noun a traditional type of English dance, in particular one performed by couples facing each other in long lines.

countryfied adjective variant spelling of COUNTRIFIED.

countryman (or **countrywoman**) noun (pl. **countrymen** or **countrywomen**) **1** a person living or born in a rural area. **2** a person from the same country as someone else.

country music noun a form of popular music originating in the rural southern US, typically featuring ballads and dance tunes accompanied by a guitar.

countryside noun the land and scenery of a rural area.

countrywide adjective & adverb extending throughout a nation.

county noun (pl. **counties**) **1** each of the main areas into which some countries are divided for the purposes of local government. **2** US a political and administrative division of a state. • adjective Brit. relating to or typical of upper-class people with an estate in a particular county: *loud county voices.*
– ORIGIN Old French *conte* 'land of a count'.

county council noun (in the UK) the elected governing body of a county.
– DERIVATIVES **county councillor** noun.

county court noun (in England and Wales) a judicial court for civil cases.

county town (N. Amer. **county seat**) noun the town that is the administrative capital of a county.

coup /koo/ noun (pl. **coups** /kooz/) **1** (also **coup d'état** /koo day-tah/) a sudden violent seizure of power from a government. [French, 'blow of state'.] **2** a successful move that achieves something difficult: *the ten-year agreement is a major coup for the company.*
– ORIGIN French.

coup de grâce /koo duh grahss/ noun (pl. **coups de grâce** pronunc. same) a final blow or shot given to kill a wounded person or animal.
– ORIGIN French, 'stroke of grace'.

coupé /koo-pay/ (also **coupe** /koop/) noun a car with a fixed roof, two doors, and a sloping rear.
– ORIGIN from French *carrosse coupé* 'cut carriage'.

couple noun **1** two people or things of the same sort considered together. **2** (treated as sing. or pl.) two people who are married or in a romantic or sexual relationship. **3** informal an indefinite small number. • verb **1** link or combine: *anger control coupled with relaxation therapy significantly lowered blood pressure.*

2 have sex.
– DERIVATIVES **coupledom** noun **coupler** noun.
– ORIGIN Latin *copula* 'connection'.

couplet noun a pair of successive lines of verse, typically rhyming and of the same length.

coupling noun a device for connecting railway vehicles or parts of machinery together.

coupon noun **1** a voucher entitling the holder to a discount or to buy something. **2** a detachable form used to send for information or to enter a competition.
– ORIGIN French, 'piece cut off'.

courage noun **1** the ability to do something that frightens one. **2** strength in the face of pain or grief.
– PHRASES **have the courage of one's convictions** act on one's beliefs despite danger or disapproval.
– ORIGIN Old French *corage.*

courageous adjective not deterred by danger or pain; brave.
– DERIVATIVES **courageously** adverb.

courgette /koor-zhet/ noun Brit. a variety of small vegetable marrow.
– ORIGIN French, 'little gourd'.

courier /kuu-ri-er/ noun **1** a person employed to deliver goods or documents quickly. **2** chiefly Brit. a person employed to guide and assist a group of tourists. • verb send goods or documents by courier.
– ORIGIN Old French *coreor* or French *courrier.*

course noun **1** a direction taken or intended to be taken. **2** the way in which something progresses or develops: *the course of history.* **3** (also **course of action**) a way of dealing with a situation: *my decision represented the wisest course open to me at the time.* **4** a dish forming one of the stages of a meal. **5** a series of lectures or lessons in a particular subject. **6** a series of repeated treatments or doses of medication. **7** an area of land or water prepared for racing, golf, or another sport. **8** a continuous horizontal layer of brick or stone in a wall. • verb **1** (of liquid) flow. **2** (often as noun **coursing**) pursue game, especially hares with greyhounds using sight rather than scent.
– PHRASES **in (the) course of 1** in the process of. **2** during. **of course 1** as expected. **2** certainly; yes.
– ORIGIN Old French *cours.*

coursebook noun Brit. a textbook designed for use on a particular course of study.

courser[1] noun literary a swift horse.
– ORIGIN Old French *corsier.*

courser[2] noun a person who goes coursing with greyhounds.

coursework noun work done during a course of study, usually counting towards a final mark.

court noun **1** (also **court of law**) the judge, jury, and law officers before whom legal cases are heard. **2** the place where a court of law meets. **3** a quadrangular area marked out for ball games such as tennis. **4** a quadrangle surrounded by a building or group of buildings. **5** the residence, councillors, and household of a sovereign. • verb **1** pay special attention to someone to try to win their support. **2** try hard to win favourable attention. **3** behave in a way that makes one vulnerable to: *he has often courted controversy.* **4** dated be involved with someone romantically, especially with a view to marriage. **5** (of a male bird or other animal) try to attract a mate.

– PHRASES **hold court** be the centre of attention. **out of court** before a legal hearing can take place. **pay court to** pay flattering attention to someone.

– ORIGIN Old French *cort*.

court card noun Brit. a playing card that is a king, queen, or jack of a suit.

– ORIGIN from *coat card*, because of the decorative dress of the figures depicted.

courteous /ker-ti-uhss/ adjective polite, respectful, and considerate.

– DERIVATIVES **courteously** adverb **courteousness** noun.

– ORIGIN Old French *corteis* 'having manners fit for a royal court'.

courtesan /kor-ti-zan/ noun a prostitute with wealthy or upper-class clients.

– ORIGIN French *courtisane*.

courtesy /ker-tuh-si/ noun (pl. **courtesies**) **1** polite and considerate behaviour. **2** something said or done for politeness in a formal social situation: *there was a ritual exchange of courtesies with the lawyers.*

– PHRASES **(by) courtesy of** given or allowed by someone.

courtesy title noun a title given to someone, especially the son or daughter of a peer, that has no legal validity.

courthouse noun **1** a building in which a court of law is held. **2** US a building containing the administrative offices of a county.

courtier /kor-ti-er/ noun a sovereign's companion or adviser.

courtly adjective (**courtlier**, **courtliest**) very polite and dignified.

– DERIVATIVES **courtliness** noun.

court martial noun (pl. **courts martial**) a court for trying members of the armed services accused of breaking military law. •verb (**court-martial**) (**court-martials**, **court-martialling**, **court-martialled**; US **court-martials**, **court-martialing**, **court-martialed**) try a member of the armed services by court martial.

court order noun a direction issued by a court or a judge requiring a person to do or not do something.

courtroom noun the room or building in which a court of law meets.

courtship noun **1** a period during which a couple develop a romantic relationship. **2** the courting of a person to win their support. **3** the behaviour of male birds and other animals aimed at attracting a mate.

court shoe noun Brit. a woman's plain, lightweight shoe that has a low-cut upper and no fastening.

courtyard noun an open area enclosed by walls or buildings, especially in a castle or large house.

couscous /kuuss-kuuss, kooss-kooss/ noun a North African dish of steamed or soaked semolina, usually served with spicy meat or vegetables.

– ORIGIN Arabic.

cousin noun **1** (also **first cousin**) a child of one's uncle or aunt. **2** a person of a similar or related people or nation: *our American cousins.*

– PHRASES **second cousin** a child of one's parent's first cousin. **third cousin** a child of one's parent's second cousin.

– DERIVATIVES **cousinly** adjective **cousinship** noun.

– ORIGIN Old French *cosin*.

couture /koo-tyoor/ noun **1** the design and manufacture of fashionable clothes to a client's specific requirements. **2** fashionable made-to-measure clothes.

– ORIGIN French, 'sewing, dressmaking'.

couturier /koo-tyoo-ri-ay/ noun (fem. **couturière** /koo-tyoo-ri-air/) a person who designs and sells fashionable made-to-measure clothes.

couverture /koo-vuh-choor/ noun chocolate with extra cocoa butter to give a high gloss, used to cover sweets and cakes.

– ORIGIN French, 'covering'.

covalent /koh-vay-luhnt/ adjective (of a chemical bond) formed by the sharing of electrons between atoms. Often contrasted with IONIC.

– DERIVATIVES **covalency** noun **covalently** adverb.

cove[1] noun **1** a small sheltered bay. **2** a concave arch or arched moulding at the junction of a wall with a ceiling.

– DERIVATIVES **coved** adjective **coving** noun.

– ORIGIN Old English, 'chamber, cave'.

cove[2] noun Brit. informal, dated a man.

– ORIGIN perhaps from a Romany word meaning 'thing or person'.

coven /kuv-uhn/ noun a group of witches who meet regularly.

– ORIGIN from Latin *convenire* 'come together'.

covenant /kuv-uh-nuhnt/ noun **1** a formal agreement, especially a written contract by which one agrees to make regular payments to a charity. **2** (in Judaism and Christianity) an agreement which brings about a commitment between God and his people. •verb agree or pay something by a formal written contract.

– DERIVATIVES **covenantal** adjective.

– ORIGIN Old French, 'agreeing'.

cover verb **1** put something over or in front of someone or something so as to protect or hide them. **2** spread or extend over: *the grounds covered eight acres.* **3** deal with or report on: *the course will cover a range of subjects.* **4** travel a specified distance. **5** (of money) be enough to pay for something. **6** (of insurance) protect against a liability, loss, or accident. **7** disguise or hide: *I laughed to cover my embarrassment.* **8** (**cover something up**) try to hide or deny something illegal or wrong. **9** (**cover for**) temporarily take over the job of a colleague. **10** aim a gun at someone. **11** protect an exposed person by shooting at the enemy. **12** (in team games) take up a position ready to defend against an opponent. **13** record or perform a cover version of a song. •noun **1** something that covers or protects. **2** a thick protective outer part or page of a book or magazine. **3** shelter or protection: *they ran for cover.* **4** military support for someone in danger. **5** a means of concealing an illegal or secret activity: *we are not using science as a cover for commercial whaling.* **6** Brit. protection by

insurance. **7** (also **cover version**) a recording or performance of a song previously recorded by a different artist. **8** a place setting at a table in a restaurant.
– PHRASES **cover one's back** informal take steps to avoid attack or criticism. **under cover of** **1** concealed by something. **2** while pretending to do something.
– DERIVATIVES **covering** noun.
– ORIGIN Latin *cooperire*.

coverage noun **1** the treatment of a subject by the media. **2** the extent to which something is covered: *eighty transmitters would give nationwide coverage.*

coverall noun (also **coveralls**) a full-length protective outer garment.

cover charge noun a service charge per person added to the bill in a restaurant.

covering letter noun an explanatory letter sent with another document or a parcel.

coverlet noun a bedspread.
– ORIGIN from Old French *covrir* 'to cover' + *lit* 'bed'.

cover note noun Brit. a temporary certificate showing that a person has a current insurance policy.

covert adjective /kuv-ert, koh-vert/ not done openly; secret. • noun /kuv-ert/ a thicket in which game can hide.
– DERIVATIVES **covertly** adverb.
– ORIGIN Old French, 'covered'.

cover-up noun an attempt to conceal a mistake or crime.

covet /kuv-it/ verb (**covets**, **coveting**, **coveted**) long to possess something belonging to someone else.
– DERIVATIVES **covetable** adjective.
– ORIGIN Old French *cuveitier*.

covetous adjective longing to possess something.
– DERIVATIVES **covetously** adverb **covetousness** noun.

covey /kuv-i/ noun (pl. **coveys**) a small flock of game birds, especially partridge.
– ORIGIN from Old French *cover* 'sit on, hatch'.

cow[1] noun **1** a fully grown female animal of a domesticated breed of ox. **2** the female of certain other large animals, such as the elephant. **3** informal, derogatory a disliked or unpleasant woman.
– PHRASES **till the cows come home** informal for an indefinitely long time.
– ORIGIN Old English.

cow[2] verb frighten someone into giving in to one's wishes.
– ORIGIN probably from Old Norse, 'oppress'.

coward noun a person who is afraid to do dangerous or unpleasant things.
– DERIVATIVES **cowardliness** noun **cowardly** adjective.
– ORIGIN Old French *couard*.

cowardice /kow-er-diss/ noun lack of courage.

cowbell noun a bell hung round a cow's neck.

cowboy noun **1** a man on horseback who herds cattle, especially in the western US. **2** Brit. informal a person in business who is dishonest or produces work of poor quality.

cowboy boot noun a high-heeled boot of a style originally worn by cowboys, typically with a pointed toe.

cowcatcher noun N. Amer. a metal frame at the front of a locomotive for pushing aside obstacles.

cower verb shrink back or crouch down in fear.
– ORIGIN German *kûren* 'lie in wait'.

cowherd noun a person who looks after grazing cattle.

cowl noun **1** a large loose hood forming part of a monk's habit. **2** a hood-shaped covering for a chimney or ventilation shaft. **3** another term for **COWLING**.
– DERIVATIVES **cowled** adjective.
– ORIGIN Latin *cucullus* 'hood of a cloak'.

cowlick noun a lock of hair hanging over the forehead.

cowling noun a removable cover for a vehicle or aircraft engine.

cow parsley noun a hedgerow plant with large heads of tiny white flowers.

cowpat noun Brit. a flat, round piece of cow dung.

cowpoke noun N. Amer. informal a cowboy.

cowpox noun a disease of cows' udders spread by a virus, which can be caught by humans and resembles mild smallpox.

cowrie /kow-ri/ noun (pl. **cowries**) a sea mollusc having a glossy, domed shell with a long, narrow opening.
– ORIGIN Hindi.

cowslip noun a wild primula with clusters of yellow flowers in spring.
– ORIGIN Old English, 'cow slime'.

Cox (in full **Cox's orange pippin**) noun an eating apple with a red-tinged green skin.
– ORIGIN named after the English fruit grower R. *Cox*.

cox noun a coxswain. • verb act as a coxswain for a racing boat or crew.
– DERIVATIVES **coxless** adjective.

coxcomb /koks-kohm/ noun old use a vain and conceited man; a dandy.
– ORIGIN variant of **COCKSCOMB**.

coxswain /kok-suhn/ noun a person who steers a boat.
– ORIGIN from former *cock* 'small boat' + **SWAIN**.

coy adjective (**coyer**, **coyest**) **1** pretending to be shy or modest. **2** reluctant to give details about something sensitive: *he's coy about his age.*
– DERIVATIVES **coyly** adverb **coyness** noun.
– ORIGIN Old French *coi*.

coyote /koy-oh-ti/ noun (pl. same or **coyotes**) a wolf-like wild dog native to North America.
– ORIGIN Nahuatl.

coypu /koy-poo/ noun (pl. **coypus**) a large beaver-like South American rodent, farmed for its fur.
– ORIGIN from a Chilean language.

coz conjunction variant spelling of **COS**[3].

cozen /kuz-uhn/ verb literary trick or deceive someone.
– ORIGIN perhaps from former Italian *cozzonare* 'to cheat'.

cozy adjective US spelling of **COSY**.

CPR abbreviation cardiopulmonary resuscitation.

CPS abbreviation (in the UK) Crown Prosecution Service.

cps (also **c.p.s.**) abbreviation **1** Computing characters per second. **2** cycles per second.

CPU abbreviation Computing central processing unit.

Cr symbol the chemical element chromium.

crab noun **1** a marine shellfish, some kinds of which are edible, with a broad shell and five pairs of legs, the first of which are modified as pincers. **2** (**crabs**) informal an infestation of crab lice. • verb (**crabs, crabbing, crabbed**) **1** move sideways or at an angle. **2** fish for crabs.
– PHRASES **catch a crab** make a faulty stroke in rowing in which the oar is jammed under the water or misses the water completely.
– DERIVATIVES **crabber** noun **crablike** adjective & adverb.
– ORIGIN Old English.

crab apple noun a small, sour kind of apple.
– ORIGIN probably Scandinavian.

crabbed adjective **1** (of writing) very small and hard to read. **2** bad-tempered; crabby.
– ORIGIN from **CRAB**, because of the crab's sideways movement and habit of snapping.

crabby adjective (**crabbier, crabbiest**) bad-tempered; irritable.
– DERIVATIVES **crabbily** adverb **crabbiness** noun.

crab louse noun a louse that infests human body hair.

crabmeat noun the flesh of a crab as food.

crabwise adverb & adjective (of movement) sideways, especially in an awkward way.

crack noun **1** a narrow opening between two parts of something which has split or been broken. **2** a sudden sharp noise. **3** a sharp blow. **4** informal a joke, especially a critical one. **5** informal an attempt to do something: *she's made the most of her first crack at stardom.* **6** (also **craic**) chiefly Irish enjoyable social activity; a good time. **7** (also **crack cocaine**) a very strong form of cocaine broken into small pieces. • verb **1** break apart or without complete separation of the parts. **2** give way under pressure or strain. **3** make a sudden sharp sound. **4** hit someone or something hard. **5** (of a person's voice) suddenly change in pitch, especially through strain. **6** informal solve or decipher: *he took less than a day to crack the code.* **7** tell a joke. • adjective very good or skilful: *he is a crack shot.*
– PHRASES **crack down on** informal take strong action against someone or something. **crack of dawn** daybreak. **crack of the whip** Brit. informal a chance to try or participate in something. **crack on** Brit. informal proceed or progress quickly. **crack up** informal **1** suffer an emotional breakdown under pressure. **2** burst into laughter. **3** (**be cracked up to be**) informal be claimed to be: *acting isn't as glamorous as it's cracked up to be.* **get cracking** informal begin immediately and work quickly.
– ORIGIN Old English.

crackbrained adjective informal very foolish.

crackdown noun a set of severe measures against undesirable or illegal behaviour.

cracked adjective **1** having cracks. **2** informal mad; crazy.

cracked wheat noun grains of wheat that have been crushed into small pieces.

cracker noun **1** a paper cylinder which, when

pulled apart, makes a sharp noise and releases a small toy or other novelty. **2** a firework that explodes with a crack. **3** a thin, dry biscuit. **4** Brit. informal an excellent example of something.

crackers adjective Brit. informal mad; crazy.

cracking adjective Brit. informal **1** excellent. **2** fast and exciting: *a cracking pace.*

crackle verb make a series of slight cracking noises. • noun a series of slight cracking noises.
– DERIVATIVES **crackly** adjective.

crackling noun the crisp fatty skin of roast pork.

cracknel /krak-nuhl/ noun a brittle sweet made from set melted sugar.

crackpot informal noun an eccentric or foolish person. • adjective eccentric; impractical.

-cracy combining form referring to a particular form of government or rule: *democracy.*
– ORIGIN from Greek *-kratia* 'power, rule'.

cradle noun **1** a baby's bed, especially one on rockers. **2** a place in which something originates or flourishes: *the Middle East is believed to be the cradle of agriculture.* **3** a supporting framework, in particular for a boat under repair or for workers on the side of a high building. • verb hold something gently and protectively.
– ORIGIN Old English.

cradle-snatcher noun informal, derogatory a person who has a sexual relationship with a much younger person.

craft noun **1** an activity involving skill in making things by hand. **2** the skill needed for one's work: *he learned his craft in Holland.* **3** (**crafts**) things made by hand. **4** skill in deceiving others; cunning. **5** (pl. same) a boat, ship, or aircraft. • verb make something skilfully.
– DERIVATIVES **crafter** noun.
– ORIGIN Old English.

craftsman (or **craftswoman**) noun (pl. **craftsmen** or **craftswomen**) a worker skilled in a particular craft.
– DERIVATIVES **craftsmanship** noun.

craftwork noun **1** the making of things by hand. **2** items produced by hand.
– DERIVATIVES **craftworker** noun.

crafty adjective (**craftier, craftiest**) clever at deceiving people; cunning.
– DERIVATIVES **craftily** adverb **craftiness** noun.
– ORIGIN Old English.

crag noun a steep or rugged cliff or rock face.
– ORIGIN Celtic.

craggy adjective (**craggier, craggiest**) **1** having many crags. **2** (of a man's face) attractively rugged.

craic noun variant spelling of **CRACK** (in sense 6).

crake noun a bird of the rail family with a short bill, such as the corncrake.
– ORIGIN Old Norse.

cram verb (**crams, cramming, crammed**) **1** force too many people or things into a place or container. **2** fill to overflowing: *the hut was crammed with sacks of wheat or maize.* **3** study intensively just before an exam.
– ORIGIN Old English.

crammer noun Brit. a college that gives students intensive preparation for exams.

cramp noun **1** painful involuntary contraction of a muscle or muscles. **2** a tool for clamping two objects together. • verb **1** restrict the development of: *tighter rules will cramp economic growth.* **2** fasten something with a cramp or cramps.
– ORIGIN German and Dutch.

cramped adjective **1** uncomfortably small or crowded. **2** (of handwriting) small and difficult to read.

crampon /kram-pon/ noun a metal plate with spikes, fixed to a boot for climbing on ice or rock.
– ORIGIN Old French.

cranberry noun (pl. **cranberries**) a small sour red berry used in cooking.
– ORIGIN German *Kranbeere* 'crane-berry'.

crane noun **1** a tall machine used for moving heavy objects by suspending them from a projecting arm. **2** a grey or white wading bird with long legs and a long neck. • verb stretch out one's neck to see something.
– ORIGIN Old English.

crane fly noun a slender fly with very long legs; a daddy-long-legs.

cranesbill noun a plant with purple, violet, or pink flowers.
– ORIGIN from the long spur on the fruit, thought to resemble a crane's beak.

cranial /kray-ni-uhl/ adjective relating to the skull or cranium.

craniosacral therapy /kray-ni-oh-say-kruhl/ noun a system of alternative medicine intended to relieve pain and tension by gentle manipulations of the skull.

cranium /kray-ni-uhm/ noun (pl. **craniums** or **crania** /kray-ni-uh/) the skull, especially the part enclosing the brain.
– ORIGIN Latin.

crank¹ verb **1** turn a crankshaft or handle to start an internal-combustion engine. **2** (**crank something up**) informal increase the intensity of something. **3** (**crank something out**) informal, derogatory produce something regularly and routinely. • noun a right-angled part of an axle or shaft, for converting linear to circular motion or vice versa.
– ORIGIN Old English.

crank² noun an eccentric or obsessive person.
– ORIGIN from **CRANKY**.

crankcase noun a case or covering enclosing a crankshaft.

crankpin noun a pin by which a connecting rod is attached to a crank.

crankshaft noun a shaft driven by a crank.

cranky adjective (**crankier**, **crankiest**) informal **1** Brit. eccentric or odd. **2** chiefly N. Amer. bad-tempered; irritable.
– DERIVATIVES **crankily** adverb **crankiness** noun.
– ORIGIN perhaps from Dutch or German *krank* 'sick'.

cranny noun (pl. **crannies**) a small, narrow space or opening.
– ORIGIN Latin *crena* 'notch'.

crap vulgar slang noun **1** excrement. **2** nonsense; rubbish. • verb (**craps**, **crapping**, **crapped**) defecate. • adjective Brit. very poor in quality.
– DERIVATIVES **crappy** adjective.
– ORIGIN related to Dutch *krappe* 'chaff'.

crape noun black silk, formerly used for mourning clothes.
– ORIGIN variant of **CRÊPE**.

craps plural noun (treated as sing.) a North American gambling game played with two dice.
– ORIGIN perhaps from **CRAB** or *crab's eyes*, referring to a throw of two ones.

crapshoot noun N. Amer. a game of craps.

crapulous /krap-yuu-luhss/ (also **crapulent**) adjective literary relating to the drinking of alcohol or to drunkenness.
– ORIGIN Latin *crapulentus* 'very drunk'.

crash verb **1** (of a vehicle) collide violently with an obstacle or another vehicle. **2** (of an aircraft) fall from the sky and hit the land or sea. **3** move with force, speed, and sudden loud noise: *the cup crashed to the floor.* **4** make a sudden loud noise. **5** (of shares) fall suddenly in value. **6** (of a computer, system, or software) fail suddenly. **7** (also **crash out**) informal fall deeply asleep. **8** informal gatecrash a party. • noun an instance or sound of crashing. • adjective rapid and concentrated: *a crash course in Italian.*
– ORIGIN imitating the sound.

crash-dive verb (of an aircraft or submarine) dive rapidly or uncontrollably.

crash helmet noun a helmet worn by a motorcyclist to protect the head.

crashing adjective informal complete; total: *a crashing bore.*
– DERIVATIVES **crashingly** adverb.

crash-land verb (of an aircraft) land roughly in an emergency.

crashworthiness noun the degree to which a vehicle will protect its occupants from the effects of a crash.
– DERIVATIVES **crashworthy** adjective

crass adjective very thoughtless and stupid.
– DERIVATIVES **crassly** adverb **crassness** noun.
– ORIGIN Latin *crassus* 'solid, thick'.

-crat combining form referring to a member or supporter of a particular form of government or rule: *democrat.*
– ORIGIN from Greek *-kratia* 'power, rule'.

crate noun **1** a slatted wooden case for transporting goods. **2** a square container divided into small individual units for holding bottles. **3** informal an old and ramshackle vehicle. • verb pack something in a crate for transportation.
– ORIGIN perhaps related to Dutch *krat* 'tailboard of a wagon'.

crater noun **1** a large hollow forming the mouth of a volcano. **2** a large bowl-shaped hollow caused by an explosion or the impact of a meteorite. • verb form a crater or craters in the ground or a planet.
– ORIGIN Greek *kratēr* 'mixing-bowl'.

-cratic combining form relating to a particular kind of government or rule: *democratic.*

cravat noun a strip of fabric worn by men round the neck and tucked inside an open-necked shirt.
– ORIGIN French *cravate.*

crave verb **1** feel a powerful desire for something. **2** old use ask for: *I must crave your indulgence.*

– ORIGIN Old English.

craven adjective lacking in courage; cowardly.
– DERIVATIVES **cravenly** adverb.
– ORIGIN perhaps from Old French *cravanter* 'crush, overwhelm'.

craving noun a powerful desire for something.

craw noun dated the crop (part of the throat) of a bird.
– PHRASES **stick in one's craw** see STICK².
– ORIGIN related to Dutch *crāghe* or German *krage* 'neck, throat'.

crawfish noun (pl. same or **crawfishes**) chiefly N. Amer. a crayfish.
– ORIGIN variant of CRAYFISH.

crawl verb 1 move forward on the hands and knees or with the body close to the ground. 2 (of an insect or small animal) move slowly along a surface. 3 move along very slowly: *the traffic was crawling along.* 4 (**be crawling with**) be unpleasantly covered or crowded with: *the place was crawling with soldiers.* 5 informal behave in an excessively friendly or submissive way to win someone's favour.
• noun 1 an act of crawling. 2 a very slow speed. 3 a swimming stroke involving alternate overarm movements and rapid kicks of the legs.
– PHRASES **make one's skin crawl** cause one to feel fear or disgust (likened to something crawling on the skin).
– DERIVATIVES **crawler** noun.
– ORIGIN perhaps related to Swedish *kravla* and Danish *kravle.*

crayfish noun (pl. same or **crayfishes**) a freshwater or sea shellfish resembling a small lobster.
– ORIGIN Old French *crevice.*

crayon noun a stick of coloured chalk or wax, used for drawing. • verb draw something with a crayon or crayons.
– ORIGIN French.

craze noun a widespread but short-lived enthusiasm for something. • verb (**be crazed**) (of a surface) be covered with a network of fine cracks.
– DERIVATIVES **crazing** noun.
– ORIGIN perhaps Scandinavian.

crazed adjective (often in combination) behaving in an uncontrolled or mad way: *drug-crazed kids.*

crazy adjective (**crazier, craziest**) 1 insane, especially in a wild way. 2 very enthusiastic: *I'm crazy about Cindy.* 3 foolish or absurd: *it was a crazy idea.* • noun (pl. **crazies**) informal, chiefly N. Amer. an insane person.
– PHRASES **like crazy** to a great degree.
– DERIVATIVES **crazily** adverb **craziness** noun.

crazy paving noun Brit. paving made of irregular pieces of flat stone.

creak verb 1 make or move with a scraping or squeaking sound. 2 show weakness under strain: *the system is creaking at the seams.* • noun a scraping or squeaking sound.
– DERIVATIVES **creaky** adjective (**creakier, creakiest**).
– ORIGIN imitating the sound.

cream noun 1 the thick fatty liquid which rises to the top when milk is left to stand. 2 a food containing cream or having a creamy consistency. 3 a thick liquid cosmetic or

medical substance that is applied to the skin. 4 the very best of a group: *the cream of American society.* 5 a very pale yellow or off-white colour. • verb 1 mash a cooked vegetable with milk or cream. 2 work butter to form a smooth soft paste. 3 (**cream something off**) take away the best part of a group: *the schools cream off the more able pupils.*
– ORIGIN Old French *cresme.*

cream cheese noun soft, rich cheese made from unskimmed milk and cream.

cream cracker noun Brit. a dry unsweetened biscuit.

creamer noun 1 a cream or milk substitute for adding to coffee or tea. 2 N. Amer. a jug for cream.

creamery noun (pl. **creameries**) a factory that produces butter and cheese.

cream of tartar noun an acidic compound produced during the fermentation of wine and used chiefly in baking powder.

cream puff noun a cake made of puff pastry filled with cream.

cream sherry noun a full-bodied mellow sweet sherry.

cream tea noun Brit. an afternoon meal consisting of tea to drink with scones, jam, and cream.

creamy adjective (**creamier, creamiest**) resembling or containing a lot of cream.
– DERIVATIVES **creamily** adverb **creaminess** noun.

crease noun 1 a line or ridge produced on paper or cloth by folding, pressing, or crushing. 2 Cricket any of a number of lines marked on the pitch at specified places. • verb 1 make or become crumpled or wrinkled. 2 (**crease up**) Brit. informal burst out laughing.
– ORIGIN probably a variant of CREST.

create verb 1 bring something into existence. 2 cause to happen: *divorce creates problems for children.* 3 appoint to a noble title or rank: *he was created a baronet.* 4 Brit. informal make a fuss; complain.
– ORIGIN Latin *creare* 'produce'.

creatine /kree-uh-teen/ noun a compound formed in protein metabolism and involved in the supply of energy for contraction of the muscles.
– ORIGIN from Greek *kreas* 'meat'.

creation noun 1 the action of bringing something into existence. 2 a thing which has been made or invented, especially something showing artistic talent. 3 (**the Creation**) the creating of the universe, regarded as an act of God. 4 (**Creation**) literary the universe.

creationism noun the belief that the universe and living creatures were created by God in accordance with the account given in the Old Testament.
– DERIVATIVES **creationist** noun & adjective.

creative adjective 1 involving the use of the imagination or original ideas in order to create something. 2 having good imagination or original ideas.
– DERIVATIVES **creatively** adverb **creativeness** noun **creativity** noun.

creative accountancy (also **creative accounting**) noun informal the exploitation of loopholes in financial regulation to gain advantage or to present figures in a misleadingly favourable light.

creator noun **1** a person or thing that creates something. **2** (**the Creator**) God.

creature noun **1** a living being, in particular an animal as distinct from a person. **2** a person viewed in a particular way: *you heartless creature!*
– ORIGIN Latin *creatura*.

creature comforts plural noun things that contribute to a comfortable life, such as good food and accommodation.

crèche /kresh/ noun Brit. a nursery where babies and young children are cared for during the working day.
– ORIGIN French.

cred noun informal short for CREDIBILITY (in sense 2).

credal /kree-duhl/ (also **creedal**) adjective relating to a statement of Christian or other religious belief.

credence /kree-duhnss/ noun **1** belief in something as true: *he gave no credence to the witness's statement.* **2** the likelihood of something being true; plausibility.
– ORIGIN from Latin *credere* 'believe'.

credential /kri-**den**-sh'l/ noun (usu. **credentials**) **1** a qualification, achievement, or quality that gives an indication of a person's suitability for something: *her academic credentials cannot be doubted.* **2** a document proving a person's identity or qualifications. **3** a letter of introduction given by a government to an ambassador before a new posting.

credibility noun **1** the quality of being trusted or believable. **2** (also **street credibility**) acceptability among fashionable young urban people.

credible adjective able to be believed; convincing.
– DERIVATIVES **credibly** adverb.
– ORIGIN from Latin *credere* 'believe'.

credit noun **1** an arrangement in which a shop or other business enables a customer to pay at a later date for goods or services supplied: *we supply quality cars on credit.* **2** money borrowed or lent under a credit arrangement. **3** public acknowledgement or praise for an achievement or quality. **4** a source of pride: *the fans are a credit to the club.* **5** a written acknowledgement of a contributor's role displayed at the beginning or end of a film or programme. **6** an entry in an account recording a sum received. **7** a unit of study counting towards a degree or diploma. **8** Brit. a grade above a pass in an exam. • verb (**credits, crediting, credited**) **1** believe that someone has done something or has a particular quality: *he is credited with coining the phrase.* **2** Brit. believe something surprising. **3** add an amount of money to an account.
– PHRASES **be in credit** (of an account) have money in it. **do someone credit** make someone worthy of praise or respect.
– ORIGIN Latin *creditum*.

creditable adjective deserving public acknowledgement and praise.
– DERIVATIVES **creditably** adverb.

credit card noun a plastic card allowing the

holder to buy things on credit.

creditor noun a person or company to whom money is owing.

credit union noun a non-profit-making cooperative whose members can borrow money at low interest rates.

creditworthy adjective considered suitable to receive financial credit.
– DERIVATIVES **creditworthiness** noun.

credo /kree-doh/ noun (pl. **credos**) a statement of a person's beliefs or aims.
– ORIGIN Latin, 'I believe'.

credulous /kred-yuu-luhss/ adjective excessively ready to believe things; gullible.
– DERIVATIVES **credulity** /kri-**dyoo**-li-ti/ noun **credulously** adverb.
– ORIGIN Latin *credulus*.

Cree /kree/ noun (pl. same or **Crees**) a member of an American Indian people of central Canada.
– ORIGIN Algonquian.

creed noun **1** a system of religious belief; a faith. **2** a statement of beliefs or principles: *nationalism is his creed.*
– ORIGIN from Latin *credo* 'I believe'.

creedal adjective variant spelling of CREDAL.

creek noun **1** chiefly Brit. a small waterway such as an inlet in a shoreline. **2** N. Amer. & Austral./NZ a stream or minor tributary of a river.
– PHRASES **up the creek** informal **1** in severe difficulty. **2** Brit. stupid or misguided.
– ORIGIN Old French *crique* or Old Norse *kriki* 'nook'.

creel noun a large basket for carrying fish.
– ORIGIN unknown.

creep verb (past and past part. **crept**) **1** move slowly and carefully to avoid being noticed. **2** progress or develop gradually: *errors crept into his game.* **3** (as adj. **creeping**) (of a plant) growing along the ground or other surface. • noun **1** informal a contemptible person, especially one who behaves in a servile way to win favour. **2** slow and gradual movement or progress.
– PHRASES **give someone the creeps** informal make someone feel disgust or fear. **make one's flesh creep** cause one to feel disgust (likened to something crawling over the skin).
– ORIGIN Old English.

creeper noun a plant that grows along the ground or another surface.

creepy adjective (**creepier, creepiest**) informal causing fear or unease.
– DERIVATIVES **creepily** adverb **creepiness** noun.

creepy-crawly noun (pl. **creepy-crawlies**) informal a spider, worm, or other small creature.

cremate verb dispose of a corpse by burning it to ashes.
– DERIVATIVES **cremation** noun.
– ORIGIN Latin *cremare* 'burn'.

crematorium /kre-muh-**tor**-i-uhm/ noun (pl. **crematoria** /kre-muh-**tor**-i-uh/ or **crematoriums**) a building where the dead are cremated.

crème brûlée /krem broo-**lay**/ noun (pl. **crèmes brûlées** pronunc. same, or **crème brûlées** /krem broo-**layz**/) a dessert of custard topped with caramelized sugar.
– ORIGIN French, 'burnt cream'.

crème caramel /krem kar-uh-**mel**/ noun (pl.

crèmes caramel or **crème caramels** pronunc. same) a custard dessert made with whipped cream and eggs and topped with caramel.
– ORIGIN French.

crème de cassis noun see CASSIS.

crème de la crème /krem duh la **krem**/ noun the best person or thing of a particular kind.
– ORIGIN French, 'cream of the cream'.

crème de menthe /krem duh **mon**-th/ noun a green peppermint-flavoured liqueur.
– ORIGIN French, 'cream of mint'.

crème fraiche /krem fresh/ noun a type of thick cream with buttermilk, sour cream, or yogurt.
– ORIGIN French, 'fresh cream'.

crenellated /kren-uhl-lay-tid/ (also **crenelated**) adjective (of a building) having battlements.
– ORIGIN from Latin *crena* 'notch'.

crenellations plural noun battlements.

Creole /**kree**-ohl/ noun 1 a person of mixed European and black descent. 2 a descendant of European settlers in the Caribbean or Central or South America. 3 a white descendant of French settlers in Louisiana. 4 a language formed from a combination of a European language and another language, especially an African language.
– ORIGIN French.

creosote noun a dark brown oil used as a wood preservative. •verb treat something with creosote.
– ORIGIN from Greek *kreas* 'flesh' + *sōtēr* 'preserver'.

crêpe /krayp/ (also **crepe**) noun 1 a light, thin fabric with a wrinkled surface. 2 hard-wearing wrinkled rubber used for the soles of shoes. 3 /also krep/ a thin pancake.
– DERIVATIVES **crêpey** (also **crêpy**) adjective.
– ORIGIN French.

crêpe de Chine /duh sheen/ noun a fine crêpe fabric of silk or a similar material.
– ORIGIN French, 'crêpe of China'.

crêpe paper noun thin, crinkled paper used for making decorations.

crêpe Suzette noun (pl. **crêpes Suzette** pronunc. same) a thin sweet pancake flamed briefly in alcohol at the table before being served.

crepitate /krep-i-tayt/ verb rare make a crackling sound.
– DERIVATIVES **crepitation** noun.
– ORIGIN Latin.

crept past and past participle of CREEP.

crepuscular /kri-**pus**-kyuu-ler/ adjective chiefly literary resembling or relating to twilight.
– ORIGIN Latin *crepusculum* 'twilight'.

crescendo /kri-**shen**-doh/ noun 1 (pl. **crescendos** or **crescendi** /kri-**shen**-di/) a gradual increase in loudness in a piece of music. 2 the loudest or climactic point: *the shrieks of laughter reached a crescendo*. •adverb & adjective Music gradually becoming louder. •verb (**crescendoes, crescendoing, crescendoed**) increase in loudness or intensity.
– ORIGIN Italian.

crescent /**krez**-uhnt/ noun 1 the form of the waxing or waning moon, seen as a narrow curved shape tapering to a point at each end.

2 chiefly Brit. a street or terrace of houses forming an arc.
– ORIGIN from Latin *crescere* 'grow'.

cress noun a plant with hot-tasting leaves, some kinds of which are eaten in salads.
– ORIGIN Old English.

crest noun 1 a tuft or growth of feathers, fur, or skin on the head of a bird or other animal. 2 a plume of feathers on a helmet. 3 the top of a ridge, wave, etc. 4 a distinctive heraldic design representing a family or organization. •verb 1 reach the top of: *he finally crested the hill.* 2 (as adj. **crested**) having a crest.
– PHRASES **on the crest of a wave** at a very successful point.
– ORIGIN from Latin *crista*.

crestfallen adjective sad and disappointed.

Cretaceous /kri-**tay**-shuhss/ adjective relating to the last period of the Mesozoic era (about 146 to 65 million years ago), at the end of which dinosaurs and many other organisms died out.
– ORIGIN from Latin *creta* 'chalk'.

Cretan /**kree**-tuhn/ noun a person from the Greek island of Crete. •adjective relating to Crete.

cretin /**kret**-in/ noun 1 a stupid person. 2 Medicine, dated a person who is deformed and has learning difficulties because of a congenital lack of thyroid hormone.
– DERIVATIVES **cretinism** noun.
– ORIGIN from Swiss French *crestin* 'Christian', apparently intended as a reminder that disabled people are human.

cretinous adjective very stupid.

cretonne /kri-**ton**/ noun a heavy cotton fabric, typically with a floral pattern, used for upholstery.
– ORIGIN French.

Creutzfeldt–Jakob disease /kroyts-felt-**yak**-ob/ noun a fatal disease which affects nerve cells in the brain, one form of which (**new variant Creutzfeldt–Jakob disease**) is possibly linked to BSE.
– ORIGIN named after the German neurologists H. G. *Creutzfeldt* and A. *Jakob*.

crevasse /kri-**vass**/ noun a deep open crack in a glacier or ice field.
– ORIGIN Old French *crevace* (see CREVICE).

crevice /**kre**-viss/ noun a narrow opening or crack in a rock or wall.
– ORIGIN Old French *crevace*, from *crever* 'to burst'.

crew[1] noun (treated as sing. or pl.) 1 a group of people who work on and operate a ship, boat, aircraft, or train. 2 a group of such people excluding the officers. 3 informal, often derogatory a group of people. •verb act as a member of a crew on a ship, boat, aircraft, etc.
– ORIGIN Old French *creue* 'increase'.

crew[2] past of CROW[2].

crew cut noun a very short haircut for men and boys.
– ORIGIN apparently first adopted by boat crews of Harvard and Yale universities.

crewel /**kroo**-uhl/ noun a thin, loosely twisted worsted yarn used for tapestry and embroidery.

– ORIGIN unknown.

crew neck noun a close-fitting round neckline.

crib noun 1 chiefly N. Amer. a child's cot. 2 a rack for animal fodder; a manger. 3 informal a translation of a text for use by students, especially in a surreptitious way. 4 informal, chiefly N. Amer. a house or flat. 5 short for CRIBBAGE. • verb (cribs, cribbing, cribbed) informal copy another person's work dishonestly or without acknowledgement.
– ORIGIN Old English.

cribbage noun a card game for two players, the objective of which is to play cards whose value reaches exactly 15 or 31.
– ORIGIN from CRIB.

crick noun a painful stiff feeling in the neck or back. • verb twist or strain one's neck or back, causing painful stiffness.
– ORIGIN unknown.

cricket¹ noun an open-air game played by two teams of eleven players with a ball, bats, and wickets, the batsmen attempting to score runs by hitting the ball and running between the wickets.
– PHRASES **not cricket** Brit. informal not fair or honourable.
– DERIVATIVES **cricketer** noun **cricketing** adjective.
– ORIGIN unknown.

cricket² noun an insect like a grasshopper but with shorter legs, the male of which produces a shrill chirping sound.
– ORIGIN from Old French criquer 'to crackle'.

cri de cœur /kree duh ker/ noun (pl. **cris de cœur** pronunc. same) a passionate appeal or complaint.
– ORIGIN French, 'cry from the heart'.

cried past and past participle of CRY.

crikey exclamation Brit. informal an expression of surprise.
– ORIGIN euphemism for CHRIST.

crime noun 1 an act or activity that is illegal and can be punished by law. 2 such acts or activities considered as a whole: the victims of violent crime. 3 something seen as immoral or shameful: such a war would be a crime against humanity.
– ORIGIN Latin crimen 'judgement, offence'.

criminal noun a person who has committed a crime. • adjective 1 relating to crime or a crime. 2 informal disgraceful and shocking: a criminal waste of taxpayers' money.
– DERIVATIVES **criminality** noun **criminally** adverb.

criminalize (or **criminalise**) verb 1 make an activity illegal. 2 turn someone into a criminal by making their activities illegal.
– DERIVATIVES **criminalization** noun.

criminology /kri-mi-nol-uh-ji/ noun the scientific study of crime and criminals.
– DERIVATIVES **criminologist** noun.

crimp verb 1 press something into small folds or ridges. 2 make curls or waves in a person's hair by pressing it with curling tongs or a similar device.
– DERIVATIVES **crimper** noun.
– ORIGIN Old English.

crimplene /krimp-leen/ noun trademark a synthetic crease-resistant fibre and fabric.
– ORIGIN probably from CRIMP + TERYLENE.

crimson /krim-z'n/ noun a rich deep red colour.

• verb (of a person's face) become flushed, especially through embarrassment.
– ORIGIN Arabic.

cringe /krinj/ verb (cringes, cringing, cringed) 1 shrink back or cower in fear or in a submissive way. 2 have a sudden feeling of embarrassment or disgust.
– ORIGIN from an Old English word meaning 'bend, yield, fall in battle'.

crinkle verb form small creases or wrinkles. • noun a small crease or wrinkle.
– DERIVATIVES **crinkly** adjective.
– ORIGIN related to CRINGE.

crinoline /krin-uh-lin/ noun a stiffened or hooped petticoat formerly worn to give a long skirt a very full and rounded shape.
– ORIGIN French, from Latin crinis 'hair' + linum 'thread'.

cripes /kryps/ exclamation informal an expression of surprise.
– ORIGIN euphemism for CHRIST.

cripple noun old use or offensive a person who is unable to walk or move properly through disability or injury. • verb 1 make someone unable to move or walk properly. 2 severely damage or weaken something: families crippled by mounting debts.
– ORIGIN Old English.

USAGE: As a noun, the word **cripple** is often regarded as offensive and should be avoided. Terms such as 'disabled person' are preferable.

crisis noun (pl. **crises**) 1 a time of extreme difficulty or danger: the current economic crisis. 2 the time when a problem or difficult situation is at its worst point.
– ORIGIN Greek krisis 'decision'.

crisp adjective 1 firm, dry, and brittle. 2 (of the weather) cool, fresh, and invigorating. 3 (of a person's way of speaking) brisk and decisive. • noun (also **potato crisp**) Brit. a thin slice of fried potato eaten as a snack. • verb give food a crisp surface by cooking it in an oven or under a grill.
– DERIVATIVES **crisply** adverb **crispness** noun.
– ORIGIN Latin crispus 'curled'.

crispbread noun a thin, crisp biscuit made from crushed rye or wheat.

crispy adjective (crispier, crispiest) firm and brittle; crisp.

criss-cross adjective with a pattern of intersecting lines. • verb 1 form a criss-cross pattern on a place. 2 move or travel around a place by going back and forth repeatedly.

criterion /kry-teer-i-uhn/ noun (pl. **criteria** /kry-teer-i-uh/) a principle or standard by which something may be judged or decided.
– ORIGIN Greek kritērion 'means of judging'.

USAGE: The singular form is **criterion** and the plural form is **criteria**. Do not use **criteria** as if it were a singular noun: say a further criterion needs to be considered not a further criteria needs to be considered.

critic noun 1 a person who expresses disapproval of someone or something. 2 a person who reviews literary or artistic works.
– ORIGIN from Greek kritēs 'a judge'.

critical adjective 1 expressing disapproving comments or judgements: the press were very

critical of him. **2** expressing or involving an assessment of a literary or artistic work. **3** at a point of danger or crisis: *the floods were rising and the situation was critical.* **4** extremely ill and at risk of death. **5** having a decisive importance in the success or failure of something; crucial: *confidence has been the critical factor in their success.* **6** Mathematics & Physics relating to a point of transition from one state to another. **7** (of a nuclear reactor or fuel) maintaining a chain reaction that can sustain itself.
– DERIVATIVES **critically** adverb.

critical mass noun **1** Physics the minimum amount of fissile material needed to maintain a nuclear chain reaction. **2** the minimum amount of resources required to start a venture or keep it going.

criticism noun **1** the expression of disapproval of someone or something. **2** the assessment of literary or artistic works.

criticize (or **criticise**) verb **1** express disapproval of someone or something. **2** assess a literary or artistic work.

critique /kri-**teek**/ noun a detailed analysis and assessment of something. •verb (**critiques**, **critiquing**, **critiqued**) analyse and assess something in detail.
– ORIGIN French.

critter noun informal or dialect, chiefly N. Amer. a living creature.

croak noun a characteristic deep hoarse sound made by a frog or a crow. •verb **1** utter a croak. **2** informal die.
– DERIVATIVES **croaky** adjective.
– ORIGIN imitating the sound.

Croatian /kroh-**ay**-sh'n/ noun (also **Croat** /**kroh**-at/) **1** a person from Croatia. **2** the language of the Croatians, almost identical to Serbian but written in the Roman alphabet. •adjective relating to Croatia or Croatian.

crochet /**kroh**-shay/ noun a handicraft in which yarn is looped into a fabric of connected stitches by means of a hooked needle. •verb (**crochets**, /**kroh**-shayz/, **crocheting** /**kroh**-shay-ing/, **crocheted** /**kroh**-shayd/) make a garment or piece of fabric in this way.
– ORIGIN French, 'little hook'.

croci plural of **CROCUS**.

crock¹ noun Brit. informal **1** an old person considered to be feeble and useless. **2** an old worn-out vehicle.
– ORIGIN probably related to **CRACK**.

crock² noun **1** an earthenware pot or jar. **2** an item of crockery.
– ORIGIN Old English.

crockery noun plates, dishes, cups, and similar items made of earthenware or china.
– ORIGIN from the former word *crocker* 'potter'.

crocodile noun **1** a large predatory tropical reptile living partly in water, with long jaws and a long tail. **2** Brit. informal a line of schoolchildren walking in pairs.
– ORIGIN from Greek *krokodilos* 'worm of the stones'.

crocodile clip noun chiefly Brit. a sprung metal clip with long, serrated teeth, used to connect an electric cable to a battery.

crocodile tears plural noun insincere tears or expressions of sorrow.
– ORIGIN from a belief that crocodiles wept while eating or luring their prey.

crocus /**kroh**-kuhss/ noun (pl. **crocuses** or **croci** /**kroh**-kee/) a small spring-flowering plant with bright yellow, purple, or white flowers.
– ORIGIN Greek *krokos*.

Croesus /**kree**-suhss/ noun a very wealthy person.
– ORIGIN from the name of a famously wealthy king of Lydia, an ancient region of Asia.

croft Brit. noun a small rented farm in Scotland or northern England. •verb farm land as a croft or crofts.
– DERIVATIVES **crofter** noun.
– ORIGIN Old English.

Crohn's disease /krohnz/ noun a disease of the intestines, especially the colon and ileum.
– ORIGIN named after the American pathologist Burrill B. *Crohn*.

croissant /**krwass**-on/ noun a crescent-shaped roll made of sweet flaky dough.
– ORIGIN French, 'crescent'.

Cro-Magnon /kroh-**man**-yon, kroh-**mag**-nuhn/ noun the earliest form of modern human in Europe, appearing *c.*35,000 years ago.
– ORIGIN the name of a hill in the Dordogne, France.

cromlech /**krom**-lek/ noun **1** (in Wales) an ancient tomb consisting of a large flat stone laid on upright ones. **2** (in Brittany) a circle of standing stones.
– ORIGIN Welsh, 'arched flat stone'.

crone noun an ugly old woman.
– ORIGIN Old French *caroigne* 'carrion'.

crony /**kroh**-ni/ noun (pl. **cronies**) informal, often derogatory a person's close friend or companion.
– ORIGIN Greek *khronios* 'long-lasting'.

cronyism (also **croneyism**) noun derogatory the practice of appointing friends and associates to positions of authority, especially when they are not suitably qualified.

crook noun **1** a shepherd's hooked staff. **2** a bishop's crozier. **3** a bend, especially at the elbow in a person's arm. **4** informal a criminal or dishonest person. •verb bend a finger or leg. •adjective Austral./NZ informal **1** bad or unwell. **2** dishonest or illegal.
– ORIGIN Old Norse, 'hook'.

crooked /**kruu**-kid/ adjective **1** bent or twisted out of shape or position. **2** informal dishonest or illegal.
– DERIVATIVES **crookedly** adverb **crookedness** noun.

croon verb hum, sing, or speak in a soft, low voice.
– DERIVATIVES **crooner** noun.
– ORIGIN German and Dutch *krōnen* 'groan, lament'.

crop noun **1** a plant, especially a cereal, fruit, or vegetable, grown for food or other use. **2** an amount of a crop harvested at one time. **3** an amount of people or things appearing at one time: *this new crop of indie bands.* **4** a very short hairstyle. **5** a riding crop. **6** a pouch in a bird's throat where food is stored or prepared for digestion. •verb (**crops**, **cropping**, **cropped**) **1** cut something very short. **2** (of an animal) bite off and eat the tops of plants. **3** (**crop up**)

appear or happen unexpectedly: *his name cropped up in the conversation.* **4** harvest a crop from an area. **5** sow or plant land with plants that will produce a crop.
– ORIGIN Old English.

crop circle noun an area of crops which has been flattened in the form of a circle or other pattern by unexplained means.

crop dusting noun the spraying of powdered insecticide or fertilizer on crops from the air.

cropper noun a plant which yields a particular crop.
– PHRASES **come a cropper** informal **1** fall over heavily. **2** experience a defeat or disaster.

crop top (also **cropped top**) noun a woman's casual garment for the upper body, cut short so that it reveals the stomach.

croque-monsieur /krok muh-**syer**/ noun a fried or grilled cheese and ham sandwich.
– ORIGIN French, 'bite a man'.

croquet /**kroh**-kay/ noun a game played on a lawn, in which wooden balls are driven through a series of hoops with a mallet.
– ORIGIN perhaps a dialect form of French *crochet* 'hook'.

croquette /kroh-**ket**/ noun a small cake or roll of vegetables, minced meat, or fish, fried in breadcrumbs.
– ORIGIN French, from *croquer* 'to crunch'.

crosier /**kroh**-zi-er/ noun variant spelling of CROZIER.

cross noun **1** a mark, object, or figure formed by two short intersecting lines or pieces (+ or ×). **2** an upright post with a bar fixed across it, as used in ancient times for crucifixion. **3** (**the Cross**) the cross on which Christ was crucified. **4** a cross-shaped medal awarded for bravery or showing rank in some orders of knighthood. **5** a thing that is unavoidable and has to be endured: *she's just a cross we have to bear.* **6** an animal or plant resulting from cross-breeding; a hybrid. **7** (**a cross between**) a mixture of two things: *a cross between a bar and a restaurant.* **8** (in football) a pass of the ball across the field towards the centre close to one's opponents' goal. • verb **1** go or extend across or to the other side of: *she crossed the street and walked down the hill.* **2** pass in an opposite or different direction; intersect. **3** place crosswise: *Michelle crossed her legs.* **4** draw a line or lines across something. **5** Brit. mark a cheque with a pair of parallel lines to indicate that it must be paid into a named bank account. **6** Football pass the ball across the field towards the centre when attacking. **7** cause an animal of one species, breed, or variety to interbreed with one of another. **8** oppose or stand in the way of: *no one dared to cross him.* • adjective annoyed.
– PHRASES **at cross purposes** misunderstanding one another. **cross one's fingers** put one finger across another as a sign of hoping for good luck. **cross the floor** Brit. join the opposing side in Parliament. **cross my heart (and hope to die)** used to emphasize the truthfulness and sincerity of what one is saying. **cross something off** delete an item from a list. **cross oneself** make the sign of the Cross in front of one's chest as a sign of Christian reverence or to call on God for protection. **cross something out/through** delete a word or phrase by

drawing a line through it. **cross swords** have an argument or dispute. **crossed line** a telephone connection that has been wrongly made with the result that another call can be heard. **get one's wires** (or **lines**) **crossed** have a misunderstanding.
– DERIVATIVES **crossly** adverb **crossness** noun.
– ORIGIN Old Irish *cros*, from Latin *crux*.

crossbar noun **1** a horizontal bar between the two upright posts of a football goal. **2** a bar between the handlebars and saddle on a bicycle.

cross-bencher noun a member of the House of Lords who is independent of any political party.

crossbill noun a finch with a beak whose upper and lower parts are crossed, enabling it to extract seeds from the cones of conifers.

crossbow noun a medieval bow fixed across a wooden support, having a groove for the bolt and a mechanism for drawing and releasing the string.

cross-breed noun an animal or plant produced by crossing two different species, breeds, or varieties. • verb produce an animal or plant in this way.

cross-check verb check figures or information by using an alternative source or method.

cross-contamination noun the process by which bacteria or other microorganisms are unintentionally transferred from one substance or object to another.
– DERIVATIVES **cross-contaminate** verb.

cross-country adjective **1** across fields or countryside, rather than keeping to roads or tracks. **2** across a region or country, in particular not keeping to main or direct routes. • noun the sport of cross-country running, riding, skiing, or motoring.

cross-current noun **1** a current in a river or sea which flows across another. **2** a situation or tendency marked by conflict with another: *political cross-currents.*

cross-cut verb **1** cut wood or stone across its main grain or axis. **2** alternate one sequence with another when editing a film.

cross-dressing noun the practice of wearing clothing usually worn by the opposite sex.

crosse /kros/ noun the stick used in women's field lacrosse.
– ORIGIN Old French *croce* 'bishop's crook'.

cross-examine verb question a witness called by the other party in a court of law to challenge or extend the testimony that they have already given.
– DERIVATIVES **cross-examination** noun.

cross-eyed adjective having one or both eyes turned inwards towards the nose, either temporarily or as a permanent condition.

cross-fertilize verb fertilize a plant using pollen from another plant of the same species.
– DERIVATIVES **cross-fertilization** noun.

crossfire noun gunfire from two or more directions passing through the same area.

cross-grained adjective **1** (of timber) having a grain that runs across the regular grain. **2** stubbornly uncooperative or bad-tempered.

cross hairs plural noun a pair of fine wires crossing at right angles at the focus of an optical instrument or gunsight.

cross-hatch verb shade an area with many intersecting parallel lines.

crossing noun 1 a place where things, especially roads or railway lines, cross. 2 a place at which one may safely cross a street or railway line. 3 a journey across water in a ship.

cross-legged adjective & adverb (of a seated person) with the legs crossed at the ankles and the knees bent outwards.

crossover noun 1 a point or place of crossing from one side to the other. 2 the production of work in a new style or combination of styles, especially in popular music: *a rock-funk crossover.*

cross-ownership noun the ownership by one corporation of different companies with related interests or commercial aims.

cross-party adjective involving or relating to two or more political parties.

crosspatch noun Brit. informal a bad-tempered person.
– ORIGIN from the former word *patch* 'fool, clown'.

crosspiece noun a beam or bar fixed or placed across something else.

cross-ply adjective Brit. (of a tyre) having fabric layers with their threads running diagonally across each other.

cross-pollinate verb pollinate a flower or plant with pollen from another flower or plant.

cross-post verb send a message to more than one Internet newsgroup at the same time. •noun a message that has been cross-posted.

cross-question verb question someone in great detail.

cross reference noun a reference to another text or part of a text, given to provide further information.
– DERIVATIVES **cross-refer** verb.

crossroads noun an intersection of two or more roads.

cross section noun 1 a surface exposed by making a straight cut through a solid object at right angles to its length. 2 a typical or representative sample of a larger group: *a cross-section of society.*

cross stitch noun an embroidery stitch formed of two stitches crossing each other.

crosstalk noun 1 unwanted transfer of signals between communication channels. 2 witty conversation.

crosstrees plural noun a pair of horizontal struts attached to a sailing ship's mast to spread the rigging.

crosswalk noun N. Amer. & Austral. a pedestrian crossing.

crosswind noun a wind blowing across one's direction of travel.

crosswise (also **crossways**) adverb 1 in the form of a cross. 2 diagonally.

crossword noun a puzzle consisting of a grid of squares and blanks into which words crossing vertically and horizontally are written according to clues.

crotch noun 1 the part of the human body between the legs where they join the torso. 2 a fork in a tree, road, or river.
– ORIGIN partly a variant of CRUTCH.

crotchet /kro-chit/ noun 1 Brit. a musical note having the time value of half a minim, represented by a large solid dot with a plain stem. 2 an odd or unfounded belief or idea.
– ORIGIN Old French *crochet* 'little hook'.

crotchety adjective irritable.

crouch verb bend the knees and bring the upper body forward and down. •noun a crouching position.
– ORIGIN perhaps from Old French *crochir* 'be bent'.

croup[1] /kroop/ noun inflammation of the throat in children, causing coughing and breathing difficulties.
– ORIGIN dialect, 'to croak'.

croup[2] /kroop/ noun the rump or hindquarters of a horse.
– ORIGIN Old French.

croupier /kroo-pi-ay/ noun the person in charge of a gambling table, gathering in and paying out money or tokens.
– ORIGIN French.

crouton /kroo-ton/ noun a small piece of fried or toasted bread served with soup or used as a garnish.
– ORIGIN French, from *croûte* 'crust'.

crow[1] noun a large bird with glossy black plumage, a heavy bill, and a harsh call.
– PHRASES **as the crow flies** in a straight line across country.
– ORIGIN Old English.

crow[2] verb (past **crowed** or **crew**) 1 (of a cock) make its characteristic loud cry. 2 express pride or triumph in a tone of gloating satisfaction. •noun the cry of a cock.
– ORIGIN Old English.

crowbar noun an iron bar with a flattened end, used as a lever.

crowd noun 1 a large number of people gathered together. 2 informal, often derogatory a group of people with a shared interest or quality: *a day at the beach with the sailing crowd.* •verb 1 (of a number of people) fill a space almost completely. 2 move or come together as a crowd: *passengers crowded into the train.* 3 move or stand too close to someone. 4 (**crowd someone/thing out**) keep someone or something out by taking their place.
– ORIGIN Old English, 'press, hasten'.

crowded adjective (of a place) filled almost completely by a large number of people.

crowd-puller noun an event or person that attracts a large audience.

crowfoot noun (pl. **crowfoots**) a water plant with white or yellow flowers.

crown noun 1 a circular ornamental headdress worn by a monarch as a symbol of authority. 2 (**the Crown**) the monarchy or reigning monarch. 3 a wreath of leaves or flowers worn as an emblem of victory. 4 an award or distinction gained by a victory or achievement: *the world championship crown.* 5 the top or highest part of something such as a person's head or a hat. 6 the part of a tooth projecting from the gum. 7 an artificial replacement for or covering for the upper part of a tooth. 8 a former British coin worth five shillings (or 25 pence). •verb 1 ceremonially place a crown on the head of someone to

c

invest them as a monarch. **2** rest on or form the top of: *a simple altar crowned by a wooden cross.* **3** be the triumphant conclusion of: *the victory which crowned his career.* **4** fit a crown on a tooth. **5** informal hit someone on the head.
– ORIGIN Latin *corona* 'wreath'.

Crown Colony noun a British colony controlled by the Crown.

Crown court noun (in England and Wales) a court which deals with serious cases referred from the magistrates' courts.

Crown Derby noun a kind of fine porcelain made at Derby in England.

crown green noun Brit. a kind of bowling green which rises slightly towards the middle.

Crown jewels plural noun the crown and other jewellery worn or carried by the sovereign on state occasions.

Crown prince noun (in some countries) a male heir to a throne.

Crown princess noun **1** the wife of a Crown prince. **2** (in some countries) a female heir to a throne.

crown wheel noun a gearwheel or cogwheel with teeth that project from the face of the wheel at right angles.

crow's feet plural noun wrinkles at the outer corner of a person's eye.

crow's nest noun a platform for a lookout at the masthead of a ship.

crozier /kroh-zi-er/ (also **crosier**) noun a hooked staff carried by a bishop.
– ORIGIN Old French *croisier* 'cross-bearer'.

CRT abbreviation cathode ray tube.

crucial /kroo-sh'l/ adjective of great importance, especially in the success or failure of something: *negotiations were at a crucial stage.*
– DERIVATIVES **crucially** adverb.
– ORIGIN Latin *crux* 'cross'.

cruciate ligament /croo-shi-ayt/ noun either of a pair of ligaments in the knee which cross each other and connect the femur (thigh bone) to the tibia (shin bone).
– ORIGIN Latin *cruciatus* 'cross-shaped'.

crucible /kroo-si-b'l/ noun **1** a container in which metals or other substances may be melted or subjected to very high temperatures. **2** a situation in which people or things are severely tested, often interacting to produce something new: *a relationship forged in the crucible of war.*
– ORIGIN Latin *crucibulum*.

cruciferous /kroo-sif-uh-ruhss/ adjective (of a plant) belonging to the cabbage family, with four equal petals arranged in a cross.
– ORIGIN from Latin *crux* 'cross' + *-fer* 'bearing'.

crucifix /kroo-si-fiks/ noun a representation of a cross with a figure of Jesus on it.
– ORIGIN from Latin *cruci fixus* 'fixed to a cross'.

crucifixion noun **1** the execution of a person by crucifying them. **2** (**the Crucifixion**) the killing of Jesus in this way.

cruciform /kroo-si-form/ adjective having the shape of a cross.

crucify /kroo-si-fy/ verb (**crucifies, crucifying, crucified**) **1** put someone to death by nailing or binding them to a cross. **2** informal criticize someone severely.

– ORIGIN from Latin *crux* 'cross' + *figere* 'fix'.

crud noun informal **1** an unpleasantly dirty or messy substance. **2** nonsense; rubbish.
– DERIVATIVES **cruddy** adjective.
– ORIGIN variant of CURD.

crude adjective **1** in a natural or raw state; not yet processed or refined: *crude oil.* **2** simple or makeshift: *crude stone tools.* **3** likely to be only approximately accurate: *a crude index of economic progress.* **4** offensively coarse or vulgar. •noun natural mineral oil.
– DERIVATIVES **crudely** adverb **crudeness** noun **crudity** noun.
– ORIGIN Latin *crudus* 'raw, rough'.

crudités /kroo-di-tay/ plural noun mixed raw vegetables served with a sauce into which they may be dipped.
– ORIGIN plural of French *crudité* 'rawness'.

cruel adjective (**crueller, cruellest** or **crueler, cruelest**) **1** taking pleasure in the pain or suffering of others. **2** causing pain or suffering.
– DERIVATIVES **cruelly** adverb.
– ORIGIN Latin *crudelis*.

cruelty noun (pl. **cruelties**) cruel behaviour or attitudes.

cruet /kroo-it/ noun a small container or set of containers for salt, pepper, oil, or vinegar for use at a dining table.
– ORIGIN Old French, 'small pot'.

cruise verb **1** sail, travel, or move slowly around without a definite destination, especially for pleasure. **2** travel smoothly at a moderate or economical speed. **3** easily achieve an objective: *the home side cruised to a 7–2 victory.* **4** informal wander about in search of a sexual partner. •noun a voyage on a ship taken as a holiday and usually calling in at several places.
– ORIGIN probably from Dutch *kruisen* 'to cross'.

cruise control noun a device in a motor vehicle which maintains a selected constant speed without requiring the driver to use the accelerator pedal.

cruise missile noun a low-flying missile which is guided to its target by an on-board computer.

cruiser noun **1** a fast warship larger than a destroyer and less heavily armed than a battleship. **2** a yacht or motorboat with passenger accommodation.

cruiserweight noun chiefly Brit. another term for LIGHT HEAVYWEIGHT.

crumb noun **1** a small fragment of bread, cake, or biscuit. **2** a very small amount: *there was only one crumb of comfort.*
– ORIGIN Old English.

crumble verb **1** break or fall apart into small fragments. **2** gradually disintegrate or fail: *the party's fragile unity began to crumble.* •noun Brit. a pudding made with fruit and a topping of flour and fat rubbed to the texture of breadcrumbs.
– ORIGIN Old English.

crumbly adjective easily breaking into small fragments.

crumbs exclamation Brit. informal an expression of dismay or surprise.
– ORIGIN euphemism for CHRIST.

crummy (also **crumby**) adjective (**crummier**, **crummiest**) informal bad, unpleasant, or of poor quality.

crumpet noun 1 a thick, flat cake with a soft, open texture, eaten toasted and buttered. 2 Brit. informal sexually attractive women.
– ORIGIN unknown.

crumple verb 1 crush something so that it becomes creased and wrinkled. 2 suddenly fall or collapse: *she crumpled to the floor.*
– ORIGIN Old English *crump* 'bent, crooked'.

crumple zone noun a part of a motor vehicle designed to crumple easily in a crash and absorb the main force of an impact.

crunch verb 1 crush something hard or brittle with the teeth, making a grinding sound. 2 make or move with a grinding sound: *the snow crunched as we walked.* •noun 1 a crunching sound. 2 (**the crunch**) informal a crucial moment or situation. 3 a sit-up.
– ORIGIN probably imitating the sound.

crunchy adjective (**crunchier**, **crunchiest**) making a crunching noise when bitten or crushed.
– DERIVATIVES **crunchiness** noun.

crupper /**krup**-per/ noun a strap buckled to the back of a saddle and looped under the horse's tail to prevent the saddle or harness from slipping forward.
– ORIGIN Old French *cropiere.*

crusade noun 1 any of a series of medieval military expeditions made by Europeans to recover the Holy Land from the Muslims. 2 an energetic organized campaign with a political, social, or religious aim: *a crusade against crime.* •verb (often as adj. **crusading**) lead or take part in a crusade.
– DERIVATIVES **crusader** noun.
– ORIGIN French *croisade,* from *croisée* 'the state of being marked with the Cross'.

cruse /krooz/ noun old use an earthenware pot or jar.
– ORIGIN Old English.

crush verb 1 press or squeeze forcefully so as to injure, squash, or break up: *the car was crushed under a lorry.* 2 violently subdue or defeat: *troops were used to crush the rebellion.* 3 make someone feel extremely disappointed or embarrassed. •noun 1 a crowd of people pressed closely together. 2 informal a strong, usually short-lived feeling of love for someone; an infatuation. 3 a drink made from the juice of crushed fruit.
– DERIVATIVES **crushable** adjective **crusher** noun.
– ORIGIN Old French *cruissir* 'crack'.

crush bar noun Brit. a bar in a theatre that sells drinks in the interval.

crush barrier noun Brit. a temporary barrier for restraining a crowd.

crushed velvet noun a type of velvet which has its nap pointing in different directions in irregular patches.

crust noun 1 the tough outer part of a loaf of bread. 2 Brit. informal a living or livelihood: *he's just trying to earn a crust.* 3 a hardened layer or coating on something soft. 4 a layer of pastry covering a pie. 5 the outermost layer of rock of which a planet consists, especially the part of the earth above the mantle. 6 a deposit formed in wine or port aged in the bottle.

•verb form into or cover with a crust.
– ORIGIN Latin *crusta.*

crustacean /kruss-**tay**-sh'n/ noun an animal with a hard outer shell, usually living in water, such as a crab, lobster, or shrimp.
– ORIGIN Latin, from *crusta* 'shell, crust'.

crusty adjective (**crustier**, **crustiest**) 1 having or consisting of a crust. 2 (of an old person) easily irritated. •noun (pl. **crusties**) informal a young person of a group having a shabby appearance and no fixed home.
– DERIVATIVES **crustiness** noun.

crutch noun 1 a long stick with a crosspiece at the top, used as a support by a person who is lame. 2 a person or thing used for support or reassurance. 3 the crotch of the body or a garment.
– ORIGIN Old English.

crux /kruks/ noun (**the crux**) the most important or difficult part of an issue or problem: *the crux of the matter is whether compensation should be paid.*
– ORIGIN Latin, 'cross'.

cry verb (**cries**, **crying**, **cried**) 1 shed tears. 2 shout or scream loudly. 3 (of a bird or other animal) make a loud distinctive call. 4 (**cry out for**) be in great need of: *a system which is crying out for fundamental change.* 5 (**cry off**) informal go back on a promise or fail to keep to an arrangement. •noun (pl. **cries**) 1 a period of shedding tears. 2 a loud shout or scream. 3 a distinctive call made by a bird or other animal.
– ORIGIN Old French *crier.*

crybaby noun (pl. **crybabies**) a person who cries frequently or readily.

crying adjective very great: *it'd be a crying shame if the country pub disappeared.*

cryogenics /kry-uh-**jen**-iks/ plural noun (treated as sing.) 1 the branch of physics concerned with the production and effects of very low temperatures. 2 another term for CRYONICS.
– DERIVATIVES **cryogenic** adjective.
– ORIGIN Greek *kruos* 'frost'.

cryonics /kry-**on**-iks/ plural noun (treated as sing.) the deep-freezing of the bodies of people who have died of an incurable disease, in the hope of a future cure.
– DERIVATIVES **cryonic** adjective.
– ORIGIN shortened form of CRYOGENICS.

cryosurgery noun a type of surgery using instruments that freeze and destroy diseased or unwanted tissue.

crypt noun an underground room or vault beneath a church, used as a chapel or burial place.
– ORIGIN from Greek *kruptos* 'hidden'.

cryptic adjective 1 mysterious or obscure in meaning: *a cryptic message.* 2 (of a crossword) having difficult clues which indicate the solutions indirectly. 3 Zoology referring to coloration or markings that camouflage an animal in its natural environment.
– DERIVATIVES **cryptically** adverb.
– ORIGIN from Greek *kruptos* 'hidden'.

cryptogram /**krip**-tuh-gram/ noun a text written in code.

cryptography /krip-**tog**-ruh-fi/ noun the art of writing or solving codes.

c

– DERIVATIVES **cryptographer** noun
cryptographic adjective.

cryptology noun the study of codes, or the art
of writing and solving them.
– DERIVATIVES **cryptological** adjective
cryptologist noun.

cryptosporidium /krip-toh-spo-**rid**-i-uhm/
noun (pl. **cryptosporidia** /krip-toh-spo-**rid**-i-uh/)
a single-celled parasite found in the intestines
of many animals, where it sometimes causes
disease.
– ORIGIN from Greek *kruptos* 'hidden' + Latin
sporidium 'small spore'.

crystal noun **1** a clear transparent mineral,
especially quartz. **2** a piece of a solid substance
with a regular internal structure with
symmetrically arranged plane faces. **3** very
clear glass. •**adjective** clear and transparent: *the
crystal waters of the lake.*
– ORIGIN Greek *krustallos* 'ice, crystal'.

crystal ball noun a solid globe of glass or rock
crystal, used for predicting the future.

crystal-gazing noun the practice of looking
intently into a crystal ball with the aim of
seeing images supposedly relating to future or
distant events.

crystalline /**kriss**-tuh-lyn/ adjective **1** having
the structure and form of a crystal. **2** literary
very clear.

crystalline lens noun the lens of the eye.

crystallize (or **crystallise**) verb **1** form crystals.
2 make or become definite and clear: *writing
can help to crystallize your thoughts.* **3** (as adj.
crystallized) (of fruit) coated with and
preserved in sugar.
– DERIVATIVES **crystallization** noun.

crystallography /kriss-tuh-**log**-ruh-fi/ noun
the branch of science concerned with the
structure and properties of crystals.
– DERIVATIVES **crystallographer** noun
crystallographic adjective.

crystal set noun a simple early form of radio
receiver which had no amplifier or
loudspeaker and so required headphones or
earphones.

Cs symbol the chemical element caesium.

c/s abbreviation cycles per second.

CSA abbreviation Child Support Agency.

CSE abbreviation historical (in England and Wales)
an exam for secondary-school pupils not
taking O levels, replaced in 1988 by the GCSE.
– ORIGIN abbreviation for *Certificate of
Secondary Education.*

CS gas noun a powerful form of tear gas used in
the control of riots.
– ORIGIN from the initials of the American
chemists Ben B. *Corson* and Roger W.
Stoughton.

CST abbreviation Central Standard Time.

CT abbreviation **1** computerized (or computed)
tomography. **2** Connecticut.

ct abbreviation **1** carat. **2** cent.

CTC abbreviation City Technology College.

CTS abbreviation carpal tunnel syndrome.

Cu symbol the chemical element copper.
– ORIGIN Latin *cuprum.*

cu. abbreviation cubic.

cub noun **1** the young of a fox, bear, lion, or
other carnivorous mammal. **2** (also **Cub Scout**)

a member of the junior branch of the Scout
Association, for boys aged about 8 to 11. •**verb**
(**cubs, cubbing, cubbed**) **1** give birth to cubs.
2 hunt fox cubs.
– ORIGIN unknown.

Cuban /**kyoo**-buhn/ noun a person from Cuba.
•**adjective** relating to Cuba.

Cuban heel noun a fairly high straight-sided
heel on a shoe or boot.

cubby noun (pl. **cubbies**) chiefly N. Amer. a
cubbyhole.

cubbyhole noun a small enclosed space or
room.
– ORIGIN from dialect *cub* 'stall, pen, hutch'.

cube noun **1** a symmetrical three-dimensional
shape with six equal square faces. **2** the
product of a number multiplied by itself
twice. •**verb 1** find the cube of a number. **2** cut
food into small cube-shaped pieces.
– ORIGIN Greek *kubos.*

cube root noun the number which, when
multiplied by itself twice, produces a
particular number.

cubic /**kyoo**-bik/ adjective **1** having the shape of
a cube. **2** referring to a volume equal to that of
a cube whose edge is a given unit of length: *a
cubic metre.* **3** involving the cube of a number.
– DERIVATIVES **cubical** adjective.

cubicle noun a small area of a room that is
partitioned off for privacy.
– ORIGIN Latin *cubiculum* 'bedroom'.

cubism noun an early 20th-century style of
painting in which objects are represented as
being made up of geometric shapes.
– DERIVATIVES **cubist** noun & adjective.

cubit /**kyoo**-bit/ noun an ancient measure of
length, approximately equal to the length of a
forearm.
– ORIGIN Latin *cubitum* 'elbow, forearm'.

cuboid /**kyoo**-boyd/ adjective having the shape
of a cube. •**noun** a solid which has six
rectangular faces at right angles to each other.

cub reporter noun informal a young or
inexperienced newspaper reporter.

cuckold /**kuk**-ohld/ noun a man whose wife has
committed adultery. •**verb** make a married
man a cuckold.
– DERIVATIVES **cuckoldry** noun.
– ORIGIN from Old French *cucu* 'cuckoo' (from
the cuckoo's habit of laying its egg in another
bird's nest).

cuckoo noun a grey or brown bird known for
the two-note call of the male and for the habit
of laying its eggs in the nests of other birds.
•**adjective** informal crazy.
– ORIGIN Old French *cucu*, imitating its call.

cuckoo clock noun a clock with a mechanical
cuckoo that pops out on the hour making a
sound like a cuckoo's call.

cuckoo pint noun a plant having a purple or
green spadix which is followed by bright red
berries.
– ORIGIN from earlier *cuckoo-pintle*, from **PINTLE**
in the former sense 'penis'.

cuckoo spit noun whitish froth found in
compact masses on leaves and plant stems,
produced by the larvae of certain insects.

cucumber noun a long green-skinned fruit
with watery flesh, eaten raw in salads.

– ORIGIN Latin *cucumis*.

cud noun partly digested food returned from the first stomach of cattle or similar animals to the mouth for further chewing.
– PHRASES **chew the cud** think or talk in a thoughtful way.
– ORIGIN Old English.

cuddle verb **1** hold someone close in one's arms as a way of showing love or affection. **2** (often **cuddle up to**) lie or sit close to someone. •noun an affectionate hug.
– ORIGIN unknown.

cuddly adjective (**cuddlier, cuddliest**) pleasantly soft or plump.

cudgel /ku-juhl/ noun a short thick stick used as a weapon. •verb (**cudgels, cudgelling, cudgelled**; US **cudgels, cudgeling, cudgeled**) beat someone with a cudgel.
– PHRASES **take up the cudgels** start to defend or support someone or something strongly.
– ORIGIN Old English.

cue¹ noun **1** a signal to an actor to enter or to begin their speech or performance. **2** an action or event that is a signal for someone to do something: *he took her words as a cue to leave.* **3** a facility for playing through an audio or video recording very quickly until a desired point is reached. •verb (**cues, cueing** or **cuing, cued**) **1** give someone a cue. **2** set a piece of audio or video equipment so that it is ready to play a particular part of a recording.
– PHRASES **on cue** at the right moment.
– ORIGIN unknown.

cue² noun a long tapering wooden rod for striking the ball in snooker, billiards, or pool. •verb (**cues, cueing** or **cuing, cued**) use a cue to strike the ball.
– ORIGIN variant of QUEUE.

cue ball noun the ball that is to be struck with the cue in snooker, billiards, etc.

cue card noun a card held beside a camera for a television broadcaster to read from while appearing to look into the camera.

cuff¹ noun **1** the end part of a sleeve, where the material is turned back or a separate band is sewn on. **2** N. Amer. a trouser turn-up. **3** (**cuffs**) informal handcuffs.
– PHRASES **off the cuff** informal without previous thought or preparation. [as if from notes jotted on one's shirt cuffs.]
– DERIVATIVES **cuffed** adjective.
– ORIGIN unknown.

cuff² verb hit someone with an open hand, especially on the head. •noun a blow given with an open hand.
– ORIGIN unknown.

cufflink noun a device for fastening together the sides of a shirt cuff.

cuirass /kwi-rass/ noun historical a piece of armour covering the chest and the back.
– ORIGIN Old French, from Latin *corium* 'leather'.

cuisine /kwi-zeen/ noun a style or method of cooking, especially as characteristic of a particular country or region: *traditional French cuisine.*
– ORIGIN French, 'kitchen'.

cul-de-sac /kul-duh-sak/ noun (pl. **cul-de-sacs** /kul-duh-saks/ or **culs-de-sac** pronunc. same) a street or passage closed at one end.

– ORIGIN French, 'bottom of a sack'.

culinary adjective of or for cooking.
– ORIGIN Latin *culina* 'kitchen'.

cull verb **1** slaughter a selected number of a certain kind of animal in order to reduce its population. **2** select or obtain from a large quantity or a variety of sources: *data culled from a number of websites.* •noun a selective slaughter of a certain kind of animal: *a seal cull.*
– ORIGIN from Latin *colligere* 'gather together'.

culminate /kul-mi-nayt/ verb reach a climax or point of highest development: *the protests culminated in a mass rally in the town hall.*
– DERIVATIVES **culmination** noun.
– ORIGIN Latin *culminare*, from *culmen* 'summit'.

culottes /kyuu-lots/ plural noun women's knee-length trousers, cut with very full legs to resemble a skirt.
– ORIGIN French, from *cul* 'rump'.

culpable /kul-puh-b'l/ adjective deserving blame.
– DERIVATIVES **culpability** noun **culpably** adverb.
– ORIGIN from Latin *culpa* 'fault, blame'.

culprit noun a person who is responsible for a crime or offence.
– ORIGIN perhaps from a misinterpretation of the written abbreviation *cul. prist* for Old French *Culpable: prest d'averrer notre bille* '(You are) guilty: (We are) ready to prove our indictment'.

cult noun **1** a system of religious worship directed towards a particular figure or object. **2** a small religious group regarded by others as strange or as having too great a control over its members. **3** (often before another noun) something popular or fashionable among a particular group of people: *a cult film.*
– DERIVATIVES **cultish** adjective **cultist** noun.
– ORIGIN Latin *cultus* 'worship'.

cultivar /kul-ti-var/ noun a plant variety that has been produced by selective breeding.
– ORIGIN blend of CULTIVATE and VARIETY.

cultivate verb **1** prepare and use land for crops or gardening. **2** grow plants or crops. **3** try to develop or gain a quality or skill: *he cultivated an air of sophistication.* **4** try to win the friendship or support of someone. **5** (as adj. **cultivated**) refined and well educated.
– DERIVATIVES **cultivable** adjective **cultivatable** adjective **cultivation** noun.
– ORIGIN Latin *cultivare*.

cultivator noun a mechanical implement for breaking up the ground.

cultural adjective **1** relating to the culture of a society. **2** relating to the arts and to intellectual achievements.
– DERIVATIVES **culturally** adverb.

culture noun **1** the arts and other instances of human intellectual achievement regarded as a whole. **2** a refined understanding or appreciation of this. **3** the art, customs, ideas, and social behaviour of a nation, people, or group: *Afro-Caribbean culture.* **4** a preparation of cells or bacteria grown in an artificial medium for scientific study, or the process of growing such cells or bacteria. **5** the growing of plants. •verb grow cells or bacteria for scientific study.

– ORIGIN Latin *cultura* 'growing'.

cultured adjective **1** well educated and able to appreciate art, literature, music, etc. **2** (of a pearl) formed round a foreign body inserted into an oyster.

culture shock noun a feeling of disorientation experienced when someone suddenly comes into contact with an unfamiliar culture or way of life.

culture vulture noun informal a person who is very interested in the arts.

culvert /kul-vert/ noun a tunnel carrying a stream or open drain under a road or railway.
– ORIGIN unknown.

cum /kum/ preposition combined with; also used as: *a study-cum-bedroom.*
– ORIGIN Latin.

Cumberland sausage noun Brit. a type of sausage traditionally made in a continuous strip and cooked as a spiral.

cumbersome adjective **1** large and heavy and so difficult to carry or use. **2** complicated and inefficient or time-consuming: *NATO's cumbersome decision-making processes.*

cumbrous /kum-bruhss/ adjective literary cumbersome.

cumin /kyoo-min/ (also **cummin**) noun the seeds of a plant of the parsley family, used as a spice in cooking.
– ORIGIN Greek *kuminon.*

cummerbund /kum-mer-bund/ noun a sash worn around the waist, especially as part of a man's formal evening suit.
– ORIGIN Urdu and Persian.

cumquat noun variant spelling of KUMQUAT.

cumulate /kyoo-myuu-layt/ verb accumulate or be accumulated.
– DERIVATIVES **cumulation** noun.
– ORIGIN from Latin *cumulus* 'a heap'.

cumulative /kyoo-myuu-luh-tiv/ adjective increasing or increased in amount, strength, or effect by successive additions: *the cumulative effect of human activities on the environment.*
– DERIVATIVES **cumulatively** adverb.

cumulonimbus /kyoo-myuu-loh-**nim**-buhss/ noun (pl. **cumulonimbi** /kyoo-myuu-loh-nim-by/) cloud forming a towering mass with a flat base, as in thunderstorms.

cumulus /kyoo-myuu-luhss/ noun (pl. **cumuli** /kyoo-myuu-lee/) cloud forming rounded masses heaped on each other above a flat base.
– ORIGIN Latin, 'heap'.

cuneiform /kyoo-ni-form, kyoo-**nay**-i-form/ adjective relating to the wedge-shaped characters used in the ancient writing systems of Mesopotamia, Persia, and Ugarit. • noun cuneiform writing.
– ORIGIN from Latin *cuneus* 'wedge'.

cunnilingus /kun-ni-**ling**-guhss/ noun stimulation of a woman's genitals using the tongue or lips.
– ORIGIN from Latin *cunnus* 'vulva' + *lingere* 'lick'.

cunning adjective **1** skilled in deceiving people to achieve one's aims. **2** ingenious; clever. • noun the ability to achieve things by using deception or cleverness.
– DERIVATIVES **cunningly** adverb.

– ORIGIN perhaps from an Old Norse word meaning 'knowledge'.

cunt noun vulgar slang **1** a woman's genitals. **2** an unpleasant or stupid person.
– ORIGIN Germanic.

cup noun **1** a small bowl-shaped container with a handle for drinking from. **2** a cup-shaped trophy with a stem and two handles, awarded as a prize in a sports contest. **3** a sports contest in which the winner is awarded a cup. **4** chiefly N. Amer. a measure of capacity used in cookery, equal to half a US pint (0.237 litre). **5** either of the two parts of a bra shaped to contain or support one breast. **6** a long mixed drink made from wine or cider and fruit juice. • verb (**cups**, **cupping**, **cupped**) **1** form one's hand or hands into the curved shape of a cup. **2** place one's curved hand or hands around something.
– PHRASES **in one's cups** informal drunk. **not one's cup of tea** informal not what one likes or is interested in.
– ORIGIN Latin *cuppa.*

cupboard noun a piece of furniture or small recess with a door and usually shelves, used for storage.

cupboard love noun Brit. affection that is pretended so as to obtain something.

cupcake noun a small iced cake baked in a cup-shaped container.

Cupid noun **1** Roman Mythology the god of love. **2** (also **cupid**) a picture or statue of a naked winged baby boy with a bow and arrow.

cupidity /kyoo-**pid**-i-ti/ noun greed for money or possessions.
– ORIGIN from Latin *cupidus* 'desirous'.

Cupid's bow noun a pronounced double curve at the top edge of a person's upper lip.

cupola /kyoo-puh-luh/ noun **1** a small rounded dome on or forming a roof. **2** a gun turret.
– ORIGIN Latin *cupula* 'small cask'.

cupro-nickel noun an alloy of copper and nickel, especially as used in 'silver' coins.

cur /ker/ noun **1** an aggressive mongrel dog. **2** informal a despicable man.
– ORIGIN perhaps from Old Norse *kurr* 'grumbling'.

curaçao /kyoo-ruh-**soh**/ noun (pl. **curaçaos**) a liqueur flavoured with bitter oranges.
– ORIGIN named after the Caribbean island of *Curaçao.*

curacy noun (pl. **curacies**) the position of a curate.

curare /kyuu-**rah**-ri/ noun a paralysing poison obtained from South American plants.
– ORIGIN Carib.

curate[1] /kyoor-uht/ noun a member of the clergy who assists a parish priest.
– PHRASES **curate's egg** Brit. something that is partly good and partly bad. [from a cartoon (1895) showing a curate who, given a stale egg when dining with the bishop, assures his host that 'parts of it are excellent'.]
– ORIGIN from Latin *cura* 'care'.

curate[2] /kyoo-**rayt**/ verb select, organize, and look after the items in a collection or exhibition.
– DERIVATIVES **curation** noun.
– ORIGIN from CURATOR.

curative adjective able to cure disease. • noun

something that is able to cure disease.

curator noun a keeper of a museum or other collection.
– DERIVATIVES **curatorial** adjective.
– ORIGIN from Latin *curare* 'take care of'.

curb verb control or put a limit on: *the new law aims to curb fraud.* •noun **1** a control or limit on something. **2** a type of bit with a strap or chain attached which passes under a horse's lower jaw. **3** US variant spelling of **KERB**.
– ORIGIN Old French *courber* 'bend'.

USAGE: Do not confuse **curb** with **kerb**. See the note at **KERB**.

curbside adjective US spelling of **KERBSIDE**.

curd (also **curds**) noun a soft, white substance formed when milk coagulates, used to make cheese.
– ORIGIN unknown.

curd cheese noun a soft, smooth cheese made from skimmed milk curd.

curdle verb (of a liquid) separate into solid and liquid parts.

cure verb **1** make a person who is ill well again. **2** end a disease or condition or solve a problem. **3** preserve meat, fish, etc. by salting, drying, or smoking. •noun **1** something that cures a disease or solves a problem. **2** the healing of a person who is unwell. **3** a Christian minister's area of responsibility.
– DERIVATIVES **curable** adjective **curer** noun.
– ORIGIN Latin *cura* 'care'.

curé /kyoo-ray/ noun a parish priest in a French-speaking country.
– ORIGIN French.

cure-all noun a remedy that will supposedly cure any ailment or problem.

curettage /kyoor-re-tij, kyoo-ri-tahzh/ noun the use of a curette, especially to scrape material from the lining of the womb.
– ORIGIN French.

curette /kyoor-ret/ noun a small surgical instrument used to scrape away material, especially from the womb.
– ORIGIN French.

curfew /ker-fyoo/ noun **1** a regulation ordering people to remain indoors between specified hours, typically at night. **2** the time at which a curfew begins.
– ORIGIN first referring to a regulation requiring fires to be put out at a fixed time: from Old French *cuvrir* 'to cover' + *feu* 'fire'.

Curia /kyoor-i-uh/ noun the papal court at the Vatican, by which the Roman Catholic Church is governed.
– DERIVATIVES **Curial** adjective.
– ORIGIN Latin.

curie /kyoor-i/ noun (pl. **curies**) a unit of radioactivity, corresponding to 3.7×10^{10} disintegrations per second.
– ORIGIN named after the French physicists Pierre and Marie *Curie*.

curio /kyoor-i-oh/ noun (pl. **curios**) an object that is interesting because it is rare or unusual.
– ORIGIN from **CURIOSITY**.

curiosity noun (pl. **curiosities**) **1** a strong desire to know or learn something. **2** an unusual or interesting object or fact.

curious adjective **1** eager to know or learn something. **2** strange; unusual.
– DERIVATIVES **curiously** adverb.
– ORIGIN Latin *curiosus* 'careful'.

curium /kyoo-ri-uhm/ noun a radioactive metallic chemical element made by high-energy atomic collisions.
– ORIGIN named after Marie and Pierre *Curie*.

curl verb **1** form or cause to form a curved or spiral shape: *her fingers curled round the microphone.* **2** (**curl up**) sit or lie with the knees drawn up. **3** move in a spiral or curved course. **4** play at the game of curling. •noun a thing forming a spiral or coil, especially a lock of hair.
– PHRASES **make someone's hair curl** informal shock or horrify someone.
– DERIVATIVES **curly** adjective (**curlier, curliest**).
– ORIGIN from Dutch *krul*.

curler noun **1** a roller or clasp around which a lock of hair is wrapped to curl it. **2** a player in the game of curling.

curlew /ker-lyoo/ noun (pl. same or **curlews**) a large brown wading bird with a long bill that curves downward.
– ORIGIN Old French *courlieu* (from the bird's call).

curlicue /ker-li-kyoo/ noun a decorative curl or twist.
– ORIGIN from **curly** + **CUE²** (in the sense 'pigtail').

curling noun a game played on ice, in which large circular flat stones are slid across the surface towards a mark.

curling tongs (also **curling iron**) plural noun a device incorporating a heated rod around which hair can be wound so as to curl it.

curmudgeon /ker-muj-uhn/ noun a bad-tempered or surly person.
– DERIVATIVES **curmudgeonly** adjective.
– ORIGIN unknown.

currant noun **1** a dried fruit made from a small seedless variety of grape. **2** a shrub producing small edible black, red, or white berries.
– ORIGIN from Old French *raisins de Corauntz* 'grapes of Corinth'.

currency noun (pl. **currencies**) **1** a system of money in general use in a country. **2** the fact or quality or period of being accepted or in use: *this minority view has now gained currency.*

current adjective **1** happening or being used or done now: *current events.* **2** in common or general use: *the other meaning of the word is still current.* •noun **1** a body of water or air moving in a definite direction through a surrounding body of water or air. **2** a flow of electrically charged particles.
– ORIGIN from Latin *currere* 'run'.

USAGE: Do not confuse **current** with **currant**. Current means 'happening now' (*current events*) or 'a flow of water, air, or electricity' (*strong ocean currents*), whereas **currant** means 'a dried grape'.

current account noun Brit. an account with a bank or building society from which money may be withdrawn without notice.

current assets plural noun cash and other assets that are expected to be converted to cash within a year. Compare with **FIXED ASSETS**.

currently adverb at the present time.

curriculum /kuh-**rik**-yuu-luhm/ noun (pl. **curricula** or **curriculums**) the subjects comprising a course of study in a school or college.
– DERIVATIVES **curricular** adjective.
– ORIGIN Latin, 'course, racing chariot'.

curriculum vitae /kuh-**rik**-yuu-luhm **vee**-ty/ noun (pl. **curricula vitae**) a summary of a person's education, qualifications, and previous jobs, sent with a job application.
– ORIGIN Latin, 'course of life'.

curry[1] noun (pl. **curries**) a dish of meat, vegetables, or fish, cooked in a hot, spicy sauce of Indian origin. •verb (**curries, currying, curried**) prepare or flavour food with a spicy sauce.
– ORIGIN Tamil.

curry[2] verb (**curries, currying, curried**) **1** chiefly N. Amer. groom a horse with a curry comb. **2** historical treat tanned leather to improve its properties.
– PHRASES **curry favour** try to gain favour by flattery and servile behaviour. [from the name (*Favel*) of a horse in a medieval French story who became a symbol of cunning; hence 'to rub down Favel' meant to use cunning.]
– ORIGIN Old French *correier*.

curry comb noun a hand-held device with serrated ridges, used for grooming horses.

curry powder noun a mixture of finely ground spices, such as turmeric and coriander, used for making curry.

curse noun **1** an appeal to a supernatural power to harm someone or something. **2** a cause of harm or misery: *the disease became the curse of cotton workers.* **3** an offensive word or phrase used to express anger or annoyance. •verb **1** use a curse against someone. **2** (**be cursed with**) be continually affected by something bad: *I'm cursed with a slow metabolism.* **3** say offensive words; swear.
– ORIGIN Old English.

cursed /**ker**-sid, kerst/ adjective informal, dated used to express annoyance or irritation.

cursive /**ker**-siv/ adjective (of writing) written with the characters joined.
– ORIGIN Latin *cursivus*.

cursor noun **1** a movable indicator on a computer screen identifying the point that will be affected by input from the user. **2** the sliding part engraved with a hairline used to locate points on a slide rule.
– ORIGIN Latin, 'runner'.

cursory /**ker**-suh-ri/ adjective hasty and therefore not thorough.
– DERIVATIVES **cursorily** adverb.

curt adjective so brief or abrupt as to be rude.
– DERIVATIVES **curtly** adverb **curtness** noun.
– ORIGIN Latin *curtus* 'cut short'.

curtail /ker-**tayl**/ verb limit or cut short: *we would not wish to curtail freedom of speech.*
– DERIVATIVES **curtailment** noun.
– ORIGIN French *courtault* 'horse with a docked tail'.

curtain noun **1** a piece of material suspended at the top to form a screen, hung at a window in pairs or between the stage and auditorium of a theatre. **2** (**the curtain**) the rise or fall of a stage curtain between acts or scenes.

3 (**curtains**) informal a disastrous outcome. •verb provide or screen something with a curtain or curtains.
– ORIGIN Latin *cortina*.

curtain call noun the appearance of one or more performers on stage after a performance to acknowledge the audience's applause.

curtain-raiser noun an event happening just before a longer or more important one.

curtain wall noun **1** a fortified wall around a medieval castle, typically one linking towers together. **2** a wall which encloses the space within a building but does not support the roof.

curtsy (also **curtsey**) noun (pl. **curtsies** or **curtseys**) a woman's or girl's respectful greeting, made by bending the knees with one foot in front of the other. •verb (**curtsies, curtsying, curtsied**; also **curtseys, curtseying, curtseyed**) perform a curtsy.
– ORIGIN variant of **COURTESY**.

curvaceous /ker-**vay**-shuhss/ adjective (especially of a woman or a woman's figure) having an attractively curved shape.

curvature /**ker**-vuh-cher/ noun the fact of being curved or the degree to which something is curved: *at that level the curvature of the earth is visible.*

curve noun **1** a line or outline which gradually bends. **2** a line on a graph showing how one quantity varies with respect to another. •verb form or move in a curve: *the path curved around the house.*
– ORIGIN from Latin *curvus* 'bent'.

curvet /ker-**vet**/ verb (**curvets, curvetting, curvetted**; also **curvets, curveting, curveted**) (especially of a horse) leap gracefully or energetically.
– ORIGIN Italian *corvetta* 'little curve'.

curvilinear /ker-vi-**lin**-i-er/ adjective contained by or consisting of a curved line or lines.

curvy adjective (**curvier, curviest**) **1** having many curves. **2** informal (of a woman's figure) curvaceous.
– DERIVATIVES **curviness** noun.

cushion noun **1** a bag of cloth stuffed with soft material, used as a comfortable support for sitting or leaning on. **2** a means of protection against impact or something unpleasant. **3** the elastic lining of the sides of a billiard table, from which the ball rebounds. •verb **1** soften the effect of an impact on someone or something. **2** lessen the adverse effects of: *he presented her with a gift to cushion the shock.*
– ORIGIN Old French *cuissin*.

cushy adjective (**cushier, cushiest**) informal (of a task or situation) easy and undemanding.
– ORIGIN from Urdu, 'pleasure'.

cusp /kusp/ noun **1** a pointed end where two curves meet, such as each of the ends of a crescent moon. **2** a cone-shaped projection on a tooth. **3** the initial point of an astrological sign or house. **4** a point of transition between two different states: *those on the cusp of adulthood.*
– DERIVATIVES **cusped** adjective.
– ORIGIN Latin *cuspis* 'point or apex'.

cuss informal noun an annoying or stubborn person or animal. •verb swear or curse.

cussed /**kuss**-id/ adjective informal awkward; annoying.
– DERIVATIVES **cussedness** noun.

custard noun 1 a sweet sauce made with milk and eggs, or milk and flavoured cornflour. 2 a baked dessert made from eggs and milk.
– ORIGIN first referring to a pie containing meat or fruit in a sauce thickened with eggs: from Old French *crouste* 'crust'.

custard apple noun a large fleshy tropical fruit with a sweet yellow pulp.

custard pie noun an open pie containing cold set custard, or a similar container of foam, as thrown in slapstick comedy.

custodian /kuss-**toh**-di-uhn/ noun a person who has responsibility for or looks after something.

custody /**kuss**-tuh-di/ noun 1 protective care of someone or something. 2 Law parental responsibility, especially as allocated to one of two parents who are getting divorced. 3 imprisonment, especially while waiting for trial.
– DERIVATIVES **custodial** /kuss-**toh**-di-uhl/ adjective.
– ORIGIN from Latin *custos* 'guardian'.

custom noun 1 a traditional way of behaving or doing something that is specific to a particular society, place, or time. 2 a thing that a person often does; a habit: *it was my custom to nap for an hour every day.* 3 Brit. regular dealings with a shop or business by customers.
– ORIGIN Old French *coustume*.

customary adjective in accordance with custom; usual.
– DERIVATIVES **customarily** adverb.

custom-built (also **custom-made**) adjective made to a particular customer's order.

customer noun 1 a person who buys goods or services from a shop or business. 2 a person of a specified kind that one has to deal with: *he's a tough customer.*

custom house (also **customs house**) noun chiefly historical the office at a port or frontier where customs duty is collected.

customize (or **customise**) verb modify to suit a particular person or task: *food manufacturers customize products for restaurant chains.*
– DERIVATIVES **customizable** adjective **customization** noun.

customs plural noun 1 the duties charged by a government on imported goods. 2 the official department that administers and collects such duties.

customs union noun a group of states that have agreed to charge the same import duties as each other and usually to allow free trade between themselves.

cut verb (**cuts, cutting, cut**) 1 make an opening, incision, or wound in something with a sharp implement. 2 make, shorten, remove, or divide with a sharp implement: *I cut his photo out of the paper.* 3 (as adj. **cut**) make or design a garment in a particular way: *an impeccably cut suit.* 4 reduce the amount or quantity of something. 5 end or interrupt the provision of a supply. 6 go across or through: *is it illegal to cut across a mini-roundabout?* 7 stop filming or recording. 8 move to another shot in a film. 9 make a sound recording. 10 divide a pack of

playing cards by lifting a portion from the top. 11 mix an illegal drug with another substance. •noun 1 an act of cutting. 2 a result of cutting: *a cut on his jaw.* 3 a reduction in amount or size. 4 the style in which a garment or the hair is cut: *the elegant cut of his jacket.* 5 a piece of meat cut from a carcass. 6 informal a share of profits. 7 a version of a film after editing: *the director's cut.*
– PHRASES **be cut from the same cloth** be of the same nature. **be cut out for** (or **to be**) informal have exactly the right qualities for a particular role. **a cut above** informal noticeably better than. **cut and dried** (of a situation) completely settled. **cut and paste** (on a word processor or computer) move an item from one part of a file to another. **cut and run** informal hastily leave a difficult situation rather than deal with it. **cut and thrust** a difficult or competitive situation. **cut both ways** 1 (of a point) serve both sides of an argument. 2 have both good and bad effects. **cut corners** do something with a lack of thoroughness to save time or money. **cut a dash** Brit. be stylish or impressive. **cut someone dead** completely ignore someone. **cut in** 1 interrupt someone. 2 pull in too closely in front of another vehicle after overtaking. 3 (of a machine) begin operating automatically. **cut someone in** informal include someone in a deal and give them a share of the profits. **cut it out** informal stop it. **cut the mustard** informal reach the required standard. **cut no ice** informal have no influence or effect. **cut someone/thing off** 1 block the usual means of access to a place. 2 deprive someone of a supply of power, water, etc. 3 break a telephone connection with someone. 4 disinherit someone. **cut out** (of an engine) suddenly stop operating. **cut someone out** exclude someone. **cut one's teeth** gain initial experience of an activity. **cut a tooth** (of a baby) have a tooth appear through the gum. **cut up** informal very upset; distressed. **cut someone up** informal (of a driver) overtake someone and pull in too closely. **cut up rough** Brit. informal behave in an aggressive or awkward way.
– ORIGIN probably Germanic.

cutaneous /kyoo-**tay**-ni-uhss/ adjective relating to or affecting the skin.
– ORIGIN from Latin *cutis* 'skin'.

cutaway adjective 1 (of a coat or jacket) having the front cut away below the waist. 2 (of a diagram of an object) having some external parts left out to reveal the interior.

cutback noun a reduction, especially in expenditure.

cute adjective 1 attractive in a charming or sweet way. 2 N. Amer. informal sexually attractive. 3 N. Amer. informal clever; shrewd.
– DERIVATIVES **cutely** adverb **cuteness** noun.
– ORIGIN shortening of ACUTE.

cutesy adjective informal excessively charming or sweet.

cut glass noun glass with decorative patterns cut into it. •adjective (of a person's accent) characterized by very precise pronunciation.

cuticle /**kyoo**-ti-k'l/ noun 1 the dead skin at the base of a fingernail or toenail. 2 the outer

cellular layer of a hair. **3** the epidermis of the body.
– ORIGIN from Latin *cuticula* 'little skin'.

cutlass /kut-luhss/ noun a short sword with a slightly curved blade, formerly used by sailors.
– ORIGIN Latin *cultellus* 'little knife'.

cutler noun a person who makes or sells cutlery.
– ORIGIN from Latin *cultellus* 'little knife'.

cutlery noun knives, forks, and spoons used for eating or serving food.

cutlet noun **1** a portion of meat, especially a chop from just behind the neck. **2** a flat cake of minced meat, nuts, or pulses, covered in breadcrumbs and fried.
– ORIGIN French *côtelette*.

cut-off noun **1** (usu. before another noun) a point or level marking a limit: *May 21 is the official cut-off date.* **2** a device for interrupting a power or fuel supply. **3** (**cut-offs**) shorts made by cutting off the legs of a pair of jeans.

cut-out noun **1** a shape cut out of board or paper. **2** a hole cut for decoration or for something to be inserted. **3** a device that automatically breaks an electric circuit for safety.

cut-price (N. Amer. also **cut-rate**) adjective for sale at a reduced price; cheap.

cutpurse noun old use a pickpocket.
– ORIGIN from the former practice of stealing purses by cutting them from a waistband.

cutter noun **1** a person or thing that cuts something. **2** a light, fast patrol boat or sailing boat.

cut-throat adjective fierce and ruthless: *a cost-cutting, cut-throat business.* •noun dated a murderer or other violent criminal.

cut-throat razor noun Brit. a razor with a long blade which folds like a penknife.

cutting noun **1** a piece cut off from something, such as a piece cut from a plant for propagation. **2** Brit. an article cut from a newspaper or magazine. **3** Brit. an open passage dug out through higher ground for a railway, road, or canal. •adjective **1** capable of cutting. **2** (of a remark) hurtful.
– DERIVATIVES **cuttingly** adverb.

cutting edge noun the latest or most advanced stage; the forefront. •adjective (**cutting-edge**) innovative; pioneering.

cuttlefish noun (pl. same or **cuttlefishes**) a marine mollusc resembling a squid, that squirts out a black liquid when attacked.
– ORIGIN Old English.

cutwater noun the forward edge of a ship's prow.

cuvée /kyoo-vay/ noun a type, blend, or batch of wine, especially champagne.
– ORIGIN French, 'vatful'.

CV abbreviation curriculum vitae.

CVS abbreviation chorionic villus sampling, a test made in early pregnancy to detect fetal abnormalities.

cwm /kuum/ noun (in Wales) a steep-sided hollow at the head of a valley or on a mountainside.
– ORIGIN Welsh.

cwt abbreviation hundredweight.
– ORIGIN from Latin *centum* 'a hundred'.

cyan /sy-uhn/ noun a greenish-blue colour which is one of the primary colours.
– ORIGIN Greek *kuaneos* 'dark blue'.

cyanide /sy-uh-nyd/ noun a highly poisonous compound containing a metal combined with carbon and nitrogen atoms.

cyanobacteria /sy-uhn-oh-bak-**teer**-i-uh/ plural noun microorganisms that are related to bacteria but capable of photosynthesis; blue-green algae.

cyanocobalamin /sy-uh-noh-kuh-**bal**-uh-min/ noun vitamin B_{12}, found in liver, fish, and eggs, a deficiency of which can cause pernicious anaemia.
– ORIGIN from Greek *kuanos* 'dark blue' + a blend of COBALT and VITAMIN.

cyanogen /sy-**an**-uh-juhn/ noun a highly poisonous gas.
– ORIGIN from Greek *kuanos* 'dark blue mineral' (because it is a constituent of Prussian blue).

cyanosis /sy-uh-**noh**-siss/ noun a bluish discoloration of the skin due to poor circulation or inadequate oxygenation of the blood.
– DERIVATIVES **cyanotic** adjective.
– ORIGIN Greek *kuanōsis* 'blueness'.

cyber- /sy-ber/ combining form relating to information technology, the Internet, and virtual reality: *cyberspace.*
– ORIGIN from CYBERNETICS.

cybercafe noun a cafe where customers can also use computer terminals and access the Internet.

cybercrime noun criminal activities carried out by means of computers or the Internet.
– DERIVATIVES **cybercriminal** noun.

cybernetics plural noun (treated as sing.) the science of communications and automatic control systems in both machines and living things.
– DERIVATIVES **cybernetic** adjective.
– ORIGIN from Greek *kubernētēs* 'steersman'.

cyberpunk noun a type of science fiction set in a lawless subculture of an oppressive society dominated by computer technology.

cyberspace noun the hypothetical environment in which communication over computer networks occurs.

cybersquatting noun the practice of registering an Internet domain name that a company or organization may later want for itself, in the hope of selling it back to them at a profit.
– DERIVATIVES **cybersquatter** noun.

cyberterrorism noun the use of computers to cause severe disruption or widespread fear in the attempt to achieve a political aim.
– DERIVATIVES **cyberterrorist** noun.

cyborg /sy-borg/ noun (in science fiction) a person having mechanical elements built into the body to extend their normal physical abilities.
– ORIGIN blend of CYBER- and ORGANISM.

cycad /sy-kad/ noun a tall, cone-bearing, palm-like plant of warm regions.
– ORIGIN Latin.

cyclamen /sik-luh-muhn/ noun (pl. same or **cyclamens**) a plant having pink, red, or white

flowers with backward-curving petals.
– ORIGIN Greek *kuklaminos*.

cycle noun **1** a series of events that are regularly repeated in the same order: *the cycle of growth and harvest*. **2** a complete sequence of changes associated with a recurring phenomenon such as an alternating electric current. **3** a bicycle. **4** a series of musical or literary works composed around a particular theme. • verb **1** ride a bicycle. **2** follow a repeated sequence of events: *on the laptop this message cycles every few seconds*.
– DERIVATIVES **cycler** noun.
– ORIGIN Greek *kuklos* 'circle'.

cyclic /**syk**-lik, **sik**-lik/ adjective **1** occurring in cycles: *the cyclic rotation of the earth and moon*. **2** having a molecular structure containing one or more closed rings of atoms.
– DERIVATIVES **cyclical** adjective **cyclically** adverb.

cyclist noun a person who rides a bicycle.

cyclone /**sy**-klohn/ noun **1** a system of winds rotating inwards to an area of low barometric pressure; a depression. **2** a tropical storm.
– DERIVATIVES **cyclonic** adjective.
– ORIGIN probably from Greek *kuklōma* 'wheel, coil of a snake'.

cyclopean /sy-kluh-**pee**-uhn, sy-**kloh**-pi-uhn/ adjective **1** relating to or resembling a Cyclops. **2** made with massive irregular stone blocks: *cyclopean walls*.

cyclopedia /sy-kloh-**pee**-di-uh/ (also **cyclopaedia**) noun (in book titles) an encyclopedia.

Cyclops /**sy**-klops/ noun (pl. same) Greek Mythology a member of a race of savage giants with only one eye.
– ORIGIN from Greek *Kuklōps* 'round-eyed'.

cyclotron /**sy**-kluh-tron/ noun a piece of equipment for accelerating charged atomic and subatomic particles by making them move spirally in a magnetic field.

cyder noun old-fashioned spelling of **CIDER**.

cygnet /**sig**-nit/ noun a young swan.
– ORIGIN Greek *kuknos* 'swan'.

cylinder /**sil**-in-der/ noun **1** a three-dimensional shape with straight parallel sides and a circular or oval cross section. **2** a piston chamber in a steam or internal-combustion engine. **3** a cylindrical container for liquefied gas under pressure.
– ORIGIN Greek *kulindros* 'roller'.

cylinder head noun the end cover of a cylinder in an internal-combustion engine, against which the piston compresses the cylinder's contents.

cylindrical /si-**lin**-dri-k'l/ adjective having the shape of a cylinder.
– DERIVATIVES **cylindrically** adverb.

cymbal /**sim**-buhl/ noun a musical instrument consisting of a slightly concave round brass plate which is either struck against another one or hit with a stick.
– ORIGIN Greek *kumbalon*.

cyme noun a flower cluster with a central stem bearing a single flower on the end that develops first. Compare with **RACEME**.
– ORIGIN Latin *cyma* 'summit'.

Cymric /**kim**-rik/ adjective (of language or

culture) Welsh. • noun the Welsh language.
– ORIGIN from Welsh *Cymru* 'Wales'.

cynic /**si**-nik/ noun **1** a person who believes that people are motivated purely by self-interest. **2** a person who raises doubts about something; a sceptic. **3** (**Cynic**) (in ancient Greece) a member of a school of philosophers who despised wealth and pleasure.
– DERIVATIVES **cynicism** noun.
– ORIGIN Greek *kunikos*.

cynical adjective **1** believing that people always act from selfish motives. **2** proceeding from self-interest, regardless of accepted standards: *a cynical foul*. **3** doubtful; sceptical: *young people are very cynical about advertising*. **4** contemptuous; mocking.
– DERIVATIVES **cynically** adverb.

cynosure /**sin**-uh-zyoor/ noun a person or thing that is the centre of attention or admiration.
– ORIGIN Greek *kunosoura* 'dog's tail', also 'Ursa Minor' (the constellation contains the Pole Star, used as a guide by sailors).

cypher noun variant spelling of **CIPHER**.

cypress noun an evergreen coniferous tree with small dark green leaves.
– ORIGIN Greek *kuparissos*.

Cypriot noun **1** a person from Cyprus. **2** the dialect of Greek used in Cyprus. • adjective relating to Cyprus.

Cyrillic /si-**ril**-lik/ adjective referring to the alphabet used for Russian, Ukrainian, Bulgarian, Serbian, and some other Slavic languages. • noun the Cyrillic alphabet.
– ORIGIN named after the 9th-century Greek missionary St *Cyril*.

cyst /sist/ noun **1** a thin-walled abnormal sac or cavity in the body, containing fluid. **2** a sac or bladder containing liquid in an animal or plant.
– ORIGIN Greek *kustis* 'bladder'.

cystic adjective **1** relating to cysts. **2** relating to the urinary bladder or the gall bladder.

cystic fibrosis noun an inherited disease in which the production of abnormally thick mucus leads to the blockage of the pancreatic ducts, intestines, and bronchi.

cystitis /si-**sty**-tiss/ noun inflammation of the urinary bladder, typically caused by infection and accompanied by frequent painful urination.

cytology /sy-**tol**-uh-ji/ noun the branch of biology concerned with the structure and function of plant and animal cells.
– DERIVATIVES **cytological** adjective **cytologist** noun.

cytomegalovirus /sy-toh-**meg**-uh-loh-vy-ruhss/ noun a kind of herpesvirus which usually produces very mild symptoms in an infected person but may cause severe neurological damage in people with weakened immune systems and in the newborn.

cytoplasm /**sy**-toh-pla-z'm/ noun the material or protoplasm within a living cell, excluding the nucleus.
– DERIVATIVES **cytoplasmic** adjective.

czar etc. noun variant spelling of **TSAR** etc.

Czech /chek/ **noun 1** a person from the Czech Republic or (formerly) Czechoslovakia. **2** the Slavic language spoken in the Czech Republic. •**adjective** relating to the Czech Republic.

Czechoslovak /chek-uh-**sloh**-vak/ (also **Czechoslovakian**) **noun** a person from the former country of Czechoslovakia, now divided between the Czech Republic and Slovakia. •**adjective** relating to the former country of Czechoslovakia.

Dd

D¹ (also **d**) noun (pl. **Ds** or **D's**) **1** the fourth letter of the alphabet. **2** referring to the fourth item in a set. **3** Music the second note of the scale of C major. **4** the Roman numeral for 500.

D² abbreviation **1** (in the US) Democrat or Democratic. **2** depth (in the sense of the dimension of an object from front to back). **3** (with a numeral) dimension(s) or dimensional. **4** (in tables of sports results) drawn.

d abbreviation **1** (in genealogies) daughter. **2** deci-. **3** (in travel timetables) departs. **4** (**d.**) died (used to indicate a date of death). **5** Brit. penny or pence (of pre-decimal currency). [from Latin *denarius* 'penny'.]

'd contraction **1** had. **2** would.

DA abbreviation US district attorney.

D/A abbreviation Electronics digital to analogue.

DAB abbreviation digital audio broadcasting.

dab¹ verb (**dabs**, **dabbing**, **dabbed**) **1** press something lightly with a cloth or sponge. **2** apply a substance with light quick strokes. •noun **1** a small amount of a substance lightly applied. **2** (**dabs**) Brit. informal fingerprints.
– ORIGIN representing a light striking movement.

dab² noun a small North Atlantic flatfish.
– ORIGIN unknown.

dabble verb **1** move one's hands or feet around gently in water. **2** take part in an activity in a casual way: *I was a vegetarian and dabbled in yoga.*
– DERIVATIVES **dabbler** noun.
– ORIGIN from former Dutch *dabbelen* or from **DAB¹**.

dabchick noun the little grebe.
– ORIGIN the first element is perhaps related to **DIP** and **DEEP**.

dab hand noun Brit. informal a person who is very skilled in a particular activity.
– ORIGIN unknown.

da capo /dah **kah**-poh/ adverb & adjective Music repeat or repeated from the beginning.
– ORIGIN Italian, 'from the head'.

dace /dayss/ noun (pl. same) a small freshwater fish related to the carp.
– ORIGIN Old French *dars* (see **DART**).

dacha /**da**-chuh/ noun (in Russia) a country house or cottage, used as a holiday home.
– ORIGIN Russian.

dachshund /dak-suhnd/ noun a breed of dog with a long body and very short legs.
– ORIGIN German, 'badger dog'.

dacoit /duh-**koyt**/ noun a member of a band of armed robbers in India or Burma (Myanmar).
– ORIGIN Hindi, 'robbery by a gang'.

dactyl /**dak**-til/ noun Poetry a metrical foot consisting of one stressed syllable followed by two unstressed syllables.
– DERIVATIVES **dactylic** adjective.
– ORIGIN Greek *daktulos* 'finger' (the three bones of the finger corresponding to the three syllables).

dad noun informal one's father.
– ORIGIN perhaps from a child's first syllables *da, da.*

Dada /dah-dah/ noun an early 20th-century movement in the arts which mocked conventions and emphasized the illogical and absurd.
– DERIVATIVES **Dadaism** noun **Dadaist** noun & adjective.
– ORIGIN French, 'hobby horse', the title of a review published in Zurich in 1916.

daddy noun (pl. **daddies**) informal one's father.

daddy-long-legs noun (pl. same) Brit. informal a crane fly.

dado /day-doh/ noun (pl. **dados**) **1** the lower part of the wall of a room, when decorated differently from the upper part. **2** Architecture the part of a pedestal between the base and the cornice.
– ORIGIN Italian, 'dice or cube'.

dado rail noun a waist-high moulding round the wall of a room.

daemon /dee-**muhn**/ noun old-fashioned spelling of **DEMON**.
– DERIVATIVES **daemonic** adjective.
– ORIGIN Greek *daimon*.

daffodil noun a plant bearing bright yellow flowers with a long trumpet-shaped centre.
– ORIGIN Latin *asphodilus* 'asphodel'.

daffy adjective (**daffier**, **daffiest**) informal silly or mildly eccentric.
– DERIVATIVES **daffiness** noun.
– ORIGIN from northern English dialect *daff* 'simpleton'.

daft adjective Brit. informal silly; foolish.
– ORIGIN Old English, 'mild, meek'.

dagger noun **1** a short pointed knife, used as a weapon. **2** another term for **OBELUS**.
– PHRASES **be at daggers drawn** Brit. (of two people) be bitterly hostile towards each other. **look daggers at** glare angrily at.
– ORIGIN perhaps from former *dag* 'pierce', influenced by Old French *dague* 'long dagger'.

dago /day-goh/ noun (pl. **dagos** or **dagoes**)

informal, offensive a Spanish, Portuguese, or Italian-speaking person.
– ORIGIN from the Spanish man's name *Diego* 'James'.

daguerreotype /duh-ger-ruh-typ/ (also **daguerrotype**) noun an early type of photograph produced by means of a silver-coated copper plate and mercury vapour.
– ORIGIN named after L.-J.-M. *Daguerre*, its French inventor.

dahlia /day-li-uh/ noun a garden plant with brightly coloured single or double flowers.
– ORIGIN named after the Swedish botanist Andreas *Dahl*.

daikon /dy-kuhn, dy-kon/ noun another term for MOOLI.
– ORIGIN Japanese.

Dáil /doyl/ (in full **Dáil Éireann** /doyl air-uhn/) noun the lower house of Parliament in the Republic of Ireland.
– ORIGIN Irish, 'assembly' (in full 'assembly of Ireland').

daily adjective done, happening, or produced every day or every weekday. •adverb every day. •noun (pl. **dailies**) informal a newspaper published every day except Sunday.

dainty adjective (**daintier**, **daintiest**) delicately small and pretty: *dainty white snowdrops*. •noun (pl. **dainties**) a small appetizing item of food.
– DERIVATIVES **daintily** adverb **daintiness** noun.
– ORIGIN from Old French *daintie* 'choice morsel, pleasure'.

daiquiri /da-ki-ri/ noun (pl. **daiquiris**) a cocktail containing rum and lime juice.
– ORIGIN from *Daiquiri*, a rum-producing district in Cuba.

dairy noun (pl. **dairies**) a building where milk and milk products are processed and distributed. •adjective 1 made from milk. 2 involved in milk production.
– DERIVATIVES **dairying** noun.
– ORIGIN Old English, 'female servant'.

dairymaid noun old use a woman employed in a dairy.

dairyman noun (pl. **dairymen**) a man who works in a dairy or who sells dairy products.

dais /day-iss/ noun a low platform for a lectern or throne.
– ORIGIN Old French *deis*.

daisy noun (pl. **daisies**) a small plant having flowers with a yellow centre and white petals.
– ORIGIN Old English, 'day's eye' (the flower opens in the morning and closes at night).

daisy chain noun a string of daisies threaded together by their stems.

daisy wheel noun a spoked disc carrying printing characters, used in word processors and typewriters.

dal noun variant spelling of DHAL.

Dalai Lama /da-ly lah-muh/ noun the spiritual head of Tibetan Buddhism.
– ORIGIN Tibetan, 'ocean monk', because he is regarded as 'the ocean of compassion'.

dalasi /dah-lah-see/ noun (pl. same or **dalasis**) the basic unit of money of Gambia.
– ORIGIN a local word.

dale noun a valley, especially in northern England.
– ORIGIN Old English.

dalliance noun 1 a casual romantic or sexual relationship. 2 a brief or casual involvement with something: *his dalliance with the far right*.

dally verb (**dallies**, **dallying**, **dallied**) 1 act or move slowly. 2 (**dally with**) have a casual sexual relationship with someone. 3 (**dally with**) show a casual interest in: *I dallied with the idea of asking her friend round too*.
– ORIGIN Old French *dalier* 'to chat'.

Dalmatian /dal-may-sh'n/ noun a breed of large dog with short white hair and dark spots.
– ORIGIN named after *Dalmatia*, a region of Croatia.

dam[1] noun a barrier built across a river to hold back water, in order to form a reservoir or prevent flooding. •verb (**dams**, **damming**, **dammed**) build a dam across a river.
– ORIGIN German or Dutch.

dam[2] noun the female parent of certain mammals, especially horses.
– ORIGIN from DAME.

damage noun 1 physical harm that affects the value, functioning, or usefulness of something. 2 harmful effects: *the damage to his reputation was considerable*. 3 (**damages**) financial compensation for a loss or injury. •verb cause harm to; have a bad effect on: *some industrial solvents can damage people's health*.
– PHRASES **what's the damage?** informal, humorous what does it cost?
– ORIGIN Old French.

damaging adjective harmful or undesirable.

damascened /dam-uh-seend/ adjective 1 (of iron or steel) given a wavy pattern by hammer-welding and repeated heating and forging. 2 (of metal) inlaid with gold or silver.
– ORIGIN from the Syrian city of *Damascus*.

damask /dam-uhsk/ noun a rich heavy fabric with a pattern woven into it. •adjective literary pink or light red.
– ORIGIN from the Syrian city of *Damascus*.

dame noun 1 (**Dame**) (in the UK) the title of a woman awarded a knighthood, equivalent to *Sir*. 2 N. Amer. informal a woman. 3 (also **pantomime dame**) Brit. a comic female character in pantomime, played by a man.
– ORIGIN Old French.

damn /dam/ verb 1 curse someone or something. 2 criticize strongly: *a company spokesman damned the plan as financially unsound*. 3 (**be damned**) (in Christian belief) be condemned by God to eternal punishment in hell. 4 (**be damned**) be doomed to misfortune or failure. •exclamation informal expressing anger or frustration. •adjective informal used to emphasize anger or frustration.
– PHRASES **damn all** Brit. informal nothing at all. **damn someone/thing with faint praise** praise someone or something so unenthusiastically as to suggest condemnation. **not be worth a damn** informal have no value.
– ORIGIN Latin *dampnare* 'inflict loss on'.

damnable adjective very bad or unpleasant.
– DERIVATIVES **damnably** adverb.

damnation /dam-nay-sh'n/ noun condemnation to eternal punishment in hell. •exclamation expressing anger or frustration.

damned /damd/ adjective used to emphasize anger or frustration.
– PHRASES **do** (or **try**) **one's damnedest** do (or

try) one's utmost.

damning adjective strongly suggestive of guilt: *damning evidence.*

damp adjective slightly wet. •noun moisture in the air, on a surface, or in a solid substance. •verb **1** make something damp. **2** (**damp something down**) control or restrain a feeling or situation. **3** (**damp something down**) make a fire burn less strongly by reducing its air supply. **4** reduce or stop the vibration of the strings of a musical instrument.
– DERIVATIVES **dampish** adjective **damply** adverb **dampness** noun.
– ORIGIN Germanic.

damp course (also **damp-proof course**) noun Brit. a layer of waterproof material in a wall near the ground, to prevent rising damp.

dampen verb **1** make something damp. **2** make less strong or intense: *nothing could dampen her enthusiasm.*
– DERIVATIVES **dampener** noun.

damper noun **1** a pad for silencing a piano string. **2** a device for reducing vibration or oscillation. **3** a movable metal plate used to regulate the air flow in a flue or chimney.
– PHRASES **put a damper on** informal have a subduing or restraining effect on.

damp squib noun Brit. something that turns out to be much less impressive than expected.

damsel /dam-z'l/ noun old use or humorous a young unmarried woman.
– ORIGIN Old French *dameisele*.

damselfly noun (pl. **damselflies**) a slender insect related to the dragonflies.

damson /dam-zuhn/ noun a small purple-black plum-like fruit.
– ORIGIN from Latin *damascenum prunum* 'plum of Damascus'.

dan noun **1** any of ten degrees of advanced proficiency in judo or karate. **2** a person who has achieved a dan.
– ORIGIN Japanese.

dance verb **1** move rhythmically to music. **2** move in a quick and lively way: *midges danced over the stream.* •noun **1** a series of steps and movements that match the rhythm of a piece of music. **2** an act of dancing. **3** a social gathering at which people dance. **4** (also **dance music**) pop music for dancing to in clubs.
– PHRASES **dance attendance on** chiefly Brit. try hard to please someone. **lead someone a merry dance** Brit. cause someone a great deal of trouble.
– DERIVATIVES **dancer** noun **dancing** noun.
– ORIGIN Old French *dancer*.

dance hall noun **1** a large public hall or building where people pay to enter and dance. **2** (**dancehall**) a style of dance music derived from reggae.

D and C abbreviation dilatation and curettage.

dandelion noun a weed with large bright yellow flowers followed by rounded heads of seeds with downy tufts.
– ORIGIN French *dent-de-lion* 'lion's tooth' (from the shape of the leaves).

dander noun (in phrase **get/have one's dander up**) informal lose one's temper.
– ORIGIN unknown.

dandified adjective (of a man) excessively concerned about his clothes and appearance.

dandle verb gently bounce a young child on one's knees or in one's arms.
– ORIGIN unknown.

dandruff noun flakes of dead skin on a person's scalp and in the hair.
– ORIGIN uncertain.

dandy noun (pl. **dandies**) a man who is excessively concerned with having a stylish and fashionable appearance. •adjective (**dandier, dandiest**) N. Amer. informal excellent.
– DERIVATIVES **dandyish** adjective.
– ORIGIN a familiar form of the man's name *Andrew.*

Dane noun a person from Denmark.
– ORIGIN Old English.

danger noun **1** the possibility of suffering harm: *her life was in danger.* **2** a cause of harm. **3** the possibility of something unpleasant or undesirable happening: *there's no danger of putting on weight in that restaurant.*
– PHRASES **be on** (or **off**) **the danger list** Brit. be critically ill (or no longer critically ill).
– ORIGIN Old French *dangier* 'jurisdiction, power to harm'.

danger money noun extra payment for working under dangerous conditions.

dangerous adjective **1** able or likely to cause harm: *dangerous chemicals like DDT.* **2** likely to cause problems.
– DERIVATIVES **dangerously** adverb **dangerousness** noun.

dangle verb **1** hang so as to swing freely. **2** offer something attractive to someone to persuade them to do something: *one firm is dangling a grand prize of a Porsche for referrals.*
– DERIVATIVES **dangler** noun **dangly** adjective.
– ORIGIN uncertain.

dangling participle noun Grammar a participle intended to refer to a noun which is not actually present.

USAGE: A **dangling participle** is one which is left 'hanging' because it does not relate to the noun it should. For example, in the sentence *arriving at the station, the sun came out,* the word **arriving** is a dangling participle, because the sentence reads grammatically as if it is **the sun** (the subject of the sentence) which is **arriving**. This is incorrect in standard English.

Danish /day-nish/ adjective relating to Denmark or the Danes. •noun the language of Denmark.

Danish blue noun a strong-flavoured blue-veined white cheese.

Danish pastry noun a cake of sweetened yeast pastry topped with icing, fruit, or nuts.

dank adjective damp and cold.
– ORIGIN probably Scandinavian.

daphnia /daf-ni-uh/ noun (pl. same) a minute semi-transparent freshwater crustacean.
– ORIGIN Latin.

dapper adjective (of a man) neat in dress and appearance.
– ORIGIN probably from a German or Dutch word meaning 'strong, stout'.

dapple verb mark with spots or small patches: *a forest clearing dappled with sunlight.* •noun a

d

patch of colour or light.
– ORIGIN perhaps from Old Norse.

dapple grey adjective (of a horse) grey or white with darker ring-like markings.

Darby and Joan noun Brit. a devoted old married couple.
– ORIGIN from a poem (1735) in the *Gentleman's Magazine*.

dare verb (3rd sing. present usu. **dare** before an expressed or implied infinitive without 'to') **1** have the courage to do something. **2** challenge to do something: *he ran his first marathon because his grandchildren dared him to.* •noun a challenge, especially to prove courage.
– PHRASES **how dare you** used to express indignation. **I dare say** (or **daresay**) it is probable.
– ORIGIN Old English.

daredevil noun a person who enjoys doing dangerous things.

daring adjective **1** willing to do dangerous or risky things; bold. **2** involving risk or danger. **3** boldly unconventional: *daring, see-through evening gowns.* •noun adventurous courage.
– DERIVATIVES **daringly** adverb.

Darjeeling /dar-jee-ling/ noun a high-quality tea grown in northern India.
– ORIGIN from *Darjeeling*, a hill station in West Bengal.

dark adjective **1** with little or no light. **2** of a deep colour: *dark green.* **3** (of skin, hair, or eyes) brown or black. **4** unpleasant or gloomy: *the dark days of the war.* **5** evil. **6** mysterious: *a dark secret.* **7** (**darkest**) humorous most remote or uncivilized. •noun **1** (**the dark**) the absence of light. **2** nightfall.
– PHRASES **in the dark** in a state of ignorance. **a shot** (or **stab**) **in the dark** a wild guess.
– DERIVATIVES **darkish** adjective **darkly** adverb **darkness** noun.
– ORIGIN Old English.

Dark Ages plural noun **1** the period in Europe between the fall of the Roman Empire and the Middle Ages, *c.*500–1100, regarded as lacking culture and knowledge. **2** a period characterized by a lack of knowledge or progress: *the dark ages of computing.*

darken verb **1** make or become darker. **2** become unhappy or angry.
– PHRASES **never darken someone's door** keep away from someone's home.

dark horse noun a person about whom little is known, especially one with unexpected talents.

darkling adjective literary **1** characterized by darkness. **2** growing darker.

dark matter noun Astronomy non-luminous material believed to exist in space.

darkroom noun a room for developing photographs, from which normal light is excluded.

darling noun **1** used as an affectionate form of address. **2** a lovable person. **3** a person popular with a particular group: *she is the darling of the media.* •adjective **1** beloved. **2** pretty; charming.
– ORIGIN Old English, from **DEAR**.

darmstadtium /darm-stat-i-uhm/ noun a radioactive chemical element produced artificially.
– ORIGIN named after the German city of

Darmstadt, where it was discovered.

darn[1] verb mend knitted material by interweaving yarn across it.
– DERIVATIVES **darning** noun.
– ORIGIN perhaps from an Old English word meaning 'to hide'.

darn[2] verb, adjective, & exclamation informal euphemism for **DAMN**.

darned adjective informal euphemism for **DAMNED**.

dart noun **1** a small pointed missile thrown or fired as a weapon. **2** a small pointed missile used in the game of darts. **3** (**darts**) (usu. treated as sing.) an indoor game in which darts are thrown at a dartboard. **4** a sudden rapid movement. **5** a tapered tuck in a garment. •verb move suddenly or rapidly.
– ORIGIN Old French.

dartboard noun a circular board used as a target in the game of darts.

Darwinism noun the theory of the evolution of species by natural selection, put forward by the English natural historian Charles Darwin.
– DERIVATIVES **Darwinian** noun & adjective **Darwinist** noun & adjective.

dash verb **1** run or travel in a great hurry. **2** strike or throw something with great force. **3** destroy or frustrate: *his political hopes were dashed.* **4** (**dash something off**) write something hurriedly. •noun **1** an act of dashing. **2** a small amount added: *whisky with a dash of soda.* **3** a horizontal stroke in writing, marking a pause or omission. **4** the longer of the signals used in Morse code. **5** style, enthusiasm, and confidence.
– ORIGIN probably symbolic of forceful movement.

dashboard noun the panel of instruments and controls facing the driver of a vehicle.
– ORIGIN first meaning a board in front of a carriage, to keep out mud.

dashiki /dah-shi-ki/ noun (pl. **dashikis**) a loose, brightly coloured shirt, originally from West Africa.
– ORIGIN Yoruba or Hausa (a West African language).

dashing adjective (of a man) attractive, adventurous, and confident.
– DERIVATIVES **dashingly** adverb.

dastardly adjective dated or humorous wicked and cruel.
– ORIGIN from the old word *dastard* 'despicable person'.

DAT abbreviation digital audiotape.

data /day-tuh/ noun **1** facts and statistics used for reference or analysis. **2** the quantities, characters, or symbols on which operations are performed by a computer.
– ORIGIN Latin, plural of **DATUM**.

USAGE: The word **data** is the plural of Latin *datum*, and in scientific use it is usually treated as a plural noun, taking a plural verb (e.g. *the data were classified*). In everyday use, however, **data** is often treated as a singular, and sentences such as *data was collected over a number of years* are now generally accepted.

databank noun a large store of data in a computer.

database noun a structured set of data held in a computer.

datable (also **dateable**) adjective able to be dated to a particular time.

data capture noun the action of gathering data and putting it into a form accessible by computer.

data protection noun legal control over access to data stored in computers.

date[1] noun **1** the day of the month or year as specified by a number. **2** a day or year when a particular event occurred or will occur. **3** a social or romantic appointment. **4** a musical or theatrical performance, especially as part of a tour. • verb **1** establish the date of something. **2** write or print the date on something. **3** (**date from** or **date back to**) start or originate at a particular time in the past. **4** (as adj. **dated**) old-fashioned. **5** informal go on a date or regular dates with someone.
– PHRASES **to date** until now.
– ORIGIN Latin *data*, from *dare* 'give'.

date[2] noun **1** a sweet, dark brown, oval fruit with a hard stone, usually eaten dried. **2** (also **date palm**) a tall palm tree which bears this fruit, native to western Asia and North Africa.
– ORIGIN Greek *daktulos* 'finger' (because of the finger-like shape of the tree's leaves).

dateable adjective variant spelling of **DATABLE**.

date rape noun rape by a person with whom the victim has gone on a date.

dating agency noun a service which arranges introductions for people seeking romantic partners or friends.

dative /day-tiv/ noun (in Latin, Greek, German, etc.) the grammatical case of nouns and pronouns that indicates an indirect object or the person or thing affected by a verb.
– ORIGIN from Latin *casus dativus* 'case of giving'.

datum /day-tuhm/ noun (pl. **data**) a piece of information.
– ORIGIN Latin, 'something given'.

datura /duh-tyoo-ruh/ noun a North American plant whose flowers contain toxic or narcotic substances.
– ORIGIN Hindi.

daub /dawb/ verb **1** carelessly coat or smear something with a thick substance. **2** spread a thick substance on a surface. • noun **1** plaster, clay, or a similar substance, especially when mixed with straw and applied to laths or wattles to form a wall. **2** a patch or smear of a thick substance. **3** a painting done without much skill.
– ORIGIN Old French *dauber*.

daube /dohb/ noun a stew of meat, typically beef, braised in wine.
– ORIGIN French.

daughter noun **1** a girl or woman in relation to her parents. **2** a female descendant.
– DERIVATIVES **daughterly** adjective.
– ORIGIN Old English.

daughterboard (also **daughtercard**) noun a small printed circuit board that attaches to a larger one.

daughter-in-law noun (pl. **daughters-in-law**) the wife of one's son.

daunt /dawnt/ verb (usu. **be daunted**) make someone feel intimidated or apprehensive.
– DERIVATIVES **daunting** adjective.
– ORIGIN Old French *danter*.

dauntless adjective fearless and determined.

dauphin /doh-fan/ noun historical the eldest son of the King of France.
– ORIGIN French.

davenport /da-vuhn-port/ noun **1** Brit. an ornamental writing desk with drawers and a sloping surface for writing. **2** N. Amer. a large upholstered sofa.
– ORIGIN sense 1 is named after a Captain *Davenport*, for whom a desk of this type was first made; sense 2 is probably a manufacturer's name.

davit /da-vit/ noun a small crane on a ship, especially one of a pair for lowering a lifeboat.
– ORIGIN Old French *daviot*.

Davy Jones's locker noun informal the bottom of the sea, regarded as the grave of those who drown.
– ORIGIN from 18th-century nautical slang *Davy Jones*, referring to the evil spirit of the sea.

Davy lamp noun historical a miner's portable safety lamp with the flame enclosed by wire gauze to reduce the risk of a gas explosion.
– ORIGIN named after the English chemist Sir Humphry *Davy*, who invented it.

dawdle verb move slowly; take one's time.
– DERIVATIVES **dawdler** noun.
– ORIGIN related to dialect *daddle*, *doddle* 'dally'.

dawn noun **1** the first appearance of light in the sky in the morning. **2** the beginning of something: *the dawn of civilization.* • verb **1** (of a day) begin. **2** come into existence: *a new era had dawned.* **3** (**dawn on**) become obvious to: *the truth began to dawn on him.*
– ORIGIN Old English.

dawn chorus noun the early-morning singing of birds.

day noun **1** a period of twenty-four hours, reckoned from midnight to midnight and corresponding to a rotation of the earth on its axis. **2** the time between sunrise and sunset. **3** (usu. **days**) a particular period of the past. **4** (**the day**) the present time or the time in question. **5** (**one's day**) the youthful or successful period of one's life. • adjective working or done during the day: *my day job.*
– PHRASES **any day** informal at any time or under any circumstances. **call it a day** decide to stop doing something. **day by day** gradually and steadily. **day in, day out** continuously or repeatedly over a long period. **day-to-day 1** happening on a daily basis. **2** involving the usual tasks or routines of every day: *the day-to-day running of the company.* **that will be the day** informal that is very unlikely. **these days** at present.
– ORIGIN Old English.

Dayak /dy-ak/ (also **Dyak**) noun (pl. same or **Dayaks**) **1** a member of a group of the native peoples inhabiting parts of Borneo. **2** the group of languages spoken by the Dayak.
– ORIGIN Malay, 'upcountry'.

daybed noun N. Amer. a couch that can be made into a bed.

day boy (or **day girl**) noun Brit. a boy (or girl) who lives at home and attends a school that also takes boarders.

daybreak noun dawn.

day centre (also **day-care centre**) noun a place providing daytime care and social facilities for elderly or disabled people.

daydream noun a series of pleasant thoughts that distract one's attention from the present. •verb have a daydream.
– DERIVATIVES **daydreamer** noun.

daylight noun 1 the natural light of the day. 2 dawn. 3 visible distance between one person or thing and another.
– PHRASES —— **the living daylights out of someone** do a particular thing to someone very strongly or severely: *you scared the living daylights out of me.*

daylight robbery noun Brit. informal blatant and unfair overcharging.

day off noun (pl. **days off**) a day's holiday from work or school.

daypack noun a small rucksack.

day release noun Brit. a system in which employees are granted days off work to go on educational courses.

day return noun Brit. a ticket at a reduced rate for a return journey on public transport within one day.

day room noun a communal room in an institution, used during the day.

day school noun 1 a school for pupils who live at home. 2 a short educational course.

day surgery noun minor surgery that does not require an overnight stay in hospital.

daytime noun 1 the time between sunrise and sunset. 2 the period of time corresponding to normal working hours.

day trip noun a journey or excursion completed in one day.
– DERIVATIVES **day tripper** noun.

daze verb make someone feel stunned or bewildered. •noun a state of stunned confusion or bewilderment.
– DERIVATIVES **dazedly** adverb.
– ORIGIN Old Norse, 'weary'.

dazzle verb 1 (of a bright light) blind someone temporarily. 2 impress someone greatly: *I was dazzled by the beauty of the exhibition.* •noun blinding brightness.
– DERIVATIVES **dazzlement** noun **dazzler** noun **dazzling** adjective.
– ORIGIN from DAZE.

Db symbol the chemical element dubnium.

dB abbreviation decibel(s).

DBE abbreviation (in the UK) Dame Commander of the Order of the British Empire.

DBS abbreviation 1 direct broadcasting by satellite. 2 direct-broadcast satellite.

DC abbreviation 1 direct current. 2 District of Columbia.

DCB abbreviation (in the UK) Dame Commander of the Order of the Bath.

DCM abbreviation (in the UK) Distinguished Conduct Medal.

DCMG abbreviation (in the UK) Dame Commander of the Order of St Michael and St George.

DD abbreviation Doctor of Divinity.

D-Day noun 1 the day (6 June 1944) in the Second World War on which Allied forces invaded northern France. 2 the day on which something important is to begin.
– ORIGIN from *D* for *day* + DAY.

DDR abbreviation historical German Democratic Republic.
– ORIGIN abbreviation of German *Deutsche Demokratische Republik.*

DDT abbreviation dichlorodiphenyltrichloro-ethane, a compound used as an insecticide but now banned in many countries.

DE abbreviation Delaware.

de- prefix forming or added to verbs or their derivatives: 1 down; away: *deduct.* 2 completely: *denude.* 3 referring to removal or reversal: *de-ice.*
– ORIGIN from Latin *de* 'off, from' or *dis-*.

deacon /dee-kuhn/ noun 1 (in Catholic, Anglican, and Orthodox Churches) a minister ranking below a priest. 2 (in some Protestant Churches) a lay officer assisting a minister.
– ORIGIN Greek *diakonos* 'servant'.

deaconess noun a woman with duties similar to those of a deacon.

deactivate verb make something inactive by disconnecting or destroying it.
– DERIVATIVES **deactivation** noun.

dead adjective 1 no longer alive. 2 (of a part of the body) numb. 3 displaying no emotion. 4 no longer relevant or important. 5 without activity or excitement. 6 (of equipment) not working. 7 complete; absolute: *dead silence.* •adverb 1 completely; exactly: *dead on time.* 2 straight; directly: *dead ahead.* 3 Brit. informal very.
– PHRASES **dead and buried** over; finished. **the dead of night** the quietest, darkest part of the night. **the dead of winter** the coldest part of winter. **dead to the world** informal fast asleep. **from the dead** from being dead; from death.
– DERIVATIVES **deadness** noun.
– ORIGIN Old English.

deadbeat adjective (**dead beat**) informal completely exhausted. •noun informal a lazy or unreliable person.

deadbolt noun a bolt secured by turning a knob or key, rather than by spring action.

dead duck noun informal an unsuccessful or useless person or thing.

deaden verb 1 make a noise or sensation less intense. 2 make something numb.

dead end noun 1 an end of a road or passage from which no exit is possible. 2 a situation in which no further progress can be made.

dead hand noun an undesirable and long-lasting influence.

deadhead noun Brit. a faded flower head. •verb remove dead flower heads from a plant.

dead heat noun a result in a race in which two or more competitors finish at exactly the same time.

dead letter noun a law or treaty which has not been repealed but is no longer applied.

deadline noun the latest time or date by which something should be completed.

deadlock noun 1 a situation in which no progress can be made. 2 Brit. a lock operated by a key, as distinct from a spring lock. •verb (**be deadlocked**) be in a situation in which no progress can be made.

dead loss noun an unproductive or useless person or thing.

deadly adjective (**deadlier**, **deadliest**) **1** causing or able to cause death. **2** (of a voice, glance, etc.) filled with hate. **3** extremely accurate or effective. **4** informal extremely boring. • adverb **1** in a way that resembles or suggests death: *her skin was deadly pale.* **2** extremely: *he was deadly serious.*
– DERIVATIVES **deadliness** noun.

deadly nightshade noun a poisonous plant with purple flowers and round black fruit.

deadly sin noun (in Christian tradition) a sin regarded as leading to damnation.

dead-nettle noun a plant of the mint family, with leaves that resemble those of a nettle but without stinging hairs.

deadpan adjective (of a person's expression) not showing any emotion.

dead reckoning noun the calculation of one's position, especially at sea, by estimating the direction and distance travelled.

dead ringer noun a person or thing that looks very like another.

deadweight noun **1** the weight of a person or thing without the strength or ability to move themselves. **2** the total weight of cargo, stores, etc. which a ship can carry.

dead wood noun useless or unproductive people or things.

dead zone noun **1** a place or period in which nothing happens. **2** a place where it is not possible to receive a mobile-phone or radio signal.

deaf adjective **1** wholly or partially unable to hear. **2** (**deaf to**) unwilling to listen or respond to: *she was deaf to all advice.*
– PHRASES **fall on deaf ears** be ignored. **turn a deaf ear** refuse to listen or respond.
– DERIVATIVES **deafness** noun.
– ORIGIN Old English.

deaf aid noun Brit. a hearing aid.

deaf-blind adjective having severely impaired hearing and vision.

deafen verb **1** make someone deaf. **2** (as adj. **deafening**) extremely loud.
– DERIVATIVES **deafeningly** adverb.

deaf mute noun a person who is deaf and unable to speak.

USAGE: As the noun **deaf mute** may be regarded as offensive, it is advisable to use terms such as **profoundly deaf** instead.

deal[1] noun **1** an agreement between two or more parties for their mutual benefit. **2** a particular form of treatment given or received: *working mothers get a bad deal.* **3** the process of distributing cards in a card game. • verb (past and past part. **dealt**) **1** (**deal something out**) distribute something. **2** (usu. **deal in**) buy and sell a product or commodity commercially. **3** buy and sell illegal drugs. **4** distribute cards to players for a game or round.
– PHRASES **a big deal** informal an important thing. **deal someone or something a blow** hit or be harmful to someone or something. **a deal of** a large amount of. **deal with 1** do business with. **2** take action to put something right. **3** cope with: *a way of helping people deal with loss.* **4** have something as a subject. **a good** (or

great) **deal 1** a large amount. **2** to a considerable extent: *a good deal better.* **a square deal** a fair bargain or treatment.
– ORIGIN Old English.

deal[2] noun fir or pine wood (as a building material).
– ORIGIN German and Dutch *dele* 'plank'.

dealer noun **1** a person who buys and sells goods. **2** a person who sells illegal drugs. **3** a player who deals cards in a card game.
– DERIVATIVES **dealership** noun.

dealt past participle of DEAL[1].

dean noun **1** the head of the governing body of a cathedral. **2** the head of a university faculty or department or of a medical school. **3** a college official who is responsible for the discipline and welfare of students.
– ORIGIN Old French *deien*.

deanery noun (pl. **deaneries**) the official house of a dean.

dear adjective **1** regarded with deep affection. **2** used in the polite introduction to a letter. **3** chiefly Brit. expensive. • noun **1** a lovable person. **2** used as an affectionate form of address. • adverb chiefly Brit. at a high cost. • exclamation used in expressions of surprise or dismay.
– ORIGIN Old English.

dearly adverb **1** very much. **2** at great cost.

dearth /derth/ noun a lack or inadequate amount of something: *a dearth of reliable information.*
– ORIGIN first meaning 'dearness and shortage of food': from DEAR.

death noun **1** the action or fact of dying. **2** an instance of a person or an animal dying. **3** the state of being dead. **4** the end of something: *the death of communism.*
– PHRASES **at death's door** so ill that one may die. **catch one's death (of cold)** informal catch a severe cold. **die a death** fail or come to an end. **do something to death** do something so often that it becomes boring. **like death warmed up** informal extremely tired or ill. **put someone to death** execute someone. **to death 1** until dead. **2** used for emphasis: *I'm sick to death of him.*
– DERIVATIVES **deathless** adjective.
– ORIGIN Old English.

deathbed noun the bed where someone is dying or has died.

death camp noun a prison camp in which many people die or are put to death.

death certificate noun an official statement, signed by a doctor, giving details of a person's death.

death duty noun former name for INHERITANCE TAX.

death knell noun an event that signals the end of something.
– ORIGIN from the ringing of a bell to mark a person's death.

deathly adjective (**deathlier**, **deathliest**) suggesting death: *a deathly silence.*

death mask noun a plaster cast of a person's face, made just after their death.

death penalty noun punishment by execution.

death rate noun the number of deaths per one thousand people per year.

death rattle noun a gurgling sound in a dying person's throat.

d

death row noun a prison block for those sentenced to death.

death toll noun the number of deaths resulting from a particular cause.

deathtrap noun a dangerous building, vehicle, etc.

death-watch beetle noun a beetle whose larvae bore into dead wood and timbers.
– ORIGIN so called because it makes a ticking sound, formerly believed to be an omen of death.

death wish noun an unconscious desire for one's own death.

deb noun informal a debutante.

debacle /day-**bah**-k'l/ noun a complete failure or disaster.
– ORIGIN French, from *débâcler* 'unleash'.

debag /dee-**bag**/ verb (**debags, debagging, debagged**) Brit. informal take the trousers off someone as a joke or punishment.

debar verb (**debars, debarring, debarred**) officially prohibit someone from doing something.
– ORIGIN Old French *desbarrer* 'unbar'.

debark verb leave a ship or aircraft.
– ORIGIN French *débarquer*.

debase /di-**bayss**/ verb lower the quality, value, or character of someone or something.
– DERIVATIVES debasement noun.

debatable adjective open to discussion or argument.

debate noun 1 a formal discussion in a public meeting or law-making body, in which opposing arguments are presented. 2 an argument. •verb 1 discuss or argue about something. 2 consider a course of action: *she debated whether or not to go for a swim.*
– PHRASES under debate being discussed.
– DERIVATIVES debater noun.
– ORIGIN Old French, from Latin *battere* 'to fight'.

debauched /di-**bawchd**/ adjective overindulging in sex, alcohol, or drugs.
– DERIVATIVES debauchery noun.
– ORIGIN from Old French *desbaucher* 'turn away from one's duty'.

debenture /di-**ben**-cher/ noun Brit. a certificate issued by a company acknowledging that it has borrowed money on which interest is being paid.
– ORIGIN Latin *debentur* 'are owing'.

debilitate /di-**bil**-i-tayt/ verb severely weaken someone or something.
– DERIVATIVES debilitation noun.
– ORIGIN from Latin *debilis* 'weak'.

debility noun (pl. **debilities**) physical weakness.

debit noun 1 an entry in an account recording a sum owed. 2 a payment made or owed. •verb (**debits, debiting, debited**) (of a bank) remove money from a customer's account.
– ORIGIN French, from Latin *debitum* 'something owed'.

debit card noun a card allowing the holder to remove money from a bank account electronically when making a purchase.

debonair adjective (of a man) confident, stylish, and charming.
– ORIGIN from Old French *de bon aire* 'of good disposition'.

debouch /di-**bowch**/ verb emerge from a confined space into a wide, open area.
– DERIVATIVES debouchment noun.
– ORIGIN French, from *bouche* 'mouth'.

debrief verb question someone in detail about a completed mission.
– DERIVATIVES debriefing noun.

debris /**deb**-ree/ noun 1 scattered pieces of rubbish or the remains of something that has been destroyed. 2 loose broken pieces of rock.
– ORIGIN French.

debt noun 1 a sum of money owed. 2 the state of owing money: *he got into debt.* 3 a feeling of gratitude for a favour or service.
– ORIGIN Latin *debitum* 'something owed'.

debt of honour noun a debt whose repayment is not legally binding but depends on a sense of moral obligation.

debtor noun a person who owes money.

debug verb (**debugs, debugging, debugged**) remove errors from computer hardware or software.
– DERIVATIVES debugger noun.

debunk verb show that a widely held belief or opinion is false or exaggerated.
– DERIVATIVES debunker noun.

deburr /dee-**ber**/ (also **debur**) verb (**deburrs, deburring, deburred**) smooth the rough edges of an object.

debut /**day**-byoo/ noun a person's first appearance or performance in a capacity or role. •adjective referring to the first recording or publication of a singer or writer: *her debut album.* •verb perform in public for the first time.
– ORIGIN from French *débuter* 'lead off'.

debutant /**deb**-yoo-ton(t)/ noun a person making a debut.

debutante /**deb**-yuh-tahnt/ noun a young upper-class woman making her first appearance in society.

Dec. abbreviation December.

decade /**dek**-ayd/ noun a period of ten years.
– ORIGIN Old French, from Greek *deka* 'ten'.

decadent adjective 1 having low moral standards and interested only in pleasure and enjoyment. 2 luxuriously self-indulgent: *a decadent soak in a scented bath.*
– DERIVATIVES decadence noun decadently adverb.
– ORIGIN French, from Latin *decadentia*.

decaffeinated /dee-**kaf**-fi-nay-tid/ adjective (of tea or coffee) having had most or all of its caffeine removed.

decagon /**dek**-uh-guhn/ noun a plane figure with ten straight sides and angles.

decahedron /dek-uh-**hee**-druhn/ noun (pl. **decahedra** or **decahedrons**) a solid figure with ten plane faces.

decal /**dee**-kal/ noun a design on prepared paper for transferring on to glass, porcelain, etc.
– ORIGIN abbreviation of *decalcomania*, from French *décalquer* 'transfer a tracing' + -*manie* '-mania'.

decalcified /dee-**kal**-si-fyd/ adjective (of rock or bone) containing a reduced quantity of calcium salts.
– DERIVATIVES decalcification noun.

decalitre noun a metric unit of capacity, equal to 10 litres.

Decalogue /dek-uh-log/ noun the Ten Commandments.
– ORIGIN from Greek *dekalogos biblos* 'book of the Ten Commandments'.

decametre (US **decameter**) noun a metric unit of length, equal to 10 metres.

decamp verb leave suddenly or secretly.

decant /di-kant/ verb 1 pour something from one container into another to separate liquid from sediment. 2 (of a vehicle) offload passengers.
– ORIGIN Latin *decanthare*.

decanter noun a glass container with a stopper into which wine or spirits are decanted.

decapitate /di-kap-i-tayt/ verb kill someone by cutting off their head.
– DERIVATIVES **decapitation** noun.
– ORIGIN Latin *decapitare*, from *caput* 'head'.

decapod /dek-uh-pod/ noun a crustacean with five pairs of walking legs, such as a shrimp.
– ORIGIN from Greek *deka* 'ten' + *pous* 'foot'.

decarbonize (or **decarbonise**) verb remove carbon deposits from an engine.

decathlon /di-kath-lon/ noun an athletic event in which each competitor takes part in the same ten events.
– DERIVATIVES **decathlete** noun.
– ORIGIN from Greek *deka* 'ten' + *athlon* 'contest'.

decay verb 1 rot as a result of the action of bacteria and fungi. 2 become progressively worse; deteriorate. 3 Physics (of a radioactive substance, particle, etc.) undergo change to a different form by emitting radiation. •noun 1 the state or process of decaying. 2 rotten matter or tissue.
– ORIGIN Old French *decair*.

decease noun formal or Law death.
– ORIGIN Latin *decessus*.

deceased formal or Law noun (**the deceased**) the recently dead person in question. •adjective recently dead.

deceit noun behaviour intended to make someone believe something that is not true.

deceitful adjective deliberately behaving in a way that makes others believe things that are not true.
– DERIVATIVES **deceitfully** adverb **deceitfulness** noun.

deceive verb 1 deliberately make someone believe something that is not true. 2 (of a thing) give a mistaken impression: *don't be deceived by the book's title.*
– DERIVATIVES **deceiver** noun.
– ORIGIN Old French *deceivre*.

decelerate /dee-sel-uh-rayt/ verb begin to move more slowly.
– DERIVATIVES **deceleration** noun.

December noun the twelfth month of the year.
– ORIGIN Latin, from *decem* 'ten' (being originally the tenth month of the Roman year).

decency noun (pl. **decencies**) 1 behaviour that follows generally accepted standards of morality or respectability. 2 (**decencies**) standards of acceptable behaviour.

decennial /di-sen-ni-uhl/ adjective lasting for or happening every ten years.
– ORIGIN from Latin *decem* 'ten' + *annus* 'year'.

decent adjective 1 following generally accepted standards of morality or respectability. 2 of an acceptable standard. 3 Brit. informal kind or generous.
– DERIVATIVES **decently** adverb.
– ORIGIN from Latin *decere* 'to be fit'.

decentralize (or **decentralise**) verb transfer authority from central to local government.
– DERIVATIVES **decentralization** noun.

deception noun 1 the action of deceiving someone. 2 a thing that deceives others into believing something that is not true.

deceptive adjective giving an impression different from the true one; misleading.

deceptively adverb 1 to a lesser extent than appears the case. 2 to a greater extent than appears the case.

USAGE: **Deceptively** can mean both one thing and also its complete opposite. A *deceptively smooth surface* is one which appears smooth but in fact is not smooth at all, while a *deceptively spacious room* is one that does not look spacious but is in fact **more** spacious than it appears. To avoid confusion, it is often better to reword a sentence rather than use **deceptively**.

deci- combining form one tenth: *decilitre*.
– ORIGIN from Latin *decimus* 'tenth'.

decibel /dess-i-bel/ noun a unit of measurement expressing the intensity of a sound or the power of an electrical signal.
– ORIGIN from **DECI-** + *bel*, a unit (= 10 decibels) named after Alexander Graham *Bell*, inventor of the telephone.

decide verb 1 consider something carefully and make a judgement or choice: *she decided to stay at home.* 2 settle an issue or contest: *the match was decided by a penalty shoot-out.* 3 give a judgement concerning a legal case.
– DERIVATIVES **decidable** adjective **deciding** adjective.
– ORIGIN Latin *decidere* 'determine'.

decided adjective definite; clear: *a decided improvement.*
– DERIVATIVES **decidedly** adverb.

decider noun a contest that settles the winner of a series of contests.

deciduous /di-sid-yoo-uhss/ adjective 1 (of a tree or shrub) shedding its leaves annually. Contrasted with **EVERGREEN**. 2 (of teeth or horns) shed after a time.
– ORIGIN Latin *deciduus*.

decilitre (US **deciliter**) noun a metric unit of capacity, equal to one tenth of a litre.

decimal adjective relating to a system of numbers based on the number ten. •noun a fractional number in the decimal system, written with figures either side of a decimal point.
– ORIGIN from Latin *decimus* 'tenth'.

decimalize (or **decimalise**) verb convert a system of coinage or weights and measures to a decimal system.
– DERIVATIVES **decimalization** noun.

decimal place noun the position of a digit to the right of a decimal point.

d

decimal point noun a full point placed after the figure representing units in a decimal fraction.

decimate /**dess**-i-mayt/ verb 1 kill or destroy a large proportion of a group. 2 drastically reduce the strength of something.
– DERIVATIVES **decimation** noun.
– ORIGIN Latin *decimare* 'take as a tenth'.

USAGE: The earliest sense of **decimate** was 'kill one in every ten of a group', a reference to the ancient Roman practice of killing one in every ten of a group of soldiers as a collective punishment. This has been more or less totally superseded by the sense 'kill or destroy a large proportion of a group', although some people argue that this later sense is wrong.

decimetre (US **decimeter**) noun a metric unit of length, equal to one tenth of a metre.

decipher /di-**sy**-fer/ verb 1 convert something written in code into normal language. 2 succeed in understanding or interpreting something: *his handwriting was difficult to decipher.*
– DERIVATIVES **decipherable** adjective **decipherment** noun.

decision noun 1 a choice or judgement made after considering something. 2 the action or process of deciding. 3 decisiveness.

decisive adjective 1 having great importance for the final result of a situation: *a decisive battle.* 2 able to make decisions quickly.
– DERIVATIVES **decisively** adverb **decisiveness** noun.

deck noun 1 a floor of a ship, especially the upper level. 2 a floor or platform, as in a bus or car park. 3 chiefly N. Amer. a pack of cards. 4 a component in sound-reproduction equipment, incorporating a player or recorder for discs or tapes. • verb 1 decorate or dress someone or something brightly or attractively: *the Morris dancers were decked out in rustic costume.* 2 informal knock someone to the ground with a punch.
– PHRASES **hit the deck** informal fall to the ground.
– DERIVATIVES **decked** adjective.
– ORIGIN Dutch *dec* 'covering, roof'.

deckchair noun a folding chair with a wooden frame and a canvas seat.

deckhand noun a member of a ship's crew performing cleaning or manual work.

decking noun material used in making a deck.

deckle /**dek**-uhl/ noun a continuous belt on either side in a paper-making machine, used for controlling the size of paper produced.
– ORIGIN German, 'small covering'.

deckle edge noun the rough uncut edge of a sheet of paper.

declaim verb speak or recite something in an emphatic or dramatic way.
– DERIVATIVES **declamatory** adjective.
– ORIGIN Latin *declamare*.

declamation noun the action of declaiming something.

declaration noun 1 a formal statement or announcement. 2 an act of declaring something.

declarative /di-**kla**-ruh-tiv/ adjective 1 making a declaration: *a declarative statement.* 2 (of a

sentence or phrase) taking the form of a simple statement.

declare verb 1 announce something solemnly or officially. 2 (**declare oneself**) reveal one's intentions or identity. 3 (as adj. **declared**) having stated something openly: *a declared atheist.* 4 acknowledge that one has income or goods on which tax or duty should be paid. 5 Cricket close an innings voluntarily with wickets remaining.
– ORIGIN Latin *declarare*, from *clarare* 'make clear'.

déclassé /day-**klas**-say/ (also **déclassée**) adjective having fallen in social status.
– ORIGIN French.

declassify verb (**declassifies, declassifying, declassified**) officially declare information or documents to be no longer secret.
– DERIVATIVES **declassification** noun.

declension /di-**klen**-sh'n/ noun the changes in the form of a noun, pronoun, or adjective that identify its grammatical case, number, and gender.
– ORIGIN from Old French *decliner* 'to decline'.

declination /dek-li-**nay**-sh'n/ noun 1 Astronomy the position of a point in the sky equivalent to latitude on the earth. 2 the angular deviation of a compass needle from true north.

decline verb 1 become smaller, weaker, or worse: *the breeding population has declined in recent years.* 2 politely refuse to accept or do something: *he declined to comment on the rumours.* 3 (especially of the sun) move downwards. 4 Grammar form a noun, pronoun, or adjective according to case, number, and gender. • noun a gradual and continuous loss of strength, numbers, or value.
– ORIGIN Latin *declinare* 'bend down, turn aside'.

declivity /di-**kliv**-i-ti/ noun (pl. **declivities**) a downward slope.
– ORIGIN Latin *declivitas*.

declutch verb disengage the clutch of a motor vehicle.

decoction noun a concentrated liquid produced by heating or boiling a substance.
– ORIGIN Latin.

decode verb 1 convert a coded message into intelligible language. 2 convert audio or video signals from analogue to digital.
– DERIVATIVES **decoder** noun.

décolletage /day-kol-i-**tahzh**/ noun 1 a low neckline on a woman's dress or top. 2 a woman's cleavage or breasts as revealed by such a neckline.
– ORIGIN French, from *décolleter* 'expose the neck'.

décolleté /day-**kol**-tay/ adjective having a low neckline. • noun a décolletage.
– ORIGIN French.

decolonize (or **decolonise**) verb withdraw from a colony, leaving it independent.
– DERIVATIVES **decolonization** noun.

decommission verb 1 take a ship out of service. 2 dismantle a nuclear reactor or weapon and make it safe.

decompose verb 1 (of organic matter) decay. 2 (of a substance) break down into its

component elements.
– DERIVATIVES **decomposition** noun.

decompress /dee-kuhm-**press**/ verb **1** expand compressed computer data to its normal size. **2** reduce the air pressure on a person who has been experiencing high pressure while deep-sea diving.
– DERIVATIVES **decompressor** noun.

decompression noun **1** reduction in air pressure. **2** a gradual reduction of air pressure on a person who has been experiencing high pressure while deep-sea diving. **3** the process of decompressing computer data.

decompression chamber noun a small room in which the air pressure can be varied, used to allow deep-sea divers to adjust to normal air pressure.

decompression sickness noun a serious condition that results when too rapid decompression causes nitrogen bubbles to form in the tissues of the body.

decongestant /dee-kuhn-**jess**-tuhnt/ noun a medicine taken to relieve a blocked nose.

deconsecrate verb officially declare that a building is no longer holy or sacred.
– DERIVATIVES **deconsecration** noun.

deconstruct /dee-kuhn-**strukt**/ verb **1** analyse something by the method of deconstruction. **2** reduce something to its constituent parts in order to reinterpret it.
– DERIVATIVES **deconstructive** adjective.

deconstruction noun a method of literary and cultural analysis which states that something has many different meanings and emphasizes the role of the subject in the production of meaning.
– DERIVATIVES **deconstructionism** noun **deconstructionist** adjective & noun.

decontaminate verb remove dangerous substances from an area or object.
– DERIVATIVES **decontamination** noun.

decontextualize (or **decontextualise**) verb consider something separately from its context.
– DERIVATIVES **decontextualization** noun.

decor /**day**-kor, **dek**-or/ noun the furnishing and decoration of a room.
– ORIGIN French.

decorate verb **1** make something more attractive by putting extra items in or on it: *the square was decorated with coloured lights.* **2** chiefly Brit. apply paint or wallpaper to the walls of a room, building, etc. **3** give an award or medal to someone. **4** (as adj. **Decorated**) referring to a stage of English Gothic church architecture of the 14th century which featured elaborate tracery.
– ORIGIN Latin *decorare* 'embellish'.

decoration noun **1** the process or art of decorating something. **2** an object or pattern that makes something look more attractive. **3** the way in which something is decorated. **4** a medal or award conferred as an honour.

decorative /**dek**-uh-ruh-tiv/ adjective **1** making something look more attractive: *decorative motifs.* **2** relating to decoration.
– DERIVATIVES **decoratively** adverb.

decorator noun a person who decorates, in particular (Brit.) a person whose job is to paint interior walls or hang wallpaper.

decorous /**dek**-uh-ruhss/ adjective in keeping with good taste; polite and restrained.
– DERIVATIVES **decorously** adverb **decorousness** noun.
– ORIGIN Latin *decorus* 'seemly'.

decorum /di-**kor**-uhm/ noun polite and socially acceptable behaviour.
– ORIGIN Latin, 'seemly thing'.

découpage /day-koo-**pahzh**, dek-oo-pahzh/ noun the decoration of a surface with paper cut-outs.
– ORIGIN French, from *découper* 'cut out'.

decouple verb separate or disengage one thing from another.

decoy noun /**dee**-koy/ **1** a real or imitation bird or mammal used by hunters to lure game. **2** a person or thing used to mislead someone or lure them into a trap. •verb /di-**koy**/ lure a person or animal by means of a decoy.
– ORIGIN from Dutch *de kooi* 'the decoy', from Latin *cavea* 'cage'.

decrease verb /di-**kreess**/ make or become smaller or fewer in size, amount, or strength. •noun /**dee**-kreess/ **1** an instance of decreasing. **2** the process of decreasing.
– ORIGIN Latin *decrescere*.

decree noun **1** an official order from a ruler or government that has the force of law. **2** a judgement or decision made by certain law courts. •verb (**decrees, decreeing, decreed**) order something by decree.
– ORIGIN Latin *decretum* 'something decided'.

decree absolute noun (pl. **decrees absolute**) English Law a final order by a court of law which officially ends a marriage.

decree nisi /**ny**-sy/ noun (pl. **decrees nisi**) English Law an order by a court of law that states the date on which a marriage will end, unless a good reason not to grant a divorce is produced.
– ORIGIN Latin *nisi* 'unless'.

decrepit /di-**krep**-it/ adjective **1** worn out or ruined because of age or neglect. **2** elderly and infirm.
– DERIVATIVES **decrepitude** noun.
– ORIGIN Latin *decrepitus*, from *crepare* 'rattle, creak'.

decriminalize (or **decriminalise**) verb change the law so that something is no longer illegal or a criminal offence.
– DERIVATIVES **decriminalization** noun.

decry /di-**kry**/ verb (**decries, decrying, decried**) express strong public disapproval of something.
– ORIGIN French *décrier* 'cry down'.

decrypt /dee-**kript**/ verb make a coded or unclear message intelligible.
– DERIVATIVES **decryption** noun.

dedicate verb **1** devote time or effort to a particular task, activity, or purpose: *Joan has dedicated her life to animals.* **2** address a book to a person as a sign of respect or affection. **3** hold an official ceremony to mark the fact that something has been built to honour a particular deity, saint, etc.: *the temple is dedicated to Krishna.*
– DERIVATIVES **dedicatee** noun **dedicator** noun **dedicatory** adjective.
– ORIGIN Latin *dedicare* 'devote or consecrate'.

d

dedicated adjective **1** devoting much time or effort to a particular task, activity, or purpose: *a dedicated musician.* **2** used or designed for one particular purpose only: *a dedicated high-speed rail link.*

dedication noun **1** the quality of devoting much time or effort to a particular task, activity, or purpose. **2** the action of dedicating a church or other building to a particular deity or saint. **3** the words with which a book is dedicated to someone.

deduce verb form an opinion or conclusion on the basis of the information or evidence available.
– DERIVATIVES **deducible** adjective.
– ORIGIN Latin *deducere* 'to take or lead away'.

deduct verb subtract an amount from a total: *the tax is deducted from your earnings.*
– ORIGIN Latin *deducere* 'to take or lead away'.

deductible adjective able to be deducted, especially from taxable income.
– DERIVATIVES **deductibility** noun.

deduction noun **1** the action of deducting an amount from a total. **2** an amount that is or may be deducted. **3** a method of reasoning in which a general rule or principle is used to draw a particular conclusion.
– DERIVATIVES **deductive** adjective.

deed noun **1** an action that is performed deliberately. **2** (usu. **deeds**) a legal document that is signed and delivered, especially one relating to property ownership or legal rights.
– ORIGIN Old English.

deed of covenant noun Brit. an agreement to pay a regular amount of money, particularly when this enables the recipient to reclaim any tax paid by the donor on the amount.

deed poll noun English Law a legal deed made and carried out by one party only, especially to formalize a change of a person's name.

deejay noun informal a disc jockey.

deem verb formal regard or consider something in a particular way: *the event was deemed a great success.*
– ORIGIN Old English.

deep adjective **1** extending far down or in from the top or surface. **2** extending a particular distance from the top, surface, or outer edge. **3** (of sound) low in pitch and full in tone. **4** (of colour) dark: *a deep blue.* **5** very intense or extreme: *a deep sleep.* **6** difficult to understand. **7** (in ball games) far down or across the field. • noun **1** (**the deep**) literary the sea. **2** (usu. **deeps**) a deep part of the sea. • adverb far down or in; deeply.
– PHRASES **go off the deep end** informal give way suddenly to an outburst of emotion. **in deep water** informal in trouble or difficulty. **jump** (or **be thrown**) **in at the deep end** informal face a difficult situation without much experience.
– DERIVATIVES **deepness** noun.
– ORIGIN Old English.

deep-dyed adjective informal complete: *a deep-dyed conservative.*

deepen verb make or become deeper.

deep freeze noun (also **deep freezer**) a freezer. • verb (**deep-freeze**) freeze or store food in a deep freeze.

deep-fry verb fry food in enough fat or oil to cover it completely.

deeply adverb **1** far down or in. **2** intensely.

deep-seated (also **deep-rooted**) adjective firmly established.

deep space noun outer space.

deep-vein thrombosis noun thrombosis in a vein lying deep below the skin, especially in the legs.

deer noun (pl. same) a hoofed animal, the male of which usually has antlers.
– ORIGIN Old English.

deerskin noun leather made from the skin of a deer.

deerstalker noun a soft cloth cap, originally worn for hunting, with ear flaps which can be tied together over the top.

de-escalate verb reduce the intensity of a conflict or crisis.
– DERIVATIVES **de-escalation** noun.

deface verb deliberately spoil the appearance of something.
– DERIVATIVES **defacement** noun.

de facto /day **fak**-toh/ adverb existing in fact, whether legally recognized or not. Compare with **DE JURE**. • adjective existing in fact but not necessarily legally recognized: *a de facto one-party system.*
– ORIGIN Latin, 'of fact'.

defalcation /dee-fal-**kay**-sh'n/ verb formal the stealing or misuse of funds placed in one's trust or under one's control.
– ORIGIN from Latin *defalcare* 'to lop'.

defame verb say or write something that damages the reputation of someone or something.
– DERIVATIVES **defamation** noun **defamatory** adjective.
– ORIGIN Latin *diffamare* 'spread evil report'.

default noun **1** failure to fulfil an obligation, especially to repay a loan or appear in a law court. **2** a previously selected option adopted by a computer program or other mechanism when no alternative is specified. • verb **1** fail to fulfil an obligation, especially to repay a loan or to appear in court. **2** (**default to**) go back automatically to a previously selected option.
– PHRASES **by default** because of a lack of opposition or positive action. **in default of** in the absence of.
– DERIVATIVES **defaulter** noun.
– ORIGIN from Old French *defaillir* 'to fail'.

defeat verb **1** win a victory over a person, team, army, etc. **2** prevent someone from achieving an aim or prevent an aim from being achieved. **3** reject or block a proposal or motion. • noun an instance of defeating someone or something or the state of being defeated.
– ORIGIN Old French *desfaire*.

defeatist noun a person who gives in to failure too readily or who expects to fail. • adjective accepting failure too readily; expecting to fail.
– DERIVATIVES **defeatism** noun.

defecate /**def**-uh-kayt/ verb expel waste matter from the bowels.
– DERIVATIVES **defecation** noun.
– ORIGIN Latin *defaecare*.

defect[1] /**dee**-fekt/ noun a fault or imperfection.
– ORIGIN Latin *defectus*.

defect[2] /di-**fekt**/ verb abandon one's country or

cause in favour of an opposing one.
- DERIVATIVES **defection** noun **defector** noun.
- ORIGIN Latin *deficere*.

defective adjective imperfect or faulty.
- DERIVATIVES **defectively** adverb **defectiveness** noun.

defence (US **defense**) noun **1** the action of defending something against attack. **2** military measures or resources for protecting a country. **3** (**defences**) fortifications against attack. **4** the attempted justification of something: *the government's defence of the police action.* **5** the case presented by or on behalf of the party being accused or sued in a lawsuit. **6** (**the defence**) the counsel for the defendant in a lawsuit. **7** (in sport) the action of defending one's goal or wicket, or the players in a team who perform this role.

defenceless (US **defenseless**) adjective without defence or protection; completely vulnerable.

defend verb **1** protect someone or something from harm or danger. **2** act as the lawyer for the party being accused or sued in a lawsuit. **3** attempt to justify: *he defended his decision to sack the strikers.* **4** compete to hold on to a title or seat in a contest or election. **5** (in sport) protect one's goal or wicket rather than attempt to score against one's opponents.
- DERIVATIVES **defendable** adjective **defender** noun.
- ORIGIN Latin *defendere*.

defendant noun a person sued or accused in a court of law. Compare with PLAINTIFF.

defenestration /dee-fe-ni-stray-sh'n/ noun formal or humorous the action of throwing someone out of a window.
- DERIVATIVES **defenestrate** verb.
- ORIGIN Latin, from *fenestra* 'window'.

defensible adjective **1** able to be justified by reasoning or argument. **2** able to be defended or protected.

defensive adjective **1** used or intended to defend or protect: *troops in defensive positions.* **2** very anxious to defend oneself against or avoid criticism.
- PHRASES **on the defensive** expecting or resisting criticism or attack.
- DERIVATIVES **defensively** adverb **defensiveness** noun.

defer[1] /di-fer/ verb (**defers, deferring, deferred**) put something off until a later time.
- DERIVATIVES **deferment** noun **deferral** noun.
- ORIGIN Latin *differre*.

defer[2] /di-fer/ verb (**defers, deferring, deferred**) (**defer to**) give in to or agree to accept: *he deferred to Tim's superior knowledge.*
- ORIGIN Latin *deferre* 'carry away, refer'.

deference /def-uh-ruhnss/ noun polite respect shown towards someone or something.

deferential adjective showing polite respect.
- DERIVATIVES **deferentially** adverb.

defiance noun open refusal to obey someone or something.
- ORIGIN Old French.

defiant adjective openly refusing to obey someone or something.
- DERIVATIVES **defiantly** adverb.

defibrillation /dee-fi-bri-lay-shuhn/ noun

Medicine the administration of a controlled electric shock to the heart to stop fibrillation of the muscles and allow the normal rhythm to be resumed.
- DERIVATIVES **defibrillate** verb **defibrillator** noun.

deficiency noun (pl. **deficiencies**) **1** a lack or shortage of something. **2** a failing or shortcoming.

deficiency disease noun a disease caused by the lack of some essential element in the diet, usually a particular vitamin or mineral.

deficient /di-fi-sh'nt/ adjective **1** not having enough of a particular quality or ingredient: *a diet deficient in vitamin A.* **2** inadequate in amount or quality: *the documentary evidence is deficient.*
- ORIGIN Latin, from *deficere* 'fail'.

deficit /def-i-sit/ noun **1** the amount by which something, especially a sum of money, falls short. **2** an excess of money spent over money earned.
- ORIGIN Latin, 'it is lacking'.

defile[1] /di-fyl/ verb **1** make something dirty or polluted. **2** treat something holy with a lack of respect.
- DERIVATIVES **defilement** noun **defiler** noun.
- ORIGIN Old French *defouler* 'trample down'.

defile[2] /dee-fyl/ noun a steep-sided narrow gorge or passage (originally one requiring troops to march in single file).
- ORIGIN French, from *file* 'column, file'.

define verb **1** state or describe the exact nature or scope of: *the contract will seek to define the client's obligations.* **2** give the meaning of a word or phrase. **3** mark out the limits or outline of something.
- DERIVATIVES **definable** adjective.
- ORIGIN Latin *definire*.

definite adjective **1** clearly stated or decided; not vague or doubtful: *a definite answer.* **2** known to be true or real: *we have no definite proof.* **3** (of a person) certain about something. **4** having exact and measurable physical limits.
- DERIVATIVES **definiteness** noun.

definite article noun Grammar the word *the*.

definitely adverb without doubt; certainly.

definition noun **1** a statement of the exact meaning of a word or the nature or scope of something. **2** the action of defining something. **3** the degree of sharpness in outline of an object or image.
- PHRASES **by definition** by its very nature.
- DERIVATIVES **definitional** adjective.

definitive adjective **1** (of a conclusion or agreement) final and not able to be changed. **2** (of a book or other text) the most accurate and trusted of its kind.
- DERIVATIVES **definitively** adverb.

deflate verb **1** let air or gas out of a tyre, balloon, etc. **2** make someone feel suddenly gloomy or discouraged. **3** reduce price levels in an economy.
- DERIVATIVES **deflator** noun.

deflation noun **1** the action or process of deflating or being deflated. **2** reduction of the general level of prices in an economy.
- DERIVATIVES **deflationary** adjective.

deflect verb **1** turn aside from a straight

course. **2** prevent something undesirable from being aimed at one: *the prime minister has sought to deflect criticism over the issue.* **3** prevent someone from following an intended course of action.
– DERIVATIVES **deflection** noun **deflective** adjective **deflector** noun.
– ORIGIN Latin *deflectere.*

deflower verb dated or literary have sex with a woman who is a virgin.

defoliant noun a chemical used to remove the leaves from trees and plants.

defoliate /dee-foh-li-ayt/ verb remove leaves from trees or plants.
– DERIVATIVES **defoliation** noun.
– ORIGIN Latin *defoliare.*

deforest verb clear an area of forest or trees.
– DERIVATIVES **deforestation** noun.

deform verb change or spoil the usual shape of someone or something.
– DERIVATIVES **deformable** adjective **deformation** noun **deformed** adjective.

deformity noun (pl. **deformities**) **1** a deformed part, especially of the body. **2** the state of being deformed.

DEFRA abbreviation (in the UK) Department for Environment, Food, and Rural Affairs.

defraud verb illegally obtain money from someone by deception.
– ORIGIN Latin *defraudare.*

defray verb provide money to pay a cost.
– ORIGIN French *défrayer.*

defrock verb officially remove a member of the Christian clergy from their job because of wrongdoing.

defrost verb **1** free a freezer or refrigerator of ice. **2** thaw frozen food.

deft adjective **1** quick and neatly skilful: *deft athletic moves.* **2** showing cleverness and skill: *a deft comedy.*
– DERIVATIVES **deftly** adverb **deftness** noun.
– ORIGIN from **DAFT**, in the former sense 'meek'.

defunct /di-fungkt/ adjective no longer existing or functioning.
– ORIGIN Latin *defunctus* 'dead'.

defuse /dee-fyooz/ verb **1** make a situation less tense or dangerous. **2** remove the fuse from an explosive device so as to prevent it from exploding.

> **USAGE: Defuse** and **diffuse** are often confused. **Defuse** means 'make a situation less tense or dangerous' (*talks were held to defuse the crisis*), while **diffuse** means 'spread over a wide area' (*this early language probably diffused across the world*).

defy verb (**defies, defying, defied**) **1** openly resist or refuse to obey someone or something. **2** be of such a kind that something is almost impossible: *his actions defy belief.* **3** challenge someone to do or prove something.
– DERIVATIVES **defier** noun.
– ORIGIN Old French *desfier.*

dégagé /day-gah-zhay, day-ga-zhay/ adjective literary not concerned with or involved in something.
– ORIGIN French, 'set free'.

degenerate verb /di-jen-uh-rayt/ become worse; deteriorate: *the meeting threatened to degenerate into a brawl.* ● adjective /di-jen-uh-ruht/ having very low moral standards. ● noun /di-jen-uh-ruht/ a person with very low moral standards.
– DERIVATIVES **degeneracy** noun **degeneration** noun.
– ORIGIN Latin *degeneratus* 'no longer of its kind'.

degenerative adjective (of a disease) becoming progressively worse, with loss of function in the organs or tissues.

deglaze verb add liquid to the cooking juices and meat sediments in a pan to make a gravy or sauce.

degradation /deg-ruh-day-sh'n/ noun **1** the state of being degraded or humiliated. **2** the process of being broken down or made worse.

degrade verb **1** cause someone to suffer a loss of dignity or self-respect: *viewers want to see reality TV that degrades participants.* **2** lower the quality of something. **3** cause something to break down or deteriorate chemically.
– DERIVATIVES **degradable** adjective **degradative** adjective.

degrading adjective causing a loss of self-respect; humiliating.

degree noun **1** the amount, level, or extent to which something happens or is present: *a degree of caution is wise.* **2** a unit of measurement of angles, equivalent to one ninetieth of a right angle. **3** a unit in a scale of temperature, intensity, hardness, etc. **4** an academic rank awarded by a college or university after examination or completion of a course. **5** a step in direct genealogical descent. **6** old use social or official rank.
– PHRASES **by degrees** gradually. **to a degree** to some extent.
– ORIGIN Old French.

de haut en bas /duh oht on bah/ adverb & adjective in a patronizing or superior way.
– ORIGIN French, 'from above to below'.

dehisce /di-hiss/ verb technical (especially of a seed case) gape or burst open.
– DERIVATIVES **dehiscence** noun **dehiscent** adjective.
– ORIGIN Latin *dehiscere.*

dehumanize (or **dehumanise**) verb deprive someone of good human qualities such as compassion or kindness.
– DERIVATIVES **dehumanization** noun.

dehumidify verb (**dehumidifies, dehumidifying, dehumidified**) remove moisture from the air or a gas.
– DERIVATIVES **dehumidification** noun **dehumidifier** noun.

dehydrate /dee-hy-drayt/ verb **1** cause someone to lose a large amount of water from their body. **2** remove water from food in order to preserve it.
– DERIVATIVES **dehydration** noun.
– ORIGIN from Greek *hudros* 'water'.

de-ice verb remove ice from something.
– DERIVATIVES **de-icer** noun.

deify /day-i-fy/ verb (**deifies, deifying, deified**) worship or treat someone as a god.
– DERIVATIVES **deification** noun.
– ORIGIN Latin *deificare.*

deign /dayn/ verb do something that one

considers to be beneath one's dignity: *celebrities often don't deign to talk to the masses.*
– ORIGIN Latin *dignare* 'deem worthy'.

deindustrialization (or **deindustrialisation**) noun the reduction of industrial activity in a region or economy.

deism /day-i-z'm, dee-i-z'm/ noun belief in the existence of an all-powerful creator who does not intervene in the universe. Compare with **THEISM**.
– DERIVATIVES **deist** noun **deistic** adjective.

deity /day-i-ti, dee-i-ti/ noun (pl. **deities**) 1 a god or goddess. 2 the state or quality of being a god or goddess.
– ORIGIN Latin *deitas*.

déjà vu /day-zhah voo/ noun a feeling of having already experienced the present situation.
– ORIGIN French, 'already seen'.

dejected adjective sad and dispirited.
– DERIVATIVES **dejectedly** adverb.

dejection noun sadness or low sprits.
– ORIGIN from Latin *deicere* 'throw down'.

de jure /day joo-ray/ adverb according to rightful entitlement; by right. Often contrasted with **DE FACTO**. • adjective existing by legal right; rightful.
– ORIGIN Latin, 'of law'.

dekko /dek-oh/ noun Brit. informal a quick look or glance.
– ORIGIN Hindi, 'look!'

delay verb 1 make or be late or slow. 2 put off to a later time; postpone: *ministers agreed to delay their decision.* • noun 1 a period of time by which someone or something is delayed. 2 the action of delaying someone or something.
– ORIGIN Old French *delayer*.

delectable adjective delicious or delightful.
– DERIVATIVES **delectably** adverb.

delectation /dee-lek-**tay**-sh'n/ noun formal, chiefly humorous pleasure and delight.
– ORIGIN from Latin *delectare* 'to charm'.

delegacy /del-i-guh-si/ noun (pl. **delegacies**) a group of delegates; a committee or delegation.

delegate noun /del-i-guht/ 1 a person sent to represent others, in particular at a conference. 2 a member of a committee. • verb /del-i-gayt/ 1 give a task or responsibility to a less senior person. 2 authorize someone to act as a representative.
– DERIVATIVES **delegator** noun.
– ORIGIN from Latin *delegare* 'send away, assign'.

delegation noun 1 a group of delegates or representatives. 2 the action of giving one's work or responsibilities to someone else.

delete verb 1 remove or cross out written or printed matter. 2 remove data from a computer's memory.
– DERIVATIVES **deletion** noun.
– ORIGIN Latin *delere* 'blot out'.

deleterious /del-i-teer-i-uhss/ adjective formal causing harm or damage.
– ORIGIN Greek *dēlētērios* 'harmful'.

delft /delft/ noun glazed earthenware, typically with blue decoration on a white background.
– ORIGIN named after the town of *Delft* in the Netherlands.

deli noun (pl. **delis**) informal a delicatessen.

deliberate adjective /di-lib-uh-ruht/ 1 done on purpose; intentional. 2 careful and unhurried: *a conscientious and deliberate worker.* • verb /di-lib-uh-rayt/ consider carefully and for a long time: *I deliberated over the menu.*
– DERIVATIVES **deliberately** adverb **deliberateness** noun.
– ORIGIN Latin *deliberare* 'consider carefully'.

deliberation noun 1 long and careful consideration. 2 carefulness and lack of haste.

deliberative adjective relating to consideration or discussion.

delicacy noun (pl. **delicacies**) 1 fineness or intricacy: *the delicacy of the palace's architecture.* 2 lack of robustness; fragility. 3 discretion and tact. 4 a delicious or expensive food.

delicate adjective 1 very fine or intricate in texture or structure: *a delicate lace shawl.* 2 easily broken or damaged; fragile. 3 tending to become ill easily. 4 requiring or showing tact, sensitivity, or skill: *a delicate issue.* 5 (of a colour or flavour) subtle and pleasant.
– DERIVATIVES **delicately** adverb.
– ORIGIN Latin *delicatus* 'delightful, charming'.

delicatessen /de-li-kuh-tess-uhn/ noun a shop selling cooked meats, cheeses, and unusual or foreign prepared foods.
– ORIGIN German or Dutch.

delicious adjective 1 very pleasant to the taste. 2 giving great pleasure; delightful: *a delicious irony.*
– DERIVATIVES **deliciously** adverb **deliciousness** noun.
– ORIGIN from Latin *deliciae* 'delight, pleasure'.

delight verb 1 please someone greatly. 2 (delight in) take great pleasure in doing something. • noun 1 great pleasure. 2 a cause of great pleasure: *the illustrations are a delight.*
– ORIGIN Latin *delectare* 'to charm'.

delighted adjective feeling or showing great pleasure.
– DERIVATIVES **delightedly** adverb.

delightful adjective causing delight; very pleasing.
– DERIVATIVES **delightfully** adverb.

delimit /di-lim-it/ verb (**delimits, delimiting, delimited**) determine the limits or boundaries of something.
– DERIVATIVES **delimitation** noun **delimiter** noun.

delineate /di-lin-i-ayt/ verb describe or indicate something precisely.
– DERIVATIVES **delineation** noun.
– ORIGIN Latin *delineare* 'to outline'.

delinquency noun (pl. **delinquencies**) 1 minor crime, especially that committed by young people. 2 formal neglect of one's duty.

delinquent /di-ling-kwuhnt/ adjective 1 (especially of young people) tending to commit crime. 2 formal failing in one's duty. • noun a person who tends to commit crime.
– ORIGIN from Latin *delinquere* 'to offend'.

deliquescent /del-i-kwess-uhnt/ adjective technical or literary becoming or having a tendency to become liquid.
– DERIVATIVES **deliquescence** noun **deliquesce** verb.
– ORIGIN Latin *deliquescere* 'dissolve'.

delirious adjective 1 in a very disturbed mental

d

state; affected by delirium. **2** very excited or happy.
– DERIVATIVES **deliriously** adverb.

delirium /di-**li**-ri-uhm/ noun a highly disturbed state of mind characterized by restlessness, illusions, and incoherent thought and speech.
– ORIGIN Latin.

delirium tremens /di-li-ri-uhm **tree**-menz/ noun a condition in which alcoholics who are trying to give up alcohol experience tremors and hallucinations.
– ORIGIN Latin, 'trembling delirium'.

deliver verb **1** bring and hand over something to the person who is to receive it. **2** provide something promised or expected: *the complex delivers all the usual attractions.* **3** state or present in a formal way: *he delivered a lecture on endangered species.* **4** launch or aim a blow or attack. **5** save or set someone free from something. **6** assist in the birth of a baby. **7** (also **be delivered of**) give birth to a baby.
– PHRASES **deliver the goods** informal provide what is promised or expected.
– DERIVATIVES **deliverable** adjective **deliverer** noun.
– ORIGIN Old French *delivrer.*

deliverance noun **1** the action of being rescued or set free. **2** a formal or authoritative statement.

delivery noun (pl. **deliveries**) **1** the action of delivering something. **2** the process of giving birth. **3** an act of throwing or bowling a ball, especially a cricket ball. **4** the way or style of giving a speech: *her delivery was stilted.*

dell noun literary a small valley.
– ORIGIN Old English.

Delphic /**del**-fik/ adjective deliberately ambiguous or hard to understand: *Delphic utterances.*
– ORIGIN from the ancient Greek oracle at *Delphi.*

delphinium /del-**fin**-i-uhm/ noun (pl. **delphiniums**) a garden plant having tall spikes of blue flowers.
– ORIGIN Greek *delphinion* 'larkspur'.

delta noun **1** a triangular area of land at the mouth of a river where it splits into several channels. **2** the fourth letter of the Greek alphabet (Δ, δ), transliterated as 'd'.

delta wing noun a single triangular swept-back wing on some aircraft.

deltoid /**del**-toid/ noun (also **deltoid muscle**) a thick triangular muscle covering the shoulder joint. • adjective technical triangular.
– ORIGIN Greek *deltoeidēs.*

delude /di-**lood**/ verb persuade someone to believe something that is not true.
– DERIVATIVES **deluded** adjective.
– ORIGIN Latin *deludere* 'to mock'.

deluge /**del**-yooj/ noun **1** a severe flood or very heavy fall of rain. **2** a great quantity of something arriving at the same time: *a deluge of angry letters.* • verb **1** overwhelm with a great quantity of something: *they've been deluged with unwanted emails.* **2** flood a place.
– ORIGIN Old French.

delusion noun a false belief or impression about oneself or one's situation: *I must get over this delusion that I know how to type.*
– DERIVATIVES **delusional** adjective **delusive**

adjective **delusory** adjective.

de luxe /di **luks**/ adjective of a higher quality and more expensive than usual.
– ORIGIN French, 'of luxury'.

delve verb **1** reach inside a receptacle and search for something. **2** investigate something in depth: *any financial company can delve into my private life.* **3** old use dig or excavate.
– ORIGIN Old English.

demagnetize (or **demagnetise**) verb remove magnetic properties from something.
– DERIVATIVES **demagnetization** noun.

demagogue /**dem**-uh-gog/ noun a political leader who appeals to the desires and prejudices of the general public.
– DERIVATIVES **demagogic** /dem-uh-**gog**-ik/ adjective **demagoguery** /dem-uh-**gog**-uh-ri/ noun **demagogy** noun.
– ORIGIN from Greek *dēmos* 'the people' + *agōgos* 'leading'.

demand noun **1** a very firm and forceful request. **2** (**demands**) things that are urgent, necessary, or difficult: *the physical and mental demands of climbing.* **3** the desire of consumers for a particular product or service: *a surge in demand for strong ales.* • verb **1** ask or ask for in a firm or forceful way. **2** need a quality, skill, action, etc.: *it was a difficult job that demanded their attention.*
– PHRASES **in demand** sought after. **on demand** as soon as or whenever required.
– ORIGIN Latin *demandare* 'hand over, entrust'.

demanding adjective requiring much skill or effort.

demarcate /**dee**-mar-kayt/ verb set the boundaries or limits of something.

demarcation noun **1** the action of fixing boundaries. **2** a dividing line.
– ORIGIN Spanish *demarcación.*

dematerialize (or **dematerialise**) verb become no longer physically present; disappear.
– DERIVATIVES **dematerialization** noun.

demean /di-**meen**/ verb **1** cause a loss of dignity or respect for: *much reality TV demeans people for the sake of ratings.* **2** (**demean oneself**) do something that is beneath one's dignity.
– DERIVATIVES **demeaning** adjective.
– ORIGIN from DE- + MEAN².

demeanour (US **demeanor**) noun a person's outward behaviour or bearing.
– ORIGIN from Old French *demener* 'to lead'.

demented adjective **1** suffering from dementia. **2** informal wild and irrational.
– DERIVATIVES **dementedly** adverb.
– ORIGIN from Latin *demens* 'insane'.

dementia /di-**men**-shuh/ noun a mental disorder marked by memory failures, personality changes, and impaired reasoning.
– ORIGIN Latin.

demerara sugar /dem-uh-**rair**-uh/ noun Brit. light brown cane sugar.
– ORIGIN from the region of *Demerara* in Guyana.

demerge verb Brit. separate a company from another with which it was merged.
– DERIVATIVES **demerger** noun.

demerit noun a fault or disadvantage.

demersal /di-**mer**-s'l/ adjective living close to the seabed.
– ORIGIN from Latin *demergere* 'submerge'.

demesne /di-**mayn**/ noun 1 historical land attached to a manor. 2 old use a region or domain.
– ORIGIN from Old French *demeine* 'belonging to a lord'.

demi- prefix 1 half: *demisemiquaver*. 2 partially; lesser: *demigod*.
– ORIGIN from Latin *dimidius* 'half'.

demigod (or **demigoddess**) noun a partly divine or lesser god (or goddess).

demijohn noun a bulbous narrow-necked bottle holding from 3 to 10 gallons of liquid.
– ORIGIN probably from French *dame-jeanne* 'Lady Jane'.

demilitarize (or **demilitarise**) verb remove all military forces from an area.
– DERIVATIVES **demilitarization** noun.

demi-monde /dem-i-**mond**/ noun a group of people on the fringes of respectable society.
– ORIGIN French, 'half-world'.

demise /di-**myz**/ noun 1 a person's death. 2 the end or failure of something.
– ORIGIN Old French.

demi-sec /de-mi-**sek**/ adjective (of wine) medium dry.
– ORIGIN French, 'half-dry'.

demisemiquaver /dem-i-**sem**-i-kway-ver/ noun chiefly Brit. a musical note having the time value of half a semiquaver.

demist /dee-**mist**/ verb Brit. clear condensation from a windscreen.
– DERIVATIVES **demister** noun.

demo informal noun (pl. **demos**) 1 chiefly Brit. a public demonstration. 2 a demonstration recording or piece of software. •verb (**demos**, **demoing**, **demoed**) demonstrate software or equipment.

demob /dee-**mob**/ verb (**demobs**, **demobbing**, **demobbed**) Brit. informal demobilize troops.

demobilize (or **demobilise**) /dee-**moh**-bi-lyz/ verb take troops out of active service.
– DERIVATIVES **demobilization** noun.

democracy /di-**mok**-ruh-si/ noun (pl. **democracies**) 1 a form of government in which the people can vote for representatives to govern the state on their behalf. 2 a state governed by elected representatives. 3 control of a group by the majority of its members.
– ORIGIN from Greek *dēmos* 'the people' + *-kratia* 'power, rule'.

democrat noun 1 a supporter of democracy. 2 (**Democrat**) (in the US) a member of the Democratic Party.

democratic adjective 1 relating to or supporting democracy. 2 based on the principle that all members of society are equal. 3 (**Democratic**) (in the US) relating to the Democratic Party.
– DERIVATIVES **democratically** adverb.

democratize (or **democratise**) verb introduce a democratic system or principles to something.
– DERIVATIVES **democratization** noun.

demodulate verb Electronics extract or separate a modulating signal from its carrier.
– DERIVATIVES **demodulation** noun **demodulator**

noun.

demographic adjective relating to the structure of populations. •noun a particular sector of a population: *the drink is popular with a young demographic.*
– DERIVATIVES **demographically** adverb.

demography /di-**mog**-ruh-fi/ noun the study of the structure of human populations using statistics of births, deaths, etc.
– DERIVATIVES **demographer** noun.

demoiselle /dem-wah-**zel**/ noun old use a young woman.
– ORIGIN French.

demolish /di-**mol**-ish/ verb 1 pull or knock down a building. 2 prove wrong or put an end to: *the authors demolish a number of old myths.* 3 informal overwhelmingly defeat someone. 4 humorous eat up food quickly.
– ORIGIN Latin *demoliri*.

demolition /de-muh-**li**-shuhn/ noun the action of demolishing something.

demon noun 1 an evil spirit or devil. 2 often humorous an evil or destructive person or thing. •adjective forceful or skilful: *she's a demon cook.*
– ORIGIN Greek *daimōn* 'deity, spirit'.

demonetize (or **demonetise**) /dee-**mun**-i-tyz/ verb make a coin or currency no longer valid as money.
– DERIVATIVES **demonetization** noun.
– ORIGIN French *démonétiser*.

demoniac /di-**moh**-ni-ak/ adjective relating to or resembling a demon or demons; demonic.
– DERIVATIVES **demoniacal** adjective.

demonic /di-**mon**-ik/ adjective relating to or resembling demons or evil spirits.
– DERIVATIVES **demonically** adverb.

demonize (or **demonise**) verb portray as wicked or threatening: *he aims to demonize smokers and make them social outcasts.*
– DERIVATIVES **demonization** noun.

demonology noun 1 the study of demons or belief in demons. 2 a set of beliefs about a group regarded as harmful or unwelcome.

demonstrable /di-**mon**-struh-b'l, de-**muhn**-struh-b'l/ adjective clearly apparent or able to be logically proved.
– DERIVATIVES **demonstrably** adverb.

demonstrate verb 1 clearly show something by giving proof or evidence: *these results demonstrate our continued strong performance.* 2 show and explain how something works or is done. 3 reveal a feeling or quality by one's actions. 4 take part in a public demonstration.
– DERIVATIVES **demonstrator** noun.
– ORIGIN Latin *demonstrare* 'point out'.

demonstration noun 1 the action of demonstrating or showing something. 2 a public meeting or march protesting against something or expressing views on an issue.

demonstrative /di-**mon**-struh-tiv/ adjective 1 tending to show one's feelings openly. 2 serving to show or prove something. 3 Grammar (of a determiner or pronoun) indicating the person or thing referred to (e.g. *this, that, those*).
– DERIVATIVES **demonstratively** adverb.

demoralize (or **demoralise**) verb cause someone to lose confidence or hope.

d

d

– DERIVATIVES **demoralization** noun **demoralized** adjective **demoralizing** adjective.
– ORIGIN French *démoraliser* 'corrupt, deprave'.

demote verb move someone to a lower rank or position.
– DERIVATIVES **demotion** noun.
– ORIGIN from DE- + a shortened form of PROMOTE.

demotic /di-**mot**-ik/ adjective (of language) used by ordinary people; colloquial. ● noun ordinary colloquial speech.
– ORIGIN Greek *dēmotikos*.

demotivate verb make someone less eager to work or make an effort.
– DERIVATIVES **demotivation** noun.

demountable adjective able to be dismantled or removed and readily reassembled or repositioned.

demur /di-**mer**/ verb (**demurs, demurring, demurred**) raise objections or show reluctance.
– PHRASES **without demur** without objecting or hesitating: *they accepted without demur.*
– DERIVATIVES **demurral** noun.
– ORIGIN Old French *demourer*.

demure /di-**myoor**/ adjective (**demurer, demurest**) (of a woman) reserved, modest, and shy.
– DERIVATIVES **demurely** adverb **demureness** noun.
– ORIGIN perhaps from Old French *demourer* 'remain'.

demutualize (or **demutualise**) verb change an organization such as a building society that is owned by its members to ownership by shareholders.

demystify verb (**demystifies, demystifying, demystified**) make a subject easier to understand.
– DERIVATIVES **demystification** noun.

demythologize (or **demythologise**) verb reinterpret a subject so that it is free of mythical elements.

den noun 1 a wild animal's lair or home. 2 informal a person's private room. 3 a place where people meet to do something wrong or forbidden: *a den of vice.*
– ORIGIN Old English.

denar /**dee**-nuh/ noun the basic unit of money of Macedonia.
– ORIGIN Latin *denarius.*

denarius /di-**nair**-i-uhss/ noun (pl. **denarii** /di-**nair**-i-I/) an ancient Roman silver coin.
– ORIGIN Latin, 'containing ten'.

denationalize (or **denationalise**) verb transfer a nationalized industry or organization to private ownership.
– DERIVATIVES **denationalization** noun.

denature /dee-**nay**-cher/ verb 1 alter the natural qualities of: *the scrambler denatured her voice.* 2 make alcohol unfit for drinking by adding poisonous or foul-tasting substances.
– DERIVATIVES **denaturation** noun.

dendrite /**den**-dryt/ noun a short extension of a nerve cell that conducts impulses to the cell body.
– DERIVATIVES **dendritic** /den-**dri**-tik/ adjective.
– ORIGIN from Greek *dendritēs* 'tree-like'.

dene /deen/ noun Brit. a deep, narrow, wooded valley.
– ORIGIN Old English.

dengue /**deng**-gi/ (also **dengue fever**) noun a tropical disease transmitted by mosquitoes, causing sudden fever and acute pains in the joints.
– ORIGIN Swahili.

deniable adjective able to be denied.
– DERIVATIVES **deniability** noun.

denial noun 1 a statement that something is not true. 2 the action of denying something. 3 refusal to accept that something unpleasant or distressing is true: *Tim was initially in denial of his illness.*

denier /**den**-yer/ noun a unit by which the fineness of yarn is measured.
– ORIGIN Latin *denarius* (see DENARIUS).

denigrate /**den**-i-grayt/ verb criticize someone or something in an unfair way.
– DERIVATIVES **denigration** noun **denigrator** noun.
– ORIGIN Latin *denigrare* 'blacken, make dark'.

denim noun 1 a hard-wearing cotton twill fabric. 2 (**denims**) jeans or other clothes made of denim.
– ORIGIN from French *serge de Nîmes*, referring to serge from the town of *Nîmes*.

denizen /**den**-i-zuhn/ noun formal or humorous an inhabitant or occupant of a particular place.
– ORIGIN from Old French *deinz* 'within'.

denominate /di-**nom**-i-nayt/ verb 1 formal give a name to: *he has denominated her 'Little Mother'.* 2 (**be denominated**) (of sums of money) be expressed in a specified unit of money.
– ORIGIN Latin *denominare.*

denomination noun 1 a recognized branch of a church or religion. 2 the face value of a banknote, coin, postage stamp, etc. 3 formal a name.

denominational adjective relating to a particular branch of a church or religion.
– DERIVATIVES **denominationalism** noun.

denominator noun Mathematics the number below the line in a fraction; a divisor.

de nos jours /duh noh **zhoor**/ adjective (after a noun) contemporary: *he is an Oscar Wilde de nos jours.*
– ORIGIN French, 'of our days'.

denote /di-**noht**/ verb 1 be a sign of or indicate something. 2 (of a word or phrase) have as a main or literal meaning (e.g. the word *mother* denotes 'a woman who is a parent').
– DERIVATIVES **denotation** noun.
– ORIGIN Latin *denotare.*

denouement /day-**noo**-mon/ (also **dénouement**) noun the final part of a play, film, or story, in which matters are explained or resolved.
– ORIGIN French.

denounce verb publicly declare someone or something to be wrong or evil.
– DERIVATIVES **denouncement** noun.
– ORIGIN Latin *denuntiare* 'give official information'.

de novo /day **noh**-voh/ adverb & adjective starting from the beginning; anew.
– ORIGIN Latin, 'from new'.

dense adjective 1 containing many people or things crowded closely together: *dense jungle.*

2 having a thick or closely packed texture: *dense rye bread.* **3** informal stupid.
– DERIVATIVES **densely** adverb **denseness** noun.
– ORIGIN Latin *densus.*

density noun (pl. **densities**) **1** the degree to which a substance is dense; mass per unit volume. **2** the quantity of people or things in a particular area: *areas of low population density.*

dent noun a slight hollow in a surface made by a blow or pressure. •verb **1** mark something with a dent. **2** have an adverse effect on something.
– ORIGIN variant of **DINT**.

dental adjective **1** relating to the teeth or to dentistry. **2** Phonetics (of a consonant) pronounced with the tip of the tongue against the upper front teeth (as *th*) or the ridge containing the sockets of the upper teeth (as *n, d, t*).
– DERIVATIVES **dentally** adverb.
– ORIGIN Latin *dentalis.*

dental surgeon noun a dentist.

dentate /den-tayt/ adjective technical having a tooth-like or serrated edge.

dentifrice /den-ti-friss/ noun a paste or powder for cleaning the teeth.
– ORIGIN from Latin *dens* 'tooth' + *fricare* 'to rub'.

dentil /den-til/ noun Architecture one of a series of small rectangular blocks used as a decoration under the moulding of a cornice.
– ORIGIN Italian *dentello* 'little tooth'.

dentine /den-teen/ noun hard dense bony tissue forming the bulk of a tooth.

dentist noun a person who is qualified to treat the diseases and conditions that affect the teeth and gums.
– DERIVATIVES **dentistry** noun.

dentition /den-ti-sh'n/ noun the arrangement or condition of the teeth in a particular species.

denture /den-cher/ noun a removable plate or frame holding one or more false teeth.

denude verb strip of covering; make bare: *the land is denuded of trees.*
– DERIVATIVES **denudation** noun.
– ORIGIN Latin *denudare.*

denunciation /di-nun-si-ay-sh'n/ noun public condemnation of someone or something.
– DERIVATIVES **denunciatory** adjective.

deny verb (**denies, denying, denied**) **1** state that something is not true. **2** refuse to admit or accept: *they denied all knowledge of the ship's sinking.* **3** refuse to give something requested or desired to someone. **4** (**deny oneself**) go without something that one desires.
– ORIGIN Old French *deneier.*

deodorant /di-oh-duh-ruhnt/ noun a substance which removes or conceals bodily smells.
– ORIGIN from Latin *odor* 'smell'.

deodorize (or **deodorise**) verb remove or conceal an unpleasant smell in a place.
– DERIVATIVES **deodorizer** noun.

deoxygenated /dee-ok-si-juh-nay-tid/ adjective having had the oxygen removed.
– DERIVATIVES **deoxygenation** noun.

deoxyribonucleic acid /di-ok-si-ry-boh-nyoo-**klay**-ik/ noun see **DNA**.

depart verb **1** leave, especially to start a

journey. **2** (**depart from**) do something different from a usual course of action.
– ORIGIN Old French *departir.*

departed adjective dead; deceased.

department noun **1** a division of a business, government, or other large organization, dealing with a specific area of activity. **2** an administrative district, especially in France. **3** (**one's department**) informal an area of special skill or responsibility: *Tiling the floor? That's your department.*
– DERIVATIVES **departmental** adjective **departmentally** adverb.

department store noun a large shop stocking many types of goods in different departments.

departure noun **1** the action of leaving. **2** a change from a usual course of action.

depend verb (**depend on**) **1** be controlled or determined by: *differences in earnings depended on a variety of factors.* **2** rely on someone or something.
– ORIGIN Latin *dependere* 'hang down'.

dependable adjective trustworthy and reliable.
– DERIVATIVES **dependability** noun **dependably** adverb.

dependant (also **dependent**) noun a person who relies on another, especially a family member, for financial support.

> USAGE: The noun **dependant** can also be spelled **dependent** (*elderly dependants* or *elderly dependents*). The adjective is always spelled **dependent** (*I was financially dependent on my parents*).

dependency noun (pl. **dependencies**) **1** a country or province controlled by another. **2** the state of being dependent on someone or something.

dependent adjective **1** (**dependent on**) determined or influenced by: *benefits will be dependent on length of service.* **2** relying on someone or something for support. **3** (**dependent on**) unable to do without something. •noun variant spelling of **DEPENDANT**.
– DERIVATIVES **dependence** noun **dependently** adverb.

depersonalize (or **depersonalise**) verb deprive someone or something of human characteristics or individuality.
– DERIVATIVES **depersonalization** noun.

depict /di-pikt/ verb **1** represent someone or something by a drawing, painting, or other art form. **2** describe something in words.
– DERIVATIVES **depiction** noun.
– ORIGIN Latin *depingere.*

depilate /dep-i-layt/ verb remove the hair from someone.
– DERIVATIVES **depilation** noun **depilator** noun.
– ORIGIN Latin *depilare.*

depilatory /di-pil-uh-tri/ adjective used to remove unwanted hair. •noun (pl. **depilatories**) a cream or lotion for removing unwanted hair.

deplete /di-pleet/ verb reduce the number or quantity of: *fish stocks are severely depleted.*
– DERIVATIVES **depleter** noun **depletion** noun.
– ORIGIN Latin *deplere* 'empty out'.

d

d

depleted uranium noun uranium from which most of the fissile isotope uranium-235 has been removed.

deplorable /di-**plor**-uh-b'l/ adjective deserving strong condemnation; shockingly bad.
– DERIVATIVES **deplorably** adverb.

deplore verb feel or express strong disapproval of something.
– ORIGIN Latin *deplorare*.

deploy /di-**ploy**/ verb **1** bring or move troops into position for military action. **2** bring into effective action: *the FBI began to deploy an Internet monitoring system*.
– DERIVATIVES **deployable** adjective **deployment** noun.
– ORIGIN French *déployer*.

depoliticize (or **depoliticise**) verb remove something from political activity or influence.
– DERIVATIVES **depoliticization** noun.

deponent /di-**poh**-nuhnt/ noun Law a person who gives a sworn statement to be used as evidence.
– ORIGIN from Latin *deponere* 'put down'.

depopulate verb substantially reduce the population of an area.
– DERIVATIVES **depopulation** noun.

deport verb **1** expel a foreigner or immigrant from a country. **2** (**deport oneself**) old use behave in a specified way.
– DERIVATIVES **deportation** noun **deportee** noun.
– ORIGIN Latin *deportare*.

deportment noun **1** Brit. the way a person stands and walks. **2** chiefly N. Amer. a person's behaviour or manners.

depose verb **1** remove someone from office suddenly and forcefully. **2** Law give evidence under oath, especially in writing.
– ORIGIN Old French *deposer*.

deposit noun **1** a sum of money paid into a bank or building society account. **2** a sum payable as a first instalment of a larger payment. **3** a returnable sum paid on the hire or rental of something, to cover possible loss or damage. **4** a layer of a substance that has accumulated or been laid down: *mineral deposits*. **5** the action of depositing something. • verb (**deposits**, **depositing**, **deposited**) **1** put down in a specific place: *he deposited her at the station*. **2** put something in a place for safekeeping. **3** pay a sum of money as a deposit. **4** (of water or another natural agency) lay down matter as a layer or covering.
– PHRASES **lose one's deposit** (of a candidate in a UK parliamentary election) receive less than a certain proportion of the votes (so losing a statutory financial deposit).
– DERIVATIVES **depositor** noun.
– ORIGIN Latin *depositum*.

deposit account noun Brit. a bank account that pays interest on money placed in it.

depositary (also **depository**) noun (pl. **depositaries**) a person to whom something is given for safekeeping.

deposition /dep-uh-**zi**-shuhn/ noun **1** the action of removing someone from office. **2** Law a sworn statement to be used as evidence. **3** the action of depositing something.

depository noun (pl. **depositories**) **1** a place where things are stored. **2** variant spelling of DEPOSITARY.

depot /**dep**-oh/ noun **1** a place for the storage of large quantities of goods. **2** a place where buses, trains, or other vehicles are housed and maintained. **3** N. Amer. a railway or bus station.
– ORIGIN French.

deprave /di-**prayv**/ verb make someone immoral or wicked.
– DERIVATIVES **depravity** /di-**prav**-i-ti/ noun.
– ORIGIN Latin *depravare*.

depraved adjective morally corrupt.

deprecate /**dep**-ri-kayt/ verb **1** express disapproval of someone or something. **2** another term for DEPRECIATE (in sense 2).
– DERIVATIVES **deprecation** noun **deprecatory** adjective.
– ORIGIN Latin *deprecari* 'pray to ward off evil'.

depreciate /di-**pree**-shi-ayt/ verb **1** reduce in value over time: *avoid buying new cars that depreciate quickly*. **2** criticize or dismiss something as unimportant.
– DERIVATIVES **depreciable** adjective **depreciation** noun.
– ORIGIN Latin *depreciare* 'lower in price, undervalue'.

depredation /dep-ri-**day**-sh'n/ noun an act that causes harm or damage: *the protection of crops from the depredations of birds*.
– ORIGIN from Latin *depraedari* 'to plunder'.

depress verb **1** make someone feel very unhappy or dispirited. **2** reduce the level of activity in a system. **3** push or pull something down.
– DERIVATIVES **depressing** adjective **depressingly** adverb.
– ORIGIN Latin *depressare*.

depressant adjective reducing activity in bodily processes. • noun a drug or other agent that reduces activity in bodily processes.

depressed adjective **1** very unhappy and dispirited. **2** suffering from clinical depression. **3** suffering from economic recession: *depressed rural areas*.

depression noun **1** severe unhappiness and dejection. **2** a medical condition in which a person experiences severe feelings of hopelessness and inadequacy. **3** a long and severe recession in an economy or market. **4** the action of lowering or depressing something. **5** a sunken place or hollow. **6** an area of low atmospheric pressure which may bring rain.

depressive adjective tending to cause depression. • noun a person who tends to suffer from depression.

depressurize (or **depressurise**) verb release the pressure inside a compartment or container.
– DERIVATIVES **depressurization** noun.

deprivation /dep-ri-**vay**-sh'n/ noun **1** hardship resulting from the lack of basic necessities. **2** the lack or denial of something necessary: *sleep deprivation*.

deprive verb prevent from having or using something: *the city was deprived of its water supply*.
– ORIGIN Latin *deprivare*.

deprived adjective suffering a harmful lack of basic material and cultural necessities.

Dept abbreviation Department.

depth noun **1** the distance from the top or surface down or from the front to back of something. **2** the quality of being intense, extreme, or complex. **3** extensive and detailed treatment or knowledge: *third-year courses go into more depth.* **4** (**the depths**) the deepest, lowest, or inmost part: *the depths of Devon.*
– PHRASES **out of one's depth 1** in water too deep to stand in. **2** in a situation beyond one's ability to cope.
– DERIVATIVES **depthless** adjective.
– ORIGIN from DEEP.

depth charge noun an explosive charge designed to explode under water, used for attacking submarines.

deputation noun a group of people who are appointed to act on behalf of a larger group.

depute verb /di-**pyoot**/ appoint someone to perform a task for which one is responsible. • noun /**dep**-yoot/ Scottish a deputy.
– ORIGIN Latin *deputare* 'consider to be, assign'.

deputize (or **deputise**) /**dep**-yuu-tyz/ verb temporarily act on behalf of someone else: *you will be required to deputize for the manager in her absence.*

deputy noun (pl. **deputies**) **1** a person appointed to undertake the duties of a more senior person in that person's absence. **2** a parliamentary representative in certain countries.

deracinated /di-**rass**-in-ay-tid/ adjective displaced from one's environment.
– DERIVATIVES **deracination** noun.
– ORIGIN French *déraciner* 'uproot'.

derail verb **1** cause a train to leave the tracks. **2** obstruct a process by diverting it from its intended course.
– DERIVATIVES **derailment** noun.

derailleur /di-**rayl**-yuh/ noun a bicycle gear which works by lifting the chain from one sprocket wheel to another.
– ORIGIN from French *dérailler* 'derail'.

derange verb **1** (usu as adj. **deranged**) make someone insane. **2** throw something into disorder.
– DERIVATIVES **derangement** noun.
– ORIGIN Old French *desrengier* 'move from orderly rows'.

Derby /**dar**-bi/ noun (pl. **Derbies**) **1** an annual flat race at Epsom in Surrey for three-year-old horses, founded by the 12th Earl of Derby. **2** (**derby**; also **local derby**) Brit. a sports match between two rival teams from the same area.

deregulate verb remove regulations from something.
– DERIVATIVES **deregulation** noun **deregulatory** adjective.

derelict adjective **1** in a very poor condition as a result of disuse and neglect. **2** chiefly N. Amer. shamefully negligent. • noun a person without a home, job, or possessions.
– ORIGIN from Latin *derelinquere* 'to abandon'.

dereliction noun **1** the state of having been abandoned and become dilapidated. **2** (**dereliction of duty**) shameful failure to fulfil one's obligations.

deride /di-**ryd**/ verb express contempt for someone or something; ridicule.
– ORIGIN Latin *deridere* 'scoff at'.

de rigueur /duh ri-**ger**/ adjective considered necessary for acceptance in fashionable society.
– ORIGIN French, 'in strictness'.

derision /di-**ri**-zh'n/ noun contemptuous ridicule or mockery.
– ORIGIN Latin.

derisive /di-**ry**-siv/ adjective expressing contempt or ridicule.
– DERIVATIVES **derisively** adverb.

derisory /di-**ry**-suh-ri/ adjective **1** ridiculously small or inadequate: *a derisory pay rise.* **2** expressing derision; derisive.

derivation noun **1** the action of obtaining something from a source or origin. **2** the formation of a word from another word.
– DERIVATIVES **derivational** adjective.

derivative /di-**riv**-uh-tiv/ adjective imitative of the work of another artist, writer, etc., and regarded as unoriginal. • noun **1** something which is based on or derived from something else: *the new drug is just a derivative of an old antibiotic.* **2** Mathematics an expression representing the rate of change of one quantity in relation to another.

derive /di-**ryv**/ verb **1** (**derive something from**) obtain or get something from: *they derived great comfort from this assurance.* **2** (**derive something from**) base something on a modification of something else. **3** (**derive from**) originate or develop from: *the word may derive from Old English.*
– DERIVATIVES **derivable** adjective.
– ORIGIN Latin *derivare* 'draw off water'.

dermatitis /der-muh-**ty**-tiss/ noun inflammation of the skin as a result of irritation or an allergic reaction.
– ORIGIN from Greek *derma* 'skin'.

dermatology noun the branch of medicine concerned with skin disorders.
– DERIVATIVES **dermatological** adjective **dermatologically** adverb **dermatologist** noun.

dermis /**der**-miss/ noun the thick layer of the skin below the epidermis, consisting of living tissue.
– DERIVATIVES **dermal** adjective.
– ORIGIN Latin.

dernier cri /der-nyay **kree**/ noun the very latest fashion: *she's wearing the dernier cri in bohemian chic.*
– ORIGIN French, 'last cry'.

derogate /**der**-uh-gayt/ verb formal **1** (**derogate from**) cause something to seem less valuable or important; detract from. **2** (**derogate from**) deviate from an agreement or rule: *one country derogated from the Rome Convention.* **3** be critical of someone or something.
– DERIVATIVES **derogation** noun.
– ORIGIN Latin *derogare* 'abrogate'.

derogatory /di-**rog**-uh-tri/ adjective showing a critical or disrespectful attitude.
– DERIVATIVES **derogatorily** adverb.

derrick /**derr**-ik/ noun **1** a kind of crane with a movable pivoted arm. **2** the framework over an oil well, holding the drilling machinery.
– ORIGIN from *Derrick*, the surname of a 17th-century hangman.

derrière /der-ri-**air**/ noun euphemistic or humorous a person's bottom.
– ORIGIN French, 'behind'.

d

derring-do /derr-ing-**doo**/ noun dated or humorous action displaying heroic courage.
– ORIGIN from the Middle English phrase *dorryng do* 'daring to do'.

derris /**der**-riss/ noun an insecticide made from the powdered roots of a tropical plant.
– ORIGIN Greek, 'leather covering' (referring to the plant's pods).

derv (also **DERV**) noun Brit. diesel oil for motor vehicles.
– ORIGIN from the initial letters of *diesel-engined road-vehicle*.

dervish /**der**-vish/ noun a member of a Muslim (specifically Sufi) religious group vowed to poverty, some orders of which are known for their wild rituals.
– ORIGIN Persian, 'religious beggar'.

desalinate /dee-**sal**-i-nayt/ verb remove salt from seawater.
– DERIVATIVES **desalination** noun.

descale verb Brit. remove deposits of scale from something.
– DERIVATIVES **descaler** noun

descant /**dess**-kant/ noun an independent treble melody sung or played above a basic melody.
– ORIGIN Latin *discantus* 'part song, refrain'.

descant recorder noun Music the most common size of recorder, with a range of two octaves above the C above middle C.

descend verb 1 move down or downwards. 2 slope or lead downwards. 3 (**descend to**) act in a shameful way that is below one's usual standards: *she began to despise herself for having descended to self-pity*. 4 (**descend on**) make a sudden attack on or unwelcome visit to someone or something. 5 (**be descended from**) be a blood relative of an ancestor. 6 pass by inheritance: *his lands descended to his eldest son*.
– DERIVATIVES **descendent** adjective **descender** noun.
– ORIGIN Latin *descendere* 'climb down'.

descendant noun 1 a person, animal, or plants that is descended from a particular ancestor. 2 something that has developed from an earlier version of something: *the instrument is a descendant of the lute*.

descent noun 1 the action of descending. 2 a downward slope. 3 a person's origin or nationality.

describe verb 1 give a detailed account in words of someone or something. 2 mark out or draw a geometrical figure.
– DERIVATIVES **describable** adjective **describer** noun.
– ORIGIN Latin *describere* 'write down'.

description noun 1 a spoken or written account. 2 the action of describing someone or something. 3 a sort, kind, or class: *people of any description*.

descriptive adjective 1 describing someone or something; giving a description. 2 describing something in an objective and non-judgemental way.
– DERIVATIVES **descriptively** adverb.

descry /di-**skry**/ verb (**descries**, **descrying**, **descried**) literary catch sight of someone or something.
– ORIGIN Old French *descrier* 'publish, proclaim'.

desecrate /**dess**-i-krayt/ verb treat something sacred with violent disrespect.
– DERIVATIVES **desecration** noun **desecrator** noun.
– ORIGIN from DE- + a shortened form of CONSECRATE.

desegregate verb end a policy of racial segregation in a school or similar institution.
– DERIVATIVES **desegregation** noun.

deselect verb Brit. reject an existing MP as a candidate in a forthcoming election.
– DERIVATIVES **deselection** noun.

desensitize (or **desensitise**) verb 1 make something less sensitive. 2 make someone less likely to be shocked or distressed by cruelty or suffering.
– DERIVATIVES **desensitization** noun.

desert[1] /di-**zert**/ verb 1 leave in a disloyal or treacherous way; abandon: *her husband deserted her long ago*. 2 (usu. as adj. **deserted**) leave a place, causing it to appear empty. 3 illegally leave the armed forces.
– DERIVATIVES **desertion** noun.
– ORIGIN Latin *desertare*.

desert[2] /**dez**-ert/ noun 1 a waterless area of land with little or no vegetation, typically covered with sand. 2 a situation or area considered dull and uninteresting: *a cultural desert*. ● adjective (of a place) like a desert.
– ORIGIN Latin *desertum* 'something left waste'.

deserter noun a member of the armed forces who deserts.

desertification /de-zer-ti-fi-**kay**-sh'n/ noun the process by which fertile land becomes desert.

desert island noun a remote, uninhabited tropical island.

deserts /di-**zerts**/ plural noun (usu. in phrase **get** or **receive one's just deserts**) the reward or punishment that a person deserves.
– ORIGIN from Old French *deservir* 'serve well, deserve'.

deserve verb do something or show qualities worthy of a reward or punishment: *Amanda deserves a lot of credit*.
– DERIVATIVES **deservedly** adverb.
– ORIGIN Latin *deservire* 'serve well'.

deserving adjective worthy of favourable treatment or assistance.

desex verb 1 deprive someone of sexual qualities. 2 castrate or spay an animal.

déshabillé /day-za-bee-**yay**/ (also **dishabille**) /diss-uh-**beel**/ noun the state of being only partly clothed.
– ORIGIN French, 'undressed'.

desiccate /**dess**-i-kayt/ verb (usu. as adj. **desiccated**) remove the moisture from something.
– DERIVATIVES **desiccation** noun.
– ORIGIN Latin *desiccare* 'make thoroughly dry'.

desideratum /di-zi-duh-**rah**-tuhm/ noun (pl. **desiderata** /di-zi-duh-**rah**-tuh/) something that is needed or wanted.
– ORIGIN Latin, 'something desired'.

design noun 1 a plan or drawing produced to show the appearance and workings of something before it is made. 2 the art or action of producing a design. 3 a decorative pattern. 4 underlying purpose or planning: *the*

appearance of design in the universe. • verb
1 produce a design for something. 2 plan or
intend for a purpose: *the reforms were
designed to stimulate economic growth.*
– PHRASES **by design** on purpose; intentionally.
have designs on aim to obtain something.
– ORIGIN Latin *designare* 'mark out, designate'.

designate verb /dez-ig-nayt/ 1 officially give a
specified status or name to: *most of the waste is
designated as hazardous.* 2 appoint someone to
a specified position. • adjective /dez-ig-nuht/
(after a noun) appointed to a post but not yet
having taken it up: *the Director designate.*
– DERIVATIVES **designator** noun.
– ORIGIN Latin *designare* 'mark out, designate'.

designated driver noun N. Amer. a person who
does not drink alcohol so as to be fit to drive
others home.

designation noun 1 the action of designating
or choosing someone or something. 2 an
official title or description.

designedly adverb on purpose; intentionally.

designer noun a person who designs things.
• adjective made by a famous fashion designer:
designer jeans.

designer baby noun a baby whose genetic
make-up has been selected in order to remove
a particular defect, or to ensure that a
particular gene is present.

designing adjective acting in a calculating,
deceitful way.

desirable adjective 1 wished for as being
attractive, useful, or necessary: *it is desirable to
have a rechargeable battery.* 2 sexually
attractive.
– DERIVATIVES **desirability** noun **desirably** adverb.

desire noun 1 a strong feeling of wanting to
have something or wishing for something to
happen: *the desire for fame.* 2 strong sexual
feeling or appetite. • verb 1 strongly wish for or
want something. 2 want someone sexually.
– ORIGIN Latin *desiderare.*

desirous /di-zy-ruhss/ adjective strongly
wishing to have: *the pope was desirous of
peace.*

desist /di-sisst/ verb stop doing something;
cease.
– ORIGIN Latin *desistere.*

desk noun 1 a piece of furniture with a flat or
sloping surface, for writing or other work. 2 a
counter in a hotel, bank, or airport. 3 a
specified section of a news organization: *the
sports desk.*
– ORIGIN Latin *discus* 'plate' (later 'desk').

deskill /dee-skil/ verb reduce the level of skill
required to carry out a job.

desktop noun 1 a microcomputer suitable for
use at an ordinary desk. 2 the working area of
a computer screen regarded as representing
the working surface of a desk.

desktop publishing noun the production of
high-quality printed matter by means of a
printer linked to a computer, with special
software.

desolate adjective /dess-uh-luht/ 1 (of a place)
empty and bleak. 2 very unhappy or lonely.
• verb /dess-uh-layt/ make someone very
unhappy.
– DERIVATIVES **desolation** noun.

– ORIGIN from Latin *desolare* 'abandon'.

despair noun the complete loss or absence of
hope. • verb lose or be without hope: *he
despaired of finding a good restaurant.*
– PHRASES **be the despair of** cause someone to
lose hope.
– ORIGIN from Latin *desperare.*

despatch verb & noun British spelling of
DISPATCH.

desperado /dess-puh-rah-doh/ noun (pl.
desperadoes or **desperados**) a desperate or
reckless criminal.
– ORIGIN pseudo-Spanish.

desperate adjective 1 full of despair;
completely without hope. 2 extremely bad or
serious: *a desperate shortage.* 3 having a great
need or desire for something: *I'm desperate for
a drink.* 4 violent or dangerous.
– DERIVATIVES **desperately** adverb.
– ORIGIN Latin *desperatus* 'deprived of hope'.

desperation noun a state of despair, especially
as resulting in extreme behaviour.

despicable /di-spik-uh-b'l/ adjective deserving
hatred and contempt.
– DERIVATIVES **despicably** adverb.
– ORIGIN from Latin *despicari* 'look down on'.

despise /di-spyz/ verb feel hatred or disgust
for someone or something.
– DERIVATIVES **despiser** noun.
– ORIGIN Latin *despicere* 'look down'.

despite /di-spyt/ preposition in spite of.
– ORIGIN first meaning 'contempt': from Latin
despectus 'looking down on'.

despoil /di-spoyl/ verb literary steal valuable
possessions from a place.
– DERIVATIVES **despoiler** noun **despoliation** /di-
spoh-li-ay-sh'n/ noun.
– ORIGIN Latin *despoliare* 'rob, plunder'.

despondent adjective in low spirits from loss
of hope or courage.
– DERIVATIVES **despondency** noun **despondently**
adverb.
– ORIGIN from Latin *despondere* 'give up,
abandon'.

despot /dess-pot/ noun a ruler with total
power, especially one who uses it in a cruel
way.
– DERIVATIVES **despotic** adjective **despotism** noun.
– ORIGIN Greek *despotēs* 'master, absolute
ruler'.

dessert /di-zert/ noun the sweet course eaten
at the end of a meal.
– ORIGIN French.

dessertspoon noun a spoon used for dessert,
smaller than a tablespoon and larger than a
teaspoon.

dessert wine noun a sweet wine drunk with
or following dessert.

destabilize (or **destabilise**) verb upset the
stability of something.
– DERIVATIVES **destabilization** noun.

destination noun the place to which someone
or something is going or being sent.

destine /des-tin/ verb (**be destined**) 1 be
intended for or certain to do something: *he
was destined to be an engineer.* 2 be bound for
a particular destination.
– ORIGIN Latin *destinare* 'make firm, establish'.

destiny noun (pl. **destinies**) 1 the events that

d

will happen to a person or thing in the future: *we share a common destiny.* **2** the power believed to control the future; fate.
– ORIGIN from Latin *destinare* 'make firm, establish'.

destitute /**dess**-ti-tyoot/ **adjective** very poor and lacking the means to provide for oneself.
– DERIVATIVES **destitution** noun.
– ORIGIN from Latin *destituere* 'forsake'.

destroy verb **1** end the existence of something by attacking or damaging it. **2** kill an animal in a quick and painless way.
– ORIGIN Latin *destruere.*

destroyer noun **1** a person or thing that destroys something. **2** a small fast warship.

destructible adjective able to be destroyed.

destruction noun **1** the action of destroying something or the state of being destroyed. **2** a cause of someone's ruin: *gambling was his destruction.*
– ORIGIN Latin.

destructive adjective **1** causing severe damage or destruction. **2** negative and unhelpful: *destructive criticism.*
– DERIVATIVES **destructively** adverb **destructiveness** noun.

desuetude /**dess**-wi-tyood/ noun formal a state of disuse.
– ORIGIN Latin *desuetudo.*

desultory /**dess**-uhl-tuh-ri/ adjective **1** lacking purpose or enthusiasm. **2** going from one subject to another in a half-hearted way: *a desultory conversation.*
– DERIVATIVES **desultorily** adverb.
– ORIGIN Latin *desultorius* 'superficial'.

detach verb **1** disconnect something and remove it. **2** (**detach oneself from**) leave or distance oneself from a group or situation. **3** (**be detached**) (of a group of soldiers) be sent on a separate mission.
– DERIVATIVES **detachable** adjective.
– ORIGIN French *détacher.*

detached adjective **1** separate or disconnected. **2** (of a house) not joined to another on either side. **3** not involved; objective: *a detached, cynical reporter.*

detachment noun **1** the state of being objective or aloof. **2** a group of troops, ships, etc. sent on a separate mission. **3** the action of detaching something.

detail noun **1** a small individual item or fact. **2** small items or facts as a whole: *attention to detail.* **3** a small part of a picture reproduced separately for close study. **4** a small detachment of troops or police officers given a special duty. • verb **1** give full information about something. **2** select someone to undertake a particular task.
– PHRASES **in detail** as regards every aspect; fully.
– ORIGIN French *détail.*

detailed adjective having many details.

detailing noun small decorative features on a building, garment, or work of art.

detain verb **1** prevent someone from proceeding; delay. **2** keep someone in official custody.
– DERIVATIVES **detainer** noun **detainment** noun.
– ORIGIN Latin *detinere* 'keep back'.

detainee /dee-tay-**nee**/ noun a person held in custody, especially for political reasons.

detect verb **1** discover the presence or existence of something. **2** notice something very slight: *I detected a hint of nervousness in him.* **3** discover or investigate a crime.
– DERIVATIVES **detectable** adjective **detectably** adverb **detection** noun.
– ORIGIN Latin *detegere* 'uncover'.

detective noun a person, especially a police officer, whose occupation is to investigate crimes.

detector noun a device designed to discover the presence of something and to send out a signal.

détente /day-**tahnt**/ noun the easing of hostility or strained relations between countries.
– ORIGIN French, 'loosening, relaxation'.

detention noun **1** the state of being detained in official custody. **2** the punishment of being kept in school after hours.

detention centre noun an institution where people, especially refugees and people awaiting trial, are detained.

deter /di-**ter**/ verb (**deters, deterring, deterred**) **1** discourage from doing something, especially by fear of the consequences: *the record heat didn't deter her from her daily run.* **2** prevent something from happening.
– ORIGIN Latin *deterrere.*

detergent noun a liquid or powder for removing dirt and grease from clothes, dishes, etc.
– ORIGIN from Latin *detergere* 'wipe away'.

deteriorate /di-**teer**-i-uh-rayt/ verb become gradually worse.
– DERIVATIVES **deterioration** noun.
– ORIGIN Latin *deteriorare.*

determinant /di-**ter**-mi-nuhnt/ noun **1** a factor which decisively affects the nature or outcome of something: *genetics may be the most important determinant of your weight.* **2** Mathematics a quantity obtained by adding products of the elements of a square matrix according to a given rule.

determinate /di-**ter**-mi-nuht/ adjective having fixed and definite limits.
– DERIVATIVES **determinacy** noun.

determination noun **1** the quality of being determined; firmness of purpose. **2** the action of establishing or deciding something.

determine verb **1** cause to happen in a particular way or to have a particular nature: *it is biological age that determines our looks.* **2** firmly decide to do something. **3** establish something by research or calculation.
– DERIVATIVES **determinable** adjective.
– ORIGIN Latin *determinare* 'limit, fix'.

determined adjective having firmness of purpose; resolute.
– DERIVATIVES **determinedly** adverb.

determiner noun **1** a person or thing that determines or decides something. **2** Grammar a word that comes before a noun to show how the noun is being used, for example *a, the, every.*

determinism noun the belief that people are not free to do as they wish because their lives are determined by factors outside their control.

– DERIVATIVES **determinist** noun & adjective **deterministic** adjective.

deterrent /di-**terr**-uhnt/ noun a thing that discourages or is intended to discourage someone from doing something. ●adjective able or intended to deter.

– DERIVATIVES **deterrence** noun.

detest verb dislike someone or something intensely.

– ORIGIN Latin *detestari* 'denounce, abhor'.

detestable adjective deserving intense dislike.

detestation /dee-tess-**tay**-sh'n/ noun intense dislike.

dethrone verb 1 remove a monarch from power. 2 remove someone from a position of authority or dominance.

– DERIVATIVES **dethronement** noun.

detonate /**det**-uh-nayt/ verb explode or cause to explode.

– DERIVATIVES **detonation** noun.
– ORIGIN Latin *detonare*.

detonator noun a device or charge used to detonate an explosive.

detour /**dee**-toor/ noun a long or roundabout route taken to avoid something or to visit something along the way. ●verb take a detour.

– ORIGIN French, 'change of direction'.

detox informal noun /**dee**-toks/ detoxification. ●verb /dee-**toks**/ detoxify.

detoxify verb (**detoxifies**, **detoxifying**, **detoxified**) 1 remove harmful or toxic substances from something. 2 abstain or help to abstain from drink or drugs until the bloodstream is free of toxins.

– DERIVATIVES **detoxification** noun **detoxifier** noun.

detract verb (**detract from**) cause something to seem less valuable or impressive.

– DERIVATIVES **detraction** noun.
– ORIGIN Latin *detrahere* 'draw away'.

detractor noun a person who is critical of someone or something.

detrain verb leave a train.

detriment /**det**-ri-muhnt/ noun harm or damage: *she fasted to the detriment of her health.*

– DERIVATIVES **detrimental** adjective **detrimentally** adjective.
– ORIGIN Latin *detrimentum*.

detritus /di-**try**-tuhss/ noun debris or waste material.

– DERIVATIVES **detrital** adjective.
– ORIGIN Latin.

de trop /duh **troh**/ adjective not wanted; unwelcome.

– ORIGIN French, 'excessive'.

detumescence /dee-tyoo-**mes**-suhnss/ noun the process of subsiding from a state of swelling or sexual arousal.

– DERIVATIVES **detumescent** adjective.
– ORIGIN Latin *detumescere*.

detune verb 1 cause a musical instrument to become out of tune. 2 reduce the performance of a motor vehicle or engine by adjustment.

deuce[1] /dyooss/ noun 1 Tennis the score of 40 all in a game, at which two consecutive points are needed to win the game. 2 chiefly N. Amer. the number two on dice or playing cards.

– ORIGIN Latin *duos* 'two'.

deuce[2] /dyooss/ noun (**the deuce**) informal used as a euphemism for 'devil' in exclamations or for emphasis.

– ORIGIN German *duus*, probably related to **DEUCE**[1] (two aces at dice being the worst throw).

deus ex machina /day-uuss eks **mak**-i-nuh/ noun an unexpected event that saves a seemingly hopeless situation.

– ORIGIN Latin, 'god from the machinery' (referring to the actors representing gods suspended above the stage in ancient Greek theatre, who intervened in the play's outcome).

deuterium /dyoo-**teer**-i-uhm/ noun Chemistry a stable isotope of hydrogen with a mass approximately twice that of the usual isotope.

– ORIGIN Latin.

Deutschmark /**doych**-mark/ noun (until the introduction of the euro in 2002) the basic unit of money of Germany.

– ORIGIN from German *deutsche Mark* 'German mark'.

devalue verb (**devalues**, **devaluing**, **devalued**) 1 reduce the worth of: *people seem to devalue my achievement.* 2 reduce the official value of a currency in relation to other currencies.

– DERIVATIVES **devaluation** noun.

devastate /**dev**-uh-stayt/ verb 1 destroy or ruin something. 2 (**be devastated**) be overwhelmed with shock and grief.

– DERIVATIVES **devastation** noun **devastator** noun.
– ORIGIN Latin *devastare*.

devastating adjective 1 highly destructive. 2 very distressing or shocking. 3 informal very impressive or attractive.

– DERIVATIVES **devastatingly** adverb.

develop verb (**develops**, **developing**, **developed**) 1 become or make larger or more advanced. 2 start to exist, experience, or possess: *he developed a passionate interest in fitness.* 3 convert land to a new purpose, especially by constructing buildings. 4 treat a photographic film with chemicals to make a visible image.

– DERIVATIVES **developable** adjective **developer** noun.
– ORIGIN French *développer* 'unfold'.

developing country noun a poor agricultural country that is seeking to become more advanced economically and socially.

development noun 1 the action of developing or the state of being developed: *she traces the development of the novel.* 2 a new product or idea. 3 a new stage in a changing situation. 4 an area with new buildings on it.

– DERIVATIVES **developmental** adjective **developmentally** adverb.

deviant adjective departing from normal standards, especially in social or sexual behaviour. ●noun a person who departs from normal standards.

– DERIVATIVES **deviance** noun **deviancy** noun.

deviate verb /**dee**-vi-ayt/ depart from an established course or from normal standards: *the vet deviated from an accepted standard of care.*

– DERIVATIVES **deviation** noun.

d

- ORIGIN Latin *deviare* 'turn out of the way'.

device noun 1 a piece of mechanical or electronic equipment made for a particular purpose. 2 a plan or method with a particular aim: *a clever marketing device*. 3 a drawing or design.
- PHRASES **leave someone to their own devices** leave someone to do as they wish.
- ORIGIN Old French *devis* 'device, intention'.

devil noun 1 (**the Devil**) (in Christian and Jewish belief) the most powerful evil spirit. 2 an evil spirit. 3 a very wicked or cruel person. 4 a mischievous person. 5 informal a person with specified characteristics: *the poor devil*. 6 (**the devil**) expressing surprise or annoyance.
- PHRASES **be a devil!** Brit. informal said to encourage a hesitant person. **between the devil and the deep blue sea** caught in a dilemma. **devil-may-care** cheerful and reckless. **the devil to pay** serious trouble to be dealt with. **like the devil** with great speed or energy. **speak** (or **talk**) **of the devil** said when a person appears just after being mentioned.
- ORIGIN Greek *diabolos* 'accuser, slanderer'.

devilish adjective 1 evil and cruel. 2 mischievous: *a devilish grin*. 3 very difficult to deal with. • adverb informal, dated very: *a devilish clever chap*.
- DERIVATIVES **devilishly** adverb **devilishness** noun.

devilled adjective cooked with hot seasoning.

devilment noun reckless mischief.

devilry noun 1 wicked activity. 2 reckless mischief.

devil's advocate noun a person who expresses an unpopular opinion in order to provoke debate.

devious /dee-vi-uhss/ adjective 1 skilful in using underhand tactics. 2 (of a route or journey) indirect.
- DERIVATIVES **deviously** adverb **deviousness** noun.
- ORIGIN Latin *devius* 'out of the way'.

devise /di-vyz/ verb plan or invent a complex procedure or device.
- DERIVATIVES **deviser** noun.
- ORIGIN Old French *deviser*.

devitalize (or **devitalise**) verb deprive someone or something of strength and energy.
- DERIVATIVES **devitalization** noun.

devoid /di-voyd/ adjective (**devoid of**) completely lacking in: *the dancers were devoid of glamour*.
- ORIGIN from Old French *devoidier* 'cast out'.

devolution /dee-vuh-loo-sh'n/ noun the transfer of power by central government to local or regional governments.
- DERIVATIVES **devolutionary** adjective **devolutionist** noun.

devolve /di-volv/ verb 1 transfer power to a lower level, especially from central to regional government. 2 (**devolve on/to**) (of duties or responsibility) pass to a deputy or successor.
- ORIGIN Latin *devolvere* 'roll down'.

Devonian /di-voh-ni-uhn/ adjective Geology relating to the fourth period of the Palaeozoic era (about 409 to 363 million years ago), when the first amphibians appeared.

devoré /duh-vor-ay/ noun a velvet fabric with a pattern formed by burning the pile away with acid.
- ORIGIN French, 'devoured'.

devote verb (**devote something to**) give time or resources to a person or activity.
- ORIGIN Latin *devovere* 'consecrate'.

devoted adjective very loving or loyal.
- DERIVATIVES **devotedly** adverb.

devotee /dev-oh-tee/ noun 1 a person who is very enthusiastic about someone or something. 2 a person with a strong belief in a particular religion or god.

devotion noun 1 great love or loyalty. 2 religious worship. 3 (**devotions**) prayers or religious observances.
- DERIVATIVES **devotional** adjective.

devour /di-vow-er/ verb 1 eat food greedily. 2 (of fire or a similar force) destroy something completely. 3 read something quickly and eagerly.
- DERIVATIVES **devourer** noun.
- ORIGIN Latin *devorare*.

devout /di-vowt/ adjective 1 deeply religious. 2 earnestly sincere: *my devout hope*.
- DERIVATIVES **devoutly** adverb.
- ORIGIN Latin *devotus* 'devoted'.

dew noun tiny drops of moisture that form on cool surfaces at night when water vapour in the air condenses.
- ORIGIN Old English.

dewberry noun (pl. **dewberries**) the edible blue-black fruit of a trailing bramble.

dewdrop noun a drop of dew.

Dewey decimal classification noun a decimal system of library classification which uses a three-figure code from 000 to 999 to represent the major branches of knowledge.
- ORIGIN named after the American librarian Melvil *Dewey*.

dewlap noun a fold of loose skin hanging from the neck or throat of an animal such as a cow.

dewy adjective wet with dew.

dewy-eyed adjective naive or sentimental: *dewy-eyed liberals*.

dexter /dek-stuh/ adjective Heraldry on or towards the bearer's right-hand side of a coat of arms. The opposite of SINISTER.
- ORIGIN Latin, 'on the right'.

dexterity /dek-ste-ri-ti/ noun 1 skill in performing tasks with the hands. 2 the ability to do something skilfully: *mental dexterity*.
- ORIGIN from Latin *dexter* 'on the right'.

dexterous /dek-stuh-ruhss/ (also **dextrous** /dek-struhss/) adjective showing skill; adroit.
- DERIVATIVES **dexterously** adverb.

dextrose noun a naturally occurring form of glucose.
- ORIGIN from Latin *dexter* 'on the right'.

DfES abbreviation (in the UK) Department for Education and Skills.

DG abbreviation director general.

dhal /dahl/ (also **dal**) noun (in Indian cookery) split pulses.
- ORIGIN Hindi.

dhansak /dun-sahk/ noun an Indian dish of meat or vegetables cooked with lentils and coriander.

– ORIGIN Gujarati.

dharma /**dar**-muh/ noun (in Indian religion) the eternal law of the universe.
– ORIGIN Sanskrit, 'decree or custom'.

dhobi /**doh**-bi/ noun (pl. **dhobis**) (in the Indian subcontinent) a person whose occupation is washing clothes.
– ORIGIN Hindi.

dhoti /**doh**-ti/ noun (pl. **dhotis**) a piece of cloth tied around the waist and covering most of the legs, worn by some Indian men.
– ORIGIN Hindi.

dhow /dow/ noun a ship with a lateen sail or sails, used in the Arabian region.
– ORIGIN Arabic.

dhurrie /**du**-ri/ noun (pl. **dhurries**) a heavy cotton rug of Indian origin.
– ORIGIN Hindi.

di- combining form twice; two-; double: *dioxide*.
– ORIGIN from Greek *dis* 'twice'.

diabetes /dy-uh-**bee**-teez/ noun a disorder of the metabolism in which a lack of the hormone insulin results in a failure to absorb sugar and starch properly.
– ORIGIN Greek, 'siphon'.

diabetic adjective having or relating to diabetes. • noun a person with diabetes.

diabolical adjective **1** (also **diabolic**) relating to or like the Devil, especially in being evil. **2** Brit. informal very bad: *an absolutely diabolical voice*.
– DERIVATIVES **diabolically** adverb.
– ORIGIN from Greek *diabolos* 'accuser, slanderer' (see **DEVIL**).

diabolism /dy-**ab**-uh-li-z'm/ noun worship of the Devil.
– DERIVATIVES **diabolist** noun.

diaconal /dy-**ak**-uh-nuhl/ adjective (in the Christian Church) relating to a deacon or deacons.
– ORIGIN from Latin *diaconus* 'deacon'.

diaconate /dy-**ak**-uh-nayt, dy-**ak**-uh-nuht/ noun **1** (in the Christian Church) the position of deacon. **2** a group of deacons.

diacritic /dy-uh-**krit**-ik/ noun a sign, such as an accent, written above or below a letter to indicate a difference in pronunciation from the same letter when unmarked.
– DERIVATIVES **diacritical** adjective.
– ORIGIN from Greek *diakrinein* 'distinguish'.

diadem /**dy**-uh-dem/ noun a jewelled crown or headband worn as a symbol of royalty.
– ORIGIN Greek *diadēma*.

diaeresis /dy-**eer**-i-siss/ (US **dieresis**) noun (pl. **diaereses** /dy-**eer**-i-seez/) a mark (¨) placed over a vowel to indicate that it is sounded separately, as in *naïve*.
– ORIGIN Greek *diairesis* 'separation'.

diagnose /dy-uhg-**nohz**/ verb **1** identify the nature of an illness or problem by examining the symptoms. **2** identify the medical condition of someone.
– DERIVATIVES **diagnosable** adjective.

diagnosis noun (pl. **diagnoses**) the identification of the nature of an illness or other problem by examination of the symptoms.
– ORIGIN Greek.

diagnostic /dy-uhg-**noss**-tik/ adjective relating to the diagnosis of illness or other problems.
• noun **1** a distinctive symptom or characteristic. **2** (**diagnostics**) (treated as sing. or pl.) the practice or techniques of diagnosis.
– DERIVATIVES **diagnostically** adverb **diagnostician** noun.

diagonal /dy-**ag**-uh-n'l/ adjective **1** (of a straight line) joining two opposite corners of a rectangle, square, or other shape. **2** (of a line) straight and at an angle; slanting. • noun a diagonal line.
– DERIVATIVES **diagonally** adverb.
– ORIGIN Greek *diagōnios* 'from angle to angle'.

diagram noun a simplified drawing showing the appearance or structure of something.
– DERIVATIVES **diagrammatic** adjective **diagrammatically** adverb.
– ORIGIN Greek *diagramma*.

dial noun **1** a disc marked to show the time on a clock or to indicate a measurement by means of a pointer. **2** a disc with numbered holes on a telephone, turned to make a call. **3** a disc turned to select a setting on a radio, cooker, etc. • verb (**dials, dialling, dialled**; US **dials, dialing, dialed**) call a telephone number by turning a dial or using a keypad.
– DERIVATIVES **dialler** (also **dialer**) noun.
– ORIGIN Latin *diale* 'clock dial'.

dialect /**dy**-uh-lekt/ noun a form of a language which is used in a specific region or by a specific social group: *Yorkshire dialect*.
– DERIVATIVES **dialectal** adjective.
– ORIGIN Greek *dialektos* 'discourse, way of speaking'.

dialectic /dy-uh-**lek**-tik/ (also **dialectics**) noun (usu. treated as sing.) Philosophy **1** the investigation of the truth of opposing opinions by logical discussion. **2** the existence of opposing social forces, concepts, etc.: *union leaders have been hidebound by the dialectic of class war*.
– DERIVATIVES **dialectical** adjective **dialectically** adverb.
– ORIGIN from Greek *dialektikē tekhnē* 'art of debate'.

dialling code noun Brit. a sequence of numbers dialled to connect a telephone to an exchange in another area or country.

dialling tone (N. Amer. **dial tone**) noun a sound produced by a telephone that indicates that a caller may start to dial.

dialog box (Brit. also **dialogue box**) noun a small area on a computer screen in which the user is prompted to provide information or select commands.

dialogic /dy-uh-**loj**-ik/ adjective relating to or in the form of dialogue.
– DERIVATIVES **dialogical** adjective.

dialogue (US also **dialog**) noun **1** conversation between two or more people as a feature of a book, play, or film. **2** a discussion intended to explore a subject or resolve a problem.
– ORIGIN Greek *dialogos*.

dial-up adjective (of a computer system or service) used remotely via a telephone line.

dialysis /dy-**al**-i-siss/ noun (pl. **dialyses** /dy-**al**-i-seez/) **1** Chemistry the separation of particles in a liquid on the basis of differences in their ability to pass through a membrane. **2** the purification of blood by dialysis, as a

substitute for the normal function of the kidney.
– ORIGIN Greek *dialusis*.

diamanté /dy-uh-**mon**-tay/ adjective decorated with glass cut to resemble diamonds.
– ORIGIN French, 'set with diamonds'.

diameter /dy-**am**-i-ter/ noun a straight line passing from side to side through the centre of a circle or sphere.
– ORIGIN from Greek *diametros grammē* 'line measuring across'.

diametrical /dy-uh-**met**-ri-k'l/ adjective **1** (of opposites) completely different: *he's the diametrical opposite of Gabriel.* **2** relating to a diameter.
– DERIVATIVES **diametrically** adverb.

diamond noun **1** a precious stone consisting of a clear and colourless crystalline form of pure carbon, the hardest naturally occurring substance. **2** a figure with four straight sides of equal length forming two opposite acute angles and two opposite obtuse angles; a rhombus. **3** (**diamonds**) one of the four suits in a pack of playing cards.
– ORIGIN Old French *diamant*.

diamond jubilee noun the sixtieth anniversary of a notable event.

diamond wedding noun Brit. the sixtieth anniversary of a wedding.

diamorphine /dy-**mor**-feen/ noun technical heroin.
– ORIGIN short for *diacetylmorphine* in the same sense.

dianthus /dy-**an**-thuhss/ noun (pl. **dianthuses**) a flowering plant of a group that includes the pinks and carnations.
– ORIGIN from Greek *Dios* 'of Zeus' + *anthos* 'flower'.

diapason /dy-uh-**pay**-suhn, dy-uh-**pay**-zuhn/ noun an organ stop sounding a main set of pipes.
– ORIGIN from Greek *dia pasōn khordōn* 'through all notes'.

diaper /dy-uh-per/ noun N. Amer. a baby's nappy.
– ORIGIN from Greek *dia* 'across' + *aspros* 'white'.

diaphanous /dy-**af**-fuh-nuhss/ adjective light, delicate, and translucent.
– ORIGIN Greek *diaphanēs*.

diaphragm /dy-uh-fram/ noun **1** a muscular partition separating the thorax from the abdomen in mammals. **2** a taut flexible membrane in mechanical or acoustic systems. **3** a thin contraceptive cap fitting over the neck of the womb. **4** a device for varying the effective aperture of the lens in a camera or other optical system.
– DERIVATIVES **diaphragmatic** adjective.
– ORIGIN Latin *diaphragma*.

diarist noun a person who writes a diary.

diarrhoea /dy-uh-**ree**-uh/ (US **diarrhea**) noun an illness in which there are frequent discharges of liquid faeces from the bowels.
– DERIVATIVES **diarrhoeal** adjective.
– ORIGIN Greek *diarrhoia*.

diary noun (pl. **diaries**) **1** a book in which one keeps a daily record of events and experiences. **2** a book marked with each day's date, in which to note appointments.

– ORIGIN Latin *diarium*.

diaspora /dy-**ass**-puh-ruh/ noun **1** (**the diaspora**) the dispersion of the Jews beyond Israel, chiefly in the 8th to 6th centuries BC. **2** the dispersion of any people from their original homeland.
– ORIGIN Greek.

diastole /dy-**ass**-tuh-li/ noun the phase of the heartbeat when the heart muscle relaxes and the chambers fill with blood. Often contrasted with SYSTOLE.
– DERIVATIVES **diastolic** /dy-uh-**stol**-ik/ adjective.
– ORIGIN Greek, 'separation, expansion'.

diatom /dy-uh-tuhm/ noun a single-celled alga which has a cell wall of silica.
– DERIVATIVES **diatomaceous** /dy-uh-tuh-may-shuhss/ adjective.
– ORIGIN from Greek *diatomos* 'cut in two'.

diatomic /dy-uh-**tom**-ik/ adjective Chemistry consisting of two atoms.

diatonic /dy-uh-**ton**-ik/ adjective Music involving only the notes of the major or minor scale, without additional sharps, flats, etc.
– ORIGIN Greek *diatonikos* 'at intervals of a tone'.

diatribe /dy-uh-tryb/ noun a harsh and forceful verbal attack.
– ORIGIN Greek, 'spending of time, discourse'.

diazepam /dy-**az**-i-pam, dy-ay-zi-pam/ noun a tranquillizing drug used to relieve anxiety. Also called VALIUM (trademark).

dibber noun Brit. another term for DIBBLE.

dibble noun a pointed hand tool for making holes in the ground for seeds or young plants.
– ORIGIN uncertain.

dice noun (pl. same; sing. also **die**) a small cube with faces bearing from one to six spots, used in games of chance. See also DIE². • verb **1** cut food into small cubes. **2** (**dice with**) take great risks with: *he enjoyed dicing with death.*
– ORIGIN Old French *des*, plural of *de*.

dicey adjective (**dicier**, **diciest**) informal unpredictable and potentially dangerous.

dichotomy /dy-**kot**-uh-mi/ noun (pl. **dichotomies**) a separation between two things that are opposed or different: *the dichotomy between good and evil.*
– DERIVATIVES **dichotomous** adjective.
– ORIGIN Greek *dikhotomia* 'a cutting in two'.

dick¹ noun vulgar slang a penis.
– ORIGIN familiar form of the man's name *Richard*.

dick² noun informal, dated, chiefly N. Amer. a detective.
– ORIGIN perhaps a shortening of DETECTIVE, or from Romany *dick* 'look'.

dickens noun informal used to express annoyance or surprise: *what the dickens is going on?*
– ORIGIN a euphemism for 'devil'.

Dickensian /di-**ken**-zi-uhn/ adjective like the novels of Charles Dickens, especially in terms of the poverty that they portray.

dickhead noun vulgar slang a stupid or ridiculous man.

dicky¹ adjective Brit. informal not strong, healthy, or functioning reliably.
– ORIGIN perhaps from the man's name *Dick*, in the old saying *as queer as Dick's hatband.*

dicky² (also **dickey**) noun (pl. **dickies** or **dickeys**) informal a false shirt front.

– ORIGIN perhaps from *Dicky,* familiar form of the man's name *Richard.*

dicky bow noun informal a bow tie.

dicotyledon /dy-kot-i-**lee**-duhn/ noun a plant with an embryo bearing two cotyledons (leaves growing from a germinating seed).

dicta plural of **DICTUM**.

dictate verb /dik-**tayt**/ **1** state or order something authoritatively. **2** control or influence: *choice is often dictated by availability.* **3** say or read aloud words to be typed or written down. •noun /**dik**-tayt/ an order or principle that must be obeyed: *those who follow the dictates of fashion.*
– DERIVATIVES **dictation** noun.
– ORIGIN Latin *dictare.*

dictator noun a ruler with total power over a country.

dictatorial /dik-tuh-**tor**-i-uhl/ adjective **1** relating to or controlled by a dictator. **2** insisting on total obedience; domineering.
– DERIVATIVES **dictatorially** adverb.

dictatorship noun **1** government by a dictator. **2** a country governed by a dictator.

diction noun **1** the choice and use of words in speech or writing. **2** a person's way of pronouncing words.
– ORIGIN Latin.

dictionary noun (pl. **dictionaries**) a book that lists the words of a language and gives their meaning, or their equivalent in a different language.
– ORIGIN from Latin *dictionarium manuale* or *dictionarius liber* 'manual or book of words'.

dictum /**dik**-tuhm/ noun (pl. **dicta** /**dik**-tuh/ or **dictums**) **1** a formal or authoritative statement. **2** a short statement that expresses a general truth.
– ORIGIN Latin, 'something said'.

did past of **DO**[1].

didactic /dy-**dak**-tik/ adjective intended to teach or give moral guidance: *a didactic religious novel.*
– DERIVATIVES **didactically** adverb **didacticism** noun.
– ORIGIN from Greek *didaskein* 'teach'.

diddle verb informal cheat or swindle someone.
– ORIGIN probably from Jeremy *Diddler,* a character in a farce who constantly borrowed small sums of money.

didgeridoo /di-juh-ri-**doo**/ noun an Australian Aboriginal wind instrument in the form of a long wooden tube, blown to produce a deep resonant sound.
– ORIGIN from an Aboriginal language.

didn't contraction did not.

didst old-fashioned second person singular past of **DO**[1].

die[1] verb (**dies, dying, died**) **1** stop living. **2** (**die out**) become extinct. **3** become less loud or strong: *the storm had died down by now.* **4** (**be dying for/to do**) informal be very eager to have or to do something.
– PHRASES **die hard** change very slowly: *old habits die hard.* **never say die** do not give up hope. **to die for** informal extremely good or desirable.
– ORIGIN Old Norse.

die[2] noun **1** singular form of **DICE**. **2** (pl. **dies**) a device for cutting or moulding metal or for stamping a design onto coins or medals.
– PHRASES **the die is cast** an event has happened that cannot be changed.
– ORIGIN Old French *de.*

dieback noun a condition in which a tree or shrub begins to die from the tip of its leaves or roots backwards.

die-cast adjective (of a metal object) formed by pouring molten metal into a mould.

diehard noun a person who strongly supports something in spite of opposition or changing circumstances.

dielectric /dy-i-**lek**-trik/ Physics adjective that does not conduct electricity; insulating. •noun an insulator.

dieresis noun US spelling of **DIAERESIS**.

diesel /**dee**-z'l/ noun **1** an internal-combustion engine in which the heat of compressed air is used to ignite the fuel. **2** (also **diesel oil**) a form of petroleum used to fuel diesel engines.
– ORIGIN named after the German engineer Rudolf *Diesel.*

diet[1] noun **1** the kinds of food that a person or animal usually eats. **2** a limited range or amount of food, eaten in order to lose weight or for medical reasons. •verb (**diets, dieting, dieted**) eat a limited range or amount of food to lose weight. •adjective (of food or drink) having a reduced fat or sugar content.
– DERIVATIVES **dietary** adjective **dieter** noun.
– ORIGIN Greek *diaita* 'a way of life'.

diet[2] noun **1** a law-making assembly in certain countries. **2** historical a regular meeting of the states of a confederation.
– ORIGIN Latin *dieta* 'day's work, meeting of councillors'.

dietetics /dy-uh-**tet**-iks/ plural noun (treated as sing.) the branch of knowledge concerned with the diet and its effects on health.
– DERIVATIVES **dietetic** adjective.

dietitian /dy-uh-**ti**-sh'n/ (also **dietician**) noun an expert on diet and nutrition.

differ verb **1** be unlike or dissimilar. **2** disagree with someone.
– PHRASES **beg to differ** politely disagree.
– ORIGIN Latin *differre.*

difference noun **1** a way in which people or things are not the same. **2** the state of being unlike: *there's little difference between the two main parties.* **3** a disagreement or quarrel. **4** the remainder left after one value is subtracted from another.

different adjective **1** not the same as another or each other. **2** separate: *he was arrested on two different occasions.* **3** informal new and unusual.
– DERIVATIVES **differently** adverb **differentness** noun.

USAGE: **Different** can be followed by **from, to,** or **than**. In British English **different from** is the most common use, while **different than** is largely found in North America.

differentiable /dif-fuh-**ren**-shi-uhb'l/ adjective able to be distinguished or differentiated.
– DERIVATIVES **differentiability** noun.

differential /dif-fuh-**ren**-sh'l/ adjective relating to or depending on a difference;

varying according to circumstances: *intense competition has not eliminated differential pricing.* •noun **1** a difference in amount, especially (Brit.) a difference in wages between industries or between categories of employees in the same industry. **2** Mathematics an infinitesimal difference between successive values of a variable. **3** a gear allowing a vehicle's driven wheels to revolve at different speeds in cornering.
– DERIVATIVES **differentially** adverb.

differential calculus noun Mathematics the part of calculus concerned with the derivatives of functions.

differential equation noun an equation involving derivatives of a function or functions.

differentiate /dif-fuh-**ren**-shi-ayt/ verb **1** recognize or identify as different; distinguish: *children can differentiate the past from the present.* **2** cause something to appear different or distinct. **3** Mathematics transform a function into its derivative.
– DERIVATIVES **differentiation** noun **differentiator** noun.

difficult adjective **1** needing much effort or skill to do or understand: *I had a difficult decision to make.* **2** causing or full of problems: *a difficult economic climate.* **3** not easy to please or satisfy; awkward.

difficulty noun (pl. **difficulties**) **1** the state of being difficult. **2** a problem. **3** a difficult or dangerous situation: *he went for a swim but got into difficulties.*
– ORIGIN Latin *difficultas*.

diffident adjective modest or shy because of a lack of self-confidence.
– DERIVATIVES **diffidence** noun **diffidently** adverb.
– ORIGIN from Latin *diffidere* 'fail to trust'.

diffraction noun Physics the process by which a beam of light or other system of waves is spread out as a result of passing through a narrow opening or across an edge.
– DERIVATIVES **diffract** verb **diffractive** adjective.
– ORIGIN from Latin *diffringere* 'break into pieces'.

diffuse verb /dif-**fyooz**/ **1** spread over a wide area: *this early language probably diffused across the world.* **2** Physics (of a gas or liquid) intermingle with another substance by movement. •adjective /dif-**fyooss**/ **1** spread out over a large area; not concentrated. **2** not clear or concise.
– DERIVATIVES **diffusely** adverb **diffuser** (also **diffusor**) noun.
– ORIGIN Latin *diffundere* 'pour out'.

USAGE: On the difference between **diffuse** and **defuse**, see the note at **DEFUSE**.

diffusion noun **1** the action of spreading over a wide area. **2** Physics the intermingling of substances by the natural movement of their particles. •adjective (of a range of garments) produced for the mass market by a fashion designer: *a revamped diffusion line.*
– DERIVATIVES **diffusive** adjective.

dig verb (**digs**, **digging**; past and past part. **dug**) **1** break up and turn over or move earth. **2** make a hole by digging. **3** remove from the ground by digging: *workmen dug the cable up.*
4 push or poke sharply: *he dug his hands in his pockets.* **5** (**dig into/through**) search or rummage in something. **6** (**dig something out/up**) discover facts. **7** (**dig in**) begin eating heartily. **8** informal, dated like or appreciate. •noun **1** an act of digging. **2** an archaeological excavation. **3** a sharp push or poke. **4** informal a mocking or critical remark. **5** (**digs**) informal lodgings.
– PHRASES **dig in one's heels** stubbornly refuse to compromise.
– ORIGIN perhaps from Old English, 'ditch'.

digerati /di-juh-**rah**-ti/ plural noun informal people with expertise in information technology.
– ORIGIN blend of **DIGITAL** and **LITERATI**.

digest verb /dy-**jest**/ **1** break down food in the stomach and intestines into substances that can be absorbed by the body. **2** reflect on and absorb information. •noun /**dy**-jest/ a compilation or summary of material or information.
– DERIVATIVES **digester** noun.
– ORIGIN Latin *digerere* 'distribute, dissolve, digest'.

digestible adjective **1** (of food) able to be digested. **2** (of information) easy to understand.
– DERIVATIVES **digestibility** noun.

digestif /dy-jes-tif, dee-zhe-**steef**/ noun a drink taken before or after a meal in order to help digestion.
– ORIGIN French, 'digestive'.

digestion noun **1** the process of digesting food. **2** a person's capacity to digest food.

digestive adjective relating to the digestion of food. •noun **1** a food or medicine that aids the digestion of food. **2** Brit. a semi-sweet wholemeal biscuit.

digger noun **1** a person, animal, or large machine that digs earth. **2** Austral./NZ informal a friendly form of address for a man.

digit /**di**-jit/ noun **1** any of the numerals from o to 9. **2** a finger or thumb.
– ORIGIN Latin *digitus* 'finger, toe'.

digital adjective **1** relating to information represented as a series of binary digits, as in a computer. **2** relating to computer technology: *the digital revolution.* **3** (of a clock or watch) showing the time by displaying numbers electronically. **4** relating to a finger or fingers.
– DERIVATIVES **digitally** adverb.

digital audiotape noun magnetic tape on which sound is recorded digitally.

digital camera noun a camera which produces digital images that can be stored in a computer and displayed on screen.

digitalis /di-ji-**tay**-liss/ noun a drug prepared from foxglove leaves, containing substances that stimulate the heart muscle.
– ORIGIN from the Latin genus name of the foxglove.

digitalize (or **digitalise**) verb another term for **DIGITIZE**.
– DERIVATIVES **digitalization** noun.

digital signature noun a digital code which is attached to an electronically transmitted document to verify its contents and the sender's identity.

digitize (or **digitise**) verb convert pictures or sound into a digital form that can be processed by a computer.
– DERIVATIVES **digitization** noun **digitizer** noun.

dignified adjective having a serious manner that is worthy of respect.

dignify verb (**dignifies, dignifying, dignified**) make something seem impressive or worthy of respect.
– ORIGIN Latin *dignificare*.

dignitary /**dig**-ni-tuh-ri/ noun (pl. **dignitaries**) a high-ranking person.

dignity noun (pl. **dignities**) **1** the state of being worthy of respect: *the dignity of labour.* **2** a calm or serious manner. **3** a sense of self-respect.
– ORIGIN Latin *dignitas*.

digraph /**dy**-grahf/ noun a combination of two letters representing one sound, as in *ph* in *phase.*

digress /dy-**gress**/ verb leave the main subject temporarily in speech or writing.
– DERIVATIVES **digression** noun **digressive** adjective.
– ORIGIN Latin *digredi* 'step away'.

dihedral /dy-**hee**-druhl/ adjective having or contained by two plane faces.

dike¹ noun variant spelling of **DYKE¹**.

dike² noun variant spelling of **DYKE²**.

diktat /**dik**-tat/ noun a decree imposed by someone in power without popular consent.
– ORIGIN German.

dilapidated /di-**lap**-i-day-tid/ adjective in a state of disrepair or ruin.
– DERIVATIVES **dilapidation** noun.
– ORIGIN from Latin *dilapidare* 'demolish'.

dilatation /dy-lay-**tay**-shuhn, di-luh-**tay**-shuhn/ noun Medicine & Physiology the action of widening a vessel or opening in the body.

dilate /dy-**layt**/ verb **1** make or become wider, larger, or more open: *her eyes dilated with horror.* **2** (**dilate on**) speak or write at length on a subject.
– DERIVATIVES **dilation** noun **dilator** noun.
– ORIGIN Latin *dilatare* 'spread out'.

dilatory /**di**-luh-tri/ adjective **1** slow to act. **2** intended to cause delay: *dilatory tactics.*
– DERIVATIVES **dilatoriness** noun.
– ORIGIN Latin *dilatorius.*

dildo noun (pl. **dildos** or **dildoes**) an object shaped like an erect penis, used for sexual stimulation.
– ORIGIN unknown.

dilemma /di-**lem**-muh/ noun **1** a situation in which a difficult choice has to be made between alternatives that are equally undesirable. **2** informal a difficult situation or problem.
– ORIGIN Greek.

dilettante /di-li-**tan**-tay/ noun (pl. **dilettanti** /di-li-**tan**-ti/ or **dilettantes**) a person who dabbles in a subject for enjoyment but without serious study.
– DERIVATIVES **dilettantish** adjective **dilettantism** noun.
– ORIGIN Italian, 'art-lover'.

diligent adjective careful and conscientious in carrying out a task or duties.

– DERIVATIVES **diligence** noun **diligently** adverb.
– ORIGIN from Latin *diligere* 'love, take delight in'.

dill noun a herb, the leaves and seeds of which are used in cookery or for medicinal purposes.
– ORIGIN Old English.

dilly-dally verb (**dilly-dallies, dilly-dallying, dilly-dallied**) informal dawdle or be indecisive.
– ORIGIN from **DALLY**.

dilute /dy-**lyoot**/ verb **1** make a liquid thinner or weaker by adding water or another solvent. **2** make weaker by modifying or adding other elements: *they rejected any attempt to dilute the law.* • adjective /also **dy**-lyoot/ **1** (of a liquid) made thinner or weaker by the addition of a solvent. **2** Chemistry (of a solution) having a relatively low concentration of solute.
– DERIVATIVES **diluter** noun **dilution** noun **dilutive** adjective.
– ORIGIN Latin *diluere* 'wash away, dissolve'.

dim adjective (**dimmer, dimmest**) **1** not bright or well lit: *the dim corridors of the building.* **2** made difficult to see by darkness or distance: *dim shapes of men passed to and fro.* **3** (of the eyes) not able to see clearly. **4** not clearly remembered. **5** informal stupid or slow to understand. • verb (**dims, dimming, dimmed**) make or become dim.
– PHRASES **take a dim view of** regard with disapproval.
– DERIVATIVES **dimly** adverb **dimmable** adjective **dimness** noun.
– ORIGIN Old English.

dime /dym/ noun N. Amer. a ten-cent coin.
– ORIGIN Old French *disme* 'tenth part'.

dimension /di-**men**-sh'n, dy-**men**-sh'n/ noun **1** a measurable extent, such as length, breadth, or height. **2** an aspect or feature: *the story has an international dimension.*
– DERIVATIVES **dimensional** adjective **dimensionally** adverb.
– ORIGIN Latin.

dimer /**dy**-mer/ noun Chemistry a molecule consisting of two identical molecules linked together.
– ORIGIN from **DI-**, on the pattern of *polymer.*

diminish verb **1** become or make smaller, weaker, or less. **2** cause to seem less impressive or valuable: *the trial has aged and diminished him.*
– ORIGIN Latin *deminuere* 'lessen'.

diminished responsibility noun English Law an unbalanced mental state considered as grounds to reduce a charge of murder to that of manslaughter.

diminuendo /di-min-yoo-**en**-doh/ adverb & adjective Music with a decrease in loudness.
– ORIGIN Italian, 'diminishing'.

diminution /di-mi-**nyoo**-sh'n/ noun a reduction in the size, extent, or importance of something.

diminutive /di-**min**-yuh-tiv/ adjective **1** very or unusually small. **2** (of a word, name, or suffix) implying smallness (e.g. *-let* in *booklet*). • noun a shortened form of a name, typically used informally.
– ORIGIN Latin *diminutivus.*

dimity /**dim**-iti/ noun a hard-wearing cotton fabric woven with stripes or checks.
– ORIGIN Greek *dimitos.*

d

dimmer (also **dimmer switch**) noun a device for varying the brightness of an electric light.

dimorphic /dy-**mor**-fik/ adjective chiefly Biology occurring in or representing two distinct forms.
– DERIVATIVES **dimorphism** noun.
– ORIGIN from Greek *dimorphos*.

dimple noun 1 a small depression formed in the fleshy part of the cheeks when one smiles. 2 a slight depression in the surface of an object. •verb produce a dimple or dimples on something.
– DERIVATIVES **dimply** adjective.
– ORIGIN Germanic.

dim sum /dim **sum**/ (also **dim sim** /dim **sim**/) noun a Chinese dish of small dumplings containing various fillings.
– ORIGIN from the Chinese words for 'dot' and 'heart'.

dimwit noun informal a stupid or silly person.
– DERIVATIVES **dim-witted** adjective.

DIN noun any of a series of international technical standards, used especially for electrical connections and film speeds.
– ORIGIN from the initial letters of German *Deutsche Industrie-Norm* 'German Industrial Standard'.

din noun a prolonged loud and unpleasant noise. •verb (**dins, dinning, dinned**) (**din something into**) put information into someone's mind by constant repetition.
– ORIGIN Old English.

dinar /**dee**-nar/ noun 1 the basic unit of money of Bosnia and the Union of Serbia and Montenegro. 2 the basic unit of money of certain countries of the Middle East and North Africa.
– ORIGIN Turkish and Serbo-Croat.

dine verb 1 eat dinner. 2 (**dine out on**) regularly entertain friends with an interesting or amusing story.
– ORIGIN Old French *disner*.

diner noun 1 a person eating a meal, especially in a restaurant. 2 a dining car on a train. 3 N. Amer. a small roadside restaurant.

dinette /dy-**net**/ noun a small room or part of a room used for eating meals.

ding verb make a metallic ringing sound.

dingbat noun N. Amer. informal a stupid or eccentric person.
– ORIGIN uncertain.

ding-dong Brit. informal noun a fierce argument or fight. •adjective (of a contest) evenly matched and hard fought.
– ORIGIN from the sound of a bell.

dinghy /**ding**-gi, **ding**-i/ noun (pl. **dinghies**) 1 a small open sailing boat for recreation or racing. 2 a small inflatable rubber boat.
– ORIGIN Hindi, 'rowing boat'.

dingle noun literary or dialect a deep wooded valley.
– ORIGIN unknown.

dingo /**ding**-goh/ noun (pl. **dingoes** or **dingos**) a wild or semi-domesticated Australian dog with a sandy-coloured coat.
– ORIGIN from an Aboriginal language.

dingy /**din**-ji/ adjective (**dingier, dingiest**) gloomy and drab.
– DERIVATIVES **dingily** adverb **dinginess** noun.
– ORIGIN perhaps from an Old English word

meaning 'dung'.

dining car noun a railway carriage equipped as a restaurant.

dining room noun a room in a house or hotel in which meals are eaten.

dinkum /**ding**-kuhm/ adjective Austral./NZ informal genuine.
– PHRASES **fair dinkum** used for emphasis or to query whether something is true.
– ORIGIN unknown.

dinky adjective (**dinkier, dinkiest**) Brit. informal attractively small and neat.
– ORIGIN from Scots and northern English dialect *dink* 'neat, trim'.

dinner noun 1 the main meal of the day, taken either around midday or in the evening. 2 a formal evening meal.
– ORIGIN from Old French *disner* 'to dine'.

dinner jacket noun a man's short jacket without tails, worn with a bow tie for formal evening occasions.

dinosaur /**dy**-nuh-sor/ noun 1 an extinct reptile of the Mesozoic era, often reaching an enormous size. 2 a thing that is outdated or has become obsolete.
– ORIGIN from Greek *deinos* 'terrible' + *sauros* 'lizard'.

dint noun a dent or hollow in a surface.
– PHRASES **by dint of** by means of.
– ORIGIN Old English, 'a blow with a weapon'.

diocese /**dy**-uh-siss/ noun (pl. **dioceses** /dy-uh-seez-iz/) (in the Christian Church) a district for which a bishop is responsible.
– DERIVATIVES **diocesan** adjective /dy-**oss**-i-z'n/.
– ORIGIN Latin *dioecesis* 'governor's jurisdiction, diocese'.

diode /**dy**-ohd/ noun 1 a semiconductor device with two terminals, typically allowing the flow of current in one direction only. 2 a thermionic valve with two electrodes.
– ORIGIN from **DI-** + a shortened form of **ELECTRODE**.

dioecious /dy-**ee**-shuhss/ adjective (of a plant or invertebrate animal) having the male and female reproductive organs in separate individuals. Compare with **MONOECIOUS**.
– ORIGIN from **DI-** + Greek *-oikos* 'house'.

Dionysian /dy-uh-**niz**-i-uhn/ (also **Dionysiac** /dy-uh-**niz**-i-ak/) adjective 1 relating to Dionysus, the Greek god of fertility and wine, associated with ecstatic religious rites. 2 wild and uninhibited.

dioptre /dy-**op**-tuh/ (US **diopter**) noun a unit of refractive power, equal to the reciprocal of the focal length (in metres) of a given lens.
– ORIGIN from Greek *di-* 'through' + *optos* 'visible'.

dioptric /dy-**op**-trik/ adjective relating to the refraction of light.
– DERIVATIVES **dioptrics** plural noun.

diorama /dy-uh-**rah**-muh/ noun 1 a model representing a scene with three-dimensional figures against a painted background. 2 chiefly historical a scenic painting, viewed through a peephole, in which changes in colour and direction of illumination simulate changes in the weather and time of day.
– ORIGIN French.

d

diorite /dy-uh-ryt/ noun a speckled, coarse-grained igneous rock.
– ORIGIN French.

dioxide /dy-ok-syd/ noun Chemistry an oxide with two atoms of oxygen to one of a metal or other element.

dioxin /dy-ok-sin/ noun a highly toxic organic compound produced as a by-product in some manufacturing processes.

Dip. abbreviation diploma.

dip verb (**dips, dipping, dipped**) 1 (**dip something in/into**) put or lower something briefly in or into liquid. 2 sink, drop, or slope downwards: *the sun had dipped below the horizon.* 3 (of a level or amount) temporarily become lower or smaller. 4 move something briefly downwards. 5 Brit. lower the beam of a vehicle's headlights. 6 (**dip into**) reach into a bag or container to take something out. 7 (**dip into**) spend from one's financial resources.
•noun 1 an act of dipping. 2 a thick sauce in which pieces of food are dipped before eating. 3 a brief swim. 4 a brief downward slope followed by an upward one.
– ORIGIN Old English.

diphtheria /dip-**theer**-i-uh, dif-**theer**-i-uh/ noun a serious contagious disease causing inflammation of the mucous membranes, especially in the throat.
– ORIGIN Greek *diphthera* 'skin, hide' (referring to the false membrane that forms in the throat).

diphthong /**dif**-thong, **dip**--thong/ noun a sound formed by the combination of two vowels in a single syllable (as in *coin*).
– ORIGIN from Greek *di-* 'twice' + *phthongos* 'sound'.

diplodocus /di-**plod**-uh-kuhss, di-ploh-**doh**-kuhss/ noun a huge plant-eating dinosaur of the late Jurassic period, with a long slender neck and tail.
– ORIGIN from Greek *diplous* 'double' + *dokos* 'wooden beam'.

diploid /**dip**-loyd/ adjective (of a cell or nucleus) containing two complete sets of chromosomes, one from each parent. Compare with HAPLOID.
– ORIGIN from Greek *diplous* 'double'.

diploma noun a certificate awarded by a school or college for successfully completing a course of study.
– ORIGIN Greek, 'folded paper'.

diplomacy noun 1 the profession, activity, or skill of managing international relations. 2 skill and tact in dealing with people.
– ORIGIN French *diplomatie*.

diplomat noun an official representing a country abroad.

diplomatic adjective 1 relating to diplomacy. 2 dealing with people in a tactful way.
– DERIVATIVES **diplomatically** adverb.

diplomatic bag noun Brit. a container in which official mail is sent to or from an embassy, which is not subject to customs inspection.

diplomatic immunity noun exemption from certain laws granted to diplomats by the state in which they are working.

dipole /**dy**-pohl/ noun 1 Physics a pair of equal and oppositely charged or magnetized poles separated by a distance. 2 an aerial consisting of a horizontal metal rod with a connecting wire at its centre.
– DERIVATIVES **dipolar** adjective.

dipper noun 1 a songbird that dives into fast-flowing streams to feed. 2 a ladle.

dippy adjective (**dippier, dippiest**) informal foolish or eccentric.
– ORIGIN unknown.

dipsomania /dip-suh-**may**-ni-uh/ noun alcoholism.
– DERIVATIVES **dipsomaniac** noun.
– ORIGIN from Greek *dipsa* 'thirst'.

dipstick noun a rod for measuring the depth of a liquid, especially oil in an engine.

diptych /**dip**-tik/ noun a painting on two hinged wooden panels, typically forming an altarpiece.
– ORIGIN Greek *diptukha* 'pair of writing tablets'.

dire adjective 1 very serious or urgent. 2 Brit. informal of a very poor quality.
– ORIGIN Latin *dirus* 'fearful, threatening'.

direct /di-**rekt**, dy-**rekt**/ adjective 1 going from one place to another without changing direction or stopping. 2 with nothing or no one in between: *I had no direct contact with Mr Clark.* 3 straightforward; frank. 4 clear; unambiguous. 5 (of descent) proceeding in continuous succession from parent to child.
•adverb in a direct way or by a direct route.
•verb 1 aim something towards: *he directed his criticism at the media.* 2 control or manage something. 3 supervise and control a film, play, or other production. 4 tell or show someone the way. 5 give an order to someone.
– DERIVATIVES **directness** noun.
– ORIGIN Latin *directus*.

direct action noun the use of strikes or other public forms of protest rather than negotiation to achieve one's aims.

direct current noun an electric current flowing in one direction only. Compare with ALTERNATING CURRENT.

direct debit noun Brit. an arrangement made with a bank that allows money to be transferred from a person's account to pay a particular person or organization.

direction /di-**rek**-sh'n, dy-**rek**-sh'n/ noun 1 a course along which someone or something moves, or which leads to a destination. 2 a point to or from which a person or thing moves or faces: *a house with views in all directions.* 3 the management or guidance of someone or something. 4 aim or purpose: *his lack of direction in life.* 5 (**directions**) instructions on how to reach a destination or how to do something.
– DERIVATIVES **directionless** adjective.

directional adjective 1 relating to or indicating direction. 2 operating or sending radio signals in one direction only: *a directional microphone.*

directive noun an official or authoritative instruction.

directly adverb 1 in a direct way. 2 exactly in a specified position: *the house directly opposite.* 3 immediately; at once. •conjunction Brit. as soon as.

direct mail noun advertising material mailed

to prospective customers without them having asked for it.

direct object noun a noun phrase that refers to a person or thing that is directly affected by the action of a transitive verb (e.g. *the dog* in *she fed the dog*).

director noun **1** a person who is in charge of a department, organization, or activity. **2** a member of the managing board of a business. **3** a person who directs a film, play, etc.
– DERIVATIVES **directorial** adjective **directorship** noun.

directorate noun **1** the board of directors of a company. **2** a section of a government department in charge of a particular activity.

director general noun (pl. **directors general**) chiefly Brit. the chief executive of a large organization.

directory noun (pl. **directories**) a book listing individuals or organizations with details such as addresses and telephone numbers.

direct speech noun the reporting of speech by repeating the actual words of a speaker, for example '*I'm going*', *she said*. Contrasted with REPORTED SPEECH.

direct tax noun a tax, such as income tax, which is charged on the income or profits of the person who pays it.

dirge /derj/ noun **1** a lament for the dead, especially one forming part of a funeral rite. **2** a mournful song or piece of music.
– ORIGIN from Latin *dirige* 'direct!', the first word of a psalm used in service for the dead.

dirham /dee-ruhm/ noun the basic unit of money of Morocco and the United Arab Emirates.
– ORIGIN Arabic.

dirigible /di-ri-ji-b'l/ noun an airship.
– ORIGIN from Latin *dirigere* 'to direct'.

dirigisme /di-ri-zhiz'm/ noun state control of economic and social matters.
– DERIVATIVES **dirigiste** adjective.
– ORIGIN French.

dirk /derk/ noun a short dagger of a kind formerly carried by Scottish Highlanders.
– ORIGIN unknown.

dirndl /dern-d'l/ noun **1** (also **dirndl skirt**) a full, wide skirt gathered into a tight waistband. **2** a woman's dress with a dirndl skirt and a close-fitting bodice.
– ORIGIN German dialect, 'little girl'.

dirt noun **1** a substance that makes something unclean. **2** soil or earth. **3** informal excrement. **4** informal scandalous or damaging information.
– ORIGIN Old Norse, 'excrement'.

dirt bike noun a motorcycle designed for use on rough terrain, especially in scrambling.

dirt cheap adjective & adverb informal very cheap.

dirt poor adjective & adverb very poor.

dirt track noun a racing track made of earth or rolled cinders.

dirty adjective (**dirtier**, **dirtiest**) **1** covered or marked with dirt; not clean. **2** concerned with sex in a lewd or obscene way: *dirty jokes.* **3** dishonest; dishonourable. **4** (of weather) rough and unpleasant. • adverb Brit. informal used for emphasis: *a dirty great slab of stone.* • verb (**dirties**, **dirtying**, **dirtied**) make someone or something dirty.

– PHRASES **do the dirty on** Brit. informal cheat or betray someone. **play dirty** informal act in a dishonest or unfair way.
– DERIVATIVES **dirtily** adverb **dirtiness** noun.

dirty bomb noun a conventional bomb that contains radioactive material.

dirty look noun informal a look expressing disapproval, disgust, or anger.

dirty weekend noun Brit. informal a weekend spent away, especially in secret, with a lover.

dirty word noun a thing regarded with dislike: *VAT is a dirty word among small businesses.*

dirty work noun unpleasant or dishonest activities that are delegated to someone else.

dis (also **diss**) verb (**disses**, **dissing**, **dissed**) informal, chiefly US speak disrespectfully to someone.

dis- prefix expressing: **1** reversal; not: *disadvantage.* **2** removal or separation: *disperse.*
– ORIGIN Latin.

disability noun (pl. **disabilities**) **1** a physical or mental condition that limits a person's movements, senses, or activities. **2** a disadvantage.

disable verb **1** (of a disease, injury, or accident) limit someone in their movements, senses, or activities. **2** put something out of action.
– DERIVATIVES **disablement** noun.

disabled adjective having a physical or mental disability.

> USAGE: **Disabled** is the standard term for people with physical or mental disabilities, and should be used instead of terms such as **crippled** or **handicapped** which often cause offence.

disabuse /diss-uh-**byooz**/ verb persuade someone that an idea or belief is mistaken: *Greg soon disabused her of this idea.*

disaccharide /dy-**sak**-uh-ryd/ noun a sugar whose molecule can be broken down to give two simple sugar molecules.

disadvantage noun something that causes a problem or that makes success or progress less likely: *women are at a disadvantage in competing for jobs with men.* • verb **1** put someone in an unfavourable position. **2** (as adj. **disadvantaged**) having less money and fewer opportunities than the rest of society.
– DERIVATIVES **disadvantageous** /dis-ad-vuhn-**tay**-juhss/ adjective.

disaffected adjective discontented through having lost one's feelings of loyalty.
– DERIVATIVES **disaffection** noun.

disagree verb (**disagrees**, **disagreeing**, **disagreed**) **1** have a different opinion. **2** fail to correspond or be consistent: *results which disagree with the findings reported so far.* **3** (**disagree with**) make someone slightly ill.
– DERIVATIVES **disagreement** noun.

disagreeable adjective **1** not pleasant or enjoyable. **2** unfriendly and bad-tempered.
– DERIVATIVES **disagreeably** adverb.

disallow verb declare something to be invalid.
– DERIVATIVES **disallowance** noun.

disambiguate /dis-am-**big**-yoo-ayt/ verb remove uncertainty of meaning from something with more than one possible

meaning.
– DERIVATIVES **disambiguation** noun.

disappear verb **1** cease to be visible. **2** cease to exist. **3** be lost or impossible to find.
– DERIVATIVES **disappearance** noun.

disappoint verb **1** fail to fulfil someone's hopes. **2** prevent hopes from becoming a reality.
– DERIVATIVES **disappointing** adjective **disappointingly** adverb.
– ORIGIN Old French *desappointer* 'deprive of a position'.

disappointed adjective sad or displeased because one's hopes have not been fulfilled.
– DERIVATIVES **disappointedly** adverb.

disappointment noun **1** sadness or displeasure caused by the failure of one's hopes to be fulfilled. **2** a cause of disappointment.

disapprobation /diss-ap-ruh-**bay**-sh'n/ noun formal strong disapproval.

disapprove verb think that someone or something is wrong or bad.
– DERIVATIVES **disapproval** noun **disapproving** adjective.

disarm verb **1** take a weapon or weapons away from a person, force, or country. **2** win over a hostile or suspicious person: *her political skills will disarm critics*. **3** remove the fuse from a bomb.

disarmament /diss-**arm**-uh-muhnt/ noun the reduction or withdrawal of military forces and weapons.

disarming adjective removing suspicion or hostility, especially through charm.
– DERIVATIVES **disarmingly** adverb.

disarrange verb make something untidy or disordered.

disarray noun a state of disorder or untidiness.

disassemble verb take something to pieces.
– DERIVATIVES **disassembly** noun.

disassociate verb another term for DISSOCIATE.
– DERIVATIVES **disassociation** noun.

disaster noun **1** a sudden accident or a natural catastrophe that causes great damage or loss of life. **2** an event or situation causing ruin or failure: *the deteriorating dollar is a disaster for the economy*.
– ORIGIN Italian *disastro* 'unlucky event'.

disastrous adjective **1** causing great damage. **2** informal highly unsuccessful.
– DERIVATIVES **disastrously** adverb.

disavow verb deny any responsibility or support for something.
– DERIVATIVES **disavowal** noun.

disband verb stop or cause to stop operating as an organized group.

disbar verb (**disbars**, **disbarring**, **disbarred**) expel a barrister from the Bar.
– DERIVATIVES **disbarment** noun.

disbelief noun **1** inability or refusal to accept that something is true or real. **2** lack of faith.

disbelieve verb **1** be unable to believe someone or something. **2** have no religious faith.
– DERIVATIVES **disbeliever** noun.

disbenefit noun Brit. a disadvantage.

disburse /diss-**berss**/ verb pay out money from a fund.

– DERIVATIVES **disbursement** noun.
– ORIGIN Old French *desbourser*.

disc (US also **disk**) noun **1** a flat, thin, circular object. **2** (**disk**) an information storage device for a computer, on which data is stored either magnetically or optically. **3** a layer of cartilage separating vertebrae in the spine. **4** dated a gramophone record.
– ORIGIN Greek *diskos* 'discus'.

discard verb /diss-**kard**/ get rid of something as useless or unwanted. •noun /**diss**-kard/ a discarded item.
– ORIGIN from DIS- + CARD[1].

disc brake noun a type of vehicle brake employing the friction of pads against a disc attached to the wheel.

discern /di-**sern**/ verb **1** recognize or find something out. **2** see or hear someone or something with difficulty.
– DERIVATIVES **discernible** adjective.
– ORIGIN Latin *discernere*.

discerning adjective having or showing good judgement.
– DERIVATIVES **discernment** noun.

discharge verb /diss-**charj**/ **1** officially tell someone that they can or must leave: *he was discharged from the RAF.* **2** cause a liquid, gas, or other substance to flow out. **3** fire a gun or missile. **4** do all that is required to fulfil a responsibility. **5** release someone from a contract or obligation. **6** Physics release or neutralize the electric charge of a battery or electric field. •noun /**diss**-charj, diss-**charj**/ **1** the action of discharging someone or something. **2** a substance that has been discharged. **3** a flow of electricity through the air or other gas.
– DERIVATIVES **discharger** noun.
– ORIGIN Latin *discarricare* 'unload'.

disciple /di-**sy**-p'l/ noun **1** a follower of Jesus during his life, especially one of the twelve Apostles. **2** a follower or pupil of a teacher, leader, or philosopher.
– DERIVATIVES **discipleship** noun.
– ORIGIN Latin *discipulus* 'learner'.

disciplinarian /diss-i-pli-**nair**-i-uhn/ noun a person who enforces firm discipline.

discipline /**diss**-i-plin/ noun **1** the training of people to obey rules or a code of behaviour. **2** controlled behaviour resulting from such training: *he was able to maintain discipline among his men.* **3** an activity providing mental or physical training: *kung fu is a discipline open to all.* **4** a branch of academic study. •verb **1** train someone to be obedient or self-controlled by punishment or imposing rules. **2** formally punish someone for an offence. **3** (as adj. **disciplined**) behaving in a controlled way.
– DERIVATIVES **disciplinary** /diss-i-**plin**-uh-ri/ adjective.
– ORIGIN Latin *disciplina* 'instruction, knowledge'.

disc jockey noun full form of DJ.

disclaim verb **1** deny responsibility for or knowledge of something. **2** Law renounce a legal claim to a property or title.

disclaimer noun a statement denying responsibility for something.

disclose verb **1** make secret or new

information known. **2** allow something hidden to be seen.

disclosure noun **1** the disclosing of new or secret information. **2** a fact that is made known.

disco noun (pl. **discos**) **1** a club or party at which people dance to pop music. **2** (also **disco music**) soul-influenced, melodic pop music.
– ORIGIN short for **DISCOTHEQUE**.

discography /diss-**kog**-ruh-fi/ noun (pl. **discographies**) **1** a descriptive catalogue of musical recordings. **2** the study of musical recordings and compilation of descriptive catalogues.

discoid /**diss**-koyd/ adjective technical shaped like a disc.
– DERIVATIVES **discoidal** adjective.

discolour (US **discolor**) verb change to a different, less attractive colour.
– DERIVATIVES **discoloration** (also **discolouration**) noun.

discomfit /diss-**kum**-fit/ verb (**discomfits**, **discomfiting**, **discomfited**) make someone uneasy or embarrassed.
– DERIVATIVES **discomfiture** noun.
– ORIGIN Old French *desconfire* 'defeat'.

discomfort noun **1** slight pain. **2** slight anxiety or embarrassment. • verb cause discomfort to someone.

discommode /diss-kuh-**mohd**/ verb formal cause someone trouble or inconvenience.
– ORIGIN former French *discommoder*.

discompose verb disturb or agitate someone.
– DERIVATIVES **discomposure** noun.

disconcert /diss-kuhn-**sert**/ verb disturb the composure of; unsettle: *troops are disconcerted by the anti-war protests*.
– DERIVATIVES **disconcerted** adjective **disconcerting** adjective.
– ORIGIN former French *desconcerter*.

disconnect verb **1** break the connection between two things. **2** detach an electrical device from a power supply.
– DERIVATIVES **disconnection** noun.

disconnected adjective (of speech, writing, or thought) lacking a logical sequence.

disconsolate /diss-**kon**-suh-luht/ adjective very unhappy and unable to be comforted.
– DERIVATIVES **disconsolately** adverb.

discontent noun lack of contentment or satisfaction.
– DERIVATIVES **discontented** adjective **discontentment** noun.

discontinue verb (**discontinues**, **discontinuing**, **discontinued**) stop doing, providing, or making something.
– DERIVATIVES **discontinuation** noun.

discontinuous adjective having intervals or gaps; not continuous.
– DERIVATIVES **discontinuity** noun (pl. **discontinuities**).

discord noun **1** lack of agreement or harmony: *financial difficulties can lead to marital discord*. **2** lack of harmony between musical notes sounding together.
– ORIGIN from Latin *discors* 'discordant'.

discordant adjective **1** not in harmony or agreement: *discordant opinions*. **2** (of a sound) harsh and unpleasant.

– DERIVATIVES **discordance** noun.

discotheque /diss-kuh-**tek**/ noun full form of **DISCO** (in sense 1).
– ORIGIN French.

discount noun /**diss**-kownt/ a deduction from the usual cost of something. • verb /diss-**kownt**/ **1** deduct a discount from the usual price of something. **2** regard something as unworthy of consideration because it seems improbable.
– DERIVATIVES **discounter** /diss-**kown**-ter/ noun.

discountenance verb **1** refuse to approve something. **2** unsettle someone.

discourage verb **1** cause someone to lose confidence or enthusiasm. **2** try to persuade someone not to do something: *we want to discourage children from smoking*.
– DERIVATIVES **discouragement** noun **discouraging** adjective.
– ORIGIN Old French *descouragier*.

discourse noun /**diss**-korss/ **1** written or spoken communication or debate. **2** a formal written or verbal discussion of a topic. • verb /diss-**korss**/ speak or write about a topic with authority.
– ORIGIN Latin *discursus* 'running to and fro'.

discourteous adjective rude and lacking consideration for others.
– DERIVATIVES **discourteously** adverb.

discourtesy noun (pl. **discourtesies**) **1** rude and inconsiderate behaviour. **2** a rude and inconsiderate act or remark.

discover verb **1** find someone or something unexpectedly or during a search. **2** become aware of a fact or situation. **3** be the first to find or observe a place, substance, or scientific phenomenon.
– DERIVATIVES **discoverable** adjective **discoverer** noun.

discovery noun (pl. **discoveries**) **1** the action of discovering something. **2** a person or thing discovered.

discredit verb (**discredits**, **discrediting**, **discredited**) **1** damage a person's good reputation. **2** make an idea or account seem false or unreliable. • noun loss or lack of respect for someone.
– DERIVATIVES **discreditable** adjective.

discreet adjective (**discreeter**, **discreetest**) careful to keep something secret or to avoid undue attention.
– DERIVATIVES **discreetly** adverb.
– ORIGIN Latin *discretus* 'separate'.

> **USAGE:** Discrete and discreet are often confused. **Discreet** means 'careful to keep something secret or to avoid attention' (*we made some discreet inquiries*), while **discrete** means 'separate' (*products are organized in discrete batches*).

discrepancy /diss-**krep**-uhn-si/ noun (pl. **discrepancies**) a difference between facts that should be the same.
– DERIVATIVES **discrepant** adjective.
– ORIGIN Latin *discrepantia*.

discrete adjective separate and distinct.
– DERIVATIVES **discretely** adverb **discreteness** noun.
– ORIGIN Latin *discretus* 'separate'.

discretion noun **1** the quality of being careful

not to reveal information or give offence.
2 the freedom to decide what should be done
in a particular situation: *you will be offered
bribes, which you may accept or decline at your
discretion.*
- ORIGIN Latin, 'separation' (later
'discernment').

discretionary adjective done or used
according to a person's judgement.

discriminate /diss-**krim**-i-nayt/ verb
1 recognize a difference: *babies can
discriminate between different facial
expressions.* **2** treat different categories of
people unfairly on the grounds of race, sex, or
age.
- DERIVATIVES **discriminative** adjective
discriminator noun.
- ORIGIN Latin *discriminare*.

discriminating adjective having or showing
good taste or judgement.

discrimination noun **1** unfair treatment of
different categories of people on the grounds
of race, sex, or age. **2** recognition of the
difference between one thing and another.
3 good judgement or taste.

discriminatory adjective showing
discrimination or prejudice.

discursive /diss-**ker**-siv/ adjective **1** wandering
from subject to subject. **2** relating to
discourse.
- DERIVATIVES **discursively** adverb **discursiveness**
noun.
- ORIGIN Latin *discursivus*.

discus noun (pl. **discuses**) a heavy disc thrown in
athletic contests.
- ORIGIN Greek *diskos*.

discuss verb **1** talk about something so as to
reach a decision. **2** talk or write about a topic
in detail.
- DERIVATIVES **discussable** adjective.
- ORIGIN Latin *discutere* 'dash to pieces,
investigate'.

discussant noun a person who takes part in a
discussion, especially a prearranged one.

discussion noun **1** the action of discussing
something. **2** a debate about or a detailed
written treatment of a topic.

disdain noun the feeling that someone or
something does not deserve one's
consideration or respect. • verb consider to be
unworthy of respect: *people disdained the
go-getters of eighties Wall Street.*
- ORIGIN Old French *desdeign*.

disdainful adjective showing contempt or lack
of respect.
- DERIVATIVES **disdainfully** adverb.

disease noun a disorder in a human, animal, or
plant, caused by infection, diet, or by faulty
functioning of a process.
- DERIVATIVES **diseased** adjective.
- ORIGIN Old French *desaise* 'lack of ease'.

diseconomy noun (pl. **diseconomies**) an
economic disadvantage such as an increase in
cost arising from an increase in the size of an
organization.

disembark verb leave a ship, aircraft, or train.
- DERIVATIVES **disembarkation** noun.

disembodied adjective **1** separated from or
existing without the body. **2** (of a sound)

coming from a person who cannot be seen.
- DERIVATIVES **disembodiment** noun.

disembowel verb (**disembowels**,
disembowelling, **disembowelled**; US
disembowels, **disemboweling**, **disemboweled**)
cut open and remove the internal organs of
someone or something.
- DERIVATIVES **disembowelment** noun.

disempower verb make someone less
powerful or confident.
- DERIVATIVES **disempowerment** noun.

disenchant verb make someone disillusioned.
- DERIVATIVES **disenchantment** noun.

disenfranchise verb deprive someone of a
right, especially the right to vote.
- DERIVATIVES **disenfranchisement** noun.

disengage verb **1** release or detach: *he
disengaged his arm from hers.* **2** remove troops
from an area of conflict. **3** (as adj. **disengaged**)
emotionally detached; uninvolved.
- DERIVATIVES **disengagement** noun.

disentangle verb free someone or something
from something they are entangled with.

disequilibrium /dis-ee-kwi-**lib**-ri-uhm, dis-
ek-wi-**lib**-ri-uhm/ noun a loss or lack of
equilibrium or stability, especially in relation
to supply, demand, and prices.

disestablish verb deprive a national Church
of its official status.
- DERIVATIVES **disestablishment** noun.

disesteem noun lack of respect or admiration.
• verb formal have a low opinion of someone or
something.

disfavour (US **disfavor**) noun **1** disapproval or
dislike. **2** the state of being disliked.

disfigure verb spoil the appearance of
someone or something.
- DERIVATIVES **disfiguration** noun **disfigurement**
noun.

disgorge verb **1** pour out; discharge: *a bus
disgorged a load of tourists.* **2** bring up food.
- ORIGIN Old French *desgorger*.

disgrace noun **1** loss of the respect of others as
the result of unacceptable behaviour: *he left
the White House in disgrace.* **2** a shamefully bad
person or thing. • verb bring disgrace to
someone or something.
- ORIGIN Italian *disgrazia*.

disgraceful adjective shockingly unacceptable.
- DERIVATIVES **disgracefully** adverb.

disgruntled adjective angry or dissatisfied.
- DERIVATIVES **disgruntlement** noun.
- ORIGIN from dialect *gruntle* 'utter little
grunts, grumble'.

disguise verb **1** change the appearance or
nature of someone or something so as to
prevent recognition: *a reporter disguised
himself as a delivery man.* **2** hide a feeling or
situation. • noun **1** a means of concealing one's
identity. **2** the state of being disguised: *the
troops were rebels in disguise.*
- ORIGIN Old French *desguisier*.

disgust noun revulsion or strong disapproval.
• verb cause someone to feel revulsion or
strong disapproval.
- DERIVATIVES **disgusted** adjective **disgustedly**
adverb.
- ORIGIN French *desgoust* or Italian *disgusto*.

d

disgusting adjective arousing revulsion or strong disapproval.
– DERIVATIVES **disgustingly** adverb **disgustingness** noun.

dish noun 1 a shallow container for cooking or serving food. 2 a particular kind of food served as part of a meal: *Thai dishes*. 3 (**the dishes**) all the crockery and utensils used for a meal. 4 a shallow, concave container: *a soap dish*. 5 informal an attractive person. •verb 1 (**dish something out/up**) put food on to a plate or plates before a meal. 2 (**dish something out**) distribute in a casual or indiscriminate way: *his dismissal brought the number of red cards dished out by referees to 21*.
– PHRASES **dish the dirt** informal reveal or spread scandal.
– ORIGIN Greek *diskos* 'discus'.

disharmony noun lack of harmony; disagreement or discord.
– DERIVATIVES **disharmonious** adjective.

dishcloth (also **dishrag**) noun a cloth for washing dishes.

dishearten verb make someone lose hope or confidence.
– DERIVATIVES **disheartening** adjective.

dishevelled /di-shev-v'ld/ (US **disheveled**) adjective (of a person's hair, clothes, or appearance) untidy; disordered.
– DERIVATIVES **dishevelment** noun.
– ORIGIN Old French *deschevele*.

dishonest adjective not honest, trustworthy, or sincere.
– DERIVATIVES **dishonestly** adverb **dishonesty** noun (pl. **dishonesties**).

dishonour (US **dishonor**) noun a state of shame or disgrace. •verb 1 bring shame or disgrace to someone or something. 2 fail to honour an agreement or cheque.

dishonourable (US **dishonorable**) adjective bringing shame or disgrace.
– DERIVATIVES **dishonourably** adverb.

dishonourable discharge noun dismissal from the armed forces as a result of criminal or morally unacceptable actions.

dishwasher noun a machine for washing dishes automatically.

dishy adjective (**dishier**, **dishiest**) informal, chiefly Brit. sexually attractive.

disillusion noun disappointment from discovering that one's beliefs are mistaken or unrealistic. •verb make someone realize that a belief is mistaken or unrealistic.
– DERIVATIVES **disillusioned** adjective **disillusionment** noun.

disincentive noun a factor that discourages a particular action: *rising house prices are a disincentive to development*.

disinclination noun a reluctance to do something.

disinclined adjective reluctant; unwilling.

disinfect verb clean something with a disinfectant in order to destroy bacteria.
– DERIVATIVES **disinfection** noun.

disinfectant noun a chemical liquid that destroys bacteria.

disinformation noun information which is intended to mislead.

disingenuous /diss-in-jen-yoo-uhss/ adjective not candid or sincere, especially in pretending ignorance about something.
– DERIVATIVES **disingenuously** adverb **disingenuousness** noun.

disinherit verb (**disinherits**, **disinheriting**, **disinherited**) prevent a person who was one's heir from inheriting one's property.

disintegrate verb 1 break up into small parts as a result of impact or decay. 2 become weaker or less united and gradually fail: *I'm afraid that our family is disintegrating*.
– DERIVATIVES **disintegration** noun **disintegrator** noun.

disinter /diss-in-ter/ verb (**disinters**, **disinterring**, **disinterred**) dig up something buried.

disinterest noun 1 the state of being impartial. 2 lack of interest.

disinterested adjective 1 not influenced by personal feelings; impartial. 2 not interested in someone or something.
– DERIVATIVES **disinterestedly** adverb **disinterestedness** noun.

USAGE: Strictly speaking, **disinterested** should only be used to mean 'impartial' (*the judgements of disinterested outsiders are likely to be more useful*) and should not be used to mean 'not interested' (in other words, the same as **uninterested**). The second meaning is very common, but should be avoided as it is not accepted by everyone.

disintermediation noun reduction in the use of intermediaries between producers and consumers, e.g. by investing directly in the securities market rather than through a bank.
– DERIVATIVES **disintermediate** verb.

disinvest verb withdraw or reduce an investment.
– DERIVATIVES **disinvestment** noun.

disjointed adjective not coherent or connected: *a disjointed, scrappy game*.

disjunction noun a difference or lack of agreement between things expected to be similar.

disjunctive adjective lacking connection or consistency.

disk noun US & Computing variant spelling of **DISC**.

disk drive noun a device which allows a computer to read from and write on to computer disks.

diskette noun another term for **FLOPPY**.

dislike verb feel distaste for or hostility towards someone or something. •noun 1 a feeling of distaste or hostility. 2 a thing that is disliked.
– DERIVATIVES **dislikable** (also **dislikeable**) adjective.

dislocate verb 1 displace a bone from its proper position in a joint. 2 disrupt something.
– DERIVATIVES **dislocation** noun.

dislodge verb remove something from a fixed position.
– DERIVATIVES **dislodgement** noun.

disloyal adjective not loyal or faithful to someone or something.
– DERIVATIVES **disloyally** adverb **disloyalty** noun.

dismal adjective **1** causing or showing gloom or depression. **2** informal disgracefully bad.
– DERIVATIVES **dismally** adverb.
– ORIGIN from Latin *dies mali* 'evil days'.

dismantle verb take something to pieces.
– DERIVATIVES **dismantlement** noun **dismantler** noun.
– ORIGIN Old French *desmanteler.*

dismast verb break or force down the mast or masts of a ship.

dismay noun concern and distress resulting from an unpleasant surprise. • verb make someone concerned and upset.
– ORIGIN Old French.

dismember verb **1** cut off the limbs of a person or animal. **2** divide up a territory or organization.
– DERIVATIVES **dismembered** adjective **dismemberment** noun.
– ORIGIN Old French *desmembrer.*

dismiss verb **1** order or allow someone to leave. **2** order an employee to leave a job. **3** treat as unworthy of serious consideration: *his comments were dismissed as a joke by the minister.* **4** refuse to allow a legal case to continue. **5** Cricket end the innings of a batsman or side.
– DERIVATIVES **dismissable** (also **dismissible**) adjective. **dismissal** noun
– ORIGIN Latin *dimittere* 'send away'.

dismissive adjective showing that something is unworthy of serious consideration.
– DERIVATIVES **dismissively** adverb.

dismount verb get off or down from a horse or bicycle.

disobedient adjective failing or refusing to obey rules or someone in authority.
– DERIVATIVES **disobedience** noun **disobediently** adverb.

disobey verb fail or refuse to obey an order, rule, or person in authority.

disobliging adjective unwilling to help or cooperate.

disorder noun **1** a lack of order; confusion. **2** the breakdown of peaceful and law-abiding behaviour. **3** an illness that disrupts normal physical or mental functions: *a skin disorder.* • verb (usu. as adj. **disordered**) bring disorder to: *a disordered room.*

disorderly adjective **1** not organized or tidy. **2** involving a breakdown of peaceful and law-abiding behaviour.
– DERIVATIVES **disorderliness** noun.

disorganized (or **disorganised**) adjective **1** not properly planned and controlled. **2** not able to plan one's activities efficiently.
– DERIVATIVES **disorganization** noun.

disorient verb another term for DISORIENTATE.

disorientate verb Brit. cause someone to lose their sense of direction or feel confused.
– DERIVATIVES **disorientated** adjective **disorientation** noun.

disown verb refuse to have anything further to do with someone.

disparage /di-**spa**-rij/ verb suggest that someone or something is worthless or unimportant.
– DERIVATIVES **disparagement** noun **disparaging** adjective.

– ORIGIN Old French *desparagier* 'marry someone of unequal rank'.

disparate /**diss**-puh-ruht/ adjective **1** very different from one another: *no small feat, blending such disparate languages into one.* **2** containing elements very different from one another: *a culturally disparate country.*
– ORIGIN from Latin *disparare* 'to separate'.

disparity noun (pl. **disparities**) a great difference.

dispassionate adjective not influenced by strong emotion; rational and impartial.
– DERIVATIVES **dispassion** noun **dispassionately** adverb.

dispatch (Brit. also **despatch**) verb **1** send someone or something to a destination or for a purpose. **2** deal with a task or opponent quickly and efficiently. **3** kill someone or something. • noun **1** the action of dispatching someone or something. **2** an official report on state or military affairs. **3** a report sent to a newspaper by a journalist working abroad. **4** promptness and efficiency: *officials believed the problem would be resolved with dispatch.*
– DERIVATIVES **dispatcher** noun.
– ORIGIN Italian *dispacciare* or Spanish *despachar* 'expedite'.

Dispatch Box noun Brit. a box in the House of Commons next to which ministers stand when speaking.

dispatch rider noun Brit. a messenger who delivers urgent business documents or military dispatches.

dispel verb (**dispels**, **dispelling**, **dispelled**) make a doubt, feeling, or belief disappear.
– ORIGIN Latin *dispellere* 'drive apart'.

dispensable adjective able to be replaced or done without.

dispensary noun (pl. **dispensaries**) a room where medicines are prepared and provided.

dispensation noun **1** permission to be exempt from a rule or usual requirement. **2** the religious or political system of a particular time: *the capitalist dispensation.* **3** the action of dispensing something.
– DERIVATIVES **dispensational** adjective.

dispense verb **1** distribute or supply something to a number of people. **2** (of a chemist) supply medicine according to a doctor's prescription. **3** (**dispense with**) get rid of or manage without: *we intend to dispense with a central heating system.*
– DERIVATIVES **dispenser** noun.
– ORIGIN Latin *dispensare* 'continue to weigh out'.

dispensing optician noun see OPTICIAN.

dispersal noun **1** the spreading of things or people over a wide area. **2** the action of causing a group to go in different directions.

dispersant noun a liquid or gas used to disperse small particles in a medium.

disperse verb **1** spread something over a wide area. **2** go in different directions: *the crowd dispersed.* **3** Physics divide light into constituents of different wavelengths.
– DERIVATIVES **disperser** noun **dispersible** adjective **dispersive** adjective.
– ORIGIN Latin *dispergere* 'scatter widely'.

dispersion noun the action of dispersing

people or things or the state of being dispersed.

dispirit verb cause someone to lose enthusiasm or hope.
– DERIVATIVES **dispiritedly** adverb **dispiriting** adjective.

displace verb **1** move something from its proper or usual position. **2** take over the position or role of: *drama, having been displaced by docusoap a couple of years ago, is back.* **3** (especially of war or natural disaster) force someone to leave their home.

displacement noun **1** the action of displacing someone or something. **2** the amount by which something is moved from its position. **3** the volume or weight of water displaced by a floating ship, used as a measure of the ship's size.

display verb **1** put something on show in a noticeable and attractive way. **2** clearly show a quality, emotion, or skill. **3** show data or an image on a screen. •noun **1** a show or other event for public entertainment. **2** an act of showing something: *a public display of affection.* **3** objects, data, or images that are displayed. **4** an electronic device for displaying data.
– ORIGIN Latin *displicare* 'scatter, disperse'.

displease verb annoy or upset someone.
– DERIVATIVES **displeased** adjective **displeasing** adjective.

displeasure noun a feeling of annoyance or dissatisfaction.

disport verb (**disport oneself**) old use enjoy oneself unrestrainedly; frolic.
– ORIGIN Old French *desporter* 'carry away'.

disposable adjective **1** (of an article) intended to be used once and then thrown away. **2** (of financial assets) available to be used when required. •noun a disposable article.
– DERIVATIVES **disposability** noun.

disposable income noun income remaining after deduction of taxes and social security charges, available to be spent or saved as one wishes.

disposal noun the action of disposing or getting rid of something.
– PHRASES **at one's disposal** available for one to use whenever or however one wishes.

dispose verb **1** (**dispose of**) get rid of something by throwing it away or by giving or selling it to someone. **2** (**dispose of**) overcome a rival, problem, or threat. **3** (usu. **be disposed to**) make someone likely to do or think something: *I am not disposed to argue about it.* **4** (as adj. **disposed**) having a specified attitude: *he was never favourably disposed towards Hitler.* **5** arrange people or things in a particular way.
– DERIVATIVES **disposer** noun.
– ORIGIN Latin *disponere* 'arrange'.

disposition noun **1** a person's natural qualities of character. **2** an inclination or tendency to do something. **3** the way in which people or things are arranged.

dispossess verb **1** deprive someone of land or property. **2** (in sport) deprive a player of the ball.
– DERIVATIVES **dispossession** noun.

disproof noun evidence that something is untrue.

disproportion noun a state of inequality between two things.
– DERIVATIVES **disproportional** adjective **disproportionally** adverb.

disproportionate adjective too large or too small in comparison with something else.
– DERIVATIVES **disproportionately** adverb.

disprove verb prove that something is false.

disputable adjective open to question.

disputation noun debate or argument.

disputatious adjective fond of having arguments.

dispute verb /diss-**pyoot**/ **1** argue about something. **2** question whether a statement or fact is true or valid. **3** compete for: *the two drivers crashed while disputing the lead.* •noun /diss-**pyoot**, diss-pyoot/ **1** an argument or disagreement. **2** a disagreement between management and employees that leads to industrial action.
– DERIVATIVES **disputant** noun.
– ORIGIN Latin *disputare* 'to estimate'.

disqualify verb (**disqualifies, disqualifying, disqualified**) prevent someone from performing an activity or taking up a job because they have broken a law or rule or are unsuitable: *he was disqualified from being a company director.*
– DERIVATIVES **disqualification** noun.

disquiet noun a feeling of worry or unease. •verb make someone worried or uneasy.
– DERIVATIVES **disquieting** adjective **disquietude** noun.

disquisition /diss-kwi-**zi**-sh'n/ noun a long or complex discussion of a topic in speech or writing.
– ORIGIN Latin, 'investigation'.

disregard verb fail to consider or pay attention to someone or something. •noun lack of attention or consideration: *they have shown utter disregard for customers.*

disrepair noun poor condition due to neglect.

disreputable /dis-**rep**-yoo-tuh-b'l/ adjective not respectable in appearance or character.

disrepute noun the state of having a bad reputation: *he was accused of bringing football into disrepute.*

disrespect noun lack of respect or courtesy. •verb informal, chiefly N. Amer. show a lack of respect for someone or something.
– DERIVATIVES **disrespectful** adjective **disrespectfully** adverb.

disrobe verb take off one's clothes.

disrupt verb interrupt the normal operation of an activity or process.
– DERIVATIVES **disrupter** (also **disruptor**) noun **disruption** noun.
– ORIGIN Latin *disrumpere* 'break apart'.

disruptive adjective disturbing or interrupting the normal operation of something.

diss verb variant spelling of **DIS**.

dissatisfaction noun lack of satisfaction.

dissatisfied adjective not content or happy.

dissect verb /di-sekt, dy-sekt/ **1** methodically cut up a body, part, or plant in order to study its internal parts. **2** analyse something in great detail. **3** (as adj. **dissected**) technical divided into separate parts.
– DERIVATIVES **dissection** noun **dissector** noun.

- ORIGIN Latin *dissecare* 'cut up'.

dissemble verb hide or disguise one's true motives or feelings.
- DERIVATIVES **dissembler** noun.
- ORIGIN Latin *dissimulare* 'disguise, conceal'.

disseminate verb spread something, especially information, widely.
- DERIVATIVES **dissemination** noun **disseminator** noun.
- ORIGIN Latin *disseminare* 'scatter'.

dissension noun disagreement that causes trouble within a group.
- ORIGIN from Latin *dissentire* 'differ in sentiment'.

dissent verb 1 express disagreement with an official or widely held view. 2 disagree with the doctrine of an established or orthodox Church. •noun disagreement with an official or widely held view.
- ORIGIN Latin *dissentire* 'differ in sentiment'.

dissenter noun 1 a person who disagrees with a widely held view. 2 (**Dissenter**) Brit. historical a member of a non-established Church; a Nonconformist.

dissentient /di-sen-shi-uhnt, di-sen-shuhnt/ adjective opposing an official or widely held opinion.

dissertation noun a long essay, especially one written for a university degree or diploma.
- ORIGIN from Latin *dissertare* 'continue to discuss'.

disservice noun a harmful action.

dissident noun a person who opposes official policy. •adjective opposing official policy.
- DERIVATIVES **dissidence** noun.
- ORIGIN from Latin *dissidere* 'sit apart, disagree'.

dissimilar adjective not similar; different: *an onion tart not dissimilar to a quiche.*
- DERIVATIVES **dissimilarity** noun.

dissimulate verb hide or disguise one's thoughts or feelings.
- DERIVATIVES **dissimulation** noun.
- ORIGIN Latin *dissimulare* 'to conceal'.

dissipate verb 1 disperse or disappear: *his anger seemed to dissipate.* 2 waste money, energy, or resources.
- DERIVATIVES **dissipative** adjective **dissipator** noun.
- ORIGIN Latin *dissipare* 'scatter'.

dissipated adjective indulging excessively in sex, drinking alcohol, and similar activities.

dissipation noun 1 dissipated living. 2 the action of dissipating something.

dissociate verb 1 disconnect or separate something from something else. 2 (**dissociate oneself from**) declare that one is not connected with someone or something.
- DERIVATIVES **dissociation** noun **dissociative** adjective.
- ORIGIN Latin *dissociare* 'separate'.

dissoluble adjective able to be dissolved, loosened, or disconnected.

dissolute /diss-uh-loot/ adjective indulging in immoral activities.
- ORIGIN Latin *dissolutus* 'disconnected, loose'.

dissolution noun 1 the formal closing down or ending of an official body or agreement. 2 the action of dissolving or decomposing.

3 immoral living.

dissolve verb 1 (of a solid) disperse into a liquid so as to form a solution. 2 close down, dismiss, or end an assembly or agreement. 3 (**dissolve into/in**) give way to strong emotion.
- DERIVATIVES **dissolvable** adjective.
- ORIGIN Latin *dissolvere*.

dissonant adjective lacking harmony; discordant.
- DERIVATIVES **dissonance** noun.
- ORIGIN from Latin *dissonare* 'be discordant'.

dissuade /dis-swayd/ verb (**dissuade someone from**) persuade or advise someone not to do something.
- DERIVATIVES **dissuasion** noun **dissuasive** adjective.
- ORIGIN Latin *dissuadere*.

distaff noun a stick or spindle on to which wool or flax is wound for spinning.
- PHRASES **the distaff side** the female side of a family.
- ORIGIN Old English.

distal adjective chiefly Anatomy situated away from the centre of the body or an area or from the point of attachment. The opposite of **PROXIMAL**.
- DERIVATIVES **distally** adverb.
- ORIGIN from **DISTANT**.

distance noun 1 the length of the space between two points. 2 the state of being distant or remote: *they are separated by decades and by distance.* 3 a far-off point or place. 4 an interval of time. 5 the full length or time of a race or other contest. 6 Brit. Horse Racing a space of more than twenty lengths between two finishers in a race. •verb 1 make someone or something far off or remote. 2 (**distance oneself from**) declare that one is not connected with someone or something.
- ORIGIN Latin *distantia*.

distance learning noun a method of studying in which lectures are broadcast and lessons are conducted by correspondence.

distant adjective 1 far away in space or time. 2 at a specified distance: *the town lay half a mile distant.* 3 far apart in resemblance or relationship: *a distant acquaintance.* 4 aloof or reserved.
- DERIVATIVES **distantly** adverb.

distaste noun dislike or mild hostility.

distasteful adjective unpleasant or disagreeable.
- DERIVATIVES **distastefully** adverb **distastefulness** noun.

distemper noun 1 a kind of paint made of powdered pigment mixed with glue or size, used on walls. 2 a disease affecting dogs, causing fever and coughing. •verb paint something with distemper.
- ORIGIN from Latin *distemperare* 'soak, mix in the wrong proportions'.

distend verb swell because of internal pressure.
- DERIVATIVES **distended** adjective **distensibility** noun **distensible** adjective **distension** noun.
- ORIGIN Latin *distendere*.

distil (US **distill**) verb (**distils, distilling, distilled**; US **distills, distilling, distilled**) 1 purify a liquid by heating it so that it vaporizes, then cooling and condensing the vapour and collecting the

d

resulting liquid. **2** make spirits by distilling. **3** extract the most important aspects of: *he distilled their comments into two-page accounts.*
– DERIVATIVES **distillation** noun **distiller** noun.
– ORIGIN Latin *distillare.*

distillate /**dis**-til-ayt/ noun a substance formed by distillation.

distillery noun (pl. **distilleries**) a place where spirits are manufactured.

distinct adjective **1** recognizably different. **2** able to be perceived clearly by the senses: *a distinct smell of vinegar.*
– DERIVATIVES **distinctly** adverb **distinctness** noun.
– ORIGIN Latin *distinctus.*

distinction noun **1** a noticeable difference or contrast. **2** the separation of people or things into different groups. **3** outstanding excellence. **4** a special honour or recognition.

distinctive adjective characteristic of a person or thing, so making it different from others: *a coffee with a distinctive caramel flavour.*
– DERIVATIVES **distinctively** adverb **distinctiveness** noun.

distinguish verb **1** recognize or treat someone or something as different. **2** manage to see or hear something barely perceptible. **3** be a distinctive characteristic of: *what distinguishes sport from games?* **4** (**distinguish oneself**) do something very well.
– DERIVATIVES **distinguishable** adjective.
– ORIGIN Latin *distinguere.*

distinguished adjective **1** very successful and greatly respected. **2** dignified in appearance.

distort verb **1** pull or twist something out of shape. **2** give a misleading account of something. **3** change the form of an electrical signal or sound wave during transmission or amplification.
– DERIVATIVES **distorted** adjective **distortion** noun.
– ORIGIN Latin *distorquere* 'twist apart'.

distract verb **1** prevent someone from concentrating on something. **2** divert attention from something.
– DERIVATIVES **distracted** adjective **distracting** adjective.
– ORIGIN Latin *distrahere* 'draw apart'.

distraction noun **1** a thing that distracts someone's attention. **2** an activity that provides entertainment. **3** mental agitation: *he loved her to distraction.*

distrain verb Law seize someone's property to obtain payment of rent or other money owed.
– ORIGIN Old French *destreindre.*

distraint /di-**straynt**/ noun Law the seizure of someone's property in order to obtain payment of rent or other money owed.

distrait /di-**stray**/ adjective distracted; absent-minded.
– ORIGIN French.

distraught adjective very worried and upset.
– ORIGIN Latin *distractus* 'pulled apart'.

distress noun **1** great anxiety, sorrow, or difficulty. **2** the state of a ship or aircraft when in danger or difficulty. **3** a state of physical strain, especially difficulty in breathing. • verb **1** make someone very worried or upset. **2** give furniture or clothing artificial marks of age and wear.
– DERIVATIVES **distressed** adjective **distressful**

adjective **distressing** adjective.
– ORIGIN Old French *destresce.*

distributary /di-**strib**-yuu-tuh-ri/ noun (pl. **distributaries**) a branch of a river that does not return to the main stream after leaving it, as in a delta.

distribute verb **1** hand or share something out to a number of people. **2** (**be distributed**) be spread over an area. **3** supply goods to retailers.
– DERIVATIVES **distributable** adjective.
– ORIGIN Latin *distribuere* 'divide up'.

distribution noun **1** the action of distributing something. **2** the way in which something is shared among a group or spread over an area: *the uneven distribution of wealth.*
– DERIVATIVES **distributional** adjective.

distributive adjective relating to distribution or things that are distributed.

distributor noun **1** an agent who supplies goods to retailers. **2** a device in a petrol engine for passing electric current to each spark plug in turn.

district noun **1** an area of a town or region, regarded as a unit for administrative purposes or because of a particular feature: *the central business district.* **2** Brit. a division of a county or region that elects its own councillors.
– ORIGIN Latin *districtus* '(territory of) jurisdiction'.

district attorney noun (in the US) a public official who acts as prosecutor for the state in a particular district.

district nurse noun (in the UK) a nurse who treats patients in their homes, operating within a particular district.

distrust noun the feeling that someone or something cannot be relied on. • verb have little trust in someone or something.
– DERIVATIVES **distrustful** adjective **distrustfully** adverb.

disturb verb **1** interfere with the normal arrangement or functioning of something. **2** interrupt the sleep, relaxation, or privacy of someone. **3** make someone anxious.
– DERIVATIVES **disturbing** adjective.
– ORIGIN Latin *disturbare.*

disturbance noun **1** the interruption or disruption of a settled or normal condition: *precautions can be taken to minimize wildlife disturbance.* **2** a breakdown of peaceful behaviour; a riot.

disturbed adjective having emotional or psychological problems.

disunited adjective lacking unity or agreement.
– DERIVATIVES **disunity** noun.

disuse noun the state of not being used.
– DERIVATIVES **disused** adjective.

disyllable /dy-**sil**-luh-b'l, **dy**-sil-luh-b'l/ noun Poetry a word or metrical foot consisting of two syllables.
– DERIVATIVES **disyllabic** adjective.
– ORIGIN from Greek *disullabos* 'of two syllables'.

ditch noun a narrow channel dug to hold or carry water. • verb **1** informal abandon or get rid of: *she had recently been ditched by her boyfriend.* **2** (with reference to an aircraft) bring or come down in a forced landing on the

sea. **3** provide a place with a ditch.
– ORIGIN Old English.

dither verb be indecisive. •noun informal a state of
agitation or indecision.
– DERIVATIVES **ditherer** noun **dithery** adjective.
– ORIGIN variant of dialect *didder* 'tremble'.

dithyramb /di-thi-ram/ noun (in ancient
Greece) an ecstatic choral hymn dedicated to
the god Dionysus.
– DERIVATIVES **dithyrambic** adjective.
– ORIGIN Greek *dithurambos*.

ditto noun **1** the same thing again (used in lists
and often indicated by a ditto mark). **2** (also
ditto mark) a symbol consisting of two
apostrophes („) placed under an item to be
repeated.
– ORIGIN Italian *detto* 'said'.

ditty noun (pl. **ditties**) a short simple song.
– ORIGIN Old French *dite* 'composition'.

ditzy (also **ditsy**) adjective N. Amer. informal silly or
scatterbrained.
– DERIVATIVES **ditziness** noun.
– ORIGIN unknown.

diuretic /dy-uh-ret-ik/ adjective causing an
increase in the flow of urine. •noun a diuretic
drug.
– ORIGIN from Greek *diourein* 'urinate'.

diurnal /dy-er-nuhl/ adjective **1** of or during the
daytime. **2** daily; of each day.
– DERIVATIVES **diurnally** adverb.
– ORIGIN Latin *diurnalis*.

diva /dee-vuh/ noun a famous female opera
singer.
– ORIGIN Latin, 'goddess'.

Divali noun variant spelling of **DIWALI**.

divan /di-van/ noun **1** Brit. a bed consisting of a
base and mattress but no footboard or
headboard. **2** a long, low sofa without a back
or arms.
– ORIGIN Persian, 'bench, court'.

dive verb (past and past part. **dived**; US also **dove**
/rhymes with rove/) **1** plunge head first and
with arms outstretched into water. **2** go to a
deeper level in water. **3** swim under water
using breathing equipment. **4** plunge steeply
downwards through the air. **5** move quickly or
suddenly: *he dived into the bushes.* **6** Football
deliberately fall as if fouled in order to
deceive the referee. •noun **1** an act of diving.
2 informal a disreputable nightclub or bar.
– ORIGIN Old English.

dive-bomb verb bomb a target while diving
steeply in an aircraft.
– DERIVATIVES **dive-bomber** noun.

diver noun **1** a person who dives under water as
a sport or as part of their work. **2** a large
diving waterbird with a straight pointed bill.

diverge verb **1** (of a road or route) separate
from another route and go in a different
direction. **2** (of opinions, theories, etc.) be
different from one another. **3** (**diverge from**)
depart from a particular pattern or standard:
individuals may well diverge from the norm.
– DERIVATIVES **divergence** noun **diverging**
adjective.
– ORIGIN Latin *divergere*.

divergent adjective different.

divers /dy-verz/ adjective old use or literary of many
different kinds.

diverse /dy-verss/ adjective widely varied:
people from diverse backgrounds.
– DERIVATIVES **diversely** adverb.
– ORIGIN Latin *diversus*.

diversify verb (**diversifies, diversifying,
diversified**) **1** make or become more varied.
2 (of a company) enlarge or vary its range of
products or field of operation.
– DERIVATIVES **diversification** noun.

diversion noun **1** an instance of diverting
something. **2** Brit. an alternative route for use
when the usual road is closed. **3** something
intended to distract attention: *a raid was
carried out at the airfield to create a diversion.*
4 a pastime or pleasant activity.
– DERIVATIVES **diversionary** adjective.

diversity noun (pl. **diversities**) **1** the state of
being varied. **2** a variety of things.

divert /dy-vert/ verb **1** change the direction or
course of: *traffic was diverted along the A69.*
2 distract someone or their attention. **3** amuse
or entertain someone.
– DERIVATIVES **diverting** adjective.
– ORIGIN Latin *divertere* 'turn in separate ways'.

diverticula plural of **DIVERTICULUM**.

diverticulitis /dy-ver-tik-yuu-ly-tiss/ noun
inflammation of a diverticulum in the
alimentary tract, causing abdominal pain and
diarrhoea or constipation.

diverticulum /dy-ver-tik-yuu-luhm/ noun (pl.
diverticula /dy-ver-tik-yuu-luh/) an abnormal
sac or pouch formed in the wall of the
alimentary tract.
– ORIGIN Latin *deverticulum* 'byway'.

divertimento /di-ver-ti-men-toh/ noun (pl.
divertimenti /di-ver-ti-men-ti/ or
divertimentos) a light and entertaining piece
of music.
– ORIGIN Italian, 'diversion'.

divertissement /dee-vair-teess-mon/ noun a
minor entertainment.
– ORIGIN French.

divest /dy-vest/ verb **1** (**divest someone/thing
of**) deprive someone or something of: *he was
divested of his property.* **2** (**divest oneself of**)
remove or get rid of: *he divested himself of his
jacket.*
– ORIGIN Old French *desvestir*, from Latin
vestire 'clothe'.

divide verb **1** separate something into parts.
2 share something out: *the house was sold and
the money divided between us.* **3** cause
disagreement between people or groups: *the
issue has divided the community.* **4** form a
boundary between two areas. **5** find
how many times a number contains another.
6 (of a law-making assembly) separate into
two groups for voting. •noun a wide difference
between two groups: *the North–South divide.*
– ORIGIN Latin *dividere* 'force apart, remove'.

dividend noun **1** a sum of money that is
divided among a number of people, such as
the part of a company's profits paid to its
shareholders or the winnings from a football
pool. **2** (**dividends**) benefits gained from
something: *the policy would pay dividends in
the future.* **3** Mathematics a number to be divided
by another number.
– ORIGIN Latin *dividendum* 'something to be
divided'.

d

divider noun **1** a screen or piece of furniture that divides a room into two separate parts. **2** (**dividers**) a measuring compass.

divination noun the use of supernatural means to find out about the future or the unknown.
– DERIVATIVES **divinatory** adjective.

divine[1] adjective (**diviner**, **divinest**) **1** relating to, from, or like God or a god. **2** informal excellent. • noun **1** dated a priest, religious leader, or theologian. **2** (**the Divine**) providence or God.
– DERIVATIVES **divinely** adverb.
– ORIGIN Latin *divinus*.

divine[2] verb **1** discover something by guesswork or intuition. **2** have supernatural insight into the future. **3** search for underground water or minerals using a pointer which is supposedly moved by unseen influences.
– DERIVATIVES **diviner** noun.
– ORIGIN Latin *divinare* 'predict'.

diving bell noun an open-bottomed chamber supplied with air, in which a person can be let down under water.

diving board noun a board projecting over a swimming pool or other body of water, from which people dive or jump in.

diving suit noun a watertight suit, typically with a helmet and an air supply, worn for working or exploring deep under water.

divining rod noun a forked stick or rod supposed to move when held over ground in which water or minerals can be found.

divinity noun (pl. **divinities**) **1** the state or quality of being divine. **2** a god or goddess. **3** (**the Divinity**) God. **4** the study of religion; theology.

divisible adjective **1** capable of being divided. **2** (of a number) containing another number a number of times without a remainder.
– DERIVATIVES **divisibility** noun.

division noun **1** the action of dividing something or the state of being divided. **2** each of the parts into which something is divided. **3** a major unit or section of an organization. **4** a number of teams or players grouped together in a sport for competitive purposes. **5** a partition that divides two groups or things.
– DERIVATIVES **divisional** adjective.

division sign noun the sign ÷, placed between two numbers showing that the first is to be divided by the second, as in $6 ÷ 3 = 2$.

divisive /di-**vy**-siv/ adjective causing disagreement or hostility between people or groups.
– DERIVATIVES **divisiveness** noun.

divisor noun Mathematics a number by which another number is to be divided.

divorce noun the legal ending of a marriage. • verb **1** legally end one's marriage with one's husband or wife. **2** (**divorce someone/thing from**) detach or separate someone or something from: *religion cannot be divorced from morality.*
– ORIGIN Old French.

divorcee /di-vor-**see**/ noun a divorced person.
– ORIGIN French *divorcé(e)* 'divorced man (or

woman)'.

divot /**di**-vuht/ noun a piece of turf cut out of the ground, especially by a golf club in making a stroke.
– ORIGIN unknown.

divulge /dy-**vulj**/ verb reveal information that is meant to be private or secret.
– ORIGIN Latin *divulgare* 'publish widely'.

divvy verb (**divvies**, **divvying**, **divvied**) informal share something out.

Diwali /di-**wah**-li/ (also **Divali**) noun a Hindu festival with lights, held in October and November to celebrate the end of the monsoon.
– ORIGIN Sanskrit, 'row of lights'.

Dixie noun an informal name for the Southern states of the US.
– ORIGIN unknown.

Dixieland noun a kind of jazz with a strong two-beat rhythm.

DIY noun chiefly Brit. the activity of decorating and making repairs in the home oneself rather than employing a professional.
– DERIVATIVES **DIY'er** noun.
– ORIGIN abbreviation of DO-IT-YOURSELF.

dizzy adjective (**dizzier**, **dizziest**) **1** having a sensation of spinning around and losing one's balance. **2** informal (of a woman) silly but attractive. • verb (**dizzies**, **dizzying**, **dizzied**) make someone feel unsteady, confused, or amazed.
– DERIVATIVES **dizzily** adverb **dizziness** noun.
– ORIGIN Old English, 'foolish'.

DJ[1] noun **1** a person who introduces and plays recorded pop music on radio or at a club. **2** a person who uses samples of recorded music to make techno or rap music. • verb (**DJ's**, **DJ'ing**, **DJ'd**) perform as a DJ.
– ORIGIN short for DISC JOCKEY.

DJ[2] noun Brit. a dinner jacket.

djellaba /**jel**-luh-buh/ (also **djellabah** or **jellaba**) noun a loose woollen hooded cloak of a kind traditionally worn by Arabs.
– ORIGIN Arabic.

Djiboutian /ji-**boo**-ti-uhn/ noun a person from Djibouti, a country on the north-east coast of Africa. • adjective relating to Djibouti.

djinn noun variant spelling of JINN.

dl abbreviation decilitre(s).

DLitt abbreviation Doctor of Letters.
– ORIGIN Latin *Doctor Litterarum.*

DM (also **D-mark**) abbreviation Deutschmark.

dm abbreviation decimetre(s).

DMA abbreviation Computing direct memory access.

DMus abbreviation Doctor of Music.

DNA noun deoxyribonucleic acid, a substance carrying genetic information which is present in the cell nuclei of nearly all living organisms.

DNA fingerprinting (also **DNA profiling**) noun another term for GENETIC FINGERPRINTING.

D notice noun Brit. a government notice requiring news editors not to publicize certain sensitive information.
– ORIGIN D for defence.

do[1] verb (**does**; past **did**; past part. **done**) **1** carry out or complete an action, duty, or task. **2** act or progress in a particular way: *the team did*

well. **3** work on something to bring it to a required state: _she's doing her hair._ **4** have a particular result or effect on: _the walk will do me good._ **5** work at for a living or take as one's subject of study: _what does she do?_ **6** make or provide something. **7** be suitable or acceptable: _he'll do._ **8** (**be/have done with**) stop being concerned about someone or something. **9** Brit. informal swindle someone • **auxiliary verb 1** used before a verb in questions and negative statements. **2** used to refer back to a verb already mentioned: _he looks better than he did before._ **3** used in commands, or to give emphasis to a positive verb: _do sit down._ • **noun** (pl. **dos** or **do's**) Brit. informal a party or other social event.
– PHRASES **can/could do with** would find useful or would like. **do away with** informal put an end to; kill. **do for 1** informal defeat, ruin, or kill. **2** be good enough for. **do someone in** informal kill someone. **dos and don'ts** rules of behaviour. **do time** informal spend a period of time in prison. **do something up 1** fasten or wrap something. **2** informal renovate or redecorate a building or room.
– DERIVATIVES **doable** adjective (informal) **doer** noun.
– ORIGIN Old English.

do² noun variant spelling of **DOH**.

Dobermann /**doh**-ber-muhn/ (also **Doberman** or **Dobermann pinscher** /**pin**-sher/) noun a large breed of dog with powerful jaws, typically black with tan markings.
– ORIGIN named after the German dog breeder Ludwig _Dobermann_ (+ German _Pinscher_ 'terrier').

doc abbreviation informal doctor.

docent /**doh**-suhnt/ noun **1** (in certain US and European universities) a member of the teaching staff immediately below professor in rank. **2** a guide in a museum, art gallery, or zoo.
– ORIGIN from Latin _docere_ 'teach'.

docile adjective willing to accept control or instruction; submissive.
– DERIVATIVES **docilely** adverb **docility** noun.
– ORIGIN Latin _docilis_, from _docere_ 'teach'.

dock¹ noun **1** an enclosed area of water in a port for the loading, unloading, and repair of ships. **2** (also **loading dock**) a platform for loading lorries or goods trains. • **verb 1** (with reference to a ship) come or bring into a dock. **2** (of a spacecraft) join with a space station or another spacecraft in space. **3** attach a piece of equipment to another.
– ORIGIN Dutch or German _docke_.

dock² noun the enclosure in a criminal court where a defendant stands or sits.
– ORIGIN probably related to Flemish _dok_ 'chicken coop, rabbit hutch'.

dock³ noun a weed with broad leaves, popularly used to relieve nettle stings.
– ORIGIN Old English.

dock⁴ verb **1** deduct money or a point in a game. **2** cut an animal's tail short.
– ORIGIN uncertain.

docker noun a person employed in a port to load and unload ships.

docket noun Brit. a document sent with a consignment of goods that lists its contents, certifies payment of duty, or entitles the holder to delivery. • **verb** (**dockets**, **docketing**, **docketed**) mark a consignment or package with a document listing the contents.
– ORIGIN perhaps from **DOCK⁴**.

docking station noun a device to which a portable computer is connected so that it can be used like a desktop computer.

dockland noun (also **docklands**) Brit. the area containing a city's docks.

dockside noun the area immediately next to a dock.

dockyard noun an area with docks and equipment for repairing and maintaining ships.

doctor noun **1** a person who is qualified to practise medicine. **2** (**Doctor**) a person who holds the highest university degree. • **verb 1** change something in order to deceive other people: _the technical data had been doctored._ **2** add a harmful or strong ingredient to food or drink. **3** Brit. remove an animal's sexual organs so that it cannot reproduce.
– PHRASES **be what the doctor ordered** informal be beneficial or desirable.
– ORIGIN Latin, 'teacher'.

doctoral adjective relating to a doctorate.

doctorate noun the highest degree awarded by a university faculty.

Doctor of Philosophy noun a person holding a doctorate in any subject except law, medicine, or sometimes theology.

doctrinaire /dok-tri-**nair**/ adjective very strict in applying beliefs or principles.
– ORIGIN French.

doctrine /**dok**-trin/ noun a set of beliefs or principles held and taught by a Church, political party, or other group.
– DERIVATIVES **doctrinal** /dok-**try**-n'l/ adjective **doctrinally** adverb.
– ORIGIN Latin _doctrina_ 'teaching, learning'.

docudrama noun a television film based on a dramatized version of real events.

document noun /**dok**-yoo-muhnt/ a piece of written, printed, or electronic matter that provides information or evidence. • **verb** /**dok**-yoo-ment/ record something in written, photographic, or other form.
– ORIGIN Latin _documentum_ 'lesson'.

documentary noun (pl. **documentaries**) a film or television or radio programme giving a factual account of something, using film, photographs, and sound recordings of real events. • **adjective** consisting of documents and other material providing a factual account of something: _documentary evidence._

documentation noun **1** documents providing official information or evidence. **2** written specifications or instructions.

docusoap noun a documentary following people in a particular occupation or location over a period of time.

dodder verb be slow and unsteady.
– DERIVATIVES **dodderer** noun **doddering** adjective **doddery** adjective.
– ORIGIN related to **DITHER**.

doddle noun Brit. informal a very easy task.
– ORIGIN unknown.

dodecagon /doh-**dek**-uh-guhn/ noun a plane figure with twelve straight sides and angles.

d

– ORIGIN Greek *dōdekagōnos* 'twelve-angled'.

dodecahedron /doh-de-kuh-**hee**-druhn/ **noun** (pl. **dodecahedra** /doh-de-kuh-**hee**-druh/ or **dodecahedrons**) a three-dimensional shape having twelve plane faces.
– ORIGIN from Greek *dōdekaedros* 'twelve-faced'.

dodge verb 1 avoid someone or something by making a sudden quick movement. **2** cunningly avoid doing or paying something. •**noun 1** an act of dodging someone or something. **2** informal a cunning trick, especially one used to avoid something.
– ORIGIN unknown.

dodgem noun a small electrically powered car with rubber bumpers, driven within an enclosure at a funfair with the aim of bumping other such cars.
– ORIGIN US trademark (as *Dodg'em*), from *dodge them*.

dodger noun informal a person who avoids doing or paying something: *a tax dodger*.

dodgy adjective (dodgier, dodgiest) Brit. informal **1** dishonest. **2** risky. **3** not working well or in good condition.

dodo /**doh**-doh/ **noun** (pl. **dodos** or **dodoes**) a large extinct flightless bird formerly found on Mauritius.
– PHRASES **as dead as a dodo** informal utterly dead or finished.
– ORIGIN Portuguese *doudo* 'simpleton' (because the birds were tame and easy to catch).

doe noun 1 a female deer or reindeer. **2** a female hare, rabbit, rat, ferret, or kangaroo.
– ORIGIN Old English.

doe-eyed adjective having large gentle dark eyes.

does third person singular present of DO¹.

doesn't contraction does not.

doff verb remove an item of clothing, especially a hat.
– ORIGIN shortened form of *do off*.

dog noun 1 a domesticated carnivorous mammal kept as a pet or used for work or hunting. **2** any member of the dog family, which includes the wolf, fox, coyote, jackal, and other species. **3** the male of an animal of the dog family. **4** (**the dogs**) Brit. informal greyhound racing. **5** dated a person of a particular kind: *you lucky dog!* •**verb** (**dogs, dogging, dogged**) **1** follow someone closely and persistently. **2** cause continual trouble for: *he was dogged by ill health in later years*.
– PHRASES **dog eat dog** used to describe an extremely competitive situation in which people are willing to harm each other in order to succeed. **a dog in the manger** a person who prevents others from having things that they do not need themselves. [from the fable of the dog that lay in a manger to prevent the ox and horse from eating the hay.] **a dog's dinner** (or **breakfast**) Brit. informal a mess. **go to the dogs** informal get into a very bad state.
– ORIGIN Old English.

dog cart noun a two-wheeled open horse-drawn cart.

dog collar noun informal a clerical collar.

dog days plural noun chiefly literary the hottest period of the year (formerly calculated from the first time Sirius, the Dog Star, rose at the same time as the sun).

doge /dohj/ **noun** historical the chief magistrate of Venice or Genoa.
– ORIGIN Italian *doze*, from Latin *dux* 'leader'.

dog-eared adjective having worn or battered corners.

dog-end noun Brit. informal a cigarette end.

dogfight noun 1 a close combat between military aircraft. **2** a ferocious struggle or fight.
– DERIVATIVES **dogfighting** noun.

dogfish noun (pl. same or **dogfishes**) a small shark with a long tail, living close to the seabed.

dogged /**dog**-gid/ **adjective** very persistent.
– DERIVATIVES **doggedly** adverb **doggedness** noun.

doggerel /**dog**-guh-ruhl/ **noun** badly written poetry, often intended to be amusing.
– ORIGIN apparently from DOG.

doggie noun variant spelling of DOGGY.

doggo adverb (in phrase **lie doggo**) informal remain still and quiet to avoid being discovered.
– ORIGIN uncertain.

doggone /**dog**-gon/ **adjective** N. Amer. informal damned.
– ORIGIN probably from *dog on it*, euphemism for *God damn it*.

doggy adjective 1 relating to or like a dog. **2** fond of dogs. •**noun** (also **doggie**) (pl. **doggies**) a child's word for a dog.

doggy bag noun a bag used to take home food left uneaten after a meal in a restaurant.

doggy-paddle noun a simple swimming stroke resembling that of a dog.

doghouse noun N. Amer. a dog's kennel.
– PHRASES **in the doghouse** informal having annoyed or displeased someone.

dog-leg noun a sharp bend.

dogma noun a principle or set of principles laid down by an authority and intended to be accepted without question.
– ORIGIN Greek, 'opinion'.

dogmatic adjective forcefully putting forward one's own beliefs or opinions and unwilling to accept those of other people.
– DERIVATIVES **dogmatically** adverb **dogmatism** noun **dogmatist** noun.

do-gooder noun a well-meaning but unrealistic or interfering person.

dog rose noun a delicately scented wild rose with pink or white flowers.

dogsbody noun (pl. **dogsbodies**) Brit. informal a person who is given boring, menial tasks.

Dog Star noun Sirius, the brightest star in the sky.
– ORIGIN so named as it appears to follow at the heels of Orion (the hunter).

dog-tired adjective extremely tired.

dog-tooth (also **dogstooth**) **noun** a small check pattern with notched corners.

dogwatch noun either of two short watches on a ship (4–6 or 6–8 p.m.).

dogwood noun a flowering shrub or small tree with red stems and hard wood.

– ORIGIN so named because the wood was formerly used to make skewers known as 'dogs'.

DoH abbreviation (in the UK) Department of Health.

doh /doh/ (also **do**) noun Music the first note of a major scale, coming before 'ray'.
– ORIGIN Italian *do*.

doily noun (pl. **doilies**) a small ornamental mat made of lace or paper.
– ORIGIN from *Doiley* or *Doyley*, a London draper.

doing noun 1 (also **doings**) a person's actions or activities. 2 (treated as sing. or pl.) informal things whose name one has forgotten.

do-it-yourself noun full form of **DIY**.

dojo /doh-joh/ noun (pl. **dojos**) a place in which judo and other martial arts are practised.
– ORIGIN from the Japanese words for 'way, pursuit' and 'a place'.

Dolby /dol-bi/ noun trademark 1 a noise-reduction system used in tape recording. 2 an electronic system providing stereophonic sound for cinemas and televisions.
– ORIGIN named after the American engineer Ray M. *Dolby*.

dolce vita /dol-chay vee-tuh/ noun a life of pleasure and luxury.
– ORIGIN Italian 'sweet life'.

doldrums /dol-druhmz/ plural noun (**the doldrums**) 1 a state of inactivity or depression. 2 a region of the Atlantic Ocean with calms, sudden storms, and unpredictable winds.
– ORIGIN perhaps from **DULL**.

dole noun (often in phrase **on the dole**) Brit. informal benefit paid by the state to the unemployed. • verb (**dole something out**) distribute something.
– ORIGIN Old English, 'division or share'.

doleful adjective 1 sorrowful. 2 causing unhappiness or misfortune.
– DERIVATIVES **dolefully** adverb.
– ORIGIN from Latin *dolere* 'grieve'.

dolerite /dol-luh-ryt/ noun a dark igneous rock.
– ORIGIN from Greek *doleros* 'deceptive' (because it resembles diorite).

doll noun 1 a small model of a human figure, used as a child's toy. 2 informal an attractive young woman. • verb (**doll oneself up**) informal dress oneself smartly and attractively.
– ORIGIN from the woman's name *Dorothy*.

dollar noun the basic unit of money of the US, Canada, Australia, and various other countries.
– ORIGIN German *Thaler*, referring to a silver coin.

dollar sign (also **dollar mark**) noun the sign $, representing a dollar.

dollop informal noun a shapeless mass or lump, especially of soft food. • verb (**dollops, dolloping, dolloped**) add or serve out soft food in a casual or careless way.
– ORIGIN perhaps Scandinavian.

doll's house (N. Amer. also **dollhouse**) noun a miniature toy house for dolls.

dolly noun (pl. **dollies**) 1 a child's word for a doll. 2 informal, dated an attractive young woman. 3 a small platform on wheels for holding heavy objects, typically film cameras.

dolly bird noun Brit. informal an attractive and fashionable young woman.

dolmades /dol-**maa**-dez/ plural noun (sing. **dolma** /dol-muh/) a Greek and Turkish dish of spiced rice and meat wrapped in vine or cabbage leaves.
– ORIGIN Turkish, from *dolmak* 'fill, be filled'.

dolman sleeve /dol-muhn/ noun a loose sleeve cut in one piece with the body of a garment.
– ORIGIN *dolman* from Turkish *dolama* 'open robe'.

dolmen /dol-men/ noun a megalithic tomb with a large flat stone laid on upright ones.
– ORIGIN Cornish, 'hole of a stone'.

dolomite /dol-uh-myt/ noun a mineral or rock consisting chiefly of a carbonate of calcium and magnesium.
– DERIVATIVES **dolomitic** adjective.
– ORIGIN named after the French geologist M. *Dolomieu*.

dolorous /dol-uh-ruhss/ adjective literary feeling great sorrow or distress.

dolour /dol-er/ (US **dolor**) noun literary a state of great sorrow or distress.
– ORIGIN Latin *dolor* 'pain, grief'.

dolphin noun a small whale with a beak-like snout and a curved fin on the back.
– ORIGIN Old French *dauphin*, from Greek *delphin*.

dolphinarium /dol-fi-**nair**-i-uhm/ noun (pl. **dolphinariums** or **dolphinaria**) an aquarium in which dolphins are kept and trained for public entertainment.

dolt noun a stupid person.
– DERIVATIVES **doltish** adjective.
– ORIGIN perhaps a variant of *dulled*, from **DULL**.

domain /duh-**mayn**/ noun 1 an area controlled by a ruler or government. 2 an area of activity or knowledge. 3 a subset of the Internet with addresses all having the same suffix.
– ORIGIN from Old French *demeine* 'belonging to a lord'.

dome noun 1 a rounded vault forming the roof of a building, typically with a circular base. 2 a sports stadium or other building with a domed roof.
– DERIVATIVES **domed** adjective.
– ORIGIN Italian *duomo* 'cathedral, dome'.

Domesday Book /doomz-day/ noun a comprehensive record of the extent, value, and ownership of land in England, made in 1086 by order of William I.
– ORIGIN variant of **DOOMSDAY**, because the book was regarded as a final authority.

domestic adjective 1 relating to a home or family. 2 of or for use in the home. 3 fond of family life and running a home. 4 (of an animal) tame and kept by humans. 5 existing or occurring within a country; not foreign. • noun a person employed to do household tasks.
– DERIVATIVES **domestically** adverb.
– ORIGIN Latin *domesticus*, from *domus* 'house'.

domesticate verb 1 tame an animal and keep it as a pet or for farm produce. 2 make someone fond of and good at family life and running a home. 3 grow a plant for food.
– DERIVATIVES **domestication** noun.

domesticity noun home or family life.

d

domestic science noun dated home economics.

domicile /dom-i-syl/ noun formal or Law **1** the country in which a person lives permanently. **2** chiefly N. Amer. a person's home. •verb (**be domiciled**) formal or Law be living in a particular place.
– ORIGIN Latin *domicilium* 'dwelling'.

domiciliary /dom-i-sil-i-uh-ri/ adjective concerned with or occurring in someone's home.

dominant adjective **1** most important, powerful, or influential. **2** (of a gene) appearing in offspring even if a contrary gene is also inherited. Compare with RECESSIVE.
– DERIVATIVES **dominance** noun **dominantly** adverb.

dominate verb **1** have power or influence over: *the economy is dominated by multinational corporations.* **2** be the most important or noticeable person or thing in: *he dominated the race from start to finish.* **3** be the tallest or largest thing in a place.
– DERIVATIVES **domination** noun **dominator** noun.
– ORIGIN Latin *dominari* 'rule', from *dominus* 'lord, master'.

dominatrix /dom-i-**nay**-triks/ noun (pl. **dominatrices** /dom-i-**nay**-tri-seez/ or **dominatrixes**) a dominating woman, especially in sadomasochistic practices.
– ORIGIN Latin.

domineering adjective arrogant and overbearing.
– ORIGIN from Latin *dominari* 'rule'.

Dominican[1] /duh-**min**-i-kuhn/ noun a member of an order of friars founded by St Dominic, or of a similar religious order for women. •adjective relating to St Dominic or the Dominicans.

Dominican[2] /duh-**min**-i-kuhn/ noun a person from the Dominican Republic in the Caribbean. •adjective relating to the Dominican Republic.

dominion noun **1** supreme power or control. **2** the territory of a sovereign or government. **3** (**Dominion**) historical a self-governing territory of the British Commonwealth.
– ORIGIN Latin *dominium*, from *dominus* 'lord'.

domino noun (pl. **dominoes**) **1** any of 28 small oblong pieces marked with 0–6 pips in each half. **2** (**dominoes**) (treated as sing.) the game played with these pieces.
– ORIGIN probably from Latin *dominus* 'lord'.

domino effect noun a situation in which one event appears to cause a series of similar events to happen elsewhere.

don[1] noun **1** a university teacher, especially a senior member of a college at Oxford or Cambridge. **2** N. Amer. informal a high-ranking member of the Mafia.
– ORIGIN Spanish, from Latin *dominus* 'lord'.

don[2] verb (**dons, donning, donned**) put on an item of clothing.
– ORIGIN shortened form of *do on*.

donate verb **1** give money, clothes, etc. to a charity or good cause. **2** allow blood or an organ to be removed from one's body for transfusion or transplantation.
– DERIVATIVES **donator** noun.
– ORIGIN Latin *donare*.

donation noun something that is given to a charity.

done past participle of DO[1]. adjective **1** (of food) cooked thoroughly. **2** no longer happening or existing. **3** informal socially acceptable: *the done thing.* •exclamation (in response to an offer) I accept!
– PHRASES **done for** informal in serious trouble. **done in** informal extremely tired.

doner kebab /**don**-er/ noun a Turkish dish consisting of spiced lamb cooked on a spit and served in slices.
– ORIGIN from Turkish *döner* 'rotating' and *kebap* 'roast meat'.

dong[1] verb (of a bell) make a deep resonant sound. •noun a deep resonant sound.

dong[2] noun the basic unit of money of Vietnam.
– ORIGIN Vietnamese, 'coin'.

donga /dong-guh/ noun S. African & Austral./NZ a dry watercourse.
– ORIGIN from Xhosa and Zulu.

dongle /dong-guhl/ noun an electronic device which must be attached to a computer in order for protected software to be used.
– ORIGIN an invented word.

donjon /don-juhn/ noun the strongest or central tower of a castle.
– ORIGIN from DUNGEON.

Don Juan /don hwahn, don joo-uhn/ noun a man who seduces many women.
– ORIGIN from the name of a legendary Spanish nobleman.

donkey noun (pl. **donkeys**) **1** a domesticated mammal of the horse family with long ears and a braying call. **2** informal a foolish person.
– PHRASES **donkey's years** Brit. informal a very long time. **talk the hind leg off a donkey** Brit. informal talk continuously.
– ORIGIN perhaps from DUN[1], or from the man's name *Duncan*.

donkey jacket noun Brit. a heavy jacket with patches of waterproof material across the shoulders.

donkey work noun Brit. informal the hard, boring part of a job.

donnish adjective like a college don; concerned with scholarly rather than practical matters.

donor noun **1** a person who donates something. **2** a substance, molecule, etc. which provides electrons for a physical or chemical process.
– ORIGIN Latin *donare* 'give'.

donor card noun a card consenting to the use of one's organs for transplant surgery in the event of one's death.

don't contraction do not.

donut noun US spelling of DOUGHNUT.

doodah (N. Amer. **doodad**) noun informal an object whose name is not known or has been forgotten.
– ORIGIN perhaps from the refrain of the song *Camptown Races*.

doodle verb draw or scribble absent-mindedly. •noun a drawing made absent-mindedly.
– DERIVATIVES **doodler** noun.
– ORIGIN German *dudeldopp* 'simpleton'.

doodlebug noun Brit. informal a V-1 bomb.

doolally /doo-lal-li/ adjective Brit. informal temporarily insane.

– ORIGIN from Indian army slang *doolally tap*, from *Deolali* (a town near Mumbai) + Urdu *tap* 'fever'.

doom noun death, destruction, or another terrible fate. •verb (**be doomed**) be fated to fail or be destroyed: *the marriage was doomed from the start.*
– DERIVATIVES **doomy** adjective.
– ORIGIN Old English, 'statute, judgement'.

doomsayer noun chiefly N. Amer. a doomster.
– DERIVATIVES **doomsaying** noun.

doomsday noun **1** the last day of the world's existence. **2** (in religious belief) the day of the Last Judgement.

doomster noun a person who predicts disaster.

door noun **1** a movable barrier at the entrance to a building, room, or vehicle, or in the framework of a cupboard. **2** the distance from one building in a row to another: *he lived two doors away.*
– PHRASES **lay something at someone's door** blame someone for something. **out of doors** in or into the open air.
– DERIVATIVES **doored** adjective.
– ORIGIN Old English.

doorbell noun a bell in a building which can be rung by visitors outside.

do-or-die adjective showing or requiring a great determination to succeed.

doorkeeper noun a person on duty at the entrance to a building.

doorknob noun a rounded door handle.

doorman noun (pl. **doormen**) a man who is on duty at the entrance to a large building.

doormat noun **1** a mat placed in a doorway for wiping the shoes. **2** informal a person who allows others to control them or treat them badly.

doornail noun (in phrase **dead as a doornail**) dead (used for emphasis).

doorstep noun **1** a step leading up to the outer door of a house. **2** Brit. informal a thick slice of bread. •verb (**doorsteps**, **doorstepping**, **doorstepped**) Brit. informal (of a journalist) try to get an interview with or photograph of someone by waiting outside their home.

doorstop (also **doorstopper**) noun an object that keeps a door open or in place.

doorway noun an entrance with a door.

doo-wop /doo-wop/ noun a style of pop music involving close harmony vocals and nonsense phrases.
– ORIGIN imitating the sound.

dopamine /doh-puh-meen/ noun a compound which exists in the body as a neurotransmitter and from which other substances including adrenalin are formed.
– ORIGIN from *dopa* (a related substance) + AMINE.

dope noun **1** informal an illegal drug, especially cannabis or (US) heroin. **2** a drug used to improve the performance of an athlete, racehorse, or greyhound. **3** informal a stupid person. **4** informal information. •verb **1** give a drug to a racehorse, greyhound, or athlete to improve their performance. **2** (**be doped up**) informal be heavily under the influence of drugs.
– ORIGIN Dutch *doop* 'sauce'.

dopey (also **dopy**) adjective (**dopier**, **dopiest**) informal **1** in a semi-conscious state from sleep or a drug. **2** stupid.
– DERIVATIVES **dopily** adverb **dopiness** noun.

doppelgänger /dop-puhl-gang-er/ noun a ghost or double of a living person.
– ORIGIN German, 'double-goer'.

Doppler effect /dop-pler/ (also **Doppler shift**) noun Physics an increase (or decrease) in the apparent frequency of sound, light, or other waves as the source and the observer move towards (or away from) each other.
– ORIGIN named after the Austrian physicist Johann Christian *Doppler*.

dorado /duh-rah-doh/ noun (pl. **dorados**) a large brightly coloured edible fish of warm seas.
– ORIGIN Spanish, 'gilded'.

Doric /dor-ik/ adjective relating to a classical order of architecture characterized by a fluted column with a square slab on top.
– ORIGIN from Greek *Dorios*, referring to a people of ancient Greece.

dork noun informal a stupid person.
– ORIGIN perhaps a variant of DICK[1].

dorm noun informal a dormitory.

dormant adjective **1** (of an animal) in or as if in a deep sleep. **2** (of a plant or bud) alive but not growing. **3** (of a volcano) temporarily inactive.
– DERIVATIVES **dormancy** noun.
– ORIGIN from Latin *dormire* 'to sleep'.

dormer (also **dormer window**) noun a window set vertically into a sloping roof.
– ORIGIN Old French *dormir* 'to sleep'.

dormitory noun (pl. **dormitories**) a bedroom for a number of people in an institution. •adjective referring to a small town or suburb from which people travel to work in a nearby city.
– ORIGIN Latin *dormitorium*.

dormouse noun (pl. **dormice**) a small mouse-like rodent with a bushy tail.
– ORIGIN unknown.

dorsal adjective technical on or relating to the upper side or back. Compare with VENTRAL.
– DERIVATIVES **dorsally** adverb.
– ORIGIN from Latin *dorsum* 'back'.

dory /rhymes with story/ noun (pl. **dories**) a narrow sea fish with a large mouth.
– ORIGIN French *dorée* 'gilded'.

DOS abbreviation Computing disk operating system.

dosage noun the size of a dose of medicine or radiation.

dose noun **1** a quantity of a medicine or drug taken at one time. **2** an amount of radiation received or absorbed at one time. **3** informal a sexually transmitted infection. •verb give someone a medicine or drug.
– PHRASES **like a dose of salts** Brit. informal very fast and efficiently. [from the use of Epsom salts as a laxative.]
– ORIGIN Greek *dosis* 'gift'.

dosh noun Brit. informal money.
– ORIGIN unknown.

dosha /dosh-uh, doh-shuh/ noun (in Ayurvedic medicine) each of three energies believed to circulate in the body and control its activity.
– ORIGIN Sanskrit, literally 'fault, disease'.

do-si-do /doh-zi-doh, doh-si-**doh**/ noun (pl. **do-si-dos**) (in country dancing) a figure in which two dancers pass round each other back to back.

– ORIGIN French *dos-à-dos* 'back to back'.

dosimeter /doh-sim-i-ter/ noun a device used to measure an absorbed dose of radiation.

– DERIVATIVES **dosimetry** noun.

doss Brit. informal verb **1** sleep in rough or makeshift conditions. **2** spend time in an idle or lazy way. • noun **1** an easy task giving plenty of time for doing nothing. **2** old use a bed in a cheap lodging house.

– DERIVATIVES **dosser** noun.

– ORIGIN perhaps related to Latin *dorsum* 'back'.

dosshouse noun Brit. informal a place providing cheap accommodation for homeless people.

dossier /doss-i-er, doss-i-ay/ noun a collection of documents about a person or subject.

– ORIGIN French.

dost /dust/ old-fashioned second person singular present of DO¹.

dot noun **1** a small round mark or spot. **2** the shorter signal of the two used in Morse code. **3** Music a dot used to indicate the lengthening of a note or rest by half, or to indicate staccato. • verb (**dots, dotting, dotted**) **1** mark something with a dot or dots. **2** scatter something over an area: *the meadow was dotted with buttercups and daisies.*

– PHRASES **dot the i's and cross the t's** informal ensure that all details are correct. **on the dot** informal exactly on time. **the year dot** Brit. informal a very long time ago.

– ORIGIN Old English, 'head of a boil'.

dotage /doh-tij/ noun the period of life in which a person is old and weak.

– ORIGIN from DOTE.

dotard /doh-terd/ noun an old person, especially one who is weak or senile.

dot-com (also **dot.com**) noun a company that conducts its business on the Internet.

– ORIGIN from '.com' in an Internet address, indicating a commercial site.

dote verb (**dote on**) be extremely and uncritically fond of: *she's a flirt but he dotes on her.*

– DERIVATIVES **doting** adjective.

– ORIGIN related to Dutch *doten* 'be silly'.

doth /duth/ old-fashioned third person singular present of DO¹.

dot matrix noun a grid of dots which are filled selectively to produce an image on a screen or on paper.

dotterel noun (pl. same or **dotterels**) a small migratory plover (bird).

– ORIGIN from DOTE (because the bird is easily caught).

dottle noun the tobacco left in a pipe after smoking.

– ORIGIN from DOT.

dotty adjective (**dottier, dottiest**) informal slightly mad or eccentric.

– DERIVATIVES **dottily** adverb **dottiness** noun.

– ORIGIN perhaps from former *dote* 'fool'.

double adjective **1** consisting of two equal, identical, or similar parts or things. **2** having twice the usual size, quantity, or strength: *a double brandy.* **3** designed to be used by two people. **4** having two different roles or interpretations: *she began a double life.* **5** (of a flower) having more than one circle of petals. • adverb twice the amount or extent. • noun **1** a thing which is twice as large as usual or is made up of two parts. **2** a person who looks exactly like another. **3** (**doubles**) a game involving sides made up of two players. **4** Brit. (**the double**) the winning of two sporting trophies in the same season. **5** Darts a hit on the ring enclosed by the two outer circles of a dartboard, scoring double. • pronoun an amount twice as large as usual. • verb **1** make or become double. **2** fold or bend over on itself. **3** (**double up**) bend over or curl up with pain or laughter. **4** (**double (up) as**) be used in or play another, different role: *a pocket-sized computer which doubles up as a mobile phone.* **5** (**double back**) go back in the direction one has come.

– PHRASES **at the double** very fast.

– DERIVATIVES **doubleness** noun **doubler** noun **doubly** adverb.

– ORIGIN Latin *duplus*, from *duo* 'two'.

double act noun a performance involving two people.

double agent noun an agent who pretends to act as a spy for one country while in fact acting for its enemy.

double-barrelled adjective **1** (of a gun) having two barrels. **2** Brit. (of a surname) having two parts joined by a hyphen.

double bass noun the largest and lowest-pitched instrument of the violin family.

double bill noun a programme of entertainment with two main items.

double bind noun a dilemma.

double-blind adjective (of a test or trial) in which information which may influence the behaviour of the tester or subject is withheld.

double bluff noun an attempt to deceive someone by telling them the truth while hoping that they believe one is lying.

double boiler noun a saucepan with an upper compartment heated by boiling water in the lower one.

double bond noun a chemical bond in which two pairs of electrons are shared between two atoms.

double-book verb accidentally reserve something for two different customers at the same time.

double-breasted adjective (of a jacket or coat) having a large overlap at the front and two rows of buttons.

double-check verb check something again to make certain.

double chin noun a roll of flesh below a person's chin.

double cream noun Brit. thick cream containing a high proportion of milk fat.

double-cross verb betray a person one is supposedly helping.

double-dealing noun deceitful behaviour. • adjective acting deceitfully.

double-decker noun a bus with two floors, one on top of the other.

double Dutch noun Brit. informal speech or writing that is difficult or impossible to understand.

double-edged adjective 1 (of a blade) having two cutting edges. 2 having two contrasting aspects or possible outcomes.

double entendre /doo-b'l on-ton-druh/ noun (pl. **double entendres** pronunc. same) a word or phrase with two possible meanings, one of which is usually rude or indecent.
– ORIGIN from former French, 'double understanding'.

double-entry adjective relating to a system of bookkeeping in which each transaction is entered as a debit in one account and a credit in another.

double exposure noun the repeated exposure of a photographic plate or film.

double fault noun Tennis an instance of two consecutive faults in serving, resulting in the loss of a point.

double figures plural noun chiefly Brit. a number between 10 and 99.

double glazing noun chiefly Brit. windows having two layers of glass with a space between them, designed to reduce heat loss and exclude noise.
– DERIVATIVES **double-glaze** verb.

Double Gloucester noun a hard cheese originally made in Gloucestershire.

double-header noun 1 a train pulled by two locomotives. 2 chiefly N. Amer. a sporting event in which two games are played in succession at the same venue.

double helix noun a pair of parallel helices intertwined about a common axis, especially that in the structure of DNA.

double jeopardy noun Law the prosecution or punishment of a person twice for the same offence.

double-jointed adjective (of a person) having unusually flexible joints.

double negative noun Grammar a negative statement containing two negative elements (e.g. *didn't say nothing*), regarded as incorrect in standard English.

> USAGE: A double negative uses two negative words in the same clause to convey a single negative, such as I *don't know nothing* (rather than I *don't know anything*). The structure is regarded as bad English because the two negative elements cancel each other out to give a positive statement, so that I *don't know nothing* could be taken to mean I *know something*.

double-park verb park a vehicle alongside one that is already parked.

double pneumonia noun pneumonia affecting both lungs.

doublespeak noun language that is deliberately unclear or ambiguous.
– ORIGIN coined by George Orwell (see **DOUBLETHINK**).

double standard noun a rule or principle applied unfairly in different ways to different people.

doublet noun 1 a man's short close-fitting padded jacket, worn from the 14th to the 17th century. 2 a pair of similar things.
– ORIGIN Old French, 'something folded'.

double take noun a second reaction to something unexpected, immediately after one's first reaction.

doublethink noun the acceptance of conflicting opinions or beliefs at the same time.
– ORIGIN coined by George Orwell in his novel *Nineteen Eighty-Four*.

double time noun a rate of pay equal to double the standard rate.

double vision noun the perception of two overlapping images of a single scene.

double whammy noun informal a blow or setback consisting of two separate elements.

doubloon /dub-loon/ noun historical a Spanish gold coin.
– ORIGIN Spanish *doblón*.

doubt noun a feeling of uncertainty. •verb 1 feel uncertain about something: I *doubt if he makes much money.* 2 disbelieve or mistrust: I *have no reason to doubt him*
– PHRASES **no doubt 1** certainly. **2** probably.
– DERIVATIVES **doubter** noun **doubting** adjective.
– ORIGIN from Latin *dubius* 'doubtful'.

doubtful adjective 1 feeling uncertain. 2 not known with certainty: *the fire was of doubtful origin.* 3 unlikely: *it's doubtful whether the council will be able to recover the money.*
– DERIVATIVES **doubtfully** adverb.

doubting Thomas noun a person who refuses to believe something without proof.
– ORIGIN referring to the apostle Thomas (Gospel of John, Chapter 20).

doubtless adverb very probably.
– DERIVATIVES **doubtlessly** adverb.

douche /doosh/ noun 1 a shower of water. 2 a jet of liquid applied to part of the body for cleansing or medicinal purposes. 3 a device for washing out the vagina as a contraceptive measure. •verb spray or clean someone or something with water.
– ORIGIN French.

dough noun 1 a thick mixture of flour and liquid, for baking into bread or pastry. 2 informal money.
– DERIVATIVES **doughy** adjective.
– ORIGIN Old English.

doughnut (also US **donut**) noun a small fried cake or ring of sweetened dough.

doughty /dow-ti/ adjective (**doughtier**, **doughtiest**) brave and determined.
– ORIGIN Old English.

Douglas fir noun a tall, slender conifer valued for its wood.
– ORIGIN named after the Scottish botanist and explorer David *Douglas*.

dour /doo-er, dow-er/ adjective very severe, stern, or gloomy.
– DERIVATIVES **dourly** adverb **dourness** noun.
– ORIGIN probably from Scottish Gaelic, 'dull, obstinate, stupid'.

douse /dowss/ (also **dowse**) verb 1 drench something with liquid. 2 extinguish a fire or light.
– ORIGIN uncertain.

dove¹ /duv/ noun 1 a stocky bird with a small head, short legs, and a cooing voice, very similar to but generally smaller than a pigeon. 2 (in politics) a person who favours a policy of peace and negotiation.

d

– DERIVATIVES **dovish** (also **doveish**) adjective.
– ORIGIN Old Norse.

dove² /dohv/ chiefly N. Amer. past and past participle of **DIVE**.

dovecote /**duv**-kot/ (also **dovecot**) noun a shelter with nest holes for domesticated pigeons.

Dover sole noun an edible flatfish.

dovetail verb **1** fit together easily or conveniently: *flights that dovetail with the working day.* **2** join things by means of a dovetail joint. ●noun a wedge-shaped joint formed by interlocking two pieces of wood.

dowager /**dow**-uh-jer/ noun **1** a widow who holds a title or property that belonged to her late husband. **2** a dignified elderly woman.
– ORIGIN Old French *douagiere.*

dowdy adjective (**dowdier, dowdiest**) (especially of a woman) unfashionable and dull in appearance.
– DERIVATIVES **dowdily** adverb **dowdiness** noun.

dowel noun a headless peg used for holding together components. ●verb (**dowels, dowelling, dowelled;** US **dowels, doweling, doweled**) fasten things with a dowel.
– ORIGIN perhaps German.

dowelling (US **doweling**) noun cylindrical rods that are cut into dowels.

dower noun **1** a widow's share for life of her husband's estate. **2** old use a dowry.
– ORIGIN Old French *douaire.*

dower house noun Brit. a house intended for a widow, typically one on her late husband's estate.

Dow Jones index /dow-**johnz**/ noun an index of figures indicating the relative price of shares on the New York Stock Exchange.
– ORIGIN named after the American financial news agency *Dow Jones & Co, Inc.*

down¹ adverb **1** towards or in a lower place or position. **2** to or at a lower level or value. **3** in or into a weaker or worse position, mood, or condition. **4** to a smaller amount or size, or a simpler or more basic state. **5** away from a central place or the north. **6** from an earlier to a later point in time or order. **7** in or into writing. **8** (of a computer system) out of action. ●preposition **1** from a higher to a lower point of. **2** at a point further along the course of. **3** along the course or extent of. **4** informal at or to a place. ●adjective **1** directed or moving towards a lower place or position. **2** unhappy. **3** (of a computer system) out of action. ●verb informal **1** knock or bring someone or something to the ground. **2** consume a drink.
– PHRASES **be** (or **have a**) **down on** Brit. informal dislike or feel hostile towards someone. **be down to 1** be caused by. **2** be left with: *I'm down to my last few pounds.* **down in the mouth** informal unhappy. **down on one's luck** informal having a period of bad luck. **down tools** Brit. informal stop work.
– ORIGIN Old English.

down² noun fine, soft feathers or hairs.
– ORIGIN Old Norse.

down³ noun **1** a gently rolling hill. **2** (**the Downs**) ridges of undulating chalk and limestone hills in southern England.
– ORIGIN Old English.

down and out adjective homeless and having no money; destitute. ●noun (**down-and-out**) a destitute person.

down at heel adjective chiefly Brit. **1** (of a shoe) with the heel worn down. **2** shabby because of a lack of money.

downbeat adjective **1** pessimistic or gloomy. **2** relaxed and understated. ●noun Music an accented beat, usually the first of the bar.

downcast adjective **1** (of a person's eyes) looking downwards. **2** feeling sad or depressed.

downcurved adjective curving downwards.

downer noun informal **1** a depressant or tranquillizing drug. **2** a sad or depressing experience.

downfall noun a loss of power, wealth, or status.

downgrade verb reduce someone or something to a lower grade, rank, or level of importance.

downhearted adjective feeling sad or discouraged.

downhill adverb & adjective **1** towards the bottom of a slope. **2** into a steadily worsening situation: *his career was rapidly going downhill.*

downland noun gently rolling hill country.

downlink noun a telecommunications link for signals coming to the earth from a satellite, spacecraft, or aircraft.

download verb copy data from one computer system to another or to a disk. ●noun **1** a downloaded computer file. **2** the process of downloading data.
– DERIVATIVES **downloadable** adjective.

downmarket adjective & adverb chiefly Brit. cheap and of low quality or status.

down payment noun an initial payment made when buying something on credit.

downpipe noun Brit. a pipe to carry rainwater from a roof to a drain or to ground level.

downplay verb make something appear less important than it really is.

downpour noun a heavy fall of rain.

downright adjective utter; complete: *a downright lie.* ●adverb extremely: *he was downright rude.*

downriver adverb & adjective towards or situated at a point nearer the mouth of a river.

downscale N. Amer. verb reduce the size or extent of something. ●adjective downmarket.

downshift verb adopt a simpler and less stressful lifestyle.

downside noun the negative aspect of something.

downsize verb reduce the number of staff employed by a company in order to cut costs.

Down's syndrome noun a medical disorder caused by a genetic defect, causing intellectual impairment and physical abnormalities.
– ORIGIN named after the English physician John L. H. *Down.*

downstage adjective & adverb at or towards the front of a stage.

downstairs adverb & adjective down a flight of stairs; on or to a lower floor. ●noun the ground floor or lower floors of a building.

downstream adverb & adjective situated or moving in the direction in which a stream or river flows.

downtempo adjective (of music) played at a slow tempo.

downtime noun time during which a computer or other machine is out of action.

down-to-earth adjective practical and realistic.

downtown chiefly N. Amer. adjective & adverb of, in, or towards the central area or main business area of a city. • noun a downtown area.
– DERIVATIVES **downtowner** noun.

downtrend noun a downward tendency, especially in economic matters: *a downtrend in the share price.*

downtrodden adjective treated badly by people in power and lacking the energy or ability to resist.

downturn noun a decline in economic or other activity.

down under informal adverb in or to Australia or New Zealand. • noun Australia and New Zealand.

downward adverb (also **downwards**) towards a lower point or level. • adjective moving towards a lower level.
– DERIVATIVES **downwardly** adverb.

downwind adverb & adjective in the direction in which the wind is blowing.

downy adjective (**downier**, **downiest**) covered with fine soft hair or feathers.

dowry /dow-ri/ noun (pl. **dowries**) property or money brought by a bride to her husband on their marriage.
– ORIGIN Old French *dowarie*.

dowse¹ /dowz/ verb search for underground water or minerals with a pointer which is supposedly moved by unseen influences.
– DERIVATIVES **dowser** noun.
– ORIGIN unknown.

dowse² verb variant spelling of DOUSE.

doxology /dok-sol-uh-ji/ noun (pl. **doxologies**) a set form of prayer praising God.
– ORIGIN Greek *doxologia*.

doxy noun (pl. **doxies**) old use 1 a man's lover or mistress. 2 a prostitute.
– ORIGIN unknown.

doyen /doy-yen/ noun (fem. **doyenne** /doy-yen, doy-**yen**/) the most respected or prominent person in a particular group or profession: *the doyenne of English cookery writers.*
– ORIGIN Old French *deien*.

doze verb sleep lightly. • noun a short light sleep.
– ORIGIN perhaps related to Danish *døse* 'make drowsy'.

dozen noun (pl. same) 1 a group or set of twelve. 2 informal a lot.
– PHRASES **talk nineteen to the dozen** Brit. talk quickly and continuously.
– DERIVATIVES **dozenth** adjective.
– ORIGIN Old French *dozeine*.

dozy adjective (**dozier**, **doziest**) 1 feeling drowsy and lazy. 2 Brit. informal not alert; stupid.
– DERIVATIVES **dozily** adverb **doziness** noun.

DP abbreviation data processing.

DPhil abbreviation (in the UK) Doctor of Philosophy.

DPP abbreviation (in the UK) Director of Public Prosecutions.

Dr abbreviation (as a title) Doctor.

dr. abbreviation 1 drachma(s). 2 dram(s).

drab adjective (**drabber**, **drabbest**) lacking brightness or interest; dull and dreary. • noun a dull light brown colour.
– DERIVATIVES **drably** adverb **drabness** noun.
– ORIGIN probably from Old French *drap* 'cloth'.

drachm /dram/ noun historical 1 a unit of weight equivalent to one eighth of an ounce. 2 (also **fluid drachm**) a liquid measure equivalent to one eighth of a fluid ounce.
– ORIGIN see DRACHMA.

drachma /drak-muh/ noun (pl. **drachmas** or **drachmae** /drak-mee/) 1 (until the introduction of the euro in 2002) the basic unit of money of Greece. 2 a silver coin of ancient Greece.
– ORIGIN Greek *drakhmē*, an ancient weight and coin.

draconian /druh-koh-ni-uhn, dray-koh-ni-uhn/ adjective (of laws or punishments) extremely harsh or severe.
– ORIGIN named after the ancient Athenian legislator *Draco*.

draft noun 1 a preliminary version of a piece of writing. 2 a plan or sketch. 3 a written order requesting a bank to pay a specified sum of money. 4 (**the draft**) US compulsory recruitment for military service. 5 US spelling of DRAUGHT. • verb 1 prepare a preliminary version of a piece of writing. 2 select a person or group and send them somewhere for a purpose: *extra police were drafted in to move the crowds away.* 3 US conscript someone for military service.
– DERIVATIVES **drafter** noun.
– ORIGIN from DRAUGHT.

> **USAGE:** Do not confuse **draft** with **draught**. **Draft** means 'a preliminary version of a piece of writing' or 'make a preliminary version of a first piece of writing' (*he drafted a letter of resignation*), while **draught** chiefly means 'a current of air' (*a cold draught from the hole in the roof*). **Draft** is the American spelling for both senses.

draftee noun US a person conscripted for military service.

draftsman noun (pl. **draftsmen**) 1 a person who drafts legal documents. 2 chiefly N. Amer. variant spelling of DRAUGHTSMAN.

drafty adjective US spelling of DRAUGHTY.

drag verb (**drags**, **dragging**, **dragged**) 1 pull something along forcefully, roughly, or with difficulty. 2 trail along the ground. 3 take someone somewhere, despite their reluctance. 4 move an image across a computer screen using a mouse. 5 (of time) pass slowly. 6 (**drag something out**) prolong something unnecessarily. 7 (**drag something up**) informal deliberately mention something unwelcome. 8 search the bottom of an area of water with grapnels or nets. 9 (**drag on**) informal inhale the smoke from a cigarette. • noun 1 informal a boring or tiresome person or thing. 2 an act of inhaling smoke from a cigarette. 3 the action of dragging. 4 the force exerted by air or water to slow down a moving object.
– PHRASES **drag one's feet 1** walk wearily or

d

with difficulty. **2** be slow or reluctant to act. **in drag** (of a man) wearing women's clothes.
– ORIGIN Old English or Old Norse.

draggle verb **1** make something dirty or wet by trailing it on the ground. **2** hang untidily.
– ORIGIN from **DRAG**.

dragnet noun **1** a net drawn through water or across ground to trap fish or game. **2** a systematic search for criminals.

dragoman /drag-oh-muhn/ noun (pl. **dragomans** or **dragomen**) an interpreter or guide in a country speaking Arabic, Turkish, or Persian.
– ORIGIN Arabic, 'interpreter'.

dragon noun **1** a mythical monster like a giant reptile, typically able to breathe out fire. **2** derogatory a fierce and intimidating woman.
– ORIGIN Greek *drakōn* 'serpent'.

dragonfly noun (pl. **dragonflies**) a fast-flying long-bodied insect with two pairs of large transparent wings.

dragoon /druh-goon/ noun **1** a member of any of several British cavalry regiments. **2** historical a mounted infantryman armed with a rifle or musket. •verb force or persuade someone do something: *she had been dragooned into helping with the housework.*
– ORIGIN French *dragon* 'dragon'.

drag queen noun informal a man who dresses up in very flamboyant or showy women's clothes.

drag race noun a short race between two cars to see which can accelerate fastest from a standstill.
– DERIVATIVES **drag racer** noun **drag racing** noun.

dragster noun a car used in drag races.

drain verb **1** make the liquid in something run out: *we drained the swimming pool.* **2** (of liquid) flow away from, out of, or into something: *the river drains into the Pacific.* **3** become dry as liquid runs off. **4** deprive of strength or vitality: *she felt drained of energy.* **5** cause a resource to be lost or used up: *my mother's hospital bills are draining my income.* **6** drink the entire contents of a glass, cup, etc. •noun **1** a channel or pipe carrying off surplus liquid. **2** a thing that uses up a resource or one's strength.
– PHRASES **go down the drain** informal be totally wasted.
– ORIGIN Old English.

drainage noun **1** the action or process of draining something. **2** a system of drains.

drainer noun **1** a rack used to hold draining crockery. **2** a draining board.

draining board noun Brit. a sloping grooved surface next to a sink, on which crockery is left to drain.

drainpipe noun **1** a pipe for carrying off rainwater from a building. **2** (**drainpipes** or **drainpipe trousers**) trousers with very narrow legs.

drake noun a male duck.
– ORIGIN Germanic.

Dralon /dray-lon/ noun trademark, chiefly Brit. a synthetic textile made from acrylic fibre.
– ORIGIN on the pattern of *nylon*.

dram noun **1** chiefly Scottish a small drink of spirits. **2** a drachm.
– ORIGIN Latin *dragma*, from Greek *drakhmē*

'drachma'.

drama noun **1** a play. **2** plays as a literary genre. **3** an exciting series of events.
– ORIGIN Greek.

dramatic adjective **1** relating to drama. **2** sudden and striking: *a dramatic increase in the prison population.* **3** exciting or impressive. **4** intended to create an effect; theatrical: *he flung out his arms in a dramatic gesture.*
– DERIVATIVES **dramatically** adverb.

dramatics plural noun **1** the study or practice of acting in and producing plays. **2** theatrically exaggerated behaviour.

dramatis personae /dra-muh-tiss per-soh-ny/ plural noun the characters of a play or novel.
– ORIGIN Latin, 'persons of the drama'.

dramatist noun a person who writes plays.

dramatize (or **dramatise**) verb **1** present a novel, event, etc. as a play or film. **2** exaggerate the excitement or seriousness of something.
– DERIVATIVES **dramatization** noun.

dramaturgy /dra-muh-ter-ji/ noun the theory and practice of writing plays.
– DERIVATIVES **dramaturgical** adjective.

Drambuie /dram-byoo-i, dram-boo-i/ noun trademark a sweet Scotch whisky liqueur.
– ORIGIN from Scottish Gaelic *dram buidheach* 'satisfying drink'.

drank past of **DRINK**.

drape verb arrange cloth or clothing loosely on or round something. •noun **1** (**drapes**) chiefly N. Amer. long curtains. **2** the way in which a garment or fabric hangs.
– ORIGIN from **DRAPERY**.

draper noun Brit. dated a person who sells fabrics.

drapery noun (pl. **draperies**) cloth, curtains, or clothing hanging in loose folds.
– ORIGIN from Old French *drap* 'cloth'.

drastic adjective having a strong or far-reaching effect.
– DERIVATIVES **drastically** adverb.
– ORIGIN Greek *drastikos*.

drat exclamation used to express mild annoyance.
– DERIVATIVES **dratted** adjective.
– ORIGIN shortening of *od rat*, a euphemism for *God rot*.

draught (US **draft**) noun **1** a current of cool air in a room or confined space. **2** a single act of drinking or breathing in. **3** literary or old use a quantity of a liquid with medicinal properties: *a sleeping draught.* **4** the depth of water needed to float a particular ship. •verb variant spelling of **DRAFT**. •adjective **1** (of beer) beer served from a cask rather than from a bottle or can. **2** (of an animal) used for pulling heavy loads.
– ORIGIN Old Norse.

USAGE: On the confusion of **draught** and **draft**, see the note at **DRAFT**.

draughtboard noun Brit. a square chequered board of sixty-four squares, used for playing draughts.

draughts noun Brit. a game played on a chequered board by two players with pieces which are moved diagonally.

– ORIGIN from DRAUGHT in the former sense 'move' (in chess).

draughtsman (or **draughtswoman**) noun (pl. **draughtsmen** or **draughtswomen**) **1** a person who makes detailed technical plans or drawings. **2** an artist skilled in drawing. **3** variant spelling of DRAFTSMAN.

– DERIVATIVES **draughtsmanship** noun.

draughty (US **drafty**) adjective (**draughtier**, **draughtiest**) (of a room, space, etc.) uncomfortable because draughts of cold air are blowing through it.

Dravidian /druh-**vid**-i-uhn/ noun **1** a family of languages spoken in southern India and Sri Lanka, including Tamil and Kannada. **2** a member of any of the peoples speaking these languages. • adjective relating to Dravidian or Dravidians.

– ORIGIN Sanskrit, 'relating to the Tamils'.

draw verb (past **drew**; past part. **drawn**) **1** produce a picture, diagram, etc. by making lines and marks on paper. **2** pull or drag a vehicle so as to make it follow behind. **3** pull or move in a particular direction: *the train drew out of the station.* **4** pull curtains shut or open. **5** arrive at a point in time: *the campaign drew to a close.* **6** take something from a container or receptacle: *he drew his gun.* **7** get or take something from a source: *he draws inspiration from ordinary scenes and places.* **8** take in a breath. **9** be the cause of a particular response: *his action drew fierce criticism.* **10** attract someone to a place or an event. **11** persuade someone to reveal or do something: *he refused to be drawn on what would happen.* **12** reach a conclusion. **13** finish a contest or game with an even score. • noun **1** an act of selecting names at random, for prizes, sporting fixtures, etc. **2** a game or match that ends with the scores even. **3** a person or thing that is very attractive or interesting. **4** an act of inhaling smoke from a cigarette. **5** Cricket a game which is left incomplete because of lack of time. Compare with TIE.

– PHRASES **draw someone's fire** attract hostile criticism away from a more important target. **draw in** (of successive days) become shorter because of the changing seasons. **draw the line at** refuse to do or tolerate something. **draw on 1** (of a period of time) pass by and approach its end. **2** suck smoke from a cigarette or pipe. **draw someone/thing out 1** make something last longer. **2** persuade someone to be more talkative. **draw up** come to a halt. **draw something up** prepare a plan or document.

– ORIGIN Old English.

> USAGE: On the confusion of **draw** and **drawer**, see the note at DRAWER.

drawback noun a disadvantage or problem.

drawbridge noun a bridge which is hinged at one end so that it can be raised.

drawer noun **1** /draw/ a storage compartment made to slide horizontally in and out of a desk or chest. **2** (**drawers**) /drawz/ dated or humorous knickers or underpants. **3** /draw-er/ a person who draws something. **4** /draw-er/ the person who writes a cheque.

> USAGE: The word **drawer**, which mainly means 'a sliding storage compartment', is often spelled incorrectly as **draw** (which, as a noun, chiefly means 'an even score at the end of a game', as in *the match ended in a goalless draw*).

drawing noun **1** a picture or diagram made with a pencil, pen, or crayon rather than paint. **2** the art or skill of making drawings.

drawing board noun a board on which paper can be spread for artists or designers to work on.

– PHRASES **back to the drawing board** a plan has failed and a new one is needed.

drawing pin noun Brit. a short flat-headed pin for fastening paper to a surface.

drawing room noun a room in a large private house in which guests can be received.

– ORIGIN abbreviation of *withdrawing-room* 'a room to withdraw to'.

drawl verb speak in a slow, lazy way with prolonged vowel sounds. • noun a drawling accent.

– ORIGIN from German or Dutch *dralen* 'delay, linger'.

drawn past participle of DRAW. adjective looking strained from illness or exhaustion.

drawn-out adjective lasting longer than is necessary.

drawstring noun a string in the seam of a garment or bag, which can be pulled to tighten or close it.

dray noun a low vehicle or cart without sides, for delivering barrels or other heavy loads.

– ORIGIN perhaps from an Old English word meaning 'dragnet'.

dread verb anticipate something with great anxiety or fear. • noun great anxiety or fear. • adjective greatly feared; dreadful: *the dread disease.*

– DERIVATIVES **dreaded** adjective.

– ORIGIN Old English.

dreadful adjective **1** extremely bad or serious. **2** used for emphasis: *I'm a dreadful hoarder.*

– DERIVATIVES **dreadfully** adverb.

dreadlocks plural noun a Rastafarian hairstyle in which the hair is twisted into tight braids or ringlets.

– DERIVATIVES **dreadlocked** adjective.

dreadnought noun historical a type of battleship of the early 20th century, equipped entirely with large-calibre guns.

– ORIGIN named after Britain's HMS *Dreadnought*.

dream noun **1** a series of thoughts, images, and sensations occurring in a person's mind during sleep. **2** a long-held ambition or ideal: *his childhood dream of climbing Everest.* **3** informal a wonderful or perfect person or thing. • verb (past and past part. **dreamed** /dremt, dreemd/ or **dreamt** /dremt/) **1** experience dreams during sleep. **2** indulge in daydreams or fantasies. **3** think of as being possible: *I never dreamed she'd take offence.* **4** (**dream something up**) imagine or invent something.

– PHRASES **like a dream** informal very easily or successfully.

– DERIVATIVES **dreamer** noun **dreamless** adjective.

– ORIGIN Germanic.

dreamboat noun informal a very attractive person, especially a man.

dreamscape noun a scene with the strangeness characteristic of dreams.

dreamy adjective (**dreamier**, **dreamiest**) 1 tending to daydream, or giving the impression that someone is daydreaming: *she had a dreamy look in her eyes.* 2 having a magical or pleasantly unreal quality.
– DERIVATIVES **dreamily** adverb **dreaminess** noun.

dreary adjective (**drearier**, **dreariest**) dull, bleak, and depressing.
– DERIVATIVES **drearily** adverb **dreariness** noun.
– ORIGIN Old English, 'gory, cruel, melancholy'.

dreck /drek/ noun informal rubbish.
– ORIGIN Yiddish, 'filth, dregs'.

dredge¹ verb 1 clean out the bed of a harbour, river, etc. with a dredge. 2 bring something up from a river or seabed with a dredge. 3 (**dredge something up**) mention something unwelcome or unpleasant that has been forgotten. •noun a piece of equipment for bringing up objects or mud from a river or seabed by scooping or dragging.
– DERIVATIVES **dredger** noun.
– ORIGIN perhaps related to Dutch *dregghe* 'grappling hook'.

dredge² verb sprinkle food with sugar or other powdered substance.
– ORIGIN from Old French *dragie*.

dregs plural noun 1 the last drops of a liquid left in a container, together with any sediment. 2 the most worthless parts: *the dregs of society.*
– ORIGIN probably Scandinavian.

drench verb 1 wet someone or something thoroughly. 2 (often as adj. **drenched**) cover with large amounts of something: *a sun-drenched clearing.* •noun a dose of medicine given to an animal.
– ORIGIN Old English.

Dresden china /drez-d'n/ noun porcelain with elaborate decoration and delicate colourings, made originally at Dresden in Germany.

dress verb 1 (also **get dressed**) put on one's clothes. 2 put clothes on someone else. 3 wear clothes in a particular way or of a particular type: *she dresses well.* 4 decorate or arrange something in an artistic or attractive way. 5 clean, treat, or apply a dressing to a wound. 6 clean and prepare food for cooking or eating. 7 add a dressing to a salad. 8 apply fertilizer to an area of ground or a plant. 9 treat or smooth the surface of leather, fabric, or stone. •noun 1 a one-piece garment for a woman or girl that covers the body and extends down over the legs. 2 clothing of a particular kind: *evening dress.* •adjective (of clothing) formal or ceremonial: *a dress suit.*
– PHRASES **dress down** informal wear informal clothes. **dressed to kill** informal wearing glamorous clothes intended to create a striking impression. **dress up** dress in smart or formal clothes, or in a special costume.
– ORIGIN Old French *dresser* 'arrange, prepare'.

dressage /dress-ahzh/ noun the art of training horses to perform a set of controlled movements at the rider's command.
– ORIGIN French, 'training'.

dress circle noun Brit. the first level of seats above the ground floor in a theatre.

dresser¹ noun 1 a sideboard with shelves above for storing and displaying crockery. 2 N. Amer. a chest of drawers.
– ORIGIN first referring a sideboard or table on which food was prepared.

dresser² noun 1 a person who dresses in a particular way: *a snappy dresser.* 2 a person who looks after theatrical costumes.

dressing noun 1 a sauce for salads, usually consisting of oil and vinegar with herbs or other flavourings. 2 N. Amer. stuffing. 3 a piece of material placed on a wound to protect it. 4 a layer of fertilizer spread over land.

dressing-down noun informal a severe reprimand.

dressing gown noun a long, loose robe worn after getting out of bed or having a bath or shower.

dressing room noun 1 a room in which actors or other performers change clothes. 2 a small room attached to a bedroom for storing clothes.

dressing table noun a table with a mirror and drawers, used while dressing or applying make-up.

dressmaker noun a person who makes women's clothes.
– DERIVATIVES **dressmaking** noun.

dress rehearsal noun a final rehearsal in which everything is done as it would be in a real performance.

dress sense noun a good instinct for selecting clothes.

dress shirt noun a man's white shirt worn with a bow tie and a dinner jacket on formal occasions.

dressy adjective (**dressier**, **dressiest**) (of clothes) suitable for a smart or formal occasion.

drew past of DRAW.

drey /dray/ noun (pl. **dreys**) a squirrel's nest of twigs in a tree.
– ORIGIN unknown.

dribble verb 1 (of a liquid) fall slowly in drops or a thin stream. 2 allow saliva to run from the mouth. 3 (in sport) take the ball forward with slight touches or (in basketball) by continuous bouncing. •noun 1 a thin stream of liquid. 2 (in sport) an act of dribbling.
– DERIVATIVES **dribbler** noun **dribbly** adjective.
– ORIGIN variant of DRIP.

driblet noun 1 a thin stream or small drop of liquid. 2 a small or insignificant amount.

dribs and drabs plural noun (in phrase **in dribs and drabs**) informal in small amounts over a period of time.

dried past and past participle of DRY.

drier¹ noun variant spelling of DRYER.

drier² adjective comparative of DRY.

drift verb 1 be carried slowly by a current of air or water. 2 walk or move slowly or casually. 3 (of snow, leaves, etc.) be blown into heaps by the wind. •noun 1 a continuous slow movement from one place to another: *the population drift from rural areas to cities.* 2 the general intention or meaning of someone's remarks: *he got her drift.* 3 a large mass of snow, leaves, etc. piled up by the wind. 4 movement away from an intended course or

direction because of currents or winds.
5 Geology deposits left by retreating ice sheets.
– ORIGIN Old Norse, 'snowdrift, something driven'.

drifter noun **1** a person who is continually moving from place to place, without any fixed home or job. **2** a fishing boat equipped with a drift net.

drift net noun a large fishing net kept upright by weights at the bottom and floats at the top and allowed to drift in the sea.

driftwood noun pieces of wood floating on the sea or washed ashore.

drill[1] noun **1** a tool or machine used for boring holes. **2** training in military exercises. **3** instruction by means of repeated exercises. **4** (**the drill**) informal the correct procedure. •verb **1** bore a hole with a drill. **2** subject someone to military training or other intensive instruction.
– DERIVATIVES **driller** noun.
– ORIGIN Dutch *drillen*.

drill[2] noun **1** a machine which makes small furrows, sows seed in them, and then covers the sown seed. **2** a small furrow made by such a machine. •verb sow seed with a drill.
– ORIGIN perhaps from DRILL[1].

drill[3] noun a strong cotton or linen fabric woven with parallel diagonal lines.
– ORIGIN from Latin *trilix* 'triple-twilled'.

drily /dry-li/ (also **dryly**) adverb in a matter-of-fact or ironically humorous way.

drink verb (past **drank**; past part. **drunk**) **1** take a liquid into the mouth and swallow. **2** consume alcohol, especially regularly or in large amounts. **3** (**drink something in**) watch or listen eagerly to something. •noun **1** a liquid for drinking. **2** a quantity of liquid swallowed at one time. **3** alcohol or an alcoholic drink.
– PHRASES **drink someone's health** (or **drink to someone**) express good wishes for someone by raising one's glass and drinking a small amount.
– DERIVATIVES **drinkable** adjective **drinker** noun.
– ORIGIN Old English.

drink-driving noun Brit. the crime of driving a vehicle with too much alcohol in the blood.

drinking chocolate noun Brit. a mixture of cocoa powder, milk solids, and sugar added to hot water to make a chocolate drink.

drinking fountain noun a device producing a small jet of water for drinking.

drip verb (**drips**, **dripping**, **dripped**) fall or let fall in small drops of liquid. •noun **1** a small drop of a liquid. **2** a piece of equipment which slowly passes fluid, nutrients, or drugs into a patient's body through a vein. **3** informal a weak and ineffectual person.
– ORIGIN Old English.

drip-dry adjective (of an item of clothing) able to dry without forming creases if hung up when wet.

drip-feed verb supply a patient with fluid through a drip.

dripping noun Brit. fat that has melted and dripped from roasting meat. •adjective extremely wet.

drippy adjective (**drippier**, **drippiest**) informal weak, ineffectual, or very sentimental.

– DERIVATIVES **drippily** adverb **drippiness** noun.

drive verb (past **drove**; past part. **driven**) **1** operate and control a motor vehicle. **2** carry someone or something in a motor vehicle. **3** propel or carry along: *the gales drove the vessel on to the rocks.* **4** urge animals or people to move. **5** make someone act in a particular way: *depression drove him to attempt suicide.* **6** provide the energy to keep an engine or machine in motion. **7** Golf hit a ball from the tee. •noun **1** a trip or journey in a car. **2** (also **driveway**) a short private road leading to a house. **3** an inborn desire or urge: *his sex drive.* **4** an organized effort to achieve a particular purpose: *a sales drive.* **5** determination and ambition. **6** the transmission of power to machinery or to the wheels of a vehicle. **7** Brit. a large organized gathering for playing a game: *a whist drive.* **8** Golf a shot from the tee.
– PHRASES **what someone is driving at** the point that someone is trying to make.
– DERIVATIVES **drivable** (also **driveable**) adjective.
– ORIGIN Old English.

drive-by shooting noun chiefly N. Amer. an incident in which a person is shot or killed by someone in a passing vehicle.

drive-in adjective (of a cinema, restaurant, etc.) that one can visit without leaving one's car.

drivel /driv-uhl/ noun nonsense; rubbish.
– ORIGIN Old English.

driven past participle of DRIVE.

driver noun **1** a person or thing that drives something. **2** a flat-faced golf club used for hitting the ball from the tee.
– PHRASES **in the driver's seat** in control.

driveshaft noun a rotating shaft which transmits torque in an engine.

driving adjective **1** having a controlling influence: *the driving force behind the plan.* **2** being blown by the wind with great force: *driving rain.*
– PHRASES **in the driving seat** in control.

driving licence (N. Amer. **driver's licence**) noun an official document permitting a person to drive a motor vehicle.

driving range noun an area where golfers can practise drives.

drizzle noun light rain falling in very fine drops. •verb **1** (**it drizzles**, **it is drizzling**, **it drizzled**) rain lightly. **2** pour a thin stream of a liquid ingredient over food.
– DERIVATIVES **drizzly** adjective.
– ORIGIN probably from an Old English word meaning 'to fall'.

drogue /drohg/ noun a device towed behind a boat or aircraft to reduce speed or improve stability, or as a target for gunnery practice.
– ORIGIN perhaps related to DRAG.

droid /droyd/ noun (in science fiction) a robot.
– ORIGIN shortening of ANDROID.

droit de seigneur /drwah duh sen-yer/ noun the alleged right of a medieval feudal lord to have sex with a vassal's bride on her wedding night.
– ORIGIN French, 'lord's right'.

droll /drohl/ adjective amusing in a strange or unexpected way.
– DERIVATIVES **drollery** noun **drolly** /drohl-li/ adverb.
– ORIGIN French.

dromedary /drom-i-duh-ri/ noun (pl. **dromedaries**) an Arabian camel, with one hump.
– ORIGIN from Latin *dromedarius camelus* 'swift camel', from Greek *dromas* 'runner'.

drone verb **1** make a continuous low humming sound. **2** (**drone on**) speak at length in a boring way. ● noun **1** a low continuous humming sound. **2** a pipe (especially in a set of bagpipes) or string used to sound a continuous low-pitched note. **3** a male bee which does no work in a colony but can fertilize a queen. **4** a lazy person. **5** a remote-controlled aircraft with no pilot.
– ORIGIN Old English, 'male bee'.

drongo /drong-goh/ noun (pl. **drongos** or **drongoes**) **1** a songbird with glossy black plumage, found in Africa, southern Asia, and Australia. **2** informal, chiefly Austral./NZ a stupid or incompetent person.
– ORIGIN from Malagasy (the language of Madagascar); sense 2 is said to be from the name of a very unsuccessful Australian racehorse.

drool verb **1** drop saliva uncontrollably from the mouth. **2** (often **drool over**) informal show great pleasure or desire. ● noun saliva falling from the mouth.
– ORIGIN from DRIVEL.

droop verb **1** bend or hang downwards limply. **2** sag down as a result of tiredness or low spirits: *the corners of his mouth drooped.* ● noun an act of drooping.
– ORIGIN Old Norse, 'hang the head'.

droopy adjective (**droopier, droopiest**) **1** hanging down limply; drooping. **2** not having much strength or spirit.
– DERIVATIVES **droopily** adverb **droopiness** noun.

drop verb (**drops, dropping, dropped**) **1** fall or cause to fall. **2** sink to the ground. **3** make or become lower, weaker, or less: *he dropped his speed.* **4** abandon or discontinue: *the charges against him were dropped.* **5** (often **drop someone off**) set down or unload a passenger or goods. **6** informal collapse from exhaustion. **7** lose a point, match, etc. **8** mention something casually. ● noun **1** a small round or pear-shaped amount of liquid. **2** an instance of falling or dropping. **3** a small drink, especially of alcohol. **4** an abrupt fall or slope. **5** a small sweet.
– PHRASES **at the drop of a hat** informal without hesitation; immediately. **drop back/behind** fall back or get left behind. **drop by/in** pay someone a brief or casual visit. **drop dead** die suddenly and unexpectedly. **drop one's guard** stop being defensive or self-protective. **a drop in the ocean** a very small amount compared with what is needed. **drop someone a line** informal send someone a note or letter. **drop off** fall asleep. **drop out 1** stop participating in something. **2** start living an unconventional lifestyle.
– ORIGIN Old English.

drop cloth noun (also **drop curtain**) a curtain or painted cloth lowered vertically on to a theatre stage. **2** N. Amer. a dust sheet.

drop-dead adverb informal used to emphasize attractiveness: *drop-dead gorgeous.*

drop goal noun Rugby a goal scored by a drop-kick of the ball over the crossbar.

drop handlebars plural noun handlebars with the handles bent below the rest of the bar, used especially on racing cycles.

drop kick noun (chiefly in rugby) a kick made by dropping the ball and kicking it as it bounces.

droplet noun a very small drop of a liquid.

drop-off noun a decline or decrease.

dropout noun **1** a person who has dropped out of society or a course of study. **2** Rugby the restarting of play with a drop kick.

dropper noun a short glass tube with a rubber bulb at one end, for measuring out drops of liquid.

droppings plural noun the excrement of animals.

drop scone noun a small, thick pancake made by dropping batter on to a heated surface.

drop shot noun (in tennis or squash) a softly hit shot which drops abruptly to the ground.

dropsy /drop-si/ noun old-fashioned or less technical term for OEDEMA.
– DERIVATIVES **dropsical** adjective.
– ORIGIN shortening of former *hydropsy*, from Greek *hudōr* 'water'.

drop waist noun a style of waistline with the seam positioned at the hips rather than the waist.

drop zone noun an area into which troops or supplies are dropped by parachute.

droshky /drosh-ki/ noun (pl. **droshkies**) historical a type of Russian four-wheeled open carriage.
– ORIGIN Russian *drozhki* 'little wagon'.

drosophila /druh-sof-i-luh/ noun a fruit fly of a kind widely used in genetic research.
– ORIGIN from Greek *drosos* 'dew, moisture' + *philos* 'loving'.

dross noun **1** rubbish. **2** scum on the surface of molten metal.
– ORIGIN Old English.

drought /drowt/ noun a very long period of abnormally low rainfall, leading to a shortage of water.
– ORIGIN Old English, 'dryness'.

drove[1] past of DRIVE.

drove[2] noun **1** a flock of animals being driven. **2** a large number of people doing the same thing: *tourists arrived in droves.*
– ORIGIN Old English.

drover noun historical a person who drove sheep or cattle to market.

drown verb **1** die as a result of submersion in water, or kill someone in this way. **2** flood an area. **3** (usu. **drown someone/thing out**) make someone or something impossible to hear by making a very loud noise.
– PHRASES **drown one's sorrows** forget one's problems by getting drunk.
– ORIGIN related to an Old Norse word meaning 'be drowned'.

drowse /drowz/ verb be half asleep; doze.

drowsy adjective (**drowsier, drowsiest**) sleepy.
– DERIVATIVES **drowsily** adverb **drowsiness** noun.
– ORIGIN probably from an Old English word meaning 'be languid or slow'.

drubbing noun **1** a beating. **2** informal a resounding defeat in a match or contest.

– DERIVATIVES **drub** verb.
– ORIGIN probably from Arabic.

drudge noun a person made to do hard, menial, or dull work.
– ORIGIN unknown.

drudgery noun hard, menial, or dull work.

drug noun **1** a substance used in the treatment or prevention of disease or infection. **2** an illegal substance taken for its narcotic or stimulant effects. •verb (**drugs, drugging, drugged**) give someone a drug, especially in order to make them unconscious.
– ORIGIN Old French *drogue*.

drugget /drug-git/ noun a floor covering made of a coarse woven fabric.
– ORIGIN French *droguet*.

druggist noun N. Amer. a pharmacist or a seller of medicinal drugs.

drugstore noun N. Amer. a pharmacy which also sells toiletries and other articles.

Druid /droo-id/ noun a priest in the ancient Celtic religion.
– DERIVATIVES **Druidic** adjective **Druidical** adjective **Druidism** noun.
– ORIGIN Gaulish (the language of the ancient Gauls).

drum noun **1** a percussion instrument with a skin stretched across a rounded frame, sounded by being struck with sticks or the hands. **2** a sound made by or resembling that of a drum. **3** a cylindrical container or part. •verb (**drums, drumming, drummed**) **1** play on a drum. **2** make a continuous rhythmic noise. **3** (**drum something into**) teach someone something by repeating it many times. **4** (**drum something up**) try to get business or support from people. **5** (**drum someone out**) expel someone from somewhere in disgrace.
– ORIGIN Dutch or German *tromme*.

drum and bass noun a type of dance music consisting largely of electronic drums and bass.

drumbeat noun a stroke or pattern of strokes on a drum.

drumhead noun the membrane or skin of a drum.

drum kit noun a set of drums, cymbals, and other percussion instruments.

drumlin /drum-lin/ noun Geology a mound or small hill consisting of compacted boulder clay.
– ORIGIN probably from Scottish Gaelic and Irish *druim* 'ridge'.

drum major noun **1** a non-commissioned officer commanding regimental drummers. **2** the male leader of a marching band, who twirls a baton.

drum majorette noun the female leader of a marching band, who twirls a baton.

drummer noun a person who plays a drum or drums.

drum roll noun a rapid succession of drumbeats.

drumstick noun **1** a stick used for beating a drum. **2** the lower joint of the leg of a cooked chicken or similar bird.

drunk past part. of DRINK. adjective affected by alcohol to such an extent that one is not in control of oneself. •noun a person who is drunk or who often drinks too much.

drunkard noun a person who is often drunk.
– ORIGIN German.

drunken adjective **1** drunk. **2** caused by or showing the effects of drink: *a drunken stupor*.
– DERIVATIVES **drunkenly** adverb **drunkenness** noun.
– ORIGIN Old English.

drupe /droop/ noun Botany a fleshy fruit with thin skin and a central stone, e.g. a plum.
– ORIGIN Latin *drupa* 'overripe olive'.

dry adjective (**drier, driest**) **1** free from moisture or liquid. **2** not producing or yielding water, oil, or milk. **3** without grease or other lubrication. **4** serious and boring. **5** (of humour) subtle and expressed in a matter-of-fact way. **6** (of wine) not sweet. **7** not allowing the sale or drinking of alcohol. •verb (**dries, drying, dried**) **1** make or become dry. **2** preserve something by evaporating the moisture from it. **3** (**dry up**) (of a supply or flow) decrease and stop. **4** (**dry up**) informal stop talking. **5** (**dry out**) informal overcome one's addiction to alcohol.
– DERIVATIVES **dryness** noun.
– ORIGIN Old English.

dryad /dry-uhd, dry-ad/ noun (in folklore and classical mythology) a nymph living in a tree or wood.
– ORIGIN from Greek *drus* 'tree'.

dry cell (also **dry battery**) noun an electric cell (or battery) in which the electrolyte is absorbed in a solid to form a paste.

dry-clean verb clean a garment with a chemical solvent rather than water.

dry dock noun a dock which can be drained of water to allow a ship's hull to be repaired.

dryer (also **drier**) noun a machine or device for drying something, especially the hair or laundry.

dry fly noun an artificial fishing fly which floats lightly on the water.

dry ice noun **1** solid carbon dioxide. **2** white mist produced with this as a theatrical effect.

dryly adverb variant spelling of DRILY.

dry rot noun a fungus causing wood to decay in conditions where there is poor ventilation.

dry run noun a rehearsal of a performance or procedure.

dry slope (also **dry ski slope**) noun an artificial ski slope.

drystone adjective Brit. (of a stone wall) built without using mortar.

drysuit noun a waterproof rubber suit for water sports, under which warm clothes can be worn.

Ds symbol the chemical element darmstadtium.

DSC abbreviation (in the UK) Distinguished Service Cross.

DSc abbreviation Doctor of Science.

DSM abbreviation (in the UK) Distinguished Service Medal.

DSO abbreviation (in the UK) Distinguished Service Order.

DSP abbreviation digital signal processor or processing.

DTI abbreviation (in the UK) Department of Trade and Industry.

DTP abbreviation desktop publishing.

DTp abbreviation (in the UK) Department of Transport.

DTs plural noun informal delirium tremens.

dual adjective consisting of two parts, elements, or aspects.
- DERIVATIVES **duality** noun **dually** adverb.
- ORIGIN Latin *dualis*, from *duo* 'two'.

dual carriageway noun Brit. a road consisting of two or more lanes in each direction, with a dividing strip separating the two directions.

dualism noun 1 division into two opposed or contrasted aspects, such as good and evil or mind and matter. 2 the quality or state of having two parts, elements, or aspects.
- DERIVATIVES **dualist** noun & adjective **dualistic** adjective.

dub[1] verb (**dubs, dubbing, dubbed**) 1 give someone an unofficial name or nickname. 2 knight someone by touching their shoulder with a sword in a special ceremony.
- ORIGIN Old French *adober* 'equip with armour'.

dub[2] verb (**dubs, dubbing, dubbed**) 1 provide a film with a soundtrack in a different language from the original. 2 add sound effects or music to a film or a recording. 3 make a copy of a recording. • noun 1 an act of dubbing sound effects or music. 2 a style of popular music originating from the remixing of recorded music (especially reggae).
- ORIGIN abbreviation of **DOUBLE**.

dubbin /dub-bin/ noun Brit. prepared grease used for softening and waterproofing leather.
- ORIGIN from *dub* 'smear leather with grease'.

dubiety /dyoo-by-i-ti/ noun formal uncertainty.

dubious /dyoo-bi-uhss/ adjective 1 hesitating or doubtful. 2 probably not honest; morally suspect: *dubious sales methods.* 3 of questionable value: *he has the dubious distinction of being Britain's top gossip columnist.*
- DERIVATIVES **dubiously** adverb **dubiousness** noun.
- ORIGIN from Latin *dubium* 'a doubt'.

Dubliner noun a person from Dublin.

dubnium /dub-ni-uhm/ noun a very unstable chemical element made by high-energy atomic collisions.
- ORIGIN from *Dubna* in Russia.

Dubonnet /dyoo-bon-nay/ noun trademark a sweet red vermouth made in France.
- ORIGIN from the name of a family of French wine merchants.

ducal /dyoo-k'l/ adjective relating to a duke or dukedom.

ducat /duk-uht/ noun a former European gold coin.
- ORIGIN Italian *ducato.*

duchess noun 1 the wife or widow of a duke. 2 a woman holding a rank equivalent to duke.
- ORIGIN Old French.

duchesse potatoes plural noun mashed potatoes mixed with egg yolk, piped into small shapes and baked.

duchesse satin /doo-shess, duch-iss/ noun a soft, heavy, glossy kind of satin.

duchy /duch-i/ noun (pl. **duchies**) the territory of a duke or duchess.
- ORIGIN Old French *duche.*

duck[1] noun (pl. same or **ducks**) 1 a waterbird with a broad blunt bill, short legs, and webbed feet. 2 a female duck. Contrasted with **DRAKE**. 3 (also **ducks**) Brit. informal a friendly form of address.
- PHRASES **like water off a duck's back** (of a critical remark) having no effect.
- ORIGIN Old English.

duck[2] verb 1 lower the head or body quickly to avoid being hit or seen. 2 push someone under water. 3 informal avoid an unwelcome duty. • noun a quick lowering of the head.
- PHRASES **duck and dive** Brit. informal use one's ingenuity to deal with or avoid something.
- DERIVATIVES **ducker** noun.
- ORIGIN Germanic.

duck[3] noun Cricket a batsman's score of nought.
- ORIGIN short for *duck's egg*, used for the figure o.

duck-billed platypus noun see **PLATYPUS**.

duckboards plural noun wooden slats joined together to form a path over muddy ground.

ducking stool noun historical a chair fastened to the end of a pole, used to plunge offenders into a pond or river as a punishment.

duckling noun a young duck.

ducks and drakes noun a game of throwing flat stones so that they skim along the surface of water.

duckweed noun a tiny flowering plant that floats in large quantities on still water.

ducky noun Brit. informal a friendly form of address.

duct noun 1 a tube or passageway in a building or machine for air, cables, etc. 2 a tube in the body through which tears or other fluids pass. • verb convey something through a duct.
- DERIVATIVES **ducting** noun.
- ORIGIN Latin *ductus* 'leading, aqueduct'.

ductile /duk-tyl/ adjective (of a metal) able to be drawn out into a thin wire.
- DERIVATIVES **ductility** noun.

duct tape noun N. Amer. strong cloth-backed waterproof adhesive tape.

dud informal noun 1 a thing that fails to work properly. 2 (**duds**) clothes. • adjective failing to work or meet a standard.
- ORIGIN unknown.

dude /dood/ noun N. Amer. informal 1 a man. 2 a stylish man.
- ORIGIN probably from German dialect *Dude* 'fool'.

dude ranch noun (in the western US) a cattle ranch converted to a holiday centre for tourists.

dudgeon /duj-uhn/ noun (in phrase **in high dudgeon**) feeling resentful or angry.
- ORIGIN unknown.

due adjective 1 expected at or planned for a certain time: *the baby's due in June.* 2 owed or deserving something: *he was due for a rise.* 3 needing to be paid; owing. 4 required as a legal or moral duty. 5 proper: *driving without due care and attention.* • noun 1 (one's **due/ dues**) a person's right. 2 (**dues**) fees. • adverb (of a point of the compass) directly.
- PHRASES **due to 1** caused by. 2 because of. **give someone their due** be fair to someone. **in due course** at the appropriate time.

– ORIGIN Old French *deu* 'owed'.

USAGE: Some people think that you should not use **due to** to mean 'because of' for the reason that **due** is an adjective and should not be used as a preposition. However, this use is now common and acceptable in standard English.

duel noun **1** historical a prearranged contest with deadly weapons between two people to settle a point of honour. **2** a contest between two parties. •verb (**duels, duelling, duelled**; US **duels, dueling, dueled**) fight a duel.
– DERIVATIVES **duellist** (US **duelist**) noun.
– ORIGIN Latin *duellum*, literary form of *bellum* 'war'.

duenna /doo-en-nuh/ noun an older woman acting as a governess and chaperone to girls in a Spanish family.
– ORIGIN Spanish.

duet noun **1** a performance by two singers, instrumentalists, or dancers. **2** a musical composition for two performers. •verb (**duets, duetting, duetted**) perform a duet.
– ORIGIN Italian *duetto*.

duff[1] adjective Brit. informal worthless or false.
– ORIGIN unknown.

duff[2] verb (**duff someone up**) Brit. informal beat someone up.
– ORIGIN uncertain.

duff[3] noun (in phrase **up the duff**) Brit. informal pregnant.
– ORIGIN uncertain.

duffel (also **duffle**) noun a coarse woollen cloth with a thick nap.
– ORIGIN from *Duffel*, a town in Belgium.

duffel bag noun a cylindrical canvas bag closed by a drawstring.

duffel coat noun a hooded coat made of duffel, typically fastened with toggles.

duffer noun informal an incompetent or stupid person.
– ORIGIN Scots *dowfart*.

dug[1] past and past participle of DIG.

dug[2] noun the udder, teat, or nipple of a female animal.
– ORIGIN perhaps Old Norse.

dugong /dyoo-gong/ noun (pl. same or **dugongs**) a sea cow (mammal) found in the Indian Ocean.
– ORIGIN Malay.

dugout noun **1** a trench that is roofed over as a shelter for troops. **2** a low shelter at the side of a sports field for a team's coaches and substitutes. **3** (also **dugout canoe**) a canoe made from a hollowed tree trunk.

duiker /dy-ker/ noun (pl. same or **duikers**) a small African antelope.
– ORIGIN Dutch, 'diver'.

du jour /dyoo zhoor/ adjective informal enjoying great but probably short-lived popularity: *black comedy is the genre du jour.*
– ORIGIN French, 'of the day'.

duke noun **1** a man holding the highest hereditary title in Britain and some other countries. **2** chiefly historical (in parts of Europe) a male ruler of a small independent state.
– DERIVATIVES **dukedom** noun.
– ORIGIN Latin *dux* 'leader'.

dulcet /dul-sit/ adjective often ironic (of a sound) sweet and soothing.
– ORIGIN Latin *dulcis* 'sweet'.

dulcimer /dul-si-mer/ noun a musical instrument with strings that are struck with hand-held hammers.
– ORIGIN Old French *doulcemer*.

dull adjective **1** not interesting or exciting: *a very dull book.* **2** lacking brightness; not shiny. **3** (of the weather) overcast. **4** slow to understand; rather stupid. **5** not clearly felt or heard: *a dull pain in his jaw.* •verb make or become dull.
– DERIVATIVES **dullness** noun **dully** adverb.
– ORIGIN Old English.

dullard /dul-lerd/ noun a slow or stupid person.

dulse noun a dark red edible seaweed with flattened fronds.
– ORIGIN from Irish and Scottish Gaelic *duileasg*.

duly adverb in accordance with what is required, appropriate, or expected.

dumb adjective **1** offensive unable to speak; lacking the power of speech. **2** temporarily unable or unwilling to speak. **3** informal, chiefly N. Amer. stupid. **4** (of a computer terminal) having no independent processing capability. •verb (**dumb something down**) informal make something less intellectually challenging so as to appeal to a wider audience.
– DERIVATIVES **dumbly** adverb **dumbness** noun.
– ORIGIN Old English.

USAGE: Avoid **dumb** in the sense meaning 'not able to speak', as it is likely to cause offence; use alternatives such as **speech-impaired**.

dumb-bell noun a short bar with a weight at each end, used for exercise or muscle-building.

dumbfound (also **dumfound**) verb greatly astonish someone.
– ORIGIN blend of DUMB and CONFOUND.

dumbo noun (pl. **dumbos**) informal a stupid person.

dumbshow noun gestures used to convey something without speech.
– ORIGIN first referring to a part of a play acted in mime.

dumbstruck adjective so shocked or surprised as to be unable to speak.

dumb waiter noun **1** a small lift for carrying food and crockery between floors. **2** Brit. a revolving circular section on a dining table.

dumdum (also **dumdum bullet**) noun a kind of soft-nosed bullet that expands on impact.
– ORIGIN from *Dum Dum*, a town and arsenal near Calcutta, India.

dum-dum noun informal a stupid person.

dummy noun (pl. **dummies**) **1** a model of a human being. **2** an object designed to resemble and act as a substitute for the real one. **3** Brit. a rubber or plastic teat for a baby to suck on. **4** (in sport) a pretended pass or kick. **5** informal, chiefly N. Amer. a stupid person. •verb (**dummies, dummying, dummied**) (in sport) pretend to pass or kick the ball.
– ORIGIN first meaning 'a person who cannot speak': from DUMB.

dummy run noun Brit. a practice or trial.

dump noun **1** a site where rubbish or waste is

left. **2** a heap of rubbish left at a dump.
3 informal an unpleasant or dreary place. **4** Military a temporary store of weaponry or provisions.
5 an act of dumping stored computer data.
• verb **1** get rid of rubbish or something unwanted. **2** put something down heavily or carelessly. **3** informal abandon someone. **4** copy stored computer data to a different location.
5 send goods to a foreign market for sale at a low price.
– ORIGIN perhaps from Old Norse.

dumper noun **1** a person or thing that dumps something. **2** (also **dumper truck**) Brit. a lorry with a body that tilts or opens at the back for unloading.

dumpling noun **1** a small savoury ball of dough boiled in water or in a stew. **2** a pudding consisting of fruit enclosed in a sweet dough and baked.
– ORIGIN probably from the former adjective *dump* 'of the consistency of dough'.

dumps plural noun (in phrase **(down) in the dumps**) informal depressed or unhappy.
– ORIGIN probably from Dutch *domp* 'haze, mist'.

dumpy adjective (**dumpier, dumpiest**) short and stout.

dun¹ noun a dull greyish-brown colour.
– ORIGIN Old English.

dun² verb (**duns, dunning, dunned**) persistently demand that someone repays a debt.
– ORIGIN perhaps from former *Dunkirk privateer* (with connotations of a pirate making aggressive demands).

dunce noun a person who is slow at learning.
– ORIGIN first referring to a follower of the Scottish theologian John *Duns* Scotus, whose followers were ridiculed as enemies of learning.

dunce's cap noun a paper cone formerly put on the head of a dunce at school as a mark of disgrace.

dunderhead noun informal a stupid person.
– DERIVATIVES **dunderheaded** adjective.
– ORIGIN perhaps from former Scots *dunder, dunner* 'resounding noise'.

dune noun a mound or ridge of sand formed by the wind, especially on the coast or in a desert.
– ORIGIN Dutch.

dung noun manure.
– ORIGIN Old English.

dungarees /dung-guh-**reez**/ plural noun chiefly Brit. a garment consisting of trousers with a bib held up by straps over the shoulders.
– ORIGIN Hindi, 'coarse calico'.

dung beetle noun a beetle whose larvae feed on dung, especially a scarab.

dungeon noun a strong underground prison cell, especially in a castle.
– ORIGIN Old French.

dunghill noun a heap of dung or refuse.

dunk verb **1** dip food into a drink or soup before eating it. **2** immerse someone or something in water.
– ORIGIN German *tunken* 'dip or plunge'.

dunlin noun (pl. same or **dunlins**) a sandpiper with a downcurved bill and (in winter) greyish-brown upper parts.
– ORIGIN probably from **DUN¹**.

dunnock /**dun**-nuhk/ noun a small songbird with a reddish-brown back.
– ORIGIN probably from **DUN¹**.

dunny noun (pl. **dunnies**) Austral./NZ informal a toilet.
– ORIGIN probably from **DUNG** + former slang *ken* 'house'.

duo noun (pl. **duos**) **1** a pair of people or things, especially in music or entertainment. **2** Music a duet.
– ORIGIN Latin, 'two'.

duodecimal /dyoo-oh-**dess**-i-m'l/ adjective relating to a system of counting that has twelve as a base.
– ORIGIN Latin *duodecimus* 'twelfth'.

duodenum /dyoo-uh-**dee**-nuhm/ noun (pl. **duodenums**) the first part of the small intestine immediately beyond the stomach.
– DERIVATIVES **duodenal** adjective.
– ORIGIN Latin.

duologue /**dyoo**-uh-log/ noun a play or part of a play with speaking roles for only two actors.

duopoly /dyoo-**op**-uh-li/ noun (pl. **duopolies**) a situation in which two suppliers dominate a market.

dupe verb deceive or trick someone. • noun a person who has been deceived or tricked.
– ORIGIN French dialect *dupe* 'hoopoe', from the bird's supposedly stupid appearance.

dupion /**dyoo**-pi-uhn/ noun a rough silk fabric woven from the threads of double cocoons.
– ORIGIN French *doupion*.

duple /**dyoo**-p'l/ adjective (of musical rhythm) based on two main beats to the bar.
– ORIGIN Latin *duplus*.

duplex /**dyoo**-pleks/ noun N. Amer. **1** a residential building divided into two apartments. **2** a flat on two floors. **3** N. Amer. & Austral. a semi-detached house. • adjective having two parts.
– ORIGIN Latin.

duplicate adjective /**dyoo**-pli-kuht/ **1** exactly like something else. **2** having two corresponding parts. • noun /**dyoo**-pli-kuht/ one of two or more identical things. • verb /**dyoo**-pli-kayt/ **1** make or be an exact copy of something. **2** multiply something by two. **3** do something again unnecessarily.
– DERIVATIVES **duplication** noun.
– ORIGIN Latin *duplicare*.

duplicator noun a machine for copying something.

duplicity /dyoo-**pli**-si-ti/ noun dishonest behaviour that is intended to deceive someone.
– DERIVATIVES **duplicitous** adjective.

durable adjective **1** hard-wearing. **2** (of goods) not for immediate consumption and so able to be kept.
– DERIVATIVES **durability** noun **durably** adverb.
– ORIGIN Latin *durabilis*.

dura mater /dyoo-ruh **may**-ter/ noun the tough outermost membrane enveloping the brain and spinal cord.
– ORIGIN Latin, 'hard mother'.

durance noun old use imprisonment.
– ORIGIN Old French.

duration noun the time during which something continues: *a flight of over eight hours' duration*.

– PHRASES **for the duration** informal for a very long time.
– ORIGIN Latin.

durbar /der-bah/ noun historical **1** the court of an Indian ruler. **2** a public reception held by an Indian prince or a British governor or viceroy in India.
– ORIGIN Persian, 'court'.

duress /dyuu-ress/ noun threats or violence used to force a person into doing something: *confessions extracted under duress.*
– ORIGIN from Latin *durus* 'hard'.

durian /doo-ri-uhn/ noun a tropical fruit with a fetid smell but pleasant taste.
– ORIGIN Malay.

during preposition **1** throughout the course of a period of time. **2** at a particular point in the course of: *he met the Prime Minister during his first visit to the country.*
– ORIGIN from Latin *durare* 'to last'.

durum wheat /dyoo-ruhm/ noun a kind of hard wheat, yielding flour from which pasta is made.
– ORIGIN from Latin *durus* 'hard'.

dusk noun the darker stage of twilight.
– ORIGIN Old English, 'dark, swarthy'.

dusky adjective (**duskier, duskiest**) **1** dark or soft in colour. **2** literary poorly lit; dim.
– DERIVATIVES **duskily** adverb **duskiness** noun.

dust noun **1** fine, dry powder consisting of tiny particles of earth or waste matter. **2** any material in the form of tiny particles: *coal dust.* • verb **1** remove dust from the surface of something. **2** cover something lightly with a powdered substance. **3** (**dust something down/off**) bring something out for use again after a long period of neglect.
– PHRASES **when the dust settles** when things quieten down.
– ORIGIN Old English.

dustbin noun Brit. a large container for household rubbish.

dust bowl noun a dry area where vegetation has been lost and soil reduced to dust and eroded.

dustcart noun Brit. a vehicle used for collecting household rubbish.

dust cover noun a dust jacket or dust sheet.

duster noun a cloth for dusting furniture.

dust jacket noun a removable paper cover on a book.

dustman noun (pl. **dustmen**) Brit. a man employed to collect household rubbish.

dustpan noun a flat hand-held container into which dust and waste can be swept.

dust sheet noun Brit. a large sheet for covering furniture to protect it from dust or while decorating.

dust storm noun a strong wind carrying clouds of fine dust and sand.

dust-up noun informal a fight or quarrel.

dusty adjective (**dustier, dustiest**) **1** covered with or resembling dust. **2** solemn and uninteresting: *the society has banished its dusty, fusty, middle-aged-male image.*
– PHRASES **dusty answer** Brit. a curt and unhelpful reply.
– DERIVATIVES **dustily** adverb **dustiness** noun.

Dutch adjective relating to the Netherlands or its language. • noun the language of the Netherlands.
– PHRASES **go Dutch** share the cost of a meal equally.
– ORIGIN Dutch *dutsch* 'Dutch, German'.

Dutch auction noun a method of selling in which the price is reduced until a buyer is found.

Dutch barn noun Brit. a farm building with a curved roof set on an open frame, used to cover hay.

Dutch cap noun **1** see CAP (sense 7). **2** a woman's lace cap with triangular flaps on each side, worn as part of Dutch traditional dress.

Dutch courage noun confidence gained from drinking alcohol.

Dutch elm disease noun a disease of elm trees, caused by a fungus.

Dutch hoe noun a hoe used with a pushing action just under the surface of the soil.

Dutchman (or **Dutchwoman**) noun (pl. **Dutchmen** or **Dutchwomen**) a person from the Netherlands, or a person of Dutch descent.

Dutch oven noun a covered earthenware or cast-iron container for cooking casseroles.

Dutch uncle noun informal, chiefly N. Amer. a person giving firm but benevolent advice.

dutiable /dyoo-ti-uh-b'l/ adjective (of goods) on which customs or other duties have to be paid.

dutiful adjective **1** doing one's duty in an obedient way. **2** done because of a feeling of obligation rather than enthusiasm: *dutiful applause greeted his speech.*
– DERIVATIVES **dutifully** adverb.

duty noun (pl. **duties**) **1** something one has to do because it is morally right or legally necessary: *it's my duty to uphold the law.* **2** a task required as part of one's job. **3** a payment charged on the import, export, manufacture, or sale of goods. **4** Brit. a payment charged on the transfer of property, for licences, and for the legal recognition of documents.
– PHRASES **on** (or **off**) **duty** doing (or not doing) one's regular work.
– ORIGIN Old French *duete.*

duty-bound adjective morally or legally obliged to do something.

duty-free adjective & adverb (of goods) exempt from payment of duty.

duvet /doo-vay/ noun chiefly Brit. a soft, thick quilt used instead of an upper sheet and blankets.
– ORIGIN French, 'down'.

DVD abbreviation digital versatile disc.

DVD-R abbreviation DVD recordable, a DVD which can be recorded on once only.

DVD-ROM abbreviation DVD read-only memory, a DVD used in a computer for displaying data.

DVD-RW (also **DVD-RAM**) abbreviation DVD rewritable (or random-access memory), a DVD on which recordings can be made and erased a number of times.

DVLA abbreviation Driver and Vehicle Licensing Agency.

dwarf noun (pl. **dwarfs** or **dwarves**) **1** a member of a mythical race of short, stocky human-like creatures. **2** a person who is unusually small. **3** (also **dwarf star**) a star of relatively small

size and low luminosity. •**adjective** (of an animal or plant) much smaller than is usual for its type or species. •**verb** cause to seem small in comparison: *the church is dwarfed by cranes.*
– DERIVATIVES **dwarfish** adjective.
– ORIGIN Old English.

> USAGE: Although the use of **dwarf** to mean 'an unusually small person' is normally considered offensive, there is no term that has been established as an alternative.

dwarfism noun unusually low stature or small size.

dweeb noun N. Amer. informal a boring, studious, or socially inept person.
– ORIGIN perhaps from **DWARF** and *feeb* 'a feeble-minded person'.

dwell verb (past and past part. **dwelt** or **dwelled**) **1** formal live in or at a place. **2** (**dwell on**) think, speak, or write at length about something.
– DERIVATIVES **dweller** noun.
– ORIGIN Old English.

dwelling (also **dwelling place**) noun formal a house or other place where someone lives.

dwindle verb gradually become smaller or weaker: *a weekly audience that's dwindled to less than nine million.*
– ORIGIN Old English, 'fade away'.

DWP abbreviation (in the UK) Department for Work and Pensions.

Dy symbol the chemical element dysprosium.

dyad /dy-ad/ noun technical something consisting of two elements or parts.
– DERIVATIVES **dyadic** adjective.
– ORIGIN from Latin *dyas*.

Dyak /dy-ak/ noun & adjective variant spelling of **DAYAK**.

dye noun a natural or synthetic substance used to colour something. •**verb** (**dyes, dyeing, dyed**) colour something with dye.
– PHRASES **dyed in the wool** having firm beliefs that will never change.
– DERIVATIVES **dyer** noun.
– ORIGIN Old English.

dyestuff noun a substance that is used as a dye or that yields a dye.

dying present participle of **DIE¹**.

dyke¹ (also **dike**) noun **1** an embankment built to prevent flooding from the sea. **2** an earthwork serving as a boundary or defence: *Offa's Dyke.* **3** a ditch or watercourse. **4** Geology an intrusion of igneous rock cutting across existing strata. Compare with **SILL**.
– ORIGIN Old Norse.

dyke² (also **dike**) noun informal a lesbian.
– DERIVATIVES **dykey** adjective.
– ORIGIN unknown.

dynamic adjective **1** (of a process or system) constantly changing or progressing: *the dynamic market in Latin America.* **2** full of energy and new ideas. **3** Physics relating to forces producing motion. Often contrasted with **STATIC**. •**noun** a force that stimulates change or progress: *evaluation is part of the basic dynamic of the project.*
– DERIVATIVES **dynamical** adjective **dynamically** adverb.
– ORIGIN Greek *dunamikos*.

dynamic range noun the range of sound intensity that occurs in a piece of music or that can be handled by a piece of equipment.

dynamics plural noun **1** (treated as sing.) the branch of mechanics concerned with the motion of bodies under the action of forces. **2** the forces which stimulate change or progress within a system or process. **3** the varying levels of volume of sound in a musical performance.

dynamism noun the quality of being full of energy, vigour, or enthusiasm: *the prosperity and dynamism of Barcelona.*

dynamite noun **1** a high explosive made of nitroglycerine. **2** informal a very impressive or potentially dangerous person or thing: *that roads policy is political dynamite.* •**verb** blow something up with dynamite.
– ORIGIN from Greek *dunamis* 'power'.

dynamo noun (pl. **dynamos**) chiefly Brit. a machine for converting mechanical energy into electrical energy.
– ORIGIN short for *dynamo-electric machine*.

dynamometer /dy-nuh-**mom**-iter/ noun an instrument which measures the power output of an engine.

dynast /**dy**-nuhst, **dy**-nast/ noun a member of a dynasty, especially a hereditary ruler.

dynasty /**di**-nuh-sti/ noun (pl. **dynasties**) **1** a series of rulers of a country who belong to the same family. **2** a succession of prominent people from the same family.
– DERIVATIVES **dynastic** adjective **dynastically** adverb.
– ORIGIN Greek *dunasteia* 'lordship'.

dyne /dyn/ noun Physics force required to give a mass of one gram an acceleration of one centimetre per second per second.
– ORIGIN Greek *dunamis* 'force, power'.

dys- combining form bad; difficult (used especially in medical terms): *dyspepsia.*
– ORIGIN from Greek *dus-*.

dysentery /**diss**-uhn-tri/ noun a disease in which the intestines are infected, resulting in severe diarrhoea.
– ORIGIN Greek *dusenteria.*

dysfunctional adjective **1** not operating normally or properly. **2** unable to deal adequately with normal relationships between people.
– DERIVATIVES **dysfunction** noun **dysfunctionally** adverb.

dyslexia /diss-**lek**-si-uh/ noun a disorder involving difficulty in learning to read or interpret words, letters, and other symbols.
– DERIVATIVES **dyslexic** adjective & noun.
– ORIGIN from **DYS-** and Greek *lexis* 'speech'.

dysmenorrhoea /diss-men-uh-**ree**-uh/ (US **dysmenorrhea**) noun Medicine painful menstruation.

dysmorphia /dis-**mor**-fi-uh/ noun Medicine deformity or abnormality in the shape or size of a part of the body.
– DERIVATIVES **dysmorphic** adjective.
– ORIGIN Greek *dusmorphia* 'misshapenness'.

dyspepsia /diss-**pep**-si-uh/ noun indigestion.
– ORIGIN Greek *duspepsia.*

dyspeptic adjective **1** relating to or having

dyspepsia (indigestion). **2** irritable; bad tempered.

dysphasia /diss-**fay**-zi-uh/ noun a disorder marked by difficulty in using language coherently, due to brain disease or damage.
– DERIVATIVES **dysphasic** adjective.
– ORIGIN from Greek *phatos* 'spoken'.

dysphoria /diss-**for**-iuh/ noun a state of unease or general dissatisfaction.
– DERIVATIVES **dysphoric** adjective.
– ORIGIN from Greek *dusphoros* 'hard to bear'.

dysplasia /diss-**play**-zi-uh/ noun the enlargement of an organ or tissue by the proliferation of abnormal cells.
– DERIVATIVES **dysplastic** adjective.
– ORIGIN from Greek *plasis* 'formation'.

dyspraxia /diss-**prak**-si-uh/ noun a disorder of the brain in childhood resulting in poor physical coordination.
– ORIGIN from Greek *dus-* 'bad or difficult' + *praxis* 'action'.

dysprosium /diss-**proh**-zi-uhm/ noun a soft silvery-white metallic chemical element of the lanthanide series.
– ORIGIN from Greek *dusprositos* 'hard to get at'.

dystopia /diss-**toh**-pi-uh/ noun an imaginary place or society in which everything is bad.
– DERIVATIVES **dystopian** adjective & noun.
– ORIGIN from DYS- + UTOPIA.

dystrophy /diss-**truh**-fi/ noun a disorder in which an organ or tissue of the body wastes away. See also MUSCULAR DYSTROPHY.
– DERIVATIVES **dystrophic** adjective.
– ORIGIN from DYS- + Greek *-trophia* 'nourishment'.

d

Ee

E¹ (also **e**) noun (pl. **Es** or **E's**) **1** the fifth letter of the alphabet. **2** referring to the fifth item in a set. **3** Music the third note of the scale of C major.

E² abbreviation **1** East or Eastern. **2** informal the drug Ecstasy or a tablet of Ecstasy. **3** Physics energy. **4** referring to products, especially food additives, which comply with EU regulations.

e symbol **1** (**€**) euro or euros. **2** (**e**) Mathematics the transcendental number that is the base of natural logarithms, approximately equal to 2.71828.

e-² prefix referring to the use of electronic data transfer, especially through the Internet.
– ORIGIN from **ELECTRONIC**, on the pattern of *email.*

each determiner & pronoun every one of two or more people or things, regarded separately.
• adverb to, for, or by every one of a group.
– ORIGIN Old English.

each other pronoun the other one or ones.

each-way adjective & adverb Brit. (of a bet) backing a horse or other competitor either to win or to finish in the first three.

eager adjective **1** strongly wanting to do or have: *I was eager to help.* **2** keenly expectant or interested.
– DERIVATIVES **eagerly** adverb **eagerness** noun.
– ORIGIN Old French *aigre* 'keen'.

eagle noun a large keen-sighted bird of prey with long broad wings and a large hooked bill.
– DERIVATIVES **eaglet** noun.
– ORIGIN Latin *aquila.*

eagle-eyed adjective sharp-sighted and very observant.

eagle owl noun a very large owl with ear tufts and a deep hoot.

ear¹ noun **1** the organ of hearing and balance in humans and other vertebrates, especially the external part of this. **2** an ability to recognize and appreciate music or language. **3** willingness to listen: *she offers a sympathetic ear to worried pet owners.*
– PHRASES **be all ears** informal be listening eagerly. **one's ears are burning** one is subconsciously aware of being talked about. **have someone's ear** have access to and influence with someone. **have** (or **keep**) **an ear to the ground** be well informed about events and trends. **be out on one's ear** informal be abruptly dismissed from a job. **up to one's ears in** informal very busy with.
– DERIVATIVES **eared** adjective.

– ORIGIN Old English.

ear² noun the seed-bearing head of a cereal plant.
– ORIGIN Old English.

earache noun pain inside the ear.

eardrum noun the membrane of the middle ear, which vibrates in response to sound waves.

earful noun informal a prolonged reprimand.

earhole noun the external opening of the ear.

earl noun a British nobleman ranking above a viscount and below a marquess.
– DERIVATIVES **earldom** noun.
– ORIGIN Old English.

Earl Grey noun a kind of China tea flavoured with bergamot.
– ORIGIN probably named after the 2nd *Earl Grey,* said to have been given the recipe by a Chinese mandarin.

ear lobe noun see **LOBE**.

early adjective (**earlier, earliest**) & adverb **1** before the usual or expected time. **2** belonging to or happening at the beginning of a particular period or sequence: *he's in his early fifties.*
– PHRASES **at the earliest** not before the time or date specified. **early bird** humorous a person who gets up or arrives early. **early** (or **earlier**) **on** at an early (or earlier) stage.
– DERIVATIVES **earliness** noun.
– ORIGIN Old English.

Early English adjective referring to a style of English Gothic architecture typical of the late 12th and 13th centuries, marked by pointed arches and narrow pointed windows.

early music noun medieval, Renaissance, and early baroque music, especially as revived and played on period instruments.

earmark verb set aside for a particular purpose: *the government has earmarked £15 million to fight hackers.* • noun **1** an identifying feature. **2** an identifying mark on the ear of a domesticated animal.

earmuffs plural noun a pair of soft fabric coverings, connected by a band, worn over the ears to protect them from cold or noise.

earn verb **1** obtain money in return for work or services. **2** receive deservedly for one's behaviour or achievements: *he earned a master's degree in English.* **3** (of capital invested) gain money as interest or profit.
– DERIVATIVES **earner** noun.
– ORIGIN Old English.

earned income noun money derived from

paid work as opposed to profit from investments.

earnest¹ adjective very serious and sincere.
– PHRASES **in earnest 1** with greater effort or intensity than before. **2** sincere and serious about one's intentions.
– DERIVATIVES **earnestly** adverb **earnestness** noun.
– ORIGIN Old English.

earnest² noun a sign or promise of what is to come.
– ORIGIN Old French *erres* 'a pledge'.

earnings plural noun money or income earned.

earphone noun an electrical device worn on the ear to listen to radio or recorded sound.

earpiece noun the part of a telephone, radio receiver, or other device that is applied to the ear during use.

ear-piercing adjective loud and shrill. •noun the piercing of the lobes or edges of the ears to allow earrings to be worn.

earplug noun a piece of wax, cotton wool, or rubber placed in the ear as protection against noise or water.

earring noun a piece of jewellery worn on the lobe or edge of the ear.

earshot noun the range or distance over which one can hear or be heard.

ear-splitting adjective very loud.

earth noun **1** (also **Earth**) the planet on which we live. **2** the substance of the land surface; soil. **3** Brit. electrical connection to the ground, regarded as having zero electrical potential. **4** the underground lair of a badger or fox. •verb Brit. connect an electrical device to earth.
– PHRASES **come back** (or **down**) **to earth** return to reality. **the earth** Brit. a very large amount: *her hat cost the earth.* **on earth** used for emphasis: *what on earth are you doing?*
– DERIVATIVES **earthward** adjective & adverb **earthwards** adverb.
– ORIGIN Old English.

earthbound adjective **1** confined to the earth or to material things. **2** moving towards the earth.

earthen adjective **1** made of compressed earth. **2** (of a pot) made of baked or fired clay.

earthenware noun pottery made of fired clay.

earthling noun (in science fiction) an inhabitant of the earth.

earthly adjective **1** relating to the earth or human life. **2** worldly rather than spiritual. **3** informal used for emphasis: *there was no earthly reason to rush.*
– DERIVATIVES **earthliness** noun.

earthquake noun a sudden violent shaking of the ground, caused by movements within the earth's crust.

earth sciences plural noun the branches of science concerned with the physical composition of the earth and its atmosphere.

earth-shattering adjective informal very important or shocking.

earthwork noun a large artificial bank of soil, especially one made as a defence in ancient times.

earthworm noun a burrowing worm that lives in the soil.

earthy adjective (**earthier, earthiest**) **1** resembling or suggestive of soil: *an earthy smell.* **2** direct and uninhibited about sex or bodily functions.
– DERIVATIVES **earthily** adverb **earthiness** noun.

ear trumpet noun a trumpet-shaped device formerly used as a hearing aid.

earwax noun the protective yellow waxy substance produced in the passage of the outer ear.

earwig noun a small insect with a pair of pincers at its rear end. •verb (**earwigs, earwigging, earwigged**) Brit. informal eavesdrop on a conversation.
– ORIGIN Old English.

ease noun **1** lack of difficulty or effort: *he beat his opponent with ease.* **2** freedom from worries or problems. •verb **1** make something less serious or severe. **2** (**ease off/up**) become less intense or unpleasant: *the gale eased off a bit.* **3** move carefully or gradually. **4** (of share prices, interest rates, etc.) decrease in value or amount.
– PHRASES **at ease** Military in a relaxed attitude with the feet apart and the hands behind the back.
– DERIVATIVES **easeful** adjective (literary).
– ORIGIN Old French *aise.*

easel /ee-z'l/ noun a wooden frame on legs for holding an artist's work in progress.
– ORIGIN Dutch *ezel* 'ass'.

easily adverb **1** without difficulty or effort. **2** without doubt; definitely. **3** very probably.

east noun (**the east**) **1** the direction in which the sun rises at the equinoxes, on the right-hand side of a person facing north. **2** the eastern part of a place. **3** (**the East**) the regions or countries lying to the east of Europe, especially China, Japan, and India. **4** (**the East**) historical the former communist states of eastern Europe. •adjective **1** lying towards, near, or facing the east. **2** (of a wind) blowing from the east. •adverb to or towards the east.
– DERIVATIVES **eastbound** adjective & adverb.
– ORIGIN Old English.

Easter (also **Easter Day** or **Easter Sunday**) noun the Christian festival celebrating the resurrection of Jesus.
– ORIGIN Old English.

Easter egg noun a chocolate egg or decorated hard-boiled egg given as a gift at Easter.

easterly adjective & adverb **1** facing or moving towards the east. **2** (of a wind) blowing from the east. •noun (pl. **easterlies**) a wind blowing from the east.

eastern adjective **1** situated in, directed towards, or facing the east. **2** (**Eastern**) relating to or characteristic of the regions to the east of Europe.
– DERIVATIVES **easternmost** adjective.

easterner noun a person from the east of a region or country.

easting noun **1** distance travelled or measured eastward, especially at sea. **2** a figure or line representing eastward distance on a map.

east-north-east noun the direction midway between east and north-east.

east-south-east noun the direction midway between east and south-east.

eastward adjective in an easterly direction. •adverb (also **eastwards**) towards the east.

e

– DERIVATIVES **eastwardly** adjective & adverb.

easy adjective (**easier, easiest**) **1** achieved without great effort; not difficult. **2** free from worry or problems: *an easy life in the New World.* **3** not anxious or awkward. **4** informal, derogatory (of a woman) very willing to have sex. • exclamation be careful!
– PHRASES **easy on the eye** (or **ear**) informal pleasant to look at (or listen to). **go** (or **be**) **easy on** informal **1** do not be too harsh with someone. **2** do not use too much of something. **take it easy** do something in a leisurely way; relax.
– DERIVATIVES **easiness** noun.

easy chair noun a large, comfortable armchair.

easy-going adjective relaxed and open-minded.

easy listening noun popular music that is tuneful and undemanding.

easy street noun informal a state of financial security.

eat verb (past **ate** /et, ayt/; past part. **eaten**) **1** put food into the mouth and chew and swallow it. **2** (**eat out** or **in**) have a meal in a restaurant (or at home). **3** (**eat something away**) gradually erode or destroy something. **4** (**eat into**) use up a part of: *my overdraft is eating into my savings.* **5** (**eat something up**) use resources in very large quantities. • noun (**eats**) informal light food or snacks.
– PHRASES **eat one's heart out** long for something that cannot be achieved. **eat one's words** admit that one was wrong. **what's eating you** (or **him** etc.)? informal what is worrying or annoying you (or him etc.)?
– DERIVATIVES **eater** noun.
– ORIGIN Old English.

eatable adjective fit to be eaten as food. • noun (**eatables**) items of food.

eatery noun (pl. **eateries**) informal a restaurant or cafe.

eating apple noun an apple suitable for eating raw.

eau de cologne /oh duh kuh-**lohn**/ noun (pl. **eaux de cologne** pronunc. same) a toilet water with a strong scent.
– ORIGIN French, 'water of Cologne'.

eau de Nil /oh duh **neel**/ noun a pale greenish colour.
– ORIGIN French, 'water of the Nile'.

eau de toilette /oh duh twah-**let**/ noun (pl. **eaux de toilette** pronunc. same) a dilute form of perfume; toilet water.
– ORIGIN French.

eau de vie /oh duh **vee**/ noun (pl. **eaux de vie** pronunc. same) brandy.
– ORIGIN French, 'water of life'.

eaves plural noun the part of a roof that meets or overhangs the walls of a building.
– ORIGIN Old English.

eavesdrop verb (**eavesdrops, eavesdropping, eavesdropped**) secretly listen to a conversation.
– DERIVATIVES **eavesdropper** noun.
– ORIGIN from former *eavesdrop* 'the ground on to which water drips from the eaves'.

ebb noun the movement of the tide out to sea. • verb **1** (of tidewater) move away from the land; recede. **2** gradually become less or

weaker: *my confidence ebbed away.*
– PHRASES **at a low ebb** in a weakened or depressed state.
– ORIGIN Old English.

Ebola fever /ee-**boh**-luh, uh-**boh**-luh/ noun an infectious, generally fatal, disease caused by a virus and marked by fever and severe internal bleeding.
– ORIGIN named after a river in the Democratic Republic of Congo.

ebonite noun another term for VULCANITE.

ebonized (or **ebonised**) adjective (of furniture) made to look like ebony.

ebony /**eb**-uh-ni/ noun **1** heavy blackish or very dark brown wood from a tree of tropical and warm regions. **2** a very dark brown or black colour.
– ORIGIN Greek *ebenos* 'ebony tree'.

e-book noun an electronic version of a printed book which can be read on a personal computer or special hand-held device.

ebullient /i-**bul**-yuhnt/ adjective cheerful and full of energy.
– DERIVATIVES **ebullience** noun **ebulliently** adverb.
– ORIGIN from Latin *ebullire* 'boil up'.

EC abbreviation **1** European Commission. **2** European Community.

eccentric /ik-**sen**-trik/ adjective **1** unconventional and slightly strange. **2** technical not placed centrally or not having its axis placed centrally. • noun a person who is unconventional and slightly strange.
– DERIVATIVES **eccentrically** adverb
– ORIGIN Greek *ekkentros.*

eccentricity /ek-sen-**triss**-i-ti/ noun (pl. **eccentricities**) **1** the quality of being unconventional and slightly strange. **2** an eccentric act or habit.

Eccles cake noun Brit. a round flat cake of sweetened pastry filled with currants.
– ORIGIN named after the town of *Eccles* near Manchester.

ecclesial /i-**klee**-zi-uhl/ adjective formal relating to a Christian Church or denomination.
– ORIGIN from Greek *ekklēsia* 'assembly, church'.

ecclesiastic /i-klee-zi-**ass**-tik/ formal noun a member of the Christian clergy. • adjective ecclesiastical.

ecclesiastical /i-klee-zi-**ass**-ti-k'l/ adjective relating to the Christian Church or its clergy.
– DERIVATIVES **ecclesiastically** adverb.
– ORIGIN Greek *ekklēsiastikos.*

ecclesiology /i-klee-zi-**ol**-uh-ji/ noun **1** the study of churches, especially church architecture. **2** theology as applied to the nature and structure of the Christian Church.
– DERIVATIVES **ecclesiological** adjective **ecclesiologist** noun.

ECG abbreviation electrocardiogram or electrocardiograph.

echelon /**esh**-uh-lon/ noun **1** a level or rank in an organization, profession, or society. **2** a formation of troops, ships, aircraft, or vehicles in parallel rows with the end of each row projecting further than the one in front.
– ORIGIN French *échelon.*

echidna /i-**kid**-nuh/ noun (pl. **echidnas**) a spiny egg-laying mammal native to Australia and

New Guinea.
- ORIGIN Greek *ekhidna* 'viper'.

echinacea /ek-i-**nay**-shuh/ noun a North American plant used in herbal medicine.
- ORIGIN Greek *ekhinos* 'hedgehog' (from the appearance of the flowers).

echinoderm /i-**ky**-nuh-derm/ noun a marine invertebrate (sea creature) of a large group which includes starfishes and sea urchins.
- ORIGIN from Greek *ekhinos* 'hedgehog, sea urchin' + *derma* 'skin'.

echo noun (pl. **echoes**) **1** a sound caused by the reflection of sound waves from a surface back to the listener. **2** a reflected radio or radar beam. **3** something suggestive of or similar to something else: *there are echoes of Thatcherism in the United States and Scandinavia.* •verb (**echoes, echoing, echoed**) **1** (of a sound) reverberate or be repeated after the original sound has stopped. **2** be suggestive of or similar to: *his choice of subject matter echoed his father's.* **3** repeat someone's words or opinions.
- DERIVATIVES **echoey** adjective
- ORIGIN Greek *ēkhō*.

echocardiography /ek-oh-kah-di-**og**-ruhfi/ noun the use of ultrasound waves to investigate the action of the heart.
- DERIVATIVES **echocardiogram** noun **echocardiograph** noun **echocardiographic** adjective.

echo chamber noun an enclosed space for producing echoes.

echoic /e-**koh**-ik/ adjective **1** relating to or like an echo. **2** representing a sound by imitation; onomatopoeic.

echolocation /ek-oh-loh-**kay**-sh'n/ noun the location of objects by reflected sound, in particular as used by animals such as dolphins and bats.

echo sounder noun a device for determining the depth of the seabed or detecting objects in water by measuring the time taken for echoes to return to the listener.

echt /ekht/ adjective authentic and typical.
- ORIGIN German.

eclair /i-**klair**/ noun a long cake of choux pastry filled with cream and topped with chocolate icing.
- ORIGIN French *éclair* 'lightning'.

eclampsia /i-**klamp**-si-uh/ noun Medicine a condition in which a pregnant woman with high blood pressure experiences convulsions.
- DERIVATIVES **eclamptic** adjective.
- ORIGIN Greek *eklampsis* 'sudden development'.

éclat /ay-**klah**/ noun brilliant or successful effect: *a few of the men landed with the same éclat as their leader.*
- ORIGIN French.

eclectic /i-**klek**-tik/ adjective using ideas from a wide variety of sources: *he thrived on an eclectic diet of rock, rap, and pop.* •noun a person whose ideas or tastes are derived from a wide variety of sources.
- DERIVATIVES **eclectically** adverb **eclecticism** noun.
- ORIGIN Greek *eklektikos*.

eclipse /i-**klips**/ noun **1** an occasion when one planet, the moon, etc. passes between another and the observer, or in front of a planet's source of light. **2** a sudden loss of significance or power. •verb **1** (of a planet, the moon, etc.) obscure the light coming from or shining on another. **2** make less significant or powerful: *he was one of the composers whose fame has been eclipsed by Mozart.*
- ORIGIN Greek *ekleipsis*.

ecliptic /i-**klip**-tik/ noun Astronomy a great circle on the celestial sphere representing the sun's apparent circular path among the stars during the year.

eco- /ee-koh/ combining form representing ECOLOGY.

eco-friendly adjective not harmful to the environment.

eco-labelling noun the use of labels to identify products that meet recognized environmental standards.
- DERIVATIVES **eco-label** noun.

E. coli /ee koh-ly/ noun the bacterium *Escherichia coli*, found in the intestines of humans and other animals, some strains of which can cause severe food poisoning.

ecology /i-**kol**-uh-ji/ noun the branch of biology concerned with the relations of organisms to one another and to their surroundings.
- DERIVATIVES **ecological** adjective **ecologically** adverb **ecologist** noun.
- ORIGIN from Greek *oikos* 'house'.

e-commerce (also **e-business**) noun commercial transactions conducted on the Internet.

econometrics /i-kon-uh-**met**-riks/ plural noun (treated as sing.) the branch of economics concerned with the use of statistical methods in describing economic systems.
- DERIVATIVES **econometric** adjective **econometrician** noun.

economic /ee-kuh-**nom**-ik, ek-uh-**nom**-ik/ adjective **1** relating to economics or the economy of a country or region. **2** profitable, or concerned with profitability: *organizations must become larger if they are to remain economic.* **3** sparing in the use of resources or money.

economical adjective **1** giving good value or return in relation to the resources used or money spent: *a small, economical car.* **2** careful not to waste resources or money.
- PHRASES **economical with the truth** euphemistic lying or deliberately withholding information.
- DERIVATIVES **economically** adverb.

economic migrant noun a person who travels from one country to another to improve their standard of living.

economics plural noun (often treated as sing.) the branch of knowledge concerned with the production, consumption, and transfer of wealth.

economist noun an expert in economics.

economize (or **economise**) verb spend less; reduce one's expenses.

economy noun (pl. **economies**) **1** the state of a country or region in terms of the production and consumption of goods and services and the supply of money. **2** the careful use of resources so as to avoid waste: *the outboard engine increases fuel economy.* **3** a financial

e

saving. **4** (also **economy class**) the cheapest class of air or rail travel. ●**adjective** offering good value for money: *an economy pack.*
– PHRASES **economy of scale** a proportionate saving in costs gained by an increased level of production.
– ORIGIN Greek *oikonomia* 'household management'.

ecosphere noun a region in which life exists or could exist; the biosphere.

ecosystem noun a biological community of interacting animals and plants and their environment.

ecotourism noun tourism directed towards unspoiled natural environments and intended to support conservation efforts.
– DERIVATIVES **ecotour** noun **ecotourist** noun.

eco-warrior noun informal a person involved in protest activities aimed at protecting the environment.

ecru /ek-roo/ **noun** a light cream or beige colour.
– ORIGIN French, 'unbleached'.

ecstasy /ek-stuh-si/ **noun** (pl. **ecstasies**) **1** an overwhelming feeling of happiness or joyful excitement. **2** (**Ecstasy**) an illegal amphetamine-based drug. **3** old use an emotional or religious frenzy or trance.
– ORIGIN from Greek *ekstasis* 'standing outside oneself'.

ecstatic /ik-stat-ik/ **adjective** very happy or excited. ●**noun** a person who is subject to mystical experiences.
– DERIVATIVES **ecstatically** adverb.

ECT abbreviation electroconvulsive therapy.

ectopic pregnancy /ek-top-ik/ **noun** a pregnancy in which the fetus develops outside the womb, typically in a Fallopian tube.
– ORIGIN Greek *ektopos* 'out of place'.

ectoplasm /ek-toh-pla-z'm/ **noun** a substance that supposedly comes out of the body of a medium during a trance.
– DERIVATIVES **ectoplasmic** adjective.
– ORIGIN from Greek *ektos* 'outside' + *plasma* 'formation'.

Ecuadorean /ek-wuh-dor-i-uhn/ (also **Ecuadorian**) **noun** a person from Ecuador. ●**adjective** relating to Ecuador.

ecumenical /ee-kyoo-men-i-k'l, ek-yoo-men-i-k'l/ **adjective** **1** representing a number of different Christian Churches. **2** promoting unity among the world's Christian Churches.
– DERIVATIVES **ecumenically** adverb.
– ORIGIN from Greek *oikoumenē* 'the inhabited earth'.

ecumenism /i-kyoo-muh-ni-z'm/ **noun** the aim of promoting unity among the world's Christian Churches.

eczema /eks-muh/ **noun** a condition in which patches of skin become rough and inflamed, causing itching and bleeding.
– ORIGIN Greek *ekzema.*

Edam /ee-dam/ **noun** a round yellow cheese with a red wax coating.
– ORIGIN from *Edam* in the Netherlands.

eddo /e-doh/ **noun** (pl. **eddoes**) a West Indian variety of taro (a plant with edible corms).
– ORIGIN West African.

eddy noun (pl. **eddies**) a circular movement of water causing a small whirlpool. ●**verb** (**eddies**,

eddying, **eddied**) (of water, air, smoke, etc.) move in a circular way.
– ORIGIN probably related to an Old English word meaning 'again, back'.

edelweiss /ay-duhl-vyss/ **noun** a mountain plant with small flowers and grey-green leaves.
– ORIGIN from German *edel* 'noble' + *weiss* 'white'.

edema noun US spelling of OEDEMA.

Eden /ee-duhn/ **noun** **1** (also **Garden of Eden**) the place where Adam and Eve lived in the biblical story of the Creation. **2** a place or state of great happiness or unspoilt beauty.
– DERIVATIVES **Edenic** /i-den-ik/ adjective.
– ORIGIN Hebrew.

edentate /ee-duhn-tayt/ **noun** a mammal of a group which has no incisor or canine teeth, including the anteaters and sloths.
– ORIGIN from Latin *edentare* 'make toothless'.

edge noun **1** the outside limit of an object, area, or surface. **2** the sharpened side of a blade. **3** the line along which two surfaces of a solid meet. **4** a slight advantage over close rivals: *Europe is losing its competitive edge.* **5** an intense or striking quality: *the chef has a fiery edge to her cooking.* ●**verb** **1** provide something with an edge or border. **2** move carefully or furtively: *I tried to edge away from her.*
– PHRASES **on edge** tense, nervous, or irritable. **set someone's teeth on edge** (especially of a sound) cause intense discomfort or irritation to someone.
– DERIVATIVES **edged** adjective **edger** noun.
– ORIGIN Old English.

edgeways (US **edgewise**) **adverb** with the edge uppermost or towards the viewer.
– PHRASES **get a word in edgeways** manage to break into a lively conversation.

edging noun something forming an edge or border.

edgy adjective (**edgier**, **edgiest**) **1** tense, nervous, or irritable. **2** informal avant-garde and unconventional.
– DERIVATIVES **edgily** adverb **edginess** noun.

EDI abbreviation electronic data interchange.

edible adjective fit to be eaten. ●**noun** (**edibles**) items of food.
– DERIVATIVES **edibility** noun.
– ORIGIN Latin *edibilis.*

edict /ee-dikt/ **noun** an official order or proclamation.
– ORIGIN Latin *edictum* 'something proclaimed'.

edifice /ed-i-fiss/ **noun** formal **1** a large, imposing building. **2** a complex system: *the edifice of economic reform degenerated into corruption.*
– ORIGIN Latin *aedificium.*

edify /ed-i-fy/ **verb** (**edifies**, **edifying**, **edified**) give educational or morally improving instruction to someone.
– DERIVATIVES **edification** noun **edifying** adjective.
– ORIGIN Latin *aedificare* 'build'.

edit verb (**edits**, **editing**, **edited**) **1** prepare written material for publication by correcting, shortening, or improving it. **2** prepare material for a film, recording, or broadcast. **3** change online text on a computer or word processor. **4** be editor of a newspaper or magazine. ●**noun** a change made as a result of editing.

– DERIVATIVES **editable** adjective.
– ORIGIN from **EDITOR**.

edition noun **1** a particular form or version of a published written work. **2** the total number of copies of a book, newspaper, etc. issued at one time. **3** a particular instance of a regular radio or television programme.
– ORIGIN Latin.

editor noun **1** a person who is in charge of a newspaper, magazine, or multi-author book. **2** a person who commissions or prepares written or recorded material for publication or broadcasting.
– DERIVATIVES **editorship** noun.
– ORIGIN Latin.

editorial adjective relating to the commissioning or preparing of material for publication. • noun a newspaper article giving an opinion on a topical issue.
– DERIVATIVES **editorialist** noun **editorially** adverb.

editorialize (or **editorialise**) verb (of a newspaper or editor) express opinions rather than just report news.

editress (also **editrix**) noun dated a female editor.

educate /ed-yuu-kayt/ verb **1** give intellectual and moral instruction to someone. **2** give someone information on a particular subject: *a campaign to educate consumers about food safety.* **3** (as adj. **educated**) showing or having had a good education: *educated, articulate elites.*
– DERIVATIVES **educable** adjective **educative** adjective **educator** noun.
– ORIGIN Latin *educare* 'lead out'.

educated guess noun a guess based on knowledge and experience.

education noun **1** the process of teaching or learning. **2** the theory and practice of teaching. **3** information about or training in a particular subject: *health education.* **4** (**an education**) an enlightening experience: *travelling has been quite an education for this former teacher.*
– DERIVATIVES **educational** adjective **educationalist** noun **educationally** adverb **educationist** noun.

Edwardian /ed-wor-di-uhn/ adjective relating to the reign of King Edward VII (1901–10). • noun a person who lived during the Edwardian period.

EEC abbreviation European Economic Community.

EEG abbreviation electroencephalogram or electroencephalograph.

eel noun a snake-like fish with a very long, thin body and small fins.
– DERIVATIVES **eel-like** adjective **eely** adjective.
– ORIGIN Old English.

e'er /air/ adverb literary form of **EVER**.

eerie /eer-i/ adjective (**eerier, eeriest**) strange and frightening.
– DERIVATIVES **eerily** adverb **eeriness** noun.
– ORIGIN probably from Old English, 'cowardly'.

efface /i-fayss/ verb **1** cause to disappear: *nothing could efface the bitter memory.* **2** (**efface oneself**) make oneself appear unimportant. **3** erase a mark from a surface.
– DERIVATIVES **effacement** noun.

– ORIGIN French *effacer*.

effect noun **1** a change which is a result of an action or other cause. **2** the state of being or becoming operative: *the agreement took effect in 2004.* **3** the extent to which something succeeds: *wind power can be used to great effect.* **4** (**effects**) personal belongings. **5** (**effects**) the lighting, sound, or scenery used in a play or film. **6** Physics a physical phenomenon, typically named after its discoverer. • verb bring about: *the prime minister effected many policy changes.*
– PHRASES **for effect** in order to impress people. **in effect** in practice, even if not formally acknowledged.
– ORIGIN Latin *effectus*.

> USAGE: On the confusion of **effect** and **affect**, see the note at **AFFECT**[1].

effective adjective **1** producing a desired or intended result. **2** (of a law or policy) operative. **3** existing in fact, though not formally acknowledged as such: *he remains in effective control of the military.*
– DERIVATIVES **effectively** adverb **effectiveness** noun.

effectual /i-fek-choo-uhl/ adjective **1** producing an intended result; effective. **2** (of a legal document) valid or binding.
– DERIVATIVES **effectually** adverb.

effeminate /i-fem-i-nuht/ adjective (of a man) having characteristics regarded as typical of a woman.
– DERIVATIVES **effeminacy** noun **effeminately** adverb.
– ORIGIN from Latin *effeminare* 'make feminine'.

effendi /e-fen-di/ noun (pl. **effendis**) a man of high education or social standing in an eastern Mediterranean or Arab country.
– ORIGIN Turkish *efendi*.

effervescent /ef-fuh-ve-suhnt/ adjective **1** (of a liquid) giving off bubbles; fizzy. **2** lively and enthusiastic.
– DERIVATIVES **effervesce** verb **effervescence** noun.
– ORIGIN from Latin *effervescere* 'boil up'.

effete /i-feet/ adjective **1** no longer effective; weak. **2** (of a man) affected or effeminate.
– DERIVATIVES **effetely** adverb **effeteness** noun.
– ORIGIN Latin *effetus* 'worn out by bearing young'.

efficacious /ef-fi-kay-shuhss/ adjective formal successful in producing an intended effect; effective.
– DERIVATIVES **efficaciously** adverb.
– ORIGIN from Latin *efficere* 'accomplish'.

efficacy /ef-fi-kuh-si/ noun formal the ability to produce an intended result.

efficiency noun (pl. **efficiencies**) **1** the quality of being efficient. **2** a means of using resources in a less wasteful way: *the firm will seek to maximize cost efficiencies.*

efficient adjective working well with minimum waste of money or effort.
– DERIVATIVES **efficiently** adverb.
– ORIGIN from Latin *efficere* 'accomplish'.

effigy /ef-fi-ji/ noun (pl. **effigies**) a sculpture or model of a person.
– ORIGIN Latin *effigies*.

efflorescence /ef-fluh-ress-uhnss/ noun
1 literary a very high stage of development: *an efflorescence of art.* 2 the crystallization of salts on a surface such as brick.
– DERIVATIVES **efflorescent** adjective.
– ORIGIN from Latin *florescere* 'begin to bloom'.

effluent noun liquid waste or sewage discharged into a river or the sea.
– ORIGIN from Latin *effluere* 'flow out'.

effluvium /i-floo-vi-uhm/ noun (pl. **effluvia** /i-floo-vi-uh/) an unpleasant or harmful smell or discharge.
– ORIGIN Latin.

effort noun 1 a vigorous or determined attempt to do something. 2 physical or mental vigour: *he put considerable effort into achieving this goal.*
– DERIVATIVES **effortful** adjective.
– ORIGIN Old French *esforcier.*

effortless adjective done or achieved without effort; natural and easy.
– DERIVATIVES **effortlessly** adverb **effortlessness** noun.

effrontery /i-frun-tuh-ri/ noun insolent or disrespectful behaviour.
– ORIGIN Latin *effrons* 'shameless, barefaced'.

effulgent /i-ful-juhnt/ adjective literary shining brightly.
– DERIVATIVES **effulgence** noun.
– ORIGIN from Latin *effulgere.*

effusion noun 1 a discharge of something, especially a liquid. 2 an unrestrained expression of feelings in speech or writing: *effusions of patriotic bigotry.*
– ORIGIN from Latin *effundere* 'pour out'.

effusive /i-fyoo-siv/ adjective expressing gratitude or approval in an unrestrained way.
– DERIVATIVES **effusively** adverb **effusiveness** noun.

e-fit noun an electronic picture of a person's face made from photographs of separate facial features, created by a computer program.

EFL abbreviation English as a foreign language.

EFTA abbreviation European Free Trade Association.

e.g. abbreviation for example.
– ORIGIN from Latin *exempli gratia* 'for the sake of example'.

egalitarian /i-gal-i-tair-i-uhn/ adjective believing in or based on the principle that all people are equal and deserve equal rights and opportunities. •noun a person who supports the principle of equality for all.
– DERIVATIVES **egalitarianism** noun.
– ORIGIN French *égalitaire.*

egg[1] noun 1 an oval or round object laid by a female bird, reptile, fish, or invertebrate and containing an ovum which can develop into a new organism. 2 an infertile egg of a chicken, used for food. 3 the cell in female humans and animals that is capable of producing young; an ovum. 4 informal, dated a person of a specified kind: *he's a good egg.*
– PHRASES **kill the goose that lays the golden eggs** destroy a reliable and valuable source of income. **with egg on one's face** informal appearing foolish or ridiculous.
– DERIVATIVES **eggy** adjective.
– ORIGIN Old English.

egg[2] verb (**egg someone on**) urge or encourage someone to do something foolish or risky.
– ORIGIN Old Norse, 'incite'.

egghead noun informal a very intelligent or studious person.

eggnog noun a drink consisting of wine or other alcohol mixed with beaten egg and milk.

eggplant noun N. Amer. another term for **AUBERGINE**.

eggshell noun the thin, brittle outer layer of an egg. •adjective 1 (of china) very thin and delicate. 2 referring to a paint that dries with a slight sheen.

egg white noun the clear substance round the yolk of an egg that turns white when cooked or beaten.

ego /ee-goh/ noun (pl. **egos**) 1 a person's sense of their own worth and importance: *keeping slim is a great boost to the ego.* 2 the part of the mind that is responsible for the interpretation of reality and a sense of personal identity. Compare with **ID** and **SUPEREGO**.
– ORIGIN Latin, 'I'.

egocentric adjective thinking only of oneself; self-centred.
– DERIVATIVES **egocentrically** adverb **egocentricity** noun **egocentrism** noun.

egoism noun another term for **EGOTISM**.
– DERIVATIVES **egoist** noun **egoistic** adjective.

egomania noun obsessive self-centredness.
– DERIVATIVES **egomaniac** noun **egomaniacal** adjective.

egotism noun the quality of being excessively conceited or self-centred.
– DERIVATIVES **egotist** noun **egotistic** adjective **egotistical** adjective.

ego trip noun informal something that a person does to feel self-important.

egregious /i-gree-juhss/ adjective outstandingly bad; shocking.
– DERIVATIVES **egregiously** adverb **egregiousness** noun.
– ORIGIN Latin *egregius* 'illustrious' (literally 'standing out from the flock').

egress /ee-gress/ noun formal 1 the action of going out of or leaving a place. 2 a way out.
– ORIGIN from Latin *egressus* 'gone out'.

egret /ee-grit/ noun a heron with mainly white plumage, having long plumes in the breeding season.
– ORIGIN Old French *aigrette.*

Egyptian noun 1 a person from Egypt. 2 the language used in ancient Egypt. •adjective relating to Egypt.

Egyptology /ee-jip-tol-uh-ji/ noun the study of the language, history, and culture of ancient Egypt.
– DERIVATIVES **Egyptological** adjective **Egyptologist** noun.

Eid /eed/ (also **Id**) noun 1 (in full **Eid ul-Fitr** /eed uul fee-truh/) the Muslim festival marking the end of the fast of Ramadan. 2 (in full **Eid ul-Adha** /eed uul aa-duh/) the festival marking the culmination of the annual pilgrimage to Mecca.
– ORIGIN Arabic, 'feast'.

eider /I-der/ (also **eider duck**) noun (pl. same or **eiders**) a northern sea duck, the male of which has mainly black-and-white plumage.

– ORIGIN Old Norse.

eiderdown noun Brit. a quilt filled with down (originally from the female eider duck) or another soft material.

eidetic /I-**det**-ik/ adjective relating to mental images that are unusually vivid and detailed.
– ORIGIN Greek *eidētikos*.

eight cardinal number **1** one more than seven; 8. (Roman numeral: **viii** or **VIII**.) **2** an eight-oared rowing boat or its crew.
– PHRASES **have one over the eight** Brit. informal have one drink too many. **pieces of eight** historical Spanish dollars, equivalent to eight reals.
– ORIGIN Old English.

eighteen cardinal number one more than seventeen; 18. (Roman numeral: **xviii** or **XVIII**.)
– DERIVATIVES **eighteenth** ordinal number.

eighth ordinal number **1** that is number eight in a sequence; 8th. **2** (**an eighth** or **one eighth**) each of eight equal parts into which something is divided.

eights plural noun a race for eight-oared rowing boats.

eightsome reel noun a lively Scottish dance for eight people.

eighty cardinal number (pl. **eighties**) ten less than ninety; 80. (Roman numeral: **lxxx** or **LXXX**.)
– DERIVATIVES **eightieth** ordinal number.

einsteinium /yn-**sty**-ni-uhm/ noun an unstable radioactive chemical element made by high-energy atomic collisions.
– ORIGIN named after the German-born physicist Albert *Einstein*.

eirenic /I-**ren**-ik/ adjective variant spelling of IRENIC.

eisteddfod /I-**steth**-vod/ noun (pl. **eisteddfods** or **eisteddfodau** /I-**steth**-vod-I/) a competitive festival of music and poetry in Wales.
– ORIGIN Welsh, 'session'.

either /**I**-ther, ee-**ther**/ conjunction & adverb **1** used before the first of two alternatives specified (the other being introduced by 'or'). **2** (adverb) used to indicate a similarity or link with a statement just made: *You don't like him, do you? I don't either.* **3** for that matter; moreover. • determiner & pronoun **1** one or the other of two people or things. **2** each of two.
– ORIGIN Old English.

USAGE: In good English, it is important that **either** and **or** are correctly placed so that the structures following each word balance each other. For example, it is better to say *I'm going to buy either a new camera or a new video* rather than *I'm either going to buy a new camera or a video.*

ejaculate verb /i-**jak**-yuu-layt/ **1** (of a man or male animal) eject semen from the penis at the moment of orgasm. **2** dated say something suddenly. • noun /i-**jak**-yuu-luht/ semen that has been ejaculated.
– DERIVATIVES **ejaculation** noun **ejaculator** noun **ejaculatory** /i-**jak**-yuu-luh-tri/ adjective.
– ORIGIN Latin *ejaculari* 'dart out'.

eject verb **1** force or throw something out violently or suddenly. **2** make someone leave a place or post. **3** (of a pilot) escape from an aircraft by means of an ejection seat.
– DERIVATIVES **ejection** noun **ejector** noun.

– ORIGIN Latin *eicere* 'throw out'.

ejection seat (also **ejector seat**) noun an aircraft seat that can throw its occupant from the craft in an emergency.

eke /eek/ verb (**eke something out**) **1** make something last longer by using it sparingly: *young mothers hunting for bargains to eke out their social security money.* **2** make a living with difficulty.
– ORIGIN Old English, 'increase'.

elaborate adjective /i-**lab**-uh-ruht/ involving many carefully arranged parts; detailed and complicated. • verb /i-**lab**-uh-rayt/ **1** develop or present a theory or policy in detail. **2** (**elaborate on**) add more detail to something already said.
– DERIVATIVES **elaborately** adverb **elaboration** noun **elaborative** adjective.
– ORIGIN from Latin *elaborare* 'work out'.

élan /ay-**lan**/ (also **elan**) noun energy and stylishness: *he played the march with great élan.*
– ORIGIN French.

eland /ee-luhnd/ noun a large African antelope with spiral horns.
– ORIGIN Dutch, 'elk'.

elapse verb (of time) pass.
– ORIGIN Latin *elabi* 'slip away'.

elastane /i-**las**-tayn/ noun a synthetic elastic material, used for close-fitting clothing.

elastic /i-**lass**-tik/ adjective **1** able to return to normal size or shape after being stretched or squeezed. **2** flexible and adaptable: *the definition of nationality is elastic.* • noun cord, tape, or fabric which returns to its original length or shape after being stretched.
– DERIVATIVES **elastically** adverb **elasticity** /i-**lass**-**tiss**-i-ti/ noun **elasticize** (or **elasticise**) verb.
– ORIGIN Greek *elastikos* 'propulsive'.

elasticated adjective Brit. (of a garment or material) made elastic with rubber thread or tape.

elastic band noun Brit. a rubber band.

elastin /i-**las**-tin/ noun an elastic, fibrous protein found in connective body tissue.

elastomer /i-**lass**-tuh-mer/ noun a natural or synthetic polymer with elastic properties, e.g. rubber.
– DERIVATIVES **elastomeric** adjective.

elated /i-**lay**-tid/ adjective very happy and excited.
– ORIGIN Latin *elatus* 'raised'.

elation /i-**lay**-sh'n/ noun great happiness and excitement.

elbow noun **1** the joint between the forearm and the upper arm. **2** a piece of piping or something similar bent through an angle. • verb **1** hit or push someone with one's elbow. **2** (often **elbow one's way**) move by pushing past people with one's elbows.
– PHRASES **give someone the elbow** Brit. informal reject or dismiss someone. **up to one's elbows in** deeply involved in something.
– ORIGIN Old English.

elbow grease noun informal hard physical work, especially vigorous cleaning.

elbow room noun informal adequate space to move or work in.

elder[1] adjective (of one or more out of a group of people) of a greater age. • noun 1 (one's elder) a person older than oneself. 2 a leader or senior figure in a community. 3 an official or minister in certain Protestant Churches.
– ORIGIN Old English.

elder[2] noun a small tree or shrub with white flowers and bluish-black or red berries.
– ORIGIN Old English.

elderberry noun (pl. **elderberries**) the berry of the elder, used for making jelly or wine.

elderflower noun the flower of the elder, used to make wines and cordials.

elderly adjective old or ageing.

elder statesman noun an experienced and respected politician or other public figure.

eldest adjective (of one out of a group of people) oldest.

El Dorado /el duh-**rah**-doh/ (also **eldorado**) noun (pl. **El Dorados**) a place of great abundance and wealth.
– ORIGIN Spanish, 'the gilded one', a country or city formerly believed to exist in South America.

eldritch /**el**-drich/ adjective literary weird and sinister or ghostly.
– ORIGIN perhaps related to ELF.

elecampane /el-i-kam-**payn**/ noun a plant with yellow daisy-like flowers and bitter roots that are used in herbal medicine.
– ORIGIN from Latin *enula* 'helenium' (a plant of the daisy family) + *campana*, probably meaning 'of the fields'.

elect verb 1 choose someone to hold public office or another position by voting. 2 choose to do something: *the manager elected to leave him out of the team.* • adjective 1 (of a person) chosen or singled out. 2 elected to a position but not yet in office: *the President Elect.*
– DERIVATIVES **electability** noun **electable** adjective.
– ORIGIN Latin *eligere* 'pick out'.

election noun 1 a formal process by which a person is elected, especially to a public office. 2 the action of electing someone.

electioneering noun the action of campaigning to be elected to a political position.

elective adjective 1 relating to or appointed by election. 2 (of a course of study, medical treatment, etc.) chosen by the person concerned; not compulsory.

elector noun 1 a person who has the right to vote in an election. 2 (**Elector**) historical a German prince entitled to take part in the election of the Holy Roman Emperor.

electoral adjective relating to elections or electors.
– DERIVATIVES **electorally** adverb.

electoral college noun a group of people chosen to represent the members of a political party in the election of a leader.

electoral roll (also **electoral register**) noun (in the UK) an official list of the people in a district who are entitled to vote in an election.

electorate /i-**lek**-tuh-ruht/ noun 1 the group of people in a country or area who are entitled to vote in an election. 2 historical the office or territories of a German elector.

electric adjective 1 relating to, worked by, or producing electricity. 2 very exciting or intense: *the atmosphere was electric.* • noun (**electrics**) Brit. the system of electric wiring and parts in a house or vehicle.
– ORIGIN from Greek *ēlektron* 'amber' (because rubbing amber causes static electricity).

electrical adjective relating to, operating by, or producing electricity.
– DERIVATIVES **electrically** adverb.

electrical storm noun a thunderstorm or other violent disturbance of the electrical condition of the atmosphere.

electric blanket noun an electrically wired blanket used for heating a bed.

electric blue noun a steely or brilliant light blue.

electric chair noun a chair in which convicted criminals are executed by electrocution.

electric eel noun a large eel-like freshwater fish of South America, which uses pulses of electricity to kill its prey.

electric fence noun a fence through which an electric current can be passed, giving an electric shock to any person or animal touching it.

electric guitar noun a guitar with a built-in pickup which converts sound vibrations into electrical signals for amplification.

electrician noun a person who installs and maintains electrical equipment.

electricity noun 1 a form of energy resulting from the existence of charged particles (such as electrons), either statically as a build-up of charge or dynamically as a current. 2 the supply of electric current to a building. 3 great excitement or intense emotion: *the atmosphere was charged with sexual electricity.*

electric shock noun a sudden discharge of electricity through a part of the body.

electrify verb (**electrifies**, **electrifying**, **electrified**) 1 pass an electric current through something. 2 convert a machine or system to the use of electrical power. 3 (as adj. **electrifying**) very exciting or impressive: *an electrifying performance.*
– DERIVATIVES **electrification** noun.

electrocardiography /i-lek-troh-kah-di-og-ruh-fi/ noun the measurement and recording of activity in the heart using electrodes placed on the skin.
– DERIVATIVES **electrocardiogram** noun **electrocardiograph** noun **electrocardiographic** adjective.

electroconvulsive adjective relating to the treatment of mental illness by applying electric shocks to the brain.

electrocute verb injure or kill someone by electric shock.
– DERIVATIVES **electrocution** noun.

electrode /i-**lek**-trohd/ noun a conductor through which electricity enters or leaves something.
– ORIGIN from ELECTRIC + Greek *hodos* 'way'.

electrodynamics plural noun (usu. treated as sing.) the branch of mechanics concerned with the interaction of electric currents with magnetic or electric fields.
– DERIVATIVES **electrodynamic** adjective.

electroencephalography /i-lek-troh-in-sef-uh-**log**-ruh-fi/ noun the measurement and recording of electrical activity in the brain.
– DERIVATIVES **electroencephalogram** noun **electroencephalograph** noun.

electrolysis /i-lek-**trol**-i-siss/ noun **1** chemical decomposition produced by passing an electric current through a conducting liquid. **2** the removal of hair roots or blemishes on the skin by means of an electric current.
– DERIVATIVES **electrolytic** /i-lek-truh-**lit**-ik/ adjective.

electrolyte /i-lek-truh-lyt/ noun a liquid or gel which contains ions and can be decomposed by electrolysis, e.g. that present in a battery.
– ORIGIN from Greek *lutos* 'released'.

electromagnet noun a metal core made into a magnet by the passage of electric current through a surrounding coil.

electromagnetic adjective relating to the interrelation of electric currents or fields and magnetic fields.
– DERIVATIVES **electromagnetically** adverb **electromagnetism** noun.

electromagnetic radiation noun a kind of radiation including visible light, radio waves, gamma rays, and X-rays, in which electric and magnetic fields vary simultaneously.

electromotive /i-lek-truh-**moh**-tiv/ adjective tending to produce an electric current.

electromotive force noun a difference in potential that tends to give rise to an electric current.

electron noun Physics a stable negatively charged subatomic particle found in all atoms and acting as the primary carrier of electricity in solids.

electronic adjective **1** having components such as microchips and transistors that control and direct electric currents. **2** relating to electrons or electronics. **3** relating to or carried out by means of a computer or other electronic device: *electronic shopping*.
– DERIVATIVES **electronically** adverb.

electronica noun a style of popular electronic music deriving from techno and rave.

electronic publishing noun the issuing of written material as electronic files rather than on paper.

electronics plural noun **1** (usu. treated as sing.) the branch of physics and technology concerned with the design of circuits using transistors and microchips, and with the behaviour and movement of electrons. **2** (treated as pl.) circuits or devices using transistors, microchips, etc.

electron microscope noun a microscope with high magnification and resolution, employing electron beams in place of light.

electrophoresis /i-lek-troh-fuh-**ree**-sis/ noun the movement of charged particles in a fluid or gel under the influence of an electric field.
– DERIVATIVES **electrophoretic** adjective.
– ORIGIN from Greek *phorēsis* 'being carried'.

electroplate /i-lek-troh-playt/ verb coat a metal object with another metal using electrolysis. •noun electroplated articles.

electroscope noun an instrument for detecting and measuring electric charge.

electroshock adjective another term for ELECTROCONVULSIVE.

electrostatic adjective relating to stationary electric charges or fields as opposed to electric currents.
– DERIVATIVES **electrostatically** adverb **electrostatics** plural noun.

electrosurgery noun surgery using a high-frequency electric current to cut tissue.
– DERIVATIVES **electrosurgical** adjective.

electrotherapy noun the use of electric currents passed through the body to treat paralysis and other disorders.

electrum /i-lek-truhm/ noun an alloy of gold with at least 20 per cent of silver, used for jewellery.
– ORIGIN Greek *ēlektron* 'amber, electrum'.

elegant adjective **1** graceful and stylish. **2** pleasingly clever but simple: *an unbelievably elegant 'theory of everything'*.
– DERIVATIVES **elegance** noun **elegantly** adverb.
– ORIGIN Latin *elegans* 'discriminating'.

elegiac /el-i-jy-uhk/ adjective **1** relating to or characteristic of an elegy. **2** sad; mournful: *the elegiac, bittersweet tone of the narrator's voice*.
– DERIVATIVES **elegiacally** adverb.

elegy /el-i-ji/ noun (pl. **elegies**) a mournful poem, typically a lament for someone who has died.
– ORIGIN Greek *elegos* 'mournful poem'.

element noun **1** an essential or typical part: *there are four elements to the proposal*. **2** (also **chemical element**) each of more than one hundred substances that cannot be chemically changed or broken down. **3** any of the four substances (earth, water, air, and fire) formerly believed to be the basic constituents of all matter. **4** a small amount: *an element of danger*. **5** a distinct group within a larger group: *right-wing elements in the army*. **6** (**the elements**) rain and other bad weather. **7** a part in an electric device consisting of a wire through which an electric current is passed to provide heat.
– PHRASES **in one's element** in a situation in which one feels happy or relaxed.
– ORIGIN Latin *elementum* 'principle, rudiment'.

elemental /el-i-**men**-t'l/ adjective **1** forming an essential or typical feature; fundamental: *the sauces are made from a few elemental ingredients*. **2** relating to or resembling the powerful forces of nature: *elemental hatred*. **3** relating to a chemical element.

elementary adjective **1** relating to the most basic aspects of a subject. **2** straightforward and simple to understand: *elementary tasks*. **3** Chemistry not able to be decomposed into elements or other primary constituents.
– DERIVATIVES **elementarily** adverb.

elementary school noun N. Amer. a primary school for the first six or eight grades.

elephant noun (pl. same or **elephants**) a very large mammal with a trunk, curved tusks, and large ears, native to Africa and southern Asia.
– ORIGIN Greek *elephas* 'ivory, elephant'.

elephantiasis /el-i-fuhn-ty-uh-sis/ noun a medical condition in which a limb becomes hugely enlarged, typically caused by a type of parasitic worm.

elephantine /el-i-**fan**-tyn/ adjective typical of or like an elephant, especially in being large or clumsy.

elevate /**el**-i-vayt/ verb **1** lift something to a higher position. **2** raise to a higher level or status: *the prize elevated her to the front rank of writers*.
– ORIGIN Latin *elevare* 'to raise'.

elevated adjective having a high intellectual or moral level.

elevation noun **1** the action of elevating someone or something: *the elevation of Bob Marley to superstar status*. **2** the height of a place above sea level. **3** the angle of something with the horizontal. **4** a particular side of a building, or a scale drawing of this.
– DERIVATIVES **elevational** adjective.

elevator noun N. Amer. a lift in a building.

eleven cardinal number **1** one more than ten; 11. (Roman numeral: **xi** or **XI**.) **2** a sports team of eleven players.
– DERIVATIVES **elevenfold** adjective & adverb.
– ORIGIN Old English.

eleven-plus noun (in the UK, especially formerly) an exam taken at the age of 11–12 to determine the type of secondary school a child should enter.

elevenses plural noun Brit. informal a mid-morning break for light refreshments.

eleventh ordinal number **1** that is number eleven in a sequence; 11th. **2** (**an eleventh/one eleventh**) each of eleven equal parts into which something is divided.
– PHRASES **the eleventh hour** the latest possible moment.

elf noun (pl. **elves**) a supernatural creature of folk tales, represented as a small human figure with pointed ears.
– DERIVATIVES **elfish** adjective **elven** adjective (literary) **elvish** adjective.
– ORIGIN Old English.

elfin adjective like an elf, especially in being small and delicate.

elicit /i-**liss**-it/ verb (**elicits, eliciting, elicited**) draw out or produce a response or reaction: *my alternative parenting choices have often elicited criticism*.
– DERIVATIVES **elicitation** noun **elicitor** noun.
– ORIGIN Latin *elicere* 'draw out by trickery'.

elide /i-**lyd**/ verb **1** omit a sound or syllable when speaking. **2** join or merge things together.
– ORIGIN Latin *elidere* 'crush out'.

eligible /**el**-i-ji-b'l/ adjective **1** meeting the conditions to do or receive something: *you may be eligible for a refund*. **2** desirable or suitable as a wife or husband.
– DERIVATIVES **eligibility** noun.
– ORIGIN Latin *eligibilis*.

eliminate /i-**lim**-i-nayt/ verb **1** completely remove or get rid of something. **2** exclude from consideration or further participation: *the team were eliminated from the cup*.
– DERIVATIVES **elimination** noun **eliminator** noun.
– ORIGIN Latin *eliminare* 'turn out of doors'.

elision /i-**li**-zh'n/ noun **1** the omission of a sound or syllable in speech. **2** the action of joining or merging things.
– ORIGIN Latin.

elite /i-**leet**/ (also **élite**) noun a group of people regarded as the best in a particular society or organization: *China's educated elite*.
– ORIGIN French, 'selection, choice'.

elitism noun **1** the belief that a society or system should be run by a group of people regarded as superior to others. **2** the superior attitude or behaviour associated with an elite: *the cosy elitism that weakened our education system for a century*.
– DERIVATIVES **elitist** adjective & noun.

elixir /i-**lik**-seer/ noun a magical potion, especially one supposedly able to make people live for ever.
– ORIGIN Arabic.

Elizabethan /i-liz-uh-**bee**-thuhn/ adjective relating to or typical of the reign of Queen Elizabeth I (1558–1603). • noun a person alive during the reign of Queen Elizabeth I.

elk /elk/ noun (pl. same or **elks**) a large northern deer with a growth of skin hanging from the neck.
– ORIGIN probably Old English.

ell noun a former measure of length used mainly for textiles, normally 45 inches in England and 37 inches in Scotland.
– ORIGIN Old English.

ellipse /i-**lips**/ noun a regular oval shape resulting when a cone is cut by an oblique plane which does not intersect the base.

ellipsis /i-**lip**-siss/ noun (pl. **ellipses** /i-**lip**-seez/) **1** the omission of words from speech or writing. **2** a set of dots indicating such an omission.
– ORIGIN Greek *elleipsis*.

ellipsoid /i-**lip**-soyd/ noun a symmetrical three-dimensional figure with a circular cross-section when viewed along one axis and elliptical cross-sections when viewed along the other axes.
– DERIVATIVES **ellipsoidal** adjective.

elliptic adjective relating to or having the shape of an ellipse.
– DERIVATIVES **ellipticity** noun.

elliptical adjective **1** (of speech or writing) having a word or words deliberately omitted: *a superficial, elliptical narrative*. **2** another term for **ELLIPTIC**.
– DERIVATIVES **elliptically** adverb.

elm noun a tall deciduous tree with rough leaves.
– ORIGIN Old English.

El Niño /el **neen**-yoh/ noun (pl. **El Niños**) an irregular and complex cycle of climatic changes affecting the Pacific region.
– ORIGIN Spanish, 'the Christ child', so called because the characteristic signs of an El Niño appear around Christmas time.

elocution /el-uh-**kyoo**-sh'n/ noun the skill of speaking clearly and pronouncing words distinctly.
– DERIVATIVES **elocutionist** noun.
– ORIGIN from Latin *eloqui* 'speak out'.

elongate /ee-long-gayt/ verb (usu. as adj. **elongated**) make or become longer: *polar bears have elongated snouts*.
– DERIVATIVES **elongation** noun.
– ORIGIN Latin *elongare* 'place at a distance'.

elope verb run away secretly in order to get

married.
- DERIVATIVES **elopement** noun.
- ORIGIN Old French *aloper*.

eloquence /el-uh-kwuhnss/ noun fluent or persuasive speaking or writing.
- ORIGIN Latin *eloquentia*.

eloquent adjective **1** fluent or persuasive in speaking or writing. **2** clearly expressing something: *an art that is eloquent of America's cultural diversity.*
- DERIVATIVES **eloquently** adverb.

else adverb **1** in addition; besides. **2** different; instead.
- PHRASES **or else** used to introduce the second of two alternatives.
- ORIGIN Old English.

elsewhere adverb in, at, or to another place or other places. • pronoun another place.

ELT abbreviation English language teaching.

elucidate /i-loo-si-dayt/ verb make something easier to understand.
- DERIVATIVES **elucidation** noun.
- ORIGIN Latin *elucidare*.

elude /i-lood/ verb **1** cleverly escape from or avoid someone or something. **2** fail to be understood or achieved by: *the logic of this eluded her.*
- ORIGIN Latin *eludere*.

elusive adjective difficult to find, catch, or achieve: *the elusive golden moon bear.*
- DERIVATIVES **elusively** adverb **elusiveness** noun.
- ORIGIN from Latin *eludere* 'elude'.

elver /el-ver/ noun a young eel.
- ORIGIN from dialect *eel-fare* 'the passage of young eels up a river', from **FARE** in its original sense 'a journey'.

elves plural of **ELF**.

Elysian /i-liz-i-uhn/ adjective relating to or like paradise.
- ORIGIN from *Elysium* or the *Elysian Fields* in Greek mythology, where heroes were taken when they died.

emaciated /i-may-si-ay-tid/ adjective abnormally thin and weak.
- DERIVATIVES **emaciation** noun.
- ORIGIN from Latin *emaciare* 'make thin'.

email (also **e-mail**) noun **1** a message sent electronically from one computer user to another or others via a network. **2** the system of sending emails. • verb mail someone or send a message using email.
- DERIVATIVES **emailer** noun.

emanate /em-uh-nayt/ verb **1** (**emanate from**) come or spread out from a source. **2** give out: *he emanated compassion.*
- ORIGIN Latin *emanare* 'flow out'.

emanation /em-uh-nay-shun/ noun **1** something which emanates or comes from a source. **2** the action of coming from a source.

emancipate /i-man-si-payt/ verb **1** set someone free, especially from legal, social, or political restrictions. **2** free someone from slavery.
- DERIVATIVES **emancipation** noun **emancipatory** adjective.
- ORIGIN Latin *emancipare* 'transfer as property'.

emasculate /i-mass-kyuu-layt/ verb **1** make weaker or less effective: *the world wars*

emasculated British power. **2** deprive a man of his male role or identity.
- DERIVATIVES **emasculation** noun.
- ORIGIN Latin *emasculare* 'castrate'.

embalm /im-bahm/ verb preserve a corpse from decay, usually by injection of a preservative.
- DERIVATIVES **embalmer** noun.
- ORIGIN Old French *embaumer*.

embankment noun **1** a wall or bank built to prevent flooding by a river. **2** a bank of earth or stone built to carry a road or railway over low ground.

embargo /em-bar-goh, im-bar-goh/ noun (pl. **embargoes**) an official ban, especially on trade or other commercial activity with a particular country. • verb (**embargoes, embargoing, embargoed**) ban something officially.
- ORIGIN Spanish.

embark verb **1** go on board a ship or aircraft. **2** (**embark on**) begin a new project or course of action.
- DERIVATIVES **embarkation** noun.
- ORIGIN French *embarquer*.

embarras de richesses /em-bar-ah duh ree-shess/ noun more resources than one knows what to do with.
- ORIGIN French, 'embarrassment of riches'.

embarrass /im-ba-ruhss, em-ba-ruhss/ verb **1** make someone feel awkward, self-conscious, or ashamed. **2** (**be embarrassed**) be put in financial difficulties.
- DERIVATIVES **embarrassed** adjective **embarrassing** adjective.
- ORIGIN French *embarrasser*.

embarrassment noun **1** a feeling of self-consciousness, shame, or awkwardness. **2** a cause of self-consciousness, shame, or awkwardness: *her extreme views might be an embarrassment to the movement.*

embassy noun (pl. **embassies**) **1** the official home or offices of an ambassador. **2** chiefly historical a deputation or mission sent by one state to another.
- ORIGIN Old French *ambasse*.

embattled adjective **1** troubled by many difficulties: *the embattled Chancellor.* **2** prepared for war because surrounded by enemy forces. **3** (of a building) having battlements.

embed (also **imbed**) verb (**embeds, embedding, embedded**) **1** fix something firmly and deeply in a surrounding mass. **2** cause an idea or feeling to be firmly lodged in a culture or someone's mind: *deeply held standards are embedded in our society.* **3** attach a journalist to a military unit during a conflict.

embellish verb **1** make something more attractive; decorate. **2** add extra, often exaggerated, details to a story to make it more interesting.
- DERIVATIVES **embellishment** noun.
- ORIGIN Old French *embellir*.

ember noun a small piece of burning wood or coal in a dying fire.
- ORIGIN Old English.

embezzle verb steal money placed in one's trust or under one's control.
- DERIVATIVES **embezzlement** noun **embezzler** noun.

e

– ORIGIN Old French *embesiler*.

embitter verb (usu. as adj. **embittered**) make someone bitter or resentful.

emblazon /im-**blay**-zuhn/ verb **1** display a design on something in a noticeable way: *T-shirts emblazoned with the names of baseball teams*. **2** depict a heraldic device on something.

emblem /**em**-bluhm/ noun **1** a heraldic design or symbol as a distinctive badge of a nation, organization, or family. **2** a symbol representing a quality or idea: *the bards wore white, as an emblem of peace*.
– ORIGIN Greek *emblēma* 'insertion'.

emblematic adjective representing a particular quality or idea: *Mill was an emblematic figure of his age*.

embodiment noun **1** a physical or visible form of an idea or quality: *I looked the embodiment of adolescent awkwardness*. **2** the representation of something in a physical or visible form.

embody verb (**embodies, embodying, embodied**) **1** give a physical or visible form to an idea or quality. **2** include or contain as a constituent part: *the changes in law embodied in the Children Act*.

embolden verb give courage or confidence to someone.

embolism /**em**-buh-li-z'm/ noun obstruction of an artery, typically by a clot of blood or an air bubble.
– ORIGIN Greek *embolismos*.

embolus /**em**-buh-luhss/ noun (pl. **emboli** /**em**-buh-lee/) a blood clot, air bubble, fatty deposit, or other object obstructing a blood vessel.
– DERIVATIVES **embolic** /em-**bo**-lik/ adjective.
– ORIGIN Greek *embolos* 'peg, stopper'.

embonpoint /em-bon-**pwan**/ noun plumpness, especially of a woman's bosom.
– ORIGIN from French *en bon point* 'in good condition'.

emboss verb carve or mould a raised design on a surface.
– DERIVATIVES **embosser** noun.
– ORIGIN from former French *embosser*.

embrace verb **1** hold someone closely in one's arms, especially to show affection. **2** include or contain something. **3** accept or support a belief or change willingly. • noun an act of embracing someone.
– DERIVATIVES **embraceable** adjective.
– ORIGIN Old French *embracer*.

embrasure /im-**bray**-sher/ noun **1** an opening or recess around a window or door forming an enlargement of the area from the inside. **2** an opening in a wall or parapet, used for shooting through.
– ORIGIN from former French *embraser* 'widen an opening'.

embrocation /em-bruh-**kay**-sh'n/ noun a liquid medication rubbed on the body to relieve pain from strains.
– ORIGIN Latin.

embroider verb **1** sew decorative needlework patterns on something. **2** add false or exaggerated details to a story.
– DERIVATIVES **embroiderer** noun.

– ORIGIN Old French *enbrouder*.

embroidery noun (pl. **embroideries**) **1** the art or pastime of embroidering. **2** embroidered cloth.

embroil verb involve someone deeply in a conflict or difficult situation.
– ORIGIN French *embrouiller* 'to muddle'.

embryo /**em**-bri-oh/ noun (pl. **embryos**) **1** an unborn animal in the process of development, especially an unborn human being in the first eight weeks from fertilization of the egg. Compare with **FETUS**. **2** the part of a seed which develops into a new plant. **3** something at an early stage of development.
– ORIGIN Greek *embruon* 'fetus'.

embryology /em-bri-**ol**-uh-ji/ noun the branch of biology and medicine concerned with the study of embryos.
– DERIVATIVES **embryological** adjective **embryologist** noun.

embryonic /em-bri-**on**-ik/ adjective **1** relating to an embryo. **2** in an early stage of development: *the plan is still in its embryonic stages*.

emcee /em-**see**/ informal noun **1** N. Amer. a master of ceremonies. **2** an MC at a club or party. • verb (**emcees, emceeing, emceed**) **1** N. Amer. act as a master of ceremonies at. **2** perform as an MC.

emend /i-**mend**/ verb correct and revise written material.
– DERIVATIVES **emendation** noun.
– ORIGIN Latin *emendare*.

emerald noun **1** a bright green precious stone consisting of a variety of beryl. **2** a bright green colour.
– ORIGIN Old French *esmeraud*.

emerge verb **1** become gradually visible. **2** begin to exist or become apparent: *the jogging boom emerged during the 1970s*. **3** (of facts) become known. **4** recover from or survive a difficult period.
– DERIVATIVES **emergence** noun.
– ORIGIN Latin *emergere*.

emergency noun (pl. **emergencies**) **1** a serious, unexpected, and often dangerous situation requiring immediate action. **2** N. Amer. the casualty department in a hospital. • adjective arising from or used in an emergency: *an emergency exit*.
– ORIGIN Latin *emergentia*.

emergent adjective in the process of coming into being: *a newly emergent middle class*.

emeritus /i-**me**-ri-tuhss/ adjective having retired but allowed to keep a title as an honour: *an emeritus professor*.
– ORIGIN Latin.

emery /**em**-uh-ri/ noun a greyish-black form of corundum (mineral), used in powdered form for smoothing and polishing.
– ORIGIN Old French *esmeri*.

emery board noun a strip of thin wood or card coated with emery or another abrasive and used as a nail file.

emetic /i-**met**-ik/ adjective (of a substance) causing vomiting. • noun a substance that causes vomiting.
– ORIGIN Greek *emetikos*.

EMF abbreviation **1** electromagnetic field(s).

2 (**emf**) electromotive force.

emigrant noun a person who emigrates to another country.

emigrate /em-i-grayt/ verb leave one's own country in order to settle permanently in another.
– DERIVATIVES **emigration** noun.
– ORIGIN Latin *emigrare*.

émigré /em-i-gray/ noun a person who has emigrated to another country, especially for political reasons.
– ORIGIN French.

eminence /em-i-nuhnss/ noun **1** the quality of being highly accomplished and respected within a particular area of activity. **2** an important or distinguished person. **3** (**His/ Your Eminence**) a title given to a Roman Catholic cardinal. **4** literary a piece of rising ground.
– ORIGIN Latin *eminentia*.

eminent adjective **1** respected; distinguished. **2** outstanding or obvious: *the eminent reasonableness of their claim.*
– DERIVATIVES **eminently** adverb.

emir /e-meer/ (also **amir**) noun a title of various Muslim (mainly Arab) rulers.
– ORIGIN Arabic, 'commander'.

emirate /em-i-ruht/ noun the rank, lands, or reign of an emir.

emissary /em-i-suh-ri/ noun (pl. **emissaries**) a person sent as a diplomatic representative on a special mission.
– ORIGIN Latin *emissarius* 'scout, spy'.

emission /i-mi-sh'n/ noun **1** the action of emitting something, especially heat, light, gas, or radiation. **2** a substance which is emitted.

emit verb (**emits, emitting, emitted**) **1** discharge or give out gas, radiation, etc. **2** make a sound.
– DERIVATIVES **emitter** noun.
– ORIGIN Latin *emittere*.

Emmental /em-uhn-tahl/ (also **Emmenthal**) noun a hard Swiss cheese with holes in it, similar to Gruyère.
– ORIGIN a valley in Switzerland where the cheese was first made.

Emmy noun (pl. **Emmys**) (in the US) a statuette awarded annually to an outstanding television programme or performer.
– ORIGIN said to be from *Immy*, short for *image orthicon tube* (a kind of television camera tube).

emollient /i-mol-li-uhnt/ adjective **1** softening or soothing the skin. **2** attempting to avoid conflict; calming. • noun a substance that softens the skin.
– ORIGIN from Latin *emollire* 'make soft'.

emolument /i-mol-yuu-muhnt/ noun formal a salary, fee, or benefit from employment.
– ORIGIN Latin *emolumentum*.

emote /i-moht/ verb show emotion in an exaggerated way: *he failed to cry, or at least emote, when Princess Diana died.*
– ORIGIN from EMOTION.

emoticon /i-moh-ti-kon, i-mo-ti-kon/ noun a representation of a facial expression such as a smile, formed with keyboard characters and used in email or texting to show the writer's feelings.
– ORIGIN blend of EMOTION and ICON.

emotion noun **1** a strong feeling, such as joy or anger. **2** instinctive feeling as distinguished from reasoning or knowledge.
– DERIVATIVES **emotionless** adjective.
– ORIGIN from Latin *emovere* 'disturb'.

emotional adjective **1** relating to a person's emotions. **2** showing intense feeling: *an emotional speech.* **3** easily affected by or openly displaying emotion: *I'm emotional, sensitive, and shy.*
– DERIVATIVES **emotionalism** noun **emotionalize** (or **emotionalise**) verb **emotionally** adverb.

emotive /i-moh-tiv/ adjective arousing intense feeling.
– DERIVATIVES **emotively** adverb.

USAGE: **Emotive** and **emotional** have similar meanings but they are not exactly the same. **Emotive** means 'arousing intense feeling' (*hunting is a highly emotive issue*), while **emotional** tends to mean 'showing intense feeling' (*an emotional speech*).

empanada /em-puh-nah-duh/ noun a Spanish or Latin American pastry turnover with a savoury filling.
– ORIGIN Spanish.

empanel (also **impanel**) verb (**empanels, empanelling, empanelled;** US **empanels, empaneling, empaneled**) enrol a jury or enrol someone on to a jury.
– DERIVATIVES **empanelment** noun.
– ORIGIN Old French *empaneller*.

empathize (or **empathise**) /em-puh-thyz/ verb understand and share the feelings of another.

empathy /em-puh-thi/ noun the ability to understand and share the feelings of another person.
– DERIVATIVES **empathetic** adjective **empathic** /em-path-ik/ adjective.
– ORIGIN Greek *empatheia*.

USAGE: Do not confuse **empathy** and **sympathy**. **Empathy** means 'the ability to understand and share the feelings of another person' (*the artist developed a considerable empathy with his elderly subject*), whereas **sympathy** means 'the feeling of being sorry for someone who is unhappy or in difficulty' (*they had great sympathy for the flood victims*).

emperor noun the ruler of an empire.
– ORIGIN Latin *imperator* 'military commander'.

emperor penguin noun the largest kind of penguin, which breeds in the Antarctic and has a yellow patch on each side of the head.

emphasis /em-fuh-siss/ noun (pl. **emphases** /em-fuh-seez/) **1** special importance, value, or prominence given to something: *management is placing greater emphasis on improving productivity.* **2** stress given to a word or words in speaking.
– ORIGIN Greek.

emphasize (or **emphasise**) verb give special importance or prominence to something.

emphatic adjective **1** showing or giving emphasis. **2** definite and clear: *an emphatic win.*
– DERIVATIVES **emphatically** adverb.

emphysema /em-fi-see-muh/ (also **pulmonary emphysema**) noun a condition in which the air sacs of the lungs are damaged

e

and enlarged, causing breathlessness.
– ORIGIN Greek *emphusēma*.

empire noun 1 a large group of states ruled over by a single monarch or ruling authority. 2 a large commercial organization under the control of one person or group: *an entertainment empire*.
– ORIGIN Latin *imperium*.

Empire line noun a style of women's clothing having a waistline cut just under the bust and a low neckline, first popular during the First Empire (1804–15) in France.

empirical /em-**pi**-rik-uhl/ (also **empiric**) adjective based on observation or experience rather than theory or logic: *empirical studies of seed dispersal*.
– DERIVATIVES **empirically** adverb.
– ORIGIN Greek *empeirikos*.

empiricism /em-**pi**-ri-si-z'm/ noun the theory that all knowledge is derived from experience and observation.
– DERIVATIVES **empiricist** noun & adjective.

emplacement noun a structure or platform where a gun is placed for firing.

employ verb 1 give work to someone and pay them for it. 2 make use of: *the methods they employed to collect the data*. 3 keep someone occupied.
– PHRASES **in the employ of** employed by.
– DERIVATIVES **employability** noun **employable** adjective.
– ORIGIN Old French *employer*.

employee noun a person employed for wages or a salary.

employer noun a person or organization that employs people.

employment noun 1 the action of employing someone or something. 2 the state of having paid work: *a fall in the numbers in full-time employment*. 3 a person's work or profession.

emporium /em-**por**-i-uhm/ noun (pl. **emporia** /em-**por**-i-uh/ or **emporiums**) a large store selling a wide variety of goods.
– ORIGIN Greek *emporion*.

empower verb 1 give authority or power to someone. 2 make someone stronger or more confident.
– DERIVATIVES **empowerment** noun.

empress /em-priss/ noun 1 a female emperor. 2 the wife or widow of an emperor.

empty adjective (**emptier**, **emptiest**) 1 containing nothing; not filled or occupied. 2 not likely to be fulfilled: *an empty threat*. 3 having no meaning or purpose: *an empty life going nowhere*. •verb (**empties**, **emptying**, **emptied**) 1 remove the contents from a container. 2 (of a place, vehicle, or container) become empty: *the bus emptied in a flash*. 3 (of a river) flow into the sea or a lake. •noun (pl. **empties**) informal a bottle or glass left empty of its contents.
– DERIVATIVES **emptily** adverb **emptiness** noun.
– ORIGIN Old English, 'at leisure, empty'.

empty-handed adjective having failed to obtain or achieve what one wanted.

empty-headed adjective unintelligent and foolish.

empty nester noun informal, chiefly N. Amer. a parent whose children have grown up and left home.

empyrean /em-py-**ree**-uhn/ noun (**the empyrean**) literary heaven or the sky.
– ORIGIN Greek *empurios*, referring to the highest part of heaven.

EMS abbreviation European Monetary System.

EMU abbreviation Economic and Monetary Union.

emu noun a large flightless fast-running Australian bird similar to an ostrich.
– ORIGIN Portuguese *ema*.

emulate /em-yuu-layt/ verb try to do as well as or better than a person or an achievement.
– DERIVATIVES **emulation** noun **emulator** noun.
– ORIGIN Latin *aemulari* 'to rival or equal'.

emulsifier noun a substance that stabilizes an emulsion, especially an additive used to stabilize processed foods.

emulsify /i-**mul**-si-fy/ verb (**emulsifies**, **emulsifying**, **emulsified**) make into or become an emulsion.
– DERIVATIVES **emulsifiable** adjective **emulsification** noun.

emulsion noun 1 a liquid in which particles of one liquid are evenly dispersed in the other. 2 a type of matt paint for walls. 3 a light-sensitive coating for photographic films and plates, containing crystals of a silver compound dispersed in a medium such as gelatin.
– ORIGIN Latin.

enable verb 1 provide someone with the ability or means to do something. 2 make something possible. 3 chiefly Computing make a device or system operational. 4 (as adj. **-enabled**) adapted for use with the specified application or system: *WAP-enabled mobile phones*.
– DERIVATIVES **enablement** noun **enabler** noun.

enact verb 1 make a bill or other proposal law. 2 act out a role or play.
– DERIVATIVES **enactor** noun.

enactment noun 1 the process of enacting something. 2 a law that has been passed.

enamel noun 1 a coloured shiny substance applied to metal, glass, or pottery for decoration or protection. 2 the hard glossy substance that covers the crown of a tooth. 3 a paint that dries to give a smooth, hard coat. •verb (**enamels**, **enamelling**, **enamelled**; US **enamels**, **enameling**, **enameled**) (usu. as adj. **enamelled**) coat or decorate something with enamel.
– DERIVATIVES **enameller** noun.
– ORIGIN Old French *amail* 'enamel'.

enamour /i-**nam**-er/ (US **enamor**) verb (**be enamoured of/with/by**) be filled with love or admiration for: *half the village are enamoured of her*.
– ORIGIN Old French *enamourer*.

en bloc /on **blok**/ adverb all together or all at once.
– ORIGIN French.

encamp verb settle in or establish a camp.

encampment noun 1 a place where a camp is set up. 2 a prehistoric enclosed or fortified site, especially an Iron Age hill fort.

encapsulate /in-**kap**-syuu-layt/ verb 1 express clearly and in few words: *can you encapsulate the idea in two sentences?* 2 enclose something

in a capsule or other container.
- DERIVATIVES **encapsulation** noun.

encase verb enclose or cover something in a case or close-fitting surround.
- DERIVATIVES **encasement** noun.

encash verb Brit. convert a cheque, money order, etc. into money.
- DERIVATIVES **encashment** noun.

encaustic /en-**kaw**-stik/ adjective (in painting and ceramics) decorated with coloured clays or pigments mixed with hot wax, which are burnt in as an inlay. • noun the art or process of encaustic painting.
- ORIGIN Greek *enkaustikos*.

encephalitis /en-sef-uh-**ly**-tiss/ noun inflammation of the brain.
- DERIVATIVES **encephalitic** adjective.
- ORIGIN from Greek *enkephalos* 'brain'.

encephalography /en-sef-uh-**log**-ruh-fi, en-kef-uh-**log**-ruh-fi/ noun any of various techniques for recording the structure or electrical activity of the brain.
- DERIVATIVES **encephalogram** /en-**sef**-uh-loh-gram, en-**kef**-uh-loh-gram/ noun.

encephalomyelitis /en-sef-uh-loh-my-uh-**ly**-tiss, en-kef-uh-loh-my-uh-**ly**-tiss/ noun inflammation of the brain and spinal cord, typically caused by acute infection with a virus.

encephalopathy /en-sef-uh-**lop**-uh-thi, en-kef-uh-**lop**-uh-thi/ noun (pl. **encephalopathies**) a disease in which the functioning of the brain is affected, especially by viral infection or toxins in the blood.

enchant verb 1 fill someone with delight. 2 put someone under a spell.
- DERIVATIVES **enchanter** noun **enchantment** noun **enchantress** noun.
- ORIGIN French *enchanter*.

enchanting adjective delightfully charming or attractive.
- DERIVATIVES **enchantingly** adverb.

enchilada /en-chi-**lah**-duh/ noun a tortilla filled with meat or cheese and served with chilli sauce.
- ORIGIN Latin American Spanish.

encipher verb convert something into a coded form.
- DERIVATIVES **encipherment** noun.

encircle verb surround or form a circle around someone or something.
- DERIVATIVES **encirclement** noun.

enclave /en-**klayv**/ noun 1 a small territory surrounded by a larger territory whose inhabitants are of a different nationality or culture. 2 a group that is different from those surrounding it: *the engineering department is a male enclave*.
- ORIGIN from Old French *enclaver* 'enclose'.

enclose verb 1 surround or close off on all sides: *breakwaters enclosed the harbour*. 2 (**enclose something in/within**) place an object inside a container. 3 place another document or an object in an envelope together with a letter.
- ORIGIN Old French *enclore*.

enclosure noun 1 an area that is enclosed by a fence, wall, or other barrier. 2 a document or object placed in an envelope together with a letter.

encode verb convert something into a coded form.
- DERIVATIVES **encoder** noun.

encomium /en-koh-mi-uhm/ noun (pl. **encomiums** or **encomia** /en-**koh**-mi-uh/) formal a speech or piece of writing praising someone or something.
- ORIGIN Greek *enkōmion* 'eulogy'.

encompass /in-**kum**-puhss/ verb 1 include a wide range or number of things. 2 surround or cover: *the estate encompasses twelve acres*.

encore /**ong**-kor/ noun a repeated or additional performance of an item at the end of a concert, as called for by an audience. • exclamation again! (as called by an audience at the end of a concert).
- ORIGIN French, 'still, again'.

encounter verb 1 unexpectedly be faced with something difficult. 2 unexpectedly meet someone. • noun 1 an unexpected or casual meeting. 2 a confrontation or difficult struggle: *his close encounter with death*.
- ORIGIN Old French *encontrer*.

encourage verb 1 give support, confidence, or hope to someone. 2 help an activity, belief, etc. to develop.
- DERIVATIVES **encourager** noun **encouraging** adjective.
- ORIGIN French *encourager*.

encouragement noun 1 the action of encouraging someone to do something. 2 something that encourages someone: *being selected as one of the best cities in Asia is a great encouragement to the city's staff*.

encroach verb 1 (**encroach on**) gradually intrude on a person's territory, rights, etc. 2 advance gradually beyond expected or acceptable limits: *the sea has encroached all round the coast*.
- DERIVATIVES **encroachment** noun.
- ORIGIN Old French *encrochier* 'seize'.

en croute /on **kroot**/ adjective & adverb in a pastry crust.
- ORIGIN French.

encrust verb cover something with a hard surface layer.
- DERIVATIVES **encrustation** noun.

encrypt /en-**kript**/ verb convert something into code.
- DERIVATIVES **encryption** noun.
- ORIGIN from Greek *kruptos* 'hidden'.

encumber /in-**kum**-ber/ verb prevent from moving or acting freely: *they were encumbered with cameras, tape recorders, and other gadgets*.
- ORIGIN Old French *encombrer* 'block up'.

encumbrance noun 1 something that prevents freedom of action or movement. 2 Law a mortgage or other claim on property or assets.

encyclical /en-**sik**-li-k'l/ noun a letter sent by the pope to all bishops of the Roman Catholic Church.
- ORIGIN from Greek *enkuklios* 'circular, general'.

encyclopedia /en-sy-kluh-**pee**-di-uh/ (also **encyclopaedia**) noun a book or set of books giving information on many subjects or on many aspects of one subject, typically

arranged alphabetically.
– ORIGIN pseudo-Greek *enkuklopaideia*, for *enkuklios paideia* 'all-round education'.

encyclopedic /en-sy-kluh-**pee**-dik/ (also **encyclopaedic**) adjective **1** having detailed information on a wide variety of subjects: *an encyclopedic knowledge of food.* **2** relating to encyclopedias or information suitable for an encyclopedia.

encyclopedist (also **encyclopaedist**) noun a person who writes, edits, or contributes to an encyclopedia.

end noun **1** the final part of something. **2** the furthest part of something. **3** the stopping of a state or situation: *they called for an end to violence.* **4** a person's death or downfall. **5** a goal or desired result. **6** a part or share of an activity: *your end of the deal.* **7** a small piece that is left after use. **8** the part of a sports field or court defended by one team or player. • verb **1** come or bring to an end; finish. **2** (**end in**) have something as its result: *the match ended in a draw.* **3** (**end up**) eventually reach or come to a particular state or place.
– PHRASES **be the end** informal be the limit of what one can tolerate. **end it all** commit suicide. **the end of one's tether** having no patience or energy left. **in the end** eventually. **keep** (or **hold**) **one's end up** Brit. informal perform well in a demanding situation. **make** (**both**) **ends meet** earn just enough money to live on. **no end** informal very much. **no end of** informal a vast number or amount of. **on end 1** continuously. **2** upright.
– ORIGIN Old English.

endanger verb put someone or something in danger.
– DERIVATIVES **endangerment** noun.

endangered adjective in danger of becoming extinct.

endear /in-**deer**/ verb make someone popular or well liked: *her personality endeared her to everyone.*

endearing adjective inspiring affection.
– DERIVATIVES **endearingly** adverb.

endearment noun **1** a word or phrase expressing love or affection. **2** love or affection.

endeavour /in-**dev**-er/ (US **endeavor**) verb try hard to do or achieve something. • noun **1** a serious attempt to achieve something. **2** serious and prolonged effort: *the museum's treasures spanned forty thousand years of human endeavour.*
– ORIGIN from the former phrase *put oneself in devoir* 'do one's utmost'.

endemic /en-**dem**-ik/ adjective **1** (of a disease or condition) regularly found among particular people or in a certain area. **2** (of a plant or animal) native or restricted to a certain area.
– DERIVATIVES **endemism** /en-di-mi-z'm/ noun.
– ORIGIN Greek *endēmios* 'native'.

endgame noun the final stage of a game such as chess or bridge, when few pieces or cards remain.

ending noun an end or final part.

endive /**en**-dyv/ noun **1** a plant with bitter curly or smooth leaves, eaten in salads. **2** (also **Belgian endive**) N. Amer. a chicory crown.

– ORIGIN Old French.

endless adjective **1** seeming to have no limits in size or amount: *the possibilities are endless.* **2** continuing indefinitely: *video screens showing endless catwalk shows.* **3** (of a belt, chain, or tape) having the ends joined to allow for continuous action.
– DERIVATIVES **endlessly** adverb **endlessness** noun.

endmost adjective nearest to the end.

endo- combining form internal; within: *endoderm.*
– ORIGIN from Greek *endon* 'within'.

endocrine /en-duh-krin/ adjective (of a gland) producing hormones or other products directly into the blood.
– ORIGIN from Greek *krinein* 'sift'.

endocrinology /en-doh-kri-**nol**-uh-ji/ noun the branch of physiology and medicine concerned with endocrine glands and hormones.
– DERIVATIVES **endocrinologist** noun.

endogenous /en-**doj**-i-nuhss, in-**doj**-i-nuhss/ adjective technical relating to an internal cause or origin. Often contrasted with **EXOGENOUS**.
– DERIVATIVES **endogenously** adverb.

endometriosis /en-doh-mee-tri-**oh**-sis/ noun a condition in which tissue from the mucous membrane lining the womb appears in other parts of the body, causing pelvic pain.

endometrium /en-doh-**mee**-tri-uhm/ noun the mucous membrane lining the womb.
– DERIVATIVES **endometrial** adjective.
– ORIGIN from Greek *mētra* 'womb'.

endorphin /en-**dor**-fin/ noun any of a group of chemical compounds produced in the body that have a painkilling effect.
– ORIGIN blend of **ENDOGENOUS** and **MORPHINE**.

endorse /in-**dorss**/ (US & Law also **indorse**) verb **1** declare one's public approval of someone or something. **2** sign a cheque on the back to specify another person as the payee or to accept responsibility for paying it. **3** Brit. enter a note on a driving licence recording the penalty for a driving offence.
– DERIVATIVES **endorsable** adjective **endorser** noun.
– ORIGIN Latin *indorsare.*

endorsement (chiefly US also **indorsement**) noun **1** a declaration of approval: *he called for the President's endorsement of the plan.* **2** (in the UK) a note on a driving licence recording the penalty points for a driving offence.

endoscope /**en**-duh-skohp/ noun an instrument which can be introduced into the body to view its internal parts.
– DERIVATIVES **endoscopic** adjective **endoscopically** adverb **endoscopy** /en-**dos**-kuh-pi/ noun.

endoskeleton noun an internal skeleton, such as that of vertebrates.

endosperm noun the part of a seed which acts as a food store for the developing plant embryo.

endothermic adjective (of a chemical reaction) accompanied by the absorption of heat.

endow /in-**dow**/ verb **1** provide a person or institution with an income or property, especially by a bequest in a will. **2** provide

with a quality, ability, or feature: *these singers are endowed with magnificent voices.* **3** establish a university post, annual prize, etc. by donating funds.
– ORIGIN Old French *endouer*.

endowment noun **1** money given to a college or other institution to provide it with an income. **2** a natural quality or ability. ● adjective referring to a form of life insurance involving payment of a fixed sum to the insured person on a specified date, or to their estate should they die before this date.

endowment mortgage noun Brit. a mortgage linked to an endowment insurance policy which is intended to repay the sum borrowed when the policy reaches the end of its term.

endpaper noun a leaf of paper at the beginning or end of a book, fixed to the inside of the cover.

endue /in-dyoo, en-dyoo/ verb (**endues, enduing, endued**) literary (usu. **be endued with**) provide someone or something with a quality or ability.
– ORIGIN Old French *enduire*.

endurance noun **1** the ability to endure something unpleasant and prolonged. **2** the capacity of something to withstand prolonged wear and tear.

endure /in-dyoor/ verb **1** suffer something unpleasant and prolonged patiently. **2** remain in existence.
– DERIVATIVES **endurable** adjective.
– ORIGIN Latin *indurare* 'harden'.

end-user noun the person who uses a particular product.

endways (also **endwise**) adverb with the end facing upwards, forwards, or towards the viewer.

ENE abbreviation east-north-east.

enema /en-i-muh/ noun a medical procedure in which fluid is injected into the rectum, especially to empty it.
– ORIGIN Greek.

enemy noun (pl. **enemies**) **1** a person who is actively opposed or hostile to someone or something. **2** (**the enemy**) (treated as sing. or pl.) a hostile nation or its armed forces in wartime. **3** a thing that damages or opposes something: *boredom is the great enemy of happiness.*
– ORIGIN Latin *inimicus*.

energetic adjective showing or involving great energy or activity.
– DERIVATIVES **energetically** adverb.
– ORIGIN from Greek *energein* 'operate, work in or upon'.

energy noun (pl. **energies**) **1** the strength and vitality required to keep active: *she had boundless energy and a zest for life.*
2 (**energies**) the physical and mental effort that is put into something. **3** power derived from physical or chemical resources to provide light and heat or to work machines. **4** Physics the capacity of matter and radiation to perform work.
– DERIVATIVES **energize** (or **energise**) verb.
– ORIGIN Greek *energeia*.

enervate /en-er-vayt/ verb make someone feel drained of energy.

– DERIVATIVES **enervation** noun.
– ORIGIN Latin *enervare* 'weaken (by extraction of the sinews)'.

enfant terrible /on-fon te-ree-bluh/ noun (pl. **enfants terribles** pronunc. same) a person who behaves in an unconventional or controversial way.
– ORIGIN French, 'terrible child'.

enfeeble verb weaken someone or something.
– DERIVATIVES **enfeeblement** noun.

enfilade /en-fi-layd/ noun a volley of gunfire directed along a line of soldiers from end to end. ● verb direct a volley of gunfire along a line of soldiers.
– ORIGIN French.

enfold verb surround or envelop someone or something.

enforce verb **1** make sure that a law, rule, or duty is obeyed or fulfilled. **2** (often as adj. **enforced**) force or require something to happen: *months of enforced idleness.*
– DERIVATIVES **enforceable** adjective **enforcement** noun **enforcer** noun.

enfranchise /in-fran-chyz/ verb **1** give the right to vote to someone. **2** historical free a slave.
– DERIVATIVES **enfranchisement** noun.

engage verb **1** attract or involve someone's interest or attention. **2** (**engage in/with**) participate or become involved in: *he was engaged in a lively conversation with the barber.* **3** employ someone. **4** promise to do something. **5** enter into combat with an enemy force. **6** (of a part of a machine or engine) move into position so as to come into operation.
– ORIGIN French *engager*.

engaged adjective **1** busy; occupied. **2** Brit. (of a telephone line) unavailable because already in use. **3** having formally agreed to marry.

engagement noun **1** a formal agreement to get married. **2** an appointment. **3** the state of being involved in something. **4** a battle between armed forces.

engaging adjective charming and attractive.
– DERIVATIVES **engagingly** adverb.

engender /in-jen-der/ verb give rise to a feeling, situation, or condition.
– ORIGIN Old French *engendrer*.

engine noun **1** a machine with moving parts that converts power into motion. **2** (also **railway engine**) a locomotive. **3** historical a mechanical device, especially one used in warfare: *a siege engine.*
– DERIVATIVES **-engined** adjective **engineless** adjective.
– ORIGIN Latin *ingenium* 'talent, device'.

engineer noun **1** a person who designs, builds, or maintains engines, machines, or structures. **2** a person who controls an engine, especially on an aircraft or ship. **3** a person who cleverly plans something. ● verb **1** design and build a machine or structure. **2** cleverly plan something: *she engineered another meeting with him.*

engineering noun **1** the branch of science and technology concerned with the design, building, and use of engines, machines, and structures. **2** an area of study or activity concerned with development in a particular area: *software engineering.*

English noun the language of England, now used in many varieties throughout the world. • adjective relating to England.
– DERIVATIVES Englishness noun.

English breakfast noun a substantial cooked breakfast, typically including bacon and eggs.

Englishman (or **Englishwoman**) noun (pl. Englishmen or Englishwomen) a person from England.

English muffin noun North American term for MUFFIN (in sense 1).

English rose noun an attractive English girl with a delicate, fair-skinned complexion.

engorge /in-gorj/ verb (often as adj. engorged) swell or cause to swell with blood, water, etc.
– DERIVATIVES engorgement noun.
– ORIGIN Old French engorgier 'feed to excess'.

engrained adjective variant spelling of INGRAINED.

engrave verb 1 cut or carve words or a design on a hard surface. 2 cut a design as lines on a metal plate for printing. 3 (be engraved on or in) be permanently fixed in one's mind.
– DERIVATIVES engraver noun.
– ORIGIN from GRAVE³.

engraving noun 1 a print made from an engraved plate, block, or other surface. 2 the process or art of cutting or carving a design on a hard surface.

engross /in-grohss/ verb involve or occupy someone completely: he was engrossed in a computer game.
– DERIVATIVES engrossing adjective.
– ORIGIN from Latin in grosso 'wholesale'.

engulf verb 1 (of a natural force) sweep over something so as to completely surround or cover it. 2 (of a feeling) powerfully affect or overwhelm someone.
– DERIVATIVES engulfment noun.

enhance /in-hahnss/ verb increase the quality, value, or extent of: the system is intended to enhance the user's online shopping experience.
– DERIVATIVES enhancement noun enhancer noun.
– ORIGIN Old French enhauncer.

enigma /i-nig-muh/ noun a person or thing that is mysterious or difficult to understand.
– ORIGIN Greek ainigma 'riddle'.

enigmatic /en-ig-mat-ik/ adjective difficult to understand; mysterious: an enigmatic smile.
– DERIVATIVES enigmatical adjective enigmatically adverb.

enjoin verb 1 instruct or urge someone to do something. 2 (enjoin someone from) Law prohibit someone from performing an action by an injunction.
– ORIGIN Old French enjoindre.

enjoy verb 1 take pleasure in an activity or occasion. 2 (enjoy oneself) have a pleasant time. 3 possess and benefit from: these professions enjoy high status.
– ORIGIN Old French enjoier 'give joy to' or enjoïr 'enjoy'.

enjoyable adjective giving delight or pleasure.
– DERIVATIVES enjoyability noun enjoyably adverb.

enjoyment noun 1 the state or process of taking pleasure in something: the weather didn't mar our enjoyment of the trip. 2 a thing that gives pleasure. 3 the fact of having and benefiting from something.

enlarge verb 1 make or become bigger. 2 (enlarge on) speak or write about something in greater detail.
– DERIVATIVES enlarger noun.

enlargement noun 1 the action of enlarging something or the state of being enlarged. 2 a photograph that is larger than the original negative or than an earlier print.

enlighten verb 1 give someone greater knowledge and understanding about something. 2 (as adj. enlightened) rational, tolerant, and well informed.

enlightenment noun 1 the gaining of knowledge and understanding. 2 (the Enlightenment) a European intellectual movement of the late 17th and 18th centuries emphasizing reason and individualism rather than tradition.

enlist verb 1 enrol or be enrolled in the armed services. 2 ask for someone's help in doing something.
– DERIVATIVES enlistee noun enlistment noun.

enlisted man noun US a member of the armed forces below the rank of officer.

enliven verb 1 make more interesting or appealing: the vegetables are enlivened by a spicy coconut sauce. 2 make someone more cheerful or lively.

en masse /on mass/ adverb all together.
– ORIGIN French, 'in a mass'.

enmesh verb (usu. be enmeshed in) entangle someone or something.

enmity noun (pl. enmities) the state of being an enemy; hostility.
– ORIGIN Old French enemistie.

ennoble verb 1 give someone a noble rank or title. 2 give greater dignity to: ennoble the mind and uplift the spirit.
– DERIVATIVES ennoblement noun.

ennui /on-wee/ noun listlessness and dissatisfaction arising from boredom.
– ORIGIN French.

enology noun US spelling of OENOLOGY.

enormity noun (pl. enormities) 1 (the enormity of) the extreme seriousness or extent of something bad. 2 great size or scale: he shook his head at the enormity of the task. 3 a serious crime or sin.
– ORIGIN Latin enormitas, from norma 'pattern, standard'.

USAGE: The earliest meaning of enormity was 'a crime' and some people therefore object to its use in modern English as another way of saying immensity (as in the enormity of the task). However, this use is now broadly accepted in standard English.

enormous adjective very large; huge.
– DERIVATIVES enormously adverb enormousness noun.

enough determiner & pronoun as much or as many as is necessary or desirable. • adverb 1 to the required degree or extent. 2 to a moderate degree.
– PHRASES enough is enough no more will be tolerated.
– ORIGIN Old English.

en passant /en pa-**sahnt**/ adverb by the way; in passing.
– ORIGIN French.

enquire verb chiefly Brit. **1** ask someone for information. **2** (**enquire after**) ask about someone's health or situation. **3** (**enquire into**) investigate something.
– DERIVATIVES **enquirer** noun
– ORIGIN Latin *inquirere*.

enquiring adjective chiefly Brit. **1** interested in learning new things: *an open, enquiring mind.* **2** (of a look) expressing a wish for information.
– DERIVATIVES **enquiringly** adverb.

enquiry noun (pl. **enquiries**) chiefly Brit. **1** an act of asking for information. **2** an official investigation.

enrage verb make someone very angry.

enrapture verb give great pleasure to someone.
– DERIVATIVES **enrapt** adjective.

enrich verb **1** improve the quality or value of: *photography has enriched my life.* **2** make someone wealthy or wealthier.
– DERIVATIVES **enrichment** noun.

enriched uranium noun uranium containing an increased proportion of the fissile isotope U-235, making it more explosive.

enrol /in-**rohl**/ (US **enroll**) verb (**enrols, enrolling, enrolled**; US **enrolls, enrolling, enrolled**) officially register or recruit someone as a member or student.
– DERIVATIVES **enrolment** (US **enrollment**) noun.
– ORIGIN Old French *enroller*.

en route /on **root**/ adverb on the way.
– ORIGIN French.

ensconce /in-**skonss**/ verb settle in a comfortable, safe, or secret place: *he was ensconced in a conference room.*
– ORIGIN from former *sconce*, referring to a small fort or earthwork.

ensemble /on-**som**-b'l/ noun **1** a group of musicians, actors, or dancers who perform together. **2** a group of items viewed as a whole, in particular a set of clothes worn together. **3** a musical passage for a whole choir or group of instruments.
– ORIGIN French.

enshrine verb **1** preserve a right, tradition, or idea in a form that ensures it will be respected: *the train operators claim that their subsidy is enshrined in European law.* **2** place a holy or precious object in an appropriate place or container.
– DERIVATIVES **enshrinement** noun.

enshroud /in-**shrowd**/ verb literary envelop something completely and hide it from view.

ensign /en-**syn**/ noun **1** a flag, especially a military or naval one indicating nationality. **2** the lowest rank of commissioned officer in the US and some other navies, above chief warrant officer and below lieutenant.
– ORIGIN Old French *enseigne*.

enslave verb **1** make someone a slave. **2** make someone completely dominated by something.
– DERIVATIVES **enslavement** noun **enslaver** noun.

ensnare verb put someone in a difficult situation or under the control of another: *fraud ensnares the poor.*

ensue verb (**ensues, ensuing, ensued**) happen afterwards or as a result: *once the auction starts, pandemonium ensues.*
– ORIGIN Old French *ensivre*.

en suite /on **sweet**/ adjective & adverb Brit. (of a bathroom) next to and directly accessible from a bedroom.
– ORIGIN French, 'in sequence'.

ensure /in-**shoor**/ verb **1** make certain that something will occur or be so. **2** (**ensure against**) make sure that a problem does not occur.
– ORIGIN Old French *enseurer*.

USAGE: On the difference between **ensure** and **insure**, see the note at **INSURE**.

ENT abbreviation ear, nose, and throat (as a department in a hospital).

entablature /en-**tab**-luh-chuh, in-**tab**-luh-chuh/ noun Architecture the upper part of a classical building supported by columns, comprising the architrave, frieze, and cornice.
– ORIGIN Italian *intavolatura* 'boarding'.

entail verb **1** involve something as an unavoidable part or consequence: *any major surgery entails a certain degree of risk.* **2** Law limit the inheritance of property over a number of generations so that ownership remains within a family or group.
– DERIVATIVES **entailment** noun.
– ORIGIN from Old French *taille* 'notch, tax'.

entangle verb (usu. **be entangled in/with**) **1** make something tangled. **2** involve someone in a complicated situation.
– DERIVATIVES **entanglement** noun.

entente /on-**tont**/ (also **entente cordiale** /on-tont kor-di-**ahl**/) noun a friendly understanding or informal alliance between countries.
– ORIGIN from French *entente cordiale* 'friendly understanding'.

enter verb **1** come or go into a place. **2** (often **enter into**) begin to be involved in or do something: *the firm entered into talks to join the consortium.* **3** join an institution or profession. **4** register as a participant in a competition, exam, etc. **5** (**enter into**) undertake to be bound by an agreement. **6** write or key information in a book, computer, etc.
– ORIGIN Old French *entrer*.

enteric /en-**terr**-ik/ adjective relating to or occurring in the intestines.
– ORIGIN Greek *enterikos*.

enteritis /en-tuh-**ry**-tis/ noun inflammation of the small intestine, usually accompanied by diarrhoea.

enterprise noun **1** a large project. **2** a business or company. **3** initiative and resourcefulness: *their success was thanks to a mixture of talent and enterprise.*
– ORIGIN Old French, 'something undertaken'.

enterprising adjective showing initiative and resourcefulness.
– DERIVATIVES **enterprisingly** adverb.

entertain verb **1** provide someone with amusement or enjoyment. **2** receive someone as a guest and give them food and drink. **3** give

consideration to: *I entertained little hope of success.*
– ORIGIN French *entretenir.*

entertainer noun a person, such as a singer or comedian, whose job is to entertain others.

entertaining adjective providing amusement or enjoyment.
– DERIVATIVES **entertainingly** adverb.

entertainment noun 1 the provision of amusement or enjoyment. 2 an event or performance designed to entertain people.

enthral /in-**thrawl**/ (US **enthrall**) verb (**enthrals**, **enthralling**, **enthralled**; US **enthralls**, **enthralling**, **enthralled**) fascinate someone and hold their attention.
– DERIVATIVES **enthralment** (US **enthrallment**) noun.

enthrone verb mark the new reign or period of office of a monarch or bishop by a ceremony in which they sit on a throne.
– DERIVATIVES **enthronement** noun.

enthuse /in-**thyooz**/ verb 1 express great enthusiasm for something: *they enthused over my new look.* 2 make someone interested and enthusiastic.

enthusiasm noun 1 great enjoyment, interest, or approval. 2 something that arouses enthusiasm.
– ORIGIN Greek *enthous* 'possessed by a god'.

enthusiast noun a person who is full of enthusiasm for something.

enthusiastic adjective having or showing great enjoyment, interest, or approval.
– DERIVATIVES **enthusiastically** adverb.

entice /in-**tyss**/ verb persuade someone to do something by offering something pleasant or beneficial.
– DERIVATIVES **enticement** noun **enticing** adjective.
– ORIGIN Old French *enticier.*

entire /in-**ty**-er/ adjective including everything, everyone, or every part; whole.
– ORIGIN Old French *entier.*

entirely adverb wholly; completely.

entirety noun (**the entirety**) the whole of something: *the ambition to acquaint oneself with the entirety of science.*
– PHRASES **in its entirety** as a whole.

entitle verb 1 give someone a right to do or receive: *employees are normally entitled to redundancy pay.* 2 give a title to a book, play, etc.
– DERIVATIVES **entitlement** noun.

entity /**en**-ti-ti/ noun (pl. **entities**) a thing which has its own distinct and independent existence.
– ORIGIN French *entité.*

entomb verb 1 place a dead body in a tomb. 2 bury in or under something: *the miners were entombed in a tunnel all night.*
– DERIVATIVES **entombment** noun.

entomology /en-tuh-**mol**-uh-ji/ noun the branch of zoology concerned with the study of insects.
– DERIVATIVES **entomological** adjective **entomologist** noun.
– ORIGIN from Greek *entomon* 'insect'.

entourage /on-toor-**ahzh**/ noun a group of people who accompany an important person.
– ORIGIN French.

entr'acte /on-**trakt**/ noun 1 an interval between two acts of a play or opera. 2 a piece of music or a dance performed during an interval.
– ORIGIN French.

entrails plural noun a person's or animal's intestines or internal organs.
– ORIGIN Latin *intralia* 'internal things'.

entrain verb formal board a train.

entrance[1] /en-**truhnss**/ noun 1 an opening through which one may enter a place. 2 an act of entering. 3 the right, means, or opportunity to enter: *he studied at home to gain entrance to London University.*

entrance[2] /in-**trahnss**/ verb 1 fill someone with wonder and delight. 2 cast a spell on someone.
– DERIVATIVES **entrancement** noun **entrancing** adjective.

entrant noun a person who enters, joins, or takes part in something.

entrap verb (**entraps**, **entrapping**, **entrapped**) 1 catch someone or something in a trap. 2 (of a police officer) trick someone into committing a crime in order to have them prosecuted.
– DERIVATIVES **entrapment** noun.

entreat verb ask someone to do something in an earnest or emotional way.
– ORIGIN Old French *entraitier.*

entreaty noun (pl. **entreaties**) an earnest or emotional request.

entrechat /on-truh-**shah**/ noun Ballet a vertical jump during which the dancer repeatedly crosses the feet and beats them together.
– ORIGIN French.

entrecôte /on-truh-**koht**/ noun a boned steak cut off the sirloin.
– ORIGIN French.

entrée /on-**tray**/ noun 1 the main course of a meal. 2 Brit. a dish served between the first and main courses at a formal dinner. 3 the right to enter a place or social group: *their veneer of respectability gave them an entrée to the business community.*
– ORIGIN French.

entrench verb 1 establish something so firmly that change is difficult: *prejudice is entrenched in our society.* 2 establish a military force in trenches or other fortified positions.
– DERIVATIVES **entrenchment** noun.

entre nous /on-truh **noo**/ adverb between ourselves.
– ORIGIN French.

entrepôt /on-truh-**poh**/ noun a port or other place which acts as a centre for import and export.
– ORIGIN French.

entrepreneur /on-truh-pruh-**ner**/ noun a person who sets up a business or businesses, taking financial risks in the hope of profit.
– DERIVATIVES **entrepreneurial** adjective **entrepreneurialism** noun **entrepreneurially** adverb **entrepreneurism** noun.
– ORIGIN French.

entropy /**en**-truh-pi/ noun Physics a quantity expressing how much of a system's thermal energy is unavailable for conversion into mechanical work.
– DERIVATIVES **entropic** /en-**trop**-ik/ adjective.

– ORIGIN from Greek *tropē* 'transformation'.

entrust verb **1** (**entrust someone with**) give a responsibility to someone. **2** (**entrust something to**) put something into someone's care.

entry noun (pl. **entries**) **1** an act of entering. **2** an entrance, such as a door. **3** the right, means, or opportunity to enter: *she was refused entry to the meeting.* **4** an item recorded in a list, diary, account book, or reference book. **5** a person who enters a competition.

entryism noun the infiltration of a political party by members of another group, to undermine its policies or objectives.
– DERIVATIVES **entryist** noun.

entry-level adjective suitable for a beginner or first-time user.

entwine verb wind or twist things together.

E-number noun Brit. a code number preceded by the letter E, given to food additives numbered in accordance with EU directives.

enumerate /i-**nyoo**-muh-rayt/ verb **1** mention a number of things one by one. **2** formal count people or things.
– DERIVATIVES **enumerable** adjective **enumeration** noun.
– ORIGIN Latin *enumerare* 'count out'.

enumerator noun a person employed in taking a census of the population.

enunciate /i-**nun**-si-ayt/ verb **1** say or pronounce something clearly. **2** set out a policy or theory precisely.
– DERIVATIVES **enunciation** noun.
– ORIGIN Latin *enuntiare* 'announce clearly'.

enuresis /en-yoo-**ree**-sis/ noun involuntary urination, especially by children at night.
– ORIGIN Latin.

envelop /in-**vel**-uhp/ verb (**envelops, enveloping, enveloped**) wrap up, cover, or surround completely: *we were enveloped in fog and rain.*
– DERIVATIVES **envelopment** noun.
– ORIGIN Old French *envoluper*.

envelope /**en**-vuh-lohp/ noun **1** a flat paper container with a sealable flap, used to enclose a letter or document. **2** a structure or layer that covers or encloses something.
– PHRASES **push the (edge of the) envelope** informal approach or extend the limits of what is possible. [from aviation slang, relating to graphs of aerodynamic performance.]
– ORIGIN from French *envelopper* 'envelop'.

enviable /**en**-vi-uh-b'l/ adjective arousing or likely to arouse envy; desirable: *he has an enviable record of success.*
– DERIVATIVES **enviably** adverb.

envious adjective feeling or showing envy.
– DERIVATIVES **enviously** adverb.

environment noun **1** the surroundings or conditions in which a person, animal, or plant lives or operates. **2** (**the environment**) the natural world, especially as affected by human activity. **3** the overall structure within which a computer, user, or program operates.
– DERIVATIVES **environmental** adjective **environmentally** adverb.

environmentalist noun a person who is concerned about protecting the environment.
– DERIVATIVES **environmentalism** noun.

environs plural noun the area surrounding a place.
– ORIGIN French.

envisage /in-**viz**-ij/ verb **1** think of something as a possible or desirable future event. **2** form a mental picture of something.
– ORIGIN French *envisager*.

envision verb imagine something as a future possibility.

envoy /**en**-voy/ noun **1** a messenger or representative, especially one on a diplomatic mission. **2** (also **envoy extraordinary**) a diplomat ranking below ambassador and above chargé d'affaires.
– ORIGIN from French *envoyé* 'sent'.

envy noun (pl. **envies**) **1** discontented longing aroused by someone else's possessions, qualities, or luck. **2** (**the envy of**) a person or thing that arouses envy: *you can have a barbecue that will be the envy of your neighbours.* • verb (**envies, envying, envied**) long to have something that belongs to someone else.
– ORIGIN Old French *envie*.

enwrap verb (**enwraps, enwrapping, enwrapped**) cover or envelop someone or something.

enzyme /**en**-zym/ noun a substance produced by a living organism that acts as a catalyst to bring about a specific biochemical reaction.
– DERIVATIVES **enzymatic** adjective **enzymic** adjective.
– ORIGIN from modern Greek *enzumos* 'leavened'.

Eocene /**ee**-oh-seen/ adjective Geology relating to the second epoch of the Tertiary period (56.5 to 35.4 million years ago), when the first horses and whales appeared.
– ORIGIN from Greek *ēōs* 'dawn' + *kainos* 'new'.

eon noun US and technical spelling of **AEON**.

EP abbreviation **1** (of a record or compact disc) extended-play. **2** European Parliament.

ep- prefix variant spelling of **EPI-** shortened before a vowel or *h*.

épater /ay-pat-ay/ verb (in phrase **épater les bourgeois**) shock people regarded as conventional or complacent.
– ORIGIN French.

epaulette /ep-uh-let/ (US also **epaulet**) noun an ornamental shoulder piece on a military uniform.
– ORIGIN French, 'little shoulder'.

épée /ay-pay, ep-pay/ noun a sharp-pointed duelling sword, used, with the end blunted, in fencing.
– ORIGIN French, 'sword'.

ephedrine /ef-uh-dreen/ noun a drug which causes constriction of the blood vessels and widening of the bronchial passages, used to relieve asthma and hay fever.
– ORIGIN from *ephedra*, a plant which is the source of the drug.

ephemera /i-fem-uh-ruh/ plural noun items of short-lived interest or usefulness, especially those later valued by collectors.
– ORIGIN Greek, 'things lasting only a day'.

ephemeral /i-fem-uh-ruhl/ adjective lasting or living for a very short time.

e

– DERIVATIVES **ephemerality** noun **ephemerally** adverb.

epi- (also **ep-** before a vowel or *h*) prefix **1** upon: *epigraph.* **2** above: *epidermis.*
– ORIGIN from Greek *epi.*

epic noun **1** a long poem describing the adventures of heroic or legendary figures or the history of a nation. **2** a long film or book portraying heroic adventures or covering a long period of time. • adjective **1** relating to an epic. **2** grand or heroic in scale: *an epic journey around the world.*
– DERIVATIVES **epical** adjective **epically** adverb.
– ORIGIN from Greek *epos* 'word, song'.

epicene /e-pi-seen/ adjective **1** having characteristics of both sexes or no characteristics of either sex. **2** effeminate.
– ORIGIN Greek *epikoinos.*

epicentre (US **epicenter**) noun the point on the earth's surface directly above the origin of an earthquake.

epicure /e-pi-kyoor/ noun a person who takes particular pleasure in fine food and drink.
– ORIGIN from *Epicurus* (see **EPICUREAN**).

Epicurean /e-pi-kyoo-ree-uhn/ noun **1** a follower of the ancient Greek philosopher Epicurus, who taught that pleasure, particularly mental pleasure, was the highest good. **2** (**epicurean**) an epicure. • adjective **1** relating to Epicurus or his ideas. **2** (**epicurean**) relating to or suitable for an epicure.
– DERIVATIVES **Epicureanism** noun.

epidemic noun **1** a widespread occurrence of an infectious disease in a community at a particular time. **2** a widespread outbreak of something undesirable: *an epidemic of violent crime.* • adjective relating to or like an epidemic.
– ORIGIN Greek *epidēmia.*

epidemiology /e-pi-dee-mi-ol-uh-ji/ noun the study of the spread and control of diseases.
– DERIVATIVES **epidemiological** adjective **epidemiologist** noun.

epidermis /e-pi-der-miss/ noun **1** the surface layer of an animal's skin, overlying the dermis. **2** the outer layer of tissue in a plant.
– DERIVATIVES **epidermal** adjective.
– ORIGIN Greek.

epidural /e-pi-**dyoor**-uhl/ noun an anaesthetic delivered into the space around the dura mater (outermost membrane) of the spinal cord, used especially in childbirth. • adjective on or around the outermost membrane of the spinal cord.

epiglottis /e-pi-**glot**-tiss/ noun a flap of cartilage behind the root of the tongue, which descends during swallowing to cover the opening of the windpipe.
– ORIGIN Greek.

epigone /ep-ig-ohn/ noun literary a follower or imitator of a distinguished artist, philosopher, musician, etc.
– ORIGIN Greek *epigonoi* 'those born afterwards'.

epigram /e-pi-gram/ noun **1** a concise and witty saying or remark. **2** a short witty poem.
– DERIVATIVES **epigrammatic** adjective.
– ORIGIN Greek *epigramma.*

epigraph /e-pi-grahf/ noun **1** an inscription on a building, statue, or coin. **2** a short quotation introducing a book or chapter.
– ORIGIN Greek *epigraphein* 'write on'.

epilation /e-pi-lay-sh'n/ noun the removal of hair by the roots.
– DERIVATIVES **epilator** noun.
– ORIGIN French *épiler.*

epilepsy /e-pi-lep-si/ noun a disorder of the nervous system causing periodic loss of consciousness or convulsions.
– DERIVATIVES **epileptic** adjective & noun.
– ORIGIN Greek *epilēpsia,* from *epilambanein* 'seize, attack'.

epilogue /e-pi-log/ (US also **epilog**) noun a section or speech at the end of a book or play which comments on or acts as a conclusion to what has happened.
– ORIGIN Greek *epilogos.*

epiphany /i-pif-uh-ni/ noun (pl. **epiphanies**) **1** (**Epiphany**) the occasion on which Jesus appeared to the Magi (Gospel of Matthew, chapter 2). **2** (**Epiphany**) the festival commemorating this, on 6 January. **3** a moment of sudden and great revelation or understanding.
– DERIVATIVES **epiphanic** adjective.
– ORIGIN from Greek *epiphainein* 'reveal'.

epiphyte /ep-i-fyt/ noun a plant that grows on a tree or other plant but is not a parasite.
– DERIVATIVES **epiphytic** /ep-i-**fit**-ik/ adjective.
– ORIGIN from Greek *epi* 'upon' + *phuton* 'plant'.

episcopacy /i-piss-kuh-puh-si/ noun (pl. **episcopacies**) **1** the government of a Church by bishops. **2** (**the episcopacy**) the bishops of a region or church as a group.

episcopal /i-piss-kuh-puhl/ adjective **1** relating to a bishop or bishops. **2** (of a Church) governed by or having bishops.
– DERIVATIVES **episcopally** adverb.
– ORIGIN Latin *episcopus* 'bishop'.

Episcopal Church noun the Anglican Church in Scotland and the US, with elected bishops.

episcopalian /i-piss-kuh-**pay**-li-uhn/ adjective **1** relating to the government of a Church by bishops. **2** of or belonging to an episcopal Church. • noun **1** a supporter of the government of a Church by bishops. **2** (**Episcopalian**) a member of the Episcopal Church.
– DERIVATIVES **episcopalianism** noun.

episcopate /i-piss-kuh-puht/ noun **1** the position or period of office of a bishop. **2** (**the episcopate**) the bishops of a church or region as a group.

episiotomy /i-pi-si-ot-uh-mi/ noun (pl. **episiotomies**) a surgical cut that may be made at the opening of the vagina during childbirth to make a difficult delivery easier.
– ORIGIN from Greek *epision* 'pubic region'.

episode noun **1** an event or a sequence of events. **2** each of the separate instalments into which a serialized story or programme is divided.
– ORIGIN Greek *epeisodion.*

episodic /e-pi-sod-ik/ adjective **1** made up of a series of separate events. **2** occurring at irregular intervals.
– DERIVATIVES **episodically** adverb.

epistemology /i-piss-ti-**mol**-uh-ji/ noun the branch of philosophy that deals with knowledge.

– DERIVATIVES **epistemic** adjective
epistemological adjective **epistemologist** noun.
– ORIGIN Greek *epistēmē* 'knowledge'.

epistle /i-**piss**-uhl/ noun **1** formal or humorous a
letter. **2** (**Epistle**) a book of the New Testament
in the form of a letter from an Apostle.
– ORIGIN Greek *epistolē*, from *epistellein* 'send
news'.

epistolary /i-**piss**-tuh-luh-ri/ adjective
1 relating to the writing of letters. **2** (of a
literary work) in the form of letters.

epitaph /e-pi-tahf/ noun **1** words written in
memory of a person who has died, especially
as an inscription on a tombstone. **2** something
which is a reminder of a person, time, or
event: *the story makes a sorry epitaph to a great
career.*
– ORIGIN Greek *epitaphion* 'funeral oration'.

epithelium /ep-i-**thee**-li-uhm/ noun (pl.
epithelia /ep-i-**thee**-li-uh/) the thin tissue
forming the outer layer of the body's surface
and lining the alimentary canal and other
hollow structures.
– ORIGIN Latin.

epithet /e-pi-thet/ noun a word or phrase
expressing a characteristic quality of the
person or thing mentioned.
– ORIGIN Greek *epitheton.*

epitome /i-**pit**-uh-mi/ noun (**the epitome of**) a
perfect example of a quality or type: *she was
the epitome of a well-bred Englishwoman.*
– ORIGIN Greek.

epitomize (or **epitomise**) verb be a perfect
example of: *the patriotic spirit was epitomized
by the poetry of Rupert Brooke.*

epoch /ee-pok/ noun **1** a long period of time
marked by particular events or characteristics:
the Victorian epoch. **2** the beginning of a period
of history. **3** Geology a division of time that is a
subdivision of a period and is itself
subdivided into ages.
– DERIVATIVES **epochal** adjective.
– ORIGIN Greek *epokhē* 'stoppage, fixed point of
time'.

epoch-making adjective very important and
likely to have a great effect on a particular
period of time.

eponym /e-puh-nim/ noun **1** a word which
comes from the name of a person. **2** a person
after whom a discovery, invention, place, etc.
is named.

eponymous /i-**pon**-i-muhss/ adjective **1** (of a
person) giving their name to something. **2** (of
a thing) named after a particular person or
group.
– ORIGIN Greek *epōnumos.*

epoxide /i-**pok**-syd/ noun an organic compound
whose molecule contains a three-membered
ring involving an oxygen atom and two carbon
atoms.
– ORIGIN from Greek *epi-* 'in addition' + OXIDE.

epoxy /i-**pok**-si/ (also **epoxy resin**) noun (pl.
epoxies) an adhesive, plastic, paint, etc. made
from synthetic polymers containing epoxide
groups.

EPROM /ee-prom/ noun Computing a read-only
memory whose contents can be erased and
reprogrammed using special means.
– ORIGIN from *erasable programmable ROM.*

Epsom salts plural noun crystals of magnesium
sulphate used as a laxative.
– ORIGIN named after the town of *Epsom* in
Surrey, where the salts were first found
occurring naturally.

equable /ek-wuh-b'l/ adjective **1** calm and
even-tempered. **2** not varying greatly: *an
equable climate.*
– DERIVATIVES **equability** noun **equably** adverb.
– ORIGIN from Latin *aequare* 'make equal'.

equal adjective **1** being the same in quantity,
size, degree, value, or status. **2** evenly or fairly
balanced: *an equal contest.* **3** (**equal to**) having
the ability or resources to meet a challenge.
•noun a person or thing that is equal to
another. •verb (**equals, equalling, equalled**; US
equals, equaling, equaled) **1** be equal or
equivalent to something. **2** match or rival: *he
equalled the championship record.*
– ORIGIN Latin *aequalis*, from *aequus* 'even,
level, equal'.

equality noun the state of being equal.

equalize (or **equalise**) verb **1** make or become
equal. **2** Brit. level the score in a match by
scoring a goal.
– DERIVATIVES **equalization** noun.

equalizer (or **equaliser**) noun **1** a thing that has
an equalizing effect. **2** Brit. a goal that levels
the score in a match.

equally adverb **1** in an equal way or to an equal
extent: *all children should be treated equally.*
2 to an equal extent: *follow-up discussion is
equally important.* **3** in amounts or parts that
are equal.

USAGE: The expression **equally as**, as in
follow-up discussion is equally as important
should be avoided: just use **equally** or **as** on its
own.

equals sign (also **equal sign**) noun the
symbol =.

equanimity /ek-wuh-**nim**-i-ti/ noun calmness
of temper; composure.
– ORIGIN Latin *aequanimitas.*

equate /i-**kwayt**/ verb **1** consider one thing as
equal or equivalent to another: *customers
equate their name with quality.* **2** make two or
more things the same or equal to each other:
we must equate supply and demand.

equation /i-**kway**-zh'n/ noun **1** Mathematics a
statement that the values of two
mathematical expressions are equal (indicated
by the sign =). **2** Chemistry a formula
representing the changes which occur in a
chemical reaction. **3** the process of equating
one thing with another.

equator /i-**kway**-ter/ noun an imaginary line
around the earth at equal distances from the
poles, dividing the earth into northern and
southern hemispheres.
– ORIGIN Latin *aequator*, in the phrase *circulus
aequator diei et noctis* 'circle equalizing day
and night'.

equatorial /ek-wuh-**tor**-i-uhl/ adjective
relating to, at, or near the equator.
– DERIVATIVES **equatorially** adverb.

equerry /ek-wuh-ri/ noun (pl. **equerries**) **1** a
male officer of the British royal household
acting as an attendant to a member of the
royal family. **2** historical an officer of a prince's

e

or nobleman's household who was responsible for the stables.
– ORIGIN Old French *esquierie* 'company of squires, prince's stables'.

equestrian /i-**kwess**-tri-uhn/ adjective
1 relating to horse riding. **2** depicting or representing a person on horseback: *an equestrian statue.* ● noun (fem. **equestrienne** /i-kwess-tri-**en**/) a person riding a horse.
– ORIGIN from Latin *equus* 'horse'.

equestrianism noun the skill or sport of horse riding.

equi- /**ee**-kwi, **ek**-wi/ combining form equal; equally: *equidistant.*
– ORIGIN Latin *aequus* 'equal'.

equidistant adjective at equal distances.
– DERIVATIVES **equidistance** noun.

equilateral /ee-kwi-**lat**-uh-ruhl, ek-wi-**lat**-uh-ruhl/ adjective (of a triangle) having all sides the same length.

equilibrium /ee-kwi-**lib**-ri-uhm, ek-wi-**lib**-ri-uhm/ noun (pl. **equilibria** /ee-kwi-**lib**-ri-uh, ek-wi-**lib**-ri-uh/) **1** a state in which opposing forces or influences are balanced. **2** the state of being physically balanced. **3** a calm state of mind.
– ORIGIN Latin *aequilibrium*, from *libra* 'balance'.

equine /**ek**-wyn/ adjective **1** relating to horses or other members of the horse family. **2** resembling a horse. ● noun a horse or other member of the horse family.
– ORIGIN from Latin *equus* 'horse'.

equinoctial /ee-kwi-**nok**-sh'l, ek-wi-**nok**-sh'l/ adjective **1** relating to or at the time of the equinox. **2** at or near the equator.

equinox /**ee**-kwi-noks, **ek**-kwi-noks/ noun the time or date (twice each year, about 22 September and 20 March) at which the sun crosses the celestial equator and when day and night are of equal length.
– ORIGIN Latin *aequinoctium*, from *aequus* 'equal' + *nox* 'night'.

equip verb (**equips**, **equipping**, **equipped**) **1** supply with the items needed for a purpose: *all bedrooms are equipped with a colour TV.* **2** prepare someone for a situation, activity, or task: *a course which equips students with the skills needed to enter the profession.*
– ORIGIN French *équiper*.

equipage /**ek**-wi-pij/ noun **1** old use equipment. **2** historical a carriage and horses with attendants.

equipment noun **1** the items needed for a particular purpose. **2** the process of supplying these items.

equipoise /**ek**-wi-poyz/ noun a state of balance between different forces or interests.

equitable /**ek**-wi-tuh-b'l/ adjective treating everyone fairly and equally.
– DERIVATIVES **equitably** adverb.

equitation /ek-wi-**tay**-sh'n/ noun formal the art and practice of horse riding.
– ORIGIN Latin.

equity /**ek**-wi-ti/ noun (pl. **equities**) **1** the quality of being fair and impartial. **2** Law a branch of law that developed alongside common law and is concerned with fairness and justice. **3** the value of a mortgaged

property after all the charges and debts secured against it have been paid. **4** the value of the shares issued by a company. **5** (**equities**) stocks and shares that do not pay a fixed amount of interest.
– ORIGIN Latin *aequitas*, from *aequus* 'equal'.

equivalent /i-**kwiv**-uh-luhnt/ adjective (often **equivalent to**) **1** equal in value, amount, function, meaning, etc. **2** having the same or a similar effect. ● noun a person or thing that is equivalent to another.
– DERIVATIVES **equivalence** noun **equivalency** noun **equivalently** adverb.
– ORIGIN from Latin *aequivalere* 'be of equal worth'.

equivocal /i-**kwiv**-uh-k'l/ adjective unclear in meaning or intention; ambiguous.
– DERIVATIVES **equivocally** adverb.
– ORIGIN from Latin *aequus* 'equal' + *vocare* 'to call'.

equivocate /i-**kwiv**-uh-kayt/ verb use ambiguous or evasive language.
– DERIVATIVES **equivocation** noun.

ER abbreviation **1** Queen Elizabeth. [from Latin *Elizabetha Regina*.] **2** N. Amer. emergency room.

Er symbol the chemical element erbium.

era /**eer**-uh/ noun **1** a long and distinct period of history. **2** Geology a major division of time that is a subdivision of an aeon and is itself subdivided into periods.
– ORIGIN Latin *aera*, plural of *aes* 'money, counter'.

eradicate /i-**rad**-i-kayt/ verb remove or destroy something completely.
– DERIVATIVES **eradication** noun **eradicator** noun.
– ORIGIN Latin *eradicare* 'tear up by the roots', from *radix* 'root'.

erase /i-**rayz**/ verb **1** rub something out. **2** remove all traces of something.
– DERIVATIVES **erasable** adjective **erasure** noun.
– ORIGIN Latin *eradere* 'scrape away'.

eraser noun a piece of rubber or plastic used to rub out something written.

erbium /**er**-bi-uhm/ noun a soft silvery-white metallic chemical element of the lanthanide series.
– ORIGIN named after *Ytterby* in Sweden (see **YTTERBIUM**).

ere /air/ preposition & conjunction literary or old use before (in time).
– ORIGIN Old English.

erect adjective **1** rigidly upright or straight. **2** (of a body part) enlarged and rigid, especially in sexual excitement. ● verb **1** construct a building, wall, etc. **2** create or establish: *the party that erected the welfare state.*
– DERIVATIVES **erectly** adverb **erectness** noun **erector** noun.
– ORIGIN Latin *erigere* 'set up'.

erectile /i-**rek**-tyl/ adjective able to become erect.

erection noun **1** the action of erecting a structure or object. **2** a building or other upright structure. **3** an erect state of the penis.

eremite /**e**-ri-myt/ noun a Christian hermit.
– DERIVATIVES **eremitic** adjective **eremitical** adjective.
– ORIGIN Latin *eremita*.

erg noun Physics a unit of work or energy.
– ORIGIN from Greek *ergon* 'work'.

ergo /er-goh/ adverb therefore.
– ORIGIN Latin.

ergonomic /er-guh-**nom**-ik/ adjective
1 relating to ergonomics. **2** designed to improve people's efficiency in their working environment.
– DERIVATIVES **ergonomically** adverb.

ergonomics plural noun (treated as sing.) the study of people's efficiency in their working environment.
– ORIGIN Greek *ergon* 'work'.

ergot /er-got/ noun a disease of rye and other cereals, caused by a fungus.
– ORIGIN French.

erica /e-ri-kuh/ noun a plant of a large genus including the heaths.
– ORIGIN Greek *ereikē*.

ericaceous /e-ri-**kay**-shuhss/ adjective relating to plants of the heather family.

Erin /e-rin/ noun old use or literary Ireland.
– ORIGIN Irish.

Eritrean /e-ri-**tray**-uhn/ noun a person from the independent state of Eritrea in NE Africa.
• adjective relating to Eritrea.

ERM abbreviation Exchange Rate Mechanism.

ermine /er-min/ noun (pl. same or **ermines**) **1** a stoat. **2** the white winter fur of the stoat, used for trimming the ceremonial robes of judges or members of the nobility.
– ORIGIN Old French *hermine*, probably from Latin *mus Armenius* 'Armenian mouse'.

Ernie noun (in the UK) the computer that randomly selects the prize-winning numbers of Premium Bonds.
– ORIGIN from *electronic random number indicator equipment*.

erode /i-rohd/ verb **1** gradually wear or be worn away. **2** gradually destroy or weaken: *the country's manufacturing base has been severely eroded.*
– ORIGIN Latin *erodere*, from *rodere* 'gnaw'.

erogenous /i-**roj**-i-nuhss/ adjective (of a part of the body) sensitive to sexual stimulation.
– ORIGIN from Greek *erōs* 'sexual love'.

erosion /i-**roh**-zh'n/ noun the process of eroding something or result of being eroded.
– DERIVATIVES **erosional** adjective **erosive** adjective.

erotic /i-**rot**-ik/ adjective relating to or arousing sexual desire or excitement.
– DERIVATIVES **erotically** adverb.
– ORIGIN Greek *erōtikos*, from *erōs* 'sexual love'.

erotica plural noun (treated as sing. or pl.) erotic literature or art.

eroticism noun **1** the quality of being erotic. **2** sexual desire or excitement.

eroticize (or **eroticise**) verb give something the quality of being able to arouse sexual desire or excitement.
– DERIVATIVES **eroticization** noun.

erotomania /i-ro-toh-**may**-ni-uh/ noun
1 excessive sexual desire. **2** a delusion in which a person believes that another person is in love with them.
– DERIVATIVES **erotomaniac** noun.

err /er/ verb **1** make a mistake. **2** (often as adj. **erring**) do wrong: *her erring husband.*
– PHRASES **err on the side of** display more

rather than less of a particular quality in one's actions: *they erred on the side of caution.*
– ORIGIN Latin *errare* 'to stray'.

errand noun a short journey made to deliver or collect something, especially on someone else's behalf.
– ORIGIN Old English, 'message, mission'.

errant /e-ruhnt/ adjective **1** formal or humorous straying from the accepted course or standards. **2** old use or literary travelling in search of adventure.
– DERIVATIVES **errantry** noun.
– ORIGIN sense 1 from Latin *errare* 'err'; sense 2 from Old French, 'travelling', from Latin *iterare*.

erratic /i-**rat**-ik/ adjective not happening at regular times or following a regular pattern; unpredictable: *her behaviour was becoming erratic.*
– DERIVATIVES **erratically** adverb.

erratum /e-**rah**-tuhm/ noun (pl. **errata** /e-**rah**-tuh/) an error in printing or writing, especially as noted in a list added to a book or published in a subsequent edition of a newspaper or journal.
– ORIGIN Latin, 'error'.

erroneous /i-**roh**-ni-uhss/ adjective wrong; incorrect.
– DERIVATIVES **erroneously** adverb.
– ORIGIN Latin *erroneus*, from *errare* 'to stray, err'.

error noun **1** a mistake. **2** the state of being wrong in behaviour or judgement: *the crash was caused by human error.* **3** technical the amount by which something is inaccurate in a calculation or measurement.
– ORIGIN Latin, from *errare* 'to stray, err'.

ersatz /er-sats/ adjective **1** (of a product) made or used as a poor-quality substitute for something else. **2** not real or genuine: *ersatz emotion.*
– ORIGIN German, 'replacement'.

Erse /erss/ noun the Scottish or Irish Gaelic language.
– ORIGIN early Scots form of **IRISH**.

erstwhile adjective former. • adverb old use formerly.

eructation /i-ruk-**tay**-shuhn/ noun formal a belch.
– ORIGIN Latin.

erudite /e-roo-dyt/ adjective having or showing knowledge or learning.
– DERIVATIVES **erudition** noun.
– ORIGIN Latin *eruditus*.

erupt verb **1** (of a volcano) forcefully eject lava, rocks, ash, or gases. **2** break out suddenly: *fierce fighting erupted.* **3** give way to feelings in a sudden and noisy way: *the crowd erupted into applause.* **4** (of a spot, rash, etc.) suddenly appear on the skin.
– DERIVATIVES **eruptive** adjective.
– ORIGIN Latin *erumpere* 'break out'.

eruption noun an act or instance of erupting.

erysipelas /e-ri-**sip**-i-luhss/ noun a skin disease causing large raised red patches on the face and legs.
– ORIGIN Greek *erusipelas*.

erythrocyte /i-**rith**-ruh-syt/ noun a blood cell

which contains haemoglobin and transports oxygen to the tissues; a red blood cell.

Es symbol the chemical element einsteinium.

ESA abbreviation **1** (in the UK) Environmentally Sensitive Area. **2** European Space Agency.

escalate /ess-kuh-layt/ verb **1** increase rapidly: *costs started to escalate.* **2** become more intense or serious: *the crisis escalated.*
– DERIVATIVES **escalation** noun.
– ORIGIN first in the sense 'travel on an escalator': from **ESCALATOR**.

escalator noun a moving staircase consisting of a circulating belt of steps driven by a motor.
– ORIGIN French *escalade*, referring to a former method of military attack using ladders.

escalope /i-ska-luhp/ noun a thin slice of meat, especially veal, coated in breadcrumbs and fried.
– ORIGIN Old French, 'shell'.

escapade /ess-kuh-payd/ noun an incident involving daring and adventure.

escape verb **1** break free from imprisonment or control. **2** elude or get free from someone. **3** succeed in avoiding something dangerous or undesirable: *she narrowly escaped death.* **4** fail to be noticed or remembered by: *his name escapes me.* **5** (of gas, liquid, or heat) leak from a container. • noun **1** an act of escaping. **2** a means of escaping. **3** (also **escape key**) Computing a key which interrupts the current operation.
– DERIVATIVES **escapee** noun **escaper** noun.
– ORIGIN Old French *eschaper*.

escape clause noun a clause in a contract which specifies the conditions under which a party can be freed from an obligation.

escapement /i-skayp-muhnt/ noun **1** a mechanism that connects and regulates the moving parts in a clock or watch. **2** the part of the mechanism in a piano that enables the hammer to fall back as soon as it has struck the string. **3** a mechanism in a typewriter that shifts the carriage a small fixed amount to the left after a key is pressed and released.

escapism noun the habit of trying to distract oneself from unpleasant realities by engaging in fantasy or forms of entertainment.
– DERIVATIVES **escapist** noun & adjective.

escapologist /ess-kuh-pol-uh-jist/ noun an entertainer who specializes in breaking free from ropes, handcuffs, and chains.
– DERIVATIVES **escapology** noun.

escarpment /i-skarp-muhnt/ noun a long, steep slope at the edge of a plateau or separating areas of land at different heights.
– ORIGIN French *escarpement*.

eschatology /ess-kuh-tol-uh-ji/ noun the part of theology concerned with death, judgement, and destiny.
– DERIVATIVES **eschatological** adjective.
– ORIGIN Greek *eskhatos* 'last'.

escheat /iss-cheet/ noun chiefly historical the return of property to the state, or (in feudal law) to a lord, if the owner should die without legal heirs.
– ORIGIN Old French *eschete*.

eschew /iss-choo/ verb deliberately avoid doing or being involved in something.
– DERIVATIVES **eschewal** noun.

– ORIGIN Old French *eschiver*.

escort noun /ess-kort/ **1** a person, vehicle, or group accompanying another in order to protect or guard them or as a mark of rank. **2** a person who accompanies a member of the opposite sex to a social event. **3** euphemistic a prostitute. • verb /i-skort/ accompany a person, vehicle, or group somewhere: *he escorted her back to her hotel.*
– ORIGIN French *escorte*.

escritoire /ess-kri-twar/ noun a small writing desk with drawers and compartments.
– ORIGIN French.

escrow /i-skroh/ noun Law a bond, deed, or other document kept by a third party and taking effect only when a specified condition has been fulfilled.
– ORIGIN Old French *escroe* 'scrap, scroll'.

escudo /ess-kyoo-doh/ noun (pl. **escudos**) the basic unit of money of Portugal and the Cape Verde Islands (replaced in Portugal by the euro in 2002).
– ORIGIN Portuguese.

esculent /es-kyuu-luhnt/ adjective formal fit to be eaten.
– ORIGIN Latin *esculentus*.

escutcheon /i-sku-chuhn/ noun **1** a shield or emblem bearing a coat of arms. **2** a flat piece of metal framing a keyhole, door handle, or light switch.
– PHRASES **a blot on one's escutcheon** something that damages one's reputation or character.
– ORIGIN Old French *escuchon*, from Latin *scutum* 'shield'.

ESE abbreviation east-south-east.

-ese suffix forming adjectives and nouns: **1** referring to an inhabitant or language of a country or city: *Chinese.* **2** often derogatory (especially with reference to language) referring to character or style: *journalese.*
– ORIGIN from Latin *-ensis*.

esker /ess-kuh/ noun Geology a long winding ridge of sediment deposited by meltwater from a retreating glacier or ice sheet.
– ORIGIN Irish *eiscir*.

Eskimo noun (pl. same or **Eskimos**) **1** a member of a people inhabiting northern Canada, Alaska, Greenland, and eastern Siberia. **2** either of the two main languages of the Eskimo (Inuit and Yupik). • adjective relating to the Eskimos or their languages.
– ORIGIN an Algonquian word, perhaps in the sense 'people speaking a different language'.

USAGE: The word **Eskimo** is now regarded by some people as offensive and the peoples inhabiting the regions of northern Canada and parts of Greenland and Alaska prefer to call themselves **Inuit**. The term **Eskimo**, however, is the only term that covers both the Inuit and the Yupik (peoples of Siberia, the Aleutian islands, and Alaska), and is still widely used.

ESL abbreviation English as a second language.
ESN abbreviation electronic serial number.
ESOL abbreviation English for speakers of other languages.
esophagus etc. noun US spelling of **OESOPHAGUS** etc.

esoteric /e-suh-**te**-rik, ee-suh-**te**-rik/ adjective intended for or understood by only a small number of people who have a specialized knowledge of something.
– DERIVATIVES **esoterically** adverb.
– ORIGIN Greek *esōterikos*.

esoterica /e-suh-**ter**-i-kuh, ee-suh-**ter**-i-kuh/ plural noun subjects or publications understood by or intended for people with a specialized knowledge of something.

ESP abbreviation extrasensory perception.

espadrille /ess-puh-**dril**/ noun a light canvas shoe with a plaited fibre sole.
– ORIGIN French.

espalier /i-**spal**-yer, e-**spal**-yer/ noun a fruit tree or ornamental shrub whose branches are trained to grow flat against a wall.
– ORIGIN French.

esparto /e-**spah**-toh, i-**spah**-toh/ (also **esparto grass**) noun (pl. **espartos**) a coarse grass native to Spain and North Africa, used to make ropes, wickerwork, and paper.
– ORIGIN Spanish.

especial adjective **1** notable; special: *the interior carvings are of especial interest.* **2** for or belonging chiefly to one person or thing.
– ORIGIN Latin *specialis.*

especially adverb **1** used to single out one person or thing over all others: *both of them were nervous, especially Geoffrey.* **2** to a great extent; very much: *he didn't especially like dancing.*

USAGE: Although similar in meaning, the words **especially** and **specially** are not interchangeable. In the broadest terms both can mean 'particularly' (*a song written especially for Jonathan* or *a song written specially for Jonathan*). However, in sentences such as *both of them were nervous, especially Geoffrey,* where **especially** means 'in particular, chiefly', **specially** is informal and should not be used in written English.

Esperanto /ess-puh-**ran**-toh/ noun an artificial language invented in 1887 as an international means of communication.
– DERIVATIVES **Esperantist** noun.
– ORIGIN from *Dr Esperanto*, a pen name of the inventor; the literal sense is 'one who hopes'.

espionage /ess-pi-uh-**nah**zh/ noun the practice of spying or of using spies.
– ORIGIN French.

esplanade /ess-pluh-**nayd**/ noun a long, open, level area, typically beside the sea, along which people may walk for pleasure.
– ORIGIN French.

espousal /i-**spow**-z'l/ noun an act of adopting or supporting a cause, belief, or way of life: *his espousal of unorthodox religious views.*

espouse /i-**spowz**/ verb adopt or support a cause, belief, or way of life.
– ORIGIN Old French *espouser.*

espresso /ess-**press**-oh/ (also **expresso** /ex-**press**-oh/) noun (pl. **espressos**) strong black coffee made by forcing steam through ground coffee beans.
– ORIGIN from Italian *caffè espresso* 'pressed out coffee'.

esprit /e-**spree**/ noun liveliness.
– ORIGIN French.

esprit de corps /e-spree duh **kor**/ noun a feeling of pride and loyalty uniting the members of a group.
– ORIGIN French, 'spirit of the body'.

espy /i-**spy**/ verb (**espies, espying, espied**) literary catch sight of someone or something.
– ORIGIN Old French *espier.*

Esq. abbreviation Esquire.

-esque suffix (forming adjectives) in the style of: *Kafkaesque.*
– ORIGIN French.

Esquimau noun (pl. **Esquimaux**) old-fashioned spelling of **ESKIMO**.

esquire /i-**skwy**-er/ noun **1** (**Esquire**) Brit. a polite title placed after a man's name when no other title is used. **2** historical a young nobleman who acted as an attendant to a knight.
– ORIGIN Old French *esquier*, from Latin *scutarius* 'shield-bearer'.

-ess suffix forming nouns referring to females: *abbess.*
– ORIGIN French *-esse.*

USAGE: In modern English, many people regard feminine forms such as **poetess** or **authoress** as old-fashioned or sexist. It is therefore often better to use the 'neutral' base form instead (e.g. *she's a famous author*).

essay noun /ess-ay/ **1** a piece of writing on a particular subject. **2** formal an attempt or effort.
• verb /e-**say**/ formal attempt: *Donald essayed a smile.*
– DERIVATIVES **essayist** noun.
– ORIGIN Old French *essai* 'trial'; the verb is an alteration of **ASSAY**.

essence noun **1** the basic or most important feature of something, which determines its character: *conflict is the essence of drama.* **2** an extract obtained from a plant or other substance and used for flavouring or perfume.
– PHRASES **in essence** basically; fundamentally. **of the essence** very important.
– ORIGIN Latin *essentia*, from *esse* 'be'.

essential adjective **1** absolutely necessary. **2** central to the nature of something; fundamental: *the essential weakness of the plaintiff's case.* • noun (**essentials**) **1** things that are absolutely necessary. **2** the fundamental elements of something: *the essentials of democracy.*
– DERIVATIVES **essentially** adverb.

essential oil noun a natural oil extracted from a plant.

EST abbreviation Eastern Standard Time.

est. abbreviation **1** established. **2** estimated.

establish verb **1** set something up on a firm or permanent basis. **2** bring about contact or communication with a person, group, or country: *the two countries established diplomatic relations.* **3** make something accepted or recognized by other people: *he had established his reputation as a journalist.* **4** discover the facts of a situation or find something out for certain: *investigators are trying to establish the cause of the fire.* **5** (as adj. **established**) recognized by the state as the national Church or religion.
– ORIGIN Old French *establir*, from Latin *stabilire* 'make firm'.

establishment noun **1** the action of

establishing something or the state of being established. **2** a business organization, institution, or household. **3 (the Establishment)** a group in a society who have power and influence in matters of policy or opinion, and who are seen as being opposed to change.

establishmentarian /i-stab-lish-muhn-**tair**-i-uhn/ adjective supporting the principle of an established Church. ●noun a person who supports the principle of an established Church.

estate noun **1** a property consisting of a large house and extensive grounds. **2** Brit. an area of land and modern buildings developed for residential, industrial, or commercial purposes. **3** a property where crops such as coffee or rubber are cultivated or where wine is produced. **4** all the money and property owned by a person at the time of their death. **5** (also **estate of the realm**) (in Britain) one of the three groups which make up Parliament, the Lords spiritual (the heads of the Church), the Lords temporal (the peerage), and the Commons. **6** old use or literary a particular state, period, or condition in life: *the holy estate of matrimony.* **7** Brit. an estate car.
– ORIGIN Old French *estat*, from Latin *status* 'state, condition'.

estate agency noun Brit. a business that sells and rents out buildings and land for clients.
– DERIVATIVES **estate agent** noun.

estate car noun Brit. a car which has a large carrying area behind the seats and an extra door at the rear.

esteem noun respect and admiration. ●verb **1** respect and admire: *he was esteemed as a philosopher.* **2** formal consider: *I should esteem it an honour if you would allow me to escort you.*
– ORIGIN Latin *aestimare* 'to estimate'.

ester /ess-ter/ noun an organic chemical compound formed by a reaction between an acid and an alcohol.

esthetic etc. adjective US spelling of **AESTHETIC** etc.

estimable adjective worthy of great respect.
– DERIVATIVES **estimably** adverb.

estimate verb /ess-ti-mayt/ roughly calculate the value, number, or amount of something: *the contract is estimated to be worth about £1 million.* ●noun /ess-ti-muht/ **1** an approximate calculation of the value, number, or amount of something. **2** a written statement indicating the likely price that will be charged for a particular piece of work. **3** a judgement or opinion.
– DERIVATIVES **estimation** noun **estimator** noun.
– ORIGIN Latin *aestimare* 'determine, appraise'.

Estonian noun a person from Estonia. ●adjective relating to Estonia.

estradiol noun US spelling of **OESTRADIOL**.

estranged adjective **1** no longer on friendly terms with someone: *she was estranged from her daughter.* **2** (of a husband or wife) no longer living with their spouse.
– DERIVATIVES **estrangement** noun.
– ORIGIN from Old French *estranger*, from Latin *extraneare* 'treat as a stranger'.

estrogen etc. noun US spelling of **OESTROGEN** etc.

estrus etc. noun US spelling of **OESTRUS** etc.

estuary /ess-tyuh-ri/ noun (pl. **estuaries**) the mouth of a large river, where it enters the sea and becomes affected by the tides.
– DERIVATIVES **estuarine** /es-tyuh-ryn/ adjective.
– ORIGIN Latin *aestuarium* 'tidal part of a shore'.

Estuary English noun (in the UK) a type of accent containing features of both standard British English pronunciation and London speech.

ET abbreviation **1** (in North America) Eastern time. **2** extraterrestrial.

ETA[1] /ee-tee-ay/ abbreviation estimated time of arrival.

ETA[2] /e-tuh/ abbreviation a Basque separatist movement in Spain.
– ORIGIN Basque, from the initial letters of *Euzkadi ta Azkatasuna* 'Basque homeland and liberty'.

e-tailer noun a retailer who sells goods via electronic transactions on the Internet.

et al. /et al/ abbreviation and others.
– ORIGIN Latin *et alii*.

etc. abbreviation et cetera.

et cetera /et set-uh-ruh/ (also **etcetera**) adverb and other similar things; and so on.
– ORIGIN Latin, from *et* 'and' and *cetera* 'the rest'.

etch verb **1** engrave metal, glass, or stone by drawing on a protective coating with a needle, and then covering it with acid to attack the exposed parts. **2** cut a text or design on a surface: *her initials were etched on the table.* **3** (**be etched**) be clearly visible: *exhaustion was etched on his face.* **4** (**be etched on/in**) be fixed permanently in someone's mind: *the date would be etched on his memory for the rest of his life.*
– DERIVATIVES **etcher** noun.
– ORIGIN Dutch *etsen*.

etching noun **1** the art or process of etching. **2** a print produced by etching.

eternal adjective **1** lasting or existing forever. **2** valid for all time: *eternal truths.*
– PHRASES **eternal triangle** a relationship between three people involving sexual rivalry.
– DERIVATIVES **eternally** adverb.
– ORIGIN Latin *aeternalis*.

eternity noun (pl. **eternities**) **1** unending time. **2** Theology endless life after death. **3** (**an eternity**) informal an undesirably long period of time.

ethane /ee-thayn/ noun a flammable hydrocarbon gas present in petroleum and natural gas.
– ORIGIN from **ETHER**.

ethanol /eth-uh-nol/ noun chemical name for **ALCOHOL** (in sense 1).

ether /ee-ther/ noun **1** a highly flammable liquid used as an anaesthetic and as a solvent. **2** (also **aether**) chiefly literary the sky or the upper regions of air.
– DERIVATIVES **etheric** adjective.
– ORIGIN Greek *aithēr* 'upper air'.

ethereal /i-theer-i-uhl/ (also **etherial**) adjective **1** extremely delicate and light. **2** heavenly or spiritual.
– DERIVATIVES **ethereality** noun **ethereally** adverb.

Ethernet noun a system for connecting a number of computer systems to form a local area network.
– ORIGIN blend of ETHER and NETWORK.

ethic noun a set of moral principles or rules of behaviour: *the Puritan work ethic.*
– ORIGIN Latin *ethice.*

ethical adjective **1** relating to moral principles or the branch of knowledge concerned with these. **2** morally correct.
– DERIVATIVES **ethically** adverb.

ethics plural noun **1** the moral principles that govern a person's behaviour or the way in which an activity is conducted. **2** the branch of knowledge concerned with moral principles.
– DERIVATIVES **ethicist** noun.

Ethiopian noun a person from Ethiopia.
● adjective relating to Ethiopia.

ethnic adjective **1** relating to a group of people who have a common national or cultural tradition. **2** referring to origin by birth rather than by present nationality: *ethnic Albanians.* **3** belonging to or characteristic of a non-Western cultural tradition: *ethnic music.*
– DERIVATIVES **ethnically** adverb **ethnicity** noun.
– ORIGIN Greek *ethnikos* 'heathen', from *ethnos* 'nation'.

ethnic cleansing noun the mass expulsion or killing of members of an ethnic or religious group in an area by those of another.

ethnic minority noun a group within a community which differs ethnically from the main population.

ethnocentric adjective assessing other cultures according to the particular values or characteristics of one's own.
– DERIVATIVES **ethnocentrically** adverb **ethnocentricity** noun **ethnocentrism** noun.

ethnography /eth-nog-ruh-fi/ noun the scientific description of peoples and cultures.
– DERIVATIVES **ethnographer** noun **ethnographic** adjective.

ethnology /eth-nol-uh-ji/ noun the study of the characteristics of different peoples and the differences and relationships between them.
– DERIVATIVES **ethnological** adjective **ethnologist** noun.

ethology /ee-thol-uh-ji/ noun **1** the science of animal behaviour. **2** the study of human behaviour from a biological perspective.
– DERIVATIVES **ethological** adjective **ethologist** noun.
– ORIGIN Greek *ēthologia.*

ethos /ee-thoss/ noun the characteristic spirit and attitudes of a culture, era, or community.
– ORIGIN Greek *ēthos* 'nature, disposition'.

ethyl /eth-yl/ noun the radical $-C_2H_5$, present in alcohol and ethane.
– ORIGIN German.

ethyl alcohol noun another term for ALCOHOL (in sense 1).

ethylene /eth-i-leen/ noun a flammable hydrocarbon gas present in natural gas and coal gas.

etiolated /ee-ti-uh-lay-tid/ adjective (of a plant) pale and weak due to a lack of light.
– ORIGIN French *étioler.*

etiology noun US spelling of AETIOLOGY.

etiquette /et-i-ket/ noun the customary rules of polite or correct behaviour in a society or among members of a profession.
– ORIGIN French, 'list of ceremonial observances of a court'.

Etruscan /i-truss-k'n/ noun **1** a person from Etruria, an ancient Italian state that was at its height *c.*500 BC. **2** the language of Etruria.
● adjective relating to Etruria.
– ORIGIN Latin *Etruscus.*

et seq. adverb and what follows (used in page references).
– ORIGIN from Latin *et sequens.*

-ette suffix forming nouns referring to: **1** small size: *kitchenette.* **2** an imitation or substitute: *leatherette.* **3** female gender: *suffragette.*
– ORIGIN Old French.

étude /ay-tyood/ noun a short musical composition or exercise.
– ORIGIN French, 'study'.

etymology /et-i-mol-uh-ji/ noun (pl. **etymologies**) an account of the origins and the developments in meaning of a word.
– DERIVATIVES **etymological** adjective **etymologically** adverb **etymologist** noun.
– ORIGIN Greek *etumologia.*

EU abbreviation European Union.

Eu symbol the chemical element europium.

eucalyptus /yoo-kuh-lip-tuhss/ (also **eucalypt**) noun (pl. **eucalyptuses**) **1** an evergreen Australasian tree valued for its wood, oil, gum, and resin. **2** the oil from eucalyptus leaves, used for its medicinal properties.
– ORIGIN Latin, from Greek *eu* 'well' + *kaluptos* 'covered', because the unopened flower is protected by a cap.

Eucharist /yoo-kuh-rist/ noun **1** the Christian ceremony commemorating the Last Supper, in which consecrated bread and wine are consumed. **2** the consecrated bread and wine used in this ceremony, especially the bread.
– DERIVATIVES **Eucharistic** adjective.
– ORIGIN Greek *eukharistia* 'thanksgiving'.

euchre /yoo-kuh/ noun a North American card game played with the thirty-two highest cards, the aim being to win at least three of the five tricks played.
– ORIGIN German dialect *Juckerspiel.*

Euclidean /yoo-klid-i-uhn/ adjective (of systems of geometry) based on the principles of the Greek mathematician Euclid (*c.* 300 BC).

eugenics /yoo-jen-iks/ plural noun the science of improving a population by controlled breeding, in such a way as to increase the occurrence of desirable mental and physical characteristics.
– DERIVATIVES **eugenic** adjective **eugenicist** noun & adjective.
– ORIGIN from Greek *eu* 'well' + *genēs* 'born'.

eulogize (or **eulogise**) /yoo-luh-jyz/ verb praise someone or something highly.
– DERIVATIVES **eulogist** noun **eulogistic** adjective.

eulogy /yoo-luh-ji/ noun (pl. **eulogies**) a speech or piece of writing that praises someone or something highly.
– ORIGIN Greek *eulogia* 'praise'.

eunuch /yoo-nuhk/ noun a man who has been castrated.

– ORIGIN Greek *eunoukhos* 'bedroom guard' (eunuchs were formerly employed to guard the women's living areas at eastern courts).

euphemism /yoo-fuh-mi-z'm/ noun (when referring to something unpleasant or embarrassing) a mild or less direct word used rather than one that is blunt or may be considered offensive.
– DERIVATIVES **euphemistic** adjective **euphemistically** adverb.
– ORIGIN Greek *euphēmismos*, from *eu* 'well' + *phēmē* 'speaking'.

euphonious /yoo-foh-ni-uhss/ adjective sounding pleasant.
– DERIVATIVES **euphoniously** adverb.

euphonium /yoo-foh-ni-uhm/ noun a brass musical instrument resembling a small tuba.
– ORIGIN from Greek *euphōnos* 'having a pleasing sound'.

euphony /yoo-fuh-ni/ noun the quality of having a pleasant sound.

euphorbia /yoo-for-bi-uh/ noun a plant of a large genus that includes the spurges.
– ORIGIN named after *Euphorbus*, an ancient Greek physician.

euphoria /yoo-for-i-uh/ noun a feeling of intense happiness.
– DERIVATIVES **euphoric** adjective **euphorically** adverb.
– ORIGIN Greek, from *euphoros* 'borne well, healthy'.

Eurasian adjective **1** of mixed European (or European-American) and Asian parentage. **2** relating to Eurasia (the land mass of Europe and Asia together). •noun a person of Eurasian parentage.

eureka /yoo-ree-kuh/ exclamation a cry of joy or satisfaction when one finds or discovers something.
– ORIGIN Greek *heurēka* 'I have found it', said to have been uttered by Archimedes when he hit on a method of determining the purity of gold.

Euro adjective informal European, especially concerned with the European Union.

euro noun (pl. **euros**) a basic unit of money of twelve member states of the European Union.

Eurocentric adjective regarding European culture as the most important; chiefly concerned with Europe.
– DERIVATIVES **Eurocentrism** noun.

Eurocrat noun informal, chiefly derogatory a bureaucrat in the administration of the European Union.

Eurodollar noun a US dollar held in Europe or elsewhere outside the US.

Euroland (also **Eurozone**) noun the economic region formed by those member countries of the European Union that have adopted the euro.

European noun **1** a person from Europe. **2** a person who is white or of European parentage. •adjective relating to Europe or the European Union.
– DERIVATIVES **Europeanism** noun **Europeanize** (or **Europeanise**) verb.

European Union noun an economic and political association of certain European countries, with free trade between member countries.

europium /yoo-roh-pi-uhm/ noun a soft silvery-white metallic element of the lanthanide series.
– ORIGIN from *Europe*.

Europop noun pop music from continental Europe with simple tunes and words, often sung in English.

Eurosceptic noun a person who is opposed to increasing the powers of the European Union.
– DERIVATIVES **Euroscepticism** noun.

Eurotrash noun informal rich European socialites, especially those living in the United States.

Eustachian tube /yoo-stay-sh'n/ noun a narrow passage leading from the pharynx to the cavity of the middle ear, which equalizes the pressure on each side of the eardrum.
– ORIGIN named after the Italian anatomist Bartolomeo *Eustachio*.

euthanasia /yoo-thuh-nay-zi-uh/ noun the painless killing of a patient who has an incurable disease or who is in an irreversible coma.
– ORIGIN from Greek *eu* 'well' + *thanatos* 'death'.

EVA abbreviation ethyl vinyl acetate.

evacuate verb **1** remove someone from a place of danger to a safer place. **2** leave a dangerous place. **3** technical remove the contents from a container. **4** empty the bowels.
– DERIVATIVES **evacuation** noun.
– ORIGIN Latin *evacuare*.

evacuee noun a person evacuated from a place of danger.

evade verb **1** escape or avoid someone or something, especially by cunning. **2** avoid dealing with or discussing: *don't try and evade the issue.* **3** avoid paying tax or duty, especially by illegitimate means.
– DERIVATIVES **evader** noun.
– ORIGIN Latin *evadere*.

evaluate verb **1** form an idea of the amount or value of something. **2** Mathematics find a numerical expression or equivalent for a formula, function, or equation.
– DERIVATIVES **evaluation** noun **evaluative** adjective **evaluator** noun.

evanescent /ev-uh-ness-uhnt/ adjective chiefly literary quickly fading from sight, memory, or existence.
– DERIVATIVES **evanesce** verb **evanescence** noun.
– ORIGIN from Latin *evanescere* 'disappear'.

evangelical /ee-van-jel-i-k'l/ adjective **1** relating to a tradition within Protestant Christianity emphasizing the authority of the Bible and salvation through personal faith in Jesus. **2** relating to the teaching of the gospel or Christianity. **3** passionate in supporting something. •noun a member of the evangelical tradition in the Christian Church.
– DERIVATIVES **evangelicalism** noun **evangelically** adverb.
– ORIGIN from Greek *euangelos* 'bringing good news'.

evangelist noun **1** a person who tries to convert others to Christianity. **2** the writer of one of the four Gospels. **3** a passionate supporter of something.
– DERIVATIVES **evangelism** noun **evangelistic**

adjective.

evangelize (or evangelise) verb **1** convert or try to convert someone to Christianity. **2** preach the gospel.
– DERIVATIVES **evangelization** noun.

evaporate verb **1** turn from liquid into vapour. **2** cease to exist: *my patience evaporated*.
– DERIVATIVES **evaporation** noun **evaporative** adjective **evaporator** noun.
– ORIGIN Latin *evaporare*.

evaporated milk noun thick sweetened milk that has had some of the liquid removed by evaporation.

evasion noun **1** the action of evading or avoiding something. **2** a statement that avoids dealing with something.

evasive adjective **1** avoiding a direct answer to a question. **2** intended to avoid or escape: *evasive action*.
– DERIVATIVES **evasively** adverb **evasiveness** noun.

eve noun **1** the day or period of time immediately before an event. **2** literary evening.
– ORIGIN short form of EVEN².

even¹ adjective **1** flat and smooth; level. **2** equal in number, amount, or value. **3** not varying much in speed, quality, etc.; regular: *just cycle at an even pace*. **4** equally balanced: *the match was even*. **5** (of a person's temper) placid; calm. **6** (of a number) able to be divided by two without a remainder. • verb make or become even. • adverb used for emphasis: *he knows even less than I do*.
– PHRASES **even as** at the very same time as. **even if** despite the possibility that. **even now** (or **then**) **1** in spite of what has (or had) happened. **2** at this (or that) very moment. **even so** nevertheless. **even though** despite the fact that.
– DERIVATIVES **evenly** adverb **evenness** noun.
– ORIGIN Old English.

even² noun old use or literary evening.
– ORIGIN Old English.

even-handed adjective fair and impartial.
– DERIVATIVES **even-handedly** adverb **even-handedness** noun.

evening noun the period of time at the end of the day.
– ORIGIN Old English.

evening primrose noun a plant with pale yellow flowers that open in the evening, used for a medicinal oil.

evening star noun (**the evening star**) the planet Venus, seen shining in the western sky after sunset.

even money noun (in betting) odds offering an equal chance of winning or losing.

evens plural noun Brit. even money.

evensong noun (especially in the Anglican Church) a service of evening prayers, psalms, and canticles.

event noun **1** a thing that happens or takes place. **2** a public or social occasion. **3** each of several contests making up a sports competition.
– PHRASES **in any event** (or **at all events**) whatever happens or may have happened. **in the event 1** as it turned out. **2** (**in the event of/that**) if the specified thing happens.
– DERIVATIVES **eventless** adjective.

– ORIGIN Latin *eventus*.

eventful adjective marked by interesting or exciting events.

event horizon noun Astronomy a hypothetical boundary around a black hole beyond which no light or other radiation can escape.

eventide noun old use or literary evening.

eventing noun a riding competition in which competitors must take part in each of several contests.
– DERIVATIVES **eventer** noun.

eventual adjective occurring at the end of a process or period of time: *he was optimistic about the eventual outcome of the talks*.
– DERIVATIVES **eventually** adverb.

eventuality noun (pl. **eventualities**) a possible event or outcome.

eventuate verb formal **1** occur as a result. **2** (**eventuate in**) lead to something as a result.

ever adverb **1** at any time. **2** used in comparisons and questions for emphasis: *I felt better than ever*. **3** at all times; always. **4** increasingly: *having to borrow ever larger sums*.
– PHRASES **ever so** (or **such**) Brit. informal very; very much.
– ORIGIN Old English.

evergreen adjective **1** (of a plant) retaining green leaves throughout the year. Contrasted with DECIDUOUS. **2** having a lasting freshness or appeal: *the timeless quality of our evergreen brand*. • noun an evergreen plant.

everlasting adjective lasting forever or a very long time.
– DERIVATIVES **everlastingly** adverb.

evermore adverb literary always; forever.

every determiner **1** used to refer to all the members of a set without exception. **2** indicating how often something happens: *every thirty minutes*. **3** all possible: *every effort was made*.
– PHRASES **every bit as** (in comparisons) quite as. **every other** each alternate in a series.

everybody pronoun every person.

everyday adjective **1** daily. **2** ordinary; commonplace.

Everyman noun an ordinary or typical person.

everyone pronoun every person.

every one pronoun each one.

everything pronoun **1** all things, or all the things of a group or class. **2** the most important thing or aspect: *money isn't everything*.

everywhere adverb **1** in or to all places. **2** in many places; very common: *sandwich bars are everywhere*.

evict verb legally force someone to leave a building or piece of land.
– DERIVATIVES **eviction** noun.
– ORIGIN from Latin *evincere* 'overcome, defeat'.

evidence noun **1** information or signs indicating whether something is true or valid. **2** information used to establish facts in a legal investigation or acceptable as testimony in a law court. • verb be or show evidence of: *the city's economic growth is evidenced by the creation of new jobs*.
– PHRASES **in evidence** noticeable; conspicuous.

– ORIGIN Latin *evidentia*.

evident adjective clear or obvious.
– DERIVATIVES **evidently** adverb.

evidential adjective formal relating to or providing evidence.

evil adjective **1** very immoral, cruel, and wicked. **2** associated with the devil: *evil spirits*. **3** very unpleasant: *an evil smell*. • noun **1** extreme wickedness. **2** something harmful or undesirable: *the evil of censorship*.
– PHRASES **the evil eye** a gaze superstitiously believed to cause harm.
– DERIVATIVES **evilly** adverb **evilness** noun.
– ORIGIN Old English.

evil-doer noun a person who does evil things.

evince verb formal reveal the presence of a quality or feeling.
– ORIGIN Latin *evincere* 'overcome, defeat'.

eviscerate /i-**viss**-uh-rayt/ verb formal disembowel someone or something.
– DERIVATIVES **evisceration** noun.
– ORIGIN Latin *eviscerare*.

evocative /i-**vok**-uh-tiv/ adjective bringing strong images, memories, or feelings to mind: *wonderfully evocative family snapshots*.

evoke /i-**vohk**/ verb **1** bring to the mind: *he said the race evoked memories of his own sporting past*. **2** obtain a response.
– DERIVATIVES **evocation** noun.
– ORIGIN Latin *evocare* 'call on a spirit'.

evolution noun **1** the process by which different kinds of living organism are believed to have developed from earlier forms. **2** the gradual development of something.
– DERIVATIVES **evolutionarily** adverb **evolutionary** adjective.
– ORIGIN Latin, 'unrolling'.

evolutionist noun a person who believes in the theories of evolution and natural selection.
– DERIVATIVES **evolutionism** noun.

evolve verb **1** develop gradually: *over the years, the business evolved into the one he runs today*. **2** (of an organism) develop from earlier forms by evolution.
– ORIGIN Latin *evolvere*.

ewe noun a female sheep.
– ORIGIN Old English.

ewer /**yoo**-er/ noun a large jug with a wide mouth.
– ORIGIN Old French *aiguiere*.

ex[1] preposition Brit. not including.

ex[2] noun informal a former husband, wife, or other partner in a relationship.

ex- (also **e-**; **ef-** before *f*) prefix **1** out: *exclude*. **2** upward: *extol*. **3** thoroughly: *excruciating*. **4** giving rise to: *exasperate*. **5** former: *ex-husband*.
– ORIGIN Latin or Greek *ex* 'out of'.

exacerbate /ig-**zass**-er-bayt/ verb make something bad worse.
– DERIVATIVES **exacerbation** noun.
– ORIGIN Latin *exacerbare* 'make harsh'.

exact adjective **1** correct in every detail: *an exact replica*. **2** not approximate; precise: *the exact time of the solstice*. **3** accurate and careful about minor details. • verb **1** demand and obtain something from someone. **2** take revenge on someone.

– DERIVATIVES **exactness** noun.
– ORIGIN from Latin *exigere* 'complete, ascertain, enforce'.

exacting adjective demanding a great deal of effort or skill.

exaction noun formal **1** the action of exacting or demanding a payment. **2** a sum of money demanded.

exactitude noun the quality of being exact.

exactly adverb **1** used to emphasize the accuracy of something: *she stayed for exactly two weeks in each state*. **2** used to confirm or agree with what has just been said.

exaggerate verb **1** make something seem larger, better, or worse than it really is. **2** (as adj. **exaggerated**) enlarged or altered beyond normal proportions.
– DERIVATIVES **exaggeratedly** adverb **exaggeration** noun.
– ORIGIN Latin *exaggerare* 'heap up'.

exalt /ig-**zawlt**/ verb **1** praise someone or something highly. **2** raise someone to a higher rank or position.
– ORIGIN Latin *exaltare*.

exaltation noun **1** extreme happiness. **2** the action of praising or elevating someone or something.

exalted adjective **1** at a high level: *the exalted rank of Inspector*. **2** (of an idea) noble; lofty.

exam noun short for **EXAMINATION** (in sense 2).

examination noun **1** a detailed inspection or investigation. **2** a formal test of knowledge or ability in a subject or skill. **3** the action of examining someone or something.

examine verb **1** inspect someone or something closely to determine their nature or condition. **2** test someone's knowledge or ability. **3** Law formally question a defendant or witness in court.
– DERIVATIVES **examinee** noun **examiner** noun.
– ORIGIN Latin *examinare* 'weigh, test'.

example noun **1** a thing that is typical of its kind or that illustrates a general rule. **2** a person or thing regarded in terms of their suitability to be imitated.
– PHRASES **for example** used to introduce something chosen as a typical case. **make an example of** punish someone as a warning to others.
– ORIGIN Latin *exemplum*.

exasperate /ig-**zass**-puh-rayt/ verb irritate someone intensely.
– DERIVATIVES **exasperated** adjective **exasperating** adjective **exasperation** noun.
– ORIGIN Latin *exasperare* 'irritate to anger'.

ex cathedra /eks kuh-**thee**-druh/ adverb & adjective with the full authority of office (especially that of the Pope).
– ORIGIN Latin, 'from the teacher's chair'.

excavate verb **1** make a hole or channel by digging. **2** carefully remove earth from an area in order to find buried remains. **3** dig out objects or material from the ground.
– DERIVATIVES **excavation** noun **excavator** noun.
– ORIGIN Latin *excavare* 'hollow out'.

exceed verb **1** be greater in number or size than: *sales for 2004 should exceed $2.1 billion*. **2** go beyond what is stipulated by a set limit. **3** be better than something; surpass.

– ORIGIN Latin *excedere*.

exceedingly adverb extremely; very.

excel verb (**excels, excelling, excelled**) **1** be exceptionally good at an activity or subject. **2** (**excel oneself**) perform exceptionally well.
– ORIGIN Latin *excellere*.

excellence noun the quality of being excellent.

Excellency noun (pl. **Excellencies**) (**His, Your**, etc. **Excellency**) a title or form of address for certain high officials of state, especially ambassadors, or of the Roman Catholic Church.

excellent adjective extremely good; outstanding.

except preposition not including; other than.
• conjunction used before a statement that is not included in one just made. • verb exclude from a category or group: *present company excepted*.
– ORIGIN from Latin *excipere* 'take out'.

> USAGE: On the confusion of **except** and **accept**, see the note at **ACCEPT**.

excepting preposition except for; apart from.

exception noun a person or thing that is not included in a general statement or that does not follow a rule.
– PHRASES **take exception to** object strongly to something.

exceptionable adjective formal open to objection; causing disapproval or offence.

exceptional adjective **1** unusually good. **2** unusual; not typical: *the drug could only be used in exceptional circumstances*.
– DERIVATIVES **exceptionally** adverb.

excerpt noun /ek-serpt/ a short extract from a film or piece of music or writing. • verb /ik-**serpt**/ take a short extract from a piece of writing.
– ORIGIN from Latin *excerpere* 'pluck out'.

excess noun /ik-**sess**/ **1** an amount that is more than necessary, permitted, or desirable. **2** extreme behaviour, especially in eating or drinking too much: *bouts of alcoholic excess*. **3** (**excesses**) unacceptable or illegal behaviour. **4** Brit. a part of an insurance claim to be paid by the insured person. • adjective /usu. **ek**-sess/ **1** exceeding a permitted or desirable amount. **2** Brit. required as extra payment.
– ORIGIN Latin *excessus*.

excess baggage noun luggage weighing more than the limit allowed on an aircraft, liable to an extra charge.

excessive adjective more than is necessary, normal, or desirable.
– DERIVATIVES **excessively** adverb **excessiveness** noun.

exchange noun **1** an act of giving something and receiving something else in return. **2** a short conversation or argument. **3** the changing of money to its equivalent in another currency. **4** a building or institution in which commodities are traded. **5** a set of equipment that connects telephone lines during a call. • verb give something and receive something else in return.
– PHRASES **exchange contracts** Brit. (of a buyer) sign a legal contract with the person selling a property or piece of land, making the purchase legally binding and enforceable.

– DERIVATIVES **exchangeable** adjective **exchanger** noun.
– ORIGIN Old French *eschangier*.

exchange rate noun the value at which one currency may be exchanged for another.

exchequer /iks-**chek**-er/ noun **1** a royal or national treasury. **2** (**Exchequer**) the account at the Bank of England into which public money is paid.
– ORIGIN Old French *eschequier* 'chessboard' (accounts were kept on a chequered tablecloth by means of counters).

excise[1] /**ek**-syz/ noun a tax charged on certain goods, such as alcohol, and licences for certain activities.
– ORIGIN Dutch *excijs*.

excise[2] /ik-**syz**/ verb **1** cut something out surgically. **2** remove a section from a piece of writing or music.
– DERIVATIVES **excision** noun.
– ORIGIN Latin *excidere* 'cut out'.

exciseman noun (pl. **excisemen**) Brit. historical an official who collected excise duty and prevented smuggling.

excitable adjective easily excited.
– DERIVATIVES **excitability** noun **excitably** adverb.

excite verb **1** make someone feel very enthusiastic and eager. **2** arouse someone sexually. **3** give rise to: *the new sauces are exciting particular interest*. **4** increase the energy or activity in a physical or biological system.
– DERIVATIVES **excitation** noun **excitatory** adjective (chiefly Physiology) **excited** adjective.
– ORIGIN Latin *excitare*.

excitement noun **1** a feeling of great enthusiasm and eagerness. **2** something that arouses great enthusiasm and eagerness. **3** sexual arousal.

exciting adjective causing great enthusiasm and eagerness.
– DERIVATIVES **excitingly** adverb.

exclaim verb cry out suddenly, especially in surprise, anger, or pain.
– ORIGIN Latin *exclamare*.

exclamation noun a sudden cry or remark.
– DERIVATIVES **exclamatory** adjective.

exclamation mark (N. Amer. **exclamation point**) noun a punctuation mark (!) indicating an exclamation.

exclude verb **1** prevent someone from entering or participating in something. **2** deliberately leave out when considering or doing something: *this information was excluded from the judicial investigation*. **3** expel a pupil from a school.
– DERIVATIVES **excludable** adjective **excluder** noun.
– ORIGIN Latin *excludere*.

excluding preposition not taking someone or something into account; except.

exclusion noun the action of excluding someone or something from something.
– DERIVATIVES **exclusionary** adjective.

exclusive adjective **1** restricted to the person, group, or area concerned: *the problem isn't exclusive to Dublin*. **2** high-class and expensive; select. **3** not including other things. **4** unable to exist or be true if something else exists or is true: *when it comes to hedges, fast growing and*

low maintenance are mutually exclusive. **5** (of a story) not published or broadcast elsewhere. ●**noun** a story published or broadcast by only one source.
– DERIVATIVES **exclusively** adverb **exclusiveness** noun **exclusivity** noun.
– ORIGIN Latin *exclusivus*.

excommunicate /eks-kuh-**myoo**-ni-kayt/ **verb** officially ban someone from the sacraments and services of the Christian Church.
– DERIVATIVES **excommunication** noun.
– ORIGIN Latin *excommunicare*.

excoriate /ik-**skor**-i-ayt/ **verb 1** formal criticize someone severely. **2** Medicine damage or remove part of the surface of the skin.
– DERIVATIVES **excoriation** noun.
– ORIGIN Latin *excoriare* 'to skin'.

excrement /**eks**-kri-muhnt/ **noun** waste matter emptied from the bowels; faeces.
– DERIVATIVES **excremental** adjective.
– ORIGIN Latin *excrementum*.

excrescence /iks-**kress**-uhnss/ **noun 1** an abnormal growth protruding from a body or plant. **2** an unattractive object or feature.
– ORIGIN from Latin *excrescere* 'grow out'.

excreta /ik-**skree**-tuh/ **noun** waste discharged from the body, especially faeces and urine.
– ORIGIN Latin.

excrete **verb** discharge a waste substance from the body.
– DERIVATIVES **excretion** noun **excretory** adjective.
– ORIGIN Latin *excernere* 'sift out'.

excruciating **adjective 1** intensely painful. **2** very embarrassing, awkward, or tedious.
– DERIVATIVES **excruciatingly** adverb.
– ORIGIN from Latin *excruciare* 'torment'.

exculpate /**eks**-kul-payt/ **verb** formal show or declare that someone is not guilty of wrongdoing.
– DERIVATIVES **exculpation** noun **exculpatory** adjective.
– ORIGIN Latin *exculpare* 'free from blame'.

excursion **noun** a short journey or trip, especially one taken for leisure.
– DERIVATIVES **excursionist** noun.
– ORIGIN from Latin *excurrere* 'run out'.

excursus /ik-**sker**-suhss, ek-**sker**-suhss/ **noun** (pl. same or **excursuses**) a detailed discussion of a particular point in a book.
– ORIGIN Latin, 'excursion'.

excuse **verb** /ik-**skyooz**/ **1** try to find reasons for a fault or offence; try to justify: *she did nothing to hide or excuse Jacob's cruelty.* **2** forgive a minor fault or a person committing one: *sit down—excuse the mess.* **3** release someone from a duty or requirement. **4** allow someone to leave a room or gathering. **5** (**excuse oneself**) say politely that one is leaving. ●**noun** /ik-**skyooss**/ **1** a reason given to justify a fault or offence. **2** something said to conceal the real reason for an action. **3** (**an excuse for**) informal a poor or inadequate example of: *you pathetic excuse for a human being!*
– PHRASES **excuse me 1** a polite apology. **2** N. Amer. used to ask someone to repeat what they have just said.
– DERIVATIVES **excusable** adjective **excusably** adverb.

– ORIGIN Latin *excusare* 'to free from blame'.

ex-directory **adjective** Brit. (of a telephone number) not listed in a telephone directory at one's own request.

execrable /**ek**-si-kruh-b'l/ **adjective** extremely bad or unpleasant.
– DERIVATIVES **execrably** adverb.
– ORIGIN Latin *execrabilis*.

execrate /**ek**-si-krayt/ **verb** feel or express great hatred for someone or something.
– DERIVATIVES **execration** noun.
– ORIGIN Latin *exsecrari* 'curse'.

execute **verb 1** put a plan, order, or course of action into effect: *the companies have executed a five-year agreement.* **2** perform a skilful action or manoeuvre. **3** carry out a sentence of death on a condemned person. **4** make a legal document valid by signing or sealing it. **5** carry out a judicial sentence, the terms of a will, or other order. **6** run a computer file or program.
– DERIVATIVES **executable** adjective.
– ORIGIN Latin *executare*.

execution **noun 1** the carrying out of a plan, order, or course of action. **2** the killing of a condemned person. **3** the way in which something is produced or carried out.

executioner **noun** an official who executes condemned criminals.

executive /ig-**zek**-yuu-tiv/ **noun 1** a senior manager in a business. **2** a decision-making committee or other group in an organization. **3** (**the executive**) the branch of a government responsible for putting decisions or laws into effect. ●**adjective** having the power to put plans, actions, or laws into effect.

executor /ig-**zek**-yuu-ter/ **noun** a person appointed by someone to carry out the terms of their will.

executrix /ig-**zek**-yoo-triks/ **noun** (pl. **executrices** /ig-**zek**-yoo-tri-seez/ or **executrixes**) a female executor of a will.

exegesis /**ek**-si-jee-siss/ **noun** (pl. **exegeses** /**ek**-si-**jee**-seez/) critical explanation of a written work, especially of the Bible.
– DERIVATIVES **exegetical** adjective.
– ORIGIN Greek.

exegete /**ek**-si-jeet/ **noun** a person who interprets a written work, especially the Bible.

exemplar /ig-**zem**-pler/ **noun** a person or thing serving as a typical example or appropriate model.
– ORIGIN Latin *exemplarium*.

exemplary **adjective 1** providing a good example to others; very good. **2** (of a punishment) serving as a warning.

exemplify /ig-**zem**-pli-fy/ **verb** (**exemplifies**, **exemplifying**, **exemplified**) be or give a typical example of: *the best dry sherry is exemplified by the fino of Jerez.*
– DERIVATIVES **exemplification** noun.

exempt /ig-**zempt**/ **adjective** free from an obligation or requirement imposed on others: *since he is only 13, he is exempt from prosecution.* ●**verb** make someone exempt from something.
– DERIVATIVES **exemption** noun.
– ORIGIN Latin *exemptus* 'taken out, freed'.

exequies /**ek**-sik-wi/ **plural noun** (sing. **exequy**)

formal funeral rites.
- ORIGIN Latin *exsequiae*.

exercise noun **1** physical activity carried out for the sake of health and fitness. **2** an activity carried out for a specific purpose: *a public relations exercise*. **3** a task set to practise or test a skill. **4 (exercises)** military drills or training manoeuvres. **5** the application of a power, right, or process: *the exercise of authority*. • verb **1** use or apply a power, right, or quality: *the industry has exercised restraint so far*. **2** do physical activity. **3** worry or perplex someone.
- DERIVATIVES **exercisable** adjective **exerciser** noun.
- ORIGIN from Latin *exercere* 'keep busy, practise'.

exercise bike noun a stationary piece of exercise equipment resembling an ordinary bicycle.

exercise book noun Brit. a booklet with blank pages for students to write in.

exert /ig-zert/ verb **1** apply or bring to bear a force, influence, or quality. **2** (**exert oneself**) make a physical or mental effort.
- ORIGIN Latin *exserere* 'put forth'.

exertion noun **1** physical or mental effort. **2** the application of a force, influence, or quality.

exeunt /ek-si-uhnt/ verb (as a stage direction) (actors) leave the stage.
- ORIGIN Latin, 'they go out'.

exfoliate /iks-foh-li-ayt/ verb **1** (of a material) be shed from a surface in scales or layers. **2** wash or rub part of the body with a granular substance to remove dead skin cells.
- DERIVATIVES **exfoliant** noun **exfoliation** noun **exfoliator** noun.
- ORIGIN Latin *exfoliare* 'strip of leaves'.

ex gratia /eks gray-shuh/ adverb & adjective (of payment) given as a gift or favour rather than because of any legal requirement.
- ORIGIN Latin, 'from favour'.

exhale verb **1** breathe out. **2** give off vapour or fumes.
- DERIVATIVES **exhalation** noun.
- ORIGIN Latin *exhalare*.

exhaust verb **1** tire someone out. **2** use up all of: *the company exhausted these funds in six months*. **3** explore a subject or possibilities so fully that there is nothing left to be said or discovered. **4** expel gas or steam from an engine or other machine. • noun **1** waste gases or air expelled from an engine or other machine. **2** the system through which waste gases are expelled.
- DERIVATIVES **exhauster** noun **exhaustible** adjective **exhausting** adjective.
- ORIGIN Latin *exhaurire* 'drain out'.

exhaustion noun **1** a state of extreme tiredness. **2** the action of using something up.

exhaustive adjective covering all aspects fully.
- DERIVATIVES **exhaustively** adverb **exhaustiveness** noun.

exhibit verb **1** publicly display an item in an art gallery or museum. **2** show a quality: *he exhibited great humility*. • noun **1** an object or collection of objects on display in an art gallery or museum. **2** Law a document or other object produced in a court as evidence.
- DERIVATIVES **exhibitor** noun.
- ORIGIN Latin *exhibere* 'hold out'.

exhibition noun **1** a public display of items in an art gallery or museum. **2** a display or demonstration of a skill or quality.
- PHRASES **make an exhibition of oneself** behave very foolishly in public.

exhibitionism noun **1** behaviour that is intended to attract attention to oneself. **2** a mental condition in which a person feels an urge to display their genitals in public.
- DERIVATIVES **exhibitionist** noun **exhibitionistic** adjective.

exhilarate verb make someone feel very happy or full of energy.
- DERIVATIVES **exhilarating** adjective **exhilaration** noun.
- ORIGIN Latin *exhilarare* 'make cheerful'.

exhort /ig-zort/ verb strongly urge someone to do something.
- DERIVATIVES **exhortation** noun.
- ORIGIN Latin *exhortari*.

exhume /ek-syoom/ verb dig out something buried, especially a corpse from the ground.
- DERIVATIVES **exhumation** noun.
- ORIGIN Latin *exhumare*.

exigency /ek-si-juhn-si/ noun (pl. **exigencies**) formal an urgent need or demand: *the exigencies of contemporary life*.
- ORIGIN Latin *exigentia*.

exigent /ek-si-juhnt/ adjective formal pressing; demanding.
- ORIGIN Latin *exigent-*.

exiguous /ig-zig-yoo-uhss/ adjective formal very small.
- ORIGIN Latin *exiguus* 'scanty'.

exile noun **1** the state of being barred from one's native country. **2** a person who lives in exile. • verb expel and bar someone from their native country.
- ORIGIN Latin *exilium* 'banishment'.

exist verb **1** be real; be present in a place or situation: *his supporters say the deal never existed*. **2** be alive; live.
- ORIGIN Latin *exsistere* 'come into being'.

existence noun **1** the fact or state of existing. **2** a way of living: *a rural existence*.

existent adjective existing.

existential /eg-zi-sten-sh'l/ adjective **1** relating to existence. **2** concerned with existentialism.
- DERIVATIVES **existentially** adverb.

existentialism noun a philosophical theory which emphasizes that human beings are free agents, responsible for their own actions.
- DERIVATIVES **existentialist** noun & adjective.

exit noun **1** a way out of a building, room, or passenger vehicle. **2** an act of leaving. **3** a place for traffic to leave a major road or roundabout. • verb (**exits, exiting, exited**) **1** go out of or leave a place. **2** terminate a computer process or program.
- ORIGIN Latin, 'he or she goes out'.

exit poll noun a poll of people leaving a polling station, asking how they voted.

ex nihilo /eks ny-hil-oh/ adverb formal out of nothing: *he created a paradise ex nihilo*.
- ORIGIN Latin.

exo- prefix external; from outside: *exoskeleton*.
- ORIGIN Greek *exō* 'outside'.

exobiology noun the branch of science concerned with the possibility and likely nature of life on other planets or in space.

– DERIVATIVES **exobiologist** noun.

exocrine /ek-soh-kryn/ adjective (of a gland) producing hormones or other products through ducts rather than directly into the blood.
– ORIGIN from Greek *krinein* 'sift'.

exodus noun a mass departure of people.
– ORIGIN Greek *exodos*.

ex officio /eks uh-fish-i-oh/ adverb & adjective by virtue of one's position or status.
– ORIGIN from Latin *ex* 'out of, from' + *officium* 'duty'.

exogenous /ik-soj-in-uhss, ek-soj-in-uhss/ adjective technical relating to an external cause or origin. Often contrasted with **ENDOGENOUS**.
– DERIVATIVES **exogenously** adverb.

exonerate /ig-zon-uh-rayt/ verb officially state that someone has not done something wrong or illegal.
– DERIVATIVES **exoneration** noun.
– ORIGIN Latin *exonerare* 'free from a burden'.

exorbitant /ig-zor-bi-tuhnt/ adjective (of a price or amount charged) unreasonably high.
– DERIVATIVES **exorbitantly** adverb.
– ORIGIN from Latin *exorbitare* 'go off the track'.

exorcize (or **exorcise**) /ek-sor-syz/ verb drive out a supposed evil spirit from a person or place.
– DERIVATIVES **exorcism** noun **exorcist** noun.
– ORIGIN Greek *exorkizein*.

exoskeleton noun the rigid external covering of the body in insects and some other invertebrate animals.

exothermic /ek-soh-ther-mik/ adjective (of a chemical reaction) accompanied by the release of heat.

exotic adjective 1 originating in or typical of a distant foreign country. 2 strikingly colourful or unusual: *youths with exotic haircuts*. •noun an exotic plant or animal.
– DERIVATIVES **exotically** adverb **exoticism** noun.
– ORIGIN Greek *exotikos* 'foreign'.

exotica /ig-zot-ik-uh/ plural noun unusual and interesting objects: *Hawaiian exotica*.

expand verb 1 make or become larger or more extensive. 2 (**expand on**) give more details about something.
– DERIVATIVES **expandability** noun **expandable** adjective **expander** noun.
– ORIGIN Latin *expandere* 'spread out'.

expanded adjective 1 (of a material) having a light cellular structure. 2 relatively broad in shape.

expanse noun a wide continuous area of something: *a vast expanse of sand dunes*.

expansion noun 1 the action of becoming larger or more extensive. 2 the political strategy of extending a state's territory by encroaching on that of other nations.
– DERIVATIVES **expansionary** adjective.

expansionism noun the policy of extending a state's territory by encroaching on that of other nations.
– DERIVATIVES **expansionist** noun & adjective.

expansive adjective 1 covering a wide area; extensive. 2 relaxed, friendly, and communicative.
– DERIVATIVES **expansively** adverb

expansiveness noun.

ex parte /eks pah-tay/ adjective & adverb Law with respect to or in the interests of one side only.
– ORIGIN Latin, 'from a side'.

expat noun & adjective informal short for **EXPATRIATE**.

expatiate /ik-spay-shi-ayt/ verb speak or write at length or in detail: *professors shuffling forth to expatiate on the American dream*.
– DERIVATIVES **expatiation** noun.
– ORIGIN Latin *exspatiari* 'move beyond one's usual bounds'.

expatriate /eks-pat-ri-uht/ noun a person who lives outside their native country. •adjective living outside one's native country.
– DERIVATIVES **expatriation** noun.
– ORIGIN Latin *expatriare*.

expect verb 1 regard something as likely to happen. 2 regard someone as likely to do or be something. 3 believe that someone will arrive soon. 4 require or demand something because it is appropriate or a person's duty: *Picasso quickly mastered the style that was expected of a fashionable portrait painter.* 5 (**be expecting**) informal be pregnant.
– DERIVATIVES **expectable** adjective.
– ORIGIN Latin *exspectare* 'look out for'.

expectancy noun (pl. **expectancies**) 1 hope or anticipation that something will happen. 2 something expected: *a life expectancy of 22 to 25 years*.

expectant adjective 1 hoping or anticipating that something is about to happen. 2 (of a woman) pregnant.
– DERIVATIVES **expectantly** adverb.

expectation noun 1 belief that something will happen or be the case. 2 a thing that is expected to happen.

expectorant noun a medicine which helps to bring up phlegm from the air passages, used to treat coughs.

expectorate /ik-spek-tuh-rayt/ verb cough or spit out phlegm from the throat or lungs.
– DERIVATIVES **expectoration** noun.
– ORIGIN Latin *expectorare* 'expel from the chest'.

expedient /ik-spee-di-uhnt/ adjective 1 convenient and practical although not always fair or right: *either side could break the agreement if it were expedient to do so.* 2 suitable or appropriate. •noun a means of achieving an end.
– DERIVATIVES **expedience** noun **expediency** noun **expediently** adverb.
– ORIGIN from Latin *expedire* (see **EXPEDITE**).

expedite /eks-pi-dyt/ verb make an action or process happen sooner or be accomplished more quickly.
– DERIVATIVES **expediter** (also **expeditor**) noun.
– ORIGIN Latin *expedire* 'extricate, put in order'.

expedition noun 1 a journey undertaken by a group of people with a particular purpose. 2 formal promptness or speed in doing something.
– DERIVATIVES **expeditionary** adjective.

expeditious /eks-pi-di-shuhss/ adjective quick and efficient.
– DERIVATIVES **expeditiously** adverb.

expel verb (**expels, expelling, expelled**) **1** force someone to leave a school, organization, or place. **2** force something out, especially from the body.
– DERIVATIVES **expellable** adjective **expellee** noun.
– ORIGIN Latin *expellere*, from *pellere* 'to drive'.

expend verb spend or use up a resource.
– ORIGIN Latin *expendere*.

expendable adjective able to be sacrificed or abandoned because of little significance when compared to an overall purpose.
– DERIVATIVES **expendability** noun.

expenditure /ik-spen-di-cher/ noun **1** the action of spending funds. **2** the amount of money spent. **3** the use of energy or other resources.

expense noun **1** the cost of something. **2** (**expenses**) specific costs spent in carrying out a job or task. **3** something on which money must be spent: *tolls are a daily expense.*
– PHRASES **at the expense of 1** paid for by someone. **2** so as to harm something.
– ORIGIN from Latin *expendere* 'weigh or pay out'.

expense account noun an arrangement under which money spent in the course of business is later repaid by one's employer.

expensive adjective costing a lot of money.
– DERIVATIVES **expensively** adverb **expensiveness** noun.

experience noun **1** practical contact with and observation of facts or events. **2** knowledge or skill gained over time. **3** an event which leaves an impression on one: *a frightening experience.* • verb **1** encounter or undergo an event or situation. **2** feel an emotion.
– ORIGIN Latin *experientia*.

experienced adjective having knowledge or skill in a particular field gained over time.

experiential /ik-speer-i-en-sh'l/ adjective involving or based on experience and observation.
– DERIVATIVES **experientially** adverb.

experiment noun **1** a scientific procedure undertaken to make a discovery, test a theory, or demonstrate a fact. **2** a new idea or method that is tried out without being sure of the outcome: *the previous experiment in democracy ended in disaster.* • verb **1** perform a scientific experiment. **2** try out new ideas or methods.
– DERIVATIVES **experimentation** noun **experimenter** noun.
– ORIGIN Latin *experimentum*.

experimental adjective **1** based on new ideas and not yet fully tested or established: *an experimental drug.* **2** relating to scientific experiments. **3** (of art, music, etc.) departing from established conventions; innovative.
– DERIVATIVES **experimentalism** noun **experimentalist** noun **experimentally** adverb.

expert noun a person who has great knowledge or skill in a particular area. • adjective having or involving great knowledge or skill.
– DERIVATIVES **expertly** adverb.
– ORIGIN Latin *expertus.*

expertise /ek-sper-teez/ noun great skill or knowledge in a particular field.

expiate /ek-spi-ayt/ verb make amends for guilt or wrongdoing.
– DERIVATIVES **expiation** noun **expiatory** /ek-spi-uh-tuh-ri/ adjective.
– ORIGIN Latin *expiare* 'appease by sacrifice'.

expire /ik-spy-er/ verb **1** (of a document or agreement) come to the end of its period of validity. **2** (of a period of time) come to an end. **3** (of a person) die. **4** technical breathe out air from the lungs.
– DERIVATIVES **expiration** noun **expiratory** adjective.
– ORIGIN Latin *exspirare* 'breathe out'.

expiry noun Brit. the time when something ends or ceases to be valid.

explain verb **1** make something clear by giving a detailed description. **2** give a reason or justification for: *Cassie found it necessary to explain her black eye.* **3** (**explain oneself**) justify one's motives or behaviour. **4** (**explain something away**) make something seem less embarrassing by giving an excuse or reason for it.
– DERIVATIVES **explainable** adjective **explainer** noun.
– ORIGIN Latin *explanare*.

explanation noun **1** a statement or description that makes something clear. **2** a reason or justification for an action or belief.

explanatory /ik-splan-uh-tuh-ri/ adjective intended to explain something.
– DERIVATIVES **explanatorily** adverb.

expletive /ik-splee-tiv/ noun an oath or swear word.
– ORIGIN from Latin *expletivus* 'acting to fill out'.

explicable /ik-splik-uh-b'l/ adjective able to be explained or understood.
– ORIGIN from Latin *explicare* 'unfold'.

explicate /eks-pli-kayt/ verb analyse and explain an idea or literary work in detail.
– DERIVATIVES **explication** noun **explicator** noun.
– ORIGIN Latin *explicare* 'unfold'.

explicit /ik-spli-sit/ adjective **1** clear and detailed, with no room for confusion or doubt. **2** describing or showing sexual activity in a direct and detailed way.
– DERIVATIVES **explicitly** adverb **explicitness** noun.
– ORIGIN from Latin *explicare* 'unfold'.

explode verb **1** burst or shatter violently as a result of the release of internal energy. **2** suddenly express an emotion. **3** increase suddenly in number or extent: *the herbal medicine market has exploded.* **4** show a belief or theory to be false. **5** (as adj. **exploded**) (of a diagram) showing parts of something in the normal relative positions but slightly separated from each other.
– DERIVATIVES **exploder** noun.
– ORIGIN Latin *explodere* 'drive out by clapping'.

exploit verb /ik-sployt/ **1** make use of a person or situation in an unfair way, so as to gain advantage for oneself: *people desperate to lose weight were being exploited by unscrupulous salesmen.* **2** make good use of a resource. • noun /ek-sployt/ a bold or daring act.
– DERIVATIVES **exploitable** adjective **exploitation** noun **exploiter** noun
– ORIGIN Old French *esploit* 'success, progress'.

exploitative (also **exploitive**) adjective treating someone unfairly so as to make money or gain an advantage.

explore verb **1** travel through an unfamiliar

area in order to learn about it. **2** inquire into or examine in detail: *she explored the possibility of converting to the Jehovah's Witnesses.* **3** examine something by touch.
– DERIVATIVES **exploration** noun **exploratory** adjective **explorer** noun.
– ORIGIN Latin *explorare* 'search out'.

explosion noun **1** an act of exploding. **2** a sudden increase in amount or extent: *an explosion in information technology.*

explosive adjective **1** able or likely to explode. **2** likely to cause an outburst of anger or controversy. **3** (of an increase) sudden and dramatic. •noun a substance which can be made to explode.
– DERIVATIVES **explosively** adverb **explosiveness** noun.

exponent /ik-spoh-nuhnt/ noun **1** a person who promotes an idea or theory. **2** a person who does a particular thing skilfully. **3** Mathematics a raised figure beside a number indicating how many times that number is to be multiplied by itself (e.g. 3 in $2^3 = 2 \times 2 \times 2$).
– ORIGIN from Latin *exponere* 'present, explain'.

exponential /eks-puh-nen-sh'l/ adjective **1** (of an increase) becoming more and more rapid. **2** relating to or expressed by a mathematical exponent.
– DERIVATIVES **exponentially** adverb.

export verb /ik-sport/ **1** send goods or services to another country for sale. **2** spread or introduce ideas or customs to another country. •noun /ek-sport/ **1** an article or service sold abroad. **2** the sale of goods or services to other countries.
– DERIVATIVES **exportable** adjective **exportation** noun **exporter** noun.
– ORIGIN Latin *exportare*.

expose verb **1** make something visible by uncovering it. **2** reveal the true nature of: *he has been exposed as a liar.* **3** (**expose someone to**) make someone vulnerable to possible harm or risk. **4** (as adj. **exposed**) unprotected from the weather. **5** (**expose oneself**) publicly and indecently display one's genitals. **6** subject photographic film to light.
– DERIVATIVES **exposer** noun.
– ORIGIN Latin *exponere* 'present, explain'.

exposé /ik-spoh-zay/ noun a report in the media that reveals something shocking.
– ORIGIN French, 'shown, set out'.

exposition noun **1** a detailed description and explanation of a theory. **2** a large public exhibition of art or trade goods. **3** Music the part of a movement in which the principal themes are first presented.
– DERIVATIVES **expositional** adjective.
– ORIGIN Latin.

expositor /ik-spoz-i-ter/ noun a person who explains complicated ideas or theories.
– DERIVATIVES **expository** adjective.

ex post facto /eks pohst fak-toh/ adjective & adverb formal with retrospective action or effect.
– ORIGIN from Latin *ex postfacto* 'in the light of subsequent events'.

expostulate /ik-sposs-tyoo-layt/ verb express strong disapproval or disagreement.
– DERIVATIVES **expostulation** noun.
– ORIGIN Latin *expostulare* 'demand'.

exposure noun **1** the state of being exposed to

something harmful: *a few simple practices can reduce exposure to bacteria.* **2** a physical condition resulting from being exposed to severe weather conditions. **3** the revelation of something secret. **4** the publicizing of information or an event. **5** the quantity of light reaching a photographic film, as determined by shutter speed and lens aperture.

expound verb present and explain a theory or idea in detail.
– DERIVATIVES **expounder** noun.
– ORIGIN Latin *exponere* 'present, explain'.

express[1] /ik-spress/ verb **1** convey a thought or feeling in words or by gestures and behaviour. **2** squeeze out liquid or air. **3** Mathematics represent something by a figure, symbol, or formula.
– DERIVATIVES **expressible** adjective.
– ORIGIN Old French *expresser*.

express[2] /ik-spress/ adjective **1** operating at high speed. **2** (of a delivery service) using a special messenger. •adverb by express train or delivery service. •noun **1** (also **express train**) a train that stops at few stations and so travels quickly. **2** a special delivery service. •verb send something by express messenger or delivery.
– ORIGIN from EXPRESS[3].

express[3] /ik-spress/ adjective **1** stated clearly and openly: *it was his express wish that the event should continue.* **2** specifically identified to the exclusion of anything else: *the league was formed with the express purpose of raising the level of football.*
– DERIVATIVES **expressly** adverb.
– ORIGIN Latin *expressus* 'distinctly presented'.

expression noun **1** the action of expressing thoughts or feelings. **2** a look on someone's face that conveys a particular feeling: *a sad expression.* **3** a word or phrase expressing an idea. **4** Mathematics a collection of symbols expressing a quantity.
– DERIVATIVES **expressionless** adjective.

expressionism noun a style in art, music, or drama in which the artist or writer seeks to express the inner world of emotion rather than external reality.
– DERIVATIVES **expressionist** noun & adjective **expressionistic** adjective.

expressive adjective **1** effectively conveying thought or feeling. **2** (**expressive of**) conveying a quality or idea.
– DERIVATIVES **expressively** adverb **expressiveness** noun **expressivity** noun.

expresso noun variant spelling of ESPRESSO.

expressway noun N. Amer. an urban motorway.

expropriate /iks-proh-pri-ayt/ verb (of the state) take property from its owner for public use or benefit.
– DERIVATIVES **expropriation** noun **expropriator** noun.
– ORIGIN Latin *expropriare*.

expulsion noun the action of expelling someone or something.
– DERIVATIVES **expulsive** adjective.
– ORIGIN Latin.

expunge /ik-spunj/ verb completely remove something undesirable or unpleasant.
– ORIGIN Latin *expungere* 'mark for deletion by means of points'.

expurgate /eks-per-gayt/ verb remove matter regarded as obscene or unsuitable from a piece of writing.
– DERIVATIVES **expurgation** noun **expurgator** noun.
– ORIGIN Latin *expurgare* 'cleanse thoroughly'.

exquisite /ik-skwi-zit, ek-skwi-zit/ adjective 1 very beautiful and delicate. 2 highly refined: *exquisite taste.* 3 intensely felt: *the exquisite pain of love.*
– DERIVATIVES **exquisitely** adverb **exquisiteness** noun.
– ORIGIN from Latin *exquirere* 'seek out'.

ex-serviceman (or **ex-servicewoman**) noun (pl. **ex-servicemen** or **ex-servicewomen**) Brit. a former member of the armed forces.

extant /ik-stant, ek-stuhnt/ adjective still in existence.
– ORIGIN from Latin *exstare* 'be visible or prominent'.

extemporaneous /ik-stem-puh-**ray**-ni-uhss/ adjective another term for **EXTEMPORARY**.
– DERIVATIVES **extemporaneously** adverb.

extemporary /ik-**stem**-puh-ruh-ri/ adjective spoken or done without preparation.
– ORIGIN from **EXTEMPORE**.

extempore /ik-stem-puh-ri/ adjective & adverb spoken or done without preparation.
– ORIGIN from Latin *ex tempore* 'on the spur of the moment'.

extemporize (or **extemporise**) /ik-**stem**-puh-ryz/ verb compose or perform something without preparation; improvise.
– DERIVATIVES **extemporization** noun.

extend verb 1 make something larger or longer in space or time. 2 occupy a specified area or continue for a specified distance: *the damage extended 40 metres either side of the shop.* 3 offer or give: *it is part of the Church's teaching to extend the warmest welcome to all.* 4 stretch out the body or a limb. 5 strain or exert someone to the utmost.
– DERIVATIVES **extendable** adjective **extender** noun **extendible** adjective **extensibility** noun **extensible** adjective.
– ORIGIN Latin *extendere*.

extended family noun a family which extends beyond the parents and children to include grandparents and other relatives.

extension noun 1 the action of extending something. 2 a part added to a building to enlarge it. 3 an additional period of time allowed for something. 4 an extra telephone on the same line as the main one. 5 (**extensions**) lengths of long artificial hair woven into a person's own hair. 6 (Brit. also **extension lead** or **cable**) an additional length of electric cable which can be plugged into a fixed socket and has another socket on the end.
– DERIVATIVES **extensional** adjective.
– ORIGIN Latin.

extensive adjective 1 covering a large area. 2 large in amount or scale: *an extensive collection of antiques.* 3 (of agriculture) obtaining a relatively small crop from a large area with a minimum of capital and labour.
– DERIVATIVES **extensively** adverb **extensiveness** noun.

extensor /ik-sten-ser/ noun a muscle whose

contraction extends a limb or other part of the body.

extent noun 1 the area covered by something. 2 the size or scale of something: *they have no idea of the extent of the problem.* 3 the degree to which something is the case: *all couples edit the truth to some extent.*
– ORIGIN Old French *extente*.

extenuating /ik-sten-yoo-ay-ting/ adjective showing reasons why an offence should be treated less seriously: *hunger and poverty are not treated by the courts as extenuating circumstances.*
– DERIVATIVES **extenuation** noun.
– ORIGIN from Latin *extenuare* 'make thin'.

exterior adjective relating to, forming, or on the outside of something. •noun the outer surface or structure of something.
– DERIVATIVES **exteriorly** adverb.
– ORIGIN Latin.

exterminate /ik-ster-mi-nayt/ verb destroy someone or something completely.
– DERIVATIVES **extermination** noun **exterminator** noun.
– ORIGIN Latin *exterminare* 'drive out'.

external adjective 1 belonging to or forming the outside of something. 2 coming from a source outside the person or thing affected: *many external factors can influence the incidence of cancer.* 3 relating to another country or institution. •noun (**externals**) the outward features of something.
– DERIVATIVES **externally** adverb.
– ORIGIN Latin.

external ear noun the parts of the ear outside the eardrum, especially the pinna.

externalize (or **externalise**) verb 1 express a thought or feeling in words or actions. 2 give external existence or physical form to something.
– DERIVATIVES **externalization** noun.

extinct adjective 1 (of a species or other large group) having no living members. 2 no longer in existence. 3 (of a volcano) not having erupted in recorded history.
– ORIGIN from Latin *exstinguere* 'extinguish'.

extinction noun the state of being or process of becoming extinct.

extinguish verb 1 put out a fire or light. 2 put an end to: *no human life should be extinguished for the benefit of another.* 3 cancel a debt by full payment.
– DERIVATIVES **extinguisher** noun.
– ORIGIN Latin *exstinguere*.

extirpate /ek-ster-payt/ verb completely destroy something.
– DERIVATIVES **extirpation** noun.
– ORIGIN Latin *exstirpare*.

extol /ik-stohl/ verb (**extols, extolling, extolled**) praise someone or something enthusiastically.
– ORIGIN Latin *extollere*.

extort /ik-stort/ verb obtain something by force, threats, or other unfair means.
– DERIVATIVES **extortion** noun **extortionist** noun.
– ORIGIN Latin *extorquere*.

extortionate /ik-stor-shuh-nuht/ adjective (of a price) much too high.
– DERIVATIVES **extortionately** adverb.

e

extra adjective added to an existing or usual amount or number. • adverb **1** to a greater extent than usual. **2** in addition. • noun **1** an item in addition to what is usual or necessary, for which an extra charge is made. **2** a person taking part in a crowd scene in a film or play.
– ORIGIN probably from EXTRAORDINARY.

extra- prefix **1** outside; beyond: *extramarital.* **2** beyond the scope of: *extra-curricular.*
– ORIGIN Latin *extra* 'outside'.

extract verb /ik-**strakt**/ **1** remove something with care or effort. **2** obtain a substance or resource from something by a special method. **3** obtain something from someone unwilling to give it: *in the Middle Ages, they would torture people to extract a false confession.* **4** select a passage from a written work, film, or piece of music for quotation, performance, or reproduction. • noun /**ek**-strakt/ **1** a short passage taken from a written work, film, or piece of music. **2** the concentrated form of the active ingredient of a substance: *vanilla extract.*
– DERIVATIVES **extractable** adjective **extractive** adjective.
– ORIGIN Latin *extrahere* 'draw out'.

extraction noun **1** the action of extracting something. **2** the ethnic origin of someone's family: *a woman of Polish extraction.*

extractor noun a machine or device used to extract something. • adjective referring to a fan used for removing unpleasant smells and stale air from a room.

extra-curricular adjective (of an activity at a school or college) done in addition to the normal curriculum.

extradite /**ek**-struh-dyt/ verb hand over a person accused or convicted of a crime in a foreign state to the legal authority of that state.
– DERIVATIVES **extradition** noun.
– ORIGIN from French *extradition.*

extramarital /eks-truh-**ma**-ri-t'l/ adjective occurring outside marriage.

extramural /eks-truh-**myoor**-uhl/ adjective **1** Brit. (of a course of study) arranged for people who are not full-time members of a university or other educational establishment. **2** outside the boundaries of a town or city.
– DERIVATIVES **extramurally** adverb.
– ORIGIN from Latin *extra muros* 'outside the walls'.

extraneous /ik-**stray**-ni-uhss/ adjective **1** unrelated to the subject; irrelevant. **2** of external origin.
– DERIVATIVES **extraneously** adverb.
– ORIGIN Latin *extraneus.*

extranet noun an intranet that can be partially accessed by authorized outside users, enabling organizations to exchange data in a secure way.

extraordinaire /ek-struh-or-di-**nair**/ adjective outstanding in a particular area: *a gardener extraordinaire.*
– ORIGIN French.

extraordinary adjective **1** very unusual or remarkable. **2** (of a meeting) specially arranged rather than being one of a regular series. **3** (of an official) specially employed: *Ambassador Extraordinary.*

– DERIVATIVES **extraordinarily** adverb **extraordinariness** noun.
– ORIGIN from Latin *extra ordinem* 'outside the normal course of events'.

extrapolate /ik-**strap**-uh-layt/ verb **1** use a fact or conclusion that is valid for one situation and apply it to a different or larger one. **2** extend a graph by inferring unknown values from trends in the known data.
– DERIVATIVES **extrapolation** noun **extrapolative** adjective.
– ORIGIN from EXTRA- + a shortened form of INTERPOLATE.

extrasensory perception /eks-truh-**sen**-suh-ri/ noun the supposed faculty of perceiving things by means other than the known senses, e.g. by telepathy.

extraterrestrial /eks-truh-tuh-**ress**-tri-uhl/ adjective relating to things beyond the earth or its atmosphere. • noun a fictional being from outer space.

extra time noun Brit. a further period of play added on to a game if the scores are equal.

extravagant /ik-**strav**-uh-guhnt/ adjective **1** lacking restraint in spending money or using resources. **2** costing a great deal. **3** exceeding what is reasonable or appropriate: *extravagant claims about the product.*
– DERIVATIVES **extravagance** noun **extravagantly** adverb.
– ORIGIN from Latin *extravagari* 'diverge greatly'.

extravaganza /ik-stra-vuh-**gan**-zuh/ noun an elaborate and spectacular entertainment.
– ORIGIN Italian *estravaganza* 'extravagance'.

extra virgin adjective (of olive oil) of a particularly fine grade, made from the first pressing of the olives.

extreme adjective **1** to the highest degree; very great. **2** highly unusual; exceptional: *in extreme cases the soldier may be discharged.* **3** very severe or serious. **4** not moderate, especially politically. **5** furthest from the centre or a given point: *the extreme north of Scotland.* **6** (of a sport) performed in a dangerous environment. • noun **1** either of two things that are as different from each other as possible. **2** the most extreme degree: *extremes of temperature.*
– DERIVATIVES **extremely** adverb.
– ORIGIN Latin *extremus* 'outermost, utmost'.

extreme unction noun (in the Roman Catholic Church) a former name for the sacrament of anointing of the sick, especially when administered to the dying.

extremist noun a person who holds extreme political or religious views.
– DERIVATIVES **extremism** noun.

extremity /ik-**strem**-i-ti/ noun (pl. **extremities**) **1** the furthest point or limit. **2** (**extremities**) the hands and feet. **3** severity or seriousness: *the extremity of the violence.* **4** extreme difficulty or hardship.

extricate /**eks**-tri-kayt/ verb free from a difficult or restrictive situation or place: *the company has to extricate itself from its current financial mess.*
– DERIVATIVES **extrication** noun.
– ORIGIN Latin *extricare* 'unravel'.

extrinsic /eks-**trin**-sik/ adjective coming or

operating from outside; not part of the essential nature of something: *population regulation probably involved both extrinsic and intrinsic factors.*
- DERIVATIVES **extrinsically** adverb.
- ORIGIN Latin *extrinsecus* 'outward'.

extrovert /ek-struh-vert/ noun **1** an outgoing, socially confident person. **2** Psychology a person predominantly concerned with external things or objective considerations. •adjective relating to or typical of an extrovert.
- DERIVATIVES **extroversion** noun **extroverted** adjective.
- ORIGIN from *extro-* (variant of EXTRA-) + Latin *vertere* 'to turn'.

extrude /ik-strood/ verb **1** thrust or force something out. **2** shape a material such as metal or plastic by forcing it through a die.
- DERIVATIVES **extrusion** noun.
- ORIGIN Latin *extrudere*.

extrusive adjective (of rock) that has been forced out at the earth's surface as lava or other volcanic deposits.

exuberant /ig-zyoo-buh-ruhnt/ adjective **1** lively and cheerful. **2** literary growing profusely.
- DERIVATIVES **exuberance** noun **exuberantly** adverb.
- ORIGIN from Latin *exuberare* 'be abundantly fruitful'.

exude /ig-zyood/ verb **1** (of liquid or a smell) discharge or be discharged slowly and steadily. **2** clearly display an emotion or quality: *silk skirts exuding elegance.*
- DERIVATIVES **exudation** noun.
- ORIGIN Latin *exsudare*, from *sudare* 'to sweat'.

exult verb show or feel triumphant elation.
- DERIVATIVES **exultation** noun.
- ORIGIN Latin *exsultare*.

exultant adjective triumphantly happy.
- DERIVATIVES **exultancy** noun **exultantly** adverb.

ex-voto /eks-voh-toh/ noun (pl. **ex-votos**) an offering given in order to fulfil a vow.
- ORIGIN from Latin *ex voto* 'from a vow'.

eye noun **1** the organ of sight in humans and animals. **2** the small hole in a needle through which the thread is passed. **3** a small metal loop into which a hook is fitted as a fastener on a garment. **4** a person's opinion or feelings: *to European eyes, the city seems overcrowded.* **5** an eye-like marking on an animal or bird. **6** a round, dark spot on a potato from which a new shoot grows. **7** the calm region at the centre of a storm. •verb (**eyes**, **eyeing** or **eying**, **eyed**) **1** look at someone or something closely or with interest. **2** (**eye someone up**) informal look at someone in a way that reveals a sexual interest.
- PHRASES **be all eyes** be watching eagerly and attentively. **an eye for an eye and a tooth for a tooth** doing the same thing in return is the appropriate way to deal with an offence or crime. [from the Book of Exodus, chapter 21.] **give someone the eye** informal look at someone with sexual interest. **have an eye for** be able to recognize and judge something wisely. **have one's eye on** aim to acquire something. **have (or keep) one's eye on** keep someone under careful observation. **have (or with) an eye to** have (or having) as one's objective. **have eyes

in the back of one's head know what is going on around one even when one cannot see it. **keep an eye out** (or **open**) look out for something. **make eyes at** look at someone with sexual interest. **one in the eye for** a disappointment or setback for someone. **open someone's eyes** cause someone to realize something. **see eye to eye** be in full agreement. **a twinkle** (or **gleam**) **in someone's eye** something that is as yet no more than an idea or dream. **up to one's eyes** informal very busy. **with one's eyes open** fully aware of possible difficulties.
- DERIVATIVES **eyed** adjective.
- ORIGIN Old English.

eyeball noun the round part of the eye of a vertebrate, within the eyelids and socket. •verb informal stare at someone or something closely.
- PHRASES **eyeball to eyeball** face to face with someone, especially in an aggressive way.

eyebrow noun the strip of hair growing on the ridge above a person's eye socket.
- PHRASES **raise one's eyebrows** (or **an eyebrow**) show surprise or mild disapproval.

eye-catching adjective immediately appealing or noticeable.

eyeful noun informal **1** a long steady look. **2** an eye-catching person or thing.

eyeglass noun **1** a single lens for correcting or assisting poor eyesight, especially a monocle. **2** (**eyeglasses**) N. Amer. another term for GLASSES.

eyelash noun each of the short hairs growing on the edges of the eyelids.

eyelet noun **1** a small round hole made in leather or cloth, used for threading a lace, string, or rope through. **2** a metal ring reinforcing an eyelet.
- ORIGIN Old French *oillet*.

eyelid noun each of the upper and lower folds of skin which cover the eye when closed.

eyeliner noun a cosmetic applied as a line round the eyes.

eye-opener noun informal an event or situation that proves to be unexpectedly revealing.

eyepatch noun a patch worn to protect an injured eye.

eyepiece noun the lens that is closest to the eye in a microscope or other optical instrument.

eye-popping adjective informal astonishingly large or blatant.

eyeshade noun a translucent visor used to protect the eyes from strong light.

eyeshadow noun a coloured cosmetic applied to the eyelids or to the skin around the eyes.

eyesight noun a person's ability to see.

eye socket noun the cavity in the skull which encloses an eyeball with its surrounding muscles.

eyesore noun a very ugly thing.

eye tooth noun a canine tooth, especially one in the upper jaw.
- PHRASES **give one's eye teeth for** (or **to do**) do anything in order to have or do something.

eyewash noun **1** liquid for cleansing a person's eye. **2** informal nonsense.

eyewitness noun a person who has seen

something happen and can give a first-hand description of it.

eyrie /eer-i, I-ri/ (US also **aerie**) **noun** a large nest of an eagle or other bird of prey, typically built high in a tree or on a cliff.

– ORIGIN probably from Old French *aire*.

eyrir /I-reer/ **noun** (pl. **aurar** /aw-rar/) a unit of money of Iceland, equal to one hundredth of a krona.

– ORIGIN Icelandic.

F[1] (also **f**) noun (pl. **Fs** or **F's**) **1** the sixth letter of the alphabet. **2** Music the fourth note of the scale of C major.

F[2] abbreviation **1** Fahrenheit. **2** farad(s). **3** (in racing results) favourite. **4** female. **5** Brit. fine (used in describing grades of pencil lead). **6** franc(s). •symbol **1** the chemical element fluorine. **2** Physics force.

f abbreviation **1** Grammar feminine. **2** (in textual references) folio. **3** Music forte. **4** (in racing results) furlong(s). •symbol **1** focal length. **2** Electronics frequency.

FA abbreviation (in the UK) Football Association.

fa noun variant spelling of **FAH**.

fab adjective informal fabulous; wonderful.

Fabian /fay-bi-uhn/ noun a member or supporter of the Fabian Society, an organization which aims to establish socialism in a gradual way that does not involve revolution. •adjective **1** relating to the Fabians. **2** using cautious delaying tactics to wear out an enemy.
– DERIVATIVES **Fabianism** noun **Fabianist** noun.
– ORIGIN from the name of the Roman general Quintus *Fabius* Maximus Verrucosus, known for his delaying tactics.

fable noun **1** a short story with a moral, typically featuring animals as characters. **2** a myth or legend.
– ORIGIN Old French, from Latin *fabula* 'story'.

fabled adjective **1** famous: *a fabled guitarist.* **2** mythical or imaginary: *a fabled beast.*

fabric noun **1** material produced by weaving or knitting textile fibres; cloth. **2** the walls, floor, and roof of a building. **3** the essential structure of a system or organization: *the fabric of society.*
– ORIGIN Latin *fabrica* 'something skilfully produced'.

fabricate verb **1** invent something, typically in order to deceive other people: *police officers had fabricated evidence to secure convictions.* **2** construct or manufacture an industrial product.
– DERIVATIVES **fabrication** noun **fabricator** noun.
– ORIGIN Latin *fabricare* 'manufacture'.

fabulist noun **1** a person who composes fables. **2** a liar.

fabulous adjective **1** very great; extraordinary: *his fabulous wealth.* **2** informal wonderful. **3** mythical.
– DERIVATIVES **fabulously** adverb **fabulousness** noun.

– ORIGIN Latin *fabulosus* 'celebrated in fable', from *fabula* 'story'.

facade /fuh-**sahd**/ noun **1** the face of a building, especially the front. **2** a deceptive outward appearance: *her facade of bravery crumbled and she burst into tears.*
– ORIGIN French, from *face* 'face'.

face noun **1** the front part of a person's head from the forehead to the chin, or the corresponding part in an animal. **2** an expression on someone's face. **3** the front or main surface of something. **4** a vertical or sloping side of a mountain or cliff. **5** an aspect: *the unacceptable face of social drinking.* •verb **1** be positioned with the face or front towards or in a particular direction: *the house faces due east.* **2** confront and deal with or accept: *I had to face the fact that I might never have a child.* **3** have a difficult event or situation ahead of one: *the president is facing a political crisis.* **4** (**face off**) chiefly N. Amer. get ready to argue or fight with someone. **5** cover the surface of something with a layer of a different material.
– PHRASES **face the music** be confronted with the unpleasant results of one's actions. **face to face** close together and looking directly at one another. **in the face of** when confronted with something. **lose** (or **save**) **face** suffer (or avoid) humiliation. **on the face of it** apparently. **set one's face against** resist something with determination. **to someone's face** used to refer to remarks made openly and directly to someone.
– DERIVATIVES **-faced** adjective.
– ORIGIN Old French, from Latin *facies* 'appearance, face'.

facecloth noun a small towelling cloth for washing one's face.

faceless adjective having no distinguishing characteristics or identity: *faceless bureaucrats.*

facelift noun **1** a surgical operation to remove unwanted wrinkles by tightening the skin of the face. **2** a procedure carried out to improve the appearance of something.

face mask noun **1** a protective mask covering the face or part of the face. **2** a face pack.

face-off noun **1** a direct confrontation. **2** Ice Hockey the start of play.

face pack noun Brit. a cosmetic preparation spread over the face to improve the skin.

face-saving adjective preserving one's reputation or dignity.

facet /fa-set/ noun **1** one of the sides of a cut

gemstone. **2** an aspect: *every facet of our business.*
- DERIVATIVES **faceted** adjective.
- ORIGIN French *facette* 'little face'.

facetious /fuh-see-shuhss/ adjective showing inappropriate humour or trying to be amusing at an inappropriate time.
- DERIVATIVES **facetiously** adverb **facetiousness** noun.
- ORIGIN French *facétieux*.

face value noun the value printed or depicted on a coin, postage stamp, etc.
- PHRASES **take something at face value** accept or believe that something is what it appears to be.

facia noun chiefly Brit. variant spelling of **FASCIA**.

facial /fay-sh'l/ adjective relating to or affecting the face. • noun a beauty treatment for the face.
- DERIVATIVES **facially** adverb.

facile /fa-syl/ adjective **1** (of an idea, remark, etc.) simplistic and lacking careful thought. **2** (of success) easily achieved.
- ORIGIN Latin *facilis* 'easy'.

facilitate /fuh-sil-i-tayt/ verb make something easy or easier.
- DERIVATIVES **facilitation** noun **facilitative** adjective **facilitator** noun.
- ORIGIN from Latin *facilis* 'easy'.

facility noun (pl. **facilities**) **1** a building, service, or piece of equipment provided for a particular purpose. **2** a natural ability to do something well and easily.

facing noun **1** a piece of material attached to the edge of a garment at the neck, armhole, etc. and turned inside, used to strengthen the edge. **2** an outer layer covering the surface of a wall. • adjective positioned so as to face something.

facsimile /fak-sim-i-li/ noun an exact copy, especially of written or printed material.
- ORIGIN from Latin *fac!* 'make!' and *simile*, from *similis* 'like'.

fact noun **1** a thing that is definitely known to be true. **2** (**facts**) information used as evidence or as part of a report.
- PHRASES **before** (or **after**) **the fact** Law before (or after) the committing of a crime. **a fact of life** something that must be accepted, even if unpleasant. **the facts of life** information about sex and reproduction. **in** (**point of**) **fact** in reality.
- ORIGIN Latin *factum* 'an act'.

faction[1] noun a small group within a larger one whose members disagree with some of the beliefs of the larger group.
- DERIVATIVES **factional** adjective **factionalism** noun.
- ORIGIN Latin *facere* 'do, make'.

faction[2] noun a type of literature or cinema in which real events are used as a basis for a fictional story or dramatization.
- ORIGIN blend of **FACT** and **FICTION**.

factious /fak-shuss/ adjective relating to or causing disagreement.
- ORIGIN Latin *factiosus*.

factitious /fak-ti-shuss/ adjective not genuine; made up.
- ORIGIN Latin *facticius* 'made by art'.

factoid noun **1** a piece of unreliable information that is repeated so often that it becomes accepted as fact. **2** N. Amer. a brief or trivial piece of information.

factor noun **1** a circumstance, fact, or influence that contributes to a result: *ill health was an important factor in his decision to retire early.* **2** Mathematics a number or quantity that when multiplied with another produces a given number or expression. **3** a level on a scale of measurement: *sun cream with a protection factor of 15.* **4** any of a number of substances in the blood which are involved in clotting. **5** a gene that determines a hereditary characteristic. **6** an agent who buys and sells goods on commission. **7** Scottish a land agent or steward. • verb (**factor something in/out**) include (or exclude) something as relevant when making a decision.
- ORIGIN Latin *facere* 'do'.

factorial Mathematics noun the product of an integer and all the integers below it, e.g. $4 \times 3 \times 2 \times 1$ (*factorial 4*, denoted by $4!$ and equal to 24). • adjective relating to a factor or factorial.

factorize (or **factorise**) verb Mathematics break down or be able to be broken down into factors.
- DERIVATIVES **factorization** noun.

factor VIII (also **factor eight**) noun a blood protein involved in the clotting of blood, a lack of which causes one of the main forms of haemophilia.

factory noun (pl. **factories**) a building where goods are manufactured or assembled chiefly by machine.
- ORIGIN Latin *factorium* 'oil press'.

factory farming noun a system of rearing poultry, pigs, or cattle indoors under strictly controlled conditions.

factory floor noun the workers in a company or industry, rather than the management.

factory outlet noun a shop in which goods, especially surplus stock, are sold directly by the manufacturers at a discount.

factotum /fak-toh-tuhm/ noun (pl. **factotums**) an employee who does all kinds of work.
- ORIGIN from Latin *fac!* 'do!' + *totum* 'the whole thing'.

factual /fak-choo-uhl/ adjective based on or concerned with fact or facts.
- DERIVATIVES **factually** adverb.

faculty noun (pl. **faculties**) **1** a basic mental or physical power: *the faculty of sight.* **2** an ability: *his faculty for taking the initiative.* **3** a group of university departments concerned with a particular area of knowledge. **4** N. Amer. the teaching or research staff of a university or college.
- ORIGIN Latin *facultas*, from *facilis* 'easy'.

fad noun **1** a craze. **2** a fussy like or dislike.
- DERIVATIVES **faddish** adjective **faddism** noun **faddist** noun.
- ORIGIN uncertain.

faddy adjective (**faddier**, **faddiest**) Brit. having many likes and dislikes about food; fussy.

fade verb **1** gradually grow faint and disappear. **2** lose or cause to lose colour. **3** (of a film or video image or recorded sound) become more or less clear or loud. • noun an act of fading.
- ORIGIN Old French *fader*.

fader noun a device for varying the volume of sound in a film or video recording, or the intensity of light.

fado /**fah**-doh/ noun (pl. **fados**) a type of popular Portuguese song, usually with a sad theme.
– ORIGIN Portuguese, 'fate'.

faeces /**fee**-seez/ (US **feces**) plural noun waste matter remaining after food has been digested, passed out of the body through the anus.
– DERIVATIVES **faecal** /**fee**-k'l/ adjective.
– ORIGIN Latin, plural of *faex* 'dregs'.

faerie /**fay**-uh-ri, **fair**-i/ (also **faery**) noun old use or literary fairyland.
– ORIGIN introduced as a variant of *fairy* by the English poet Edmund Spenser in *The Faerie Queene*.

Faeroese noun & adjective variant spelling of **FAROESE**.

faff Brit. informal verb (usu. **faff about/around**) spend time doing things in a disorganized or ineffectual way. •noun disorganized or ineffectual activity.
– ORIGIN dialect 'blow in puffs', describing the wind.

fag[1] noun Brit. informal a cigarette.
– ORIGIN from **FAG END**.

fag[2] Brit. noun **1** informal a tiring or unwelcome task. **2** a junior pupil at a public school who does minor chores for a senior pupil. •verb (**fags, fagging, fagged**) **1** (of a public-school pupil) act as a fag. **2** (as adj. **fagged out**) informal exhausted. **3** informal work hard.
– ORIGIN unknown.

fag[3] noun N. Amer. informal, derogatory a male homosexual.
– DERIVATIVES **faggy** adjective.
– ORIGIN short for **FAGGOT** (in sense 3).

fag end noun Brit. informal **1** a cigarette end. **2** the last and least important part of something: *the fag end of the campaign.*
– ORIGIN from former *fag* 'a flap'.

faggot /**fag**-guht/ noun **1** Brit. a ball of seasoned chopped liver, baked or fried. **2** (US **fagot**) a bundle of sticks bound together as fuel. **3** N. Amer. informal, derogatory a male homosexual.
– DERIVATIVES **faggoty** adjective.
– ORIGIN Old French *fagot*, from Greek *phakelos* 'bundle'.

faggoting (US **fagoting**) noun embroidery in which threads are fastened together in bundles.

fah (also **fa**) noun Music the fourth note of a major scale, coming after 'me' and before 'soh'.
– ORIGIN the first syllable of *famuli*, taken from a Latin hymn.

Fahr. abbreviation Fahrenheit.

Fahrenheit /**fa**-ruhn-hyt/ adjective relating to a scale of temperature on which water freezes at 32° and boils at 212°.
– ORIGIN named after the German physicist Gabriel Daniel *Fahrenheit*.

faience /fy-**ahnss**/ noun a type of glazed ceramic earthenware.
– ORIGIN from *Faenza*, a town in Italy.

fail verb **1** be unsuccessful in achieving something. **2** be unable to meet the standards set by a test. **3** neglect to do something: *she failed to keep the appointment.* **4** not happen in the way expected: *chaos has failed to materialize.* **5** stop working properly. **6** become weaker or less good: *his sight was failing.* **7** let someone down: *her courage failed her.* **8** go out of business. •noun a mark which is not high enough to pass an exam or test.
– PHRASES **without fail** whatever happens.
– ORIGIN from Latin *fallere* 'deceive'.

failing noun a weakness in a person's character. •preposition if not.

fail-safe adjective **1** causing machinery to return to a safe condition if a breakdown occurs. **2** unlikely or unable to fail.

failure noun **1** lack of success. **2** an unsuccessful person or thing. **3** an instance of not doing something that is expected: *their failure to comply with the rules.* **4** an instance of something not functioning properly.

fain old use adverb gladly. •adjective willing or obliged to do something.
– ORIGIN Old English, 'happy'.

faint adjective **1** not clearly seen, heard, or smelt. **2** (of a hope, chance, or idea) slight. **3** close to losing consciousness. •verb briefly lose consciousness because of an inadequate supply of oxygen to the brain. •noun a sudden loss of consciousness.
– DERIVATIVES **faintly** adverb **faintness** noun.
– ORIGIN Old French *faindre* 'feign'.

USAGE: Do not confuse **faint** with **feint**. Faint means 'not clearly seen, heard, or smelt' (*the faint murmur of voices*) or 'lose consciousness', whereas **feint** means 'a pretended attacking movement' or 'make a pretended attacking movement'.

faint-hearted adjective timid.

fair[1] adjective **1** treating people equally. **2** just or appropriate in the circumstances. **3** considerable in size or amount: *I do a fair bit of business travelling.* **4** moderately good. **5** (of hair or complexion) light; blonde. **6** (of weather) fine and dry. **7** old use beautiful. •adverb **1** in a fair way. **2** dialect very: *she'll be fair delighted to see you.*
– PHRASES **fair and square 1** with absolute accuracy. **2** honestly and straightforwardly. **fair dinkum** see **DINKUM**. **the fair sex** (also **the fairer sex**) dated or humorous women.
– DERIVATIVES **fairish** adjective **fairness** noun.
– ORIGIN Old English.

fair[2] noun **1** a gathering of sideshows, rides, and other amusements for public entertainment. **2** an event at which people, businesses, etc. display and sell goods. **3** an exhibition held to promote particular products.
– ORIGIN Latin *feria*, from *feriae* 'holy days' (on which fairs were often held).

fair copy noun a copy of written or printed matter produced after final corrections have been made.

fair game noun a person or thing regarded as a reasonable target for criticism or exploitation.

fairground noun an outdoor area where a fair is held.

fairing noun a structure added to increase the streamlining on a vehicle, boat, or aircraft.

Fair Isle noun a traditional multicoloured geometric design used in woollen knitwear.

– ORIGIN *Fair Isle* in the Shetlands, where the design was first devised.

fairly adverb **1** with justice. **2** moderately. **3** used for emphasis: *he fairly snarled at her.*

fair-minded adjective judging things in a fair and impartial way.

fair play noun respect for the rules or equal treatment for all.

fair trade noun trade in which fair prices are paid to producers in developing countries.

fairway noun **1** the part of a golf course between a tee and a green. **2** a channel in a river or harbour which can be used by shipping.

fair-weather friend noun a person whose friendship cannot be relied on in times of difficulty.

fairy noun (pl. **fairies**) **1** a small imaginary being of human form that has magical powers. **2** informal, derogatory a male homosexual.
– ORIGIN Old French *faerie* 'fairyland', from *fae* 'a fairy'.

fairy cake noun Brit. a small iced sponge cake.

fairy godmother noun a female character in fairy stories who brings unexpected good fortune to the hero or heroine.

fairyland noun the imaginary home of fairies.

fairy lights plural noun Brit. small coloured electric lights used for decoration, especially on a Christmas tree.

fairy ring noun a ring of dark grass caused by the growth of certain fungi, once believed to have been made by fairies dancing.

fairy story noun **1** a children's tale about magical and imaginary beings and lands. **2** an untrue account.

fairy tale noun a fairy story. • adjective magical, idealized, or perfect: *a fairy-tale romance.*

fait accompli /fayt uh-**kom**-pli/ noun a thing that has been done or decided and cannot now be altered.
– ORIGIN French, 'accomplished fact'.

faith noun **1** complete trust or confidence in someone or something. **2** strong belief in a religion. **3** a system of religious belief.
– ORIGIN from Latin *fides*.

faithful adjective **1** remaining loyal. **2** remaining sexually loyal to a lover or to a husband or wife. **3** true to the facts or the original: *a faithful copy.* • noun (**the faithful**) those who are faithful to a particular religion or political party.
– DERIVATIVES **faithfully** adverb **faithfulness** noun.

faith healing noun a method of treating a sick person through the power of religious faith and prayer, rather than by medical means.

faithless adjective **1** disloyal, especially to a lover, husband, or wife. **2** without religious faith.
– DERIVATIVES **faithlessness** noun.

fajitas /fuh-**hee**-tuhz/ plural noun a Mexican dish consisting of strips of spiced meat with vegetables and cheese, wrapped in a soft tortilla.
– ORIGIN Mexican Spanish, 'little strips'.

fake adjective not genuine. • noun a person or thing that is not genuine. • verb **1** make something that seems genuine in order to deceive other people: *she faked her spouse's*

signature. **2** pretend to have a particular feeling or illness.
– DERIVATIVES **faker** noun **fakery** noun.
– ORIGIN uncertain.

fakir /**fay**-keer/ noun a Muslim (or, loosely, a Hindu) holy man who lives on charitable donations.
– ORIGIN Arabic, 'needy man'.

falafel /fuh-**la**-fuhl/ (also **felafel**) noun a Middle Eastern dish of spiced mashed chickpeas formed into balls and deep-fried.
– ORIGIN Arabic, 'pepper'.

falcon /**fawl**-k'n/ noun a fast-flying bird of prey with long pointed wings.
– ORIGIN Old French *faucon.*

falconry noun the skill of keeping birds of prey and training them to hunt.
– DERIVATIVES **falconer** noun.

fall verb (past **fell**; past part. **fallen**) **1** move downwards quickly and without control. **2** collapse to the ground. **3** (**fall off**) become detached and drop to the ground. **4** hang or slope down: *the land fell away in a steep bank.* **5** (of someone's face) show dismay or disappointment. **6** decrease: *the level of unemployment is falling.* **7** become: *she fell silent.* **8** occur: *her birthday fell on a Sunday.* **9** be captured or defeated in a battle or contest. **10** (**fall to**) become someone's duty. • noun **1** an act of falling. **2** a thing which falls or has fallen. **3** a waterfall. **4** a decrease. **5** a defeat or downfall. **6** N. Amer. autumn.
– PHRASES **fall back** retreat. **fall back on** turn to something when in difficulty. **fall for** informal **1** fall in love with. **2** be deceived by. **fall foul of** come into conflict with. **fall in** (or **into**) **line** do what one is told or what other people do. **fall into place** begin to make sense. **fall in with 1** meet someone by chance and become involved with them. **2** agree to something. **fall on 1** attack someone fiercely or unexpectedly. **2** be someone's duty. **fall out** have an argument. **fall short** (**of**) **1** (of a missile) fail to reach its target. **2** fail to reach a required standard. **fall through** (of a plan, project, etc.) not happen or be completed.
– ORIGIN Old English.

fallacious /fuh-**lay**-shuss/ adjective based on a mistaken belief; wrong: *a fallacious argument.*

fallacy /**fal**-luh-si/ noun (pl. **fallacies**) **1** a mistaken belief. **2** a mistake in reasoning which makes an argument invalid.
– ORIGIN from Latin *fallere* 'deceive'.

fallback noun an alternative plan for use in an emergency.

fallen past participle of **FALL**. adjective **1** dated (of a woman) regarded as having lost her honour as a result of an extramarital sexual relationship. **2** killed in battle.

fallen angel noun (in Christian, Jewish, and Muslim tradition) an angel who rebelled against God and was cast out of heaven.

fall guy noun informal a person who is blamed for something that is not their fault; a scapegoat.

fallible /**fal**-li-b'l/ adjective capable of making mistakes or being wrong.
– DERIVATIVES **fallibility** noun.
– ORIGIN from Latin *fallere* 'deceive'.

falling-out noun a quarrel.

falling star noun a meteor or shooting star.

fall-off (also **falling-off**) noun a decrease.

Fallopian tube /fuh-**loh**-pi-uhn/ noun (in a female mammal) either of a pair of tubes along which eggs travel from the ovaries to the womb.
– ORIGIN named after the Italian anatomist Gabriello *Fallopio*.

fallout noun 1 radioactive particles spread over a wide area after a nuclear explosion. 2 the bad results of a situation or action: *the political fallout from his decision.*

fallow¹ adjective 1 (of farmland) ploughed but left for a period of time without being planted with crops. 2 (of a period of time) when nothing is done or achieved.
– ORIGIN Old English.

fallow² noun a pale brown or reddish yellow colour.
– ORIGIN Old English.

fallow deer noun a small deer which has a white-spotted reddish-brown coat in summer.
– ORIGIN Old English, 'pale brown'.

false adjective 1 not correct or true; wrong. 2 invalid or illegal: *false imprisonment.* 3 not genuine; artificial: *false eyelashes.* 4 based on something that is not true or correct: *a false sense of security.* 5 literary (of a person) not faithful.
– DERIVATIVES **falsely** adverb **falseness** noun **falsity** noun.
– ORIGIN from Latin *falsum* 'fraud'.

false alarm noun a warning given about something that does not happen.

false dawn noun a promising situation which comes to nothing.

false economy noun an apparent financial saving that in fact leads to greater expenditure.

falsehood noun 1 the state of being untrue. 2 a lie.

false memory noun an apparent memory of an event, especially one of childhood sexual abuse, which did not actually happen, arising from techniques used in psychoanalysis.

false move noun an unwise action that could have dangerous consequences.

false pretences plural noun behaviour intended to deceive other people.

false start noun an occasion when a competitor in a race starts before the official signal has been given, so that the race has to be started again.

false step noun 1 a slip or stumble. 2 a mistake.

falsetto /fawl-**set**-toh/ noun (pl. **falsettos**) a high-pitched voice above a person's natural range, used by male singers.
– ORIGIN Italian, from *falso* 'false'.

falsify /**fawl**-si-fy/ verb (**falsifies, falsifying, falsified**) alter information or evidence so as to mislead others.
– DERIVATIVES **falsifiable** adjective **falsification** noun.

falter /**fawl**-ter/ verb 1 lose strength or momentum. 2 move or speak hesitantly.
– DERIVATIVES **faltering** adjective.
– ORIGIN perhaps from **FOLD¹**.

fame noun the state of being famous.

famed adjective famous; well known.

familiar adjective 1 well known as a result of long or close association: *a familiar figure.* 2 frequently encountered; common: *the situation was all too familiar.* 3 (**familiar with**) having a good knowledge of: *he's familiar with the property market.* 4 friendly. 5 more friendly or informal than is appropriate. •noun 1 (also **familiar spirit**) a spirit supposedly attending and obeying a witch. 2 a close friend or associate.
– DERIVATIVES **familiarity** noun (pl. **familiarities**) **familiarly** adverb.
– ORIGIN from Latin *familia* 'household servants, family'.

familiarize (or **familiarise**) verb (**familiarize someone with**) give someone better knowledge or understanding of something.
– DERIVATIVES **familiarization** noun.

family noun (pl. **families**) 1 a group consisting of parents and their children living together as a unit. 2 a group of people related by blood or marriage. 3 the children of a person or couple. 4 all the descendants of a common ancestor: *the house has been in the family for 300 years.* 5 a group of things that are alike in some way. 6 Biology a main category into which animals and plants are divided, ranking above genus and below order. •adjective designed to be suitable for children as well as adults: *family entertainment.*
– PHRASES **in the family way** informal pregnant.
– DERIVATIVES **familial** adjective.
– ORIGIN Latin *familia* 'household servants, family'.

family credit noun (in the UK) a regular payment made by the state to a family with an income below a certain level.

family name noun a surname.

family planning noun the control of the number of children in a family by means of contraception.

family tree noun a diagram showing the relationship between people in several generations of a family.

family values plural noun values supposedly characteristic of a traditional family unit, typically those of high moral standards and discipline.

famine /**famm**-in/ noun a severe shortage of food.
– ORIGIN from Latin *fames*.

famished adjective informal extremely hungry.
– ORIGIN Latin *fames* 'hunger'.

famous adjective 1 known about by many people. 2 informal magnificent.
– DERIVATIVES **famously** adverb.
– ORIGIN from Latin *fama* 'fame'.

fan¹ noun 1 a device with rotating blades that creates a current of air for cooling or ventilation. 2 a hand-held device that is waved so as to cool the user. •verb (**fans, fanning, fanned**) 1 wave something so as to drive a current of air towards someone or something. 2 (of an air current) increase the strength of a fire. 3 make a belief or emotion stronger: *his scathing tones had fanned her curiosity.* 4 (**fan out**) spread out from a central point to cover a wide area.
– ORIGIN Latin *vannus*.

fan² noun a person who has a strong interest in

or admiration for a particular sport, art form, famous person, etc.
– DERIVATIVES **fandom** noun.
– ORIGIN abbreviation of **FANATIC**.

fanatic noun **1** a person who holds extreme or dangerous religious or political opinions. **2** informal a person with an obsessive enthusiasm for a pastime or hobby.
– DERIVATIVES **fanatical** adjective **fanatically** adverb **fanaticism** noun.
– ORIGIN from Latin *fanaticus* 'of a temple, inspired by a god'.

fan belt noun a belt driving the fan that cools the radiator of a motor vehicle.

fancier noun a person who has a special interest in or breeds a particular animal.

fanciful adjective **1** over-imaginative and unrealistic. **2** existing only in the imagination. **3** highly ornamental or imaginative in design.
– DERIVATIVES **fancifully** adverb **fancifulness** noun.

fan club noun an organized group of fans of a famous person or team.

fancy verb (**fancies, fancying, fancied**) chiefly Brit. **1** informal want or want to do. **2** informal find someone sexually attractive. **3** regard someone or something as a likely winner. **4** think: *I fancied I could hear their laughter.* **5** used to express surprise: *fancy that!* ● adjective (**fancier, fanciest**) **1** elaborate or highly decorated. **2** sophisticated or expensive: *a fancy Italian restaurant.* ● noun (pl. **fancies**) **1** a superficial or brief feeling of attraction. **2** the power of imagining things. **3** something that is imagined.
– PHRASES **take someone's fancy** appeal to someone. **take a fancy to** become fond of someone or something.
– DERIVATIVES **fanciable** adjective (informal) **fancily** adverb **fanciness** noun.
– ORIGIN from **FANTASY**.

fancy dress noun a costume worn to make someone look like a famous person, a well-known fictional character, an animal, etc.

fancy-free adjective not emotionally involved with anyone.

fancy man noun informal, often derogatory a woman's lover.

fancy woman noun informal, often derogatory a married man's mistress.

fandango /fan-dang-goh/ noun (pl. **fandangoes** or **fandangos**) a lively Spanish dance for two people.
– ORIGIN Spanish.

fanfare noun **1** a short ceremonial tune or flourish played on brass instruments. **2** great media attention surrounding the introduction of something.
– ORIGIN French.

fang noun **1** a large sharp tooth, especially a canine tooth of a dog or wolf. **2** a tooth with which a snake injects poison. **3** the biting mouthpart of a spider.
– DERIVATIVES **fanged** adjective.
– ORIGIN from Old Norse, 'capture, grasp'.

fanlight noun a small semicircular window over a door or another window.

fanny noun (pl. **fannies**) **1** Brit. vulgar slang a woman's genitals. **2** N. Amer. informal a person's bottom.

– ORIGIN unknown.

Fanny Adams (also **sweet Fanny Adams**) noun Brit. informal nothing at all.
– ORIGIN first used as a nautical term for tinned meat or stew (a reference to the name of a murder victim c.1870), now often understood as a euphemism for *fuck all.*

fantabulous /fan-**tab**-yuu-luhss/ adjective informal excellent; wonderful.
– ORIGIN blend of **FANTASTIC** and **FABULOUS**.

fantail noun **1** a fan-shaped tail or end of something. **2** a domestic pigeon of a broad-tailed variety.
– DERIVATIVES **fan-tailed** adjective.

fantasia /fan-**tay**-zi-uh/ noun **1** a musical composition that does not follow a conventional form. **2** a musical composition based on several familiar tunes.
– ORIGIN Italian, 'fantasy'.

fantasize (or **fantasise**) verb daydream about desirable but unlikely situations or events: *she fantasized about living on a boat in the Caribbean.*
– DERIVATIVES **fantasist** noun.

fantastic adjective **1** hard to believe or unlikely to happen: *fantastic schemes.* **2** informal very good, attractive, or large.
– DERIVATIVES **fantastical** adjective **fantastically** adverb.

fantasy noun (pl. **fantasies**) **1** the imagining of unlikely or impossible things. **2** a daydream about a situation or event which is desirable but unlikely to happen. **3** a type of imaginative fiction involving magic and adventure.
– ORIGIN Greek *phantasia* 'imagination, appearance'.

fanzine /fan-zeen/ noun a magazine for fans of a particular team, performer, activity, etc.
– ORIGIN blend of **FAN²** and **MAGAZINE**.

FAO abbreviation for the attention of.

FAQ abbreviation Computing frequently asked questions.

far adverb (**further, furthest** or **farther, farthest**) **1** at, to, or by a great distance. **2** over a long time. **3** by a great deal. ● adjective **1** situated at a great distance. **2** distant from the centre. **3** more distant than another object of the same kind: *the far corner.*
– PHRASES **as far as** to the extent that. **be a far cry from** be very different to. **by far** by a great amount. **far and away** by a very large amount. **far and wide** over a large area. **far gone 1** in a bad or worsening state. **2** advanced in time. **go far 1** achieve a great deal. **2** be worth or amount to much. **go too far** go beyond what is reasonable or acceptable. **(in) so far as** (or **that**) to the extent that.
– ORIGIN Old English.

farad /fa-rad/ noun the SI unit of electrical capacitance.
– ORIGIN from the name of the English physicist Michael *Faraday.*

faraway adjective **1** distant in space or time. **2** seeming remote from one's present situation; dreamy: *a faraway look.*

farce noun **1** a comic play involving ridiculously improbable situations and events. **2** this type of play or performance. **3** an absurd or ridiculous event: *the debate turned into a*

drunken farce.
- ORIGIN French, 'stuffing' (from the former practice of 'stuffing' comic interludes into religious plays).

farceur /fah-**ser**/ noun a person who writes or performs in farces.
- ORIGIN French.

farcical adjective absurd or ridiculous.
- DERIVATIVES **farcically** adverb.

fare noun **1** the money a passenger on public transport has to pay. **2** a passenger in a taxi. **3** a range of food. •verb perform in a particular way: *the party fared badly in the April elections.*
- ORIGIN Old English.

Far East noun China, Japan, and other countries of east Asia.
- DERIVATIVES **Far Eastern** adjective.

farewell exclamation goodbye. •noun an act of parting or of marking someone's departure.

far-fetched adjective very difficult to believe.

far-flung adjective distant or remote.

farinaceous /fa-ri-**nay**-shuhss/ adjective containing or resembling starch.
- ORIGIN Latin *farina* 'flour'.

farl noun an unsweetened roll made of oatmeal or flour, usually triangular in shape.
- ORIGIN from former *fardel* 'quarter', shortening of *fourth deal*.

farm noun **1** an area of land and its buildings used for growing crops and rearing animals. **2** a farmhouse. **3** a place for breeding or growing something: *a fish farm.* •verb **1** make one's living by growing crops or keeping livestock. **2** (**farm something out**) send out or subcontract work to others.
- DERIVATIVES **farming** noun.
- ORIGIN Old French *ferme*, from Latin *firmare* 'fix, settle'.

farmer noun a person who owns or manages a farm.

farmhand noun a worker on a farm.

farmhouse noun a house attached to a farm.

farmland noun (also **farmlands**) land used for farming.

farmstead noun a farm and its buildings.

farmyard noun a yard or small area of land surrounded by or next to farm buildings.

faro /**fair**-oh/ noun a gambling card game in which players bet on the order in which the cards will appear.
- ORIGIN French *pharaon* 'pharaoh', said to have been the name of the king of hearts.

Faroese /fair-oh-**eez**/ (also **Faeroese**) noun (pl. same) **1** a person from the Faroe Islands. **2** the language of the Faroe Islands.

far-off adjective distant in time or space.

farouche /fuh-**roosh**/ adjective sullen or shy in the company of other people.
- ORIGIN Old French *forache*.

far out adjective **1** unconventional. **2** informal excellent.

farrago /fuh-**rah**-goh/ noun (pl. **farragos** or US **farragoes**) a confused mixture.
- ORIGIN Latin, 'mixed fodder'.

far-reaching adjective having many important effects or implications.

farrier /**fa**-ri-er/ noun a smith who shoes horses.
- DERIVATIVES **farriery** noun.

- ORIGIN from Latin *ferrum* 'iron, horseshoe'.

farrow noun a litter of pigs. •verb (of a sow) give birth to piglets.
- ORIGIN Old English, 'young pig'.

far-seeing adjective having foresight; far-sighted.

Farsi /**far**-see/ noun the modern form of the Persian language, spoken in Iran.
- ORIGIN from the Persian word for 'Persia'.

far-sighted adjective **1** having or showing an awareness of what may happen in the future. **2** N. Amer. long-sighted.

fart informal verb **1** emit wind from the anus. **2** (**fart about/around**) waste time on silly or unimportant things. •noun **1** an act of emitting wind from the anus. **2** a boring or unpleasant person.
- ORIGIN Old English.

farther adverb & adjective variant form of **FURTHER**.

> USAGE: On the difference in use between **farther** and **further**, see the note at **FURTHER**.

farthermost adjective variant form of **FURTHERMOST**.

farthest adjective & adverb variant form of **FURTHEST**.

farthing noun **1** a former coin of the UK, equal to a quarter of an old penny. **2** the least possible amount: *she didn't care a farthing.*
- ORIGIN Old English, 'fourth'.

farthingale /**far**-thing-gayl/ noun historical a hooped petticoat or circular pad of fabric around the hips, formerly worn under women's skirts to extend and shape them.
- ORIGIN French *verdugale.*

fasces /**fas**-eez/ plural noun historical a bundle of rods with a projecting axe blade, used as a symbol of a magistrate's power in ancient Rome.
- ORIGIN Latin, from *fascis* 'bundle'.

fascia /**fay**-shuh/ (also chiefly Brit. **facia**) noun **1** a board covering the ends of rafters or other fittings. **2** Brit. a signboard on a shopfront. **3** Brit. the dashboard of a motor vehicle. **4** a detachable covering for the front of a mobile phone. **5** (in classical architecture) a long flat surface between mouldings on an architrave.
- ORIGIN Latin, 'band, door frame'.

fascinate verb attract or interest someone very much.
- DERIVATIVES **fascinating** adjective **fascinatingly** adverb.
- ORIGIN Latin *fascinare* 'bewitch'.

fascination noun **1** the state of being very attracted to and interested in someone or something. **2** the power of something to attract or interest someone.

> USAGE: Be careful to distinguish between the expressions **fascination with** and **fascination for**. A person has a **fascination with** something they are very interested in (*her fascination with the royal family*), whereas something interesting holds a **fascination for** a person (*circuses have a fascination for children*).

fascism /**fash**-i-z'm/ noun **1** a right-wing system of government characterized by extreme nationalistic beliefs and strict obedience to a

leader or the state. **2** extreme right-wing or intolerant views or practices.
– DERIVATIVES **fascist** noun & adjective **fascistic** adjective.
– ORIGIN Italian *fascismo*, from Latin *fascis* 'bundle'.

fashion noun **1** a style of clothing, hair, behaviour, etc. that is currently popular. **2** the production and marketing of new styles of clothing and cosmetics. **3** a way of doing something: *they strolled across in a leisurely fashion.* • verb form or make something: *a bench fashioned out of a fallen tree trunk.*
– PHRASES **after a fashion** to a certain extent but not perfectly. **in** (or **out of**) **fashion** fashionable (or unfashionable).
– ORIGIN Old French *façon*, from Latin *facere* 'do, make'.

fashionable adjective in or influenced by a style that is currently popular.
– DERIVATIVES **fashionability** noun **fashionably** adverb.

fashionista /fash-uh-**nis**-tuh/ noun informal **1** a designer at a leading fashion house. **2** a devoted follower of fashion.

fast¹ adjective **1** moving or capable of moving at high speed. **2** taking place or acting rapidly. **3** (of a clock or watch) ahead of the correct time. **4** firmly fixed or attached. **5** (of a dye) not fading in light or when washed. **6** (of photographic film) needing only a short exposure. **7** involving or engaging in exciting or immoral activities. • adverb **1** at high speed. **2** within a short time. **3** firmly or securely.
– PHRASES **fast aleep** in a deep sleep. **pull a fast one** informal try to gain an unfair advantage.
– ORIGIN Old English.

fast² verb go without food or drink, especially for religious reasons. • noun an act or period of fasting.
– ORIGIN Old English.

fast breeder noun a nuclear reactor using high-speed neutrons.

fasten verb **1** close or do up securely. **2** fix or hold something in place. **3** (**fasten on**) pick out and concentrate on something: *critics fastened on two sections of the report.*
– DERIVATIVES **fastener** noun **fastening** noun.
– ORIGIN Old English, 'make sure, confirm'.

fast food noun cooked food sold in snack bars and restaurants as a quick meal.

fast forward noun a control on a tape or video player for moving the tape forward rapidly. • verb (**fast-forward**) move a tape forward with this control.

fastidious /fa-**stid**-i-uhss/ adjective **1** very careful about accuracy and detail. **2** very concerned about cleanliness.
– DERIVATIVES **fastidiously** adverb **fastidiousness** noun.
– ORIGIN Latin *fastidium* 'loathing'.

fastness noun **1** a secure place well protected by natural features. **2** the ability of a dye to maintain its colour.

fast-talk verb informal pressurize someone into doing something by using rapid or misleading speech.

fast track noun a rapid way of achieving something. • verb (**fast-track**) speed up the development or progress of something.

fat noun **1** a natural oily substance found in animal bodies, deposited under the skin or around certain organs. **2** such a substance, or a similar one made from plants, used in cooking. **3** Chemistry any of a group of organic compounds of glycerol and acids which form the main constituents of animal and vegetable fat. • adjective (**fatter, fattest**) **1** (of a person or animal) having much excess fat. **2** (of food) containing much fat. **3** informal large or substantial: *fat profits.* **4** informal very little: *fat chance.*
– PHRASES **live off the fat of the land** have the best of everything.
– DERIVATIVES **fatness** noun **fattish** adjective.
– ORIGIN Old English.

fatal adjective **1** causing death. **2** leading to failure or disaster: *a fatal mistake.*
– DERIVATIVES **fatally** adverb.
– ORIGIN from Latin *fatum* (see **FATE**).

fatalism noun **1** the belief that all events are decided in advance by a supernatural power and that humans have no control over them. **2** an attitude characterized by the belief that nothing can be done to prevent something from happening.
– DERIVATIVES **fatalist** noun **fatalistic** adjective.

fatality noun (pl. **fatalities**) an occurrence of death by accident, in war, or from disease.

fat cat noun derogatory a wealthy and powerful businessman or politician.

fate noun **1** the development of events outside a person's control, regarded as decided in advance by a supernatural power. **2** the outcome of a situation for someone or something: *England suffered the same fate in the second Test Match.* **3** (**the Fates**) Greek & Roman Mythology the three goddesses (Clotho, Lachesis, and Atropos) who controlled the lives of humans. • verb (**be fated**) be destined to happen or act in a particular way: *it was as if they were fated to meet again.*
– ORIGIN Latin *fatum* 'that which has been spoken'.

fateful adjective having far-reaching and usually disastrous consequences.
– DERIVATIVES **fatefully** adverb.

fathead noun informal a stupid person.

father noun **1** a male parent. **2** an important male figure in the origin and early history of something: *Jung was one of the fathers of modern psychoanalysis.* **3** literary a male ancestor. **4** (often as a title or form of address) a priest. **5** (**the Father**) (in Christian belief) God. • verb be the father of someone.
– DERIVATIVES **fatherhood** noun **fatherless** adjective.
– ORIGIN Old English.

Father Christmas noun Brit. an imaginary being said to bring presents for children on Christmas Eve.

father-in-law noun (pl. **fathers-in-law**) the father of one's husband or wife.

fatherland noun a person's native country.

fatherly adjective like a father, especially in being protective and affectionate.
– DERIVATIVES **fatherliness** noun.

Father's Day noun a day of the year on which fathers are honoured with gifts and greetings cards (in Britain usually the third Sunday in

June).

fathom noun a unit of length equal to six feet (1.8 metres), used in measuring the depth of water. • verb 1 understand or find an explanation for: *he couldn't fathom why she was so anxious.* 2 measure the depth of water.
– DERIVATIVES **fathomable** adjective **fathomless** adjective.
– ORIGIN Old English, 'something which embraces' (the original measurement was based on the span of a person's outstretched arms).

fatigue noun 1 extreme tiredness. 2 brittleness in metal or other materials caused by repeated stress. 3 (**fatigues**) loose-fitting clothing of a sort worn by soldiers. 4 (**fatigues**) menial non-military tasks performed by a soldier. • verb (**fatigues, fatiguing, fatigued**) make someone extremely tired.
– ORIGIN from Latin *fatigare* 'tire out'.

fatso noun (pl. **fatsos**) informal, derogatory a fat person.

fatten verb make or become fat or fatter.

fatty adjective (**fattier, fattiest**) 1 containing a large amount of fat. 2 Medicine involving abnormal amounts of fat being deposited in a part of the body: *fatty degeneration of the arteries.* • noun (pl. **fatties**) informal a fat person.
– DERIVATIVES **fattiness** noun.

fatty acid noun an organic acid whose molecule contains a hydrocarbon chain.

fatuity /fuh-tyoo-i-ti/ noun (pl. **fatuities**) 1 a silly or pointless remark. 2 the quality of being silly or pointless.

fatuous adjective silly and pointless.
– DERIVATIVES **fatuously** adverb **fatuousness** noun.
– ORIGIN Latin *fatuus* 'foolish'.

fatwa /fat-wah/ noun an authoritative ruling on a point of Islamic law.
– ORIGIN Arabic, 'decide a point of law'.

faucet /faw-sit/ noun N. Amer. a tap.
– ORIGIN Old French *fausset*.

fault noun 1 an unattractive or unsatisfactory feature; a defect or mistake. 2 responsibility for an accident or misfortune: *it's not my fault he's in this mess.* 3 (in tennis) a service that breaks the rules. 4 an extended break in the continuity of layers of rock formation, caused by movement of the earth's crust. • verb criticize someone or something for being unsatisfactory: *her colleagues could not fault her dedication to the job.*
– PHRASES **find fault** make a criticism or objection. —— **to a fault** to an excessive extent: *he was generous to a fault.*
– DERIVATIVES **faultless** adjective **faultlessly** adverb.
– ORIGIN Latin *fallere* 'deceive'.

faulty adjective (**faultier, faultiest**) 1 not working or made correctly. 2 (of thinking or reasoning) containing mistakes.

faun /fawn/ noun Roman Mythology a lustful god of woods and fields, represented as a man with a goat's horns, ears, legs, and tail.
– ORIGIN from the name of the god *Faunus.*

fauna /faw-nuh/ noun (pl. **faunas**) the animals of a particular region, habitat, or period of time. Compare with FLORA.
– DERIVATIVES **faunal** adjective.
– ORIGIN Latin, from *Fauna*, a goddess of woods and fields.

Faustian /fowst-i-uhn/ adjective relating to the German astronomer Johann Faust, who was reputed to have sold his soul to the Devil.

Fauve /fohv/ noun a member of a group of early 20th-century French artists who painted in very bright colours.
– DERIVATIVES **Fauvism** noun **Fauvist** noun & adjective.
– ORIGIN French, 'wild beast', with reference to a remark by the art critic Louis Vauxcelles.

faux /foh/ adjective made in imitation; artificial.
– ORIGIN French, 'false'.

faux pas /foh pah/ noun (pl. same) an embarrassing blunder in a social situation.
– ORIGIN French, 'false step'.

fava bean /fah-vuh/ noun North American term for BROAD BEAN.
– ORIGIN from Latin *faba* 'bean'.

favela /fa-vel-uh/ noun (in Brazil) a shack or shanty town.
– ORIGIN Portuguese.

favour (US **favor**) noun 1 approval or liking: *training is looked upon with favour by many employers.* 2 an act of kindness beyond what is due or usual: *I've come to ask you a favour.* 3 special treatment given to one person at the expense of another. 4 old use a thing such as a badge that is worn as a mark of favour or support. • verb 1 regard with approval or liking: *slashing public spending is a policy few politicians favour.* 2 give unfairly preferential treatment to: *conservatives said the treaty favoured the USA.* 3 work to someone's or something's advantage: *natural selection has favoured females that are best at competing.* 4 informal look like a parent or other relative. 5 (**favour someone with**) give someone something they wish for.
– PHRASES **in favour of 1** to be replaced by. 2 in support or to the advantage of.
– ORIGIN Latin *favor*, from *favere* 'show kindness to'.

favourable (US **favorable**) adjective 1 expressing approval or agreement: *a favourable response.* 2 advantageous or helpful: *favourable economic conditions.* 3 suggesting a good outcome: *a favourable prognosis.*
– DERIVATIVES **favourably** adverb.

favourite (US **favorite**) adjective preferred to all others of the same kind. • noun 1 a favourite person or thing. 2 the competitor thought most likely to win.

favouritism (US **favoritism**) noun the unfair favouring of one person or group at the expense of another.

fawn¹ noun 1 a young deer in its first year. 2 a light brown colour.
– ORIGIN Old French *faon.*

fawn² verb 1 try to please someone by flattering them or paying them too much attention. 2 (of a dog) show extreme devotion, especially by rubbing against someone.
– DERIVATIVES **fawning** adjective.
– ORIGIN Old English, 'make or be glad'.

fax noun 1 an exact copy of a document made by electronic scanning and sent by telecommunications links. 2 the making or sending of documents in this way. 3 (also **fax**

machine) a machine for sending and receiving such documents. • verb **1** send a document by fax. **2** contact someone by fax.
– ORIGIN abbreviation of **FACSIMILE**.

fayre noun mock old-fashioned spelling of **FAIR²**.

faze verb informal disconcert or unsettle someone.
– ORIGIN dialect *feeze* 'drive off', from Old English.

FBI abbreviation (in the US) Federal Bureau of Investigation.

FC abbreviation Football Club.

FCO abbreviation (in the UK) Foreign and Commonwealth Office.

FDA abbreviation (in the US) Food and Drug Administration.

FDI abbreviation foreign direct investment, investment by a company in a country other than that in which the company is based.

FE abbreviation (in the UK) further education.

Fe symbol the chemical element iron.
– ORIGIN from Latin *ferrum*.

fealty /fee-uhl-ti/ noun historical the loyalty sworn to a feudal lord by a tenant or vassal.
– ORIGIN Old French *feaulte*.

fear noun **1** an unpleasant emotion caused by the threat of danger, pain, or harm. **2** the likelihood of something unwelcome happening: *she observed them without fear of attracting attention.* • verb **1** be afraid of someone or something. **2** (**fear for**) be anxious about: *she feared for her son's safety.*
– PHRASES **no fear** Brit. informal certainly not. **without fear or favour** in a fair and impartial way.
– ORIGIN Old English, 'danger'.

fearful adjective **1** showing or causing fear. **2** informal very great.
– DERIVATIVES **fearfully** adverb **fearfulness** noun.

fearless adjective without fear; brave.
– DERIVATIVES **fearlessly** adverb **fearlessness** noun.

fearsome adjective frightening, especially in appearance.
– DERIVATIVES **fearsomely** adverb.

feart /fi-uht/ adjective Scottish afraid.

feasible adjective **1** able to be done easily. **2** likely; probable.
– DERIVATIVES **feasibility** noun **feasibly** adverb.
– ORIGIN Old French *faisible*, from Latin *facere* 'do, make'.

USAGE: Some people object to the use of **feasible** to mean 'likely' or 'probable' (as in *the most feasible explanation*). This sense has been in the language for centuries, however, and is generally considered to be acceptable.

feast noun **1** a large meal, especially one marking a special occasion. **2** an annual religious celebration. **3** a day dedicated to a particular saint. • verb **1** have a feast. **2** (**feast on**) eat large quantities of something.
– PHRASES **feast one's eyes on** gaze at someone or something with pleasure.
– ORIGIN from Latin *festus* 'joyous'.

feast day noun a day on which an annual Christian celebration is held.

feat noun an achievement requiring great courage, skill, or strength.
– ORIGIN Old French *fait*.

feather noun any of the flat structures growing from a bird's skin, consisting of a partly hollow horny shaft fringed with fine strands. • verb **1** turn an oar so that the blade passes through the air edgeways. **2** (as adj. **feathered**) covered or decorated with feathers.
– PHRASES **a feather in one's cap** an achievement to be proud of. **feather one's nest** make oneself richer, usually at someone else's expense.
– DERIVATIVES **feathery** adjective.
– ORIGIN Old English.

feather bed noun a bed with a mattress stuffed with feathers. • verb (**feather-bed**) provide someone or something with very favourable economic or working conditions.

feather-brained adjective silly or absent-minded.

feathering noun **1** a bird's plumage. **2** the feathers of an arrow. **3** feather-like markings.

featherweight noun **1** a weight in boxing between bantamweight and lightweight. **2** a person or thing of little or no importance.

feature noun **1** a distinctive element or aspect: *the market town has many interesting features.* **2** a part of the face, such as the mouth or nose. **3** a newspaper or magazine article or a broadcast programme devoted to a particular topic. **4** (also **feature film**) a full-length film forming the main item in a cinema programme. • verb **1** have as a feature: *the hotel features a swimming pool and spacious gardens.* **2** have as an important actor or participant. **3** have an important or notable part in: *floral designs feature prominently in Persian rugs.*
– DERIVATIVES **featured** adjective **featureless** adjective.
– ORIGIN Old French *faiture* 'form'.

Feb. abbreviation February.

febrile /fee-bryl/ adjective **1** having or showing the symptoms of a fever. **2** overactive and excitable: *her febrile imagination.*
– ORIGIN Latin *febrilis*, from *febris* 'fever'.

February /feb-yuu-ri, feb-ruu-uh-ri/ noun (pl. **Februaries**) the second month of the year.
– ORIGIN Latin *februarius*, from *februa*, a purification feast held in this month.

feces noun US spelling of **FAECES**.

feckless adjective irresponsible and lacking strength of character.
– DERIVATIVES **fecklessly** adverb **fecklessness** noun.
– ORIGIN from Scots and northern English dialect *effeck*, variant of **EFFECT**.

fecund /fek-uhnd/ adjective **1** very fertile: *a lush and fecund garden.* **2** producing many new and creative ideas: *her fecund imagination.*
– DERIVATIVES **fecundity** noun.
– ORIGIN Latin *fecundus*.

Fed noun US informal a member of the FBI or other federal official.

fed past and past participle of **FEED**.

federal adjective **1** relating to a system of government in which several states unite under a central authority but remain independent in internal affairs. **2** relating to the central government of a federation: *federal laws.* **3** (**Federal**) US historical relating to the Northern States in the Civil War.
– DERIVATIVES **federally** adverb.
– ORIGIN Latin *foedus* 'league, covenant'.

federalism noun the federal principle or system of government.
– DERIVATIVES **federalist** noun & adjective.

Federal Reserve noun (in the US) the banking authority that has the functions of a central bank.

federate /fed-uh-rayt/ verb (of a number of states or organizations) unite on a federal basis.

federation noun **1** a group of states that have a central government but are independent in internal affairs. **2** an organization within which smaller divisions have some internal independence.

fedora /fi-**dor**-uh/ noun a soft felt hat with a curled brim and the crown creased lengthways.
– ORIGIN from *Fédora*, a play written by the French dramatist Victorien Sardou.

fed up adjective informal annoyed or bored.

fee noun **1** a payment given for professional advice or services. **2** a sum of money paid in order to join an organization, gain admission to somewhere, etc.
– ORIGIN Old French *feu* 'an estate held on condition of feudal service'.

feeble adjective (**feebler**, **feeblest**) **1** lacking physical or mental strength. **2** not convincing or impressive: *a feeble excuse*.
– DERIVATIVES **feebleness** noun **feebly** adverb.
– ORIGIN from Latin *flebilis* 'lamentable'.

feeble-minded adjective **1** foolish; stupid. **2** dated having less than average intelligence.

feed verb (past and past part. **fed**) **1** give food to a person or animal. **2** provide enough food for: *she needed money to feed and clothe her family*. **3** eat: *slugs and snails feed at night*. **4** supply with material, power, water, etc.: *a lake fed by waterfalls*. **5** pass something gradually through a confined space. **6** prompt an actor with a line. • noun **1** an act of feeding or of being fed. **2** food for domestic animals. **3** a device or pipe for supplying material to a machine. **4** the supply of raw material to a machine or device. **5** a broadcast distributed by a satellite or network from a central source to a large number of radio or television stations.
– ORIGIN Old English.

feedback noun **1** comments about a product or a person's performance, used as a basis for improvement. **2** the return of a fraction of the output of an amplifier, microphone, or other device to the input of the same device, causing distortion or a whistling sound.

feeder noun **1** a person or animal that eats a particular food or in a particular way. **2** a thing that feeds or supplies something. **3** a road or rail route linking outlying districts with a main system.

feeding frenzy noun **1** an aggressive group attack on prey by a number of sharks or piranhas. **2** an episode of frantic and unscrupulous competition for something, especially on the part of journalists covering a sensational story.

feedstock noun raw material used to supply a machine or industrial process.

feel verb (past and past part. **felt**) **1** notice, be aware of, or examine by touch or through physical sensation: *she felt her hand on his shoulder*. **2** give a sensation of a particular quality when touched: *his hair felt rough*. **3** experience an emotion or sensation: *I felt angry and upset*. **4** be affected by: *investors who have felt the effects of the recession*. **5** have a belief, attitude, or impression: *I felt that he hated me*. **6** (**feel up to**) have the strength or energy to do something. • noun **1** an act of feeling. **2** the sense of touch. **3** a sensation given by something when touched. **4** an impression given by something: *a cafe with a European feel*.
– PHRASES **get a feel for** become familiar with something. **have a feel for** have a sensitive appreciation or understanding of something.
– ORIGIN Old English.

feeler noun **1** an animal organ such as an antenna that is used for testing things by touch. **2** a tentative proposal intended to find out someone's attitude or opinion.

feel-good adjective informal causing a feeling of happiness and well-being: *a feel-good movie*.

feeling noun **1** an emotional state or reaction. **2** (**feelings**) the emotional side of a person's character: *I don't want to hurt her feelings*. **3** strong emotion. **4** the capacity to experience the sense of touch: *she lost all feeling in her leg*. **5** the sensation of touching or being touched: *the feeling of silk next to your skin*. **6** a belief or opinion. **7** (**feeling for**) a sensitivity to or intuitive understanding of something: *he had a feeling for poetry*. • adjective showing emotion or sensitivity.
– DERIVATIVES **feelingly** adverb.

fee simple noun (pl. **fees simple**) Law a permanent and absolute tenure in land with freedom to dispose of it at will.

feet plural of FOOT.

feign /fayn/ verb pretend to feel or have: *he feigned surprise*.
– ORIGIN Old French *feindre*.

feint[1] /faynt/ noun a deceptive or pretended attacking movement in boxing or fencing. • verb make a feint.
– ORIGIN from French *feindre* 'feign'.

> USAGE: On the confusion of **feint** and **faint**, see the note at FAINT.

feint[2] /faynt/ adjective (of paper) printed with faint lines as a guide for handwriting.
– ORIGIN variant of FAINT.

feisty /fy-sti/ adjective (**feistier**, **feistiest**) lively and spirited.
– DERIVATIVES **feistily** adverb **feistiness** noun.
– ORIGIN from former *feist* 'small dog'.

felafel /fuh-**la**-fuhl, fuh-**lah**-fuhl/ noun variant spelling of FALAFEL.

Feldenkrais method /**fel**-duhn-krys/ noun a system designed to promote well-being through exercises which improve flexibility and coordination.
– ORIGIN named after the Russian-born physicist Moshe *Feldenkrais*.

feldspar /**feld**-spar/ (also **felspar**) noun a mineral forming igneous rocks, consisting chiefly of aluminium silicates.
– ORIGIN German *Feldspat* 'field spar'.

felicitations plural noun formal congratulations.

felicitous /fuh-**liss**-i-tuhss/ adjective well chosen or appropriate: *a felicitous phrase*.

– DERIVATIVES **felicitously** adverb.

felicity noun (pl. **felicities**) **1** great happiness. **2** the ability to express oneself in an appropriate way. **3** an appropriate or well-chosen feature of a work of literature.
– ORIGIN Latin *felicitas*.

feline adjective relating to or resembling a cat or cats. •noun a cat or other animal of the cat family.
– ORIGIN from Latin *feles* 'cat'.

fell[1] past of **FALL**.

fell[2] verb **1** cut down a tree. **2** knock someone down. **3** stitch down the edge of a seam to lie flat.
– DERIVATIVES **feller** noun.
– ORIGIN Old English.

fell[3] noun a hill or area of high moorland, especially in northern England.
– ORIGIN Old Norse.

fell[4] adjective literary very evil or fierce.
– PHRASES **in** (or **at**) **one fell swoop** all in one go. [from Shakespeare's *Macbeth* (IV. iii. 219).]
– ORIGIN Old French *fel*.

fellatio /fe-**lay**-shi-oh/ noun stimulation of a man's penis with the mouth.
– DERIVATIVES **fellate** verb.
– ORIGIN from Latin *fellare* 'to suck'.

felloes /**fell**-ohz/ (also **fellies** /**fell**-iz/) plural noun the outer rim of a wheel, to which the spokes are fixed.
– ORIGIN Old English.

fellow noun **1** a man or boy. **2** a person in the same situation or associated with another: *they raised money for their fellows in need.* **3** a thing of the same kind as another. **4** a member of a learned society. **5** Brit. a member of the governing body of certain colleges. **6** (also **research fellow**) an elected graduate receiving funds for a period of research. •adjective sharing a particular activity, situation, or condition: *a fellow sufferer.*
– ORIGIN Old English, 'partner, colleague'.

fellow feeling noun sympathy based on shared experiences.

fellowship noun **1** friendliness and companionship based on shared interests. **2** a group of people meeting to pursue a shared interest or aim. **3** the position of a fellow of a college or society.

fellow-traveller noun chiefly historical a person who sympathizes with the Communist Party but is not a member of it.
– DERIVATIVES **fellow-travelling** adjective.

felon /**fe**-luhn/ noun a person who has committed a felony.
– ORIGIN Old French, 'wicked, a wicked person'.

felony /**fe**-luh-ni/ noun (pl. **felonies**) (in the US and many other judicial systems) a crime regarded as more serious than a misdemeanour.
– DERIVATIVES **felonious** /fi-**loh**-ni-uhss/ adjective **feloniously** adverb.

felspar /**fel**-spar/ noun variant spelling of **FELDSPAR**.

felt[1] noun cloth made by rolling and pressing wool, which causes the fibres to mat together. •verb **1** mat together or become matted. **2** (as adj. **felted**) covered with felt.
– ORIGIN Old English.

felt[2] past and past participle of **FEEL**.

felt-tip pen (also **felt-tipped pen**) noun a pen with a writing point made of felt or tightly packed fibres.

felucca /fe-**lu**-kuh/ noun a small boat propelled by oars or sails, used especially on the Nile.
– ORIGIN Arabic.

female adjective **1** referring to the sex that can bear offspring or produce eggs. **2** relating to or typical of women or female animals. **3** (of a plant or flower) having a pistil but no stamens. **4** (of a fitting) manufactured hollow so that a corresponding male part can be inserted. •noun a female person, animal, or plant.
– DERIVATIVES **femaleness** noun.
– ORIGIN from Latin *femina* 'woman'.

feminine adjective **1** having qualities traditionally associated with women, especially delicacy and prettiness. **2** relating to women; female. **3** Grammar (of a gender of nouns and adjectives in certain languages) treated as female.
– DERIVATIVES **femininely** adverb **femininity** noun.
– ORIGIN from Latin *femina* 'woman'.

feminism noun a movement or theory supporting women's rights on the grounds of equality of the sexes.
– DERIVATIVES **feminist** noun & adjective.

feminize (or **feminise**) verb make something more feminine or female.
– DERIVATIVES **feminization** noun.

femme fatale /fam fuh-**tahl**/ noun (pl. **femmes fatales** pronunc. same) an attractive and seductive woman.
– ORIGIN French, 'disastrous woman'.

femto- combining form referring to a factor of one thousand million millionth (10^{-15}).
– ORIGIN from Danish or Norwegian *femten* 'fifteen'.

femur /**fee**-mer/ noun (pl. **femurs** or **femora** /**fem**-uh-ruh/) the bone of the thigh.
– DERIVATIVES **femoral** /**fem**-uh-ruhl/ adjective.
– ORIGIN Latin, 'thigh'.

fen[1] noun a low and marshy or frequently flooded area of land.
– DERIVATIVES **fenny** adjective.
– ORIGIN Old English.

fen[2] noun (pl. same) a unit of money of China, equal to one hundredth of a yuan.
– ORIGIN Chinese, 'a hundredth part'.

fence noun **1** a barrier enclosing an area, typically consisting of posts connected by wire, wood, etc. **2** a large upright obstacle in steeplechasing, showjumping, or cross-country races. **3** informal a dealer in stolen goods. **4** a guard or guide on a plane or other tool. •verb **1** surround or protect something with a fence. **2** informal deal in stolen goods. **3** practise the sport of fencing.
– PHRASES **sit on the fence** avoid making a decision.
– DERIVATIVES **fencer** noun.
– ORIGIN shortening of **DEFENCE**.

fencing noun **1** the sport of fighting with blunted swords in order to score points. **2** a series of fences. **3** material for making fences.

fend verb **1** (**fend for oneself**) look after and provide for oneself. **2** (**fend someone/thing off**) defend oneself from an attack or attacker.

– ORIGIN shortening of DEFEND.

fender noun 1 a low frame around a fireplace to keep in falling coals. 2 a cushioning device hung over a ship's side to protect it against impact. 3 N. Amer. the mudguard or area around the wheel well of a vehicle.

fenestration /fen-i-stray-shuhn/ noun Architecture the arrangement of windows in a building.
– ORIGIN from Latin *fenestra* 'window'.

feng shui /feng shoo-i, fung shway/ noun an ancient Chinese system of designing buildings and positioning objects inside buildings to ensure a favourable flow of energy.
– ORIGIN from the Chinese words for 'wind' and 'water'.

Fenian /fee-ni-uhn/ noun 1 a member of the Irish Republican Brotherhood, a 19th-century revolutionary nationalist organization. 2 informal, offensive (chiefly in Northern Ireland) a Protestant name for a Catholic.
– ORIGIN from an Old Irish name of an ancient Irish people.

fenland noun (also **fenlands**) land consisting of fens.

fennel /fen-n'l/ noun a plant whose leaves and seeds are used as a herb, and whose base is eaten as a vegetable.
– ORIGIN Latin *faeniculum*.

fenugreek /fen-yuu-greek/ noun a white-flowered plant with seeds that are used as a spice.
– ORIGIN from Latin *faenum graecum* 'Greek hay' (the Romans used it as fodder).

feral /fe-ruhl/ adjective 1 (of an animal or plant) wild, especially after having been domesticated. 2 resembling a wild animal.
– ORIGIN from Latin *fera* 'wild animal'.

ferment verb /fer-ment/ 1 undergo or cause to undergo fermentation. 2 stir up disorder.
• noun /fer-ment/ a state of unrest or excitement, especially among a large group of people: *the creative ferment of post-war Britain.*
– DERIVATIVES **fermentable** adjective **fermenter** noun.
– ORIGIN from Latin *fermentum* 'yeast'.

fermentation noun the chemical breakdown of a substance by bacteria, yeasts, or other microorganisms, such as when sugar is converted into alcohol.
– DERIVATIVES **fermentative** adjective.

fermion /fer-mi-on/ noun Physics a subatomic particle, such as a nucleon, which has a spin of a half integer.
– ORIGIN named after the Italian physicist Enrico *Fermi*.

fermium /fer-mi-uhm/ noun an unstable radioactive chemical element made by high-energy atomic collisions.

fern noun (pl. same or **ferns**) a flowerless plant which has feathery or leafy fronds and reproduces by spores.
– DERIVATIVES **fernery** noun (pl. **ferneries**) **ferny** adjective.
– ORIGIN Old English.

ferocious adjective 1 savagely fierce, cruel, or violent. 2 informal very great; extreme.
– DERIVATIVES **ferociously** adverb **ferocity** /fuh-ross-i-ti/ noun.
– ORIGIN from Latin *ferox* 'fierce'.

-ferous (usu. **-iferous**) combining form having or containing a specified thing: *Carboniferous.*
– ORIGIN from Latin *-fer* 'producing'.

ferret /ferr-it/ noun 1 a domesticated albino or brown polecat, used for catching rabbits. 2 informal a search. • verb (**ferrets, ferreting, ferreted**) 1 search for something in a place or container. 2 (**ferret something out**) discover something by determined searching. 3 (usu. as noun **ferreting**) hunt with ferrets.
– DERIVATIVES **ferreter** noun **ferrety** adjective.
– ORIGIN Old French *fuiret.*

ferric /ferr-ik/ adjective Chemistry relating to iron with a valency of three.
– ORIGIN from Latin *ferrum* 'iron'.

Ferris wheel noun a fairground ride consisting of a giant vertical revolving wheel with passenger cars suspended on its outer edge.
– ORIGIN named after the American engineer George W. G. *Ferris.*

ferroconcrete noun concrete reinforced with steel.

ferroelectric adjective displaying permanent electric polarization which varies in strength with the applied electric field.
– DERIVATIVES **ferroelectricity** noun.

ferrous /ferr-uhss/ adjective 1 (of metals) containing iron. 2 Chemistry relating to iron with a valency of two.

ferruginous /fe-roo-jin-uhss/ adjective 1 containing iron oxides or rust. 2 rust-coloured.
– ORIGIN from Latin *ferrugo* 'rust, dark red'.

ferrule /ferr-ool/ noun a metal ring or cap used to strengthen the end of a handle, stick, or tube.
– ORIGIN Old French *virelle.*

ferry noun (pl. **ferries**) a boat or ship for carrying passengers and goods, especially as a regular service. • verb (**ferries, ferrying, ferried**) carry someone or something by ferry or other transport.
– DERIVATIVES **ferryman** noun (pl. **ferrymen**).
– ORIGIN Old Norse.

fertile adjective 1 (of soil or land) producing or capable of producing abundant vegetation or crops. 2 (of a person, animal, or plant) able to conceive young or produce seed. 3 producing new and inventive ideas: *a fertile imagination.*
– DERIVATIVES **fertility** noun.
– ORIGIN Latin *fertilis.*

fertilize (or **fertilise**) verb 1 introduce sperm or pollen into an egg, female animal, or plant to develop a new individual. 2 add fertilizer to soil or land.
– DERIVATIVES **fertilization** noun.

fertilizer (or **fertiliser**) noun a chemical or natural substance added to soil to increase its fertility.

fervent /fer-vuhnt/ adjective intensely passionate.
– DERIVATIVES **fervency** noun **fervently** adverb.
– ORIGIN from Latin *fervere* 'boil'.

fervid adjective intensely or excessively enthusiastic.
– DERIVATIVES **fervidly** adverb.
– ORIGIN Latin *fervidus.*

fervour (US **fervor**) noun intense and

passionate feeling: *the party swept to power on a tide of patriotic fervour.*

fescue /fes-kyoo/ **noun** a narrow-leaved grass, some kinds of which are used for pasture and fodder.
– ORIGIN Old French *festu.*

-fest **combining form** informal in nouns referring to a festival or large gathering of a specified kind: *a media-fest.*
– ORIGIN from German *Fest* 'festival'.

festal **adjective** relating to a festival; festive.
– ORIGIN from Latin *festa* 'feast'.

fester **verb 1** (of a wound or sore) become septic. **2** (of food or rubbish) become rotten. **3** (of a negative feeling or problem) become worse or more intense: *hate can breed and fester for centuries.*
– ORIGIN Old French *festrir.*

festival **noun 1** a day or period of celebration, typically for religious reasons. **2** an organized series of concerts, films, etc.
– ORIGIN Latin *festa* 'feast'.

festive **adjective 1** relating to a festival. **2** typical of a festival or celebration; happy.
– DERIVATIVES **festively** adverb.

festivity **noun** (pl. **festivities**) **1** joyful celebration. **2** (**festivities**) activities or events celebrating a special occasion.

festoon /fess-toon/ **verb** decorate something with chains of flowers, lights, etc. • **noun** a decorative chain of flowers, leaves, or ribbons, hung in a curve.
– ORIGIN Italian *festone* 'festive ornament'.

feta /fet-uh/ (also **feta cheese**) **noun** a salty Greek cheese made from the milk of ewes or goats.
– ORIGIN modern Greek *pheta.*

fetal /fee-t'l/ **adjective 1** relating to a fetus. **2** (of a posture) typical of a fetus, with the limbs folded in front of the body.

fetch **verb 1** go for and bring back someone or something. **2** sell for a particular price. **3** (**fetch up**) informal arrive or come to rest: *Steve fetched up in Ireland in 1985.* **4** informal land a blow on someone.
– PHRASES **fetch and carry** perform a series of menial tasks for someone.
– DERIVATIVES **fetcher** noun.
– ORIGIN Old English.

fetching **adjective** attractive: *a fetching black miniskirt.*
– DERIVATIVES **fetchingly** adverb.

fete /fayt/ (also **fête**) **noun** Brit. an outdoor public event to raise funds for a charity, typically involving entertainment and the sale of goods. • **verb** praise, welcome, or entertain publicly: *in New York, she was feted like royalty.*
– ORIGIN French.

fetid /fet-id/ (also **foetid**) **adjective** smelling very unpleasant.
– ORIGIN Latin *fetidus.*

fetish **noun 1** an object worshipped for its supposed magical powers. **2** a form of sexual desire in which sexual pleasure is gained from an object, part of the body, or activity. **3** something which a person is obsessively devoted to: *a fetish for detail.*
– DERIVATIVES **fetishism** noun **fetishist** noun

fetishistic adjective.
– ORIGIN French *fétiche.*

fetishize (or **fetishise**) **verb 1** make something the object of a sexual fetish. **2** have an excessive and irrational commitment to: *an author who fetishizes privacy.*
– DERIVATIVES **fetishization** noun.

fetlock **noun** a joint of a horse's leg between the knee and the hoof.
– ORIGIN Germanic.

fetor /fee-ter/ **noun** a strong, foul smell.
– ORIGIN Latin.

fetter **verb 1** restrict the freedom of: *like most schools, it just rolls on, fettered by routine.* **2** restrain someone with chains or shackles. • **noun 1** (**fetters**) restraints or controls. **2** a chain or shackle placed around a prisoner's ankles.
– ORIGIN Old English.

fettle **noun** condition: *I was in fine fettle.*
– ORIGIN Old English, 'strip of material'.

fettuccine /fet-tuh-chee-ni/ **plural noun** pasta made in ribbons.
– ORIGIN Italian, 'little ribbons'.

fetus /fee-tuhss/ (Brit. (in non-technical use) also **foetus**) **noun** (pl. **fetuses**) an unborn mammal, in particular an unborn human more than eight weeks after conception.
– ORIGIN Latin, 'pregnancy, childbirth, offspring'.

feud **noun 1** a prolonged and bitter dispute. **2** a state of prolonged hostility and violence between two groups. • **verb** take part in a feud.
– ORIGIN Old French *feide* 'hostility'.

feudal **adjective** relating to feudalism.
– ORIGIN from Latin *feodum* 'fee'.

feudalism **noun** the social system in medieval Europe, in which the nobility held lands from the Crown in exchange for military service, and those at a lower level in society worked and fought for the nobles in exchange for land and protection.

fever **noun 1** an abnormally high body temperature, usually accompanied by shivering, headache, and in severe instances, delirium. **2** great excitement or agitation: *World Cup fever.*
– DERIVATIVES **feverish** adjective **feverishly** adverb **feverishness** noun.
– ORIGIN Latin *febris.*

fevered **adjective 1** having or showing the symptoms of fever. **2** nervously excited or agitated: *my fevered imagination.*

feverfew **noun** an aromatic plant with feathery leaves and daisy-like flowers, used as a herbal remedy for headaches.
– ORIGIN Latin *febrifuga*, from *febris* 'fever' + *fugare* 'drive away'.

fever pitch **noun** a state of extreme excitement.

few **determiner, pronoun, & adjective 1** (**a few**) a small number of. **2** not many. • **noun** (**the few**) a select minority of people.
– PHRASES **few and far between** scarce. **a good few** Brit. a fairly large number of. **no fewer than** a surprisingly large number of. **quite a few** a fairly large number.
– ORIGIN Old English.

fey adjective **1** unworldly and vague. **2** able to see into the future; clairvoyant.
– ORIGIN Old English, 'fated to die soon'.

fez noun (pl. **fezzes**) a flat-topped conical red hat, worn by men in some Muslim countries.
– ORIGIN Turkish *fes*, named after the city of *Fez* in Morocco.

ff abbreviation Music fortissimo.

ff. abbreviation **1** folios. **2** following pages.

fiancé /fi-on-say/ noun (fem. **fiancée** pronunc. same) a person to whom another is engaged to be married.
– ORIGIN French.

fiasco /fi-**ass**-koh/ noun (pl. **fiascos**) a ridiculous or humiliating failure.
– ORIGIN from Italian *far fiasco* 'fail in a performance', literally 'make a bottle'.

fiat /fy-at/ noun an official order or authorization.
– ORIGIN Latin, 'let it be done'.

fib noun a trivial lie. • verb (**fibs, fibbing, fibbed**) tell a fib.
– DERIVATIVES **fibber** noun.
– ORIGIN perhaps from former *fible-fable* 'nonsense', from **FABLE**.

fiber etc. noun US spelling of **FIBRE** etc.

Fibonacci series /fib-uh-**nah**-chi/ noun Mathematics a series of numbers in which each number (**Fibonacci number**) is the sum of the two preceding numbers (e.g. the series 1, 1, 2, 3, 5, 8, etc.).
– ORIGIN named after the Italian mathematician Leonardo *Fibonacci*.

fibre (US **fiber**) noun **1** a thread or strand from which a plant or animal tissue, mineral substance, or textile is formed. **2** a substance formed of fibres. **3** substances in vegetables, fruit, and some other foods, that are difficult to digest and therefore help the passage of food through the body. **4** strength of character: *a lack of moral fibre*.
– ORIGIN Latin *fibra* 'fibre, entrails'.

fibreboard (US **fiberboard**) noun a building material made of wood fibres compressed into boards.

fibreglass (US **fiberglass**) noun **1** a reinforced plastic material composed of glass fibres embedded in a resin matrix. **2** a textile fabric made from woven glass fibres.

fibre optics plural noun (treated as sing.) the use of thin flexible transparent fibres to transmit light signals, chiefly for telecommunications or for internal inspection of the body.
– DERIVATIVES **fibre-optic** adjective.

fibril /fy-bril/ noun technical a small or slender fibre.
– ORIGIN Latin *fibrilla* 'little fibre'.

fibrillate /fy-bri-layt, fib-ri-layt/ verb (of a muscle, especially in the heart) make a quivering movement due to uncoordinated contraction of the individual fibres.
– DERIVATIVES **fibrillation** noun.

fibrin /fy-brin/ noun an insoluble protein formed as a fibrous mesh during the clotting of blood.

fibrinogen /fy-**brin**-uh-juhn/ noun a soluble protein present in blood plasma, from which fibrin is produced.

fibroblast /fy-broh-blast/ noun a cell in connective tissue which produces collagen and other fibres.

fibroid adjective relating to fibres or fibrous tissue. • noun a non-cancerous tumour of fibrous tissues, typically developing in the wall of the womb.

fibrosis /fy-broh-siss/ noun the thickening and scarring of connective tissue, usually as a result of injury.
– DERIVATIVES **fibrotic** /fy-bro-tik/ adjective.

fibrous adjective consisting of or characterized by fibres.

fibula /fib-yuu-luh/ noun (pl. **fibulae** /fib-yuu-lee/ or **fibulas**) the outer of the two bones between the knee and the ankle, parallel with the tibia.
– ORIGIN Latin, 'brooch'.

fichu /fee-shoo/ noun a small triangular shawl, worn round a woman's shoulders and neck.
– ORIGIN French.

fickle adjective changeable, especially as regards one's loyalties.
– DERIVATIVES **fickleness** noun.
– ORIGIN Old English, 'deceitful'.

fiction noun **1** literary works in prose describing imaginary events and people. **2** something that is invented or untrue: *keeping up the fiction that they were happily married*. **3** a false belief or statement, accepted as true for the sake of convenience.
– DERIVATIVES **fictionist** noun.
– ORIGIN Latin.

fictional adjective relating to fiction.
– DERIVATIVES **fictionality** noun **fictionally** adverb.

fictionalize (or **fictionalise**) verb make a true story into a fictional one.

fictitious /fik-**tish**-uhss/ adjective **1** imaginary or invented; not real or true. **2** referring to the characters and events found in fiction.

fictive adjective created by the imagination.
– DERIVATIVES **fictiveness** noun.

fiddle noun informal **1** a violin. **2** chiefly Brit. an act of fraud or cheating. **3** Brit. a minor task that seems awkward or needlessly complex. • verb **1** touch or fidget with something restlessly or nervously. **2** informal, chiefly Brit. falsify figures, data, or records. **3** informal play the violin.
– PHRASES **fit as a fiddle** in very good health. **play second fiddle to** take a subordinate role to someone or something.
– DERIVATIVES **fiddler** noun.
– ORIGIN Old English *fithele* 'violin'.

fiddle-faddle noun trivial matters; nonsense.

fiddler crab noun a small amphibious crab, the males of which have one greatly enlarged claw.

fiddlesticks exclamation informal, dated nonsense.

fiddling adjective informal annoyingly trivial.

fiddly adjective Brit. informal complicated and awkward to do or use.

fidelity /fi-del-i-ti/ noun 1 continuing faithfulness to a person, cause, or belief. 2 the degree of exactness with which something is copied or reproduced.
– ORIGIN from Latin *fidelis* 'faithful'.

fidget /fi-jit/ verb (**fidgets, fidgeting, fidgeted**) make small movements through nervousness or impatience. • noun 1 a person who fidgets. 2 (**fidgets**) mental or physical restlessness.
– DERIVATIVES **fidgety** adjective.
– ORIGIN from former *fidge* 'to twitch'.

fiduciary /fi-dyoo-shuh-ri/ Law adjective involving trust, especially with regard to the relationship between a trustee and a beneficiary. • noun (pl. **fiduciaries**) a trustee.

fie /fy/ exclamation old use used to express disgust or outrage.
– ORIGIN Latin *fi*, an exclamation of disgust at an unpleasant smell.

fief /feef/ noun 1 a person's area of operation or control. 2 historical an estate of land held on condition of feudal service.
– DERIVATIVES **fiefdom** noun.
– ORIGIN Old French, variant of *feu* 'fee'.

field noun 1 an area of open land, especially one planted with crops or pasture. 2 a piece of land used for a sport or game. 3 a subject of study or area of activity: *experts in the field of design.* 4 a region or space with a particular property: *a magnetic field.* 5 a range within which objects are visible from a particular viewpoint or through a piece of equipment: *the webcam's field of view.* 6 (**the field**) all the participants in a contest or sport. 7 a scene of a battle or a military campaign. • verb 1 chiefly Cricket & Baseball attempt to catch or stop the ball and return it after it has been hit. 2 select someone to play in a game or to stand in an election. 3 deal with a difficult question, problem, etc. • adjective 1 carried out or working in the natural environment, rather than in a laboratory or office. 2 (of military equipment) light and mobile for use on campaign.
– PHRASES **in the field 1** (of troops) engaged in combat or manoeuvres. **2** engaged in practical work in the natural environment. **play the field** informal have a series of casual sexual relationships.
– DERIVATIVES **fielder** noun.
– ORIGIN Old English.

fieldcraft noun the techniques involved in living in or making military or scientific observations in the field.

field day noun an opportunity for action or success, especially at the expense of others: *he's having a field day bossing people about.*

field events plural noun athletic sports other than races, such as throwing and jumping events.

fieldfare noun a large northern thrush with a grey head.
– ORIGIN Old English.

field glasses plural noun binoculars for outdoor use.

field hockey noun hockey played on grass or a hard pitch, as opposed to ice hockey.

field hospital noun a temporary hospital set up near a battlefield.

field marshal noun the highest rank of officer in the British army.

field mouse noun a common dark brown mouse with a long tail and large eyes.

field mushroom noun the common edible mushroom.

field officer noun a major, lieutenant colonel, or colonel.

field sports plural noun hunting, shooting, and fishing.

field test noun (also **field trial**) a test carried out in the environment in which a product is to be used. • verb (**field-test**) test a product in the environment in which it is to be used.

field trip noun an expedition made by students or research workers to study something at first hand.

fieldwork noun practical work conducted by a researcher in the field rather than in a laboratory or office.

fiend /feend/ noun 1 an evil spirit or demon. 2 a very wicked or cruel person. 3 informal a person who is very interested in something: *an exercise fiend.*
– ORIGIN Old English, 'an enemy, the devil'.

fiendish adjective 1 very cruel or unpleasant. 2 informal very complex.
– DERIVATIVES **fiendishly** adverb.

fierce adjective 1 violent or aggressive; ferocious. 2 intense or powerful: *her fierce determination never to lose the new order in her life.*
– DERIVATIVES **fiercely** adverb **fierceness** noun.
– ORIGIN Latin *ferus* 'untamed'.

fiery adjective (**fierier, fieriest**) 1 resembling or consisting of fire. 2 quick-tempered or passionate.
– DERIVATIVES **fierily** adverb **fieriness** noun.

fiesta /fi-ess-tuh/ noun 1 (in Spanish-speaking countries) a religious festival. 2 a special public event.
– ORIGIN Spanish.

FIFA /fee-fuh/ abbreviation Fédération Internationale de Football Association, the international governing body of football.

fife noun a small shrill flute played in military bands.
– ORIGIN German *Pfeife* 'pipe'

fifteen cardinal number 1 one more than fourteen; 15. (Roman numeral: **xv** or **XV**.) 2 a team of fifteen players, especially in rugby.
– DERIVATIVES **fifteenth** ordinal number.
– ORIGIN Old English.

fifth ordinal number 1 that is number five in a sequence; 5th. 2 (a **fifth**/**one fifth**) each of five equal parts into which something is divided. 3 a musical interval spanning five consecutive notes in a scale, in particular (also **perfect fifth**) an interval of three tones and a semitone.
– PHRASES **take the fifth** (in the US) exercise the right guaranteed by the Fifth Amendment to the Constitution to refuse to answer questions in order to avoid incriminating oneself.
– DERIVATIVES **fifthly** adverb.

fifth column noun a group within a country at war who are working for its enemies.
– DERIVATIVES **fifth columnist** noun.

– ORIGIN from the Spanish Civil War, when General Mola, leading four columns of troops towards Madrid, declared that he had a fifth column inside the city.

fifty cardinal number (pl. **fifties**) ten less than sixty; 50. (Roman numeral: **l** or **L**.)
– DERIVATIVES **fiftieth** ordinal number.
– ORIGIN Old English.

fifty-fifty adjective & adverb with equal shares or chances.

fig[1] noun a soft pear-shaped fruit with sweet flesh and many small seeds.
– PHRASES **not give** (or **care**) **a fig** not care at all.
– ORIGIN Old French *figue*.

fig[2] noun (in phrase **in full fig**) informal wearing the complete set of clothes appropriate to a particular occasion or profession.
– ORIGIN from former *feague* 'whip', later 'liven up'.

fight verb (past and past part. **fought**) **1** take part in a violent struggle involving physical force or weapons. **2** take part in a war or contest. **3** (**fight someone/thing off**) defend oneself against an attack by someone or something. **4** quarrel or argue. **5** struggle to overcome, end, or prevent: *he came to power with a pledge to fight corruption.* **6** try very hard to obtain or do something: *doctors fought to save her life.* • noun **1** an act of fighting. **2** a vigorous struggle or campaign.
– PHRASES **fight fire with fire** use the weapons or tactics of one's opponent, even if one finds them distasteful. **fight shy of** be unwilling to do something. **fight one's way** move forward with difficulty.
– ORIGIN Old English.

fightback noun Brit. a great effort to recover the lead made by a person or group who seem likely to lose a contest.

fighter noun **1** a person or animal that fights. **2** a fast military aircraft designed for attacking other aircraft.

fighting chance noun a possibility of success if great effort is made.

fighting fit adjective in excellent health.

fig leaf noun a leaf of a fig tree, used to conceal the genitals of naked people in paintings and sculpture.
– ORIGIN with reference to the story of Adam and Eve in the Bible, who made clothes out of fig leaves after becoming aware of their nakedness.

figment /fig-muhnt/ noun a thing that exists only in a person's imagination.
– ORIGIN Latin *figmentum*.

figural /fig-yoor-uhl/ adjective another term for FIGURATIVE.

figuration /fig-uh-ray-shuhn/ noun **1** decoration using designs. **2** the representation of people or things in art as they appear in real life. **3** Music use of elaborate counterpoint.

figurative adjective **1** not using words in their literal sense; metaphorical. **2** (of art) representing people or things as they appear in real life.
– DERIVATIVES **figuratively** adverb.

figure noun **1** a number or numerical symbol. **2** an amount of money. **3** a person's bodily shape, especially that of a woman. **4** an important or distinctive person: *he became something of a cult figure.* **5** an artistic representation of a person or animal. **6** a geometrical shape defined by one or more lines. **7** a diagram or illustrative drawing. **8** a short succession of musical notes from which longer passages are developed. • verb **1** play a significant part in something. **2** (**figure someone/thing out**) informal understand someone or something. **3** N. Amer. calculate an amount arithmetically. **4** informal, chiefly N. Amer. think or consider: *I figured I was safe here.* **5** (**figure on**) N. Amer. informal expect something to happen or be the case.
– ORIGIN Latin *figura* 'figure, form'.

figurehead noun **1** a person who is leader in name only, lacking real power. **2** a carved bust or full-length figure set at the prow of an old-fashioned sailing ship.

figure-hugging adjective (of an item of clothing) fitting closely to the contours of a woman's body.

figure of speech noun a word or phrase used in a non-literal sense to create a particular effect in speech or writing.

figure skating noun a type of ice skating in which the skater combines a number of movements including steps, jumps, and turns.

figurine /fi-guh-reen/ noun a small statue of a person.
– ORIGIN Italian *figurina* 'small figure'.

Fijian /fee-jee-uhn/ noun a person from Fiji. • adjective relating to Fiji.

filagree noun variant spelling of FILIGREE.

filament /fil-uh-muhnt/ noun **1** a slender thread-like object or fibre. **2** a metal wire in an electric light bulb, which glows white-hot when an electric current is passed through it. **3** Botany the slender part of a stamen that supports the anther.
– DERIVATIVES **filamentary** adjective **filamentous** adjective.
– ORIGIN Latin *filamentum*.

filariasis /fil-air-i-ay-siss, fil-uh-ry-uh-siss/ noun a disease caused by infestation with parasitic worms, transmitted by biting flies and mosquitoes in the tropics.
– ORIGIN from Latin *Filaria*, former name of a genus of nematode worms.

filbert noun a cultivated hazelnut.
– ORIGIN from French *noix de filbert* (so named because it ripens around 20 August, the feast day of St *Philibert*).

filch verb informal steal something.
– ORIGIN unknown.

file[1] noun **1** a folder or box for keeping loose papers together and in order. **2** Computing a collection of data or programs stored under a single identifying name. **3** a line of people or things one behind another. **4** Military a small detachment of troops. • verb **1** place a document in a file. **2** officially place a legal document, application, or charge on record. **3** walk one behind the other.
– ORIGIN Latin *filum* 'a thread'.

file[2] noun a tool with a roughened surface or surfaces, used for smoothing or shaping a hard material. • verb smooth or shape something with a file.

– ORIGIN Old English.

filename noun an identifying name given to a computer file.

filial /fil-i-uhl/ adjective relating to or due from a son or daughter: *no one can accuse me of neglecting my filial duty.*
– ORIGIN from Latin *filius* 'son', *filia* 'daughter'.

filibuster /fil-i-buss-ter/ noun prolonged speaking which obstructs progress in a law-making assembly. • verb obstruct the progress of legislation by prolonged speaking.
– ORIGIN French *flibustier*, first applied to pirates in the West Indies.

filicide /fil-i-syd/ noun 1 the killing of one's child or children. 2 a person who kills their child or children.
– ORIGIN from Latin *filius* 'son', *filia* 'daughter'.

filigree /fil-i-gree/ (also **filagree**) noun delicate ornamental work of fine gold, silver, or copper wire.
– DERIVATIVES **filigreed** adjective.
– ORIGIN from Latin *filum* 'thread' + *granum* 'seed'.

filings plural noun small particles rubbed off by a file.

Filipino /fi-li-pee-noh/ noun (pl. **Filipinos**; fem. **Filipina**, pl. **Filipinas**) 1 a person from the Philippines. 2 the national language of the Philippines. • adjective relating to Filipinos or their language.

fill verb 1 make or become full: *his wardrobe is filled with designer clothes.* 2 block up a hole or gap. 3 be an overwhelming presence in: *the smell of garlic filled the air.* 4 cause someone to experience a feeling. 5 satisfy a need. 6 occupy a period of time. 7 hold and perform the duties of a position or role. • noun (**one's fill**) as much as one wants or can bear.
– PHRASES **fill in** act as a substitute. **fill someone in** give someone information. **fill something in** Brit. complete a form by adding information. **fill out** put on weight. **fill someone's shoes** (or **boots**) informal take over someone's role and fulfil it satisfactorily.
– ORIGIN Old English.

filler[1] noun 1 something used to fill a gap or cavity, or to increase bulk. 2 an item serving only to fill space or time in a broadcast, conversation, etc.

filler[2] /fi-ler/ noun (pl. same) a unit of money of Hungary, equal to one hundredth of a forint.
– ORIGIN Hungarian.

filler cap noun a cap closing the pipe leading to the petrol tank of a motor vehicle.

fillet noun 1 a boneless piece of meat from near the loins or ribs of an animal. 2 a boned side of a fish. 3 a band or ribbon binding the hair. 4 Architecture a narrow flat band separating two mouldings. • verb (**fillets, filleting, filleted**) 1 remove the bones from a fish. 2 cut meat or fish into boneless strips.
– ORIGIN Old French *filet* 'thread'.

filling noun a quantity or piece of material that fills or is used to fill something. • adjective (of food) leaving one feeling pleasantly full.

filling station noun a petrol station.

fillip /fil-lip/ noun a stimulus or boost: *the latest EU initiative will bring a fillip to the area's economy.*

– ORIGIN in imitation of making a flick with the fingers.

filly noun (pl. **fillies**) 1 a young female horse, especially one less than four years old. 2 humorous a lively girl or young woman.
– ORIGIN Old Norse.

film noun 1 a thin, flexible strip of plastic or other material coated with a light-sensitive substance, used in a camera to produce photos or motion pictures. 2 a story or event recorded by a camera as a series of moving images and shown in a cinema or on television. 3 motion pictures considered as an art or industry. 4 material in the form of a very thin flexible sheet. 5 a thin layer covering a surface. • verb 1 make a film of a story, event, etc. 2 become covered with a thin layer of something.
– ORIGIN Old English, 'membrane'.

filmic adjective relating to films or cinematography.

film noir /film nwah/ noun a style of film marked by a mood of pessimism, fatalism, and menace.
– ORIGIN French, 'black film'.

filmography noun (pl. **filmographies**) a list of films by one director or actor, or on one subject.

filmstrip noun a series of transparencies in a strip for projection.

filmy adjective (**filmier, filmiest**) 1 thin and translucent: *a flowing robe of filmy chiffon.* 2 covered with a thin film.

filo /fee-loh/ (also **phyllo**) noun a kind of flaky pastry in the form of very thin sheets.
– ORIGIN modern Greek *phullo* 'leaf'.

Filofax /fy-loh-faks/ noun trademark a loose-leaf notebook for recording appointments, addresses, and notes.
– ORIGIN representing an informal pronunciation of *file of facts.*

filovirus /fee-loh-vy-ruhss/ noun an RNA virus of a group which causes certain severe fevers characterized by haemorrhages.

fils /feess/ noun used after a surname to distinguish a son from a father of the same name.
– ORIGIN French, 'son'.

filter noun 1 a device or substance that allows liquid or gas to pass through it, but holds back any solid particles. 2 a screen, plate, or layer which absorbs some of the light passing through it. 3 Brit. an arrangement at a junction whereby vehicles may turn while traffic waiting to go straight ahead is stopped by a red light. 4 a piece of computer software that processes data before passing it to another application, for example to remove unwanted material. • verb 1 pass something through a filter. 2 move gradually in or out of somewhere: *the sun filtered through the window.* 3 (of information) gradually become known.
– DERIVATIVES **filterable** adjective **filtration** noun.
– ORIGIN Latin *filtrum* 'felt used as a filter'.

filter tip noun a filter attached to a cigarette for removing impurities from the inhaled smoke.

filth noun 1 disgusting dirt. 2 obscene and offensive language or printed material.
– ORIGIN Old English.

filthy adjective (**filthier**, **filthiest**) **1** disgustingly dirty. **2** obscene and offensive. **3** informal very unpleasant or disagreeable: *filthy weather.*
• adverb informal extremely: *she's filthy rich.*
– DERIVATIVES **filthily** adverb **filthiness** noun.

filtrate noun a liquid which has passed through a filter.

fin noun **1** a flattened part that projects from the body of a fish or other aquatic animal, used for propelling, steering, and balancing. **2** an underwater swimmer's flipper. **3** a projection on an aircraft, rocket, or car, for providing aerodynamic stability.
– DERIVATIVES **finned** adjective.
– ORIGIN Old English.

finagle /fi-**nay**-guhl/ verb informal, chiefly US obtain something in a dishonest or devious way.
– DERIVATIVES **finagler** noun.
– ORIGIN from dialect *fainaigue* 'cheat'.

final adjective **1** coming at the end; last.
2 allowing no further doubt or dispute: *the decision of the judges is final.* • noun **1** the last game in a tournament, which will decide the overall winner. **2** (**finals**) a series of games forming the final stage of a competition.
3 (**finals**) Brit. a series of exams at the end of a degree course.
– ORIGIN from Latin *finis* 'end'.

finale /fi-**nah**-li/ noun the last part of a piece of music, an entertainment, or a public event.
– ORIGIN Italian.

finalist noun a person or team competing in a final or finals.

finality noun (pl. **finalities**) the fact or quality of being final and unable to be changed.

finalize (or **finalise**) verb complete or decide on a final version of a plan or agreement.
– DERIVATIVES **finalization** noun.

finally adverb **1** after a long time and much difficulty or delay. **2** as a final point in a series.

final solution noun the Nazi policy (1941–5) of exterminating Jews.

finance /fy-**nanss**/ noun **1** the management of large amounts of money by governments or large organizations. **2** funds to support an enterprise. **3** (**finances**) the money available to a state, organization, or person. • verb provide funding for a person or enterprise.
– ORIGIN Old French.

finance company (also **finance house**) noun a company concerned primarily with providing money, e.g. for hire-purchase transactions.

financial adjective relating to finance.
– DERIVATIVES **financially** adverb.

financial year noun a year as reckoned for taxing or accounting purposes, especially the British tax year reckoned from 6 April.

financier /fy-**nan**-si-er/ noun a person who manages the finances of governments or other large organizations.
– ORIGIN French.

finch noun a songbird of a large group including the chaffinch and goldfinch, most of which have short stubby bills.
– ORIGIN Old English.

find verb (past and past part. **found**) **1** discover someone or something by chance or by searching. **2** recognize or discover to be

present or to be the case: *vitamin B12 is found in dairy products.* **3** confirm something by research or calculation. **4** reach or arrive at a state or point by a natural or normal process.
5 Law (of a court) officially declare to be the case: *he was found guilty of fraud.* **6** (**find against** or **for**) Law (of a court) make a decision against (or in favour of) someone. • noun a valuable or interesting discovery.
– PHRASES **find one's feet** become confident in a new situation. **find someone out** discover that someone has lied or been dishonest. **find something out** discover information or a fact.
– DERIVATIVES **findable** adjective.
– ORIGIN Old English.

finder noun **1** a person who finds someone or something. **2** a small telescope attached to a large one to locate an object for observation. **3** a viewfinder in a camera.

fin de siècle /fan duh sy-**ek**-luh/ adjective relating to or typical of the end of a century, especially the 19th century.
– ORIGIN French, 'end of century'.

finding noun a conclusion reached as a result of an inquiry, investigation, or trial.

fine[1] adjective **1** of very high quality.
2 satisfactory. **3** healthy and feeling well. **4** (of the weather) bright and clear. **5** very thin: *fine hair.* **6** of delicate or intricate workmanship.
7 difficult to distinguish because precise or subtle: *the ear makes fine distinctions between different noises.* • adverb informal in a satisfactory or pleasing way. • verb **1** (usu. **fine down**) make or become thinner. **2** clarify beer or wine by causing the precipitation of sediment.
– PHRASES **cut it fine** allow a very small margin of time. **not to put too fine a point on it** to speak bluntly.
– DERIVATIVES **finely** adverb **fineness** noun.
– ORIGIN Old French *fin.*

fine[2] noun a sum of money imposed as a punishment by a court of law or other authority. • verb punish someone by a fine.
– ORIGIN Old French *fin* 'end, payment'.

fine art noun art intended to appeal mainly or solely to the sense of beauty, such as painting.
– PHRASES **have something down to a fine art** achieve a high level of skill in something through experience.

fine print noun another term for SMALL PRINT.

finery /fy-nuh-ri/ noun showy clothes or decoration.

fines herbes /feenz **airb**/ plural noun mixed herbs used in cooking.
– ORIGIN French, 'fine herbs'.

finesse noun **1** impressive delicacy and skill: *his acting showed considerable dignity and finesse.*
2 subtle skill in handling people or situations.
3 (in bridge and whist) an attempt to win a trick with a card that is not a certain winner.
• verb **1** do something with great subtlety and skill. **2** chiefly N. Amer. slyly attempt to avoid blame when dealing with a situation.
– ORIGIN French.

fine-tooth comb (also **fine-toothed comb**) noun (in phrase **with a fine-tooth comb**) with a very thorough search or analysis.

fine-tune verb make small adjustments to something in order to achieve the best performance.

finger noun **1** each of the four slender jointed parts attached to either hand (or five, if the thumb is included). **2** a measure of liquor in a glass, based on the breadth of a finger. **3** a long, narrow object. • verb **1** touch or feel someone or something with the fingers. **2** informal, chiefly N. Amer. inform on someone. **3** Music play a passage with a particular sequence of positions of the fingers.
– PHRASES **be all fingers and thumbs** Brit. informal be clumsy. **get one's fingers burnt** suffer unpleasant consequences as a result of one's actions. **have a finger in every pie** be involved in a large number of activities. **have one's finger on the pulse** be aware of the latest trends. **lay a finger on** touch someone with the intention of harming them. **pull one's finger out** Brit. informal stop hesitating and start to act. **put the finger on** informal inform on someone. **put one's finger on** identify something exactly.
– DERIVATIVES **fingered** adjective **fingerless** adjective.
– ORIGIN Old English.

fingerboard noun a flat strip on the neck of a stringed instrument, against which the strings are pressed in order to vary the pitch.

finger bowl noun a small bowl holding water for rinsing the fingers at a meal.

finger food noun food that can conveniently be eaten with the fingers.

fingering noun a way or technique of using the fingers to play a musical instrument.

fingermark noun a mark left on a surface by a dirty or greasy finger.

fingernail noun the nail on the upper surface of the tip of each finger.

finger paint noun thick paint designed to be applied with the fingers, used by young children.

fingerpick verb play a guitar or similar instrument using the fingernails or plectrums worn on the fingertips.

fingerpost noun a post at a road junction from which signs project in the direction of the place indicated.

fingerprint noun a mark made on a surface by a person's fingertip, useful for identification. • verb record a person's fingerprints.

fingerstall noun a cover to protect a finger.

fingertip adjective using or operated by the fingers.
– PHRASES **at one's fingertips** (of information) readily available.

finial /fin-i-uhl/ noun **1** a distinctive section or ornament at the highest point of a roof, pinnacle, or similar structure. **2** an ornament at the top, end, or corner of an object.
– ORIGIN from Latin *finis* 'end'.

finicky adjective **1** fussy about one's requirements: *a finicky eater.* **2** excessively detailed and elaborate.
– DERIVATIVES **finickiness** noun.
– ORIGIN probably from FINE¹.

fining noun a substance used for clarifying beer or wine.

finis /fee-nis, fi-nis, fy-nis/ noun the end (printed at the end of a book or shown at the end of a film).

– ORIGIN Latin.

finish verb **1** bring or come to an end. **2** consume the whole or the remainder of food or drink. **3** (**finish with**) Brit. have no more need for something. **4** (**finish with**) Brit. end a relationship with someone. **5** reach the end of a race or other competition. **6** (**finish up**) end by doing something or being in a particular position: *some of the guests finished up dead.* **7** (**finish someone off**) kill or comprehensively defeat someone. **8** complete the manufacture or decoration of something by giving it an attractive surface appearance. • noun **1** an end or final stage. **2** the place at which a race or competition ends. **3** the way in which a manufactured article is finished: *nylon with a shiny finish.*
– DERIVATIVES **finisher** noun.
– ORIGIN Latin *finire*.

finishing school noun a private college where girls are taught how to behave correctly in fashionable society.

finishing touch noun a final detail that completes and improves a piece of work.

finite /fy-nyt/ adjective limited in size or extent.
– DERIVATIVES **finitely** adverb **finiteness** noun.
– ORIGIN Latin *finitus* 'finished'.

finito /fi-nee-toh/ adjective informal finished: *his door closed, and that was it—the end, finito.*
– ORIGIN Italian.

fink noun N. Amer. informal an unpleasant or contemptible person.
– ORIGIN unknown.

Finn noun a person from Finland.

finnan haddock noun haddock cured with the smoke of green wood, turf, or peat.
– ORIGIN from the Scottish village of *Findon*.

Finnish noun the language of the Finns. • adjective relating to the Finns or their language.

fino /fee-noh/ noun (pl. **finos**) a light-coloured dry sherry.
– ORIGIN Spanish, 'fine'.

fiord noun variant spelling of FJORD.

fir noun an evergreen coniferous tree with upright cones and flat needle-shaped leaves.
– ORIGIN probably Old Norse.

fir cone noun Brit. the dry fruit of a fir tree or other conifer.

fire noun **1** the state of burning, in which substances combine chemically with oxygen from the air and give out bright light, heat, and smoke. **2** an instance of burning in which something is destroyed. **3** wood or coal burnt in a hearth or stove for heating or cooking. **4** (also **electric fire** or **gas fire**) chiefly Brit. a domestic heating appliance that uses electricity or gas as fuel. **5** passionate emotion or enthusiasm. **6** the firing of guns. **7** strong criticism: *he turned his fire on Labour for heaping regulations on small businesses.* • verb **1** shoot a bullet or projectile from a gun or other weapon. **2** direct a rapid succession of questions or statements towards someone. **3** informal dismiss someone from a job. **4** stimulate: *this personal testimony fired the girls' imagination.* **5** (**fire someone up**) fill someone with enthusiasm. **6** supply a furnace, power station, etc. with fuel. **7** bake or dry pottery or bricks in a kiln. **8** old use set fire to

something.
- PHRASES **catch fire** begin to burn. **fire away** informal go ahead. **firing on all cylinders** functioning at a peak level. **on fire 1** burning. **2** very excited. **set fire to** (or **set something on fire**) cause something to burn. **set the world on fire** do something remarkable or sensational. **under fire 1** being shot at. **2** being strongly criticized.
- ORIGIN Old English.

fire alarm noun a device making a loud noise that gives warning of a fire.

firearm noun a rifle, pistol, or other portable gun.

fireball noun **1** a ball of flame or fire. **2** a large bright meteor. **3** an energetic or hot-tempered person.

fire blanket noun a sheet of flexible material used to smother a fire.

firebomb noun a bomb designed to cause a fire. •verb attack something with a firebomb.

firebrand noun a passionate supporter of a particular cause.

firebreak noun an obstacle that prevents fire from spreading, especially a strip of open space in a forest.

firebrick noun a brick capable of withstanding intense heat, used especially to line furnaces and fireplaces.

fire brigade noun Brit. an organized body of firefighters employed to extinguish fires.

fireclay noun clay capable of withstanding high temperatures, used for making firebricks.

firecracker noun a firework that explodes with a loud bang.

firedamp noun a gas, chiefly methane, that forms an explosive mixture with air in coal mines.

firedog noun each of a pair of decorative metal supports for wood burning in a fireplace.

fire door noun a fire-resistant door to prevent the spread of fire.

fire drill noun a practice of the emergency procedures to be used in case of fire.

fire-eater noun an entertainer who appears to eat fire.

fire engine noun a vehicle carrying firefighters and their equipment.

fire escape noun a staircase or ladder used for escaping from a burning building.

fire extinguisher noun a portable device that discharges a jet of liquid, foam, or gas to extinguish a fire.

firefight noun Military a battle using guns rather than bombs or other weapons.

firefighter noun a person whose job is to extinguish fires.

firefly noun (pl. **fireflies**) a kind of beetle which glows in the dark.

fireguard noun a protective screen or grid placed in front of an open fire.

firehouse noun N. Amer. a fire station.

fire irons plural noun tongs, a poker, and a shovel for tending a domestic fire.

firelight noun light from a fire in a fireplace.

firelighter noun Brit. a piece of flammable material used to help start a fire.

fireman noun (pl. **firemen**) a male firefighter.

fireplace noun a partially enclosed space at the base of a chimney for a domestic fire.

firepower noun the destructive capacity of guns, missiles, or a military force.

fire practice noun Brit. a fire drill.

fireproof adjective able to withstand fire or great heat.

fire-raiser noun Brit. an arsonist.

fireside noun the part of a room round a fireplace.

fireside chat noun an informal and intimate conversation.

fire station noun the headquarters of a fire brigade.

firestorm noun a very intense and destructive fire, fanned by strong currents of air drawn in from the surrounding area.

firetrap noun a building without any or enough fire exits.

firewall noun **1** a wall or partition designed to stop the spread of fire. **2** a part of a computer system or network that blocks unauthorized access to a network while allowing outward communication.

firewater noun informal strong alcohol.

firewood noun wood that is burnt as fuel.

firework noun **1** a device containing chemicals that burn or explode when it is ignited, producing spectacular coloured lights and loud noises. **2** (**fireworks**) an outburst of anger or a display of great skill or energy.

firing line noun **1** the front line of troops in a battle. **2** a position where one is likely to be criticized or blamed: *the prime minister is in the firing line again.*

firing squad noun a group of soldiers appointed to shoot a condemned person.

firkin /fer-kin/ noun chiefly historical a small cask used chiefly for liquids, butter, or fish.
- ORIGIN probably from Dutch *vierde* 'fourth' (a firkin originally contained a quarter of a barrel).

firm¹ adjective **1** having a surface or structure that does not give way or sink under pressure. **2** solidly in place and stable. **3** having steady power or strength: *a firm grip.* **4** showing determination and strength of character. **5** fixed or definite: *she had no firm plans.* •verb **1** make something firm. **2** (often **firm something up**) make an agreement or plan explicit and definite. •adverb in a determined way: *he vowed to stand firm.*
- PHRASES **a firm hand** strict discipline or control.
- DERIVATIVES **firmly** adverb **firmness** noun.
- ORIGIN Latin *firmus.*

firm² noun a business organization.
- ORIGIN Latin *firmare* 'confirm by signature, settle'.

firmament /fer-muh-muhnt/ noun literary the heavens; the sky.
- ORIGIN Latin *firmamentum.*

firmware noun Computing software permanently programmed into a read-only memory.

first ordinal number **1** coming before all others in time or order; 1st. **2** before doing something else. **3** before all others in position, rank, or importance. **4** Brit. a place in the top grade in an exam for a degree. **5** informal something never

previously achieved or occurring.
– PHRASES **at first** at the beginning. **first past the post 1** winning a race by being the first to reach the finishing line. **2** Brit. referring to an electoral system in which a candidate or party is selected by the achievement of a simple majority. **of the first order** (or **magnitude**) of the highest quality or degree: *a soprano of the first order.*
– ORIGIN Old English.

first aid noun emergency medical help given to a sick or injured person until full treatment is available.
– DERIVATIVES **first-aider** noun.

firstborn noun the first child to be born to someone.

first class noun **1** a set of people or things grouped together as the best. **2** the best accommodation in an aircraft, train, or ship. **3** Brit. the highest division in the results of the exams for a university degree. • adjective & adverb relating to the first class; of the best quality.

first-day cover noun an envelope with one or more stamps postmarked on their day of issue.

first-degree adjective **1** (of burns) affecting only the surface of the skin and causing reddening. **2** Law, chiefly N. Amer. (of crime, especially murder) in the most serious category.

first-foot verb be the first person to cross someone's threshold in the New Year. • noun (also **first-footer**) the first person to cross a threshold in this way.

first fruits plural noun **1** the first agricultural produce of a season. **2** the first results of an enterprise or undertaking.

first-hand adjective & adverb from the original source or personal experience; direct: *first-hand knowledge.*
– PHRASES **at first hand** directly or from personal experience.

first lady noun the wife of the President of the US or other head of state.

firstly adverb in the first place; first.

first mate noun the officer second in command to the master of a merchant ship.

first minister noun the leader of the ruling political party in some regions or countries.

first name noun a personal name given to someone at birth or baptism and used before a family name.
– PHRASES **be on first-name terms** have a friendly and informal relationship.

first night noun the first public performance of a play or show.

first offender noun a person who is convicted of a criminal offence for the first time.

first officer noun **1** the first mate on a merchant ship. **2** the second in command to the captain on an aircraft.

first person noun the form of a pronoun or verb used to refer to oneself, or to a group including oneself.

first principles plural noun the basic or fundamental concepts or assumptions on which a theory, system, or method is based.

first-rate adjective of the best class, quality, or condition; excellent.

first reading noun the first presentation of a bill to a law-making assembly.

first refusal noun the privilege of deciding whether to accept or reject something before it is offered to others.

first school noun Brit. a school for children from five to eight or nine years old.

first strike noun an opening attack with nuclear weapons.

First World noun the industrialized capitalist countries of western Europe, North America, Japan, Australia, and New Zealand.

firth noun a narrow inlet of the sea.
– ORIGIN Old Norse.

fiscal /fiss-k'l/ adjective **1** relating to the income received by a government, especially as raised through taxes. **2** chiefly N. Amer. relating to financial matters.
– DERIVATIVES **fiscally** adverb.
– ORIGIN Latin *fiscalis.*

fiscal year noun North American term for FINANCIAL YEAR.

fish¹ noun (pl. same or **fishes**) **1** a cold-blooded animal with a backbone, gills, and fins, living in water. **2** the flesh of fish as food. **3** informal a person who is slightly strange: *he's an odd fish.* • verb **1** catch fish with a net or hook and line. **2** (**fish something out**) pull or take something out of water or a container. **3** grope or feel for something hidden. **4** (**fish for**) try to get a response or information by indirect means: *I wasn't fishing for compliments.*
– PHRASES **a big fish** an important person. **a cold fish** a person who is unfriendly or shows little emotion. **a fish out of water** a person who feels out of place in their surroundings. **have other** (or **bigger**) **fish to fry** have more important matters to deal with.
– DERIVATIVES **fishable** adjective **fishing** noun.
– ORIGIN Old English.

USAGE: The normal plural of **fish** is **fish** (*he caught two huge fish*), but the older form **fishes** is still used when referring to different kinds of fish: *freshwater fishes of France.*

fish² noun **1** (also **fishplate**) a flat piece fixed across a joint to strengthen or connect it, e.g. in railway track. **2** a long curved piece of wood lashed to a ship's damaged mast or spar as a temporary repair.
– ORIGIN probably from French *ficher* 'to fix'.

fishbowl noun a round glass bowl for keeping pet fish in.

fishcake noun a patty of shredded fish and mashed potato.

fisher noun old use a fisherman.

fisherman noun (pl. **fishermen**) a person who catches fish for a living or for sport.

fishery noun (pl. **fisheries**) **1** a place where fish are reared, or caught in large numbers. **2** the occupation or industry of catching or rearing fish.

fisheye noun a very wide-angle lens with a field of vision covering up to 180°, the scale being reduced towards the edges.

fish finger noun Brit. a small oblong piece of flaked or minced fish coated in batter or breadcrumbs.

fishing line noun a long thread of silk or nylon attached to a baited hook and used for catching fish.

fishing rod noun a long, tapering rod to which a fishing line is attached.

fish kettle noun an oval pan for boiling fish.

fishmeal noun ground dried fish used as fertilizer or animal feed.

fishmonger noun a person or shop that sells fish for food.

fishnet noun an open mesh fabric resembling a fishing net.

fishplate noun another term for FISH² (in sense 1).

fish slice noun Brit. a kitchen utensil with a broad flat blade for lifting fish and fried foods.

fishtail noun a thing that is forked like a fish's tail. • verb (of a vehicle) travel with its rear end sliding uncontrollably from side to side.

fishwife noun (pl. **fishwives**) a woman with a loud, harsh voice.

fishy adjective (**fishier, fishiest**) 1 referring to or resembling a fish or fish. 2 informal causing feelings of doubt or suspicion.

fissile /fiss-yl/ adjective 1 (of an atom or element) able to undergo nuclear fission. 2 (chiefly of rock) easily split. – ORIGIN Latin *fissilis*.

fission /fi-sh'n/ noun 1 the action of splitting into two or more parts. 2 a reaction in which an atomic nucleus splits in two, releasing much energy. 3 Biology reproduction by means of a cell dividing into two or more new cells. • verb (of atoms) undergo fission. – DERIVATIVES **fissionable** adjective.

fissure /fish-er/ noun a long, narrow crack. • verb split; crack. – ORIGIN Latin *fissura*.

fist noun a person's hand when the fingers are bent in towards the palm and held there tightly. – PHRASES **make a —— fist of** informal do something to a particular degree of success: *he's made a decent fist of running the business.* – DERIVATIVES **fisted** adjective **fistful** noun. – ORIGIN Old English.

fisticuffs plural noun fighting with the fists.

fistula /fis-tyoo-luh/ noun (pl. **fistulas** or **fistulae** /fis-tyoo-lee/) an abnormal or surgically made passage between a hollow or tubular organ and the body surface, or between two hollow or tubular organs. – ORIGIN Latin, 'pipe, flute, fistula'.

fit¹ adjective (**fitter, fittest**) 1 of a suitable quality, standard, or type: *food fit for human consumption.* 2 having the necessary qualities or skills to do something competently. 3 in good health, especially through regular physical exercise. 4 Brit. informal sexually attractive. • verb (**fits, fitting, fitted** (US also **fit**)) 1 be of the right shape and size for someone or something. 2 be of the right size, shape, or number to occupy a position or place: *we can all fit in her car.* 3 fix something into place. 4 (often **be fitted with**) provide something with a component or article. 5 join together to form a whole. 6 be suitable for; match: *the punishment should fit the crime.* 7 make someone suitable for a role or task: *an MSc fits the student for a professional career.* 8 (usu. **be fitted for**) try clothing on someone

in order to make or alter it to the correct size. • noun the way in which something fits. – PHRASES **fit in** be compatible with other members of a group or in harmony with other elements of a situation. **fit someone/thing in** (or **into**) manage to find time to see someone or do something. **fit someone/thing out** (or **up**) provide someone or something with necessary items. **fit to bust** informal with great energy. **fit someone up** Brit. informal incriminate someone by falsifying evidence against them. **see** (or **think**) **fit** consider it correct or acceptable. – DERIVATIVES **fitly** adverb **fitness** noun **fitter** noun. – ORIGIN unknown.

fit² noun 1 a sudden attack of an illness, such as epilepsy, in which a person makes violent, uncontrolled movements and often loses consciousness. 2 a sudden short period of coughing, laughter, etc. 3 a sudden burst of intense feeling: *a fit of jealous rage.* • verb (**fits, fitting, fitted**) have an epileptic fit. – PHRASES **in** (or **by**) **fits and starts** with irregular bursts of activity. – ORIGIN Old English, 'conflict'.

fitful adjective not continuous, regular, or steady: *a few hours' fitful sleep.* – DERIVATIVES **fitfully** adverb **fitfulness** noun.

fitment noun Brit. a fixed item of furniture or piece of equipment.

fitted adjective 1 made to fill a space or to cover something closely. 2 chiefly Brit. (of a room) equipped with matching units of furniture.

fitting noun 1 a small part attached to a piece of furniture or equipment. 2 (**fittings**) chiefly Brit. items which are fixed in a building but can be removed when the owner moves. 3 an occasion when one tries on a garment that is being made or altered. • adjective appropriate; right or proper. – DERIVATIVES **fittingly** adverb.

fitting room noun a room in a shop where one can try on clothes before buying them.

five cardinal number one more than four; 5. (Roman numeral: **v** or **V**.) – DERIVATIVES **fivefold** adjective & adverb. – ORIGIN Old English.

five-a-side noun Brit. a form of football with five players in each team.

five o'clock shadow noun a slight growth of beard visible on a man's chin several hours after he has shaved.

fiver noun 1 Brit. informal a five-pound note. 2 N. Amer. a five-dollar bill.

fives plural noun (treated as sing.) a game in which a ball is hit with a gloved hand or a bat against a wall. – ORIGIN plural of FIVE; the significance is unknown.

five-spice noun a blend of five powdered spices, typically fennel seeds, cinnamon, cloves, star anise, and peppercorns, used in Chinese cooking.

fix verb 1 attach or position something securely. 2 (**fix on**) direct or be directed unwaveringly toward: *her gaze fixed on Jess.* 3 decide or settle on: *no date has yet been fixed.* 4 make unchanging or permanent: *the rate of interest is fixed for two years* 5 repair something. 6 make arrangements for something. 7 informal

influence the outcome of something in an underhand way. **8** informal, chiefly N. Amer. provide someone with food or drink. • noun informal **1** a difficult or awkward situation. **2** a dose of a narcotic drug to which one is addicted. **3** an act of fixing something.
– PHRASES **fix someone up** informal provide someone with something. **fix something up** arrange or organize something. **get a fix on** find out the position, nature, or facts of.
– DERIVATIVES **fixable** adjective **fixer** noun.
– ORIGIN Latin *fixus* 'fixed'.

fixate /fik-sayt/ verb (**fixate on** or **be fixated on**) be obsessively interested in someone or something.

fixation noun **1** an obsessive interest in someone or something. **2** the process by which some plants and microorganisms combine chemically with nitrogen or carbon dioxide in the air to form solid compounds.

fixative /fiks-uh-tiv/ noun a substance used to fix, protect, or stabilize something.

fixed adjective **1** fastened securely in position. **2** not changing or able to be changed. **3** (**fixed for**) informal situated in terms of: *how are you fixed for money?*
– DERIVATIVES **fixedly** adverb.

fixed assets plural noun assets which are bought for long-term use and are not likely to be converted quickly into cash, such as land, buildings, and equipment. Compare with CURRENT ASSETS.

fixed-wing adjective (of aircraft) of the conventional type as opposed to those with rotating wings, such as helicopters.

fixings plural noun Brit. screws, bolts, or other items used to fix or assemble building material, furniture, or equipment.

fixity noun the state of being unchanging or permanent.

fixture /fiks-cher/ noun **1** a piece of equipment or furniture which is fixed in position in a building or vehicle. **2** (**fixtures**) articles attached to a house or land and considered legally part of it so that they normally remain in place when an owner moves. **3** Brit. a sporting event which takes place on a particular date. **4** informal a person or thing that has become firmly established in a particular place.

fizz verb **1** (of a liquid) produce bubbles of gas and make a hissing sound. **2** make a buzzing or crackling sound. • noun **1** the quality of being fizzy. **2** informal a fizzy drink, especially sparkling wine. **3** liveliness.
– ORIGIN imitating the sound.

fizzle verb **1** make a feeble hissing or spluttering sound. **2** (**fizzle out**) gradually become less successful; end in a disappointing way.
– ORIGIN probably imitating the sound.

fizzog noun variant of PHIZ.

fizzy adjective (**fizzier, fizziest**) (of a drink) containing bubbles of gas.
– DERIVATIVES **fizziness** noun.

fjord /fyord, fee-ord/ (also **fiord**) noun a long, narrow, deep inlet of the sea between high cliffs, found especially in Norway.
– ORIGIN Norwegian.

FL abbreviation Florida.

fl. abbreviation **1** floruit. **2** fluid.

flab noun informal soft, loose excess flesh on a person's body.

flabbergast /flab-ber-gahst/ verb (usu. as adj. **flabbergasted**) informal surprise someone greatly.
– ORIGIN unknown.

flabby adjective (**flabbier, flabbiest**) **1** (of a part of a person's body) soft, loose, and fleshy. **2** lacking force, strength, or tight control; not impressive or effective: *a flabby script.*
– DERIVATIVES **flabbiness** noun.
– ORIGIN alteration of earlier *flappy.*

flaccid /flass-id, flak-sid/ adjective soft and limp.
– DERIVATIVES **flaccidity** noun.
– ORIGIN from Latin *flaccus* 'flabby'.

flack noun variant spelling of FLAK.

flag[1] noun **1** an oblong piece of cloth that is attached to a pole and used as a symbol of a country or organization or as a signal. **2** a device or symbol resembling a flag, used as a marker. **3** a small paper badge given to people who donate to a charity appeal. • verb (**flags, flagging, flagged**) **1** mark something for attention. **2** direct or alert someone by waving a flag or using hand signals. **3** (**flag someone down**) signal to a driver to stop.
– PHRASES **fly the flag 1** (of a ship) be registered in a particular country and sail under its flag. **2** represent one's country or show that one is a member of a party or organization. **put the flags out** celebrate.
– ORIGIN unknown.

flag[2] noun a flat rectangular or square stone slab, used for paving.
– DERIVATIVES **flagged** adjective.
– ORIGIN probably Scandinavian.

flag[3] noun a plant of the iris family, with long sword-shaped leaves.
– ORIGIN unknown.

flag[4] verb (**flags, flagging, flagged**) **1** become tired or less enthusiastic. **2** (as adj. **flagging**) becoming weaker or less dynamic: *the country's flagging economy.*
– ORIGIN related to former *flag* 'drooping'.

flag day noun Brit. a day on which money is collected in the street for a charity and contributors give flags to wear.

flagellate[1] /fla-juh-layt/ verb whip someone, either as a form of religious punishment or for sexual pleasure.
– DERIVATIVES **flagellation** noun.
– ORIGIN Latin *flagellare* 'whip'.

flagellate[2] /fla-juh-luht/ adjective (of a single-celled organism) having one or more flagella used for swimming.

flagellum /fluh-jel-luhm/ noun (pl. **flagella** /fluh-jel-luh/) Biology a long, thin projection which enables many single-celled organisms to swim.
– ORIGIN Latin, 'little whip'.

flageolet[1] /fla-juh-let/ noun a very small flute-like instrument resembling a recorder.
– ORIGIN French.

flageolet[2] /flaj-uh-lay/ noun a small variety of French kidney bean.
– ORIGIN French.

flagon /fla-guhn/ noun a large bottle or other container in which wine, cider, or beer is sold or served.
– ORIGIN from Latin *flasco*.

flagpole noun a pole used for flying a flag.

flagrant /flay-gruhnt/ adjective very obvious and unashamed: *a flagrant violation of the law*.
– DERIVATIVES **flagrantly** adverb.
– ORIGIN Latin *flagrare* 'blaze'.

flagship noun 1 the ship in a fleet which carries the commanding admiral. 2 the best or most important thing owned or produced by an organization.

flagstaff noun a flagpole.

flagstone noun a flat square or rectangular stone slab, used for paving.

flag-waving noun a display of extreme patriotism.

flail /flayl/ verb 1 swing or wave one's arms or legs wildly. 2 (usu. **flail about/around**) struggle to move while swinging one's arms and legs wildly. • noun a tool or machine with a swinging action, used for threshing.
– ORIGIN Latin *flagellum* 'little whip'.

flair noun 1 a natural ability or talent. 2 stylishness.
– ORIGIN French.

USAGE: On the confusion of **flair** with **flare**, see the note at **FLARE**.

flak (also **flack**) noun 1 anti-aircraft fire. 2 strong criticism.
– ORIGIN abbreviation of German *Fliegerab-wehrkanone* 'aviator-defence gun'.

flake¹ noun a small, flat, very thin piece of something. • verb 1 come away from a surface in flakes. 2 separate something into flakes.
– ORIGIN probably Germanic.

flake² verb (**flake out**) informal fall asleep or drop from exhaustion.
– ORIGIN from **FLAG⁴**.

flak jacket noun a sleeveless jacket made of heavy fabric reinforced with metal, worn as protection against bullets and shrapnel.

flaky adjective (**flakier**, **flakiest**) 1 breaking or separating easily into flakes. 2 informal, chiefly N. Amer. unconventional or eccentric.
– DERIVATIVES **flakiness** noun.

flaky pastry noun pastry consisting of a number of layers.

flambé /flom-bay/ adjective (after a noun) (of food) covered with spirits and set alight briefly: *steak flambé*. • verb (**flambés**, **flambéing**, **flambéed**) cover food with spirits and set it alight briefly.
– ORIGIN French, 'singed'.

flambeau /flam-boh/ noun (pl. **flambeaus** or **flambeaux** /flam-bohz/) 1 a flaming torch. 2 a branched candlestick.
– ORIGIN French, from *flambe* 'a flame'.

flamboyant /flam-boy-uhnt/ adjective 1 confident and lively in a way that attracts the attention of other people. 2 brightly coloured or highly decorated.
– DERIVATIVES **flamboyance** noun **flamboyantly** adverb.
– ORIGIN French, 'flaming, blazing'.

flame noun 1 a hot glowing body of ignited gas produced by something on fire. 2 a brilliant orange-red colour. • verb 1 give off flames. 2 set something alight. 3 (of a strong emotion) appear suddenly and fiercely. 4 (of a person's face) become red with embarrassment or anger. 5 informal send an abusive email message to someone.
– PHRASES **old flame** informal a former lover.
– ORIGIN Latin *flamma*.

flamenco /fluh-meng-koh/ noun a style of Spanish guitar music accompanied by singing and dancing.
– ORIGIN Spanish, 'like a Gypsy' (literally 'Fleming', i.e. 'a Flemish person').

flameproof adjective 1 (of fabric) treated so as to be non-flammable. 2 (of cookware) able to be used either in an oven or on a hob.

flame-thrower noun a weapon that sprays out burning fuel.

flaming adjective 1 sending out flames. 2 very hot. 3 full of anger: *a flaming row*. 4 informal expressing annoyance: *that flaming dog!*

flamingo /fluh-ming-goh/ noun (pl. **flamingos** or **flamingoes**) a wading bird with mainly pink or scarlet plumage and a long neck and legs.
– ORIGIN Spanish *flamengo*.

flammable /flam-muh-b'l/ adjective easily set on fire.
– DERIVATIVES **flammability** noun.

USAGE: For advice on the words **flammable** and **inflammable**, see the note at **INFLAMMABLE**.

flan noun a baked dish consisting of an open-topped pastry case with a savoury or sweet filling.
– ORIGIN Old French *flaon*.

flange /flanj/ noun a projecting flat rim on an object for strengthening it or attaching it to something.
– DERIVATIVES **flanged** adjective.
– ORIGIN perhaps from Old French *flanchir* 'to bend'.

flank noun 1 the side of a person's or animal's body between the ribs and the hip. 2 the side of something such as a building or mountain. 3 the left or right side of a group of people. • verb be situated on each or on one side of: *the road is flanked by avenues of trees*.
– ORIGIN Old French *flanc*.

flanker noun 1 Rugby a wing forward. 2 Military a fortification to the side of a force or position.

flannel noun 1 a kind of soft-woven woollen or cotton fabric. 2 (**flannels**) men's trousers made of woollen flannel. 3 Brit. a small piece of towelling for washing oneself. 4 Brit. informal empty or insincere talk used to avoid dealing with a difficult subject. • verb (**flannels**, **flannelling**, **flannelled**) Brit. informal use empty or insincere talk to avoid dealing with a difficult subject.
– ORIGIN probably from Welsh *gwlanen* 'woollen article'.

flannelette /flan-nuh-let/ noun a cotton fabric resembling flannel.

flap verb (**flaps**, **flapping**, **flapped**) 1 move or be moved up and down or from side to side. 2 Brit. informal behave in an anxious or agitated way. • noun 1 a piece of something attached on one side only, that covers an opening. 2 a hinged or sliding section of an aircraft wing, used to

control upward movement. **3** a single flapping movement. **4** informal a state of worry or panic.
– DERIVATIVES **flappy** adjective.
– ORIGIN uncertain.

flapjack noun **1** Brit. a soft, thick biscuit made from oats and butter. **2** N. Amer. a pancake.
– ORIGIN from **FLAP** (in the dialect sense 'toss a pancake') + **JACK**[1].

flapper noun informal (in the 1920s) a fashionable and unconventional young woman.

flare noun **1** a sudden brief burst of flame or light. **2** a device producing a very bright flame as a signal or marker. **3** a gradual widening towards the hem of a garment. **4** (**flares**) trousers whose legs widen from the knees down. •verb **1** burn or shine with a sudden intensity. **2** (usu. **flare up**) suddenly start or become stronger or more violent: *rioting flared up in other towns and cities.* **3** (**flare up**) suddenly become angry. **4** gradually become wider at one end.
– ORIGIN unknown.

> **USAGE:** Do not confuse **flare** with **flair**: **flare** means 'burn' or 'gradually become wider', whereas **flair** means 'a natural ability or talent'. Trousers whose legs widen from the knees down are **flared** not **flaired**.

flash verb **1** shine or cause to shine with a bright but brief or irregular light. **2** move or pass swiftly: *the scenery flashed by.* **3** display or be displayed briefly or repeatedly: *a message flashed up on the screen.* **4** informal display something in an obvious way so as to impress people: *they flash their money about.* **5** informal (of a man) show the genitals in public. •noun **1** a sudden brief burst of bright light. **2** a camera attachment that produces a flash of light, for taking photographs in poor light. **3** a sudden or brief occurrence: *a flash of inspiration.* **4** a bright patch of colour. **5** Brit. a coloured patch of cloth worn on a uniform to identify a regiment, country, etc. •adjective informal, chiefly Brit. stylish or expensive in a way designed to attract attention and impress people.
– PHRASES **flash in the pan** a sudden but brief success. **in a flash** very quickly.
– DERIVATIVES **flasher** noun.
– ORIGIN uncertain.

flashback noun **1** a scene in a film or novel set in a time earlier than the main story. **2** a sudden vivid memory of a past event.

flashbulb noun a bulb for a flashgun.

flashcard noun a card containing a clear display of a word or words, used in teaching reading.

flash flood noun a sudden local flood resulting from extreme rainfall.

flashgun noun a device which gives a brief flash of intense light, used for taking photographs in poor light.

flashing noun a strip of metal used to seal the junction of a roof with another surface.

flashlight noun **1** an electric torch with a strong beam. **2** a flashgun.

flash memory noun Computing memory that retains data in the absence of a power supply.

flashpoint noun **1** a point or place at which

anger or violence flares up. **2** Chemistry the temperature at which a flammable compound gives off enough vapour to ignite in air.

flashy adjective (**flashier**, **flashiest**) stylish or expensive in a way designed to attract attention and impress other people.
– DERIVATIVES **flashily** adverb **flashiness** noun.

flask noun **1** a conical or round bottle with a narrow neck. **2** Brit. a vacuum flask. **3** a hip flask. **4** a lead-lined container for radioactive nuclear waste.
– ORIGIN Latin *flasca.*

flat[1] adjective (**flatter**, **flattest**) **1** having a level and even surface. **2** not sloping; horizontal. **3** with a level surface and little height or depth: *a flat cap.* **4** (of shoes) without high heels. **5** without liveliness or interest: *a flat voice.* **6** (of a sparkling drink) no longer fizzy. **7** (of something kept inflated) having lost some or all of its air. **8** Brit. (of a battery) having used up its charge. **9** (of a fee, charge, or price) unvarying; fixed. **10** (of a negative statement) definite and firm: *a flat denial.* **11** (of musical sound) below true or normal pitch. **12** (after a noun) (of a note or key) lower by a semitone than a particular note or key: *E flat.* •adverb **1** in or to a horizontal position. **2** so as to become level and even. **3** informal completely; absolutely: *she turned him down flat.* **4** emphasizing the speed of an action: *in ten minutes flat.* •noun **1** the flat part of something. **2** (**flats**) an area of low level ground, especially near water. **3** informal a flat tyre. **4** (**the Flat**) Brit. flat racing. **5** an upright section of stage scenery. **6** a musical note that is a semitone lower than the corresponding one of natural pitch, indicated by the sign ♭.
– PHRASES **fall flat** fail to produce the intended effect. **flat out** as fast or as hard as possible.
– DERIVATIVES **flatly** adverb **flatness** noun **flattish** adjective.
– ORIGIN Old Norse.

flat[2] noun chiefly Brit. a set of rooms forming an individual home within a larger building.
– ORIGIN related to **FLAT**[1].

flatbed adjective referring to a vehicle whose body consists of an open platform without raised sides or ends, used for carrying loads. •noun Computing a scanner or other device which keeps paper flat during use.

flat feet plural noun feet with arches that are lower than usual.

flatfish noun (pl. same or **flatfishes**) a sea fish, such as a plaice or sole, that swims on its side with both eyes on the upper side of its flattened body.

flat-footed adjective **1** having flat feet. **2** informal clumsy.

flat iron noun historical an iron heated on a hotplate or fire.

flatlet noun a small flat.

flatline verb informal die.
– DERIVATIVES **flatliner** noun.
– ORIGIN with reference to the continuous straight line displayed on a heart monitor when a person dies.

flatmate noun Brit. a person with whom one shares a flat.

flat-pack adjective Brit. referring to furniture or equipment that is sold in pieces and assembled by the buyer.

flat race noun a horse race over a course with no jumps, as opposed to a steeplechase or hurdles.

flatten verb **1** make or become flat or flatter. **2** informal knock someone down.
– DERIVATIVES **flattener** noun.

flatter verb **1** praise or compliment someone excessively or insincerely. **2** (**be flattered**) feel honoured and pleased. **3** (**flatter oneself**) believe something good about oneself, especially something which has no basis in reality. **4** (of clothing or a colour) make someone appear attractive. **5** (often as adj. **flattering**) paint or draw someone so that they appear more attractive than in reality.
– PHRASES **flatter to deceive** appear promising but fail to live up to expectations.
– DERIVATIVES **flatterer** noun.
– ORIGIN Old French *flater*.

flattery noun (pl. **flatteries**) excessive or insincere praise.

flatulent /flat-yuu-luhnt/ adjective suffering from a build-up of gas in the intestines or stomach.
– DERIVATIVES **flatulence** noun.
– ORIGIN Latin *flatus* 'blowing'.

flatware noun **1** items of crockery such as plates and saucers. **2** N. Amer. domestic cutlery.

flatworm noun a type of worm, such as a tapeworm, with a flattened body that lacks blood vessels.

flaunt verb display something proudly or in a way intended to attract attention.
– ORIGIN unknown.

> USAGE: Be careful not to confuse **flaunt** with **flout**. Flaunt means 'display something in a way intended to attract attention' (*some students liked to flaunt their wealth*), while flout means 'openly fail to follow a rule or convention' (*the tendency of some athletes to flout regulations*).

flautist /flaw-tist/ noun a flute player.
– ORIGIN Italian *flautista*.

flavonoid /flay-vuh-noyd/ noun any of a group of naturally occurring chemical compounds including several white or yellow plant pigments.
– ORIGIN from Latin *flavus* 'yellow'.

flavour (US **flavor**) noun **1** the distinctive taste of a food or drink. **2** a particular quality or atmosphere: *the resort has a distinctly Italian flavour.* • verb alter or add to the taste of food or drink by adding a particular ingredient: *cottage cheese flavoured with chives.*
– PHRASES **flavour of the month** a person or thing that is currently popular.
– DERIVATIVES **flavourful** adjective **flavourless** adjective **flavoursome** adjective.
– ORIGIN Old French *flaor* 'a smell'.

flavouring (US **flavoring**) noun a substance used to add to or alter the flavour of a food or drink.

flaw noun **1** a mark or flaw that spoils something. **2** a fundamental weakness or mistake. • verb (usu. as adj. **flawed**) spoil or weaken: *a flawed genius.*
– DERIVATIVES **flawless** adjective **flawlessly** adverb.
– ORIGIN perhaps from an Old Norse word meaning 'stone slab'.

flax noun **1** a blue-flowered plant that is grown for its seed (linseed) and for thread made from its stalks. **2** thread made from flax, used to make linen.
– ORIGIN Old English.

flaxen adjective literary (of hair) pale yellow.

flaxseed noun another term for LINSEED.

flay verb **1** strip the skin from a body or carcass. **2** whip or beat someone so hard that some of their skin is removed. **3** criticize someone harshly.
– ORIGIN Old English.

flea noun a small wingless jumping insect which feeds on the blood of mammals and birds.
– PHRASES **a flea in one's ear** a sharp reprimand.
– ORIGIN Old English.

flea-bitten adjective **1** bitten by or infested with fleas. **2** shabby or run-down.

fleadh /flah/ noun a festival of Irish or Celtic music, dancing, and culture.
– ORIGIN from Irish *fleadh ceoil* 'music festival'.

flea market noun a street market selling second-hand goods at low prices.

fleapit noun Brit. informal a dirty, run-down cinema.

fleck noun **1** a very small patch of colour or light. **2** a small particle: *flecks of dust.* • verb mark or dot with small areas of a particular colour or small pieces of something: *her brown hair was flecked with grey.*
– ORIGIN perhaps from Old Norse, or from German, Dutch *vlecke*.

fled past and past participle of FLEE.

fledge verb **1** (of a young bird) develop wing feathers that are large enough for flight. **2** (as adj. **fledged**) having just taken on a particular role: *a newly fledged Detective Inspector.*
– ORIGIN from Old English, 'ready to fly'.

fledgling (also **fledgeling**) noun a young bird that has just developed wing feathers that are large enough for flight. • adjective new and inexperienced: *a fledgling democracy.*

flee verb (**flees, fleeing**; past and past part. **fled**) run away.
– ORIGIN Old English.

fleece noun **1** the wool coat of a sheep. **2** a soft, warm fabric with a texture similar to sheep's wool, or a jacket made from this. • verb informal swindle someone by charging them too much money.
– DERIVATIVES **fleecy** adjective.
– ORIGIN Old English.

fleet[1] noun **1** a group of ships sailing together. **2** (**the fleet**) a country's navy. **3** a number of vehicles or aircraft operating together.
– ORIGIN Old English.

fleet[2] adjective fast and nimble.
– PHRASES **fleet of foot** able to walk or move swiftly.
– DERIVATIVES **fleetness** noun.
– ORIGIN probably from Old Norse.

fleet[3] verb literary move or pass quickly.
– ORIGIN Old English.

fleeting adjective lasting for a very short time.
– DERIVATIVES **fleetingly** adverb.

Fleming /flem-ing/ noun **1** a Flemish person. **2** a member of the Flemish-speaking people living in northern and western Belgium.
– ORIGIN Old English.

Flemish /flem-ish/ noun 1 (the Flemish) the people of Flanders, a region divided between Belgium, France, and the Netherlands. 2 the Dutch language as spoken in Flanders. •adjective relating to the Flemish people or language.
– ORIGIN Dutch *Vlāmisch*.

flense /flens/ verb slice the skin or fat from a carcass, especially that of a whale.
– ORIGIN Danish *flensa*.

flesh noun 1 the soft substance in the body consisting of muscle tissue and fat. 2 the edible soft part of a fruit or vegetable. 3 (the flesh) the physical aspects and needs of the human body: *pleasures of the flesh*. •verb (flesh something out) give more information or details about something: *the chancellor fleshed out his economic philosophy*.
– PHRASES **one's flesh and blood** a close relative; one's family. **in the flesh** in person or (of a thing) in its actual state. **make someone's flesh creep** (or **crawl**) make someone feel fear, horror, or disgust.
– ORIGIN Old English.

fleshly adjective (**fleshlier, fleshliest**) relating to the body and its needs.

fleshpots plural noun places where people can satisfy their sexual desires.
– ORIGIN from the *fleshpots of Egypt* mentioned in the Bible (Book of Exodus).

flesh wound noun a wound that breaks the skin but does not damage bones or vital organs.

fleshy adjective (**fleshier, fleshiest**) 1 having a lot of flesh; plump. 2 (of leaves or fruit) soft and thick. 3 resembling flesh.
– DERIVATIVES **fleshiness** noun.

fleur-de-lis /fler-duh-lee/ (also **fleur-de-lys**) noun (pl. **fleurs-de-lis** pronunc. same) a representation of a lily made up of three petals bound together near their bases.
– ORIGIN Old French *flour de lys* 'flower of the lily'.

flew past of FLY¹.

flex¹ verb 1 bend a limb or joint. 2 tighten a muscle. 3 warp or bend and then return to the proper shape.
– ORIGIN Latin *flectere*.

flex² noun Brit. a flexible insulated cable used for carrying electric current to an appliance.
– ORIGIN abbreviation of FLEXIBLE.

flexible adjective 1 capable of bending easily without breaking. 2 able to change or be changed to respond to different circumstances.
– DERIVATIVES **flexibility** noun **flexibly** adverb.

flexion /flek-sh'n/ (also **flection**) noun the action of bending or the condition of being bent.

flexitime noun a system by which employees work an agreed total number of hours but have some flexibility as to when they start and finish work each day.

flexor /flek-suh/ noun a muscle whose contraction bends a limb or other part of the body.

flibbertigibbet /flib-ber-ti-jib-bit/ noun a frivolous or irresponsible person.
– ORIGIN probably imitating idle chatter.

flick verb 1 make a sudden sharp movement. 2 hit or remove something with a flick of the fingers: *she flicked some ash off her sleeve*. 3 (flick through) look quickly through a book or a collection of papers. •noun 1 a sudden sharp movement up and down or from side to side. 2 the sudden release of a finger or thumb held bent against another finger. 3 informal a cinema film. 4 (the flicks) Brit. informal the cinema.
– ORIGIN representing sudden movement.

flicker verb 1 shine or burn unsteadily. 2 (of a feeling) be felt or shown briefly. 3 make small, quick movements. •noun 1 a flickering movement or light. 2 a brief feeling or indication of emotion: *a flicker of alarm*.
– ORIGIN Old English, 'to flutter'.

flick knife noun Brit. a knife with a blade that springs out from the handle when a button is pressed.

flier noun variant spelling of FLYER.

flight noun 1 the action or process of flying. 2 a journey made in an aircraft or in space. 3 the path of something through the air. 4 the action of running away: *the enemy were in flight*. 5 a very imaginative idea or story: *a flight of fancy*. 6 a flock of birds flying together. 7 a series of steps between floors or levels. 8 a unit of about six aircraft operating together. 9 the tail of an arrow or dart.
– PHRASES **take flight 1** (of a bird) take off and fly. 2 run away.
– ORIGIN Old English; related to FLY¹.

flight attendant noun a steward or stewardess on an aircraft.

flight deck noun 1 the cockpit of a large aircraft. 2 the deck of an aircraft carrier, used as a runway.

flight feather noun any of the large feathers in a bird's wing which support it during flight.

flightless adjective (of a bird or insect) naturally unable to fly.

flight lieutenant noun a rank of officer in the RAF, above flying officer and below squadron leader.

flight path noun the route taken by an aircraft or spacecraft.

flight recorder noun an electronic device in an aircraft that records technical details during a flight, used in the event of an accident to discover its cause.

flight sergeant noun a rank of non-commissioned officer in the RAF, above sergeant and below warrant officer.

flighty adjective (**flightier, flightiest**) irresponsible and uninterested in serious things.
– DERIVATIVES **flightiness** noun.

flimflam noun informal 1 insincere and unconvincing talk. 2 a confidence trick.
– ORIGIN an invented word.

flimsy adjective (**flimsier, flimsiest**) 1 weak and fragile. 2 (of clothing) light and thin. 3 unconvincing: *a flimsy excuse*.
– DERIVATIVES **flimsily** adverb **flimsiness** noun.
– ORIGIN probably from FLIMFLAM.

flinch verb 1 make a quick, nervous movement as an instinctive reaction to fear or pain. 2 (flinch from) avoid something through fear or anxiety.

– ORIGIN Old French *flenchir* 'turn aside'.

fling verb (past and past part. **flung**) **1** throw something forcefully. **2** move or go suddenly and forcefully: *he flung out his arm.* **3** (**fling oneself into**) take part in an activity or enterprise with great enthusiasm. **4** (**fling something on/off**) put on or take off clothes carelessly and rapidly. •noun **1** a short period of enjoyment or wild behaviour. **2** a short sexual relationship. **3** a Highland fling.
– ORIGIN perhaps related to an Old Norse word meaning 'flog'.

flint noun **1** a hard grey rock consisting of nearly pure silica. **2** a piece of this rock. **3** a piece of flint or a metal alloy, used to produce a spark in a cigarette lighter.
– ORIGIN Old English.

flintlock noun an old-fashioned type of gun fired by a spark from a flint.

flinty adjective (**flintier**, **flintiest**) **1** relating to, containing, or resembling flint. **2** stern and showing no emotion: *a flinty stare.*
– DERIVATIVES **flintily** adverb **flintiness** noun.

flip verb (**flips**, **flipping**, **flipped**) **1** turn over with a sudden, quick movement: *the plane flipped over.* **2** press a button or switch in order to turn a machine or device on or off. **3** move or toss something with a quick action. **4** (**flip through**) look through a book, magazine, etc. **5** (also **flip one's lid**) informal suddenly become very angry or lose one's self-control. •noun a flipping action or movement. •adjective not serious or respectful.
– ORIGIN probably a shortened form of **FILLIP**.

flip chart noun a very large pad of paper bound so that pages can be turned over at the top, used on a stand at presentations.

flip-flop noun a light sandal with a thong that passes between the big and second toes.

flippant adjective not treating something with the appropriate seriousness or respect.
– DERIVATIVES **flippancy** noun **flippantly** adverb.
– ORIGIN from **FLIP**.

flipper noun **1** a broad, flat limb without fingers, used for swimming by sea animals such as seals and turtles. **2** each of a pair of flat rubber attachments worn on the feet for underwater swimming. **3** a pivoted arm in a pinball machine.

flipping adjective informal, chiefly Brit. used for emphasis or to express mild annoyance.

flippy adjective (of a flared, relatively short, skirt) that flicks up as the wearer walks.

flip side noun informal **1** the B-side of a pop single. **2** the reverse or less pleasant aspect of a situation.

flirt verb **1** behave as if one finds another person sexually attractive but without intending to have a relationship with them. **2** (**flirt with**) show a casual interest in an idea or activity. **3** (**flirt with**) deliberately behave in such a way as to risk danger or death. •noun a person who likes to flirt.
– DERIVATIVES **flirtation** noun **flirty** adjective.
– ORIGIN uncertain.

flirtatious adjective liking to flirt with people.
– DERIVATIVES **flirtatiously** adverb.

flit verb (**flits**, **flitting**, **flitted**) **1** move swiftly and lightly. **2** chiefly Scottish & N. English move house

or leave one's home, especially secretly.
– PHRASES **do a (moonlight** or **midnight) flit** Brit. informal leave one's home secretly at night, especially to avoid paying one's debts.
– ORIGIN Old Norse.

flitch /flich/ noun **1** a slab of wood cut from a tree trunk. **2** chiefly dialect a side of bacon.
– ORIGIN Old English.

flitter verb move quickly here and there.
– ORIGIN from **FLIT**.

float verb **1** rest on the surface of a liquid without sinking. **2** move slowly, hover, or be suspended in a liquid or the air: *clouds floated across the sky.* **3** put forward an idea as a suggestion or to test other people's reactions. **4** (as adj. **floating**) not settled or living permanently in one place: *the region's floating population.* **5** offer the shares of a company for sale on the stock market for the first time. **6** allow a currency to have a variable rate of exchange against other currencies. •noun **1** a lightweight object or device designed to float on water. **2** a small floating object attached to a fishing line that moves when a fish bites. **3** Brit. a small vehicle powered by electricity: *a milk float.* **4** a platform mounted on a lorry and carrying a display in a procession. **5** Brit. a sum of money used for change at the beginning of selling a shop, stall, etc. **6** a hand tool with a rectangular blade used for smoothing plaster.
– DERIVATIVES **floater** noun.
– ORIGIN Old English.

floatation noun variant spelling of **FLOTATION**.

floating-point adjective Computing referring to a method of encoding numbers as two sequences of bits, one representing the number's significant digits and the other an exponent.

floating rib noun any of the lower ribs which are not attached directly to the breastbone.

floating voter noun Brit. a person who does not consistently vote for the same party.

floatplane noun a seaplane.

floaty adjective (of a woman's garment or a fabric) light and flimsy.

flocculent /flok-kyuu-luhnt/ adjective having or resembling tufts of wool.
– ORIGIN Latin *flocculus* 'tuft of wool'.

flock¹ noun **1** a number of birds moving or resting together. **2** a number of domestic animals, especially sheep, that are kept together. **3** (**a flock/flocks**) a large number or crowd: *a flock of children.* **4** a Christian congregation under the charge of a particular minister. •verb gather or move in a flock or crowd: *tourists flocked to the area.*
– ORIGIN Old English.

flock² noun a soft material for stuffing cushions and quilts, made of wool refuse or torn-up cloth.
– ORIGIN Latin *floccus.*

flock wallpaper noun wallpaper with a velvety raised pattern made from powdered cloth.

floe /floh/ noun a sheet of floating ice.
– ORIGIN probably from Norwegian *flo* 'layer'.

flog verb (**flogs**, **flogging**, **flogged**) **1** beat someone with a whip or stick as a punishment. **2** Brit. informal sell something. **3** informal talk about

or promote something repeatedly or at excessive length: *the issue has been flogged to death already.*
– PHRASES **flog a dead horse** Brit. waste energy on something that can never be successful.
– DERIVATIVES **flogger** noun.
– ORIGIN perhaps from Latin *flagellare* 'to whip'.

flokati /flo-**kah**-ti/ noun (pl. **flokatis**) a Greek woven woollen rug with a thick loose pile.
– ORIGIN modern Greek *phlokatē* 'peasant's blanket'.

flood noun **1** an overflow of a large amount of water over dry land. **2 (the Flood)** the flood described in the Bible, brought by God because of the wickedness of the human race. **3** an overwhelming quantity of things or people appearing at once: *a flood of refugees.* **4** an outpouring of tears or emotion. **5** the rising of the tide. • verb **1** cover or become covered with water in a flood. **2** (of a river) become swollen and overflow its banks. **3** arrive in very large numbers: *letters of support and sympathy flooded in.* **4** fill completely: *she flooded the room with light.* **5** overfill the carburettor of an engine with petrol.
– ORIGIN Old English.

floodgate noun **1** a gate that can be opened or closed to control a flow of water, especially the lower gate of a lock. **2 (the floodgates)** controls or restraints holding something back: *the case could open the floodgates for thousands of similar claims.*

floodlight noun a large, powerful light used to illuminate a stage, sports ground, etc. • verb (past and past part. **floodlit**) (usu. as adj. **floodlit**) light up a stage, sports ground, etc. with floodlights.

flood plain noun an area of low-lying ground next to a river that regularly becomes flooded.

flood tide noun an incoming tide.

floor noun **1** the lower surface of a room. **2** a storey of a building. **3** the bottom of the sea, a cave, etc. **4** a minimum level of prices or wages. **5 (the floor)** the part of a law-making body in which members sit and from which they speak. **6 (the floor)** the right to speak in a debate: *other speakers have the floor.* • verb **1** provide a room with a floor. **2** informal knock someone to the ground. **3** informal completely baffle someone.
– DERIVATIVES **flooring** noun.
– ORIGIN Old English.

floorboard noun a long plank making up part of a wooden floor.

floor manager noun **1** the stage manager of a television production. **2** a supervisor of shop assistants in a large store.

floor show noun an entertainment presented on the floor of a nightclub or restaurant.

floozy (also **floozie**) noun (pl. **floozies**) informal, chiefly humorous a girl or woman who has sexual relationships with many different men.
– ORIGIN uncertain.

flop verb (**flops, flopping, flopped**) **1** hang or swing loosely. **2** sit or lie down heavily and clumsily. **3** informal fail totally. • noun **1** a heavy, clumsy fall. **2** informal a total failure.
– ORIGIN variant of FLAP.

-flop combining form Computing floating-point operations per second.

flophouse noun informal, chiefly N. Amer. a dosshouse.

floppy adjective (**floppier, floppiest**) not firm or rigid; flopping or hanging loosely. • noun (pl. **floppies**) (also **floppy disk**) Computing a flexible removable magnetic disk used for storing data.

flora noun (pl. **floras**) **1** the plants of a particular region, habitat, or period of time. Compare with FAUNA. **2** the bacteria found naturally in the intestines.
– ORIGIN Latin *flos* 'flower'.

floral adjective relating to or decorated with flowers.
– DERIVATIVES **florally** adverb.

Florentine /flo-ruhn-tyn/ adjective relating to the city of Florence in Italy. • noun **1** a person from Florence. **2** a biscuit consisting mainly of nuts and preserved fruit, coated on one side with chocolate.

floret /flo-rit/ noun **1** one of the small flowers making up a composite flower head. **2** one of the flowering stems making up a head of cauliflower or broccoli.
– ORIGIN Latin *flos* 'flower'.

floribunda /flo-ri-**bun**-duh/ noun a plant, especially a rose, which has dense clusters of flowers.
– ORIGIN Latin, from *floribundus* 'freely flowering'.

floriculture /flo-ri-kulch-er/ noun the growing of flowers.

florid /flo-rid/ adjective **1** having a red or flushed complexion. **2** too elaborate or ornate: *florid prose.*
– DERIVATIVES **floridly** adverb.
– ORIGIN Latin *floridus*.

floriferous /flo-**rif**-uh-ruhss/ adjective producing many flowers.

florin /flo-rin/ noun **1** a former British coin worth two shillings. **2** an English gold coin of the 14th century. **3** a Dutch guilder.
– ORIGIN Italian *fiorino* 'little flower' (originally referring to a Florentine coin bearing a fleur-de-lis).

florist noun a person who sells and arranges cut flowers.
– DERIVATIVES **floristry** noun.

floruit /flo-ruu-it/ verb used to indicate when a historical figure lived, worked, or was most active.
– ORIGIN Latin, 'he or she flourished'.

floss noun **1** (also **dental floss**) a soft thread used to clean between the teeth. **2** untwisted silk threads used in embroidery. **3** the rough silk enveloping a silkworm's cocoon. • verb clean between one's teeth with dental floss.
– DERIVATIVES **flossy** adjective.
– ORIGIN Old French *flosche* 'down, nap of velvet'.

flotation /floh-**tay**-sh'n/ (also **floatation**) noun **1** the action of floating. **2** the process of offering a company's shares for sale on the stock market for the first time.

flotation tank noun a lightproof, soundproof tank of salt water in which a person floats as a form of deep relaxation.

flotilla /fluh-til-luh/ noun a small fleet of ships or boats.
– ORIGIN Spanish.

flotsam /flot-suhm/ noun wreckage found floating on the sea.
– PHRASES **flotsam and jetsam** useless or discarded objects.
– ORIGIN Old French *floteson*.

flounce[1] verb move in a way that draws attention to oneself in order to emphasize one's impatience or annoyance. • noun an exaggerated action expressing annoyance or impatience.
– ORIGIN perhaps related to Norwegian *flunsa* 'hurry'.

flounce[2] noun a wide ornamental strip of material gathered and sewn to a skirt or dress; a frill.
– DERIVATIVES **flounced** adjective **flouncy** adjective.
– ORIGIN from an alteration of former *frounce* 'a fold or pleat', from Old French *fronce*.

flounder[1] verb 1 stagger clumsily in mud or water. 2 have trouble doing or understanding something.
– ORIGIN perhaps a blend of FOUNDER[3] and BLUNDER.

USAGE: On the confusion of **flounder** and **founder**, see the note at FOUNDER[3].

flounder[2] noun a small flatfish of shallow coastal waters.
– ORIGIN Old French *flondre*.

flour noun a powder produced by grinding grain, used to make bread, cakes, and pastry. • verb sprinkle something with flour.
– ORIGIN from FLOWER in the sense 'the best part', first used to mean 'the finest quality of ground wheat'.

flourish verb 1 grow or develop in a healthy or vigorous way. 2 be working or at the height of one's career during a particular period. 3 wave something about dramatically. • noun 1 an exaggerated gesture or movement, made especially to attract attention. 2 an ornamental flowing curve in handwriting. 3 a fanfare played by brass instruments.
– ORIGIN Old French *florir*.

floury adjective 1 covered with flour. 2 (of a potato) having a soft, fluffy texture when cooked.

flout /flowt/ verb openly fail to follow a rule, law, or convention.
– ORIGIN perhaps from Dutch *fluiten* 'play the flute, hiss scornfully'.

USAGE: On the confusion of **flout** and **flaunt**, see the note at FLAUNT.

flow verb 1 move steadily and continuously in a current or stream. 2 move steadily and freely: *people flowed into the courtyard*. 3 (often as adj. **flowing**) hang loosely and elegantly: *a long flowing gown*. 4 (of the sea or a tidal river) move towards the land; rise. • noun 1 the action of flowing. 2 a steady, continuous stream: *the flow of traffic*. 3 the rise of a tide or a river.
– PHRASES **in full flow** talking or performing fluently and enthusiastically.
– ORIGIN Old English.

flow chart (also **flow diagram**) noun a diagram showing a sequence of operations or functions making up a complex process or computer program.

flower noun 1 the part of a plant from which the seed or fruit develops, usually having brightly coloured petals. 2 (often in phrase **in flower**) the state or period in which a plant's flowers have developed and opened. 3 (**the flower of**) the best of a group: *the flower of Ireland's youth*. • verb 1 produce flowers. 2 develop richly and fully: *a musical form which flowered in the nineteenth century*.
– ORIGIN Old French *flour, flor*, from Latin *flos*.

flowered adjective decorated with patterns of flowers.

flower head noun a compact mass of flowers at the top of a stem, especially a dense flat cluster of florets.

flowerpot noun an earthenware or plastic container in which to grow a plant.

flower power noun the promotion by hippies of peace and love as means of changing the world.

flowery adjective 1 full of, decorated with, or resembling flowers. 2 (of speech or writing) elaborate.

flown past participle of FLY[1].

flu noun influenza.

fluctuate /fluk-chuu-ayt/ verb rise and fall irregularly in number or amount: *her weight has fluctuated between eight and eleven stones*.
– DERIVATIVES **fluctuation** noun.
– ORIGIN Latin *fluctuare* 'undulate'.

flue /floo/ noun 1 a duct in a chimney for smoke and waste gases. 2 a pipe or passage for conveying heat.
– ORIGIN unknown.

fluent /floo-uhnt/ adjective 1 speaking or writing in an articulate and natural way. 2 (of a language) used easily and accurately. 3 smoothly graceful and easy: *a runner in fluent motion*.
– DERIVATIVES **fluency** noun **fluently** adverb.
– ORIGIN from Latin *fluere* 'to flow'.

fluff noun 1 soft fibres gathered in small light clumps. 2 the soft fur or feathers of a young mammal or bird. 3 informal a mistake. • verb 1 (usu. **fluff something up/out**) make something fuller and softer by shaking or patting. 2 informal fail to accomplish properly: *he fluffed his only line*.
– ORIGIN probably from Flemish *vluwe*.

fluffy adjective (**fluffier, fluffiest**) 1 resembling or covered with fluff. 2 (of food) light in texture. 3 informal frivolous, silly, or vague: *fluffy game shows*.
– DERIVATIVES **fluffiness** noun.

flugelhorn /floo-g'l-horn/ noun a brass musical instrument like a cornet but with a fuller tone.
– ORIGIN from German *Flügel* 'wing' + *Horn* 'horn'.

fluid noun a substance, such as a liquid or gas, that has no fixed shape and yields easily to external pressure. • adjective 1 able to flow easily. 2 not settled or stable: *today's fluid social environment*. 3 (of movement) smoothly elegant or graceful.
– DERIVATIVES **fluidity** noun **fluidly** adverb.
– ORIGIN Latin *fluidus*.

fluid ounce noun **1** Brit. a unit of capacity equal to one twentieth of a pint (approximately 0.028 litre). **2** US a unit of capacity equal to one sixteenth of a US pint (approximately 0.03 litre).

fluke[1] noun a lucky chance occurrence.
– DERIVATIVES **fluky** (also **flukey**) adjective.
– ORIGIN perhaps a dialect word.

fluke[2] noun a parasitic flatworm which typically has suckers and hooks for attachment to the host.
– ORIGIN Old English.

fluke[3] noun **1** a broad triangular plate on the arm of an anchor. **2** either of the lobes of a whale's tail.
– ORIGIN perhaps from **FLUKE**[2] (because of the shape).

flume /floom/ noun **1** an artificial channel for water. **2** a water slide at a swimming pool or amusement park.
– ORIGIN Latin *flumen* 'river'.

flummery /**flum**-muh-ri/ noun (pl. **flummeries**) empty talk; nonsense.
– ORIGIN Welsh *llymru*.

flummox /**flum**-muhks/ verb informal baffle or bewilder someone.
– ORIGIN probably dialect.

flump verb fall or sit down heavily.
– ORIGIN imitating the sound.

flung past and past participle of **FLING**.

flunk verb informal, chiefly N. Amer. fail an exam.
– ORIGIN perhaps related to **FUNK**[1].

flunkey (also **flunky**) noun (pl. **flunkeys** or **flunkies**) chiefly derogatory **1** a uniformed manservant or footman. **2** a person who performs menial tasks.
– ORIGIN perhaps from **FLANK** in the sense 'a person who stands at one's flank'.

fluoresce /fluu-uh-**ress**/ verb shine or glow brightly due to fluorescence.

fluorescence /fluu-uh-**ress**-uhnss/ noun **1** light given out by a substance when it is exposed to radiation such as ultraviolet light or X-rays. **2** the property of giving out light in this way.
– ORIGIN from **FLUORSPAR** (which fluoresces).

fluorescent adjective **1** having or showing fluorescence. **2** (of lighting) based on fluorescence from a substance illuminated by ultraviolet light. **3** vividly colourful.

fluoridate /**fluu**-uh-ri-dayt/ verb add traces of fluorides to something.
– DERIVATIVES **fluoridation** noun.

fluoride /**fluu**-uh-ryd/ noun **1** a compound of fluorine with another element or group. **2** a fluorine-containing salt added to water supplies or toothpaste to reduce tooth decay.

fluorinate /**fluu**-uh-ri-nayt/ verb **1** introduce fluorine into a compound. **2** another term for **FLUORIDATE**.
– DERIVATIVES **fluorination** noun.

fluorine /**fluu**-uh-reen/ noun a poisonous, extremely reactive, pale yellow gaseous chemical element.
– ORIGIN from *fluor* (see **FLUORSPAR**).

fluorite noun a mineral form of calcium fluoride.

fluoroscope noun an instrument used for viewing X-ray images without taking and developing X-ray photographs.
– DERIVATIVES **fluoroscopic** adjective **fluoroscopy** noun.

fluorspar /**fluu**-uh-spar/ noun another term for **FLUORITE**.
– ORIGIN from Latin *fluor* 'a flow' + **SPAR**[3].

flurried adjective agitated, confused, or anxious.

flurry noun (pl. **flurries**) **1** a small swirling mass of snow, leaves, etc. moved by a gust of wind. **2** a sudden short spell of activity or excitement. **3** a number of things arriving suddenly and at the same time: *a flurry of emails*.
– ORIGIN from former *flurr* 'fly up, flutter', probably influenced by **HURRY**.

flush[1] verb **1** (of a person's skin or face) become red and hot, typically through illness or emotion. **2** (**be flushed with**) be excited or very pleased by: *flushed with success, I was getting into my stride*. **3** clean something by passing large quantities of water through it. **4** remove or dispose of something by flushing with water. **5** force a person or animal out of hiding: *their task was to flush out the rebels*. • noun **1** a reddening of the face or skin. **2** a sudden rush of intense emotion. **3** a period of freshness and vigour: *the first flush of youth*. **4** an act of flushing something with water.
– DERIVATIVES **flusher** noun.
– ORIGIN perhaps influenced by **FLASH** and **BLUSH**.

flush[2] adjective (usu. **flush with**) **1** completely level with another surface. **2** informal having plenty of something, especially money.
– ORIGIN probably related to **FLUSH**[1].

flush[3] noun (in poker or brag) a hand of cards all of the same suit.
– ORIGIN Latin *fluxus* 'flux'.

fluster verb (often as adj. **flustered**) make someone agitated or confused. • noun a flustered state.
– ORIGIN perhaps Scandinavian.

flute noun **1** a high-pitched wind instrument consisting of a tube with holes along it. **2** a tall, narrow wine glass. **3** Architecture an ornamental vertical groove in a column. • verb speak in a melodious way.
– DERIVATIVES **fluting** noun **fluty** (also **flutey**) adjective.
– ORIGIN Old French *flahute*.

fluted adjective (of an object) having a series of decorative grooves.

flutist noun US term for **FLAUTIST**.

flutter verb **1** fly unsteadily by flapping the wings quickly and lightly. **2** move with a light irregular motion: *flags fluttered in the breeze*. **3** (of a pulse or heartbeat) beat irregularly. • noun **1** an act of fluttering. **2** a state of nervous excitement. **3** Brit. informal a small bet. **4** Electronics rapid variation in the pitch or amplitude of a signal, especially of recorded sound. Compare with **WOW**[2].
– DERIVATIVES **fluttery** adjective.
– ORIGIN Old English.

fluvial /**floo**-vi-uhl/ adjective chiefly Geology relating to or found in a river.
– ORIGIN from Latin *fluvius* 'river'.

flux /fluks/ noun **1** continuous change: *urban life is in a constant state of flux*. **2** technical the action of flowing. **3** Medicine an abnormal discharge

from or within the body. **4** Physics the total amount of radiation, or of electric or magnetic field lines, passing through an area. **5** a substance mixed with a solid to lower the melting point, used in soldering or smelting.
– ORIGIN Latin *fluxus*.

fly[1] verb (**flies, flying, flew**; past part. **flown**) **1** (of a winged creature or aircraft) move through the air. **2** control the flight of an aircraft. **3** carry or accomplish in an aircraft: *by 22 June, the squadron had flown 207 sorties.* **4** go or move quickly: *his fingers flew across the keyboard.* **5** move or be thrown quickly through the air. **6** wave or flutter in the wind. **7** (of a flag) be displayed on a flagpole. **8** (**fly at**) attack someone verbally or physically. **9** old use run away; flee. • noun (pl. **flies**) **1** (Brit. also **flies**) an opening at the crotch of a pair of trousers, closed with a zip or buttons. **2** a flap of material covering the opening of a tent. **3** (**the flies**) the space over the stage in a theatre.
– PHRASES **fly in the face of** oppose or be the opposite of what is usual or expected. **fly into a rage** (or **temper**) become suddenly angry. **fly off the handle** informal lose one's temper suddenly.
– DERIVATIVES **flyable** adjective.
– ORIGIN Old English.

fly[2] noun (pl. **flies**) **1** a flying insect with a single pair of transparent wings and sucking or piercing mouthparts. **2** used in names of other flying insects, e.g. **dragonfly**. **3** a fishing bait consisting of a natural or artificial flying insect.
– PHRASES **a fly in the ointment** a minor irritation that spoils the enjoyment of something. **fly on the wall** an unnoticed observer. **there are no flies on ——** the person specified is quick and shrewd.
– ORIGIN Old English.

fly[3] adjective (**flyer, flyest**) informal **1** Brit. knowing and clever; worldly-wise. **2** N. Amer. stylish and fashionable.
– ORIGIN unknown.

fly agaric noun a poisonous toadstool which has a red cap with fluffy white spots.

flyaway adjective (of hair) fine and difficult to control.

flyblown adjective contaminated by contact with flies and their eggs and larvae.

fly-by-night adjective unreliable or untrustworthy, especially in financial matters.

fly-by-wire adjective referring to a semi-automatic computer-regulated system for controlling an aircraft or spacecraft.

flycatcher noun a perching bird that catches flying insects.

flyer (also **flier**) noun **1** a person or thing that flies. **2** informal a fast-moving person or thing. **3** a small leaflet advertising an event or product. **4** a flying start.

fly-fishing noun the sport of fishing using a rod and an artificial fly as bait.

fly half noun Rugby another term for **STAND-OFF HALF**.

flying adjective **1** able to move through the air. **2** hasty; brief: *a flying visit.*
– PHRASES **with flying colours** very well; with particular merit.

flying boat noun a large seaplane that lands with its fuselage in the water.

flying buttress noun Architecture a buttress slanting from a separate column, typically forming an arch with the wall it supports.

flying fish noun a fish of warm seas which leaps out of the water and uses its wing-like pectoral fins to glide for some distance.

flying fox noun a large fruit bat with a foxlike face, found in Madagascar, SE Asia, and northern Australia.

flying officer noun a rank of commissioned officer in the RAF, above pilot officer and below flight lieutenant.

flying picket noun Brit. a person who travels to picket any workplace where there is an industrial dispute.

flying saucer noun a disc-shaped flying craft supposedly piloted by aliens.

flying squad noun Brit. a division of a police force which is capable of reaching an incident quickly.

flying start noun **1** a start of a race in which the competitors are already moving at speed as they pass the starting point. **2** a good beginning giving an advantage over competitors.

flyleaf noun (pl. **flyleaves**) a blank page at the beginning or end of a book.

flyover noun chiefly Brit. a bridge carrying one road or railway line over another.

flypaper noun sticky, poison-treated strips of paper that are hung indoors to catch and kill flies.

fly-past noun Brit. a ceremonial flight of aircraft past a person or a place.

fly-post verb Brit. put up advertising posters in unauthorized places.

flysheet noun Brit. a fabric cover pitched over a tent to give extra protection against bad weather.

fly-tip verb Brit. dump waste illegally.

flyweight noun a weight in boxing and other sports intermediate between light flyweight and bantamweight.

flywheel noun a heavy wheel in a machine which is used to increase momentum and thereby provide greater stability or a reserve of available power.

FM abbreviation **1** Field Marshal. **2** frequency modulation.

Fm symbol the chemical element fermium.

fm abbreviation fathom(s).

f-number noun the ratio of the focal length of a camera lens to the diameter of the aperture being used for a particular shot.

FO abbreviation Foreign Office.

foal noun a young horse or related animal. • verb (of a mare) give birth to a foal.
– ORIGIN Old English.

foam noun **1** a mass of small bubbles formed on or in liquid. **2** a liquid substance containing many small bubbles: *shaving foam.* **3** a lightweight form of rubber or plastic made by solidifying foam. • verb form or produce foam.
– PHRASES **foam at the mouth** informal be very angry.
– DERIVATIVES **foamy** adjective.
– ORIGIN Old English.

fob[1] noun **1** a chain attached to a watch for carrying in a waistcoat or waistband pocket. **2** (also **fob pocket**) a small pocket for carrying a watch. **3** a tab on a key ring.
– ORIGIN probably related to German dialect *Fuppe* 'pocket'.

fob[2] verb (**fobs, fobbing, fobbed**) **1** (**fob someone off**) try to deceive someone into accepting excuses or something inferior. **2** (**fob something off on**) give something inferior to someone.
– ORIGIN perhaps related to German *foppen* 'deceive, banter'.

fob watch noun a pocket watch.

focaccia /fuh-**kach**-uh/ noun a type of flat Italian bread made with olive oil and flavoured with herbs.
– ORIGIN Italian.

focal /**foh**-k'l/ adjective relating to a focus, especially the focus of a lens.
– DERIVATIVES **focally** adverb.

focal length noun the distance between the centre of a lens or curved mirror and its focus.

focal point noun **1** the point at which rays or waves from a lens or mirror meet, or the point from which rays or waves going in different directions appear to proceed. **2** the centre of interest or activity: *a fireplace serves as the focal point of any room*.

fo'c's'le /**fohk**-s'l/ noun variant spelling of FORECASTLE.

focus /**foh**-kuhss/ noun (pl. **focuses** or **foci** /**foh**-sy/) **1** the centre of interest or activity. **2** the state or quality of having or producing a clear, well-defined image: *his face is out of focus*. **3** the point at which an object must be situated in order for a lens or mirror to produce a clear image of it. **4** a focal point. **5** the point of origin of an earthquake. Compare with EPICENTRE. **6** Geometry a fixed point with reference to which an ellipse, parabola, or other curve is drawn. •verb (**focuses, focusing, focused** or **focusses, focussing, focussed**) **1** (of a person or their eyes) adapt to the prevailing level of light and become able to see clearly. **2** (**focus on**) pay particular attention to: *I was able to focus on a single project*. **3** adjust the focus of a telescope, camera, etc. **4** (of rays or waves) meet or cause to meet at a single point.
– DERIVATIVES **focuser** noun.
– ORIGIN Latin, 'domestic hearth'.

focus group noun a group of people assembled to assess a new product, political campaign, etc.

fodder noun **1** food for cattle and other livestock. **2** people or things regarded only as material to satisfy a need: *young people ending up as factory fodder*.
– ORIGIN Old English.

foe noun formal or literary an enemy or opponent.
– ORIGIN from Old English, 'hostile'.

foehn noun variant spelling of FÖHN.

foetid adjective variant spelling of FETID.

foetus noun variant spelling of FETUS (chiefly in British non-technical use).
– DERIVATIVES **foetal** adjective.

fog noun **1** a thick cloud of tiny water droplets suspended in the atmosphere at or near the earth's surface which restricts visibility. **2** a state or cause of confusion. **3** Photography cloudiness obscuring the image on a developed negative or print. •verb (**fogs, fogging, fogged**) **1** cover or become covered with steam. **2** bewilder or confuse: *the sedative still fogged Jack's mind.* **3** Photography make a film, negative, or print cloudy.
– ORIGIN perhaps from FOGGY.

fogbound adjective surrounded or hidden by fog.

fogey /**foh**-gi/ (also **fogy**) noun (pl. **fogeys** or **fogies**) a very old-fashioned or conservative person.
– DERIVATIVES **fogeydom** noun **fogeyish** adjective **fogeyism** noun.
– ORIGIN unknown.

foggy adjective (**foggier, foggiest**) **1** full of fog. **2** confused or unclear: *my memories of the event are foggy*.
– PHRASES **not have the foggiest** (**idea**) informal, chiefly Brit. have no idea at all.
– ORIGIN perhaps from Norwegian *fogg* 'grass which grows in a field after a crop of hay has been cut'.

foghorn noun a device making a loud, deep sound as a warning to ships in fog.

fogy noun variant spelling of FOGEY.

föhn /fern/ (also **foehn**) noun a hot southerly wind on the northern slopes of the Alps.
– ORIGIN German.

foible /**foy**-b'l/ noun a minor weakness or eccentricity.
– ORIGIN from former French form of Old French *fieble* 'feeble'.

foie gras /fwah grah/ (also **pâté de foie gras**) noun a pâté made from the liver of a fattened goose.

foil[1] verb **1** prevent something wrong or undesirable from succeeding. **2** prevent someone from doing something.
– ORIGIN first meaning 'trample down': perhaps from Old French *fouler* 'to full cloth, trample'.

foil[2] noun **1** metal hammered or rolled into a thin, flexible sheet. **2** a person or thing that contrasts with and so emphasizes the qualities of another: *silver foliage provides the perfect foil for bright flower colours*.
– ORIGIN Latin *folium* 'leaf'.

foil[3] noun a light, blunt-edged fencing sword with a button on its point.
– ORIGIN unknown.

foist /foysst/ verb (**foist someone/thing on**) impose an unwelcome person or thing on: *electricity privatization was foisted on the public*.
– ORIGIN Dutch dialect *vuisten* 'take in the hand'.

fold[1] verb **1** bend something over on itself so that one part of it covers another. **2** (often as adj. **folding**) be able to be folded into a flatter shape. **3** cover or wrap something in a flexible material. **4** affectionately hold someone in one's arms. **5** informal (of a company) go out of business. **6** (**fold something in/into**) mix an ingredient gently with another ingredient. •noun **1** a folded part or thing: *drooping folds of skin*. **2** a line or crease produced by folding. **3** chiefly Brit. a slight hill or hollow. **4** Geology a bend or curvature of strata.
– PHRASES **fold one's arms** cross one's arms over

one's chest.
– DERIVATIVES **foldable** adjective.
– ORIGIN Old English.

fold² noun **1** a pen or enclosure for sheep. **2** (**the fold**) a group with shared aims and values: *Churchill went back into the Tory fold.*
– ORIGIN Old English.

-fold suffix forming adjectives and adverbs from cardinal numbers: **1** in an amount multiplied by: *threefold.* **2** consisting of a specified number of parts: *twofold.*
– ORIGIN Old English.

foldaway adjective designed to be folded up for easy storage or transport.

folder noun **1** a folding cover or holder for storing loose papers. **2** Computing a directory containing related files.

folderol /fol-duh-rol/ noun trivial or nonsensical fuss.
– ORIGIN from a meaningless refrain in old songs.

foliage /foh-li-ij/ noun the leaves of a plant.
– ORIGIN Old French *feuillage.*

foliar /foh-li-uh/ adjective technical relating to leaves.

foliate /foh-li-ayt/ adjective decorated with leaves or a leaf-like pattern.

folic acid /foh-lik/ noun a vitamin of the B complex found especially in leafy green vegetables, liver, and kidney.
– ORIGIN from Latin *folium* 'leaf'.

folie à deux /fol-i a der/ noun (pl. **folies à deux**) delusion or mental illness shared by two people in a close relationship.
– ORIGIN French, 'shared madness'.

folie de grandeur /fol-i duh gron-der/ noun delusions of grandeur.
– ORIGIN French.

folio /foh-li-oh/ noun (pl. **folios**) **1** a sheet of paper folded once to form two leaves (four pages) of a book. **2** a book made up of such sheets. **3** an individual leaf of paper numbered on the front side only. **4** the page number in a printed book.
– ORIGIN from Latin *folium* 'leaf'.

folk /fohk/ plural noun **1** (also **folks**) informal people in general. **2** (**one's folks**) chiefly N. Amer. one's family, especially one's parents. **3** (also **folk music**) traditional music of unknown authorship, passed on by word of mouth. • adjective originating from the beliefs, culture, and customs of ordinary people: *folk wisdom.*
– DERIVATIVES **folkish** adjective.
– ORIGIN Old English.

folk dance noun a traditional dance of a particular people or area.

folk etymology noun **1** a popular but mistaken account of the origin of a word or phrase. **2** the process by which the form of an unfamiliar or foreign word is adapted to a more familiar form through popular use.

folkie noun informal a singer, player, or fan of folk music.

folklore noun the traditional beliefs, stories, and customs of a community, passed on by word of mouth.
– DERIVATIVES **folkloric** adjective **folklorist** noun.

folksy adjective (**folksier**, **folksiest**) traditional and homely, especially in an artificial way: *his carefully cultivated, folksy image.*
– DERIVATIVES **folksiness** noun.

folk tale noun a traditional story originally passed on by word of mouth.

folky adjective (**folkier**, **folkiest**) resembling or typical of folk music.

follicle /fol-li-k'l/ noun a small cavity in the body, especially one in which the root of a hair develops.
– DERIVATIVES **follicular** /fol-lik-yuu-ler/ adjective.
– ORIGIN Latin *folliculus* 'little bag'.

follow verb **1** move or travel behind someone or something. **2** go after someone so as to observe them. **3** go along a route or path. **4** come after in time or order: *the six years that followed his death.* **5** (also **follow on from**) happen as a result of something else. **6** be a logical consequence. **7** act according to an instruction or example. **8** accept someone as a guide, example, or leader of a movement. **9** take an interest in or pay close attention to: *supporters who have followed the club through thick and thin.* **10** understand someone or something. **11** practise or undertake a career or course of action. **12** (**follow something through**) continue an action or task to its conclusion. **13** (**follow something up**) pursue or investigate something further.
– PHRASES **follow one's nose 1** trust to one's instincts. **2** go straight ahead. **follow on** (of a cricket team) be required to bat again immediately after failing to reach a certain score in their first innings. **follow suit 1** do the same as someone else. **2** (in card games) play a card of the suit led.
– ORIGIN Old English.

follower noun **1** a supporter, fan, or disciple. **2** a person who follows someone or something.
– DERIVATIVES **followership** noun.

following preposition coming after or as a result of. • noun a group of supporters or admirers. • adjective next in time or order.

follow-through noun the continuing of an action or task to its conclusion.

follow-up noun **1** an activity carried out to monitor or further develop earlier work. **2** a work that follows or builds on an earlier work.

folly noun (pl. **follies**) **1** lack of good sense; foolishness. **2** a foolish act or idea. **3** an ornamental building with no practical purpose, built in a large garden.
– ORIGIN Old French *folie* 'madness'.

foment /foh-ment/ verb stir up trouble or violence.
– DERIVATIVES **fomentation** noun.
– ORIGIN Latin *fomentare* 'bathe part of the body with warm or medicated lotions'.

fond adjective **1** (**fond of**) feeling affection for someone or having a liking for something. **2** affectionate; loving: *fond memories of our childhood.* **3** (of a hope or belief) not likely to be fulfilled; foolishly optimistic.
– DERIVATIVES **fondly** adverb **fondness** noun.
– ORIGIN unknown.

fondant /fon-duhnt/ noun **1** a thick paste made of sugar and water, used in making sweets and icing cakes. **2** a sweet made of fondant.
– ORIGIN French, 'melting'.

fondle verb stroke or caress someone lovingly

or erotically. •noun an act of fondling.

– DERIVATIVES **fondler** noun.

– ORIGIN from **FOND**.

fondue /fon-doo/ noun a dish in which small pieces of food are dipped into melted cheese, a hot sauce, or hot oil.

– ORIGIN French, 'melted'.

font¹ noun a large stone bowl in a church that holds the water used in baptism.

– ORIGIN Latin *fons* 'spring, fountain'.

font² (Brit. also **fount**) noun Printing a set of type of a particular face and size.

– ORIGIN French *fonte* 'casting'.

fontanelle /fon-tuh-nel/ (US **fontanel**) noun a soft area between the bones of the skull in a baby or fetus, where the sutures are not yet fully formed.

– ORIGIN Old French, 'little fountain'.

fontina /fon-tee-nuh/ noun a pale yellow Italian cheese.

– ORIGIN Italian.

food noun any nutritious substance that people or animals eat or drink or that plants absorb to maintain life and growth.

– PHRASES **food for thought** something that merits serious consideration.

– ORIGIN Old English.

food chain noun a series of organisms each dependent on the next as a source of food.

foodie (also **foody**) noun (pl. **foodies**) informal a person with a strong interest in food.

food mile noun Brit. a mile over which an item of food is transported from producer to consumer, as a unit of measurement of the fuel used to do this.

food poisoning noun illness caused by bacteria or other toxins in food, typically with vomiting and diarrhoea.

foodstuff noun a substance suitable to be eaten as food.

fool¹ noun **1** a person who acts unwisely. **2** historical a jester or clown. •verb **1** trick or deceive someone. **2** (**fool about/around**) act in a joking or silly way. **3** (**fool around**) N. Amer. engage in casual or extramarital sex.

– DERIVATIVES **foolery** noun.

– ORIGIN Old French *fol* 'fool, foolish'.

fool² noun chiefly Brit. a cold dessert made of puréed fruit served with cream or custard.

– ORIGIN perhaps from **FOOL¹**.

foolhardy adjective bold in a reckless way.

– DERIVATIVES **foolhardily** adverb **foolhardiness** noun.

– ORIGIN from Old French *fol* 'foolish' + *hardi* 'emboldened'.

foolish adjective lacking good sense or judgement; silly or unwise.

– DERIVATIVES **foolishly** adverb **foolishness** noun.

foolproof adjective incapable of going wrong or being misused.

foolscap /foolz-kap/ noun Brit. a size of paper, about 330 × 200 (or 400) mm.

– ORIGIN said to be from a former watermark representing a fool's cap.

fool's errand noun a task or activity that has no hope of success.

fool's gold noun a brassy yellow mineral that can be mistaken for gold, especially pyrite.

fool's paradise noun a state of happiness based on not knowing about or ignoring

potential trouble.

foot noun (pl. **feet**) **1** the part of the leg below the ankle, on which a person walks. **2** the base or bottom of something vertical. **3** the end of a bed where the occupant's feet normally rest. **4** a unit of length equal to 12 inches (30.48 cm). **5** Poetry a group of syllables making up a basic unit of metre. •verb informal **1** pay a bill. **2** (**foot it**) go somewhere on foot.

– PHRASES **feet of clay** a flaw or weakness in a person otherwise admired. **get** (or **start**) **off on the right** (or **wrong**) **foot** make a good (or bad) start. **have** (or **keep**) **one's feet on the ground** be (or remain) practical and sensible. **have** (or **get**) **a foot in the door** have (or gain) a first introduction to a profession or organization. **have one foot in the grave** humorous be very old or ill. **land** (or **fall**) **on one's feet** have good luck or success. **on** (or **by**) **foot** walking rather than using transport. **put one's best foot forward** begin with as much effort and determination as possible. **put one's foot down** informal **1** be firm when faced with opposition or disobedience. **2** Brit. accelerate a motor vehicle by pressing the accelerator. **put one's foot in it** informal say or do something tactless or embarrassing. **put a foot wrong** make a mistake. **under one's feet** in one's way. **under foot** on the ground.

– DERIVATIVES **footless** adjective.

– ORIGIN Old English.

footage noun **1** a length of film made for cinema or television. **2** size or length measured in feet.

foot-and-mouth disease noun a disease caused by a virus in cattle and sheep, causing ulcers on the hoofs and around the mouth.

football noun **1** a team game involving kicking a ball, in particular (in the UK) soccer or (in the US) American football. **2** a large inflated ball used in football.

– DERIVATIVES **footballer** noun **footballing** adjective (Brit.).

footboard noun **1** an upright panel forming the foot of a bed. **2** a board acting as a step up to a vehicle such as a train.

footbrake noun a foot-operated brake lever in a motor vehicle.

footbridge noun a bridge for pedestrians.

footer noun **1** a person or thing of a specified number of feet in length or height: *a six-footer*. **2** a kick of a football performed with a specified foot: *a low left-footer*. **3** variant of **FOOTY**. **4** a line of writing appearing at the foot of each page of a book or document.

footfall noun **1** the sound of a footstep or footsteps. **2** the number of people entering a shop or shopping area in a given time: *footfall in post offices is decreasing dramatically.*

foot fault noun (in tennis, squash, etc.) an infringement of the rules made by overstepping the baseline when serving.

foothill noun a low hill at the base of a mountain or mountain range.

foothold noun **1** a secure position from which further progress may be made: *the company has failed to gain a foothold in Japan.* **2** a place where one can place a foot to give support while climbing.

footie noun variant spelling of **FOOTY**.

footing noun **1** (**one's footing**) a secure grip

with one's feet. **2** the basis on which something is established or operates: *we are on equal footing with our competitors in the market.* **3** the foundations of a wall.

footle /foo-t'l/ **verb** chiefly Brit. potter or mess about.
– ORIGIN uncertain.

footlights plural noun a row of spotlights along the front of a stage at the level of the actors' feet.

footling /foot-ling/ **adjective** trivial and irritating.

footloose adjective free to go where one likes and do as one pleases.

footman noun (pl. **footmen**) a uniformed servant whose duties include admitting visitors.

footmark noun a footprint.

footnote noun an additional piece of information printed at the bottom of a page.

footpad noun historical a highwayman operating on foot rather than riding a horse.

footpath noun a path for people to walk along.

footplate noun chiefly Brit. the platform for the crew in the cab of a locomotive.

footprint noun the mark left by a foot or shoe on a surface or the ground.

footrest noun a support for the feet, used when sitting.

footsie /fuut-si/ noun (in phrase **play footsie**) informal touch someone's feet lightly with one's own as a playful expression of romantic interest.

foot soldier noun **1** a soldier who fights on foot. **2** a low-ranking person who nevertheless does valuable work.

footsore adjective having sore feet from much walking.

footstep noun a step taken in walking, especially as heard by another person.
– PHRASES **follow** (or **tread**) **in someone's footsteps** do as another person did before.

footstool noun a low stool for resting the feet on when sitting.

foot-tapping adjective having a strong rhythmical musical beat.

footwear noun shoes, boots, and other coverings for the feet.

footwell noun a space for the feet in front of a seat in a vehicle.

footwork noun the way in which one moves one's feet in dancing and sport.

footy (also **footie** or **footer**) noun Brit. informal football.

fop noun a man who is excessively concerned with his clothes and appearance.
– DERIVATIVES **foppery** noun **foppish** adjective.
– ORIGIN perhaps related to FOB².

for preposition **1** affecting or relating to. **2** in favour of. **3** on behalf of. **4** because of. **5** so as to get, have, or do. **6** in the direction of. **7** over a distance or during a period of time. **8** in exchange for or in place of. **9** in relation to the expected norm of: *she was tall for her age.* **10** indicating an occasion in a series.
• **conjunction** literary because; since.
– PHRASES **be for it** Brit. informal be about to be punished or get into trouble.
– ORIGIN Old English.

fora plural of FORUM (in sense 3).

forage /fo-rij/ **verb 1** search for food. **2** search for something: *she foraged in her pocket for a paper hanky.* • **noun** food for horses and cattle.
– DERIVATIVES **forager** noun.
– ORIGIN Old French *fourrager*.

forage cap noun a soldier's peaked cap.

foramen /fuh-ray-men/ noun (pl. **foramina** /fuh-ram-in-uh/) Anatomy an opening, hole, or passage, especially in a bone.
– ORIGIN Latin.

forasmuch as conjunction old use because; since.

foray /fo-ray/ noun **1** a sudden attack or raid into enemy territory. **2** a spirited attempt to become involved in a new activity: *this is the firm's first foray into cookbook publishing.* • **verb** attempt a new activity.
– DERIVATIVES **forayer** noun.
– ORIGIN from Old French *forrier* 'forager'.

forbade (also **forbad**) past of FORBID.

forbear¹ /for-bair/ **verb** (past **forbore**; past part. **forborne**) stop oneself from doing something.
– ORIGIN Old English.

> **USAGE:** Do not confuse **forbear** with **forebear**. **Forbear** means 'stop oneself from doing something' (*he doesn't forbear to write about the bad times*), while **forebear** (which is also sometimes spelled **forbear**) means 'an ancestor' (*our Stone Age forebears*).

forbear² /for-bair/ noun variant spelling of FOREBEAR.

forbearance noun the quality of being patient and tolerant towards others.

forbearing adjective patient and restrained.

forbid /for-bid/ **verb** (**forbids**, **forbidding**, **forbade** /for-bad, for-bayd/ or **forbad**; past part. **forbidden**) **1** refuse to allow something. **2** order someone not to do something.
– PHRASES **forbidden fruit** a thing that is desired all the more because it is not allowed. [with reference to the Book of Genesis, chapter 2.]
– ORIGIN Old English.

forbidding adjective appearing unfriendly or threatening.
– DERIVATIVES **forbiddingly** adverb.

forbore past of FORBEAR¹.

forborne past participle of FORBEAR¹.

force noun **1** physical strength or energy accompanying action or movement: *we had to lean against the force of the wind.* **2** strong pressure on someone to do something backed by the use or threat of violence. **3** influence or power: *the force of public opinion.* **4** a person or thing having power or influence. **5** an organized group of military personnel, police, or workers. **6** (**the forces**) Brit. the army, navy, and air force. **7** Physics an influence that changes the motion of a body or produces motion or stress in a stationary body. • **verb 1** make a way through or into something by force. **2** push into a specified position using force: *thieves tried to force open the cash register.* **3** achieve something by effort. **4** make someone do something against their will. **5** (**force something on**) impose something on: *the new technology is being forced on retailers by the banks.* **6** make a plant develop or mature

more quickly than normal.
- PHRASES **force someone's hand** make someone do something. **in force 1** in great strength or numbers. **2 (in/into force)** in or into effect.
- DERIVATIVES **forcer** noun.
- ORIGIN Old French.

forced landing noun the abrupt landing of an aircraft in an emergency.

forced march noun a fast march by soldiers over a long distance.

force-feed verb force someone to eat food.

forceful adjective powerful, assertive, or vigorous.
- DERIVATIVES **forcefully** adverb **forcefulness** noun.

force majeure /fors ma-**zher**/ noun **1** Law unforeseeable circumstances that prevent someone from fulfilling a contract. **2** superior strength.
- ORIGIN French.

forcemeat noun a mixture of chopped and seasoned meat or vegetables used as a stuffing or garnish.

forceps /**for**-seps/ plural noun **1** a pair of pincers used in surgery or in a laboratory. **2** a large surgical instrument with broad blades, used to assist in the delivery of a baby.
- ORIGIN Latin, 'tongs, pincers'.

forcible adjective done by force.
- DERIVATIVES **forcibly** adverb.

ford noun a shallow place in a river or stream where it can be crossed. ●verb cross a river or stream at a ford.
- DERIVATIVES **fordable** adjective.
- ORIGIN Old English.

fore adjective situated or placed in front. ●noun the front part of something, especially a ship. ●exclamation called out as a warning to people in the path of a golf ball.
- PHRASES **to the fore** in or to a prominent or leading position.
- ORIGIN Old English.

fore- combining form **1** before; in advance: *foreshorten*. **2** in or at the front of: *forecourt*.

fore and aft adjective **1** backwards and forwards. **2** (of a ship's sail or rigging) set lengthwise, not on the yards.

forearm[1] /**for**-arm/ noun the part of a person's arm from the elbow to the wrist.

forearm[2] /for-**arm**/ verb **(be forearmed)** be prepared in advance for danger or attack.

forebear (also **forbear**) noun an ancestor.
- ORIGIN from FORE + former *beer* 'someone who exists'.

USAGE: Forebear (meaning 'an ancestor') can also be spelled **forbear** and is often confused with the verb **forbear**. See the note at **FORBEAR**.

forebode verb old use act as an advance warning of something bad.

foreboding noun a feeling that something bad is going to happen. ●adjective suggesting that something bad is going to happen.

forebrain noun the front part of the brain.

forecast verb (past and past part. **forecast** or **forecasted**) predict or estimate a future event or trend. ●noun a prediction or estimate,

especially of the weather or a financial trend.
- DERIVATIVES **forecaster** noun.

forecastle /**fohk**-s'l/ (also **fo'c's'le**) noun the front part of a ship below the deck.

foreclose verb **1** take possession of a mortgaged property when a person fails to keep up with their mortgage payments. **2** rule out or prevent a course of action.
- DERIVATIVES **foreclosure** noun.
- ORIGIN Old French *forclore* 'shut out'.

forecourt noun an open area in front of a large building or petrol station.

foredoom verb **(be foredoomed)** literary be condemned beforehand to certain failure.

forefather (or **foremother**) noun an ancestor.

forefinger noun the finger next to the thumb.

forefoot noun (pl. **forefeet**) each of the two front feet of a four-footed animal.

forefront noun the leading position or place: *he has always been at the forefront of research.*

foregather (also **forgather**) verb formal assemble or gather together.

forego[1] verb variant spelling of FORGO.

forego[2] verb (foregoes, foregoing, forewent; past part. **foregone**) old use come before someone or something in place or time.

foregoing adjective previously mentioned.

foregone past participle of FOREGO[1], FOREGO[2].
- PHRASES **a foregone conclusion** an easily predictable result.

foreground noun **1** the part of a view or picture nearest to the observer. **2** the most prominent or important position. ●verb make something the most important feature.

forehand noun (in tennis and other racket sports) a stroke played with the palm of the hand facing in the direction of the stroke.

forehead /**for**-hed/ noun the part of the face above the eyebrows.

foreign /**fo**-rin, **fo**-ruhn/ adjective **1** relating to or typical of a country or language other than one's own. **2** dealing with or involving other countries. **3** coming or introduced from outside: *the difficulty of introducing foreign genes into plants.* **4** (**foreign to**) not familiar to or typical of: *aisles of food and cosmetics entirely foreign to the British consumer.*
- DERIVATIVES **foreignness** noun.
- ORIGIN Old French *forein, forain.*

Foreign and Commonwealth Office (also **Foreign Office**) noun the British government department dealing with foreign affairs.

foreign body noun an unwanted object that has entered the body from outside.

foreigner noun **1** a person from a foreign country. **2** informal a stranger or outsider.

foreign exchange noun the currency of other countries.

Foreign Legion noun a military formation of the French army composed chiefly of non-Frenchmen.

Foreign Secretary noun (in the UK) the government minister who heads the Foreign and Commonwealth Office.

foreknowledge noun awareness of something before it happens or exists.

foreland noun **1** an area of land in front of a

particular feature. **2** a piece of land that juts out into the sea; a promontory.

foreleg noun either of the front legs of a four-footed animal.

forelimb noun either of the front limbs of an animal.

forelock noun a lock of hair growing just above the forehead.
– PHRASES **touch** (or **tug**) **one's forelock** Brit. raise a hand to one's forehead to show respect to a person of higher social rank.

foreman (or **forewoman**) noun (pl. **foremen** or **forewomen**) **1** a worker who supervises other workers. **2** (in a law court) a leader of a jury, who speaks on its behalf.

foremast noun the mast of a ship nearest the bow.

foremost adjective highest in rank, importance, or position. • adverb in the first place.

forename noun another term for FIRST NAME.

forenoon noun N. Amer. or Nautical the morning.

forensic /fuh-ren-sik/ adjective **1** relating to the use of scientific methods to investigate crime. **2** relating to courts of law. • noun (**forensics**) forensic tests or techniques.
– DERIVATIVES **forensically** adverb.
– ORIGIN Latin *forensis* 'in open court, public'.

forensic medicine noun the application of medical knowledge to the investigation of crime, particularly in establishing the causes of injury or death.

foreordain /for-or-**dayn**/ verb (of God or fate) appoint or determine something beforehand.

foreplay noun sexual activity that precedes intercourse.

forerun verb (**foreruns**, **forerunning**, **foreran**; past part. **forerun**) literary go before or indicate the coming of someone or something.

forerunner noun a person or thing that comes before and influences someone or something else.

foresail /for-sayl, for-s'l/ noun the main sail on a foremast.

foresee verb (**foresees**, **foreseeing**, **foresaw**; past part. **foreseen**) be aware of something beforehand; predict.
– DERIVATIVES **foreseeable** adjective **foreseeably** adverb.

foreshadow verb be a warning or indication of: *changes have begun that could foreshadow a new workplace structure.*

foreshore noun the part of a shore between high- and low-water marks, or between the water and cultivated or developed land.

foreshorten verb **1** depict an object or view as being closer or shallower than in reality, so as to convey an effect of perspective. **2** reduce something in time or scale.

foresight noun **1** the ability to predict and prepare for future events and needs. **2** the front sight of a gun.
– DERIVATIVES **foresighted** adjective.

foreskin noun the retractable roll of skin covering the end of the penis.

forest noun **1** a large area covered with trees and undergrowth. **2** a mass of vertical or tangled objects: *a forest of pillars.* • verb (usu. as adj. **forested**) plant land with trees.

– DERIVATIVES **forestation** noun.
– ORIGIN from Latin *forestis silva* 'outside wood'.

forestall /for-**stawl**/ verb **1** prevent or delay something anticipated by taking action before it happens: *he forestalled the Board's plans by obtaining an injunction.* **2** prevent someone from doing something by anticipating what they are going to do.
– ORIGIN from Old English, 'an ambush'.

forester noun a person in charge of a forest or skilled in forestry.

forestry noun the science or practice of planting, managing, and caring for forests.

foretaste noun a sample of something that is to come: *it had been an exceptionally warm day, a foretaste of heatwaves to come.*

foretell verb (past and past part. **foretold**) predict the future.

forethought noun careful consideration of what will be necessary or may happen in the future.

foretoken verb literary be a sign of a future event.

foretold past and past participle of FORETELL.

forever adverb **1** (also **for ever**) for all future time. **2** a very long time. **3** continually; all the time.

forewarn verb warn someone of a possible future danger or problem.

forewent past of FOREGO¹, FOREGO².

forewing noun either of the two front wings of a four-winged insect.

foreword noun a short introduction to a book.

forex abbreviation foreign exchange.

forfeit /for-fit/ verb (**forfeits**, **forfeiting**, **forfeited**) **1** lose or be deprived of property or a right as a penalty for a fault or mistake. **2** lose or give up as a necessary result: *she had forfeited her studies after marriage.* • noun **1** a penalty for a fault or mistake. **2** Law a right, privilege, or item of property lost as a result of wrongdoing. • adjective lost as a penalty for wrongdoing.
– DERIVATIVES **forfeiture** noun.
– ORIGIN Old French *forfaire* 'transgress'.

forgather verb variant spelling of FOREGATHER.

forgave past of FORGIVE.

forge¹ verb **1** make or shape a metal object by heating and hammering the metal. **2** create something strong or successful: *the two women forged a close bond.* **3** produce a fraudulent copy or imitation of a banknote, work of art, signature, etc. • noun **1** a blacksmith's workshop. **2** a furnace or hearth for melting or refining metal.
– DERIVATIVES **forger** noun.
– ORIGIN Old French *forger.*

forge² verb **1** move forward gradually or steadily. **2** (**forge ahead**) make progress.
– ORIGIN perhaps from a pronunciation of FORCE.

forgery noun (pl. **forgeries**) **1** the action of forging a banknote, work of art, etc. **2** a forged or copied item.

forget verb (**forgets**, **forgetting**, **forgot**; past part. **forgotten** or chiefly US **forgot**) **1** fail to remember something. **2** accidentally fail to do something. **3** deliberately cease to think of

someone or something. **4** (**forget oneself**) fail to behave in an appropriate way.
– DERIVATIVES **forgettable** adjective.
– ORIGIN Old English.

forgetful adjective apt or likely not to remember.
– DERIVATIVES **forgetfully** adverb **forgetfulness** noun.

forget-me-not noun a low-growing plant with bright blue flowers.
– ORIGIN translating Old French *ne m'oubliez mye*; said to ensure that the wearer of the flower would never be forgotten by a lover.

forgive verb (past **forgave**; past part. **forgiven**) **1** stop feeling angry or resentful towards someone for an offence or mistake. **2** no longer feel angry about or wish to punish an offence, flaw, or mistake.
– DERIVATIVES **forgivable** adjective **forgiving** adjective.
– ORIGIN Old English.

forgiveness noun the action of forgiving or the state of being forgiven.

forgo (also **forego**) verb (**forgoes**, **forgoing**, **forwent**; past part. **forgone**) go without something desirable.
– ORIGIN Old English.

forgot past of FORGET.

forgotten past participle of FORGET.

forint /for-int/ noun the basic unit of money of Hungary.
– ORIGIN Hungarian.

fork noun **1** a small implement with two or more prongs used for lifting or holding food. **2** a farm or garden tool with prongs, used for digging or lifting. **3** each of a pair of supports in which a bicycle or motorcycle wheel revolves. **4** the point where a road, path, or river divides into two parts. **5** either of the parts where a road, path, or river divides. •verb **1** divide into two parts. **2** take one route or the other at a fork. **3** dig or lift something with a fork. **4** (**fork something out/up**) informal pay money for something, especially reluctantly.
– ORIGIN Latin *furca* 'pitchfork, forked stick'.

forked adjective having a divided or pronged end.

forked lightning noun lightning seen as a zigzag or branching line across the sky.

forklift truck noun a vehicle with a pronged device in front for lifting and carrying heavy loads.

forlorn /fer-**lorn**/ adjective **1** pitifully sad and lonely. **2** unlikely to succeed or be fulfilled: *a forlorn attempt to escape.*
– PHRASES **forlorn hope** a persistent hope that is unlikely to be fulfilled. [from Dutch *verloren hoop* 'lost troop', originally referring to a band of soldiers picked to begin an attack, many of whom would not survive.]
– DERIVATIVES **forlornly** adverb **forlornness** noun.
– ORIGIN Old English, 'depraved, lost'.

form noun **1** the visible shape or arrangement of something. **2** a particular way in which a thing exists or appears: *a press release in the form of an eight-page booklet.* **3** a type of something. **4** a printed document with blank spaces for information to be inserted. **5** the state of a sports player with regard to their current play: *illness has affected her form.* **6** details of previous performances by a racehorse or greyhound. **7** a person's mood and state of health: *she was on good form.* **8** the usual or correct method or procedure. **9** chiefly Brit. a class or year in a school. **10** Brit. a long bench without a back. •verb **1** bring together parts to create something. **2** go to make up: *the ideas that form the basis of the book.* **3** establish or develop something. **4** make or be made into a certain form: *form the dough into balls.*
– PHRASES **in** (or Brit. **on**) **form** playing or performing well. **off** (or Brit. **out of**) **form** not playing or performing well.
– DERIVATIVES **formable** adjective **formless** adjective.
– ORIGIN Latin *forma* 'a mould or form'.

formal adjective **1** suitable for or referring to an official or important occasion: *formal evening wear.* **2** officially recognized: *a formal complaint.* **3** having a recognized form, structure, or set of rules: *he had little formal education.* **4** (of language) characterized by more elaborate grammatical structures and conservative vocabulary. **5** concerned with outward form rather than content.
– DERIVATIVES **formally** adverb.

formaldehyde /for-mal-di-hyd/ noun a colourless pungent gas, used in solution as a preservative for biological specimens.
– ORIGIN blend of FORMIC ACID and ALDEHYDE.

formalin /for-muh-lin/ noun a solution of formaldehyde in water.

formalism noun (in art, music, literature, etc.) concern or excessive concern with rules and outward form rather than the content of something.
– DERIVATIVES **formalist** noun.

formality noun (pl. **formalities**) **1** a thing done to follow convention or rules: *a statutory declaration that all the formalities have been complied with.* **2** correct and formal behaviour. **3** (**a formality**) a thing done or occurring as a matter of course.

formalize (or **formalise**) verb **1** give something legal or official status. **2** give something a definite form or shape.
– DERIVATIVES **formalization** noun.

format noun **1** the way in which something is arranged or presented. **2** the shape, size, and presentation of a book, document, etc. **3** the medium in which a sound recording is made available: *LP and CD formats.* **4** Computing a defined structure for the processing, storage, or display of data. •verb (**formats**, **formatting**, **formatted**) (especially in computing) arrange or put something into a particular format.
– ORIGIN from Latin *formatus liber* 'shaped book'.

formation noun **1** the action of forming or the process of being formed. **2** a structure or arrangement: *strange rock formations.* **3** a formal arrangement of aircraft in flight or troops.
– DERIVATIVES **formational** adjective.

formative adjective having an important influence on the development of someone or something: *his formative years in Victorian Scotland.*
– DERIVATIVES **formatively** adverb.

former[1] adjective **1** having previously been: *her former husband.* **2** relating to or occurring in the past. **3** (**the former**) referring to the first of two things mentioned.
– ORIGIN Old English.

former[2] noun **1** a person or thing that forms something. **2** Brit. a person in a particular school year: *a fifth-former.*

formerly adverb in the past.

Formica /for-**my**-kuh/ noun trademark a hard plastic laminate used for worktops, cupboard doors, etc.
– ORIGIN unknown.

formic acid /**for**-mik/ noun an acid present in the fluid produced by some ants.
– ORIGIN from Latin *formica* 'ant'.

formidable /**for**-mi-duh-b'l, for-**mid**-uh-b'l/ adjective inspiring fear or respect through being impressively large, powerful, or capable.
– DERIVATIVES **formidably** adverb.
– ORIGIN Latin *formidabilis.*

formula /**for**-myuu-luh/ noun (pl. **formulae** /**for**-myuu-lee/ (in senses 1 and 2) or **formulas**) **1** a mathematical relationship or rule expressed in symbols. **2** (also **chemical formula**) a set of chemical symbols showing the elements present in a compound and their relative proportions. **3** a method for achieving something: *at ZDC, we stick to our proven formula for success.* **4** a fixed form of words used in a particular situation. **5** a list of ingredients with which something is made. **6** a baby's liquid food preparation based on cow's milk or soya protein. **7** a classification of racing car: *Formula One.*
– ORIGIN Latin, 'small shape or mould'.

formulaic /for-myuu-**lay**-ik/ adjective **1** made up of or containing a set form of words. **2** following a rule or style too closely: *formulaic, disposable pop.*
– DERIVATIVES **formulaically** adverb.

formulary /**form**-yuu-luh-ri/ noun (pl. **formularies**) **1** an official list giving details of prescribable medicines. **2** a collection of set forms for use in religious ceremonies.
– ORIGIN French *formulaire* 'book of formulae'.

formulate /**for**-myuu-layt/ verb **1** create or prepare something methodically. **2** express an idea in a concise or systematic way.
– DERIVATIVES **formulator** noun.

formulation noun **1** the action of creating or preparing something. **2** a mixture prepared according to a formula.

fornicate verb formal or humorous have sexual intercourse with someone one is not married to.
– DERIVATIVES **fornication** noun **fornicator** noun.
– ORIGIN from Latin *fornix* 'vaulted chamber', later 'brothel'.

forsake verb (past **forsook**; past part. **forsaken**) chiefly literary **1** abandon someone. **2** give up something valued or pleasant.
– ORIGIN Old English.

forsooth /fer-**sooth**/ adverb old use or humorous indeed.

forswear verb (past **forswore**; past part. **forsworn**) formal agree to give up or do without something.

forsythia /for-**sy**-thi-uh/ noun a shrub whose bright yellow flowers appear in early spring before its leaves.
– ORIGIN named after the Scottish botanist William *Forsyth.*

fort noun a building constructed to defend a place against attack.
– PHRASES **hold the fort** take responsibility for something while someone is away.
– ORIGIN from Latin *fortis* 'strong'.

forte[1] /**for**-tay/ noun a thing at which someone excels: *photo sessions are not his forte*
– ORIGIN French, 'strong'.

forte[2] /**for**-tay/ adverb & adjective Music loud or loudly.
– ORIGIN Italian, 'strong, loud'.

Fortean /**for**-ti-uhn/ adjective relating to paranormal phenomena.
– DERIVATIVES **Forteana** plural noun.
– ORIGIN from the American student of paranormal phenomena Charles H. *Fort.*

fortepiano /for-tay-**pyan**-noh/ noun (pl. **fortepianos**) a piano, especially one of the kind made in the 18th and early 19th centuries.
– ORIGIN from FORTE[2] + PIANO[2].

forth adverb formal or literary **1** out and away from a starting point. **2** so as to be revealed. **3** onwards in time.
– PHRASES **and so forth** and so on.
– ORIGIN Old English.

forthcoming adjective **1** about to happen or appear. **2** ready or made available when required: *help was not forthcoming.* **3** willing to reveal information.

forthright adjective direct and outspoken.
– DERIVATIVES **forthrightly** adverb **forthrightness** noun.
– ORIGIN Old English.

forthwith adverb without delay.

fortification noun **1** a defensive wall or other structure built to strengthen a place against attack. **2** the action of fortifying something.

fortify /**for**-ti-fy/ verb (**fortifies**, **fortifying**, **fortified**) **1** provide a place with defensive structures as protection against attack. **2** encourage or strengthen someone. **3** add spirits to wine to make port, sherry, etc. **4** make food more nutritious by adding vitamins.
– DERIVATIVES **fortifier** noun.
– ORIGIN Latin *fortificare.*

fortissimo /for-**tiss**-i-moh/ adverb & adjective Music very loud or loudly.
– ORIGIN Italian.

fortitude /**for**-ti-tyood/ noun courage and strength in bearing pain or trouble.
– ORIGIN Latin *fortitudo.*

fortnight noun Brit. a period of two weeks.
– ORIGIN Old English, 'fourteen nights'.

fortnightly Brit. adjective happening or produced every two weeks. • adverb every two weeks.

fortress noun a fort or a strongly fortified town.
– ORIGIN Old French *forteresse* 'strong place'.

fortuitous /for-**tyoo**-i-tuhss/ adjective **1** happening by chance rather than intention. **2** happening by a lucky chance; fortunate.
– DERIVATIVES **fortuitously** adverb

fortuitousness noun **fortuity** noun (pl. **fortuities**).
– ORIGIN Latin *fortuitus*.

fortunate adjective **1** having or happening by good luck; lucky. **2** favourable; advantageous: *in the fortunate position of being headhunted to join a major firm.*

fortunately adverb it is fortunate that.

fortune noun **1** chance as a force affecting people's lives. **2** luck, especially good luck. **3** (**fortunes**) the success or failure of a person or enterprise. **4** a large amount of money or assets.
– PHRASES **a small fortune** informal a large amount of money. **tell someone's fortune** predict a person's future by palmistry or similar methods.
– ORIGIN Latin *Fortuna*, a goddess personifying luck or chance.

fortune-teller noun a person who predicts what will happen in people's lives.
– DERIVATIVES **fortune-telling** noun.

forty cardinal number (pl. **forties**) ten less than fifty; 40. (Roman numeral: **xl** or **XL**.)
– PHRASES **forty winks** informal a short daytime sleep.
– DERIVATIVES **fortieth** ordinal number.
– ORIGIN Old English.

forty-five noun a gramophone record played at 45 rpm.

forum /for-uhm/ noun (pl. **forums**) **1** a meeting or medium for an exchange of views. **2** (pl. **fora** /for-uh/) (in ancient Roman cities) a public square or marketplace used for judicial and other business.
– ORIGIN Latin, 'what is out of doors'.

forward adverb (also **forwards**) **1** in the direction that one is facing or travelling. **2** onward so as to make progress. **3** ahead in time. **4** in or near the front of a ship or aircraft. •adjective **1** towards the direction that one is facing or travelling. **2** relating to the future. **3** bold or overfamiliar. **4** progressing towards a successful conclusion: *the decision is a forward step.* **5** situated in or near the front of a ship or aircraft. •noun an attacking player in football, hockey, or other sports. •verb **1** send a letter or email on to a further address. **2** send a document or goods. **3** help something to develop or progress.
– DERIVATIVES **forwarder** noun **forwardly** adverb **forwardness** noun.
– ORIGIN Old English.

forward-looking (also **forward-thinking**) adjective favouring innovation; progressive.

forwent past of FORGO.

fossick /fo-sik/ verb Austral./NZ informal **1** rummage; search. **2** search for gold in abandoned workings.
– DERIVATIVES **fossicker** noun.
– ORIGIN probably from the English dialect sense 'obtain by asking'.

fossil /foss-uhl/ noun **1** the remains or impression of a prehistoric plant or animal that have become hardened into rock. **2** humorous an old or outdated person or thing.
– ORIGIN from Latin *fossilis* 'dug up'.

fossil fuel noun a natural fuel such as coal or gas, formed in the geological past from the remains of animals and plants.

fossiliferous /fos-i-lif-uh-ruhss/ adjective (of a rock or stratum) containing fossils or organic remains.

fossilize (or **fossilise**) verb (**fossilizes**, **fossilizing**, **fossilized**) preserve an animal or plant so that it becomes a fossil.
– DERIVATIVES **fossilization** noun.

foster verb **1** promote the development of: *they hope the visit will foster improved relations between the two countries.* **2** bring up a child that is not one's own by birth.
– DERIVATIVES **fosterage** noun **fosterer** noun.
– ORIGIN Old English, 'feed, nourish'.

fought past and past participle of FIGHT.

foul adjective **1** having a very unpleasant smell or taste; disgusting. **2** very unpleasant: *he was in a foul mood.* **3** wicked or obscene. **4** not allowed by the rules of a sport. **5** polluted or contaminated. •noun (in sport) a piece of play that is not allowed by the rules. •verb **1** make something foul or polluted. **2** (of an animal) dirty something with excrement. **3** (in sport) commit a foul against an opponent. **4** (**foul something up**) make a mistake with or spoil something. **5** cause a cable or anchor to become entangled or jammed.
– DERIVATIVES **foully** adverb **foulness** noun.
– ORIGIN Old English.

foulard /foo-lahd/ noun a thin, soft material of silk or silk and cotton.
– ORIGIN French.

foul-mouthed adjective using bad language.

foul play noun **1** unfair play in a game or sport. **2** criminal or violent activity, especially murder.

foul-up noun a problem caused by a stupid mistake.

found¹ past and past participle of FIND.

found² verb **1** establish an institution or organization. **2** (**be founded on**) be based on a particular principle or idea.
– ORIGIN Old French *fonder*.

found³ verb **1** melt and mould metal. **2** fuse materials to make glass. **3** make an object by melting and moulding metal.
– ORIGIN Latin *fundere* 'melt, pour'.

foundation noun **1** the lowest load-bearing part of a building, typically below ground level. **2** a basis for something: *the Chinese laid the scientific foundation for many modern discoveries.* **3** justification or reason: *there was no foundation for the claim.* **4** an institution or organization. **5** the establishment of an institution or organization. **6** a cream or powder applied to the face as a base for other make-up.
– DERIVATIVES **foundational** adjective.

foundation course noun Brit. a course taken at some colleges and universities, preparing students for more advanced study.

foundation garment noun a woman's supportive undergarment, such as a corset.

foundation stone noun a stone laid at a ceremony to celebrate the laying of a building's foundations.

founder¹ noun a person who founds an institution or settlement.

founder² noun the owner or operator of a foundry.

founder³ verb **1** (of a plan or undertaking) fail;

come to nothing. **2** (of a ship) fill with water and sink. **3** (of a horse) stumble or fall.
– ORIGIN Old French *fondrer* 'submerge, collapse'.

> USAGE: The words **founder** and **flounder** are often confused. **Founder** chiefly means 'fail' (*a proposed merger between the two airlines foundered last year*), while **flounder** means 'have trouble doing or understanding something' (*the school was floundering in confusion about its role in the world*).

foundling noun a young child that has been abandoned by its parents and is found and cared for by others.

foundry noun (pl. **foundries**) a workshop or factory for casting metal.

fount[1] noun **1** a source of a desirable quality: *he was a fount of wisdom*. **2** literary a spring or fountain.
– ORIGIN from **FOUNTAIN**.

fount[2] noun Brit. variant spelling of **FONT**[2].

fountain noun **1** an ornamental structure in a pool or lake from which a jet of water is pumped into the air. **2** a source of something desirable: *Susan is a fountain of knowledge about the area*. **3** literary a natural spring of water. • verb spurt or cascade like a fountain.
– ORIGIN Old French *fontaine*.

fountainhead noun an original source of something.

fountain pen noun a pen with a container from which ink flows continuously to the nib.

four cardinal number **1** one more than three; 4. (Roman numeral: **iv** or **IV**.) **2** Cricket a hit that reaches the boundary after first striking the ground, scoring four runs. **3** a four-oared rowing boat or its crew.
– DERIVATIVES **fourfold** adjective & adverb.
– ORIGIN Old English.

four-by-four (also **4 × 4**) noun a vehicle with four-wheel drive.

four-dimensional adjective having the three dimensions of space (length, breadth, and depth) plus time.

four-in-hand noun a vehicle with four horses driven by one person.

four-letter word noun any of several short words referring to sex or excretion, regarded as rude or offensive.

four-poster (also **four-poster bed**) noun a bed with a post at each corner supporting a canopy.

fourscore cardinal number old use eighty.

foursome noun a group of four people.

four-square adjective **1** (of a building) having a square shape and solid appearance. **2** firm and resolute. • adverb in a firm and resolute way: *the public is four-square behind the prime minister*.

four-stroke adjective (of an internal-combustion engine) having a cycle of four strokes (intake, compression, combustion, and exhaust).

fourteen cardinal number one more than thirteen; 14. (Roman numeral: **xiv** or **XIV**.)
– DERIVATIVES **fourteenth** ordinal number.

fourth ordinal number **1** that is number four in a sequence; 4th. **2** (**a fourth**/**one fourth**) chiefly N.

Amer. a quarter. **3** Music an interval spanning four consecutive notes in a diatonic scale.
– PHRASES **the fourth estate** the press; journalism.
– DERIVATIVES **fourthly** adverb.

fourth dimension noun time regarded as a dimension comparable to the three linear dimensions.

Fourth World noun those countries considered to be the poorest and most underdeveloped of the Third World.

4WD abbreviation four-wheel drive.

four-wheel drive noun a transmission system which provides power directly to all four wheels of a vehicle.

fowl noun (pl. same or **fowls**) **1** (also **domestic fowl**) a domesticated bird kept for its eggs or flesh; a cock or hen. **2** any domesticated bird, e.g. a turkey. **3** birds as a group, especially as the quarry of hunters.
– DERIVATIVES **fowler** noun **fowling** noun.
– ORIGIN Old English.

fox noun **1** an animal of the dog family with a pointed muzzle, bushy tail, and a reddish coat. **2** a cunning or sly person. • verb informal baffle or deceive someone.
– ORIGIN Old English.

foxed adjective (of the paper of old books or prints) discoloured with brown spots.
– DERIVATIVES **foxing** noun.

foxglove noun a tall plant with pinkish-purple or white bell-shaped flowers growing up the stem.

foxhole noun a hole in the ground used by troops as a shelter against enemy fire or as a firing point.

foxhound noun a breed of dog with smooth hair and drooping ears, trained to hunt foxes in packs.

fox-hunting noun the sport of hunting a fox across country with a pack of hounds, carried out by people on foot and horseback.

foxtrot noun a ballroom dance with alternation of slow and quick steps.

foxy adjective (**foxier**, **foxiest**) **1** resembling a fox. **2** cunning or sly. **3** informal (of a woman) sexually attractive.
– DERIVATIVES **foxily** adverb **foxiness** noun.

foyer /foy-ay/ noun a large entrance hall in a hotel or theatre.
– ORIGIN French, 'hearth, home'.

Fr abbreviation Father (as a courtesy title of priests).
– ORIGIN from French *frère* 'brother'.

fr. abbreviation franc(s).

fracas /fra-kah/ noun (pl. same, pronounced /fra-kahz/) a noisy disturbance or quarrel.
– ORIGIN French.

fractal /frak-tuhl/ noun Mathematics a curve or geometrical figure, each part of which has the same statistical character as the whole.
– ORIGIN French.

fraction /frak-sh'n/ noun **1** a numerical quantity that is not a whole number (e.g. ½, 0.5). **2** a very small part, amount, or proportion. **3** Chemistry each of the parts into which a mixture may be separated by the process of fractionation.
– ORIGIN Latin.

fractional adjective **1** relating to or expressed

as a fraction. **2** very small in amount.
- DERIVATIVES **fractionally** adverb.

fractionation noun Chemistry separation of a mixture into its constituent parts by using the fact that they condense or vaporize at different temperatures.

fractious /frak-shuhss/ adjective **1** easily irritated. **2** difficult to control.
- DERIVATIVES **fractiously** adverb **fractiousness** noun.
- ORIGIN from FRACTION, probably on the pattern of *faction, factious*.

fracture noun **1** a crack or break, especially in a bone or layer of rock. **2** the cracking or breaking of a hard object or material. •verb **1** break or cause to break. **2** (of a group) split up or fragment.
- ORIGIN Latin *fractura*.

fragile adjective **1** easily broken, damaged, or destroyed. **2** (of a person) not strong; delicate.
- DERIVATIVES **fragility** noun.
- ORIGIN Latin *fragilis*.

fragment noun /frag-muhnt/ **1** a small part broken off or detached. **2** an isolated or incomplete part: *a fragment of conversation.* •verb /frag-ment/ break into fragments.
- ORIGIN Latin *fragmentum*.

fragmentary /frag-muhn-tri/ adjective consisting of small disconnected or incomplete parts.
- DERIVATIVES **fragmentarily** adverb.

fragmentation noun the process of breaking or the state of being broken into fragments.

fragrance /fray-gruhnss/ noun **1** a pleasant, sweet smell. **2** a perfume or aftershave.
- DERIVATIVES **fragranced** adjective.

fragrant adjective having a pleasant, sweet smell.
- DERIVATIVES **fragrantly** adverb.
- ORIGIN from Latin *fragrare* 'smell sweet'.

frail adjective **1** (of a person) weak and delicate. **2** easily damaged or broken.
- DERIVATIVES **frailness** noun.
- ORIGIN Old French *fraile*.

frailty noun (pl. **frailties**) **1** the condition of being frail or weak. **2** weakness in a person's character or morals.

frame noun **1** a rigid structure surrounding a picture, door, etc. **2** (**frames**) a metal or plastic structure holding the lenses of a pair of glasses. **3** the rigid supporting structure of a vehicle, building, or other object. **4** a person's body with reference to its size or build: *her slim frame.* **5** the underlying structure of a system, concept, or written work: *the novels rested on a frame of moral truth.* **6** a single complete picture in a series forming a cinema or video film. **7** the triangular structure for positioning the red balls in snooker. **8** a single game of snooker. •verb **1** place a picture in a frame. **2** surround so as to create an attractive image: *a short style cut to frame the face.* **3** formulate or develop a plan or system. **4** informal produce false evidence against an innocent person to make them appear guilty of a crime.
- PHRASES **be in** (or **out of**) **the frame 1** be (or not be) eligible. **2** be wanted (or not wanted) by the police. **frame of mind** a particular mood. **frame of reference** a set of values

according to which judgements can be made.
- DERIVATIVES **framed** adjective **frameless** adjective **framer** noun.
- ORIGIN Old English, 'be useful', later 'prepare timber for building'.

frame-up noun informal a conspiracy to incriminate someone falsely.

framework noun a supporting or underlying structure.

franc /frangk/ noun the basic unit of money of France, Belgium, Switzerland, Luxembourg, and several other countries (replaced in France, Belgium, and Luxembourg by the euro in 2002).
- ORIGIN from Latin *Francorum Rex* 'king of the Franks', the inscription on 14th-century gold coins.

franchise /fran-chyz/ noun **1** formal permission granted by a government or company to a person or group enabling them to sell certain products or provide a service. **2** a business or service run under a franchise. **3** the right to vote in public elections. •verb **1** grant a franchise to someone. **2** grant a franchise for goods or a service.
- DERIVATIVES **franchisee** noun **franchiser** (also **franchisor**) noun.
- ORIGIN Old French.

Franciscan /fran-siss-kuhn/ noun a monk or nun of a Christian religious order following the rule of the Italian monk St Francis of Assisi. •adjective relating to St Francis or the Franciscans.

francium /fran-si-uhm/ noun an unstable radioactive chemical element of the alkali-metal group.
- ORIGIN from *France*.

Franco- (also **franco-**) combining form **1** French; French and ...: *francophone.* **2** relating to France: *Francophile.*
- ORIGIN from Latin *Francus* 'Frank'.

Francoist noun a supporter of the Spanish dictator General Francisco Franco or his policies. •adjective relating to Franco's regime or policies.
- DERIVATIVES **Francoism** noun.

francolin /frang-koh-lin/ noun a large game bird resembling a partridge, native to Africa and South Asia.
- ORIGIN Italian *francolino*.

Francophile noun a person who is fond of or greatly admires France or the French.

francophone /frang-koh-fohn/ adjective French-speaking. •noun a French-speaking person.

frangible /fran-ji-b'l/ adjective literary or technical fragile; brittle.
- ORIGIN Latin *frangibilis*.

frangipane /fran-zhi-payn/ noun an almond-flavoured cream or paste, used to fill tarts.
- ORIGIN first referring to the frangipani plant, which was used to flavour frangipane.

frangipani /fran-zhi-pah-ni/ noun (pl. **frangipanis**) **1** a tropical American tree or shrub with fragrant white, pink, or yellow flowers. **2** perfume obtained from the frangipani plant.
- ORIGIN named after the Marquis Muzio *Frangipani*, an Italian nobleman who invented a perfume for gloves.

franglais /frong-glay/ noun a blend of French and English, either French that makes excessive use of English expressions, or unidiomatic French spoken by an English person.
– ORIGIN a blend of French *français* 'French' and *anglais* 'English'.

Frank noun a member of a Germanic people that conquered Gaul in the 6th century.
– DERIVATIVES **Frankish** adjective & noun.
– ORIGIN Old English *Franca*.

frank¹ adjective 1 honest and direct, especially when dealing with unpleasant matters. 2 open or undisguised: *he looked at her with frank admiration*.
– DERIVATIVES **frankness** noun.
– ORIGIN Latin *francus* 'free'.

frank² verb stamp an official mark on a letter or parcel to indicate that postage has been paid or does not need to be paid. •noun a franking mark on a letter or parcel.
– ORIGIN from **FRANK**¹, in the former sense 'free of obligation'.

Frankenfood /frang-kuhn-food/ noun informal, derogatory a genetically modified food.
– ORIGIN from **FRANKENSTEIN**.

Frankenstein /frang-kuhn-styn/ (also **Frankenstein's monster**) noun a thing that becomes terrifying or destructive to its maker.
– ORIGIN from Victor *Frankenstein*, a character in a novel by Mary Shelley, who creates a manlike monster.

frankfurter noun a seasoned smoked sausage made of beef and pork.
– ORIGIN from German *Frankfurter Wurst* 'Frankfurt sausage'.

frankincense /frang-kin-senss/ noun an aromatic resinous substance obtained from an African tree and burnt as incense.
– ORIGIN from Old French *franc encens* 'high-quality incense'.

frankly adverb 1 in an honest and direct way. 2 to be frank.

frantic adjective 1 distraught with fear, anxiety, or other emotion. 2 done in a hurried and chaotic way: *frantic efforts to put out the fires*.
– DERIVATIVES **frantically** adverb **franticness** noun.
– ORIGIN Old French *frenetique* 'violently mad'.

frappé /frap-pay/ adjective (of a drink) iced or chilled. •noun a drink served with ice or frozen to a slushy consistency.
– ORIGIN French.

Frascati /fra-skah-ti/ noun a white wine produced in the Frascati region of Italy.

fraternal /fruh-ter-n'l/ adjective 1 relating to or like a brother; brotherly. 2 relating to a fraternity. 3 (of twins) developed from separate ova (female reproductive cells) and therefore not identical.
– DERIVATIVES **fraternally** adverb.
– ORIGIN Latin *frater* 'brother'.

fraternity /fruh-ter-ni-ti/ noun (pl. **fraternities**) 1 a group of people sharing the same profession or interests: *the medical fraternity*. 2 N. Amer. a male students' society in a university or college. 3 friendship and shared support within a group.

fraternize (or **fraternise**) /frat-er-nyz/ verb (usu. **fraternize with**) be on friendly terms, especially with someone that one is not supposed to be friendly with.
– DERIVATIVES **fraternization** noun.

fratricide /frat-ri-syd/ noun 1 the killing of one's brother or sister. 2 the accidental killing of one's own forces in war.
– DERIVATIVES **fratricidal** adjective.
– ORIGIN from Latin *frater* 'brother' + **-CIDE**.

Frau /frow/ noun a title or form of address for a married or widowed German woman.
– ORIGIN German.

fraud /frawd/ noun 1 the crime of deceiving someone to gain money or personal advantage. 2 a person who deceives others into believing that they have certain qualities or abilities.
– ORIGIN Latin *fraus* 'deceit, injury'.

fraudster noun Brit. a person who commits fraud.

fraudulent /fraw-dyuu-luhnt/ adjective 1 done by or involving fraud. 2 intended to deceive.
– DERIVATIVES **fraudulence** noun **fraudulently** adverb.

fraught /frawt/ adjective 1 (**fraught with**) filled with something undesirable. 2 causing or feeling anxiety or stress.
– ORIGIN from Dutch *vracht* 'ship's cargo'.

Fräulein /froy-lyn/ noun a title or form of address for an unmarried German woman.
– ORIGIN German.

fray¹ verb 1 (of a fabric, rope, or cord) unravel or become worn at the edge. 2 (of a person's nerves or temper) show the effects of strain.
– ORIGIN Old French *freiier*.

fray² noun (**the fray**) 1 a very competitive or demanding situation: *with new manufacturers entering the fray, the competition is certain to intensify*. 2 a battle or fight.
– ORIGIN from Old French *afrayer* 'disturb, startle'.

frazzle informal verb 1 (as adj. **frazzled**) completely exhausted. 2 make something shrivel up with burning. •noun (**a frazzle**) 1 an exhausted state. 2 a burnt state.
– ORIGIN perhaps from **FRAY**¹ and former *fazle* 'ravel out'.

freak noun 1 informal a person who is obsessed with a particular activity or interest: *a fitness freak*. 2 a very unusual and unexpected event. 3 (also **freak of nature**) a person, animal, or plant with a physical abnormality. 4 informal a person regarded as strange because of their unusual appearance or behaviour. •adjective very unusual and unexpected: *a freak accident*. •verb (usu. **freak out**) informal react or cause to react in a wild, shocked, or excited way.
– DERIVATIVES **freakish** adjective.
– ORIGIN probably from a dialect word.

freaky adjective (**freakier**, **freakiest**) informal very odd or strange.
– DERIVATIVES **freakily** adverb **freakiness** noun.

freckle noun a small light brown spot on the skin. •verb cover or become covered with freckles.
– DERIVATIVES **freckly** adjective.
– ORIGIN Old Norse.

free adjective (**freer**, **freest**) 1 able to do what one wants; not under the control of anyone else. 2 not confined, obstructed, or fixed: *they set the birds free*. 3 not having or filled with

things to do: *I spent my free time shopping.*
4 not occupied or in use. **5** (**free of**/**from**) not containing or affected by something undesirable. **6** available without charge. **7** (usu. **free with**) using or spending something without restraint. **8** behaving or speaking without restraint. **9** (of art, music, etc.) not following the normal conventions. **10** (of a translation) conveying the general meaning; not literal. • adverb without cost or payment. • verb (**frees, freeing, freed**) **1** make someone or something free. **2** make something available for a purpose.

– PHRASES **free and easy** informal and relaxed. **a free hand** freedom to act completely as one wishes. **a free ride** a situation in which someone benefits without making a fair contribution. **the free world** the non-communist countries of the world, as formerly opposed to the Soviet bloc. **make free with** treat something without proper respect.

– DERIVATIVES **freeness** noun.

– ORIGIN Old English.

-free combining form free of or from: *tax-free.*

freebase noun cocaine that has been purified by heating with ether, taken by inhaling the fumes or smoking the residue. • verb take cocaine in this way.

freebie noun informal a thing given free of charge.

freeboard noun the height of a ship's side between the waterline and the deck.

freebooter noun a person who behaves in an illegal way for their own advantage.

– DERIVATIVES **freebooting** adjective.

– ORIGIN Dutch *vrijbuiter.*

freeborn adjective not born in slavery.

Free Church noun a Christian Church which has separated from an established Church.

freedom noun **1** the power or right to act, speak, or think as one wants. **2** the state of being free: *clothing that allows maximum freedom of movement.* **3** (**freedom from**) the state of not being subject to or affected by something undesirable. **4** unrestricted use of something: *the dog had the freedom of the house.* **5** Brit. a special privilege, especially that of full citizenship of a city given to someone as an honour.

freedom fighter noun a person who takes part in a struggle to achieve political freedom.

free enterprise noun an economic system in which private businesses compete with each other with little state control.

free fall noun **1** downward movement under the force of gravity. **2** a rapid decline that cannot be stopped: *the euro was in free fall.* • verb (**free-fall**) fall rapidly.

free-for-all noun a disorganized or unrestricted situation or event in which everyone may take part.

free-form adjective not in a regular or formal structure.

freehand adjective & adverb done by hand without the aid of instruments such as rulers.

freehold noun chiefly Brit. permanent and absolute ownership of land or property with the freedom to sell it when one wishes.

– DERIVATIVES **freeholder** noun.

free house noun Brit. a pub not controlled by a brewery and therefore not restricted to selling that brewery's products.

free kick noun (in football and rugby) an unimpeded kick of the stationary ball awarded when the opposing team has broken the rules.

freelance /free-lahnss/ adjective self-employed and hired to work for different companies on particular assignments. • adverb earning one's living as a freelance. • noun (also **freelancer**) a freelance worker. • verb earn one's living as a freelance.

– ORIGIN first referring to a mercenary: from FREE + LANCE.

freeloader noun informal a person who takes advantage of others' generosity without giving anything in return.

– DERIVATIVES **freeload** verb.

free love noun dated the practice of having sexual relationships freely, without being faithful to one partner.

freely adverb **1** not under the control of someone else. **2** without restriction or restraint: *a world where people cannot speak freely.* **3** in abundant amounts. **4** willingly and readily.

freeman noun (pl. **freemen**) **1** Brit. a person who has been given the freedom of a city or borough. **2** historical a person who is not a slave or serf.

free market noun an economic system in which prices are determined by supply and demand rather than controlled by a government.

Freemason noun a member of an international order whose members help each other and hold secret ceremonies.

– DERIVATIVES **Freemasonry** noun.

free pardon noun Brit. an official decision that cancels the legal consequences of an offence or conviction.

free port noun **1** a port open to all traders. **2** a port area where goods in transit are exempt from customs duty.

free radical noun a highly reactive molecule with one odd electron not paired up in a chemical bond.

free-range adjective (of livestock or their produce) kept or produced in natural conditions, where the animals may move around freely.

freesia /free-zi-uh/ noun a small plant with fragrant, colourful, tubular flowers, native to southern Africa.

– ORIGIN named after the German physician Friedrich H. T. *Freese.*

free-standing adjective not attached to or supported by another structure.

freestyle noun (usu. before another noun) a contest, race, or type of sport in which there are few restrictions on the style or technique that competitors employ. • verb perform or compete in an unrestricted or improvised fashion.

– DERIVATIVES **freestyler** noun.

freethinker noun a person who questions or rejects accepted opinions, especially those concerning religious belief.

free trade noun international trade left to its natural course without tariffs or other restrictions.

free verse noun poetry that does not rhyme or have a regular rhythm.

free vote noun chiefly Brit. a vote in which members of parliament cast their votes independently of party policy.

freeway noun N. Amer. a dual-carriageway main road.

freewheel verb 1 ride on a bicycle without using the pedals. 2 (as adj. **freewheeling**) not concerned with rules or the results of one's actions. •noun a bicycle wheel which is able to revolve freely when no power is being applied to the pedals.
– DERIVATIVES **freewheeler** noun.

free will noun the power to act according to one's own wishes.

freeze verb (past **froze**; past part. **frozen**) 1 (with reference to a liquid) turn or be turned into ice or another solid as a result of extreme cold. 2 block or become blocked or rigid with ice. 3 be or make very cold. 4 store something at a very low temperature in order to preserve it. 5 become suddenly motionless with fear or shock. 6 hold at a fixed level or in a fixed state: *the Act has given the police powers to freeze the assets of suspects.* 7 (of a computer screen) suddenly become locked. 8 (**freeze someone out**) informal make someone feel left out by being hostile or cold towards them. •noun 1 an act of holding something at a fixed level or in a fixed state. 2 a period of very cold weather.
– DERIVATIVES **freezable** adjective.
– ORIGIN Old English.

freeze-dry verb preserve something by rapidly freezing it and then removing the ice in a vacuum.

freeze-frame noun 1 a single frame forming a motionless image from a film or videotape. 2 the facility or process of stopping a film or videotape to obtain a freeze-frame.

freezer noun a refrigerated cabinet or room for preserving food at very low temperatures.

freezing adjective 1 below 0°C. 2 very cold. 3 (of fog or rain) consisting of droplets which freeze rapidly on contact with a surface. •noun the freezing point of water (0°C).

freezing point noun the temperature at which a liquid turns into a solid when cooled.

freight /frayt/ noun 1 transport of goods in bulk by lorry, train, ship, or aircraft. 2 goods transported by freight. •verb 1 transport goods by freight. 2 (**be freighted with**) be laden or burdened with: *each word was freighted with anger.*
– ORIGIN Dutch and German *vrecht.*

freighter noun a large ship or aircraft designed to carry freight.

French adjective relating to France or its people or language. •noun the language of France, also used in parts of Belgium, Switzerland, Canada, and elsewhere.
– PHRASES **excuse (or pardon) my French** informal used to apologize for swearing.
– DERIVATIVES **Frenchness** noun.

French bean noun Brit. an edible green bean.

French bread noun white bread in a long, crisp loaf.

French Canadian noun a Canadian whose native language is French. •adjective relating to French Canadians.

French chalk noun a kind of steatite (talc) used for marking cloth and removing grease.

French dressing noun a salad dressing of vinegar, oil, and seasonings.

French fries plural noun chiefly N. Amer. potato chips.

French horn noun a brass instrument with a coiled tube, valves, and a wide bell.

Frenchify verb (**Frenchifies, Frenchifying, Frenchified**) often derogatory make someone or something French in form or character.

French kiss noun a kiss with contact between tongues.
– DERIVATIVES **French kissing** noun.

French knickers plural noun women's loose-fitting, wide-legged knickers.

French letter noun Brit. informal, dated a condom.

Frenchman (or **Frenchwoman**) noun (pl. **Frenchmen** or **Frenchwomen**) a person who is French by birth or descent.

French polish noun a kind of polish that produces a high gloss on wood. •verb (**french-polish**) treat wood with French polish.

French stick noun a loaf of French bread.

French toast noun bread coated in egg and milk and fried.

French window noun each of a pair of glazed doors in an outside wall.

Frenchy (also **Frenchie**) noun (pl. **Frenchies**) informal, chiefly derogatory a French person.

frenetic /fruh-net-ik/ adjective fast and energetic in a disorganized or uncontrolled way.
– DERIVATIVES **frenetically** adverb **freneticism** noun.
– ORIGIN from Greek *phrenitis* 'delirium'.

frenzy noun (pl. **frenzies**) a state or period of uncontrolled excitement or wild behaviour.
– DERIVATIVES **frenzied** adjective **frenziedly** adverb.
– ORIGIN Latin *phrenesia.*

frequency noun (pl. **frequencies**) 1 the rate at which something occurs in a given period or sample: *the lightning strikes seemed to increase in frequency.* 2 the fact or state of being frequent. 3 the number of cycles per second of a sound, light, or radio wave. 4 the particular waveband at which radio signals are broadcast or transmitted.

frequency modulation noun the varying of the frequency of a wave, used as a means of broadcasting an audio signal by radio.

frequent adjective /free-kwuhnt/ 1 occurring or done many times at short intervals. 2 doing something often; regular: *he was a frequent visitor to Paris.* •verb /fri-kwent/ visit a place often or regularly.
– DERIVATIVES **frequenter** noun **frequently** adverb.
– ORIGIN Latin *frequens* 'crowded, frequent'.

fresco /fress-koh/ noun (pl. **frescoes** or **frescos**) a painting done on wet plaster on a wall or ceiling, in which the colours become fixed as the plaster dries.
– DERIVATIVES **frescoed** adjective.
– ORIGIN Italian, 'cool, fresh'.

fresh adjective **1** not previously known or used; new or different: *a fresh approach to treating problem skin.* **2** (of food) recently made or picked; not frozen or preserved. **3** recently created and so not impaired: *the memory was fresh in their minds.* **4** pleasantly clean and cool: *fresh air.* **5** (of the wind) cool and fairly strong. **6** (of water) not salty. **7** full of energy. **8** informal too familiar towards someone, especially in a sexual way. ● adverb newly; recently.
– DERIVATIVES **freshly** adverb **freshness** noun.
– ORIGIN Old English, 'not salt, fit for drinking'.

freshen verb **1** make or become fresh. **2** chiefly N. Amer. top up a drink.
– DERIVATIVES **freshener** noun.

fresher noun Brit. informal a first-year student at college or university.

freshet noun **1** the flood of a river from heavy rain or melted snow. **2** a rush of fresh water flowing into the sea.
– ORIGIN probably from Old French *freschete*.

freshman noun (pl. **freshmen**) a first-year student at university or (N. Amer.) at high school.

freshwater adjective relating to or found in fresh water; not of the sea.

fret¹ verb (**frets, fretting, fretted**) **1** be constantly or visibly anxious. **2** gradually wear away something. ● noun chiefly Brit. a state of anxiety.
– ORIGIN Old English, 'devour, consume'.

fret² noun each of a sequence of ridges on the fingerboard of some stringed instruments, used for fixing the positions of the fingers. ● verb (**frets, fretting, fretted**) provide a stringed instrument with frets.
– ORIGIN unknown.

fret³ noun an ornamental design of vertical and horizontal lines. ● verb (**frets, fretting, fretted**) decorate something with fretwork.
– ORIGIN Old French *frete* 'trelliswork'.

fretful adjective anxious or upset.
– DERIVATIVES **fretfully** adverb **fretfulness** noun.

fretsaw noun a saw with a narrow blade for cutting designs in thin wood or metal.

fretwork noun decorative patterns cut in wood with a fretsaw.

Freudian /froy-di-uhn/ adjective **1** relating to or influenced by the Austrian psychotherapist Sigmund Freud and his methods of psychoanalysis. **2** able to be analysed in terms of unconscious thoughts or desires: *a Freudian slip.* ● noun a follower of Freud or his methods.
– DERIVATIVES **Freudianism** noun.

Fri. abbreviation Friday.

friable /fry-uh-b'l/ adjective easily crumbled.
– DERIVATIVES **friability** noun.
– ORIGIN from Latin *friare* 'to crumble'.

friar noun a member of certain religious orders of men.
– ORIGIN Old French *frere*.

friary noun (pl. **friaries**) a building or community occupied by friars.

fricassée /fri-kuh-say/ noun a dish of stewed or fried pieces of meat served in a thick white sauce.
– DERIVATIVES **fricasséed** adjective.
– ORIGIN French.

fricative /frik-uh-tiv/ adjective referring to a type of consonant (e.g. *f*) made by the friction of breath in a narrow opening.
– ORIGIN from Latin *fricare* 'to rub'.

friction noun **1** the resistance that one surface or object encounters when moving over another. **2** the action of one surface or object rubbing against another. **3** conflict or disagreement: *a number of issues are causing friction between the two countries.*
– DERIVATIVES **frictional** adjective **frictionless** adjective.
– ORIGIN from Latin *fricare* 'to rub'.

Friday noun the day of the week before Saturday and following Thursday.
– ORIGIN Old English, named after the Germanic goddess *Frigga*.

fridge noun a refrigerator.

fridge-freezer noun an upright unit made up of a separate refrigerator and freezer.

fried past and past participle of **FRY**¹.

friend noun **1** a person that one likes and knows well. **2** a person who supports a particular cause or organization. **3** (**Friend**) a Quaker.
– DERIVATIVES **friendless** adjective **friendship** noun.
– ORIGIN Old English.

friendly adjective (**friendlier, friendliest**) **1** kind and pleasant. **2** on good terms; not hostile. **3** (in combination) not harmful to a specified thing: *environment-friendly.* **4** Military relating to or allied with one's own forces: *two soldiers were killed by friendly fire.* ● noun (pl. **friendlies**) Brit. a game or match not forming part of a serious competition.
– DERIVATIVES **friendlily** adverb **friendliness** noun.

friendly society noun (in the UK) an association owned by its members and providing sickness benefits, life assurance, and pensions.

Friesian /free-zh'n/ noun Brit. an animal of a black-and-white breed of dairy cattle originally from Friesland in the Netherlands.

frieze /freez/ noun **1** a broad horizontal band of sculpted or painted decoration. **2** Architecture the part of an entablature between the architrave and the cornice.
– ORIGIN Latin *frisium*.

frigate /fri-guht/ noun a warship with a mixed armament, generally lighter than a destroyer.
– ORIGIN Italian *fregata*.

frigate bird noun a tropical seabird with a deeply forked tail and a long hooked bill.

fright noun **1** a sudden intense feeling of fear. **2** a shock.
– PHRASES **look a fright** informal look ridiculous or very dishevelled. **take fright** suddenly become frightened.
– ORIGIN Old English.

frighten verb **1** make someone afraid. **2** (**frighten someone/thing off**) make someone or something too afraid to do something.
– DERIVATIVES **frightened** adjective **frightening** adjective **frighteningly** adverb.

frightener noun a frightening thing.
– PHRASES **put the frighteners on** Brit. informal threaten or intimidate someone.

frightful adjective **1** very unpleasant, serious, or shocking. **2** informal terrible; awful.
– DERIVATIVES **frightfully** adverb **frightfulness**

noun.

fright wig noun a wig with the hair arranged sticking out, as worn by a clown.

frigid /fri-jid/ adjective **1** very cold. **2** (of a woman) unable to be sexually aroused. **3** stiff or formal in style: *the house is no frigid art museum.*
– DERIVATIVES **frigidity** noun **frigidly** adverb.
– ORIGIN Latin *frigidus.*

frigid zone noun each of the two regions of the earth respectively north of the Arctic Circle and south of the Antarctic Circle.

frill noun **1** a strip of gathered or pleated material used as a decorative edging. **2** a frill-like fringe of feathers, hair, skin, etc. on a bird or other animal. **3** (frills) unnecessary extra features: *a comfortable flat with no frills.*
– DERIVATIVES **frilled** adjective **frilly** adjective.
– ORIGIN Flemish *frul.*

fringe noun **1** a border of threads, tassels, or twists, used to edge clothing or material. **2** chiefly Brit. the front part of someone's hair, cut so as to hang over the forehead. **3** a natural border of hair or fibres in an animal or plant. **4** an outer part or edge of an area, group, or activity: *loners living on the fringes of society.* • adjective not part of the mainstream; unconventional: *fringe theatre.* • verb provide with or form a fringe: *the sea is fringed by palm trees.*
– DERIVATIVES **fringing** noun **fringy** adjective.
– ORIGIN Old French *frenge.*

fringe benefit noun an additional benefit, especially one given to an employee.

frippery noun (pl. **fripperies**) **1** showy or unnecessary ornament. **2** a frivolous or trivial thing.
– ORIGIN Old French *freperie* 'second-hand clothes'.

frisbee noun trademark a plastic disc designed for skimming through the air as an outdoor game.
– ORIGIN said to be named after the pie tins of the *Frisbie* bakery in Connecticut.

frisée /free-zay/ noun a kind of endive with curled leaves.
– ORIGIN from French *chicorée frisée* 'curly endive'.

Frisian /free-zi-uhn, free-zhuhn/ noun **1** a person from Frisia or Friesland in the Netherlands. **2** the Germanic language spoken in northern parts of the Netherlands and adjacent islands. • adjective relating to Frisia or Friesland.

frisk verb **1** pass the hands over someone in a search for hidden weapons or drugs. **2** skip or move playfully; frolic.
– ORIGIN Old French *frisque* 'alert, lively'.

frisky adjective (**friskier**, **friskiest**) playful and full of energy.

frisson /free-son/ noun a sudden strong feeling of excitement or fear; a thrill.
– ORIGIN French.

fritillary /fri-til-luh-ri/ noun (pl. **fritillaries**) **1** a plant with hanging bell-like flowers. **2** a butterfly with orange-brown wings chequered with black.
– ORIGIN Latin *fritillaria.*

frittata /fri-tah-tuh/ noun an Italian dish made with fried beaten eggs, resembling a Spanish omelette.
– ORIGIN Italian.

fritter[1] verb (**fritter something away**) waste time, money, or energy on trivial matters.
– ORIGIN from former *fitter* 'break into fragments'.

fritter[2] noun a piece of fruit, vegetable, or meat that is coated in batter and deep-fried.
– ORIGIN Old French *friture.*

frivolous adjective **1** not having any serious purpose or value. **2** (of a person) not serious or responsible.
– DERIVATIVES **frivolity** noun **frivolously** adverb.
– ORIGIN Latin *frivolus* 'silly, trifling'.

frizz verb (of hair) form into a mass of tight curls. • noun a mass of tightly curled hair.
– ORIGIN French *friser.*

frizzle[1] verb fry something until crisp or burnt.
– ORIGIN from FRY[1], probably influenced by SIZZLE.

frizzle[2] verb form hair into tight curls.
– ORIGIN from FRIZZ.

frizzy adjective (**frizzier**, **frizziest**) formed of a mass of small, tight curls.
– DERIVATIVES **frizziness** noun.

fro adverb see TO AND FRO.
– ORIGIN Old Norse.

frock noun **1** chiefly Brit. a dress. **2** a loose outer garment, especially a long gown worn by monks or priests.
– ORIGIN Old French *froc.*

frock coat noun a man's double-breasted, long-skirted coat, now worn chiefly on formal occasions.

frog[1] noun **1** a tailless amphibian with a short squat body and very long hind legs for leaping. **2** (Frog) informal, derogatory a French person.
– PHRASES **have a frog in one's throat** informal find it hard to speak because of hoarseness.
– DERIVATIVES **froggy** adjective **froglet** noun.
– ORIGIN Old English: sense 2 is partly from the reputation of the French for eating frogs' legs.

frog[2] noun **1** a thing used to hold or fasten something. **2** an ornamental coat fastener consisting of a spindle-shaped button and a loop.
– ORIGIN perhaps from FROG[1], influenced by Italian *forchetta* or French *fourchette* 'small fork'.

frog[3] noun an elastic horny pad in the sole of a horse's hoof.
– ORIGIN perhaps from FROG[1]; perhaps also influenced by Italian *forchetta* or French *fourchette* (see FROG[2]).

frogman noun (pl. **frogmen**) a diver equipped with a rubber suit, flippers, and breathing equipment.

frogmarch verb force someone to walk forward by pinning their arms from behind.

frogspawn noun a mass of frogs' eggs surrounded by transparent jelly.

froideur /frwah-der/ noun coolness or reserve between people.
– ORIGIN French.

frolic verb (**frolics**, **frolicking**, **frolicked**) play or move about in a cheerful and lively way. • noun a lively or playful act or activity.
– DERIVATIVES **frolicker** noun.
– ORIGIN from Dutch *vrolijk* 'merry, cheerful'.

frolicsome adjective lively and playful.

from preposition **1** indicating the point at which a journey, process, or action starts. **2** indicating the source of something. **3** indicating the starting point of a range. **4** indicating separation, removal, or prevention. **5** indicating a cause. **6** indicating a difference.
– PHRASES **from time to time** occasionally.
– ORIGIN Old English.

fromage blanc /from-ahzh blonk/ noun a type of soft French cheese with a creamy sour taste.
– ORIGIN French, 'white cheese'.

fromage frais /from-ahzh fray/ noun a type of smooth, soft fresh cheese.
– ORIGIN French, 'fresh cheese'.

frond noun the leaf or leaf-like part of a palm, fern, or similar plant.
– ORIGIN Latin *frons* 'leaf'.

front noun **1** the side or part of an object that presents itself to view or that is normally seen first. **2** the position directly ahead. **3** the forward-facing part of a person's body. **4** any face of a building, especially that of the main entrance: *the west front of the Cathedral.* **5** the furthest position that an armed force has reached. **6** Meteorology the forward edge of an advancing mass of air. **7** a particular situation or area of activity: *good news on the jobs front.* **8** an organized political group. **9** a deceptive appearance or way of behaving: *I put on a brave front.* **10** a person or organization serving as a cover for secret or illegal activities. **11** boldness and confidence. • adjective of or at the front. • verb **1** have the front facing towards something. **2** place or be placed at the front of something. **3** provide something with a front or facing. **4** lead or be prominent in: *the group is fronted by two girl singers.* **5** present or host a television or radio programme. **6** act as a front for secret or illegal activity.
– PHRASES **front of house** Brit. **1** the parts of a theatre in front of the stage. **2** the business of a theatre that concerns the audience. **in front of** in the presence of.
– DERIVATIVES **frontward** adjective & adverb **frontwards** adverb.
– ORIGIN Latin *frons* 'forehead, front'.

frontage noun **1** the facade of a building. **2** a piece of land adjoining a street or waterway.

frontal adjective **1** relating to or at the front. **2** relating to the forehead or front part of the skull.
– DERIVATIVES **frontally** adverb.

frontal lobe noun each of the paired lobes of the brain lying immediately behind the forehead.

frontbencher noun a member of the cabinet or shadow cabinet who sits in the front benches in the House of Commons.
– DERIVATIVES **front-bench** adjective.

front-end adjective **1** informal (of money) paid or charged at the beginning of a transaction. **2** Computing (of a device or program) directly accessed by the user and allowing access to further devices or programs.

frontier noun **1** a border separating two countries. **2** the extreme limit of settled land beyond which lies wilderness. **3** the limit of knowledge or achievement in a particular area: *fundamental problems at the frontiers of cosmology.*
– ORIGIN Old French *frontiere*.

frontiersman (or **frontierswoman**) noun (pl. **frontiersmen** or **frontierswomen**) a man (or woman) living in the region of a frontier.

frontispiece /frun-tiss-peess/ noun an illustration facing the title page of a book.
– ORIGIN Latin *frontispicium* 'facade'.

front line noun **1** the part of an army that is closest to the enemy. **2** the most important position in an area of activity: *we're on the front line of world theatre.*

frontman noun (pl. **frontmen**) **1** the leader of a band. **2** a person who represents an illegal organization to give it an appearance of legitimacy.

front runner noun the leading contestant in a race or other competition.

front-wheel drive noun a transmission system that provides power to the front wheels of a motor vehicle.

frost noun **1** a deposit of white ice crystals formed on surfaces when the temperature falls below freezing. **2** a period of cold weather when frost forms. • verb cover or be covered with frost.
– ORIGIN Old English.

frostbite noun injury to body tissues, especially the nose, fingers, or toes, caused by exposure to extreme cold.
– DERIVATIVES **frostbitten** adjective.

frosted adjective **1** covered with frost. **2** (of glass) having a textured surface so that it is difficult to see through.

frosting noun N. Amer. icing.

frosty adjective (**frostier, frostiest**) **1** (of the weather) very cold with frost forming on surfaces. **2** cold and unfriendly.
– DERIVATIVES **frostily** adverb **frostiness** noun.

froth noun **1** a mass of small bubbles in liquid. **2** worthless or superficial talk, ideas, or activities: *the BBC has to explain the substance rather than the froth of politics.* • verb **1** form or produce froth. **2** be very angry or agitated.
– ORIGIN Old Norse.

frothy adjective (**frothier, frothiest**) **1** full of or covered with a mass of small bubbles. **2** light and entertaining but of little substance: *lots of frothy interviews.*
– DERIVATIVES **frothily** adverb **frothiness** noun.

frou-frou /froo-froo/ noun (usu. before another noun) frills or other ornamentation: *a little frou-frou skirt.*
– ORIGIN French.

frown verb **1** furrow one's brows to show disapproval, displeasure, or concentration. **2** (**frown on**) disapprove of: *casual sex is still frowned upon.* • noun an act of frowning.
– ORIGIN Old French *froignier*.

frowsty /frow-sti/ adjective Brit. having a stale, warm, and stuffy atmosphere.
– ORIGIN from **FROWZY**.

frowzy /frow-zi/ (also **frowsy**) adjective scruffy, dingy, and neglected in appearance.
– ORIGIN unknown.

froze past of **FREEZE**.

frozen past participle of **FREEZE**.

FRS abbreviation (in the UK) Fellow of the Royal Society.

fructify /fruk-ti-fy/ verb (**fructifies, fructifying, fructified**) formal 1 make or become fruitful. 2 bear fruit.
– ORIGIN Latin *fructificare*.

fructose /fruk-tohz/ noun a simple sugar found chiefly in honey and fruit.
– ORIGIN from Latin *fructus* 'fruit'.

frugal /froo-g'l/ adjective 1 using only as much money or food as is necessary: *a frugal way of life*. 2 (of a meal) simple, plain, and costing little.
– DERIVATIVES **frugality** noun **frugally** adverb.
– ORIGIN Latin *frugalis*.

frugivore /froo-ji-vor/ noun an animal that feeds on fruit.
– DERIVATIVES **frugivorous** /froo-**jiv**-uh-ruhss/ adjective.
– ORIGIN from Latin *frux* 'fruit'.

fruit noun 1 the sweet and fleshy product of a tree or other plant that contains seed and can be eaten as food. 2 Botany the seed-bearing structure of a plant, e.g. an acorn. 3 the result or reward of work or activity: *the state is encouraging people to enjoy the fruits of their labour*. •verb (of a plant) produce fruit.
– ORIGIN Latin *fructus* 'enjoyment of produce, harvest'.

fruitarian noun a person who eats only fruit.
– DERIVATIVES **fruitarianism** noun.

fruit bat noun a large bat which feeds chiefly on fruit or nectar.

fruitcake noun informal an eccentric or mad person.

fruit cocktail noun a finely chopped fruit salad, sold in tins.

fruiterer noun chiefly Brit. a person who sells fruit.

fruit fly noun a small fly which feeds on fruit in both its adult and larval stages.

fruitful adjective 1 producing much fruit; fertile. 2 producing good results: *fruitful research*.
– DERIVATIVES **fruitfully** adverb **fruitfulness** noun.

fruiting body noun the spore-producing organ of a fungus, often seen as a toadstool.

fruition /fruu-i-sh'n/ noun 1 the fulfilment of a plan or project. 2 literary the state or action of producing fruit.
– ORIGIN from Latin *frui* 'enjoy'.

fruitless adjective 1 failing to achieve the desired results; unproductive: *a fruitless search for contentment*. 2 not producing fruit.
– DERIVATIVES **fruitlessly** adverb **fruitlessness** noun.

fruitlet noun an immature or small fruit.

fruit machine noun Brit. a coin-operated gambling machine that generates combinations of symbols (typically representing fruit), certain combinations winning money for the player.

fruit salad noun a mixture of different types of chopped fruit served in syrup or juice.

fruit sugar noun another term for **FRUCTOSE**.

fruity adjective (**fruitier, fruitiest**) 1 relating to, resembling, or containing fruit. 2 (of a voice) deep and rich. 3 Brit. informal sexually suggestive.
– DERIVATIVES **fruitiness** noun.

frump noun an unattractive woman who wears dowdy old-fashioned clothes.
– DERIVATIVES **frumpy** adjective.
– ORIGIN probably from Dutch *verrompelen* 'wrinkle'.

frustrate verb 1 prevent a plan or action from progressing or succeeding. 2 prevent someone from doing or achieving something. 3 make someone annoyed or dissatisfied as a result of being unable to do something.
– DERIVATIVES **frustrated** adjective **frustrating** adjective.
– ORIGIN Latin *frustrare* 'disappoint'.

frustration noun 1 the feeling of being upset or annoyed as a result of being unable to do something. 2 a cause of dissatisfaction or annoyance: *the frustrations of travel*. 3 the prevention of the progress, success, or fulfilment of something.

fry[1] verb (**fries, frying, fried**) 1 cook or be cooked in hot fat or oil. 2 informal (of a person) burn or overheat. •noun (pl. **fries**) 1 a fried dish or meal. 2 (**fries**) French fries.
– ORIGIN Old French *frire*.

fry[2] plural noun young fish, especially when newly hatched.
– ORIGIN Old Norse.

fryer noun a large, deep container for frying food.

frying pan (also **frypan**) noun a shallow pan with a long handle, used for frying food.
– PHRASES **out of the frying pan into the fire** from a bad situation to one that is worse.

fry-up noun Brit. informal a dish or meal of fried food.

f-stop noun a camera setting corresponding to a particular f-number.

ft abbreviation foot or feet.

FTP abbreviation Computing file transfer protocol, a standard for the exchange of program and data files across a network.

FTSE index (also **FT index**) noun a figure (published by the *Financial Times*) indicating the relative prices of shares on the London Stock Exchange.
– ORIGIN abbreviation of *Financial Times Stock Exchange*.

fuchsia /fyoo-shuh/ noun 1 an ornamental shrub with drooping tubular flowers that are typically of two different colours. 2 a vivid purplish-red colour.
– ORIGIN named after the German botanist Leonhard *Fuchs*.

fuck vulgar slang verb 1 have sexual intercourse with someone. 2 damage or ruin something. •noun an act of sexual intercourse. •exclamation a strong expression of annoyance or contempt.
– PHRASES **fuck off** go away. **fuck someone/ thing up** 1 damage someone emotionally. 2 do something badly.
– ORIGIN Germanic.

fuddled adjective unable to think clearly, especially as a result of drinking alcohol.
– ORIGIN unknown.

fuddy-duddy noun (pl. **fuddy-duddies**) informal a person who is old-fashioned and who often disapproves of modern ideas, behaviour, etc.
– ORIGIN unknown.

fudge noun **1** a soft sweet made from sugar, butter, and milk or cream. **2** an attempt to fudge an issue. •verb **1** present or deal with an issue in a vague way, especially to conceal the truth or mislead people. **2** manipulate facts or figures so as to present a more desirable picture.
– ORIGIN probably from former *fadge* 'to fit'.

fuehrer noun variant spelling of FÜHRER.

fuel noun **1** material such as coal, gas, or oil that is burned to produce heat or power. **2** food, drink, or drugs as a source of energy. **3** something that stirs up argument or strong emotion. •verb (**fuels, fuelling, fuelled**; US **fuels, fueling, fueled**) **1** supply something with fuel. **2** stir up or strengthen: *the slide in share prices fuelled demands for government intervention.*
– ORIGIN Old French *fouaille.*

fuel cell noun a cell producing an electric current direct from a chemical reaction.

fuel injection noun the direct introduction of fuel under pressure into the combustion units of an internal-combustion engine, as a way of improving a car's performance.

fug noun Brit. informal a warm, stuffy atmosphere.
– DERIVATIVES **fuggy** adjective.
– ORIGIN unknown.

fugal /fyoo-guhl/ adjective relating to a fugue.

fugitive noun a person who has escaped from captivity or is in hiding. •adjective quick to disappear; fleeting: *a fugitive glimpse.*
– ORIGIN from Latin *fugere* 'flee'.

fugue /fyoog/ noun **1** a musical composition in which a short melody or phrase is introduced by one part and successively taken up by others. **2** Psychiatry a period during which someone loses their memory or sense of identity and may leave their home or usual surroundings.
– ORIGIN Latin *fuga* 'flight'.

führer /fyoo-uh-ruh/ (also **fuehrer**) noun the title used by Hitler as leader of Germany.
– ORIGIN German, 'leader'.

fulcrum /fuul-kruhm/ noun (pl. **fulcra** /fuul-kruh/ or **fulcrums**) the point on which a lever turns or is supported.
– ORIGIN Latin, 'post of a couch'.

fulfil (US **fulfill**) verb (**fulfils, fulfilling, fulfilled**) **1** achieve or realize something desired, promised, or predicted: *I fulfilled a childhood dream when I became champion.* **2** satisfy or meet a requirement or condition. **3** (**fulfil oneself**) gain happiness or satisfaction by fully developing one's abilities.
– DERIVATIVES **fulfilled** adjective **fulfilling** adjective.
– ORIGIN Old English, 'fill up, make full'.

fulfilment (US **fulfillment**) noun **1** a feeling of satisfaction or happiness as a result of fully developing one's abilities. **2** the action of fulfilling something.

full[1] adjective **1** containing or holding as much or as many as possible; having no empty space. **2** (**full of**) having a large number or quantity of something. **3** not lacking or omitting anything; complete: *I don't know the full story.* **4** (**full of**) unable to stop talking or thinking about: *they had their photographs taken and he was full of it.* **5** plump or rounded. **6** (of flavour, sound, or colour) strong or rich.

•adverb **1** straight; directly. **2** very.
– PHRASES **full of oneself** very self-satisfied and proud of oneself. **full on 1** running at or providing maximum power or capacity. **2** so as to make a direct impact. **3** (**full-on**) informal unrestrained: *hours of full-on fun.* **full steam** (or **speed**) **ahead** proceeding with as much speed or energy as possible. **full up** filled to capacity. **to the full** to the greatest possible extent.
– ORIGIN Old English.

full[2] verb clean, shrink, and thicken cloth using heat, pressure, and moisture.
– ORIGIN probably from FULLER.

full back noun a player in a defensive position near the goal in a ball game such as football.

full-blooded adjective wholehearted and enthusiastic.

full-blown adjective fully developed.

full board noun Brit. a type of accommodation at a hotel or guest house which includes all meals.

full-bodied adjective rich and satisfying in flavour or sound.

full bore adverb at full speed or maximum capacity. •adjective referring to firearms with a relatively large calibre.

fuller noun a person whose occupation is fulling cloth.
– ORIGIN Old English *fullere.*

fullerene /fuu-luh-reen/ noun Chemistry a form of carbon having a molecule consisting of atoms joined together in a hollow structure.
– ORIGIN shortening of *buckminsterfullerene* (the first known example, named after the American architect Richard Buckminster Fuller).

fuller's earth noun a type of clay used in fulling cloth.

full-fledged adjective North American term for FULLY FLEDGED.

full-frontal adjective fully exposing the front of the body, especially the genitals.

full house noun **1** a theatre or meeting that is filled to capacity. **2** a winning card at bingo. **3** a poker hand with three of a kind and a pair.

full marks plural noun the maximum award in an exam or assessment.

full moon noun the phase of the moon in which its whole disc is illuminated.

fullness (also **fulness**) noun **1** the state of being full. **2** richness or abundance.
– PHRASES **in the fullness of time** after a due length of time has passed.

full-scale adjective **1** (of a model or representation) of the same size as the thing represented. **2** as complete and thorough as possible: *a full-scale search of the area.*

full stop noun Brit. a punctuation mark (.) used at the end of a sentence or an abbreviation.

full-time adjective using the whole of a person's available working time. •adverb on a full-time basis. •noun (**full time**) Brit. the end of a sports match.
– DERIVATIVES **full-timer** noun.

fully adverb **1** completely or entirely. **2** no less or fewer than: *fully 65 per cent.*

fully fashioned adjective (of women's clothing) shaped and seamed to fit the body.

fully fledged adjective **1** (of a bird) having fully developed wing feathers and able to fly. **2** Brit. completely developed or established: *a fully fledged welfare state*.

fulmar /**fuul**-mer/ noun a large grey and white northern seabird.
– ORIGIN from Old Norse, 'stinking gull' (because of its habit of regurgitating its stomach contents when disturbed).

fulminate /**fuul**-mi-nayt/ verb protest strongly about something.
– DERIVATIVES **fulmination** noun.
– ORIGIN Latin *fulminare* 'strike with lightning'.

fulness noun variant spelling of **FULLNESS**.

fulsome adjective **1** excessively complimentary or flattering. **2** of large size or quantity; generous or plentiful: *fulsome details*.
– DERIVATIVES **fulsomely** adverb **fulsomeness** noun.

> USAGE: Although the earliest sense of fulsome was 'plentiful', this meaning was replaced by the negative sense 'excessively flattering', and is now generally thought to be incorrect. The word is often in heard in phrases such as **fulsome praise**, however, where the speaker just means that the praise is abundant rather than excessively flattering .

fumarole /**fyoo**-muh-rohl/ noun an opening in or near a volcano, through which hot sulphurous gases emerge.
– ORIGIN Latin *fumariolum* 'vent, hole for smoke'.

fumble verb **1** use the hands clumsily while doing or handling something. **2** (of the hands) do or handle something clumsily. **3** (**fumble about/around**) move about clumsily using the hands to find one's way. **4** express oneself or deal with something clumsily or nervously. **5** (in ball games) fail to catch or field the ball cleanly. •noun an act of fumbling.
– DERIVATIVES **fumbler** noun **fumbling** adjective.
– ORIGIN German *fommeln* or Dutch *fommelen*.

fume noun a gas or vapour that smells strongly or is dangerous to inhale. •verb **1** send out fumes. **2** feel extremely angry.
– DERIVATIVES **fuming** adjective.
– ORIGIN Latin *fumus* 'smoke'.

fumigate verb use the fumes of certain chemicals to disinfect a contaminated area.
– DERIVATIVES **fumigant** noun **fumigation** noun **fumigator** noun.
– ORIGIN Latin *fumigare*.

fun noun **1** light-hearted enjoyment. **2** a source of this: *exercise can be great fun*. **3** playfulness: *she's full of fun*. •adjective informal enjoyable.
– PHRASES **make fun of** tease or laugh at in a mocking way.
– ORIGIN unknown.

function noun **1** an activity that is natural to or the purpose of a person or thing. **2** a large or formal social event or ceremony. **3** a computer operation corresponding to a single instruction from the user. **4** Mathematics a relationship between one element and another, or between several elements and one another. •verb **1** work or operate in a proper or particular way. **2** (**function as**) fulfil the purpose or task of: *the building functions as a youth centre*.
– ORIGIN French *fonction*.

functional adjective **1** relating to or having a function. **2** designed to be practical and useful, rather than attractive. **3** working or operating. **4** (of a disease) affecting the operation rather than the structure of an organ.
– DERIVATIVES **functionally** adverb.

functional food noun a food containing health-giving additives.

functionalism noun the theory that the design of an object should be governed by its use rather than an attractive appearance.
– DERIVATIVES **functionalist** noun & adjective.

functionality noun **1** the quality of being functional. **2** the range of operations that can be run on a computer or other electronic system.

functionary noun (pl. **functionaries**) an official.

function key noun a key on a computer keyboard which can be assigned a particular function or operation.

fund noun **1** a sum of money saved or made available for a purpose. **2** (**funds**) financial resources. **3** a large stock of something. •verb provide money for something: *a project funded by the Arts Council*.
– DERIVATIVES **funder** noun **funding** noun.
– ORIGIN Latin *fundus* 'bottom, piece of landed property'.

fundament noun **1** the foundation or basis of something. **2** humorous a person's bottom.
– ORIGIN Latin *fundamentum*, from *fundare* 'to found'.

fundamental adjective of central importance: *a fundamental difference of opinion*. •noun a central or basic rule or principle.
– DERIVATIVES **fundamentally** adverb.

fundamentalism noun **1** a form of Protestant Christianity which promotes the belief that everything written in the Bible is literally true. **2** the strict following of the basic underlying doctrines of any religion or ideology.
– DERIVATIVES **fundamentalist** noun & adjective.

fundamental note noun Music the lowest note of a chord.

fundholding noun (in the UK) a former system of state funding in which a general practitioner was allocated a budget with which they could buy hospital services.
– DERIVATIVES **fundholder** noun.

fund-raiser noun **1** a person who raises money for an organization or cause. **2** an event held to raise money for an organization or cause.
– DERIVATIVES **fund-raising** noun.

funeral noun a ceremony held shortly after a person's death, usually including the person's burial or cremation.
– PHRASES **it's your funeral** informal said to warn someone that the consequences of an unwise act are their own responsibility.
– ORIGIN Latin *funeralia*.

funeral director noun an undertaker.

funeral parlour (also **funeral home**) noun an establishment where people who have died are prepared for burial or cremation.

funerary /fyoo-nuh-ruh-ri/ **adjective** relating to a funeral or to other rites in which people who have died are commemorated.

funereal /fyoo-neer-i-uhl/ **adjective** having the sombre quality or atmosphere appropriate to a funeral.

funfair **noun** chiefly Brit. a fair consisting of rides, sideshows, and other amusements.

fungi plural of **FUNGUS**.

fungicide /fun-ji-syd, fung-gi-syd/ **noun** a chemical that destroys fungus.
– DERIVATIVES **fungicidal** adjective.

fungus /fung-guhss/ **noun** (pl. **fungi** /fung-gy/) a spore-producing organism, such as a mushroom, that has no leaves or flowers and grows on other plants or on decaying matter.
– DERIVATIVES **fungal** adjective **fungoid** adjective.
– ORIGIN Latin, perhaps from Greek *spongos* 'sponge'.

funicular /fuh-nik-yuu-ler/ **adjective** (of a railway on a steep slope) operated by cables attached to cars which balance each other while one goes up and the other goes down.
• **noun** a funicular railway.
– ORIGIN from Latin *funiculus* 'little rope'.

funk¹ informal, chiefly Brit. **noun** (also **blue funk**) a state of panic or fear. • **verb** avoid something out of fear.
– ORIGIN perhaps from **FUNK²** in the informal sense 'tobacco smoke'.

funk² **noun** a style of popular dance music of US black origin, having a strong rhythm.
– ORIGIN perhaps from French dialect *funkier* 'blow smoke on'.

funky **adjective** (**funkier, funkiest**) informal **1** (of music) having a strong dance rhythm. **2** unconventionally modern and stylish.
– DERIVATIVES **funkily** adverb **funkiness** noun.

funnel **noun 1** a utensil that is wide at the top and narrow at the bottom, used for guiding liquid or powder into a small opening. **2** a metal chimney on a ship or steam engine.
• **verb** (**funnels, funnelling, funnelled**; US **funnels, funneling, funneled**) guide or move through a funnel or narrow space: *the wind was funnelling through the gorge.*
– ORIGIN Provençal *fonilh*.

funny **adjective** (**funnier, funniest**) **1** causing laughter or amusement. **2** strange; peculiar. **3** suspicious: *there's something funny going on.* **4** informal slightly unwell.
– DERIVATIVES **funnily** adverb.

funny bone **noun** informal the part of the elbow over which a sensitive nerve passes.

funny farm **noun** informal, derogatory a psychiatric hospital.

fun run **noun** informal an uncompetitive run for sponsored runners, held in support of a charity.

fur **noun 1** the short, soft hair of certain animals. **2** the skin of an animal with fur on it, used in making clothes. **3** a coat made from fur. **4** a coating formed on the tongue as a symptom of sickness. **5** Brit. a coating formed by hard water on the inside surface of a pipe, kettle, etc.
• **verb** (**furs, furring, furred**) Brit. coat or clog something up.
– PHRASES **the fur will fly** informal there will be a dramatic argument.
– DERIVATIVES **furred** adjective.
– ORIGIN from Old French *forrer* 'to line, sheathe'.

furbelow **noun 1** a strip of gathered or pleated material attached to a skirt or petticoat. **2** (**furbelows**) showy ornaments or trimmings.
– ORIGIN French *falbala* 'trimming, flounce'.

furious **adjective 1** extremely angry. **2** full of energy, intensity, or anger: *he strode off at a furious pace.*
– DERIVATIVES **furiously** adverb.
– ORIGIN Latin *furiosus*, from *furia* 'fury'.

furl **verb** roll or fold something up neatly and securely.
– DERIVATIVES **furled** adjective.
– ORIGIN French *ferler*.

furlong **noun** an eighth of a mile, 220 yards.
– ORIGIN from the Old English words for 'furrow' + 'long' (originally referring to the length of a furrow in a field).

furlough /fer-loh/ **noun** leave of absence, especially from military duty.
– ORIGIN Dutch *verlof*.

furnace **noun 1** an enclosed chamber in which material can be heated to very high temperatures. **2** a very hot place.
– ORIGIN from Latin *fornus* 'oven'.

furnish **verb 1** provide a room or building with furniture and fittings. **2** (**furnish someone with**) supply someone with equipment or information: *she was able to furnish me with details of the incident.* **3** be a source of something.
– DERIVATIVES **furnished** adjective **furnisher** noun.
– ORIGIN Old French *furnir*.

furnishing **noun 1** (**furnishings**) furniture and fittings in a room or building. **2** referring to fabrics used for curtains or upholstery: *furnishing fabrics.*

furniture **noun 1** the movable articles that are used to make a room or building suitable for living or working in, such as tables, chairs, or desks. **2** the small accessories or fittings that are required for a particular task or function: *door furniture.*
– ORIGIN French *fourniture*.

furore /fyoo-ror-i/ (US **furor** /fyoo-ror/) **noun** an outbreak of public anger or excitement.
– ORIGIN Italian.

furrier /furr-i-er/ **noun** a person who prepares or deals in furs.

furrow **noun 1** a long, narrow trench made in the ground by a plough. **2** a rut or groove. **3** a deep wrinkle on a person's face. • **verb 1** make a furrow in the ground or the surface of something. **2** (of a person's forehead) become wrinkled: *his brow furrowed in concentration.*
– ORIGIN Old English.

furry **adjective** (**furrier, furriest**) covered with or like fur.
– DERIVATIVES **furriness** noun.

fur seal **noun** a seal whose thick underside fur is used commercially as sealskin.

further used as comparative of **FAR**. **adverb** (also **farther**) **1** at, to, or by a greater distance. **2** over a greater expanse of space or time. **3** beyond the point already reached. **4** at or to a more advanced or desirable stage. **5** in addition; also. • **adjective 1** (also **farther**) more

distant in space. **2** additional. •verb help the progress or development of something.
– PHRASES **further to** formal following on from (used especially at the beginning of a letter).
– ORIGIN Old English, related to FORTH.

> USAGE: Is there any difference between **further** and **farther**? When talking about distance, either form can be used: *she moved further down the train* and *she moved farther down the train* are both correct. However you should use **further** when you mean 'beyond or in addition to what has already been done (*have you anything further to say?*) or 'additional' (*phone for further information*).

furtherance noun the action of helping a scheme or plan to progress.

further education noun Brit. education below degree level for people above school age.

furthermore adverb in addition; besides.

furthermost (also **farthermost**) adjective at the greatest distance from something.

furthest (also **farthest**) used as superlative of FAR. adjective **1** situated at the greatest distance. **2** covering the greatest area or distance. •adverb **1** at or by the greatest distance. **2** over the greatest distance or area. **3** to the most extreme or advanced point.

furtive adjective done in a secretive or guilty way.
– DERIVATIVES **furtively** adverb **furtiveness** noun.
– ORIGIN Latin *furtivus*, from *furtum* 'theft'.

fury noun (pl. **furies**) **1** extreme anger. **2** extreme strength or violence: *the fury of the storm.* **3** (**Furies**) Greek Mythology three goddesses who punished wrongdoers.
– ORIGIN from Latin *furere* 'be mad, rage'.

furze noun another term for GORSE.
– ORIGIN Old English.

fuse¹ verb **1** join or blend to form a single entity. **2** melt a material or object with intense heat, so as to join it with something else. **3** Brit. (of an electrical appliance) stop working when a fuse melts. **4** provide a circuit or electrical appliance with a fuse. •noun a safety device consisting of a strip of wire that melts and breaks an electric circuit if the current exceeds a safe level.
– ORIGIN from Latin *fundere* 'pour, melt'.

fuse² (also **fuze**) noun **1** a length of material along which a small flame moves to explode a bomb or firework. **2** a device in a bomb that controls the timing of the explosion. •verb fit a fuse to a bomb.
– ORIGIN Latin *fusus* 'spindle'.

fuse box noun a box or board containing the fuses for electrical circuits in a building.

fuselage /fyoo-zuh-lahzh/ noun the main body of an aircraft.
– ORIGIN French, from *fuseler* 'shape into a spindle'.

fusible adjective able to be fused or melted easily.

Fusilier /fyoo-zi-leer/ noun a member of any of several British regiments formerly armed with fusils (light muskets).

fusillade /fyoo-zi-layd/ noun a series of shots fired at the same time or in rapid succession.
– ORIGIN French.

fusion noun **1** the process or result of fusing things to form a single entity. **2** a reaction in which light atomic nuclei fuse to form a heavier nucleus, releasing much energy. **3** popular music that is a mixture of different styles, especially jazz and rock. •adjective referring to food or cooking which combines elements of both eastern and western cuisine.
– ORIGIN Latin, from *fundere* 'pour, melt'.

fuss noun **1** a display of unnecessary or excessive excitement or activity. **2** a protest or complaint. •verb **1** show unnecessary or excessive concern about something. **2** pay too much attention to someone: *his mother fussed over him all the time.*
– ORIGIN perhaps Anglo-Irish.

fusspot noun informal a fussy person.

fussy adjective (**fussier, fussiest**) **1** too concerned about one's requirements and therefore hard to please. **2** full of unnecessary detail or decoration.
– DERIVATIVES **fussily** adverb **fussiness** noun.

fustian /fuss-ti-uhn/ noun a thick, hard-wearing twilled cloth.
– ORIGIN from Latin *pannus fustaneus* 'cloth from *Fostat*', a suburb of Cairo.

fusty adjective (**fustier, fustiest**) **1** smelling stale and damp or stuffy. **2** old-fashioned.
– DERIVATIVES **fustiness** noun.
– ORIGIN Old French *fuste* 'smelling of the cask'.

futile adjective producing no useful results; pointless.
– DERIVATIVES **futilely** adverb **futility** noun.
– ORIGIN Latin *futilis*.

futon /foo-ton/ noun a Japanese padded mattress with no springs, able be rolled up when not in use.
– ORIGIN Japanese.

future noun **1** (**the future**) time that is still to come. **2** events or conditions occurring or existing in time still to come. **3** a prospect of success or happiness: *I might have a future as an artist.* **4** Grammar a tense of verbs expressing events that have not yet happened. **5** (**futures**) contracts for assets bought at agreed prices but delivered and paid for later. •adjective **1** existing or occurring in the future. **2** planned or destined to hold a particular position: *his future wife.* **3** Grammar (of a tense) expressing an event yet to happen.
– PHRASES **in future** from now onwards.
– ORIGIN from Latin *futurus* 'going to be'.

future perfect noun Grammar a tense of verbs expressing an action expected to be completed in the future, in English exemplified by *will have done.*

future shock noun a state of distress or disorientation caused by rapid social or technological change.

Futurism noun an early 20th-century artistic movement, which strongly rejected traditional forms and embraced modern technology.
– DERIVATIVES **Futurist** adjective.

futuristic adjective **1** having or involving very modern technology or design. **2** (of a film or book) set in the future.
– DERIVATIVES **futuristically** adverb.

futurity /fyoo-tyoor-i-ti/ noun (pl. **futurities**) **1** the future time. **2** a future event.

futurology noun the prediction of future events based on present trends.
- DERIVATIVES **futurologist** noun.

fuze noun variant spelling of FUSE².

fuzz¹ noun a frizzy mass of hair or fibre. • verb make or become fuzzy.
- ORIGIN probably German or Dutch.

fuzz² noun (**the fuzz**) informal the police.
- ORIGIN unknown.

fuzzy adjective (**fuzzier, fuzziest**) 1 having a frizzy texture or appearance. 2 indistinct or vague: *a fuzzy picture.*
- DERIVATIVES **fuzzily** adverb **fuzziness** noun.

fuzzy logic noun a form of logic in which predicates can have fractional values rather than simply being true or false.

F-word noun euphemistic the word 'fuck'.

FX abbreviation visual or sound effects.
- ORIGIN from the pronunciation of *effects.*

FYI abbreviation for your information.

Gg

G[1] (also **g**) noun (pl. **Gs** or **G's**) **1** the seventh letter of the alphabet. **2** referring to the next item after F in a set. **3** Music the fifth note in the scale of C major.

G[2] abbreviation **1** giga- (10^9). **2** N. Amer. informal grand (a thousand dollars). **3** the force exerted by the earth's gravitational field.

g abbreviation **1** Chemistry gas. **2** gram(s). •symbol Physics the acceleration due to gravity (9.81 m s^{-2}).

G8 abbreviation Group of Eight, a group of eight industrial nations whose heads of government meet regularly.

GA abbreviation Georgia.

Ga symbol the chemical element gallium.

gab verb (**gabs, gabbing, gabbed**) informal talk at length.
– PHRASES **the gift of the gab** the ability to speak fluently and persuasively.
– DERIVATIVES **gabby** adjective.
– ORIGIN from **GOB**[1].

gabble verb talk rapidly and in a way that is hard to understand. •noun rapid, unintelligible talk.
– DERIVATIVES **gabbler** noun.
– ORIGIN Dutch *gabbelen*.

gabbro /gab-broh/ noun (pl. **gabbros**) a dark, coarse-grained rock.
– ORIGIN Italian, from Latin *glaber* 'smooth'.

gaberdine /ga-ber-deen/ (also **gabardine**) noun a smooth, hard-wearing worsted or cotton cloth, used especially for making raincoats.
– ORIGIN Old French *gauvardine*.

gable noun **1** the triangular upper part of a wall at the end of a ridged roof. **2** a gable-shaped canopy over a window or door.
– DERIVATIVES **gabled** adjective.
– ORIGIN Old Norse.

Gabonese /ga-buh-neez/ noun (pl. same) a person from Gabon, a country in West Africa. •adjective relating to Gabon.

gad verb (**gads, gadding, gadded**) (**gad about/around**) informal enjoy oneself by visiting many different places or travelling from one place to another.
– ORIGIN from former *gadling* 'wanderer'.

gadabout noun informal a person who is always travelling from one place to another enjoying themselves.

gadfly noun (pl. **gadflies**) **1** a large fly that bites livestock. **2** an annoying person.
– ORIGIN from **GAD**, or former *gad* 'goad, spike'.

gadget noun a small mechanical device or tool.

– DERIVATIVES **gadgetry** noun.
– ORIGIN probably from French *gâchette* 'lock mechanism'.

gadolinium /gad-uh-lin-i-uhm/ noun a soft silvery-white metallic chemical element of the lanthanide series.
– ORIGIN named after the Finnish mineralogist Johan *Gadolin*.

gadzooks /gad-zooks/ exclamation old use expressing surprise or annoyance.
– ORIGIN alteration of *God's hooks*, i.e. the nails by which Christ was fastened to the cross.

Gael /gayl/ noun a Gaelic-speaking person.
– ORIGIN Scottish Gaelic *Gaidheal*.

Gaelic /gay-lik, ga-lik/ noun **1** (also **Scottish Gaelic**) a Celtic language spoken in western Scotland, brought from Ireland in the 5th and 6th centuries AD. **2** (also **Irish Gaelic**) the Celtic language of Ireland; Irish. •adjective relating to the Celtic languages and their speakers.

Gaelic coffee noun coffee served with cream and whisky.

gaff[1] noun **1** a stick with a hook or barbed spear, for landing large fish. **2** Sailing a spar to which the head of a fore-and-aft sail is bent.
– ORIGIN Provençal *gaf* 'hook'.

gaff[2] noun (in phrase **blow the gaff**) Brit. informal reveal a plot or secret.
– ORIGIN unknown.

gaff[3] noun Brit. informal a person's home.
– ORIGIN unknown.

gaffe /gaf/ (also **gaff**) noun an embarrassing blunder or mistake.
– ORIGIN French.

gaffer noun **1** Brit. informal a person's supervisor or boss. **2** informal an old man. **3** the chief electrician in a film or television production unit.
– ORIGIN probably from **GODFATHER**.

gaffer tape noun strong waterproof adhesive tape with a cloth backing.

gag[1] noun **1** a piece of cloth put in or over a person's mouth to prevent them from speaking. **2** a restriction on free speech. •verb (**gags, gagging, gagged**) **1** put a gag on someone. **2** prevent someone from speaking freely. **3** choke or retch.
– ORIGIN perhaps imitating a person choking.

gag[2] noun a joke or funny story.
– ORIGIN unknown.

gaga /gah-gah/ adjective informal rambling in speech or thought, especially as a result of old age.
– ORIGIN French.

gage[1] /gayj/ **noun** old use **1** a valued object given as a guarantee of someone's good faith. **2** a glove or other object thrown down as a challenge to fight.
– ORIGIN Old French.

gage[2] **noun & verb** US spelling of **GAUGE**.

gaggle noun 1 a flock of geese. **2** informal a noisy group of people: *a gaggle of children.*
– ORIGIN imitating the noise that a goose makes.

Gaia /gy-uh/ **noun** the earth viewed as a vast self-regulating organism.
– ORIGIN coined by the English scientist James Lovelock, from the name of the Greek goddess *Gaia.*

gaiety (US also **gayety**) **noun** (pl. **gaieties**) **1** the state or quality of being light-hearted and cheerful. **2** lively celebrations or festivities.
– ORIGIN French *gaieté.*

gaily adverb 1 in a light-hearted and cheerful way. **2** without thinking of the consequences of one's actions. **3** with a bright appearance.

gain verb 1 obtain or secure: *troops gained control of the town.* **2** reach or arrive at a place. **3** (**gain on**) come closer to a person or thing being chased. **4** increase the amount or rate of weight or speed. **5** increase in value. **6** (**gain in**) improve or progress in some way: *she has gained in confidence.* **7** benefit: *both of them stood to gain from the relationship.* **8** (of a clock or watch) become fast. ● **noun 1** a thing that is gained. **2** an increase in wealth or resources.
– DERIVATIVES **gainer** noun.
– ORIGIN Old French *gaignier.*

gainful adjective (of employment) useful and for which one is paid.
– DERIVATIVES **gainfully** adverb.

gainsay /gayn-**say**/ **verb** (past and past part. **gainsaid**) formal deny or contradict a fact or statement.
– ORIGIN from former *gain-* 'against' + **SAY**.

gait /gayt/ **noun 1** a person's way of walking. **2** the pattern of steps of a horse or dog at a particular speed.
– ORIGIN Old Norse, 'street'.

gaiter noun 1 a covering of cloth or leather for the ankle and lower leg. **2** chiefly US a shoe or overshoe extending to the ankle or above.
– DERIVATIVES **gaitered** adjective.
– ORIGIN French *guêtre.*

gal noun informal, chiefly N. Amer. a girl or young woman.

gal. abbreviation gallon(s).

gala /gah-luh/ **noun 1** a social occasion with special entertainments. **2** Brit. a special sports event, especially a swimming competition.
– ORIGIN Old French *gale* 'rejoicing'.

galactic /guh-**lak**-tik/ **adjective** relating to a galaxy or galaxies.
– DERIVATIVES **galactically** adverb.

galangal /ga-luhn-gal/ (also **galingale**) **noun** an Asian plant of the ginger family, used in cookery and herbal medicine.
– ORIGIN Old French *galingale.*

galantine /ga-luhn-teen/ **noun** a dish of cooked meat or fish served cold in aspic.
– ORIGIN Latin *galatina.*

galaxy noun (pl. **galaxies**) **1** a system of millions or billions of stars held together by gravitational attraction. **2** (**the Galaxy**) the galaxy of which the solar system is a part; the Milky Way. **3** a large and impressive group of people or things: *a galaxy of celebrities.*
– ORIGIN from Greek *galaxias kuklos* 'milky vault' (referring to the Milky Way).

gale noun 1 a very strong wind. **2** an outburst of laughter.
– ORIGIN perhaps related to an Old Norse word meaning 'mad, frantic'.

galena /guh-lee-nuh/ **noun** a metallic grey or black mineral consisting of lead sulphide.
– ORIGIN Latin, 'lead ore'.

galia melon /gah-lee-uh/ **noun** a small round melon of a variety with rough skin and fragrant orange flesh.
– ORIGIN from the Hebrew name *Galia.*

Galilean[1] /ga-li-**lay**-uhn/ **adjective** relating to the Italian astronomer and physicist Galileo Galilei.

Galilean[2] /ga-li-**lee**-uhn/ **noun** a person from Galilee, the region of ancient Palestine associated with the ministry of Jesus and now part of Israel. ● **adjective** relating to Galilee.

galingale /ga-lin-gayl/ **noun** variant spelling of **GALANGAL**.

gall[1] /gawl/ **noun** bold and disrespectful behaviour: *she had the gall to ask him for money.*
– ORIGIN Old English.

gall[2] /gawl/ **noun 1** annoyance or resentment. **2** a sore on the skin made by rubbing. ● **verb 1** make someone feel annoyed or resentful. **2** make the skin sore by rubbing.
– DERIVATIVES **galling** adjective.
– ORIGIN Old English.

gall[3] /gawl/ **noun** an abnormal growth on plants and trees, caused by the presence of insect larvae, mites, or fungi.
– ORIGIN Latin *galla.*

gall. abbreviation gallon(s).

gallant adjective 1 /**gal**-luhnt/ brave or heroic. **2** /guh-**lant**/ (of a man) polite and charming to women. ● **noun** /guh-**lant**/ a man who is charmingly attentive to women.
– DERIVATIVES **gallantly** adverb.
– ORIGIN Old French *galant.*

gallantry noun (pl. **gallantries**) **1** courageous behaviour. **2** polite attention paid by men to women.

gall bladder noun a small sac-shaped organ beneath the liver, in which bile is stored.

galleon noun historical a large square-rigged sailing ship with three or more decks and masts.
– ORIGIN French *galion* or Spanish *galeón.*

gallery noun (pl. **galleries**) **1** a room or building in which works of art are displayed. **2** a balcony or upper floor projecting from a back or side wall inside a hall or church. **3** the highest balcony in a theatre, having the cheapest seats. **4** a long room or passage forming a portico or colonnade. **5** a horizontal underground passage in a mine.
– PHRASES **play to the gallery** do something intended to win approval or make oneself popular.
– DERIVATIVES **galleried** adjective.

– ORIGIN Italian *galleria*.

galley noun (pl. **galleys**) **1** historical a low, flat ship with one or more sails and up to three banks of oars, often manned by slaves or criminals. **2** a narrow kitchen in a ship or aircraft. **3** (also **galley proof**) a printer's proof in the form of long single-column strips.
– ORIGIN Greek *galaia*; sense 3 is from French *galée* referring to an oblong tray for holding set-up type.

galliard /ga-li-ahd/ noun historical a lively dance in triple time for two people.
– ORIGIN Old French *gaillard* 'valiant'.

Gallic /gal-lik/ adjective **1** relating to or characteristic of France or the French. **2** relating to the Gauls.
– DERIVATIVES **Gallicize** (or **Gallicise**) verb.
– ORIGIN Latin *Gallicus*, from *Gallus* 'a Gaul'.

Gallicism /ga-li-siz-uhm/ noun a French word or phrase adopted in another language.

gallimaufry /gal-li-maw-fri/ noun a jumble or mixture.
– ORIGIN former French *galimafrée* 'unappetizing dish'.

gallium /gal-li-uhm/ noun a soft silvery-white metallic chemical element which melts just above normal room temperature.
– ORIGIN from Latin *Gallia* 'France' or *gallus* 'cock'.

gallivant /gal-li-vant/ verb informal go from place to place enjoying oneself.
– ORIGIN perhaps from GALLANT.

gallon /gal-luhn/ noun **1** a unit of volume for measuring liquids, equal to eight pints: in Britain (also **imperial gallon**), equivalent to 4.55 litres; in the US, equivalent to 3.79 litres. **2** (**gallons**) informal large quantities of something.
– ORIGIN Old French *galon*.

gallop noun **1** the fastest pace of a horse, with all the feet off the ground together in each stride. **2** a ride on a horse at a gallop. • verb (**gallops, galloping, galloped**) **1** go at the pace of a gallop. **2** move or progress very rapidly.
– ORIGIN Old French *galoper*.

gallows plural noun (usu. treated as sing.) **1** a structure consisting of two uprights and a crosspiece, used for hanging a person. **2** (**the gallows**) execution by hanging.
– ORIGIN Old English.

gallows humour noun grim and ironical humour in a desperate or hopeless situation.

gallstone /gawl-stohn/ noun a small hard mass formed abnormally in the gall bladder or bile ducts, causing pain and obstruction.

Gallup poll /gal-luhp/ noun trademark an assessment of public opinion by questioning a representative sample of the population, used in forecasting voting results in an election.
– ORIGIN named after the American statistician George H. *Gallup*.

galoot /guh-loot/ noun N. Amer. & Scottish informal a clumsy or stupid person.
– ORIGIN unknown.

galore adjective in large quantities: *there were prizes galore.*
– ORIGIN from Irish *go leor* 'to sufficiency'.

galosh /guh-losh/ noun a waterproof rubber overshoe.

– ORIGIN from Latin *gallica solea* 'Gallic shoe'.

galumph /guh-lumf/ verb informal move in a clumsy, heavy, or noisy way.
– ORIGIN coined by Lewis Carroll in *Through the Looking-Glass*; perhaps a blend of GALLOP and TRIUMPH.

galvanic /gal-van-ik/ adjective **1** relating to or involving electric currents produced by chemical action. **2** sudden and dramatic.
– DERIVATIVES **galvanically** adverb.
– ORIGIN French *galvanique*, from the name of the Italian physiologist Luigi *Galvani*, known for his discovery of the twitching of frogs' legs in an electric field.

galvanize (or **galvanise**) /gal-vuh-nyz/ verb **1** make someone do something by shocking or exciting them: *a bang on the door galvanized her into action.* **2** (as adj. **galvanized**) (of iron or steel) coated with a protective layer of zinc.
– DERIVATIVES **galvanization** noun.
– ORIGIN from the name of the Italian physiologist Luigi *Galvani*.

galvanometer /gal-vuh-nom-i-ter/ noun an instrument for detecting and measuring small electric currents.

Gamay /ga-may/ noun a variety of black wine grape native to the Beaujolais district of France.
– ORIGIN from the name of a hamlet in Burgundy, eastern France.

Gambian /gam-bi-uhn/ noun a person from Gambia, a country in West Africa. • adjective relating to Gambia.

gambit noun **1** an opening action or remark intended to gain someone an advantage. **2** (in chess) an opening move in which a player makes a sacrifice for the sake of some compensating advantage.
– ORIGIN Italian *gambetto* 'tripping up'.

gamble verb **1** play games of chance for money. **2** bet a sum of money. **3** take risky action in the hope of a successful result: *they are gambling on a turnaround in the company's fortunes.* • noun a risky undertaking.
– DERIVATIVES **gambler** noun.
– ORIGIN from former *gamel* 'play games', or from the verb GAME¹.

gamboge /gam-bohzh/ noun a resinous substance produced by certain East Asian trees, used as a yellow pigment and in medicine as a laxative.
– ORIGIN Latin *gambaugium*, from *Cambodia*.

gambol verb (**gambols, gambolling, gambolled**; US **gambols, gamboling, gamboled**) run or jump about playfully. • noun an act of gambolling.
– ORIGIN Italian *gambata* 'trip up'.

game¹ noun **1** an activity taken part in for amusement. **2** a form of competitive activity or sport played according to rules. **3** a complete period of play, ending in a final result. **4** a single portion of play, forming a scoring unit within a game. **5** (**games**) a meeting for sporting contests. **6** the equipment used in playing a board game, computer game, etc. **7** informal a type of activity or business: *he was in the restaurant game.* **8** a secret plan or trick. **9** wild mammals or birds hunted for sport or food. • adjective eager and willing to do something new or challenging:

g

they were game for anything. •**verb** play at games of chance for money.
– PHRASES **ahead of the game** ahead of one's competitors. **beat someone at their own game** use someone's own methods to outdo them. **the game is up** the deception or crime is revealed and so cannot succeed. **on the game** Brit. informal working as a prostitute. **play the game** behave in a fair or honourable way.
– DERIVATIVES **gamely** adverb **gameness** noun **gamester** noun.
– ORIGIN Old English, 'amusement, fun'.

game[2] **adjective** dated (of a person's leg) lame.
– ORIGIN unknown.

game bird noun **1** a bird shot for sport or food. **2** a bird of a large group that includes pheasants, grouse, quails, guineafowl, etc.

game fish noun (pl. same) a fish caught by anglers for sport, especially (in fresh water) salmon and trout and (in the sea) marlins, sharks, bass, and mackerel.

gamekeeper noun a person employed to breed and protect game for a large estate.

gamelan /ga-muh-lan/ noun a traditional instrumental group in Java and Bali, including many bronze percussion instruments.
– ORIGIN Javanese.

game plan noun a plan for success in sport, politics, or business.

game point noun (in tennis and other sports) a point which if won by a player or side will also win them the game.

gamer noun a participant in a computer or role-playing game.

game show noun a programme on television in which people compete to win prizes.

gamesmanship noun the art of winning games by using tactics to make one's opponent less confident.
– DERIVATIVES **gamesman** noun.

gamete /gam-eet/ noun a cell which is able to unite with another of the opposite sex in sexual reproduction to form a zygote.
– ORIGIN Greek *gametē* 'wife', *gametēs* 'husband', from *gamos* 'marriage'.

game theory noun the mathematical study of strategies for dealing with competitive situations where the outcome of a participant's choice of action depends critically on the actions of other participants.

gamey adjective variant spelling of GAMY.

gamine /ga-meen/ adjective (of a girl) attractively boyish in appearance. •noun a girl who is attractively boyish in appearance.
– ORIGIN French.

gamma /gam-muh/ noun **1** the third letter of the Greek alphabet (Γ, γ), represented as 'g'. **2** Brit. a third-class mark. •adjective relating to gamma rays.

gamma globulin noun a mixture of blood proteins, mainly immunoglobulins, often given to boost immunity.

gamma rays (also **gamma radiation**) plural noun penetrating electromagnetic radiation of shorter wavelength than X-rays.

gammon noun Brit. **1** ham which has been cured like bacon. **2** the bottom piece of a side of bacon, including a hind leg.
– ORIGIN Old French *gambon*.

gammy adjective Brit. informal (of a person's leg or knee) injured or painful.
– ORIGIN dialect form of GAME[2].

gamut /gam-uht/ noun **1** the complete range or scope of something: *the whole gamut of human emotion.* **2** a complete scale of musical notes; the range of a voice or instrument. **3** historical a musical scale consisting of seven overlapping scales, containing all the recognized notes used in medieval music.
– PHRASES **run the gamut** experience, display, or perform the complete range of something: *they ran the gamut of electronic dance music.*
– ORIGIN from Latin *gamma ut* the lowest musical note in the medieval scale.

gamy (also **gamey**) adjective (**gamier**, **gamiest**) (of meat) having the strong flavour or smell of game when it is slightly decomposed and so ready to cook.
– DERIVATIVES **gaminess** noun.

gander /gan-der/ noun **1** a male goose. **2** informal a look or glance.
– ORIGIN Old English.

gang[1] noun **1** an organized group of criminals or rowdy young people. **2** informal a group of people who regularly meet and do things together. **3** an organized group of people doing manual work. **4** a set of switches, sockets, or other devices grouped together. •verb **1** (**gang together**) form a group or gang. **2** (**gang up**) join together to oppose or intimidate someone: *the other children ganged up on him.*
– ORIGIN Old Norse, 'gait, course, going'.

gang[2] verb Scottish go; proceed.
– ORIGIN Old English.

gang bang noun informal **1** a gang rape. **2** a sexual orgy.

gangbusters plural noun (in phrase **go** (or **like**) **gangbusters**) N. Amer. informal used to refer to great energy, speed, or success: *four-wheel-drive sales are going gangbusters.*

ganger noun Brit. the foreman of a gang of labourers.

gangland noun the world of criminal gangs.

gangling (also **gangly**) adjective (of a person) tall, thin, and awkward in their movements.
– ORIGIN from GANG[2].

ganglion /gang-gli-uhn/ noun (pl. **ganglia** /gang-gli-uh/ or **ganglions**) Anatomy & Medicine **1** a structure containing a number of nerve cells, often forming a swelling on a nerve fibre. **2** a mass of grey matter within the central nervous system. **3** an abnormal but harmless swelling on the sheath of a tendon.
– DERIVATIVES **ganglionic** adjective.
– ORIGIN Greek.

gangmaster noun Brit. a person who organizes and oversees the work of casual manual labourers.

gangplank noun a movable plank used to board or leave a ship or boat.

gang rape noun the rape of one person by a group of other people.

gangrene /gang-green/ noun the death and decomposition of body tissue, caused by an obstructed blood supply or bacterial infection.
– DERIVATIVES **gangrenous** /gang-grin-uhss/ adjective.

g

– ORIGIN Greek *gangraina*.

gangster noun a member of an organized gang of violent criminals.
– DERIVATIVES **gangsterism** noun.

gangway noun **1** Brit. a passage between rows of seats in an auditorium, aircraft, etc. **2** a movable bridge linking a ship to the shore. **3** a raised platform or walkway providing a passage.

ganja /gan-juh/ noun cannabis.
– ORIGIN Hindi.

gannet /gan-nit/ noun **1** a large seabird with mainly white plumage. **2** Brit. informal a greedy person.
– ORIGIN Old English.

gantry noun (pl. **gantries**) a bridge-like overhead structure supporting equipment such as a crane or railway signals.
– ORIGIN probably from **GALLON** + **TREE**.

gaol noun Brit. variant spelling of **JAIL**.

gap noun **1** a break or hole in an object or between two objects. **2** a space, interval, or break.
– DERIVATIVES **gappy** adjective.
– ORIGIN Old Norse, 'chasm'.

gape verb **1** stare with one's mouth open wide in amazement or wonder. **2** (often as adj. **gaping**) be or become wide open: *a gaping wound*. •noun **1** an open-mouthed stare. **2** a wide opening.
– ORIGIN Old Norse.

gap year noun a period taken by a student as a break from education between leaving school and starting a university or college course.

garage /ga-rahj, ga-rij/ noun **1** a building in which a car or other motor vehicle is kept. **2** an establishment which sells fuel or which repairs and sells motor vehicles. **3** (also UK **garage**) a form of pop music incorporating elements of drum and bass, house music, and soul. •verb put or keep a motor vehicle in a garage.
– ORIGIN French, from *garer* 'to shelter'.

garage sale noun chiefly N. Amer. a sale of unwanted goods held in a garage or front garden.

garam masala /ga-ruhm muh-**sah**-luh/ noun a spice mixture used in Indian cookery.
– ORIGIN Urdu, 'pungent spice'.

garb noun clothing of a particular kind: *women in riding garb*. •verb dress in distinctive clothes: *a motorcyclist garbed in black leather*.
– ORIGIN Italian *garbo* 'elegance'.

garbage noun chiefly N. Amer. **1** domestic rubbish or waste. **2** something worthless or meaningless.
– ORIGIN Old French.

garble verb reproduce a message or transmission in a confused and distorted way.
– DERIVATIVES **garbler** noun.
– ORIGIN Arabic, 'sift'.

garçon /**gah**-son/ noun a waiter in a French restaurant.
– ORIGIN French, 'boy'.

Garda /gar-duh/ noun **1** the state police force of the Irish Republic. **2** (pl. **Gardai** /gaar-di/) a member of the Irish police force.
– ORIGIN from Irish *Garda Síochána* 'Civic Guard'.

garden noun **1** chiefly Brit. a piece of ground next to a house, typically with a lawn and flower beds. **2** (**gardens**) ornamental grounds laid out for public enjoyment. •verb cultivate or work in a garden.
– DERIVATIVES **gardener** noun.
– ORIGIN Old French *jardin*.

garden centre noun Brit. a place where plants and gardening equipment are sold.

garden city noun Brit. a new town designed as a whole with much open space and greenery.

gardenia /gar-**dee**-ni-uh/ noun a tree or shrub of warm climates, with large fragrant white or yellow flowers.
– ORIGIN named after the Scottish naturalist Dr Alexander *Garden*.

garden party noun a social event held on a lawn in a garden.

garden-variety adjective N. Amer. of the usual or ordinary type; commonplace.

gargantuan /gar-gan-tyuu-uhn/ adjective very large; enormous.
– ORIGIN from *Gargantua*, a giant in a book by the French writer Rabelais.

gargle verb wash one's mouth and throat with a liquid that is kept in motion by breathing through it. •noun **1** a liquid used for gargling. **2** an act of gargling.
– ORIGIN from Old French *gargouille* 'throat'.

gargoyle /gar-goyl/ noun a spout in the form of a grotesque carved face or figure, set below the roof of a building to carry rainwater away.
– ORIGIN Old French *gargouille* 'throat', also 'gargoyle'.

garibaldi /ga-ri-**borl**-di, ga-ri-**bal**-di/ noun (pl. **garibaldis**) Brit. a thin biscuit containing a compressed layer of currants.
– ORIGIN named after the Italian patriot Giuseppe *Garibaldi*.

garish /gair-ish/ adjective unpleasantly bright and showy; lurid.
– DERIVATIVES **garishly** adverb **garishness** noun.
– ORIGIN unknown.

garland noun a wreath of flowers and leaves, worn on the head or hung as a decoration. •verb decorate someone or something with a garland.
– ORIGIN Old French *garlande*.

garlic noun the bulb of a plant of the onion family, having a strong taste and smell and used as a flavouring in cookery.
– DERIVATIVES **garlicky** adjective.
– ORIGIN Old English, from *gār* 'spear' + *lēac* 'leek'.

garment noun an item of clothing.
– ORIGIN Old French *garnement* 'equipment'.

garner verb gather or collect: *the series has garnered more than thirty five awards*.
– ORIGIN Old French *gernier*.

garnet /gar-nit/ noun a deep red semi-precious stone.
– ORIGIN perhaps from Latin *granatum*, as in *pomum granatum* 'pomegranate', because the garnet is similar in colour to the fruit.

garnish verb decorate food with a small amount of another food: *pheasant breast garnished with truffles*. •noun a small amount of food used to decorate other food.
– ORIGIN Old French *garnir* 'equip, arm'.

garret noun a top-floor or attic room.
– ORIGIN Old French *garite* 'watchtower'.

garrison noun a group of troops stationed in a fortress or town to defend it. • verb provide a place with a garrison.
– ORIGIN Old French *garison*.

garrotte /guh-**rot**/ (also **garotte**; US **garrote**) verb strangle someone with a wire or cord. • noun a wire, cord, or other implement used to strangle someone.
– ORIGIN Spanish *garrote* 'cudgel, garrotte'.

garrulous /**ga**-ryuh-luhss/ adjective excessively talkative.
– DERIVATIVES **garrulity** /guh-**roo**-li-ti/ noun **garrulously** adverb.
– ORIGIN Latin *garrulus*.

garter noun 1 a band worn around the leg to keep up a stocking or sock. 2 N. Amer. a suspender for a sock or stocking.
– ORIGIN Old French *gartier*.

garter snake noun 1 a common harmless North American snake with longitudinal stripes. 2 a venomous burrowing African snake, typically dark with lighter bands.

garter stitch noun knitting in which all of the rows are knitted in plain stitch, rather than alternating with purl rows.

gas noun (pl. **gases** or chiefly US **gasses**) 1 an air-like fluid substance which expands freely to fill any space available. 2 a flammable gas used as a fuel. 3 a gas used as an anaesthetic. 4 N. Amer. informal petrol. 5 (**a gas**) informal an entertaining or amusing person or thing. 6 Mining an explosive mixture of firedamp with air. • verb (**gases, gassing, gassed**) 1 harm or kill someone or something with gas. 2 informal talk excessively about trivial things.
– DERIVATIVES **gasser** noun.
– ORIGIN invented by the Belgian chemist J. B. van Helmont; suggested by Greek *khaos* 'chaos'.

gasbag noun informal a person who talks excessively about trivial things.

gas chamber noun an airtight room that can be filled with poisonous gas to kill people or animals.

gaseous /**gass**-i-uhss/ adjective relating to or having the characteristics of a gas.

gash noun a long, deep cut or wound. • verb make a gash in something.
– ORIGIN from Old French *garcer* 'to chap, crack'.

gasify verb (**gasifies, gasifying, gasified**) convert a solid or liquid into a gas.
– DERIVATIVES **gasification** noun.

gasket /**gass**-kit/ noun a sheet or ring of rubber or other material sealing the junction between two surfaces in an engine or other device.
– ORIGIN perhaps from French *garcette* 'thin rope'.

gaslight noun light from a lamp which uses a jet of burning gas.
– DERIVATIVES **gaslit** adjective.

gas mask noun a protective mask used to cover the face as a defence against poison gas.

gasoline noun N. Amer. petrol.

gasometer /gass-**om**-i-ter/ noun a large tank in which gas is stored before being distributed to consumers.

gasp verb 1 take a quick breath with the mouth open, from pain, breathlessness, or astonishment. 2 (**gasp for**) struggle for air by gasping. 3 (**be gasping for**) Brit. informal be desperate to have: *I'm gasping for a drink!* • noun a sudden quick breath.
– PHRASES **the last gasp** the point of exhaustion, death, or completion.
– ORIGIN Old Norse, 'to yawn'.

gasper noun Brit. informal a cigarette.

gassy adjective (**gassier, gassiest**) resembling or full of gas.

gastric adjective relating to the stomach.
– ORIGIN from Greek *gastēr* 'stomach'.

gastric flu noun a short-lived stomach disorder of unknown cause.

gastric juice noun an acid fluid produced by the stomach glands, which helps digestion.

gastritis /gas-**try**-tiss/ noun inflammation of the lining of the stomach.

gastroenteritis /gas-troh-en-tuh-**ry**-tis/ noun inflammation of the stomach and intestines, causing diarrhoea and vomiting.

gastroenterology /gas-troh-en-tuh-**rol**-uh-ji/ noun the branch of medicine which deals with disorders of the stomach and intestines.
– DERIVATIVES **gastroenterologist** noun.
– ORIGIN from Greek *gastēr* 'stomach' and *enteron* 'intestine'.

gastronome /**gas**-truh-nohm/ noun a gourmet.

gastronomy /gass-**tron**-uh-mi/ noun the practice or art of choosing, cooking, and eating good food.
– DERIVATIVES **gastronomic** adjective.
– ORIGIN Greek *gastronomia*.

gastropod /**gass**-truh-pod/ noun Zoology any of a large class of molluscs including snails, slugs, and whelks.
– ORIGIN from Greek *gastēr* 'stomach' + *pous* 'foot'.

gastropub noun Brit. a pub that specializes in serving high-quality food.

gasworks plural noun (treated as sing.) a place where gas is manufactured and processed.

gate noun 1 a hinged barrier used to close an opening in a wall, fence, or hedge. 2 an exit from an airport building to an aircraft. 3 a hinged or sliding barrier for controlling the flow of water on a waterway. 4 the number of people who pay to attend a sports event. 5 an electric circuit with an output which depends on the combination of several inputs. • verb Brit. confine a pupil or student to school or college.
– DERIVATIVES **gated** adjective.
– ORIGIN Old English.

-gate combining form in nouns referring to a scandal, especially one involving a cover-up: *Irangate*.
– ORIGIN suggested by the *Watergate* scandal in the US, 1972.

gateau /**gat**-oh/ noun (pl. **gateaus** or **gateaux** /**gat**-ohz/) chiefly Brit. a rich cake with layers of cream or fruit.
– ORIGIN French.

gatecrash verb enter a party without an invitation or ticket.
– DERIVATIVES **gatecrasher** noun.

gatefold noun an oversized folded page in a

book or magazine, intended to be opened out for reading.

gatehouse noun **1** a house standing by the gateway to a country estate. **2** historical a room over a city or palace gate, often used as a prison.

gatekeeper noun an attendant at a gate.

gateleg table noun a table with hinged legs that may be swung out from the centre to support folding leaves.

gatepost noun a post on which a gate is hinged or against which it shuts.

gateway noun **1** an opening in a wall or fence that can be closed by a gate. **2** (**gateway to**) a means of entering somewhere or achieving something: *college education is a gateway to the middle class.* **3** a device used to connect two different computer networks, especially a connection to the Internet.

gather verb **1** come or bring together; assemble or collect. **2** increase in speed, force, etc. **3** understand something to be the case as a result of information or evidence: *I gather he's resigned.* **4** collect plants or fruits for food. **5** harvest a crop. **6** draw together or towards oneself: *she gathered the child in her arms.* **7** pull fabric together in a series of folds by drawing thread through it. •noun (**gathers**) a part of a garment that is gathered.
– DERIVATIVES **gatherer** noun.
– ORIGIN Old English.

gathering noun a group of people assembled for a purpose.

gauche /gohsh/ adjective unsophisticated and awkward when dealing with others.
– DERIVATIVES **gauchely** adverb **gaucheness** noun.
– ORIGIN French, 'left'.

gaucherie /goh-shuh-ri/ noun awkward or unsophisticated ways.
– ORIGIN French.

gaucho /gow-choh/ noun (pl. **gauchos**) a cowboy from the South American plains.
– ORIGIN Latin American Spanish.

gaudy /gaw-di/ adjective (**gaudier, gaudiest**) tastelessly bright or showy: *gaudy multicoloured shorts.*
– DERIVATIVES **gaudily** adverb **gaudiness** noun.
– ORIGIN probably from Old French *gaudir* 'rejoice'.

gauge /gayj/ (chiefly US also **gage**) noun **1** an instrument that measures and gives a visual display of the amount, level, or contents of something. **2** the thickness, size, or capacity of a wire, tube, bullet, etc., especially as a standard measure. **3** the distance between the rails of a railway track. •verb **1** judge or assess a situation or mood: *it is difficult to gauge his true feelings.* **2** estimate or measure the amount or level of something. **3** measure the dimensions of an object with a gauge.
– DERIVATIVES **gauger** noun.
– ORIGIN Old French.

Gaul /gawl/ noun a person from the ancient European region of Gaul.
– ORIGIN Latin *Gallus*.

Gaulish noun the Celtic language of the ancient Gauls. •adjective relating to the ancient Gauls.

Gaullist /goh-list/ noun a supporter of the

principles and policies of the French statesman Charles de Gaulle, characterized chiefly by conservatism and nationalism. •adjective relating to Gaullists or Gaullism.
– DERIVATIVES **Gaullism** noun.

gaunt adjective **1** lean and haggard, especially through suffering or age. **2** (of a place) grim or desolate.
– DERIVATIVES **gauntly** adverb **gauntness** noun.
– ORIGIN unknown.

gauntlet[1] noun **1** a strong glove with a long, loose wrist. **2** a leather glove with steel plates, worn as part of medieval armour.
– PHRASES **take up** (or **throw down**) **the gauntlet** accept (or issue) a challenge. [from the medieval custom of issuing a challenge by throwing one's gauntlet to the ground; a person accepted the challenge by picking it up.]
– ORIGIN Old French *gantelet*.

gauntlet[2] noun (in phrase **run the gauntlet**) **1** go through an intimidating crowd or experience in order to reach a goal. **2** historical undergo the military punishment of receiving blows while running between two rows of men with sticks.
– ORIGIN from Swedish *gata* 'lane' + *lopp* 'course', influenced by **GAUNTLET**[1].

gauss /rhymes with house/ noun (pl. same or **gausses**) a unit of magnetic flux density, equal to one ten-thousandth of a tesla.
– ORIGIN named after the German mathematician Karl Friedrich *Gauss*.

gauze /gawz/ noun **1** thin transparent fabric. **2** thin, loosely woven cloth used for dressing wounds. **3** (also **wire gauze**) a fine wire mesh.
– DERIVATIVES **gauzy** adjective.
– ORIGIN French *gaze*.

gave past of GIVE.

gavel /gav-uhl/ noun a small hammer with which an auctioneer, judge, or chair of a meeting hits a surface to call for attention or order.
– ORIGIN unknown.

gavial noun variant spelling of **GHARIAL**.

gavotte /guh-vot/ noun a medium-paced French dance, popular in the 18th century.
– ORIGIN Provençal *gavoto* 'dance of the mountain people'.

gawk verb stare in a stupid or rude way. •noun an awkward or shy person.
– DERIVATIVES **gawker** noun.
– ORIGIN perhaps from Old Norse, 'to heed'.

gawky adjective nervously awkward and ungainly.
– DERIVATIVES **gawkily** adverb **gawkiness** noun.

gawp verb Brit. informal stare in a stupid or rude way.
– DERIVATIVES **gawper** noun.
– ORIGIN perhaps from GAPE.

gay adjective (**gayer, gayest**) **1** (especially of a man) homosexual. **2** relating to homosexuals. **3** dated light-hearted and carefree. **4** dated brightly coloured; showy. •noun a homosexual person, especially a man.
– DERIVATIVES **gayness** noun.
– ORIGIN Old French *gai*.

gaydar noun informal the supposed ability of homosexuals to recognize one another by

interpreting very slight indications.
– ORIGIN from **GAY** + **RADAR**.

gayety noun US variant spelling of **GAIETY**.

gaze verb look steadily and intently. • noun a steady intent look.
– DERIVATIVES **gazer** noun.
– ORIGIN perhaps related to **GAWK**.

gazebo /guh-zee-boh/ noun (pl. **gazebos**) a summer house or similar structure with a wide view of the surrounding area.
– ORIGIN perhaps from **GAZE**, in imitation of Latin future tenses ending in -ebo.

gazelle noun a small antelope with curved horns and white underparts.
– ORIGIN French.

gazette noun a journal or newspaper, especially the official journal of an organization.
– ORIGIN from Venetian gazeta de la novità 'a halfpennyworth of news'.

gazetteer /ga-zuht-teer/ noun a list of place names published as a book or part of a book.
– ORIGIN Italian gazzetta 'gazette'.

gazpacho /guhs-pach-oh/ noun (pl. **gazpachos**) a cold Spanish soup made chiefly from tomatoes and peppers.
– ORIGIN Spanish.

gazump /guh-zump/ verb Brit. informal make a higher offer for a house than someone whose offer has already been accepted by the seller and thus succeed in buying the property.
– DERIVATIVES **gazumper** noun.
– ORIGIN Yiddish, 'overcharge'.

GB abbreviation 1 Great Britain. 2 (also **Gb**) Computing gigabyte(s) or gigabit(s).

GBH abbreviation Brit. grievous bodily harm.

GC abbreviation George Cross.

GCE abbreviation General Certificate of Education.

GCHQ abbreviation Government Communications Headquarters.

GCSE abbreviation (in the UK except Scotland) General Certificate of Secondary Education (the lower of the two main levels of the GCE exam).

Gd symbol the chemical element gadolinium.

GDP abbreviation gross domestic product.

GDR abbreviation historical German Democratic Republic.

Ge symbol the chemical element germanium.

gear noun 1 (**gears**) a set of toothed wheels that connect the engine to the wheels of a vehicle and work together to alter its speed. 2 a particular setting of gears in a vehicle: I never leave third gear. 3 informal equipment, possessions, or clothing. • verb 1 design or adjust gears to give a particular speed or power output. 2 adapt something for a particular purpose: an activity programme geared towards senior citizens. 3 (**gear someone/thing up**) prepare someone or something to do something.
– PHRASES **in** (or **out of**) **gear** with a gear (or no gear) engaged.
– ORIGIN Scandinavian.

gearbox noun a set of gears with its casing, especially in a motor vehicle; the transmission.

gearing noun 1 the set or arrangement of gears in a machine. 2 Brit. the ratio of a company's loan capital (debt) to the value of its ordinary shares (equity).

gear lever (also **gearstick**) noun Brit. a lever used to engage or change gear in a motor vehicle.

gearwheel noun 1 a toothed wheel in a set of gears. 2 (on a bicycle) a cogwheel driven directly by the chain.

gecko /gek-koh/ noun (pl. **geckos** or **geckoes**) a lizard of warm regions, with adhesive pads on the feet.
– ORIGIN Malay.

gee[1] (also **gee whiz**) exclamation informal, chiefly N. Amer. a mild expression of surprise, enthusiasm, or sympathy.
– ORIGIN perhaps an abbreviation of **JESUS**.

gee[2] exclamation (**gee up**) a command to a horse to go faster. • verb (**gees, geeing, geed**) (**gee someone up**) encourage someone to put more effort into something.
– ORIGIN unknown.

geek /geek/ noun informal 1 a person who is unfashionable or awkward in the company of other people. 2 an obsessive enthusiast: a computer geek.
– DERIVATIVES **geekdom** noun **geeky** adjective.
– ORIGIN from English dialect geck 'fool'.

geese plural of **GOOSE**.

geezer /gee-zer/ noun Brit. informal a man.
– ORIGIN from a dialect pronunciation of earlier guiser 'mummer'.

Geiger counter /gy-ger/ noun a device for measuring radioactivity.
– ORIGIN named after the German physicist Hans Geiger.

geisha /gay-shuh/ noun (pl. same or **geishas**) a Japanese hostess trained to entertain men with conversation, dance, and song.
– ORIGIN Japanese, 'entertainer'.

gel[1] /jel/ noun 1 a jelly-like substance, especially one used in cosmetic or medicinal products. 2 Chemistry a semi-solid suspension of a solid dispersed in a liquid. • verb (**gels, gelling, gelled**) 1 Chemistry form into a gel. 2 smooth or style the hair with gel.
– ORIGIN from **GELATIN**.

gel[2] /jel/ (also **jell**) verb 1 (of jelly or a similar substance) set or become firmer. 2 take definite form or begin to work well: we had new players and it took some time for the team to gel.

gelatin /jel-uh-tin/ (also **gelatine** /jel-uh-teen/) noun a clear water-soluble protein obtained from animal bones, used in food preparation, in photographic processing, and in glue.
– DERIVATIVES **gelatinous** /ji-lat-i-nuhss/ adjective.
– ORIGIN French gélatine.

geld verb castrate a male animal.
– ORIGIN from an Old Norse word meaning 'barren'.

gelding noun a castrated male horse.

gelid /jel-id/ adjective chiefly literary very cold; icy.
– ORIGIN Latin gelidus.

gelignite /jel-ig-nyt/ noun a high explosive made from nitroglycerine and nitrocellulose in a base of wood pulp and sodium.

– ORIGIN probably from **GELATIN** + Latin *lignis* 'wood'.

gelt /gelt/ noun informal money.
– ORIGIN German *Geld*.

gem noun **1** a precious or semi-precious stone, especially one that has been cut and polished. **2** an outstanding person or thing: *a gem of a book*.
– ORIGIN Latin *gemma* 'bud, jewel'.

Gemini /jem-in-ee/ noun a constellation (the Twins) and sign of the zodiac, which the sun enters about 21 May.
– DERIVATIVES **Geminian** /je-mi-**nee**-uhn/ noun & adjective.
– ORIGIN Latin, 'twins'.

gemsbok /**khemz**-bok, **khems**-bok/ noun a large African antelope with black-and-white head markings and long straight horns.
– ORIGIN Dutch, 'chamois'.

gemstone noun a gem used in a piece of jewellery.

gen /jen/ Brit. informal noun information. • verb (**gens, genning, genned**) (**gen up on**) find out about something.
– ORIGIN perhaps from *general information*.

-gen combining form referring to a substance that produces something: *allergen*.
– ORIGIN from Greek *genēs* '-born, of a specified kind'.

gendarme /**zhon**-darm/ noun a paramilitary police officer in French-speaking countries.
– ORIGIN French, from *gens d'armes* 'men of arms'.

gendarmerie /zhon-**dah**-muh-ri/ noun **1** the headquarters of a force of gendarmes. **2** a force of gendarmes.

gender noun **1** Grammar a class (usually masculine, feminine, common, or neuter) into which nouns and pronouns are placed in some languages. **2** the state of being male or female (with reference to social or cultural differences). **3** the members of one or other sex.
– DERIVATIVES **gendered** adjective.
– ORIGIN Old French *gendre*.

> **USAGE:** The words **gender** and **sex** both have the sense 'the state of being male or female', but they are used in different ways: **sex** usually refers to biological differences, while **gender** tends to refer to cultural or social ones.

gene /jeen/ noun a distinct sequence of DNA forming part of a chromosome, by which offspring inherit characteristics from a parent.
– ORIGIN German *Gen*.

genealogy /jee-ni-**al**-uh-ji/ noun (pl. **genealogies**) **1** a line of descent traced continuously from an ancestor. **2** the study of lines of descent.
– DERIVATIVES **genealogical** adjective **genealogist** noun.
– ORIGIN from Greek *genea* 'race, generation' + *logos* 'account'.

gene pool noun the stock of different genes in a particular species of animal or plant.

genera plural of **GENUS**.

general adjective **1** affecting or concerning all or most people or things; not specialized or limited: *books of general interest*. **2** involving only the main features or elements; not detailed. **3** chief or principal: *the general manager*. • noun **1** a commander of an army, or an army officer ranking above lieutenant general. **2** short for **LIEUTENANT GENERAL** or **MAJOR GENERAL**.
– PHRASES **in general 1** usually; mainly. **2** as a whole.
– ORIGIN Latin *generalis*.

general anaesthetic noun an anaesthetic that affects the whole body and causes a loss of consciousness.

general election noun the election of representatives to a legislature from constituencies throughout the country.

generalissimo /jen-uh-ruh-**lis**-i-moh/ noun (pl. **generalissimos**) the commander of a combined military force consisting of army, navy, and air force units.
– ORIGIN from Italian, 'having greatest authority'.

generalist noun a person who is competent in several different fields or activities.

generality noun (pl. **generalities**) **1** a statement or principle that is general rather than specific: *you're talking in generalities*. **2** the quality or state of being general. **3** (**the generality**) the majority.

generalize (or **generalise**) verb **1** make a general or broad statement based on specific cases: *you cannot generalize about the actions of one set of employees*. **2** make something more common or more widely applicable. **3** (as adj. **generalized**) (of a disease) affecting much or all of the body; not localized.
– DERIVATIVES **generalizable** adjective **generalization** noun.

generally adverb **1** in most cases. **2** without regard to details or exceptions. **3** by or to most people; widely.

general meeting noun a meeting open to all members of an organization.

general practitioner noun a doctor based in a local community, who treats patients with minor or long-lasting illnesses.
– DERIVATIVES **general practice** noun.

general-purpose adjective having a range of potential uses or functions.

general staff noun the staff assisting a military commander.

general strike noun a strike of workers in all or most industries.

generate verb create or produce: *the article generated much reader interest*.
– ORIGIN Latin *generare*.

generation noun **1** all of the people born and living at about the same time: *he was one of the cleverest entrepreneurs of his generation*. **2** the average period in which children grow up and have children of their own (reckoned as about thirty years). **3** a set of members of a family regarded as a single stage in descent. **4** a group of people of similar age involved in an activity: *a new generation of actors*. **5** a stage in the development of a product: *the next generation of mobile phones*. **6** the production or creation of something.
– DERIVATIVES **generational** adjective.

generation gap noun a difference in

attitudes between people of different generations, leading to lack of understanding.

Generation X noun the generation born between the mid 1960s and the mid 1970s, typically seen as lacking a sense of direction and feeling that they have no role in society.
– DERIVATIVES **Generation Xer** noun.

generative adjective capable of production or reproduction.

generator noun **1** a person or thing that generates something. **2** a dynamo or similar machine for converting mechanical energy into electricity.

generic /ji-**ne**-rik/ adjective **1** referring to a class, group, or genus; not specific: *Indians are fond of saag* (*a generic term for leafy greens*). **2** (of goods) having no brand name.
– DERIVATIVES **generically** adverb.
– ORIGIN from Latin *genus* 'stock, race'.

generosity /jen-uh-**ros**-it-i/ noun **1** the quality of being kind and generous. **2** the fact of being plentiful or large: *diners cannot complain about the generosity of portions.*

generous adjective **1** freely giving more than is necessary or expected. **2** kind towards others. **3** larger or more plentiful than is usual: *a generous helping of rice.*
– DERIVATIVES **generously** adverb.
– ORIGIN Latin *generosus* 'noble, magnanimous'.

genesis /**jen**-i-siss/ noun **1** the origin of something. **2** (**Genesis**) the first book of the Bible, which includes the story of the creation of the world.
– ORIGIN Greek, 'generation, creation'.

gene therapy noun the introduction of normal genes into cells in place of missing or defective ones in order to correct genetic disorders.

genetic adjective **1** relating to genes or heredity. **2** relating to genetics. **3** relating to the origin of something.
– DERIVATIVES **genetical** adjective **genetically** adverb.
– ORIGIN from **GENESIS**.

genetically modified adjective (of a plant or animal) containing genetic material that has been artificially altered so as to produce a desired characteristic.

genetic code noun the means by which DNA and RNA molecules carry genetic information.

genetic engineering noun the deliberate modification of a plant or animal by altering its genetic material.

genetic fingerprinting noun the analysis of DNA from samples of body tissues or fluids in order to identify individuals.

genetics plural noun (treated as sing.) the study of the way in which inherited characteristics are passed from one generation to another.
– DERIVATIVES **geneticist** noun.

genial adjective friendly and cheerful.
– DERIVATIVES **geniality** noun **genially** adverb.
– ORIGIN Latin *genialis* 'nuptial, productive'.

-genic combining form **1** producing or produced by: *carcinogenic.* **2** well suited to: *photogenic.*

genie /**jee**-ni/ noun (pl. **genii** /**jee**-ni-I/ or **genies**) (in Arabian folklore) a spirit, especially one capable of granting wishes when summoned.
– ORIGIN Latin *genius* (see **GENIUS**).

genii plural of **GENIE**.

genital adjective referring to the human or animal reproductive organs. • noun (**genitals**) a person or animal's external reproductive organs.
– DERIVATIVES **genitally** adverb.
– ORIGIN Latin *genitalis*.

genitalia /jen-i-**tay**-li-uh/ plural noun formal or technical a person or animal's genitals.
– ORIGIN Latin.

genitive noun the grammatical case of a word that is used to show possession or close association.
– ORIGIN from Latin *genitivus casus* 'case of production or origin'.

genito-urinary adjective relating to the genital and urinary organs.

genius /**jee**-ni-uhss/ noun (pl. **geniuses**) **1** exceptional intellectual power or other natural ability: *a painter of genius.* **2** an exceptionally intelligent or able person. **3** the prevalent character of a nation, period, etc.
– ORIGIN Latin, also in the sense 'spirit present at one's birth'.

genocide /**jen**-uh-syd/ noun the deliberate killing of a very large number of people from a particular ethnic group or nation.
– DERIVATIVES **genocidal** adjective.
– ORIGIN from Greek *genos* 'race' + -**CIDE**.

genome /**jee**-nohm/ noun **1** the full set of the chromosomes of an animal, plant, or other life form. **2** the complete set of genetic material present in an animal, plant, or other life form.
– ORIGIN blend of **GENE** and **CHROMOSOME**.

genomics /ji-**noh**-miks, ji-**no**-miks/ plural noun the branch of biology concerned with the structure, function, evolution, and mapping of genomes.
– DERIVATIVES **genomic** adjective.

genotype /**jen**-uh-typ/ noun the genetic make-up of an individual animal, plant, or other life form.
– DERIVATIVES **genotypic** adjective.

genre /**zhon**-ruh/ noun a style or category of art or literature. • adjective referring to a style of painting showing scenes from ordinary life.
– ORIGIN French, 'a kind'.

gent noun informal **1** a gentleman. **2** (**the Gents**) Brit. a men's public toilet.

genteel adjective polite and refined in an affected or exaggerated way.
– DERIVATIVES **genteelly** adverb.
– ORIGIN French *gentil* 'well-born'.

gentian /**jen**-sh'n/ noun a plant of temperate and mountainous regions with violet or blue trumpet-shaped flowers.
– ORIGIN Latin *gentiana*.

gentian violet noun a synthetic violet dye used as an antiseptic.

Gentile /**jen**-tyl/ adjective not Jewish. • noun a person who is not Jewish.
– ORIGIN Latin *gentilis* 'relating to a family or nation'.

gentility noun polite and refined behaviour, especially as typical of a high social class: *the ideal of Victorian gentility was to distance oneself from the taint of commerce.*
– ORIGIN from Old French *gentil* 'high-born, noble'.

gentle adjective (**gentler, gentlest**) **1** mild or kind; not rough or violent: *a gentle and loving mother.* **2** not harsh or severe. **3** old use noble or courteous.
– DERIVATIVES **gentleness** noun **gently** adverb.
– ORIGIN Old French *gentil* 'high-born, noble'.

gentlefolk plural noun old use people of noble birth or good social position.

gentleman noun (pl. **gentlemen**) **1** a courteous or honourable man. **2** a man of good social position. **3** (in polite or formal use) a man.
– DERIVATIVES **gentlemanly** adjective.

gentleman's agreement noun an arrangement which is based on trust rather than on a legal contract.

gentlewoman noun (pl. **gentlewomen**) old use a woman of noble birth or good social position.

gentrify verb (**gentrifies, gentrifying, gentrified**) renovate or improve a house or district so that it is in keeping with middle-class taste.
– DERIVATIVES **gentrification** noun **gentrifier** noun.

gentry noun (**the gentry**) people of good social position, specifically the class next below the nobility.
– ORIGIN Old French *genterie*.

genuflect /jen-yuu-flekt/ verb lower the body briefly by bending one knee to the ground in worship or as a sign of respect.
– DERIVATIVES **genuflection** noun.
– ORIGIN Latin *genuflectere*.

genuine adjective **1** truly what it is said to be; authentic: *a genuine leather strap.* **2** able to be trusted; sincere.
– DERIVATIVES **genuinely** adverb **genuineness** noun.
– ORIGIN Latin *genuinus*.

genus /jee-nuhss/ noun (pl. **genera** /jen-uh-ruh/) **1** a category in the classification of animals and plants that ranks above species and below family, shown by a capitalized Latin name, e.g. *Leo.* **2** a class of things which have common characteristics.
– ORIGIN Latin, 'birth, race, stock'.

geo- /jee-oh/ combining form relating to the earth: *geology.*
– ORIGIN from Greek *gē* 'earth'.

geocentric adjective **1** having the earth as the centre, as in former astronomical systems. Compare with **HELIOCENTRIC**. **2** Astronomy measured from or considered in relation to the centre of the earth.

geode /jee-ohd/ noun **1** a small cavity in rock lined with crystals or other mineral matter. **2** a rock containing such a cavity.
– ORIGIN from Greek *geōdēs* 'earthy'.

geodesic /jee-oh-dess-ik/ adjective **1** referring to the shortest possible line between two points on a sphere or other curved surface. **2** (of a dome) constructed from struts which follow geodesic lines and form an open framework of triangles and polygons.

geodesy /ji-od-i-si/ noun the branch of mathematics concerned with the shape and area of the earth.
– DERIVATIVES **geodesist** noun.
– ORIGIN Greek *geōdaisia*.

geodetic /jee-oh-de-tik/ adjective relating to geodesy, especially as applied to land surveying.

geographical adjective relating to geography.
– DERIVATIVES **geographic** adjective **geographically** adverb.

geography noun **1** the study of the physical features of the earth and of human activity as it relates to these. **2** the way in which the physical features of a place are arranged: *the rugged geography of British Columbia.*
– DERIVATIVES **geographer** noun.

geology noun **1** the science which deals with the physical structure and substance of the earth. **2** the geological features of a district.
– DERIVATIVES **geologic** adjective **geological** adjective **geologically** adverb **geologist** noun.

geomancy /jee-oh-man-si/ noun the art of siting buildings so as to encourage good fortune.
– DERIVATIVES **geomancer** noun **geomantic** adjective.

geometric /ji-uh-met-rik/ adjective **1** relating to geometry. **2** (of a design) consisting of regular lines and shapes.
– DERIVATIVES **geometrical** adjective **geometrically** adverb.

geometric mean noun the central number in a geometric progression (e.g. 9 in 3, 9, 27).

geometric progression (also **geometric series**) noun a sequence of numbers with a constant ratio between each number and the one before (e.g. 1, 3, 9, 27, 81).

geometry /ji-om-uh-tri/ noun (pl. **geometries**) **1** the branch of mathematics concerned with the properties and relations of points, lines, surfaces, and solids. **2** the shape and relative arrangement of the parts of something.
– DERIVATIVES **geometrician** noun.
– ORIGIN Greek *geometria*.

geomorphology /jee-oh-mor-fol-uh-ji/ noun the study of the physical features of the surface of the earth and their relation to its geological structures.
– DERIVATIVES **geomorphological** adjective **geomorphologist** noun.

geophysics plural noun (treated as sing.) the physics of the earth.
– DERIVATIVES **geophysical** adjective **geophysicist** noun.

geopolitical adjective relating to politics, especially international relations, as influenced by geographical factors.
– DERIVATIVES **geopolitics** noun.

Geordie noun Brit. informal a person from Tyneside.
– ORIGIN from the man's name *George.*

georgette /jor-jet/ noun a thin silk or crêpe dress material.
– ORIGIN named after the French dressmaker *Georgette* de la Plante.

Georgian[1] adjective **1** relating to or characteristic of the reigns of the British Kings George I–IV (1714–1830). **2** relating to British neoclassical architecture of this period.

Georgian[2] noun **1** a person from the country of Georgia. **2** the official language of Georgia.
• adjective relating to Georgians or Georgian.

g

geostationary adjective (of an artificial satellite) orbiting in such a way that it appears to be stationary above a fixed point on the earth's surface.

geostrategic adjective relating to the strategy required in dealing with international political problems.

geosynchronous /jee-oh-sing-kruh-nuhss/ adjective another term for **synchronous** (in sense 2).

geothermal adjective relating to or produced by the internal heat of the earth.

geranium noun 1 a garden plant with red, pink, or white flowers; a pelargonium. 2 a plant or small shrub of a genus that comprises the cranesbills.
– ORIGIN Greek *geranion*.

gerbera /**jer**-buh-ruh/ noun a tropical plant of the daisy family, with large brightly coloured flowers.
– ORIGIN named after the German naturalist Traugott *Gerber*.

gerbil noun a mouse-like desert rodent, often kept as a pet.
– ORIGIN Latin *gerbillus* 'little jerboa'.

geriatric /je-ri-at-rik/ adjective 1 relating to old people. 2 informal very old or out of date; decrepit. • noun an old person, especially one receiving special care.
– ORIGIN from Greek *gēras* 'old age' + *iatros* 'doctor'.

USAGE: **Geriatric** is the normal term used to refer to the health care of old people (*a geriatric ward*). When used outside such situations, it carries overtones of being decrepit and can be offensive if used with reference to people.

geriatrics plural noun (treated as sing. or pl.) the branch of medicine or social science concerned with the health and care of old people.
– DERIVATIVES **geriatrician** noun.

germ noun 1 a microorganism, especially one which causes disease. 2 a portion of an organism capable of developing into a new one or part of one. 3 an initial stage from which something may develop: *the germ of an idea*.
– ORIGIN Latin *germen* 'seed, sprout'.

German noun 1 a person from Germany. 2 the language of Germany, Austria, and parts of Switzerland. • adjective relating to Germany or German.
– DERIVATIVES **Germanize** (or **Germanise**) verb.

germane /jer-**mayn**/ adjective relevant to a subject under consideration: *considerations germane to a foreign policy decision*.
– ORIGIN Latin *germanus* 'genuine, of the same parents'.

Germanic adjective 1 referring to the language family that includes English, German, Dutch, Frisian, and the Scandinavian languages. 2 referring to the peoples of ancient northern and western Europe speaking such languages. 3 characteristic of Germans or Germany. • noun 1 the Germanic languages. 2 the ancient language from which the Germanic languages developed.

germanium /jer-**may**-ni-uhm/ noun a shiny

grey chemical element with semiconducting properties.
– ORIGIN from Latin *Germanus* 'German'.

German measles plural noun (usu. treated as sing.) another term for **rubella**.

German shepherd noun a large breed of dog often used as guard dogs or for police work; an Alsatian.

germ cell noun Biology a cell which is able to unite with another of the opposite sex in sexual reproduction; a gamete.

germicide noun a substance which destroys harmful microorganisms.
– DERIVATIVES **germicidal** adjective.

germinal adjective 1 relating to a germ cell or embryo. 2 in the earliest stage of development: *a germinal idea*. 3 providing material for future development.
– ORIGIN from Latin *germen* 'sprout, seed'.

germinate verb (of a seed or spore) begin to grow and put out shoots after a period of being dormant.
– DERIVATIVES **germination** noun.
– ORIGIN Latin *germinare* 'sprout forth, bud'.

germ warfare noun the use of disease-spreading microorganisms as a military weapon.

Geronimo /juh-**ron**-i-moh/ exclamation used to express exhilaration when leaping or moving quickly.
– ORIGIN used as a slogan by American paratroopers, by association with the Apache chief *Geronimo*.

gerontocracy /je-ruhn-**tok**-ruh-si/ noun 1 a state, society, or group governed by old people. 2 government based on rule by old people.
– DERIVATIVES **gerontocrat** noun **gerontocratic** adjective.

gerontology /je-ruhn-**tol**-uh-ji/ noun the scientific study of old age and old people.
– DERIVATIVES **gerontological** adjective **gerontologist** noun.

gerrymander verb alter the boundaries of a constituency so as to favour one political party in an election.
– ORIGIN from Governor Elbridge *Gerry* of Massachusetts + **salamander**, from the similarity between a salamander and the shape of a voting district created when he was in office.

gerund /je-ruhnd/ noun Grammar a verb form which functions as a noun, in English ending in *-ing* (e.g. *asking* in *do you mind my asking you?*).
– ORIGIN Latin *gerundum*.

gesso /jess-oh/ noun a hard compound of plaster of Paris or whiting in glue, used in sculpture.
– ORIGIN Italian.

gestalt /guh-**shtahlt**/ noun Psychology an organized whole that is perceived as more than the sum of its parts.
– ORIGIN German, 'form, shape'.

Gestapo /ge-**stah**-poh/ noun the German secret police under Nazi rule.
– ORIGIN German, from *Geheime Staatspolizei* 'secret state police'.

gestation /je-**stay**-sh'n/ noun 1 the process of

developing in the womb between conception and birth. **2** the development of something over a period of time: *the gestation of a musical can take months.*
– DERIVATIVES **gestate** verb **gestational** adjective.
– ORIGIN from Latin *gestare* 'carry, carry in the womb'.

gesticulate /jess-tik-yuu-layt/ verb gesture dramatically instead of or to emphasize speech.
– DERIVATIVES **gesticulation** noun.
– ORIGIN Latin *gesticulari*.

gesture noun **1** a movement of part of the body to express an idea or meaning. **2** an action performed to convey one's feelings or intentions: *the prisoners were released as a gesture of goodwill.* **3** an action performed for show in the knowledge that it will have no effect. •verb make a gesture.
– DERIVATIVES **gestural** adjective.
– ORIGIN Latin *gestura*.

get verb (**gets**, **getting**, **got**; past part. **got**, N. Amer. **gotten**) **1** come to have or hold something. **2** succeed in obtaining, achieving, or experiencing something. **3** experience or suffer something. **4** pick up, fetch, or deal with something. **5** reach a particular state or condition: *she'd got thinner.* **6** move to or from a specified position or place. **7** persuade someone to do something. **8** begin to be or do something, especially gradually or by chance: *we got talking.* **9** catch or thwart someone. **10** travel by or catch a form of transport. **11** informal punish, injure, or kill someone. **12** used with past participle to form the passive: *the cat got drowned.*
– PHRASES **get something across** manage to communicate an idea clearly. **get at 1** reach or gain access to somewhere. **2** informal imply something. **3** Brit. informal criticize someone. **get away** escape or leave. **get away with** escape blame or punishment for something. **get back at** take revenge on someone. **get by** manage with difficulty to live. **get down to** begin to do or give serious attention to something. **get off** informal escape a punishment. **get off with** Brit. informal have a sexual encounter with someone. **get on 1** make progress with a task. **2** chiefly Brit. have a friendly relationship. **3** (**be getting on**) informal be old or comparatively old. **get over** recover from an illness or an unpleasant experience. **get something over** manage to communicate something. **get something over with** deal with an unpleasant but necessary task promptly. **get one's own back** informal have one's revenge. **get round 1** persuade someone to do or allow something. **2** deal successfully with a problem. **get round to** find the time to deal with a task. **get through 1** pass or endure a difficult experience or period. **2** chiefly Brit. use up a large amount or number of something. **3** make contact by telephone. **4** succeed in communicating with someone. **getting on for** chiefly Brit. almost a specified time, age, or amount. **get to** informal annoy or upset someone. **get together** gather socially or to cooperate. **get up** rise from bed after sleeping. **get up to** Brit. informal be involved in something.
– ORIGIN Old Norse, 'obtain, beget, guess'.

getaway noun **1** an escape, especially after committing a crime. **2** a short holiday.

get-out noun Brit. a means of avoiding something.

get-together noun an informal social gathering.

get-up noun informal an outfit, especially an unusual one.

gewgaw /gyoo-gaw/ noun a showy object, especially one that is useless or worthless.
– ORIGIN unknown.

geyser /gee-zer, gy-zer/ noun **1** a hot spring in which water intermittently boils, sending a tall column of water and steam into the air. **2** Brit. a gas-fired water heater.
– ORIGIN named after a spring in Iceland.

Ghanaian /gah-nay-uhn/ noun a person from Ghana. •adjective relating to Ghana.

gharial /gar-i-ahl, gur-i-ahl/ (also **gavial** /gay-vi-uhl/) noun a large fish-eating crocodile, native to the Indian subcontinent.
– ORIGIN Hindi.

ghastly adjective (**ghastlier**, **ghastliest**) **1** causing great horror or fear. **2** informal very unpleasant. **3** very white.
– DERIVATIVES **ghastliness** noun.
– ORIGIN Old English, 'terrify'.

ghat /gaht/ noun **1** (in the Indian subcontinent) a flight of steps leading down to a river. **2** (in the Indian subcontinent) a mountain pass.
– ORIGIN Hindi.

GHB abbreviation (sodium) gamma-hydroxybutyrate, a designer drug with anaesthetic properties.

ghee /gee/ noun clarified butter used in Indian cooking.
– ORIGIN from Sanskrit, 'sprinkled'.

gherkin /ger-kin/ noun a small pickled cucumber.
– ORIGIN Greek *angourion* 'cucumber'.

ghetto /get-toh/ noun (pl. **ghettos** or **ghettoes**) **1** a part of a city occupied by people of a particular race, nationality, or ethnic group. **2** historical the Jewish quarter in a city.
– ORIGIN perhaps from Italian *getto* 'foundry' (because the first ghetto was established on the site of a foundry in Venice), or from Italian *borghetto* 'small borough'.

ghetto blaster noun informal a large portable radio and cassette or CD player.

ghettoize (also **ghettoise**) verb put in an isolated or segregated place, group, or situation: *they were black and quickly ghettoized in northern cities.*
– DERIVATIVES **ghettoization** noun.

ghillie noun variant spelling of GILLIE.

ghost noun **1** an apparition of a dead person which is believed to appear to the living. **2** a faint trace: *the ghost of a smile.* •verb act as ghost writer of a book.
– PHRASES **give up the ghost** die or stop functioning.
– ORIGIN Old English, 'spirit, soul'.

ghosting noun the appearance of a secondary image on a television or other display screen.

ghostly adjective (**ghostlier**, **ghostliest**) relating to or like a ghost; eerie.

ghost town noun a town with few or no remaining inhabitants.

ghost writer noun a person employed to write

material for another person who is the named author.

– DERIVATIVES **ghostwrite** verb.

ghoul /gool/ noun 1 an evil spirit, especially one supposed to rob graves and feed on dead bodies. 2 a person with an unhealthy interest in death or disaster.

– DERIVATIVES **ghoulish** adjective **ghoulishly** adverb **ghoulishness** noun.

– ORIGIN Arabic.

GHQ abbreviation General Headquarters.

GHz (also **gHz**) abbreviation gigahertz.

GI noun (pl. **GIs**) a private soldier in the US army.

– ORIGIN abbreviation of *government* (or *general*) *issue* (referring to military equipment).

giant noun 1 an imaginary or mythical being of human form but superhuman size. 2 an unusually tall or large person or thing. 3 a star of relatively great size and luminosity. • adjective very large; gigantic.

– DERIVATIVES **giantess** noun.

– ORIGIN Greek *gigas*.

giant-killer noun a person or team that defeats a much more powerful opponent.

– DERIVATIVES **giant-killing** noun.

gibber /jib-ber/ verb speak rapidly and in a way that is difficult to understand.

– ORIGIN imitating the sound.

gibberish /jib-buh-rish/ noun speech or writing that is meaningless or difficult to understand.

gibbet /jib-bit/ noun historical 1 a gallows. 2 an upright post with an arm on which the bodies of executed criminals were left hanging.

– ORIGIN Old French *gibet* 'little staff, cudgel, gallows'.

gibbon noun a small ape with long, powerful arms, native to the forests of SE Asia.

– ORIGIN from an Indian dialect word.

gibbous /gib-buhss/ adjective (of the moon) having the illuminated part greater than a semicircle and less than a circle.

– ORIGIN Latin *gibbosus*.

gibe /jyb/ noun & verb variant spelling of JIBE¹.

giblets /jib-lits/ plural noun the liver, heart, gizzard, and neck of a chicken or other fowl.

– ORIGIN Old French *gibelet* 'game bird stew'.

giddy adjective (**giddier**, **giddiest**) 1 having or causing a sensation of spinning and losing one's balance; dizzy. 2 excitable and not interested in serious things.

– DERIVATIVES **giddily** adverb **giddiness** noun.

– ORIGIN Old English, 'insane'.

giddy-up exclamation said to make a horse start moving or go faster.

– ORIGIN from a pronunciation of *get up*.

GIF noun Computing 1 a format for image files. 2 a file in this format.

– ORIGIN from the initial letters of *graphic interchange format*.

gift noun 1 a thing given willingly to someone without payment; a present. 2 a natural ability or talent: *she has a gift for maths.* 3 informal a very easy task. • verb 1 give something as a gift. 2 (**gift someone with**) provide someone with an ability or talent. 3 (as adj. **gifted**) having exceptional talent or ability.

– DERIVATIVES **giftedness** noun.

– ORIGIN Old Norse.

gift token (also **gift voucher**) noun Brit. a voucher which can be exchanged for goods in a shop, given as a present.

gift wrap noun decorative paper for wrapping gifts. • verb (**gift-wrap**) wrap a gift in decorative paper.

gig¹ /gig/ informal noun 1 a live performance by a musician or other performer. 2 a task or assignment: *spotting whales seemed like a great gig.* • verb (**gigs, gigging, gigged**) perform a gig or gigs.

– ORIGIN unknown.

gig² /gig/ noun chiefly historical a light two-wheeled carriage pulled by one horse.

– ORIGIN probably from former *gig* 'a flighty girl'.

giga- /gig-uh, jig-uh/ combining form 1 referring to a factor of one thousand million (10^9). 2 Computing referring to a factor of 2^{30}.

– ORIGIN from Greek *gigas* 'giant'.

gigabit /gig-uh-bit, jig-uh-bit/ noun a unit of information stored in a computer equal to one thousand million (10^9) or (strictly) 2^{30} bits.

gigabyte /gig-uh-byt, jig-uh-byt/ noun a unit of information stored in a computer equal to one thousand million (10^9) or (strictly) 2^{30} bytes.

gigaflop noun Computing a unit of computing speed equal to one thousand million floating-point operations per second.

gigahertz noun a unit of frequency equivalent to one thousand million hertz.

gigantic adjective very great in size or extent.

– DERIVATIVES **gigantically** adverb.

– ORIGIN from Latin *gigas* 'giant'.

gigantism noun chiefly Biology unusual or abnormal largeness.

gigawatt noun a unit of power equal to one thousand million watts.

giggle verb laugh lightly in a nervous or silly way. • noun 1 a nervous or silly laugh. 2 Brit. informal an amusing person or thing.

– DERIVATIVES **giggler** noun **giggly** adjective.

– ORIGIN imitating the sound.

gigolo /jig-uh-loh/ noun (pl. **gigolos**) a young man paid by an older woman to be her escort or lover.

– ORIGIN French, 'male dancing partner'.

gigot /ji-guht/ noun a leg of mutton or lamb.

– ORIGIN French.

gild verb 1 cover something thinly with gold. 2 (as adj. **gilded**) wealthy and privileged: *gilded youth.*

– PHRASES **gild the lily** try to improve what is already beautiful or excellent. [misquotation of a line from Shakespeare's *King John* VI. ii.]

– DERIVATIVES **gilder** noun **gilding** noun.

– ORIGIN Old English.

gilet /zhi-lay/ noun (pl. **gilets** pronunc. same) a light sleeveless padded jacket.

– ORIGIN French, 'waistcoat'.

gill¹ /gil/ noun 1 the breathing organ of fish and some amphibians. 2 the vertical plates on the underside of mushrooms and many toadstools. • verb gut or clean a fish.

– PHRASES **to the gills** until completely full.

– DERIVATIVES **gilled** adjective.

– ORIGIN Old Norse.

gill² /jil/ **noun** a unit of measure for liquids, equal to a quarter of a pint.
– ORIGIN Old French *gille* 'measure or container for wine'.

gillie /gil-li/ (also **ghillie**) **noun** (in Scotland) a person who assists someone who is hunting or fishing for sport.
– ORIGIN Scottish Gaelic *gille* 'lad, servant'.

gillyflower /jil-li-flow-er/ (also **gilliflower**) **noun** any of a number of fragrant flowers, such as the wallflower.
– ORIGIN Old French *gilofre, girofle*.

gilt **adjective** covered thinly with gold leaf or gold paint. ● **noun 1** gold leaf or gold paint applied in a thin layer to a surface. **2** (**gilts**) fixed-interest loan securities issued by the UK government.
– ORIGIN from GILD.

gilt-edged **adjective** referring to stocks or securities (such as gilts) that are regarded as very reliable investments.

gimbal /jim-buhl/ (also **gimbals**) **noun** a device for keeping an instrument such as a compass horizontal in a moving vessel or aircraft.
– ORIGIN Old French *gemel* 'twin'.

gimcrack /jim-krak/ **adjective** showy but flimsy or poorly made. ● **noun** a cheap and showy ornament.
– DERIVATIVES **gimcrackery** noun.
– ORIGIN unknown.

gimlet /gim-lit/ **noun** a small T-shaped tool with a screw-tip for boring holes.
– ORIGIN Old French *guimbelet* 'little drill'.

gimmick **noun** something intended to attract attention rather than fulfil a useful purpose.
– DERIVATIVES **gimmickry** noun **gimmicky** adjective.
– ORIGIN unknown.

gin¹ **noun 1** a clear alcoholic spirit distilled from grain or malt and flavoured with juniper berries. **2** (also **gin rummy**) a form of the card game rummy.
– ORIGIN abbreviation of *genever*, a kind of Dutch gin.

gin² **noun 1** a machine for separating cotton from its seeds. **2** a trap for catching small game.
– ORIGIN Old French *engin* 'engine'.

ginger **noun 1** a hot spice made from the rhizome of a SE Asian plant. **2** a light reddish-yellow colour. ● **verb 1** (**ginger someone/thing up**) make someone or something more lively or exciting. **2** flavour something with ginger.
– DERIVATIVES **gingery** adjective.
– ORIGIN Latin *gingiber*.

ginger ale **noun** a fizzy soft drink flavoured with ginger.

ginger beer **noun** a fizzy drink made by fermenting a mixture of ginger and syrup.

gingerbread **noun** cake made with treacle or syrup and flavoured with ginger.
– PHRASES **take the gilt off the gingerbread** Brit. make something no longer attractive or desirable.

ginger group **noun** Brit. an active and more radical group within a political party or movement.

gingerly **adverb** in a careful or cautious way.
– ORIGIN perhaps from Old French *gensor*

'delicate'.

ginger nut **noun** Brit. a hard ginger-flavoured biscuit.

gingham /ging-uhm/ **noun** lightweight cotton cloth with a check pattern.
– ORIGIN from a Malay word meaning 'striped'.

gingivitis /jin-ji-vy-tiss/ **noun** inflammation of the gums.
– ORIGIN from Latin *gingiva* 'gum'.

ginkgo /ging-koh/ (also **gingko**) **noun** (pl. **ginkgos** or **ginkgoes**) a Chinese tree with fan-shaped leaves and yellow flowers.
– ORIGIN Chinese.

ginormous **adjective** Brit. informal very large.
– ORIGIN blend of GIANT and ENORMOUS.

ginseng /jin-seng/ **noun** the tuber of an east Asian and North American plant, believed to have medicinal properties.
– ORIGIN from Chinese 'man' + the name of a kind of herb.

gip **noun** variant spelling of GYP¹.

Gipsy **noun** variant spelling of GYPSY.

giraffe **noun** (pl. same or **giraffes**) a large African mammal with a very long neck and legs, the tallest living animal.
– ORIGIN French *girafe*, from Arabic.

gird **verb** (past and past part. **girded** or **girt**) literary encircle or secure something with a belt or band.
– PHRASES **gird (up) one's loins** prepare and strengthen oneself for something difficult.
– ORIGIN Old English.

girder **noun** a large metal beam used in building bridges and large buildings.
– ORIGIN from GIRD.

girdle **noun 1** a belt or cord worn round the waist. **2** a woman's elasticated corset extending from waist to thigh. ● **verb** encircle something with a girdle or belt.
– ORIGIN Old English, related to GIRD and GIRTH.

girl **noun 1** a female child. **2** a young woman. **3** a person's girlfriend.
– DERIVATIVES **girlhood** noun **girlish** adjective **girlishly** adverb.
– ORIGIN perhaps related to German *gör* 'child'.

girlfriend **noun 1** a person's regular female companion in a romantic or sexual relationship. **2** a woman's female friend.

Girl Guide **noun** Brit. a member of the Guides Association.

girlie (also **girly**) **adjective 1** often derogatory typical of or resembling a girl. **2** depicting nude or partially nude young women in erotic poses: *girlie magazines*. ● **noun** (pl. **girlies**) informal a girl or young woman.

giro **noun** (pl. **giros**) **1** a system of electronic credit transfer involving banks, post offices, and public utilities. **2** Brit. a social security payment or cheque by giro.
– ORIGIN Italian, 'circulation (of money)'.

girt past participle of GIRD.

girth **noun 1** the measurement around the middle of something. **2** a band attached to a saddle and fastened around a horse's belly.
– ORIGIN Old Norse.

gist /jist/ **noun** the main or general meaning of a speech or piece of writing.
– ORIGIN from Old French *cest action gist* 'this action lies', meaning that there were

sufficient grounds to proceed in a legal case.

git noun Brit. informal an unpleasant or contemptible person.
– ORIGIN variant of GET in the dialect sense 'a stupid or unpleasant person'.

gîte /zheet/ noun a furnished holiday house in France.
– ORIGIN French.

give verb (**gives, giving, gave**; past part. **given**) 1 cause someone to receive or have something. 2 cause to experience or suffer: *you gave me a fright.* 3 carry out an action or make a sound. 4 present an appearance or impression. 5 state or put forward information. 6 alter in shape under pressure rather than resist or break. 7 concede that someone deserves something. • noun the capacity of something to bend under pressure.
– PHRASES **give oneself airs** act pretentiously or snobbishly. **give and take** willingness on both sides of a relationship to make concessions. **give something away** reveal something secret. **give the game away** accidentally reveal something secret. **give in** stop fighting or arguing. **give or take** —— informal to within a specified amount. **give out** stop operating. **give something off/out** produce and send out a smell, heat, etc. **give rise to** cause something to happen. **give up** stop making an effort and accept that one has failed. **give someone up** hand over a wanted person. **give something up** stop doing, eating, or drinking something regularly.
– DERIVATIVES **giver** noun.
– ORIGIN Old English.

giveaway noun informal 1 something that reveals the truth about something: *the shape of the parcel was a dead giveaway.* 2 something given free, especially for promotional purposes.

given past participle of GIVE. adjective 1 specified or stated. 2 (**given to**) inclined to. • preposition taking into account. • noun an established fact or situation.

given name noun another term for FIRST NAME.

gizmo noun (pl. **gizmos**) informal a clever device; a gadget.
– ORIGIN unknown.

gizzard noun a muscular, thick-walled part of a bird's stomach for grinding food.
– ORIGIN Old French.

GLA abbreviation Greater London Authority.

glacé /gla-say/ adjective (of fruit) preserved in sugar.
– ORIGIN French, 'iced'.

glacé icing noun icing made with icing sugar and water.

glacial /glay-si-uhl/ adjective 1 relating to ice, especially in the form of glaciers. 2 very cold or unfriendly.
– DERIVATIVES **glacially** adverb.
– ORIGIN Latin *glacialis* 'icy'.

glacial period noun an ice age.

glaciated /glay-si-ay-tid/ adjective covered or having been covered by glaciers or ice sheets.

glaciation noun 1 the state or result of being covered by glaciers or ice sheets. 2 an ice age.

glacier /gla-si-er, glay-si-er/ noun a slowly moving mass of ice formed by the accumulation of snow on mountains or near the poles.
– ORIGIN French, from *glace* 'ice'.

glad adjective (**gladder, gladdest**) 1 feeling pleasure or happiness. 2 grateful: *he'll be glad of a short break at home.* 3 causing happiness.
– DERIVATIVES **gladly** adverb **gladness** noun.
– ORIGIN Old English, 'bright, shining'.

gladden verb make someone glad.

glade noun an open space in a wood or forest.
– ORIGIN unknown.

glad-hand verb chiefly N. Amer. (especially of a politician) greet or welcome someone warmly.
– DERIVATIVES **glad-hander** noun.

gladiator noun (in ancient Rome) a man trained to fight with weapons against other men or wild animals in an arena.
– DERIVATIVES **gladiatorial** adjective.
– ORIGIN Latin.

gladiolus /glad-i-oh-luhss/ noun (pl. **gladioli** /glad-i-oh-ly/) a plant with sword-shaped leaves and tall stems of brightly coloured flowers.
– ORIGIN Latin.

glad rags plural noun informal clothes for a party or special occasion.

Gladstone bag noun a bag having two equal compartments joined by a hinge.
– ORIGIN named after the British Liberal statesman W. E. *Gladstone.*

Glam. abbreviation Glamorgan.

glam informal adjective glamorous. • verb (**glams, glamming, glammed**) (**glam someone up**) make oneself look glamorous.

glamorize (or **glamorise**) verb make something, especially something bad, seem attractive or desirable.
– DERIVATIVES **glamorization** noun.

glamorous adjective excitingly attractive and appealing.
– DERIVATIVES **glamorously** adverb.

glamour (US also **glamor**) noun an attractive and exciting quality. • adjective referring to erotic photography or publications: *a glamour model.*
– ORIGIN first meaning 'magic': from GRAMMAR, with reference to the occult practices associated with learning in medieval times.

glance verb 1 take a brief or hurried look. 2 hit something and bounce off at an angle. • noun a brief or hurried look.
– DERIVATIVES **glancing** adjective.
– ORIGIN Old French *glacier* 'to slip'.

gland noun 1 an organ of the body which produces particular chemical substances. 2 a lymph node.
– ORIGIN from Latin *glandulae* 'throat glands'.

glandular adjective relating to or affecting a gland or glands.

glandular fever noun Brit. an infectious disease caused by a virus that causes swelling of the lymph glands and prolonged lack of energy.

glans /glanz/ noun (pl. **glandes** /glan-deez/) the rounded part forming the end of the penis or clitoris.
– ORIGIN Latin, 'acorn'.

glare verb 1 stare in an angry way. 2 shine with a dazzling light. 3 (as adj. **glaring**) highly

obvious: *a glaring error*. • **noun 1** an angry stare. **2** dazzling light. **3** overwhelming public attention: *his visit will be conducted in the full glare of publicity*.
– DERIVATIVES **glaringly** adverb **glary** adjective.
– ORIGIN from Dutch and German *glaren* 'to gleam or glare'.

glasnost /glaz-nosst/ noun (in the former Soviet Union) the policy or practice of more open government.
– ORIGIN Russian *glasnost* 'the fact of being public, openness'.

glass noun **1** a hard, brittle, transparent substance made by fusing sand with soda and lime. **2** a drinking container made of glass. **3** chiefly Brit. a mirror. **4** a lens or optical instrument, in particular a monocle or a magnifying lens. • **verb** cover or enclose something with glass.
– DERIVATIVES **glassful** noun **glassware** noun.
– ORIGIN Old English.

glass-blowing noun the craft of making glassware by blowing semi-molten glass through a long tube.

glass ceiling noun a situation in which certain groups, especially women and minorities, find that progress in a profession is blocked although there are no official barriers to advancement.

glasses plural noun a pair of lenses set in a frame that rests on the nose and ears, used to correct defective eyesight.

glass fibre noun chiefly Brit. a strong material containing embedded glass filaments for reinforcement.

glasshouse noun Brit. a greenhouse.

glasspaper noun paper covered with powdered glass, used for smoothing and polishing.

glass wool noun glass in the form of fine fibres used for packing and insulation.

glassy adjective (**glassier, glassiest**) **1** resembling glass. **2** (of a person's eyes or expression) showing no interest or liveliness.
– DERIVATIVES **glassily** adverb.

Glaswegian /glaz-wee-j'n/ noun a person from Glasgow. • **adjective** relating to Glasgow.

glaucoma /glaw-koh-muh/ noun a condition of increased pressure within the eyeball, causing gradual loss of sight.
– ORIGIN Greek *glaukōma*.

glaucous /glaw-kuhss/ adjective technical or literary **1** dull greyish-green or blue in colour. **2** covered with a powdery bloom like that on grapes.
– ORIGIN Greek *glaukos*.

glaze verb **1** fit panes of glass into a window frame or similar structure. **2** enclose or cover something with glass. **3** cover something with a glaze. **4** lose brightness and liveliness: *transactions complex enough to make an accountant's eyes glaze over*. • **noun 1** a glass-like substance fused on to the surface of pottery to form an impervious decorative coating. **2** a liquid such as milk or beaten egg, used to form a shiny coating on food. **3** Art a thin topcoat of transparent paint used to modify the tone of an underlying colour.
– DERIVATIVES **glazing** noun.
– ORIGIN from GLASS.

glazier /glay-zi-er/ noun a person whose trade is fitting glass into windows and doors.

gleam verb shine brightly, especially with reflected light. • **noun 1** a faint or brief light. **2** a brief or faint sign of a quality or emotion: *there was a gleam of mischief in her eyes*.
– PHRASES **a gleam in someone's eye** see EYE.
– DERIVATIVES **gleaming** adjective.
– ORIGIN Old English.

glean verb **1** collect information or objects gradually from various sources. **2** historical gather leftover grain after a harvest.
– DERIVATIVES **gleaner** noun.
– ORIGIN Latin *glennare*.

gleanings plural noun things gathered from various sources.

glebe /gleeb/ noun historical a piece of land serving as part of a clergyman's benefice and providing income.
– ORIGIN Latin *gleba* 'clod, land, soil'.

glee noun **1** great delight. **2** a song for men's voices in three or more parts.
– ORIGIN Old English, 'entertainment, music, fun'.

gleeful adjective very happy, especially in a gloating way.
– DERIVATIVES **gleefully** adverb.

glen noun a narrow valley, especially in Scotland or Ireland.
– ORIGIN Scottish Gaelic and Irish *gleann*.

glib adjective (**glibber, glibbest**) using words easily, but without much thought or sincerity.
– DERIVATIVES **glibly** adverb **glibness** noun.
– ORIGIN Germanic.

glide verb **1** move with a smooth, quiet, continuous motion. **2** fly without power or in a glider. • **noun** an instance of gliding.
– DERIVATIVES **gliding** noun.
– ORIGIN Old English.

glider noun a light aircraft designed to fly without using an engine.

glimmer verb shine faintly with a wavering light. • **noun 1** a faint or wavering light. **2 a** faint sign of a feeling or quality: *a glimmer of hope*.
– DERIVATIVES **glimmering** adjective & noun.
– ORIGIN probably Scandinavian.

glimpse noun a brief or partial view. • **verb** see someone or something briefly or partially.
– ORIGIN probably Germanic.

glint verb give out or reflect small flashes of light. • **noun 1** a small flash of reflected light. **2** an expression of an emotion in a person's eyes: *the unmistakable glint of interest in her eye*.
– ORIGIN probably Scandinavian.

glissade /gli-sahd, gli-sayd/ noun **1** a slide down a steep slope of snow or ice, typically on the feet with the support of an ice axe. **2** Ballet a gliding movement. • **verb** slide down a slope of snow or ice.
– ORIGIN from French *glisser* 'to slip, slide'.

glissando /glis-san-doh/ noun (pl. **glissandi** /glis-san-di/ or **glissandos**) Music a continuous slide upwards or downwards between two notes.
– ORIGIN Italian.

glisten verb (of something wet or greasy) shine or sparkle. • **noun** a sparkling light

g

reflected from something wet.
– ORIGIN Old English.

glister literary **verb** sparkle; glitter. •**noun** a sparkle.
– ORIGIN probably from German *glistern* or Dutch *glisteren.*

glitch noun informal **1** a sudden fault or failure of equipment. **2** an unexpected setback in a plan.
– ORIGIN unknown.

glitter verb 1 shine with a bright, shimmering reflected light. **2** (as adj. **glittering**) impressively successful or glamorous: *a glittering career.* •**noun 1** bright, shimmering reflected light. **2** tiny pieces of sparkling material used for decoration. **3** an attractive but superficial quality: *a stylist's life is not all glitter and glamour.*
– DERIVATIVES **glittery** adjective.
– ORIGIN Old Norse.

glitterati /glit-tuh-**rah**-ti/ **plural noun** informal fashionable people involved in show business or other glamorous activity.
– ORIGIN blend of **GLITTER** and **LITERATI.**

glitz noun informal showy but superficial display.
– DERIVATIVES **glitzy** adjective.
– ORIGIN from **GLITTER,** suggested by **RITZY.**

gloaming noun (**the gloaming**) literary twilight; dusk.
– ORIGIN Old English.

gloat verb be smug or pleased about one's own success or another person's misfortune.
– DERIVATIVES **gloater** noun **gloating** adjective & noun.
– ORIGIN uncertain.

glob noun informal a lump of a semi-liquid substance.
– ORIGIN perhaps a blend of **BLOB** and **GOB²**.

global adjective 1 relating to the whole world; worldwide. **2** relating to or including the whole of something, or of a group of things. **3** Computing operating or applying through the whole of a file or program.
– DERIVATIVES **globally** adverb.

globalism noun the operation or planning of economic and foreign policy on a global basis.
– DERIVATIVES **globalist** noun & adjective.

globalization (or **globalisation**) **noun** the process by which businesses start operating on a global scale.
– DERIVATIVES **globalize** verb.

global village noun the world considered as a single community linked by telecommunications.

global warming noun the gradual increase in the overall temperature of the earth's atmosphere due to the greenhouse effect caused by increased levels of pollutants.

globe noun 1 a spherical or rounded object. **2** (**the globe**) the earth. **3** a spherical representation of the earth.
– DERIVATIVES **globose** adjective.
– ORIGIN Latin *globus.*

globetrotter noun informal a person who travels widely.
– DERIVATIVES **globetrotting** noun & adjective.

globular adjective 1 globe-shaped; spherical. **2** composed of globules.

globule noun a small round particle of a substance; a drop.

– ORIGIN Latin *globulus* 'little globe'.

globulin /glob-yuu-lin/ **noun** any of a group of simple proteins found in blood serum.

glockenspiel /glok-uhn-shpeel/ **noun** a musical percussion instrument containing tuned metal pieces which are struck with small hammers.
– ORIGIN German, 'bell play'.

gloom noun 1 partial or total darkness. **2** a state of depression or despondency.
– ORIGIN unknown.

gloomy adjective (**gloomier, gloomiest**) **1** dark or poorly lit. **2** causing or feeling depression or despondency: *despite the gloomy forecasts, a political crisis looks unlikely.*
– DERIVATIVES **gloomily** adverb **gloominess** noun.

gloop noun informal sloppy or sticky semi-fluid matter.
– DERIVATIVES **gloopy** adjective.
– ORIGIN uncertain.

glorify verb (**glorifies, glorifying, glorified**) **1** represent something as admirable, especially undeservedly. **2** (as adj. **glorified**) made to appear more important or special than is the case: *he was nothing more than a glorified janitor.* **3** praise and worship God.
– DERIVATIVES **glorification** noun.

glorious adjective 1 having or bringing glory: *his glorious career with Chelsea is coming to an end.* **2** very beautiful or impressive. **3** very enjoyable.
– DERIVATIVES **gloriously** adverb **gloriousness** noun.

glory noun (pl. **glories**) **1** great fame or honour won by notable achievements: *he began his pursuit of Olympic glory with the 100 metres.* **2** magnificence; great beauty. **3** a very beautiful or impressive thing. **4** worship and thanksgiving offered to God. •**verb** (**glory in**) take great pride or pleasure in: *he gloried in the power of public office.*
– ORIGIN Latin *gloria.*

glory box noun Austral./NZ a box in which a woman stores clothes and household items in preparation for marriage.

glory hole noun informal an untidy room or cupboard used for storage.

Glos. abbreviation Gloucestershire.

gloss¹ noun 1 the shine on a smooth surface. **2** (also **gloss paint**) a type of paint which dries to a shiny surface. **3** an attractive appearance that conceals something ordinary or unpleasant: *the gloss of suburban life.* •**verb 1** apply a glossy substance to something. **2** (**gloss over**) try to conceal or pass over something by mentioning it briefly or misleadingly.
– ORIGIN unknown.

gloss² noun a translation or explanation of a word, phrase, or passage. •**verb** provide a translation or explanation of a word, phrase, or passage.
– ORIGIN Old French *glose.*

glossary noun (pl. **glossaries**) an alphabetical list of words relating to a specific subject, dialect, or written work, with explanations.
– ORIGIN Latin *glossarium.*

glossolalia /glos-uh-**lay**-li-uh/ **noun** the phenomenon of apparently speaking in an

unknown language during religious worship, regarded as a gift of the Holy Spirit.
– ORIGIN from Greek *glōssa* 'language, tongue' + *lalia* 'speech'.

glossy adjective (**glossier**, **glossiest**) **1** shiny and smooth. **2** superficially attractive and stylish. • noun (pl. **glossies**) informal a magazine printed on glossy paper with many colour photographs.
– DERIVATIVES **glossily** adverb **glossiness** noun.

glottal adjective relating to the glottis (part of the larynx).

glottal stop noun a speech sound made by opening and closing the glottis, sometimes used instead of a properly sounded *t*.

glottis /glot-tiss/ noun the part of the larynx consisting of the vocal cords and the slit-like opening between them.
– ORIGIN Greek.

glove noun **1** a covering for the hand with separate parts for each finger and the thumb. **2** a padded protective covering for the hand used in boxing and other sports.
– PHRASES **fit like a glove** (of clothes) fit exactly.
– DERIVATIVES **gloved** adjective.
– ORIGIN Old English.

glove compartment (also **glovebox**) noun a small storage compartment in the dashboard of a motor vehicle.

glove puppet noun Brit. a cloth puppet fitted on the hand and worked by the fingers.

glow verb **1** give out a steady light without flame. **2** look or feel warm or pink: *she was glowing with excitement*. **3** look very pleased or happy. • noun **1** a steady light. **2** a feeling or appearance of warmth. **3** a strong feeling of pleasure or well-being: *a glow of pride*.
– ORIGIN Old English.

glower /glow-er/ verb have an angry or sullen expression. • noun an angry or sullen look.
– ORIGIN perhaps from Scandinavian.

glowing adjective expressing great praise: *a glowing report*.
– DERIVATIVES **glowingly** adverb.

glow-worm noun a type of beetle, the wingless female of which glows to attract males.

gloxinia /glok-sin-i-uh/ noun a tropical American plant with large, velvety, bell-shaped flowers.
– ORIGIN named after the German botanist Benjamin P. *Gloxin*.

glucose /gloo-kohz/ noun a simple sugar which is an important energy source in living organisms.
– ORIGIN Greek *gleukos* 'sweet wine'.

glue noun an adhesive substance used for sticking objects or materials together. • verb (**glues**, **gluing** or **glueing**, **glued**) **1** fasten or join things with glue. **2** (**be glued to**) informal be paying very close attention to something.
– DERIVATIVES **gluey** adjective.
– ORIGIN Latin *gluten*.

glue ear noun Brit. blocking of the Eustachian tube in the ear by mucus, occurring especially in children.

glue-sniffing noun the practice of inhaling intoxicating fumes from some types of glue.

glug informal verb (**glugs**, **glugging**, **glugged**) pour or drink liquid with a hollow gurgling sound. • noun a hollow gurgling sound.
– DERIVATIVES **gluggable** adjective.
– ORIGIN imitating the sound.

glum adjective (**glummer**, **glummest**) sad or dejected.
– DERIVATIVES **glumly** adverb.
– ORIGIN variant of **GLOOM**.

glut noun an excessively abundant supply. • verb (**gluts**, **glutting**, **glutted**) supply or fill something to excess.
– ORIGIN probably from Latin *gluttire* 'to swallow'.

gluten /gloo-tuhn/ noun a substance containing a number of proteins that is found in wheat and other cereal grains.
– ORIGIN Latin, 'glue'.

gluteus /gloo-ti-uhss/ noun (pl. **glutei** /gloo-ti-I/) any of three muscles in each buttock which move the thigh.
– DERIVATIVES **gluteal** adjective.
– ORIGIN Greek *gloutos* 'buttock'.

glutinous /gloo-ti-nuhss/ adjective **1** like glue in texture; sticky. **2** excessively sentimental; sickly: *glutinous ballads*.
– ORIGIN Latin *glutinosus*.

glutton noun **1** an excessively greedy eater. **2** a person who is very eager for something difficult or challenging: *I was a glutton for punishment*.
– DERIVATIVES **gluttonous** adjective.
– ORIGIN Latin *glutto*.

gluttony noun the habit or fact of eating excessively.

glycerine /gli-suh-reen/ (US **glycerin** /gli-suh-rin/) noun another term for **GLYCEROL**.
– ORIGIN French *glycerin*.

glycerol /gli-suh-rol/ noun a colourless, sweet liquid formed as a by-product in soap manufacture, used in making cosmetics, explosives, and antifreeze.

glycogen /gly-kuh-juhn/ noun a substance deposited in bodily tissues as a store of glucose.

glycolysis /gly-kol-is-iss/ noun the breakdown of glucose by enzymes, releasing energy.

glyph /glif/ noun **1** a hieroglyphic character. **2** Architecture an ornamental carved groove, as on a Greek frieze. **3** Computing a small graphic symbol.
– ORIGIN Greek *gluphē* 'carving'.

glyphosate /gly-fos-ayt/ noun a synthetic compound which is a systemic herbicide.

GM abbreviation **1** general manager. **2** genetically modified. **3** George Medal. **4** (of a school) grant-maintained.

gm abbreviation gram(s).

G-man noun informal US an FBI agent.
– ORIGIN probably an abbreviation of *Government man*.

GMO abbreviation genetically modified organism.

GMT abbreviation Greenwich Mean Time.

gnarled adjective knobbly, rough, and twisted, especially with age.
– ORIGIN from former *knarre* 'rugged rock or stone'.

gnarly adjective (**gnarlier**, **gnarliest**) **1** gnarled.

g

2 N. Amer. informal dangerous, challenging, or unpleasant.

gnash /nash/ verb grind one's teeth together, especially as a sign of anger.
– ORIGIN perhaps from Old Norse.

gnashers plural noun Brit. informal teeth.

gnat /nat/ noun a small two-winged fly resembling a mosquito.
– ORIGIN Old English.

gnaw /naw/ verb **1** bite at or nibble something persistently. **2** cause persistent anxiety or pain: *his conscience gnawed at him.*
– ORIGIN Old English.

gneiss /nyss/ noun a metamorphic rock with a banded or layered structure, typically consisting of feldspar, quartz, and mica.
– ORIGIN German.

gnocchi /nyok-ki/ plural noun (in Italian cooking) small dumplings made from potato, semolina, or flour.
– ORIGIN Italian.

gnome noun **1** an imaginary creature like a tiny man, supposed to guard the earth's treasures underground. **2** a small garden ornament in the form of a bearded man with a pointed hat.
– DERIVATIVES **gnomish** adjective.
– ORIGIN Latin *gnomus.*

gnomic /noh-mik/ adjective clever but often difficult to understand: *I had to have the gnomic response interpreted for me.*
– DERIVATIVES **gnomically** adverb.
– ORIGIN from Greek *gnōmē* 'thought, opinion'

gnosis /noh-sis/ noun knowledge of spiritual mysteries.
– ORIGIN Greek, 'knowledge'.

Gnosticism /noss-ti-si-z'm/ noun a heretical movement of the 2nd-century Christian Church, teaching that mystical knowledge (gnosis) of the supreme divine being enabled the human spirit to be redeemed.
– DERIVATIVES **Gnostic** adjective & noun.

GNP abbreviation gross national product.

gnu /noo/ noun a large African antelope with a long head and a beard and mane.
– ORIGIN from Khoikhoi and San.

GNVQ abbreviation General National Vocational Qualification.

go verb (**goes, going, went**; past part. **gone**)
1 move to or from a place. **2** pass into or be in a specified state: *my mind went blank.* **3** (often **go into**) start an activity or course of action: *she decided to go into business.* **4** engage in an activity on a regular basis. **5** lie or extend in a certain direction. **6** come to an end; cease to exist. **7** disappear or be used up. **8** (of time) pass. **9** pass time in a particular way: *they went for months without talking.* **10** have a particular outcome. **11** (**be going to be/do**) used to express a future tense. **12** function or operate. **13** be matching. **14** be acceptable or permitted: *anything goes.* **15** fit into or be regularly kept in a particular place. **16** make a specified sound. **17** informal say. **18** (**go by/under**) be known or called by a specified name. •noun (pl. **goes**) informal, chiefly Brit. **1** an attempt: *give it a go.* **2** a turn to do or use something. **3** a single item, action, or spell of activity: *the remedies cost up to five quid a go.* **4** spirit or energy.
– PHRASES **go about** begin or carry on with an

activity. **go along with** agree to something. **go at** energetically attack or tackle something. **go back on** fail to keep a promise. **go down 1** be defeated in a contest. **2** obtain a specified reaction: *the show went down well.* **go for 1** decide on something. **2** attempt to gain something. **3** attack someone. **go in for 1** Brit. enter a contest as a competitor. **2** like or regularly take part in something. **going!, gone!** an auctioneer's announcement that bidding is closing or closed. **go into 1** investigate or enquire into something. **2** (of a whole number) be capable of dividing another, typically without a remainder. **go off 1** (of a bomb or gun) explode or fire. **2** (of food) begin to decompose. **3** Brit. informal begin to dislike someone or something. **go on 1** continue or persevere. **2** take place. **go out 1** stop shining or burning. **2** (of the tide) ebb. **3** carry on a regular romantic relationship with someone. **go over** examine or check the details of something. **go round** be sufficient to supply everybody present. **go through 1** undergo a difficult experience. **2** examine something carefully. **3** informal use up or spend something. **go under** become bankrupt. **go without** suffer lack or hardship. **have a go at** chiefly Brit. attack or criticize someone. **have** – **going for one** informal be in one's favour. **make a go of** informal be successful in something. **on the go** informal very active or busy. **to go** N. Amer. (of food or drink from a restaurant or cafe) to be eaten or drunk off the premises.
– ORIGIN Old English.

USAGE: For information on the use of **go** followed by **and** (as in *I must go and change*), see the note at AND.

goad /gohd/ verb **1** keep annoying or criticizing someone until they react. **2** urge on cattle with a goad. •noun **1** a thing that stimulates someone into action. **2** a spiked stick used for driving cattle.
– ORIGIN Old English.

go-ahead informal noun (**the go-ahead**) permission to proceed. •adjective enterprising and ambitious.

goal noun **1** (in football, rugby, etc.) a pair of posts linked by a crossbar and forming a space into or over which the ball has to be sent to score. **2** an instance of sending the ball into or over a goal. **3** an aim or desired result: *my goal is to make movies.*
– DERIVATIVES **goalless** adjective.
– ORIGIN unknown.

goal average noun Football the ratio of the numbers of goals scored for and against a team in a series of matches.

goal difference noun Football the difference between the number of goals scored for and against a team in a series of matches.

goalie noun informal a goalkeeper.

goalkeeper noun a player in football or field hockey whose role is to stop the ball from entering the goal.

goal kick noun **1** Football a free kick taken by the defending side after attackers send the ball over the byline. **2** Rugby an attempt to kick a goal.

goal line noun a line across a football or

hockey field on which the goal is placed or which acts as the boundary beyond which a try or touchdown is scored.

goalpost noun either of the two upright posts of a goal.
– PHRASES **move the goalposts** unfairly alter the conditions or rules of something while it is still happening.

goalscorer noun a player who scores a goal.
– DERIVATIVES **goalscoring** adjective.

goat noun 1 a hardy domesticated mammal that has backward-curving horns and (in the male) a beard. 2 a wild mammal related to the goat, such as the ibex. 3 informal a lecherous man.
– PHRASES **act the goat** informal fool around; act stupidly. **get someone's goat** informal irritate someone.
– DERIVATIVES **goatish** adjective **goaty** adjective.
– ORIGIN Old English.

goat-antelope noun a mammal of a group including the chamois, with characteristics of both goats and antelopes.

goatee /goh-tee/ noun a small pointed beard like that of a goat.
– DERIVATIVES **goateed** adjective.

goatherd noun a person who looks after goats.

goatskin noun leather made from the skin of a goat.

gob[1] noun Brit. informal a person's mouth.
– ORIGIN perhaps from Scottish Gaelic.

gob[2] informal noun a lump of a slimy or thick semi-liquid substance. •verb (**gobs, gobbing, gobbed**) Brit. spit.
– ORIGIN Old French *gobe* 'mouthful, lump'.

gobbet /gob-bit/ noun a piece or lump of flesh, food, or other matter.
– ORIGIN Old French *gobet* 'little lump or mouthful'.

gobble[1] verb 1 eat hurriedly and noisily. 2 use a large amount of something very quickly: *impractical ventures gobbled up the rock star's cash.*
– DERIVATIVES **gobbler** noun.
– ORIGIN probably from GOB[2].

gobble[2] verb (of a turkeycock) make a swallowing sound in the throat.
– DERIVATIVES **gobbler** noun.
– ORIGIN imitating the sound.

gobbledegook /gob-b'l-di-gook/ (also **gobbledygook**) noun informal language that is difficult to understand because of excessive use of technical terms.
– ORIGIN probably imitating a turkey's gobble.

go-between noun an intermediary or negotiator.

goblet noun 1 a drinking glass with a foot and a stem. 2 Brit. a container forming part of a liquidizer.
– ORIGIN Old French *gobelet* 'little cup'.

goblin noun (in fairy stories) a small, ugly, mischievous creature.
– ORIGIN Old French *gobelin*.

gobsmacked adjective Brit. informal completely astonished.
– DERIVATIVES **gobsmacking** adjective.

gobstopper noun chiefly Brit. a large, hard spherical sweet.

goby /goh-bi/ noun (pl. **gobies**) a small sea fish, typically with a sucker on the underside.

– ORIGIN Greek *kōbios*.

go-cart noun variant spelling of GO-KART.

God noun 1 (in Christianity and other religions which believe in only one God) the creator and supreme ruler of the universe. 2 (**god**) a superhuman being or spirit worshipped as having power over nature and human life. 3 (**god**) a greatly admired or influential person. 4 (**the gods**) informal the gallery in a theatre. •exclamation used to express surprise, anger, etc. or for emphasis.
– PHRASES **God the Father, Son, and Holy Ghost** (in Christian doctrine) the persons of the Trinity. **God's gift** chiefly ironic the best possible person for someone: *he thought he was God's gift to women.*
– DERIVATIVES **godhood** noun **godlike** adjective.
– ORIGIN Old English.

godchild noun (pl. **godchildren**) a person in relation to a godparent.

god-daughter noun a female godchild.

goddess noun 1 a female god. 2 a woman who is greatly admired, especially for her beauty.

godet /goh-det, goh-day/ noun a triangular piece of material inserted in a garment to make it flared or for decoration.
– ORIGIN French.

godetia /goh-dee-shuh/ noun a North American plant with showy lilac to red flowers.
– ORIGIN named after the Swiss botanist Charles H. *Godet*.

godfather noun 1 a male godparent. 2 a male leader of the American Mafia.

God-fearing adjective earnestly religious.

godforsaken adjective (of a place) unattractive, remote, or depressing.

godhead noun 1 (**the Godhead**) God. 2 divine nature.

godless adjective 1 not believing in a god or God. 2 wicked; very bad.

godly adjective (**godlier, godliest**) devoutly religious; pious.
– DERIVATIVES **godliness** noun.

godmother noun a female godparent.

godown /goh-down/ noun (in east Asia, especially India) a warehouse.
– ORIGIN Tamil.

godparent noun a person who presents a child at baptism and promises to take responsibility for their religious education.

godsend noun something very helpful or welcome at a particular time.

godson noun a male godchild.

Godspeed exclamation dated an expression of good wishes to a person starting a journey.

godwit noun a large long-legged wading bird with a long bill.
– ORIGIN unknown.

goer noun 1 a person who regularly attends a specified place or event: *a theatregoer.* 2 Brit. informal a sexually unrestrained woman.

goes third person singular present of GO.

gofer /goh-fer/ (also **gopher**) noun informal a person who runs errands; a dogsbody.
– ORIGIN from *go for* (i.e. go and fetch).

go-getter noun informal an energetic and very enterprising person.
– DERIVATIVES **go-getting** adjective.

g

goggle verb **1** look with wide open eyes. **2** (of the eyes) protrude or open wide. • noun (**goggles**) close-fitting protective glasses with side shields.
– ORIGIN probably representing oscillating movement.

goggle-box noun Brit. informal a television set.

goggle-eyed adjective having wide-open eyes, especially through astonishment.

go-go adjective referring to an unrestrained and erotic style of dancing to pop music.

going noun **1** the condition of the ground viewed in terms of suitability for horse racing or walking. **2** conditions for, or progress in, an activity or enterprise: *the company sold its advertising airtime for $500m, good going in a recession.* • adjective **1** chiefly Brit. existing or available: *any jobs going?* **2** (of a price) usual or current.

going concern noun a thriving business.

going-over noun informal **1** a thorough cleaning or inspection. **2** an attack or heavy defeat.

goings-on plural noun informal suspect or unusual activities.

goitre /goy-ter/ (US **goiter**) noun a swelling of the neck resulting from enlargement of the thyroid gland.
– DERIVATIVES **goitrous** adjective.
– ORIGIN French, or from Old French *goitron* 'gullet'.

go-kart (also **go-cart**) noun a small racing car with a lightweight body.

gold noun **1** a yellow precious metal, used in jewellery and decoration and to guarantee the value of currencies. **2** a deep yellow or yellow-brown colour. **3** coins or articles made of gold.
– ORIGIN Old English.

goldcrest noun a very small warbler with a yellow or orange crest.

gold-digger noun informal a woman who forms relationships with men purely for financial gain.

gold disc noun a framed golden disc awarded to a recording artist or group for sales exceeding a specified figure.

gold dust noun fine particles of gold.
– PHRASES **be like gold dust** Brit. be very rare and valuable.

golden adjective **1** made of or resembling gold. **2** (of a period) very happy and prosperous. **3** excellent: *a golden opportunity.*
– DERIVATIVES **goldenly** adverb.

golden age noun the period when something is most successful: *the golden age of cinema.*

golden boy (or **golden girl**) noun informal a very popular or successful young person.

Golden Delicious noun a variety of eating apple with a greenish-yellow skin.

golden eagle noun a large eagle with yellow-tipped head feathers.

golden goose noun a continuing source of wealth or profit that may be exhausted if it is misused.

golden handcuffs plural noun informal benefits provided by an employer to discourage an employee from working elsewhere.

golden handshake noun informal a payment given to someone who is made redundant or retires early.

golden jubilee noun the fiftieth anniversary of a significant event.

golden mean noun the ideal moderate position between two extremes.

golden oldie noun informal an old song or film that is still well known and popular.

golden retriever noun a breed of retriever with a thick golden-coloured coat.

goldenrod noun a plant with tall spikes of small bright yellow flowers.

golden rule noun a basic principle which should always be followed.

golden syrup noun Brit. a pale treacle.

golden wedding noun Brit. the fiftieth anniversary of a wedding.

goldfield noun a district in which gold is found as a mineral.

goldfinch noun a brightly coloured finch with a yellow patch on each wing.

goldfish noun (pl. same or **goldfishes**) a small reddish-golden carp popular in ponds and aquaria.

goldfish bowl noun **1** a spherical glass container for goldfish. **2** a place or situation lacking privacy.

gold leaf noun gold beaten into a very thin sheet, used in gilding.

gold medal noun a medal made of or coloured gold, awarded for first place in a competition.

gold mine noun **1** a place where gold is mined. **2** a source of wealth or resources.

gold plate noun **1** a thin layer of gold applied as a coating to another metal. **2** plates, dishes, etc. made of or plated with gold.

gold rush noun a rapid movement of people to a newly discovered goldfield.

goldsmith noun a person who makes gold articles.

gold standard noun historical the system by which the value of a currency was defined in terms of gold.

golem /goh-luhm, goy-luhm/ noun (in Jewish legend) a clay figure brought to life by magic.
– ORIGIN Hebrew, 'shapeless mass'.

golf noun a game played on an outdoor course, the aim of which is to strike a small hard ball with a club into a series of small holes with the fewest possible strokes. • verb (usu. as noun **golfing**) play golf.
– DERIVATIVES **golfer** noun.
– ORIGIN perhaps related to Dutch *kolf* 'club'.

Goliath noun a person or thing of enormous size or strength.
– ORIGIN from the name of a giant in the Bible, killed by David.

golliwog noun a soft doll with a black face and fuzzy hair.
– ORIGIN from *Golliwogg*, a doll character in books by the US writer Bertha Upton.

golly exclamation informal used to express surprise or delight.
– ORIGIN euphemism for **God**.

gonad /goh-nad/ noun a bodily organ that produces gametes; a testis or ovary.
– DERIVATIVES **gonadal** /goh-nay-d'l/ adjective.
– ORIGIN Latin *gonades*, plural of *gonas*.

gondola /gon-duh-luh/ noun **1** a flat-bottomed boat used on Venetian canals, having a high

point at each end and worked by one oar at the stern. **2** a cabin on a ski lift, or suspended from an airship or balloon.
– ORIGIN Venetian Italian.

gondolier /gon-duh-**leer**/ noun a person who propels and steers a gondola.

gone past participle of GO. adjective **1** no longer present, available, or in existence. **2** informal having reached a specified time in a pregnancy: *she's four months gone.* • preposition Brit. **1** (of time) past. **2** (of age) older than.

goner /gon-er/ noun informal a person or thing that is doomed or cannot be saved.

gong noun **1** a metal disc with a turned rim, giving a resonant note when struck. **2** Brit. informal a medal or decoration.
– ORIGIN Malay.

gonorrhoea /gon-uh-**ree**-uh/ (US **gonorrhea**) noun a sexually transmitted disease causing discharge from the urethra or vagina.
– ORIGIN from Greek *gonos* 'semen' + *rhoia* 'flux'.

goo noun informal a sticky or slimy substance.
– ORIGIN perhaps from *burgoo*, a nautical slang term for porridge.

good adjective (**better**, **best**) **1** having the required qualities; of a high standard. **2** morally right, polite, or obedient. **3** enjoyable, pleasant, or satisfying. **4** appropriate or suitable. **5** (**good for**) beneficial to. **6** thorough: *have a good look around.* **7** at least. • noun **1** behaviour that is right or acceptable. **2** something beneficial: *he resigned for the good of the country.* **3** (**goods**) products or possessions. **4** (**goods**) Brit. freight.
– PHRASES **as good as** very nearly. **be —— to the good** have a specified net profit or advantage. **come up with** (or **deliver**) **the goods** informal do what is expected or required. **do someone good** be beneficial to someone. **for good** forever. **the Good Book** the Bible. **good for** (or **on**) **you!** well done! **a good word** words recommending or defending a person. **in good time 1** with no risk of being late. **2** (also **all in good time**) in due course but without haste. **make something good 1** compensate for loss, damage, or expense. **2** fulfil a promise or claim. **take something in good part** not be offended.
– ORIGIN Old English.

goodbye (US also **goodby**) exclamation used to express good wishes when parting or ending a conversation. • noun (pl. **goodbyes**; US also **goodbys**) an instance of saying 'goodbye'; a parting.
– ORIGIN contraction of *God be with you!*

good faith noun honesty or sincerity of intention.

good form noun behaviour that is socially acceptable.

good-for-nothing adjective worthless and lazy. • noun a worthless and lazy person.

Good Friday noun the Friday before Easter Sunday, on which the Crucifixion of Jesus is commemorated in the Christian Church.

good-hearted adjective kind and well meaning.

good-humoured adjective friendly or cheerful.

goodie noun variant spelling of GOODY.

goodish adjective **1** fairly good. **2** fairly large.

good-looking adjective physically attractive.

goodly adjective (**goodlier**, **goodliest**) considerable in size or quantity.

good-natured adjective kind and unselfish.

goodness noun **1** the quality of being good. **2** the nutritious element of food. • exclamation expressing surprise, anger, etc.

goodnight exclamation expressing good wishes on parting at night or before going to bed.

goods and chattels plural noun all kinds of personal possessions.

good-tempered adjective not easily angered.

good-time adjective interested in pleasure more than anything else.

goodwill noun **1** friendly or helpful feelings or attitude. **2** the established reputation of a business regarded as an asset and calculated as part of its value when it is sold.

goody noun (also **goodie**) (pl. **goodies**) informal **1** Brit. a good person, especially a hero in a story or film. **2** (**goodies**) tasty things to eat. • exclamation expressing childish delight.

goody-goody informal noun a person who behaves well so as to impress other people.

gooey adjective (**gooier**, **gooiest**) informal **1** soft and sticky. **2** excessively sentimental: *gooey nostalgia.*
– DERIVATIVES **gooeyness** noun.

goof informal, chiefly N. Amer. noun **1** a mistake. **2** a foolish or stupid person. • verb **1** fool around. **2** make a mistake.
– ORIGIN unknown.

goofy adjective (**goofier**, **goofiest**) informal **1** chiefly N. Amer. foolish; harmlessly eccentric. **2** having protruding front teeth.
– DERIVATIVES **goofily** adverb **goofiness** noun.

googly noun (pl. **googlies**) Cricket an off break bowled with an apparent leg-break action.
– ORIGIN unknown.

gook noun N. Amer. informal, offensive a person of SE Asian descent.
– ORIGIN unknown.

goolie (also **gooly**) noun (pl. **goolies**) Brit. vulgar slang a testicle.
– ORIGIN perhaps related to a Hindi word meaning 'bullet, ball, pill'.

goon noun informal **1** a foolish or eccentric person. **2** a thug.
– ORIGIN perhaps from dialect *gooney* 'stupid person'.

goosander /goo-**san**-der/ noun (pl. same or **goosanders**) a large merganser (diving duck), the male of which has a dark green head and whitish underparts.
– ORIGIN probably from GOOSE + *-ander* as in dialect *bergander* 'shelduck'.

goose noun (pl. **geese**) **1** a large waterbird with a long neck and webbed feet. **2** a female goose. **3** informal a foolish person. • verb informal poke someone in the bottom.
– ORIGIN Old English.

gooseberry noun (pl. **gooseberries**) **1** a round edible yellowish-green berry with a hairy skin. **2** Brit. informal a third person in the company of two lovers, who would rather be alone.
– ORIGIN the first element perhaps from GOOSE, or perhaps from Old French *groseille*.

g

gooseflesh (also **goosepimples**) noun a pimply state of the skin with the hairs erect, produced by cold or fright.

goose step noun a military marching step in which the legs are not bent at the knee. • verb (**goose-step**) march with the legs kept straight.

gopher /goh-fer/ noun 1 (also **pocket gopher**) a burrowing American rodent with pouches on its cheeks. 2 variant spelling of **GOFER**.
– ORIGIN perhaps from Canadian French *gaufre* 'honeycomb' (because the gopher 'honeycombs' the ground with its burrows).

Gordian knot /gor-di-uhn/ noun (in phrase **cut the Gordian knot**) solve a difficult problem in a direct or forceful way.
– ORIGIN from the legendary knot tied by King *Gordius* and cut through by Alexander the Great in response to the prophecy that whoever untied it would rule Asia.

gore[1] noun blood that has been shed, especially as a result of violence.
– ORIGIN Old English, 'dung, dirt'.

gore[2] verb (of an animal such as a bull) pierce or stab someone with a horn or tusk.
– ORIGIN unknown.

gore[3] noun a triangular or tapering piece of material used in making a garment, sail, or umbrella.
– DERIVATIVES **gored** adjective.
– ORIGIN Old English, 'triangular piece of land'.

gorge noun a steep, narrow valley or ravine. • verb eat a large amount greedily.
– PHRASES **one's gorge rises** one is sickened or disgusted.
– DERIVATIVES **gorger** noun.
– ORIGIN Old French, 'throat'.

gorgeous adjective 1 beautiful; very attractive. 2 informal very pleasant.
– DERIVATIVES **gorgeously** adverb **gorgeousness** noun.
– ORIGIN Old French *gorgias* 'fine, elegant'.

gorget /gor-jit/ noun 1 historical an article of clothing or piece of armour covering the throat. 2 a patch of colour on the throat of a bird.
– ORIGIN Old French *gorgete*.

gorgio /gor-ji-oh/ noun (pl. **gorgios**) the Gypsy name for a non-Gypsy.
– ORIGIN Romany.

gorgon /gor-guhn/ noun 1 Greek Mythology each of three sisters with snakes for hair, who had the power to turn anyone who looked at them to stone. 2 a fierce or repulsive woman.
– ORIGIN Greek *gorgos* 'terrible'.

Gorgonzola /gor-guhn-**zoh**-luh/ noun a rich, strong-flavoured Italian cheese with bluish-green veins.
– ORIGIN named after the Italian village of *Gorgonzola*.

gorilla noun 1 a powerfully built great ape of central Africa, the largest living primate. 2 informal a heavily built aggressive-looking man.
– ORIGIN Greek.

gormless adjective Brit. informal stupid or slow-witted.
– DERIVATIVES **gormlessly** adverb.
– ORIGIN from dialect *gaum* 'understanding'.

gorse noun a yellow-flowered shrub with thin prickly leaves.
– ORIGIN Old English.

gory adjective (**gorier, goriest**) 1 involving violence and bloodshed. 2 covered in blood.
– PHRASES **the gory details** humorous explicit details.
– DERIVATIVES **goriness** noun.

gosh exclamation informal used to express surprise or for emphasis.
– ORIGIN euphemism for **GOD**.

goshawk /goss-hawk/ noun a short-winged hawk resembling a large sparrowhawk.
– ORIGIN Old English, 'goose-hawk'.

gosling noun a young goose.
– ORIGIN Old Norse.

go-slow noun Brit. a form of industrial action in which work is done more slowly than usual.

gospel noun 1 the teachings of Jesus. 2 (**Gospel**) the record of Jesus's life and teaching in the first four books of the New Testament. 3 (**Gospel**) each of the first four books of the New Testament. 4 (also **gospel truth**) something absolutely true. 5 (also **gospel music**) a style of black American evangelical religious singing.
– ORIGIN Old English, 'good news'.

gossamer noun a fine, filmy substance consisting of cobwebs spun by small spiders. • adjective very fine and insubstantial.
– ORIGIN probably from **GOOSE** + **SUMMER**, perhaps from the time around St Martin's day (11 November) when geese were eaten and gossamer is seen.

gossip noun 1 casual conversation or unproven reports about other people. 2 chiefly derogatory a person who likes talking about other people's private lives. • verb (**gossips, gossiping, gossiped**) engage in gossip.
– DERIVATIVES **gossiper** noun **gossipy** adjective.
– ORIGIN Old English, 'godfather or godmother', later 'a close friend'.

gossip column noun a section of a newspaper devoted to gossip about well-known people.

got past and past participle of **GET**.

Goth /goth/ noun 1 a member of a Germanic people that invaded the Roman Empire between the 3rd and 5th centuries. 2 (**goth**) a young person of a group favouring black clothing and a style of rock music having apocalyptic or mystical lyrics.
– ORIGIN Greek *Gothoi*.

Gothic adjective 1 relating to the style of architecture prevalent in western Europe in the 12th–16th centuries, characterized by pointed arches and elaborate tracery. 2 very gloomy or horrifying. 3 (of lettering) derived from the angular style of handwriting with broad vertical downstrokes used in medieval western Europe. 4 relating to the ancient Goths. • noun 1 Gothic architecture. 2 the extinct language of the Goths.

gothic novel noun an English type of fiction popular in the 18th to early 19th centuries, characterized by an atmosphere of mystery and horror.

gotten N. Amer. or old use past participle of **GET**.

gouache /goo-ash/ noun 1 a method of painting using watercolours thickened with a

type of glue. **2** watercolours thickened with a type of glue.
– ORIGIN French.

Gouda /gow-duh/ **noun** a flat round Dutch cheese with a yellow rind.
– ORIGIN made in *Gouda* in the Netherlands.

gouge /gowj/ **verb 1** make a rough hole or groove in a surface. **2 (gouge something out)** cut or force something out roughly or brutally. • **noun 1** a chisel with a concave blade. **2** a hole or groove made by gouging.
– DERIVATIVES **gouger** noun.
– ORIGIN Old French.

goujons /goo-zhuhnz/ **plural noun** Brit. deep-fried strips of chicken or fish.
– ORIGIN French *goujon* 'gudgeon'.

goulash /goo-lash/ **noun** a Hungarian stew of meat and vegetables, flavoured with paprika.
– ORIGIN from Hungarian *gulyás* 'herdsman' + *hús* 'meat'.

gourami /guu-uh-**rah**-mi, goor-uh-mi/ **noun** (pl. same or **gouramis**) an Asian fish of a large group including many kinds popular in aquaria.
– ORIGIN Malay.

gourd /gord/ **noun 1** the large hard-skinned fleshy fruit of a climbing or trailing plant. **2** a container made from the hollowed and dried skin of a gourd.
– ORIGIN Old French *gourde*.

gourmand /gor-muhnd/ **noun 1** a person who enjoys eating, sometimes to excess. **2** a person who is knowledgeable about good food; a gourmet.
– ORIGIN Old French.

gourmandize (or **gourmandise**) **verb** eat good food, especially to excess.

gourmet /gor-may/ **noun** a person who is knowledgeable about good food. • **adjective** (of food or a meal) high quality.
– ORIGIN French.

gout /gowt/ **noun 1** a disease that causes the joints to swell and become painful. **2** literary a drop or spot.
– DERIVATIVES **gouty** adjective.
– ORIGIN Latin *gutta* 'drop'.

govern **verb 1** conduct the policy and affairs of a state, organization, or people. **2** control or influence: *the wines are governed by strict regulations.* **3** Grammar (of a word) require that another word or group of words be in a particular case.
– DERIVATIVES **governability** noun **governable** adjective.
– ORIGIN Greek *kubernan* 'to steer'.

governance **noun** the action or style of governing something.

governess **noun** a woman employed to teach children in a private household.

governing body **noun** a group of people who govern an institution such as a school in partnership with the managers.

government **noun 1** (treated as sing. or pl.) the group of people who govern a state. **2** the system by which a state or community is governed. **3** the action or way of governing a state or organization: *he believed in strong government.*
– DERIVATIVES **governmental** adjective.

governor **noun 1** an official appointed to govern a town or region. **2** the elected executive head of a US state. **3** the representative of the British Crown in a colony or in a Commonwealth state that regards the monarch as head of state. **4** the head of a public institution. **5** a member of a governing body. **6** Brit. informal a person's employer or manager.
– DERIVATIVES **governorship** noun.

Governor General **noun** (pl. **Governors General**) the chief representative of the Crown in a Commonwealth country of which the British monarch is head of state.

gown **noun 1** a long dress worn on formal occasions. **2** a protective garment worn in hospital by surgical staff or patients. **3** a loose cloak indicating a person's profession or status, worn by a lawyer, academic, or university student. **4** the members of a university as distinct from the residents of a town. • **verb** (**be gowned**) be dressed in a gown.
– ORIGIN Latin *gunna* 'fur garment'.

goy /goy/ **noun** (pl. **goyim** /goy-im/ or **goys**) informal, derogatory a Jewish name for a non-Jew.
– DERIVATIVES **goyish** adjective.
– ORIGIN Hebrew, 'people, nation'.

GP **abbreviation 1** Brit. general practitioner. **2** Grand Prix.

GPRS **abbreviation** general packet radio services, a technology for radio transmission of small packets of data, especially between mobile phones and the Internet.

GPS **abbreviation** Global Positioning System (a satellite navigational system).

gr. **abbreviation 1** grain(s). **2** gram(s). **3** gross.

grab **verb** (**grabs, grabbing, grabbed**) **1** seize someone or something suddenly and roughly. **2** informal obtain quickly or when an opportunity arises: *the concerts are very popular, so get into town early to grab a parking space.* **3** informal impress: *how does that grab you?* • **noun 1** a quick sudden attempt to seize something. **2** a mechanical device for moving loads.
– PHRASES **up for grabs** informal available.
– DERIVATIVES **grabber** noun.
– ORIGIN German and Dutch *grabben*.

grace **noun 1** elegance of movement. **2** polite good will: *she had the grace to look sheepish.* **3** (**graces**) attractive qualities or behaviour. **4** (in Christian belief) the free and unearned favour of God. **5** a person's favour. **6** a period officially allowed for an obligation to be met: *the sport has three years' grace before the ban comes into force.* **7** a short prayer of thanks said before or after a meal. **8** (**His, Her,** or **Your Grace**) used as forms of description or address for a duke, duchess, or archbishop. • **verb 1** bring honour to something by one's presence. **2** make more attractive: *a fresh wreath graced an upstairs window.*
– PHRASES **the (Three) Graces** Greek Mythology three beautiful goddesses believed to personify charm, grace, and beauty. **with good** (or **bad**) **grace** in a willing (or reluctant) way.
– ORIGIN Latin *gratia*.

grace and favour **adjective** Brit. (of accommodation) occupied free or at a low rent by permission of a sovereign or government.

graceful adjective having or showing grace or elegance.
– DERIVATIVES **gracefully** adverb **gracefulness** noun.

graceless adjective lacking grace, elegance, or charm.
– DERIVATIVES **gracelessly** adverb **gracelessness** noun.

grace note noun Music an extra note added to ornament a melody.

gracious adjective **1** polite, kind, and pleasant. **2** elegant in a way associated with upper-class status or wealth: *magazines devoted to gracious living.* **3** (in Christian belief) showing God's grace. •**exclamation** expressing polite surprise.
– DERIVATIVES **graciously** adverb **graciousness** noun.

gradation /gruh-**day**-sh'n/ noun **1** a scale of successive changes, stages, or degrees. **2** a stage in a such a scale.
– DERIVATIVES **gradational** adjective.

grade noun **1** a specified level of rank, quality, proficiency, or value: *the worst grade of coffee.* **2** a mark indicating the quality of a student's work. **3** N. Amer. a class in a school comprising children grouped according to age or ability. •**verb 1** arrange people or things in groups according to quality, size, ability, etc.: *caviar is graded according to the size of its grains.* **2** pass gradually from one level to another.
– PHRASES **make the grade** informal succeed.
– DERIVATIVES **grader** noun.
– ORIGIN Latin *gradus* 'step'.

grade crossing noun N. Amer. a level crossing.

grade school noun N. Amer. elementary school.

gradient /**gray**-di-uhnt/ noun **1** a sloping part of a road or railway. **2** the degree to which the ground slopes. **3** a change in the magnitude of a property (e.g. temperature) observed in passing from one point or moment to another.
– ORIGIN from GRADE.

gradual adjective **1** taking place in stages over an extended period. **2** (of a slope) not steep.
– DERIVATIVES **gradually** adverb **gradualness** noun.
– ORIGIN Latin *gradualis.*

gradualism noun a policy or theory of gradual rather than sudden change.
– DERIVATIVES **gradualist** noun.

graduand /**grad**-juu-and/ noun Brit. a person who is about to receive an academic degree.

graduate noun /**grad**-yuu-uht/ a person who has been awarded a first academic degree, or (N. Amer.) a high-school diploma. •**verb** /**grad**-yoo-ayt/ **1** successfully complete a degree, course, or (N. Amer.) high school. **2** (**graduate to**) move up to something more advanced. **3** arrange or mark out something in a scale in gradations. **4** change gradually.
– DERIVATIVES **graduation** noun.
– ORIGIN from Latin *graduare* 'take a degree'.

Graeco- /**gree**-koh/ (also **Greco-**) combining form Greek; Greek and ...: *Graeco-Roman.*
– ORIGIN Latin *Graecus* 'Greek'.

graffiti /gruh-**fee**-ti/ plural noun (treated as sing. or pl.) writing or drawings on a surface in a public place. •**verb** write or draw graffiti on a surface.

– DERIVATIVES **graffitist** noun.
– ORIGIN Italian.

graft¹ noun **1** a shoot or twig inserted into a slit on the trunk or stem of a living plant, from which it receives sap. **2** a piece of living body tissue that is transplanted surgically to replace diseased or damaged tissue. **3** an operation in which tissue is transplanted. •**verb 1** insert or transplant something as a graft. **2** add or attach to something else, especially inappropriately: *plate glass windows had been grafted on to an eighteenth-century building.*
– ORIGIN Greek *graphion* 'writing implement'.

graft² Brit. informal noun hard work. •**verb** work hard.
– DERIVATIVES **grafter** noun.
– ORIGIN perhaps from *spade's graft* 'the amount of earth that one stroke of a spade will move'.

graft³ informal noun bribery and other corrupt measures adopted to gain power or money in politics or business.
– DERIVATIVES **grafter** noun.
– ORIGIN unknown.

Grail (also **Holy Grail**) noun (in medieval legend) the cup or platter used by Jesus at the Last Supper, especially as the object of quests by knights.
– ORIGIN Old French *graal.*

grain noun **1** wheat or other cultivated cereal used as food. **2** a single seed or fruit of a cereal. **3** a small hard particle of a substance such as sand. **4** the smallest unit of weight in the troy and avoirdupois systems. **5** the smallest possible amount: *there wasn't a grain of truth in the rumours.* **6** the lengthwise arrangement of fibres, particles, or layers in wood, paper, rock, etc.
– PHRASES **against the grain** contrary to one's nature or instinct.
– DERIVATIVES **grained** adjective.
– ORIGIN Latin *granum.*

grainy adjective (**grainier, grainiest**) **1** consisting of grains; granular. **2** (of a photograph) showing visible grains of emulsion.
– DERIVATIVES **graininess** noun.

gram (Brit. also **gramme**) noun a metric unit of mass equal to one thousandth of a kilogram.
– ORIGIN Greek *gramma* 'small weight'.

grammar noun **1** the whole structure of a language, including the rules for the way words are formed and their relationship to each other in a sentence. **2** knowledge and use of the rules or principles of grammar: *bad grammar.* **3** a book on grammar.
– ORIGIN from Greek *grammatikē tekhnē* 'art of letters'.

grammarian /gruh-**mair**-i-uhn/ noun a person who studies and writes about grammar.

grammar school noun **1** (in the UK, especially formerly) a state secondary school which admits pupils on the basis of their ability. **2** US another term for ELEMENTARY SCHOOL.

grammatical /gruh-**mat**-i-k'l/ adjective relating to or following the rules of grammar.
– DERIVATIVES **grammaticality** noun **grammatically** adverb.

gramme noun variant spelling of **GRAM**.

Grammy noun (pl. **Grammys** or **Grammies**) an annual award given by the American National Academy of Recording Arts and Sciences for achievement in the record industry.
– ORIGIN blend of **GRAMOPHONE** and **EMMY**.

gramophone noun dated a record player.
– ORIGIN formed by reversing the elements of *phonogram* 'sound recording'.

gramophone record noun fuller form of **RECORD** (in sense 2).

grampus /gram-puhss/ noun (pl. **grampuses**) a killer whale or other dolphin-like sea animal.
– ORIGIN Old French *grapois* (influenced by **GRAND**).

gran noun Brit. informal one's grandmother.

granary noun (pl. **granaries**) 1 a storehouse for threshed grain. 2 a region supplying large quantities of corn.
– ORIGIN Latin *granarium*.

granary bread noun Brit. trademark a type of brown bread containing whole grains of wheat.

grand adjective 1 magnificent and impressive. 2 large or ambitious in scope or scale: *a grand plan to bring Las Vegas to Blackpool.* 3 of the highest importance or rank. 4 dignified, noble, or proud. 5 informal excellent. 6 (in combination) (in names of family relationships) referring to one generation removed in ascent or descent: *a grand-niece.* • noun 1 (pl. same) informal a thousand dollars or pounds. 2 a grand piano.
– DERIVATIVES **grandly** adverb **grandness** noun.
– ORIGIN Latin *grandis* 'full-grown, great'.

grandad (also **granddad**) noun informal one's grandfather. • adjective (of a shirt) having a collar in the form of a narrow upright band.

grandchild noun (pl. **grandchildren**) a child of one's son or daughter.

granddaughter noun a daughter of one's son or daughter.

grand duchess noun 1 the wife or widow of a grand duke. 2 a woman holding the rank of grand duke in her own right.

grand duke noun 1 (in Europe, especially formerly) a prince or nobleman ruling over a small independent state. 2 historical a son (or grandson) of a Russian tsar.

grande dame /grond dam/ noun a woman who is influential within a particular area of activity.
– ORIGIN French, 'grand lady'.

grandee /gran-dee/ noun 1 a Spanish or Portuguese nobleman of the highest rank. 2 a high-ranking or eminent man.
– ORIGIN from Spanish and Portuguese *grande* 'grand'.

grandeur /gran-dyer/ noun 1 the quality of being grand and impressive: *the wild grandeur of the mountains.* 2 high rank or social importance.

grandfather noun 1 the father of one's father or mother. 2 a founder or originator of something.

grandfather clock noun a clock in a tall free-standing wooden case, driven by weights.

Grand Guignol /gron gee-ny-ol/ noun dramatic entertainment of a sensational or horrific nature.
– ORIGIN *Guignol* was the bloodthirsty chief character in a French puppet show; the entertainment originated at the *Grand Guignol* theatre in Paris.

grandiflora /gran-di-flor-uh/ adjective (of a cultivated plant) bearing large flowers.
– ORIGIN from Latin *grandis* 'great' + *flos* 'flower'.

grandiloquent /gran-dil-uh-kwuhnt/ adjective using long or difficult words in order to impress.
– DERIVATIVES **grandiloquence** noun **grandiloquently** adverb.
– ORIGIN Latin *grandiloquus* 'grand-speaking'.

grandiose /gran-di-ohss/ adjective very large or ambitious, especially in a way which is intended to impress: *the city was built on a vast and grandiose scale.*
– DERIVATIVES **grandiosely** adverb **grandiosity** /gran-di-os-it-i/ noun.
– ORIGIN Italian *grandioso*.

grand jury noun US Law a jury selected to examine the validity of an accusation prior to trial.

grandma noun informal one's grandmother.

grand mal /gron mal/ noun a serious form of epilepsy with muscle spasms and prolonged loss of consciousness. Compare with **PETIT MAL**.
– ORIGIN French, 'great sickness'.

grand master noun 1 (also **grandmaster**) a chess player of the highest class. 2 (**Grand Master**) the head of an order of chivalry or of Freemasons.

grandmother noun the mother of one's father or mother.
– PHRASES **teach one's grandmother to suck eggs** have the audacity to advise a more experienced person.

Grand National noun an annual steeplechase held at Aintree, Liverpool.

grand opera noun an opera on a serious theme in which the entire libretto (including dialogue) is sung.

grandpa noun informal one's grandfather.

grandparent noun a grandmother or grandfather.

grand piano noun a large full-toned piano which has the body, strings, and soundboard arranged horizontally and is supported by three legs.

Grand Prix /gron pree/ noun (pl. **Grands Prix** /gron pree/) a race forming part of a motor-racing or motorcycling world championship.
– ORIGIN French, 'great or chief prize'.

grandsire noun old use one's grandfather.

grand slam noun 1 the winning of each of a group of major championships or matches in a particular sport in the same year. 2 Bridge the bidding and winning of all thirteen tricks.

grandson noun the son of one's son or daughter.

grandstand noun the main stand at a racecourse or sports ground.

grand total noun the final amount after everything is added up.

grand tour noun a cultural tour of Europe formerly undertaken by upper-class young men.

grange noun Brit. 1 a country house with farm

g

buildings attached. **2** *old use* a barn.
- ORIGIN Old French.

granita /gra-**nee**-tuh/ **noun** (pl. **granitas**) a coarse Italian-style water ice.
- ORIGIN Italian.

granite /**gran**-it/ **noun** a very hard rock consisting mainly of quartz, mica, and feldspar.
- DERIVATIVES **granitic** adjective.
- ORIGIN from Italian *granito* 'grained'.

granny (also **grannie**) **noun** (pl. **grannies**) *informal* one's grandmother.

granny flat noun *informal, chiefly Brit.* a part of a house made into self-contained accommodation suitable for an elderly relative.

granny knot noun a reef knot with the ends crossed the wrong way and therefore liable to slip.

Granny Smith noun a bright green variety of apple with crisp, sharp-flavoured flesh.
- ORIGIN named after Maria Ann (*Granny*) *Smith*, who first produced such apples.

granola /gra-**noh**-luh/ **noun** *N. Amer.* a kind of breakfast cereal resembling muesli.

grant verb 1 agree to give something to someone or allow them to do something. **2** give something formally or legally to: *someone with a fear of torture would be granted asylum.* **3** admit to someone that something is true. •**noun 1** a sum of money given by a government or public body for a particular purpose. **2** the action of granting something.
- PHRASES **take someone/thing for granted 1** fail to appreciate someone or something as a result of overfamiliarity. **2** assume that something is true.
- DERIVATIVES **grantee** noun **grantor** (also **granter**) noun.
- ORIGIN Old French *granter* 'consent to support'.

grant aid noun *Brit.* financial assistance granted by central government to local government or an institution.

granted adverb admittedly; it is true. •**conjunction** (**granted that**) even assuming that.

grant-maintained adjective *Brit.* (of a school) funded by central rather than local government, and self-governing.

granular adjective 1 resembling or consisting of granules. **2** having a roughened surface.
- DERIVATIVES **granularity** noun.

granulated adjective 1 in the form of granules. **2** *technical* having a roughened surface.
- DERIVATIVES **granulation** noun.

granule /**gran**-yool/ **noun** a small hard particle of a substance.
- ORIGIN Latin *granulum* 'little grain'.

grape noun a green, purple, or black berry growing in clusters on a vine, eaten as fruit and used in making wine.
- DERIVATIVES **grapey** adjective.
- ORIGIN Old French, 'bunch of grapes'.

grapefruit noun (pl. same) a large round yellow citrus fruit with a slightly bitter taste.

grape hyacinth noun a small plant with clusters of small globular blue flowers.

grapeshot noun *historical* ammunition consisting of a number of small iron balls fired together from a cannon.

grapevine noun 1 a vine bearing grapes. **2** (**the grapevine**) *informal* the spreading of information through rumour and informal conversation: *I heard on the grapevine that he'd been very impressive in a reserve match.*

graph noun a diagram showing the relation between two or more sets of numbers or quantities, typically plotted along a pair of lines at right angles.
- ORIGIN abbreviation of *graphic formula*.

-graph combining form 1 referring to something written or drawn in a specified way: *autograph.* **2** referring to an instrument that records something: *seismograph.*
- ORIGIN from Greek *graphos* 'written, writing'.

graphic adjective 1 relating to visual art, especially involving drawing, engraving, or lettering. **2** giving vividly explicit detail: *graphic descriptions of sexual practices.* **3** in the form of a graph. •**noun** a visual image displayed on a computer screen or stored as data.
- ORIGIN Greek *graphē* 'writing, drawing'.

graphical adjective 1 relating to or in the form of a graph. **2** relating to visual art or computer graphics.
- DERIVATIVES **graphically** adverb.

graphical user interface noun a visual way of interacting with a computer using items such as windows and icons.

graphic arts plural noun visual arts based on the use of line and tone rather than three-dimensional work or the use of colour.

graphic design noun the art of combining words and pictures in advertisements, magazines, or books.

graphic equalizer noun a device for controlling the strength and quality of selected frequency bands.

graphic novel noun a novel in comic-strip format.

graphics plural noun (usu. treated as sing.) the use of drawings, designs, or pictures to illustrate books, magazines, etc.

graphite noun a grey form of carbon used as pencil lead and as a solid lubricant in machinery.
- DERIVATIVES **graphitic** adjective.
- ORIGIN from Greek *graphein* 'write'.

graphology noun the study of handwriting, especially as used to analyse a person's character.
- DERIVATIVES **graphological** adjective **graphologist** noun.
- ORIGIN from Greek *graphē* 'writing'.

graph paper noun paper printed with a network of small squares, used for drawing graphs or other diagrams.

-graphy combining form forming nouns referring to: **1** a descriptive science: *geography.* **2** a technique of producing images: *radiography.* **3** a style of writing or drawing: *calligraphy.* **4** writing about a specified subject: *hagiography.* **5** a written or printed list: *filmography.*
- DERIVATIVES **-graphic** combining form.

– ORIGIN Greek -*graphia* 'writing'.

grapnel /grap-nuhl/ noun a device with iron claws, attached to a rope and used for dragging or grasping.
– ORIGIN Old French *grapon*.

grappa /gra-puh/ noun a brandy distilled from the fermented residue of grapes after they have been pressed in winemaking.
– ORIGIN Italian, 'grape stalk'.

grapple verb **1** take a firm hold of someone and struggle to overcome them. **2 (grapple with)** struggle to deal with or understand: *Europe is grappling with a fuel crisis.*
– DERIVATIVES **grappler** noun.
– ORIGIN from Old French *grapil* 'small hook'.

grappling hook (also **grappling iron**) noun a grapnel.

grasp /graasp/ verb **1** seize and hold someone or something firmly. **2** take an opportunity eagerly. **3** understand something fully. •noun **1** a firm grip. **2** a person's capacity to achieve or understand something: *the top job was within her grasp.*
– DERIVATIVES **graspable** adjective **grasper** noun.
– ORIGIN perhaps related to **GROPE**.

grasping adjective greedy for wealth.

grass noun **1** vegetation consisting of short plants with long, narrow leaves. **2** ground covered with grass. **3** informal cannabis. **4** Brit. informal a police informer. •verb **1** cover an area with grass. **2** (often **grass on**) Brit. informal inform the police of someone's criminal activity.
– PHRASES **not let the grass grow under one's feet** not delay in taking action. **put someone/thing out to grass 1** put an animal out to graze. **2** informal force someone to retire.
– ORIGIN Old English; sense 4 is perhaps related to rhyming slang *grasshopper* 'copper'.

grasshopper noun an insect with long hind legs which are used for jumping and for producing a chirping sound.

grassland noun (also **grasslands**) a large area of grass-covered land, especially one used for grazing.

grass roots plural noun the most basic level of an activity or organization.

grass snake noun a harmless grey-green snake with a yellowish band around the neck.

grass widow noun a woman whose husband is away often or for a long time.
– ORIGIN first referring to an unmarried woman with a child: perhaps from the idea of a couple having lain on the grass instead of in bed.

grassy adjective (**grassier, grassiest**) covered with or resembling grass.

grate¹ verb **1** shred food by rubbing it on a grater. **2** make an unpleasant scraping sound. **3** have an irritating effect: *the fly's buzzing grated on my nerves.*
– ORIGIN Old French *grater*.

grate² noun **1** a metal frame for holding fuel in a fireplace. **2** the recess of a fireplace.
– ORIGIN Old French.

grateful adjective feeling or showing one's appreciation of something that has been done for one.
– DERIVATIVES **gratefully** adverb.
– ORIGIN Latin *gratus* 'pleasing, thankful'.

grater noun a device having a surface covered with sharp-edged holes, used for grating food.

gratification noun **1** pleasure, especially when gained from the satisfaction of a desire: *a thirst for sexual gratification.* **2** a source of pleasure.

gratify verb (**gratifies, gratifying, gratified**) **1** give pleasure or satisfaction to: *he was gratified that they liked the book.* **2** indulge or satisfy a desire.
– ORIGIN Latin *gratificari* 'give or do as a favour'.

gratin /gra-tan/ noun a dish with a light browned crust of breadcrumbs or melted cheese.
– ORIGIN French.

gratiné /gra-ti-nay/ adjective another term for **AU GRATIN**.
– ORIGIN French.

grating¹ adjective **1** sounding harsh and unpleasant. **2** irritating: *his grating confrontational personality.*
– DERIVATIVES **gratingly** adverb.

grating² noun a framework of parallel or crossed bars that covers an opening.

gratis /grah-tiss/ adverb & adjective free of charge.
– ORIGIN Latin.

gratitude noun the quality of being grateful; appreciation of kindness.
– ORIGIN Latin *gratitudo*.

gratuitous /gruh-tyoo-i-tuhss/ adjective **1** having no justifiable reason or purpose: *studios were under pressure to tone down gratuitous violence.* **2** free of charge.
– DERIVATIVES **gratuitously** adverb.
– ORIGIN Latin *gratuitus* 'given freely, spontaneous'.

gratuity /gruh-tyoo-i-ti/ noun (pl. **gratuities**) formal a sum of money given to someone who has provided a service; a tip.
– ORIGIN Latin *gratuitas* 'gift'.

gravadlax /grav-uhd-laks/ noun variant spelling of **GRAVLAX**.

grave¹ noun **1** a hole dug in the ground for a coffin or a corpse. **2 (the grave)** death.
– PHRASES **dig one's own grave** do something foolish which causes one's downfall. **turn in one's grave** (of a dead person) be likely to have been angry or distressed about something had they been alive.
– ORIGIN Old English.

grave² adjective **1** giving cause for alarm or concern: *he was in grave danger.* **2** solemn or serious: *her face was grave.*
– DERIVATIVES **gravely** adverb.
– ORIGIN Latin *gravis* 'heavy, serious'.

grave³ verb (past part. **graven** or **graved**) **1** literary fix something firmly in the mind. **2** old use engrave something on a surface.
– ORIGIN Old English, 'dig'.

grave accent /grahv/ noun a mark (`) placed over a vowel in some languages to indicate a change in its sound quality.
– ORIGIN French *grave* 'heavy, serious'.

gravedigger noun a person who digs graves.

gravel noun a loose mixture of small stones and coarse sand, used for paths and roads. •verb (**gravels, gravelling, gravelled; US gravels,**

graveling, graveled) cover something with gravel.
– ORIGIN Old French.

gravelly adjective **1** resembling, containing, or consisting of gravel. **2** (of a voice) deep and rough-sounding.

graven image noun a carved figure of a god used as an idol.
– ORIGIN with reference to the Book of Exodus, chapter 20.

graver noun an engraving tool.

Graves /grahv/ noun a red or white wine from Graves, a district of SW France.

gravestone noun an inscribed headstone marking a grave.

graveyard noun a burial ground beside a church.

graveyard shift noun a work shift that runs from midnight to 8 a.m.

gravid /**gra**-vid/ adjective **1** technical pregnant. **2** literary full of meaning or a specified quality: *the scene appears gravid with unease.*
– ORIGIN Latin *gravidus* 'laden, pregnant'.

gravimeter /gruh-**vim**-i-ter/ noun an instrument for measuring the force of gravity at different places.

gravimetric /gra-vi-**met**-rik/ adjective **1** relating to the measurement of weight. **2** relating to the measurement of gravity.

gravitas /**gra**-vi-tass/ noun a dignified and serious manner.
– ORIGIN Latin.

gravitate /**gra**-vi-tayt/ verb **1** be drawn towards a place, person, or thing: *Taureans often gravitate towards careers in music.* **2** Physics move, or tend to move, towards a centre of gravity.

gravitation noun **1** movement, or a tendency to move, towards a centre of gravity. **2** Physics gravity.
– DERIVATIVES **gravitational** adjective **gravitationally** adverb.

gravity noun **1** the force that attracts a body towards the centre of the earth, or towards any other physical body having mass. **2** extreme importance or seriousness: *the gravity of environmental crimes.* **3** a solemn or serious manner.
– ORIGIN Latin *gravitas* 'weight, seriousness'.

gravlax /**grav**-laks/ (also **gravadlax**) noun a Scandinavian dish of dry-cured salmon marinated in herbs.
– ORIGIN Swedish.

gravure /gruh-**vyoor**/ noun short for **PHOTOGRAVURE**.

gravy noun (pl. **gravies**) a sauce made by adding stock, flour, and seasoning to the fat and juices that come out of meat during cooking.
– ORIGIN perhaps from Old French *grané.*

gravy boat noun a long, narrow jug used for serving gravy.

gravy train noun informal a situation in which someone can easily make a lot of money.

gray adjective US spelling of **GREY**.

graylag noun US spelling of **GREYLAG**.

grayling noun an edible silvery-grey freshwater fish with horizontal violet stripes.

graze[1] verb **1** (of cattle, sheep, etc.) eat grass in a field. **2** informal eat frequent snacks at irregular intervals.
– DERIVATIVES **grazer** noun.
– ORIGIN Old English.

graze[2] verb **1** scrape and break the skin on part of the body. **2** touch something lightly in passing. • noun a slight injury caused by grazing the skin.
– ORIGIN perhaps from **GRAZE**[1].

grazier /**gray**-zi-uh/ noun a person who rears or fattens cattle or sheep for market.

grazing noun grassland suitable for use as pasture.

grease noun **1** a thick oily substance, especially one used to lubricate machinery. **2** animal fat used or produced in cooking. • verb smear or lubricate something with grease.
– PHRASES **grease the palm of** informal bribe someone. **like greased lightning** informal very rapidly.
– ORIGIN Old French *graisse.*

grease gun noun a device for pumping grease under pressure to a particular point.

greasepaint noun a waxy substance used as make-up by actors.

greaseproof paper noun Brit. paper that does not allow grease to pass through it, used in cooking.

greaser noun **1** informal a long-haired young man belonging to a motorcycle gang. **2** a motor mechanic or unskilled engineer on a ship.

greasy adjective (**greasier, greasiest**) **1** covered with or resembling grease. **2** polite or friendly in a way that seems excessive and insincere.
– DERIVATIVES **greasily** adverb **greasiness** noun.

greasy spoon noun informal a shabby cafe serving cheap fried meals.

great adjective **1** much higher than average in amount, extent, or intensity. **2** much higher than average in ability, quality, or importance: *a great Italian composer.* **3** informal excellent. **4** used to emphasize a description: *I was a great fan of Hank's.* **5** (**Greater**) referring to an area that includes the centre of a city and a large urban area round it: *Greater London.* **6** (in combination) (in names of family relationships) referring to one degree further removed upwards or downwards: *a great-aunt.* • noun **1** a famous and successful person. **2** (**Greats**) the honours course in classics, philosophy, and ancient history at Oxford University. • adverb informal very well.
– DERIVATIVES **greatness** noun.
– ORIGIN Old English.

great ape noun a large ape of a family closely related to humans, including the gorilla and chimpanzees.

great-aunt noun an aunt of one's father or mother.

great circle noun a circle on the surface of a sphere which lies in a plane passing through the sphere's centre.

greatcoat noun a long, heavy overcoat.

Great Dane noun a very large and powerful dog with short hair.

greatly adverb very much.

great-nephew noun a son of one's nephew or niece.

great-niece noun a daughter of one's nephew or niece.

great tit noun a common songbird with a black

and white head, grey back, and yellow breast.

great-uncle noun an uncle of one's mother or father.

Great War noun the First World War.

greave noun historical a piece of armour for the shin.
– ORIGIN Old French *greve* 'shin, greave'.

grebe /greeb/ noun a diving waterbird with a long neck and a very short tail.
– ORIGIN French.

Grecian adjective relating to ancient Greece, especially its architecture.

greed noun **1** a strong and selfish desire for possessions, wealth, or power. **2** a desire to eat more food than is necessary.

greedy adjective (**greedier**, **greediest**) **1** having an excessive desire for food. **2** having or showing a strong and selfish desire for wealth or power: *people driven from their land by greedy developers.*
– DERIVATIVES **greedily** adverb **greediness** noun.
– ORIGIN Old English.

Greek noun **1** a person from Greece. **2** the ancient or modern language of Greece. • adjective relating to Greece.
– PHRASES **it's all Greek to me** informal I can't understand it at all.

Greek coffee noun very strong black coffee served with the fine grounds in it.

Greek cross noun a cross of which all four arms are of equal length.

Greek Orthodox Church noun the national Church of Greece.

green adjective **1** of the colour between blue and yellow in the spectrum; coloured like grass. **2** covered with grass or other vegetation. **3** (**Green**) concerned with or supporting protection of the environment. **4** (of a plant or fruit) young or unripe. **5** inexperienced or naive. **6** in an untreated or original state; not cured, seasoned, etc. • noun **1** green colour or material. **2** a piece of common grassy land, especially in the centre of a village. **3** an area of smooth, very short grass immediately surrounding a hole on a golf course. **4** (**greens**) green vegetables. **5** (**Green**) a member or supporter of an environmentalist group or party. • verb **1** make or become green. **2** make something less harmful to the environment.
– PHRASES **the green-eyed monster** jealousy personified. [from Shakespeare's *Othello*.]
– DERIVATIVES **greenish** adjective **greenness** noun.
– ORIGIN Old English.

greenback noun US informal a dollar.

green belt noun an area of open land around a city, on which building is restricted.

Green Beret noun informal a British commando or a member of the US Army Special Forces.

green card noun (in the US) a permit that allows a foreign national to live and work permanently in the US.

greenery noun green foliage or vegetation.

greenfield adjective (of a site) previously undeveloped or built on.

greenfinch noun a large finch with green and yellow plumage.

green fingers plural noun Brit. informal natural ability in growing plants.

greenfly noun (pl. **greenflies**) a green aphid.

greengage noun a sweet greenish fruit resembling a small plum.
– ORIGIN named after the English botanist Sir William *Gage*.

greengrocer noun Brit. a person who sells fruit and vegetables.
– DERIVATIVES **greengrocery** noun.

greenhorn noun informal, chiefly N. Amer. an inexperienced or naive person.

greenhouse noun a glass building in which plants that need protection from cold weather are grown.

greenhouse effect noun the trapping of the sun's warmth in a planet's lower atmosphere, because visible radiation from the sun passes through the atmosphere more readily than infrared radiation coming from the planet's surface.

greenhouse gas noun a gas, such as carbon dioxide, that contributes to the greenhouse effect by absorbing infrared radiation.

greenkeeper noun a person employed to look after a golf course.

Greenlander noun a person from Greenland.

green light noun **1** a green traffic light giving permission to proceed. **2** permission to go ahead with a project.

Green Paper noun (in the UK) a preliminary report containing government proposals on a particular subject, intended for general discussion.

green pepper noun an unripe sweet pepper, green in colour and eaten as a vegetable.

green revolution noun a large increase in crop production in developing countries achieved by the use of artificial fertilizers, pesticides, and high-yield crop varieties.

green room noun a room in a theatre or studio in which performers can relax when they are not performing.

greensand noun a greenish kind of sandstone.

greenshank noun a large grey and white sandpiper with long greenish legs.

greenstick fracture noun a fracture of the bone, occurring typically in children, in which one side of the bone is broken and the other only bent.

greenstone noun **1** a greenish igneous rock containing feldspar and hornblende. **2** chiefly NZ a variety of jade.

greensward /green-sword/ noun literary grass-covered ground.

green tea noun tea made from unfermented leaves, produced mainly in China and Japan.

Greenwich Mean Time /gren-ich/ noun the time measured at the Greenwich meridian, used as the standard time in a zone that includes the British Isles.
– ORIGIN from *Greenwich* in London, former site of the Royal Observatory.

Greenwich meridian noun the meridian of zero longitude, passing through Greenwich.

greenwood noun old use a wood or forest in leaf, especially as a refuge for medieval outlaws.

green woodpecker noun a large green and yellow woodpecker with a red crown and a laughing call.

g

greet[1] verb 1 give a word or sign of welcome when meeting someone. 2 react to or acknowledge in a particular way: 3 (of a sight or sound) become apparent to a person arriving somewhere.
– DERIVATIVES **greeter** noun.
– ORIGIN Old English.

greet[2] verb Scottish weep; cry.
– ORIGIN Old English.

greeting noun 1 a word or sign of welcome when meeting someone. 2 (usu. **greetings**) a formal expression of good wishes.

greetings card (N. Amer. **greeting card**) noun a decorative card sent to express good wishes on a particular occasion.

gregarious /gri-**gair**-i-uhss/ adjective 1 fond of company; sociable. 2 (of animals) living in flocks or colonies.
– DERIVATIVES **gregariously** adverb **gregariousness** noun.
– ORIGIN Latin *gregarius*, from *grex* 'a flock'.

Gregorian calendar /gri-**gor**-i-uhn/ noun the modified form of the Julian calendar introduced in 1582 by Pope Gregory XIII, and still used today.

Gregorian chant noun medieval church plainsong.
– ORIGIN named after St *Gregory* the Great.

gremlin noun a mischievous creature regarded as responsible for unexplained mechanical or electrical faults.
– ORIGIN a Second World War term: perhaps suggested by GOBLIN.

Grenache /gruh-**nash**/ noun a variety of black wine grape native to the Languedoc-Roussillon region of France.
– ORIGIN French.

grenade /gruh-**nayd**/ noun a small bomb thrown by hand or launched mechanically.
– ORIGIN from Old French *pome grenate* 'pomegranate'; the bomb was regarded as resembling a pomegranate.

Grenadian /gri-**nay**-di-uhn/ noun a person from the Caribbean country of Grenada.
• adjective relating to Grenada.

grenadier /gren-uh-**deer**/ noun 1 historical a soldier armed with grenades. 2 (**Grenadiers** or **Grenadier Guards**) the first regiment of the royal household infantry.

grenadine /**gren**-uh-deen/ noun a sweet cordial made in France from pomegranates.
– ORIGIN French.

grew past of GROW.

grey (US **gray**) adjective 1 of a colour between black and white, as of ashes or lead. 2 (of hair) turning grey or white with age. 3 (of the weather) cloudy and dull; without sun. 4 dull and nondescript: *grey, faceless men*. 5 not accounted for in official statistics: *the grey economy*. • noun grey colour. • verb (especially of hair) become grey.
– DERIVATIVES **greyish** adjective **greyness** noun.
– ORIGIN Old English.

grey area noun an area of activity that does not easily fit into an existing category and is difficult to deal with.

greybeard noun humorous an old man.

Grey Friar noun a friar of the Franciscan order (who wear grey habits).

greyhound noun a swift, slender breed of dog used in racing.
– ORIGIN Old English.

greylag noun a large goose with mainly grey plumage, the ancestor of the domestic goose.
– ORIGIN probably from dialect *lag* 'goose'.

grey matter noun 1 the darker tissue of the brain and spinal cord. 2 informal intelligence.

grey seal noun a large North Atlantic seal with a spotted greyish coat.

grey squirrel noun a tree squirrel with mainly grey fur, native to eastern North America and introduced to Britain and elsewhere.

grid noun 1 a framework of bars that are parallel to or cross each other. 2 a network of lines that cross each other to form a series of squares or rectangles. 3 a network of cables or pipes for distributing power, especially high-voltage electricity. 4 a pattern of lines marking the starting places on a motor-racing track.
– ORIGIN from GRIDIRON.

griddle noun a heavy, flat iron plate that is heated and used for cooking food. • verb cook food on a griddle.
– ORIGIN Old French *gredil*.

gridiron /**grid**-I-uhn/ noun 1 a frame of parallel metal bars used for grilling meat or fish over an open fire. 2 a grid pattern, especially of streets. 3 a field for American football, marked with regularly spaced parallel lines.
– ORIGIN alteration of former *gredile* 'griddle'.

gridlock noun a traffic jam affecting a whole network of intersecting streets.
– DERIVATIVES **gridlocked** adjective.

grief noun 1 intense sorrow, especially caused by someone's death. 2 informal trouble or annoyance.
– PHRASES **come to grief** have an accident; meet with disaster.
– ORIGIN Old French.

grievance noun a real or imagined cause for complaint.

grieve verb 1 feel intense sorrow, especially as a result of someone's death. 2 cause great distress to someone.
– DERIVATIVES **griever** noun.
– ORIGIN Old French *grever* 'burden, encumber'.

grievous /**gree**-vuhss/ adjective formal (of something bad) very severe or serious: *the loss of his father was a grievous blow*.
– DERIVATIVES **grievously** adverb.

grievous bodily harm noun Law, Brit. serious physical injury inflicted on a person by the deliberate action of another, considered more serious than actual bodily harm.

griffin (also **gryphon** or **griffon**) noun a mythical creature with the head and wings of an eagle and the body of a lion.
– ORIGIN Old French *grifoun*.

griffon /**grif**-fuhn/ noun 1 a dog of a small terrier-like breed. 2 a large vulture with pale brown plumage.
– ORIGIN variant of GRIFFIN.

grig noun dialect 1 a small eel. 2 a grasshopper or cricket.
– ORIGIN unknown.

grill noun Brit. 1 a device on a cooker that radiates heat downwards for cooking food. 2 a

gridiron used for cooking food on an open fire. **3** a dish of food cooked using a grill. **4** a restaurant serving grilled food. **5** variant form of **GRILLE**. • verb **1** cook food using a grill. **2** informal question someone in a relentless or aggressive way.
– ORIGIN Old French *graille* 'grille'.

grille (also **grill**) noun a grating or screen of metal bars or wires.
– ORIGIN French.

grilse /grilss/ noun a salmon that has returned to fresh water after a single winter at sea.
– ORIGIN unknown.

grim adjective (**grimmer, grimmest**) **1** very serious or gloomy; forbidding. **2** horrifying, depressing, or worrying: *the grim realities of warfare.*
– PHRASES **like** (or **for**) **grim death** Brit. with great determination.
– DERIVATIVES **grimly** adverb **grimness** noun.
– ORIGIN Old English.

grimace /gri-mayss, gri-muhss/ noun a twisted expression on a person's face, expressing disgust, pain, or wry amusement. • verb make a grimace.
– ORIGIN French.

grime noun dirt ingrained on a surface. • verb make something black or dirty with grime.
– DERIVATIVES **grimy** adjective.
– ORIGIN German and Dutch.

grin verb (**grins, grinning, grinned**) smile broadly. • noun a broad smile.
– PHRASES **grin and bear it** Brit. suffer pain or misfortune without complaining.
– ORIGIN Old English.

Grinch noun N. Amer. informal a spoilsport or killjoy.
– ORIGIN the name of a character in the children's story *How the Grinch Stole Christmas* by Dr Seuss.

grind verb (past and past part. **ground**) **1** reduce something to small particles or powder by crushing it. **2** make something sharp or smooth by rubbing it against a hard or abrasive surface or tool. **3** rub together or move gratingly. **4** (**grind someone down**) weaken someone by treating them harshly over a long period of time. **5** (**grind something out**) produce something slowly and laboriously. **6** (as adj. **grinding**) (of a difficult situation) oppressive and seemingly endless: *grinding poverty.* **7** informal (of a dancer) rotate the hips. • noun hard, dull work: *the daily grind.*
– PHRASES **grind to a halt** (or **come to a grinding halt**) slow down gradually and then stop completely.
– DERIVATIVES **grinder** noun **grindingly** adverb.
– ORIGIN Old English.

grindstone noun **1** a thick revolving disc of abrasive material used for sharpening or polishing metal objects. **2** a millstone.
– PHRASES **keep one's nose to the grindstone** work hard and continuously.

gringo /gring-goh/ noun (pl. **gringos**) informal, derogatory (in Latin America) a white English-speaking person.
– ORIGIN Spanish, 'foreign, foreigner'.

griot /gree-oh/ noun a West African travelling poet, musician, and storyteller.
– ORIGIN French.

grip verb (**grips, gripping, gripped**) **1** take and

keep a firm hold of something. **2** affect deeply: *she was gripped by a feeling of panic.* **3** (often as adj. **gripping**) hold someone's attention or interest: *a gripping drama.* • noun **1** a firm hold. **2** an understanding of something. **3** a part or attachment by which something is held in the hand. **4** a travelling bag. **5** a member of a camera crew responsible for moving and setting up equipment.
– PHRASES **come** (or **get**) **to grips with** begin to deal with or understand. **lose one's grip** become unable to understand or control one's situation.
– DERIVATIVES **gripper** noun.
– ORIGIN Old English.

gripe verb **1** informal complain or grumble. **2** (as adj. **griping**) (of pain in the stomach or intestines) sudden and acute. • noun **1** informal a minor complaint. **2** pain in the stomach or intestines; colic.
– ORIGIN Old English, 'grasp, clutch'.

gripe water noun Brit. trademark a solution given to babies for the relief of colic, wind, and indigestion.

grisaille /gri-zyl, gri-zayl/ noun a method of painting using only various shades of grey.
– ORIGIN French.

grisly /griz-li/ adjective (**grislier, grisliest**) causing horror or disgust.
– DERIVATIVES **grisliness** noun.
– ORIGIN Old English.

> **USAGE:** Grisly and grizzly are often confused. Grisly means 'causing horror or disgust', as in *a grisly murder*, whereas a **grizzly** is a kind of large American bear.

grist noun **1** corn that is ground to make flour. **2** malt crushed to make mash for brewing.
– PHRASES **grist to the mill** useful experience or knowledge.
– ORIGIN Old English, 'grinding'.

gristle /griss-uhl/ noun tough inedible cartilage in meat.
– DERIVATIVES **gristly** adjective.
– ORIGIN Old English.

grit noun **1** small loose particles of stone or sand. **2** (also **gritstone**) a coarse sandstone. **3** courage and determination. • verb (**grits, gritting, gritted**) spread grit on an icy road.
– PHRASES **grit one's teeth 1** clench one's teeth. **2** be determined to do or continue to do something difficult or unpleasant.
– DERIVATIVES **gritter** noun.
– ORIGIN Old English.

grits plural noun US coarsely ground maize kernels, served boiled with water or milk.
– ORIGIN Old English, 'bran, mill dust'.

gritty adjective (**grittier, grittiest**) **1** containing or covered with grit. **2** showing courage and determination. **3** showing something unpleasant as it really is; uncompromising: *a gritty prison drama.*
– DERIVATIVES **grittily** adverb **grittiness** noun.

grizzle verb Brit. informal (of a child) cry or whimper fretfully.
– ORIGIN unknown.

grizzled adjective having grey or grey-streaked hair.
– ORIGIN Old French *gris* 'grey'.

grizzly (also **grizzly bear**) noun (pl. **grizzlies**) a

g

large variety of brown bear often having white-tipped fur, native to western North America.
– ORIGIN from GRIZZLED.

> USAGE: On the confusion of grizzly and grisly, see the note at GRISLY.

groan verb 1 make a deep sound of pain or despair. 2 make a low creaking sound when pressure or weight is applied. 3 (**groan under**) be weighed down by: *a table groaning under an assortment of richly spiced dishes.* •noun a groaning sound.
– DERIVATIVES **groaner** noun.
– ORIGIN Old English.

groat noun historical an English silver coin worth four old pence.
– ORIGIN from Dutch *groot* or German *grōte* 'great, thick'.

groats plural noun hulled or crushed grain, especially oats.
– ORIGIN Old English.

grocer noun a person who sells food and small household items.
– ORIGIN Old French *grossier*.

grocery noun (pl. **groceries**) 1 a grocer's shop or business. 2 (**groceries**) items of food sold in a grocer's shop or supermarket.

grockle noun Brit. informal, derogatory a holiday-maker, especially one in the West Country.
– ORIGIN an invented word.

grog noun 1 spirits (originally rum) mixed with water. 2 informal or Austral./NZ alcoholic drink.
– ORIGIN said to be from the nickname of Admiral Vernon, who ordered diluted (instead of neat) rum to be served out to sailors.

groggy adjective (**groggier, groggiest**) feeling dazed, weak, or unsteady.
– DERIVATIVES **groggily** adverb **grogginess** noun.

groin¹ noun 1 the area between the abdomen and the thigh on either side of the body. 2 informal the region of the genitals. 3 Architecture a curved edge formed by two intersecting roof arches.
– ORIGIN perhaps from an Old English word meaning 'depression, abyss'.

groin² noun US spelling of GROYNE.

grommet /grom-mit/ noun 1 a protective eyelet in a hole that a rope or cable passes through. 2 Brit. a tube surgically implanted in the eardrum to drain fluid from the middle ear.
– ORIGIN from former French *gourmer* 'to curb'.

groom verb 1 brush and clean a horse's or dog's coat. 2 (often as adj. **groomed**) keep oneself neat and tidy in appearance: *a beautifully groomed woman.* 3 prepare or train someone for a particular purpose or activity: *she had been groomed to take over her father's business* 4 (of a paedophile) prepare a child for a meeting, especially via an Internet chat room. •noun 1 a person employed to take care of horses. 2 a bridegroom.
– ORIGIN unknown.

groove noun 1 a long, narrow cut in a hard material. 2 a spiral track cut in a gramophone record, into which the stylus fits. 3 an established routine or habit. 4 informal a rhythmic pattern in popular or jazz music. •verb 1 make a groove or grooves in

something. 2 informal dance to or play pop or jazz music.
– DERIVATIVES **grooved** adjective **groover** noun.
– ORIGIN Dutch *groeve* 'furrow, pit'.

groovy adjective (**groovier, grooviest**) informal, dated or humorous fashionable and exciting.
– DERIVATIVES **groovily** adverb **grooviness** noun.

grope verb 1 feel about uncertainly with one's hands. 2 informal fondle someone for sexual pleasure, especially against their will. •noun informal an act of groping someone.
– DERIVATIVES **groper** noun.
– ORIGIN Old English.

grosbeak /grohs-beek/ noun a songbird with a stout conical bill and brightly coloured plumage.
– ORIGIN from French *gros* 'big, fat' + *bec* 'beak'.

grosgrain /groh-grayn/ noun a heavy ribbed fabric, typically of silk or rayon.
– ORIGIN French, 'coarse grain'.

gros point /groh pwan/ noun a type of needlepoint embroidery consisting of stitches crossing two or more threads of the canvas in each direction.
– ORIGIN French, 'large stitch'.

gross adjective 1 unattractively large. 2 very obvious and unacceptable: *gross misconduct.* 3 informal very unpleasant; repulsive. 4 rude or vulgar. 5 (of income, profit, or interest) without deduction of tax or other contributions. Often contrasted with NET². 6 (of weight) including contents or other variable items. •adverb without tax or other contributions having been deducted. •verb 1 produce or earn an amount of money as gross profit or income. 2 (**gross someone out**) N. Amer. informal disgust someone. •noun 1 (pl. same) an amount equal to twelve dozen; 144. 2 (pl. **grosses**) a gross profit or income.
– DERIVATIVES **grossly** adverb **grossness** noun.
– ORIGIN Old French *gros* 'large'; sense 1 of the noun is from French *grosse douzaine* 'large dozen'.

gross domestic product noun the total value of goods produced and services provided within a country during one year.

gross national product noun the total value of goods produced and services provided by a country during one year, equal to the gross domestic product plus the net income from foreign investments.

grosz /grorsh/ noun (pl. **groszy** or **grosze** /gror-shi/) a unit of money of Poland, equal to one hundredth of a zloty.
– ORIGIN Polish.

grotesque /groh-tesk/ adjective 1 comically or repulsively ugly or distorted. 2 shocking or offensive: *a grotesque waste of money.* •noun 1 a grotesque figure or image. 2 a style of decorative painting or sculpture in which human and animal forms are interwoven with flowers and foliage.
– DERIVATIVES **grotesquely** adverb **grotesqueness** noun.
– ORIGIN from Italian *opera* or *pittura grottesca* 'work or painting like that found in a grotto'.

grotesquerie /groh-tesk-uh-ri/ noun (pl. **grotesqueries**) the quality of being grotesque, or things that are grotesque.

grotto noun (pl. **grottoes** or **grottos**) a small picturesque cave, especially an artificial one in a park or garden.
– ORIGIN Italian *grotta*.

grotty adjective (**grottier, grottiest**) Brit. informal **1** unpleasant and of poor quality. **2** unwell.
– DERIVATIVES **grottiness** noun.
– ORIGIN from **GROTESQUE**.

grouch /growch/ informal noun **1** a person who is often grumpy. **2** a complaint or grumble. • verb complain; grumble.
– ORIGIN from Old French *grouchier* 'to grumble, murmur'.

grouchy adjective (**grouchier, grouchiest**) irritable and bad-tempered; grumpy.
– DERIVATIVES **grouchily** adverb.

ground¹ noun **1** the solid surface of the earth. **2** land or soil of a particular kind: *marshy ground*. **3** an area of land or sea with a particular use: *fishing grounds*. **4** (**grounds**) an area of enclosed land surrounding a large house. **5** (**grounds**) reasons for doing or believing something. **6** a prepared surface to which paint or other decoration is applied. **7** (**grounds**) small pieces of solid matter in a liquid, especially coffee, which settle at the bottom. • verb **1** ban or prevent a pilot or aircraft from flying. **2** run a ship aground. **3** (**be grounded in/on**) have as a firm theoretical or practical basis: *an area of research grounded in classical physics*. **4** informal (of a parent) refuse to allow a child to go out socially, as a punishment.
– PHRASES **be thick** (or **thin**) **on the ground** exist in large (or small) numbers or amounts. **break new ground** achieve or create something new. **gain ground** become more popular or accepted. **get off the ground** start happening or functioning successfully. **give** (or **lose**) **ground** retreat or lose one's advantage. **go to ground** (of a fox or other animal) enter its earth or burrow. **hold** (or **stand**) **one's ground** not retreat or lose one's advantage. **on the ground** in a place where real, practical work is done.
– ORIGIN Old English.

ground² past and past participle of **GRIND**.

groundbreaking adjective involving completely new methods or discoveries.

ground control noun (treated as sing. or pl.) the personnel and equipment that monitor and direct the flight and landing of aircraft or spacecraft.

ground elder noun a common weed with leaves that resemble those of the elder and spreading underground stems.

ground floor noun the floor of a building at ground level.

ground frost noun Brit. frost formed on the surface of the ground or in the top layer of soil.

ground glass noun **1** glass with a smooth ground surface that makes it non-transparent. **2** glass ground into an abrasive powder.

groundhog noun North American term for **WOODCHUCK**.

grounding noun basic training or instruction in a subject.

groundless adjective not based on any good reason.

groundling noun a spectator or reader whose taste is unsophisticated or uneducated.
– ORIGIN first referring to a member of the part of a theatre audience that stood in the pit beneath the stage: with reference to Shakespeare's *Hamlet* III. ii. 11.

groundnut noun another term for **PEANUT**.

ground rent noun Brit. rent paid by the owner of a building to the owner of the land on which it is built.

ground rules plural noun basic principles controlling the way in which something is done.

groundsel /grownd-s'l/ noun a plant of the daisy family with small yellow flowers.
– ORIGIN Old English.

groundsheet noun a waterproof sheet spread on the ground inside a tent.

groundsman (N. Amer. **groundskeeper**) noun (pl. **groundsmen**) Brit. a person who maintains a sports ground or the grounds of a large building.

ground speed noun an aircraft's speed relative to the ground.

ground squirrel noun a burrowing squirrel of a large group including the chipmunks.

groundswell /grownd-swel/ noun a build-up of opinion in a large section of the population.

groundwater noun water held underground in the soil or in rock.

groundwork noun preliminary or basic work.

ground zero noun the point on the earth's surface directly below an exploding nuclear bomb.

group noun (treated as sing. or pl.) **1** a number of people or things located, gathered, or classed together. **2** a number of musicians who play popular music together. **3** a division of an air force. **4** Chemistry a set of elements occupying a column in the periodic table and having broadly similar properties. **5** Chemistry a combination of atoms having a recognizable identity in a number of compounds. • verb place in or form a group or groups: *sofas and chairs were grouped around a low table*.
– ORIGIN Italian *gruppo*.

group captain noun a rank of officer in the RAF, above wing commander and below air commodore.

grouper noun a large heavy-bodied fish found in warm seas.
– ORIGIN Portuguese *garoupa*.

groupie noun informal a young woman who follows a pop group or celebrity, especially in the hope of a sexual relationship with them.

grouping noun a group of people with a shared interest or aim, especially within a larger organization.

group therapy noun a form of psychiatric therapy in which patients meet to discuss their problems.

grouse¹ noun (pl. same) a medium-sized game bird with a plump body and feathered legs.
– ORIGIN perhaps related to Latin *gruta* or to Old French *grue* 'crane'.

grouse² verb complain or grumble. • noun a grumble or complaint.
– ORIGIN unknown.

grout /growt/ noun a mortar or paste for filling

g

crevices, especially the gaps between wall or floor tiles. •verb fill in crevices with grout.
– ORIGIN perhaps related to French dialect *grouter* 'grout a wall'.

grove noun a small wood, orchard, or group of trees.
– ORIGIN Old English.

grovel verb (**grovels, grovelling, grovelled**; US **grovels, groveling, groveled**) **1** crouch or crawl on the ground. **2** act in a very humble way in an attempt to gain forgiveness or favourable treatment.
– DERIVATIVES **groveller** noun.
– ORIGIN from an Old Norse word meaning 'face downwards'.

grow verb (past **grew**; past part. **grown**) **1** (of a living thing) undergo natural development by increasing in size and changing physically. **2** (of a plant) germinate and develop. **3** become larger or greater over a period of time; increase. **4** become gradually or increasingly: *we grew braver.* **5** (**grow up**) become an adult. **6** (**grow on**) become gradually more appealing to: *the tune grows on you.* **7** (**grow out of**) become too mature to continue to do something: *she had long since grown out of her disco phase.*
– DERIVATIVES **grower** noun.
– ORIGIN Old English.

growbag noun Brit. a bag containing potting compost, in which plants can be grown.

growing pains plural noun **1** pains which can occur in the limbs of young children. **2** difficulties experienced in the early stages of an enterprise.

growl verb **1** (especially of a dog) make a low sound of hostility in the throat. **2** say something in a low, angry voice. **3** make a low rumbling sound. •noun a growling sound.
– ORIGIN probably imitating the sound.

growler noun **1** a person or thing that growls. **2** a small iceberg.

grown past participle of GROW.

grown-up adjective adult. •noun informal an adult.

growth noun **1** the process of growing. **2** something that has grown or is growing. **3** a tumour or other abnormal formation.

growth hormone noun a hormone which stimulates growth in animal or plant cells.

growth industry noun an industry that is developing particularly rapidly.

growth ring noun a concentric layer of wood, shell, or bone developed during a regular period of growth.

growth stock noun a company stock that tends to increase in capital value rather than yield high income.

groyne (US **groin**) noun a low wall or barrier built out into the sea from a beach to prevent the beach from shifting or being eroded.
– ORIGIN from Latin *grunium* 'pig's snout'.

GRP abbreviation glass-reinforced plastic.

grub noun **1** the larva of an insect, especially a beetle. **2** informal food. •verb (**grubs, grubbing, grubbed**) **1** dig shallowly in soil. **2** (**grub something up**) dig something up. **3** search clumsily and unmethodically: *I began grubbing about in the waste-paper basket.*

– DERIVATIVES **grubber** noun.
– ORIGIN perhaps related to Dutch *grobbelen*, also to GRAVE[1].

grubby adjective (**grubbier, grubbiest**) **1** dirty, grimy. **2** involving activities that are dishonest or immoral: *a grubby affair.*
– DERIVATIVES **grubbiness** noun.

Grub Street noun the world or class of impoverished journalists and writers.
– ORIGIN the name of a London street in which such writers lived in the 17th century.

grudge noun a long-lasting feeling of resentment or dislike: *he held a grudge against his former boss.* •verb **1** be resentfully unwilling to give or allow something: *he grudged the money spent on her.* **2** feel resentful that someone has achieved something: *I don't grudge him his moment of triumph.*
– ORIGIN related to GROUCH.

grudging adjective given or allowed only reluctantly or resentfully: *a grudging apology.*

gruel noun a thin liquid food of oatmeal boiled in milk or water.
– ORIGIN Old French.

gruelling (US **grueling**) adjective extremely tiring and demanding.
– DERIVATIVES **gruellingly** adverb.
– ORIGIN from former *gruel* 'exhaust, punish'.

gruesome adjective causing disgust or horror.
– DERIVATIVES **gruesomely** adverb **gruesomeness** noun.
– ORIGIN from Scots *grue* 'feel horror, shudder'.

gruff adjective **1** (of a person's voice) rough and low in pitch. **2** abrupt or unfriendly in manner.
– DERIVATIVES **gruffly** adverb **gruffness** noun.
– ORIGIN from Flemish and Dutch *grof* 'coarse, rude'.

grumble verb **1** complain in a bad-tempered but muted way. **2** make a low rumbling sound. •noun a complaint.
– DERIVATIVES **grumbler** noun.
– ORIGIN probably Germanic.

grump noun informal **1** a grumpy person. **2** a period of sulking.

grumpy adjective (**grumpier, grumpiest**) bad-tempered and sulky.
– DERIVATIVES **grumpily** adverb **grumpiness** noun.
– ORIGIN imitating sounds expressing displeasure.

grunge noun **1** a style of rock music with a loud, harsh guitar sound. **2** a casual, deliberately untidy style of fashion including loose, layered clothing and ripped jeans. **3** informal grime; dirt.
– DERIVATIVES **grungy** adjective.
– ORIGIN perhaps from by GRUBBY and DINGY.

grunt verb **1** (of an animal, especially a pig) make a low, short guttural sound. **2** make a low sound as a result of physical effort or to show agreement. •noun a grunting sound.
– DERIVATIVES **grunter** noun.
– ORIGIN Old English.

Gruyère /groo-yair/ noun a Swiss cheese with a firm texture.
– ORIGIN named after *Gruyère*, a district in Switzerland.

gryphon noun variant spelling of GRIFFIN.

GSM abbreviation Global System (or Standard) for Mobile.

GSOH abbreviation good sense of humour.

G-spot noun a sensitive area of the wall of the vagina believed by some to be very sensitive to sexual stimulation.
– ORIGIN first as *Gräfenberg spot*, from *Gräfenberg* and Dickinson, the American gynaecologists who first described it.

GST abbreviation (in New Zealand and Canada) Goods and Services Tax.

G-string noun a skimpy undergarment covering the genitals, consisting of a narrow strip of cloth attached to a waistband.

G-suit noun a garment with inflatable pressurized pouches, worn by fighter pilots and astronauts to enable them to withstand high gravitational forces.
– ORIGIN abbreviation of *gravity*-suit.

GT noun a high-performance car.
– ORIGIN short for Italian *gran turismo* 'great touring'.

GTi noun a GT car with a fuel-injection engine.

guacamole /gwa-kuh-**moh**-lay/ noun a dish of mashed avocado mixed with chilli peppers, tomatoes, and other ingredients.
– ORIGIN Nahuatl, 'avocado sauce'.

guaiacum /**gwy**-uh-kuhm/ noun an evergreen tree of the Caribbean and tropical America, formerly important for its hard, heavy, oily wood.
– ORIGIN Latin.

guanaco /gwuh-**nah**-koh/ noun (pl. **guanacos**) a wild mammal native to the Andes of South America, similar to the llama.
– ORIGIN Quechua.

guano /**gwah**-noh/ noun the excrement of seabirds, used as a fertilizer.
– ORIGIN Quechua.

guarana /gwuh-**rah**-nuh/ noun a substance prepared from the seeds of a Brazilian shrub, believed to have medicinal properties.
– ORIGIN Tupi.

Guarani /gwah-ruh-**nee**/ noun (pl. same) **1** a member of an American Indian people of Paraguay and adjacent regions. **2** the language of the Guarani. **3** (**guarani**) the basic unit of money of Paraguay.
– ORIGIN Spanish.

guarantee noun **1** an assurance that certain conditions will be fulfilled or that certain things will be done. **2** an assurance that a product will remain in working order for a particular length of time. **3** something that makes an outcome certain: *a degree is no guarantee of a fast-track career.* **4** money or a valuable item given or promised as an assurance that something will be done. •verb (**guarantees, guaranteeing, guaranteed**) **1** provide a guarantee for something: *the company guarantees to refund your money.* **2** promise with certainty: *no one can guarantee a profit on stocks and shares.* **3** provide financial security for something.
– ORIGIN perhaps from Spanish *garante*.

guarantor /ga-ruhn-**tor**/ noun a person or organization that gives or acts as a guarantee.

guard verb **1** watch over someone or something in order to protect or control them. **2** protect

against damage or harm: *the company fiercely guarded its independence.* **3** (**guard against**) take precautions against: *farmers must guard against sudden changes in the market.* •noun **1** a person, especially a soldier, assigned to protect a person or to control access to somewhere. **2** (treated as sing. or pl.) a body of soldiers guarding a place or person. **3** (**Guards**) the household troops of the British army. **4** a defensive posture taken up in a fight. **5** a state of looking out for possible dangers or difficulties: *he let his guard slip.* **6** a device worn or fitted on something to prevent injury or damage: *a retractable blade guard.* **7** Brit. an official who rides on and is in general charge of a train. **8** N. Amer. a prison warder.
– PHRASES **guard of honour** a group of soldiers ceremonially welcoming an important visitor. **on** (or **off**) **guard** prepared (or unprepared) for a surprise or difficulty.
– ORIGIN Old French *garder*.

guarded adjective cautious and having possible reservations: *the proposals were given a guarded welcome.*
– DERIVATIVES **guardedly** adverb.

guard hair noun long, coarse hair forming an animal's outer fur.

guardhouse (also **guardroom**) noun a building for soldiers guarding the entrance to a military camp or for the detention of military prisoners.

guardian noun **1** a person who defends or protects something. **2** a person legally responsible for someone unable to manage their own affairs, especially a child whose parents have died.
– DERIVATIVES **guardianship** noun.
– ORIGIN Old French *garden*.

guardian angel noun a spirit believed to watch over and protect a person or place.

guardsman noun (pl. **guardsmen**) **1** (in the UK) a soldier of a regiment of Guards. **2** (in the US) a member of the National Guard.

guard's van noun Brit. a carriage or wagon occupied by the guard on a train.

guar gum /gwaar/ noun a gum used in the food and paper industries, obtained from the seeds of an African and Asian bean plant.
– ORIGIN Hindi.

Guatemalan /gwah-tuh-**mah**-luhn/ noun a person from Guatemala in Central America. •adjective relating to Guatemala.

guava /**gwah**-vuh/ noun a tropical American fruit with pink juicy flesh.
– ORIGIN probably from Taino (an extinct Caribbean language).

gubbins plural noun Brit. informal **1** (treated as sing. or pl.) an assortment of miscellaneous items. **2** (treated as sing.) a gadget.
– ORIGIN Old French.

gubernatorial /goo-ber-nuh-**tor**-i-uhl/ adjective relating to a governor, particularly of a US state.
– ORIGIN Latin *gubernator* 'governor'.

gudgeon[1] /**guj**-uhn/ noun a small freshwater fish often used as bait by anglers.
– ORIGIN Old French *goujon*.

gudgeon[2] /**guj**-uhn/ noun **1** a pivot or spindle on which something swings or rotates. **2** the tubular part of a hinge into which the pin fits.

g

g

3 a socket at the stern of a boat, into which the rudder is fitted. **4** a pin holding two blocks of stone together.
– ORIGIN from Old French *gouge* 'chisel'.

guelder rose /gel-der/ noun a shrub with heads of fragrant creamy-white flowers followed by translucent red berries.
– ORIGIN from Dutch *geldersche roos* 'rose of *Gelderland*' (a province of the Netherlands).

guerdon /ger-duhn/ noun old use a reward or compensation for something.
– ORIGIN Old French.

Guernsey /gern-zi/ noun (pl. **Guernseys**) **1** a breed of dairy cattle from Guernsey in the Channel Islands, noted for producing rich, creamy milk. **2** (**guernsey**) a thick sweater made from oiled wool.

guerrilla /guh-ril-luh/ (also **guerilla**) noun a member of a small independent group fighting against the government or regular forces.
– ORIGIN Spanish, 'little war'.

guess verb **1** estimate or suppose something without having enough information to be sure of being right. **2** correctly estimate: *she's guessed where we're going.* **3** (**I guess**) informal I suppose: *I guess I'd better tell you.* • noun an estimate or conclusion formed by guessing.
– DERIVATIVES **guesser** noun.
– ORIGIN perhaps from Dutch *gissen*.

guesstimate (also **guestimate**) informal noun /gess-ti-muht/ an estimate based on a mixture of guesswork and calculation. • verb /gess-ti-mayt/ estimate something by using a mixture of guesswork and calculation.

guesswork noun the process or results of guessing.

guest noun **1** a person invited to visit someone's home or to a social occasion. **2** a person invited to take part in a broadcast or entertainment. **3** a person staying at a hotel or guest house. • verb appear as a guest in a broadcast or entertainment.
– PHRASES **guest of honour** the most important guest at an occasion.
– ORIGIN Old Norse.

guest beer noun Brit. a draught beer offered temporarily or in addition to those produced by the parent brewery.

guest house noun a private house offering accommodation to paying guests.

guest worker noun a person with temporary permission to work in another country.

guff noun informal ridiculous talk or ideas; nonsense.
– ORIGIN first meaning 'whiff of a bad smell'.

guffaw /guhf-faw/ noun a loud, deep laugh. • verb give a loud, deep laugh.
– ORIGIN imitating the sound.

GUI abbreviation Computing graphical user interface.

guidance noun **1** advice or information aimed at solving a problem or difficulty. **2** the directing of the movement or position of something.

guide noun **1** a person who advises or shows the way to other people. **2** something which helps a person make a decision or form an opinion: *your resting pulse rate is a rough guide to your* *physical condition.* **3** a book providing information on a subject. **4** a structure or marking which directs the movement or positioning of something. **5** (**Guide**) a member of the Guides Association, a girls' organization corresponding to the Scouts. • verb **1** show someone the way to a place. **2** direct the positioning or movement of something. **3** (as adj. **guided**) directed by remote control or internal equipment: *a guided missile.* **4** direct or influence the behaviour or development of: *his entire life was guided by his religious beliefs.*
– ORIGIN Old French.

guidebook noun a book containing information about a place for visitors or tourists.

guide dog noun a dog that has been trained to lead a blind person.

guideline noun a general rule, principle, or piece of advice.

guild noun **1** a medieval association of craftsmen or merchants. **2** an association of people who do the same work or have the same interests or aims.
– ORIGIN Old English.

guilder /gil-der/ noun (pl. same or **guilders**) **1** (until the introduction of the euro in 2002) the basic unit of money of the Netherlands. **2** historical a gold or silver coin formerly used in the Netherlands, Germany, and Austria.
– ORIGIN Dutch.

guildhall noun **1** the meeting place of a guild or corporation. **2** Brit. a town hall. **3** (**the Guildhall**) the hall of the Corporation of the City of London.

guile /gyl/ noun clever but dishonest or devious behaviour.
– DERIVATIVES **guileful** adjective.
– ORIGIN Old French.

guileless adjective innocent, honest, and sincere.
– DERIVATIVES **guilelessly** adverb.

guillemot /gil-li-mot/ noun an auk (seabird) with a narrow pointed bill, nesting on cliff ledges.
– ORIGIN French.

guillotine /gil-luh-teen/ noun **1** a machine with a heavy blade that slides down a frame, used for beheading people. **2** a device with a descending or sliding blade used for cutting paper or sheet metal. **3** Brit. (in parliament) a procedure used to limit the discussion of a legislative bill by fixing times at which various parts of it must be voted on. • verb execute someone with a guillotine.
– ORIGIN named after the French physician Joseph-Ignace *Guillotin*, who recommended its use for executions.

guilt noun **1** the fact of having committed an offence or crime. **2** a feeling of having done something wrong.
– ORIGIN Old English.

guiltless adjective having no guilt; innocent.
– DERIVATIVES **guiltlessly** adverb.

guilt trip noun informal a feeling of guilt about something, especially when this feeling is self-indulgent or deliberately provoked by another person.

guilty adjective (**guiltier**, **guiltiest**) **1** responsible for a particular wrongdoing, fault, or mistake:

he was found guilty of manslaughter. **2** having or showing a feeling of guilt: *a guilty conscience.*
– DERIVATIVES **guiltily** adverb **guiltiness** noun.

guinea /gi-ni/ noun Brit. **1** a former British gold coin with a value of 21 shillings (now £1.05). **2** the sum of £1.05, used mainly for determining professional fees and auction prices.
– ORIGIN named after *Guinea* in West Africa (the source of the gold from which the first guineas were minted).

guineafowl noun (pl. same) a large African game bird with slate-coloured, white-spotted plumage.

guinea pig noun **1** a tailless South American rodent, often kept as a pet. **2** a person or thing used in an experiment.

guipure /gi-pyoor/ noun heavy lace consisting of embroidered motifs held together by large connecting stitches.
– ORIGIN French.

guise /gyz/ noun an outward form, appearance, or way of presenting someone or something: *the country has carried on whaling under the guise of scientific research.*
– ORIGIN Old French.

guitar noun a stringed musical instrument with six (or occasionally twelve) strings, played by plucking or strumming with the fingers or a plectrum.
– DERIVATIVES **guitarist** noun.
– ORIGIN Spanish *guitarra.*

Gujarati /goo-juh-**rah**-ti/ (also **Gujerati**) noun (pl. **Gujaratis**) **1** a person from the Indian state of Gujarat. **2** the language of the Gujaratis. •adjective relating to the Gujaratis or their language.

Gulag /goo-lag/ noun (**the Gulag**) a system of harsh labour camps maintained in the Soviet Union 1930–1955.
– ORIGIN Russian.

gulch /gulch/ noun N. Amer. a narrow, steep-sided ravine.
– ORIGIN perhaps from dialect *gulch* 'to swallow'.

gules /gyoolz/ noun red, as a conventional heraldic colour.
– ORIGIN from Latin *gula* 'throat'.

gulf noun **1** a deep inlet of the sea almost surrounded by land, with a narrow mouth. **2** a deep ravine. **3** a substantial difference between two people, ideas, or situations: *the gulf between rich and poor.*
– ORIGIN Italian *golfo.*

Gulf War syndrome noun an unexplained medical condition affecting some veterans of the 1991 Gulf War, characterized by fatigue, chronic headaches, and skin and breathing disorders.

gull[1] noun a long-winged seabird having white plumage with a grey or black back.
– ORIGIN Celtic.

gull[2] verb fool or deceive someone. •noun a person who is fooled or deceived.
– ORIGIN unknown.

Gullah /gul-luh/ noun (pl. same or **Gullahs**) **1** a member of a black people living on the coast of South Carolina and nearby islands. **2** the

Creole language of the Gullah, having an English base with West African elements.
– ORIGIN perhaps a shortening of *Angola.*

gullet noun the passage by which food passes from the mouth to the stomach; the oesophagus.
– ORIGIN Old French *goulet* 'little throat'.

gullible adjective easily persuaded to believe something.
– DERIVATIVES **gullibility** noun.
– ORIGIN from GULL[2].

gull-wing noun (of a door on a car or aircraft) opening upwards.

gully noun (pl. **gullies**) **1** (also **gulley**) a ravine or deep channel caused by the action of running water. **2** (also **gulley**) a gutter or drain. **3** Cricket a fielding position on the off side between point and the slips.
– ORIGIN French *goulet* (see GULLET).

gulp verb **1** swallow drink or food quickly or in large mouthfuls. **2** swallow with difficulty as a result of strong emotion: *she gulped, trying hard to stop crying.* •noun **1** an act of gulping. **2** a large mouthful of liquid drunk quickly.
– ORIGIN probably from Dutch *gulpen.*

gum[1] noun **1** a thick sticky substance produced by some trees and shrubs. **2** glue used for sticking paper or other light materials together. **3** chewing gum or bubble gum. •verb (**gums, gumming, gummed**) **1** cover or fasten something with gum or glue. **2** (**gum something up**) clog up a mechanism and prevent it from working properly.
– ORIGIN Old French *gomme.*

gum[2] noun the firm area of flesh around the roots of the teeth in the upper or lower jaw.
– ORIGIN Old English.

gum arabic noun a gum produced by some kinds of acacia tree, and used as glue and in incense.

gumbo noun (pl. **gumbos**) N. Amer. (in Cajun cooking) a spicy chicken or seafood soup thickened with okra or rice.
– ORIGIN Angolan.

gumboil noun a small swelling formed on the gum over an abscess at the root of a tooth.

gumboot noun a long rubber boot; a wellington.

gumdrop noun a firm, jelly-like sweet.

gummy[1] adjective (**gummier, gummiest**) sticky.

gummy[2] adjective (**gummier, gummiest**) toothless: *a gummy grin.*

gumption /gump-sh'n/ noun informal initiative and resourcefulness.
– ORIGIN unknown.

gumshield noun a pad or plate used by a sports player to protect the teeth and gums.

gumshoe noun N. Amer. informal a detective.
– ORIGIN from *gumshoes* in the sense 'sneakers', suggesting stealth.

gum tree noun a tree that produces gum, especially a eucalyptus.
– PHRASES **up a gum tree** Brit. informal in a predicament.

gun noun **1** a weapon incorporating a metal tube from which bullets or shells are propelled by explosive force. **2** a device using pressure to send out a substance or object: *a grease gun.* **3** N. Amer. a gunman: *a hired gun.* •verb (**guns,**

gunning, gunned) **1** (**gun someone down**) shoot someone with a gun. **2** (**be gunning for**) be actively looking for an opportunity to blame or attack someone. **3** informal make a vehicle's engine operate at excessive speed.
– PHRASES **go great guns** informal proceed forcefully or successfully. **jump the gun** informal act before the proper or appropriate time. **stick to one's guns** informal refuse to compromise or change.
– ORIGIN perhaps from a familiar form of the Scandinavian name *Gunnhildr*, from *gunnr* + *hildr*, both meaning 'war'.

gunboat noun a small ship armed with guns.

gunboat diplomacy noun foreign policy supported by the use or threat of military force.

gun carriage noun a framework with wheels used to support a piece of artillery.

guncotton noun an explosive made by steeping cotton or wood pulp in a mixture of nitric and sulphuric acids.

gun dog noun a dog trained to retrieve game that has been shot.

gunfight noun a fight involving an exchange of gunfire.
– DERIVATIVES **gunfighter** noun

gunfire noun the repeated firing of a gun or guns.

gunge noun Brit. informal an unpleasantly sticky or messy substance.
– DERIVATIVES **gungy** adjective.
– ORIGIN perhaps suggested by GOO and GUNK.

gung-ho /gung-**hoh**/ adjective too eager to take part in fighting or warfare.
– ORIGIN from a Chinese word taken to mean 'work together' and adopted as a slogan by US Marines.

gunk noun informal an unpleasantly sticky or messy substance.
– ORIGIN the trademark of a US detergent.

gunman noun (pl. **gunmen**) a man who uses a gun to commit a crime or terrorist act.

gunmetal noun **1** a grey corrosion-resistant form of bronze containing zinc. **2** a dull bluish-grey colour.

gunnel noun variant spelling of GUNWALE.

gunner noun **1** a person who operates a gun. **2** a British artillery soldier (an official term for a private).

gunnery noun the design, manufacture, or firing of heavy guns.

gunplay noun chiefly N. Amer. the use of guns.

gunpoint noun (in phrase **at gunpoint**) while threatening someone or being threatened with a gun.

gunpowder noun an explosive consisting of a powdered mixture of saltpetre, sulphur, and charcoal.

gunrunner noun a person involved in the illegal sale or importing of firearms.
– DERIVATIVES **gunrunning** noun.

gunship noun a heavily armed helicopter.

gunshot noun a shot fired from a gun.

gun-shy adjective (especially of a hunting dog) alarmed at the sound of a gun.

gunsight noun a device on a gun enabling it to be aimed accurately.

gunslinger noun informal a man who carries a gun.

gunsmith noun a person who makes and sells small firearms.

gunwale /gun-n'l/ (also **gunnel**) noun the upper edge or planking of the side of a boat.
– PHRASES **to the gunwales** informal so as to be almost overflowing.
– ORIGIN from GUN + WALE (because it was formerly used to support guns).

guppy /gup-pi/ noun (pl. **guppies**) a small freshwater fish native to tropical America, popular in aquariums.
– ORIGIN named after the Trinidadian clergyman R. J. Lechmere *Guppy*, who sent the first specimen to the British Museum.

gurdwara /goor-**dwah**-ruh/ noun a Sikh place of worship.
– ORIGIN from Sanskrit words meaning 'teacher' and 'door'.

gurgle verb make a hollow bubbling sound.
● noun a gurgling sound.
– ORIGIN perhaps from Latin *gurgulio* 'gullet'.

Gurkha /ger-kuh/ noun **1** a member of a Nepalese people noted for their ability as soldiers. **2** a member of a regiment in the British army established for Nepalese recruits.
– ORIGIN a Nepalese place name.

gurn /gern/ (also **girn**) verb Brit. pull a grotesque face.
– ORIGIN dialect variant of GRIN.

gurnard /ger-nerd/ noun a small sea fish with three finger-like bony parts to its fins with which it searches for food and walks on the seabed.
– ORIGIN Old French *gornart* 'grunter'.

gurney noun (pl. **gurneys**) chiefly N. Amer. a stretcher on wheels for transporting hospital patients.
– ORIGIN apparently named after J. T. *Gurney* of Boston, Massachusetts.

guru /guu-roo/ noun **1** a Hindu spiritual teacher. **2** each of the ten first leaders of the Sikh religion. **3** an influential teacher or expert on a particular subject: *a management guru.*
– ORIGIN Sanskrit, 'weighty, grave'.

Guru Granth Sahib noun the main sacred scripture of Sikhism.

gush verb **1** flow in a strong, fast stream. **2** express approval in a very enthusiastic way.
● noun a strong, fast stream.
– DERIVATIVES **gushing** adjective.
– ORIGIN probably imitating the sound.

gusher noun an oil well from which oil gushes without being pumped.

gushy adjective (**gushier, gushiest**) expressing approval in very enthusiastic way.

gusset /guss-it/ noun **1** a piece of material sewn into a garment to strengthen or enlarge a part of it. **2** a bracket strengthening an angle of a structure.
– ORIGIN Old French *gousset* 'small pod or shell'.

gust noun **1** a brief, strong rush of wind. **2** a sudden burst of rain, sound, etc. ● verb blow in gusts.
– DERIVATIVES **gusty** adjective.
– ORIGIN Old Norse.

gustatory /gu-**stay**-tuh-ri/ adjective formal concerned with tasting or the sense of taste.
– ORIGIN Latin.

gusto noun enthusiasm and energy.
– ORIGIN Italian.

gut noun **1** the stomach or intestine. **2 (guts)** internal organs that have been removed or exposed. **3 (guts)** the internal parts or essence of something. **4 (guts)** informal courage and determination. **5** fibre from the intestines of animals, used for violin or racket strings. ●verb **(guts, gutting, gutted) 1** take out the internal organs of a fish or other animal before cooking it. **2** remove or destroy the internal parts of: *the building was gutted by fire.* ●adjective informal instinctive: *a gut feeling.*
– ORIGIN Old English.

gutless adjective informal lacking courage or determination.
– DERIVATIVES **gutlessness** noun.

gutsy adjective **(gutsier, gutsiest)** informal **1** showing courage and determination. **2** (of food or drink) having a strong flavour.
– DERIVATIVES **gutsiness** noun.

gutta-percha /gu-tuh-per-chuh/ noun a hard, tough substance resembling rubber, obtained from certain Malaysian trees.
– ORIGIN Malay.

gutted adjective Brit. informal bitterly disappointed or upset.

gutter noun **1** a shallow trough beneath the edge of a roof, or a channel at the side of a street, for carrying off rainwater. **2 (the gutter)** a very poor or squalid environment. ●verb (of a flame) flicker and burn unsteadily.
– ORIGIN Old French *gotiere*.

guttering noun chiefly Brit. the gutters of a building.

gutter press noun chiefly Brit. newspapers that focus on scandalous or sensational stories rather than serious news.

guttersnipe noun a scruffy, badly behaved child who spends most of their time on the street.

guttural /gut-tuh-ruhl/ adjective **1** (of a speech sound) produced in the throat and harsh-sounding. **2** (of a way of speaking) characterized by guttural sounds.
– DERIVATIVES **gutturally** adverb.
– ORIGIN from Latin *guttur* 'throat'.

guv (also **guv'nor**) noun Brit. informal (as a form of address) sir.
– ORIGIN abbreviation of GOVERNOR.

guy¹ noun **1** informal a man. **2 (guys)** informal, chiefly N. Amer. people of either sex. **3** Brit. a figure representing the Catholic conspirator Guy Fawkes, burnt on a bonfire on 5 November to commemorate a plot to blow up Parliament in 1605. ●verb make fun of someone.

guy² noun a rope or line fixed to the ground to secure a tent.
– ORIGIN probably German.

Guyanese /gy-uh-neez/ noun (pl. same) a person from Guyana, a country on the NE coast of South America. ●adjective relating to Guyana.

Guy Fawkes Night noun another term for BONFIRE NIGHT.

guzzle verb eat or drink something greedily.
– DERIVATIVES **guzzler** noun.
– ORIGIN perhaps from Old French *gosillier* 'chatter, vomit'.

gybe /jyb/ (US **jibe**) Sailing verb **1** change course by swinging the sail across a following wind. **2** (of a sail or boom) swing across the wind. ●noun an act of gybing.
– ORIGIN from former Dutch *gijben*.

gym noun **1** a gymnasium. **2** a private club with facilities for improving or maintaining physical fitness. **3** gymnastics.

gymkhana /jim-kah-nuh/ noun an event consisting of a series of competitions on horseback, typically for children.
– ORIGIN Urdu, 'racket court'.

gymnasium /jim-nay-zi-uhm/ noun (pl. **gymnasiums** or **gymnasia** /jim-nay-zi-uh/) a hall or building equipped for gymnastics and other physical exercise.
– ORIGIN from Greek *gumnazein* 'exercise naked'.

gymnast noun a person trained in gymnastics.

gymnastics plural noun (also treated as sing.) exercises involving physical agility, flexibility, and coordination.
– DERIVATIVES **gymnastic** adjective.

gymnosperm /jim-noh-sperm/ noun a plant of a large group that have seeds which are not protected by an ovary or fruit, such as conifers.
– ORIGIN from Greek *gumnos* 'naked'.

gymslip noun Brit. a belted pinafore dress reaching from the shoulder to the knee, formerly worn by schoolgirls.

gynaecology /gy-ni-kol-uh-ji/ (US **gynecology**) noun the branch of medicine concerned with conditions and diseases specific to women and girls, especially those affecting the reproductive system.
– DERIVATIVES **gynaecological** adjective **gynaecologically** adverb **gynaecologist** noun.
– ORIGIN Greek *gunē* 'woman, female'.

gyp¹ /jip/ (also **gip**) noun Brit. informal pain or discomfort.
– ORIGIN perhaps from *gee-up* (see GEE²).

gyp² /jip/ verb (**gyps, gypping, gypped**) informal cheat or swindle someone.
– ORIGIN unknown.

gypsophila /jip-sof-fi-luh/ noun a garden plant with small pink or white flowers.
– ORIGIN Latin.

gypsum /jip-suhm/ noun a soft white or grey mineral used to make plaster of Paris and in the building industry.
– ORIGIN Latin.

Gypsy (also **Gipsy**) noun (pl. **Gypsies**) a member of a travelling people speaking the Romany language.
– DERIVATIVES **Gypsyish** adjective.
– ORIGIN from *gipcyan*, short for EGYPTIAN (because Gypsies were believed to have come from Egypt).

gyrate verb **1** move in a circle or spiral. **2** dance by rotating the hips in a suggestive way.
– DERIVATIVES **gyration** noun **gyrator** noun.
– ORIGIN Latin *gyrare* 'revolve'.

gyratory /jy-ray-tuh-ri, jy-ruh-tuh-ri/ adjective involving circular or spiral movement.

gyre /jy-uh, gy-uh/ verb literary whirl. ●noun a spiral or vortex.
– ORIGIN Latin *gyrare*.

g

gyrfalcon /jer-fawl-kuhn/ noun a large arctic falcon, with mainly grey or white plumage.
– ORIGIN probably related to German *gēr* 'spear'.

gyro /jy-roh/ noun (pl. **gyros**) a gyroscope or gyrocompass.

gyrocompass noun a compass in which the direction of true north is maintained by a

gyroscope rather than magnetism.
– ORIGIN from Greek *guros* 'a ring'.

gyroscope noun a device used to provide stability or maintain a fixed direction, consisting of a wheel or disc spinning rapidly about an axis which is itself free to alter in direction.
– DERIVATIVES **gyroscopic** adjective.

Hh

H¹ (also **h**) noun (pl. **Hs** or **H's**) the eighth letter of the alphabet.

H² abbreviation **1** (of a pencil lead) hard. **2** height. **3** Physics henry(s). ∙symbol the chemical element hydrogen.

h abbreviation **1** (in measuring the height of horses) hand(s). **2** hour(s).

ha abbreviation hectare(s).

habeas corpus /hay-bi-uhss **kor**-puhss/ noun Law a writ requiring that a person who has been arrested be brought before a judge or into court, to decide whether their detention is lawful.
– ORIGIN Latin, 'you shall have the body (in court)'.

haberdasher /**hab**-er-dash-er/ noun **1** Brit. a person who sells dressmaking and sewing goods. **2** N. Amer. a person who sells men's clothing.
– DERIVATIVES **haberdashery** noun.
– ORIGIN probably from Old French *hapertas*, perhaps the name of a fabric.

habiliment /huh-**bil**-i-muhnt/ noun old use clothing.
– ORIGIN Old French *habillement*.

habit noun **1** something that a person does regularly. **2** informal an addiction to a drug. **3** a long, loose garment worn by a monk or nun.
– ORIGIN Latin *habitus* 'condition, appearance'.

habitable adjective of a good enough condition to live in.
– DERIVATIVES **habitability** noun.
– ORIGIN Latin *habitabilis*.

habitat noun the natural home or environment of an animal or plant.
– ORIGIN Latin, 'it inhabits'.

habitation noun **1** the fact of living somewhere. **2** formal a house or home.

habit-forming adjective (of a drug) addictive.

habitual /huh-**bit**-yuu-uhl/ adjective **1** done regularly and in a way that is difficult to stop: *her father's habitual complaints.* **2** regular; usual: *his habitual dress.*
– DERIVATIVES **habitually** adverb.

habituate verb make or become used to something.
– DERIVATIVES **habituation** noun.

habitué /huh-**bit**-yuu-ay/ noun a person who regularly goes to a particular place.
– ORIGIN French, 'accustomed'.

háček /**hah**-chek, ha-chek/ noun a mark (ˇ) placed over a letter to alter the sound in Slavic and other languages.
– ORIGIN Czech, 'little hook'.

hachures /ha-**shyoorz**/ plural noun parallel lines used on maps to shade in hills, the steepness being shown by how close the lines are together.
– DERIVATIVES **hachured** adjective.
– ORIGIN French, from *hacher* (see HATCH³).

hacienda /ha-si-**en**-duh/ noun (in Spanish-speaking countries) a large estate with a house.
– ORIGIN Spanish.

hack¹ verb **1** cut something with rough or heavy blows. **2** kick something wildly or roughly. **3** use a computer to gain unauthorized access to data in another system. **4** (**hack it**) informal manage; cope. **5** (**hack someone off**) informal annoy someone. ∙noun a rough cut or blow.
– DERIVATIVES **hacker** noun.
– ORIGIN Old English.

hack² noun **1** a writer, especially a journalist, who produces mediocre or unoriginal work. **2** a horse for ordinary riding, or one that can be hired. **3** a ride on a horse. ∙verb ride a horse.
– DERIVATIVES **hackery** noun.
– ORIGIN abbreviation of HACKNEY.

hacking cough noun a dry, frequent cough.

hacking jacket noun a riding jacket with slits at the side or back.

hackle noun **1** (**hackles**) hairs along an animal's back which rise when it is angry or alarmed. **2** a long, narrow feather on the neck or lower back of a domestic cock or other bird.
– PHRASES **make someone's hackles rise** make someone angry or indignant.
– ORIGIN Germanic.

hackney noun (pl. **hackneys**) chiefly historical **1** a horse with a high-stepping trot, used in harness. **2** a horse-drawn vehicle kept for hire.
– ORIGIN probably from *Hackney* in East London, where horses were formerly kept.

hackney carriage noun Brit. the official term for a taxi.

hackneyed adjective (of a phrase or idea) unoriginal and used too often.
– ORIGIN from the former verb *hackney* 'use a horse for general purposes'.

hacksaw noun a saw with a narrow blade set in a frame, used for cutting metal.

had past and past participle of HAVE.

haddock noun (pl. same) a silvery-grey edible fish of North Atlantic coastal waters.
– ORIGIN Old French *hadoc*.

Hades /**hay**-deez/ noun **1** Greek Mythology the underworld; the home of the spirits of the dead. **2** informal hell.

– ORIGIN Greek *Haidēs*, a name of Pluto, the god of the dead.

Hadith /ha-deeth/ noun (pl. same or **Hadiths**) a collection of Islamic traditions containing sayings of the prophet Muhammad.
– ORIGIN Arabic, 'tradition'.

hadn't contraction had not.

hadron /had-ron/ noun Physics a subatomic particle of a type that is held in atomic nuclei, such as a baryon or meson.
– ORIGIN from Greek *hadros* 'bulky'.

hadst old-fashioned second person singular past of **HAVE**.

haematite /hee-muh-tyt/ (US **hematite**) noun a reddish-black mineral consisting of iron oxide.
– ORIGIN from Greek *haimatitēs lithos* 'blood-like stone'.

haematology /hee-muh-tol-uh-ji/ (US **hematology**) noun the branch of medicine concerned with the study and treatment of the blood.
– DERIVATIVES **haematological** adjective **haematologist** noun.
– ORIGIN from Greek *haima* 'blood'.

haematoma /hee-muh-toh-muh/ (US **hematoma**) noun a solid swelling of clotted blood within the tissues.
– ORIGIN from Greek *haima* 'blood'.

haemoglobin /hee-muh-gloh-bin/ (US **hemoglobin**) noun a red protein containing iron, responsible for transporting oxygen in the blood.
– ORIGIN a shortened form of *haematoglobulin*, in the same sense, from Greek *haima* 'blood' + **GLOBULE**.

haemophilia /hee-muh-fi-li-uh/ (US **hemophilia**) noun a medical condition in which the ability of the blood to clot is severely reduced, causing severe bleeding from even a slight injury.
– ORIGIN from Greek *haima* 'blood' + **-PHILIA**.

haemophiliac (US **hemophiliac**) noun a person with haemophilia.

haemorrhage /hem-uh-rij/ (US **hemorrhage**) noun **1** a severe loss of blood from a ruptured blood vessel. **2** a damaging loss of valuable people or resources: *the continuing haemorrhage of doctors.* •verb **1** bleed heavily from a ruptured blood vessel. **2** use or spend something valuable in large amounts: *the business was haemorrhaging cash.*
– ORIGIN from Greek *haima* 'blood' + *rhēgnunai* 'burst'.

haemorrhoid /hem-uh-royd/ (US **hemorrhoid**) noun a swollen vein or group of veins (piles) in the region of the anus.
– ORIGIN from Greek *haimorrhoides phlebes* 'bleeding veins'.

hafnium /haf-ni-uhm/ noun a hard silver-grey metal resembling zirconium.
– ORIGIN from *Hafnia*, the Latin form of *Havn*, a former name of Copenhagen.

haft /hahft/ noun the handle of a knife, axe, or spear.
– ORIGIN Old English.

hag noun **1** an ugly old woman. **2** a witch.
– ORIGIN perhaps from Old English.

hagfish noun (pl. same or **hagfishes**) a primitive jawless sea fish with a slimy eel-like body and

a rasping tongue used for feeding on dead or dying fish.

haggard adjective looking exhausted and ill.
– ORIGIN French *hagard*.

haggis noun (pl. same) a Scottish dish consisting of seasoned sheep's or calf's offal mixed with suet and oatmeal, boiled in a bag traditionally made from the animal's stomach.
– ORIGIN probably from earlier *hag* 'hack, hew', from Old Norse.

haggle verb argue or negotiate with someone about the price of something.
– DERIVATIVES **haggler** noun.
– ORIGIN Old Norse.

hagiography /ha-gi-og-ruh-fi/ noun **1** literature concerned with the lives of saints. **2** a biography which idealizes its subject.
– DERIVATIVES **hagiographer** noun **hagiographic** adjective **hagiographical** adjective.

hag-ridden adjective suffering from nightmares or feeling great anxiety.

ha-ha noun a ditch with a wall on its inner side below ground level, forming a boundary to a park or garden without interrupting the view.
– ORIGIN said to be from the cry of surprise uttered on coming across such an obstacle.

haiku /hy-koo/ noun (pl. same or **haikus**) a Japanese poem of seventeen syllables, in three lines of five, seven, and five.
– ORIGIN Japanese.

hail¹ noun **1** pellets of frozen rain falling in showers. **2** a large number of things hurled forcefully through the air: *a hail of missiles.* •verb (**it hails, it is hailing, it hailed**) hail falls.
– ORIGIN Old English.

hail² verb **1** call out to someone to attract attention. **2** describe enthusiastically: *he was hailed as a literary genius.* **3** (**hail from**) have one's home or origins in: *she hails from Scotland.* •exclamation old use expressing greeting or praise.
– ORIGIN from former *hail* 'healthy'.

hail-fellow-well-met adjective showing too much friendliness or familiarity.

Hail Mary noun (pl. **Hail Marys**) a prayer to the Virgin Mary used chiefly by Roman Catholics.

hailstone noun a pellet of hail.

hair noun **1** any of the fine thread-like strands growing from the skin of mammals and other animals, or from the outer layer of a plant. **2** strands of hair collectively, especially on a person's head.
– PHRASES **hair of the dog** informal an alcoholic drink taken to cure a hangover. [from *hair of the dog that bit you*, formerly recommended as a remedy for the bite of a mad dog.] **a hair's breadth** a very small margin. **let one's hair down** informal enjoy oneself in an uninhibited way. **make someone's hair stand on end** alarm someone. **not turn a hair** remain apparently unmoved by something. **split hairs** make small and unnecessary distinctions.
– DERIVATIVES **haired** adjective **hairless** adjective.
– ORIGIN Old English.

hairball noun a ball of hair which collects in the stomach of an animal as a result of the animal licking its coat.

hairband noun a band worn over the top of the head and behind the ears to keep the hair off the face.

hairbrush noun a brush for smoothing one's hair.

haircut noun 1 the style in which someone's hair is cut. 2 an act of cutting someone's hair.

hairdo noun (pl. **hairdos**) informal the style of a person's hair.

hairdresser noun a person who cuts and styles hair.

– DERIVATIVES **hairdressing** noun.

hairdryer (also **hairdrier**) noun an electrical device for drying the hair with warm air.

hairgrip noun Brit. a flat hairpin with the ends close together.

hairline noun the edge of a person's hair. •adjective very thin or fine: a hairline fracture.

hairnet noun a small piece of fine net used to hold the hair in place.

hairpiece noun a patch or bunch of false hair used to add to a person's natural hair.

hairpin noun a U-shaped pin for fastening the hair.

hairpin bend noun a sharp U-shaped bend in a road.

hair-raising adjective extremely alarming or frightening.

hair shirt noun a shirt made of stiff cloth woven from horsehair, formerly worn as a penance for doing wrong.

hairslide noun Brit. a clip for keeping a woman's hair in position.

hair-splitting noun the making of small and unnecessary distinctions.

hairspray noun a solution sprayed on to hair to keep it in place.

hairspring noun a flat coiled spring which regulates the timekeeping in some clocks and watches.

hairstyle noun a way in which someone's hair is cut or arranged.

– DERIVATIVES **hairstyling** noun **hairstylist** noun.

hair trigger noun a firearm trigger set for release at the slightest pressure.

hairy adjective (**hairier**, **hairiest**) 1 covered with or resembling hair. 2 informal dangerous or frightening: a hairy mountain road.

– DERIVATIVES **hairiness** noun.

Haitian /hay-shi-uhn, hay-shuhn/ noun a person from Haiti. •adjective relating to Haiti.

haji /ha-jee/ (also **hajji**) noun (pl. **hajis**) a Muslim who has been to Mecca as a pilgrim.

– ORIGIN Arabic.

hajj /haj/ (also **haj**) noun the pilgrimage to Mecca which all Muslims are expected to make at least once if they can afford to do so.

– ORIGIN Arabic, 'pilgrimage'.

haka /hah-kuh/ noun a ceremonial Maori war dance involving chanting.

– ORIGIN Maori.

hake noun a long-bodied edible fish with strong teeth.

– ORIGIN perhaps from Old English, 'hook'.

halal /huh-**lahl**/ adjective (of meat) prepared as prescribed by Muslim law.

– ORIGIN Arabic, 'according to religious law'.

halala /huh-**lah**-luh/ noun (pl. same or **halalas**) a unit of money of Saudi Arabia, equal to one hundredth of a rial.

– ORIGIN Arabic.

halberd /hal-berd/ (also **halbert**) noun historical a combined spear and battleaxe.

– ORIGIN German helmbarde.

halberdier /hal-buh-**di**-uh/ noun historical a man armed with a halberd.

halcyon /hal-si-uhn/ adjective (of a past time) idyllically happy and peaceful: halcyon days.

– ORIGIN first referring to a mythical bird (usually identified with a species of kingfisher) said to breed in a nest floating at sea and to calm the wind and waves: from Greek alkuōn 'kingfisher'.

hale¹ adjective (of an old person) strong and healthy.

– ORIGIN Old English, 'whole'.

hale² verb old use haul.

– ORIGIN Old French haler.

haler /haa-luh/ noun (pl. same or **halers**) a unit of money of the Czech Republic, equal to one hundredth of a koruna.

– ORIGIN Czech haléř.

half noun (pl. **halves**) 1 either of two equal or matching parts into which something is or can be divided. 2 either of two equal periods into which a match or performance is divided. 3 Brit. informal half a pint of beer. 4 informal a half-price fare or ticket. 5 a halfback. •predeterminer & pronoun an amount equal to a half. •adjective forming a half. •adverb 1 to the extent of half. 2 partly: half-cooked.

– PHRASES **at half mast** (of a flag) flown halfway down its mast, as a mark of respect for a person who has died. **half a chance** informal the slightest opportunity. **not do things by halves** do things thoroughly. **not half** 1 not nearly. 2 informal not at all. 3 Brit. informal to an extreme degree: she didn't half flare up! **too —— by half** excessively ——: he's too charming by half.

– ORIGIN Old English.

half-and-half adverb & adjective in equal parts.

half-arsed adjective vulgar slang done without much skill or effort.

halfback noun a player in a ball game whose position is between the forwards and full backs.

half-baked adjective informal not well planned or considered.

half binding noun a type of bookbinding in which the spine and corners are bound in a different material to the rest of the cover.

half board noun Brit. a type of accommodation at a hotel or guest house which includes breakfast and one main meal.

half-breed noun offensive a person whose parents are of different races.

half-brother (or **half-sister**) noun a brother (or sister) with whom one has only one parent in common.

half-caste noun offensive a person whose parents are of different races.

half-cock noun the partly raised position of the cock of a gun.

– PHRASES **at half-cock** when only partly ready.

– DERIVATIVES **half-cocked** adjective.

half-crown (also **half a crown**) noun a former British coin and unit of money equal to two shillings and sixpence (12½p).

half-cut adjective Brit. informal drunk.

half-dozen (also **half a dozen**) noun a group of six.

half-hardy adjective (of a plant) able to grow outdoors except in severe frost.

half-hearted adjective without enthusiasm or energy.
– DERIVATIVES **half-heartedly** adverb **half-heartedness** noun.

half hitch noun a knot formed by passing the end of a rope round itself and then through the loop created.

half-hour noun 1 (also **half an hour**) a period of thirty minutes. 2 a point in time thirty minutes after the beginning of an hour of the clock.
– DERIVATIVES **half-hourly** adjective & adverb.

half-hunter noun a pocket watch with a small opening in the cover allowing one to read the approximate time.

half-inch verb Brit. informal steal.
– ORIGIN rhyming slang for 'pinch'.

half landing noun Brit. a landing where a flight of stairs turns through 180 degrees.

half-life noun the time taken for the radioactivity of a substance to fall to half its original value.

half-light noun dim light, such as that at dusk.

half measures plural noun actions or policies that are not forceful or decisive enough.

half-moon noun 1 the moon when only half its surface is visible from the earth. 2 a semicircular or crescent-shaped object.

half nelson noun see NELSON.

halfpenny /hayp-ni/ (also **ha'penny**) noun (pl. **halfpennies** (for separate coins); **halfpence** (for a sum of money) /hay-p'nss/) a former British coin equal to half an old or new penny.

halfpennyworth /hay-puhth, hayp-ni-wuhth/ (also **ha'p'orth** /hay-puhth/) noun Brit. 1 as much as could be bought for a halfpenny. 2 (**ha'p'orth**) informal a trivial amount: *he's never been a ha'p'orth of bother.*

half-term noun Brit. a short holiday halfway through a school term.

half-timbered adjective having walls with a timber frame and a brick or plaster filling.

half-time noun (in sport) a short interval between two halves of a match.

half-title noun the title of a book, printed on the right-hand page before the title page.

half-tone noun a reproduction of a photographic image in which the different shades are produced by dots of varying sizes.

half-track noun a vehicle with wheels at the front and caterpillar tracks at the rear.

half-truth noun a statement that is only partly true.

half-volley noun (in sport) a strike or kick of the ball immediately after it bounces.

halfway adverb & adjective 1 at or to a point equal in distance between two others. 2 (as adverb) to some extent: *halfway decent.*

halfway house noun 1 the halfway point in a process. 2 Brit. a compromise. 3 a place where discharged prisoners or psychiatric patients can stay for a short time to prepare themselves for a return to normal life.

halfwit noun informal a stupid person.

– DERIVATIVES **half-witted** adjective.

halibut noun (pl. same) a large edible marine flatfish.
– ORIGIN from former *haly* 'holy' + *butt* 'flatfish' (because it was often eaten on holy days).

halide /hay-lyd/ noun a chemical compound formed from a halogen and another element or group: *silver halide.*

halier /hal-yair/ noun (pl. same or **haliers**) a unit of money of Slovakia, equal to one hundredth of a koruna.
– ORIGIN Slovak.

halitosis /ha-li-toh-siss/ noun unpleasant-smelling breath.
– ORIGIN Latin *halitus* 'breath'.

hall noun 1 the room or space just inside the front entrance of a house. 2 a large room for meetings, concerts, etc. 3 (also **hall of residence**) Brit. a university building in which students live. 4 the dining room of a college, university, or school. 5 Brit. a large country house. 6 the main living room of a medieval house.
– ORIGIN Old English.

hallelujah /hal-li-loo-yuh/ (also **alleluia**) exclamation God be praised.
– ORIGIN Hebrew, 'praise ye the Lord'.

hallmark noun 1 an official mark stamped on articles made of gold, silver, or platinum as a guarantee of their purity. 2 a distinctive feature of something: *tiny bubbles are the hallmark of fine champagne.* • verb stamp an object with a hallmark.
– ORIGIN from *Goldsmiths' Hall* in London, where articles were tested and stamped.

hallo exclamation variant spelling of HELLO.

Hall of Fame noun the group of people who have performed exceptionally well in a particular area of activity.

halloo exclamation used to encourage dogs during a hunt.
– ORIGIN probably from Old French *haloer* 'pursue or urge on with shouts'.

halloumi /huh-loo-mi/ noun a mild Cypriot cheese made from goats' or ewes' milk.
– ORIGIN from an Arabic word meaning 'to be mild'.

hallowed /hal-ohd/ adjective 1 made holy: *a hallowed shrine.* 2 greatly honoured and respected: *the hallowed turf of Wimbledon.*
– ORIGIN Old English, related to HOLY.

Halloween (also **Hallowe'en**) noun the night of 31 October, the eve of All Saints' Day.
– ORIGIN shortened form of *All Hallow Even*, from *hallow* 'saint, holy person' + EVEN².

hallucinate /huh-loo-si-nayt/ verb seem to see something that is not actually present.
– DERIVATIVES **hallucination** noun.
– ORIGIN Latin *hallucinari* 'go astray in thought'.

hallucinatory /huh-loo-si-nuh-tuh-ri/ adjective resembling or causing hallucinations: *hallucinatory drugs.*

hallucinogen /huh-loo-si-nuh-juhn/ noun a drug causing hallucinations.
– DERIVATIVES **hallucinogenic** adjective.

hallway noun another term for HALL (in sense 1).

halo /hay-loh/ noun (pl. **haloes** or **halos**) 1 (in a

painting) a circle of light surrounding the head of a holy person. **2** a circle of light round the sun or moon, refracted through ice crystals in the atmosphere. •**verb** (**haloes, haloing, haloed**) surround someone or something with a halo, or with something resembling a halo.
– ORIGIN Greek *halōs* 'disc of the sun or moon'.

halogen /**hal**-uh-juhn/ **noun** any of the non-metallic chemical elements fluorine, chlorine, bromine, iodine, and astatine. •**adjective** using a filament surrounded by iodine vapour or that of another halogen: *a halogen bulb.*
– ORIGIN from Greek *hals* 'salt'.

halon /**hay**-lon/ **noun** any of a number of gaseous compounds of carbon with halogens, used in fire extinguishers.
– ORIGIN from HALOGEN.

halt¹ verb bring or come to an abrupt stop. •**noun 1** a stopping of movement or activity. **2** Brit. a minor stopping place on a railway line.
– PHRASES **call a halt** stop something: *he decided to call a halt to all further discussions.*
– ORIGIN German *halten* 'to hold'.

halt² adjective old use lame.
– ORIGIN Old English.

halter noun 1 a rope or strap placed around the head of an animal and used to lead or tether it. **2** old use a noose for hanging a person. •**verb** put a halter on an animal.
– ORIGIN Old English.

halter neck noun a style of woman's top that is fastened behind the neck, leaving the shoulders, upper back, and arms bare.

halting adjective slow and hesitant.
– DERIVATIVES **haltingly** adverb.

halva /**hal**-vuh/ (also **halvah**) **noun** a Middle Eastern sweet made of sesame flour and honey.
– ORIGIN Arabic and Persian, 'sweetmeat'.

halve verb 1 divide something into two parts of equal size. **2** reduce or be reduced by half: *pre-tax profits halved to £5 m.*

halves plural of HALF.

halyard /**hal**-yerd/ **noun** a rope used for raising and lowering a sail, yard, or flag on a ship.
– ORIGIN from HALE².

ham¹ noun 1 meat from the upper part of a pig's leg which has been salted and dried or smoked. **2** (**hams**) the back of the thigh or the thighs and buttocks.
– ORIGIN from a Germanic word meaning 'be crooked'.

ham² noun 1 a bad actor, especially one who overacts. **2** (also **radio ham**) informal an amateur radio operator. •**verb** (**hams, hamming, hammed**) informal overact.
– ORIGIN perhaps from the first syllable of AMATEUR.

hamadryad /ha-muh-**dry**-uhd, ha-muh-**dry**-ad/ **noun** (in classical mythology) a nymph who lives in a tree and dies when it dies.
– ORIGIN from Greek *hama* 'together' + *drus* 'tree'.

hamburger noun a small flat cake of minced beef, fried or grilled and typically served in a bread roll.
– ORIGIN German, from the city of *Hamburg* in Germany.

ham-fisted (also **ham-handed**) **adjective** informal clumsy; awkward.

hamlet noun a small village, especially (in Britain) one without a church.
– ORIGIN Old French *hamelet*.

hammam /ha-**mam**, huh-**mahm**/ **noun** a Turkish bath.
– ORIGIN from Turkish or Arabic, 'bath'.

hammer noun 1 a tool consisting of a heavy metal head mounted at the end of a handle, used for breaking things and driving in nails. **2** an auctioneer's mallet, tapped to indicate a sale. **3** a part of a mechanism that hits another, e.g. one exploding the charge in a gun. **4** a heavy metal ball attached to a wire for throwing in an athletic contest. •**verb 1** hit something repeatedly. **2** (**hammer away**) work hard and persistently. **3** (**hammer something in/into**) make something stick in someone's mind by constant repetition: *a story that has been hammered into her since childhood.* **4** (**hammer something out**) laboriously work out the details of a plan or agreement. **5** informal utterly defeat a person or team in a contest.
– PHRASES **come** (or **go**) **under the hammer** be sold at an auction. **hammer and tongs** informal with great energy or enthusiasm.
– ORIGIN Old English.

hammer and sickle noun the symbols of the industrial worker and the peasant used as the emblem of the former Soviet Union and of international communism.

hammer beam noun a short wooden beam projecting from a wall to support a main rafter or one end of an arch.

hammer drill noun a power drill that delivers a rapid succession of blows.

hammerhead noun a shark with flattened extensions on either side of the head.

hammerlock noun an armlock in which a person's arm is bent up behind their back.

hammer toe noun a toe that is bent permanently downwards, typically as a result of pressure from footwear.

hammock noun a wide strip of canvas or rope mesh suspended at both ends, used as a bed.
– ORIGIN from Taino (an extinct Caribbean language).

Hammond organ noun trademark a type of electronic organ.
– ORIGIN named after the American mechanical engineer Laurens *Hammond*.

hammy adjective (**hammier, hammiest**) informal (of acting) exaggerated or over-theatrical.

hamper¹ noun 1 a basket with a handle and a hinged lid, used for food, cutlery, etc. on a picnic. **2** Brit. a box containing a selection of food and drink, given as a gift.
– ORIGIN Old French *hanaper* 'case for a goblet'.

hamper² verb slow down or prevent the movement or progress of: *their work is hampered by lack of funds.*
– ORIGIN perhaps related to German *hemmen* 'restrain'.

hamster noun a burrowing rodent with a short tail and large cheek pouches, native to Europe and North Asia.
– ORIGIN German *hamustro* 'corn-weevil'.

hamstring noun 1 any of five tendons at the

h

back of a person's knee. **2** the large tendon at the back of the hind leg of a horse or other four-legged animal. • verb (past and past part. **hamstrung**) **1** cripple a person or animal by cutting their hamstrings. **2** prevent someone or something from taking action or making progress.
– ORIGIN from **HAM**[1] + **STRING**.

Han noun **1** the Chinese dynasty that ruled almost continuously from 206 BC until AD 220. **2** the dominant ethnic group in China.

hand noun **1** the end part of the arm beyond the wrist. **2** a pointer on a clock or watch indicating the passing of units of time. **3** (**hands**) a person's power or control: *taking the law into their own hands.* **4** an active role: *he had a big hand in organizing the event.* **5** help in doing something: *do you need a hand?* **6** a person who does physical work, especially in a factory, on a farm, or on board a ship. **7** informal a round of applause. **8** the set of cards dealt to a player in a card game. **9** a person's handwriting or workmanship. **10** a unit of measurement of a horse's height, equal to 4 inches (10.16 cm). [referring to the breadth of a hand.] **11** dated a promise of marriage made by or on behalf of a woman. • verb give something to someone. • adjective **1** operated by or held in the hand: *hand luggage.* **2** done or made manually: *hand signals.*
– PHRASES **at hand** easy to reach; near. **by hand** by a person or not a machine. **get** (or **keep**) **one's hand in** become (or remain) practised in something. **hand something down** pass something on to a successor. **hand in glove** in close association. **hand in hand** closely associated or connected. **hand something out** distribute something among a group. (**from**) **hand to mouth** satisfying only one's immediate needs; with no money in reserve. **hands down** easily and decisively. **hands-on** involving or offering direct participation in something. **in hand 1** in progress or receiving attention. **2** ready for use if required. **in safe hands** protected by someone trustworthy. **make** (or **lose** or **spend**) **money hand over fist** informal make (or lose or spend) money very rapidly. **on hand** present and available. **on someone's hands** as someone's responsibility. **2** at someone's disposal. **on the one** (or **the other**) **hand** used to present factors for (and against) something. **out of hand 1** not under control. **2** without taking time to think: *the proposal was rejected out of hand.* **to hand** within easy reach. **turn one's hand to** do something which is different from one's usual occupation.
– ORIGIN Old English.

handbag noun Brit. a small bag used by a woman to carry everyday personal items.

handball noun **1** a game similar to fives, in which the ball is hit with the hand in a walled court. **2** Football unlawful touching of the ball with the hand or arm.

handbell noun a small bell, especially one of a set tuned to a range of notes and played by a group of people.

handbill noun a small printed advertisement or other notice distributed by hand.

handbook noun a book giving basic information or instructions.

handbrake noun chiefly Brit. a brake operated by hand, used to hold a vehicle that is already stationary.

handcart noun a small cart pushed or drawn by hand.

handclap noun a clapping of the hands.

handcrafted adjective made skilfully by hand.

handcuff noun (**handcuffs**) a pair of lockable linked metal rings for securing a prisoner's wrists. • verb put handcuffs on someone.

handful noun (pl. **handfuls**) **1** a quantity that fills the hand. **2** a small number or amount. **3** informal a person who is difficult to deal with or control.

hand grenade noun a hand-thrown grenade.

handgun noun a gun designed for use with one hand.

handhold noun something for a hand to grip on.

handicap noun **1** a condition that restricts a person's ability to function physically, mentally, or socially. **2** something that makes progress or success difficult: *not being able to drive was something of a handicap.* **3** a disadvantage placed on a superior competitor in a sport in order to make the chances more equal, such as the extra weight given to a racehorse on the basis of its previous form. **4** the number of strokes by which a golfer normally exceeds par for a course. • verb (**handicaps**, **handicapping**, **handicapped**) make it difficult for someone or something to progress or succeed: *the industry was handicapped by an acute manpower shortage.*
– ORIGIN from the phrase *hand in cap*, an old gambling game which involved players putting their hands into a cap in which money had been deposited.

handicapped adjective (of a person) having a condition that restricts their ability to function physically, mentally, or socially.

> **USAGE:** Until quite recently the word **handicapped** was the standard term used in British English to refer to people with physical and mental disabilities. However it has been superseded by terms such as **disabled**, or, in reference to mental disability, **having learning disabilities**, and is now best avoided.

handicraft noun **1** an activity involving the making of decorative objects by hand. **2** decorative objects made by hand.

handiwork noun **1** (**one's handiwork**) something that one has made or done. **2** the making of things by hand.

handkerchief /hang-ker-cheef/ noun (pl. **handkerchiefs** or **handkerchieves**) a square of cotton or other material for wiping one's nose.

handle verb **1** feel or manipulate something with the hands. **2** deal or cope with a situation, person, or problem: *he handled the interview brilliantly.* **3** control or manage something commercially. **4** (**handle oneself**) behave oneself in a particular way. **5** (of a vehicle) respond in a particular way when being driven: *the new model does not handle well.* • noun **1** the part by which a thing is held,

carried, or controlled. **2** a way of understanding, controlling, or approaching a person or situation: *they seem unable to get a handle on the problem.* **3** informal the name of a person or place.
– DERIVATIVES **handled** adjective **handling** noun.
– ORIGIN Old English.

handlebar (also **handlebars**) noun the steering bar of a bicycle or motorbike.

handlebar moustache noun a wide, thick moustache with the ends curving slightly upwards.

handler noun **1** a person who handles a particular type of article: *baggage handlers.* **2** a person who trains or has charge of an animal. **3** a person who trains or manages another person.

handmade adjective made by hand rather than machine.

handmaid (also **handmaiden**) noun **1** old use a female servant. **2** something that supports and helps something else: *shipping is the handmaiden of trade and commerce.*

hand-me-down noun a garment or other item that has been passed on from another person.

handout noun **1** an amount of money or other aid given to a person or organization. **2** a piece of printed information provided free of charge, especially to accompany a lecture.

handover noun an act of handing something over.

hand-pick verb select someone or something carefully.

handprint noun the mark left by the impression of a hand.

handrail noun a rail fixed to posts or a wall for people to hold on to for support.

handset noun **1** the part of a telephone that is held up to speak into and listen to. **2** a hand-held control device for a piece of electronic equipment.

hands-free adjective (especially of a telephone) designed to be operated without using the hands.

handshake noun an act of shaking a person's hand.
– DERIVATIVES **handshaking** noun.

handsome adjective (**handsomer**, **handsomest**) **1** (of a man) good-looking. **2** (of a woman) striking and strong-featured rather than conventionally pretty. **3** (of a thing) well made and of obvious quality. **4** (of an amount) large: *a handsome profit.*
– DERIVATIVES **handsomely** adverb **handsomeness** noun.
– ORIGIN from HAND, first meaning 'easy to handle or use'.

handspan noun see SPAN (in sense 5).

handspring noun a jump through the air on to one's hands followed by another on to one's feet.

handstand noun an act of balancing upside down on one's hands.

hand-to-hand adjective (of fighting) at close quarters and involving physical contact between the opponents.

handwriting noun **1** writing with a pen or pencil rather than by typing or printing. **2** a person's particular style of writing.

handwritten adjective written with a pen or pencil.

handy adjective (**handier**, **handiest**) **1** convenient to handle or use; useful. **2** in a convenient place or position. **3** skilful with one's hands.
– DERIVATIVES **handily** adverb **handiness** noun.

handyman noun (pl. **handymen**) a person employed to do general decorating or domestic repairs.

hang verb (past and past part. **hung** except in sense 2) **1** suspend or be suspended from above with the lower part not attached. **2** (past and past part. **hanged**) kill someone by suspending them from a rope tied around the neck (used as a form of capital punishment). **3** attach something so as to allow free movement about the point of attachment (such as a hinge): *hanging a door.* **4** (of fabric or a garment) fall or drape in a particular way. **5** attach meat or game to a hook and leave it until it is ready to cook. **6** paste wallpaper to a wall. **7** remain static in the air: *a cloud of smoke hung over the city.* **8** (of something bad or unwelcome) be oppressively present or imminent: *a sense of dread hung over him.* •noun the way in which something hangs or is hung. •exclamation dated used in expressions as a mild oath.
– PHRASES **get the hang of** informal learn how to operate or do something. **hang around 1** wait around; loiter. **2** (**hang around with**) associate with someone. **hang back** remain behind. **hang fire** delay taking action. **hang on 1** hold tightly. **2** informal wait for a short time. **3** be dependent on: *so much hangs on exam results.* **4** listen closely to something. **hang out** informal spend time relaxing or enjoying oneself. **hang up** end a telephone conversation by cutting the connection.
– ORIGIN Old English.

> USAGE: **Hang** has two past tense and past participle forms: **hanged** and **hung**. Use **hung** in general situations (*they hung out the washing*), but use **hanged** to refer to execution of someone by hanging (*the prisoner was hanged*).

hangar /hang-er/ noun a large building in which aircraft are kept.
– ORIGIN French.

hangdog adjective having a dejected or guilty appearance; shamefaced.

hanger noun **1** a person who hangs something. **2** (also **coat hanger**) a curved frame of wood, plastic, or metal with a hook at the top, for hanging clothes from a rail.

hanger-on noun (pl. **hangers-on**) someone who tries to associate with a rich or powerful person in order to benefit from the relationship.

hang-glider noun an unpowered flying device for a single person, consisting of a frame with fabric stretched over it from which the operator is suspended.
– DERIVATIVES **hang-glide** verb **hang-gliding** noun.

hanging noun **1** the practice of hanging condemned criminals as a form of capital punishment. **2** a decorative piece of fabric hung on the wall of a room or around a bed.

● **adjective** suspended in the air.

hanging valley noun a valley that ends in a very steep descent to a main valley, the main valley having been deepened through erosion by a glacier.

hangman noun (pl. **hangmen**) an executioner who hangs condemned people.

hangnail noun a piece of torn skin at the root of a fingernail.
– ORIGIN Old English.

hang-out noun informal a place where someone spends a great deal of time.

hangover noun 1 a severe headache or other after-effects caused by drinking too much alcohol. 2 a custom, feeling, etc. that has survived from the past: *this feeling of insecurity was a hangover from her schooldays.*

hang-up noun informal an emotional problem or inhibition.

hank noun a coil or length of wool, hair, or other material.
– ORIGIN Old Norse.

hanker verb (**hanker after/for/to do**) feel a desire for or to do: *she hankered after a traditional white wedding.*
– ORIGIN probably related to **HANG**.

hanky (also **hankie**) noun (pl. **hankies**) informal a handkerchief.

hanky-panky noun informal behaviour considered to be slightly improper.
– ORIGIN uncertain.

Hanoverian /han-uh-**veer**-i-uhn/ adjective relating to the royal house of Hanover, who ruled as monarchs in Britain from 1714 to 1901.

Hansard /**han**-sard/ noun the official word-for-word record of debates in the British, Canadian, Australian, New Zealand, or South African parliament.
– ORIGIN named after the English printer Thomas C. *Hansard.*

Hansen's disease noun another term for **LEPROSY**.
– ORIGIN named after the Norwegian physician Gerhard H. A. *Hansen.*

hansom /**han**-suhm/ (also **hansom cab**) noun historical a two-wheeled horse-drawn cab for two passengers, with the driver seated behind.
– ORIGIN named after the English architect Joseph A. *Hansom.*

hantavirus /**han**-tuh-vy-ruhss/ noun a virus carried by rodents which can cause various diseases in humans.
– ORIGIN from *Hantaan* (a river in Korea where the virus was first isolated).

Hants abbreviation Hampshire.

Hanukkah /**han**-uu-kuh/ (also **Chanukkah**) noun an eight-day Jewish festival of lights held in December, commemorating the rededication of the Jewish Temple in Jerusalem.
– ORIGIN Hebrew, 'consecration'.

hap noun old use luck; fortune.
– ORIGIN Old Norse.

ha'penny noun variant spelling of **HALFPENNY**.

haphazard adjective having no particular order or plan; disorganized.
– DERIVATIVES **haphazardly** adverb.

hapless adjective unlucky; unfortunate.
– DERIVATIVES **haplessly** adverb.

haploid /**hap**-loyd/ adjective (of a cell or nucleus) containing a single set of unpaired chromosomes. Compare with **DIPLOID**.

happen verb 1 take place; occur. 2 come about by chance: *it just so happened that she turned up that afternoon.* 3 (**happen on**) come across something by chance: *I happened on a street with a few restaurants.* 4 chance to do something or come about. 5 (**happen to**) be experienced by: *the same thing happened to me.* 6 (**happen to**) become of: *I don't care what happens to the money.*
– PHRASES **as it happens** actually; as a matter of fact.
– ORIGIN from **HAP**.

happening noun an event or occurrence.
● adjective informal fashionable.

happenstance noun chiefly N. Amer. coincidence.
– ORIGIN blend of **HAPPEN** and **CIRCUMSTANCE**.

happy adjective (**happier, happiest**) 1 feeling or showing pleasure or contentment. 2 willing to do something. 3 fortunate and convenient: *a happy coincidence.* 4 (in combination) inclined to use a particular thing too readily or at random: *trigger-happy.*
– DERIVATIVES **happily** adverb **happiness** noun.
– ORIGIN from **HAP**.

happy-go-lucky adjective cheerfully unconcerned about the future.

happy hour noun a period of the day when drinks are sold at reduced prices in a bar or pub.

happy hunting ground noun a place where success or enjoyment can be found.
– ORIGIN referring to the optimistic hope of American Indians for good hunting grounds in the afterlife.

haptic /**hap**-tik/ adjective technical relating to the sense of touch.
– ORIGIN Greek *haptikos* 'able to touch or grasp'.

hara-kiri /ha-ruh-**ki**-ri/ noun a method of ritual suicide involving cutting open the stomach with a sword, formerly practised in Japan by samurai.
– ORIGIN from the Japanese words for 'belly' + 'cutting'.

haram /hah-**rahm**/ adjective forbidden by Islamic law.
– ORIGIN Arabic.

harangue /huh-**rang**/ verb address a person or group in a loud and aggressive or critical way.
● noun a forceful and aggressive or critical speech.
– ORIGIN Latin *harenga.*

harass /**ha**-ruhss, huh-**rass**/ verb 1 torment someone by putting constant pressure on them or by saying or doing unpleasant things to them: *he had been harassed by the KGB.* 2 (as adj. **harassed**) feeling tired or tense as a result of too many demands made on one: *harassed parents.* 3 make repeated small-scale attacks on an enemy in order to wear down their resistance.
– DERIVATIVES **harasser** noun **harassment** noun.
– ORIGIN French *harasser*, from *harer* 'set a dog on'.

harbinger /**har**-bin-jer/ noun a person or thing that announces or signals the approach of

something: *the plant is the first harbinger of spring.*
– ORIGIN Old French *herbergier* 'provide lodging for'.

harbour (US **harbor**) noun a place on the coast where ships may moor in shelter. • verb **1** keep a thought or feeling secretly in one's mind. **2** give a refuge or shelter to someone or something. **3** carry the germs of a disease.
– ORIGIN Old English, 'shelter'.

hard adjective **1** solid, firm, and rigid; not easily broken, bent, or pierced. **2** requiring or showing a great deal of endurance or effort; difficult. **3** (of a person) not showing any signs of weakness; tough. **4** done with a great deal of force or strength: *a hard whack.* **5** harsh or unpleasant to the senses: *the hard light of morning.* **6** (of information or a subject of study) concerned with precise facts that can be proved. **7** (of drink) strongly alcoholic. **8** (of a drug) very addictive. **9** (of pornography) very obscene and explicit. **10** referring to an extreme faction within a political party: *the hard left.* **11** (of water) containing mineral salts. • adverb **1** with a great deal of effort or force. **2** so as to be solid or firm. **3** to the fullest extent possible.
– PHRASES **be hard put (to it)** find it very difficult. **hard and fast** (of a rule or distinction) fixed and definitive. **hard at it** informal busily working. **hard done by** Brit. harshly or unfairly treated. **hard feelings** feelings of resentment. **hard luck** (or **lines**) Brit. informal used to express sympathy or commiserations. **hard of hearing** not able to hear well. **hard on** following soon after. **hard up** informal short of money. **play hard to get** informal deliberately adopt an uninterested attitude.
– DERIVATIVES **hardish** adjective **hardness** noun.
– ORIGIN Old English.

hardback noun a book bound in stiff covers.

hardbitten adjective tough and cynical.

hardboard noun stiff board made of compressed and treated wood pulp.

hard-boiled adjective **1** (of an egg) boiled until solid. **2** (of a person) tough and cynical.

hard cash noun coins and banknotes as opposed to other forms of payment.

hard copy noun a printed version on paper of data held in a computer.

hard core noun **1** the most committed or uncompromising members of a group. **2** very explicit pornography. **3** (usu. **hardcore**) a type of rock or dance music that is experimental, loud, and played aggressively. **4** Brit. broken bricks and rubble used as a filling or foundation in building.

hardcover noun chiefly N. Amer. another term for HARDBACK.

hard disk (also **hard drive**) noun Computing a rigid non-removable magnetic disk with a large data storage capacity.

harden verb **1** make or become hard or harder. **2** (as adj. **hardened**) fixed in a bad habit or way of life: *hardened criminals.*
– DERIVATIVES **hardener** noun.

hard-headed adjective tough and realistic.

hard-hearted adjective unsympathetic or uncaring.

hard-hitting adjective uncompromisingly direct and honest.

hardihood noun dated or US boldness; daring.

hard labour noun a type of punishment that takes the form of heavy physical work.

hard line noun a strict and uncompromising policy or attitude: *he takes a hard line on most moral issues.* • adjective uncompromising; strict.
– DERIVATIVES **hardliner** noun.

hardly adverb **1** almost no; almost not; almost none: *there was hardly any wind.* **2** no or not. **3** only with great difficulty. **4** only a very short time before: *the party had hardly started when the police arrived.*

hard-nosed adjective informal realistic and tough-minded.

hard-on noun vulgar slang an erection of the penis.

hard palate noun the bony front part of the roof of the mouth.

hardpan noun a hardened layer, occurring in or below the soil, that resists penetration by water and plant roots.

hard-pressed adjective in difficulties or under pressure: *she'd be hard-pressed to find anyone else who'd put up with her.*

hard rock noun very loud rock music with a heavy beat.

hard sell noun a policy or technique of aggressive selling or advertising.

hardship noun severe suffering or difficulty.

hard shoulder noun Brit. a hardened strip alongside a motorway for use in an emergency.

hardstanding noun Brit. ground surfaced with a hard material for parking vehicles on.

hard tack noun old use hard dry bread or biscuit, especially as rations for sailors or soldiers.

hardtop noun a motor vehicle with a rigid roof which in some cases is detachable.

hardware noun **1** tools and other items used in the home and in activities such as gardening. **2** the machines, wiring, and other physical components of a computer. **3** heavy military equipment such as tanks and missiles.

hard-wearing adjective able to stand much wear.

hard-wired adjective Electronics involving permanently connected circuits rather than software.

hardwood noun the wood from broadleaved trees as opposed to that of conifers.

hardy adjective (**hardier**, **hardiest**) **1** capable of enduring difficult conditions; robust. **2** (of a plant) able to survive outside during winter.
– DERIVATIVES **hardiness** noun.
– ORIGIN Old French *hardi*.

hare noun a fast-running, long-eared mammal resembling a large rabbit, with very long hind legs. • verb chiefly Brit. run very fast.
– ORIGIN Old English.

harebell noun a plant with pale blue bell-shaped flowers.

hare-brained adjective foolish and unlikely to succeed: *steer clear of hare-brained schemes.*

Hare Krishna /ha-ri krish-nuh/ noun a member of a religious sect based on the worship of the Hindu god Krishna.

- ORIGIN Sanskrit, 'O Vishnu Krishna', a devotional chant.

harelip noun offensive term for CLEFT LIP.

> USAGE: The word **harelip** can cause offence and should be avoided; use **cleft lip** instead.

harem /**hah**-reem/ noun 1 the separate part of a Muslim household reserved for women. 2 the wives and concubines of a polygamous Muslim man.
- ORIGIN Arabic, 'prohibited place'.

haricot /**ha**-ri-koh/ noun chiefly Brit. a round white variety of French bean.
- ORIGIN French.

harissa /**har**-i-suh/ noun a hot sauce or paste used in North African cuisine, made from chilli peppers, paprika, and olive oil.
- ORIGIN Arabic.

hark verb 1 literary listen. 2 (**hark back to**) recall or remind one of something in the past.
- ORIGIN Germanic.

harken verb variant spelling of HEARKEN.

harlequin /**har**-li-kwin/ noun (**Harlequin**) a character in traditional pantomime, wearing a mask and a diamond-patterned costume.
• adjective in varied colours; variegated.
- ORIGIN former French *Herlequin*, the leader of a legendary troop of demon horsemen.

harlequinade /har-li-kwi-**nayd**/ noun 1 historical the section of a traditional pantomime in which Harlequin played a leading role. 2 dated a piece of foolish behaviour.

harlot noun old use a prostitute or promiscuous woman.
- DERIVATIVES **harlotry** noun.
- ORIGIN Old French, 'young man, knave'.

harm noun 1 physical injury to a person. 2 damage done to something. 3 an adverse effect: *there was no harm in looking was there?*
• verb 1 physically injure someone. 2 damage or have an adverse effect on: *when we use products that waste energy, we harm the environment.*
- ORIGIN Old English.

harmful adjective causing or likely to cause harm.
- DERIVATIVES **harmfully** adverb **harmfulness** noun.

harmless adjective not able or likely to cause harm.
- DERIVATIVES **harmlessly** adverb **harmlessness** noun.

harmonic /har-**mon**-ik/ adjective 1 relating to or characterized by harmony. 2 Music relating to a harmonic. • noun Music a tone produced by vibration of a string in any of certain fractions (half, third, etc.) of its length.
- DERIVATIVES **harmonically** adverb.

harmonica noun a small rectangular wind instrument with a row of metal reeds that produce different notes.

harmonious adjective 1 tuneful; not discordant. 2 arranged in a pleasing way so that each part goes well with the others: *dishes providing a harmonious blend of colour, flavour, and aroma.* 3 free from disagreement or conflict.
- DERIVATIVES **harmoniously** adverb **harmoniousness** noun.

harmonium noun a keyboard instrument in which the notes are produced by air driven through metal reeds by foot-operated bellows.
- ORIGIN from Greek *harmonios* 'harmonious'.

harmonize (or **harmonise**) verb 1 add notes to a melody to produce harmony. 2 sing or play in harmony. 3 make or be harmonious or in agreement: *unsweetened coconut harmonizes well with many Indian dishes.* 4 make things consistent with each other.
- DERIVATIVES **harmonization** noun **harmonizer** noun.

harmony noun (pl. **harmonies**) 1 the combination of musical notes sounded at the same time to produce a pleasing effect. 2 a pleasing quality when things are arranged together well. 3 a state of agreement and peaceful existence: *images of racial harmony.*
- ORIGIN Latin *harmonia* 'joining, concord'.

harness noun 1 a set of straps and fittings by which a horse or other animal is fastened to a cart, plough, etc. and is controlled by its driver. 2 an arrangement of straps for fastening something such as a parachute to a person's body or for restraining a young child.
• verb 1 fit a horse or other animal with a harness. 2 control and use so as to achieve or produce something: *we will harness new technology to keep the police ahead of the criminals.*
- PHRASES **in harness** in the routine of daily work.
- ORIGIN Old French *harneis* 'military equipment'.

harp noun a musical instrument consisting of a frame supporting a series of parallel strings of different lengths, played by plucking with the fingers. • verb (**harp on**) keep talking or writing about something in a boring way.
- DERIVATIVES **harpist** noun.
- ORIGIN Old English.

harpoon noun a barbed spear-like missile attached to a long rope and thrown by hand or fired from a gun, used for catching whales and other large sea creatures. • verb spear something with a harpoon.
- DERIVATIVES **harpooner** noun.
- ORIGIN Greek *harpē* 'sickle'.

harpsichord noun a keyboard instrument similar in shape to a grand piano, with horizontal strings plucked by points operated by pressing the keys.
- DERIVATIVES **harpsichordist** noun.
- ORIGIN from Latin *harpa* 'harp' + *chorda* 'string'.

harpy noun (pl. **harpies**) 1 Greek & Roman Mythology a monster with a woman's head and body and a bird's wings and claws. 2 an unpleasant woman.
- ORIGIN Greek *harpuiai* 'snatchers'.

harquebus /**har**-kwi-buhss/ (also **arquebus**) noun a former type of portable gun supported on a tripod or a forked rest.
- ORIGIN French *harquebuse.*

harridan noun a bossy or aggressive old woman.
- ORIGIN perhaps from French *haridelle* 'old horse'.

harrier[1] noun a long-winged, slender bird of prey.

– ORIGIN from **HARRY**.

harrier² noun a hound of a breed used for hunting hares.
– ORIGIN from **HARE**.

harrier³ noun a person who harries or harasses others.

harrow noun an implement consisting of a heavy frame set with teeth which is dragged over ploughed land to break up or spread the soil. •verb **1** use a harrow to break up soil. **2** (as adj. **harrowing**) very distressing.
– ORIGIN Old Norse.

harrumph verb **1** clear the throat noisily. **2** grumpily express disapproval.
– ORIGIN imitating the sound.

harry verb (**harries**, **harrying**, **harried**) **1** carry out repeated attacks on an enemy. **2** harass someone continuously.
– ORIGIN Old English.

harsh adjective **1** unpleasantly rough or intense to the senses: *a harsh white light*. **2** cruel or severe. **3** (of climate or conditions) difficult to survive in; hostile.
– DERIVATIVES **harshen** verb **harshly** adverb **harshness** noun.
– ORIGIN German *harsch* 'rough'.

hart noun an adult male deer, especially a red deer over five years old.
– ORIGIN Old English.

hartebeest /har-ti-beest/ noun a large African antelope with a long head and sloping back.
– ORIGIN from Dutch *hert* 'hart' + *beest* 'beast'.

harum-scarum adjective reckless or impetuous.
– ORIGIN from **HARE** and **SCARE**.

harvest noun **1** the process or period of gathering in crops. **2** the season's yield or crop. •verb gather a crop as a harvest.
– DERIVATIVES **harvestable** adjective **harvester** noun.
– ORIGIN Old English, 'autumn'.

harvestman noun (pl. **harvestmen**) a creature like a spider, with a globular body and very long, thin legs.

harvest moon noun the full moon that is seen closest to the time of the autumn equinox.

harvest mouse noun a small mouse that nests among the stalks of growing cereals.

has third person singular present of **HAVE**.

has-been noun informal a person or thing that is outdated or no longer significant.

hash¹ noun a dish of diced cooked meat reheated with potatoes.
– PHRASES **make a hash of** informal make a mess of something. **settle someone's hash** informal deal with someone in a forceful and decisive way.
– ORIGIN French *hache* 'axe'.

hash² noun informal hashish.

hash³ noun Brit. the symbol #.
– ORIGIN probably from **HATCH³**.

hash browns plural noun chiefly N. Amer. a dish of chopped and fried cooked potatoes.

hashish /ha-sheesh/ noun cannabis.
– ORIGIN Arabic, 'dry herb, powdered hemp leaves'.

Hasid /hass-id/ (also **Chasid**, **Chassid**, or **Hassid**) noun (pl. **Hasidim**) a follower of Hasidism, a mystical Jewish movement founded in the eighteenth century and represented today by fundamentalist communities in Israel and New York.
– DERIVATIVES **Hasidic** /ha-si-dik/ adjective **Hasidism** noun.
– ORIGIN from Hebrew, 'pious'.

haslet /haz-lit/ noun chiefly Brit. a cold meat consisting of chopped and compressed pork offal.
– ORIGIN Old French *hastelet*.

hasn't contraction has not.

hasp noun a hinged metal plate that forms part of a fastening for a door or lid and is fitted over a metal loop and secured by a pin or padlock.
– ORIGIN Old English.

Hassid noun variant spelling of **HASID**.

hassium /hass-i-uhm/ noun a very unstable chemical element made by high-energy atomic collisions.
– ORIGIN from *Hassias*, the Latin name for the German state of *Hesse*.

hassle informal noun **1** annoying inconvenience. **2** a situation of conflict or disagreement: *with no job and no money, she gets hassle from her dad*. •verb harass or pester someone.
– ORIGIN unknown.

hassock noun a cushion for kneeling on in church.
– ORIGIN Old English, 'clump of grass in marshy ground'.

hast old-fashioned second person singular present of **HAVE**.

haste noun speed or urgency in doing something: *the note was clearly written in haste*.
– ORIGIN Old French.

hasten verb **1** be quick to do something; move quickly. **2** make something happen sooner than expected.

hasty adjective (**hastier**, **hastiest**) **1** done with speed or urgency. **2** acting too quickly and without much thought: *the medics were a little hasty in predicting an early death for him*.
– DERIVATIVES **hastily** adverb **hastiness** noun.

hat noun a shaped covering for the head, typically with a brim and a crown.
– PHRASES **keep something under one's hat** keep something a secret. **pass the hat round** collect contributions of money. **take one's hat off to someone** used to express admiration or praise for someone. **talk through one's hat** informal talk foolishly or ignorantly.
– DERIVATIVES **hatful** noun **hatless** adjective **hatted** adjective.
– ORIGIN Old English.

hatband noun a decorative ribbon around a hat, just above the brim.

hatch¹ noun **1** a small opening in a floor, wall, or roof allowing access from one area to another. **2** a door in an aircraft, spacecraft, or submarine.
– ORIGIN Old English, referring to the lower half of a divided door.

hatch² verb **1** (of a young bird, fish, or reptile) emerge or cause to emerge from its egg. **2** (of an egg) open and produce a young animal. **3** think up a plot or plan. •noun a newly hatched brood.
– ORIGIN unknown.

h

hatch[3] verb (in technical drawing) shade an area with closely drawn parallel lines.
- DERIVATIVES **hatching** noun.
- ORIGIN Old French *hacher*.

hatchback noun a car with a door across the full width at the back end that opens upwards.

hatchery noun (pl. **hatcheries**) an establishment where fish or poultry eggs are hatched.

hatchet noun a small axe with a short handle.
- PHRASES **bury the hatchet** end a quarrel or conflict. [referring to an American Indian custom.]
- ORIGIN Old French *hachette* 'little axe'.

hatchet-faced adjective informal sharp-featured and grim-looking.

hatchet job noun informal a fierce spoken or written attack.

hatchet man noun informal a person employed to carry out unpleasant tasks on behalf of someone else.

hatchling noun a newly hatched young animal.

hatchway noun an opening or hatch, especially in a ship's deck.

hate verb feel intense dislike for someone or something. • noun **1** intense dislike. **2** informal a disliked thing: *her pet hate is filling in tax forms.* • adjective (of a hostile act) motivated by intense dislike or prejudice: *a hate crime.*
- DERIVATIVES **hater** noun.
- ORIGIN Old English.

hateful adjective arousing or deserving hate; very unpleasant.
- DERIVATIVES **hatefully** adverb **hatefulness** noun.

hath old-fashioned third person singular present of **HAVE**.

hatha yoga /hut-uh, hath-uh/ noun a system of physical exercises used in yoga.
- ORIGIN *hatha* from Sanskrit, 'force'.

hatred noun very strong hate.

hatter noun a person who makes and sells hats.
- PHRASES **(as) mad as a hatter** informal completely insane.

hat-trick noun three successes of the same kind, especially (in football) three goals scored by the same player in a game or (in cricket) three wickets taken by a bowler with successive balls.
- ORIGIN first referring to the presentation of a new hat to a bowler taking a hat-trick.

hauberk /hor-berk/ noun historical a full-length coat of mail.
- ORIGIN Old French *hauberc*.

haughty adjective (**haughtier**, **haughtiest**) behaving in an arrogant and superior way toward others.
- DERIVATIVES **haughtily** adverb **haughtiness** noun.
- ORIGIN Old French *hault* 'high'.

haul verb **1** pull or drag something with effort. **2** transport something in a lorry or cart. • noun **1** a quantity of something obtained, especially illegally: *they escaped with a haul of antiques.* **2** a number of fish caught at one time. **3** a distance to be travelled: *the thirty-mile haul to Boston.*
- PHRASES **haul someone over the coals** reprimand someone severely.
- DERIVATIVES **hauler** noun.
- ORIGIN variant of **HALE**[2].

haulage noun Brit. the commercial transport of goods.

haulier noun Brit. a person or company employed in the commercial transport of goods by road.

haulm /hawm/ noun a plant stalk or stem.
- ORIGIN Old English.

haunch noun **1** the buttock and thigh of a human or animal. **2** the leg and loin of an animal, as food.
- ORIGIN Old French *hanche*.

haunt verb **1** (of a ghost) appear regularly in a place. **2** (of a person) visit a place often. **3** be persistently and disturbingly present in the mind: *both men are haunted by memories of death.* • noun a place frequented by a specified person: *the bar was a favourite haunt of artists.*
- DERIVATIVES **haunter** noun.
- ORIGIN Old French *hanter*.

haunted adjective **1** (of a place) visited by a ghost. **2** having or showing signs of great distress.

haunting adjective beautiful or sad in a way that is hard to forget: *the haunting sound of the flutes.*
- DERIVATIVES **hauntingly** adverb.

hautboy /hoh-boy/ noun old-fashioned form of **OBOE**.
- ORIGIN French *hautbois*.

haute couture /oht kuu-tyoor/ noun the designing and making of high-quality clothes by leading fashion houses.
- ORIGIN French, 'high dressmaking'.

haute cuisine /oht kwi-zeen/ noun high-quality cooking in the traditional French style.
- ORIGIN French, 'high cookery'.

hauteur /oh-ter/ noun proud haughtiness of manner.
- ORIGIN French.

Havana noun a cigar made in Cuba or from Cuban tobacco.
- ORIGIN named after *Havana*, the capital of Cuba.

have verb (**has**, **having**, **had**) **1** possess, own, or hold something. **2** experience: *I had difficulty keeping awake.* **3** be able to make use of something. **4** (**have to**) be obliged to; must. **5** perform a particular action: *he had a look round.* **6** show a personal quality or characteristic. **7** suffer from an illness or disability. **8** cause to be or be done: *she had dinner ready.* **9** place, hold, or keep something in a particular position. **10** receive something from someone. **11** take or invite someone into one's home. **12** eat or drink something. **13** (**not have**) refuse to allow or accept something. **14** (**be had**) informal be cheated or deceived. • auxiliary verb used with a past participle to form the perfect, pluperfect, and future perfect tenses, and the conditional mood.
- PHRASES **have had it** informal be beyond repair or revival. **have (got) it in for someone** informal behave in a hostile way towards someone. **have it out** informal attempt to settle a dispute by confrontation. **have someone on** informal try to make someone believe something untrue, especially as a joke. **the haves and the have-nots** informal people with plenty of money and

those who are poor. **have someone up** Brit. informal bring someone before a court for an alleged offence.
– ORIGIN Old English.

> **USAGE:** Be careful not to write **of** when you mean **have** or **'ve**: *I could've told you that* not *I could of told you that.* The mistake occurs because the pronunciation of **have** can sound the same as that of **of**, so that the words are confused when they are written down.

haven noun **1** a place of safety. **2** a harbour or small port.
– ORIGIN Old English.

haven't contraction have not.

haver /hay-ver/ verb **1** Scottish talk foolishly; babble. **2** Brit. act in an indecisive way.
– ORIGIN unknown.

haversack noun a small, strong bag carried on the back or over the shoulder.
– ORIGIN from former German *Habersack* 'bag used to carry oats'.

havoc noun **1** widespread destruction. **2** great confusion or disorder.
– PHRASES **play havoc with** completely disrupt something.
– ORIGIN Old French *havot*.

haw¹ noun the red fruit of the hawthorn.
– ORIGIN Old English.

haw² verb see hum and haw at HUM.

Hawaiian /huh-wy-uhn/ noun **1** a person from Hawaii. **2** the language of Hawaii. •adjective relating to Hawaii.

Hawaiian shirt noun a brightly coloured and gaily patterned shirt.

hawfinch noun a large finch with a massive bill for cracking open hard seeds.
– ORIGIN from HAW¹ + FINCH.

hawk¹ noun **1** a fast-flying bird of prey with broad rounded wings and a long tail. **2** any bird of prey used in falconry. **3** a person who advocates aggressive policies in foreign affairs. •verb hunt game with a trained hawk.
– DERIVATIVES **hawkish** adjective.
– ORIGIN Old English.

hawk² verb offer goods for sale in the street.
– ORIGIN probably from HAWKER.

hawk³ verb **1** clear the throat noisily. **2** (**hawk something up**) bring phlegm up from the throat.
– ORIGIN probably imitating the sound.

hawker noun a person who travels about selling goods.
– ORIGIN probably from German or Dutch.

hawser /haw-zer/ noun a thick rope or cable for mooring or towing a ship.
– ORIGIN from Old French *haucier* 'to hoist'.

hawthorn noun a thorny shrub or tree with white, pink, or red blossom and small dark red fruits (haws).
– ORIGIN Old English.

hay noun grass that has been mown and dried for use as fodder.
– PHRASES **hit the hay** informal go to bed. **make hay (while the sun shines)** make good use of an opportunity while it lasts.
– DERIVATIVES **haying** noun.
– ORIGIN Old English.

haycock noun a conical heap of hay left in the field to dry.

hay fever noun an allergy to pollen or dust, causing sneezing and watery eyes.

hayloft noun a loft over a stable used for storing hay or straw.

haymaker noun **1** a person involved in making hay. **2** informal a forceful blow.
– DERIVATIVES **haymaking** noun.

hayrick noun a haystack.

hayseed noun informal, chiefly N. Amer. a simple, unsophisticated country person.

haystack noun a large packed pile of hay.

haywire adjective informal out of control: *everybody's weather is going haywire.*
– ORIGIN from the use of hay-baling wire in makeshift repairs.

hazard noun **1** a danger or risk of danger: *many people viewed GM food as a health hazard.* **2** an obstacle, such as a bunker, on a golf course. **3** literary chance; probability. •verb **1** say something in a tentative way. **2** put something at risk of being lost.
– ORIGIN Persian or Turkish, 'dice'.

hazard lights plural noun flashing indicator lights on a vehicle, used to warn that the vehicle is stationary or unexpectedly slow.

hazardous adjective risky; dangerous.
– DERIVATIVES **hazardously** adverb.

haze noun **1** a thin mist typically caused by fine particles of dust, pollutants, or water vapour. **2** a state of mental confusion: *I went to bed in an alcoholic haze.* •verb cover or conceal with a haze.
– ORIGIN probably from HAZY.

hazel noun **1** a shrub or small tree bearing catkins in spring and edible nuts in autumn. **2** a rich reddish-brown colour.
– ORIGIN Old English.

hazelnut noun the round brown edible nut of the hazel.

hazy adjective (**hazier, haziest**) **1** covered by a haze. **2** vague, unclear, or confused: *those days are a hazy memory.*
– DERIVATIVES **hazily** adverb **haziness** noun.
– ORIGIN unknown.

HB abbreviation **1** half board. **2** (also **hb**) hardback. **3** hard black (as a medium grade of pencil lead).

H-bomb noun short for HYDROGEN BOMB.

HDTV abbreviation high-definition television.

He symbol the chemical element helium.

he pronoun (third person sing.) **1** used to refer to a man, boy, or male animal previously mentioned or easily identified. **2** used to refer to a person or animal of unspecified sex. •noun a male; a man.
– ORIGIN Old English.

> **USAGE:** Until recently, **he** was used to refer to both males and females when a person's sex was not specified; this is now regarded as outdated and sexist. One solution is to use **he or she**, but this can be awkward if used repeatedly. An alternative is to use **they**, especially where it occurs after an indefinite pronoun such as **everyone** or **someone** (as in *everyone needs to feel that they matter*): this is becoming more and more accepted both in speech and in writing.

h

head noun 1 the upper part of the body, containing the brain, mouth, and sense organs. 2 a person in charge of something. 3 the front, forward, or upper part or end of something. 4 a person considered as a unit: *they paid fifty pounds a head*. 5 (treated as pl.) a specified number of animals: *seventy head of cattle*. 6 a compact mass of leaves or flowers at the top of a stem. 7 the cutting or operational end of a tool or mechanism. 8 a part of a computer or a tape or video recorder which transfers information to and from a tape or disk. 9 the source of a river or stream. 10 the foam on top of a glass of beer. 11 (**heads**) the side of a coin bearing the image of a head. 12 pressure of water or steam in an engine or other confined space: *a good head of steam*. • adjective chief; principal. • verb 1 be or act as the head of: *the foreign policy team is headed by an academic*. 2 (also **be headed**) move in a specified direction: *I headed for the exit*. 3 give a title or heading to something. 4 (**head someone/thing off**) intercept someone or something and force them to turn aside. 5 Football shoot or pass the ball with the head.
− PHRASES **come to a head** reach a crisis. **give someone his** (or **her**) **head** allow someone complete freedom of action. **go to someone's head 1** (of alcohol) make someone slightly drunk. **2** (of success) make someone conceited. **head first 1** with the head in front of the rest of the body. **2** without thinking beforehand. **a head for** a talent for or an ability to cope with something: *a head for heights*. —— **one's head off** informal talk, laugh, shout, scream, etc. unrestrainedly. **head over heels 1** turning over completely in forward motion. **2** madly in love. **a head start** an advantage granted or gained at the beginning. **keep** (or **lose**) **one's head** remain (or fail to remain) calm. **keep one's head above water** avoid falling into debt or difficulty. **make head or tail of** understand something at all. **off** (or **out of**) **one's head** Brit. informal crazy. **off the top of one's head** without careful thought. **over someone's head 1** (also **above someone's head**) beyond someone's ability to understand. **2** without consulting someone. **turn someone's head** make someone conceited.
− DERIVATIVES **headed** adjective **headless** adjective.
− ORIGIN Old English.

headache noun 1 a continuous pain in the head. 2 informal a cause of worry or trouble.
− DERIVATIVES **headachy** adjective.

headband noun a band of fabric worn around the head as a decoration or to keep the hair off the face.

headbanger noun informal a fan or performer of heavy metal music.

headboard noun an upright panel at the head of a bed.

headbutt verb attack someone by hitting them hard with the head. • noun an act of head-butting.

headcase noun informal a mentally ill or unstable person.

headcount noun a count of the number of people present or available.

headdress noun an ornamental covering for the head.

header noun 1 Football a shot or pass made with the head. 2 informal a headlong fall or dive. 3 a line of writing at the top of each page of a book or document. 4 (also **header tank**) a raised tank of water maintaining pressure in a plumbing system. 5 a brick or stone laid at right angles to the face of a wall.

headgear noun hats and other items worn on the head.

headhunt verb 1 approach someone already employed elsewhere to fill a vacant post. 2 (as noun **headhunting**) the practice among some peoples of collecting the heads of dead enemies as trophies.
− DERIVATIVES **headhunter** noun.

heading noun 1 a title at the top of a page or section of a book. 2 a direction or bearing. 3 the top of a curtain extending above the hooks or wire by which it is suspended.

headland noun a narrow piece of land projecting into the sea.

headlight (also **headlamp**) noun a powerful light at the front of a motor vehicle or railway engine.

headline noun 1 a heading at the top of an article or page in a newspaper or magazine. 2 (**the headlines**) a summary of the most important items of news. • verb 1 provide an article with a headline. 2 appear as the star performer at a concert.
− DERIVATIVES **headliner** noun.

headlock noun a method of restraining someone by holding an arm firmly around their head.

headlong adverb & adjective 1 with the head first. 2 in a rush.

headman noun (pl. **headmen**) the leader of a tribe.

headmaster (or **headmistress**) noun chiefly Brit. a head teacher.

head of state noun a president, monarch, or other official leader of a country, who may also be the head of government.

head-on adjective & adverb 1 with or involving the front of a vehicle. 2 with or involving direct confrontation.

headphones plural noun a pair of earphones joined by a band placed over the head.

headpiece noun a device worn on the head.

headquarter verb (**be headquartered**) have headquarters at a specified place.

headquarters noun (treated as sing. or pl.) 1 the managerial and administrative centre of an organization. 2 the premises occupied by a military commander and the commander's staff.

headrest noun a padded support for the head on the back of a seat.

headroom noun the space between the top of a vehicle or a person's head and the ceiling or other structure above.

headscarf noun (pl. **headscarves**) a square of fabric worn as a covering for the head.

headset noun a set of headphones with a microphone attached.

headship noun 1 the position of leader. 2 chiefly Brit. the position of head teacher in a school.

headshrinker noun informal, chiefly N. Amer. a psychiatrist.

headstone noun an inscribed stone slab set up at the head of a grave.

headstrong adjective determined to do things in one's own way, regardless of advice to the contrary.

head teacher noun chiefly Brit. the teacher in charge of a school.

head-to-head adjective & adverb involving two parties confronting each other in a dispute or contest.

head-turning adjective very noticeable or attractive.

headwaters plural noun the tributary streams of a river close to or forming its source.

headway noun (in phrase **make headway**) make progress.

headwind noun a wind blowing from directly in front.

headword noun a word which begins a separate entry in a reference book such as a dictionary.

heady adjective (**headier, headiest**) **1** exciting or exhilarating: *the heady days after Independence.* **2** (of alcohol) intoxicating.
– DERIVATIVES **headily** adverb.

heal verb **1** make or become sound or healthy again. **2** put right an undesirable situation.
– DERIVATIVES **healer** noun.
– ORIGIN Old English.

health noun **1** the state of being free from illness or injury. **2** a person's mental or physical condition.
– ORIGIN Old English.

health centre noun an establishment housing local medical services.

health club noun a private club with exercise facilities and health and beauty treatments.

health farm noun chiefly Brit. a place where people stay to improve their health by dieting, exercising, and having various treatments.

health food noun natural food that is thought to be good for the health.

healthful adjective good for the health.
– DERIVATIVES **healthfully** adverb **healthfulness** noun.

health service noun a public service providing medical care.

health tourism noun the practice of travelling abroad in order to receive medical treatment.

health visitor noun Brit. a nurse who visits patients or parents of very young children in their homes.

healthy adjective (**healthier, healthiest**) **1** having or promoting good health. **2** normal, sensible, or desirable. **3** of a very satisfactory size or amount: *a healthy profit.*
– DERIVATIVES **healthily** adverb **healthiness** noun.

heap noun **1** a pile of a substance or of a number of objects. **2** informal a large amount or number: *we have heaps of room.* **3** informal an old vehicle in bad condition. • verb **1** put in or form a heap. **2** (**heap something with**) load something with a large amount of something. **3** (**heap something on**) give much praise, abuse, etc. to: *the press heaped abuse on him.*
– ORIGIN Old English.

hear verb (past and past part. **heard**) **1** perceive a sound with the ear. **2** be told about something.

3 (**have heard of**) be aware of the existence of: *nobody had heard of my college.* **4** (**hear from**) receive a letter or phone call from someone. **5** listen to someone or something. **6** listen to and judge a case or person bringing a case in a law court.
– PHRASES **hear! hear!** used to express full agreement with something in a speech. **will** (or **would**) **not hear of** will (or would) not allow or agree to.
– DERIVATIVES **hearable** adjective **hearer** noun.
– ORIGIN Old English.

hearing noun **1** the faculty of perceiving sounds. **2** the range within which sounds may be heard; earshot. **3** an opportunity to state one's case: *a fair hearing.* **4** an act of listening to evidence before an official or in a law court.

hearing aid noun a small amplifying device worn on the ear by a partially deaf person.

hearken /har-k'n/ (also **harken**) verb (usu. **hearken to**) old use listen.
– ORIGIN Old English.

hearsay noun information received from others which cannot be proved.

hearse /herss/ noun a vehicle for carrying the coffin at a funeral.
– ORIGIN Old French *herce* 'harrow, frame'.

heart noun **1** the hollow muscular organ in the chest that pumps the blood around the body. **2** the central, innermost, or vital part: *the heart of the city.* **3** a person's capacity for feeling love or compassion. **4** mood or feeling: *a change of heart.* **5** courage or enthusiasm. **6** a shape representing a heart with two equal curves meeting at a point at the bottom and a cusp at the top. **7** (**hearts**) one of the four suits in a pack of playing cards.
– PHRASES **after one's own heart** sharing one's tastes. **at heart** in one's real nature, in contrast to how one may appear. **break someone's heart** overwhelm someone with sadness. **by heart** from memory. **close** (or **dear**) **to one's heart** very important to one. **from the** (or **the bottom of one's**) **heart** in a very sincere way. **have a heart of gold** have a very kind nature. **have the heart to do something** be hard-hearted enough to do something. **have one's heart in one's mouth** be very alarmed or apprehensive. **in one's heart of hearts** in one's innermost feelings. **tug** (or **pull**) **at one's heartstrings** arouse strong feelings of love or pity. **take something to heart** be very upset by criticism. **wear one's heart on one's sleeve** show one's feelings openly.
– ORIGIN Old English.

heartache noun distress or grief.

heart attack noun a sudden occurrence of coronary thrombosis.

heartbeat noun a pulsation of the heart.
– PHRASES **a heartbeat away** very close.

heartbreak noun overwhelming distress.
– DERIVATIVES **heartbreaker** noun **heartbreaking** adjective **heartbroken** adjective.

heartburn noun a form of indigestion felt as a burning sensation in the chest, caused by acid regurgitation into the oesophagus.

hearten verb make more cheerful or confident: *he was heartened by the increase in party membership.*
– DERIVATIVES **heartening** adjective.

heart failure noun severe failure of the heart to function properly, especially as a cause of death.

heartfelt adjective deeply and strongly felt.

hearth /harth/ noun the floor or surround of a fireplace.
– ORIGIN Old English.

hearthrug noun a rug laid in front of a fireplace.

heartily adverb 1 in a hearty way. 2 very: *I'm heartily sick of them.*

heartland noun the central or most important part of a country or area.

heartless adjective lacking any pity for others; very unkind or unfeeling.
– DERIVATIVES **heartlessly** adverb **heartlessness** noun.

heart-rending adjective very sad or distressing.

heart-searching noun thorough examination of one's feelings and motives.

heartsease /harts-eez/ noun a wild pansy with purple and yellow flowers.

heartsick (also **heartsore**) adjective literary very downhearted from grief or loss of love.

heart-stopping adjective very exciting.

heart-throb noun informal a well-known man who is very good-looking.

heart-to-heart adjective (of a conversation) intimate and personal.

heart-warming adjective emotionally rewarding or uplifting.

heartwood noun the dense inner part of a tree trunk, yielding the hardest wood.

hearty adjective (**heartier**, **heartiest**) 1 enthusiastic and friendly. 2 cheerful and full of energy: *a big bluff hearty man.* 3 (of a feeling or opinion) deeply felt. 4 (of a meal) wholesome and filling.
– DERIVATIVES **heartiness** noun.

heat noun 1 the quality of being hot; high temperature. 2 heat as a form of energy arising from the random movement of molecules. 3 a source or level of heat for cooking. 4 intensity of feeling: *an attempt to take some heat out of the debate.* 5 (**the heat**) informal great pressure to do or achieve something: *the heat is on.* 6 a preliminary round in a race or contest. ● verb 1 make or become hot or warm. 2 (**heat up**) become more intense and exciting. 3 (as adj. **heated**) passionate: *a heated argument.*
– PHRASES **in the heat of the moment** while temporarily angry or excited and without stopping to think. **on heat** (of a female mammal) in a sexual state of readiness for mating.
– DERIVATIVES **heatedly** adverb.
– ORIGIN Old English.

heater noun a device for heating something.

heath noun 1 chiefly Brit. an area of open uncultivated land, typically on sandy soil and covered with heather, gorse, and coarse grasses. 2 a dwarf shrub with small pink or purple bell-shaped flowers, found on heaths and moors.
– ORIGIN Old English.

heathen /hee-*th*uhn/ noun derogatory a person who does not belong to a widely held religion (especially Christianity, Judaism, or Islam) as regarded by those who do. ● adjective relating to heathens.
– DERIVATIVES **heathenish** adjective **heathenism** noun.
– ORIGIN Old English.

heather noun a dwarf shrub with purple flowers, found on moors and heaths.
– DERIVATIVES **heathery** adjective.
– ORIGIN Old English.

heathland noun an extensive area of heath.

Heath Robinson adjective Brit. (of a device) ingeniously or ridiculously over-complicated in design.
– ORIGIN named after the English cartoonist William *Heath Robinson.*

heating noun equipment or devices used to provide heat, especially to a building.

heatproof adjective able to resist great heat.

heat-seeking adjective (of a missile) able to detect and home in on heat produced by a target.

heatstroke noun a feverish condition caused by failure of the body's temperature-regulating mechanism when exposed to very high temperatures.

heatwave noun a long period of unusually hot weather.

heave verb (past and past part. **heaved** or Nautical **hove**) 1 lift, haul, or throw something heavy with great effort. 2 rise and fall with a steady movement: *his shoulders heaved as he panted.* 3 produce a sigh noisily. 4 try to vomit. 5 (**heave to**) (of a ship) come to a stop. ● noun an act of heaving something.
– PHRASES **heave in sight** (or **into view**) (especially of a ship) come into view.
– DERIVATIVES **heaver** noun.
– ORIGIN Old English.

heave-ho noun (**the heave-ho**) informal dismissal from a job or contest.

heaven noun 1 (in various religions) the place where God or the gods live and where good people go after death. 2 (**the heavens**) literary the sky. 3 a place or state of great happiness. 4 (also **heavens**) used in exclamations as a substitute for 'God'.
– PHRASES **the heavens open** it suddenly starts to rain very heavily. **in seventh heaven** very happy; ecstatic.
– DERIVATIVES **heavenward** adjective & adverb **heavenwards** adverb.
– ORIGIN Old English.

heavenly adjective 1 relating to heaven; divine. 2 relating to the sky. 3 informal very pleasant; wonderful.

heavenly body noun a planet, star, or other object in space.

heaven-sent adjective happening unexpectedly and at a very favourable time.

heaving adjective Brit. informal (of a place) very crowded.

heavy adjective (**heavier**, **heaviest**) 1 weighing a great deal. 2 very dense, thick, or substantial: *heavy grey clouds.* 3 of more than the usual size, amount, or force. 4 doing something to excess: *a heavy smoker.* 5 striking or falling with force: *he felt a heavy blow on his shoulder.* 6 needing much physical effort. 7 not delicate

or graceful. **8** serious or difficult to understand: *a heavy discussion.* **9** informal full of anger or other strong emotion and difficult to deal with: *things were getting heavy.* **10** (of music, especially rock) having a strong bass component and a forceful rhythm. **11** (of ground) muddy or full of clay. • **noun** (pl. **heavies**) informal a large, strong man, especially one hired for protection.
– DERIVATIVES **heavily** adverb **heaviness** noun.
– ORIGIN Old English.

heavy-duty adjective designed to withstand a great deal of use or wear.

heavy-handed adjective clumsy, insensitive, or overly forceful.

heavy-hearted adjective depressed or melancholy.

heavy hitter (also **big hitter**) noun informal an important or powerful person.

heavy hydrogen noun another term for DEUTERIUM.

heavy industry noun the manufacture of large, heavy articles and materials in bulk.

heavy metal noun **1** a type of very loud harsh-sounding rock music with a strong beat. **2** a metal of relatively high density, or of high relative atomic weight.

heavy petting noun sexual activity between two people that stops short of intercourse.

heavyset noun (of a person) broad and strongly built.

heavy water noun water in which the hydrogen in the molecules is partly or wholly replaced by the isotope deuterium, used especially in nuclear reactors.

heavyweight noun **1** a weight in boxing and other sports, typically the heaviest category. **2** informal an influential person. • adjective **1** of above-average weight. **2** informal serious or influential: *heavyweight news coverage.*

hebe /hee-bi/ noun an evergreen flowering shrub with mauve, pink, or white flowers, native to New Zealand.
– ORIGIN named after the Greek goddess *Hebe*, cup-bearer of the gods.

Hebraic /hi-**bray**-ik/ adjective relating to Hebrew or the Hebrew people.

Hebrew /hee-broo/ noun **1** a member of an ancient people living in what is now Israel and Palestine, who established the kingdoms of Israel and Judah. **2** the language of the Hebrews, in its ancient or modern form.
– ORIGIN from a Hebrew word understood to mean 'one from the other side (of the river)'.

Hebridean /heb-ri-**dee**-uhn/ noun a person from the Hebrides off the NW coast of Scotland. • adjective relating to the Hebrides.

heck exclamation used for emphasis, or to express surprise, annoyance, etc.
– ORIGIN euphemistic alteration of HELL.

heckle verb interrupt a public speaker with derisive comments or abuse.
– DERIVATIVES **heckler** noun.
– ORIGIN from a dialect form of HACKLE.

hectare /hek-tair/ noun a metric unit of area, equal to 10,000 square metres (2.471 acres).
– ORIGIN from Greek *hekaton* 'hundred'.

hectic adjective full of frantic activity.
– DERIVATIVES **hectically** adverb.

– ORIGIN Greek *hektikos* 'habitual'.

hector /**hek**-ter/ verb talk to someone in a bullying way.
– DERIVATIVES **hectoring** adjective.
– ORIGIN from the Trojan warrior *Hector* in Homer's *Iliad.*

he'd contraction **1** he had. **2** he would.

hedge noun **1** a fence or boundary formed by closely growing bushes. **2** a way of protecting oneself against financial loss or another adverse situation: *index-linked gilts are a useful hedge against inflation.* • verb **1** surround something with a hedge. **2** avoid making a definite statement or commitment. **3** protect an investor or investment against loss by making compensating contracts or transactions.
– PHRASES **hedge one's bets** avoid committing oneself when faced with a difficult choice.
– DERIVATIVES **hedger** noun.
– ORIGIN Old English.

hedgehog noun a small mammal with a spiny coat, able to roll itself into a ball for defence.

hedge-hop verb fly an aircraft at a very low altitude.

hedgerow noun a hedge of wild bushes and occasional trees bordering a field.

hedge sparrow noun another term for DUNNOCK.

hedging noun **1** the planting or trimming of hedges. **2** bushes planted to form hedges.

hedonism /hee-duh-ni-z'm/ noun behaviour based on the belief that pleasure is the most important thing in life.
– DERIVATIVES **hedonist** noun **hedonistic** adjective.
– ORIGIN from Greek *hēdonē* 'pleasure'.

heebie-jeebies plural noun (**the heebie-jeebies**) informal a state of nervous fear or anxiety.
– ORIGIN unknown.

heed verb pay attention to someone or something.
– PHRASES **pay** (or **take**) **heed** pay careful attention.
– DERIVATIVES **heedful** adjective.
– ORIGIN Old English.

heedless adjective showing a reckless lack of care or attention.
– DERIVATIVES **heedlessly** adverb **heedlessness** noun.

hee-haw noun the loud, harsh cry of a donkey or mule.

heel[1] noun **1** the back part of the foot below the ankle. **2** the part of a shoe or boot supporting the heel. **3** the part of the palm of the hand next to the wrist. **4** informal, dated an inconsiderate or untrustworthy man.
• exclamation a command to a dog to walk close behind its owner. • verb fit a new heel on a shoe or boot.
– PHRASES **at** (or **on**) **the heels of** following closely after someone or something. **bring someone to heel** bring someone under control. **cool** (or Brit. **kick**) **one's heels** be kept waiting. **take to one's heels** run away.
– DERIVATIVES **heeled** adjective.
– ORIGIN Old English.

heel[2] verb (of a ship) lean over owing to the pressure of wind or an uneven load.
– ORIGIN Germanic.

heel³ verb (**heel something in**) set a plant in the ground and cover its roots.
– ORIGIN Old English, 'cover, hide'.

heelball noun a mixture of hard wax and lampblack used by shoemakers for polishing or in brass rubbing.

heft verb **1** lift or carry something heavy. **2** lift or hold something to test its weight.
– ORIGIN probably from HEAVE.

hefty adjective (**heftier, heftiest**) **1** large and heavy. **2** (of a number or amount) considerable: *she could face a hefty fine.* **3** done with vigour or force.
– DERIVATIVES **heftily** adverb.

Hegelian /hi-**gay**-li-uhn/ adjective relating to the German philosopher Georg Hegel or his philosophy. ●noun a follower of Hegel.
– DERIVATIVES **Hegelianism** noun.

hegemony /hi-**jem**-uh-ni, hi-**gem**-uh-ni/ noun dominance of one social group or state over others.
– DERIVATIVES **hegemonic** adjective.
– ORIGIN from Greek *hēgemōn* 'leader'.

Hegira /**hej**-i-ruh/ (also **Hejira** or **Hijra**) noun **1** Muhammad's departure from Mecca to Medina in AD 622, marking the consolidation of the first Muslim community. **2** the Muslim era reckoned from this date.
– ORIGIN Arabic, 'departure'.

heifer /**hef**-fer/ noun a young cow that has not had a calf, or has had only one calf.
– ORIGIN Old English.

height noun **1** the measurement of someone or something from head to foot or from base to top. **2** the distance of something above ground or sea level. **3** the quality of being tall or high. **4** a high place. **5** the most intense part or period: *the height of the attack.* **6** an extreme example: *it would be the height of bad manners not to attend the wedding.*
– ORIGIN Old English.

heighten verb **1** make or become more intense. **2** make something higher.

heightism noun prejudice or discrimination against someone on the basis of their height.
– DERIVATIVES **heightist** adjective & noun.

Heimlich manoeuvre /**hym**-lik/ noun a first-aid procedure for dislodging an obstruction from a person's windpipe, in which a sudden strong pressure is applied on the abdomen between the navel and the ribcage.
– ORIGIN named after the American physician Henry J. *Heimlich.*

heinous /**hay**-nuhss, **hee**-nuhss/ adjective very wicked: *a heinous crime.*
– DERIVATIVES **heinously** adverb **heinousness** noun.
– ORIGIN Old French *haineus.*

heir /air/ noun **1** a person who is legally entitled to the property or rank of another on that person's death. **2** a person who continues the work of a predecessor.
– DERIVATIVES **heirship** noun.
– ORIGIN Old French.

heir apparent noun (pl. **heirs apparent**) **1** an heir whose rights cannot be taken away by the birth of another heir. **2** a person who is most likely to take on the job or role of another.

heiress noun a female heir.

heirloom noun a valuable object that has belonged to a family for several generations.
– ORIGIN from HEIR + LOOM¹ (in the former senses 'tool, heirloom').

heir presumptive noun (pl. **heirs presumptive**) an heir whose rights may be taken away by the birth of another heir.

heist /hysst/ informal noun a robbery. ●verb steal something.
– ORIGIN from a pronunciation of HOIST.

Hejira noun variant spelling of HEGIRA.

held past and past participle of HOLD¹.

helical /**hel**-i-k'l/ adjective having the shape or form of a helix; spiral.
– DERIVATIVES **helically** adverb.

helices plural of HELIX.

helicopter noun a type of aircraft powered by one or two sets of horizontally revolving rotors.
– ORIGIN from Greek *helix* 'spiral' + *pteron* 'wing'.

heliocentric /hee-li-oh-**sen**-trik/ adjective **1** having the sun as the centre, as in the accepted astronomical model of the solar system. Compare with GEOCENTRIC. **2** Astronomy measured from or considered in relation to the centre of the sun.
– ORIGIN from Greek *hēlios* 'sun'.

heliograph noun **1** a device which reflects sunlight in flashes from a movable mirror, used to send signals. **2** a message sent using a heliograph.
– DERIVATIVES **heliographic** adjective.
– ORIGIN from Greek *hēlios* 'sun'.

heliosphere /**hee**-li-oh-sfeer/ noun the region of space, including the solar system, in which the solar wind has a significant influence.
– DERIVATIVES **heliospheric** /hee-li-oh-**sfer**-ik/ adjective.
– ORIGIN from Greek *hēlios* 'sun'.

heliotrope /**hee**-li-uh-trohp/ noun a plant of the borage family with fragrant purple or blue flowers.
– ORIGIN from Greek *hēlios* 'sun' + *trepein* 'to turn'.

helipad noun a landing and take-off area for helicopters.

heliport noun an airport or landing place for helicopters.

heli-skiing noun skiing in which the skier is taken up the mountain by helicopter.

helium /**hee**-li-uhm/ noun a light colourless gas that does not burn.
– ORIGIN from Greek *hēlios* 'sun'.

helix /**hee**-liks/ noun (pl. **helices** /**hee**-li-seez/) an object with a three-dimensional spiral shape like that of a wire wound in a single layer around a cylinder or cone.
– ORIGIN Greek.

hell noun **1** (in various religions) a place of evil and everlasting suffering to which the wicked are sent after death. **2** a state or place of great suffering. ●exclamation used to express annoyance or surprise or for emphasis.
– PHRASES **all hell breaks** (or **is let**) **loose** informal suddenly there is chaos. **come hell or high water** whatever difficulties may occur. **for the hell of it** informal just for fun. **give someone hell**

informal reprimand someone severely. **hell for leather** as fast as possible. **like hell** informal very fast, much, hard, etc. **not a hope in hell** informal no chance at all. **until hell freezes over** forever.
– DERIVATIVES **hellward** adverb & adjective.
– ORIGIN Old English.

he'll contraction he shall or he will.

hell-bent adjective determined to achieve something at all costs.

hellcat noun a spiteful, violent woman.

hellebore /**hel**-i-bor/ noun a poisonous winter-flowering plant with large white, green, or purplish flowers.
– ORIGIN Greek *helleboros*.

Hellene /**hel**-een/ noun a Greek.
– ORIGIN named after *Hellen*, who was held in Greek mythology to be the ancestor of all the Greeks.

Hellenic /hel-**len**-ik/ adjective **1** Greek. **2** relating to ancient Greek culture between *c*.1050 BC and *c*.300 BC. •noun the Greek language.

Hellenism noun **1** the national character or culture of Greece, especially ancient Greece. **2** the study or imitation of ancient Greek culture.
– DERIVATIVES **Hellenist** noun **Hellenize** (or **Hellenise**) verb.

Hellenistic adjective relating to ancient Greek culture from the death of Alexander the Great (323 BC) to the defeat of Cleopatra and Mark Antony by Octavian in 31 BC.

hellfire noun the fire said to exist in hell.

hellhole noun a very unpleasant place.

hellhound noun a demon in the form of a dog.

hellish adjective **1** relating to or like hell. **2** informal extremely difficult or unpleasant.
– DERIVATIVES **hellishly** adverb **hellishness** noun.

hello (also **hallo** or **hullo**) exclamation **1** used as a greeting. **2** Brit. used to express surprise or to attract someone's attention.
– ORIGIN from French *ho* 'ho!' + *là* 'there'.

hellraiser noun a person who causes trouble by violent, drunken, or outrageous behaviour.

Hell's Angel noun a member of a gang of male motorcycle enthusiasts, originally known for their lawless behaviour.

helm noun **1** a tiller or wheel for steering a ship or boat. **2** (**the helm**) a position of leadership. •verb **1** steer a boat or ship. **2** manage the running of something.
– ORIGIN Old English.

helmet noun a hard or padded protective hat.
– DERIVATIVES **helmeted** adjective.
– ORIGIN Old French, 'little helmet'.

helmsman noun (pl. **helmsmen**) a person who steers a boat.

helot /**hel**-uht/ noun **1** (in part of ancient Greece) a member of a class of people having a status in between slaves and citizens. **2** a serf or slave.
– ORIGIN Greek *Heilōtes*.

help verb **1** make it easier for someone to do something. **2** improve a situation or problem. **3** (**help someone to**) serve someone with food or drink. **4** (**help oneself**) take something without asking permission. **5** (**can/could not help**) cannot or could not stop oneself doing: *he couldn't help laughing*. •noun **1** the action of

helping someone. **2** a person or thing that helps someone. **3** a person employed to do household tasks.
– DERIVATIVES **helper** noun.
– ORIGIN Old English.

helpful adjective **1** giving or ready to give help. **2** useful.
– DERIVATIVES **helpfully** adverb **helpfulness** noun.

helping noun a portion of food served to one person at one time.

helpless adjective **1** unable to defend oneself or to act without help. **2** uncontrollable: *helpless laughter.*
– DERIVATIVES **helplessly** adverb **helplessness** noun.

helpline noun a telephone service providing help with problems.

helpmate (also **helpmeet**) noun a helpful companion or partner.

helter-skelter adjective & adverb in a hasty and confused or disorganized way. •noun Brit. a tall spiral slide winding around a tower at a fair.
– ORIGIN perhaps symbolic of running feet or from former *skelte* 'hasten'.

hem[1] noun the edge of a piece of cloth or item of clothing which has been turned under and stitched down. •verb (**hems, hemming, hemmed**) **1** make a hem on a piece of cloth or item of clothing. **2** (**hem someone/thing in**) surround someone or something and restrict their space or movement.
– ORIGIN Old English.

hem[2] exclamation expressing the sound made when coughing or clearing the throat to attract attention or show hesitation.
– PHRASES **hem and haw** chiefly N. Amer. another way of saying **hum and haw** (see **HUM**).

he-man noun informal a very well-built, masculine man.

hematite etc. noun US spelling of **HAEMATITE** etc.

hemi- prefix half: *hemisphere*.
– ORIGIN Greek *hēmi-*.

hemidemisemiquaver /hem-i-dem-i-**sem**-i-kway-vuh/ noun chiefly Brit. a musical note with the time value of half a demisemiquaver.

hemiplegia /he-mi-**plee**-juh/ noun paralysis of one side of the body.
– DERIVATIVES **hemiplegic** noun & adjective.

hemisphere /**he**-mi-sfeer/ noun **1** a half of a sphere. **2** a half of the earth, usually as divided into northern and southern halves by the equator, or into western and eastern halves by an imaginary line passing through the North and South Poles. **3** (also **cerebral hemisphere**) each of the two parts of the cerebrum (the main part of the brain) of a vertebrate.
– DERIVATIVES **hemispheric** /he-mi-**sfer**-ik/ adjective **hemispherical** adjective.

hemline noun the level of the lower edge of a garment such as a skirt or coat.

hemlock noun **1** a very poisonous plant of the parsley family, with fern-like leaves and small white flowers. **2** a poison obtained from hemlock.
– ORIGIN Old English.

hemp noun **1** the cannabis plant. **2** the fibre of the cannabis plant, extracted from the stem

and used to make rope, strong fabrics, paper, etc. **3** the drug cannabis.
– ORIGIN Old English.

hen noun **1** a female bird, especially of a domestic fowl. **2** (**hens**) domestic fowls of either sex.
– ORIGIN Old English.

henbane /hen-bayn/ noun a poisonous plant of the nightshade family, with sticky hairy leaves and an unpleasant smell.

hence adverb **1** as a consequence; for this reason. **2** from now; in the future. **3** (also **from hence**) old use from here.
– ORIGIN Old English.

henceforth (also **henceforward**) adverb from this or that time on.

henchman noun (pl. **henchmen**) **1** chiefly derogatory a faithful supporter or assistant, especially one prepared to engage in criminal or dishonest activities. **2** historical a squire or page attending a prince or nobleman.
– ORIGIN from Old English *hengest* 'male horse' + **MAN**, the first sense being probably 'a groom'.

hendecagon /hen-**dek**-uh-guhn/ noun a plane figure with eleven straight sides and angles.
– ORIGIN from Greek *hendeka* 'eleven'.

henge /henj/ noun a prehistoric monument consisting of a circle of stone or wooden uprights.
– ORIGIN from *Stonehenge*, a monument of this type in Wiltshire, from two Old English words meaning 'stone' + 'to hang'.

henna noun a reddish-brown dye made from the powdered leaves of a tropical shrub, used especially to colour the hair and decorate the body. • verb (**hennas, hennaing, hennaed**) dye the hair with henna.
– ORIGIN Arabic.

hen night noun Brit. informal a celebration held for a woman who is about to get married, attended only by women.

hen party noun informal a social gathering for women only.

henpeck verb (usu. as adj. **henpecked**) (of a woman) continually criticize and nag her husband.

henry noun (pl. **henries** or **henrys**) Physics the SI unit of inductance.
– ORIGIN named after the American physicist Joseph *Henry*.

heparin /hep-uh-rin/ noun a compound found in the liver and other tissues which prevents blood clotting or coagulating, used in the treatment of thrombosis.
– ORIGIN from Greek *hēpar* 'liver'.

hepatic /hi-**pat**-ik/ adjective relating to the liver.
– ORIGIN from Greek *hēpar* 'liver'.

hepatitis /hep-uh-ty-tiss/ noun a disease in which the liver becomes inflamed, causing jaundice and other symptoms, mainly spread by a series of viruses (**hepatitis A, B,** and **C**) transmitted in blood or food.

hepcat noun informal, dated a stylish or fashionable person.
– ORIGIN from *hep* (variant of **HIP³**) + *cat* (an informal term for a man, especially among jazz enthusiasts).

hepta- combining form seven; having seven: *heptathlon*.
– ORIGIN Greek *hepta* 'seven'.

heptagon /hep-tuh-guhn/ noun a plane figure with seven straight sides and angles.

heptahedron /hep-tuh-**hee**-druhn/ noun (pl. **heptahedra** or **heptahedrons**) a solid figure with seven plane faces.

heptathlon /hep-**tath**-lon/ noun an athletic contest for women that consists of seven separate events.
– DERIVATIVES **heptathlete** noun.
– ORIGIN from **HEPTA-** + Greek *athlon* 'contest'.

her pronoun (third person sing.) **1** used as the object of a verb or preposition to refer to a female person or animal previously mentioned. **2** referring to a ship, country, or other thing regarded as female. • possessive determiner **1** belonging to or associated with a female person or animal previously mentioned. **2** (**Her**) used in titles.
– ORIGIN Old English.

herald noun **1** an official employed to oversee matters concerning state ceremonies and the use of coats of arms. **2** historical a person who carried official messages, made proclamations, and oversaw tournaments. **3** a person or thing viewed as a sign that something is about to happen: *primroses are the herald of spring.* **4** (in the UK) an official of the College of Arms ranking above a pursuivant. • verb **1** be a sign that something is about to happen: *the speech heralded a change in policy.* **2** describe in enthusiastic terms: *he was heralded as the next Sinatra.*
– ORIGIN Old French *herault*.

heraldic /hi-**ral**-dik/ adjective relating to heraldry.
– DERIVATIVES **heraldically** adverb.

heraldry noun the system by which coats of arms are drawn up, described, and regulated.

herb noun **1** any plant whose leaves, seeds, or flowers are used for flavouring food or in medicine. **2** Botany any seed-bearing plant which does not have a woody stem and dies down to the ground after flowering.
– DERIVATIVES **herby** adjective.
– ORIGIN Latin *herba* 'grass, green crops'.

herbaceous /her-**bay**-shuhss/ adjective relating to herbs (in the botanical sense).

herbaceous border noun a garden border consisting mainly of flowering plants that live for several years.

herbage noun herbaceous plants, especially grass used for grazing.

herbal adjective relating to or made from herbs. • noun a book that describes herbs and their culinary and medicinal properties.

herbalism noun the study or practice of using herbs for medicinal or therapeutic purposes.

herbalist noun a person who practises herbalism, or one who grows or sells herbs for medicinal purposes.

herbarium /her-**bair**-i-uhm/ noun (pl. **herbaria** /her-**bair**-i-uh/) a collection of dried plants organized in a systematic way.

herbed adjective cooked or flavoured with herbs.

herbert /her-buht/ noun Brit. informal an

unimpressive or foolish man or youth: *a bunch of spotty herberts.*
– ORIGIN from the man's name *Herbert.*

herbicide /her-bi-syd/ noun a poisonous substance used to destroy unwanted plants.

herbivore /her-bi-vor/ noun an animal that feeds on plants.
– DERIVATIVES **herbivorous** /her-biv-uh-ruhss/ adjective.

Herculean /her-kyuu-lee-uhn/ adjective requiring great strength or effort: *a Herculean task.*
– ORIGIN named after *Hercules*, a hero of Roman and Greek mythology famed for his strength.

herd noun 1 a large group of animals, especially hoofed mammals, that live or are kept together. 2 derogatory a large group of people: *herds of tourists.* •verb 1 move in a large group. 2 keep or look after livestock.
– DERIVATIVES **herder** noun.
– ORIGIN Old English.

herd instinct noun an inclination or natural tendency to behave or think like the majority of a group.

herdsman noun (pl. **herdsmen**) the owner or keeper of a herd of domesticated animals.

here adverb 1 in, at, or to this place or position. 2 (usu. **here is/are**) used when introducing or handing over something or someone. 3 used when indicating a time, point, or situation that has arrived or is happening. •exclamation used to attract someone's attention.
– PHRASES **here and now** at the present time. **here and there** in various places. **here's to** used to wish someone health or success before raising one's glass and drinking a small amount. **neither here nor there** of no importance or relevance.
– ORIGIN Old English.

hereabouts (also **hereabout**) adverb near this place.

hereafter adverb formal 1 from now on or at some time in the future. 2 after death. •noun (**the hereafter**) life after death.

hereby adverb formal as a result of this.

hereditary /hi-red-i-tuh-ri/ adjective 1 passed on by or relating to inheritance. 2 (of a characteristic or disease) able to be passed on genetically from parents to their offspring.
– DERIVATIVES **hereditarily** adverb.

heredity /hi-red-i-ti/ noun 1 the passing on of physical or mental characteristics genetically from one generation to another. 2 the inheriting of a title, office, or right.
– ORIGIN Latin *hereditas* 'heirship'.

Hereford /he-ri-fuhd/ noun an animal of a breed of red and white beef cattle.
– ORIGIN from *Hereford* in west central England.

herein adverb formal in this document, book, or matter.

hereinafter adverb formal further on in this document.

hereof adverb formal of this document.

heresy /he-ri-si/ noun (pl. **heresies**) 1 belief or opinion which goes against traditional religious doctrine. 2 opinion which differs greatly from that which is generally accepted.

– ORIGIN Greek *hairesis* 'choice, sect'.

heretic /he-ri-tik/ noun 1 a person who holds beliefs or opinions which go against traditional religious doctrine. 2 a person whose opinion differs greatly from that which is generally accepted.
– DERIVATIVES **heretical** /hi-ret-i-k'l/ adjective **heretically** adverb.

hereto adverb formal to this matter or document.

heretofore adverb formal before now.

hereunder adverb formal 1 as provided for under the terms of this document. 2 further on in this document.

hereupon adverb old use after or as a result of this.

herewith adverb formal with this letter or document.

heritable adjective able to be inherited.
– DERIVATIVES **heritability** noun **heritably** adverb.

heritage noun 1 property that is or may be inherited; an inheritance. 2 valued things such as historic buildings that have been passed down from previous generations. •adjective relating to things of historic or cultural value that are worthy of being preserved: *a heritage site.*
– ORIGIN Old French, from *heriter* 'inherit'.

hermaphrodite /her-maf-ruh-dyt/ noun 1 a person or animal with both male and female sex organs or characteristics. 2 Botany a plant having stamens and pistils in the same flower.
– DERIVATIVES **hermaphroditic** adjective **hermaphroditism** noun.
– ORIGIN Greek *hermaphroditos*, first the name of the son of Hermes and Aphrodite who became joined in one body with the nymph Salmacis.

hermeneutic /her-mi-nyoo-tik/ adjective relating to interpretation, especially of the Bible or literary texts.
– DERIVATIVES **hermeneutical** adjective.
– ORIGIN Greek *hermēneutikos.*

hermeneutics plural noun (usu. treated as sing.) the branch of knowledge that deals with interpretation, especially of the Bible or literary texts.

hermetic /her-met-ik/ adjective 1 (of a seal or closure) complete and airtight. 2 insulated or protected from outside influences: *a hermetic society.*
– DERIVATIVES **hermetically** adverb.
– ORIGIN from Latin *Hermes Trismegistus* 'thrice-greatest Hermes', the legendary founder of alchemy and astrology identified with the Greek god Hermes.

hermit noun 1 a person living in solitude for religious reasons. 2 a person who prefers to live alone.
– DERIVATIVES **hermitic** adjective.
– ORIGIN from Greek *erēmos* 'solitary'.

hermitage noun the home of a hermit, especially when small and remote.

hermit crab noun a crab with a soft abdomen which lives in shells cast off by other shellfish.

hernia /her-ni-uh/ noun (pl. **hernias**) a condition in which part of an organ (typically the intestine) protrudes through the wall of the cavity containing it.

– DERIVATIVES **herniated** adjective **herniation** noun.
– ORIGIN Latin.

hero noun (pl. **heroes**) **1** a person who is admired for their courage or outstanding achievements. **2** the chief male character in a book, play, or film. **3** (in mythology and folklore) a person of superhuman qualities.
– ORIGIN Greek *hērōs*.

heroic adjective **1** relating to or like a hero or heroine; very brave. **2** grand or ambitious in size or intention: *this is film-making on a heroic scale.* • noun (**heroics**) brave or dramatic behaviour or talk.
– DERIVATIVES **heroically** adverb.

heroin noun a highly addictive painkilling drug obtained from morphine.
– ORIGIN German, from Latin *heros* 'hero' (because of its effects on the user's self-esteem).

heroine noun **1** a woman admired for her courage or outstanding achievements. **2** the chief female character in a book, play, or film.

heroism noun great bravery.

heron noun a large fish-eating wading bird with long legs, a long neck, and a long pointed bill.
– ORIGIN Old French.

heronry noun (pl. **heronries**) a breeding colony of herons, typically in a group of trees.

hero worship noun extreme admiration for someone. • verb (**hero-worship**) admire someone very much.

herpes /**her**-peez/ noun a disease caused by a virus, affecting the skin (often with blisters) or the nervous system.
– DERIVATIVES **herpetic** adjective.
– ORIGIN Greek *herpēs* 'shingles'.

herpes simplex noun a form of herpes which can produce cold sores, genital inflammation, or conjunctivitis.

herpesvirus /**her**-peez-vy-rus/ noun any of a group of viruses causing herpes and other diseases.

herpes zoster /zos-tuh/ noun medical name for SHINGLES.
– ORIGIN Greek *herpēs* 'shingles' and *zōstēr* 'girdle, belt'.

herpetology /her-pi-**tol**-uh-ji/ noun the branch of zoology concerned with reptiles and amphibians.
– DERIVATIVES **herpetological** adjective **herpetologist** noun.
– ORIGIN Greek *herpeton* 'creeping thing'.

Herr /hair/ noun a title or form of address for a German-speaking man, corresponding to *Mr.*
– ORIGIN from German *hērro* 'more exalted'.

herring noun an edible silvery fish which is found in shoals in coastal waters.
– ORIGIN Old English.

herringbone noun a zigzag pattern consisting of columns of short parallel lines, with all the lines in one column sloping one way and all the lines in the next column sloping the other way.

herring gull noun a common northern gull with grey black-tipped wings.

hers possessive pronoun used to refer to a thing or things belonging to or associated with a female person or animal previously mentioned.

USAGE: There is no apostrophe: the spelling should be hers not *her's*.

herself pronoun (third person sing.) **1** (reflexive) used as the object of a verb or preposition to refer to a female person or animal previously mentioned as the subject of the clause. **2** (emphatic) she or her personally.

Herts. /harts/ abbreviation Hertfordshire.

hertz /herts/ noun (pl. same) the SI unit of frequency, equal to one cycle per second.
– ORIGIN named after the German physicist H. R. *Hertz*.

he's contraction **1** he is. **2** he has.

hesitant adjective slow to act or speak as a result of indecision or reluctance.
– DERIVATIVES **hesitance** noun **hesitancy** noun **hesitantly** adverb.

hesitate verb **1** pause indecisively. **2** be reluctant to do something: *please do not hesitate to contact me.*
– DERIVATIVES **hesitation** noun.
– ORIGIN Latin *haesitare* 'stick fast'.

hessian noun chiefly Brit. a strong, coarse fabric made from hemp or jute, used especially to make sacks and in upholstery.
– ORIGIN from *Hesse*, a state of western Germany.

hetero- combining form other; different: *heterosexual.*
– ORIGIN Greek *heteros* 'other'.

heterodox /**het**-uh-ruh-doks/ adjective not following the usual or accepted standards or beliefs.
– DERIVATIVES **heterodoxy** noun.
– ORIGIN from Greek *heteros* 'other' + *doxa* 'opinion'.

heterogeneous /het-uh-ruh-**jee**-ni-uhss/ adjective consisting of many different kinds of people or things; varied: *a heterogeneous collection.*
– DERIVATIVES **heterogeneity** /het-uh-ruh-juh-**nee**-i-ti/ noun **heterogeneously** adverb.
– ORIGIN from Greek *heteros* 'other' + *genos* 'a kind'.

heterosexism noun discrimination or prejudice against homosexuals on the assumption that heterosexuality is the norm.
– DERIVATIVES **heterosexist** adjective.

heterosexual adjective **1** sexually attracted to the opposite sex. **2** (of a sexual relationship) between a man and a woman. • noun a heterosexual person.
– DERIVATIVES **heterosexuality** noun **heterosexually** adverb.
– ORIGIN from Greek *heteros* 'other'.

het up adjective informal angry and agitated.
– ORIGIN from dialect *het* 'heated, hot'.

heuristic /hyuu-uh-**riss**-tik/ adjective **1** allowing a person to discover or learn something for themselves. **2** Computing proceeding to a solution by trial and error or by rules that are only loosely defined. • noun **1** (**heuristics**) (usu. treated as sing.) the study and use of heuristic techniques. **2** a heuristic process or method.
– DERIVATIVES **heuristically** adverb.
– ORIGIN Greek *heuriskein* 'to find'.

hew /hyoo/ verb (past part. **hewn** or **hewed**) **1** chop or cut wood, coal, etc. with an axe, pick, or other tool. **2** (**be hewn**) be cut or formed from a hard material: *a seat hewn out of a fallen tree trunk*.
– ORIGIN Old English.

hex N. Amer. verb cast a spell on someone. • noun **1** a magic spell. **2** a witch.
– ORIGIN German *hexen*.

hexa- (also **hex-** before a vowel) combining form six; having six: *hexagon*.
– ORIGIN Greek *hex* 'six'.

hexadecimal /hek-suh-**des**-i-muhl/ adjective Computing relating to or using a system of numerical notation that has 16 rather than 10 as its base.

hexagon /**hek**-suh-guhn/ noun a plane figure with six straight sides and angles.
– DERIVATIVES **hexagonal** adjective.

hexagram noun a six-pointed star formed by two intersecting equilateral triangles.

hexahedron /hek-suh-**hee**-druhn/ noun (pl. **hexahedra** or **hexahedrons**) a solid figure with six plane faces.
– DERIVATIVES **hexahedral** adjective.

hexameter /hek-**sam**-i-ter/ noun a line of verse consisting of six metrical feet.

hey exclamation used to attract attention or to express surprise, interest, etc.

heyday noun (**one's heyday**) the period of someone's or something's greatest success, popularity, activity, etc.: *the paper has lost millions of readers since its heyday in 1964*.
– ORIGIN first used as an exclamation of joy or surprise.

hey presto exclamation Brit. announcing the successful completion of a conjuring trick or other surprising achievement.

HF abbreviation Physics high frequency.

Hf symbol the chemical element hafnium.

Hg symbol the chemical element mercury.
– ORIGIN abbreviation of Latin *hydrargyrum*.

HGV abbreviation Brit. heavy goods vehicle.

HH abbreviation extra hard (as a grade of pencil lead).

HI abbreviation Hawaii.

hi exclamation informal used as a friendly greeting.

hiatus /hy-**ay**-tuhss/ noun (pl. **hiatuses**) a pause or gap in a series or sequence: *there was a brief hiatus in the war*.
– ORIGIN Latin, 'gaping'.

hiatus hernia noun a condition in which an organ (usually the stomach) protrudes through the diaphragm at the opening for the oesophagus.

Hib noun a bacterium that causes meningitis in very young children or babies.
– ORIGIN from the initial letters of *Haemophilus influenzae type B*.

hibernate verb (of an animal) spend the winter in a state like deep sleep.
– DERIVATIVES **hibernation** noun **hibernator** noun.
– ORIGIN Latin *hibernare*.

Hibernian /hy-**ber**-ni-uhn/ adjective Irish (now chiefly used in names). • noun an Irish person (now chiefly used in names).
– ORIGIN Latin *Hibernia*, from Celtic.

hibiscus /hi-**biss**-kuhss/ noun a plant of the mallow family with large brightly coloured flowers.
– ORIGIN Greek *hibiskos* 'marsh mallow'.

hiccup (also **hiccough** pronunc. same) noun **1** a gulping sound in the throat caused by an involuntary spasm of the diaphragm and respiratory organs. **2** a minor difficulty or setback. • verb (**hiccups**, **hiccuping**, **hiccuped**) make the sound of a hiccup or series of hiccups.
– DERIVATIVES **hiccupy** adjective.
– ORIGIN imitating the sound.

hick noun informal, chiefly N. Amer. an unsophisticated person from the country.
– ORIGIN informal form of the man's name *Richard*.

hickey noun (pl. **hickeys**) N. Amer. informal a love bite.
– ORIGIN unknown.

hickory noun **1** a tree found in chiefly in North America with tough, heavy wood and edible nuts. **2** a stick made of hickory wood.
– ORIGIN from *pohickery*, the local Virginian name, from Algonquian.

hid past of **HIDE**[1].

hidden past participle of **HIDE**[1].
– DERIVATIVES **hiddenness** noun.

hidden agenda noun a secret motive or plan.

hide[1] verb (past **hid**; past part. **hidden**) **1** put or keep out of sight: *I hid the key under a flowerpot*. **2** conceal oneself. **3** keep something secret. • noun Brit. a camouflaged shelter used to watch wild animals or birds at close quarters.
– PHRASES **hide one's light under a bushel** keep quiet about one's talents or accomplishments. [with biblical reference to the Gospel of Matthew, chapter 15.]
– ORIGIN Old English.

hide[2] noun the skin of an animal, especially when made into leather.
– PHRASES **neither hide nor hair of** not the slightest trace of.
– ORIGIN Old English.

hide-and-seek noun a children's game in which one or more players hide and the other or others have to look for them.

hideaway noun a place where one can hide or be alone.

hidebound adjective unwilling or unable to abandon old-fashioned ideas or customs in favour of new ways of thinking.

hideous adjective **1** extremely ugly. **2** extremely unpleasant.
– DERIVATIVES **hideously** adverb **hideousness** noun.
– ORIGIN Old French *hidos*, *hideus*.

hideout noun a hiding place, especially one used by someone who has broken the law.

hidey-hole (also **hidy-hole**) noun informal a hiding place.

hiding[1] noun **1** a physical beating. **2** informal a severe defeat.
– PHRASES **be on a hiding to nothing** Brit. be unlikely to succeed.
– ORIGIN from **HIDE**[2].

hiding[2] noun the action of hiding or the state of being hidden: *he had gone into hiding*.

hie /hi/ verb (**hies, hieing** or **hying, hied**) old use go quickly.
– ORIGIN Old English, 'strive, pant'.
hierarchical /hy-uh-**rar**-ki-k'l/ adjective arranged in order of rank or status.
– DERIVATIVES **hierarchically** adverb.
hierarchy /**hy**-uh-rar-ki/ noun (pl. **hierarchies**)
1 a system in which people are ranked one above the other according to their status or authority. **2** a classification of things according to their relative importance.
– ORIGIN from Greek *hierarkhēs* 'sacred ruler'.
hieratic /hy-uh-**rat**-ik/ adjective relating to priests.
– ORIGIN Greek *hieratikos*.
hieroglyph /**hy**-ruh-glif/ noun a picture of an object representing a word, syllable, or sound, especially as found in the ancient Egyptian writing system.
hieroglyphic noun (**hieroglyphics**) writing consisting of hieroglyphs. •adjective relating to or written in hieroglyphs.
– ORIGIN from Greek *hieros* 'sacred' + *gluphē* 'carving'.
hierophant /**hy**-roh-fant/ noun a person, especially a priest, who interprets sacred mysteries or other things that are very difficult to understand.
– DERIVATIVES **hierophantic** adjective.
– ORIGIN from Greek *hieros* 'sacred' + *phainein* 'show'.
hi-fi informal adjective relating to the reproduction of high-fidelity sound. •noun (pl. **hi-fis**) a set of equipment for reproducing high-fidelity sound.
higgledy-piggledy adverb & adjective in confusion or disorder.
– ORIGIN probably with reference to the irregular herding together of pigs.
high adjective **1** extending far upwards. **2** of a specified height. **3** far above ground or sea level. **4** great or greater than normal in amount, value, size, or intensity: *high blood pressure.* **5** (of a period or movement) at its peak: *high summer.* **6** great in rank or status; important. **7** culturally or morally superior: *a man with high ideals.* **8** (of a sound or note) at or near the top of a musical scale; not deep or low. **9** informal under the influence of drugs or alcohol. **10** (of food) strong-smelling because beginning to go bad. **11** (of game) slightly decomposed and so ready to cook. •noun **1** a high point, level, or figure. **2** an area of high atmospheric pressure. **3** informal a state of intense happiness. •adverb **1** at or to a high or specified level or position. **2** at a high price. **3** (of a sound) at or to a high pitch.
– PHRASES **high and dry 1** stranded by the sea as it retreats. **2** in a very difficult position. **high and low** in many different places. **high and mighty** informal arrogant. **high days and holidays** special occasions. **the high ground** a position of superiority. **it is high time that ——** it is past the time when something should have happened or been done. **on one's high horse** informal behaving arrogantly or pompously. **run high 1** (of a river) be full and close to overflowing, with a strong current. **2** (of feelings) be intense.
– ORIGIN Old English.

high altar noun the chief altar of a church.
highball noun N. Amer. a long drink consisting of a spirit and a mixer such as soda, served with ice.
highbrow adjective often derogatory concerned with serious artistic or cultural ideas; intellectual or refined.
high chair noun a small chair with long legs for a baby or small child, fitted with a tray and used at mealtimes.
High Church noun a tradition within the Anglican Church which emphasizes the importance of ritual and the authority of bishops and priests.
high-class adjective of a high standard, quality, or social class.
high command noun the commander-in-chief and associated senior staff of an army, navy, or air force.
high commission noun an embassy of one Commonwealth country in another.
– DERIVATIVES **high commissioner** noun.
high court noun a supreme court of justice.
Higher noun (in Scotland) the more advanced of the two main levels of the Scottish Certificate of Education. Compare with ORDINARY GRADE.
higher court noun Law a court that can overrule the decision of another.
higher education noun education to degree level or equivalent, provided at universities or colleges.
highest common factor noun the highest number that can be divided exactly into each of two or more numbers.
high explosive noun a powerful chemical explosive of the kind used in shells and bombs.
highfalutin /hy-fuh-**loo**-tin/ adjective informal grand or self-important in a pompous or pretentious way.
– ORIGIN perhaps from HIGH + *fluting*.
high fashion noun another term for HAUTE COUTURE.
high fidelity noun the reproduction of sound with little distortion.
high finance noun financial transactions involving large sums of money.
high five noun informal, chiefly N. Amer. a gesture of celebration or greeting in which two people slap each other's palms with their arms raised.
high-flown adjective (especially of language) extravagant or intended to impress.
high-flyer (also **high-flier**) noun a very successful person.
high frequency noun (in radio) a frequency of 3–30 megahertz.
high gear noun a gear that makes a wheeled vehicle move fast.
High German noun the standard literary and spoken form of German, originally used in the highlands in the south of Germany.
high-handed adjective using one's authority forcefully and without considering the feelings of other people.
high-impact adjective (of physical exercises, especially aerobics) very strenuous.
high jinks plural noun high-spirited fun.

high jump noun (**the high jump**) an athletic event in which competitors jump as high as possible over a bar which is raised after each round.
– PHRASES **be for the high jump** Brit. informal be about to be severely reprimanded.
– DERIVATIVES **high jumper** noun.

highland noun (also **highlands**) 1 an area of high or mountainous land. 2 (**the Highlands**) the mountainous northern part of Scotland.
– DERIVATIVES **highlander** noun.

Highland cattle plural noun a shaggy-haired breed of cattle with long curved horns.

Highland dress noun the kilt and other clothing in the traditional style of the Scottish Highlands.

Highland fling noun an energetic solo Scottish dance consisting of a series of complex steps.

high-level adjective 1 involving senior people; of relatively high importance: *high-level negotiations*. 2 (of a computer programming language) having instructions resembling an existing language such as English, making it relatively easy to use.

high life noun an extravagant social life as enjoyed by wealthy people.

highlight noun 1 an outstanding part of an event or period of time: *that season was the highlight of his career*. 2 a bright or reflective area in a painting, picture, or design. 3 (**highlights**) bright tints in the hair, produced by bleaching or dyeing. • verb 1 draw attention to: *the issues highlighted by the report*. 2 mark something with a highlighter. 3 create highlights in hair.

highlighter noun 1 a broad marker pen used to mark transparent fluorescent colour on a part of a text or plan. 2 a powder or cream used to emphasize the cheekbones or other facial features.

highly adverb 1 to a high degree or level. 2 favourably.

highly strung adjective Brit. very nervous and easily upset.

High Mass noun a Roman Catholic or Anglo-Catholic mass with full ritual procedure, including music and incense.

high-minded adjective having strong moral principles.

highness noun 1 (**His, Her, Your Highness**) a title given to a person of royal rank, or used in addressing them. 2 the state of being high.

high-octane adjective 1 (of petrol) having a high octane number and therefore allowing an engine to run smoothly. 2 powerful or dynamic: *a high-octane career*.

high-powered adjective informal (of a person) dynamic and forceful.

high priest noun 1 a chief priest of a non-Christian religion. 2 (also **high priestess**) the leader of a cult or movement.

high-profile adjective attracting much attention or publicity: *a high-profile court case*.

high relief noun see RELIEF (sense 8).

high-rise adjective (of a building) having many storeys.

high road noun a main road.

high roller noun informal, chiefly N. Amer. a person who gambles or spends large sums of money.

high school noun 1 N. Amer. a secondary school. 2 (in the UK except Scotland) used chiefly in names of grammar schools or independent fee-paying secondary schools.

high seas plural noun (**the high seas**) the areas of the sea that are not under the control of any one country.

high season noun chiefly Brit. the most popular time of year for a holiday, when prices are highest.

high sheriff noun see SHERIFF.

high spirits plural noun lively and cheerful behaviour or mood.
– DERIVATIVES **high-spirited** adjective.

high spot noun the most enjoyable part of an experience or period of time.

high street noun Brit. the main street of a town. • adjective (**high-street**) catering to the needs of the ordinary public: *high-street fashion*.

high table noun Brit. a high table in a dining hall at which high-ranking people, such as the fellows of a college, sit.

hightail verb informal, chiefly N. Amer. move or travel fast.

high tea noun Brit. a meal eaten in the late afternoon or early evening, typically consisting of a cooked dish and tea.

high-tech (also **hi-tech**) adjective 1 using, needing, or involved in high technology. 2 (of architecture and interior design) functional in style and using materials such as steel, plastic, and glass.

high technology noun advanced technological development, especially in electronics.

high-tensile adjective (of metal) very strong under tension.

high tide (also **high water**) noun the time when the sea is closest to the land.

high-top adjective referring to a soft-soled sports shoe with a laced upper that extends above the ankle. • noun (**high-tops**) a pair of such shoes.

high treason noun see TREASON.

high-water mark noun the level reached by the sea at high tide, or by a lake or river during a flood.

highway noun 1 chiefly N. Amer. a main road. 2 (chiefly in official use) a public road.

highwayman noun (pl. **highwaymen**) historical a man, typically on horseback, who held up and robbed travellers.

high wire noun a high tightrope.

hijab /hi-jaab/ noun a head covering worn in public by some Muslim women.
– ORIGIN from an Arabic word meaning 'to veil'.

hijack verb 1 illegally seize control of an aircraft, ship, etc. while it is travelling somewhere. 2 take over something and use it for a new purpose: *the organization had been hijacked by extremists*. • noun an instance of hijacking an aircraft, ship, etc.
– DERIVATIVES **hijacker** noun.
– ORIGIN unknown.

Hijra /hij-ruh/ noun variant spelling of HEGIRA.

hike noun 1 a long walk or walking tour. 2 a sharp increase, especially in price. • verb 1 go

h

on a hike. **2** pull or lift up clothing. **3** increase a price sharply.
- DERIVATIVES **hiker** noun.
- ORIGIN unknown.

hilarious /hi-**lair**-i-uhss/ adjective extremely funny.
- DERIVATIVES **hilariously** adverb.
- ORIGIN Greek *hilaros* 'cheerful'.

hilarity /hi-**lar**-i-ti/ noun a state of great amusement causing loud laughter.

hill noun a naturally raised area of land, not as high or craggy as a mountain.
- PHRASES **over the hill** informal old and past one's best.
- ORIGIN Old English.

hillbilly noun (pl. **hillbillies**) N. Amer. informal, chiefly derogatory an unsophisticated country person.
- ORIGIN from **HILL** + *Billy* (informal form of the man's name *William*).

hill fort noun a fort built on a hill, in particular an Iron Age system of defensive banks and ditches.

hillock noun a small hill or mound.
- DERIVATIVES **hillocky** adjective.

hillside noun the sloping side of a hill.

hill station noun a town in the low mountains of the Indian subcontinent, popular as a holiday resort during the hot season.

hilltop noun the summit of a hill.

hillwalking noun the pastime of walking in hilly country.

hilly adjective (**hillier, hilliest**) having many hills.
- DERIVATIVES **hilliness** noun.

hilt noun the handle of a sword, dagger, or knife.
- PHRASES **to the hilt** completely.
- ORIGIN Old English.

him pronoun (third person sing.) used as the object of a verb or preposition to refer to a male person or animal previously mentioned.
- ORIGIN Old English.

USAGE: Why is it often said that you should say *I could never be as good as he* rather than *I could never be as good as him*? For a discussion of this issue, see the note at **PERSONAL PRONOUN**.

Himalayan /him-uh-**lay**-uhn/ adjective relating to the Himalayas, a mountain system in southern Asia.

himself pronoun (third person sing.) **1** (reflexive) used as the object of a verb or preposition to refer to a male person or animal previously mentioned as the subject of the clause. **2** (emphatic) he or him personally.

hind[1] adjective situated at the back.
- ORIGIN perhaps from Old English, 'behind'.

hind[2] noun a female deer.
- ORIGIN Old English.

hinder[1] /**hin**-der/ verb delay or impede someone or something.
- ORIGIN Old English, 'damage'.

hinder[2] /**hyn**-der/ adjective situated at or towards the back.
- ORIGIN perhaps from Old English, 'backward'.

Hindi /**hin**-di/ noun a language of northern India derived from Sanskrit. •adjective relating to Hindi.
- ORIGIN Urdu.

hindlimb noun either of the two back limbs of an animal.

hindmost adjective furthest back.

hindquarters plural noun the hind legs and adjoining parts of a four-legged animal.

hindrance /**hin**-druhnss/ noun a thing that delays or impedes someone or something.

hindsight noun understanding of a situation or event after it has happened.

Hindu /**hin**-doo/ noun (pl. **Hindus**) a follower of Hinduism. •adjective relating to Hinduism.
- ORIGIN Urdu.

Hinduism noun a major religious and cultural tradition of the Indian subcontinent, including belief in reincarnation and the worship of a large number of gods and goddesses.
- DERIVATIVES **Hinduize** (or **Hinduise**) verb.

Hindustani /hin-duu-**stah**-ni/ noun a group of languages and dialects spoken in NW India which includes Hindi and Urdu.

hindwing noun either of the two back wings of a four-winged insect.

hinge noun a movable joint or mechanism by which a door, gate, or lid opens and closes or which connects linked objects. •verb (**hinges, hingeing** or **hinging, hinged**) **1** attach or join something with a hinge. **2** (**hinge on**) depend entirely on: *contests for the mayorship are likely to hinge on local issues.*
- ORIGIN related to **HANG**.

hinny noun (pl. **hinnies**) the offspring of a female donkey and a male horse.
- ORIGIN Greek *hinnos.*

hint noun **1** a slight or indirect indication. **2** a very small trace of something. **3** a small item of practical information. •verb **1** indicate something indirectly. **2** (**hint at**) be a slight indication of: *a sound that hinted at deep power.*
- ORIGIN probably from an Old English word meaning 'grasp'.

hinterland /**hin**-ter-land/ noun **1** the remote areas of a country, away from the coast and major rivers. **2** the area around or beyond a major town or port.
- ORIGIN German.

hip[1] noun a projection of the pelvis and upper thigh bone on each side of the body.
- PHRASES **be joined at the hip** informal (of two people) be inseparable.
- DERIVATIVES **hipped** adjective.
- ORIGIN Old English.

hip[2] noun the fruit of a rose.
- ORIGIN Old English.

hip[3] adjective (**hipper, hippest**) informal **1** very fashionable. **2** (**hip to**) aware of or informed about something.
- DERIVATIVES **hipness** noun.
- ORIGIN unknown.

hip[4] exclamation introducing a communal cheer.
- ORIGIN unknown.

hip bath noun a bath shaped to sit rather than lie down in.

hip bone noun a large bone forming the main part of the pelvis on each side of the body.

hip flask noun a small flask for spirits, carried in a hip pocket.

hip hop noun a style of pop music of US black and Hispanic origin, featuring rap with an electronic backing.

- DERIVATIVES **hip-hopper** noun.
- ORIGIN probably from **HIP³**.

hippie noun variant spelling of **HIPPY¹**.

hippo noun (pl. same or **hippos**) informal a hippopotamus.

Hippocratic oath /hip-puh-**krat**-ik/ noun an oath formerly taken by medical doctors to observe a code of professional behaviour (parts of which are still used in some medical schools).
- ORIGIN from the name of the ancient Greek physician *Hippocrates*.

hippodrome /**hip**-puh-drohm/ noun **1** a theatre or concert hall. **2** (in ancient Greece or Rome) a course for chariot or horse races.
- ORIGIN from Greek *hippos* 'horse' + *dromos* 'race, course'.

hippopotamus /hip-puh-**pot**-uh-muhss/ noun (pl. **hippopotamuses** or **hippopotami** /hip-puh-**pot**-uh-my/) a large African mammal with a thick skin and massive jaws, living partly on land and partly in water.
- ORIGIN from Greek *hippos ho potamios* 'river horse'.

hippy¹ (also **hippie**) noun (pl. **hippies**) (especially in the 1960s) a young person who advocates peace and free love and dresses unconventionally.
- DERIVATIVES **hippiedom** noun **hippyish** adjective.
- ORIGIN from **HIP³**.

hippy² adjective (of a woman) having large hips.

hipster noun informal a person who follows the latest trends and fashions.
- ORIGIN from **HIP³**.

hipsters plural noun Brit. trousers cut to fit and fasten at the hips rather than the waist.
- ORIGIN from **HIP¹**.

hire verb **1** chiefly Brit. pay to be allowed to use something for an agreed period. **2** (**hire something out**) allow something to be used for an agreed period in return for payment. **3** appoint someone as an employee. **4** employ someone for a short time to do a particular job. •noun the action of hiring someone or something.
- PHRASES **for hire** available to be hired.
- DERIVATIVES **hireable** adjective **hirer** noun.
- ORIGIN Old English.

hireling noun chiefly derogatory a person who is willing to undertake any kind of work provided that they are paid.

hire purchase noun Brit. a system by which someone pays for a thing in regular instalments while having the use of it.

hirsute /**her**-syoot/ adjective having a great deal of hair on the face or body; hairy.
- DERIVATIVES **hirsuteness** noun.
- ORIGIN Latin *hirsutus*.

his possessive determiner **1** belonging to or associated with a male person or animal previously mentioned. **2** (**His**) used in titles. •possessive pronoun used to refer to a thing belonging to or associated with a male person or animal previously mentioned.
- ORIGIN Old English.

Hispanic /hi-**span**-ik/ adjective relating to Spain or the Spanish-speaking countries of Central and South America. •noun a Spanish-speaking person, especially one of Latin American descent, living in the US.
- DERIVATIVES **Hispanicize** (or **Hispanicise**) verb.
- ORIGIN from Latin *Hispania* 'Spain'.

hiss verb **1** make a sharp sound like that made when pronouncing the letter *s*, often as a sign of disapproval or mockery. **2** whisper something in an urgent or angry way. •noun **1** a hissing sound. **2** electrical interference at audio frequencies.
- ORIGIN imitating the sound.

histamine /**hiss**-tuh-meen/ noun a compound which is released by cells in response to injury and in allergic reactions.
- ORIGIN from Greek *histos* 'web, tissue' and **AMINE**.

histology /hi-**stol**-uh-ji/ noun the branch of biology concerned with the microscopic structure of tissues.
- DERIVATIVES **histological** adjective **histologist** noun.
- ORIGIN from Greek *histos* 'web, tissue'.

histopathology /his-toh-puh-**thol**-uh-ji/ noun the branch of medicine concerned with the changes in tissues caused by disease.
- DERIVATIVES **histopathological** adjective **histopathologist** noun.
- ORIGIN from Greek *histos* 'web, tissue'.

historian noun an expert in history.

historic adjective **1** famous or important in history, or likely to be so in the future: *a historic occasion*. **2** Grammar (of a tense) used in describing past events.

> USAGE: **Historic** and **historical** do not have the same meaning. **Historic** means 'famous or important in history' (*a historic occasion*), whereas **historical** chiefly means 'relating to history' (*historical evidence*).

historical adjective **1** relating to history: *historical evidence*. **2** belonging to or set in the past. **3** (of the study of a subject) based on an analysis of its development over a period.
- DERIVATIVES **historically** adverb.

historicism noun **1** the theory that social and cultural developments are determined by history. **2** excessive regard for past styles of art and architecture.
- DERIVATIVES **historicist** noun **historicize** (or **historicise**) verb.

historicity /his-tuh-**ris**-i-ti/ noun historical authenticity.

historic present noun Grammar the present tense used instead of the past in vivid narrative or informal speech.

historiography /hi-sto-ri-og-ruh-fi/ noun **1** the study of the writing of history and of written histories. **2** the writing of history.
- DERIVATIVES **historiographer** noun **historiographic** adjective **historiographical** adjective.

history noun (pl. **histories**) **1** the study of past events. **2** the past considered as a whole. **3** the past events connected with someone or something: *a patient with a complicated medical history*. **4** a continuous record of past events or trends.
- PHRASES **be history** informal be dismissed or dead; be finished.
- ORIGIN Greek *historia* 'narrative, history'.

h

histrionic /hiss-tri-on-ik/ adjective
1 excessively theatrical or dramatic. 2 formal
relating to actors or acting. • noun (**histrionics**)
exaggerated behaviour designed to attract
attention.
– DERIVATIVES **histrionically** adverb.
– ORIGIN from Latin *histrio* 'actor'.

hit verb (**hits, hitting, hit**) 1 strike someone or
something with the hand or a tool, bat,
weapon, etc. 2 come into contact with
someone or something quickly and forcefully.
3 strike a target. 4 cause harm or distress to:
the area was badly hit by pit closures. 5 (**hit out**)
make a strongly worded criticism or attack.
6 be suddenly realized by: *it hit me that I was
successful.* 7 (**hit on**) suddenly discover or
think of something. 8 informal reach or arrive at
a place, level, or figure. • noun 1 an instance of
hitting or being hit. 2 a successful film, pop
record, etc. 3 Computing an instance of
identifying an item of data which matches the
requirements of a search. 4 an instance of a
particular website being accessed by a user.
5 informal, chiefly N. Amer. a murder carried out by a
criminal organization. 6 informal a dose of an
addictive drug.
– PHRASES **hit-and-miss** done or occurring at
random. **hit-and-run** (of a road accident) from
which the driver responsible leaves rapidly
without helping the other people involved. **hit
someone below the belt** 1 Boxing give one's
opponent an illegal low blow. 2 behave
unfairly towards someone. **hit someone for six**
Brit. affect someone very severely. **hit the
ground running** informal start something new
with energy and enthusiasm. **hit it off** informal
be naturally well suited. **hit the nail on the
head** find exactly the right answer. **hit-or-miss**
as likely to be unsuccessful as successful. **hit
the road** (or N. Amer. **trail**) informal set out on a
journey.
– DERIVATIVES **hitter** noun.
– ORIGIN Old Norse, 'come upon, meet with'.

hitch verb 1 move something into a different
position with a jerk: *she hitched up her skirt
and ran.* 2 fasten or tether an animal with a
rope. 3 informal travel or obtain a lift by hitch-
hiking. • noun 1 a temporary difficulty. 2 a
temporary knot used to fasten one thing to
another.
– PHRASES **get hitched** informal get married.
– ORIGIN unknown.

hitcher noun a hitch-hiker.

hitch-hike verb travel by getting free lifts in
passing vehicles.
– DERIVATIVES **hitch-hiker** noun.

hither adverb old use to or towards this place.
– PHRASES **hither and thither** (also **hither and
yon**) to and fro.
– ORIGIN Old English.

hitherto adverb until the point in time under
discussion.

Hitlerian /hit-leer-i-uhn/ adjective relating to
or characteristic of the Austrian-born Nazi
leader and Chancellor of Germany Adolf
Hitler.

hit list noun a list of people to be killed for
criminal or political reasons.

hit man noun informal a hired assassin.

Hittite /hi-tyt/ noun 1 a member of an ancient

people who established an empire in the
western peninsula of Asia and Syria *c.*1700–
1200 BC. 2 the language of the Hittites.
• adjective relating to the Hittites.

HIV abbreviation human immunodeficiency virus
(the virus which causes Aids).

hive noun 1 a beehive. 2 a place full of people
working hard. • verb 1 (**hive something off**)
chiefly Brit. transfer part of a business to new
ownership. 2 place bees in a hive.
– ORIGIN Old English.

hives plural noun (treated as sing. or pl.) another
term for URTICARIA.
– ORIGIN unknown.

HIV-positive adjective having had a positive
result in a blood test for HIV.

HK abbreviation Hong Kong.

HM abbreviation (in the UK) Her (or His)
Majesty or Majesty's.

HMG abbreviation (in the UK) Her or His
Majesty's Government.

HMI abbreviation historical (in the UK) Her or His
Majesty's Inspector (of Schools).

HMS abbreviation Her or His Majesty's Ship.

HMSO abbreviation (in the UK) Her or His
Majesty's Stationery Office, which publishes
government documents and legislation.

HNC abbreviation (in the UK) Higher National
Certificate.

HND abbreviation (in the UK) Higher National
Diploma.

Ho symbol the chemical element holmium.

hoar /hor/ adjective old use or literary grey or grey-
haired.
– ORIGIN Old English.

hoard noun 1 a secret store of money or
valuables. 2 a store of useful information.
• verb gradually collect something and store it
away.
– DERIVATIVES **hoarder** noun.
– ORIGIN Old English.

USAGE: Hoard and horde are sometimes
confused. A **hoard** is 'a secret store' (*a hoard of
treasure*), while **horde** is a word showing
disapproval when talking about 'a large group
of people' (*hordes of greedy shareholders*).

hoarding noun Brit. 1 a large board used to
display advertisements. 2 a temporary board
fence around a building site.
– ORIGIN probably from Old French *hourd.*

hoar frost noun a greyish-white feathery
deposit of frost.

hoarse adjective (of a voice) rough and harsh.
– DERIVATIVES **hoarsely** adverb **hoarsen** verb
hoarseness noun.
– ORIGIN Old English.

hoary adjective (**hoarier, hoariest**) 1 old and
having grey or white hair. 2 old and
unoriginal: *a hoary old adage.*
– DERIVATIVES **hoarily** adverb **hoariness** noun.

hoax noun a humorous or cruel trick. • verb
deceive someone with a hoax.
– DERIVATIVES **hoaxer** noun.
– ORIGIN probably from HOCUS-POCUS.

hob noun Brit. the flat top part of a cooker, with
hotplates or burners.
– ORIGIN alteration of HUB.

hobbit noun a member of an imaginary race

similar to humans, of small size and with hairy feet.
- ORIGIN invented by the British writer J. R. R. Tolkien, and said by him to mean 'hole-dweller'.

hobble verb **1** walk awkwardly, typically because of pain. **2** strap together the legs of a horse to prevent it from straying. •noun an awkward way of walking.
- DERIVATIVES **hobbler** noun.
- ORIGIN probably related to Dutch *hobbelen* 'rock from side to side'.

hobbledehoy /hob-uhl-di-hoy/ noun informal, dated a clumsy or awkward youth.
- ORIGIN unknown.

hobby¹ noun (pl. **hobbies**) a leisure activity that a person does regularly for pleasure.
- ORIGIN from a familiar form of the man's name *Robin*.

hobby² noun (pl. **hobbies**) a small falcon which hunts birds and insects in flight.
- ORIGIN Old French *hobet* 'little falcon'.

hobby horse noun **1** a child's toy consisting of a stick with a model of a horse's head at one end. **2** a rocking horse. **3** a person's favourite topic of conversation.

hobbyist noun a person with a particular hobby.

hobgoblin noun a mischievous imp.
- ORIGIN from *hob*, familiar form of the names *Robin* and *Robert*, used in the sense 'country fellow'.

hobnail noun a short heavy-headed nail used to reinforce the soles of boots.
- DERIVATIVES **hobnailed** adjective.
- ORIGIN from HOB + NAIL.

hobnob verb (**hobnobs, hobnobbing, hobnobbed**) informal spend time socially with rich or important people.
- ORIGIN from former *hob or nob*, or *hob and nob*, probably meaning 'give and take'.

hobo noun (pl. **hoboes** or **hobos**) N. Amer. a homeless person; a tramp.
- ORIGIN unknown.

Hobson's choice noun a choice of taking what is offered or nothing at all.
- ORIGIN named after Thomas *Hobson*, who hired out horses, making the customer take the one nearest the door or none at all.

hock¹ noun **1** the joint in the hind leg of a four-legged animal, between the knee and the fetlock. **2** a knuckle of pork or ham.
- ORIGIN from an Old English word meaning 'heel'.

hock² noun Brit. a dry white wine from the German Rhineland.
- ORIGIN from German *Hochheimer Wein* 'wine from Hochheim'.

hock³ verb informal pawn an object.
- PHRASES **in hock 1** having been pawned. **2** in debt.
- ORIGIN from Dutch *hok* 'hutch, prison, debt'.

hockey /hok-ki/ noun a game played between two teams of eleven players each, using hooked sticks to drive a small hard ball towards a goal.
- ORIGIN unknown.

hocus-pocus noun **1** meaningless talk used to deceive someone. **2** a form of words used by a

conjuror.
- ORIGIN from *hax pax max Deus adimax*, a mock Latin phrase used by conjurors.

hod noun **1** a builder's V-shaped open trough attached to a short pole, used for carrying bricks. **2** a coal scuttle.
- ORIGIN Old French *hotte* 'pannier'.

hodgepodge noun N. Amer. variant of HOTCHPOTCH.

Hodgkin's disease noun a cancerous disease causing enlargement of the lymph nodes, liver, and spleen.
- ORIGIN named after the English physician Thomas *Hodgkin*.

hoe noun a long-handled gardening tool with a thin metal blade, used mainly for weeding.
•verb (**hoes, hoeing, hoed**) use a hoe to turn earth or cut through weeds.
- DERIVATIVES **hoer** noun.
- ORIGIN Old French *houe*.

hoedown noun N. Amer. a gathering for lively folk dancing.

hog noun **1** a castrated male pig reared for slaughter. **2** informal a greedy person. •verb (**hogs, hogging, hogged**) informal take or use most or all of something selfishly.
- PHRASES **go the whole hog** informal do something completely or thoroughly.
- DERIVATIVES **hogger** noun **hoggish** adjective.
- ORIGIN Old English.

hogback (also **hog's back**) noun a long steep hill or mountain ridge.

hogget noun Brit. a sheep that is one year old.

Hogmanay /hog-muh-nay/ noun (in Scotland) New Year's Eve.
- ORIGIN perhaps from Old French *aguillanneuf* 'last day of the year, new year's gift'.

hogshead noun **1** a large cask. **2** a measure of liquid volume for wine or beer.

hogwash noun informal nonsense.
- ORIGIN first meaning 'kitchen swill for pigs'.

hogweed noun a large white-flowered weed of the parsley family.

hoick verb Brit. informal lift or pull something with a jerk.
- ORIGIN perhaps from HIKE.

hoi polloi /hoy puh-loy/ plural noun derogatory the ordinary people.
- ORIGIN Greek, 'the many'.

hoisin sauce /hoy-zin/ noun a sweet, spicy dark red sauce made from soya beans, used in Chinese cooking.
- ORIGIN from two Cantonese words meaning 'sea' + 'fresh'.

hoist verb **1** raise something by means of ropes and pulleys. **2** haul or lift something up. •noun **1** an act of hoisting something. **2** a device for hoisting something.
- DERIVATIVES **hoister** noun.
- ORIGIN probably from Dutch *hijsen* or German *hiesen*.

hoity-toity adjective snobbish or haughty.
- ORIGIN from former *hoit* 'romp'.

hokey adjective (**hokier, hokiest**) N. Amer. informal excessively sentimental or artificial.
- ORIGIN from HOKUM.

hoki /hoh-ki/ noun an edible marine fish found off the southern coasts of New Zealand.
- ORIGIN Maori.

h

hokum /hoh-kuhm/ **noun** informal **1** nonsense; rubbish. **2** unoriginal or sentimental material in a film, book, etc.
– ORIGIN unknown.

hold[1] **verb** (past and past part. **held**) **1** grasp, carry, or support someone or something. **2** contain or be able to contain: *the tank held twenty-four gallons.* **3** have, own, or occupy something. **4** keep or detain someone. **5** stay or keep at a certain value or level: *MCI shares held at 99p.* **6** have a belief or opinion. **7** (**hold someone/thing in**) regard someone or something in a particular way: *the speed limit is held in contempt by many drivers.* **8** (**hold someone to**) make someone keep a promise. **9** continue to follow a course. **10** arrange and take part in a meeting or conversation. **11** N. Amer. informal refrain from adding or using something. • **noun 1** an act or way of grasping someone or something. **2** a handhold. **3** a degree of power or control: *Tom had some kind of hold over his father.*
– PHRASES **get hold of 1** grasp something. **2** informal find or contact someone. **hold something against someone** continue to feel resentful for something that someone has done. **hold back** hesitate. **hold something down** informal succeed in keeping a job. **hold fast 1** remain tightly secured. **2** continue to believe in a principle. **hold forth** talk at length. **hold good** (or **true**) remain true or valid. **hold it** informal wait or stop doing something. **hold off** (of bad weather) fail to occur. **hold someone/thing off 1** resist an attacker or challenge. **2** postpone an action or decision. **hold on 1** wait; stop. **2** keep going in difficult circumstances. **hold out 1** resist difficult circumstances. **2** continue to be enough. **hold out for** continue to demand something. **hold something over** postpone something. **hold up** remain strong. **hold someone/thing up 1** delay someone or something. **2** rob someone using the threat of violence. **3** present someone or something as an example. **no holds barred** without rules or restrictions. **on hold** waiting to be dealt with or connected by telephone. **take hold** start to have an effect.
– DERIVATIVES **holder** noun.
– ORIGIN Old English.

hold[2] **noun** a storage space in the lower part of a ship or aircraft.
– ORIGIN from HOLE.

holdall **noun** Brit. a large bag with handles and a shoulder strap.

holding **noun 1** an area of land held by lease. **2** (**holdings**) stocks and other financial assets owned by a person or organization.

holding company **noun** a company created to buy shares in other companies, which it then controls.

holding pattern **noun** the flight path maintained by an aircraft awaiting permission to land.

hold-up **noun 1** a cause of delay. **2** a robbery carried out with the threat of violence. **3** a stocking held up by an elasticated top.

hole **noun 1** a hollow space in a solid object or surface. **2** an opening or gap in or passing through something. **3** (in golf) a hollow in the ground into which the ball must be hit.

4 informal an awkward or unpleasant place or situation. • **verb 1** make a hole or holes in something. **2** Golf hit the ball into a hole. **3** (**hole up**) informal hide oneself.
– PHRASES **hole-and-corner** trying to avoid notice; secret. **hole-in-one** (pl. **holes-in-one**) Golf a shot that enters the hole from the tee. **make a hole in** use a large amount of something.
– DERIVATIVES **holey** adjective.
– ORIGIN Old English.

hole in the heart **noun** an abnormal opening present from birth in the wall between the chambers of the heart, resulting in inadequate circulation of oxygenated blood.

Holi /hoh-li/ **noun** a Hindu spring festival celebrated in honour of Krishna.
– ORIGIN Sanskrit.

holiday chiefly Brit. **noun 1** an extended period of leisure, especially away from home. **2** a day of national or religious celebration when no work is done. **3** a short period during which the payment of instalments, tax, etc. may be suspended. • **verb** spend a holiday in a particular place.
– ORIGIN Old English, 'holy day'.

holiday camp **noun** Brit. a camp for holidaymakers with accommodation and entertainments.

holidaymaker **noun** Brit. a tourist.

holier-than-thou **adjective** offensively certain that one is morally superior to others.

holiness **noun 1** the state of being holy. **2** (**His/Your Holiness**) the title of the Pope, Orthodox patriarchs, and the Dalai Lama.

holism /hoh-li-z'm/ **noun** Medicine the treating of the whole person, taking into account mental and social factors, rather than just the symptoms of a disease.
– DERIVATIVES **holistic** adjective.
– ORIGIN from Greek *holos* 'whole'.

hollandaise sauce /hol-uhn-**dayz**/ **noun** a creamy sauce made of butter, egg yolks, and vinegar.
– ORIGIN French *hollandais* 'Dutch'.

holler informal **verb** give a loud shout. • **noun** a loud shout.
– ORIGIN related to HALLOO.

hollow **adjective 1** having a hole or empty space inside. **2** curving inwards; concave: *hollow cheeks.* **3** (of a sound) echoing. **4** worthless or insincere: *hollow election promises.* • **noun 1** a hole or depression. **2** a small valley. • **verb 1** form by making a hole: *the pond was hollowed out by hand.* **2** make something hollow.
– PHRASES **beat someone hollow** defeat someone thoroughly.
– DERIVATIVES **hollowly** adverb **hollowness** noun.
– ORIGIN Old English, 'cave'.

holly **noun** an evergreen shrub with prickly dark green leaves and red berries.
– ORIGIN Old English.

hollyhock **noun** a tall plant of the mallow family, with large showy flowers.
– ORIGIN from HOLY + former *hock* 'mallow'.

holmium /hohl-mi-uhm/ **noun** a soft silvery-white metallic element.
– ORIGIN from *Holmia*, Latinized form of *Stockholm*, the capital of Sweden.

holm oak noun an evergreen oak with dark green glossy leaves.
– ORIGIN from Old English, 'holly'.

holocaust /hol-uh-kawst/ noun **1** destruction or killing on a mass scale. **2** (**the Holocaust**) the mass murder of Jews under the German Nazi regime in World War II.
– ORIGIN from Greek *holos* 'whole' + *kaustos* 'burnt'.

Holocene /hol-uh-seen/ adjective Geology relating to the present epoch (from about 10,000 years ago, following the Pleistocene).
– ORIGIN from Greek *kainos* 'new'.

hologram /hol-uh-gram/ noun a photographic image formed in such a way that it looks three-dimensional when it is lit up.
– DERIVATIVES **holographic** adjective **holography** noun.
– ORIGIN from Greek *holos* 'whole'.

holograph /hol-uh-grahf/ noun a manuscript handwritten by its author.

hols plural noun Brit. informal holidays.

holster /hohl-ster/ noun a holder for carrying a handgun, worn on a belt or under the arm.
• verb put a gun into its holster.
– ORIGIN unknown.

holt /hohlt/ noun the den of an otter.
– ORIGIN from HOLD¹.

holy adjective (**holier**, **holiest**) **1** dedicated to God or a religious purpose. **2** morally and spiritually excellent.
– ORIGIN Old English.

holy day noun a religious festival.

Holy Father noun the Pope.

holy of holies noun **1** historical the inner chamber of the sanctuary in the Jewish Temple in Jerusalem. **2** a place regarded as most sacred or special.

holy orders plural noun see ORDER (in sense 10 of the noun).

Holy Roman Empire noun the western part of the Roman Empire, as revived by Charlemagne in 800.

Holy Scripture noun the Bible.

Holy See noun the office of Pope or those associated with the Pope in governing the Roman Catholic Church.

Holy Spirit (or **Holy Ghost**) noun (in Christianity) the third person of the Trinity; God as spiritually active in the world.

holy war noun a war waged in support of a religious cause.

Holy Week noun the week before Easter.

Holy Writ noun sacred writings as a whole, especially the Bible.

homage /hom-ij/ noun honour or respect shown publicly to someone: *they paid homage to the local boy who became President.*
– ORIGIN Old French.

homburg /hom-berg/ noun a man's felt hat having a narrow curled brim and a lengthwise indentation in the crown.
– ORIGIN named after the German town of *Homburg.*

home noun **1** the place where someone lives. **2** an institution for people needing professional care. **3** a place where something flourishes or from which it originated: *Barcelona became the home of Modernism.*

4 the finishing point in a race. **5** (in games) the place where a player is free from attack.
• adjective **1** relating to the home. **2** made, done, or intended for use in the home. **3** relating to someone's own country. **4** (in sport) referring to a team's own ground. • adverb **1** to or at someone's home. **2** to the end of something. **3** to the intended or correct position: *he slid the bolt home noisily.* • verb **1** (of an animal) return by instinct to its territory. **2** (**home in on**) move or be aimed towards a target or destination.
– PHRASES **at home 1** comfortable and at ease. **2** ready to receive visitors. **bring something home to** make someone realize the significance of something. **close to home** (of a remark) uncomfortably accurate. **home and dry** Brit. having achieved one's objective.
– ORIGIN Old English.

homeboy (or **homegirl**) noun informal, chiefly US **1** a person from one's own town or neighbourhood. **2** (especially among urban black people) a member of a peer group or gang.

home brew noun beer or other alcoholic drink brewed at home.

homebuyer noun a person who buys a house or flat.

homecoming noun an instance of returning home.

home economics plural noun (often treated as sing.) the study of cookery and household management.

home farm noun Brit. & S. African a farm on an estate that provides produce for the owner.

home-grown adjective grown or produced in one's own garden or country.

Home Guard noun the British volunteer force organized in 1940 to defend the UK against invasion.

home help noun Brit. a person employed to help with household work.

homeland noun **1** a person's native land. **2** a self-governing state occupied by a particular people. **3** historical any of ten partially self-governing areas in South Africa assigned to particular African peoples.

homeless adjective not having anywhere to live.
– DERIVATIVES **homelessness** noun.

homely adjective (**homelier**, **homeliest**) **1** Brit. simple but comfortable: *a modern hotel with a homely atmosphere.* **2** Brit. unsophisticated or ordinary. **3** N. Amer. (of a person) unattractive.
– DERIVATIVES **homeliness** noun.

home-made adjective made at home.

homemaker noun chiefly N. Amer. a person who manages a home.

Home Office noun the British government department dealing with law and order, immigration, etc. in England and Wales.

homeopath /hoh-mi-uh-path/ (also **homoeopath**) noun a person who practises homeopathy.

homeopathy /hoh-mi-op-uh-thi/ (also **homoeopathy**) noun a system of complementary medicine in which disease is treated by minute doses of natural substances

that would normally produce symptoms of the disease.
- DERIVATIVES **homeopathic** adjective.
- ORIGIN from Greek *homoios* 'like' + *patheia* 'suffering, feeling'.

homeostasis /hoh-mi-uh-**stay**-siss/ (also **homoeostasis**) noun the tendency of the body to keep its own temperature, blood pressure, etc. at a constant level.
- DERIVATIVES **homeostatic** adjective.
- ORIGIN from Greek *homoios* 'like' + *stasis* 'stoppage, standing'.

homeowner noun a person who owns their own home.

home page noun a person's or organization's introductory document on the Internet.

Homeric /hoh-**merr**-ik/ adjective relating to the ancient Greek poet Homer or to the epic poems that he is thought to have written.

home rule noun the government of a place by its own citizens.

home run noun Baseball a hit that allows the batter to make a complete circuit of the bases.

Home Secretary noun (in the UK) the Secretary of State in charge of the Home Office.

homesick adjective missing one's home during a time away from it.

homespun adjective **1** simple and unsophisticated. **2** (of cloth or yarn) made or spun at home. •noun homespun cloth.

homestead noun a farmhouse with surrounding land and outbuildings.
- DERIVATIVES **homesteader** noun **homesteading** noun.

home straight (also **home stretch**) noun the final stretch of a racecourse.

home truth noun an unpleasant fact about oneself, pointed out by someone else.

home unit noun Austral./NZ a flat that is one of several in a building.

homeward adverb (also **homewards**) towards home. •adjective going or leading towards home.

homework noun **1** school work that a pupil is required to do at home. **2** preparation for an event or situation. **3** paid work done in one's own home.
- DERIVATIVES **homeworker** noun.

homey (also **homy**) adjective (**homier**, **homiest**) chiefly N. Amer. **1** comfortable and cosy. **2** unsophisticated. •noun variant of **HOMIE**.

homicide noun chiefly N. Amer. the killing of another person.
- DERIVATIVES **homicidal** adjective.
- ORIGIN from Latin *homo* 'man' + -**CIDE**.

homie (also **homey**) noun (pl. **homies** or **homeys**) informal, chiefly US a homeboy or homegirl.

homiletic /hom-i-**let**-ik/ adjective relating to or like a homily; morally uplifting.

homily /hom-i-li/ noun (pl. **homilies**) **1** a talk on a religious subject that is intended to be spiritually uplifting. **2** a tedious talk on a moral issue.
- DERIVATIVES **homilist** noun.
- ORIGIN Greek *homilia* 'discourse'.

homing adjective **1** (of a pigeon or other animal) able to return home from a great distance. **2** (of a weapon) able to find and hit a target electronically.

hominid /hom-i-nid/ noun a member of a family of primates which includes humans and their fossil ancestors.
- ORIGIN from Latin *homo* 'man'.

hominoid /hom-in-oyd/ noun Zoology a primate of a group that includes humans, their fossil ancestors, and the great apes.

hominy /hom-in-i/ noun US coarsely ground maize used to make grits.
- ORIGIN Algonquian.

homo /hoh-moh/ informal, chiefly derogatory noun (pl. **homos**) a homosexual man. •adjective homosexual.

homo- combining form **1** same: *homogeneous*. **2** relating to homosexual love: *homoerotic*.
- ORIGIN from Greek *homos* 'same'.

homoeopath noun variant spelling of **HOMEOPATH**.

homoeopathy noun variant spelling of **HOMEOPATHY**.

homoeostasis noun variant spelling of **HOMEOSTASIS**.

homoerotic /hoh-moh-i-**rot**-ik, hom-oh-i-**rot**-ik/ adjective concerning or arousing sexual desire centred on a person of the same sex.
- DERIVATIVES **homoeroticism** noun.

homogeneous /hom-uh-jee-ni-uhss/ adjective **1** of the same kind; alike. **2** consisting of parts all of the same kind: *a homogeneous society*.
- DERIVATIVES **homogeneity** /hom-uh-ji-nee-i-ti/ noun **homogeneously** adverb **homogeneousness** noun.
- ORIGIN from Greek *homos* 'same' + *genos* 'race, kind'.

homogenize (or **homogenise**) verb **1** treat milk so that the particles of fat are broken down and the cream does not separate. **2** make different things more similar or uniform.
- DERIVATIVES **homogenization** noun **homogenizer** noun.

homograph noun each of two or more words having the same spelling but different meanings and origins (e.g. **BOW**[1] and **BOW**[2] in this dictionary).

homologate /huh-**mol**-uh-gayt/ verb formal approve something, especially a vehicle for sale or use in a class of racing.
- DERIVATIVES **homologation** noun.
- ORIGIN Latin *homologare* 'agree'.

homologous /huh-**mol**-uh-guhss/ adjective **1** having a similar relative position or structure; corresponding. **2** Biology (of organs) similar in position, structure, and evolutionary origin.
- DERIVATIVES **homologize** (or **homologise**) verb **homology** noun.
- ORIGIN Greek *homologos* 'agreeing, consistent'.

homologue /hom-uh-log/ (US **homolog**) noun technical a thing that has the same relative position or structure as another.

homonym /hom-uh-nim/ noun each of two or more words having the same spelling or pronunciation but different meanings and origins (e.g. **CAN**[1] and **CAN**[2] in this dictionary).
- DERIVATIVES **homonymous** adjective.
- ORIGIN Greek *homōnumos* 'having the same

name'.

homophobia noun an extreme and irrational hatred or fear of homosexuality and homosexuals.
– DERIVATIVES **homophobe** noun **homophobic** adjective.

homophone noun each of two or more words having the same pronunciation but different meanings, origins, or spelling (e.g. *new* and *knew*).
– ORIGIN from Greek *phōnē* 'sound, voice'.

Homo sapiens /hoh-moh **sap**-i-enz/ noun the primate species to which modern humans belong.
– ORIGIN Latin, 'wise man'.

homosexual adjective feeling or involving sexual attraction to people of one's own sex. ● noun a homosexual person.
– DERIVATIVES **homosexuality** noun **homosexually** adverb.

homunculus /huh-**mung**-kyoo-luhss/ noun (pl. **homunculi** /huh-**mung**-kyoo-li/) a very small human or human-like creature.
– ORIGIN Latin, 'little man'.

homy adjective variant spelling of **HOMEY**.

Hon. abbreviation **1** (in official job titles) Honorary. **2** (in titles of the British nobility, members of parliament, and (in the US) judges) Honourable.

honcho /**hon**-choh/ noun (pl. **honchos**) informal a leader.
– ORIGIN Japanese, 'group leader'.

Honduran /hon-**dyoor**-uhn/ noun a person from Honduras, a country in Central America. ● adjective relating to Honduras.

hone verb **1** make better or more efficient: *she honed her singing skills.* **2** sharpen a tool with a whetstone.
– ORIGIN Old English, 'stone'.

honest adjective **1** truthful and sincere. **2** fairly earned through hard work: *an honest living.* **3** simple and unpretentious. ● adverb informal genuinely; really.
– ORIGIN Latin *honestus.*

honestly adverb **1** in an honest way. **2** really (used for emphasis).

honest-to-God adjective informal genuine; real.

honest-to-goodness adjective genuine and straightforward.

honesty noun **1** the quality of being honest and sincere: *they spoke with honesty about their fears.* **2** a plant with round, flat translucent seed pods.

honey noun (pl. **honeys**) **1** a sweet, sticky yellowish-brown fluid made by bees from flower nectar. **2** darling; sweetheart. **3** informal an excellent something of: *it's a honey of a movie.* **4** informal an attractive girl.
– ORIGIN Old English.

honeybee noun the common bee.

honeycomb noun **1** a structure of six-sided cells of wax, made by bees to store honey and eggs. **2** a structure resembling a bee's honeycomb. ● verb fill an area with cavities or tunnels.

honeydew noun a sweet, sticky substance produced by aphids (small insects) feeding on the sap of plants.

honeydew melon noun a variety of melon with pale skin and sweet green flesh.

honeyed adjective **1** containing or coated with honey. **2** soothing and soft: *honeyed words.* **3** having a warm yellow colour.

honeymoon noun **1** a holiday taken by a newly married couple. **2** an initial period of enthusiasm or goodwill. ● verb go on honeymoon.
– DERIVATIVES **honeymooner** noun.
– ORIGIN first referring to affection waning like the moon, then to the first month after marriage.

honeypot noun a place to which many people are attracted.

honeysuckle noun a climbing shrub with fragrant yellow and pink flowers.

honeytrap noun a plan in which an attractive person entices another person into revealing information or doing something unwise.

hongi /**hong**-i/ noun NZ the traditional Maori greeting in which people press their noses together.
– ORIGIN Maori.

honk noun **1** the cry of a goose. **2** the sound of a car horn. ● verb make a honk.
– ORIGIN imitating the sound.

honky noun (pl. **honkies**) N. Amer. informal, derogatory (among black people) a white person.
– ORIGIN unknown.

honky-tonk noun informal **1** chiefly N. Amer. a cheap or disreputable bar or club. **2** ragtime piano music.
– ORIGIN unknown.

honor noun & verb US spelling of **HONOUR**.

honorable adjective US spelling of **HONOURABLE**.

honorarium /on-uh-**rair**-i-uhm/ noun (pl. **honorariums** or **honoraria** /on-uh-**rair**-i-uh/) a voluntary payment for professional services which are offered without charge.
– ORIGIN Latin, referring to a gift made to someone entering public office.

honorary adjective **1** (of a title or position) given as an honour. **2** Brit. (of an office or its holder) unpaid.

honorific adjective given as a mark of respect.

honour (US **honor**) noun **1** great respect. **2** a clear sense of what is morally right. **3** something that is a privilege and a pleasure: *he had the honour of being received by the Queen.* **4** a person or thing that brings credit to something. **5** an award or title given as a reward for achievement. **6** (**honours**) a course of degree studies more specialized than for an ordinary pass. **7** (**His, Your,** etc. **Honour**) a title of respect for a circuit judge. **8** dated a woman's chastity. **9** Bridge an ace, king, queen, jack, or ten. ● verb **1** regard someone or something with great respect. **2** pay public respect to: *talented writers were honoured at a special ceremony.* **3** fulfil a duty or keep an agreement.
– PHRASES **do the honours** informal serve food or drink to a guest. **in honour of** as an expression of respect for. **on one's honour** morally obliged to behave in a particular way.
– ORIGIN Latin *honor.*

honourable (US **honorable**) adjective **1** bringing or worthy of honour. **2** (**Honourable**) a title given to certain high officials, members of the nobility, and MPs.

– DERIVATIVES **honourably** adverb.

honourable mention noun a commendation for a candidate in an exam or competition who is not awarded a prize.

honours list noun a public list of people to be awarded honours.

hooch /hooch/ (also **hootch**) noun informal strong alcoholic drink, especially inferior or illicit whisky.
– ORIGIN abbreviation of *Hoochinoo*, an Alaskan Indian people who made alcoholic spirits.

hood[1] noun 1 a covering for the head and neck with an opening for the face. 2 Brit. a folding waterproof cover of a vehicle or pram. 3 N. Amer. the bonnet of a vehicle. 4 a protective canopy. •verb put a hood on or over someone.
– DERIVATIVES **hooded** adjective.
– ORIGIN Old English.

hood[2] noun informal, chiefly N. Amer. a gangster or violent criminal.
– ORIGIN abbreviation of **HOODLUM**.

hood[3] noun informal, chiefly US a neighbourhood.

-hood suffix forming nouns referring to: 1 a condition or quality: *womanhood*. 2 a collection or group: *brotherhood*.
– ORIGIN Old English.

hoodlum /hood-luhm/ noun a gangster or other violent criminal.
– ORIGIN unknown.

hoodoo noun 1 a run or cause of bad luck. 2 voodoo. •verb (**hoodoos, hoodooing, hoodooed**) bring bad luck to someone or something.
– ORIGIN alteration of **VOODOO**.

hoodwink verb deceive or trick someone.
– ORIGIN from **HOOD**[1] + **WINK** in the former sense 'close the eyes'.

hoody (also **hoodie**) noun (pl. **hoodies**) a hooded sweatshirt or other top.

hooey noun informal, chiefly N. Amer. nonsense.
– ORIGIN unknown.

hoof noun (pl. **hoofs** or **hooves**) the horny part of the foot of a horse, cow, etc.
– PHRASES **hoof it** informal 1 go on foot. 2 dance. **on the hoof** Brit. informal without great thought or preparation.
– DERIVATIVES **hoofed** adjective.
– ORIGIN Old English.

hoofer noun informal a professional dancer.

hoo-ha noun Brit. informal a commotion or fuss.
– ORIGIN unknown.

hook noun 1 a piece of curved metal or other material for catching hold of things or hanging things on. 2 a short swinging punch made with the elbow bent and rigid. 3 a thing designed to catch people's attention. 4 a catchy passage in a song. •verb 1 attach or fasten something with a hook. 2 bend into a curved shape: *he hooked his thumbs in his belt*. 3 catch a fish with a hook. 4 (**be hooked**) informal be very interested or addicted. 5 (in cricket or golf) hit the ball in a curving path.
– PHRASES **by hook or by crook** by any possible means. **hook, line, and sinker** completely. **hook up 1** link to electronic equipment. **2** meet or join another person or people. **off the hook 1** informal no longer in trouble. **2** (of a telephone receiver) not on its rest. **sling one's hook** Brit. informal leave.
– ORIGIN Old English.

hookah /huuk-uh/ noun an oriental tobacco pipe with a long, flexible tube which draws the smoke through water in a bowl.
– ORIGIN Urdu.

hook and eye noun a small metal hook and loop used to fasten a garment.

hooked adjective having or resembling a hook or hooks.

hooker noun 1 informal, chiefly N. Amer. a prostitute. 2 Rugby the player in the middle of the front row of the scrum.

hookey (also **hooky**) noun (in phrase **play hookey**) N. Amer. informal play truant.
– ORIGIN unknown.

hook-up noun a connection to mains electricity, a communications system, etc.

hookworm noun a parasitic worm with hook-like mouthparts which can infest the intestines.

hooligan noun a violent young troublemaker.
– DERIVATIVES **hooliganism** noun.
– ORIGIN perhaps from *Hooligan*, the surname of a fictional rowdy Irish family in a music-hall song.

hoop noun 1 a circular band of a rigid material. 2 a large ring used as a toy or for circus performers to jump through. 3 a metal arch through which the balls are hit in croquet. 4 a contrasting horizontal stripe on a sports shirt or cap. •verb bind or surround with hoops.
– DERIVATIVES **hooped** adjective.
– ORIGIN Old English.

hoopla /hoop-lah/ noun Brit. a game in which rings are thrown in an attempt to encircle a prize.

hoopoe /hoo-poo, hoo-poh/ noun a salmon-pink bird with a long bill, a large crest, and black-and-white wings and tail.
– ORIGIN Latin *upupa*, imitating the bird's call.

hooray exclamation hurrah.

Hooray Henry noun (pl. **Hooray Henrys** or **Hooray Henries**) Brit. informal a lively but ineffectual young upper-class man.

hoot noun 1 a low sound made by owls or a similar sound made by a horn, siren, etc. 2 a shout of scorn or disapproval. 3 an outburst of laughter. 4 (**a hoot**) informal an amusing person or thing. •verb make or cause to make a hoot.
– PHRASES **not care** (or **give**) **a hoot** (or **two hoots**) informal not care at all.
– ORIGIN perhaps imitating the sound.

hootch noun variant spelling of **HOOCH**.

hooter noun 1 Brit. a siren, steam whistle, or horn. 2 informal a person's nose.

Hoover Brit. noun trademark a vacuum cleaner. •verb (**hoover**) 1 clean something with a vacuum cleaner. 2 (usu. **hoover something up**) eat, drink, or use all of something very quickly and eagerly.
– ORIGIN named after the American industrialist William H. *Hoover*.

hooves plural of **HOOF**.

hop[1] verb (**hops, hopping, hopped**) 1 jump along on one foot. 2 (of a bird or animal) jump along with two or all feet at once. 3 jump over or off something. 4 informal move or go somewhere quickly: *hop in then and we'll be*

off. **5** (**hop it**) Brit. informal go away quickly. •**noun 1** a hopping movement. **2** a short journey or distance. **3** an informal dance.
– PHRASES **hopping mad** informal very angry. **on the hop** Brit. informal **1** unprepared. **2** busy.
– ORIGIN Old English.

hop² noun a climbing plant whose dried flowers (**hops**) are used in brewing to give beer a bitter flavour.
– DERIVATIVES **hoppy** adjective.
– ORIGIN from German or Dutch.

hope noun **1** a feeling of expectation and desire for something to happen. **2** a cause or source of hope: *her only hope is surgery.* •**verb 1** expect and want something to happen. **2** intend if possible to do something.
– DERIVATIVES **hoper** noun.
– ORIGIN Old English.

hopeful adjective feeling or inspiring hope. •**noun** a person likely or hoping to succeed.
– DERIVATIVES **hopefulness** noun.

hopefully adverb **1** in a hopeful way. **2** it is to be hoped that.

> USAGE: The traditional sense of **hopefully** is 'in a hopeful way'. The newer use, meaning 'it is to be hoped that' (as in *hopefully, it should be finished next year*) is now the most common, although some people still think that it is incorrect.

hopeless adjective **1** feeling or causing despair. **2** chiefly Brit. very bad or incompetent.
– DERIVATIVES **hopelessly** adverb **hopelessness** noun.

Hopi /hoh-pi/ noun (pl. same or **Hopis**) **1** a member of an American Indian people living chiefly in NE Arizona. **2** the language of the Hopi.
– ORIGIN Hopi.

hopper noun **1** a container that tapers downwards and discharges its contents at the bottom. **2** a person or thing that hops.

hopsack noun a coarse clothing fabric of a loose weave.

hopscotch noun a children's game of hopping into and over squares marked on the ground to retrieve a marker.
– ORIGIN from HOP¹ + SCOTCH in the sense 'put and end to, stop'.

horde noun **1** chiefly derogatory a large group of people. **2** an army or tribe of nomadic warriors.
– ORIGIN Turkish *ordu* 'royal camp'.

> USAGE: On the confusion of **horde** and **hoard**, see the note at **HOARD**.

horehound /hor-hownd/ noun a plant of the mint family, traditionally used as a medicinal herb.
– ORIGIN Old English.

horizon noun **1** the line at which the earth's surface and the sky appear to meet. **2** the limit of a person's knowledge, experience, or interest: *she wanted to leave home and broaden her horizons.*
– PHRASES **on the horizon** about to happen; imminent.
– ORIGIN from Greek *horizōn* 'limiting'.

horizontal adjective parallel to the plane, of the horizon; at right angles to the vertical.

•**noun** a horizontal line, plane, or structure.
– DERIVATIVES **horizontality** noun **horizontally** adverb.

hormonal /hor-moh-n'l/ adjective **1** relating to a hormone or hormones. **2** informal affected by one's sex hormones: *giggly, hormonal fourth formers.*

hormone noun a substance produced by a living thing and carried by blood or sap to regulate the action of specific cells or tissues.
– ORIGIN Greek *hormōn* 'setting in motion'.

hormone replacement therapy noun treatment with certain hormones to make symptoms of the menopause or osteoporosis less severe.

horn noun **1** a hard bony outgrowth, often curved and pointed, found in pairs on the heads of cattle, sheep, and other animals. **2** the substance of which horns are composed. **3** a brass wind instrument, conical in shape or wound into a spiral. **4** an instrument sounding a signal. **5** a pointed projection or object.
– PHRASES **draw** (or **pull**) **in one's horns** become less assertive or ambitious. **horn in** informal interfere or intrude. **on the horns of a dilemma** faced with a decision involving equally unfavourable alternatives.
– DERIVATIVES **horned** adjective.
– ORIGIN Old English.

hornbeam noun a deciduous tree with hard pale wood.

hornbill noun a tropical bird with a horn-like structure on its large curved bill.

hornblende /horn-blend/ noun a dark brown, black, or green mineral present in many rocks.
– ORIGIN German.

hornet noun a kind of large wasp, typically red and yellow or red and black.
– PHRASES **stir up a hornets' nest** cause a situation full of difficulties or angry feelings.
– ORIGIN Old English.

horn of plenty noun a cornucopia.

hornpipe noun **1** a lively solo dance traditionally performed by sailors. **2** a piece of music for a hornpipe.

horn-rimmed adjective (of glasses) having rims made of horn or a similar substance.

horny adjective (**hornier, horniest**) **1** made of or resembling horn. **2** hard and rough. **3** informal sexually aroused or arousing.
– DERIVATIVES **horniness** noun.

horology /ho-rol-uh-ji/ noun **1** the study and measurement of time. **2** the art of making clocks and watches.
– DERIVATIVES **horological** adjective **horologist** noun.
– ORIGIN from Greek *hōra* 'time'.

horoscope /hor-uh-skohp/ noun a forecast of a person's future based on the relative positions of the stars and planets at the time of their birth.
– ORIGIN from Greek *hōra* 'time' + *skopos* 'observer'.

horrendous adjective highly unpleasant or horrifying.
– DERIVATIVES **horrendously** adverb.
– ORIGIN Latin *horrendus*.

h

horrible adjective 1 causing or likely to cause horror. 2 very unpleasant.
– DERIVATIVES **horribly** adverb.

horrid adjective 1 causing horror. 2 very unpleasant.
– DERIVATIVES **horridly** adverb **horridness** noun.

horrific adjective causing horror.
– DERIVATIVES **horrifically** adverb.

horrify verb (**horrifies**, **horrifying**, **horrified**) fill someone with horror.
– DERIVATIVES **horrified** adjective **horrifying** adjective.
– ORIGIN Latin *horrificare*.

horror noun 1 an intense feeling of fear, shock, or disgust. 2 a cause of horror. 3 intense dislike: *he had a horror of modernity.* 4 informal a badly behaved or mischievous child.
– ORIGIN from Latin *horrere* 'shudder, (of hair) stand on end'.

hors de combat /or duh kom-bah/ adjective out of action due to injury or damage.
– ORIGIN French, 'out of the fight'.

hors d'oeuvre /or derv/ noun (pl. same or **hors d'oeuvres** pronunc. same or /or dervz/) a savoury appetizer.
– ORIGIN French, 'outside the work'.

horse noun 1 a large four-legged mammal with a flowing mane and tail, used for riding and for pulling heavy loads. 2 an adult male horse, as opposed to a mare or colt. 3 (treated as sing. or pl.) cavalry. 4 a structure on which something is mounted or supported: *a clothes horse.* • verb (**horse around/about**) informal fool about.
– PHRASES **from the horse's mouth** from the person directly concerned in the matter. **hold one's horses** informal wait a moment.
– ORIGIN Old English.

horseback noun (in phrase **on horseback**) & adjective mounted on a horse.

horsebox noun Brit. a motorized vehicle or a trailer for transporting horses.

horse chestnut noun 1 a large deciduous tree producing nuts (conkers) enclosed in a spiny case. 2 a conker.
– ORIGIN horse chestnuts are said to have been an Eastern remedy for chest diseases in horses.

horseflesh noun horses considered as a group.

horsefly noun (pl. **horseflies**) a large fly that bites horses and other large mammals.

horsehair noun hair from the mane or tail of a horse, used in furniture for padding.

horse latitudes plural noun a belt of calm air and sea occurring in both the northern and southern hemispheres between the trade winds and the westerlies.
– ORIGIN uncertain.

horse laugh noun a loud, coarse laugh.

horseman (or **horsewoman**) noun (pl. **horsemen** or **horsewomen**) a rider on horseback, especially a skilled one.
– DERIVATIVES **horsemanship** noun.

horseplay noun rough, boisterous play.

horsepower noun (pl. same) an imperial unit of power equal to 550 foot-pounds per second (about 750 watts), especially as a measurement of engine power.

horseradish noun a plant grown for its strong-tasting root which is often made into a sauce.

horse sense noun informal common sense.

horseshoe noun a U-shaped iron band attached to the base of a horse's hoof.

horsetail noun a flowerless plant with a jointed stem and narrow leaves.

horse-trading noun informal hard and shrewd bargaining.

horsewhip noun a long whip used for driving and controlling horses. • verb (**horsewhips**, **horsewhipping**, **horsewhipped**) beat someone or something with a horsewhip.

horsey (also **horsy**) adjective 1 relating to or resembling a horse. 2 very interested in horses or horse racing.

horst noun Geology a raised elongated block of the earth's crust lying between two faults.
– ORIGIN German, 'heap'.

hortatory /hor-tuh-tuh-ri/ adjective formal strongly urging someone to do something.
– ORIGIN from Latin *hortari* 'exhort'.

horticulture /hor-ti-kul-cher/ noun the art or practice of garden cultivation and management.
– DERIVATIVES **horticultural** adjective **horticulturist** (also **horticulturalist**) noun.
– ORIGIN from Latin *hortus* 'garden'.

hosanna (also **hosannah**) noun & exclamation a biblical cry of praise or joy.
– ORIGIN from a Hebrew phrase meaning 'save, we pray'.

hose noun 1 (Brit. also **hosepipe**) a flexible tube conveying water. 2 (treated as pl.) stockings, socks, and tights. • verb water or spray something with a hose.
– ORIGIN Old English.

hosiery noun stockings, socks, and tights.

hospice noun 1 a home providing care for people who are sick or terminally ill. 2 old use a lodging for travellers, especially one run by a religious order.
– ORIGIN Latin *hospitium*.

hospitable adjective 1 friendly and welcoming to guests or strangers. 2 (of an environment) pleasant and favourable for living in.
– DERIVATIVES **hospitably** adverb.

hospital noun an institution providing medical and surgical treatment and nursing care for sick or injured people.
– ORIGIN Latin *hospitale*.

hospitality noun the friendly and generous treatment of guests or strangers.

hospitalize (or **hospitalise**) verb admit someone to hospital for treatment.
– DERIVATIVES **hospitalization** noun.

hospitaller (US **hospitaler**) noun a member of a charitable religious order.

hospital trust noun a UK National Health Service hospital which has opted to withdraw from local authority control and be managed by a trust instead.

Host noun (**the Host**) the bread consecrated in the Christian Eucharist (Holy Communion).
– ORIGIN Latin *hostia* 'victim'.

host¹ noun 1 a person who receives or entertains guests. 2 the presenter of a television or radio programme. 3 a place or organization that holds and organizes an event to which others are invited. 4 a

computer which mediates multiple access to databases or provides other services to a network. **5** an animal or plant on or in which a parasite lives. • **verb** act as host at an event or for a television or radio programme.
– ORIGIN Latin *hospes* 'host, guest'.

host² noun (**a host/hosts of**) a large number of people or things.
– ORIGIN Latin *hostis* 'stranger, enemy', later 'army'.

hosta /hos-tuh/ noun a shade-tolerant plant with ornamental foliage.
– ORIGIN named after the Austrian physician Nicolaus T. *Host*.

hostage noun a person held prisoner in an attempt to make others give in to a demand.
– PHRASES **a hostage to fortune** an act or remark regarded as unwise because it invites trouble in the future.
– ORIGIN Latin *obsidatus* 'the state of being a hostage'.

hostel noun an establishment which provides cheap food and lodging for a particular group of people.
– ORIGIN Old French.

hostelling (US **hosteling**) noun the practice of staying in youth hostels when travelling.
– DERIVATIVES **hosteller** noun.

hostelry noun (pl. **hostelries**) old use or humorous an inn or pub.
– ORIGIN Old French *hostelerie* .

hostess noun **1** a female host. **2** a woman employed to welcome and entertain customers at a nightclub or bar.

hostile adjective **1** showing or feeling dislike or opposition. **2** relating to a military enemy. **3** (of a takeover bid) opposed by the company to be bought.
– DERIVATIVES **hostilely** adverb.
– ORIGIN from Latin *hostis* 'stranger, enemy'.

hostility noun (pl. **hostilities**) **1** hostile behaviour. **2** (**hostilities**) acts of warfare: *a cessation of hostilities*.

hot adjective (**hotter**, **hottest**) **1** having a high temperature. **2** feeling or producing an uncomfortable sensation of heat. **3** feeling or showing anger, lust, or other strong emotion. **4** informal currently popular, fashionable, or interesting: *they know the hottest dance moves*. **5** informal very knowledgeable or skilful: *she's very hot on local history*. **6** (**hot on**) informal strict about something. **7** informal (of goods) stolen. • **verb** (**hots**, **hotting**, **hotted**) (**hot up** or **hot something up**) Brit. informal become or make more intense or exciting.
– PHRASES **have the hots for** informal be sexually attracted to someone. **hot under the collar** informal angry or resentful. **in hot water** informal in trouble. **make it** (or **things**) **hot for** informal stir up trouble for someone.
– DERIVATIVES **hotly** adverb **hotness** noun.
– ORIGIN Old English.

hot air noun informal empty or boastful talk.

hot-air balloon noun another term for **BALLOON** (in sense 2).

hotbed noun **1** an environment where a particular activity happens or flourishes: *the country was a hotbed of revolt*. **2** a bed of earth heated by fermenting manure, for raising or forcing plants.

hot-blooded adjective lustful; passionate.

hot button noun N. Amer. informal a political or social issue that arouses passionate emotions or debate.

hotchpotch (N. Amer. **hodgepodge**) noun a confused mixture.
– ORIGIN Old French *hochepot*.

hot cross bun noun a bun marked with a cross, traditionally eaten on Good Friday.

hot-desking noun the allocation of desks to office workers when they are required or on a rota system.

hot dog noun a hot sausage served in a long, soft roll. • **verb** (**hotdog**) (**hotdogs**, **hotdogging**, **hotdogged**) N. Amer. informal perform stunts.

hotel noun an establishment providing accommodation and meals for travellers and tourists.
– ORIGIN French *hôtel*.

> USAGE: It is better to say **a hotel** rather than **an hotel** because the normal pronunciation of **hotel** sounds the **h-**. The pronunciation of **hotel** without the **h-** is still sometimes heard, giving rise to the use of **an** instead of **a**, but many people now think that this is rather old fashioned.

hotelier noun a person who owns or manages a hotel.

hot flush (N. Amer. also **hot flash**) noun a sudden feeling of heat in the skin or face, often as a symptom of the menopause.

hotfoot adverb in eager haste. • **verb** (**hotfoot it**) hurry eagerly.

hothead noun a rash or quick-tempered person.
– DERIVATIVES **hot-headed** adjective.

hothouse noun **1** a heated greenhouse. **2** an environment that encourages rapid growth or development. • **verb** educate a child to a higher level than is usual for their age.

hot key noun Computing a key or combination of keys providing quick access to a function within a program.

hotline noun a direct telephone line set up for a specific purpose.

hot money noun capital which is frequently transferred between financial institutions in an attempt to maximize interest or profit.

hot pants plural noun women's tight, brief shorts.

hotplate noun a flat heated metal or ceramic surface on an electric cooker.

hotpot (also **Lancashire hotpot**) noun Brit. a casserole of meat and vegetables with a covering layer of sliced potato.

hot potato noun informal a controversial issue that is difficult to deal with.

hot rod noun a motor vehicle that has been specially modified to give it extra power and speed. • **verb** (**hot-rod**) **1** modify a vehicle or other device to make it faster or more powerful. **2** drive a hot rod.
– DERIVATIVES **hot-rodder** noun.

hot seat noun (**the hot seat**) informal **1** the position of a person who carries full responsibility for something. **2** N. Amer. the electric chair.

hot shoe noun a socket on a camera with direct

h

electrical contacts for an attached flashgun or other accessory.

hotshot noun informal an important or exceptionally able person.

hot spot noun 1 a place of significant activity or danger. **2** a small area with a high temperature in comparison to its surroundings.

hot stuff noun informal **1** a person or thing of outstanding talent or interest. **2** a sexually exciting person, book, etc.

hot-tempered adjective easily angered.

Hottentot /hot-tuhn-tot/ **noun & adjective** offensive formerly used to refer to the Khoikhoi peoples of South Africa and Namibia.
– ORIGIN Dutch.

hot ticket noun informal a person or thing that is in great demand.

hot tub noun a large tub filled with hot bubbling water, used for recreation or therapy.

hot-water bottle (US also **hot-water bag**) **noun** a rubber container that is filled with hot water and used for warming a bed or part of the body.

hot-wire verb informal start the engine of a vehicle by bypassing the ignition switch.

Houdini /hoo-**dee**-ni/ **noun** a person skilled at escaping from difficult situations.
– ORIGIN named after the American magician and escape artist Harry *Houdini* (Erik Weisz).

houmous noun variant spelling of HUMMUS.

hound noun a dog of a breed used for hunting.
●**verb** harass or pursue relentlessly: *she was hounded by the media.*
– ORIGIN Old English.

houndstooth noun a large check pattern with notched corners.

hour noun 1 a period of 60 minutes, one of the twenty-four equal parts that a day is divided into. **2** a time of day specified as an exact number of hours from midnight or midday. **3** a period set aside for a particular purpose or activity: *leisure hours.* **4** a point in time: *the shop is half-full even at this hour.*
– PHRASES **on the hour 1** at an exact hour, or on each hour, of the day or night. **2** after a period of one hour.
– ORIGIN Greek *hōra* 'season, hour'.

hourglass noun a device with two connected glass bulbs containing sand that takes an hour to fall from the upper to the lower bulb.
●**adjective** shaped like an hourglass: *her hourglass figure.*

houri /**hoo**-ri/ **noun** (pl. **houris**) a beautiful young woman, especially one of the virgin companions of the faithful in the Muslim Paradise.
– ORIGIN from an Arabic word meaning 'having eyes with a marked contrast of black and white'.

hourly adjective 1 done or occurring every hour. **2** calculated hour by hour. ●**adverb 1** every hour. **2** by the hour.

house noun /howss/ **1** a building for people to live in. **2** a building devoted to a particular activity or purpose: *a house of prayer.* **3** a firm or institution: *a fashion house.* **4** a religious community that occupies a particular

building. **5** chiefly Brit. a group of pupils living in the same building at a boarding school. **6** a law-making assembly. **7** a dynasty: *the House of Stewart.* **8** (also **house music**) a style of fast electronic dance music. **9** Astrology a twelfth division of the celestial sphere. ●**adjective** /howss/ **1** (of an animal or plant) kept in or infesting buildings. **2** relating to medical staff resident at a hospital. **3** relating to a firm, institution, or society: *a house journal.* ●**verb** /howz/ **1** provide someone with shelter or accommodation. **2** provide space for: *the museum houses a collection of Roman sculpture.* **3** enclose or encase something.
– PHRASES **get on like a house on fire** informal have a very good and friendly relationship. **keep house** run a household. **on the house** at the management's expense. **put one's house in order** make necessary reforms.
– DERIVATIVES **houseful noun.**
– ORIGIN Old English.

house arrest noun the state of being kept as a prisoner in one's own house.

houseboat noun a boat which is fitted for use as a home.

housebound adjective unable to leave one's house, often due to illness or old age.

houseboy noun a boy or man employed to undertake domestic duties.

housebreaking noun the action of breaking into a building to commit a crime.
– DERIVATIVES **housebreaker noun.**

housecoat noun a woman's long, loose robe for casual wear around the house.

housefly noun (pl. **houseflies**) a common small fly often found in and around houses.

household noun a house and its occupants regarded as a unit.
– DERIVATIVES **householder noun.**

household name (also **household word**) **noun** a famous person or thing.

house-hunting noun the process of seeking a house to buy or rent.
– DERIVATIVES **house-hunter noun.**

house husband noun a man who lives with a partner and carries out the household duties traditionally done by a housewife.

housekeeper noun a person, typically a woman, employed to manage a household.
– DERIVATIVES **housekeeping noun.**

houseleek noun a succulent plant that grows on walls, with rosettes of fleshy leaves and small pink flowers.

house lights plural noun the lights in the auditorium of a theatre.

housemaid noun a female employee who cleans rooms.

housemaid's knee noun inflammation of the fluid-filled cavity covering the kneecap, often due to excessive kneeling.

houseman noun (pl. **housemen**) Brit. a house officer in a hospital.

house martin noun a black-and-white bird of the swallow family, nesting on buildings.

housemaster (or **housemistress**) **noun** chiefly Brit. a teacher in charge of a house at a boarding school.

housemate noun a person with whom one shares a house.

house mouse noun a greyish-brown mouse found abundantly as a scavenger in houses.

House of Commons noun the part of Parliament in the UK whose members are elected by voters.

house officer noun Brit. a recent medical graduate receiving supervised training in a hospital and acting as an assistant physician or surgeon.

House of Keys noun the part of Tynwald, the parliament of the Isle of Man, whose members are elected by voters.

House of Lords noun 1 the part of Parliament in the UK whose members are peers and bishops and are not elected by voters. 2 a committee of specially qualified members of the House of Lords, appointed as the ultimate judicial appeal court of England and Wales.

House of Representatives noun the lower house of the US Congress.

house-proud adjective very concerned with the cleanliness and appearance of one's home.

houseroom noun space or accommodation in one's house.
– PHRASES **not give something houseroom** Brit. be unwilling to have or consider something.

house-sit verb live in and look after a house while its owner is away.
– DERIVATIVES **house-sitter** noun.

Houses of Parliament plural noun the Houses of Lords and Commons in the UK regarded together.

house sparrow noun a common brown and grey sparrow that nests in the eaves and roofs of houses.

house style noun a company's preferred manner of presentation and layout of written material.

house-to-house adjective & adverb performed at or taken to each house in turn.

house-train verb train a pet to urinate and defecate outside the house.

housewares noun kitchen utensils and similar household items.

house-warming noun a party celebrating a move to a new home.

housewife noun (pl. **housewives**) a married woman whose main occupation is caring for her family and running the household.
– DERIVATIVES **housewifely** adjective **housewifery** /howss-**wif**-uh-ri/ noun.

housework noun cleaning and other work done in running a home.

housey-housey noun Brit. old-fashioned term for **BINGO**.

housing noun 1 houses and flats as a whole. 2 the provision of accommodation. 3 a rigid casing for a piece of equipment.

housing estate noun Brit. a residential area planned and built as a unit.

hove Nautical past tense of **HEAVE**.

hovel noun a small squalid or run-down dwelling.
– ORIGIN unknown.

hover verb 1 remain in one place in the air. 2 linger close at hand in an uncertain way. 3 remain near a particular level or between two states: *the temperature hovered around ten degrees.* • noun an act of hovering.

– DERIVATIVES **hoverer** noun.
– ORIGIN unknown.

hovercraft noun (pl. same) a vehicle or craft that travels over land or water on a cushion of air.

hoverfly noun (pl. **hoverflies**) a black and yellow fly which hovers in the air and feeds on nectar.

how adverb 1 in what way or by what means. 2 in what condition or health. 3 to what extent or degree. 4 the way in which.
– PHRASES **how about?** would you like? **how do you do?** said when meeting a person for the first time in a formal situation. **how many** what number. **how much** what amount or price. **how's that?** Cricket is the batsman out or not? (said to an umpire).
– ORIGIN Old English.

howbeit adverb old use nevertheless.

howdah /how-duh/ noun a seat for riding on the back of an elephant, usually having a canopy.
– ORIGIN Urdu.

howdy exclamation N. Amer. an informal friendly greeting.
– ORIGIN alternative of *how d'ye.*

how-d'ye-do (also **how-de-do**) noun informal an awkward or annoying situation.

however adverb 1 used to introduce a statement that contrasts with a previous one. 2 in whatever way or to whatever extent.

howitzer /how-it-ser/ noun a short gun for firing shells at a high angle.
– ORIGIN Dutch *houwitser.*

howl noun 1 a long wailing cry made by an animal. 2 a loud cry of pain, amusement, etc. • verb make a howling sound.
– ORIGIN probably imitating the sound.

howler noun informal a stupid mistake.

howling adjective informal great: *the meal was a howling success.*

howsoever formal or old use adverb to whatever extent. • conjunction in whatever way.

howzat exclamation Cricket shortened form of **how's that** (see **HOW**).

hoy exclamation used to attract someone's attention.

hoya /hoy-uh/ noun an evergreen climbing shrub with waxy flowers, native to SE Asia and the Pacific.
– ORIGIN named after the English gardener Thomas *Hoy.*

hoyden /hoy-duhn/ noun dated a girl who behaves in a high-spirited or wild way.
– DERIVATIVES **hoydenish** adjective.
– ORIGIN probably from Dutch *heiden* 'heathen'.

h.p. (also **HP**) abbreviation 1 high pressure. 2 Brit. hire purchase. 3 horsepower.

HQ abbreviation headquarters.

hr abbreviation hour.

HRH abbreviation Brit. Her (or His) Royal Highness.

HRT abbreviation hormone replacement therapy.

Hs symbol the chemical element hassium.

HST abbreviation (in the UK) high-speed train.

HTML abbreviation Computing Hypertext Markup Language.

HTTP abbreviation Computing Hypertext Transport (or Transfer) Protocol.

hub noun **1** the central part of a wheel, rotating on or with the axle. **2** the centre of an activity, region, or network.
– ORIGIN related to **HOB**.

hubbub noun **1** a loud, confused noise caused by a crowd. **2** a busy, noisy situation.
– ORIGIN perhaps Irish.

hubby noun (pl. **hubbies**) informal a husband.

hubcap noun a cover for the hub of a motor vehicle's wheel.

hubris /hyoo-briss/ noun excessive pride or self-confidence.
– DERIVATIVES **hubristic** adjective.
– ORIGIN Greek.

huckster noun **1** a person who sells small items, either door-to-door or from a stall. **2** a person who uses aggressive selling techniques.
– DERIVATIVES **hucksterism** noun.
– ORIGIN probably German.

huddle verb **1** crowd together. **2** curl one's body into a small space. •noun a number of people or things grouped closely together.
– ORIGIN perhaps German.

hue noun **1** a colour or shade. **2** technical the quality of a colour, dependent on its dominant wavelength, by virtue of which it is discernible as red, green, etc. **3** an aspect: *men of all political hues*.
– ORIGIN Old English.

hue and cry noun clamour or public outcry.
– ORIGIN from Old French *hu e cri* 'outcry and cry'.

huff verb (often in phrase **huff and puff**) **1** breathe out noisily. **2** show one's annoyance in an obvious way. •noun a fit of petty annoyance.
– ORIGIN imitating the sound.

huffy adjective (**huffier, huffiest**) easily offended.
– DERIVATIVES **huffily** adverb **huffiness** noun.

hug verb (**hugs, hugging, hugged**) **1** hold someone or something tightly in one's arms or against one's body. **2** keep close to: *a few craft hugged the shore.* •noun an act of hugging.
– DERIVATIVES **huggable** adjective **hugger** noun.
– ORIGIN probably Scandinavian.

huge adjective (**huger, hugest**) very large; enormous.
– DERIVATIVES **hugely** adverb **hugeness** noun.
– ORIGIN Old French *ahuge*.

hugger-mugger noun **1** confusion or disorder. **2** secrecy. •adjective **1** confused or disorderly. **2** secret.
– ORIGIN probably related to **HUDDLE** and to dialect *mucker* 'hoard money, conceal'.

Huguenot /hyoo-guh-noh/ noun a French Protestant of the 16th–17th centuries.
– ORIGIN French.

huh exclamation used to express scorn or surprise, or in questions to invite agreement.

hula /hoo-luh/ (also **hula-hula**) noun a dance performed by Hawaiian women, in which the dancers sway their hips.
– ORIGIN Hawaiian.

hula hoop (also US trademark **Hula-Hoop**) noun a large hoop spun round the body by gyrating the hips.

hulk noun **1** an old ship stripped of fittings and permanently moored. **2** a large or clumsy person or thing.
– ORIGIN Old English, 'fast ship'.

hulking adjective informal very large or clumsy.

hull[1] noun the main body of a ship or other vessel.
– DERIVATIVES **hulled** adjective.
– ORIGIN perhaps the same word as **HULL**[2], or related to **HOLD**[2].

hull[2] noun **1** the outer covering of a fruit or seed. **2** the cluster of leaves and stalk on a strawberry or raspberry. •verb remove the hulls from strawberries or raspberries.
– ORIGIN Old English.

hullabaloo noun informal a commotion or uproar.
– ORIGIN from *hallo, hullo*, etc.

hullo exclamation variant spelling of **HELLO**.

hum verb (**hums, humming, hummed**) **1** make a low continuous sound like that of a bee. **2** sing with closed lips. **3** informal be in a very busy state. **4** Brit. informal smell unpleasant. •noun a low continuous sound.
– PHRASES **hum and haw** Brit. be unable to make up one's mind.
– DERIVATIVES **hummable** adjective **hummer** noun.
– ORIGIN imitating the sound.

human adjective **1** relating to or characteristic of human beings. **2** showing the better qualities of human beings, such as kindness. •noun (also **human being**) a person.
– DERIVATIVES **humanly** adverb **humanness** noun.
– ORIGIN from Latin *homo* 'man, human being'.

humane /hyuu-**mayn**/ adjective **1** kind or considerate towards people or animals. **2** formal (of a branch of learning) intended to civilize people.
– DERIVATIVES **humanely** adverb **humaneness** noun.

human interest noun the aspect of a news story that interests people because it describes other people's experiences or emotions.

humanism noun **1** a system of thought that regards people as capable of using their intelligence to live their lives, rather than relying on religious belief. **2** a Renaissance cultural movement which revived interest in ancient Greek and Roman thought.
– DERIVATIVES **humanist** noun & adjective **humanistic** adjective.

humanitarian /hyuu-man-i-**tair**-i-uhn/ adjective concerned with or seeking to improve human welfare: *humanitarian aid.* •noun a humanitarian person.
– DERIVATIVES **humanitarianism** noun.

USAGE: Sentences such as *this is the worst humanitarian disaster this country has seen* are a loose use of **humanitarian** to mean 'human'. This use is especially common in journalism but is best avoided in careful writing.

humanity noun (pl. **humanities**) **1** human beings as a whole. **2** the condition of being human. **3** sympathy and kindness towards other people. **4** (**humanities**) studies concerned with human culture, such as literature, art, or history.

humanize (or **humanise**) verb **1** make something more pleasant or suitable for people. **2** give a human character to something.
– DERIVATIVES **humanization** noun.

humankind noun human beings as a whole.

human nature noun the general characteristics and feelings shared by all people.

humanoid /hyoo-muh-noyd/ adjective resembling a human in appearance or character. • noun a being resembling a human.

human rights plural noun basic rights to which every person is entitled, such as freedom.

humble adjective (**humbler**, **humblest**) **1** having or showing a modest or low estimate of one's own importance. **2** of low rank. **3** not large or special: *a small, humble chalet.* • verb make someone feel less important or proud.
– PHRASES **eat humble pie** make a humble apology and accept humiliation. [from former *umbles* meaning 'offal', considered inferior food.]
– DERIVATIVES **humbly** adverb.
– ORIGIN Latin *humilis* 'low, lowly'.

humblebee noun dated another term for **BUMBLEBEE**.
– ORIGIN probably from German *hummel* 'to buzz' + *bē* 'bee'.

humbug noun **1** false or misleading talk or behaviour. **2** a person who is not sincere or honest. **3** Brit. a boiled peppermint sweet.
– DERIVATIVES **humbuggery** noun.
– ORIGIN unknown.

humdinger /hum-ding-er/ noun informal a remarkable or outstanding person or thing.
– ORIGIN unknown.

humdrum adjective lacking excitement or variety; dull.
– ORIGIN probably from **HUM**.

humectant /hyuu-mek-tuhnt/ adjective retaining or preserving moisture. • noun a substance used to reduce the loss of moisture.
– ORIGIN from Latin *humectare* 'moisten'.

humerus /hyoo-muh-ruhss/ noun (pl. **humeri** /hyoo-muh-ry/) the bone of the upper arm, between the shoulder and the elbow.
– DERIVATIVES **humeral** adjective.
– ORIGIN Latin, 'shoulder'.

humid /hyoo-mid/ adjective (of the air or weather) damp and warm.
– DERIVATIVES **humidly** adverb **humidity** noun.
– ORIGIN Latin *humidus*.

humidify verb (**humidifies**, **humidifying**, **humidified**) (often as adj. **humidified**) increase the level of moisture in air.
– DERIVATIVES **humidification** noun **humidifier** noun.

humidor /hyoo-mi-dor/ noun an airtight container for keeping cigars or tobacco moist.

humiliate verb make someone feel ashamed or foolish in front of another.
– DERIVATIVES **humiliating** adjective **humiliation** noun **humiliator** noun.
– ORIGIN Latin *humiliare* 'make humble'.

humility noun the quality of having a modest view of one's importance.

hummingbird noun a small long-billed tropical American bird able to hover by beating its wings extremely fast.

hummock noun a small hill or mound.
– DERIVATIVES **hummocky** adjective.
– ORIGIN unknown.

hummus /huu-muhss/ (also **houmous**) noun a thick Middle Eastern dip made from chickpeas puréed with olive oil and garlic.
– ORIGIN Arabic.

humongous /hyoo-mung-guhss/ (also **humungous**) adjective informal, chiefly N. Amer. very large; enormous.
– ORIGIN perhaps from **HUGE** and **MONSTROUS**.

humor noun US spelling of **HUMOUR**.

humorist noun a writer or speaker who is known for being amusing.

humorous adjective **1** causing amusement. **2** having or showing a sense of humour.
– DERIVATIVES **humorously** adverb **humorousness** noun.

humour (US **humor**) noun **1** the quality of being amusing. **2** a state of mind: *her good humour vanished.* **3** (also **cardinal humour**) each of four fluids of the body that were formerly believed to determine a person's physical and mental qualities. • verb agree with someone's wishes so as to keep the person in a good mood.
– PHRASES **out of humour** in a bad mood.
– DERIVATIVES **humourless** adjective.
– ORIGIN Latin *humor* 'moisture'.

hump noun **1** a rounded raised mass of earth or land. **2** a rounded part projecting from the back of a camel or other animal or as an abnormality on a person's back. • verb **1** informal, chiefly Brit. lift or carry something heavy with difficulty. **2** (as adj. **humped**) having a hump. **3** vulgar slang have sex with someone.
– PHRASES **get the hump** Brit. informal become annoyed or sulky. **over the hump** informal past the most difficult part of something.
– DERIVATIVES **humpless** adjective **humpy** adjective.
– ORIGIN probably related to German *humpe* 'hump'.

humpback noun another term for **HUNCHBACK**.
– DERIVATIVES **humpbacked** adjective.

humpback bridge noun Brit. a small road bridge that slopes steeply on both sides.

humungous adjective variant spelling of **HUMONGOUS**.

humus /hyoo-muhss/ noun the organic component of soil, formed from dead and dying leaves and other plant material.
– ORIGIN Latin, 'soil'.

Hun noun **1** a member of an Asiatic people who invaded Europe in the 4th–5th centuries. **2** informal, derogatory a German (especially during the First and Second World Wars).
– ORIGIN Greek *Hounnoi*.

hunch verb raise one's shoulders and bend the top of one's body forward. • noun a belief that something is true, based on a feeling rather than evidence.
– ORIGIN unknown.

hunchback noun offensive a person with a hump on his or her back.
– DERIVATIVES **hunchbacked** adjective.

hundred cardinal number **1** ten more than ninety; 100. (Roman numeral: **c** or **C**.) **2** (**hundreds**) informal an unspecified large number. **3** used to express whole hours in the

h

twenty-four-hour system.
- PHRASES **a** (or **one**) **hundred per cent**
1 entirely. **2** informal completely fit and healthy.
3 informal maximum effort and commitment.
- DERIVATIVES **hundredfold** adjective & adverb
hundredth ordinal number.
- ORIGIN Old English.

hundreds and thousands plural noun Brit.
tiny coloured sugar strands used for
decorating cakes and desserts.

hundredweight noun (pl. same or
hundredweights) **1** (also **long
hundredweight**) Brit. a unit of weight equal to
112 lb (about 50.8 kg). **2** (also **short
hundredweight**) US a unit of weight equal to
100 lb (about 45.4 kg). **3** (also **metric
hundredweight**) a unit of weight equal to
50 kg.

hung past and past participle of **HANG**. adjective
1 (of an elected body in the UK and Canada)
having no political party with an overall
majority. **2** (of a jury) unable to agree on a
verdict. **3** (**hung up**) informal emotionally
confused or disturbed.

Hungarian /hung-**gair**-i-uhn/ noun **1** a person
from Hungary. **2** the official language of
Hungary. •adjective relating to Hungary.

hunger noun **1** a feeling of discomfort and a
need to eat, caused by a lack of food. **2** a strong
desire: *his hunger for money.* •verb (**hunger
after/for**) have a strong desire for someone or
something.
- ORIGIN Old English.

hunger strike noun a prolonged refusal to eat,
carried out as a protest by a prisoner.

hungover adjective suffering from a hangover.

hungry adjective (**hungrier, hungriest**) **1** feeling
or showing hunger. **2** having a strong desire: *a
party hungry for power.*
- DERIVATIVES **hungrily** adverb **hungriness** noun.

hunk noun **1** a large piece cut or broken from
something larger. **2** informal a strong, sexually
attractive man.
- DERIVATIVES **hunky** adjective.
- ORIGIN probably Dutch or German.

hunker verb **1** squat or crouch down low.
2 (**hunker down**) approach a task seriously.
- ORIGIN probably related to German *hocken.*

hunkers plural noun informal a person's haunches.
- ORIGIN from **HUNKER**.

hunky-dory adjective informal excellent.
- ORIGIN *hunky* from Dutch *honk* 'home'; the
origin of *dory* is unknown.

hunt verb **1** chase and kill a wild animal for
sport or food. **2** try to find by thorough
searching: *he desperately hunted for a new job.*
3 (**hunt someone down**) chase and capture
someone. **4** (as adj. **hunted**) appearing alarmed
or harassed. •noun **1** an act of hunting. **2** a
group of people who meet regularly to hunt
animals as a sport.
- DERIVATIVES **hunting** noun.
- ORIGIN Old English.

hunter noun **1** a person or animal that hunts.
2 a watch with a hinged cover protecting the
glass.
- DERIVATIVES **huntress** noun.

hunter-gatherer noun a member of a
nomadic people who live chiefly by hunting

and fishing, and harvesting wild food.

hunting ground noun a place where people
are likely to find what they are looking for.

Huntington's disease noun a hereditary
disease marked by degeneration of brain cells,
causing chorea (disorder of the nervous
system) and progressive dementia.
- ORIGIN named after the American neurologist
George *Huntington.*

huntsman noun (pl. **huntsmen**) **1** a person who
hunts. **2** an official in charge of hounds during
a fox hunt.

hurdle noun **1** one of a series of upright frames
which athletes in a race must jump over.
2 (**hurdles**) a hurdle race. **3** a problem or
difficulty that must be overcome: *the project
must still clear several hurdles before work can
start.* **4** a portable rectangular frame used as a
temporary fence. •verb **1** run in a hurdle race.
2 jump over a hurdle or other obstacle while
running.
- DERIVATIVES **hurdler** noun.
- ORIGIN Old English.

hurdy-gurdy /her-di-ger-di/ noun (pl. **hurdy-
gurdies**) **1** a musical instrument with a
droning sound played by turning a handle,
with keys worked by the other hand. **2** informal a
barrel organ.
- ORIGIN probably imitating the instrument's
sound.

hurl verb **1** throw someone or something with
great force. **2** shout abuse or insults.
- ORIGIN probably influenced by German
hurreln.

hurley noun **1** a stick used in the game of
hurling. **2** another term for **HURLING**.
- ORIGIN from **HURL**.

hurling noun an Irish game resembling hockey,
played with a shorter stick.

hurly-burly noun busy and noisy activity.
- ORIGIN from **HURL**.

hurrah (also **hooray, hurray**) exclamation used
to express joy or approval.
- ORIGIN alteration of **HUZZA**.

hurricane noun a severe storm with a violent
wind, in particular a tropical cyclone in the
Caribbean.
- ORIGIN Spanish *huracán.*

hurricane lamp noun an oil lamp in which the
flame is protected from the wind by a glass
tube.

hurry verb (**hurries, hurrying, hurried**) **1** move
or act quickly. **2** do quickly or too quickly:
guided tours tend to be hurried. •noun **1** great
speed or urgency in doing something. **2** a need
for speed or haste; urgency: *relax, what's the
hurry?*
- PHRASES **in a hurry** informal easily; readily: *you
won't forget that in a hurry.*
- DERIVATIVES **hurried** adjective **hurriedly** adverb.
- ORIGIN imitating the movement.

hurt verb (past and past part. **hurt**) **1** cause pain or
injury to someone. **2** feel pain. **3** upset or
distress someone. •noun **1** injury or pain.
2 unhappiness or distress.
- ORIGIN Old French *hurter* 'to strike'.

hurtful adjective causing mental pain or
distress.
- DERIVATIVES **hurtfully** adverb.

hurtle verb move at great speed, especially in

an uncontrolled way.
– ORIGIN from **HURT**.

husband noun a married man considered in relation to his wife. •verb use resources economically.
– ORIGIN Old Norse, 'master of a house'.

husbandman noun (pl. **husbandmen**) old use a farmer.

husbandry noun **1** the care, cultivation, and breeding of crops and animals; farming. **2** management and careful use of resources.

hush verb **1** make or become quiet. **2** (**hush something up**) prevent something from becoming public. •noun a silence.
– ORIGIN from former *husht* 'silent', 'be quiet!'

hush-hush adjective informal highly secret or confidential.

hush money noun informal money paid to someone to prevent them from revealing information.

husk noun the dry outer covering of some fruits or seeds. •verb remove the husk or husks from fruit or seeds.
– ORIGIN probably from German *hüske* 'sheath'.

husky¹ adjective (**huskier**, **huskiest**) **1** sounding low-pitched and slightly hoarse: *her deliciously husky voice.* **2** big and strong.
– DERIVATIVES **huskily** adverb **huskiness** noun.

husky² noun (pl. **huskies**) a powerful dog of a breed with a thick double coat, used in the Arctic for pulling sledges.
– ORIGIN from a North American dialect word meaning 'Eskimo'.

huss /hus/ noun Brit. a dogfish.
– ORIGIN unknown.

hussar /huu-**zar**/ noun (now only in titles) a soldier in a light cavalry regiment which adopted a dress uniform modelled on that of the Hungarian light horsemen of the 15th century.
– ORIGIN Hungarian *huszár*.

hussy noun (pl. **hussies**) an immoral or cheeky girl or woman.
– ORIGIN from **HOUSEWIFE**.

hustings noun (treated as pl. or sing.) (**the hustings**) the political meetings and other campaigning that take place before an election.
– ORIGIN Old Norse, 'household assembly held by a leader'.

hustle verb **1** push roughly; jostle. **2** (**hustle someone into**) pressure someone into doing something without time for consideration. **3** informal, chiefly N. Amer. obtain something dishonestly or by aggressive methods. **4** N. Amer. informal work as a prostitute. •noun busy movement and activity: *the hustle and bustle of the big city.*
– DERIVATIVES **hustler** noun.
– ORIGIN Dutch *hutselen* 'shake, toss'.

hut noun a small simple house or shelter.
– ORIGIN German *hütte*.

hutch noun a box with a wire mesh front, used for keeping rabbits or other small domesticated animals.
– ORIGIN Latin *hutica* 'storage chest'.

Hutu /**hoo**-too/ noun (pl. same or **Hutus** or **Bahutu** /buh-**hoo**-too/) a member of a people forming the majority population in Rwanda

and Burundi.

huzza /huu-**zah**/ (also **huzzah**) exclamation old use used to express approval or delight.
– ORIGIN perhaps first used as a sailor's cry.

hyacinth /**hy**-uh-sinth/ noun a plant with fragrant bell-shaped flowers.
– ORIGIN named after *Hyacinthus*, a youth loved by the god Apollo in Greek mythology.

hyaena noun variant spelling of **HYENA**.

hybrid /**hy**-brid/ noun **1** the offspring of two plants or animals of different species or varieties, such as a mule. **2** a thing made by combining two different elements: *tae-bo, a hybrid of aerobics and Thai kick-boxing.*
– DERIVATIVES **hybridity** noun.
– ORIGIN Latin *hybrida* 'offspring of a tame sow and wild boar, child of a freeman and slave, etc.'

hybridize (or **hybridise**) verb breed individuals of two different species or varieties to produce hybrids.
– DERIVATIVES **hybridization** noun.

hydra noun a minute freshwater invertebrate animal with a tubular body and a ring of tentacles around the mouth.
– ORIGIN named after the *Hydra* of Greek mythology, a snake with many heads that grew again if they were cut off.

hydrangea /hy-**drayn**-juh/ noun a shrub with large white, blue, or pink clusters of flowers.
– ORIGIN from Greek *hudro-* 'water' + *angeion* 'container'.

hydrant /**hy**-druhnt/ noun a water pipe with a nozzle to which a fire hose can be attached.

hydrate noun /**hy**-drayt/ a compound in which water molecules are chemically bound to another compound or an element. •verb /hy-**drayt**/ cause something to absorb or combine with water.
– DERIVATIVES **hydration** noun.

hydraulic /hy-**dro**-lik/ adjective relating to or operated by a liquid moving in a confined space under pressure.
– DERIVATIVES **hydraulically** adverb.
– ORIGIN from Greek *hudro-* 'water' + *aulos* 'pipe'.

hydraulics plural noun (usu. treated as sing.) the branch of science concerned with the use of liquids moving under pressure to provide mechanical force.

hydride /**hy**-dryd/ noun Chemistry a compound of hydrogen with a metal.

hydro noun (pl. **hydros**) **1** Brit. a hotel or health farm providing hydropathic and other treatment. **2** a hydroelectric power plant.

hydro- (also **hydr-**) combining form **1** relating to water or fluid: *hydraulic.* **2** combined with hydrogen: *hydrocarbon.*
– ORIGIN from Greek *hudōr* 'water'.

hydrocarbon noun a compound of hydrogen and carbon, such as any of those which are the chief components of petroleum and natural gas.

hydrocephalus /hy-druh-**sef**-uh-luhss/ noun a condition in which fluid accumulates in the brain.
– DERIVATIVES **hydrocephalic** adjective **hydrocephaly** noun.

h

– ORIGIN from Greek *hudro-* 'water' + *kephalē* 'head'.

hydrochloric acid noun a corrosive acid containing hydrogen and chlorine.

hydrochloride noun a compound of an organic base with hydrochloric acid.

hydrocortisone /hy-druh-**kor**-ti-zohn/ noun a steroid hormone used to treat inflammation and rheumatism.

hydrocyanic acid /hy-droh-sy-**an**-ik/ noun a highly poisonous acidic solution of hydrogen cyanide.

hydrodynamics plural noun (treated as sing.) the branch of science concerned with the forces acting on or exerted by fluids (especially liquids).
– DERIVATIVES **hydrodynamic** adjective **hydrodynamically** adverb.

hydroelectric adjective relating to the generation of electricity using flowing water to drive a turbine which powers a generator.
– DERIVATIVES **hydroelectricity** noun.

hydrofoil noun 1 a boat fitted with structures (known as foils) which lift the hull clear of the water at speed. 2 each of the foils of a hydrofoil.

hydrogen /**hy**-druh-juhn/ noun a colourless, odourless, highly flammable gas which is the lightest of the chemical elements.

hydrogenate /hy-**droj**-uh-nayt/ verb combine a substance with hydrogen.
– DERIVATIVES **hydrogenation** noun.

hydrogen bomb noun a nuclear bomb whose destructive power comes from the fusion of isotopes of hydrogen (deuterium and tritium).

hydrogen peroxide noun a colourless liquid used in some disinfectants and bleaches.

hydrogen sulphide noun a colourless poisonous gas with a smell of bad eggs, made by the action of acids on sulphides.

hydrography /hy-**drog**-ruh-fi/ noun the science of surveying and charting seas, lakes, and rivers.
– DERIVATIVES **hydrographer** noun **hydrographic** adjective.

hydrology noun the branch of science concerned with the properties and distribution of water on the earth's surface.
– DERIVATIVES **hydrologic** adjective **hydrological** adjective **hydrologist** noun.

hydrolyse /**hy**-druh-lyz/ (or US **hydrolyze**) verb break down a compound by chemical reaction with water.

hydrolysis /hy-**drol**-i-siss/ noun Chemistry the chemical breakdown of a compound due to reaction with water.
– DERIVATIVES **hydrolytic** adjective.

hydrometer /hy-**drom**-i-ter/ noun an instrument for measuring the density of liquids.

hydropathy /hy-**drop**-uh-thi/ noun the treatment of illness through the use of water, either internally or by external means such as steam baths.
– DERIVATIVES **hydropathic** adjective.

hydrophilic /hy-druh-**fil**-ik/ adjective having a tendency to mix with or dissolve in water.

hydrophobia noun 1 extreme fear of water,

especially as a symptom of rabies. 2 rabies.

hydrophobic adjective 1 tending to repel or fail to mix with water. 2 relating to or suffering from hydrophobia.

hydrophone noun a microphone which detects sound waves under water.

hydroplane noun 1 a light, fast motorboat designed to skim over the surface of water. 2 a fin-like attachment which enables a moving submarine to rise or fall in the water. 3 US a seaplane. ● verb N. Amer. another term for **AQUAPLANE**.

hydroponics /hy-druh-**pon**-iks/ plural noun (treated as sing.) the growing of plants in sand, gravel, or liquid, with added nutrients but without soil.
– DERIVATIVES **hydroponic** adjective **hydroponically** adverb.
– ORIGIN from Greek *hudōr* 'water' + *ponos* 'labour'.

hydrosphere noun the seas, lakes, and other waters of the earth's surface, considered as a group.

hydrostatic adjective relating to the pressure and other characteristics of liquid that is not in motion.
– DERIVATIVES **hydrostatics** plural noun.

hydrotherapy noun 1 the use of exercises in a pool to treat conditions such as arthritis. 2 another term for **HYDROPATHY**.

hydrothermal adjective relating to the action of heated water in the earth's crust.
– DERIVATIVES **hydrothermally** adverb.

hydrothermal vent noun an opening in the sea floor out of which heated mineral-rich water flows.

hydrous adjective containing water.

hydroxide noun a compound containing OH negative ions together with a metallic element.

hydroxyl /hy-**drok**-syl, hy-**drok**-sil/ noun Chemistry the radical −OH, present in alcohols and many other organic compounds.

hyena (also **hyaena**) noun a doglike carnivorous African mammal with an erect mane.
– ORIGIN Greek *huaina* 'female pig'.

hygiene noun conditions or practices that help to prevent illness or disease, especially the keeping of oneself and one's surroundings clean.
– ORIGIN from Greek *hugieinē tekhnē* 'art of health'.

hygienic adjective clean and free of the organisms which spread disease.
– DERIVATIVES **hygienically** adverb.

hygienist noun a person working with a dentist who specializes in scaling and polishing teeth and giving advice on oral hygiene.

hygrometer /hy-**grom**-i-ter/ noun an instrument for measuring humidity.
– ORIGIN Greek *hugros* 'wet'.

hygroscopic /hy-groh-**skop**-ik/ adjective tending to absorb moisture from the air.

hying present participle of **HIE**.

hymen /**hy**-muhn/ noun a membrane which partially closes the opening of the vagina and is usually broken on the first occasion a

woman or girl has sex.
– ORIGIN Greek *humēn* 'membrane'.

hymeneal /hy-mi-**nee**-uhl/ adjective literary relating to marriage.
– ORIGIN from *Hymen*, the Greek god of marriage.

hymenopterous /hy-muh-**nop**-tuh-ruhss/ noun (of an insect) belonging to a large group that includes the bees, wasps, and ants, having four transparent wings.
– ORIGIN Greek *humenopteros* 'membrane-winged'.

hymn noun a religious song of praise, especially a Christian song in praise of God. •verb praise or celebrate something.
– ORIGIN Greek *humnos* 'ode or song in praise'.

hymnal /**him**-nuhl/ noun a book of hymns.

hymnody /**him**-nuh-di/ noun the singing or composing of hymns.
– ORIGIN Greek *humnōidia*.

hyoid /**hy**-oyd/ noun a U-shaped bone in the neck which supports the tongue. •adjective relating to this bone.
– ORIGIN from Greek *huoeidēs* 'shaped like the letter upsilon (υ)'.

hyoscine /**hy**-uh-seen/ noun a poisonous substance found in plants, used especially to prevent travel sickness.
– ORIGIN from Greek *huoskamos* 'henbane'.

hype[1] informal noun extravagant or excessive publicity or sales promotion. •verb publicize something in an excessive or extravagant way.
– ORIGIN unknown.

hype[2] verb (**be hyped up**) informal be stimulated or very excited.
– ORIGIN abbreviation of **HYPODERMIC**.

hyper adjective informal full of nervous energy; hyperactive.

hyper- prefix 1 over; beyond; above: *hypersonic*. 2 excessively; above normal: *hyperactive*.
– ORIGIN Greek *huper* 'over, beyond'.

hyperactive adjective abnormally or extremely active.
– DERIVATIVES **hyperactivity** noun.

hyperbaric /hy-puh-**bar**-ik/ adjective relating to or involving a gas at a pressure greater than normal.
– ORIGIN from Greek *barus* 'heavy'.

hyperbola /hy-**per**-buh-luh/ noun (pl. **hyperbolas** or **hyperbolae** /hy-**per**-buh-li/) a symmetrical curve formed when a cone is cut by a plane nearly parallel to the cone's axis.
– ORIGIN from Greek *huperbolē* 'excess'.

hyperbole /hy-**per**-buh-li/ noun a way of speaking or writing that deliberately exaggerates things for effect.
– ORIGIN Greek *huperbolē* 'excess'.

hyperbolic /hy-per-**bol**-ik/ adjective 1 (of language) deliberately exaggerated. 2 relating to a hyperbola.
– DERIVATIVES **hyperbolically** adverb.

hypercritical adjective excessively and unreasonably critical.

hyperdrive noun (in science fiction) a supposed propulsion system for travel in hyperspace.

hyperglycaemia /hy-per-gly-**see**-mi-uh/ (US **hyperglycemia**) noun an excess of glucose in the bloodstream, often associated with the commonest form of diabetes.
– DERIVATIVES **hyperglycaemic** adjective.

hypericin /hy-**per**-i-sin/ noun a substance found in the leaves and flowers of St John's wort, believed to have properties similar to those of antidepressant drugs.
– ORIGIN from **HYPERICUM**.

hypericum /hy-**per**-i-kuhm/ noun a yellow-flowered plant of a family that includes St John's wort.
– ORIGIN Greek *hupereikon*.

hyperinflation noun inflation of prices or wages occurring at a very high rate.

hyperlink noun Computing a link from a hypertext document to another location, activated by clicking on a highlighted word or image.

hypermarket noun Brit. a very large supermarket.

hypermedia noun Computing an extension to hypertext providing multimedia facilities, such as sound and video.

hyperreal adjective 1 exaggerated in comparison to reality. 2 (of art) extremely realistic.

hypersensitive adjective abnormally or excessively sensitive.

hypersonic adjective 1 relating to speeds of more than five times the speed of sound (Mach 5). 2 relating to sound frequencies above about a thousand million hertz.

hyperspace noun 1 space of more than three dimensions. 2 (in science fiction) a notional space–time continuum in which it is possible to travel faster than light.

hypertension noun abnormally high blood pressure.
– DERIVATIVES **hypertensive** adjective.

hypertext noun Computing a software system allowing users to move quickly between related documents or sections of text.

hyperthermia /hy-puh-**ther**-mi-uh/ noun the condition of having an abnormally high body temperature.

hyperthyroidism /hy-puh-**thy**-roy-di-z'm/ noun overactivity of the thyroid gland, resulting in an increased rate of metabolism.
– DERIVATIVES **hyperthyroid** adjective.

hypertrophy /hy-**per**-truh-fi/ noun abnormal enlargement of an organ or tissue resulting from an increase in size of its cells.
– DERIVATIVES **hypertrophic** adjective **hypertrophied** adjective.
– ORIGIN from Greek *-trophia* 'nourishment'.

hyperventilate verb 1 breathe at an abnormally rapid rate. 2 be or become overexcited.
– DERIVATIVES **hyperventilation** noun.

hypha /**hy**-fuh/ noun (pl. **hyphae** /**hy**-fi/) Botany each of the filaments that make up the mycelium of a fungus.
– ORIGIN Greek *huphē* 'web'.

hyphen /**hy**-fuhn/ noun the sign (-) used to join words to show that they have a combined meaning or that they are grammatically linked, or to divide a word into parts between one part and the next.
– ORIGIN from Greek *huphen* 'together'.

h

USAGE: When a phrasal verb such as **build up** is made into a noun it is usually written with a hyphen (a *build-up of pressure*). However, a normal phrasal verb should not have a hyphen: *continue to build up your pension.*

hyphenate verb write words with a hyphen.
– DERIVATIVES **hyphenation** noun.

hypnosis noun the practice of causing a person to enter a state of consciousness in which they lose the power of voluntary action and respond readily to suggestions or commands.
– ORIGIN Greek *hupnos* 'sleep'.

hypnotherapy noun the use of hypnosis to treat physical or mental problems.
– DERIVATIVES **hypnotherapist** noun.

hypnotic adjective 1 producing or relating to hypnosis. 2 causing one to feel very relaxed or drowsy. 3 (of a drug) causing sleep.
– DERIVATIVES **hypnotically** adverb.

hypnotism noun the study or practice of hypnosis.
– DERIVATIVES **hypnotist** noun.

hypnotize (or **hypnotise**) verb put someone into a state of hypnosis.

hypo- (also **hyp-**) prefix 1 under: *hypodermic*. 2 below normal: *hypoglycaemia*.
– ORIGIN from Greek *hupo* 'under'.

hypoallergenic adjective unlikely to cause an allergic reaction.

hypocaust /hy-per-kawst/ noun an ancient Roman heating system, consisting of a hollow space under the floor into which hot air was directed.
– ORIGIN Greek *hupokauston* 'place heated from below'.

hypochondria /hy-puh-**kon**-dri-uh/ noun excessive anxiety about one's health.
– ORIGIN Greek *hupokhondria*, referring to the soft body area below the ribs, once thought to be the seat of melancholy.

hypochondriac noun a person who is excessively worried about their health.

hypocrisy noun (pl. **hypocrisies**) the practice of claiming to have higher moral standards than is the case.
– ORIGIN Greek *hupokrisis* 'acting of a theatrical part'.

hypocrite noun a person who claims to have higher moral standards than is the case.
– DERIVATIVES **hypocritical** adjective **hypocritically** adverb.

hypodermic adjective 1 (of a needle or syringe) used to inject a drug or other substance beneath the skin. 2 relating to the region immediately beneath the skin. • noun a hypodermic syringe or injection.
– DERIVATIVES **hypodermically** adverb.
– ORIGIN from Greek *derma* 'skin'.

hypoglycaemia /hy-poh-gly-**see**-mi-uh/ (US **hypoglycemia**) noun lack of glucose in the bloodstream.
– DERIVATIVES **hypoglycaemic** adjective.

hypotension noun abnormally low blood pressure.
– DERIVATIVES **hypotensive** adjective.

hypotenuse /hy-**pot**-uh-nyooz/ noun the longest side of a right-angled triangle,

opposite the right angle.
– ORIGIN from Greek *hupoteinousa grammē* 'subtending line'.

hypothalamus /hy-puh-**thal**-uh-muhss/ noun (pl. **hypothalami** /hy-puh-**thal**-uh-my/) a region of the front part of the brain below the thalamus, controlling body temperature, thirst, and hunger, and involved in sleep and emotional activity.
– DERIVATIVES **hypothalamic** adjective.

hypothecate /hy-**poth**-i-kayt/ verb pledge money by law to be spent in a particular way.
– DERIVATIVES **hypothecation** noun.
– ORIGIN Latin *hypothecare* 'give as a pledge'.

hypothermia /hy-puh-**ther**-mi-uh/ noun the condition of having an abnormally low body temperature.
– ORIGIN from Greek *thermē* 'heat'.

hypothesis /hy-**poth**-i-siss/ noun (pl. **hypotheses** /hy-**poth**-i-seez/) a proposed explanation of something made on the basis of limited evidence, used as a starting point for further investigation.
– ORIGIN Greek *hupothesis* 'foundation'.

hypothesize (or **hypothesise**) verb put forward an explanation as a hypothesis.

hypothetical /hy-puh-**thet**-i-k'l/ adjective based on an assumption or imagined situation rather than fact.
– DERIVATIVES **hypothetically** adverb.

hypothyroidism /hy-poh-**thy**-roy-di-z'm/ noun abnormally low activity of the thyroid gland, resulting in retarded growth and mental development.
– DERIVATIVES **hypothyroid** adjective.

hypoxia /hy-**pok**-si-uh/ noun a situation in which not enough oxygen reaches the body tissues.
– DERIVATIVES **hypoxic** adjective.

hyrax /**hy**-raks/ noun a small mammal with a short tail, found in Africa and Arabia.
– ORIGIN Greek *hurax* 'shrew-mouse'.

hyssop /**hiss**-uhp/ noun a small bushy plant whose bitter minty leaves are used in cookery and herbal medicine.
– ORIGIN Greek *hyssōpos*.

hysterectomy /hiss-tuh-**rek**-tuh-mi/ noun (pl. **hysterectomies**) a surgical operation to remove all or part of the womb.
– ORIGIN from Greek *hustera* 'womb'.

hysteria noun 1 extreme or uncontrollable emotion or excitement: *a note of hysteria crept into his voice.* 2 dated a psychological disorder involving a change in self-awareness or the conversion of psychological stress into physical symptoms.
– ORIGIN Greek *hustera* 'womb' (hysteria once being thought to be caused by a disorder of the womb).

hysteric noun 1 (**hysterics**) wildly emotional behaviour. 2 (**hysterics**) informal uncontrollable laughter. 3 a person suffering from hysteria.

hysterical adjective 1 in a state of uncontrolled excitement or other strong emotion. 2 informal very funny.
– DERIVATIVES **hysterically** adverb.

Hz abbreviation hertz.

I¹ (also **i**) noun (pl. **Is** or **I's**) **1** the ninth letter of the alphabet. **2** the Roman numeral for one.

I² pronoun (first person sing.) used by a speaker to refer to himself or herself.
– ORIGIN Old English.

I³ abbreviation (**I.**) Island(s) or Isle(s). ●symbol the chemical element iodine.

IA abbreviation Iowa.

IAEA abbreviation International Atomic Energy Agency.

iambic /I-**am**-bik/ Poetry adjective (of poetry or poetic metre) using iambuses. ●noun (**iambics**) verse using iambuses.

iambus /I-**am**-buhss/ (also **iamb**) noun (pl. **iambuses** or **iambi** /I-**am**-by/) Poetry a metrical foot consisting of one short (or unstressed) syllable followed by one long (or stressed) syllable.
– ORIGIN Greek *iambos*.

iatrogenic /I-at-roh-**jen**-ik/ adjective (of illness) caused by medical treatment.
– ORIGIN Greek *iatros* 'physician'.

IBA abbreviation Independent Broadcasting Authority.

I-beam noun a girder which has the shape of a capital I when viewed in section.

Iberian adjective relating to Iberia (the peninsula that consists of modern Spain and Portugal). ●noun a person from Iberia.

ibex /**I**-beks/ noun (pl. **ibexes**) a wild mountain goat with long curved horns.
– ORIGIN Latin.

IBF abbreviation International Boxing Federation.

ibid. /**ib**-id/ adverb in the same source (referring to a work previously referred to).
– ORIGIN abbreviation of Latin *ibidem* 'in the same place'.

ibis /**I**-biss/ noun (pl. same or **ibises**) a large wading bird with a long downcurved bill, long neck, and long legs.
– ORIGIN Greek.

Ibizan /i-**beeth**-uhn/ noun a person from Ibiza. ●adjective relating to Ibiza.

IBM abbreviation International Business Machines.

IBS abbreviation irritable bowel syndrome.

ibuprofen /I-byoo-**proh**-fen/ noun a synthetic compound used as a painkiller and to reduce inflammation.
– ORIGIN from the chemical name.

IC abbreviation integrated circuit.

i/c abbreviation **1** in charge of. **2** in command.

ICBM abbreviation intercontinental ballistic missile.

ICC abbreviation International Cricket Council.

ice noun **1** frozen water, a brittle transparent crystalline solid. **2** chiefly Brit. an ice cream or water ice. ●verb **1** decorate something with icing. **2** (usu. **ice up/over**) become covered or blocked with ice.
– PHRASES **break the ice** start the conversation at the beginning of a social gathering so as to make people feel more relaxed. **on thin ice** in a precarious or risky situation.
– DERIVATIVES **iced** adjective.
– ORIGIN Old English.

ice age noun a period when ice sheets covered much of the earth's surface, in particular during the Pleistocene period.

ice beer noun a type of strong lager matured at a low temperature after the main fermentation is complete.

iceberg noun a large mass of ice floating in the sea.
– PHRASES **the tip of the iceberg** the small noticeable part of a much larger situation or problem.
– ORIGIN Dutch *ijsberg*.

iceberg lettuce noun a kind of lettuce having a closely packed round head of crisp pale leaves.

icebox noun **1** a chilled container for keeping food cold. **2** Brit. a compartment in a refrigerator for making and storing ice. **3** US dated a refrigerator.

icebreaker noun a ship designed for breaking a channel through ice.

ice cap noun a permanent covering of ice over a large area, especially at the North and South Poles.

ice cream noun a semi-soft frozen dessert made with sweetened and flavoured milk fat.

ice dancing noun a form of ice skating involving choreographed dance moves based on ballroom dances.

iced tea noun a chilled drink of sweetened black tea.

ice field noun a large permanent expanse of ice, especially at the North and South Poles.

ice hockey noun a form of hockey played on an ice rink between two teams of six skaters.

Icelander noun a person from Iceland.

Icelandic /Is-**lan**-dik/ noun the language of Iceland. ●adjective relating to Iceland or its language.

ice lolly noun Brit. a piece of flavoured water ice

or ice cream on a stick.

Iceni /I-**see**-ni, I-**see**-ny/ plural noun a tribe of ancient Britons living in an area of SE England, whose queen was Boudicca (Boadicea).
– ORIGIN Latin.

ice pack noun a bag filled with ice and held against part of the body to reduce swelling or lower temperature.

ice pick noun a small pick used by climbers or for breaking ice.

ice skate noun a boot with a blade attached to the sole, used for skating on ice. • verb (**ice-skate**) skate on ice as a sport or pastime.
– DERIVATIVES **ice skater** noun **ice skating** noun.

I Ching /ee ching/ noun an ancient Chinese manual for foretelling the future.
– ORIGIN Chinese, 'book of changes'.

ichneumon /ik-**nyoo**-muhn/ noun **1** a slender parasitic wasp which lays its eggs in or on the larvae of other insects. **2** the Egyptian mongoose.
– ORIGIN Greek *ikhneumōn* 'tracker'.

ichor /I-kor/ noun Greek Mythology the fluid said to flow like blood in the veins of the gods.
– ORIGIN Greek *ikhōr*.

ichthyology /ik-thi-**ol**-uh-ji/ noun the branch of zoology concerned with fish.
– DERIVATIVES **ichthyological** adjective **ichthyologist** noun.
– ORIGIN from Greek *ikhthus* 'fish'.

ichthyosaur /ik-thi-uh-sor/ (also **ichthyosaurus** /ik-thi-uh-**sor**-uhss/) noun a fossil marine reptile with a long pointed head, four flippers, and a vertical tail.

icicle noun a hanging, tapering piece of ice formed when dripping water freezes.
– ORIGIN from Old English.

icing noun a mixture of sugar with liquid or fat, used as a coating or filling for cakes or biscuits.
– PHRASES **the icing on the cake** an additional thing which makes something already good even better.

icing sugar noun Brit. finely powdered sugar used to make icing.

icky adjective informal, chiefly N. Amer. **1** unpleasantly sticky. **2** distastefully sentimental.
– ORIGIN perhaps related to SICK¹ or to the child's word *ickle* 'little'.

icon /I-kon/ noun **1** (also **ikon**) (in the Orthodox Church) a painting of Jesus or another holy figure, typically on wood, which is itself treated as holy and used as an aid to prayer. **2** a person or thing admired as a symbol of a particular idea, quality, time, etc.: *an iron-jawed icon of American manhood*. **3** a small symbol on a computer screen that represents a program, option, or window.
– ORIGIN Greek *eikōn* 'image'.

iconic /I-**kon**-ik/ adjective referring to someone or something regarded as a symbol of a particular idea, quality, period, etc.: *he became an iconic figure for directors around the world*.
– DERIVATIVES **iconically** adverb.

iconify verb (**iconifies, iconifying, iconified**) Computing reduce a window on a computer screen to an icon.

iconoclast /I-**kon**-uh-klast/ noun **1** a person

who attacks cherished beliefs or established values and practices. **2** (in the past) a person who destroyed images used in religious worship.
– DERIVATIVES **iconoclasm** noun **iconoclastic** adjective.
– ORIGIN from Greek *eikōn* 'image' + *klan* 'to break'.

iconography /I-kuh-**nog**-ruh-fi/ noun (pl. **iconographies**) **1** the use or study of images or symbols in visual arts. **2** the images or symbols associated with a person or movement. **3** the illustration of a subject by drawings or figures.
– DERIVATIVES **iconographer** noun **iconographic** adjective.

iconostasis /I-kuh-**nos**-tuh-siss/ noun (pl. **iconostases** /I-kuh-**nos**-tuh-seez/) a screen bearing icons, separating the sanctuary of many Eastern churches from the nave.
– ORIGIN from Greek *eikōn* 'image' + *stasis* 'standing'.

icosahedron /I-koss-uh-**hee**-druhn/ noun (pl. **icosahedra** /I-koss-uh-**hee**-druh/or **icosahedrons**) a three-dimensional shape with twenty plane faces.
– DERIVATIVES **icosahedral** adjective.
– ORIGIN from Greek *eikosaedros* 'twenty-faced'.

ICT abbreviation information and computing technology.

ICU abbreviation intensive-care unit.

icy adjective (**icier, iciest**) **1** covered with or consisting of ice. **2** very cold: *an icy wind.* **3** very unfriendly or hostile: *her voice was icy.*
– DERIVATIVES **icily** adverb **iciness** noun.

ID abbreviation **1** identification or identity. **2** Idaho.

Id noun variant spelling of **EID**.

I'd contraction **1** I had. **2** I should or I would.

id /id/ noun Psychoanalysis the part of the unconscious mind consisting of a person's basic inherited instinct, needs, and feelings. Compare with **EGO** and **SUPEREGO**.
– ORIGIN Latin, 'that'.

id. abbreviation idem.

idea noun **1** a thought or suggestion about a possible course of action. **2** a mental impression: *shop around to get an idea of what things cost.* **3** a belief: *nineteenth-century ideas about drinking.* **4** (**the idea**) the aim or purpose: *the idea was to bring people into bookshops.*
– ORIGIN Greek, 'form, pattern'.

ideal adjective **1** most suitable; perfect: *an ideal opportunity to brush up on her French.* **2** desirable or perfect but existing only in the imagination: *in an ideal world, we might have made a different decision.* • noun **1** a person or thing regarded as perfect. **2** a principle or standard that is worth trying to achieve: *tolerance and freedom, the liberal ideals.*
– DERIVATIVES **ideally** adverb.

idealism noun **1** the belief that ideals can be achieved, even when this is unrealistic. **2** (in art or literature) the representation of things as perfect or better than in reality.
– DERIVATIVES **idealist** noun **idealistic** adjective **idealistically** adverb.

idealize (or **idealise**) **verb** (often as adj. **idealized**) regard or represent as perfect or better than in reality: *her idealized accounts of their life together.*
– DERIVATIVES **idealization** noun.

idée fixe /ee-day feeks/ noun (pl. **idées fixes** pronunc. same) an idea that dominates someone's mind; an obsession.
– ORIGIN French, 'fixed idea'.

idem /i-dem/ adverb used in quotations to indicate an author or word that has just been mentioned.
– ORIGIN Latin, 'the same'.

ident /I-dent, I-dent/ noun a short sequence shown on television between programmes to identify the channel.

identical adjective **1** exactly alike or the same: *four girls in identical green outfits.* **2** (of twins) developed from a single fertilized ovum, and therefore of the same sex and very similar in appearance.
– DERIVATIVES **identically** adverb.
– ORIGIN Latin *identicus.*

identification noun **1** the action of identifying someone or something or the fact of being identified. **2** an official document or other proof of one's identity.

identify verb (**identifies, identifying, identified**) **1** prove or recognize who or what a person or thing is: *he couldn't identify his attackers.* **2** recognize something as being worthy of attention: *a system that ensures that the pupil's needs are identified.* **3** (**identify with**) feel that one understands or shares the feelings of another person. **4** (**identify with**) associate someone or something closely with.
– DERIVATIVES **identifiable** adjective **identifiably** adverb **identifier** noun.

identikit noun trademark a picture of a person wanted by the police, put together from a set of typical facial features according to witnesses' descriptions. ● adjective often derogatory very typical and ordinary; having few unique features: *identikit chain hotels.*

identity noun (pl. **identities**) **1** the fact of being who or what a person or thing is: *he knows the identity of the bombers.* **2** the characteristics determining who or what a person or thing is and distinguishing them from others: *a sense of national identity.* **3** a close similarity or feeling of understanding.
– ORIGIN Latin *identitas,* from *idem* 'same'.

identity parade noun Brit. a group of people assembled so that an eyewitness may identify a suspect for a crime from among them.

identity theft noun the fraudulent practice of using another person's name and personal information in order to obtain credit, loans, etc.

ideogram /id-i-uh-gram/ (also **ideograph**) noun a character used in a writing system to symbolize the idea of a thing rather than the sounds used to say it (e.g. a numeral).

ideologue /I-di-uh-log/ noun a person who follows a system of ideas and principles in a strict and inflexible way.

ideology /I-di-ol-uh-ji/ noun (pl. **ideologies**) **1** a system of ideas and principles forming the basis of an economic or political theory. **2** the set of beliefs held by a particular social group: *bourgeois ideology.*

– DERIVATIVES **ideological** adjective **ideologically** adverb **ideologist** noun.
– ORIGIN from Greek *idea* 'form'.

ides /rhymes with hides/ plural noun (in the ancient Roman calendar) a day falling roughly in the middle of each month, from which other dates were calculated.
– ORIGIN Latin *idus* (plural).

idiocy noun (pl. **idiocies**) extremely stupid behaviour.

idiolect /i-di-uh-lekt/ noun the way that a particular person uses language.
– ORIGIN from Greek *idios* 'own, distinct'.

idiom noun **1** a group of words whose meaning is different from the meanings of the individual words (e.g. *over the moon*). **2** a form of language and grammar used by particular people at a particular time or place. **3** a style of expression in music or art that is characteristic of a particular group or place: *a restrained classical idiom.*
– ORIGIN Greek *idiōma* 'private property'.

idiomatic adjective using or relating to expressions that are natural to a native speaker: *he spoke fluent, idiomatic English.*
– DERIVATIVES **idiomatically** adverb.

idiosyncrasy /id-i-oh-sing-kruh-si/ noun (pl. **idiosyncrasies**) **1** a distinctive or unusual way of behaving or thinking peculiar to a particular person. **2** a distinctive characteristic of something: *the idiosyncrasies of the prison system.*
– ORIGIN Greek *idiosunkrasia.*

idiosyncratic /id-i-oh-sing-krat-ik/ adjective peculiar or distinctively individual: *her idiosyncratic diet.*
– DERIVATIVES **idiosyncratically** adverb.

idiot noun **1** informal a stupid person. **2** old use a person of low intelligence.
– ORIGIN Greek *idiōtēs* 'layman, ignorant person'.

idiotic adjective very stupid or foolish.
– DERIVATIVES **idiotically** adverb.

idiot savant /i-di-oh sa-von/ noun (pl. **idiot savants** or **idiots savants** pronunc. same) a person who has a mental disability or learning difficulties but is gifted in a particular way, such as the ability to perform feats of memory.
– ORIGIN French, 'knowledgeable idiot'.

idle adjective (**idler, idlest**) **1** tending to avoid work; lazy. **2** not working or in use. **3** having no purpose or effect: *she did not make idle threats.* ● verb **1** spend time doing nothing. **2** (of an engine) run slowly while out of gear.
– DERIVATIVES **idleness** noun **idler** noun **idly** adverb.
– ORIGIN Old English, 'empty, useless'.

idol noun **1** a statue or picture of a god which is itself worshipped. **2** a person who is greatly admired: *a soccer idol.*
– ORIGIN Greek *eidōlon.*

idolatry /I-dol-uh-tri/ noun **1** the practice of worshipping statues or pictures of a god or gods. **2** extreme admiration or devotion.
– DERIVATIVES **idolater** noun **idolatrous** adjective.
– ORIGIN from Greek *eidōlon* 'idol' + *-latreia* 'worship'.

idolize (or **idolise**) **verb** admire or love someone greatly or excessively.
– DERIVATIVES **idolization** noun.

idyll /i-dil/ noun 1 a very happy or peaceful period or situation. 2 a short poem or piece or writing describing a picturesque country scene or incident.
– ORIGIN Greek *eidullion* 'little form'.
idyllic adjective extremely happy, peaceful, or picturesque.
– DERIVATIVES **idyllically** adverb.
i.e. abbreviation that is to say.
– ORIGIN from Latin *id est* 'that is'.
IF abbreviation intermediate frequency.
if conjunction 1 on the condition or in the event that. 2 despite the possibility or fact that. 3 whether. 4 every time that; whenever. 5 expressing a polite request or tentative opinion. 6 expressing surprise or regret. •noun a situation that is not certain: *if we can get promotion, and it's a big if since only one club goes up.*
– ORIGIN Old English.

> USAGE: **If** and **whether** are more or less interchangeable in sentences like *I'll see if he left an address* and *I'll see whether he left an address,* although **whether** is more formal and more suitable for written use.

iffy adjective (**iffier, iffiest**) informal 1 uncertain. 2 seeming bad or wrong in some way.
igloo noun a dome-shaped Eskimo house, typically built from blocks of solid snow.
– ORIGIN Inuit, 'house'.
igneous /ig-ni-uhss/ adjective Geology (of rock) formed when molten rock cools and solidifies.
– ORIGIN Latin *ignis* 'fire'.
ignite /ig-nyt/ verb 1 catch fire or set on fire. 2 provoke or stir up: *the words ignited new fury in him.*
– DERIVATIVES **igniter** noun.
– ORIGIN Latin *ignis* 'fire'.
ignition noun 1 the action of catching fire or setting something on fire. 2 the process of starting the combustion of fuel in the cylinders of an internal-combustion engine. 3 the mechanism for bring this about.
ignoble adjective (**ignobler, ignoblest**) 1 not good or honest; dishonourable. 2 of humble origin or social status.
– DERIVATIVES **ignobly** adverb.
– ORIGIN Latin *ignobilis.*
ignominious /ig-nuh-**min**-i-uhss/ adjective deserving or causing public disgrace or shame: *an ignominious defeat.*
– DERIVATIVES **ignominiously** adverb.
– ORIGIN Latin *ignominiosus.*
ignominy /ig-nuh-mi-ni/ noun public shame or disgrace.
ignoramus /ig-nuh-**ray**-muhss/ noun (pl. **ignoramuses**) an ignorant or stupid person.
– ORIGIN Latin, 'we do not know'.
ignorance noun lack of knowledge or information.
ignorant adjective 1 lacking knowledge or education. 2 (often **ignorant of**) not informed about or aware of a particular subject or fact: *I was ignorant of the effects of radiotherapy.* 3 informal not polite; rude.
– DERIVATIVES **ignorantly** adverb.
– ORIGIN from Latin *ignorare* 'not know'.
ignore verb 1 deliberately take no notice of: *I shouted to her but she ignored me.* 2 fail to consider something important.
– ORIGIN Latin *ignorare* 'not know'.
iguana /i-**gwah**-nuh/ noun a large tropical American lizard with a spiny crest along the back.
– ORIGIN Arawak.
ikat /ee-kat, i-kat/ noun fabric made using an Indonesian technique in which threads are tie-dyed before weaving.
– ORIGIN from Malay, 'fasten, tie'.
ikebana /i-ki-**bah**-nuh/ noun the art of Japanese flower arrangement.
– ORIGIN Japanese, 'living flowers'.
ikon noun variant spelling of **ICON** (in sense 1).
IL abbreviation Illinois.
ileum /il-i-uhm/ noun (pl. **ilea** /il-i-uh/) the third and lowest part of the small intestine, between the jejunum and the caecum.
– ORIGIN Latin, variant of **ILIUM.**
ilex /I-leks/ noun 1 the holm oak. 2 a tree or shrub of a family that includes holly.
– ORIGIN Latin.
iliac /il-i-ak/ adjective relating to the ilium or the nearby regions of the lower body.
ilium /il-i-uhm/ noun (pl. **ilia** /il-i-uh/) the large broad bone forming the upper part of each half of the pelvis.
– ORIGIN Latin.
ilk noun a type: *fascists, racists, and others of that ilk.*
– ORIGIN Old English, related to **ALIKE.**
I'll contraction I shall; I will.
ill adjective 1 not in good health; unwell. 2 bad, harmful, or unfavourable: *she suffered no ill effects.* •adverb 1 badly, wrongly, or imperfectly: *ill-chosen.* 2 only with difficulty: *she could ill afford the cost.* •noun 1 a problem or misfortune. 2 evil or harm.
– PHRASES **ill at ease** uncomfortable or embarrassed.
– ORIGIN Old Norse, 'evil, difficult'.
ill-advised adjective unwise or badly thought out.
ill-assorted adjective not well matched.
ill-bred adjective badly brought up or rude.
ill-conceived adjective not carefully planned or considered.
ill-disposed adjective unfriendly or unsympathetic.
illegal adjective against the law.
– DERIVATIVES **illegality** (pl. **illegalities**) noun **illegally** adverb.

> USAGE: **Illegal** and **unlawful** have slightly different meanings. An illegal act is against the law, but an **unlawful** one only goes against the rules that apply in a particular situation. For example, handball in football is **unlawful**, but not **illegal.**

illegible /il-**lej**-i-b'l/ adjective not clear enough to be read.
– DERIVATIVES **illegibility** noun **illegibly** adverb.
illegitimate /il-li-**jit**-i-muht/ adjective 1 not allowed by law or a particular set of rules: *the strike was condemned as illegitimate.* 2 (of a child) having parents who are not married to each other.

- DERIVATIVES **illegitimacy** noun **illegitimately** adverb.

ill-equipped adjective not having the necessary equipment or resources.

ill-fated adjective destined to fail or have bad luck.

ill-favoured (US **ill-favored**) adjective unattractive.

ill-founded adjective not based on fact or reliable evidence.

ill-gotten adjective acquired by illegal or unfair means.

illiberal adjective restricting freedom of thought or behaviour.

illicit adjective forbidden by law, rules, or accepted standards: *an illicit relationship.*
- DERIVATIVES **illicitly** adverb.
- ORIGIN Latin *illicitus.*

illimitable adjective having no limits or end.
- DERIVATIVES **illimitably** adverb.

illiterate /il-**lit**-uh-ruht/ adjective **1** unable to read or write. **2** having no knowledge of a particular subject or activity: *voters who are politically illiterate.*
- DERIVATIVES **illiteracy** noun.

ill-judged adjective lacking careful thought; unwise.

ill-natured adjective bad-tempered and sullen.

illness noun a disease or period of sickness.

illogical adjective not sensible or based on sound reasoning.
- DERIVATIVES **illogicality** noun (pl. **illogicalities**) **illogically** adverb.

ill-omened adjective accompanied by bad omens.

ill-starred adjective unlucky.

ill-tempered adjective irritable or surly.

ill-treat verb treat someone or something cruelly.

illuminate /il-**lyoo**-mi-nayt/ verb **1** light something up. **2** (usu. as adj. **illuminating**) help to clarify or explain something: *a most illuminating discussion.* **3** decorate a page or initial letter in a manuscript with gold, silver, or coloured designs.
- DERIVATIVES **illuminator** noun.
- ORIGIN Latin *illuminare* 'illuminate', from *lumen* 'light'.

illuminati /i-lyoom-i-**nah**-ti/ plural noun people claiming to possess special knowledge or understanding.
- ORIGIN plural of Italian *illuminato* or Latin *illuminatus* 'enlightened'.

illumination noun **1** lighting or light. **2** (**illuminations**) lights used in decorating a building or other structure. **3** understanding or enlightenment: *he had moments of intense spiritual illumination.*

illumine verb literary light something up.

ill-use verb treat someone badly.

illusion /il-**lyoo**-zh'n/ noun **1** a false or unreal idea or belief: *he had no illusions about her.* **2** something that seems to exist but does not, or that seems to be something it is not: *he uses colour to give an illusion of space.*
- ORIGIN Latin, from *illudere* 'to mock'.

illusionism noun the use of perspective in art to give a three-dimensional appearance.
- DERIVATIVES **illusionistic** adjective.

illusionist noun a magician or conjuror.

illusive /i-**loo**-siv/ adjective chiefly literary deceptive; illusory.

illusory /il-**lyoo**-suh-ri/ adjective apparently real but not actually so.
- DERIVATIVES **illusorily** adverb.

illustrate verb **1** provide a book, magazine, etc. with pictures. **2** make something clear by using examples, charts, or pictures. **3** act as an example of: *the World Cup illustrated what high standards our players must achieve.*
- DERIVATIVES **illustrator** noun.
- ORIGIN Latin *illustrare* 'light up'.

illustration noun **1** a picture illustrating a book, magazine, etc. **2** the action of illustrating something. **3** an example that proves something or helps to explain it: *the case provides a good illustration of the legal problems.*

illustrative /il-luh-struh-tiv/ adjective **1** serving as an example or explanation. **2** relating to pictorial illustration.
- DERIVATIVES **illustratively** adverb.

illustrious /il-**luss**-tri-uhss/ adjective famous and admired for past achievements.
- ORIGIN Latin *illustris* 'clear, bright'.

ill will noun hostility or animosity towards someone.

I'm contraction I am.

im- prefix variant spelling of **IN-¹**, **IN-²** before *b*, *m*, *p* (as in *imbibe, impart*).

image noun **1** a likeness of a person or thing in the form of a picture or statue. **2** a picture of someone or something seen on a television or computer screen, through a lens, or as a reflection. **3** the impression that a person, organization, or product presents to the public: *the band have tarnished their squeaky-clean image.* **4** a picture in the mind. **5** a person or thing that closely resembles another: *he's the image of his father.* **6** a simile or metaphor.
• verb make or form an image of someone or something.
- DERIVATIVES **imageless** adjective.
- ORIGIN Latin *imago.*

imager noun an electronic or other device which records images.

imagery noun **1** language using similes and metaphors that produces images in the mind. **2** visual symbolism. **3** visual images as a whole.

imaginable adjective possible to be thought of or believed.
- DERIVATIVES **imaginably** adverb.

imaginary adjective **1** existing only in the imagination. **2** Mathematics expressed in terms of the square root of -1 (represented by *i* or *j*): *imaginary numbers.*
- DERIVATIVES **imaginarily** adverb.

imagination noun **1** the faculty or action of forming ideas or images in the mind: *her story captured the public's imagination.* **2** the ability of the mind to be creative or resourceful.

imaginative adjective having or showing creativity or inventiveness.
- DERIVATIVES **imaginatively** adverb **imaginativeness** noun.

imagine verb **1** form a mental image of someone or something. **2** believe that something unreal exists. **3** suppose or assume: *we*

imagined that Mabel would move away after Ned died.
- DERIVATIVES **imaginer** noun.
- ORIGIN from Latin *imaginare* 'form an image of' and *imaginari* 'picture to oneself'.

imaginings plural noun thoughts or fantasies.

imagism /im-i-jiz-uhm/ noun a movement in early 20th-century English and American poetry which aimed to achieve clarity of expression through the use of precise images.
- DERIVATIVES **imagist** noun.

imago /i-may-goh/ noun (pl. **imagos** or **imagines** /i-may-ji-neez/) the final and fully developed adult stage of an insect.
- ORIGIN Latin, 'image'.

imam /i-mahm/ noun **1** the person who leads prayers in a mosque. **2** (**Imam**) a title of various Muslim leaders.
- DERIVATIVES **imamate** noun.
- ORIGIN Arabic, 'leader'.

imbalance noun a lack of proportion or balance.

imbecile /im-bi-seel/ noun informal a stupid person. ● adjective stupid; idiotic.
- DERIVATIVES **imbecilic** adjective **imbecility** noun (pl. **imbecilities**).
- ORIGIN from Latin *imbecillus* 'weak, without a supporting staff'.

imbed verb variant spelling of **EMBED**.

imbibe /im-byb/ verb **1** formal or humorous drink alcohol. **2** literary absorb ideas or knowledge.
- DERIVATIVES **imbiber** noun.
- ORIGIN Latin *imbibere*.

imbroglio /im-broh-li-oh/ noun (pl. **imbroglios**) a very confused or complicated situation.
- ORIGIN Italian.

imbue /im-byoo/ verb (**imbues, imbuing, imbued**) fill with a feeling or quality: *we were imbued with a sense of purpose*.
- ORIGIN Latin *imbuere* 'moisten'.

IMF abbreviation International Monetary Fund.

imitate verb **1** follow someone or something as a model. **2** copy a person's speech or behaviour, especially to amuse people. **3** make a copy of or simulate something.
- DERIVATIVES **imitable** adjective **imitator** noun.
- ORIGIN Latin *imitari*.

imitation noun **1** a copy. **2** the action of imitating someone or something.

imitative /im-i-tuh-tiv/ adjective **1** following a model or example. **2** (of a word) reproducing a natural sound (e.g. *fizz*); onomatopoeic.
- DERIVATIVES **imitatively** adverb.

immaculate adjective **1** completely clean, neat, or tidy. **2** free from flaws or mistakes: *an immaculate safety record*.
- DERIVATIVES **immaculacy** noun **immaculately** adverb.
- ORIGIN Latin *immaculatus*.

Immaculate Conception noun (in the Roman Catholic Church) the doctrine that the Virgin Mary was free of the sin common to all human beings from the moment she was conceived by her mother.

immanent /im-muh-nuhnt/ adjective **1** present as a natural part of something; inherent: *love is a force immanent in the world*. **2** (of God) permanently present throughout the universe.
- DERIVATIVES **immanence** noun.

- ORIGIN from Latin *immanere* 'remain within'.

immaterial adjective **1** unimportant under the circumstances; irrelevant. **2** spiritual rather than physical.
- DERIVATIVES **immateriality** noun.

immature adjective **1** not fully developed. **2** lacking the emotional or intellectual development of an adult or mature person; childish.
- DERIVATIVES **immaturely** adverb **immaturity** noun.

immeasurable adjective too large or extreme to measure.
- DERIVATIVES **immeasurably** adverb.

immediacy /i-mee-di-uh-si/ noun **1** the quality of providing direct and instant involvement with something: *the immediacy of television images*. **2** lack of delay; speed.

immediate adjective **1** occurring or done at once. **2** most urgent: *the immediate concern was how to avoid taxes*. **3** nearest in time, space, or relationship. **4** direct: *a coronary was the immediate cause of death*.
- ORIGIN Latin *immediatus*.

immediately adverb **1** at once. **2** very close in time, space, or relationship. ● conjunction chiefly Brit. as soon as.

immemorial adjective existing from before what can be remembered or found in records: *they had lived there from time immemorial*.
- DERIVATIVES **immemorially** adverb.

immense adjective very large or great.
- DERIVATIVES **immensity** noun.
- ORIGIN Latin *immensus* 'immeasurable'.

immensely adverb to a great extent; extremely.

immerse verb **1** dip or submerge someone or something in a liquid. **2** (**immerse oneself** or **be immersed**) involve oneself deeply in an activity or interest.
- ORIGIN Latin *immergere* 'dip into'.

immersion noun **1** the action of immersing someone or something in a liquid. **2** deep involvement in an interest or activity.

immersion heater noun an electric device that is positioned in a domestic water tank to heat the water.

immersive adjective (of a computer display) generating a three-dimensional image which appears to surround the user.

immigrant noun a person who comes to live permanently in a foreign country.

immigration noun the action of coming to live permanently in a foreign country.
- DERIVATIVES **immigrate** verb (chiefly N. Amer.).
- ORIGIN Latin *immigrare*.

imminent adjective about to happen.
- DERIVATIVES **imminence** noun **imminently** adverb.
- ORIGIN from Latin *imminere* 'overhang, impend'.

immiscible /im-miss-i-b'l/ adjective (of liquids) not forming a homogeneous mixture when mixed.

immobile adjective **1** not moving; motionless. **2** unable to move or be moved.
- DERIVATIVES **immobility** noun.

immobilize (or **immobilise**) verb prevent

someone or something from moving or operating as normal.
– DERIVATIVES **immobilization** noun **immobilizer** noun.

immoderate adjective not sensible or restrained; excessive.
– DERIVATIVES **immoderately** adverb.

immodest adjective **1** tending to be boastful. **2** tending to show off one's body.
– DERIVATIVES **immodestly** adverb **immodesty** noun.

immolate /im-muh-layt/ verb kill or offer something as a sacrifice, especially by burning.
– DERIVATIVES **immolation** noun.
– ORIGIN Latin *immolare* 'sprinkle with sacrificial meal'.

immoral adjective not following accepted standards of morality.
– DERIVATIVES **immorality** noun (pl. **immoralities**) **immorally** adverb.

> USAGE: On the difference between **immoral** and **amoral**, see the note at **AMORAL**.

immoral earnings plural noun earnings from prostitution.

immortal adjective **1** living forever. **2** deserving to be remembered forever: *the immortal children's classic, 'The Wind in the Willows'.* •noun **1** an immortal being, especially a Greek or Roman god. **2** a person who will remain famous for a long time.
– DERIVATIVES **immortality** noun.

immortalize (or **immortalise**) verb (**immortalizes, immortalizing, immortalized**) cause someone or something to be remembered for a very long time.

immovable adjective **1** not able to be moved. **2** not able to be changed or persuaded: *an immovable truth.* **3** Law (of property) consisting of land, buildings, or other permanent items.
– DERIVATIVES **immovably** adverb.

immune adjective **1** having a natural resistance to a particular infection. **2** relating to such resistance: *the immune system.* **3** not affected or influenced by something: *no one is immune to her charm.* **4** protected or exempt from a duty or penalty.
– ORIGIN Latin *immunis* 'exempt from public service or charge'.

immune response noun the reaction of the cells and fluids of the body to the presence of an antigen (harmful substance).

immune system noun the organs and processes of the body that provide resistance to infection and toxins.

immunity noun (pl. **immunities**) **1** the ability of an organism to resist a particular infection. **2** exemption from a duty or penalty: *the rebels were given immunity from prosecution.*

immunize (or **immunise**) verb make a person or animal immune to infection, typically by inoculation.
– DERIVATIVES **immunization** noun.

immunodeficiency /im-yuu-noh-di-fi-sh'n-si/ noun failure of the immune system to protect the body from infection.

immunoglobulin /im-yuu-noh-**glob**-yuu-lin/ noun a protein produced in the blood which functions as an antibody.

immunology /im-yuu-**nol**-uh-ji/ noun the branch of medicine and biology concerned with immunity to infection.
– DERIVATIVES **immunologic** adjective **immunological** adjective **immunologist** noun.

immunosuppression noun prevention of a person's natural response to infection, especially as induced to help the survival of an organ after a transplant operation.
– DERIVATIVES **immunosuppressant** noun **immunosuppressed** adjective.

immunotherapy noun the prevention or treatment of disease with substances that stimulate the body's resistance to infection.

immure /im-**myoor**/ verb confine or imprison someone.
– ORIGIN Latin *immurare*.

immutable /im-**myoo**-tuh-b'l/ adjective not changing or able to be changed.
– DERIVATIVES **immutability** noun **immutably** adverb.

i-Mode noun a technology that allows data to be transferred to and from Internet sites via mobile phones.

imp noun **1** a small, mischievous devil. **2** a mischievous child.
– ORIGIN from an Old English word meaning 'a young shoot'.

impact noun /**im**-pakt/ **1** an act of one object hitting another. **2** a marked effect or influence: *man's impact on the environment.* •verb /im-**pakt**/ **1** hit another object. **2** have a strong effect: *high interest rates have impacted on retail spending* **3** press something firmly into something else.
– DERIVATIVES **impactor** noun.
– ORIGIN from Latin *impingere* 'drive in'.

impacted adjective (of a tooth) wedged between another tooth and the jaw.
– DERIVATIVES **impaction** noun.

impair verb **1** weaken or damage something. **2** (as adj. **impaired**) having a disability of a specified kind: *hearing-impaired.*
– DERIVATIVES **impairment** noun.
– ORIGIN Old French *empeirier*.

impala /im-**pah**-luh/ noun (pl. same) an antelope of southern and East Africa, with lyre-shaped horns.
– ORIGIN Zulu.

impale verb pierce someone or something with a sharp object.
– DERIVATIVES **impalement** noun **impaler** noun.
– ORIGIN Latin *impalare*.

impalpable adjective **1** unable to be felt by touch. **2** not easily understood.
– DERIVATIVES **impalpably** adverb.

impanel verb variant spelling of **EMPANEL**.

impart verb **1** communicate information. **2** give a quality: *the mushrooms impart a woody flavour to the salad.*
– ORIGIN Latin *impartire* 'give a share of'.

impartial adjective treating everyone equally; not biased.
– DERIVATIVES **impartiality** noun **impartially** adverb.

impassable adjective impossible to travel along or over.
– DERIVATIVES **impassability** noun.

impasse /am-**pahss**/ noun a situation in which

progress is impossible; a deadlock.
– ORIGIN French.

impassioned adjective filled with or showing great emotion.

impassive adjective not feeling or showing emotion.
– DERIVATIVES **impassively** adverb **impassivity** noun.

impasto /im-**pass**-toh/ noun the process or technique of laying on paint thickly so that it stands out from the surface of a painting.
– ORIGIN Italian.

impatient adjective 1 lacking patience or tolerance. 2 restlessly eager: *they were impatient for change.*
– DERIVATIVES **impatience** noun **impatiently** adverb.

impeach verb 1 chiefly US charge the holder of a public office with misconduct. 2 Brit. charge someone with treason or another crime against the state. 3 question the validity or worth of something.
– DERIVATIVES **impeachable** adjective **impeachment** noun.
– ORIGIN Old French *empecher* 'impede'.

impeccable /im-**pek**-kuh-b'l/ adjective without any faults or mistakes; perfect.
– DERIVATIVES **impeccability** noun **impeccably** adverb.
– ORIGIN Latin *impeccabilis* 'not liable to sin'.

impecunious /im-pi-**kyoo**-ni-uhss/ adjective having little or no money.
– DERIVATIVES **impecuniosity** noun.
– ORIGIN from IN-¹ + Latin *pecuniosus* 'wealthy'.

impedance /im-**pee**-duhnss/ noun the total resistance of an electric circuit to the flow of alternating current.

impede /im-**peed**/ verb delay or block the progress or action of: *matters which would impede progress.*
– ORIGIN Latin *impedire* 'shackle the feet of'.

impediment /im-**ped**-i-muhnt/ noun 1 a hindrance or obstruction. 2 (also **speech impediment**) a defect in a person's speech, such as a lisp or stammer.

impedimenta /im-ped-i-**men**-tuh/ plural noun equipment for an activity or expedition, especially when regarded as hindering progress.
– ORIGIN Latin, 'impediments'.

impel /im-**pel**/ verb (**impels, impelling, impelled**) 1 drive or urge someone to do something. 2 drive someone or something forward.
– DERIVATIVES **impeller** noun.
– ORIGIN Latin *impellere*.

impending adjective (especially of something bad or important) be about to happen: *a sense of impending danger.*
– ORIGIN from Latin *impendere* 'overhang'.

impenetrable /im-**pen**-i-truh-b'l/ adjective 1 impossible to get through or into. 2 impossible to understand.
– DERIVATIVES **impenetrability** noun **impenetrably** adverb.

impenitent adjective not feeling shame or regret.
– DERIVATIVES **impenitence** noun **impenitently** adverb.

imperative adjective 1 vitally important; essential. 2 giving an authoritative command. 3 Grammar (of a mood of a verb) expressing a command, as in *come here!* ● noun an essential or urgent thing.
– DERIVATIVES **imperatively** adverb.
– ORIGIN Latin *imperativus* 'specially ordered'.

imperceptible adjective too slight or gradual to be seen, heard, or felt.
– DERIVATIVES **imperceptibly** adverb.

imperfect adjective 1 faulty or incomplete. 2 (of a tense) referring to a past action in progress but not completed at the time in question.
– DERIVATIVES **imperfection** noun **imperfectly** adverb.

imperial adjective 1 relating to an empire or an emperor. 2 typical of an emperor; majestic. 3 (of weights and measures) based on a non-metric system formerly used for all measures in the UK, and still used for some.
– DERIVATIVES **imperially** adverb.
– ORIGIN Latin *imperialis*.

imperialism noun a policy of extending a country's power and influence through establishing colonies or by military force.
– DERIVATIVES **imperialist** noun & adjective **imperialistic** adjective.

imperil verb (**imperils, imperilling, imperilled**; US **imperils, imperiling, imperiled**) put someone or something in danger.

imperious /im-**peer**-i-uhss/ adjective expecting to be obeyed without question; arrogant and domineering.
– DERIVATIVES **imperiously** adverb **imperiousness** noun.
– ORIGIN Latin *imperiosus*.

imperishable adjective lasting forever.
– DERIVATIVES **imperishably** adverb.

impermanent adjective not lasting or unchanging.
– DERIVATIVES **impermanence** noun **impermanently** adverb.

impermeable /im-**per**-mi-uh-b'l/ adjective not allowing fluid to pass through.
– DERIVATIVES **impermeability** noun.

impermissible adjective not permitted or allowed.

impersonal adjective 1 not influenced by or involving personal feelings. 2 lacking human qualities; cold or anonymous: *an impersonal tower block.* 3 Grammar (of a verb) used only with *it* as a subject (as in *it is snowing*).
– DERIVATIVES **impersonality** noun **impersonally** adverb.

impersonal pronoun noun the pronoun *it* when not referring to a thing, as in *it was snowing.*

impersonate verb pretend to be another person to entertain or deceive people.
– DERIVATIVES **impersonation** noun **impersonator** noun.
– ORIGIN from IN-² + Latin *persona* 'person'.

impertinent adjective 1 not showing proper respect. 2 formal not relevant or pertinent.
– DERIVATIVES **impertinence** noun **impertinently** adverb.

imperturbable /im-per-**ter**-buh-b'l/ adjective not easily upset or excited.

- DERIVATIVES **imperturbability** noun **imperturbably** adverb.

impervious /im-**per**-vi-uhss/ adjective **1** not allowing fluid to pass through. **2 (impervious to)** unable to be affected by: *he worked, apparently impervious to the heat.*
- DERIVATIVES **imperviously** adverb **imperviousness** noun.

impetigo /im-pi-**ty**-goh/ noun a skin infection caused by a bacterium and forming spots and yellow crusty sores.
- ORIGIN Latin.

impetuous adjective acting or done quickly and without thought or care.
- DERIVATIVES **impetuosity** noun **impetuously** adverb **impetuousness** noun.
- ORIGIN Latin *impetuosus.*

impetus noun **1** the force or energy with which a body moves. **2** something that makes a process happen or happen more quickly: *the main impetus for change has been the enforcement of legislation.*
- ORIGIN Latin, 'assault, force'.

impi /im-pi/ noun (pl. **impis**) a group of Zulu warriors.
- ORIGIN Zulu.

impiety /im-**py**-i-ti/ noun lack of religious respect or reverence.

impinge verb (**impinges, impinging, impinged**) **1** have an effect: *these laws clearly impinge on freedom of speech.* **2** advance over an area belonging to another; encroach.
- DERIVATIVES **impingement** noun.
- ORIGIN Latin *impingere* 'drive something in or at'.

impious /im-pi-uhss/ adjective not showing respect or reverence.
- DERIVATIVES **impiously** adverb.

impish adjective inclined to do naughty things for fun; mischievous.
- DERIVATIVES **impishly** adverb **impishness** noun.

implacable adjective **1** unwilling to stop opposing someone or something: *an implacable enemy of the arts.* **2** unable to be stopped; relentless.
- DERIVATIVES **implacability** noun **implacably** adverb.
- ORIGIN from **IN-¹** + Latin *placabilis* 'easily calmed'.

implant verb /im-**plahnt**/ **1** insert tissue or an artificial object into the body for medical purposes. **2** establish an idea in the mind. **3** (of a fertilized egg) become attached to the wall of the womb. • noun /im-plahnt/ a thing that has been implanted.
- DERIVATIVES **implantation** noun.
- ORIGIN Latin *implantare* 'engraft'.

implausible adjective not seeming reasonable or probable.
- DERIVATIVES **implausibility** noun **implausibly** adverb.

implement noun /im-pli-muhnt/ a tool, utensil, or other piece of equipment that is used for a particular purpose. • verb /im-pli-ment/ put a decision, plan, or agreement into effect.
- DERIVATIVES **implementation** noun **implementer** noun.
- ORIGIN from Latin *implere* 'fill up, employ'.

implicate /im-pli-kayt/ verb **1** show someone to be involved in a crime. **2 (be implicated in)** bear some of the responsibility for: *he was implicated in the bombing of the hotel.* **3** convey a meaning indirectly; imply something.
- DERIVATIVES **implicative** /im-**plik**-uh-tiv/ adjective.
- ORIGIN Latin *implicare* 'fold in, involve, imply'.

implication noun **1** the conclusion that can be drawn from something although it is not stated directly. **2** a likely consequence of something. **3** the state of being involved in something.
- DERIVATIVES **implicational** adjective.

implicit /im-**pliss**-it/ adjective **1** suggested though not directly stated. **2 (implicit in)** always to be found in: *the problems implicit in all social theory.* **3** with no qualification or question: *an implicit faith.*
- DERIVATIVES **implicitly** adverb **implicitness** noun.
- ORIGIN Latin *implicitus.*

implode /im-**plohd**/ verb collapse violently inwards.
- DERIVATIVES **implosion** noun **implosive** adjective.
- ORIGIN from **IN-²** + Latin *plodere, plaudere* 'to clap'.

implore verb beg someone earnestly or desperately to do something.
- ORIGIN Latin *implorare* 'invoke with tears'.

imply verb (**implies, implying, implied**) **1** suggest something rather than state it directly. **2** suggest something as a likely consequence: *the forecast traffic increase implied more pollution.*
- ORIGIN Latin *implicare* 'fold in, involve'.

> USAGE: The words **imply** and **infer** can describe the same situation, but from different points of view. If a person **implies** something, as in *he implied that the General was a traitor,* it means that they are suggesting something but not saying it directly. If you **infer** something from what has been said, as in *we inferred from his words that the General was a traitor,* this means that you come to the conclusion that this is what they really mean.

impolite adjective not having or showing good manners.
- DERIVATIVES **impolitely** adverb **impoliteness** noun.

impolitic adjective not wise or prudent.

imponderable adjective difficult or impossible to assess. • noun a factor that is difficult or impossible to assess.

import verb **1** bring goods or services into a country from abroad. **2** transfer data into a computer file or document. • noun **1** an article or service imported from abroad. **2** the action of importing goods or services. **3** the implied meaning of something. **4** importance.
- DERIVATIVES **importable** adjective **importation** noun **importer** noun.
- ORIGIN Latin *importare* 'bring in'.

important adjective **1** of great significance or value. **2** having great authority or influence: *important modern writers.*
- DERIVATIVES **importance** noun **importantly** adverb.

importunate /im-**por**-tyuu-nuht/ adjective

very persistent.
- DERIVATIVES **importunately** adverb
importunity noun (pl. **importunities**).
- ORIGIN Latin *importunus* 'inconvenient'.
importune /im-por-**tyoon**/ verb harass
someone with persistent requests.
- ORIGIN Latin *importunus* (see **IMPORTUNATE**).
impose verb 1 introduce something that must
be obeyed or done: *they plan to impose a tax on
fuel.* 2 force something to be accepted. 3 take
unreasonable advantage of someone: *she had
imposed on Mark's kindness.*
- ORIGIN Latin *imponere* 'inflict, deceive'.
imposing adjective grand and impressive.
- DERIVATIVES **imposingly** adverb.
imposition noun 1 the action of introducing
something that must be obeyed or done.
2 something that has been imposed; an
unwelcome demand or burden.
impossible adjective 1 not able to occur, exist,
or be done. 2 very difficult to deal with: *I was
in an impossible situation.*
- DERIVATIVES **impossibility** noun (pl.
impossibilities) **impossibly** adverb.
impostor (also **imposter**) noun a person who
pretends to be someone else in order to
deceive or defraud others.
- ORIGIN Latin.
imposture noun an act of pretending to be
someone else in order to deceive others.
impotent /im-puh-tuhnt/ adjective 1 unable to
take effective action; powerless. 2 (of a man)
unable to achieve an erection or orgasm.
- DERIVATIVES **impotence** noun **impotency** noun
impotently adverb.
impound verb 1 seize and take legal
possession of something. 2 shut up domestic
animals in an enclosure. 3 (of a dam) hold
back water.
- DERIVATIVES **impoundment** noun.
impoverish verb (often as adj. **impoverished**)
1 make a person or area poor. 2 make worse in
quality: *impoverished soil.*
- DERIVATIVES **impoverishment** noun.
- ORIGIN Old French *empoverir*.
impracticable adjective impossible to be done
in practice: *it was impracticable to widen the
road here.*
- DERIVATIVES **impracticability** noun
impracticably adverb.
impractical adjective not adapted for use or
action; not sensible: *impractical high heels.*
- DERIVATIVES **impracticality** noun **impractically**
adverb.
imprecation noun formal a spoken curse.
- ORIGIN from Latin *imprecari* 'invoke evil'.
imprecise adjective not exact or detailed.
- DERIVATIVES **imprecisely** adverb **imprecision**
noun.
impregnable adjective 1 unable to be
captured or broken into. 2 unable to be
overcome: *Liverpool forged an impregnable
lead.*
- DERIVATIVES **impregnability** noun **impregnably**
adverb.
- ORIGIN Old French *imprenable*.
impregnate /im-preg-nayt/ verb 1 soak or
saturate something with a substance. 2 fill
with a feeling or quality: *an atmosphere

impregnated with tension. 3 make someone
pregnant.
- DERIVATIVES **impregnation** noun.
- ORIGIN Latin *impregnare*.
impresario /im-pri-**sah**-ri-oh/ noun (pl.
impresarios) a person who organizes and often
finances theatrical or musical productions.
- ORIGIN Italian.
impress verb /im-**press**/ 1 make someone feel
admiration and respect. 2 (**impress something
on**) emphasize the importance of something
to someone. 3 make a mark or design on
something using a stamp or seal. ● noun /im-
press/ 1 an act of impressing a mark. 2 a mark
made by pressure. 3 a person's characteristic
quality: *his desire to put his own impress on the
films he made.*
- ORIGIN Old French *empresser* 'press in'.
impression noun 1 an idea, feeling, or opinion.
2 an effect produced on someone: *his quick wit
made a good impression.* 3 an imitation of a
person or thing, done to entertain. 4 a mark
impressed on a surface. 5 the printing of a
number of copies of a publication for issue at
one time. 6 chiefly Brit. a particular printed
version of a book, especially one reprinted
with no or only minor alteration.
impressionable adjective easily influenced.
- DERIVATIVES **impressionability** noun.
Impressionism noun a style or movement in
painting concerned with showing the visual
impression of a particular moment, especially
the shifting effects of light.
- DERIVATIVES **Impressionist** noun & adjective.
- ORIGIN from French *impressionniste*.
impressionist noun an entertainer who
impersonates famous people.
impressionistic adjective 1 based on personal
impressions or reactions. 2 (**Impressionistic**) in
the style of Impressionism.
- DERIVATIVES **impressionistically** adverb.
impressive adjective arousing admiration
through size, quality, or skill.
- DERIVATIVES **impressively** adverb
impressiveness noun.
imprimatur /im-pri-**mah**-ter/ noun 1 a
person's authoritative approval. 2 an official
licence issued by the Roman Catholic Church
to print a religious book.
- ORIGIN Latin, 'let it be printed'.
imprint verb 1 make a mark on an object by
pressure. 2 make an impression or effect on:
*he'd always have this ghastly image imprinted
on his mind.* ● noun 1 a mark made by pressure.
2 a printer's or publisher's name and other
details in a publication. 3 a brand name under
which books are published.
- ORIGIN Latin *imprimere* 'impress, imprint'.
imprison verb put or keep someone in prison.
- DERIVATIVES **imprisonment** noun.
improbable adjective not likely to be true or to
happen.
- DERIVATIVES **improbability** noun (pl.
improbabilities) **improbably** adverb.
impromptu /im-**promp**-tyoo/ adjective & adverb
done without being planned or rehearsed.
● noun (pl. **impromptus**) a short piece of
instrumental music, especially a solo, similar
to an improvisation.
- ORIGIN from Latin *in promptu* 'in readiness'.

improper adjective **1** not following accepted standards of behaviour. **2** not modest or decent.
– DERIVATIVES **improperly** adverb.

improper fraction noun a fraction in which the numerator is greater than the denominator, such as ⁵⁄₄.

impropriety /im-pruh-**pry**-uh-ti/ noun (pl. **improprieties**) behaviour that fails to conform to standards of morality or honesty.

improve verb **1** make or become better. **2** (**improve on**) achieve or produce something better than something else. **3** (as adj. **improving**) giving moral or intellectual benefit.
– DERIVATIVES **improvability** noun **improvable** adjective **improver** noun.
– ORIGIN Old French *emprower*.

improvement noun **1** the action of making or becoming better. **2** a thing that improves something or is better than something else: *home improvements*.

improvident adjective not providing for future needs.
– DERIVATIVES **improvidence** noun **improvidently** adverb.

improvisation noun **1** the action of improvising something. **2** a piece of music, drama, or verse created without preparation.
– DERIVATIVES **improvisational** adjective.

improvise verb **1** create and perform music, drama, or verse without preparation. **2** make something from whatever is available.
– DERIVATIVES **improvisatory** adjective **improviser** noun.
– ORIGIN from Latin *improvisus* 'unforeseen'.

imprudent adjective not thinking about the results of an action; rash.
– DERIVATIVES **imprudence** noun **imprudently** adverb.

impudent /im-**pyuu**-duhnt/ adjective not showing proper respect to someone; cheeky.
– DERIVATIVES **impudence** noun **impudently** adverb.
– ORIGIN Latin *impudens* 'shameless'.

impugn /im-**pyoon**/ verb express doubts about the honesty or validity of a fact or statement.
– ORIGIN Latin *impugnare* 'assail'.

impulse noun **1** a sudden strong urge to act, without thinking about the results. **2** something that causes something to happen; an impetus: *the impulse for the book came from personal experience*. **3** a pulse of electrical energy. **4** Physics a force acting briefly on a body and producing a change of momentum.
– ORIGIN Latin *impulsus* 'a push'.

impulsion noun **1** a strong urge to do something. **2** the influence behind an action or process.

impulsive adjective acting or done without thinking ahead.
– DERIVATIVES **impulsively** adverb **impulsiveness** noun **impulsivity** noun.

impunity /im-**pyoo**-ni-ti/ noun freedom from punishment or from the harmful results of an action: *rebels crossed the border with impunity*.
– ORIGIN Latin *impunitas*.

impure adjective **1** mixed with unwanted substances. **2** morally wrong, especially in sexual matters.

impurity noun (pl. **impurities**) **1** the quality or state of being impure. **2** a substance which spoils the purity of something.

impute /im-**pyoot**/ verb believe that something undesirable has been done or caused by someone or something: *madness among the troops was imputed to shell shock*.
– DERIVATIVES **imputable** adjective **imputation** noun.
– ORIGIN Latin *imputare* 'enter in the account'.

IN abbreviation Indiana.

In symbol the chemical element indium.

in preposition **1** so as to be enclosed, surrounded, or inside. **2** expressing a period of time during which an event takes place. **3** expressing the length of time before an event is expected to happen. **4** expressing a state, condition, or quality. **5** expressing inclusion or involvement. **6** indicating the means of expression used: *put it in writing*. **7** indicating a person's occupation or profession. **8** expressing a value as a proportion of a whole. • adverb **1** expressing movement that results in being inside or surrounded. **2** expressing the state of being enclosed or surrounded. **3** present at one's home or office. **4** expressing arrival at a destination. **5** (of the tide) rising or at its highest level. • adjective informal fashionable.
– PHRASES **be in for** be going to experience something, especially something unpleasant. **in on** knowing a secret. **in that** for the reason that. **in with** informal enjoying friendly relations with. **the ins and outs** informal all the details.
– ORIGIN Old English.

in. abbreviation inch(es).

in-¹ prefix **1** (added to adjectives) not: *infertile*. **2** (added to nouns) without; a lack of: *inaction*.
– ORIGIN Latin.

in-² prefix in; into; towards; within: *influx*.
– ORIGIN from **in** or Latin *in*.

inability noun the state of being unable to do something.

in absentia /in ab-**sen**-ti-uh/ adverb while not present.
– ORIGIN Latin, 'in absence'.

inaccessible adjective **1** unable to be reached or used. **2** difficult to understand or appreciate. **3** (of a person) not open to advances; unapproachable.
– DERIVATIVES **inaccessibility** noun **inaccessibly** adverb.

inaccurate adjective not accurate or correct.
– DERIVATIVES **inaccuracy** noun (pl. **inaccuracies**) **inaccurately** adverb.

inaction noun lack of action where some is expected or appropriate.

inactivate verb make something inactive or inoperative.
– DERIVATIVES **inactivation** noun.

inactive adjective not active or working.
– DERIVATIVES **inactivity** noun.

inadequate adjective **1** not enough or not good enough: *inadequate funding*. **2** unable to deal with a situation or with life.
– DERIVATIVES **inadequacy** noun (pl. **inadequacies**) **inadequately** adverb.

inadmissible adjective **1** (especially of

evidence in court) not accepted as valid. **2** not to be allowed.

inadvertent adjective not deliberate or intentional.
– DERIVATIVES **inadvertence** noun **inadvertently** adverb.
– ORIGIN from **IN-**¹ + Latin *advertere* 'turn the mind to'.

inadvisable adjective likely to have undesirable results; unwise.
– DERIVATIVES **inadvisability** noun.

inalienable adjective unable to be taken away from or given away by the possessor: *inalienable rights*.
– DERIVATIVES **inalienably** adverb.

inamorato /i-nam-uh-**rah**-toh/ noun (pl. **inamoratos**; fem. **inamorata**, pl. **inamoratas**) a person's lover.
– ORIGIN Italian, 'enamoured'.

inane adjective lacking sense or meaning; silly.
– DERIVATIVES **inanely** adverb **inanity** noun (pl. **inanities**).
– ORIGIN Latin *inanis* 'empty, vain'.

inanimate adjective not alive: *inanimate objects like stones*.

inanition /in-uh-**nish**-uhn/ noun formal exhaustion caused by lack of nourishment.
– ORIGIN Latin.

inapplicable adjective not relevant or appropriate.
– DERIVATIVES **inapplicability** noun.

inapposite /in-**ap**-uh-zit/ adjective out of place; inappropriate.

inappropriate adjective not suitable or appropriate.
– DERIVATIVES **inappropriately** adverb **inappropriateness** noun.

inapt adjective not suitable or appropriate.
– DERIVATIVES **inaptly** adverb.

inarticulate /in-ar-**tik**-yuu-luht/ adjective **1** unable to express one's ideas or feelings clearly or easily. **2** not expressed in words.
– DERIVATIVES **inarticulacy** noun **inarticulately** adverb **inarticulateness** noun.

inasmuch adverb (**inasmuch as**) **1** to the extent that. **2** considering that; since.

inattentive adjective not paying attention.
– DERIVATIVES **inattention** noun **inattentively** adverb **inattentiveness** noun.

inaudible adjective unable to be heard.
– DERIVATIVES **inaudibility** noun **inaudibly** adverb.

inaugural /in-**aw**-gyuu-ruhl/ adjective marking the beginning of an organization or period of office.

inaugurate /in-**aw**-gyuu-rayt/ verb **1** introduce a new system, project, or period. **2** admit someone formally to a position or office. **3** mark the opening of an organization or the first public use of a service with a special ceremony.
– DERIVATIVES **inauguration** noun **inaugurator** noun.
– ORIGIN from Latin *inauguratus* 'consecrated after interpreting omens'.

inauspicious adjective not likely to lead to success; unpromising.
– DERIVATIVES **inauspiciously** adverb **inauspiciousness** noun.

inauthentic noun not authentic, genuine, or sincere.
– DERIVATIVES **inauthenticity** noun.

inboard adverb & adjective within or towards the centre of a ship, aircraft, or vehicle.

inborn adjective existing from birth.

inbound adjective & adverb travelling back towards an original point of departure.

in-box noun the window on a computer screen in which received emails are displayed.

inbred adjective **1** produced by breeding from closely related people or animals. **2** existing from birth; inborn.

inbreed verb (past and past part. **inbred**) (often as noun **inbreeding**) breed from closely related people or animals.

inbuilt adjective present as an original or essential part: *his inbuilt sense of direction*.

Inc. abbreviation N. Amer. Incorporated.

Inca noun **1** a member of a South American Indian people living in the central Andes before the Spanish conquest in the early 1530s. **2** the supreme ruler of the Incas.
– DERIVATIVES **Incan** adjective.
– ORIGIN Quechua, 'lord, royal person'.

incalculable adjective **1** too great to be calculated or estimated. **2** not able to be calculated or estimated.
– DERIVATIVES **incalculability** noun **incalculably** adverb.

in camera adverb see **CAMERA**.

incandescent /in-kan-**des**-uhnt/ adjective **1** glowing as a result of being heated. **2** (of an electric light) containing a filament which glows white-hot when heated by a current passed through it. **3** informal very angry.
– DERIVATIVES **incandescence** noun **incandescently** adverb.
– ORIGIN from Latin *incandescere* 'glow'.

incantation /in-kan-**tay**-sh'n/ noun words said as a magic spell or charm.
– DERIVATIVES **incantatory** adjective.
– ORIGIN from Latin *incantare* 'chant, bewitch'.

incapable adjective **1** (**incapable of**) lacking the ability or required quality to do something. **2** unable to behave rationally or take care of oneself.
– DERIVATIVES **incapability** noun.

incapacitate /in-kuh-**pa**-si-tayt/ verb prevent someone from functioning in a normal way.
– DERIVATIVES **incapacitant** noun **incapacitation** noun.
– ORIGIN from **INCAPACITY**.

incapacity noun (pl. **incapacities**) **1** inability to do something or to function normally. **2** legal disqualification.

incarcerate /in-**kar**-suh-rayt/ verb imprison or confine someone.
– DERIVATIVES **incarceration** noun.
– ORIGIN Latin *incarcerare*.

incarnate adjective /in-**kar**-nuht/ **1** (of a god or spirit) in human form. **2** represented in physical form: *she was beauty incarnate*. • verb /**in**-kar-nayt/ **1** be the living embodiment of a quality. **2** embody or represent a god or spirit in human form.
– ORIGIN from Latin *incarnare* 'make flesh'.

incarnation noun **1** a physical embodiment of a god, spirit, or quality: *they regarded the* *dictator as the incarnation of evil.* **2 (the Incarnation)** (in Christian belief) the embodiment of God the Son in human flesh as Jesus. **3** (with reference to reincarnation) each of a series of earthly lifetimes or forms.

incautious adjective not concerned about potential problems or risks.
– DERIVATIVES **incaution** noun **incautiously** adverb.

incendiary /in-sen-di-uh-ri/ **adjective 1** (of a bomb) designed to cause fires. **2** tending to stir up conflict. •**noun** (pl. **incendiaries**) a bomb designed to cause fires.
– DERIVATIVES **incendiarism** noun.
– ORIGIN Latin *incendiarius*.

incense[1] /in-senss/ **noun** a gum, spice, or other substance that is burned for the sweet smell it produces. •**verb** perfume with incense.
– ORIGIN Latin *incensum* 'something burnt, incense'.

incense[2] /in-senss/ **verb** make someone very angry.
– ORIGIN Latin *incendere* 'set fire to'.

incentive noun a thing that motivates or encourages someone to do something.
– DERIVATIVES **incentivize** (or **incentivise**) verb.
– ORIGIN Latin *incentivum* 'something that incites'.

inception noun the establishment or starting point of an institution or activity.
– ORIGIN from Latin *incipere* 'begin'.

incertitude noun a state of uncertainty.

incessant adjective continuing without stopping.
– DERIVATIVES **incessantly** adverb.
– ORIGIN from Latin *in-* 'not' + *cessare* 'cease'.

incest noun sexual intercourse between people classed as being too closely related to marry each other.
– ORIGIN from Latin *in-* 'not' + *castus* 'chaste'.

incestuous /in-sess-tyoo-uhss/ **adjective 1** involving sex between people who are too closely related to marry each other. **2** excessively close and resistant to outside influence: *a small, incestuous legal community.*
– DERIVATIVES **incestuously** adverb.

inch noun 1 a unit of length equal to one twelfth of a foot (2.54 cm). **2** a quantity of rainfall that would cover a horizontal surface to a depth of one inch. **3** a very small amount or distance: *don't yield an inch.* •**verb** move along slowly and carefully.
– PHRASES **every inch 1** the whole area or distance. **2** entirely; very much so. **(to) within an inch of one's life** almost to the point of death.
– ORIGIN Latin *uncia* 'twelfth part'.

inchoate adjective /in-koh-uht/ just begun and so not fully formed or developed.
– DERIVATIVES **inchoately** adverb.
– ORIGIN from Latin *incohare* 'begin'.

incidence noun 1 the occurrence, rate, or frequency of something undesirable: *an increased incidence of cancer.* **2** Physics the intersection of a line or ray with a surface.

incident noun 1 an instance of something happening; an event. **2** a violent event, such as an attack. **3** the occurrence of dangerous or exciting events: *the plane landed without incident.* •**adjective 1** (**incident to**) resulting from. **2** (of light or other radiation) falling on

a surface. **3** Physics relating to the intersection of a line or ray with a surface.
– ORIGIN from Latin *incidere* 'fall upon, happen to'.

incidental adjective 1 occurring in connection with or as a result of something else: *the risks incidental to a firefighter's job.* **2** occurring as a minor accompaniment to something else: *incidental expenses.* •**noun** an incidental detail or expense.

incidentally adverb **1** by the way. **2** in an incidental way.

incidental music noun music used in a film or play as a background.

incinerate /in-sin-uh-rayt/ **verb** destroy something by burning.
– DERIVATIVES **incineration** noun.
– ORIGIN Latin *incinerare* 'burn to ashes'.

incinerator noun a device for burning waste material.

incipient /in-sip-i-uhnt/ **adjective** beginning to happen or develop.
– DERIVATIVES **incipiently** adverb.
– ORIGIN from Latin *incipere* 'undertake, begin'.

incise verb 1 make a cut or cuts in a surface. **2** cut a mark or decoration into a surface.
– ORIGIN Latin *incidere* 'cut into'.

incision noun 1 a cut made as part of a surgical operation. **2** the action of cutting into something.

incisive adjective 1 showing or having clear thought and sharp insight: *incisive questions.* **2** (of an action) quick and direct.
– DERIVATIVES **incisively** adverb **incisiveness** noun.

incisor noun a narrow-edged tooth at the front of the mouth, adapted for cutting.

incite verb 1 encourage or stir up violent or unlawful behaviour. **2** urge someone to act in a violent or unlawful way.
– DERIVATIVES **incitement** noun **inciter** noun.
– ORIGIN Latin *incitare*.

incivility noun (pl. **incivilities**) rude or offensive speech or behaviour.

inclement /in-klem-uhnt/ **adjective** (of the weather) unpleasantly cold or wet.
– DERIVATIVES **inclemency** noun (pl. **inclemencies**).

inclination noun 1 a person's natural tendency to act or feel in a particular way: *Jack was a scientist by inclination.* **2** (**inclination for/ to/towards**) an interest in or liking for something. **3** a slope or slant. **4** the angle at which a straight line or plane slopes away from another.

incline verb /in-klyn/ **1** tend or be willing to think or do: *I was inclined to accept her offer.* **2** (**be inclined**) have a specified tendency or talent: *Sam was mathematically inclined.* **3** lean or turn away from the vertical or horizontal. **4** bend the head forwards and downwards. •**noun** /in-klyn/ an inclined surface or plane; a slope.
– ORIGIN Latin *inclinare* 'to bend towards'.

inclined plane noun a plane inclined at an angle to the horizontal, used to make it easier to raise a load.

include verb 1 have or contain something as part of a whole: *the price includes bed and breakfast.* **2** make or treat someone or

something as part of a whole or group.
– ORIGIN Latin *includere* 'shut in'.

including preposition containing someone or something as part of a whole or group.

inclusion noun 1 the action of including or the state of being included. 2 a person or thing that is included.
– DERIVATIVES **inclusionary** adjective.

inclusive adjective 1 including all the expected or required services or items. 2 (**inclusive of**) containing a specified element as part of a whole. 3 (after a noun) including the limits stated: *the ages of 55 to 59 inclusive*. 4 not excluding any section of society or any party: *an inclusive peace process*.
– DERIVATIVES **inclusively** adverb **inclusiveness** noun.

incognito /in-kog-**nee**-toh/ adjective & adverb having one's true identity concealed. ● noun (pl. **incognitos**) a false identity.
– ORIGIN Italian, 'unknown'.

incoherent adjective 1 (of language or a speaker) difficult to understand. 2 not logical or well organized.
– DERIVATIVES **incoherence** noun **incoherency** noun (pl. **incoherencies**) **incoherently** adverb.

incombustible adjective (especially of a building material) not inflammable.

income noun money received during a particular period for work or from investments.

incomer noun Brit. a person who has come to live in an area in which they have not grown up.

income support noun (in the UK and Canada) payment made by the state to people on a low income.

income tax noun tax levied directly on personal income.

incoming adjective 1 coming in. 2 (of an official or administration) having just been elected or appointed to succeed another. ● noun (**incomings**) revenue; income.

incommensurable /in-kuh-**men**-shuh-ruh-b'l/ adjective 1 not able to be judged or measured by the same standards. 2 Mathematics (of numbers) in a ratio that cannot be expressed by means of integers.
– DERIVATIVES **incommensurability** noun.

incommensurate /in-kuh-**men**-shuh-ruht/ adjective 1 (**incommensurate with**) not in keeping or in proportion with something. 2 another term for **INCOMMENSURABLE** (in sense 1).

incommode verb formal cause inconvenience to someone.
– ORIGIN Latin *incommodare*.

incommodious adjective formal or dated causing inconvenience or discomfort.

incommunicable adjective not able to be communicated to others.

incommunicado /in-kuh-myoo-ni-**kah**-doh/ adjective & adverb not able to communicate with other people.
– ORIGIN Spanish *incomunicado*.

incomparable /in-**kom**-puh-ruh-b'l/ adjective so good or impressive that nothing can be compared to it: *the furnishings are of incomparable beauty*.

– DERIVATIVES **incomparably** adverb.

incompatible adjective 1 (of two things) not able to exist or be used together. 2 (of two people) not able to live or work together without disagreeing.
– DERIVATIVES **incompatibility** noun (pl. **incompatibilities**).

incompetent adjective 1 not sufficiently skilful to do something successfully. 2 Law not qualified to act in a particular capacity. ● noun an incompetent person.
– DERIVATIVES **incompetence** noun **incompetency** noun **incompetently** adverb.

incomplete adjective not finished or having all the necessary parts.
– DERIVATIVES **incompletely** adverb **incompleteness** noun **incompletion** noun.

incomprehensible adjective not able to be understood.
– DERIVATIVES **incomprehensibility** noun **incomprehensibly** adverb **incomprehension** noun.

inconceivable adjective not able to be imagined or grasped mentally.
– DERIVATIVES **inconceivably** adverb.

inconclusive adjective not leading to a firm conclusion or result.
– DERIVATIVES **inconclusively** adverb **inconclusiveness** noun.

incongruent /in-**kong**-groo-uhnt/ adjective out of place; incongruous.
– DERIVATIVES **incongruence** noun **incongruently** adverb.

incongruous /in-**kong**-groo-uhss/ adjective out of place or not appropriate in a particular situation.
– DERIVATIVES **incongruity** noun (pl. **incongruities**) **incongruously** adverb.

inconsequent adjective 1 not connected or following logically. 2 not important; inconsequential.
– DERIVATIVES **inconsequence** noun **inconsequently** adverb.

inconsequential adjective not important or significant.
– DERIVATIVES **inconsequentiality** noun **inconsequentially** adverb.

inconsiderable adjective small in size, amount, extent, etc.: *a not inconsiderable number*.

inconsiderate adjective thoughtlessly causing hurt or inconvenience to others.
– DERIVATIVES **inconsiderately** adverb **inconsiderateness** noun.

inconsistent adjective 1 having parts or elements that differ from or contradict each other. 2 (**inconsistent with**) not in keeping with.
– DERIVATIVES **inconsistency** noun (pl. **inconsistencies**) **inconsistently** adverb.

inconsolable adjective not able to be comforted or consoled.
– DERIVATIVES **inconsolably** adverb.

inconspicuous adjective not clearly visible or noticeable.
– DERIVATIVES **inconspicuously** adverb **inconspicuousness** noun.

inconstant adjective frequently changing; variable or irregular.
– DERIVATIVES **inconstancy** noun.

incontestable adjective not able to be disputed.
– DERIVATIVES **incontestably** adverb.

incontinent adjective 1 unable to control when one urinates or defecates. 2 lacking self-control.
– DERIVATIVES **incontinence** noun **incontinently** adverb.

incontrovertible adjective not able to be denied or disputed.
– DERIVATIVES **incontrovertibly** adverb.

inconvenience noun the state of being slightly troublesome or difficult. •verb cause someone slight trouble or difficulty.

inconvenient adjective causing trouble, difficulties, or discomfort.
– DERIVATIVES **inconveniently** adverb.

incorporate verb 1 take in or contain as part of a whole: *some schemes incorporated all these variations.* 2 combine ingredients into one substance. 3 (often as adj. **incorporated**) form a company or other organization as a legal corporation.
– DERIVATIVES **incorporation** noun **incorporative** adjective **incorporator** noun.
– ORIGIN Latin *incorporare* 'embody'.

incorporeal /in-kor-**por**-i-uhl/ adjective not having a physical body or form.

incorrect adjective 1 not true or factually accurate; wrong: *the doctor gave you incorrect advice.* 2 not following accepted standards or rules.
– DERIVATIVES **incorrectly** adverb **incorrectness** noun.

incorrigible /in-**kor**-i-ji-b'l/ adjective not able to be changed or reformed: *he's an incorrigible liar.*
– DERIVATIVES **incorrigibility** noun **incorrigibly** adverb.
– ORIGIN Latin *incorrigibilis.*

incorruptible adjective 1 not able to be corrupted, especially by taking bribes. 2 not subject to death or decay; everlasting.
– DERIVATIVES **incorruptibility** noun.

increase verb /in-**kreess**/ become or make greater in size, amount, or intensity: *car use is increasing at an alarming rate.* •noun /**in**-kreess/ a rise in size, amount, or intensity.
– DERIVATIVES **increasing** adjective **increasingly** adverb.
– ORIGIN Latin *increscere.*

incredible adjective 1 impossible or hard to believe. 2 informal very good.
– DERIVATIVES **incredibility** noun **incredibly** adverb.

incredulous adjective unwilling or unable to believe something.
– DERIVATIVES **incredulity** noun **incredulously** adverb.

increment /**ing**-kri-muhnt/ noun an increase or addition, especially one of a series on a fixed scale.
– DERIVATIVES **incremental** adjective **incrementally** adverb.
– ORIGIN Latin *incrementum.*

incriminate /in-**krim**-i-nayt/ verb make someone appear guilty of a crime or wrongdoing.
– DERIVATIVES **incrimination** noun **incriminatory** adjective.

– ORIGIN Latin *incriminare* 'accuse'.

in-crowd noun (**the in-crowd**) informal a small group of people that are particularly fashionable or popular.

incubate /**ing**-kyuu-bayt/ verb 1 (of a bird) sit on eggs to keep them warm and hatch them. 2 keep bacteria, cells, etc. at a suitable temperature so that they develop. 3 (of an infectious disease) develop slowly without noticeable signs.
– DERIVATIVES **incubation** noun.
– ORIGIN Latin *incubare* 'lie on'.

incubator noun 1 a machine used to hatch eggs or grow microorganisms under controlled conditions. 2 an enclosed machine providing a controlled and protective environment for the care of premature babies.

incubus /**ing**-kyuu-buhss/ noun (pl. **incubi** /**ing**-kyuu-by/) 1 a male demon believed to have sex with sleeping women. 2 literary a cause of difficulty or anxiety.
– ORIGIN Latin *incubo* 'nightmare'.

inculcate /in-**kul**-kayt/ verb fix an idea in someone's mind by constantly repeating it.
– DERIVATIVES **inculcation** noun.
– ORIGIN Latin *inculcare* 'press in'.

incumbency noun (pl. **incumbencies**) the period during which an office is held.

incumbent /in-**kum**-buhnt/ adjective 1 (**incumbent on**) necessary for someone as a duty. 2 currently holding an office or post. •noun 1 the holder of an office or post. 2 (in the Christian Church) the holder of a benefice.
– ORIGIN from Latin *incumbere* 'lie or lean on'.

incur verb (**incurs**, **incurring**, **incurred**) do something that results in one experiencing something unpleasant or unwelcome: *he incurred the crowd's anger.*
– ORIGIN Latin *incurrere* 'run into or towards'.

incurable adjective 1 not able to be cured. 2 not able to be changed: *he's an incurable romantic.* •noun an incurable person.
– DERIVATIVES **incurably** adverb.

incurious adjective not eager to know something; lacking curiosity.
– DERIVATIVES **incuriosity** noun **incuriously** adverb.

incursion noun a sudden or brief invasion or attack.
– ORIGIN from Latin *incurrere* 'run into or towards'.

indebted adjective 1 owing gratitude to someone: *Alex obviously feels indebted to his rescuer.* 2 owing money.
– DERIVATIVES **indebtedness** noun.
– ORIGIN from Old French *endetter* 'involve in debt'.

indecent adjective 1 not following accepted standards of behaviour in relation to sexual matters. 2 not appropriate in the circumstances: *he was buried with indecent haste.*
– DERIVATIVES **indecency** noun (pl. **indecencies**) **indecently** adverb.

indecent assault noun sexual assault that does not involve rape.

indecent exposure noun the crime of intentionally showing one's genitals in public.

indecipherable /in-di-sy-fuh-ruh-b'l/

i

adjective not able to be read or understood.

indecisive adjective 1 not able to make decisions quickly. 2 not settling an issue: *an indecisive battle.*
– DERIVATIVES **indecision** noun **indecisively** adverb **indecisiveness** noun.

indecorous adjective not in keeping with good taste and propriety; improper.

indeed adverb 1 used to emphasize a statement or answer. 2 used to introduce a further and stronger or more surprising point.
– ORIGIN from *in deed.*

indefatigable /in-di-**fat**-i-guh-b'l/ adjective never tiring or stopping.
– DERIVATIVES **indefatigably** adverb.
– ORIGIN Latin *indefatigabilis,* from *fatigare* 'wear out'.

indefensible adjective not able to be justified or defended.
– DERIVATIVES **indefensibly** adverb.

indefinable adjective not able to be defined or described exactly.
– DERIVATIVES **indefinably** adverb.

indefinite adjective 1 not clearly expressed or defined; vague. 2 lasting for an unknown or unstated length of time.
– DERIVATIVES **indefinitely** adverb **indefiniteness** noun.

indefinite article noun Grammar the words *a* or *an.*

indefinite pronoun noun Grammar a pronoun that does not refer to any person or thing in particular, e.g. *anything, everyone.*

indelible /in-**del**-i-b'l/ adjective 1 unable to be forgotten: *the beauty of the valley made an indelible impression on him.* 2 (of ink or a mark) unable to be removed.
– DERIVATIVES **indelibly** adverb.
– ORIGIN Latin *indelebilis.*

indelicate adjective 1 lacking sensitive understanding or tact. 2 slightly indecent.
– DERIVATIVES **indelicacy** noun **indelicately** adverb.

indemnify /in-**dem**-ni-fy/ verb (**indemnifies, indemnifying, indemnified**) 1 compensate someone for harm or loss. 2 protect or insure someone against legal responsibility for their actions.
– DERIVATIVES **indemnification** noun **indemnifier** noun.

indemnity /in-**dem**-ni-ti/ noun (pl. **indemnities**) 1 security or protection against a loss. 2 security against or exemption from legal responsibility for one's actions. 3 a sum of money paid to compensate for damage or loss, especially by a country defeated in war.
– ORIGIN from Latin *indemnis* 'unhurt, free from loss'.

indent verb /in-**dent**/ 1 form hollows, dents, or notches in something. 2 begin a line of writing further from the margin than the other lines. 3 Brit. make a written order for something.
• noun /**in**-dent/ 1 Brit. an official order for goods or stores. 2 a space left by indenting writing.
– DERIVATIVES **indenter** (also **indentor**) noun.
– ORIGIN Latin *indentare.*

indentation noun 1 a deep recess or notch on an edge or surface. 2 the action of indenting something, especially a line of writing.

indenture /in-**den**-cher/ noun 1 a formal agreement or contract, such as one formerly binding an apprentice to work for an employer. 2 historical a contract by which a person agreed to work for a set period for a colonial landowner in exchange for passage to the colony. • verb chiefly historical bind someone by an indenture as an apprentice or labourer.
– DERIVATIVES **indentureship** noun.

independence noun the fact or state of being independent.

independent adjective 1 free from outside control or influence: *you should take independent advice.* 2 (of a country) self-governing. 3 having or earning enough money to support oneself. 4 not connected with another person or thing; separate. 5 (of broadcasting, a school, etc.) not supported by public funds. • noun an independent person or organization.
– DERIVATIVES **independency** noun **independently** adverb.

in-depth adjective comprehensive and thorough.

indescribable adjective too unusual, extreme, or vague to be adequately described.
– DERIVATIVES **indescribably** adverb.

indestructible adjective not able to be destroyed.
– DERIVATIVES **indestructibility** noun **indestructibly** adverb.

indeterminable adjective not able to be determined.

indeterminate /in-di-**ter**-mi-nuht/ adjective 1 not exactly known, established, or defined: *a woman of indeterminate age.* 2 Mathematics (of a quantity) having no definite or definable value.
– DERIVATIVES **indeterminacy** noun **indeterminately** adverb.

index /**in**-deks/ noun (pl. **indexes** or especially in technical use **indices** /**in**-di-seez/) 1 an alphabetical list of names or subjects with references to the places in a book where they occur. 2 an alphabetical list or catalogue of books or documents. 3 a sign or measure of something: *national security was no longer an index of weaponry.* 4 a number representing the relative value or magnitude of something in terms of a standard: *a price index.* 5 Mathematics an exponent or other superscript or subscript number appended to a quantity.
• verb 1 record items in or provide something with an index. 2 link the value of prices, wages, etc. automatically to the value of a price index.
– DERIVATIVES **indexable** adjective **indexation** noun **indexer** noun.
– ORIGIN Latin, 'forefinger, informer, sign'.

index finger noun the forefinger.

index-linked adjective Brit. (of wages, pensions, etc.) adjusted according to the value of a retail price index.

Indiaman noun (pl. **Indiamen**) historical a ship engaged in trade with India or the East or West Indies.

Indian noun 1 a person from India. 2 dated an American Indian. • adjective 1 relating to India. 2 dated relating to American Indians.
– DERIVATIVES **Indianism** noun **Indianize** (or **Indianise**) verb **Indianness** noun.

USAGE: Do not use **Indian** or **Red Indian** to refer to American native peoples, as these terms are now outdated; use **American Indian** instead.

Indian club noun each of a pair of bottle-shaped clubs swung to exercise the arms in gymnastics.

Indian corn noun chiefly N. Amer. a type of maize.

Indian file noun single file.

Indian ink noun deep black ink used especially in drawing and technical graphics.
– ORIGIN first used of Chinese and Japanese pigments imported to Europe via India.

Indian summer noun a period of dry, warm weather occurring in late autumn.

India rubber noun natural rubber.

indicate verb **1** point out or show something. **2** be a sign of: *sales indicate a growing market for such art.* **3** mention something briefly or indirectly. **4** (**be indicated**) be necessary or recommended: *treatment for shock may be indicated.* **5** Brit. (of a driver) use an indicator to signal an intention to change lanes or turn.
– DERIVATIVES **indication** noun.
– ORIGIN Latin *indicare*.

indicative /in-**dik**-uh-tiv/ adjective **1** acting as a sign: *having recurrent dreams is not necessarily indicative of any psychological problem.* **2** Grammar (of a form of a verb) expressing a simple statement of fact (e.g. *she left*). •noun Grammar an indicative verb.

indicator noun **1** a thing that shows a state or level: *assessment tasks are an indicator of the teacher's performance.* **2** a gauge or meter that gives particular information: *a speed indicator.* **3** Brit. a flashing light on a vehicle used to show that it is about to change lanes or turn. **4** a chemical compound which changes colour at a specific pH value or in the presence of a particular substance, and can be used to monitor a chemical change.

indices plural of **INDEX**.

indict /in-**dyt**/ verb chiefly N. Amer. formally accuse someone of or charge them with a crime.
– ORIGIN Latin *indicere* 'proclaim, appoint'.

indictable /in-**dyt**-uh-b'l/ adjective (of an offence) making the person who commits it liable to be charged with a crime that warrants a trial by jury.

indictment /in-**dyt**-muhnt/ noun **1** Law, chiefly N. Amer. a formal charge or accusation of a crime. **2** an indication that a system or situation is bad and deserves to be condemned: *these escalating crime figures are an indictment of our society.*

indie adjective informal (of a pop group or record label) not belonging or linked to a major record company.

indifferent adjective **1** having no particular interest in or feelings about something. **2** not particularly good; mediocre.
– DERIVATIVES **indifference** noun **indifferently** adverb.
– ORIGIN Latin, 'making no difference'.

indigenize (or **indigenise**) /in-**dij**-i-nyz/ verb bring something under the control or influence of native people.
– DERIVATIVES **indigenization** noun.

indigenous /in-**dij**-in-uhss/ adjective originating or occurring naturally in a particular place; native.
– ORIGIN Latin *indigena* 'a native'.

indigent /in-di-juhnt/ adjective very poor. •noun a person who is very poor.
– DERIVATIVES **indigence** noun.
– ORIGIN Latin, from *indigere* 'to lack'.

indigestible adjective **1** difficult or impossible to digest. **2** difficult to read or understand.
– DERIVATIVES **indigestibility** noun **indigestibly** adverb.

indigestion noun pain or discomfort in the stomach caused by difficulty in digesting food.

indignant adjective feeling or showing offence and annoyance.
– DERIVATIVES **indignantly** adverb.
– ORIGIN Latin, from *indignari* 'regard as unworthy'.

indignation noun annoyance caused by what is seen as unfair treatment.

indignity noun (pl. **indignities**) treatment or circumstances that cause one to feel ashamed or embarrassed.

indigo /in-di-goh/ noun (pl. **indigos** or **indigoes**) **1** a dark blue dye obtained from a tropical plant. **2** a dark blue colour.
– ORIGIN Portuguese, from Greek *indikos* 'Indian (dye)'.

indirect adjective **1** not direct: *an indirect route.* **2** (of taxation) charged on goods and services rather than income or profits. **3** (of costs) arising from the regular expenses involved in running a business or from subsidiary work.
– DERIVATIVES **indirection** noun **indirectly** adverb **indirectness** noun.

indirect object noun Grammar a person or thing that is affected by the action of a transitive verb but is not the main object (e.g. *him* in *give him the book*).

indirect question noun Grammar a question in reported speech (e.g. *they asked who I was*).

indirect speech noun another term for REPORTED SPEECH.

indiscernible /in-di-**ser**-ni-b'l/ adjective impossible to see or distinguish clearly.

indiscipline noun disorderly or uncontrolled behaviour.

indiscreet adjective too ready to reveal things that should remain secret or private.
– DERIVATIVES **indiscreetly** adverb.

indiscretion noun behaviour or an act or remark that is indiscreet or shows a lack of good judgement.

indiscriminate /in-dis-**krim**-in-uht/ adjective done or acting at random or without careful judgement.
– DERIVATIVES **indiscriminately** adverb.

indispensable adjective absolutely necessary.
– DERIVATIVES **indispensability** noun.

indisposed adjective **1** slightly unwell. **2** unwilling to do something.

indisposition noun a slight illness.

indisputable adjective unable to be challenged or denied.
– DERIVATIVES **indisputability** noun **indisputably** adverb.

indissoluble /in-dis-**sol**-yuu-b'l/ adjective unable to be destroyed; lasting.

indistinct adjective not clear or sharply defined.
– DERIVATIVES **indistinctly** adverb **indistinctness** noun.

indistinguishable adjective not able to be identified as different or distinct.
– DERIVATIVES **indistinguishably** adverb.

indium /in-di-uhm/ noun a soft silvery-white metallic chemical element resembling zinc, used in some alloys and semiconductor devices.
– ORIGIN from **INDIGO**.

individual adjective **1** single; separate. **2** relating to or for one particular person: *the individual needs of the children.* **3** striking or unusual; original: *a highly individual musical style.* • noun **1** a single person or item as distinct from a group. **2** a person of a particular kind: *a selfish individual.* **3** a person who is unusual or different from other people.
– DERIVATIVES **individually** adverb.
– ORIGIN from Latin *in-* 'not' + *dividere* 'to divide'.

individualism noun **1** independence and self-reliance. **2** a social theory which favours the idea that individual people should have freedom of action rather than be controlled by society or the state.
– DERIVATIVES **individualist** noun & adjective **individualistic** adjective.

individuality noun the quality or character of a person or thing that makes them different from others.

individualize (or **individualise**) verb make or alter something in such a way as to suit the needs or wishes of a particular person.

individuate verb distinguish someone or something from other people or things of the same kind.
– DERIVATIVES **individuation** noun.

indivisible adjective **1** unable to be divided or separated. **2** (of a number) unable to be divided by another number exactly without leaving a remainder.
– DERIVATIVES **indivisibility** noun **indivisibly** adverb.

indoctrinate /in-dok-tri-nayt/ verb make someone accept a set of beliefs, without allowing them to consider any alternatives.
– DERIVATIVES **indoctrination** noun.
– ORIGIN from **DOCTRINE**.

Indo-European noun **1** the family of languages spoken over the greater part of Europe and Asia as far as northern India. **2** a person who speaks an Indo-European language. • adjective relating to Indo-European languages.

indolent /in-duh-luhnt/ adjective wanting to avoid activity or exertion; lazy.
– DERIVATIVES **indolence** noun **indolently** adverb.
– ORIGIN Latin, 'not giving pain'.

indomitable /in-dom-i-tuh-b'l/ adjective impossible to subdue or defeat.
– DERIVATIVES **indomitability** noun **indomitably** adverb.
– ORIGIN Latin *indomitabilis* 'unable to be tamed'.

Indonesian noun **1** a person from Indonesia. **2** the group of languages spoken in Indonesia. • adjective relating to Indonesia.

indoor adjective situated, done, or used inside a building or under cover.

indoors adverb into or within a building. • noun the area or space inside a building.

indorse verb US & Law variant spelling of **ENDORSE**.

indorsement noun US & Law variant spelling of **ENDORSEMENT**.

indrawn adjective **1** (of breath) taken in. **2** (of a person) shy and introspective.

indubitable /in-dyoo-bi-tuh-b'l/ adjective formal impossible to doubt; unquestionable.
– DERIVATIVES **indubitably** adverb.
– ORIGIN Latin *indubitabilis*.

induce /in-dyooss/ verb **1** persuade or influence someone to do something. **2** bring about or cause: *herbs to induce sleep.* **3** cause a pregnant woman to go into labour by the use drugs or other artificial means. **4** produce an electric charge or current or a magnetic state by induction.
– DERIVATIVES **inducer** noun **inducible** adjective.
– ORIGIN Latin *inducere* 'lead in'.

inducement noun **1** a thing that persuades or influences someone to do something. **2** a bribe.

induct verb **1** formally admit someone to an organization or establish them in a position. **2** US enlist someone for military service.
– DERIVATIVES **inductee** noun.
– ORIGIN Latin *inducere* 'lead in'.

inductance noun Physics the property of an electric conductor or circuit that causes an electromotive force to be generated by a change in the current flowing.

induction noun **1** the action or process of introducing someone to an organization or establishing them in a position. **2** the action or process of inducing something. **3** a method of reasoning in which a general rule or conclusion is drawn from particular facts or examples. **4** the production of an electric or magnetic state in an object by bringing an electrified or magnetized object close to it (without touching it). **5** the drawing of the fuel mixture into the cylinders of an internal-combustion engine.

induction coil noun a coil for generating intermittent high voltage from a direct current.

induction loop noun a sound system in which a loop of wire around an area in a building produces an electromagnetic signal received directly by hearing aids.

inductive adjective **1** using a method of reasoning that draws general conclusions from particular facts or examples. **2** relating to electric or magnetic induction. **3** Physics possessing inductance.
– DERIVATIVES **inductively** adverb **inductivism** noun **inductivist** noun & adjective.

inductor noun a component of an electric circuit which possesses inductance.

indulge verb **1** (**indulge in**) allow oneself to enjoy the pleasure of something: *we indulged in a cream tea.* **2** satisfy a desire or interest: *she was able to indulge a growing passion for literature.* **3** allow someone to do or have whatever they wish.

– ORIGIN Latin *indulgere* 'give free rein to'.

indulgence noun **1** the action of allowing oneself to do something pleasurable. **2** a thing that is indulged in; a luxury. **3** a willingness to tolerate someone's faults. **4** an extension of the time in which a bill or debt has to be paid. **5** chiefly historical (in the Roman Catholic Church) the setting aside or cancellation by the Pope of the punishment still due for sins after absolution.

indulgent adjective **1** readily indulging someone or overlooking their faults. **2** self-indulgent.
– DERIVATIVES **indulgently** adverb.

industrial adjective relating to or used in industry, or having many industries.
– DERIVATIVES **industrially** adverb.

industrial action noun Brit. action taken by employees of a company as a protest, especially striking or working to rule.

industrial estate (N. Amer. **industrial park**) noun chiefly Brit. an area of land developed as a site for factories and other industrial use.

industrialism noun a social or economic system based on manufacturing industries.

industrialist noun a person who owns or controls a manufacturing business.

industrialize (or **industrialise**) verb (often as adj. **industrialized**) develop industries in a country or region on a wide scale.
– DERIVATIVES **industrialization** noun.

industrial relations plural noun the relations between management and workers in industry.

industrial-strength adjective very strong or powerful.

industrious adjective hard-working.
– DERIVATIVES **industriously** adverb **industriousness** noun.

industry noun (pl. **industries**) **1** economic activity concerned with the processing of raw materials and manufacture of goods in factories. **2** a particular branch of economic or commercial activity: *the tourist industry.* **3** hard work.
– ORIGIN Latin *industria* 'diligence'.

inebriate verb /i-nee-bri-ayt/ (usu. as adj. **inebriated**) make someone drunk. • adjective /i-nee-bri-uht/ drunk.
– DERIVATIVES **inebriation** noun.
– ORIGIN Latin *inebriare*.

inedible adjective not fit for eating.

ineducable /in-ed-yuu-kuh-b'l/ adjective considered incapable of being educated.

ineffable /in-ef-fuh-b'l/ adjective **1** too great or extreme to be expressed in words: *the ineffable beauty of the Everglades.* **2** too sacred to be spoken.
– DERIVATIVES **ineffability** noun **ineffably** adverb.
– ORIGIN Latin *ineffabilis*

ineffective adjective not producing any or the desired effect.
– DERIVATIVES **ineffectively** adverb **ineffectiveness** noun.

ineffectual adjective **1** not producing any or the desired effect. **2** lacking the necessary forcefulness in a role or situation.
– DERIVATIVES **ineffectually** adverb.

inefficient adjective failing to make the best use of time or resources.
– DERIVATIVES **inefficiency** noun **inefficiently** adverb.

inelastic adjective (of a material) not elastic.
– DERIVATIVES **inelastically** adverb **inelasticity** noun.

inelegant adjective not elegant or graceful.
– DERIVATIVES **inelegance** noun **inelegantly** adverb.

ineligible adjective not eligible.
– DERIVATIVES **ineligibility** noun.

ineluctable /in-i-luk-tuh-b'l/ adjective unable to be resisted or avoided; inescapable.
– DERIVATIVES **ineluctably** adverb.
– ORIGIN Latin *ineluctabilis*.

inept adjective awkward or clumsy; incompetent.
– DERIVATIVES **ineptitude** noun **ineptly** adverb **ineptness** noun.
– ORIGIN Latin *ineptus* 'not suitable'.

inequality noun (pl. **inequalities**) lack of equality.

inequitable adjective unfair; unjust.
– DERIVATIVES **inequitably** adverb.

inequity noun (pl. **inequities**) lack of fairness or justice.

ineradicable /in-i-rad-i-kuh-b'l/ adjective unable to be destroyed or removed.
– DERIVATIVES **ineradicably** adverb.

inert adjective **1** lacking the ability or strength to move. **2** without active chemical properties.
– DERIVATIVES **inertly** adverb **inertness** noun.
– ORIGIN Latin *iners*, 'unskilled, inactive'.

inert gas noun another term for **NOBLE GAS**.

inertia /i-ner-shuh/ noun **1** lack of desire or ability to move or change. **2** Physics a property of matter by which it continues in its existing state of rest or continues moving in a straight line, unless changed by an external force.
– DERIVATIVES **inertial** adjective.

inertia reel noun a device which allows a vehicle seat belt to unwind freely but which locks under force of impact or rapid deceleration.

inescapable adjective unable to be avoided or denied.
– DERIVATIVES **inescapability** noun **inescapably** adverb.

inessential adjective not absolutely necessary. • noun an inessential thing.

inestimable adjective too great to be measured.
– DERIVATIVES **inestimably** adverb.

inevitable adjective certain to happen; unavoidable. • noun (**the inevitable**) a situation that is unavoidable.
– DERIVATIVES **inevitability** noun **inevitably** adverb.
– ORIGIN Latin *inevitabilis*.

inexact adjective not quite accurate.
– DERIVATIVES **inexactitude** noun **inexactly** adverb **inexactness** noun.

inexcusable adjective too bad to be justified or tolerated.
– DERIVATIVES **inexcusably** adverb.

inexhaustible adjective (of an amount or supply of something) available in unlimited quantities.
– DERIVATIVES **inexhaustibly** adverb.

i

inexorable /in-ek-suh-ruh-b'l/ adjective
1 impossible to stop or prevent: *the inexorable march of new technology.* 2 (of a person) impossible to persuade; unrelenting.
– DERIVATIVES **inexorability** noun **inexorably** adverb.
– ORIGIN Latin *inexorabilis.*

inexpensive adjective not costing a great deal; cheap.
– DERIVATIVES **inexpensively** adverb **inexpensiveness** noun.

inexperience noun lack of experience.
– DERIVATIVES **inexperienced** adjective.

inexpert adjective lacking skill or knowledge in a particular field.
– DERIVATIVES **inexpertly** adverb.

inexplicable /in-ik-splik-uh-b'l/ adjective unable to be explained or accounted for.
– DERIVATIVES **inexplicability** noun **inexplicably** adverb.

inexpressible adjective (of a feeling) too strong to be described or expressed in words.
– DERIVATIVES **inexpressibly** adverb.

inexpressive adjective showing no expression.
– DERIVATIVES **inexpressively** adverb **inexpressiveness** noun.

inextinguishable adjective unable to be extinguished.

in extremis /in ek-stree-miss/ adverb 1 in an extremely difficult situation. 2 at the point of death.
– ORIGIN Latin.

inextricable /in-ik-strik-uh-b'l/ adjective impossible to disentangle or separate: *the past and the present are inextricable.*
– DERIVATIVES **inextricably** adverb.

infallible /in-fal-li-b'l/ adjective 1 incapable of making mistakes or being wrong. 2 never failing; always effective.
– DERIVATIVES **infallibility** noun **infallibly** adverb.

infamous /in-fuh-muhss/ adjective 1 well known for some bad quality or deed. 2 morally bad; wicked.
– DERIVATIVES **infamously** adverb.

infamy /in-fuh-mi/ noun (pl. **infamies**) 1 the state of being known for something bad. 2 a wicked act.

infancy noun 1 the state or period of being a baby or very young child. 2 the early stage in the development or growth of something: *opinion polls were in their infancy.*

infant noun 1 a baby or very young child. 2 Brit. a schoolchild between the ages of about four and eight.
– ORIGIN from Latin *infans* 'unable to speak'.

infanta /in-fan-tuh/ noun historical a daughter of the king or queen of Spain or Portugal.
– ORIGIN Spanish and Portuguese.

infanticide /in-fan-ti-syd/ noun the killing of a baby or very young child.

infantile /in-fuhn-tyl/ adjective 1 relating to or affecting babies and very young children. 2 derogatory childish.

infantilism /in-fan-ti-li-z'm/ noun 1 childish behaviour. 2 Psychology a condition in which characteristics or behaviour of babies or very young children persist into adult life.

infantry noun soldiers who fight on foot.
– DERIVATIVES **infantryman** noun (pl. infantrymen).
– ORIGIN Italian *infanteria*, from *infante* 'youth, infantryman'.

infarct /in-fahkt, in-fahkt/ noun Medicine a small area of dead tissue resulting from a failure of the blood supply.
– DERIVATIVES **infarction** noun.
– ORIGIN Latin *infarctus.*

infatuate verb (**be infatuated with**) have an intense but usually short-lived passion for someone.
– DERIVATIVES **infatuation** noun.
– ORIGIN Latin *infatuare* 'make foolish'.

infect verb 1 affect a person, part of the body, etc. with an organism that causes disease. 2 contaminate something.
– ORIGIN Latin *inficere* 'to taint'.

infection noun 1 the process of infecting someone or something or the state of being infected. 2 an infectious disease.

infectious adjective 1 (of a disease or disease-causing organism) liable to be transmitted through the environment. 2 (of a person or animal) likely to spread infection. 3 likely to spread to or influence other people: *her enthusiasm is infectious.*
– DERIVATIVES **infectiously** adverb **infectiousness** noun.

infective adjective capable of causing infection.

infelicitous adjective unfortunate; inappropriate.
– DERIVATIVES **infelicitously** adverb.

infelicity noun (pl. **infelicities**) 1 an inappropriate remark or action. 2 old use unhappiness or misfortune.

infer verb (**infers, inferring, inferred**) work something out from evidence and reasoning rather than from direct statements.
– DERIVATIVES **inferable** (also **inferrable**) adjective.
– ORIGIN Latin *inferre* 'bring in, bring about'.

USAGE: On the use of **imply** and **infer**, see the note at **IMPLY**.

inference /in-fuh-ruhnss/ noun 1 a conclusion reached on the basis of evidence and reasoning. 2 the process of reaching a conclusion in this way.
– DERIVATIVES **inferential** adjective.

inferior adjective 1 lower in rank, status, or quality. 2 of low standard or quality. 3 chiefly Anatomy low or lower in position. 4 (of a letter or symbol) written or printed below the line.
• noun a person lower than another in rank, status, or ability.
– DERIVATIVES **inferiority** noun.
– ORIGIN Latin, from *inferus* 'low'.

inferiority complex noun a feeling that one is of lower status or has less ability than other people, resulting in aggressive or withdrawn behaviour.

infernal adjective 1 relating to hell or the underworld. 2 informal very annoying: *an infernal nuisance.*
– DERIVATIVES **infernally** adverb.
– ORIGIN Latin *infernus* 'underground'.

inferno noun (pl. **infernos**) 1 a large uncontrollable fire. 2 (**Inferno**) hell.

- ORIGIN Italian, from Latin *infernus* 'underground'.

infertile adjective 1 unable to have children or (of an animal) bear young. 2 (of land) unable to produce crops or vegetation.
- DERIVATIVES **infertility** noun.

infest verb (of insects or organisms) be present in large numbers, typically so as to cause damage or disease.
- DERIVATIVES **infestation** noun.
- ORIGIN Latin *infestare* 'assail'.

infidel /in-fi-duhl/ noun chiefly old use a person who has no religion or whose religion is not that of the majority.
- ORIGIN Latin *infidelis*.

infidelity noun (pl. **infidelities**) 1 the action or state of being sexually unfaithful. 2 lack of religious faith.

infield noun Cricket the part of the field closer to the wicket. • adverb into or towards the infield.
- DERIVATIVES **infielder** noun.

infighting noun conflict within a group or organization.

infill noun (also **infilling**) material or buildings used to fill a space or hole. • verb fill or block up a space or hole.

infiltrate /in-fil-trayt/ verb 1 enter or gain access to an organization or place in a gradual and surreptitious way. 2 pass slowly into or through something.
- DERIVATIVES **infiltration** noun **infiltrator** noun.

infinite /in-fi-nit/ adjective 1 without limits and impossible to measure or calculate: *the infinite number of stars in the universe.* 2 very great in amount or degree: *he bathed the wound with infinite care.*
- DERIVATIVES **infinitely** adverb **infinitude** noun.
- ORIGIN Latin *infinitus*.

infinitesimal /in-fi-ni-tess-i-m'l/ adjective extremely small.
- DERIVATIVES **infinitesimally** adverb.
- ORIGIN Latin *infinitesimus*.

infinitive /in-fin-i-tiv/ noun the basic form of a verb, normally occurring in English with the word *to*, as in *to see, to ask*.
- ORIGIN from Latin *infinitus*.

infinity noun (pl. **infinities**) 1 the state or quality of having no limit and being impossible to measure or calculate. 2 a very great number or amount. 3 Mathematics a number greater than any assignable quantity or countable number (symbol ∞).

infirm adjective physically weak.
- ORIGIN Latin *infirmus*.

infirmary noun (pl. **infirmaries**) a hospital or place set aside for the care of sick or injured people.

infirmity noun (pl. **infirmities**) physical or mental weakness.

in flagrante delicto /in fluh-gran-tay di-lik-toh/ adverb in the very act of doing something wrong, especially having illicit sex.
- ORIGIN Latin, 'in the heat of the crime'.

inflame verb 1 make something stronger or worse: *comments that inflamed what was already a sensitive situation.* 2 arouse strong feelings in someone. 3 cause inflammation in a part of the body.

inflammable adjective easily set on fire.

- DERIVATIVES **inflammability** noun.

USAGE: The words **inflammable** and **flammable** both mean 'easily set on fire'. It is, however, safer to use **flammable** to avoid ambiguity, as the *in-* part of **inflammable** can give the impression that the word means 'non-flammable'.

inflammation noun a condition in which an area of the skin or body becomes reddened, swollen, hot, and often painful, especially as a reaction to injury or infection.

inflammatory adjective 1 relating to or causing inflammation. 2 arousing or intended to arouse angry or violent feelings.

inflatable adjective capable of being inflated. • noun a plastic or rubber object that is inflated before use.

inflate verb 1 expand something by filling it with air or gas. 2 increase something by a large or excessive amount. 3 (as adj. **inflated**) exaggerated: *an inflated view of her own importance.* 4 bring about inflation of a currency or in an economy.
- ORIGIN Latin *inflare* 'blow into'.

inflation noun 1 the action of inflating something. 2 a general increase in prices and fall in the value of money.
- DERIVATIVES **inflationary** adjective.

inflect verb 1 Grammar (of a word) change by inflection. 2 vary the intonation or pitch of the voice.
- ORIGIN Latin *inflectere*.

inflection (chiefly Brit. also **inflexion**) noun 1 Grammar a change in the form of a word (typically the ending) to show a grammatical function or quality such as tense, mood, person, number, case, and gender. 2 a variation in intonation or pitch of the voice. 3 chiefly Mathematics a change of curvature from convex to concave.
- DERIVATIVES **inflectional** adjective.

inflexible adjective 1 not able to be altered or adapted. 2 unwilling to change or compromise. 3 not able to be bent; stiff.
- DERIVATIVES **inflexibility** noun **inflexibly** adverb.

inflict verb (**inflict something on**) 1 cause someone to suffer something unpleasant: *they inflicted serious injuries on the other men.* 2 impose something unwelcome on someone: *she is wrong to inflict her beliefs on everyone else.*
- DERIVATIVES **infliction** noun.
- ORIGIN Latin *infligere* 'strike against'.

in-flight adjective occurring or provided during an aircraft flight.

inflorescence /in-fluh-ress-uhnss/ noun 1 the complete flower head of a plant, including stems, stalks, bracts, and flowers. 2 the process of flowering.
- ORIGIN Latin *inflorescere* 'come into flower'.

inflow noun 1 the movement of liquid or air into a place. 2 the movement of a lot of money, people, or things into a place.

influence noun 1 the power or ability to have an effect on someone's beliefs or actions. 2 a person or thing with the power or ability to do this. 3 the power arising out of one's status, contacts, or wealth. • verb have an effect on: *feminist ideas have influenced the lawmakers.*

– PHRASES **under the influence** informal affected by alcohol or drugs.
– DERIVATIVES **influencer** noun.
– ORIGIN Latin *influere* 'flow in'.

influential adjective having great influence.
– DERIVATIVES **influentially** adverb.

influenza noun a highly contagious infection of the nose, throat, and lungs, spread by a virus and causing fever, severe aching, and catarrh.
– ORIGIN Italian, 'influence'.

influx noun 1 the arrival or entry of large numbers of people or things. 2 an inflow of water into a river, lake, or the sea.
– ORIGIN Latin *influxus*.

info noun informal information.

infomercial noun chiefly N. Amer. a long television advertisement which gives a great deal of information about a product in a supposedly objective way.
– ORIGIN blend of INFORMATION and COMMERCIAL.

inform verb 1 give facts or information to someone. 2 **(inform on)** give information about someone's involvement in a crime to the police. 3 have an important influence on; determine the nature of: *religion informs every aspect of their lives.*
– ORIGIN Latin *informare* 'shape, describe'.

informal adjective 1 relaxed, friendly, or unofficial. 2 (of clothes) suitable for everyday wear; casual. 3 referring to the language of everyday speech and writing, rather than that used in official and formal situations.
– DERIVATIVES **informality** noun **informally** adverb.

informant noun 1 a person who gives information to someone else. 2 an informer.

informatics /in-fuh-**mat**-iks/ plural noun (treated as sing.) Computing the science of processing data for storage and retrieval.

information noun 1 facts or knowledge provided or learned. 2 what is conveyed or represented by a particular arrangement of sequence of things: *genetically transmitted information.*
– DERIVATIVES **informational** adjective.

information superhighway noun an extensive electronic network such as the Internet, used for the rapid transfer of information in digital form.

information technology noun the study or use of systems such as computers and telecommunications for storing, retrieving, and sending information.

informative adjective providing useful information.
– DERIVATIVES **informatively** adverb.

informed adjective 1 having or showing knowledge: *an informed readership.* 2 (of a decision or judgement) based on an understanding of the facts.

informer noun a person who informs on another person to the police or other authority.

infotainment noun broadcast programmes which present news and serious subjects in an entertaining way.
– ORIGIN blend of INFORMATION and ENTERTAINMENT.

infra- prefix below: *infrasonic.*

– ORIGIN Latin *infra* 'below'.

infraction noun chiefly Law a breaking of a law or agreement.
– ORIGIN Latin, from *infringere* 'infringe'.

infra dig /in-fruh **dig**/ adjective informal, chiefly Brit. beneath one's dignity.
– ORIGIN from Latin *infra dignitatem.*

infrared noun electromagnetic radiation having a wavelength just greater than that of red light but less than that of microwaves, emitted particularly by heated objects.
• adjective relating to such radiation.

infrasonic adjective relating or referring to sound waves with a frequency below the range that can be heard by the human ear.

infrasound noun infrasonic sound waves.

infrastructure noun the basic physical and organizational structures (e.g. buildings, roads, or power supplies) needed for a society or enterprise to function.
– DERIVATIVES **infrastructural** adjective.

infrequent adjective not occurring often; rare.
– DERIVATIVES **infrequency** noun **infrequently** adverb.

infringe verb 1 break the terms of a law, agreement, etc. 2 limit or restrict someone's rights: *such widespread surveillance could infringe personal liberties.*
– DERIVATIVES **infringement** noun.
– ORIGIN Latin *infringere.*

infuriate /in-**fyoor**-i-ayt/ verb make someone very irritated or angry.
– DERIVATIVES **infuriating** adjective.
– ORIGIN Latin *infuriare.*

infuse verb 1 fill something with a quality: *a play infused with humour.* 2 soak tea, herbs, etc. to extract the flavour or healing properties. 3 Medicine allow a liquid to flow into a vein or tissue.
– DERIVATIVES **infuser** noun.
– ORIGIN Latin *infundere* 'pour in'.

infusible adjective not able to be melted or fused.

infusion noun 1 a drink or remedy prepared by soaking tea or herbs. 2 a new or additional element introduced into something: *the company needs a serious infusion of cash.* 3 the action of infusing something.

ingenious /in-**jee**-ni-uhss/ adjective clever, original, and inventive.
– DERIVATIVES **ingeniously** adverb.
– ORIGIN Latin *ingeniosus.*

ingénue /an-zhuh-nyoo/ noun an innocent or unsophisticated young woman.
– ORIGIN French.

ingenuity /in-ji-**nyoo**-i-ti/ noun the quality of being clever, original, and inventive.
– ORIGIN Latin *ingenuitas* 'ingenuousness'.

ingenuous /in-**jen**-yoo-uhss/ adjective innocent and unsuspecting.
– DERIVATIVES **ingenuously** adverb **ingenuousness** noun.
– ORIGIN Latin *ingenuus* 'native, inborn'.

ingest verb take food or drink into the body by swallowing or absorbing it.
– DERIVATIVES **ingestion** noun.
– ORIGIN Latin *ingerere* 'bring in'.

inglenook noun a space on either side of a large fireplace.

– ORIGIN from dialect *ingle* 'fire, fireplace' + NOOK.

inglorious adjective causing shame; dishonourable.

ingoing adjective going towards or into.

ingot /ing-guht/ noun a rectangular block of steel, gold, or other metal.
– ORIGIN perhaps from an Old English word meaning 'pour, cast'.

ingrained (also **engrained**) adjective 1 (of a habit or attitude) firmly established and hard to change. 2 (of dirt) deeply embedded.
– ORIGIN from the old use of *grain* to mean 'kermes, cochineal' (the first meaning was 'dyed with cochineal').

ingrate /in-grayt/ formal or literary noun an ungrateful person. • adjective ungrateful.
– ORIGIN Latin *ingratus*.

ingratiate /in-gray-shi-ayt/ verb (**ingratiate oneself**) try to gain favour with someone by flattering or trying to please them.
– DERIVATIVES **ingratiating** adjective **ingratiation** noun.
– ORIGIN from Latin *in gratiam* 'into favour'.

ingratitude noun a lack of gratitude for something that has been done for one.

ingredient noun 1 any of the substances that are combined to make a particular dish. 2 one of the parts or elements of something: *their romance had all the ingredients of a fairy tale.*
– ORIGIN Latin *ingredi* 'enter'.

ingress /in-gress/ noun 1 the action entering or coming in. 2 a place or means of access.
– ORIGIN Latin *ingressus*.

ingrowing adjective (of a toenail) growing inwards into the flesh of the toe.
– DERIVATIVES **ingrown** adjective.

inguinal /ing-gwi-nuhl/ adjective relating to the groin.
– ORIGIN Latin *inguinalis*.

inhabit verb (**inhabits, inhabiting, inhabited**) live in or occupy a place.
– DERIVATIVES **inhabitable** adjective.
– ORIGIN Latin *inhabitare*.

inhabitant noun a person or animal that lives in or occupies a place.

inhalant noun a drug or medicine that is inhaled.

inhale /in-hayl/ verb breathe in air, gas, smoke, etc.
– DERIVATIVES **inhalation** noun.
– ORIGIN Latin *inhalare*.

inhaler noun a portable device used for inhaling a drug.

inharmonious adjective not forming a pleasing whole; discordant.

inhere /in-heer/ verb (**inhere in/within**) formal be an essential or permanent part of something.
– ORIGIN Latin *inhaerere* 'stick to'.

inherent /in-herr-uhnt/ adjective existing in someone or something as a permanent or essential part or quality: *the risks inherent in our business.*
– DERIVATIVES **inherently** adverb.

inherit verb (**inherit, inheriting, inherited**) 1 receive money, property, or a title as an heir at the death of the previous holder. 2 have a quality or characteristic that one's parents or

ancestors also possessed: *she inherited her mother's strong-willed nature.* 3 receive or be left with a situation, object, etc. from a predecessor or former owner.
– DERIVATIVES **inheritable** adjective **inheritor** noun.
– ORIGIN Latin *inhereditare* 'appoint as heir'.

inheritance noun 1 money, property, or a title received on the death of the previous owner. 2 the action of inheriting something.

inheritance tax noun (in the UK) tax levied on property and money acquired by gift or inheritance.

inhibit verb (**inhibits, inhibiting, inhibited**) 1 hinder or restrict an action or process: *cold inhibits plant growth.* 2 make someone unable to act in a relaxed and natural way.
– DERIVATIVES **inhibited** adjective.
– ORIGIN Latin *inhibere*.

inhibition noun 1 a feeling that makes someone unable to act in a relaxed and natural way. 2 the action of inhibiting something.

inhibitor noun a substance which slows down or prevents a particular chemical reaction or other process.
– DERIVATIVES **inhibitory** adjective.

inhospitable adjective 1 (of an environment) harsh and difficult to live in. 2 unwelcoming.

in-house adjective & adverb within an organization.

inhuman adjective 1 lacking good human qualities; cruel or brutal. 2 not human in nature or character.
– DERIVATIVES **inhumanly** adverb.

inhumane adjective showing no compassion for the misery or suffering of other people; cruel.
– DERIVATIVES **inhumanely** adverb.

inhumanity noun (pl. **inhumanities**) cruel or brutal behaviour.

inhumation /in-hyuu-may-shuhn/ noun chiefly Archaeology 1 the action or practice of burying the dead. 2 a burial or buried corpse.
– ORIGIN Latin *inhumare* 'bury'.

inimical /i-nim-i-k'l/ adjective harmful or unfavourable: *the policy was inimical to Britain's real interests.*
– DERIVATIVES **inimically** adverb.
– ORIGIN from Latin *inimicus* 'enemy'.

inimitable /in-im-i-tuh-b'l/ adjective impossible to imitate; unique.
– DERIVATIVES **inimitably** adverb.

iniquity /i-ni-kwi-ti/ noun (pl. **iniquities**) highly unfair or immoral behaviour.
– DERIVATIVES **iniquitous** adjective.
– ORIGIN Latin *iniquitas*.

initial adjective existing or occurring at the beginning: *our initial impression was favourable.* • noun the first letter of a name or word. • verb (**initials, initialling, initialled;** US **initials, initialing, initialed**) mark a document with one's initials as a sign of approval or authorization.
– DERIVATIVES **initially** adverb.
– ORIGIN from Latin *initium* 'beginning'.

initialism noun an abbreviation consisting of initial letters pronounced separately (e.g. BBC).

initiate verb /i-ni-shi-ayt/ 1 cause a process or action to begin. 2 admit someone into a

society or group with a formal ceremony or ritual. **3** (**initiate someone into**) introduce someone to a new activity or skill: *they were initiated into the mysteries of mathematics.* • **noun** /i-**nish**-i-uht/ a person who has been initiated into a society, group, or new activity.
– DERIVATIVES **initiation** noun **initiator** noun **initiatory** adjective.
– ORIGIN Latin *initiare* 'begin'.

initiative noun **1** the ability to act independently and with a fresh approach. **2** the power or opportunity to act before others do: *we have lost the initiative.* **3** a new development or fresh approach to a problem: *a new initiative against car crime.*
– PHRASES **on one's own initiative** without being prompted by other people.

inject verb **1** introduce a drug or other substance into the body with a syringe: *the doctor injected a painkilling drug.* **2** administer a drug or medicine to a person or animal with a syringe: *he injected himself with adrenalin.* **3** introduce something under pressure into a passage, cavity, or solid material. **4** introduce a new or different element into something: *she tried to inject scorn into her tone.*
– DERIVATIVES **injectable** adjective & noun **injector** noun.
– ORIGIN Latin *inicere* 'throw in'.

injection noun **1** an act of giving a person or animal a drug using a syringe. **2** a substance that is injected. **3** a large sum of additional money used to help a situation, business, etc.

in-joke noun a joke that is shared exclusively by a small group.

injudicious adjective showing poor judgement; unwise.
– DERIVATIVES **injudiciously** adverb.

injunction noun **1** an order made by a court of law stating that a person must or must not do something. **2** an authoritative warning.
– DERIVATIVES **injunctive** adjective.
– ORIGIN Latin.

injure verb **1** do physical harm to someone or something. **2** harm or damage: *a company's reputation could be injured by a libel.*

injured adjective **1** physically harmed. **2** offended or upset: *his injured pride.*

injurious /in-**joor**-i-uhss/ adjective **1** causing or likely to cause harm or damage. **2** (of language) libellous.

injury noun (pl. **injuries**) **1** an instance of being physically harmed. **2** the fact of being injured; harm or damage.
– ORIGIN Latin *injuria* 'a wrong'.

injury time noun Brit. (in football and other sports) extra playing time allowed to make up for time lost as a result of injuries.

injustice noun **1** lack of justice or fairness. **2** an unjust act or occurrence.

ink noun **1** a coloured fluid used for writing, drawing, or printing. **2** a black liquid squirted by a cuttlefish, octopus, or squid to confuse a predator. • verb **1** write or mark words or a design with ink. **2** cover metal type or a stamp with ink before printing.
– ORIGIN Old French *enque.*

inkjet printer noun a printer in which the characters are formed by minute jets of ink.

inkling noun a slight suspicion; a hint.
– ORIGIN from former *inkle* 'say in an undertone'.

inkstand noun a stand for ink bottles, pens, and other items of stationery.

inkwell noun a container for ink, usually fitted into a hole in a desk.

inky adjective (**inkier, inkiest**) **1** as dark as ink. **2** stained with ink.

INLA abbreviation Irish National Liberation Army.

inlaid past and past participle of INLAY.

inland adjective & adverb **1** in or into the interior of a country. **2** (as adj.) chiefly Brit. carried on within a country; domestic: *inland trade.* • noun the interior of a country or region.
– DERIVATIVES **inlander** noun.

Inland Revenue noun (in the UK) the government department responsible for assessing and collecting income tax and some other taxes.

in-law noun a relative by marriage. • **combining form** related by marriage: *father-in-law.*

inlay verb (past and past part. **inlaid**) decorate an object by embedding pieces of a different material in its surface. • noun **1** inlaid decoration. **2** a material or substance used for inlaying. **3** a filling shaped to fit a cavity in a tooth.

inlet noun **1** a small arm of the sea, a lake, or a river. **2** a place or means of entry: *an air inlet.* **3** (in tailoring and dressmaking) an inserted piece of material.

in-line adjective **1** having parts arranged in a line. **2** forming an integral part of a continuous sequence of operations or machines.

in-line skate noun a type of roller skate in which the wheels are fixed in a single line along the sole.

in loco parentis /in loh-koh puh-**ren**-tiss/ adverb (of a teacher or other adult) in the place of a parent.
– ORIGIN Latin.

inmate noun a person living in an institution such as a prison or hospital.
– ORIGIN probably from INN + MATE¹.

in memoriam /in mi-**mor**-i-am/ preposition in memory of a dead person.
– ORIGIN Latin.

inmost adjective closest to the centre; innermost.

inn noun a pub, traditionally one that also provides food and accommodation.
– ORIGIN Old English.

innards plural noun informal **1** internal organs; entrails. **2** the internal workings of a device or machine.
– ORIGIN representing a dialect pronunciation of INWARDS.

innate /in-**nayt**/ adjective inborn; natural.
– DERIVATIVES **innately** adverb **innateness** noun.
– ORIGIN Latin *innatus.*

inner adjective **1** situated inside; close to the centre. **2** mental or spiritual: *inner strength.* **3** private; not expressed. • noun an inner part.

inner city noun an area in or near the centre of a city, especially when associated with social and economic problems.

inner ear noun the part of the ear embedded in the temporal bone, consisting of the semicircular canals and the cochlea.

innermost adjective **1** furthest in; closest to the centre. **2** (of thoughts) most private and deeply felt.

inner tube noun a separate inflatable tube inside a tyre casing.

inning noun Baseball each division of a game during which both sides have a turn at batting.
– ORIGIN Old English, 'a putting or getting in'.

innings noun (pl. same) (treated as sing.) Cricket each of the divisions of a game during which one side has a turn at batting.
– PHRASES **a good innings** Brit. informal a long and fulfilling life or career.

innkeeper noun chiefly old use a person who runs an inn.

innocent adjective **1** not guilty of a crime or offence. **2** having had little experience of life, especially of sexual matters. **3** not intended to cause offence: *an innocent remark.* **4** (**innocent of**) without experience or knowledge of something: *a man innocent of war's cruelties.* • noun an innocent person.
– DERIVATIVES **innocence** noun **innocently** adverb.
– ORIGIN Latin, 'not harming'.

innocuous /in-nok-yoo-uhss/ adjective not harmful or offensive.
– DERIVATIVES **innocuously** adverb.
– ORIGIN Latin *innocuus*.

Inn of Court noun (in the UK) each of the four legal societies having the exclusive right of admitting people to the English Bar.

innovate /in-nuh-vayt/ verb introduce new methods, ideas, or products.
– DERIVATIVES **innovator** noun **innovatory** adjective.
– ORIGIN Latin *innovare* 'renew, alter'.

innovation noun **1** the action of introducing new methods, ideas, or products. **2** a new method, idea, or product.

innovative /in-nuh-vuh-tiv/ adjective **1** featuring new ideas or methods; advanced and original: *innovative designs.* **2** (of a person) original and creative in their thinking.

innuendo /in-yuu-en-doh/ noun (pl. **innuendoes** or **innuendos**) a remark which makes an indirect reference to something, typically something rude or unpleasant.
– ORIGIN Latin, 'by nodding at, by pointing to'.

innumerable adjective too many to be counted.

innumerate adjective without a basic knowledge of mathematics and arithmetic.
– DERIVATIVES **innumeracy** noun.

inoculate /i-nok-yuu-layt/ verb **1** another term for VACCINATE. **2** introduce cells or microorganisms into a substance in which they can be grown.
– DERIVATIVES **inoculation** noun **inoculator** noun.
– ORIGIN Latin *inoculare*.

inoffensive adjective not objectionable or harmful.
– DERIVATIVES **inoffensively** adverb **inoffensiveness** noun.

inoperable adjective **1** not able to be safely treated or removed by a surgical operation: *an inoperable brain tumour.* **2** not able to be used. **3** impractical; unworkable.

inoperative adjective not working or taking effect.

inopportune adjective happening at an inconvenient time.

inordinate /in-or-di-nuht/ adjective unusually large; excessive.
– DERIVATIVES **inordinately** adverb.
– ORIGIN Latin *inordinatus*.

inorganic adjective **1** not consisting of or coming from living matter. **2** Chemistry relating or referring to compounds that do not contain carbon.
– DERIVATIVES **inorganically** adverb.

inpatient noun a patient who is staying day and night in a hospital while receiving treatment.

input noun **1** what is put or taken in or operated on by any process or system. **2** a person's contribution: *I'd value your input.* **3** energy supplied to a device or system; an electrical signal. **4** a place or device from which electricity, data, etc. enters a system. • verb (**inputs, inputting**; past and past part. **input** or **inputted**) put data into a computer.
– DERIVATIVES **inputter** noun.

inquest noun **1** a judicial inquiry to find out the facts relating to a particular incident. **2** Brit. an inquiry by a coroner's court into the cause of a death.
– ORIGIN Old French *enqueste*.

inquire verb another term for ENQUIRE.
– DERIVATIVES **inquirer** noun.

inquiry noun (pl. **inquiries**) another term for ENQUIRY.

inquisition noun **1** a period of long and intensive questioning or investigation. **2** the verdict of a coroner's jury.
– ORIGIN Latin, 'examination'.

inquisitive adjective **1** eager to learn things. **2** too curious about other people's affairs; prying.
– DERIVATIVES **inquisitively** adverb **inquisitiveness** noun.

inquisitor /in-kwiz-i-ter/ noun a person conducting a long, intensive, or relentless period of questioning or investigation.
– DERIVATIVES **inquisitorial** adjective.

inquorate /in-kwor-uht, in-kwor-ayt/ adjective Brit. (of a meeting) not having enough members present to make its business valid.

inroad noun (usu. in phrase **make inroads in/into**) a gradual entry into or effect on a place or situation: *the firm is beginning to make inroads into the UK market.*

inrush noun a sudden inward rush or flow.
– DERIVATIVES **inrushing** adjective & noun.

insalubrious /in-suh-loo-bri-uhss/ adjective not clean or well kept; seedy or squalid.

insane adjective **1** seriously mentally ill. **2** extremely foolish; irrational.
– DERIVATIVES **insanely** adverb **insanity** noun (pl. **insanities**).
– ORIGIN Latin *insanus*.

insanitary adjective so dirty or germ-ridden as to be a danger to health.

insatiable /in-say-shuh-b'l/ adjective impossible to satisfy.

- DERIVATIVES **insatiability** noun **insatiably** adverb.

inscribe verb **1** write or carve words or symbols on a surface. **2** write a dedication to someone in a book. **3** Geometry draw a figure within another so that their boundaries touch but do not intersect.
- ORIGIN Latin *inscribere*.

inscription noun **1** words or symbols inscribed on a monument, in a book, etc. **2** the action of inscribing something.
- DERIVATIVES **inscriptional** adjective.

inscrutable /in-skroo-tuh-b'l/ adjective impossible to understand or interpret.
- DERIVATIVES **inscrutability** noun **inscrutably** adverb.
- ORIGIN Latin *inscrutabilis*.

insect noun a small invertebrate animal with a body divided into three segments (head, thorax, and abdomen), six legs, two antennae, and usually one or two pairs of wings.
- ORIGIN from Latin *animal insectum* 'segmented animal'.

insecticide noun a substance used for killing insects.
- DERIVATIVES **insecticidal** adjective.

insectile adjective resembling an insect.

insectivore /in-sek-ti-vor/ noun **1** an animal that feeds on insects and other invertebrates. **2** Zoology a mammal of an order that includes the shrews, moles, and hedgehogs.
- DERIVATIVES **insectivorous** /in-sek-tiv-uh-ruhss/ adjective.

insecure adjective **1** not confident or self-assured. **2** not firm or firmly fixed. **3** (of a place) easily broken into; not protected.
- DERIVATIVES **insecurely** adverb **insecurity** noun (pl. **insecurities**).

inseminate /in-sem-i-nayt/ verb introduce semen into the vagina of a woman or a female animal.
- DERIVATIVES **insemination** noun **inseminator** noun.
- ORIGIN Latin *inseminare* 'sow'.

insensate adjective **1** lacking physical sensation. **2** lacking sympathy for other people; unfeeling. **3** completely lacking sense or reason.

insensible adjective **1** unconscious. **2** numb; without feeling. **3** (**insensible of/to**) unaware of or indifferent to something. **4** too small or gradual to be noticed.
- DERIVATIVES **insensibly** adverb **insensibility** noun.

insensitive adjective **1** showing or having no concern for the feelings of other people. **2** not able to feel something physically: *she was remarkably insensitive to pain.* **3** not aware of or able to respond to something: *politicians had been insensitive to local issues.*
- DERIVATIVES **insensitively** adverb **insensitivity** noun.

insentient adjective incapable of feeling; inanimate.
- DERIVATIVES **insentience** noun.

inseparable adjective **1** unable to be separated or treated separately. **2** very friendly and close.
- DERIVATIVES **inseparability** noun **inseparably** adverb.

insert verb /in-sert/ **1** place or fit something into something else: *she inserted her key into the lock.* **2** include text in a piece of writing. •noun /in-sert/ **1** a loose page or section in a magazine. **2** an ornamental section of cloth inserted into a garment. **3** a shot inserted in a film or video.
- DERIVATIVES **insertable** adjective **inserter** noun.
- ORIGIN Latin *inserere* 'put in'.

insertion noun **1** the action of inserting something. **2** a change or new item inserted in a piece of writing. **3** each appearance of an advertisement in a newspaper or magazine.

in-service adjective (of training) intended to take place during the course of employment.

inset noun /in-set/ **1** a thing inserted; an insert. **2** a small picture or map inserted within the border of a larger one. •verb /in-set/ (**insets, insetting;** past and past part. **inset** or **insetted**) **1** put something in as an inset. **2** decorate something with an inset: *tables inset with ceramic tiles.*

inshore adjective **1** at sea but close to the shore. **2** operating at sea but near the coast. •adverb towards or closer to the shore.

inside noun **1** the inner side, surface, or part of something. **2** (**insides**) informal the stomach and bowels. **3** the part of a road furthest from the centre. **4** the side of a bend where the edge is shorter. •adjective **1** situated on or in, or coming from, the inside. **2** (in some sports) referring to positions nearer to the centre of the field. **3** known or done by someone within an organization: *inside information.* •preposition & adverb **1** situated or moving within. **2** within a person's body or mind. **3** informal in prison. **4** (in some sports) closer to the centre of the field than. **5** in less than the period of time specified.
- PHRASES **on the inside** informal in a position in which one can get private information.

inside job noun informal a crime committed by or with the help of a person associated with the place where it occurred.

inside leg noun the length of a person's leg or trouser leg from crotch to ankle.

inside out adverb with the inner surface turned outwards.
- PHRASES **know something inside out** know something very thoroughly.

insider noun a person within an organization, especially someone who has information unavailable to those outside it.

insider dealing (also **insider trading**) noun the illegal practice of trading on the stock exchange to one's own advantage as a result of having access to confidential information.

insidious /in-sid-i-uhss/ adjective proceeding or spreading gradually or without being noticed, but causing serious harm.
- DERIVATIVES **insidiously** adverb **insidiousness** noun.
- ORIGIN Latin *insidiosus* 'cunning'.

insight noun **1** the ability to see and understand the truth about someone or something. **2** an understanding of the nature of someone or something: *a fascinating insight into the town's industrial heritage.*
- DERIVATIVES **insightful** adjective.

insignia /in-sig-ni-uh/ noun (pl. same or

insignias) a badge or emblem of someone's rank, position, or membership of a group or organization.
– ORIGIN Latin, 'signs, badges'.

insignificant adjective having little or no importance or value.
– DERIVATIVES **insignificance** noun **insignificantly** adverb.

insincere adjective not expressing one's true feelings.
– DERIVATIVES **insincerely** adverb **insincerity** noun (pl. **insincerities**).

insinuate /in-sin-yuu-ayt/ verb 1 suggest or hint at something bad in an indirect and unpleasant way. 2 (**insinuate oneself into**) manoeuvre oneself gradually into a favourable position: *he insinuated himself into the king's confidence.*
– DERIVATIVES **insinuating** adjective.
– ORIGIN Latin *insinuare*, from *sinuare* 'to curve'.

insinuation noun an unpleasant hint or suggestion.

insipid /in-si-pid/ adjective 1 lacking flavour. 2 not interesting or exciting.
– DERIVATIVES **insipidity** noun **insipidly** adverb.
– ORIGIN Latin *insipidus*.

insist verb 1 demand or state something forcefully, without accepting refusal. 2 (**insist on**) persist in doing something.
– ORIGIN Latin *insistere* 'persist'.

insistent adjective 1 demanding something and not allowing refusal: *she was very insistent that I call her.* 2 repeated and demanding attention.
– DERIVATIVES **insistence** noun **insistency** noun **insistently** adverb.

in situ /in sit-yoo/ adverb & adjective in the original or appropriate position.
– ORIGIN Latin.

insobriety noun drunkenness.

insole noun 1 a removable sole worn inside a shoe for warmth or to improve the fit. 2 the fixed inner sole of a boot or shoe.

insolent adjective rude and disrespectful.
– DERIVATIVES **insolence** noun **insolently** adverb.
– ORIGIN Latin, 'immoderate, arrogant'.

insoluble adjective 1 impossible to solve. 2 (of a substance) unable to be dissolved.
– DERIVATIVES **insolubility** noun.

insolvent adjective not having enough money to pay debts owed.
– DERIVATIVES **insolvency** noun.

insomnia noun the condition of being unable to sleep.
– DERIVATIVES **insomniac** noun & adjective.
– ORIGIN Latin.

insomuch adverb (**insomuch that/as**) to the extent that.

insouciant /in-soo-si-uhnt/ adjective casually unconcerned.
– DERIVATIVES **insouciance** noun **insouciantly** adverb.
– ORIGIN French.

inspect verb 1 look at someone or something closely. 2 examine someone or something to ensure that they reach an official standard.
– DERIVATIVES **inspection** noun.
– ORIGIN Latin *inspicere* 'look into, examine'.

inspector noun 1 an official who ensures that

regulations are obeyed. 2 a police officer ranking below a chief inspector.
– DERIVATIVES **inspectorate** noun **inspectorial** adjective **inspectorship** noun.

inspiration noun 1 the process of being filled with a feeling or with the urge to do something: *the Malvern Hills have provided inspiration for many artists.* 2 a person or thing that inspires other people. 3 a sudden clever idea. 4 the process of breathing in.
– DERIVATIVES **inspirational** adjective.

inspire verb 1 give someone the desire, enthusiasm, or confidence to do something. 2 create a feeling in a person. 3 give rise to: *the film was successful enough to inspire a sequel.* 4 breathe in air; inhale.
– DERIVATIVES **inspiratory** adjective **inspirer** noun **inspiring** adjective.
– ORIGIN Latin *inspirare* 'breathe or blow into'.

inspired adjective 1 displaying creativity or excellence: 2 (of air or another substance) that has been breathed in.

inspiriting adjective giving encouragement or inspiration.

inspissate /in-spi-sayt/ verb chiefly technical thicken or congeal something.
– ORIGIN Latin *inspissare*.

instability noun (pl. **instabilities**) lack of stability.

install verb (**installs, installing, installed**) 1 place or fix equipment in position ready for use. 2 establish someone in a new place or role.
– DERIVATIVES **installer** noun.
– ORIGIN Latin *installare*.

installation noun 1 the action of installing or establishing someone or something. 2 a large piece of equipment installed for use. 3 a military or industrial establishment. 4 an art exhibit constructed within a gallery.

instalment (US also **installment**) noun 1 a sum of money due as one of several payments made over a period of time. 2 one of several parts of something published or broadcast at intervals.
– ORIGIN Old French *estalement*.

instance noun 1 an example or single occurrence of something. 2 a particular case: *she hired a writer, in this instance Christopher Jones.* • verb give something as an example.
– PHRASES **for instance** as an example. **in the first instance** in the first stage of a series of actions.
– ORIGIN Latin *instantia* 'presence, urgency'.

instant adjective 1 happening immediately. 2 (of food) processed to allow quick preparation. 3 dated urgent; pressing. • noun 1 a precise moment of time. 2 a very short time.
– DERIVATIVES **instantly** adverb.
– ORIGIN Latin.

instantaneous /in-stuhn-tay-ni-uhss/ adjective occurring or done immediately.
– DERIVATIVES **instantaneity** noun **instantaneously** adverb.

instantiate /in-stan-shi-ayt/ verb represent something by a particular instance or example.
– DERIVATIVES **instantiation** noun.

instead adverb 1 as an alternative or substitute. 2 (**instead of**) in place of.

instep noun the part of a person's foot between the ball and the ankle.
– ORIGIN unknown.

instigate /in-sti-gayt/ verb 1 cause something to happen or begin. 2 (**instigate someone to/to do**) encourage someone to do something, especially something bad.
– DERIVATIVES **instigation** noun **instigator** noun.
– ORIGIN Latin *instigare* 'urge, incite'.

instil /in-stil/ (also **instill**) verb (**instils, instilling, instilled**) 1 gradually establish an idea or attitude in someone's mind: *her mother instilled in Harriet a love for cooking.* 2 put a liquid into something in drops.
– DERIVATIVES **instillation** noun.
– ORIGIN Latin *instillare*.

instinct noun 1 an inborn tendency to behave in a certain way. 2 a natural ability or skill. 3 a feeling based on intuition rather than facts or reasoning.
– DERIVATIVES **instinctual** adjective.
– ORIGIN Latin *instinctus* 'impulse'.

instinctive adjective based on instinct rather than conscious thought or training.
– DERIVATIVES **instinctively** adverb.

institute noun an organization for the promotion of science, education, culture, or a particular profession. •verb 1 begin or establish a scheme, policy, legal proceedings, etc. 2 appoint someone to a position, especially as a cleric.
– ORIGIN from Latin *instituere* 'establish'.

institution noun 1 an important organization such as a university, bank, hospital, or Church. 2 an organization providing residential care for people with special needs. 3 an established law or custom. 4 informal a well-established and familiar person or thing. 5 the establishment or introduction of something.

institutional adjective 1 relating to an institution. 2 typical of an institution, especially in being impersonal or unimaginative.
– DERIVATIVES **institutionally** adverb.

institutionalize (or **institutionalise**) verb 1 establish as an accepted part of an organization or culture: *claims that racism is institutionalized in education.* 2 place someone in a residential institution. 3 (**be/become institutionalized**) be or become apathetic and dependent after a long period in a residential institution.
– DERIVATIVES **institutionalization** noun.

instruct verb 1 tell or order someone to do something. 2 teach someone a subject or skill. 3 inform someone of a fact or situation. 4 Brit. authorize a solicitor or barrister to act on one's behalf.
– ORIGIN Latin *instruere* 'construct, equip, teach'.

instruction noun 1 an act of telling someone to do something; an order. 2 (**instructions**) detailed information about how something should be done. 3 teaching or education. 4 a code in a computer program which defines and carries out an operation.
– DERIVATIVES **instructional** adjective.

instructive adjective useful and informative.
– DERIVATIVES **instructively** adverb.

instructor (or **instructress**) noun 1 a teacher. 2 N. Amer. a university teacher ranking below assistant professor.

instrument noun 1 a tool or implement, especially for precision work. 2 a measuring device, especially in a vehicle or aircraft. 3 (also **musical instrument**) a device for producing musical sounds. 4 a means of pursuing an aim: *her car is the instrument of her freedom.* 5 a person who is exploited by another. 6 a formal or legal document.
– ORIGIN Latin *instrumentum*.

instrumental adjective 1 serving as a means of achieving something. 2 (of music) performed on instruments. 3 relating to an implement or measuring device. •noun a piece of music performed by instruments, with no vocals.
– DERIVATIVES **instrumentality** noun **instrumentally** adverb.

instrumentalist noun a player of a musical instrument.

instrumentation noun 1 the instruments used in a piece of music. 2 the arrangement of a piece of music for particular instruments. 3 measuring instruments as a group.

insubordinate adjective disobedient to orders or authority.
– DERIVATIVES **insubordination** noun.

insubstantial adjective lacking strength and solidity.
– DERIVATIVES **insubstantiality** noun **insubstantially** adverb.

insufferable adjective 1 too extreme to bear; intolerable. 2 unbearably arrogant or conceited.
– DERIVATIVES **insufferably** adverb.
– ORIGIN from Latin *sufferre* 'suffer'.

insufficient adjective not enough for a purpose.
– DERIVATIVES **insufficiency** noun **insufficiently** adverb.

insulant noun an insulating material.

insular adjective 1 ignorant of or uninterested in cultures, ideas, or peoples outside one's own experience. 2 relating to an island.
– DERIVATIVES **insularity** noun.
– ORIGIN from Latin *insula* 'island'.

insulate verb 1 place material between one thing and another to prevent loss of heat or intrusion of sound. 2 cover something with non-conducting material to prevent the passage of electricity. 3 protect someone from something unpleasant.
– DERIVATIVES **insulator** noun.
– ORIGIN from Latin *insula* 'island'.

insulation noun 1 material used to insulate something. 2 the action of insulating or state of being insulated: *his comparative insulation from the world.*

insulin noun a hormone produced in the pancreas, which regulates glucose levels in the blood, and the lack of which causes diabetes.
– ORIGIN from Latin *insula* 'island' (with reference to the islets of Langerhans in the pancreas).

insult verb /in-sult/ speak to or treat someone with disrespect or abuse. •noun /in-sult/ 1 a disrespectful or abusive remark or action. 2 a thing so worthless as to be offensive: *the pay offer is an absolute insult.*
– ORIGIN Latin *insultare* 'jump or trample on'.

insuperable /in-soo-puh-ruh-b'l/ adjective impossible to overcome.
– DERIVATIVES **insuperably** adverb.
– ORIGIN Latin *insuperabilis*.

insupportable adjective 1 unable to be supported or justified. 2 unable to be endured; intolerable.
– DERIVATIVES **insupportably** adverb.

insurance noun 1 an arrangement by which a company or the state guarantees to provide compensation for loss, damage, illness, or death in return for payment of a specified premium. 2 money paid as compensation under an insurance policy. 3 a thing providing protection against a possible event: *jackets hung on their chairs, insurance against the air conditioning.*

> USAGE: There is a technical distinction between **insurance** and **assurance**: see the note at **ASSURANCE**.

insurance policy noun a contract of insurance.

insure verb 1 arrange for compensation in the event of damage to or loss of property, life, or a person, in exchange for regular payments to a company. 2 (**insure someone against**) protect someone against a possible event. 3 another term for **ENSURE**.
– DERIVATIVES **insurable** adjective **insurer** noun.
– ORIGIN alteration of **ENSURE**.

> USAGE: There is considerable overlap between the meaning and use of **insure** and **ensure**. In both British and US English the main meaning of **insure** is 'arrange for compensation in the event of damage or loss'; **ensure** is not used at all in this sense. For the general senses, **insure** and **ensure** are often interchangeable, but **insure** tends to be more common in US English.

insurgent /in-ser-juhnt/ noun a rebel or revolutionary. • adjective relating to rebels.
– DERIVATIVES **insurgence** noun **insurgency** noun (pl. **insurgencies**).
– ORIGIN from Latin *insurgere* 'rise up'.

insurmountable /in-ser-mown-tuh-b'l/ adjective too great to be overcome.
– DERIVATIVES **insurmountably** adverb.

insurrection /in-suh-rek-sh'n/ noun a violent uprising against authority.
– DERIVATIVES **insurrectionary** adjective **insurrectionist** noun & adjective.
– ORIGIN Latin, from *insurgere* 'rise up'.

insusceptible adjective not likely to be affected by something.
– DERIVATIVES **insusceptibility** noun.

intact adjective not damaged in any way.
– DERIVATIVES **intactness** noun.
– ORIGIN Latin *intactus* 'untouched'.

intaglio /in-ta-li-oh/ noun (pl. **intaglios**) 1 an incised or engraved design. 2 a gem with an incised design.
– ORIGIN Italian.

intake noun 1 an amount or quantity taken in. 2 an act of taking something in. 3 a place or structure through which something is taken in.

intangible adjective 1 unable to be touched; not physical: *the intangible gift of joy.* 2 vague and abstract. • noun an abstract or intangible thing.
– DERIVATIVES **intangibility** noun **intangibly** adverb.

intarsia /in-tah-si-uh/ noun 1 a method of knitting in which a separate length or ball of yarn is used for each area of colour. 2 elaborate marquetry or inlaid work.
– ORIGIN Italian *intarsio*.

integer /in-ti-jer/ noun a whole number.
– ORIGIN from Latin, 'intact, whole'.

integral adjective /in-ti-gruhl, in-teg-ruhl/ 1 necessary to make a whole complete; fundamental: *games are an integral part of the curriculum.* 2 included as part of a whole. 3 forming a whole; complete. 4 Mathematics relating to an integer or integers. • noun /in-ti-gruhl/ Mathematics a function of which a given function is the derivative, and which may express the area under the curve of a graph of the function.
– DERIVATIVES **integrally** adverb.

integral calculus noun Mathematics the part of calculus concerned with the integrals of functions.

integrate verb /in-ti-grayt/ 1 combine or be combined to form a whole: *transport planning should be integrated with energy policy.* 2 make or become accepted as a member of a social group. 3 Mathematics find the integral of a function.
– DERIVATIVES **integrable** /in-tig-ruh-b'l/ adjective **integrative** /in-tig-ruh-tiv/ adjective **integrator** noun.
– ORIGIN Latin *integrare* 'make whole'.

integrated circuit noun an electronic circuit on a small piece of semiconducting material, performing the same function as a larger circuit of separate components.

integration noun 1 the action of combining things to form a whole. 2 the mixing of peoples or groups who were previously segregated.
– DERIVATIVES **integrationist** noun.

integrity /in-teg-ri-ti/ noun 1 the quality of being honest and having strong moral principles. 2 the state of being whole or unified. 3 the quality of being sound in construction.
– ORIGIN Latin *integritas*.

integument /in-teg-yuu-muhnt/ noun a tough outer protective layer, especially of an animal or plant.
– ORIGIN Latin *integumentum*.

intellect noun 1 the faculty of using the mind to think logically and understand things. 2 an intelligent person.
– ORIGIN Latin *intellectus* 'understanding'.

intellectual /in-tuh-lek-chyuu-uhl/ adjective 1 having a highly developed ability to think logically and understand things. 2 relating or appealing to the intellect. • noun a person with a highly developed intellect.
– DERIVATIVES **intellectually** adverb.

intellectualism noun the use of the intellect at the expense of the emotions.
– DERIVATIVES **intellectualist** noun.

intellectualize (or **intellectualise**) verb 1 make something seem rational or logical. 2 talk or write in a logical or intellectual way.

intellectual property noun Law intangible property that is the result of creativity, e.g. patents or copyrights.

intelligence noun 1 the ability to gain and apply knowledge and skills. 2 the collection of secret information of military or political value. 3 secret information collected about an enemy or competitor.
– ORIGIN Latin *intelligentia*.

intelligence quotient noun a number representing a person's reasoning ability, compared to the statistical norm, 100 being average.

intelligent adjective 1 having intelligence, especially of a high level. 2 (of a device) able to vary its state or action in response to varying situations and past experience. 3 (of a computer terminal) having its own processing capability.
– DERIVATIVES **intelligently** adverb.

intelligentsia /in-tel-li-**jent**-si-uh/ noun (treated as sing. or pl.) intellectuals or highly educated people as a class.

intelligible /in-**tel**-li-ji-b'l/ adjective able to be understood.
– DERIVATIVES **intelligibility** noun **intelligibly** adverb.
– ORIGIN Latin *intelligibilis*.

intemperate adjective 1 lacking self-control. 2 characterized by excessive drinking of alcohol.
– DERIVATIVES **intemperance** noun **intemperately** adverb.

intend verb 1 have a course of action as one's aim or plan. 2 plan that something should be, do, or mean something: *the book was intended as a satire.* 3 (**intend for/to do**) design or plan something for a particular purpose. 4 (**be intended for**) be meant for the use of someone.
– DERIVATIVES **intender** noun.
– ORIGIN Latin *intendere* 'intend, extend, direct'.

intended adjective planned or meant. • noun (**one's intended**) informal one's fiancé(e).

intense adjective (**intenser, intensest**) 1 very great in force, degree, or strength: *the job demands intense concentration.* 2 very earnest or serious.
– DERIVATIVES **intensely** adverb **intenseness** noun.
– ORIGIN Latin *intensus* 'stretched tightly, strained'.

intensifier noun 1 a thing that makes something more intense. 2 Grammar an adverb used to give force or emphasis (e.g. *really* in *my feet are really cold*).

intensify verb (**intensifies, intensifying, intensified**) increase in degree, force, or strength: *the war has intensified.*
– DERIVATIVES **intensification** noun.

intensity noun (pl. **intensities**) 1 the quality of being great in force, degree, or strength: *the pain grew in intensity.* 2 chiefly Physics the measurable amount of a property, such as force or brightness.

intensive adjective 1 concentrated on a single subject or into a short time: *an intensive course in Arabic.* 2 (of agriculture) aiming to achieve maximum production within a limited area. 3 (in combination) concentrating on or making

much use of something: *labour-intensive methods.*
– DERIVATIVES **intensively** adverb **intensiveness** noun.

intensive care noun special medical treatment given to a dangerously ill patient.

intent noun something intended; a plan or intention. • adjective 1 (**intent on**) determined to do something. 2 (**intent on**) concentrating hard on something. 3 showing earnest and eager attention.
– PHRASES **to all intents and purposes** in all important respects. **with intent** Law with the intention of committing a crime.
– DERIVATIVES **intently** adverb **intentness** noun.
– ORIGIN Latin *intendere* 'intend'.

intention noun 1 an aim or plan. 2 (**one's intentions**) a man's plans in respect to marriage.
– DERIVATIVES **intentioned** adjective.

intentional adjective done on purpose; deliberate.
– DERIVATIVES **intentionality** noun **intentionally** adverb.

inter /in-**ter**/ verb (**inters, interring, interred**) place a corpse in a grave or tomb.
– ORIGIN Old French *enterrer*.

inter- prefix 1 between; among: *interbreed.* 2 so as to affect both; mutually: *interaction.*
– ORIGIN Latin *inter*.

interact verb (of two people or things) act so as affect each other.
– DERIVATIVES **interaction** noun.

interactive adjective 1 influencing each other. 2 (of a computer or other electronic device) allowing a two-way flow of information between it and a user.
– DERIVATIVES **interactively** adverb **interactivity** noun.

inter alia /in-ter **ay**-li-uh/ adverb among other things.
– ORIGIN Latin.

interbreed verb (past and past part. **interbred**) breed or cause to breed with an animal of a different race or species.

intercede /in-ter-**seed**/ verb intervene on behalf of someone.
– ORIGIN Latin *intercedere*.

intercellular adjective located or occurring between cells.

intercept verb /in-ter-**sept**/ stop a person, vehicle, or communication so as to prevent them from continuing to a destination. • noun /in-ter-sept/ 1 an act of intercepting someone or something. 2 Mathematics the point at which a line cuts the axis of a graph.
– DERIVATIVES **interception** noun **interceptor** noun.
– ORIGIN Latin *intercipere* 'catch between'.

intercession /in-ter-**sesh**-uhn/ noun 1 the action of intervening on behalf of someone. 2 the saying of a prayer on behalf of another person.
– DERIVATIVES **intercessor** noun **intercessory** adjective.
– ORIGIN Latin.

interchange verb /in-ter-**chaynj**/ 1 exchange things with each other. 2 put each of two things in the other's place. • noun /in-ter-chaynj/ **1** the action of exchanging people or things. **2** an exchange of words. **3** a road junction on several levels so that traffic streams do not intersect.

interchangeable adjective **1** (of things) able to be interchanged. **2** very similar: *interchangeable disco divas.*
– DERIVATIVES **interchangeability** noun **interchangeably** adverb.

intercity adjective existing or travelling between cities.

intercom noun an electrical device allowing one-way or two-way communication.
– ORIGIN short for *intercommunication*.

intercommunicating adjective (of two rooms) having a shared connecting door.

intercommunication noun the process of communicating between people or groups.

interconnect verb connect with each other.
– DERIVATIVES **interconnection** noun.

intercontinental adjective relating to or travelling between continents.

intercooler noun a device for cooling gas between successive compressions, especially in a supercharged engine.
– DERIVATIVES **intercool** verb.

intercourse noun **1** communication or dealings between people. **2** sexual intercourse.
– ORIGIN Latin *intercursus*.

intercrop verb (intercrops, intercropping, intercropped) (often as noun **intercropping**) grow a crop among plants of a different kind.

intercut verb (intercuts, intercutting, intercut) alternate scenes with contrasting scenes in a film.

interdenominational adjective relating to more than one religious denomination.

interdepartmental adjective relating to more than one department.

interdependent adjective dependent on each other.
– DERIVATIVES **interdependence** noun **interdependency** noun.

interdict noun /in-ter-dikt/ **1** an authoritative order forbidding something. **2** (in the Roman Catholic Church) a sentence barring a person or place from ecclesiastical functions and privileges. • verb /in-ter-**dikt**/ chiefly N. Amer. prohibit or forbid something.
– DERIVATIVES **interdiction** noun.
– ORIGIN from Latin *interdicere* 'interpose, forbid by decree'.

interdisciplinary adjective relating to more than one branch of knowledge.

interest noun **1** the state of wanting to know about something or someone. **2** the quality of arousing curiosity or holding the attention: *a tale full of interest.* **3** a subject which one enjoys doing or studying. **4** money paid for the use of money that is lent. **5** a person's advantage or benefit. **6** a share, right, or stake in property or a financial undertaking. **7** a group in politics or business having a common concern. • verb **1** arouse someone's curiosity or attention. **2** (**interest someone in**) persuade someone to do or obtain something. **3** (as adj. **interested**) involved in something and so not impartial: *interested parties.*
– DERIVATIVES **interestedly** adverb.

– ORIGIN Latin *interesse* 'differ, be important'.

interesting adjective arousing curiosity or interest.
– DERIVATIVES **interestingly** adverb.

interface noun **1** a point where two things meet and interact. **2** a device or program enabling a user to communicate with a computer, or for connecting two items of hardware or software. **3** chiefly Physics a surface forming a boundary between two portions of matter or space. • verb (**interface with**) **1** interact with another person, system, etc. **2** Computing connect with something by an interface.

interfacing noun an extra layer of material or an adhesive stiffener, applied to the facing of a garment to add support.

interfaith adjective relating to or between different religions.

interfere verb **1** (**interfere with**) prevent something from continuing or being carried out properly. **2** (**interfere with**) handle or adjust something without permission. **3** become involved in something without being asked or required to do so: *she tried not to interfere in her children's lives.* **4** (**interfere with**) Brit. euphemistic fondle or assault someone sexually. **5** Physics (of waves of the same wavelength) interact to produce interference.
– DERIVATIVES **interferer** noun **interfering** adjective.
– ORIGIN Old French *s'entreferir* 'strike each other'.

interference noun **1** the action of interfering with someone or something. **2** disturbance to radio signals caused by unwanted signals from other sources. **3** Physics the combination of waves of the same wavelength from two or more sources, producing a new wave pattern.
– DERIVATIVES **interferential** adjective.

interferon /in-ter-feer-on/ noun a protein released by animal cells which prevents a virus from reproducing.

interfuse verb literary join or mix things together.
– DERIVATIVES **interfusion** noun.

intergalactic adjective relating to or situated between galaxies.

interglacial adjective Geology relating to a period of milder climate between two glacial periods.

intergovernmental adjective relating to or conducted between governments.

interim /in-tuh-rim/ noun (**the interim**) the time between two events. • adjective in or for the time between two events; provisional.
– ORIGIN from Latin, 'meanwhile'.

interior adjective **1** situated within or inside something; inner. **2** remote from the coast or frontier; inland. **3** relating to a country's internal affairs. **4** within the mind or soul: *an interior monologue.* • noun **1** the interior part of a building, country, etc. **2** the internal affairs of a country.
– DERIVATIVES **interiorize** (or **interiorise**) verb **interiorly** adverb.
– ORIGIN Latin, 'inner'.

interior angle noun the angle between adjacent sides of a straight-sided figure.

interior decoration noun the decoration of the interior of a building or room, with regard for colour combination and artistic effect.

interior design noun the design, decoration, and furnishings of the interior of a room or building.

interiority noun the quality of being interior or inward.

interject /in-ter-jekt/ verb say something suddenly as an interruption.
– ORIGIN Latin *interjicere* 'interpose'.

interjection noun an exclamation or interruption.

interlace verb 1 cross or be crossed together; interweave. 2 (**interlace something with**) mingle or intersperse something with: *discussion interlaced with mathematics.*

interlard verb (**interlard something with**) intersperse speech or writing with contrasting words and phrases.

interleave verb 1 place something between the layers of something else. 2 insert blank leaves between the pages of a book.

interline verb put an extra lining in a garment or curtain.

interlinear adjective written between the lines of another piece of writing.

interlining noun material used to interline a garment or curtain.

interlink verb join or connect things together.
– DERIVATIVES **interlinkage** noun.

interlock verb (of two or more things) engage with each other by overlapping or fitting together. • noun 1 a device for connecting or coordinating the function of components. 2 (also **interlock fabric**) a fabric with closely interlocking stitches allowing it to stretch.

interlocutor /in-ter-lok-yuu-ter/ noun formal a person who takes part in a conversation.
– DERIVATIVES **interlocution** noun.
– ORIGIN from Latin *interloqui* 'interrupt (with speech)'.

interlocutory /in-ter-lok-yuu-tuh-ri/ adjective 1 Law (of a decree or judgement) given provisionally during the course of a legal action. 2 relating to dialogue.

interloper /in-ter-loh-per/ noun a person who is present in a place or situation where they are not wanted or do not belong.
– ORIGIN from INTER- + -*loper*, from Dutch *landlooper* 'vagabond'.

interlude noun 1 a period of time or activity that contrasts with what goes before or after it: *a romantic interlude.* 2 a pause between the acts of a play. 3 a piece of music played between other pieces or between the verses of a hymn.
– ORIGIN Latin *interludium.*

intermarry verb (**intermarries, intermarrying, intermarried**) (of people of different races, castes, or religions) marry each other.
– DERIVATIVES **intermarriage** noun.

intermediary /in-ter-mee-di-uh-ri/ noun (pl. **intermediaries**) a person who acts as a link between people in order to try to bring about an agreement. • adjective intermediate.

intermediate /in-ter-mee-di-uht/ adjective 1 coming between two things in time, place, or character: *an intermediate stage of development.* 2 having a level of knowledge or skill between basic and advanced. • noun a thing coming between other things in time, place, or character.
– DERIVATIVES **intermediacy** noun **intermediation** noun.
– ORIGIN from Latin *inter-* 'between' + *medius* 'middle'.

interment /in-ter-muhnt/ noun the burial of a corpse in a grave or tomb.

intermezzo /in-ter-met-zoh/ noun (pl. **intermezzi** /in-ter-met-zi/ or **intermezzos**) 1 a short connecting instrumental movement in an opera or other musical work. 2 a short piece for a solo instrument. 3 a light dramatic or other performance between the acts of a play.
– ORIGIN Italian.

interminable adjective endless or seemingly endless.
– DERIVATIVES **interminably** adverb.
– ORIGIN Latin *interminabilis.*

intermingle verb mix or mingle together.

intermission noun 1 a pause or break. 2 an interval between parts of a play or film.
– ORIGIN Latin.

intermittent adjective occurring at irregular intervals: *intermittent rain.*
– DERIVATIVES **intermittency** noun **intermittently** adverb.
– ORIGIN Latin, 'ceasing'.

intermix verb mix together.
– DERIVATIVES **intermixable** adjective **intermixture** noun.

intermodal adjective involving two or more different modes of transport.

intermolecular adjective existing or occurring between molecules.

intern verb /in-tern/ confine someone as a prisoner. • noun /in-tern/ (also **interne**) N. Amer. 1 a recent medical graduate receiving supervised training in a hospital and acting as an assistant physician or surgeon. 2 a student or trainee who does a job to gain work experience.
– DERIVATIVES **internment** noun **internship** noun.
– ORIGIN from Latin *internus* 'inward, internal'.

internal adjective 1 relating to or situated on the inside. 2 inside the body. 3 relating to affairs and activities within a country. 4 existing or used within an organization. 5 in one's mind or soul. • noun (**internals**) inner parts or features.
– DERIVATIVES **internality** noun **internally** adverb.
– ORIGIN Latin *internalis.*

internal-combustion engine noun an engine in which power is generated by the expansion of hot gases from the burning of fuel with air inside the engine.

internal exile noun banishment from a part of one's own country as a punishment.

internalize (or **internalise**) verb unconsciously make an attitude or belief part of one's behaviour.
– DERIVATIVES **internalization** noun.

internal market noun 1 another term for SINGLE MARKET. 2 a system within an organization whereby departments buy each other's services.

international adjective 1 existing or occurring

between nations. 2 agreed on or used by all or many nations. • noun 1 Brit. a game or contest between teams from different countries. 2 Brit. a player who has taken part in a contest between teams from different countries. 3 (**International**) any of four associations founded (1864–1936) to promote socialism or communism.
– DERIVATIVES **internationality** noun **internationally** adverb.

International Date Line noun an imaginary North–South line through the Pacific Ocean, chiefly along the meridian furthest from Greenwich, to the east of which the date is a day earlier than it is to the west.

internationalism noun the belief in or promotion of cooperation and understanding between nations.
– DERIVATIVES **internationalist** noun.

internationalize (or **internationalise**) verb make something international in scope or nature.
– DERIVATIVES **internationalization** noun.

international law noun a set of rules established by custom or treaty and recognized by nations as binding in their relations with one another.

international style noun a style of 20th-century architecture characterized by the use of steel and reinforced concrete, simple lines, and strict geometric forms.

interne noun variant spelling of **INTERN**.

internecine /in-ter-nee-syn/ adjective 1 destructive to both sides in a conflict. 2 relating to conflict within a group: *internecine rivalries.*
– ORIGIN Latin *internecinus.*

internee noun a prisoner.

Internet noun a global computer network providing a variety of information and communication facilities.

interoperable adjective (of computer systems or software) able to exchange and make use of information.
– DERIVATIVES **interoperability** noun.

interpenetrate verb (of different things) mix or merge together.
– DERIVATIVES **interpenetration** noun.

interpersonal adjective relating to relationships between people.
– DERIVATIVES **interpersonally** adverb.

interplanetary adjective situated or travelling between planets.

interplay noun the way in which things interact: *the painting has a dramatic interplay of light and shade.*

Interpol /in-ter-pol/ noun an international organization that coordinates investigations made by the police forces of member countries into international crimes.
– ORIGIN from *Inter(national) pol(ice).*

interpolate /in-ter-puh-layt/ verb 1 insert something different or additional into something else. 2 add a remark to a conversation. 3 Mathematics insert an intermediate term into a series by estimating it from surrounding known values.
– DERIVATIVES **interpolation** noun **interpolator** noun.

– ORIGIN Latin *interpolare* 'refurbish, alter'.

interpose verb 1 insert between one thing and another: *she interposed herself between the newcomers.* 2 intervene between parties. 3 say something as an interruption.
– DERIVATIVES **interposition** noun.
– ORIGIN Latin *interponere* 'put in'.

interpret verb (**interprets, interpreting, interpreted**) 1 explain the meaning of something. 2 translate aloud the words of a person speaking a different language. 3 understand as having a particular meaning: *he interpreted her silence as indifference.* 4 perform a creative work in a way that conveys one's understanding of the creator's ideas.
– DERIVATIVES **interpretable** adjective **interpretative** (also **interpretive**) adjective.
– ORIGIN Latin *interpretari* 'explain, translate'.

interpretation noun 1 the action of explaining the meaning of something. 2 an explanation. 3 the way in which a performer expresses a creative work.
– DERIVATIVES **interpretational** adjective.

interpreter noun a person who interprets foreign speech aloud as it is spoken.

interracial adjective existing between or involving different races.
– DERIVATIVES **interracially** adverb.

interregnum /in-ter-reg-nuhm/ noun (pl. **interregnums**) a period between reigns or political regimes when normal government is suspended.
– ORIGIN Latin.

interrelate verb relate or connect to one other.
– DERIVATIVES **interrelation** noun **interrelationship** noun.

interrogate /in-ter-oh-gayt/ verb ask someone questions in a detailed or aggressive way.
– DERIVATIVES **interrogation** noun **interrogator** noun.
– ORIGIN Latin *interrogare* 'question'.

interrogative /in-ter-rog-uh-tiv/ adjective 1 expressing a question: *a hard, interrogative stare.* 2 Grammar used in questions. • noun a word used in questions, e.g. *how* or *what.*
– DERIVATIVES **interrogatively** adverb.

interrogatory /in-ter-rog-uh-tuh-ri/ adjective expressing a question; questioning.

interrupt verb 1 stop the continuous progress of something. 2 stop a person who is speaking by saying or doing something. 3 break the continuity of a line, surface, or view.
– DERIVATIVES **interrupter** (also **interruptor**) noun **interruptible** adjective **interruptive** adjective.
– ORIGIN Latin *interrumpere* 'break, interrupt'.

interruption noun 1 an act, remark, or period that stops the progress of something. 2 the action of interrupting someone or something.

intersect verb 1 divide something by passing or lying across it. 2 (of lines, roads, etc.) cross or cut each other.
– ORIGIN Latin *intersecare* 'cut, intersect'.

intersection noun 1 a point at which roads intersect or cross each other. 2 a point or line common to lines or surfaces that intersect.
– DERIVATIVES **intersectional** adjective.

intersex noun the condition of being between male and female; hermaphroditism.

intersexual adjective **1** existing or occurring between the sexes. **2** relating to the condition of being between male and female; hermaphroditic.
– DERIVATIVES **intersexuality** noun.

interspace noun a space between objects.

intersperse verb scatter or place things among or between other things.
– DERIVATIVES **interspersion** noun.
– ORIGIN Latin *interspergere* 'scatter between'.

interstate adjective existing or carried on between states, especially of the US. •noun one of a system of motorways running between US states.

interstellar /in-ter-**stel**-ler/ adjective occurring or situated between stars.

interstice /in-ter-**stiss**/ noun a small space between things.
– ORIGIN Latin *interstitium*.

interstitial /in-ter-**sti**-sh'l/ adjective relating to or found in small spaces between things.
– DERIVATIVES **interstitially** adverb.

intertextuality noun the relationship between pieces of writing.
– DERIVATIVES **intertextual** adjective.

intertribal adjective existing or occurring between different tribes.

intertwine verb twist or twine together.

interval noun **1** a period of time between two events. **2** a pause in activity, especially (Brit.) a pause between parts of a performance or a sports match. **3** a space or gap between things: *the path is marked with rocks at intervals.* **4** the difference in pitch between two sounds.
– ORIGIN Latin *intervallum* 'space between ramparts, interval'.

intervene verb **1** come between people or things so as to prevent or alter a situation: *he intervened in the dispute.* **2** (usu. as adj. **intervening**) occur or be between events or things.
– DERIVATIVES **intervener** (also **intervenor**) noun.
– ORIGIN Latin *intervenire* 'come between'.

intervention noun **1** the action of intervening between people or things to influence or control a situation. **2** action taken to improve a medical disorder.
– DERIVATIVES **interventional** adjective.

interventionist adjective favouring intervention to influence or control a situation. •noun a person who favours intervening to influence or control a situation.
– DERIVATIVES **interventionism** noun.

interview noun **1** an occasion on which a journalist or broadcaster puts questions to a person. **2** a formal meeting at which a person is asked questions to assess their suitability for a job or college place. **3** a session of formal questioning of a person by the police. •verb hold an interview with someone.
– DERIVATIVES **interviewee** noun **interviewer** noun.
– ORIGIN French *entrevue*.

interwar adjective existing in the period between two wars, especially the two world wars.

interweave verb (past **interwove**; past part. **interwoven**) weave or become woven together.

intestate /in-**tess**-tayt/ adjective not having made a will before dying.
– DERIVATIVES **intestacy** /in-**tes**-tuh-si/ noun.

intestine (also **intestines**) noun the long tubular organ leading from the end of the stomach to the anus.
– DERIVATIVES **intestinal** /in-tes-**ty**-n'l/ adjective.
– ORIGIN Latin *intestinum*.

intifada /in-ti-**fah**-duh/ noun the Palestinian uprising against Israeli occupation of the West Bank and Gaza Strip, beginning in 1987.
– ORIGIN Arabic.

intimacy noun (pl. **intimacies**) **1** close familiarity or friendship. **2** a familiar or private act or remark.

intimate[1] /**in**-ti-muht/ adjective **1** close and friendly: *they're on intimate terms.* **2** private and personal. **3** euphemistic having a sexual relationship. **4** involving very close connection: *her intimate involvement with the community.* **5** (of knowledge) detailed. **6** having a relaxed and cosy atmosphere. •noun a very close friend.
– DERIVATIVES **intimately** adverb.
– ORIGIN from Latin *intimare* 'impress, make familiar'.

intimate[2] /**in**-ti-mayt/ verb state something, especially in an indirect way.
– DERIVATIVES **intimation** noun.
– ORIGIN Latin *intimare* (see **INTIMATE**[1]).

intimidate verb frighten someone, especially so as to force them into doing something.
– DERIVATIVES **intimidation** noun **intimidator** noun **intimidatory** adjective.
– ORIGIN Latin *intimidare* 'make timid'.

into preposition **1** expressing movement or direction to a point on or within. **2** expressing a change of state or the result of an action. **3** so as to turn towards. **4** about or concerning. **5** expressing division. **6** informal very interested in.

intolerable adjective unable to be endured.
– DERIVATIVES **intolerably** adverb.

intolerant adjective not tolerant of views of behaviour that differ from one's own.
– DERIVATIVES **intolerance** noun **intolerantly** adverb.

intonation noun **1** the rise and fall of the voice in speaking. **2** the action of saying something with little rise and fall of the voice. **3** accuracy of musical pitch.
– DERIVATIVES **intonational** adjective.

intone /in-**tohn**/ verb say or recite something with little rise and fall of the pitch of the voice.
– ORIGIN Latin *intonare*.

in toto /in toh-toh/ adverb as a whole.
– ORIGIN Latin.

intoxicant noun a substance that causes someone to lose their self-control.

intoxicate verb **1** (of alcoholic drink or a drug) cause someone to lose their self-control. **2** excite or exhilarate someone.
– DERIVATIVES **intoxication** noun.
– ORIGIN Latin *intoxicare*.

intra- /**in**-truh/ prefix (added to adjectives) on the inside; within: *intramural.*
– ORIGIN Latin, 'inside'.

intractable /in-**trak**-tuh-b'l/ adjective **1** hard to

solve or deal with. **2** (of a person) stubborn.
– DERIVATIVES **intractability** noun **intractably**
adverb.

intramural /in-truh-**myoor**-uhl/ adjective
1 situated or done within a building. **2** chiefly N.
Amer. forming part of normal university or
college studies.
– ORIGIN from **INTRA-** + Latin *murus* 'wall'.

intranet /**in**-truh-net/ noun a private
communications network created with
Internet software.

intransigent /in-**tran**-zi-juhnt/ adjective
refusing to change one's views. ● noun a person
who refuses to change their views.
– DERIVATIVES **intransigence** noun **intransigency**
noun **intransigently** adverb.
– ORIGIN from Spanish *los intransigentes* (a
name adopted by extreme republicans).

intransitive /in-**tran**-zi-tiv/ adjective (of a
verb) not taking a direct object, e.g. *die* in *he
died suddenly*. The opposite of **TRANSITIVE**.
– DERIVATIVES **intransitively** adverb **intransitivity**
noun.

intrauterine /in-truh-**yoo**-tuh-ryn/ adjective
within the womb.

intrauterine device noun a contraceptive
device fitted inside the womb, which prevents
the implantation of fertilized eggs.

intravenous /in-truh-**vee**-nuhss/ adjective
within or into a vein or veins.
– DERIVATIVES **intravenously** adverb.

in tray noun chiefly Brit. a tray on a desk for
incoming documents.

intrepid adjective not afraid of danger or
difficulty; brave or bold.
– DERIVATIVES **intrepidity** noun **intrepidly** adverb.
– ORIGIN Latin *intrepidus* 'not alarmed'.

intricacy /**in**-tri-kuh-si/ noun (pl. **intricacies**)
1 the quality of being complicated or detailed.
2 (**intricacies**) complicated details.

intricate adjective very complicated or
detailed.
– DERIVATIVES **intricately** adverb.
– ORIGIN from Latin *intricare* 'entangle'.

intrigue verb /in-**treeg**/ (**intrigues**, **intriguing**,
intrigued) **1** arouse someone's curiosity or
interest. **2** plot something illegal or harmful.
● noun /**in**-treeg/ **1** the plotting of something
illegal or harmful. **2** a secret love affair.
– DERIVATIVES **intriguer** noun **intriguing** adjective.
– ORIGIN French *intriguer* 'tangle, plot'.

intrinsic /in-**trin**-sik/ adjective belonging to the
basic nature of someone or something;
essential: *the club was an intrinsic part of
Liverpool nightlife*.
– DERIVATIVES **intrinsically** adverb.
– ORIGIN Latin *intrinsecus* 'inwardly, inwards'.

intro- prefix into; inwards: *introvert*.
– ORIGIN Latin *intro* 'to the inside'.

introduce verb **1** bring something into use or
operation for the first time. **2** present
someone by name to another. **3** (**introduce
something to**) cause someone to learn about a
subject or experience an activity for the first
time. **4** insert something. **5** occur at the start
of: *a longer opening which introduces a courting
song*. **6** provide an opening announcement for
a television or radio programme. **7** present
new legislation for debate in a law-making

assembly.
– DERIVATIVES **introducer** noun.
– ORIGIN Latin *introducere*.

introduction noun **1** the action of introducing
someone or something. **2** a thing newly
brought in. **3** an act of introducing one person
to another. **4** a thing that introduces another,
such as a section at the beginning of a book.
5 a book or course of study intended for
people who are beginning to study a subject.
6 a person's first experience of a subject or
activity.

introductory adjective serving as an
introduction; basic or preliminary.

introit /in-**troyt**/ noun (in the Christian
Church) a psalm or antiphon sung or said
while the priest approaches the altar for Holy
Communion.
– ORIGIN Latin *introitus*.

introspection noun the examination of one's
own thoughts or feelings.
– DERIVATIVES **introspective** adjective
introspectively adverb.
– ORIGIN from Latin *introspicere* 'look into' or
from *introspectare* 'keep looking into'.

introvert noun a shy, quiet person who is
mainly concerned with their own thoughts
and feelings. ● adjective relating to an introvert.
– DERIVATIVES **introversion** noun **introverted**
adjective.
– ORIGIN from Latin *intro-* 'to the inside' +
vertere 'to turn'.

intrude verb **1** enter a place or situation where
one is unwelcome or uninvited. **2** interrupt
and disturb: *the noise began to intrude into her
thoughts*.
– ORIGIN Latin *intrudere*.

intruder noun a person who intrudes,
especially one who enters a building with
criminal intent.

intrusion noun **1** the action of entering a place
or situation where one is unwelcome or
uninvited. **2** a thing that intrudes.

intrusive adjective **1** unwelcome or uninvited
and causing disturbance or annoyance: *an
intrusive question*. **2** (of igneous rock) that has
been forced when molten into cracks in
neighbouring rocks.
– DERIVATIVES **intrusively** adverb **intrusiveness**
noun.

intuit /in-**tyoo**-it/ verb understand or work
something out by intuition.
– ORIGIN Latin *intueri* 'contemplate'.

intuition /in-tyoo-**ish**-uhn/ noun the ability to
understand or know something immediately,
without conscious reasoning.

intuitive /in-**tyoo**-it-iv/ adjective **1** based on
what one feels to be true; instinctive.
2 (chiefly of computer software) easy to use
and understand.
– DERIVATIVES **intuitively** adverb **intuitiveness**
noun.

Inuit /**in**-yuu-it/ noun **1** (pl. same or **Inuits**) a
member of a people of northern Canada and
parts of Greenland and Alaska. **2** the language
of the Inuit.
– ORIGIN Inuit, 'people'.

USAGE: For an explanation of the terms **Inuit**
and **Eskimo**, see the note at **Eskimo**.

Inuktitut /i-**nuuk**-tit-uut/ noun the Inuit language.
– ORIGIN Inuit, 'the Inuit way'.

inundate /in-uhn-dayt/ verb **1** overwhelm with things to be dealt with: *we've been inundated with complaints.* **2** flood something.
– DERIVATIVES **inundation** noun.
– ORIGIN Latin *inundare* 'flood'.

inure /i-**nyoor**/ verb (**be inured to**) become used to something, especially something unpleasant.
– ORIGIN from an Old French phrase meaning 'in use or practice'.

in utero /in yoo-tuh-roh/ adverb & adjective in a woman's womb; before birth.
– ORIGIN Latin.

invade verb **1** (of an armed force) enter a country so as to conquer or occupy it. **2** enter somewhere in large numbers. **3** intrude on: *his privacy was being invaded.* **4** (of a parasite or disease) spread into the body.
– DERIVATIVES **invader** noun.
– ORIGIN Latin *invadere*.

invalid[1] /in-vuh-lid/ noun a person made weak or disabled by illness or injury. •verb (**be invalided**) be removed from active service in the armed forces because of injury or illness.
– DERIVATIVES **invalidism** noun.
– ORIGIN from **INVALID**[2].

invalid[2] /in-**val**-id/ adjective **1** not valid or officially recognized. **2** not true because based on incorrect information or faulty reasoning.
– DERIVATIVES **invalidly** adverb.
– ORIGIN Latin *invalidus* 'not strong'.

invalidate verb **1** make or prove an argument or theory to be incorrect or faulty. **2** make an official document or procedure no longer legally valid.
– DERIVATIVES **invalidation** noun.

invalidity noun **1** Brit. the condition of being an invalid. **2** the fact of being invalid.

invaluable adjective very useful.
– DERIVATIVES **invaluably** adverb.

invariable adjective **1** never changing. **2** Mathematics (of a quantity) constant.
– DERIVATIVES **invariability** noun.

invariably adverb in every case or on every occasion; always.

invasion noun **1** an instance of invading a country. **2** the arrival of a large number of people or things. **3** an intrusion: *random drug testing is an invasion of privacy.*

invasive adjective **1** tending to invade or intrude: *invasive grasses.* **2** (of medical procedures) involving the introduction of instruments or other objects into the body.

invective noun strongly abusive or critical language.
– ORIGIN Latin *invectivus* 'attacking'.

inveigh /in-**vay**/ verb (**inveigh against**) speak or write about someone with great hostility.
– ORIGIN Latin *invehi* 'be carried into, attack'.

inveigle /in-**vay**-g'l/ verb persuade someone to do something by deception or flattery: *he can inveigle any woman into bed in minutes.*
– ORIGIN Old French *aveugler* 'to blind'.

invent verb **1** create or design a new device or process. **2** make up a false story, name, etc.
– DERIVATIVES **inventor** noun.

– ORIGIN Latin *invenire* 'contrive, discover'.

invention noun **1** the action of inventing something. **2** a newly created device or process. **3** a false story. **4** a person's creative ability.

inventive adjective having or showing creativity or original thought.
– DERIVATIVES **inventively** adverb **inventiveness** noun.

inventory /in-vuh-tuh-ri/ noun (pl. **inventories**) **1** a complete list of items such as goods in stock or the contents of a building. **2** a quantity of goods in stock. •verb (**inventories, inventorying, inventoried**) make an inventory of items.
– ORIGIN Latin *inventarium* 'a list of what is found'.

inverse /in-verss/ adjective opposite in position, direction, order, or effect. •noun **1** a thing that is the opposite or reverse of another. **2** Mathematics a reciprocal quantity.
– DERIVATIVES **inversely** adverb.
– ORIGIN Latin *inversus*.

inverse proportion (also **inverse ratio**) noun a relation between two quantities such that one increases in proportion as the other decreases.

inversion noun **1** the action of inverting something or the state of being inverted. **2** (also **temperature** or **thermal inversion**) a reversal of the normal decrease of air temperature with altitude, or of water temperature with depth.
– DERIVATIVES **inversive** adjective.

invert /in-vert/ verb put something upside down or in the opposite position, order, or arrangement.
– DERIVATIVES **inverter** noun **invertible** adjective.
– ORIGIN Latin *invertere* 'turn inside out'.

invertebrate /in-ver-ti-bruht/ noun an animal having no backbone, such as a mollusc. •adjective relating to invertebrates.

inverted comma noun chiefly Brit. a quotation mark.

inverted snobbery noun Brit. derogatory an attitude which criticizes anything associated with high social status, while valuing those things associated with low social status.

invest verb **1** put money into financial schemes, shares, or property with the expectation of making a profit. **2** devote time or energy to an undertaking with the expectation of a worthwhile result. **3** (**invest in**) informal buy something whose usefulness will repay the cost. **4** (**invest someone/thing with**) provide someone or something with a quality: *these weapons are invested with an almost mystical value by collectors.* **5** formally appoint someone to a rank or office.
– DERIVATIVES **investable** adjective **investor** noun.
– ORIGIN Latin *investire* 'clothe'; sense 1 is influenced by Italian *investire*.

investigate verb **1** carry out a systematic or formal inquiry into an incident or allegation so as to establish the truth. **2** carry out research into a subject. **3** make a search or systematic inquiry.
– DERIVATIVES **investigator** noun **investigatory** adjective.
– ORIGIN Latin *investigare* 'trace out'.

investigation noun **1** the action of investigating something or someone. **2** a formal inquiry or systematic study.

investigative /in-vess-ti-guh-tiv/ adjective **1** relating to investigation or research. **2** (of journalism or a journalist) investigating and seeking to expose dishonesty or injustice.

investiture /in-vess-ti-cher/ noun **1** the action of formally investing a person with honours or rank. **2** a ceremony at which this takes place.

investment noun **1** the action of investing money in something for profit. **2** a thing worth buying because it may be profitable or useful in the future.

investment trust noun a limited company which buys and sells shares in selected companies to make a profit for its members.

inveterate /in-vet-uh-ruht/ adjective **1** having a long-standing and firmly established habit or interest: *an inveterate gambler.* **2** (of a feeling or habit) firmly established.
– DERIVATIVES **inveteracy** noun **inveterately** adverb.
– ORIGIN Latin *inveteratus* 'made old'.

invidious /in-vid-i-uhss/ adjective unacceptable, unfair, and likely to arouse resentment or anger in others.
– DERIVATIVES **invidiously** adverb **invidiousness** noun.
– ORIGIN Latin *invidiosus*, from *invidia* 'hostility'.

invigilate /in-vij-i-layt/ verb Brit. supervise candidates during an exam.
– DERIVATIVES **invigilation** noun **invigilator** noun.
– ORIGIN Latin *invigilare* 'watch over'.

invigorate /in-vig-uh-rayt/ verb give strength or energy to someone or something.
– DERIVATIVES **invigorating** adjective **invigoration** noun.
– ORIGIN Latin *invigorare* 'make strong'.

invincible /in-vin-si-b'l/ adjective too powerful to be defeated or overcome.
– DERIVATIVES **invincibility** noun **invincibly** adverb.
– ORIGIN from Latin *in-* 'not' + *vincibilis* 'able to be overcome'.

inviolable /in-vy-uh-luh-b'l/ adjective never to be broken, infringed or violated: *inviolable rules.*
– DERIVATIVES **inviolability** noun **inviolably** adverb.

inviolate /in-vy-uh-luht/ adjective that is or should be free from injury or attack.
– ORIGIN from Latin *in-* 'not' + *violare* 'violate'.

invisible adjective **1** unable to be seen, either by nature or because hidden. **2** relating to earnings which a country makes from the sale of services rather than tangible commodities.
– DERIVATIVES **invisibility** noun **invisibly** adverb.

invitation noun **1** a written or spoken request inviting someone to go somewhere or to do something. **2** the action of inviting someone to go somewhere or to do something. **3** a situation or action that is likely to result in a particular outcome: *his tactics were an invitation to disaster.*

invite verb **1** ask someone in a friendly or formal way to go somewhere or to do something. **2** request something formally or politely. **3** tend to result in a particular outcome. •noun informal an invitation.
– DERIVATIVES **invitee** noun **inviter** noun.
– ORIGIN Latin *invitare.*

inviting adjective tempting or attractive.
– DERIVATIVES **invitingly** adverb.

in vitro /in vee-troh/ adjective & adverb (of biological processes) taking place in a test tube or elsewhere outside a living organism.
– ORIGIN Latin, 'in glass'.

in vivo /in vee-voh/ adverb & adjective (of biological processes) taking place in a living organism.
– ORIGIN Latin, 'in a living thing'.

invocation /in-vuh-kay-sh'n/ noun **1** the action of appealing to someone or something as an authority or in support of an argument. **2** an appeal to a god or spirit.

invoice noun a list of goods or services provided, with a statement of the sum due. •verb send an invoice to someone for goods or services.
– ORIGIN from French *envoyer* 'send'.

invoke /in-vohk/ verb **1** appeal to someone or something as an authority or in support of an argument. **2** call on a god or spirit in prayer or as a witness. **3** call earnestly for something. **4** give rise to: *how could she explain the accident without invoking his wrath?*
– ORIGIN Latin *invocare.*

involuntary adjective **1** done without conscious control. **2** (especially of muscles or nerves) involved in processes that are not consciously controlled. **3** done against someone's will.
– DERIVATIVES **involuntarily** adverb.

involute /in-vuh-lyoot/ adjective **1** (also **involuted**) formal complicated or intricate. **2** technical curled spirally.
– ORIGIN Latin *involutus* 'wrapped up'.

involve verb **1** (of a situation or event) include something as a necessary part or result. **2** cause to experience or participate in an activity or situation: *his car was stolen and involved in a crash.* **3** (**be/get involved**) be or become occupied or engrossed in something. **4** (**be involved**) be in a romantic relationship with someone.
– DERIVATIVES **involvement** noun.
– ORIGIN Latin *involvere* 'entangle, enfold'.

involved adjective difficult to understand; complicated.

invulnerable adjective impossible to harm or damage.
– DERIVATIVES **invulnerability** noun **invulnerably** adverb.

-in-waiting combining form **1** referring to a position as attendant to a royal person: *lady-in-waiting.* **2** awaiting a turn or about to happen: *a political administration-in-waiting.*

inward adjective **1** directed or proceeding towards the inside. **2** mental or spiritual. •adverb variant of **INWARDS**.
– DERIVATIVES **inwardly** adverb **inwardness** noun.

inwards (also **inward**) adverb **1** towards the inside. **2** into or towards the mind or spirit.

in-your-face adjective informal blatantly aggressive or provocative.
– ORIGIN from *in your face*, used as an insult.

I/O abbreviation Electronics input-output.

iodide /I-uh-dyd/ noun a compound of iodine with another element or group.

iodine /I-uh-deen/ noun 1 a black crystalline non-metallic chemical element of the halogen group. 2 an antiseptic solution of iodine in alcohol.
- DERIVATIVES **iodize** (or **iodise**) verb.
- ORIGIN from Greek *iōdēs* 'violet-coloured'.

IOM abbreviation Isle of Man.

ion /I-uhn/ noun an atom or molecule with a net electric charge through loss or gain of electrons, either positive (a **cation**) or negative (an **anion**).
- ORIGIN Greek, 'going'.

ion exchange noun the exchange of ions of the same charge between an insoluble solid and a solution in contact with it, used in water-softening and other purification processes.

Ionian /I-oh-ni-uhn/ noun a person from the Ionian Islands, a chain of islands off the western coast of mainland Greece. • adjective relating to the Ionians or the Ionian Islands.

Ionic /I-on-ik/ adjective relating to a classical order of architecture characterized by a column with scroll shapes on the top.
- ORIGIN Greek *Iōnikos*.

ionic /I-on-ik/ adjective 1 relating to ions. 2 (of a chemical bond) formed by the attraction of ions with opposite charges. Often contrasted with **COVALENT**.
- DERIVATIVES **ionically** adverb.

ionize (or **ionise**) /I-uh-nyz/ verb convert an atom, molecule, or substance into an ion or ions, typically by removing one or more electrons.
- DERIVATIVES **ionizable** adjective **ionization** noun.

ionizer noun a device which produces ions, especially one used to improve the quality of the air in a room.

ionosphere /I-on-uh-sfeer/ noun the layer of the atmosphere above the mesosphere, which contains a high concentration of ions and electrons and is able to reflect radio waves.
- DERIVATIVES **ionospheric** /I-on-uhss-**fer**-ik/ adjective.

iota /I-oh-tuh/ noun 1 the ninth letter of the Greek alphabet (Ι, ι), represented as 'i'. 2 an extremely small amount: *it won't make an iota of difference*.
- ORIGIN Greek.

IOU noun a signed document acknowledging a debt.
- ORIGIN representing the pronunciation of *I owe you*.

IOW abbreviation Isle of Wight.

IP abbreviation Computing Internet Protocol.

IPA abbreviation International Phonetic Alphabet.

ipecacuanha /ip-i-kak-yoo-**an**-uh/ noun the dried root of a South American shrub, used to cause vomiting.
- ORIGIN Tupi-Guarani.

IPO abbreviation initial public offering, the first issue of a company's shares to the public, used as a means of raising start-up or expansion capital.

ipso facto /ip-soh **fak**-toh/ adverb by that very fact or act.

- ORIGIN Latin.

IQ abbreviation intelligence quotient.

Ir symbol the chemical element iridium.

IRA abbreviation Irish Republican Army.

Iranian noun a person from Iran. • adjective relating to Iran.

Iraqi noun (pl. **Iraqis**) 1 a person from Iraq. 2 the form of Arabic spoken in Iraq. • adjective relating to Iraq.

irascible /i-rass-i-b'l/ adjective hot-tempered; irritable.
- DERIVATIVES **irascibility** noun **irascibly** adverb.
- ORIGIN Latin *irascibilis*, from *ira* 'anger'.

irate /I-rayt/ adjective very angry.
- DERIVATIVES **irately** adverb.
- ORIGIN Latin *iratus*.

IRC abbreviation Computing Internet Relay Chat.

ire /rhymes with fire/ noun chiefly literary anger.
- ORIGIN Latin *ira*.

irenic /I-ren-ik/ (also **eirenic**) adjective formal intended or intending to maintain or bring about peace.
- ORIGIN from Greek *eirēnē* 'peace'.

iridescent /i-ri-dess-uhnt/ adjective showing bright colours that seem to change when seen from different angles.
- DERIVATIVES **iridescence** noun **iridescently** adverb.
- ORIGIN from Latin *iris* 'rainbow'.

iridium /i-rid-i-uhm/ noun a hard, dense silvery-white metallic element.
- ORIGIN from Latin *iris* 'rainbow' (so named because it forms compounds of various colours).

iridology /I-ri-**dol**-uh-ji/ noun (in alternative medicine) a method of diagnosing illnesses or conditions by examining the iris of the eye.
- DERIVATIVES **iridologist** noun.

iris noun 1 a coloured ring-shaped membrane behind the cornea of the eye, with the pupil in the centre. 2 a plant with sword-shaped leaves and purple or yellow flowers.
- ORIGIN Greek, 'rainbow, iris'.

Irish noun (also **Irish Gaelic**) the Celtic language of Ireland. • adjective relating to Ireland or Irish.
- DERIVATIVES **Irishman** noun (pl. **Irishmen**) **Irishness** noun **Irishwoman** noun (pl. **Irish-women**).
- ORIGIN Old English.

Irish coffee noun coffee mixed with a dash of Irish whisky and served with cream on top.

Irish moss noun another term for **CARRAGEEN**.

Irish setter noun a breed of setter (dog) with a long, silky dark red coat and a long feathered tail.

Irish stew noun a stew made with mutton, potatoes, and onions.

Irish wolfhound noun a large greyish hound with a rough coat.

irk /erk/ verb irritate or annoy someone.
- ORIGIN perhaps from Old Norse, 'to work'.

irksome adjective irritating or annoying.
- DERIVATIVES **irksomely** adverb.

iron noun 1 a strong, hard magnetic silvery-grey metal, used in construction and manufacturing. 2 a tool made of iron. 3 a hand-held implement with a flat heated steel base, used to smooth clothes. 4 a golf club

used for hitting the ball at a high angle.
5 (**irons**) handcuffs or chains used as a
restraint. •**verb 1** smooth clothes with an iron.
2 (**iron something out**) settle a difficulty or
problem.
– PHRASES **have many** (or **other**) **irons in the
fire** have a range of options or be involved in
several activities. **an iron hand** (or **fist**) **in a
velvet glove** firmness or ruthlessness covered
by an outward appearance of gentleness.
– ORIGIN Old English.

Iron Age noun the period that followed the
Bronze Age, when weapons and tools came to
be made of iron.

ironclad adjective **1** covered or protected with
iron. **2** impossible to weaken or change: *an
ironclad guarantee.*

Iron Curtain noun (**the Iron Curtain**) a barrier
regarded as separating the former Soviet bloc
and the West before the decline of
communism in eastern Europe.

ironic /I-**ron**-ik/ adjective **1** expressing an idea
with words that usually mean the opposite in
order to be humorous or emphasize a point.
2 happening in the opposite way to what is
expected.
– DERIVATIVES **ironical** adjective **ironically** adverb.

ironing noun clothes that need to be or have
just been ironed.

ironing board noun a long, narrow board with
folding legs, on which clothes are ironed.

ironist noun a person who uses irony.
– DERIVATIVES **ironize** (or **ironise**) verb.

iron lung noun a rigid case fitted over a
patient's body, used to provide artificial
respiration by means of mechanical pumps.

iron maiden noun a former instrument of
torture consisting of a coffin-shaped box lined
with iron spikes.

iron man noun **1** an exceptionally strong man.
2 a sporting contest involving several events
and requiring a great deal of stamina.

ironmonger noun Brit. a person who sells tools
and other hardware.
– DERIVATIVES **ironmongery** noun.

iron rations plural noun a small emergency
supply of food.

ironstone noun **1** sedimentary rock containing
iron compounds. **2** a kind of dense opaque
stoneware.

ironwork noun things made of iron.

ironworks noun a place where iron is smelted
or iron goods are made.

irony /I-ruh-ni/ noun (pl. **ironies**) **1** the
expression of meaning through the use of
words which normally mean the opposite,
typically in order to be humorous or
emphasize a point. **2** a situation that is the
opposite to what is expected.
– ORIGIN Greek *eirōneia* 'pretended ignorance'.

Iroquois /i-ruh-kwoy, i-ruh-koy/ noun (pl.
same) a member of a former group of six
American Indian peoples who lived mainly in
southern Ontario and Quebec and northern
New York State.
– ORIGIN French, from an Algonquian language.

irradiate verb **1** expose someone or something
to radiation. **2** shine light on something, or
appear to do so: *happiness filled her, irradiating*

her whole face.
– DERIVATIVES **irradiation** noun.
– ORIGIN Latin *irradiare.*

irrational adjective not logical or reasonable.
– DERIVATIVES **irrationality** noun **irrationally**
adverb.

irreconcilable adjective **1** incompatible: *the
two points of view were irreconcilable.* **2** not
able to be resolved: *irreconcilable differences.*
– DERIVATIVES **irreconcilably** adverb.

irrecoverable adjective not able to be
recovered or remedied.
– DERIVATIVES **irrecoverably** adverb.

irredeemable adjective not able to be saved,
improved, or corrected.
– DERIVATIVES **irredeemably** adverb.

irredentist /ir-ri-**den**-tist/ noun a person
believing that territory formerly belonging to
their own country should be restored to it.
– DERIVATIVES **irredentism** noun.
– ORIGIN Italian *irredentista.*

irreducible adjective not able to be reduced or
simplified.
– DERIVATIVES **irreducibly** adverb.

irrefutable /ir-ri-**fyoo**-tuh-b'l/ adjective
impossible to deny or disprove.
– DERIVATIVES **irrefutably** adverb.

irregardless adjective & adverb informal
regardless.
– ORIGIN probably a blend of **IRRESPECTIVE** and
REGARDLESS.

irregular adjective **1** not even or regular in
shape, arrangement, or occurrence: *an
irregular heartbeat.* **2** contrary to the rules or
to that which is normal or established:
irregular financial dealings. **3** (of troops) not
belonging to regular army units. **4** Grammar (of
a word) having inflections that do not
conform to the usual rules. •noun a member of
an irregular military force.
– DERIVATIVES **irregularity** noun (pl.
irregularities) **irregularly** adverb.

irrelevant adjective not relevant to the subject
or matter in question.
– DERIVATIVES **irrelevance** noun **irrelevancy** noun
(pl. **irrelevancies**) **irrelevantly** adverb.

irreligious adjective without religious belief,
or showing no respect for religion.
– DERIVATIVES **irreligion** noun.

irremediable /ir-ri-**mee**-di-uh-b'l/ adjective
impossible to remedy.
– DERIVATIVES **irremediably** adverb.

irremovable adjective not able to be removed.

irreparable /ir-**rep**-uh-ruh-b'l/ adjective
impossible to repair or put right: *irreparable
brain damage.*
– DERIVATIVES **irreparably** adverb.

irreplaceable adjective impossible to replace
if lost or damaged.

irrepressible adjective not able to be
controlled or restrained.
– DERIVATIVES **irrepressibly** adverb.

irreproachable adjective not able to be
criticized; faultless.
– DERIVATIVES **irreproachably** adverb.

irresistible adjective too tempting or powerful
to be resisted.
– DERIVATIVES **irresistibly** adverb.

irresolute adjective uncertain.

i

- DERIVATIVES **irresolutely** adverb **irresolution** noun.

irresolvable adjective impossible to solve.

irrespective adjective (**irrespective of**) regardless of.

irresponsible adjective not showing a proper sense of responsibility.
- DERIVATIVES **irresponsibility** noun **irresponsibly** adverb.

irretrievable adjective not able to be improved or put right.
- DERIVATIVES **irretrievably** adverb.

irreverent adjective disrespectful.
- DERIVATIVES **irreverence** noun **irreverently** adverb.

irreversible adjective impossible to be reversed or altered.
- DERIVATIVES **irreversibility** noun **irreversibly** adverb.

irrevocable /ir-**rev**-uh-kuh-b'l/ adjective not able to be changed, reversed, or recovered: *an irrevocable decision.*
- DERIVATIVES **irrevocability** noun **irrevocably** adverb.
- ORIGIN Latin *irrevocabilis*.

irrigate /**ir**-ri-gayt/ verb 1 supply water to land or crops by means of channels. 2 Medicine apply a flow of water or medication to an organ or wound.
- DERIVATIVES **irrigable** adjective **irrigation** noun **irrigator** noun.
- ORIGIN Latin *irrigare* 'moisten'.

irritable adjective 1 easily annoyed or angered. 2 Medicine abnormally sensitive.
- DERIVATIVES **irritability** noun **irritably** adverb.

irritable bowel syndrome noun a condition involving recurrent abdominal pain and diarrhoea or constipation.

irritant noun 1 a substance that irritates part of the body. 2 a source of continual annoyance. • adjective causing irritation to the body.

irritate verb 1 make someone annoyed or angry. 2 cause inflammation in a part of the body.
- DERIVATIVES **irritating** adjective **irritation** noun.
- ORIGIN Latin *irritare*.

irruption /i-**rup**-sh'n/ noun a sudden forcible entry.
- DERIVATIVES **irrupt** verb **irruptive** adjective.
- ORIGIN Latin *irrumpere* 'break into'.

IRS abbreviation Internal Revenue Service.

is third person singular present of **BE**.

ISA abbreviation 1 (in the UK) individual savings account. 2 Computing industry standard architecture.

ISBN abbreviation international standard book number.

ischaemia /i-**skeem**-i-uh/ (US **ischemia**) noun an inadequate blood supply to a part of the body, especially the heart muscles.
- DERIVATIVES **ischaemic** adjective.
- ORIGIN Greek *iskhaimos* 'stopping blood'.

ISDN abbreviation integrated services digital network, a telecommunications network through which sound, images, and data can be transmitted as digitized signals.

-ise suffix variant spelling of **-IZE**.

USAGE: For advice on the use of -ise or -ize, see the note at -IZE.

isinglass /**I**-zing-glahs/ noun a kind of gelatin obtained from fish.
- ORIGIN from Dutch *huysenblas* 'sturgeon's bladder'.

Islam /iz-**lahm**/ noun 1 the religion of the Muslims, based on belief in one God and regarded by them to have been revealed through Muhammad as the Prophet of Allah. 2 the Muslim world.
- DERIVATIVES **Islamize** (or **Islamise**) verb.
- ORIGIN Arabic, 'submission'.

Islamic /iz-**lam**-ik/ adjective relating to Islam.
- DERIVATIVES **Islamicize** (or **Islamicise**) verb.

Islamism noun Islamic extremism or fundamentalism.
- DERIVATIVES **Islamist** (also **Islamicist**) noun & adjective.

Islamophobia noun a hatred or fear of Islam or Muslims.

island noun 1 a piece of land surrounded by water. 2 a thing that is isolated, detached, or surrounded: *the last island of democracy in this country.*
- DERIVATIVES **islander** noun.
- ORIGIN Old English.

isle noun literary (except in place names) an island.
- ORIGIN Old French *ile*.

islet /**I**-lit/ noun a small island.

islets of Langerhans /lang-er-hanz/ plural noun groups of cells in the pancreas that produce insulin.
- ORIGIN named after the German anatomist Paul *Langerhans*.

ism /i-zuhm/ noun informal, chiefly derogatory a distinctive system, philosophy, or ideology.

isn't contraction is not.

isobar /**I**-soh-bar/ noun a line on a map connecting points having the same atmospheric pressure.
- DERIVATIVES **isobaric** adjective.
- ORIGIN Greek *isobaros* 'of equal weight'.

isolate verb 1 place someone or something apart or alone. 2 Chemistry & Biology obtain or extract a compound, microorganism, etc. in a pure form. 3 cut off the electrical or other connection to something. • noun an isolated person or thing.
- DERIVATIVES **isolator** noun.
- ORIGIN from **ISOLATED**.

isolated adjective 1 remote; lonely: *isolated villages.* 2 single; exceptional: *isolated incidents of unrest.*
- ORIGIN French *isolé*, from Latin *insulatus* 'made into an island'.

isolation noun the process of isolating someone or something or the fact of being isolated.
- PHRASES **in isolation** without relation to others; separately.

isolationism noun a policy of remaining apart from the political affairs of other countries.
- DERIVATIVES **isolationist** noun.

isomer /**I**-suh-mer/ noun 1 Chemistry each of two or more compounds with the same formula but a different arrangement of atoms and different properties. 2 Physics each of two or

more atomic nuclei with the same atomic number and mass number but different energy states.
– DERIVATIVES **isomeric** adjective **isomerism** noun **isomerize** (or **isomerise**) verb.
– ORIGIN Greek *isomerēs* 'sharing equally'.

isometric /I-suh-met-rik/ adjective **1** having equal dimensions. **2** Physiology involving an increase in muscle tension but no contraction of the muscle. **3** (of perspective drawing) having the three main dimensions represented by axes 120° apart.
– DERIVATIVES **isometrically** adverb.
– ORIGIN Greek *isometria* 'equality of measure'.

isometrics plural noun a system of physical exercises in which muscles are made to act against each other or against a fixed object.

isomorphic /I-soh-mor-fik/ adjective having a similar form and relationship.
– DERIVATIVES **isomorphism** noun **isomorphous** adjective.

isosceles /I-soss-i-leez/ adjective (of a triangle) having two sides of equal length.
– ORIGIN Greek *isoskelēs*.

isotherm /I-soh-therm/ noun a line on a map or diagram connecting points having the same temperature.
– DERIVATIVES **isothermal** adjective & noun.
– ORIGIN from Greek *isos* 'equal' + *thermē* 'heat'.

isotonic /I-soh-ton-ik/ adjective **1** Physiology (of a muscle action) taking place with normal contraction. **2** (of a drink) containing essential salts and minerals in the same concentration as in the body.
– ORIGIN Greek *isotonos*.

isotope /I-suh-tohp/ noun Chemistry each of two or more forms of the same element that contain equal numbers of protons but different numbers of neutrons in their nuclei.
– DERIVATIVES **isotopic** adjective.
– ORIGIN from Greek *isos* 'equal' + *topos* 'place', because the isotopes occupy the same place in the periodic table.

isotropic /I-soh-trop-ik/ adjective Physics having the same size or properties when measured in different directions.
– ORIGIN from Greek *isos* 'equal' + *tropos* 'a turn'.

ISP abbreviation Internet service provider.

Israeli /iz-ray-li/ noun (pl. **Israelis**) a person from Israel. • adjective relating to the modern country of Israel.

Israelite /iz-ruh-lyt/ noun a member of the ancient Hebrew nation.

issue noun **1** an important topic or problem to be discussed or resolved: *environmental issues*. **2** (**issues**) personal problems or difficulties. **3** the action of supplying or distributing something. **4** each of a regular series of publications. **5** formal or Law children of one's own. • verb (**issues, issuing, issued**) **1** supply or distribute something. **2** formally send out or make known: *the minister issued a statement*. **3** (**issue from**) come, go, or flow out from: *exotic smells issued from a nearby building*.
– PHRASES **at issue** under discussion. **make an issue of** treat something too seriously or as a problem. **take issue with** disagree with or challenge.
– DERIVATIVES **issuer** noun.

– ORIGIN Old French.

isthmus /iss-muhss/ noun (pl. **isthmuses**) a narrow strip of land with sea on either side, linking two larger areas of land.
– ORIGIN Greek *isthmos*.

IT abbreviation information technology.

it pronoun (third person sing.) **1** used to refer to a thing previously mentioned or easily identified. **2** referring to an animal or child of unspecified sex. **3** used to identify a person: *it's me*. **4** used as a subject in statements about time, distance, or weather: *it is raining*. **5** used to refer to something specified later in the sentence: *it is impossible to get there today*. **6** used to refer the situation or circumstances: *if it's convenient*. **7** exactly what is needed or desired.
– ORIGIN Old English, neuter of **HE**.

Italian noun **1** a person from Italy. **2** the language of Italy, descended from Latin. • adjective relating to Italy or Italian.
– DERIVATIVES **Italianize** (or **Italianise**) verb.

Italianate adjective Italian in character or appearance.

italic /i-tal-ik/ adjective referring to the sloping typeface used especially for emphasis and in foreign words. • noun (also **italics**) an italic typeface or letter.
– ORIGIN Greek *Italikos* 'Italian'.

itch noun **1** an uncomfortable sensation that causes a desire to scratch the skin. **2** informal an impatient desire. • verb **1** have an itch. **2** informal feel an impatient desire to do something: *he was itching to get outside*.
– ORIGIN Old English.

itchy adjective (**itchier, itchiest**) having or causing an itch.
– PHRASES **have itchy feet** informal have a strong urge to travel.
– DERIVATIVES **itchiness** noun.

it'd contraction **1** it had. **2** it would.

item noun an individual article or unit: *an item of clothing*.
– PHRASES **be an item** informal (of a couple) be in a romantic or sexual relationship.
– ORIGIN Latin, 'in like manner, also'.

itemize (or **itemise**) verb present something as a list of individual items or parts.

iterate /it-uh-rayt/ verb **1** do or say something repeatedly. **2** make repeated use of a mathematical or computational procedure, applying it each time to the result of the previous application.
– DERIVATIVES **iteration** noun **iterative** adjective.
– ORIGIN Latin *iterare*.

itinerant /I-tin-uh-ruhnt/ adjective travelling from place to place. • noun an itinerant person.
– ORIGIN Latin *itinerari* 'travel'.

itinerary /I-tin-uh-ruh-ri/ noun (pl. **itineraries**) a planned route or journey.

-itis suffix forming names of diseases which cause inflammation: *cystitis*.
– ORIGIN Greek *-itēs*.

it'll contraction **1** it shall. **2** it will.

ITN abbreviation (in the UK) Independent Television News.

its possessive determiner **1** belonging to or associated with a thing previously mentioned or easily identified. **2** belonging to or associated with a child or animal of unspecified sex.

USAGE: A common error in writing is to confuse the possessive **its** (as in *turn the camera on its side*) with the form **it's** (short for either **it is** or **it has**, as in *it's my fault; it's been a hot day*).

it's contraction **1** it is. **2** it has.

itself pronoun (third person sing.) **1** (reflexive) used to refer to something previously mentioned as the subject of the clause: *his horse hurt itself.* **2** (emphatic) used to emphasize a particular thing or animal mentioned: *she wanted him more than life itself.*
– PHRASES **in itself** viewed in its essential qualities.

itsy-bitsy (also **itty-bitty**) adjective informal very small.
– ORIGIN from a child's form of LITTLE + *bitsy*, from BIT¹.

ITU abbreviation Brit. intensive therapy unit.

ITV abbreviation Independent Television.

IUD abbreviation intrauterine device.

IV abbreviation intravenous or intravenously.

I've contraction I have.

IVF abbreviation in vitro fertilization.

ivied adjective covered in ivy.

Ivorian /I-**vor**-i-uhn/ noun a person from the Ivory Coast, a country in West Africa.
● adjective relating to the Ivory Coast.

ivory noun (pl. **ivories**) **1** a hard creamy-white substance which forms the main part of the tusks of an elephant or walrus. **2** the creamy-white colour of ivory. **3** (**the ivories**) informal the keys of a piano.

– ORIGIN Old French *ivurie.*

ivory tower noun a privileged or secluded existence in which someone does not have to face the normal difficulties of life.

ivy noun a woody evergreen climbing plant, typically with shiny five-pointed leaves.
– ORIGIN Old English.

Ivy League noun a group of long-established and prestigious universities in the eastern US.
– ORIGIN with reference to the ivy traditionally growing over their walls.

Iyengar /i-**yen**-gah/ noun a type of yoga focusing on the correct alignment of the body, making use of straps, wooden blocks, and other objects to help achieve the correct postures.
– ORIGIN named after the Indian yoga teacher B. K. S. *Iyengar.*

-ize (or **-ise**) suffix forming verbs meaning: **1** make or become: *privatize.* **2** cause to resemble: *Americanize.* **3** treat in a specified way: *pasteurize.* **4** treat or cause to combine with a specified substance: *carbonize.* **5** perform or subject someone to a specified practice: *hospitalize.*
– ORIGIN Greek *-izein.*

USAGE: Many verbs that end in **-ize** can also end in **-ise**: in such cases both endings are equally acceptable. However, there are a small number of verbs that must always be spelled with **-ise** at the end. This is either because **-ise** forms part of a larger word element, such as *-mise* in **compromise**, or because the verb corresponds to a noun which has **-s-** in the stem, such as **televise** (from *television*).

Jj

J¹ (also **j**) **noun** (pl. **Js** or **J's**) the tenth letter of the alphabet.

J² **abbreviation 1** (in card games) jack. **2** Physics joule(s).

jab **verb** (**jabs, jabbing, jabbed**) poke someone or something roughly or quickly with a sharp or pointed object. • **noun 1** a quick, sharp poke or blow. **2** Brit. informal an injection, especially a vaccination.
– ORIGIN apparently symbolic of the action.

jabber **verb** talk rapidly and excitedly. • **noun** rapid, excited talk.
– ORIGIN imitating the sound.

jabiru /**jab**-i-roo/ **noun** a large stork with a black neck and an upturned bill.
– ORIGIN Tupi-Guarani.

jabot /**zha**-boh/ **noun** an ornamental ruffle on the front of a shirt or blouse.
– ORIGIN French.

jacaranda /ja-kuh-**ran**-duh/ **noun** a tropical American tree with blue trumpet-shaped flowers and sweet-smelling wood.
– ORIGIN Tupi-Guarani.

jack¹ **noun 1** a device for lifting heavy objects, especially one for raising the axle of a motor vehicle off the ground **2** a playing card with a picture of a soldier, page, or knave on it, normally ranking next below a queen. **3** (also **jack socket**) a socket designed to receive a jack plug. **4** the small white ball at which bowls players aim. **5** a small metal piece used in games of tossing and catching. **6** (**jacks**) a game played by tossing and catching jacks. **7** a small national flag flown at the bow of a vessel in harbour. **8** the male of various animals, e.g. the donkey. **9** used in names of animals and plants that are smaller than similar kinds, e.g. **jack pine**. • **verb 1** (**jack something up**) raise something with a jack. **2** (**jack something up**) informal increase something by a considerable amount: *the hotels have jacked up their prices.* **3** (**jack something in**) Brit. informal give something up: *he jacked in his day job as a waiter.*
– PHRASES **every man jack** informal every single person. **jack of all trades** (**and master of none**) a person who can do many different types of work (but has no special skill in none).
– ORIGIN from *Jack*, familiar form of the man's name *John*.

jack² **verb** informal, chiefly N. Amer. steal something.

jackal /ja-k'l/ **noun** a wild dog that feeds on the decaying flesh of dead animals, found in Africa and southern Asia.
– ORIGIN Turkish *çakal*.

jackanapes /jak-uh-nayps/ **noun** dated a rude or cheeky person.
– ORIGIN first as *Jack Napes*, perhaps from a playful name for a tame monkey.

jackaroo /jak-**uh**-roo/ **noun** Austral./NZ informal a young, inexperienced worker on a sheep or cattle station.
– ORIGIN perhaps a blend of **JACK** and **KANGAROO**.

jackass **noun 1** a stupid person. **2** a male ass or donkey.

jackboot **noun** a large leather military boot reaching to the knee.
– DERIVATIVES **jackbooted** adjective.

jackdaw **noun** a small grey-headed crow, noted for its inquisitiveness.
– ORIGIN from **JACK** + earlier *daw* (of Germanic origin).

jacket **noun 1** an outer garment extending to the waist or hips, with sleeves. **2** an outer covering placed around something for protection or insulation. **3** Brit. the skin of a potato. • **verb** (**jackets, jacketing, jacketed**) cover something with a jacket.
– ORIGIN Old French *jaquet*.

jacket potato **noun** Brit. a baked potato served with the skin on.

Jack Frost **noun** frost represented as a human being.

jackfruit **noun** the very large edible fruit of an Asian tree, resembling a breadfruit.
– ORIGIN from Portuguese *jaca* + **FRUIT**.

jackhammer chiefly N. Amer. **noun** a portable pneumatic hammer or drill. • **verb** beat or hammer something heavily or loudly and repeatedly.

jack-in-the-box **noun** a toy consisting of a box containing a figure on a spring which pops up when the lid is opened.

jackknife **noun** (pl. **jackknives**) **1** a large knife with a folding blade. **2** a dive in which the body is bent at the waist and then straightened. • **verb** (**jacknives, jackknifing, jackknifed**) **1** move one's body into a bent or doubled-up position. **2** (of a lorry or other articulated vehicle) bend into a V-shape in an uncontrolled skidding movement. **3** (of a diver) perform a jackknife.

jack-o'-lantern **noun** a lantern made from a hollowed-out pumpkin or turnip in which holes are cut to represent facial features.

jack pine **noun** a small, hardy North American pine with short needles.

jack plug **noun** a plug consisting of a single

jackpot noun a large cash prize in a game or lottery.
- PHRASES **hit the jackpot** informal have great or unexpected success.
- ORIGIN first used in a form of poker, where the pot, or bets made, accumulated until a player could open the bidding with two jacks or better.

jackrabbit noun a North American prairie hare.
- ORIGIN abbreviation of *jackass-rabbit*, because of its long ears.

Jack Russell (also **Jack Russell terrier**) noun a small breed of terrier with short legs.
- ORIGIN named after the English clergyman Revd John (*Jack*) *Russell*.

jacksie (also **jacksy**) noun Brit. informal a person's bottom.
- ORIGIN from **JACK**.

Jack Tar noun Brit. informal, dated a sailor.

Jack the Lad noun Brit. informal a cocky young man.
- ORIGIN nickname of *Jack* Sheppard, 18th-century thief.

Jacobean /jak-uh-bee-uhn/ adjective relating to or characteristic of the reign of James I of England (1603–1625). •noun a person who lived in the Jacobean period.
- ORIGIN from Latin *Jacobus* 'James'.

Jacobite /jak-uh-byt/ noun a supporter of the deposed James II and his descendants in their claim to the British throne after the Revolution of 1688.
- DERIVATIVES **Jacobitism** noun.

Jacob's ladder noun a plant with blue or white flowers and slender pointed leaves formed in ladder-like rows.
- ORIGIN with biblical reference to Jacob's dream of a ladder reaching to heaven (Book of Genesis, chapter 28).

jacquard /ja-kard/ noun 1 a piece of equipment consisting of perforated cards, fitted to a loom for weaving patterned and brocaded fabrics. 2 a fabric made on a jacquard loom.
- ORIGIN named after the French weaver Joseph M. *Jacquard*.

jacuzzi /juh-koo-zi/ noun (pl. **jacuzzis**) trademark a large bath with jets of water which massage the body.
- ORIGIN named after the Italian-born American inventor Candido *Jacuzzi*.

jade¹ noun 1 a hard bluish-green stone used for ornaments and jewellery. 2 a light bluish-green colour.
- ORIGIN French, from Spanish *piedra de ijada* 'stone for colic', which it was believed to cure.

jade² noun old use 1 a bad-tempered or disreputable woman. 2 an old or worn-out horse.
- ORIGIN unknown.

jaded adjective tired or lacking enthusiasm after having had too much of something.
- ORIGIN from **JADE**².

jadeite /jayd-yt/ noun a green, blue, or white form of jade.

Jaffa /ja-fuh/ noun Brit. trademark a large thick-skinned variety of orange.
- ORIGIN from the city of *Jaffa* in Israel.

jag¹ verb (**jags, jagging, jagged**) stab, pierce, or prick something. •noun 1 a sharp projection. 2 chiefly Scottish a prick or injection.
- DERIVATIVES **jaggy** adjective.
- ORIGIN perhaps representing sudden movement or unevenness.

jag² noun informal, chiefly N. Amer. a period of unrestrained activity or emotion: *a crying jag.*
- ORIGIN unknown.

jagged /jagg-id/ adjective with rough, sharp points sticking out.
- DERIVATIVES **jaggedly** adverb **jaggedness** noun.

jaguar /jag-yuu-er/ noun a large, heavily built cat that has a yellowish-brown coat with black spots, found mainly in Central and South America.
- ORIGIN Tupi-Guarani.

Jah /jah, yah/ noun the Rastafarian name for God.
- ORIGIN representing a Hebrew abbreviation of **YAHWEH**.

jail (Brit. also **gaol**) noun a place for holding people accused or convicted of a crime. •verb put someone in jail.
- DERIVATIVES **jailer** noun.
- ORIGIN Old French *jaiole* and *gayole*.

jailbait noun (treated as sing. or pl.) informal a young woman, or young women as a group, regarded as sexually attractive but under the legal age of consent.

jailbird noun informal a person who is or has repeatedly been in prison.

jailbreak noun an escape from jail.

jailhouse noun N. Amer. a prison.

Jain /jayn/ noun a follower of Jainism. •adjective relating to Jainism.
- ORIGIN Sanskrit.

Jainism noun an Indian religion characterized by non-violence and strict self-discipline.

jake adjective N. Amer. & Austral./NZ informal all right; satisfactory.
- ORIGIN unknown.

jalapeño /ha-luh-pay-nyoh, ha-luh-pee-noh/ noun (pl. **jalapeños**) a very hot green chilli pepper.
- ORIGIN Mexican Spanish, from the Mexican city of *Jalapa.*

jalfrezi /jal-fray-zi/ noun (pl. **jalfrezis**) a medium-hot Indian dish consisting of chicken or lamb with fresh chillies, tomatoes, and onions.
- ORIGIN Bengali.

jalopy /juh-lop-i/ noun (pl. **jalopies**) informal a dilapidated old car.
- ORIGIN unknown.

jalousie /zha-loo-zee/ noun a blind or shutter made of a row of angled slats.
- ORIGIN French, 'jealousy'.

jam¹ verb (**jams, jamming, jammed**) 1 squeeze or pack tightly into a space: *four of us were jammed in one compartment.* 2 push something roughly and forcibly into position: *he jammed his hat on.* 3 crowd on to a road or area so as to block it. 4 become or make unable to function due to a part becoming stuck: *the photocopier jammed.* 5 (**jam something on**) apply something forcibly: *he jammed on the brakes.*

6 make a radio transmission unintelligible by causing interference. **7** informal improvise with other musicians. •**noun 1** an instance of something jamming or becoming stuck. **2** informal an awkward situation. **3** informal an improvised performance by a group of musicians.
– ORIGIN probably symbolic of the action.

jam² noun chiefly Brit. a thick spread made from fruit and sugar.
– ORIGIN perhaps from JAM¹.

Jamaican /juh-**may**-kuhn/ noun a person from Jamaica. •**adjective** relating to Jamaica.

jamb /jam/ noun a side post of a doorway, window, or fireplace.
– ORIGIN French *jambe* 'leg, vertical support'.

jambalaya /jam-buh-**ly**-uh/ noun a Cajun dish of rice with shrimps, chicken, and vegetables.
– ORIGIN Provençal *jambalaia*.

jamboree /jam-buh-**ree**/ noun **1** a lavish or noisy celebration or party. **2** a large rally of Scouts or Guides.
– ORIGIN unknown.

jammy adjective (**jammier, jammiest**) **1** covered, filled with, or like jam. **2** Brit. informal lucky.

jam-packed adjective informal extremely crowded or full to capacity.

Jan. abbreviation January.

jangle verb **1** make or cause to make a ringing metallic sound. **2** (of a person's nerves) be set on edge. •**noun** a ringing metallic sound.
– DERIVATIVES **jangly** adjective.
– ORIGIN Old French *jangler*.

janissary /**jan**-is-uh-ri/ noun (pl. **janissaries**) historical a Turkish infantryman in the Sultan's guard.
– ORIGIN French *janissaire*.

janitor /**jan**-i-ter/ noun chiefly N. Amer. a caretaker of a building.
– DERIVATIVES **janitorial** adjective.
– ORIGIN Latin, from *janua* 'door'.

January noun (pl. **Januaries**) the first month of the year.
– ORIGIN from Latin *Januarius mensis* 'month of *Janus*' (the Roman god of beginnings).

Jap noun & adjective informal, offensive short for JAPANESE.

japan noun a black glossy varnish originating in Japan. •**verb** (**japans, japanning, japanned**) varnish something with japan.

Japanese noun (pl. same) **1** a person from Japan. **2** the language of Japan. •**adjective** relating to Japan.

jape noun a practical joke.
– ORIGIN probably from Old French *japer* 'to yelp, yap' and *gaber* 'to mock'.

japonica /juh-**pon**-i-kuh/ noun an Asian shrub of the rose family, with bright red flowers.
– ORIGIN Latin, 'Japanese'.

jar¹ noun **1** a wide-mouthed cylindrical container made of glass or pottery. **2** Brit. informal a glass of beer.
– ORIGIN French *jarre*.

jar² verb (**jars, jarring, jarred**) **1** send a painful or uncomfortable shock through a part of the body. **2** strike against something with an unpleasant vibration or jolt. **3** have an unpleasant or annoying effect: *a laugh which*

jarred on the ears. **4** conflict or clash with something: *the play's symbolism jarred with the realism of its setting.* •**noun** an instance of jarring.
– DERIVATIVES **jarring** adjective.
– ORIGIN probably imitating the sensation.

jardinière /zhar-din-**yair**/ noun **1** an ornamental pot or stand for displaying plants. **2** a garnish of mixed vegetables.
– ORIGIN French, 'female gardener'.

jargon noun words or expressions used by a particular group that are difficult for other people to understand.
– DERIVATIVES **jargonistic** adjective **jargonize** (or **jargonise**) verb.
– ORIGIN Old French *jargoun*.

jasmine noun a shrub or climbing plant with sweet-smelling white, pink, or yellow flowers.
– ORIGIN French *jasmin*, from Persian.

jasper noun an opaque reddish-brown variety of quartz.
– ORIGIN Old French *jasp(r)e*.

jaundice /**jawn**-diss/ noun **1** yellowing of the skin or whites of the eyes, caused especially by a liver disorder. **2** bitterness or resentment.
– DERIVATIVES **jaundiced** adjective.
– ORIGIN Old French *jaunice* 'yellowness'.

jaunt noun a short trip for pleasure.
– ORIGIN unknown.

jaunty adjective (**jauntier, jauntiest**) having a lively and self-confident manner.
– DERIVATIVES **jauntily** adverb **jauntiness** noun.
– ORIGIN French *gentil* 'well-born'.

Java /**jah**-vuh/ noun trademark a computer programming language designed to work across different computer systems.

Javan noun a person from the Indonesian island of Java. •**adjective** relating to Java.

Javanese noun (pl. same) **1** a person from Java. **2** the language of central Java. •**adjective** relating to Java.

javelin /**jav**-lin/ noun a long, light spear thrown in a competitive sport or as a weapon.
– ORIGIN Old French *javeline*.

jaw noun **1** each of the upper and lower bony structures in vertebrates forming the framework of the mouth and containing the teeth. **2** (**jaws**) the grasping, biting, or crushing mouthparts of an invertebrate. **3** (**jaws**) the gripping parts of a tool such as a wrench or vice. •**verb** informal talk or gossip at length.
– DERIVATIVES **jawed** adjective.
– ORIGIN Old French *joe* 'cheek, jaw'.

jawbone noun a bone of the jaw, especially that of the lower jaw.

jaw-dropping adjective informal amazing.

jawline noun the contour of the lower edge of a person's jaw.

jay noun a noisy bird of the crow family with boldly patterned plumage.
– ORIGIN Latin *gaius, gaia*.

jaywalk verb chiefly N. Amer. walk along or across a road without paying attention to the traffic.
– DERIVATIVES **jaywalker** noun.
– ORIGIN from JAY in the former sense 'silly person'.

jazz noun a type of music of black American origin, typically instrumental and characterized by improvisation. •**verb** (**jazz**

j

something up) make something more lively or attractive.
- PHRASES **and all that jazz** informal and other similar things.
- ORIGIN unknown.

jazzy adjective (**jazzier, jazziest**) **1** relating to or like jazz. **2** bright, colourful, and showy.

JCB noun Brit. trademark a type of mechanical excavator with a shovel at the front and a digging arm at the rear.
- ORIGIN the initials of *J. C.* Bamford, the makers.

J-cloth noun trademark (in the UK) a type of cloth used for household cleaning.
- ORIGIN *J* from Johnson and Johnson, the original makers.

jealous adjective **1** envious of someone else's achievements or advantages. **2** having a resentful suspicion that one's partner is sexually attracted to or involved with someone else: *a jealous husband.* **3** very protective of one's rights or possessions: *they kept a jealous eye over their interests.*
- DERIVATIVES **jealously** adverb **jealousy** noun (pl. **jealousies**).
- ORIGIN Old French *gelos.*

jeans plural noun casual trousers made of denim.
- ORIGIN from Latin *Janua* 'Genoa', where *jean,* a type of hard-wearing cotton cloth, was originally made.

jeep noun trademark a sturdy motor vehicle with four-wheel drive.
- ORIGIN probably from the vehicle's model code *GP,* influenced by 'Eugene the Jeep', a creature in the *Popeye* comic strip.

jeer verb make rude and mocking remarks to someone. • noun a rude and mocking remark.
- ORIGIN unknown.

jehad noun variant spelling of **JIHAD**.

Jehovah /ji-**hoh**-vuh/ noun a form of the Hebrew name of God.
- ORIGIN Hebrew.

Jehovah's Witness noun a member of a Christian sect that denies many traditional Christian doctrines and preaches that Jesus will return to earth at the Last Judgement.

jejune /ji-**joon**/ adjective **1** naive and simplistic. **2** (of ideas or writings) dull.
- ORIGIN Latin *jejunus* 'fasting, barren'.

jejunum /ji-**joo**-nuhm/ noun the part of the small intestine between the duodenum and ileum.
- ORIGIN Latin, 'fasting' (because it is usually found to be empty after death).

Jekyll /**je**-k'l/ noun (in phrase **a Jekyll and Hyde**) a person who displays alternately good and evil personalities.
- ORIGIN after the central character in Robert Louis Stevenson's story *The Strange Case of Dr Jekyll and Mr Hyde.*

jell verb (**jells, jelling, jelled**) variant spelling of **GEL²**.

jellaba noun variant spelling of **DJELLABA**.

jellied adjective (of food) set in a jelly.

jello (also trademark **Jell-O**) noun N. Amer. a fruit-flavoured gelatin dessert made up from a powder.

jelly noun (pl. **jellies**) **1** chiefly Brit. a dessert consisting of a sweet, fruit-flavoured liquid set with gelatin to form a semi-solid mass. **2** a substance or preparation with a similar semi-solid consistency. **3** a small sweet made with gelatin.
- ORIGIN Old French *gelee* 'frost, jelly'.

jellyfish noun (pl. same or **jellyfishes**) a sea animal with a soft bell- or saucer-shaped body that has stinging tentacles around the edge.

jemmy (also **jimmy**) noun (pl. **jemmies**) a short crowbar. • verb (**jemmies, jemmying, jemmied**) informal force open a window or door with a jemmy.
- ORIGIN familiar form of the man's name *James.*

je ne sais quoi /zhuh nuh say **kwah**/ noun a quality that is hard to describe or define.
- ORIGIN French, 'I do not know what'.

jenny noun (pl. **jennies**) a female donkey or ass.
- ORIGIN familiar form of the woman's name *Janet.*

jeopardize (or **jeopardise**) /**jep**-er-dyz/ verb put someone or something into a situation where there is a risk of loss, harm, or failure.

jeopardy /**jep**-er-di/ noun danger of loss, harm, or failure.
- ORIGIN from Old French *ieu parti* '(evenly) divided game'.

jerboa /jer-**boh**-uh/ noun a rodent with very long hind legs found in deserts from North Africa to central Asia.
- ORIGIN Arabic.

jeremiad /je-ri-**my**-ad/ noun a long, mournful complaint.
- ORIGIN French *jérémiade,* with reference to the Lamentations of Jeremiah in the Old Testament.

jerk¹ noun **1** a quick, sharp, sudden movement. **2** informal a stupid person. • verb **1** move or raise something with a jerk. **2** (**jerk someone around**) N. Amer. informal deal with someone dishonestly or unfairly.
- DERIVATIVES **jerker** noun.
- ORIGIN uncertain.

jerk² verb prepare pork or chicken by marinating it in spices and barbecuing it over a wood fire. • noun meat that has been marinated and barbecued over a wood fire.
- ORIGIN Spanish *charquear.*

jerkin noun a sleeveless jacket.
- ORIGIN unknown.

jerky adjective (**jerkier, jerkiest**) moving in abrupt stops and starts.
- DERIVATIVES **jerkily** adverb **jerkiness** noun.

jeroboam /je-ruh-**boh**-uhm/ noun a wine bottle with a capacity four times larger than that of an ordinary bottle.
- ORIGIN named after *Jeroboam,* a king of Israel (Book of Kings 1, chapters 11 and 14).

Jerry noun (pl. **Jerries**) Brit. informal, derogatory a German or Germans.
- ORIGIN probably from **GERMAN**.

jerry-built adjective badly or hastily built.
- DERIVATIVES **jerry-builder** noun.
- ORIGIN uncertain: perhaps from the name of a firm of builders in Liverpool.

jerrycan (also **jerrican**) noun a large flat-sided metal container for storing or transporting liquids.

– ORIGIN from **Jerry** + **can²**, because first used in Germany.

jersey noun (pl. **jerseys**) **1** a knitted garment with long sleeves. **2** a distinctive shirt worn by a player in certain sports. **3** a soft knitted fabric. **4** (**Jersey**) an animal of a breed of light brown dairy cattle.
– ORIGIN first referring to fabric made in the Channel Island of *Jersey*.

Jerusalem artichoke noun a knobbly root vegetable with white flesh.
– ORIGIN from Italian *girasole* 'sunflower'.

jess noun Falconry a short leather strap that is fastened round each leg of a hawk, to which a leash may be attached.
– ORIGIN Old French *ges*.

jessie (also **jessy**) noun (pl. **jessies**) Brit. informal, derogatory an effeminate or weak man.
– ORIGIN from the woman's name *Jessie*.

jest noun a joke. •verb speak or act in a joking way.
– ORIGIN Latin *gesta* 'actions, exploits'.

jester noun historical a professional joker or 'fool' at a medieval court.

Jesuit /jez-yuu-it/ noun a member of the Society of Jesus, a Roman Catholic order of priests founded by St Ignatius Loyola.

Jesuitical adjective **1** relating to the Jesuits. **2** using evasive language, in a way once associated with Jesuits.

Jesus (also **Jesus Christ**) noun the central figure of the Christian religion, believed by Christians to be the Messiah and the Son of God. •exclamation informal expressing irritation, dismay, or surprise.

jet¹ noun **1** a rapid stream of liquid or gas forced out of a small opening. **2** an aircraft powered by jet engines. •verb (**jets, jetting, jetted**) **1** spurt out in a jet. **2** travel by jet aircraft.
– ORIGIN from French *jeter* 'to throw'.

jet² noun **1** a hard black semi-precious mineral. **2** (also **jet black**) a glossy black colour.
– ORIGIN Old French *jaiet*.

jetboat noun a motorboat propelled by a jet of water pumped forcefully out from below the waterline at the back of the boat.

jeté /zhe-tay/ noun Ballet a spring from one foot to the other, with the following leg extended backwards while in the air.
– ORIGIN French.

jet engine noun an aircraft engine which provides force for forward movement by ejecting a high-speed jet of gas obtained by burning fuel in air.

jetfoil noun a type of passenger-carrying hydrofoil.
– ORIGIN from **jet¹** and **hydrofoil**.

jet lag noun extreme tiredness and other effects felt by a person after a long flight across different time zones.
– DERIVATIVES **jet-lagged** adjective.

jetliner noun a large jet aircraft carrying passengers.

jetsam /jet-suhm/ noun unwanted material or goods that have been thrown overboard from a ship and washed ashore.
– ORIGIN from **jettison**.

jet set noun (**the jet set**) informal fashionable and wealthy people who frequently travel abroad for pleasure.
– DERIVATIVES **jet-setter** noun **jet-setting** adjective.

jet ski noun trademark a small jet-propelled vehicle which skims across the surface of water and is ridden in a similar way to a motorcycle.
– DERIVATIVES **jet-skier** noun **jet-skiing** noun.

jet stream noun any of several narrow bands of very strong predominantly westerly air currents encircling the globe several miles above the earth.

jettison /jet-i-suhn/ verb **1** throw or drop something from an aircraft or ship. **2** abandon or discard an unwanted person or thing.
– ORIGIN Old French *getaison*.

jetty noun (pl. **jetties**) **1** a landing stage or small pier for boats. **2** a construction built out into the water to protect a harbour, riverbank, or coastline.
– ORIGIN Old French *jetee*.

jeunesse dorée /zher-nes dor-ay/ noun fashionable, wealthy, and stylish young people.
– ORIGIN French, 'gilded youth'.

Jew noun a member of the people whose traditional religion is Judaism and who trace their origins to the ancient Hebrew people of Israel.
– ORIGIN Hebrew, 'Judah'.

jewel noun **1** a precious stone. **2** (**jewels**) pieces of jewellery. **3** a hard precious stone used as a bearing in a watch or other device. **4** a highly valued person or thing: *she was a jewel of a nurse.*
– DERIVATIVES **jewelled** (US **jeweled**) adjective.
– PHRASES **the jewel in the crown** the most valuable or successful part of something.
– ORIGIN Old French *joel*.

jeweller (US **jeweler**) noun a person who makes or sells jewellery.

jewellery (US also **jewelry**) noun personal ornaments such as necklaces, rings, or bracelets.

Jewess noun usu. offensive a Jewish woman or girl.

Jewish adjective relating to Jews or Judaism.
– DERIVATIVES **Jewishness** noun.

Jewish New Year noun another term for **Rosh Hashana**.

Jewry /joo-ri/ noun Jews as a group.

Jew's harp noun a small musical instrument like a U-shaped harp, held between the teeth and struck with a finger.

Jezebel /jez-uh-bel/ noun a shameless or immoral woman.
– ORIGIN the name of the wife of King Ahab in the Bible.

jiao /jow/ noun (pl. same) a unit of money of China, equal to one tenth of a yuan.
– ORIGIN Chinese.

jib¹ noun **1** Sailing a triangular sail set in front of the mast. **2** the projecting arm of a crane.
– ORIGIN unknown.

jib² verb (**jibs, jibbing, jibbed**) (usu. **jib at**) **1** be unwilling to do or accept something. **2** (of a horse) stop and refuse to go on.
– ORIGIN perhaps related to French *regimber* 'buck, rear'.

jibe¹ (also **gibe**) noun an insulting or mocking remark. •verb make insulting or mocking remarks.

– ORIGIN perhaps from Old French *giber* 'handle roughly'.

jibe² verb & noun US variant of GYBE.

jibe³ verb (usu. **jibe with**) N. Amer. informal be in accordance or agree with something.
– ORIGIN unknown.

jiffy (also **jiff**) noun informal a moment.
– ORIGIN unknown.

jig noun **1** a lively dance with leaping movements. **2** a device that holds a piece of work and guides the tool operating on it. • verb (**jigs, jigging, jigged**) **1** move up and down jerkily. **2** dance a jig.
– ORIGIN unknown.

jigger¹ noun **1** a machine or vehicle with a part that rocks or moves to and fro. **2** a measure of spirits or wine. • verb Brit. informal **1** rearrange or tamper with something. **2** (as adj. **jiggered**) damaged, broken, or exhausted.

jigger² noun variant spelling of CHIGGER.

jiggery-pokery noun informal, chiefly Brit. dishonest or suspicious behaviour.
– ORIGIN probably from Scots *jouk* 'dodge, skulk'.

jiggle verb move lightly and quickly from side to side or up and down. • noun an instance of jiggling.
– DERIVATIVES **jiggly** adjective.
– ORIGIN from JOGGLE and JIG.

jiggy adjective US informal **1** uninhibited, especially in a sexual way. **2** trembling or nervous, especially as the result of drug withdrawal.

jigsaw noun **1** a puzzle consisting of a picture printed on cardboard or wood and cut into many interlocking shapes that have to be fitted together. **2** a machine saw with a fine blade enabling it to cut curved lines.

jihad /ji-**hahd**/ (also **jehad**) noun (in Islam) a war or struggle against unbelievers.
– DERIVATIVES **jihadist** noun.
– ORIGIN Arabic, 'effort'.

jihadi /ji-**hah**-di/ (also **jehadi**) noun (pl. **jihadis**) a person involved in a jihad.

jilt verb abruptly break off a relationship with a lover.
– ORIGIN unknown.

Jim Crow noun US **1** the former practice of segregating black people in the US. **2** offensive a black person.
– DERIVATIVES **Jim Crowism** noun.
– ORIGIN a black character in a plantation song.

jim-jams plural noun Brit. informal pyjamas.

jimmy noun & verb US spelling of JEMMY.

jingle noun **1** a light ringing sound such as that made by metal objects being shaken together. **2** a short, easily remembered slogan, verse, or tune. • verb make a light ringing sound.
– DERIVATIVES **jingler** noun **jingly** adjective.
– ORIGIN imitating the sound.

jingoism noun chiefly derogatory extreme patriotism in the form of aggressive foreign policy.
– DERIVATIVES **jingoist** noun **jingoistic** adjective.
– ORIGIN from *by jingo!* in a song adopted by those who supported the sending of a British fleet into Turkish waters to resist Russia in 1878.

jink verb change direction suddenly and nimbly. • noun a sudden quick change of direction.
– ORIGIN from Scots *high jinks*, referring to

antics at drinking parties.

jinn /jin/ (also **djinn**) noun (pl. same or **jinns**) (in Arabian and Muslim mythology) an intelligent spirit able to appear in human or animal form.
– ORIGIN Arabic.

jinx noun a person or thing that brings bad luck. • verb bring bad luck to someone or something.
– ORIGIN probably from Latin *jynx* 'wryneck' (because the bird was used in witchcraft).

jitter informal noun **1** (**the jitters**) a feeling of extreme nervousness. **2** slight irregular variation in an electrical signal. • verb act nervously.
– DERIVATIVES **jitteriness** noun **jittery** adjective.
– ORIGIN unknown.

jitterbug noun a fast dance performed to swing music, popular in the 1940s. • verb (**jitterbugs, jitterbugging, jitterbugged**) dance the jitterbug.

jiu-jitsu noun variant spelling of JU-JITSU.

jive noun a style of lively dance popular in the 1940s and 1950s, performed to swing music or rock and roll. • verb dance the jive.
– DERIVATIVES **jiver** noun.
– ORIGIN unknown.

joanna noun Brit. rhyming slang a piano.

job noun **1** a paid position of regular employment. **2** a task or piece of work. **3** informal a crime, especially a robbery. **4** informal a procedure to improve the appearance of something: *a nose job.* • verb (**jobs, jobbing, jobbed**) (usu. as adj. **jobbing**) do casual or occasional work.
– PHRASES **a good job** informal, chiefly Brit. a fortunate fact or circumstance. **just the job** Brit. informal exactly what is needed.
– ORIGIN unknown.

jobber noun **1** a person who does casual or occasional work. **2** (in the UK) a principal or wholesaler dealing only on the Stock Exchange with brokers, not directly with the public (term officially replaced by **broker-dealer** in 1986).

jobbery noun the practice of using a public office or position of trust for one's own benefit.

jobcentre noun (in the UK) a government office of a local area, giving information about available jobs and administering benefits to unemployed people.

jobless adjective without a paid job.
– DERIVATIVES **joblessness** noun.

job lot noun a batch of articles sold or bought at one time, especially at a discount.

job-share verb (of two part-time employees) share a single full-time job. • noun an arrangement in which two part-time employees share a full-time job.
– DERIVATIVES **job-sharer** noun.

jobsworth noun Brit. informal an official who upholds petty rules regardless of common sense.
– ORIGIN from 'it's more than my *job's worth* (not) to...'.

Jock noun informal, often offensive a Scotsman.
– ORIGIN Scots form of the man's name *Jack*.

jock noun N. Amer. informal an enthusiast or participant in a particular sport or other activity.

jockey noun (pl. **jockeys**) a professional rider in horse races. ● verb (**jockeys, jockeying, jockeyed**) struggle to gain or achieve something: *drivers are constantly jockeying for position*.
– ORIGIN from **Jock**, formerly referring to a mounted courier.

jockstrap noun a support or pouch worn to protect a man's genitals, especially in sport.
– ORIGIN from slang *jock* 'genitals'.

jocose /juh-**kohss**/ adjective formal playful or humorous.
– DERIVATIVES **jocosely** adverb **jocosity** /juh-**koss**-it-i/ noun (pl. **jocosities**).
– ORIGIN from Latin *jocus* 'jest, joke'.

jocular /**jok**-yuu-ler/ adjective humorous or amusing.
– DERIVATIVES **jocularity** noun **jocularly** adverb.
– ORIGIN Latin *jocularis*.

jocund /**jok**-uhnd/ adjective formal cheerful and light-hearted.
– ORIGIN Latin *jucundus* 'pleasant, agreeable'.

jodhpurs /**jod**-perz/ plural noun trousers worn for horse riding that are close-fitting below the knee.
– ORIGIN named after the Indian city of *Jodhpur*.

jog verb (**jogs, jogging, jogged**) **1** run at a steady, gentle pace, especially for exercise. **2** (**jog along/on**) continue in a steady, uneventful way. **3** knock something slightly. ● noun **1** a spell of jogging. **2** a gentle running pace. **3** a slight push or knock.
– PHRASES **jog someone's memory** make someone remember something.
– ORIGIN from **JAG**[1].

jogger noun **1** a person who jogs. **2** (**joggers**) tracksuit trousers worn for jogging.

joggle verb move with repeated small jerks.
– ORIGIN from **JOG**.

jogtrot noun a slow trot.

john noun informal **1** chiefly N. Amer. a toilet. **2** a prostitute's client.
– ORIGIN from the man's name *John*.

John Bull noun a character representing England or the typical Englishman.
– ORIGIN from a character in John Arbuthnot's satire *Law is a Bottomless Pit; or, the History of John Bull*.

John Dory noun (pl. **John Dories**) an edible dory (fish) of the eastern Atlantic and Mediterranean, with a black oval mark on each side.

johnny noun (pl. **johnnies**) Brit. informal **1** a man. **2** (also **rubber johnny**) a condom.
– ORIGIN familiar form of the man's name *John*.

johnny-come-lately noun informal a newcomer to or late starter at a place or area of activity.

joie de vivre /zhwah duh **vee**-vruh/ noun lively enjoyment of life.
– ORIGIN French.

join verb **1** link or become linked to. **2** unite to form a whole: *they joined up with local environmentalists*. **3** become a member or employee of an organization. **4** (also **join in**) take part in an activity. **5** meet or go somewhere with someone. **6** (**join up**) become a member of the armed forces. ● noun a place where things are connected or fastened

together.
– PHRASES **join forces** combine efforts.
– DERIVATIVES **joinable** adjective.
– ORIGIN Old French *joindre*.

joiner noun chiefly Brit. a person who constructs the wooden parts of a building.

joinery noun **1** the wooden parts of a building. **2** the work of a joiner.

joint noun **1** a point at which parts are joined. **2** a structure in the body by which two bones are fitted together. **3** the part of a plant stem from which a leaf or branch grows. **4** Brit. a large piece of meat. **5** informal a place for eating, drinking, or entertainment: *a burger joint*. **6** informal a cannabis cigarette. ● adjective **1** shared, held, or made by two or more people: *a joint account*. **2** sharing in an achievement or activity. ● verb **1** (usu. as adj. **jointed**) provide or fasten something with joints. **2** cut the body of an animal into joints.
– PHRASES **out of joint 1** (of a joint of the body) dislocated. **2** in a state of disorder.
– DERIVATIVES **jointly** adverb.
– ORIGIN from Old French *joindre* 'to join'.

jointer noun a plane for preparing a wooden edge for joining to another.

joist /joysst/ noun a length of timber or steel supporting the floor or ceiling of a building.
– ORIGIN Old French *giste* 'beam supporting a bridge'.

jojoba /hoh-**hoh**-buh/ noun an oil extracted from the seeds of a North American shrub, used in cosmetics.
– ORIGIN Mexican Spanish.

joke noun **1** a thing that someone says to cause amusement or laughter. **2** a trick played for fun. **3** informal a ridiculously inadequate person or thing: *public transport is a joke*. ● verb make jokes.
– DERIVATIVES **jokey** (also **joky**) adjective.
– ORIGIN perhaps from Latin *jocus*.

joker noun **1** a person who is fond of joking. **2** informal a foolish or ridiculous person. **3** a playing card with the figure of a jester, used as a wild card.
– PHRASES **the joker in the pack** a person or factor likely to have an unpredictable effect.

jollification noun lively celebration with others; merrymaking.

jollity noun (pl. **jollities**) **1** lively and cheerful activity. **2** the quality of being cheerful.

jolly[1] adjective (**jollier, jolliest**) **1** happy and cheerful. **2** lively and entertaining. ● verb (**jollies, jollying, jollied**) informal encourage in a friendly way: *he jollied her along*. ● adverb Brit. informal very. ● noun (pl. **jollies**) Brit. informal a party or celebration.
– DERIVATIVES **jollily** adverb **jolliness** noun.
– ORIGIN Old French *jolif* 'pretty'.

jolly[2] (also **jolly boat**) noun (pl. **jollies**) a ship's boat that is smaller than a cutter.
– ORIGIN perhaps related to **YAWL**.

Jolly Roger noun a pirate's flag with a white skull and crossbones on a black background.
– ORIGIN unknown.

jolt verb **1** push or shake someone or something abruptly and roughly. **2** shock someone into taking action. ● noun **1** a sudden or violent movement. **2** a surprise or shock.
– ORIGIN unknown.

j

jonquil /jong-kwil/ noun a narcissus with small sweet-smelling yellow flowers.
– ORIGIN Spanish *junquillo*.

Jordanian noun a person from Jordan. • adjective relating to Jordan.

josh verb informal tease someone playfully.
– DERIVATIVES **josher** noun.
– ORIGIN unknown.

Joshua tree noun a tall branching yucca of SW North America, with clusters of spiky leaves.
– ORIGIN probably from *Joshua* in the Bible, the plant being likened to a man with a spear.

joss stick noun a thin stick of a sweet-smelling substance, burnt as incense.
– ORIGIN from *joss*, referring to a Chinese religious statue or idol.

jostle verb 1 push or bump against someone roughly. 2 (**jostle for**) struggle or compete forcefully for: *they jostled for control of the bathroom.*
– ORIGIN from **JOUST**.

jot verb (**jots, jotting, jotted**) write something quickly. • noun a very small amount: *his rich voice has not lost a jot of its power.*
– ORIGIN from Greek *iōta*, the smallest letter of the Greek alphabet (see **IOTA**).

jotter noun Brit. a small notebook.

jotting noun a brief note.

joule /jool/ noun the unit of work or energy in the SI system.
– ORIGIN named after the English physicist James P. *Joule*.

jounce /*rhymes with* bounce/ verb jolt or bounce.
– ORIGIN uncertain.

journal noun 1 a newspaper or magazine dealing with a particular subject. 2 a diary or daily record. • verb (**journals, journaling, journaled**) write in a journal or diary.
– ORIGIN Old French *jurnal*.

journalese noun informal an unoriginal and poor writing style supposedly typical of journalists.

journalism noun the activity or profession of being a journalist.

journalist noun a person who writes for newspapers or magazines or prepares news or features to be broadcast on radio or television.
– DERIVATIVES **journalistic** adjective.

journey noun (pl. **journeys**) an act of travelling from one place to another. • verb (**journeys, journeying, journeyed**) travel somewhere.
– DERIVATIVES **journeyer** noun.
– ORIGIN Old French *jornee* 'day, a day's travel, a day's work'.

journeyman noun (pl. **journeymen**) 1 a skilled worker who is employed by another. 2 a worker who is reliable but not outstanding.
– ORIGIN from **JOURNEY** in the former sense 'day's work'.

joust /jowsst/ verb 1 (of a medieval knight) fight an opponent on horseback with lances. 2 (usu. as noun **jousting**) compete for superiority with someone: *he ignored Sam's verbal jousting.* • noun a medieval contest in which knights on horseback fought with lances.
– DERIVATIVES **jouster** noun.
– ORIGIN Old French *jouster* 'bring together'.

Jove /johv/ noun (in phrase **by Jove**) dated used for emphasis or to indicate surprise.
– ORIGIN another name for the Roman god Jupiter.

jovial /joh-vi-uhl/ adjective cheerful and friendly.
– DERIVATIVES **joviality** noun **jovially** adverb.
– ORIGIN Latin *jovialis* 'of Jupiter' (referring to the influence of the planet Jupiter).

jowl noun 1 the lower part of a person's cheek, especially when fleshy. 2 the loose skin at the throat of cattle.
– DERIVATIVES **jowled** adjective **jowly** adjective.
– ORIGIN Old English.

joy noun 1 great pleasure and happiness. 2 a cause of great pleasure and happiness. 3 Brit. informal success or satisfaction: *you'll get no joy out of her.*
– ORIGIN Old French *joie*.

joyful adjective feeling or causing great pleasure or happiness.
– DERIVATIVES **joyfully** adverb **joyfulness** noun.

joyless adjective not giving or feeling any pleasure or satisfaction; grim or dismal.

joyous adjective chiefly literary full of happiness and joy.
– DERIVATIVES **joyously** adverb **joyousness** noun.

joypad noun a device for a computer games console which uses buttons to control an image on the screen.

joyride noun informal 1 a fast ride in a stolen vehicle. 2 a ride for enjoyment.
– DERIVATIVES **joyrider** noun **joyriding** noun.

joystick noun informal 1 the control column of an aircraft. 2 a lever for controlling the movement of an image on a computer screen.

JP abbreviation Justice of the Peace.

JPEG /jay-peg/ noun Computing a format for compressing images.
– ORIGIN abbreviation of *Joint Photographic Experts Group*.

jubilant adjective happy and triumphant.
– DERIVATIVES **jubilantly** adverb.

jubilation /joo-bi-lay-sh'n/ noun a feeling of great happiness and triumph.
– ORIGIN from Latin *jubilare* 'shout for joy'.

jubilee noun a special anniversary, especially one celebrating twenty-five or fifty years of something.
– ORIGIN from a Hebrew word meaning 'ram's-horn trumpet', with which a year of emancipation and restoration, kept every fifty years, was proclaimed.

Judaeo- /joo-dee-oh/ (US **Judeo-**) combining form Jewish; Jewish and ...: *Judaeo-Christian*.
– ORIGIN from Latin *Judaeus* 'Jewish'.

Judaic /joo-day-ik/ adjective relating to Judaism or the ancient Jews.

Judaism /joo-day-i-z'm/ noun the religion of the Jews, based on the Old Testament and the Talmud.
– DERIVATIVES **Judaist** noun.
– ORIGIN Greek *Ioudaïsmos*.

Judaize (or **Judaise**) /joo-day-yz/ verb make someone or something Jewish.
– DERIVATIVES **Judaization** noun.

Judas /joo-duhss/ noun a person who betrays a friend.
– ORIGIN from *Judas* Iscariot, the disciple who betrayed Christ.

judder verb shake rapidly and forcefully.
– DERIVATIVES **juddery** adjective.
– ORIGIN imitating the sound.

Judeo- combining form US spelling of **Judaeo-**.

judge noun 1 a public officer appointed to decide cases in a law court. 2 a person who decides the results of a competition. 3 a person with the necessary knowledge or skill to give an opinion. • verb 1 form an opinion about: *a work should be judged on its own merits.* 2 give a verdict on a case or person in a law court. 3 decide the results of a competition.
– ORIGIN Latin *judex.*

judgement (also **judgment**) noun 1 the ability to make considered decisions or form sensible opinions: *an error of judgement.* 2 an opinion or conclusion. 3 a decision of a law court or judge.
– PHRASES **against one's better judgement** opposite to what one feels to be wise. **sit in judgement** assume the right to judge or criticize someone.

USAGE: In British English the normal spelling is **judgement**. The spelling **judgment** is used in legal situations and in American English.

judgemental (also **judgmental**) adjective 1 relating to the use of judgement. 2 excessively critical.
– DERIVATIVES **judgementally** adverb.

Judgement Day noun the time of the Last Judgement; the end of the world.

judicature /joo-dik-uh-cher, joo-**dik**-uh-cher/ noun 1 the administration of a country's justice system. 2 (**the judicature**) judges as a group.
– ORIGIN from Latin *judicare* 'to judge'.

judicial /joo-**di**-sh'l/ adjective relating to a law court or judge.
– DERIVATIVES **judicially** adverb.
– ORIGIN from Latin *judicium* 'judgement'.

USAGE: On the difference between **judicial** and **judicious**, see the note at **judicious**.

judiciary /joo-**di**-shuh-ri/ noun (pl. **judiciaries**) (usu. **the judiciary**) the system of judges of a country.

judicious /joo-**di**-shuhss/ adjective having or done with good judgement; sensible.
– DERIVATIVES **judiciously** adverb **judiciousness** noun.

USAGE: **Judicious** and **judicial** do not mean the same thing. **Judicious** means 'having or done with good judgement, sensible' (*the judicious use of public investment*), whereas **judicial** means 'relating to a law court or judge' (*the judicial system*).

judo noun a sport of unarmed combat using holds and leverage to unbalance the opponent.
– ORIGIN Japanese, 'gentle way'.

jug noun 1 Brit. a container with a handle and a lip, for holding and pouring liquids. 2 N. Amer. a large container for liquids, with a narrow mouth. 3 (**the jug**) informal prison.
– ORIGIN perhaps from *Jug,* familiar form of the woman's names *Joan, Joanna,* and *Jenny.*

jug band noun a group of jazz, blues, or folk musicians using simple or improvised instruments such as jugs and washboards.

jugged adjective (of a hare) stewed in a covered container.

juggernaut /**jug**-ger-nawt/ noun Brit. a large heavy lorry.
– ORIGIN Sanskrit, 'Lord of the world', referring to an image of the Hindu god Krishna carried on a heavy chariot.

juggle verb 1 continuously throw up and catch a number of objects so as to keep at least one in the air at any time. 2 manage to deal with several activities at the same time. 3 organize or manipulate facts to as to present them in the most effective or favourable way.
– DERIVATIVES **juggler** noun.
– ORIGIN Old French *jogler.*

jugular /**jug**-yuu-ler/ adjective relating to the neck or throat. • noun (also **jugular vein**) any of several large veins in the neck, carrying blood from the head.
– PHRASES **go for the jugular** attack an opponent's weakest point in an aggressive way.
– ORIGIN from Latin *jugulum* 'collarbone, throat'.

juice noun 1 the liquid present in fruit or vegetables, often made into a drink. 2 (**juices**) fluid produced by the stomach. 3 (**juices**) liquid coming from meat or other food in cooking. 4 informal fuel or electrical energy. 5 (**juices**) informal a person's creative abilities. • verb extract the juice from fruit or vegetables.
– ORIGIN Latin *jus* 'broth, vegetable juice'.

juicer noun a device for extracting juice from fruit and vegetables.

juicy adjective (**juicier, juiciest**) 1 full of juice. 2 informal interestingly scandalous: *a juicy bit of gossip.* 3 informal likely to be rewarding or profitable: *juicy projects.*
– DERIVATIVES **juicily** adverb **juiciness** noun.

ju-jitsu /joo-**jit**-soo/ (also **jiu-jitsu**) noun a Japanese system of unarmed combat and physical training.
– ORIGIN Japanese, 'gentle skill'.

juju /**joo**-joo/ noun 1 a charm or fetish, especially as used by some West African peoples. 2 supernatural power believed to be possessed by a charm or fetish.
– ORIGIN West African.

jujube /**joo**-joob/ noun 1 an edible berry-like fruit of a shrub, formerly eaten as a cough cure. 2 N. Amer. a jujube-flavoured lozenge or sweet.
– ORIGIN Latin *jujuba.*

jukebox noun a machine that plays a selected musical recording when a coin is inserted.
– ORIGIN *juke* is from a word in a Creole language meaning 'disorderly'.

Jul. abbreviation July.

julep /**joo**-lep/ noun a sweet drink made from sugar syrup.
– ORIGIN Latin *julapium.*

Julian calendar noun a calendar introduced by the Roman general Julius Caesar, in which the year consisted of 365 days, every fourth year having 366 (replaced by the Gregorian calendar).

julienne /joo-li-**en**/ noun a portion of food cut into short, thin strips.
– ORIGIN French.

j

July noun (pl. **Julys**) the seventh month of the year.
– ORIGIN from Latin *Julius mensis* 'month of July', named after the Roman general Julius Caesar.

jumble noun 1 an untidy collection of things. 2 Brit. articles collected for a jumble sale. •verb mix things up in a confused way.
– ORIGIN uncertain.

jumble sale noun Brit. a sale of various second-hand goods, especially for charity.

jumbo informal noun (pl. **jumbos**) 1 a very large person or thing. 2 (also **jumbo jet**) a very large airliner. •adjective very large.
– ORIGIN probably from MUMBO-JUMBO.

jumbuck /jum-buk/ noun Austral. informal a sheep.
– ORIGIN perhaps Australian pidgin for *jump up*.

jump verb 1 push oneself off the ground using the muscles in one's legs and feet. 2 move over, onto, or down from somewhere by jumping. 3 move suddenly and quickly: *I jumped to my feet.* 4 make an uncontrolled movement in surprise. 5 (**jump at/on**) accept an opportunity or offer eagerly. 6 (**jump on**) informal attack or criticize someone suddenly. 7 pass abruptly from one subject or state to another. 8 rise suddenly and by a large amount: *prices jumped two per cent in two weeks.* 9 (**be jumping**) informal (of a place) be very lively. •noun 1 an act of jumping. 2 a large or sudden change or increase. 3 an obstacle to be jumped by a horse.
– PHRASES **jump down someone's throat** informal respond to someone in a sudden and angry way. **jump the queue** move ahead of one's proper place in a queue of people. **jump ship** (of a sailor) leave a ship without permission. **jump through hoops** go through a complicated procedure in order to achieve something. **one jump ahead** one stage ahead of a rival.
– DERIVATIVES **jumpable** adjective.
– ORIGIN probably imitating the sound of feet landing on the ground.

jumped-up adjective informal considering oneself to be more important than one really is.

jumper¹ noun 1 Brit. a pullover or sweater. 2 N. Amer. a pinafore dress.
– ORIGIN perhaps from Old French *jupe* 'loose jacket or tunic'.

jumper² noun a person or animal that jumps.

jump jet noun a jet aircraft that can take off and land vertically.

jump lead noun Brit. each of a pair of cables for recharging a battery in a motor vehicle by connecting it to the battery in another.

jump-off noun a deciding round in a showjumping competition.

jump-start verb 1 start a car with a flat battery with jump leads or by a sudden release of the clutch while it is being pushed. 2 give impetus to something that is progressing slowly or has stopped. •noun an act of jump-starting something.

jumpsuit noun a one-piece garment incorporating trousers and a sleeved top.
– ORIGIN first referring to a garment worn when parachuting.

jumpy adjective (**jumpier, jumpiest**) informal 1 anxious and uneasy. 2 stopping and starting abruptly.
– DERIVATIVES **jumpily** adverb **jumpiness** noun.

Jun. abbreviation June.

junction noun 1 a point where two or more things meet or are joined. 2 a place where roads or railway lines meet. 3 the action of joining things or the state of being joined.
– ORIGIN from Latin *jungere* 'to join'.

junction box noun a box containing a junction of electric wires or cables.

juncture /jungk-cher/ noun 1 a particular point in time. 2 a place where things join.
– ORIGIN Latin *junctura* 'joint'.

June noun the sixth month of the year.
– ORIGIN from Latin *Junius mensis* 'month of June', from *Junonius* 'sacred to the goddess Juno'.

Jungian /yuung-i-uhn/ adjective relating to the Swiss psychologist Carl Jung or his work. •noun a follower of Jung or his work.

jungle noun 1 an area of land with dense forest and tangled vegetation, typically in the tropics. 2 a very complex or competitive situation: *a jungle of competing technologies.* 3 a style of dance music with very fast electronic drum tracks and slower synthesized bass lines.
– PHRASES **the law of the jungle** the principle that people who are strongest and most selfish will be most successful.
– DERIVATIVES **junglist** noun & adjective **jungly** adjective.
– ORIGIN Sanskrit, 'rough and arid terrain'.

junior adjective 1 relating to young or younger people. 2 Brit. relating to schoolchildren aged 7–11. 3 N. Amer. relating to students in the third year of a four-year course at college or high school. 4 (after a name) referring to the younger of two people with the same name in a family. 5 low or lower in rank or status: *a junior minister.* •noun 1 a person who is a specified number of years younger than someone else: *he's five years her junior.* 2 Brit. a child at a junior school. 3 N. Amer. a student in the third year at college or high school. 4 (in sport) a competitor who is not yet an adult. 5 a person with low rank or status.
– ORIGIN Latin.

junior college noun (in the US) a college offering courses for two years beyond high school.

junior common room noun Brit. a room used for social purposes by the undergraduates of a college.

junior high school noun (in the US and Canada) a school intermediate between an elementary school and a high school.

junior school noun a school for young children, especially (in England and Wales) for those aged 7–11.

juniper /joo-ni-per/ noun an evergreen shrub or small tree with berries that are used to flavour gin.
– ORIGIN Latin *juniperus*.

junk¹ noun informal 1 useless or worthless articles or material; rubbish. 2 heroin. •verb informal get rid of something regarded as worthless or useless.
– ORIGIN unknown.

junk² noun a flat-bottomed sailing boat used in China and the East Indies.
– ORIGIN Malay.

junk bond noun a high-yielding high-risk security, typically issued to finance a takeover.

junket /jung-kit/ noun 1 a dish of sweetened curds of milk. 2 informal an extravagant trip enjoyed by officials at public expense. •verb (**junkets, junketing, junketed**) informal take part in an extravagant trip at public expense.
– ORIGIN first referring to a cream cheese made in a rush basket: from Old French *jonquette* 'rush basket'.

junk food noun pre-prepared food with little nutritional value.

junkie (also **junky**) noun informal 1 a drug addict. 2 a person with an obsessive interest in or enthusiasm for something: *a media junkie*.
– ORIGIN from **JUNK¹**.

junk mail noun informal advertising material received in the post which has not been requested.

junky noun (pl. **junkies**) variant spelling of **JUNKIE**.

Junoesque /joo-noh-esk/ adjective (of a woman) tall and shapely.
– ORIGIN named after the Roman goddess *Juno*.

junta /jun-tuh/ noun a military or political group that rules a country after taking power by force.
– ORIGIN Spanish and Portuguese, 'deliberative or administrative council'.

Jupiter noun the largest planet in the solar system, fifth in order from the sun.

Jurassic /juu-rass-ik/ adjective Geology relating to the second period of the Mesozoic era (about 208 to 146 million years ago), when large reptiles were dominant and the first birds appeared.
– ORIGIN French *jurassique*, from the *Jura* Mountains between France and Switzerland.

juridical /juu-rid-i-kuhl/ adjective Law relating to judicial proceedings and the law.
– DERIVATIVES **juridically** adverb.
– ORIGIN Latin *juridicus*.

jurisdiction /joo-riz-dik-sh'n, joo-riss-dik-sh'n/ noun 1 the official power to make legal decisions and judgements: *the English court had no jurisdiction over the defendants.* 2 the area or sphere of activity over which the legal authority of a court or other institution extends. 3 a system of law courts.
– DERIVATIVES **jurisdictional** adjective.
– ORIGIN Latin.

jurisprudence /joo-riss-proo-duhnss/ noun 1 the theory or philosophy of law. 2 a legal system.
– DERIVATIVES **jurisprudential** adjective.
– ORIGIN Latin *jurisprudentia*.

jurist /joor-ist/ noun 1 an expert in law. 2 N. Amer. a lawyer or a judge.
– DERIVATIVES **juristic** adjective.
– ORIGIN Latin *jurista*.

juror noun a member of a jury.

jury noun (pl. **juries**) 1 a group of people (typically twelve) sworn to give a verdict in a legal case on the basis of evidence given in court. 2 a group of people judging a competition.

– PHRASES **the jury is out** a decision has not yet been reached.
– ORIGIN Old French *juree* 'oath, inquiry'.

jury-rigged adjective 1 (of a ship) having makeshift rigging. 2 chiefly N. Amer. makeshift; improvised.
– ORIGIN *jury* perhaps from Old French *ajurie* 'aid'.

jus /zhoo/ noun (especially in French cuisine) a thin gravy or sauce made from meat juices.
– ORIGIN French, 'juice'.

just adjective 1 morally right and fair. 2 appropriate or deserved: *we got our just deserts.* 3 (of an opinion) well founded; justifiable. •adverb 1 exactly. 2 exactly or nearly at this or that moment. 3 very recently. 4 by a small amount. 5 simply; only.
– PHRASES **just in case** as a precaution. **just so** 1 arranged or done very carefully. 2 formal expressing agreement.
– DERIVATIVES **justly** adverb **justness** noun.
– ORIGIN Latin *justus*.

justice noun 1 behaviour or treatment that is morally right and fair. 2 the quality of being right and fair: *the justice of his case.* 3 the administration of law in a way that is fair and morally right. 4 a judge or magistrate.
– PHRASES **bring someone to justice** arrest and try someone in court for a crime. **do oneself justice** perform as well as one is able. **do someone/thing justice** treat someone or something with due fairness.
– ORIGIN Old French *justise* 'administration of the law'.

Justice of the Peace noun (in the UK) a non-professional magistrate appointed to hear minor cases, grant licences, etc., in a town or county.

justiciable /ju-stish-uh-b'l/ adjective Law subject to trial in a court of law.

justifiable adjective able to be shown to be right or reasonable: *the paper takes justifiable pride in its political coverage.*
– DERIVATIVES **justifiability** noun **justifiably** adverb.

justification noun 1 the action of justifying something. 2 good reason for something that exists or has been done: *there's no justification for the job losses.*

justify verb (**justifies, justifying, justified**) 1 prove something to be right or reasonable. 2 be a good reason for: *the situation was grave enough to justify further investigation.* 3 adjust written words so that the lines of type form straight edges at both sides.
– DERIVATIVES **justificatory** adjective **justifier** noun.
– ORIGIN Latin *justificare* 'do justice to'.

jut verb (**juts, jutting, jutted**) extend out, over, or beyond the main body or line of something.
– ORIGIN from **JET¹**.

Jute /joot/ noun a member of a Germanic people that settled in southern Britain in the 5th century.
– DERIVATIVES **Jutish** adjective.
– ORIGIN Old English.

jute /joot/ noun rough fibre made from the stems of a tropical plant, used for making rope or sacking.
– ORIGIN Bengali.

juvenile /joo-vuh-nyl/ adjective 1 relating to

young people or animals. **2** childish; immature. • **noun 1** a young person or animal. **2** Law a person below the age at which ordinary criminal prosecution is possible (18 in most countries).
– DERIVATIVES **juvenility** noun.
– ORIGIN Latin *juvenilis*.

juvenile delinquency noun the regular committing of criminal acts by a young person.

– DERIVATIVES **juvenile deliquent** noun.

juvenilia /joo-vuh-**nil**-i-uh/ plural noun works produced by an author or artist when young.
– ORIGIN Latin.

juxtapose /juk-stuh-**pohz**/ verb place things close together, especially so as to show a contrast: *a world of obscene extravagance juxtaposed with abject poverty.*
– DERIVATIVES **juxtaposition** noun.
– ORIGIN French *juxtaposer.*

j

Kk

K[1] (also **k**) noun (pl. **Ks** or **K's**) the eleventh letter of the alphabet.

K[2] abbreviation **1** kelvin(s). **2** Computing kilobyte(s). **3** kilometre(s). **4** (in card games and chess) king. **5** Köchel (catalogue of Mozart's works). **6** informal thousand. [from KILO-.] •symbol the chemical element potassium. [from Latin *kalium*.]

k abbreviation kilo-.

Kabbalah /kuh-**bah**-luh/ (also **Kabbala, Cabbala, Cabala,** or **Qabalah**) noun the ancient Jewish tradition of mystical interpretation of the Bible.
– DERIVATIVES **Kabbalism** noun **Kabbalist** noun **Kabbalistic** adjective.
– ORIGIN Hebrew, 'tradition'.

kabob noun US spelling of KEBAB.

kabuki /kuh-**boo**-ki/ noun a form of traditional Japanese drama performed by men, with stylized song, mime, and dance.
– ORIGIN Japanese.

Kaddish /**kad**-ish/ noun **1** an ancient Jewish prayer sequence recited in the synagogue service. **2** a form of the Kaddish recited for the dead.
– ORIGIN from Aramaic, 'holy'.

Kaffir /**kaf**-fer/ noun offensive, chiefly S. African a black African.
– ORIGIN Arabic, 'infidel'.

> USAGE: The word **Kaffir** is a racially abusive and offensive term, and in South Africa its use is actionable.

kaffiyeh noun variant spelling of KEFFIYEH.

Kafkaesque /kaf-kuh-**esk**/ adjective relating to the Czech novelist Franz Kafka or his nightmarish fictional world.

kaftan /**kaf**-tan/ (also **caftan**) noun **1** a woman's long, loose dress. **2** a man's long belted tunic, worn in the Near East.
– ORIGIN Persian.

kagoul noun variant spelling of CAGOULE.

kahuna /kuh-**hoo**-nuh/ noun N. Amer. informal an important person.
– ORIGIN Hawaiian, 'wise man, shaman'.

kai /ky/ noun NZ informal food.
– ORIGIN Maori.

kail noun variant spelling of KALE.

kaiser /**ky**-zer/ noun historical the German Emperor, the Emperor of Austria, or the head of the Holy Roman Empire.
– ORIGIN German.

kakapo /**kah**-kuh-poh/ noun (pl. **kakapos**) a flightless New Zealand parrot with greenish plumage.
– ORIGIN Maori.

kalanchoe /ka-luhn-**koh**-i/ noun a tropical succulent plant with clusters of tubular flowers.
– ORIGIN Chinese.

Kalashnikov /kuh-**lash**-ni-kof/ noun a type of rifle or sub-machine gun made in Russia.
– ORIGIN named after the Russian designer Mikhail T. *Kalashnikov*.

kale (also **kail**) noun a variety of cabbage with large leaves and a loosely packed head.
– ORIGIN Latin *caulis* 'stem, cabbage'.

kaleidoscope /kuh-**ly**-duh-skohp/ noun **1** a toy consisting of a tube containing mirrors and pieces of coloured glass or paper, whose reflections produce changing patterns when the tube is rotated. **2** a constantly changing pattern: *the dancers moved in a kaleidoscope of colour.*
– DERIVATIVES **kaleidoscopic** adjective.
– ORIGIN from Greek *kalos* 'beautiful' + *eidos* 'form' + -SCOPE.

kalends plural noun variant spelling of CALENDS.

Kama Sutra /kah-muh **soo**-truh/ noun an ancient Sanskrit work on the art of love and sexual technique.
– ORIGIN Sanskrit, 'love thread'.

kameez /kuh-**meez**/ noun (pl. same or **kameezes**) a long tunic worn by people from the Indian subcontinent.
– ORIGIN Arabic.

kamikaze /ka-mi-**kah**-zi/ noun (in the Second World War) a Japanese aircraft loaded with explosives and making a deliberate suicidal crash on an enemy target. •adjective reckless or potentially self-destructive.
– ORIGIN from the Japanese words for 'divinity' and 'wind'.

kampong /**kam**-pong/ noun a Malaysian enclosure or village.
– ORIGIN Malay.

kangaroo noun a large Australian marsupial with a long, powerful tail and strong hind legs that enable it to travel by leaping.
– ORIGIN from an Aboriginal language.

kangaroo court noun an unofficial court formed by a group of people to try someone regarded as guilty of an offence.

Kantian /**kant**-i-uhn/ adjective relating to the German philosopher Immanuel Kant or his philosophy. •noun a follower of Kant's philosophy.
– DERIVATIVES **Kantianism** noun.

k

kaolin /**kay**-uh-lin/ noun a fine soft white clay, used for making china and in medicine.
– ORIGIN from a Chinese word meaning 'high hill'.

kapok /**kay**-pok/ noun a substance resembling cotton wool which grows around the seeds of a tropical tree, used as stuffing for cushions, soft toys, etc.
– ORIGIN Malay.

kaput /kuh-**puut**/ adjective informal broken and useless.
– ORIGIN German *kaputt*.

karabiner /ka-ruh-**bee**-nuh/ (also **carabiner**) noun a coupling link with a safety closure, used by rock climbers.
– ORIGIN from German *Karabiner-haken* 'spring hook'.

karakul /**kar**-uh-kuul/ (also **caracul**) noun **1** a breed of Asian sheep with a dark curled fleece when young. **2** cloth or fur made from or resembling the fleece of the karakul.
– ORIGIN Russian.

karaoke /ka-ri-**oh**-ki/ noun a form of entertainment in which people sing popular songs over pre-recorded backing tracks.
– ORIGIN Japanese, 'empty orchestra'.

karat noun US spelling of **CARAT** (in sense 2).

karate /kuh-**rah**-ti/ noun an oriental system of unarmed combat using the hands and feet to deliver and block blows.
– ORIGIN Japanese, 'empty hand'.

karma /**kar**-muh/ noun **1** (in Hinduism and Buddhism) the sum of a person's actions in this and previous lives, viewed as affecting their fate in future existences. **2** informal good or bad luck, viewed as resulting from one's actions.
– DERIVATIVES **karmic** adjective.
– ORIGIN Sanskrit, 'action, effect, fate'.

karst /*rhymes with* cast/ noun Geology a limestone region with underground streams and many cavities in the rock.
– DERIVATIVES **karstic** adjective.
– ORIGIN from German *der Karst*, a limestone region in Slovenia.

kart noun a small racing car with a tubular frame, no suspension, and with the engine at the back.
– DERIVATIVES **karting** noun.
– ORIGIN shortening of **GO-KART**.

kasbah /**kaz**-bah/ (also **casbah**) noun a fortress in the old part of a North African city, and the narrow streets that surround it.
– ORIGIN Arabic.

Kashmiri /kash-**meer**-i/ noun **1** a person from Kashmir. **2** the language of Kashmir. • adjective relating to Kashmir.

katydid /**kay**-ti-did/ noun a large North American insect related to the grasshoppers, the male of which makes a sound which resembles its name.

kauri /**kow**-ri/ (also **kauri pine**) noun (pl. **kauris**) a tall coniferous tree native to New Zealand, which produces valuable wood and resin.
– ORIGIN Maori.

kava /**kah**-vuh/ noun a Polynesian drink which causes drowsiness, made from the crushed roots of a plant of the pepper family.
– ORIGIN Tongan.

kayak /**ky**-ak/ noun a canoe made of a light frame with a watertight covering. • verb (**kayaks**, **kayaking**, **kayaked**) travel in a kayak.
– DERIVATIVES **kayaker** noun.
– ORIGIN Inuit.

kazoo /kuh-**zoo**/ noun a musical instrument consisting of a pipe with a hole in it, over which is a membrane that produces a buzzing sound when the player hums into it.
– ORIGIN probably imitating the sound produced.

KB (also **Kb**) abbreviation kilobyte(s).

KBE abbreviation (in the UK) Knight Commander of the Order of the British Empire.

KC abbreviation King's Counsel.

kcal abbreviation kilocalorie(s).

KCB abbreviation (in the UK) Knight Commander of the Order of the Bath.

KCMG abbreviation (in the UK) Knight Commander of the Order of St Michael and St George.

kea /**kee**-uh/ noun a New Zealand parrot with a long, narrow bill and mainly olive-green plumage.
– ORIGIN Maori.

kebab /ki-**bab**/ (N. Amer. also **kabob**) noun a dish of pieces of meat, fish, or vegetables roasted or grilled on a skewer or spit.
– ORIGIN Arabic.

kecks plural noun Brit. informal trousers.
– ORIGIN respelling of former *kicks*.

kedge /kej/ verb move a boat by hauling in a hawser attached at a distance to an anchor. • noun a small anchor used for kedging a boat.
– ORIGIN perhaps from dialect *cadge* 'bind, tie'.

kedgeree /**kej**-uh-ree/ noun Brit. a dish of smoked fish, rice, and hard-boiled eggs.
– ORIGIN Sanskrit.

keel noun a lengthwise structure along the base of a ship, often extended downwards to increase stability. • verb (**keel over**) **1** fall over; collapse. **2** (of a boat or ship) turn over on its side; capsize.
– ORIGIN Old Norse.

keelboat noun **1** a yacht built with a permanent keel rather than a centreboard. **2** a large, flat freight boat used on American rivers.

keelhaul verb **1** humorous punish or reprimand someone severely. **2** historical punish someone by dragging them through the water under the keel of a ship.

keelson /**keel**-suhn/ (also **kelson**) noun a structure running the length of a ship, that fastens the timbers or plates of the floor to the keel.
– ORIGIN from German *kiel* 'keel' + *swīn* 'swine' (used as the name of a timber).

keen[1] adjective **1** chiefly Brit. eager and enthusiastic. **2** (**keen on**) interested in: *the school was very keen on sports.* **3** (of a blade) sharp. **4** (of a sense) highly developed. **5** quick to understand things: *her keen intellect.* **6** Brit. (of prices) very low.
– DERIVATIVES **keenly** adverb **keenness** noun.
– ORIGIN Old English, 'clever, brave'.

keen[2] verb **1** wail in grief for a dead person. **2** make an eerie wailing sound. • noun an Irish

funeral song accompanied with wailing as a lament for the dead.
– ORIGIN from Irish *caoinim* 'I wail'.

keep verb (past and past part. **kept**) **1** continue to have something. **2** continue in a specified condition, position, or activity: *I should have kept quiet, but I blundered on.* **3** save or retain something for use in the future. **4** store something in a regular place. **5** do something promised, agreed, or necessary: *I have to go and keep another appointment soon.* **6** (of food) remain in good condition. **7** make a note about something or write a diary. **8** make someone late. **9** provide accommodation and food for someone. **10** own and look after an animal. **11** (as adj. **kept**) (of a woman) supported financially in return for sex. ● noun **1** food, clothes, and other essentials for living. **2** the strongest or central tower of a castle.
– PHRASES **for keeps** informal permanently. **keep from** avoid doing something. **keep someone from** prevent someone from doing something. **keep something from** cause something to remain a secret from someone. **keep on** continue to do something. **keep someone/thing on** continue to use or employ someone or something. **keep to 1** avoid leaving a path, road, or place. **2** stay on schedule or to the point being discussed. **3** fulfil a promise. **keep up** move at the same rate as someone or something else. **keep something up** continue a course of action. **keep up with 1** be aware of current events. **2** continue to be in contact with someone. **keep up with the Joneses** try hard not to be outdone by one's neighbours or friends.
– ORIGIN Old English.

keeper noun **1** a person who manages or looks after something or someone. **2** a goalkeeper or wicketkeeper. **3** an object which protects or secures another.

keep-fit noun chiefly Brit. regular exercises to improve personal fitness and health.

keeping noun (in phrase **in** (or **out of**) **keeping with**) harmonious or suitable (or inharmonious or unsuitable) in a particular situation: *the cuisine is in keeping with the hotel's Edwardian character.*

keepsake noun a small item kept in memory of the person who gave it or originally owned it.

keffiyeh /kuh-fee-yuh/ (also **kaffiyeh**) noun a headdress worn by Arab men, consisting of a square of fabric fastened by a band round the head.
– ORIGIN Arabic.

keg noun a small barrel. ● adjective Brit. (of beer) supplied in a keg, to which carbon dioxide has been added.
– ORIGIN Old Norse.

kelim noun variant spelling of **KILIM**.

keloid /kee-loyd/ noun an area of fibrous tissue formed at the site of a scar or injury.
– ORIGIN from Greek *khēlē* 'crab's claw'.

kelp noun a very large brown seaweed with broad fronds divided into strips.
– ORIGIN unknown.

kelpie /kel-pi/ noun a water spirit of Scottish folklore, typically taking the form of a horse.
– ORIGIN perhaps from Scottish Gaelic *cailpeach, colpach* 'bullock, colt'.

kelson /kel-suhn/ noun variant spelling of **KEELSON**.

kelt noun a salmon or sea trout after spawning and before returning to the sea.
– ORIGIN unknown.

kelvin noun the SI base unit of thermodynamic temperature, equal to one degree Celsius.
– ORIGIN named after the British physicist William T. *Kelvin.*

Kelvin scale noun the scale of temperature with absolute zero as zero and the freezing point of water as 273.15 kelvins.

ken noun (**one's ken**) one's range of knowledge or understanding. ● verb (**kens, kenning;** past and past part. **kenned** or **kent**) Scottish & N. English **1** know someone or something. **2** recognize someone or something.
– ORIGIN from Old English, 'tell, make known'.

kendo /ken-doh/ noun a Japanese form of fencing with two-handed bamboo swords.
– ORIGIN Japanese, 'sword way'.

kennel noun **1** a small shelter for a dog. **2** (**kennels**) (treated as sing. or pl.) a boarding or breeding establishment for dogs. ● verb (**kennels, kennelling, kennelled;** US **kennels, kenneling, kenneled**) put or keep a dog in a kennel or kennels.
– ORIGIN Old French *chenil*.

kent past and past participle of **KEN**.

Kenyan /ken-yuhn/ noun a person from Kenya. ● adjective relating to Kenya.

kepi /kep-i/ noun (pl. **kepis**) a French military cap with a horizontal peak.
– ORIGIN French *képi*.

kept past and past participle of **KEEP**.

keratin /ke-ruh-tin/ noun a fibrous protein forming the main constituent of hair, feathers, hoofs, claws, and horns.
– ORIGIN from Greek *keras* 'horn'.

kerb (US **curb**) noun a stone edging to a pavement or raised path.
– ORIGIN variant of **CURB**.

USAGE: Do not confuse **kerb** with **curb**. **Kerb** means 'the stone edging of a pavement', while **curb** means 'control or limit something' (*she promised to curb her temper*) or 'a control or limit'. In American English, the spelling **curb** is used for all these senses.

kerb-crawling noun Brit. the action of driving slowly along the edge of the road in search of a prostitute.
– DERIVATIVES **kerb-crawler** noun.

kerb drill noun Brit. a set of rules followed in order to cross a road safely, as taught to children.

kerbside (US **curbside**) noun the side of a road or pavement that is nearer to the kerb.

kerbstone noun a long, narrow stone or concrete block, laid end to end with others to form a kerb.

kerchief /ker-chif/ noun **1** a piece of fabric used to cover the head. **2** dated a handkerchief.
– ORIGIN Old French *cuevrechief*.

kerf noun **1** a slit made by cutting with a saw. **2** the cut end of a felled tree.
– ORIGIN Old English.

kerfuffle /ker-fuf-f'l/ noun Brit. informal a commotion or fuss.

k

– ORIGIN perhaps from Scots *curfuffle*, or related to Irish *cior thual* 'confusion, disorder'.

kermes /ker-miz/ noun a red dye obtained from the dried bodies of a type of insect.
– ORIGIN Arabic.

kernel /ker-n'l/ noun **1** the softer part of a nut, seed, or fruit stone contained within its hard shell. **2** the seed and hard husk of a cereal, especially wheat. **3** the central or most important part of something: *there is a kernel of truth in what he asserted.*
– ORIGIN Old English, 'small corn'.

kerosene /ke-ruh-seen/ (also **kerosine**) noun chiefly N. Amer. paraffin oil.
– ORIGIN from Greek *kēros* 'wax'.

Kerry noun (pl. **Kerries**) an animal of a breed of small black dairy cattle.
– ORIGIN from *Kerry* in Ireland.

kestrel noun a small falcon that hovers with rapidly beating wings while searching for prey.
– ORIGIN perhaps from Old French *crecerelle*.

ketamine /kee-tuh-meen/ noun a medical drug used as an anaesthetic and painkiller and also illegally as a hallucinogen.
– ORIGIN blend of **KETONE** and **AMINE**.

ketch noun a type of two-masted sailing boat.
– ORIGIN probably from **CATCH**.

ketchup (US also **catsup**) noun a spicy sauce made chiefly from tomatoes and vinegar.
– ORIGIN perhaps from Chinese, 'tomato juice'.

ketone /kee-tohn/ noun any of a class of organic chemical compounds including acetone.
– ORIGIN from German *Aketon* 'acetone'.

kettle noun a metal or plastic container with a lid, spout, and handle, used for boiling water.
– PHRASES **a different kettle of fish** informal something completely different from the one just mentioned. **the pot calling the kettle black** used to say that a person is criticizing someone for faults that they have themselves. **a pretty** (or **fine**) **kettle of fish** informal an awkward situation.
– ORIGIN Latin *catillus* 'little pot'.

kettledrum noun a large drum shaped like a bowl, with adjustable pitch.

key[1] noun (pl. **keys**) **1** a small piece of shaped metal which is inserted into a lock and turned to open or close it. **2** an instrument for grasping and turning a screw, peg, or nut. **3** a lever pressed down by the finger in playing an instrument such as the organ, piano, or flute. **4** each of several buttons on a panel for operating a typewriter or computer terminal. **5** a means of achieving or understanding something: *discipline seems to be the key to her success.* **6** an explanatory list of symbols used in a map or table. **7** a word or system for solving a code. **8** a group of musical notes based on a particular note and comprising a scale. **9** roughness on a surface, provided to assist adhesion of plaster or other material. • adjective vitally important: *he was a key figure in the civil war.* • verb (**keys, keying, keyed**) **1** enter or operate on data through a computer keyboard. **2** (**be keyed up**) be nervous, tense, or excited. **3** (**key something to**) chiefly N. Amer. make something suitable for

or in harmony with: *courses keyed to the needs of health professionals.*
– ORIGIN Old English.

key[2] noun a low-lying island or reef in the Caribbean or off the coast of Florida.
– ORIGIN Spanish *cayo* 'reef'.

keyboard noun **1** a panel of keys for use with a computer or typewriter. **2** a set of keys on a piano or similar musical instrument. **3** an electronic musical instrument with keys arranged as on a piano. • verb enter data by means of a keyboard.
– DERIVATIVES **keyboarder** noun.

key grip noun the person in a film crew who is in charge of the camera equipment.

keyhole noun a hole in a lock into which the key is inserted.

keyhole surgery noun surgery carried out through a very small cut made in the affected area.

key money noun Brit. a payment required from a new tenant of a rented house or flat in exchange for a key to the premises.

Keynesian /kayn-zi-uhn/ adjective relating to the theories of the English economist John Maynard Keynes, who believed that government spending on public works is necessary to stimulate the economy and provide employment.
– DERIVATIVES **Keynesianism** noun.

keynote noun **1** a central theme: *individuality was the keynote of the Nineties.* **2** the note on which a musical key is based. • adjective (of a speech) setting out the central theme of a conference.

keypad noun a small keyboard or set of buttons for operating a portable electronic device or telephone.

keypunch noun a device for transferring data by means of punched holes or notches on a series of cards or paper tape.

key ring noun a metal ring for holding keys together in a bunch.

key signature noun Music a combination of sharps or flats after the clef at the beginning of each stave, indicating the key of a composition.

keystone noun **1** the central part of a policy or system: *he has made tax cuts the keystone of his domestic policy.* **2** a central stone at the summit of an arch, locking the whole together.

keystroke noun a single pressing of a key on a keyboard.

keyword noun **1** a word or idea of great significance: *homes and jobs are the keywords in the campaign.* **2** a word used in a computer system to indicate the content of a document. **3** a significant word mentioned in an index.

KG abbreviation (in the UK) Knight of the Order of the Garter.

kg abbreviation kilogram(s).

khaki /kah-ki/ noun (pl. **khakis**) **1** a cotton or wool fabric of a dull brownish-yellow colour, used especially in military clothing. **2** a dull greenish- or yellowish-brown colour.
– ORIGIN from Urdu, 'dust-coloured'.

Khalsa /kul-suh/ noun the company of fully initiated Sikhs to which devout orthodox Sikhs are ritually admitted at puberty.

k

– ORIGIN from Arabic, 'pure, belonging to'.

khan /kahn/ noun a title given to rulers and officials in central Asia, Afghanistan, and some other Muslim countries.
– DERIVATIVES **khanate** noun.
– ORIGIN Turkic, 'lord, prince'.

khat /kaht/ noun the leaves of an Arabian shrub, which are chewed (or drunk as an infusion) as a stimulant.
– ORIGIN Arabic.

khazi /**kah**-zi/ noun (pl. **khazies**) Brit. informal a toilet.
– ORIGIN Italian *casa* 'house'.

Khmer /kmair/ noun (pl. same or **Khmers**) 1 a person from Cambodia. 2 the official language of Cambodia.

Khoikhoi /**koy**-koy/ (also **Khoi**) noun (pl. same) a member of a group of peoples of South Africa and Namibia.
– ORIGIN Nama (a Khoikhoi language), 'men of men'.

kHz abbreviation kilohertz.

kia ora /ki-uh **or**-uh/ exclamation (in New Zealand) a greeting wishing good health.
– ORIGIN Maori.

kibbutz /kib-**buts**/ noun (pl. **kibbutzim** /kib-**buts**-im/) a farming settlement in Israel in which work is shared between the whole community.
– ORIGIN modern Hebrew, 'gathering'.

kibbutznik /ki-**buts**-nik/ noun a member of a kibbutz.

kibosh /**ky**-bosh/ (also **kybosh**) noun (in phrase **put the kibosh on**) informal put a decisive end to: *he put the kibosh on the deal.*
– ORIGIN unknown.

kick verb 1 hit or propel someone or something forcibly with the foot. 2 strike out with the foot or feet. 3 informal succeed in giving up a habit or addiction. 4 (of a gun) recoil when fired. • noun 1 an instance of kicking. 2 informal a thrill of pleasurable excitement: *rich kids turning to crime just for kicks.* 3 informal the strong stimulating effect of alcohol or a drug.
– PHRASES **kick against** resist or disagree with something. **kick around** (or **about**) lie unwanted or unused. **kick someone around** treat someone roughly or without respect. **kick something around** discuss an idea informally. **kick the bucket** informal die. **kick in** come into effect or operation. **a kick in the teeth** informal a serious setback. **kick off** 1 (of a football match) be started or resumed by a player kicking the ball from the centre spot. 2 (also **kick something off**) begin or cause something to begin. **kick oneself** be annoyed with oneself. **kick someone out** informal expel or dismiss someone.
– DERIVATIVES **kicker** noun.
– ORIGIN unknown.

kickback noun 1 a sudden forceful recoil. 2 informal an underhand payment made to someone in return for help in arranging a business or political deal.

kick-boxing noun a form of martial art which combines boxing with elements of karate, in particular kicking with bare feet.

kicking adjective informal (especially of music) lively and exciting.

kick-off noun 1 the start or resumption of a football match, with a kick from the centre spot. 2 informal the start of an event or activity.

kick-pleat noun an inverted pleat in a narrow skirt to allow freedom of movement.

kickstand noun a rod attached to a bicycle or motorcycle that may be kicked into a vertical position to support the vehicle when it is stationary.

kick-start verb 1 start a motorcycle engine with a downward thrust of a pedal. 2 provide an impetus to start or boost a process: *the government could kick-start the economy by cutting interest rates.* • noun 1 an act of kick-starting something. 2 a device to kick-start an engine.

kid¹ noun 1 informal a child or young person. 2 a young goat.
– PHRASES **handle** (or **treat**) **someone/thing with kid gloves** deal with someone or something very carefully. **kids' stuff** informal something that is easy or simple to do.
– ORIGIN Old Norse.

kid² verb (**kids, kidding, kidded**) informal 1 fool someone into believing something. 2 (**kid around**) behave in a silly way.
– ORIGIN perhaps from KID¹, expressing the idea 'make a child or goat of'.

kid brother (or **kid sister**) noun informal a younger brother or sister.

kiddie (also **kiddy**) noun (pl. **kiddies**) informal a young child.

kiddush /**kid**-uush/ noun a Jewish ceremony of prayer and blessing over wine, performed at a meal preceding the Sabbath or a holy day.
– ORIGIN Hebrew, 'sanctification'.

kidnap verb (**kidnaps, kidnapping, kidnapped**; US also **kidnaps, kidnaping, kidnaped**) take someone by force and keep them captive, typically to obtain a ransom for their release. • noun an instance of kidnapping someone.
– DERIVATIVES **kidnapper** noun.
– ORIGIN from KID¹ + slang *nap* 'seize'.

kidney noun (pl. **kidneys**) 1 each of a pair of organs in the abdominal cavity that remove waste products from the blood and excrete urine. 2 the kidney of a sheep, ox, or pig as food.
– ORIGIN unknown.

kidney bean noun a dark red kidney-shaped bean, eaten as a vegetable.

kidney machine noun a machine that performs the functions of a person's kidney when one or both organs are damaged.

kidney stone noun a hard mass formed in the kidneys, typically consisting of insoluble calcium compounds.

kidology /kid-**ol**-uh-ji/ noun Brit. informal the deliberate deception or teasing of people.

kif (also **kef**) noun a substance, especially cannabis, smoked to produce a drowsy state.
– ORIGIN Arabic, 'enjoyment, well-being'.

kilim /ki-**leem**/ (also **kelim**) noun a carpet or rug woven without a pile, made in Turkey, Kurdistan, and neighbouring areas.
– ORIGIN Persian.

kill verb 1 cause the death of someone or something. 2 put an end to or defeat something. 3 informal overwhelm someone with

k

an emotion: *the suspense is killing me.* **4** informal cause pain or distress to someone. **5** pass time, typically while waiting for an event. • **noun 1** an act of killing, especially of one animal by another. **2** an animal or animals killed by a hunter or another animal.
- PHRASES **be in at the kill** be present at or benefit from the successful completion of an enterprise.
- ORIGIN probably Germanic.

killer noun **1** a person or thing that kills. **2** informal a very impressive or difficult thing. **3** informal a hilarious joke.

killer whale noun a large toothed whale with black-and-white markings and a prominent fin on its back.

killifish noun (pl. same or **killifishes**) a small, brightly coloured fish of fresh or brackish water.
- ORIGIN probably from KILL and FISH¹.

killing noun an act of causing death. • **adjective** informal exhausting or unbearable.
- PHRASES **make a killing** make a great deal of money out of something.

killing field noun a place where many people have been killed, especially during a war.

killjoy noun a person who spoils the enjoyment of others by behaving very seriously or disapprovingly.

kiln noun a furnace or oven for burning, baking, or drying pottery, bricks, or lime.
- ORIGIN Latin *culina* 'kitchen, cooking stove'.

kilo noun (pl. **kilos**) a kilogram.

kilo- /ki-loh, kee-loh/ combining form referring to a factor of one thousand (10³): *kilometre*.
- ORIGIN from Greek *khilioi* 'thousand'.

kilobyte noun a unit of information stored in a computer equal to 1,024 bytes.

kilocalorie noun a unit of energy of one thousand calories (equal to one large calorie).

kilogram (also **kilogramme**) noun the SI unit of mass, equal to 1,000 grams (approximately 2.205 lb).

kilohertz noun a measure of frequency equivalent to 1,000 cycles per second.

kilojoule noun 1,000 joules, especially as a measure of the energy value of foods.

kilolitre (US **kiloliter**) noun 1,000 litres (equivalent to 220 imperial gallons).

kilometre /kil-uh-mee-ter, ki-lom-i-ter/ (US **kilometer**) noun a metric unit of measurement equal to 1,000 metres (approximately 0.62 miles).
- DERIVATIVES **kilometric** adjective.

USAGE: The first pronunciation of kilometre, with the stress on the **kil-** is considered the correct one, especially in British English.

kiloton (also **kilotonne**) noun a unit of explosive power equivalent to 1,000 tons of TNT.

kilovolt noun 1,000 volts.

kilowatt noun 1,000 watts.

kilowatt-hour noun a measure of electrical energy equivalent to a power consumption of one thousand watts for one hour.

kilt noun a knee-length skirt of pleated tartan cloth, traditionally worn by men as part of Scottish Highland dress. • **verb 1** (usu. as adj.

kilted) arrange a garment or material in pleats. **2** (**kilt something up**) tuck up one's skirt around one's body.
- DERIVATIVES **kilted** adjective.
- ORIGIN Scandinavian.

kilter noun (in phrase **out of kilter**) out of harmony or balance.
- ORIGIN unknown.

kimchi /**kim**-chi/ noun a Korean dish of spicy pickled cabbage.
- ORIGIN Korean.

kimono /ki-**moh**-noh/ noun (pl. **kimonos**) a long, loose Japanese robe having wide sleeves and tied with a sash.
- ORIGIN Japanese, 'wearing thing'.

kin noun (treated as pl.) one's family and relations. • **adjective** (of a person) related.
- ORIGIN Old English.

kind¹ noun **1** a group or type of people or things with similar characteristics: *all kinds of music.* **2** character; nature: *the US is different in kind from other countries.* **3** (in the Christian Church) each of the elements (bread and wine) consumed during Holy Communion.
- PHRASES **in kind 1** in the same way. **2** (of payment) in goods or services as opposed to money. **kind of** informal rather. **of a kind** only partly deserving the name. **one of a kind** unique. **two** (or **three, four,** etc.) **of a kind** the same or very similar.
- ORIGIN Old English.

USAGE: When using kind to refer to a plural noun, it is incorrect to say *these kind of questions are not relevant* (that is, to have kind in the singular): you should use kinds instead (*these kinds of questions are not relevant*).

kind² adjective caring, friendly, and generous.
- ORIGIN Old English, 'natural, native'.

kindergarten /**kin**-der-gar-tuhn/ noun a nursery school.
- ORIGIN German, 'children's garden'.

kind-hearted adjective having a kind and sympathetic nature.
- DERIVATIVES **kind-heartedly** adverb **kind-heartedness** noun

kindle /**kin**-d'l/ verb **1** light a flame or set something on fire. **2** arouse an emotion or reaction: *his enthusiasm for politics was kindled by his wife.*
- ORIGIN from Old Norse, 'candle, torch'.

kindling noun small sticks or twigs used for lighting fires.

kindly adverb **1** in a kind way. **2** please (used in a polite request). • **adjective** (**kindlier, kindliest**) kind; warm-hearted.
- PHRASES **not take kindly to** not welcome or be pleased by something.
- DERIVATIVES **kindliness** noun.

kindness noun **1** the quality of being caring, friendly, and generous. **2** a kind act.

kindred /**kin**-drid/ noun **1** (treated as pl.) one's family and relations. **2** relationship by blood. • **adjective** having similar qualities: *books on kindred subjects.*
- ORIGIN Old English.

kindred spirit noun a person whose interests or attitudes are similar to one's own.

kine /kyn/ **plural noun** old use cows as a group; cattle.

kinematics /kin-i-**mat**-iks/ **plural noun** (treated as sing.) the branch of mechanics concerned with the motion of objects without reference to the forces which cause the motion.
– DERIVATIVES **kinematic** adjective.
– ORIGIN from Greek *kinēma* 'motion'.

kinesiology /ki-nee-si-**ol**-uh-ji/ **noun** the study of the mechanics of body movements.

kinesis /ki-**nee**-siss/ **noun** technical movement; motion.
– ORIGIN Greek.

kinetic /ki-**net**-ik/ **adjective** 1 relating to or resulting from motion. 2 (of a work of art) depending on movement for its effect.
– DERIVATIVES **kinetically** adverb.
– ORIGIN Greek *kinētikos*.

kinetic energy noun Physics energy which a body possesses as a result of being in motion. Compare with **POTENTIAL ENERGY**.

kinetics /ki-**net**-iks/ **plural noun** (treated as sing.) 1 the branch of chemistry concerned with the rates of chemical reactions. 2 Physics another term for **DYNAMICS** (in sense 1).

kinetoscope /ki-**nee**-toh-skohp/ **noun** an early motion-picture device in which the images were viewed through a peephole.

kinfolk plural noun another term for **KINSFOLK**.

king noun 1 the male ruler of an independent state, especially one who inherits the position by birth. 2 the best or most important person or thing in an area of activity or group: *India's king of fruits, the mango.* 3 a playing card bearing a picture of a king, ranking next below an ace. 4 the most important chess piece, which the opponent has to checkmate in order to win. 5 a piece in draughts with extra capacity for moving, made by crowning an ordinary piece that has reached the opponent's baseline.
– DERIVATIVES **kingly** adjective **kingship** noun.
– ORIGIN Old English.

King Charles spaniel noun a small breed of spaniel with a white, black, and tan coat.
– ORIGIN named after King Charles II of England, Scotland, and Ireland.

king cobra noun a brownish cobra native to the Indian subcontinent, the largest of all venomous snakes.

kingcup noun British term for **MARSH MARIGOLD**.

kingdom noun 1 a country, state, or territory ruled by a king or queen. 2 an area associated with or dominated by a particular person or thing: *the world they came upon was far from being a kingdom of brotherly love.* 3 the spiritual reign or authority of God. 4 each of the three divisions (animal, vegetable, and mineral) in which natural objects are classified.
– PHRASES **to kingdom come** informal into the next world.

King Edward noun a variety of potato having a white skin mottled with red.
– ORIGIN named after King Edward VII.

kingfisher noun a colourful bird with a long sharp beak which dives to catch fish in rivers and ponds.

King James Bible (also **King James Version**) noun another name for **AUTHORIZED VERSION**.

kingmaker noun a person who uses their political influence to bring a leader to power.
– ORIGIN first used with reference to the Earl of Warwick (1428–71).

King of Arms noun Heraldry (in the UK) a chief herald.

king of beasts noun the lion.

King of Kings noun (in the Christian Church) God.

kingpin noun 1 a main or large bolt in a central position. 2 a vertical bolt used as a pivot. 3 a person or thing that is essential to the success of an organization or operation.

king post noun an upright post in the centre of a roof truss, extending from the tie beam to the apex of the truss.

king prawn noun a large edible prawn.

king-sized (also **king-size**) **adjective** of a larger size than normal; very large.

kink noun 1 a sharp twist or curve in something that is otherwise straight. 2 a flaw or obstacle in a plan or operation. 3 a quirk in a person's character. •**verb** form a kink in something.
– ORIGIN German *kinke*.

kinkajou /**king**-kuh-joo/ **noun** a mammal with a tail that can grasp things, found in the tropical forests of Central and South America.
– ORIGIN Algonquian.

kinky adjective (**kinkier**, **kinkiest**) 1 informal relating to or liking unusual sexual activities. 2 having kinks or twists.
– DERIVATIVES **kinkily** adverb **kinkiness** noun.

kinsfolk (also **kinfolk**) **plural noun** a person's family and other blood relations.

kinship noun 1 family or blood relationship. 2 a sharing of characteristics or origins: *they felt a kinship with architects.*

kinsman (or **kinswoman**) **noun** (pl. **kinsmen** or **kinswomen**) one of a person's blood relations.

kiosk /**kee**-ossk/ **noun** 1 a small open-fronted cubicle from which newspapers, refreshments, or tickets are sold. 2 Brit. a public telephone booth.
– ORIGIN Turkish *köşk* 'pavilion'.

kip Brit. informal **noun** a sleep; a nap. •**verb** (**kips**, **kipping**, **kipped**) sleep.
– ORIGIN perhaps related to Danish *kippe* 'hovel, tavern'.

kipper noun a herring that has been split open, salted, and dried or smoked. •**verb** cure a herring by splitting it open and salting and drying or smoking it.
– ORIGIN Old English, referring to a male salmon in the spawning season.

kipper tie noun a brightly coloured and very wide tie.

kirby grip (also trademark **Kirbigrip**) **noun** Brit. a hairgrip consisting of a thin folded and sprung metal strip.
– ORIGIN named after *Kirby*, Beard, & Co. Ltd, the manufacturers.

kirk noun Scottish & N. English 1 a church. 2 (**the Kirk** or **the Kirk of Scotland**) the Church of Scotland.
– ORIGIN from the same Old English root as **CHURCH**.

Kirk session noun the lowest court in the Church of Scotland.

k

kirsch /keersh/ noun brandy distilled from the fermented juice of cherries.
– ORIGIN German.

kirtle /ker-tuhl/ noun old use 1 a woman's gown or outer petticoat. 2 a man's tunic or coat.
– ORIGIN Old English.

kismet /kiz-met/ noun destiny or fate.
– ORIGIN Arabic, 'division, portion, lot'.

kiss verb 1 touch or caress someone with the lips as a sign of love, affection, or greeting. 2 Billiards & Snooker (of a ball) lightly touch another ball. • noun a touch or caress with the lips.
– PHRASES **kiss of death** an action that ensures that an enterprise will fail. **kiss of life** 1 mouth-to-mouth resuscitation. 2 something that revives a failing enterprise. **kiss of peace** a ceremonial kiss given as a sign of unity, especially during the Christian Eucharist (Holy Communion).
– DERIVATIVES **kissable** adjective.
– ORIGIN Old English.

kiss curl noun a small curl of hair on the forehead, at the nape of the neck, or in front of the ear.

kisser noun 1 a person who kisses someone. 2 informal a person's mouth.

kissing cousin noun a relative known well enough to greet with a kiss.

kissogram noun a novelty greeting delivered by a person who accompanies it with a kiss.

Kiswahili /kee-swuh-**hee**-li, ki-swah-**hee**-li/ noun another term for **Swahili** (the language).

kit¹ noun 1 a set of articles or equipment for a specific purpose. 2 Brit. the clothing and other items needed for an activity: *football kit.* 3 a set of all the parts needed to assemble something. • verb (**kit someone/thing out**) provide someone or something with appropriate clothing or equipment.
– PHRASES **get one's kit off** Brit. informal take off one's clothes.
– ORIGIN Dutch *kitte* 'wooden container'.

kit² noun the young of certain animals, e.g. the beaver, ferret, and mink.

kitbag noun a long cylindrical canvas bag for carrying a soldier's possessions.

kitchen noun 1 a room where food is prepared and cooked. 2 a set of fitments and units installed in a kitchen.
– ORIGIN Old English.

kitchen cabinet noun informal a group of unofficial political advisers considered to be too influential.

kitchenette noun a small kitchen or part of a room equipped as a kitchen.

kitchen garden noun a garden where vegetables and fruit are grown for household use.

kitchen paper (also **kitchen roll**) noun Brit. absorbent paper used for drying and cleaning in a kitchen.

kitchen-sink adjective (of drama) dealing with working-class life in a very realistic way.

kitchenware noun kitchen utensils.

kite noun 1 a toy consisting of a light frame with thin material stretched over it, flown in the wind at the end of a long string. 2 a long-winged bird of prey with a forked tail and a soaring flight. 3 Geometry a quadrilateral figure having two pairs of equal sides next to each other. • verb (usu. as noun **kiting**) fly a kite.
– ORIGIN Old English.

Kitemark noun trademark (in the UK) an official kite-shaped mark on goods approved by the British Standards Institution.

kitesurfing (also **kiteboarding**) noun the sport of riding on a surfboard while harnessed or holding on to a specially designed kite, using the wind for propulsion.

kith /kith/ noun (in phrase **kith and kin**) one's family and other relations.
– ORIGIN Old English.

kitsch /rhymes with rich/ noun art, objects, or design considered to be tastelessly showy or sentimental.
– DERIVATIVES **kitschiness** noun **kitschy** adjective.
– ORIGIN German.

kitten noun 1 a young cat. 2 the young of certain other animals, such as the rabbit and beaver. • verb give birth to kittens.
– PHRASES **have kittens** Brit. informal be very nervous or upset.
– ORIGIN Old French *chitoun*.

kitten heel noun a type of low stiletto heel.

kittenish adjective playful, lively, or flirtatious.
– DERIVATIVES **kittenishly** adverb.

kittiwake /kit-ti-wayk/ noun a small gull that nests in colonies on sea cliffs and has a loud call that resembles its name.

kitty¹ noun (pl. **kitties**) 1 a fund of money for use by a group of people. 2 a pool of money in some card games. 3 (in bowls) the jack.
– ORIGIN unknown.

kitty² noun (pl. **kitties**) a pet name for a cat.

kiwi noun (pl. **kiwis**) 1 a flightless, tailless New Zealand bird with hair-like feathers and a long downcurved bill. 2 (**Kiwi**) informal a New Zealander.
– ORIGIN Maori.

kiwi fruit noun (pl. same) the fruit of an Asian climbing plant, with a thin hairy skin, green flesh, and black seeds.

kJ abbreviation kilojoule(s).

KKK abbreviation Ku Klux Klan.

kl abbreviation kilolitre(s).

Klansman (or **Klanswoman**) noun (pl. **Klansmen** or **Klanswomen**) a member of the Ku Klux Klan, an extremist right-wing secret society in the US.

klaxon /klak-suhn/ noun trademark a vehicle horn or warning hooter.
– ORIGIN the name of the manufacturers.

kleptomania /klep-tuh-**may**-ni-uh/ noun a recurrent urge to steal things.
– DERIVATIVES **kleptomaniac** noun & adjective.
– ORIGIN from Greek *kleptēs* 'thief'.

klieg light /kleeg/ noun a powerful electric lamp used in filming.
– ORIGIN named after the American brothers, Anton T. and John H. *Kliegl*, who invented it.

klipspringer noun a small antelope native to rocky regions of southern Africa.
– ORIGIN Dutch, 'rock jumper'.

kludge /kluj/ noun informal something hastily or badly put together.
– ORIGIN invented word.

klutz /kluts/ noun informal, chiefly N. Amer. a clumsy,

awkward, or foolish person.
- DERIVATIVES **klutzy** adjective.
- ORIGIN Yiddish, 'wooden block'.

km abbreviation kilometre(s).

knack noun **1** a skill at performing a task. **2** a tendency to do something: *he had the knack of falling asleep anywhere.*
- ORIGIN probably from former *knack* 'sharp blow or sound'.

knacker Brit. noun **1** a person who disposes of dead or unwanted animals. **2** (**knackers**) vulgar slang testicles. •verb (usu. as adj. **knackered**) informal **1** exhaust someone. **2** damage something.
- ORIGIN uncertain: perhaps from former *knack* 'trinket'; sense 2 may be from dialect *knacker* 'castanet'.

knacker's yard noun Brit. a place where old or injured animals are slaughtered.

knapsack noun a small rucksack used by soldiers and hikers.
- ORIGIN Dutch *knapzack*.

knapweed noun a plant with purple thistle-like flower heads.
- ORIGIN from *knop* 'knob' (because of its rounded flower heads).

knave noun **1** old use a dishonest or unscrupulous man. **2** (in cards) a jack.
- DERIVATIVES **knavery** noun **knavish** adjective.
- ORIGIN Old English, 'boy, servant'.

knead verb **1** work dough or clay with the hands. **2** massage a part of the body by squeezing and pressing it.
- ORIGIN Old English.

knee noun **1** the joint between the thigh and the lower leg. **2** the upper surface of a person's thigh when in a sitting position. •verb (**knees, kneeing, kneed**) hit someone with the knee.
- PHRASES **bring someone to their knees** defeat someone or force them to submit.
- ORIGIN Old English.

kneecap noun the convex bone in front of the knee joint. •verb (**kneecaps, kneecapping, kneecapped**) shoot someone in the knee or leg as a punishment.

knee-jerk noun an involuntary kick caused by a blow on the tendon just below the knee. •adjective automatic and unthinking: *a knee-jerk reaction.*

kneel verb (past and past part. **knelt** or chiefly N. Amer. also **kneeled**) fall or rest on a knee or the knees.
- ORIGIN Old English.

kneeler noun a cushion or bench for kneeling on.

knees-up noun Brit. informal a lively party.

knell /nel/ literary noun the sound of a bell, especially when rung solemnly for a death or funeral. •verb (of a bell) ring solemnly.
- ORIGIN Old English.

knelt past and past participle of **KNEEL**.

knew past of **KNOW**.

Knickerbocker Glory noun Brit. a dessert consisting of ice cream, fruit, and cream in a tall glass.

knickerbockers plural noun short loose-fitting trousers gathered in at or just below the knee.
- ORIGIN from Diedrich *Knickerbocker*, the pretended author of Washington Irving's

History of New York, the Dutch settlers in the book wearing short trousers which fastened at the knee.

knickers plural noun Brit. a woman's or girl's undergarment covering the body from the waist or hips to the top of the thighs and having two holes for the legs.
- ORIGIN abbreviation of *knickerbockers*.

knick-knack noun a small ornament, usually one of little value.
- ORIGIN from **KNACK**.

knife noun (pl. **knives**) **1** a cutting instrument consisting of a blade fixed into a handle. **2** a cutting blade on a machine. •verb stab someone with a knife.
- PHRASES **at knifepoint** under threat of injury from a knife.
- ORIGIN Old Norse.

knife-edge noun the cutting edge of a knife.
- PHRASES **on a knife-edge** in a very tense or dangerous situation: *investors could be living on a knife-edge for the next twelve months.*

knife pleat noun a sharp, narrow pleat on a skirt.

knight noun **1** (in the Middle Ages) a man raised to military rank after serving his sovereign or lord as a page and squire. **2** (in the UK) a man awarded a non-hereditary title by the sovereign and entitled to use 'Sir' in front of his name. **3** a chess piece, typically shaped like a horse's head, that moves by jumping to the opposite corner of a rectangle two squares by three. •verb give a man the title of knight.
- PHRASES **knight in shining armour** a gallant man who helps a woman in a difficult situation.
- DERIVATIVES **knightly** adjective.
- ORIGIN Old English, 'boy, youth, servant'.

knight commander noun a very high class in some orders of knighthood.

knight errant noun a medieval knight who wandered in search of opportunities to perform acts of chivalry and courage.

knighthood noun the title, rank, or status of a knight.

knit verb (**knits, knitting**; past and past part. **knitted** or (especially in sense 3) **knit**) **1** make a garment by interlocking loops of yarn with knitting needles or on a machine. **2** make a plain stitch in knitting. **3** unite or join together: *their two clans are knit together by common traditions.* **4** tighten one's eyebrows in a frown. •noun (**knits**) knitted garments.
- DERIVATIVES **knitter** noun **knitting** noun.
- ORIGIN Old English.

knitting needle noun a long, thin, pointed rod used as part of a pair for hand knitting.

knitwear noun knitted garments.

knives plural of **KNIFE**.

knob noun **1** a rounded lump or ball at the end or on the surface of something. **2** a ball-shaped handle on a door or drawer. **3** a round control switch on a machine. **4** a small lump of something: *a knob of butter.* **5** vulgar slang a man's penis.
- DERIVATIVES **knobbed** adjective **knobby** adjective.
- ORIGIN German *knobbe* 'knot, knob'.

knobble noun Brit. a small lump on something.

k

- DERIVATIVES **knobbly** adjective.
- ORIGIN shortened form of **KNOB**.

knobkerrie /nob-ke-ri/ noun a short stick with a rounded head, used as a weapon by peoples native to South Africa.
- ORIGIN from **KNOB** + a Nama word meaning 'knobkerrie'.

knock verb 1 strike a surface noisily to attract attention. 2 collide forcefully with someone or something. 3 strike someone or something so that they move or fall. 4 make a hole, dent, etc. in something by striking it. 5 informal criticize someone or something. 6 (of a motor) make a thumping or rattling noise. • noun 1 a sudden short sound caused by a blow. 2 a blow or collision. 3 a setback.
- PHRASES **knock about** (or **around**) informal 1 travel or spend time without a specific purpose. 2 happen to be present. **knock something back** informal consume a drink quickly. **knock something down** informal 1 reduce the price of an article. 2 (at an auction) confirm a sale to a bidder by a knock with a hammer. **knock it off** informal stop doing something. **knock off** informal stop work. **knock something off** informal 1 produce a piece of work quickly and easily. 2 Brit. steal something. **be knocking on** informal be growing old. **knock something on the head** informal put an end to an idea, plan, etc. **knock someone out** 1 make someone unconscious. 2 informal astonish or greatly impress someone. 3 eliminate a competitor in a knockout competition. **knock spots off** Brit. informal easily outdo. **knock something up** Brit. make something hurriedly. **the school of hard knocks** painful or difficult but useful life experiences.
- ORIGIN Old English.

knockabout adjective (of comedy) rough and slapstick.

knock-back noun informal a refusal or setback.

knock-down adjective 1 informal (of a price) very low. 2 (of furniture) easily dismantled.

knocker noun 1 a hinged object fixed to a door and rapped by visitors to attract attention. 2 informal a person who continually finds fault. 3 (**knockers**) informal a woman's breasts.

knocking shop noun Brit. informal a brothel.

knock-kneed adjective having legs that curve inwards at the knee.

knock-off noun informal a copy or imitation of a product.

knock-on effect noun chiefly Brit. a secondary or indirect result of an action or decision.

knockout noun 1 an act of making someone unconscious. 2 Brit. a tournament in which the loser in each round is eliminated. 3 informal an extremely attractive or impressive person or thing.

knock-up noun Brit. (in racket sports) a period of practice play before a game.

knoll /nol/ noun a small hill or mound.
- ORIGIN Old English.

knot noun 1 a fastening made by looping a piece of string, rope, etc. on itself and tightening it. 2 a tangled mass in hair, wool, or other fibres. 3 a hard mass in wood at the point where the trunk and a branch join. 4 a hard lump of tissue in the body. 5 a small group of people: a

knot of spectators. 6 a unit of speed equivalent to one nautical mile per hour, used of ships, aircraft, or winds. • verb (**knots**, **knotting**, **knotted**) 1 fasten something with a knot: scarves were knotted loosely around their throats. 2 make something tangled. 3 cause a muscle to become tense and hard. 4 (of the stomach) tighten as a result of tension.
- PHRASES **at a rate of knots** Brit. informal very fast. **tie someone (up) in knots** informal completely confuse someone. **tie the knot** informal get married.
- ORIGIN Old English; sense 6 comes from the former practice of measuring a ship's speed by using a float attached to a long knotted line.

knot garden noun a formal garden laid out in a complex design.

knotgrass noun a common plant with jointed creeping stems and small pink flowers.

knothole noun a hole in a piece of wood where a knot has fallen out.

knotty adjective (**knottier**, **knottiest**) 1 full of knots. 2 extremely difficult or complex: a knotty problem.

knotweed noun knotgrass or a related plant.

know verb (past **knew**; past part. **known**) 1 be aware of something through observation, inquiry, or information. 2 be absolutely sure of something. 3 be familiar or friendly with someone. 4 have a good command of a subject or language. 5 have personal experience of: a man who had known better times. 6 (usu. **be known as**) think of as having a particular characteristic, or give a particular name or title to: the boss was universally known as 'Sir'. 7 old use have sex with someone.
- PHRASES **be in the know** informal be aware of something known only to a few people. **know no bounds** have no limits. **know one's own mind** be decisive and certain. **know the ropes** have experience of the correct way of doing something. **know what's what** informal be experienced and competent in a particular area.
- DERIVATIVES **knowable** adjective.
- ORIGIN Old English, 'recognize, identify'.

know-all (N. Amer. **know-it-all**) noun informal a person who behaves as if they know everything.

know-how noun practical knowledge or skill.

knowing adjective 1 suggesting that one has secret knowledge: a knowing smile. 2 chiefly derogatory experienced or shrewd.
- PHRASES **there is no knowing** no one can tell whether something is the case.
- DERIVATIVES **knowingly** adverb **knowingness** noun.

knowledge noun 1 information and skills gained through experience or education. 2 the total of what is known. 3 awareness of or familiarity with a fact or situation: he denied all knowledge of the incident.
- PHRASES **to (the best of) my knowledge** 1 so far as I know. 2 as I know for certain.

knowledgeable (also **knowledgable**) adjective intelligent and well informed.
- DERIVATIVES **knowledgeably** adverb.

knowledge base noun 1 a store of information or data that is available to draw on. 2 the underlying set of facts and rules which a computer system has available to solve a problem.

knowledge worker noun a person whose job involves handling or using information.

known past participle of **KNOW**. adjective **1** recognized, familiar, or within the scope of knowledge: *a subject little known to English readers.* **2** publicly acknowledged to be: *a known criminal.* **3** Mathematics (of a quantity or variable) having a value that can be stated.

know-nothing noun an ignorant person.

knuckle noun **1** each of the joints of a finger. **2** a knee-joint of a four-legged animal, or the part joining the leg to the foot. **3** a joint of meat consisting of the knuckle of a four-legged animal. •verb rub or press something with the knuckles.
– PHRASES **knuckle down 1** apply oneself seriously to a task. **2** (also **knuckle under**) submit to someone's authority. **near the knuckle** Brit. informal close to being being indecent or offensive. **rap someone on** (or **over**) **the knuckles** rebuke or criticize someone.
– ORIGIN German or Dutch *knökel* 'little bone'.

knuckleduster noun a metal fitting worn over the knuckles in fighting to increase the effect of blows.

knucklehead noun informal a stupid person.

knuckle sandwich noun informal a punch in the mouth.

knurl /*rhymes with* curl/ noun a small projecting knob or ridge.
– DERIVATIVES **knurled** adjective.
– ORIGIN apparently from German *knorre* 'knob'.

KO[1] abbreviation kick-off.

KO[2] noun a knockout in a boxing match. •verb (**KO's, KO'ing, KO'd**) knock someone out in a boxing match.

koala /koh-**ah**-luh/ noun a bear-like tree-dwelling Australian marsupial that has thick grey fur and feeds on eucalyptus leaves.
– ORIGIN Dharuk (an Aboriginal language).

koan /ko-hahn, ko-han/ noun (in Zen Buddhism) a paradox or puzzle that cannot be understood or answered in conventional terms, requiring a pupil to abandon ordinary ways of understanding in order to move towards enlightenment.
– ORIGIN Japanese, 'matter for public thought'.

kobo /koh-boh/ noun (pl. same) a unit of money of Nigeria, equal to one hundredth of a naira.
– ORIGIN from **COPPER**[1].

kofta /kof-tuh, kohf-tuh/ noun (pl. same or koftas) (in Middle Eastern and Indian cookery) a savoury ball of minced meat or vegetables.
– ORIGIN Urdu and Persian, 'pounded meat'.

kohl /kohl/ noun a black powder used as eye make-up.
– ORIGIN Arabic.

kohlrabi /kohl-**rah**-bi/ noun (pl. **kohlrabies**) a variety of cabbage with an edible turnip-like stem.
– ORIGIN German.

koi /koy/ noun (pl. same) a large common Japanese carp.
– ORIGIN Japanese.

kola noun variant spelling of **COLA** (in sense 2).

kolkhoz /kol-koz, kulk-**horz**/ noun (pl. same or kolkhozes) a collective farm in the former Soviet Union.
– ORIGIN Russian.

Komodo dragon /kuh-**moh**-doh/ noun a very large lizard native to Komodo and neighbouring Indonesian islands.

kook noun N. Amer. informal a mad or eccentric person.
– DERIVATIVES **kooky** adjective.
– ORIGIN probably from **CUCKOO**.

kookaburra /kuu-kuh-bur-ruh/ noun a very large, noisy Australasian kingfisher that feeds on reptiles and birds.
– ORIGIN Wiradhuri (an Aboriginal language).

kopek /koh-pek/ (also **copeck** or **kopeck**) noun a unit of money of Russia and some other countries of the former Soviet Union, equal to one hundredth of a rouble.
– ORIGIN Russian *kopeïka* 'small lance'.

kora /kor-uh/ noun a West African musical instrument shaped like a lute and played like a harp.
– ORIGIN a local word.

Koran /ko-**rahn**/ (also **Quran** or **Qur'an** /kuu-**rahn**/) noun the sacred book of Islam, believed to be the word of God as dictated to Muhammad and written down in Arabic.
– DERIVATIVES **Koranic** /ko-**ran**-ik/ adjective.
– ORIGIN Arabic, 'recitation'.

Korean noun **1** a person from Korea. **2** the language of Korea. •adjective relating to Korea.

korma /kor-muh/ noun a mild Indian curry of meat or fish marinated in yogurt or curds.
– ORIGIN Urdu, from Turkish *kavurma*.

koruna /ko-ruu-nuh, kuh-**roo**-nuh/ noun the basic unit of money of the Czech Republic and Slovakia.
– ORIGIN Czech, 'crown'.

kosher /koh-sher/ adjective **1** (of food) prepared according to the requirements of Jewish law. **2** informal genuine and legitimate.
– ORIGIN Hebrew, 'proper'.

Kosovar /koss-uh-var/ noun a person from Kosovo, a province of Serbia whose population is largely of Albanian descent.
– DERIVATIVES **Kosovan** noun & adjective.

kowtow /kow-**tow**/ verb **1** be excessively meek and obedient in one's behaviour towards someone: *she didn't have to kowtow to a boss.* **2** historical kneel and touch the ground with the forehead as a gesture of deference or submission, as part of Chinese custom.
– ORIGIN Chinese.

kph abbreviation kilometres per hour.

Kr symbol the chemical element krypton.

kraal /krahl/ S. African noun **1** a traditional African village of huts. **2** an enclosure for sheep and cattle.
– ORIGIN Dutch.

kraft /krahft/ (also **kraft paper**) noun a kind of strong, smooth brown wrapping paper.
– ORIGIN Swedish, 'strength'.

kraken /krah-kuhn/ noun a mythical sea monster said to appear off the coast of Norway.
– ORIGIN Norwegian.

Kraut /krowt/ noun informal, offensive a German.
– ORIGIN shortening of **SAUERKRAUT**.

kremlin /krem-lin/ noun **1** a citadel within a Russian town. **2** (**the Kremlin**) the citadel in Moscow, housing the Russian government.
– ORIGIN Russian *kreml'*.

krill plural noun small shrimp-like crustaceans which are the main food of baleen whales.
– ORIGIN Norwegian *kril* 'small fish fry'.

kris /krees/ noun a Malay or Indonesian dagger with a wavy-edged blade.
– ORIGIN Malay.

krona /kroh-nuh/ noun **1** (pl. **kronor** pronunc. same) the basic unit of money of Sweden. **2** (pl. **kronur** pronunc. same) the basic unit of money of Iceland.
– ORIGIN Swedish and Icelandic, 'crown'.

krone /kroh-nuh/ noun (pl. **kroner** pronunc. same) the basic unit of money of Denmark and Norway.
– ORIGIN Danish and Norwegian, 'crown'.

kroon noun (pl. **kroons** or **krooni**) the basic unit of money of Estonia.
– ORIGIN Estonian, 'crown'.

krugerrand /kroo-ger-rand/ (also **Kruger**) noun a South African gold coin bearing a portrait of President Kruger.

krypton /krip-ton/ noun an inert gaseous chemical element, present in trace amounts in the air
– ORIGIN Greek *krupton* 'hidden'.

Kshatriya /ksha-tri-uh/ noun a member of the second-highest Hindu caste, that of the military.
– ORIGIN Sanskrit, 'rule, authority'.

KStJ abbreviation Knight of the Order of St John.

KT abbreviation (in the UK) Knight of the Order of the Thistle.

kt abbreviation knot(s).

kudos /kyoo-doss/ noun praise, admiration, and respect.
– ORIGIN Greek.

USAGE: Despite appearances, **kudos** is not a plural word. The use of it as if it were a plural, as in *he received many kudos for his work*, is wrong (the correct use is *he received much kudos for his work*).

kudu /koo-doo/ noun (pl. same or **kudus**) a striped African antelope, the male of which has long, spirally curved horns.
– ORIGIN Afrikaans.

Ku Klux Klan /koo kluks klan/ noun an extremist right-wing secret society in the US whose members believe in the supremacy of white people.
– ORIGIN perhaps from Greek *kuklos* 'circle' and CLAN.

kukri /koo-kri/ noun (pl. **kukris**) a curved knife which broadens towards the point, used by Gurkhas.
– ORIGIN Nepalese.

kulak /koo-lak/ noun historical a peasant in Russia wealthy enough to own a farm and hire workers.
– ORIGIN Russian, 'fist, tight-fisted person'.

kümmel /kuu-muhl/ noun a sweet liqueur flavoured with caraway and cumin seeds.
– ORIGIN German.

kumquat /kum-kwot/ (also **cumquat**) noun an East Asian fruit like a small orange, with an edible sweet rind and acid pulp.
– ORIGIN Chinese, 'little orange'.

kuna /koo-nuh/ noun (pl. **kune**) the basic unit of money of Croatia.
– ORIGIN Serbo-Croat, 'marten' (the fur of the marten was once used as a form of currency).

kundalini /kun-duh-li-ni/ noun (in yoga) latent female energy believed to lie coiled at the base of the spine.
– ORIGIN Sanskrit, 'snake'.

kung fu /kung foo/ noun a Chinese martial art resembling karate.
– ORIGIN Chinese, from words meaning 'merit' and 'master'.

Kurd /kerd/ noun a member of a mainly Islamic people living in Kurdistan, an area composed of parts of Turkey, Iraq, Iran, Syria, Armenia, and Azerbaijan.
– ORIGIN the name in Kurdish.

Kurdish /ker-dish/ noun the Iranian language of the Kurds. • adjective relating to the Kurds.

kurta /ker-tuh/ noun a loose collarless shirt worn by people from the Indian subcontinent.
– ORIGIN Urdu and Persian.

kurus /kuh-roosh/ noun (pl. same) a unit of money of Turkey, equal to one hundredth of a lira.
– ORIGIN Turkish.

Kuwaiti /koo-way-ti/ noun a person from Kuwait. • adjective relating to Kuwait.

kV abbreviation kilovolt(s).

kvetch /kvech/ N. Amer. informal noun **1** a person who complains a great deal. **2** a complaint. • verb complain.
– ORIGIN Yiddish.

kW abbreviation kilowatt(s).

kwacha /kwah-chuh/ noun the basic unit of money of Zambia and Malawi.
– ORIGIN Bantu, 'dawn'.

kwaito /kwy-toh/ noun S. African a style of popular music similar to hip hop, in which words are recited over an instrumental backing.
– ORIGIN named after the *Amakwaito*, a group of gangsters in Johannesburg, from Afrikaans *kwaai* 'angry, vicious'.

kwanza noun (pl. same or **kwanzas**) the basic unit of money of Angola.
– ORIGIN perhaps from a Kiswahili word meaning 'first'.

kwashiorkor /kwo-shi-or-kor/ noun a form of malnutrition caused by a lack of protein in the diet, typically affecting young children in certain parts of Africa.
– ORIGIN a local word in Ghana.

kWh abbreviation kilowatt-hour(s).

KY abbreviation Kentucky.

kyat /kee-aht/ noun (pl. same or **kyats**) the basic unit of money of Burma (Myanmar).
– ORIGIN Burmese.

kybosh noun variant spelling of KIBOSH.

kyle /kyl/ noun Scottish a narrow sea channel.
– ORIGIN Scottish Gaelic *caol* 'strait'.

Kyrie /kir-ri-ay/ (also **Kyrie eleison** /kir-ri-ay i-lay-i-zon/) noun (in the Christian Church) a short repeated appeal to God used in many set forms of public worship.
– ORIGIN Greek *Kuriē eleēson* 'Lord, have mercy'.

Effective Writing for College and Career

Introduction

This section of the dictionary has been specially written to help students to improve their writing and study skills. It has two main aims: first, to enable you to improve your overall use of English and, second, to give specific guidance on writing and preparing college coursework and compiling CVs/résumés and job applications. There are two main parts (**Brush up your English** and **Writing for college and career**), each of which is divided into a number of separate sections, allowing you to find the information you need quickly and easily. Using the information given in this section will help you to do better in your studies and to get a good start in your chosen career.

SECTION 1: *Brush up your English*   3

　　　　　　Introduction   3

　　1.1　*Essentials of spelling, grammar,*   4
　　　　　and punctuation

　　　　　■ Spelling   4
　　　　　■ Grammar   9
　　　　　■ Punctuation   17
　　　　　■ Common spelling errors   21
　　　　　■ Commonly confused words   23

　　1.2　*Striking the right note:*   25
　　　　　appropriate language

　　　　　■ Register, style, and tone   25
　　　　　■ Email guidelines   34

SECTION 2: *Writing for college and career* 36

Introduction 36

2.1 *College* 37

- Essays and dissertations 37
- Effective note-taking 45
- References and bibliographies 49
  - referencing websites and electronic sources 52
- Writing in exams 53
- Other types of writing: 56
  - reports 56
  - summaries 60
  - reviews 62
- Plagiarism 63

2.2 *Career* 65

- Writing CVs/résumés 65
- Job application letters and emails 69
  - for a specific job 69
  - speculative applications 72

SECTION 1:
Brush up your English

Introduction

This section takes the form of a quick-reference guide to the aspects of English that you will need for most situations at college or university in which a piece of writing is required, from essays and exams to reports and job application letters. All of these situations require the ability to write well-formed English, so as to create the right impression, prevent confusion, and avoid losing marks. There is advice on improving your spelling, grammar, and punctuation, together with guidance on choosing the most suitable level, tone, and vocabulary for different types of writing.

Many people find that their knowledge of English is such that they feel confident in some areas (e.g. punctuation) but that there are other areas where they need to build up their knowledge (e.g. spelling). The information in this section is therefore presented in a way that enables you to pinpoint the particular aspects of English with which you need help or guidance. There are two main parts, each of which is divided into several sections dealing with different language topics.

You can also access lots of extra information, including samples of good writing, language links, and self-assessment tests at:

- the Online Resource Centre (www.oup.com/uk/dictionaries/coedfs)
- www.AskOxford.com.

1.1 Essentials of spelling, grammar, and punctuation

Spelling, grammar, and punctuation are important. They can make the difference between a piece of writing that is clear and well-presented and one that is careless and difficult to understand. The best approach is to check your spelling, grammar, and punctuation after you have written your assignment and established the overall content, argument, and structure.

▶ SPELLING

Correct spelling matters: if you present an assignment that contains spelling errors, it could create the impression that you are careless and may well prevent you from getting the intended meaning across. Even more seriously, many employers faced with hundreds of job applications routinely discard any CVs/résumés and letters that contain spelling and grammatical mistakes.

In addition, while you may use a spellchecker when writing coursework assignments, you will not be able to rely on such 'props' in exams. Another disadvantage of spellcheckers is that they usually cannot help you to distinguish between pairs of words that are often confused with each other because they sound the same, such as *pour* and *pore*.

The first part of this section contains some ideas on how to identify your spelling weak spots, while section two gives you a selection of helpful spelling rules and advice. If you already know that you have difficulty with a particular type of spelling, then you could go straight to the latter section.

1. Self-evaluation: recognizing the problem

As a start, you may find it helpful to assess the areas in which your spelling needs improvement and then to focus on developing ways in which you can achieve this. Even the best spellers are likely to have a few 'spelling weak spots'. Being able to identify the particular areas which cause you problems is invaluable in taking steps to improve.

Here are some general suggestions to help you identify problem areas and develop an awareness of correct spelling.

- **Keep a list of words** that you always spell incorrectly or have to look up in the dictionary. You might find it useful to keep one list of frequent spelling errors (with the right spellings) and one of confusable words, as set out on pages 21 and 23.

- **Make a habit of checking words you are unsure of.** Keep an online or print dictionary to hand whenever you write, look up any words that you are uncertain about, then note the correct spellings in your list as suggested above.

- **Develop your proofreading skills.** Look at the spelling in both your own writing and printed and online material such as newspapers, websites, brochures, etc. with a critical eye. Highlight words which you think may be spelled incorrectly and then check them in a dictionary.

- **Pinpoint your problem areas.** Once you have begun to keep such lists, you may see patterns emerging, e.g. words which are spelled with *ei* or *ie* in the middle (*receive, achieve,* etc.).

After you have identified your spelling strengths and weaknesses, you can select those rules and tips in section 2 below that are relevant to you. For instance, you might have particular difficulty in knowing when to double or drop letters when adding word endings, in which case, go to the **Adding other endings** section.

Be proactive

Work on your problem areas and invent your own spelling strategies. Base these on ways of learning that work for you: some people learn best by constant repetition (whether writing the words repeatedly or spelling them in your head), while others find methods such as mnemonics helpful. A mnemonic is a brief easy-to-remember sentence (e.g. *rhythm really has your two hips moving*). There is a selection of mnemonics at the end of the **Spelling rules and guidelines** section, but it can be fun (and more memorable) to think up your own as well.

2. Spelling rules and guidelines

There are some words, such as *necessary* and *Caribbean*, where you just have to learn the spelling. Using mnemonics and the other ways outlined above can help in such cases, as can the list of common spelling mistakes on page 21. However, there are plenty of other words which follow special rules. Here are some of the main guidelines:

Plurals of nouns

Adding -s

Most nouns form their plurals by simply adding -s to the end: *book, books*; *journey, journeys*.

Adding -es

Does the noun end with -ch, -s, -sh, -x, or -z? If so, add -es to make the plural: *church, churches; bus, buses; box, boxes.*

Nouns ending in -o

These can add either -s or -es in the plural.

- As a rule, nouns ending in -o behave in the same way as most other nouns and add -s to make the plural (e.g. *solos, zeros*), so you are more likely to be correct if you choose -s (but check in the dictionary if you're not sure)
- Nouns which end in a vowel (including y) before the final o always add -s to make the plural (e.g. *studios, videos, zoos, embryos*)
- Some nouns always have -es in the plural. Here are a few of the most common ones:

SINGULAR	PLURAL	SINGULAR	PLURAL
echo	echoes	potato	potatoes
embargo	embargoes	tomato	tomatoes
hero	heroes	veto	vetoes
mosquito	mosquitoes		

Changing endings

- If the noun ends with a consonant plus -y, make the plural by changing the -y to -ies: *berry, berries.*
- For nouns which end in a consonant or a single vowel plus -f or -fe, make the plural by changing the -f or -fe to -ves: *half, halves; knife, knives.*
- Nouns which end in -is usually come from Latin; the plurals of these are made by changing the -is to -es: *crisis, crises; neurosis, neuroses.*

Nouns from Latin, Greek, and other foreign languages

- The plurals of words which have come into English from a foreign language such as Latin often have two possible spellings: the foreign plural spelling and an English one. For example, the plural of *aquarium* (from Latin) can be spelled *aquaria* (as in Latin) or *aquariums*, and the plural of *chateau* (from French) can be written as *chateaux* (as in French) or *chateaus*. If you want to check which one is correct, look up the word in the main part of the dictionary.

Adding other endings (suffixes)

-ed and -ing

- The basic, unchanged part of a verb is called the *infinitive*; it normally occurs with the word 'to', as in 'to ask'. To make the form of the verb referring to things that happened in the past (the past tense), add the ending -ed to the infinitive (*asked*), and to make the form of the verb referring to things that are still happening (the present participle), add the ending -ing (*asking*).

■ Although there is usually no need to make any other changes to the infinitive, here are some of the main cases where spelling changes do occur:

□ If the verb ends with a silent (unspoken) -e (as in *bake*), then drop this before -ed and -ing: *baked, baking*. There are some exceptions to this rule:

— verbs ending in -ee, -ye, and -oe, such as *free, dye,* and *hoe*, do not drop the final -e when adding -ing: *freeing, dyeing, hoeing*.

— there are a few verbs (such as *singe*) that keep the final -e when adding -ing (*singeing*) to distinguish them from similar words without the -e (such as *sing*).

□ If the verb ends with a vowel plus -l (as in *travel*), then double this before -ed and -ing: *travelled, travelling*.

Note that this rule does not apply in American spelling; you will find the alternative US spelling for such words in the main part of the dictionary

□ If the verb ends with a single vowel plus a consonant and the stress is at the end of the word (as in *refer* or *admit*), then double the final consonant before -ed and -ing: *referred, referring; admitted, admitting*.

□ If the verb ends with a single vowel plus a consonant and the stress is not at the end of the word (as in *target*), do not double the final consonant: *targeted, targeting*.

Other endings (suffixes) beginning with vowels

■ These include -able, -ion, -ous, -er, -or, -ance, -ent, -ish, and -al. They are generally used to form adjectives and nouns, and their spelling rules are similar to those outlined above for adding -ed and -ing to verbs.

□ If adding such a suffix to a word that ends with a consonant, the spelling is often straightforward: *adapt, adaptable; addict, addiction; mountain, mountainous; black, blackish*.

□ When adding such an ending to a word that ends with a final silent -e, drop the final -e: *inflate, inflation; advise, advisable*.

□ Keep the final -e when adding suffixes to words that end with a soft -ce or -ge sound: *notice, noticeable; courage, courageous*.

□ When adding these endings to verbs ending in a vowel plus -l, double the -l: *counsel, counsellor; excel, excellent*.

□ Double the final consonant when adding these endings to verbs that end with a single vowel plus a consonant, where the stress is at the end of the word: *refer, referral; begin, beginner*.

□ When adding the suffixes -ous, -ious, -ary, -ation, -ific, -ize, and -ise to a word which ends in -our, you should change the -our to -or before adding the suffix: *humour, humorous*; *glamour, glamorize*; *honour, honorary*; *labour, laborious*.

Note that the ending should remain as -our before other suffixes: *colourful, favourite, odourless*.

Other spelling rules

- The ending -ful can form nouns or adjectives. It is always spelled with one l: *faithful, scornful*. The related suffix -fully is always spelled with a double l: *scornfully, faithfully*.

- When adding suffixes to words that end with a consonant plus -y, change the final y to i (unless the suffix already begins with an i), for example:

  □ *pretty, prettier, prettiest*
  □ *ready, readily*
  □ *beauty, beautiful*

  This rule also applies when adding the -s, -ed, and -ing endings to verbs ending in -y: *defy, defies, defying, defied*.

- When adding suffixes that begin with a consonant (such as -ment, -ful, and -ly) to words which end in a double l, drop the final l before adding the ending: *install, instalment*; *skill, skilful*; *chill, chilly*.

  The ending -ness is an exception to this rule: *small, smallness*; *ill, illness*.

- Most people know the rule i before e except after c; this only applies when the sound is *ee*. So you should spell *receive, ceiling*, and *conceive* with -ei- because the *ee* sound follows the letter c, whereas *piece*, *believe*, and *thief* are spelled -ie- because the *ee* sound does not follow a c.

  There are a few exceptions to this rule (such as *seize*); you should just learn how to spell these.

Mnemonics

Mnemonics are brief, memorable sentences or phrases that help you to remember spellings. They may consist of a sentence that contains all the letters in a tricky word in order (*rhythm really has your two hips moving*) or they may focus on the part of the word that causes difficulty: the sentence *the Arctic has a cold climate* draws your attention to the fact that there are two cs in Arctic.

The following list contains a few suggestions, based on words that people often have trouble with. It may give you some ideas in making up your own mnemonics. The letters in bold colour show the parts of the word that you need to remember.

WORD	MNEMONIC
address	add your address
Arctic	the Arctic has a cold climate
necessary	it was necessary to cut some services
rhythm	rhythm really has your two hips moving
stationary	the car was stationary
stationery	stationery is paper

▶ GRAMMAR

Grammar is the way in which words are put together to form sentences. If you do not write in well-formed, grammatical sentences, it is likely that the reader will be confused or the impact of your argument will be reduced. This section is divided into three main units: **Parts of speech**; **Sentences, clauses, and phrases**; and **Agreement**. If you feel uncertain about grammar in general, it is a good idea to read through the whole section, otherwise you may not understand all the terms discussed.

Parts of speech (word classes)

Words can be categorized according to the task they do. These categories are called **parts of speech** or **word classes**. There are eight main parts of speech in English: noun, verb, adjective, adverb, pronoun, preposition, conjunction, and exclamation. This section introduces some of the essential points and terms relating to parts of speech.

Nouns

A noun is the name of a person or thing. There are two main kinds:

- **Common nouns** include the words for people, creatures, and objects, such as *shoe, woman, dog,* or *house*. Common nouns can be divided into three more kinds, **abstract nouns**, **concrete nouns**, and **collective nouns**. Abstract nouns are words for qualities, concepts, and states, which have no physical reality (for example, *truth, danger, warmth,* or *happiness*), while concrete nouns are those which refer to tangible people, animals, or things (*house, woman, coffee, dog*).

  Collective nouns are words for groups of things or people (for example, *family, audience, herd*). They can be treated as singular or plural, with either a singular or plural verb: *the whole family was at the table or the whole family were at the table*. For more information, see the section on **Agreement** on page 15.

- **Proper nouns** are names of particular people, places, organizations, and events (for example, *Sam, India, Charles Dickens,* the *American Civil War*). They should always begin with a capital letter.

Verbs

A verb describes what a person or thing does or what happens (such as *run, follow, rain,* or *grow*) or a state (such as *be*). The basic form of a verb, which often appears with the word 'to', is called the **infinitive** (e.g. *to hit, to be*).

Tenses

The tense of a verb tells you when a person did something or when something took place. In English, the main tenses are the **present** (*I am, she laughs, they like*), the **past** (*I was, she laughed, they liked*), and the **future** (*I shall, she will laugh, they will like*).

Different tenses are usually made either by adding *-ed* or *-ing* to the end of the verb, or by using words like *am, was, have, had,* and *will* (which are known as **auxiliary verbs**), or by doing both. Verbs whose tenses are formed in this way, like *laugh,* are called **regular verbs**, while those which form tenses by changing the main part of the verb (the *stem*), such as *sit, buy,* or *drink,* are known as **irregular verbs**. In this dictionary the spellings used in the different tenses of irregular verbs are shown in the dictionary entry for the verb.

Active and passive

Depending on the way in which you word a sentence, a verb can be either **active** or **passive**. All verbs have a **subject**, which is the person or thing which comes before the verb. For example, *Sam* and *France* are the subjects of the verbs in the examples below:

Sam took the dog home France beat Brazil in the final

When the verb is active (*took* and *beat* in these examples) the subject of the verb is doing the action. The person or thing affected by the verb (*the dog* and *Brazil* in these sentences) is called the **object**.

When the verb is passive, the subject is the person or thing affected by the verb:

the dog was taken home **Brazil** were beaten by France in the final

The passive is often used in more formal writing, such as reports or official documents. You will find more information about this in the section on **Register, style, and tone** on page 25.

Participles

A participle is a word formed from a verb and used to make compound verb tenses such as the **present continuous** (*she is laughing*) and the **past perfect** (*she had laughed*) with the auxiliary verbs described in **Tenses** above. Participles can also be used as adjectives (**burnt** *toast*) or nouns (*good* **breeding**).

There are two kinds of participle in English:

■ the **present participle**, which ends with *-ing* (*we are* **going**)

■ the **past participle**, which ends with -*d* or -*ed* for regular verbs (*have you decided?*) and with -*t* or -*en* (*new houses are being built*; *it's not broken*) or some other form for irregular ones. This dictionary always shows irregular participles.

Participles are often used to introduce less important or 'subordinate' clauses (see page 14 for more on **Clauses**) where the participle is attached to other words in a sentence, for example:

Her mother,   opening the door quietly,   came into the room.
[subject]   [subordinate clause]

Here, you can see that the subordinate clause refers to the subject of the sentence (*her mother*) and the sentence makes sense. However, you should avoid 'dangling' participles, when the participle does not refer to the noun to which it is attached, normally the subject of the sentence:

⊠ Recently converted into apartments, I passed by the house where I grew up.

In the incorrect example above, the sentence technically means that it is 'I' who is 'recently converted into apartments'. You need to make 'the house' the subject of the sentence rather than 'I' so that the participle (*converted*) matches the subject; a correct sentence would be:

☑ Recently converted into apartments, the house where I grew up was unrecognizable.

Subjunctive

The subjunctive is a special form (or *mood*) of a verb that expresses a wish or possibility instead of fact. It has a limited role in English compared to other languages such as French, but it is important to get its use right in formal written contexts:

It was suggested he wait till the next morning.
Her religion decrees that men and women be strictly segregated.

In these sentences, the verbs *wait* and *be* are in the **subjunctive**; the ordinary forms (called the **indicative**) would be *waits* and *are*.

You should also use the subjunctive in sentences that state a hypothetical situation, after *if*, *as if*, *as though*, and *unless*:

If I were taller, I would have been a model.

Adjectives

An adjective is a word, such as *sweet*, *red*, or *technical*, that is used to describe a noun.

Most adjectives can be used in two positions: either before the noun they describe, where they are called **attributive**, as in *a black cat* and *a gloomy outlook*, or after a verb such as *be*, *become*, *grow*, *look*, or *seem*, where they are called **predicative**, as in *the cat was black* and *the outlook is gloomy*. You will find more information on using commas between two or more attributive adjectives in the section on **Punctuation** below.

Adverbs

An adverb is a word, such as *gently*, *lazily*, *there*, or *very*, which is typically used to give information about a verb, adjective, or other adverb. An adverb can describe how, when, or where something happens (*we ran **quickly***; *he lives **there***) or it can make the meaning of another word, such as an adjective or verb, stronger or weaker (*she **really** meant it*; *they're **very** clever*).

Adverbs normally come between the subject and its verb, or between an auxiliary verb (such as *be* or *have*) and a main verb:

She carefully avoided my eye.
Roosevelt's financial policy was roundly criticized in 1933.

But if you want to change the emphasis of a sentence, you can alter the position of an adverb accordingly, as in the following examples:

The student will happily answer any questions.
(the student will be happy to answer any questions)

The student will answer any questions happily.
(the student will answer any questions in a happy way)

Happily, the student will answer any questions. [sentence adverb]
(it is fortunate that the student will answer any questions)

Sentence adverbs

As you can see from the final example above, some adverbs (such as *clearly*, *happily*, *hopefully*, *thankfully*) refer to a whole statement, and indicate the attitude of the speaker or writer rather than relating to what is said. In this role they are called **sentence adverbs**. Sentence adverbs often stand at the beginning of the sentence:

Clearly, we will have to think about this. [sentence adverb]
(it is clear that we will have to think about this)

Compare this with:

We will have to think clearly about this. [adverb]
(we will have to think in a clear way about this)

Sentence adverbs are well established in English, although the use of *thankfully* and (in particular) *hopefully* can arouse controversy:

⚑ Hopefully the road should be finished by June 2007.

Although there is no good reason for regarding such usage as bad grammar, you should be aware that some people object to this: in more formal written contexts it is better to avoid such adverbs.

Pronouns

A pronoun is a word such as *I*, *we*, *they*, *me*, *you*, *she*, or *them*, and other forms such as the **possessive pronouns** *hers* and *theirs* and the **reflexive pronouns** *myself* and *themselves*. They are used to refer to (and take the place of) a noun that has already been mentioned or is known, especially to avoid repeating the noun again:

Kate was tired so *she* went to bed.

Harris and others like *him* suffer from Information Fatigue Syndrome.

Personal pronouns

I, we, he, she, and *they* are **subjective pronouns**, which means they act as the subjects of verbs, while *me, us, him, her,* and *them* are **objective pronouns**, which means that they act as the objects of verbs and prepositions.

I or me?

These two personal pronouns are often used incorrectly, usually in sentences in which 'I' is used with another noun. If the pronoun is the subject of the verb, then you should use 'I':

Mira and I had a cup of tea

If the pronoun is the object of the verb, then you should use 'me':

She nodded towards Dad and me
It's a tiny bit boring, between you and me.

A common mistake in spoken English is to say:

⊠ It's a tiny bit boring, between you and I.

This is incorrect because 'between' is a preposition that should be followed by the objective pronoun 'me'.

Prepositions

Prepositions are used in front of nouns or pronouns. They describe:

- the position of something: *the cat was **under** the chair.*
- the time when something happens: *they arrived **on** Sunday.*
- the way in which something is done: *we went **by** train.*

Conjunctions

A conjunction (sometimes also called a *connective*) is a word such as *and, because, but, for, if, or,* and *when* that is used to connect words, phrases, clauses, and sentences.

Sentences, phrases, and clauses

What is the difference between these terms?

- a **sentence** is a group of words that makes complete sense, contains a main verb, and begins with a capital letter and ends with a full stop, question mark, or exclamation mark:

  I drew some money from the bank.   What's wrong with her?

- a **clause** is a group of words that contains a verb and usually other components and forms part of a sentence:

  I went to the bank   and drew out some money.
  [clause]   [clause]

■ a **phrase** is a group of words that forms part of a clause:

I went   to the bank   and drew out   some money.
[phrase]   [phrase]   [phrase]   [phrase]

Sentences

There are three kinds of sentence:

■ a **simple sentence** normally contains one statement:

The train should be here soon.

■ a **compound sentence** contains two or more clauses of equal status (**main clauses**), normally joined by a conjunction such as *and* or *but*:

He became bored with teaching   and   looked for a new career.
[clause]   [conjunction]   [clause]

■ a **complex sentence** is also made up of clauses, but in these sentences the clauses are not equally balanced. They contain a **main clause** and one or more **subordinate clauses**. The terms used to describe the different types of clauses are explained in the **Clauses** section below. Here are some examples of complex sentences:

The story would make headlines   if it ever became public.
[main clause]   [subordinate clause]

It was hard to hear   what he said.
[main clause]   [subordinate clause]

In academic writing, it can be tempting to use many clauses in a sentence and many complex sentences so as to try to give a more formal or learned impression. However, you will usually express your meaning better if you aim for shorter sentences with fewer subordinate clauses. You will find more information on this in section 1.2 **Striking the right note: register, style, and tone (page 25)**.

Clauses

Here are the main types of clauses:

■ a **main clause** forms part of a compound or complex sentence, but makes sense on its own:

I went to a restaurant   and treated myself to lunch.
[main clause]   [main clause]

■ a **subordinate clause** depends on a main clause for its meaning: together with a main clause, a subordinate clause or clauses form part of a complex sentence. Subordinate clauses can be categorized into further types:

□ a **conditional clause** is one that usually begins with *if* or *unless* and describes something that is possible, probable, or hypothetical:

If it looks like rain,   a simple shelter can be made out of a plastic sheet.
[conditional clause]   [main clause]

□ a **relative clause** is one connected to a main clause by a word such as *which, that, whom, whose, when, where* or *who*:

I first saw her in Paris,	where I lived in the early nineties
[main clause]	[relative clause]
She wants to be with Thomas,	who is best suited to take care of her.
[main clause]	[relative clause]

More about relative clauses: using words like *who*, *that*, and *which*

Some people are uncertain about when you should use *that* and when you should use *which* or *who*. As the following examples show, for much of the time *that* is interchangeable with either of these words, and it is the usual choice in everyday writing and conversation:

It is a film *that* should be seen by everyone.

It is a film *which* should be seen by everyone.

You're the only person *who* has ever listened to me.

You're the only person *that* has ever listened to me.

However, there are cases when it is not good English to use *that*. This is related to the fact that there are two types of relative clause:

■ a **restrictive** (or **defining**) **relative clause** gives essential information about a noun that comes before it. It can be introduced by *that*, *which*, *who*, or *whose* and does not normally have a comma before it:

she held out the hand	which was hurt
she held out the hand	that was hurt.
[main clause]	[restrictive relative clause]

You can also leave out *that* or *which* in some restrictive relative clauses:

It reminded him of the house that he used to live in.

It reminded him of the house he used to live in.

■ a **non-restrictive** (or **non-defining**) **relative clause** gives extra information that could be left out without affecting the structure or meaning of the sentence. It is normally introduced by *which*, *who*, or *whose* (but never *that*), and should be preceded by a comma:

she held out her hand,	which Rob shook.
[main clause]	[non-restrictive relative clause]

A non-restrictive relative clause should also be followed by a comma if it is in the middle of a sentence:

Bill,	who had fallen asleep,	suddenly roused himself.
	[non-restrictive relative clause]	

Agreement

Agreement is the process of making words match up with each other in a sentence, for example, ensuring that the singular form of a verb accompanies a singular subject. Mostly we do this instinctively, but problems can arise in sentences in certain contexts: for example, is it right to say *the government are doing a good job* or *the government is doing a good job*? Here are some guidelines.

Compound subjects

Two nouns joined by *and* are normally treated as plural and take a plural verb:

Speed and accuracy *are* top of the list.

But if the two nouns combine to make a phrase that can be regarded as a single unit, they are sometimes treated as singular, even when one of them is plural:

Fish and chips *is* my favourite meal.

When the subject is a single noun followed by an additional element tagged on by a phrase such as *as well as, accompanied by,* or *together with,* then the verb should be singular and not plural, since the singular noun is by itself the true subject:

The little girl, together with her friend Kerry, *was* busy filling her bucket with sand.
[subject]   [singular verb]

Your booking form, accompanied by a cheque, *needs* to reach us by Monday.
[subject]   [singular verb]

One easy way to check the agreement in these cases is to think of the sentence without the extra element: *The little girl ... was ...; Your booking form ... needs ...*

Singular nouns treated as plural

Some singular nouns are used with either a singular or plural verb, and some are always used with a plural verb. The commonest of these are the **collective nouns** which stand for a group or collection of people or things. These include words such as *audience, committee, crew, family, government, group, team,* and many others.

The general rule with words like these is to treat them as singular when the emphasis is on the group as a whole and as plural when the emphasis is on the individuals that form the group:

A group of lads *was* gathered around the pub. (singular)
The jury retired to consider *their* verdict. (plural)

However, some collective nouns are always used with a plural verb:

By and large the police *do* a good job.

If you are unsure about whether to treat collective nouns as singular or plural, then you should look them up in the dictionary, where you will see the words 'treated as pl.' in brackets before the definitions.

Plural nouns treated as singular

Some plural nouns are treated as singular, either always or in some meanings. These include the names of branches of knowledge or science, such as *acoustics* and *mathematics*, activities such as *billiards* and *gymnastics*, and diseases such as *measles*:

Acoustics *is* taught as part of the extended course.
The figures show that measles *is* on the increase.

You will also find that some other plural nouns, such as *data* and *media* (which are Latin plural forms), are now often treated as singular. *Data* is a special case. In scientific writing data is usually treated as a plural:

The data *were* tested for reliability.

However, in everyday use, it is acceptable to treat *data* as a singular, with a singular verb:

Raw data by itself *is* of no value to the business decision-maker.

▶ PUNCTUATION

The purpose of punctuation is to make your writing clear, by making the structure of continuous writing plain and showing how words relate to each other. If your written work is badly punctuated, you run the risk of failing to say what you mean or confusing the reader.

This section gives practical guidance on how to use punctuation such as commas and apostrophes accurately and in a way that makes the meaning of your writing easy to understand. As many people find that particular aspects are harder to grasp than others, the section is divided into units dealing with the major types of punctuation so that you can go directly to the areas that you need guidelines on if you prefer.

Full stop

The use of the full stop is quite straightforward.

■ It is mainly used to mark the end of a sentence, however long, that is a complete statement:

My name's Beth and I was 18 in July.

I am sceptical about in-car navigation aids, partly because I think that display screens and electronic voices are distracting for drivers, partly because some early attempts were hopeless when it came to things like pedestrian areas.

■ You should also use a full stop after some abbreviations:

Dec. (December)   etc. (et cetera)   pp. (pages)

If you are not sure when to use a full stop with an abbreviation, look the word up in the dictionary.

Comma

The role of the comma is to give detail to the structure of sentences and to make their meaning clear by grouping or separating words. It usually represents the natural breaks and pauses that you make when speaking, and can be used to mark off phrases or words.

Many people are unsure as to when to use commas, often sprinkling them throughout their written work without knowing the basic rules. Here are the main cases when you should use a comma:

- **To separate items in a list:**

  We sat down to eggs, bacon, and fried tomatoes.

(The final comma before *and*, called the **serial comma**, is not essential and is not used by all writers or publishers: this dictionary does include one.)

- **To introduce or end direct speech:**

  'Yes, mama,' she said, 'and you men would do well to watch your step from now on.'

- **To separate clauses in a sentence:**

A **clause** is a group of words in a sentence that has its own verb. If the clause makes sense on its own, it is called a **main clause** (e.g. *we went back to work* in the example below). If the clause depends on the main clause to make sense it is known as a **subordinate clause** (e.g. *having had lunch*). There is more information on clauses in the **Grammar** section on page 14.

  Having had lunch, we went back to work

  She decided to take the company to an employment tribunal, but the company paid a week before the hearing.

You should use a comma before and after a clause beginning with 'who', 'which', or 'whom' that adds extra and non-essential information to a sentence (known as a **non-restrictive relative clause**: see page 15 of the **Grammar** section):

  Mary, who has two young children, has a part-time job in the library.

But do not use a comma if the clause beginning with 'who', 'which', or 'whom' is necessary to understand the meaning of the sentence:

  Passengers who have young children may board the aircraft first.

- **To separate a part of a sentence that is an optional 'aside':**

It may help to see if you can replace the pair of commas with brackets, or leave out the part without the commas and still be able to understand the sentence:

  Gunpowder is not, of course, a chemical compound.

  His sister, Alicia, was nothing but a crashing bore.

- **To follow 'however':**

(but only when *however* means 'by contrast' or 'on the other hand'):

  However, a good deal of discretion is left in the hands of area managers.

Semicolon

The main role of the semicolon is to highlight a break that is stronger than a comma but not as final as a full stop. It is used between two main clauses that balance each other and are too closely linked to be made into separate sentences:

  The sky grew bright with sunset; the earth glowed.

Honey looked up and glared; the man scurried away.

Colon

There are three main uses of the colon:

■ Between two main clauses in cases where the second clause explains or follows from the first:

He was being made to feel more part of the family: the children kissed him goodnight, like a third parent.

It wasn't easy: to begin with, I had to find the right house.

■ To introduce a list:

The price includes the following: travel to London, flight to Venice, hotel accommodation, and excursions.

■ Before a quotation and sometimes before direct speech:

The headline read: 'Nuclear scientist goes missing'.

Apostrophes

Many people are unsure about when to use apostrophes, but if you understand the three main instances when they should be used, it will be easier to get them right.

■ To show belonging

Use an apostrophe to show that a thing or person belongs or relates to someone or something (called the possessive); so instead of saying *the book of Sara* or *the weather of yesterday*, you can write *Sara's book* and *yesterday's weather*.

◻ with a singular noun or most personal names, add an apostrophe plus s: *Sara's book*; *the cat's paws*; *yesterday's weather*

◻ for personal names that end in -s, add an apostrophe plus s when you would naturally pronounce an extra s in speech: *Charles's house*; *Dickens's novels*; *Thomas's brother*.

Note that there are some exceptions to this rule, especially in names of places, for example: *St Thomas' Hospital*; *Barclays Bank*.

◻ for personal names that end in -s but are not spoken with an extra s, just add an apostrophe after the -s: *Bridges' poems*; *Connors' sister*; *Herodotus' writings*.

◻ with a plural noun that already ends in -s, add an apostrophe after the s: *a boys' school*; *two weeks' newspapers*; *the horses' stables*

◻ with a plural noun that does not end in -s, add an apostrophe plus s: *the children's coats*; *men's clothing*

◻ the only case in which you do not need an apostrophe to show belonging is in the group of words called **possessive pronouns**: these are the words *hers, its, ours, theirs, yours* (meaning 'belonging to her, it, us, them, or you').

Remember that *its* (without an apostrophe) means 'belonging to it' (*the dog wagged its tail*), but *it's* (with an apostrophe) is short for 'it is' or 'it has' (*it's cold outside*): always think what meaning you want before writing these words.

■ **To show that letters or numbers have been omitted**

□ An apostrophe can show that letters have been omitted: for example, *I'm* (short for *I am*); *he'll* (short for *he will*); *pick 'n' mix* (short for *pick and mix*).

□ It also shows that numbers have been omitted, especially in dates: for example, *the winter of '89* (short for *1989*).

■ **To show plurals of letters or numbers**

Do not use an apostrophe for ordinary plurals of nouns such as *pizzas*, *euros*, *cats*, etc. However, some special plurals do need an apostrophe, usually to make their meaning clear:

□ to show the plurals of letters or numbers, use an apostrophe before the *s*: *there are two p's in appear*; *find all the number 7's*

□ use an apostrophe to show the plurals of some very short words, especially when they end with a vowel: *he was taken aback when the no's overwhelmed the yeses*

In the past people often used to put an apostrophe in plurals of abbreviations such as *MP's*, or in dates made up of numbers such as *1970's*, but nowadays it is more usual to write them without: *MPs*; *1970s*.

Hyphens

Although hyphens are not as common today as they used to be, there are three main cases where you should use them:

■ **To join two or more words so as to form a compound word:**

The hyphen shows that the words have a combined meaning (e.g. a *pick-me-up*, *mother-in-law*, *good-hearted*) or that there is a relationship between the words that make up the compound: for example, *rock-forming minerals* are minerals that form rocks.

□ With compound adjectives such as *well known*, you should use a hyphen when the compound comes before the noun (*a well-known woman*), but not when the compound comes after the noun (*the woman is well known*).

□ Do not put a hyphen between an adverb ending in *-ly* and a linked adjective, even when they come before the noun: *a highly competitive market*; *recently published books*.

□ Hyphens are often used to link words to avoid confusion (e.g. a *great-aunt* is not the same as a *great aunt*); this happens especially when a compound expression comes before a noun (e.g. *twenty-odd people came to the meeting* means something very different from *twenty odd people came to the meeting*).

- ☐ Do not put a hyphen between parts of verbs made up of more than one word (called **phrasal verbs**), such as *build up* in *continue to build up your pension*. However, when such a verb is made into a noun, such as *build-up* in a *build-up of traffic*, then you should use a hyphen.

■ **To join a prefix to another word:**

- ☐ Hyphens can be used to join a prefix (an added beginning) that ends in a vowel (such as *co-* and *neo-*) to another word, especially if that word begins with a vowel (e.g. *co-opt, neo-Impressionism*), although one-word forms are becoming more usual (*cooperate, neoclassical*). They are also used to join a prefix to a proper name (*half-Italian*).

- ☐ Use a hyphen to avoid confusion with another word: for example, to distinguish *re-cover* (= provide something with a new cover) from *recover* (= get well again)

■ **To show word breaks:**

Hyphens can also be used to divide words that are not usually hyphenated for the following reasons:

- ☐ to show where a word is to be divided at the end of a line of writing. Always try to split the word in a sensible place, so that the first part does not mislead the reader: for example, *hel-met* not *he-lmet*; *dis-abled* not *disa-bled*.

- ☐ to stand for a common second element in all but the last word of a list, e.g. *two-, three-,* or *fourfold*.

▶ COMMON SPELLING ERRORS

The following list provides a quick-reference guide to some English words which people often misspell, together with short notes to help you remember the right spelling and avoid mistakes. All the words follow the accepted British English spelling; alternative American spellings can be found at the relevant words within the main dictionary.

The list is not intended to be exhaustive (there is a larger one on the Online Resource Centre, www.oup.com/uk/dictionaries/coedfs): everyone has particular words that they have difficulty with, so you might find it helpful to personalize the list by copying it and adding the words that cause you problems, together with ways to memorize the correct spellings.

accommodate, accommodation, etc.	two *c*s, two *m*s	aggressive, aggression, etc.	two *g*s, two *s*'s
		all right	two words (not *alright*)
achieve	*i* before *e*		
address	two *d*s	a lot	two words (not *alot*)

Antarctic	remember the *c* after the *r*	humorous, humorist	-*mor*- in the middle (no *u*)
Arctic	remember the *c* after the *r*	hygiene, hygienic	*i* before *e*
argument	no *e* after the *u*	inadvertent	ends with -*ent* (not -*ant*)
belief, believe	*i* before *e*	independent	ends with -*ent* (not -*ant*)
besiege	*i* before *e*	instalment	one *l*
biased	only one *s*	introvert	begins with *intro*- (not *intra*-)
bigoted	only one *t*		
broccoli	two *cs*, one *l*	judgement	use *judgement* in general contexts, *judgment* in legal use
Caribbean	one *r*, two *bs*		
ceiling	*e* before *i*	knowledge	remember the *d*
cemetery	3 vowels, all *es*	liaise, liaison	remember the second *i*: *liais*-
commitment	two *ms*, one *t* in the middle		
committee	two *ms*, two *ts*	lightning	*lightn*- (no *e*)
consensus	-*sensus* (not -*census*)	liquefy	-*efy* (not -*ify*)
cursor	ends with -*or* (not -*er*)	manoeuvre	-*oeu*- in the middle, ends with -*vre*
deceive	*e* before *i*	medicine	begins with *medi*- (not *mede*-)
definite	-*ite* (not -*ate*)		
eighth	two *hs*, ends with -*hth*	Mediterranean	one *d*, one *t*, two *rs*
embarrass, embarrassment, etc.	two *rs*, two *s's*	miniature	remember the *a* after the *i*: *minia*-
		minuscule	-*uscule* (not -*iscule*)
estuary	-*tuary* (not -*taury*)	mischievous	*i* before *e*, ends with -*vous* (not -*vious*)
exaggerate, exaggeration	two *gs*, one *r*		
		necessary, necessity, etc.	one *c*, two *s's*
extrovert	begins with *extro*- (not *extra*-)		
		noticeable	remember the middle *e*
familiar	only one *l*	occasion	two *cs*, one *s*
February	two *rs* (-*ruary* not -*uary*)	omission, omit	one *m*
		ours	no apostrophe
fluorescent	*fluor*- (not *flour*-)	parallel	two *ls* in the middle, ends with one *l*
forty	begins with *for*- (no *u*)		
fulfil, fulfilment	two single *ls*	parliament	-*lia*- in the middle
gauge	-*au*- (not -*ua*-)	perceive	*e* before *i*
glamorous, glamorize	-*mor*- in the middle (no *u*)	Portuguese	ends with -*guese* (remember the 2nd *u*)
government	remember the *n* before the *m*	privilege	ends with -*lege* (not -*ledge*)
grateful	begins with *grate*- (not *great*-)	pronunciation	-*nunc*- in the middle (no *o*)
harass, harassment, etc.	one *r*, two *s's*	protein	*e* before *i*
		publicly	ends with -*cly* (not -*cally*)
hers	no apostrophe	questionnaire	two *ns*, one *r*
homogeneous	the ending is -*eous*, with an *e*	rarefied	*rare*- (not *rari*-)
honorary	-*nor*- in the middle (no *u*)	receive	*e* before *i*

recommend, recommendation, etc.	one c, two ms	supersede	-sede (not -cede)
relief, relieve	i before e	surprise	begins with sur- (not sup-)
rhythm	begins with rhy-, ends with -thm	theirs	no apostrophe
		thief	i before e
rigorous	-gor- in the middle (no u)	threshold	one h in the middle
		truly	no e
sacrilege	-rilege (not -relige)	underrate	two rs in the middle
Scandinavian	-din- in the middle (not -dan-)	until	just one l at the end
		weird	e before i
seize	e before i	wield	l before e
separate	-par- in the middle (not -per-)	withhold	two hs in the middle
		yield	i before e
skilful	two single ls	yours	no apostrophe
success, successful, etc.	two cs, two s's		

▶ COMMONLY CONFUSED WORDS

There are many words in English which look or sound alike but have quite different meanings. It is important to choose the right word, otherwise you will not be saying what you mean and your written work will suffer as a result. Most spellcheckers are not helpful here, as you will have spelled the word correctly, but chosen the wrong word of the pair for the particular context. All the words below follow the accepted British English spelling; alternative American spellings can be found at the relevant words within the main dictionary.

The following list provides a quick-reference guide to the differences between some pairs of words that are often confused (there is a longer list on the Online Resource Centre www.oup.com/uk/dictionaries/coedfs). You may also find it useful to keep your own list of confusable words.

WORD 1	MEANING	WORD 2	MEANING
affect	to change or make a difference to	effect	a result; to bring about a result
amoral	not concerned with right or wrong	immoral	not following accepted moral standards
bated	with **bated** breath (in great suspense)	baited	taunted
born	having started life	borne	carried
chord	a group of musical notes	cord	a length of string; a cord-like body part
complement	to add to so as to improve; an addition that improves something	compliment	to politely congratulate or praise; a polite expression of praise
complementary	combining to form a whole or to improve something	complimentary	praising; given free of charge

WORD 1	MEANING	WORD 2	MEANING
defuse	to make a situation less tense	diffuse	to spread over a wide area
discreet	careful to keep something secret or to avoid attention	discrete	separate and distinct
disinterested	impartial	uninterested	not interested
ensure	to make certain that something will happen	insure	to provide compensation if a person dies or property is damaged
flaunt	to display in a way intended to attract attention	flout	to openly fail to follow a rule
grisly	causing horror or disgust	grizzly	a type of bear
hoard	a secret store	horde	a large crowd of people
imply	to suggest indirectly	infer	to draw a conclusion about something not directly stated
its	belonging to it	it's	short for *it is* or *it has*
licence	a permit to own or do something	license	to grant a licence or authorize something
loath	reluctant, unwilling	loathe	to hate
militate	to be a powerful factor in preventing	mitigate	to make less severe
pedal	a foot-operated lever; to work the pedals of a bicycle	peddle	to sell goods or promote an idea
peninsula	piece of land jutting out into the sea	peninsular	relating to a peninsula
pore	a minute opening; to study or read something closely	pour	to flow in a steady stream
practice	the use of an idea or method; the work or business of a doctor, dentist, etc.	practise	to do repeatedly to gain skill; to carry out regularly
principal	most important; the most important person in an organization	principle	a fundamental law; a belief
reign	period that a monarch rules; to rule as a monarch	rein	strap used to control a horse; also used in the phrase **a free rein**
silicon	element used in electronics	silicone	material used in cosmetic implants
stationary	not moving	stationery	paper and writing materials
their	belonging to them	there	in, at, or to that place
to	in the direction of	too	excessively; in addition
who's	short for *who is* or *who has*	whose	belonging to which person
your	belonging to you	you're	short for *you are*

1.2 Striking the right note: appropriate language

Introduction

People use many different varieties of English, depending on the situation and purpose of the speech or writing. As a student, you may well be asked to present different kinds of writing, from essays and dissertations to reviews, summaries, and reports. You will also need to ensure that CVs/résumés are written in a way that is acceptable to potential employers. Whatever the type of writing you are required to produce, it should be clear, readable, and convey your intended message in the most appropriate way for the particular purpose and audience.

▶ REGISTER, STYLE, AND TONE

Many college and university courses involve different types of written assignment. The following guidelines are intended as a general introduction to register, tone, and good writing style, but your particular course or assignment may have its own requirements: check with your tutor before embarking on any written work.

Register

In general, everyone naturally varies the type or level of language that they use in different situations, whether they are writing a college essay, emailing a friend, or phoning a company to inquire about career opportunities. No particular style of vocabulary and grammar is better than another; it is how appropriate it is to the occasion that matters.

Consider the following two extracts:

> When the bank seeks to abrogate its agreement and to combine the accounts upon the customer's insolvency, its interests do not conflict with the customer's but with the claims of his general creditors.

> er hello ... EMO! and the dude that dissed the get up kids, seriously man, what the fxxxs that about? honestly ... this country ... I mean, that's no bad thing—it clearly has a lot of people excited, just not me, innit

One is taken from a legal textbook, the other from a chat room: it is not difficult to tell which is which. They represent different levels of

English, one formal and the other very informal. Even at a glance, you can see that they differ in the following broad ways:

- vocabulary
- grammar and sentence structure
- punctuation

However, one is not superior to the other: they are both appropriate for the context in which they occur.

The technical term for a particular level of language use, such as **formal** or **informal**, is **register**. Register is not the same as accent or dialect: a person with a strong regional accent may speak standard English, and anyone, whatever their accent, may use the latest street slang.

Here are two ways in which you can build up your awareness of levels of language:

- Read and listen to a variety of different types of English, from textbooks, fiction, and instruction manuals to television and radio shows, newspapers, adverts, and blogs. Try to classify the levels of language involved and think about the ways in which they are different.
- Make your dictionary really work for you. It contains much more information about words than how to spell them and what they mean. In this case, it can tell you what level of language a word belongs to: it does this by giving markers or 'labels' to words and senses that are not part of standard English. The main labels are set out in the front of the dictionary; they include *formal*, *informal*, and *dialect*, as well as those that classify different global varieties of English, such as American and Indian.

The main registers of English are set out below. When writing for college or university you are likely to encounter situations in which it is appropriate to use a mixture of standard English, formal, and technical language. You are unlikely to have to employ dialect, informal, or dated language unless you are taking an English course and are specifically required to write in these ways, but it is still useful to have a broad understanding of these categories.

Standard English

Unless otherwise stated, the words and senses in this dictionary are classed as standard English. Standard English is generally appropriate in most written and spoken situations: you will find it particularly in business, broadcasting, and printed matter.

The advantages of using the everyday vocabulary of standard English in your assignments are that it provides the clearest, simplest, and most accessible use of the language and it enables you to get your message across effectively. It is also more permanent than some other forms of language such as slang, which often go out of use or fashion from one generation to the next.

Many students believe that their written college work should be similar to that found in textbooks or academic journals, full of highly specialist vocabulary and often hard to grasp at first reading. While you should certainly be developing your understanding of the specialist terms particular to your subject and be able to use them appropriately, it is more important to aim for clarity and simplicity in your assignments.

Here is an example of a clear, well-written sentence. Although it is taken from a sociology textbook, all the vocabulary is part of standard English:

> In the first scheme, presented in 1961, there are four types of organization corresponding to four stages of evolution: the band, the tribe, the chiefdom, and the state.

This demonstrates that writing for a particular subject area need not always be phrased in highly formal language or specialist terminology: you should focus on conveying your message in a clear and straightforward way whenever possible. As you become more familiar with the subject you are studying, you will develop an appreciation as to when technical terms are necessary and appropriate and when they are not.

It is also important to use standard English when applying for jobs: prospective employers will not be impressed if your application or CV/résumé contains informal vocabulary or grammar. In particular, never use the type of abbreviations and spelling used in informal emails and texting in a job application.

Formal language

Compared with standard English, formal, technical, and informal kinds of language tend to contain more exclusive vocabulary, that is, they use words which are common among specific groups of people. By using these forms of language, the user signals that they belong to that particular group.

Formal writing brings a certain seriousness to its contents and may be found in academic journals, reports, official letters, etc. Here are some examples of formal words with their equivalents in standard English:

FORMAL	STANDARD ENGLISH	FORMAL	STANDARD ENGLISH
cogitate	to think deeply	penurious	having no money
purview	the scope or concerns of something	opine	to state an opinion
		abode	a home
appellation	a name or title		

If you are unfamiliar with the requirements of college and university writing, you may think that formal language is necessary to make your essays and other written work sound learned or sophisticated. While such terms may be appropriate in legal and other official contexts, they could make your writing sound pompous or even rather amusing if you use them excessively or inappropriately: many people deliberately use formal words to create a humorous effect. You also run the risk of not choosing the right word if you sprinkle your work with formal terms that you are not completely familiar with.

Personal or impersonal?

Academic writing is often written from an impersonal standpoint, avoiding the use of the personal word 'I': this gives it a more formal tone. Nevertheless, requirements can vary from subject to subject or from one piece of work to another. Conventions are changing all the time, and in some subjects, the use of 'I' is actively encouraged: always check with your tutor as to what is suitable.

In general, however, it is still not usual at college and university to write from a directly personal point of view. Using an impersonal approach is a way of giving your work authority and shows that you can distance yourself from your subject matter and discuss it objectively and rationally (see also the section on **Tone** below).

For instance, in scientific reports the conventional practice is always to write objectively, as in the extract from a botanical journal below. Instead of saying *I subjected the plants to gradual cooling ...*, the author has distanced himself or herself by using passive verbs (*the plants were subjected ...*).

> On the fourth day the plants were subjected to gradual cooling over a 6 min period, using a Peltier cooling element.

Most essays and dissertations take a similar approach:

> This essay argues that international law neither endorses nor prohibits espionage, but rather preserves the practice as a tool by which to facilitate international cooperation.

As the above example shows, it is important to understand that avoiding the word 'I' does not mean that you should not express your own views (the writer here is clearly proposing a particular opinion). However, you can choose less subjective ways of expressing yourself: replace phrases such as 'I think that ...' or 'I discovered that ...' with impersonal words such as 'it' and passive verbs, or just omit them completely, as in the examples shown below:

> It is clear that an ideal system of co-ordinated central planning will perform better than a chaotic market economy.
> [rather than *I think that...*]

An analysis of a typical sample of the crude licorice extract showed 11.4 per cent glycyrrhizic acid.
[rather than *I analysed a typical sample…*]
The two phenomena may be related.
[rather than *I feel that the two phenomena…*]

Note that, unless you are writing a scientific report, you should not overuse passive verbs, as your writing can end up sounding over-formal, remote, or too complicated.

Technical language

All subjects have their own technical terminology, often called jargon. For example, *gravid*, meaning 'pregnant', occurs mainly in medicine and biology, and it would be appropriate to use it in those fields:

Gravid females from each of the three populations were brought into the laboratory.

Conversely, if you used *gravid* instead of *pregnant* in the following sentence, you would be aiming to amuse:

The *Gladiator* star arrived at the screening with his pregnant wife.

The section on **Standard English** above gives some guidelines on when the use of technical language is appropriate in your writing. Always bear in mind your intended audience and the impression that you are trying to convey. Remember that your written work should be clearly expressed and straightforward to grasp; while you need to be precise in what you say and show an understanding of your subject and its vocabulary, you should not be attempting to sound superior by using many obscure technical terms.

Informal language

Informal language, sometimes called *slang* or *colloquial language*, is used more in conversation than in writing (apart from emails and texting), especially among people who know each other, or by particular social groups (such as teenagers) or occupations (such as the army). Informal language also includes taboo language (called *vulgar slang* in this dictionary). This typically refers to sex or bodily functions and should not be used in writing or formal situations as it is likely to cause offence.

Much informal vocabulary is short-lived and relatively few words and uses pass into standard English: for instance, many informal words for 'excellent' are being coined all the time, but many of them will never be recorded in a dictionary. This dictionary includes a selection of well-known informal vocabulary, shown with the marker *informal*. Always look a word up if you are not sure if it is informal or not: you might be surprised to find out that words such as *comedown* and *write-off* are not part of standard English.

Apart from vocabulary, informality is also conveyed by the use of contractions (in which words are shortened by omitting letters, as in *they're*, *it's*, and *he'd*), short sentences, active verbs, non-standard spelling, and leaving out the subject of a sentence (*Wanna go for a drink?*).

As a rule, you should avoid all informal vocabulary, spelling, and grammar in your written work and in job applications. Although there may be a few special instances where informal language is required in a college assignment (for example, if you were asked to write advertising copy as part of an English course), it is usually not appropriate in student writing. Informal language seems less serious and scholarly than standard English, and implies that you have not given proper consideration for the intended audience or purpose of the writing. Furthermore, you also run the risk of failing to communicate with the reader, as informal language can be exclusive to certain groups in society.

Old uses and literary language

Some expressions which were once common are no longer in ordinary use but remain in our stock of words. Today, they are often used to give a deliberately old-fashioned effect, for example in historical novels or to amuse people. This dictionary distinguishes between expressions classified as *old use*, which have generally not been in everyday use for a century or more (e.g. *fain* or *bedchamber*), and those that are *dated*: these may still be used occasionally, especially by older people or in writing from the past, such as *gramophone* (a record player) or *wizard* (excellent).

Some words are found chiefly in literature or poetry written in an elevated style, such as *coruscate*, *dolorous*, or *eve*. These are marked as *literary* in the dictionary.

As with informal language and dialect, you should avoid using these types of language in your writing unless your tutor specifically asks you to do so.

Dialect

A dialect is a non-standard form of language that is used in a particular local region. Examples of English dialects are those of NE England (known as *Geordie*) and of Liverpool (known as *Scouse*). You should avoid regional terms in formal academic writing and job applications, although of course you can use them in speaking or writing to people you know.

Style

Style is a way of describing the overall way in which a piece of work is written, or the characteristic way in which a person writes. Factors such as vocabulary, grammar, register, and tone all contribute to a particular style of writing.

There are many different styles of writing: it is important to assess the purpose and intended readership of a piece of writing and develop a style that is appropriate. It will also be helpful if you increase your awareness of different writing styles by reading a wide variety of material, both academic and general.

Everyone is an individual and writes in a particular way: evaluate your own style and think about how it can be tailored to suit a particular purpose. Your style is likely to evolve over the course of your studies as you become familiar with your subject and also as you come into contact with the writing styles of different authors (although you should not try to imitate another writer's style).

As a general rule, you should always aim in your writing to be as clear and direct as possible, while respecting the particular conventions of your subject or the specific assignment (if any). Here are some points to bear in mind.

Simplicity versus complexity

Consider the following sentence from a palaeontology textbook:

> The subject of the nomenclature, or naming of fossils, is productive of irritation and of sarcastic utterances among some field geologists, to whom the time spent by many palaeontologists on the accurate determination of the names of fossils appears wasteful.

Although it is not inappropriate for the context of a scientific textbook, the sentence is rather complex and wordy and most people would not understand it on first reading. It would be far easier to grasp if expressed along these lines:

> Some field geologists regard the amount of time that many palaeontologists spend on the accurate naming of fossils as unnecessary.

The sentence has been shortened and the number of clauses reduced, while the subject has been switched from the naming of fossils to focus on what some field geologists think about this (which is the main point that the writer is trying to convey).

On the whole, a greater number of shorter, succinct sentences is preferable to a small number of very long ones that are full of clauses. Develop your understanding of the effective use of full stops, commas, colons, and other punctuation to convey your meaning in the most simple and direct way.

Building up sentences and paragraphs into a text

Once you have addressed the matter of simplicity at sentence level, you can then work on the way your sentences and paragraphs relate to each other and how they build up to form a complete piece of writing.

A reader is more likely to understand a piece of writing easily if the different elements of a text (sentences, paragraphs, etc.) relate to each other in a clearly structured and coherent way, with each point following logically from the one before it. There are two main methods of linking sentences and paragraphs:

- **Reference.** Everyone does this automatically: they use pronouns to refer back to people or things that have already been mentioned. This not only links a sentence closely to the one before it, but it also avoids repetition:

   I have never seen Mr Asher up close before. **He's** very old and a real gentleman.

   The purpose of job costing is the keeping of separate cost records for each individual job. **This** is done on a job order cost sheet.

   However, you should be careful to ensure that your reader can follow all these pronouns without losing track of who or what you are referring to: too many 'he's', 'she's', or 'this's' can become confusing, so sometimes it is better to go back to using a proper noun or a short phrase instead.

- **Connecting words and phrases.** You can use these to:

   □ **Make lists:** itemize the points you are making by using words such as *firstly, secondly, finally*, etc.

   □ **Explain connections and effects:** show how one point is related to another by using words and phrases such as *as a result, consequently, although, therefore, however*, etc.

   □ **Give examples:** give the reader instances that illustrate your point by using phrases and words such as *for instance, as an example, such as, namely*, etc.

Finally, always read through your work carefully: you may need to reorder paragraphs to ensure a logical flow of ideas or reword sentences to ensure that the reader is not confused. Make sure that you begin a new paragraph when you want to introduce a new idea, theme, or argument: this helps the reader to grasp what you are saying more quickly. At this stage you should also check that you have not over-used certain words or phrases, or repeated the same word or phrase in the same sentence: keep a good thesaurus to hand and get into the habit of using it.

Tone

The term tone refers to the overall character, mood, or feeling that is conveyed by a speaker or writer. It may convey qualities and emotions such as seriousness, joy, disapproval, anger, or irony. When writing assignments or job applications, it is important to use an appropriate tone. In the majority of cases at college or university, this is likely to be one that is objective, serious, and detached. Your essays, reports, and dissertations should not be written in an emotional or passionate way, even though you may hold very strong views about your topic. Remember that you can take a critical or analytical approach without showing obvious emotion.

Students taking some courses may be asked to produce different types of writing where they are required to write from a particular standpoint, such as writing advertising copy, reviews, or letters. In such cases it is acceptable to convey qualities such as humour or annoyance in your writing. If you are unsure about what is required, discuss the assignment with your tutor.

As regards job application letters, the case is rather different from writing student assignments. While you should use standard English, you can certainly put yourself forward in a confident and persuasive way, highlighting your strengths and skills to a potential employer.

To sum up:

To develop an appropriate style for your academic writing, concentrate on expressing yourself in as clear and straightforward a way as possible. The main ways to achieve this are:

- always be aware of the intended audience and purpose of your writing and tailor your register, style, and tone accordingly
- keep to standard English wherever possible
- use technical terms and jargon appropriately
- aim for an impersonal approach without being pompous or over-formal
- use punctuation judiciously to aid understanding
- avoid overlong and complex sentences
- make clear, concise statements that focus on the main points of your argument
- structure your work with paragraphs to help your reader to follow your theme
- ensure that each point follows on from the other in a logical way

▶ EMAIL GUIDELINES

Nowadays, everyone is so familiar with email, texting, and similar forms of electronic communication that we tend to do it unthinkingly. These new ways of communicating have generated new forms of English, with many features that are more usually found in informal conversations rather than writing.

While such informality is acceptable between friends and people you know well, it is not appropriate in more formal situations, such as when contacting college or university staff for the first time or potential employers. These sorts of emails need to be similar in style and tone to a business letter, although they need not always reach that level of formality, as you will see from the guidelines below. As with other forms of writing, it is essential that you think about your intended reader and develop an awareness of an appropriate approach for different situations.

Here are some guidelines on sending more formal emails (as opposed to those to friends):

■ **Starting and finishing:** always fill in the subject line so that the person you are emailing can easily see what the message is about. Although many emails do not require a formal opening, it is still best to avoid being too familiar unless you have had previous contact with the person and know that this is suitable. If you are making a first approach to a tutor or employer, do not begin with *Hi* or *Hello*. If you know the person's name you could either use the *Dear Mr/Ms/Dr/ Professor* etc. form as you would in a letter or, if not, you could just omit the opening greeting.

If you begin the email with *Dear Mr/Ms* etc., you can end it with 'Yours sincerely' (as you would do in a letter) or just with your name. If appropriate, you could use a sentence such as 'I look forward to hearing from you' or' Best wishes' instead. Always give your full name (rather than just your first name) if making a first contact: it cannot always be deduced from your email address.

■ **Tone and register:** you may associate email with chatting to your friends but remember that your tone when emailing a tutor or employer should be formal rather than familiar. Express yourself in language that is clear, polite, and to the point. As it is easy to create the wrong impression, avoid attempts at humour unless you know the person you are emailing. Use standard English rather than informal language or slang (see the section on **Register** on page 25).

■ **Spelling and grammar:** once you have written the email, read it carefully to make sure that there are no spelling mistakes and typing errors and that your grammar is correct. You should write in conventional sentences and brief paragraphs and use standard English spelling. Do not use informal abbreviations such as 2 (instead of 'to'), U (instead of 'you') or *nxt* (instead of 'next'). Avoid peppering your message with exclamation marks, 'smileys' or other emoticons and do not write whole words or sentences in capital letters.

■ **Pause and think:** emails are quick and convenient, but that very speed can also be a disadvantage. Letters give time for reflection which emails do not, so be careful not to hit the 'send' button until you have given your message due consideration, especially if you are annoyed or upset. If you have said that you are sending an attachment with the email, make sure that you have actually attached it.

Here is a sample showing a formal email to a tutor:

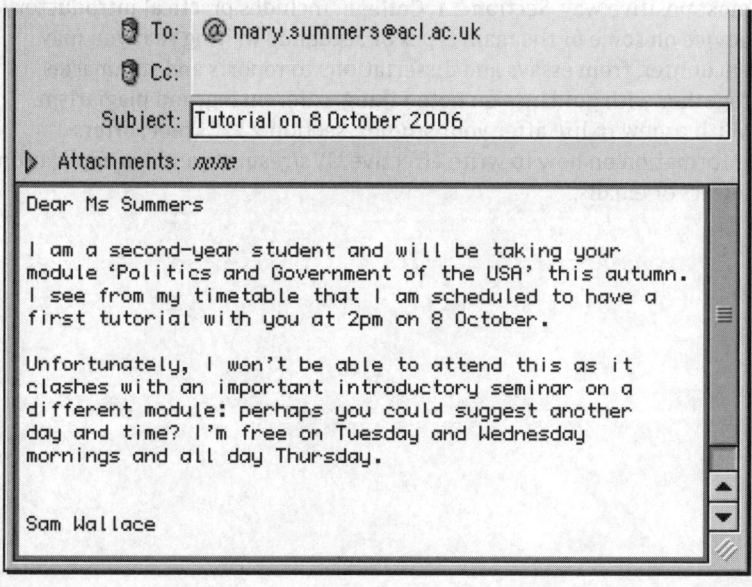

```
   To:  @ mary.summers@acl.ac.uk

   Cc:

Subject: Tutorial on 8 October 2006

▷ Attachments: none

Dear Ms Summers

I am a second-year student and will be taking your
module 'Politics and Government of the USA' this autumn.
I see from my timetable that I am scheduled to have a
first tutorial with you at 2pm on 8 October.

Unfortunately, I won't be able to attend this as it
clashes with an important introductory seminar on a
different module: perhaps you could suggest another
day and time? I'm free on Tuesday and Wednesday
mornings and all day Thursday.


Sam Wallace
```

SECTION 2:
Writing for College and Career

Introduction

This section provides a range of information that will equip you with the essentials for tackling written college and university assignments and advise you on presenting yourself to a potential employer in the most positive way. Section 2.1, **College**, includes practical introductory advice on some of the main types of academic writing that you may encounter, from essays and dissertations to reports and summaries, together with guidance on note-taking, referencing, and plagiarism. With a view to life after your studies, section 2.2, **Career**, offers information on how to write effective CVs/résumés and job application letters or emails.

2.1 College

This section provides an introduction to some of the main types of writing that you will encounter at college and university. It will help you to prepare well-planned essays, reports, summaries, and other assignments, and also offers useful advice on note-taking, referencing, and plagiarism.

▶ ESSAYS AND DISSERTATIONS

As a student, you will find that it is essential to master the skill of writing well-reasoned, articulate, and well-presented essays. You will usually need to write essays as part of your coursework and in exams, and you may also be required to submit a dissertation (also called an *extended essay* or a *thesis*) in order to achieve a degree or similar qualification.

As you progress in your course of study, you will realize that, in addition to being crucial to gaining good grades and therefore a good qualification, successful essay-writing is also vital to successful learning. Once you have developed the ability to analyse an issue, research it, outline an argument and consider opposing arguments in a coherent way, give evidence for your viewpoint, and reach a conclusion, you should have gained a much clearer understanding of your subject in the process. You will also find that such skills will stand you in good stead in your working life.

Coursework essays

The main purpose of an essay is to provide a formal framework which will enable your tutors to assess your ability to construct a reasoned argument and to evaluate your understanding of an aspect of your subject. You are likely to be asked to write essays as part of your coursework or in an exam (there is more information on **Writing in Exams** on page 53).

It is likely that you will need to complete a number of essays during a course of study. Many tutors will give you instructions as to the length of an essay, and you should follow a structured format; you will find guidelines on this in the **Writing the essay** section below. Of course, different subjects require different approaches; there is no one way of writing in higher education and tutors may often have their own ideas as to what constitutes a good essay. If you are unsure as to what is expected of you, it is a good idea to discuss what your tutor is looking for in your writing before you begin. The following guidelines are intended to serve as a general model for essays which can be adapted to the specific needs of your course.

Writing an essay can be thought of as a process, and as such you may find it helpful to break down the task of essay-writing into a number of stages. Here is a suggested approach to follow.

Planning your time

Writing is a complex developmental process as well as a final product and everyone constructs an essay in different ways. Some students find that they have actually to start writing a first draft before they have a concept of what the final essay will be like, in order to discover what they are thinking. Others find that they can make notes and construct a plan from those notes at an earlier stage in their thinking.

Whatever kind of a writer you are, writing a schedule or action plan for each essay will help you to manage your time. The following example of a schedule gives you an outline of the types of activities you need to consider and it is particularly useful for someone who is able to prepare an essay in specific stages.

WEEK/DATE	ACTIVITY	NOTES
7–8 November	Preparation: think about question/discuss with tutor/ assemble reading list	Appointment 10.30 am on Monday 7th
9–18 November	Library and other research	Need to book Simpson and Jarvis textbooks from Restricted Loan (try Thursday or Friday pm)
18/19 November	Assemble all notes/materials; write essay plan.	
20–25 November	Write essay	Two drafts; leave gap between 1 and 2
26 November	Final read through; final tweaks if necessary.	**Check references/bibliography. Ask Anna or Mark to read essay too if they have time!
27 November	Hand in essay	

As you become more experienced in academic study you will come to develop your own learning style and be able to assess how long you need to spend on these tasks. However, you should always leave yourself plenty of time for preparing and completing the essay.

Understanding the essay question

As your first step in preparing for the essay, take some time to think about what the question means and what you are being asked to do. You may think that the question looks straightforward and want to charge straight in and begin reading, or even writing a first draft of your essay.

Although some people take this approach, it is likely that they will fail to grasp the full implications of the question and not produce a good essay. If you work in the way suggested below, your essay should take the right approach to the topic from the outset.

Essay questions are usually worded in one of a number of standard ways: they often start with words and phrases such as *discuss, analyse, assess,* and *to what extent?* which give you a hint as to how to deal with the question. Here are some typical instructions and what they mean:

INSTRUCTION	MEANING
analyse/examine/investigate	break down an issue into its main features and look at them in detail
assess/evaluate/how far?/ to what extent?	present your judgement as to how far something is the case, supported by evidence
compare	identify the similarities between the stated items
contrast	identify the differences between the stated items
describe/give an account of/state	present a detailed account of
discuss/do you agree?	present the arguments for and against something
explore	look at the issue from different points of view

One way to get to grips with a question is to write it out and highlight or underline these instructions and any other words which seem important. Make sure you understand all the words you have highlighted: look them up in a dictionary or your lecture notes or ask your tutor if you are not sure what they mean.

For instance, if answering an essay question which asked you to 'Assess the risks of global war during the Cuban missile crisis', you might highlight the key words as follows:

Assess the risks of global war during the Cuban missile crisis

Once you have thought about or investigated each highlighted word, then you should be able to make sense of the question and understand exactly what is expected in your essay. In addition to thinking about the key words, another useful strategy is to write in your own words what you think the question is asking you to do.

Research

The next step in the essay-writing process is selecting your reading material and deciding on any other research that you need to carry out.

Carrying out systematic research is one of the key aspects of academic life. When investigating your topic, it is essential to bear in mind that you are not expected to know (and cannot know) all there is about the subject, nor should you try to cover everything in your essay. Target your research to what is relevant from the outset and always try to keep focused on the essay question and what it is asking you to do.

Some of the considerations you might want to address are:

- reading list/subject literature—how much reading is necessary?
- arranging access to restricted-loan library books
- use of Internet or audio/visual sources
- use of primary sources/gathering original data
- planning museum or similar visits

The reading list for your course or essay will provide a starting point for your study, but your essay should demonstrate that you have also carried out your own research into relevant texts and other sources. You can do this by:

- Looking at the bibliographies in the texts in the reading list: if an author is cited in several different books their works may well be relevant and worth investigating.

- Read through handouts or lecture notes: they are useful for background information and tutors may have recommended additional reading in them.

- Familiarize yourself with the library section or sections relevant to your subject: browse through the titles on the shelves.

- Use key word, author, or subject searches in the library's online catalogue: ask library staff to help if necessary.

- Investigate the printed or electronic journals for your subject: they contain the most recent thinking and research. Read abstracts of articles to check whether they contain useful material.

- Use the Internet to search websites or within online books or journals. Library staff should be able to direct you to relevant and authoritative sites.

- Keep abreast of current affairs as they relate to the background issues surrounding your subject as a whole.

Once you have identified a selection of key texts and sources, you should then read each one and take notes in the targeted and accurate way described in the **Effective note-taking section** on page 45.

Organizing your material

You should now have all the material you need to write your essay, but it is a good idea to go back to the question to check that you have covered every key aspect of it before you begin to plan your essay and how to incorporate your research into it.

As you were carrying out your research, you will have been evaluating the issues and arguments involved. You should now think carefully about your approach to the essay question, the main theme or themes that are emerging, what arguments you will use, and the evidence you need to support them.

The next step is planning the essay: you will doubtless know that essays should have an introductory paragraph, a main section, and a conclusion. You now need to expand this basic format into a specific essay plan. Here is a suggested approach:

- Identify the main theme or themes of the essay and the key points that you want to make.

- Use these themes and points as headings in your plan and write brief notes as to what you want to include under each heading. These headings will help you plan out the paragraphs in the main body of the essay.

- Think about how your material relates to these points and organize your notes and other reference sources accordingly.

- You might find it helpful to use colour coding or different folders to categorize your notes, and relate these to the headings and points in your essay plan.

- Once you have drafted a plan, check it again to confirm that you have covered the key points raised by the question, then critically reassess the order in which you have developed your arguments.

Remember that the most effective essays are those which enable the reader to trace your reasoning through structured arguments to the conclusion: the introduction should set out your approach to the question and the key points that you will be considering, the main section should present your arguments and evidence in a rational order, and the conclusion should follow logically from the main section.

Writing the essay

Although everyone has a preferred way of writing, here are some guidelines that should be useful.

First draft:

- Before you begin to write, you might find it helpful to read the sections on **Register, style, and tone** on page 25 so as to refresh your mind as to the level of language you should use and how to build up a text in a coherent way.

- Write a first, rough draft of your essay, using the points made in your plan as the basis for paragraphs or sections. Always try to keep to one main point per paragraph: make the point at the outset, then support it with arguments, evidence, or discussion.

- You may not keep strictly to your original plan since your thoughts will develop as your writing proceeds, but make sure that you have an introduction, a main section, and conclusion as outlined in **Organizing your material** above.

- Once you have written a first draft, you might find it helpful to read it through quickly to check that you have addressed all the points raised by the question and that you have not wandered off the subject.

- Do not worry about grammar, punctuation, and spelling at this stage: these are matters to be addressed at the end of the essay-writing process.
- Put your first draft aside for a day or so. This will give your mind a rest and allow you to look at the essay with a fresh eye later on.

Final draft:

- This is essentially an assessment, redrafting, and checking process. Look at your first draft critically: think of your reader, and rewrite or sharpen up passages that seem unclear, rambling, or badly worded.
- Assess the structure for logical order and coherence: link sentences and paragraphs in the ways suggested in the **Style** section on page 31.
- You may wish to reconsider the beginning and end of the essay in the light of what you have written or revised in the main body of it: does the introduction still clearly state your approach and does the final conclusion incorporate and sum up your key arguments?
- Check your facts and evidence. Have you provided all the relevant supporting data and referenced all your sources in a consistent and accurate way?
- Write a *Bibliography* or *References* section (see page 49 for advice on these topics).
- If you have been asked to keep to a particular word count for the essay, then now is the time to count the words and reduce or expand your text as necessary.
- When you have finished writing and refining it, read the whole essay once more for clarity, logical structure, and relevance to the question.

Final checks

The final stage of the essay-writing process should be a thorough proofread from a printed copy (rather than looking at your text on a computer screen). This is the point at which you must check your grammar, spelling, punctuation, and formatting very carefully. You should read the essay more than once for such mistakes, and might find it useful to ask a friend to proofread your essay as well if they have time: another person can often spot errors that you might have missed.

Lastly, check that you have attached any supplementary or supporting material, such as graphs, tables, or diagrams, and that you have put your name, the date, the essay question or title, and any other necessary information (such as a module or course title) at the top.

Dissertations

A *dissertation, thesis,* or *extended essay* is much longer than an essay (usually between 10,000 to 15,000 words): you will typically be given a whole term, semester, or academic year in which to complete it. Although it is similar to an essay in some respects, a dissertation gives you the opportunity to choose an aspect of your subject which particularly interests you and to research it in far more depth than a coursework essay. A dissertation serves as a formal framework to prove your ability to conduct extensive research, to build on existing studies with original work of your own, to organize your workload over a sustained period, and to produce a logical, structured discussion of your findings.

The process of writing a dissertation can be divided into stages similar to those which should be followed for an essay (as outlined in the previous section). Although requirements for dissertations vary from subject to subject and you should always work closely with your supervisor, here are some considerations that you should take into account:

First stages: planning and research

Given the fact that a dissertation is longer and more complex than an essay and may well involve original research, it is important that you organize your workload efficiently and allocate plenty of time for each stage of the process.

- **The topic and approach:** first of all, you need to decide what topic to write about rather than being given a set essay question to answer. You should do this in conjunction with your dissertation supervisor, who will be able to offer advice on the type of topic that students on the course have already covered and suggest fruitful avenues of research. There may be dissertations in your library written by former students for you to consult for ideas.

- **Planning:** decide what activities you need to undertake and then assess the time you will need to spend on each one. You should also consider how your dissertation workload fits in with your other study and personal commitments.

- **Research:** it is likely that you will need to conduct a review of the relevant literature so as to assess the existing theories and issues regarding your topic. Although your supervisor may suggest basic approaches, you will need to carry out much more independent research than for an essay, and to read more widely. You will have to consult relevant journals, search electronic catalogues and indexes, and may also need to visit specialist libraries or similar institutions. The methods suggested in the **Research** part of the **Coursework essays** section above will provide a starting point and you should also consult with specialist subject librarians. You may also need to initiate your own research in order to obtain data and evidence for your arguments. Your supervisor should be able to offer advice on methods of undertaking this.

■ Note-taking: as with an essay, ensure that you take careful notes and reference all your sources. As you will be dealing with a large amount of material it is particularly important that you make well-organized and accurate notes: you might find it helpful to set up different folders for different topics and to write index cards for each source you use.

Writing the dissertation

The guidelines on organizing your material and writing given in the **Coursework essays** section above can form a basis to writing your dissertation. Essentially, you need to identify your key themes and arguments and develop these in an in-depth, logical, and coherent way. Of course, there is a greater amount of material to deal with than in an essay, so it is important to plan out what you want to say under headings and subheadings, and arrange your arguments and evidence accordingly.

Check with your supervisor as to how often they will want to monitor your progress and what form this will take. They may wish to have regular discussions with you or to read some sections or chapters before the whole dissertation is complete, or they may want to read the first draft and provide feedback on it (although the last two procedures are not allowed by some colleges and universities).

You should also be aware that there are usually some differences between the structure of an essay and that of a dissertation. As requirements vary from course to course, make sure that you are aware of any specifications as to the dissertation's structure or presentation before you begin. In general, a dissertation should contain some or all of the following sections:

■ Title

■ Contents

■ Abstract: this is a brief summary of the main points of the dissertation.

■ Introductory chapter: this should comprise an explanation of your approach and your key arguments and themes, and a brief overview of current thinking on your topic.

■ Review of literature: this should show your researches into the relevant literature and your critical evaluation of it.

■ Methodology: if you undertook other research, state how this was carried out.

■ Results/findings: detail what you found out in your research, using tables and graphics if necessary.

- Discussion/evaluation: develop your own arguments, supported by your research. Compare what you have found with the work of others as presented in the literature review.

- Conclusion: sum up your arguments, based on the findings and your evaluation of them.

- Bibliography/references: list all your sources here (see the **References and Bibliographies** section on page 49).

- Appendices: attach supporting statistical data, any questionnaires used, etc.

Once you have written a first draft of your dissertation and received feedback on it (if permitted), then write the final version and proceed through the final checking stages as outlined in the **Coursework essays** section above.

▶ EFFECTIVE NOTE-TAKING

The ability to take notes, whether during a listening/discussion situation such as a lecture or study group or when reading a book, is fundamental to successful study and learning. Notes record the significant points of reading, lectures, or group sessions and will form the basis of essays and similar assignments as well as being important for exam revision. Note-taking skills are also valuable for many situations outside college and university, such as minuting meetings or recording verbal instructions.

With regard to college, effective notes are those which identify and sum up all the main points of a lecture, study group, or text and record them in a clear, concise, and well-organized way.

Although there are different ways of making notes, there are two main types of skill that you will need to develop: the ability to evaluate material while reading or listening and the ability to summarize and organize it. In other words, you need to take a proactive approach towards reading and listening, rather than being simply a passive consumer of information. Remember that note-taking is a skill that you will gradually develop over the course of your studies: you will also find that you come to adopt note-taking strategies that are compatible with your individual style of learning.

Making notes from texts

You will need to read many different books, articles, and other texts during your studies: these may be printed or accessible in electronic form. Reading what authors have written about your subject enables you to learn the facts, appreciate the range of opinions or approaches involved, and to form your own opinions and arguments.

Reading for learning involves the ability to read in a much more focused and proactive way than reading for leisure. It is essential that you select what you read, evaluate material as you are reading it, identify key points, and make concise and accurate notes. The information that you record could be used in a number of ways: for specific assignments, when revising for exams, or for broadening your knowledge. Taking care at the outset to ensure that notes are clear, brief, and relevant will ensure that you will quickly be able to identify the key points when you need them. Here are some guidelines that will help you to take effective notes from texts:

Preparation

- Start by thinking about why you are reading: this will help you to choose what to study. For example if you have to write an assignment on a specific question or topic, then spend some time assessing what books or articles are essential to your understanding of it (there is more about research in the **Essays and dissertations** section on page 39).

- If you are not working from a reading list, or need to research around a subject, scan introductions to books or abstracts of articles to gain a quick idea of whether they are relevant or not.

- If you need to consult online journals or websites, library staff should be able to direct you to relevant and authoritative sites.

- When you have selected the most appropriate texts, look at the contents, index, and chapter headings: you might well only need to read a particular section or paragraph rather than the whole text.

- You could then make a list of texts that include relevant sections and page numbers or you could use annotated page markers such as strips of paper or colour-coded adhesive notes to enable you to refer quickly to these later on.

- Do not write on books or other texts at any point in the reading and note-taking process unless they are your own copies. If you want to mark relevant passages in a library book or journal, it should be possible to photocopy selected pages for private study, but always check with a librarian to avoid infringing copyright laws.

- If making notes from electronic sources, you could print out relevant pages and highlight key passages in the same way.

Reading and note-taking

- Before taking any notes, record the title, author, date, edition, etc. of the text or online source. Be precise: the standard ways of recording this information are given in the **References and Bibliographies** section on page 49.

▪ Read each section that you identified in your preparatory work, breaking it down into smaller subsections if necessary.

▪ Evaluate each passage as you read it, rereading it if you do not understand it: many academic texts are complex. Have a good dictionary to hand to look up any unfamiliar words.

▪ Select the main points that the author is making and summarize them, noting them down in your own words and giving the relevant page number for each point. This will enable you to refer quickly to the right passages when writing an assignment or revising.

▪ If you want to use the author's actual words in your assignment, then write the quotation down exactly as it appears in the text, with the correct page number. Remember that you must acknowledge your sources for both direct quotes and reusing an author's ideas (there is more about **Plagiarism** on page 63).

▪ If you find that several themes are emerging as you read, it may help to use a fresh sheet of paper for each theme.

▪ Try to remain focused on your particular task. It is counterproductive to take a great deal of time making pages of notes that contain so much irrelevant information that you subsequently have to spend further hours reading them so as to extract the most important points.

Making notes from lectures and study groups

Note-taking from lectures, seminars, and other spoken situations primarily involves the development of effective listening skills. As with reading, you are aiming to build up your ability to listen in a proactive way: to engage with what is being said, evaluate it, and summarize it in note form.

To develop active listening skills at college or university, you will be building on the skills that you already use in everyday situations, for example, when listening to the radio, TV, or friends' conversations: we all automatically focus on certain points, process what we are hearing, and either store it in our minds or discard it. If you think about how you do this and practise evaluating and summarizing what you hear in such situations, it will help you to listen proactively in lectures or study groups. Like any skill, the more you practise, the easier it will become.

Here are some strategies that will help you to take effective lecture and study group notes:

Preparation

▪ You may be asked to prepare for a lecture or study group by carrying out recommended reading of texts or handouts: make sure that you do this, or else you may not understand the issues involved or the terminology used.

■ Even if you are not specifically asked to do such preparation, it is worth taking a little time beforehand to think about the topic that will be presented. The sorts of questions you might consider are: what do you already know about this topic? How does it relate to your course as a whole?

In the lecture/study group

■ Adopt a Listen Evaluate Select approach (less is more). *Listen* carefully to what is being said and divide it up into smaller items of information in your mind; *evaluate* what you have heard (is it an important point or not?); if so, *select* key words and phrases that sum up the point and then write them down. Make intelligent use of the way the lecture is given; the speaker will often repeat important points or write them on a board as they go along.

■ Some people think that if the tutor provides handouts summing up the key points of a session, there is no need to take notes at all. Handouts are helpful, but it is much better to use them as a basis for your own notes, jotting down points that strike you as significant during the session and putting your own interpretation on what has been said. Also, tutors may diverge from handouts, sometimes just to check that you are concentrating or else because they have thought of something new and valid while they are speaking.

■ On the other hand, some people try to write down everything that is being said. This approach is likely to be unsuccessful on two counts: unless you can write very fast shorthand you will never record everything; secondly, even if you can jot down everything it will not help you when you come to read the notes later on, as you will have recorded superfluous information in a disorganized way which will not help with focused learning or revision.

■ Make sure your writing is as legible as possible: also, scribbling might be a sign that you are trying to record too much information.

■ How you organize your written notes is a matter of choice. Some people prefer to record points in a sequence that roughly follows the course of the lecture, while others find that taking what are sometimes called *pattern notes* is a more effective method for them. This involves writing a key word or phrase in the middle or at the top of a sheet of paper, and then jotting down more key words or phrases around this, with lines linking related topics. You may also find it useful to colour-code or highlight notes, as suggested in the **Making notes from texts** section above.

Follow-up action

- Get into the habit of reading through your notes as soon as you can after the lecture or study group. Now is a good time to underline, circle, or highlight important points. It is also a good idea to spend a few minutes writing about the topic in your own words (without referring back to your notes).

- If you do not understand something, or you cannot read what you have written, or there are gaps in your notes, then talk to your friends or your tutor to find out the information you need.

- You may find it helpful (if you have the time) to write out a fair copy of your initial notes. If you are new to selective note-taking this is the point at which you can cut out unnecessary material and organize your notes in a clear and logical way.

- Carry out any recommended follow-up reading and use this to supplement your lecture notes.

▶ REFERENCES AND BIBLIOGRAPHIES

The citing of sources to support your arguments and the accurate documenting of these is essential to successful academic study and writing. References record the fact that you have used another person's words or ideas and bibliographies list the texts and other sources that you have used for a particular piece of work. As well as supporting your ideas, both references and bibliographies allow the reader to identify the exact sources of what you have written: failure to do this is bad academic practice and could also lead to accusations of plagiarism.

References

During your studies you will read many different books, articles, and other texts in order to learn more about your subject and prepare coursework. It is vital to keep accurate notes of everything you read so as to compile full references and bibliographies. When writing, it is your responsibility as an author to make sure that your work is properly supported by appropriate sources, that the sources are correctly quoted or interpreted, and that the citations are accurate and complete. Remember that you must reference all points taken from other authors, whether you quote them directly or put them in your own words.

There are a number of accepted systems or styles of referencing, some of which are more appropriate to certain subjects than others. You should always check with your tutor as to which one is preferred or required for your subject or course before completing any coursework. Whichever system you use, it is important to be consistent, thorough, and accurate.

This section outlines the main elements of one widely used style of referencing, the **author-date** system. Information on the footnote/endnote and the Vancouver (author-number) systems is available on the Online Resource Centre (www.oup.com/uk/dictionaries/coedfs).

There are several versions of the **author-date** system: the following guidelines contain the essential features of what is known as the **Harvard** style of referencing, which is used especially in the social sciences, physical sciences, and related fields.

The Harvard system involves giving brief notes in the text containing the author's name and the date of the work in brackets, which take the reader to the appropriate point in a list of full citations, generally known as the *References* section rather than a *Bibliography*. Strictly speaking, a **References** section includes only those works that are cited in the text, whereas a more general list of works of related interest should be called the *Bibliography* or *Further Reading*. The **Bibliography** section below gives more information on how to give full citations in the *References* list.

A typical reference in the text should consist of an author's name and the date of their publication enclosed within brackets, with or without a comma separating the name and date, according to the style adopted. Punctuation can vary within the Harvard system: always check the correct style for your course or college and be consistent. The reference is placed immediately after the statement to which it relates. Here are some examples of the Harvard referencing style:

Reference in text

While there was an extraordinary sense of optimism among people establishing their own farms in the early years of independence (Unwin 1994), this is rapidly withering away.

Reference section

Unwin, T. (1994), 'Structural Change in Estonian Agriculture: From Command Economy to Privatisation', *Geography*, 79, 3: 246–61.

If the author's name is given in open text it need not be repeated within the bracketed note, where you need only to give the date:

Reference in text

For years, most textbooks referred to the five stages of economic integration as defined by Balassa (1961).

If you use a direct quotation from an author, then the reference should follow the closing punctuation. Some subjects require that you also give a page number for your source, in which case you should show it as follows, with a colon separating the date and the page number:

Reference in text

In Uppsala 'the main aim is to create sustainable development, although there is no true consensus as to what this means' (Peterson 2005: 439).

More than one reference may be included within the same set of brackets, separated by semicolons:

Reference in text

They are also used to detect segmental hypermobility (Magarey 1988; Maitland 2001).

Reference section

Magarey, M. E. 1988 'Examination of the Cervical and Thoracic Spine'. In: Grant R (ed.) *Physical Therapy of the Cervical and Thoracic Spine*, pp. 81–109. Churchill Livingstone: New York.

Maitland, G. 2001 *Maitland's Vertebral Manipulation*, 6th edn. Butterworth-Heinemann: Oxford.

Many scientific publications have multiple authors. You can use the abbreviation 'et al.' (short for Latin *et alii* and meaning 'and others') in the text reference to save listing all the authors, but these must be given in full in the reference section.

Reference in text

Prototypical birds, for instance, seem to be birds of average size and average predacity (Rips et al., 1973).

Reference section

Rips, L. J., Shoben, E. J., and Smith, E. E. (1973). 'Semantic Distance and the Verification of Semantic Relations'. *Journal of Verbal Learning and Verbal Behaviour* 12: 1–20.

Bibliographies

A bibliography (or in the author-date system, a *References* section) should contain a list of all the texts or other sources that you have used for a piece of coursework. You should cite all your sources in a consistent and accurate way, so as to provide enough key material for readers to be able to identify the work and locate it in a library or on the Internet.

The format of citations in a bibliography is determined by the referencing system that you are using. Styles of punctuation may vary, so it is best to check with a style guide or your tutor as to which you should use. Do not mix different styles within the same bibliography or reference list and always be accurate.

Here are some guidelines for the **author-date** referencing system outlined above. There is information about the format used for the footnote/endnote style of bibliography on the Online Resource Centre (www.com/uk/dictionaries/coedfs).

If using an author-date style of referencing, your list of cited sources should be titled *References* rather than *Bibliography*. All the texts and other sources you have referred to in your text should be listed in alphabetical order. Broadly speaking, the information given in each reference should appear in the following order:

author, date, title, place of publication, publisher

Here is a simple citation for a single-author book:

Lakoff, R. (1975). *Language and Women's Place*. New York: Harper and Row.

If a text is produced by an organization, the reference should start with the name of the organization:

World Bank (1993). *Vietnam: Transition to the Market*. Washington, DC: The World Bank.

If citing from an academic journal the citation should appear in this form:

Stookey, R. W., 1974. 'Social Structure and Politics in the Yemen Arab Republic'. *Middle East Journal*, 28/3: 248–60.

Note that the title of the article should appear within single quotation marks, with the title of the journal in italics (or underlined). The year that the journal was published should come after the author's name and you should give the volume number of the journal after the title, together with the page numbers of the whole article.

If a book or article has several authors, then these should appear in the order that they are given on the title page of the book or the heading of the article:

Rips, L. J., Shoben, E. J., and Smith, E. E. (1973). 'Semantic Distance and the Verification of Semantic Relations'. *Journal of Verbal Learning and Verbal Behaviour* 12: 1–20.

If you are referencing a chapter of a book containing contributions from a number of authors, the citation should be:

Jessop, B. (1997) 'The Governance of Complexity and Complexity of Governance', in A. Amin and J. Hausner (eds) *Beyond Markets and Hierarchy*, Aldershot: Edward Elgar.

Referencing websites and electronic sources

When using the Internet, it is important that you follow the same principles as when referencing printed sources: always provide enough details to ensure that the reader can accurately identify the source you are citing. The basic template for citing websites might include some, or all, of the following classes of information:

- author's or editor's name
- title of the article or other subsection used (in quotes)
- general title or title of the complete work (italic)
- volume or page numbers (when citing electronic journals that have no volumes the date may be cited here)
- general information, including type of medium (in square brackets)
- date on which the material was created or on which it was published or posted (day month year, in round brackets)

- institution or organization responsible for maintaining or publishing the information
- address of electronic source (within angle brackets)
- page number or online equivalent
- date accessed.

As far as possible, you should use the same style when citing electronic texts as you would for citing printed sources, as described in the **References** and **Bibliography** sections above.

Here are some examples of website references: note that you should always record the date that you last accessed the website, as information on the Internet can often change:

Internet sites

Strunk, William, *The Elements of Style* (Geneva, NY, 1918; pubd online July 1999) <http://www.bartleby.com/141> accessed 14 Dec 2006.

Online books

Maury, M. F., *The Physical Geography of the Sea* [online facsimile] (Harper: New York, 1855), Making of America digital library <http://moa.umdl.umich.edu/cgi/sgml/moa-idx?notisid=AFK9140> accessed 1 Sept. 2007.

Online journal articles

'University Performance, 2001 League Tables: Firsts and Upper Seconds', *Times Higher Education Supplement*, Statistics page (published online 31 May 2001) <http://www.thesis.co.uk/main.asp> accessed 31 May 2006.

▶ WRITING IN EXAMS

Although some college and university courses may be assessed on coursework alone, there are many in which assessment is by a combination of exams and coursework or by exams only. It is therefore important to understand what is required of you in exam situations and to be able to adapt your writing skills accordingly so as to increase your chances of success.

This section offers some guidelines on developing your own techniques for writing effectively in exams. You can find strategies for revision on the Online Resource Centre (www.oup.com/uk/dictionaries/coedfs).

Preparation

You will find that if you allocate enough time to preparing for an exam, you will gain confidence in your knowledge and feel more in control of the situation, allowing you to write more effectively on the actual day. Points to consider are:

- Make your revision as active as possible to keep your mind alert.

- Begin revising in good time before the exam; plan your revision and target it towards specific topics rather than trying to revise and learn everything.

- Familiarize yourself with past question papers, including:

  □ likely topics and wording of questions

  □ type and duration of the exam (for example, there may be multiple-choice questions, you may be required to give short answers rather than essays, or it may be an open-book exam in which you are allowed to take specified texts into the exam)

- Read through relevant coursework and handouts and identify and note key facts.

- Read through lecture or study group and reading notes; collate these with your coursework notes and draw up overall summaries of key points and facts under likely exam topic headings.

- Practise answering questions from past exam papers under timed conditions.

- Attend any revision or other exam preparation sessions organized by your tutors.

- Make sure you know your way around any books that you are allowed to take into an open-book exam.

In the exam

The following guidelines are based on the type of exam that requires answers in an essay format. While there are some similarities to writing essays for coursework, there are also some important differences. The purpose of a coursework essay is to demonstrate your ability to research around a particular topic and develop structured arguments about it, whereas exam essays enable examiners to assess your knowledge and understanding of a subject and your ability to tailor this knowledge so as to answer questions clearly, logically, and concisely within a limited period of time.

Before you begin to write

- Always read the instructions at the top of the question paper very carefully to make sure you know how many questions you need to answer, how long you have to do this, and any other specific requirements.

- Read each question and then select the ones you are going to answer.

- Allocate a set amount of time for each question; if all questions carry the same number of marks you should devote the same amount of time to each. If not, then allocate your time to each question proportionately.

■ Think about the order in which you will answer the questions. It is advisable to answer the questions you feel most knowledgeable about first, but do not spend more time on them than you have allocated.

■ Approach exam questions in the same way as coursework essay questions. Think carefully about what the question means, what information it is asking for, and the approach you need to take: you might find it helpful to circle or underline key words (as suggested in the section on **Essays and dissertations** on page 39).

Answering the questions

The process of answering each exam question can be divided into three parts:

■ **Planning:** once you have decided what the question means, then write short notes as to what information and areas you will need to cover and in what order. You should try to structure exam essays in the same way as coursework essays, with an introduction, a main section, and a conclusion, but you are not expected to write the same amount as in a coursework essay.

■ **Writing:** once you have sketched out an essay plan, focus on setting out the main elements of the essay in a clear and logical way, bearing in mind the following points:

  □ Remember that your time is limited and be selective: concentrate on including the essential facts and discussing the major issues rather than trying to write down everything you know.

  □ Back up key points with selected evidence; cite authors or give statistics, examples, etc.

  □ You do not need to give a bibliography at the end of your essay, but you should provide references to any works and authors cited in a recognized style.

  □ Check how long you are taking to answer the question and keep to your allocated timings as closely as possible. Be disciplined with yourself: if you have not finished one question but your time allocation for it has run out, go on to the next one.

  □ If you run out of time to complete the essay, submitting a clear outline as evidence of how you would have argued your case will create a good impression and may well gain you a few marks.

■ **Checking:** allow yourself some time (for example 5 minutes for each question) to read through what you have written. Check that you have answered all the issues raised in the question, included all the main points in your essay outline, and that your spelling, punctuation, and grammar are correct.

▶ OTHER TYPES OF WRITING

The previous sections have given you some guidelines on writing effective essays and dissertations. While all courses have individual requirements, it is likely that you will also be asked to submit other kinds of coursework, such as reports, summaries, or reviews. These are typically quite distinct from academic essays; they are written for a different purpose or audience and follow a different structure.

This section provides you with a broad introduction to tackling some different types of college and university writing, but you should bear in mind that individual subjects usually require specific approaches: always check with your tutor as to what is expected from an assignment before you begin.

Reports

A report is a formal written account of a specific matter that a person has observed or investigated in some depth. The process of compiling a report will typically involve the collection of information or evidence, the evaluation of that information, and the presentation of the findings in an objective and conventional way. Most reports also offer recommendations for discussion or future action, although a scientific report will typically focus on the methods used to gather the data and the reporting of the results of experiments.

As a student, you may need to write a report as part of your coursework, especially if you are studying for a scientific or business qualification, or you may be asked to prepare one for an employer during an extended work placement. Here are some general guidelines for writing reports, but remember that the format, content, and tone of the report will vary according to the subject you are studying or the context in which the report is written, so always check with the person who has asked for the report before you begin.

Preparation

Scope and purpose of the report

Firstly, make sure that you know exactly what you have been asked to investigate. If the report is a piece of coursework you will probably have been given a written assignment, but if you are writing a report for an employer, you may only have received a verbal briefing. If you are unsure about the report's scope or purpose, always discuss what is required before you begin and look at previous reports compiled for the same subject field.

Background work

Careful planning at this stage will ensure that you investigate the situation in an organized and thorough way. Think about how what information you need, how you will obtain it, who you should approach, and any background reading or other research you might have to carry out. If you need statistical data or illustrations to back up your research, think about how best to source them. If you are writing a scientific report, then you should plan what experiments you need to conduct.

You will now have a number of tasks to complete, so you might find it helpful to draw up a schedule, listing key actions and the dates by which they should be achieved.

Collecting the information

How you gather your information depends on what you are investigating. Do any background reading or other research at any early stage to familiarize yourself with the issues involved, taking careful notes. If you need to ascertain people's views, decide who you need to approach and prepare a list of questions. Write up any interviews or experiments as soon as possible after conducting them, while they are fresh in your mind.

Compiling the report

Organizing and evaluating the information

Once you have researched a situation and obtained all the information you need, you can then begin to organize your findings with a view to writing the report. Think about the structure of the report and how your information corresponds to the various headings. Refresh your mind as to the original brief: have you stayed within its parameters? Now is the time to discard any irrelevant material: the report should be concise and focused on the issue in question.

You should also consider the most effective ways to display data (as graphs, tables, charts, etc.) and also decide whether it is supporting information that should appear in an appendix or central to a point that you are making and therefore to be inserted in the main body of the report.

Structure

Although specific subjects may have differing approaches, a report can generally be structured as follows (note that you will not always need to use every section):

- **Title and contents:** base the title on the essentials of the brief you were given, and give your name and the date of the report. You only need to include a Contents page if the report is a long or complex one.

- **Summary/abstract:** this is a paragraph that sums up the main points of the report. Although some subjects require this, it is not always obligatory; check with the person who has asked for the report.

- **Introduction/terms of reference:** state the details of the brief you were given or any other reason for writing the report.

- **Procedure/method/methodology:** describe your method of gathering information.

- **Findings:** present the outcome of your research in a succinct and logical way, making sure that you include enough information to demonstrate that you have investigated the matter thoroughly. You can summarize the opinions of people you have approached, present statistics in support of your points, or describe any other relevant research. It will help the reader if you organize these findings under further headings, subheadings, or numbered subsections. Use graphics or illustrations if appropriate.

- **Conclusions:** this section should sum up your assessment of the current situation, based on your findings.

- **Recommendations:** propose recommendations to be considered for future action, based on your conclusions.

- **Bibliography:** list any books, periodicals, or articles that you consulted, using one of the standard referencing systems.

- **Appendices:** this section, if used, should contain supporting data, any questionnaires used, etc.

Language and tone

In general, the language and tone of a report should be more formal and impersonal than that of an essay, reflecting the fact that it is essentially an objective assessment of a situation.

For example, a scientific report is written for a particular audience (other scientists in the field) and its purpose is to present the results of an experiment in an objective and very concise way. As a result, the language is formal and technical, with passive verbs used in preference to active ones, and the tone is brisk and highly impersonal, as in this extract from a psychology journal:

> The temperature of the copper stage was controlled with Peltier cells powered by a feedback-regulated, adjustable DC power source (PTC-10; ALA Instruments). Temperature in the recording chamber was maintained within [+ or -] 0.5 degrees C. Electrode filling solution was freshly prepared … .

Other types of report, however, may be less formal, depending on the context in which they are written: find out what is appropriate before you begin. If you are writing a report for a general audience, always explain any technical terms that you use. Whatever the situation, your reader needs to grasp the main points of the report quickly and easily, so keep to standard English, avoid very long sentences, and generally present your information in a clear and concise way.

Final stages

Once you have written your report:

- read it through for clarity, logical flow, and relevance
- check grammar, spelling, and punctuation
- check that any documents that you are using to support your case are given in the relevant appendices

Here is an example of a well-structured, clear, and concise report that would be appropriate for a business studies course:

Report on Central Purchasing Policy
Matthew Nash
3 February 2007

Summary

A report into the central purchasing policy of Smith and Co in order to assess current purchasing practice and address concerns about the recent decline in regional sales.

Introduction

This report addresses branch managers' concerns with the central purchasing policy, which have arisen following a steady decline in regional sales. It has been suggested that the previous purchasing system be reintroduced to prevent a further drop in sales: this report will assess the current situation and make recommendations as to appropriate action.

Method

Interviews were carried out with each of our 20 branch managers within the last month. They were questioned as to their objections to the central policy and asked to identify its main failings.

Research into our main competitors' practices and sales was also undertaken by personal visits to stores and assessment of sales figures in the trade press.

Findings

1. Existing situation
The central purchasing policy was implemented in January 2005. It replaced the previous system whereby regional managers were responsible for purchasing and could select lines likely to appeal to customers in their area. Since the central purchasing policy was implemented there has been a steady reduction in regional sales (see Appendix A) and a subsequent demand from our branches to return to the previous system.

However, the central purchasing policy has proved to be efficient and cost-effective over the past year, especially in terms of reducing storage overheads (see Appendix B).

2. Branch managers' concerns
Interviews with managers indicated that dissatisfaction with the existing policy reached a peak after the Christmas 2006 sales period, when regional sales were significantly lower year-on-year, as managers had predicted.

In every shop, managers highlighted lines that were previously stocked because they had a specific appeal for customers in their area but which had not been ordered by central purchasing this year because they were unlikely to do well

---

across the country as a whole. Managers also reported that many customers had requested such lines, especially over the Christmas period. Conversely, there were many examples of stock received by branches which were of no interest to customers in their area and which subsequently remained unsold.

3. Competitors' practice
Visits to competitors' stores revealed that they all held stock with a regional appeal. A review of sales figures for these lines in the *Monthly Trade Journal* during the period July 2005 to January 2007 shows that we have missed out on a sizeable amount of revenue by not stocking such items. (Statistics are attached in Appendix C.)

Conclusions

While savings have been made, the existing situation is unsatisfactory and could seriously damage the company's market share if allowed to continue. Action should be taken to address managers' concerns and prevent a further decline in sales. There are three possible courses of action:

1. to continue with the central purchasing policy
2. to modify this system to address its drawbacks
3. to return to the former system of regional buying

Recommendations

1. Given that the central purchasing policy, although cost-effective, has resulted in a decline in sales, it would appear that continuing with this system without modification is not advisable.

2. Consideration should be given to allotting regional managers a small proportion of the annual budget to allow them to buy in lines with known local appeal. This could be trialled and sales could be monitored for a fixed period, following which the situation could be reviewed again if necessary.

3. A return to the previous system of regional buying would seem undesirable, given that the central purchasing policy is both efficient and cost-effective.

Summaries

The ability to summarize is essential: it demonstrates that you understand what you have read and that you can condense the information into a set of focused points. During your studies, you might be asked to write a summary of an article, a book, or part of a book for an assignment. You will also need to be able to summarize in situations such as note-taking, writing an abstract or review of an article, or minuting the points raised at a meeting.

A good summary should:

- be brief (you will usually have to keep to a stipulated number of words or pages)
- present all the significant points in a clear and well-structured way
- be written in your own words
- be written from an objective standpoint, whatever the tone of the original text (unless the assignment specifically asks you to do otherwise)
- be written in full sentences (do not use lists or bullet points unless asked to do so)

Here are some guidelines for writing a summary:

- Read the whole text quickly so as to gain an overall impression of what it is about. It is best not to try to take notes at this stage, although you will probably start to think about some of the main points that the author is making.

- Read the text again, but this time you should focus on identifying all the significant information and take notes accordingly. You can do this in several ways, depending on the size and complexity of the original. You could just highlight or underline relevant points at first, or jot them down on a separate sheet of paper. If the original text is a long one, it may be useful to break it down into more manageable sections, and write a sentence that summarizes each section.

- Write a rough draft of your summary, based on your notes. It is important to convey the main points of the text in your own words, but you should not put forward your own opinions: be objective. There is no need to count words exactly at this stage, but bear in mind that you are aiming for conciseness and clarity. You can omit examples, explanations, descriptions, asides, quotations, irrelevant details, and references.

- Edit your rough draft, deleting any superfluous material. Now is the time to focus on achieving your word limit, so look critically at everything you have written and cut all unnecessary words and phrases. Remember that it is not always desirable to give the points in the same sequence as the original text; you might need to reorganize your material in order for it to make better sense.

- Check that your spelling, grammar, and punctuation are correct, and that the summary gives the reader all the necessary information in a clear and accessible way.

Here is a 353-word article from the UK Department for Education and Skills website (<http://www.standards.dfes.gov.uk/academies/what_are_academies/?> accessed March 2006) and a suggested 86-word summary:

What are Academies?

Academies are a new type of school. They bring a distinctive approach to school leadership drawing on the skills of sponsors and other supporters. They give Principals and staff new opportunities to develop educational strategies to raise standards and contribute to diversity in areas of disadvantage.

Academies are all ability schools established by sponsors from business, faith or voluntary groups working in highly innovative partnerships with central Government and local education partners. Sponsors and the Department for Education and Skills (DfES) provide the capital costs for the Academy. Running costs are met in full by the DfES.

The Academies programme aims to challenge the culture of educational underattainment and to deliver real improvements in standards. All Academies are located in areas of disadvantage. They either replace one or more existing schools facing challenging circumstances or are established where there is a need for additional school places. The Department expects Local Authorities (LAs) to consider the scope for the establishment of Academies as part of their strategic plans to increase diversity in secondary provision and improve educational opportunities.

Each Academy will provide an excellent environment for teaching and learning that is comparable with the best available in the maintained sector. It will offer a broad and balanced curriculum to pupils of all abilities focusing especially on one or more subject areas. As the Academy becomes successfully established it will share its expertise and facilities with other schools and the wider community.

As well as providing the best opportunities for their pupils, Academies have a key part to play in the regeneration of communities. A new Academy will be a significant focus for learning for its pupils, their families and other local people. Academies will help break the cycle of underachievement in areas of social and economic deprivation whether in inner cities, suburban or rural areas.

Each Academy will offer local solutions for local needs. Each will be different, drawing on the expertise of its sponsors to help develop its own distinctive ethos and mission. Whether they involve new buildings, refurbishment, or both, Academies will be innovative in design and built to high environmental standards.

Summary

Academies are a type of school that will be established by the government in partnership with sponsors from business, religious, or voluntary groups. They will be located in socially or economically disadvantaged areas where it is necessary to raise educational standards. Each Academy will offer a broad curriculum with a focus on particular subjects appropriate to the sponsor's area of knowledge or interest. Academies will help to regenerate local communities by sharing their facilities and teaching expertise with other schools and the area as a whole.

Reviews

Broadly speaking, a review is a short critical appraisal of something, such as a book, film, play, or restaurant, which is written for a particular audience and published in a newspaper or magazine. In academic contexts, you may be asked to review a book, play, film, or TV programme as an assignment for English or Media Studies. On other courses, you may be required to write a review of a journal article or scholarly book to demonstrate that you understand the points that the author is making and that you can adopt a critical approach to what you read.

Here are some factors that you should consider when writing a critical academic review of an article or book:

- You will typically be expected to sum up the main themes or arguments in your own words and to provide a brief critical commentary on them.

- Ensure you are clear as to what is expected of you before you begin: you can also find examples of reviews in academic journals for your subject which may be helpful to use as a guide.

- The review should be concise and to the point; the skills that you develop in writing summaries will be useful here.

- Although you are making a personal assessment of the article or book, you should adopt an objective approach, as you would in a coursework essay.

- Unlike a coursework essay, it is not usually necessary to develop your own arguments.

- You should use standard English vocabulary, with technical terminology as appropriate (see the section on **Register** on page 25).

▶ PLAGIARISM

Plagiarism is the taking of another person's work or ideas and passing them off as your own. Most educational institutions have their own regulations and policies regarding plagiarism, so it is important to familiarize yourself with these or discuss the issue with your tutor before you embark on any academic writing. Penalties for using someone else's work without acknowledgement may range from being downgraded in a piece of coursework to being dismissed from your course of study in the most serious cases.

Whatever the regulations at your college or university, it is vital to have a clear understanding as to what plagiarism is and how to avoid it. There are two ways in which plagiarism may arise:

Deliberate copying

This can be regarded as 'stealing' an author's intellectual property. The creator of an original text holds the legal copyright to that work: it belongs to them. If you intentionally incorporate sentences or longer passages from published texts in your essays without acknowledging the source or try to pass off authors' arguments as your own, you are likely to be punished and even dismissed from your course. If you do this in a published article, then you could be sued for infringement of copyright.

The temptation to deliberately copy another person's work or ideas in this way may be increased when using the Internet, which provides access to huge amounts of information that are easy to cut and paste into your own work. However, just because the material is in an electronic form rather than a printed one does not mean that you can copy it without giving the source (see the **References and bibliography** section on page 49 for details about citing online sources). Additionally, there are many websites selling whole essays and dissertations for students to download and pretend that they have written themselves. However, it is not difficult for tutors to spot such plagiarism, either by

Internet searches for key phrases used in the essays, or by using dedicated plagiarism-recognition software. Tutors will also be familiar with your individual style of writing: passages or whole assignments written in another person's style will be immediately obvious to them. Furthermore, copying in this way will be to the detriment of your education, as such shortcuts will not actually help you to understand your subject or to do well in exams.

Unintentional oversights in crediting sources

This is far more common than deliberate copying and can be more difficult to avoid, because it is an integral part of academic study and writing to assess the current literature on the subject and make informed judgements about it. Essays and other assignments involve reading and assimilating a range of other people's ideas and using them as a basis to develop your own opinions and arguments. It is often the case that students simply forget to note where ideas originated or fail to realize that their ideas are not original ones. It is also difficult to know what counts in any subject as 'common knowledge' that need not be referenced.

The safest way to avoid accusations of this type of unintentional plagiarism is to reference your work thoroughly. It is essential to realise that this means not only referencing direct quotations from a text, but also when you reword (paraphrase) what an author has written: you are still using their ideas and you must acknowledge this fact.

Methodical referencing can only be achieved by paying attention to your sources from the outset. This means that when reading and making notes, whether from texts or websites, you must record the title, author, date, edition, etc. of each text (see the **References and bibliography** section on page 49). Be accurate: if using the author's actual words in your assignment, then write the quotation down exactly as it appears in the original text, with the correct page number. If you are rewording or summarizing an author's argument or idea, make sure that you record its origin in the same way: you could leave yourself a reminder or highlight the item to make sure that you reference it when writing your assignment.

Careful note-taking should ensure that when writing your coursework you have a clear record of which ideas and quotes can be attributed to particular authors. If you are unsure, always go back to the text and check. Tutors are familiar with the main authors in their subject and will find it easy to identify uncredited ideas and arguments.

Finally, some colleges and universities are now recommending that students keep their reading notes and essay drafts to demonstrate that their coursework has not been copied wholesale from elsewhere: this is another reason for keeping careful records of what you read.

2.2 Career

This section gives advice on how to write effective CVs/résumés and job application letters. When applying for a job, your chances of success will be greatly improved if you are able to write a good CV/résumé that contains your personal information in a concise, focused, and structured way, accompanied by a well-written and relevant letter of application.

Additional examples of CVs/résumés and application letters can be found on the Online Resource Centre (www.oup.com/uk/dictionaries/coed.fs). It is also important that you ask for advice from your careers adviser, who should have a range of sample CVs/résumés and who will be able to help you with writing specific applications.

▶ WRITING CVS/RÉSUMÉS

A CV (curriculum vitae), also called a résumé, is a brief, structured account that presents your education, previous employment, and qualifications to a potential employer. Employers may receive hundreds of applications for every job, so it is vital to make sure that your CV/résumé presents your personal information in the most advantageous way.

As a student, you may either be embarking on your career and not have been in full-time permanent employment before college or university, or you may have worked for several years and be intending to return to full-time employment after your studies. It is best to tailor the structure of your CV/résumé to each situation, as employers will expect students who have not worked before to focus on their education and qualifications rather than their experience.

This section provides advice on writing a CV/résumé for a person starting out on a career. If you come to college or university directly from school, sixth-form college, or after a gap year, you are likely to be applying for your first full-time permanent job when your course ends. You should therefore focus on your education and qualifications to date and then any work experience, part-time or temporary jobs, and other skills.

Preparation

Firstly, make sure you have all the relevant information to hand, such as the dates when you gained your qualifications, and the beginning and end dates for any jobs. It is also vital to approach people who could act as your referees and confirm that they are happy to provide a reference for you.

You should also read the advert carefully to familiarize yourself with the specific requirements of the job that you are applying for. While many people know that they should tailor their application letter to a particular post, they are not always aware that it creates a good impression with employers if applicants can focus on relevant aspects of their experience or qualifications in the CV/résumé as well.

Structure

An effective CV/résumé should be clear and well structured, with a limited number of main sections that will enable an employer to quickly pinpoint the information they are seeking. Always start with your **personal details:**

- name
- address (home and college address if different)
- telephone number (home/mobile/college if applicable)
- email address
- personal profile

It is not necessary to include your date of birth, your marital status, or your nationality unless the job advert has specifically asked you to do so.

Nowadays, it is usual to include a brief summary outlining who you are and why you are a worthwhile employment prospect (often called a *personal profile*): it offers a good opportunity to tailor your CV/résumé at the outset to correspond with the requirements of a particular job.

As this is your first job, you should now include a section listing your education and qualifications, with any employment experience given in a separate section after that.

- **Education and qualifications:** if you are currently studying for a qualification in higher education, start with this, making it clear that your studies are ongoing and when the course is due to end. If you have completed any other further or higher education, this should then be given next, followed by your secondary school education.

  State your school or schools and the dates you attended them. List your A-level subjects and grades first. Unless the employer has specifically asked for them or the subjects are relevant to the job in question, it is not usually necessary to give full details of all your GCSEs or equivalent qualifications: the number and the grades achieved should be sufficient.

- **Employment history:** if you have worked in several temporary or part-time jobs, you can list the most important of these in chronological order, beginning with the most recent. Give a very brief summary of your role and responsibilities, focusing on those most relevant to the post for which you are applying. It is not necessary to go into great detail about all your jobs: if you have worked in a variety of short-term jobs with no relevance to your current application, it is acceptable to summarize these as, for example, 'various temporary retail posts'.

Avoid leaving gaps in your employment history as this can give a negative impression. It is better to add a sentence explaining any periods that are unaccounted for, such as a gap year. You can even use this to your advantage, by highlighting relevant aspects of your experiences.

- **Any other skills, achievements, or training:** if you have undertaken any relevant courses or training you can list these now. These might include IT qualifications or proficiency in a foreign language. You might also want to give details of any achievements or to mention positions of responsibility at college.

Although this is not obligatory, most people include a section on their **interests or pastimes**. The final part of the CV/résumé should always be the names, titles, and addresses of **referees**.

- **Interests or pastimes:** a brief overview of your interests or hobbies will help to give your potential employer an insight into the type of person you are.

- **Referees:** you can either supply the names of two people who would be willing to give a reference for you or state that references are available on request. If you are providing specific names and this is your first job, you could use a tutor, teacher, or anyone (apart from your family) who knows you well enough to vouch for your character.

There is an example of a CV/résumé for a student starting out on her career on the next page. She is applying for a job as a Business Analyst with an international company (her covering letter of application is on page 72).

Sara Anne Green

Address (college):	26 Windmill Road Bristol, BS2 6DP Telephone (mobile): 0778 6050912
Address (home):	47 Gerrard Street Manchester, M20 4LZ Telephone: 0121 423170
Email:	sara.green@amail.com

A well-organized and outgoing Business Economics student graduating in June 2007 with good communication and analytical skills, looking to develop a career as an economist within an international business environment. Fluent Spanish speaker experienced in the use of spreadsheets, databases, and similar business software.

Education and qualifications:

September 2004 to present:	BA (Hons) in Business Economics City University, Bristol (graduating in June 2007)
September 1996–June 2003	Manchester School 4 A Levels: Economics (A), Information and Communication Technology (A), English (A), Spanish (B) 9 GCSEs (including A* grades in Economics, Spanish, English, Mathematics, ICT, and German)

Employment history:

July–September 2006	Administrative Assistant MKL Smith & Co (Accountants), Manchester Duties included: • using spreadsheets to sort and chart financial information • administering client database • assisting PA with routine admin tasks
July–September 2005	English Language Teaching Assistant EFL International, Seville, Spain Duties included: • assisting teachers in preparing lessons • administering student database • liaising with local companies to organize student activities
July 2003–August 2004	Various jobs (including voluntary and hotel work) and travel in Spain and Latin America, gaining a valuable insight into the culture and spoken language of those countries.

Other qualifications and skills:	Advanced Certificate in MS Word, MS Excel, and MS Access (evening course, September–July 2006) Full driving licence
Interests:	Netball, travel, swimming
References:	Dr Thomas Clark Senior Lecturer in Business and Management Department of Business Organization and Strategy City University Bristol BS1 2ER Ms Susan Hunter Senior Partner MKL Smith & Co (Accountants) 231 Parker Street Manchester M20 6QR

General guidelines for successful CVs/résumés

- **Length:** try to keep your CV/résumé as brief as possible (one to two sides of A4 paper), although the length will depend on how old you are and your career to date. Remember that a CV/résumé should provide a clear and concise overview that avoids excessive detail.

- **Style:** keep to brief, informative sentences, short paragraphs, and standard English. When describing your duties, it creates more impact if you begin with an action verb, as in the example CVs/résumés above.

- **Layout:** today, most people use a word processor to write a CV/résumé. Do not use many different typefaces: keep to one or two that are clear and easy to read. It is acceptable to use bold type or bullet points to highlight key points. Do not try to brighten your CV up with inappropriate colour, photos, or graphics.

- **Sequence:** make sure you have followed the most straightforward and logical sequence for your individual situation, as outlined above.

- **Checking:** after you have completed your CV/résumé, read it very carefully, paying particular attention to spelling, grammar, and punctuation. Many employers routinely discard job applications that contain such errors.

- **Updating:** keep your CV/résumé on file so that it can be updated as necessary. When applying for a job, review your CV/résumé to see how you can tailor it to match the needs of the advertised post.

▶ JOB APPLICATION LETTERS AND EMAILS

When applying for a job it is usual to include a covering letter or email with your CV/résumé. This gives you an opportunity to say why you want the job and it also forms a prospective employer's first impression of you, so it is vital to get it right.

This section provides a set of general guidelines on writing a well-structured covering letter or email, both for applying for a specific job and for a speculative approach to an organization. It is also worthwhile checking with a careers adviser before you begin, as different organizations or sectors of the jobs market may require slightly different approaches.

Applying for a specific job

Preparation

Before starting your covering letter:

- **Read the advert closely:** if you study the requirements you will then be able to tailor your application, so you can take in the relevant information and omit details of skills not specifically asked for. Also make sure that you include any information requested by the advert, for example when you would be able to begin work.

- **Think about why you want the job:** this will focus your mind so you can outline your reason for applying in a concise and coherent way.

- **Find out what you can about the organization:** check any website that the organization may have or search for information in the national or local press. If you can show in your letter that you have knowledge of the organization it shows prospective employers that you are interested in them.

Composing the letter

You are aiming for a logical, polite, and concise letter written in well-formed standard English. Here are the main guidelines that you should bear in mind:

Style and content

- **Keep it brief:** you do not need to give a full record of your life to date (your CV/résumé does that). What you are aiming for is a clear explanation of your suitability for the post.

- **Keep it coherent:** make sure your letter follows a logical sequence (see below for advice on ordering the information).

- **Keep it relevant:** check that you are not including details which are irrelevant or superfluous. If it is not relevant, leave it out.

- **Avoid inappropriate language:** your letter should be in standard English (see the section on Register on page 25) and you should avoid the use of slang or the inclusion of technical jargon and obscure abbreviations (unless you explain them).

- **Check that your grammar and spelling are correct:** read the letter very carefully once you have drafted it and do not rely on your computer's spellchecker. Nothing will put off a prospective employer more than a letter full of careless spelling or grammatical errors.

Structure

The usual order of a job application letter is as follows:

- heading/position applied for
- current situation
- reasons for wanting advertised job
- closing statement/signature

Heading or first paragraph

Unless you are writing a letter for a speculative application, give the title of the job you are applying for as a heading, or refer to it in the first paragraph of the letter. Human Resource departments of large companies often deal with many different posts at the same time, so stating the job at the outset will ensure that your letter is passed directly to the correct person. It is also a good idea to include the source of the job advert: this may be a newspaper, periodical, or website, or you may have heard of the post through someone you know in the company (if so, mention their name and position).

Current situation

Next, state your current situation. If you are still studying make this clear, and give the date that your course ends. If you are working, describe your job and the company that you work for. There is no need to go into too much detail: just give a brief outline of what your job entails. Whether you are studying or working you should pick up on the job requirements outlined in the advert and focus on any of your course elements, skills, or experience that correspond to those requested. For example, if the advert states that leadership skills are desirable, then you could mention that you are the captain of a student sports team.

Reasons for wanting advertised job

You can now lead into why you want this job. Your reasons should appear positive, for example you feel that you have always been interested in pursuing a career that develops your particular skills or that you wish to use your studies to bring about a change of career direction. It is also important to say what you feel you would be able to bring to the job or company.

Closing statement/signature

End the letter with a short closing paragraph: you could say when you are available for work or suggest that the company keep your CV/résumé on file if they decide that you are not suitable for the current job. Remember to sign your letter (people often forget to do this). However, always include your typed name underneath.

When you have finished writing your letter, read it a couple of times, firstly for logical order and relevance of the information, and secondly for grammar and spelling. You could also show it to a careers adviser, along with your CV/résumé.

Layout

Set out your information in a clear and attractive way. You can write your letter in traditional paragraphs or if you prefer you could use bullet points. Nowadays nearly all letters are word-processed; use clear and conventional typefaces, picking out the heading in bold.

Occasionally an advert may request a handwritten letter; if this is the case you must ensure that your writing is neat and, above all, legible.

Here is an example of a covering letter for the CV/résumé shown on page 68:

26 Windmill Road
Bristol
BS2 6DP

2 May 2007

Ms Kate Roberts
Human Resources Manager
Business Solutions International
Ambassador House
Marcham Way
LONDON
WC2 9TP

Dear Ms Roberts

Vacancy for Business Analyst

I am writing in reply to your advert for the above post, which appeared in *The Guardian* on Tuesday 30 April 2007, and I enclose my CV in application.

I am currently in the final year of a BA (Hons) course in Business Economics at City University, Bristol, and will graduate next month. I have always wanted to pursue a career as an economist within an international environment and have been able to tailor my studies to that end. I have obtained A grades in the Economic Data Analysis, International Economics, and Economics of Business Strategy modules, and am currently completing a dissertation on the growth of e-commerce in the European Union. I am fluent in spoken and written Spanish, having built on my A-level proficiency in that subject when working in Spain and Mexico.

In addition to the qualifications and abilities outlined above, I have kept my IT skills fully up to date (including MS Excel and Access) and am competent in a wide range of business data analysis operations. The post also requires someone with good communications skills who is able to negotiate with corporate clients: I enjoy making new contacts and establishing relationships with a wide range of people, and have successfully liaised with Spanish companies when arranging student activities while working in Seville.

I feel that the position offered would be ideal in giving me the opportunity to use my education and skills to provide a high level of service for the international client profile you describe. I look forward to hearing from you.

Yours sincerely

Sara Green

Speculative job applications

If you know that you want to work for a particular company but you have not seen an advert for a suitable vacancy, then you can submit a speculative job application. This will consist of your CV/résumé, tailored appropriately to the type of job you are interested in, together with a covering letter of application.

Preparation

When approaching a prospective employer with a speculative application, it is vital first to build up a thorough background knowledge of the company and the types of career opportunities it can offer. You can do this by a number of means:

- watching out for job adverts that the company publishes in the local, national, or trade press
- visiting its website
- searching for articles about the company or its sector of the industry in the press or on the Internet
- talking to people who already work there (your careers adviser may well be able to put you in touch with former students who have joined a particular organization)

Once you have done this, you should also find out the name of the correct person or department to send your application to: you could find this out by phoning the company or consulting its website. This will ensure that your letter or email does not get mislaid or passed over.

Composing the application letter/email

Read through the advice given in **Composing the letter** on page 70: all these points also apply for a speculative job application letter or email. In addition, you will need to:

- state at the outset who you are and what type of job you are interested in
- say why you are particularly interested in working for the organization
- outline what you can offer, focusing on specific skills, qualifications, or personal qualities

You could then finish your letter by stating when you would be available for work or for interview, or, in the event of no suitable vacancies being currently available, by asking the company to keep your details on file should any arise in the future. If you are applying by letter, you could enclose a stamped, self-addressed envelope to increase your chances of a response.

Further action

If you are making a number of speculative applications to different organizations, make sure that you keep a copy of each letter/email and CV/résumé. You should also keep a list of companies whom you have contacted, together with a note of when you contacted them and what the outcome of your approach was, if any. If you are offered a job, it is polite to inform any other employers that you contacted that you are no longer available for work.

Here is an example of a speculative letter of application:

478 Barton Avenue
Coventry
CV6 2LK

12 September 2007

Mr T R Fowler
Head of Graduate Recruitment
Human Resources Department
The Library of Political Science
LONDON
WC1 4HY

Dear Mr Fowler

Vacancies for Librarians

I am writing to enquire if you have any vacancies for librarians at graduate entry level and enclose my CV in application.

As you will see from my CV, I have just completed an MA in Library and Information Studies at City University, London, and I also hold a BA (Hons) in Politics from Oxford Brookes University. I am now keen to combine my knowledge of Politics with a career in librarianship: your organization has a high reputation as one of the world's leading specialist subject libraries and I believe that I could make a real contribution to managing its collections and promoting their use.

My MA, which is recognized by the Chartered Institute of Library and Information Professionals, has equipped me with an in-depth knowledge of modern information services and I would welcome the opportunity to be involved in the management and development of your collections of e-journals and other electronic publications. I am conscientious, hardworking, and a good communicator and am particularly interested in enhancing my skills as a librarian in an institution which encourages very high standards of personal development.

I would be happy to attend for interview at your convenience and would be able to start work from early October onwards. If you do not have any suitable openings at present, I would be grateful if you would keep my CV on file should any future vacancies arise.

Yours sincerely

Jenny Harrison

LL

L¹ (also **l**) noun (pl. **Ls** or **L's**) **1** the twelfth letter of the alphabet. **2** the Roman numeral for 50. [first a symbol similar in form to the letter *L*.]

L² abbreviation **1** (**L.**) Lake, Loch, or Lough. **2** large (as a clothes size). **3** Brit. learner driver. **4** (in tables of sports results) lost.

l abbreviation **1** left. **2** (in horse racing) length(s). **3** (**l.**) line. **4** litre(s). **5** (**l.**) old use pound(s). •symbol (in mathematical formulae) length.

£ abbreviation pound(s).
– ORIGIN the initial letter of Latin *libra* 'pound, balance'.

LA abbreviation **1** Los Angeles. **2** Louisiana.

La symbol the chemical element lanthanum.

la noun Music variant spelling of LAH.

laager /lah-guh/ noun S. African historical an encampment formed by a circle of wagons.
– ORIGIN South African Dutch.

lab noun informal a laboratory.

label noun **1** a small piece of paper, fabric, etc. attached to an object and giving information about it. **2** the name or trademark of a fashion company. **3** a company that produces recorded music. **4** a classifying name given to a person or thing: *young women who dislike the feminist label.* •verb (**labels, labelling, labelled**; US **labels, labeling, labeled**) **1** attach a label to something. **2** place someone or something in a category: *he was labelled as an anarchist.*
– ORIGIN Old French, 'ribbon'.

labia /lay-bi-uh/ plural noun (sing. **labium** /lay-bi-uhm/) the inner and outer folds of the vulva (the female external genitals).
– ORIGIN Latin, 'lips'.

labial /lay-bi-uhl/ adjective **1** chiefly Anatomy & Biology relating to the labia or lips. **2** Phonetics (of a consonant) produced with the lips partially or completely closed (e.g. *p* or *w*), or (of a vowel) produced with rounded lips (e.g. *oo*).

labiate /lay-bi-uht/ adjective relating to plants of the mint family, which have distinctive two-lobed flowers.
– ORIGIN Latin *labiatus.*

labile /lay-byl/ adjective **1** technical liable to change; easily altered. **2** Chemistry easily broken down or displaced.
– ORIGIN Latin *labilis.*

labium noun singular of LABIA.

labor etc. noun US spelling of LABOUR etc.

laboratory noun (pl. **laboratories**) a room or building for scientific experiments, research, or teaching, or for the manufacture of drugs or chemicals.

– ORIGIN Latin *laboratorium.*

laborious /luh-bor-i-uhss/ adjective **1** requiring considerable time and effort. **2** showing obvious signs of effort: *a slow, laborious speech.*
– DERIVATIVES **laboriously** adverb.

labour (US **labor**) noun **1** work, especially hard physical work. **2** workers as a group. **3** (**Labour**) the Labour Party. **4** the process of childbirth. •verb **1** work hard. **2** work at an unskilled manual job. **3** try hard to do something in the face of difficulty: *biologists have laboured for years to develop hardier crops.* **4** move with difficulty. **5** (**labour under**) believe something that is not true: *you've been labouring under a misapprehension.*
– PHRASES **a labour of love** a task done for pleasure, not reward. **labour the point** repeat or emphasize something that has already been said and understood.
– ORIGIN Latin *labor* 'toil, trouble'.

labour camp noun a prison camp in which punishment takes the form of heavy manual work.

Labour Day noun a public holiday held in honour of working people in some countries on 1 May, or (in the US and Canada) on the first Monday in September.

laboured (US **labored**) adjective **1** done with great difficulty: *laboured breathing.* **2** not natural or spontaneous: *a rather laboured joke.*

labourer (US **laborer**) noun a person doing unskilled manual work.

labour exchange noun former term for JOBCENTRE.

labour force noun the members of a population who are able to work.

labour-intensive adjective needing a large workforce or a large amount of work in relation to what is produced.

Labourite (US **Laborite**) noun a member or supporter of the Labour Party.

Labour Party noun a British left-of-centre political party formed to represent the interests of ordinary working people.

labour-saving adjective designed to reduce the amount of work needed to carry out a task.

labour union noun N. Amer. a trade union.

Labrador /lab-ruh-dor/ (also **Labrador retriever**) noun a breed of retriever with a black or yellow coat, used also as a guide dog.
– ORIGIN named after the *Labrador* Peninsula of eastern Canada.

laburnum /luh-ber-nuhm/ noun a small hardwood tree with hanging clusters of yellow flowers followed by pods of poisonous seeds.
– ORIGIN Latin.

labyrinth /lab-i-rinth/ noun 1 a complicated irregular network of passages or paths. 2 an intricate and confusing arrangement: *the labyrinth of immigration laws.* 3 a complex bony structure in the inner ear which contains the organs of hearing and balance.
– DERIVATIVES **labyrinthine** /lab-i-rin-thyn/ adjective.
– ORIGIN Greek *laburinthos*, referring to the maze built to house the Minotaur in Greek mythology.

lac noun a resinous substance produced by an Asian insect (the **lac insect**), used to make varnish, shellac, etc.
– ORIGIN Hindi or Persian.

lace noun 1 a delicate open fabric of cotton or silk made by looping, twisting, or knitting thread in patterns. 2 a cord or leather strip used to fasten a shoe or garment. • verb 1 fasten a shoe or garment with a lace or laces. 2 twist or tangle things together. 3 add an ingredient, especially alcohol, to a drink or dish to improve the flavour or to make it stronger: *coffee laced with brandy.*
– ORIGIN Old French *laz.*

lacerate /lass-uh-rayt/ verb tear or cut the flesh or skin.
– DERIVATIVES **laceration** noun.
– ORIGIN Latin *lacerare.*

lacewing noun a delicate insect with large, clear membranous wings.

lachrymal /lak-ri-muhl/ (also **lacrimal**) adjective 1 formal or literary connected with weeping or tears. 2 Physiology & Anatomy concerned with the production of tears.
– ORIGIN from Latin *lacrima* 'tear'.

lachrymose /lak-ri-mohss/ adjective formal or literary 1 tending to cry easily; tearful. 2 causing tears; sad.

lacing noun 1 a laced fastening of a shoe or garment. 2 a dash of spirits added to a drink.

lack noun the state of being without or not having enough of something: *the lack of funds available for research.* • verb (also **lack for**) be without or or without enough of: *he lacked imagination.*
– ORIGIN perhaps partly from German *lak*, Dutch *laken.*

lackadaisical /lak-uh-day-zi-k'l/ adjective lacking enthusiasm and thoroughness.
– DERIVATIVES **lackadaisically** adverb.
– ORIGIN from the former exclamation *lackaday*, expressing surprise or grief.

lackey noun (pl. **lackeys**) 1 a servant. 2 a person who is too willing to serve or obey others.
– ORIGIN French *laquais.*

lacking adjective missing or not having enough of something: *she was shy and lacking in confidence.*

lacklustre (US **lackluster**) adjective 1 lacking energy or inspiration: *a lacklustre performance.* 2 (of the hair or eyes) not shining.

laconic /luh-kon-ik/ adjective using very few words: *his laconic reply suggested a lack of interest in the subject.*

– DERIVATIVES **laconically** adverb.
– ORIGIN Greek *Lakōnikos* 'Spartan', the inhabitants of Sparta being known for their terse speech.

lacquer /lak-ker/ noun 1 a varnish made of shellac or of synthetic substances. 2 the sap of an East Asian tree (the **lacquer tree**) used as a varnish. 3 a chemical substance sprayed on hair to keep it in place.
– DERIVATIVES **lacquered** adjective.
– ORIGIN from Hindi or Persian (see **LAC**).

lacrimal adjective variant spelling of **LACHRYMAL**.

lacrosse /luh-kross/ noun a team game in which a ball is thrown, carried, and caught with a long-handled stick which has a net at one end.
– ORIGIN from French (*le jeu de*) *la crosse* '(the game of) the hooked stick'.

lacrymal adjective variant spelling of **LACHRYMAL**.

lactate[1] /lak-tayt/ verb (of a female mammal) produce milk.
– ORIGIN Latin *lactare* 'suckle'.

lactate[2] /lak-tayt/ noun Chemistry a salt or ester of lactic acid.

lactation noun 1 the producing of milk by the mammary glands. 2 the process of suckling a baby or young animal.

lactic /lak-tik/ adjective relating to or obtained from milk.
– ORIGIN Latin *lac* 'milk'.

lactic acid noun an organic acid present in sour milk and produced in the muscles during strenuous exercise.

lactose /lak-tohz/ noun Chemistry a compound sugar present in milk.

lacto-vegetarian noun a person who eats only dairy products and vegetables.

lacuna /luh-kyoo-nuh/ noun (pl. **lacunae** /luh-kyoo-nee/ or **lacunas**) a gap or missing portion: *there are a few lacunae in the historical record.*
– ORIGIN Latin, 'pool'.

lacustrine /luh-kuss-tryn, luh-kuss-trin/ adjective technical or literary relating to lakes.
– ORIGIN from Latin *lacus* 'lake'.

lacy adjective (**lacier**, **laciest**) made of, resembling, or trimmed with lace.

lad noun informal 1 a boy or young man. 2 (**lads**) Brit. a group of men sharing leisure or working interests. 3 Brit. a boisterously macho or high-spirited man.
– DERIVATIVES **laddish** adjective.
– ORIGIN unknown.

ladder noun 1 a structure consisting of a series of bars or steps between two uprights, used for climbing up or down. 2 a series of stages by which progress can be made: *the career ladder.* 3 Brit. a vertical strip of unravelled fabric in tights or stockings. • verb Brit. develop or cause to develop a ladder in tights or stockings.
– ORIGIN Old English.

ladder-back noun an upright chair with a back resembling a ladder.

laddie noun informal, chiefly Scottish a boy or young man.

lade /layd/ verb (past part. **laden**) old use put cargo

on board a ship.
– ORIGIN Old English.

laden adjective loaded or weighed down.

ladette noun Brit. informal a young woman who behaves boisterously or crudely and engages in heavy drinking sessions.
– ORIGIN from **LAD** + **-ETTE**

la-di-da (also **lah-di-dah**) adjective informal pretentious or snobbish.
– ORIGIN imitating an affected way of speaking.

ladies plural of **LADY**.

ladies' fingers plural noun Brit. another term for **OKRA**.

ladies' man (also **lady's man**) noun informal a man who enjoys spending time and flirting with women.

ladies' room noun N. Amer. a women's toilet in a public building.

Ladino /luh-**dee**-noh/ noun (pl. **Ladinos**) 1 the language of some Sephardic Jews, based on medieval Spanish. 2 (in Latin America) a person of mixed race or a Spanish-speaking white person.
– ORIGIN Spanish.

ladle noun a large long-handled spoon with a cup-shaped bowl, for serving soup, stew, or a sauce. •verb 1 serve or transfer soup or sauce with a ladle. 2 (**ladle something out**) distribute something in large amounts.
– DERIVATIVES **ladleful** noun.
– ORIGIN Old English.

lady noun (pl. **ladies**) 1 (in polite or formal use) a woman. 2 a woman of high social position. 3 (**Lady**) (in the UK) a title used by peeresses, female relatives of peers, the wives and widows of knights, etc. 4 a polite and well-educated woman. 5 (**the Ladies**) Brit. a women's public toilet.
– PHRASES **My Lady** a polite form of address to female judges and certain noblewomen.
– ORIGIN Old English, from words meaning 'loaf' and 'knead'; compare with **LORD**.

ladybird noun a small beetle having a red or yellow back with black spots.

ladybug noun N. Amer. a ladybird.

Lady chapel noun a chapel dedicated to the Virgin Mary in a church or cathedral.

Lady Day noun the Christian feast of the Annunciation, 25 March.

lady-in-waiting noun (pl. **ladies-in-waiting**) a woman who attends a queen or princess.

ladykiller noun informal a charming man who habitually seduces women.

ladylike adjective appropriate for or typical of a well-mannered woman or girl.

lady of the night noun euphemistic a prostitute.

Ladyship noun (**Her/Your Ladyship**) a respectful way of referring to or addressing a Lady.

lady's maid noun chiefly historical a maid who attended to the personal needs of her mistress.

lady's man noun variant spelling of **LADIES' MAN**.

lady's mantle noun a plant with greenish flowers, formerly used in herbal medicine.

lady's slipper noun an orchid whose flower has a pouch- or slipper-shaped lip.

lag¹ verb (**lags, lagging, lagged**) move or develop more slowly than another or others: *the country was lagging behind its European competitors.* •noun (also **time lag**) a period of time between two events; a delay.
– ORIGIN perhaps Scandinavian.

lag² verb (**lags, lagging lagged**) cover a water tank, pipes, etc. with material designed to prevent heat loss.
– ORIGIN from earlier *lag* 'piece of insulating cover'.

lag³ noun Brit. informal a person who has frequently been convicted and sent to prison.
– ORIGIN unknown.

lager noun a light effervescent beer.
– ORIGIN from German *Lagerbier* 'beer brewed for keeping'.

lager lout noun Brit. informal a young man who behaves offensively as a result of drinking too much alcohol.

laggard /**lag**-gerd/ noun a person who falls behind others. •adjective slower than desired or expected.
– ORIGIN from **LAG¹**.

lagging noun material providing heat insulation for a water tank, pipes, etc.

lagoon noun 1 a stretch of salt water separated from the sea by a low sandbank or coral reef. 2 N. Amer. & Austral./NZ a small freshwater lake near a larger lake or river.
– ORIGIN Italian and Spanish *laguna*.

lah (also **la**) noun Music the sixth note of a major scale, coming after 'soh' and before 'te'.
– ORIGIN the first syllable of *labii*, a word taken from a Latin hymn.

lah-di-dah noun variant spelling of **LA-DI-DA**.

laicize (or **laicise**) /**lay**-i-syz/ verb formal withdraw clerical or ecclesiastical character or status from someone or something.
– DERIVATIVES **laicism** noun **laicization** noun.
– ORIGIN Latin *laicus*.

laid past and past participle of **LAY¹**.

laid-back adjective informal relaxed and easy-going.

lain past participle of **LIE¹**.

lair noun 1 a wild animal's resting place. 2 a person's hiding place or den.
– ORIGIN Old English.

laird /*rhymes with* scared/ noun (in Scotland) a person who owns a large estate.
– ORIGIN Scots form of **LORD**.

lairy adjective (**lairier, lairiest**) Brit. informal aggressive or rowdy.
– ORIGIN alteration of **LEERY**.

laissez-faire /less-ay-**fair**/ noun a policy of allowing things to take their course without interfering, especially non-intervention by governments in the workings of the free market.
– ORIGIN French, 'allow to do'.

laity /**lay**-i-ti/ noun (**the laity**) people who are not members of the clergy.
– ORIGIN from **LAY²**.

lake¹ noun 1 a large area of water surrounded by land. 2 (**the Lakes**) the Lake District.
– DERIVATIVES **lakeside** noun.
– ORIGIN Latin *lacus* 'pool, lake'.

lake² noun a purplish-red pigment, originally made with lac.
– ORIGIN variant of **LAC**.

Lake District noun a region of lakes and mountains in Cumbria.

lakh /lak, lahk/ noun Indian a hundred thousand.
– ORIGIN Sanskrit.

lam¹ verb (**lams, lamming, lammed**) (often **lam into**) informal hit someone or something hard or repeatedly.
– ORIGIN perhaps Scandinavian.

lam² noun (in phrase **on the lam**) N. Amer. informal in the process of running away or escaping.
– ORIGIN from **LAM¹**.

lama /lah-muh/ noun 1 a title given to a spiritual leader in Tibetan Buddhism as a mark of respect. 2 a Tibetan or Mongolian Buddhist monk.
– ORIGIN Tibetan, 'superior one'.

Lamarckism /la-**mark**-i-z'm/ noun the theory of evolution devised by the French naturalist Jean Baptiste de Lamarck (1744–1829), based on the proposition that characteristics acquired by an animal or plant in order to survive can be passed on to its offspring.
– DERIVATIVES **Lamarckian** noun & adjective.

lamasery /lah-muh-suh-ri, luh-**mah**-suh-ri/ noun (pl. **lamaseries**) a monastery of lamas.

lamb noun 1 a young sheep. 2 a mild-mannered, gentle, or innocent person. • verb 1 (of a ewe) give birth to lambs. 2 tend ewes during the period when lambs are born.
– PHRASES **the Lamb of God** a title of Jesus.
– DERIVATIVES **lambing** noun.
– ORIGIN Old English.

lambada /lam-**bah**-duh/ noun a fast Brazilian dance which couples perform in close physical contact.
– ORIGIN Portuguese, 'a beating'.

lambaste /lam-**baysst**/ (also **lambast** /lam-**bast**/) verb criticize someone or something harshly.
– ORIGIN from **LAM¹** + dated *baste*, also meaning 'beat'.

lambent /lam-buhnt/ adjective literary glowing or flickering with a soft radiance.
– ORIGIN Latin *lambere* 'to lick'.

Lambrusco /lam-**bruuss**-koh/ noun a sparkling red or white wine made from grapes grown in the Emilia-Romagna region of northern Italy.
– ORIGIN Italian, 'grape of the wild vine'.

lamb's lettuce noun a small plant with soft roundish leaves that are eaten in salads.

lamb's-tails plural noun Brit. catkins from the hazel tree.

lambswool noun soft, fine wool from lambs, used to make knitted garments.

lame adjective 1 walking with difficulty as the result of an injury or illness affecting the leg or foot. 2 (of an explanation or excuse) unconvincingly feeble. 3 dull and uninspiring: *a lame, predictable storyline.* • verb make a person or animal lame.
– DERIVATIVES **lamely** adverb **lameness** noun.
– ORIGIN Old English.

lamé /lah-may/ noun fabric with interwoven gold or silver threads.
– ORIGIN French.

lamebrain adjective informal a stupid person.

lame duck noun 1 an ineffectual or unsuccessful person or thing. 2 chiefly N. Amer. a President or administration in the final period

of office, after a successor has been elected.

lamella /luh-**mel**-luh/ noun (pl. **lamellae** /luh-**mel**-lee/) technical a thin layer, membrane, or plate of tissue, especially in bone.
– DERIVATIVES **lamellar** adjective **lamellate** adjective.
– ORIGIN Latin, 'small, thin plate'.

lament /luh-**ment**/ noun 1 a passionate expression of grief. 2 a song, piece of music, or poem expressing grief or regret. • verb 1 mourn a person's death. 2 (as adj. **lamented** or **late lamented**) a conventional way of referring to a dead person. 3 express regret or disappointment about something: *he lamented the modernization of the old buildings.*
– DERIVATIVES **lamentation** noun.
– ORIGIN from Latin *lamenta* 'weeping'.

lamentable /la-muhn-tuh-b'l/ adjective 1 (of circumstances or conditions) very bad: *the industry is in a lamentable state.* 2 (of an event or attitude) regrettable: *her prejudice showed lamentable immaturity.*
– DERIVATIVES **lamentably** adverb.

lamina /lam-i-nuh/ noun (pl. **laminae** /lam-i-nee/) technical a thin layer, plate, or scale of sedimentary rock, organic tissue, or other material.
– DERIVATIVES **laminar** adjective.
– ORIGIN Latin.

laminate verb /lam-i-nayt/ 1 cover a flat surface with a layer of protective material. 2 manufacture something by sticking layers of material together. 3 split into layers or leaves. 4 beat or roll metal into thin plates. • noun /lam-i-nuht/ a laminated structure or material. • adjective /lam-i-nuht/ consisting or made of many layers of material stuck together.
– DERIVATIVES **lamination** noun

Lammas /lam-muhss/ (also **Lammas Day**) noun the first day of August, formerly observed as harvest festival.
– ORIGIN Old English, 'loaf mass'.

lammergeier /lam-mer-gy-er/ (also **lammergeyer**) noun a long-winged, long-tailed vulture, noted for dropping bones to break them and get at the marrow.
– ORIGIN German, from *Lämmer* 'lambs' + *Geier* 'vulture'.

lamp noun 1 an electric, oil, or gas device for giving light. 2 an electrical device producing ultraviolet or other radiation, especially for therapeutic purposes.
– ORIGIN Greek *lampas* 'torch'.

lampblack noun a black pigment made from soot.

lamplight noun the light cast by a lamp.
– DERIVATIVES **lamplit** adjective.

lampoon /lam-**poon**/ verb publicly ridicule or mock someone or something. • noun a speech or piece of writing which ridicules or mocks someone or something.
– ORIGIN French *lampon*.

lamp post noun a tall pole with a light at the top, used to light a street.

lamprey /lam-pri/ noun (pl. **lampreys**) an eel-like jawless fish that has a sucker mouth with horny teeth and a rasping tongue.
– ORIGIN Latin *lampreda*.

lampshade noun a cover for a lamp, used to

LAN abbreviation local area network.

Lancashire hotpot noun a stew of meat and vegetables, covered with a layer of sliced potato.

Lancastrian /lang-**kass**-tri-uhn/ noun **1** a person from Lancashire or Lancaster. **2** a follower of the House of Lancaster in the Wars of the Roses. ●adjective relating to Lancashire or Lancaster, or the House of Lancaster.

lance noun **1** a long weapon with a wooden shaft and a pointed steel head, formerly used by a horseman in charging. **2** a metal pipe supplying a jet of oxygen to a furnace or to make a very hot flame for cutting. ●verb **1** prick or cut open an abscess or boil with a lancet or other sharp instrument. **2** pierce something.
– ORIGIN Latin *lancea*.

lance corporal noun a rank of non-commissioned officer in the British army, above private and below corporal.

lancelet /**lahnss**-lit/ noun a small invertebrate marine animal.

lanceolate /**lahn**-si-uh-luht/ adjective technical having a narrow oval shape tapering to a point at each end.
– ORIGIN from Latin *lanceola* 'a small lance'.

lancer noun a soldier of a cavalry regiment armed or formerly armed with lances.

lancet /**lahn**-sit/ noun a small, broad two-edged surgical knife with a sharp point.
– ORIGIN Old French *lancette* 'small lance'.

lancet window noun a slender window with a pointed arch, especially in a medieval church.

Lancs. abbreviation Lancashire.

Land /land/ noun (pl. **Länder** /**len**-duh/) a province of Germany or Austria.
– ORIGIN German, 'land'.

land noun **1** the part of the earth's surface that is not covered by water. **2** an area of ground in terms of its ownership or use: *waste land.* **3** (**the land**) ground or soil as a basis for agriculture. **4** a country or state. ●verb **1** go ashore. **2** put someone or something on land from a boat. **3** come down to the ground, or bring an aircraft or spacecraft to the ground. **4** bring a fish to land with a net or rod. **5** informal succeed in obtaining or achieving something desirable: *she landed a contract with a major film studio.* **6** (**land up**) reach a place or destination. **7** (**land up with**) end up with an unwelcome situation. **8** (**land someone in**) informal put someone in a difficult situation: *his exploits landed him in trouble.* **9** (**land someone with**) inflict something unwelcome on someone: *the mistake landed the company with a massive bill.* **10** informal inflict a blow on someone.
– PHRASES **how the land lies** Brit. what the situation is. **the land of Nod** humorous a state of sleep. [with reference to the biblical place name *Nod*, mentioned in the Book of Genesis, chapter 4.]
– DERIVATIVES **landless** adjective.
– ORIGIN Old English.

land agent noun Brit. **1** a person employed to manage an estate on behalf of its owners. **2** a person who deals with the sale of land.

landau /**lan**-dor/ noun a four-wheeled enclosed horse-drawn carriage.
– ORIGIN named after *Landau* in Germany, where it was first made.

land bridge noun an area of land formerly connecting two land masses which are now separate.

landed adjective **1** owning much land, especially through inheritance. **2** consisting of or relating to land owned through inheritance.

Länder plural of **LAND**.

lander noun a spacecraft designed to land on the surface of a planet or moon.

landfall noun **1** an arrival at land on a sea or air journey. **2** a collapse of a mass of land.

landfill noun **1** the disposal of waste material by burying it. **2** waste material that has been buried.

landform noun a natural feature of the earth's surface.

land girl noun (in the UK) a woman doing farm work during the Second World War.

landholder noun a landowner.

landing noun **1** a level area at the top of a staircase or between flights of stairs. **2** the action of coming to land or bringing something to land. **3** a place where people and goods can be landed from a boat.

landing craft noun a boat specially designed for putting troops and military equipment ashore on a beach.

landing gear noun the undercarriage of an aircraft.

landing stage noun a platform on to which passengers or cargo can be landed from a boat.

landlady noun (pl. **landladies**) **1** a woman who rents out land or property. **2** a woman who owns or runs lodgings, a guest house, or (Brit.) a pub.

landline noun a conventional telecommunications connection by cable laid across land.

landlocked adjective almost or entirely surrounded by land: *a landlocked country.*

landlord noun **1** a man (in legal use also a woman) who rents out land or property. **2** a man who owns or runs lodgings, a guest house, or (Brit.) a pub.

landlordism noun the system whereby land or property is owned by landlords to whom tenants pay a fixed rent.

landlubber noun informal a person who is not used to the sea or sailing.

landmark noun **1** an object or feature of a landscape or settlement that is easily seen and recognized from a distance. **2** an event, discovery, or change marking an important stage or turning point: *a landmark in civil aviation technology.*

land mass noun a continent or other large body of land.

landmine noun an explosive mine laid on or just under the surface of the ground.

landowner noun a person who owns land.
– DERIVATIVES **landownership** noun **landowning** adjective & noun.

landscape noun **1** all the visible features of an area of land. **2** a picture of an area of

countryside. **3** the distinctive features of an area of intellectual activity: *the political landscape.* • **verb** improve the appearance of a piece of land by changing its contours, planting trees and shrubs, etc. • **adjective** referring to a format for printed material which is wider than it is high. Compare with **PORTRAIT**.
– DERIVATIVES **landscaper** noun **landscapist** noun.
– ORIGIN Dutch *lantscap.*

landscape architecture noun the art and practice of designing the outdoor environment, especially so as to make parks or gardens harmonize with buildings or roads.

landscape gardening noun the art and practice of laying out grounds in a way which is ornamental or which imitates natural scenery.

landside noun the area of an airport terminal to which the general public has unrestricted access.

landslide noun **1** (chiefly Brit. also **landslip**) the sliding down of a mass of earth or rock from a mountain or cliff. **2** an overwhelming majority of votes for one party in an election.

landsman noun (pl. **landsmen**) a person unfamiliar with the sea or sailing.

landward adverb (also **landwards**) towards land. • **adjective** facing towards land as opposed to sea.

lane noun **1** a narrow road, especially in a rural area. **2** a division of a road intended to separate single lines of traffic according to speed or direction. **3** each of a number of parallel strips of track or water for competitors in a race. **4** a route or course regularly followed by ships or aircraft.
– ORIGIN Old English.

langoustine /long-goo-steen/ noun a small European lobster.
– ORIGIN French.

language noun **1** the method of human communication, either spoken or written, consisting of the use of words in a structured and conventional way. **2** the system of communication used by a particular community or country. **3** a particular style of speaking or writing: *legal language.* **4** the manner or style of a piece of writing or speech. **5** a system of symbols and rules for writing computer programs.
– ORIGIN Old French *langage*, from Latin *lingua* 'tongue'.

language laboratory noun a room equipped with audio and visual equipment for learning a foreign language.

languid /lang-gwid/ adjective **1** relaxed and not inclined to exert oneself physically. **2** weak or faint from illness or tiredness.
– DERIVATIVES **languidly** adverb.

languish /lang-gwish/ verb **1** grow weak or feeble. **2** be kept in an unpleasant place or situation: *he was languishing in jail.*
– ORIGIN Old French *languir.*

languor /lang-ger/ noun tiredness or inactivity, especially when pleasurable.
– DERIVATIVES **languorous** adjective **languorously** adverb.

langur /lang-ger, lan-goor/ noun a long-tailed Asian monkey with a loud call.

– ORIGIN Sanskrit.

laniard noun variant spelling of **LANYARD**.

lank adjective **1** (of hair) long, limp, and straight. **2** lanky.
– ORIGIN Old English, 'thin'.

lanky adjective (**lankier**, **lankiest**) awkwardly thin and tall.
– DERIVATIVES **lankiness** noun.

lanolin noun a fatty substance found naturally on sheep's wool and used as a base for ointments.
– ORIGIN from Latin *lana* 'wool' + *oleum* 'oil'.

lantern noun **1** a lamp enclosed in a metal frame with glass panels. **2** the light chamber at the top of a lighthouse. **3** a square, curved, or polygonal structure on the top of a dome or a room, with glass or open sides.
– ORIGIN Latin *lanterna.*

lantern-jawed adjective having long, thin jaws.

lantern slide noun historical a photographic slide for use in a magic lantern.

lanthanide /lan-thuh-nyd/ noun any of the series of fifteen rare-earth elements from lanthanum to lutetium in the periodic table.

lanthanum /lan-thuh-nuhm/ noun a silvery-white rare-earth metallic chemical element.
– ORIGIN from Greek *lanthanein* 'escape notice' (because the element was not at first detected in cerium oxide).

lanyard /lan-yerd/ (also **laniard**) noun **1** a rope used to secure or raise and lower something such as a ship's sails. **2** a cord passed round the neck, shoulder, or wrist for holding a whistle or similar object.
– ORIGIN Old French *laniere.*

Laodicean /lay-oh-di-see-uhn/ adjective old use half-hearted or indifferent about something, especially religion or politics.
– ORIGIN referring to the early Christians of *Laodicea* in Asia Minor (Book of Revelation, chapter 3).

Laotian /low-shuhn/ noun a person from the country of Laos in SE Asia. • **adjective** relating to Laos.

lap¹ noun the flat area between the waist and knees of a seated person.
– PHRASES **in someone's lap** as someone's responsibility. **in the lap of the gods** open to chance. **in the lap of luxury** in conditions of great comfort and wealth.
– ORIGIN Old English, 'fold, flap'.

lap² noun **1** one circuit of a track or racetrack. **2** a part of a journey or other undertaking: *the last lap of their four-day tour.* **3** an overlapping or projecting part. **4** a single turn of rope, thread, or cable round a drum or reel. • **verb** (**laps**, **lapping**, **lapped**) **1** overtake a competitor in a race to become one or more laps ahead. **2** (**lap someone/thing in**) literary enfold someone or something protectively in something soft: *he was lapped in blankets.*
– ORIGIN from **LAP**¹.

lap³ verb (**laps**, **lapping**, **lapped**) **1** (of an animal) take up liquid with the tongue. **2** (**lap something up**) accept something with obvious pleasure: *she's lapping up all the attention.* **3** (of water) wash against something with a gentle rippling sound: *a sun-kissed island lapped by an*

azure sea. • **noun** the action of water lapping.
– ORIGIN Old English.

laparoscopy /la-puh-**ros**-kuh-pi/ **noun** (pl. **laparoscopies**) a surgical procedure in which a fibre-optic instrument is inserted through the wall of the abdomen to enable the internal organs to be viewed.
– DERIVATIVES **laparoscope** noun **laparoscopic** adjective.
– ORIGIN from Greek *lapara* 'flank'.

laparotomy /la-puh-**rot**-uh-mi/ **noun** (pl. **laparotomies**) a surgical incision into the abdomen, to make a diagnosis or in preparation for major surgery.

lap dancing **noun** erotic dancing in which the dancer performs a striptease near to or on the lap of a paying customer.
– DERIVATIVES **lap dance** noun **lap dancer** noun.

lapdog **noun 1** a small pampered pet dog. **2** a person who is completely under the influence of another.

lapel **noun** the part on each side of a coat or jacket immediately below the collar which is folded back against the front opening.
– ORIGIN from **LAP**¹.

lapidary /la-pi-duh-ri/ **adjective 1** relating to the engraving, cutting, or polishing of stones and gems. **2** (of language) elegant and concise. • **noun** (pl. **lapidaries**) a person who cuts, polishes, or engraves stones and gems.
– ORIGIN from Latin *lapis* 'stone'.

lapis lazuli /la-piss **laz**-yuu-li/ (also **lapis**) **noun 1** a bright blue rock used in jewellery. **2** the pigment ultramarine, originally made by crushing lapis lazuli.
– ORIGIN Latin, 'stone of lapis lazuli'.

lap joint **noun** a joint between shafts, rails, etc., made by halving the thickness of each part at the joint and fitting them together.

Laplander /**lap**-land-er/ **noun** a person from Lapland, a region in northern Europe.

lap of honour **noun** a celebratory circuit of a sports field, track, etc. by the victorious person or team.

Lapp **noun 1** a member of a people of the extreme north of Scandinavia. **2** the language of the Lapps.
– ORIGIN Swedish.

USAGE: Although the term **Lapp** is still widely used and is the most familiar term to many people, the people themselves prefer to be called **Sami**.

lappet /**lap**-pit/ **noun 1** a fold or hanging piece of flesh in some animals. **2** a loose or overlapping part of a garment.
– ORIGIN from **LAP**¹.

lapse **noun 1** a brief failure of concentration, memory, or judgement. **2** a decline from previously high standards: *his lapse into petty crime.* **3** a period of time between two events. **4** Law the termination of a right or privilege through disuse or failure to follow the appropriate procedures. • **verb 1** (of a right, privilege, or agreement) become invalid because it is not used, claimed, or renewed. **2** (usu. as adj. **lapsed**) stop following the rules and practices of a religion or doctrine: *a lapsed Catholic.* **3** (**lapse into**) pass gradually into a different, often worse state or condition: *the*

country lapsed into chaos.
– ORIGIN Latin *lapsus*.

laptop **noun** a portable microcomputer suitable for use while travelling.

lapwing **noun** a large crested plover (bird) with a dark green back, black-and-white head, and a loud call.
– ORIGIN Old English, from words meaning 'to leap' and 'move from side to side'.

larboard /**lar**-bord, **lar**-berd/ **noun** Nautical old-fashioned term for **PORT**³.
– ORIGIN from **LADE**, referring to the side of a ship on which cargo was loaded.

larceny /**lar**-suh-ni/ **noun** (pl. **larcenies**) N. Amer. or dated theft of personal property.
– DERIVATIVES **larcenous** adjective.
– ORIGIN Old French *larcin*.

larch **noun** a northern coniferous tree with bunches of deciduous bright green needles and tough wood.
– ORIGIN German *larche*.

lard **noun** fat from the abdomen of a pig, prepared for use in cooking. • **verb 1** insert strips of fat or bacon in meat before cooking. **2** add many obscure or technical expressions to talk or writing: *his conversation is larded with references to Coleridge.*
– ORIGIN Latin *lardum*.

larder **noun** a room or large cupboard for storing food.
– ORIGIN Latin *lardarium*.

lardon /**lar**-duhn/ **noun** a chunk or strip of bacon inserted in meat before it is cooked.
– ORIGIN French.

lardy **adjective** informal (of a person) fat.

lardy cake **noun** Brit. a cake made with bread dough, lard, and currants.

large **adjective 1** of great or relatively great size, extent, or capacity. **2** of wide range or scope: *we can afford to take a larger view of the situation.* • **verb** (**large it**) Brit. informal go out and have a good time.
– PHRASES **at large 1** escaped or not yet captured. **2** as a whole: *society at large.*
– DERIVATIVES **largeness** noun **largish** adjective.
– ORIGIN Latin *larga* 'copious'.

large intestine **noun** the part of the alimentary canal which consists of the caecum, colon, and rectum collectively.

largely **adverb** on the whole; mostly.

large-scale **adjective** involving large numbers or a large area; extensive.

largesse /lar-**zhess**/ (also **largess**) **noun 1** generosity. **2** money or gifts given generously.
– ORIGIN Old French.

largo /**lar**-goh/ **adverb & adjective** Music in a slow tempo and dignified style.
– ORIGIN Italian.

lari /**lah**-ree/ **noun** (pl. same or **laris**) a unit of money of the Maldives, equal to one hundredth of a rufiyaa.
– ORIGIN Persian.

lariat /la-ri-uht/ **noun** a rope used as a lasso or for tethering animals.
– ORIGIN from Spanish *la reata*.

lark¹ **noun** a brown songbird that sings while in flight.
– PHRASES **be up with the lark** Brit. get out of bed

very early in the morning.
– ORIGIN Old English.

lark² informal noun **1** an amusing adventure or escapade. **2** Brit. an activity regarded as foolish or a waste of time: *he's serious about this music lark*. • verb (**lark about/around**) Brit. behave in a playful and mischievous way.
– ORIGIN perhaps from dialect *lake* 'play'.

larkspur noun a Mediterranean plant resembling a delphinium.

larrikin /lar-ri-kin/ noun Austral./NZ **1** a boisterous, often badly behaved young man. **2** a person who disregards convention.
– ORIGIN perhaps from the name *Larry*.

larva /lar-vuh/ noun (pl. **larvae** /lar-vee/) an immature form of an insect or other animal that undergoes metamorphosis, e.g. a caterpillar or tadpole.
– DERIVATIVES **larval** adjective.
– ORIGIN Latin, 'ghost, mask'.

laryngeal /luh-rin-jee-uhl/ adjective relating to the larynx.

laryngitis /la-rin-jy-tiss/ noun inflammation of the larynx.

larynx /la-ringks/ noun (pl. **larynxes** or **larynges** /luh-rin-jeez/) the hollow muscular organ forming an air passage to the lungs and containing the vocal cords.
– ORIGIN Greek *larunx*.

lasagne /luh-zan-yuh, luh-zahn-yuh/ noun **1** pasta in the form of sheets or wide strips. **2** an Italian dish consisting of lasagne baked with meat or vegetables and a cheese sauce.
– ORIGIN Italian.

lascivious /luh-siv-i-uhss/ adjective feeling or showing obvious sexual desire.
– DERIVATIVES **lasciviously** adverb **lasciviousness** noun.
– ORIGIN Latin *lascivia* 'lustfulness'.

laser noun a device that produces an intense narrow beam of light.
– ORIGIN from the initial letters of *light amplification by stimulated emission of radiation*.

laserdisc noun a disc resembling a large compact disc, used for high-quality video and for interactive multimedia.

laser printer noun a computer printer in which a laser is used to form a pattern of electrically charged dots on a light-sensitive drum, which attracts toner.

lash verb **1** beat a person or animal with a whip or stick. **2** beat forcefully against: *waves lashed the coast*. **3** (**lash out**) attack someone or something verbally or physically. **4** (of an animal) move its tail quickly and violently. **5** fasten something securely with a cord or rope. **6** (**lash out**) Brit. spend money extravagantly. • noun **1** a sharp blow or stroke with a whip or stick. **2** the flexible leather part of a whip. **3** an eyelash.
– ORIGIN probably imitating the sound.

lashing noun **1** a whipping or beating. **2** a cord used to fasten something securely.

lashings plural noun Brit. informal a large amount of something, especially food or drink.

lash-up noun informal, chiefly Brit. a makeshift improvised structure or arrangement.

LASIK /lay-zik/ noun corrective eye surgery in which a flap of the cornea's surface is raised and a thin layer of underlying tissue is removed using a laser.
– ORIGIN from the initial letters of *laser-assisted in situ keratomileusis*.

lass (also **lassie**) noun chiefly Scottish & N. English a girl or young woman.
– ORIGIN Old Norse, 'unmarried'.

Lassa fever /lass-uh/ noun an acute and often fatal disease transmitted by a virus and occurring chiefly in West Africa.
– ORIGIN named after the village of *Lassa* in Nigeria, where it was first reported.

lassi /lass-ee/ noun a sweet or savoury Indian drink made from a yogurt or buttermilk base with water.
– ORIGIN Hindi.

lassitude /lass-i-tyood/ noun physical or mental weariness; lack of energy.
– ORIGIN Latin *lassitudo*.

lasso /luh-soo/ noun (pl. **lassos** or **lassoes**) a rope with a noose at one end, used especially in North America for catching cattle. • verb (**lassoes, lassoing, lassoed**) catch an animal with a lasso.
– ORIGIN Spanish *lazo*.

last¹ adjective **1** coming after all others in time or order. **2** most recent in time: *last year*. **3** immediately preceding something in order: *their last album*. **4** lowest in importance or rank. **5** (**the last**) the least likely or suitable. **6** only remaining: *it's our last hope*. • adverb **1** on the last occasion before the present: *she was last seen on Friday evening*. **2** (in combination) after all others in order: *the last-named film*. **3** (in stating numbered points) lastly. • noun (pl. same) **1** the last person or thing. **2** (**the last of**) the only remaining part of.
– PHRASES **at last** (or **at long last**) in the end; after much delay. **the last minute** the latest possible time before an event. **the last word 1** a final statement on a subject. **2** the most modern or advanced example of something: *the hotel is the last word in luxury*. **to the last** up to the last moment of a person's life.
– ORIGIN Old English.

last² verb **1** continue for a specified period of time. **2** remain operating or usable for a considerable or specified length of time: *the car is built to last*. **3** (of provisions or resources) be enough for someone for a specified period of time: *there was only enough food to last them three months*. **4** (often **last something out**) manage to survive or endure something.
– ORIGIN Old English.

last³ noun a shaped stand used by a shoemaker for shaping or repairing a shoe or boot.
– ORIGIN Old English.

last-ditch adjective referring to a final desperate attempt to achieve something.

last-gasp adjective done or happening at the last possible moment.

lasting adjective enduring or able to endure for a long time: *a lasting impression*.

Last Judgement noun the judgement of humankind expected in some religions to take place at the end of the world.

lastly adverb as a final point; last.

last name noun a person's surname.

last post noun (in the British armed forces) the second of two bugle calls indicating the time for retiring at night, played also at military funerals and acts of remembrance.

last rites plural noun (in the Christian Church) a religious ceremony performed for and in the presence of a person who is about to die.

Last Supper noun the meal eaten by Jesus and his disciples on the night before the Crucifixion.

last trump noun the trumpet blast that in some religions is thought will wake the dead on Judgement Day.

lat /lat/ noun (pl. **lati** /lat-ee/ or **lats**) the basic unit of money of Latvia.
– ORIGIN from *Latvija* 'Latvia'.

lat. abbreviation latitude.

latch noun 1 a bar with a catch and lever used for fastening a door or gate. 2 a spring lock for an outer door, which catches when the door is closed and can only be opened from the outside with a key. •verb fasten a door or gate with a latch.
– PHRASES **latch on to** informal 1 join someone and remain with them as a constant and usually unwelcome companion. 2 take up an idea or trend enthusiastically: *Californians had a reputation for latching on to fads.* 3 understand the meaning of something. **on the latch** (of a door or gate) closed but not locked.
– ORIGIN Old English, 'take hold of, grasp'.

latchkey noun (pl. **latchkeys**) a key of a house's outer door.

latchkey child noun a child who is alone at home after school until a parent returns from work.

late adjective 1 acting, arriving, or happening after the proper or usual time. 2 belonging or taking place far on in a particular time or period: *a woman in her late fifties.* 3 far on in the day or night. 4 (**the/one's late**) (of a person) no longer alive: *his late wife.* 5 (**latest**) of most recent date or origin. •adverb 1 after the proper or usual time. 2 towards the end of a period. 3 far on in the day or night. 4 (**later**) at a time in the near future; afterwards. 5 (**late of**) formerly but not now living or working in a place. •noun (**the latest**) the most recent news or fashion.
– PHRASES **at the latest** no later than the time specified. **of late** recently.
– DERIVATIVES **lateness** noun **latish** (also **lateish**) adjective & adverb.
– ORIGIN Old English.

latecomer noun a person who arrives late.

lateen sail /la-teen/ noun a triangular sail on a long yard at an angle of 45° to the mast.
– ORIGIN from French *voile Latine* 'Latin sail'.

lately adverb recently; not long ago.

latent adjective existing but not yet developed, apparent, or active: *her latent talent.*
– DERIVATIVES **latency** noun **latently** adverb.
– ORIGIN Latin *latere* 'be hidden'.

latent heat noun the heat required to convert a solid into a liquid or vapour, or a liquid into a vapour, without change of temperature.

latent image noun an image on exposed photographic film that has not yet been made visible by developing.

lateral /lat-uh-ruhl/ adjective relating to, towards, or from the side or sides. •noun a lateral part, especially a shoot or branch growing out from the side of a stem.
– DERIVATIVES **laterally** adverb.
– ORIGIN Latin *lateralis*.

lateral thinking noun chiefly Brit. the solving of problems by taking an indirect and creative approach.

laterite /lat-tuh-ryt/ noun a reddish clayey topsoil found in tropical regions, sometimes used to make roads.
– ORIGIN from Latin *later* 'brick'.

latex /lay-teks/ noun 1 a milky fluid found in many plants, notably the rubber tree, which coagulates on exposure to the air. 2 a synthetic product resembling latex, used to make paints, coatings, etc.
– ORIGIN Latin, 'liquid, fluid'.

lath /lath/ noun (pl. **laths**) a thin, flat strip of wood, especially one of a series forming a foundation for the plaster of a wall.
– ORIGIN Old English.

lathe /rhymes with bathe/ noun a machine for shaping wood or metal by means of a rotating drive which turns the piece being worked on against changeable cutting tools.
– ORIGIN probably from Danish *lad* 'structure, frame'.

lather /lah-ther, la-ther/ noun 1 a frothy white mass of bubbles produced by soap when mixed with water. 2 heavy sweat visible on a horse's coat as a white foam. 3 (**a lather**) informal a state of agitation or nervous excitement. •verb 1 form a lather. 2 rub something with soap until a lather is produced. 3 spread a substance thickly or liberally: *we lathered cream on our scones.*
– ORIGIN Old English.

lathi /lah-tee/ noun (pl. **lathis**) (in the Indian subcontinent) a long metal-bound bamboo stick used as a weapon, especially by police.
– ORIGIN Hindi.

Latin noun 1 the language of ancient Rome and its empire. 2 a person from a country whose language developed from Latin. •adjective 1 relating to the Latin language. 2 relating to countries using languages that developed from Latin, especially Latin America. 3 relating to the Western or Roman Catholic Church.
– DERIVATIVES **Latinism** noun **Latinist** noun **Latinity** noun.
– ORIGIN Latin *Latinus* 'of Latium' (an ancient region in central Italy).

Latina /luh-tee-nuh/ noun fem. of **LATINO**.

Latin American adjective relating to the parts of the American continent where Spanish or Portuguese is the main national language. •noun a person from Latin America.

Latinate /lat-i-nayt/ adjective (of language) having the character of Latin.

Latinize (or **Latinise**) verb give a Latin or Latinate form to a word.
– DERIVATIVES **Latinization** noun.

Latino /luh-tee-noh/ noun (pl. **Latinos**; fem. **Latina**, pl. **Latinas**) chiefly N. Amer. a Latin American inhabitant of the United States. •adjective relating to Latinos or Latinas.

– ORIGIN Latin American Spanish.

latitude /la-ti-tyood/ noun **1** the angular distance of a place north or south of the equator. **2** (**latitudes**) regions with reference to their temperature and distance from the equator: *northern latitudes*. **3** scope for freedom of action or thought: *journalists have considerable latitude in criticizing public figures.*
– DERIVATIVES **latitudinal** adjective **latitudinally** adverb.
– ORIGIN Latin *latitudo* 'breadth'.

latitudinarian /lat-i-tyoo-di-**nair**-i-uhn/ adjective liberal in religious views. • noun a person with a liberal religious outlook.
– DERIVATIVES **latitudinarianism** noun.

latrine /luh-**treen**/ noun a communal toilet in a camp or barracks.
– ORIGIN Latin *latrina*.

latte /**lat**-tay/ (also **caffè latte**) noun a drink of frothy steamed milk with a shot of espresso coffee.
– ORIGIN from Italian *caffè latte* 'milk coffee'.

latter adjective **1** nearer to the end than to the beginning. **2** recent: *in latter years*. **3** (**the latter**) referring to the second or second-mentioned of two people or things.
– ORIGIN Old English, 'slower'.

latter-day adjective modern or contemporary, especially when resembling a person or thing of the past: *a latter-day Noah.*

Latter-Day Saints plural noun the Mormons' name for themselves.

latterly adverb **1** recently. **2** in the later stages of a period of time.

lattice noun **1** a structure or pattern consisting of strips crossing each other with square or diamond-shaped spaces left between. **2** a regular repeated three-dimensional arrangement of atoms, ions, or molecules in a metal or other crystalline solid.
– DERIVATIVES **latticed** adjective **latticework** noun.
– ORIGIN Old French *lattis*.

Latvian noun **1** a person from Latvia. **2** the language of Latvia. • adjective relating to Latvia.

laud /lawd/ verb formal praise someone or something highly.
– DERIVATIVES **laudation** noun.
– ORIGIN Latin *laudare*.

laudable adjective deserving praise.
– DERIVATIVES **laudably** adverb.

laudanum /**law**-duh-nuhm/ noun a solution prepared from opium and formerly used as a painkiller.
– ORIGIN Latin.

laudatory /**law**-duh-tuh-ri/ adjective expressing praise.

laugh verb **1** make the sounds that express lively amusement. **2** (**laugh at**) make fun of. **3** (**laugh something off**) dismiss something by treating it light-heartedly. **4** (**be laughing**) informal be in a fortunate or successful position. • noun **1** an act of laughing. **2** (**a laugh**) informal a cause of laughter.
– PHRASES **have the last laugh** be eventually proved right or at an advantage. **laugh someone/thing out of court** dismiss someone or something as being obviously ridiculous. **laugh up one's sleeve** be secretly amused.

– DERIVATIVES **laugher** noun.
– ORIGIN Old English.

laughable adjective so ridiculous as to be amusing.
– DERIVATIVES **laughably** adverb.

laughing gas noun non-technical term for NITROUS OXIDE.

laughing hyena noun a southern African hyena with a loud laughing call.

laughing stock noun a person who is ridiculed by everyone.

laughter noun the action or sound of laughing.

launch[1] verb **1** move a boat or ship from land into the water. **2** send a rocket or missile on its course. **3** hurl or move forcefully: *I launched myself out of bed*. **4** begin an enterprise or introduce a new product. **5** (**launch into**) begin something energetically and enthusiastically. • noun **1** an act of launching something. **2** an occasion at which a new product or publication is introduced to the public.
– ORIGIN Old French *lancier* 'to lance'.

launch[2] noun a large motorboat.
– ORIGIN Spanish *lancha* 'pinnace'.

launcher noun a structure that holds a rocket or missile during launching.

launder verb **1** wash and iron clothes or linen. **2** informal pass illegally obtained money through legitimate businesses or foreign banks to conceal its origins.
– DERIVATIVES **launderer** noun.
– ORIGIN from Latin *lavanda* 'things to be washed'.

launderette (also **laundrette**) noun Brit. a place with coin-operated washing machines and dryers for public use.

laundress noun a woman employed to launder clothes and linen.

laundromat noun N. Amer. (trademark in the US) a launderette.

laundry noun (pl. **laundries**) **1** clothes and linen that need to be washed or that have been newly washed. **2** a room or building where clothes and linen are washed and ironed.

laureate /**lo**-ri-uht/ noun **1** a person given an award for outstanding creative or intellectual achievement. **2** a Poet Laureate.
– DERIVATIVES **laureateship** noun.
– ORIGIN from Latin *laurea* 'laurel wreath'.

laurel noun **1** an evergreen shrub or small tree with dark green glossy leaves. **2** (**laurels**) a crown woven from bay leaves and awarded as a sign of victory or mark of honour in classical times. **3** (**laurels**) honour or praise for an achievement.
– PHRASES **rest on one's laurels** be so satisfied with what one has already achieved that one makes no further effort.
– ORIGIN Latin *laurus*.

lava noun hot molten or semi-fluid rock that erupts from a volcano or fissure, or solid rock formed when this cools.
– ORIGIN Italian.

lava lamp noun a transparent electric lamp containing a viscous liquid in which a suspended waxy substance rises and falls in constantly changing shapes.

lavatorial adjective **1** relating to or resembling lavatories. **2** chiefly Brit. (of conversation or humour) referring excessively to lavatories and excretion.

lavatory noun (pl. **lavatories**) a toilet.
– ORIGIN Latin *lavatorium* 'place for washing'.

lave /layv/ verb literary wash something.
– ORIGIN Latin *lavare* 'to wash'.

lavender noun **1** a small evergreen shrub with narrow strong-smelling leaves and bluish-purple flowers. **2** a pale bluish-purple colour.
– ORIGIN Latin *lavandula*.

lavender water noun a perfume made from distilled lavender.

laver /lah-ver/ (also **purple laver**) noun an edible seaweed with thin reddish-purple and green fronds.
– ORIGIN Latin.

lavish adjective **1** very rich, elaborate, or luxurious. **2** giving or given in large amounts: *lavish funding from abroad.* ●verb give in abundant or extravagant quantities: *he lavished money and attention on the family.*
– DERIVATIVES **lavishly** adverb **lavishness** noun.
– ORIGIN from Old French *lavasse* 'deluge of rain'.

law noun **1** a rule or system of rules recognized by a country or community as regulating the actions of its members and enforced by the imposition of penalties. **2** such rules as a subject of study or as the basis of the legal profession. **3** statute law and the common law as distinct from equity. **4** a rule that controls correct behaviour in a sport. **5** a statement of the fact that a particular natural or scientific phenomenon always occurs if certain conditions are present. **6** something that has binding force or effect: *his word was law.* **7** (**the law**) informal the police.
– PHRASES **be a law unto oneself** behave in an unconventional or unpredictable way. **lay down the law** issue instructions in a domineering way. **take the law into one's own hands** illegally punish someone according to one's own ideas of justice.
– ORIGIN Old Norse, 'something laid down or fixed'.

law-abiding adjective obedient to the laws of society.

lawbreaker noun a person who breaks the law.

law centre noun (in the UK) an independent publicly funded advisory service on legal matters.

law court noun a court of law.

lawful adjective following, permitted by, or recognized by the law or a set of rules.
– DERIVATIVES **lawfully** adverb **lawfulness** noun.

lawgiver noun a person who draws up and enacts laws.

lawless adjective not governed by or obedient to laws.
– DERIVATIVES **lawlessly** adverb **lawlessness** noun.

law lord noun (in the UK) a member of the House of Lords qualified to perform its legal work.

lawmaker noun a member of a government who draws up laws.

lawman noun (pl. **lawmen**) (in the US) a law-enforcement officer, especially a sheriff.

lawn¹ noun an area of mown grass in a garden or park.
– ORIGIN Old French *launde* 'wooded district,

heath'.

lawn² noun a fine linen or cotton fabric.
– ORIGIN probably from *Laon*, a French city important for linen manufacture.

lawnmower noun a machine for cutting the grass on a lawn.

lawn tennis noun dated or formal tennis.

law of averages noun the supposed principle that future events are likely to turn out so that they balance any past events.

Law Officer (in full **Law Officer of the Crown**) noun (in England and Wales) the Attorney General or the Solicitor General, or (in Scotland) the Lord Advocate or the Solicitor General for Scotland.

law of nature noun another term for NATURAL LAW.

lawrencium /lo-ren-si-uhm/ noun a very unstable chemical element made by high-energy collisions.
– ORIGIN named after the American physicist Ernest O. *Lawrence*.

lawsuit noun a claim or dispute brought to a law court to be decided.

lawyer noun a person who practises or studies law, especially (in the UK) a solicitor or a barrister or (in the US) an attorney.
– DERIVATIVES **lawyering** noun **lawyerly** adjective.

lax adjective **1** not strict, severe, or careful enough: *lax security arrangements.* **2** (of limbs or muscles) relaxed.
– DERIVATIVES **laxity** noun **laxly** adverb **laxness** noun.
– ORIGIN Latin *laxus* 'loose, lax'.

laxative noun a medicine that causes a person to empty their bowels. ●adjective causing the bowels to empty.
– ORIGIN from Latin *laxare* 'loosen'.

lay¹ verb (past and past part. **laid**) **1** put something down gently or carefully. **2** put something down and set it in position for use. **3** assign or place: *they tried to lay the blame on others.* **4** (**lay something before**) present material for consideration and action to someone. **5** (of a female bird, reptile, etc.) produce an egg from inside the body. **6** stake an amount of money in a bet. **7** cause a ghost to stop appearing. **8** vulgar slang have sex with someone. ●noun **1** the general appearance of an area of land. **2** the position or direction in which something lies. **3** vulgar slang a sexual partner or act of sex.
– PHRASES **lay claim** to claim that one has a right to something or possesses a skill or quality. **lay something down 1** formulate and enforce a rule or principle. **2** build up a deposit of a substance. **3** store wine in a cellar. **4** pay or bet money. **lay something in/up** build up a stock in case of need. **lay into** informal attack someone violently. **lay off** informal give something up. **lay someone off** discharge a worker because of a shortage of work. **lay something on** Brit. provide a service or amenity. **lay something on thick** (or **with a trowel**) informal greatly exaggerate or overemphasize something. **lay someone open to** expose someone to the risk of something. **lay someone out** prepare someone for burial after death. **lay something out 1** construct or arrange buildings or gardens according to a plan. **2** arrange and present material for

printing and publication. **3** informal spend a sum of money. **lay something to rest 1** bury a body in a grave. **2** put an end to fear, anxiety, etc. **lay someone up** put someone out of action through illness or injury.
– ORIGIN Old English.

> USAGE: The words **lay** and **lie** are often used incorrectly. **Lay** generally means 'put something down' (*they are going to lay the carpet*), whereas **lie** means 'be in a horizontal position to rest' (*why don't you lie down?*). The past tense and past participle of **lay** is **laid** (*they laid the carpet*); the past tense of **lie** is **lay** (*he lay on the floor*) and the past participle is **lain** (*she had lain awake for hours*).

lay² adjective **1** not belonging to the clergy. **2** not having professional qualifications or expert knowledge in a particular subject.
– ORIGIN Latin *laicus*.

lay³ noun **1** a short lyric or narrative poem intended to be sung. **2** literary a song.
– ORIGIN Old French *lai*.

lay⁴ past of **LIE¹**.

layabout noun derogatory, chiefly Brit. a person who does little or no work.

lay brother (or **lay sister**) noun a person who has taken the vows of a religious order but is not ordained and is employed in ancillary or manual work.

lay-by noun (pl. **lay-bys**) Brit. an area at the side of a road where vehicles may pull off the road and stop.

layer noun **1** a sheet or thickness of material, typically one of several, covering a surface. **2** (in combination) a person or thing that lays something: *a cable-layer*. **3** a shoot fastened down to take root while attached to the parent plant. • verb (often as adj. **layered**) arrange or cut something in a layer or layers.
– ORIGIN from **LAY¹**.

layette noun a set of clothing and bedclothes for a newborn child.
– ORIGIN French.

layman (or **laywoman** or **layperson**) noun (pl. **laymen**, **laywomen**, **laypersons**, or **laypeople**) **1** a member of a Church who is not a priest or minister. **2** a person without professional or specialized knowledge in a particular subject.

lay-off noun **1** an instance of discharging a worker or workers because of a shortage of work. **2** a temporary break from an activity.

layout noun **1** the way in which something, especially a page, is laid out. **2** a thing set out in a particular way.

lay reader noun (in the Anglican Church) a layperson licensed to preach and to conduct some services but not to celebrate Holy Communion.

laywoman noun see **LAYMAN**.

laze verb spend time relaxing or doing very little. • noun a spell of lazing.

lazy adjective (**lazier**, **laziest**) **1** unwilling to work or use energy. **2** showing a lack of effort or care: *a lazy investigation*.
– DERIVATIVES **lazily** adverb **laziness** noun.
– ORIGIN perhaps related to German *lasich* 'languid, idle'.

lazybones noun (pl. same) informal a lazy person.

lazy eye noun an eye with poor vision due to underuse, especially the unused eye in a squint.

lb abbreviation pound(s) (in weight).
– ORIGIN from Latin *libra*.

lbw abbreviation Cricket leg before wicket.

l.c. abbreviation **1** in the passage cited. [from Latin *loco citato*.] **2** lower case.

LCD abbreviation **1** Electronics & Computing liquid crystal display. **2** Mathematics lowest (or least) common denominator.

LCM abbreviation Mathematics lowest (or least) common multiple.

L-driver noun Brit. a learner driver.

LEA abbreviation (in the UK) Local Education Authority.

lea noun literary an open area of grassy land.
– ORIGIN Old English.

leach verb (of a soluble substance) drain away from soil or other material by the action of water passing through it.
– ORIGIN Old English, 'to water'.

lead¹ /leed/ verb (past and past part. **led**) **1** draw, guide, or take a person or animal with one. **2** be a route or means of access: *the street led into the square.* **3** (**lead** (**up**) **to**) result in. **4** influence to do or believe something: *that may lead them to reconsider.* **5** be in charge of other people. **6** be in first place in a competition or contest. **7** be best in an area of activity: *these companies lead the way in new technological developments.* **8** have a particular way of life. **9** (often **lead** (**off**) **with**) begin with a particular action or item. **10** (**lead up to**) come before: *the weeks leading up to the election.* **11** (**lead someone on**) deceive someone into believing that one is attracted to them. **12** (in card games) play the first card in a trick or round of play. • noun **1** an example for others to follow: *others followed our lead.* **2** (**the lead**) first place in a competition or contest. **3** an amount by which a competitor is ahead of the others: *a one-goal lead.* **4** the chief part in a play or film. **5** a clue to be followed in solving a problem. **6** Brit. a strap or cord for restraining and guiding a dog. **7** Brit. a wire conveying electric current from a source to an appliance, or connecting two points of a circuit together. • adjective **1** playing the chief part in a musical group: *the lead singer.* **2** referring to the main item in a newspaper, magazine, or broadcast: *the lead article.*
– PHRASES **lead someone up the garden path** informal give someone misleading clues or signals.
– ORIGIN Old English.

lead² /led/ noun **1** a heavy bluish-grey soft metallic element. **2** graphite used as the part of a pencil that makes a mark. **3** (**leads**) lead frames holding the glass of a lattice or stained-glass window. **4** (**leads**) Brit. sheets or strips of lead covering a roof. **5** Nautical a lump of lead suspended on a line to determine the depth of water. **6** Printing a blank space between lines of print.
– ORIGIN Old English.

lead crystal (also **lead glass**) noun glass containing a substantial proportion of lead oxide, making it more refractive.

leaded adjective **1** framed, covered, or weighted

with lead. **2** (of petrol) containing lead.

leaden adjective **1** dull, heavy, or slow: *he hoped sleep would loosen his leaden legs.* **2** dull grey in colour.
– DERIVATIVES **leadenly** adverb.

leader noun **1** a person or thing that leads. **2** a person or thing that is the most successful or advanced in a particular area. **3** the principal player in a music group. **4** Brit. a leading article in a newspaper. **5** (also **Leader of the House**) Brit. a member of the government officially responsible for initiating business in Parliament. **6** a short strip of non-functioning material at each end of a reel of film or recording tape for connection to the spool.
– DERIVATIVES **leaderless** adjective **leadership** noun.

leader board noun a scoreboard showing the names and current scores of the leading competitors, especially in a golf match.

lead-in noun an introduction to something.

leading /lee-ding/ adjective most important or in first place.

leading aircraftman (or **leading aircraftwoman**) noun a rank in the RAF immediately above aircraftman (or aircraftwoman).

leading article noun Brit. a newspaper article giving the editorial opinion.

leading edge noun the forefront of technological development.

leading light noun a person who is prominent or influential in a particular field or organization.

leading question noun a question that prompts the answer wanted.

leading seaman noun a rank in the Royal Navy immediately above able seaman.

lead time noun the time between the beginning and completion of a production process.

lead-up noun an event or sequence that leads up to something else.

leaf noun (pl. **leaves**) **1** a flat, typically green structure that grows from the stem of a plant. **2** the state of having leaves: *the trees were in leaf.* **3** a single sheet of paper, especially in a book. **4** gold, silver, or other metal in the form of very thin foil. **5** a hinged or detachable part, especially of a table. •verb **1** (of a plant) put out new leaves. **2** (**leaf through**) turn over pages or papers, reading them quickly or casually.
– PHRASES **turn over a new leaf** start to act or behave in a better way.
– DERIVATIVES **leafage** noun **leafed** (also **leaved**) adjective **leafless** adjective.
– ORIGIN Old English.

leaflet noun **1** a printed sheet of paper containing information or advertising and usually distributed free. **2** a small leaf, especially a component of a compound leaf. •verb (**leaflets, leafleting, leafleted**) distribute leaflets to people or an area.

leaf mould noun soil consisting chiefly of decayed leaves.

leafy adjective (**leafier, leafiest**) **1** having many leaves. **2** full of trees and shrubs: *a leafy avenue.*

– DERIVATIVES **leafiness** noun.

league[1] noun **1** a collection of people, countries, or groups that combine to help each other or promote something. **2** a group of sports clubs which play each other over a period for a championship. **3** a class of quality or excellence: *the two men were not in the same league.* •verb (**leagues, leaguing, leagued**) join in a league or alliance.
– PHRASES **in league** (of people) conspiring with each other.
– ORIGIN Italian *lega*.

league[2] noun a former measure of distance, usually about three miles.
– ORIGIN Latin *leuga, leuca*.

league table noun Brit. **1** a list of the competitors in a league ranked according to performance. **2** a list in order of merit or achievement.

leak verb **1** (of a container or covering) accidentally allow contents to escape or enter through a hole or crack. **2** (of liquid, gas, etc.) escape or enter accidentally through a hole or crack. **3** deliberately disclose secret information. •noun **1** a hole or crack through which contents leak. **2** an instance of leaking.
– PHRASES **have** (or **take**) **a leak** informal urinate.
– DERIVATIVES **leakage** noun **leaker** noun **leaky** adjective.
– ORIGIN probably from German or Dutch.

lean[1] verb (past and past part. **leaned** or chiefly Brit. **leant**) **1** be in or move into a sloping position. **2** (**lean against/on**) slope and rest against. **3** (**lean on**) rely on someone for support. **4** (**lean to/towards**) favour a point of view. **5** (**lean on**) informal intimidate someone into doing something. •noun an instance of leaning or sloping.
– ORIGIN Old English.

lean[2] adjective **1** (of a person) having no unwanted fat; thin. **2** (of meat) containing little fat. **3** (of a period of time) difficult because money or food is scarce: *the lean years of the Depression.* **4** informal (of an industry or organization) efficient and with no wastage. **5** (of a vaporized fuel mixture) having a high proportion of air. •noun the lean part of meat.
– DERIVATIVES **leanness** noun.
– ORIGIN Old English.

leaning noun a tendency or preference: *communist leanings.*

lean-to noun (pl. **lean-tos**) a building sharing a wall with a larger building and having a roof that leans against that wall.

leap verb (past or past part. **leaped** or **leapt**) **1** jump high, far, or across something. **2** move quickly and suddenly: *Ann leapt to her feet.* **3** (**leap at**) accept something eagerly. **4** (especially of a price or amount) increase dramatically. **5** (**leap out**) be immediately noticeable. •noun **1** an instance of leaping. **2** a sudden change or increase.
– PHRASES **a leap in the dark** a daring step or enterprise with an unpredictable outcome. **by** (or **in**) **leaps and bounds** with very rapid progress.
– DERIVATIVES **leaper** noun.
– ORIGIN Old English.

leapfrog noun a game in which players in turn vault with parted legs over others who are bending down. • verb (**leapfrogs, leapfrogging, leapfrogged**) **1** vault over someone in the game of leapfrog. **2** reach a leading position by overtaking others or omitting a stage in a process: *the firm has leapfrogged over all its rivals.*

leap year noun a year, occurring once every four years, which has 366 days (29 February being the additional day).

learn verb (past and past part. **learned** or chiefly Brit. **learnt**) **1** gain knowledge of or skill in something through study or experience or by being taught. **2** become aware of something by information or from observation. **3** memorize something. **4** informal teach someone.
– DERIVATIVES **learnable** adjective **learner** noun.
– ORIGIN Old English.

learned /ler-nid/ adjective having or showing much knowledge gained by studying.

learning noun knowledge or skills gained through study or by being taught.

learning curve noun the rate of a person's progress in gaining experience or new skills.

learning difficulties plural noun Brit. difficulties in gaining knowledge and skills to the normal level expected of those of the same age.

USAGE: The term **learning difficulties** covers general conditions such as Down's syndrome as well as more specific conditions such as dyslexia. In Britain, it has now replaced terms such as **mentally handicapped** in official situations.

lease noun a contract by which one party lets land, property, services, etc. to another for a specified time, in return for payment. • verb let or rent something on lease.
– PHRASES **a new lease of life** a greatly improved prospect of life or use after recovery or repair.
– ORIGIN from Old French *lesser, laissier* 'let, leave'.

leasehold noun **1** the holding of property by a lease. **2** a piece of land or property held by a lease.
– DERIVATIVES **leaseholder** noun.

leash noun a dog's lead. • verb put a lead on a dog.
– ORIGIN from Old French *laissier* in the sense 'let an animal run on a slack lead'.

least determiner & pronoun (usu. **the least**) smallest in amount, extent, or significance. • adverb to the smallest extent or degree.
– PHRASES **at least 1** not less than. **2** if nothing else. **3** anyway. **at the least** (or **very least**) **1** not less than. **2** taking the most pessimistic view. **not in the least** not at all. **not least** in particular.
– ORIGIN Old English.

leastways (also **leastwise**) adverb dialect or informal at least.

leather noun **1** a material made from the skin of an animal by tanning or a similar process. **2** a piece of leather as a polishing cloth. **3** (**leathers**) leather clothes worn by a motorcyclist. • verb **1** (as adj. **leathered**) covered with leather. **2** informal beat or thrash someone.
– ORIGIN Old English.

leatherback turtle noun a very large black turtle with a thick leathery shell, living chiefly in tropical seas.

leatherette noun imitation leather.

leatherjacket noun Brit. the tough-skinned larva of a large crane fly.

leathern adjective old use made of leather.

leathery adjective having a tough, hard texture like leather.
– DERIVATIVES **leatheriness** noun.

leave¹ verb (past and past part. **left**) **1** go away from someone or something. **2** stop living at, attending, or working for: *he left home at 16.* **3** allow something to remain; go away without taking something. **4** (**be left**) remain to be used or dealt with: *drink left over from the wedding.* **5** cause to be in a particular state or position: *leave the door open.* **6** let someone do something without help or interference. **7** (**leave something to**) let someone deal with or be responsible for something. **8** deposit something to be collected or dealt with. **9** have someone as a surviving relative after one's death. **10** give something to someone in a will.
– PHRASES **leave someone/thing be** informal avoid disturbing or interfering with someone or something. **leave go** Brit. informal remove one's hold or grip. **leave off** stop doing something. **leave someone/thing out** fail to include someone or something.
– DERIVATIVES **leaver** noun.
– ORIGIN Old English.

leave² noun **1** (also **leave of absence**) time when one has permission to be absent from work or duty. **2** formal permission: *seeking leave to appeal.*
– PHRASES **take one's leave** formal say goodbye.
– ORIGIN Old English.

leaven /lev-uhn/ noun **1** a substance, typically yeast, added to dough to make it ferment and rise. **2** an influence or quality that modifies or improves something: *John's humour was the leaven of his charm.* • verb **1** (usu. as adj. **leavened**) make dough or bread ferment and rise by adding yeast or another leaven. **2** make an addition to improve something: *the debate was leavened by humour.*
– ORIGIN Latin *levamen* 'relief'.

leaves plural of LEAF.

leave-taking noun an act of saying goodbye.

leavings plural noun things that have been left as worthless.

Lebanese /le-buh-**neez**/ noun (pl. same) a person from Lebanon. • adjective relating to Lebanon.

Lebensraum /**lay**-buhnz-rowm/ noun territory which a state or nation believes is needed for its natural development.
– ORIGIN German, 'living space'.

lecher noun a lecherous man.
– DERIVATIVES **lechery** noun.

lecherous adjective having or showing excessive or offensive sexual desire.
– DERIVATIVES **lecherously** adverb **lecherousness** noun.
– ORIGIN from Old French *lechier* 'live in debauchery or gluttony'.

lecithin /**les**-i-thin/ noun a substance found in egg yolk and other animal and plant tissues, often used as an emulsifier in food processing.

– ORIGIN from Greek *lekithos* 'egg yolk'.

lectern /lek-tern/ noun a tall stand with a sloping top from which a speaker can read while standing up.
– ORIGIN Latin *lectrum*, from *legere* 'to read'.

lecture noun 1 an educational talk to an audience, especially one of students in a university. 2 a lengthy reprimand or warning. ● verb 1 give an educational talk or talks. 2 criticize or reprimand someone.
– ORIGIN Latin *lectura*.

lecturer noun a person who gives lectures, especially (Brit.) as a teacher in higher education.

lectureship noun a post as a lecturer.

LED abbreviation light-emitting diode, a semiconductor diode which glows when a voltage is applied.

led past and past participle of LEAD¹.

lederhosen /lay-duh-hoh-zuhn/ plural noun leather shorts with braces, traditionally worn by men in the Alps.
– ORIGIN German.

ledge noun 1 a narrow horizontal surface projecting from a wall, cliff, or other vertical surface. 2 an underwater ridge, especially one of rocks near the seashore.
– ORIGIN perhaps from LAY¹.

ledger noun a book in which financial accounts are kept.
– ORIGIN probably from variants of LAY¹ and LIE¹, influenced by Dutch *legger* and *ligger*.

ledger line (also **leger line**) noun Music a short line added for notes above or below the range of a stave.

lee noun 1 (also **lee side**) the side of something sheltered from the wind. Contrasted with WEATHER. 2 shelter from wind or weather given by an object.
– ORIGIN Old English, 'shelter'.

leech¹ noun 1 a worm that sucks the blood of animals or people, formerly used in medicine for bloodletting. 2 a person who lives off others.
– ORIGIN Old English.

leech² noun old use a doctor or healer.
– ORIGIN Old English.

leek noun a vegetable related to the onion, with flat overlapping leaves forming an elongated cylindrical bulb.
– ORIGIN Old English.

leer verb look or gaze in a lustful or unpleasant way. ● noun a lustful or unpleasant look.
– ORIGIN perhaps from an Old English word meaning 'cheek'.

leery adjective (**leerier, leeriest**) informal cautious or wary: *a city leery of gang violence.*
– DERIVATIVES **leeriness** noun.
– ORIGIN from LEER.

lees plural noun the sediment of wine in the bottom of the barrel.
– ORIGIN Latin *liae*.

lee shore noun a shore lying on the side of a ship that is sheltered from the wind (and on to which the ship could be blown).

leeward /lee-werd, loo-erd/ adjective & adverb on or towards the side sheltered from the wind or towards which the wind is blowing. Contrasted with WINDWARD. ● noun the leeward side.

leeway noun 1 the amount of freedom to move or act that is available: *we have a lot of leeway in how we do our jobs.* 2 the sideways drift of a ship to leeward of the desired course.

left¹ adjective 1 on, towards, or relating to the side of a person or thing which is to the west when the person or thing is facing north. 2 relating to a left-wing person or group. ● adverb on or to the left side. ● noun 1 (**the left**) the left-hand part, side, or direction. 2 a left turn. 3 a person's left fist, or a blow given with it. 4 (often **the Left**) (treated as sing. or pl.) a group or party with radical, reforming, or socialist views.
– PHRASES **have two left feet** be clumsy or awkward.
– DERIVATIVES **leftish** adjective **leftmost** adjective **leftward** adjective & adverb **leftwards** adverb.
– ORIGIN Old English, 'weak'.

left² past and past participle of LEAVE¹.

left back noun a defender in football or field hockey who plays mainly on the left of the field.

left-field adjective informal unconventional or experimental.

left hand noun the region or direction on the left side of someone or something. ● adjective 1 on or towards the left side. 2 done with or using the left hand.

left-hand drive noun a motor-vehicle steering system with the steering wheel and other controls fitted on the left side, for use in countries where vehicles drive on the right.

left-handed adjective 1 using or done with the left hand. 2 turning to the left; towards the left. 3 (of a screw) that is to be turned anticlockwise.

left-hander noun 1 a left-handed person. 2 a blow struck with a person's left hand.

leftie noun variant spelling of LEFTY.

leftism noun the political views or policies of the Left.
– DERIVATIVES **leftist** noun & adjective.

left luggage noun Brit. travellers' luggage left in temporary storage at a railway station, bus station, or airport.

leftover noun (**leftovers**) something, especially food, remaining after the rest has been used. ● adjective remaining; surplus.

left wing noun 1 the radical, reforming, or socialist section of a political party or system. [with reference to the National Assembly in France (1789–91), where the nobles sat to the president's right and the commoners to the left.] 2 the left side of a sports team on the field or of an army.
– DERIVATIVES **left-winger** noun.

lefty (also **leftie**) noun (pl. **lefties**) informal 1 chiefly Brit. a left-wing person. 2 chiefly N. Amer. a left-handed person.

leg noun 1 each of the limbs on which a person or animal moves and stands. 2 a long, thin support or prop, especially of a chair or table. 3 a section of a journey, process, or race. 4 (in sport) each of two or more games or stages that make up a round or match. 5 (**legs**) informal sustained popularity or success: *some books have legs, others don't.* 6 (also **leg side**) Cricket

the half of the field away from which the batsman's feet are pointed when standing to receive the ball. The opposite of **OFF**.
– PHRASES **leg before wicket** Cricket (of a batsman) judged to be out through obstructing the ball with the leg (or other part of the body) when the ball would otherwise have hit the wicket. **leg it** Brit. informal **1** travel by foot; walk. **2** run away. **not have a leg to stand on** be unable to justify one's arguments or actions. **on one's** (or **its**) **last legs** near the end of life, usefulness, or existence.
– DERIVATIVES **legged** adjective.
– ORIGIN Old Norse.

legacy noun (pl. **legacies**) **1** an amount of money or property left to someone in a will. **2** a situation that exists because of a past event or action: *all the ills in the country are the legacy of military rule*. •**adjective** (of computer hardware or software) that has been superseded but is difficult to replace because of its wide use.
– ORIGIN Old French *legacie*.

legal adjective **1** relating to or required by the law. **2** permitted by law.
– DERIVATIVES **legally** adverb.
– ORIGIN Latin *legalis*.

legal aid noun payment from public funds given to people who cannot afford to pay for legal advice or proceedings.

legalese /lee-guh-**leez**/ noun informal the formal and technical language of legal documents.

legalism noun the practice of keeping strictly to the law.
– DERIVATIVES **legalist** noun & adjective **legalistic** adjective.

legality noun (pl. **legalities**) **1** the quality or state of being legal. **2** (**legalities**) rules and duties imposed by law.

legalize (or **legalise**) verb make something that was illegal allowed by the law.
– DERIVATIVES **legalization** noun.

legal separation noun an arrangement by which a husband or wife remain married but live apart, following a court order.

legal tender noun coins or banknotes that must be accepted if offered in payment of a debt.

legate /**leg**-uht/ noun a member of the clergy who represents the Pope.
– ORIGIN Latin *legatus*.

legatee /leg-uh-**tee**/ noun a person who receives a legacy.
– ORIGIN from Latin *legare* 'delegate, bequeath'.

legation /li-**gay**-sh'n/ noun **1** a diplomatic minister and their staff. **2** the official residence of a diplomat.

legato /li-**gah**-toh/ adverb & adjective Music in a smooth, flowing way.
– ORIGIN Italian, 'bound'.

leg break noun Cricket a ball which spins from the leg side towards the off side after pitching.

legend noun **1** a traditional story about the past which may or may not have a factual basis. **2** a very famous person: *a screen legend*. **3** an inscription or explanatory wording. •**adjective** very well known: *his speed and ferocity in attack were legend*.
– ORIGIN from Latin *legenda* 'things to be read'.

legendary adjective **1** relating to or based on traditional stories about the past. **2** remarkable enough to be famous: *France's legendary chefs*.
– DERIVATIVES **legendarily** adverb.

legerdemain /lej-er-di-**mayn**/ noun **1** skilful use of the hands when performing conjuring tricks. **2** deception; trickery.
– ORIGIN from French *léger de main* 'dexterous' (literally 'light of hand').

leggings plural noun **1** tight-fitting stretchy trousers worn by women. **2** strong protective coverings for the legs from knee to ankle.

leggy adjective (**leggier, leggiest**) **1** long-legged. **2** (of a plant) having a long and straggly stem or stems.

legible adjective (of handwriting or print) clear enough to read.
– DERIVATIVES **legibility** noun **legibly** adverb.
– ORIGIN Latin *legibilis*.

legion noun **1** a division of 3,000–6,000 men in the ancient Roman army. **2** (**a legion/legions of**) a vast number of people or things. •**adjective** great in number: *her fans are legion*.
– ORIGIN Latin.

legionary noun (pl. **legionaries**) a soldier in an ancient Roman legion.

legionnaire /lee-juh-**nair**/ noun **1** a member of the Foreign Legion. **2** a member of a national association for former servicemen and servicewomen.

legionnaires' disease noun a form of pneumonia spread chiefly in water droplets through air conditioning systems.
– ORIGIN because identified after an outbreak at an American Legion meeting.

leg iron noun a metal band or chain placed around a prisoner's ankle as a restraint.

legislate /**lej**-iss-layt/ verb **1** make laws. **2** (**legislate for/against**) provide or prepare for: *you can't legislate for bad luck like that*.

legislation noun laws as a whole.
– ORIGIN Latin, 'proposing of a law'.

legislative /**lej**-iss-luh-tiv/ adjective **1** having the power to make laws. **2** relating to laws or a law-making body.
– DERIVATIVES **legislatively** adverb.

legislator noun a person who makes laws; a member of a legislature.

legislature /**lej**-iss-luh-cher/ noun the law-making body of a state.

legitimate adjective /li-**jit**-i-muht/ **1** in accordance with the law or rules. **2** (of a child) born of parents lawfully married to each other. **3** able to be defended or justified: *a legitimate excuse for being late*. **4** (of a sovereign) having a title based on strict hereditary right. •**verb** /li-**jit**-i-mayt/ make something lawful.
– DERIVATIVES **legitimacy** noun **legitimately** adverb **legitimation** noun.
– ORIGIN from Latin *legitimare* 'make legal'.

legitimize (or **legitimise**) verb make something lawful or legitimate.
– DERIVATIVES **legitimization** noun.

legless adjective **1** having no legs. **2** Brit. informal very drunk.

Lego noun trademark a toy consisting of interlocking plastic building blocks.

– ORIGIN from Danish *leg godt* 'play well'.

leg-of-mutton sleeve noun a sleeve which is full on the upper arm but close-fitting on the forearm and wrist.

legroom noun space in which a seated person can put their legs.

legume /leg-yoom/ noun 1 a plant of the pea family grown as a crop. 2 a seed, pod, or other edible part of a plant of the pea family.
– ORIGIN Latin *legumen*.

leguminous /li-gyoo-mi-nuhss/ adjective relating to plants of the pea family, typically having seeds in pods and root nodules containing nitrogen-fixing bacteria.

leg-up noun 1 an act of helping someone to mount a horse or high object. 2 a boost to improve one's position.

leg warmers plural noun a pair of knitted garments covering the legs from ankle to knee or thigh.

legwork noun work that involves tiring or boring travel from place to place.

lei /lay/ noun a Polynesian garland of flowers.
– ORIGIN Hawaiian.

Leicester /les-ter/ noun (also **Red Leicester**) a kind of mild, firm orange cheese originally made in Leicestershire.

Leics. abbreviation Leicestershire.

leishmaniasis /leesh-muh-ny-uh-sis/ noun a tropical and subtropical disease transmitted by the bite of sandflies.
– ORIGIN named after the British pathologist William B. *Leishman*.

leisure noun time spent in or free for relaxation or enjoyment.
– PHRASES **at leisure 1** not occupied; free. **2** in an unhurried way. **at one's leisure** when convenient.
– DERIVATIVES **leisured** adjective.
– ORIGIN Old French *leisir*.

leisure centre (or **complex**) noun Brit. a public building or complex offering facilities for sport and recreation.

leisurely adjective relaxed and unhurried. ●adverb without hurry.
– DERIVATIVES **leisureliness** noun.

leisurewear noun casual clothes worn for leisure activities.

leitmotif /lyt-moh-teef/ (also **leitmotiv**) noun a recurring theme in a musical or literary work.
– ORIGIN German *Leitmotiv*.

lemming noun 1 a short-tailed Arctic rodent which periodically migrates in large numbers. 2 a person who unthinkingly joins a mass movement, especially a rush to destruction.
– ORIGIN Norwegian and Danish.

lemon noun 1 a pale yellow oval citrus fruit with thick skin and acidic juice. 2 a drink made from or flavoured with lemon juice. 3 a pale yellow colour. 4 informal a feeble or unsatisfactory person or thing.
– DERIVATIVES **lemony** adjective.
– ORIGIN Old French *limon*.

lemonade noun a sweetened drink made from lemon juice or lemon flavouring and still or fizzy water.

lemon balm noun a bushy lemon-scented herb of the mint family.

lemon curd noun a sweet spread made from lemons, butter, eggs, and sugar.

lemon grass noun a tropical grass which yields an oil that smells of lemon, used in Asian cooking.

lemon sole noun a common flatfish of the plaice family.
– ORIGIN French *limande*.

lemur /lee-mer/ noun a primate with a pointed snout and a long tail that lives in trees in Madagascar.
– ORIGIN from Latin *lemures* 'spirits of the dead' (from the animal's face).

lend verb (past and past part. **lent**) 1 allow someone to use something on the understanding that it will be returned. 2 allow someone to use a sum of money under an agreement to pay it back later, typically with interest. 3 contribute or add a quality to: *the smile lent his face a boyish charm.* 4 (**lend itself to**) (of a thing) be suitable for something.
– PHRASES **lend an ear** listen sympathetically or attentively.
– DERIVATIVES **lender** noun.
– ORIGIN Old English.

> USAGE: Pairs of words such as **lend** and **borrow** are often confused. Although uses such as *can I lend your pen?* (meaning 'borrow') are common in a number of British dialects, the correct standard use is *can I borrow your pen?*

lending library noun a public library from which books may be borrowed for a limited time.

length noun 1 the measurement or extent of something from end to end. 2 the amount of time occupied by something: *schools have reduced the length of break times.* 3 the quality of being long. 4 the full distance that a thing extends for. 5 the extent of a garment downwards when worn. 6 the length of a horse or boat as a measure of the lead in a race. 7 a stretch or piece of something. 8 a degree to which a course of action is taken: *they go to great lengths to avoid the press.*
– PHRASES **at length 1** in detail; fully. **2** after a long time.
– ORIGIN Old English.

lengthen verb make or become longer.

lengthways adverb in a direction parallel with the length of something.

lengthwise adverb lengthways. ●adjective lying or moving lengthways.

lengthy adjective (**lengthier**, **lengthiest**) very or excessively long in time or extent.
– DERIVATIVES **lengthily** adverb.

lenient /lee-ni-uhnt/ adjective not as strict or severe as expected: *a lenient one-year sentence.*
– DERIVATIVES **lenience** noun **leniency** noun **leniently** adverb.
– ORIGIN from Latin *lenire* 'soothe'.

Leninism noun Marxism as interpreted and applied by the Soviet premier Vladimir Ilich Lenin.
– DERIVATIVES **Leninist** noun & adjective.

lens noun 1 a piece of glass or other transparent material with one or both sides curved for concentrating or dispersing light rays. 2 the light-gathering device of a camera, containing a group of compound lenses. 3 the transparent

structure behind the iris in the eye, by which light is focused on to the retina.
– ORIGIN Latin, 'lentil'.

lensman noun (pl. **lensmen**) a professional photographer or cameraman.

Lent noun (in the Christian Church) the period preceding Easter, during which some people give up food or other things that they enjoy.
– ORIGIN abbreviation of **LENTEN**.

lent past and past participle of **LEND**.

Lenten adjective relating to Lent.
– ORIGIN Old English, 'spring, Lent'.

lenticular /len-**tik**-yuu-luh/ adjective **1** shaped like a lentil, especially by having two curved edges. **2** relating to the lens of the eye.

lentil noun a pulse (edible seed) which is dried and then soaked and cooked before eating.
– ORIGIN Latin *lens* 'lentil'.

lento adverb & adjective Music slow or slowly.
– ORIGIN Italian.

Leo noun a constellation (the Lion) and sign of the zodiac, which the sun enters about 23 July.
– ORIGIN Latin.

leonine /**lee**-uh-nyn/ adjective relating to or resembling a lion or lions.
– ORIGIN from Latin *leo* 'lion'.

leopard noun (fem. **leopardess**) a large solitary cat with a black-spotted fawn or brown coat, found in the forests of Africa and southern Asia.
– ORIGIN Greek *leopardos*.

leotard noun a close-fitting, stretchy one-piece garment covering the body to the top of the thighs, worn for dance, gymnastics, and exercise.
– ORIGIN named after the French trapeze artist Jules *Léotard*.

leper noun **1** a person with leprosy. **2** a person who is rejected or avoided by others: *the story suggested she was a social leper.*
– ORIGIN from Greek *lepros* 'scaly'.

Lepidoptera /lep-i-**dop**-tuh-ruh/ plural noun an order of insects comprising the butterflies and moths.
– DERIVATIVES **lepidopteran** adjective & noun **lepidopterist** noun **lepidopterous** adjective.
– ORIGIN from Greek *lepis* 'scale' + *pteron* 'wing'.

leprechaun /**lep**-ruh-kawn/ noun (in Irish folklore) a small, mischievous sprite.
– ORIGIN Old Irish *luchorpán*.

leprosy noun a contagious disease that causes discoloration and lumps on the skin and, in severe cases, disfigurement and deformities.

leprous adjective referring to or suffering from leprosy.

lepton noun Physics a subatomic particle of a type that is not held in atomic nuclei, such as an electron or neutrino.
– ORIGIN from Greek *leptos* 'small'.

lesbian noun a woman who is sexually attracted to other women. ● adjective referring to lesbians or homosexuality in women.
– DERIVATIVES **lesbianism** noun.
– ORIGIN from *Lesbos*, Greek island and home of Sappho, who expressed affection for women in her poetry.

lese-majesty /leez ma-jis-ti/ (also **lèse-majesté**) /layz ma-jis-ti/ noun **1** the insulting of a monarch; treason. **2** arrogant or disrespectful behaviour.
– ORIGIN from Latin *laesa majestas* 'injured sovereignty'.

lesion /lee-**zh**uhn/ noun a region in an organ or tissue which has been damaged through injury or disease.
– ORIGIN from Latin *laedere* 'injure'.

less determiner & pronoun **1** a smaller amount of; not as much. **2** fewer in number. ● adverb to a smaller extent; not so much. ● preposition minus.
– ORIGIN Old English.

> USAGE: On the difference in use between **less** and **fewer**, see the note at **FEW**.

lessee noun a person who holds the lease of a property.
– ORIGIN Old French *lesse*.

lessen verb make or become less; diminish.

lesser adjective not so great, large, or important as the other or the rest.

lesson noun **1** a period of learning or teaching. **2** a thing learned by teaching or experience. **3** a thing that acts as a warning or encouragement. **4** a passage from the Bible read aloud during a church service.
– ORIGIN Old French *leçon*.

lessor noun a person who lets a property to another.
– ORIGIN Old French.

lest conjunction formal **1** to avoid the risk of. **2** because of the possibility of.
– ORIGIN Old English, 'whereby less that'.

> USAGE: The word **lest** takes the *subjunctive* mood of a verb, meaning that the correct use is *she was worrying lest he be attacked* (not … *lest he was attacked*).

let[1] verb (**lets**, **letting**, **let**) **1** allow someone to do something or something to happen. **2** used to express an intention, proposal, or instruction: *let's have a drink.* **3** chiefly Brit. allow someone to have the use of a room or property in return for payment. **4** used to express an assumption on which a theory or calculation is to be based. ● noun Brit. a period during which a room or property is rented.
– PHRASES **let alone** not to mention. **let someone down** fail to support or help someone. **let fly** attack someone. **let someone/ thing go 1** allow a person or animal to go free. **2** release one's grip on someone or something. **let oneself go 1** act in an uninhibited way. **2** become careless in one's habits or appearance. **let someone off 1** refrain from punishing someone. **2** excuse someone from a task or duty. **let something off** cause a gun, firework, or bomb to fire or explode. **let on** informal reveal information. **let something out 1** make a sound or cry. **2** make a piece of clothing looser or larger. **let up** informal become less intense. **to let** available for rent.
– DERIVATIVES **letting** noun.
– ORIGIN Old English, 'leave behind, leave out'.

let[2] noun (in racket sports) a situation in which a point is not counted and is played for again.
– PHRASES **without let or hindrance** formal without obstruction; freely.
– ORIGIN Old English, 'hinder'.

let-down noun a disappointment.

lethal adjective **1** able or enough to cause death. **2** very harmful or destructive.
– DERIVATIVES **lethality** noun **lethally** adverb.
– ORIGIN Latin *lethalis*.

lethargy /leth-er-ji/ noun a lack of energy and enthusiasm.
– DERIVATIVES **lethargic** adjective **lethargically** adverb.
– ORIGIN from Greek *lēthargos* 'forgetful'.

let-off noun informal an instance of unexpectedly escaping or avoiding something.

let-out noun Brit. informal an opportunity to escape from or avoid a difficult situation.

let's contraction let us.

letter noun **1** a symbol representing one or more of the sounds used in speech; any of the symbols of an alphabet. **2** a written, typed, or printed communication, sent by post or messenger. **3** the precise terms of a statement or requirement: *adherence to the letter of the law.* **4** (**letters**) literature. •verb carve or write letters on something.
– PHRASES **to the letter** precisely or exactly.
– DERIVATIVES **lettering** noun.
– ORIGIN Latin *litera* 'letter of the alphabet', (plural) 'epistle, literature, culture'.

letter bomb noun an explosive device hidden in a small package, which explodes when the package is opened.

letter box noun Brit. a slot in a door through which mail is delivered.

letterhead noun a printed heading on stationery, stating the sender's name and address.

letter of credit noun a letter issued by one bank to another to serve as a guarantee for payments made to a specified person.

letterpress noun printing from a hard raised image under pressure, using viscous ink.

letters of administration plural noun Law authority to administer the estate of someone who has died without making a will.

letters patent plural noun an open document issued by a monarch or government granting a patent or other right.
– ORIGIN from Latin *litterae patentes*, 'letters lying open'.

lettuce noun **1** a cultivated plant with edible leaves that are eaten in salads. **2** used in names of other plants with edible green leaves, e.g. **lamb's lettuce**.
– ORIGIN Old French *letues*.

let-up noun informal a brief time when something becomes less intense, difficult, or tiring.

leu /lay-oo/ noun (pl. **lei** /lay/) the basic unit of money of Romania.
– ORIGIN Romanian, 'lion'.

leucocyte /loo-koh-syt/ (also **leukocyte**) noun a colourless cell which circulates in the blood and body fluids and acts against foreign substances and disease; a white blood cell.
– ORIGIN from Greek *leukos* 'white' + *kutos* 'vessel'.

leukaemia /loo-kee-mi-uh/ (US **leukemia**) noun a serious disease in which increased numbers of immature or abnormal white cells are produced, stopping the production of normal blood cells.

– DERIVATIVES **leukaemic** adjective.
– ORIGIN from Greek *leukos* 'white' + *haima* 'blood'.

lev /lev/ noun (pl. **levs**) the basic unit of money of Bulgaria.
– ORIGIN Bulgarian, 'lion'.

Levant /li-vant/ noun (**the Levant**) historical the eastern part of the Mediterranean.
– DERIVATIVES **Levantine** noun & adjective.
– ORIGIN from French, 'rising' (used to mean 'point of sunrise, east').

levee[1] /lev-ay/ noun N. Amer. or old use a formal reception of visitors or guests.
– ORIGIN French, 'rising' (first referring to a reception held by a monarch after rising from bed).

levee[2] /lev-i/ noun **1** an embankment built to prevent a river from overflowing. **2** a ridge of sediment deposited naturally alongside a river. **3** N. Amer. a landing place; a quay.
– ORIGIN French, 'rising, lifting'.

level noun **1** a position or stage on a scale of quantity, extent, rank, or quality: *a high level of unemployment.* **2** a horizontal line or surface. **3** a height or distance from the ground or another base point: *storms caused river levels to rise.* **4** a floor of a multi-storey building. **5** a flat area of land. **6** an instrument giving a line parallel to the plane of the horizon for testing whether things are horizontal. •adjective **1** having a flat, horizontal surface. **2** having the same height, position, or value as someone or something else: *her face was level with his own.* **3** chiefly Brit. having the same score. **4** calm and steady. •verb (**levels, levelling, levelled**; US **levels, leveling, leveled**) **1** make or become level or flat. **2** make or become equal or similar. **3** aim or direct a weapon, criticism, or accusation. **4** (**level with**) informal be frank or honest with someone.
– PHRASES **be level pegging** Brit. be equal during a contest. **a level playing field** a situation in which everyone has an equal chance of succeeding. **on the level** informal honest; truthful.
– DERIVATIVES **levelly** adverb **levelness** noun.
– ORIGIN Old French *livel*.

level crossing noun Brit. a place where a railway and a road cross at the same level.

level-headed adjective calm and sensible.
– DERIVATIVES **level-headedly** adverb **level-headedness** noun.

leveller (US **leveler**) noun **1** a person or thing that levels something. **2** a situation or activity in which distinctions of class, age, or ability do not matter: *he valued the sport because it was a great leveller.*

lever noun **1** a rigid bar resting on a pivot, used to move a load with one end when pressure is applied to the other. **2** an arm or handle that is moved to operate a mechanism. •verb **1** lift or move something with a lever. **2** move with effort: *she levered herself up.*
– ORIGIN from Old French *lever* 'to lift'.

leverage /lee-ver-ij/ noun **1** the exertion of force by means of a lever. **2** the power to influence: *states trying to regain their former leverage.*

leveraged buyout noun the purchase of a controlling share in a company by its management using capital borrowed from outside the company.

leveret /lev-uh-rit/ noun a young hare in its first year.
– ORIGIN Old French.

leviathan /li-vy-uh-thuhn/ noun **1** a very large or powerful thing. **2** (in biblical use) a sea monster.
– ORIGIN Hebrew.

levitate verb rise or cause to rise and hover in the air.
– DERIVATIVES **levitation** noun.
– ORIGIN from Latin *levis* 'light'.

levity noun the treatment of a serious matter with humour or lack of respect.
– ORIGIN Latin *levitas*.

levy verb (**levies, levying, levied**) **1** impose a tax, fee, or fine. **2** old use enlist someone for military service. • noun (pl. **levies**) **1** an act of imposing a tax, fee, or fine: *a levy on energy-intensive industries.* **2** a sum of money raised by a tax, fee, or fine. **3** old use a body of enlisted troops.
– ORIGIN Old French *lever* 'raise'.

lewd adjective crude and offensive in a sexual way.
– DERIVATIVES **lewdly** adverb **lewdness** noun.
– ORIGIN Old English.

lexical adjective **1** relating to the words of a language. **2** relating to a lexicon or dictionary.
– DERIVATIVES **lexically** adverb.
– ORIGIN from Greek *lexikos* 'of words'.

lexicography /leks-i-kog-ruh-fi/ noun the practice of compiling dictionaries.
– DERIVATIVES **lexicographer** noun **lexicographic** adjective.

lexicon noun **1** the vocabulary of a person, language, or subject area. **2** a dictionary.
– ORIGIN from Greek *lexikon biblion* 'book of words'.

ley[1] /rhymes with pay/ noun a piece of land where grass or clover is grown for a limited time.
– ORIGIN Old English, 'fallow'.

ley[2] /rhymes with pay or pea/ (also **ley line**) noun a supposed straight line connecting ancient sites, believed by some people to be associated with lines of energy and other paranormal phenomena.
– ORIGIN variant of LEA.

Leyden jar /ly-duhn/ noun an early form of capacitor (device storing electric charge) consisting of a glass jar with layers of metal foil on the outside and inside.
– ORIGIN named after the city of *Leyden* (or *Leiden*) in the Netherlands.

leylandii /lay-lan-di-I/ noun (pl. same) a fast-growing conifer, grown as a screening plant or for shelter.
– ORIGIN named after the British horticulturalist Christopher J. *Leyland*.

LF abbreviation low frequency.

LGV abbreviation Brit. large goods vehicle.

Li symbol the chemical element lithium.

liability noun (pl. **liabilities**) **1** the state of being legally responsible for something. **2** a thing for which someone is legally responsible, especially a debt. **3** a person or thing likely to cause embarrassment or difficulty: *the party*

has become a liability to green politics.

liable adjective **1** responsible by law. **2** (**liable to**) legally required to do something. **3** (**liable to do**) likely to do, be, or experience: *areas liable to flooding.*
– ORIGIN perhaps from French *lier* 'to bind'.

liaise verb **1** cooperate on a matter of shared concern. **2** (**liaise between**) act as a link to assist communication between people.
– ORIGIN from LIAISON.

liaison noun **1** communication or cooperation between people or organizations. **2** a sexual relationship, especially a secret one.
– ORIGIN from French *lier* 'to bind'.

liana /li-ah-nuh/ (also **liane** /li-ahn/) noun a woody climbing plant that hangs from trees, especially in tropical rainforests.
– ORIGIN French *liane* 'clematis, liana'.

liar noun a person who tells lies.

lias /ly-uhss/ (also **blue lias**) noun a blue-grey clayey limestone found chiefly in SW England.
– ORIGIN Old French *liais* 'hard limestone'.

lib noun informal (in the names of political movements) the liberation of a specified group: *women's lib.*
– DERIVATIVES **libber** noun.

libation /ly-bay-sh'n/ noun **1** a drink poured out as an offering to a god. **2** humorous an alcoholic drink.
– ORIGIN from Latin *libare* 'pour as an offering'.

Lib Dem noun informal (in the UK) Liberal Democrat.

libel noun **1** the crime of publishing a false statement that is damaging to a person's reputation. Compare with SLANDER. **2** a published false statement that damages a person's reputation. • verb (**libels, libelling, libelled**; US **libels, libeling, libeled**) publish a false and damaging statement about someone.
– DERIVATIVES **libellous** (US also **libelous**) adjective.
– ORIGIN Latin *libellus* 'little book'.

liberal adjective **1** willing to respect and accept behaviour or opinions different from one's own. **2** (of a society, law, etc.) favourable to individual rights and freedoms. **3** (in politics favouring individual liberty, free trade, and moderate reform. **4** (**Liberal**) relating to Liberals or a Liberal Party, especially (in the UK) relating to the Liberal Democrat party. **5** (of an interpretation) broadly understood; not strictly literal. **6** given, used, or giving in generous amounts: *liberal amounts of wine were consumed.* **7** (of education) concerned with broadening general knowledge and experience. • noun **1** a person of liberal views. **2** (**Liberal**) a supporter or member of a Liberal Party, especially (in the UK) a Liberal Democrat.
– DERIVATIVES **liberalism** noun **liberality** noun **liberally** adverb.
– ORIGIN Latin *liberalis*.

Liberal Democrat noun (in the UK) a member of a party formed from the Liberal Party and members of the Social Democratic Party.

liberalize (or **liberalise**) verb remove or loosen restrictions on something, typically an economic or political system.

– DERIVATIVES **liberalization** noun.

liberate verb **1** set someone free, especially from imprisonment or oppression. **2** (as adj. **liberated**) free from social conventions, especially with regard to sexual roles.
– DERIVATIVES **liberation** noun **liberationist** noun **liberator** noun **liberatory** adjective.
– ORIGIN Latin *liberare*.

liberation theology noun a movement in Christian belief which attempts to address the problems of poverty and social injustice.

Liberian /ly-beer-i-uhn/ noun a person from Liberia, a country in in West Africa. •adjective relating to Liberia.

libertarian /lib-er-tair-i-uhn/ noun a person who believes that the state should intervene only minimally in the lives of its citizens.
– DERIVATIVES **libertarianism** noun.

libertine /li-ber-teen/ noun a man who behaves without moral principles, especially in sexual matters.
– DERIVATIVES **libertinism** noun.
– ORIGIN Latin *libertinus* 'freed slave'.

liberty noun (pl. **liberties**) **1** the state of being free; freedom. **2** a right or privilege. **3** the power or scope to act as one pleases: *he's not at liberty to discuss his real work.* **4** informal a disrespectful remark or action.
– PHRASES **take liberties with 1** behave in an excessively familiar way towards someone. **2** treat something without strict faithfulness to the facts or to an original. **take the liberty** do something without first asking permission.
– ORIGIN Latin *libertas*.

libidinous /li-bid-i-nuhss/ adjective having or showing a strong sex drive.
– ORIGIN from Latin *libido* 'desire, lust'.

libido /li-bee-doh/ noun (pl. **libidos**) sexual desire.
– DERIVATIVES **libidinal** adjective.
– ORIGIN Latin, 'desire, lust'.

Libra /lee-bruh/ noun a constellation (the Scales) and sign of the zodiac, which the sun enters about 23 September.
– DERIVATIVES **Libran** noun & adjective.
– ORIGIN Latin.

librarian noun a person in charge of or assisting in a library.
– DERIVATIVES **librarianship** noun.

library noun (pl. **libraries**) **1** a building or room containing a collection of books and periodicals for use by the public or the members of an institution. **2** a private collection of books. **3** an organized collection of films, recorded music, etc., kept for research or borrowing. **4** (also **software library**) a collection of computer programs and software packages made generally available.
– ORIGIN Latin *libraria* 'bookshop'.

libretto /li-bret-toh/ noun (pl. **libretti** /li-bret-ti/ or **librettos**) the text of an opera or other long vocal work.
– DERIVATIVES **librettist** noun.
– ORIGIN Italian, 'small book'.

Libyan noun a person from Libya. •adjective relating to Libya.

lice plural of LOUSE.

licence (US **license**) noun **1** a permit from an authority to own, use, or do something.

2 freedom to behave without restraint: *the government has given the army too much licence.* **3** the freedom of a writer or artist to deviate from facts or accepted rules.
– ORIGIN Latin *licentia* 'freedom, licentiousness'.

license (also **licence**) verb **1** grant a licence to someone. **2** authorize or permit something.
– DERIVATIVES **licensable** adjective **licenser** (also **licensor**) noun.
– ORIGIN from LICENCE.

licensee noun the holder of a licence, especially to sell alcoholic drinks.

license plate noun North American term for NUMBER PLATE.

licentiate /ly-sen-shi-uht/ noun **1** the holder of a certificate of competence to practise a particular profession. **2** (in certain universities) a degree between that of bachelor and master or doctor.
– DERIVATIVES **licentiateship** noun.
– ORIGIN from Latin *licentiatus* 'having freedom'.

licentious /ly-sen-shuhss/ adjective promiscuous and unprincipled in sexual matters.
– DERIVATIVES **licentiously** adverb **licentiousness** noun.
– ORIGIN Latin *licentiosus*.

lichen /ly-kuhn, li-chuhn/ noun a simple plant consisting of a fungus living in close association with an alga, typically growing on rocks, walls, and trees.
– DERIVATIVES **lichened** adjective.
– ORIGIN Greek *leikhēn*.

licit /lis-it/ adjective formal not forbidden; lawful.
– ORIGIN Latin *licitus* 'allowed'.

lick verb **1** pass the tongue over something in order to taste, moisten, or clean it. **2** move lightly and quickly: *the flames licked around the wood.* **3** informal overcome someone decisively. •noun **1** an act of licking. **2** informal a small amount or quick application of something: *a lick of paint.* **3** informal a short phrase or solo in jazz or popular music.
– PHRASES **at a lick** informal at a fast pace. **a lick and a promise** informal a hasty wash. **lick someone's boots** (or vulgar slang **arse**) be excessively flattering or servile towards someone.
– ORIGIN Old English.

lickspittle noun a person who behaves in a flattering or servile way to those in power.

licorice noun US spelling of LIQUORICE.

lid noun **1** a removable or hinged cover for the top of a container. **2** an eyelid.
– DERIVATIVES **lidded** adjective **lidless** adjective.
– ORIGIN Old English.

lido /lee-doh/ noun (pl. **lidos**) Brit. a public open-air swimming pool or bathing beach.
– ORIGIN Italian, 'shore'.

lie[1] verb (**lies**, **lying**, **lay**; past part. **lain**) **1** be in or take up a horizontal or resting position on a supporting surface. **2** be or remain in a particular state: *many buildings were lying empty.* **3** be situated in a specified position or direction. **4** be found: *the solution lies in a return to traditional values.* •noun the way, direction, or position in which something lies or comes to rest.

– PHRASES **let something lie** take no action on a problematic matter. **lie in** Brit. remain in bed later than usual. **lie in state** (of the corpse of a person of national importance) be laid in a public place of honour before burial. **lie low** keep out of sight; avoid attention. **the lie** (N. Amer. **lay**) **of the land 1** the features of an area. **2** the current situation. **lie with** old use have sex with. **take something lying down** accept an insult or reprimand without protest.
– ORIGIN Old English.

USAGE: For the correct use of **lay** and **lie**, see the note at **LAY¹**.

lie² noun **1** a deliberately false statement. **2** a situation involving deception or based on a mistaken impression. • verb (**lies, lying, lied**) **1** tell a lie or lies. **2** present a false impression: *the camera cannot lie*.
– PHRASES **give the lie to** show that something assumed to be true is not true.
– ORIGIN Old English.

Liebfraumilch /leeb-frow-milsh/ noun a light white wine from the Rhine region.
– ORIGIN from German *lieb* 'dear' + *Frau* 'lady' (referring to the Virgin Mary) + *Milch* 'milk'.

lied /leed/ noun (pl. **lieder** /lee-der/) a type of German song, typically for solo voice with piano accompaniment.
– ORIGIN German.

lie detector noun a device for determining whether a person is telling the truth.

lie-down noun Brit. a short rest on a bed or sofa.

lief /leef/ adverb (**as lief**) old use as happily.
– ORIGIN Old English, 'dear, pleasant'.

liege /leej/ noun historical **1** (also **liege lord**) a lord or sovereign under the feudal system. **2** a person who served a lord in the feudal system.
– ORIGIN Old French.

lie-in noun Brit. a prolonged stay in bed in the morning.

lien /lee-uhn/ noun Law a right to keep the property of another person until a debt owed by that person is paid.
– ORIGIN Old French *loien*.

lieu /loo/ noun (in phrase **in lieu**) instead: *rum was used by local merchants in lieu of cash*.
– ORIGIN French.

lieutenant /lef-ten-uhnt/ noun **1** a person who acts as a deputy or substitute for a superior. **2** a rank of officer in the British army or in the navy.
– DERIVATIVES **lieutenancy** noun (pl. **lieutenancies**).
– ORIGIN Old French, 'place-holding'.

lieutenant colonel noun a rank of officer in the army and the US air force, above major and below colonel.

lieutenant commander noun a rank of officer in the navy, above lieutenant and below commander.

lieutenant general noun a high rank of officer in the army, above major general and below general.

life noun (pl. **lives**) **1** the condition that distinguishes animals and plants from inorganic matter, including the ability to grow, breathe, and reproduce. **2** the existence of an individual human being or animal. **3** a particular type or aspect of people's existence: *school life*. **4** living things and their activity. **5** the period during which something continues to exist, function, or be valid. **6** vitality or energy. **7** informal a sentence of imprisonment for life. **8** a biography. • adjective (in art) based on a living rather than an imagined form: *a life drawing*.
– PHRASES **as large as** (or **larger than**) **life** informal noticeably present. **not on your life** informal definitely not. **take one's life in one's hands** risk being killed.
– ORIGIN Old English.

life assurance noun Brit. another term for **LIFE INSURANCE**.

lifebelt noun an inflatable or buoyant ring used to help a person who has fallen into water to stay afloat.

lifeblood noun a vital factor or force: *intelligence is the lifeblood of anti-terrorist operations*.

lifeboat noun **1** a type of boat launched from land to rescue people at sea. **2** a small boat kept on a ship for use in an emergency.

lifebuoy noun a buoyant support such as a lifebelt for keeping a person afloat in water.

life cycle noun the series of changes in the life of an organism.

life expectancy noun the period that a person may expect to live.

life force noun the force that gives something its vitality or strength.

life form noun any living thing.

lifeguard noun a person employed to rescue bathers who get into difficulty at a beach or swimming pool.

life imprisonment noun a long term of imprisonment which (in the UK) is now the only sentence for murder and the maximum for any crime.

life insurance noun insurance that pays out a sum of money either on the death of the insured person or after a set period.

life jacket noun a sleeveless inflatable jacket for keeping a person afloat in water.

lifeless adjective **1** dead or apparently dead. **2** not containing living things. **3** lacking vitality or excitement.
– DERIVATIVES **lifelessly** adverb **lifelessness** noun.

lifelike adjective very similar to the person or thing represented.

lifeline noun **1** a thing on which someone or something depends or which provides a means of escape: *as a forest manager, my mobile is my lifeline*. **2** a rope thrown to rescue someone in water or used by sailors to secure themselves to a boat. **3** (in palmistry) a line on the palm of a person's hand, regarded as indicating how long they will live.

lifelong adjective lasting in a particular state throughout a person's life.

life peer (or **peeress**) noun (in the UK) a peer (or peeress) whose title cannot be inherited.

lifer noun informal a person serving a life sentence.

life raft noun an inflatable raft for use in an emergency at sea.

lifesaver noun **1** informal a thing that saves someone from serious difficulty. **2** Austral./NZ a lifeguard.

life sciences plural noun the sciences concerned with the study of living organisms, including biology, botany, and zoology.

life sentence noun a punishment of life imprisonment.

life-size (also **life-sized**) adjective of the same size as the person or thing represented.

lifespan noun the length of time for which a person or animal lives or a thing functions.

lifestyle noun the way in which someone lives.

life support noun the maintenance of a patient's vital functions following an injury or serious illness.

life-threatening adjective potentially fatal.

lifetime noun **1** the length of time that a person lives or a thing lasts. **2** informal a very long time.

lift verb **1** raise or be raised to a higher position or level. **2** pick someone or something up and move them to a different position. **3** formally remove or end a legal restriction, decision, or ban. **4** (**lift off**) (of an aircraft, spacecraft, or rocket) take off, especially vertically. **5** win a prize or event. **6** informal steal something. • noun **1** Brit. a platform or compartment housed in a shaft for raising and lowering people or things. **2** an act of lifting. **3** a free ride in another person's vehicle. **4** a device for carrying people up or down a mountain. **5** a feeling of increased cheerfulness: *winning the match has given everyone a lift.* **6** upward force exerted by the air on an aerofoil.
– PHRASES **not lift a finger** refuse to make the slightest effort.
– DERIVATIVES **liftable** adjective **lifter** noun.
– ORIGIN Old Norse.

lift-off noun the vertical take-off of a spacecraft, rocket, or aircraft.

lig Brit. informal verb (**ligs**, **ligging**, **ligged**) take advantage of free parties, shows, or travel offered by companies for publicity purposes. • noun a free party or show provided for publicity.
– DERIVATIVES **ligger** noun.
– ORIGIN from a dialect form of LIE¹ meaning 'lie about, loaf'.

ligament noun **1** a short band of tough, flexible fibrous tissue which connects two bones or cartilages or holds together a joint. **2** a fold of membrane that supports a body organ and keeps it in position.
– DERIVATIVES **ligamentous** adjective.
– ORIGIN Latin *ligamentum* 'bond'.

ligature noun **1** a thing used for tying something tightly, especially a cord used in surgery to tie up a bleeding artery. **2** Music a slur or tie. **3** Printing a character consisting of two or more joined letters, e.g. æ. • verb bind or connect something with a ligature.
– ORIGIN Latin *ligatura*.

light¹ noun **1** the natural form of energy that makes things visible; electromagnetic radiation from about 390 to 740 nm in wavelength. **2** a source of illumination such as a lamp. **3** (**lights**) traffic lights. **4** a device producing a flame or spark. **5** an expression in someone's eyes. **6** understanding: *light dawned in her eyes.* **7** an area that is brighter or paler than its surroundings. **8** a window or

section of a window. • verb (past **lit**; past part. **lit** or **lighted**) **1** provide something with light. **2** ignite or be ignited. • adjective **1** having a considerable amount of natural light. **2** (of a colour) pale.
– PHRASES **bring** (or **come**) **to light** make (or become) widely known or evident. **in a —— light** in the way specified. **in (the) light of** taking something into consideration. **light at the end of the tunnel** an indication that a period of difficulty is ending. **the light of day** general public attention. **light up 1** become illuminated. **2** become lively or happy. **light something up** ignite a cigarette, pipe, or cigar before smoking it. **see the light** understand or realize something. **throw** (or **cast** or **shed**) **light on** help to explain something by providing further information.
– DERIVATIVES **lightless** adjective **lightness** noun.
– ORIGIN Old English.

light² adjective **1** not heavy or heavy enough. **2** not strongly or heavily built or made. **3** relatively low in density, amount, or intensity: *traffic was light.* **4** carrying or suitable for small loads. **5** gentle or delicate. **6** not serious or challenging: *light entertainment.* **7** (of sleep or a sleeper) easily disturbed. **8** easily done. **9** cheerful or carefree.
– PHRASES **make light of** treat something as unimportant. **make light work of** accomplish something quickly and easily.
– DERIVATIVES **lightish** adjective **lightly** adverb **lightness** noun.
– ORIGIN Old English.

light³ verb (past and past part. **lit** or **lighted**) (**light on**) come upon or discover someone or something by chance.
– ORIGIN Old English, 'descend, alight'.

light bulb noun a glass bulb containing inert gas, fitted into a lamp or ceiling socket, which provides light when an electric current is passed through it.

lighten¹ verb **1** make or become lighter in weight. **2** make or become less serious.

lighten² verb make or become brighter.

lighter¹ noun a device producing a small flame, used to light cigarettes.

lighter² noun a flat-bottomed barge used to transfer goods to and from ships in harbour.
– ORIGIN from LIGHT² (in the sense 'unload'), or from German *luchter*.

light-fingered adjective informal prone to steal.

light flyweight noun the lowest weight in amateur boxing.

light-footed adjective fast and nimble on one's feet.

light-headed adjective dizzy and slightly faint.

light-hearted adjective **1** amusing and entertaining. **2** cheerful or carefree.
– DERIVATIVES **light-heartedly** adverb.

light heavyweight noun a weight in boxing and other sports between middleweight and heavyweight.

lighthouse noun a tower or other structure containing a light to warn ships at sea.

light industry noun the manufacture of small or light articles.

lighting noun **1** equipment for producing light. **2** the arrangement or effect of lights.

lighting-up time noun Brit. the time at which motorists are required by law to switch their vehicles' lights on.

light meter noun an instrument measuring the intensity of light, used when taking photographs.

light middleweight noun a weight in amateur boxing between welterweight and middleweight.

lightning noun a high-voltage electrical discharge between a cloud and the ground or within a cloud, accompanied by a bright flash. •adjective very quick: *lightning speed*.
– ORIGIN from LIGHTEN².

USAGE: Do not confuse **lightning** with **lightening**. Lightning means 'a high-voltage electrical discharge and bright flash in the sky' (*thunder and lightning*) or 'very quick', whereas **lightening** is part of the verb **lighten** and means 'getting lighter' (*the sea was lightening from black to grey*).

lightning conductor (also chiefly N. Amer. **lightning rod**) noun Brit. a metal rod or wire fixed in a high and exposed place to divert lightning into the ground.

light pen noun **1** a hand-held pen-like photosensitive device used for passing information to a computer. **2** a hand-held device for reading bar codes.

light pollution noun excessive brightening of the night sky by street lights and other man-made sources.

lights plural noun the lungs of sheep, pigs, or bullocks as food for pets.
– ORIGIN from LIGHT² (because of their lightness).

lightship noun an anchored boat with a light to warn ships at sea.

lightweight noun **1** a weight in boxing and other sports between featherweight and welterweight. **2** informal a person of little importance. •adjective **1** of thin material or build. **2** lacking seriousness or importance: *lightweight magazine essays*.

light welterweight noun a weight in amateur boxing between lightweight and welterweight.

light year noun Astronomy a unit of distance equivalent to the distance that light travels in one year, 9.4607×10^{12} km (nearly 6 million million miles).

ligneous /lig-ni-uhss/ adjective consisting of or resembling wood.
– ORIGIN Latin *ligneus* 'relating to wood'.

lignin noun a complex organic substance found in the cell walls of many plants, making them rigid and woody.
– ORIGIN from Latin *lignum* 'wood'.

lignite noun a type of soft brownish coal.
– ORIGIN from Latin *lignum* 'wood'.

lignum vitae /lig-nuhm vy-tee, lig-nuhm vee-ty/ noun another term for GUAIACUM.
– ORIGIN Latin, 'wood of life'.

likable adjective variant spelling of LIKEABLE.

like¹ preposition **1** similar to. **2** in the same way as. **3** in a way appropriate to. **4** in this way.

5 such as. **6** used to ask about the nature of someone or something. •conjunction informal **1** in the same way that. **2** as if. •noun **1** a similar person or thing. **2** (**the like**) things of the same kind. •adjective having similar characteristics.
– PHRASES **like so** informal in this way.
– ORIGIN Old Norse.

USAGE: When writing formal English, do not use **like** to mean 'as if', as in *he's behaving like he owns the place*; use **as if** or **as though** instead.

like² verb **1** find someone or something pleasant or satisfactory. **2** wish for or want something. •noun (**likes**) the things one likes.
– ORIGIN Old English, 'be pleasing'.

likeable (also **likable**) adjective pleasant; easy to like.
– DERIVATIVES **likeably** adverb.

likelihood noun the state or fact of being likely or probable.

likely adjective (**likelier**, **likeliest**) **1** such as well might be the case; probable. **2** apparently suitable; promising. •adverb probably.
– PHRASES **a likely story!** used to express disbelief. **not likely!** informal certainly not.

like-minded adjective having similar tastes or opinions.

liken verb (**liken someone/thing to**) point out that someone or something is similar to; compare: *he likened the election to a job interview*.

likeness noun **1** the fact of being alike; resemblance. **2** outward appearance: *humans are made in God's likeness*. **3** a portrait or other representation of a person.

likewise adverb **1** also; moreover. **2** in a similar way.

liking noun **1** a regard or fondness for someone or something. **2** a person's taste: *the coffee was just to his liking*.

lilac noun **1** a shrub or small tree with fragrant violet, pink, or white blossom. **2** a pale pinkish-violet colour.
– ORIGIN from Persian, 'bluish'.

Lilliputian /lil-li-**pyoo**-sh'n/ adjective very small or unimportant. •noun a very small or unimportant person or thing.
– ORIGIN from *Lilliput* in Jonathan Swift's *Gulliver's Travels*, a country inhabited by 6-inch high people.

lilo (also trademark **Li-lo**) noun (pl. **lilos**) Brit. an inflatable mattress used for floating on water or as a bed.
– ORIGIN alteration of *lie low*.

lilt noun **1** a characteristic rising and falling of the voice when speaking. **2** a gentle rhythm in a tune. •verb speak, sing, or sound with a lilt.
– ORIGIN unknown.

lily noun (pl. **lilies**) a plant with large trumpet-shaped flowers on a tall, slender stem.
– ORIGIN Greek *leirion*.

lily-livered adjective weak and cowardly.

lily of the valley noun a plant of the lily family, with broad leaves and small white bell-shaped flowers.

lily pad noun a leaf of a water lily.

lily-white adjective **1** pure white. **2** totally innocent or pure.

lima bean /**lee**-muh/ noun an edible flat whitish bean.
– ORIGIN from *Lima*, the capital of Peru.

limb[1] noun **1** an arm, leg, or wing. **2** a large branch of a tree. **3** a projecting part of a structure, object, or natural feature.
– PHRASES **out on a limb** in a position where one is not supported by anyone else.
– DERIVATIVES **limbed** adjective **limbless** adjective.
– ORIGIN Old English.

limb[2] noun Astronomy a specified edge of the disc of the sun, moon, or other celestial object.
– ORIGIN Latin *limbus* 'hem, border'.

limber[1] verb (**limber up**) warm up in preparation for exercise or activity. • adjective supple; flexible.
– ORIGIN perhaps from LIMBER[2] in the dialect sense 'cart shaft'.

limber[2] noun the detachable front part of a gun carriage.
– ORIGIN probably related to Latin *limonarius*.

limbic system noun a complex system of nerves and networks in the brain, controlling the basic emotions and drives such as fear and hunger.
– ORIGIN from Latin *limbus* 'edge, border'.

limbo[1] noun **1** (in some Christian beliefs) the place between heaven and hell where the souls of people who have not been baptized go to when they die. **2** an uncertain period of waiting for a decision.
– ORIGIN from Latin *limbus* 'hem, border, limbo'.

limbo[2] noun (pl. **limbos**) a West Indian dance in which the dancer bends backwards to pass under a horizontal bar which is progressively lowered toward the ground. • verb dance the limbo.
– ORIGIN from LIMBER[1].

lime[1] noun **1** a product obtained from burning chalk or limestone, used in agriculture or in traditional building to make mortar and plaster. **2** any salt or alkali containing calcium. • verb treat soil or water with lime.
– DERIVATIVES **limy** adjective.
– ORIGIN Old English.

lime[2] noun **1** a rounded green citrus fruit similar to a lemon. **2** a bright light green colour. **3** a drink made from lime juice.
– ORIGIN French.

lime[3] (also **lime tree**) noun a deciduous tree with heart-shaped leaves and yellowish blossom.
– ORIGIN Old English.

limeade noun a drink made from lime juice sweetened with sugar.

limekiln noun a kiln for burning limestone to produce quicklime.

limelight noun **1** (**the limelight**) the focus of public attention. **2** an intense white light produced by heating lime, formerly used in theatres.

limerick noun a humorous five-line poem with a rhyme scheme *aabba*.
– ORIGIN said to be from the chorus 'will you come up to Limerick?', sung between improvised verses at a party.

limescale noun Brit. a hard white substance consisting chiefly of calcium carbonate,

deposited by water on the inside of pipes, kettles, etc.

limestone noun a hard sedimentary rock composed mainly of calcium carbonate.

limewash noun a mixture of lime and water for coating walls.

Limey noun (pl. **Limeys**) N. Amer. & Austral. informal a British person.
– ORIGIN from the former practice of giving lime juice to sailors in the British navy.

liminal /**lim**-in-uhl/ adjective technical **1** relating to a transitional or initial stage. **2** at or on a boundary or threshold.
– DERIVATIVES **liminality** noun.
– ORIGIN from Latin *limen* 'threshold'.

limit noun **1** a point beyond which something does not or may not pass. **2** a restriction on the size or amount of something that is allowed or possible: *an age limit*. **3** the furthest extent of one's endurance. • verb (**limits, limiting, limited**) set a limit on; restrict: *try to limit the amount you drink*.
– PHRASES **be the limit** informal be very annoying. **off limits** out of bounds. **within limits** up to a point.
– DERIVATIVES **limiter** noun.
– ORIGIN Latin *limes* 'boundary, frontier'.

limitation noun **1** a rule or condition that limits someone or something; a restriction. **2** a fault or failing. **3** the act of limiting something.

limited adjective **1** restricted in size, amount, extent, or ability. **2** (of a monarchy or government) operating under limitations of power set down in a constitution. **3** (**Limited**) Brit. referring to a limited company.

limited company noun Brit. a private company whose owners are legally responsible for its debts only to the extent of the amount of capital they invested.

limited liability noun Brit. the condition of being legally responsible for the debts of a company only to the extent of the value of one's shares when they were issued.

limitless adjective without a limit; very large or extensive: *limitless possibilities*.
– DERIVATIVES **limitlessly** adverb **limitlessness** noun.

limn /lim/ verb literary depict or describe someone or something in painting or words.
– DERIVATIVES **limner** noun.
– ORIGIN Latin *luminare* 'make light'.

limo noun (pl. **limos**) informal a limousine.

Limousin /**lim**-uu-zan/ noun a French breed of beef cattle.
– ORIGIN named after the French region of *Limousin*.

limousine noun a large, luxurious car.
– ORIGIN French, first referring to a caped cloak worn in the region of *Limousin*; the car originally had an outside driving compartment, covered with a canopy.

limp[1] verb **1** walk with difficulty because of an injured leg or foot. **2** (of a damaged ship or aircraft) move with difficulty. • noun a walk hampered by an injury.
– ORIGIN related to former *limphalt* 'lame'.

limp[2] adjective **1** not stiff or firm. **2** lacking energy or vigour.

– DERIVATIVES **limply** adverb **limpness** noun.
– ORIGIN perhaps related to LIMP¹.

limpet noun a marine shellfish with a conical shell and a muscular foot for clinging tightly to rocks.
– ORIGIN Latin *lampreda* 'limpet, lamprey'.

limpet mine noun a mine that attaches magnetically to a ship's hull and explodes after a certain time.

limpid adjective 1 (of a liquid or the eyes) clear. 2 (especially of writing or music) clear or melodious.
– DERIVATIVES **limpidity** noun **limpidly** adverb.
– ORIGIN Latin *limpidus*.

limp-wristed adjective informal weak, feeble, or effeminate.

linage /ly-nij/ noun the number of lines in printed or written matter.

linchpin (also **lynchpin**) noun 1 a vital or essential person or thing. 2 a pin through the end of an axle to keep a wheel in position.
– ORIGIN Old English.

Lincs. abbreviation Lincolnshire.

linctus noun Brit. thick liquid medicine, especially cough mixture.
– ORIGIN Latin.

lindane noun a synthetic insecticide, now restricted in use owing to its persistence in the environment.
– ORIGIN named after the Dutch chemist Teunis van der *Linden*.

linden noun a lime tree.
– ORIGIN Old English.

line¹ noun 1 a long, narrow mark or band. 2 a row or series of people or things. 3 a row of written or printed words. 4 a direction, course, or channel. 5 a telephone connection. 6 a railway track or route. 7 a limit or boundary: *the issue cut across class lines.* 8 a range of products. 9 an area of activity: *the stresses unique to their line of work.* 10 a wrinkle in the skin. 11 a shape or outline. 12 a length of cord, wire, etc. 13 a connected series of military defences facing an enemy force. 14 (also **line of battle**) an arrangement of troops for action in battle. 15 informal a remark intended to achieve a purpose: *a cheesy chat-up line.* 16 (**lines**) the words of an actor's part. 17 (**lines**) Brit. a number of repetitions of a sentence written out as a school punishment.
•verb 1 stand or be positioned at intervals along a route. 2 (**line someone/thing up**) arrange people or things in a row. 3 (**line someone/thing up**) have someone or something prepared. 4 (as adj. **lined**) marked or covered with lines.
– PHRASES **come** (or **bring**) **into line** conform (or cause to conform) with something. **in line** under control. **in line for** likely to receive something. **in** (or **out of**) **line with** in (or not in) alignment or accordance with something. **lay it on the line** speak frankly. **line of fire** the expected path of gunfire or a missile. **on the line** at serious risk. **out of line** informal behaving inappropriately or badly.
– ORIGIN Old English; later influenced by Old French *ligne*.

line² verb cover the inner surface of something with a layer of different material.
– PHRASES **line one's pocket** make money,

especially by dishonest means.
– ORIGIN from former *line* 'flax', with reference to the use of linen for linings.

lineage /lin-i-ij/ noun a person's ancestry or pedigree.

lineal /lin-i-uhl/ adjective 1 in a direct line of descent or ancestry. 2 consisting of lines; linear.
– DERIVATIVES **lineally** adverb.

lineament /lin-i-uh-muhnt/ noun (usu. **lineaments**) literary a distinctive feature of the face.
– ORIGIN Latin *lineamentum*.

linear /lin-i-er/ adjective 1 arranged in or extending along a straight line. 2 consisting of lines. 3 progressing in a series of stages: *a linear narrative.* 4 involving one dimension only. 5 Mathematics able to be represented by a straight line on a graph.
– DERIVATIVES **linearity** noun **linearly** adverb.

linear equation noun an equation between two variables that gives a straight line when plotted on a graph.

lineation /lin-i-ay-sh'n/ noun 1 a line or linear marking. 2 the action of drawing lines or marking with lines.

line dancing noun a type of country and western dancing in which a line of dancers follow a choreographed pattern of steps.
– DERIVATIVES **line dance** noun **line dancer** noun.

line drawing noun a drawing based on the use of line rather than shading.

line manager noun chiefly Brit. a manager to whom an employee is directly responsible.
– DERIVATIVES **line management** noun.

linen noun 1 cloth woven from flax. 2 articles such as sheets or clothes that were traditionally made of linen.
– ORIGIN Old English.

linen basket noun chiefly Brit. a basket for dirty clothing.

line-out noun 1 Rugby Union a formation of parallel lines of opposing forwards at right angles to the touchline when the ball is thrown in. 2 an output socket in an electrical device.

liner¹ noun 1 a large passenger ship. [because such a ship travelled on a regular line or route.] 2 a cosmetic for outlining or accentuating the eyes or lips.

liner² noun a lining of a garment, container, etc.

linesman noun (pl. **linesmen**) 1 (in sport) an official who assists the referee or umpire in deciding whether the ball is out of play. 2 Brit. a person who repairs and maintains telephone or electricity power lines.

line-up noun a group of people or things assembled for a purpose.

ling¹ noun a long-bodied edible sea fish of the cod family.
– ORIGIN probably from Dutch.

ling² noun the common heather.
– ORIGIN Old Norse.

lingam /ling-gam/ noun Hinduism a phallus or phallic object as a symbol of Shiva, the god of reproduction.
– ORIGIN Sanskrit, 'mark, sexual characteristic'.

linger verb 1 be slow or reluctant to leave. 2 (**linger over**) spend a long time over

something. **3** be slow to fade, disappear, or die: *the tradition seems to linger on.*
– DERIVATIVES **lingerer** noun.
– ORIGIN Germanic.

lingerie /lan-zhuh-ri/ noun women's underwear and nightclothes.
– ORIGIN French.

lingo noun (pl. **lingos** or **lingoes**) informal **1** a foreign language. **2** the jargon of a particular subject or group.
– ORIGIN probably from Latin *lingua* 'tongue'.

lingua franca /ling-gwuh frang-kuh/ noun (pl. **lingua francas**) a language used as a common language between speakers whose native languages are different.
– ORIGIN Italian, 'Frankish tongue'.

lingual /ling-gwuhl/ adjective technical **1** relating to the tongue. **2** relating to speech or language.
– DERIVATIVES **lingually** adverb.
– ORIGIN Latin *lingualis*.

linguine /ling-gwee-ni/ plural noun small ribbons of pasta.
– ORIGIN Italian, 'little tongues'.

linguist noun **1** a person skilled in foreign languages. **2** a person who studies linguistics.
– ORIGIN from Latin *lingua* 'language'.

linguistic adjective relating to language or linguistics.
– DERIVATIVES **linguistically** adverb.

linguistics plural noun (treated as sing.) the scientific study of language and its structure.

liniment noun an ointment rubbed on the body to relieve pain or bruising.
– ORIGIN Latin *linimentum*.

lining noun a layer of different material covering or attached to the inside of something.

link noun **1** a relationship or connection between people or things. **2** something that enables people to communicate with each other. **3** a means of contact or transport between two places. **4** a code or instruction connecting one part of a computer program, website, etc. to another. **5** a loop in a chain.
● verb make, form, or suggest a link with or between: *a network of routes linking towns and villages.*
– DERIVATIVES **linker** noun.
– ORIGIN Old Norse.

linkage noun **1** the action of linking people or things. **2** a system of links.

linkman noun (pl. **linkmen**) Brit. **1** a person serving as a connection between others. **2** a person providing continuity between items on radio or television.

links (also **golf links**) plural noun (treated as sing. or pl.) a golf course, especially one on sandy grassland near the sea.
– ORIGIN Old English, 'rising ground'.

link-up noun **1** an instance of people or things linking. **2** a connection enabling people or machines to communicate with each other.

Linnaean /li-nee-uhn/ (also **Linnean**) adjective relating to the Swedish botanist Linnaeus (Latinized name of Carl von Linné) or his classification of animals and plants.

linnet noun a mainly brown and grey finch with a reddish breast and forehead.

– ORIGIN from Old French *lin* 'flax' (because the bird feeds on flaxseeds).

lino noun (pl. **linos**) informal, chiefly Brit. linoleum.

linocut noun a design carved in relief on a block of linoleum, used for printing.

linoleic acid /lin-oh-lee-ik, lin-oh-lay-ik/ noun a polyunsaturated fatty acid present in linseed oil and other oils and essential in the diet.
– ORIGIN from Latin *linum* 'flax'.

linoleum /li-noh-li-uhm/ noun a floor covering consisting of a canvas backing thickly coated with a preparation of linseed oil and powdered cork.
– ORIGIN from Latin *linum* 'flax' + *oleum* 'oil'.

linseed noun the seeds of the flax plant.
– ORIGIN Old English.

linseed oil noun oil extracted from linseed, used especially in paint and varnish.

lint noun **1** short, fine fibres which separate from cloth or yarn during processing. **2** a fabric with a raised nap on one side, used for dressing wounds.
– DERIVATIVES **linty** adjective.
– ORIGIN perhaps from Old French *linette* 'linseed'.

lintel noun a horizontal support across the top of a door or window.
– DERIVATIVES **lintelled** (US **linteled**) adjective.
– ORIGIN Old French.

lion noun (fem. **lioness**) **1** a large tawny cat of Africa and NW India, the male of which has a shaggy mane. **2** a brave, strong, or fierce person. **3** (also literary **lion**) a famous author.
– PHRASES **the lion's share** Brit. the largest part of something.
– ORIGIN Greek *leōn*.

lion-hearted adjective brave and determined.

lionize (or **lionise**) verb treat someone as a celebrity.
– DERIVATIVES **lionization** noun.

lip noun **1** either of the two fleshy parts forming the edges of the mouth opening. **2** the edge of a hollow container or an opening. **3** informal disrespectful talk.
– PHRASES **bite one's lip** stop oneself from saying something or laughing. **pass one's lips** be eaten, drunk, or spoken. **pay lip service to** express superficial respect or support for something.
– DERIVATIVES **lipless** adjective **lipped** adjective.
– ORIGIN Old English.

lipa /lee-puh/ noun (pl. same or **lipas**) a unit of money of Croatia, equal to one hundredth of a kuna.
– ORIGIN Serbo-Croat, 'lime tree'.

lipase /lip-ayz/ noun an enzyme produced by the pancreas that promotes the breakdown of fats.
– ORIGIN from Greek *lipos* 'fat'.

lipgloss noun a glossy cosmetic applied to the lips.

lipid /lip-id/ noun any of a class of fats that are insoluble in water and include many natural oils, waxes, and steroids.
– ORIGIN from Greek *lipos* 'fat'.

lipoprotein /lip-oh-proh-teen, ly-poh-proh-teen/ noun a soluble protein that transports lipids (a type of fat) in the blood.

liposome /lip-uh-sohm, ly-puh-sohm/ noun a

tiny artificial container of insoluble fat enclosing a water droplet, used to carry drugs into body tissues.
– ORIGIN from Greek *lipos* 'fat' + *sôma* 'body'.

liposuction /lip-oh-suk-sh'n/ noun a technique in cosmetic surgery for removing excess fat from under the skin by suction.

lippy informal adjective (**lippier, lippiest**) disrespectful; cheeky. ● noun (also **lippie**) lipstick.

lip-read verb understand speech from watching a speaker's lip movements.
– DERIVATIVES **lip-reader** noun.

lip salve noun Brit. a preparation to prevent or relieve sore or chapped lips.

lipstick noun coloured cosmetic applied to the lips from a small solid stick.

lip-sync (also **lip-synch**) verb (of an actor or singer) move the lips silently in time to pre-recorded music or speech.

liquefy /lik-wi-fy/ verb (**liquefies, liquefying, liquefied**) make or become liquid.
– DERIVATIVES **liquefaction** noun.
– ORIGIN Latin *liquefacere*.

liqueur /li-kyoor/ noun a strong, sweet flavoured alcoholic spirit.
– ORIGIN French.

liquid noun a substance that flows freely but remains at constant volume, such as water or oil. ● adjective **1** relating to or in the form of a liquid. **2** clear, like water: *liquid dark eyes.* **3** (of a sound) pure and flowing. **4** (of assets) held in or easily converted into cash.
– DERIVATIVES **liquidly** adverb **liquidness** noun.
– ORIGIN Latin *liquidus*.

liquidate verb **1** close a business and sell what it owns in order to pay its debts. **2** sell something in order to get money. **3** pay off a debt. **4** informal kill someone.
– DERIVATIVES **liquidation** noun **liquidator** noun.
– ORIGIN Latin *liquidare* 'make clear'.

liquid crystal display noun an electronic visual display in which the application of an electric current to a liquid crystal layer makes it opaque.

liquidity /li-kwid-i-ti/ noun the availability of assets that are held in or easily converted to cash to a market or company.

liquidize (or **liquidise**) verb Brit. convert solid food into a liquid or purée.
– DERIVATIVES **liquidizer** noun.

liquid paraffin noun chiefly Brit. a colourless oily liquid obtained from petroleum, used as a laxative.

liquify verb variant spelling of LIQUEFY.

liquor /lik-er/ noun **1** alcoholic drink, especially spirits. **2** liquid that has been produced in or used for cooking.
– ORIGIN Latin.

liquorice /lik-uh-riss, lik-uh-rish/ (US **licorice**) noun a chewy black substance made from the juice of a root and used in making sweets and medicine.
– ORIGIN Old French *licoresse*.

lira /leer-uh/ noun (pl. **lire** /leer-uh, leer-ay/) **1** (until the introduction of the euro in 2002) the basic monetary unit of Italy. **2** the basic unit of money of Turkey.
– ORIGIN Italian.

-lish suffix forming nouns referring to a blend of a language with English, as used by native speakers of the first language: *Japlish.*

lisle /lyl/ noun a fine, smooth cotton thread formerly used for stockings.
– ORIGIN from *Lisle*, former spelling of the French city *Lille*.

lisp noun a speech defect in which *s* is pronounced like *th* in *thick* and *z* is pronounced like *th* in *this*. ● verb speak with a lisp.
– DERIVATIVES **lisper** noun.
– ORIGIN Old English.

lissom (also **lissome**) adjective slim, supple, and graceful.
– DERIVATIVES **lissomness** noun.
– ORIGIN from LITHE + -*some* 'characterized by being'.

list[1] noun **1** a number of connected items or names written one below or one after the other. **2** a selvedge of a piece of fabric. **3** (**lists**) historical a fence of stakes enclosing an area for a tournament. ● verb **1** make a list of people or things. **2** include someone or something in a list.
– PHRASES **enter the lists** issue or accept a challenge.
– ORIGIN sense 1 of the noun from French *liste*; sense 2 from Old English; sense 3 from Old French *lisse*.

list[2] verb (of a ship) lean over to one side. ● noun an instance of leaning to one side.
– ORIGIN unknown.

list[3] old use verb want or like. ● noun desire or inclination.
– ORIGIN Old English.

listed adjective **1** (of a building in the UK) officially classified as being of historical importance and so protected. **2** referring to companies whose shares are quoted on the main market of the London Stock Exchange.

listen verb **1** give one's attention to a sound. **2** make an effort to hear something. **3** (**listen in**) listen to a private conversation. **4** respond to advice or a request: *politicians should listen to popular opinion.* ● noun an act of listening.
– DERIVATIVES **listener** noun.
– ORIGIN Old English, 'pay attention to'.

listenable adjective easy or pleasant to listen to.
– DERIVATIVES **listenability** noun.

listening post noun a station for intercepting electronic communications.

listeria /li-steer-i-uh/ noun a type of bacterium which infects humans and other animals through contaminated food.
– ORIGIN named after the English surgeon Joseph *Lister*.

listeriosis /li-steer-i-oh-siss/ noun disease caused by infection with listeria, which can resemble influenza or meningitis and may cause miscarriage.

listing noun **1** a list or catalogue. **2** an entry in a list.

listless adjective lacking energy or enthusiasm.
– DERIVATIVES **listlessly** adverb **listlessness** noun.
– ORIGIN from LIST[3].

list price noun the price of an article as listed by the manufacturer.

lit[1] past and past participle of **LIGHT**[1], **LIGHT**[3].

lit[2] noun short for **LITERATURE**: *chick lit*.

litany /li-tuh-ni/ noun (pl. **litanies**) **1** a series of prayers in church services, usually recited by the clergy and responded to by the people. **2** a long and boring list of complaints, reasons, etc.
– ORIGIN Greek *litaneia* 'prayer'.

litas /lee-tass/ noun (pl. same) the basic unit of money of Lithuania.
– ORIGIN Lithuanian.

litchi noun variant spelling of **LYCHEE**.

lite adjective **1** relating to low-fat or low-sugar versions of food or drink products. **2** (often in combination) informal referring to a simplified or less challenging version of something: *schmaltzy reggae-lite*.
– ORIGIN respelling of **LIGHT**[2].

liter noun US spelling of **LITRE**.

literacy noun **1** the ability to read and write. **2** ability or knowledge in a particular area: *computer literacy*.

literal adjective **1** using or interpreting words in their usual or most basic sense. **2** (of a translation) representing the exact words of the original text. **3** informal absolute (used for emphasis): *fifteen years of literal hell*. •noun Brit. a misprint of a letter.
– DERIVATIVES **literalness** noun.
– ORIGIN Latin *litera* 'letter of the alphabet'.

literalism noun the interpretation of words in their usual or most basic sense.
– DERIVATIVES **literalist** noun **literalistic** adjective.

literally adverb **1** in a literal way or sense. **2** informal used for emphasis rather than being actually true: *we were literally killing ourselves laughing*.

literary adjective **1** concerning the writing, study, or content of literature. **2** (of language) typical of or suitable for works of literature or formal writing.
– DERIVATIVES **literariness** noun.
– ORIGIN Latin *litera* 'letter of the alphabet'.

literary criticism noun the art or practice of judging the qualities and character of works of literature.

literate adjective **1** able to read and write. **2** knowledgeable in a particular field: *computer literate*.

literati /li-tuh-rah-ti/ plural noun educated people who are interested in literature.
– ORIGIN Latin.

literature noun **1** written works such as novels, plays, and poems that are regarded as having artistic merit. **2** books and writings on a particular subject. **3** leaflets and other material giving information or advice.

lithe /lyth/ adjective slim, supple, and graceful.
– DERIVATIVES **lithely** adverb **litheness** noun.
– ORIGIN Old English, 'gentle, meek, mellow'.

lithium /lith-i-uhm/ noun **1** a light, soft, silver-white metallic chemical element. **2** a lithium salt used as a drug in the treatment of manic-depressive illness or depression.
– ORIGIN from Greek *lithos* 'stone'.

lithograph /li-thuh-grahf/ noun a print made by lithography. •verb print text or pictures by lithography.
– DERIVATIVES **lithographic** adjective.

lithography /li-thog-ruh-fi/ noun the process of printing from a flat metal (formerly stone) surface treated so as to repel the ink except where it is required for printing.
– DERIVATIVES **lithographer** noun.
– ORIGIN Greek *lithos* 'stone'.

lithology /li-thol-uh-ji/ noun the study of the physical characteristics of rocks.
– DERIVATIVES **lithological** adjective.

lithosphere /li-thuh-sfeer/ noun the rigid outer part of the earth, consisting of the crust and upper mantle.
– DERIVATIVES **lithospheric** /li-thuhss-fer-ik/ adjective.

Lithuanian noun **1** a person from Lithuania. **2** the language of Lithuania. •adjective relating to Lithuania.

litigant noun a person involved in a dispute or claim being heard in a court of law.

litigate /lit-i-gayt/ verb take a dispute or claim to a court of law.
– DERIVATIVES **litigation** noun **litigator** noun.
– ORIGIN Latin *litigare*.

litigious /li-ti-juhss/ adjective having a tendency to take legal action to settle disputes.
– DERIVATIVES **litigiousness** noun.

litmus /lit-muhss/ noun a dye obtained from certain lichens that is red under acid conditions and blue under alkaline conditions.
– ORIGIN from Old Norse words meaning 'dye' and 'moss'.

litmus paper noun paper stained with litmus, used as a test for acids or alkalis.

litmus test noun a reliable test of the truth or value of something.

litotes /ly-toh-teez/ noun ironical under-statement in which something is expressed by the negative of its opposite (e.g. *I shan't be sorry* for *I shall be glad*).
– ORIGIN Greek.

litre (US **liter**) noun a metric unit of capacity equal to 1,000 cubic centimetres (about 1.75 pints).
– ORIGIN French, from Greek *litra*, a Sicilian unit of money.

LittD abbreviation Doctor of Letters.
– ORIGIN from Latin *Litterarum Doctor*.

litter noun **1** small items of rubbish left lying in a public place. **2** an untidy collection of things. **3** a number of young born to an animal at one time. **4** (also **cat litter**) absorbent material lining a tray for a cat to urinate and defecate in indoors. **5** straw or other plant matter used as animal bedding. **6** (also **leaf litter**) decomposing leaves and other matter forming a layer on top of soil. **7** historical a vehicle containing a bed or seat enclosed by curtains and carried by men or animals. •verb make a place or area untidy with scattered articles: *clothes and newspapers littered the floor*.
– ORIGIN Old French *litiere*, from Latin *lectus* 'bed'.

litterbug (Brit. also **litter lout**) noun informal a person who carelessly drops rubbish in public places.

little adjective **1** small in size, amount, or degree. **2** (of a person) young or younger: *my little brother*. **3** short in time or distance.

4 relatively unimportant. • **determiner & pronoun**
1 (a **little**) a small amount of something. 2 (a
little) a short time or distance. 3 not much.
• **adverb** (**less**, **least**) 1 (a **little**) to a small
extent. 2 hardly or not at all.
- PHRASES **little by little** gradually.
- DERIVATIVES **littleness** noun.
- ORIGIN Old English.

Little Englander noun informal a person
opposed to an international role or policy for
Britain.

little finger noun the smallest finger, at the
outer side of the hand.
- PHRASES **twist** (or **wind** or **wrap**) **someone
around one's little finger** be able to make
someone do whatever one wants.

little people plural noun 1 the ordinary people
of a country or organization. 2 fairies or
leprechauns.

littoral /lit-tuh-ruhl/ adjective relating to the
shore of the sea or a lake. • noun a region lying
along a shore.
- ORIGIN Latin *littoralis*.

liturgical /li-tur-ji-k'l/ adjective relating to
liturgy or public worship.
- DERIVATIVES **liturgically** adverb **liturgist** /lit-ter-
jist/ noun.

liturgy /lit-er-ji/ noun (pl. **liturgies**) a set form
of public worship used in the Christian
Church.
- ORIGIN Greek *leitourgia* 'public service,
worship of the gods'.

livable adjective variant spelling of **LIVEABLE**.

live[1] /liv/ verb 1 remain alive. 2 be alive at a
particular time. 3 spend one's life in a
particular way or under particular
circumstances: *they are living in fear.* 4 make
one's home in a particular place or with a
particular person. 5 (**live in/out**) have one's
home at (or away from) the place where one
works or studies. 6 supply oneself with the
means of staying alive: *they live by hunting and
fishing.* 7 (**live for**) regard something as the
most important aspect of one's life: *he lived for
his painting.* 8 survive in someone's mind: *her
name lived on.*
- PHRASES **live something down** succeed in
making other people forget something
embarrassing or regrettable. **live it up** informal
lead a very enjoyable life, usually by being
extravagant and having an exciting social life.
live off (or **on**) 1 depend on someone or
something as a source of income or support.
2 eat as a major part of one's diet. **live rough**
live outdoors as a result of being homeless.
live together (of a couple not married to each
other) share a home and have a sexual
relationship. **live up to** fulfil expectations, a
commitment, etc.: *the president lived up to his
promise.* **live with** 1 share a home and have a
sexual relationship with a person to whom
one is not married. 2 accept or tolerate
something unpleasant.
- ORIGIN Old English.

live[2] /lyv/ adjective 1 living. 2 (of a musical
performance) played in front of an audience.
3 (of a broadcast) transmitted at the time it
occurs; not recorded. 4 of current or
continuing interest and importance: *a live
issue.* 5 (of a wire or device) connected to a

source of electric current. 6 containing or
using explosive that has not been detonated:
live ammunition. 7 (of coals) burning. 8 (of
yogurt) containing the living microorganisms
by which it is formed. • adverb at the time of
something's occurrence or performance: *the
match will be televised live.*
- ORIGIN shortening of **ALIVE**.

liveable (US also **livable**) adjective 1 worth
living. 2 fit to live in. 3 (**liveable with**) informal
easy to live with.
- DERIVATIVES **liveability** noun.

live-bearing adjective bearing live young
rather than laying eggs.
- DERIVATIVES **livebearer** noun.

lived-in adjective (of a room or building)
showing comforting signs of wear and
habitation.

live-in adjective 1 (of a domestic employee)
living in an employer's house. 2 living with
someone as their sexual partner: *his live-in
girlfriend.* 3 (of a course of study, treatment,
etc.) residential.

livelihood noun a means of earning money in
order to live.
- ORIGIN Old English, 'way of life'.

livelong /liv-long/ adjective literary (of a period
of time) entire: *all this livelong day.*

lively adjective (**livelier**, **liveliest**) 1 full of life
and energy. 2 (of a place) full of activity.
3 intellectually stimulating: *a lively debate.*
4 mentally quick and active: *her lively mind.*
- PHRASES **look lively** informal move more quickly
and energetically.
- DERIVATIVES **liveliness** noun.

liven verb (**liven someone/thing up** or **liven up**)
make or become more lively or interesting.

liver[1] noun 1 a large organ in the abdomen that
produces bile and neutralizes toxins. 2 the
flesh of an animal's liver as food.
- ORIGIN Old English.

liver[2] noun a person who lives in a particular
way: *a clean liver.*

liverish adjective 1 feeling slightly ill, as
though having a liver disorder. 2 unhappy and
bad-tempered.

Liverpudlian /li-ver-pud-li-uhn/ noun 1 a
person from the city of Liverpool in NW
England. 2 the dialect or accent of people from
Liverpool. • adjective relating to Liverpool.
- ORIGIN from *Liverpool* + **PUDDLE**.

liver sausage noun chiefly Brit. a savoury meat
paste in the form of a sausage containing
cooked liver, or a mixture of liver and pork.

liver spot noun a small brown spot on the skin.

liverwort /li-ver-wert/ noun a small flowerless
green plant that grows in moist habitats.

livery noun (pl. **liveries**) 1 a special uniform
worn by an official or a servant such as a
footman. 2 a distinctive design and colour
scheme used on the vehicles or products of a
company.
- PHRASES **at livery** (of a horse) kept for the
owner and fed and cared for at a fixed charge.
- DERIVATIVES **liveried** adjective.
- ORIGIN first meaning 'the giving of food,
provisions, or clothing to servants': from Old
French *livree* 'delivered'.

livery stable noun a stable where horses are

kept at livery or may be hired out.

lives plural of **LIFE**.

livestock noun farm animals.

live wire noun informal an energetic and lively person.

livid adjective **1** informal furiously angry. **2** dark bluish-grey in colour.
- DERIVATIVES **lividity** noun.
- ORIGIN Latin *lividus*.

living noun **1** a way or style of life: *the benefits of country living.* **2** an income which is enough to live on, or the means of earning it. •adjective **1** alive. **2** (of a place) for living rather than working in: *living quarters.* **3** (of a language) still spoken and used.
- PHRASES **in** (or **within**) **living memory** within or during a time that is remembered by people still alive. **the living image of** an exact copy or likeness of someone.

living room noun a room in a house for general everyday use.

living wage noun a wage which is high enough to enable someone to maintain a normal standard of living.

living will noun a written statement giving details of a person's wishes regarding their future medical treatment should they become unable to give informed consent.

lizard noun a four-legged reptile with a long body and tail and a rough, scaly, or spiny skin.
- ORIGIN Old French *lesard*.

LJ abbreviation (pl. **L JJ**) (in the UK) Lord Justice.

ll. abbreviation (in textual references) lines.

'll contraction shall; will.

llama /lah-muh/ noun a domesticated animal of the camel family found in the Andes, used for carrying loads and valued for its soft woolly fleece.
- ORIGIN Spanish.

LLB abbreviation Bachelor of Laws.
- ORIGIN from Latin *legum baccalaureus*.

LLD abbreviation Doctor of Laws.
- ORIGIN from Latin *legum doctor*.

LLM abbreviation Master of Laws.
- ORIGIN from Latin *legum magister*.

Lloyd's noun **1** an incorporated society of insurance underwriters in London, made up of private syndicates. **2** short for **LLOYD'S REGISTER**.
- ORIGIN named after the coffee house of Edward *Lloyd*, in which underwriters and merchants congregated.

Lloyd's Register (in full **Lloyd's Register of Shipping**) noun a classified list of merchant ships over a certain tonnage, published annually in London.

lm abbreviation lumen(s).

LMS abbreviation (in the UK) local management of schools.

ln abbreviation Mathematics natural logarithm.
- ORIGIN from Latin *logarithmus naturalis*.

LNB abbreviation low noise blocker, a circuit on a satellite dish which selects the required signal from the transmission.

LNG abbreviation liquefied natural gas.

lo exclamation old use used to draw attention to an interesting event.
- PHRASES **lo and behold** used to present a new scene or situation.

- ORIGIN first recorded in Old English.

loach /lohch/ noun a small freshwater fish with several long, thin growths (barbels) near the mouth.
- ORIGIN Old French *loche*.

load noun **1** a heavy or bulky thing being or about to be carried. **2** the total number or amount carried in a vehicle or container. **3** a weight or source of pressure. **4** (**a load/loads of**) informal a large quantity or amount of something. **5** the amount of work to be done by a person or machine. **6** the amount of power supplied by a source. **7** a burden of responsibility, worry, or grief: *their offer took a load off my mind.* •verb **1** put a load or large quantity of something on or in a vehicle or container. **2** insert something into a device so that it will operate. **3** put ammunition into a firearm. **4** transfer data or a program into a computer's memory. **5** bias something so that a particular outcome is likely: *the odds were loaded against them before the match.*
- PHRASES **get a load of** informal take a look at (used to draw attention to someone or something). **load the dice against** (or **in favour of**) put someone or something at a disadvantage (or an advantage).
- DERIVATIVES **loader** noun.
- ORIGIN Old English, 'journey, conveyance'.

loaded adjective **1** carrying a load. **2** (of dice) weighted so that they will always fall in the same way when thrown. **3** having an underlying meaning or implication: *a loaded question.* **4** informal wealthy. **5** informal, chiefly N. Amer. drunk.

load factor noun the ratio of the average or actual amount of some quantity and the maximum possible or permissible.

loading noun **1** the application of a load to something. **2** the amount of load applied. **3** an increase in an insurance premium due to a factor which increases the risk involved.

load line noun another term for **PLIMSOLL LINE**.

loadmaster noun the member of an aircraft's crew responsible for the cargo.

loadstone noun variant spelling of **LODESTONE**.

loaf¹ noun (pl. **loaves**) a quantity of bread that is shaped and baked in one piece.
- PHRASES **use one's loaf** Brit. informal use one's common sense. [probably from *loaf of bread*, rhyming slang for 'head'.]
- ORIGIN Old English.

loaf² verb spend time in an idle or aimless way.
- ORIGIN probably from **LOAFER**.

loafer noun **1** a person who spends their time in an idle or aimless way. **2** trademark a casual leather shoe with a flat heel.
- ORIGIN perhaps from German *Landläufer* 'tramp'.

loam noun **1** a fertile soil of clay and sand containing humus. **2** a paste of clay and water with sand and chopped straw, used in making bricks and plastering walls.
- DERIVATIVES **loamy** adjective.
- ORIGIN Old English, 'clay'.

loan noun **1** a thing that is borrowed, especially a sum of money that is expected to be paid back with interest. **2** the action of lending something. •verb give something as a loan.
- PHRASES **on loan** being borrowed.

– ORIGIN Old Norse.

loan shark noun informal a moneylender who charges extremely high rates of interest.

loath /lohth/ (also **loth**) adjective reluctant; unwilling.
– ORIGIN Old English, 'hostile'.

> USAGE: Do not confuse **loath** and **loathe**. **Loath** is an adjective meaning 'reluctant or unwilling' (*I was loath to leave*), whereas **loathe** is a verb meaning 'feel hatred or disgust for' (*she loathed him on sight*).

loathe /loh*th*/ verb feel hatred or disgust for someone or something.
– ORIGIN Old English, related to **LOATH**.

loathsome adjective causing hatred or disgust.

loaves plural of **LOAF**[1].

lob verb (**lobs, lobbing, lobbed**) throw or hit something in a high arc. • noun 1 (in football or tennis) a ball lobbed over an opponent or a stroke producing this result. 2 (in cricket) a ball bowled with a slow underarm action.
– ORIGIN probably from German or Dutch.

lobar /loh-buh/ adjective relating to or affecting a lobe, especially a lobe of a lung.

lobate /loh-bayt/ adjective having a lobe or lobes.

lobby noun (pl. **lobbies**) 1 a room out of which one or more other rooms or corridors lead, typically one near the entrance of a public building. 2 (in the UK) any of several large halls in the Houses of Parliament in which MPs meet members of the public. 3 (also **division lobby**) each of two corridors in the Houses of Parliament to which MPs go to vote. 4 a group of people trying to influence politicians on a particular issue: *members of the anti-abortion lobby.* 5 an organized attempt by members of the public to influence politicians. • verb (**lobbies, lobbying, lobbied**) try to influence a politician on an issue.
– DERIVATIVES **lobbyist** noun.
– ORIGIN Latin *lobia* 'covered walk'.

lobe noun 1 a roundish projection or division of something. 2 (also **ear lobe**) the rounded fleshy part at the lower edge of the outer ear. 3 a major division of an organ such as the brain.
– DERIVATIVES **lobed** adjective.
– ORIGIN Greek *lobos.*

lobelia /luh-bee-li-uh/ noun a garden plant with blue or scarlet flowers.
– ORIGIN named after the Flemish botanist Matthias de *Lobel.*

lobotomize (or **lobotomise**) verb perform a lobotomy on someone.

lobotomy /luh-bot-uh-mi/ noun (pl. **lobotomies**) a surgical operation involving cutting into part of the brain, formerly used to treat mental illness.

lobster noun 1 a large edible shellfish with large pincers. 2 the flesh of this animal as food.
– ORIGIN Old English.

lobster pot noun a basket-like trap in which lobsters are caught.

lobster thermidor noun a dish of lobster cooked in a cream sauce, returned to its shell, sprinkled with cheese, and browned under the grill.
– ORIGIN *thermidor* from *Thermidor,* the eleventh month of the French Republican calendar.

local adjective 1 relating to a particular area or to the area in which a person lives: *the local post office.* 2 (in technical use) relating to a particular region or part: *a local infection.* 3 Computing referring to a device that can be accessed without the use of a network. • noun 1 a person who lives in a particular area. 2 Brit. informal a pub near to a person's home.
– DERIVATIVES **locally** adverb.
– ORIGIN Latin *localis,* from *locus* 'place'.

local anaesthetic noun an anaesthetic that affects only a part of the body.

local area network noun a computer network that links devices within a building or group of adjacent buildings.

local authority noun Brit. an administrative body in local government.

local derby noun see **DERBY**.

locale /loh-kahl/ noun a place where something happens or is set.
– ORIGIN French *local* 'locality'.

local government noun the administration of a particular county or district, with representatives elected by those who live there.

locality noun (pl. **localities**) 1 an area or neighbourhood. 2 the position or site of something.

localize (or **localise**) verb 1 (often as adj. **localized**) restrict or assign something to a particular place: *a localized infection.* 2 make something local in character: *a more localized news service.*
– DERIVATIVES **localizable** adjective **localization** noun **localizer** noun.

local time noun time as reckoned in a particular region or time zone.

locate verb 1 discover the exact place or position of: *engineers were working to locate the fault.* 2 (**be located**) be situated in a particular place.
– DERIVATIVES **locatable** adjective **locator** noun.
– ORIGIN Latin *locare* 'to place'.

location noun 1 a particular place or position. 2 the action of locating someone or something. 3 an actual place in which a film or broadcast is made, outside a studio.
– DERIVATIVES **locational** adjective.

loc. cit. abbreviation in the passage already quoted.
– ORIGIN Latin *loco citato.*

loch /lokh/ noun Scottish 1 a lake. 2 a narrow strip of sea, almost surrounded by land.
– ORIGIN Scottish Gaelic.

loci plural of **LOCUS**.

loci classici plural of **LOCUS CLASSICUS**.

lock[1] noun 1 a mechanism for keeping a door or container fastened, operated by a key. 2 a similar device used to prevent the operation of a vehicle or other machine. 3 a short section of a canal or river with gates and sluices at each end which can be opened or closed to change the water level, used for raising and lowering boats. 4 (also **full lock**) the maximum extent that the front wheels of a vehicle can

be turned. **5** (in wrestling and martial arts) a hold that prevents an opponent from moving a limb. **6** (also **lock forward**) Rugby a player in the second row of a scrum. **7** old use a mechanism for exploding the charge of a gun. • verb **1** fasten or secure something with a lock. **2** (**lock something up**) shut and secure a building by fastening its doors with locks. **3** enclose or shut in by locking a door, fastening a lid, etc.: *the prisoners are locked in overnight.* **4** (**lock someone up/away**) imprison someone. **5** make or become fixed in one position or unable to to move: *the brakes locked.* **6** (**be locked in**) be deeply involved in a difficult situation: *they were locked in a legal battle.* **7** (**lock on to**) locate and then track a target by radar or similar means.
– PHRASES **lock horns** become involved in a conflict or dispute. **lock, stock, and barrel** including everything. [referring to the complete mechanism of a firearm.]
– DERIVATIVES **lockable** adjective.
– ORIGIN Old English.

lock² noun **1** a section of a person's hair that coils or hangs in a piece. **2** (**locks**) literary a person's hair.
– ORIGIN Old English.

lockdown noun N. Amer. the confining of prisoners to their cells.

locker noun a small lockable cupboard or compartment in which belongings may be left temporarily.

locker room noun a sports changing room containing rows of lockers.

locket noun a small ornamental case worn on a chain round a person's neck, used to hold an item of sentimental value such as a tiny photograph or a lock of hair.
– ORIGIN Old French *locquet* 'small latch or lock'.

lock forward noun another term for LOCK¹ (in sense 6).

lock-in noun **1** an arrangement which obliges a person or company to negotiate or trade only with a specific company. **2** Brit. a period during which some customers remain in a bar or pub after the doors are locked at closing time, in order to continue drinking privately.

lockjaw noun spasm of the jaw muscles, causing the mouth to remain tightly closed, typically as a symptom of tetanus.

locknut noun **1** a nut screwed down on another to keep it tight. **2** a nut designed so that, once tightened, it cannot be accidentally loosened.

lockout noun a situation in which an employer refuses to allow employees to enter their place of work until certain terms are agreed to.

locksmith noun a person who makes and repairs locks.

lock-up noun **1** a makeshift jail. **2** Brit. a garage or small shop separate from living quarters, that can be locked up.

loco¹ noun (pl. **locos**) informal a locomotive.

loco² adjective informal crazy.
– ORIGIN Spanish, 'insane'.

locomotion noun movement or the ability to move from one place to another.
– ORIGIN from Latin *loco* 'from a place' + *motio*

'motion'.

locomotive noun a powered railway vehicle used for pulling trains. • adjective relating to locomotion.

locomotor (also **locomotory**) adjective chiefly Biology relating to locomotion.

locum /loh-kuhm/ noun Brit. a doctor or priest standing in for another who is temporarily away.
– ORIGIN from Latin *locum tenens* 'one holding a place'.

locus /loh-kuhss/ noun (pl. **loci** /loh-sy/)
1 technical a particular position, point, or place. **2** Mathematics a curve or other figure formed by all the points satisfying a particular condition.
– ORIGIN Latin, 'place'.

locus classicus /loh-kuhss klas-i-kuhss/ noun (pl. **loci classici** /loh-sy klas-i-sy/) the best known or most authoritative passage on a particular subject.
– ORIGIN Latin, 'classical place'.

locust noun a large tropical grasshopper which migrates in vast swarms and is very destructive to vegetation.
– ORIGIN Latin *locusta*.

locution /luh-kyoo-sh'n/ noun **1** a word or phrase. **2** a person's particular style of speech.
– ORIGIN from Latin *loqui* 'speak'.

lode /rhymes with rode/ noun a vein of metal ore in the earth.
– ORIGIN Old English, 'way, course'.

loden /loh-duhn/ noun **1** a thick waterproof woollen cloth. **2** the dark green colour in which such cloth is often made.
– ORIGIN German.

lodestar noun a star that is used to guide the course of a ship, especially the Pole Star.

lodestone (also **loadstone**) noun **1** a piece of magnetite or other naturally magnetic mineral, able to be used as a magnet. **2** a person or thing that is a focus of attention or attraction.

lodge noun **1** a small house at the gates of a large house with grounds, occupied by a gatekeeper or other employee. **2** a small country house occupied by people engaged in hunting and shooting. **3** a porter's room or rooms at the entrance of a college or other large building. **4** a branch or meeting place of an organization such as the Freemasons. **5** a beaver's den. **6** an American Indian tent or other dwelling. • verb **1** formally present a complaint, appeal, etc. to the proper authorities. **2** make or become firmly fixed or embedded in a place: *he had a bullet lodged in his skull.* **3** rent accommodation in another person's house. **4** provide someone with rented accommodation. **5** (**lodge something in/with**) leave money or a valuable item in a place or with a person for safekeeping.
– ORIGIN Old French *loge* 'arbour, hut'.

lodgement noun **1** chiefly literary a place in which a person or thing is lodged. **2** the depositing of money in a particular bank or account.

lodger noun chiefly Brit. a person who pays rent to live in a property with the owner.

lodging noun **1** temporary accommodation. **2** (**lodgings**) a rented room or rooms, usually in the same house as the owner.

lodging house noun a private house providing rented accommodation.

loess /loh-iss/ noun a loosely fine soil originally deposited by the wind.
– ORIGIN Swiss German *lösch* 'loose'.

lo-fi (also **low-fi**) adjective relating to or using sound reproduction of a lower quality than hi-fi.
– ORIGIN from LOW¹ + *-fi* on the pattern of *hi-fi*.

loft noun 1 a room or storage space directly under the roof of a house or other building. 2 a large, open living area in a converted warehouse or other large building. 3 a gallery in a church or hall. 4 a shelter with nest holes for pigeons. 5 Golf upward movement given to the ball in a stroke. 6 the thickness of an insulating material such as that in a sleeping bag. • verb kick, hit, or throw a ball or missile high into the air.
– ORIGIN Old Norse, 'air, upper room'.

lofty adjective (**loftier, loftiest**) 1 tall and impressive. 2 morally good or admirable; noble: *lofty ideals*. 3 haughty and aloof.
– DERIVATIVES **loftily** adverb **loftiness** noun.

log¹ noun 1 a part of the trunk or a large branch of a tree that has fallen or been cut off. 2 (also **logbook**) an official record of events during the voyage of a ship or aircraft. 3 a piece of equipment for measuring the speed of a ship, originally one consisting of a float attached to a knotted line. • verb (**logs, logging, logged**) 1 enter information in an official record: *customs officials logged the contents of every ship*. 2 achieve a certain distance, speed, or time. 3 (**log in/on** or **out/off**) go through the procedures to begin (or finish) using a computer. 4 cut down an area of forest to use the wood commercially.
– DERIVATIVES **logger** noun **logging** noun.
– ORIGIN unknown.

log² noun short for LOGARITHM.

loganberry noun (pl. **loganberries**) an edible soft red fruit, similar to a raspberry.
– ORIGIN from the name of the American horticulturalist John H. *Logan*.

logarithm /log-uh-ri-*th*uhm/ noun one of a series of numbers, representing the power to which a fixed number (the base) must be raised to produce a given number, used to simplify calculations.
– DERIVATIVES **logarithmic** adjective.
– ORIGIN from Greek *logos* 'reckoning, ratio' + *arithmos* 'number'.

logbook noun 1 a log of a ship or aircraft. 2 Brit. an official document recording details about a vehicle and its owner.

loggerhead noun (also **loggerhead turtle**) a large-headed reddish-brown turtle of warm seas.
– PHRASES **at loggerheads** engaged in strong dispute or disagreement. [perhaps from a use of *loggerhead* in a former sense 'long-handled iron instrument for heating liquids' (when used as a weapon).]
– ORIGIN from dialect *logger* 'block of wood for hobbling a horse' + HEAD.

loggia /loj-uh/ noun a gallery or room with one or more open sides, especially one having facing a garden.
– ORIGIN Italian, 'lodge'.

logic noun 1 the science of reasoning. 2 good or valid reasoning: *the logic of the argument is faulty*. 3 an underlying system or set of principles used in preparing a computer or electronic device to perform a particular task.
– DERIVATIVES **logician** noun.
– ORIGIN from Greek *logikē tekhnē* 'art of reason'.

logical adjective 1 relating to or following the rules of logic. 2 capable of or showing rational thought. 3 expected or sensible under the circumstances: *the polar expedition is a logical extension of his Arctic travels*.
– DERIVATIVES **logically** adverb.

logic bomb noun Computing a set of instructions secretly incorporated into a program so that if a particular condition is satisfied they will be carried out, usually with harmful effects.

login (also **logon**) noun an act of logging in to a computer, or the password needed to do so.

logistics /luh-jiss-tiks/ plural noun (treated as sing. or pl.) 1 the detailed coordination of a large and complex project or event. 2 the commercial activity of transporting goods to customers.
– DERIVATIVES **logistic** adjective **logistical** adjective.
– ORIGIN French *logistique* 'movement and supply of troops and equipment'.

logjam noun 1 a situation that seems unable to be settled; deadlock. 2 a backlog.

logo /loh-goh/ noun (pl. **logos**) a design or symbol adopted by an organization to identify its products.
– ORIGIN Greek *logos* 'word'.

loin noun 1 the part of the body on both sides of the spine between the lowest ribs and the hip bones. 2 a joint of meat from the back or sides of an animal, near the tail. 3 (**loins**) literary a person's sexual organs.
– ORIGIN Old French *loigne*.

loincloth noun a piece of cloth wrapped round the hips, worn by men in some hot countries as their only garment.

loiter verb stand around without any obvious purpose.
– DERIVATIVES **loiterer** noun.
– ORIGIN perhaps from Dutch *loteren* 'wag about'.

Lolita /loh-lee-tuh/ noun (a **Lolita**) a sexually precocious young girl.
– ORIGIN a character in the novel *Lolita* by Vladimir Nabokov.

loll verb 1 sit, lie, or stand in a lazy, relaxed way. 2 hang loosely: *he let his head loll back*.
– ORIGIN probably symbolic of dangling.

lollapalooza /lol-luh-puh-loo-zuh/ noun N. Amer. informal a very impressive or attractive person or thing.
– ORIGIN an invented word.

lollipop noun a large, flat, rounded boiled sweet on the end of a stick.
– ORIGIN perhaps from dialect *lolly* 'tongue' + POP¹.

lollipop lady (or **lollipop man**) noun Brit. informal a person employed to help children cross the road safely near a school by holding up a circular sign on a pole to stop the traffic.

lollop verb (**lollops, lolloping, lolloped**) move in a series of clumsy bounding steps.

– ORIGIN probably from **LOLL**.

lollo rosso /lol-oh ros-oh/ noun a variety of lettuce with red-edged leaves.
– ORIGIN Italian, from *lolla* 'husk' + *rosso* 'red'.

lolly noun (pl. **lollies**) Brit. informal **1** a lollipop. **2** money.

lollygag verb (**lollygags, lollygagging, lollygagged**) N. Amer. informal spend time in an aimless way.
– ORIGIN unknown.

Lombard /lom-bard/ noun **1** a member of a Germanic people who invaded Italy in the 6th century. **2** a person from Lombardy in northern Italy.
– DERIVATIVES **Lombardic** adjective.
– ORIGIN Italian *lombardo*.

Londoner noun a person from London.

London pride noun a rock plant with rosettes of fleshy leaves and pink starlike flowers.

lone adjective **1** having no companions; solitary. **2** lacking the support of other people: *I am by no means a lone voice.* **3** literary (of a place) remote and rarely visited.
– ORIGIN shortening of **ALONE**.

lonely adjective (**lonelier, loneliest**) **1** sad because one has no friends or company. **2** spent without company: *long, lonely hours.* **3** (of a place) remote and rarely visited.
– DERIVATIVES **loneliness** noun.

lonely hearts plural noun people looking for a lover or friend through the personal columns of a newspaper.

loner noun a person who prefers to be alone.

lonesome adjective chiefly N. Amer. lonely.

long[1] adjective (**longer, longest**) **1** of a great distance or duration. **2** having a particular length, distance, or duration: *the ship will be 150 metres long.* **3** relatively great in extent: *a long list.* **4** (of a ball in sport) travelling a great distance, or further than expected. **5** Phonetics (of a vowel) pronounced in a way that takes longer than a short vowel in the same position (e.g. in standard British English the vowel /oo/ in *food*). **6** (of odds in betting) reflecting a low level of probability. **7** (**long on**) informal well supplied with something: *an industry that's long on ideas but short on cash.* • noun a long time. • adverb (**longer, longest**) **1** for a long time. **2** at a distant time: *long ago.* **3** throughout a particular period of time: *all day long.* **4** (with reference to the ball in sport) at, to, or over a great distance.
– PHRASES **as** (or **so**) **long as 1** during the whole time that. **2** provided that. **in the long run** (or **term**) eventually. **the long and the short of it** all that can or need be said. **long in the tooth** rather old. [originally said of horses, from the receding of the gums with age.]
– DERIVATIVES **longish** adjective.
– ORIGIN Old English.

long[2] verb (**long for/to do**) have a strong wish for or to do something.
– ORIGIN Old English, 'grow long', also 'yearn'.

long. abbreviation longitude.

longboat noun **1** historical a large boat which could be launched from a sailing ship. **2** another term for **LONGSHIP**.

longbow noun historical a large bow drawn by hand and shooting a long feathered arrow.

long-distance adjective **1** travelling or operating between distant places. **2** Athletics referring to a race distance of 6 miles or 10,000 metres (6 miles 376 yds), or longer. • adverb between distant places.

long division noun the process of dividing one number by another with the calculations written down.

long-drawn (also **long-drawn-out**) adjective lasting a very long time, or too long.

longe noun variant of **LUNGE**[2].

longevity /lon-jev-i-ti/ noun long life.
– ORIGIN from Latin *longus* 'long' + *aevum* 'age'.

long face noun an unhappy or disappointed expression.

longhand noun ordinary handwriting (as opposed to shorthand, typing, or printing).

long haul noun **1** a relatively long distance in terms of travel or the transport of goods. **2** a lengthy and difficult task.

longhorn noun a breed of cattle with long horns.

longhouse noun a large communal house in parts of Malaysia and Indonesia or among some North American Indians.

longing noun a strong wish to do or have something. • adjective having or showing a strong wish to do or have something: *a longing look.*
– DERIVATIVES **longingly** adverb.

longitude /long-i-tyood/ noun the distance of a place east or west of the Greenwich meridian, measured in degrees.
– ORIGIN Latin *longitudo*.

longitudinal /long-i-tyoo-di-n'l/ adjective **1** running lengthwise. **2** relating to the distance of a place east or west of the Greenwich meridian.
– DERIVATIVES **longitudinally** adverb.

long johns plural noun informal underpants with closely fitted legs reaching to the ankles.

long jump noun (**the long jump**) an athletic event in which competitors jump as far as possible along the ground in one leap.
– DERIVATIVES **long jumper** noun.

long leg noun Cricket a fielding position far behind the batsman on the leg side.

long-life adjective (of perishable goods) treated so as to stay fresh for longer than usual.

longline noun a deep-sea fishing line with a large number of hooks attached to it.

long-lived adjective living or lasting a long time.

long off noun Cricket a fielding position far behind the bowler and towards the off side.

long on noun Cricket a fielding position far behind the bowler and towards the on side.

long-playing adjective (of a record) 12 inches (about 30 cm) in diameter and designed to rotate at 33⅓ revolutions per minute.

long-range adjective **1** able to be used or be effective over long distances. **2** relating to a period of time far into the future.

longship noun a long, narrow warship with oars and a sail, used by the Vikings.

longshore adjective relating to or moving along the seashore.
– ORIGIN from *along shore*.

longshore drift noun the movement of material along a coast by waves which approach at an angle to the shore but recede directly away from it.

longshoreman noun (pl. **longshoremen**) N. Amer. a docker.

long shot noun an attempt or guess that has only the slightest chance of succeeding or being accurate.
– PHRASES **not by a long shot** informal not at all.

long-sighted adjective Brit. unable to see things clearly if they are relatively close to the eyes.

long-standing adjective having existed for a long time.

longstop noun Cricket a fielding position directly behind the wicketkeeper.

long-suffering adjective bearing problems or annoying behaviour patiently.

long suit noun 1 (in bridge or whist) a situation in which a player holds several cards of one suit in a hand. 2 an outstanding personal quality or achievement: *tact was not his long suit.*

longueur /long-ger/ noun a tedious period of time or passage in a book or piece of music.
– ORIGIN French, 'length'.

long wave noun 1 a radio wave of a wavelength above one kilometre (and a frequency below 300 kilohertz). 2 broadcasting using radio waves of 1 to 10 kilometre wavelength.

longways adverb lengthways.

long-winded adjective lengthy and boring.

Lonsdale belt noun an ornate belt awarded to a professional boxer winning a British title fight.
– ORIGIN named after the fifth Earl of *Lonsdale*, Hugh Cecil Lowther, who presented the first one.

loo noun Brit. informal a toilet.
– ORIGIN uncertain: one theory suggests the source is *Waterloo*, a trade name for iron cisterns in the early 20th century.

loofah /loo-fuh/ noun a long, rough, fibrous object used like a bath sponge, consisting of the dried inner parts of a tropical fruit.
– ORIGIN Egyptian Arabic.

look verb 1 direct one's gaze in a particular direction. 2 have the appearance or give the impression of being: *he looked unhappy.* 3 face in a particular direction: *the rooms look out over the harbour.* • noun 1 an act of looking at someone or something. 2 an expression of a feeling or thought by looking at someone: *he gave me a funny look.* 3 the appearance of someone or something: *the contemporary look of the city skyline.* 4 (**looks**) a person's facial appearance. 5 a style or fashion: *Italian designers unveiled their latest looks.* • exclamation (also **look here!**) used to call attention to what one is going to say.
– PHRASES **look after** take care of. **look at** 1 think of something in a particular way. 2 examine a matter and consider what action to take. **look down on** (also **look down one's nose at**) regard someone or something with a feeling of superiority. **look for** attempt to find. **look in** make a short visit. **look into**

investigate. **look lively** (or **sharp**) informal be quick; get moving. **look on** watch without getting involved. **look out** be alert for possible trouble or danger. **look something out** Brit. search for and produce something. **look to** 1 rely on someone to do something. 2 hope or expect to do something. **look up** improve. **look something up** search for and find a piece of information in a reference work. **look someone up** informal visit or contact someone. **look up to** have a great deal of respect for.
– ORIGIN Old English.

lookalike noun a person or thing that looks very similar to another.

looker noun 1 a person with a particular appearance: *she's not a bad looker.* 2 informal a very attractive person.

look-in noun Brit. informal a chance to take part or succeed in something.

looking glass noun a mirror.

lookout noun 1 a place from which to keep watch. 2 a person stationed to keep watch for danger or trouble. 3 (**one's lookout**) Brit. informal one's own responsibility or problem: *if they let him in that's their lookout.* 4 informal, chiefly Brit. a good or bad prospect or outcome.
– PHRASES **be on the lookout** (or **keep a lookout**) **for 1** be alert to possible danger or trouble. 2 keep searching for something.

look-see noun informal a brief look or inspection.

lookup noun systematic retrieval of electronic information.

loom[1] noun a piece of equipment for weaving fabric.
– ORIGIN Old English, 'tool'.

loom[2] verb 1 appear as a vague shape, especially one that is large or threatening: *vehicles loomed out of the darkness.* 2 (of an unwelcome event) seem about to happen: *there is a crisis looming.*
– ORIGIN probably from German or Dutch.

loon[1] noun informal a silly or foolish person.
– ORIGIN from LOON[2] (referring to the bird's actions when escaping from danger), perhaps influenced by LOONY.

loon[2] noun North American term for DIVER (in sense 2).
– ORIGIN probably from Shetland dialect *loom*.

loons (also **loon pants**) plural noun Brit. dated close-fitting casual trousers with wide flares.
– ORIGIN unknown.

loony informal noun (pl. **loonies**) a mad or silly person. • adjective (**loonier**, **looniest**) mad or silly.
– DERIVATIVES **looniness** noun.
– ORIGIN from LUNATIC.

loony bin noun informal, derogatory an institution for people with mental illnesses.

loop noun 1 a shape produced by a curve that bends round and crosses itself. 2 an endless strip of tape or film allowing sounds or images to be continuously repeated. 3 a complete circuit for an electric current. 4 Computing a programmed sequence of instructions that is repeated until or while a particular condition is satisfied. 5 (also **loop line**) Brit. a length of railway track which is connected at either end to the main line. • verb 1 form into a loop or loops: *she looped her arms around his neck.*

2 follow a course that forms a loop or loops.
– PHRASES **in** (or **out of**) **the loop** informal aware (or unaware) of information known to only a privileged few. **loop the loop** (of an aircraft) fly in a vertical circle.
– ORIGIN unknown.

loophole noun an inexact wording or omission in a law or contract that enables someone to avoid doing something.
– ORIGIN from former *loop* 'opening in a wall' + HOLE.

loopy adjective (**loopier**, **loopiest**) informal mad or silly.
– DERIVATIVES **loopiness** noun.

loose /looss/ adjective **1** not firmly or tightly fixed in place. **2** not held, tied, or packaged together. **3** not tied up or shut in: *the bull was loose in the field.* **4** (of a garment) not fitting tightly or closely. **5** not dense or compact in structure. **6** relaxed: *her loose, easy stride.* **7** not strict; inexact: *a loose interpretation.* **8** careless and indiscreet: *loose talk.* **9** dated promiscuous or immoral. **10** (of the ball in a game) in play but not in any player's possession. •verb **1** release someone or something. **2** relax one's grip. **3** (usu. **loose something off**) fire a shot, bullet, etc.
– PHRASES **on the loose** having escaped from prison or confinement.
– DERIVATIVES **loosely** adverb **looseness** noun.
– ORIGIN Old Norse.

USAGE: Do not confuse **loose** and **lose**; **loose** means 'not fixed in place or tied up' (*a loose tooth*), while **lose** means 'have something taken away' (*she might lose her job*) or 'become unable to find someone or something'.

loose box noun Brit. a stable or stall in which a horse is kept without being tied up.

loose cannon noun an unpredictable person who may cause unintentional harm or damage.

loose cover noun Brit. a removable fitted cloth cover for a chair or sofa.

loose end noun a detail that is not yet settled or explained.
– PHRASES **be at a loose end** (or N. Amer. **at loose ends**) have nothing specific to do.

loose forward noun Rugby a forward who plays at the back of the scrum.

loose-leaf adjective (of a folder) having pages that can be taken out and put in separately.

loosen verb **1** make or become loose. **2** (**loosen up**) warm up in preparation for an activity.
– PHRASES **loosen someone's tongue** make someone talk freely.
– DERIVATIVES **loosener** noun.

loose scrum noun Rugby a scrum formed by the players round the ball during play, not ordered by the referee.

loosestrife /looss-stryf/ noun a waterside plant with a tall upright spike of purple or yellow flowers.
– ORIGIN Greek *lusimakheion*.

loot noun **1** goods stolen from empty buildings during a war or riot. **2** goods stolen by a thief. **3** informal money. •verb steal goods from empty buildings during a war or riot.
– DERIVATIVES **looter** noun.

– ORIGIN Sanskrit, 'rob'.

lop verb (**lops**, **lopping**, **lopped**) **1** cut off a branch or limb from a tree or body. **2** informal make something smaller or less by a particular amount: *the new rail link lops an hour off journey times.*
– DERIVATIVES **lopper** noun.
– ORIGIN unknown.

lope verb run with a long bounding stride. •noun a long bounding stride.
– ORIGIN Old Norse, 'leap'.

lop-eared adjective (of an animal) having drooping ears.
– DERIVATIVES **lop ears** plural noun.
– ORIGIN from former *lop* 'hang loosely or limply'.

lopsided adjective with one side lower or smaller than the other.
– DERIVATIVES **lopsidedly** adverb **lopsidedness** noun.

loquacious /luh-kway-shuhss/ adjective talkative.
– DERIVATIVES **loquacity** noun.
– ORIGIN from Latin *loqui* 'to talk'.

loquat /loh-kwot/ noun a small egg-shaped yellow fruit from an East Asian tree.
– ORIGIN Chinese dialect, 'rush orange'.

lord noun **1** a man of noble rank. **2** (**Lord**) a title given formally to a baron, less formally to a marquess, earl, or viscount, and as a courtesy title to a younger son of a duke or marquess. **3** (**the Lords**) the House of Lords, or its members. **4** a master or ruler. **5** (**Lord**) a name for God or Jesus. •exclamation (**Lord**) used in exclamations expressing surprise or worry, or for emphasis. •verb (**lord it over**) act in an arrogant and bullying way towards someone.
– PHRASES **the Lord's Day** Sunday. **the Lord's Prayer** the prayer taught by Jesus to his disciples, beginning 'Our Father'.
– ORIGIN Old English, 'bread-keeper'; compare with LADY.

Lord Advocate noun the principal Law Officer of the Crown in Scotland.

Lord Chamberlain noun (in the UK) the official in charge of the royal household.

Lord Chancellor noun (in the UK) the highest judge, who also presides over the House of Lords.

Lord Chief Justice noun (in the UK) the second highest judge.

Lord Justice noun (pl. **Lords Justices**) (in the UK) a judge in the Court of Appeal.

Lord Lieutenant noun (in the UK) the representative of the Queen and head of magistrates in each county.

lordly adjective (**lordlier**, **lordliest**) characteristic of or suitable for a lord.
– DERIVATIVES **lordliness** noun.

Lord Mayor noun the title of the mayor in London and some other large cities.

Lord of Appeal (in full **Lord of Appeal in Ordinary**) noun formal term for LAW LORD.

Lord Privy Seal noun (in the UK) a senior cabinet minister without specified official duties.

Lord Provost noun the head of a municipal corporation or borough in certain Scottish cities.

lordship noun **1** (**His/Your Lordship**) a form of address to a judge, bishop, or nobleman. **2** supreme power or rule.

Lords spiritual plural noun the bishops in the House of Lords.

Lords temporal plural noun the members of the House of Lords other than the bishops.

Lord Treasurer noun see **TREASURER**.

lore noun a body of traditions and knowledge relating to a particular subject: *farming lore*.
– ORIGIN Old English, 'instruction'.

lorgnette /lor-nyet/ (also **lorgnettes**) noun a pair of glasses or opera glasses held by a long handle at one side.
– ORIGIN French, from *lorgner* 'to squint'.

lorikeet /lor-ri-keet/ noun a small bird of the lory family, found chiefly in New Guinea.
– ORIGIN from **LORY**.

loris /lor-ris/ noun (pl. **lorises**) a small, slow-moving primate that lives in thick vegetation in South Asia.
– ORIGIN French.

lorry noun (pl. **lorries**) Brit. a large, heavy motor vehicle for transporting goods or troops.
– ORIGIN uncertain.

lory /lor-ri/ noun (pl. **lories**) a small Australasian or SE Asian parrot.
– ORIGIN Malay.

lose /looz/ verb (past and past part. **lost**) **1** no longer have or keep: *I've lost my appetite.* **2** have something taken away: *she was upset about losing her job.* **3** become unable to find something or someone. **4** fail to win a game or contest. **5** earn less money than one is spending. **6** waste or fail to take advantage of: *he may have lost his chance.* **7** (**be lost**) be destroyed or killed. **8** escape from a pursuer. **9** (**lose oneself in/be lost in**) be or become deeply absorbed in: *he had been lost in thought.* **10** (of a watch or clock) become slow by a particular amount of time.
– PHRASES **lose face** become less well respected. **lose heart** become discouraged. **lose it** informal lose control of one's temper or emotions. **lose out** not get a full chance or opportunity. **lose one's** (or **the**) **way** become lost.
– ORIGIN Old English, 'perish, destroy', also 'become unable to find'.

USAGE: On the confusion of **lose** and **loose**, see the note at **LOOSE**.

loser noun **1** a person or thing that loses or has lost a game or contest. **2** informal a person who is generally unsuccessful in life.

losing battle noun a struggle in which failure seems certain.

loss noun **1** the fact or process of losing something or someone. **2** a person, thing, or amount lost. **3** the feeling of grief after losing a valued person or thing. **4** a person or thing that is badly missed when lost.
– PHRASES **at a loss 1** uncertain or puzzled. **2** making less money than is spent in operating or producing something.
– ORIGIN Old English, 'destruction'.

loss adjuster noun Brit. an insurance agent who assesses the amount of compensation that should be paid to a person making a claim.

loss-leader noun a product sold at a loss to attract customers.

lost past and past participle of **LOSE**. adjective unable to find one's way; not knowing where one is.
– PHRASES **be lost for words** be so surprised or upset that one cannot think what to say. **be lost on** fail to be noticed or understood by: *the irony is lost on him.*

lost cause noun a person or thing that can no longer have hope to succeed or be improved.

lost generation noun the generation reaching maturity during and just after the First World War, many of whose men were killed during those years.

lot pronoun informal **1** (**a lot** or **lots**) a large number or amount of something. **2** (**the lot**) the whole number or amount. • adverb (**a lot** or **lots**) informal a great deal. • noun **1** (treated as sing. or pl.) informal a particular group or set of people or things: *you lot think you're so clever.* **2** an item or set of items for sale at an auction. **3** a method of deciding something by choosing an item at random, especially one piece of paper from a number of pieces. **4** a person's destiny, luck, or situation in life: *many housewives are not happy with their lot.* **5** chiefly N. Amer. an area of land: *a parking lot.*
– PHRASES **draw** (or **cast**) **lots** decide something by choosing one piece of paper from a number of other pieces. **fall to someone's lot** become someone's task or responsibility. **throw in one's lot with** decide to join a person or group and share their fate.

USAGE: Although **a lot of** and **lots of** are very common in speech, they still have an informal feel and it is better to avoid them in formal English; use alternatives such as **many** or a **large number** instead.
The correct spelling is **a lot**; do not spell it as one word (*alot*).

– ORIGIN Old English.

loth adjective variant spelling of **LOATH**.

Lothario /luh-thair-i-oh/ noun (pl. **Lotharios**) a man who has many casual sexual relationships with women; a womanizer.
– ORIGIN from a character in Nicholas Rowe's tragedy *The Fair Penitent*.

lotion noun a thick creamy liquid applied to the skin as a medicine or cosmetic.
– ORIGIN Latin.

lottery noun (pl. **lotteries**) **1** a means of raising money by selling numbered tickets and giving prizes to the holders of numbers drawn at random. **2** something whose success is governed by chance: *the Grand Prix was made a lottery by heavy rain.*
– ORIGIN probably from Dutch *loterij*.

lotto noun **1** a children's game similar to bingo, using illustrated counters or cards. **2** a lottery.
– ORIGIN Italian.

lotus noun **1** a kind of large water lily. **2** (in Greek mythology) a legendary fruit that causes dreamy forgetfulness and an unwillingness to leave.
– ORIGIN Greek *lōtos*.

lotus-eater noun a person who indulges in pleasure and luxury rather than dealing with practical concerns.

lotus position noun a cross-legged position for meditation, with the feet resting on the thighs.

louche /loosh/ adjective having a bad reputation but still attractive: *a louche rock star.*
– ORIGIN French, 'squinting'.

loud adjective **1** producing or capable of producing much noise. **2** expressed forcefully: *the bold decision to introduce change despite loud protests from all.* **3** very bright and tasteless: *a loud checked suit.* •adverb with much noise.
– PHRASES **out loud** so as to be heard; aloud.
– DERIVATIVES **louden** verb **loudly** adverb **loudness** noun.
– ORIGIN Old English.

loudhailer noun Brit. an electronic device for amplifying the voice; a megaphone.

loudmouth noun informal a person who talks too much or makes tactless remarks.

loudspeaker noun a device that converts electrical impulses into sound.

lough /lokh/ noun (in Ireland) a loch.

lounge verb lie, sit, or stand in a relaxed or lazy way. •noun **1** Brit. a sitting room. **2** a room in a hotel, theatre, or airport in which to relax or wait.
– ORIGIN unknown.

lounge bar noun Brit. a bar in a pub or hotel that is more comfortable or smarter than the public bar.

lounge lizard noun informal an idle man who spends his time among rich and fashionable people.

lounger noun **1** a comfortable chair, especially an outdoor chair that allows a person to lie back. **2** a person who spends their time in a lazy or relaxed way.

lounge suit noun Brit. a man's suit for ordinary day wear.

lour /rhymes with flour/ (also **lower**) verb **1** (of the sky) look dark and threatening. **2** look angry or sullen; scowl.
– ORIGIN unknown.

louse noun **1** (pl. **lice**) a small wingless insect which lives as a parasite on humans, animals, and plants. **2** (pl. **louses**) informal an unpleasant person. •verb (**louse something up**) informal spoil something.
– ORIGIN Old English.

lousy adjective (**lousier**, **lousiest**) **1** informal very poor or bad. **2** infested with lice. **3** (**lousy with**) informal full of or teeming with something undesirable.
– DERIVATIVES **lousily** adverb **lousiness** noun.

lout noun a rough or aggressive man or boy.
– DERIVATIVES **loutish** adjective.
– ORIGIN perhaps from an Old English word meaning 'bow down'.

louvre /loo-ver/ (US also **louver**) noun each of a set of slanting slats fixed at intervals in a door, shutter, or cover to allow air or light through.
– DERIVATIVES **louvred** adjective.
– ORIGIN Old French *lover*, *lovier* 'skylight'.

lovable (also **loveable**) adjective inspiring love or affection.
– DERIVATIVES **lovableness** noun **lovably** adverb.

lovage /luv-ij/ noun a large white-flowered plant used as a herb in cookery.
– ORIGIN Old French *luvesche*.

lovat /luv-uht/ noun a muted green colour used especially in tweed garments.
– ORIGIN from *Lovat*, a place in Highland Scotland.

love noun **1** a strong feeling of affection. **2** strong affection linked with sexual attraction. **3** a great interest and pleasure in something. **4** a person or thing that one loves: *she was the love of his life.* **5** (in tennis, squash, etc.) a score of zero. •verb **1** feel love for someone. **2** like or enjoy something very much. **3** (as adj. **loving**) showing love or great care.
– PHRASES **make love 1** have sex. **2** (**make love to**) dated pay romantic attention to someone. **there's no love lost between** the people mentioned dislike each other.
– DERIVATIVES **loveless** adjective **lovingly** adverb.
– ORIGIN Old English.

loveable adjective variant spelling of **LOVABLE**.

love affair noun **1** a romantic or sexual relationship between two people who are not married to each other. **2** an intense enthusiasm for something.

lovebird noun **1** a very small African or Madagascan parrot that shows affection for its mate. **2** (**lovebirds**) informal an openly affectionate couple.

love bite noun Brit. a temporary red mark on the skin caused by biting or sucking during sexual play.

love child noun a child born to parents who are not married to each other.

love handles plural noun informal excess fat at a person's waistline.

love-in noun informal (especially among hippies in the 1960s) a gathering at which people are encouraged to express friendship and physical attraction.

love-in-a-mist noun a plant whose blue flowers are surrounded by thread-like green bracts (modified leaves).

love-lies-bleeding noun a South American plant with long drooping tassels of crimson flowers.

love life noun the part of a person's life concerning their relationships with lovers.

lovelorn adjective unhappy because one loves someone who does not feel the same in return.
– ORIGIN from **LOVE** + a former word meaning 'lost'.

lovely adjective (**lovelier**, **loveliest**) **1** very beautiful. **2** very pleasant. •noun (pl. **lovelies**) informal a beautiful woman or girl.
– DERIVATIVES **loveliness** noun.

lovemaking noun sexual intercourse and other sexual activity.

love nest noun informal a private place where two lovers spend time together.

lover noun **1** a person in a sexual or romantic relationship with someone. **2** a person who enjoys a specified thing: *a music lover.*

love seat noun a sofa designed in an S-shape so that two people can face each other.

lovesick adjective in love, or missing the person

one loves, so much that one is unable to act normally.
- DERIVATIVES **lovesickness** noun.

lovey-dovey adjective informal very affectionate or romantic.

loving cup noun a two-handled cup passed round at banquets.

low[1] adjective 1 not high or tall; of less than average height. 2 not far above the ground, horizon, or sea level. 3 below average in amount, extent, or intensity. 4 ranking below others in importance: *training was given low priority.* 5 lacking quality; inferior. 6 (of a sound) deep or quiet. 7 unfavourable: *she had a low opinion of herself.* 8 depressed or lacking energy. 9 lacking moral principles; unscrupulous or dishonest. • noun 1 a low point, level, or figure. 2 an area of low atmospheric pressure. • adverb 1 in or into a low position or state. 2 quietly or at a low pitch.
- DERIVATIVES **lowish** adjective **lowness** noun.
- ORIGIN Old Norse.

low[2] verb (of a cow) moo. • noun a moo.
- ORIGIN Old English.

lowbrow adjective chiefly derogatory not intellectual or interested in culture.

Low Church noun a tradition within the Anglican Church that places relatively little emphasis on ritual and the authority of bishops and priests.

low comedy noun comedy bordering on farce.

low-down informal adjective unfair or dishonest. • noun (**the low-down**) the true or most important facts about something.

lower[1] adjective comparative of **LOW**[1]. 1 less high in position, importance, or amount. 2 (of a geological period or formation) older (and hence forming more deeply buried strata): *the Lower Cretaceous.* 3 (in place names) situated to the south.
- DERIVATIVES **lowermost** adjective.

lower[2] verb 1 move someone or something downward. 2 make or become less in amount, intensity, or value: *I lowered my voice to a whisper.* 3 (**lower oneself**) behave in a way that is humiliating.

lower[3] verb variant spelling of **LOUR**.

lower case noun small letters as opposed to capitals.

lower class (also **lower classes**) noun the working class.

lower court noun Law a court whose decisions may be overruled by another on appeal.

lower house (also **lower chamber**) noun 1 the larger section of a parliament with two chambers, typically with elected members. 2 (**the Lower House**) (in the UK) the House of Commons.

lowest common denominator noun 1 Mathematics the lowest common multiple of the denominators of several fractions. 2 derogatory the level of the least discriminating audience or other group.

lowest common multiple noun Mathematics the lowest quantity that is a multiple of two or more given quantities.

low-fi adjective variant spelling of **LO-FI**.

low frequency noun (in radio) 30–300

kilohertz.

low gear noun a gear that causes a vehicle to move slowly.

Low German noun a German dialect spoken in much of northern Germany.

low-impact adjective 1 (of exercises) putting little stress on the body. 2 affecting the environment as little as possible.

low-key (also **low-keyed**) adjective not elaborate, showy, or intensive; restrained.

lowland /loh-luhnd/ noun 1 (also **lowlands**) low-lying country. 2 (**the Lowlands**) the part of Scotland lying south and east of the Highlands.
- DERIVATIVES **lowlander** noun.

low-level adjective 1 of relatively little importance. 2 (of a computer programming language) similar to machine code in form.

low life noun 1 dishonest or immoral people or activities. 2 (**lowlife**) informal a dishonest or immoral person.

lowlight noun 1 (**lowlights**) darker dyed streaks in the hair. 2 informal a disappointing or dull event or feature.

low-loader noun Brit. a lorry with a low floor and no sides, for heavy loads.

lowly adjective (**lowlier**, **lowliest**) low in status or importance. • adverb to a low degree: *lowly paid workers.*
- DERIVATIVES **lowliness** noun.

low-lying adjective (of land) not far above sea level.

low-profile adjective avoiding attention or publicity: *a low-profile campaign.*

low relief noun see **RELIEF** (sense 8).

low-rise adjective 1 (of a building) having few storeys. 2 (of trousers) cut so as to fit low on the hips rather than on the waist.

low season noun Brit. the least popular time of year for a holiday, when prices are lowest.

low-slung adjective 1 lower in height or closer to the ground than usual. 2 (of clothes) cut to fit low on the hips rather than the waist.

low spirits plural noun a feeling of sadness and gloom.

low technology noun less advanced technological development or equipment.

low tide (also **low water**) noun the state of the tide when at its lowest level.

low-water mark noun the level reached by the sea at low tide.

lox /loks/ noun N. Amer. smoked salmon.
- ORIGIN Yiddish.

loyal adjective showing firm and constant support for a person, an organization, or one's country.
- DERIVATIVES **loyally** adverb.
- ORIGIN French.

loyalist noun 1 a person who remains loyal to the established ruler or government. 2 (**Loyalist**) a supporter of union between Great Britain and Northern Ireland.
- DERIVATIVES **loyalism** noun.

loyalty noun (pl. **loyalties**) 1 the state of being loyal or faithful to a person, an organization, or one's country. 2 a strong feeling of support or commitment: *rows with in-laws can cause divided loyalties.*

loyalty card noun Brit. a card issued by a retailer to its customers, on which credits are accumulated for future discounts every time a purchase is recorded.

lozenge /loz-inj/ noun 1 a small tablet of medicine that is sucked to soothe a sore throat. 2 a diamond shape; a rhombus.
– ORIGIN Old French *losenge*.

LP abbreviation long-playing (gramophone record).

LPG abbreviation liquefied petroleum gas.

L-plate noun Brit. a sign with the letter L on it, attached to a vehicle to show that the driver is a learner.

Lr symbol the chemical element lawrencium.

LSD noun lysergic acid diethylamide, a powerful drug that causes hallucinations.

Lt abbreviation Lieutenant.

Ltd abbreviation Brit. (after a company name) Limited.

Lu symbol the chemical element lutetium.

lubber noun old use or dialect a big, clumsy person.
– DERIVATIVES **lubberly** adjective & adverb.
– ORIGIN perhaps from Old French *lobeor* 'swindler, parasite'.

lubricant noun a substance for lubricating machinery or part of the body.

lubricate /loo-bri-kayt/ verb apply a substance such as oil or grease to machinery or part of the body to allow smooth movement.
– DERIVATIVES **lubrication** noun **lubricator** noun.
– ORIGIN Latin *lubricare* 'make slippery'.

lubricious /loo-bri-shuhss/ adjective referring to sexual matters in a rude or offensive way.
– DERIVATIVES **lubriciously** adverb **lubricity** noun.
– ORIGIN Latin *lubricus* 'slippery'.

lucent /loo-suhnt/ adjective literary glowing with or giving off light; shining.
– DERIVATIVES **lucency** noun.
– ORIGIN from Latin *lucere* 'shine'.

lucerne /loo-sern/ noun another term for ALFALFA.
– ORIGIN modern Provençal *luzerno* 'glow-worm' (with reference to its shiny seeds).

lucid /loo-sid/ adjective 1 easy to understand; clear: *a lucid account.* 2 showing an ability to think clearly. 3 literary bright or luminous.
– DERIVATIVES **lucidity** noun **lucidly** adverb.
– ORIGIN Latin *lucidus*.

Lucifer /loo-si-fer/ noun 1 the Devil. 2 (**lucifer**) old use a match.
– ORIGIN Latin, 'light-bringing, morning star'.

luck noun 1 good things that happen by chance: *it was just luck that the first goal went in.* 2 chance considered as a force that causes success or failure: *we both had bad luck and lost five thousand dollars.* • verb informal (**luck into/upon**) find or obtain something by good luck.
– PHRASES **no such luck** informal unfortunately not. **try one's luck** attempt something risky. **worse luck** informal unfortunately.
– ORIGIN German *lucke*.

luckily adverb it is fortunate that.

luckless adjective having bad luck; unfortunate.

lucky adjective (**luckier**, **luckiest**) having, bringing, or resulting from good luck: *seven's my lucky number.*

lucky dip noun Brit. a game in which small prizes are concealed in a container for people to pick out at random.

lucrative /loo-kruh-tiv/ adjective producing a great deal of profit; profitable.
– DERIVATIVES **lucratively** adverb.
– ORIGIN Latin *lucrativus*.

lucre /loo-ker/ noun literary money, especially when gained in an underhand or dishonourable way.
– ORIGIN Latin *lucrum*.

lucubration /loo-kyuu-bray-sh'n/ noun literary a scholarly or pedantic piece of writing.
– ORIGIN from Latin *lucubrare* 'work by lamplight'.

lud noun (**m'lud** or **my lud**) Brit. used to address a judge in court.
– ORIGIN alteration of LORD.

Luddite /lud-dyt/ noun 1 derogatory a person opposed to industrialization or new technology. 2 a member of any of the bands of English workers who opposed mechanization and destroyed machinery in the early 19th century.
– DERIVATIVES **Luddism** noun **Ludditism** noun.
– ORIGIN perhaps named after Ned *Lud*, a worker who destroyed machinery.

ludic /loo-dik/ adjective formal spontaneous; playful.
– ORIGIN French *ludique*.

ludicrous /loo-dik-ruhss/ adjective absurd; ridiculous.
– DERIVATIVES **ludicrously** adverb **ludicrousness** noun.
– ORIGIN Latin *ludicrus*.

ludo noun Brit. a board game in which players move counters according to throws of a dice.
– ORIGIN Latin, 'I play'.

luff verb steer a sailing ship nearer the wind.
– ORIGIN Old French *lof*.

Luftwaffe /luuft-wa-fuh/ noun the German air force until the end of the Second World War.
– ORIGIN from German *Luft* 'air' + *Waffe* 'weapon'.

lug[1] verb (**lugs**, **lugging**, **lugged**) carry or drag a heavy object with great effort.
– ORIGIN probably Scandinavian.

lug[2] noun 1 Brit. informal an ear. 2 a projection on an object by which it may be carried or fixed in place.
– ORIGIN probably Scandinavian.

luge /loozh/ noun a light toboggan ridden in a sitting or lying position.
– ORIGIN Swiss French.

Luger /loo-ger/ noun (trademark in the US) a type of German automatic pistol.
– ORIGIN named after the German firearms expert George *Luger*.

luggage noun suitcases or other bags for a traveller's belongings.
– ORIGIN from LUG[1].

lugger noun a small ship with two or three masts and a four-sided sail on each.

lughole noun Brit. informal an ear.

lugubrious /luu-goo-bri-uhss/ adjective sad and dismal; mournful.
– DERIVATIVES **lugubriously** adverb **lugubriousness** noun.
– ORIGIN Latin *lugubris*.

lugworm noun a worm that lives in muddy

sand, used as fishing bait.
– ORIGIN unknown.

lukewarm adjective **1** only slightly warm. **2** not enthusiastic or interested: *a lukewarm response*.
– ORIGIN from dialect *luke* 'tepid'.

lull verb **1** calm someone or send them to sleep with soothing sounds or movements. **2** make someone feel secure or confident, even if they are at risk. **3** (of noise or a storm) become quiet or calm. •noun a temporary period of quiet or inactivity.
– ORIGIN imitating sounds used to quieten a child.

lullaby noun (pl. **lullabies**) a soothing song sung to send a child to sleep.
– ORIGIN from LULL + *bye-bye*.

lumbago /lum-**bay**-goh/ noun pain in the lower back.
– ORIGIN Latin.

lumbar /**lum**-ber/ adjective relating to the lower back.
– ORIGIN Latin *lumbaris*.

lumbar puncture noun Medicine, Brit. the taking of spinal fluid from the lower back through a hollow needle, usually for diagnosis.

lumber[1] verb move in a slow, heavy, awkward way.
– ORIGIN uncertain.

lumber[2] noun **1** Brit. disused articles of furniture that take up space. **2** chiefly N. Amer. partly prepared timber. •verb **1** Brit. informal burden with an unwanted responsibility: *he's lumbered with an ex-wife and a truculent daughter.* **2** chiefly N. Amer. cut and prepare forest timber for transport and sale.
– ORIGIN perhaps from LUMBER[1]; later associated with former *lumber* 'pawnbroker's shop'.

lumberjack (also **lumberman**) noun a person who fells trees, cuts them into logs, or transports them.

lumberjack shirt noun a shirt of brushed cotton or flannel, typically with a check pattern.

lumen /**loo**-muhn/ noun Physics the SI unit of flux of light.
– ORIGIN Latin, 'light'.

luminaire /loo-min-**air**/ noun a complete electric light unit.
– ORIGIN French.

luminance /**loo**-min-uhns/ noun **1** the component of a television signal which carries information on the brightness of the image. **2** Physics the intensity of light emitted from a surface per unit area in a given direction.

luminary /**loo**-mi-nuh-ri/ noun (pl. **luminaries**) **1** a person who is influential or famous within an area of activity: *culinary luminaries.* **2** old use the sun or moon.

luminesce /loo-mi-**ness**/ verb produce light by luminescence.

luminescence /loo-mi-**ness**-uhnss/ noun the production of light by a substance that has not been heated, as in fluorescence.
– DERIVATIVES **luminescent** adjective.

luminosity noun (pl. **luminosities**) the quality of being bright or shining.

luminous /**loo**-mi-nuhss/ adjective **1** bright or shining, especially in the dark. **2** Physics relating to visible light.
– DERIVATIVES **luminously** adverb.
– ORIGIN Latin *luminosus*.

lummox /**lum**-uhks/ noun informal, chiefly N. Amer. a clumsy, stupid person.
– ORIGIN unknown.

lump[1] noun **1** an irregular mass or piece of something hard or solid. **2** a swelling under the skin. **3** informal a heavy, clumsy, or slow-witted person. **4** (**the lump**) Brit. informal casual employment in the building trade. •verb **1** treat as alike, regardless of details: *Hong Kong and Bangkok tend to be lumped together in holiday brochures.* **2** Brit. carry a heavy load with difficulty.
– PHRASES **a lump in the throat** a feeling of tightness in the throat caused by strong emotion.
– ORIGIN perhaps Germanic.

lump[2] verb (**lump it**) informal accept or put up with something whether one likes it or not.
– ORIGIN uncertain.

lumpectomy /lum-**pek**-tuh-mi/ noun (pl. **lumpectomies**) a surgical operation in which a lump, typically a tumour, is removed from the breast.

lumpen adjective **1** lumpy and misshapen. **2** uncultured and stupid.
– ORIGIN abbreviation of LUMPENPROLETARIAT.

lumpenproletariat /lum-puhn-proh-li-**tair**-i-uht/ noun (in Marxism) the lower orders of society who are not interested in politics or revolutionary advancement.
– ORIGIN from German *Lumpen* 'rag, rogue' + PROLETARIAT.

lumpfish noun (pl. same or **lumpfishes**) a North Atlantic fish with edible roe.
– ORIGIN from German *lumpen*, Dutch *lompe*.

lumpish adjective **1** stupid or slow-witted. **2** roughly or clumsily formed.
– DERIVATIVES **lumpishly** adverb **lumpishness** noun.

lump sum noun a single payment made at one time, as opposed to several instalments.

lumpy adjective (**lumpier**, **lumpiest**) full of or covered with lumps.
– DERIVATIVES **lumpily** adverb **lumpiness** noun.

lunacy noun (pl. **lunacies**) **1** insanity (not in technical use). **2** great foolishness.
– ORIGIN from LUNATIC.

lunar /**loo**-ner/ adjective relating to, determined by, or resembling the moon.
– ORIGIN from Latin *luna* 'moon'.

lunar eclipse noun an eclipse in which the moon passes into the earth's shadow.

lunar month noun **1** a month measured between successive new moons (roughly 29½ days). **2** (in general use) four weeks.

lunatic noun **1** a person who is mentally ill (not in technical use). **2** a very foolish person.
– ORIGIN from Latin *luna* 'moon' (from the former belief that changes of the moon caused insanity).

lunatic asylum noun dated a psychiatric hospital.

lunatic fringe noun a small section within a group with extreme or eccentric views.

lunch noun a meal eaten in the middle of the day. •verb eat lunch.

– DERIVATIVES **luncher** noun.
– ORIGIN abbreviation of **LUNCHEON**.

luncheon noun formal lunch.
– ORIGIN perhaps from Spanish *lonja* 'slice'.

luncheon meat noun finely minced cooked pork mixed with cereal, sold in a tin.

luncheon voucher noun Brit. a voucher given to employees and exchangeable for food at restaurants and shops.

lunchtime noun the time when lunch is eaten.

lunette /loo-**net**/ noun **1** an arched window or other aperture in a domed ceiling. **2** a crescent-shaped or semicircular alcove containing a painting or statue.
– ORIGIN French, 'little moon'.

lung noun each of the pair of organs within the ribcage of humans and most vertebrates, into which air is drawn in breathing.
– DERIVATIVES **lunged** adjective **lungful** noun.
– ORIGIN Old English.

lunge¹ noun **1** a sudden forward movement of the body. **2** a thrust in fencing, in which the leading leg is bent while the back leg remains straightened. ● verb (**lunges, lunging** or **lungeing, lunged**) make a sudden forward movement or thrust.
– ORIGIN from French *allonger* 'lengthen'.

lunge² (also **longe**) noun a long rein on which a horse is made to move in a circle round its trainer.
– ORIGIN French *longe*.

lungfish noun (pl. same or **lungfishes**) a freshwater fish with one or two sacs which function as lungs, enabling it to breathe air and live dormant in mud to survive drought.

lungi /**luung**-gee/ noun (pl. **lungis**) an item of clothing like a sarong, wrapped around the waist and extending to the ankles, worn in India and Burma (Myanmar).
– ORIGIN Urdu.

lunk (also **lunkhead**) noun informal a slow-witted person.
– ORIGIN probably from **LUMP**¹.

lupin /**loo**-pin/ noun a plant with a tall stem bearing many small colourful flowers.
– ORIGIN Latin *lupinus*.

lupine /**loo**-pyn/ adjective relating to or like a wolf or wolves.
– ORIGIN from Latin *lupus* 'wolf'.

lupus /**loo**-puhss/ noun an ulcerous skin disease, especially (**lupus vulgaris**) one due to direct infection with tuberculosis.
– ORIGIN Latin, 'wolf'.

lupus erythematosus /e-ri-thee-muh-**toh**-suhss/ noun an inflammatory disease causing scaly red patches on the skin.
– ORIGIN from **LUPUS** + Greek *eruthēma* 'reddening'.

lurch¹ verb make a sudden unsteady movement; stagger. ● noun a sudden unsteady movement.
– ORIGIN unknown.

lurch² noun (in phrase **leave someone in the lurch**) leave someone in a difficult situation without assistance or support.
– ORIGIN from French *demeurer lourche* 'be discomfited' (*lourche* referring to a game resembling backgammon).

lurcher noun Brit. a dog that is a cross between a greyhound and a retriever, collie, or sheepdog.
– ORIGIN first referring to a petty thief: related

to **LURK**.

lure /lyoor/ verb tempt someone to do something or to go somewhere. ● noun **1** the attractive or tempting qualities of a person or thing: *the lure of the city.* **2** a type of bait used in fishing or hunting. **3** a bunch of feathers with a piece of meat attached to a long string, which a falconer swings around their head to recall a hawk.
– ORIGIN Old French *luere*.

lurex /**lyoo**-reks/ noun trademark yarn or fabric incorporating a glittering metallic thread.
– ORIGIN unknown.

lurgy /**ler**-gi/ noun (pl. **lurgies**) Brit. informal, humorous an unspecified illness.
– ORIGIN unknown.

lurid /**lyoor**-id/ adjective **1** unpleasantly vivid in colour. **2** deliberately shocking or sensational: *lurid accounts of murders.*
– DERIVATIVES **luridly** adverb **luridness** noun.
– ORIGIN Latin *luridus* 'yellow, sallow'.

lurk verb **1** wait in hiding so as to attack someone or something. **2** be present in an underlying or hidden way: *danger lurks beneath the surface.*
– DERIVATIVES **lurker** noun.
– ORIGIN perhaps from **LOUR**.

luscious adjective **1** having a pleasingly rich, sweet taste. **2** very pleasing to the senses: *luscious harmonies.* **3** (of a woman) sexually attractive.
– DERIVATIVES **lusciously** adverb **lusciousness** noun.
– ORIGIN perhaps from **DELICIOUS**.

lush¹ adjective **1** (of vegetation) growing thickly. **2** rich and pleasing to the senses: *the album's lush production.* **3** Brit. informal sexually attractive.
– DERIVATIVES **lushly** adverb **lushness** noun.
– ORIGIN perhaps from Old French *lasche* 'lax'.

lush² noun informal, chiefly N. Amer. a drunkard.
– ORIGIN perhaps from **LUSH**¹.

lust noun **1** strong sexual desire. **2** a passionate desire for something: *a lust for power.* ● verb (usu. **lust for/after**) feel strong desire for someone or something.
– ORIGIN Old English.

lustful adjective filled with strong sexual desire.
– DERIVATIVES **lustfully** adverb **lustfulness** noun.

lustre (US **luster**) noun **1** a soft sheen or glow. **2** prestige or distinction: *a celebrity player will add lustre to the line-up.* **3** a thin metallic coating used to give an iridescent glaze to ceramics.
– DERIVATIVES **lustred** adjective **lustreless** adjective.
– ORIGIN Latin *lustrare* 'illuminate'.

lustrous adjective having a soft glow or sheen.
– DERIVATIVES **lustrously** adverb **lustrousness** noun.

lusty adjective (**lustier, lustiest**) healthy and strong; vigorous.
– DERIVATIVES **lustily** adverb **lustiness** noun.

lute noun a stringed instrument with a long neck and a rounded body with a flat front, played by plucking.
– ORIGIN Old French *lut, leut*.

lutenist /**loo**-tuh-nist/ (also **lutanist**) noun a lute player.

lutetium /loo-**tee**-shi-uhm/ noun a rare silvery-white metallic chemical element of the lanthanide series.
– ORIGIN from Latin *Lutetia*, the ancient name of Paris, where its discoverer lived.

Lutheran noun a member of the Lutheran Church, a Protestant Church based on the beliefs and teachings of the German theologian Martin Luther. ● adjective relating to the teachings of Martin Luther or to the Lutheran Church.
– DERIVATIVES **Lutheranism** noun.

luthier /loo-ti-er/ noun a maker of stringed instruments.
– ORIGIN from French *luth* 'lute'.

luvvie (also **luvvy**) noun (pl. **luvvies**) Brit. informal a pretentious actor or actress.

lux /luks/ noun (pl. same) the SI unit of illumination.
– ORIGIN Latin, 'light'.

luxe /luks, luuks/ noun luxury.
– ORIGIN French.

Luxembourger /**luk**-suhm-ber-ger/ noun a person from Luxembourg.

luxuriant /lug-**zhoor**-i-uhnt/ adjective **1** (of vegetation or hair) growing thickly and strongly. **2** rich and pleasing to the senses: *the novel's luxuriant prose.*
– DERIVATIVES **luxuriance** noun **luxuriantly** adverb.
– ORIGIN from Latin *luxuriare* 'grow rankly'.

luxuriate /lug-**zhoor**-i-ayt/ verb (**luxuriate in/over**) take pleasure in something enjoyable.

luxurious adjective **1** very elegant, comfortable, and expensive. **2** giving sensual pleasure: *long, luxurious baths.*
– DERIVATIVES **luxuriously** adverb **luxuriousness** noun.

luxury noun (pl. **luxuries**) **1** a state of great comfort and elegance, especially when involving great expense. **2** an item that is expensive and enjoyable but not essential. ● adjective expensive and elegant; luxurious: *a luxury yacht.*
– ORIGIN Latin *luxuria* 'lechery'.

LW abbreviation long wave.

lwei /luh-**way**/ noun (pl. same) a unit of money of Angola, equal to one hundredth of a kwanza.
– ORIGIN a local word.

lx abbreviation Physics lux.

lycanthrope /**ly**-kuhn-throhp/ noun a werewolf.

lycanthropy /ly-**kan**-thruh-pi/ noun the mythical transformation of a person into a wolf.
– DERIVATIVES **lycanthropic** adjective.
– ORIGIN from Greek *lukos* 'wolf' + *anthrōpos* 'man'.

lychee /**ly**-chee/ (also **litchi**) noun a small round fruit with sweet white flesh, a large stone, and thin rough skin.
– ORIGIN Chinese.

lychgate /**lich**-gayt/ noun a roofed gateway to a churchyard.
– ORIGIN from Old English *līc* 'body' (from the former practice of using such a gateway to shelter a coffin before burial).

lycopene /**ly**-koh-peen/ noun a red pigment related to carotene and present in tomatoes and many berries and fruits.
– ORIGIN from Latin *Lycopersicon* a genus name including the tomato.

Lycra /**ly**-kruh/ noun trademark a synthetic elastic fibre or fabric used for close-fitting clothing.
– ORIGIN unknown.

lye noun a strongly alkaline solution, especially of potassium hydroxide, used for washing or cleaning.
– ORIGIN Old English.

lying¹ present participle of LIE¹.

lying² present participle of LIE².

Lyme disease /lym/ noun a form of arthritis caused by bacteria that are transmitted by ticks.
– ORIGIN named after the US town of *Lyme*, where an outbreak occurred.

lymph /limf/ noun a colourless fluid containing white blood cells, which bathes the tissues of the body.
– ORIGIN Latin *lympha, limpa* 'water'.

lymphatic adjective relating to lymph or its production. ● noun a structure like a vein that conveys lymph in the body.
– ORIGIN Greek *numpholēptos* 'seized by nymphs'; now associated with LYMPH.

lymphatic system noun the network of vessels through which lymph drains from the body tissues into the blood.

lymph node (also **lymph gland**) noun each of a number of small swellings in the body's lymphatic system where lymph is filtered and lymphocytes are formed.

lymphocyte /**lim**-fuh-syt/ noun a form of small leucocyte (white blood cell) with a single round nucleus, occurring especially in the lymphatic system.

lymphoma /lim-**foh**-muh/ noun (pl. **lymphomas**) cancer of the lymph nodes.

lynch verb (of a group) kill someone for an alleged crime without a legal trial, especially by hanging.
– DERIVATIVES **lyncher** noun.
– ORIGIN named after Captain William *Lynch* of Virginia, head of an unofficial court of justice.

lynchpin noun variant spelling of LINCHPIN.

lynx noun a wild cat with a short tail and tufted ears.
– ORIGIN Greek *lunx*.

lynx-eyed adjective keen-sighted.

lyonnaise /lee-uh-**nayz**/ adjective (especially of sliced potatoes) cooked with onions or with a white wine and onion sauce.
– ORIGIN French, 'characteristic of the city of Lyons'.

lyre noun a stringed instrument like a small U-shaped harp with strings fixed to a crossbar, used especially in ancient Greece.
– ORIGIN Greek *lura*.

lyrebird noun a large Australian songbird, the male of which has a long lyre-shaped tail.

lyric noun **1** (also **lyrics**) the words of a song. **2** a fairly short poem expressing the writer's emotions or mood. ● adjective **1** (of poetry) expressing the writer's emotions or mood, usually briefly. **2** (of a singing voice) light.

– ORIGIN from Greek *lura* 'lyre'.

lyrical adjective **1** (of literature, art, or music) expressing the writer's emotions in an imaginative and pleasing way. **2** (of poetry) expressing the writer's emotions or mood; lyric. **3** relating to the words of a popular song.

– PHRASES **wax lyrical** talk in a very enthusiastic and unrestrained way.

– DERIVATIVES **lyrically** adverb.

lyricism /li-ri-si-z'm/ noun the expression of emotion in literature or music in an imaginative and pleasing way.

lyricist noun a person who writes the words to popular songs.

Mm

M[1] (also **m**) noun (pl. **Ms** or **M's**) **1** the thirteenth letter of the alphabet. **2** the Roman numeral for 1,000. [from Latin *mille*.]

M[2] abbreviation **1** male. **2** medium. **3** mega-. **4** Monsieur. **5** motorway.

m abbreviation **1** married. **2** masculine. **3** Physics mass. **4** Chemistry meta-. **5** metre(s). **6** mile(s). **7** milli-. **8** million(s). **9** minute(s).

m- prefix referring to commercial activity carried out electronically by means of mobile phones: *m-commerce*.

MA abbreviation **1** Massachusetts. **2** Master of Arts.

ma noun informal a person's mother.

ma'am noun madam.

mac noun Brit. informal a mackintosh.

macabre /muh-**kah**-bruh/ adjective disturbing and horrifying because concerned with death or injury.
– ORIGIN French.

macadam /muh-**kad**-uhm/ noun broken stone used with tar or bitumen for surfacing roads and paths.
– ORIGIN named after the British surveyor John L. *McAdam*.

macadamia /ma-kuh-**day**-mi-uh/ noun the round edible nut of an Australian tree.
– ORIGIN named after the Australian chemist John *Macadam*.

macaque /muh-**kak**/ noun a medium-sized monkey with a long face and cheek pouches for holding food.
– ORIGIN from Bantu *makaku* 'some monkeys'.

macaroni noun **1** pasta in the form of narrow tubes. **2** (pl. **macaronies**) an 18th-century British dandy who imitated continental fashions.
– ORIGIN Italian *maccaroni*.

macaroon noun a light biscuit made with egg white and ground almonds or coconut.
– ORIGIN French *macaron*.

macaw /muh-**kaw**/ noun a large brightly coloured parrot with a long tail, native to Central and South America.
– ORIGIN Portuguese *macau*.

McCarthyism noun a campaign against alleged communists in the US government and other organizations carried out under Senator Joseph McCarthy from 1950–4.
– DERIVATIVES **McCarthyite** adjective & noun.

macchiato /ma-ki-**ah**-toh/ noun espresso coffee with a dash of frothy steamed milk.
– ORIGIN Italian, 'stained, marked'.

McCoy noun (in phrase **the real McCoy**) informal the real thing.
– ORIGIN uncertain.

mace[1] noun **1** a ceremonial staff carried as a symbol of authority by certain officials. **2** historical a heavy club with a spiked metal head. **3** (**Mace**) trademark an irritant chemical sprayed from an aerosol to disable attackers.
– ORIGIN Old French *masse* 'large hammer'.

mace[2] noun a spice consisting of the dried outer covering of the nutmeg.
– ORIGIN Latin *macir*.

macédoine /**mass**-i-dwahn/ noun a mixture of vegetables or fruit cut into small pieces.
– ORIGIN French, 'Macedonia', with reference to the mixture of peoples in the Macedonian Empire of Alexander the Great.

Macedonian noun a person from the republic of Macedonia (formerly part of Yugoslavia), ancient Macedonia, or the modern Greek region of Macedonia. ● adjective relating to Macedonia.

macerate /**mass**-uh-rayt/ verb soften or break up food by soaking in a liquid.
– DERIVATIVES **maceration** noun.
– ORIGIN Latin *macerare*.

McGuffin noun an object or device in a film or a book which serves merely as a trigger for the plot.
– ORIGIN a Scottish surname, said to have been borrowed by the English film director Alfred Hitchcock from a story involving such a factor.

Mach /mak/ noun used with a numeral (as **Mach 1**, **Mach 2**, etc.) to indicate the speed of sound, twice the speed of sound, etc.
– ORIGIN named after the Austrian physicist Ernst *Mach*.

machete /muh-**shet**-i/ noun a broad, heavy knife used as an implement or weapon.
– ORIGIN Spanish.

Machiavellian /ma-ki-uh-**vel**-li-uhn/ adjective cunning, scheming, and unscrupulous.
– ORIGIN from the Italian statesman and philosopher Niccolò *Machiavelli*.

machicolation /muh-chik-uh-**lay**-sh'n/ noun (in medieval fortifications) an opening between the supports of a projecting structure, through which stones or burning objects could be dropped on attackers.
– DERIVATIVES **machicolated** adjective.
– ORIGIN from Provençal *macar* 'to crush' + *col* 'neck'.

machinable adjective (of a material) able to be worked by a machine tool.
– DERIVATIVES **machinability** noun.

machinations /mash-i-**nay**-sh'nz/ plural noun

secret plots; scheming.
- ORIGIN from Latin *machinari* 'contrive'.

machine noun **1** a device using mechanical power and having several parts, for performing a particular task. **2** a well-organized group of influential people: *the council's publicity machine.* •verb make or operate on something with a machine.
- ORIGIN Greek *mēkhos* 'contrivance'.

machine code (also **machine language**) noun a computer programming language consisting of instructions which a computer can respond to directly.

machine gun noun an automatic gun that fires bullets in rapid succession for as long as the trigger is pressed. •verb (**machine-gun**) shoot someone with a machine gun.

machine-readable adjective in a form that a computer can process.

machinery noun **1** machines as a whole, or the components of a machine. **2** an organized system or structure: *the machinery of the state.*

machine tool noun a fixed powered tool for cutting or shaping metal, wood, etc.

machine translation noun translation carried out by a computer.

machinist noun a person who operates a machine or who makes machinery.

machismo /muh-**kiz**-moh/ noun strong or aggressive masculine pride.
- ORIGIN Mexican Spanish.

macho /**mach**-oh/ adjective showing aggressive pride in one's masculinity.
- ORIGIN Mexican Spanish.

mackerel noun an edible sea fish with a greenish-blue back.
- ORIGIN Old French *maquerel*.

mackintosh (also **macintosh**) noun Brit. a full-length waterproof coat.
- ORIGIN named after the Scottish inventor Charles *Macintosh*.

macramé /muh-**krah**-may/ noun the craft of knotting cord or string in patterns to make decorative articles.
- ORIGIN French.

macro noun (pl. **macros**) Computing a single instruction that expands automatically into a set of instructions to perform a particular task.

macro- combining form large; large-scale: *macroeconomics.*
- ORIGIN from Greek *makros* 'long, large'.

macrobiotic /mak-roh-by-**ot**-ik/ adjective (of diet) consisting of unprocessed organic foods, based on Buddhist principles of the balance of yin and yang.
- ORIGIN from Greek *makros* 'long' + *bios* 'life'.

macrocarpa /mak-roh-**kar**-puh/ noun a Californian cypress tree with a large spreading crown of horizontal branches.
- ORIGIN from Greek *makros* 'long' + *karpos* 'fruit'.

macrocosm noun the whole of a complex structure (such as the world) contrasted with a small or representative part of it (a microcosm).
- DERIVATIVES **macrocosmic** adjective.
- ORIGIN from Greek *makros kosmos* 'big world'.

macroeconomics plural noun (treated as sing.) the branch of economics concerned with large-scale economic factors, such as interest rates.

macro lens noun a camera lens suitable for taking photographs unusually close to the subject.

macromolecule noun a molecule containing a very large number of atoms, such as a protein.
- DERIVATIVES **macromolecular** adjective.

macron noun a written or printed mark (ˉ) used to indicate a long vowel in some languages, or a stressed vowel in verse.

macroscopic /mak-roh-**skop**-ik/ adjective **1** visible to the naked eye; not microscopic. **2** relating to large-scale or general analysis.

macula /**mak**-yuu-luh/ (also **macule**) noun (pl. maculae /**mak**-yuu-lee/) Medicine an area of skin discoloration.
- ORIGIN Latin.

macumba /muh-**kuum**-buh/ noun a religious cult practised among black people in Brazil, using sorcery, ritual dance, and fetishes.
- ORIGIN Portuguese.

mad adjective (**madder, maddest**) **1** mentally ill. **2** very foolish; not sensible. **3** impulsive, confused, or frenzied: *it was a mad dash to get away.* **4** informal very enthusiastic about something. **5** informal very angry. **6** (of a dog) having rabies.
- DERIVATIVES **madly** adverb **madness** noun.
- ORIGIN Old English.

Madagascan /mad-uh-**gass**-k'n/ noun a person from Madagascar. •adjective relating to Madagascar.

madam noun **1** a polite form of address for a woman. **2** Brit. informal a bossy or cheeky girl. **3** a woman who runs a brothel.
- ORIGIN from French *ma dame* 'my lady'.

Madame /muh-**dam**/ noun (pl. **Mesdames** /may-**dam**/) a title or form of address for a French-speaking woman.

madcap adjective foolish or reckless.

mad cow disease noun informal term for **BSE**.

madden verb **1** drive someone insane. **2** make someone very annoyed.

madder noun a red dye or pigment obtained from the roots of a plant.
- ORIGIN Old English.

madding adjective literary acting madly; frenzied: *far from the madding crowd.*

made past and past participle of **MAKE**.

Madeira noun a strong sweet white wine from the island of Madeira in the Atlantic Ocean.

Madeira cake noun Brit. a rich kind of sponge cake.
- ORIGIN because formerly eaten with Madeira wine.

madeleine noun a small rich sponge cake decorated with coconut and jam.
- ORIGIN probably named after *Madeleine Paulmier*, a French pastry cook.

Mademoiselle /ma-duh-mwah-**zel**/ noun (pl. **Mesdemoiselles** /may-duh-mwa-**zel**/) a title or form of address for an unmarried French-speaking woman.
- ORIGIN from French *ma demoiselle* 'my damsel'.

made to measure adjective specially made to

fit a particular person or thing: *made-to-measure curtains.*

made-up adjective 1 wearing make-up.
2 invented; untrue.

madhouse noun 1 informal a scene of great confusion or uproar. 2 historical an institution for the mentally ill.

madman (or **madwoman**) noun (pl. **madmen** or **madwomen**) 1 a person who is mentally ill. 2 a foolish or reckless person.

Madonna noun (**the Madonna**) the Virgin Mary.
– ORIGIN from Italian *ma donna* 'my lady'.

madras noun 1 a colourful striped or checked cotton fabric. 2 a hot spiced curry dish.
– ORIGIN named after the Indian city of *Madras*.

madrigal noun a 16th- or 17th-century song for several voices without instrumental accompaniment.
– ORIGIN Italian *madrigale.*

maelstrom /**mayl**-struhm/ noun 1 a powerful whirlpool. 2 a state or situation of confused movement or turmoil: *they were caught up in a maelstrom of change.*
– ORIGIN Dutch.

maenad /**mee**-nad/ noun (in ancient Greece) a female follower of the god Bacchus, associated with frenzied rites.
– ORIGIN Greek *Mainas.*

maestro /**my**-stroh/ noun (pl. **maestri** /**my**-stri/ or **maestros**) 1 a distinguished male conductor or performer of classical music. 2 a distinguished man in any area of activity.
– ORIGIN Italian, 'master'.

Mafia noun 1 (**the Mafia**) an international criminal organization originating in Sicily.
2 (**mafia**) a powerful group who secretly influence matters: *the top tennis mafia.*
– ORIGIN Italian.

Mafioso /ma-fi-**oh**-soh/ noun (pl. **Mafiosi** /ma-fi-**oh**-si/) a member of the Mafia.

magazine noun 1 a periodical publication containing articles and illustrations. 2 a regular television or radio programme dealing with a variety of items. 3 a chamber holding cartridges to be fed automatically to the breech of a gun. 4 a store for arms, ammunition, and explosives.
– ORIGIN Arabic, 'storehouse'.

magenta /muh-**jen**-tuh/ noun a light reddish-purple colour.
– ORIGIN named after *Magenta* in Italy.

maggot noun a soft-bodied legless larva of a fly or other insect, found in decaying matter.
– ORIGIN perhaps from Old Norse.

magi plural of **MAGUS.**

magic noun 1 the power of apparently using mysterious or supernatural forces to make things happen. 2 conjuring tricks performed to entertain. 3 a mysterious and fascinating quality: *the magic of the theatre.* 4 informal exceptional skill or talent. • adjective
1 apparently having supernatural powers.
2 Brit. informal very good. • verb (**magics, magicking, magicked**) do or create by or as if by magic: *they magicked their island out of sight.*
– ORIGIN from Greek *magikē tekhnē* 'art of a magus'.

magical adjective 1 relating to or using magic.
2 very pleasant or enjoyable.
– DERIVATIVES **magically** adverb.

magic carpet noun (especially in Arabian stories) a carpet that is able to transport people through the air.

magician noun 1 a person with magic powers.
2 a conjuror.

magic lantern noun an early form of projector for showing photographic slides.

magic mushroom noun informal a toadstool that causes hallucinations if eaten.

magic realism (also **magical realism**) noun a type of literature in which realistic narrative is combined with surreal elements of dream or fantasy.

magisterial /ma-ji-**steer**-i-uhl/ adjective
1 having or showing great authority: *a magisterial volume.* 2 relating to a magistrate.
– DERIVATIVES **magisterially** adverb.
– ORIGIN from Latin *magister* 'master'.

magistracy noun (pl. **magistracies**) 1 the position or authority of a magistrate.
2 magistrates as a group.

magistrate noun an official who administers the law, especially one with authority to judge minor cases and hold preliminary hearings.
– ORIGIN Latin *magistratus* 'administrator'.

maglev noun a transport system in which trains glide above a track, supported by magnetic repulsion.
– ORIGIN short for *magnetic levitation.*

magma /**mag**-muh/ noun very hot fluid or semi-fluid material within the earth's crust from which lava and other igneous rock is formed by cooling.
– ORIGIN Greek.

Magna Carta noun a charter of liberty and political rights signed by King John of England in 1215.
– ORIGIN Latin, 'great charter'.

magnanimous /mag-**nan**-i-muhss/ adjective generous or forgiving, especially towards a rival or less powerful person.
– DERIVATIVES **magnanimity** noun **magnanimously** adverb.
– ORIGIN from Latin *magnus* 'great' + *animus* 'soul'.

magnate noun a wealthy and influential businessman or businesswoman.
– ORIGIN Latin *magnas* 'great man'.

magnesia /mag-**nee**-zhuh, mag-**nee**-zi-uh/ noun a compound of magnesium used to reduce stomach acid and as a laxative.
– ORIGIN Greek, referring to a mineral from Magnesia in Asia Minor.

magnesium /mag-**nee**-zi-uhm/ noun a silvery-white metallic element which burns with a brilliant white flame.

magnet noun 1 a piece of iron or other material that can attract iron-containing objects and that points north and south when suspended. 2 a person or thing that has a powerful attraction: *the beach is a magnet for sun-worshippers.*
– ORIGIN from Greek *magnēs lithos* 'lodestone'.

magnetic adjective 1 having the property of magnetism. 2 very attractive.
– DERIVATIVES **magnetically** adverb.

magnetic field noun a region around a magnet within which the force of magnetism acts.

magnetic mine noun a mine that detonates when it comes near to a magnetized body such as a ship or tank.

magnetic north noun the direction in which the north end of a compass needle will point in response to the earth's magnetic field.

magnetic pole noun each of the points near the geographical North and South Poles, indicated by the needle of a magnetic compass.

magnetic resonance imaging noun a technique for producing images of bodily organs by measuring the response of the atomic nuclei of body tissues to high-frequency radio waves when placed in a strong magnetic field.

magnetic storm noun a disturbance of the magnetic field of the earth.

magnetic tape noun tape used in recording sound, pictures, or computer data.

magnetism noun 1 the property displayed by magnets and produced by the motion of electric charges, which results in objects being attracted or pushed away. 2 the ability to attract and charm people.

magnetite noun a grey-black magnetic mineral which is an important form of iron ore.

magnetize (or **magnetise**) verb give magnetic properties to something.

magneto /mag-nee-toh/ noun (pl. **magnetos**) a small electric generator containing a permanent magnet and used to provided high-voltage pulses, especially (formerly) in the ignition systems of internal-combustion engines.

magnetometer /mag-ni-tom-i-ter/ noun an instrument used for measuring magnetic forces, especially the earth's magnetism.

magnetron noun an electron tube for amplifying or generating microwaves, with the flow of electrons controlled by an external magnetic field.

Magnificat /mag-nif-i-kat/ noun the hymn of the Virgin Mary (Gospel of Luke, chapter 1), sung as a regular part of a Christian service.
– ORIGIN Latin, 'magnifies', from the opening words, which translate as 'my soul magnifies the Lord'.

magnification noun 1 the action of magnifying something with a lens or microscope. 2 the degree to which something can be made to appear larger by means of a lens or microscope.

magnificence noun the quality of being very impressive or attractive: *the magnificence of nature.*

magnificent adjective 1 very beautiful, impressive, or elaborate. 2 very good; excellent.
– DERIVATIVES **magnificently** adverb.
– ORIGIN Latin *magnificus.*

magnifico /mag-nif-i-koh/ noun (pl. **magnificoes**) informal an important or powerful person.
– ORIGIN from Italian, 'high-minded, excellent'.

magnify verb (**magnifies**, **magnifying**, **magnified**) 1 make something appear larger than it is, especially with a lens or microscope. 2 intensify or increase: *the city magnified the heat like a kiln.* 3 old use praise someone or something highly.
– DERIVATIVES **magnifier** noun.
– ORIGIN Latin *magnificare.*

magnifying glass noun a lens that produces an enlarged image, used to examine small or finely detailed things.

magniloquent /mag-ni-luh-kwuhnt/ adjective formal using language that is excessively elaborate or pompous.

magnitude noun 1 great size, extent, or importance: *events of tragic magnitude.* 2 the size of something. 3 the degree of brightness of a star.
– ORIGIN Latin *magnitudo.*

magnolia noun 1 a tree or shrub with large creamy-pink or -white waxy flowers. 2 a pale creamy-white colour.
– ORIGIN named after the French botanist Pierre *Magnol.*

magnox noun a magnesium-based alloy used to enclose uranium fuel elements in some nuclear reactors.

magnum noun (pl. **magnums**) 1 a wine bottle of twice the standard size, normally 1½ litres. 2 (trademark in the US) a gun designed to fire cartridges that are more powerful than its calibre would suggest.
– ORIGIN Latin, 'great thing'.

magnum opus /mag-nuhm oh-puhss, mag-nuhm op-uhss/ noun a work of art, music, or literature that is the most important that a person has produced.
– ORIGIN Latin, 'great work'.

magpie noun 1 a black and white bird with a long tail and a noisy cry. 2 a person who obsessively collects unimportant things.
– ORIGIN probably from dialect *maggot the pie*, *maggoty-pie*, from *Magot*, a former form of the woman's name *Marguerite*, + Latin *pica* 'magpie'.

magus /may-guhss/ noun (pl. **magi** /may-jy/) 1 a priest of ancient Persia. 2 a sorcerer. 3 (**the Magi**) the three wise men from the East who brought gifts to the infant Jesus.
– ORIGIN Latin.

Magyar /mag-yar/ noun 1 a member of the predominant people in Hungary. 2 the Hungarian language.
– ORIGIN Hungarian.

maharaja /mah-huh-rah-juh/ (also **maharajah**) noun historical an Indian prince.
– ORIGIN Hindi.

maharani /mah-huh-rah-ni/ noun historical a maharaja's wife or widow.
– ORIGIN Hindi.

Maharishi /mah-huh-ri-shi/ noun a great Hindu wise man or spiritual leader.
– ORIGIN Sanskrit.

mahatma /muh-hat-muh/ noun (in the Indian subcontinent) a holy or wise person regarded with love and respect.
– ORIGIN Sanskrit, 'great soul'.

Mahayana /mah-huh-yah-nuh/ noun one of the two major traditions of Buddhism (the

other being Theravada), practised especially in China, Tibet, Japan, and Korea.
– ORIGIN Sanskrit, 'great vehicle'.

Mahican /ma-hi-kuhn/ (also **Mohican**) noun a member of an American Indian people formerly inhabiting the Upper Hudson Valley. •adjective relating to the Mahicans.
– ORIGIN the name in the extinct Mahican language.

mah-jong /mah-jong/ (also **mah-jongg**) noun a Chinese game played with 136 or 144 small rectangular tiles.
– ORIGIN Chinese dialect, 'sparrows'.

mahogany noun **1** hard reddish-brown wood from a tropical tree, used for furniture. **2** a rich reddish-brown colour.
– ORIGIN unknown.

mahout /muh-**howt**/ noun (in the Indian subcontinent and SE Asia) a person who works with and rides an elephant.
– ORIGIN Hindi.

maid noun **1** a female domestic servant. **2** old use a girl or young woman.

maiden noun **1** old use an unmarried girl or young woman, especially a virgin. **2** (also **maiden over**) Cricket an over in which no runs are scored. •adjective **1** (of an older woman) unmarried. **2** first of its kind: *a maiden voyage.*
– ORIGIN Old English.

maidenhair fern noun a fern with fine stems and delicate fronds.

maidenhead noun old use **1** a girl's or woman's virginity. **2** the hymen.

maiden name noun the surname of a married woman before her marriage.

maid of honour noun **1** an unmarried noblewoman attending a queen or princess. **2** N. Amer. a principal bridesmaid.

maidservant noun dated a female servant.

mail[1] noun **1** letters and parcels sent by post. **2** the postal system. **3** email. •verb **1** send a letter or parcel by post. **2** send email to someone.
– ORIGIN Old French *male* 'wallet'.

mail[2] noun historical flexible armour made of metal rings or plates.
– ORIGIN Old French *maille*.

mailbag noun a large sack or bag for carrying mail.

mailbox noun **1** N. Amer. a box for mail at the entrance to a person's house. **2** N. Amer. a post box. **3** a computer file in which emails are stored.

mailer noun **1** N. Amer. the sender of a letter or package by post. **2** a computer program that sends emails.

mailing noun an item of advertising posted to a large number of people.

mailing list noun a list of the names and addresses of people to whom advertising matter or information may be mailed regularly.

mailman noun (pl. **mailmen**) N. Amer. a postman.

mail order noun the ordering of goods by post.

mailshot noun Brit. a piece of advertising material sent to a large number of addresses.

maim verb injure someone so that part of the body is permanently damaged.
– ORIGIN Old French *mahaignier*.

main adjective chief in size or importance. •noun **1** a chief water or gas pipe or electricity cable. **2** (**the mains**) Brit. public water, gas, or electricity supply through pipes or cables. **3** (**the main**) old use or literary the open ocean.
– PHRASES **in the main** on the whole.
– ORIGIN from Old English, 'physical force'.

mainboard noun another term for **MOTHERBOARD**.

main brace noun the rope attached to the main yard (spar) of a sailing ship.

main clause noun Grammar a clause that can form a complete sentence standing alone, having a subject and a verb.

main drag noun informal, chiefly N. Amer. the main street of a town.

mainframe noun a large high-speed computer, especially one supporting numerous workstations.

mainland noun the main area of land of a country, not including islands and separate territories.

main line noun **1** a chief railway line. **2** informal a principal vein as a site for a drug injection. •verb (**mainline**) informal inject a drug into a vein.

mainly adverb for the most part; chiefly.

main man noun N. Amer. informal a close and trusted friend.

mainmast noun the principal mast of a ship.

mainsail /mayn-sayl, mayn-s'l/ noun the chief sail of a ship, especially the lowest sail on the mainmast of a square-rigged ship.

mainspring noun **1** the most influential or important part: *faith was the mainspring of her life.* **2** the chief spring in a watch, clock, etc.

mainstay noun **1** a thing on which something else is based or depends: *cotton is the mainstay of the economy.* **2** a rope or wire that extends from the top of the mainmast of a sailing ship to the foot of the mast nearest the front.

mainstream noun the ideas, attitudes, or activities that are shared by most people. •adjective belonging to or typical of the mainstream. •verb bring into the mainstream: *vegetarianism has been mainstreamed.*

maintain verb **1** cause to continue in the same state or at the same level: *she maintained close links with India.* **2** keep a building, machine, or road in good condition by checking or repairing it regularly. **3** provide enough money to support someone. **4** strongly state that something is the case: *he has always maintained his innocence.*
– DERIVATIVES **maintainability** noun **maintainable** adjective **maintainer** noun.
– ORIGIN Old French *maintenir*.

maintained school noun Brit. a school financed with public money.

maintenance noun **1** the process of keeping something in the same state or in good condition. **2** Brit. the provision of financial support for a former husband or wife after divorce.

maiolica /muh-**yol**-i-kuh, my-**ol**-i-kuh/ noun fine Italian earthenware with coloured decoration on an opaque white glaze.
– ORIGIN from Italian *Maiolica* 'Majorca'.

maisonette noun a flat on two storeys of a

larger building.
- ORIGIN French *maisonnette* 'small house'.

maître d'hôtel /may-truh doh-**tel**/ **noun** (pl. **maîtres d'hôtel** pronunc. same) the head waiter of a restaurant.
- ORIGIN French, 'master of the house'.

maize noun Brit. a cereal plant with large grains (corn or sweetcorn) set in rows on a cob.
- ORIGIN Spanish *maíz*.

majestic adjective impressively grand or beautiful.
- DERIVATIVES **majestically** adverb.

majesty noun (pl. **majesties**) **1** impressive grandeur or beauty. **2** royal power. **3** (**His, Your,** etc. **Majesty**) a title given to a sovereign or their wife or widow.
- ORIGIN Latin *majestas*.

majolica /muh-**yol**-i-kuh, muh-**jol**-i-kuh/ **noun** a kind of earthenware made in England in imitation of Italian maiolica.

major adjective 1 important, serious, or significant. **2** greater or more important; main: *he got the major share of the profit.* **3** (of a musical scale) having intervals of a semitone between the third and fourth, and seventh and eighth notes. Contrasted with **MINOR**.
 • **noun 1** a rank of officer in the army and the US air force, above captain and below lieutenant colonel. **2** an officer in charge of a section of band instruments. **3** Music a major key, interval, or scale. **4** N. Amer. a student's main subject or course. **5** N. Amer. a student specializing in a specified subject. • **verb** (**major in**) N. Amer. & Austral./NZ specialize in a particular subject at college or university.
- ORIGIN Latin, 'greater'.

Majorcan /muh-**yor**-k'n/ **noun** a person from Majorca. • **adjective** relating to Majorca.

major-domo noun (pl. **major-domos**) the chief steward of a large household.
- ORIGIN Latin *major domus* 'highest official of the household'.

major general noun a rank of officer in the army and the US air force, above brigadier or brigadier general and below lieutenant general.

majoritarian /muh-jor-i-**tair**-i-uhn/ **adjective** governed by or believing in decision by a majority.

majority noun (pl. **majorities**) **1** the greater number. **2** Brit. the number of votes by which one party or candidate in an election defeats the opposition. **3** the age when a person is legally a full adult, usually 18 or 21.

> USAGE: The main meaning of **majority** is 'the greater number' and it should be used with plural nouns: *the majority of cases.* It is not good English to use **majority** with nouns that do not take a plural to mean 'the greatest part', as in *she ate the majority of the meal.*

majority rule noun the principle that the greater number of people should exercise greater power.

majority verdict noun English Law a verdict agreed by all but one or two of the members of a jury.

majuscule /**maj**-uhss-kyool/ **noun** a capital letter.
- ORIGIN from Latin *majuscula littera*

'somewhat greater letter'.

make verb (past and past part. **made**) **1** form something by putting parts together or combining substances. **2** cause or bring about something. **3** force someone to do something. **4** (**make something into**) alter something so that it forms something else. **5** add up to: *one and one makes two.* **6** estimate, decide, or calculate something. **7** gain or earn money or profit. **8** be suitable for: *this fern makes a good house plant.* **9** manage to arrive at or achieve something. **10** prepare to go in a particular direction or do a particular thing: *I made towards the car.* **11** (**make it**) become successful. **12** arrange bedclothes tidily on a bed ready for use. • **noun** the manufacturer or trade name of a product.
- PHRASES **have (got) it made** informal be in a position where success is certain. **make away with** kill someone. **make do** manage with the limited means available. **make for 1** move towards. **2** tend to result in. **3** (**be made for**) be very suitable for. **make it up to** compensate someone for unfair treatment. **make something of 1** give attention or importance to. **2** understand the meaning of. **make off** leave hurriedly. **make off with** steal something. **make or break** be the factor which decides whether something will succeed or fail. **make someone/thing out 1** manage with difficulty to see, hear, or understand someone or something. **2** pretend to be or do something. **3** draw up a list or document. **make out** informal **1** make progress; get on. **2** N. Amer. engage in sexual activity. **make someone over** give someone a new image with cosmetics, hairstyling, and clothes. **make something over** transfer the possession of something. **make sail** spread a sail or sails, especially to begin a voyage. **make time** find the time to do something. **make up** become friendly again after a quarrel. **make someone up** apply cosmetics to someone. **make something up 1** put something together from parts or ingredients. **2** invent a story. **3** (also **make up for**) compensate for something. **make up one's mind** make a decision. **make way** allow room for someone or something else. **on the make** informal trying to make money or gain an advantage.
- ORIGIN Old English.

make-believe noun a state of fantasy or pretence. • **adjective** imitating something real; pretend.

make-do adjective makeshift or temporary.

makeover noun a complete transformation of the appearance of someone or something.

maker noun 1 a person or thing that makes something. **2** (**our, the,** etc. **Maker**) God.
- PHRASES **meet one's Maker** chiefly humorous die.

makeshift adjective acting as a temporary substitute or measure.

make-up noun 1 cosmetics applied to the face. **2** the way in which something is formed or put together: *the make-up of the rock.* **3** the arrangement of written matter, illustrations, etc. on a printed page.

makeweight noun 1 an unimportant person or thing that is only included to complete something. **2** something added to make up a required weight.

making noun 1 (in phrase **be the making of**) bring about the success of. 2 (**makings**) the necessary qualities: *she had the makings of a great teacher.*

mako /**mah**-koh, **mak**-oh/ noun (pl. **makos**) a large shark with a deep blue back and white underparts.
– ORIGIN Maori.

mal- combining form 1 bad; badly: *malodorous.* 2 wrong or incorrectly: *malfunction.* 3 not: *maladroit.*
– ORIGIN from Latin *male* 'badly'.

malachite /**mal**-uh-kyt/ noun a bright green mineral that contains copper.
– ORIGIN Greek *malakhē* 'mallow'.

maladjusted adjective failing to cope with normal social situations.

maladministration noun formal dishonest or inefficient management or administration.
– DERIVATIVES **maladminister** verb.

maladroit /mal-uh-**droyt**/ adjective inefficient or clumsy.

malady noun (pl. **maladies**) literary a disease or illness.
– ORIGIN from Old French *malade* 'ill'.

Malagasy /ma-luh-**gass**-i/ noun (pl. same or **Malagasies**) 1 a person from Madagascar. 2 the language of Madagascar.

malaise noun a general feeling of unease, bad health, or low spirits.
– ORIGIN French.

malapropism /**mal**-uh-prop-i-z'm/ (US also **malaprop**) noun the mistaken use of a word in place of a similar-sounding one (e.g. 'dance a *flamingo*' instead of *flamenco*).
– ORIGIN named after Mrs *Malaprop* in Richard Sheridan's play *The Rivals.*

malaria noun a disease that causes recurrent attacks of fever, caused by a parasite that is transmitted by mosquitoes.
– DERIVATIVES **malarial** adjective.
– ORIGIN from Italian *mala aria* 'bad air' (the disease was formerly thought to be caused by vapours given off by marshes).

malarkey /muh-**lar**-ki/ noun informal nonsense.
– ORIGIN unknown.

malathion /ma-luh-**thy**-uhn/ noun a synthetic insecticide containing phosphorus.
– ORIGIN from its chemical name.

Malawian /muh-**lah**-wi-uhn/ noun a person from Malawi in south central Africa. •adjective relating to Malawi.

Malay noun 1 a member of a people inhabiting Malaysia and Indonesia. 2 the language of the Malays. •adjective relating to the Malays or their language.

Malayan noun another term for **MALAY**.
•adjective relating to Malays or Malaya (now part of Malaysia).

Malaysian /muh-**lay**-zi-uhn, muh-**lay**-zh'n/ noun a person from Malaysia. •adjective relating to Malaysia.

malcontent noun a person who is dissatisfied and rebellious.

Maldivian /mawl-**div**-i-uhn/ noun a person from the Maldives, a country consisting of a chain of islands in the Indian Ocean. •adjective relating to the Maldives.

male adjective 1 relating to the sex that can

fertilize or inseminate the female to give rise to offspring. 2 relating to or typical of men: *a deep male voice.* 3 (of a plant or flower) having stamens but not functional pistils. 4 (of a fitting) manufactured to fit inside a corresponding female part. •noun a male person, animal, or plant.
– DERIVATIVES **maleness** noun.
– ORIGIN Old French *masle.*

malediction /mal-i-**dik**-sh'n/ noun a curse.
– ORIGIN from Latin *maledicere* 'speak evil of'.

malefactor /**mal**-i-fak-ter/ noun formal a criminal or other wrongdoer.
– ORIGIN from Latin *malefacere* 'do wrong'.

malefic /muh-**lef**-ik/ adjective literary causing harm or destruction.
– DERIVATIVES **maleficent** adjective.
– ORIGIN from Latin *male* 'ill' + *-ficus* 'doing'.

malevolent /muh-**lev**-uh-luhnt/ adjective wishing evil to others.
– DERIVATIVES **malevolence** noun **malevolently** adverb.
– ORIGIN from Latin *male* 'ill' + *velle* 'to wish'.

malfeasance /mal-**fee**-zuhnss/ noun Law wrongdoing, especially (US) by a public official.
– ORIGIN Old French *malfaisance.*

malformation noun 1 a part of the body that is not formed correctly. 2 the state of being abnormally shaped or formed.
– DERIVATIVES **malformed** adjective.

malfunction verb (of equipment or machinery) fail to function normally. •noun a failure to function normally.

Malian /**mah**-li-uhn/ noun a person from Mali, a country in West Africa. •adjective relating to Mali.

malice noun the desire to harm someone.
– ORIGIN Old French.

malice aforethought noun Law the intention to kill or harm, which distinguishes murder from unlawful killing.

malicious adjective intending or intended to do harm: *his talent for malicious gossip.*
– DERIVATIVES **maliciously** adverb **maliciousness** noun.

malign /muh-**lyn**/ adjective harmful or evil.
•verb criticize someone in a spiteful way.
– DERIVATIVES **malignity** /muh-**lig**-ni-ti/ noun **malignly** adverb.
– ORIGIN Latin *malignus* 'tending to evil'.

malignancy noun (pl. **malignancies**) 1 the presence of a malignant tumour; cancer. 2 a cancerous growth. 3 the quality of being harmful or evil.

malignant adjective 1 harmful or evil. 2 (of a tumour) tending to grow uncontrollably or to recur after removal; cancerous.
– ORIGIN from Latin *malignare* 'plan maliciously'.

malinger verb pretend to be ill in order to avoid duty or work.
– DERIVATIVES **malingerer** noun.
– ORIGIN from French *malingre* 'weak, sickly'.

mall /mal, mawl/ noun 1 a large enclosed pedestrian shopping area. 2 a sheltered walk or promenade.
– ORIGIN probably from *The Mall*, a walk in St

James's Park, London.

mallard noun a wild duck, the male of which has a dark green head and white collar.
– ORIGIN Old French, 'wild drake'.

malleable adjective **1** able to be hammered or pressed into shape without breaking or cracking. **2** easily influenced: *a malleable youth*.
– DERIVATIVES **malleability** noun.
– ORIGIN from Latin *malleus* 'a hammer'.

mallee /mal-i/ noun a low-growing bushy Australian eucalyptus tree.
– ORIGIN from an Aboriginal language.

mallet noun **1** a hammer with a large wooden head. **2** a long-handled wooden stick with a head like a hammer, for hitting a croquet or polo ball.
– ORIGIN Latin *malleus*.

mallow noun a plant with pink or purple flowers.
– ORIGIN Latin *malva*.

malmsey /mahm-zi/ noun a very sweet Madeira wine.
– ORIGIN from *Monemvasia*, a port in Greece.

malnourished adjective suffering from lack of food or of the right foods.
– DERIVATIVES **malnourishment** noun.

malnutrition noun the state of not having enough food or not eating enough of the right foods.

malodorous adjective smelling very unpleasant.

malpractice noun illegal, corrupt, or negligent professional behaviour.

malt noun barley or other grain that has been soaked in water, allowed to sprout, and dried, used for brewing or distilling. • verb **1** convert grain into malt. **2** (as adj. **malted**) mixed with malt or a malt extract.
– ORIGIN Old English.

Maltese noun (pl. same) a person from Malta. • adjective relating to Malta.

Maltese cross noun a cross with arms of equal length which broaden from the centre and have their ends indented in a shallow V-shape.
– ORIGIN so named because the cross was formerly worn by the Knights Hospitallers, a religious order based in Malta.

Malthusian /mal-thyoo-zi-uhn/ adjective relating to the theory of the English economist Thomas Malthus that, if unchecked, the population tends to increase at a greater rate than its food supplies. • noun a person who supports this theory.

maltose /mawl-tohz/ noun a sugar produced by the breakdown of starch, e.g. by enzymes found in malt and saliva.

maltreat verb treat a person or animal badly or cruelly.
– DERIVATIVES **maltreatment** noun.

maltster noun Brit. a person who makes malt.

malt whisky noun whisky made only from malted barley.

malversation /mal-vuh-say-sh'n/ noun formal corrupt behaviour by a person in public office.
– ORIGIN from Latin *male* 'badly' + *versari* 'behave'.

mama (also **mamma**) noun dated or N. Amer. one's mother.
– ORIGIN imitating a child's first syllables *ma, ma*.

mamba noun a large, highly venomous African snake.
– ORIGIN Zulu.

mambo noun (pl. **mambos**) a Latin American dance similar to the rumba.
– ORIGIN American Spanish.

mammal noun a warm-blooded vertebrate animal that has hair or fur, produces milk, and (typically) bears live young.
– DERIVATIVES **mammalian** adjective.
– ORIGIN from Latin *mamma* 'breast'.

mammary adjective relating to the breasts or the milk-producing organs of other mammals: *a mammary gland*. • noun (pl. **mammaries**) informal a breast.
– ORIGIN from Latin *mamma* 'breast'.

mammogram /mam-uh-gram/ noun an image obtained by mammography.

mammography /ma-mog-ruh-fi/ noun a technique using X-rays to diagnose and locate tumours of the breasts.

Mammon noun wealth regarded as an evil influence or false object of worship.
– ORIGIN from an Aramaic word meaning 'riches'; see Gospel of Matthew, chapter 6 and Gospel of Luke, chapter 16.

mammoth noun a large extinct form of elephant with a hairy coat and long curved tusks. • adjective huge; enormous.
– ORIGIN Russian.

mammy noun (pl. **mammies**) informal a child's name for their mother.

man noun (pl. **men**) **1** an adult human male. **2** a male member of a workforce, team, etc. **3** a husband or lover. **4** a person. **5** human beings in general: *places untouched by man*. **6** a piece or token used in a board game. • verb (**mans, manning, manned**) provide a place or machine with the personnel to run, operate, or defend it. • exclamation informal, chiefly N. Amer. used for emphasis or to express surprise, admiration, or delight.
– PHRASES **man about town** a fashionable and sociable man. **man and boy** from childhood. **the man in the street** the average man. **man of the cloth** a clergyman. **man of letters** a male scholar or author. **man to man** in a direct and frank way between two men. **to a man** with no exceptions.
– ORIGIN Old English.

USAGE: Many people now think that the use of **man** to refer to 'human beings in general' is old-fashioned or sexist. Alternative terms such as **the human race** or **humankind** may be used in some situations, but elsewhere there are no established alternatives, for example for the term **manpower**.

-man combining form forming nouns referring to: **1** a man of a specified nationality or origin: *Frenchman*. **2** a person belonging to a specified group or having a specified occupation or role: *chairman*. **3** a ship of a specified kind: *merchantman*.

USAGE: The use of the form **-man** to create words referring to an occupation or role, as in **fireman** and **policeman**, is now often regarded as outdated and sexist. As a result, there has been a move away from **-man** compound words except where it is known that a man rather than a woman is being referred to. Alternative non-specific terms which can be used instead include **firefighter** and **police officer**.

manacle noun a metal band or chain fastened around a person's hands or ankles to restrict their movement. • verb restrict someone with a manacle or manacles.
– ORIGIN Old French *manicle* 'handcuff'.

manage verb 1 be in charge of people or an organization. 2 control the use of money, time, or other resources. 3 succeed in doing or dealing with: *she eventually managed to buy a house.* 4 succeed or cope despite difficulties. 5 be free to attend an appointment.
– DERIVATIVES **managing** adjective.
– ORIGIN Italian *maneggiare* 'train a horse'.

manageable adjective able to be dealt with or controlled without difficulty.

management noun 1 the process of managing people or things. 2 the managers of an organization.

management accounting noun the provision of financial data and advice to a company for use in the organization and development of its business.
– DERIVATIVES **management accountant** noun.

manager noun 1 a person who manages an organization, a group of staff, or a sports team. 2 a person in charge of the business affairs of a sports player, actor, or performer.
– DERIVATIVES **managerial** adjective **managership** noun.

manageress noun Brit. a female manager.

mañana /man-yah-nuh/ adverb tomorrow, or at some time in the future.
– ORIGIN Spanish.

man-at-arms noun old use a soldier.

manatee /man-uh-tee/ noun a large mammal that lives in the sea near tropical Atlantic coasts.
– ORIGIN Carib.

Manchego /man-chay-goh/ noun a Spanish cheese traditionally made with sheep's milk.
– ORIGIN Spanish.

Manchu /man-choo/ noun a member of a people originally living in Manchuria in NE China, who formed the last imperial dynasty of China (1644–1912).
– ORIGIN Manchu, 'pure'.

Mancunian /man-kyoo-ni-uhn/ noun a person from Manchester. • adjective relating to Manchester.
– ORIGIN Latin *Mancunium* 'Manchester'.

mandala /man-duh-luh/ noun an intricate circular design symbolizing the universe in Hinduism and Buddhism.
– ORIGIN Sanskrit, 'disc, circle'.

mandarin noun 1 (**Mandarin**) the official form of the Chinese language. 2 a high-ranking official in the former imperial Chinese civil service. 3 a powerful official or senior bureaucrat. 4 a small citrus fruit with a loose yellow-orange skin.
– ORIGIN Hindi *mantri* 'counsellor'.

mandarin collar noun a close-fitting upright collar.

mandarin duck noun a small East Asian duck, the male of which has an orange ruff and sail-like feathers on each side of the body.

mandate noun /man-dayt/ 1 an official order or authorization. 2 the authority to carry out a policy, regarded as given by a country's voters to the winner of an election: *a government with a popular mandate.* 3 historical a commission from the League of Nations (the forerunner of the UN) to a member state to administer a territory. • verb /man-dayt/ authorize someone to do something.
– ORIGIN Latin *mandatum* 'something commanded'.

mandatory /man-duh-tuh-ri/ adjective required by law or mandate; compulsory.
– DERIVATIVES **mandatorily** adverb.

mandible noun 1 the lower jawbone in a mammal or fish. 2 either of the upper and lower parts of a bird's beak. 3 either half of the crushing organ in an insect's mouthparts.
– ORIGIN from Latin *mandere* 'to chew'.

mandolin noun 1 a musical instrument resembling a lute, having paired metal strings plucked with a plectrum. 2 (also **mandoline**) a kitchen implement consisting of a frame with adjustable blades, for slicing vegetables.
– DERIVATIVES **mandolinist** noun.
– ORIGIN Italian *mandolino* 'little mandola' (a *mandola* being an early form of mandolin).

mandragora /man-drag-uh-ruh/ noun literary the mandrake, especially when used to bring drowsiness or unconsciousness.
– ORIGIN Latin.

mandrake noun a plant with a forked fleshy root supposedly resembling the human form, used in herbal medicine and magic.
– ORIGIN Latin *mandragora*.

mandrel noun 1 a shaft or spindle in a lathe to which work is fixed while being turned. 2 a cylindrical rod round which metal or other material is forged or shaped.
– ORIGIN unknown.

mandrill noun a large West African baboon with a red and blue face, the male having a blue rump.
– ORIGIN probably from **MAN** + a local word.

mane noun 1 a growth of long hair on the neck of a horse, lion, or other mammal. 2 a person's long flowing hair.
– ORIGIN Old English.

man-eater noun 1 an animal that can kill and eat people. 2 informal a dominant woman who has many sexual partners.
– DERIVATIVES **man-eating** adjective.

manège /ma-nezh/ noun 1 a riding school. 2 the movements in which a horse is trained in a riding school.
– ORIGIN French.

maneuver noun & verb US spelling of **MANOEUVRE**.

manful adjective brave and determined.
– DERIVATIVES **manfully** adverb.

manga noun Japanese cartoons, comic books,

and animated films with a science-fiction or fantasy theme.
– ORIGIN Japanese.

mangabey /mang-guh-bay/ noun a long-tailed monkey from West and central Africa.
– ORIGIN by wrong association with *Mangabey*, a region of Madagascar.

manganese noun a hard grey metallic element used in special steels and magnetic alloys.
– ORIGIN Italian, alteration of *magnesia*.

mange /rhymes with range/ noun a skin disease in some animals that is caused by mites and results in severe itching and hair loss.
– ORIGIN from Old French *mangier* 'eat'.

mangel-wurzel /mang-g'l wer-z'l/ noun another term for **MANGOLD**.

manger noun a long trough from which horses or cattle feed.
– ORIGIN Old French *mangeure*, from Latin *manducare* 'to chew'.

mangetout /monzh-too/ noun (pl. same or **mangetouts** pronunc. same) Brit. a variety of pea with an edible pod.
– ORIGIN French, 'eat all'.

mangle¹ noun Brit. a machine with two or more cylinders turned by a handle, between which wet laundry is squeezed to remove water.
– ORIGIN from Greek *manganon* 'axis, engine'.

mangle² verb 1 destroy or severely damage something by tearing or crushing. 2 spoil or do something badly: *he was mangling Bach on the piano*.
– ORIGIN Old French *mahaignier* 'maim'.

mango noun (pl. **mangoes** or **mangos**) an oval tropical fruit with yellow flesh.
– ORIGIN Portuguese *manga*.

mangold noun a variety of beet with a large root, grown as feed for farm animals.
– ORIGIN German *Mangoldwurzel*.

mangosteen /mang-guh-steen/ noun a tropical fruit with juicy white flesh inside a thick reddish-brown rind.
– ORIGIN Malay.

mangrove noun a tropical tree or shrub found in tropical coastal swamps, with tangled roots that grow above ground.
– ORIGIN probably from Taino (an extinct Caribbean language).

mangy adjective (**mangier**, **mangiest**) 1 having mange. 2 in poor condition; shabby.

manhandle verb 1 move a heavy object with effort. 2 drag or push someone roughly.

manhattan noun a cocktail made of vermouth and whisky.
– ORIGIN named after the New York island and borough of *Manhattan*.

manhole noun a covered opening allowing access to a sewer or other underground structure.

manhood noun 1 the state or period of being a man. 2 the men of a country or society. 3 the qualities traditionally associated with men, such as strength and sexual potency.

manhunt noun an organized search for a suspect, criminal, or escaped prisoner.

mania noun 1 mental illness characterized by an overactive imagination and excited activity. 2 an excessive enthusiasm; an obsession.
– ORIGIN Greek, 'madness'.

-mania combining form 1 referring to a specified type of mental abnormality or obsession: *kleptomania*. 2 referring to extreme enthusiasm: *Beatlemania*.
– DERIVATIVES **-maniac** combining form.

maniac /may-ni-ak/ noun 1 a person who behaves in an extremely wild or violent way. 2 informal a person with an extreme enthusiasm for something.
– DERIVATIVES **maniacal** /muh-ny-uh-k'l/ adjective **maniacally** adverb.

manic adjective 1 relating to a mental illness characterized by an overactive imagination and excited activity. 2 showing wild excitement and energy: *a manic grin*.
– DERIVATIVES **manically** adverb.

manic depression noun a mental disorder marked by alternating periods of excited activity and depression.
– DERIVATIVES **manic-depressive** adjective & noun.

Manichaean /ma-ni-kee-uhn/ (also **Manichean**) adjective 1 chiefly historical relating to Manichaeism. 2 relating to a contrast or conflict between opposites.
– DERIVATIVES **Manichaeanism** noun.

Manichaeism /ma-ni-kee-i-z'm/ (also **Manicheism**) noun a religious system with Christian, Gnostic, and pagan elements, founded in Persia in the 3rd century by Manes and based on a belief in an ancient conflict between light and darkness.
– ORIGIN from Latin *Manichaeus* 'of Manes'.

manicure noun a cosmetic treatment of the hands and nails. •verb 1 give a manicure to a person or the hands. 2 (as adj. **manicured**) (of a lawn or garden) neatly trimmed and maintained.
– DERIVATIVES **manicurist** noun.
– ORIGIN from Latin *manus* 'hand' + *cura* 'care'.

manifest¹ adjective clear and obvious. •verb 1 show or display: *she manifested signs of severe depression*. 2 (of an illness or disorder) become apparent. 3 (of a ghost) appear.
– DERIVATIVES **manifestly** adverb.
– ORIGIN Latin *manifestus* 'caught in the act, flagrant'.

manifest² noun 1 a document listing a ship's contents, cargo, crew, and passengers. 2 a list of passengers or cargo in an aircraft.
– ORIGIN Italian *manifesto* 'manifesto'.

manifestation noun a sign that something exists or is happening: *graffiti was a manifestation of bored youth*. 2 an appearance of a god or spirit in physical form.

manifesto noun (pl. **manifestos**) a public declaration of the policy and aims of a political party or other group.
– ORIGIN Italian.

manifold adjective 1 many and various. 2 having many different forms or aspects. •noun a pipe with several openings that connect to other parts, especially one in an internal-combustion engine conveying air and fuel from the carburettor to the cylinders or leading from the cylinders to the exhaust pipe.
– ORIGIN Old English.

manikin (also **mannikin**) noun 1 a very small person. 2 a jointed model of the human body.
– ORIGIN Dutch *manneken* 'little man'.

m

Manila (also **Manilla**) noun **1** strong brown paper, originally made from a Philippine plant. **2** a cigar or cheroot made in Manila.
– ORIGIN from *Manila*, the capital of the Philippines.

manioc /man-i-ok/ noun another term for CASSAVA.
– ORIGIN Tupi.

manipulate verb **1** handle or control a tool, device, etc. in a skilful way. **2** control or influence someone in a clever or underhand way. **3** alter or present information so as to mislead someone. **4** examine or treat part of the body by feeling or moving it with the hand.
– DERIVATIVES **manipulable** adjective **manipulation** noun **manipulator** noun.
– ORIGIN from Latin *manipulus* 'handful'.

manipulative adjective **1** controlling a person or situation in a clever or underhand way. **2** relating to manipulation of an object or part of the body.

mankind noun human beings as a whole; the human race.

manky adjective (**mankier, mankiest**) Brit. informal **1** dirty and unpleasant. **2** of poor quality.
– ORIGIN probably from former *mank* 'mutilated, defective'.

manly adjective (**manlier, manliest**) **1** having qualities traditionally associated with men, such as courage and strength. **2** suitable for a man: *manly sports.*
– DERIVATIVES **manliness** noun.

man-made adjective made or caused by human beings.

manna noun **1** (in the Bible) the substance miraculously supplied as food to the Israelites in the wilderness (Book of Exodus, chapter 16). **2** something unexpected and very welcome or beneficial.
– ORIGIN Hebrew and Arabic.

manned adjective having a human crew.

mannequin /man-i-kin, man-i-kwin/ noun **1** a dummy used to display clothes in a shop window. **2** dated a fashion model.
– ORIGIN French, from Dutch *manneken* 'little man'.

manner noun **1** a way in which something is done or happens. **2** a person's outward behaviour or attitude towards other people: *his relaxed, easy manner.* **3** (**manners**) polite social behaviour. **4** a style in literature or art. **5** literary a kind or sort.
– PHRASES **all manner of** many different kinds of. **in a manner of speaking** in some sense. **to the manner born** naturally at ease in a particular job or situation.
– ORIGIN from Latin *manuarius* 'of the hand', from *manus* 'hand'.

mannered adjective **1** behaving in a specified way: *well mannered.* **2** (of behaviour, art, literary style, etc.) marked by distinctive or exaggerated features intended to be impressive.

mannerism noun **1** a habitual gesture or way of speaking or behaving. **2** the use of a very distinctive style in art, literature, or music. **3** (**Mannerism**) a style of 16th-century Italian art characterized by distortions in scale and perspective.

– DERIVATIVES **mannerist** noun & adjective.

mannerly adjective well mannered; polite.

mannikin noun variant spelling of MANIKIN.

mannish adjective (of a woman) looking or behaving like a man.

manoeuvrable (US **maneuverable**) adjective (of a boat or aircraft) able to be manoeuvred easily.
– DERIVATIVES **manoeuvrability** noun.

manoeuvre (US **maneuver**) noun **1** a movement or series of moves requiring skill and care. **2** a carefully planned scheme or action. **3** (**manoeuvres**) a large-scale military exercise. • verb (**manoeuvres, manoeuvring, manoeuvred**) **1** move skilfully or carefully. **2** carefully manipulate someone or something in order to achieve an aim.
– ORIGIN French *manœuvrer*, from Latin *manus* 'hand' + *operari* 'to work'.

man-of-war (also **man-o'-war**) noun historical an armed sailing ship.

manometer /muh-nom-i-ter/ noun an instrument for measuring the pressure of fluids.
– ORIGIN from Greek *manos* 'thin, rarefied'.

manor noun **1** a large country house with lands. **2** (in medieval times) an area of land controlled by a lord.
– DERIVATIVES **manorial** adjective.
– ORIGIN Old French *maner* 'dwelling'.

manpower noun the number of people working or available for work or service.

manqué /mong-kay/ adjective having never become what one might have been; unfulfilled: *an actor manqué.*
– ORIGIN French, from *manquer* 'to lack'.

mansard noun a roof with four sides, in each of which the lower part of the slope is steeper than the upper part.
– ORIGIN named after the French architect François *Mansart*.

manse noun a house provided for a minister of certain Christian churches, especially the Scottish Presbyterian Church.
– ORIGIN Latin *mansus* 'house'.

manservant noun (pl. **menservants**) a male servant.

mansion noun a large, impressive house.
– ORIGIN Latin, 'place where someone stays'.

mansion block noun Brit. a large block of flats.

manslaughter noun the crime of killing a person without intending to do so.

manta noun a very large ray (fish) of tropical seas.
– ORIGIN Latin American Spanish, 'large blanket'.

mantel (also **mantle**) noun a mantelpiece or mantelshelf.
– ORIGIN from MANTLE.

mantelpiece noun **1** a structure surrounding a fireplace. **2** a mantelshelf.

mantelshelf noun a shelf forming the top of a mantelpiece.

mantilla /man-til-luh/ noun (in Spain) a lace or silk scarf traditionally worn by women over the hair and shoulders.
– ORIGIN Spanish, 'little mantle or shawl'.

mantis (also **praying mantis**) noun (pl. same or **mantises**) a slender insect with a triangular head, typically waiting motionless for prey

with its forelegs folded like hands in prayer.
– ORIGIN Greek, 'prophet'.

mantle noun **1** a woman's loose sleeveless cloak or shawl. **2** a covering layer of something: *a mantle of snow.* **3** (also **gas mantle**) a mesh cover fixed round a gas jet to give a glowing light when heated. **4** an important role or responsibility that passes from one person to another. **5** the region of the earth's interior between the crust and the core, consisting of hot, dense silicate rock. • verb literary cover or envelop something.
– ORIGIN Latin *mantellum* 'cloak'.

mantra noun **1** (originally in Hinduism and Buddhism) a word or sound repeated to help concentration while meditating. **2** a Vedic hymn. **3** a frequently repeated statement or slogan.
– ORIGIN Sanskrit, 'instrument of thought'.

mantrap noun a trap for catching people.

manual adjective **1** relating to or operated with the hands: *a manual typewriter.* **2** using or working with the hands: *a manual worker.* • noun **1** a book giving instructions or information. **2** an organ keyboard played with the hands not the feet.
– DERIVATIVES **manually** adverb.
– ORIGIN from Latin *manus* 'hand'.

manufactory noun (pl. **manufactories**) old use a factory.

manufacture verb **1** make something on a large scale using machinery. **2** make up evidence or a story. • noun the process of making goods on a large scale using machinery.
– DERIVATIVES **manufacturer** noun.
– ORIGIN French, from Italian *manifattura*, influenced by Latin *manu factum* 'made by hand'.

manuka /ma-**noo**-kuh, mah-**nuu**-kuh/ noun a small tree with aromatic leaves, native to New Zealand and Tasmania.
– ORIGIN Maori.

manumit verb (**manumits, manumitting, manumitted**) historical free someone from slavery.
– DERIVATIVES **manumission** noun.
– ORIGIN Latin *manumittere* 'send forth from the hand'.

manure noun animal dung used for fertilizing land. • verb spread manure on land.
– ORIGIN Old French.

manuscript noun **1** a handwritten book, document, or piece of music. **2** an author's handwritten or typed work, submitted for printing and publication.
– ORIGIN from Latin *manu* 'by hand' + *scriptus* 'written'.

Manx noun the Celtic language formerly spoken in the Isle of Man, still used for some ceremonial purposes. • adjective relating to the Isle of Man.
– ORIGIN from Old Irish *Manu* 'Isle of Man'.

Manx cat noun a breed of cat without a tail.

many determiner, pronoun, & adjective (**more, most**) a large number of people or things. • noun (**the many**) the majority of people.
– ORIGIN Old English.

manzanilla /man-zuh-**nil**-luh, man-zuh-**neel**-yuh/ noun a pale, very dry Spanish sherry.

– ORIGIN Spanish, 'chamomile' (because the flavour is considered similar to that of chamomile).

Maoism /**mow**-i-z'm/ noun the communist policies and theories of the former Chinese head of state Mao Zedong.
– DERIVATIVES **Maoist** noun & adjective.

Maori /**mow**-ri/ noun (pl. same or **Maoris**) **1** a member of the aboriginal people of New Zealand. **2** the Polynesian language of the Maori.

map noun **1** a flat diagram of an area of land or sea showing physical features, cities, roads, etc. **2** a diagram or collection of data showing the arrangement, distribution, or sequence of something. • verb (**maps, mapping, mapped**) **1** represent or record something on a map. **2** (**map something out**) plan something in detail.
– PHRASES **off the map** very distant or remote. **put someone/thing on the map** make someone or something famous.
– ORIGIN Latin *mappa* 'sheet, napkin'.

maple noun a tree or shrub with five-pointed leaves, winged fruits, and syrupy sap.
– ORIGIN Old English.

maple leaf noun the leaf of the maple, used as the Canadian national emblem.

maple syrup noun sugary syrup produced from the sap of a maple tree.

maquette /ma-**ket**/ noun a small model or sketch made by a sculptor as a basis for a larger work.
– ORIGIN French.

maquis /ma-**kee**/ noun (pl. same) **1** (**the Maquis**) the French resistance movement during the German occupation of France in the Second World War. **2** dense evergreen vegetation characteristic of coastal regions in the Mediterranean.
– ORIGIN French, 'brushwood'.

Mar. abbreviation March.

mar verb (**mars, marring, marred**) damage or spoil: *violence marred a number of New Year celebrations.*
– ORIGIN Old English.

marabou /**ma**-ruh-boo/ noun **1** an African stork with a massive bill and large neck pouch. **2** down feathers from the marabou used as trimming for hats or clothing.
– ORIGIN French, from Arabic, 'holy man'.

maraca /muh-**rak**-uh/ noun a hollow gourd or gourd-shaped container filled with small beans, stones, etc., shaken as a musical instrument.
– ORIGIN Portuguese, from Tupi.

marae /muh-**ry**/ noun (pl. same) the courtyard of a Maori meeting house, especially as a place for ceremonies or social gatherings.
– ORIGIN Polynesian, referring to a sacrificial altar or sacred enclosure.

maraschino /ma-ruh-**skee**-noh, ma-ruh-**shee**-noh/ noun (pl. **maraschinos**) a strong, sweet liqueur made from a kind of cherry.
– ORIGIN Italian, from *marasca* (the name of the cherry).

maraschino cherry noun a cherry preserved in maraschino.

marathon noun **1** a long-distance running

race, strictly one of 26 miles 385 yards (42.195 km). **2** a long and very difficult task.
– ORIGIN from *Marathōn* in Greece, the scene of a victory over the Persians in 490 BC; the modern race is based on the tradition that a messenger ran from Marathon to Athens (22 miles) with the news.

maraud /muh-**rawd**/ verb go about in search of goods to steal or people to attack.
– DERIVATIVES **marauder** noun.
– ORIGIN from French *maraud* 'rogue'.

marble noun **1** a hard form of limestone, typically with streaks of colour running through it, which may be polished and used in sculpture and building. **2** a small ball of coloured glass used as a toy. **3 (marbles)** (treated as sing.) a game in which marbles are rolled along the ground. **4 (one's marbles)** informal one's mental faculties. •verb stain or streak something so that it looks like marble.
– DERIVATIVES **marbled** adjective.
– ORIGIN Greek *marmaros* 'shining stone'.

marbling noun **1** colouring or marking that resembles marble. **2** streaks of fat in lean meat.

marc noun **1** the skins and other remains from grapes that have been pressed for winemaking. **2** an alcoholic spirit distilled from this.
– ORIGIN French, from *marcher* in the early sense 'to tread or trample'.

marcasite /mar-kuh-syt, mar-kuh-zeet/ noun **1** a semi-precious stone consisting of iron pyrites. **2** a piece of polished metal cut as a gem.
– ORIGIN Latin *marcasita*.

March noun the third month of the year.
– ORIGIN from Latin *Martius mensis* 'month of Mars'.

march verb **1** walk in time with other people and with regular paces, like a soldier. **2** proceed quickly and with determination. **3** force someone to walk somewhere quickly. **4** take part in an organized procession to make a protest. •noun **1** an act of marching. **2** a procession organized as a protest. **3** a piece of music written to accompany marching.
– PHRASES **on the march 1** engaged in marching. **2** making progress.
– DERIVATIVES **marcher** noun.
– ORIGIN French *marcher* 'to walk'.

Marches plural noun an area of land on the border between two countries or territories.
– ORIGIN Old French *marche*, related to MARK¹.

March hare noun informal a brown hare in the breeding season, noted for its wild behaviour.

marching orders noun **1** instructions for troops to depart. **2** informal a dismissal from a place, job, etc.

marchioness /mar-shuh-**ness**/ noun **1** the wife or widow of a marquess. **2** a woman holding the rank of marquess in her own right.
– ORIGIN Latin *marchionissa*, 'female ruler of a border territory'.

marchpane noun old use marzipan.

Mardi Gras /mar-di **grah**/ noun a carnival held in some countries on Shrove Tuesday.
– ORIGIN French, 'fat Tuesday', referring to the last day of feasting before the fast and penitence of Lent.

mare¹ /mair/ noun the female of a horse or related animal.
– ORIGIN Old English.

mare² /**mah**-ray/ noun (pl. **maria** /**mah**-ri-uh/) a large plain of volcanic rock on the surface of the moon.
– ORIGIN Latin *mare* 'sea'; these areas were once thought to be seas, as they appear dark by contrast with surrounding highland areas.

mare's nest noun **1** a complicated situation. **2** a discovery that turns out to be illusory or worthless.

mare's tail noun **1** a water plant with whorls of narrow leaves around a tall thick stem. **2** (**mare's tails**) long straight streaks of cirrus cloud.

margarine noun a butter substitute made from vegetable oils or animal fats.
– ORIGIN French, from Greek *margaron* 'pearl' (because the crystals of the compounds from which it was first made had a pearly lustre).

margarita noun a cocktail made with tequila and citrus fruit juice.
– ORIGIN Spanish equivalent of the woman's name *Margaret*.

marge noun Brit. informal margarine.

margin noun **1** an edge or border. **2** the blank border on each side of the print on a page. **3** an amount by which something is won: **4** an amount included or allowed for so as to ensure success or safety: *there was no margin for error.* **5** the furthest reach or limit: *the margins of acceptability.*
– ORIGIN Latin *margo* 'edge'.

marginal adjective **1** relating to or situated on an edge or border. **2** of minor importance. **3** (of a decision or distinction) very narrow. **4** Brit. (of a parliamentary seat) held by a small majority and so at risk in an election. •noun Brit. a marginal parliamentary seat.
– DERIVATIVES **marginality** noun.

marginalia /mar-ji-**nay**-li-uh/ plural noun notes written or printed in the margin of a book or manuscript.

marginalize (or **marginalise**) verb treat a person, group, or idea as unimportant.
– DERIVATIVES **marginalization** noun.

marginally adverb to only a limited extent.

margrave noun historical the hereditary title of some princes of the Holy Roman Empire.
– ORIGIN Dutch, from *marke* 'boundary' + *grave* 'count'.

marguerite /mar-guh-**reet**/ noun another term for OX-EYE DAISY.
– ORIGIN French form of the woman's name *Margaret*.

maria plural of MARE².

mariachi /ma-ri-**ah**-chi/ noun (pl. **mariachis**) (in Mexico) a musician performing traditional folk music.
– ORIGIN Mexican Spanish, 'street singer'.

marigold noun a plant of the daisy family with yellow or orange flowers.
– ORIGIN from the woman's name *Mary* + dialect *gold* 'marigold'.

marijuana /ma-ri-**hwah**-nuh/ noun cannabis.
– ORIGIN Latin American Spanish.

marimba noun a deep-toned xylophone of African origin.

marina noun a purpose-built harbour with moorings for yachts and small boats.
- ORIGIN Italian or Spanish, from Latin *mare* 'sea'.

marinade noun /ma-ri-**nayd**/ a mixture of oil, vinegar, and spices, in which meat, fish, or other food is soaked before cooking in order to flavour or soften it. • verb /**ma**-ri-nayd/ another term for MARINATE.
- ORIGIN French, from Spanish *marinar* 'pickle in brine'.

marinara /ma-ri-**nah**-ruh/ noun (in Italian cooking) a sauce made from tomatoes, onions, and herbs.
- ORIGIN from Italian *alla marinara* 'sailor-style'.

marinate verb soak meat, fish, or other food in a marinade.
- DERIVATIVES **marination** noun.

marine adjective 1 relating to the sea. 2 relating to shipping or a navy. • noun a member of a body of troops trained to serve on land or sea, in particular (in the UK) a member of the Royal Marines or (in the US) a member of the Marine Corps.
- ORIGIN Latin *marinus*, from *mare* 'sea'.

mariner noun formal or literary a sailor.

marionette noun a puppet worked by strings.
- ORIGIN French, from the woman's name *Marion*.

marital adjective relating to marriage or the relations between husband and wife.
- DERIVATIVES **maritally** adverb.
- ORIGIN Latin *maritus* 'husband'.

maritime adjective 1 relating to shipping or other activity taking place at sea. 2 living or found in or near the sea. 3 (of a climate) moist and mild owing to the influence of the sea.
- ORIGIN Latin *maritimus*, from *mare* 'sea'.

marjoram noun a plant of the mint family whose sweet-scented leaves are used as a herb in cooking.
- ORIGIN Latin *majorana*.

mark¹ noun 1 a small area on a surface having a different colour from its surroundings. 2 something that indicates position or acts as a pointer. 3 a line, figure, or symbol made to identify or record something. 4 a sign or indication of a quality or feeling: *a mark of respect.* 5 a characteristic feature of something: *it is the mark of a civilized society to treat its elderly members well.* 6 a level or stage: *unemployment had passed the two million mark.* 7 chiefly Brit. a point awarded for a correct answer or for good performance in an exam. 8 a particular model or type of a vehicle or machine. • verb 1 make a mark on something. 2 write a word or symbol on an object to identify it. 3 indicate the position of something. 4 (**mark someone/thing out**) distinguish someone or something from other people or things: *his sword marked him out as an officer.* 5 indicate or acknowledge a significant event: *a ceremony was held to mark the occasion.* 6 (**mark something up** or **down**) increase or reduce the price of an item. 7 assess a written work and give it a mark. 8 notice or pay careful attention to something.

9 Brit. (in team games) stay close to an opponent in order to prevent them getting or passing the ball.
- PHRASES **be quick off the mark** be fast in responding. **make its** (or **one's** or **a**) **mark** have a lasting or significant effect. **mark time** 1 (of troops) march on the spot without moving forward. 2 pass one's time in routine activities while waiting for something to happen. **near** (or **close**) **to the mark** almost accurate. **off** (or **wide of**) **the mark** wrong or inaccurate. **on your marks** be ready to start (used to instruct competitors in a race). **up to the mark** up to the required standard.
- ORIGIN Old English.

mark² noun (until the introduction of the euro in 2002) the basic unit of money of Germany.
- ORIGIN Old Norse.

marked adjective 1 having a visible mark or other identifying feature. 2 clearly noticeable: *a marked increase in UK sales.* 3 singled out as a target for attack: *a marked man.*
- DERIVATIVES **markedly** adverb.

marker noun 1 an object used to indicate a position, place, or route. 2 a felt-tip pen with a broad tip. 3 Brit. (in team games) a player who marks an opponent. 4 a person who marks a test or exam.

market noun 1 a regular gathering for the buying and selling of food, livestock, or other goods. 2 an outdoor space or hall where people offer goods for sale. 3 a particular area of commercial or competitive activity: *the export market.* 4 demand for a particular product or service: *the rapidly growing market for Internet software.* • verb (**markets, marketing, marketed**) advertise or promote something.
- PHRASES **on the market** available for sale.
- DERIVATIVES **marketable** adjective **marketer** noun.
- ORIGIN Latin *mercatus*.

marketeer noun 1 a person who sells products or services in a market. 2 a person who is in favour of a particular system of trade: *a free marketeer.*

market garden noun Brit. a place where vegetables and fruit are grown for sale.
- DERIVATIVES **market gardener** noun.

marketing noun the promotion and selling of products or services.

market-maker noun Stock Exchange a dealer in securities or other assets who undertakes to buy or sell at specified prices at all times.

marketplace noun 1 an open space where a market is held. 2 a competitive or commercial area of activity: *the global marketplace.*

market research noun the activity of gathering information about consumers' needs and preferences.

market town noun a town of moderate size where a regular market is held.

market value noun the amount for which something can be sold in an open market.

marking noun 1 an identifying mark. 2 (also **markings**) a pattern of marks on an animal's fur, feathers, or skin.

markka /**mah**-kah, **mah**-kuh/ noun (until the introduction of the euro in 2002) the basic unit of money of Finland.
- ORIGIN Finnish.

m

marksman noun (pl. **marksmen**) a person skilled in shooting.
- DERIVATIVES **marksmanship** noun.

markup noun **1** the amount added to the cost price of goods to cover overheads and profit. **2** a set of codes given to different elements of a body of computer data to indicate their relationship to the rest of the data.

marl[1] noun rock or soil consisting of clay and lime, formerly used as fertilizer.
- ORIGIN Old French *marle*.

marl[2] noun a yarn or fabric with differently coloured threads.
- ORIGIN shortening of *marbled*.

marlin noun a large edible fish of warm seas, with a pointed snout.
- ORIGIN from **MARLINSPIKE** (with reference to its pointed snout).

marlinspike (also **marlinespike**) noun a pointed metal tool used by sailors to separate strands of rope or wire.
- ORIGIN from Dutch *marlen* 'keep binding'.

marmalade noun a preserve made from citrus fruit, especially bitter oranges.
- ORIGIN Portuguese *marmelada* 'quince jam', from *marmelo* 'quince'.

Marmite noun Brit. trademark a dark savoury spread made from yeast extract and vegetable extract.

marmite /**mah**-myt, mah-**meet**/ noun a cooking pot.
- ORIGIN from Old French *marmite* 'hypocritical' (with reference to the hidden contents of the pot).

marmoreal /mar-**mor**-i-uhl/ adjective literary made of or resembling marble.
- ORIGIN from Latin *marmor* 'marble'.

marmoset /**mar**-muh-zet/ noun a small tropical American monkey with a silky coat and a long tail.
- ORIGIN Old French *marmouset* 'grotesque image'.

marmot noun a heavily built burrowing rodent.
- ORIGIN French *marmotte*.

Maronite /**ma**-ruh-nyt/ noun a member of a Christian sect living chiefly in Lebanon.
- ORIGIN from the name of John *Maro*, a 5th-century Syrian religious leader.

maroon[1] noun **1** a dark brownish-red colour. **2** chiefly Brit. a firework that makes a loud bang, used as a signal or warning.
- ORIGIN from French *marron* 'chestnut'; sense 2 is so named because the firework makes the noise of a chestnut bursting in the fire.

maroon[2] verb leave someone alone in a remote or inaccessible place.
- ORIGIN from *Maroon*, a member of a group of black people descended from runaway slaves and living in parts of Suriname and the West Indies, from Spanish *cimarrón* 'runaway slave'.

marque noun a make of car, as distinct from a specific model.
- ORIGIN French.

marquee noun **1** chiefly Brit. a large tent used for social or business events. **2** N. Amer. a roof-like projection over the entrance to a theatre, hotel, or other building.

- ORIGIN from **MARQUISE** (formerly a synonym for *marquee*).

marquess noun a British nobleman ranking above an earl and below a duke.
- ORIGIN variant of **MARQUIS**.

marquetry /**mar**-ki-tri/ noun inlaid work made from small pieces of coloured wood, used to decorate furniture.
- ORIGIN French *marqueter* 'become variegated'.

marquis /**mar**-kwiss/ noun **1** (in some European countries) a nobleman ranking above a count and below a duke. **2** variant spelling of **MARQUESS**.
- ORIGIN Old French *marchis*.

marquise /mar-**keez**/ noun **1** the wife or widow of a marquis, or a woman holding the rank of marquis in her own right. **2** a ring set with a pointed oval gem or cluster of gems.
- ORIGIN French, feminine of **MARQUIS**.

marram grass noun a coarse grass of coastal sand dunes.
- ORIGIN Old Norse.

marriage noun **1** the formal union of a man and a woman, by which they become husband and wife. **2** a combination of two or more elements: *her music is a marriage of funk, jazz, and hip hop.*
- ORIGIN Old French *mariage*.

marriageable adjective suitable for marriage, especially in terms of age.

married adjective united by marriage. •noun (**marrieds**) married people.

marron glacé /ma-ron gla-**say**/ noun (pl. **marrons glacés** pronunc. same) a chestnut preserved in and coated with sugar.
- ORIGIN French, 'iced chestnut'.

marrow noun **1** Brit. a long vegetable with a thin green skin and white flesh. **2** (also **bone marrow**) a soft fatty substance in the cavities of bones, in which blood cells are produced.
- PHRASES **to the marrow** to one's innermost being.
- ORIGIN Old English.

marrowbone noun a bone containing edible marrow.

marrowfat pea noun a pea of a large variety which is processed and sold in cans.

marry[1] verb (**marries**, **marrying**, **married**) **1** take someone as one's wife or husband in marriage. **2** join two people in marriage. **3** (**marry into**) become a member of a family by marriage. **4** join two things together in a harmonious way: *the show marries poetry with art.*
- ORIGIN Old French *marier*.

marry[2] exclamation old use expressing surprise, indignation, etc.
- ORIGIN variant of *Mary* (mother of Jesus).

Mars noun a small planet of the solar system, fourth in order from the sun and the nearest to the earth.

Marsala /mah-**sah**-luh/ noun a dark, sweet fortified dessert wine made in Sicily.
- ORIGIN named after *Marsala*, a town in Sicily.

marsh noun an area of low-lying land which is flooded in wet seasons or at high tide and typically remains waterlogged.
- DERIVATIVES **marshy** adjective.
- ORIGIN Old English.

marshal noun **1** an officer of the highest rank in the armed forces of some countries. **2** (in the US) a federal or municipal law-enforcement officer. **3** an official responsible for supervising public events. **4** Brit. historical a high-ranking officer of state. **5** (in the UK) an official accompanying a judge on circuit. • verb (**marshals, marshalling, marshalled;** US **marshals, marshaling, marshaled**) **1** assemble a group of people, especially soldiers, in an orderly way. **2** bring facts, information, etc. together in an organized way. **3** direct the movement of an aircraft on the ground at an airport.
– ORIGIN Old French *mareschal* 'farrier, commander'.

marshalling yard noun a large railway yard in which freight wagons are organized into trains.

Marshal of the Royal Air Force noun the highest rank of officer in the RAF.

Marsh Arab noun a member of a semi-nomadic Arab people living in marshland in southern Iraq.

marsh gas noun gas, mainly methane, produced by decaying matter in marshes.

marshland noun (also **marshlands**) land consisting of marshes.

marshmallow noun a spongy sweet made from a mixture of sugar, egg white, and gelatin.

marsh mallow noun a tall pink-flowered plant growing in marshes, whose roots were formerly used to make marshmallow.

marsh marigold noun a plant with large yellow flowers which grows in damp ground and shallow water.

marsupial /mar-soo-pi-uhl/ noun a mammal, such as a kangaroo, whose young are born before they are fully developed and are carried and suckled in a pouch on the mother's belly.
– ORIGIN Greek *marsupion* 'little purse'.

mart noun **1** N. Amer. a shop. **2** a market.
– ORIGIN Dutch, variant of *marct* 'market'.

Martello tower noun any of a number of small circular defensive forts built along the coasts of Britain during the Napoleonic Wars.
– ORIGIN alteration of Cape *Mortella* in Corsica, where such a tower proved difficult for the English to capture in 1794.

marten noun a weasel-like forest mammal that is hunted for fur in some countries.
– ORIGIN from Old French *peau martrine* 'marten fur'.

martial adjective relating to or appropriate to war; warlike.
– DERIVATIVES **martially** adverb.
– ORIGIN Latin *martialis*, from *Mars*, the name of the Roman god of war.

martial arts plural noun various sports or skills which originated mainly in Japan, Korea, and China as forms of self-defence or attack, such as judo, karate, and kung fu.

martial law noun government by the military forces of a country, during which ordinary laws are suspended.

Martian noun a supposed inhabitant of the planet Mars. • adjective relating to Mars.

martin noun used in names of small short-tailed swallows, e.g. **house martin**.
– ORIGIN probably from the name of St *Martin* of Tours.

martinet noun a person who enforces strict discipline.
– ORIGIN named after Jean *Martinet*, a French soldier.

martingale noun a strap or set of straps running from the noseband or reins to the girth of a horse, used to prevent the horse from raising its head too high.
– ORIGIN French.

Martiniquan /mah-ti-**nee**-kuhn/ (also **Martinican**) noun a person from Martinique, a French island in the Lesser Antilles. • adjective relating to Martinique.

Martinmas noun St Martin's Day, 11 November.

martyr /**mar**-tuh/ noun **1** a person who is killed because of their religious or political beliefs. **2** a person who exaggerates their difficulties in order to obtain sympathy. • verb make someone a martyr.
– DERIVATIVES **martyrdom** noun.
– ORIGIN Greek *martur* 'witness'.

martyrology noun (pl. **martyrologies**) **1** the study of martyrs. **2** a list of martyrs.

marvel verb (**marvels, marvelling, marvelled;** US **marvels, marveling, marveled**) be filled with wonder: *she marvelled at the beauty of the scenery.* • noun a person or thing that causes a feeling of wonder.
– ORIGIN Old French *merveille*.

marvellous (US **marvelous**) adjective **1** causing great wonder; extraordinary. **2** extremely good or pleasing.
– DERIVATIVES **marvellously** adverb.

Marxism noun the political and economic theories of Karl Marx and Friedrich Engels, later developed by their followers as the basis for communism.
– DERIVATIVES **Marxian** noun & adjective **Marxist** noun & adjective.

Marxism–Leninism noun the doctrines of Marx as interpreted and put into effect by Lenin in the Soviet Union.

marzipan noun a sweet paste of ground almonds, sugar, and egg whites, used to coat cakes or to make confectionery.
– ORIGIN Italian *marzapane*.

Masai /mah-sy, muh-**sy**/ (also **Maasai**) noun (pl. same or **Masais**) a member of a pastoral people living in Tanzania and Kenya.
– ORIGIN the Masai's name for themselves.

masala /muh-**sah**-luh/ noun a mixture of spices ground into a paste or powder and used in Indian cookery.
– ORIGIN Urdu.

mascara noun a cosmetic for darkening and thickening the eyelashes.
– ORIGIN Italian, 'mask'.

mascarpone /mas-kuh-**poh**-nay, mas-kuh-**poh**-ni/ noun a soft, mild Italian cream cheese.
– ORIGIN Italian.

mascot noun a person, animal, or object that is identified with a person, group, team, etc. and supposed to bring good luck.

m

– ORIGIN French *mascotte*.

masculine adjective 1 having the qualities or appearance traditionally associated with men. **2** relating to men; male. **3** Grammar (of a gender of nouns and adjectives in certain languages) treated as male.
– DERIVATIVES **masculinity** noun.
– ORIGIN from Latin *masculus* 'male'.

maser /**may**-zer/ **noun** a form of laser generating a beam of microwaves.
– ORIGIN from the initial letters of *microwave amplification (by the) stimulated emission (of) radiation*.

mash verb 1 crush or beat something to a soft mass. **2** (in brewing) mix powdered malt with hot water to form wort. **3** N. English (with reference to tea) brew or infuse. • **noun 1** a soft mass made by crushing a substance into a pulp. **2** Brit. informal boiled and mashed potatoes. **3** bran mixed with hot water, given as a food to horses. **4** (in brewing) a mixture of powdered malt and hot water, which is left standing until the sugars dissolve to form the wort.
– ORIGIN Old English.

mask noun 1 a covering for all or part of the face, worn as a disguise, for protection or hygiene, or for theatrical effect. **2** a device used to filter inhaled air or to supply gas for breathing. **3** a likeness of a person's face moulded or sculpted in clay or wax. **4** a face pack. • **verb 1** cover someone's face or part of their face with a mask. **2** conceal or disguise: *brandy did not mask the bitter taste*. **3** cover an object or surface so as to protect it during painting or similar work.
– DERIVATIVES **masked** adjective.
– ORIGIN French *masque*, from Italian *maschera* or *mascara*.

masked ball noun a ball at which participants wear masks to conceal their faces.

masking tape noun adhesive tape used in painting to cover areas on which paint is not wanted.

masochism /**mass**-uh-ki-z'm/ **noun** the tendency to enjoy one's own pain or humiliation.
– DERIVATIVES **masochist** noun **masochistic** adjective.
– ORIGIN named after the Austrian novelist Leopold von Sacher-*Masoch*.

mason noun 1 a builder and worker in stone. **2** (**Mason**) a Freemason.
– ORIGIN Old French *masson*.

Masonic adjective relating to Freemasons.

masonry noun 1 stonework. **2** (**Masonry**) Freemasonry.

masque /mahsk/ **noun** a form of dramatic entertainment popular in the 16th and 17th centuries, consisting of dancing and acting performed by players wearing masks.
– ORIGIN probably from *masker* 'person wearing a mask'.

masquerade noun 1 an attempt to hide the truth or one's real feelings. **2** chiefly N. Amer. a masked ball. • **verb 1** pretend to be someone that one is not. **2** be disguised or passed off as something else: *the idle gossip that masquerades as news*.
– ORIGIN French *mascarade*.

Mass noun 1 the Christian service of the Eucharist or Holy Communion, especially in the Roman Catholic Church. **2** a musical setting of parts of the liturgy used in the Mass.
– ORIGIN Latin *missa*, from *mittere* 'dismiss', perhaps from the last words of the service, *Ite, missa est* 'Go, it is the dismissal'.

mass noun 1 a body of matter with no definite shape. **2** a large number of people or objects gathered together. **3** (**the masses**) ordinary people. **4** (**the mass of**) the majority of. **5** (**a mass of**) a large amount of. **6** Physics the quantity of matter which a body contains, as measured by its acceleration under a given force or by the force exerted on it by a gravitational field. • **adjective** done by or affecting large numbers of people or things: *a mass exodus*. • **verb** gather together into a single body or mass: *both countries began massing troops in the region*.
– ORIGIN Latin *massa*.

massacre noun 1 a brutal slaughter of a large number of people. **2** informal a very heavy defeat. • **verb 1** brutally kill a large number of people. **2** informal inflict a heavy defeat on an opponent.
– ORIGIN French.

massage noun the rubbing and kneading of parts of the body with the hands to relieve tension or pain. • **verb 1** give someone a massage. **2** manipulate figures to give a more acceptable result.
– ORIGIN French.

massage parlour noun 1 a place where one can pay to have a massage. **2** euphemistic a brothel.

masseur noun (fem. **masseuse**) a person who provides massage professionally.
– ORIGIN French.

massif /ma-**seef**/ **noun** a compact group of mountains.
– ORIGIN French, 'massive'.

massive adjective 1 large and heavy or solid. **2** exceptionally large, intense, or severe: *a massive heart attack*. **3** forming a solid or continuous mass.
– DERIVATIVES **massively** adverb **massiveness** noun.
– ORIGIN French *massif*.

mass-market adjective (of goods) produced in large quantities for many people.

mass media noun television, radio, and newspapers considered as a group; the media.

mass noun noun a noun referring to something which cannot be counted, in English usually a noun which has no plural form and is not used with *a* or *an*, e.g. *luggage*, *happiness*. Contrasted with **COUNT NOUN**.

mass number noun Physics the total number of protons and neutrons in a nucleus.

mass-produce verb produce goods in large quantities, using machinery.
– DERIVATIVES **mass production** noun.

mast¹ noun 1 a tall upright post or spar on a boat, generally carrying a sail or sails. **2** any tall upright post, especially a flagpole or a television or radio transmitter.
– PHRASES **nail one's colours to the mast** openly declare one's beliefs or intentions.
– ORIGIN Old English.

mast[2] noun the fruit of beech and other forest trees, especially as food for pigs.
– ORIGIN Old English.

mastectomy /ma-stek-tuh-mi/ noun (pl. **mastectomies**) a surgical operation to remove a breast.
– ORIGIN from Greek *mastos* 'breast'.

master noun 1 a man in a position of authority, control, or ownership. 2 a person who is skilled in a particular art or activity: *a master of disguise*. 3 the head of a college or school. 4 Brit. a male schoolteacher. 5 a person who holds a second or further degree. 6 an original film, recording, or document from which copies can be made. 7 (**Master**) a title placed before a boy's name. ●adjective 1 (of an artist) having great skill or expertise: *a master painter*. 2 skilled in a particular trade and able to teach others: *a master builder*. 3 main; principal: *the master bedroom*. ●verb 1 gain complete knowledge of or skill in a subject, technique, etc. 2 gain control of: *I managed to master my fears*. 3 make a master copy of a film or record.
– ORIGIN Latin *magister*.

master-at-arms noun a warrant officer responsible for police duties on board a ship.

masterclass noun a class given to students by an expert musician.

masterful adjective 1 powerful and able to control others. 2 performed or performing very skilfully.
– DERIVATIVES **masterfully** adverb.

master key noun a key that opens several locks, each of which also has its own key.

masterly adjective performed or performing very skilfully.

mastermind noun 1 a person who is extremely intelligent. 2 a person who plans and directs a complex scheme or enterprise. ●verb plan and direct a complex scheme or enterprise.

master of ceremonies noun a person in charge of procedure at a state occasion, formal event, or entertainment, who introduces the speakers or performers.

Master of the Rolls noun (in England and Wales) the judge who presides over the Court of Appeal.

masterpiece noun a work of outstanding skill.

masterstroke noun an outstandingly skilful or clever move.

masterwork noun a masterpiece.

mastery noun 1 complete knowledge or command of a subject or skill. 2 control or superiority: *man's mastery over nature*.

masthead noun 1 the highest part of a ship's mast. 2 the name of a newspaper or magazine printed at the top of the first page.

mastic noun 1 an aromatic gum from the bark of a Mediterranean tree, used in making varnish and chewing gum and as a flavouring. 2 a putty-like waterproof substance used as a filler and sealant in building.
– ORIGIN Greek *mastikhē*.

masticate verb chew food.
– DERIVATIVES **mastication** noun.
– ORIGIN Latin *masticare*.

mastiff noun a dog of a large, strong breed with drooping ears and lips.
– ORIGIN Old French *mastin*.

mastitis /ma-sty-tiss/ noun inflammation of the mammary gland in the breast or udder.
– ORIGIN from Greek *mastos* 'breast'.

mastodon /mass-tuh-don/ noun a large extinct elephant-like mammal.
– ORIGIN from Greek *mastos* 'breast' + *odous* 'tooth' (with reference to nipple-shaped projections on the crowns of its molar teeth).

mastoid (also **mastoid process**) noun a conical projection of the temporal bone behind the ear, to which neck muscles are attached, and which has air spaces linked to the middle ear.

masturbate verb stimulate one's genitals with one's hand for sexual pleasure.
– DERIVATIVES **masturbation** noun **masturbator** noun **masturbatory** adjective.
– ORIGIN Latin *masturbari*.

mat noun 1 a thick piece of material placed on the floor to protect it from dirt or as a decoration. 2 a piece of thick material for landing on in gymnastics or similar sports. 3 a small piece of material placed on a surface to protect it from the heat or moisture of an object placed on it. 4 (also **mouse mat**) Brit. a small piece of rigid material on which a computer mouse is moved. 5 a thick, untidy layer of hairy or woolly material.
– ORIGIN Old English.

Matabele /ma-tuh-bee-li/ noun the Ndebele people, particularly those of Zimbabwe.
– ORIGIN Sotho (a Bantu language).

matador noun a bullfighter whose task is to kill the bull.
– ORIGIN Spanish, 'killer'.

match[1] noun 1 a contest in which people or teams compete against each other. 2 a person or thing that can compete with another as an equal in quality or strength. 3 an exact equivalent. 4 a pair of things which are very similar or combine together well. 5 a potential husband or wife. 6 a marriage. ●verb 1 correspond in appearance; combine together well: *the jacket and trousers do not match*. 2 be equal to someone or something in quality or strength. 3 place one person or group in competition with another.
– ORIGIN Old English, 'mate, companion'.

match[2] noun 1 a short, thin stick tipped with a mixture that ignites when rubbed against a rough surface. 2 historical a piece of wick or cord used for lighting gunpowder.
– ORIGIN Old French *meche*.

matchboard noun interlocking boards joined together by tongue and groove.

matchbox noun a small box in which matches are sold.

matchless adjective so good that no one or nothing is an equal.

matchlock noun historical a type of gun with a lock in which a piece of wick or cord was placed for igniting the powder.

matchmaker noun a person who tries to bring about marriages or relationships between other people.

match play noun golf in which the score is reckoned by the number of holes won. Compare with STROKE PLAY.

match point noun (in tennis and some other sports) a point which if won by one

m

of the players will also win them the match.

matchstick noun the stem of a match.
 • adjective Brit. drawn using thin straight lines: *matchstick men.*

matchwood noun very small pieces or splinters of wood.

mate[1] noun 1 Brit. informal a friend or companion. 2 (in combination) a fellow member or occupant: *his teammates.* 3 the sexual partner of an animal. 4 chiefly Brit. an assistant to a skilled worker. 5 an officer on a merchant ship below the master. • verb 1 (of animals or birds) come together for breeding. 2 join or connect two things.
 – ORIGIN German, 'comrade'.

mate[2] noun & verb Chess short for CHECKMATE.

matelot /mat-loh/ noun Brit. informal a sailor.
 – ORIGIN French, from Dutch *mattenoot* 'bed companion' (because sailors had to share hammocks).

mater /may-ter/ noun Brit. informal, dated mother.
 – ORIGIN Latin.

materfamilias /may-ter-fuh-mi-li-ass/ noun (pl. **matresfamilias** /may-treez-fuh-mi-li-ass/) the female head of a family or household.
 – ORIGIN Latin.

material noun 1 the substance from which something is or can be made. 2 items needed for doing or creating something. 3 cloth or fabric. • adjective 1 consisting of or referring to physical objects rather than the mind or spirit: *the material world.* 2 essential or relevant: *evidence material to the case.*
 – DERIVATIVES **materiality** noun **materially** adverb.
 – ORIGIN Latin *materia* 'matter'.

materialism noun 1 a tendency to consider material possessions and physical comfort as more important than spiritual values. 2 Philosophy the doctrine that nothing exists except matter.
 – DERIVATIVES **materialist** noun & adjective **materialistic** adjective.

materialize (or **materialise**) verb 1 become fact; happen: *the hoped-for investment boom did not materialize.* 2 appear.
 – DERIVATIVES **materialization** noun.

materiel /muh-teer-i-el/ noun military materials and equipment.
 – ORIGIN French *matériel.*

maternal adjective 1 relating to or characteristic of a mother. 2 related through the mother's side of the family.
 – DERIVATIVES **maternally** adverb.
 – ORIGIN French *maternel*, from Latin *mater* 'mother'.

maternity noun motherhood. • adjective relating to the period during pregnancy and shortly after childbirth: *maternity clothes.*

mateship noun Austral./NZ informal companionship or friendship.

matey adjective (**matier, matiest**) Brit. informal familiar and friendly.
 – DERIVATIVES **mateyness** (also **matiness**) noun **matily** adverb.

mathematics plural noun (usu. treated as sing.) the branch of science concerned with number, quantity, and space, either as abstract ideas (**pure mathematics**) or as applied to physics, engineering, and other subjects (**applied mathematics**).
 – DERIVATIVES **mathematical** adjective **mathematically** adverb **mathematician** noun.
 – ORIGIN from Greek *mathēma* 'science'.

maths (N. Amer. **math**) noun mathematics.

matinee /mat-i-nay/ noun an afternoon performance in a theatre or cinema.
 – ORIGIN from French *matin* 'morning'.

matinee coat noun Brit. a baby's short coat.

matinee idol noun informal, dated a handsome actor admired chiefly by women.

matins noun a service of morning prayer, especially in the Anglican Church.
 – ORIGIN Old French *matines* 'mornings'.

matriarch /may-tri-ark/ noun 1 a woman who is the head of a family or tribe. 2 a powerful older woman.
 – DERIVATIVES **matriarchal** adjective.
 – ORIGIN from Latin *mater* 'mother'.

matriarchy noun 1 a form of social organization in which the mother or eldest female is the head of the family. 2 a society in which women hold most or all of the power.

matrices plural of MATRIX.

matricide /ma-tri-syd/ noun 1 the killing of one's mother. 2 a person who kills their mother.
 – DERIVATIVES **matricidal** adjective.
 – ORIGIN from Latin *mater* 'mother' + *-cidium* 'killing'.

matriculate verb enrol or be enrolled at a college or university.
 – DERIVATIVES **matriculation** noun.
 – ORIGIN Latin *matriculare.*

matrilineal adjective based on relationship with the mother or the female line of descent.
 – DERIVATIVES **matrilineally** adverb.

matrimony noun the state of being married, or the ceremony of marriage.
 – DERIVATIVES **matrimonial** adjective.
 – ORIGIN Latin *matrimonium.*

matrix /may-triks/ noun (pl. **matrices** /may-tri-seez/ or **matrixes**) 1 an environment or material in which something develops. 2 a mould in which something is cast or shaped. 3 Mathematics a rectangular arrangement of quantities in rows and columns that is manipulated according to particular rules. 4 a grid-like array of elements; a lattice. 5 a mass of rock in which gems, crystals, or fossils are embedded.
 – ORIGIN Latin, 'womb'.

matron noun 1 a woman in charge of domestic and medical arrangements at a boarding school. 2 a dignified or sedate married woman. 3 Brit. dated a woman in charge of nursing in a hospital. 4 chiefly US a female prison officer.
 – DERIVATIVES **matronly** adjective.
 – ORIGIN Latin *matrona*, from *mater* 'mother'.

USAGE: In sense 3, the official term is now **senior nursing officer.**

matron of honour noun a married woman attending the bride at a wedding.

matt (also **matte**) adjective (of a surface, paint, etc.) not shiny: *matt white paint.* • noun 1 a matt colour, paint, or finish. 2 a sheet of cardboard placed on the back of a picture, as a mount or

to form a border.
– ORIGIN French *mat*.

matted adjective (of hair or fur) tangled into a thick mass.

matter noun **1** physical substance or material in general, as distinct from mind and spirit; (in physics) that which occupies space and possesses mass. **2** a subject or situation under consideration: *complicated financial matters.* **3** (**the matter**) the reason for a problem: *what's the matter?* **4** written or printed material. **5** Law something to be tried or proved in court; a case. ● verb be important or significant: *it doesn't matter what she thinks.*
– PHRASES **as a matter of fact** in reality; in fact. **in the matter of** regarding. **a matter of 1** no more than a particular period of time: *they were shown the door in a matter of minutes.* **2** a question of. **a matter of course** the natural or expected thing. **no matter 1** regardless of. **2** it is of no importance.
– ORIGIN Latin *materia*.

matter-of-fact adjective unemotional and practical.

mattify /mat-i-fy/ verb (**mattifies, mattifying, mattified**) (of a cosmetic) reduce the shine or oiliness of the complexion.
– DERIVATIVES **mattifier** noun.

matting noun material used for mats, especially coarse fabric woven from a natural fibre.

mattock noun an agricultural tool similar to a pickaxe, but with one arm of the head curved like an adze and the other like a chisel edge.
– ORIGIN Old English.

mattress noun a fabric case filled with soft, firm, or springy material used for sleeping on.
– ORIGIN Arabic, 'carpet or cushion'.

maturation noun **1** the action or process of maturing. **2** the formation of pus in a boil, abscess, etc.

mature adjective **1** fully grown or physically developed; adult. **2** like an adult in mental or emotional development. **3** (of thought or planning) careful and thorough. **4** (of certain foods or drinks) ready for consumption. **5** due for payment. ● verb **1** become mature. **2** (of an insurance policy) reach the end of its term and so become payable.
– DERIVATIVES **maturely** adverb.
– ORIGIN Latin *maturus* 'timely, ripe'.

maturity noun **1** the state, fact, or period of being mature. **2** the time when an insurance policy reaches the end of its term and so becomes payable.

matutinal /ma-tyuu-ty-n'l/ adjective formal relating to or happening in the morning.
– ORIGIN Latin *matutinus* 'early'.

matzo /mat-soh/ (also **matzoh**) noun (pl. **matzos**) a crisp biscuit of unleavened bread, traditionally eaten by Jews during Passover.
– ORIGIN Yiddish, from Hebrew.

maudlin adjective sentimental in a tearful or self-pitying way.
– ORIGIN from the name of Mary *Magdalen* in the Bible, typically represented weeping.

maul verb **1** (of an animal) wound a person or other animal by scratching and tearing. **2** handle or treat someone or something savagely or roughly. ● noun **1** Rugby Union a loose

scrum formed around a player with the ball off the ground. **2** another term for **BEETLE²**.
– ORIGIN from Latin *malleus* 'hammer'.

maunder verb talk or act in a rambling or aimless way.
– ORIGIN perhaps from former *maunder* 'to beg'.

Maundy noun a public ceremony on the Thursday before Easter (**Maundy Thursday**) at which the British monarch distributes specially minted coins (**Maundy money**) to a group of people.
– ORIGIN Old French *mande*, from Latin *mandatum novum* 'new commandment' (referring to Christ's words in the Gospel of John, chapter 13).

Mauritanian /mor-i-**tay**-ni-uhn/ noun a person from Mauritania, a country in West Africa. ● adjective relating to Mauritania.

Mauritian /muh-**rish**-uhn/ noun a person from the island of Mauritius in the Indian Ocean. ● adjective relating to Mauritius.

mausoleum /maw-suh-**lee**-uhm/ noun (pl. **mausolea** /maw-suh-**lee**-uh/ or **mausoleums**) a building containing a tomb or tombs.
– ORIGIN Greek *Mausōleion*, from *Mausōlos*, the name of a king to whose tomb the name was originally applied.

mauve noun a pale purple colour.
– ORIGIN French, 'mallow'.

maven /**may**-vuhn/ noun N. Amer. informal an expert or connoisseur.
– ORIGIN Yiddish.

maverick noun **1** an unconventional or independent-minded person. **2** N. Amer. an unbranded calf or yearling.
– ORIGIN from Samuel A. *Maverick*, a Texas rancher who did not brand his cattle.

maw noun the jaws or throat, especially of a voracious animal.
– ORIGIN Old English.

mawkish adjective expressing emotion in an exaggerated or embarrassing way: *a mawkish ode to parenthood.*
– ORIGIN from former *mawk* 'maggot'.

max abbreviation maximum.

maxi noun (pl. **maxis**) a skirt or coat reaching to the ankle.

maxilla /mak-**sil**-luh/ noun (pl. **maxillae** /mak-**sil**-lee/) **1** the bone of the upper jaw. **2** (in an insect or other arthropod) each of a pair of chewing mouthparts.
– DERIVATIVES **maxillary** adjective.
– ORIGIN Latin, 'jaw'.

maxim noun a short statement expressing a general truth or rule of behaviour.
– ORIGIN from Latin *propositio maxima* 'most important proposition'.

maximize (or **maximise**) verb **1** make as great or large as possible: *the company is aiming to maximize profits.* **2** make the best use of something.
– DERIVATIVES **maximization** noun **maximizer** noun.

maximum noun (pl. **maxima** or **maximums**) the greatest amount, size, or intensity possible or achieved. ● adjective greatest in amount, size, or intensity.
– DERIVATIVES **maximal** adjective.
– ORIGIN Latin, 'greatest thing'.

m

maxwell noun a unit used in measuring the strength of a magnetic field.
– ORIGIN named after the Scottish physicist J. C. Maxwell.

May noun **1** the fifth month of the year. **2** (**may**) the hawthorn or its blossom.
– ORIGIN from Latin *Maius mensis* 'month of the goddess *Maia*'.

may modal verb (3rd sing. present **may**; past **might**) **1** expressing possibility. **2** expressing permission. **3** expressing a wish or hope.
– PHRASES **be that as it may** nevertheless.
– ORIGIN Old English.

> USAGE: For an explanation of the difference in use between **may** and **can**, see the note at **CAN**.

Maya /my-uh/ noun (pl. same or **Mayas**) a member of a Central American people whose civilization died out *c*.900 AD.
– DERIVATIVES **Mayan** adjective & noun.
– ORIGIN the Maya's name for themselves.

maybe adverb perhaps; possibly.

May Day noun 1 May, celebrated as a springtime festival or as a holiday in honour of workers.

Mayday noun an international radio distress signal used by ships and aircraft.
– ORIGIN from the pronunciation of French *m'aider*, from *venez m'aider* 'come and help me'.

mayfly noun (pl. **mayflies**) an insect with transparent wings which lives as an adult for only a very short time.

mayhem noun violent disorder; chaos.
– ORIGIN first meaning 'the crime of maliciously injuring someone': from Old French.

mayn't contraction may not.

mayonnaise /may-uh-**nayz**/ noun a thick creamy dressing made from egg yolks, oil, and vinegar.
– ORIGIN French.

mayor noun the elected head of a city or borough council.
– DERIVATIVES **mayoral** adjective **mayorship** noun.
– ORIGIN from Latin *major* 'greater'.

mayoralty noun (pl. **mayoralties**) the position or term of office of a mayor.

mayoress noun **1** the wife of a mayor. **2** a woman elected as mayor.

maypole noun a decorated pole with long ribbons attached to the top, traditionally used for dancing round on May Day.

maze noun **1** a puzzle consisting of a network of paths and walls or hedges through which one has to find a way. **2** a confusing mass of information.
– ORIGIN related to **AMAZE**.

mazurka /muh-**zer**-kuh/ noun a lively Polish dance in triple time.
– ORIGIN Polish, 'folk dance from Mazovia' (a region of Poland).

MB abbreviation **1** Bachelor of Medicine. [Latin *Medicinae Baccalaureus*.] **2** Manitoba. **3** (also **Mb**) Computing megabyte(s).

MBA abbreviation Master of Business Administration.

MBE abbreviation Member of the Order of the British Empire.

MBO abbreviation management buyout.

MC abbreviation **1** Master of Ceremonies. **2** (in the US) Member of Congress. **3** Military Cross. •noun a person who provides entertainment at a club or party by instructing the DJ and performing rap music. •verb (**MC's**, **MC'ing**, **MC'd**) perform as an MC.

MCC abbreviation Marylebone Cricket Club.

m-commerce noun commercial dealings carried out electronically by mobile phone.

MD abbreviation **1** Doctor of Medicine. [Latin *Medicinae Doctor*.] **2** Brit. Managing Director. **3** Maryland.

Md symbol the chemical element mendelevium.

MDF abbreviation medium density fibreboard.

MDMA abbreviation methylenedioxymethamphetamine, the drug Ecstasy.

ME abbreviation **1** myalgic encephalomyelitis, a medical condition of unknown cause, with fever, aching, and prolonged tiredness and depression. **2** Maine.

me¹ pronoun (first person sing.) used as the object of a verb or preposition or after 'than', 'as', or the verb 'to be', to refer to the speaker himself or herself.
– ORIGIN Old English.

> USAGE: The pronoun **me** should be used as the object of a verb or preposition, as in *John hates me*. It is wrong to use **me** as the subject of a verb, as in *John and me went to the shops*; in this case **I** should be used instead.

me² (also **mi**) noun Music the third note of a major scale, coming after 'ray' and before 'fah'.
– ORIGIN taken from the first syllable of *mira*, in a Latin hymn.

mea culpa /may-uh **kuul**-puh/ exclamation an acknowledgement that one is wrong or at fault.
– ORIGIN Latin, 'by my fault'.

mead¹ noun an alcoholic drink of fermented honey and water.
– ORIGIN Old English.

mead² noun literary a meadow.

meadow noun **1** an area of grassland, especially one used for hay. **2** a piece of low ground near a river.
– ORIGIN Old English.

meadowsweet noun a tall meadow plant with heads of creamy-white fragrant flowers.

meagre (US **meager**) adjective lacking in quantity or quality: *a meagre diet of bread and beans.*
– DERIVATIVES **meagreness** noun.
– ORIGIN Latin *macer*.

meal¹ noun **1** any of the regular daily occasions when food is eaten. **2** the food eaten during a meal.
– PHRASES **make a meal of** Brit. informal carry out a task with unnecessary effort or carefulness.
– ORIGIN Old English.

meal² noun the edible part of any grain or pulse ground to a powder, used to make flour or to feed animals.
– ORIGIN Old English.

mealie noun S. African a maize plant or cob.
– ORIGIN Afrikaans *mielie*.

meal ticket noun a person or thing that is exploited as a source of money.

mealtime noun the time at which a meal is eaten.

mealy adjective (**mealier, mealiest**) **1** relating to or containing ground grain or pulses. **2** pale in colour.

mealy bug noun a sap-sucking scale insect which is coated with a white powdery wax and which can be a serious pest.

mealy-mouthed adjective reluctant to speak frankly.
– ORIGIN perhaps from German *Mehl im Maule behalten* 'carry meal in the mouth' (i.e. be indirect in speech).

mean¹ verb (past and past part. **meant**) **1** intend to express or refer to something. **2** (of a word) have something as its explanation in the same language or its equivalent in another language. **3** intend to do or be the case: *they mean no harm.* **4** have something as a result. **5** intend or design for a particular purpose: *the coat was meant for a much larger person.* **6** be of specified importance to someone.
– PHRASES **mean business** be in earnest. **mean well** have good intentions, but not always carry them out.
– ORIGIN Old English.

mean² adjective **1** chiefly Brit. unwilling to give or share things; not generous. **2** unkind or unfair. **3** N. Amer. vicious or aggressive. **4** poor in quality and appearance: *her home was mean and small.* **5** dated coming from a low social class. **6** informal excellent.
– DERIVATIVES **meanly** adverb **meanness** noun.
– ORIGIN first meaning 'common to two or more people': from Old English.

mean³ noun **1** the average value of a set of quantities. **2** something in the middle of two extremes. ● adjective **1** calculated as a mean; average. **2** equally far from two extremes.
– ORIGIN Latin *medianus* 'middle'.

meander /mi-an-der/ verb **1** (of a river or road) follow a winding course. **2** wander or progress in a leisurely or aimless way. ● noun a bend of a river that curves back on itself.
– ORIGIN from the river *Maeander* in Turkey.

meaning noun **1** what is meant by a word, idea, or action. **2** a sense of purpose.

meaningful adjective **1** having meaning. **2** important or worthwhile. **3** expressing something without words: *they exchanged meaningful glances.*
– DERIVATIVES **meaningfully** adverb **meaningfulness** noun.

meaningless adjective having no meaning or significance.
– DERIVATIVES **meaninglessly** adverb **meaninglessness** noun.

means plural noun (also treated as sing.) **1** an action or method for achieving a result: *language is a means of communication.* **2** a person's financial resources; income.
– PHRASES **by all means** of course. **by means of** by using. **by no means** certainly not. **a man (or woman) of means** a rich man (or woman). **a means to an end** a thing that is not valued in itself but is useful in achieving an aim.
– ORIGIN plural of **mean**³.

means test noun an official investigation into a person's finances to determine whether they qualify for state benefits. ● verb (**means-test**) base a state benefit on a means test.

meant past and past participle of **mean**¹.

meantime adverb (also **in the meantime**) in the period of time between two events; meanwhile.

meanwhile adverb **1** (also **in the meanwhile**) in the period of time between two events. **2** at the same time.

measles plural noun (treated as sing.) an infectious disease spread by a virus, causing fever and a red rash.
– ORIGIN probably from Dutch *masel* 'spot'.

measly adjective (**measlier, measliest**) informal ridiculously small or few.

measure verb **1** determine the size, amount, or degree of something by comparing it with a standard unit. **2** be of a specified size. **3** (**measure something out**) take an exact quantity of something. **4** assess the importance or value of: *it is hard to measure teaching ability.* **5** (**measure up**) reach the required standard. ● noun **1** a means of achieving a purpose: *cost-cutting measures.* **2** a standard unit used to express size, amount, or degree. **3** a measuring device marked with standard units of size, amount, or degree. **4** (**a measure of**) a certain amount or degree of. **5** (**a measure of**) an indication of the extent or quality of. **6** a proposal for a law. **7** (**measures**) a group of rock strata: *coal measures.* **8** a unit of metre in poetry.
– PHRASES **for good measure** as an amount or item that is additional to what is strictly required. **have the measure of** understand the character or abilities of.
– DERIVATIVES **measurable** adjective **measurably** adverb **measurer** noun.
– ORIGIN Latin *mensura*, from *metiri* 'to measure'.

measured adjective **1** slow and regular in rhythm. **2** (of language) carefully considered.

measureless adjective literary having no limits.

measurement noun **1** the action of measuring. **2** an amount, size, or extent found by measuring. **3** a standard unit used in measuring.

meat noun **1** the flesh of an animal as food. **2** the chief part: *let's get to the meat of the matter.*
– PHRASES **easy meat** informal a person who is easily overcome or outwitted.
– ORIGIN Old English, 'food', 'article of food'.

meatball noun a ball of minced or chopped meat.

meat loaf noun minced or chopped meat baked in the shape of a loaf.

meaty adjective (**meatier, meatiest**) **1** resembling or full of meat. **2** fleshy or muscular. **3** full of substance or interest: *a meaty, scholarly book.*
– DERIVATIVES **meatiness** noun.

Mecca noun a place which attracts many people: *the area is a Mecca for skiers.*
– ORIGIN from the city of *Mecca* in Saudi Arabia, the holiest city for Muslims.

mechanic noun a skilled worker who repairs and maintains machinery.

– ORIGIN from Greek *mēkhanē* 'machine'.

mechanical adjective 1 relating to or operated by a machine or machinery. 2 done without thought; automatic. 3 relating to physical forces or motion.
– DERIVATIVES **mechanically** adverb.

mechanical drawing noun a scale drawing done with precision instruments.

mechanical engineering noun the branch of engineering concerned with the design, construction, and use of machines.

mechanics plural noun 1 (treated as sing.) the branch of study concerned with motion and forces producing motion. 2 machinery or working parts. 3 the practical aspects of something: *the mechanics of cello playing*.

mechanism noun 1 a piece of machinery. 2 the way in which something works or is brought about.

mechanistic adjective relating to the theory that all natural processes can be explained in purely physical terms.

mechanize (or **mechanise**) verb equip a process or place with machines or automatic devices.
– DERIVATIVES **mechanization** noun.

meconium /mi-koh-ni-uhm/ noun the dark green substance forming the first faeces of a newborn infant.
– ORIGIN Latin, 'poppy juice'.

med. abbreviation 1 medium. 2 informal medical.

medal noun a metal disc with an inscription or design, awarded for achievement or to mark an event.
– ORIGIN Latin *medalia* 'half a denarius'.

medallion noun 1 a piece of jewellery in the shape of a medal, worn as a pendant. 2 a decorative oval or circular painting, panel, or design. 3 a small flat round or oval cut of meat or fish.

medallist (US **medalist**) noun a person awarded a medal.

meddle verb interfere in something that is not one's concern.
– DERIVATIVES **meddler** noun **meddlesome** adjective.
– ORIGIN Old French.

media noun 1 television, radio, and newspapers as the means of mass communication. 2 plural of **MEDIUM**.

USAGE: The word media comes from the Latin plural of medium. In the normal sense 'television, radio, and newspapers', it often behaves as a collective noun (one referring to a group of people or things, such as **staff**), and can correctly be used with either a singular or a plural verb: *the media was informed* or *the media were informed*.

mediaeval adjective variant spelling of **MEDIEVAL**.

medial adjective situated in the middle.
– DERIVATIVES **medially** adverb.
– ORIGIN Latin *medialis*.

median adjective 1 technical situated in the middle. 2 having a value in the middle of a series of values arranged in order of magnitude. •noun 1 a median value. 2 Geometry a straight line drawn from one of the angles of a triangle to the middle of the opposite side.
– ORIGIN Latin *medianus*.

mediate verb 1 try to settle a dispute between other people or groups. 2 formal be a means of conveying or influencing: *the meaning of poems is mediated by the language employed*.
– DERIVATIVES **mediation** noun **mediator** noun.
– ORIGIN Latin *mediare* 'to place in the middle'.

medic noun informal, chiefly Brit. a doctor or medical student.

medical adjective relating to the science or practice of medicine. •noun an examination to assess a person's physical health.
– DERIVATIVES **medically** adverb.
– ORIGIN from Latin *medicus* 'physician'.

medical certificate noun a doctor's certificate confirming that a person is either unfit or fit to work.

medical officer noun a doctor in charge of the health services of a local authority or other organization.

medicament /muh-dik-uh-muhnt/ noun a medicine.

medicate verb 1 give medicine or a drug to someone. 2 (as adj. **medicated**) containing a medicinal substance.
– ORIGIN Latin *medicari* 'give remedies to'.

medication noun 1 a medicine or drug. 2 treatment with medicines.

medicinal adjective 1 having healing properties. 2 relating to medicines.
– DERIVATIVES **medicinally** adverb.

medicine noun 1 the science or practice of the treatment and prevention of disease. 2 a drug or other substance taken by mouth in order to treat or prevent disease.
– ORIGIN from Latin *medicus* 'physician'.

medicine ball noun a large, heavy solid ball thrown and caught for exercise.

medicine man noun (especially among North American Indians) a person believed to have magical powers of healing.

medico noun (pl. **medicos**) another term for **MEDIC**.

medieval (also **mediaeval**) adjective 1 relating to the Middle Ages. 2 informal outdated, primitive, or unsophisticated: *a country which is medieval in outlook*.
– DERIVATIVES **medievalize** (or **medievalise**) verb **medievally** adverb.
– ORIGIN from Latin *medium aevum* 'middle age'.

medievalist (also **medievalist**) noun a scholar of medieval history or literature.

medina /me-dee-nuh/ noun the old quarter of a North African town.
– ORIGIN Arabic, 'town'.

mediocre /mee-di-oh-ker/ adjective of only average quality; not very good.
– ORIGIN Latin *mediocris* 'of middle height or degree'.

mediocrity noun (pl. **mediocrities**) 1 the state of being average in quality. 2 a person of average ability and lacking originality.

meditate verb 1 focus one's mind for a time for spiritual purposes or for relaxation. 2 (**meditate on/about**) think carefully about.
– ORIGIN Latin *meditari* 'contemplate'.

meditation noun 1 the action or practice of

meditating. 2 a speech or piece of writing expressing considered thoughts on a subject.

meditative adjective involving or absorbed in focused thought or deep reflection.
– DERIVATIVES **meditatively** adverb.

Mediterranean adjective relating to the Mediterranean Sea or the countries around it.
– ORIGIN Latin *mediterraneus* 'inland'.

Mediterranean climate noun a climate that has warm, wet winters and calm, hot, dry summers, characteristic of the Mediterranean region and parts of California, South Africa, and SW Australia.

medium noun (pl. **media** or **mediums**) 1 a means by which something is expressed, communicated, or achieved: *using the latest technology as a medium for job creation.* 2 a substance through which a force or other influence is transmitted. 3 a form of storage for computer software, such as magnetic tape or disks. 4 a liquid with which pigments are mixed to make paint. 5 (pl. **mediums**) a person claiming to be able to communicate between the dead and the living. 6 the middle state between two extremes. 7 the substance in which an organism lives or is grown for scientific study. ▪ adjective between two extremes; average.
– ORIGIN Latin, 'middle'.

medium wave noun chiefly Brit. a radio wave of a frequency between 300 kilohertz and 3 megahertz.

medlar noun a small brown apple-like fruit.
– ORIGIN Old French *medler*.

medley noun (pl. **medleys**) 1 a varied mixture. 2 a collection of musical items performed as a continuous piece.
– ORIGIN Old French *medlee* 'melee'.

Médoc /**may**-dok/ noun (pl. same or **Médocs**)a red wine produced in the Médoc area of SW France.

medulla /mi-**dul**-luh/ noun 1 a distinct inner region of a body organ or tissue. 2 the soft internal tissue of a plant.
– ORIGIN Latin, 'pith or marrow'.

medulla oblongata /mi-dul-luh ob-long-**gah**-tuh/ noun the part of the spinal cord extending into the brain.

medusa /mi-**dyoo**-zuh/ noun (pl. **medusae** /mi-**dyoo**-zee/ or **medusas**) the free-swimming stage in the life cycle of a jellyfish or related organism.
– ORIGIN from *Medusa*, a gorgon in Greek mythology with snakes in her hair.

meek adjective quiet, gentle, and submissive.
– DERIVATIVES **meekly** adverb **meekness** noun.
– ORIGIN Old Norse, 'soft, gentle'.

meerkat noun a small southern African mongoose.
– ORIGIN Dutch, 'sea cat'.

meerschaum /**meer**-shuhm, meer-shawm/ noun 1 a soft white clay-like material. 2 a tobacco pipe with a bowl made from meerschaum.
– ORIGIN German, 'sea foam'.

meet[1] verb (past and past part. **met**) 1 come together with someone at the same place and time. 2 see or be introduced to someone for the first time. 3 touch or join: *the wall curved*

to meet the ceiling. 4 experience a situation. 5 (**meet with**) receive a reaction. 6 fulfil or satisfy a need or requirement. ▪ noun a meeting for races or (Brit.) fox-hunting.
– ORIGIN Old English.

meet[2] adjective old use suitable or proper.
– ORIGIN related to **METE**.

meeting noun 1 an organized gathering of people for a discussion or other purpose. 2 a situation in which people meet by chance or arrangement.

mega adjective informal 1 very large. 2 excellent.

mega- combining form 1 large: *megalith*. 2 referring to a factor of one million (10^6): *megabyte.*
– ORIGIN Greek *megas* 'great'.

megabucks plural noun informal a huge sum of money.

megabyte noun a unit of information stored in a computer equal to one million or (strictly) 1,048,576 bytes.

megaflop noun Computing a unit of computing speed equal to one million or (strictly) 1,048,576 floating-point operations per second.

megahertz noun (pl. same) a unit of frequency equal to one million hertz.

megalith noun a large stone that forms a prehistoric monument or part of one.
– DERIVATIVES **megalithic** adjective.

megalomania /meg-uh-luh-**may**-ni-uh/ noun 1 the false belief that one is very powerful or important. 2 a strong desire for power.
– DERIVATIVES **megalomaniac** noun & adjective.

megalopolis /meg-uh-**lop**-uh-lis/ noun a very large, densely populated city.
– ORIGIN from Greek *polis* 'city'.

megaphone noun a large cone-shaped device for amplifying the voice.

megapixel noun Computing a unit of graphic resolution equivalent to 2^{20} or (strictly) 1,048,576 pixels.

megapode /**meg**-uh-pohd/ noun a large Australasian or SE Asian bird that lives on the ground and builds a mound of plant debris to incubate its eggs.
– ORIGIN from Greek *pous* 'foot'.

megastar noun informal a very famous entertainer or sports player.

megaton noun a unit of explosive power equivalent to one million tons of TNT.

megavolt noun one million volts.

megawatt noun a unit of power equal to one million watts.

meiosis /my-**oh**-siss/ noun (pl. **meioses** /my-oh-seez/) Biology the division of a cell that results in four cells, each with half the number of chromosomes of the original cell. Compare with **MITOSIS**.
– DERIVATIVES **meiotic** adjective.
– ORIGIN Greek *meiōsis* 'lessening'.

Meissen /**my**-s'n/ noun fine porcelain produced at Meissen in Germany since 1710.

-meister /my-ster/ combining form referring to a person who is skilled or prominent in a particular area of activity: *a media-meister.*
– ORIGIN from German *Meister* 'master'.

meitnerium /myt-**neer**-i-uhm/ noun a very unstable chemical element made by high-

energy atomic collisions.
- ORIGIN named after the Swedish physicist Lise *Meitner*.

melamine /mel-uh-meen/ noun a hard, heat-resistant plastic used to coat surfaces.
- ORIGIN German *Melamin*, from AMINE.

melancholia /me-luhn-**koh**-li-uh/ noun dated severe depression.

melancholy noun deep and long-lasting sadness. • adjective feeling or causing sadness.
- DERIVATIVES **melancholic** adjective.
- ORIGIN Greek *melankholia*.

Melanesian adjective relating to the islands that make up Melanesia in the western Pacific. • noun a person from Melanesia.

melange /may-**lonzh**/ noun a varied mixture.
- ORIGIN French *mélange*.

melanin /mel-uh-nin/ noun a dark pigment in the hair and skin, responsible for tanning of skin exposed to sunlight.
- ORIGIN from Greek *melas* 'black'.

melanoma /mel-uh-**noh**-muh/ noun a form of skin cancer which develops in melanin-forming cells.

Melba toast noun very thin crisp toast.
- ORIGIN named after the Australian opera singer Dame Nellie *Melba*.

meld verb combine something with something else.
- ORIGIN perhaps a blend of MELT and WELD.

melee /mel-ay/ noun 1 a confused fight. 2 a confused crowd of people.
- ORIGIN French *mêlée*.

mellifluous /mel-**lif**-luu-uhsss/ adjective pleasingly smooth and musical to hear.
- DERIVATIVES **mellifluously** adverb **mellifluousness** noun.
- ORIGIN from Latin *mel* 'honey' + *fluere* 'to flow'.

mellotron noun an electronic keyboard instrument in which each key controls the playback of a single pre-recorded musical sound.
- ORIGIN from MELLOW + -*tron*, from ELECTRONIC.

mellow adjective 1 pleasantly smooth or soft in sound, taste, or colour. 2 relaxed and good-humoured. • verb make or become mellow.
- ORIGIN perhaps related to MEAL².

melodeon /mel-**oh**-di-uhn/ noun 1 a small accordion. 2 a small organ similar to the harmonium.

melodic /muh-**lod**-ik/ adjective 1 relating to melody. 2 pleasant-sounding.
- DERIVATIVES **melodically** adverb.

melodious /mi-**loh**-di-uhss/ adjective pleasant-sounding; tuneful.

melodrama noun 1 a play full of exciting events and with exaggerated characters and emotions. 2 exaggerated or extreme behaviour or events.
- ORIGIN first referring to a play interspersed with songs and music: from Greek *melos* 'music' + French *drame* 'drama'.

melodramatic adjective overdramatic or exaggerated: *he flung the door open with a melodramatic flourish*.
- DERIVATIVES **melodramatically** adverb.

melody noun (pl. **melodies**) 1 a sequence of notes that is musically satisfying; a tune. 2 the

arrangement of musical notes to form a tune. 3 the main part in harmonized music.
- ORIGIN from Greek *melos* 'song'.

melon noun a large round fruit with sweet pulpy flesh and many seeds.
- ORIGIN Greek *mēlopepōn*.

melt verb 1 make or become liquid by heating. 2 gradually disappear or disperse: *most of the crowd had melted away*. 3 become or make more tender or loving.
- ORIGIN Old English.

meltdown noun 1 a disastrous collapse: *the coming economic meltdown*. 2 an accident in a nuclear reactor in which the fuel overheats and melts the reactor core.

melting point noun the temperature at which a solid will melt.

melting pot noun a place where different peoples, ideas, or styles are mixed together.
- PHRASES **in the melting pot** Brit. in a process of change and with an uncertain outcome.

meltwater (also **meltwaters**) noun water formed by the melting of snow and ice.

member noun 1 a person or organization belonging to a group or society. 2 a part of a complex structure. 3 old use a part of the body, especially a limb.
- ORIGIN Latin *membrum* 'limb'.

membership noun 1 the fact of being a member of a group. 2 the members or the number of members in a group.

membrane noun 1 a skin-like structure that lines, connects, or covers a cell or part of the body. 2 a thin pliable sheet of material forming a barrier or lining.
- DERIVATIVES **membraneous** adjective **membranous** adjective.
- ORIGIN Latin *membrum* 'limb'.

memento noun (pl. **mementos** or **mementoes**) an object kept as a reminder of a person or event.
- ORIGIN Latin, 'remember!'

memento mori /mi-men-toh **mor**-i/ noun (pl. same) an object kept as a reminder that death is inevitable.
- ORIGIN Latin, 'remember (that you have) to die'.

memo noun (pl. **memos**) a memorandum.

memoir /mem-war/ noun 1 a historical account or biography written from personal knowledge. 2 (**memoirs**) an account written by a public figure of their life and experiences.
- ORIGIN French *mémoire* 'memory'.

memorabilia /mem-uh-ruh-**bil**-i-uh/ plural noun objects kept or collected because of their associations with memorable people or events.

memorable adjective worth remembering or easily remembered.
- DERIVATIVES **memorably** adverb.

memorandum noun (pl. **memoranda** or **memorandums**) 1 a note sent from one person to another in an organization. 2 a note recording something for future use.
- ORIGIN Latin, 'something to be brought to mind'.

memorial noun an object or structure established in memory of a person or event. • adjective in memory of someone.
- DERIVATIVES **memorialist** noun **memorialize**

(or **memorialise**) verb.

memorize (or **memorise**) verb learn something by heart.

memory noun (pl. **memories**) 1 the faculty by which the mind stores and remembers information. 2 a person or thing remembered. 3 the length of time over which people's memory extends. 4 a computer's equipment or capacity for storing information.
- PHRASES **in memory of** so as to honour and remind people of a dead person.
- ORIGIN Latin *memoria*.

memsahib /mem-sahb, mem-suh-heeb/ noun dated (in the Indian subcontinent) a respectful form of address for a married white woman.
- ORIGIN from an Indian pronunciation of *ma'am* + SAHIB.

men plural of MAN.

menace noun 1 a dangerous or harmful person or thing. 2 a threatening quality. •verb put someone or something at risk; threaten.
- DERIVATIVES **menacing** adjective.
- ORIGIN from Latin *minax* 'threatening'.

ménage à trois /may-nahzh ah trwah/ noun an arrangement in which a married couple and the lover of one of them live together.
- ORIGIN French, 'household of three'.

menagerie /muh-**naj**-uh-ri/ noun a collection of wild animals kept in captivity for showing to the public.
- ORIGIN French.

menaquinone /men-uh-**kwin**-ohn/ noun a member of the vitamin K group, a compound produced by bacteria in the intestines, essential for blood-clotting.
- ORIGIN from its chemical name.

mend verb 1 restore something to its correct or working condition. 2 improve an unpleasant situation. •noun a repair in a material.
- PHRASES **mend fences** resolve a disagreement with someone. **on the mend** improving in health or condition.
- DERIVATIVES **mendable** adjective **mender** noun.
- ORIGIN shortening of AMEND.

mendacious /men-**day**-shuss/ adjective lying; untruthful.
- DERIVATIVES **mendaciously** adverb **mendacity** noun.
- ORIGIN Latin *mendax* 'lying'.

mendelevium /men-duh-**lee**-vi-uhm/ noun a very unstable chemical element made by high-energy collisions.
- ORIGIN named after the Russian chemist Dimitri *Mendeleev*.

Mendelian /men-**dee**-li-uhn/ adjective relating to the theory of heredity based on characteristics transmitted as genes, as developed by the Austrian botanist G. J. Mendel.
- DERIVATIVES **Mendelism** noun.

mendicant /**men**-di-kuhnt/ adjective 1 living by begging. 2 (of a religious order) originally dependent on charitable donations. •noun 1 a beggar. 2 a member of a mendicant religious order.
- ORIGIN from Latin *mendicus* 'beggar'.

menfolk plural noun the men of a family or community.

menhir /men-heer/ noun a tall upright stone erected as a monument in prehistoric times.
- ORIGIN from Breton *men* 'stone' + *hir* 'long'.

menial adjective (of work) of low status and requiring little skill. •noun a person with a menial job.
- ORIGIN Old French.

meninges /mi-**nin**-jeez/ plural noun (sing. **meninx**) the three membranes that enclose the brain and spinal cord.
- ORIGIN from Greek *mēninx* 'membrane'.

meningitis /men-in-**jy**-tiss/ noun a serious disease in which the meninges around the brain and spinal cord become inflamed owing to infection with a bacterium or virus.

meniscus /muh-**niss**-kuhss/ noun (pl. **menisci** /muh-**niss**-I/) 1 Physics the curved upper surface of a liquid in a tube. 2 a thin lens that curves outwards on one side and inwards on the other.
- ORIGIN Greek *mēniskos* 'crescent'.

menopause noun the ending of menstruation or the period in a woman's life (typically between 45 and 50) when this occurs.
- DERIVATIVES **menopausal** adjective.
- ORIGIN from Greek *mēn* 'month' + PAUSE.

menorah /mi-**nor**-uh/ noun a candelabrum used in Jewish worship, typically with eight branches.
- ORIGIN Hebrew.

menses /**men**-seez/ plural noun blood discharged from the womb at menstruation.
- ORIGIN Latin, plural of *mensis* 'month'.

menstrual adjective relating to menstruation.
- ORIGIN Latin *menstrualis*.

menstruate verb (of a woman) discharge blood from the lining of the womb each month.

menstruation noun the process in a woman of discharging blood from the lining of the womb each month from puberty until the menopause, except during pregnancy.

mensuration noun 1 the measurement of something. 2 the part of geometry concerned with measuring lengths, areas, and volumes.
- ORIGIN from Latin *mensurare* 'to measure'.

menswear noun clothes for men.

mental adjective 1 relating to or done by the mind. 2 relating to disorders or illnesses of the mind. 3 informal mad.
- DERIVATIVES **mentally** adverb.
- ORIGIN from Latin *mens* 'mind'.

> USAGE: The use of **mental** in sense 2 (as in **mental hospital**) is now regarded as old-fashioned, even offensive, and has been largely replaced by **psychiatric**.

mental age noun a person's mental ability expressed as the age at which an average person reaches the same ability.

mental block noun an inability to remember something.

mental handicap noun a condition in which a person's intellectual ability is underdeveloped and prevents them functioning normally in society.
- DERIVATIVES **mentally handicapped** adverb.

m

USAGE: In Britain, the terms **mental handicap** and **mentally handicapped** have been largely replaced in official situations by the term **learning difficulties**.

mentalist noun Brit. informal an eccentric or mad person.

mentality noun (pl. **mentalities**) a typical way of thinking of a person or group.

menthol noun a minty substance found chiefly in peppermint oil, used as a flavouring and in decongestants.
– DERIVATIVES **mentholated** adjective.
– ORIGIN Latin *mentha* 'mint'.

mention verb **1** refer to something briefly. **2** refer to someone as being noteworthy: *he is regularly mentioned as a possible Cabinet minister.* • noun **1** a reference to someone or something. **2** a formal acknowledgement of something noteworthy.
– PHRASES **be mentioned in dispatches** Brit. be praised for one's actions by name in an official military report.
– ORIGIN Latin.

mentor noun **1** an experienced and trusted adviser. **2** an experienced person in an organization or educational institution who trains and advises new employees or students.
– ORIGIN from *Mentor*, the adviser of Telemachus in Homer's *Odyssey*.

menu noun **1** a list of dishes available in a restaurant. **2** the food to be served at a meal. **3** a list of commands or facilities displayed on a computer screen.
– ORIGIN French, 'detailed list'.

meow noun & verb variant spelling of MIAOW.

MEP abbreviation Member of the European Parliament.

Mephistophelian /me-fis-to-**fee**-li-uhn/ (also **Mephistophelean**) adjective wicked or evil.
– ORIGIN from *Mephistopheles*, an evil spirit to whom Faust, in the German legend, sold his soul.

mephitic /mi-**fi**-tik/ adjective literary smelling very unpleasant.
– ORIGIN from Latin *mephitis* 'foul vapour'.

mercantile adjective relating to trade or commerce.
– ORIGIN from Italian *mercante* 'merchant'.

Mercator projection noun a world map projection made on to a cylinder in such a way that all parallels of latitude have the same length as the equator.
– ORIGIN from *Mercator*, Latinized name of the Flemish geographer G. Kremer.

mercenary adjective motivated chiefly by the desire to make money. • noun (pl. **mercenaries**) a professional soldier hired to serve in a foreign army.
– ORIGIN from Latin *mercenarius* 'hireling'.

mercerized (or **mercerised**) adjective (of cotton) chemically treated to make it strong and shiny.
– ORIGIN named after J. *Mercer*, said to have invented the process.

merchandise noun /**mer**-chuhn-dyss/ goods for sale. • verb /**mer**-chuhn-dyz/ (or **merchandize**) promote the sale of goods.

– DERIVATIVES **merchandiser** noun.
– ORIGIN from Old French *marchand* 'merchant'.

merchandising noun **1** products used to promote a particular film, pop group, etc. **2** the promotion of goods in shops and other retail outlets.

merchant noun **1** a wholesale trader. **2** N. Amer. & Scottish a retail trader. **3** informal, derogatory a person fond of a particular activity: *a speed merchant.* • adjective (of sailors or shipping) involved with commerce.
– ORIGIN Old French *marchant*.

merchantable adjective suitable for sale.

merchant bank noun a bank dealing in commercial loans and investment.

merchantman noun (pl. **merchantmen**) a ship carrying merchandise.

merchant navy (N. Amer. **merchant marine**) noun a country's commercial shipping.

merciful adjective **1** showing compassion and forgiveness. **2** giving relief from suffering: *her death was a merciful release.*

mercifully adverb **1** in a merciful way. **2** to one's great relief; fortunately.

merciless adjective showing no mercy.
– DERIVATIVES **mercilessly** adverb **mercilessness** noun.

mercurial /mer-**kyoor**-i-uhl/ adjective **1** tending to change mood suddenly. **2** relating to the element mercury.
– ORIGIN Latin *mercurialis* 'relating to the god Mercury'.

Mercury noun a small planet that is the closest to the sun in the solar system.
– DERIVATIVES **Mercurian** adjective.

mercury noun a heavy silvery-white liquid metallic element used in some thermometers and barometers.
– DERIVATIVES **mercuric** adjective **mercurous** adjective.
– ORIGIN from *Mercury*, the Roman messenger of the gods.

mercy noun (pl. **mercies**) **1** compassion or forgiveness shown towards someone in one's power to punish or harm. **2** something to be grateful for. • adjective done from a desire to relieve suffering: *a mercy killing.* • exclamation old use used to express surprise or fear.
– PHRASES **at the mercy of** completely in the power of.
– ORIGIN Latin *merces* 'reward, pity'.

mere[1] adjective **1** that is nothing more than what is specified: *questions that cannot be answered by mere mortals.* **2** (**the merest**) the smallest or slightest.
– ORIGIN Latin *merus* 'pure, undiluted'.

mere[2] noun literary (except in place names) a lake or pond.
– ORIGIN Old English.

merely adverb just; only.

merengue /muh-**reng**-gay/ noun **1** a Caribbean style of dance music typically in duple and triple time. **2** a dance style associated with merengue, with alternating long and short stiff-legged steps.
– ORIGIN probably American Spanish.

meretricious /me-ri-**tri**-shuhss/ adjective appearing attractive but having no real value.

– ORIGIN from Latin *meretrix* 'prostitute'.

merganser /mer-**gan**-zer/ noun a fish-eating diving duck with a long, thin jagged and hooked bill.
– ORIGIN from Latin *mergus* 'diver' + *anser* 'goose'.

merge verb **1** combine or be combined into a whole: *the merchant bank merged with another.* **2** blend gradually into something else.
– ORIGIN Latin *mergere* 'to dip, plunge'.

merger noun a merging of two things, especially companies, into one.

merguez /mer-**gez**/ noun (pl. same) a spicy beef and lamb sausage coloured with red peppers, originally made in North Africa.
– ORIGIN French, from Arabic.

meridian noun **1** a circle of constant longitude passing through a given place on the earth's surface and the poles. **2** any of twelve pathways in the body, believed by practitioners of Chinese medicine to be a channel for vital energy.
– ORIGIN from Latin *meridianum* 'noon' (because the sun crosses a meridian at noon).

meridional /muh-**rid**-i-uh-nuhl/ adjective **1** relating to the south, especially southern Europe. **2** relating to a meridian.

meringue /muh-**rang**/ noun **1** beaten egg whites and sugar baked until crisp. **2** a small cake made of meringue.
– ORIGIN French.

merino /muh-**ree**-noh/ noun (pl. **merinos**) **1** a breed of sheep with long, fine wool. **2** a soft woollen or wool-and-cotton material.
– ORIGIN Spanish.

meristem /**me**-ri-stem/ noun a region of plant tissue consisting of actively dividing cells.
– ORIGIN from Greek *meristos* 'divisible'.

merit noun **1** the quality of being particularly good; excellence. **2** a good point or quality. • verb (**merits**, **meriting**, **merited**) deserve or be worthy of: *offences regarded as serious enough to merit dismissal.*
– ORIGIN Latin *meritum* 'due reward'.

meritocracy /mer-i-**tok**-ruh-si/ noun (pl. **meritocracies**) a society in which power is held by the people with the greatest ability.
– DERIVATIVES **meritocrat** noun **meritocratic** adjective.

meritorious adjective deserving reward or praise.

merlin noun a small dark falcon.
– ORIGIN Old French *merilun*.

Merlot /**mer**-loh, **mer**-lot/ noun a red wine made from a variety of grape originally from the Bordeaux region of France.
– ORIGIN French.

mermaid noun a mythical sea creature with a woman's head and trunk and a fish's tail.
– ORIGIN from MERE² (in the former sense 'sea') + MAID.

merman noun (pl. **mermen**) a mythical sea creature with the head and trunk of a man and a fish's tail.

merriment noun cheerfulness and fun.

merry adjective (**merrier**, **merriest**) **1** cheerful and lively. **2** informal slightly drunk.
– PHRASES **make merry** enjoy oneself with other people by dancing and drinking.

– DERIVATIVES **merrily** adverb **merriness** noun.
– ORIGIN Old English, 'pleasing, delightful'.

merry-go-round noun **1** a revolving machine with model horses or cars on which people ride for amusement. **2** a continuous cycle of activities or events.

merrymaking noun cheerful celebration and fun.

mesa /**may**-suh/ noun an isolated flat-topped hill with steep sides.
– ORIGIN Spanish, 'table'.

mésalliance /me-**zal**-i-uhns/ noun a marriage to a person of a lower social class.
– ORIGIN French, 'misalliance'.

mescal noun **1** an alcoholic spirit distilled from a type of agave (plant). **2** a peyote cactus.
– ORIGIN Nahuatl.

mescaline /**mes**-kuh-lin, **mes**-kuh-leen/ (also **mescalin**) noun a drug which causes hallucinations, made from the peyote cactus.

Mesdames plural of MADAME.

Mesdemoiselles plural of MADEMOISELLE.

mesembryanthemum /mi-zem-bri-**an**-thi-muhm/ noun a succulent plant with brightly coloured daisy-like flowers.
– ORIGIN from Greek *mesēmbria* 'noon' + *anthemon* 'flower'.

mesh noun **1** material made of a network of wire or thread. **2** the spacing of the strands of a net. **3** a complex or constricting situation: *people caught in the mesh of history.* • verb **1** become entangled or entwined. **2** (**mesh with**) be in harmony with. **3** (of a gearwheel) lock together with another.
– ORIGIN probably from Old English.

mesmeric adjective completely capturing a person's attention so that they become unaware of their surroundings; hypnotic.
– DERIVATIVES **mesmerically** adverb.

mesmerism noun historical a therapeutic technique involving hypnotism.
– DERIVATIVES **mesmerist** noun.
– ORIGIN named after the Austrian physician Franz A. *Mesmer.*

mesmerize (or **mesmerise**) verb capture a person's attention completely.

Mesolithic /me-soh-**lith**-ik, me-zoh-**lith**-ik/ adjective relating to the middle part of the Stone Age, between the end of the glacial period and the beginnings of agriculture.
– ORIGIN from Greek *mesos* 'middle' + *lithos* 'stone'.

meson /**mee**-zon, **me**-zon/ noun Physics a subatomic particle that is intermediate in mass between an electron and a proton.
– ORIGIN from Greek *mesos* 'middle'.

Mesopotamian /mess-uh-puh-**tay**-mi-uhn/ adjective relating to Mesopotamia, an ancient region of what is now Iraq. • noun a person from Mesopotamia.

mesosphere noun the region of the earth's atmosphere above the stratosphere and below the thermosphere.
– ORIGIN from Greek *mesos* 'middle'.

Mesozoic /mes-oh-**zoh**-ik/ adjective Geology relating to the era between the Palaeozoic and Cenozoic eras, about 245 to 65 million years ago, with evidence of the first mammals, birds, and flowering plants.

m

– ORIGIN from Greek *mesos* 'middle' + *zōion* 'animal'.

mesquite /mes-keet, me-skeet/ noun a spiny tree of the south-western US and Mexico, yielding wood, medicinal products, and edible pods.
– ORIGIN Mexican Spanish *mezquite*.

mess noun 1 a dirty or untidy state. 2 a state of confusion or difficulty. 3 euphemistic a dog's or cat's excrement. 4 a place providing meals and recreational facilities for members of the armed forces. 5 a portion of semi-solid food.
● verb 1 make something untidy or dirty. 2 (mess about/around) behave in a silly or playful way. 3 (mess someone about/around) Brit. informal cause someone problems. 4 mess something up informal handle something badly. 5 (mess with) informal meddle with. 6 eat in an armed forces' mess.
– ORIGIN Old French *mes* 'portion of food'.

message noun 1 a spoken, written, or electronic communication. 2 a significant point or central theme of a novel, speech, etc.
● verb send a message to someone, especially by email.
– PHRASES **get the message** informal understand what is meant. **on** (or **off**) **message** (of a politician) following (or not following) the official party line.
– ORIGIN Old French.

Messeigneurs plural of **Monseigneur**.

messenger noun a person who carries a message.

messenger RNA noun the form of RNA in which genetic information transcribed from DNA is transferred to a ribosome.

messiah noun 1 (the Messiah) the person sent by God to save the Jewish people, as prophesied in the Hebrew Bible (the Old Testament). 2 (the Messiah) Jesus regarded by Christians as the Messiah of the Hebrew prophecies. 3 a leader regarded as a saviour of a country, group, etc.
– ORIGIN Hebrew, 'anointed'.

messianic /mess-i-an-ik/ adjective 1 relating to the Messiah. 2 passionate or fervent: *messianic zeal*.
– DERIVATIVES **messianism** noun.

Messieurs plural of **Monsieur**.

Messrs plural of **Mr**.
– ORIGIN abbreviation of **Messieurs**.

messy adjective (messier, messiest) 1 untidy or dirty. 2 confused and difficult to deal with.
– DERIVATIVES **messily** adverb **messiness** noun.

mestizo /me-stee-zoh/ noun (pl. **mestizos**; fem. **mestiza**, pl. **mestizas**) a Latin American of mixed race, especially one of Spanish and American Indian parentage.
– ORIGIN Spanish, 'mixed'.

Met abbreviation informal 1 meteorological. 2 (the Met) the Metropolitan Police in London.

met past and past participle of **meet**[1].

meta- (also **met-** before a vowel or h) combining form forming words referring to: 1 a change of position or condition: *metamorphosis*. 2 position behind, after, or beyond: *metacarpus*. 3 something of a higher or second-order kind: *metalanguage*.
– ORIGIN from Greek *meta* 'with, across, after'.

metabolism /mi-tab-uh-li-z'm/ noun the chemical processes in a living organism by which food is used for tissue growth or energy production.
– DERIVATIVES **metabolic** adjective.
– ORIGIN from Greek *metabolē* 'change'.

metabolize (or **metabolise**) /mi-tab-uh-lyz/ verb (of the body or an organ) process a substance by metabolism.

metacarpus /met-uh-kar-puhss/ noun (pl. **metacarpi** /met-uh-kar-pi/) the group of five bones of the hand between the wrist and the fingers.
– DERIVATIVES **metacarpal** adjective & noun.
– ORIGIN Greek *metakarpion*.

metal noun 1 a solid material which is typically hard, shiny, and able to be shaped and which can conduct electricity and heat, e.g. iron, copper, and gold. 2 (also **road metal**) broken stone used in road-making.
– ORIGIN Greek *metallon* 'mine, metal'.

metalanguage noun a form of language used to describe or analyse another language.

metal detector noun an electronic device that gives a signal when it is close to metal.

metalled (US **metaled**) adjective 1 made from or coated with metal. 2 Brit. surfaced with road metal.

metallic adjective 1 relating to or resembling metal. 2 (of sound) sharp and ringing.
– DERIVATIVES **metallically** adverb.

metalliferous adjective containing or producing metal.

metallize (or **metallise**, US also **metalize**) verb 1 coat something with a layer of metal. 2 make something metallic.

metallography /met-uh-log-ruh-fi/ noun the descriptive science of the structure and properties of metals.
– DERIVATIVES **metallographic** adjective.

metallurgy /mi-tal-ler-ji, met-uh-ler-ji/ noun the scientific study of the properties, production, and purification of metals.
– DERIVATIVES **metallurgical** adjective **metallurgist** noun.

metalwork noun 1 the art of making things from metal. 2 objects made from metal.

metamorphic adjective (of rock) having been changed by heat, pressure, or other natural agencies.
– DERIVATIVES **metamorphism** noun.

metamorphose /met-uh-mor-fohz/ verb 1 (of an insect or amphibian) undergo metamorphosis. 2 change completely in form or nature.

metamorphosis /met-uh-mor-fuh-siss/ noun (pl. **metamorphoses** /met-uh-mor-fuh-seez/) 1 the transformation of an insect or amphibian from an immature form or larva to an adult form in distinct stages. 2 a change in form or nature.
– ORIGIN Greek, from *metamorphoun* 'transform, change shape'.

metaphor noun 1 a figure of speech in which a word or phrase is used of something to which it does not literally apply (e.g. *the long arm of the law*). 2 a thing seen as symbolic of something else.
– ORIGIN from Greek *metapherein* 'to transfer'.

metaphorical (also **metaphoric**) adjective relating to or making use of metaphors.
– DERIVATIVES **metaphorically** adverb.

metaphysic noun a system of metaphysics.

metaphysical adjective **1** relating to metaphysics. **2** beyond physical matter: *the metaphysical battle between Good and Evil.* **3** referring to a group of 17th-century English poets (in particular John Donne, George Herbert, Andrew Marvell, and Henry Vaughan) known for their complex imagery.
– DERIVATIVES **metaphysically** adverb.

metaphysics plural noun (usu. treated as sing.) **1** philosophy concerned with abstract ideas such as the nature of existence or of truth and knowledge. **2** abstract theory with no basis in reality.
– DERIVATIVES **metaphysician** noun.
– ORIGIN from Greek *ta meta ta phusika* 'the things after the Physics', referring to the sequence of subjects treated in the works of Aristotle.

metastasis /mi-**tas**-tuh-siss/ noun (pl. **metastases** /mi-**tas**-tuh-seez/) the development of secondary tumours elsewhere in the body from the primary site of cancer.
– ORIGIN Greek, 'removal or change'.

metatarsal noun any of the bones of the foot.

metatarsus noun (pl. **metatarsi**) the group of bones in the foot, between the ankle and the toes.

metazoan /me-tuh-**zoh**-uhn/ noun an animal other than a protozoan or sponge.
– ORIGIN from META- + Greek *zōion* 'animal'.

mete verb (**mete something out**) deal out justice, punishment, etc. to someone.
– ORIGIN Old English, 'measure'.

meteor /**mee**-ti-or/ noun a small body of matter from outer space that glows as a result of friction with the earth's atmosphere and appears as a shooting star.
– ORIGIN from Greek *meteōros* 'lofty'.

meteoric adjective **1** relating to meteors or meteorites. **2** (of change or development) very rapid: *her meteoric rise to the top of her profession.*

meteorite noun a piece of rock or metal that has fallen to the earth from space.

meteoroid noun a small body that would become a meteor if it entered the earth's atmosphere.

meteorology /mee-ti-uh-**rol**-uh-ji/ noun the study of atmospheric processes and conditions, especially for weather forecasting.
– DERIVATIVES **meteorological** adjective **meteorologist** noun.

meter[1] noun a device that measures and records the quantity, degree, or rate of something. •verb measure the quantity, degree, or rate of something with a meter.
– ORIGIN from METE.

USAGE: Do not confuse **meter** with **metre**. A **meter** is a device that measures and records something (*a gas meter*), while a **metre** is a unit of measurement or the rhythm of a poem.

meter[2] noun US spelling of METRE[1], METRE[2].

-meter combining form **1** in names of measuring instruments: *thermometer.* **2** in nouns referring to lines of poetry with a specified number of metrical feet: *hexameter.*
– ORIGIN from Greek *metron* 'measure'.

methadone noun a powerful painkiller, used as a substitute for morphine and heroin in the treatment of addiction.
– ORIGIN from its chemical name.

methamphetamine /meth-am-**fet**-uh-meen/ noun a drug related to amphetamine, used illegally as a stimulant.

methane /**mee**-thayn/ noun a colourless, odourless flammable gas which is the main constituent of natural gas.
– ORIGIN from METHYL.

methanol noun a poisonous flammable alcohol, used to make methylated spirit.

methedrine /meth-uh-drin/ noun (trademark in the UK) another term for METHAMPHETAMINE.

methinks verb (past **methought**) old use or humorous it seems to me.
– ORIGIN Old English.

method noun **1** a way of doing something. **2** the quality of being well organized and systematic in one's thinking and behaviour.
– ORIGIN Greek *methodos* 'pursuit of knowledge'.

method acting noun an acting technique in which an actor tries to identify completely with a character's emotions.

methodical (also **methodic**) adjective well organized and systematic.
– DERIVATIVES **methodically** adverb.

Methodist noun a member of a Christian Protestant denomination originating in the 18th century and based on the ideas of Charles and John Wesley. •adjective relating to Methodists or their beliefs.
– DERIVATIVES **Methodism** noun.
– ORIGIN probably from the idea of following a specified 'method' of Bible study.

methodology noun (pl. **methodologies**) a system of methods used in a particular activity or area of study.
– DERIVATIVES **methodological** adjective.

methought past of METHINKS.

meths noun Brit. informal methylated spirit.

Methuselah /mi-**thoo**-zuh-luh/ noun **1** humorous a very old person. **2** (**methuselah**) a wine bottle of eight times the standard size.
– ORIGIN named after the biblical patriarch *Methuselah,* said to have lived for 969 years (Book of Genesis, chapter 5).

methyl /**mee**-thyl/ noun Chemistry the radical –CH₃, derived from methane.
– ORIGIN from Greek *methu* 'wine' + *hulē* 'wood'.

methyl alcohol noun methanol.

methylate verb **1** mix or impregnate something with methanol or methylated spirit. **2** Chemistry introduce a methyl group into a molecule or compound.
– DERIVATIVES **methylation** noun.

methylated spirit (also **methylated spirits**) noun alcohol for use as a solvent or fuel, made unfit for drinking by the addition of methanol and a violet dye.

metical /me-ti-kal/ noun (pl. **meticais** /me-ti-**kysh**/) the basic unit of money of Mozambique.
– ORIGIN Portuguese.

m

meticulous adjective very careful and precise.
- DERIVATIVES **meticulously** adverb **meticulousness** noun.
- ORIGIN Latin *meticulosus* 'fearful'.

métier /**may**-ti-ay/ noun **1** a profession or occupation. **2** an occupation or activity that someone is good at.
- ORIGIN French.

metonym /met-uh-nim/ noun a word or phrase used as a substitute for something with which it is closely associated, e.g. *Washington* for the US government.
- DERIVATIVES **metonymic** adjective **metonymy** noun.
- ORIGIN Greek *metōnumia* 'change of name'.

me-too adjective informal **1** (of a product) designed to imitate or compete with another which has already been successful: *me-too drugs*. **2** (of a person or course of action) adopting the views or policies of another person, especially a competitor.

metre[1] (US **meter**) noun the basic unit of length in the metric system, equal to 100 centimetres (approx. 39.37 inches).
- ORIGIN French, from Greek *metron* 'measure'.

USAGE: On the confusion of **metre** and **meter**, see the note at **METER**[1].

metre[2] (US **meter**) noun **1** the rhythm of a piece of poetry, determined by the number and length of feet in a line. **2** the basic rhythmic pattern of a piece of music.
- ORIGIN Greek *metron* 'measure'.

metric adjective relating to the metric system.

metrical adjective **1** relating to or composed in poetic metre. **2** relating to measurement.
- DERIVATIVES **metrically** adverb.

metricate verb convert something to a metric system of measurement.
- DERIVATIVES **metrication** noun.

metric system noun the decimal measuring system based on the metre, litre, and gram as units of length, capacity, and weight or mass.

metric ton (also **metric tonne**) noun a unit of weight equal to 1,000 kilograms (2,205 lb).

metro noun (pl. **metros**) an underground railway system in a city, especially Paris.
- ORIGIN French, from *Chemin de Fer Métropolitain* 'Metropolitan Railway'.

metronome noun a musicians' device that marks time at a selected rate by giving a regular tick.
- DERIVATIVES **metronomic** adjective.
- ORIGIN from Greek *metron* 'measure' + *nomos* 'law'.

metropolis /mi-trop-uh-liss/ noun the main city of a country or region.
- ORIGIN Greek, from *mētēr* 'mother' + *polis* 'city'.

metropolitan adjective **1** relating to a large or capital city. **2** relating to the parent state of a colony. **3** Christian Church relating to a metropolitan or his see. • noun **1** a person living in a large or capital city. **2** Christian Church a bishop having authority over the bishops of a province.

metropolitan county noun (in England) each of six units of local government centred on a large urban area (established in 1974, although their councils were abolished in

1986).

metrosexual noun informal a heterosexual urban man who enjoys shopping, fashion, and similar interests usually associated with women or homosexual men.
- ORIGIN from **METROPOLITAN** and **HETEROSEXUAL**.

mettle noun spirit and strength in the face of difficulty.
- PHRASES **be on one's mettle** be ready to show one's ability or courage.
- ORIGIN variant spelling of **METAL**.

meunière /mern-yair/ adjective (after a noun) cooked or served in lightly browned butter with lemon juice and parsley: *sole meunière*.
- ORIGIN from French *à la meunière* 'in the manner of a miller's wife'.

mew[1] verb (of a cat or gull) make a characteristic high-pitched crying noise. • noun a high-pitched crying noise.
- ORIGIN imitating the sound.

mew[2] noun Falconry a cage or building for trained hawks, especially while they are moulting.
• verb (**mew someone up**) keep someone confined in a place.
- ORIGIN from Old French *muer* 'to moult'.

mewl verb **1** cry feebly. **2** make a high-pitched crying noise.
- ORIGIN imitating the sound.

mews noun (pl. same) Brit. a row of houses or flats converted from stables in a small street or square.
- ORIGIN from **MEW**[2]: first referring to the royal stables on the site of the hawk mews at Charing Cross, London.

Mexican noun a person from Mexico. • adjective relating to Mexico.

Mexican wave noun an effect resembling a moving wave produced by successive sections of a stadium crowd standing, raising their arms, lowering them, and sitting down again.
- ORIGIN because first seen at the 1986 football World Cup in Mexico City.

meze /may-zay/ (also **mezze**) noun (pl. same or **mezes**) (in Turkish, Greek, and Middle Eastern cookery) a selection of hot and cold hors d'oeuvres.
- ORIGIN Turkish, 'appetizer'.

mezzanine /mez-zuh-neen, mets-uh-neen/ noun **1** a low storey between two others, typically between the ground and first floors of a building. **2** N. Amer. the lowest balcony of a theatre or the front rows of the balcony.
- ORIGIN from Italian *mezzano* 'middle'.

mezzo /met-zoh/ (also **mezzo-soprano**) noun (pl. **mezzos**) a female singer with a voice pitched between soprano and contralto.
- ORIGIN Italian, 'half, middle'.

mezzotint /met-soh-tint/ noun a print made from an engraved metal plate, the surface of which has been scraped and polished to give areas of shade and light respectively.
- ORIGIN from Italian *mezzo* 'half' + *tinto* 'tint'.

MF abbreviation medium frequency.

Mg symbol the chemical element magnesium.

mg abbreviation milligram(s).

Mgr abbreviation **1** (**mgr**) manager. **2** Monseigneur. **3** Monsignor.

MHR abbreviation (in the US and Australia) Member of the House of Representatives.

MHz abbreviation megahertz.

MI abbreviation Michigan.

mi noun variant spelling of **ME**[2].

mi. abbreviation mile(s).

MI5 abbreviation Military Intelligence section 5, the former name for the UK government agency responsible for internal security and counter-espionage on British territory (now officially named the Security Service).

MI6 abbreviation Military Intelligence section 6, the former name for the UK government agency responsible for counter-espionage overseas (now officially named the Secret Intelligence Service).

MIA abbreviation N. Amer. missing in action.

miaow (also **meow**) noun the characteristic cry of a cat. ●verb make a miaow.
– ORIGIN imitating the sound.

miasma /mi-**az**-muh, my-**az**-muh/ noun literary
1 an unpleasant or unhealthy smell or vapour.
2 an oppressive or unpleasant atmosphere: *a miasma of despair.*
– ORIGIN Greek, 'defilement'.

mic /rhymes with bike/ noun informal a microphone.

mica /my-kuh/ noun a mineral found as minute shiny scales in granite and other rocks.
– ORIGIN Latin, 'crumb'.

mice plural of **MOUSE**.

Michaelmas /mi-k'l-muhss/ noun the day of the Christian festival of St Michael, 29 September.
– ORIGIN Old English, 'Saint Michael's Mass'.

Michaelmas daisy noun a garden plant with numerous pinkish-lilac daisy-like flowers which bloom in autumn.

mickey noun (in phrase **take the mickey**) Brit. informal tease or make fun of someone.
– DERIVATIVES **mickey-taking** noun.
– ORIGIN unknown.

Mickey Finn noun informal a drink to which a drug has been secretly added.
– ORIGIN probably the name of a notorious Chicago bar owner.

Mickey Mouse adjective informal not of high quality.
– ORIGIN from the name of the character created by the cartoonist Walt Disney.

mickle (also **muckle**) old use or Scottish & N. English noun a large amount. ●adjective very large.
– ORIGIN Old English.

Micmac /mik-mak/ noun (pl. same or **Micmacs**) a member of an American Indian people living in the Maritime Provinces of Canada.
– ORIGIN the Micmacs' name for themselves.

micro noun (pl. **micros**) a microcomputer or microprocessor. ●adjective extremely small or small-scale.

micro- combining form **1** very small or of reduced size: *microchip.* **2** referring to a factor of one millionth (10^{-6}): *microfarad.*
– ORIGIN Greek *mikros* 'small'.

microanalysis noun the analysis of chemical compounds using a sample of a few milligrams.

microbe /my-krohb/ noun a microorganism, especially a bacterium causing disease.
– DERIVATIVES **microbial** adjective.
– ORIGIN from Greek *mikros* 'small' + *bios* 'life'.

microbiology noun the scientific study of microorganisms.

microbrewery noun (pl. **microbreweries**) chiefly N. Amer. a brewery producing limited quantities of beer.
– DERIVATIVES **microbrewer** noun.

microchip noun a tiny wafer of silicon or similar material used to make an integrated circuit. ●verb (**microchips, microchipping, microchipped**) implant a microchip under the skin of a cat or dog so that they can be identified.

microcircuit noun a minute electric circuit, especially an integrated circuit.

microclimate noun the climate of a very small or restricted area.

microcode noun a very low-level set of instructions controlling the operation of a computer.

microcomputer noun a small computer with a microprocessor as its central processor.

microcosm /my-kroh-ko-z'm/ noun a thing seen as a miniature representation of something much larger: *the city's population is a microcosm of modern Malaysia.*
– DERIVATIVES **microcosmic** adjective.
– ORIGIN from Greek *mikros kosmos* 'little world'.

microdermabrasion /my-kroh-der-muh-**bray**-zh'n/ noun a cosmetic treatment in which the face is sprayed with granular crystals to remove dead skin cells.

microdot noun **1** a photograph, especially of a printed document, reduced to a very small size. **2** a tiny tablet of LSD.

microeconomics plural noun (treated as sing.) the part of economics concerned with single factors and the effects of individual decisions.

microelectronics plural noun (usu. treated as sing.) the design, manufacture, and use of microchips and microcircuits.

microfibre noun a very fine synthetic yarn.

microfiche /my-kroh-feesh/ noun a flat piece of film containing greatly reduced photographs of the pages of a newspaper, catalogue, or other document.
– ORIGIN from **MICRO-** + French *fiche* 'slip of paper'.

microfilm noun a length of film containing greatly reduced photographs of a newspaper, catalogue, or other document.

microgram noun one millionth of a gram.

micrograph noun a photograph taken using a microscope.

microgravity noun very weak gravity, as in an orbiting spacecraft.

microlight noun chiefly Brit. a very small, light, one- or two-seater aircraft.

microlitre (US also **microliter**) noun one millionth of a litre.

micrometer /my-**krom**-i-ter/ noun a gauge which measures small distances or thicknesses.

micrometre (US **micrometer**) noun one millionth of a metre.

micron noun one millionth of a metre.

Micronesian noun a person from Micronesia, an island group in the western Pacific. ●adjective relating to Micronesia.

micronutrient noun a chemical element or

substance required in trace amounts by living things.

microorganism noun a microscopic organism, especially a bacterium or virus.

micropayment noun a very small payment made each time a user accesses an Internet page or service.

microphone noun a device for converting sound waves into electrical energy which can then be amplified, transmitted, or recorded.

microprocessor noun an integrated circuit which can perform the role of a central processing unit of a computer.

microscooter noun a small two-wheeled foldable aluminium scooter for both children and adults.

microscope noun an instrument used in scientific study for magnifying very small objects.
– ORIGIN from **MICRO-** + *skopein* 'look at'.

microscopic adjective 1 so small as to be visible only with a microscope. 2 very small. 3 relating to a microscope.
– DERIVATIVES **microscopically** adverb.

microscopy /my-kross-kuh-pi/ noun the use of a microscope.

microsecond noun one millionth of a second.

microstructure noun the fine structure in a material which can be made visible and examined with a microscope.

microsurgery noun intricate surgery performed using very small instruments and a microscope.

microwave noun 1 an electromagnetic wave with a wavelength in the range 0.001–0.3 m, shorter than that of a normal radio wave but longer than those of infrared radiation. 2 (also **microwave oven**) an oven that uses microwaves to cook or heat food. • verb cook food in a microwave oven.

micturate /mik-tyoo-rayt/ verb formal urinate.
– DERIVATIVES **micturition** noun.
– ORIGIN Latin *micturire*.

mid adjective relating to or in the middle point of a range. • preposition literary in the middle of; amid.

mid- combining form 1 referring to the middle of: *midsection*. 2 in the middle; medium; half: *midway*.
– ORIGIN Old English.

mid-air noun a part of the air above ground level.

Midas touch noun the ability to make money out of anything one does.
– ORIGIN from *Midas*, king of Phrygia, who in Greek mythology was given the power to turn everything he touched into gold.

midbrain noun a small central part of the brainstem, developing from the middle of the embryonic brain.

midday noun the middle of the day; noon.

midden noun a dunghill or rubbish heap.
– ORIGIN Scandinavian.

middle adjective 1 at an equal distance from the edges or ends of something; central. 2 intermediate in rank, quality, or ability. • noun 1 a middle point or position. 2 informal a person's waist and stomach.
– ORIGIN Old English.

middle age noun the period after early adulthood and before old age, about 45 to 60.
– DERIVATIVES **middle-aged** adjective.

Middle Ages plural noun the period of European history from the fall of the Roman Empire in the West (5th century) to the fall of Constantinople (1453), or, more narrowly, from c.1000 to 1453.

Middle America noun the conservative middle classes of the United States, characterized as living in the Midwest.

middlebrow adjective informal needing or involving only a moderate level of intellectual effort.

middle C noun the C near the middle of the piano keyboard, written on the first ledger line below the treble stave or the first ledger line above the bass stave.

middle class noun the social group made up of business and professional people, between the upper and working classes.

middle distance noun 1 the part of a real or painted landscape between the foreground and the background. 2 Athletics a race distance between 800 and 5,000 metres.

middle ear noun the air-filled central cavity of the ear, behind the eardrum.

Middle East noun an area of SW Asia and northern Africa, stretching from the Mediterranean to Pakistan, in particular Iran, Iraq, Israel, Jordan, Lebanon, and Syria.
– DERIVATIVES **Middle Eastern** adjective.

Middle England noun the conservative middle classes in England.

Middle English noun the English language from c.1150 to c.1470.

middle ground noun an area of compromise or possible agreement between two opposing positions or groups.

middleman noun (pl. **middlemen**) 1 a person who buys goods from producers and sells them to retailers or consumers. 2 a person who arranges business or political deals between other people.

middle name noun a person's name placed after the first name and before the surname.

middle-of-the-road adjective 1 (of views) not extreme; moderate. 2 (of music) popular with a wide range of people but rather bland or unadventurous.

middle school noun (in the UK) a school for children from about 9 to 13 years old.

middleweight noun a weight in boxing and other sports intermediate between welterweight and light heavyweight.

middling adjective moderate or average. • adverb informal fairly or moderately.

Middx abbreviation Middlesex.

midfield noun 1 (chiefly in football) the central part of the field. 2 the players who play in a central position between attack and defence.
– DERIVATIVES **midfielder** noun.

midge noun a small two-winged fly that forms swarms near water, of which many kinds feed on blood.
– ORIGIN Old English.

midget noun a very small person or thing. • adjective very small: *a midget submarine*.

m

MIDI noun a standard for interconnecting electronic musical instruments and computers.
– ORIGIN from the initial letters of *musical instrument digital interface.*

midi noun (pl. **midis**) a woman's calf-length skirt, dress, or coat.

midi- combining form of medium size or length.

midi system noun Brit. a set of compact stacking hi-fi equipment components.

midland noun 1 the middle part of a country. 2 (**the Midlands**) the inland counties of central England. •adjective (also **midlands**) relating to or in the middle part of a country or the Midlands.
– DERIVATIVES **midlander** noun.

midlife noun the central period of a person's life, between around 45 and 60 years old.

midnight noun twelve o'clock at night; the middle of the night.

midnight blue noun a very dark blue.

midnight sun noun the sun when seen at midnight during the summer within either the Arctic or Antarctic Circle.

mid-off noun Cricket a fielding position on the off side near the bowler.

mid-on noun Cricket a fielding position on the on side near the bowler.

midpoint noun 1 a point halfway through a period or process. 2 the exact middle point of something.

midrib noun a large strengthened vein running down the centre of a leaf.

midriff noun the front of the body between the chest and the waist.
– ORIGIN Old English.

midship noun the middle part of a ship or boat.

midshipman noun (pl. **midshipmen**) 1 a rank of officer in the Royal Navy, above naval cadet and below sub lieutenant. 2 a naval cadet in the US navy.

midships adverb & adjective another term for AMIDSHIPS.

midst old use or literary preposition in the middle of. •noun the middle point or part.
– PHRASES **in our** (or **your** or **their**) **midst** among us (or you or them).

midstream noun the middle of a stream or river.
– PHRASES **in midstream** in the middle of doing something.

midsummer noun 1 the middle part of summer. 2 the summer solstice.

Midsummer Day (Brit. also **Midsummer's Day**) noun 24 June.

midterm noun the middle of a period of office, an academic term, or a pregnancy.

midway adverb & adjective in or towards the middle.

midweek noun the middle of the week. •adjective & adverb in the middle of the week.

Midwest noun the region of northern states of the US from Ohio west to the Rocky Mountains.
– DERIVATIVES **Midwestern** adjective **Midwesterner** noun.

midwicket noun Cricket a fielding position on the leg side, level with the middle of the pitch.

midwife /mid-wyf/ noun (pl. **midwives**) a nurse who is trained to help women in childbirth.
– DERIVATIVES **midwifery** /mid-wif-uh-ri/ noun.
– ORIGIN probably from former *mid* 'with' + WIFE (in the sense 'woman').

midwinter noun 1 the middle part of winter. 2 the winter solstice.

mien /meen/ noun a person's look or manner.
– ORIGIN probably from French *mine* 'expression'.

miffed adjective informal offended or irritated.
– ORIGIN uncertain.

might[1] modal verb (3rd sing. present **might**) past of MAY. 1 used to express possibility or make a suggestion. 2 used politely or tentatively in questions and requests.

might[2] noun great power or strength.
– PHRASES **with might and main** with all one's strength or power.
– ORIGIN Old English.

mightn't contraction might not.

mighty adjective (**mightier, mightiest**) 1 very powerful or strong. 2 informal very large. •adverb informal, chiefly N. Amer. extremely.
– DERIVATIVES **mightily** adverb **mightiness** noun.

mignonette /min-yuh-net/ noun a plant with spikes of small fragrant greenish flowers.
– ORIGIN French.

migraine /mee-grayn, my-grayn/ noun a throbbing headache, typically affecting one side of the head and often accompanied by nausea and disturbed vision.
– ORIGIN French, from Greek *hēmi-* 'half' + *kranion* 'skull'.

migrant noun 1 a person who moves from one place to another to find work. 2 an animal that migrates. •adjective tending to migrate or having migrated: *migrant workers.*

migrate verb 1 (of an animal) move from one habitat to another according to the seasons. 2 move to settle in a new area in order to find work. 3 Computing change or transfer from one system to another.
– DERIVATIVES **migration** noun **migratory** adjective.
– ORIGIN Latin *migrare* 'to move, shift'.

mihrab /meer-ahb/ noun a niche in the wall of a mosque at the point nearest to Mecca, towards which the congregation faces to pray.
– ORIGIN Arabic, 'place for prayer'.

mikado /mi-kah-doh/ noun historical a title given to the emperor of Japan.
– ORIGIN Japanese.

mike noun informal a microphone.

mil abbreviation informal millions.

milady noun historical or humorous used to address or refer to an English noblewoman.

milage noun variant spelling of MILEAGE.

milch adjective (of a domestic mammal) giving or kept for milk.
– ORIGIN from Old English *-milce* in *thrimilce* 'May' (when cows could be milked three times a day).

milch cow noun a source of easy profit.

mild adjective 1 not severe, harsh, or extreme: *mild criticism.* 2 (of weather) fairly warm. 3 not sharp or strong in flavour. 4 gentle and calm: *his mild manner.* •noun Brit. a kind of dark beer not strongly flavoured with hops.
– DERIVATIVES **mildly** adverb **mildness** noun.

m

– ORIGIN Old English.

mildew noun a coating of minute fungi that grows on plants or on materials such as paper or leather when they are damp.
– DERIVATIVES **mildewed** adjective.
– ORIGIN Old English.

mild steel noun strong, tough steel containing a small percentage of carbon.

mile noun 1 (also **statute mile**) a unit of length equal to 1,760 yards (approximately 1.609 kilometres). 2 (**miles**) informal a very long way. • adverb (**miles**) informal by a great amount or a long way: *the second tape is miles better.*
– PHRASES **be miles away** informal be lost in thought. **go the extra mile** try particularly hard to achieve something. **stand** (or **stick**) **out a mile** informal be very obvious or noticeable.
– ORIGIN Latin *milia*, plural of *mille* 'thousand'; a Roman 'mile' consisted of 1,000 paces (approximately 1,620 yards).

mileage (also **milage**) noun 1 a number of miles travelled or covered. 2 informal actual or potential benefit or advantage: *she got plenty of mileage out of the rumour.*

mileometer noun variant spelling of **MILOMETER**.

milepost noun chiefly N. Amer. 1 a milestone. 2 a post one mile from the finishing post of a race.

miler noun informal a person or horse trained to run over races of a mile.

milestone noun 1 a stone set up beside a road to mark the distance in miles to a particular place. 2 an event marking a significant new development or stage.

milfoil noun 1 another term for **YARROW**. 2 a water plant with whorls of submerged leaves.
– ORIGIN from Latin *mille* 'thousand' + *folium* 'leaf'.

milieu /**mee**-lyer/ noun (pl. **milieux** or **milieus** pronunc. same or /**mee**-lyers/) a person's social environment: *his working-class milieu.*
– ORIGIN French, from *mi* 'mid' + *lieu* 'place'.

militant adjective prepared to take aggressive action in support of a political or social cause. • noun a militant person.
– DERIVATIVES **militancy** noun **militantly** adverb.

militaria plural noun military articles of historical interest.

militarism noun the belief that a country should maintain and readily use strong armed forces.
– DERIVATIVES **militarist** noun & adjective **militaristic** adjective.

militarize (or **militarise**) verb (often as adj. **militarized**) 1 supply a place with soldiers and other military resources. 2 make something military in nature or similar to an army: *militarized police forces.*
– DERIVATIVES **militarization** noun.

military adjective relating to or characteristic of soldiers or armed forces. • noun (**the military**) the armed forces of a country.
– DERIVATIVES **militarily** adverb.
– ORIGIN Latin *militaris*, from *miles* 'soldier'.

Military Cross noun (in the UK and Commonwealth) a decoration awarded for distinguished active service on land (originally for officers).

military honours plural noun ceremonies performed by troops as a mark of respect at the burial of a member of the armed forces.

military-industrial complex noun a country's military establishment and arms industries, regarded as a strong influence on government.

Military Medal noun (in the UK and Commonwealth) a decoration awarded for distinguished active service on land (originally for enlisted men).

military police noun a military body responsible for policing and disciplinary duties in the armed forces.

militate verb (**militate against**) be a powerful or decisive factor in preventing something: *these differences will militate against the two communities coming together.*
– ORIGIN Latin *militare* 'wage war'.

> USAGE: On the confusion between **militate** and **mitigate**, see the note at **MITIGATE**.

militia /mi-li-shuh/ noun 1 a military force made up of civilians, used to supplement a regular army in an emergency. 2 a rebel force opposing a regular army.
– DERIVATIVES **militiaman** noun (pl. **militiamen**).
– ORIGIN Latin, 'military service'.

milk noun 1 an opaque white fluid produced by female mammals to feed their young. 2 the milk of cows as a food and drink for humans. 3 the milk-like juice of certain plants, such as the coconut. • verb 1 draw milk from a cow or other animal. 2 exploit or defraud by taking small amounts of money over a period of time: *he had milked his grandmother of all her money.* 3 take full advantage of a situation.
– ORIGIN Old English.

milk-and-water adjective feeble or ineffective.

milk chocolate noun solid chocolate that has been made with milk.

milk fever noun an acute illness in cows or other female animals that have just produced young.

milk float noun Brit. an open-sided electrically powered van used for delivering milk to houses.

milkmaid noun (in the past) a girl or woman who worked in a dairy.

milkman noun (pl. **milkmen**) a man who delivers milk to houses.

milk pudding noun Brit. a baked pudding made of milk and a grain such as rice, sago, or tapioca.

milk round noun Brit. a series of visits to universities and colleges by staff from large companies looking to recruit students.

milk run noun a routine, uneventful journey, especially by aircraft.
– ORIGIN RAF slang in the Second World War for a sortie that was as simple as a milkman's round.

milkshake noun a cold drink made from milk whisked with a flavouring such as syrup or fruit.

milksop noun a timid and indecisive person.

milk thistle noun a thistle with a solitary purple flower and glossy leaves, used in herbal medicine.

milk tooth noun a temporary tooth in a child or young mammal.

milky adjective (**milkier**, **milkiest**) **1** containing milk. **2** having a soft white colour or clouded appearance.
– DERIVATIVES **milkily** adverb **milkiness** noun.

Milky Way noun the galaxy of which our solar system is a part, visible at night as a faint band of light crossing the sky.

mill noun **1** a building equipped with machinery for grinding grain into flour. **2** a device or piece of machinery for grinding solid substances, such as peppercorns. **3** a building fitted with machinery for a manufacturing process: *a steel mill*. • verb **1** grind something in a mill. **2** cut or shape metal with a rotating tool. **3** (usu. as adj. **milled**) produce regular ribbed markings on the edge of a coin. **4** (**mill about/around**) move around in a confused mass.
– PHRASES **go** (or **put someone**) **through the mill** undergo (or make someone undergo) an unpleasant experience.
– ORIGIN Latin *mola* 'grindstone, mill'.

millefeuille /meel-**fuh**-i/ noun a cake consisting of thin layers of puff pastry filled with jam and cream.
– ORIGIN French, 'thousand-leaf'.

millenarian /mi-li-**nair**-ri-uhn/ adjective relating to or believing in Christian millenarianism. • noun a person who believes in millenarianism.
– ORIGIN Latin *millenarius* 'having a thousand'.

millenarianism noun the belief in a future thousand-year age of blessedness, beginning with or culminating in the Second Coming of Jesus.
– DERIVATIVES **millenarianist** noun & adjective.

millenary /mil-**len**-uh-ri/ noun (pl. **millenaries**) **1** a period of a thousand years. **2** a thousandth anniversary. • adjective consisting of a thousand.

millennial adjective relating to a millennium.

millennialism noun another term for MILLENARIANISM.
– DERIVATIVES **millennialist** noun & adjective.

millennium /mil-**len**-i-uhm/ noun (pl. **millennia** or **millenniums**) **1** a period of a thousand years, especially when calculated from the traditional date of the birth of Jesus. **2** (**the millennium**) the point at which one period of a thousand years ends and another begins. **3** (**the millennium**) Christian Theology the prophesied forthcoming thousand-year reign of Jesus. **4** an anniversary of a thousand years.
– ORIGIN from Latin *mille* 'thousand' + *annus* 'year'.

> USAGE: The correct spelling is **millennium**, with a double **l** and a double **n**. The spelling with one **n** is a common mistake, arising from confusion with other similar words such as **millenarian**, correctly spelled with only one **n**.

millennium bug noun an inability in older computing software to deal correctly with dates of 1 January 2000 or later.

miller noun a person who owns or works in a grain mill.

millet noun a cereal which bears a large crop of small seeds, used to make flour or alcoholic drinks.
– ORIGIN French.

milli- combining form a thousand, especially a factor of one thousandth (10^{-3}): *milligram*.
– ORIGIN from Latin *mille* 'thousand'.

milliard noun Brit., dated one thousand million; a billion.

millibar noun one thousandth of a bar, a unit of atmospheric pressure equivalent to 100 pascals.

milligram (also **milligramme**) noun one thousandth of a gram.

millilitre (US **milliliter**) noun one thousandth of a litre.

millimetre (US **millimeter**) noun one thousandth of a metre.

milliner noun a person who makes or sells women's hats.
– DERIVATIVES **millinery** noun.
– ORIGIN from the name of the Italian city *Milan*, first meaning 'a native of Milan', later 'a seller of fancy goods from Milan'.

million cardinal number (pl. **millions** or (with numeral or quantifying word) same) **1** the number equivalent to a thousand multiplied by a thousand; 1,000,000 or 10^6. **2** (also **millions**) informal a very large number or amount.
– DERIVATIVES **millionth** ordinal number.

millionaire noun (fem. **millionairess**) a person whose money and property are worth one million pounds or dollars or more.

millipede noun a small invertebrate animal with a long body composed of many segments, most of which have two pairs of legs.
– ORIGIN from Latin *mille* 'thousand' + *pes* 'foot'.

millisecond noun one thousandth of a second.

millpond noun **1** an artificial pool providing a head of water to power a watermill. **2** a very still and calm stretch of water.

mill race noun the channel carrying the swift current of water that drives a mill wheel.

millstone noun **1** each of a pair of circular stones used for grinding grain. **2** a heavy and inescapable responsibility.

millstream noun the flowing water that drives a mill wheel.

mill wheel noun a wheel used to drive a watermill.

milo noun a drought-resistant variety of sorghum, an important cereal in the central US.
– ORIGIN Sesotho (an African language).

milometer /my-**lom**-i-ter/ (also **mileometer**) noun Brit. an instrument on a vehicle for recording the number of miles travelled.

milord noun historical or humorous used to address or refer to an English nobleman.

Milquetoast /milk-**tohst**/ noun chiefly N. Amer. a timid or submissive person.
– ORIGIN from the name of an American cartoon character, Caspar *Milquetoast*, created by H. T. Webster.

milt noun **1** the semen of a male fish. **2** the reproductive gland of a male fish.
– ORIGIN Old English.

mime noun the use of silent gestures and facial

m

expressions to tell a story or convey a feeling, especially as a form of theatrical performance. •**verb 1** use mime to act out a story or convey a feeling. **2** pretend to sing or play an instrument as a recording is being played.
– ORIGIN Greek *mimos.*

mimeograph noun a duplicating machine which produces copies from a stencil, now superseded by the photocopier.
– ORIGIN from Greek *mimeomai* 'I imitate'.

mimesis /mi-**mee**-siss/ **noun 1** imitation of reality in art and literature. **2** the quality of resembling another animal or plant.
– ORIGIN Greek.

mimetic /mi-**met**-ik/ **adjective 1** imitating reality in art or literature. **2** resembling another animal or plant.

mimic verb (mimics, mimicking, mimicked) 1 imitate someone in order to make fun of them or to entertain others. **2** (of an animal or plant) take on the appearance of another for protection. **3** imitate or copy something. •**noun** a person skilled in mimicking others.

mimicry noun 1 imitation of someone or something. **2** the close external resemblance of an animal or plant to another.

mimosa /mi-**moh**-zuh/ **noun 1** an acacia tree with delicate fern-like leaves and yellow flowers. **2** a plant of a genus that includes the sensitive plant.
– ORIGIN probably from Latin *mimus* 'mime' (because the plant mimics an animal's sensitivity to touch).

mimsy adjective rather feeble and prim.
– ORIGIN coined by Lewis Carroll from MISERABLE and FLIMSY.

min. abbreviation 1 minimum. **2** minute(s).

minaret noun a slender tower of a mosque, with a balcony from which Muslims are called to prayer.
– ORIGIN Arabic.

minatory /**min**-uh-tuh-ri/ **adjective** formal threatening.
– ORIGIN from Latin *minari* 'threaten'.

mince verb 1 cut up meat into very small pieces. **2** walk in an affected way with short, quick steps and swinging hips. •**noun** Brit. minced meat.
– PHRASES **not mince (one's) words** speak in a direct way.
– DERIVATIVES **mincer** noun.
– ORIGIN Old French *mincier.*

mincemeat noun a mixture of currants, raisins, apples, candied peel, sugar, spices, and suet.
– PHRASES **make mincemeat of** informal defeat someone decisively.

mince pie noun chiefly Brit. a small tart containing mincemeat, typically eaten at Christmas.

mind noun 1 a person's faculty of consciousness and thought. **2** a person's ability to reason or remember things. **3** a person's attention or will. **4** an intelligent person. •**verb 1** be distressed or annoyed by someone or something. **2** feel concern about something. **3** take care with or watch out for: *mind your head on that cupboard!* **4** take care of someone or something temporarily. **5** (**be minded**) be inclined to do something.

– PHRASES **be in two minds** be unable to decide between alternatives. **give someone a piece of one's mind** informal rebuke someone. **have a (or a good) mind to do** be inclined to do. **in one's mind's eye** in one's imagination. **mind one's Ps & Qs** be careful to be polite and avoid giving offence. **never mind 1** do not be concerned or distressed. **2** let alone. **out of one's mind** not thinking sensibly; mad. **put one in mind of** remind one of. **to my mind** in my opinion.
– ORIGIN Old English.

mind-bending adjective informal altering one's state of mind.

mind-blowing adjective informal overwhelmingly impressive.

mind-boggling adjective informal overwhelming; startling.

minded adjective (often in combination) inclined to think in a particular way: *liberal-minded.*

minder noun 1 a person employed to look after someone or something. **2** informal a bodyguard.

mindful adjective 1 (**mindful of/that**) aware of or recognizing that. **2** formal inclined to do something.

mind game noun a series of actions intended to unsettle someone or to gain an advantage over them.

mindless adjective 1 acting or done without justification and with no concern for the consequences. **2** (**mindless of**) not thinking of or concerned about. **3** (of an activity) simple and repetitive.
– DERIVATIVES **mindlessly** adverb **mindlessness** noun.

mindset noun a person's established set of attitudes.

mine[1] **possessive pronoun** referring to a thing or things belonging to or associated with the speaker.
– ORIGIN Old English.

mine[2] **noun 1** a hole or passage dug in the earth for extracting coal or other minerals. **2** an abundant source: *the book is a mine of information.* **3** a type of bomb placed on or in the ground or water, which detonates on contact. •**verb 1** extract coal and other minerals from a mine. **2** lay explosive mines on or in the ground or water. **3** exploit a source of information or skill: *his body of work should be mined for its fresh ideas.*
– ORIGIN Old French.

minefield noun 1 an area planted with explosive mines. **2** a subject or situation presenting hidden risks.

miner noun a person who works in a mine.

mineral noun 1 a solid inorganic substance that occurs naturally, such as copper. **2** an inorganic substance needed by the human body for good health, such as calcium. **3** a substance obtained by mining. **4** (**minerals**) Brit. fizzy soft drinks.
– ORIGIN Latin *minera* 'ore'.

mineralogy noun the scientific study of minerals.
– DERIVATIVES **mineralogical** adjective **mineralogist** noun.

mineral oil noun petroleum, or a product produced by distilling petroleum.

mineral water noun water that naturally

contains some dissolved salts.

mineshaft noun a deep, narrow shaft that gives access to a mine.

minestrone /mi-ni-**stroh**-ni/ noun an Italian soup containing vegetables and pasta.
– ORIGIN from Italian *minestrare* 'serve at table'.

minesweeper noun a warship equipped for detecting and removing tethered explosive mines.

Ming adjective (of Chinese porcelain) made during the Ming dynasty (1368–1644), having vivid colours and elaborate designs.
– ORIGIN Chinese, 'clear or bright'.

minger /ming-er/ noun Brit. informal, derogatory an unattractive person or thing.

minging /ming-ing/ adjective Brit. informal very bad or unpleasant.
– ORIGIN perhaps from Scots dialect *ming* 'excrement'.

mingle verb 1 mix together. 2 move around and chat at a social function.
– ORIGIN from former *meng* 'mix or blend'.

mingy /min-ji/ adjective informal mean; not generous.
– ORIGIN perhaps from MEAN² and STINGY.

mini adjective referring to a very small version of something. •noun (pl. **minis**) a very short skirt or dress.

mini- combining form very small of its kind; miniature: *minibus*.

miniature adjective much smaller than normal in size. •noun 1 a thing that is much smaller than normal. 2 a very small bottle of spirits. 3 a very small and highly detailed portrait.
– DERIVATIVES **miniaturize** (or **miniaturise**) verb.
– ORIGIN from Latin *minium* 'red lead' (formerly used to mark words in manuscripts).

miniaturist noun an artist who paints miniatures.

minibar noun a refrigerator in a hotel room containing a selection of drinks.

minibus noun a small bus for about ten to fifteen passengers.

minicab noun Brit. an ordinary car that is used as a taxi but which must be ordered in advance.

minicam noun a hand-held video camera.

minicomputer noun a computer of medium power, more than a microcomputer but less than a mainframe.

minidisc noun a disc similar to a small CD but able to record sound or data as well as play it back.

minidress noun a very short dress.

minim noun 1 Brit. a musical note having the time value of two crotchets or half a semibreve, represented by a ring with a stem. 2 one sixtieth of a fluid drachm, about one drop of liquid.
– ORIGIN from Latin *minimus* 'smallest'.

minima plural of MINIMUM.

minimal adjective 1 of a minimum amount, quantity, or degree. 2 (of art) using simple forms or structures. 3 (of music) characterized by the repetition and gradual alteration of short phrases.
– DERIVATIVES **minimally** adverb.

minimalist adjective 1 relating to minimal art or music. 2 deliberately simple or basic in design. •noun a person who creates minimal art or music.
– DERIVATIVES **minimalism** noun.

mini-me noun informal a person who closely resembles a smaller or younger version of another.
– ORIGIN the name of a cloned character in the film *Austin Powers: The Spy Who Shagged Me*.

minimize (or **minimise**) verb 1 reduce something to the smallest possible amount or degree. 2 represent something as less important than it really is.
– DERIVATIVES **minimization** noun **minimizer** noun.

minimum noun (pl. **minima** or **minimums**) the least or smallest amount, extent, or intensity possible or recorded: *they checked passports with the minimum of fuss.* •adjective smallest or lowest in amount, extent, or intensity.
– ORIGIN Latin.

minimum wage noun the lowest wage permitted by law or by agreement.

minion noun a lowly employee or assistant of a powerful person.
– ORIGIN from French *mignon* 'pretty, dainty'.

mini-pill noun a contraceptive pill containing a progestogen and not oestrogen.

miniseries noun a television drama shown in a small number of episodes.

miniskirt noun a very short skirt.
– DERIVATIVES **miniskirted** adjective.

minister noun 1 a head of a government department. 2 a member of the clergy, especially in the Presbyterian and Nonconformist Churches. 3 a diplomat, usually ranking below an ambassador, representing a state or sovereign in a foreign country. •verb 1 (**minister to**) attend to the needs of. 2 act as a minister of religion.
– ORIGIN Latin, 'servant'.

ministerial /min-is-**teer**-i-uhl/ adjective relating to a minister or ministers.
– DERIVATIVES **ministerially** adverb.

Minister of State noun (in the UK) a government minister ranking below a Secretary of State.

Minister of the Crown noun (in the UK and Canada) a member of the cabinet.

Minister without Portfolio noun (in the UK and some other countries) a government minister with cabinet status but not in charge of a specific department of state.

ministrations plural noun 1 formal or humorous the provision of help or care. 2 the services of a minister of religion.
– DERIVATIVES **ministrant** noun.

ministry noun (pl. **ministries**) 1 a government department headed by a minister. 2 a period of government under one Prime Minister. 3 the work or office of a minister of religion.

minivan (also trademark **Mini Van**) noun a small van fitted with seats for passengers.

mink noun a small stoat-like mammal farmed for its fur.
– ORIGIN Swedish.

minke /ming-kuh/ noun a small rorqual whale with a dark grey back and white underparts.

– ORIGIN probably named after *Meincke*, a Norwegian whaler.

minnow noun 1 a small freshwater fish of the carp family. **2** a minor or unimportant person.
– ORIGIN probably from Old English.

Minoan /mi-**noh**-uhn/ **adjective** relating to a Bronze Age civilization centred on Crete (*c.*3000–1050 BC).
– ORIGIN named after the legendary Cretan king *Minos*.

minor adjective 1 lesser in importance, seriousness, or significance: *minor alterations.* **2** (of a musical scale) having intervals of a semitone between the second and third, and (usually) the fifth and sixth, and the seventh and eighth notes. Contrasted with **MAJOR.** ● **noun 1** a person under the age of full legal responsibility. **2** Music a minor key, interval, or scale. **3** N. Amer. a student's subsidiary subject or course. ● **verb (minor in)** N. Amer. study a subsidiary subject at college or university.
– ORIGIN Latin, 'smaller, less'.

Minorcan /mi-**nor**-k'n/ **noun** a person from Minorca. ● **adjective** relating to Minorca.

minority noun (pl. **minorities**) **1** the smaller number or part. **2** a relatively small group of people differing from the majority in race, religion, etc. **3** the state of being under the age of full legal responsibility.

Minotaur /**mi**-nuh-tor, **my**-nuh-tor/ **noun** Greek Mythology a creature who was half-man and half-bull, kept in a labyrinth on Crete by King Minos.
– ORIGIN Greek *Minōtauros* 'bull of Minos'.

minster noun Brit. a large or important church, typically one of cathedral status that was built as part of a monastery.
– ORIGIN from Greek *monastērion* 'monastery'.

minstrel noun a medieval singer or musician.
– ORIGIN Old French *menestral* 'entertainer, servant'.

minstrelsy noun the activity of performing as a minstrel.

mint¹ noun 1 a plant used as a herb in cookery. **2** the flavour of mint, especially peppermint. **3** a peppermint sweet.
– DERIVATIVES **minty** adjective.
– ORIGIN Greek *minthē.*

mint² noun 1 a place where coins are made. **2 (a mint)** informal a large sum of money. ● **adjective** as new; in perfect condition. ● **verb 1** make a coin by stamping metal. **2** produce something for the first time.
– ORIGIN from Latin *moneta* 'money'.

Minton noun trademark pottery made at Stoke-on-Trent from 1793 onwards by Thomas Minton or his factory.

mint sauce noun chopped spearmint in vinegar and sugar, traditionally eaten with lamb.

minuet noun a slow ballroom dance in triple time, popular in the 18th century.
– ORIGIN from French *menuet* 'fine, delicate'.

minus preposition 1 with the subtraction of. **2** (of temperature) falling below zero by: *minus 40° centigrade.* **3** informal lacking: *he was minus a finger.* ● **adjective 1** (before a number) below zero; negative. **2** (after a grade) slightly below: *C minus.* **3** having a negative electric

charge. ● **noun 1** (also **minus sign**) the symbol –, indicating subtraction or a negative value. **2** informal a disadvantage.
– ORIGIN Latin, neuter of *minor* 'less'.

minuscule adjective very small. ● **noun** a lower-case letter.
– ORIGIN from Latin *minuscula littera* 'somewhat smaller letter'.

USAGE: The correct spelling is **minuscule** (not *miniscule*).

minute¹ /min-it/ **noun 1** a period of time equal to sixty seconds or a sixtieth of an hour. **2 (a minute)** informal a very short time. **3** (also **arc minute** or **minute of arc**) a measurement of an angle equal to one sixtieth of a degree.
– PHRASES **up to the minute** up to date.
– ORIGIN from Latin *pars minuta prima* 'first very small part'.

minute² /my-**nyoot**/ **adjective** (**minutest**) **1** very small. **2** very detailed or thorough: *he made a minute examination of the area.*
– DERIVATIVES **minutely** adverb **minuteness** noun.
– ORIGIN Latin *minutus* 'lessened, made small'.

minute³ /min-it/ **noun 1 (minutes)** a written summary of the points discussed at a meeting. **2** an official written message. ● **verb** record the points discussed at a meeting.
– ORIGIN French *minute*, from the idea of a rough copy in 'small writing'.

minute steak noun a thin slice of steak cooked very quickly.

minutiae /mi-**nyoo**-shi-ee/ **plural noun** small or precise details.
– ORIGIN Latin.

minx noun chiefly humorous a cheeky, cunning, or flirtatious girl or young woman.
– DERIVATIVES **minxy** adjective.
– ORIGIN unknown.

Miocene /**my**-oh-seen/ **adjective** Geology relating to the fourth epoch of the Tertiary period (23.3 to 5.2 million years ago), when the first apes appeared.
– ORIGIN from Greek *meiōn* 'less' + *kainos* 'new'.

mirabile dictu /mi-rah-bi-lay **dik**-too/ **adverb** wonderful to relate.
– ORIGIN Latin.

miracle noun 1 an extraordinary and welcome event believed to be the work of God or a saint. **2** a remarkable and welcome event: *it was a miracle that more people hadn't been killed.* **3** an outstanding example or achievement.
– ORIGIN Latin *miraculum* 'object of wonder'.

miracle play noun a mystery play.

miraculous adjective like a miracle; very surprising and welcome.
– DERIVATIVES **miraculously** adverb.

mirage /mi-**rahzh**/ **noun 1** an optical illusion caused by the refraction of light by heated air, in which a sheet of water seems to appear in a desert or on a hot road. **2** something that seems real or possible but is not in fact so: *such promised happiness is only a mirage.*
– ORIGIN French.

mire noun 1 a stretch of swampy or boggy ground. **2** a difficult situation from which it is hard to escape. ● **verb (be mired) 1** become stuck in mud. **2** become involved in a difficult situation.

– ORIGIN Old Norse.

mirepoix /meer-pwah/ noun a mixture of chopped sautéed vegetables used in various sauces.
– ORIGIN named after the French general Duc de *Mirepoix*.

mirror noun 1 a piece of glass coated with metal which reflects a clear image. 2 something that accurately represents something else. •verb 1 reflect someone or something. 2 correspond to: *the expansion in the Far East has been mirrored in the loss of investment to Eastern Europe.*
– ORIGIN Old French *mirour*.

mirrorball noun a revolving ball covered with small mirrored facets, used to provide lighting effects at discos.

mirror image noun an image which is identical in form to another but has the structure reversed, as if seen in a mirror.

mirror site noun an Internet site which stores contents copied from another site.

mirth noun amusement, especially as expressed in laughter.
– DERIVATIVES **mirthful** adjective
– ORIGIN Old English.

mirthless adjective (of a smile or laugh) lacking real amusement.
– DERIVATIVES **mirthlessly** adverb.

MIRV abbreviation multiple independently targeted re-entry vehicle, an intercontinental nuclear missile with several independent warheads.

miry adjective very muddy or boggy.

MIS abbreviation Computing management information systems.

mis- prefix 1 (added to verbs and their derivatives) wrongly, badly, or unsuitably: *mismanage.* 2 (added to some nouns) expressing a negative sense: *misadventure.*
– ORIGIN Old English.

misadventure noun 1 (also **death by misadventure**) English Law death caused accidentally by a person while performing a legal act without negligence or intent to harm. 2 a mishap.

misaligned adjective incorrectly aligned.
– DERIVATIVES **misalignment** noun.

misalliance noun an unsuitable or unhappy alliance or marriage.

misanthrope /miz-uhn-throhp/ noun a person who dislikes and avoids other people.
– DERIVATIVES **misanthropic** adjective **misanthropy** noun.
– ORIGIN from Greek *misein* 'to hate' + *anthrōpos* 'man'.

misapply verb (**misapplies, misapplying, misapplied**) use something for the wrong purpose or in the wrong way.
– DERIVATIVES **misapplication** noun.

misapprehension noun a mistaken belief.

misappropriate verb dishonestly take something for one's own use.
– DERIVATIVES **misappropriation** noun.

misbegotten adjective 1 badly designed or planned. 2 old use (of a child) illegitimate.

misbehave verb behave badly.
– DERIVATIVES **misbehaviour** noun.

miscalculate verb calculate or assess

something wrongly.
– DERIVATIVES **miscalculation** noun.

miscall verb call something by a wrong or inappropriate name.

miscarriage noun 1 the early and unplanned birth of a fetus, before it is able to survive independently. 2 an unsuccessful outcome; a failure.

miscarriage of justice noun a failure of a court or judicial system to achieve justice.

miscarry verb (**miscarries, miscarrying, miscarried**) 1 (of a pregnant woman) have a miscarriage. 2 (of a plan) fail to achieve an intended result.

miscast verb (**be miscast**) (of an actor) be given an unsuitable role.

miscegenation /mi-si-ji-**nay**-sh'n/ noun the interbreeding of people of different races.
– ORIGIN from Latin *miscere* 'to mix' + *genus* 'race'.

miscellanea /mi-suh-**lay**-ni-uh/ plural noun different items collected together.

miscellaneous /mi-suh-**lay**-ni-uhss/ adjective 1 (of a number of things or people) of various types. 2 composed of things of different kinds: *a miscellaneous collection of problems.*
– DERIVATIVES **miscellaneously** adverb.
– ORIGIN Latin *miscellus* 'mixed'.

miscellany /mi-**sel**-luh-ni/ noun (pl. **miscellanies**) a collection of different things.

mischance noun bad luck.

mischief noun 1 playful misbehaviour. 2 harm or trouble caused by someone or something.
– ORIGIN Old French *meschief.*

mischievous /**miss**-chi-vuhss/ adjective 1 misbehaving or fond of misbehaving in a playful way. 2 intended to cause trouble.
– DERIVATIVES **mischievously** adverb **mischievousness** noun.

miscible /**miss**-i-b'l/ adjective (of liquids) capable of being mixed together.
– ORIGIN from Latin *miscere* 'to mix'.

miscommunication noun failure to communicate properly.

misconceive verb 1 fail to understand something correctly. 2 (**be misconceived**) be badly judged or planned.

misconception noun a false or mistaken idea or belief.

misconduct /miss-**kon**-dukt/ noun unacceptable or improper behaviour, especially by a professional person.

misconstruction noun the action of misinterpreting something.

misconstrue verb (**misconstrues, misconstruing, misconstrued**) interpret something wrongly.

miscount verb count something incorrectly.

miscreant /**miss**-kri-uhnt/ noun a person who has done something wrong or unlawful.
– ORIGIN Old French *mescreant* 'disbelieving'.

miscue verb (**miscues, miscueing or miscuing, miscued**) (in billiards and snooker) fail to cue the ball properly. •noun an act of miscueing the ball.

misdeed noun a wrong or unlawful act.

misdemeanour (US **misdemeanor**) noun 1 a minor wrongdoing. 2 Law (in the US and formerly in the UK) an offence regarded as less serious than a felony.

misdiagnose verb make an incorrect diagnosis of an illness.
– DERIVATIVES **misdiagnosis** noun.

misdial verb (**misdials, misdialling, misdialled;** US **misdials, misdialing, misdialed**) dial a telephone number incorrectly.

misdirect verb direct or instruct someone wrongly.
– DERIVATIVES **misdirection** noun.

mise en scène /meez on sen/ noun **1** the arrangement of scenery and stage props in a play. **2** the setting of an event.
– ORIGIN French, 'putting on stage'.

miser noun a person who hoards wealth and spends as little as possible.
– ORIGIN from Latin, 'wretched'.

miserabilism /miz-ruh-bil-iz'm/ noun a gloomily pessimistic or negative attitude.
– DERIVATIVES **miserabilist** noun & adjective.

miserable adjective **1** deeply unhappy or depressed. **2** causing unhappiness or discomfort. **3** gloomy and humourless. **4** too small; inadequate: *all they pay me is a miserable £10,000 a year.*
– DERIVATIVES **miserableness** noun **miserably** adverb.

misericord /mi-ze-ri-kord/ noun a ledge projecting from the underside of a hinged seat in a choir stall in a church, giving support to someone standing when the seat is folded up.
– ORIGIN from Latin *misericors* 'compassionate'.

miserly adjective **1** unwilling to spend money; mean. **2** (of a quantity) too small; inadequate.
– DERIVATIVES **miserliness** noun.

misery noun (pl. **miseries**) **1** great unhappiness or distress. **2** a cause of misery. **3** Brit. informal a person who is always miserable.

misfire verb **1** (of a gun) fail to fire properly. **2** (of an internal-combustion engine) fail to ignite the fuel correctly. **3** fail to produce the intended result: *he didn't know that his plan had misfired.*

misfit noun a person whose behaviour or attitude sets them apart from others.

misfortune noun **1** bad luck. **2** an unfortunate event.

misgivings plural noun feelings of doubt or anxiety about what might happen.

misgovern verb govern a country unfairly or poorly.

misguided adjective showing poor judgement or reasoning.

mishandle verb handle or deal with something unwisely or wrongly.

mishap noun an unlucky accident.

mishear verb (past and past part. **misheard**) hear something spoken incorrectly.

mishit verb (**mishits, mishitting, mishit**) hit or kick a ball badly.

mishmash noun a confused mixture.
– ORIGIN from **MASH**.

misidentify verb (**misidentifies, misidentifying, misidentified**) identify someone or something incorrectly.
– DERIVATIVES **misidentification** noun.

misinform verb give someone false or inaccurate information.
– DERIVATIVES **misinformation** noun.

misinterpret verb (**misinterprets, misinterpreting, misinterpreted**) interpret something wrongly.
– DERIVATIVES **misinterpretation** noun.

misjudge verb **1** form an incorrect opinion of someone or something. **2** estimate wrongly: *the horse misjudged the fence and Joe was thrown off.*
– DERIVATIVES **misjudgement** (also **misjudgment**) noun.

mislay verb (past and past part. **mislaid**) lose an object by temporarily forgetting where one has left it.

mislead verb (past and past part. **misled**) give someone inaccurate or false information.
– DERIVATIVES **misleading** adjective.

mismanage verb manage something badly or wrongly.
– DERIVATIVES **mismanagement** noun.

mismatch noun a failure to correspond or match: *a huge mismatch between supply and demand.* • verb match people or things unsuitably or incorrectly.

misname verb give a wrong or inappropriate name to someone or something.

misnomer noun **1** an inaccurate or misleading name. **2** the wrong use of a name or term.
– ORIGIN from Old French *mesnommer* 'misname'.

miso /mee-soh/ noun paste made from fermented soya beans and barley or rice malt, used in Japanese cookery.
– ORIGIN Japanese.

misogynist /mi-soj-uh-nist/ noun a man who hates women.
– DERIVATIVES **misogynistic** adjective.

misogyny /mi-soj-uh-ni/ noun hatred of women.
– ORIGIN from Greek *misos* 'hatred' + *gunē* 'woman'.

misplace verb put something in the wrong place.

misplaced adjective **1** not appropriate in the circumstances. **2** (of a feeling) directed to an inappropriate person or thing: *a misplaced faith in the ability of scientists.*

misprint noun an error in a printed work. • verb print something incorrectly.

mispronounce verb pronounce something wrongly.
– DERIVATIVES **mispronunciation** noun.

misquote verb quote someone or something inaccurately.
– DERIVATIVES **misquotation** noun.

misread verb (past and past part. **misread**) read or interpret something wrongly.

misrepresent verb give a false or misleading account of someone or something.
– DERIVATIVES **misrepresentation** noun.

misrule noun **1** unfair or inefficient government of a country. **2** disruption of peace; disorder. • verb govern a country badly.

miss[1] verb **1** fail to hit, reach, or come into contact with something aimed at. **2** fail to notice, hear, or understand: *she had shrewd eyes that missed nothing.* **3** (**miss someone/ thing out**) Brit. omit someone or something. **4** fail to attend or take advantage of something. **5** avoid someone or something.

6 be too late for a passenger vehicle or the post. **7** notice or feel the loss or absence of: *he missed all his old friends.* •noun **1** a failure to hit, catch, or reach something. **2** an unsuccessful record or film.
– PHRASES **give something a miss** Brit. informal decide not to do or have something. **miss the boat** informal be too slow to take advantage of something.
– ORIGIN Old English.

miss² noun **1** (**Miss**) a title used before the name of an unmarried woman or girl. **2** (**Miss**) used as a form of address to a female teacher. **3** a girl or young woman, especially one regarded as headstrong.
– ORIGIN abbreviation of *mistress*.

missal noun a book that contains the set forms of worship used in the Catholic Mass.
– ORIGIN from Latin *missa* 'Mass'.

misshapen adjective not having the normal or natural shape.

missile noun **1** an object which is forcibly propelled at a target. **2** an explosive weapon that is self-propelled or directed by remote control.
– ORIGIN Latin, from *mittere* 'send'.

missing adjective **1** absent and unable to be found. **2** not present when expected or supposed to be.

missing link noun a supposed fossil form believed to be a link between humans and apes.

mission noun **1** an important assignment, typically involving travel abroad. **2** an organization involved in a long-term assignment abroad. **3** a military or scientific operation or expedition. **4** the work carried out by a religious organization to spread its faith. **5** an aim or task that a person feels to be their duty to do: *his mission in life has been to cut unemployment.*
– ORIGIN Latin.

missionary noun (pl. **missionaries**) a person sent on a religious mission. •adjective relating to a missionary or religious mission.

mission creep noun a gradual shift in objectives during a military campaign, often resulting in a longer involvement than was planned.

mission statement noun a formal summary of the aims and values of an organization.

missis noun variant spelling of **MISSUS**.

missive noun formal a letter.
– ORIGIN Latin *missivus*.

misspell verb (past and past part. **misspelt** or **misspelled**) spell a word wrongly.

misspend verb (past and past part. **misspent**) spend time or money foolishly or wastefully.

misstate verb state something wrongly or inaccurately.
– DERIVATIVES **misstatement** noun.

misstep noun a badly judged step.

missus (also **missis**) noun informal or humorous a person's wife.

missy noun (pl. **missies**) an affectionate or scornful form of address to a young girl.

mist noun **1** a cloud of tiny water droplets in the atmosphere that limits visibility to a lesser extent than fog. **2** a condensed vapour settling on a surface. •verb cover or become covered with mist.
– ORIGIN Old English.

mistake noun **1** a thing that is incorrect. **2** an error of judgement. •verb (past **mistook**; past part. **mistaken**) **1** be wrong about: *I mistook the nature of our relationship.* **2** (**mistake someone/thing for**) confuse someone or something with.
– ORIGIN Old Norse, 'take in error'.

mistaken adjective **1** wrong in one's opinion or judgement. **2** based on a misunderstanding or faulty judgement.
– DERIVATIVES **mistakenly** adverb.

mister noun **1** variant form of **MR**. **2** informal a form of address to a man.

mistime verb choose an inappropriate moment to do or say something.

mistle thrush noun a large thrush with a spotted breast.
– ORIGIN because of the bird's fondness for mistletoe berries.

mistletoe noun a plant which grows as a parasite on trees, and bears white berries in winter.
– ORIGIN Old English.

mistook past of **MISTAKE**.

mistral /miss-truhl/ noun a strong, cold north-westerly wind that blows through the Rhône valley and southern France.
– ORIGIN French.

mistranslate verb translate something incorrectly.
– DERIVATIVES **mistranslation** noun.

mistreat verb treat a person or animal badly or unfairly.
– DERIVATIVES **mistreatment** noun.

mistress noun **1** a woman who controls or owns something. **2** a woman skilled in a particular subject or activity: *she's a mistress of the sound bite.* **3** a woman in a sexual relationship with a man who is married to someone else. **4** Brit. a female schoolteacher. **5** (**Mistress**) old use Mrs.
– ORIGIN Old French *maistresse*.

mistrial noun a trial that is made invalid through an error in the proceedings.

mistrust verb have no trust in someone or something. •noun lack of trust.
– DERIVATIVES **mistrustful** adjective.

misty adjective (**mistier**, **mistiest**) **1** full of or covered with mist. **2** not clear or distinct: *a few misty memories.*
– DERIVATIVES **mistily** adverb **mistiness** noun.

misunderstand verb (past and past part. **misunderstood**) fail to understand someone or something correctly.

misunderstanding noun **1** a failure to understand something correctly. **2** a disagreement with someone.

misuse verb /mis-yooz/ **1** use something wrongly. **2** treat someone badly or unfairly. •noun /mis-yoos/ the action of misusing something.

mite¹ noun a very tiny creature like a spider, several kinds of which live as parasites on animals or plants.
– ORIGIN Old English.

mite² noun **1** a small child or animal. **2** a very small amount. •adverb (**a mite**) informal slightly.

m

– ORIGIN Dutch (first referring to a Flemish copper coin of low value).

miter noun & verb US spelling of **MITRE**.

mither /my-*th*uh/ verb dialect, chiefly N. English **1** make a fuss. **2** pester someone.
– ORIGIN unknown.

mitigate verb **1** make something bad less severe or serious. **2** (as adj. **mitigating**) (of a fact or circumstance) lessening the seriousness of or blame attached to an action.
– DERIVATIVES **mitigation** noun.
– ORIGIN Latin *mitigare* 'soften, alleviate'.

> USAGE: Do not confuse mitigate and militate.
> Mitigate means 'make something bad less severe' (*drainage schemes helped to mitigate the problem*), while **militate** is used with **against** to mean 'be a powerful factor in preventing' (*laws that militate against personal freedom*).

mitochondrion /my-tuh-**kon**-dri-uhn/ noun (pl. **mitochondria** /my-tuh-**kon**-dri-uh/) Biology a structure found in large numbers in most cells, in which respiration and energy production occur.
– DERIVATIVES **mitochondrial** adjective.
– ORIGIN from Greek *mitos* 'thread' + *khondrion* 'small granule'.

mitosis /my-**toh**-siss/ noun (pl. **mitoses** /my-**toh**-seez/) Biology the division of a cell that results in two daughter cells, each with the same number and kind of chromosomes as the original cell. Compare with **MEIOSIS**.
– ORIGIN from Greek *mitos* 'thread'.

mitre (US **miter**) noun **1** a tall headdress that tapers to a point at front and back, worn by bishops and senior abbots. **2** a joint made between two pieces of wood cut at an angle so as to form a corner of 90°. • verb join pieces of wood by means of a mitre joint.
– ORIGIN Greek *mitra* 'belt or turban'.

mitt noun **1** a mitten. **2** a fingerless glove. **3** informal a person's hand.

mitten noun a glove having a single section for all four fingers, with a separate section for the thumb.
– ORIGIN Old French *mitaine*.

mix verb **1** combine or be combined to form a whole. **2** make something by combining ingredients. **3** (**mix something up**) spoil the order or arrangement of a group of things. **4** (**mix someone/thing up**) confuse a person or thing with another. **5** combine signals or soundtracks into one to produce a recording. **6** enjoy meeting other people socially. • noun **1** a mixture. **2** the proportion of different people or things making up a mixture. **3** a version of a sound recording mixed in a different way from the original.
– PHRASES **be mixed up in** (or **with**) be involved in dishonest or underhand activity.
– ORIGIN from **MIXED**.

mixed adjective **1** consisting of different kinds, qualities or elements. **2** relating to or intended for both men and women.
– ORIGIN from Latin *miscere* 'to mix'.

mixed bag noun a varied assortment of things or people.

mixed blessing noun a thing that has both advantages and disadvantages.

mixed economy noun an economic system in which some business enterprises are owned by the state and some are owned by independent companies.

mixed farming noun farming of both crops and livestock.

mixed grill noun a dish of various grilled meats, mushrooms, and tomatoes.

mixed marriage noun a marriage between people of different races or religions.

mixed metaphor noun a combination of metaphors that produces a ridiculous effect (e.g. *this tower of strength will forge ahead*).

mixed-up adjective informal suffering from psychological or emotional problems.

mixer noun **1** a device for mixing things. **2** a person considered in terms of their ability to mix socially. **3** a soft drink that can be mixed with alcohol.

mixer tap noun a single tap through which both hot and cold water can flow at the same time.

mixologist noun informal a person who is skilled at mixing cocktails and other drinks.
– DERIVATIVES **mixology** noun.

mixture noun **1** a substance made by mixing other substances together. **2** (**a mixture of**) a combination of different things in which each part is distinct: *the area is a bizarre mixture of ancient and modern*. **3** a combination of two or more substances that mix together without any chemical reaction occurring.

mix-up noun informal a confusion or misunderstanding.

mizuna /my-**zoo**-nuh/ noun an oriental plant of the rape family, with leaves that are eaten in salads.
– ORIGIN from Japanese.

mizzen (also **mizzenmast**) noun the mast behind a ship's mainmast.
– ORIGIN from Italian *mezzano* 'middle'.

mizzle chiefly dialect noun light rain; drizzle. • verb (**it mizzles, it is mizzling, it mizzled**) rain lightly.
– ORIGIN probably from **MIST**.

ml abbreviation **1** mile or miles. **2** millilitre or millilitres.

MLA abbreviation Canadian & Indian Member of the Legislative Assembly.

MLitt abbreviation Master of Letters.
– ORIGIN from Latin *Magister Litterarum*.

Mlle abbreviation (pl. **Mlles**) Mademoiselle.

mm abbreviation millimetre or millimetres.

Mme abbreviation (pl. **Mmes**) Madame.

MMR abbreviation measles, mumps, and rubella (a vaccination given to children).

MMS abbreviation Multimedia Messaging Service, a system that enables mobile phones to send and receive colour pictures and sound clips as well as text messages.

MN abbreviation Minnesota.

Mn symbol the chemical element manganese.

mnemonic /ni-**mon**-ik/ noun a pattern of letters or words which helps one to remember something. • adjective helping or designed to help the memory.
– ORIGIN from Greek *mnēmōn* 'mindful'.

MO abbreviation **1** Medical Officer. **2** Missouri.

3 modus operandi. **4** money order.
Mo symbol the chemical element molybdenum.
mo noun informal, chiefly Brit. a moment.

moa /moh-uh/ noun a large extinct flightless bird resembling the emu, formerly found in New Zealand.
– ORIGIN Maori.

moan noun **1** a low mournful sound, usually expressing suffering. **2** informal a minor complaint. • verb **1** make a moan. **2** complain or grumble.
– DERIVATIVES moaner noun.
– ORIGIN unknown.

moat noun a deep, wide ditch filled with water, surrounding and protecting a castle.
– DERIVATIVES moated adjective.
– ORIGIN Old French mote 'mound'.

mob noun **1** a disorderly crowd of people. **2** Brit. informal a group of people. **3** (the Mob) N. Amer. the Mafia. **4** (the mob) derogatory the ordinary people. • verb (mobs, mobbing, mobbed) crowd round someone or into somewhere in an unruly way.
– ORIGIN from Latin mobile vulgus 'excitable crowd'.

mob cap noun a large, soft hat covering the hair, worn indoors by women in the 18th and early 19th centuries.
– ORIGIN from former mab 'slut'.

mobe (also mobey) noun informal a mobile phone.

mob-handed adverb Brit. informal in considerable numbers.

mobile adjective **1** able to move or be moved freely or easily. **2** (of a shop or other service) set up in a vehicle so as to travel around. **3** able or willing to move between occupations, homes, or social classes. **4** (of the features of the face) readily changing expression. • noun **1** a decorative structure hung so as to turn freely in the air. **2** a mobile phone.
– PHRASES upwardly (or downwardly) mobile moving to a higher (or lower) social class.
– ORIGIN Latin mobilis.

mobile home noun a large caravan used as permanent living accommodation.

mobile phone noun a portable telephone using a cellular radio system.

mobility noun the ability to move or be moved freely and easily.

mobilize (or mobilise) verb **1** prepare and organize troops for active service. **2** organize people or resources for a particular task.
– DERIVATIVES mobilization noun.

Möbius strip /mer-bi-uhss/ noun a surface with one continuous side formed by joining the ends of a rectangle after twisting one end through 180°.
– ORIGIN named after the German mathematician August F. Möbius.

mobster noun informal a gangster.

moccasin noun a soft leather shoe with the sole turned up and sewn to the upper, originally worn by North American Indians.
– ORIGIN Virginia Algonquian.

mocha /mok-uh/ noun **1** a fine-quality coffee. **2** a drink or flavouring made with mocha and chocolate.

– ORIGIN named after Mocha, a port in Yemen on the Red Sea.

mochaccino /mok-uh-chee-noh/ noun (pl. mochaccinos) a cappuccino containing chocolate syrup or flavouring.
– ORIGIN blend of MOCHA and CAPPUCCINO.

mock verb **1** tease or laugh at someone scornfully. **2** imitate someone in an unkind way. **3** (mock something up) make a replica or imitation of something. • adjective **1** not authentic or real: a mock-Georgian house. **2** (of an exam, battle, etc.) arranged for training or practice. • noun (mocks) Brit. informal exams taken in school as training for public exams.
– ORIGIN Old French mocquer 'deride'.

mocker noun a person who mocks.
– PHRASES put the mockers on Brit. informal thwart or bring bad luck to.

mockery noun (pl. mockeries) **1** scornful teasing; ridicule. **2** an absurd or worthless version of something: after a mockery of a trial, he was executed.
– PHRASES make a mockery of make something seem foolish or absurd.

mock-heroic adjective imitating the grandiose style of heroic literature in order to mock an ordinary subject.

mockingbird noun a long-tailed American songbird, noted for its mimicry of the calls of other birds.

mockney noun Brit. informal a form of speech regarded as an affected imitation of cockney.

mock orange noun a bushy shrub with white flowers whose perfume resembles that of orange blossom.

mock turtle soup noun imitation turtle soup made from a calf's head.

mock-up noun a model of a machine or structure that is used for teaching or testing.

MOD abbreviation (in the UK) Ministry of Defence.

mod noun Brit. (especially in the 1960s) a young person of a group who wore smart clothes and rode motor scooters. • adjective informal modern.

modal /moh-d'l/ adjective **1** relating to the way in which something is done. **2** Grammar relating to the mood of a verb. **3** (of music) using melodies or harmonies based on modes other than the ordinary major and minor scales.
– DERIVATIVES modality noun (pl. modalities) modally adverb.

modal verb noun Grammar an auxiliary verb that expresses necessity or possibility, e.g. must, shall, will.

mod cons plural noun modern conveniences, the equipment and features typical of a well-equipped modern house.

mode noun **1** a way in which something occurs or is done: his preferred mode of travel was a kayak. **2** a style or fashion in clothes, art, etc. **3** a set of musical notes forming a scale and from which melodies and harmonies are constructed. **4** Statistics the value that occurs most frequently in a given set of data.
– ORIGIN Latin modus 'measure, manner'.

model noun **1** a three-dimensional copy of a person or thing, typically on a smaller scale. **2** something used as an example. **3** an excellent example of a quality: she was a model

m

of self-control. **4** a person employed to display clothes by wearing them. **5** a person employed to pose for an artist or photographer. **6** a particular design or version of a product. **7** a simplified mathematical description of a system or process, used to assist calculations and predictions. •verb (**models, modelling, modelled**; US **models, modeling, modeled**) **1** make or shape a figure in clay, wax, etc. **2** (**model something on**) use something as an example to follow. **3** display clothes by wearing them. **4** work as an artist's or photographer's model. **5** make a mathematical model of something. **6** (in drawing or painting) make something appear three-dimensional.
– DERIVATIVES **modeller** noun.

modem /**moh**-dem/ noun a device for converting digital and analogue signals, especially to enable a computer to be connected to a telephone line.
– ORIGIN blend of *modulator* and *demodulator.*

moderate adjective /**mod**-uh-ruht/ **1** average in amount, intensity, or degree: *we walked at a moderate pace.* **2** (of a political position) not radical or extreme. •noun /**mod**-uh-ruht/ a person with moderate political views. •verb /**mod**-uh-rayt/ **1** make or become less extreme or intense. **2** Brit. review exam papers or results to ensure that marking is consistent. **3** be in charge of a decision-making body or a debate. **4** monitor an Internet bulletin board or chat room for inappropriate or offensive content.
– DERIVATIVES **moderately** adverb.
– ORIGIN from Latin *moderare* 'reduce, control'.

moderation noun **1** the avoidance of extremes in one's actions or opinions. **2** the action of making something less intense or extreme.

moderato /mod-uh-**rah**-toh/ adverb & adjective Music at a moderate pace.
– ORIGIN Italian, 'moderate'.

moderator noun **1** a person who helps people to settle a dispute. **2** a chairman of a debate. **3** Brit. a person who moderates exam papers.

modern adjective **1** relating to the present or to recent times. **2** having or using the most up-to-date techniques or equipment. **3** (in the arts) marked by a significant departure from traditional styles and values. •noun a person who believes in a departure from traditional styles or values.
– DERIVATIVES **modernity** noun **modernly** adverb **modernness** noun.
– ORIGIN Latin *modernus.*

modernism noun **1** modern ideas, methods, or styles. **2** a movement in the arts that aims to depart significantly from traditional styles or ideas.
– DERIVATIVES **modernist** noun & adjective **modernistic** adjective.

modernize (or **modernise**) verb bring something up to date with modern equipment, techniques, or ideas.
– DERIVATIVES **modernization** noun **modernizer** noun.

modern languages plural noun European languages as a subject of study, as contrasted with classical Latin and Greek.

modest adjective **1** viewing one's abilities or achievements in a humble way. **2** relatively moderate, limited, or small: *drink modest amounts of alcohol.* **3** not showing off the body; decent.
– DERIVATIVES **modestly** adverb.
– ORIGIN Latin *modestus* 'keeping due measure'.

modesty noun the quality or state of being humble, decent, or moderate.

modicum /**mod**-i-kuhm/ noun a small quantity of something.
– ORIGIN from Latin *modicus* 'moderate'.

modification noun **1** the action of modifying something. **2** a change made.

modifier noun **1** a person or thing that modifies something. **2** Grammar a word that qualifies the sense of a noun (e.g. *good* and *family* in *a good family house*).

modify verb (**modifies, modifying, modified**) make partial or minor changes to something.
– ORIGIN Latin *modificare.*

modish /**moh**-dish/ adjective currently fashionable.
– DERIVATIVES **modishly** adverb **modishness** noun.

modiste /mo-**deest**/ noun dated a fashionable milliner or dressmaker.
– ORIGIN French.

modular adjective **1** made up of separate units. **2** Mathematics relating to a modulus.
– DERIVATIVES **modularity** noun.

modulate verb **1** control or regulate something. **2** vary the strength, tone, or pitch of the voice. **3** adjust the amplitude or frequency of an oscillation or signal. **4** Music change from one key to another.
– DERIVATIVES **modulation** noun **modulator** noun.
– ORIGIN Latin *modulari* 'to measure'.

module noun **1** each of a set of parts or units that can be used to make a more complex structure. **2** each of a set of independent units of study forming part of a course. **3** an independent self-contained unit of a spacecraft.
– ORIGIN Latin *modulus.*

modulus /**mod**-yuu-luhss/ noun (pl. **moduli** /**mod**-yuu-li/) **1** Mathematics the magnitude of a number irrespective of whether it is positive or negative. **2** Physics a constant factor relating a physical effect to the force producing it.

modus operandi /moh-duhss op-uh-**ran**-di/ noun (pl. **modi operandi** /moh-di op-uh-**ran**-di/) a way of operating or doing something.
– ORIGIN Latin.

modus vivendi /moh-duhss vi-**ven**-di/ noun (pl. **modi vivendi** /moh-di vi-**ven**-di/) an arrangement allowing differing or conflicting groups to exist together peacefully.
– ORIGIN Latin.

moggie (also **moggy**) noun (pl. **moggies**) Brit. informal a cat.
– ORIGIN variant of *Maggie*, familiar form of the woman's name *Margaret.*

Mogul /**moh**-guhl/ (also **Moghul** or **Mughal**) noun **1** a member of the Muslim dynasty of Mongol origin which ruled much of India in the 16th–19th centuries. **2** (**mogul**) an important or powerful person.
– ORIGIN Persian, 'Mongol'.

MOH abbreviation Ministry of Health.

mohair noun a yarn or fabric made from the hair of the angora goat.

– ORIGIN Arabic, 'cloth made of goat's hair'.

Mohammedan noun & adjective variant spelling of **MUHAMMADAN**.

Mohawk noun (pl. same or **Mohawks**) a member of an American Indian people originally inhabiting parts of what is now upper New York State.
– ORIGIN from an American Indian language meaning 'maneaters'.

Mohegan /moh-**hee**-guhn/ noun a member of an American Indian people fformerly inhabiting western parts of Connecticut and Massachusetts. • adjective relating to the Mohegans.
– ORIGIN Mohegan, 'people of the tidal waters'.

Mohican[1] /moh-**hee**-kuhn/ noun a hairstyle in which the sides of the head are shaved and a central strip of hair is made to stand up.
– ORIGIN wrongly associated with the American Indian people.

Mohican[2] adjective & noun old-fashioned variant of **MAHICAN** or **MOHEGAN**.

moiety /**moy**-i-ti/ noun (pl. **moieties**) formal or technical each of two parts into which a thing is or can be divided.
– ORIGIN from Old French moite.

moire /mwar/ (also **moiré** /**mwah**-ray/) noun silk fabric treated to give it an appearance like that of rippled water.
– ORIGIN French moiré 'mohair' (the treatment first being used on mohair).

moist adjective slightly wet; damp.
– DERIVATIVES **moistly** adverb **moistness** noun.
– ORIGIN Old French moiste.

moisten verb make or become slightly wet.

moisture noun tiny drops of water or other liquid in the air, in a substance, or condensed on a surface.

moisturize (or **moisturise**) verb make something, especially the skin, less dry.
– DERIVATIVES **moisturizer** noun.

mojo noun (pl. **mojos**) chiefly US **1** a magic charm or spell. **2** power or influence.
– ORIGIN probably African.

moke noun Brit. informal a donkey.
– ORIGIN unknown.

mol /mohl/ noun Chemistry short for **MOLE**[4].

molar[1] noun a grinding tooth at the back of a mammal's mouth.
– ORIGIN from Latin mola 'millstone'.

molar[2] adjective Chemistry **1** relating to one mole of a substance. **2** (of a solution) containing one mole of solute per litre of solvent.

molasses noun **1** a thick dark brown liquid obtained from raw sugar. **2** N. Amer. golden syrup.
– ORIGIN from Latin mellacium 'must'.

mold noun & verb US spelling of **MOULD**[1], **MOULD**[2], and **MOULD**[3].

Moldavian noun a person from Moldavia, a former principality of SE Europe. • adjective relating to Moldavia.

molder verb & noun US spelling of **MOULDER**.

molding noun US spelling of **MOULDING**.

Moldovan /mol-**doh**-vuhn/ noun a person from Moldova, a country in SE Europe. • adjective relating to Moldova.

moldy adjective US spelling of **MOULDY**.

mole[1] noun **1** a small burrowing mammal with dark velvety fur, a long muzzle, and very small eyes. **2** a spy who manages to gain an important position within the security defences of a country. **3** someone within an organization who secretly passes on confidential information to another organization or country.
– ORIGIN Germanic.

mole[2] noun a small dark brown mark on the skin where there is a high concentration of melanin.
– ORIGIN Old English.

mole[3] noun **1** a large solid structure acting as a pier, breakwater, or causeway. **2** a harbour formed by a mole.
– ORIGIN Latin moles 'mass'.

mole[4] noun Chemistry the SI unit of amount of substance.
– ORIGIN from German Molekul 'molecule'.

molecular /muh-**lek**-yuu-ler/ adjective relating to or consisting of molecules.

molecular biology noun the branch of biology concerned with the macromolecules (e.g. proteins and DNA) essential to life.

molecular weight noun another term for **RELATIVE MOLECULAR MASS**.

molecule /**mol**-i-kyool/ noun a group of atoms chemically bonded together, representing the smallest fundamental unit of a compound that can take part in a chemical reaction.
– ORIGIN French, from Latin molecula 'small mass'.

molehill noun a small mound of earth thrown up by a burrowing mole.
– PHRASES **make a mountain out of a molehill** exaggerate the importance of a small problem.

moleskin noun **1** the skin of a mole used as fur. **2** a thick cotton fabric with a soft pile surface.

molest verb **1** assault or abuse someone sexually. **2** dated pester or harass someone in a hostile way.
– DERIVATIVES **molestation** noun **molester** noun.
– ORIGIN Latin molestare 'annoy'.

moll noun informal **1** a gangster's girlfriend. **2** dated a prostitute.
– ORIGIN familiar form of the woman's name Mary.

mollify verb (**mollifies**, **mollifying**, **mollified**) make someone feel less angry or anxious.
– DERIVATIVES **mollification** noun.
– ORIGIN Latin mollis 'soft'.

mollusc /**mol**-luhsk/ (US **mollusk**) noun an invertebrate animal of a large group including snails, slugs, and mussels, with a soft unsegmented body and often an external shell.
– DERIVATIVES **molluscan** adjective.
– ORIGIN from Latin mollis 'soft'.

molly (also **mollie**) noun (pl. **mollies**) a small fish which is bred for aquaria in many colours, especially black.
– ORIGIN from the name of Count Mollien, a French statesman.

mollycoddle verb treat someone in an indulgent or overprotective way.
– ORIGIN from molly 'girl' + **CODDLE**.

Molotov cocktail noun a simple incendiary device thrown by hand, consisting of a bottle of flammable liquid ignited by means of a wick.
– ORIGIN named after the Soviet statesman

m

Vyacheslav *Molotov*, who led the Soviet campaign against Finland in World War II, when such weapons were used by the Finns.

molt verb & noun US spelling of **MOULT**.

molten adjective (especially of metal, rock, or glass) liquefied by heat.
– ORIGIN old-fashioned past participle of **MELT**.

molto adverb Music very.
– ORIGIN Italian.

molybdenum /muh-**lib**-duh-nuhm/ noun a brittle silver-grey metallic element used in some steels and other alloys.
– ORIGIN Greek *molubdos* 'lead'.

mom noun N. Amer. informal one's mother.

moment noun 1 a brief period of time. 2 an exact point in time. 3 formal importance: *the issues were of little moment.* 4 Physics a turning effect produced by a force on an object, expressed as the product of the force and the distance from its line of action to a given point.
– PHRASES **have one's** (or **its**) **moments** be very good at times. **moment of truth** a time when a person or thing is tested or a crisis has to be faced. **of the moment** currently popular, famous, or important.
– ORIGIN Latin *momentum* (see **MOMENTUM**).

momentarily adverb 1 for a very short time. 2 N. Amer. very soon.

momentary adjective very brief or short-lived.

momentous adjective very important or significant: *a momentous decision.*
– DERIVATIVES **momentously** adverb **momentousness** noun.

momentum noun (pl. **momenta**) 1 the force gained by a moving object. 2 the driving force caused by the development of something: *the investigation gathered momentum.* 3 Physics the quantity of motion of a moving body, equal to the product of its mass and velocity.
– ORIGIN Latin *movimentum*, from *movere* 'to move'.

mommy noun (pl. **mommies**) N. Amer. informal one's mother.

Mon. abbreviation Monday.

monad /**mo**-nad, **moh**-nad/ noun technical a single unit; the number one.
– ORIGIN Greek *monas* 'unit'.

monarch noun 1 a king, queen, or emperor who rules a country or empire. 2 a large orange and black butterfly.
– DERIVATIVES **monarchical** adjective.
– ORIGIN from Greek *monos* 'alone' + *arkhein* 'to rule'.

monarchism noun support for the principle that a monarch should rule a country.
– DERIVATIVES **monarchist** noun & adjective.

monarchy noun (pl. **monarchies**) 1 rule by a monarch. 2 a state ruled by a monarch.

monastery noun (pl. **monasteries**) a community of monks living under religious vows.
– ORIGIN Greek *monastērion*, from *monazein* 'live alone'.

monastic adjective 1 relating to monks or nuns or their communities. 2 resembling monks or their way of life, especially in being simple, plain, or solitary.
– DERIVATIVES **monastically** adverb **monasticism**

noun.

Monday noun the day of the week before Tuesday and following Sunday.
– ORIGIN Old English, 'day of the moon'.

Monégasque /mo-nay-**gask**/ noun a person from Monaco. ● adjective relating to Monaco.
– ORIGIN French.

monetarism noun the theory that inflation is best controlled by limiting the supply of money circulating in an economy.
– DERIVATIVES **monetarist** noun & adjective.

monetary adjective relating to money or currency.
– DERIVATIVES **monetarily** adverb.

monetize (or **monetise**) /**mun**-i-tyz/ verb 1 convert something into currency. 2 (as adj. **monetized**) (of a society) adapted to the use of money.
– DERIVATIVES **monetization** noun.

money noun 1 a means of payment in the form of coins and banknotes. 2 the assets, property, etc. owned by someone or something: *the college is very short of money.* 3 payment or profit: *he's making a lot of money.* 4 (**moneys** or **monies**) formal sums of money.
– PHRASES **for my money** informal in my opinion. **put one's money where one's mouth is** informal take action to support one's statements.
– ORIGIN Latin *moneta* 'mint, money', originally a title of the goddess Juno, in whose temple in ancient Rome money was minted.

moneybags noun informal a wealthy person.

moneyed (also **monied**) adjective having much money; wealthy.

money-grubbing adjective informal greedily concerned with making money.

moneylender noun a person whose business is lending money, usually at a high rate of interest.

moneymaker noun a person or thing that earns a lot of money.
– DERIVATIVES **moneymaking** noun & adjective.

money market noun the trade in short-term loans between banks and other financial institutions.

money order noun a printed order for payment of a specified sum, issued by a bank or post office.

money spider noun a very small black spider, supposed to bring financial luck.

money-spinner noun chiefly Brit. a thing that brings in a large profit.

money supply noun the total amount of money in circulation or in existence in a country.

-monger combining form 1 referring to someone who trades in a particular thing: *fishmonger.* 2 chiefly derogatory referring to a person engaging in a particular activity: *rumour-monger.*
– ORIGIN Latin *mango* 'dealer'.

Mongol noun 1 a person from Mongolia. 2 (**mongol**) offensive a person with Down's syndrome.
– DERIVATIVES **mongolism** noun (offensive).

USAGE: The use of the term **mongol** to refer to a person with Down's syndrome is now unacceptable and considered offensive.

Mongolian noun 1 a person from Mongolia.

2 the language of Mongolia. •adjective relating to Mongolia.

Mongoloid adjective **1** relating to the division of humankind which includes the peoples native to east Asia, SE Asia, and Arctic North America. **2** (**mongoloid**) offensive affected with Down's syndrome.

> USAGE: The term **Mongoloid** is associated with outdated ideas about racial types; it is potentially offensive and best avoided.

mongoose noun (pl. **mongooses**) a small carnivorous mammal with a long body and tail, native to Africa and Asia.
– ORIGIN Marathi (a central Indian language).

mongrel noun a dog of a mixed breed.
– ORIGIN apparently related to MINGLE and AMONG.

monied adjective variant spelling of MONEYED.

monies plural of MONEY, used in financial contexts.

moniker (also **monicker**) noun informal a name.
– DERIVATIVES **monikered** adjective.
– ORIGIN unknown.

monism /mo-ni-z'm, moh-ni-z'm/ noun Philosophy a theory or doctrine that denies the existence of a distinction between things such as matter and mind.
– DERIVATIVES **monist** noun & adjective.
– ORIGIN from Greek *monos* 'single'.

monitor noun **1** a person or device that monitors something. **2** a display screen used to view a picture from a particular camera or a display from a computer. **3** a loudspeaker used by performers to hear what is being played or recorded. **4** a school pupil with disciplinary or other special duties. **5** (also **monitor lizard**) a large tropical lizard. •verb keep someone or something under observation, especially so as to regulate or record their activity or progress.
– ORIGIN from Latin *monere* 'warn'.

monk noun a man belonging to a religious community, typically one living under vows of poverty, chastity, and obedience.
– DERIVATIVES **monkish** adjective.
– ORIGIN from Greek *monakhos* 'solitary'.

monkey noun (pl. **monkeys**) **1** a primate which typically has a long tail and lives in trees in tropical countries. **2** a mischievous child. **3** Brit. informal a sum of £500. •verb (**monkeys, monkeying, monkeyed**) **1** (**monkey about/around**) behave in a silly or playful way. **2** (**monkey with**) tamper with something.
– PHRASES **make a monkey of** (or **out of**) make a fool of. **not give a monkey's** Brit. informal not care at all.
– ORIGIN unknown.

monkey business noun informal mischievous or underhand behaviour.

monkey nut noun Brit. a peanut.

monkey puzzle noun a coniferous tree with branches covered in spirals of tough spiny leaves.

monkey suit noun informal a man's evening dress or formal suit.

monkey wrench noun an adjustable spanner with large jaws.

monkfish noun (pl. same or **monkfishes**) an anglerfish, especially when used as food.

monkshood noun a poisonous plant with blue or purple flowers.

mono adjective **1** (of sound reproduction) using only one transmission channel. **2** monochrome. •noun **1** sound reproduction which uses only one transmission channel. **2** monochrome colour reproduction.

mono- (also **mon-** before a vowel) combining form **1** one; single: *monochromatic.* **2** (forming names of chemical compounds) containing one atom or group of a specified kind.
– ORIGIN Greek *monos* 'alone'.

monobasic adjective Chemistry (of an acid) having one replaceable hydrogen atom.

monobloc adjective made as or contained in a single casting.

monochromatic adjective **1** containing only one colour. **2** (of light or other radiation) of a single wavelength or frequency.

monochrome noun representation or reproduction of images in black and white or in varying tones of one colour. •adjective consisting of or displaying images in black and white or in varying tones of one colour.
– ORIGIN Greek *monokhrōmatos* 'of a single colour'.

monocle noun a single lens worn to improve sight in one eye.
– ORIGIN Latin *monoculus* 'one-eyed'.

monoclonal /mo-noh-**kloh**-nuhl/ adjective Biology relating to a clone or line of clones produced from a single individual or cell.

monocoque /**mon**-oh-kok/ noun an aircraft or vehicle structure in which the chassis and the body are built as a single piece.
– ORIGIN French, from *mono-* 'single' + *coque* 'shell'.

monocotyledon /mon-oh-kot-i-**lee**-duhn/ noun a flowering plant whose seeds have a single cotyledon (seed leaf).

monocular adjective with, for, or using one eye.
– ORIGIN Latin *monoculus* 'having one eye'.

monoculture noun the cultivation of a single crop in a particular area.

monocycle noun a unicycle.

monody /**mon**-uh-di/ noun (pl. **monodies**) **1** an ode sung by a single actor in a Greek tragedy. **2** music with only one melodic line.
– ORIGIN Greek *monōdos* 'singing alone'.

monoecious /muh-**nee**-shuhss/ adjective (of a plant or invertebrate animal) having both the male and female reproductive organs in the same individual. Compare with DIOECIOUS.
– ORIGIN from Greek *monos* 'single' + *oikos* 'house'.

monogamy /muh-**nog**-uh-mi/ noun the state of having only one husband, wife, or sexual partner at any one time.
– DERIVATIVES **monogamist** noun **monogamous** adjective.
– ORIGIN from Greek *monos* 'single' + *gamos* 'marriage'.

monoglot adjective using or speaking only one language.
– ORIGIN from Greek *monos* 'single' + *glōtta* 'tongue'.

monogram noun a motif of two or more

m

interwoven letters, typically a person's initials.
– DERIVATIVES **monogrammed** adjective.

monograph noun a scholarly written study of a single subject.
– DERIVATIVES **monographic** adjective.

monohull noun a boat with only one hull, as opposed to a catamaran or multihull.

monolingual adjective speaking or expressed in only one language.

monolith noun **1** a large single upright block of stone, especially a pillar or monument. **2** a very large organization or institution that is seen as impersonal and slow to change.
– ORIGIN from Greek *monos* 'single' + *lithos* 'stone'.

monolithic adjective **1** formed of a single large block of stone. **2** (of an organization or institution) large, impersonal, and slow to change.

monologue noun **1** a long speech by one actor in a play or film. **2** a long, boring speech by one person during a conversation.
– ORIGIN Greek *monologos* 'speaking alone'.

monomania noun an obsessive preoccupation with one thing.
– DERIVATIVES **monomaniac** noun.

monomer /mon-uh-mer/ noun a molecule that can be linked to other identical molecules to form a polymer.

monophonic adjective full form of **MONO** (in sense 1).

monoplane noun an aircraft with one pair of wings.

monopolist noun a person or organization that has exclusive control of the supply of a particular product or service.
– DERIVATIVES **monopolistic** adjective.

monopolize (or **monopolise**) verb dominate or take control of: *bigger clubs monopolize the most profitable TV deals.*
– DERIVATIVES **monopolization** noun.

monopoly noun (pl. **monopolies**) **1** the exclusive possession or control of the supply of a product or service. **2** an organization having a monopoly, or a product or service controlled by one. **3** exclusive possession or control of something: *men don't have a monopoly on unrequited love.*
– ORIGIN from Greek *monos* 'single' + *pōlein* 'sell'.

monorail noun a railway in which the track consists of a single rail.

monosaccharide /mon-oh-sak-uh-ryd/ noun a sugar (e.g. glucose) that cannot be broken down to give a simpler sugar.

monosodium glutamate noun a compound used to add flavour to food.

monosyllabic adjective **1** consisting of one syllable. **2** saying only brief words, or saying very little.

monosyllable noun a word of one syllable.

monotheism /mon-oh-thee-i-z'm/ noun the belief that there is a single god.
– DERIVATIVES **monotheist** noun & adjective **monotheistic** adjective.

monotone noun a continuing sound that is unchanging in pitch.

monotonous adjective **1** boring because of lack of change or variety: *a monotonous job.* **2** (of a sound) lacking variation of tone or pitch.
– DERIVATIVES **monotonously** adverb **monotony** noun.

monotreme /mon-uh-treem/ noun a mammal which possesses a cloaca and lays eggs, i.e. a platypus or echidna.
– ORIGIN from Greek *monos* 'single' + *trēma* 'hole'.

monounsaturated adjective referring to fats whose molecules are saturated except for one multiple bond, believed to be healthier in the diet than polyunsaturated fats.

monoxide noun an oxide containing one atom of oxygen.

Monseigneur /mon-sen-yer/ noun (pl. **Messeigneurs** /mess-en-yer/) a title or form of address for a French-speaking prince, cardinal, archbishop, or bishop.
– ORIGIN French, 'my lord'.

Monsieur /muh-syer/ noun (pl. **Messieurs** /mess-yer/) a title or form of address for a French-speaking man, corresponding to *Mr* or *sir.*
– ORIGIN French, 'my lord'.

Monsignor /mon-seen-yer/ noun (pl. **Monsignori** /mon-seen-yor-i/) the title of various senior Roman Catholic priests and officials.
– ORIGIN Italian.

monsoon noun **1** a seasonal wind in the region of the Indian subcontinent and SE Asia, bringing rain when blowing from the south-west. **2** the rainy season (typically May to September) accompanying the monsoon.
– DERIVATIVES **monsoonal** adjective.
– ORIGIN Arabic, 'season'.

mons pubis /monz pyoo-biss/ noun the rounded mass of fatty tissue lying over the joint of the pubic bones.
– ORIGIN Latin, 'mount of the pubes'.

monster noun **1** a large, ugly, and frightening imaginary creature. **2** a very cruel or wicked person. • adjective informal extraordinarily large: *a monster 36 lb carp.*
– ORIGIN Latin *monstrum.*

monstrance /mon-struhnss/ noun (in the Roman Catholic Church) a container in which the consecrated Host is displayed for veneration.
– ORIGIN from Latin *monstrare* 'to show'.

monstrosity noun (pl. **monstrosities**) **1** a very large and ugly building or other object. **2** a thing that is evil.

monstrous adjective **1** very large and ugly or frightening. **2** very evil or wrong: *a monstrous crime.* **3** extraordinarily large: *a monstrous tidal wave.*
– DERIVATIVES **monstrously** adverb.

mons Veneris /monz ven-uh-riss/ noun (in women) the mons pubis.
– ORIGIN Latin, 'mount of Venus'.

montage /mon-tahzh/ noun **1** the technique of making a picture or film by putting together pieces from other pictures or films. **2** a picture or film resulting from this.
– ORIGIN French.

montane /mon-tayn/ adjective relating to or

inhabiting mountainous country.
- ORIGIN Latin, from *mons* 'mountain'.

Montenegrin /mon-ti-nee-grin/ noun a person from Montenegro, a republic in the Balkans that is part of the Union of Serbia and Montenegro. •adjective relating to Montenegro.

Montessori /mon-ti-sor-ri/ noun a system of education that aims to develop a child's natural interests and activities rather than use formal teaching methods.
- ORIGIN named after the Italian educationist Maria *Montessori*.

month noun 1 each of the twelve named periods into which a year is divided. 2 a period of time between the same dates in successive calendar months. 3 a period of 28 days or four weeks.
- PHRASES **a month of Sundays** informal a very long time.
- ORIGIN Old English, related to MOON (since in many early civilizations the calendar month was calculated as beginning with the new moon).

monthly adjective done, produced, or happening once a month. •adverb once a month. •noun (pl. **monthlies**) a magazine published once a month.

monty noun (**the full monty**) Brit. informal the full amount expected, desired, or possible.
- ORIGIN unknown; perhaps from *the full Montague Burton*, apparently meaning 'Sunday-best three-piece suit' (from the name of a tailor), or in reference to 'the full cooked English breakfast' insisted on by Field Marshal *Montgomery*.

monument noun 1 a statue or structure built to commemorate a person or event. 2 a structure or site of historical importance. 3 a lasting and memorable example of something: *the house is a monument to timeless elegance*.
- ORIGIN Latin *monumentum*.

monumental adjective 1 very large or impressive: *a monumental achievement*. 2 acting as a monument.
- DERIVATIVES **monumentality** noun **monumentally** adverb.

monumental mason noun Brit. a person who makes tombstones and similar items.

moo verb (**moos, mooing, mooed**) (of a cow) make a long, deep sound. •noun (pl. **moos**) the long, deep sound made by a cow.
- ORIGIN imitating the sound.

mooch verb Brit. informal stand or walk around in a bored or listless way.
- ORIGIN probably from Old French *muscher* 'hide, skulk'.

mood noun 1 a temporary state of mind. 2 an angry, irritable, or sulky state of mind: *she's in a mood*. 3 the atmosphere or overall tone of something: *the mood of modern times*. 4 Grammar a form or category of a verb expressing a fact, command, question, wish, or condition.
- ORIGIN Old English.

moody adjective (**moodier, moodiest**) 1 tending to become bad-tempered or sulky. 2 giving a sad or mysterious impression.
- DERIVATIVES **moodily** adverb **moodiness** noun.

moolah noun informal money.

- ORIGIN unknown.

mooli /moo-li/ noun a variety of large white slender radish.
- ORIGIN from Sanskrit, 'root'.

moon noun 1 (also **Moon**) the natural satellite of the earth, orbiting it every 28 days and shining by reflected light from the sun. 2 a natural satellite of any planet. 3 literary or humorous a month. •verb 1 (usu. **moon about/around**) behave in a listless or dreamy way. 2 informal expose one's buttocks to someone as an insult or joke.
- PHRASES **over the moon** informal delighted.
- ORIGIN Old English, related to MONTH.

moonbeam noun a ray of moonlight.

moon boot noun a thickly padded boot with a fabric or plastic outer surface.

moon-faced adjective having a round face.

Moonie noun informal, often derogatory a member of the Unification Church.
- ORIGIN named after its founder, the Korean religious leader Sun Myung *Moon*.

moonlight noun the light of the moon. •verb (past and past part. **moonlighted**) informal do a second job, especially at night, without declaring it for tax purposes.
- DERIVATIVES **moonlighter** noun **moonlit** adjective.

moonscape noun a rocky and barren landscape resembling the moon's surface.

moonshine noun informal 1 foolish talk or ideas. 2 N. Amer. alcoholic drink that has been made illicitly or smuggled.

moonstone noun a pearly white semi-precious form of the mineral feldspar.

moonstruck adjective unable to think or act normally, especially as a result of being in love.

moonwalk verb 1 walk on the moon. 2 move or dance in a way reminiscent of the weightless movement of walking on the moon.

moony adjective (**moonier, mooniest**) dreamy, especially as a result of being in love.

Moor noun a member of a Muslim people of NW Africa.
- DERIVATIVES **Moorish** adjective.
- ORIGIN Greek *Mauros* 'inhabitant of Mauretania' (an ancient region of N. Africa).

moor¹ noun chiefly Brit. a stretch of open uncultivated upland.
- ORIGIN Old English.

moor² verb secure a boat by attaching it by cable or rope to the shore or to an anchor.
- ORIGIN probably from Germanic.

moorhen noun a water bird with blackish plumage and a red and yellow bill.

mooring (also **moorings**) noun 1 a place where a boat is moored. 2 the ropes or cables by which a boat is moored.

moorland noun (also **moorlands**) chiefly Brit. an extensive area of moor.

moose noun (pl. same) North American term for ELK.
- ORIGIN from Abnaki (an American Indian language).

moot adjective debatable or uncertain: *a moot point*. •verb raise a question or topic for discussion: *the scheme was first mooted last*

October. • noun (in Anglo-Saxon and medieval England) an assembly held for debate.
– ORIGIN Old English, 'assembly or meeting'.

mop noun 1 a bundle of thick loose strings or a sponge attached to a handle, used for wiping floors. 2 a thick mass of untidy hair. • verb (**mops, mopping, mopped**) 1 clean or soak up liquid from something by wiping: *she mopped the floor.* 2 (**mop something up**) complete or put an end to something by dealing with the remaining parts: *troops mopped up the last pockets of resistance.*
– ORIGIN perhaps related to Latin *mappa* 'napkin'.

mope verb be listless and gloomy.
– ORIGIN perhaps Scandinavian.

moped /moh-ped/ noun a light motorcycle with an engine capacity below 50 cc.
– ORIGIN from Swedish *trampcykel med motor och pedaler* 'pedal cycle with motor and pedals'.

moppet noun informal an endearing small child.
– ORIGIN from former *moppe* 'baby or rag doll'.

moptop noun a man's hairstyle in the form of a long shaggy bob.

moquette /mo-ket/ noun a thick pile fabric used for carpets and upholstery.
– ORIGIN French.

MOR abbreviation (of music) middle-of-the-road.

moraine /muh-rayn/ noun a mass of rocks and sediment carried down and deposited by a glacier.
– ORIGIN from French dialect *morre* 'snout'.

moral adjective 1 concerned with the principles of right and wrong behaviour. 2 based on or following the code of behaviour that is considered socially right or acceptable: *they have a moral obligation to pay the money back.* 3 psychological rather than physical or practical: *moral support.* • noun 1 a lesson about right or wrong that can be learned from a story or experience. 2 (**morals**) standards of behaviour, or principles of right and wrong.
– DERIVATIVES **morally** adverb.
– ORIGIN Latin *moralis.*

morale /muh-rahl/ noun the level of a person's or group's confidence or enthusiasm at a particular time: *the extra pay is aimed at boosting morale.*
– ORIGIN French *moral.*

moralist noun 1 a teacher or student of morality. 2 a person with a tendency to moralize.
– DERIVATIVES **moralistic** adjective.

morality noun (pl. **moralities**) 1 principles concerning the distinction between right and wrong or good and bad behaviour. 2 a particular system of values and moral principles. 3 the extent to which an action is right or wrong.

morality play noun a kind of play, popular in the 15th and 16th centuries, which presents a lesson about right and wrong behaviour in which characters represent qualities such as good or evil.

moralize (or **moralise**) verb comment on issues of right or wrong behaviour, especially in a disapproving way.
– DERIVATIVES **moralizer** noun.

moral majority noun 1 the part of society in favour of strict moral standards. 2 (**Moral Majority**) a right-wing Christian movement in the US.

moral philosophy noun the branch of philosophy concerned with ethics.

moral victory noun a situation in which one's ideas or principles are shown to be fair or justified, even if one has not achieved one's aim.

morass /muh-rass/ noun 1 an area of muddy or boggy ground. 2 a complicated or confused situation: *a morass of lies.*
– ORIGIN Dutch *moeras.*

moratorium /mo-ruh-tor-i-uhm/ noun (pl. **moratoriums** or **moratoria** /mo-ruh-tor-i-uh/) 1 a temporary ban on an activity. 2 a legal authorization to debtors to postpone payment.
– ORIGIN Latin.

Moravian /muh-ray-vi-uhn/ noun 1 a person from Moravia in the Czech Republic. 2 a member of a Protestant Church founded by emigrants from Moravia. • adjective relating to Moravia or the Moravian Church.

moray (also **moray eel**) noun an eel-like predatory fish of warm seas.
– ORIGIN Portuguese *moréia.*

morbid adjective 1 having or showing an unhealthy interest in unpleasant subjects, especially about death and disease. 2 Medicine relating to or indicating disease.
– DERIVATIVES **morbidity** noun **morbidly** adverb.
– ORIGIN Latin *morbus* 'disease'.

mordant adjective (especially of humour) sharply sarcastic. • noun 1 a substance that combines with a dye, used to fix it in a material. 2 a corrosive liquid used to etch the lines on a printing plate.
– ORIGIN Latin *mordere* 'to bite'.

more determiner & pronoun a greater or additional amount or degree. • adverb 1 forming the comparative of adjectives and adverbs. 2 to a greater extent. 3 again. 4 (**more than**) extremely: *I'm more than happy to oblige.*
– PHRASES **more or less** 1 to a certain extent. 2 approximately. **no more** 1 nothing or no further. 2 (**be no more**) no longer exist.
– ORIGIN Old English.

USAGE: Do not use **more** with an adjective that is already in a comparative (**-er**) form (as in *more better, more hungrier*); the correct use is *better* or *hungrier* (or *more hungry*).

moreish adjective Brit. informal so pleasant to eat that one wants more.

morel /muh-rel/ noun an edible fungus having a brown oval or pointed cap with an irregular honeycombed surface.
– ORIGIN French *morille.*

morello noun (pl. **morellos**) a kind of sour dark cherry used in cooking.
– ORIGIN Italian, 'blackish'.

moreover adverb in addition to what has been said; besides.

mores /mor-ayz/ plural noun the customs and conventions of a community.
– ORIGIN Latin, plural of *mos* 'custom'.

morganatic /mor-guh-nat-ik/ adjective (of a marriage) between a man of high rank and a

woman of low rank who keeps her former status, their children having no claim to the father's possessions or title.
– ORIGIN from Latin *matrimonium ad morganaticam* 'marriage with a morning gift' (because a gift given by a husband on the morning after the marriage was the wife's only entitlement).

morgue noun **1** a mortuary. **2** informal a newspaper's archive or library or cuttings, photographs, or other reference material.
– ORIGIN French, originally the name of a building in Paris where bodies were kept until identified.

MORI /mor-ri/ (also **Mori**) abbreviation trademark Market and Opinion Research International.

moribund adjective **1** at the point of death. **2** in decline or lacking vitality or effectiveness: *the country's moribund economy.*
– ORIGIN from Latin *mori* 'to die'.

Mormon noun a member of the Church of Jesus Christ of Latter-Day Saints, a religion founded in the US in 1830 by Joseph Smith Jr.
– DERIVATIVES **Mormonism** noun.
– ORIGIN the name of a prophet to whom Smith attributed *The Book of Mormon*, a collection of supposed revelations.

morn noun literary morning.
– ORIGIN Old English.

mornay adjective referring to or served in a cheese-flavoured white sauce: *cauliflower mornay.*
– ORIGIN perhaps named after *Mornay*, the eldest son of the French cook Joseph Voiron, the inventor of the sauce.

morning noun **1** the period of time between midnight and noon, especially from sunrise to noon. **2** sunrise. • adverb (**mornings**) informal every morning.
– ORIGIN from **MORN**, on the pattern of *evening*.

morning-after pill noun a contraceptive pill that is effective up to about seventy-two hours after having sex.

morning coat noun a man's tailcoat.

morning dress noun a man's formal dress of morning coat and striped trousers.

morning glory noun a climbing plant of the convolvulus family with trumpet-shaped flowers.

morning sickness noun nausea occurring in the mornings during early pregnancy.

morning star noun the planet Venus when visible in the east before sunrise.

Moroccan noun a person from Morocco in North Africa. • adjective relating to Morocco.

morocco noun fine flexible leather made (originally in Morocco) from goatskins.

moron noun informal a stupid person.
– DERIVATIVES **moronic** adjective.
– ORIGIN Greek *mōros* 'foolish'.

morose adjective sullen and bad-tempered.
– DERIVATIVES **morosely** adverb **moroseness** noun.
– ORIGIN Latin *morosus* 'peevish'.

morph verb (in computer animation) change smoothly and gradually from one image to another.
– ORIGIN from **METAMORPHOSIS**.

morpheme /mor-feem/ noun Linguistics the smallest unit of meaning into which a word can be divided (e.g. *in*, *come*, *-ing*, forming *incoming*).

morphia noun dated morphine.

morphine noun a drug obtained from opium and used medicinally to relieve pain.
– ORIGIN named after the Roman god of sleep, *Morpheus*.

morphology noun (pl. **morphologies**) **1** the branch of biology concerned with the forms and structures of living organisms. **2** the study of the forms of words. **3** the form, shape, or structure of something.
– DERIVATIVES **morphological** adjective **morphologist** noun.

morris dancing noun traditional English folk dancing performed outdoors by groups of dancers wearing costumes with small bells attached and carrying handkerchiefs or sticks.
– ORIGIN from *Moorish* (see **MOOR**).

morrow noun (**the morrow**) old use or literary the following day.
– ORIGIN Old English.

Morse (also **Morse code**) noun a code in which letters are represented by combinations of long and short light or sound signals.
– ORIGIN named after its American inventor Samuel F. B. *Morse*.

morsel noun a small piece of food.
– ORIGIN Old French, 'little bite'.

mortadella /mor-tuh-del-luh/ noun a type of smooth-textured Italian sausage containing pieces of fat.
– ORIGIN from Latin *murtatum* 'sausage seasoned with myrtle berries'.

mortal adjective **1** having to die at some time. **2** causing death: *a mortal wound.* **3** (of fear, pain, etc.) intense. **4** (of conflict or an enemy) lasting until death; never to be reconciled. **5** informal conceivable or imaginable: *every mortal thing.* **6** Christian Theology (of a sin) regarded as depriving the soul of divine grace. Often contrasted with **VENIAL**. • noun a human being.
– DERIVATIVES **mortally** adverb.
– ORIGIN from Latin *mors* 'death'.

mortality noun **1** the state of having to die at some time. **2** death, especially on a large scale. **3** (also **mortality rate**) the number of deaths in a particular area or period, or from a particular cause.

mortar noun **1** a mixture of lime with cement, sand, and water, used to hold bricks or stones together. **2** a cup-shaped container in which substances are crushed or ground with a pestle. **3** a short cannon for firing shells at high angles. • verb **1** join bricks or stones together with mortar. **2** attack someone or something with shells fired from a mortar.
– ORIGIN Latin *mortarium* 'container in which substances are crushed or ground'; sense 1 is probably a transferred use of sense 2, the mortar being mixed in a trough or other container.

mortar board noun **1** a hat with a stiff, flat square top and a tassel, worn as part of formal academic dress. **2** a small square board held horizontally by a handle on the underside, used for holding mortar.

mortgage noun **1** a legal agreement by which a person takes out a loan using property as security (usually a house which is being

m

purchased). **2** an amount of money borrowed in a mortgage. •**verb** give a bank or building society the right to hold a person's house as security for the loan borrowed from them.
– ORIGIN Old French, 'dead pledge'.

mortgagee noun the lender in a mortgage.

mortgagor noun the borrower in a mortgage.

mortician noun N. Amer. an undertaker.

mortify verb (**mortifies, mortifying, mortified**) **1** make someone feel embarrassed or humiliated. **2** use self-discipline to control one's physical desires. **3** (of flesh) become gangrenous.
– DERIVATIVES **mortification** noun **mortifying** adjective.
– ORIGIN Old French *mortifier*.

mortise (also **mortice**) noun a hole or recess designed to receive a corresponding projection (a tenon) so that the two are held together. •**verb 1** join two things together using a mortise and tenon. **2** cut a mortise in something.
– ORIGIN Old French *mortaise*.

mortise lock noun a lock set into the framework of a door in a recess or mortise.

mortuary noun (pl. **mortuaries**) a room or building in which dead bodies are kept until burial or cremation. •**adjective** relating to burial or tombs.
– ORIGIN from Latin *mortuus* 'dead'.

Mosaic adjective relating to or associated with the biblical prophet Moses.

mosaic noun a picture or pattern produced by arranging together smaller pieces of stone, tile, or glass of different colours.
– DERIVATIVES **mosaicist** noun.
– ORIGIN French *mosaïque*.

Moselle /moh-**zel**/ (also **Mosel**) noun a light medium-dry white wine from the valley of the River Moselle.

mosey verb (**moseys, moseying, moseyed**) informal walk or move in a leisurely way.
– ORIGIN unknown.

mosh verb informal dance to rock music in a violent way that involves jumping up and down and deliberately colliding with other dancers.
– ORIGIN perhaps from MASH or MUSH¹.

Moslem noun & adjective variant spelling of MUSLIM.

mosque noun a Muslim place of worship.
– ORIGIN French, from Arabic.

mosquito noun (pl. **mosquitoes**) a small fly, some kinds of which transmit diseases through the bite of the female.
– ORIGIN Spanish and Portuguese, 'little fly'.

mosquito net noun a fine net hung across a door or window or around a bed to keep mosquitoes away.

moss noun **1** a small flowerless spreading green plant which grows in damp habitats and reproduces by means of spores. **2** Scottish & N. English a peat bog.
– DERIVATIVES **mossy** adjective.
– ORIGIN Old English.

moss stitch noun alternate plain and purl stitches in knitting.

most determiner & pronoun **1** greatest in amount or degree. **2** the majority of. •**adverb 1** to the greatest extent. **2** forming the superlative of adjectives and adverbs. **3** very.
– PHRASES **at (the) most** not more than. **for the most part** in most cases; usually. **make the most of** use something to the best advantage.
– ORIGIN Old English.

mostly adverb **1** on the whole; mainly. **2** usually.

Most Reverend noun the title of an Anglican archbishop or an Irish Roman Catholic bishop.

MOT noun (in the UK) a compulsory annual test of motor vehicles of more than a specified age.
– ORIGIN abbreviation of *Ministry of Transport*.

mote noun a speck.
– ORIGIN Old English.

motel noun a roadside hotel for motorists.
– ORIGIN blend of MOTOR and HOTEL.

motet /moh-**tet**/ noun a short piece of sacred choral music.
– ORIGIN Old French, 'little word'.

moth noun an insect resembling a butterfly but holding its wings flat when at rest and mainly active at night.
– ORIGIN Old English.

mothball noun a small ball of a strong-smelling substance such as naphthalene, placed among stored clothes to keep clothes moths away. •**verb** put something into storage or on hold for an indefinite period: *plans to invest in four superstores have been mothballed.*

moth-eaten adjective damaged or apparently damaged by clothes moths; shabby or threadbare.

mother noun **1** a female parent. **2** (**Mother**) (especially as a title or form of address) the head of a female religious community. **3** informal an extreme or very large example of something: *the mother of all traffic jams.* •**verb 1** bring up a child with care and affection. **2** look after someone kindly and protectively.
– DERIVATIVES **motherhood** noun **motherless** adjective.
– ORIGIN Old English.

motherboard (also **mainboard**) noun a printed circuit board containing the main components of a microcomputer.

mother country noun a country in relation to its colonies.

Mothering Sunday noun Brit. the fourth Sunday in Lent, traditionally a day for honouring one's mother.

mother-in-law noun (pl. **mothers-in-law**) the mother of one's husband or wife.

motherland noun a person's native country.

mother lode noun a principal vein of an ore or mineral.

motherly adjective relating to or like a mother, especially in being caring, protective, and kind.
– DERIVATIVES **motherliness** noun.

mother-of-pearl noun a smooth pearly substance lining the shells of oysters and certain other molluscs.

Mother's Day noun a day of the year on which children honour their mothers (in Britain Mothering Sunday, and in North America and South Africa the second Sunday in May).

mother ship noun a large spacecraft or ship from which smaller craft are launched or maintained.

mother's ruin noun Brit. informal gin.

Mother Superior noun the head of a community of nuns.

mother tongue noun a person's native language.

motif /moh-teef/ noun **1** a single or repeated image forming a design. **2** a theme that is repeated in an artistic, musical, or literary work.
– ORIGIN French.

motile /moh-tyl/ adjective (of cells and single-celled organisms) capable of motion.
– DERIVATIVES **motility** noun.
– ORIGIN from Latin *motus* 'motion'.

motion noun **1** the action of moving. **2** a movement or gesture. **3** a formal proposal put to a law-making body or committee. **4** Brit. an emptying of the bowels. ● verb direct someone by making a gesture: *he motioned her towards the sofa.*
– PHRASES **go through the motions** do something with little effort or care.
– DERIVATIVES **motionless** adjective.
– ORIGIN from Latin *movere* 'to move'.

motion picture noun chiefly N. Amer. a cinema film.

motivate verb **1** give someone a motive for doing something: *he was motivated by the desire for profit.* **2** stimulate someone's interest: *it is the teacher's job to motivate the child at school.*
– DERIVATIVES **motivator** noun.

motivation noun **1** the reason or reasons behind someone's actions or behaviour. **2** desire or willingness to do something; enthusiasm.
– DERIVATIVES **motivational** adjective.

motive noun a factor influencing a person to act in a particular way. ● adjective producing physical or mechanical motion.
– DERIVATIVES **motiveless** adjective.
– ORIGIN Latin *motivus.*

motive power noun the energy used to drive machinery.

mot juste /moh zhoost/ noun (pl. **mots justes** pronunc. same) (**the mot juste**) the most appropriate word or expression.
– ORIGIN French, 'appropriate word'.

motley adjective made up of a variety of very different people or things: *a motley collection of cars.* ● noun a varied mixture.
– ORIGIN unknown.

motocross noun cross-country racing on motorcycles.

motor noun **1** a machine that supplies the power to drive a vehicle or other device. **2** Brit. informal a car. ● adjective **1** relating to motor vehicles. **2** giving or producing motion or action. **3** relating to muscular movement or the nerves activating it. ● verb travel in a car.
– ORIGIN Latin, 'mover', from *movere* 'to move'.

motorbike noun a motorcycle.

motorboat noun a boat powered by a motor.

motorcade noun a procession of motor vehicles.
– ORIGIN from **MOTOR**, on the pattern of *cavalcade.*

motor car noun Brit. a car.

motorcycle noun a two-wheeled vehicle that is powered by a motor and has no pedals.
– DERIVATIVES **motorcycling** noun **motorcyclist** noun.

motorhome noun chiefly N. Amer. a motor vehicle that is fitted out as a caravan.

motorist noun the driver of a car.

motorize (or **motorise**) verb (usu. as adj. **motorized**) **1** equip a vehicle or device with a motor to operate or propel it. **2** equip troops with motor transport.
– DERIVATIVES **motorization** noun.

motorman noun (pl. **motormen**) the driver of a train or tram.

motormouth noun informal a person who talks rapidly and continuously.

motor neuron disease noun a disease in which the nerve cells carrying messages to the muscles from the brain gradually deteriorate, causing muscle loss and eventual death.

motor racing noun the sport of racing in specially developed fast cars.

motor vehicle noun a road vehicle powered by an internal-combustion engine.

motorway noun Brit. a road designed for fast traffic, typically with three lanes in each direction.

motte /mot/ noun historical a mound forming the site of a castle or camp.
– ORIGIN French, 'mound'.

mottle verb (usu. as adj. **mottled**) mark something with patches of a different colour. ● noun a patch of colour.
– ORIGIN probably from **MOTLEY**.

motto noun (pl. **mottoes** or **mottos**) a short sentence or phrase expressing a belief or aim of a person or group.
– ORIGIN Italian, 'word'.

moue /moo/ noun a pout.
– ORIGIN French.

mould[1] (US **mold**) noun **1** a hollow container used to give shape to molten or hot liquid material when it cools and hardens. **2** a jelly or mousse. **3** a distinctive type, style, or character: *he's a leader in the mould of Winston Churchill.* ● verb **1** form an object out of a soft substance. **2** influence the development of something.
– PHRASES **break the mould** end a restrictive pattern of events or behaviour by doing things differently.
– ORIGIN probably from Old French *modle.*

mould[2] (US **mold**) noun a furry growth of minute fungi occurring in moist warm conditions on organic matter.
– ORIGIN probably from former *moul* 'grow mouldy'.

mould[3] (US **mold**) noun chiefly Brit. soft loose earth, especially when rich in organic matter.
– ORIGIN Old English.

mouldboard noun the board or plate in a plough that turns the earth over.

moulder (US **molder**) verb slowly decay.
– ORIGIN perhaps from **MOULD**[3].

moulding (US **molding**) noun a shaped strip of wood, stone, or plaster as a decorative architectural feature.

mouldy (US **moldy**) adjective (**mouldier**, **mouldiest**) **1** covered with or smelling of

mould. **2** informal boring or worthless.
– DERIVATIVES **mouldiness** noun.

moult (US **molt**) verb shed old feathers, hair, or skin, to make way for a new growth. ●noun a period of moulting.
– ORIGIN from Latin *mutare* 'to change'.

mound noun **1** a raised rounded mass of earth or other material. **2** a small hill. **3** a large pile or quantity of something. ●verb heap something up into a rounded pile.
– ORIGIN uncertain.

mount[1] verb **1** climb up or on to something. **2** get up on an animal or bicycle to ride it. **3** (**be mounted**) be on horseback. **4** increase in size, number, or intensity: *the costs mount up when you buy a home.* **5** organize and begin a course of action. **6** put or fix something in place or on a support. **7** set in or attach a picture to a backing. ●noun **1** (also **mounting**) something on which an object is mounted for support or display. **2** a horse used for riding.
– PHRASES **mount guard** keep watch.
– DERIVATIVES **mountable** adjective.
– ORIGIN Old French *munter*.

mount[2] noun old use or in place names a mountain or hill.
– ORIGIN Old English.

mountain noun **1** a very high, steep hill. **2** a large pile or quantity. **3** a surplus stock of a commodity.
– PHRASES **move mountains** achieve spectacular and apparently impossible results.
– ORIGIN Old French *montaigne*.

mountain ash noun a rowan tree.

mountain bike noun a sturdy bicycle having broad tyres with deep treads and multiple gears.

mountaineering noun the sport or activity of climbing mountains.
– DERIVATIVES **mountaineer** noun.

mountain goat noun a goat that lives on mountains, known for its agility.

mountain lion noun N. Amer. a puma.

mountainous adjective **1** having many mountains. **2** huge; enormous.
– DERIVATIVES **mountainously** adverb.

mountain sickness noun altitude sickness.

mountainside noun the sloping surface of a mountain.

mountebank /mown-ti-bangk/ noun a person who deceives others.
– ORIGIN from Italian *monta in banco!* 'climb on the bench!', referring to the raised platform used by people who sold patent medicines in public.

Mountie noun informal a member of the Royal Canadian Mounted Police.

mourn verb **1** feel deep sorrow following the death of someone. **2** feel regret or sadness about the loss of something.
– ORIGIN Old English.

mourner noun a person who attends a funeral as a relative or friend of the dead person.

mournful adjective feeling, showing, or causing sadness or grief.
– DERIVATIVES **mournfully** adverb **mournfulness** noun.

mourning noun **1** the expression of deep sorrow for someone who has died. **2** black clothes worn in a period of mourning.

mouse noun (pl. **mice**) **1** a small rodent with a pointed snout and a long thin tail. **2** a timid and quiet person. **3** (pl. also **mouses**) a small hand-held device which controls cursor movements on a computer screen. ●verb **1** hunt for or catch mice. **2** informal use a mouse to move a cursor on a computer screen.
– DERIVATIVES **mouser** noun.
– ORIGIN Old English.

mousetrap noun **1** a trap for catching mice, traditionally baited with cheese. **2** Brit. informal poor-quality cheese.

moussaka /moo-sah-kuh/ noun a Greek dish of minced lamb layered with aubergines and tomatoes and topped with a cheese sauce.
– ORIGIN Turkish, 'that which is fed liquid'.

mousse noun **1** a light sweet or savoury dish made with whipped cream or egg white and flavoured with fruit, fish, etc. **2** a foamy substance for styling the hair or applied to the skin.
– ORIGIN French, 'moss or froth'.

mousseline /moos-leen/ noun **1** a fine fabric similar to muslin. **2** a light sweet or savoury mousse.
– ORIGIN French.

moustache (US also **mustache**) noun a strip of hair left to grow above a man's upper lip.
– DERIVATIVES **moustached** adjective.
– ORIGIN French.

mousy (also **mousey**) adjective (**mousier**, **mousiest**) **1** (of hair) light brown. **2** timid and quiet.

mouth noun **1** the opening in the body through which food is taken and sounds are made. **2** an opening or entrance of a structure, container, etc. **3** the place where a river enters the sea. **4** informal cheeky or excessive talk. ●verb **1** move the lips as if to form words. **2** say something in an insincere way. **3** (**mouth off**) informal express one's opinions in an unpleasantly loud or assertive way.
– ORIGIN Old English.

mouthful noun **1** a quantity of food or drink that fills or can be put in the mouth. **2** a long or complicated word or phrase.
– PHRASES **give someone a mouthful** Brit. informal talk to someone in an angry or abusive way.

mouth organ noun a harmonica.

mouthpart noun any of the projecting parts surrounding the mouth of an insect or similar creature and adapted for feeding.

mouthpiece noun **1** a part of a musical instrument, telephone, or breathing apparatus that is designed to be put in or against the mouth. **2** chiefly derogatory a person or publication that expresses the views of another person or an organization.

mouth-to-mouth adjective (of artificial respiration) in which a person breathes into someone's lungs through their mouth.

mouthwash noun an antiseptic liquid for rinsing the mouth or gargling.

mouth-watering adjective **1** smelling or looking delicious. **2** very attractive or tempting.

mouthy adjective (**mouthier**, **mouthiest**) informal inclined to talk a lot, especially in a cheeky way.

movable (also **moveable**) adjective 1 capable of being moved. 2 (of a religious festival) occurring on a different date each year.

move verb 1 go or cause to go in a specified direction or way. 2 change or cause to change position. 3 change one's home or place of work. 4 change from one state or activity to another. 5 take or cause to take action. 6 make progress: *aircraft design has moved forward a long way.* 7 arouse sympathy, sadness, or other feelings in: *he was genuinely moved by the tragedy.* 8 propose something for discussion and resolution at a meeting or law-making assembly. • noun 1 an instance of moving. 2 an action taken towards achieving a purpose: *my next move is to talk to Mark.* 3 a player's turn during a board game.
– PHRASES **get a move on** informal hurry up. **make a move 1** take action. **2** Brit. set off. **move in** (or **out**) start (or cease) living or working in a place.
– DERIVATIVES **mover** noun.
– ORIGIN Latin *movere*.

movement noun 1 an act or the process of moving. 2 a group of people who share the same aims or ideas: *the women's movement.* 3 a trend or development. 4 (**movements**) a person's activities during a particular period of time. 5 a main division of a musical work. 6 the moving parts of a mechanism, especially a clock or watch.

movie noun chiefly N. Amer. a cinema film.

moving adjective 1 in motion. 2 arousing sadness or sympathy.
– DERIVATIVES **movingly** adverb.

mow verb (past part. **mowed** or **mown**) 1 cut down grass or a cereal crop. 2 (**mow someone down**) kill someone by gunfire or by knocking them down with a motor vehicle.
– DERIVATIVES **mower** noun.
– ORIGIN Old English.

Mozambican /moh-zam-bee-kuhn/ noun a person from Mozambique. • adjective relating to Mozambique.

mozzarella /mot-suh-rel-luh/ noun a firm white Italian cheese made from buffalo's or cow's milk.
– ORIGIN Italian.

MP abbreviation 1 Member of Parliament. 2 military police.

mpg abbreviation miles per gallon.

mph abbreviation miles per hour.

MPhil abbreviation Master of Philosophy.

MP3 noun a means of compressing a sound sequence into a very small file, used as a way of downloading audio files from the Internet.
– ORIGIN from *MPEG* (an encoding standard) + *Audio Layer-3*.

MPV abbreviation multi-purpose vehicle.

Mr noun 1 a title used before a man's surname or full name. 2 a title used to address the male holder of an office.
– ORIGIN abbreviation of **MASTER**.

MRI abbreviation magnetic resonance imaging.

Mrs noun a title used before a married woman's surname or full name.
– ORIGIN abbreviation of **MISTRESS**.

Mrs Grundy noun a person with very conventional standards of proper moral behaviour.
– ORIGIN a person repeatedly mentioned in T. Morton's comedy *Speed the Plough*.

MS abbreviation 1 manuscript. 2 Mississippi. 3 multiple sclerosis.

Ms noun a title used before the surname or full name of a married or unmarried woman (a neutral alternative to **Mrs** or **Miss**).

MSc abbreviation Master of Science.

MS-DOS abbreviation Computing, trademark Microsoft disk operating system.

MSG abbreviation monosodium glutamate.

MSP abbreviation Member of the Scottish Parliament.

MT abbreviation Montana.

Mt abbreviation (in place names) Mount. • symbol the chemical element meitnerium.

much determiner & pronoun (**more**, **most**) a large amount. • adverb 1 to a great extent; a great deal. 2 often.
– PHRASES **a bit much** informal rather excessive or unreasonable. (**as**) **much as** even though. **not much of a** not a good example of: *I'm not much of a gardener.* **so much the better** (or **worse**) that is even better (or worse). **too much** too difficult or exhausting to tolerate.
– ORIGIN Old English.

muchness noun (in phrase (**much**) **of a muchness**) very similar.

mucilage /myoo-si-lij/ noun 1 a thick bodily fluid. 2 a thick or sticky solution extracted from plants, used in medicines and adhesives.
– DERIVATIVES **mucilaginous** /myoo-si-laj-i-nuhss/ adjective.
– ORIGIN Latin *mucilago* 'musty juice'.

muck noun 1 dirt or waste matter. 2 manure. 3 informal something unpleasant or worthless. • verb 1 (**muck something up**) informal spoil something. 2 (**muck about/around**) Brit. informal behave in a silly or aimless way. 3 (**muck about/around with**) Brit. informal interfere with. 4 (**muck in**) Brit. informal share tasks or accommodation. 5 (**muck something out**) chiefly Brit. remove manure from a stable.
– ORIGIN probably Scandinavian.

mucker noun Brit. informal a friend or companion.

muckle noun & adjective variant form of **MICKLE**.

muckraking noun the searching out and publicizing of scandal about famous people.
– ORIGIN coined by President Theodore Roosevelt in a speech referring to the man with the *muck rake* in Bunyan's *Pilgrim's Progress*.

muck sweat noun informal a state of perspiring heavily.

mucky adjective (**muckier**, **muckiest**) 1 covered with muck; dirty. 2 informal sordid or indecent.

mucosa /myoo-koh-suh/ noun (pl. **mucosae** /myoo-koh-see/) a mucous membrane.

mucous /myoo-kuhss/ adjective relating to or covered with mucus.

mucous membrane noun a tissue that produces mucus, lining many body cavities and tubular organs.

mucus noun a slimy substance produced by the mucous membranes and glands of animals for lubrication, protection, etc.
– ORIGIN Latin.

mud noun **1** wet earth that is soft and sticky. **2** damaging information or allegations.
– PHRASES **drag someone through the mud** slander or criticize someone publicly. **someone's name is mud** informal someone is in disgrace or unpopular.
– ORIGIN probably from German *mudde*.

mudbank noun a bank of mud on the bed of a river or the bottom of the sea.

mudbath noun **1** a very muddy place. **2** a bath in the mud of mineral springs, taken to relieve rheumatic complaints.

muddle verb **1** bring something into a disordered or confusing state. **2** confuse someone. **3** (**muddle something up**) confuse two or more things with each other. **4** (**muddle through** or Brit. **along**) cope fairly well. ● noun a confused or disordered state.
– DERIVATIVES **muddled** adjective.
– ORIGIN perhaps from Dutch *modden* 'dabble in mud'.

muddle-headed adjective disorganized or confused.

muddy adjective (**muddier**, **muddiest**) **1** covered in or full of mud. **2** not bright or clear. ● verb (**muddies**, **muddying**, **muddied**) **1** make something muddy. **2** make something difficult to understand.

mudflap noun a flap hung behind the wheel of a vehicle to protect against mud and stones thrown up from the road.

mudflat noun a stretch of muddy land left uncovered at low tide.

mudguard noun a curved strip fitted over a wheel of a bicycle or motorcycle to protect against water and dirt thrown up from the road.

mud pack noun a paste applied to the face to improve the condition of the skin.

mud-slinging noun informal the use of insults and accusations to damage an opponent's reputation.

muesli /myooz-li/ noun (pl. **mueslis**) a breakfast cereal consisting of oats, dried fruit, and nuts.
– ORIGIN Swiss German.

muezzin /moo-ez-zin/ noun a man who calls Muslims to prayer from the minaret of a mosque.
– ORIGIN from Arabic, 'proclaim'.

muff[1] noun a short tube made of fur or other warm material into which the hands are placed for warmth.
– ORIGIN Dutch *mof*.

muff[2] informal verb handle something clumsily or badly.
– ORIGIN unknown.

muffin noun **1** (N. Amer. **English muffin**) a flat circular bread roll eaten split, toasted, and buttered. **2** a small spongy cake with a rounded top.
– ORIGIN unknown.

muffle verb **1** wrap or cover someone or something for warmth. **2** make a sound quieter or less distinct by covering its source.
– ORIGIN from Old French *moufle* 'thick glove'.

muffler noun **1** a scarf worn around the neck and face. **2** a device for deadening the sound of a drum or other instrument. **3** N. Amer. a silencer for a motor vehicle exhaust.

mufti[1] /muf-ti/ noun (pl. **muftis**) a Muslim legal expert empowered to give rulings on religious matters.
– ORIGIN from Arabic, 'decide a point of law'.

mufti[2] /muf-ti/ noun civilian clothes when worn by a person who wears a uniform for their job.
– ORIGIN perhaps from **MUFTI**[1].

mug[1] noun **1** a large cylindrical cup with a handle. **2** informal a person's face. **3** Brit. informal a stupid or gullible person. ● verb (**mugs**, **mugging**, **mugged**) **1** attack and rob someone in a public place. **2** informal make faces in front of an audience or a camera.
– PHRASES **a mug's game** informal an activity likely to be unsuccessful or dangerous.
– DERIVATIVES **mugger** noun.
– ORIGIN probably Scandinavian.

mug[2] verb (**mugs**, **mugging**, **mugged**) (**mug something up**) Brit. informal learn or revise a subject quickly and intensively.
– ORIGIN unknown.

muggins noun Brit. informal a foolish and gullible person.
– ORIGIN perhaps a use of the surname *Muggins*, with reference to **MUG**[1].

muggy adjective (**muggier**, **muggiest**) (of the weather) unpleasantly warm and humid.
– ORIGIN from dialect *mug* 'mist, drizzle'.

Mughal noun variant spelling of **MOGUL**.

mugshot noun informal a photograph of a person's face made for an official purpose, especially police records.

mugwort noun a plant with aromatic leaves that are dark green above and whitish below.
– ORIGIN Old English.

Muhammadan (also **Mohammedan**) noun & adjective old-fashioned term for **MUSLIM** (not favoured by Muslims).
– ORIGIN from the name of the Arab prophet and founder of Islam *Muhammad*.

mujahedin /muu-jah-hi-deen/ (also **mujaheddin**, **mujahideen**) plural noun Islamic guerrilla fighters.
– ORIGIN Persian and Arabic, 'people who fight a holy war'.

mukluk /muk-luk/ noun N. Amer. a high, soft sealskin boot worn in the American Arctic.
– ORIGIN from Yupik (an Eskimo language), 'bearded seal'.

mulatto /muu-lat-toh/ noun (pl. **mulattoes** or **mulattos**) offensive a person with one white and one black parent.
– ORIGIN Spanish *mulato* 'young mule, mulatto'.

mulberry noun (pl. **mulberries**) **1** a dark red or white fruit resembling the loganberry. **2** a dark red or purple colour.
– ORIGIN Latin *morum* 'mulberry'.

mulch noun a mass of leaves, bark, or compost spread around or over a plant for protection or to enrich the soil. ● verb cover soil or the base of a plant with mulch.
– ORIGIN probably from dialect *mulch* 'soft'.

mule[1] noun **1** the offspring of a male donkey and a female horse, typically sterile. **2** informal a courier for illegal drugs. **3** historical a kind of spinning machine producing yarn on spindles.
– ORIGIN Latin *mulus, mula*.

mule[2] noun a slipper or light shoe without a

back.
- ORIGIN French, 'slipper'.

muleteer /myoo-li-**teer**/ noun a person who drives mules.

mulga /**mul**-guh/ noun a small Australian acacia tree or shrub which forms dense scrubby growth.
- ORIGIN from an Aboriginal language.

mulish adjective stubborn (like a mule).

mull[1] verb (**mull something over**) think about something at length.
- ORIGIN uncertain.

mull[2] verb (usu. as adj. **mulled**) warm wine or beer and add sugar and spices to it.
- ORIGIN unknown.

mull[3] noun (in Scottish place names) a narrow piece of land projecting into the sea or a lake.
- ORIGIN perhaps from Scottish Gaelic or Icelandic.

mullah /**muul**-luh/ noun a Muslim who is learned in Islamic theology and sacred law.
- ORIGIN Arabic.

mullein /**mul**-in/ noun a plant with woolly leaves and tall spikes of yellow flowers.
- ORIGIN Celtic.

mullet noun any of various sea fish that are caught for food.
- ORIGIN Greek *mullos*.

mulligatawny /mul-li-guh-**taw**-ni/ noun a spicy meat soup originally made in India.
- ORIGIN Tamil, 'pepper water'.

mullion noun a vertical bar between the panes of glass in a window.
- DERIVATIVES **mullioned** adjective.
- ORIGIN probably from Old French *moinel* 'middle'.

multi- combining form more than one; many: *multicultural.*
- ORIGIN from Latin *multus* 'much, many'.

multicast verb (past and past part. **multicast**) send data across a computer network to several users at the same time. •noun a set of multicast data.

multicoloured (also **multicolour**; US **multicolored, multicolor**) adjective having many colours.

multicultural adjective relating to or made up of several cultural or ethnic groups.
- DERIVATIVES **multiculturalism** noun **multiculturalist** noun & adjective.

multidisciplinary adjective involving several academic disciplines or professional specializations.

multifaceted adjective having many facets or aspects.

multifarious /mul-ti-**fair**-i-uhss/ adjective having many different kinds; very varied: *multifarious talents.*
- ORIGIN Latin *multifarius*.

multiform adjective existing in many forms or kinds.

multihull noun a boat with two or more, especially three, hulls.

multilateral adjective involving three or more participants.
- DERIVATIVES **multilateralism** noun **multilaterally** adverb.

multilayered adjective consisting of several or many layers.

multilingual adjective in or using several languages.

multimedia adjective using more than one medium of expression or communication. •noun a system for linking sound and images to text on a computer screen.

multimillion adjective consisting of several million of a currency.

multimillionaire noun a person with assets worth several million pounds or dollars.

multinational adjective 1 involving several countries or nationalities. 2 operating in several countries. •noun a company operating in several countries.
- DERIVATIVES **multinationally** adverb.

multipack noun a package containing a number of similar or identical products.

multiparty adjective relating to or involving several political parties.

multiple adjective 1 having or involving several or many people or things: *multiple occupancy.* 2 (of a disease or injury) affecting several parts of the body. •noun 1 a number that may be divided by another a certain number of times without a remainder. 2 Brit. a shop with several branches.
- ORIGIN Latin *multiplus*.

multiple-choice adjective (of a question in an exam) accompanied by several possible answers, from which the candidate must choose the correct one.

multiple sclerosis noun see SCLEROSIS.

multiplex noun (also **multiplex cinema**) a cinema having several separate screens within one building. •adjective 1 consisting of many elements in a complex relationship. 2 involving simultaneous transmission of several messages along a single channel of communication.
- ORIGIN Latin.

multiplicand /mul-ti-pli-**kand**, **mul**-ti-pli-kand/ noun a quantity which is to be multiplied by another (the multiplier).

multiplication noun 1 the process of multiplying. 2 Mathematics the process of combining matrices, vectors, or other quantities under specific rules to obtain their product.

multiplication sign noun the sign $\times$, used to indicate that one quantity is to be multiplied by another.

multiplication table noun a list of multiples of a particular number, typically from 1 to 12.

multiplicity /mul-ti-**pli**-si-ti/ noun (pl. **multiplicities**) a large number or variety.

multiplier noun 1 a quantity by which a given number (the multiplicand) is to be multiplied. 2 a device for increasing the intensity of an electric current, force, etc. to a measurable level.

multiply[1] /**mul**-ti-ply/ verb (**multiplies, multiplying, multiplied**) 1 add a number to itself a specified number of times. 2 increase in number or quantity: *the problems facing the industry have multiplied alarmingly.* 3 (of an organism) increase in number by reproducing.
- ORIGIN Latin *multiplicare*.

multiply[2] /**mul**-ti-pli/ adverb in different ways or respects.

m

multiprocessing (also **multiprogramming**) noun the execution of more than one program or task by a computer at the same time.

multiprocessor noun a computer with more than one central processor.

multi-purpose adjective having several purposes.

multiracial adjective relating to or involving people of many races.

multistage adjective 1 consisting of or involving several stages or processes. 2 (of a rocket) having at least two sections which contain their own motor and are jettisoned as their fuel runs out.

multi-storey adjective (of a building) having several storeys.

multitask verb (usu. as noun **multitasking**) 1 (of a computer) execute more than one program or task at the same time. 2 (of a person) deal with more than one task at the same time.
- DERIVATIVES **multitasker** noun.

multitrack adjective relating to or made by the mixing of several separately recorded tracks of sound.

multitude noun 1 a large number of people or things. 2 (**the multitude**) ordinary people.
- ORIGIN Latin *multitudo*.

multitudinous /mul-ti-**tyoo**-di-nuhss/ adjective 1 very large in number. 2 consisting of many parts or elements.

multi-utility noun a former public utility which is now in private ownership and has extended its business to offer additional services.

multivalent /mul-ti-**vay**-luhnt/ adjective having many interpretations, uses, or values.

multiverse noun a hypothetical space or realm consisting of a number of universes, of which our own universe is only one.

mum¹ noun Brit. informal one's mother.

mum² adjective (in phrase **keep mum**) informal say nothing so as not to reveal a secret.
- PHRASES **mum's the word** do not reveal a secret.
- ORIGIN imitating a sound made with closed lips.

mumble verb say something indistinctly and quietly. • noun something said quietly and indistinctly.
- ORIGIN from MUM².

mumbo-jumbo noun informal language or a ceremony that seems complicated but has no real meaning.
- ORIGIN from *Mumbo Jumbo*, the supposed name of an African idol.

mummer noun an actor in a traditional English folk play.
- ORIGIN from Old French *momer* 'act in a mime'.

mummers' play (also **mumming play**) noun a traditional English folk play typically featuring Saint George.

mummery noun (pl. **mummeries**) 1 a performance of a traditional English folk play. 2 ridiculous or excessive ceremonial procedures.

mummify verb (**mummifies, mummifying, mummified**) 1 (especially in ancient Egypt) preserve a body by embalming and wrapping

it. 2 dry up a body and so preserve it.
- DERIVATIVES **mummification** noun.

mummy¹ noun (pl. **mummies**) Brit. informal one's mother.
- ORIGIN uncertain.

mummy² noun (pl. **mummies**) (especially in ancient Egypt) a body that has been preserved for burial by embalming and wrapping in cloth.
- ORIGIN Arabic, 'embalmed body'.

mumps plural noun (treated as sing.) an infectious disease spread by a virus, causing swelling of the salivary glands at the sides of the face.
- ORIGIN from former *mump* 'grimace'.

mumsy adjective Brit. informal (of a woman) homely and unfashionable.

munch verb eat food with a steady and noticeable chewing action.
- ORIGIN imitating the sound of eating.

Munchausen's syndrome /muunch-how-z'nz/ noun a mental disorder in which a person pretends to be severely ill so as to obtain medical attention.
- ORIGIN from Baron *Munchausen*, the hero of a book of fantastic tales.

munchies plural noun informal 1 snacks or small items of food. 2 (**the munchies**) a sudden strong desire for food.

mundane /mun-**dayn**/ adjective 1 lacking interest or excitement: *his mundane, humdrum existence*. 2 relating to the physical world rather than a heavenly or spiritual one.
- DERIVATIVES **mundanely** adverb **mundanity** /mun-**dan**-it-i/ noun.
- ORIGIN from Latin *mundus* 'world'.

mung bean noun a small round green bean grown in the tropics, chiefly as a source of bean sprouts.
- ORIGIN Hindi.

municipal adjective relating to a town or district or its governing body.
- DERIVATIVES **municipally** adverb.
- ORIGIN from Latin *municipium* 'free city'.

municipality noun (pl. **municipalities**) a town or district that has local government.

munificent /myoo-**nif**-i-suhnt/ adjective very generous.
- DERIVATIVES **munificence** noun **munificently** adverb.
- ORIGIN Latin *munificus*.

muniments /**myoo**-ni-muhnts/ plural noun Law title deeds or other documents proving a person's right of ownership of land.
- ORIGIN from Latin *munimentum* 'defence', later 'title deed'.

munitions plural noun military weapons, ammunition, equipment, and stores.
- ORIGIN Latin, 'fortification'.

muntjac /**munt**-jak/ noun a small SE Asian deer with a doglike bark and small tusks.
- ORIGIN Sundanese.

muon /**myoo**-on/ noun Physics an unstable subatomic particle of the same class as an electron, but with a mass around 200 times greater.
- ORIGIN from the earlier name *mu-meson*.

muppet noun Brit. informal an incompetent or

foolish person.
- ORIGIN from the name given to various puppets created for the children's television programmes *Sesame Street* and *The Muppet Show*.

mural noun a picture or design painted directly on a wall. • adjective relating to or resembling a wall.
- ORIGIN from Latin *murus* 'wall'.

murder noun 1 the unlawful and deliberate killing of one person by another. 2 informal a very difficult or unpleasant situation or experience. • verb 1 kill someone unlawfully and deliberately. 2 informal spoil by lack of skill: *couples were shuffling around to a band murdering Beatles songs.* 3 (**could murder**) informal, chiefly Brit. one would like to eat or drink something very much.
- PHRASES **get away with murder** informal succeed in doing whatever one chooses without being punished. **scream blue murder** informal protest strongly and noisily.
- DERIVATIVES **murderer** noun **murderess** noun.
- ORIGIN Old English.

murderous adjective 1 capable of or involving murder or extreme violence. 2 informal very difficult or unpleasant.
- DERIVATIVES **murderously** adverb **murderousness** noun.

murk noun darkness or fog causing poor visibility.
- ORIGIN Old English.

murky adjective (**murkier, murkiest**) 1 dark and gloomy. 2 (of water) dirty or cloudy. 3 unclear so as to conceal dishonesty or immorality: *an MP with a murky past.*
- DERIVATIVES **murkily** adverb **murkiness** noun.

murmur verb 1 say something quietly. 2 make a low continuous sound. 3 complain in a subdued way. • noun 1 something that is said quietly. 2 a low continuous background noise. 3 a complaint: *she paid for the meal without a murmur.* 4 a recurring sound heard in the heart through a stethoscope and usually indicating disease or damage.
- ORIGIN Latin.

Murphy's Law noun a supposed law of nature, to the effect that anything that can go wrong will go wrong.

murrain /**mu**-rin/ noun 1 an infectious disease affecting cattle. 2 old use a plague or crop blight.
- ORIGIN Old French *morine*.

Muscadet /**muss**-kuh-day, **muuss**-kuh-day/ noun a dry white wine from the Loire region of France.
- ORIGIN French.

muscat /**muss**-kat/ noun 1 a variety of grape with a musky scent. 2 a sweet or fortified white wine made from muscat grapes.
- ORIGIN from Provençal *musc* 'musk'.

muscatel /**muss**-kuh-**tel**/ noun a sweet wine made from muscat grapes.

muscle noun 1 a band of tissue in the body that is able to contract so as to move or hold the position of a part of the body. 2 power, influence, or strength: *the plan is designed to increase Japan's financial muscle.* • verb (**muscle in/into**) informal interfere in another's affairs.
- DERIVATIVES **muscly** adjective.
- ORIGIN Latin *musculus*.

USAGE: Do not confuse **muscle** with **mussel**. Muscle means 'the tissue that moves a body part' (*tone up your thigh muscles*), whereas mussel means 'a shellfish'.

muscle-bound adjective having overdeveloped muscles.

muscleman noun (pl. **musclemen**) a large, strong man, especially a bodyguard or hired thug.

muscovado /muss-kuh-**vah**-doh/ noun unrefined sugar made from sugar cane.
- ORIGIN from Portuguese *mascabado açúcar* 'sugar of the lowest quality'.

Muscovite noun a person from Moscow. • adjective relating to Moscow.

Muscovy /**muss**-kuh-vi/ noun old use Russia.
- ORIGIN Russian *Moskva* 'Moscow'.

muscular adjective 1 relating to the muscles. 2 having well-developed muscles.
- DERIVATIVES **muscularity** noun **muscularly** adverb.

muscular dystrophy noun an inherited condition in which the muscles gradually become weaker and waste away.

musculature noun the muscular system or arrangement of a body or an organ.

muse[1] noun 1 (**Muse**) (in Greek and Roman mythology) each of nine goddesses who encouraged the arts and sciences. 2 a woman who is the inspiration for a creative artist.
- ORIGIN Greek *mousa*.

muse[2] verb 1 be absorbed in thought. 2 say something to oneself in a thoughtful way.
- ORIGIN Old French *muser* 'meditate, waste time'.

museum noun a building in which important or interesting objects are stored and exhibited.
- ORIGIN Greek *mouseion* 'seat of the Muses'.

museum piece noun an old-fashioned or useless person or object.

mush[1] noun 1 a soft, wet mass. 2 excessive sentimentality. • verb crush or mash something to form a soft, wet mass.
- ORIGIN probably from MASH.

mush[2] exclamation a command urging on dogs that pull a dog sled.
- ORIGIN probably from French *marchez!* or *marchons!* 'advance!'

mushroom noun 1 a spore-producing body of a fungus, typically having the form of a domed cap at the top of a stalk and often edible. 2 a pale pinkish-brown colour. • verb increase or develop rapidly.
- ORIGIN Old French *mousseron*.

mushroom cloud noun a mushroom-shaped cloud of dust and debris formed after a nuclear explosion.

mushy adjective (**mushier, mushiest**) 1 soft and pulpy. 2 excessively sentimental.
- DERIVATIVES **mushiness** noun.

music noun 1 the art of combining vocal or instrumental sounds in a pleasing way. 2 the sound so produced. 3 the signs in which music is written or printed.
- PHRASES **music to one's ears** something very pleasant to hear or learn.
- ORIGIN from Greek *mousikē tekhnē* 'art of the Muses'.

musical adjective **1** relating to or accompanied by music. **2** fond of or skilled in music. **3** pleasant-sounding. •noun a play or film in which singing and dancing play an essential part.
– DERIVATIVES **musicality** noun **musically** adverb.

musical box noun Brit. a small box which plays a tune when the lid is opened.

musical chairs plural noun (treated as sing.) **1** a party game in which players compete for a decreasing number of chairs when the accompanying music is stopped. **2** a situation in which people frequently exchange jobs or positions.

music centre noun Brit. a combined radio, cassette player, and record or compact disc player.

music hall noun **1** a form of entertainment involving singing, dancing, and comedy, popular in Britain from about 1850–1918. **2** a theatre where music-hall shows took place.

musician noun a person who plays a musical instrument or composes music.
– DERIVATIVES **musicianly** adjective **musicianship** noun.

musicology noun the study of music as an academic subject.
– DERIVATIVES **musicological** adjective **musicologist** noun.

musk noun a strong-smelling substance produced by the male musk deer, used in making perfume.
– DERIVATIVES **muskiness** noun **musky** adjective.
– ORIGIN Persian.

musk deer noun a small East Asian deer, the male of which produces musk.

muskeg noun a swamp or bog in northern North America.
– ORIGIN from an American Indian language.

musket noun historical a light gun with a long barrel, typically fired from the shoulder.
– ORIGIN Italian *moschetto* 'crossbow bolt'.

musketeer noun historical **1** a soldier armed with a musket. **2** a member of the household troops of the French king in the 17th and 18th centuries.

musketry noun **1** musket fire. **2** soldiers armed with muskets. **3** the art or technique of handling a musket.

musk ox noun a large heavily built goat-antelope with a thick shaggy coat, native to the tundra of North America and Greenland.

muskrat noun a large North American rodent with a musky smell that lives partly in water and is valued for its fur.

Muslim (also **Moslem**) noun a follower of Islam. •adjective relating to Muslims or Islam.
– ORIGIN Arabic.

muslin noun lightweight cotton cloth in a plain weave.
– ORIGIN from Italian *Mussolo* 'Mosul' (the place in Iraq where it was made).

muso noun (pl. **musos**) Brit. informal a musician or keen music fan.

musquash /muss-kwosh/ noun Brit. the fur of the muskrat.
– ORIGIN from an American Indian language.

muss verb informal, chiefly N. Amer. make something untidy or messy.

– ORIGIN probably from **MESS**.

mussel noun an edible shellfish with a dark brown or purplish-black shell, found in the sea or in fresh water.
– ORIGIN Latin *musculus* 'muscle'.

USAGE: On the confusion of **mussel** with **muscle**, see the note at **MUSCLE**.

must¹ modal verb (past **had to** or in reported speech **must**) **1** be obliged to; should. **2** used to insist on something. **3** expressing an opinion about something that is very likely. •noun informal something that should be done or bought.
– ORIGIN Old English.

must² noun grape juice before or during fermentation.
– ORIGIN from Latin *mustus* 'new'.

must- combining form used to form adjectives referring to things that are essential or highly recommended: *a must-read book.*

mustache noun US spelling of **MOUSTACHE**.

mustachios /muh-stah-shi-ohz/ plural noun a long or elaborate moustache.
– ORIGIN Italian *mostaccio*.

mustang noun a small wild horse of the south-western US.
– ORIGIN from a blend of Spanish *mestengo* and *mostrenco*, both meaning 'wild cattle'.

mustard noun **1** a hot-tasting yellow or brown paste made from the crushed seeds of a plant, eaten with meat. **2** a brownish-yellow colour.
– ORIGIN Old French *moustarde*.

mustard gas noun a liquid whose vapour causes severe irritation and blistering, used in chemical weapons.

muster verb **1** achieve a feeling, attitude, or reaction: *with all the courage I could muster, I came to my decision.* **2** bring troops together, especially for inspection or military action. **3** (of people) gather together. •noun **1** a formal gathering of troops. **2** Austral./NZ a rounding up of livestock.
– PHRASES **pass muster** be accepted as satisfactory.
– ORIGIN Old French *moustrer*.

must-have adjective essential or highly desirable. •noun an essential or highly desirable item.

mustn't contraction must not.

musty adjective (**mustier**, **mustiest**) **1** having a stale or mouldy smell or taste. **2** not fresh or original; outdated.
– DERIVATIVES **mustiness** noun.
– ORIGIN perhaps from former *moisty* 'moist'.

mutable /myoo-tuh-b'l/ adjective liable to change; changeable.
– DERIVATIVES **mutability** noun.
– ORIGIN Latin *mutabilis*.

mutagen /myoo-tuh-juhn/ noun a substance which causes genetic mutation.

mutant adjective resulting from or showing the effect of a change in genetic structure. •noun an organism that has undergone a change in genetic structure.

mutate verb change in form or nature; undergo mutation.

mutation noun **1** a change in form or structure. **2** a change in the structure of a gene which results in a variant form and may be

transmitted to subsequent generations. **3** a distinct form resulting from a change in genetic structure.
– DERIVATIVES **mutational** adjective.
– ORIGIN from Latin *mutare* 'to change'.

mutatis mutandis /moo-tah-tiss moo-**tan**-diss/ **adverb** (used when comparing two or more cases) making necessary alterations while not affecting the main point.
– ORIGIN Latin, 'things being changed that have to be changed'.

mute **adjective 1** not speaking or temporarily speechless. **2** lacking the power of speech. **3** (of a letter in a word) not pronounced. • **noun 1** dated a person who is unable to speak. **2** a clamp placed over the bridge of a stringed instrument to deaden the resonance of the strings. **3** a pad or cone placed in the opening of a wind instrument. • **verb 1** deaden or muffle the sound of something. **2** reduce the strength or intensity of: *his sharp wit was muted by good nature.* **3** (as adj. **muted**) (of colour or lighting) not bright; subdued.
– DERIVATIVES **mutely** adverb **muteness** noun.
– ORIGIN Latin *mutus*.

> USAGE: To describe a person without the power of speech as **mute** (especially as in **deaf mute**) is today likely to cause offence. Since there are no accepted alternative terms in general use, the solution may be to use a longer description, such as *she is both deaf and unable to speak.*

mute swan **noun** the commonest Eurasian swan, having an orange-red bill with a black knob at the base.

mutilate **verb 1** cause a severe and disfiguring injury to someone. **2** cause serious damage to something.
– DERIVATIVES **mutilation** noun **mutilator** noun.
– ORIGIN Latin *mutilare* 'maim'.

mutineer **noun** a person who refuses to obey a person in authority.

mutinous **adjective** tending to mutiny or be disobedient; rebellious.
– DERIVATIVES **mutinously** adverb.

mutiny **noun** (pl. **mutinies**) an open rebellion against authority, especially by soldiers or sailors against their officers. • **verb** (**mutinies**, **mutinying**, **mutinied**) refuse to obey a person in authority.
– ORIGIN from French *mutin* 'mutineer, rebellious'.

mutt **noun** informal **1** a dog, especially a mongrel. **2** a stupid or incompetent person.
– ORIGIN abbreviation of **MUTTONHEAD**.

mutter **verb 1** say something in a very quiet voice. **2** talk or grumble in secret or in private. • **noun** something said very quietly.
– ORIGIN imitating the sound of muttering.

mutton **noun** the flesh of mature sheep used as food.
– PHRASES **mutton dressed as lamb** Brit. informal, derogatory an older woman dressed in a style suitable for a much younger woman.
– ORIGIN Old French *moton*.

mutton-chop whiskers **plural noun** whiskers on a man's cheek that are narrow at the top and broad and rounded at the bottom.

muttonhead **noun** informal a stupid person.

mutual **adjective 1** experienced or done by two or more people equally: *a partnership based on mutual respect.* **2** (of two or more people) having the same specified relationship to each other. **3** shared by two or more people: *a mutual friend.* **4** (of a building society or insurance company) owned by its members and dividing its profits between them.
– DERIVATIVES **mutuality** noun **mutually** adverb.
– ORIGIN Old French *mutuel.*

muumuu /moo-moo/ **noun** a loose, brightly coloured dress as traditionally worn by Hawaiian women.
– ORIGIN Hawaiian, 'cut off'.

muzak **noun** trademark recorded light background music played in public places.
– ORIGIN alteration of **MUSIC**.

muzzle **noun 1** the projecting part of an animal's face, including the nose and mouth. **2** a guard fitted over an animal's muzzle to stop it biting or feeding. **3** the open end of the barrel of a firearm. • **verb 1** put a guard over an animal's muzzle. **2** prevent someone expressing their opinions freely.
– ORIGIN Latin *musum.*

muzzy **adjective** (**muzzier**, **muzziest**) **1** dazed or confused. **2** blurred or indistinct: *a slightly muzzy picture.*
– DERIVATIVES **muzzily** adverb **muzziness** noun.
– ORIGIN unknown.

MW **abbreviation 1** medium wave. **2** megawatt(s).

my **possessive determiner 1** belonging to or associated with the speaker. **2** used in various expressions of surprise.
– PHRASES **My Lady** (or **Lord**) a polite form of address to certain titled people.
– ORIGIN Old English.

myalgia /my-**al**-juh/ **noun** pain in a muscle or group of muscles.
– DERIVATIVES **myalgic** adjective.
– ORIGIN from Greek *mus* 'muscle' + *algos* 'pain'.

myalgic encephalomyelitis **noun** full form of **ME**.

mycelium /my-**see**-li-uhm/ **noun** (pl. **mycelia**) Botany a network of fine white filaments (hyphae) making up the main part of a fungus, usually invisible above ground.
– ORIGIN from Greek *mukēs* 'fungus'.

Mycenaean /my-si-**nee**-uhn/ **adjective** relating to a late Bronze Age civilization in Greece represented by archaeological discoveries at Mycenae and other ancient cities of the Peloponnese.

mycology /my-**kol**-uh-ji/ **noun** the scientific study of fungi.
– DERIVATIVES **mycological** adjective **mycologist** noun.
– ORIGIN from Greek *mukēs* 'fungus'.

myelin /**my**-uh-lin/ **noun** a whitish fatty substance forming a sheath around many nerve fibres.
– ORIGIN from Greek *muelos* 'marrow'.

myeloid /**my**-uh-loyd/ **adjective** relating to bone marrow or the spinal cord.
– ORIGIN from Greek *muelos* 'marrow'.

myeloma /my-uh-**loh**-muh/ **noun** (pl. **myelomas**) a malignant tumour of the bone marrow.

mynah (also **mynah bird**) **noun** a southern

Asian or Australasian starling with a loud call, some kinds of which can mimic human speech.
– ORIGIN Hindi.

myocardium /my-oh-**kar**-di-uhm/ noun the muscular tissue of the heart.
– DERIVATIVES **myocardial** adjective.
– ORIGIN from Greek *mus* 'muscle' + *kardia* 'heart'.

myopia /my-**oh**-pi-uh/ noun **1** short-sightedness. **2** failure or inability to foresee the future consequences of an action, decision, etc.
– DERIVATIVES **myopic** adjective.
– ORIGIN from Greek *muein* 'shut' + *ōps* 'eye'.

myriad /**mi**-ri-uhd/ noun **1** (also **myriads**) a countless or very great number of people or things: *myriads of insects danced around the light.* **2** (in classical times) a unit of ten thousand. •adjective countless: *the myriad lights of the city.*
– ORIGIN Greek *murias*, from *murioi* '10,000'.

myriapod /**mi**-ri-uh-pod/ noun a centipede, millipede, or other insect having a long body with numerous leg-bearing segments.
– ORIGIN from Greek *murioi* '10,000' + *pous* 'foot'.

myrmidon /**mer**-mi-duhn/ noun a follower or subordinate of a powerful person, especially one who is willing to engage in dishonest activities.
– ORIGIN from Greek *Murmidones*, a warlike people of Thessaly who accompanied Achilles to Troy.

myrrh /mer/ noun a sweet-smelling resin obtained from certain trees and used in perfumes, medicines, and incense.
– ORIGIN Greek *murra*.

myrtle noun an evergreen shrub with glossy leaves and white flowers followed by purple-black berries.
– ORIGIN Greek *murtos*.

myself pronoun (first person sing.) **1** (reflexive) used by a speaker to refer to himself or herself as the object of a verb or preposition when he or she is the subject of the clause: *I hurt myself.* **2** (emphatic) I or me personally: *I wrote it myself.*
– ORIGIN Old English.

mysterious adjective **1** difficult or impossible to understand, explain, or identify: *he vanished in mysterious circumstances.* **2** deliberately not saying much about something that interests other people: *he was rather mysterious about you.*
– DERIVATIVES **mysteriously** adverb **mysteriousness** noun.

mystery noun (pl. **mysteries**) **1** something that is difficult or impossible to understand or explain. **2** the quality of being secret or difficult to explain: *much of her past is shrouded in mystery.* **3** a novel, play, or film dealing with a puzzling crime. **4** (**mysteries**) the secret rites or ceremonies of an ancient religion. **5** chiefly Christian Theology a religious belief based on divine revelation. **6** an incident in the life of Jesus or of a saint as a focus of devotion in the Roman Catholic Church.
– ORIGIN Greek *mustērion*.

mystery play noun a popular medieval play based on biblical stories or the lives of saints.

mystery tour noun Brit. a trip to an unspecified destination.

mystic noun a person who devotes their time to prayer and meditation in order to become closer to God and to reach truths beyond human understanding. •adjective mystical.
– ORIGIN Greek *mustēs* 'initiated person'.

mystical adjective **1** relating to mystics or mysticism. **2** having a spiritual significance that goes beyond human understanding. **3** inspiring a sense of spiritual mystery, awe, and fascination: *the mystical city of Kathmandu.*
– DERIVATIVES **mystically** adverb.

mysticism noun **1** the belief that knowledge of God and truths beyond human understanding can be gained by prayer and meditation. **2** religious or spiritual belief that is not clearly defined.

mystify verb (**mystifies, mystifying, mystified**) **1** utterly bewilder: *I was mystified by his disappearance.* **2** make something seem obscure or mysterious.
– DERIVATIVES **mystification** noun **mystifying** adjective.
– ORIGIN French *mystifier.*

mystique noun **1** a quality of mystery, glamour, and power surrounding a person or thing. **2** an air of secrecy surrounding an activity or subject, making it impressive or baffling to those people not involved in it.
– ORIGIN French.

myth noun **1** a traditional story about the early history of a people or explaining a natural or social phenomenon, typically involving supernatural beings or events. **2** a widely held but false belief. **3** a fictitious or imaginary person or thing.
– ORIGIN Greek *muthos.*

mythical adjective **1** occurring in or characteristic of myths or folk tales. **2** fictitious or imaginary.
– DERIVATIVES **mythic** adjective **mythically** adverb.

mythological adjective relating to or found in myths or mythology.
– DERIVATIVES **mythologically** adverb.

mythologize (or **mythologise**) verb make someone or something the subject of a myth.

mythology noun (pl. **mythologies**) **1** a collection of myths. **2** a set of widely held but exaggerated or false stories or beliefs. **3** the study of myths.
– DERIVATIVES **mythologist** noun.

mythomania noun an abnormal tendency to exaggerate or tell lies.
– DERIVATIVES **mythomaniac** noun & adjective.

mythopoeia /mith-oh-**pee**-uh/ noun the making of a myth or myths.
– DERIVATIVES **mythopoeic** adjective **mythopoetic** adjective.
– ORIGIN Greek.

myxomatosis /mik-suh-muh-**toh**-siss/ noun a highly infectious and usually fatal disease of rabbits, spread by a virus and causing inflammation and discharge around the eyes.
– ORIGIN from Greek *muxa* 'slime, mucus'.

Nn

N[1] (also **n**) noun (pl. **Ns** or **N's**) the fourteenth letter of the alphabet.

N[2] abbreviation **1** (used in recording moves in chess) knight. **2** (chiefly in place names) New. **3** Physics newton(s). **4** North or Northern. • symbol the chemical element nitrogen.

n abbreviation **1** nano- (10^{-9}). **2** Grammar neuter. **3** Grammar noun. • symbol an unspecified or variable number.

'n' (also **'n**) contraction informal and (e.g. *rock 'n' roll*).

Na symbol the chemical element sodium.
– ORIGIN from Latin *natrium*.

n/a abbreviation **1** not applicable. **2** not available.

NAAFI /na-fi/ Brit. abbreviation Navy, Army, and Air Force Institutes. • noun a canteen or shop run by the NAAFI.

naan noun variant spelling of NAN².

nab verb (**nabs, nabbing, nabbed**) informal **1** catch someone doing something wrong. **2** take or grab something suddenly.
– ORIGIN unknown.

nabob /nay-bob/ noun **1** historical a Muslim official or governor under the Mogul empire. **2** a very rich or important person.
– ORIGIN Urdu.

nacelle /nuh-sel/ noun the streamlined outer casing of an aircraft engine.
– ORIGIN French.

nacho /nach-oh/ noun (pl. **nachos**) a small piece of tortilla topped with melted cheese, peppers, etc.
– ORIGIN perhaps from Mexican Spanish *Nacho*, familiar form of *Ignacio*, first name of the chef credited with creating the dish.

nacre /nay-ker/ noun mother-of-pearl.
– DERIVATIVES **nacreous** adjective.
– ORIGIN French.

nada /nah-duh/ pronoun N. Amer. informal nothing.
– ORIGIN Spanish.

nadir /nay-deer/ noun **1** the lowest or most unsuccessful point: *the nadir of my career*. **2** Astronomy the point in the sky directly opposite the zenith and below an observer.
– ORIGIN from Arabic, 'opposite to the zenith'.

naevus /nee-vuhss/ (US **nevus**) noun (pl. **naevi** /nee-vy/) a birthmark or a mole on the skin.
– ORIGIN Latin.

naff Brit. informal verb (**naff off**) go away. • adjective lacking taste or style.
– DERIVATIVES **naffness** noun.
– ORIGIN the verb is a euphemism for FUCK; the source of the adjective is uncertain.

NAFTA (also **Nafta**) abbreviation North American Free Trade Agreement.

nag[1] verb (**nags, nagging, nagged**) **1** constantly ask someone to do something that they are reluctant to do. **2** (often as adj. **nagging**) be persistently painful or worrying to someone: *I was left with nagging doubts*. • noun a persistent feeling of anxiety.
– ORIGIN perhaps Scandinavian or German.

nag[2] noun informal, often derogatory a horse, especially one that is old or in poor condition.
– ORIGIN unknown.

Nahuatl /nah-wah-t'l, nah-**wah**-t'l/ noun (pl. same or **Nahuatls**) **1** a member of a group of peoples native to southern Mexico and Central America, including the Aztecs. **2** the language of the Nahuatl.
– ORIGIN Nahuatl.

naiad /ny-ad/ noun (in classical mythology) a water nymph.
– ORIGIN Greek *Naias*.

naif /ny-eef/ adjective naive. • noun a naive person.
– ORIGIN French.

nail noun **1** a small metal spike with a broadened flat head, hammered in to join things together or to serve as a hook. **2** a thin hard layer covering the upper surface of the tip of the fingers and toes. • verb **1** fasten something with a nail or nails. **2** informal catch someone, especially a suspected criminal. **3** (**nail someone down**) force someone to commit themselves to something: *I can't nail her down to a specific date*. **4** (**nail something down**) identify something precisely.
– PHRASES **a nail in the coffin** an action or event likely to have a bad or destructive effect on someone or something. **on the nail** (of payment) without delay.
– ORIGIN Old English.

nail-biting adjective causing great tension or anxiety.

nail file noun a small file or emery board for smoothing and shaping the fingernails and toenails.

nail polish (also **nail varnish**) noun a glossy coloured substance applied to the fingernails or toenails.

naira /ny-ruh/ noun the basic unit of money of Nigeria.
– ORIGIN from *Nigeria*.

naive /ny-eev/ (also **naïve**) adjective **1** lacking experience, wisdom, or judgement. **2** (of art or an artist) produced in or using a simple,

childlike style which deliberately rejects sophisticated techniques.
- DERIVATIVES **naively** adverb.
- ORIGIN French, from Latin *nativus* 'native, natural'.

naivety /ny-eev-ti, ny-ee-vi-ti/ (also **naiveté** /ny-eev-tay/) noun lack of experience, wisdom, or judgement.

naked adjective 1 without clothes. 2 (of an object) without the usual covering or protection: *a naked light bulb.* 3 not hidden or concealed: *naked aggression.* 4 helpless or vulnerable.
- PHRASES **the naked eye** the normal power of the eye, without using a telescope, microscope, or other optical instrument.
- DERIVATIVES **nakedly** adverb **nakedness** noun.
- ORIGIN Old English.

Nama /nah-muh/ noun (pl. same or **Namas**) 1 a member of one of the Khoikhoi peoples of South Africa and SW Namibia. 2 the language of the Nama.
- ORIGIN Nama.

namby-pamby adjective weak and ineffectual.
- ORIGIN from the name of *Ambrose* Philips, an English writer ridiculed for his bad poetry.

name noun 1 a word or words by which someone or something is known. 2 a famous person. 3 a reputation, especially a good one: *he made a name for himself in the theatre.* 4 (in the UK) an insurance underwriter belonging to a Lloyd's syndicate. • verb 1 give someone or something a name. 2 identify or mention by name: *the dead man has been named as John Mackintosh.* 3 specify a time, place, or sum of money.
- PHRASES **call someone names** insult someone verbally. **have to one's name** have in one's possession. **in all but name** existing in practice but not formally recognized as such. **in someone's name** 1 formally registered as belonging to or reserved for someone. 2 on behalf of someone. **in the name of** for the sake of. **name names** mention specific names, especially of people accused of wrongdoing. **the name of the game** informal the main purpose or most important aspect of a situation.
- ORIGIN Old English.

namecheck noun a public mention of someone's name, especially to express gratitude or for publicity purposes. • verb publicly mention someone's name.

name day noun the feast day of a saint after whom a person is named.

name-dropping noun the casual mentioning of famous people as if one knows them, so as to impress others.

nameless adjective 1 having no name. 2 not identified by name; anonymous. 3 too horrific or unpleasant to be described.

namely adverb that is to say.

nameplate noun a plate attached to something and bearing the name of the owner, occupier, or the thing itself.

namesake noun a person or thing with the same name as another.
- ORIGIN from the phrase *for the name's sake.*

Namibian /nuh-mib-i-uhn/ noun a person from Namibia, a country in southern Africa.
• adjective relating to Namibia.

nan[1] /nan/ noun Brit. informal one's grandmother.
- ORIGIN abbreviation of **NANNY**, or a child's pronunciation of **GRAN**.

nan[2] /nahn/ (also **naan**) noun a type of soft, flat Indian bread.
- ORIGIN Urdu and Persian.

nana[1] /nah-nuh/ noun Brit. informal a silly person.
- ORIGIN perhaps a shortening of *banana.*

nana[2] /na-nuh/ (Brit. also **nanna**) noun informal one's grandmother.
- ORIGIN child's pronunciation of **NANNY** or **GRAN**.

nancy (also **nance, nancy boy**) noun (pl. **nancies**) informal, derogatory an effeminate or homosexual man.
- ORIGIN familiar form of the name *Ann.*

nankeen /nang-keen, nan-keen/ noun a yellowish cotton cloth.
- ORIGIN named after the city of *Nanking* in China, where it was first made.

nanny noun (pl. **nannies**) 1 a woman employed to look after a child in its own home. 2 (also **nanny goat**) a female goat. • adjective interfering and overprotective: *the nanny state.* • verb (**nannies, nannying, nannied**) (usu. as noun **nannying**) 1 work as a nanny. 2 treat someone in an overprotective way.
- ORIGIN familiar form of the name *Ann.*

nano- /na-noh/ combining form 1 referring to a factor of one thousand millionth (10^{-9}): *nanosecond.* 2 extremely small; submicroscopic: *nanotechnology.*
- ORIGIN from Greek *nanos* 'dwarf'.

nanobot noun a submicroscopic self-propelled machine, especially one that has some freedom of action and can reproduce.

nanometre /nan-oh-mee-ter/ (US **nanometer**) noun one thousand millionth of a metre.

nanosecond noun one thousand millionth of a second.

nanotechnology noun technology on an atomic or molecular scale, concerned with dimensions of less than 100 nanometres.

nap[1] noun a short sleep, especially during the day. • verb (**naps, napping, napped**) have a nap.
- ORIGIN Old English.

nap[2] noun short raised hairs or threads on the surface of materials such as velvet or suede.
- ORIGIN Dutch or German *noppe.*

nap[3] noun 1 a card game similar to whist. 2 Brit. a tipster's prediction of the most likely winner of a race. • verb (**naps, napping, napped**) Brit. name a horse or greyhound as a likely winner of a race.
- ORIGIN abbreviation of *napoleon*, the original name of the card game.

napalm /nay-pahm/ noun a highly flammable jelly-like form of petrol, used in firebombs and flame-throwers.
- ORIGIN from *naphthenic* and *palmitic acids* (compounds used in its manufacture).

nape noun the back of a person's neck.
- ORIGIN unknown.

napery /nay-puh-ri/ noun tablecloths, napkins, and similar articles.
- ORIGIN Old French *naperie.*

naphtha /naf-thuh/ noun a flammable oil

distilled from coal, shale, or petroleum.
– ORIGIN Greek.

naphthalene /naf-thuh-leen/ noun a white crystalline substance used in mothballs and for chemical manufacture.

napkin noun **1** a square piece of cloth or paper used at a meal to wipe the fingers or lips and to protect clothes. **2** Brit. dated a baby's nappy.
– ORIGIN Old French *nappe* 'tablecloth'.

Napoleonic /nuh-poh-li-on-ik/ adjective relating to or characteristic of the French emperor Napoleon I or his time.

napper noun Brit. informal a person's head.
– ORIGIN unknown.

nappy noun (pl. **nappies**) Brit. a piece of absorbent material wrapped round a baby's bottom and between its legs to absorb and retain urine and faeces.
– ORIGIN abbreviation of NAPKIN.

narcissism /nar-siss-i-z'm/ noun excessive interest in or admiration of oneself and one's physical appearance.
– DERIVATIVES **narcissist** noun **narcissistic** adjective.
– ORIGIN from *Narcissus*, a beautiful youth in Greek mythology who fell in love with his reflection in a pool.

narcissus /nar-siss-uhss/ noun (pl. **narcissi** /nar-siss-I/ or **narcissuses**) a daffodil with a flower that has white or pale outer petals and a shallow orange or yellow centre.
– ORIGIN Greek *narkissos*.

narcolepsy /nar-kuh-lep-si/ noun a condition characterized by an extreme tendency to fall asleep whenever in relaxing surroundings.
– DERIVATIVES **narcoleptic** adjective & noun.
– ORIGIN from Greek *narkē* 'numbness'.

narcosis /nar-koh-siss/ noun a state of drowsiness or unconsciousness produced by drugs.
– ORIGIN from Greek *narkoun* 'make numb'.

narcotic noun **1** an addictive drug, especially an illegal one, which affects mood or behaviour. **2** Medicine a drug which causes drowsiness or unconsciousness, and relieves pain. ●adjective relating to narcotics.

nark Brit. informal noun a police informer. ●verb annoy someone.
– ORIGIN Romany *nāk* 'nose'.

narrate verb **1** give an account of something. **2** provide a commentary for a film, television programme, etc.
– DERIVATIVES **narration** noun **narrator** noun.
– ORIGIN Latin *narrare*.

narrative noun **1** an account of connected events; a story. **2** the part of a fictional work that tells the story, as distinct from the dialogue. ●adjective in the form of a narrative or relating to the narration of something.
– DERIVATIVES **narratively** adverb.

narrow adjective (**narrower**, **narrowest**) **1** of small width in comparison to length. **2** limited in extent, amount, or scope: *a narrow range of skills.* **3** only just achieved: *a narrow escape.* ●verb **1** become or make narrower. **2** (**narrow something down**) reduce the number of possibilities or options. ●noun (**narrows**) a narrow channel connecting two larger areas of water.
– DERIVATIVES **narrowly** adverb **narrowness** noun.
– ORIGIN Old English.

narrowboat noun Brit. a canal boat less than 7 ft (2.1 metres) wide and steered with a tiller rather than a wheel.

narrowcast (past and past part. **narrowcast** or **narrowcasted**) transmit a television programme, especially by cable, to a comparatively small or specialist audience.

narrow gauge noun a railway gauge which is narrower than the standard gauge of 4 ft 8½ inches (1.435 metres).

narrow-minded adjective unwilling to listen to or accept the views of other people.

narthex /nar-theks/ noun an antechamber or large porch in a church.
– ORIGIN Greek.

narwhal /nar-wuhl/ noun a small Arctic whale, the male of which has a long spirally twisted tusk.
– ORIGIN Danish *narhval*, perhaps from an Old Norse word meaning 'corpse', with reference to the whale's skin colour.

nary /nair-i/ adjective informal or dialect form of NOT.
– ORIGIN from *ne'er a* 'never a'.

NASA /na-suh/ abbreviation (in the US) National Aeronautics and Space Administration.

nasal adjective **1** relating to the nose. **2** (of a speech sound) produced by the breath passing through the nose, e.g. *m*, *n*, *ng*. **3** (of speech) having an intonation caused by the breath passing through the nose.
– DERIVATIVES **nasally** adverb.
– ORIGIN from Latin *nasus* 'nose'.

nasalize (or **nasalise**) verb pronounce something nasally.
– DERIVATIVES **nasalization** noun.

nascent /nay-suhnt/ adjective just coming into existence and beginning to develop: *the nascent economic recovery.*
– ORIGIN from Latin *nasci* 'be born'.

NASDAQ abbreviation (in the US) National Association of Securities Dealers Automated Quotations, a computerized system for trading in securities.

nasturtium /nuh-ster-sh'm/ noun a trailing garden plant with round leaves and bright orange, yellow, or red flowers.
– ORIGIN Latin.

nasty adjective (**nastier**, **nastiest**) **1** unpleasant or disgusting. **2** spiteful, violent, or bad-tempered. **3** dangerous or serious: *a nasty bang on the head.* ●noun (pl. **nasties**) informal an unpleasant or harmful person or thing.
– DERIVATIVES **nastily** adverb **nastiness** noun.
– ORIGIN unknown.

Nat. abbreviation **1** national. **2** nationalist.

natal /nay-t'l/ adjective relating to the place or time of one's birth.
– ORIGIN Latin *natalis*.

nation noun a large group of people sharing the same culture, language, or history, and inhabiting a particular state or territory.
– ORIGIN Latin, from *nasci* 'be born'.

national adjective **1** relating to or characteristic of a nation. **2** owned, controlled, or financially supported by the state. ●noun a citizen of a particular country: *French nationals.*
– DERIVATIVES **nationally** adverb.

national curriculum noun a curriculum of

study that must be taught in state schools.

national debt noun the total amount of money which a country's government has borrowed.

national grid noun Brit. 1 the network of high-voltage power lines between major power stations. 2 the metric system of geographical coordinates used in maps of the British Isles.

National Guard noun (in the US) the main reserve military force partly maintained by the states but also available for federal use.

National Hunt (also **National Hunt Committee**) noun the organization controlling steeplechasing and hurdle racing in Great Britain.

National Insurance noun (in the UK) a system of compulsory payments by employees and employers to provide state assistance for people who are sick, unemployed, or retired.

nationalism noun 1 strong support for and pride in one's own country, often to an extreme degree. 2 belief in political independence for a particular country.
– DERIVATIVES **nationalist** noun & adjective **nationalistic** adjective.

nationality noun (pl. **nationalities**) 1 the status of belonging to a particular nation. 2 an ethnic group forming a part of one or more political nations.

nationalize (or **nationalise**) verb transfer an industry or business from private to state ownership or control.
– DERIVATIVES **nationalization** noun.

national park noun an area of natural beauty or environmental importance which is protected by the state and may be visited by the public.

national service noun a period of compulsory service in the armed forces during peacetime.

National Socialism noun historical the political doctrine of the Nazi Party of Germany.

nation state noun a sovereign state most of whose citizens or subjects are united by factors such as a shared language or culture.

nationwide adjective & adverb throughout the whole nation.

native noun 1 a person born in a specified place: *she's a native of Boston.* 2 a local inhabitant. 3 an animal or plant that lives or grows naturally in a place. 4 dated, offensive a non-white original inhabitant of a country as regarded by European colonists or travellers. • adjective 1 associated with a person's place of birth: *her native country.* 2 (of a plant or animal) living or growing naturally in a place. 3 relating to the original inhabitants of a place. 4 naturally in a person's character: *his native wit.*
– ORIGIN Latin *nativus.*

USAGE: In sentences such as *she's a native of Boston* the use of the noun **native** is quite acceptable. When it is used to refer to non-white original inhabitants of a country, however, it has an old-fashioned feel and may cause offence.

Native American noun a member of any of the peoples who were the original inhabitants of North and South America and the Caribbean Islands. • adjective relating to Native Americans.

USAGE: In the US, **Native American** is now the current accepted term in many contexts. See also **AMERICAN INDIAN.**

native speaker noun a person who has spoken the language in question from their earliest childhood.

nativity noun (pl. **nativities**) 1 a person's birth. 2 (**the Nativity**) the birth of Jesus.

nativity play noun a play performed at Christmas based on the events surrounding the birth of Jesus.

NATO (also **Nato**) abbreviation North Atlantic Treaty Organization.

natter informal verb chat casually. • noun a chat.
– ORIGIN first meaning 'grumble, fret'.

natterjack toad noun a small toad with a bright yellow stripe down its back.
– ORIGIN perhaps from **NATTER** (because of its loud croak) + **JACK.**

natty adjective (**nattier, nattiest**) informal smart and fashionable.
– DERIVATIVES **nattily** adverb.
– ORIGIN perhaps related to **NEAT.**

natural adjective 1 existing in or obtained from nature; not made or caused by humans: *natural disasters such as earthquakes.* 2 in accordance with nature; normal or to be expected: *he died of natural causes.* 3 born with a particular skill or quality: *a natural leader.* 4 relaxed and unaffected. 5 (of a parent or child) related by blood. 6 old use illegitimate. 7 Music (of a note) not sharp or flat. • noun 1 a person with an inborn gift or talent for a particular task or activity. 2 an off-white colour. 3 Music a natural note or a sign (♮) indicating one.
– DERIVATIVES **naturalness** noun.
– ORIGIN Middle English.

natural gas noun flammable gas, consisting largely of methane, occurring naturally underground and used as fuel.

natural history noun the scientific study of animals or plants, especially as concerned with observation rather than carrying out experiments.

naturalism noun an artistic or literary movement or style based on the highly detailed and realistic portrayal of daily life.

naturalist noun 1 an expert in or student of natural history. 2 a person who practises naturalism in art or literature.

naturalistic adjective 1 closely imitating real life or nature. 2 based on the theory of naturalism in art or literature.
– DERIVATIVES **naturalistically** adverb.

naturalize (or **naturalise**) verb 1 make someone who was not born in a particular country a citizen of that country. 2 establish a plant or animal in a region where it does not occur naturally. 3 alter an adopted foreign word so that it conforms more closely to the language which has adopted it.
– DERIVATIVES **naturalization** noun.

natural law noun 1 a body of unchanging moral principles regarded as common to all human beings and forming a basis for human behaviour. 2 an observable law relating to natural phenomena.

natural logarithm noun a logarithm to the base e (2.71828 ...).

naturally adverb **1** in a natural way. **2** of course.

natural numbers plural noun the sequence of whole numbers 1, 2, 3, etc., used for counting.

natural philosophy noun old use natural science.

natural resources plural noun naturally occurring materials such as coal or oil.

natural science noun a branch of science which deals with the physical world, e.g. physics, chemistry, geology, biology.

natural selection noun the evolutionary process by which those animals and plants that are better adapted to their environment tend to survive and produce more offspring.

nature noun **1** the physical world, including plants, animals, the landscape, and natural phenomena, as opposed to people or things made by people. **2** the inborn qualities or characteristics of a person or thing: *it's not in her nature to listen to advice.* **3** a kind, sort, or class: *topics of a religious nature.* **4** hereditary characteristics as a factor which determines someone's personality. Often contrasted with **NURTURE**.
– PHRASES **in the nature of things** inevitable or inevitably.
– DERIVATIVES **natured** adjective.
– ORIGIN Latin *natura* 'birth, nature, quality', from *nasci* 'be born'.

nature reserve noun an area of land managed so as to preserve its plants, animals, and physical features.

nature trail noun a signposted path through the countryside designed to draw attention to natural features.

naturism noun chiefly Brit. nudism.
– DERIVATIVES **naturist** noun & adjective.

naturopathy /nay-chuh-**rop**-uh-thi/ noun a system of alternative medicine involving the treatment or prevention of diseases by diet, exercise, and massage rather than by using drugs.
– DERIVATIVES **naturopath** noun **naturopathic** adjective.

naught pronoun old use nothing.
– ORIGIN Old English.

naughty adjective (**naughtier, naughtiest**) **1** (especially of a child) disobedient; badly behaved. **2** informal mildly rude or indecent.
– DERIVATIVES **naughtily** adverb **naughtiness** noun.
– ORIGIN from **NAUGHT**: first meaning 'possessing nothing'.

nausea /naw-zi-uh/ noun **1** a feeling of sickness and being about to vomit. **2** disgust or revulsion.
– ORIGIN Greek *nausia* 'seasickness'.

nauseate verb make someone feel sick or disgusted.

nauseous adjective **1** feeling sick. **2** causing a feeling of sickness.
– DERIVATIVES **nauseously** adverb.

nautical adjective relating to sailors or navigation.
– DERIVATIVES **nautically** adverb.
– ORIGIN Greek *nautikos*, from *nautēs* 'sailor'.

nautical mile noun a unit used in measuring distances at sea, equal to 1,852 metres (approximately 2,025 yards).

nautilus /**naw**-ti-luhss/ noun (pl. **nautiluses** or nautili /**naw**-ti-ly/) a swimming mollusc with a spiral shell and many short tentacles around the mouth.
– ORIGIN Greek *nautilos* 'sailor'.

Navajo /**na**-vuh-hoh/ (also **Navaho**) noun (pl. same or **Navajos**) **1** a member of an American Indian people of New Mexico and Arizona. **2** the language of the Navajo.
– ORIGIN from an American Indian word meaning 'fields adjoining a dry gully'.

naval adjective relating to a navy or navies.
– ORIGIN from Latin *navis* 'ship'.

navarin /**na**-vuh-rin, **na**-vuh-ran/ noun a casserole of lamb or mutton with vegetables.
– ORIGIN French.

nave¹ noun the central part of a church apart from the side aisles, chancel, and transepts.
– ORIGIN Latin *navis* 'ship'.

nave² noun the hub of a wheel.
– ORIGIN Old English.

navel noun the small hollow in the centre of a person's belly where the umbilical cord was cut at birth.
– ORIGIN Old English.

navel-gazing noun self-satisfied concentration on oneself or a single issue.

navel orange noun a variety of orange having a navel-like hollow at the top containing a small secondary fruit.

navigable adjective **1** wide and deep enough to be used by boats and ships. **2** (of a website) easy to move around in.
– DERIVATIVES **navigability** noun.

navigate verb **1** plan and direct the route of a ship, aircraft, or other form of transport. **2** sail or travel over a stretch of water or terrain. **3** guide a ship, boat, or vehicle over a particular route: *she navigated the car safely through the traffic.* **4** move around a website, the Internet, etc.
– ORIGIN Latin *navigare* 'to sail'.

navigation noun **1** the process or activity of navigating. **2** the movement of ships.
– DERIVATIVES **navigational** adjective.

navigator noun **1** a person who navigates a ship, aircraft, etc. **2** historical a person who explored by sea. **3** a browser program for accessing data on the World Wide Web or another information system.

navvy noun (pl. **navvies**) Brit. dated a labourer employed in the building of a road, canal, or railway.
– ORIGIN abbreviation of **NAVIGATOR** in the former sense 'builder of a *navigation*' (a dialect word for a canal).

navy noun (pl. **navies**) **1** the branch of a country's armed services which carries out military operations at sea. **2** (also **navy blue**) a dark blue colour.
– ORIGIN Old French *navie* 'ship, fleet', from Latin *navis* 'ship'.

nawab /nu-**wahb**/ noun Indian **1** a native governor during the time of the Mogul empire. **2** a Muslim nobleman or person of high status.

n

– ORIGIN Urdu, from Arabic, 'deputy'.

nay adverb **1** or rather: *it will take months, nay years.* **2** old use or dialect no. •noun a negative answer.

– ORIGIN Old Norse.

Nazarene /**na**-zuh-reen, na-zuh-**reen**/ noun **1** a native or inhabitant of the town of Nazareth in Israel. **2** (**the Nazarene**) Jesus. **3** a member of an early sect of Jewish Christians. •adjective relating to Nazareth or Nazarenes.

Nazi /**naht**-si/ noun (pl. **Nazis**) historical a member of the far-right National Socialist German Workers' Party.

– DERIVATIVES **Nazism** noun.

– ORIGIN German, representing the pronunciation of *Nati-* in *Nationalsozialist*.

NB abbreviation **1** New Brunswick. **2** (used to draw attention to what follows) take special notice. [Latin *nota bene* 'note well!']

Nb symbol the chemical element niobium.

nb abbreviation Cricket no-ball.

NC abbreviation **1** network computer. **2** North Carolina.

NCO abbreviation non-commissioned officer.

ND abbreviation North Dakota.

Nd symbol the chemical element neodymium.

Ndebele /uhn-duh-**bee**-li, uhn-duh-**bay**-li/ noun (pl. same or **Ndebeles**) a member of a people of Zimbabwe and NE South Africa.

– ORIGIN Nguni (a Bantu language).

NE abbreviation **1** Nebraska. **2** north-east or north-eastern.

Ne symbol the chemical element neon.

Neanderthal /ni-**an**-der-tahl/ noun **1** (also **Neanderthal man**) an extinct human living in ice age Europe between *c.*120,000 and 35,000 years ago. **2** informal a man who is uncouth or who holds very old-fashioned views.

– ORIGIN from *Neanderthal*, a region in Germany where remains of Neanderthal man were found.

neap /neep/ (also **neap tide**) noun a tide just after the first or third quarters of the moon when there is least difference between high and low water.

– ORIGIN Old English.

Neapolitan /ni-uh-**pol**-i-tuhn/ noun a person from the Italian city of Naples. •adjective **1** relating to Naples. **2** (of ice cream) made in layers of different colours and flavours.

near adverb **1** at or to a short distance in space or time. **2** almost: *a near perfect fit.* •preposition (also **near to**) **1** at or to a short distance in space or time from. **2** close to a state or condition; verging on: *she was near tears.* •adjective **1** at a short distance away in space or time. **2** close to being: *a near disaster.* **3** closely related. **4** located on the nearside of a vehicle. •verb approach: *he was nearing retirement.*

– DERIVATIVES **nearness** noun.

– ORIGIN Old Norse.

nearby adjective & adverb not far away.

Near East noun the countries of SW Asia between the Mediterranean and India (including the Middle East).

– DERIVATIVES **Near Eastern** adjective.

nearly adverb very close to; almost.

– PHRASES **not nearly** nothing like; far from.

near miss noun **1** a narrowly avoided collision or accident. **2** a bomb or shot that just misses its target.

nearside noun Brit. **1** the side of a vehicle nearest the kerb. **2** the left side of a horse.

nearsighted adjective chiefly N. Amer. short-sighted.

neat adjective **1** tidy or carefully arranged. **2** done with or showing skill or efficiency: *a neat bit of deduction.* **3** (of a drink of spirits) not diluted or mixed with anything else. **4** N. Amer. informal excellent.

– DERIVATIVES **neatly** adverb **neatness** noun.

– ORIGIN French *net*, from Latin *nitidus* 'shining'.

neaten verb make something neat.

neath preposition literary beneath.

neat's-foot oil noun oil obtained by boiling the feet of cattle, used to treat leather.

– ORIGIN from *neat*, an old word for a cow or ox.

neb noun Scottish & N. English a nose, snout, or bird's beak.

– ORIGIN Old English.

Nebuchadnezzar /neb-yuu-kuhd-**nez**-zer/ noun a very large wine bottle, equal in capacity to about twenty regular bottles.

– ORIGIN from *Nebuchadnezzar* II, king of Babylon in the 6th century BC.

nebula /**neb**-yuu-luh/ noun (pl. **nebulae** /**neb**-yuu-lee/ or **nebulas**) a cloud of gas or dust in outer space, visible in the night sky either as a bright patch or as a dark silhouette against other glowing matter.

– DERIVATIVES **nebular** adjective.

– ORIGIN Latin, 'mist'.

nebulizer /**neb**-yuu-ly-zer/ (or **nebuliser**) noun a device for producing a fine spray of liquid, used for inhaling a medicinal drug.

– DERIVATIVES **nebulize** verb.

nebulous adjective **1** in the form of a cloud or haze; hazy: *a nebulous glow.* **2** not clearly defined; vague: *nebulous concepts.*

– DERIVATIVES **nebulosity** noun.

necessarily adverb as a necessary result; unavoidably.

necessary adjective **1** needing to be done, achieved, or present: *major structural changes are necessary.* **2** that must be; unavoidable: *a necessary consequence.* •noun **1** (**necessaries**) the basic requirements of life, such as food and warmth. **2** (**the necessary**) informal the action, item, or money required.

– ORIGIN Latin *necessarius*.

necessitate verb **1** make necessary: *the rain necessitated a change of plan.* **2** force someone to do something.

necessitous adjective formal lacking the basic requirements of life; poor.

necessity noun (pl. **necessities**) **1** the state or fact of being needed or essential. **2** a thing that is essential: *a good book is a necessity when travelling.* **3** a situation that requires a particular course of action: *a system born out of political necessity.*

neck noun **1** the part of the body connecting the head to the rest of the body. **2** a narrow connecting or end part, such as the part of a bottle near the mouth. **3** the part of a violin, guitar, or other instrument that bears the fingerboard. **4** the length of a horse's head and

neck as a measure of its lead in a race. • verb informal **1** kiss and caress passionately. **2** Brit. swallow a drink.
– PHRASES **get it in the neck** Brit. informal be severely criticized or punished. **neck and neck** level in a race or competition. **neck of the woods** informal a particular place. **up to one's neck in** informal heavily or busily involved in something.
– ORIGIN Old English, 'nape of the neck'.

neckband noun a strip of material round the neck of a garment.

neckerchief noun a square of cloth worn round the neck.

necklace noun **1** an ornamental chain or string of beads, jewels, or links worn round the neck. **2** (in South Africa) a tyre soaked with petrol, placed round a victim's neck and set alight in order to burn them to death.

necklet noun a close-fitting, typically rigid ornament worn around the neck.

neckline noun the edge of a dress or top at or below the neck.

necktie noun N. Amer. or dated a tie worn around the neck.

necromancy /nek-ruh-man-si/ noun **1** prediction of the future by supposedly communicating with the dead. **2** witchcraft or black magic.
– DERIVATIVES **necromancer** noun **necromantic** adjective.
– ORIGIN from Greek *nekros* 'corpse'.

necrophilia /nek-ruh-fil-i-uh/ noun sexual intercourse with or attraction towards dead bodies.
– DERIVATIVES **necrophiliac** noun.

necrophobia noun extreme or irrational fear of death or dead bodies.

necropolis /ne-krop-uh-liss/ noun a cemetery, especially a large ancient one.
– ORIGIN from Greek *nekros* 'corpse' + *polis* 'city'.

necropsy /nek-rop-si, ne-krop-si/ noun (pl. **necropsies**) another term for AUTOPSY.

necrosis /ne-kroh-siss/ noun the death of most or all of the cells in an organ or tissue due to disease or injury.
– DERIVATIVES **necrotic** adjective.
– ORIGIN from Greek *nekros* 'corpse'.

necrotizing /nek-ruh-ty-zing/ (also **necrotising**) adjective causing or accompanied by necrosis.

nectar noun **1** a sugary fluid produced by flowers to encourage pollination by insects, made into honey by bees. **2** (in Greek and Roman mythology) the drink of the gods. **3** a delicious drink.
– ORIGIN Greek *nektar*.

nectarine /nek-tuh-reen/ noun a variety of peach with smooth skin.
– ORIGIN from NECTAR.

ned noun Scottish informal a hooligan or troublemaker.
– ORIGIN perhaps from *Ned*, familiar form of the man's name *Edward*.

née /nay/ adjective born (used in giving a married woman's maiden name): *Mrs. Hargreaves, née Liddell*.
– ORIGIN French.

need verb **1** want something because it is essential or very important: *I need help.* **2** used to express what should or must be done: *need I say more?* • noun **1** circumstances in which something is necessary or must be done: *he was in need of medical care.* **2** a thing that is wanted or required: *his day-to-day needs.* **3** a state of being poor or in great difficulty: *children in need.*
– ORIGIN Old English.

needful adjective formal necessary.

needle noun **1** a very thin pointed piece of metal with a hole or eye for thread at the blunter end, used in sewing. **2** a long thin metal or plastic rod with a pointed end, used in knitting. **3** the pointed hollow end of a hypodermic syringe. **4** a stylus used to play records. **5** a thin pointer on a dial, compass, etc. **6** the thin, sharp, stiff leaf of a fir or pine tree. **7** Brit. informal hostility or antagonism caused by rivalry between two people, teams, etc. • verb informal deliberately provoke or annoy someone.
– ORIGIN Old English.

needlecord noun Brit. corduroy fabric with narrow ridges.

needlepoint noun **1** closely stitched embroidery worked over canvas. **2** lace made by hand using a needle rather than bobbins.

needless adjective unnecessary; avoidable.
– PHRASES **needless to say** of course.
– DERIVATIVES **needlessly** adverb.

needlewoman noun (pl. **needlewomen**) a woman who has particular sewing skills or who sews for a living.

needlework noun sewing or embroidery.

needn't contraction need not.

needy adjective (**needier**, **neediest**) **1** lacking the necessities of life; very poor. **2** insecure and needing emotional support.
– DERIVATIVES **neediness** noun.

neem /neem/ noun a tropical tree from which wood, oil, medicinal products, and insecticide are obtained.
– ORIGIN Sanskrit.

neep noun Scottish & N. English a turnip.
– ORIGIN Latin *napus*.

ne'er /nair/ contraction literary or dialect never.

ne'er-do-well noun a person who is lazy and irresponsible.

nefarious /ni-fair-i-uhss/ adjective wicked or criminal.
– ORIGIN from Latin *nefas* 'wrong'.

negate /ni-gayt/ verb **1** prevent something from having an effect: *alcohol negates the effects of the drug.* **2** deny that something exists.
– ORIGIN Latin *negare* 'deny'.

negation noun **1** the contradiction or denial of something. **2** the absence or opposite of something: *evil is not merely the negation of goodness.* **3** Mathematics replacement of positive by negative.

negative adjective **1** characterized by the absence rather than the presence of particular features: *a negative test result.* **2** expressing or implying denial, disagreement, or refusal. **3** not optimistic, encouraging, or desirable: *his negative attitude.* **4** (of a quantity) less than

n

zero. **5** relating to, containing, or producing the kind of electric charge carried by electrons. **6** (of a photographic image) showing light and shade or colours reversed from those of the original. **7** Grammar stating that something is not the case. •noun **1** a word or statement expressing denial or refusal. **2** a negative photographic image from which positive prints may be made.
– DERIVATIVES **negatively** adverb **negativity** noun.

negative equity noun a situation in which the market value of a property is less than the outstanding amount of the mortgage secured on it.

negative pole noun the south-seeking pole of a magnet.

neglect verb **1** fail to give proper care or attention to: *she neglected her children.* **2** fail to do something: *he neglected to write to her.* •noun the action of neglecting someone or something, or the state of being neglected.
– ORIGIN Latin *neglegere* 'disregard'.

neglectful adjective failing to give proper care or attention to someone or something.

negligee /neg-li-zhay/ noun a woman's dressing gown made of very thin fabric.
– ORIGIN French, 'given little thought or attention'.

negligence noun **1** failure to take proper care over something. **2** Law breach of a duty of care which results in damage.
– DERIVATIVES **negligent** adjective.

negligible /neg-li-juh-b'l/ adjective so small or unimportant that it is not worth considering.
– DERIVATIVES **negligibly** adverb.
– ORIGIN from French *négliger* 'to neglect'.

negotiable adjective **1** able to be changed as a result of discussion: *the fee may be negotiable.* **2** (of a route) able to be travelled on; passable. **3** (of a document) able to be transferred or given to the legal ownership of another person.
– DERIVATIVES **negotiability** noun.

negotiate verb **1** try to reach an agreement or compromise by discussion. **2** obtain or bring about by discussion: *he negotiated a new contract.* **3** find a way over an obstacle or through a difficult path. **4** transfer a cheque, bill, etc. to the legal ownership of another person.
– DERIVATIVES **negotiator** noun.
– ORIGIN Latin *negotiari* 'do in the course of business'.

negotiation (also **negotiations**) noun discussion aimed at reaching an agreement or compromise.

Negress /nee-gress/ noun dated a woman or girl of black African origin.

Negro noun (pl. **Negroes**) a member of a group of black peoples originally native to Africa.
– ORIGIN from Latin *niger* 'black'.

USAGE: The terms **Negro** and **Negress** are now regarded as old-fashioned or even offensive; **black** is the preferred term.

neigh noun a high whinnying sound made by a horse. •verb make a high whinnying sound.
– ORIGIN imitating the sound.

neighbour (US **neighbor**) noun **1** a person living next door to or very near to another. **2** a

person or place next to or near another. •verb (usu. as adj. **neighbouring**) be situated next to or very near: *neighbouring countries.*
– DERIVATIVES **neighbourly** adjective.
– ORIGIN Old English.

neighbourhood (US **neighborhood**) noun **1** a district within a town or city. **2** the area surrounding a place, person, or object.
– PHRASES **in the neighbourhood of** about; approximately.

neighbourhood watch noun a scheme in which local groups of householders watch each other's homes to discourage burglary and other crimes.

neither /ny-ther, nee-ther/ determiner & pronoun not either. •adverb **1** used to show that a negative statement is true of two things: *I am neither a liberal nor a conservative.* **2** used to show that a negative statement is also true of something else.
– ORIGIN Old English.

nelly noun (pl. **nellies**) informal a silly person.
– PHRASES **not on your nelly** Brit. certainly not. [from *not on your Nelly Duff*, rhyming slang for 'puff' (i.e. breath of life).]
– ORIGIN from the woman's name *Nelly.*

nelson noun a wrestling hold in which one arm is passed under the opponent's arm from behind and the hand is applied to the neck (**half nelson**), or both arms and hands are applied (**full nelson**).
– ORIGIN probably from the surname *Nelson.*

nematode /nem-uh-tohd/ noun a worm of a group with slender, unsegmented, cylindrical bodies, such as a roundworm or threadworm.
– ORIGIN from Greek *nēma* 'thread'.

nemesia /ni-mee-zhuh/ noun a plant related to the snapdragon, grown for its colourful funnel-shaped flowers.
– ORIGIN Latin.

nemesis /nem-i-siss/ noun (pl. **nemeses** /nem-i-seez/) **1** a means of punishment or downfall that is deserved or unavoidable: *it was in New York that she first met her future husband and ultimately her nemesis.* **2** downfall caused by an unavoidable agent.
– ORIGIN Greek, 'retribution'.

neo- /nee-oh/ combining form **1** new: *neonate.* **2** a new or revived form of: *neoclassicism.*
– ORIGIN from Greek *neos* 'new'.

neoclassical (also **neoclassic**) adjective relating to the revival of a classical style in the arts.
– DERIVATIVES **neoclassicism** noun **neoclassicist** noun & adjective.

neocolonialism noun the use of economic, political, or cultural pressures to control or influence other countries.
– DERIVATIVES **neocolonial** adjective **neocolonialist** noun & adjective.

neodymium /nee-oh-dim-i-uhm/ noun a silvery-white metallic element of the lanthanide series.
– ORIGIN from NEO- + *didymium*, a mixture of the elements praseodymium and neodymium, from Greek *didumos* 'twin'.

neo-Impressionism noun an artistic movement which aimed to improve on Impressionism through a systematic approach to form and colour.

– DERIVATIVES **neo-Impressionist** adjective & noun.

Neolithic /nee-uh-**lith**-ik/ adjective relating to the later part of the Stone Age, when agriculture was introduced and ground or polished stone weapons and implements were used.
– ORIGIN from **NEO-** + Greek *lithos* 'stone'.

neologism /ni-**ol**-uh-ji-z'm/ noun a newly coined word or expression.
– ORIGIN from **NEO-** + Greek *logos* 'word'.

neon noun an inert gas that gives an orange glow when electricity is passed through it, used in fluorescent lighting. • adjective very bright or fluorescent in colour: *bold neon colours*.
– ORIGIN Greek, 'something new'.

neonatal /nee-uh-**nay**-t'l/ adjective relating to newborn children.
– DERIVATIVES **neonatology** noun.

neonate /**nee**-oh-nayt/ noun a newborn child or mammal.
– ORIGIN from Greek *neos* 'new' + Latin *nasci* 'be born'.

neo-Nazi noun (pl. **neo-Nazis**) a person with extreme racist or nationalist views. • adjective relating to neo-Nazis.
– DERIVATIVES **neo-Nazism** noun.

neophobia noun extreme or irrational fear or dislike of anything new or unfamiliar.
– DERIVATIVES **neophobic** adjective.

neophyte /**nee**-uh-fyt/ noun **1** a person who is new to a subject, skill, or belief. **2** a novice in a religious order, or a newly ordained priest.
– ORIGIN from Greek *neophutos* 'newly planted'.

neoplasm noun a new and abnormal growth of tissue in the body, especially a cancerous tumour.
– ORIGIN from **NEO-** + Greek *plasma* 'formation'.

neoprene /**nee**-oh-preen/ noun a synthetic substance resembling rubber.
– ORIGIN from **NEO-** + *prene*, of uncertain origin.

Nepalese /ne-puh-**leez**/ noun a person from Nepal. • adjective relating to Nepal.

Nepali /ni-**paw**-li/ noun (pl. same or **Nepalis**) **1** a person from Nepal. **2** the language of Nepal. • adjective relating to Nepal or Nepali.

nephew noun a son of a person's brother or sister.
– ORIGIN Latin *nepos* 'grandson, nephew'.

nephrite /**nef**-ryt/ noun a pale green or white form of jade.
– ORIGIN from Greek *nephros* 'kidney' (with reference to its supposed ability to treat kidney disease).

nephritis /ni-**fry**-tiss/ noun inflammation of the kidneys.
– ORIGIN from Greek *nephros* 'kidney'.

ne plus ultra /nay pluuss **uul**-trah/ noun (**the ne plus ultra**) the perfect example of its kind: *the ne plus ultra of editors.*
– ORIGIN Latin, 'not further beyond', the supposed inscription on the Pillars of Hercules (at the Strait of Gibraltar) banning ships from going further.

nepotism /**nep**-uh-ti-z'm/ noun favouritism shown to relatives or friends, especially by giving them jobs.
– DERIVATIVES **nepotistic** adjective.
– ORIGIN from Italian *nipote* 'nephew' (with reference to privileges given to the 'nephews' of popes, often their illegitimate sons).

Neptune noun a planet of the solar system, eighth in order from the sun.
– DERIVATIVES **Neptunian** adjective.

neptunium noun a rare radioactive metallic element produced from uranium.
– ORIGIN from *Neptune*, on the pattern of *uranium* (Neptune being the next planet beyond Uranus).

nerd noun informal a person who is obsessively interested in something and finds it difficult to get on with people.
– DERIVATIVES **nerdish** adjective **nerdy** adjective.
– ORIGIN unknown.

Nereid /**neer**-i-id/ noun Greek Mythology a sea nymph.

nerve noun **1** a fibre or bundle of fibres in the body that transmits impulses of sensation between the brain or spinal cord and other parts of the body. **2** (**nerves** or **one's nerve**) steadiness and courage in a demanding situation: *the journey tested her nerves to the full.* **3** (**nerves**) nervousness. **4** informal cheeky or excessively bold behaviour. • verb (**nerve oneself**) brace oneself for a demanding situation.
– PHRASES **get on someone's nerves** informal irritate someone.
– ORIGIN Latin *nervus*.

nerve cell noun a neuron.

nerve centre noun **1** the control centre of an organization or operation. **2** a group of connected nerve cells performing a particular function.

nerve gas noun a poisonous gas which attacks the nervous system, causing death or disablement.

nerveless adjective **1** lacking strength or feeling. **2** not nervous; confident.

nerve-racking (also **nerve-wracking**) adjective causing stress or anxiety.

nervous adjective **1** easily frightened or worried. **2** apprehensive or anxious: *he's nervous of speaking in public.* **3** relating to the nerves.
– DERIVATIVES **nervously** adverb **nervousness** noun.

nervous breakdown noun a period of mental illness resulting from severe depression or stress.

nervous system noun the network of nerve cells and fibres which transmits nerve impulses between parts of the body.

nervous wreck noun informal a person suffering from stress or emotional exhaustion.

nervy adjective (**nervier, nerviest**) Brit. nervous or tense.
– DERIVATIVES **nervily** adverb **nerviness** noun.

ness noun a headland or promontory.
– ORIGIN Old English.

-ness suffix forming nouns referring to: **1** a state or condition: *liveliness.* **2** something in a certain state: *wilderness.*
– ORIGIN Old English.

nest noun **1** a structure made by a bird for laying eggs and sheltering its young. **2** a place where an animal or insect breeds or shelters. **3** a place filled with undesirable people or

things: *a nest of spies.* **4** a set of similar objects of graduated sizes, fitting together for storage. •**verb 1** (of a bird or animal) use or build a nest. **2** fit an object or objects inside a larger one. **3** (often as adj. **nested**) (especially in computing) place something in a lower position in a hierarchy.
– DERIVATIVES **nester** noun.
– ORIGIN Old English.

nest egg noun a sum of money saved for the future.

nestle verb **1** settle comfortably within or against something. **2** (of a place) lie in a sheltered position.
– ORIGIN Old English.

nestling noun a bird that is too young to leave the nest.

net¹ noun **1** a material made of strands of twine or cord woven or knotted together to form open squares. **2** a piece or structure of net for catching fish, surrounding a goal, etc. **3** a fine fabric with a very open weave. **4** (**the net**) the goal in football. **5** a means of catching or securing someone or something: *passengers and luggage go through several checks to make sure no one slips through the net.* **6** (**the Net**) the Internet. **7** a communications or computer network. •**verb** (**nets, netting, netted**) **1** catch something in a net. **2** catch or obtain in a skilful way: *customs have netted large caches of drugs.* **3** (in sport) score a goal. **4** cover something with a net.
– ORIGIN Old English.

net² (Brit. also **nett**) adjective **1** (of an amount, value, or price) remaining after tax, discounts, or expenses have been deducted. Often contrasted with GROSS. **2** (of a weight) not including that of the packaging. **3** (of an effect or result) remaining after other factors have been taken into account; overall. •**verb** (**nets, netting, netted**) gain a sum of money as clear profit.
– ORIGIN French *net* 'neat'.

netball noun a team game in which goals are scored by throwing a ball through a net hanging from a hoop.

nether /ne**th**-er/ adjective lower in position.
– DERIVATIVES **nethermost** adjective.
– ORIGIN Old English.

Netherlander noun a person from the Netherlands.
– DERIVATIVES **Netherlandish** adjective.

nether regions plural noun **1** hell; the underworld. **2** euphemistic a person's genitals and bottom.

netherworld noun **1** the underworld; hell. **2** an area of activity that is hidden, underhand, or poorly defined.

net profit noun the actual profit after working expenses have been paid.

netsuke /net-ski, net-suu-ki/ noun (pl. same or **netsukes**) a carved ornament of wood or ivory, formerly worn in Japan to suspend items from the sash of a kimono.
– ORIGIN Japanese.

nett adjective & verb Brit. variant spelling of NET².

netting noun material made of net.

nettle noun a plant with jagged leaves covered with stinging hairs. •**verb** annoy someone.

– PHRASES **grasp the nettle** Brit. tackle a difficulty boldly.
– ORIGIN Old English.

nettlerash noun another term for URTICARIA.

network noun **1** an arrangement of horizontal and vertical lines that cross each other. **2** a system of railways, roads, etc., that connect with each other. **3** a group of broadcasting stations that connect to broadcast a programme at the same time. **4** a number of interconnected computers or operations. **5** a group of people who keep in contact to exchange information. •**verb 1** Brit. broadcast a programme on a network. **2** interact with other people to exchange information and develop contacts.
– DERIVATIVES **networker** noun.

neural adjective relating to a nerve or the nervous system.
– DERIVATIVES **neurally** adverb.

neuralgia /nyoo-ral-juh/ noun intense pain along a nerve, especially in the head or face.
– DERIVATIVES **neuralgic** adjective.

neuritis /nyoo-ry-tiss/ noun inflammation of a peripheral nerve or nerves.

neuro- combining form relating to nerves or the nervous system: *neurosurgery.*
– ORIGIN from Greek *neuron* 'nerve, sinew, tendon'.

neurochemistry noun the branch of biochemistry concerned with the processes occurring in nerve tissue and the nervous system.
– DERIVATIVES **neurochemical** adjective **neurochemist** noun.

neuroleptic /nyoo-ruh-lep-tik/ adjective (of a drug) tending to lower nervous tension by reducing nerve functions.
– ORIGIN from NEURO- + Greek *lēpsis* 'seizing'.

neurology noun the branch of medicine and biology concerned with the nervous system.
– DERIVATIVES **neurologic** adjective **neurological** adjective **neurologist** noun.

neuron (also **neurone**) noun a specialized cell that transmits nerve impulses.
– DERIVATIVES **neuronal** adjective.
– ORIGIN Greek *neuron* 'sinew, tendon, nerve'.

neurosis /nyoo-roh-siss/ noun (pl. **neuroses** /nyoo-roh-seez/) a relatively mild mental illness involving symptoms such as depression, anxiety, obsessive behaviour, or hypochondria.

neurosurgery noun surgery performed on the nervous system.
– DERIVATIVES **neurosurgeon** noun **neurosurgical** adjective.

neurotic adjective **1** having or relating to neurosis. **2** informal abnormally sensitive, anxious, or obsessive. •**noun** a neurotic person.
– DERIVATIVES **neurotically** adverb **neuroticism** noun.

neurotoxin /nyoo-roh-tok-sin/ noun a poison which acts on the nervous system.

neurotransmitter noun a chemical substance released from a nerve fibre and bringing about the transfer of an impulse to another nerve, muscle, etc.

neuter adjective **1** Grammar (of a noun) not masculine or feminine. **2** (of an animal or

plant) having no sexual or reproductive organs. ●verb 1 castrate or spay a domestic animal. 2 take away the power of: *their only purpose is to neuter local democracy.*
– ORIGIN Latin, 'neither'.

neutral adjective 1 not supporting either side in a dispute or conflict; impartial. 2 deliberately not expressing or provoking strong feeling: *her tone was neutral, devoid of sentiment.* 3 pale grey, cream, or beige in colour. 4 Chemistry neither acid nor alkaline; having a pH of about 7. 5 electrically neither positive nor negative. ●noun 1 a country or person that does not take sides in a conflict or dispute. 2 pale grey, cream, or beige. 3 a position of a gear mechanism in which the engine is disconnected from the driven parts.
– DERIVATIVES **neutrality** noun **neutrally** adverb.
– ORIGIN Latin *neutralis* 'of neuter gender'.

neutralize (or **neutralise**) verb 1 prevent something from having an effect by counteracting it with something else: *never try to neutralize odours with air fresheners.* 2 make an acid or alkaline chemically neutral. 3 euphemistic kill or destroy someone or something.
– DERIVATIVES **neutralization** noun.

neutrino /nyoo-tree-noh/ noun (pl. **neutrinos**) Physics a subatomic particle with a mass close to zero and no electric charge.
– ORIGIN Italian.

neutron noun a subatomic particle of about the same mass as a proton but without an electric charge.
– ORIGIN from **NEUTRAL**.

neutron bomb noun a nuclear weapon that produces large numbers of neutrons, destroying life but not property.

neutron star noun a very dense star composed mainly of neutrons.

névé /ne-vay/ noun compacted or hardened snow, especially as found on the upper part of a glacier.
– ORIGIN Swiss French, 'glacier'.

never adverb 1 not ever. 2 not at all. 3 Brit. informal (expressing surprise) surely not.
– PHRASES **the never-never** Brit. informal hire purchase. **never-never land** an imaginary perfect place. [the ideal country in J. M. Barrie's *Peter Pan*.] **well I never!** informal expressing great surprise.
– ORIGIN Old English.

never-ending adjective (especially of something unpleasant) having or seeming to have no end.

nevermore adverb literary never again.

nevertheless adverb in spite of that.

nevus noun (pl. **nevi**) US spelling of **NAEVUS**.

new adjective 1 not existing before; made, introduced, or discovered recently: *she was signing copies of her new book.* 2 not previously used or owned. 3 obtained or experienced recently: *her new coat.* 4 (**new to/at**) not familiar or experienced at. 5 better than before; renewed or transformed: *the pills would make him a new man.* ●adverb newly.
– DERIVATIVES **newness** noun.
– ORIGIN Old English.

New Age noun a movement concerned with

alternative approaches to traditional Western culture, religion, medicine, etc.

newborn adjective recently born. ●noun a newborn child.

newbuild noun a newly constructed house or ship.
– DERIVATIVES **newbuilding** noun.

newcomer noun 1 a person who has recently arrived. 2 a person who is new to an activity or situation.

newel /nyoo-uhl/ noun 1 (also **newel post**) the top or bottom supporting post of a stair rail. 2 the central supporting pillar of a spiral staircase.
– ORIGIN Old French *nouel* 'knob'.

newfangled adjective derogatory new and different from what one is used to.
– ORIGIN from dialect *newfangle* 'liking what is new'.

Newfoundland /nyoo-fuhnd-luhnd/ noun a dog of a very large breed with a thick coarse coat.
– ORIGIN named after *Newfoundland* in Canada.

New Guinean noun a person from New Guinea. ●adjective relating to New Guinea.

newly adverb 1 recently. 2 again; afresh: *confidence for the newly single.*

newly-wed noun a recently married person.

new man noun a man who rejects traditional male attitudes, often taking on childcare and housework.

new maths (N. Amer. **new math**) plural noun (usu. treated as sing.) a system of teaching mathematics to children, with emphasis on investigation by them and on set theory.

new moon noun the phase of the moon when it first appears as a slender crescent.

news noun 1 new or important information about recent events. 2 (**the news**) a broadcast or published news report. 3 (**news to**) informal information not previously known to someone.

news agency noun an organization that collects and distributes news items to the media.

newsagent noun Brit. a person or shop selling newspapers, magazines, etc.

newscast noun N. Amer. a broadcast news report.
– DERIVATIVES **newscaster** noun.

news conference noun N. Amer. a press conference.

newsfeed noun 1 a service by which news items are provided on a regular or continuous basis for onward distribution or broadcasting. 2 a system by which data is transferred or exchanged between central computers to provide newsgroup access to networked users.

newsflash noun a short broadcast of important news that often interrupts other programmes.

newsgroup noun a group of Internet users who exchange information online on a particular topic.

newsletter noun a bulletin issued periodically to the members of a society or other organization.

newsman noun (pl. **newsmen**) a male reporter or journalist.

newspaper noun a daily or weekly publication

n

consisting of folded sheets and containing news, articles, and advertisements.

newspeak noun deliberately misleading and indirect language, used by politicians.
– ORIGIN an official language in George Orwell's novel *Nineteen Eighty-Four*.

newsprint noun cheap, low-quality printing paper used for newspapers.

newsreader noun 1 Brit. a person who reads the news on radio or television. 2 a computer program for reading emails posted to newsgroups.

newsreel noun a short cinema film of news and current affairs.

newsroom noun the area in a newspaper or broadcasting office where news is processed.

news-stand noun a stand for the sale of newspapers.

New Stone Age noun the Neolithic period.

New Style noun the method of calculating dates using the Gregorian calendar.

newswire noun an Internet news service.

newsworthy adjective important enough to be mentioned as news.

newsy adjective informal full of news.

newt noun a small animal with a thin body and a long tail, that can live in water or on land.
– ORIGIN from *an ewt* (from Old English *efeta* 'eft'), interpreted as *a newt*.

New Testament noun the second part of the Christian Bible, recording the life and teachings of Jesus and his earliest followers.

newton noun Physics the SI unit of force.
– ORIGIN named after the English scientist Sir Isaac *Newton*.

Newtonian adjective relating to or arising from the work of Sir Isaac Newton; behaving according to the principles of classical physics.

new town noun a town planned and built in an undeveloped or rural area.

new wave noun 1 a group of people who introduce new styles and ideas in art, cinema, literature, etc. 2 a style of rock music popular in the late 1970s, deriving from punk.

New World noun North and South America in contrast to Europe, Asia, and Africa.

new year noun 1 the calendar year just begun or about to begin. 2 the period immediately before and after 31 December.

New Year's Day noun 1 January.

New Year's Eve noun 31 December.

New Yorker noun a person from the state or city of New York.

New York minute noun US informal a very short time; a moment.

New Zealander noun a person from New Zealand.

next adjective 1 coming immediately after the present one in time, space, or order. 2 (of a day of the week) nearest (or the nearest but one) after the present. • adverb 1 immediately afterwards. 2 following in the specified order: *Joe was the next oldest after Martin.* • noun the next person or thing.
– PHRASES **next of kin** a person's closest living relative or relatives. **next to 1** beside. **2** following in order or importance. **3** almost. **the next world** (in some religious beliefs) the

place where people go after death.
– ORIGIN Old English.

next door adverb & adjective in or to the next house or room.

nexus /nek-suhss/ noun (pl. same or **nexuses**) 1 a connection or series of connections: *the nexus between birth and privilege.* 2 a connected group. 3 a central or focal point.
– ORIGIN Latin.

NF abbreviation 1 National Front. 2 Newfoundland.

NFL abbreviation (in the US) National Football League.

NGO abbreviation non-governmental organization.

ngwee /uhng-gway/ noun (pl. same) a unit of money of Zambia, equal to one hundredth of a kwacha.
– ORIGIN a local word.

NH abbreviation New Hampshire.

NHS abbreviation (in the UK) National Health Service.

NI abbreviation 1 (in the UK) National Insurance. 2 Northern Ireland.

Ni symbol the chemical element nickel.

niacin /ny-uh-sin/ noun another term for NICOTINIC ACID.

nib noun the pointed end part of a pen, which distributes the ink.
– ORIGIN probably from Dutch *nib* or German *nibbe* 'beak'.

nibble verb 1 take small bites out of something. 2 bite a part of the body gently. 3 gradually reduce: *the fringes of the region have been nibbled away by development.* • noun 1 an instance of nibbling. 2 a small piece of food bitten off. 3 (**nibbles**) informal small savoury snacks.
– ORIGIN probably German or Dutch.

niblet noun a small piece of food.

niblick /nib-lik/ noun Golf, dated an iron with a heavy head, used for playing out of bunkers.
– ORIGIN unknown.

nibs noun (**his nibs**) informal a mock title used to refer to a man who thinks he is important.
– ORIGIN unknown.

NiCad /ny-kad/ (also US trademark **Nicad**) noun a battery or cell containing nickel, cadmium, and potassium hydroxide.
– ORIGIN blend of NICKEL and CADMIUM.

Nicam /ny-kam/ noun a digital system used in British television to provide video signals with high-quality stereo sound.
– ORIGIN from the initial letters of *near instantaneously companded audio multiplex.*

Nicaraguan /ni-kuh-rag-yuu-uhn, ni-kuh-rag-wuhn/ noun a person from Nicaragua in Central America. • adjective relating to Nicaragua.

nice adjective 1 pleasant, agreeable, or attractive. 2 good-natured; kind. 3 fine or subtle: *a nice distinction.*
– DERIVATIVES **nicely** adverb **niceness** noun.
– ORIGIN early senses included 'stupid' and 'coy': from Latin *nescius* 'ignorant'.

nicety noun (pl. **niceties**) 1 a fine detail or distinction: *legal niceties are wasted on him.* 2 a detail of polite social behaviour. 3 accuracy or precision.

- PHRASES **to a nicety** precisely.

niche /neesh, nich/ **noun 1** a shallow recess, especially one in a wall to display an ornament. **2 (one's niche)** a position or role in life that suits someone: *he found his niche as a writer.* **3** a particular group seen as a potential market for a product: *targeting the urban youth niche.*
- ORIGIN French.

nick **noun 1** a small cut or notch. **2 (the nick)** Brit. informal prison or a police station. **3** Brit. informal condition: *in good nick.* • **verb 1** make a small cut in something. **2** Brit. informal steal something. **3** Brit. informal arrest someone.
- PHRASES **in the nick of time** only just in time.
- ORIGIN unknown.

nickel **noun 1** a silvery-white metallic chemical element resembling iron, used in alloys. **2** N. Amer. informal a five-cent coin. • **verb** (**nickels, nickelling, nickelled**; US **nickels, nickeling, nickeled**) coat something with nickel.
- ORIGIN German *Kupfernickel* (the copper-coloured ore from which nickel was first obtained).

nickelodeon /ni-kuh-**loh**-di-uhn/ **noun** N. Amer. informal, dated a jukebox.
- ORIGIN from **NICKEL** + **MELODEON**.

nickel silver **noun** an alloy of nickel, zinc, and copper.

nickel steel **noun** stainless steel containing chromium and nickel.

nicker **noun** (pl. same) Brit. informal a pound sterling.
- ORIGIN unknown.

nickname **noun** an informal, often amusing name for a person or thing. • **verb** give a nickname to someone or something.
- ORIGIN from *an eke-name* (*eke* meaning 'addition'), misinterpreted as *a neke name.*

nicotiana /ni-ko-ti-**ah**-nuh, ni-koh-shi-**ah**-nuh/ **noun** an ornamental plant related to tobacco, with tubular sweet-smelling flowers.

nicotine **noun** a toxic oily liquid found in tobacco.
- ORIGIN named after Jean *Nicot*, a diplomat who introduced tobacco to France.

nicotine patch **noun** a patch containing nicotine, worn on the skin by a person trying to give up smoking.

nicotinic acid **noun** a vitamin of the B complex, found in milk, wheat germ, meat, and other foods.

nictitating membrane **noun** a whitish membrane forming an inner eyelid in birds, reptiles, and some mammals.
- ORIGIN from Latin *nictare* 'to blink'.

nidification /ni-di-fi-**kay**-sh'n/ **noun** Zoology nest-building.
- ORIGIN Latin, from *nidus* 'nest'.

niece **noun** a daughter of a person's brother or sister.
- ORIGIN Old French.

niello /ni-**el**-loh/ **noun 1** a black compound of sulphur with silver, lead, or copper, used for filling in engraved designs in metals. **2** objects decorated with niello.
- ORIGIN Italian.

Nietzschean /neech-i-uhn/ **adjective** relating to the German philosopher Friedrich Wilhelm Nietzsche.

niff Brit. informal **noun** an unpleasant smell. • **verb** smell unpleasant; stink.
- DERIVATIVES **niffy** adjective.
- ORIGIN perhaps from **SNIFF**.

nifty **adjective** (**niftier, niftiest**) informal particularly good, effective, or stylish.
- DERIVATIVES **niftily** adverb.
- ORIGIN unknown.

Nigerian /ny-**jeer**-i-uhn/ **noun** a person from Nigeria. • **adjective** relating to Nigeria.

niggard /**nig**-gerd/ **noun** a miserly person.
- ORIGIN Scandinavian.

niggardly **adjective** not generous; mean: *I was kept on a niggardly allowance.*

nigger **noun** offensive a black person.
- ORIGIN from Spanish *negro* 'black'.

> USAGE: The word **nigger** is very offensive and should not be used.

niggle **verb 1** worry or annoy someone slightly but persistently. **2** criticize someone in a petty way. • **noun** a minor worry or criticism.
- DERIVATIVES **niggly** adjective.
- ORIGIN probably Scandinavian.

nigh **adverb, preposition, & adjective 1** old use or literary near. **2** almost; nearly.
- ORIGIN Old English.

night **noun 1** the time from sunset to sunrise. **2** the darkness of night. **3** an evening until bedtime. **4** literary dusk; nightfall. • **adverb** (**nights**) informal at night.
- ORIGIN Old English.

nightcap **noun 1** a hot or alcoholic drink taken at bedtime. **2** historical a cap worn in bed.

nightclothes **plural noun** clothes worn in bed.

nightclub **noun** a club that is open at night, with a bar and music.

nightdress **noun** a light, loose garment worn by a woman or girl in bed.

nightfall **noun** dusk.

nightgown **noun** a nightdress.

nightie **noun** informal a nightdress.

nightingale **noun** a small brownish thrush noted for its tuneful song, often heard at night.
- ORIGIN from **NIGHT** and an Old English word meaning 'sing'.

nightjar **noun** a grey-brown bird with a distinctive call, active at night.

nightlife **noun** social activities or entertainment available at night.

night light **noun** a lamp or candle providing a dim light during the night.

nightly **adjective 1** happening or done every night. **2** happening or done during the night. • **adverb** every night.

nightmare **noun 1** a frightening or unpleasant dream. **2** a very unpleasant or difficult experience or situation: *acne is every teenager's nightmare.*
- DERIVATIVES **nightmarish** adjective.
- ORIGIN from an Old English word meaning 'male demon believed to have sex with sleeping women'.

night owl **noun** informal a person who enjoys staying up late at night.

night safe **noun** Brit. a safe that can be accessed from the outer wall of a bank, used for

n

depositing money when the bank is closed.

night school noun evening classes provided for people who work during the day.

nightshirt noun a long, loose shirt worn in bed.

nightside noun the side of a planet or moon facing away from the sun and therefore in darkness.

night soil noun human excrement collected at night from cesspools and basic toilets.

nightspot noun informal a nightclub.

nightstick noun N. Amer. a police officer's truncheon.

night-time noun the time between evening and morning.

nightwatchman noun (pl. **nightwatchmen**) a person who guards a building at night.

nightwear noun clothing worn in bed.

nihilism /ny-hi-li-z'm/ noun the rejection of all religious and moral principles, often in the belief that life is meaningless.
– DERIVATIVES **nihilist** noun **nihilistic** adjective.
– ORIGIN from Latin *nihil* 'nothing'.

-nik suffix (forming nouns) referring to a person associated with a specified thing: *beatnik*.
– ORIGIN from Russian and Yiddish.

Nikkei index /nik-kay/ (also **Nikkei average**) noun an index of figures indicating the relative price of shares on the Tokyo Stock Exchange.
– ORIGIN abbreviation of *Ni(hon) Kei(zai Shimbun)* 'Japanese Economic Journal'.

nil noun nothing; zero. •adjective non-existent.
– ORIGIN Latin.

nil desperandum /nil dess-puh-**ran**-duhm/ exclamation do not despair.
– ORIGIN from Latin *nil desperandum Teucro duce* 'no need to despair with Teucer as your leader', from Horace's *Odes* 1.vii.27.

Nilotic /ny-**lot**-ik/ adjective relating to the River Nile or to the Nile region of Africa.

nimble adjective (**nimbler, nimblest**) quick and agile in movement or thought.
– DERIVATIVES **nimbly** adverb.
– ORIGIN Old English.

nimbus /**nim**-buhss/ noun (pl. **nimbi** /**nim**-by/ or **nimbuses**) 1 a large grey rain cloud. 2 a luminous cloud or a halo surrounding a supernatural being or saint.
– ORIGIN Latin, 'cloud, aureole'.

Nimby /**nim**-bi/ noun (pl. **Nimbys**) informal a person who objects to the siting of unpleasant developments in their neighbourhood.
– DERIVATIVES **Nimbyism** noun.
– ORIGIN from the initial letters of *not in my back yard*.

niminy-piminy adjective prim in an affected way.
– ORIGIN unknown.

nincompoop /**ning**-kuhm-poop/ noun a foolish or stupid person.
– ORIGIN perhaps from the man's name *Nicholas*.

nine cardinal number one less than ten; 9. (Roman numeral: **ix** or **IX**.)
– PHRASES **to** (or Brit. **up to**) **the nines** to a great or elaborate extent: *the women were dressed to the nines*.
– ORIGIN Old English.

ninepins plural noun (usu. treated as sing.) the

traditional form of the game of skittles, using nine pins.
– PHRASES **go down** (or **fall**) **like ninepins** Brit. be overcome in large numbers.

nineteen cardinal number one more than eighteen; 19. (Roman numeral: **xix** or **XIX**.)
– DERIVATIVES **nineteenth** ordinal number.

nineteenth hole noun humorous the bar in a golf clubhouse, as reached after a round of eighteen holes.

ninety cardinal number (pl. **nineties**) ten less than one hundred; 90. (Roman numeral: **xc** or **XC**.)
– DERIVATIVES **ninetieth** ordinal number.

ninja /**nin**-juh/ noun a person skilled in ninjutsu (the Japanese technique of espionage).
– ORIGIN Japanese, 'spy'.

ninjutsu /nin-**jut**-soo/ noun the traditional Japanese art of stealth, camouflage, and sabotage, first developed for espionage and now popular as a martial art.
– ORIGIN Japanese, 'art or science of stealth'.

ninny noun (pl. **ninnies**) informal a foolish and weak person.
– ORIGIN perhaps from **INNOCENT**.

ninth ordinal number **1** that is number nine in a sequence; 9th. **2** (**a ninth/one ninth**) each of nine equal parts into which something is divided. **3** a musical interval spanning nine consecutive notes in a scale.
– DERIVATIVES **ninthly** adverb.

niobium /ny-**oh**-bi-uhm/ noun a silver-grey metallic chemical element.
– ORIGIN from *Niobe*, daughter of Tantalus in Greek mythology.

nip[1] verb (**nips, nipping, nipped**) **1** pinch or bite someone or something sharply. **2** (of cold or frost) hurt or damage someone or something. **3** Brit. informal go somewhere quickly. •noun **1** a sharp bite or pinch. **2** a feeling of sharp coldness.
– PHRASES **nip something in the bud** stop something at an early stage.
– ORIGIN probably German or Dutch.

nip[2] noun a small quantity or sip of spirits.
– ORIGIN probably from former *nipperkin* 'small measure'.

nip and tuck adverb & adjective closely contested; neck and neck. •noun informal a cosmetic surgical operation.

nipper noun **1** informal a child. **2** (**nippers**) pliers, pincers, or a similar tool.

nipple noun **1** a small projection in the centre of each breast, containing (in females) the outlets of the organs that produce milk. **2** a small projection on a machine from which oil or other fluid is dispensed.
– ORIGIN perhaps from **NEB**.

nippy adjective (**nippier, nippiest**) informal **1** Brit. quick; nimble. **2** (of the weather) chilly.
– DERIVATIVES **nippily** adverb **nippiness** noun.

nirvana /neer-**vah**-nuh/ noun **1** the ultimate goal of Buddhism, a state in which there is no suffering or desire, and no sense of self. **2** a perfect or very happy state or place: *Toronto is a restaurant-goer's nirvana*.
– ORIGIN Sanskrit.

Nissen hut /**niss**-uhn/ noun Brit. a tunnel-shaped hut of corrugated iron.
– ORIGIN named after the British engineer

Peter N. *Nissen*.

nit noun informal **1** the egg of a human head louse. **2** Brit. a stupid person.
– ORIGIN Old English.

niterie /ny-ter-ri/ noun (pl. **niteries**) informal a nightclub.

nit-picking noun informal fussy fault-finding.
– DERIVATIVES **nit-pick** verb **nit-picker** noun.

nitrate noun /ny-trayt/ a salt or ester of nitric acid. ● verb /ny-**trayt**/ treat a substance with nitric acid.
– DERIVATIVES **nitration** noun.

nitre /ny-ter/ (US **niter**) noun potassium nitrate; saltpetre.
– ORIGIN Greek *nitron*.

nitric acid noun a very corrosive acid.

nitride /ny-tryd/ noun a compound of nitrogen with another element or group.

nitrify /ny-tri-fy/ verb (**nitrifies, nitrifying, nitrified**) convert ammonia or another nitrogen compound into nitrites or nitrates.
– DERIVATIVES **nitrification** noun.

nitrite /ny-tryt/ noun a salt or ester of nitrous acid.

nitro- /ny-troh/ combining form relating to or containing nitric acid, nitrates, or nitrogen: *nitroglycerine*.

nitrocellulose noun a highly flammable material used to make explosives and celluloid.

nitrogen /ny-truh-juhn/ noun a colourless, odourless gas forming about 78 per cent of the earth's atmosphere.
– DERIVATIVES **nitrogenous** /ny-**troj**-i-nuhss/ adjective.
– ORIGIN French *nitrogène* (from **NITRE**).

nitrogen cycle noun the series of processes by which nitrogen from the air is converted into compounds that are deposited in the soil, absorbed by plants, and eaten by animals, then returned to the atmosphere when these organic substances decay.

nitrogen dioxide noun a reddish-brown poisonous gas formed when many metals dissolve in nitric acid.

nitrogen fixation noun the chemical processes by which nitrogen in the atmosphere is absorbed into organic compounds.

nitroglycerine (US also **nitroglycerin**) noun an explosive yellow liquid used in dynamite.

nitrous /ny-truhss/ adjective relating to or containing nitrogen.

nitrous acid noun a weak acid made by the action of acids on nitrites.

nitrous oxide noun a gas with a sweetish smell, used as an anaesthetic.

nitty-gritty noun informal the most important aspects or basic details of a matter.
– ORIGIN unknown.

nitwit noun informal a silly or foolish person.
– ORIGIN probably from **NIT** + **WIT**[1].

nix informal pronoun nothing. ● verb chiefly N. Amer. put an end to or cancel something.
– ORIGIN German, variant of *nichts* 'nothing'.

NJ abbreviation New Jersey.

NM abbreviation New Mexico.

nm abbreviation **1** nanometre. **2** (also **n.m.**)

nautical mile.

NNE abbreviation north-north-east.

NNW abbreviation north-north-west.

No[1] noun variant spelling of **NOH**.

No[2] symbol the chemical element nobelium.

no determiner **1** not any. **2** quite the opposite of: *he's no fool.* **3** hardly any. ● exclamation used to refuse, deny, or disagree with something. ● adverb **1** (with comparative) not at all. **2** Scottish not. ● noun (pl. **noes**) a vote or decision against something.
– PHRASES **no place** N. Amer. nowhere. **no way** informal certainly not; not at all.
– ORIGIN Old English.

no. abbreviation (pl. **nos**) number.
– ORIGIN from Latin *numero* 'by number'.

n.o. abbreviation Cricket not out.

nob noun Brit. informal an upper-class or wealthy person.
– DERIVATIVES **nobby** adjective.
– ORIGIN unknown.

no-ball noun a ball in cricket that is unlawfully bowled, counting as an extra run to the batting side.

nobble verb Brit. informal **1** try to influence or thwart by underhand methods: *an attempt to nobble the jury.* **2** tamper with a racehorse to prevent it from winning a race. **3** stop someone so as to talk to them. **4** steal something.
– ORIGIN probably from dialect *knobble*, *knubble* 'knock, strike with the knuckles'.

nobelium /noh-bee-li-uhm/ noun a very unstable chemical element made by high-energy collisions.
– ORIGIN named after Alfred *Nobel* (see **NOBEL PRIZE**).

Nobel Prize noun any of six international prizes awarded annually for outstanding work in physics, chemistry, physiology or medicine, literature, economics, and the promotion of peace.
– ORIGIN named after the Swedish chemist and engineer Alfred *Nobel*.

nobility noun **1** the quality of being noble. **2** the aristocracy.

noble adjective (**nobler, noblest**) **1** belonging to the aristocracy. **2** having admirable personal qualities or high moral principles: *fighting for a noble cause.* **3** impressive; magnificent. ● noun **1** (especially in former times) a member of the aristocracy. **2** a former English gold coin.
– DERIVATIVES **nobly** adverb.
– ORIGIN Latin *nobilis* 'noted, high-born'.

noble gas noun any of the gases helium, neon, argon, krypton, xenon, and radon, which seldom or never combine with other elements to form compounds.

nobleman (or **noblewoman**) noun (pl. **noblemen** or **noblewomen**) a man (or woman) who belongs to the aristocracy.

noble rot noun a grey mould deliberately cultivated on grapes in order to perfect certain wines.

noble savage noun a representative of primitive mankind as idealized in Romantic literature.

noblesse oblige /noh-bless oh-**bleezh**/ noun

n

noble or wealthy people should help those who are less fortunate.
– ORIGIN French, 'nobility obliges'.

nobody pronoun no person; no one. • noun (pl. **nobodies**) an unimportant person.

no-brainer noun informal something that involves little or no mental effort.

nock Archery noun a notch at either end of a bow or at the end of an arrow, for receiving the string of the bow. • verb fit an arrow to the string of the bow.
– ORIGIN perhaps from Dutch *nocke* 'point, tip'.

no-claims bonus noun Brit. a reduction in an insurance premium when no claim has been made during an agreed period.

noctule /**nok**-tyool/ noun a large golden-brown bat.
– ORIGIN Italian *nottola* 'bat'.

nocturnal adjective done, occurring, or active at night.
– DERIVATIVES **nocturnally** adverb.
– ORIGIN from Latin *nocturnus* 'of the night'.

nocturne /**nok**-tern/ noun a short musical composition of a romantic and dreamy nature.
– ORIGIN French.

nod verb (**nods, nodding, nodded**) 1 lower and raise one's head slightly and briefly to show agreement or as a greeting or signal. 2 let one's head fall forward when drowsy or asleep. 3 (**nod off**) informal fall asleep. 4 (**nod something through**) informal approve something by general agreement and without discussion. 5 Football head the ball without great force. • noun 1 an act of nodding. 2 a gesture acknowledging something: *Lord British was a pseudonym he chose as a nod to his English birth.*
– PHRASES **be on nodding terms** know someone slightly. **give someone/thing the nod** 1 approve someone or something. 2 give someone a signal. **a nodding acquaintance** a slight acquaintance. **on the nod** Brit. informal by general agreement and without discussion.
– ORIGIN perhaps German.

noddle noun informal, dated a person's head.
– ORIGIN unknown.

noddy noun (pl. **noddies**) 1 dated a silly or foolish person. 2 a tropical tern with mainly dark plumage.
– ORIGIN sense 2 perhaps refers to the birds' nodding during courtship.

node noun technical 1 a point in a network at which lines cross or branch. 2 the part of a plant stem from which one or more leaves grow. 3 a small mass of distinct body tissue. 4 Physics & Mathematics a point at which the amplitude of vibration of a wave is zero.
– DERIVATIVES **nodal** adjective.
– ORIGIN Latin *nodus* 'knot'.

nodule noun 1 a small swelling or cluster of cells in the body. 2 a swelling on a root of a plant of the pea family, containing nitrogen-fixing bacteria. 3 a small rounded lump of matter distinct from its surroundings.
– DERIVATIVES **nodular** adjective.
– ORIGIN Latin *nodulus* 'little knot'.

Noel noun Christmas.
– ORIGIN French.

noggin noun informal 1 a person's head. 2 a small quantity of alcoholic drink.

– ORIGIN unknown.

no-go area noun Brit. an area which is dangerous to enter, or to which entry is banned.

Noh /noh/ (also **No**) noun traditional Japanese masked drama with dance and song.
– ORIGIN Japanese.

no-hoper noun informal a person who is not expected to be successful.

noir /nwah/ noun a type of crime film or fiction marked by a mood of cynicism, fatalism, and a lack of moral certainty.
– DERIVATIVES **noirish** adjective.
– ORIGIN from FILM NOIR.

noise noun 1 a loud or unpleasant sound or series of sounds. 2 (**noises**) conventional remarks without real meaning: *the government made tough noises about defending sterling.* 3 disturbances that accompany and interfere with an electrical signal. • verb (usu. **be noised about**) dated talk about or make something known publicly.
– DERIVATIVES **noiseless** adjective.
– ORIGIN Old French.

noise pollution noun harmful or annoying levels of noise.

noisette /nwah-**zet**/ noun 1 a small round piece of meat. 2 a chocolate made with hazelnuts.
– ORIGIN French, 'little nut'.

noisome /**noy**-suhm/ adjective literary 1 having a very unpleasant smell. 2 very unpleasant.
– ORIGIN from ANNOY.

noisy adjective (**noisier, noisiest**) full of or making a lot of noise.
– DERIVATIVES **noisily** adverb **noisiness** noun.

nomad noun a member of a people that travels from place to place to find fresh pasture for its animals.
– DERIVATIVES **nomadism** noun.
– ORIGIN Greek *nomas*.

nomadic adjective having the life of a nomad; wandering.
– DERIVATIVES **nomadically** adverb.

no-man's-land noun an area between two opposing armies that is not controlled by either.

nom de guerre /nom duh **gair**/ noun (pl. **noms de guerre** pronunc. same) a name used by a person to engage in combat.
– ORIGIN French, 'war name'.

nom de plume /nom duh **ploom**/ noun (pl. **noms de plume** pronunc. same) a name used by a writer instead of their real name; a pen name.
– ORIGIN French.

nomenclature /noh-**men**-kluh-cher/ noun 1 a system of names used in a particular subject. 2 the selecting of names for things in a particular subject. 3 formal a name or term given to someone or something.
– DERIVATIVES **nomenclatural** /noh-men-**kla**-chuh-ruhl/ adjective.
– ORIGIN Latin *nomenclatura*.

nomenklatura /noh-men-kluh-**tyoo**-ruh/ noun (in the former Soviet Union) the holders of influential public positions, appointed by the Communist Party.
– ORIGIN Russian.

nominal adjective 1 existing in name but not in reality: *a purely nominal Arsenal fan.* 2 (of a sum of money) very small, but charged or paid

as a sign that payment is necessary. **3** Grammar relating to or functioning as a noun.
– DERIVATIVES **nominally** adverb.
– ORIGIN Latin *nominalis*.

nominalism noun Philosophy the theory that general terms or ideas are mere names without any corresponding reality. Often contrasted with **REALISM**.
– DERIVATIVES **nominalist** noun.

nominal value noun **1** the value that is stated on a coin, note, etc. **2** the price of a share, bond, or stock when it was issued, rather than its current market value.

nominate verb **1** put someone forward as a candidate for election or for an honour or award. **2** appoint someone to a job or position. **3** specify something formally.
– DERIVATIVES **nomination** noun **nominator** noun.
– ORIGIN Latin *nominare* 'to name'.

nominative /nom-i-nuh-tiv/ noun the grammatical case used for the subject of a verb.

nominee noun **1** a person who is nominated for a post, award, etc. **2** a person or company in whose name a company, stock, or bond is registered.

non- prefix expressing negation or absence; not: *non-recognition*.
– ORIGIN Latin, 'not'.

USAGE: The prefixes (word beginnings) **non-** and **un-** both mean 'not', but they tend to be used in slightly different ways. **Non-** is more neutral, while **un-** often suggests a particular bias or standpoint. For example, **unnatural** means that something is not natural in a bad way, whereas **non-natural** simply means 'not natural'.

nonagenarian /non-uh-juh-**nair**-i-uhn, noh-nuh-juh-**nair**-i-uhn/ noun a person between 90 and 99 years old.
– ORIGIN Latin *nonagenarius*.

nonagon /non-uh-guhn/ noun a plane figure with nine straight sides and nine angles.

non-alcoholic adjective (of a drink) not containing alcohol.

non-aligned adjective (of a country during the cold war) not allied to any of the major world powers.

non-allergenic (also **non-allergic**) adjective not causing an allergic reaction.

non-being noun the state of not being; non-existence.

non-believer noun a person who does not believe in something, especially one who has no religious faith.

non-belligerent adjective not engaged in a war or conflict.

nonce[1] /nonss/ adjective (of a word or expression) coined for one occasion.
– PHRASES **for the nonce** for the present; temporarily.
– ORIGIN wrong division of former *then anes* 'the one (purpose)'.

nonce[2] /nonss/ noun Brit. informal a person convicted of a sexual offence, especially against a child.
– ORIGIN unknown.

nonchalant /**non**-shuh-luhnt/ adjective

casually calm and relaxed.
– DERIVATIVES **nonchalance** noun **nonchalantly** adverb.
– ORIGIN French, 'not being concerned'.

non-combatant noun a person who is not engaged in fighting during a war, especially a civilian or an army chaplain or doctor.

non-commissioned adjective (of a military officer) appointed from the lower ranks rather than holding a commission.

non-committal adjective not expressing an opinion.
– DERIVATIVES **non-committally** adverb.

non compos mentis /non kom-poss **men**-tiss/ adjective mentally unbalanced or insane.
– ORIGIN Latin, 'not having control of one's mind'.

non-conductor noun a substance that does not conduct heat or electricity.
– DERIVATIVES **non-conducting** adjective.

nonconformist noun **1** a person who does not follow accepted ideas or behaviour. **2** (**Nonconformist**) a member of a Protestant Church which does not follow the beliefs of the established Church of England. • adjective not following accepted ideas or behaviour.
– DERIVATIVES **nonconformism** noun **nonconformity** noun.

non-contributory adjective (of a pension) funded by regular payments by the employer, not the employee.

non-cooperation noun failure to cooperate, especially as a form of protest.

non-denominational adjective open or acceptable to people of any recognized branch of Christianity.

nondescript adjective lacking distinctive or interesting features: *a nondescript suburban apartment block*.
– ORIGIN from **NON-** + former *descript* 'described, engraved'.

non-drinker noun a person who does not drink alcohol.

none pronoun **1** not any. **2** no one. • adverb (**none the**) (with comparative) not at all: *none the wiser*.
– ORIGIN Old English.

USAGE: When you use **none of** with a plural noun or pronoun (such as *them*), or with a singular noun that refers to a group of people or things, you can correctly use either a singular or plural verb: *none of them is coming* or *none of them are coming*; *none of the family was present* or *none of the family were present*.

nonentity /non-**en**-ti-ti/ noun (pl. **nonentities**) an unimportant person or thing.
– ORIGIN Latin *nonentitas* 'non-existence'.

non-essential adjective not absolutely necessary. • noun a non-essential thing.

nonet /no-**net**, noh-**net**/ noun **1** a group of nine people or things. **2** a musical composition for nine voices or instruments.
– ORIGIN Italian *nonetto*.

nonetheless (also **none the less**) adverb in spite of that; nevertheless.

non-event noun an event which is not as interesting or important as it was expected to be.

n

non-existent adjective not existing or not real or present.
– DERIVATIVES **non-existence** noun.
non-ferrous adjective (of metal) other than iron or steel.
non-fiction noun prose writing that deals with real people, facts, or events.
– DERIVATIVES **non-fictional** adjective.
non-flammable adjective not catching fire easily.

USAGE: The terms **non-flammable** and **non-inflammable** both mean 'not catching fire easily'. See the note at INFLAMMABLE.

non-functional adjective 1 not having a particular function. 2 not in working order.
non-governmental adjective not belonging to or associated with any government.
non-inflammable adjective not catching fire easily.

USAGE: The terms **non-inflammable** and **non-flammable** have the same meaning. See the note at INFLAMMABLE.

non-interference noun failure or refusal to intervene, especially in political matters.
non-intervention noun the policy of not becoming involved in the affairs of other countries.
– DERIVATIVES **non-interventionist** adjective & noun.
non-invasive adjective (of medical procedures) not involving the introduction of instruments into the body.
non-judgemental adjective avoiding moral judgements.
non-linear adjective not linear or arranged in a straight line.
non-member noun a person, group, or country that is not a member of a particular organization.
non-metal noun an element or substance that is not a metal.
– DERIVATIVES **non-metallic** adjective.
non-native adjective 1 (of a person, animal, or plant) not native to a particular place. 2 (of a speaker) not having spoken the language in question from earliest childhood.
non-natural adjective not produced by or involving natural processes.
non-negotiable adjective 1 not open to discussion or modification. 2 not able to be transferred to the legal ownership of another person.
no-no noun (pl. **no-nos**) informal a thing that is not possible or acceptable.
no-nonsense adjective simple and straightforward; sensible.
non-operational adjective 1 not working or in use. 2 not involving active duties.
nonpareil /non-puh-**rayl**/ adjective better than anyone or anything else; unrivalled: *he's a nonpareil storyteller.* ● noun a person or thing that is unrivalled in a particular area.
– ORIGIN French, 'not equal'.
non-payment noun failure to pay an amount of money that is owed.
non-person noun a person who is ignored or forgotten.

nonplussed /non-**plusst**/ adjective surprised and confused and not knowing how to react.
– ORIGIN from Latin *non plus* 'not more'.
non-productive adjective not producing or able to produce something.
– DERIVATIVES **non-productively** adverb.
non-professional adjective 1 relating to or holding a job that does not need advanced education or training. 2 engaged in an activity that is not one's main paid job: *non-professional actors.* ● noun a non-professional person.
non-profit adjective not making or intended to make a profit.
non-proliferation noun the prevention of an increase in the number of nuclear weapons that are produced.
non-resident adjective not living in a particular country or a place of work. ● noun a person not living in a particular place.
nonsense noun 1 words that make no sense. 2 foolish or unacceptable behaviour. 3 an unwise or impractical scheme, situation, etc.: *the proposal would make a nonsense of their plans.*
nonsensical adjective making no sense; ridiculous.
– DERIVATIVES **nonsensically** adverb.
non sequitur /non sek-wi-ter/ noun a conclusion that does not logically follow from the previous statement.
– ORIGIN Latin, 'it does not follow'.
non-slip adjective designed to prevent slipping.
non-smoker noun a person who does not smoke tobacco.
– DERIVATIVES **non-smoking** adjective.
non-specific adjective not detailed or exact; general.
non-specific urethritis noun inflammation of the urethra due to infection by organisms other than those which cause gonorrhoea.
non-standard adjective 1 not average or usual. 2 (of language) not considered correct by most educated speakers.
non-starter noun 1 a person or animal that fails to take part in a race. 2 informal something that has no chance of succeeding.
non-stick adjective (of a pan or surface) covered with a substance that prevents food sticking to it during cooking.
non-stop adjective 1 continuing without stopping. 2 having no stops on the way to a destination. ● adverb without stopping.
non-technical adjective 1 not relating to or involving science or technology. 2 not using technical terms or requiring specialized knowledge.
non-toxic adjective not poisonous or toxic.
non-U adjective Brit. informal (of language or behaviour) not characteristic of the upper social classes.
non-uniform adjective not uniform or regular; varying.
non-verbal adjective not involving or using words or speech.
non-violent adjective 1 using peaceful means rather than force to bring about political or social change. 2 not involving violence: *non-violent films.*

- DERIVATIVES **non-violence** noun.

non-white adjective (of a person) not white or not of European origin. •noun a non-white person.

noodle[1] noun (usu. **noodles**) a very thin, long strip of pasta or a similar flour paste.
- ORIGIN German *Nudel*.

noodle[2] noun informal **1** a silly person. **2** a person's head.
- ORIGIN unknown.

noodle[3] verb informal improvise or play casually on a musical instrument.
- ORIGIN unknown.

nook noun a small corner or other place that is sheltered or hidden.
- PHRASES **every nook and cranny** every part of something.
- ORIGIN unknown.

nooky (also **nookie**) noun informal sexual activity or intercourse.
- ORIGIN perhaps from NOOK.

noon noun twelve o'clock in the day; midday.
- ORIGIN from Latin *nona hora* 'ninth hour' (from sunrise).

noonday adjective happening or appearing in the middle of the day.

no one pronoun no person; not a single person.

noontime (also literary **noontide**) noun noon.

noose noun a loop with a knot which tightens as the rope or wire is pulled, used to hang people or trap animals.
- ORIGIN probably from Old French *nous*.

nor conjunction & adverb and not; and not either.
- ORIGIN Old English.

noradrenaline /nor-uh-**dren**-uh-lin/ noun a hormone which functions as a neuro-transmitter and is also used as a drug to raise blood pressure.

Nordic adjective **1** relating to Scandinavia, Finland, and Iceland. **2** referring to a tall, blonde type of person associated with northern Europe.
- ORIGIN French *nordique*.

Nordic skiing noun cross-country skiing and ski jumping.

Norfolk jacket noun a loose belted jacket with box pleats, typically made of tweed.

nori /**nor**-i/ noun (in Japanese cuisine) seaweed, eaten fresh or dried in sheets.
- ORIGIN Japanese.

norm noun **1** (**the norm**) the usual or standard thing: *strikes were the norm*. **2** a required or acceptable standard: *the norms of good behaviour*.
- ORIGIN Latin *norma* 'rule, carpenter's square'.

normal adjective **1** usual, typical, or expected. **2** technical (of a line) intersecting a given line or surface at right angles. •noun **1** the normal state or condition: *her temperature was above normal*. **2** technical a line at right angles to a given line or surface.
- DERIVATIVES **normality** (N. Amer. also **normalcy**) noun **normally** adverb.

normalize (or **normalise**) verb bring or return to a normal or standard state.
- DERIVATIVES **normalization** noun.

Norman noun **1** a member of a people of Normandy in northern France who conquered England in 1066. **2** (also **Norman French**) the

form of Old French spoken by the Normans. **3** a person from modern Normandy. •adjective **1** relating to the Normans or Normandy. **2** relating to the style of Romanesque architecture used in Britain under the Normans.

normative adjective formal relating to or setting a standard or norm: *a normative theory of world politics*.

Norse noun an ancient or medieval form of Norwegian or a related Scandinavian language. •adjective relating to Norse or ancient or medieval Norway or Scandinavia.
- DERIVATIVES **Norseman** noun (pl. **Norsemen**).
- ORIGIN Dutch *noordsch*.

north noun **1** the direction in which a compass needle normally points, on the left-hand side of a person facing east. **2** the northern part of a place. •adjective **1** lying towards, near, or facing the north. **2** (of a wind) blowing from the north. •adverb to or towards the north.
- DERIVATIVES **northbound** adjective & adverb.
- ORIGIN Old English.

North American noun a person from North America, especially a citizen of the US or Canada. •adjective relating to North America.

Northants abbreviation Northamptonshire.

north-east noun the direction or region halfway between north and east. •adjective **1** lying towards, near, or facing the north-east. **2** (of a wind) from the north-east. •adverb to or towards the north-east.
- DERIVATIVES **north-eastern** adjective.

north-easterly adjective & adverb in a north-eastward position or direction. •noun (pl. **north-easterlies**) a wind blowing from the north-east.

north-eastward adverb (also **north-eastwards**) towards the north-east. •adjective in, towards, or facing the north-east.

northerly adjective & adverb **1** facing or moving towards the north. **2** (of a wind) blowing from the north. •noun (pl. **northerlies**) a north wind.

northern adjective **1** situated in, directed towards, or facing the north. **2** (usu. **Northern**) relating to or typical of the north.
- DERIVATIVES **northernmost** adjective.

northerner noun a person from the north of a region or country.

Northern Lights plural noun the aurora borealis.

northing noun **1** distance travelled or measured northward, especially at sea. **2** a figure or line representing northward distance on a map.

northland noun (also **northlands**) literary the northern part of a country or region.

north-north-east noun the direction midway between north and north-east.

north-north-west noun the direction midway between north and north-west.

North Star noun the Pole Star.

Northumb. abbreviation Northumberland.

northward adjective in a northerly direction. •adverb (also **northwards**) towards the north.
- DERIVATIVES **northwardly** adjective & adverb.

north-west noun the direction or region halfway between north and west. •adjective **1** lying towards or facing the north-west. **2** (of

n

a wind) from the north-west. • adverb to or towards the north-west.
– DERIVATIVES **north-western** adjective.

north-westerly adjective & adverb in a north-westward position or direction. • noun (pl. **north-westerlies**) a wind blowing from the north-west.

north-westward adverb (also **north-westwards**) towards the north-west. • adjective in, towards, or facing the north-west.

Norwegian /nor-wee-juhn/ noun 1 a person from Norway. 2 the language spoken in Norway. • adjective relating to Norway.
– ORIGIN from Latin *Norvegia* 'Norway'.

nose noun 1 the part of the face above the mouth, containing the nostrils and used in breathing and smelling. 2 the front part of an aircraft or other vehicle. 3 the sense of smell. 4 a natural talent for detecting something: *he has a nose for a good script.* 5 the characteristic smell of a wine. 6 an act of looking around somewhere. • verb 1 move slowly forward: *they nosed out of the parking place.* 2 look around or pry into something. 3 (of an animal) thrust its nose against or into something.
– PHRASES **by a nose** (of a victory) by a very narrow margin. **cut off one's nose to spite one's face** do something which is supposed to harm someone else but which also puts oneself at a disadvantage. **get up someone's nose** Brit. informal irritate someone. **keep one's nose clean** informal stay out of trouble. **keep one's nose out of** refrain from interfering in another person's business. **put someone's nose out of joint** informal offend someone or hurt their pride. **turn one's nose up at** informal show distaste or contempt for. **under someone's nose** informal directly in front of someone, typically without being noticed by them.
– ORIGIN Old English.

nosebag noun Brit. a bag containing fodder, hung from a horse's head.

noseband noun the strap of a bridle that passes over the horse's nose and under its chin.

nosebleed noun an instance of bleeding from the nose.

nosedive noun 1 a sudden dramatic decline: *my fortunes took a nosedive.* 2 a steep downward plunge by an aircraft. • verb 1 fall or decline suddenly: *prices nosedived after the market collapsed.* 2 (of an aircraft) make a nosedive.

nosegay noun a small bunch of flowers.
– ORIGIN from GAY in the former sense 'ornament'.

nosey adjective & verb variant spelling of NOSY.

nosh informal noun Brit. food. • verb eat enthusiastically or greedily.
– ORIGIN Yiddish.

no-show noun a person who has made a reservation or appointment but neither keeps nor cancels it.

nosh-up noun Brit. informal a large meal.

nostalgia /no-stal-juh/ noun wistful longing or affection for a happier or better time in the past: *touches of nostalgia for the 70s.*
– DERIVATIVES **nostalgic** adjective **nostalgically** adverb.

– ORIGIN from Greek *nostos* 'return home' + *algos* 'pain'.

nostril noun either of two external openings of the nose through which air passes to the lungs.
– ORIGIN Old English, 'nose hole'.

nostrum noun 1 a favourite method for improving something: *right-wing nostrums such as cutting public spending.* 2 a medicine that is prepared by an unqualified person and is not effective.
– ORIGIN Latin, 'something of our own making'.

nosy (also **nosey**) adjective (**nosier, nosiest**) informal too inquisitive about other people's business.
– DERIVATIVES **nosily** adverb **nosiness** noun.

nosy parker noun Brit. informal a very inquisitive person.
– ORIGIN from a picture postcard caption, 'The adventures of Nosey Parker', referring to a peeping Tom.

not adverb 1 used to form or express a negative. 2 less than: *not ten feet away.*
– ORIGIN from NOUGHT.

notability noun (pl. **notabilities**) dated a famous or important person.

notable adjective worthy of attention or notice. • noun a famous or important person.

notably adverb 1 in particular. 2 in a way that is noticeable or remarkable.

notarize (or **notarise**) verb have a signature on a document confirmed as legal by a notary.

notary (in full **notary public**) noun (pl. **notaries**) a lawyer who is officially authorized to draw up and witness the signing of contracts and other documents.
– DERIVATIVES **notarial** adjective.
– ORIGIN Latin *notarius* 'secretary'.

notation noun 1 a system of written symbols used to represent numbers, amounts, or elements in a subject such as music or mathematics. 2 a note or annotation.
– DERIVATIVES **notate** verb **notational** adjective.

notch noun 1 a V-shaped cut or indentation on an edge or surface. 2 a point or level on a scale: *her opinion of him dropped a few notches.* • verb 1 make notches in something. 2 (**notch something up**) score or achieve something.
– ORIGIN Old French *osche.*

note noun 1 a brief written record of something, used as an aid to memory. 2 a short written message or document. 3 Brit. a banknote. 4 a single sound of a particular pitch and length made by a musical instrument or voice, or a symbol representing this. 5 a particular quality or tone: *there was a note of scorn in his voice.* 6 a bird's song or call. 7 a basic component of a perfume or flavour. • verb 1 pay attention to or notice something. 2 record something in writing.
– PHRASES **hit the right (or wrong) note** say or do something in the right (or wrong) way. **of note** important. **take note** pay attention.
– ORIGIN from Latin *nota* 'a mark' and *notare* 'to mark'.

notebook noun 1 a small book for writing notes in. 2 a portable computer smaller than a laptop.

noted adjective well known; famous.

notelet noun Brit. a small folded sheet of notepaper with a decorative design on the front.

notepad noun **1** a pad of paper for writing notes on. **2** a pocket-sized personal computer in which text is input by writing with a stylus on the screen.

notepaper noun paper for writing letters on.

noteworthy adjective interesting or significant.

nothing pronoun **1** not anything. **2** something of no importance or concern. **3** nought; no amount. • adverb not at all.
– PHRASES **for nothing 1** without payment or charge. **2** to no purpose. **nothing but** only. **nothing doing** informal there is no chance of success. **sweet nothings** words of affection exchanged by lovers.
– ORIGIN Old English.

nothingness noun the state of not existing or a state where nothing exists.

notice noun **1** the fact of being aware of or paying attention to something: *his silence did not escape my notice*. **2** information or warning that something is going to happen: *interest rates may change without notice*. **3** a formal statement that someone is going to leave a job or end an agreement. **4** a sheet or placard put on display to give information. **5** a small announcement or advertisement published in a newspaper. **6** a short published review of a new film, play, or book. • verb **1** become aware of: *I noticed the youths behaving suspiciously*. **2 (be noticed)** be recognized as worthy of attention.
– PHRASES **at short notice** with little warning. **take (no) notice (of)** pay (no) attention (to).
– ORIGIN Latin *notitia*.

noticeable adjective easily seen; clear or apparent.
– DERIVATIVES **noticeably** adverb.

noticeboard noun Brit. a board for displaying notices.

notifiable adjective (of an infectious disease) so serious that it must be reported to the health authorities.

notify verb (**notifies, notifying, notified**) formally inform someone about something.
– DERIVATIVES **notification** noun.
– ORIGIN Latin *notificare* 'make known'.

notion noun **1** a concept or belief. **2** a person's understanding of something. **3** an impulse or whim.
– ORIGIN Latin, 'idea'.

notional adjective based on an estimate or theory; hypothetical.
– DERIVATIVES **notionally** adverb.

notoriety /noh-tuh-**ry**-i-ti/ noun the state of being famous for a bad quality or action.

notorious adjective famous for a bad quality or action.
– DERIVATIVES **notoriously** adverb.
– ORIGIN Latin *notus* 'known'.

Notts. abbreviation Nottinghamshire.

notwithstanding preposition in spite of. • adverb nevertheless.

nougat /**noo**-gah, **nug**-uht/ noun a sweet made from sugar or honey, nuts, and egg white.
– ORIGIN Provençal *noga* 'nut'.

nought noun Brit. the figure 0. • pronoun variant spelling of **NAUGHT**.
– PHRASES **noughts and crosses** Brit. a game in which two players try to complete a row of either three noughts or three crosses drawn alternately in the spaces of a grid of nine squares.

noughties /**naw**-tiz/ plural noun informal the decade from 2000 to 2009.
– ORIGIN from **NOUGHT**.

noun noun a word (other than a pronoun) that refers to a person, place, or thing.
– ORIGIN Latin *nomen* 'name'.

nourish verb **1** provide someone or something with the food or other substances necessary for growth and health. **2** keep a feeling or belief in the mind for a long time.
– ORIGIN Latin *nutrire*.

nourishment noun **1** the food or other substances necessary for growth, health, and good condition. **2** the action of nourishing someone or something.

nous /nowss/ noun Brit. informal common sense.
– ORIGIN Greek, 'mind, intelligence'.

nouveau riche /noo-voh **reesh**/ noun (treated as pl.) people who have recently become rich and who like to display their wealth in an obvious or tasteless way.
– ORIGIN French, 'new rich'.

nouvelle cuisine /noo-vel kwi-**zeen**/ noun a modern style of cookery that avoids rich foods and emphasizes the presentation of the dishes.
– ORIGIN French, 'new cookery'.

Nov. abbreviation November.

nova /**noh**-vuh/ noun (pl. **novae** /**noh**-vee/ or **novas**) a star that suddenly becomes very bright and then slowly returns to normal.
– ORIGIN from Latin *novus* 'new'.

novel¹ noun a story about imaginary people and events, long enough to fill a complete book.
– ORIGIN from Italian *novella storia* 'new story'.

novel² adjective new in an interesting or unusual way: *a novel approach to architecture*.
– ORIGIN Latin *novus* 'new'.

novelette noun a short novel, especially a romantic novel regarded as poorly written.

novelist noun a person who writes novels.
– DERIVATIVES **novelistic** adjective.

novelize (or **novelise**) verb convert a story, screenplay, or play into a novel.
– DERIVATIVES **novelization** noun.

novella /nuh-**vel**-luh/ noun a short novel or long short story.
– ORIGIN Italian.

novelty noun (pl. **novelties**) **1** the quality of being new and unusual: *the novelty of being a married woman wore off*. **2** a new or unfamiliar thing. **3** a small and inexpensive toy or ornament. • adjective intended to be amusingly unusual: *a novelty teapot*.

November noun the eleventh month of the year.
– ORIGIN from Latin *novem* 'nine' (November being originally the ninth month of the Roman year).

novena /noh-**vee**-nuh/ noun (in the Roman Catholic Church) a form of worship consisting

of special prayers or services on nine successive days.
– ORIGIN Latin.

novice noun 1 a person who is new to and lacks experience in a job or situation. 2 a person who has entered a religious order and is under probation, before taking vows. 3 a racehorse that has not yet won a major prize or reached a qualifying level of performance.
– ORIGIN Latin *novicius*.

novitiate /noh-vi-shi-uht/ (also **noviciate**) noun 1 the period or state of being a novice in a religious order. 2 a religious novice.

now adverb 1 at the present time. 2 at or from this precise moment. 3 under the present circumstances. •conjunction as a result of the fact.
– PHRASES **now and again** (or **then**) from time to time.
– ORIGIN Old English.

nowadays adverb at the present time, in contrast with the past.

nowhere adverb not anywhere. •pronoun no place.
– PHRASES **from** (or **out of**) **nowhere** appearing or happening suddenly and unexpectedly. **get** (or **go**) **nowhere** make no progress. **nowhere near** not nearly.

no-win adjective (of a situation) in which success or a favourable outcome is impossible.

nowt pronoun & adverb N. English nothing.

noxious /nok-shuhss/ adjective harmful, poisonous, or very unpleasant.
– ORIGIN from Latin *noxa* 'harm'.

nozzle noun a spout used to control a jet of liquid or gas.
– ORIGIN from **NOSE**.

Np symbol the chemical element neptunium.

NS abbreviation 1 (in calculating dates) New Style. 2 Nova Scotia.

n/s abbreviation (in personal advertisements) non-smoker; non-smoking.

NSPCC abbreviation (in the UK) National Society for the Prevention of Cruelty to Children.

NSU abbreviation Medicine non-specific urethritis.

NSW abbreviation New South Wales.

NT abbreviation 1 National Trust. 2 New Testament. 3 Northern Territory. 4 Northwest Territories.

-n't contraction not, used with auxiliary verbs (e.g. *can't*).

nth /enth/ adjective 1 referring to the last or latest item in a long series. 2 Mathematics referring to an unspecified term in a series.
– PHRASES **to the nth degree** to the utmost.

nuance /nyoo-ahnss/ noun a subtle difference in meaning, expression, sound, etc.: *the nuances of facial expression.* •verb (often as adj. **nuanced**) give subtle differences to: *an intricate and nuanced portrait.*
– ORIGIN French.

nub noun 1 (**the nub**) the central point of a matter. 2 a small lump.
– DERIVATIVES **nubby** adjective.
– ORIGIN probably from German *knubbe*, *knobbe* 'knob'.

Nubian /nyoo-bi-uhn/ adjective relating to Nubia, an ancient region corresponding to southern Egypt and northern Sudan. •noun 1 a person from Nubia. 2 the language of the Nubians.

nubile /nyoo-byl/ adjective (of a girl or young woman) sexually attractive.
– DERIVATIVES **nubility** noun.
– ORIGIN from Latin *nubilis* 'fit for marriage'.

nubuck /nyoo-buk/ noun leather which has been rubbed on the flesh side of the skin to give a suede-like effect.

nuclear adjective 1 relating to the nucleus of an atom or cell. 2 using energy released in the fission (splitting) or fusion of atomic nuclei. 3 referring to or involving nuclear weapons.

nuclear family noun a couple and their children, regarded as a basic unit of society.

nuclear fuel noun a substance that will undergo nuclear fission (splitting) and can be used as a source of nuclear energy.

nuclear physics plural noun (treated as sing.) the science of atomic nuclei and the way in which they interact.

nuclear power noun power generated by a nuclear reactor.

nuclear waste noun radioactive waste material, especially from the use or reprocessing of nuclear fuel.

nuclear winter noun a period of abnormal cold and darkness predicted to follow a nuclear war, caused by smoke and dust blocking the sun's rays.

nucleate verb /nyoo-kli-ayt/ (usu. as adj. **nucleated**) form a nucleus. •adjective /nyoo-kli-uht/ chiefly Biology having a nucleus.
– DERIVATIVES **nucleation** noun.

nuclei plural of **NUCLEUS**.

nucleic acid /nyoo-klee-ik, nyoo-**klay**-ik/ noun a complex organic substance, especially DNA or RNA, that is present in all living cells.

nucleon /nyoo-kli-on/ noun a proton or neutron (type of subatomic particle).

nucleus /nyoo-kli-uhss/ noun (pl. **nuclei** /nyoo-kli-I/) 1 the central and most important part of an object or group: *the family is the nucleus of Islamic society.* 2 Physics the positively charged central core of an atom, containing nearly all its mass. 3 Biology a structure present in most cells, containing the genetic material.
– ORIGIN Latin, 'kernel, inner part'.

nude adjective wearing no clothes. •noun a painting, sculpture, or photograph of a naked human figure.
– DERIVATIVES **nudity** noun.
– ORIGIN Latin *nudus* 'plain, explicit'.

nudge verb 1 prod someone with one's elbow to attract their attention. 2 touch or push something gently. 3 gently encourage someone to do something. •noun a light touch or push.
– ORIGIN unknown.

nudist noun a person who goes naked wherever possible.
– DERIVATIVES **nudism** noun.

nugatory /nyoo-guh-tuh-ri/ adjective formal having no purpose or value.
– ORIGIN Latin *nugatorius*.

nugget noun 1 a small lump of gold or other precious metal found in the earth. 2 a small but valuable fact.

– ORIGIN unknown.

nuisance noun a cause of inconvenience or annoyance.
– ORIGIN Old French, 'hurt'.

nuke informal noun a nuclear weapon. • verb attack or destroy something with nuclear weapons.

null adjective 1 (in phrase **null and void**) having no legal force; invalid. 2 Mathematics having or associated with the value zero.
– ORIGIN Latin *nullus* 'none'.

nullify verb (**nullifies, nullifying, nullified**) 1 make something legally invalid. 2 cancel out the effect of something.
– DERIVATIVES **nullification** noun.

nullity noun (pl. **nullities**) 1 the state of being legally invalid. 2 an unimportant or worthless thing.

numb adjective 1 (of a part of the body) having no sensation. 2 lacking the power to feel, think, or react: *the tragic events left us shocked and numb.* • verb make someone or something numb.
– DERIVATIVES **numbly** adverb **numbness** noun.
– ORIGIN from Germanic.

number noun 1 a quantity or value expressed by a word, symbol, or figure. 2 a quantity or amount: *the exhibition attracted vast numbers of visitors.* 3 (**a number of**) several. 4 chiefly Brit. a single issue of a magazine. 5 a song, dance, or other piece of music. 6 informal an item of clothing regarded with approval: *a little black number.* 7 a grammatical classification of words that depends on whether one or more people or things are being referred to. • verb 1 amount to a specified figure or quantity. 2 give a number to each thing in a series. 3 count things or people. 4 include as a member of a group: *she wanted to be numbered among the more fashionable novelists.*
– PHRASES **by numbers** following a set of simple instructions identified by numbers. **have someone's number** informal understand a person's real motives or character. **someone's days are numbered** someone will not survive for much longer. **someone's number is up** informal someone is finished or certain to die. **without number** too many to count.
– ORIGIN Latin *numerus.*

number cruncher noun informal 1 a computer or program for performing complicated calculations. 2 often derogatory an accountant, statistician, or other person whose job involves dealing with large amounts of numerical data.

numberless adjective too many to be counted; innumerable.

number one noun 1 the most important person or thing in a particular area or activity. 2 informal oneself. • adjective most important; top: *a number-one priority.*

number plate noun Brit. a sign on the front and rear of a vehicle displaying its registration number.

numbskull (also **numskull**) noun informal a stupid or foolish person.

numen /nyoo-muhn/ noun (pl. **numina** /nyoo-mi-nuh/) literary a spirit or divine power that presides over a place.
– ORIGIN Latin.

numeral /nyoo-muh-ruhl/ noun a figure or symbol representing a number.

numerate /nyoo-muh-ruht/ adjective having a good basic knowledge of arithmetic.
– DERIVATIVES **numeracy** noun.
– ORIGIN from Latin *numerus* 'a number'.

numeration noun the action of calculating or giving a number to something.

numerator noun Mathematics the number above the line in a fraction.

numerical adjective relating to or expressed as a number or numbers.
– DERIVATIVES **numeric** adjective **numerically** adverb.

numerology noun the study of the supposed magical power of numbers.
– DERIVATIVES **numerological** adjective **numerologist** noun.

numerous adjective 1 great in number; many. 2 consisting of many members.
– DERIVATIVES **numerously** adverb.

numina plural of NUMEN.

numinous /nyoo-mi-nuhss/ adjective having a strong religious or spiritual quality.
– ORIGIN from Latin *numen* (see NUMEN).

numismatics /nyoo-miz-mat-iks/ plural noun (usu. treated as sing.) the study or collection of coins, banknotes, and medals.
– DERIVATIVES **numismatic** adjective **numismatist** noun.

numskull noun variant spelling of NUMBSKULL.

nun noun a member of a female religious community, typically one who has taken vows of poverty, chastity, and obedience.
– ORIGIN Latin *nonna.*

nuncio /nun-si-oh/ noun (pl. **nuncios**) (in the Roman Catholic Church) an official representative of the pope in a foreign country.
– ORIGIN Latin *nuntius* 'messenger'.

nunnery noun (pl. **nunneries**) a convent.

nuptial /nup-sh'l/ adjective relating to marriage or weddings. • noun (**nuptials**) a wedding.
– ORIGIN from Latin *nuptiae* 'wedding'.

nurse[1] noun 1 a person trained to care for sick or injured people. 2 dated a person employed to look after young children. • verb 1 give medical and other care to a sick or injured person. 2 treat or hold carefully or protectively: *he nursed his small case on his lap.* 3 cling to a belief or feeling for a long time: *she nursed the hope that their relationship would improve.* 4 feed a baby at the breast.
– DERIVATIVES **nursing** noun.
– ORIGIN Old French *nourice*, from Latin *nutrire* 'nourish'.

nurse[2] (also **nurse shark**) noun a slow-moving Australian shark.
– ORIGIN probably from HUSS, as a result of a mistaken division of *an huss.*

nursemaid noun dated a woman or girl employed to look after a young child or children.

nursery noun (pl. **nurseries**) 1 a room in a house in which young children sleep or play. 2 (also **day nursery**) a nursery school. 3 a place where young plants and trees are grown for sale or for planting elsewhere.

nurseryman noun (pl. **nurserymen**) a person

n

who works in or owns a plant or tree nursery.

nursery nurse noun Brit. a person trained to look after young children and babies in a nursery or crèche.

nursery rhyme noun a simple traditional song or poem for children.

nursery school noun a school for young children, mainly between the ages of three and five.

nursery slope noun a gentle ski slope suitable for beginners.

nursing home noun a small private institution providing accommodation and health care for elderly people.

nursling noun dated a baby that is being breastfed.

nurture verb 1 care for and protect someone or something while they are growing and developing. 2 have a long-standing hope, belief, or ambition. • noun 1 the action of nurturing someone or something. 2 upbringing, education, and environment as a factor determining someone's personality. Often contrasted with **NATURE**.
– ORIGIN Old French *noureture* 'nourishment', from Latin *nutrire* 'nourish, cherish'.

nut noun 1 a fruit consisting of a hard shell around an edible kernel. 2 the hard kernel of such a fruit. 3 a small flat piece of metal or other material, typically square or hexagonal, with a threaded hole through the centre for screwing on to a bolt. 4 informal a crazy or eccentric person. 5 informal a person who is extremely interested in or enthusiastic about something: *a football nut.* 6 informal a person's head. 7 a small lump of something hard or solid, especially coal. 8 (**nuts**) vulgar slang a man's testicles.
– PHRASES **do one's nut** Brit. informal be extremely angry. **nuts and bolts** informal the basic practical details of a subject or activity. **a tough (or hard) nut to crack** informal a difficult problem or an opponent that is hard or overcome.
– DERIVATIVES **nutty** adjective.
– ORIGIN Old English.

nutcase noun informal a mad or foolish person.

nutcrackers plural noun a device for cracking the shells of nuts.

nuthatch noun a small grey-backed songbird which climbs up and down tree trunks.
– ORIGIN from a former word related to **HACK**[1], from the bird's habit of hacking at nuts with its beak.

nut loaf noun a baked vegetarian dish made from ground or chopped nuts, vegetables, and herbs.

nutmeg noun a spice made from the seed of a tropical tree.
– ORIGIN partial translation of Old French *nois muguede* 'musky nut'.

nutria /nyoo-tri-uh/ noun the skin or fur of the coypu (a large rodent).
– ORIGIN Spanish, 'otter'.

nutrient noun a substance that provides

nourishment essential for life, growth, and health.
– ORIGIN from Latin *nutrire* 'nourish'.

nutriment /nyoo-tri-muhnt/ noun the food or other substances necessary for growth and health.

nutrition noun 1 the process of taking in and absorbing nutrients. 2 the branch of science concerned with this process.
– DERIVATIVES **nutritional** adjective **nutritionist** noun.
– ORIGIN Latin, from *nutrire* 'nourish'.

nutritious adjective (of food) full of nutrients and so helping the body to grow or stay healthy.
– DERIVATIVES **nutritiously** adverb.

nutritive adjective 1 relating to nutrition. 2 nutritious.

nuts adjective informal mad.

nutshell noun (in phrase **in a nutshell**) in the fewest possible words.

nutter noun Brit. informal a mad or eccentric person.

nux vomica /nuks vom-i-kuh/ noun a southern Asian tree with berry-like fruit and toxic seeds that contain strychnine.
– ORIGIN Latin, 'nut causing vomiting'.

nuzzle verb rub or push against gently with the nose and mouth: *the foal nuzzled at its mother.*
– ORIGIN from **NOSE**.

NV abbreviation Nevada.

nvCJD abbreviation new variant Creutzfeldt–Jakob disease.

NVQ abbreviation (in the UK) National Vocational Qualification.

NW abbreviation 1 north-west. 2 north-western.

NY abbreviation New York.

NYC abbreviation New York City.

nylon noun 1 a tough, lightweight synthetic material which can be made into fabric, yarn, and many other products. 2 (**nylons**) nylon stockings or tights.
– ORIGIN an invented word.

nymph noun 1 (in Greek and Roman mythology) a spirit of nature in the form of a beautiful young woman. 2 literary a beautiful young woman. 3 an immature form of an insect such as a dragonfly.
– DERIVATIVES **nymphal** adjective.
– ORIGIN Greek *numphē* 'nymph, bride'.

nymphet noun an attractive and sexually mature young girl.

nympho noun (pl. **nymphos**) informal a nymphomaniac.

nymphomania noun uncontrollable or abnormally strong sexual desire in a woman.
– DERIVATIVES **nymphomaniac** noun.

nystagmus /ni-stag-muhss/ noun rapid involuntary movements of the eyes.
– ORIGIN Greek *nustagmos* 'nodding, drowsiness'.

NZ abbreviation New Zealand.

Oo

O¹ (also **o**) noun (pl. **Os** or **O's**) **1** the fifteenth letter of the alphabet. **2** (also **oh**) zero.

O² symbol the chemical element oxygen.

O³ exclamation old-fashioned spelling of **OH¹**.

oaf noun a stupid, rude, or clumsy man.
– DERIVATIVES **oafish** adjective.
– ORIGIN from Old Norse, 'elf'.

oak noun **1** a large tree which produces acorns and a hard wood used for building and furniture. **2** a smoky flavour characteristic of wine which has been aged in oak barrels.
– DERIVATIVES **oaken** adjective (old use) **oaky** adjective.
– ORIGIN Old English.

oak apple noun a spongy growth which forms on oak trees, caused by wasp larvae.

oakum noun chiefly historical loose fibre obtained by untwisting old rope, used especially to fill in cracks in wooden ships.
– ORIGIN Old English, 'off-combings'.

OAP abbreviation Brit. old-age pensioner.

oar noun a pole with a flat blade, used for rowing or steering a boat.
– PHRASES **put** (or **stick**) **one's oar in** informal, chiefly Brit. give an opinion without being asked.
– ORIGIN Old English.

oarsman (or **oarswoman**) noun (pl. **oarsmen** or **oarswomen**) a rower.

oasis /oh-**ay**-siss/ noun (pl. **oases** /oh-**ay**-seez/) **1** a fertile place in a desert where water rises to ground level. **2** a calm and pleasant area or period in the midst of a difficult or hectic place or situation.
– ORIGIN Greek.

oast house noun a building containing an oven for drying hops (an **oast**), typically conical in shape.
– ORIGIN Old English.

oat noun **1** a cereal plant grown in cool climates. **2** (**oats**) the edible grain of this plant.
– PHRASES **sow one's wild oats** (especially of a young man) have many casual sexual relationships while young.
– DERIVATIVES **oaty** adjective.
– ORIGIN Old English.

oatcake noun a savoury oatmeal biscuit.

oath noun (pl. **oaths**) **1** a solemn promise about one's future actions or behaviour. **2** a sworn declaration, such as the promise to tell the truth, made in a court of law. **3** a swear word.
– PHRASES **under** (or **on**) **oath** having sworn to tell the truth, especially in a court of law.
– ORIGIN Old English.

oatmeal noun meal made from ground oats,

used in making porridge and oatcakes.

obbligato /ob-bli-**gah**-toh/ (US also **obligato**) noun (pl. **obbligatos** or **obbligati** /ob-bli-**gah**-ti/) an accompanying instrumental part which is necessary to a piece of music and must not be left out of a performance.
– ORIGIN from Italian, 'obligatory'.

obdurate /ob-dyuu-ruht/ adjective stubbornly refusing to change one's mind.
– DERIVATIVES **obduracy** noun **obdurately** adverb.
– ORIGIN Latin *obduratus*.

OBE abbreviation Officer of the Order of the British Empire.

obeah /oh-bi-uh/ noun a kind of magic or witchcraft practised especially in the Caribbean.
– ORIGIN from an African language.

obedient adjective willing to do what one is told.
– DERIVATIVES **obedience** noun **obediently** adverb.
– ORIGIN from Latin *oboedire* 'obey'.

obeisance /oh-**bay**-suhnss/ noun **1** deferential respect for someone. **2** a gesture expressing this, such as a bow.
– ORIGIN Old French *obeissance*.

obelisk noun a four-sided stone pillar that tapers to a point, set up as a monument or landmark.
– ORIGIN Greek *obeliskos* 'small pointed pillar'.

obelus /ob-uh-luhss/ noun (pl. **obeli** /ob-uh-lee/) a symbol (†) used in printed material as a reference mark or to indicate that a person is dead.
– ORIGIN Greek *obelos* 'pointed pillar', also 'critical mark'.

obese adjective very fat.
– DERIVATIVES **obesity** noun.
– ORIGIN Latin *obesus*.

obey verb **1** do what one is told to do. **2** carry out an order. **3** behave in accordance with a general principle or natural law.
– ORIGIN Old French *obeir*.

obfuscate /ob-fuss-kayt/ verb make something hard to understand.
– DERIVATIVES **obfuscation** noun **obfuscatory** adjective.
– ORIGIN Latin *obfuscare* 'darken'.

obi /oh-bi/ noun (pl. **obis**) a broad sash worn round the waist of a Japanese kimono.
– ORIGIN Japanese, 'belt'.

obituarist noun a writer of obituaries.

obituary /oh-**bi**-chuu-ri, oh-**bi**-tyuu-ri/ noun (pl. **obituaries**) a short biography of a person,

published in a newspaper soon after their death.
– ORIGIN Latin *obitus* 'death'.

object noun /ob-jikt/ **1** a physical thing that can be seen and touched. **2** a person or thing to which an action or feeling is directed: *he hated being the object of public attention.* **3** a goal or purpose: *the object of the exercise was to shock the audience.* **4** Grammar a noun acted on by a transitive verb or by a preposition. • verb /uhb-**jekt**/ express disapproval or opposition: *residents objected to the noise.*
– PHRASES **no object** not influencing or restricting choices or decisions: *money is no object.*
– DERIVATIVES **objector** noun.
– ORIGIN Latin *objectum* 'thing presented to the mind'.

objectify verb (**objectifies, objectifying, objectified**) **1** express something abstract in a concrete form: *good poetry objectifies feeling.* **2** treat someone merely as an object rather than a person.
– DERIVATIVES **objectification** noun.

objection noun an expression of disapproval or opposition.

objectionable adjective unpleasant or offensive.

objective adjective **1** not influenced by personal feelings or opinions: *historians try to be objective.* **2** having actual existence outside the mind: *a matter of objective fact.* **3** Grammar relating to a case of nouns and pronouns used for the object of a transitive verb or a preposition. • noun **1** a goal or aim: *his main objective was to combat inflation.* **2** the lens in a telescope or microscope nearest to the object observed.
– DERIVATIVES **objectively** adverb **objectivity** noun.

object lesson noun a striking practical example of what should or should not be done in a particular situation: *they responded to emergencies in a way that was an object lesson to us all.*

objet d'art /ob-zhay **dar**/ noun (pl. **objets d'art** pronunc. same) a small decorative or artistic object.
– ORIGIN French, 'object of art'.

objurgation /ob-jer-**gay**-sh'n/ noun rare a severe rebuke.
– DERIVATIVES **objurgate** verb.
– ORIGIN Latin.

oblate /ob-layt/ adjective Geometry (of a sphere-shaped body) flattened at each pole.
– ORIGIN Latin *oblatus* 'carried inversely'.

oblation noun **1** a thing presented or offered to a god. **2** Christian Church the presentation of bread and wine to God in the service of Holy Communion.
– ORIGIN Latin.

obligate verb (**be obligated**) have a moral or legal duty to do something: *the hospital is obligated to provide health care.*
– ORIGIN Latin *obligare.*

obligation noun **1** something a person must do because it is morally right or legally necessary; a duty or commitment: *I have an obligation to look after her.* **2** the state of having to do something because it is morally right or legally necessary: *they are under no obligation*

to stick to the scheme. **3** a feeling of gratitude for a service or favour.

obligato noun US variant spelling of **OBBLIGATO**.

obligatory /uh-**blig**-uh-tri/ adjective required by a law, rule, or custom; compulsory.

oblige verb **1** compel someone to do something because it is a law, necessity, or duty: *he was obliged to do military service.* **2** do as someone asks in order to help or please them. **3** (**be obliged**) be indebted or grateful.
– ORIGIN Latin *obligare.*

obliging adjective willing to help someone or do as they ask.
– DERIVATIVES **obligingly** adverb.

oblique /uh-**bleek**/ adjective **1** neither parallel nor at right angles; slanting. **2** not explicit or direct: *an oblique reference to the US.* **3** Geometry (of a line, plane figure, or surface) inclined at other than a right angle. • noun Brit. another term for **SLASH** (in sense 3).
– DERIVATIVES **obliquely** adverb **obliqueness** noun **obliquity** /uh-**blik**-wi-ti/ noun.
– ORIGIN Latin *obliquus.*

obliterate /uh-**blit**-uh-rayt/ verb **1** destroy something completely. **2** completely cover: *clouds obliterated the moon.*
– DERIVATIVES **obliteration** noun.
– ORIGIN Latin *obliterare* 'strike out, erase'.

oblivion noun **1** the state of being unaware of what is happening around one. **2** the state of being forgotten: *his name will fade into oblivion.* **3** the state of being completely destroyed.
– ORIGIN Latin, from *oblivisci* 'forget'.

oblivious adjective not aware of what is happening around one: *he was oblivious to his surroundings.*
– DERIVATIVES **obliviously** adverb **obliviousness** noun.

oblong adjective having a rectangular shape. • noun an oblong object or shape.
– ORIGIN Latin *oblongus* 'longish'.

obloquy /ob-luh-kwi/ noun **1** strong public criticism. **2** disgrace brought about by strong public criticism.
– ORIGIN from Latin *obloqui* 'speak against'.

obnoxious /uhb-**nok**-shuhss/ adjective extremely unpleasant.
– DERIVATIVES **obnoxiously** adverb **obnoxiousness** noun.
– ORIGIN from Latin *obnoxius* 'exposed to harm'.

oboe /oh-boh/ noun a woodwind instrument of treble pitch, played with a double reed.
– DERIVATIVES **oboist** noun.
– ORIGIN Italian, or from French *hautbois*, from *haut* 'high' + *bois* 'wood'.

obscene adjective **1** (of the portrayal or description of sexual matters) offensive or disgusting according to accepted standards of morality or decency. **2** (especially of an amount of money) unacceptably large: *obscene pay rises.*
– DERIVATIVES **obscenely** adverb.
– ORIGIN Latin *obscaenus* 'ill-omened, hateful'.

obscenity noun (pl. **obscenities**) **1** obscene language or behaviour. **2** an obscene act or word.

obscurantism /ob-skyuu-**rant**-i-z'm/ noun the practice of deliberately preventing the facts or

full details of something from becoming known or understood.
- DERIVATIVES **obscurantist** noun & adjective.
- ORIGIN from Latin *obscurare* 'make dark'.

obscure adjective (**obscurer, obscurest**) **1** not discovered or known about; uncertain. **2** not well known: *a relatively obscure actor.* **3** not clearly expressed or easily understood: *obscure references to Proust.* **4** hard to see or make out. •verb make something difficult to see or understand.
- DERIVATIVES **obscuration** noun **obscurely** adverb.
- ORIGIN Latin *obscurus* 'dark'.

obscurity noun (pl. **obscurities**) **1** the state of being unknown or forgotten. **2** the quality of being hard to understand.

obsequies /ob-si-kwiz/ plural noun funeral rites.
- ORIGIN Latin.

obsequious /uhb-see-kwi-uhss/ adjective trying too hard to please someone; excessively obedient or respectful.
- DERIVATIVES **obsequiously** adverb **obsequiousness** noun.
- ORIGIN from Latin *obsequium* 'compliance'.

observance noun **1** the obeying of a law or rule, or the following of a custom. **2** (**observances**) acts performed for religious or ceremonial reasons.

observant adjective **1** quick to notice things. **2** following the rules of a religion.

observation noun **1** the action of watching someone or something closely: *he was brought into hospital for observation.* **2** the ability to notice important or significant details: *she was famous for her powers of observation.* **3** a comment based on something one has seen, heard, or noticed.
- DERIVATIVES **observational** adjective.

observatory noun (pl. **observatories**) a building housing a telescope or other scientific equipment for studying natural phenomena such as the stars and the weather.

observe verb **1** notice someone or something. **2** watch carefully; monitor: *many patients were observed for long periods.* **3** make a remark. **4** obey a law or rule. **5** celebrate or take part in a festival or ritual
- DERIVATIVES **observable** adjective **observer** noun.
- ORIGIN Latin *observare* 'to watch'.

obsess verb **1** preoccupy someone to a disturbing extent: *he was obsessed with thoughts of suicide.* **2** be constantly talking or worrying about something.
- ORIGIN Latin *obsidere* 'besiege'.

obsession noun **1** the state of being obsessed. **2** a person or thing that someone is unable to stop thinking about: *her career had become an obsession.*
- DERIVATIVES **obsessional** adjective.

obsessive adjective **1** thinking continually about someone or something: *he was obsessive about cleanliness.* **2** preoccupying a person's mind to a disturbing extent: *obsessive jealousy.*
- DERIVATIVES **obsessively** adverb **obsessiveness** noun.

obsessive-compulsive adjective relating to a mental condition in which a person feels compelled to carry out certain actions over and over again.

obsidian /uhb-sid-i-uhn/ noun a dark glass-like volcanic rock formed when lava solidifies rapidly without crystallizing.
- ORIGIN Latin *obsidianus*.

obsolescent /ob-suh-less-uhnt/ adjective becoming obsolete.
- DERIVATIVES **obsolescence** noun.
- ORIGIN from Latin *obsolescere* 'fall into disuse'.

obsolete adjective no longer produced or used; out of date.
- ORIGIN Latin *obsoletus* 'grown old, worn out'.

obstacle noun a thing that blocks one's way or makes it difficult to do or achieve something.
- ORIGIN Latin *obstaculum*.

obstetrician /ob-stuh-tri-sh'n/ noun a doctor qualified to practise in obstetrics.

obstetrics plural noun the branch of medicine and surgery concerned with childbirth.
- DERIVATIVES **obstetric** adjective.
- ORIGIN from Latin *obstetrix* 'midwife'.

obstinate adjective **1** stubbornly refusing to change one's mind. **2** hard to deal with or overcome: *an obstinate problem.*
- DERIVATIVES **obstinacy** noun **obstinately** adverb.
- ORIGIN Latin *obstinatus*.

obstreperous /uhb-strep-uh-ruhss/ adjective noisy and difficult to control.
- DERIVATIVES **obstreperously** adverb **obstreperousness** noun.
- ORIGIN from Latin *obstrepere* 'clamour against'.

obstruct verb **1** be in the way of; block: *she was obstructing the entrance.* **2** make it difficult to achieve something: *they promised not to obstruct the peace process.*
- DERIVATIVES **obstructor** noun.
- ORIGIN Latin *obstruere*.

obstruction noun **1** an obstacle or blockage. **2** the action of obstructing someone or something.

obstructionism noun the practice of deliberately blocking or delaying the progress of law-making or other procedures.
- DERIVATIVES **obstructionist** noun & adjective.

obstructive adjective deliberately causing difficulties or delays.

obtain verb **1** come into possession of; get. **2** formal be established or usual: *the standards which obtain in this school.*
- DERIVATIVES **obtainable** adjective.
- ORIGIN Latin *obtinere*.

obtrude verb **1** become obtrusive. **2** impose or force something on someone.
- ORIGIN Latin *obtrudere*.

obtrusive adjective noticeable in an unwelcome or unpleasant way.
- DERIVATIVES **obtrusively** adverb **obtrusiveness** noun.

obtuse adjective **1** annoyingly insensitive or slow to understand. **2** (of an angle) more than 90° and less than 180°. **3** not sharp or pointed; blunt.
- DERIVATIVES **obtusely** adverb **obtuseness** noun.
- ORIGIN Latin *obtusus*.

obverse noun **1** the side of a coin or medal with the head or main design. **2** the opposite or counterpart of a fact or truth.
- ORIGIN Latin *obversus* 'turned towards'.

obviate /ob-vi-ayt/ verb remove or prevent a need or difficulty.
– ORIGIN Latin *obviare*.

obvious adjective easily seen or understood; clear.
– DERIVATIVES **obviously** adverb **obviousness** noun.
– ORIGIN from Latin *ob viam* 'in the way'.

OC abbreviation Officer Commanding.

ocarina /ok-uh-ree-nuh/ noun a small egg-shaped wind instrument with holes for the fingers.
– ORIGIN Italian, 'little goose' (referring to its shape).

Occam's razor (also **Ockham's razor**) noun the principle that in explaining something no more assumptions should be made than are necessary.
– ORIGIN named after the English philosopher William of *Occam*.

occasion noun 1 a particular event, or the time at which it takes place. 2 a special event or celebration. 3 a suitable time for doing something: *this is not the occasion for a detailed analysis of the proposals.* 4 formal reason or justification: *we have occasion to rejoice.* • verb formal cause something.
– PHRASES **on occasion** from time to time. **rise to the occasion** perform well in response to a special situation.
– ORIGIN Latin, 'juncture, reason'.

occasional adjective 1 occurring infrequently or irregularly. 2 produced on or intended for particular occasions: *occasional verse.*
– DERIVATIVES **occasionally** adverb.

Occident /ok-si-duhnt/ noun (**the Occident**) literary the countries of the West.
– ORIGIN from Latin *occidere* 'go down, set', with reference to the setting of the sun.

occidental literary adjective relating to the countries of the West. • noun (**Occidental**) a person from the West.

occiput /ok-si-put/ noun Anatomy the back of the head.
– DERIVATIVES **occipital** /ok-si-pi-t'l/ adjective.
– ORIGIN Latin, from *caput* 'head'.

Occitan /ok-si-tuhn/ noun the medieval or modern language of Languedoc (southern France), including Provençal.
– ORIGIN French.

occlude /uh-klood/ verb technical 1 close up or block an opening or passage. 2 (of a tooth) come into contact with another in the opposite jaw.
– ORIGIN Latin *occludere*.

occluded front noun a weather front produced when a cold front catches up with a warm front, so that the warm air in between them is forced upwards.

occlusion noun technical the process of blocking something up.
– DERIVATIVES **occlusive** adjective.

occult /ok-kult, ok-kult/ noun (**the occult**) supernatural or magical powers, practices, or phenomena. • adjective 1 relating to the occult. 2 beyond ordinary knowledge or experience. 3 Medicine (of blood) abnormally present, but detectable only microscopically or by chemical testing.
– DERIVATIVES **occultism** noun **occultist** noun.

– ORIGIN from Latin *occulere* 'conceal'.

occupancy noun 1 the action or fact of occupying a place. 2 the proportion of accommodation occupied or used.

occupant noun 1 a person who occupies a place at a given time. 2 the holder of a job.

occupation noun 1 a job or profession. 2 a way of spending time. 3 the action of occupying a place or the state of being occupied: *the Roman occupation of Britain.*

occupational adjective relating to a job or profession: *an occupational pension scheme.*
– DERIVATIVES **occupationally** adverb.

occupational hazard noun a risk arising as a consequence of a particular job or profession.

occupational therapy noun the use of particular activities to help someone recover from an illness.
– DERIVATIVES **occupational therapist** noun.

occupy verb (**occupies, occupying, occupied**) 1 live or work in a place. 2 fill or take up a space, time, or position. 3 keep someone busy and active: *he has occupied himself with research.* 4 enter and take control of a place, especially by military force.
– DERIVATIVES **occupier** noun.
– ORIGIN Latin *occupare* 'seize'.

occur verb (**occurs, occurring, occurred**) 1 happen; take place. 2 be found or present: *radon occurs in rocks such as granite.* 3 (**occur to**) come into someone's mind.
– ORIGIN Latin *occurrere* 'go to meet, present itself'.

occurrence /uh-ku-ruhnss/ noun 1 a thing that happens; an incident or event. 2 the fact or frequency of something happening or existing: *the occurrence of cancer increases with age.*

ocean noun 1 a very large expanse of sea, specifically each of the Atlantic, Pacific, Indian, Arctic, and Antarctic Oceans. 2 (**the ocean**) N. Amer. the sea.
– ORIGIN Greek *ōkeanos* 'great stream encircling the earth's disc'.

oceanarium /oh-shuh-nair-i-uhm/ noun (pl. **oceanariums** or **oceanaria** /oh-shuh-nair-i-uh/) a large seawater aquarium.

Oceanian /oh-si-ah-ni-uhn, oh-shi-ah-ni-uhn/ adjective relating to Oceania, the islands of the Pacific Ocean and the adjacent seas. • noun a person from Oceania.

oceanic /oh-si-an-ik, oh-shi-an-ik/ adjective 1 relating to the ocean. 2 (**Oceanic**) Oceanian.

oceanography noun the branch of science concerned with the study of the sea.
– DERIVATIVES **oceanographer** noun **oceanographic** adjective.

ocelot /oss-i-lot/ noun a medium-sized striped and spotted wild cat, native to South and Central America.
– ORIGIN French.

och /ok, okh/ exclamation Scottish & Irish expressing surprise, regret, or disbelief.

oche /o-ki/ noun Brit. the line behind which darts players stand when throwing.
– ORIGIN perhaps related to Old French *ocher* 'cut a notch in'.

ochre /oh-ker/ (US also **ocher**) noun a type of earth which varies in colour from light yellow

to brown or red, used as a pigment.
- DERIVATIVES **ochreous** /oh-kri-uhss/ adjective.
- ORIGIN Greek *ōkhra*.

Ockham's razor noun variant spelling of **OCCAM'S RAZOR**.

o'clock adverb used to specify the hour when telling the time.
- ORIGIN from *of the clock*.

OCR abbreviation optical character recognition.

Oct. abbreviation October.

octa- (also **oct-** before a vowel) combining form eight; having eight: *octahedron.*
- ORIGIN Greek *oktō* 'eight'.

octagon noun a plane figure with eight straight sides and eight angles.
- DERIVATIVES **octagonal** adjective.

octahedron /ok-tuh-**hee**-druhn/ noun (pl. **octahedra** /ok-tuh-**hee**-druh/ or **octahedrons**) a three-dimensional shape having eight plane faces, in particular eight equal triangular faces.
- DERIVATIVES **octahedral** adjective.

octane noun a liquid hydrocarbon present in petroleum spirit.

octane number (or **octane rating**) noun a figure indicating the quality of a fuel, based on a comparison with a standard mixture.

octave /ok-tiv/ noun **1** a series of eight musical notes occupying the interval between (and including) two notes, one having twice or half the pitch of the other. **2** the interval between two such notes, or the notes themselves sounding together.
- ORIGIN from Latin *octava dies* 'eighth day', first referring to a period of eight days following and including a Church festival.

octavo /ok-**tah**-voh/ noun (pl. **octavos**) a size of book page that results from folding each printed sheet into eight leaves (sixteen pages).
- ORIGIN from Latin *in octavo* 'in an eighth'.

octet noun **1** a group of eight musicians. **2** a musical composition for eight voices or instruments. **3** a group of eight lines of verse.

octo- (also **oct-** before a vowel) combining form eight; having eight: *octopus.*
- ORIGIN Latin *octo* or Greek *oktō* 'eight'.

October noun the tenth month of the year.
- ORIGIN from Latin *octo* 'eight', October being originally the eighth month of the Roman year.

octogenarian /ok-tuh-ji-**nair**-i-uhn/ noun a person who is between 80 and 89 years old.
- ORIGIN from Latin *octoginta* 'eighty'.

octopus noun (pl. **octopuses**) a sea animal with a soft body and eight long tentacles with suckers.
- DERIVATIVES **octopoid** adjective.
- ORIGIN Greek, from *oktō* 'eight' + *pous* 'foot'.

> USAGE: The standard plural in English of **octopus** is **octopuses**, but as the word comes from Greek, the Greek plural form **octopodes** is still occasionally used. The plural form **octopi**, formed according to rules for Latin plurals, is incorrect.

octoroon /ok-tuh-**roon**/ noun dated a person who is one-eighth black by descent.

octuple /ok-tyuu-p'l, ok-**tyoo**-p'l/ adjective

1 consisting of eight parts or things. **2** eight times as many or as much.
- ORIGIN from Latin *octo* 'eight' + *-plus* (as in *duplus* 'double').

octuplet /ok-tyuu-plit, ok-**tyoo**-plit/ noun each of eight children born at one birth.

ocular /ok-yuu-ler/ adjective relating to the eyes or vision.
- ORIGIN from Latin *oculus* 'eye'.

oculist /ok-yuu-list/ noun dated a person who specializes in the medical treatment of diseases or defects of the eye.
- ORIGIN from Latin *oculus* 'eye'.

oculus /ok-yuu-luhss/ noun (pl. **oculi** /ok-yuu-lee/) Architecture **1** a circular window. **2** an opening at the top of a dome.
- ORIGIN Latin, 'eye'.

OD informal verb (**OD's, OD'ing, OD'd**) take an overdose of a drug. • noun an overdose.

odalisque /oh-duh-lisk/ noun historical a female slave or concubine in a harem.
- ORIGIN French.

odd adjective **1** unusual or unexpected; strange. **2** (of whole numbers such as 3 and 5) having one left over as a remainder when divided by two. **3** (in combination) in the region of: *fifty-odd years.* **4** occasional: *we have the odd drink together.* **5** spare or available: *an odd five minutes.* **6** separated from a pair or set: *an odd sock.*
- PHRASES **odd one out** a person or thing differing in some way from the other members of a group or set. **odds and ends** various small items that are not part of a larger set.
- DERIVATIVES **oddly** adverb **oddness** noun.
- ORIGIN Old Norse.

oddball noun informal a strange or eccentric person.

oddity noun (pl. **oddities**) **1** the quality of being strange. **2** a strange person or thing.

odd-job man noun Brit. a man who does small domestic or manual jobs on a casual basis.

oddment noun an item or piece left over from a larger piece or set.

odds plural noun **1** the ratio between the amounts placed as a bet and the money that would be received if the bet was won: *odds of 8–1.* **2** (**the odds**) the chances of something happening or being the case. **3** (**the odds**) the advantage thought to be possessed by one person compared to another; superiority in strength, power, or resources: *she clung to the lead against all the odds.*
- PHRASES **at odds** in conflict or disagreement. **it makes no odds** informal, chiefly Brit. it does not matter. **over the odds** Brit. (of a price) above what is generally thought acceptable.

odds-on adjective **1** (especially of a horse) rated as more likely than evens to win. **2** very likely to happen or succeed.

ode noun a poem addressed to a person or thing, or celebrating an event.
- ORIGIN Greek *ōidē* 'song'.

odiferous /oh-**dif**-uh-ruhss/ adjective variant spelling of **ODORIFEROUS**.

odious adjective extremely unpleasant; repulsive.
- DERIVATIVES **odiously** adverb **odiousness** noun.

– ORIGIN from Latin *odium* 'hatred'.

odium noun general or widespread hatred or disgust.
– ORIGIN Latin.

odometer /oh-**dom**-i-ter/ noun an instrument for measuring the distance travelled by a vehicle.
– ORIGIN French *odomètre*.

odontology /o-don-**tol**-uh-ji, oh-don-**tol**-uh-ji/ noun the scientific study of the structure and diseases of teeth.
– DERIVATIVES **odontologist** noun.
– ORIGIN from Greek *odous* 'tooth'.

odorant noun a substance used to give a scent or smell to a product.

odoriferous /oh-duh-**rif**-uh-ruhss/ adjective giving off a smell, especially an unpleasant one.
– ORIGIN from Latin *odorifer* 'odour-bearing'.

odour (US **odor**) noun **1** a distinctive smell. **2** a lingering quality or impression: *an odour of suspicion.*
– DERIVATIVES **odorous** adjective **odourless** adjective.
– ORIGIN Latin *odor*.

odyssey /**od**-i-si/ noun (pl. **odysseys**) a long, eventful journey.
– DERIVATIVES **odyssean** /o-**dis**-i-uhn/ adjective.
– ORIGIN the title of a Greek epic poem attributed to Homer, describing the adventures of Odysseus.

OECD abbreviation Organization for Economic Cooperation and Development.

oedema /i-**dee**-muh/ (US **edema**) noun an excess of watery fluid in the cavities or tissues of the body.
– ORIGIN Greek *oidēma*.

Oedipus complex /**ee**-di-puhss/ noun (in the theory of Sigmund Freud) the emotions aroused in a young child by an unconscious sexual desire for the parent of the opposite sex.
– DERIVATIVES **Oedipal** adjective.
– ORIGIN from *Oedipus* in Greek mythology, who unknowingly killed his father and married his mother.

OEM abbreviation original equipment manufacturer.

oenology /ee-**nol**-uh-ji/ (US also **enology**) noun the study of wines.
– DERIVATIVES **oenological** adjective **oenologist** noun.
– ORIGIN from Greek *oinos* 'wine'.

oenophile /**ee**-nuh-fyl/ (US also **enophile**) noun a connoisseur of wines.

o'er adverb & preposition old-fashioned or literary form of OVER.

oesophagus /i-**sof**-fuh-guhss/ (US **esophagus**) noun (pl. **oesophagi** /i-**sof**-fuh-jy/) the muscular tube which connects the throat to the stomach.
– DERIVATIVES **oesophageal** /i-so-fuh-**jee**-uhl/ adjective.
– ORIGIN Greek *oisophagos*.

oestradiol /ee-struh-**dy**-ol/ (US **estradiol**) noun a major oestrogen produced in the ovaries.

oestrogen /**ee**-struh-juhn, **ess**-truh-juhn/ (US **estrogen**) noun any of a group of hormones which produce and maintain female physical and sexual characteristics.
– ORIGIN from OESTRUS.

oestrus /**ee**-struhss, **ess**-truhss/ (US **estrus**) noun a regularly occurring period of time during which many female mammals are fertile and sexually receptive to males.
– ORIGIN Greek *oistros* 'gadfly or frenzy'.

oeuvre /**er**-vruh/ noun the works of an artist, composer, author, etc., considered as a whole.
– ORIGIN French.

of preposition **1** expressing the relationship between a part and a whole. **2** belonging to; coming from. **3** expressing the relationship between a scale or measure and a value. **4** made from. **5** expressing the relationship between a direction and a point of reference. **6** expressing the relationship between a general category and something which belongs to such a category. **7** N. Amer. expressing time in relation to the following hour.
– ORIGIN Old English.

USAGE: Be careful not to write the word **of** instead of **have** in sentences such as *I could have told you*. For more information, see the note at **HAVE**.

Ofcom abbreviation (in the UK) Office of Communications.

off adverb **1** away from the place in question. **2** so as to be removed or separated. **3** starting a journey or race. **4** so as to finish or be discontinued. **5** (of an electrical appliance or power supply) not functioning or so as to stop functioning. **6** having a particular level of wealth: *badly off.* •preposition **1** moving away and often down from. **2** situated or leading in a direction away from. **3** so as to be removed, separated, or absent from. **4** having a temporary dislike of. •adjective **1** unsatisfactory or inadequate: *an off day.* **2** (of food) no longer fresh. **3** located on the side of a vehicle that is normally furthest from the kerb. **4** Brit. informal annoying or unfair. •noun **1** (also **off side**) Cricket the half of the field towards which the batsman's feet are pointed when standing to receive the ball. The opposite of LEG. **2** Brit. informal the start of a race or journey.
– PHRASES **off and on** not regularly or all the time.
– ORIGIN Old English.

USAGE: The use of **off of** rather than **off** is considered wrong in standard modern English: you should say *the cup fell off the table* rather than *the cup fell off of the table*.

Offa abbreviation (in the UK) Office for Fair Access (to higher education).

offal noun the internal organs of an animal used as food.
– ORIGIN probably from Dutch *afval*.

offbeat adjective unconventional; unusual. •noun Music any of the normally unaccented beats in a bar.

off break noun Cricket a ball which spins from the off side towards the leg side after pitching.

off-colour adjective **1** Brit. slightly unwell. **2** slightly indecent or obscene.

offcut noun Brit. a piece of wood, fabric, etc. that is left behind after a larger piece has been cut off.

offence (US **offense**) noun **1** an act that breaks a law or rule. **2** a feeling of hurt or annoyance: *I didn't mean to give offence.* **3** the action of making a military attack. **4** N. Amer. the attacking players in a team.

offend verb **1** make someone feel upset, resentful, or annoyed. **2** be displeasing to: *the smell of ash offended him.* **3** commit an illegal act.
– DERIVATIVES **offender** noun.
– ORIGIN Latin *offendere* 'strike against'.

offensive adjective **1** making someone feel upset, resentful, or annoyed. **2** involved in an attack, or meant for use in an attack: *an offensive weapon.* **3** chiefly N. Amer. relating to the team in possession of the ball or puck in a game. • noun **1** an attacking military campaign. **2** a forceful campaign to achieve something: *the need to launch an offensive against crime.*
– PHRASES **be on the offensive** be ready to act aggressively.
– DERIVATIVES **offensively** adverb **offensiveness** noun.

offer verb **1** present something for someone to accept or reject as they wish. **2** express willingness to do something for someone: *he offered to fix the gate.* **3** provide: *the hotel offers direct access to a spa and pool.* **4** present something to God or another deity as an act of worship: *a monk offered prayers for their health and happiness.* • noun **1** an expression of readiness to do or give something. **2** an amount of money that someone is willing to pay for something. **3** a specially reduced price.
– PHRASES **on offer 1** available. **2** for sale at a reduced price.
– ORIGIN Latin *offerre* 'bestow, present'.

offering noun something that is offered; a gift or contribution.

offertory /of-fer-tuh-ri/ noun (pl. **offertories**) Christian Church **1** the offering of the bread and wine in the service of Holy Communion. **2** a collection of money made at a church service.
– ORIGIN Latin *offertorium.*

offhand adjective rudely casual or cool in manner. • adverb without previous thought or consideration: *I can't think of a better answer offhand.*

office noun **1** a room, set of rooms, or building in which business or clerical work is carried out. **2** a position of authority: *the office of Director General.* **3** the holding of an official position: *the President took office in 1980.* **4** (**offices**) services done for other people: *the good offices of the rector.* **5** (also **Divine Office**) Christian Church the services of prayers and psalms said daily by Catholic priests or other clergy.
– ORIGIN Latin *officium* 'performance of a task'.

officer noun **1** a person holding a position of authority in the armed forces. **2** a policeman or policewoman. **3** a person holding a position of authority in the government or a large organization.

official adjective **1** relating to an authority or public organization and its activities and responsibilities. **2** permitted or done by a person or group in a position of authority: *an official inquiry.* • noun a person holding public office or having official duties.
– DERIVATIVES **officialdom** noun **officially** adverb.

officialese noun formal or complicated language typical of that used in official documents.

official secret noun Brit. a piece of information that is important for national security and is officially classified as confidential.

officiant /uh-fish-i-uhnt/ noun a priest or minister who performs a religious service or ceremony.

officiate /uh-fish-i-ayt/ verb **1** act as an official in charge of something, especially a sporting event. **2** perform a religious service or ceremony.
– DERIVATIVES **officiation** noun **officiator** noun.
– ORIGIN Latin *officiare* 'perform divine service'.

officious adjective too ready to assert one's authority or interfere.
– DERIVATIVES **officiously** adverb **officiousness** noun.

offing noun the more distant part of the sea in view.
– PHRASES **in the offing** likely to happen or appear soon.

offish adjective informal aloof or unfriendly in manner.

off-key adjective & adverb **1** Music not in the correct key or of the correct pitch. **2** not suitable or appropriate.

off-licence noun Brit. a shop selling alcoholic drinks that are to be drunk elsewhere.

off-limits adjective out of bounds.

offline adjective not connected to a computer.

offload verb **1** unload a cargo. **2** get rid of something by passing it on to someone else.

off-peak adjective & adverb at a time when demand is less.

off-piste adjective & adverb Skiing away from prepared ski runs.

offprint noun a printed copy of an article that originally appeared as part of a larger publication.

off-putting adjective unpleasant or disconcerting.

off-ramp noun N. Amer. an exit road from a motorway.

off-road adjective (of a vehicle or bicycle) for use on rough terrain rather than on public roads.

off season noun a time of year when people do not take part in a particular activity or a business is quiet.

offset verb (**offsetting**; past and past part. **offset**) **1** counteract something by having an equal and opposite force or effect: *many costs can be offset by productivity savings.* **2** place something out of line. **3** transfer an impression by means of offset printing. • noun **1** a consideration or amount that reduces or balances the effect of an opposite one. **2** the amount by which something is out of line. **3** a side shoot from a plant which can be used for propagation. **4** a method of printing in which ink is transferred from a plate or stone to a rubber surface and from that to the paper.

offshoot noun 1 a side shoot on a plant. 2 a thing that develops from something else.

offshore adjective & adverb 1 situated at sea some distance from the shore. 2 (of the wind) blowing towards the sea from the land. 3 relating to the business of extracting oil or gas from the seabed. 4 made, situated, or registered abroad. 5 relating to a foreign country.

offshoring noun the practice of basing some of a company's processes or services overseas, to take advantage of lower costs.

offside adjective & adverb (of a player in games such as football, rugby, or hockey) occupying a position on the field where playing the ball or puck is not allowed. • noun 1 the fact of being offside. 2 Brit. the side of a vehicle furthest from the kerb. 3 the right side of a horse.

offspring noun (pl. same) a person's child or children, or the young of an animal.

offstage adjective & adverb (in a theatre) not on the stage and so not visible to the audience.

off-white noun a white colour with a grey or yellowish tinge.

Ofgem abbreviation (in the UK) Office of Gas and Electricity Markets.

Ofsted abbreviation (in the UK) Office for Standards in Education.

OFT abbreviation (in the UK) Office of Fair Trading.

oft (also **oft-times**) adverb old use or literary often.
– ORIGIN Old English.

Oftel abbreviation (in the UK) Office of Telecommunications.

often (also old use or N. Amer. **oftentimes**) adverb (**oftener**, **oftenest**) 1 frequently. 2 in many cases.

Ofwat abbreviation (in the UK) Office of Water Services.

ogee /oh-jee, oh-jee/ noun Architecture an S-shaped line or moulding.
– ORIGIN uncertain.

ogee arch noun Architecture a pointed arch with two S-shaped curves meeting at the top.

ogle verb stare at someone in a lecherous way.
– DERIVATIVES **ogler** noun.
– ORIGIN probably from German or Dutch.

ogre /oh-guh/ noun (fem. **ogress**) 1 (in folklore) a man-eating giant. 2 a cruel or terrifying person.
– DERIVATIVES **ogreish** (also **ogrish**) adjective.
– ORIGIN French.

OH abbreviation Ohio.

oh[1] exclamation expressing surprise, disappointment, joy, acknowledgement, etc.

oh[2] noun variant spelling of **O**[1] (in sense 2).

ohm noun the SI unit of electrical resistance. (Symbol: Ω)
– ORIGIN named after the German physicist G. S. *Ohm*.

OHMS abbreviation on Her (or His) Majesty's Service.

OHP abbreviation Brit. overhead projector.

OIEO abbreviation Brit. offers in excess of.

oik (also **oick**) noun Brit. informal an uncouth, rude, or unpleasant person.
– ORIGIN unknown.

oil noun 1 a thick, sticky liquid obtained from petroleum, used especially as a fuel or lubricant. 2 petroleum. 3 any of various thick liquids which cannot be dissolved in water and are obtained from animals or plants. 4 Chemistry any of a group of organic compounds of glycerol and acids which are liquid at room temperature. 5 (also **oils**) oil paint. • verb lubricate, coat, or treat something with oil.
– ORIGIN Old French *oile*, from Latin *oleum* 'oil, olive oil'.

oilcan noun a can with a long nozzle used for applying oil to machinery.

oilcloth noun cotton fabric treated with oil to make it waterproof.

oilfield noun an area where oil is found beneath the ground or the seabed.

oil paint noun artists' paint made from ground pigment mixed with linseed or other oil.

oil painting noun 1 the art of painting in oil paint. 2 a picture painted in oil paint.

oil palm noun a tropical West African palm whose fruit yields a kind of oil.

oil rig (or **oil platform**) noun a structure designed to stand on the seabed to provide a stable base above water for drilling oil wells.

oilseed noun any of various seeds from crops from which oil is obtained, e.g. rape, peanut, or cotton.

oilskin noun 1 heavy cotton cloth waterproofed with oil. 2 (**oilskins**) a set of garments made of oilskin.

oil slick noun a film or layer of oil floating on an area of water.

oilstone noun a fine-grained flat stone used with oil for sharpening chisels, planes, or other tools.

oil well noun a shaft bored in rock so as to extract oil.

oily adjective (**oilier**, **oiliest**) 1 containing, covered with, or soaked in oil. 2 resembling oil. 3 (of a person) polite or flattering in an insincere and unpleasant way.
– DERIVATIVES **oiliness** noun.

oink noun the characteristic grunting sound made by a pig. • verb (of a pig) grunt.
– ORIGIN imitating the sound.

ointment noun a smooth substance that is rubbed on the skin for medicinal purposes.
– ORIGIN Old French *oignement*.

OIRO abbreviation Brit. offers in the region of.

Ojibwa /oh-jib-way/ noun (pl. same or **Ojibwas**) a member of an American Indian people of the area around Lake Superior.
– ORIGIN Ojibwa, said to mean 'puckered' (with reference to their moccasins).

OK[1] (also **okay**) informal exclamation expressing agreement or acceptance. • adjective 1 satisfactory, but not especially good. 2 permissible; allowed. • adverb in a satisfactory way. • noun approval or permission. • verb (**OK's**, **OK'ing**, **OK'd**) approve or agree to something.
– ORIGIN probably an abbreviation of *orl korrect*, humorous form of *all correct*.

OK[2] abbreviation Oklahoma.

okapi /oh-kah-pi/ noun (pl. same or **okapis**) a large African mammal of the giraffe family, having a dark chestnut coat with stripes on the hindquarters and upper legs.

- ORIGIN a local word.

okra /**ok**-ruh, **oh**-kruh/ noun the long seed pods of a tropical plant, eaten as a vegetable.
- ORIGIN a West African word.

old adjective (**older**, **oldest**) **1** having lived for a long time. **2** made or built long ago. **3** possessed or used for a long time: *I gave my old clothes away.* **4** long-established or known. **5** former; previous: *they moved back to their old house.* **6** of a specified age. **7** informal expressing affection or contempt.
- PHRASES **of old 1** in or belonging to the past. **2** for a long time. **the old days** a period in the past. **the old school** the traditional form or type: *a gentleman of the old school.*
- DERIVATIVES **oldish** adjective **oldness** noun.
- ORIGIN Old English.

old age noun the later part of normal life.

old-age pensioner noun Brit. an old person receiving a retirement pension.

old boy (or **old girl**) noun Brit. a former student of a school or college.

old boy network (also **old boys' network**) noun an informal system through which men use their positions of influence to help others who went to the same school or university.

olde /ohld, **ohl**-di/ (also Brit. **olde worlde**) adjective mock old-fashioned attractively old-fashioned; quaint.

olden adjective relating to former times.

Old English noun the language of the Anglo-Saxons (up to about 1150).

Old English sheepdog noun a large breed of sheepdog with a shaggy blue-grey and white coat.

old-fashioned adjective **1** no longer current or modern; outdated. **2** disapproving: *an old-fashioned look.*

Old French noun the French language up to about 1400.

Old Glory noun US informal the US national flag.

old gold noun a dull brownish-gold colour.

old guard noun the long-standing members of a group, who are typically unwilling to accept change.

old hand noun a very experienced person.

old hat noun informal something that is boringly familiar or outdated.

oldie noun informal an old person or thing.

old lady noun informal a person's mother, wife, or girlfriend.

old maid noun **1** derogatory a single woman regarded as too old for marriage. **2** a prim and fussy person.

old man noun **1** informal a person's father, husband, or male lover. **2** Brit. informal an affectionate form of address between men or boys.

old man's beard noun a wild clematis with grey fluffy hairs around the seeds.

old master noun a great artist of the past, especially of the 13th–17th century in Europe.

old moon noun the phase of the moon in its last quarter, before the new moon.

Old Nick noun informal the Devil.

Old Norse noun the language of medieval Norway, Iceland, Denmark, and Sweden.

old salt noun informal an experienced sailor.

old stager noun informal a very experienced or long-serving person.

oldster noun informal, chiefly N. Amer. an older person.

Old Stone Age noun the Palaeolithic period.

Old Style noun the former method of calculating dates using the Julian calendar.

Old Testament noun the first part of the Christian Bible, comprising the sacred writings of Judaism in thirty-nine books.

old-time adjective **1** relating to or typical of the past. **2** (of ballroom dancing) in which a sequence of steps is repeated throughout, as opposed to modern dancing in which steps may be varied.

old-timer noun informal a very experienced or long-serving person.

old wives' tale noun a widely held traditional belief that is now thought to be unscientific or incorrect.

old woman noun **1** informal a person's mother, wife, or female lover. **2** derogatory a fussy or timid person.

Old World noun Europe, Asia, and Africa, regarded as the part of the world known before the discovery of the Americas.

old-world adjective belonging to or associated with past times; quaint.

olé /oh-**lay**/ exclamation bravo!
- ORIGIN Spanish.

oleaginous /oh-li-**aj**-i-nuhss/ adjective **1** oily or greasy. **2** excessively flattering; obsequious: *oleaginous speeches praising government policies.*
- ORIGIN Latin *oleaginus* 'of the olive tree'.

oleander /oh-li-**an**-der/ noun an evergreen shrub of warm countries with clusters of white, pink, or red flowers.
- ORIGIN Latin.

oleograph /**oh**-li-uh-grahf/ noun a type of print that has been textured to resemble an oil painting.
- ORIGIN from Latin *oleum* 'oil'.

O level noun historical (in the UK except Scotland) the lower of the two main levels of the GCE exam.
- ORIGIN short for ORDINARY LEVEL.

olfaction /ol-**fak**-sh'n/ noun technical the sense of smell.

olfactory /ol-**fak**-tuh-ri/ adjective relating to the sense of smell.
- ORIGIN from Latin *olfacere* 'to smell'.

oligarch /**ol**-i-gark/ noun a ruler in a state governed by a small group of people.

oligarchy /**ol**-i-gar-ki/ noun (pl. **oligarchies**) **1** a small group of people having control of a state. **2** a state governed by a small group of people.
- DERIVATIVES **oligarchic** adjective.
- ORIGIN from Greek *oligoi* 'few' + *arkhein* 'to rule'.

Oligocene /**ol**-i-goh-seen/ adjective Geology relating to the third epoch of the Tertiary period (35.4 to 23.3 million years ago), when the first primates appeared.
- ORIGIN from Greek *oligos* 'few' + *kainos* 'new'.

oligopoly /oli-**gop**-uh-li/ noun (pl. **oligopolies**) a state of limited competition, in which a

O

market is shared by a small number of producers or sellers.
- DERIVATIVES **oligopolist** noun **oligopolistic** adjective.

olive noun **1** a small oval fruit with a hard stone and bitter flesh, green when unripe and black when ripe. **2** the small evergreen tree which produces olives. **3** (also **olive green**) a greyish-green colour. **4** a slice of beef or veal made into a roll with stuffing inside and stewed. • adjective (of a person's complexion) yellowish brown.
- ORIGIN Latin *oliva*.

olive branch noun an offer to restore friendly relations.
- ORIGIN with reference to the story of Noah in the Book of Genesis, to whom a dove returned with an olive branch after the Flood.

olive drab noun a dull olive-green colour, used in some military uniforms.

olive oil noun an oil obtained from olives, used in cookery and salad dressings.

Olmec /ol-mek/ noun (pl. same or **Olmecs**) **1** a member of a prehistoric people who lived on the Gulf of Mexico. **2** an unrelated people inhabiting this area during the 15th and 16th centuries.
- ORIGIN Nahuatl, 'inhabitants of the rubber country'.

oloroso /ol-uh-roh-soh/ noun (pl. **olorosos**) a heavy, dark, medium-sweet sherry.
- ORIGIN from Spanish, 'fragrant'.

Olympiad /uh-lim-pi-ad/ noun **1** a staging of the Olympic Games. **2** a major international contest in a particular game, sport, or scientific subject.

Olympian adjective **1** relating to the Olympic Games. **2** like a god, especially in being powerful or aloof: *an editorial filled with Olympian disdain for the President.* **3** associated with Mount Olympus in Greece, traditional home of the Greek gods. • noun **1** a competitor in the Olympic Games. **2** a person who is greatly admired or superior to others. **3** any of the twelve main Greek gods.

Olympic adjective relating to the Olympic Games. • noun (**the Olympics**) the Olympic Games.

Olympic Games plural noun **1** a sports festival held every four years in different countries, established in 1896. **2** an ancient Greek festival with athletic, literary, and musical competitions, held every four years at Olympia in Greece.

OM abbreviation (in the UK) Order of Merit.

om /ohm, om/ noun Hinduism & Tibetan Buddhism a mystic syllable, considered the most sacred mantra.
- ORIGIN Sanskrit.

Omani /oh-mah-ni/ noun a person from Oman in the Arabian peninsula. • adjective relating to Oman.

ombudsman /om-buudz-muhn/ noun (pl. **ombudsmen**) an official appointed to investigate people's complaints against an organization.
- ORIGIN Swedish, 'legal representative'.

omega /oh-mi-guh/ noun **1** the last letter of the Greek alphabet (Ω, ω). **2** (usu. before another noun) the last of a series.

omega-3 fatty acid noun an unsaturated fatty acid of a kind occurring chiefly in fish oils.

omelette (US also **omelet**) noun a dish of beaten eggs cooked in a frying pan and usually served with a savoury filling.
- ORIGIN French.

omen noun **1** an event regarded as a sign of future good or bad luck. **2** indication of the future: *a bird of evil omen.*
- ORIGIN Latin.

omertà /oh-mair-tah/ noun the Mafia code of silence about criminal activity.
- ORIGIN Italian, 'humility'.

ominous adjective giving the impression that something bad is going to happen: *the first ominous signs of mental torment soon emerged.*
- DERIVATIVES **ominously** adverb **ominousness** noun.
- ORIGIN Latin *ominosus*.

omission noun **1** the action of leaving something out. **2** something that has been left out or not done. **3** a failure to fulfil a duty.

omit verb (**omits, omitting, omitted**) **1** leave out or exclude someone or something. **2** fail to do: *he modestly omits to mention that he was a pole-vault champion.*
- DERIVATIVES **omissible** adjective.
- ORIGIN Latin *omittere* 'let go'.

omni- combining form **1** all; of all things: *omniscient.* **2** in all ways or places: *omnipresent.*
- ORIGIN from Latin *omnis* 'all'.

omnibus noun **1** a book containing several works previously published separately. **2** Brit. a television or radio programme consisting of two or more programmes previously broadcast separately. **3** dated a bus.
- ORIGIN Latin, 'for all'.

omnicompetent adjective able to deal with all matters.
- DERIVATIVES **omnicompetence** noun.

omnidirectional adjective Telecommunications receiving signals from or transmitting in all directions.

omnipotent /om-ni-puh-tuhnt/ adjective having unlimited or very great power.
- DERIVATIVES **omnipotence** noun.
- ORIGIN Latin *omnipotens*.

omnipresent adjective **1** widely or constantly encountered: *omnipresent military checkpoints.* **2** (of God) present everywhere at the same time.
- DERIVATIVES **omnipresence** noun.

omniscient /om-niss-i-uhnt/ adjective knowing everything.
- DERIVATIVES **omniscience** noun **omnisciently** adverb.
- ORIGIN Latin *omnisciens*.

omnisexual adjective relating to or engaging in sexual activity with all kinds of people.

omnivore /om-ni-vor/ noun an animal that eats both plants and meat.

omnivorous /om-niv-uh-ruhss/ adjective **1** (of an animal) eating both plants and meat. **2** taking in or using whatever is available; not selective: *an omnivorous reader.*
- DERIVATIVES **omnivorously** adverb.

ON abbreviation Ontario.

on preposition **1** in contact with and supported by a surface. **2** on to. **3** in the possession of. **4** forming a noticeable part of the surface of: *a scratch on her arm.* **5** about; concerning. **6** as a member of a committee, jury, etc. **7** having the thing mentioned as a target, aim, or focus: *thousands marched on Washington.* **8** stored in or broadcast by. **9** in the course of a journey or while travelling in a vehicle. **10** indicating the day or time of an event. **11** engaged in. **12** regularly taking a drug or medicine. **13** paid for by. **14** added to. •adverb **1** in contact with and supported by a surface. **2** (of clothing) being worn. **3** further forward; with continued movement or action: *I drove on.* **4** (of an event) taking place or being presented. **5** (of an electrical appliance or power supply) functioning. **6** on duty or on stage. •noun (also **on side**) Cricket the leg side.
– PHRASES **be on about** Brit. informal talk about something at length. **be on at** Brit. informal nag someone. **be on to** informal **1** be close to discovering that someone has done something wrong. **2** have an idea that is likely to lead to an important discovery. **on and on** continually; without stopping. **on to** moving to a place on the surface of or aboard something.
– ORIGIN Old English.

onager /on-uh-ger/ noun a wild ass native to northern Iran.
– ORIGIN Greek *onagros* 'wild ass'.

onanism /oh-nuh-ni-z'm/ noun formal **1** masturbation. **2** sexual intercourse in which the penis is withdrawn before ejaculation.
– DERIVATIVES **onanist** noun **onanistic** adjective.
– ORIGIN from *Onan* in the Bible (Book of Genesis, chapter 38).

once adverb **1** on one occasion or for one time only. **2** on even one occasion: *he never once complained.* **3** in the past; formerly. **4** multiplied by one. •conjunction as soon as; when.
– PHRASES **all at once** suddenly. **at once 1** immediately. **2** at the same time; simultaneously. **for once** (or **this once**) on this occasion only. **once and for all** (or **once for all**) now and for the last time; finally. **once** (or **every once**) **in a while** occasionally. **once or twice** a few times. **once upon a time** at some time in the past.

once-over noun informal a rapid inspection, search, or piece of work.

oncogene /ong-koh-jeen/ noun a gene which in certain circumstances can transform a cell into a tumour cell.
– DERIVATIVES **oncogenic** /ong-koh-jen-ik/ adjective.
– ORIGIN from Greek *onkos* 'mass'.

oncology /ong-kol-uh-ji/ noun the study and treatment of tumours.
– DERIVATIVES **oncological** adjective **oncologist** noun.

oncoming adjective approaching from the front; moving towards one.

one cardinal number **1** the lowest cardinal number; 1. (Roman numeral: **i** or **I**.) **2** a single person or thing. **3** single; sole. **4** identical; the same. **5** (before a person's name) a certain. **6** informal, chiefly N. Amer. a noteworthy example of: *he was was one smart-mouthed troublemaker.*
•pronoun **1** used to refer to a person or thing previously mentioned or easily identified. **2** a person of a specified kind: *her loved ones.* **3** (third person sing.) used to refer to the speaker, or any person, as representing people in general.
– PHRASES **at one** in agreement or harmony. **be one up on** informal have an advantage over someone. **one and all** everyone. **one and only** unique; single. **one another** each other. **one by one** separately and following each other. **one day** at an unspecified time in the past or future. **one or two** informal a few.
– ORIGIN Old English.

USAGE: In modern English the use of **one** to mean 'anyone' or 'me and people in general' (*one must try one's best*) is chiefly restricted to formal situations and writing, and can be regarded as pompous or over-formal. In informal and spoken contexts the normal alternative is **you** (*you have to do what you can, don't you?*).

one-armed bandit noun informal a fruit machine operated by pulling a long handle at the side.

one-dimensional adjective not complex or deep; superficial.

one-horse race noun a contest in which one competitor is clearly better than all the others.

one-horse town noun informal a small town with few and poor facilities.

oneiric /oh-ny-rik/ adjective formal relating to dreams or dreaming.
– ORIGIN from Greek *oneiros* 'dream'.

one-liner noun informal a short joke or witty remark.

one-man band noun **1** a street entertainer who plays many instruments at the same time. **2** a person who runs a business alone.

oneness noun **1** the state of being unified, whole, or in harmony: *the oneness of man and nature.* **2** the state of being one in number.

one-night stand (also **one-nighter**) noun **1** informal a sexual relationship lasting only one night. **2** a single performance of a play or show in a particular place.

one-off Brit. informal adjective done, made, or happening only once. •noun **1** something done, made, or happening only once. **2** a remarkable person.

onerous /oh-nuh-ruhss/ adjective involving great effort and difficulty: *the onerous task of running a country.*
– ORIGIN Latin *onerosus.*

oneself pronoun (third person sing.) **1** (reflexive) used as the object of a verb or preposition when this is the same as the subject of the clause and the subject is 'one'. **2** (emphatic) used to emphasize that one does something individually or without help. **3** in one's normal state of body or mind.

one-shot adjective informal, chiefly N. Amer. achieved with a single attempt or action.

one-sided adjective **1** giving only one point of view; biased. **2** (of a contest or conflict) not involving participants of equal ability.

one-time adjective former.

one-to-one adjective & adverb referring to a situation in which two people come into direct contact or opposition. • noun informal a face-to-face meeting or conversation.

one-track mind noun informal a mind preoccupied with one subject, especially sex.

one-trick pony noun informal a person or thing with only one special feature or talent.

one-two noun 1 a pair of punches in quick succession with alternate hands. 2 chiefly Football a move in which a player plays a short pass to a teammate and moves forward to receive an immediate return pass.

one-upmanship noun informal the technique of gaining an advantage over someone else.

one-way adjective moving or allowing movement in one direction only.

ongoing adjective continuing; still in progress.

onion noun a vegetable consisting of a bulb with a strong taste and smell.
– PHRASES **know one's onions** informal be very knowledgeable.
– DERIVATIVES **oniony** adjective.
– ORIGIN Old French *oignon*.

online adjective & adverb 1 controlled by or connected to a computer. 2 available on or carried out via the Internet: *online banking*. 3 in or into operation.

onlooker noun a person who watches something without getting involved in it.
– DERIVATIVES **onlooking** adjective.

only adverb 1 and no one or nothing more besides. 2 no longer ago than. 3 not until. 4 with the negative result that: *he turned, only to find his way blocked*. • adjective 1 alone of its or their kind; single or solitary. 2 alone deserving consideration. • conjunction informal except that.
– PHRASES **only just 1** by a very small margin. 2 very recently. **only too** —— to an extreme or regrettable extent.
– ORIGIN Old English.

> USAGE: The traditional view is that, to avoid confusion, you should place the adverb **only** next to the word or words whose meaning it restricts: *I have seen him only once* rather than *I have only seen him once*. In practice, people tend to state **only** as early as possible in the sentence, generally just before the main verb, and the result is usually clear.

o.n.o. abbreviation Brit. or nearest offer.

onomastic /on-uh-**mas**-tik/ adjective relating to the study of the history and origin of proper names.
– DERIVATIVES **onomastics** noun.
– ORIGIN from Greek *onoma* 'name'.

onomatopoeia /on-uh-mat-uh-**pee**-uh/ noun the use or formation of words that sound similar to the noise described (e.g. *cuckoo*, *sizzle*).
– DERIVATIVES **onomatopoeic** adjective **onomatopoeically** adverb.
– ORIGIN Greek *onomatopoiia* 'word-making'.

onrush noun a surging rush forward.
– DERIVATIVES **onrushing** adjective.

onset noun the beginning of something, especially something unpleasant: *the technology is effective in detecting the onset of heart disease*.

onshore adjective & adverb 1 situated or occurring on land. 2 (of the wind) blowing from the sea towards the land.

onside adjective & adverb 1 (of a player in football, rugby, etc.) occupying a position where playing the ball is allowed. 2 informal in or into agreement.

onslaught noun 1 a fierce or destructive attack. 2 an overwhelmingly large quantity of people or things: *the onslaught of cars far exceeds capacity*.
– ORIGIN Dutch *aenslag*.

onstage adjective & adverb (in a theatre) on the stage and so visible to the audience.

onto preposition variant form of **on to** (see **ON**).

> USAGE: Although the spelling **onto** is widely used, it is still not fully accepted in standard British English and it is best to use **on to** in formal writing. In the US, the spelling **onto** is standard.

ontology /on-**tol**-uh-ji/ noun the branch of philosophy concerned with the nature of being.
– DERIVATIVES **ontological** adjective **ontologist** noun.

onus /**oh**-nuhss/ noun a duty or responsibility: *the onus is on you to spot mistakes*.
– ORIGIN Latin, 'load or burden'.

onward adverb (also **onwards**) 1 in a continuing forward direction; ahead. 2 so as to make progress. • adjective moving forward.

onyx /**on**-iks/ noun a semi-precious variety of agate with different colours in layers.
– ORIGIN Greek *onux* 'fingernail, onyx'.

oodles plural noun informal a very great number or amount.
– ORIGIN unknown.

oolite /**oh**-uh-lyt/ noun limestone consisting of rounded granules, each consisting of calcium carbonate surrounding a grain of sand.
– DERIVATIVES **oolitic** adjective.
– ORIGIN Latin *oolites* 'egg stone'.

oolong /**oo**-long/ noun a kind of dark-coloured partly fermented China tea.
– ORIGIN Chinese, 'black dragon'.

oompah noun informal the sound of deep-toned brass instruments in a band.
– ORIGIN imitating the sound.

oomph (also **umph**) noun informal the quality of being exciting, vigorous, or sexually attractive: *add oomph to your personal style*.
– ORIGIN uncertain.

oops exclamation informal used to show recognition of a mistake or minor accident.

ooze verb 1 (of a fluid) slowly trickle or seep out. 2 give a powerful impression of: *she oozes sex appeal*. • noun 1 wet mud or slime, especially that found at the bottom of a river, lake, or sea. 2 the sluggish flow of a fluid.
– DERIVATIVES **oozy** adjective.
– ORIGIN Old English, 'juice or sap'.

Op. (also **op.**) abbreviation Music (before a number given to each work of a composer) opus.

op noun informal 1 a surgical operation. 2 (**ops**) military operations.

opacity /oh-pa-si-ti/ **noun 1** the state of being opaque or difficult to see through. **2** the quality of being difficult to understand.

opal **noun** a semi-transparent gemstone in which many small points of shifting colour can be seen.
– ORIGIN Latin *opalus*.

opalescent **adjective** showing many small points of shifting colour: *opalescent eyes.*
– DERIVATIVES **opalescence** noun.

opaline /oh-puh-lyn, oh-puh-lin/ **adjective** showing many points of shifting colour; opalescent.

opaque /oh-**payk**/ **adjective** (**opaquer**, **opaquest**) **1** not able to be seen through; not transparent. **2** difficult or impossible to understand.
– DERIVATIVES **opaquely** adverb.
– ORIGIN Latin *opacus* 'darkened'.

op art **noun** a form of abstract art that gives the illusion of movement by its use of pattern and colour.
– ORIGIN abbreviation of *optical art*.

op. cit. **adverb** in the work already cited.
– ORIGIN from Latin *opere citato*.

OPEC /oh-pek/ **abbreviation** Organization of the Petroleum Exporting Countries.

open **adjective 1** not closed, fastened, or restricted. **2** exposed to view or attack; not covered or protected. **3** (**open to**) likely to suffer from or be affected by: *the system is open to abuse.* **4** spread out, expanded, or unfolded. **5** admitting customers or visitors; available for business. **6** accessible or available. **7** frank and communicative. **8** not disguised or hidden: *his eyes showed open admiration.* **9** not finally decided. **10** (**open to**) making possible: *a message open to different interpretations.* **11** (of a string of a musical instrument) allowed to vibrate along its whole length. **12** (of an electric circuit) having a break in the conducting path. • **verb 1** make or become open. **2** formally begin or establish: *he opened his own restaurant.* **3** make something available or more widely known. **4** (**open on to/into**) give access to. **5** (**open out/up**) become more frank or communicative. **6** break the conducting path of an electric circuit. • **noun 1** (**the open**) outdoors or in the countryside. **2** (**Open**) a competition with no restrictions on who may compete.
– PHRASES **the open air** an unenclosed space outdoors. **in open court** in a court of law, before the judge and the public. **in** (or **into**) **the open** not concealed or secret. **open-and-shut** not disputed; straightforward. **open up** (or **open fire**) begin shooting.
– DERIVATIVES **openable** adjective **openness** noun.
– ORIGIN Old English.

opencast **adjective** (of mining) in which coal or ore is extracted from a level near the earth's surface, rather than from shafts.

open day **noun** Brit. a day when members of the public may visit a place to which they do not usually have access.

open-ended **adjective** having no limit decided in advance.

opener **noun 1** a device for opening something. **2** a person or thing that opens or begins something, for example the first goal in a match.

– PHRASES **for openers** informal to start with.

open-handed **adjective 1** (of a blow) delivered with the palm of the hand. **2** giving freely; generous.

open-hearted **adjective** friendly and kind.

open-heart surgery **noun** surgery in which the heart is exposed and the blood made to bypass it.

open house **noun 1** a place or situation in which all visitors are welcome. **2** N. Amer. an open day.

opening **noun 1** a space or gap that allows access or passage. **2** a beginning. **3** a ceremony at which a building, show, etc. is declared to be open. **4** an opportunity or available job: *there are few openings for an ex-footballer.* • **adjective** coming at the beginning; initial.

open letter **noun** a letter addressed to a particular person but intended for publication in a newspaper or journal.

openly **adverb** in a frank, honest, or public way.

open market **noun** a situation in which people or companies can trade without restrictions.

open marriage **noun** a marriage in which both partners agree that each may have other sexual partners.

open-minded **adjective** willing to consider new ideas.

open-necked **adjective** (of a shirt) worn with the collar unbuttoned and without a tie.

open-plan **adjective** (of a room or building) having few or no dividing walls.

open prison **noun** Brit. a prison with the minimum of restrictions on prisoners' movements and activities.

open season **noun** the annual period when restrictions on the killing of certain types of wildlife are lifted.

open secret **noun** a supposed secret that is in fact known to many people.

open-source **adjective** referring to computer software for which the original source code is made freely available.

open-toed **adjective** (of a shoe) not covering the toes.

open-topped (also **open-top**) **adjective** (of a vehicle) having no roof, or having a folding or detachable roof.

open verdict **noun** Law a verdict of a coroner's jury which states that a suspicious death has occurred but the cause is not known.

openwork **noun** ornamental work in cloth, leather, etc. with regular patterns of openings and holes.

opera¹ **noun 1** a dramatic work set to music for singers and musicians. **2** a building in which operas are performed.
– ORIGIN Italian.

opera² plural of **OPUS**.

operable **adjective 1** able to be used. **2** able to be treated by a surgical operation.

opera buffa /op-uh-ruh boo-fuh/ **noun** (pl. **opere buffe** /op-uh-ray boo-fay/) a comic opera, especially in Italian.
– ORIGIN Italian.

opera glasses plural noun small binoculars for

use at the opera or theatre.

opera house noun a theatre designed for the performance of opera.

operand /op-uh-rand/ noun Mathematics the quantity on which an operation is to be done.
– ORIGIN Latin *operandum* 'thing to be operated on'.

opera seria /op-uh-ruh seer-i-uh/ noun (pl. **opere serie** /op-uh-ray seer-i-ay/) an opera, especially one of the 18th century in Italian, on a serious theme.
– ORIGIN Italian.

operate verb 1 (of a machine, process, or system) be in action; function. 2 control a machine, process, or business. 3 (of an organization) carry on its activities in a particular way or from a particular place: *they operate from a New York office.* 4 (of an armed force) carry on military activities in a particular place. 5 be in effect: *a powerful law operates in politics.* 6 perform a surgical operation.
– ORIGIN Latin *operari*.

operatic adjective 1 relating to opera. 2 melodramatic or exaggerated: *she wrung her hands in operatic despair.*
– DERIVATIVES **operatically** adverb.

operating profit noun a gross profit before expenses are deducted.

operating system noun the low-level software that supports a computer's basic functions.

operating table noun a table on which a patient is placed during a surgical operation.

operating theatre (N. Amer. **operating room**) noun a room in which surgical operations are performed.

operation noun 1 the action or process of operating: *we have a lot of security measures in operation.* 2 an act of surgery performed on a patient to remove or repair a damaged body part. 3 an organized action involving a number of people: *a rescue operation.* 4 a business organization. 5 Mathematics a process in which a number, quantity, expression, etc. is altered according to formal rules.

operational adjective 1 being used or ready for use. 2 relating to the functioning of an organization.
– DERIVATIVES **operationally** adverb.

operations room noun a room from which military or police operations are controlled.

operative adjective 1 functioning or having effect. 2 (of a word) having the most importance in a phrase. 3 relating to surgery. •noun 1 a worker. 2 chiefly N. Amer. a private detective or secret agent.
– DERIVATIVES **operatively** adverb.

operator noun 1 a person who operates equipment or a machine. 2 a person who works at the switchboard of a telephone exchange. 3 a person or company that runs a business. 4 informal a person who acts in a clever or manipulative way: *a smooth operator.* 5 a mathematical symbol or function referring to an operation (e.g. ×, +).

operculum /oh-**per**-kyuu-luhm/ noun (pl. **opercula** /oh-**per**-kyuu-luh/) Zoology 1 a flap of skin protecting a fish's gills. 2 a plate that

closes the opening of a mollusc's shell.
– ORIGIN Latin, 'lid, covering'.

operetta noun a short opera on a light or humorous theme.
– ORIGIN Italian, 'little opera'.

ophidian /oh-**fid**-i-uhn/ adjective literary resembling or typical of a snake: *a soft, ophidian hiss.*
– ORIGIN Greek *ophis* 'snake'.

ophthalmia /off-**thal**-mi-uh/ noun inflammation of the eye, especially conjunctivitis.
– ORIGIN from Greek *ophthalmos* 'eye'.

ophthalmic adjective relating to the eye and its diseases.

ophthalmic optician noun see OPTICIAN.

ophthalmology /off-thal-**mol**-uh-ji/ noun the study and treatment of disorders and diseases of the eye.
– DERIVATIVES **ophthalmological** adjective **ophthalmologist** noun.

ophthalmoscope /off-**thal**-muh-skohp/ noun an instrument for inspecting the retina and other parts of the eye.
– DERIVATIVES **ophthalmoscopic** adjective **ophthalmoscopy** noun.

opiate /oh-pi-uht/ noun 1 a drug containing or related to opium. 2 something that causes a false sense of contentment: *movies are the opiate of the people.* •adjective relating to or containing opium.
– DERIVATIVES **opiated** adjective.

opine verb formal state something as one's opinion.
– ORIGIN Latin *opinari* 'think, believe'.

opinion noun 1 a personal view not necessarily based on fact or knowledge. 2 the views of people in general: *public opinion.* 3 an estimate of quality or worth: *he had a high opinion of himself.* 4 a formal statement of advice by an expert or professional.
– PHRASES **a matter of opinion** something not capable of being proven either way.
– ORIGIN Latin.

opinionated adjective tending to state one's views forcefully and to be unwilling to change them.

opinion poll noun the questioning of a small sample of people in order to assess wider public opinion.

opioid /oh-pi-oyd/ noun a compound resembling opium. •adjective relating to opioids.

opium noun an addictive drug prepared from the juice of a poppy, used to alter mood or behaviour and in medicine as a painkiller.
– ORIGIN Greek *opion* 'poppy juice'.

opossum /uh-**poss**-uhm/ noun 1 an American marsupial mammal with a tail which it can use for grasping. 2 Austral./NZ a possum.
– ORIGIN Algonquian, 'white dog'.

oppo noun (pl. **oppos**) Brit. informal a colleague or friend.
– ORIGIN abbreviation of *opposite number.*

opponent noun 1 a person who opposes or competes with another in a contest, argument, or fight. 2 a person who disagrees with a proposal or practice.
– ORIGIN from Latin *opponere* 'set against'.

opportune /op-per-tyoon, op-per-**tyoon**/ adjective **1** (of a time) especially convenient or appropriate for something: *he chose an opportune moment to get away.* **2** done or occurring at an especially convenient or appropriate time.
– DERIVATIVES **opportunely** adverb.
– ORIGIN Latin *opportunus.*

opportunist noun a person who takes advantage of opportunities when they arise, regardless of whether or not they are right to do so. • adjective taking advantage of opportunities when they arise; opportunistic.
– DERIVATIVES **opportunism** noun.

opportunistic adjective **1** taking advantage of opportunities when they arise, especially in a selfish way. **2** (of an infection) occurring when the immune system is depressed.
– DERIVATIVES **opportunistically** adverb.

opportunity noun (pl. **opportunities**) **1** a favourable time or set of circumstances for doing something. **2** a career opening: *job opportunities.*

opposable adjective (of the thumb of a primate mammal) capable of facing and touching the other digits on the same hand.

oppose verb **1** (also **be opposed to**) disagree with and try to prevent or resist: *Ross was rabidly opposed to the plan.* **2** compete with or fight someone. **3** (as adj. **opposed**) (of two or more things) contrasting or conflicting. **4** (as adj. **opposing**) opposite.
– DERIVATIVES **opposer** noun.
– ORIGIN Latin *opponere* 'set against'

opposite adjective **1** situated on the other or further side; facing. **2** completely different. **3** being the other of a contrasted pair: *the opposite ends of the price range.* **4** (of angles) between opposite sides of the intersection of two lines. • noun a person or thing that is completely different from or the reverse of another. • adverb in an opposite position. • preposition in a position opposite to.
– DERIVATIVES **oppositely** adverb.
– ORIGIN Latin *oppositus.*

opposite number noun a person's counterpart in another organization.

opposite sex noun (**the opposite sex**) women in relation to men or vice versa.

opposition noun **1** resistance or disagreement: *there was considerable opposition to the plan.* **2** a group of opponents. **3** (**the Opposition**) Brit. the main party in parliament that is opposed to the one in office. **4** a contrast or complete opposite.
– DERIVATIVES **oppositional** adjective **oppositionist** adjective & noun.

oppress verb **1** treat or govern someone in a very harsh and unfair way. **2** make someone feel distressed or anxious.
– DERIVATIVES **oppression** noun **oppressor** noun.
– ORIGIN Old French *oppresser.*

oppressive adjective **1** harsh and demanding strict obedience: *an oppressive dictatorship.* **2** causing anxiety or distress. **3** (of weather) hot and close.
– DERIVATIVES **oppressively** adverb **oppressiveness** noun.

opprobrious /uh-**proh**-bri-uhss/ adjective formal expressing criticism or scorn.
– DERIVATIVES **opprobriously** adverb.

opprobrium /uh-**proh**-bri-uhm/ noun formal **1** criticism or scorn. **2** public disgrace arising from bad behaviour.
– ORIGIN Latin, 'infamy'.

oppugn /uh-**pyoon**/ verb formal question the truth or validity of something.
– ORIGIN Latin *oppugnare* 'attack, besiege'.

opt verb make a choice: *the couple opted for a traditional marriage.*
– PHRASES **opt out 1** choose not to participate in something. **2** Brit. (of a school or hospital) decide to withdraw from local authority control.
– ORIGIN Latin *optare* 'choose, wish'.

optic adjective relating to the eye or vision. • noun Brit. trademark a device fastened to the neck of an inverted bottle for measuring out spirits.
– ORIGIN Greek *optikos.*

optical adjective relating to vision, light, or optics.
– DERIVATIVES **optically** adverb.

optical character recognition noun the identification of printed characters using photoelectric devices and computer software.

optical fibre noun a thin glass fibre through which light can be transmitted.

optical illusion noun a thing that deceives the eye by appearing to be something that it is not.

optician noun Brit. a person qualified to prescribe and dispense glasses and contact lenses, and to detect eye diseases (**ophthalmic optician**), or to make and supply glasses and contact lenses (**dispensing optician**).

optic nerves plural noun the pair of nerves transmitting impulses from the eyes to the brain.

optics plural noun (usu. treated as sing.) the branch of science concerned with vision and the behaviour of light.

optimal adjective best or most favourable.
– DERIVATIVES **optimality** noun **optimally** adverb.

optimism noun **1** hopefulness and confidence about the future or success of something. **2** Philosophy the belief that this world is the best of all possible worlds.
– DERIVATIVES **optimist** noun.
– ORIGIN French *optimisme.*

optimistic adjective hopeful and confident about the future.
– DERIVATIVES **optimistically** adverb.

optimize (or **optimise**) verb make the best use of a situation or resource.
– DERIVATIVES **optimization** noun **optimizer** noun.

optimum adjective most likely to lead to a favourable outcome: *the units combine high quality with optimum performance.* • noun (pl. **optima** or **optimums**) the most favourable conditions for growth or success.
– ORIGIN from Latin, 'best thing'.

option noun **1** a thing that is or may be chosen. **2** the freedom or right to choose: *she was given the option of resigning or being dismissed.* **3** a right to buy or sell something at a specified price within a set time.
– PHRASES **keep** (or **leave**) **one's options open** not commit oneself.

optional adjective available to be chosen but not compulsory.
– DERIVATIVES **optionality** noun **optionally** adverb.

optometrist noun chiefly N. Amer. an ophthalmic optician.

optometry noun the occupation of measuring eyesight, prescribing corrective lenses, and detecting eye disease.

opulent /op-yuu-luhnt/ adjective expensive and luxurious: *opulent furnishings.*
– DERIVATIVES **opulence** noun **opulently** adverb.
– ORIGIN Latin *opulens* 'wealthy, splendid'.

opus /oh-puhss, op-uhss/ noun (pl. **opuses** or **opera** /op-uh-ruh/) **1** a musical composition or set of compositions. **2** an artistic work.
– ORIGIN Latin, 'work'.

OR abbreviation Oregon.

or¹ conjunction **1** used to link alternatives. **2** introducing a word that means the same as a preceding word or phrase, or that explains it. **3** otherwise.
– ORIGIN Old English.

or² noun gold or yellow, as a conventional heraldic colour.
– ORIGIN French.

-or suffix **1** forming nouns referring to a person or thing performing the action of a verb: *escalator.* **2** forming nouns referring to a state: *terror.*
– ORIGIN Latin.

orache /o-ruhch/ (also **orach**) noun a plant with red, yellow, or green leaves sometimes eaten as a vegetable.
– ORIGIN Old French *arasche.*

oracle noun **1** (in ancient Greece or Rome) a priest or priestess who acted as a channel for advice or prophecy from the gods. **2** an authority which is always correct.
– ORIGIN Latin *oraculum.*

oracular /o-rak-yuu-ler/ adjective **1** relating to an oracle. **2** hard to interpret. **3** having the authority of an oracle.

oracy /o-ruh-si/ noun Brit. the ability to express oneself fluently and grammatically in speech.
– ORIGIN from Latin *os* 'mouth'.

oral adjective **1** spoken rather than written. **2** relating to the mouth. **3** done or taken by the mouth. •noun a spoken exam or test.
– DERIVATIVES **orally** adverb.
– ORIGIN Latin *oralis.*

USAGE: On the confusion of **oral** and **aural**, see the note at AURAL.

oral history noun the collection and study of historical information from people's personal memories.

oralism noun the teaching of deaf people to communicate by the use of speech and lip-reading rather than sign language.
– DERIVATIVES **oralist** adjective & noun.

orality noun the quality of being communicated by speech rather than by writing.

orange noun **1** a large round citrus fruit with a tough reddish-yellow rind. **2** a drink made from or flavoured with orange juice. **3** a bright reddish-yellow colour. •adjective reddish yellow.
– DERIVATIVES **orangey** (also **orangy**) adjective.

– ORIGIN Old French *orenge.*

orangeade noun Brit. a fizzy soft drink flavoured with orange.

Orangeman noun (pl. **Orangemen**) a member of the Orange Order.

Orange Order noun a Protestant political society in Northern Ireland.
– ORIGIN named after the Protestant king William of *Orange* (William III of Great Britain and Ireland).

orange pekoe /pee-koh/ noun a type of black tea made from young leaves.
– ORIGIN *pekoe* from a Chinese dialect word meaning 'white down'.

orangery noun (pl. **orangeries**) a type of large conservatory where orange trees are grown.

orange stick noun a thin pointed stick for manicuring the fingernails.

orang-utan /uh-rang-oo-tan/ (also **orang-utang** /uh-rang-oo-tang/) noun a large ape with long red hair, native to forests in Borneo and Sumatra.
– ORIGIN Malay, 'forest person'.

orate verb make a speech, especially a long or pompous one.

oration noun a formal speech made on a public occasion.
– ORIGIN from Latin *orare* 'speak, pray'.

orator noun a skilful public speaker.
– DERIVATIVES **oratorial** adjective.

oratorio /o-ruh-tor-i-oh/ noun (pl. **oratorios**) a large-scale musical work on a religious theme for orchestra and voices.
– ORIGIN Italian.

oratory¹ /o-ruh-tri/ noun (pl. **oratories**) a small chapel for private worship.

oratory² /o-ruh-tri/ noun powerful and persuasive public speaking.
– DERIVATIVES **oratorical** /o-ruh-to-ri-k'l/ adjective.

orb noun **1** a spherical object or shape. **2** a golden globe with a cross on top, carried by a monarch on ceremonial occasions.
– ORIGIN Latin *orbis* 'ring'.

orbit noun **1** the regularly repeated elliptical course of a planet, moon, spacecraft, etc. around a star or planet. **2** an area of activity or influence: *they brought many friends within the orbit of our lives.* **3** the path of an electron round an atomic nucleus. **4** Anatomy the eye socket. •verb (**orbits, orbiting, orbited**) move in orbit round a star or planet.
– DERIVATIVES **orbiter** noun.
– ORIGIN Latin *orbita* 'course, track'.

orbital adjective **1** relating to an orbit or orbits. **2** Brit. (of a road) passing round the outside of a town.
– DERIVATIVES **orbitally** adverb.

orbital sander noun a sander in which the sanding surface has a minute circular motion without rotating relative to the object being worked on.

orca /or-kuh/ noun a killer whale.
– ORIGIN French *orque* or Latin *orca.*

Orcadian /or-kay-di-uhn/ adjective relating to the Orkney Islands. •noun a person from the Orkney Islands.
– ORIGIN Latin *Orcades* 'Orkney Islands'.

orchard noun a piece of enclosed land planted

with fruit trees.
– ORIGIN Old English.

orchestra noun 1 (treated as sing. or pl.) a large group of musicians with string, woodwind, brass, and percussion sections. 2 (also **orchestra pit**) the part of a theatre where the orchestra plays, typically in front of the stage and on a lower level. 3 N. Amer. the stalls in a theatre. 4 the semicircular space in front of an ancient Greek theatre stage where the chorus danced and sang.
– DERIVATIVES **orchestral** adjective **orchestrally** adverb.
– ORIGIN Greek *orkhēstra*, from *orkheisthai* 'to dance'.

orchestrate verb 1 adapt a musical composition so that it can be performed by an orchestra. 2 organize a complicated event or situation carefully or secretly: *a nationwide campaign orchestrated by conservationists.*
– DERIVATIVES **orchestration** noun **orchestrator** noun.

orchid noun a plant of a large family with complex showy flowers.
– DERIVATIVES **orchidaceous** adjective.
– ORIGIN Greek *orkhis* 'testicle' (because of the shape of the tuber).

ordain verb 1 make someone a priest or minister. 2 order something officially: *the king ordained that the courts should be revived.* 3 (of God or fate) decide something in advance.
– ORIGIN Latin *ordinare.*

ordeal noun 1 a prolonged painful or unpleasant experience. 2 an ancient test of guilt or innocence in which the accused person was subjected to severe pain, survival of which was taken as divine proof of their innocence.
– ORIGIN Old English.

order noun 1 the arrangement of people or things according to a particular sequence or method: *I filed the cards in alphabetical order.* 2 a state in which everything is in its right place. 3 a state in which the laws and rules regulating public behaviour are followed: *a breakdown of law and order.* 4 an instruction which must be obeyed; a command. 5 a request for something to be made, supplied, or served. 6 the set procedure followed in a meeting, law court, or religious service. 7 quality or nature: *poetry of the highest order.* 8 a social class or system. 9 a rank in the Christian ministry. 10 (**orders** or **holy orders**) the rank of an ordained minister of the Church. 11 a society of monks, nuns, or friars living under the same rule. 12 an institution founded by a king or queen to honour good conduct: *the Order of the Garter.* 13 Biology a main category into which animals and plants are divided that ranks below class and above family. 14 any of the five classical styles of architecture (Doric, Ionic, Corinthian, Tuscan, and Composite). • verb 1 give a command: *she ordered me to leave.* 2 request that something be made, supplied, or served: *I ordered a fillet steak.* 3 arrange something methodically.
– PHRASES **in order 1** in the right condition for operation or use. **2** appropriate in the circumstances. **in order for** (or **that**) so that. **in order to** with the purpose of doing. **of** (or **in or on**) **the order of** approximately. **on order** (of goods) requested but not yet received. **the order of the day 1** the current situation. **2** the day's business to be considered in a meeting or parliament. **out of order 1** not working properly or at all. **2** Brit. informal unacceptable or wrong.
– ORIGIN Latin *ordo* 'row, series'.

orderly adjective 1 neatly and methodically arranged. 2 well behaved. • noun (pl. **orderlies**) 1 a hospital worker responsible for cleaning and other non-medical tasks. 2 a soldier who carries orders or performs minor tasks for an officer.
– DERIVATIVES **orderliness** noun.

order of magnitude noun 1 a level in a system of classifying things by size, typically where each level is higher by a factor of ten. 2 size or quantity.

Order Paper noun Brit. a paper on which the day's parliamentary business is entered.

ordinal adjective relating to order in a series.
– ORIGIN Latin *ordinalis.*

ordinal number noun a number defining a thing's position in a series, such as 'first' or 'second'.

ordinance noun formal 1 an official order. 2 a religious rite.
– ORIGIN Old French *ordenance.*

ordinand /or-di-nand/ noun a person who is training to be ordained as a priest or minister.
– ORIGIN Latin *ordinandus.*

ordinary adjective 1 having no distinctive features; normal or usual. 2 not interesting or exceptional: *a very ordinary piece of work.* • noun (pl. **ordinaries**) 1 (**Ordinary**) those parts of a Roman Catholic service, especially the Mass, which do not vary from day to day. 2 a rule or book laying down the order of divine service. 3 Heraldry any of the simplest main emblems or devices used in coats of arms.
– PHRASES **out of the ordinary** unusual.
– DERIVATIVES **ordinarily** adverb **ordinariness** noun.
– ORIGIN Latin *ordinarius* 'orderly'.

ordinary grade noun (in Scotland) the lower of the two main levels of the Scottish Certificate of Education exam. Compare with HIGHER.

ordinary level noun full form of O LEVEL.

ordinary seaman noun the lowest rank of sailor in the Royal Navy, below able seaman.

ordinary share noun Brit. a share which entitles the holder to dividends that are in proportion to the company's profits. Compare with PREFERENCE SHARE.

ordinate /or-di-nuht/ noun Mathematics a straight line from a point on a graph drawn parallel to the vertical axis and meeting the other; the *y*-coordinate.
– ORIGIN from Latin *linea ordinata applicata* 'line applied parallel'.

ordination noun the action of ordaining someone as a priest or minister.

ordnance /ord-nuhnss/ noun 1 large guns mounted on wheels. 2 US military equipment and stores. 3 a government department dealing with military supplies.
– ORIGIN variant of ORDINANCE.

Ordnance Survey noun (in the UK) an official survey organization preparing large-scale detailed maps of the whole country.
– ORIGIN first prepared by the government department dealing with military supplies.

Ordovician /or-duh-vish-i-uhn/ adjective Geology relating to the second period of the Palaeozoic era (about 510 to 439 million years ago), when the first vertebrates appeared.
– ORIGIN from *Ordovices*, the Latin name of an ancient British tribe in North Wales.

ordure /or-dyuur/ noun excrement or dung.
– ORIGIN Old French.

ore noun a naturally occurring material from which a metal or valuable mineral can be extracted.
– ORIGIN Old English, 'unwrought metal'.

øre /er-uh/ noun (pl. same) a monetary unit of Denmark and Norway, equal to one hundredth of a krone.
– ORIGIN Danish and Norwegian.

öre /er-uh/ noun (pl. same) a monetary unit of Sweden, equal to one hundredth of a krona.
– ORIGIN Swedish.

oregano /o-ri-gah-noh/ noun a sweet-smelling plant whose leaves are used as a herb in cookery.
– ORIGIN Spanish.

orfe /orf/ noun a silvery freshwater fish of the carp family.
– ORIGIN German.

organ noun 1 a part of an animal or plant that is adapted for a particular function, for example the heart or kidneys. 2 a large musical keyboard instrument with rows of pipes supplied with air from bellows. 3 a smaller keyboard instrument producing similar sounds electronically. 4 a newspaper or journal which puts forward the views of a political party or movement.
– DERIVATIVES organist noun.
– ORIGIN Greek *organon* 'tool, sense organ'.

organdie /or-guhn-di/ (US also organdy) noun a fine, translucent, stiff cotton muslin.
– ORIGIN French *organdi*.

organelle /or-guh-nel/ noun Biology a specialized structure within a cell.
– ORIGIN Latin *organella* 'little tool'.

organ-grinder noun a street musician who plays a barrel organ.

organic adjective 1 relating to or obtained from living matter. 2 not involving or produced with artificial chemicals such as fertilizers: *organic farming*. 3 (of a chemical compound) containing carbon and chiefly or ultimately of biological origin. 4 relating to or affecting an organ or organs of the body. 5 (of the parts of a whole) fitting together in a harmonious way. 6 (of development or change) continuous or natural. • noun (usu. **organics**) 1 a food produced by organic farming. 2 an organic compound.
– DERIVATIVES organically adverb.

organism noun 1 an individual animal, plant, or other life form. 2 a whole made up of interdependent parts.

organization (or **organisation**) noun 1 an organized group of people with a particular purpose, e.g. a business. 2 the action of organizing something. 3 a systematic arrangement or approach.
– DERIVATIVES organizational adjective organizationally adverb.

organize (or **organise**) verb 1 arrange something in a systematic way: *the book is organized into nine thematic chapters.* 2 make arrangements or preparations for an event or activity: *social programmes are organized by the school.* 3 form people into a trade union or other political group.
– DERIVATIVES organizer noun.
– ORIGIN Latin *organizare*.

organophosphate /or-guh-noh-foss-fayt/ noun any of a group of organic compounds whose molecules contain phosphates, especially a pesticide of this kind.

organza /or-gan-zuh/ noun a thin, stiff transparent fabric made of silk or a synthetic yarn.
– ORIGIN uncertain.

orgasm noun the climax of sexual excitement, when feelings of sexual pleasure are most intense. • verb have an orgasm.
– DERIVATIVES orgasmic adjective.
– ORIGIN Greek *orgasmos*.

orgiastic adjective relating to or like an orgy.

orgy noun (pl. **orgies**) 1 a wild party involving a great deal of drinking and indiscriminate sexual activity. 2 an instance of engaging in a particular activity to an extreme or excessive degree: *an orgy of spending.*
– ORIGIN Greek *orgia* 'secret rites or revels'.

oriel /or-ri-uhl/ noun a large upper-storey bay with a window (an **oriel window**), supported by brackets or projections from the wall.
– ORIGIN Old French *oriol* 'gallery'.

orient noun /or-i-uhnt/ (**the Orient**) literary the countries of the East, especially east Asia.
• adjective /or-i-uhnt/ literary oriental. • verb /or-i-ent/ 1 align or position something in relation to the points of a compass or other specified positions. 2 (**orient oneself**) find one's position in relation to unfamiliar surroundings. 3 tailor or adapt something to particular needs or circumstances: *magazines oriented to the business community.*
– ORIGIN from Latin *oriens* 'rising or east'.

oriental adjective relating to or from the Far East. • noun often offensive a person of Far Eastern descent.
– DERIVATIVES orientalism noun orientalist noun orientally adverb.

USAGE: The term **oriental** is now regarded as old-fashioned and potentially offensive as a term referring to people from the Far East. In US English, **Asian** is the standard accepted term in modern use; in British English, where **Asian** tends to refer to people from the Indian subcontinent, specific terms such as **Chinese** or **Japanese** are more likely to be used.

orientate verb another term for ORIENT.

orientation noun 1 the action of orienting someone or something. 2 the relative position or direction of something. 3 a person's basic attitude, beliefs, or feelings about something: *a bill outlawing job discrimination on the basis of sexual orientation.*
– DERIVATIVES orientational adjective.

orienteering noun a competitive sport in

which runners have to find their way across rough country with the aid of a map and compass.
– DERIVATIVES **orienteer** noun & verb.

orifice /o-ri-fiss/ noun an opening, particularly one in the body such as a nostril.
– ORIGIN French.

origami /o-ri-gah-mi/ noun the Japanese art of folding paper into decorative shapes and figures.
– ORIGIN Japanese.

origin noun **1** the point or place where something begins: *the origin of the universe.* **2** a person's social background or ancestry: *his Italian origins.* **3** Mathematics a fixed point from which coordinates are measured.
– ORIGIN Latin *origo*, from *oriri* 'to rise'.

original adjective **1** existing from the beginning; first or earliest: *a Tudor fireplace with original oak beams.* **2** produced by an artist, author, etc.; not a copy. **3** new and different from what has been done before; inventive: *an unusual and original idea.* •noun the earliest form of something, from which copies can be made.
– DERIVATIVES **originally** adverb.

originality noun **1** the ability to think independently or creatively. **2** the quality of being new or inventive.

original sin noun (in Christian theology) the tendency to be sinful that is thought to be present in all human beings as a consequence of Adam and Eve's disobedience.

originate verb **1** begin in a particular place or situation: *the word originated as a marketing term.* **2** create or initiate something.
– DERIVATIVES **origination** noun **originator** noun.

oriole /or-i-ohl/ noun a brightly coloured bird with a musical call.
– ORIGIN Latin *oriolus*.

orison /o-ri-zuhn/ noun literary a prayer.
– ORIGIN Old French *oreison*.

ormolu /or-muh-loo/ noun a gold-coloured alloy of copper, zinc, and tin used in decoration.
– ORIGIN from French *or moulu* 'powdered gold'.

ornament noun **1** an object designed to make something look more attractive but usually having no practical purpose. **2** decorative items as a whole. **3** (**ornaments**) Music embellishments made to a melody. •verb make something more attractive by adding decorative items: *large rooms ornamented with marble and gilt columns.*
– DERIVATIVES **ornamentation** noun.
– ORIGIN Latin *ornamentum*.

ornamental adjective acting or intended as an ornament; decorative. •noun a plant grown for its attractive appearance.
– DERIVATIVES **ornamentally** adverb.

ornate adjective elaborately or highly decorated.
– DERIVATIVES **ornately** adverb **ornateness** noun.
– ORIGIN from Latin *ornare* 'adorn'.

ornery /or-nuh-ri/ adjective N. Amer. informal bad-tempered.
– ORIGIN representing a dialect pronunciation of ORDINARY.

ornithology /or-ni-thol-uh-ji/ noun the scientific study of birds.
– DERIVATIVES **ornithological** adjective **ornithologist** noun.
– ORIGIN from Greek *ornis* 'bird'.

ornithopter noun chiefly historical a flying machine with flapping wings.
– ORIGIN French *ornithoptère.*

orotund /o-roh-tund/ adjective **1** (of a person's voice) resonant and impressive. **2** (of writing or style) pompous.
– ORIGIN from Latin *ore rotundo* 'with rounded mouth'.

orphan noun a child whose parents are dead. •verb (**be orphaned**) (of a child) be made an orphan.
– ORIGIN from Greek *orphanos* 'bereaved'.

orphanage noun a residential institution where orphans are cared for.

orpiment /or-pi-muhnt/ noun a bright yellow mineral formerly used as a dye and artist's pigment.
– ORIGIN Latin *auripigmentum.*

orrery /o-ruh-ri/ noun (pl. **orreries**) a clockwork model of the solar system.
– ORIGIN named after the fourth Earl of *Orrery,* for whom one was made.

orris (also **orris root**) noun a preparation made from the fragrant root of a kind of iris, used in perfumery.
– ORIGIN alteration of IRIS.

ortho- combining form **1** straight; rectangular; upright: *orthodontics.* **2** correct: *orthography.*
– ORIGIN from Greek *orthos* 'straight, right'.

orthodontics /or-thuh-don-tiks/ plural noun (treated as sing.) the treatment of irregularities in the teeth and jaws.
– DERIVATIVES **orthodontic** adjective **orthodontist** noun.
– ORIGIN from Greek *odous* 'tooth'.

orthodox adjective **1** following traditional or generally accepted beliefs: *orthodox medical treatment.* **2** conventional or normal. **3** (**Orthodox**) relating to Orthodox Judaism or the Orthodox Church.
– ORIGIN Greek *orthodoxos.*

Orthodox Church noun any of the ancient branches of the Christian Church which originated in eastern Europe and the Middle East and which do not accept the authority of the Pope of Rome.

Orthodox Judaism noun a branch of Judaism which teaches that the requirements of Jewish law and traditional custom regarding religious and everyday life must be strictly followed.

orthodoxy noun (pl. **orthodoxies**) **1** traditional or generally accepted theories, beliefs, or practices. **2** the state of being orthodox. **3** the whole community of Orthodox Jews or Orthodox Christians.

orthography /or-thog-ruh-fi/ noun (pl. **orthographies**) the conventional spelling system of a language.
– DERIVATIVES **orthographic** adjective.

orthopaedics /or-thuh-pee-diks/ (US **orthopedics**) plural noun (treated as sing.) the branch of medicine concerned with the correction of deformities caused by disease of or damage to bones or joints.

- DERIVATIVES **orthopaedic** adjective.
- ORIGIN from Greek *paideia* 'rearing of children'.

orthotics /or-thot-iks/ plural noun (treated as sing.) the branch of medicine concerned with the design and fitting of surgical appliances such as braces or splints.
- DERIVATIVES **orthotic** adjective & noun.

ortolan /or-tuh-luhn/ noun a small songbird formerly eaten as a delicacy.
- ORIGIN Provençal, 'gardener' (because the bird frequents gardens).

Orwellian adjective relating to the work of the British novelist George Orwell, especially the totalitarian state depicted in *Nineteen Eighty-Four*.

oryx /o-riks/ noun a large antelope with long horns, found in arid regions of Africa and Arabia.
- ORIGIN Greek *orux* 'stonemason's pickaxe' (because of its pointed horns).

OS abbreviation **1** Computing operating system. **2** Ordinary Seaman. **3** (in the UK) Ordnance Survey. **4** (as a size of clothing) outsize.

Os symbol the chemical element osmium.

Oscar noun (trademark in the US) the nickname for a gold statuette given as an Academy award.
- ORIGIN one explanation claims that the statuette reminded an executive director of the Academy of Motion Picture Arts and Sciences of her uncle Oscar.

oscillate /oss-i-layt/ verb **1** move or swing back and forth in a regular rhythm. **2** waver between extremes of opinion or emotion: *he was oscillating between fear and bravery.*
- DERIVATIVES **oscillation** noun **oscillator** noun **oscillatory** /o-sil-luh-tri, oss-i-lay-tuh-ri/ adjective.
- ORIGIN Latin *oscillare* 'to swing'.

oscilloscope /o-sil-luh-skohp/ noun a device for showing changes in electrical current as a display on the screen of a cathode ray tube.

osculation /oss-kyuu-lay-sh'n/ noun humorous kissing.
- ORIGIN from Latin *osculari* 'to kiss'.

osier /oh-zi-er/ noun a small willow tree with long flexible shoots used in making baskets.
- ORIGIN Old French.

osmium /oz-mi-uhm/ noun a hard, dense silvery-white metallic element.
- ORIGIN from Greek *osmē* 'smell' (from the strong smell of one of its oxides).

osmoregulation noun Biology the control of water content and salt concentration in the body of an organism.

osmosis /oz-moh-siss/ noun **1** a process by which molecules of a solvent pass through a semipermeable membrane from a less concentrated solution into a more concentrated one. **2** the gradual absorbing of ideas or information.
- DERIVATIVES **osmotic** adjective.
- ORIGIN Greek *ōsmos* 'a push'.

osprey noun (pl. **ospreys**) a large fish-eating bird of prey with a brown back and white underside.
- ORIGIN apparently from Latin *ossifraga*, from *os* 'bone' + *frangere* 'to break'.

osseous /oss-i-uhss/ adjective chiefly Zoology &

Medicine consisting of or turned into bone.
- ORIGIN Latin *osseus* 'bony'.

ossicle noun a very small bone, especially one of those which transmit sounds within the middle ear.
- ORIGIN Latin *ossiculum* 'little bone'.

ossify /oss-i-fy/ verb (**ossifies, ossifying, ossified**) **1** turn into bone or bony tissue. **2** (usu. as adj. **ossified**) stop developing: *ossified political institutions.*
- DERIVATIVES **ossification** noun.
- ORIGIN from Latin *os* 'bone'.

ossuary /oss-yuu-ri/ noun (pl. **ossuaries**) a container or room for the bones of dead people.
- ORIGIN from Latin *os* 'bone'.

ostensible adjective apparently true, but not necessarily so.
- DERIVATIVES **ostensibly** adverb.
- ORIGIN Latin *ostensibilis*.

ostentation noun a showy display of wealth, knowledge, etc. which is intended to impress other people.
- ORIGIN from Latin *ostendere* 'stretch out to view'.

ostentatious adjective expensive or showy in a way that is intended to impress other people: *ostentatious gold jewellery.*
- DERIVATIVES **ostentatiously** adverb.

osteo- combining form relating to the bones: *osteoporosis.*
- ORIGIN from Greek *osteon* 'bone'.

osteoarthritis /oss-ti-oh-ar-thry-tiss/ noun a condition in which cartilage in the joints deteriorates, causing pain and stiffness.

osteology /oss-ti-ol-uh-ji/ noun the study of the skeleton and bone.
- DERIVATIVES **osteological** adjective **osteologist** noun.

osteomyelitis /oss-ti-oh-my-i-ly-tiss/ noun inflammation of bone or bone marrow.

osteopathy /oss-ti-op-uh-thi/ noun a system of complementary medicine involving the manipulation of the bones and muscles.
- DERIVATIVES **osteopath** noun **osteopathic** adjective.

osteoporosis /oss-ti-oh-puh-roh-siss/ noun a medical condition in which the bones become brittle and fragile, typically as a result of hormonal changes, or lack of calcium or vitamin D.
- ORIGIN from Greek *poros* 'passage, pore'.

osteospermum /oss-ti-oh-sper-muhm/ noun a plant or shrub of the daisy family, native to Africa and the Middle East.

ostinato /oss-ti-nah-toh/ noun (pl. **ostinatos** or **ostinati** /oss-ti-nah-ti/) a continually repeated musical phrase or rhythm.
- ORIGIN from Italian, 'obstinate'.

ostler /oss-ler/ (also **hostler**) noun historical a man employed at an inn to look after customers' horses.
- ORIGIN Old French *hostelier* 'innkeeper'.

ostracize (or **ostracise**) /oss-truh-syz/ verb exclude someone from a society or group; refuse to meet or speak to someone.
- DERIVATIVES **ostracism** noun.
- ORIGIN Greek *ostrakizein*, from *ostrakon* 'shell or piece of broken pottery' (on which names

were written in voting to banish unpopular citizens).

ostrich noun 1 a large flightless swift-running African bird with a long neck and long legs. 2 a person who refuses to accept unpleasant truths. [from the popular belief that ostriches bury their heads in the sand if pursued.]
– ORIGIN Old French *ostriche*.

Ostrogoth /oss-truh-goth/ noun a member of the eastern branch of the Goths, who conquered Italy in the 5th-6th centuries AD.
– ORIGIN Latin *Ostrogothi* 'East Goths'.

OT abbreviation 1 occupational therapist; occupational therapy. 2 Old Testament.

OTC abbreviation 1 (in the UK) Officers' Training Corps. 2 over the counter.

other adjective & pronoun 1 used to refer to a person or thing that is different from one already mentioned or known: *other people found her difficult.* 2 additional: *one other word of advice.* 3 alternative of two: *the other side of the page.* 4 those not already mentioned.
– PHRASES **the other day** (or **night**, **week**, etc.) a few days (or nights, weeks, etc.) ago.
– ORIGIN Old English.

other half noun Brit. informal one's wife, husband, or partner.

otherness noun the quality or fact of being different.

other place noun Brit. humorous 1 hell, as opposed to heaven. 2 the House of Lords as regarded by the House of Commons, and vice versa.

other ranks plural noun Brit. (in the armed forces) all those who are not commissioned officers.

otherwise adverb 1 in different circumstances; or else. 2 in other respects. 3 in a different way. 4 alternatively. • adjective in a different state or situation.

other woman noun the mistress of a married man.

other-worldly adjective 1 relating to an imaginary or spiritual world. 2 not aware of the realities of life; unworldly.

otiose /oh-ti-ohss/ adjective serving no practical purpose; pointless.
– ORIGIN Latin *otiosus*.

otitis /oh-ty-tiss/ noun inflammation of part of the ear, especially the middle ear (**otitis media**).
– ORIGIN from Greek *ous* 'ear'.

OTT abbreviation Brit. informal over the top.

otter noun a fish-eating mammal with a long body, dense fur, and webbed feet, living partly in water and partly on land.
– ORIGIN Old English.

Ottoman adjective historical 1 relating to the Turkish dynasty of Osman I (Othman I), founded in about 1300. 2 relating to the Ottoman Empire, the Turkish empire ruled by the successors of Osman I. 3 Turkish. • noun (pl. **Ottomans**) a Turk, especially of the Ottoman period.
– ORIGIN Arabic.

ottoman noun (pl. **ottomans**) a low upholstered seat without a back or arms which can also be used as a box or chest, the seat being hinged to form a lid.

OU abbreviation (in the UK) Open University.

oubliette /oo-bli-et/ noun a secret dungeon which can only be accessed through a trapdoor in its ceiling.
– ORIGIN French, from *oublier* 'forget'.

ouch exclamation used to express pain.

ought modal verb (3rd sing. present and past **ought**) 1 used to indicate duty or correctness. 2 used to indicate something that is probable. 3 used to indicate a desirable or expected state. 4 used to give or ask advice.
– ORIGIN Old English.

> USAGE: The correct way of forming negative sentences with **ought** is *he ought not to have gone.* The sentences *he didn't ought to have gone* and *he hadn't ought to have gone* are found in dialect but are not acceptable in standard modern English.

oughtn't contraction ought not.

Ouija board /wee-juh/ noun trademark a board with letters, numbers, and other signs around its edge, to which a pointer moves, supposedly in answer to questions at a seance.
– ORIGIN from French *oui* 'yes' + German *ja* 'yes'.

ounce noun 1 a unit of weight of one sixteenth of a pound avoirdupois (approximately 28 grams). 2 a unit of one twelfth of a pound troy, equal to 480 grains (approximately 31 grams). 3 a very small amount: *a girl without an ounce of ambition.*
– ORIGIN Latin *uncia* 'twelfth part'.

our possessive determiner 1 belonging to or connected with the speaker and one or more other people. 2 belonging to or associated with people in general. 3 used in formal contexts by a royal person to refer to something belonging to himself or herself.
– ORIGIN Old English.

Our Father noun 1 God. 2 the Lord's Prayer.

Our Lady noun the Virgin Mary.

Our Lord noun God or Jesus.

ours possessive pronoun used to refer to something belonging to or connected with the speaker and one or more other people.

> USAGE: There is no apostrophe: the spelling should be **ours** not *our's.*

ourself pronoun (first person pl.) used instead of 'ourselves', typically when 'we' refers to people in general.

> USAGE: The standard reflexive pronoun (a word such as 'myself' or 'himself') corresponding to **we** and **us** is **ourselves**, as in *we enjoyed ourselves.* The singular form **ourself** is sometimes used, but it is not widely accepted in standard English.

ourselves pronoun (first person pl.) 1 used as the object of a verb or preposition when this is the same as the subject of the clause and the subject is the speaker and one or more other people considered together. 2 (emphatic) we or us personally.

ousel noun variant spelling of OUZEL.

oust /owsst/ verb force out of a job or position of power: *three directors have been ousted from the board.*

– ORIGIN Old French *ouster* 'take away'.

out adverb **1** moving away from a place, especially from one that is enclosed to one that is open. **2** away from one's home or place of work. **3** outdoors. **4** so as to be revealed, heard, or known. **5** at or to an end: *the romance fizzled out.* **6** at a specified distance away from the target. **7** to sea, away from the land. **8** (of the tide) falling or at its lowest level. **9** no longer in prison. **10** (of a light or fire) so as to be extinguished or no longer burning. •**preposition** non-standard contraction of **out of**. •**adjective 1** not at home or one's place of work. **2** made public or available. **3** open about one's homosexuality. **4** not possible or worth considering. **5** no longer existing or current. **6** unconscious. **7** mistaken. **8** (of the ball in tennis, squash, etc.) outside the playing area. **9** Cricket & Baseball no longer batting. •**verb** informal reveal that someone is homosexual.

– PHRASES **out for** intent on having: *he was out for revenge.* **out of 1** from. **2** not having a stock or supply of something. **out to do** trying hard to do something: *they were out to impress.*

– ORIGIN Old English.

> USAGE: It is better to write **out of** rather than simply **out** in sentences such as *he threw it out of the window.*

out- prefix **1** to the point of surpassing or going beyond: *outperform.* **2** external; separate; from outside: *outbuildings.* **3** away from: *outpost.*

outage noun a period when a power supply or other service is not available.

out-and-out adjective in every way; complete: *an out-and-out lie.*

outback noun (**the outback**) the remote inland area of Australia that has very few inhabitants.

outbid verb (**outbids, outbidding**; past and past part. **outbid**) bid more for something than someone else.

outboard adjective & adverb on, towards, or near the outside of a ship or aircraft. •**noun 1** an outboard motor. **2** a boat with an outboard motor.

outboard motor noun a portable motor which can be attached to the outside of a boat.

outbound adjective & adverb travelling from a place rather than arriving in it.

outbreak noun a sudden or violent occurrence of war, disease, etc.

outbuilding noun a smaller building near to but separate from a main building.

outburst noun **1** a sudden release of strong emotion: *an angry outburst from the Prime Minister.* **2** a sudden violent occurrence of something: *outbursts of fighting*

outcast noun a person rejected by their society or social group.

outclass verb be far better than someone or something.

outcome noun the result or consequence of an action or event: *his remarks did not affect the outcome of the trial.*

outcrop noun a part of a rock formation that is visible above the surface of the ground.

outcry noun (pl. **outcries**) a strong expression of public disapproval.

outdated adjective no longer used or fashionable.

outdistance verb leave a competitor or pursuer far behind.

outdo verb (**outdoes, outdoing**; past **outdid**; past part. **outdone**) be better than someone else.

outdoor adjective **1** done, situated, or used outdoors. **2** fond of being outdoors.

outdoors adverb in or into the open air. •**noun** any area outside buildings or shelter.

outer adjective **1** outside; external. **2** further from the centre or the inside. •**noun** Brit. the division of a target furthest from the bullseye.

outermost adjective furthest from the centre.

outer space noun the universe beyond the earth's atmosphere.

outface verb disconcert or defeat someone by confronting them boldly.

outfall noun the place where a river, drain, or sewer empties into the sea, a river, or a lake.

outfield noun the outer part of a cricket or baseball field.

outfit noun **1** a set of clothes worn together. **2** informal a group of people working together as a business, team, etc. •**verb** (**outfits, outfitting, outfitted**) provide someone with a set of clothes.

outfitter (also **outfitters**) noun Brit. dated a shop selling men's clothing.

outflank verb **1** move round the side of an enemy, especially so as to attack them from behind. **2** outwit someone.

outflow noun a large amount of something that moves or is transferred out of a place.

outfox verb informal defeat someone by being more clever or cunning than them.

outgas verb (**outgases, outgassing, outgassed**) release or give off a substance as a gas or vapour.

outgoing adjective **1** friendly and confident. **2** leaving a job or position. **3** going out or away from a place. •**noun** Brit. (**outgoings**) money that has to be spent regularly.

outgrow verb (past **outgrew**; past part. **outgrown**) **1** grow too big for something. **2** stop doing or having an interest in something as one matures: *she had outgrown her collection of china kittens.* **3** grow faster or taller than someone or something else.

outgrowth noun **1** something that grows out of something else. **2** a natural development or result.

outgun verb (**outguns, outgunning, outgunned**) have more or better weapons than another person or group.

outhouse noun a smaller building built on to or in the grounds of a house.

outing noun **1** a short trip taken for pleasure. **2** informal an occasion when a competitor takes part in a sporting event, or an actor appears in a film, play, etc.: *an actress in her first screen outing.* **3** the practice of revealing someone's homosexuality.

outlandish adjective extremely unusual or unconventional; bizarre.

– ORIGIN Old English, 'not native'.

outlast verb last longer than: *the kind of beauty that will outlast youth.*

outlaw noun 1 a person who has broken the law, especially one who has escaped captivity or is in hiding. 2 historical a person who has been deprived of legal rights or protection. • verb 1 make something illegal: *secondary picketing has been outlawed.* 2 historical deprive someone of legal rights or protection.
– DERIVATIVES **outlawry** noun.

outlay noun an amount of money spent.

outlet noun 1 a pipe or hole through which water or gas may escape. 2 a point from which goods are sold or distributed: *a fast-food outlet.* 3 a means of expressing one's talents, energy, or emotions: *boxing provided a perfect outlet for his aggression.* 4 the mouth of a river. 5 an output socket in an electrical device.

outlier /owt-ly-er/ noun 1 a thing which is separate or detached from a main body or system. 2 a younger rock formation among older rocks.

outline noun 1 a drawing or diagram showing the shape of an object. 2 the contours or outer edges of an object. 3 a brief description of the main points of something. • verb 1 draw or define the outer edge or shape of something. 2 give a summary of: *she outlined the case briefly.*

outlive verb live or last longer than someone or something else.

outlook noun 1 a person's point of view or attitude to life. 2 a view. 3 what is likely to happen in the future.

outlying adjective situated far from a centre.

outmanoeuvre verb evade or gain an advantage over an opponent by using skill and cunning.

outmatch verb be better than someone or something else.

outmoded adjective old-fashioned.

outnumber verb be more numerous than: *women outnumbered men by three to one.*

out-of-body experience noun a sensation of being outside one's body, typically of observing oneself from a distance.

out-of-court adjective (of a settlement) made without the involvement of a court of law.

out of date adjective 1 old-fashioned. 2 no longer valid.

outpace verb go, rise, or improve faster than someone or something else.

outpatient noun a patient attending a hospital for treatment without staying overnight.

outperform verb perform better than someone or something else.

outplacement noun the action of helping workers who have been made redundant to find new employment.

outplay verb play better than another person or team.

outpost noun 1 a small military camp at a distance from the main army. 2 a remote part of a country or empire.

outpouring noun 1 something that streams out rapidly. 2 an outburst of strong emotion: *an outpouring of grief.*

output noun 1 the amount of something produced. 2 the process of producing something. 3 the power, energy, etc. supplied by a device or system. 4 Electronics a place where power or information leaves a system. • verb (**outputting**; past and past part. **output** or **outputted**) (of a computer) produce data.

outrage noun 1 an extremely strong reaction of anger, shock, or indignation. 2 an extremely cruel, wicked, or shocking act: *some of the worst terrorist outrages.* • verb make someone feel extremely angry, shocked, or indignant.
– ORIGIN Old French, from Latin *ultra* 'beyond'.

outrageous adjective 1 shockingly bad or unacceptable: *an outrageous waste of time and money.* 2 very unusual and slightly shocking: *her outrageous costumes.*
– DERIVATIVES **outrageously** adverb **outrageousness** noun.

outran past of OUTRUN.

outrank verb 1 have a higher rank than someone else. 2 be better or more important than something else.

outré /oo-tray/ adjective unusual and typically rather shocking.
– ORIGIN French, 'exceeded'.

outreach noun an organization's involvement with the community, especially in providing a service or advice outside its usual centres of operation.

outrider noun a person in a vehicle or on horseback who escorts or guards another vehicle.

outrigger noun 1 a spar or framework projecting from or over a boat's side. 2 a float fixed parallel to a canoe or small ship to help keep it stable. 3 a boat fitted with an outrigger.

outright adverb 1 altogether: *unions rejected the offer outright.* 2 in an open and direct way. 3 immediately or instantly. • adjective 1 open and direct: *an outright refusal.* 2 complete and total: *an outright ban.*

outrun verb (**outruns, outrunning**; past **outran**; past part. **outrun**) 1 run or travel faster or further than someone or something else. 2 go beyond or exceed something.

outsell verb (past and past part. **outsold**) be sold in greater quantities than another product.

outset noun the start or beginning.

outshine verb (past and past part. **outshone**) 1 shine more brightly than something else. 2 be much better than: *his technical expertise far outshone that of his rivals.*

outside noun 1 the external side or surface of something. 2 the external appearance of someone or something. 3 the side of a bend or curve where the edge is longer. • adjective 1 situated on or near the outside. 2 not of or belonging to a particular group, organization, etc.: *outside contractors.* 3 (in hockey, football, etc.) referring to positions nearer to the sides of the field. • preposition & adverb 1 situated or moving beyond the boundaries of something. 2 (in hockey, football, etc.) closer to the side of the field than. 3 beyond the limits or scope of something. 4 not being a member of a particular group.
– PHRASES **at the outside** at the most. **an outside chance** a remote possibility.

outside broadcast noun Brit. a radio or television programme recorded or broadcast live on location.

outside interest noun an interest not connected with one's work or studies.

outsider noun 1 a person who does not belong to a particular group. 2 a competitor thought to have little chance of success.

outsize adjective (also **outsized**) exceptionally large.

outskirts plural noun the outer parts of a town or city.

outsmart verb defeat or get the better of someone by being clever or cunning.

outsold past and past participle of **outsell**.

outsole noun the outer sole of a boot or shoe.

outsource verb 1 obtain goods from an outside supplier. 2 arrange for work to be done outside one's own company.

outspoken adjective stating one's opinions in a frank and direct way.
– DERIVATIVES **outspokenness** noun.

outspread adjective extended or stretched out as far as possible.

outstanding adjective 1 exceptionally good. 2 clearly noticeable. 3 not yet dealt with or paid.
– DERIVATIVES **outstandingly** adverb.

outstation noun 1 a branch of an organization situated far from its headquarters. 2 Austral./NZ a part of a farming estate that is separate from the main estate.

outstay verb stay somewhere for longer than the expected or permitted time.

outstretched adjective extended or stretched out.

outstrip verb (**outstrips, outstripping, outstripped**) 1 move faster than and overtake someone or something else. 2 exceed or go beyond: *demand is outstripping supply.* 3 be better than: *the company outstripped its competitors.*

out-take noun a scene or sequence filmed for a film or television programme but not included in the final version.

outvote verb defeat someone or something by winning a larger number of votes.

outward adjective 1 of, on, or from the outside. 2 going out or away from a place. •adverb outwards.
– DERIVATIVES **outwardly** adverb.

outwards adverb chiefly Brit. towards the outside; away from the centre or a place.

outweigh verb be heavier, greater, or more significant than: *the advantages greatly outweigh the disadvantages.*

outwit verb (**outwits, outwitting, outwitted**) defeat or gain an advantage over someone as a result of greater cleverness or ingenuity.

outwith preposition Scottish outside; beyond.

outwork noun 1 an outer section of a fortification. 2 Brit. work done outside the factory or office which provides it.
– DERIVATIVES **outworker** noun.

ouzel /oo-z'l/ (also **ousel**) noun used in names of birds resembling the blackbird, e.g. **ring ouzel**.
– ORIGIN Old English, 'blackbird'.

ouzo /oo-zoh/ noun an aniseed-flavoured Greek alcoholic drink.
– ORIGIN modern Greek.

ova plural of **ovum**.

oval adjective having a rounded and slightly elongated outline; egg-shaped. •noun 1 an oval object or design. 2 an oval sports field or track.
– ORIGIN from Latin *ovum* 'egg'.

Oval Office noun the office of the US President in the White House.

ovarian adjective relating to the ovaries.

ovary noun (pl. **ovaries**) 1 a female reproductive organ in which eggs or ova are produced. 2 the base of the reproductive organ of a flower, containing one or more ovules.
– ORIGIN from Latin *ovum* 'egg'.

ovate /oh-vayt/ adjective oval; egg-shaped.
– ORIGIN Latin *ovatus*.

ovation noun a long and enthusiastic round of applause.
– ORIGIN Latin, from *ovare* 'exult'.

oven noun 1 an enclosed compartment in which food is cooked or heated. 2 a small furnace or kiln.
– ORIGIN Old English.

ovenproof adjective suitable for use in an oven.

oven-ready adjective (of food) sold as a prepared dish, ready for cooking in an oven.

over preposition 1 extending upwards from or above. 2 above so as to cover or protect. 3 expressing movement or a route across. 4 beyond and falling or hanging from. 5 expressing length of time. 6 at a higher level, layer, or intensity than. 7 higher or more than. 8 expressing authority or control. 9 on the subject of. •adverb 1 expressing movement or a route across an area. 2 beyond and falling or hanging from a point. 3 in or to the place indicated. 4 expressing action and result: *the car flipped over.* 5 finished. 6 expressing repetition of a process. •noun Cricket a sequence of six balls bowled by a bowler from one end of the pitch.
– PHRASES **be over** be no longer affected by something. **over and above** in addition to.
– ORIGIN Old English.

over- prefix 1 excessively: *overambitious.* 2 completely: *overjoyed.* 3 upper; outer; extra: *overcoat.* 4 over; above: *overcast.*

overachieve verb do better than expected.
– DERIVATIVES **overachievement** noun **overachiever** noun.

overact verb act a role in a play or film in an exaggerated way.

overactive adjective more active than is normal or desirable.
– DERIVATIVES **overactivity** noun.

overall adjective taking everything into account; total. •adverb taken as a whole. •noun (also **overalls**) Brit. a loose-fitting garment worn over ordinary clothes for protection.

overambitious adjective too ambitious.

overarch verb 1 form an arch over something. 2 (as adj. **overarching**) covering or dealing with everything: *a single overarching principle.*

overarm adjective & adverb chiefly Brit. (of a throw, stroke with a racket, etc.) made with the hand brought forward and down from above shoulder level.

overate past of **overeat**.

overawe verb impress someone so much that

they are silent or nervous.

overbalance verb fall or cause to fall due to loss of balance.

overbearing adjective trying to impose one's views or control other people in a forceful and unpleasant way.

overbite noun the overlapping of the lower teeth by the upper.

overblown adjective 1 made to seem more important or impressive than is really the case: *an overblown action thriller.* 2 (of a flower) past its prime.

overboard adverb from a ship into the water.
– PHRASES **go overboard 1** be very enthusiastic. **2** react in an extreme way.

overbook verb accept more reservations for a flight or hotel than there is room for.

overbridge noun a bridge over a railway or road.

overburden verb give someone or something more work or pressure than it is possible to deal with.

overcame past of OVERCOME.

overcapacity noun a situation in which an industry or factory cannot sell as much as it is designed to produce.

overcast adjective (of the sky or weather) cloudy; dull.

overcautious adjective excessively cautious.

overcharge verb charge someone too high a price for something.

overclass noun a privileged, wealthy, or powerful section of society.

overcoat noun 1 a long warm coat. 2 a top layer of paint or varnish.

overcome verb (past **overcame**; past part. **overcome**) 1 succeed in dealing with a problem. 2 defeat an opponent. 3 (of an emotion) overwhelm: *she was overcome with excitement.*

overcommit verb (**overcommits**, **overcommitting, overcommitted**) (**overcommit oneself**) undertake to do more than one is capable of doing.

overcompensate verb do something which is too extreme in an attempt to correct a problem.
– DERIVATIVES **overcompensation** noun.

overconfident adjective excessively confident.
– DERIVATIVES **overconfidence** noun.

overcook verb cook food for too long.

overcrowded adjective filled with more people or things than is usual or comfortable.
– DERIVATIVES **overcrowding** noun.

overdetermine verb formal determine or account for something in more than one way or with more conditions than are necessary.
– DERIVATIVES **overdetermination** noun.

overdevelop verb (**overdevelops, overdeveloping, overdeveloped**) develop something too much.
– DERIVATIVES **overdevelopment** noun.

overdo verb (**overdoes, overdoing, overdid**; past part. **overdone**) 1 do something excessively or in an exaggerated way. 2 use too much of: *I'd overdone the garlic in the curry.* 3 (**overdo it/things**) exhaust oneself. 4 (as adj. **overdone**) overcooked.

overdose noun an excessive and dangerous dose of a drug. ●verb take an overdose.
– DERIVATIVES **overdosage** noun.

overdraft noun an arrangement with a bank that allows someone to take out more money than there is in their account.

overdramatize (or **overdramatise**) verb react to or portray something in an excessively dramatic way.
– DERIVATIVES **overdramatic** adjective.

overdrawn adjective 1 (of a bank account) in a state in which more money has been taken out than the account holds. 2 having an overdrawn bank account.

overdressed adjective wearing clothes that are too elaborate or formal for a particular occasion.

overdrink verb (past **overdrank**; past part. **overdrunk**) drink too much alcohol.

overdrive noun 1 a mechanism in a motor vehicle providing an extra gear above the usual top gear. 2 a state of great or excessive activity: *my heart had gone into overdrive.*
– DERIVATIVES **overdriven** adjective.

overdue adjective not having arrived, happened, or been done at the expected or required time.

overeager adjective excessively eager.

overeat verb (past **overate**; past part. **overeaten**) eat too much.

over-egg verb (usu. in phrase **over-egg the pudding**) go too far in doing something; exaggerate.

over-elaborate adjective excessively elaborate.

overemotional adjective excessively emotional.

overemphasize (or **overemphasise**) verb place excessive emphasis or importance on something.
– DERIVATIVES **overemphasis** noun.

overenthusiastic adjective excessively enthusiastic.
– DERIVATIVES **overenthusiasm** noun.

overestimate verb estimate as better or greater than in reality: *has the record company overestimated the popularity of these new stars?* ●noun an excessively high estimate.
– DERIVATIVES **overestimation** noun.

overexcited adjective too excited to behave sensibly.
– DERIVATIVES **overexcitable** adjective **overexcitement** noun.

overexert verb (**overexert oneself**) exhaust oneself by making too much physical effort.
– DERIVATIVES **overexertion** noun.

overexpose verb 1 subject photographic film to too much light. 2 (as adj. **overexposed**) seen too much on television, in the newspapers, etc.
– DERIVATIVES **overexposure** noun.

overextend verb 1 involve someone in excessive work or financial commitments: *the major chains overextended themselves in the 1980s.* 2 make something too long.

overfall noun a turbulent stretch of open water caused by a strong current over a submarine ridge, or by a meeting of currents.

overfamiliar adjective 1 too well known.

2 behaving or speaking in an inappropriately informal way.
– DERIVATIVES **overfamiliarity** noun.

overfeed verb (past and past part. **overfed**) feed someone or something too much.

overfill verb put more into a container than there is room for.

overfish verb take too many fish from the sea or a river or lake, greatly reducing the stock.

overflow verb 1 flow over the brim of a container. 2 be excessively full or crowded. 3 (**overflow with**) be very full of an emotion. •noun 1 the overflowing of a liquid. 2 the people or things that do not fit into a particular space. 3 (also **overflow pipe**) an outlet for excess water.

overgarment noun an item of clothing worn over others.

overgeneralize (or **overgeneralise**) verb express something in a way that is too general.

overgenerous adjective excessively generous.

overgraze verb graze grassland too heavily.

overground adverb & adjective on or above the ground.

overgrown adjective 1 covered with plants that have been allowed to grow wild. 2 having grown too large.

overgrowth noun excessive growth of something.

overhand adjective & adverb 1 with the palm of the hand downward or inward. 2 chiefly N. Amer. overarm.

overhang verb (past and past part. **overhung**) hang outwards over something. •noun a part that hangs outwards over something.

overhaul verb 1 examine and repair equipment or machinery. 2 analyse and improve a system or process. 3 Brit. overtake someone. •noun a thorough examination of machinery or a system, with repairs or changes made if necessary.

overhead adverb above the head. •adjective 1 situated above the head. 2 (of a driving mechanism) above the object driven. •noun 1 (**overheads**) the regular expenses involved in running a business or organization, such as rent, electricity, wages, etc. 2 a transparency for use with an overhead projector.

overhead projector noun a device that projects an enlarged image of a transparency by means of an overhead mirror.

overhear verb (past and past part. **overheard**) hear someone or something accidentally or secretly.

overheat verb 1 make or become too hot. 2 (of a country's economy) show marked inflation when increased demand results in rising prices.

overhung past and past participle of **OVERHANG**.

overhype verb informal make exaggerated claims about the good qualities of product, idea, or event, in order to get public attention.

overindulge verb 1 have too much of something enjoyable. 2 give in to someone's wishes too readily.
– DERIVATIVES **overindulgence** noun **overindulgent** adjective.

overinflated adjective 1 (of a price or value) excessive. 2 exaggerated: *overinflated claims*. 3 filled with too much air.

overjoyed adjective very happy.

overkill noun too much of something: *the heavy security has raised concerns of overkill*.

overladen adjective carrying too large a load.

overlaid past and past participle of **OVERLAY**[1].

overlain past participle of **OVERLIE**.

overland adjective & adverb by land.

overlander noun a person who travels a long distance overland.

overlap verb (**overlaps, overlapping, overlapped**) 1 extend over something so as to partly cover it. 2 (of two events) occur at the same time for part of their duration. 3 cover part of the same area of interest or responsibility: *the union's commitments overlapped with those of NATO.* •noun 1 an overlapping part or amount. 2 a common area of interest or responsibility.

overlarge adjective too large.

overlay[1] verb (past and past part. **overlaid**) 1 coat the surface of something. 2 (of a quality or feeling) become more noticeable than a previous one: *the concern in his voice was overlaid with annoyance.* •noun 1 a covering. 2 a transparent sheet over artwork or a map, giving additional detail.

overlay[2] past of **OVERLIE**.

overleaf adverb on the other side of the page.

overlie verb (**overlies, overlying, overlay**; past part. **overlain**) lie on top of something.

overload verb 1 load something too heavily. 2 put too great a demand on: *the staff are heavily overloaded with work.* •noun an excessive amount.

overlock verb prevent fraying of an edge of cloth by oversewing it.
– DERIVATIVES **overlocker** noun.

overlong adjective & adverb too long.

overlook verb 1 fail to notice: *she's overlooked one important fact.* 2 choose to ignore a fault or wrongdoing. 3 have a view of something from above.

overlord noun a person who rules or controls many people.

overly adverb excessively; too.

overlying present participle of **OVERLIE**.

overman verb (**overmans, overmanning, overmanned**) provide an organization with more employees than necessary.

overmantel noun an ornamental structure over a mantelpiece.

overmaster verb literary overcome someone or something.

overmuch adverb, determiner, & pronoun too much.

overnight adverb 1 for the duration of a night. 2 during a night. 3 very quickly. •adjective 1 done, happening, or for use overnight. 2 very quick; instant: *Tom became an overnight celebrity.* •verb stay in a place overnight.
– DERIVATIVES **overnighter** noun.

over-optimistic adjective having a feeling of optimism about something that is unlikely to be justified.

overpaint verb cover something with paint.

overpass noun a bridge by which a road or railway line passes over another.

overpay verb (past and past part. **overpaid**) pay someone too much.
– DERIVATIVES **overpayment** noun.

overplay verb give too much importance or emphasis to something.
– PHRASES **overplay one's hand** spoil one's chance of success by being too confident.

overpopulated adjective (of an area or city) having too many people living in it.
– DERIVATIVES **overpopulation** noun.

overpower verb 1 defeat someone with superior strength. 2 have an overwhelming effect on: *he was overpowered by the fumes.*
– DERIVATIVES **overpowering** adjective.

overpriced adjective too expensive.

overproduce verb 1 produce too much of something. 2 record or produce a song or film in an excessively elaborate way.
– DERIVATIVES **overproduction** noun.

overprotective adjective excessively protective.

overqualified adjective too highly qualified.

overran past of **OVERRUN**.

overrate verb (often as adj. **overrated**) have too high an opinion of someone or something.

overreach verb (**overreach oneself**) fail as a result of being too ambitious or trying too hard.

overreact verb react to something more strongly or emotionally than is justified.
– DERIVATIVES **overreaction** noun.

override verb (past **overrode**; past part. **overridden**) 1 use one's authority to reject or cancel another's decision or order. 2 be more important than: *teachers' professionalism should override personal feelings.* 3 interrupt the action of an automatic device. •noun a device on a machine for overriding an automatic process.
– DERIVATIVES **overriding** adjective.

overripe adjective too ripe.

overrule verb use one's superior authority to reverse or disallow another's decision or order.

overrun verb (**overruns, overrunning, overran**; past part. **overrun**) 1 spread over or occupy a place in large numbers. 2 go beyond a set time, cost, or limit.

overseas adverb in or to a foreign country. •adjective relating to a foreign country.

oversee verb (**oversees, overseeing, oversaw**; past part. **overseen**) supervise a person or their work.
– DERIVATIVES **overseer** noun.

oversell verb (past and past part. **oversold**) 1 exaggerate the quality or worth of someone or something. 2 sell more of something than is available.

oversensitive adjective excessively sensitive.
– DERIVATIVES **oversensitivity** noun.

oversew verb (past part. **oversewn** or **oversewed**) sew the edges of two pieces of fabric together, having the stitches passing over the join.

oversexed adjective having unusually strong sexual desires.

overshadow verb 1 appear more important or successful than: *he was overshadowed by his brilliant brother.* 2 cast gloom over something.

3 tower above and cast a shadow over something.

overshirt noun a loose shirt worn over other clothes.

overshoe noun a protective shoe worn over a normal shoe.

overshoot verb (past and past part. **overshot**) 1 accidentally go past an intended stopping or turning point. 2 exceed a financial target or limit.

oversight noun an unintentional failure to notice or do something.

oversimplify verb (**oversimplifies, oversimplifying, oversimplified**) simplify something so much that an inaccurate impression is given.
– DERIVATIVES **oversimplification** noun.

oversized (also **oversize**) adjective bigger than the usual size.

overskirt noun an outer skirt, worn over the skirt of a dress.

oversleep verb (past and past part. **overslept**) sleep longer or later than one intended.

oversold past and past participle of **OVERSELL**.

overspecialize (or **overspecialise**) verb concentrate too much on one aspect of something.
– DERIVATIVES **overspecialization** noun.

overspend verb (past and past part. **overspent**) spend too much.

overspill noun Brit. part of the population of a city or town moving from an overcrowded area to live elsewhere.

overstaffed adjective having more members of staff than are necessary.

overstate verb state something too strongly; exaggerate something.
– DERIVATIVES **overstatement** noun.

overstay verb stay longer than an allowed or expected time.

oversteer verb (of a vehicle) turn more sharply than is desirable.

overstep verb (**oversteps, overstepping, overstepped**) go beyond a set or accepted limit.
– PHRASES **overstep the mark** behave in an unacceptable way.

overstimulate verb stimulate someone or something excessively.
– DERIVATIVES **overstimulation** noun.

overstock verb stock something with more of something than is necessary or required. •noun a supply or quantity that exceeds demand.

overstrain verb place too much strain on someone or something.

overstress verb 1 cause too much stress to someone or something. 2 lay too much emphasis on something.

overstretch verb 1 make excessive demands on: *classes are large and facilities are overstretched.* 2 stretch something too much.

overstuffed adjective 1 (of a container) excessively full. 2 (of furniture) covered completely with a thick layer of stuffing.

oversubscribed adjective 1 (of something for sale) applied for in greater quantities than are available. 2 (of a course, college, etc.) having more applications than available places.

oversupply noun (pl. **oversupplies**) an

excessive supply of something. • **verb**
(**oversupplies, oversupplying, oversupplied**)
supply with too much or too many of
something: *the country was oversupplied with
lawyers.*

overt /oh-**vert**, oh-vert/ adjective done or shown
openly: *an overt act of aggression.*
– DERIVATIVES **overtly** adverb **overtness** noun.
– ORIGIN Old French, 'opened'.

overtake verb (past **overtook**; past part.
overtaken) **1** chiefly Brit. catch up with and pass
someone while travelling in the same
direction. **2** become greater or more
successful than someone or something.
3 suddenly affect: *weariness overtook him.*

overtax verb **1** make excessive demands on a
person's strength or abilities. **2** require people
to pay too much tax.

overthrow verb (past **overthrew**; past part.
overthrown) **1** forcibly remove someone from
power. **2** put an end to something through
force. • **noun** the forcible removal of someone
from power.

overtime noun **1** time worked in addition to
one's normal working hours. **2** N. Amer. extra
time played at the end of a tied game. • **adverb**
in addition to normal working hours.

overtired adjective excessively tired;
exhausted.

overtone noun **1** a subtle additional quality or
implication: *the decision had political
overtones.* **2** a musical tone which is a part of
the harmonic series above a fundamental
note, and may be heard with it.

overtop verb (**overtops, overtopping,
overtopped**) be higher or taller than someone
or something.

overtrousers plural noun protective or
waterproof trousers worn over other trousers.

overture noun **1** an orchestral piece at the
beginning of a musical work. **2** an
independent orchestral composition in one
movement. **3** (**overtures**) approaches made
with the aim of opening negotiations or
establishing a relationship: *he began making
overtures to merchant banks.* **4** an introduction
to something more substantial.
– ORIGIN Old French, 'aperture'.

overturn verb **1** turn over and come to rest
upside down. **2** abolish or reverse a decision,
system, etc.

overuse verb /oh-ver-**yooz**/ use something too
much. • **noun** /oh-ver-**yooss**/ excessive use.

overvalue verb (**overvalues, overvaluing,
overvalued**) **1** overestimate the importance of
something. **2** fix the value of something,
especially a currency at too high a level.
– DERIVATIVES **overvaluation** noun.

overview noun a general summary or survey.

overwear noun outer clothing.

overweening adjective (especially of a
quality) excessive: *overweening pride.*
– ORIGIN from Old English, 'think or suppose'.

overweight adjective above a normal,
desirable, or permitted weight.

overwhelm verb **1** have a strong emotional
effect on: *she was overwhelmed by guilt.* **2** give
someone too much of something. **3** defeat
someone or something completely. **4** cover

something completely with a huge mass of
water.
– DERIVATIVES **overwhelming** adjective.
– ORIGIN from Old English, 'engulf or
submerge'.

overwinter verb **1** spend the winter in a
particular place. **2** (of an insect, plant, etc.)
survive through the winter.

overwork verb **1** work or cause to work too
hard. **2** use a word or idea too much and so
make it less effective. • **noun** excessive work.

overwrite verb (past **overwrote**; past part.
overwritten) **1** write on top of other writing.
2 destroy computer data by entering new data
in its place. **3** write something too elaborately.

overwrought adjective **1** in a state of nervous
excitement or anxiety. **2** (of a piece of writing
or a work of art) too elaborate.

overzealous adjective excessively
enthusiastic.

oviduct /oh-vi-dukt/ noun the tube through
which an ovum (female reproductive cell)
passes from an ovary.
– ORIGIN from Latin *ovum* 'egg'.

ovine /oh-vyn/ adjective relating to sheep.
– ORIGIN Latin *ovinus.*

oviparous /oh-**vip**-uh-ruhss/ adjective (of an
animal such as a bird) producing young by
means of eggs which are hatched after they
have been laid by the parent. Compare with
VIVIPAROUS.

ovipositor /oh-vi-**poz**-i-ter/ noun a tubular
organ through which a female insect or fish
deposits eggs.
– ORIGIN from Latin *ovum* 'egg' + *ponere* 'to
place'.

ovoid /oh-voyd/ adjective **1** egg-shaped. **2** (of a
plane figure) oval. • **noun** an oval or egg-shaped
object or shape.
– ORIGIN Latin *ovoides.*

ovulate /ov-yuu-layt/ verb (of a woman or
female animal) discharge ova (reproductive
cells) from the ovary.
– DERIVATIVES **ovulation** noun.

ovule noun the part of the ovary of seed plants
that becomes the seed after fertilization.
– DERIVATIVES **ovular** adjective.
– ORIGIN Latin *ovulum* 'little egg'.

ovum noun (pl. **ova**) a mature female
reproductive cell, which can divide to develop
into an embryo if fertilized by a male cell.
– ORIGIN Latin, 'egg'.

owe verb **1** be required to pay money or goods
to someone in return for something received.
2 be morally obliged to do or give something
to: *you owe me an apology.* **3** (**owe something
to**) have something because of: *I owe my life to
you.*
– ORIGIN Old English.

owing adjective chiefly Brit. (of money or goods)
yet to be paid or supplied.
– PHRASES **owing to** because of.

owl noun a bird of prey with large eyes, a
hooked beak, and a hooting call, active at
night.
– ORIGIN Old English.

owlet noun a young or small owl.

owlish adjective **1** like an owl, especially in
appearing to be wise or solemn. **2** (of glasses)

resembling the large round eyes of an owl.
– DERIVATIVES **owlishly** adverb.

own adjective & pronoun **1** (with a possessive) belonging or relating to the person specified: *I saw it with my own eyes.* **2** done or produced by the person specified. **3** particular to the person or thing specified; individual. • verb **1** possess something. **2** formal admit or acknowledge that something is the case. **3** (**own up**) admit to having done something wrong or embarrassing.
– PHRASES **come into its** (or **one's**) **own** become fully effective. **hold one's own** remain in a strong position in a demanding situation.
– ORIGIN Old English.

own brand noun Brit. a product manufactured specially for a retailer and bearing the retailer's name.

owner noun a person who owns something.

owner-occupier noun Brit. a person who owns the house or flat in which they live.

ownership noun the act, state, or right of possessing something.

own goal noun **1** (in football) a goal scored when a player accidentally hits the ball into their own team's goal. **2** Brit. informal an act that unintentionally harms one's own interests: *government scores own goal by assisting organized crime.*

owt pronoun N. English anything.
– ORIGIN variant of **AUGHT**.

ox noun (pl. **oxen**) **1** a cow or bull. **2** a castrated bull, used for pulling heavy loads.
– ORIGIN Old English.

oxalic acid /ok-**sal**-ik/ noun a poisonous acid found in rhubarb leaves and other plants.
– ORIGIN from Greek *oxalis* 'wood sorrel'.

oxbow noun a loop formed by a horseshoe bend in a river.
– ORIGIN first referring to the U-shaped collar of an ox-yoke.

oxbow lake noun a curved lake formed from a horseshoe bend in a river where the main stream has cut across the neck and no longer flows around the loop of the bend.

Oxbridge noun Oxford and Cambridge universities regarded together.

oxen plural of **ox**.

ox-eye daisy noun a daisy which has large white flowers with yellow centres.

oxford noun a type of lace-up shoe with a low heel.
– ORIGIN named after the city of *Oxford*.

Oxford bags plural noun Brit. wide baggy trousers.

oxidant noun Chemistry a substance that brings about oxidation.

oxidation noun Chemistry the process of oxidizing or the result of being oxidized.
– DERIVATIVES **oxidative** adjective.

oxide noun a compound of oxygen with another element or group.

oxidize (or **oxidise**) verb **1** combine or cause to combine with oxygen. **2** Chemistry cause a substance to undergo a reaction in which electrons are lost to another substance or molecule. The opposite of **REDUCE**.
– DERIVATIVES **oxidization** noun **oxidizer** noun.

Oxon abbreviation **1** Oxfordshire. **2** (in degree titles) of Oxford University.
– ORIGIN from *Oxonia*, Latinized form of Oxford.

Oxonian /ok-**soh**-ni-uhn/ adjective relating to Oxford or Oxford University. • noun **1** a person from Oxford. **2** a member of Oxford University.

oxtail noun the tail of an ox (used in making soup).

ox tongue noun the tongue of an ox (used as meat).

oxyacetylene /ok-si-uh-**set**-i-leen/ adjective (of welding or cutting techniques) using a very hot flame produced by mixing acetylene and oxygen.

oxygen noun a colourless, odourless, gaseous chemical element, forming about 20 per cent of the earth's atmosphere and essential to life.
– ORIGIN from French *principe oxygène* 'acidifying constituent' (because at first it was believed to be the essential component of acids).

oxygenate verb (often as adj. **oxygenated**) supply or enrich with oxygen: *oxygenated blood.*
– DERIVATIVES **oxygenation** noun **oxygenator** noun.

oxygen bar noun a place where people pay to inhale pure oxygen for its reputedly therapeutic effects.

oxygen mask noun a mask placed over the nose and mouth and connected to an oxygen supply, used when the body is not able to gain enough oxygen by breathing air.

oxymoron /ok-si-**mor**-on/ noun a figure of speech in which apparently contradictory terms appear together (e.g. *a deafening silence*).
– DERIVATIVES **oxymoronic** adjective.
– ORIGIN from Greek *oxumōros* 'pointedly foolish'.

oxytocin /ok-si-**toh**-sin/ noun a hormone released by the pituitary gland that in women causes contraction of the womb during labour and stimulates the flow of milk into the breasts.
– ORIGIN from Greek *oxutokia* 'sudden delivery'.

oyez /oh-yez/, oh-yay/ (also **oyes**) exclamation a call given by a town crier or court official to ask for silence before an announcement.
– ORIGIN Old French, 'hear!'

oyster noun **1** a shellfish with two hinged oval shells, several kinds of which are farmed for food or pearls. **2** a shade of greyish white.
– PHRASES **the world is your oyster** you have a wide range of opportunities available to you. [from Shakespeare's *Merry Wives of Windsor* (II. ii. 5).]
– ORIGIN Greek *ostreon*.

oystercatcher noun a wading bird with black or black-and-white plumage and a strong orange-red bill, feeding chiefly on shellfish.

oyster mushroom noun an edible fungus with a greyish-brown oval cap.

Oz noun & adjective informal Australia or Australian.
– ORIGIN from the abbreviation of *Australia*.

O

oz abbreviation ounce(s).
– ORIGIN Italian *onza* 'ounce'.

ozone noun 1 a strong-smelling, toxic form of oxygen, formed in electrical discharges or by ultraviolet light. 2 Brit. informal fresh invigorating air.
– ORIGIN Greek *ozein* 'to smell'.

ozone hole noun an area of the ozone layer where the ozone is greatly reduced, due to CFCs and other pollutants.

ozone layer noun a layer in the earth's stratosphere containing a high concentration of ozone, which absorbs most of the ultraviolet radiation reaching the earth from the sun.

Ozzie noun & adjective variant spelling of **Aussie**.

Pp

P[1] (also **p**) noun (pl. **Ps** or **P's**) the sixteenth letter of the alphabet.

P[2] abbreviation **1** (in tables of sports results) games played. **2** (on road signs and street plans) parking. • symbol the chemical element phosphorus.

p abbreviation **1** page. **2** Brit. penny or pence.

PA abbreviation **1** Pennsylvania. **2** Brit. personal assistant. **3** public address.

Pa abbreviation pascal(s). • symbol the chemical element protactinium.

pa noun informal father.
– ORIGIN abbreviation of PAPA.

p.a. abbreviation per annum.

paan /pahn/ (also **pan**) noun Indian betel leaves prepared and chewed as a stimulant.
– ORIGIN Sanskrit, 'feather, leaf'.

pabulum /pab-yuu-luhm/ (also **pablum** /pab-luhm/) noun literary bland intellectual matter or entertainment: *predictable pop pabulum*.
– ORIGIN Latin, 'food, fodder'.

paca /pa-kuh/ noun a large South American rodent that has a reddish-brown coat with rows of white spots.
– ORIGIN Tupi.

pace[1] /payss/ noun **1** a single step taken when walking or running. **2** speed in walking, running, or moving. **3** the speed or rate at which something happens or develops: *the communications revolution gathered pace.* **4** a way in which a horse is trained to run or walk. • verb **1** walk up and down in a small area, typically as an expression of anxiety. **2** (**pace something out**) measure a distance by walking it and counting the number of steps taken. **3** set the speed or rate at which something happens or develops: *they paced their drinking throughout the week.* **4** lead another runner in a race in order to establish a competitive speed. **5** (**pace oneself**) do something at a controlled and steady rate.
– PHRASES **keep pace with** progress at the same speed as. **put someone through their paces** make someone demonstrate their abilities. **stand** (or **stay**) **the pace** be able to keep up with others.
– ORIGIN Latin *passus* 'stretch (of the leg)'.

pace[2] /pah-chay, pay-si/ preposition with due respect to someone.
– ORIGIN Latin, 'in peace'.

pacemaker noun **1** an artificial device for stimulating and regulating the heart muscle. **2** (also **pacesetter**) a competitor who sets the pace at the beginning of a race.

pacey adjective variant spelling of PACY.

pacha noun variant spelling of PASHA.

pachyderm /pak-i-derm/ noun a very large mammal with thick skin, especially an elephant, rhinoceros, or hippopotamus.
– ORIGIN from Greek *pakhus* 'thick' + *derma* 'skin'.

pacific adjective **1** peaceful or pacifying: *a pacific gesture.* **2** (**Pacific**) relating to the Pacific Ocean. • noun (**the Pacific**) the Pacific Ocean.
– DERIVATIVES **pacifically** adverb.
– ORIGIN Latin *pacificus* 'peacemaking'.

pacifier noun N. Amer. a baby's dummy.

pacifism noun the belief that disputes should be settled peacefully and that war and violence are always wrong.
– DERIVATIVES **pacifist** noun & adjective.

pacify verb (**pacifies, pacifying, pacified**) **1** make someone less angry or upset. **2** bring peace to a country or groups in conflict.
– DERIVATIVES **pacification** noun.
– ORIGIN Latin *pacificare*.

pack[1] noun **1** a cardboard or paper container and the items inside it. **2** Brit. a set of playing cards. **3** a collection of related documents. **4** a group of animals that live and hunt together. **5** chiefly derogatory a group of similar things or people: *the reports were a pack of lies.* **6** (**the pack**) the main body of competitors following the leader in a race. **7** Rugby a team's forwards. **8** (**Pack**) an organized group of Cub Scouts or Brownies. **9** a rucksack. **10** a hot or cold pad of absorbent material, used for treating an injury. • verb **1** fill a suitcase or bag with clothes and other items needed for travel. **2** place something in a container for transport or storage. **3** be capable of being folded up for transport or storage: *a tent that packs away compactly.* **4** cram a large number of things into something. **5** cover, surround, or fill something. **6** informal carry a gun.
– PHRASES **pack a punch 1** be capable of hitting with skill or force. **2** have a powerful effect. **pack something in** informal give up an activity or job. **pack someone off** informal send someone somewhere without much notice. **pack up** Brit. informal (of a machine) break down. **send someone packing** informal dismiss someone abruptly.
– DERIVATIVES **packable** adjective **packer** noun.
– ORIGIN German *pak*.

pack[2] verb fill a jury or committee with people likely to support a particular verdict or decision.

p

– ORIGIN probably from former *pact* 'enter into an agreement with'.

package noun 1 an object or group of objects wrapped in paper or packed in a box. 2 N. Amer. a packet. 3 (also **package deal**) a set of proposals or terms offered or agreed as a whole. 4 informal a package holiday. 5 a collection of related computer programs or sets of instructions. •verb 1 put something into a box or wrapping. 2 present in a favourable way: *school science is packaged to appeal to boys.* 3 combine various products for sale as one unit.
– DERIVATIVES **packaged** adjective **packager** noun.

package holiday (also **package tour**) noun a holiday organized by a travel agent, the price of which includes arrangements for transport and accommodation.

packaging noun materials used to wrap or protect goods.

packed (also Brit. **packed out**) adjective very crowded.

packed lunch noun Brit. a cold lunch carried in a bag or box to work or school or on a journey.

packet noun 1 a paper or cardboard container. 2 (**a packet**) informal, chiefly Brit. a large sum of money. 3 Computing a block of data transmitted across a network. •verb (**packets, packeting, packeted**) wrap something up in a packet.
– ORIGIN from **PACK**[1].

packet boat noun dated a boat travelling at regular intervals between two ports, originally carrying mail and later taking passengers.

packhorse noun a horse used to carry loads.

pack ice noun a mass of ice floating in the sea, formed by smaller pieces freezing together.

packing noun material used to protect fragile goods in transit.

packing case noun a large, strong box used for transporting or storing things.

packsack noun N. Amer. a rucksack.

pact noun a formal agreement between people or parties.
– ORIGIN Latin *pactum* 'something agreed'.

pacy (also **pacey**) adjective (**pacier, paciest**) fast-moving: *a pacy wartime thriller.*

pad[1] noun 1 a thick piece of soft or absorbent material. 2 the fleshy underpart of an animal's foot or of a human finger. 3 a protective guard worn over a part of the body by a sports player. 4 a number of sheets of blank paper fastened together at one edge. 5 a flat-topped structure or area used for helicopter take-off and landing or for rocket-launching. 6 informal a person's home. •verb (**pads, padding, padded**) 1 fill or cover something with a pad or padding. 2 (**pad something out**) make a speech or piece of writing longer by adding unnecessary material.
– ORIGIN uncertain.

pad[2] verb (**pads, padding, padded**) walk with steady steps making a soft, dull sound.
– ORIGIN German *padden*.

padding noun 1 soft material used to pad or stuff something. 2 unnecessary material added to a speech or piece of writing to make it longer.

paddle[1] noun 1 a short pole with a broad blade at one or both ends, used to move a small boat

through the water. 2 an implement or part of a machine shaped like a paddle, used for stirring or mixing. 3 each of the boards fitted around the outside edge of a paddle wheel or mill wheel. •verb 1 move a boat with a paddle or paddles. 2 (of a bird or other animal) swim with short fast strokes.
– DERIVATIVES **paddler** noun.
– ORIGIN unknown.

paddle[2] verb walk with bare feet in shallow water. •noun an act of paddling.
– DERIVATIVES **paddler** noun.
– ORIGIN uncertain.

paddle steamer (also **paddle boat**) noun a boat powered by steam and propelled by paddle wheels.

paddle wheel noun a large steam-driven wheel with paddles round its edge, attached to the side or stern of a ship and moving the ship as it turns.

paddling pool noun Brit. a shallow artificial pool for children to paddle in.

paddock noun 1 a small field or enclosure for horses. 2 an enclosure next to a racecourse or track where horses or cars are displayed before a race.
– ORIGIN unknown.

Paddy noun (pl. **Paddies**) informal, chiefly offensive an Irishman.
– ORIGIN informal form of the Irish man's name *Padraig*.

paddy[1] noun (pl. **paddies**) 1 (also **paddy field**) a field where rice is grown. 2 rice before threshing or still in the husk.
– ORIGIN Malay.

paddy[2] noun (pl. **paddies**) Brit. informal a fit of temper.
– ORIGIN from **Paddy**.

padlock noun a detachable lock hanging by a hinged hook on the object fastened. •verb secure something with a padlock.
– ORIGIN *pad-* is of unknown origin.

padre /pah-dray, pah-dri/ noun informal a chaplain in the armed services.
– ORIGIN from Italian, Spanish, and Portuguese, 'father, priest'.

padrone /pa-droh-nay, pa-droh-ni/ noun a patron or master, especially a Mafia boss.
– ORIGIN Italian.

padsaw noun a small saw with a narrow blade, for cutting curves.

paean /pee-uhn/ noun a song of praise or triumph.
– ORIGIN Greek *paian* 'hymn of thanksgiving to Apollo'.

paediatrics /pee-di-at-riks/ (US **pediatrics**) plural noun (treated as sing.) the branch of medicine concerned with children and their diseases.
– DERIVATIVES **paediatric** adjective **paediatrician** noun.
– ORIGIN from Greek *pais* 'child' + *iatros* 'physician'.

paedophile (US **pedophile**) noun a person who is sexually attracted to children.
– DERIVATIVES **paedophilia** noun **paedophiliac** adjective & noun.
– ORIGIN from Greek *pais* 'child'.

paella /py-el-luh/ noun a Spanish dish of rice, saffron, chicken, seafood, and vegetables,

cooked in a large shallow pan.
– ORIGIN Catalan.

paeony noun variant spelling of **PEONY**.

pagan noun a person who holds religious beliefs other than those of the main world religions. •adjective relating to pagans or their beliefs.
– DERIVATIVES **paganism** noun.
– ORIGIN Latin *paganus* 'villager', later 'civilian' (i.e. a person who was not a 'soldier' in Christ's army).

page¹ noun **1** one side of a leaf of a book, magazine, or newspaper, or the material on it. **2** both sides of such a leaf considered as a single unit. **3** a section of data displayed on a computer screen at one time. **4** a particular event considered as part of a longer history: *the vote will form a page in the world's history.* •verb (**page through**) **1** look through the pages of a book, magazine, etc. **2** move through and display information on a computer screen one page at a time.
– ORIGIN Latin *pagina*.

page² noun **1** a boy or young man employed in a hotel or club to run errands, open doors, etc. **2** a young boy attending a bride at a wedding. **3** historical a boy who entered the service of a knight while training to be a knight himself. •verb summon someone over a public address system or by means of a pager.
– ORIGIN Old French.

pageant /paj-uhnt/ noun **1** a public entertainment consisting of a procession of people in elaborate costumes, or an outdoor performance of a historical scene. **2** (also **beauty pageant**) N. Amer. a beauty contest.
– ORIGIN unknown.

pageantry noun elaborate display or ceremony.

pageboy noun **1** a page in a hotel or attending a bride at a wedding. **2** a woman's hairstyle consisting of a shoulder-length bob with the ends rolled under.

pager noun a small radio device which bleeps or vibrates to inform the wearer that someone wishes to contact them or that it has received a short text message.

page-turner noun informal an exciting book.
– DERIVATIVES **page-turning** adjective.

paginate /paj-i-nayt/ noun give numbers to the pages of a book, journal, document, etc.
– DERIVATIVES **pagination** noun.

pagoda /puh-goh-duh/ noun a Hindu or Buddhist temple, typically having a tower with several tiers.
– ORIGIN Portuguese *pagode*.

paid past and past participle of **PAY**.
– PHRASES **put paid to** informal stop or end something abruptly.

paid-up adjective **1** (of a member of an organization) with all subscriptions paid in full. **2** committed to a cause or group: *a fully paid-up postmodernist.*

pail noun a bucket.
– ORIGIN uncertain.

pain noun **1** a very unpleasant feeling caused by illness or injury. **2** mental suffering or distress. **3** (**pains**) great care or trouble: *she took pains to see that everyone ate well.* **4** (also **pain in the neck** or vulgar slang **pain in the arse**)

informal an annoying or boring person or thing. •verb cause pain to someone.
– PHRASES **on** (or **under**) **pain of** the punishment for wrongdoing being: *we must not, on pain of death, utter a sound.*
– ORIGIN Latin *poena* 'penalty, pain'.

USAGE: Do not confuse **pain** with **pane**. **Pain** means 'an unpleasant feeling caused by illness or injury' (*agonizing stomach pains*), whereas **pane** means 'a sheet of glass' (*a window pane*).

pained adjective showing annoyance or distress: *a pained expression came over his face.*

painful adjective **1** affected with or causing pain. **2** informal very bad: *their attempts at reggae are painful.*
– DERIVATIVES **painfully** adverb **painfulness** noun.

painkiller noun a medicine for relieving pain.
– DERIVATIVES **painkilling** adjective.

painless adjective **1** not causing pain. **2** involving little effort or stress.
– DERIVATIVES **painlessly** adverb **painlessness** noun.

painstaking adjective very careful and thorough.
– DERIVATIVES **painstakingly** adverb.

paint noun **1** a coloured substance which is spread over a surface to give a thin decorative or protective coating. **2** dated cosmetic make-up. •verb **1** apply paint to something. **2** apply a liquid to a surface with a brush. **3** produce a picture with paint. **4** give a description of: *the city isn't as bad as it's painted.*
– PHRASES **be like watching paint dry** be very boring. **paint oneself into a corner** leave oneself no means of escape or room to manoeuvre. **paint the town red** informal go out and enjoy oneself in a lively way.
– ORIGIN from Latin *pingere* 'to paint'.

paintball noun a combat game in which participants shoot capsules of paint at each other with air guns.

paintbox noun a box holding a palette of dry paints for painting pictures.

paintbrush noun a brush for applying paint.

painted lady noun a butterfly with mainly orange-brown wings and darker markings.

painter¹ noun **1** an artist who paints pictures. **2** a person who paints buildings.

painter² noun a rope attached to the bow of a boat for tying it to a quay.
– ORIGIN uncertain.

painterly adjective **1** relating to or like a painter; artistic. **2** (of a painting) characterized by qualities of colour, brushstroke, and texture rather than of line.

painting noun **1** the action of painting. **2** a painted picture.

paintwork noun chiefly Brit. painted surfaces in a building or on a vehicle.

pair noun **1** a set of two things used together or regarded as a unit. **2** an article consisting of two joined or corresponding parts: *a pair of jeans.* **3** two people or animals that are related or considered together. **4** two opposing members of a parliament who agree to be absent for a particular vote, leaving the relative position of the parties unaffected. •verb **1** join or put together to form a pair: *a cardigan paired with a matching skirt.* **2** (**pair**

p

off/**up**) form a romantic or sexual relationship.
– ORIGIN Latin *par* 'equal'.

paisa /py-sah/ noun (pl. **paise** /py-say/) a unit of money of India, Pakistan, and Nepal, equal to one hundredth of a rupee.
– ORIGIN Hindi.

paisley /**payz**-li/ noun an intricate pattern on fabric, consisting of curved shapes resembling feathers.
– ORIGIN named after the town of *Paisley* in Scotland.

Paiute /py-oot/ noun (pl. same or **Paiutes**) a member of either of two American Indian peoples (the **Southern Paiute** and the **Northern Paiute**) of the western US.
– ORIGIN Spanish *Payuchi, Payuta.*

pajamas plural noun US spelling of PYJAMAS.

pak choi /pak **choy**/ (also N. Amer. **bok choy**) noun a variety of Chinese cabbage with smooth-edged tapering leaves.
– ORIGIN Chinese, 'white vegetable'.

Pakeha /**pah**-ki-hah/ noun NZ a white New Zealander, as opposed to a Maori.
– ORIGIN Maori.

Paki noun (pl. **Pakis**) Brit. informal, offensive a Pakistani person.

Pakistani /pak-i-**stah**-ni, pak-i-**sta**-ni/ noun (pl. **Pakistanis**) a person from Pakistan. ● adjective relating to Pakistan.

pakora /puh-**kor**-uh/ noun (in Indian cookery) a piece of battered and deep-fried vegetable or meat.
– ORIGIN Hindi, referring to a dish of vegetables in gram flour.

pal informal noun a friend. ● verb (**pals, palling, palled**) (**pal up**) form a friendship.
– ORIGIN Romany, 'brother, mate'.

palace noun a large, impressive building forming the official residence of a sovereign, president, archbishop, etc.
– ORIGIN Old French *paleis.*

palace coup noun the non-violent overthrow of a sovereign or government by senior officials within the ruling group.

paladin /**pa**-luh-din/ noun **1** literary a brave, chivalrous knight. **2** historical any of the twelve most famous warriors of Charlemagne's court.
– ORIGIN French.

palaeo- /**pa**-li-oh, **pay**-li-oh/ (US **paleo-**) combining form older or ancient: *Palaeolithic.*
– ORIGIN from Greek *palaios* 'ancient'.

Palaeocene /**pa**-li-oh-seen, **pay**-li-oh-seen/ (US **Paleocene**) adjective Geology relating to the earliest epoch of the Tertiary period (about 65 to 56.5 million years ago), a time of rapid development of mammals.
– ORIGIN from Greek *palaios* 'ancient' + *kainos* 'new'.

palaeography /pa-li-og-ruh-fi, pay-li-og-ruh-fi/ (US **paleography**) noun the study of ancient writing systems and manuscripts.
– DERIVATIVES **palaeographer** noun **palaeographic** adjective.

Palaeolithic /pa-li-uh-**li**-thik, pay-li-uh-**li**-thik/ (US **Paleolithic**) adjective Archaeology relating to the early phase of the Stone Age, up to the end of the glacial period.
– ORIGIN from Greek *palaios* 'ancient' + *lithos*

'stone'.

palaeontology /pa-li-on-**tol**-uh-ji, pay-li-on-**tol**-uh-ji/ (US **paleontology**) noun the branch of science concerned with fossil animals and plants.
– DERIVATIVES **palaeontological** adjective **palaeontologist** noun.
– ORIGIN from Greek *palaios* 'ancient' + *onta* 'beings'.

Palaeozoic /pa-li-uh-**zoh**-ik, pay-li-uh-**zoh**-ik/ (US **Paleozoic**) adjective Geology relating to the era between the Precambrian aeon and the Mesozoic era, about 570 to 245 million years ago, which ended with the rise to dominance of the reptiles.
– ORIGIN from Greek *palaios* 'ancient' + *zōē* 'life'.

palais /**pa**-lay/ noun Brit. a public hall for dancing.
– ORIGIN from French *palais de danse* 'dancing hall'.

palanquin /pa-luhn-**keen**/ noun (in India and the East) a seat with a canopy, carried on poles and used as a form of transport for one passenger.
– ORIGIN Portuguese *palanquim.*

palatable /**pa**-luh-tuh-b'l/ adjective **1** pleasant to taste. **2** pleasant or acceptable to someone.
– DERIVATIVES **palatability** noun.

palatal /**pal**-uh-tuhl/ adjective **1** relating to the palate. **2** Phonetics (of a speech sound) made by placing the blade of the tongue against or near the hard palate (e.g. *y* in *yes*).

palate noun **1** the roof of the mouth, separating the cavities of the mouth and nose in vertebrates. **2** a person's ability to distinguish between and appreciate different flavours: *a cocktail created for the discerning palates of the international jet set.*
– ORIGIN Latin *palatum.*

USAGE: On the confusion of **palate** with **palette** or **pallet**, see the note at PALLET².

palatial adjective resembling a palace, especially in being impressively spacious or grand.
– DERIVATIVES **palatially** adverb.

palatinate /puh-**lat**-i-nuht/ noun historical a territory under the jurisdiction of a palatine official or feudal lord.

palatine /**pa**-luh-tyn/ adjective chiefly historical **1** (of an official or feudal lord) having local authority that elsewhere belongs only to a king or queen. **2** (of a territory) subject to such authority.
– ORIGIN French.

palaver /puh-**lah**-ver/ noun informal a lengthy or boring fuss about something; an unnecessarily long-drawn-out process.
– ORIGIN Portuguese *palavra* 'word'.

palazzo /puh-**lat**-soh/ noun (pl. **palazzos** or **palazzi** /puh-**lat**-see/) a large, grand building, especially in Italy.
– ORIGIN Italian, 'palace'.

palazzo pants plural noun women's loose wide-legged trousers.

pale¹ adjective **1** of a light shade or colour. **2** (of a person's face) having little colour, through shock, fear, illness, etc. **3** not very good or impressive: *a pale imitation of the real thing.*

p

•**verb 1** become pale in one's face. **2** seem or become less good or important: *his version of the song pales in comparison to the original.*
– DERIVATIVES **palely** adverb **paleness** noun.
– ORIGIN Old French.

pale² noun **1** a wooden stake used with others to form a fence. **2** a boundary or limit. **3** old use or historical an area within set boundaries or subject to a particular jurisdiction.
– PHRASES **beyond the pale** outside the boundaries of acceptable behaviour.
– ORIGIN Old French *pal*.

paleface noun a name supposedly used by North American Indians for a white person.

paleo- combining form US spelling of **PALAEO-**.

Palestinian /pa-li-**stin**-i-uhn/ adjective relating to Palestine. •noun a member of the native Arab population of Palestine.

palette /**pa**-lit/ noun **1** a thin board on which an artist lays and mixes paints. **2** the range of colours used by an artist.
– ORIGIN French, 'little shovel'.

USAGE: On the confusion of **palette**, **palate**, and **pallet**, see the note at **PALLET²**.

palette knife noun **1** a thin steel blade with a handle for mixing paints or for applying or removing paint. **2** Brit. a kitchen knife with a long, blunt, flexible, round-ended blade.

palfrey /**porl**-fri, **pal**-fri/ noun (pl. **palfreys**) old use a docile horse ridden especially by women.
– ORIGIN Old French *palefrei*.

palimony /**pa**-li-muh-ni/ noun informal, chiefly N. Amer. financial support given by one member of an unmarried couple to the other after separation.
– ORIGIN from **PAL** + **ALIMONY**.

palimpsest /**pa**-limp-sesst/ noun **1** a parchment or other surface on which writing has been applied over earlier writing which has been erased. **2** something altered or used again but still bearing visible traces of its earlier form: *the house is a palimpsest of the taste of successive owners.*
– ORIGIN from Greek *palin* 'again' + *psēstos* 'rubbed smooth'.

palindrome /**pal**-in-drohm/ noun a word or sequence of words that reads the same backwards as forwards, e.g. *madam.*
– DERIVATIVES **palindromic** /pal-in-**drom**-ik/ adjective.
– ORIGIN from Greek *palindromos* 'running back again'.

paling /**pay**-ling/ noun **1** a fence made from stakes. **2** a stake used in such a fence.

palisade /pa-li-**sayd**/ noun a fence of stakes or iron railings forming an enclosure or defence.
– ORIGIN French *palissade*.

pall¹ /pawl/ noun **1** a cloth spread over a coffin, hearse, or tomb. **2** a dark cloud of smoke or dust. **3** a general atmosphere of gloom or fear: *the murder had cast a pall of terror over the village.*
– ORIGIN Latin *pallium* 'covering, cloak'.

pall² /pawl/ verb become less appealing or interesting as a result of being too familiar: *the thrill of flouting her father's wishes began to pall.*
– ORIGIN shortening of **APPAL**.

Palladian /puh-**lay**-di-uhn/ adjective referring to a neoclassical style of architecture based on that of the Italian architect Andrea Palladio.

palladium /puh-**lay**-di-uhm/ noun a rare silvery-white metallic element resembling platinum.
– ORIGIN from *Pallas*, an asteroid discovered just before the element.

pall-bearer noun a person helping to carry or escorting a coffin at a funeral.

pallet¹ noun a straw mattress or makeshift bed.
– ORIGIN Old French *paillete*.

pallet² noun a portable platform on which goods can be moved, stacked, and stored.
– DERIVATIVES **palletize** (or **palletise**) verb.
– ORIGIN French, 'little blade'.

USAGE: Do not confuse **pallet** with **palate** or **palette**. A **pallet** is 'a portable platform for moving goods' or 'a makeshift bed', **palate** means 'the roof of the mouth' or 'a person's ability to distinguish between different flavours', and a **palette** is 'an artist's board for mixing paints'.

palliasse /pal-li-**ass**/ noun a straw mattress.
– ORIGIN French *paillasse*.

palliate /**pal**-li-ayt/ verb **1** make the symptoms of a disease less severe without curing it. **2** cause something bad to seem less serious: *there is no way to palliate his offence.*
– DERIVATIVES **palliation** noun.
– ORIGIN Latin *palliare* 'to cloak'.

palliative /**pal**-li-uh-tiv/ adjective **1** (of a medicine or medical care) relieving pain without curing the condition which is causing it. **2** (of an action) intended to make a problem less severe without dealing with its underlying cause. •noun a palliative medicine or remedy.

pallid adjective **1** pale, especially because of poor health. **2** weak or insipid: *a pallid ray of winter sun.*
– ORIGIN Latin *pallidus* 'pale'.

pallor noun an unhealthy pale appearance.
– ORIGIN Latin.

pally adjective informal having a close, friendly relationship.

palm¹ noun **1** (also **palm tree**) an evergreen tree with a crown of very long feathered or fan-shaped leaves, growing in warm regions. **2** a leaf of a palm tree awarded as a prize or viewed as a symbol of victory.
– ORIGIN Latin *palma* 'palm (of a hand)', its leaf being likened to a spread hand.

palm² noun the inner surface of the hand between the wrist and fingers. •verb **1** hide a small object in the hand, especially as part of a trick. **2** (**palm something off**) sell or get rid of something dishonestly, especially by misrepresenting its quality or worth. **3** (**palm someone off**) informal persuade someone to accept something that is unwanted or has little value.
– PHRASES **in the palm of one's hand** under one's control or influence. **read someone's palm** tell someone's fortune by looking at the lines on their palm.
– ORIGIN Latin *palma.*

palmate /**pal**-mayt/ adjective shaped like an open hand with a number of sections

p

resembling fingers: *palmate leaves.*

palmer noun historical a pilgrim, especially one who had returned from the Holy Land with a palm branch or leaf as a sign of having undertaken the pilgrimage.
– ORIGIN Latin *palmarius* 'pilgrim'.

palmetto /pal-**met**-toh/ noun (pl. **palmettos**) an American palm with large fan-shaped leaves.
– ORIGIN Spanish *palmito* 'small palm'.

palmier /**pal**-mi-ay/ noun (pl. pronounced same) a sweet pastry shaped like the leaf of a palm tree.
– ORIGIN French, 'palm tree'.

palmistry noun the supposed interpretation of a person's character or prediction of their future by examining their hand.
– DERIVATIVES **palmist** noun.

Palm Sunday noun the Sunday before Easter, on which Jesus's entry into Jerusalem is celebrated by processions in which palm tree branches are carried.

palmtop noun a computer small and light enough to be held in one hand.

palmy adjective (**palmier, palmiest**) comfortable and prosperous: *the palmy days of the 1970s.*

palomino /pa-luh-**mee**-noh/ noun (pl. **palominos**) a pale golden or tan-coloured horse with a white mane and tail.
– ORIGIN Latin American Spanish, from Spanish, 'young pigeon'.

palp /*rhymes with* scalp/ noun each of a pair of long segmented feelers near the mouth of some insects and crustaceans.
– ORIGIN Latin *palpus.*

palpable /**pal**-puh-b'l/ adjective **1** able to be touched or felt. **2** (of a feeling or atmosphere) so intense that one seems to experience it as a physical sensation: *a palpable sense of loss.*
– DERIVATIVES **palpably** adverb.
– ORIGIN Latin *palpabilis.*

palpate /pal-**payt**/ verb examine a part of the body by touch, especially for medical purposes.
– DERIVATIVES **palpation** noun.

palpitate /**pal**-pi-tayt/ verb **1** (of the heart) beat rapidly or irregularly. **2** shake or tremble.
– ORIGIN Latin *palpitare* 'tremble, throb'.

palpitation noun **1** throbbing or trembling. **2** (**palpitations**) a noticeably rapid, strong, or irregular heartbeat.

palsy /**pawl**-zi/ noun (pl. **palsies**) dated paralysis, especially when accompanied by involuntary shaking of the limbs. • verb (**be palsied**) suffer from palsy.
– ORIGIN Old French *paralisie*, from Latin *paralysis.*

paltry adjective (**paltrier, paltriest**) **1** (of an amount) very small. **2** petty or trivial.
– DERIVATIVES **paltriness** noun.
– ORIGIN probably from dialect *pelt* 'rubbish'.

pampas /**pam**-puhss/ noun (treated as sing. or pl.) large treeless plains in South America.
– ORIGIN Quechua, 'plain'.

pampas grass noun a tall South American grass with silky flowering plumes.

pamper verb lavish care and attention on someone; spoil someone.
– ORIGIN probably from German or Dutch, first meaning 'cram with food'.

pamphlet /**pam**-flit/ noun a small booklet or leaflet containing information about a particular subject. • verb (**pamphlets, pamphleting, pamphleted**) distribute pamphlets to people.
– ORIGIN from *Pamphilet*, the name given to a 12th-century Latin love poem *Pamphilus, seu de Amore.*

pamphleteer noun a person who writes pamphlets, especially ones that deal with political issues.
– DERIVATIVES **pamphleteering** noun.

pan¹ noun **1** a metal container for cooking food in. **2** a bowl fitted at either end of a pair of scales. **3** Brit. the bowl of a toilet. **4** a shallow bowl in which gravel and mud are shaken and washed by people looking for gold. **5** a hollow in the ground in which water collects or in which salt is deposited after evaporation. **6** a part of the lock that held the priming in old types of gun. **7** a steel drum. • verb (**pans, panning, panned**) **1** informal criticize someone or something severely. **2** (**pan out**) informal end up or conclude: *he's happy with the way the deal panned out.* **3** wash gravel in a pan to separate out gold.
– PHRASES **go down the pan** Brit. informal fail or be totally useless.
– ORIGIN Old English.

pan² verb (**pans, panning, panned**) swing a video or film camera on a horizontal plane to give a panoramic effect or follow a subject. • noun a panning movement.
– ORIGIN abbreviation of **PANORAMA.**

pan³ /pahn/ noun variant spelling of **PAAN.**

pan- combining form including everything or everyone, especially the whole of a continent, people, etc.: *pan-African.*
– ORIGIN Greek.

panacea /pan-uh-**see**-uh/ noun a solution or remedy for all difficulties or diseases.
– ORIGIN Greek *panakeia.*

panache /puh-**nash**/ noun an impressively confident and stylish way of doing something.
– ORIGIN French, 'plume of feathers'.

panama noun a man's wide-brimmed hat of straw-like material, originally made from the leaves of a tropical palm tree.
– ORIGIN named after the country of *Panama.*

Panamanian /pa-nuh-**may**-ni-uhn/ noun a person from Panama. • adjective relating to Panama.

panatella /pan-uh-**tel**-luh/ noun a long thin cigar.
– ORIGIN Latin American Spanish *panatela* 'long thin biscuit'.

pancake noun **1** a thin, flat cake of batter, fried and turned in a pan. **2** theatrical make-up consisting of a flat solid layer of compressed powder.

Pancake Day noun Shrove Tuesday, when pancakes are traditionally eaten.

pancetta /pan-**chet**-uh/ noun Italian cured belly of pork.
– ORIGIN Italian, 'little belly'.

panchromatic adjective (of black-and-white photographic film) sensitive to all visible colours of the spectrum.

pancreas /**pang**-kri-uhss/ noun (pl. **pancreases**)

a large gland behind the stomach which produces digestive enzymes and releases them into the duodenum.
– DERIVATIVES **pancreatic** adjective.
– ORIGIN from Greek *pan* 'all' + *kreas* 'flesh'.

pancreatitis /pang-kri-uh-**ty**-tiss/ noun inflammation of the pancreas.

panda noun **1** (also **giant panda**) a large black-and-white bear-like mammal native to bamboo forests in China. **2** (also **red panda**) a raccoon-like Himalayan mammal with thick reddish-brown fur and a bushy tail.
– ORIGIN Nepali.

panda car noun Brit. informal a police patrol car (originally black and white or blue and white).

pandanus /pan-**day**-nuhss, pan-**dan**-uhss/ noun a tropical tree or shrub with a twisted stem and long, narrow spiny leaves from which fibre is obtained.
– ORIGIN Malay.

pandemic /pan-**dem**-ik/ adjective (of a disease) widespread over a whole country or large part of the world. • noun an outbreak of such a disease.
– ORIGIN from Greek *pan* 'all' + *dēmos* 'people'.

pandemonium /pan-di-**moh**-ni-uhm/ noun a state of wild and noisy disorder or confusion; uproar.
– ORIGIN first meaning 'the place of all demons', in Milton's *Paradise Lost*: from Greek *pan* 'all' + *daimōn* 'demon'.

pander verb (**pander to**) satisfy or indulge someone's desires or tastes, especially when these are unreasonable or distasteful: *newspapers are pandering to people's baser instincts.* • noun dated a pimp.
– ORIGIN from *Pandare*, a character in Chaucer's *Troilus and Criseyde* who acts as a lovers' go-between.

pandit (also **pundit**) noun a Hindu scholar learned in Sanskrit and Hindu philosophy and religion.
– ORIGIN from Sanskrit, 'learned'.

Pandora's box noun a process that once begun creates many complicated problems.
– ORIGIN from *Pandora* in Greek mythology, who was sent to earth with a jar or box of evils and contrary to instructions opened it, letting the evils escape.

p. & p. abbreviation Brit. postage and packing.

pane noun **1** a single sheet of glass in a window or door. **2** a sheet or page of stamps.
– ORIGIN Latin *pannus* 'piece of cloth'.

USAGE: On the confusion of **pane** and **pain**, see the note at **PAIN**.

paneer /pa-**ni**-uh/ noun a type of milk curd cheese used in Indian and Iranian cooking.
– ORIGIN Hindi or Persian, 'cheese'.

panegyric /pa-ni-**ji**-rik/ noun a speech or piece of writing in praise of someone or something.
– ORIGIN from Greek *panēgurikos* 'of public assembly'.

panel noun **1** a distinct, usually rectangular section of a door, vehicle, item of clothing, etc. **2** a flat board on which instruments or controls are fixed. **3** a small group of people brought together to investigate, discuss, or decide on something. **4** chiefly N. Amer. a jury, or a list of available jurors.

– DERIVATIVES **panelled** (US **paneled**) adjective.
– ORIGIN Latin *pannus* 'piece of cloth'.

panel beater noun Brit. a person whose job is to beat out the bodywork of motor vehicles.

panel game noun Brit. a broadcast quiz played by a team of people.

panelling (US **paneling**) noun wooden panels as a decorative wall covering.

panellist (US **panelist**) noun a member of a panel taking part in a broadcast game or discussion.

panel pin noun Brit. a light, thin nail with a very small head.

panel saw noun Brit. a light saw with small teeth, for cutting thin wood.

panel truck noun N. Amer. a small enclosed delivery lorry.

pan-fry verb fry food in a pan in shallow fat.

pang noun a sudden sharp pain or painful emotion: *pangs of remorse.*
– ORIGIN perhaps an alteration of **PRONG**.

Panglossian /pang-**gloss**-i-uhn/ adjective literary unrealistically optimistic.
– ORIGIN from *Pangloss*, the tutor and philosopher in Voltaire's *Candide*.

pangolin /pang-**guh**-lin/ noun an insect-eating mammal whose body is covered with horny overlapping scales.
– ORIGIN Malay, 'roller' (from the animal's habit of rolling into a ball).

panhandle N. Amer. noun a narrow strip of territory projecting from the main territory of one state into another. • verb informal beg in the street.
– DERIVATIVES **panhandler** noun.

panic noun **1** sudden uncontrollable fear or anxiety. **2** informal frenzied hurry to do something. • verb (**panics**, **panicking**, **panicked**) feel sudden uncontrollable fear or anxiety, or make someone feel this: *the crowd panicked and stampeded for the exit.*
– DERIVATIVES **panicky** adjective.
– ORIGIN from the name of the Greek god *Pan*, noted for causing terror.

panic attack noun a sudden overwhelming feeling of acute anxiety, making someone unable to function normally.

panic button noun a button for summoning help in an emergency.

panicle /**pan**-i-k'l/ noun a loose branching cluster of flowers, as in oats.
– ORIGIN Latin *panicula*.

panic stations plural noun (treated as sing.) Brit. informal a state of alarm or emergency.

panino /pa-**nee**-noh/ noun (pl. **panini** /pa-**nee**-ni/) a sandwich made with a baguette or with Italian bread, typically toasted.
– ORIGIN Italian, 'bread roll'.

Panjabi noun (pl. **Panjabis**) & adjective variant spelling of **PUNJABI**.

panjandrum /pan-**jan**-druhm/ noun a pompous, self-important person in a position of authority.
– ORIGIN from *Grand Panjandrum*, an invented phrase in a nonsense verse by Samuel Foote.

panne /pan/ (also **panne velvet**) noun a glossy fabric resembling velvet, with a flattened pile.
– ORIGIN French.

pannier noun **1** a bag or box fitted on either

p

side of the rear wheel of a bicycle or motorcycle. **2** a basket, especially each of a pair carried by a donkey or mule.
– ORIGIN Old French *panier*.

pannikin noun a small metal drinking cup.

panoply /pan-uh-pli/ noun a large or impressive collection or display of something.
– ORIGIN from Greek *pan* 'all' + *hopla* 'weapons, armour'.

panoptic /pan-op-tik/ adjective showing or seeing the whole of something at one view.
– ORIGIN Greek *panoptos* 'seen by all'.

panorama noun **1** an unbroken view of the whole region surrounding an observer. **2** a complete survey of a subject or sequence of events: *a full panorama of 20th-century art.*
– DERIVATIVES **panoramic** adjective **panoramically** adverb.
– ORIGIN from Greek *pan* 'all' + *horama* 'view'.

pan pipes plural noun a musical instrument made from a row of short pipes fixed together.
– ORIGIN from the name of the Greek god *Pan*.

pansexual adjective another term for OMNISEXUAL.

panstick noun a kind of matt cosmetic foundation in stick form, used in theatrical make-up.
– ORIGIN from PANCAKE + STICK¹.

pansy noun **1** a plant of the viola family, with brightly coloured flowers. **2** informal, derogatory an effeminate or homosexual man.
– ORIGIN French *pensée* 'thought, pansy'.

pant verb **1** breathe with short, quick breaths, typically as a result of physical exertion. **2** (**pant for**) long for something. •noun a short, quick breath.
– ORIGIN Old French *pantaisier* 'be agitated, gasp'.

pantalettes plural noun women's long underpants with a frill at the bottom of each leg, worn in the 19th century.

pantaloons plural noun **1** women's baggy trousers gathered at the ankles. **2** historical men's close-fitting breeches fastened below the calf or at the foot.
– ORIGIN from *Pantalone*, a character in Italian comic theatre represented as a foolish old man wearing pantaloons.

pantechnicon /pan-tek-ni-kuhn/ noun Brit. a large van for transporting furniture.
– ORIGIN from Greek *pan* 'all' + *tekhnikon* 'piece of art', originally the name of a London market selling artistic work, later converted into a furniture warehouse.

pantheism /pan-thee-i-z'm/ noun **1** the belief that God is present in all things in the universe. **2** the worship or tolerance of many gods.
– DERIVATIVES **pantheist** noun **pantheistic** adjective.

pantheon /pan-thi-uhn/ noun **1** all the gods of a people or religion. **2** an ancient temple dedicated to all the gods. **3** a collection of famous or important people: *the pantheon of powerful Washington journalists.*
– ORIGIN from Greek *pan* 'all' + *theion* 'holy'.

panther noun **1** a leopard, especially a black one. **2** N. Amer. a puma or a jaguar.
– ORIGIN Greek *panthēr*.

panties plural noun informal underpants worn by women and girls; knickers.

pantihose plural noun variant spelling of PANTYHOSE.

pantile /pan-tyl/ noun a roof tile curved to form an S-shaped section, fitted to overlap its neighbour.
– ORIGIN from PAN¹ + TILE.

panto noun (pl. **pantos**) Brit. informal a pantomime.

pantograph noun **1** an instrument for copying a plan or drawing on a different scale by a system of hinged and jointed rods. **2** a jointed framework conveying a current to an electric train or tram from overhead wires.

pantomime noun **1** Brit. a theatrical entertainment involving music, topical jokes, and slapstick comedy, usually produced around Christmas. **2** a ridiculous or confused action or situation.
– ORIGIN Greek *pantomimos* 'imitator of all', first meaning 'actor using mime'.

pantothenic acid /pan-tuh-then-ik/ noun a vitamin of the B complex, found in rice, bran, and other foods, and essential for the oxidation of fats and carbohydrates.
– ORIGIN from Greek *pantothen* 'from every side' (referring to its widespread occurrence).

pantry noun (pl. **pantries**) a small room or cupboard in which food, crockery, and cutlery are kept.
– ORIGIN from Old French *paneter* 'baker'.

pants plural noun **1** Brit. underpants or knickers. **2** chiefly N. Amer. trousers.
– PHRASES **fly** (or **drive**) **by the seat of one's pants** informal rely on instinct rather than logic or knowledge. **scare** (or **bore** etc.) **the pants off** informal make someone extremely scared, bored, etc.
– ORIGIN abbreviation of PANTALOONS.

pantsuit (also **pants suit**) noun N. Amer. a trouser suit.

pantyhose (also **pantihose**) plural noun N. Amer. women's thin nylon tights.

panzer /pan-zuh/ noun a German armoured military unit.
– ORIGIN German, 'coat of mail'.

pap¹ noun **1** bland soft or semi-liquid food suitable for babies or invalids. **2** books, magazines, television programmes, or other forms of entertainment that require no intellectual effort.
– DERIVATIVES **pappy** adjective.
– ORIGIN probably from Latin *pappare* 'eat'.

pap² noun old use or dialect a woman's breast or nipple.
– ORIGIN probably Scandinavian.

papa /puh-pah, pop-puh/ noun N. Amer. or dated one's father.
– ORIGIN French.

papacy /pay-puh-si/ noun (pl. **papacies**) the position or period of office of the pope.
– ORIGIN Latin *papa* 'pope'.

papal /pay-p'l/ adjective relating to the pope or the papacy.
– DERIVATIVES **papally** adverb.

paparazzo /pa-puh-rat-zoh/ noun (pl. **paparazzi** /pa-puh-rat-zi/) a freelance photographer who pursues celebrities to get photographs of them.

– ORIGIN Italian, the name of a character in Fellini's film *La Dolce Vita*.

papaw /puh-**por**/ noun variant spelling of **PAWPAW**.

papaya /puh-**py**-uh/ noun a tropical fruit with edible orange flesh and small black seeds.
– ORIGIN Spanish and Portuguese.

paper noun 1 material manufactured in thin sheets from the pulp of wood or other fibrous substances, used for writing or printing on or as wrapping material. 2 (**papers**) sheets of paper covered with writing or printing; documents. 3 a newspaper. 4 a government report or policy document. 5 an essay or dissertation read at a conference or published in a journal. 6 Brit. a set of exam questions. • verb 1 cover a wall with wallpaper. 2 (**paper something over**) disguise an awkward problem instead of resolving it. • adjective officially recorded but having no real existence or use: *a paper profit.*
– PHRASES **on paper 1** in writing. **2** in theory rather than in reality.
– DERIVATIVES **paperless** adjective **papery** adjective.
– ORIGIN Old French *papir*, from Latin *papyrus* (see **PAPYRUS**).

paperback noun a book bound in stiff paper or flexible card.

paper boy (or **paper girl**) noun a boy (or girl) who delivers newspapers to people's homes.

paper clip noun a piece of bent wire or plastic used for holding several sheets of paper together.

paperknife noun a blunt knife used for opening envelopes.

paper money noun money in the form of banknotes.

paper round (N. Amer. **paper route**) noun a job of regularly delivering newspapers.

paper-thin adjective very thin or insubstantial.

paper tiger noun a person or thing that appears threatening but is actually weak or ineffectual.

paper trail noun chiefly N. Amer. the total amount of written evidence of someone's activities.

paperweight noun a small, heavy object for keeping loose papers in place.

paperwork noun routine work involving written documents.

papier mâché /pa-pi-ay **mash**-ay/ noun a mixture of paper and glue that is easily moulded but becomes hard when dry.
– ORIGIN French, 'chewed paper'.

papilla /puh-**pil**-luh/ noun (pl. **papillae** /puh-**pil**-lee/) a small rounded protuberance on a part of the body or on a plant.
– DERIVATIVES **papillary** adjective.
– ORIGIN Latin, 'nipple'.

papilloma /pa-pil-**loh**-muh/ noun (pl. **papillomas** or **papillomata** /pa-pil-**loh**-muh-tuh/) a small, usually benign wart-like growth.

papillon /pa-pil-lon, pa-pi-yon/ noun a breed of toy dog with ears suggesting the form of a butterfly.
– ORIGIN French, 'butterfly'.

papist /**pay**-pist/ chiefly derogatory noun a Roman Catholic. • adjective Roman Catholic.

papoose /puh-**poos**/ noun offensive a young North American Indian child.

– ORIGIN Algonquian.

paprika /**pap**-ri-kuh, puh-**pree**-kuh/ noun a deep orange-red powdered spice made from certain varieties of sweet pepper.
– ORIGIN Hungarian.

Pap test noun a smear test carried out to detect cancer of the cervix or womb.
– ORIGIN named after the American scientist George N. *Papanicolaou*.

Papuan noun 1 a person from Papua or Papua New Guinea. 2 a group of languages spoken in Papua New Guinea and neighbouring islands. • adjective relating to Papua or its languages.

papule /**pap**-yool/ noun a small pimple or swelling on the skin, often forming part of a rash.
– ORIGIN Latin *papula*.

papyrus /puh-**py**-ruhss/ noun (pl. **papyri** /puh-**py**-ry/ or **papyruses**) 1 a material made in ancient Egypt from the stem of a kind of water plant, used for writing or painting on. 2 the plant from which papyrus was obtained.
– ORIGIN Greek *papuros*.

par noun 1 Golf the number of strokes a first-class player should normally require for a particular hole or course. 2 Stock Exchange the face value of a share or other security. • verb (**pars, parring, parred**) Golf play a hole in a score equal to par.
– PHRASES **above** (or **below** or **under**) **par** above (or below) the usual or expected level. **on a par with** equal to. **par for the course** what is normal or expected in any given circumstances.
– ORIGIN Latin, 'equal, equality'.

para[1] /**pa**-ruh/ noun informal a paratrooper.

para[2] /**pa**-ruh/ noun (pl. same or **paras**) a unit of money of Bosnia, Montenegro, and Serbia, equal to one hundredth of a dinar.
– ORIGIN Turkish, 'money'.

para- (also **par-**) prefix 1 beside; adjacent to: *parallel.* 2 beyond or distinct from, but comparable to: *paramilitary.*
– ORIGIN from Greek *para* 'beside, beyond'.

parable noun a simple story used to illustrate a moral or spiritual lesson.
– ORIGIN Latin *parabola* 'comparison'.

parabola /puh-**rab**-uh-luh/ noun (pl. **parabolas** or **parabolae** /puh-**rab**-uh-lee/) a symmetrical open plane curve of the kind formed by the intersection of a cone with a plane parallel to its side.
– DERIVATIVES **parabolic** /pa-ruh-**bol**-ik/ adjective.
– ORIGIN Latin.

paracetamol /pa-ruh-**see**-tuh-mol, pa-ruh-**set**-uh-mol/ noun (pl. same or **paracetamols**) Brit. a drug used to relieve pain and reduce fever.
– ORIGIN from its chemical name.

parachute noun a cloth canopy which allows a person or heavy object attached to it to descend slowly through the air when dropped from a high position. • verb 1 drop from an aircraft by parachute. 2 appoint someone in an emergency or from outside the existing management structure: *he was parachuted in as chief executive in May.*
– DERIVATIVES **parachutist** noun.
– ORIGIN from French *para-* 'protection against' + *chute* 'fall'.

p

parade noun **1** a public procession. **2** a formal march or gathering of troops for inspection or display. **3** a series or succession: *the parade of celebrities who troop on to his show.* **4** a boastful or obvious display of something. **5** Brit. a public promenade or row of shops. •verb **1** walk, march, or display something in a parade. **2** display something in order to impress other people or attract attention: *he enjoyed being able to parade his knowledge.* **3** (**parade as**) appear to be something that is not the case: *these untruths parading as history.*
– ORIGIN French, 'a showing'.

parade ground noun a place where troops gather for parade.

paradiddle /pa-ruh-did-d'l/ noun Music a simple drum roll consisting of four even strokes.
– ORIGIN imitating the sound.

paradigm /pa-ruh-dym/ noun a typical example, pattern, or model of something: *society's paradigm of the 'ideal woman'.*
– DERIVATIVES **paradigmatic** /pa-ruh-dig-mat-ik/ adjective **paradigmatically** adverb.
– ORIGIN Greek *paradeigma.*

paradigm shift noun a fundamental change in approach or in the assumptions underlying something.

paradise noun **1** (in some religions) heaven as the place where the good live after death. **2** the Garden of Eden. **3** an ideal or very beautiful place or state: *the surrounding countryside is a walker's paradise.*
– DERIVATIVES **paradisal** adjective **paradisiacal** /pa-ruh-di-sy-uh-k'l/ adjective.
– ORIGIN Old French *paradis.*

parador /pa-ruh-dor/ noun (in Spain) a hotel which is owned and managed by the government.
– ORIGIN Spanish.

paradox noun **1** a statement that sounds absurd or seems to contradict itself but may in fact be true. **2** a person or thing that combines contradictory features or qualities.
– DERIVATIVES **paradoxical** adjective **paradoxically** adverb.
– ORIGIN Greek *paradoxon* 'contrary opinion'.

paraffin noun **1** (also **paraffin wax**) chiefly Brit. a flammable waxy solid obtained from petroleum or shale and used for sealing and waterproofing and in candles. **2** (also **paraffin oil** or **liquid paraffin**) Brit. a liquid fuel made in a similar way, especially kerosene.
– ORIGIN German.

paragliding noun a sport in which a person glides through the air attached to a wide parachute after jumping from or being hauled to a height.
– DERIVATIVES **paraglide** verb **paraglider** noun.

paragon noun a person or thing seen as perfect, or as a perfect example of a particular quality: *he was a paragon of blond male beauty.*
– ORIGIN Italian *paragone* 'touchstone'.

paragraph noun a distinct section of a piece of writing, beginning on a new line and often indented.
– ORIGIN French *paragraphe.*

paragraph mark noun a symbol (usually ¶) used to mark a new paragraph or as a reference mark.

Paraguayan /pa-ruh-gwy-uhn/ noun a person

from Paraguay. •adjective relating to Paraguay.

parakeet /pa-ruh-keet/ (also **parrakeet**) noun a small parrot with mainly green plumage and a long tail.
– ORIGIN Old French *paroquet*, Italian *parrocchetto*, and Spanish *periquito.*

paralegal noun N. Amer. a person trained in certain legal matters but not fully qualified as a lawyer.

parallax /pa-ruh-laks/ noun **1** the apparent difference in the position of an object when viewed from different positions, e.g. through the viewfinder and the lens of a camera. **2** Astronomy the angular difference in the apparent positions of a star observed from opposite sides of the earth's orbit.
– DERIVATIVES **parallactic** adjective.
– ORIGIN Greek *parallaxis* 'a change'.

parallel adjective **1** (of lines, planes, or surfaces) side by side and having the same distance continuously between them. **2** occurring or existing at the same time or in a similar way: *a parallel universe.* •noun **1** a person or thing that is similar or comparable to another. **2** a similarity or comparison: *there are interesting parallels between the 1960s and the 1940s.* **3** (also **parallel of latitude**) each of the imaginary parallel circles of latitude on the earth's surface. **4** Printing two parallel lines (‖) used as a reference mark for footnotes. •verb (**parallels, paralleling, paralleled**) **1** run or lie parallel to something. **2** be similar or corresponding to: *changes in 20th century art have paralleled changes in society.*
– PHRASES **in parallel 1** taking place at the same time and having some connection. **2** (of electrical components or circuits) connected to common points at each end, so that the current is divided between them.
– DERIVATIVES **parallelism** noun.
– ORIGIN Greek *parallēlos.*

parallel bars plural noun a pair of parallel rails on posts, used in gymnastics.

parallel imports plural noun goods imported by unlicensed distributors for sale at less than the manufacturer's official retail price.

parallelogram /pa-ruh-lel-uh-gram/ noun a plane figure with four straight sides and opposite sides parallel.

Paralympics plural noun (usu. treated as sing.) an international athletic competition for athletes with disabilities.
– DERIVATIVES **Paralympic** adjective.
– ORIGIN blend of *paraplegic* and *Olympics.*

paralyse (chiefly US also **paralyze**) verb **1** cause a person or part of the body to become partly or wholly incapable of movement. **2** prevent someone or something from functioning: *the regional capital was paralysed by a general strike.*

paralysis /puh-ral-i-siss/ noun (pl. **paralyses** /puh-ral-i-seez/) **1** the loss of the ability to move part or most of the body. **2** inability to act or function.
– ORIGIN Greek *paralusis.*

paralytic adjective **1** relating to paralysis. **2** Brit. informal extremely drunk.
– DERIVATIVES **paralytically** adverb.

paramecium /pa-ruh-mee-si-uhm/ noun (pl. **paramecia** /pa-ruh-mee-si-uh/) a single-celled freshwater animal which has a slipper-like

p

shape.
– ORIGIN Latin.

paramedic noun a person who is trained to do medical work, especially emergency first aid, but is not a fully qualified doctor.
– DERIVATIVES **paramedical** adjective.

parameter /puh-**ram**-i-ter/ noun **1** a limit or boundary which dictates the scope of a particular process or activity: *the parameters within which the media work.* **2** technical a numerical or other measurable factor forming one of a set that defines a system or sets the conditions of its operation. **3** Mathematics a quantity which is fixed for the case in question but may vary in other cases.
– DERIVATIVES **parametric** adjective **parametrically** adverb.
– ORIGIN from Greek *para-* 'beside' + *metron* 'measure'.

paramilitary adjective organized on similar lines to a military force. ●noun (pl. **paramilitaries**) a member of a paramilitary organization.

paramount adjective **1** more important than anything else: *the safety of the staff is paramount.* **2** having supreme power.
– DERIVATIVES **paramountcy** noun.
– ORIGIN from Old French *par* 'by' + *amont* 'above'.

paramour noun old use a person's lover, especially the illicit lover of someone who is married.
– ORIGIN from Old French *par amour* 'by love'.

paranoia /pa-ruh-**noy**-uh/ noun **1** a mental condition characterized by delusions of persecution, unfounded jealousy, or exaggerated self-importance. **2** unjustified suspicion and mistrust of other people.
– DERIVATIVES **paranoiac** /pa-ruh-**noy**-ik/ (also **paranoic** /pa-ruh-**noh**-ik/) adjective & noun **paranoiacally** adverb.
– ORIGIN Latin, from Greek *para* 'irregular' + *noos* 'mind'.

paranoid adjective **1** relating to or suffering from paranoia. **2** unreasonably or obsessively anxious, suspicious, or mistrustful: *he was paranoid about being overcharged.*

paranormal adjective beyond the scope of normal scientific understanding.
– DERIVATIVES **paranormally** adverb.

parapente /pa-ruh-**pont**/ verb (usu. as noun **parapenting**) glide while suspended from a wing-like parachute launched from high ground. ●noun a parachute used for this purpose.
– DERIVATIVES **parapenter** noun.
– ORIGIN French, from *para*(*chute*) + *pente* 'slope'.

parapet /**pa**-ruh-pit/ noun **1** a low protective wall along the edge of a roof, bridge, or balcony. **2** a protective wall or bank along the top of a military trench.
– ORIGIN French, or from Italian *parapetto*, 'chest-high wall'.

paraphernalia /pa-ruh-fer-**nay**-li-uh/ noun (treated as sing. or pl.) miscellaneous items, especially the equipment needed for a particular activity.
– ORIGIN Latin, first meaning 'property owned by a married woman'.

paraphrase verb express the meaning of something written or spoken using different words. ●noun a rewording of something written or spoken.

paraplegia /pa-ruh-**plee**-juh/ noun paralysis of the legs and lower body.
– DERIVATIVES **paraplegic** adjective & noun.
– ORIGIN Greek, from *paraplēssein* 'strike at the side'.

parapsychology noun the study of mental phenomena that cannot be explained by scientific knowledge, such as hypnosis or telepathy.
– DERIVATIVES **parapsychological** adjective **parapsychologist** noun.

paraquat /**pa**-ruh-kwot, **pa**-ruh-kwat/ noun a poisonous fast-acting weedkiller.
– ORIGIN from **PARA-** + **QUATERNARY**.

parasailing noun the sport of gliding through the air wearing an open parachute while being towed by a motorboat.
– DERIVATIVES **parasail** noun & verb.

parascending noun Brit. paragliding or parasailing.
– DERIVATIVES **parascend** verb **parascender** noun.

parasite noun **1** an animal or plant which lives in or on another animal or plant from which it obtains food. **2** derogatory a person who lives off or exploits other people.
– DERIVATIVES **parasitism** noun.
– ORIGIN Greek *parasitos* 'person eating at another's table'.

parasitic /pa-ruh-**sit**-ik/ adjective **1** (of an animal or plant) living in or on another animal or plant. **2** resulting from infestation by a parasite: *a parasitic disease.* **3** derogatory (of a person) habitually relying on or exploiting other people.
– DERIVATIVES **parasitical** adjective **parasitically** adverb.

parasitize (or **parasitise**) /pa-ruh-sy-tyz, pa-ruh-si-tyz/ verb live in or on another animal or plant as a parasite.

parasitology noun the study of parasitic animals and plants.
– DERIVATIVES **parasitologist** noun.

parasol noun a light umbrella used to give shade from the sun.
– ORIGIN Italian *parasole*.

parasympathetic adjective relating to a system of nerves arising from the brain and the lower end of the spinal cord and supplying the internal organs, blood vessels, and glands.

paratha /puh-**rah**-tuh/ noun (in Indian cookery) a flat, thick piece of unleavened bread fried on a griddle.
– ORIGIN Hindi.

parathyroid noun a gland next to the thyroid which produces a hormone that regulates calcium levels in a person's body.

paratroops plural noun troops equipped to be dropped by parachute from aircraft.
– DERIVATIVES **paratrooper** noun.

paratyphoid noun a fever resembling typhoid, caused by related bacteria.

parboil verb partly cook something by boiling it.
– ORIGIN Latin *perbullire* 'boil thoroughly'.

parcel noun **1** an object or collection of objects

wrapped in paper in order to be carried or sent by post. **2** a quantity or amount of something: *a parcel of land.* • verb (**parcels, parcelling, parcelled;** US **parcels, parceling, parceled**) **1** make something into a parcel by wrapping it. **2** (**parcel something out**) divide something into portions and then share it out.
– ORIGIN Old French *parcelle.*

parch verb **1** make something dry through intense heat. **2** (as adj. **parched**) informal extremely thirsty.
– ORIGIN unknown.

parchment noun **1** a stiff material made from the skin of a sheep or goat, formerly used for writing on. **2** (also **parchment paper**) stiff translucent paper treated to resemble parchment.
– ORIGIN Old French *parchemin.*

pardon noun **1** the action of forgiving someone for a mistake or offence. **2** an official cancellation of the legal consequences of an offence. **3** Christian Church, historical an indulgence. • verb **1** forgive or excuse a person, mistake, or offence. **2** give an offender an official pardon. • exclamation used to ask a speaker to repeat something because one did not hear or understand it.
– DERIVATIVES **pardonable** adjective.
– ORIGIN Latin *perdonare* 'concede'.

pardoner noun historical a person licensed to sell papal pardons or indulgences.

pare verb **1** trim something by cutting away its outer edges. **2** (often **pare something away/ down**) reduce or diminish something in a number of small successive stages: *the company's domestic operations were pared down.*
– ORIGIN Old French *parer.*

parent noun **1** a father or mother. **2** an animal or plant from which younger ones are derived. **3** an organization which owns or controls a number of smaller organizations. **4** old use a forefather or ancestor. • verb (often as noun **parenting**) be or act as a parent to someone: *institutions cannot provide good parenting.*
– DERIVATIVES **parental** adjective **parentally** adverb **parenthood** noun.
– ORIGIN from Latin *parere* 'bring forth'.

parentage noun the identity and origins of one's parents.

parenthesis /puh-**ren**-thi-siss/ noun (pl. **parentheses** /puh-**ren**-thi-seez/) **1** a word or phrase inserted as an explanation or afterthought, in writing usually marked off by brackets, dashes, or commas. **2** (**parentheses**) a pair of round brackets () used to include such a word or phrase.
– ORIGIN Greek.

parenthetic adjective added as an explanation or afterthought.
– DERIVATIVES **parenthetical** adjective **parenthetically** adverb.

par excellence /par ek-suh-**lonss**/ adjective (after a noun) better or more than all others of the same kind: *a designer par excellence.*
– ORIGIN French, 'by excellence'.

parfait /par-**fay**/ noun **1** a rich cold dessert made with whipped cream, eggs, and fruit. **2** a dessert consisting of layers of ice cream, meringue, and fruit, served in a tall glass.

– ORIGIN from French, 'perfect'.

pargeting /par-ji-ting/ noun patterned or decorative plaster or mortar.
– DERIVATIVES **pargeted** adjective.
– ORIGIN from Old French *parjeter.*

parhelion /par-**hee**-li-uhn/ noun (pl. **parhelia** /par-**hee**-li-uh/) a bright spot in the sky on either side of the sun, formed by the refraction of sunlight through ice crystals high in the atmosphere.
– ORIGIN from Greek *para-* 'beside' + *hēlios* 'sun'.

pariah /puh-**ry**-uh/ noun **1** an outcast: *they were treated as social pariahs.* **2** historical a member of a low caste or of no caste in southern India.
– ORIGIN from a Tamil word meaning 'hereditary drummers'.

parietal /puh-**ry**-i-tuhl/ adjective relating to the walls of a body cavity.
– ORIGIN from Latin *paries* 'wall'.

parietal bone noun a bone forming the central side and upper back part of each side of the skull.

parietal lobe noun either of the paired lobes of the brain at the top of the head.

parings plural noun thin strips pared off from something.

parish noun **1** (in the Christian Church) a small administrative district with its own church and clergy. **2** (also **civil parish**) Brit. the smallest unit of local government in rural areas.
– ORIGIN Old French *paroche.*

parish council noun the administrative body in a civil parish.

parishioner noun a person who lives in a particular church parish.

parish-pump adjective Brit. of only local importance; parochial.

parish register noun a book recording christenings, marriages, and burials at a parish church.

Parisian /puh-**ri**-zi-uhn/ adjective relating to Paris. • noun a person from Paris.

Parisienne /pa-ri-zi-**en**/ noun a Parisian girl or woman.

parity /pa-ri-ti/ noun **1** the state of being equal or equivalent: *the euro's slide to parity with the dollar.* **2** Mathematics the fact of being an even or an odd number.
– ORIGIN Latin *paritas.*

park noun **1** a large public garden in a town, where people go to walk, relax, play games, etc. **2** a large area of woodland and pasture attached to a country house. **3** an area devoted to a particular purpose: *a wildlife park.* **4** an area in which vehicles may be parked. **5** (**the park**) Brit. informal a football pitch. • verb **1** stop and leave a vehicle somewhere for a period of time. **2** informal leave something in a convenient place until required. **3** (**park oneself**) informal sit down.
– ORIGIN Old French *parc.*

parka noun a large windproof jacket with a hood.
– ORIGIN Russian.

parkin noun Brit. soft, dark gingerbread made with oatmeal and treacle or molasses.
– ORIGIN perhaps from the family name *Parkin.*

parking meter noun a machine next to a

parking space in a street, into which coins are inserted to pay for parking a vehicle.

parking ticket noun a notice informing a driver of a fine for parking illegally.

Parkinson's disease noun a progressive disease of the brain and nervous system marked by involuntary trembling, muscular rigidity, and slow, imprecise movement.
– DERIVATIVES **Parkinsonism** noun.
– ORIGIN named after the English surgeon James *Parkinson*.

Parkinson's law noun the idea that work expands so as to fill the time available for its completion.
– ORIGIN named after the English writer Cyril Northcote *Parkinson*.

parkland (also **parklands**) noun open land consisting of fields and scattered groups of trees.

parkway noun N. Amer. a highway or main road with trees, grass, etc. planted alongside.

parky adjective Brit. informal chilly.
– ORIGIN unknown.

parlance /par-luhnss/ noun a way of using words associated with a particular subject: *medical parlance*.
– ORIGIN Old French, from *parler* 'speak'.

parlay /par-lay/ verb (**parlay something into**) N. Amer. turn an asset, situation, etc. into something much better or more valuable: *a banker who parlayed a sizeable inheritance into a financial empire*.
– ORIGIN from French *paroli* 'cumulative series of bets'.

parley /par-li/ noun (pl. **parleys**) a meeting between opponents or enemies to discuss terms for a truce. •verb (**parleys, parleying, parleyed**) hold a parley.
– ORIGIN perhaps from Old French *parlee* 'spoken'.

parliament /par-luh-muhnt/ noun 1 (**Parliament**) (in the UK) the highest law-making body, consisting of the king or queen, the House of Lords, and the House of Commons. 2 a similar body in other countries.
– ORIGIN Old French *parlement* 'speaking'.

parliamentarian noun 1 a member of parliament who is experienced in parliamentary procedures and debates. 2 historical a supporter of Parliament in the English Civil War; a Roundhead. •adjective relating to parliament or parliamentarians.

parliamentary /par-luh-men-tri/ adjective relating to, enacted by, or suitable for a parliament.

parliamentary private secretary noun (in the UK) a Member of Parliament assisting a government minister.

parlour (US **parlor**) noun 1 dated a sitting room. 2 a shop or business providing particular goods or services: *an ice-cream parlour*. 3 a room or building equipped for milking cows.
– ORIGIN Old French *parlur* 'place for speaking'.

parlour game noun an indoor game, especially a word game.

parlourmaid noun historical a maid employed to serve food at the table.

parlous /par-luhss/ adjective old use or humorous dangerously uncertain; precarious: *the parlous state of the economy*.
– ORIGIN from PERILOUS.

Parma ham noun a strongly flavoured Italian cured ham, eaten uncooked and thinly sliced.
– ORIGIN named after the Italian city of *Parma*.

Parmesan /par-mi-zan/ noun a hard, dry Italian cheese used chiefly in grated form.
– ORIGIN from Italian *Parmigiano* 'of Parma'.

parochial /puh-roh-ki-uhl/ adjective 1 relating to a parish. 2 having a narrow outlook or range: *parochial attitudes*.
– DERIVATIVES **parochialism** noun.
– ORIGIN Latin *parochialis*.

parody noun (pl. **parodies**) 1 a piece of writing or music that deliberately copies the style of another, exaggerating it in order to be funny or ironical. 2 an imitation of something that falls far short of the real thing. •verb (**parodies, parodying, parodied**) produce a parody of something.
– DERIVATIVES **parodic** adjective **parodist** noun.
– ORIGIN Greek *parōidia* 'burlesque poem or song'.

parole noun 1 the temporary or permanent release of a prisoner before the end of a sentence, on condition that they behave well. 2 historical a prisoner of war's word of honour not to escape or, if released, to return to custody under certain specified conditions. •verb release a prisoner on parole.
– DERIVATIVES **parolee** noun.
– ORIGIN Old French, 'word'.

parotid /puh-rot-id/ adjective relating to a pair of large salivary glands situated just in front of each ear.
– ORIGIN Greek.

paroxysm /pa-ruhk-si-z'm/ noun a sudden attack or outburst: *a paroxysm of weeping*.
– DERIVATIVES **paroxysmal** adjective.
– ORIGIN Greek *paroxusmos*.

parquet /par-kay, par-ki/ noun flooring composed of wooden blocks arranged in a geometric pattern.
– DERIVATIVES **parquetry** noun.
– ORIGIN French, 'small compartment'.

parr noun (pl. same) a young salmon or trout up to two years old.
– ORIGIN unknown.

parrakeet noun variant spelling of PARAKEET.

parricide /pa-ri-syd/ noun 1 the killing of a parent or other near relative. 2 a person who commits parricide.
– DERIVATIVES **parricidal** adjective.
– ORIGIN Latin *parricidium*.

parrot noun a mainly tropical bird with brightly coloured plumage and a strong hooked bill, some kinds of which are able to mimic human speech. •verb (**parrots, parroting, parroted**) repeat something mechanically.
– ORIGIN probably from French dialect *perrot*, from the man's name *Pierre* 'Peter'.

parrot-fashion adverb Brit. without thought or understanding.

parrotfish noun (pl. same or **parrotfishes**) a brightly coloured sea fish with a parrot-like beak.

parry verb (**parries, parrying, parried**) 1 ward off a weapon or attack. 2 say something to

p

avoid answering a question directly. • **noun** (pl.
parries) an act of parrying.
– ORIGIN probably from French *parer* 'ward off'.

parse /parz/ **verb** divide a sentence into parts
and describe the grammar of each word or
part.
– ORIGIN perhaps from Old French *pars* 'parts'.

parsec **noun** a unit of astronomical distance
equal to about 3.25 light years.
– ORIGIN blend of **PARALLAX** and **SECOND**².

Parsee /par-see, par-see/ **noun** a descendant of
a group of Zoroastrian Persians who fled to
India during the 7th–8th centuries.
– ORIGIN from a Persian word meaning
'Persian'.

parsimony /par-si-muh-ni/ **noun** extreme
unwillingness to spend money or use
resources.
– DERIVATIVES **parsimonious** adjective.
– ORIGIN Latin *parsimonia, parcimonia*.

parsley **noun** a herb with crinkly or flat leaves,
used for seasoning or garnishing food.
– ORIGIN Greek *petroselinon*.

parsnip **noun** a long tapering cream-coloured
root vegetable.
– ORIGIN Old French *pasnaie*.

parson **noun 1** (in the Church of England) a
parish priest. **2** informal any clergyman.
– ORIGIN Latin *persona* 'person', later 'rector'.

parsonage **noun** a church house provided for a
parson.

parson's nose **noun** informal the piece of fatty
flesh at the rump of a cooked fowl.

part **noun 1** a piece or section which is
combined with others to make up a whole.
2 some but not all of something. **3** a specified
fraction of a whole: *a twentieth part*. **4** a role
played by an actor or actress. **5** a person's
contribution to something: *he played a key
part in ending the revolt*. **6** (**parts**) informal a
region. **7** a measure allowing comparison
between the amounts of different ingredients
used in a mixture: *a mix of one part cement to
five parts ballast*. **8** a melody or other
constituent of harmony given to a particular
voice or instrument. • **verb 1** move apart or
divide to leave a central space: *her lips parted
in a smile*. **2** (also **be parted**) leave someone's
company. **3** (**part with**) give up possession of.
• **adverb** partly: *part jazz, part blues*.
– PHRASES **be part and parcel of** be an essential
element of. **for my** (or **his, her,** etc.) **part** as far
as I am (or he, she, etc. is) concerned. **in part**
to some extent. **on the part of** used to say that
someone is responsible for something. **part
company** go in different directions or end a
relationship. **take part** join in an activity. **take
the part of** give support to someone in a
dispute.
– ORIGIN Latin *pars*; the verb is from Latin
partire 'divide, share'.

partake **verb** (past **partook**; past part. **partaken**)
formal **1** (**partake of**) eat or drink something.
2 (**partake in**) participate in an activity.
– ORIGIN from earlier *partaker* 'person who
takes a part'.

parterre /par-**tair**/ **noun** a group of flower beds
laid out in a formal pattern.
– ORIGIN French.

part exchange **noun** Brit. a way of buying

something in which one gives an article that
one already owns as part of the payment for a
more expensive one, paying the balance in
money.

parthenogenesis /par-thi-noh-jen-i-siss/
noun Biology reproduction from an ovum
without fertilization, especially in some
invertebrate animals and lower plants.
– DERIVATIVES **parthenogenetic** adjective.
– ORIGIN from Greek *parthenos* 'virgin' + *genesis*
'creation'.

Parthian shot /par-thi-uhn/ **noun** another
term for **PARTING SHOT**.
– ORIGIN from the practice among horsemen
from the ancient Asian kingdom of Parthia of
shooting arrows backwards while fleeing.

partial **adjective 1** existing only in part;
incomplete. **2** favouring one side in a dispute
above the other; biased. **3** (**partial to**) having a
liking for.
– DERIVATIVES **partiality** noun **partially** adverb.

participant **noun** a person who takes part in
something.

participate **verb** take part in an activity or
event.
– DERIVATIVES **participation** noun **participative**
adjective **participator** noun **participatory** adjective.
– ORIGIN Latin *participare* 'share in'.

participle /par-**tiss**-i-p'l/ **noun** Grammar a word
formed from a verb (e.g. *going, gone, being,
been*) and used as an adjective or noun (as in
burnt toast, good breeding) or used to make
compound verb forms (*is going, has been*).
– DERIVATIVES **participial** /par-ti-**sip**-i-uhl/
adjective.
– ORIGIN from Latin *participium* 'sharing'.

particle **noun 1** a minute piece of a substance.
2 Physics a component of the physical world
smaller than an atom, such as an electron or
proton. **3** Grammar an adverb or preposition that
has comparatively little meaning, e.g. *in, up,
off,* or *over,* used with verbs to make phrasal
verbs.
– ORIGIN Latin *particula* 'little part'.

particle board **noun** another term for
CHIPBOARD.

particoloured (US **particolored**) **adjective**
having two or more different colours.

particular **adjective 1** relating to an individual
member of a group or class. **2** more than is
usual; special: *he had dressed with particular
care.* **3** insisting that something should be
correct or suitable in every detail; fastidious:
she is very particular about cleanliness. • **noun** a
detail.
– PHRASES **in particular** especially.
– ORIGIN Latin *particularis*.

particularity **noun** (pl. **particularities**) **1** the
quality of being individual. **2** attention to
detail in the treatment of something.
3 (**particularities**) small details.

particularize (or **particularise**) **verb** formal treat
something individually or in detail.
– DERIVATIVES **particularization** noun.

particularly **adverb 1** more than is usual;
especially or very. **2** in particular; specifically.

particulate /par-**tik**-yuu-luht, par-**tik**-yuu-
layt/ **adjective** relating to or in the form of
minute particles. • **noun** (**particulates**) matter
in the form of minute particles.
– ORIGIN from Latin *particula* 'particle'.

parting noun Brit. a line of scalp revealed by combing the hair away in opposite directions on either side.

parting shot noun a cutting remark made by someone as they are leaving.

partisan /par-ti-zan, par-ti-**zan**/ noun **1** a strong supporter of a party, cause, or person. **2** a member of an armed group fighting secretly against an occupying force. • adjective prejudiced in favour of a particular cause, party, or person.
– DERIVATIVES **partisanship** noun.
– ORIGIN Italian *partigiano*.

partition noun **1** a light interior wall or other structure dividing a space into parts. **2** the division of something into parts, especially a country. • verb **1** divide into parts: *an agreement was reached to partition the country.* **2** divide a room with a partition.
– DERIVATIVES **partitionist** noun.
– ORIGIN from Latin *partiri* 'divide into parts'.

partitive /par-ti-tiv/ adjective (of a grammatical construction) indicating that only a part of a whole is referred to (e.g. *a slice of bacon, some of the children*). • noun a noun or pronoun used as the first term in a partitive construction (e.g. *slice, some*).

partly adverb to some extent; not completely.

partner noun **1** a person who takes part in an undertaking with another or others, especially in a business with shared risks and profits. **2** either of two people doing something as a pair. **3** either member of a couple in a marriage or a romantic or sexual relationship. • verb be the partner of someone.
– ORIGIN Old French *parcener*.

partnership noun **1** the state of being a partner or partners. **2** an association of two or more people as partners.

part of speech noun a category in which a word is placed according to its grammatical function, e.g. noun, pronoun, adjective, verb.

partook past of **PARTAKE**.

partridge noun (pl. same or **partridges**) a short-tailed game bird with mainly brown plumage.
– ORIGIN Latin *perdix*.

part song noun a song with three or more voice parts, typically without musical accompaniment.

part-time adjective & adverb for only part of the usual working day or week.

parturient /par-**tyoor**-i-uhnt/ adjective technical about to give birth; in labour.

parturition /par-tyuu-**ri**-sh'n/ noun formal or technical the action of giving birth; childbirth.
– ORIGIN from Latin *parturire* 'be in labour'.

partway adverb part of the way.

party noun (pl. **parties**) **1** a social gathering of invited guests. **2** a political organization that puts forward candidates for election for local or national office. **3** a group of people taking part in an activity or trip. **4** a person or group forming one side in an agreement or dispute. **5** informal, dated a person of a particular type: *an old party came in to clean.* • verb (**parties, partying, partied**) informal enjoy oneself by going out socially and typically also drinking and dancing.
– PHRASES **be party** (or **a party**) **to** be involved in.

– ORIGIN Old French *partie*.

party line noun **1** a policy or policies officially adopted by a political party. **2** a telephone line shared by two or more subscribers.

party politics plural noun (treated as sing. or pl.) politics that relate to political parties rather than to the good of the general public.

party-pooper noun informal a person who spoils other people's fun.

party wall noun a wall shared by two adjoining buildings or rooms.

parvenu /par-vuh-nyoo/ noun chiefly derogatory a person from a humble background who has recently become rich or famous.
– ORIGIN from French, 'arrived'.

parvovirus /par-voh-vy-ruhss/ noun any of a class of very small viruses causing contagious disease in dogs and other animals.
– ORIGIN from Latin *parvus* 'small'.

pascal /pass-kuhl/ noun the SI unit of pressure, equal to one newton per square metre.
– ORIGIN named after the French scientist Blaise Pascal.

paschal /pass-kuhl, pahss-kuhl/ adjective **1** relating to Easter. **2** relating to the Jewish Passover.
– ORIGIN from Latin *pascha* 'feast of Passover'.

pas de deux /pah duh **der**/ noun (pl. same) Ballet a dance for a couple.
– ORIGIN French, 'step of two'.

pasha /rhymes with rasher/ (also **pacha**) noun historical the title of a Turkish officer of high rank.
– ORIGIN Turkish.

pashmina /pash-**mee**-nuh/ noun a shawl made from fine-quality goat's wool.
– ORIGIN Persian, 'wool, down'.

Pashto /pash-toh, puush-toh/ noun the official language of Afghanistan, also spoken in northern Pakistan.
– ORIGIN the name in Pashto.

paso doble /pa-soh **doh**-blay/ noun (pl. **paso dobles**) a fast-paced ballroom dance based on a Latin American marching style.
– ORIGIN Spanish, 'double step'.

pasque flower /passk, pahsk/ noun a spring-flowering plant with purple flowers.
– ORIGIN French *passe-fleur*; later associated with former *pasque* 'Easter'.

pass[1] verb **1** move or go onward, past, through, or across. **2** change from one state or condition to another: *those who have just passed from middle-aged to elderly.* **3** transfer something to someone. **4** kick, hit, or throw the ball to a teammate. **5** (of time) go by. **6** occupy or spend time. **7** be done or said: *not another word passed between them.* **8** come to an end. **9** be successful in an exam, test, or course. **10** declare something to be satisfactory. **11** approve or put into effect a proposal or law by voting. **12** formally state a judgement or sentence. **13** choose not to do or have something that is offered: *we'll pass on pudding and have coffee.* **14** discharge urine or faeces from the body. • noun **1** an act of passing. **2** a success in an exam. **3** an official document authorizing the holder to go somewhere or use something. **4** (also **a pretty pass**) an undesirable situation: *things came to such a pass that mothers feared for their daughters'*

p

safety. **5** a single scan through a set of computer data or a program.

– PHRASES **make a pass at** informal make a sexual approach to someone. **pass as/for** be accepted as. **pass away/on** (of a person) die. **pass off** happen in a specified, usually satisfactory, way. **pass something off** lightly dismiss an awkward remark. **pass someone/thing off as** present someone or something in a way that gives a false impression. **pass out 1** become unconscious. **2** Brit. complete one's initial training in the armed forces. **pass someone over** ignore someone's claims to be promoted. **pass something over** avoid mentioning or considering something. **pass something up** choose not to take up an opportunity.

– DERIVATIVES **passer** noun.
– ORIGIN Old French *passer.*

pass² noun a route over or through mountains.
– ORIGIN from **PACE¹**, influenced by **PASS¹**.

passable adjective **1** just good enough to be accepted. **2** (of a route) able to be travelled along or on.
– DERIVATIVES **passably** adverb.

passage noun **1** the action of passing: *the feeling will fade with the passage of time.* **2** a way through something. **3** a journey by sea or air. **4** the right to pass through somewhere: *a permit for safe passage.* **5** a short section from a written work or musical composition.

passageway noun a corridor or other narrow passage between buildings or rooms.

passata /puh-**sah**-tuh/ noun a thick paste made from sieved tomatoes.
– ORIGIN Italian.

passbook noun a book issued by a bank or building society to an account holder, recording amounts deposited and withdrawn.

passé /**pass**-ay/ adjective no longer fashionable; out of date.
– ORIGIN French, 'gone by'.

passenger noun **1** a person travelling in a vehicle, ship, or aircraft other than the driver, pilot, or crew. **2** chiefly Brit. a member of a team who does very little effective work.
– ORIGIN from Old French *passager* 'passing, transitory'.

passer-by noun (pl. **passers-by**) a person who happens to be walking past something or someone.

passerine /**pass**-uh-ryn, **pass**-uh-reen/ adjective referring to birds of a large group distinguished by having feet adapted for perching and including all songbirds.
– ORIGIN from Latin *passer* 'sparrow'.

passim /**pass**-im/ adverb (of references) at various places throughout a written work.
– ORIGIN Latin, 'everywhere'.

passing adjective **1** done quickly and casually. **2** (of a resemblance or similarity) slight. •noun **1** the end of something. **2** euphemistic a person's death.
– PHRASES **in passing** while doing or saying something else; briefly.

passion noun **1** very strong emotion. **2** intense sexual love. **3** an intense enthusiasm for something: *the English have a passion for gardens.* **4** (**the Passion**) the suffering and death of Jesus.
– DERIVATIVES **passionless** adjective.

– ORIGIN Latin.

passionate adjective having or showing intense emotion, sexual love, or enthusiasm: *a passionate belief in freedom.*
– DERIVATIVES **passionately** adverb.

passion flower noun a climbing plant with a flower whose parts are said to suggest objects associated with Jesus's Crucifixion.

passion fruit noun the edible purple fruit of some species of passion flower.

Passion play noun a play about Jesus's crucifixion.

passive adjective **1** accepting or allowing what happens or what others do, without reacting or resisting: *he takes on a passive role in the story.* **2** Grammar (of verbs) in which the subject undergoes the action of the verb (e.g. *they were killed* as opposed to the active form *he killed them*). **3** (of a circuit or device) containing no source of energy or electromotive force. **4** Chemistry (of a metal) unreactive because of a thin inert surface layer of oxide. •noun a passive form of a verb.
– DERIVATIVES **passively** adverb **passiveness** noun **passivity** noun.
– ORIGIN Latin *passivus.*

passive resistance noun non-violent opposition to authority, especially a refusal to cooperate with legal requirements.

passive smoking noun breathing in smoke from other people's cigarettes, cigars, or pipes.

pass key noun **1** a key given only to those who are officially allowed access. **2** a master key.

Passover noun the major Jewish spring festival, commemorating the liberation of the Israelites from slavery in Egypt.
– ORIGIN from *pass over,* with reference to the exemption of the Israelites from the death of their firstborn (Book of Exodus, chapter 12).

passport noun **1** an official government document certifying the holder's identity and citizenship and entitling them to travel abroad. **2** a thing that enables someone to do or achieve something: *qualifications are a passport to success.*

password noun **1** a secret word or phrase used to gain entry to somewhere. **2** a series of words or numbers allowing someone to use a computer system.

past adjective **1** gone by in time and no longer existing: *the danger is now past.* **2** belonging to a former time. **3** (of time) occurring before and leading up to the present: *he's been in form over the past six months.* **4** (of a tense of a verb) expressing an action that has happened or a state that used to exist. •noun **1** a past period or the events in it. **2** a person's or thing's history or earlier life: *the country's colourful past.* **3** a past tense or form of a verb. •preposition **1** beyond in time or space. **2** in front of or from one side to the other of. **3** beyond the scope, limits, or power of: *I was long past caring.* •adverb **1** so as to pass from one side to the other. **2** used to indicate the passage of time.
– PHRASES **not put it past** believe someone to be capable of doing something wrong or rash. **past it** informal too old to be any good at anything.
– ORIGIN from *passed,* past participle of **PASS¹**.

pasta noun dough formed into various shapes

(e.g. spaghetti, lasagne), cooked as part of a dish or in boiling water.
- ORIGIN Italian, 'paste'.

paste noun **1** a thick, soft, moist substance. **2** a savoury spread: *salmon paste*. **3** a glue made from water and starch. **4** a hard glassy substance used in making imitation gems. • verb **1** coat or stick something with paste. **2** Computing insert a section of data into a document. **3** informal beat or defeat someone severely.
- ORIGIN Latin *pasta* 'paste'.

pasteboard noun thin board made by pasting together sheets of paper.

pastel noun **1** a crayon made of powdered pigments bound with gum or resin. **2** a picture drawn with pastels. **3** a pale shade of a colour. • adjective (of a colour) pale.
- DERIVATIVES **pastellist** (also **pastelist**) noun.
- ORIGIN Italian *pastello*.

pastern /pass-tern/ noun the part of a horse's or other animal's foot between the fetlock and the hoof.
- ORIGIN Old French *pasturon*.

paste-up noun a document prepared for copying or printing by pasting various sections on a backing.

pasteurize (or **pasteurise**) /pahss-tyuu-ryz, pahss-chuu-ryz/ verb make milk or other food safe to eat by heating it to destroy most of the microorganisms in it.
- DERIVATIVES **pasteurization** noun.
- ORIGIN named after the French chemist Louis *Pasteur*.

pastiche /pa-steesh/ noun an artistic work in a style that imitates that of another work, artist, or period.
- DERIVATIVES **pasticheur** /pa-sti-sher/ noun.
- ORIGIN Italian *pasticcio*.

pastie noun variant spelling of **PASTY**.

pastille /pass-tuhl/ noun chiefly Brit. a small sweet or lozenge.
- ORIGIN Latin *pastillus* 'little loaf, lozenge'.

pastime noun an activity done regularly for enjoyment; a hobby.
- ORIGIN from **PASS**[1] + **TIME**.

pastis /pass-teess, pass-tiss/ noun (pl. same) an aniseed-flavoured aperitif.
- ORIGIN French.

past master noun a person who is skilled in an activity.

pastor /pah-ster/ noun a minister in charge of a Christian church or congregation.
- ORIGIN Latin, 'shepherd'.

pastoral /pahss-tuh-ruhl/ adjective **1** relating to or portraying country life: *the property is located in a beautiful pastoral setting*. **2** relating to the farming or grazing of sheep or cattle. **3** (in the Christian Church) relating to the giving of spiritual guidance by the clergy. **4** relating to a teacher's responsibility for the general well-being of students. • noun a literary work portraying an idealized version of country life.
- DERIVATIVES **pastoralism** noun.

past participle noun the form of a verb which is used in forming perfect and passive tenses and sometimes as an adjective, e.g. *looked* in *have you looked?*, *lost* in *lost property*.

pastrami /pass-trah-mi/ noun highly seasoned

smoked beef.
- ORIGIN Yiddish.

pastry noun (pl. **pastries**) **1** a dough of flour, fat, and water, used as a base and covering in baked dishes such as pies. **2** a cake consisting of sweet pastry with a cream, jam, or fruit filling.
- ORIGIN from **PASTE**.

pasturage noun **1** land used for grazing cattle or sheep. **2** the occupation of pasturing cattle or sheep.

pasture noun land covered with grass, suitable for grazing cattle or sheep. • verb put animals to graze in a pasture.
- PHRASES **pastures new** somewhere offering new opportunities. [from 'Tomorrow to fresh woods and pastures new' (Milton's *Lycidas*).] **put someone out to pasture** force someone to retire.
- ORIGIN Latin *pastura* 'grazing'.

pasty[1] /pass-ti/ (also **pastie**) noun (pl. **pasties**) Brit. a folded pastry case filled with meat and vegetables.
- ORIGIN Old French *pastee*.

pasty[2] /pay-sti/ adjective (**pastier**, **pastiest**) (of a person's skin) unhealthily pale.

pat[1] verb (**pats**, **patting**, **patted**) **1** tap someone or something quickly and gently with the flat of the hand. **2** mould or position something with gentle taps. • noun **1** an act of patting. **2** a compact mass of a soft substance.
- PHRASES **a pat on the back** an expression of congratulation or encouragement.
- ORIGIN probably imitating the sound.

pat[2] adjective too quick and easy and not convincing: *there are no pat answers to these questions*.
- PHRASES **have something off pat** have something memorized perfectly.
- ORIGIN related to **PAT**[1].

Patagonian /pa-tuh-goh-ni-uhn/ noun a person from the South American region of Patagonia. • adjective relating to Patagonia.

patch noun **1** a piece of material used to mend a hole or strengthen a weak point. **2** a small area that is different from its surroundings. **3** a small plot of land: *a cabbage patch*. **4** Brit. informal a brief period of time: *she's going through a bad patch*. **5** Brit. informal an area for which someone is responsible or in which they operate. **6** a shield worn over a sightless or injured eye. **7** an adhesive piece of material containing a drug and worn on the skin so that the drug may be gradually absorbed. **8** a temporary electrical or telephone connection. **9** a small piece of code inserted to correct or improve a computer program. • verb **1** mend, strengthen, or protect something with a patch. **2** (**patch someone/thing up**) informal treat an injured person or repair something temporarily. **3** (**patch something up**) informal settle a quarrel or dispute. **4** (**patch something together**) make something hastily. **5** connect someone by a temporary electrical, radio, or telephonic connection.
- PHRASES **not a patch on** Brit. informal not nearly as good as.
- DERIVATIVES **patcher** noun.
- ORIGIN perhaps from Old French dialect *pieche* 'piece'.

p

patchouli /puh-**choo**-li/ noun a scented oil obtained from a SE Asian shrub, used in perfumery, insecticides, and medicine.
– ORIGIN Tamil.

patch pocket noun a pocket made of a separate piece of cloth sewn on to the outside of a garment.

patch test noun an allergy test in which a range of substances are applied to the skin in light scratches or under a plaster.

patchwork noun 1 needlework in which small pieces of cloth in different designs are sewn together to form a larger piece of fabric. 2 a thing composed of many different elements: *a patchwork of educational courses.*
– DERIVATIVES **patchworked** adjective.

patchy adjective (**patchier, patchiest**) 1 existing or happening in small, isolated areas: *patchy fog.* 2 not complete or even throughout: *his memory of what happened was patchy.*
– DERIVATIVES **patchily** adverb **patchiness** noun.

pate /rhymes with gate/ noun old use or humorous a person's head.
– ORIGIN unknown.

pâté /pa-tay/ noun a rich savoury paste made from finely minced or mashed meat, fish, or other ingredients.
– ORIGIN French.

pâté de foie gras /pa-tay duh fwah **grah**/ noun fuller form of **FOIE GRAS**.

patella /puh-**tel**-luh/ noun (pl. **patellae** /puh-**tel**-lee/) the kneecap.
– DERIVATIVES **patellar** adjective.
– ORIGIN Latin, 'small dish'.

paten /**pa**-tuhn/ noun a plate for holding the bread during the Eucharist (Holy Communion).
– ORIGIN Greek *patanē* 'a plate'.

patent /**pay**-t'nt, **pa**-t'nt/ noun a government licence giving a person or body the sole right to make, use, or sell an invention for a set period. • adjective /**pay**-t'nt/ 1 easily recognizable; obvious: *she smiled with patent insincerity.* 2 made and marketed under a patent. • verb obtain a patent for an invention.
– DERIVATIVES **patentable** adjective **patently** /**pay**-t'nt-li/ adverb.
– ORIGIN from Latin *patere* 'lie open'; see also **LETTERS PATENT**.

patentee /pay-t'n-**tee**, pa-t'n-**tee**/ noun a person or body that obtains or holds a patent.

patent leather noun glossy varnished leather.

patent medicine noun a medicine made and sold under a patent and available without prescription.

pater /**pay**-ter/ noun Brit. informal, dated father.
– ORIGIN Latin.

paterfamilias /pay-ter-fuh-**mi**-li-ass/ noun (pl. **patresfamilias** /pay-treez-fuh-**mi**-li-ass/) the male head of a family.
– ORIGIN Latin, 'father of the family'.

paternal adjective 1 relating to or like a father. 2 related through the father.
– DERIVATIVES **paternally** adverb.

paternalism noun the policy of people in authority protecting those who are governed or employed by them, but also restricting their freedom or responsibilities.
– DERIVATIVES **paternalist** noun & adjective

paternalistic adjective.

paternity noun 1 the state of being a father. 2 a person's descent from a father.

paternity suit noun chiefly N. Amer. a court case held to establish the identity of a child's father.

paternoster /pa-ter-**noss**-ter/ noun (in the Roman Catholic Church) the Lord's Prayer.
– ORIGIN from Latin *pater noster* 'our father', the first words of the Lord's Prayer.

path noun 1 a way or track laid down for walking or made by continual treading. 2 the direction in which a person or thing moves. 3 a course of action: *a chosen career path.*
– ORIGIN Old English.

path-breaking adjective pioneering; innovative.

pathetic adjective 1 arousing pity. 2 informal completely inadequate.
– DERIVATIVES **pathetically** adverb.
– ORIGIN Greek *pathētikos* 'sensitive'.

pathetic fallacy noun (in art and literature) the depiction of inanimate things or animals as having human feelings.

pathfinder noun a person who goes ahead and discovers or shows others a way.

patho- combining form relating to disease: *pathology.*
– ORIGIN from Greek *pathos* 'suffering, disease'.

pathogen /**pa**-thuh-juhn/ noun a microorganism that can cause disease.
– DERIVATIVES **pathogenic** adjective.

pathological (US **pathologic**) adjective 1 relating to or caused by a disease. 2 informal possessing a quality to an extreme or uncontrollable degree: *a pathological liar.* 3 relating to pathology.
– DERIVATIVES **pathologically** adverb.

pathology noun 1 the branch of medicine concerned with the causes and effects of diseases. 2 the typical behaviour of a disease.
– DERIVATIVES **pathologist** noun.

pathos /**pay**-thoss/ noun a quality that arouses pity or sadness.
– ORIGIN Greek, 'suffering'.

pathway noun a path or its course.

patience noun 1 the ability to accept delay, trouble, or suffering without becoming angry or upset. 2 Brit. a card game for one player.
– ORIGIN Latin *patientia.*

patient adjective able to accept delay, trouble, or suffering without becoming angry or upset: *supporters have been patient and understanding.* • noun a person receiving or registered to receive medical treatment.
– DERIVATIVES **patiently** adverb.

patina /**pa**-ti-nuh/ noun 1 a green or brown film on the surface of old bronze. 2 a sheen on wooden furniture produced by age and polishing.
– DERIVATIVES **patinated** adjective **patination** noun.
– ORIGIN Latin, 'shallow dish'.

patio noun (pl. **patios**) 1 a paved outdoor area adjoining a house. 2 a roofless inner courtyard in a Spanish or Spanish-American house.
– ORIGIN Spanish.

patio door noun a large glass sliding door leading to a patio or balcony.

patisserie /puh-**tiss**-uh-ri, puh-**tee**-suh-ri/ noun **1** a shop where pastries and cakes are sold. **2** pastries and cakes.
– ORIGIN French.

patois /**pat**-wah/ noun (pl. same /**pat**-wahz/) the local dialect of a region, especially one with low status in relation to the standard language of the country.
– ORIGIN French, 'rough speech'.

patresfamilias plural of PATERFAMILIAS.

patriarch /**pay**-tri-ark/ noun **1** the male head of a family or tribe. **2** a biblical figure regarded as a father of the human race, such as Abraham, Isaac, or Jacob. **3** a powerful or respected older man. **4** a high-ranking bishop in certain Christian churches. **5** the head of an independent Orthodox Church.
– DERIVATIVES **patriarchal** adjective **patriarchate** noun.
– ORIGIN Greek *patriarkhēs*.

patriarchy noun (pl. **patriarchies**) **1** a system of society in which men hold most or all of the power. **2** a form of social organization in which the father or eldest male is the head of the family.

patrician /puh-**tri**-sh'n/ noun **1** an aristocrat. **2** a member of the nobility in ancient Rome. •adjective relating to or typical of aristocrats; upper-class.
– ORIGIN Latin *patricius* 'having a noble father'.

patricide /**pa**-tri-syd/ noun **1** the killing of a father by his child. **2** a person who kills their father.
– ORIGIN Latin *patricidium*.

patrimony /**pa**-tri-muh-ni/ noun (pl. **patrimonies**) **1** property inherited from a person's father or male ancestor. **2** valued things passed down from previous generations; heritage.
– ORIGIN Latin *patrimonium*.

patriot /**pa**-tri-uht, **pay**-tri-uht/ noun a person who strongly supports their country and is prepared to defend it.
– DERIVATIVES **patriotism** noun.
– ORIGIN Latin *patriota* 'fellow countryman'.

patriotic adjective devoted to and vigorously supporting one's country.
– DERIVATIVES **patriotically** adverb.

patristic /puh-**triss**-tik/ adjective relating to the early Christian theologians or their writings.
– ORIGIN German *patristisch*.

patrol noun **1** a person or group that keeps watch over an area by walking or travelling around it at regular intervals. **2** the action of patrolling an area. **3** a unit of six to eight Scouts or Guides forming part of a troop. •verb (**patrols, patrolling, patrolled**) keep watch over an area by regularly walking or travelling around it.
– DERIVATIVES **patroller** noun.
– ORIGIN from French *patrouiller* 'paddle in mud'.

patrolman noun (pl. **patrolmen**) N. Amer. a patrolling police officer.

patron noun **1** a person who gives financial or other support to a person, organization, or cause. **2** a regular customer of a restaurant, hotel, or shop.
– DERIVATIVES **patroness** noun.
– ORIGIN Latin *patronus* 'protector of clients,

defender'.

patronage /**pa**-truh-nij, **pay**-truh-nij/ noun **1** support given by a patron: *the arts could no longer depend on private patronage.* **2** the system by which a powerful person gives a job or privilege to someone in return for their support. **3** the regular custom attracted by a restaurant, hotel, or shop. **4** a patronizing way of behaving.

patronize (or **patronise**) verb **1** treat someone in a way that suggests they are inferior. **2** be a regular customer of a restaurant, hotel, or shop.

patron saint noun the protecting or guiding saint of a person or place.

patronymic /**pa**-truh-**nim**-ik/ noun a name derived from the name of a father or ancestor, e.g. *Johnson, O'Brien.*
– ORIGIN Greek *patrōnumikos.*

patsy noun (pl. **patsies**) informal, chiefly N. Amer. a person who is easily taken advantage of.
– ORIGIN unknown.

patten /**pa**-tuhn/ noun historical a shoe with a raised sole or set on an iron ring, worn to raise the feet above wet ground.
– ORIGIN Old French *patin.*

patter[1] verb **1** make a repeated light tapping sound. **2** run with quick light steps. •noun a repeated light tapping sound.
– ORIGIN from PAT[1].

patter[2] noun **1** rapid continuous talk, such as that used by a comedian. **2** the jargon of a group or profession: *the patter of an urban street culture.*
– ORIGIN from PATERNOSTER (from the rapid and mechanical way in which the prayer was often said).

pattern noun **1** a repeated decorative design. **2** a regular form or order in which a series of things occur: *a change in working patterns.* **3** a model, design, or set of instructions for making something. **4** an example for others to follow. **5** a sample of cloth or wallpaper. •verb **1** decorate something with a pattern. **2** (**pattern something on/after**) use something as a model for something else: *the clothing is patterned on athletes' wear.*
– ORIGIN from PATRON in the former sense 'something serving as a model'.

patty noun (pl. **patties**) **1** N. Amer. a small flat cake of minced food, especially meat. **2** a small pie or pasty.
– ORIGIN French *pâté.*

paua /**pah**-wuh, **pow**-uh/ noun a large New Zealand abalone (shellfish), whose shell is used to make ornaments and jewellery.
– ORIGIN Maori.

paucity /**paw**-si-ti/ noun the presence of something in only small or insufficient quantities or amounts: *a paucity of information.*
– ORIGIN from Latin *paucus* 'few'.

Pauline /**paw**-lyn/ adjective relating to St Paul.

paunch noun a belly or abdomen that is large or sticks out.
– DERIVATIVES **paunchy** adjective.
– ORIGIN Old French *paunche.*

pauper noun **1** a very poor person. **2** historical a person who received public charity.

- DERIVATIVES **pauperism** noun **pauperize** (or **pauperise**) verb.
- ORIGIN from Latin, 'poor'.

pause verb stop temporarily: *he paused for a moment, as if he was going to say more.* • noun **1** a temporary stop in action or speech. **2** a mark (⌒) over a musical note or rest that is to be lengthened by an unspecified amount.
- PHRASES **give pause to someone** (or **give someone pause for thought**) cause someone to stop and think before doing something.
- ORIGIN Greek *pausis*.

pavane /puh-**van**/ (also **pavan** /pa-vuhn/) noun a stately dance in slow duple time, popular in the 16th and 17th centuries.
- ORIGIN French.

pave verb cover a piece of ground with flat stones or bricks.
- PHRASES **pave the way for** create the circumstances to enable something to happen.
- DERIVATIVES **paver** noun **paving** noun.
- ORIGIN Old French *paver*.

pavement noun **1** Brit. a raised path surfaced with stones or asphalt at the side of a road. **2** N. Amer. the hard surface of a road or street. **3** Geology a horizontal expanse of bare rock with cracks or joints.
- ORIGIN Latin *pavimentum* 'trodden down floor'.

pavilion noun **1** Brit. a building at a sports ground used for changing and taking refreshments. **2** a summer house or other decorative shelter in a park or large garden. **3** a large marquee used at a show or fair. **4** a temporary display stand or other structure at a trade exhibition.
- ORIGIN Old French *pavillon*.

paving stone noun a large flat piece of stone or similar material, used in paving.

pavlova noun a dessert consisting of a meringue filled with whipped cream and fruit.
- ORIGIN named after the Russian ballerina Anna *Pavlova*.

Pavlovian /pav-**loh**-vi-uhn/ adjective relating to trained reflexes as described by the Russian physiologist Ivan P. Pavlov, famous for training dogs to respond instantly to various stimuli.

paw noun **1** an animal's foot having claws and pads. **2** informal a person's hand. • verb **1** feel or scrape something with a paw or hoof. **2** informal touch or handle someone or something clumsily or sexually.
- ORIGIN Old French *poue*.

pawl /pawl/ noun a pivoted bar or lever whose free end engages with the teeth of a cogwheel or ratchet, allowing it to move or turn in one direction only.
- ORIGIN perhaps from German and Dutch *pal*.

pawn¹ noun **1** a chess piece of the smallest size and value. **2** a person used by others for their own purposes.
- ORIGIN Old French *poun*.

pawn² verb place an object with a pawnbroker as security for money lent.
- PHRASES **in pawn** (of an object) held as security by a pawnbroker.
- ORIGIN from Old French *pan* 'pledge, security'.

pawnbroker noun a person licensed to lend

money in exchange for an article left with them, which they can sell if the borrower fails to pay the money back.

Pawnee /paw-**nee**/ noun (pl. same or **Pawnees**) a member of an American Indian confederacy now living mainly in Oklahoma.
- ORIGIN from a North American Indian language.

pawnshop noun a pawnbroker's shop.

pawpaw /paw-paw/ (also **papaw** /puh-**paw**/) noun a papaya (fruit).
- ORIGIN Spanish and Portuguese *papaya*.

pay verb (past and past part. **paid**) **1** give someone money owed to them for work, goods, or as a debt. **2** be profitable or advantageous: *crime doesn't pay.* **3** suffer as a result of an action: *someone's got to pay for all that grief.* **4** give someone attention, respect, or a compliment. **5** visit or call on someone. **6** give what is due or deserved to someone. • noun money paid for work.
- PHRASES **in the pay of** employed by. **pay someone back** take revenge on someone. **pay dearly** suffer for wrongdoing or failure. **pay one's last respects** show respect towards a dead person by attending their funeral. **pay off** informal yield good results. **pay someone off** dismiss someone with a final payment. **pay something out** let out a rope by slackening it. **pay through the nose** informal pay much more than a fair price.
- DERIVATIVES **payer** noun.
- ORIGIN Old French *payer* 'appease'.

payable adjective **1** that must be paid. **2** able to be paid.

payback noun **1** profit from an investment equal to the initial amount invested. **2** informal an act of revenge.

pay bed noun (in the UK) a hospital bed for private patients in a National Health Service hospital.

PAYE abbreviation (in the UK and South Africa) pay as you earn, a system whereby an employer deducts income tax from an employee's wages to be paid directly to the government.

payee noun a person to whom money is paid or to be paid.

paying guest noun a lodger.

payload noun **1** passengers and cargo as the part of a vehicle's load which earns money. **2** an explosive warhead carried by an aircraft or missile. **3** the load carried by a spacecraft.

paymaster noun **1** a person who pays another and therefore controls them. **2** an official who pays troops or workers.

payment noun **1** the action of paying or the process of being paid. **2** an amount paid.

pay-off noun informal **1** a payment, especially as a bribe or on leaving a job. **2** the return on investment or on a bet. **3** a final outcome.

payola /pay-**oh**-luh/ noun chiefly N. Amer. the practice of bribing someone in return for the unofficial promotion of a product.
- ORIGIN from **PAY** + *-ola* as in *Victrola*, a make of gramophone (the term first referred to the bribery of a disc jockey to promote a record).

payout noun a large payment of money.

pay-per-view noun a television service in

which viewers have to pay a fee to watch a particular programme.

payphone noun a public telephone operated by coins or by a credit or prepaid card.

payroll noun a list of a company's employees and the amount of money they are to be paid.

payslip noun chiefly Brit. a note given to an employee, detailing the amount of pay and any deductions.

Pb symbol the chemical element lead.
– ORIGIN from Latin *plumbum*.

pb abbreviation paperback.

PC abbreviation 1 personal computer. 2 Brit. police constable. 3 (also **pc**) politically correct; political correctness.

p.c. abbreviation per cent.

PCB abbreviation 1 Electronics printed circuit board. 2 Chemistry polychlorinated biphenyl, a poisonous compound formed as waste in some industrial processes.

PCV abbreviation Brit. passenger-carrying vehicle.

Pd symbol the chemical element palladium.

PDA abbreviation personal digital assistant, a basic palmtop computer.

PDF noun Computing 1 a file format for capturing and sending electronic documents in exactly the intended format. 2 a file in this format.
– ORIGIN abbreviation of *Portable Document Format*.

PDQ abbreviation informal pretty damn quick.

PDSA abbreviation (in the UK) People's Dispensary for Sick Animals.

PDT abbreviation Pacific Daylight Time.

PE abbreviation physical education.

pea noun 1 a round green seed eaten as a vegetable. 2 the climbing plant which has pods containing peas.
– ORIGIN Old English.

peace noun 1 freedom from noise or anxiety; tranquillity. 2 freedom from or the ending of war. 3 (**the peace**) an action such as a handshake, signifying Christian unity and performed during the Eucharist (Holy Communion).
– PHRASES **at peace** 1 free from anxiety or distress. 2 euphemistic dead. **hold one's peace** remain silent. **keep the peace** refrain or prevent others from disturbing civil order. **make (one's) peace** re-establish friendly relations with someone.
– ORIGIN Latin *pax*.

peaceable adjective 1 inclined to avoid conflict. 2 free from conflict; peaceful.
– DERIVATIVES **peaceably** adverb.

peace dividend noun a sum of public money available for other purposes when spending on defence is reduced.

peaceful adjective 1 free from noise or anxiety: *her peaceful mood vanished.* 2 not involving war or violence. 3 inclined to avoid conflict; peaceable.
– DERIVATIVES **peacefully** adverb **peacefulness** noun.

peacekeeping noun the practice of using an international military force to maintain a truce.
– DERIVATIVES **peacekeeper** noun.

peacemaker noun a person who brings about peace.

– DERIVATIVES **peacemaking** noun.

peacenik noun informal, often derogatory a member of a pacifist movement.

peace offering noun a gift that is given in an attempt to re-establish friendly relations.

peacetime noun a period when a country is not at war.

peach[1] noun 1 a round fruit with juicy yellow flesh, downy red and yellow skin, and a stone inside. 2 a pinkish-orange colour. 3 informal an exceptionally good or attractive person or thing: *it was another peach of a day.*
– DERIVATIVES **peachy** adjective.
– ORIGIN Old French *pesche*.

peach[2] verb (**peach on**) informal inform on.
– ORIGIN related to **IMPEACH**.

peach Melba noun ice cream and peaches with a raspberry sauce.
– ORIGIN named after Dame Nellie *Melba* (see **MELBA TOAST**).

peacock noun a large male bird of the pheasant family, having very long tail feathers with eye-like markings that can be fanned out in display.
– ORIGIN Old English.

peacock blue noun a greenish-blue colour like that of a peacock's neck.

peacock butterfly noun a brightly coloured butterfly with characteristic eye-like markings.

peafowl noun a peacock or peahen.

pea green noun a bright green colour.

peahen noun a female peafowl, which has mainly brown plumage and a shorter tail than a peacock.

pea jacket (also **pea coat**) noun a short double-breasted overcoat of coarse woollen cloth.
– ORIGIN Dutch *pijjakker*.

peak noun 1 the pointed top of a mountain. 2 a mountain with a pointed top. 3 Brit. a stiff brim at the front of a cap. 4 the point of highest activity, achievement, intensity, etc.: *he was at his peak as a cricketer.* ◆verb reach a highest point or maximum. ◆adjective characterized by maximum activity or demand.
– ORIGIN probably from dialect *picked* 'pointed'.

peaked[1] adjective (of a cap) having a peak.

peaked[2] adjective North American term for **PEAKY**.

peak load noun the maximum of electrical power demand.

peaky adjective (**peakier, peakiest**) Brit. pale from illness or exhaustion.
– ORIGIN from former *peak* 'decline in health'.

peal noun 1 a loud ringing of a bell or bells. 2 a loud repeated or resounding sound of thunder or laughter. 3 a set of bells. ◆verb (of a bell or sound) ring or resound loudly.
– ORIGIN shortening of **APPEAL**.

peanut noun 1 the oval edible seed of a plant native to South America, whose seeds develop in underground pods. 2 (**peanuts**) informal a very small sum of money.

peanut butter noun a spread made from ground roasted peanuts.

pear noun a yellow or green edible fruit that is narrow at the stalk and widens towards the bottom.

p

– PHRASES **go pear-shaped** Brit. informal go wrong. [RAF slang.]
– ORIGIN Old English, from Latin *pirum*.

pear drop noun a boiled sweet in the shape of a pear, with a distinctive flavour.

pearl noun 1 a small, hard, shiny white or bluish-grey ball formed inside the shell of an oyster or other mollusc and having great value as a gem. 2 a highly valued person or thing: *pearls of wisdom*. 3 a very pale bluish grey or white colour.
– PHRASES **cast pearls before swine** offer valuable things to people who do not appreciate them. [with reference to the Gospel of Matthew, chapter 7.]
– ORIGIN Old French *perle*.

pearl barley noun barley reduced to small round grains by grinding.

pearled adjective literary decorated with or wearing pearls.

pearlescent adjective having a soft glow resembling that of mother-of-pearl.

pearly adjective (**pearlier, pearliest**) resembling a pearl in lustre or colour. • noun (**pearlies**) (also **pearly whites**) informal a person's teeth.

Pearly Gates plural noun informal the gates of heaven.
– ORIGIN from the Book of Revelation in the Bible.

pearly king (or **pearly queen**) noun a London costermonger wearing traditional ceremonial clothes covered with pearl buttons.

pear-shaped adjective having hips that are disproportionately wide in relation to the upper part of the body.

peasant noun 1 a poor smallholder or farm labourer of low social status. 2 informal an ignorant, rude, or unsophisticated person.
– DERIVATIVES **peasantry** noun.
– ORIGIN Old French *paisent*.

pease pudding noun chiefly Brit. a dish of split peas boiled with onion and carrot and mashed to a pulp.

peashooter noun a toy weapon consisting of a small tube out of which dried peas are blown.

pea-souper noun Brit. a very thick yellowish fog.

peat noun partly decomposed vegetable matter forming a deposit on acidic, boggy ground, dried for use in gardening and as fuel.
– DERIVATIVES **peaty** adjective.
– ORIGIN Anglo-Latin *peta*.

peatland noun (also **peatlands**) land consisting largely of peat or peat bogs.

pebble noun a small stone made smooth and round by the action of water or sand.
– DERIVATIVES **pebbly** adjective.
– ORIGIN Old English.

pebble-dash noun Brit. mortar with pebbles in it, used as a coating for external walls.

pec noun informal a pectoral muscle.

pecan /pee-k'n, pi-**kan**/ noun a smooth pinkish-brown nut with a kernel similar to a walnut, obtained from a tree of the southern US.
– ORIGIN from an American Indian language.

peccadillo /pek-kuh-**dil**-loh/ noun (pl. **peccadilloes** or **peccadillos**) a minor fault.
– ORIGIN Spanish.

peccary /pek-kuh-ri/ noun (pl. **peccaries**) a piglike mammal found from the southwestern US to Paraguay.
– ORIGIN Carib.

peck[1] verb 1 (of a bird) strike or bite something with its beak. 2 kiss someone lightly and briefly. 3 (**peck at**) informal eat food without enthusiasm. 4 type something slowly and laboriously. • noun 1 an act of pecking. 2 a quick, light kiss.
– ORIGIN unknown.

peck[2] noun a measure of capacity for dry goods, equal to a quarter of a bushel.
– ORIGIN Old French *pek*.

pecker noun (in phrase **keep your pecker up**) Brit. informal remain cheerful.

pecking order noun a strict order of importance among members of a group.

peckish adjective informal hungry.

pecorino /pe-kuh-**ree**-noh/ noun an Italian cheese made from ewes' milk.
– ORIGIN from Italian, 'of ewes'.

pectin noun a soluble jelly-like substance present in ripe fruits, used to set jams and jellies.
– ORIGIN from Greek *pektos* 'congealed'.

pectoral /**pek**-tuh-ruhl/ adjective relating to or worn on the breast or chest. • noun a pectoral muscle.
– ORIGIN Latin *pectoralis*.

pectoral muscle noun each of four large paired muscles which cover the front of the ribcage.

peculation /pek-yuu-**lay**-sh'n/ noun formal embezzlement of public funds.
– ORIGIN from Latin *peculari* 'embezzle'.

peculiar adjective 1 different to what is normal or expected; strange. 2 (**peculiar to**) belonging exclusively to. 3 particular; special: *the peculiar difficulties faced by West African women*.
– DERIVATIVES **peculiarly** adverb.
– ORIGIN Latin *peculiaris* 'of private property'.

peculiarity noun (pl. **pecularities**) 1 an unusual or distinctive feature or habit. 2 the state of being strange or odd.

pecuniary adjective formal relating to money.
– ORIGIN Latin *pecuniarius*.

pedagogue /**ped**-uh-gog/ noun formal or humorous a teacher.
– ORIGIN Greek *paidagōgos*, referring to a slave who accompanied a child to school.

pedagogy /**ped**-uh-go-gi/ noun the profession or theory of teaching.
– DERIVATIVES **pedagogic** (also **pedagogical**) adjective.

pedal[1] /**ped**-uhl/ noun 1 each of a pair of foot-operated levers for powering a bicycle or other vehicle. 2 a foot-operated throttle, brake, or clutch control. 3 a foot-operated lever on a piano, organ, etc. for sustaining or softening the tone. • verb (**pedals, pedalling, pedalled**; US **pedals, pedaling, pedaled**) work the pedals of a bicycle or pedalo to move along.
– DERIVATIVES **pedaller** (US **pedaler**) noun.
– ORIGIN Latin *pedalis* 'a foot in length'.

pedal² /ped-uhl, pee-d'l/ adjective chiefly Medicine & Zoology relating to the foot or feet.
– ORIGIN Latin *pedalis*.

pedalo /ped-uh-loh/ noun (pl. **pedalos** or **pedaloes**) Brit. a small pedal-operated pleasure boat.

pedal pushers plural noun women's calf-length trousers.

pedant /ped-uhnt/ noun a person who is excessively concerned with minor detail or with displaying academic learning.
– DERIVATIVES **pedantic** adjective **pedantically** adverb **pedantry** noun.
– ORIGIN French *pédant*.

peddle verb **1** sell goods by going from place to place. **2** sell an illegal drug or stolen item. **3** promote an idea persistently or widely.
– ORIGIN from **PEDLAR**.

peddler noun variant spelling of **PEDLAR**.

pederasty /ped-uh-rass-ti/ noun sexual intercourse between a man and a boy.
– DERIVATIVES **pederast** noun **pederastic** adjective.
– ORIGIN Greek *paiderastia*.

pedestal noun **1** the base or support on which a statue or column is mounted. **2** the supporting column of a washbasin or toilet pan.
– PHRASES **put someone on a pedestal** admire someone greatly and uncritically.
– ORIGIN Italian *piedestallo*.

pedestrian noun a person walking rather than travelling in a vehicle. • adjective not exciting or interesting: *a pedestrian task*.
– DERIVATIVES **pedestrianly** adverb.
– ORIGIN from Latin *pedester* 'going on foot'.

pedestrianize (or **pedestrianise**) verb make a street or area accessible only to pedestrians.
– DERIVATIVES **pedestrianization** noun.

pediatrics plural noun US spelling of **PAEDIATRICS**.

pedicure noun a cosmetic treatment of the feet and toenails.
– DERIVATIVES **pedicurist** noun.
– ORIGIN French.

pedigree noun **1** the record of an animal's origins, showing that all the animals from which it is descended are of the same breed. **2** a person's family background or ancestry. **3** the history or origin of a person or thing: *the scheme has a long pedigree*.
– ORIGIN from Old French *pé de grue* 'crane's foot', a mark used to show succession in pedigrees.

pediment noun the triangular upper part above the entrance to a classical building.
– ORIGIN perhaps from **PYRAMID**.

pedlar (chiefly US also **peddler**) noun **1** a travelling trader who sells small goods. **2** a person who sells illegal drugs or stolen goods.

3 a person who promotes an idea or view persistently.
– ORIGIN perhaps from dialect *ped* 'pannier'.

pedometer /pi-dom-i-ter/ noun an instrument for estimating the distance travelled on foot by recording the number of steps taken.
– ORIGIN from Latin *pes* 'foot'.

pedophile noun US spelling of **PAEDOPHILE**.

peduncle /pi-dung-k'l/ noun **1** Botany the stalk carrying a flower or fruit. **2** Zoology a stalk-like connecting structure.
– DERIVATIVES **pedunculate** adjective.
– ORIGIN Latin *pedunculus*.

pee informal verb (**pees, peeing, peed**) urinate. • noun **1** an act of urinating. **2** urine.
– ORIGIN from the initial letter of **PISS**.

peek verb **1** look quickly or furtively. **2** stick out slightly so as to be just visible: *his socks were so full of holes his toes peeked through*. • noun a quick or furtive look.
– ORIGIN unknown.

peekaboo adjective (of an item of clothing) made of transparent fabric or having a pattern of small holes.

peel verb **1** remove the outer covering or skin from a fruit or vegetable. **2** (of a surface or object) lose parts of its outer layer or covering in small pieces. **3** (**peel something away/off**) remove a thin outer covering. **4** (**peel off**) leave a group by veering away. • noun the outer skin or rind of a fruit or vegetable.
– DERIVATIVES **peelable** adjective **peelings** plural noun.
– ORIGIN Latin *pilare* 'to strip hair from'.

peeler¹ noun a knife or device for peeling fruit and vegetables.

peeler² noun Brit. informal, old use a police officer.
– ORIGIN from the name of the British Prime Minister Sir Robert *Peel*, who established the Metropolitan Police.

peen (also **pein**) noun the rounded or wedge-shaped end of a hammer head opposite the face.
– ORIGIN probably Scandinavian.

peep¹ verb **1** look quickly and furtively. **2** (**peep out**) come slowly or partially into view. • noun **1** a quick or furtive look. **2** a glimpse of something: *a peep of gold earring*.

peep² noun a weak or brief high-pitched sound. • verb make a peep.
– PHRASES **not a peep** not the slightest sound or complaint.
– ORIGIN imitating the sound.

peeper noun **1** a person who looks quickly or furtively. **2** (**peepers**) informal a person's eyes.

peephole noun a small hole in a door through which callers may be identified.

peeping Tom noun a person who gains sexual pleasure from secretly watching people undress or have sex.
– ORIGIN the name of the tailor said to have watched Lady Godiva ride naked through Coventry.

peep show noun a form of entertainment in which pictures are viewed through a lens or hole set into a box.

peer¹ verb **1** look with difficulty or concentration. **2** be just visible: *the towers peer over the roofs*.
– ORIGIN uncertain.

p

peer² noun **1** a member of the nobility in Britain or Ireland, comprising the ranks of duke, marquess, earl, viscount, and baron. **2** a person of the same age, status, or ability as another specified person: *his astute management is better than any of his peers.*
– PHRASES **without peer** better than all others; unrivalled.
– ORIGIN Old French.

peerage noun **1** the title and rank of peer or peeress. **2** (**the peerage**) peers as a group.

peeress noun **1** a woman holding the rank of a peer in her own right. **2** the wife or widow of a peer.

peer group noun a group of people of approximately the same age, status, and interests.

peerless adjective better than all others; unrivalled.

peeve informal verb annoy or irritate someone: *he was peeved at being left out.* •noun a cause of annoyance.
– ORIGIN from PEEVISH.

peevish adjective easily annoyed; irritable.
– DERIVATIVES **peevishly** adverb **peevishness** noun.
– ORIGIN unknown.

peewit noun Brit. a lapwing (bird).
– ORIGIN imitating its call.

peg noun **1** a short projecting pin or bolt used for hanging things on, securing something in place, or marking a position. **2** a clothes peg. **3** informal a person's leg. **4** chiefly Indian a measure of spirits. •verb (**pegs, pegging, pegged**) **1** fix, attach, or mark something with a peg or pegs. **2** fix a price, rate, or amount at a particular level. **3** (**peg out**) informal die. **4** (**peg away**) informal work hard over a long period.
– PHRASES **off the peg** Brit. (of clothes) not made to order. **a peg to hang something on** something used as an excuse or opportunity to discuss or explain something. **a square peg in a round hole** a person in a situation unsuited to their abilities or character. **take** (or **bring**) **someone down a peg or two** make someone less arrogant.
– ORIGIN probably German.

pegboard noun a board with a regular pattern of small holes for pegs.

peg leg noun informal an artificial leg.

peignoir /pay-nwar/ noun a woman's light dressing gown or negligee.
– ORIGIN French.

pein noun variant spelling of PEEN.

pejorative /pi-jo-ruh-tiv/ adjective (of a word or phrase) expressing contempt or disapproval.
– DERIVATIVES **pejoratively** adverb.
– ORIGIN French *péjoratif*.

Pekinese /pee-ki-neez/ (also **Pekingese**) noun (pl. same) a small dog of a short-legged breed with long hair and a snub nose. •adjective relating to Beijing (Peking).

Peking duck noun a Chinese dish consisting of strips of roast duck served with shredded vegetables and a sweet sauce.

pelagic /pi-la-jik/ adjective technical **1** relating to the open sea. **2** (chiefly of fish) inhabiting the upper layers of the open sea.
– ORIGIN Greek *pelagikos*.

pelargonium /pe-luh-goh-ni-uhm/ noun a garden plant with red, pink, or white flowers.
– ORIGIN Latin.

pelf noun literary money, especially when gained dishonestly.
– ORIGIN Old French *pelfre* 'spoils'.

pelican noun a large waterbird with a long bill and a pouch hanging from its throat.
– ORIGIN Greek *pelekan*.

pelican crossing noun (in the UK) a pedestrian crossing with traffic lights operated by pedestrians.
– ORIGIN from *pe(destrian) li(ght) con(trolled)*, altered to conform with the bird's name.

pelisse /pi-leess/ noun historical a woman's long cloak with armholes or sleeves.
– ORIGIN French.

pellagra /pel-lag-ruh, pel-lay-gruh/ noun a disease that results from a lack of a vitamin, causing inflamed skin, diarrhoea, and mental disturbance.
– ORIGIN Italian.

pellet noun **1** a small, rounded, compressed mass of a substance. **2** a piece of small shot or other lightweight bullet. •verb (**pellets, pelleting, pelleted**) form a substance into pellets.
– DERIVATIVES **pelletize** (or **pelletise**) verb.
– ORIGIN Old French *pelote* 'metal ball'.

pell-mell adjective & adverb in a confused, rushed, or disorderly way.
– ORIGIN French *pêle-mêle*.

pellucid /pel-lyoo-sid/ adjective literary **1** transparent or semi-transparent. **2** easily understood: *pellucid answers.*
– ORIGIN Latin *pellucidus*.

pelmet noun a narrow border fitted across the top of a door or window to conceal the curtain fittings.
– ORIGIN probably from French *palmette* 'small palm leaf'.

pelota /pi-loh-tuh, pi-lo-tuh/ noun a Basque or Spanish ball game played in a walled court with basket-like rackets.
– ORIGIN Spanish, 'ball'.

peloton /pel-uh-ton/ noun the main group of cyclists in a race.
– ORIGIN French, 'small ball'.

pelt¹ verb **1** hurl missiles at someone or something. **2** (**pelt down**) (chiefly of rain) fall very heavily. **3** run very quickly.
– PHRASES (**at**) **full pelt** as fast as possible.
– ORIGIN unknown.

pelt² noun the skin of an animal with the fur, wool, or hair still on it.
– ORIGIN Latin *pellis* 'skin'.

pelvic floor noun the muscles around the base of the abdomen, attached to the pelvis.

pelvic girdle noun (in vertebrates) the enclosing structure formed by the pelvis.

pelvis /pel-viss/ noun (pl. **pelvises** or **pelves** /pel-veez/) the large bony frame at the base of the spine to which the lower limbs are attached.
– DERIVATIVES **pelvic** adjective.
– ORIGIN Latin, 'basin'.

Pembs. abbreviation Pembrokeshire.

pen¹ noun **1** an instrument for writing or drawing with ink. **2** an electronic device used

with a writing surface to enter commands into a computer. •verb (**pens, penning, penned**) write or compose something.
– ORIGIN Latin *penna* 'feather' (pens were originally made from a quill feather).

pen² noun **1** a small enclosure for farm animals. **2** a covered dock for a submarine or other warship. •verb (**pens, penning, penned**) **1** put or keep an animal in a pen. **2** (**pen someone up/in**) confine someone in a restricted space.
– ORIGIN Old English.

pen³ noun a female swan.
– ORIGIN unknown.

penal /pee-n'l/ adjective **1** relating to the punishment of offenders under the legal system. **2** very severe: *penal rates of interest*.
– ORIGIN from Latin *poena* 'pain, penalty'.

penalize (or **penalise**) verb **1** give a penalty or punishment to someone who has broken the law or a rule. **2** make an action punishable by law. **3** put in an unfavourable position: *single people are often penalized by hotels by being charged a supplement*.
– DERIVATIVES **penalization** noun.

penal servitude noun imprisonment with hard labour.

penalty noun (pl. **penalties**) **1** a punishment for breaking a law, rule, or contract. **2** a disadvantage suffered as a result of an action or situation: *feeling cold is one of the penalties of old age*. **3** a penalty kick or shot.

penalty area (also **penalty box**) noun Football the rectangular area marked out in front of each goal, within which a foul by a defender involves the award of a penalty kick.

penalty kick noun **1** Football a free shot at the goal awarded to the attacking team after a foul within the penalty area. **2** Rugby a place kick awarded to a team after an offence by an opponent.

penance noun **1** punishment inflicted on oneself to show that one is sorry for wrongdoing: *he had done public penance for those hasty words*. **2** (chiefly in the Roman Catholic and Orthodox Church) a religious act in which a person confesses their sins to a priest and is asked to perform a religious duty before being given formal forgiveness. **3** a religious duty that a priest asks a person to do to show repentance for a sin.
– ORIGIN Latin *paenitentia* 'repentance'.

pence Brit. plural of **PENNY** (used for sums of money).

penchant /pon-shon/ noun a strong liking for or tendency to do something: *a penchant for champagne*.
– ORIGIN French, 'leaning, inclining'.

pencil noun an instrument for writing or drawing, typically consisting of a thin stick of graphite enclosed in a wooden case. •verb (**pencils, pencilling, pencilled**; US **pencils, penciling, penciled**) **1** write, draw, or colour something with a pencil. **2** (**pencil something in**) arrange or note something down provisionally.
– ORIGIN Old French *pincel* 'paintbrush'.

pencil skirt noun a very narrow straight skirt.

pendant noun **1** a piece of jewellery that hangs from a necklace chain. **2** a light designed to hang from the ceiling. •adjective hanging

downwards.
– ORIGIN from Old French, 'hanging'.

pendent adjective literary hanging down or overhanging.

pending adjective **1** awaiting decision or settlement. **2** about to happen. •preposition until something happens.
– ORIGIN anglicized spelling of French *pendant* 'hanging'.

pendulous adjective hanging down; drooping.

pendulum noun a weight hung from a fixed point so that it can swing freely, especially one regulating the mechanism of a clock.
– DERIVATIVES **pendular** adjective.
– ORIGIN Latin, 'thing hanging down'.

peneplain /pee-ni-playn/ noun a level land surface produced by erosion over a long period.
– ORIGIN from Latin *paene* 'almost'.

penes plural form of **PENIS**.

penetrate verb **1** go into or through something, especially with force or effort. **2** gain access to an organization, place, or system, especially in an underhand way: *MI5 had been penetrated by Russian intelligence*. **3** (of a company) begin to sell its products in a new market or area. **4** understand something complex. **5** (as adj. **penetrating**) (of a sound) clearly heard through or above other sounds. **6** (of a man) insert the penis into the vagina or anus of a sexual partner.
– DERIVATIVES **penetrable** adjective **penetrative** adjective **penetrator** noun.
– ORIGIN Latin *penetrare* 'go into'.

penetration noun **1** the action of penetrating. **2** the extent to which a product is recognized and bought by customers in a particular market: *the company achieved remarkable market penetration*. **3** understanding of complex matters.

penfriend noun Brit. a person with whom one becomes friendly by exchanging letters.

penguin noun a flightless black and white seabird of the southern hemisphere, with wings used as flippers.
– ORIGIN unknown.

penicillin noun an antibiotic produced naturally by certain blue moulds and now usually made synthetically.
– ORIGIN from Latin *penicillum* 'paintbrush' (from the shape of the fruiting bodies in the mould).

peninsula noun a long, narrow piece of land projecting out into a sea or lake.
– DERIVATIVES **peninsular** adjective.
– ORIGIN Latin.

USAGE: Do not confuse **peninsula** and **peninsular**. Peninsula is a noun meaning 'a long piece of land jutting out into a sea or lake' (*the Italian peninsula*), whereas **peninsular** is an adjective that means 'relating to a peninsula' (*the peninsular part of Malaysia*).

penis /pee-niss/ noun (pl. **penises** or **penes** /pee-neez/) the male organ that is used for sexual intercourse and urinating.
– DERIVATIVES **penile** adjective.
– ORIGIN Latin, 'tail'.

penitent adjective feeling sorrow and regret

p

for having done wrong. •**noun** a person who repents their sins or does a religious duty required by a priest.
- DERIVATIVES **penitence** noun **penitential** adjective **penitently** adverb.
- ORIGIN from Latin *paenitere* 'repent'.

penitentiary /pen-i-ten-shuh-ri/ noun (pl. **penitentiaries**) (in North America) a prison for people convicted of serious crimes.

penknife noun (pl. **penknives**) a small knife with a blade which folds into the handle.

penlight noun a small electric torch shaped like a pen.

penman noun (pl. **penmen**) **1** a person with a specified ability in handwriting. **2** historical a person employed to write or copy documents; a clerk.
- DERIVATIVES **penmanship** noun.

pen name noun a name used by a writer instead of their real name.

pennant noun **1** a long, narrow pointed flag, especially one flown by a ship and used for signalling. **2** N. Amer. a flag identifying a sports team, club, etc.
- ORIGIN blend of PENDANT and PENNON.

penne /pen-nay/ plural noun pasta in the form of short wide tubes.
- ORIGIN Italian, 'quills'.

penniless adjective having no money; very poor.

pennon noun less common term for PENNANT.
- ORIGIN Old French.

penny noun (pl. **pennies** (for separate coins); **pence** (for a sum of money)) **1** a British bronze coin worth one hundredth of a pound. **2** a former British coin worth one twelfth of a shilling and 240th of a pound. **3** N. Amer. informal a one-cent coin.
- PHRASES **be two** (or **ten**) **a penny** be plentiful and therefore of little value. **in for a penny, in for a pound** used to say that since one has started something one may as well spend as much time or money as is necessary to complete it. **not a penny** no money at all. **the penny dropped** informal someone has finally realized something. **penny wise and pound foolish** economical in small matters but extravagant in large ones.
- ORIGIN Old English.

penny black noun the world's first adhesive postage stamp, issued in Britain in 1840.

penny dreadful noun historical or humorous a cheap, sensational comic or storybook.

penny-farthing noun Brit. an early type of bicycle with a very large front wheel and a small rear wheel.

penny-pinching adjective unwilling to spend money; mean. •**noun** unwillingness to spend money; meanness.
- DERIVATIVES **penny-pincher** noun.

pennyroyal noun a small-leaved plant of the mint family, used in herbal medicine.
- ORIGIN from Old French *puliol real* 'royal thyme'.

penny whistle noun another term for TIN WHISTLE.

pennywort noun a plant with small rounded leaves, growing in crevices or marshy places.

pennyworth noun Brit. **1** an amount of

something worth a penny. **2** (**one's pennyworth**) one's contribution to a discussion.

penology /pee-nol-uh-ji, pi-nol-uh-ji/ noun the study of the punishment of crime and of prison management.
- DERIVATIVES **penological** adjective **penologist** noun.
- ORIGIN from Latin *poena* 'penalty'.

pen pal noun a penfriend.

pen-pusher noun informal an office worker who deals with routine paperwork.

pensée /pon-say/ noun a thought written down in a concise or witty form.
- ORIGIN French.

pension¹ /pen-sh'n/ noun **1** a regular payment made to retired people and to some widows and disabled people, either by the state or from an investment fund. **2** historical a regular payment made to a favourite of a monarch or to an artist or scholar. •**verb** (**pension someone off**) dismiss someone from employment and pay them a pension.
- DERIVATIVES **pensionable** adjective **pensioner** noun.
- ORIGIN Latin, 'payment'.

pension² /pon-syon/ noun a small hotel or guest house in France and other European countries.
- ORIGIN French.

pensione /pen-si-oh-nay/ noun (pl. **pensioni** /pen-si-oh-ni/) a small hotel or guest house in Italy.
- ORIGIN Italian.

pensive adjective engaged in deep or serious thought.
- DERIVATIVES **pensively** adverb **pensiveness** noun.
- ORIGIN Old French *pensif*.

penstemon /pen-sti-muhn, pen-stee-muhn/ noun a North American plant with snapdragon-like flowers.
- ORIGIN Latin.

penta- combining form five; having five: *pentagon*.
- ORIGIN Greek *pente* 'five'.

pentacle /pen-tuh-k'l/ noun a pentagram.
- ORIGIN Latin *pentaculum*.

pentad noun a group or set of five.

pentagon noun **1** a plane figure with five straight sides and five angles. **2** (**the Pentagon**) the headquarters of the US Department of Defense, near Washington DC.
- DERIVATIVES **pentagonal** adjective.

pentagram noun a five-pointed star drawn using a continuous line, often used as a mystic and magical symbol.

pentameter /pen-tam-i-ter/ noun a line of verse consisting of five metrical feet.

pentangle noun a pentagram.
- ORIGIN perhaps from Latin *pentaculum* 'pentacle'.

pentaprism noun a five-sided prism that deviates light from any direction, used chiefly in camera viewfinders.

Pentateuch /pen-tuh-tyook/ noun the first five books of the Old Testament and Hebrew Scriptures (Genesis, Exodus, Leviticus, Numbers, and Deuteronomy).

p

– ORIGIN Greek.

pentathlon noun an athletic event consisting of five different events for each competitor, in particular (**modern pentathlon**) an event involving fencing, shooting, swimming, riding, and cross-country running.
– DERIVATIVES **pentathlete** noun.
– ORIGIN Greek.

pentatonic /pen-tuh-**ton**-ik/ adjective relating to or consisting of a musical scale of five notes.

Pentecost noun **1** the Christian festival celebrating the coming of the Holy Spirit to the disciples of Jesus after his Ascension, held on Whit Sunday. **2** the Jewish festival of Shavuoth, held on the fiftieth day after the second day of Passover.
– ORIGIN from Greek *pentēkostē hēmera* 'fiftieth day'.

Pentecostal adjective **1** relating to a Christian movement which emphasizes the gifts of the Holy Spirit, such as 'speaking in tongues' and healing of the sick. **2** relating to the Christian festival of Pentecost.
– DERIVATIVES **Pentecostalism** noun **Pentecostalist** adjective & noun.

penthouse noun a flat on the top floor of a tall building.
– ORIGIN Old French *apentis* 'outhouse', changed by association with *house*.

Pentothal /pen-tuh-thal/ noun trademark an anaesthetic and sedative drug.

pent-up adjective not expressed or released: *pent-up anger.*
– ORIGIN former past participle of PEN².

penultimate adjective last but one in a series.
– ORIGIN from Latin *paene* 'almost' + *ultimus* 'last'.

penumbra /pi-**num**-bruh/ noun (pl. **penumbrae** /pi-**num**-bree/ or **penumbras**) the partially shaded outer region of the shadow cast by an object.
– DERIVATIVES **penumbral** adjective.
– ORIGIN from Latin *paene* 'almost' + *umbra* 'shadow'.

penurious /pi-**nyoor**-i-uhss/ adjective formal **1** having no money; very poor. **2** unwilling to spend money; mean.
– DERIVATIVES **penuriously** adverb.

penury /**pen**-yuu-ri/ noun the state of having no money; great poverty.
– ORIGIN Latin *penuria.*

peon /pee-uhn, pay-**on**/ noun an unskilled Spanish-American farm worker.
– ORIGIN from Portuguese *peão* and Spanish *peón.*

peony /**pee**-uh-ni/ (also **paeony**) noun a plant grown for its large white, pink, or red flowers.
– ORIGIN Greek *Paiōn*, the physician of the gods.

people plural noun **1** human beings in general or as a whole. **2** (**the people**) the ordinary citizens of a country. **3** (pl. **peoples**) (treated as sing. or pl.) the members of a particular nation, community, or ethnic group. **4** (**one's people**) one's employees or supporters. **5** (**one's people**) dated one's relatives. •verb inhabit a place: *a mountain region peopled by warring clans.*
– ORIGIN Latin *populus* 'populace'.

people carrier noun Brit. a large motor vehicle with three rows of seats.

PEP abbreviation Brit. personal equity plan.

pep informal verb (**peps, pepping, pepped**) (**pep someone/thing up**) make someone or something more lively or interesting. •noun liveliness or energy.
– DERIVATIVES **peppy** adjective.
– ORIGIN abbreviation of PEPPER.

peplum /**pep**-luhm/ noun a short flared strip of fabric attached at the waist of a woman's jacket, dress, or blouse.
– ORIGIN Greek *peplos* 'woman's outer tunic or shawl'.

pepper noun **1** a hot-tasting powder made from peppercorns, used to flavour food. **2** the fruit of a tropical American plant, of which sweet peppers and chilli peppers are varieties. •verb **1** season food with pepper. **2** cover or fill with a large amount of scattered items: *the script is peppered with four-letter words.* **3** hit someone or something repeatedly with small missiles or gunshot.
– DERIVATIVES **peppery** adjective.
– ORIGIN Greek *peperi.*

pepper-and-salt adjective speckled with a mixture of dark and light shades.

peppercorn noun the dried berry of a climbing vine, used whole as a spice or crushed or ground to make pepper.

peppercorn rent noun Brit. a very low rent, charged as a sign that payment is necessary.

peppermint noun **1** a plant of the mint family which produces aromatic leaves and oil, used as a flavouring in food. **2** a sweet flavoured with peppermint oil.

pepperoni /pep-puh-**roh**-ni/ noun beef and pork sausage seasoned with pepper.
– ORIGIN Italian *peperone* 'chilli'.

pepper spray noun an aerosol spray containing oils obtained from cayenne pepper which irritate the eyes, used to disable an attacker.

pep pill noun informal a pill containing a stimulant drug.

pepsin noun the chief digestive enzyme in the stomach, which breaks down proteins.
– ORIGIN from Greek *pepsis* 'digestion'.

pep talk noun informal a talk intended to make someone feel braver or more enthusiastic.

peptic adjective relating to digestion.
– ORIGIN Greek *peptikos* 'able to digest'.

peptic ulcer noun an ulcer in the lining of the stomach or small intestine.

peptide noun a chemical compound consisting of two or more linked amino acids.
– ORIGIN German *Peptid.*

per preposition **1** for each. **2** by means of.
– PHRASES **as per** in accordance with. **as per usual** as usual.
– ORIGIN Latin, 'through, by means of'.

per- prefix **1** through; all over: *pervade.* **2** completely; very: *perfect.* **3** Chemistry having the maximum proportion of a particular element in combination: *peroxide.*

peradventure adverb old use perhaps. •noun uncertainty or doubt.
– ORIGIN from Old French *per* (or *par*) *auenture* 'by chance'.

p

perambulate /puh-ram-byuu-layt/ verb formal walk or travel from place to place.
– DERIVATIVES **perambulation** noun **perambulatory** adjective.
– ORIGIN Latin *perambulare* 'walk about'.

perambulator noun dated a pram.

per annum adverb for each year.
– ORIGIN Latin.

percale /per-kayl/ noun a closely woven fine cotton fabric.
– ORIGIN French.

per capita /per ka-pi-tuh/ adverb & adjective for each person.
– ORIGIN Latin, 'by heads'.

perceive verb 1 become aware of something through the senses. 2 come to realize: *her mouth fell open as she perceived the truth.* 3 regard in a particular way: *the couple were perceived as arrogant.*
– DERIVATIVES **perceivable** adjective **perceiver** noun.
– ORIGIN Latin *percipere* 'seize, understand'.

per cent (also US **percent**) adverb by a specified amount in or for every hundred. • noun one part in every hundred.

percentage noun 1 a rate, number, or amount in each hundred. 2 any proportion or share in relation to a whole: *camera phones are making up a huge percentage of all mobile phone sales.* 3 a share in the profits of something, granted as a commission.

percentile /per-sen-tyl/ noun Statistics each of 100 equal groups into which a large group of people can be divided, according to their place on a scale measuring a particular value.

perceptible adjective able to be seen or noticed: *a perceptible decline in public confidence.*
– DERIVATIVES **perceptibly** adverb.

perception noun 1 the ability to see, hear, or become aware of something through the senses. 2 the process of perceiving something. 3 a way of understanding or interpreting something: *the public perception of him seems distorted.* 4 intuitive understanding; insight.
– ORIGIN Latin.

perceptive adjective having or showing sensitive insight.
– DERIVATIVES **perceptively** adverb **perceptiveness** noun.

perceptual adjective relating to the ability to perceive things through the senses.
– DERIVATIVES **perceptually** adverb.

perch[1] noun 1 an object on which a bird rests or roosts. 2 a high or narrow seat or resting place. • verb 1 sit, rest, or place somewhere. 2 (**be perched**) (of a building) be situated above or on the edge of something.
– DERIVATIVES **percher** noun.
– ORIGIN from PERCH[3].

perch[2] noun (pl. same or **perches**) a freshwater fish with a spiny fin on its back and dark vertical bars on the body.
– ORIGIN Greek *perkē*.

perch[3] noun historical a measure of length equal to a quarter of a chain or 5½ yards (approximately 5.029 metres).
– ORIGIN Latin *pertica* 'measuring rod, pole'.

perchance adverb old use or literary by some chance; perhaps.
– ORIGIN from Old French *par cheance* 'by chance'.

percheron /per-shuh-ron/ noun a powerful breed of grey or black horse, used for pulling loads.
– ORIGIN French (the animal was originally bred in le *Perche* in northern France).

percipient /per-sip-i-uhnt/ adjective having a sensitive understanding; perceptive.
– DERIVATIVES **percipience** noun **percipiently** adverb.

percolate verb 1 (of a liquid or gas) filter through a porous surface or substance. 2 (of information or ideas) spread gradually through a group of people: *this attitude is starting to percolate down to the masses.* 3 prepare coffee in a percolator.
– DERIVATIVES **percolation** noun.
– ORIGIN Latin *percolare* 'strain through'.

percolator noun a machine for making coffee, consisting of a pot in which boiling water is circulated through a small chamber that holds the ground beans.

percuss /per-kuss/ verb gently tap a part of the body as part of a medical diagnosis.

percussion noun 1 musical instruments that are played by being struck or shaken, such as drums or cymbals. 2 the striking of one solid object with or against another.
– DERIVATIVES **percussionist** noun **percussive** adjective.
– ORIGIN Latin.

percussion cap noun full form of CAP (in sense 8).

per diem /per dee-em, per dy-em/ adverb & adjective for each day.
– ORIGIN Latin.

perdition /per-di-sh'n/ noun 1 (in Christian belief) a state of eternal damnation into which a sinful person who has not repented passes after death. 2 complete and utter ruin: *the spending plan dooms the state to fiscal perdition.*
– ORIGIN Latin.

perdurable /per-dyoor-uh-b'l/ adjective literary enduring continuously; permanent.

père /pair/ noun used after a surname to distinguish a father from a son of the same name.
– ORIGIN French, 'father'.

peregrination /pe-ri-gri-nay-sh'n/ noun literary a long or rambling journey: *a secret diary of their boozy peregrinations.*
– DERIVATIVES **peregrinate** /pe-ri-gri-nayt/ verb (old use).
– ORIGIN from Latin *peregrinari* 'travel abroad'.

peregrine /pe-ri-grin/ noun a powerful falcon with a bluish-grey back and wings and pale underparts.
– ORIGIN Latin, 'pilgrim falcon'.

peremptory /puh-remp-tuh-ri/ adjective 1 insisting on immediate attention or obedience, especially in an abrupt way: *she had come to dread his peremptory orders.* 2 Law not open to appeal or challenge; final.
– DERIVATIVES **peremptorily** adverb.
– ORIGIN Latin *peremptorius* 'deadly, decisive'.

perennial adjective 1 lasting or doing

something for a long time or for ever: *his perennial distrust of the media.* 2 (of a plant) living for several years. •noun a plant that lives for several years.
- DERIVATIVES **perennially** adverb.
- ORIGIN from Latin *perennis* 'lasting the year through'.

perestroika /pe-ri-**stroy**-kuh/ noun the economic and political reforms established in the former Soviet Union during the 1980s.
- ORIGIN Russian, 'restructuring'.

perfect adjective /**per**-fikt/ 1 having all the required elements or qualities: *she strove to be the perfect wife.* 2 free from any flaws or defects. 3 complete; absolute: *they were perfect strangers to him.* 4 Grammar (of a tense) describing a completed action or a state in the past, formed in English with *have* or *has* and the past participle, as in *they have eaten.* 5 Mathematics (of a number) equal to the sum of its positive divisors, e.g. the number 6, whose divisors (1, 2, 3) also add up to 6. •verb /per-**fekt**/ make something perfect or as good as possible: *she perfected her English by tuning in to American television.*
- DERIVATIVES **perfecter** noun **perfectible** adjective.
- ORIGIN Latin *perfectus* 'completed'.

perfection noun 1 the state of being excellent, complete, or flawless: *all the food was cooked to perfection.* 2 the action of making something perfect.

perfectionist noun a person who refuses to be satisfied with something unless it is perfect.
- DERIVATIVES **perfectionism** noun.

perfectly adverb 1 in a perfect way. 2 completely; absolutely (used for emphasis).

perfect pitch noun the ability to recognize the pitch of a note or produce any given note.

perfervid /per-**fer**-vid/ adjective literary intensely passionate or enthusiastic.
- ORIGIN from Latin *per-* 'utterly' + *fervidus* 'glowing hot, fiery'.

perfidious adjective literary deceitful and untrustworthy.
- DERIVATIVES **perfidiously** adverb **perfidiousness** noun.

perfidy /**per**-fi-di/ noun literary the state of being deceitful and untrustworthy.
- ORIGIN Latin *perfidia.*

perforate /**per**-fuh-rayt/ verb pierce and make a hole or holes in something.
- DERIVATIVES **perforation** noun **perforator** noun.
- ORIGIN Latin *perforare* 'pierce through'.

perforce adverb formal necessarily; inevitably.
- ORIGIN from Old French *par force* 'by force'.

perform verb 1 carry out or complete an action or function. 2 function or do something to a specified standard: *the car performs well at low speeds.* 3 present entertainment to an audience.
- DERIVATIVES **performable** adjective **performer** noun.
- ORIGIN Old French *parfournir.*

performance noun 1 the action of performing a task or function. 2 an act of performing a play, concert, song, etc. 3 the standard of functioning achieved by a machine or product. 4 informal an act that involves a great deal of time and effort, often when exaggerated or unnecessary: *she stayed behind, making a*

performance of wiping her shoes.

performance art noun an art form that combines visual art with dramatic performance.

performing arts plural noun forms of creative activity that are performed in front of an audience, such as drama, music, and dance.

perfume noun /per-fyoom/ 1 a fragrant liquid used to give a pleasant smell to one's body. 2 a pleasant smell. •verb /per-**fyoom**/ 1 give a pleasant smell to something. 2 put perfume or a sweet-smelling ingredient on or into something.
- DERIVATIVES **perfumed** adjective.
- ORIGIN French *parfum.*

perfumery noun (pl. **perfumeries**) 1 the process of producing and selling perfumes. 2 a shop that sells perfumes.
- DERIVATIVES **perfumer** noun.

perfunctory /per-**fungk**-tuh-ri/ adjective carried out with very little effort or interest: *they exchanged a perfunctory handshake.*
- DERIVATIVES **perfunctorily** adverb.
- ORIGIN Latin *perfunctorius* 'careless'.

perfuse verb literary spread a liquid, colour, quality, etc. throughout something; permeate.
- DERIVATIVES **perfusion** noun.
- ORIGIN Latin *perfundere* 'pour through'.

pergola /**per**-guh-luh/ noun an arched structure forming a framework for climbing plants.
- ORIGIN Latin *pergula* 'projecting roof'.

perhaps adverb 1 expressing uncertainty or possibility. 2 used when making a polite request or suggestion.
- ORIGIN from PER + HAP.

peri- prefix round; about: *perimeter.*
- ORIGIN Greek *peri* 'about, around'.

perianth /**pe**-ri-anth/ noun the outer part of a flower, consisting of the calyx (sepals) and corolla (petals).
- ORIGIN from Greek *peri* 'around' + *anthos* 'flower'.

pericardium /pe-ri-**kar**-di-uhm/ noun (pl. **pericardia** /pe-ri-**kar**-di-uh/) the membrane enclosing the heart.
- DERIVATIVES **pericardial** adjective.
- ORIGIN Latin.

pericarp noun the part of a fruit formed from the wall of the ripened ovary.
- ORIGIN from Greek *peri-* 'around' + *karpos* 'fruit'.

peridot /**pe**-ri-dot/ noun a green semi-precious stone.
- ORIGIN French.

peridotite /**pe**-ri-do-tyt/ noun a dense rock that is rich in magnesium and iron, thought to be the main constituent of the earth's mantle.

perigee /**pe**-ri-jee/ noun the point in the orbit of the moon or a satellite at which it is nearest to the earth. The opposite of APOGEE.
- ORIGIN from Greek *peri-* 'around' + *gē* 'earth'.

perihelion /pe-ri-**hee**-li-uhn/ noun (pl. **perihelia** /pe-ri-**hee**-li-uh/) the point in the orbit of a planet, asteroid, or comet at which it is closest to the sun. The opposite of APHELION.
- ORIGIN from Greek *peri-* 'around' + *hēlios* 'sun'.

peril noun 1 a situation of serious and

p

immediate danger. **2** the risks or difficulties of a situation or activity.
– PHRASES **at one's peril** at one's own risk. **in peril of** very likely to suffer from; at risk of.
– ORIGIN Latin *periculum* 'danger'.

perilous adjective full of danger or risk.
– DERIVATIVES **perilously** adverb **perilousness** noun.

perimeter noun **1** the outermost parts or boundary of an area or object: *I drove round the perimeter of the car park.* **2** the continuous line forming the boundary of a closed geometrical figure.
– ORIGIN from Greek *peri-* 'around' + *metron* 'measure'.

perinatal /per-i-**nay**-t'l/ adjective relating to the time immediately before and after a birth.
– DERIVATIVES **perinatally** adverb.

perineum /pe-ri-**nee**-uhm/ noun (pl. **perinea** /pe-ri-**nee**-uh/) the area between the anus and the scrotum or vulva.
– DERIVATIVES **perineal** adjective.
– ORIGIN Greek *perinaion*.

period noun **1** a length or portion of time. **2** a portion of time with particular characteristics: *the early medieval period.* **3** a major division of geological time, forming part of an era. **4** a lesson in a school. **5** (also **menstrual period**) a monthly flow of blood and other material from the lining of the womb, occurring in women between puberty and the menopause who are not pregnant. **6** N. Amer. a full stop. **7** Physics the interval of time between recurrences of a phenomenon. ● adjective belonging to or typical of a past historical time: *period furniture.*
– ORIGIN Greek *periodos* 'orbit, recurrence, course'.

periodic /peer-i-**od**-ik/ adjective appearing or occurring at intervals.
– DERIVATIVES **periodicity** noun.

periodical adjective occurring or appearing at intervals. ● noun a magazine or newspaper published at regular intervals.
– DERIVATIVES **periodically** adverb.

periodic table noun a table of the chemical elements arranged in order of atomic number, usually in rows, with elements having similar atomic structure appearing in vertical columns.

period piece noun an object or work that is set in or typical of an earlier historical period.

peripatetic /pe-ri-puh-**tet**-ik/ adjective **1** travelling from place to place. **2** (of a teacher) working in more than one school or college.
– DERIVATIVES **peripatetically** adverb.
– ORIGIN Greek *peripatētikos* 'walking up and down'.

peripheral /puh-**rif**-uh-ruhl/ adjective **1** relating to or situated on the outer limits of something. **2** of secondary importance: *she saw their problems as peripheral to her own.* **3** (of a device) able to be attached to and used with a computer. ● noun a device that is able to be attached to and used with a computer.
– DERIVATIVES **peripherality** noun **peripherally** adverb.

peripheral nervous system noun the nervous system outside the brain and spinal cord.

periphery /puh-**rif**-uh-ri/ noun (pl. **peripheries**) **1** the outer limits or edge of an area or object. **2** a part of a subject, group, or area of activity that is of secondary importance: *she's content to stay on the periphery of music.*
– ORIGIN Greek *periphereia* 'circumference'.

periphrasis /puh-**rif**-ruh-siss/ noun (pl. **periphrases** /puh-**rif**-ruh-seez/) the use of indirect and roundabout language.
– DERIVATIVES **periphrastic** adjective.
– ORIGIN from Greek *peri-* 'around' + *phrazein* 'declare'.

periscope noun a tube attached to a set of mirrors or prisms, by which an observer in a submerged submarine or behind an obstacle can see things that are otherwise out of sight.

perish verb **1** literary die, especially in a violent or sudden way. **2** literary be completely ruined or destroyed. **3** (of rubber, food, etc.) rot or decay. **4** (**be perished**) Brit. informal feel very cold.
– PHRASES **perish the thought** informal used to say that a suggestion or idea is ridiculous or unwelcome.
– ORIGIN Latin *perire* 'pass away'.

perishable adjective (of food) likely to rot quickly. ● noun (**perishables**) perishable foods.

perisher noun Brit. informal a mischievous or awkward person, especially a child.

perishing adjective Brit. informal **1** very cold. **2** dated used for emphasis or to express annoyance.
– DERIVATIVES **perishingly** adverb.

peristalsis /pe-ri-**stal**-siss/ noun the contraction and relaxation of the muscles of the intestines, creating movements which push the contents of the intestines forward.
– DERIVATIVES **peristaltic** adjective.
– ORIGIN from Greek *peristallein* 'wrap around'.

peristyle noun a row of columns surrounding a courtyard or internal garden or edging a veranda or porch.
– ORIGIN from Greek *peri-* 'around' + *stulos* 'pillar'.

peritoneum /pe-ri-tuh-**nee**-uhm/ noun (pl. **peritoneums** or **peritonea** /pe-ri-tuh-**nee**-uh/) the membrane lining the cavity of the abdomen and covering the abdominal organs.
– DERIVATIVES **peritoneal** adjective.
– ORIGIN Latin.

peritonitis /pe-ri-tuh-**ny**-tiss/ noun inflammation of the peritoneum (the membrane lining the cavity of the abdomen).

periwig noun a wig of a kind worn in the 17th and 18th centuries.
– ORIGIN from **PERUKE**.

periwinkle[1] noun a plant with flat five-petalled flowers and glossy leaves.
– ORIGIN Latin *pervinca*.

periwinkle[2] noun another term for **WINKLE**.
– ORIGIN unknown.

perjure verb **1** (**perjure oneself**) deliberately tell a lie in a a court of law after one has sworn to tell the truth. **2** (as adj. **perjured**) (of evidence) involving deliberate untruth.
– DERIVATIVES **perjurer** noun.
– ORIGIN Latin *perjurare* 'swear falsely'.

perjury /**per**-juh-ri/ noun the offence of deliberately telling a lie in a court of law when having sworn to be truthful.

perk[1] verb (**perk up** or **perk someone/thing up**) become or make more cheerful or lively.
– ORIGIN perhaps from Old French *percher* 'to perch'.

perk[2] noun informal a benefit, especially one which a person receives from their job.
– ORIGIN abbreviation of PERQUISITE.

perk[3] verb informal (of coffee) percolate.

perky adjective (**perkier, perkiest**) cheerful and lively.
– DERIVATIVES **perkily** adverb **perkiness** noun.

perlite /per-lyt/ noun a form of obsidian (volcanic rock) consisting of glassy globules, used as insulation or in a mixture with plant compost.
– ORIGIN French.

perm[1] noun (also **permanent wave**) a method of setting the hair in curls and treating it with chemicals so that the style lasts for several months. • verb set the hair in a perm.

perm[2] noun Brit. informal a selection of a specified number of matches in a football pool; a permutation.

permaculture noun the development of agricultural ecosystems that are intended to be sustainable and self-sufficient.
– ORIGIN blend of PERMANENT and AGRICULTURE.

permafrost noun a thick layer beneath the surface of the soil that remains frozen throughout the year.

permanent adjective lasting or intending to last for a long time or forever: *he had never settled down in a permanent job.*
– DERIVATIVES **permanence** noun **permanency** noun **permanently** adverb.
– ORIGIN from Latin *permanere* 'remain to the end'.

Permanent Undersecretary (also **Permanent Secretary**) noun (in the UK) a senior civil servant who is a permanent adviser to a Secretary of State.

permanent wave noun see PERM[1].

permanent way noun Brit. the finished foundation of a railway together with the track.

permanganate /per-mang-guh-nuht, per-mang-guh-nayt/ noun a salt of manganese, oxygen, and another element such as potassium, used as an oxidizing agent in some tanning preparations and disinfectants.

permeable adjective allowing liquids or gases to pass through.
– DERIVATIVES **permeability** noun.

permeate verb spread throughout something: *the aroma of soup permeated the air.*
– DERIVATIVES **permeation** noun.
– ORIGIN Latin *permeare* 'pass through'.

Permian /per-mi-uhn/ adjective Geology relating to the last period of the Palaeozoic era, about 290 to 245 million years ago, a time when reptiles increased rapidly in number.
– ORIGIN from *Perm*, a Russian province with deposits from this period.

permissible adjective allowable; permitted.
– DERIVATIVES **permissibility** noun.

permission noun the action of officially allowing something; authorization.

permissive adjective allowing or characterized

by freedom of behaviour, especially in sexual matters: *the permissive society of the 60s.*
– DERIVATIVES **permissively** adverb **permissiveness** noun.

permit verb /per-mit/ (**permits, permitting, permitted**) 1 officially allow someone to do something. 2 (also formal **permit of**) make possible: *the car park was too rutted to permit ball games.* • noun /per-mit/ an official document allowing someone to do something.
– ORIGIN Latin *permittere*.

permutation noun 1 each of several possible ways in which things can be ordered or arranged. 2 Mathematics the action of changing the arrangement of a set of items. 3 Brit. a selection of a specified number of matches in a football pool.
– DERIVATIVES **permutational** adjective.
– ORIGIN from Latin *permutare* 'change completely'.

permute (also **permutate**) verb technical alter the sequence of a set or group of things.

pernicious /per-nish-uhss/ adjective having a harmful effect, especially in a gradual or subtle way: *the pernicious influences of the mass media.*
– DERIVATIVES **perniciously** adverb **perniciousness** noun.
– ORIGIN Latin *perniciosus* 'destructive'.

pernicious anaemia noun a deficiency in the production of red blood cells through a lack of vitamin B_{12}.

pernickety adjective Brit. informal 1 placing excessive emphasis on minor details; fussy. 2 requiring a precise or careful approach.
– ORIGIN unknown.

peroration /pe-ruh-ray-sh'n/ noun the concluding part of a speech; the summing up.
– ORIGIN Latin *perorare* 'speak at length'.

peroxide noun 1 Chemistry a compound containing two oxygen atoms bonded together. 2 hydrogen peroxide, a chemical used as a bleach for the hair. • verb bleach hair with peroxide.

perpendicular /per-puhn-dik-yuu-ler/ adjective 1 at an angle of 90° to a given line, plane, or surface, or to the ground. 2 (**Perpendicular**) referring to the latest stage of English Gothic architecture (late 14th to mid 16th centuries), characterized by large windows with vertical tracery. • noun a straight line at an angle of 90° to a given line, plane, or surface.
– DERIVATIVES **perpendicularity** noun **perpendicularly** adverb.
– ORIGIN Latin *perpendicularis*.

perpetrate /per-pi-trayt/ verb carry out a bad or illegal act.
– DERIVATIVES **perpetration** noun **perpetrator** noun.
– ORIGIN Latin *perpetrare* 'perform'.

USAGE: Do not confuse **perpetrate** and **perpetuate**. **Perpetrate** means 'carry out a bad or illegal act' (*a crime has been perpetrated against a sovereign state*), whereas **perpetuate** means 'make something continue for a considerable time' (*a monument to perpetuate the memory of those killed in the war*).

perpetual /per-pet-yoo-uhl/ adjective 1 never

p

ending or changing. **2** so frequent as to seem continual: *their perpetual money worries.*
– DERIVATIVES **perpetually** adverb.
– ORIGIN Latin *perpetualis.*

perpetual motion noun the motion of a hypothetical machine which, once activated, would run forever unless subject to an external force or to wear.

perpetuate verb make something continue for a considerable time.
– DERIVATIVES **perpetuation** noun **perpetuator** noun.
– ORIGIN Latin *perpetuare* 'make permanent'.

USAGE: On the difference between **perpetuate** and **perpetrate**, see the note at **PERPETRATE**.

perpetuity /per-pi-**tyoo**-i-ti/ noun (pl. **perpetuities**) **1** the state or quality of lasting forever. **2** a bond or other security with no fixed maturity date.
– PHRASES **in** (or **for**) **perpetuity** for ever.

perplex verb make someone feel baffled or very puzzled.
– ORIGIN from Latin *perplexus* 'entangled'.

perplexity noun (pl. **perplexities**) **1** the state of being puzzled. **2** a puzzling thing.

perquisite /per-kwi-zit/ noun formal a benefit or right enjoyed as a result of one's job or position.
– ORIGIN Latin *perquisitum* 'acquisition'.

perry noun (pl. **perries**) an alcoholic drink made from the fermented juice of pears.
– ORIGIN Latin *pirum* 'pear'.

per se /per **say**/ adverb by or in itself or themselves.
– ORIGIN Latin.

persecute verb **1** treat someone in a cruel or unfair way, especially because of their race or beliefs. **2** persistently harass someone.
– DERIVATIVES **persecution** noun **persecutor** noun.
– ORIGIN Latin *persequi* 'follow with hostility'.

persevere verb continue in a course of action in spite of difficulty or lack of success: *he persevered with subjects which he found disagreeable.*
– DERIVATIVES **perseverance** noun.
– ORIGIN Latin *perseverare* 'abide by strictly'.

Persian noun **1** a person from Persia (now Iran). **2** the language of ancient Persia or modern Iran. **3** a long-haired breed of domestic cat. •adjective relating to Persia or Iran.

Persian carpet noun a carpet or rug with a traditional Persian design incorporating stylized symbolic designs.

Persian lamb noun the silky, tightly curled fleece of the karakul (an Asian sheep), used to make clothing.

persiflage /per-si-flahzh/ noun formal light mockery or banter.
– ORIGIN from French *persifler* 'to banter'.

persimmon /per-sim-muhn/ noun an edible fruit resembling a large tomato, with very sweet flesh.
– ORIGIN Algonquian.

persist verb **1** continue doing something in spite of difficulty or opposition: *the minority of drivers who persist in drinking.* **2** continue to exist.
– ORIGIN Latin *persistere* 'continue steadfastly'.

persistent adjective **1** continuing to do something in spite of difficulty or opposition. **2** continuing or recurring for a long time.
– DERIVATIVES **persistence** noun **persistently** adverb.

persistent vegetative state noun a condition in which a patient is kept alive by medical means but displays no sign of higher brain function.

person noun (pl. **people** or **persons**) **1** a human being regarded as an individual. **2** a human being's body: *a bottle of wine concealed on his person.* **3** Grammar a category used to classify pronouns or verb forms according to whether they indicate the speaker (**first person**), the person spoken to (**second person**), or a third party (**third person**).
– PHRASES **in person** with the presence or action of the person specified.
– ORIGIN Latin *persona* 'actor's mask, character in a play'.

USAGE: The words **people** and **persons** are not used in exactly the same way. **People** is by far the most common and is used in ordinary writing (*a group of people*). However, **persons** is now found chiefly in official or formal writing: *this vehicle is authorized to carry twenty persons.*

-person combining form used as a neutral alternative to -man in nouns referring to role or status: *salesperson.*

persona /per-**soh**-nuh/ noun (pl. **personas** or **personae** /per-**soh**-nee/) **1** the aspect of a person's character that is presented to others: *her public persona.* **2** a role or character adopted by an author or actor.
– ORIGIN Latin, 'mask, character in a play'.

personable adjective having a pleasant appearance and character.
– DERIVATIVES **personably** adverb.

personage noun an important or high-ranking person.
– ORIGIN Old French.

personal adjective **1** relating or belonging to a particular person. **2** done by a particular person rather than someone else: *a personal appearance.* **3** concerning a person's private rather than professional life. **4** referring to a person's character or appearance in an offensive way: *he had the cheek to make personal remarks.* **5** relating to a person's body. **6** Grammar relating to one of the three persons. •noun (**personals**) chiefly N. Amer. advertisements or messages in the personal column of a newspaper.

personal assistant noun a secretary or administrative assistant working for one particular person.

personal column noun a section of a newspaper containing private advertisements or messages.

personal computer noun a microcomputer designed for use by one person.

personal equity plan noun (in the UK) a former scheme whereby a person could invest a limited sum in shares each year without liability for tax on dividends or capital gains.

p

personal identification number noun a number allocated to a person and used with a bank card to validate electronic transactions.

personality noun (pl. **personalities**) 1 the characteristics or qualities that form a person's character. 2 lively or interesting personal qualities: *she's always had loads of personality.* 3 a celebrity.

personality disorder noun Psychiatry a deeply ingrained pattern of behaviour causing long-term difficulties in relationships or in functioning in society.

personalize (or **personalise**) verb 1 design or produce something to meet someone's individual requirements. 2 mark something to show that it belongs to a particular person. 3 cause an issue or argument to become concerned with personalities or feelings: *the media's tendency to personalize politics.*
– DERIVATIVES **personalization** noun.

personally adverb 1 in person. 2 from one's own viewpoint.
– PHRASES **take something personally** interpret a remark or action as directed against oneself and be upset by it.

personal organizer noun a loose-leaf notebook with a diary and address book.

personal pension noun a pension scheme that is independent of the contributor's employer.

personal pronoun noun each of the pronouns in English (*I, you, he, she, it, we, they, me, him, her, us,* and *them*) that show person, gender, number, and case.

> USAGE: **I, we, they, he,** and **she** are **subjective** personal pronouns, which means they are used as the subject of a sentence, often coming before the verb (*she lives in Paris*). **Me, us, them, him,** and **her** are **objective** personal pronouns, which means that they are used as the object of a verb or preposition (*John hates me*). This explains why it is wrong to use *me* in *John and me went to the shops*: the personal pronoun is in the subject position, so it must be **I**.
> Where a personal pronoun is used alone, the situation is more difficult. Some people say that statements such as *she's younger than me* are wrong and that the correct form is *she's younger than I*. This is based on the fact that *than* is a conjunction and so the personal pronoun is still in the subject position even though there is no verb (in full it would be *she's younger than I am*). Yet for most people the supposed 'correct' form does not sound natural and it is mainly found in very formal writing; it is usually perfectly acceptable to say *she's younger than me.*

personal property noun Law all of someone's property except land and buildings. Compare with REAL PROPERTY.

personal stereo noun a small portable cassette or compact disc player, used with headphones.

personalty /per-suh-nuhl-ti/ noun Law a person's personal property. Compare with REALTY.

persona non grata /per-soh-nuh nohn grah-tuh/ noun (pl. **personae non gratae** /per-soh-

nee nohn **grah**-tee/) a person who is not welcome somewhere because they have done something unacceptable.
– ORIGIN Latin.

personate verb formal pretend to be someone else, especially for fraudulent purposes.
– DERIVATIVES **personation** noun.

personify verb (**personifies, personifying, personified**) 1 represent a quality or concept by a figure in human form: *dramas in which vices and virtues were personified.* 2 give a personal nature or human characteristics to something non-human.
– DERIVATIVES **personification** noun.

personnel /per-suh-**nel**/ plural noun people who work for an organization or one of the armed forces.
– ORIGIN from French, 'personal'.

personnel carrier noun an armoured vehicle for transporting troops.

perspective noun 1 the art of representing three-dimensional objects on a two-dimensional surface so as to convey the impression of height, width, depth, and relative distance. 2 a particular point of view. 3 understanding of the relative importance of things: *we must keep a sense of perspective about what he's done.*
– DERIVATIVES **perspectival** adjective.
– ORIGIN from Latin *perspectiva ars* 'science of optics'.

perspex noun trademark a tough transparent plastic used as a substitute for glass.
– ORIGIN from Latin *perspicere* 'look through'.

perspicacious /per-spi-**kay**-shuhss/ adjective quickly gaining insight into and understanding of things.
– DERIVATIVES **perspicaciously** adverb **perspicacity** noun.
– ORIGIN from Latin *perspicax* 'seeing clearly'.

perspicuous /per-**spik**-yuu-uhss/ adjective 1 clearly expressed and easily understood; lucid. 2 expressing things clearly.
– DERIVATIVES **perspicuity** noun **perspicuously** adverb.
– ORIGIN Latin *perspicuus* 'transparent, clear'.

perspiration noun 1 sweat. 2 the process of sweating.

perspire verb give out sweat through the pores of the skin.
– ORIGIN Latin *perspirare*, from *spirare* 'breathe'.

persuade verb use reasoning or argument to make someone do or believe something: *he persuaded her to go out with him.*
– DERIVATIVES **persuadable** adjective **persuader** noun.
– ORIGIN Latin *persuadere*.

persuasion noun 1 the process of persuading someone or of being persuaded. 2 a belief or set of beliefs: *writers of all political persuasions.* 3 a group or sect holding a particular religious belief.

persuasive adjective 1 good at persuading someone to do or believe something. 2 providing sound reasons or arguments: *an informative and persuasive speech.*
– DERIVATIVES **persuasively** adverb **persuasiveness** noun.

pert adjective 1 attractively lively or cheeky. 2 (especially of a part of the body) attractively

p

small and well shaped. **3** impudent or cheeky.
- DERIVATIVES **pertly** adverb **pertness** noun.
- ORIGIN from Latin *apertus* 'opened'.

pertain verb **1** (**pertain to**) be relevant or appropriate to: *matters pertaining to the organization of government.* **2** formal be in effect or existence at a particular place or time.
- ORIGIN Latin *pertinere* 'extend to'.

pertinacious /per-ti-nay-shuhss/ adjective formal persistent and determined.
- DERIVATIVES **pertinaciously** adverb **pertinacity** noun.
- ORIGIN Latin *pertinax* 'holding fast'.

pertinent adjective relevant or appropriate: *she asked a lot of pertinent questions.*
- DERIVATIVES **pertinence** noun **pertinently** adverb.
- ORIGIN from Latin *pertinere* 'extend to'.

perturb verb **1** make someone anxious or unsettled. **2** alter the normal or regular state or path of a system, moving object, etc.
- ORIGIN Latin *perturbare*.

perturbation noun **1** anxiety or uneasiness. **2** an alteration in the normal or regular state or path of a system, moving object, etc.

pertussis /per-tuss-iss/ noun medical term for WHOOPING COUGH.
- ORIGIN Latin, from *tussis* 'a cough'.

peruke /puh-rook/ noun old use a wig or periwig.
- ORIGIN French *perruque*.

peruse /puh-rooz/ verb formal read or examine something thoroughly or carefully.
- DERIVATIVES **perusal** noun **peruser** noun.
- ORIGIN perhaps from PER- + USE.

USAGE: The verb **peruse** means 'read something thoroughly and carefully'. It is sometimes taken to mean 'read through something quickly', but this is a mistake.

Peruvian /puh-roo-vi-uhn/ noun a person from Peru. •adjective relating to Peru.

perv (also **perve**) noun informal a sexual pervert.
- DERIVATIVES **pervy** adjective.

pervade verb spread or be present throughout: *a smell of cabbage pervaded the air.*
- ORIGIN Latin *pervadere* 'go or come through'.

pervasive adjective spreading widely through an area or group of people; widespread: *ageism is pervasive in our society.*
- DERIVATIVES **pervasively** adverb **pervasiveness** noun.

perverse adjective **1** showing a deliberate desire to behave in a way that other people find difficult or unacceptable. **2** contrary to what is accepted or expected. **3** sexually perverted.
- DERIVATIVES **perversely** adverb **perverseness** noun **perversity** noun (pl. **perversities**).

perversion noun **1** the action of perverting something. **2** abnormal or unacceptable sexual behaviour.

pervert verb **1** change the original form or meaning of something so that it is no longer what it should be. **2** lead someone away from doing what is right, natural, or acceptable. •noun a person whose sexual behaviour is abnormal and unacceptable.
- ORIGIN Latin *pervertere* 'turn about'.

perverted adjective sexually abnormal or unacceptable.

pervious /per-vi-uhss/ adjective allowing water to pass through; permeable.
- ORIGIN Latin *pervius* 'having a passage through'.

Pesach /pay-sahk/ noun the Passover festival.
- ORIGIN from Hebrew.

peseta /puh-say-tuh/ noun (until the introduction of the euro in 2002) the basic unit of money of Spain.
- ORIGIN Spanish, 'little weight'.

pesky adjective (**peskier, peskiest**) informal, chiefly N. Amer. annoying.
- ORIGIN perhaps related to PEST.

peso /pay-soh/ noun (pl. **pesos**) the basic unit of money of several Latin American countries and of the Philippines.
- ORIGIN Spanish, 'weight'.

pessary /pess-uh-ri/ noun (pl. **pessaries**) **1** a small solid block of a medical preparation designed to dissolve after being inserted into the vagina, used to treat an infection or as a contraceptive. **2** a device inserted into the vagina to support the womb.
- ORIGIN Latin *pessarium*.

pessimism noun **1** lack of hope or confidence in the future. **2** Philosophy a belief that this world is as bad as it could be or that evil will ultimately triumph over good.
- DERIVATIVES **pessimist** noun **pessimistic** adjective **pessimistically** adverb.
- ORIGIN from Latin *pessimus* 'worst'.

pest noun **1** a destructive animal or insect that attacks crops, food, or livestock. **2** informal an annoying person or thing.
- ORIGIN French *peste* or Latin *pestis* 'plague'.

pester verb trouble or annoy someone with persistent requests or interruptions.
- ORIGIN French *empestrer* 'encumber'.

pesticide noun a substance for destroying insects or other pests.

pestiferous adjective **1** literary carrying infection and disease. **2** humorous annoying.
- ORIGIN Latin *pestifer* 'bringing pestilence'.

pestilence noun old use a deadly epidemic disease, especially bubonic plague.
- ORIGIN Latin *pestilentia*.

pestilent adjective **1** deadly. **2** informal, dated annoying.

pestilential adjective **1** relating to or tending to cause infectious diseases. **2** very widespread and troublesome: *pestilential weeds.* **3** informal annoying.

pestle /pess-uhl/ noun a heavy implement with a rounded end, used for crushing and grinding substances in a mortar.
- ORIGIN Latin *pistillum*.

pesto /pess-toh/ noun a sauce of crushed basil leaves, pine nuts, garlic, Parmesan cheese, and olive oil, served with pasta.
- ORIGIN Italian.

pet[1] noun **1** an animal or bird kept for companionship or pleasure. **2** a person treated with special favour or affection: *the teacher's pet.* •adjective **1** relating to or kept as a pet. **2** treated with special attention or arousing particularly strong feelings: *my pet hate.* •verb (**pets, petting, petted**) **1** stroke or pat an animal. **2** caress someone sexually.

– ORIGIN unknown.

pet² noun a fit of sulking or bad temper.
– ORIGIN unknown.

peta- /pet-uh/ combining form referring to a factor of one thousand million million (10¹⁵).
– ORIGIN alteration of **PENTA-**.

petal noun each of the segments forming the outer part of a flower.
– ORIGIN Greek *petalon* 'leaf'.

pétanque /puh-tongk/ noun a game similar to boule, played chiefly in Provence.
– ORIGIN French.

petard /pi-tard/ noun historical a small bomb made of a metal or wooden box filled with powder.
– PHRASES **be hoist with** (or **by**) **one's own petard** find that one's schemes to cause trouble for other people backfire on one. [from Shakespeare's *Hamlet* (III. iv. 207); *hoist* is in the sense 'lifted and removed'.]
– ORIGIN French, from *péter* 'break wind'.

peter verb (usu. **peter out**) gradually come to an end: *the storm had petered out.*
– ORIGIN unknown.

Peter Pan noun a person who continues to look young, or one who is immature.
– ORIGIN the hero of J. M. Barrie's play of the same name.

petersham noun a kind of thick tape used to stiffen dresses and hats.
– ORIGIN named after the English army officer Lord *Petersham*.

Peters projection noun a world map projection in which areas are shown in the correct proportion at the expense of distorted shape.
– ORIGIN named after the German historian Arno *Peters*.

pethidine /peth-i-deen/ noun a painkiller used especially for women giving birth.

pétillant /pet-i-yon/ adjective (of wine) slightly sparkling.
– ORIGIN French.

petiole /pee-ti-ohl/ noun the stalk that joins a leaf to a stem.
– ORIGIN Latin *petiolus* 'little foot, stalk'.

petit bourgeois adjective characteristic of the lower middle class, especially in being conventional and conservative. ▪noun (pl. **petits bourgeois** pronunc. same) a petit bourgeois person.
– ORIGIN French, 'little citizen'.

petite /puh-teet/ adjective (of a woman) attractively small and slim.
– ORIGIN French, feminine of *petit* 'small'.

petite bourgeoisie (also **petit bourgeoisie**) noun the lower middle class.
– ORIGIN French, 'little townsfolk'.

petit four /puh-ti for/ noun (pl. **petits fours** /puh-ti forz/) a very small fancy cake, biscuit, or sweet.
– ORIGIN French, 'little oven'.

petition noun 1 a formal written appeal or request concerning a particular cause, signed by many people and presented to an authority. 2 an appeal or prayer to a deity or someone in authority. 3 Law an application to a court for a writ, judicial action, etc.: *a divorce petition.* ▪verb make or present a petition to: *they petitioned the government for a total ban on pesticide use.*
– DERIVATIVES **petitioner** noun.
– ORIGIN Latin.

petit mal /puh-ti mal/ noun a mild form of epilepsy with only very brief spells of unconsciousness. Compare with **GRAND MAL**.
– ORIGIN French, 'little sickness'.

petit point /puh-ti poynt, puh-ti pwan/ noun embroidery on canvas, using small diagonal stitches.
– ORIGIN French, 'little stitch'.

petits pois /puh-ti pwah/ plural noun small, fine peas.
– ORIGIN French, 'small peas'.

pet name noun a name used to express affection or familiarity.

petrel /pet-ruhl/ noun a black-and-white seabird that typically flies far from land.
– ORIGIN from the name of St *Peter*, because of the bird's habit of flying low with legs dangling, and so appearing to walk on the water (as St Peter did in the Gospel of Matthew).

Petri dish /pet-ri, pee-tri/ noun a shallow transparent dish with a flat lid, used in laboratories for the culture of microorganisms.
– ORIGIN named after the German bacteriologist Julius R. *Petri*.

petrify verb (**petrifies, petrifying, petrified**) 1 make someone so frightened that they are unable to move. 2 change organic matter into stone by encrusting or replacing its original substance with a mineral deposit.
– DERIVATIVES **petrifaction** noun **petrification** noun.
– ORIGIN from Latin *petra* 'rock'.

petrochemical adjective relating to the chemical properties and processing of petroleum and natural gas. ▪noun a chemical obtained from petroleum and natural gas.
– ORIGIN from **PETROLEUM**.

petrodollar noun a unit of currency used for calculating the money earned by a country from the export of petroleum.

petroglyph /pet-ruh-glif/ noun a rock carving.
– ORIGIN from Greek *petros* 'rock' + *glyphē* 'carving'.

petrography /pe-trog-ruh-fi/ noun the study of the composition and properties of rocks.
– DERIVATIVES **petrographer** noun **petrographic** adjective.

petrol noun Brit. 1 a light fuel obtained by distilling petroleum and used in internal-combustion engines. 2 (also **petrol blue**) a shade of greenish or greyish blue.

petrolatum /pe-truh-lay-tuhm/ noun another term for **PETROLEUM JELLY**.
– ORIGIN Latin, from **PETROL**.

petrol bomb noun Brit. a simple bomb consisting of a bottle containing petrol and a cloth wick.

petroleum noun a hydrocarbon oil found in layers of rock and extracted and refined to produce fuels including petrol, paraffin, and diesel oil.
– ORIGIN Latin, from *petra* 'rock' + *oleum* 'oil'.

petroleum jelly noun a translucent solid

substance obtained from petroleum, used as a lubricant or ointment.

petrology /pi-trol-uh-ji/ noun the study of the origin, structure, and composition of rocks.
– DERIVATIVES **petrological** adjective **petrologist** noun.

petticoat noun a woman's light, loose undergarment in the form of a skirt or dress.
– ORIGIN from former *petty coat* 'small coat'.

pettifog verb (**pettifogs, pettifogging, pettifogged**) old use quibble about trivial points.
– DERIVATIVES **pettifoggery** noun.

pettifogging adjective petty or trivial.
– ORIGIN from **PETTY** + former *fogger* 'underhand dealer'.

pettish adjective childishly sulky.
– DERIVATIVES **pettishly** adverb.

petty adjective (**pettier, pettiest**) **1** of little importance; trivial. **2** (of a person's behaviour) small-minded. **3** of secondary or lesser importance, rank, or scale: *petty theft.*
– DERIVATIVES **pettily** adverb **pettiness** noun.
– ORIGIN from the pronunciation of French *petit* 'small'.

petty bourgeois noun variant of **PETIT BOURGEOIS.**

petty bourgeoisie noun variant of **PETITE BOURGEOISIE.**

petty cash noun a small amount of money kept in an office for minor payments.

petty officer noun a rank of non-commissioned officer in the navy, above leading seaman and below chief petty officer.

petulant /pet-yuu-luhnt/ adjective childishly sulky or bad-tempered.
– DERIVATIVES **petulance** noun **petulantly** adverb.
– ORIGIN Latin *petulans* 'impudent'.

petunia noun a South American plant with white, purple, or red funnel-shaped flowers.
– ORIGIN from an American Indian word meaning 'tobacco' (to which these plants are related).

pew noun **1** (in a church) a long bench with a back. **2** Brit. informal a seat.
– ORIGIN Old French *puye* 'balcony'.

pewter noun a grey alloy of tin with copper and antimony (formerly, tin and lead).
– ORIGIN Old French *peutre*.

peyote /pay-oh-ti/ noun **1** a small cactus native to Mexico and the southern US. **2** a hallucinogenic drug prepared from this, containing mescaline.
– ORIGIN Nahuatl.

pfennig /pfen-nig/ noun (pl. same or **pfennigs**) a former unit of money of Germany, equal to one hundredth of a mark.
– ORIGIN German, related to **PENNY.**

PFI abbreviation (in the UK) Private Finance Initiative, a scheme whereby public services such as the National Health Service raise funds for projects from commercial organizations.

PG abbreviation (in the UK) parental guidance, a film classification indicating that some parents may find the film unsuitable for their children.

PGCE abbreviation Brit. Postgraduate Certificate of Education.

pH noun Chemistry a figure expressing how acid or alkaline a substance is (7 is neutral, lower values are more acid, and higher values are more alkaline).
– ORIGIN from *p* representing German *Potenz* 'power' + *H*, the symbol for hydrogen.

phaeton /fay-tuhn/ noun historical a light, open four-wheeled horse-drawn carriage.
– ORIGIN from *Phaethon*, son of the sun god Helios in Greek mythology, who was allowed to drive the chariot of the sun for a day.

phage /fayj, fahzh/ noun a kind of virus which acts as a parasite of bacteria, infecting them and reproducing inside them.
– ORIGIN short for *bacteriophage*, from **BACTERIUM** + Greek *phagein* 'eat'.

phagocyte /fag-uh-syt/ noun a type of body cell which surrounds and absorbs bacteria and other small particles.
– DERIVATIVES **phagocytic** adjective.
– ORIGIN from Greek *phago-* 'eating' + *kutos* 'vessel'.

phalange /fa-lanj/ noun Anatomy another term for **PHALANX** (in sense 3).

phalangeal adjective Anatomy relating to a phalanx or the phalanges.

phalanger /fuh-lan-jer/ noun a tree-dwelling marsupial native to Australia and New Guinea.
– ORIGIN Greek *phalangion* 'spider's web' (because of the animal's webbed toes).

phalanx /fa-langks/ noun (pl. **phalanxes**) **1** a group of similar people or things: *the phalanx of waiting reporters.* **2** a body of troops or police officers in close formation. **3** (pl. **phalanges** /fa-lan-jeez/) Anatomy a bone of the finger or toe.
– ORIGIN Greek.

phalarope /fa-luh-rohp/ noun a small wading or swimming bird with a straight bill.
– ORIGIN French.

phallic adjective relating to or resembling a penis, especially when erect.

phallocentric /fa-loh-sen-trik/ adjective focused on the penis as a symbol of male dominance.

phallus /fal-luhss/ noun (pl. **phalli** /fal-ly/or **phalluses**) **1** a penis, especially when erect. **2** a representation of an erect penis as a symbol of fertility or potency.
– ORIGIN Greek *phallos*.

phantasm /fan-ta-z'm/ noun literary a thing that exists only in the imagination.
– DERIVATIVES **phantasmal** adjective.
– ORIGIN Greek *phantasma*.

phantasmagoria /fan-taz-muh-gor-i-uh/ noun a sequence of real or imaginary images like that seen in a dream.
– DERIVATIVES **phantasmagoric** adjective **phantasmagorical** adjective.
– ORIGIN probably from French *fantasmagorie.*

phantom noun **1** a ghost. **2** a thing that exists only in the imagination. • adjective apparently real but not actually so: *a phantom conspiracy.*
– ORIGIN Greek *phantasma.*

phantom limb noun a sensation experienced by a person who has had a limb amputated that the limb is still there.

phantom pregnancy noun a condition in

which signs of pregnancy are present in a woman who is not pregnant.

pharaoh /**fair**-oh/ noun a ruler in ancient Egypt.
– DERIVATIVES **pharaonic** /fair-ay-**on**-ik/ adjective.
– ORIGIN Greek *Pharaō*, from an Egyptian word meaning 'great house'.

Pharisee /**fa**-ri-see/ noun 1 a member of an ancient Jewish sect noted for following traditional and written Jewish law very strictly. 2 a self-righteous or hypocritical person.
– DERIVATIVES **Pharisaic** /fa-ri-**say**-ik/ adjective **Pharisaical** adjective.
– ORIGIN Greek *Pharisaios*.

pharmaceutical /far-muh-**syoo**-ti-k'l/ adjective relating to medicinal drugs. •noun a manufactured medicinal drug.
– DERIVATIVES **pharmaceutically** adverb.
– ORIGIN from Greek *pharmakon* 'drug'.

pharmacist noun a person qualified to prepare and dispense medicinal drugs.

pharmacology noun the branch of science concerned with the uses, effects, and action of drugs.
– DERIVATIVES **pharmacologic** adjective **pharmacological** adjective **pharmacologist** noun.
– ORIGIN from Greek *pharmakon* 'drug'.

pharmacopoeia /far-muh-kuh-**pee**-uh/ (US also **pharmacopeia**) noun 1 a book containing a list of medicinal drugs with directions for their use. 2 a stock of medicinal drugs.
– ORIGIN Greek *pharmakopoiia* 'art of preparing drugs'.

pharmacy noun (pl. **pharmacies**) 1 a place where medicinal drugs are prepared or sold. 2 the science or practice of preparing and dispensing medicinal drugs.
– ORIGIN Old French *farmacie*, from Greek *pharmakon* 'drug'.

pharyngeal /fuh-**rin**-ji-uhl, fa-rin-**jee**-uhl/ adjective relating to the pharynx.

pharyngitis /fa-rin-**jy**-tiss/ noun inflammation of the pharynx.

pharynx /**fa**-ringks/ noun (pl. **pharynges** /fa-**rin**-jeez/) the cavity behind the nose and mouth, connecting them to the oesophagus.
– ORIGIN Greek *pharunx*.

phase noun 1 a distinct period or stage in a process of change or development: *the final phases of the war.* 2 each of the forms in which the moon or a planet appears, according to the amount that is lit up. 3 Physics the stage that a regularly varying quantity (e.g. an alternating electric current) has reached in relation to zero or another chosen value. •verb 1 carry something out in gradual stages. 2 (**phase something in/out**) gradually introduce or withdraw something: *the changes will be phased in over 10 years.*
– PHRASES **in** (or **out of**) **phase** working (or not working) together in the correct or a harmonious way.
– ORIGIN French.

phatic /**fat**-ik/ adjective (of words) used for general social interaction rather than to convey information or ask questions.
– ORIGIN Greek *phatos* 'spoken'.

PhD abbreviation Doctor of Philosophy.
– ORIGIN from Latin *philosophiae doctor*.

pheasant noun a large long-tailed game bird, the male of which has brightly coloured plumage.
– ORIGIN Greek *phasianos* 'bird of Phasis', a river in the Caucasus from which the bird is said to have spread westwards.

phencyclidine /fen-**sy**-kli-deen/ noun a drug used in veterinary medicine as an anaesthetic and in hallucinogenic drugs such as angel dust.

phenobarbitone /fee-noh-**bar**-bi-tohn/ (US **phenobarbital** /fee-noh-**bar**-bi-t'l/) noun a sedative drug used to treat epilepsy.

phenol /**fee**-nol/ noun a poisonous white crystalline solid obtained from coal tar. Also called **CARBOLIC ACID**.
– DERIVATIVES **phenolic** adjective.
– ORIGIN French *phène* 'benzene'.

phenomenal adjective 1 remarkable or outstanding: *the town expanded at a phenomenal rate.* 2 able to be perceived by the senses: *the phenomenal world.*
– DERIVATIVES **phenomenally** adverb.

phenomenology /fi-no-mi-**nol**-uh-ji/ noun Philosophy 1 the study of phenomena (things that can be observed) as distinct from that of the nature of being (ontology). 2 an approach that concentrates on the study of consciousness and the objects of direct experience.
– DERIVATIVES **phenomenological** adjective **phenomenologist** noun.

phenomenon noun (pl. **phenomena**) 1 a fact or situation that is observed to exist or happen: *natural phenomena such as clouds or the wind.* 2 a remarkable person or thing: *the band was a pop phenomenon for their sales figures alone.* 3 Philosophy the object of a person's perception.
– ORIGIN Greek *phainomenon* 'thing appearing to view'.

USAGE: The singular form is **phenomenon** and the plural form is **phenomena**. Do not use **phenomena** as if it were a singular form; say *this is a strange phenomenon* not *this is a strange phenomena.*

phenotype /**fee**-noh-typ/ noun Biology the observable characteristics of an individual determined by its genetic make-up and the environment.
– ORIGIN from Greek *phainein* 'to show'.

phenyl /**fee**-nyl, **fen**-il/ noun Chemistry the radical $-C_6H_5$, obtained from benzene.
– ORIGIN French *phényle*.

pheromone /**fe**-ruh-mohn/ noun a chemical substance produced by an animal and causing a response in others of its species.
– ORIGIN from Greek *pherein* 'convey' + **HORMONE**.

phew exclamation informal expressing relief.
– ORIGIN in imitation of puffing.

phial /**fy**-uhl/ noun a small cylindrical glass bottle, typically used for holding medicine or perfume.
– ORIGIN Greek *phialē* 'broad flat container'.

philadelphus /fi-luh-**del**-fuhss/ noun a mock orange (shrub).

- ORIGIN Latin, from Greek *philadelphos* 'loving one's brother'.

philander /fi-**lan**-der/ verb (of a man) have many casual sexual relationships with women.
- DERIVATIVES **philanderer** noun.
- ORIGIN from an earlier meaning 'man, husband', from Greek *philandros* 'fond of men'.

philanthropist noun a person who helps other people, especially by giving money to good causes.

philanthropy noun the practice of helping other people, especially by giving money to good causes.
- DERIVATIVES **philanthropic** adjective **philanthropically** adverb.
- ORIGIN from Greek *philanthrōpos* 'man-loving'.

philately /fi-**lat**-uh-li/ noun the collection and study of postage stamps.
- DERIVATIVES **philatelic** adjective **philatelist** noun.
- ORIGIN from Greek *philo-* 'loving' + *ateleia* 'exemption from payment', used to mean a franking mark or postage stamp exempting the recipient from payment.

-phile combining form referring to a person or thing having a liking for a particular thing: *bibliophile*.
- ORIGIN from Greek *philos* 'loving'.

philharmonic adjective (in the names of orchestras) devoted to music.

-philia combining form referring to a liking for something, especially an abnormal love for or inclination towards something: *paedophilia*.
- ORIGIN from Greek *philia* 'fondness'.

philippic /fi-**lip**-pik/ noun a bitter verbal attack.
- ORIGIN from Greek *philippikos*, the name given to Demosthenes' speeches against Philip II of Macedon, and Cicero's against Mark Antony.

Philippine /fi-lip-peen/ adjective relating to the Philippines.

Philistine /**fil**-i-styn/ noun 1 a member of a people of ancient Palestine who came into conflict with the Israelites. 2 (philistine) a person who is hostile towards or uninterested in culture and the arts.
- DERIVATIVES **philistinism** /**fil**-i-stin-i-z'm/ noun.
- ORIGIN Greek *Philistinos*.

Phillips adjective trademark referring to a screw with a cross-shaped slot for turning, or a corresponding screwdriver.
- ORIGIN the name of the American manufacturer Henry F. *Phillips*.

philodendron /fi-luh-**den**-druhn/ noun (pl. **philodendrons** or **philodendra** /fi-luh-den-druh/) a tropical American climbing plant grown as a greenhouse or indoor plant.
- ORIGIN from Greek *philos* 'loving' + *dendron* 'tree'.

philology noun the study of the structure and historical development of languages.
- DERIVATIVES **philological** adjective **philologist** noun.
- ORIGIN Greek *philologia*.

philosopher noun a person engaged or learned in philosophy.

philosopher's stone noun a mythical substance supposed to change any metal into gold or silver.

philosophical adjective 1 relating to the study of philosophy. 2 calm in difficult circumstances.
- DERIVATIVES **philosophic** adjective **philosophically** adverb.

philosophize (or philosophise) verb talk about serious issues, especially in a boring or pompous way.

philosophy noun (pl. **philosophies**) 1 the study of the fundamental nature of knowledge, reality, and existence. 2 the theories of a particular philosopher. 3 a theory or attitude that guides a person's behaviour. 4 the study of the theoretical basis of a branch of knowledge or experience: *the philosophy of science.*
- ORIGIN Greek *philosophia* 'love of wisdom'.

philtre /**fil**-ter/ (US philter) noun a love potion.
- ORIGIN Greek *philtron*.

phishing noun a type of Internet fraud in which a person impersonates a reputable company in order to persuade others to reveal personal information, such as passwords and credit card numbers, online.
- ORIGIN respelling of fishing (see FISH¹).

phiz /fiz/ (also phizog, fizzog /**fiz**-zog/) noun Brit. informal a person's face or expression.
- ORIGIN abbreviation of PHYSIOGNOMY.

phlebitis /fli-by-tiss/ noun inflammation of the walls of a vein.
- ORIGIN from Greek *phleps* 'vein'.

phlebotomy /fli-bo-tuh-mi/ noun (pl. **phlebotomies**) the surgical opening or puncture of a vein to withdraw blood or introduce a fluid.
- DERIVATIVES **phlebotomist** noun.

phlegm /flem/ noun 1 a thick substance produced by the mucous membranes of the nose and throat, especially when one has a cold. 2 (in medieval science and medicine) one of the four bodily humours, believed to be associated with a calm or apathetic temperament. 3 calmness of temperament.
- DERIVATIVES **phlegmy** adjective.
- ORIGIN Greek *phlegma* 'inflammation'.

phlegmatic /fleg-**mat**-ik/ adjective calm and unemotional.
- DERIVATIVES **phlegmatically** adverb.

phloem /**floh**-em/ noun the tissue in plants which conducts nutrients downwards from the leaves.
- ORIGIN from Greek *phloos* 'bark'.

phlox /floks/ noun a plant with clusters of colourful scented flowers.
- ORIGIN Greek, 'flame'.

-phobe combining form referring to a person having a fear or dislike of a specified thing: *technophobe*.
- ORIGIN from Greek *phobos* 'fear'.

phobia noun an extreme or irrational fear of something.
- DERIVATIVES **phobic** adjective & noun.

-phobia combining form extreme or irrational fear or dislike of a specified thing: *arachnophobia*.
- DERIVATIVES **-phobic** combining form.

Phoenician /fuh-**nee**-sh'n, fuh-**ni**-sh'n/ noun a

member of an ancient people living in Phoenicia in the eastern Mediterranean.
● **adjective** relating to Phoenicia.

phoenix /fee-niks/ **noun** (in classical mythology) a bird that periodically burned itself on a funeral pyre and was born again from the ashes.
– ORIGIN Greek *phoinix*.

phone noun a telephone. ● **verb** make a telephone call to someone.

-phone combining form 1 referring to an instrument using or connected with sound: *megaphone*. **2** referring to a person who uses a specified language: *francophone*.
– ORIGIN from Greek *phōnē* 'sound, voice'.

phone book noun a telephone directory.

phonecard noun a prepaid card allowing the user to make calls on a public telephone.

phone-in noun a radio or television programme during which listeners or viewers can make comments or ask questions by telephoning the studio.

phoneme /foh-neem/ **noun** any of the distinct units of sound that distinguish one word from another, e.g. *p*, *b*, *d*, and *t* in *pad*, *pat*, *bad*, and *bat*.
– ORIGIN Greek *phōnēma* 'sound, speech'.

phonetic adjective 1 relating to speech sounds. **2** (of a system of spelling) closely matching the sounds represented.
– DERIVATIVES **phonetically** adverb.
– ORIGIN Greek *phōnētikos*.

phonetics plural noun (treated as sing.) the study and classification of speech sounds.

phoney (chiefly N. Amer. also **phony**) informal **adjective** (**phonier**, **phoniest**) not genuine.
● **noun** (pl. **phoneys** or **phonies**) a person or thing that is not genuine.
– DERIVATIVES **phoniness** noun.
– ORIGIN unknown.

phonic /fon-ik, foh-nik/ **adjective** relating to speech sounds.

phonics plural noun (treated as sing.) a method of teaching people to read by associating letters or groups of letters with particular sounds.

phono adjective referring to a type of plug used with audio and video equipment, in which one conductor is cylindrical and the other is a central prong that extends beyond it.
– ORIGIN abbreviation of **PHONOGRAPH**.

phono- combining form relating to sound: *phonograph*.
– ORIGIN from Greek *phōnē* 'sound, voice'.

phonograph noun 1 Brit. an early form of gramophone. **2** N. Amer. a record player.
– DERIVATIVES **phonographic** adjective.

phonology /fuh-**nol**-uh-ji/ **noun** the system of relationships between the basic speech sounds of a language.
– DERIVATIVES **phonological** adjective.

phony adjective & noun variant spelling of **PHONEY**.

phooey informal **exclamation** used to express scorn or disbelief. ● **noun** nonsense.
– ORIGIN imitating the sound of a scornful exclamation.

phosgene /foz-jeen/ **noun** a poisonous gas formerly used in warfare.
– ORIGIN from Greek *phōs* 'light'.

phosphate /foss-fayt/ **noun** Chemistry a salt or ester of phosphoric acid.

phosphine /foss-feen/ **noun** a foul-smelling gas formed from phosphorus and hydrogen.

phosphor /foss-fer/ **noun 1** a synthetic fluorescent or phosphorescent substance. **2** old-fashioned term for **PHOSPHORUS**.

phosphorescence noun light given out by a substance without burning or heat, or with so little heat that it cannot be felt.
– DERIVATIVES **phosphoresce** verb **phosphorescent** adjective.

phosphoric /foss-fo-rik/ **adjective** relating to or containing phosphorus.

phosphoric acid noun a crystalline acid obtained by treating phosphates with sulphuric acid.

phosphorus /foss-fuh-ruhss/ **noun** a poisonous non-metallic chemical element in the form of a yellowish waxy solid which ignites spontaneously in air and glows in the dark.
– DERIVATIVES **phosphorous** adjective.
– ORIGIN Greek *phōsphoros*.

photo noun (pl. **photos**) a photograph.

photo- combining form 1 relating to light. **2** relating to photography.
– ORIGIN sense 1 from Greek *phōs* 'light'.

photocall noun Brit. a prearranged occasion on which famous people pose for photographers.

photocell noun short for **PHOTOELECTRIC CELL**.

photochemistry noun the branch of chemistry concerned with the chemical effects of light.
– DERIVATIVES **photochemical** adjective.

photochromic adjective (of glass, lenses, etc.) undergoing a reversible change in colour when exposed to bright light.

photocopier noun a machine for making photocopies.

photocopy noun (pl. **photocopies**) a photographic copy of something produced by a process involving the action of light on a specially prepared surface. ● **verb** (**photocopies**, **photocopying**, **photocopied**) make a photocopy of something.
– DERIVATIVES **photocopiable** adjective.

photoelectric adjective involving the emission of electrons from a surface by the action of light.

photoelectric cell noun a device using a photoelectric effect to generate current.

photo finish noun a close finish of a race in which the winner can be identified only from a photograph of competitors crossing the line.

photofit noun Brit. a picture of a person made up from existing photographs of separate facial features.

photogenic /foh-tuh-jen-ik/ **adjective** **1** looking attractive in photographs. **2** Biology producing or giving out light.

photograph noun a picture made with a camera, in which an image is focused on to film and then made visible and permanent by chemical treatment. ● **verb** take a photograph of someone or something.
– DERIVATIVES **photographer** noun **photographic** adjective.

photographic memory noun an ability to

p

remember information or visual images in great detail.

photography noun the taking and processing of photographs.

photogravure /foh-toh-gra-**vyoor**/ noun a printing process in which the type or image is produced from a photographic negative transferred to a metal plate and etched in.
– ORIGIN French, 'photo-engraving'.

photojournalism noun the taking and publishing of photographs as a means of communicating news.
– DERIVATIVES **photojournalist** noun.

photometer /foh-**tom**-i-ter/ noun an instrument for measuring the strength of light.
– DERIVATIVES **photometric** adjective **photometry** noun.

photomicrograph noun another term for MICROGRAPH.

photomontage /foh-toh-mon-**tahzh**/ noun a picture consisting of a number of separate photographs placed together or overlapping.

photon /**foh**-ton/ noun Physics a particle representing a quantum of light or other electromagnetic radiation.
– DERIVATIVES **photonic** adjective.

photo opportunity noun a photocall.

photorealism noun a style of art and sculpture characterized by a very detailed and unidealized portrayal of ordinary life.
– DERIVATIVES **photorealist** noun & adjective **photorealistic** adjective.

photoreceptor noun a structure in an animal or plant that responds to light.

photosensitive adjective responding to light.
– DERIVATIVES **photosensitivity** noun.

photostat noun trademark **1** a type of machine for making photocopies on special paper. **2** a copy made by a photostat. • verb (**photostats, photostatting, photostatted**) copy something with a photostat.

photosynthesis noun the process by which green plants use sunlight to form nutrients from carbon dioxide and water.
– DERIVATIVES **photosynthesize** (or **photosynthesise**) verb **photosynthetic** adjective.

phototropism /foh-toh-**troh**-pi-z'm/ noun the turning of a plant or other organism either towards or away from a source of light.
– DERIVATIVES **phototropic** adjective.

photovoltaic /foh-toh-vol-**tay**-ik/ adjective relating to the production of electric current at the junction of two substances exposed to light.

phrasal verb noun a verb combined with an adverb or preposition to give a new meaning that cannot be worked out from the individual parts, e.g. *break down* or *see to*.

phrase noun **1** a small group of words forming a unit within a clause. **2** Music a group of notes forming a distinct unit within a longer passage. **3** a group of words which have a particular meaning when used together. • verb **1** put into a particular form of words: *it's important to phrase the question correctly.* **2** (often as noun **phrasing**) divide music into phrases in a particular way.
– PHRASES **turn of phrase** a particular or

characteristic manner of expression.
– DERIVATIVES **phrasal** adjective.
– ORIGIN Greek *phrasis.*

phrase book noun a book listing useful expressions in a foreign language and their translations.

phraseology /fray-zi-**ol**-uh-ji/ noun (pl. **phraseologies**) a particular or characteristic way in which words are used: *legal phraseology.*

phrenology /fri-**nol**-uh-ji/ noun chiefly historical the study of the shape and size of a person's skull as a supposed indication of their character.
– DERIVATIVES **phrenologist** noun.
– ORIGIN from Greek *phrēn* 'mind'.

Phrygian /**fri**-ji-uhn/ noun a person from Phrygia, an ancient region of west central Asia Minor (the western peninsula of Asia).
• adjective relating to Phrygia.

phthisis /**fthy**-siss/ noun old use tuberculosis or a similar disease.
– ORIGIN Greek.

phut exclamation used to represent a dull abrupt sound like that of a slight impact or explosion.
– ORIGIN perhaps from a Hindi word meaning 'to burst'.

phyla plural of PHYLUM.

phylactery /fi-**lak**-tuh-ri/ noun (pl. **phylacteries**) a small leather box containing biblical passages written in Hebrew, worn by Jewish men at morning prayer.
– ORIGIN Greek *phulaktērion* 'amulet'.

phyllo noun variant spelling of FILO.

phylloquinone /fi-loh-**kwi**-nohn/ noun vitamin K₁, a compound found in cabbage, spinach, and other leafy green vegetables, and essential for blood-clotting.
– ORIGIN from Greek *phullon* 'leaf' + QUINONE.

phylloxera /fi-lok-**serr**-uh, fi-**lok**-suh-ruh/ noun an insect that is a pest of vines.
– ORIGIN from Greek *phullon* 'leaf' + *xēros* 'dry'.

phylum /**fy**-luhm/ noun (pl. **phyla** /**fy**-luh/) a category in the classification of animals and plants that ranks above class and below kingdom.
– ORIGIN Greek *phulon* 'race'.

physalis /fi-**say**-liss/ noun a plant of a genus that includes the Cape gooseberry and Chinese lantern.
– ORIGIN Greek *phusallis* 'bladder'.

physic noun old use medicinal drugs or medical treatment.
– ORIGIN Latin *physica.*

physical adjective **1** relating to the body as opposed to the mind. **2** relating to things that can be seen, heard, or touched. **3** involving bodily contact or activity: *a physical relationship.* **4** relating to physics or the operation of natural forces. • noun a medical examination to establish how fit a person is.
– DERIVATIVES **physicality** noun **physically** adverb.

physical chemistry noun the branch of chemistry concerned with the application of the techniques and theories of physics to the study of chemical systems.

physical education noun instruction in physical exercise and games, especially in schools.

physical geography noun the branch of geography concerned with natural features.

physical sciences plural noun the sciences concerned with the study of inanimate natural objects, including physics, chemistry, and astronomy.

physical therapy noun US term for PHYSIOTHERAPY.
– DERIVATIVES **physical therapist** noun.

physician noun a person qualified to practise medicine.

physics plural noun (treated as sing.) **1** the branch of science concerned with the nature and properties of matter and energy. **2** the physical properties and nature of something.
– DERIVATIVES **physicist** noun.
– ORIGIN Latin *physica* 'natural things'.

physio noun (pl. **physios**) Brit. informal physiotherapy or a physiotherapist.

physiognomy /fi-zi-og-nuh-mi, fi-zi-on-uh-mi/ noun (pl. **physiognomies**) a person's facial features or expression, especially when seen as an indication of character.
– ORIGIN Greek *phusiognōmonia*.

physiology noun **1** the branch of biology concerned with the normal functions of living organisms and their parts. **2** the way in which a living organism or bodily part functions.
– DERIVATIVES **physiological** adjective **physiologist** noun.

physiotherapy (US **physical therapy**) noun the treatment of disease or injury, by physical methods such as massage and exercise.
– DERIVATIVES **physiotherapist** noun.

physique noun the form, size, and development of a person's body.
– ORIGIN French, 'physical' (used as a noun).

phytochemical /fy-toh-**kem**-i-k'l/ noun any of a group of compounds found in plants that are believed to have beneficial effects.
– ORIGIN from Greek *phuton* 'a plant'.

phytoplankton /fy-toh-**plangk**-tuhn/ noun plankton consisting of microscopic plants.
– ORIGIN from Greek *phuton* 'a plant'.

pi /py/ noun **1** the sixteenth letter of the Greek alphabet (Π, π), transliterated as 'p'. **2** the numerical value of the ratio of the circumference of a circle to its diameter (approximately 3.14159).
– ORIGIN Greek: sense 2 from the initial letter of *periphereia* 'circumference'.

pia /py-uh, pee-uh/ (in full **pia mater** /may-tuh/) noun the delicate innermost membrane enveloping the brain and spinal cord.
– ORIGIN Latin, (in full) 'tender mother'.

pianism noun skill or artistry in playing the piano or composing music for the piano.
– DERIVATIVES **pianistic** adjective.

pianissimo /pi-uh-**niss**-i-moh/ adverb & adjective Music very soft or softly.
– ORIGIN Italian, 'softest'.

piano[1] /pi-**an**-oh/ noun (pl. **pianos**) a large keyboard musical instrument with metal strings, which are struck by hammers when the keys are pressed.
– DERIVATIVES **pianist** noun.
– ORIGIN Italian, abbreviation of PIANOFORTE.

piano[2] /pi-**ah**-noh/ adverb & adjective Music soft or softly.

– ORIGIN Italian, 'soft'.

piano accordion noun an accordion with a small vertical keyboard like that of a piano.

pianoforte /pi-an-oh-**for**-tay/ noun formal term for PIANO[1].
– ORIGIN from Italian *piano e forte* 'soft and loud'.

pianola /pi-uh-**noh**-luh/ noun trademark a piano equipped to be played automatically with a roll of perforated paper which controls the movement of the keys to produce a tune.

piano nobile /pi-ah-noh **noh**-bi-lay/ noun the main storey of a large house, usually the first floor.
– ORIGIN Italian, 'noble floor'.

piastre /pi-**ass**-ter/ (US also **piaster**) noun a unit of money of several Middle Eastern countries.
– ORIGIN from Italian *piastra d'argento* 'plate of silver'.

piazza /pi-**at**-zuh/ noun a public square or marketplace, especially in Italy.
– ORIGIN Italian.

pibroch /**pee**-brok/ noun a form of music for the Scottish bagpipes involving elaborate variations on a theme.
– ORIGIN Scottish Gaelic *piobaireachd* 'art of piping'.

pic noun informal a photograph or cinema film.

pica /**py**-kuh/ noun Printing **1** a unit of type size and line length equal to 12 points (about ⅙ inch or 4.2 mm). **2** a size of letter in typewriting, with 10 characters to the inch (about 3.9 to the centimetre).
– ORIGIN Latin.

picador /**pik**-uh-dor/ noun (in bullfighting) a person on horseback who goads the bull with a lance.
– ORIGIN Spanish.

picaresque /pi-kuh-**resk**/ adjective relating to fiction dealing with the adventures of a dishonest but appealing hero.
– ORIGIN from Spanish *pícaro* 'rogue'.

picayune /pi-kuh-**yoon**/ N. Amer. informal adjective of little value or importance. • noun an unimportant person or thing.
– ORIGIN French *picaillon*, referring to a copper coin from Piedmont.

piccalilli /pik-kuh-**lil**-li/ noun (pl. **piccalillies** or **piccalillis**) a pickle made of chopped vegetables, mustard, and hot spices.
– ORIGIN probably from a blend of PICKLE and CHILLI.

piccaninny /pik-kuh-**nin**-ni/ (US **pickaninny**) noun (pl. **piccaninnies**) offensive a small black child.
– ORIGIN from Spanish *pequeño* or Portuguese *pequeno* 'little'.

piccolo noun (pl. **piccolos**) a small flute an octave higher than the ordinary one.
– ORIGIN Italian, 'small flute'.

pick[1] verb **1** (also **pick something up**) take hold of something and move it: *he picked a match out of the ash tray.* **2** remove a flower or fruit from where it is growing. **3** choose someone or something from a number of alternatives: *he was picked for the England squad.* **4** remove unwanted matter from one's nose or teeth with a finger or a pointed instrument. • noun **1** an act of selecting something: *take your pick*

p

from our extensive menu. **2 (the pick of**) informal
the best person or thing in a particular group:
he was the pick of the bunch.
– PHRASES **pick and choose** select only the best
from among a number of alternatives. **pick at**
1 repeatedly pull at something with one's
fingers. **2** eat food in small amounts. **pick**
someone's brains informal obtain information by
questioning someone who is better informed
about a subject. **pick a fight** provoke an
argument or fight. **pick holes in** find fault
with. **pick a lock** open a lock with an
instrument other than the proper key. **pick**
someone/thing off shoot one of a group from
a distance. **pick on** single someone out for
unfair treatment. **pick someone/thing out**
1 distinguish someone or something from
among a group. **2** play a tune slowly or with
difficulty on a guitar or similar instrument.
pick over (or **pick through**) sort through a
number of items carefully. **pick someone's**
pockets steal something from a person's
pocket. **pick up** improve or increase. **pick**
someone/thing up 1 go to collect someone.
2 informal casually strike up a relationship with
someone with a sexual purpose in mind.
3 return to an earlier point or topic. **4** obtain,
acquire, or learn something: *he had picked up a*
little Russian from his father. **5** become aware of
or sensitive to something. **6** detect or receive a
signal or sound. **pick one's way** walk slowly
and carefully.
– DERIVATIVES **picker** noun.
– ORIGIN unknown.
pick[2] (also **pickaxe**) noun **1** a tool consisting of a
curved iron bar with one or both ends pointed,
fixed at right angles to its handle, used for
breaking up hard ground or rock. **2** a plectrum.
– ORIGIN variant of PIKE[2].
picket noun **1** a person or group of people
standing outside a workplace with the aim of
persuading other people not to work during a
strike. **2** a soldier or small group of troops sent
out to watch for the enemy. **3** a pointed
wooden stake driven into the ground. •verb
(**pickets, picketing, picketed**) act as a picket
outside a workplace.
– ORIGIN French *piquet* 'pointed stake', first
meaning a pointed stake, on which a soldier
had to stand on one foot as a military
punishment.
pickings plural noun profits or gains, especially
those made easily or dishonestly.
pickle noun **1** vegetables or fruit preserved in
vinegar, brine, or mustard, served cold with
other food to add flavour. **2** liquid used to
preserve food or other perishable items. **3 (a**
pickle) informal a difficult situation. •verb
1 preserve food in pickle. **2** (as adj. **pickled**)
informal drunk.
– ORIGIN Dutch or German *pekel.*
pick-me-up noun informal a thing that makes
one feel more energetic or cheerful.
pickpocket noun a person who steals from
people's pockets.
pickup noun **1** (also **pickup truck**) a small van or
lorry with low sides, for carrying small loads.
2 an act of picking up or collecting a person or
goods. **3** an improvement. **4** a device on an
electric guitar which converts sound

vibrations into electrical signals for
amplification. **5** the cartridge of a record
player, carrying the stylus.
picky adjective (**pickier, pickiest**) informal fussy: *a*
picky eater.
picnic noun a packed meal eaten outdoors, or an
occasion when such a meal is eaten. •verb
(**picnics, picnicking, picnicked**) have or take
part in a picnic.
– PHRASES **be no picnic** informal be difficult or
unpleasant.
– DERIVATIVES **picnicker** noun.
– ORIGIN French *pique-nique.*
pico- combining form referring to a factor of one
million millionth (10^{-12}): *picosecond.*
– ORIGIN from Spanish *pico,* 'beak, little bit'.
picot /pee-koh/ noun a small decorative loop or
series of loops in lace or embroidery, typically
used to decorate a border.
– ORIGIN French, 'small peak or point'.
Pict noun a member of an ancient people living
in northern Scotland in Roman times.
– ORIGIN Latin *Picti,* perhaps from *pingere* 'to
paint or tattoo'.
pictograph (also **pictogram**) noun **1** a picture
or symbol representing a word or phrase. **2** a
pictorial representation of statistics on a
chart, graph, or computer screen.
– DERIVATIVES **pictographic** adjective.
– ORIGIN from Latin *pingere* 'to paint'.
pictorial adjective relating to or using pictures.
•noun a newspaper or magazine which has
pictures as a main feature.
– DERIVATIVES **pictorially** adverb.
– ORIGIN Latin *pictorius.*
picture noun **1** a painting, drawing, or
photograph. **2** an image on a television screen.
3 a cinema film. **4 (the pictures)** the cinema.
5 an impression formed from an account or
description of something: *a full picture of the*
disaster had not yet emerged. •verb **1** represent
someone or something in a picture. **2** form a
mental image of; visualize: *she pictured him*
waiting and smiled.
– PHRASES **(as) pretty as a picture** very pretty. **in**
the picture informal informed about something.
– ORIGIN Latin *pictura,* from *pingere* 'to paint'.
picture messaging noun a system that
enables digital photos and animated graphics
to be sent and received by mobile phone.
picture-postcard adjective (of a view)
prettily picturesque.
picture rail noun a horizontal strip of wood on
a wall from which pictures can be hung.
picturesque adjective attractive in a quaint or
charming way: *miles of picturesque beaches.*
– DERIVATIVES **picturesquely** adverb
picturesqueness noun.
picture window noun a large window
consisting of one pane of glass.
piddle verb informal **1** urinate. **2** (**piddle about/**
around) spend time in unimportant activities.
– ORIGIN probably from PISS and PUDDLE.
piddling (also **piddly**) adjective informal
ridiculously small or unimportant.
pidgin noun a simplified form of a language
with elements taken from local languages,
used for communication between people not
sharing a common language.

– ORIGIN Chinese alteration of English *business*.

pie noun a baked dish of savoury or sweet ingredients encased in or topped with pastry.
– PHRASES **pie in the sky** informal a pleasant future event or idea that is very unlikely to happen.
– ORIGIN probably the same word as former *pie* 'magpie', the combinations of ingredients being compared to objects collected by a magpie.

piebald adjective (of a horse) having irregular patches of two colours, typically black and white. •noun a piebald horse.
– ORIGIN from *pie* in *magpie* + *bald* in the former sense 'streaked with white'.

piece noun 1 a portion separated from the whole. 2 an item used in constructing something or forming part of a set: *a piece of luggage*. 3 a musical or written work. 4 a figure or token used to make moves in a board game. 5 a coin of specified value. 6 informal, chiefly N. Amer. a firearm. •verb (**piece something together**) assemble something from individual parts.
– PHRASES **go to pieces** become so upset that one cannot function normally. **in one piece** not harmed or damaged. (**all**) **of a piece** completely the same. **say one's piece** give one's opinion.
– ORIGIN Old French.

pièce de résistance /pyess duh ray-**ziss**-tonss/ noun the most important or impressive feature of something: *the garden was her pièce de résistance*.
– ORIGIN French, 'piece (i.e. means) of resistance'.

piecemeal adjective & adverb done in stages over a period of time.
– ORIGIN from PIECE + an Old English word meaning 'measure, quantity taken at one time'.

piecework noun work paid for according to the amount produced.

pie chart noun a diagram in which a circle is divided into sectors that each represent a proportion of the whole.

pied /rhymes with ride/ adjective having two or more different colours.
– ORIGIN first meaning 'black and white like a magpie'.

pied-à-terre /pyay-dah-**tair**/ noun (pl. **pieds-à-terre** pronunc. same) a small flat or house kept for occasional use, one's permanent home being elsewhere.
– ORIGIN French, 'foot to earth'.

Pied Piper noun a person who entices others to follow them in a course of action, especially one with disastrous results.
– ORIGIN from the piper in German legend who rid the town of Hamelin of rats by enticing them away with his music, and when refused the promised payment lured away the town's children.

pie-eyed adjective informal very drunk.

pier noun 1 a structure leading out to sea and used as a landing stage for boats or as a place of entertainment. 2 the pillar of an arch or supporting a bridge. 3 a wall between windows or other adjoining openings.
– ORIGIN Latin *pera*.

pierce verb 1 make a hole in or through something with a sharp object. 2 force a way through: *a shrill voice pierced the air.* 3 (as adj. **piercing**) very sharp, cold, or high-pitched.
– DERIVATIVES **piercer** noun.
– ORIGIN Old French *percer*.

pier glass noun a large mirror, used originally to fill wall space between windows.

Pierrot /**peer**-oh, pyair-oh/ noun a male character in French pantomime, with a sad white-painted face, a loose white costume, and a pointed hat.
– ORIGIN French, familiar form of the man's name *Pierre* 'Peter'.

piety /**py**-uh-ti/ noun (pl. **pieties**) 1 the quality of being deeply religious. 2 a conventional belief that is accepted without thinking.
– ORIGIN Latin *pietas* 'dutifulness'.

piezo /**py**-ee-zoh, pee-zoh/ adjective piezoelectric.

piezoelectric /py-ee-zoh-i-**lek**-trik/ adjective relating to electric polarization produced in certain crystals by the application of mechanical stress.
– ORIGIN from Greek *piezein* 'press, squeeze'.

piffle noun informal nonsense.
– ORIGIN uncertain.

piffling adjective informal trivial; unimportant.

pig noun 1 a domesticated mammal with sparse bristly hair and a flat snout, kept for its meat. 2 informal a greedy, dirty, or unpleasant person. 3 informal, derogatory a police officer. 4 an oblong mass of iron or lead from a smelting furnace. •verb (**pigs, pigging, pigged**) informal (often **pig out**) gorge oneself with food.
– PHRASES **make a pig of oneself** informal overeat. **make a pig's ear of** Brit. informal handle something clumsily. **a pig in a poke** something that is bought without first being seen.
– DERIVATIVES **piglet** noun.
– ORIGIN probably from an Old English word meaning 'acorn' or 'pig bread'.

pigeon noun a fat bird with a small head and a cooing voice.
– ORIGIN Old French *pijon* 'young bird'.

pigeonhole noun 1 each of a set of small compartments where letters or messages may be left for people. 2 a category into which someone or something is placed. •verb place in a particular category, especially a restrictive one: *I was pigeonholed as a 'youth writer'.*

pigeon-toed adjective having the toes or feet turned inwards.

piggery noun (pl. **piggeries**) 1 a farm or enclosure where pigs are kept. 2 greed or unpleasantness, regarded as characteristic of pigs.

piggish adjective greedy, dirty, or unpleasant.

piggy noun (pl. **piggies**) a child's word for a pig. •adjective resembling a pig, especially in features or appetite.

piggyback noun a ride on someone's back and shoulders. •adverb on the back and shoulders of another person. •verb link to or take advantage of an existing system or body of work: *they have piggybacked their own networks on to the system.*

piggy bank noun a money box shaped like a pig.

p

pig-headed adjective stupidly obstinate.

pig iron noun crude iron as first obtained from a smelting furnace.

pigment noun 1 a natural substance that gives animal or plant tissue its colour. 2 a substance used for colouring or painting.
– DERIVATIVES **pigmentary** adjective **pigmentation** noun.
– ORIGIN Latin *pigmentum*.

pigmented adjective having a natural colour.

pigmy noun variant spelling of PYGMY.

pigskin noun leather made from the hide of a pig.

pigsty noun (pl. **pigsties**) 1 an enclosure for a pig or pigs. 2 a very dirty or untidy house or room.

pigswill noun kitchen refuse and scraps fed to pigs.

pigtail noun a plaited length of hair worn singly at the back or on each side of the head.
– DERIVATIVES **pigtailed** adjective.

pike¹ noun (pl. same) a predatory freshwater fish with a long body and sharp teeth.
– ORIGIN from PIKE² (because of the fish's pointed jaw).

pike² noun historical a weapon with a pointed metal head on a long wooden shaft.
– ORIGIN French *pique*.

pike³ noun a jackknife position in diving or gymnastics.
– ORIGIN unknown.

pikelet noun a thin kind of crumpet.
– ORIGIN from Welsh *bara pyglyd* 'pitchy bread'.

pikestaff noun historical the wooden shaft of a pike.
– PHRASES (**as**) **plain as a pikestaff** very obvious. [alteration of *as plain as a packstaff*, the staff being that of a pedlar, on which he rested his pack of wares.]

pilaf /pi-**laf**/ (also **pilau** /pi-**low**/, **pulao**) noun a Middle Eastern or Indian dish of spiced rice, often with vegetables or meat added.
– ORIGIN Turkish.

pilaster /pi-**lass**-ter/ noun a rectangular column incorporated within and projecting slightly from a wall.
– ORIGIN Latin *pilastrum*.

Pilates /pi-**lah**-teez/ noun a system of exercises designed to improve physical strength, flexibility, and posture, and enhance mental awareness.
– ORIGIN named after Joseph *Pilates*, its German inventor.

pilchard noun a small edible sea fish of the herring family.
– ORIGIN unknown.

pile¹ noun 1 a heap of things laid or lying one on top of another. 2 informal a large amount. 3 a large imposing building. • verb 1 place things one on top of the other. 2 (**pile up**) form a pile or very large quantity. 3 (**pile something on**) informal exaggerate something for effect. 4 (**pile into/out of**) get into or out of a vehicle in a disorganized way.
– ORIGIN Latin *pila* 'pillar, pier'.

pile² noun a heavy stake or post driven into the ground to support foundations.
– ORIGIN Old English.

pile³ noun the soft projecting surface of a carpet or a fabric, consisting of the cut ends of many small threads.
– ORIGIN Latin *pilus* 'hair'.

piledriver noun 1 a machine for driving piles into the ground. 2 Brit. informal a forceful act, blow, or shot.

piles plural noun haemorrhoids.
– ORIGIN probably from Latin *pila* 'ball'.

pile-up noun 1 a crash involving several vehicles. 2 a large collection of something.

pilfer verb steal things of little value.
– DERIVATIVES **pilferage** noun.
– ORIGIN Old French *pelfrer* 'to pillage'.

pilgrim noun a person who journeys to a holy place for religious reasons.
– ORIGIN Provençal *pelegrin*.

pilgrimage noun 1 a pilgrim's journey to a holy place. 2 a journey to a place of interest or importance.

pill noun 1 a small round mass of solid medicine for swallowing whole. 2 (**the pill**) a contraceptive pill.
– PHRASES a **bitter pill** something that is unpleasant but must be accepted. **sugar** (or **sweeten**) **the pill** make an unpleasant necessity easier to accept.
– ORIGIN Latin *pilula* 'little ball'.

pillage verb rob a place or steal something with violence, especially in wartime. • noun the action of pillaging a place or property.
– DERIVATIVES **pillager** noun.
– ORIGIN Old French.

pillar noun 1 a tall vertical structure used as a support for a building or as an ornament. 2 a person or thing providing reliable support: *he was a pillar of his local community.*
– PHRASES **from pillar to post** from one place to another in an unsatisfactory way.
– DERIVATIVES **pillared** adjective.
– ORIGIN Latin *pila* 'pillar'.

pillar box noun (in the UK) a large red cylindrical public postbox.

pillbox noun 1 a woman's hat with straight sides, a flat top, and no brim. 2 a small round box for holding pills. 3 a small, partly underground, concrete fort.

pillion noun a seat for a passenger behind a motorcyclist.
– ORIGIN Irish *pillín* 'small cushion'.

pillock noun Brit. informal a stupid person.
– ORIGIN from former *pillicock* 'penis'.

pillory noun (pl. **pillories**) a wooden framework with holes for the head and hands, in which offenders were formerly imprisoned and exposed to public abuse. • verb (**pillories, pillorying, pilloried**) 1 attack or ridicule someone publicly. 2 put someone in a pillory.
– ORIGIN Old French *pilori*.

pillow noun a rectangular cloth bag stuffed with soft material, used to support the head when lying or sleeping. • verb support the head on something soft.
– DERIVATIVES **pillowy** adjective.
– ORIGIN Latin *pulvinus* 'cushion'.

pillowcase (also **pillowslip**) noun a removable cloth cover for a pillow.

pillow talk noun intimate conversation between lovers in bed.

pilot noun 1 a person who operates the flying

controls of an aircraft. **2** a person with local knowledge who is qualified to take charge of a ship entering or leaving a harbour. **3** something done or produced as a test before introducing it more widely: *a pilot for a Channel 4 sitcom.* ●verb (**pilots, piloting, piloted**) **1** act as a pilot of an aircraft or ship. **2** test a scheme, programme, etc. before introducing it more widely.
– DERIVATIVES **pilotage** noun.
– ORIGIN Latin *pilotus*.

pilot light noun **1** a small gas burner kept alight permanently to light a larger burner when needed. **2** an electric indicator light or control light.

pilot officer noun the lowest rank of officer in the RAF.

pilot whale noun a black toothed whale with a square bulbous head.

Pilsner /**pilz**-ner, **pilss**-ner/ noun a lager beer with a strong hop flavour, originally brewed at Pilsen (Plzeň) in the Czech Republic.

PIM abbreviation personal information manager.

pimento /pi-**men**-toh/ (also **pimiento** /pi-**myen**-toh/) noun (pl. **pimentos**) a red sweet pepper.
– ORIGIN Spanish.

pimp noun a man who controls prostitutes and arranges clients for them, taking a percentage of their earnings in return. ●verb act as a pimp.
– ORIGIN unknown.

pimpernel noun a low-growing plant with bright five-petalled flowers.
– ORIGIN Old French *pimpernelle*.

pimple noun a small, hard inflamed spot on the skin.
– DERIVATIVES **pimpled** adjective **pimply** adjective.
– ORIGIN related to an Old English word meaning 'break out in pustules'.

PIN (also **PIN number**) abbreviation personal identification number.

pin noun **1** a thin piece of metal with a sharp point at one end and a round head at the other, used for fastening pieces of cloth, paper, etc. **2** a metal projection from an electric plug or an integrated circuit. **3** a small brooch or badge. **4** a steel rod used to join the ends of fractured bones while they heal. **5** Golf a stick with a flag placed in a hole to mark its position. **6** a metal peg in a hand grenade that prevents it from exploding. **7** a skittle in bowling. **8** (**pins**) informal legs. ●verb (**pins, pinning, pinned**) **1** attach or fasten something with a pin or pins. **2** hold someone firmly so they are unable to move. **3** (**pin someone down**) force someone to be specific about their intentions. **4** (**pin someone down**) restrict the actions of an enemy by firing at them. **5** (**pin something on**) place blame or responsibility on someone.
– PHRASES **pin one's hopes on** rely heavily on.
– ORIGIN Latin *pinna* 'point, tip, edge'.

pina colada /pee-nuh kuh-**lah**-duh/ noun a cocktail made with rum, pineapple juice, and coconut.
– ORIGIN Spanish, 'strained pineapple'.

pinafore noun **1** (also Brit. **pinafore dress**) a collarless, sleeveless dress worn over a blouse or jumper. **2** Brit. a loose sleeveless piece of clothing worn over other clothes to keep them clean.
– ORIGIN from **PIN** + **AFORE**.

pinball noun a game in which small metal balls are shot across a sloping board and score points by striking targets.

pince-nez /panss-**nay**/ noun (treated as sing. or pl.) a pair of glasses with a nose clip instead of earpieces.
– ORIGIN French, 'that pinches the nose'.

pincer noun **1** (**pincers**) a tool made of two pieces of metal with blunt inward-curving jaws, used for gripping and pulling things. **2** a front claw of a lobster or similar type of shellfish.
– ORIGIN from Old French *pincier* 'to pinch'.

pincer movement noun an attack in which an army approaches the enemy from two sides at the same time.

pinch verb **1** grip flesh tightly between the finger and thumb. **2** (of a shoe) hurt a foot by being too tight. **3** informal steal something. **4** Brit. informal arrest someone. ●noun **1** an act of pinching. **2** an amount of an ingredient that can be held between the fingers and thumb: *a pinch of salt.*
– PHRASES **at a pinch** if absolutely necessary. **feel the pinch** experience financial hardship.
– ORIGIN Old French *pincier* 'to pinch'.

pinchbeck noun an alloy of copper and zinc resembling gold, used in cheap jewellery. ●adjective appearing valuable, but actually cheap or tawdry.
– ORIGIN named after the English watchmaker Christopher *Pinchbeck*.

pincushion noun a small pad for holding pins.

pine[1] noun (also **pine tree**) an evergreen coniferous tree having clusters of long needle-shaped leaves.
– ORIGIN Latin *pinus*.

pine[2] verb **1** (often **pine away**) feel very distressed or weak because one misses someone so much. **2** (**pine for**) miss or long for: *some Communist Party members still pine for the old days.*
– ORIGIN Old English.

pineal gland /py-nee-uhl, pin-i-uhl/ (also **pineal body**) noun a small gland at the back of the skull within the brain, producing a hormone-like substance in some mammals.
– ORIGIN from Latin *pinea* 'pine cone'.

pineapple noun a large tropical fruit with juicy yellow flesh surrounded by a tough skin and topped with a tuft of leaves.
– ORIGIN from **PINE**[1] + **APPLE**.

pine cone noun the conical or rounded woody fruit of a pine tree.

pine marten noun a dark brown weasel-like mammal that lives in trees.

pine nut noun the edible seed of various pine trees.

ping noun an abrupt high-pitched ringing sound. ●verb make an abrupt high-pitched ringing sound.
– ORIGIN imitating the sound.

ping-pong (also US trademark **Ping-Pong**) noun informal table tennis.
– ORIGIN imitating the sound of a bat striking a ball.

pinhead noun **1** the flattened head of a pin.

p

2 informal a stupid person.

pinhole noun a very small hole.

pinion[1] /pin-yuhn/ noun the outer part of a bird's wing including the flight feathers. • verb **1** tie or hold someone by the arms or legs. **2** cut off the pinion of a bird to prevent it from flying.
– ORIGIN Old French *pignon*.

pinion[2] /pin-yuhn/ noun a small cogwheel or spindle that engages with a large cogwheel.
– ORIGIN French *pignon*.

pink[1] adjective **1** of a colour between red and white. **2** informal, often derogatory left-wing. **3** relating to homosexuals: *the pink economy*. • noun **1** pink colour or material. **2** (the pink) informal the best condition: *he's in the pink of health.*
– DERIVATIVES **pinkish** adjective **pinky** adjective.
– ORIGIN from **PINK**[2].

pink[2] noun a plant with sweet-smelling pink or white flowers and narrow grey-green leaves.
– ORIGIN uncertain.

pink[3] verb cut a zigzag edge on something.
– ORIGIN perhaps from German *pinken* 'strike, peck'.

pink[4] verb Brit. (of a vehicle engine) make rattling sounds as a result of over-rapid combustion in the cylinders.
– ORIGIN imitating the sound.

pinking shears plural noun scissors with a serrated blade, used to cut a zigzag edge in fabric.

pinko noun (pl. **pinkos** or **pinkoes**) informal, derogatory, chiefly N. Amer. a left-wing or liberal person.

pinky (also **pinkie**) noun (pl. **pinkies**) informal the little finger.
– ORIGIN partly from Dutch *pink*.

pin money noun a small sum of money for spending on small items that are not essential.
– ORIGIN first referring to an allowance to a woman from her husband for personal expenses.

pinna /pin-nuh/ noun (pl. **pinnae** /pin-nee/) the external part of the ear; the auricle.
– ORIGIN Latin.

pinnace /pin-niss/ noun chiefly historical a small boat forming part of the equipment of a larger ship.
– ORIGIN French *pinace*.

pinnacle noun **1** the most successful point: *the pinnacle of his career.* **2** a high pointed piece of rock. **3** a small pointed turret on a roof.
– ORIGIN Latin *pinnaculum*.

pinnate adjective Botany & Zoology having leaflets or other parts arranged on either side of a stem or axis.
– ORIGIN Latin *pinnatus* 'feathered'.

PIN number noun see **PIN**.

pinny noun (pl. **pinnies**) Brit. informal a pinafore.

Pinot /pee-noh/ noun any of several varieties of black (**Pinot Noir**) or white (**Pinot Blanc**) wine grape.
– ORIGIN French.

pinpoint verb find or identify exactly: *it is difficult to pinpoint a single cause for violence like this.* • noun a tiny dot or point. • adjective absolutely precise.

pinprick noun **1** a prick caused by a pin. **2** a very small dot.

pins and needles plural noun (treated as sing.) a tingling sensation in a limb recovering from numbness.

pinstripe noun a very narrow stripe in cloth, used especially for suits.
– DERIVATIVES **pinstriped** adjective.

pint noun **1** a unit of liquid or dry capacity equal to one eighth of a gallon, in Britain equal to 0.568 litre and in the US equal to 0.473 litre (for liquid measure) or 0.551 litre (for dry measure). **2** Brit. informal a pint of beer.
– ORIGIN Old French *pinte*.

pintail noun a duck with a long pointed tail.

pintle noun a pin or bolt on which a rudder turns.
– ORIGIN Old English, 'penis'.

pinto /pin-toh/ noun (pl. **pintos**) N. Amer. a piebald horse.
– ORIGIN from Spanish, 'mottled'.

pinto bean noun a medium-sized speckled variety of kidney bean.

pint-sized (also **pint-size**) adjective informal very small.

pin-tuck noun a very narrow ornamental tuck in an item of clothing.

pin-up noun a poster featuring a sexually attractive person.

pinwheel noun chiefly N. Amer. a small Catherine wheel firework.

Pinyin /pin-yin/ noun the standard system for transliterating Chinese characters into the roman alphabet.
– ORIGIN Chinese, 'spell-sound'.

pion /py-on/ noun Physics a meson (subatomic particle) with a mass around 270 times that of the electron.
– ORIGIN from the earlier name *pi-meson*.

pioneer noun **1** a person who explores or settles in a new region. **2** a person who develops new ideas or techniques. • verb develop or be the first to use: *the company pioneered the use of the computer in the courtroom.*
– ORIGIN French *pionnier* 'foot soldier'.

pious adjective **1** deeply religious. **2** pretending to be good or religious so as to impress. **3** (of a hope) sincere but unlikely to be fulfilled.
– DERIVATIVES **piously** adverb **piousness** noun.
– ORIGIN Latin *pius* 'dutiful'.

pip[1] noun a small hard seed in a fruit.
– ORIGIN abbreviation of **PIPPIN**.

pip[2] noun (the pips) Brit. a series of short high-pitched sounds used as a signal on the radio or within the telephone system.
– ORIGIN imitating the sound.

pip[3] noun **1** Brit. a star indicating rank on the shoulder of an army officer's uniform. **2** any of the spots on a playing card, dice, or domino.
– ORIGIN unknown.

pip[4] noun a disease of poultry or other birds causing thick mucus in the throat.
– PHRASES **give someone the pip** informal, dated annoy someone.
– ORIGIN Dutch *pippe*.

pip[5] verb (in phrase **be pipped at the post**) Brit. informal be defeated by a small margin or at the last moment.
– ORIGIN from **PIP**[1] or **PIP**[3].

pipe noun **1** a tube used to carry water, gas, oil, etc. **2** a device for smoking tobacco, consisting of a narrow tube that opens into a small bowl in which the tobacco is burned. **3** a wind instrument consisting of a single tube with holes along its length that are covered by the fingers to produce different notes. **4** one of the tubes by which notes are produced in an organ. **5** (**pipes**) bagpipes. •verb **1** convey something through a pipe. **2** transmit music, a programme, or a signal by wire or cable. **3** play a tune on a pipe. **4** sing or say something in a high, shrill voice. **5** decorate food, clothing, or furnishings with piping.
– PHRASES **pipe down** informal be less noisy. **pipe up** say something suddenly. **put that in your pipe and smoke it** informal said to emphasize that someone will have to accept a particular situation, even if it is unwelcome.
– ORIGIN from Latin *pipare* 'to peep, chirp'.

pipeclay noun a fine white clay, used for making tobacco pipes or for whitening leather.

pipe cleaner noun a piece of wire covered with fibre, used to clean a tobacco pipe.

piped music noun pre-recorded background music played through loudspeakers.

pipe dream noun a hope or scheme that will never be realized.
– ORIGIN referring to a dream experienced when smoking an opium pipe.

pipeline noun a long pipe for carrying oil, gas, or water over a long distance. •verb carry oil, gas, or water by a pipeline.
– PHRASES **in the pipeline** in the process of being developed.

pipe organ noun an organ using pipes instead of or as well as reeds.

piper noun a person who plays a pipe or bagpipes.

pipette /pi-**pet**/ noun a narrow tube used in a laboratory for handling small quantities of liquid, the liquid being drawn into the tube by suction.
– ORIGIN French, 'little pipe'.

pipework noun pipes that make up a network in a house, heating system, etc.

piping noun **1** lengths of pipe. **2** lines of icing or cream, used to decorate cakes and desserts. **3** thin cord covered in fabric and inserted along a seam or hem for decoration.
– PHRASES **piping hot** (of food or water) very hot. [with reference to the whistling sound made by very hot liquid or food.]

pipistrelle /pi-pi-**strel**, **pip**-i-strel/ noun a small insect-eating bat.
– ORIGIN French.

pipit /**pi**-pit/ noun a songbird of open country, typically having brown streaky plumage.
– ORIGIN probably imitating its call.

pippin noun a red and yellow dessert apple.
– ORIGIN Old French *pepin* 'seed of a fruit'.

pipsqueak noun informal an insignificant person.

piquant /**pee**-kuhnt, **pee**-kont/ adjective **1** having a pleasantly sharp or spicy taste. **2** stimulating or interesting: *legal arguments punctuated by piquant asides.*
– DERIVATIVES **piquancy** noun **piquantly** adverb.

– ORIGIN French, 'stinging, pricking'.

pique /peek/ noun irritation or resentment arising from hurt pride. •verb (**piques, piquing, piqued**) **1** arouse someone's interest. **2** (**be piqued**) feel irritated or resentful.
– ORIGIN French *piquer* 'prick, irritate'.

piqué /**pee**-kay/ noun stiff cotton fabric woven in a ribbed or raised pattern.
– ORIGIN French, 'backstitched'.

piquet /pi-**ket**/ noun a trick-taking card game for two players.
– ORIGIN French.

piracy noun **1** the practice of attacking and robbing ships at sea. **2** the use or reproduction of a film, recording, or other material without permission and in order to make a profit.

piranha /pi-**rah**-nuh/ noun a freshwater fish with very sharp teeth.
– ORIGIN Portuguese.

pirate noun **1** a person who attacks and robs ships at sea. **2** a person who reproduces film or other material for profit without permission. •adjective **1** (of a film, recording, or other material) that has been reproduced and used for profit without permission: *pirate videos.* **2** (of an organization) broadcasting without official permission: *a pirate radio station.* •verb **1** reproduce film or other material for profit without permission. **2** dated rob or plunder a ship.
– DERIVATIVES **piratic** adjective.
– ORIGIN Greek *peiratēs*.

pirogue /pi-**rohg**/ noun (in Central America and the Caribbean) a long narrow canoe made from a single tree trunk.
– ORIGIN French.

pirouette /pi-ruu-**et**/ noun (especially in ballet) an act of spinning on one foot. •verb spin round on one foot.
– ORIGIN French, 'spinning top'.

piscatorial /piss-kuh-**tor**-i-uhl/ (also **piscatory**) adjective formal relating to fishing.
– ORIGIN from Latin *piscator* 'fisherman'.

Pisces /**py**-seez/ noun a constellation (the Fish or Fishes) and sign of the zodiac, which the sun enters about 20 February.
– DERIVATIVES **Piscean** /**py**-see-uhn/ noun & adjective.
– ORIGIN Latin, 'fishes'.

pisciculture /**pi**-si-kul-cher/ noun the controlled breeding and rearing of fish.
– ORIGIN from Latin *piscis* 'fish'.

piscina /pi-**see**-nuh/ noun (pl. **piscinas** or **piscinae** /pi-**see**-nee/) a stone basin near the altar in some churches, for draining water used in the Mass.
– ORIGIN Latin, 'fish pond'.

piscine /**pi**-syn/ adjective relating to fish.

piscivorous /pi-**siv**-uh-ruhss/ adjective (of an animal) feeding on fish.
– DERIVATIVES **piscivore** noun.

piss vulgar slang verb urinate. •noun **1** urine. **2** an act of urinating.
– PHRASES **be on the piss** Brit. be engaged in a heavy drinking session. **piss about/around** Brit. mess around. **piss off** go away. **piss someone off** annoy someone. **take the piss** Brit. mock someone or something.
– DERIVATIVES **pisser** noun.

p

– ORIGIN Old French *pisser*.
pissed adjective vulgar slang **1** Brit. drunk. **2** (**pissed off** or N. Amer. **pissed**) very annoyed.
pissoir /pee-swar, piss-war/ noun a public urinal.
– ORIGIN French.
pistachio /pi-sta-shi-oh/ noun (pl. **pistachios**) the edible pale green seed of an Asian tree.
– ORIGIN Greek *pistakion*.
piste /peesst/ noun a course or run for skiing.
– ORIGIN French, 'racetrack'.
pistil /piss-til/ noun the female organs of a flower, comprising the stigma, style, and ovary.
– ORIGIN Latin *pistillum* 'pestle'.
pistol noun a small gun designed to be held in one hand.
– ORIGIN French *pistole*.
pistol-whip verb (**pistol-whips, pistol-whipping, pistol-whipped**) hit or beat someone with the butt of a pistol.
piston noun **1** a disc or short cylinder fitting closely inside a tube in which it moves up and down, used especially in an internal-combustion engine to make other parts of the engine move. **2** a valve in a brass instrument, which is pressed down to alter the pitch of a note.
– ORIGIN Italian *pestone* 'large pestle'.
pistou /pee-stoo/ noun a paste made from crushed basil, garlic, and cheese, used in Provençal dishes.
– ORIGIN Provençal.
pit¹ noun **1** a large hole in the ground. **2** a mine or quarry for coal, chalk, etc. **3** a hollow in a surface. **4** a sunken area in a workshop floor allowing access to a car's underside. **5** an area at the side of a track where racing cars are serviced and refuelled. **6** a part of a theatre where an orchestra plays. **7** a part of the floor of an exchange in which a particular stock or commodity is traded. **8** historical an enclosure in which animals were made to fight as a form of entertainment. **9** (**the pits**) informal a very bad place or situation. **10** (**the pit**) literary hell. •verb (**pits, pitting, pitted**) **1** (**pit someone/thing against**) test someone or something in a contest or struggle against: *pit your wits against the world champions.* **2** make a hollow in the surface of something.
– PHRASES **the pit of the stomach** the lower part of the abdomen.
– DERIVATIVES **pitted** adjective.
– ORIGIN Old English, from Latin *puteus* 'well, shaft'.
pit² chiefly N. Amer. noun the stone of a fruit. •verb (**pits, pitting, pitted**) remove the stone from fruit.
– ORIGIN probably from Dutch.
pit-a-pat (also **pitapat**) adverb with a sound like quick light taps.
– ORIGIN imitating the sound.
pit bull terrier noun a fierce American type of bull terrier.
pitch¹ noun **1** Brit. an area of ground marked out for playing outdoor team games. **2** the extent to which a sound or tone is high or low. **3** a particular level of intensity: *he's keyed up to the highest pitch of concentration.* **4** particular words used to sell or promote something: *a*

sales pitch. **5** the steepness of a roof. **6** Brit. a place where a street vendor or performer is situated. **7** the movement up and down of the front of a ship or aircraft. •verb **1** throw or fall heavily or roughly. **2** set one's voice or a piece of music at a particular pitch. **3** set or aim at a particular level, target, or audience: *he should pitch his talk at a suitable level.* **4** set up and fix something in position. **5** (**pitch in**) informal join in enthusiastically with a task or activity. **6** (**pitch up**) informal arrive somewhere. **7** (of the front of a moving ship or aircraft) move up and down. **8** (as adj. **pitched**) (of a roof) sloping.
– PHRASES **make a pitch** make an attempt at or bid for something.
– ORIGIN uncertain.
pitch² noun a sticky black substance which hardens on cooling, made from tar or turpentine and used for waterproofing.
– ORIGIN Old English.
pitch-black (also **pitch-dark**) adjective completely dark.
pitchblende /pich-blend/ noun a mineral found in dark pitch-like masses and containing radium.
– ORIGIN German *Pechblende*.
pitched battle noun a fierce fight between a large number of people.
pitcher¹ noun a large jug.
– ORIGIN Old French *pichier* 'pot'.
pitcher² noun Baseball the player who throws the ball for the batter to hit.
pitcher plant noun a plant with a deep pitcher-shaped pouch containing fluid in which insects are trapped and absorbed.
pitchfork noun a farm tool with a long handle and two sharp metal prongs, used for lifting hay. •verb **1** lift something with a pitchfork. **2** thrust suddenly into an unexpected and difficult situation: *he was pitchforked into the job for six months.*
– ORIGIN from former *pickfork*, influenced by **PITCH**¹.
pitch pine noun a pine tree with hard, heavy, resinous wood.
pitchy adjective (**pitchier, pitchiest**) resembling pitch, especially in being sticky or dark.
piteous adjective deserving or arousing pity: *piteous cries.*
– DERIVATIVES **piteously** adverb **piteousness** noun.
– ORIGIN Old French *piteus*.
pitfall noun **1** a hidden or unsuspected danger or difficulty: *the pitfalls of setting up an office at home.* **2** a covered pit used to trap animals.
pith noun **1** spongy white tissue lining the rind of citrus fruits. **2** spongy tissue in the stems and branches of many plants. **3** the essential part of something: *puzzling over the pith of the problem.* **4** conciseness and clarity in expressing a point.
– ORIGIN Old English.
pithead noun the top of a mineshaft and the area around it.
pith helmet noun a head covering made from the dried pith of a tropical plant, used for protection from the sun.
pithy adjective (**pithier, pithiest**) **1** (of language or style) concise and expressing a point

clearly. **2** (of a fruit or plant) containing much pith.
– DERIVATIVES **pithily** adverb **pithiness** noun.

pitiable adjective **1** deserving or arousing pity. **2** ridiculously poor or small.
– DERIVATIVES **pitiably** adverb.

pitiful adjective **1** deserving or arousing pity. **2** very small or poor; inadequate.
– DERIVATIVES **pitifully** adverb **pitifulness** noun.

pitiless adjective showing no pity; harsh or cruel.
– DERIVATIVES **pitilessly** adverb **pitilessness** noun.

piton /pee-ton/ noun a peg or spike driven into a crack to support a climber or a rope.
– ORIGIN French, 'eye bolt'.

pitta /pit-tuh/ noun a type of flat bread which can be split open to hold a filling.
– ORIGIN modern Greek, 'cake or pie'.

pittance noun a very small or inadequate amount of money.
– ORIGIN Old French *pitance* 'pity, pittance'.

pitter-patter noun a sound of quick light steps or taps. • adverb with a sound of quick light steps or taps.

pituitary gland /pi-tyoo-i-tuh-ri/ (also **pituitary body**) noun a pea-sized gland attached to the base of the brain, important in controlling growth and development.
– ORIGIN Latin *pituitarius* 'secreting phlegm'.

pity noun (pl. **pities**) **1** a feeling of sorrow and sympathy caused by the sufferings of others. **2** a cause for regret or disappointment: *what a pity we can't be friends.* • verb (**pities, pitying, pitied**) feel pity for someone.
– ORIGIN Old French *pite* 'compassion'.

pivot noun **1** the central point, pin, or shaft on which a mechanism turns or balances. **2** a person or thing playing a central part in an activity or organization. • verb (**pivots, pivoting, pivoted**) **1** turn on a central point. **2** (**pivot on**) depend on: *the government's reaction pivoted on the response of the Prime Minister.*
– DERIVATIVES **pivotable** adjective.
– ORIGIN French.

pivotal adjective **1** of central importance; vital: *Japan's pivotal role in the world economy.* **2** fixed or turning on a pivot.

pixel noun any of the tiny areas of light on a display screen which make up an image.
– ORIGIN abbreviation of *picture element.*

pixelate /pik-suh-layt/ (also **pixellate** or **pixilate**) verb **1** divide an image into pixels, for display or for storage in a digital format. **2** display a person's image as a small number of large pixels in order to disguise their identity.
– DERIVATIVES **pixelation** noun.

pixie (also **pixy**) noun (pl. **pixies**) a supernatural being in folklore, portrayed as a tiny man with pointed ears and a pointed hat.
– DERIVATIVES **pixieish** adjective.
– ORIGIN unknown.

pizza noun a dish consisting of a flat, round base of dough baked with a topping of tomatoes, cheese, and other ingredients.
– ORIGIN Italian, 'pie'.

pizzazz (also **pizazz** or **pzazz**) noun informal a combination of liveliness and style.

– ORIGIN said to have been invented by Diana Vreeland, fashion editor of *Harper's Bazaar* in the 1930s.

pizzeria /peet-zuh-ree-uh/ noun a pizza restaurant.
– ORIGIN Italian.

pizzicato /pit-zi-kah-toh/ adverb & adjective plucking the strings of a violin or other stringed instrument with the finger.
– ORIGIN Italian, 'pinched'.

PJs abbreviation pyjamas.

pl. abbreviation **1** (also **Pl.**) place. **2** plural.

placard /pla-kard/ noun a sign for public display, either fixed on a wall or carried during a demonstration. • verb cover something with placards.
– ORIGIN Old French *placquart.*

placate /pluh-kayt/ verb make someone less angry or hostile.
– DERIVATIVES **placatory** adjective.
– ORIGIN Latin *placare.*

place noun **1** a particular position or area; a location. **2** a portion of space occupied by or set aside for someone or something: *Jack had saved her a place.* **3** a vacancy, especially on a course of study. **4** a position in a sequence: *I finished in second place.* **5** the position of a figure in a decimal number. **6** (in place names) a square or short street. **7** informal a person's home. • verb **1** put in a particular position or situation: *enemy officers were placed under arrest.* **2** find an appropriate place or role for someone or something. **3** allocate a specified position in a sequence to: *a survey placed the company 13th for achievement.* **4** remember where one has seen someone or something. **5** arrange for an order, bet, etc. to be carried out.
– PHRASES **go places** informal be increasingly successful. **in place** established and working or ready. **in place of** instead of. **keep someone in his** (or **her**) **place** keep someone from becoming too self-important. **out of place 1** not in the proper position. **2** in a situation where one does not fit in. **put someone in his** (or **her**) **place** make someone feel less proud or arrogant. **take place** happen; occur. **take the place of** replace someone or something.
– DERIVATIVES **placer** noun.
– ORIGIN Old French.

placebo /pluh-see-boh/ noun (pl. **placebos**) **1** a medicine given to a patient to make them feel better psychologically rather than for any physical effect. **2** a substance that has no medicinal effect, used as a control in testing new drugs.
– ORIGIN Latin, 'I shall be acceptable or pleasing'.

place kick American Football, Rugby, & Football noun a kick made after the ball is first placed on the ground. • verb (**place-kick**) take a place kick.
– DERIVATIVES **place-kicker** noun.

placeman noun (pl. **placemen**) Brit. derogatory a person appointed to a position chiefly for personal profit and as a reward for political support.

placement noun **1** the action of placing someone or something. **2** Brit. a temporary job undertaken to gain work experience.

placenta /pluh-sen-tuh/ noun (pl. **placentae**

/pluh-**sen**-tee/ or **placentas**) an organ that forms in the womb of a pregnant mammal and which supplies blood and nourishment to the fetus through the umbilical cord.
– DERIVATIVES **placental** adjective.
– ORIGIN Latin.

placid adjective **1** not easily upset or excited. **2** with little movement or activity; calm: *the placid waters of the lake.*
– DERIVATIVES **placidity** noun **placidly** adverb.
– ORIGIN Latin *placidus.*

placing noun a ranking given to a competitor.

placket noun **1** an opening in an item of clothing, covering fastenings or for access to a pocket. **2** a flap of material used to strengthen such an opening.
– ORIGIN from **PLACARD** in the former sense 'garment worn under an open coat'.

plagiarize (or **plagiarise**) /**play**-juh-ryz/ verb take the work or idea of someone else and pass it off as one's own.
– DERIVATIVES **plagiarism** noun **plagiarist** noun **plagiarizer** noun.
– ORIGIN from Latin *plagiarius* 'kidnapper'.

plague noun **1** a contagious disease spread by bacteria and causing fever and delirium. **2** an unusually large quantity of destructive insects or animals. • verb (**plagues, plaguing, plagued**) **1** cause continual trouble to: *he grew up on an estate plagued by crime.* **2** pester someone continually.
– ORIGIN Latin *plaga* 'stroke, wound'.

plaice noun (pl. same) an edible brown marine flatfish with orange spots.
– ORIGIN Old French *plaiz.*

plaid /plad/ noun fabric woven in a chequered or tartan design.
– ORIGIN Scottish Gaelic *plaide* 'blanket'.

plain adjective **1** not decorated or elaborate; simple or ordinary: *good plain food.* **2** without a pattern or in only one colour. **3** without identification; unmarked: *a plain envelope.* **4** easy to see or understand; clear. **5** (of language) clearly expressed, without the use of difficult terms. **6** (of a woman or girl) not beautiful or attractive. **7** sheer; simple: *the problem was plain exhaustion.* **8** (of a knitting stitch) made by putting the needle through the front of the stitch from left to right. Compare with **PURL¹**. • adverb informal used for emphasis: *that's plain stupid.* • noun a large area of flat land with few trees.
– DERIVATIVES **plainly** adverb **plainness** noun.
– ORIGIN Latin *planus* 'flat, plain'.

plain chocolate noun Brit. dark, slightly bitter chocolate without added milk.

plain clothes plural noun ordinary clothes rather than uniform, especially when worn by police officers.

plain flour noun Brit. flour that does not contain a raising agent.

plain sailing noun smooth and easy progress.

plainsong (also **plainchant**) noun unaccompanied medieval church music sung by a number of voices together.

plain-spoken adjective outspoken; blunt.

plaint noun **1** Law, Brit. an accusation or charge. **2** chiefly literary a complaint or lament.
– ORIGIN Old French *plainte.*

plaintiff noun a person who brings a case against another in a court of law. Compare with **DEFENDANT**.
– ORIGIN Old French *plaintif* 'plaintive'.

plaintive adjective sounding sad and mournful.
– DERIVATIVES **plaintively** adverb **plaintiveness** noun.
– ORIGIN Old French.

plait noun Brit. a single length of hair, rope, or other material made up of three or more interlaced strands. • verb form hair or other material into a plait or plaits.
– ORIGIN Old French *pleit* 'a fold'.

plan noun **1** a detailed proposal for doing or achieving something. **2** an intention or decision about what one is going to do. **3** a scheme for making regular payments towards a pension, insurance policy, etc. **4** a map or diagram. **5** a scale drawing of a horizontal section of a building. • verb (**plans, planning, planned**) **1** decide on and arrange something in advance. **2** (**plan for**) make preparations for. **3** make a plan of something to be made or built.
– DERIVATIVES **planner** noun.
– ORIGIN French.

planar /**play**-ner/ adjective Mathematics relating to or in the form of a plane.

planchette /plahn-**shet**/ noun a small board on castors and fitted with a vertical pencil, used in seances to convey supposed messages from spirits.
– ORIGIN French, 'small plank'.

plane¹ noun **1** technical a flat surface on which a straight line joining any two points would wholly lie. **2** a level of existence or thought: *many believe there is a higher plane of existence.* • adjective **1** completely level or flat. **2** relating to two-dimensional surfaces or magnitudes. • verb **1** (especially of a bird) soar without moving the wings; glide. **2** (of a boat, surfboard, etc.) skim over the surface of water.
– ORIGIN Latin *planum* 'flat surface'.

plane² noun an aeroplane.

plane³ (also **planer**) noun a tool consisting of a block with a projecting steel blade, used to smooth a wooden surface by paring shavings from it. • verb smooth a surface with a plane.
– ORIGIN Latin *plana.*

plane⁴ (also **plane tree**) noun a tall spreading tree with maple-like leaves and a peeling bark.
– ORIGIN Old French.

planet noun **1** a large round object in space that orbits round a star. **2** (**the planet**) the earth.
– DERIVATIVES **planetary** adjective **planetology** noun.
– ORIGIN Greek *planētēs* 'wanderer, planet'.

planetarium /plan-i-**tair**-i-uhm/ noun (pl. **planetariums** or **planetaria** /plan-i-**tair**-i-uh/) a building in which images of stars, planets, and constellations are projected on to a domed ceiling.
– ORIGIN Latin.

planetoid noun another term for **ASTEROID**.

plangent /**plan**-juhnt/ adjective literary (of a sound) resonant and mournful.
– DERIVATIVES **plangency** noun **plangently** adverb.
– ORIGIN from Latin *plangere* 'to lament'.

plank noun **1** a long, flat piece of timber, used in

flooring. **2** a fundamental part of a political or other programme: *crime reduction is a central plank of the manifesto.*
– PHRASES **walk the plank** (formerly) be forced by pirates to walk blindfold along a plank over the side of a ship to one's death in the sea.
– DERIVATIVES **planked** adjective.
– ORIGIN Latin *planca* 'board'.

planking noun planks used for flooring or as part of a boat.

plankton noun small and microscopic organisms living in the sea or fresh water.
– DERIVATIVES **planktic** adjective **planktonic** adjective.
– ORIGIN from Greek *planktos* 'wandering'.

planned economy noun an economy in which production, investment, prices, and incomes are determined centrally by the government.

planning noun **1** the process of making plans for something. **2** the control of development in cities and towns by local government.

planning permission noun Brit. formal permission from a local authority for the erection or alteration of buildings.

plant noun **1** a living organism that grows in the ground, having roots with which it absorbs substances and leaves in which it makes nutrients by photosynthesis. **2** a place where an industrial or manufacturing process takes place. **3** machinery used in an industrial or manufacturing process. **4** a person placed in a group as a spy. **5** a thing put among someone's belongings to make them appear guilty of wrongdoing. •verb **1** place a seed, bulb, or plant in the ground so that it can grow. **2** place or fix someone or something in a specified position. **3** secretly place a bomb somewhere. **4** put or hide something among someone's belongings to make them appear guilty of wrongdoing. **5** send someone to join a group to act as a spy. **6** establish an idea in someone's mind.
– DERIVATIVES **plantlet** noun.
– ORIGIN from Latin *planta* 'sprout, cutting' and *plantare* 'plant, fix in place'.

Plantagenet /plan-**taj**-uh-nuht/ noun a member of the English royal dynasty which ruled from 1154 until 1485.
– ORIGIN from Latin *planta genista* 'sprig of broom', said to be worn as a crest by Geoffrey, count of Anjou, the father of Henry II.

plantain[1] /**plan**-tin, **plan**-tayn/ noun a low-growing plant, with a rosette of leaves and green flowers.
– ORIGIN Old French.

plantain[2] /**plan**-tin, **plan**-tayn/ noun a type of banana which is harvested green and cooked as a vegetable.
– ORIGIN Spanish *plá(n)tano* 'plane tree'.

plantation noun **1** a large estate on which crops such as coffee, sugar, and tobacco are grown. **2** an area in which trees have been planted.

planter noun **1** a manager or owner of a plantation. **2** a decorative container in which plants are grown.

plaque /plak, plahk/ noun **1** an ornamental tablet fixed to a wall in commemoration of a person or event. **2** a sticky deposit on teeth, which encourages the growth of bacteria.
– ORIGIN French.

plash noun a splashing sound. •verb make or hit with a splash.
– DERIVATIVES **plashy** adjective.
– ORIGIN probably imitating the sound.

plasma /**plaz**-muh/ noun **1** the colourless fluid part of blood, lymph, or milk, in which corpuscles or fat globules are suspended. **2** Physics a gas of positive ions and free electrons with little or no overall electric charge.
– DERIVATIVES **plasmatic** adjective **plasmic** adjective.
– ORIGIN Greek.

plasma screen noun a flat display screen which uses an array of cells containing a gas plasma to produce different colours in each cell.

plaster noun **1** a soft mixture of lime with sand or cement and water for spreading on walls and ceilings to form a smooth hard surface when dried. **2** (also **plaster of Paris**) a hard white substance made by adding water to powdered gypsum, used for setting broken bones and making sculptures and casts. **3** (also **sticking plaster**) Brit. an adhesive strip of material for covering cuts and wounds. •verb **1** cover a wall or ceiling with plaster. **2** coat thickly with a substance: *a face plastered in heavy make-up.* **3** make hair lie flat by damping it. **4** display widely and prominently: *her story was plastered all over the December issue.*
– DERIVATIVES **plasterer** noun.
– ORIGIN Latin *plastrum*.

plasterboard noun board made of plaster set between two sheets of paper, used to line interior walls and ceilings.

plastered adjective informal very drunk.

plasterwork noun plaster as part of the interior of a building, especially when formed into decorative shapes.

plastic noun **1** a material produced by chemical processes that can be moulded into shape while soft and then set into a rigid or slightly elastic form. **2** informal credit cards or other plastic cards that can be used as money. •adjective **1** made of plastic. **2** easily shaped or moulded. **3** artificial or false: *a holiday rep with a plastic smile.* **4** relating to moulding or modelling in three dimensions: *the plastic arts.*
– DERIVATIVES **plastically** adverb **plasticity** noun.
– ORIGIN Greek *plastikos.*

plastic bullet noun a bullet made of PVC or another plastic, used for riot control.

plastic explosive noun a putty-like explosive capable of being moulded by hand.

plasticine (also **Plasticine**) noun trademark a soft modelling material.

plasticize (or **plasticise**) verb **1** treat or coat something with plastic. **2** make something plastic or able to be moulded.
– DERIVATIVES **plasticization** noun **plasticizer** noun.

plasticky adjective **1** resembling plastic. **2** artificial or of poor quality.

plastic surgery noun surgery performed to repair or reconstruct parts of the body damaged by injury or for cosmetic reasons.

plastique /pla-**steek**/ noun plastic explosive.

p

– ORIGIN French, 'plastic'.

plate noun **1** a flat dish from which food is eaten or served. **2** bowls, cups, and other utensils made of gold or silver. **3** a thin, flat piece of metal used to join or strengthen something or forming part of a machine. **4** a small, flat piece of metal with a name or other writing on it, fixed to a wall or door. **5** a sheet of metal or other material with an image of type or illustrations on it, from which multiple copies are printed. **6** a printed photograph or illustration in a book. **7** a thin, flat structure in a plant or animal. **8** each of the several rigid pieces of the earth's crust and upper mantle which together make up the earth's surface. • verb cover a metal object with a thin coating of a different metal.
– PHRASES **on a plate** informal with little or no effort. **on one's plate** chiefly Brit. occupying one's time or energy.
– DERIVATIVES **plater** noun.
– ORIGIN from Old French *plat* 'platter' or *plate* 'sheet of metal'.

plateau /plat-oh/ noun (pl. **plateaux** /plat-ohz/ or **plateaus**) **1** an area of fairly level high ground. **2** a period of little or no change following a period of activity or progress. • verb (**plateaus**, **plateauing**, **plateaued**) reach a period of little or no change following activity or progress: *after making a huge jump in the rankings his game has really plateaued.*
– ORIGIN French.

plate glass noun thick fine-quality glass used for shop windows and doors.

platelet noun a small disc-shaped cell fragment without a nucleus, found in large numbers in blood and involved in clotting.

platen /plat-uhn/ noun **1** a cylindrical roller in a typewriter against which the paper is held. **2** a plate in a small letterpress printing press which presses the paper against the type.
– ORIGIN French *platine* 'flat piece'.

platform noun **1** a raised level surface on which people or things can stand. **2** a raised structure along the side of a railway track where passengers get on and off trains. **3** a raised structure standing in the sea from which oil or gas wells can be drilled. **4** the declared policy of a political party or group: *seeking election of a platform of low taxes.* **5** an opportunity for the expression or exchange of views. **6** a very thick sole on a shoe. **7** a standard for the hardware of a computer system, which determines the kinds of software it can run.
– ORIGIN French *plateforme* 'ground plan'.

platinum /plat-i-nuhm/ noun a precious silvery-white metallic chemical element used in jewellery and in some electrical and laboratory equipment. • adjective greyish-white or silvery.
– ORIGIN Spanish *platina.*

platinum blonde adjective (of hair) silvery-blonde.

platinum disc noun a framed platinum disc awarded to a recording artist or group for sales exceeding a specified high figure.

platitude noun a remark or statement that has been used too often to be interesting or thoughtful.

– DERIVATIVES **platitudinous** adjective.
– ORIGIN French.

Platonic /pluh-ton-ik/ adjective **1** relating to the ancient Greek philosopher Plato or his ideas. **2** (**platonic**) (of love or friendship) intimate and affectionate but not sexual.
– DERIVATIVES **platonically** adverb.

Platonism /play-tuh-ni-z'm/ noun the philosophy of Plato, especially his theories on the relationship between abstract ideas or entities and their corresponding objects or forms in the material world.
– DERIVATIVES **Platonist** noun & adjective.

platoon noun a subdivision of a company of soldiers, usually commanded by a subaltern or lieutenant and divided into three sections.
– ORIGIN French *peloton* 'platoon', literally 'small ball'.

platter noun **1** a large flat serving dish. **2** a selection of food served on a platter: *a seafood platter.*
– PHRASES **on a (silver) platter** informal with little or no effort.
– ORIGIN Old French *plater.*

platypus /plat-i-puhss/ (also **duck-billed platypus**) noun (pl. **platypuses**) an egg-laying Australian mammal with a duck-like bill and webbed feet, living partly on land and partly in water.
– ORIGIN from Greek *platupous* 'flat-footed'.

plaudits plural noun enthusiastic approval; praise.
– ORIGIN from Latin *plaudite* 'applaud!'

plausible adjective **1** seeming reasonable or probable. **2** skilled at producing persuasive arguments: *a plausible liar.*
– DERIVATIVES **plausibility** noun **plausibly** adverb.
– ORIGIN from Latin *plaudere* 'applaud'.

play verb **1** take part in games or other activities for enjoyment. **2** take part in a sport or contest. **3** compete against another player or team. **4** take a specified position in a sports team: *he played in goal.* **5** act the role of a character in a play or film. **6** perform on a musical instrument or perform a piece of music. **7** move a piece or display a playing card in one's turn in a game. **8** make a CD, tape, or record produce sounds. **9** be cooperative: *he needs financial backing, but the banks won't play.* **10** move lightly and quickly; flicker: *a smile played about her lips.* • noun **1** games and other activities that one takes part in for enjoyment. **2** the progress of a sporting match: *bad weather stopped play.* **3** a move or manoeuvre in a sport or game. **4** the state of being active or effective: *luck came into play.* **5** a dramatic work written for the stage or to be broadcast. **6** freedom of movement in a mechanism. **7** constantly changing movement: *the play of light across the surface.*
– PHRASES **make great play of** draw attention to something in an exaggerated way. **make a play for** informal attempt to attract someone or gain something. **play about** (or **around**) behave in a casual or irresponsible way. **play along** pretend to cooperate with someone. **play something by ear 1** perform music without having seen a score. **2** (**play it by ear**) informal proceed according to circumstances rather than following rules or a plan. **play something down** disguise the importance of something.

play fast and loose behave irresponsibly or immorally. **play for time** use excuses or unnecessary activities to gain time. **play into someone's hands** give someone an advantage without meaning to do so. **play someone off against another** cause someone to compete with or oppose another for one's own advantage. **play on** exploit someone's weak point. **a play on words** a pun. **play** (or **play it**) **safe** avoid taking risks. **play up 1** Brit. informal fail to function properly. **2** (**play up to**) humour or flatter someone. **play something up** emphasize the extent or importance of something. **play with** treat someone inconsiderately for one's own amusement. **play with fire** take foolish risks.
– DERIVATIVES **playable** adjective.
– ORIGIN Old English, 'to exercise'.

play-acting noun behaviour that is exaggerated for pretence.

playback noun the replaying of previously recorded sound or moving images.

playboy noun a wealthy man who spends his time enjoying himself.

player noun **1** a person taking part in a sport or game. **2** a person who plays a musical instrument. **3** a device for playing compact discs, tapes, or records. **4** a person who is influential in an area of activity: *a major player in political circles.* **5** an actor.

playful adjective **1** fond of playing; full of fun. **2** made or done in fun; not serious: *a playful punch on the arm.*
– DERIVATIVES **playfully** adverb **playfulness** noun.

playground noun an outdoor area provided for children to play on.

playgroup (also **playschool**) noun Brit. a regular play session for preschool children, organized by parents.

playhouse noun **1** a theatre. **2** a toy house for children to play in.

playing card noun each of a set of rectangular pieces of card with numbers and symbols on one side, used to play various games.

playing field noun a field used for outdoor team games.

playlist noun a list of songs or pieces of music chosen to be broadcast on a radio station.

playmaker noun a player in a team game who leads attacks or brings teammates into attacking positions.

playmate noun a friend with whom a child plays.

play-off noun an additional match played to decide the outcome of a contest.

playpen noun a small portable enclosure in which a baby or small child can play safely.

playscheme noun a local project providing recreational facilities and activities for children.

playschool noun another term for PLAYGROUP.

playsuit noun an all-in-one stretchy garment for a baby or toddler.

plaything noun **1** a person who is treated as amusing but unimportant. **2** a toy.

playtime noun a period in the school day when children are allowed to go outside and play.

playwright noun a person who writes plays.

plaza noun **1** a public square or similar open space in a town or city. **2** N. Amer. a shopping centre.
– ORIGIN Spanish, 'place'.

plc (also **PLC**) abbreviation Brit. public limited company.

plea noun **1** a request made in an urgent and emotional way. **2** a formal statement made by or on behalf of a person charged with an offence in a law court. **3** a claim that one should not be blamed for or have to do something because of particular circumstances.
– ORIGIN Old French *plait, plaid* 'agreement, discussion'.

plea-bargaining noun Law an arrangement between a prosecutor and a person charged with an offence in which the latter pleads guilty to a lesser charge in the expectation of a less severe sentence.

pleach /pleech/ verb (usu as adj. **pleached**) entwine tree branches to form a hedge or provide cover for a path.
– ORIGIN Old French *plaissier*.

plead verb (past and past part. **pleaded** or US & dialect **pled**) **1** make an urgent and emotional request. **2** argue in support of: *he visited the country to plead his cause.* **3** state formally in a court of law whether one is guilty or not guilty of the offence with which one is charged. **4** Law give a reason or a point of law as an accusation or defence. **5** present an excuse for doing or not doing something: *she pleaded family commitments as a reason for not attending.*
– DERIVATIVES **pleader** noun.
– ORIGIN Old French *plaidier* 'go to law'.

USAGE: In a law court a person can **plead guilty** or **plead not guilty.** The phrase **plead innocent** is not a legal term, although it is found in general use.

pleading adjective earnestly appealing. ●noun (usu. **pleadings**) a formal statement of a case presented by each party in a lawsuit.
– DERIVATIVES **pleadingly** adverb.

pleasant adjective **1** enjoyable, pleasing, or attractive: *a pleasant town on a river.* **2** friendly and likeable.
– DERIVATIVES **pleasantly** adverb **pleasantness** noun.
– ORIGIN Old French *plaisant.*

pleasantry noun (pl. **pleasantries**) **1** a conventional remark made as part of a polite conversation. **2** a mildly amusing joke.

please verb **1** make someone feel happy and satisfied. **2** wish or desire: *do as you please.* **3** (**please oneself**) do as one wishes, without considering anyone else. ●adverb used in polite requests or questions, or to accept an offer.
– ORIGIN Old French *plaisir.*

pleased adjective **1** feeling or showing pleasure and satisfaction. **2** (**pleased to do**) willing or glad to do something.

pleasing adjective pleasant, satisfying, or attractive.
– DERIVATIVES **pleasingly** adverb.

pleasurable adjective pleasing; enjoyable.
– DERIVATIVES **pleasurably** adverb.

pleasure noun **1** a feeling of happy satisfaction and enjoyment. **2** an enjoyable event or

activity. **3** sexual satisfaction. • **adjective**
intended for entertainment rather than
business: *pleasure boats.* • **verb** arouse someone
sexually.
- PHRASES **at someone's pleasure** formal as and
when someone wishes.
- ORIGIN from Old French *plaisir* 'to please'.

pleat **noun** a fold in fabric or an item of
clothing, held by stitching the top or side.
• **verb** fold or form fabric into pleats.
- ORIGIN from **PLAIT**.

pleb **noun** informal, derogatory a lower-class person.
- DERIVATIVES **plebby** adjective.
- ORIGIN abbreviation of **PLEBEIAN**.

plebeian /pli-bee-uhn/ **adjective** lower-class or
unsophisticated: *I've got very plebeian tastes.*
• **noun 1** a lower-class person. **2** (in ancient
Rome) a commoner.
- ORIGIN from Latin *plebs* 'the common people'.

plebiscite /pleb-i-syt/ **noun** a vote made by all
the members of an electorate on an important
public issue.
- DERIVATIVES **plebiscitary** /ple-**bi**-si-tuh-ri/
adjective.
- ORIGIN French *plébiscite.*

plectrum **noun** (pl. **plectrums** or **plectra**) a thin
flat piece of plastic or tortoiseshell used to
pluck the strings of a guitar or similar musical
instrument.
- ORIGIN Greek *plēktron* 'something with which
to strike'.

pled US or dialect past and past participle of
PLEAD.

pledge **noun 1** a solemn promise to do
something. **2** something valuable given as a
guarantee that a debt will be paid or a promise
kept. **3** (**the pledge**) a solemn vow not to drink
alcohol. **4** a thing given as a token of love,
favour, or loyalty. • **verb 1** solemnly promise to
do or give something. **2** give something
valuable as a guarantee on a loan.
- ORIGIN Old French *plege* 'person acting as
surety for another'.

Pleistocene /ply-stuh-seen/ **adjective** Geology
relating to the first epoch of the Quaternary
period (from 1.64 million to about 10,000
years ago), a time which included the ice ages
and the appearance of humans.
- ORIGIN from Greek *pleistos* 'most' + *kainos*
'new'.

plenary /plee-nuh-ri/ **adjective 1** full; absolute:
plenary powers. **2** (of a meeting at a conference
or assembly) to be attended by all
participants. • **noun** a meeting attended by all
participants at a conference or assembly.
- ORIGIN Latin *plenus* 'full'.

plenipotentiary /plen-i-puh-**ten**-shuh-ri/
noun (pl. **plenipotentiaries**) a person given full
power by a government to act on its behalf.
• **adjective 1** having full power to take
independent action. **2** (of power) absolute.
- ORIGIN from Latin *plenus* 'full' + *potentia*
'power'.

plenitude **noun** formal a large amount of
something; an abundance.
- ORIGIN Old French.

plenteous **adjective** literary plentiful; abundant.

plentiful **adjective** existing in great quantities;
abundant: *countries with plentiful supplies of
oil.*

- DERIVATIVES **plentifully** adverb.

plentitude **noun** another term for **PLENITUDE**.

plenty **pronoun** a large amount or quantity, or
as much as is needed. • **noun** a situation in
which food and other necessities are available
in large quantities. • **adverb** informal used to
emphasize the degree or extent of something:
she has plenty more ideas.
- ORIGIN Old French *plente.*

plenum /plee-nuhm/ **noun 1** an assembly of all
the members of a group or committee. **2** Physics
a space completely filled with matter, or the
whole of space regarded in such a way.
- ORIGIN Latin, 'full space'.

pleonasm /plee-oh-na-z'm/ **noun** the use of
more words than are necessary to express
meaning (e.g. *I saw her with my own eyes*).
- DERIVATIVES **pleonastic** adjective.
- ORIGIN Greek *pleonasmos.*

plethora /pleth-uh-ruh/ **noun** an excessive
amount: *a plethora of complaints.*
- ORIGIN Latin.

pleura /ploor-uh/ **noun** (pl. **pleurae** /ploor-ee/)
each of a pair of membranes covering the
lungs.
- DERIVATIVES **pleural** adjective.
- ORIGIN Greek, 'side of the body, rib'.

pleurisy /ploor-i-si/ **noun** inflammation of the
membranes around the lungs, causing pain
during breathing.

plexus **noun** (pl. same or **plexuses**) **1** a network
of nerves or vessels in the body. **2** an intricate
network or web-like formation.
- ORIGIN Latin, 'plaited formation'.

pliable **adjective 1** easily bent; flexible. **2** easily
influenced: *pliable teenage minds.*
- DERIVATIVES **pliability** noun.
- ORIGIN French.

pliant **adjective** easily bent or influenced;
pliable.
- DERIVATIVES **pliancy** noun **pliantly** adverb.

plié /plee-ay/ **noun** Ballet a movement in which a
dancer bends the knees and straightens them
again, having the feet turned right out and
heels firmly on the ground.
- ORIGIN French, 'bent'.

pliers **plural noun** pincers with parallel flat jaws,
used for gripping small objects or bending
wire.
- ORIGIN from French *plier* 'to bend'.

plight¹ **noun** a dangerous or difficult situation.
- ORIGIN Old French *plit* 'fold'.

plight² **verb** old use **1** solemnly promise faith or
loyalty. **2** (**be plighted to**) be engaged to be
married to.
- ORIGIN Old English.

plimsoll (also **plimsole**) **noun** Brit. a light
rubber-soled canvas sports shoe.
- ORIGIN probably from the resemblance of the
side of the sole to a **PLIMSOLL LINE**.

Plimsoll line **noun** a marking on a ship's side
showing the limit to which the ship may be
legally submerged in the water when loaded
with cargo.
- ORIGIN named after the English politician
Samuel *Plimsoll*, responsible for the Merchant
Shipping Act.

plink **verb** make a short, sharp, metallic ringing
sound. • **noun** a short, sharp, metallic ringing
sound.

p

- DERIVATIVES **plinky** adjective.
- ORIGIN imitating the sound.

plinth noun **1** a heavy base supporting a statue or vase. **2** the lower square slab at the base of a column.
- ORIGIN Greek *plinthos* 'tile, brick, squared stone'.

Pliocene /ply-uh-seen/ adjective Geology relating to the last epoch of the Tertiary period (5.2 to 1.64 million years ago), when the first hominids appeared.
- ORIGIN from Greek *pleiōn* 'more' + *kainos* 'new'.

PLO abbreviation Palestine Liberation Organization.

plod verb (**plods, plodding, plodded**) **1** walk slowly with heavy steps. **2** work slowly but determinedly at a dull task. • noun **1** a slow, heavy walk. **2** (also **PC Plod**) Brit. informal a police officer.
- DERIVATIVES **plodder** noun.
- ORIGIN probably imitating the sound of a heavy walk.

plonk¹ informal, chiefly Brit. verb **1** set something down heavily or carelessly. **2** play unskilfully on a musical instrument. • noun a sound like that of something being set down heavily.
- ORIGIN imitating the sound.

plonk² noun Brit. informal cheap wine.
- ORIGIN probably from French *blanc* in *vin blanc* 'white wine'.

plonker noun Brit. informal a foolish or incompetent person.
- ORIGIN from **PLONK**¹.

plop noun a sound like that of a small solid object dropping into water. • verb (**plops, plopping, plopped**) fall or drop with a plop.
- ORIGIN imitating the sound.

plosive adjective referring to a consonant (e.g. *d* and *p*) that is produced by stopping the flow of air from the mouth with the lips, teeth, or palate and then suddenly releasing it.
- ORIGIN from **EXPLOSIVE**.

plot noun **1** a secret plan to do something illegal or wrong. **2** the main sequence of events in a play, novel, or film. **3** a small piece of ground marked out for building, gardening, etc. **4** a graph showing the relation between two variables. • verb (**plots, plotting, plotted**) **1** secretly make plans to carry out something illegal or wrong. **2** invent the plot of a play, novel, or film. **3** mark a route or position on a chart or graph.
- DERIVATIVES **plotless** adjective **plotter** noun.
- ORIGIN Old English, 'small piece of ground'; sense 1 is associated with Old French *complot* 'dense crowd, secret project'.

plough (US **plow**) noun **1** a large farming implement with one or more blades fixed in a frame, drawn over soil to turn it over and cut furrows. **2** (**the Plough**) Brit. a formation of seven stars in the constellation Ursa Major (the Great Bear). • verb **1** turn up earth with a plough. **2** (**plough through/into**) (of a vehicle) move in a fast or uncontrolled way through or into someone or something. **3** move forward or progress with difficulty: *the students are ploughing through grammar exercises.*
4 (**plough something in**) invest money in a business.

- DERIVATIVES **ploughable** adjective **ploughman** noun (pl. **ploughmen**).
- ORIGIN Old English.

ploughman's lunch noun Brit. a meal of bread and cheese with pickle and salad.

ploughshare noun the main cutting blade of a plough.

plover /*rhymes with* lover/ noun a wading bird with a short bill.
- ORIGIN Old French.

plow noun & verb US spelling of **PLOUGH**.

ploy noun a cunning plan or action intended to gain an advantage.
- ORIGIN unknown.

pluck verb **1** take hold of something and quickly remove it from its place. **2** pull out a hair, feather, etc. **3** pull the feathers from a bird's carcass to prepare it for cooking. **4** catch hold of: *she plucked at his sleeve.* **5** sound a stringed musical instrument with the finger or a plectrum. • noun **1** spirited and determined courage. **2** the heart, liver, and lungs of an animal as food.
- PHRASES **pluck up courage** summon up enough courage to do something frightening.
- ORIGIN Old English.

plucky adjective (**pluckier, pluckiest**) determined and brave in the face of difficulties.
- DERIVATIVES **pluckily** adverb **pluckiness** noun.

plug noun **1** a piece of solid material fitting tightly into and blocking a hole. **2** a device consisting of an insulated casing with metal pins that fit into holes in a socket to make an electrical connection. **3** informal an electrical socket. **4** informal a piece of publicity promoting a product or event. **5** a piece of tobacco cut from a larger cake for chewing. • verb (**plugs, plugging, plugged**) **1** block or fill in a hole or gap. **2** (**plug something in**) connect an electrical appliance to the mains by means of a socket. **3** (**plug into**) gain access to an information system or area of activity.
4 informal promote a product or event by mentioning it publicly: *during the show she plugged her new record.* **5** informal shoot or hit someone or something. **6** (**plug away**) informal proceed steadily with a task.
- DERIVATIVES **plugger** noun.
- ORIGIN Dutch and German *plugge*.

plughole noun Brit. a hole at the lowest point of a bath or sink, through which the water drains away.

plug-in noun a module or piece of software which can be added to an existing computer system to give extra features.

plum noun **1** a soft oval fruit with purple, reddish, or yellow skin, containing a flattish stone. **2** a reddish-purple colour. • adjective informal highly desirable: *a plum job.*
- ORIGIN Latin *prunum*.

plumage /ploo-mij/ noun a bird's feathers.
- ORIGIN Old French.

plumb¹ verb **1** explore or experience fully or to extremes: *using the Bible to plumb the spiritual depths of the human heart.* **2** measure the depth of water. **3** test an upright surface to find out if it is vertical. • noun a lead ball or other heavy object attached to a line for finding the depth of water or whether an upright surface is vertical. • adverb informal

1 exactly: *plumb in the centre*. **2** N. Amer. extremely or completely. •**adjective** vertical.
– ORIGIN Latin *plumbum* 'lead'.

plumb² verb (**plumb something in**) Brit. install a bath, washing machine, etc. and connect it to water and drainage pipes.
– ORIGIN from **PLUMBER**.

plumbago /plum-**bay**-goh/ noun (pl. **plumbagos**) an evergreen shrub or climber with grey or blue flowers.
– ORIGIN from Latin *plumbum* 'lead'.

plumber noun a person who fits and repairs the pipes and fittings of water supply, sanitation, or heating systems.
– ORIGIN Old French *plommier* 'person working with lead'.

plumbing noun **1** the system of pipes, tanks, and fittings required for the water supply, heating, and sanitation in a building. **2** the occupation of a plumber.

plumb line noun a line with a heavy weight attached to it, used to find the depth of water or to check that something is vertical.

plum duff noun dated a plum pudding.

plume noun **1** a long, soft feather or arrangement of feathers. **2** a long spreading cloud of smoke or vapour. •**verb 1** (as adj. **plumed**) decorated with feathers. **2** (of smoke or vapour) spread out in a plume.
– ORIGIN Latin *pluma* 'down'.

plummet verb (**plummets, plummeting, plummeted**) **1** fall or drop straight down at high speed. **2** decrease rapidly in value or amount: *foreign sales have plummeted*. •**noun 1** a steep and rapid fall or drop. **2** a plumb line or weight.
– ORIGIN from Old French *plommet* 'small sounding lead'.

plummy adjective (**plummier, plummiest**) **1** resembling a plum. **2** Brit. informal (of a person's voice) typical of the English upper classes. **3** Brit. informal highly desirable.

plump¹ adjective **1** rather fat. **2** full and rounded in shape. •**verb** (**plump something up**) make a cushion or pillow full and rounded.
– DERIVATIVES **plumpish** adjective **plumpness** noun.
– ORIGIN related to Dutch *plomp*, German *plump* 'blunt, obtuse'.

plump² verb **1** set or sit down heavily and suddenly. **2** (**plump for**) make a definite choice: *offered drinks, he plumped for brandy*. •**adverb** informal with a sudden or heavy fall.
– ORIGIN uncertain.

plum pudding noun a rich suet pudding containing raisins, currants, and spices.

plum tomato noun a plum-shaped variety of tomato.

plumy adjective resembling or decorated with feathers.

plunder verb steal goods from a place by force, especially during war or rioting. •**noun 1** goods obtained illegally and by force. **2** the forcible theft of goods.
– DERIVATIVES **plunderer** noun.
– ORIGIN German *plündern*, 'rob of household goods'.

plunge verb **1** fall or move suddenly and uncontrollably. **2** jump or dive quickly and

energetically. **3** (**plunge in**) begin a course of action without much thought. **4** (**be plunged into**) suddenly be brought into a specified condition or state: *the area was plunged into darkness*. **5** push or thrust something quickly. •**noun 1** an act of plunging. **2** a sudden and marked fall in value or amount: *a 75% plunge in profits*.
– PHRASES **take the plunge** informal decide on a course of action which one feels nervous about.
– ORIGIN Old French *plungier* 'thrust down'.

plunge pool noun **1** a small, deep swimming pool. **2** a deep basin at the foot of a waterfall formed by the action of the falling water.

plunger noun **1** a part of a device that can be pushed down. **2** a rubber cup on a long handle, used to clear blocked pipes by means of suction.

plunk informal verb play a keyboard or pluck a stringed instrument in a heavy-handed way. •**noun** the sound of a stringed instrument being plucked.
– ORIGIN probably imitating the sound.

pluperfect adjective Grammar (of a tense) referring to an action completed before a past point of time, formed in English by *had* and the past participle (as in *he had gone by then*).
– ORIGIN from Latin *plus quam perfectum* 'more than perfect'.

plural adjective **1** more than one in number. **2** Grammar (of a word or form) referring to more than one. **3** containing diverse elements: *a plural society*. •**noun** Grammar a plural word or form.
– DERIVATIVES **plurally** adverb.
– ORIGIN Latin *pluralis*.

pluralism noun **1** a political system of power-sharing among a number of political parties. **2** the existence or toleration in society of a number of different ethnic groups, cultures, and beliefs. **3** the holding of more than one ecclesiastical office or position at the same time by one person.
– DERIVATIVES **pluralist** noun & adjective **pluralistic** adjective.

plurality noun (pl. **pluralities**) **1** the state of being plural or more than one. **2** a large number of people or things.

pluralize (or **pluralise**) verb **1** make something more numerous. **2** give a plural form to a word.
– DERIVATIVES **pluralization** noun.

plus preposition **1** with the addition of. **2** informal together with. •**adjective 1** (after a number or amount) at least: *companies put losses at $500,000 plus*. **2** (after a grade) rather better than: *B plus*. **3** (before a number) above zero: *plus 60 degrees centigrade*. **4** having a positive electric charge. •**noun 1** (also **plus sign**) the symbol +, indicating addition or a positive value. **2** informal an advantage. •**conjunction** informal furthermore; also.
– ORIGIN Latin, 'more'.

plus ça change /ploo sa shonzh/ exclamation used to acknowledge that certain things remain essentially unchanged.
– ORIGIN from French *plus ça change, plus c'est la même chose* 'the more it changes, the more it stays the same'.

p

plus fours plural noun men's short baggy trousers that fit closely below the knee, formerly worn for hunting and golf.
- ORIGIN so named because the overhang at the knee added four inches of material.

plush noun a rich fabric of silk, cotton, or wool, with a long, soft nap. •adjective informal expensively luxurious.
- DERIVATIVES **plushy** adjective.
- ORIGIN former French *pluche*.

plus-size adjective N. Amer. (of a woman or women's clothing) of a larger size than normal; outsize.

Pluto noun the most remote known planet of the solar system, ninth in order from the sun.
- DERIVATIVES **Plutonian** adjective.

plutocracy /ploo-**tok**-ruh-si/ noun (pl. **plutocracies**) **1** government by wealthy people. **2** a society governed by wealthy people. **3** a ruling class whose power is based on their wealth.
- DERIVATIVES **plutocratic** adjective.
- ORIGIN from Greek *ploutos* 'wealth' + *kratos* 'strength, authority'.

plutocrat noun often derogatory a person who is powerful because they are wealthy.

plutonic adjective (of igneous rock) formed by solidification at considerable depth beneath the earth's surface.

plutonium noun a radioactive metallic element used as a fuel in nuclear reactors and as an explosive in atomic weapons.
- ORIGIN from **Pluto**.

pluvial adjective technical relating to rainfall.
- ORIGIN Latin *pluvialis*.

ply¹ noun (pl. **plies**) **1** a thickness or layer of a folded or laminated material. **2** each of a number of multiple layers or strands of which something is made.
- ORIGIN French *pli* 'fold'.

ply² verb (**plies**, **plying**, **plied**) **1** work steadily with a tool or at one's job. **2** (of a ship or vehicle) travel regularly over a route. **3** (**ply someone with**) provide someone with food or drink in a continuous way. **4** (**ply someone with**) repeatedly ask someone questions.
- ORIGIN shortening of **APPLY**.

plywood noun thin strong board consisting of two or more layers of wood glued together.

PM abbreviation **1** post-mortem. **2** Prime Minister.

Pm symbol the chemical element promethium.

p.m. abbreviation after noon.
- ORIGIN from Latin *post meridiem*.

PMS abbreviation premenstrual syndrome.

PMT abbreviation chiefly Brit. premenstrual tension.

pneumatic /nyoo-**mat**-ik/ adjective containing or operated by air or gas under pressure: *a pneumatic drill.*
- DERIVATIVES **pneumatically** adverb.
- ORIGIN Greek *pneumatikos*.

pneumatics plural noun (treated as sing.) the science of the mechanical properties of gases.

pneumococcus /nyoo-muh-**kok**-kuhss/ noun (pl. **pneumococci** /nyoo-muh-**kok**-ky/) a bacterium associated with pneumonia and some forms of meningitis.
- DERIVATIVES **pneumococcal** adjective.

pneumonia /nyoo-**moh**-ni-uh/ noun an infection causing inflammation of one or both lungs.
- DERIVATIVES **pneumonic** adjective.
- ORIGIN from Greek *pneumōn* 'lung'.

PNG abbreviation Papua New Guinea.

PO abbreviation **1** postal order. **2** Post Office.

Po symbol the chemical element polonium.

poach¹ verb cook food by simmering it in a small amount of liquid.
- ORIGIN Old French *pochier* 'poach, enclose in a bag'.

poach² verb **1** take game or fish illegally from private or protected areas. **2** take or obtain in an unfair or underhand way: *they tried to poach passengers by offering better seats.*
- ORIGIN probably related to **POKE**¹.

poacher¹ noun a pan for poaching eggs or other food.

poacher² noun a person who poaches game or fish.

PO box noun short for **POST OFFICE BOX**.

pochard /**poh**-cherd, **po**-cherd/ noun a diving duck, the male of which has a reddish-brown head.
- ORIGIN unknown.

pock noun a pockmark.
- DERIVATIVES **pocked** adjective.
- ORIGIN Old English.

pocket noun **1** a small bag sewn into or on clothing, used for carrying small articles. **2** a small group or area that is set apart or different from its surroundings: *a patchwork of prairie interspersed with pockets of poverty.* **3** informal a person's financial resources: *gifts to suit every pocket.* **4** a pouch-like storage compartment in a suitcase, car door, etc. **5** (in billiards and snooker) an opening at the corner or on the side of a billiard table into which balls are struck. •adjective of a suitable size for carrying in a pocket. •verb (**pockets**, **pocketing**, **pocketed**) **1** put something into one's pocket. **2** take something belonging to someone else. **3** earn or win money: *he pocketed $4m for a few months' work.* **4** Billiards & Snooker drive a ball into a pocket.
- PHRASES **in someone's pocket** dependent on someone financially and therefore under their influence. **out of** (or **in**) **pocket** having lost (or gained) money.
- DERIVATIVES **pocketable** adjective.
- ORIGIN Old French *pokete* 'little bag'.

pocketbook noun **1** Brit. a notebook. **2** US a wallet, purse, or handbag.

pocket borough noun (in the UK, before the 1832 Reform Act) a borough in which the election of political representatives was controlled by one person or family.

pocketknife noun (pl. **pocketknives**) a penknife.

pocket money noun Brit. **1** a small sum of money given regularly to a child by their parents. **2** a small amount of money for minor expenses.

pocket watch noun a watch on a chain, intended to be carried in a jacket or waistcoat pocket.

pockmark noun **1** a hollow scar or mark on the skin left by a pustule or spot. **2** a hollow mark on a surface. •verb cover something with hollow scars or marks.

P

pod¹ noun 1 a long seed-case of a pea, bean, or related plant. **2** a self-contained or detachable unit on an aircraft or spacecraft. • **verb (pods, podding, podded) 1** remove peas or beans from their pods before cooking. **2** (of a plant) form pods.
– ORIGIN unknown.

pod² noun a small group of whales or similar sea mammals.
– ORIGIN unknown.

podcast noun a digital recording of a radio broadcast or similar programme, made available on the Internet for downloading to a personal computer or audio player.
– DERIVATIVES **podcasting** noun.
– ORIGIN from *iPod*, a proprietary name for a personal audio player.

podgy adjective (podgier, podgiest) Brit. informal rather fat; chubby.
– ORIGIN unknown.

podiatry /puh-**dy**-uh-tri/ **noun** chiropody.
– DERIVATIVES **podiatrist** noun.
– ORIGIN from Greek *pous* 'foot' + *iatros* 'physician'.

podium /poh-di-uhm/ **noun** (pl. **podiums** or **podia** /poh-di-uh/) a small platform on which a person stands when giving a speech or conducting an orchestra.
– ORIGIN Greek *podion* 'little foot'.

poem noun a piece of imaginative writing arranged in a particular rhythm and also often in rhyme.
– ORIGIN Greek *poiēma* 'fiction, poem'.

poesy /poh-i-zi/ **noun** old use or literary poetry.
– ORIGIN Greek *poēsis, poiēsis* 'making, poetry'.

poet noun 1 a person who writes poems. **2** a person possessing special powers of imagination or expression.
– DERIVATIVES **poetess** noun.

poetaster /poh-i-**tass**-ter/ **noun** a person who writes very bad poetry.

poetic (also **poetical**) **adjective** relating to or resembling poetry.
– DERIVATIVES **poetically** adverb.

poeticize (or **poeticise**) **verb 1** make something poetic. **2** write or speak poetically.
– DERIVATIVES **poeticism** noun.

poetic justice noun suitable or deserved punishment or reward.

poetic licence noun freedom to depart from the facts of a matter or from the accepted rules of language for artistic effect.

poetics plural noun (treated as sing.) the study of linguistic techniques in poetry and literature.

Poet Laureate noun (pl. **Poets Laureate**) a poet appointed as a member of the British royal household, formerly responsible for writing poems for state occasions.

poetry noun 1 poems as a whole or as a form of literature. **2** a quality of beauty or emotional intensity: *vocals that are poetry in motion.*

po-faced adjective Brit. humourless and disapproving.
– ORIGIN perhaps from *po* 'chamber pot', influenced by *poker-faced*.

pogo verb (pogoes, pogoing, pogoed) informal jump up and down as if on a pogo stick as a form of dancing to rock music.

pogo stick noun a toy for bouncing around on, consisting of a spring-loaded pole with a handle at the top and a bar to stand on near the bottom.

pogrom /**pog**-rom/ **noun** an organized massacre of an ethnic group, originally that of Jews in Russia or eastern Europe.
– ORIGIN Russian, 'devastation'.

poignant /**poy**-nyuhnt/ **adjective** arousing a feeling of sadness or regret: *a poignant moment's silence for the dead footballer.*
– DERIVATIVES **poignancy** noun **poignantly** adverb.
– ORIGIN from Old French *poindre* 'to prick'.

poinsettia /poyn-**set**-ti-uh/ **noun** a small shrub with large showy scarlet modified leaves (bracts) surrounding the small yellow flowers.
– ORIGIN named after the American diplomat and botanist Joel R. *Poinsett*.

point noun 1 the tapered, sharp end of a tool, weapon, or other object. **2** a particular place or moment: *at one point a shouting match broke out.* **3** an item, detail, or idea in a discussion, written work, etc. **4** (**the point**) the most important or relevant part of what is being discussed. **5** the advantage or purpose of something: *what's the point of it all?* **6** a particular feature or quality: *the building has its good points.* **7** a unit of scoring or of measuring value, achievement, or extent. **8** a full stop or a decimal point. **9** a very small dot or mark on a surface. **10** (in geometry) something having position but not spatial extent, magnitude, dimension, or direction. **11** each of thirty-two directions marked at equal distances round a compass. **12** a narrow piece of land jutting out into the sea. **13** (**points**) Brit. a junction of two railway lines, with a pair of linked rails that can be moved sideways to allow a train to pass from one line to the other. **14** Printing a unit of measurement for type sizes and spacing (in the UK and US 0.351 mm, in Europe 0.376 mm). **15** Brit. an electrical socket. **16** (**points**) a set of electrical contacts in the distributor of a motor vehicle. **17** Cricket a fielding position on the off side near the batsman. • **verb 1** direct someone's attention in a particular direction by extending one's finger. **2** direct or aim something. **3** face in or indicate a particular direction: *a sign pointing left.* **4** (**point something out**) make someone aware of something. **5** (**point to**) indicate that something is likely to happen: *everything pointed to an enemy attack.* **6** (**point something up**) reveal the true nature or importance of something. **7** give a sharp point to something. **8** fill in the joints of brickwork or tiling with mortar or cement.
– PHRASES **a case in point** an example that illustrates what is being discussed. **make a point of** make a special effort to do something. **on the point of** on the verge of. **take someone's point** chiefly Brit. accept that what someone is saying is valid. **up to a point** to some extent.
– ORIGIN from Old French *pointe* or *point*.

point-blank adjective & adverb 1 (of a shot or missile) fired from very close to its target. **2** in a blunt way, without explanation.

point duty noun Brit. the duties of a police officer stationed at a junction to control traffic.

pointed adjective 1 having a sharpened or tapered tip or end. **2** (of a remark or look)

directed towards a particular person and expressing a clear message.
– DERIVATIVES **pointedly** adverb.

pointer noun **1** a long, thin piece of metal on a scale or dial which moves to give a reading. **2** a rod used for pointing to features on a map or chart. **3** a hint or tip. **4** a breed of dog that on scenting game stands rigid looking towards it. **5** Computing a cursor or a link.

pointillism /pwan-ti-li-z'm/ noun a technique of neo-Impressionist painting using tiny dots of various pure colours, which become blended in the viewer's eye.
– DERIVATIVES **pointillist** noun & adjective.
– ORIGIN from French *pointiller* 'mark with dots'.

pointing noun mortar or cement used to fill the joints of brickwork or tiling.

pointless adjective having little or no sense or purpose.
– DERIVATIVES **pointlessly** adverb **pointlessness** noun.

point of order noun (pl. **points of order**) a query in a formal debate or meeting as to whether correct procedure is being followed.

point of view noun (pl. **points of view**) **1** a particular attitude or opinion. **2** the position from which something or someone is observed.

point-to-point noun (pl. **point-to-points**) Brit. an amateur cross-country steeplechase for horses used in hunting.

pointy adjective (**pointier, pointiest**) informal having a pointed tip or end.

poise noun **1** a graceful and elegant way of holding the body. **2** calmness and confidence: *he had a moment to think, to recover his poise.* •verb **1** be or cause to be balanced or suspended: *the world was poised between peace and war.* **2** (**be poised to do**) be ready and prepared to do something. **3** (as adj. **poised**) calm and elegant or confident.
– ORIGIN Old French *pois*.

poisha /poy-shuh/ noun (pl. same) a unit of money of Bangladesh, equal to one hundredth of a taka.
– ORIGIN Bengali.

poison noun **1** a substance that causes death or injury when swallowed or absorbed by a living organism. **2** a destructive influence: *the poison of fear.* •verb **1** harm or kill a person or animal with poison. **2** contaminate something with poison. **3** have a destructive or harmful effect on: *the bad professors who poisoned the minds of a generation.*
– DERIVATIVES **poisoner** noun.
– ORIGIN Old French, 'magic potion'.

poisoned chalice noun something offered which seems attractive but which is likely to cause problems to the person receiving it.

poison ivy noun a North American climbing plant which produces an irritant oil in its leaves.

poisonous adjective **1** (of an animal) producing poison. **2** (of a plant or substance) causing or capable of causing death or illness if taken into the body. **3** very unpleasant or spiteful.
– DERIVATIVES **poisonously** adverb.

poison pen letter noun an anonymous letter that is spiteful or abusive.

poison pill noun a tactic used by a company threatened with an unwelcome takeover bid to make itself unattractive to the bidder.

poke¹ verb **1** prod someone or something with a finger or a sharp object. **2** make a hole by jabbing or prodding. **3** (**poke about/around**) look or search around . **4** push or stick out: *she poked her tongue out at him.* •noun an act of poking.
– PHRASES **poke fun at** tease or make fun of. **poke one's nose into** informal take an unwelcome interest in.
– ORIGIN uncertain.

poke² noun chiefly Scottish a bag or small sack.
– ORIGIN Old French *poche* 'pocket'.

poke bonnet noun a woman's bonnet with a projecting brim, popular in the early 19th century.

poker¹ noun a metal rod with a handle, used for prodding and stirring an open fire.

poker² noun a card game in which the players bet on the value of the hands dealt to them, sometimes using bluff.
– ORIGIN perhaps related to German *pochen* 'to brag', *Pochspiel* 'bragging game'.

poker face noun an emotionless expression that hides one's true feelings.

pokerwork noun Brit. the art of decorating wood or leather by burning a design on the surface with a heated metallic point.

poky (also **pokey**) adjective (**pokier, pokiest**) (of a room or building) uncomfortably small and cramped.
– ORIGIN from **POKE**¹ (in the former sense 'confine').

polar adjective **1** relating to the North or South Poles of the earth or the areas around them. **2** having an electrical or magnetic field. **3** completely opposite in type.

polar bear noun a large white arctic bear which lives mainly on the pack ice.

polarity noun (pl. **polarities**) **1** the state of having poles or opposites. **2** the direction of a magnetic or electric field.

polarize (or **polarise**) verb **1** divide into two groups with sharply contrasting opinions: *the nation's media are polarized in the controversy.* **2** Physics restrict the vibrations of a transverse wave, especially light, to one direction. **3** give magnetic or electric polarity to something.
– DERIVATIVES **polarization** noun.

Polaroid noun trademark **1** a composite material that polarizes the light passing through it, produced in thin plastic sheets and used in sunglasses. **2** a type of camera that produces a finished print rapidly after each exposure. **3** a photograph taken with a Polaroid camera.

polder /pohl-der/ noun an area reclaimed from the sea or a river, especially in the Netherlands.
– ORIGIN Dutch.

Pole noun a person from Poland.

pole¹ noun **1** a long, thin rounded piece of wood or metal, used as a support. **2** Brit. historical another term for **PERCH**³. •verb move a boat along with a pole.
– PHRASES **up the pole** Brit. informal mad.
– ORIGIN Old English.

pole² noun **1** either of the two locations (**North Pole** or **South Pole**) at opposite ends of the

earth's axis. **2** each of two opposing qualities or ideas: *these discs represent the opposite poles of rave culture.* **3** each of the two opposite points of a magnet at which magnetic forces are strongest. **4** the positive or negative terminal of an electric cell or battery.
– PHRASES **be poles apart** have nothing in common.
– ORIGIN Greek *polos* 'pivot, axis, sky'.

poleaxe (US also **poleax**) verb **1** knock down or stun someone with a heavy blow. **2** shock someone greatly: *she was poleaxed by the news.* • noun **1** a battleaxe. **2** a butcher's axe used to slaughter animals.
– ORIGIN from **POLL + AXE.**

polecat noun **1** a weasel-like mammal with dark brown fur and an unpleasant smell. **2** N. Amer. a skunk.
– ORIGIN perhaps from Old French *pole* 'chicken' + **CAT.**

pole dancing noun erotic dancing which involves swinging around a fixed pole.
– DERIVATIVES **pole dancer** noun.

polemic /puh-**lem**-ik/ noun **1** a strong verbal or written attack: *a polemic against liberalism.* **2** (also **polemics**) the practice of engaging in fierce discussion. • adjective (also **polemical**) relating to fierce discussion.
– DERIVATIVES **polemicist** noun **polemicize** (or **polemicise**) verb.
– ORIGIN Greek *polemos* 'war'.

polenta /puh-**len**-tuh/ noun (in Italian cookery) maize flour or a dough made from this, which is boiled and then fried or baked.
– ORIGIN Latin, 'pearl barley'.

pole position noun the most favourable position at the start of a motor race.
– ORIGIN from the use of *pole* in horse racing to mean the starting position next to the inside boundary fence.

Pole Star noun a fairly bright star located in the part of the sky above the North Pole.

pole vault noun an athletic event in which competitors attempt to vault over a high bar with the aid of a long flexible pole.

police noun (treated as pl.) **1** an official state organization responsible for preventing and solving crime and maintaining public order. **2** the members of a police force. • verb **1** maintain law and order in an area. **2** ensure that a law, rule, agreement, etc. is obeyed.
– ORIGIN Latin *politia* 'policy, government'.

policeman (or **policewoman**) noun (pl. **policemen** or **policewomen**) a member of a police force.

police officer noun a policeman or policewoman.

police state noun a state in which the police are required by the government to keep secret watch over and control citizens' activities.

police station noun a building housing a local police force.

policy[1] noun (pl. **policies**) **1** a course of action adopted or proposed by a political party, business, or other organization. **2** a principle that influences one's behaviour: *his was a policy of live and let live.*
– ORIGIN Greek *politeia* 'citizenship'.

policy[2] noun (pl. **policies**) a contract of insurance.

– DERIVATIVES **policyholder** noun.
– ORIGIN French *police* 'bill of lading, contract of insurance'.

polio noun short for **POLIOMYELITIS.**

poliomyelitis /poh-li-oh-my-uh-**ly**-tiss/ noun an infectious disease that affects the central nervous system and can cause temporary or permanent paralysis.
– ORIGIN from Greek *polios* 'grey' + *muelos* 'marrow'.

Polish /**poh**-lish/ noun the language of Poland. • adjective relating to Poland.

polish /**po**-lish/ verb **1** make the surface of something smooth and shiny by rubbing. **2** improve or refine: *she's got to polish up her French for the job.* **3** (**polish something off**) finish or consume something quickly. • noun **1** a substance rubbed on something to make it smooth and shiny. **2** an act of polishing something. **3** smoothness or glossiness produced by polishing. **4** the quality of being skilful, elegant, or refined: *she has the confidence and polish of a veteran gymnast.*
– DERIVATIVES **polisher** noun.
– ORIGIN Latin *polire.*

politburo /**pol**-it-byuu-roh/ noun (pl. **politburos**) the chief policy-making committee of a communist party, especially that of the former Soviet Union.
– ORIGIN from Russian *politicheskoe byuro* 'political bureau'.

polite adjective (**politer**, **politest**) **1** respectful and considerate towards other people; courteous. **2** cultured or well bred: *polite society.*
– DERIVATIVES **politely** adverb **politeness** noun.
– ORIGIN Latin *politus* 'polished, made smooth'.

politesse /po-li-**tess**/ noun formal politeness.
– ORIGIN French.

politic adjective **1** (of an action) sensible and wise in the circumstances. **2** (also **politick**) old use (of a person) prudent and shrewd. • verb (**politics**, **politicking**, **politicked**) (usu. as noun **politicking**) often derogatory take part in political activity.
– ORIGIN Greek *politikos.*

political adjective **1** relating to the government or public affairs of a country. **2** related to or interested in politics. **3** chiefly derogatory concerned with power or status within an organization rather than matters of principle: *snooker is paying the price for years of political infighting.*
– DERIVATIVES **politically** adverb.

political correctness noun the avoidance of language or behaviour considered to be discriminatory or offensive to certain groups of people.

politically correct (or **incorrect**) adjective showing (or failing to show) political correctness.

political prisoner noun a person imprisoned for their political beliefs or actions.

political science noun the study of political activity and behaviour.

politician noun a person who is involved in politics as a job, as either a holder of or a candidate for an elected office.

politicize (or **politicise**) verb **1** make someone politically aware; involve someone in politics.

p

2 make an issue or activity political in nature.
– DERIVATIVES **politicization** noun.

politick adjective old-fashioned spelling of POLITIC.

politico noun (pl. **politicos**) informal, chiefly derogatory a politician.
– ORIGIN Spanish and Italian, 'politic' or 'political person'.

politics plural noun (usu. treated as sing.) **1** the activities associated with governing a country or area, and with the political relations between states. **2** the political beliefs of a person or organization. **3** activities aimed at gaining power within an organization: *office politics*. **4** the principles relating to or underlying a sphere or activity, especially when concerned with power and status.

polity noun (pl. **polities**) **1** a particular form of government. **2** a state as having a distinct political existence.
– ORIGIN Greek *politeia* 'citizenship, government'.

polka /pol-kuh/ noun a lively dance for couples in duple time.
– ORIGIN Czech *půlka* 'half-step'.

polka dot noun each of a number of round dots repeated to form a regular pattern.

poll /rhymes with pole or doll/ noun **1** the process of voting in an election. **2** a record of the number of votes cast. **3** dialect a person's head. •verb **1** record the opinion or vote of a number of people. **2** (of a candidate in an election) receive a specified number of votes. **3** Telecommunications & Computing check the status of a device, especially as part of a repeated cycle. **4** cut the horns off a young cow.
– ORIGIN perhaps from German.

pollack /pol-luhk/ (also **pollock**) noun (pl. same or **pollacks**) an edible greenish-brown fish of the cod family.
– ORIGIN perhaps from Celtic.

pollard /pol-lerd/ verb cut off the top and branches of a tree to encourage new growth. •noun a pollarded tree.
– ORIGIN from POLL.

pollen noun a powdery substance produced by the male part of a flower, containing the fertilizing agent.
– ORIGIN Latin, 'fine powder'.

pollen count noun a measure of the amount of pollen in the air.

pollinate verb carry pollen to a flower or plant and so fertilize it.
– DERIVATIVES **pollination** noun **pollinator** noun.

pollock noun variant spelling of POLLACK.

pollster /pohl-ster/ noun a person who carries out or analyses opinion polls.

poll tax noun a tax paid at the same rate by every adult, regardless of their income or resources.

pollutant noun a substance that creates unpleasant or harmful effects in the air, soil, or water.

pollute verb **1** add harmful or unpleasant substances to soil, air, or water. **2** spoil or harm: *a society polluted by racism*.
– DERIVATIVES **polluter** noun.
– ORIGIN Latin *polluere*.

pollution noun the presence in the air, soil, or water of a substance with unpleasant or harmful effects.

Pollyanna noun an excessively cheerful or optimistic person.
– ORIGIN the name of the optimistic heroine created by the American author Eleanor H. Porter.

polo noun a game similar to hockey, played on horseback with a long-handled mallet.
– ORIGIN from a word in a Tibetan language meaning 'ball'.

polonaise /pol-uh-nayz/ noun a slow stately dance of Polish origin in triple time. •adjective (of a dish) garnished with chopped hard-boiled egg yolk, breadcrumbs, and parsley.
– ORIGIN from French, 'Polish'.

polo neck noun Brit. a high, close-fitting turned-over collar on a sweater.

polonium /puh-loh-ni-uhm/ noun a rare radioactive metallic element.
– ORIGIN from Latin *Polonia* 'Poland' (the native country of Marie Curie, the element's co-discoverer).

polo shirt noun a casual short-sleeved shirt with a collar and two or three buttons at the neck.

poltergeist /pol-ter-gyst/ noun a supernatural being supposedly responsible for throwing objects about.
– ORIGIN from German *poltern* 'create a disturbance' + *Geist* 'ghost'.

poltroon /pol-troon/ noun old use a coward.
– ORIGIN Italian *poltrone*.

poly noun (pl. **polys**) informal **1** polythene. **2** Brit. historical a polytechnic.

poly- combining form many; much: *polychrome*.
– ORIGIN from Greek *polus* 'much', *polloi* 'many'.

polyamide /po-li-ay-myd, po-li-a-myd/ noun a polymer of a type that includes many synthetic fibres such as nylon.

polyandry /po-li-an-dri/ noun the practice of having more than one husband at the same time.
– DERIVATIVES **polyandrous** adjective.
– ORIGIN from Greek *anēr* 'male'.

polyanthus /po-li-an-thuss/ noun (pl. same) a flowering garden plant that is a hybrid from the wild primrose.
– ORIGIN from Greek *anthos* 'flower'.

polycarbonate noun a synthetic resin of a type that includes many moulding materials and films.

polychromatic adjective having several colours; multicoloured.

polychrome adjective painted, printed, or decorated in several colours. •noun varied colouring.
– DERIVATIVES **polychromy** noun.
– ORIGIN from Greek *khrōma* 'colour'.

polycotton noun fabric made from a mixture of cotton and polyester fibre.

polyester noun a synthetic resin of a type that is used chiefly to make textile fibres.

polyethylene /po-li-eth-i-leen/ noun another term for POLYTHENE.

polygamy /puh-lig-uh-mi/ noun the practice of having more than one wife or husband at the same time.

- DERIVATIVES **polygamist** noun **polygamous** adjective.
- ORIGIN from Greek *polugamos* 'often marrying'.

polyglot /**po**-li-glot/ adjective knowing, using, or written in several languages. • noun a person who knows or uses several languages.
- ORIGIN Greek *poluglōttos* 'many-tongued'.

polygon /**po**-li-guhn/ noun a plane figure with three or more straight sides and angles.
- DERIVATIVES **polygonal** /puh-**li**-guh-n'l/ adjective.

polygraph noun a machine which records changes in a person's physiological characteristics, such as pulse and breathing rates, used especially as a lie detector.

polygyny /puh-**li**-ji-ni/ noun the practice of having more than one wife at the same time.
- DERIVATIVES **polygynous** /puh-**li**-ji-nuhss/ adjective.
- ORIGIN from Greek *gunē* 'woman'.

polyhedron /po-li-**hee**-druhn/ noun (pl. **polyhedra** /po-li-**hee**-druh/ or **polyhedrons**) a solid figure with many plane faces, typically more than six.
- DERIVATIVES **polyhedral** adjective.

polymath /**po**-li-math/ noun a person with a wide knowledge of many different subjects.
- DERIVATIVES **polymathic** adjective.
- ORIGIN from Greek *polumathēs* 'having learned much'.

polymer /**po**-li-mer/ noun a substance with a molecular structure formed from many identical small molecules bonded together.
- DERIVATIVES **polymeric** adjective.
- ORIGIN from Greek *polumeros* 'having many parts'.

polymerase /po-li-muh-rayz, po-li-**lim**-uh-rayz/ noun an enzyme which brings about the formation of a particular polymer, especially DNA or RNA.

polymerize (or **polymerise**) verb combine or cause to combine to form a polymer.
- DERIVATIVES **polymerization** noun.

polymorphism noun the occurrence of something in several different forms.
- DERIVATIVES **polymorphic** adjective **polymorphous** adjective.

Polynesian noun **1** a person from Polynesia, a large group of Pacific islands including New Zealand, Hawaii, and Samoa. **2** a group of languages spoken in Polynesia. • adjective relating to Polynesia.

polynomial /po-li-**noh**-mi-uhl/ noun Mathematics an expression consisting of several terms, especially terms containing different powers of the same variable.
- ORIGIN from POLY-, on the pattern of *binomial*.

polyp /**po**-lip/ noun **1** a simple sea creature which remains fixed in the same place, such as coral. **2** Medicine a small growth protruding from a mucous membrane.
- ORIGIN Greek *polupous* 'cuttlefish, polyp'.

polypeptide noun a peptide consisting of many amino acids bonded together in a chain, e.g. in a protein.

polyphonic adjective **1** having many sounds or voices. **2** (especially of vocal music) in two or more parts each having a melody of its own.

- ORIGIN from Greek *phōnē* 'voice, sound'.

polyphony /puh-**li**-fuh-ni/ noun (pl. **polyphonies**) the combination in harmony of a number of musical parts, each forming an individual melody.

polyploid /**po**-li-ployd/ adjective (of a cell or nucleus) containing more than two matching sets of chromosomes.

polypropylene /po-li-**proh**-pi-leen/ noun a synthetic resin which is a polymer of propylene.

polyptych /**po**-lip-tik/ noun a painting, especially an altarpiece, consisting of more than three panels joined by hinges or folds.
- ORIGIN from Greek *poluptukhos* 'having many folds'.

polyrhythm noun Music the use of two or more different rhythms simultaneously.
- DERIVATIVES **polyrhythmic** adjective.

polysaccharide /po-li-**sak**-uh-ryd/ noun a carbohydrate (e.g. starch or cellulose) whose molecules consist of long chains of monosaccharide units.

polystyrene /po-li-**sty**-reen/ noun a light synthetic material used especially as packaging.
- ORIGIN blend of POLYMER + STYRENE.

polysyllabic adjective having more than one syllable.

polytechnic noun a college offering courses at degree level or below (little used after 1992, when British polytechnics became able to call themselves 'universities').

polytheism /**po**-li-thee-i-z'm/ noun the belief in or worship of more than one god.
- DERIVATIVES **polytheist** noun **polytheistic** adjective.
- ORIGIN from Greek *polutheos* 'of many gods'.

polythene noun Brit. a tough, light, flexible plastic, chiefly used for packaging.
- ORIGIN shortened form of *polyethylene*.

polytunnel noun a long polythene-covered frame under which plants are grown outdoors.

polyunsaturated adjective referring to fats whose molecules contain several double or triple bonds, believed to be less healthy in the diet than monounsaturated fats.
- DERIVATIVES **polyunsaturates** plural noun.

polyurethane /po-li-**yoor**-i-thayn/ noun a synthetic resin used in paints and varnishes.
- ORIGIN blend of POLYMER + URETHANE.

polyvalent /po-li-**vay**-luhnt/ adjective having many different functions, forms, or aspects.

polyvinyl chloride noun full form of **PVC**.

Pom noun short for POMMY.

pomade /puh-**mayd**, puh-**mahd**/ noun a scented oil or cream for making the hair smooth and glossy.
- DERIVATIVES **pomaded** adjective.
- ORIGIN French *pommade*.

pomander /puh-**man**-der, **pom**-uhn-der/ noun a ball or perforated container of mixed sweet-smelling substances used to perfume a room or cupboard.
- ORIGIN from Latin *pomum de ambra* 'apple of ambergris'.

pomegranate /**pom**-i-gran-it/ noun a round tropical fruit with a tough golden-orange skin and sweet red flesh containing many seeds.

– ORIGIN from Latin *pomum granatum* 'apple having many seeds'.

pomelo /pom-uh-loh/ noun (pl. **pomelos**) a large citrus fruit similar to a grapefruit, with a thick yellow skin and bitter pulp.
– ORIGIN unknown.

Pomeranian noun a small breed of dog with long silky hair and a pointed muzzle.
– ORIGIN from *Pomerania*, a region of central Europe.

pommel /pom-m'l/ noun 1 the upward curving or projecting front part of a saddle. 2 a rounded knob on the end of the handle of a sword, dagger, or old-fashioned gun.
– ORIGIN Old French *pomel.*

pommes frites /pom freet/ plural noun very thin chips.
– ORIGIN French.

Pommy (also **Pommie**) noun (pl. **Pommies**) Austral./NZ informal, chiefly derogatory a British person.
– ORIGIN said by some to be short for *pomegranate*, as a near rhyme to *immigrant.*

pomp noun 1 the impressive clothes, music, and traditions that are part of a grand public ceremony. 2 (also **pomps**) old use a showy display of something, intended to impress other people.
– ORIGIN Greek *pompē* 'procession'.

pompadour /pom-puh-dor/ noun a woman's hairstyle in which the hair is turned back off the forehead in a roll.
– ORIGIN named after Madame de *Pompadour*, the mistress of Louis XV of France.

pompom (also **pompon**) noun 1 a small woollen ball attached to a garment for decoration. 2 a dahlia, chrysanthemum, or aster with small tightly clustered petals.
– ORIGIN French *pompon* 'tuft, topknot'.

pom-pom noun Brit. an automatic quick-firing cannon of the Second World War period.
– ORIGIN imitating the sound of the discharge.

pompous adjective affectedly solemn or self-important.
– DERIVATIVES **pomposity** noun **pompously** adverb.

ponce Brit. informal noun 1 a man who lives off a prostitute's earnings. 2 derogatory an effeminate man. • verb (**ponce about/around**) behave in a way that wastes time or looks affected or foolish.
– DERIVATIVES **poncey** (also **poncy**) adjective.
– ORIGIN perhaps from **POUNCE**[1].

poncho noun (pl. **ponchos**) a garment made of a large piece of woollen cloth with a slit in the middle for the head.
– ORIGIN Latin American Spanish.

pond noun 1 a fairly small area of still water. 2 (**the pond**) humorous the Atlantic Ocean.
– ORIGIN alteration of **POUND**[3].

ponder verb consider something carefully.
– ORIGIN Latin *ponderare* 'weigh'.

ponderable adjective literary worthy of consideration; thought-provoking.

ponderosa /pon-duh-roh-zuh, pon-duh-roh-suh/ (also **ponderosa pine**) noun a tall North American pine tree, grown for its wood and as an ornamental.
– ORIGIN feminine of Latin *ponderosus* 'massive'.

ponderous adjective 1 slow and clumsy because of great weight. 2 tediously solemn or long-winded: *the play's ponderous dialogue.*
– DERIVATIVES **ponderously** adverb.
– ORIGIN Latin *ponderosus.*

pondweed noun a plant that grows in still or running water.

pong Brit. informal noun a strong, unpleasant smell. • verb smell strongly and unpleasantly.
– DERIVATIVES **pongy** adjective.
– ORIGIN unknown.

poniard /pon-yerd/ noun historical a small, slim dagger.
– ORIGIN French *poignard.*

pons /ponz/ noun (pl. **pontes** /pon-teez/) the part of the brainstem that links the medulla oblongata and the thalamus.
– ORIGIN Latin, 'bridge'.

Pontefract cake /pon-ti-frakt/ noun Brit. a flat, round liquorice sweet.
– ORIGIN named after *Pontefract* (earlier *Pomfret*), a town in Yorkshire where the sweets were first made.

pontiff noun the Pope.
– ORIGIN Latin *pontifex* 'high priest'.

pontifical /pon-ti-fi-k'l/ adjective 1 relating to the Pope; papal. 2 speaking as if one's own opinions are always correct; pompously dogmatic.
– DERIVATIVES **pontifically** adverb.

pontificate verb /pon-ti-fi-kayt/ 1 express one's opinions in a pompous and overbearing or dogmatic way. 2 (in the Roman Catholic Church) officiate as bishop, especially at Mass. • noun /pon-ti-fi-kuht/ (also **Pontificate**) (in the Roman Catholic Church) the office or period of office of pope or bishop.
– DERIVATIVES **pontificator** noun.

pontoon[1] noun Brit. a card game in which players try to obtain cards with a value totalling twenty-one.
– ORIGIN probably an alteration of French *vingt-et-un* 'twenty-one'.

pontoon[2] noun 1 a flat-bottomed boat or hollow metal cylinder used with others to support a temporary bridge or floating landing stage. 2 a bridge or landing stage supported by pontoons.
– ORIGIN French *ponton.*

pony noun (pl. **ponies**) 1 a horse of a small breed, especially one below 15 hands. 2 Brit. informal twenty-five pounds sterling.
– ORIGIN probably from French *poulenet* 'small foal'.

ponytail noun a hairstyle in which the hair is drawn back and tied at the back of the head.

pony-trekking noun Brit. the leisure activity of riding across country on a pony or horse.

poo exclamation & noun variant spelling of **POOH**.

pooch noun informal a dog.
– ORIGIN unknown.

poodle noun 1 a breed of dog with a curly coat that is usually clipped. 2 Brit. a person who is too ready to do what someone else tells them to do.
– ORIGIN German *Pudelhund*, from *puddeln* 'splash in water'.

p

poof /puuf/ (also **pouf, poofter**) noun Brit. informal, derogatory an effeminate or homosexual man.
- DERIVATIVES **poofy** adjective.
- ORIGIN perhaps an alteration of *puff* in the former sense 'boastful person'.

pooh (also **poo**) informal **exclamation 1** expressing disgust at an unpleasant smell. **2** expressing impatience or contempt. ●noun excrement.

pooh-bah /poo-bah/ noun a pompous or self-important person who has a great deal of influence or holds many posts at the same time.
- ORIGIN named after a character in W. S. Gilbert's *The Mikado*.

pooh-pooh verb informal dismiss an idea or suggestion as being foolish or impractical.

pool¹ noun **1** a small area of still water. **2** (also **swimming pool**) an artificial pool for swimming in. **3** a small, shallow patch of liquid lying on a surface: *a pool of blood*. **4** a deep place in a river.
- ORIGIN Old English.

pool² noun **1** a shared supply of vehicles, people, goods, or funds that is available when needed. **2** the total amount of players' stakes in gambling or sweepstakes. **3** (**the pools** or **football pools**) a form of gambling on the results of football matches, the winners receiving large sums accumulated from entry money. **4** a game played on a billiard table using 16 balls. **5** an arrangement between competing commercial organizations to fix prices and share business so as to eliminate competition. ●verb put money or other resources into a common fund to be used by a number of people: *they pooled their wages and bought food*.
- ORIGIN French *poule* 'stake, kitty'.

poolside noun the area immediately next to a swimming pool.

poop (also **poop deck**) noun a raised deck at the stern of a ship, especially a sailing ship.
- ORIGIN Latin *puppis* 'stern'.

pooped adjective N. Amer. informal exhausted.
- ORIGIN unknown.

poor adjective **1** not having enough money to live at a comfortable or normal standard. **2** of a low standard or quality: *poor working conditions*. **3** (**poor in**) lacking in: *an acid soil which is poor in nutrients*. **4** deserving pity or sympathy: *he's driven the poor woman away*.
- PHRASES **the poor man's —** an inferior or cheaper substitute for the thing specified: *herring roe—the poor man's caviar*. **poor relation** a person or thing that is considered less good than others of the same type. **take a poor view of** regard someone or something with disapproval.
- ORIGIN Old French *poure*.

poorhouse noun Brit. a workhouse.

poorly adverb in a poor way: *schools that were performing poorly*. ●adjective chiefly Brit. unwell.

poor white noun derogatory a white person, especially in the southern US, who lacks money, education, or social status.

pootle verb Brit. informal move or travel in a leisurely way.
- ORIGIN blend of **TOOTLE** and *poodle* in the same sense.

pop¹ verb (**pops, popping, popped**) **1** make or cause to make a sudden short explosive sound. **2** go or come quickly or unexpectedly: *I might pop round later*. **3** quickly put something somewhere: *he popped a sweet into his mouth*. **4** (of a person's eyes) open wide and appear to bulge. **5** informal take or inject a drug. ●noun **1** a sudden short explosive sound. **2** informal, dated a sweet fizzy soft drink.
- PHRASES **have** (or **take**) **a pop at** informal attack. **pop the question** informal propose marriage.
- ORIGIN imitating the sound.

pop² noun (also **pop music**) popular modern commercial music, typically with a strong melody and beat. ●adjective **1** relating to pop music. **2** often derogatory (especially of a scientific or academic subject) presented in a way that the general public will easily understand: *pop psychology*.

pop³ noun chiefly US informal term for FATHER.
- ORIGIN abbreviation of POPPA.

popadom noun variant spelling of POPPADOM.

pop art noun art that uses styles and images from modern popular culture.

popcorn noun maize kernels which swell up and burst open when heated and are then eaten as a snack.

pope noun (**the Pope**) the Bishop of Rome as head of the Roman Catholic Church.
- ORIGIN Greek *papas* 'bishop, patriarch'.

popery noun derogatory, chiefly old use Roman Catholicism.

pop-eyed adjective informal having bulging or staring eyes.

popgun noun a child's toy gun which shoots a harmless pellet or cork.

popinjay /pop-in-jay/ noun dated a conceited person who is extremely concerned with their clothes and appearance.
- ORIGIN Old French *papingay* 'parrot'.

popish adjective derogatory Roman Catholic.

poplar noun a tall, slender tree with soft wood.
- ORIGIN Latin *populus*.

poplin noun a cotton fabric with a finely ribbed surface.
- ORIGIN former French *papeline*.

popliteal /po-pli-ti-uhl, po-pli-tee-uhl/ adjective relating to or situated in the hollow at the back of the knee.
- ORIGIN Latin *popliteus*.

poppa noun N. Amer. informal term for FATHER.
- ORIGIN alteration of PAPA.

poppadom /pop-puh-duhm/ (also **poppadum** or **popadom**) noun (in Indian cookery) a large thin circular piece of unleavened spiced bread made from ground lentils and fried in oil until crisp.
- ORIGIN Tamil.

popper noun informal **1** Brit. a press stud. **2** a small vial of amyl nitrite which is inhaled, making a popping sound when opened.

poppet noun Brit. informal a pretty or endearing child.
- ORIGIN Latin *puppa* 'girl, doll'.

popping crease noun Cricket a line across the pitch in front of the stumps, behind which the batsman must keep the bat or one foot on the ground to avoid the risk of being stumped or run out.

– ORIGIN from **POP**[1].

poppy[1] noun a plant with showy red, pink, or orange flowers and large seed capsules, including species which produce drugs such as opium and codeine.
– ORIGIN Old English.

poppy[2] adjective (of popular music) tuneful and immediately appealing.

poppycock noun informal nonsense.
– ORIGIN Dutch dialect *pappekak*, literally 'soft dung'.

Poppy Day noun Brit. another name for **REMEMBRANCE SUNDAY**.

popsy (also **popsie**) noun (pl. **popsies**) informal, chiefly Brit. an attractive young woman.
– ORIGIN alteration of **POPPET**.

populace /pop-yuu-luhss/ noun (treated as sing. or pl.) the general public.
– ORIGIN Italian *popolaccio* 'common people'.

popular adjective **1** liked or admired by many people or by a particular group: *one of the most popular girls in the school.* **2** intended for or suited to the taste or means of the general public: *the popular press.* **3** (of a belief or attitude) widely held among the general public. **4** (of political activity) carried on by the people as a whole: *a popular revolt.*
– DERIVATIVES **popularity** noun **popularly** adverb.
– ORIGIN Latin *popularis*, from *populus* 'people'.

popular front noun a political party or coalition representing left-wing elements.

popularize (or **popularise**) verb **1** make something popular: *his books have done much to popularize the sport.* **2** present something scientific or academic in a way that the general public will find interesting and understandable.
– DERIVATIVES **popularization** noun **popularizer** noun.

populate verb **1** live in a place and form its population: *the island is populated by scarcely 40,000 people.* **2** cause people to settle in a place. **3** add data to a computer database.
– ORIGIN Latin *populare* 'supply with people'.

population noun **1** all the inhabitants of a place. **2** a particular group within this: *the country's immigrant population.* **3** Biology a community of animals or plants that interbreed.

populist adjective intended to appeal to or represent the interests and views of ordinary people. ●noun a member of a political party that seeks to appeal to or represent the interests and views of ordinary people.
– DERIVATIVES **populism** noun.

populous adjective having a large population.

pop-up noun **1** (of a book or greetings card) containing folded pictures that rise up to form a three-dimensional scene or figure when opened. **2** (of a computer menu or other feature) able to be superimposed on the screen being worked on and suppressed rapidly. ●noun **1** a pop-up computer menu or other feature. **2** an Internet browser window that appears without having been requested, especially one containing an advertisement.

porbeagle /por-bee-g'l/ noun a large shark found chiefly in the open seas of the North Atlantic and in the Mediterranean.

– ORIGIN Cornish dialect.

porcelain /por-suh-lin/ noun **1** a type of fine translucent china. **2** articles made of porcelain.
– ORIGIN Italian *porcellana* 'cowrie shell, china'.

porch noun **1** a covered shelter projecting over the entrance of a building. **2** N. Amer. a veranda.
– ORIGIN Old French *porche*.

porcine /por-syn/ adjective relating to or resembling a pig or pigs.
– ORIGIN from Latin *porcus* 'pig'.

porcini /por-chee-ni/ plural noun ceps (edible wild mushrooms).
– ORIGIN Italian, 'little pigs'.

porcupine noun a large rodent with protective spines or quills on the body and tail.
– ORIGIN from Latin *porcus* 'pig' + *spina* 'thorn'.

pore[1] noun a tiny opening in the skin or other surface through which gases, liquids, or microscopic particles may pass.
– ORIGIN Greek *poros*.

pore[2] verb (**pore over/through**) study or read something with close attention.
– ORIGIN perhaps related to **PEER**[1].

USAGE: Do not confuse **pore** and **pour**. **Pore** is used with **over** or **through** and means 'study or read something closely' (*I spend hours poring over cookery books*), while **pour** means 'flow in a steady stream' (*water poured off the roof*).

pork noun the flesh of a pig used as food.
– ORIGIN Latin *porcus* 'pig'.

pork barrel noun N. Amer. informal referring to the use of government funds for projects designed to win votes.
– ORIGIN from the farmers' practice of keeping a reserve supply of meat in a barrel, later meaning 'a supply of money'.

porker noun **1** a young pig raised and fattened for food. **2** informal, derogatory a fat person.

pork pie noun Brit. a raised pie made with minced cooked pork, eaten cold.

pork-pie hat noun a hat with a flat crown and a brim turned up all round.

porky informal adjective (**porkier, porkiest**) fat. ●noun (pl. **porkies**) (also **porky pie**) Brit. rhyming slang a lie.

porn (also **porno**) informal noun pornography. ●adjective pornographic.

pornography noun photographs, writing, films, etc. intended to cause sexual excitement.
– DERIVATIVES **pornographer** noun **pornographic** adjective.
– ORIGIN Greek *pornographos* 'writing about prostitutes'.

porous adjective (of a rock or other material) having tiny spaces through which liquid or air may pass.
– DERIVATIVES **porosity** noun.
– ORIGIN from Latin *porus* 'pore'.

porphyria /por-fi-ri-uh/ noun a rare hereditary disease in which the body fails to break down haemoglobin properly, causing mental disturbance, extreme sensitivity to light, and excretion of dark pigments in the urine.
– ORIGIN from *porphyrin* (a pigment made by breakdown of haemoglobin).

p

porphyry /por-fi-ri/ noun (pl. **porphyries**) a hard reddish igneous rock containing crystals of feldspar.
– ORIGIN Greek *porphurītēs*.

porpoise /por-puhss, por-poyz/ noun a small toothed whale with a blunt rounded snout.
– ORIGIN Old French *porpois*.

porridge noun **1** chiefly Brit. a dish consisting of oats or oatmeal boiled with water or milk. **2** Brit. informal time spent in prison.
– ORIGIN alteration of **POTTAGE**.

porringer /po-rin-jer/ noun historical a small bowl, often with a handle, used for soup or similar food.
– ORIGIN Old French *potager*.

port[1] noun **1** a town or city with a harbour. **2** a harbour.
– PHRASES **port of call** a place where a ship or person stops on a journey.
– ORIGIN Latin *portus* 'harbour'.

port[2] (also **port wine**) noun a sweet dark red fortified wine from Portugal.
– ORIGIN shortened form of *Oporto*, a port in Portugal from which the wine is shipped.

port[3] noun the side of a ship or aircraft that is on the left when one is facing forward. The opposite of **STARBOARD**. • verb turn a ship or its helm to the port side.
– ORIGIN probably originally the side turned towards the port or quayside for loading.

port[4] noun **1** an opening in the side of a ship for boarding or loading. **2** a porthole. **3** an opening for the passage of steam, liquid, or gas. **4** an opening in the body of an aircraft or in a wall or armoured vehicle through which a gun may be fired. **5** a socket in a computer network into which a device can be plugged.
– ORIGIN Latin *porta* 'gate'.

port[5] verb **1** Computing transfer software from one system or machine to another. **2** Military carry a weapon diagonally across and close to the body with the barrel or blade near the left shoulder. • noun **1** Military the position required by an order to port a weapon. **2** Computing a transfer of software from one system or machine to another.
– ORIGIN from French *porter* 'carry' or Old French *port* 'bearing, gait'.

portable adjective **1** able to be easily carried or moved. **2** (of a loan or pension) capable of being transferred or adapted. **3** Computing (of software) able to be ported.
– DERIVATIVES **portability** noun.

portage /por-tij/ noun **1** the carrying of a boat or its cargo overland between two navigable waterways. **2** a place at which this is necessary. • verb carry a boat or its cargo in this way.
– ORIGIN French.

portal noun **1** a large and imposing doorway, gate, or gateway. **2** an Internet site providing a directory of links to other sites.
– ORIGIN Latin *porta*.

portal vein noun a vein carrying blood to the liver from the spleen, stomach, pancreas, and intestines.

portamento /por-tuh-men-toh/ noun (pl. **portamentos** or **portamenti** /por-tuh-men-ti/) Music a slide from one note to another, especially in singing or playing the violin.
– ORIGIN Italian, 'carrying'.

portcullis noun a strong, heavy grating that can be lowered to block a gateway to a castle.
– ORIGIN from Old French *porte coleice* 'sliding door'.

portend verb be a sign or warning that something important or disastrous is likely to happen.
– ORIGIN Latin *portendere*.

portent /por-tent, por-tuhnt/ noun a sign or warning that something important or disastrous is likely to happen: *many birds are regarded as portents of death*.
– ORIGIN Latin *portentum*.

portentous adjective **1** important as a sign or warning of what is likely to happen; of great significance: *this portentous year in their history*. **2** done in a pompous or excessively solemn way.
– DERIVATIVES **portentously** adverb **portentousness** noun.

porter[1] noun **1** a person employed to carry luggage and other loads. **2** a hospital employee who moves equipment or patients. **3** dark brown bitter beer brewed from charred or browned malt. [so called because it was originally made for porters.]
– DERIVATIVES **porterage** noun.
– ORIGIN Old French *porteour*.

porter[2] noun Brit. an employee in charge of the entrance of a large building.
– ORIGIN Old French *portier*.

porterhouse steak noun a thick steak cut from the thick end of a sirloin.
– ORIGIN from *porterhouse*, formerly an establishment where porter and other drinks and sometimes steaks were served.

portfolio noun (pl. **portfolios**) **1** a thin, flat case for carrying drawings, maps, etc. **2** a set of pieces of creative work intended to demonstrate a person's ability. **3** a range of investments held by a person or organization. **4** the position and duties of a government minister.
– ORIGIN Italian *portafogli*.

porthole noun **1** a small window on the outside of a ship or aircraft. **2** historical an opening for firing a cannon through.

portico /por-ti-koh/ noun (pl. **porticoes** or **porticos**) a roof supported by columns at regular intervals, built over the entrance to a building.
– ORIGIN Latin *porticus* 'porch'.

portion noun **1** a part or a share. **2** an amount of food suitable for or served to one person. **3** old use a person's destiny or fate. **4** old use a dowry. • verb divide something into portions and share it out.
– ORIGIN Latin, from *pro portione* 'in proportion'.

Portland cement noun cement which resembles Portland stone when hard.

Portland stone noun limestone from the Isle of Portland in Dorset, valued as a building material.

portly adjective (**portlier**, **portliest**) (especially of a man) rather fat.
– DERIVATIVES **portliness** noun.
– ORIGIN from Old French *port* 'bearing, gait'.

portmanteau /port-man-toh/ noun (pl. **portmanteaus** or **portmanteaux** /port-man-

tohz/) a large travelling bag made of stiff leather and opening into two equal parts. •**adjective** consisting of two or more aspects or qualities: *a portmanteau movie.*
– ORIGIN French *portemanteau.*

portmanteau word noun a word blending the sounds and combining the meanings of two others, e.g. *brunch* from *breakfast* and *lunch.*

portrait noun **1** a painting, drawing, or photograph of a person, especially one depicting only the face or head and shoulders. **2** a written or filmed description. **3** a format of printed matter which is higher than it is wide. Compare with LANDSCAPE.
– DERIVATIVES **portraitist** noun **portraiture** noun.
– ORIGIN Old French *portraire* 'portray'.

portray verb **1** show or describe in a work of art or literature: *the Oxbridge dons portrayed by Evelyn Waugh.* **2** describe in a particular way: *the book portrayed him as a relentless careerist.* **3** (of an actor) play the part of someone in a film or play.
– DERIVATIVES **portrayal** noun **portrayer** noun.
– ORIGIN Old French *portraire.*

Portuguese /port-yuu-**geez**, por-chuu-**geez**/ noun (pl. same) **1** a person from Portugal. **2** the language of Portugal and Brazil. •**adjective** relating to Portugal.

Portuguese man-of-war noun a floating sea creature like a jellyfish, with long stinging tentacles.

pose verb **1** present or be a problem, danger, question, etc.: *the sheer number of visitors is posing a threat to the area.* **2** sit or stand in a particular position in order to be photographed, painted, or drawn. **3** (**pose as**) pretend to be: *two women posing as social workers stole her pension book.* **4** behave in a way intended to impress other people. •**noun 1** a position taken up in order to be painted, drawn, or photographed. **2** a way of behaving adopted in order to impress other people or give a false impression.
– ORIGIN Old French *poser.*

poser noun **1** a person who behaves or dresses in a way intended to impress other people. **2** a puzzling question or problem.

poseur /poh-**zer**/ noun a person who dresses or behaves in a way intended to impress others.
– ORIGIN French.

posey (also **posy**) adjective informal trying to impress other people; pretentious.

posh informal adjective **1** very elegant or luxurious. **2** chiefly Brit. upper-class.
– DERIVATIVES **poshly** adverb **poshness** noun.
– ORIGIN perhaps from former slang *posh* 'a dandy'; there is no evidence for the well-known theory that *posh* is formed from the initials of *port out starboard home* (referring to the more comfortable accommodation, out of the heat of the sun, on ships between England and India).

posit /**poz**-it/ verb (**posits, positing, posited**) put something forward as a fact or as a basis for argument.
– ORIGIN Latin, 'placed'.

position noun **1** a place where someone or something is located or has been put. **2** the correct place. **3** a way in which someone or something is placed or arranged: *he raised himself to a sitting position.* **4** a situation: *the company's financial position is grim.* **5** a person's place or level of importance in relation to other people: *she finished in second position.* **6** high rank or social standing. **7** a job. **8** a point of view or attitude: *the party's position on abortion.* **9** a place where part of a military force is posted. •**verb** put or arrange in a particular position: *she positioned herself near the fireplace.*
– DERIVATIVES **positional** adjective **positionally** adverb.
– ORIGIN Latin, from *ponere* 'to place'.

positive adjective **1** characterized by the presence rather than the absence of distinguishing features: *a positive test result.* **2** expressing or implying confirmation, agreement, or permission. **3** constructive, optimistic, or confident: *a positive outlook on life.* **4** with no possibility of doubt; certain. **5** (of a quantity) greater than zero. **6** relating to, containing, or producing the kind of electric charge opposite to that carried by electrons. **7** (of a photographic image) showing light and shade or colours true to the original. **8** (of an adjective or adverb) expressing the basic degree of a quality. Contrasted with COMPARATIVE and SUPERLATIVE. •**noun** a positive quality, attribute, or image.
– DERIVATIVES **positively** adverb **positiveness** noun **positivity** noun.
– ORIGIN from Old French *positif* or Latin *positivus.*

positive discrimination noun Brit. the policy of employing or favouring people belonging to groups which suffer from discrimination.

positive pole noun the north-seeking pole of a magnet.

positive vetting noun Brit. the investigation of the background and character of a candidate for a Civil Service post that involves access to secret material.

positivism noun a system of philosophy recognizing only that which can be scientifically verified or logically proved.
– DERIVATIVES **positivist** noun & adjective **positivistic** adjective.

positron /**poz**-i-tron/ noun Physics a subatomic particle with the same mass as an electron and a numerically equal but positive charge.

posse /**poss**-i/ noun **1** N. Amer. historical a group of men summoned by a sheriff to enforce the law. **2** informal a group of people: *a posse of medical students.*
– ORIGIN from Latin, 'be able', later 'power'.

possess verb **1** have as property; own. **2** (also **be possessed of**) have as an ability, quality, or characteristic: *he did not possess a sense of humour.* **3** (of a demon or spirit) have complete power over someone. **4** (of an emotion, idea, etc.) dominate someone's mind.
– DERIVATIVES **possessor** noun.
– ORIGIN from Latin *possidere* 'occupy, hold'.

possession noun **1** the state of having or owning something: *the book came into his possession.* **2** a thing owned: *my most precious possession.* **3** the state of being possessed by a demon, emotion, etc. **4** (in sport) temporary control of the ball by a player or team.

possessive adjective **1** demanding someone's total attention and love. **2** unwilling to share one's possessions with other people. **3** Grammar expressing possession.
– DERIVATIVES **possessively** adverb **possessiveness** noun.

possessive determiner noun Grammar a determiner showing possession, for example *my.*

possessive pronoun noun Grammar a pronoun showing possession, for example *mine.*

posset /poss-it/ noun a drink made of hot milk curdled with ale or wine and flavoured with spices, formerly drunk as a delicacy or as a remedy for colds.
– ORIGIN unknown.

possibility noun (pl. **possibilities**) **1** a thing that is possible. **2** the state of being possible. **3** (**possibilities**) general qualities of a promising nature: *the house had possibilities.*

possible adjective **1** capable of existing, happening, or being done. **2** that may be so, but that is not certain: *the possible cause of the plane crash.* • noun a possible candidate for a job or member of a team.
– ORIGIN Latin *possibilis.*

possibly adverb **1** perhaps. **2** in accordance with what is possible: *I try to do the job as well as I possibly can.*

possum noun **1** an Australasian marsupial that lives in trees. **2** N. Amer. informal an opossum.
– PHRASES **play possum** pretend to be unconscious, asleep, or unaware of something in order to trick someone.
– ORIGIN shortening of OPOSSUM.

post¹ noun **1** a long, strong, upright piece of timber or metal used as a support or a marker. **2** (**the post**) a starting post or winning post in a race. **3** a message sent to an Internet bulletin board or newsgroup. • verb **1** display a notice in a public place. **2** announce or publish something: *the company posted a £460,000 loss.* **3** send a message to an Internet bulletin board or newsgroup. **4** achieve or record a particular score or result.
– ORIGIN Latin *postis* 'doorpost'.

post² noun chiefly Brit. **1** the official service or system that delivers letters and parcels. **2** letters and parcels delivered. **3** a single collection or delivery of post. • verb **1** chiefly Brit. send a letter or parcel via the postal system. **2** (in bookkeeping) enter an item in a ledger.
– PHRASES **keep someone posted** keep someone informed of the latest developments or news.
– ORIGIN French *poste* 'station, stand'.

post³ noun **1** a place where someone is on duty or where an activity is carried out. **2** a job. • verb **1** station a soldier, police officer, etc. in a particular place. **2** send someone to a place to take up a job.
– ORIGIN Italian *posto.*

post- prefix after in time or order: *post-date.*
– ORIGIN Latin *post* 'after, behind'.

postage noun **1** the sending of letters and parcels by post. **2** the amount required to send something by post.

postage stamp noun an adhesive stamp stuck on a letter or parcel to show the amount of postage paid.

postal adjective relating to the post or carried out by post: *a postal vote.*

postal code noun another term for POSTCODE.

postal order noun Brit. a document that can be bought from a post office and sent to someone to be exchanged for money.

postbag noun British term for MAILBAG.

postbellum adjective occurring or existing after a war, in particular the American Civil War.
– ORIGIN from Latin *post* 'after' + *bellum* 'war'.

postbox noun a large public box into which letters are posted for collection by the post office.

postcard noun a card for sending a message by post without an envelope.

post-chaise /pohst-shayz/ noun (pl. **post-chaises** pronunc. same) historical a horse-drawn carriage used for transporting passengers or mail.

postcode noun Brit. a group of letters and numbers added to a postal address to assist the sorting of mail.

post-coital adjective occurring or done after sex.
– DERIVATIVES **post-coitally** adverb.

post-date verb **1** put a date later than the actual one on a document or document. **2** occur or come at a later date than: *Stonehenge was believed to post-date these structures.*

postdoctoral adjective (of research) undertaken after the completion of a doctorate.

poster noun a large printed picture or notice used for decoration or advertisement.

poste restante /pohst ress-tuhnt/ noun Brit. a department in a post office that keeps letters until they are collected by the person they are addressed to.
– ORIGIN French, 'mail remaining'.

posterior adjective **1** chiefly Anatomy further back in position; at or nearer the rear or hind end. The opposite of ANTERIOR. **2** formal coming after in time or order; later. • noun humorous a person's buttocks.
– ORIGIN Latin, from *posterus* 'following'.

posterity noun all future generations of people.
– ORIGIN from Latin *posterus* 'following'.

postern /poss-tern/ noun old use a back or side entrance.
– ORIGIN Old French *posterne.*

poster paint noun a thick opaque paint used for posters and children's paintings.

post-feminist adjective moving beyond or rejecting some of the earlier ideas of feminism as out of date.

postgraduate adjective relating to study undertaken after completing a first degree. • noun a person engaged in postgraduate study.

post-haste adverb with great speed.
– ORIGIN from the direction 'haste, post, haste', formerly given on letters.

posthumous /poss-tyuu-muhss/ adjective happening, awarded, or appearing after the person involved has died: *he was granted a posthumous pardon.*
– DERIVATIVES **posthumously** adverb.
– ORIGIN Latin *postumus* 'last'.

p

postilion /po-stil-i-uhn/ (also **postillion**) noun chiefly historical the rider of the leading nearside horse of a team or pair drawing a coach, when there is no coachman.
– ORIGIN French *postillon*.

post-Impressionism noun a late 19th-century and early 20th-century style of art in which emphasis was placed on the emotions of the artist, as expressed by colour, line, and shape.
– DERIVATIVES **post-Impressionist** noun & adjective.

post-industrial adjective (of an economy or society) no longer relying on heavy industry.

posting[1] noun chiefly Brit. an appointment to a job, especially one abroad or in the armed forces.

posting[2] noun a message sent to an Internet bulletin board or newsgroup.

postlude noun a concluding piece of music.
– ORIGIN from POST-, on the pattern of *prelude*.

postman (or **postwoman**) noun (pl. **postmen** or **postwomen**) Brit. a person who is employed to deliver or collect post.

postmark noun an official mark stamped on a letter or parcel, giving the date of posting and cancelling the postage stamp. •verb stamp a letter or parcel with a postmark.

postmaster (or **postmistress**) noun a person in charge of a post office.

postmodernism noun a style and movement in the arts characterized by distrust of theories and ideologies and by the deliberate mixing of different styles.
– DERIVATIVES **postmodern** adjective **postmodernist** noun & adjective **postmodernity** noun.

post-mortem noun 1 an examination of a dead body to establish the cause of death. 2 an analysis of an event made after it has happened: *an election post-mortem*. •adjective happening after death.
– ORIGIN Latin, 'after death'.

post-natal adjective happening in or relating to the period after childbirth.

post office noun 1 the public department or corporation responsible for postal services and (in some countries) telecommunications. 2 a building where postal business is carried out.

post office box noun a numbered box in a post office where letters for a person or organization are kept until called for.

post-operative adjective relating to the period following a surgical operation.

post-partum /pohsst-par-tuhm/ adjective relating to the period following childbirth or the birth of young.
– ORIGIN from Latin *post partum* 'after childbirth'.

postpone verb arrange for something to take place at a time later than that first planned.
– DERIVATIVES **postponement** noun.
– ORIGIN Latin *postponere*.

postpositive adjective (of a word) placed after the word that it relates to.

postprandial adjective formal or humorous during or relating to the period after a meal.
– ORIGIN from Latin *prandium* 'a meal'.

postscript noun an additional remark at the end of a letter, following the signature.
– ORIGIN Latin *postscriptum*.

post-traumatic stress disorder noun a condition of persistent stress occurring as a result of injury or severe psychological shock.

postulant /poss-tyuu-luhnt/ noun a person who wishes to enter a religious order.

postulate verb /poss-tyuu-layt/ suggest or assume that something exists or is true, as a basis for a theory or discussion. •noun /poss-tyuu-luhnt/ a thing that is postulated.
– DERIVATIVES **postulation** noun.
– ORIGIN Latin *postulare* 'ask'.

posture noun 1 a particular position of the body. 2 the usual way in which a person holds their body: *muscle tension can be the result of bad posture*. 3 an approach or attitude towards something: *trade unions adopted a more militant posture in wage negotiations*. •verb behave in a way that is intended to impress or mislead other people.
– DERIVATIVES **postural** adjective.
– ORIGIN Latin *positura* 'position'.

postviral syndrome (also **postviral fatigue syndrome**) noun myalgic encephalomyelitis (ME) following infection by a virus.

post-war adjective occurring or existing after a war.

posy[1] noun (pl. **posies**) a small bunch of flowers.
– ORIGIN first meaning 'motto or line of verse inscribed inside a ring': from POESY.

posy[2] adjective variant spelling of POSEY.

pot[1] noun 1 a rounded or cylindrical container used for storage or cooking. 2 a container designed to hold a particular thing: *a yogurt pot*. 3 (**the pot**) the total sum of the bets made on a round in poker, brag, etc. 4 Billiards & Snooker a shot in which a player strikes a ball into a pocket. •verb (**pots**, **potting**, **potted**) 1 plant something in a flowerpot. 2 preserve food in a sealed pot or jar. 3 Billiards & Snooker strike a ball into a pocket. 4 informal hit or kill someone or something by shooting.
– PHRASES **go to pot** informal deteriorate as a result of neglect.
– ORIGIN Old English.

pot[2] noun informal cannabis.
– ORIGIN probably from Mexican Spanish *potiguaya* 'cannabis leaves'.

potable /poh-tuh-b'l/ adjective formal (especially of water) safe to drink.
– DERIVATIVES **potability** noun.
– ORIGIN from Latin *potare* 'to drink'.

potage /po-tahzh/ noun thick soup.
– ORIGIN French.

potager /po-tuh-jer/ noun a kitchen garden.
– ORIGIN from French *jardin potager* 'garden providing vegetables for the pot'.

potash noun an alkaline potassium compound, used especially in making fertilizers.
– ORIGIN from *pot-ashes*, because first obtained from a solution made from ashes that was evaporated in an iron pot.

potassium /puh-tass-i-uhm/ noun a soft silvery-white reactive metallic element.
– ORIGIN from POTASH.

potassium hydroxide noun a strongly alkaline white compound used in many industrial processes, e.g. soap manufacture.

p

potation /poh-**tay**-sh'n/ noun old use or humorous **1** the action of drinking alcohol. **2** an alcoholic drink.
– ORIGIN Latin, from *potare* 'to drink'.

potato noun (pl. **potatoes**) a starchy plant tuber which is cooked and eaten as a vegetable.
– ORIGIN Spanish *patata* 'sweet potato', from Taino (an extinct Caribbean language).

pot-au-feu /pot-oh-**fer**/ noun (pl. same) a French soup of meat and vegetables cooked in a large pot.
– ORIGIN French, 'pot on the fire'.

pot belly noun a large protruding stomach.

potboiler noun informal a book, film, etc. produced purely to earn money quickly by appealing to popular taste.

pot-bound adjective (of a plant) having roots which fill the flowerpot, leaving no room for them to expand.

poteen /po-**teen**/ noun (in Ireland) whisky that is made illicitly.
– ORIGIN from Irish *fuisce poitín* 'little pot of whisky'.

potent adjective **1** having great power, influence, or effect: *a potent drug*. **2** (of a male) able to achieve an erection or to reach an orgasm.
– DERIVATIVES **potency** noun (pl. **potencies**) **potently** adverb.
– ORIGIN from Latin *posse* 'be powerful, be able'.

potentate noun a monarch or ruler.
– ORIGIN Latin *potentatus* 'dominion'.

potential adjective having the capacity to develop into something in the future: *a potential problem*. • noun **1** qualities or abilities that may be developed and lead to future success or usefulness: *he showed great potential as an actor*. **2** (often **potential for/to do**) the possibility of something happening or of someone doing something in the future. **3** Physics the difference in voltage between two points in an electric field or circuit.
– DERIVATIVES **potentiality** noun **potentially** adverb.
– ORIGIN from Latin *potentia* 'power'.

potential difference noun Physics the difference of electrical potential between two points.

potential energy noun Physics energy possessed by a body as a result of its position or state. Compare with **KINETIC ENERGY**.

potentiate /poh-**ten**-shi-ayt/ verb increase the power or effect of a drug, physiological reaction, etc.

potentilla /poh-tuhn-**til**-luh/ noun a small shrub with yellow or red flowers.
– ORIGIN from Latin *potent*- 'being powerful' (with reference to its herbal qualities).

potentiometer /poh-ten-shi-**om**-i-ter/ noun an instrument for measuring or adjusting an electromotive force.

pother /po-*ther*/ noun a commotion or fuss.
– ORIGIN unknown.

pothole noun **1** a deep underground cave formed by water eroding the rock. **2** a hole in a road surface. • verb (usu. as noun **potholing**) Brit. explore underground potholes as a pastime.
– DERIVATIVES **potholed** adjective **potholer** noun.

– ORIGIN from dialect *pot* 'pit'.

potion noun a liquid with healing, magical, or poisonous properties.
– ORIGIN Latin, 'drink'.

potlatch noun (among some North American Indian peoples) a ceremonial feast at which possessions are given away or destroyed as an indication of wealth.
– ORIGIN from an American Indian language.

pot luck noun the chance that whatever is available will prove to be good or acceptable.

pot plant noun Brit. a plant suitable for growing in a flowerpot, especially indoors.

potpourri /poh-**poor**-i, poh-puh-**ree**/ noun (pl. **potpourris**) **1** a mixture of dried petals and spices placed in a bowl to perfume a room. **2** a mixture of things.
– ORIGIN French, 'rotten pot', first meaning 'stew made of different kinds of meat'.

pot roast noun a piece of meat cooked slowly in a covered pot.

potsherd /**pot**-sherd/ noun a piece of broken pottery.
– ORIGIN from **POT¹** + **SHERD**.

potshot noun a shot aimed unexpectedly or at random.
– ORIGIN first meaning a *shot* at an animal intended for the *pot*, i.e. for food, rather than for display (which would require skilled shooting).

pottage /**pot**-ij/ noun old use soup or stew.
– ORIGIN Old French *potage* 'that which is put into a pot'.

potted adjective **1** grown or preserved in a pot. **2** (of an account of something) put into a short, understandable form: *a potted history of psychology*.

potter¹ verb **1** occupy oneself by doing minor, pleasant tasks in a relaxed way. **2** move or go in a casual, unhurried way.
– ORIGIN from dialect *pote* 'to push, kick, or poke'.

potter² noun a person who makes pottery.

potter's wheel noun a flat revolving disc on which wet clay is shaped into pots, bowls, etc.

pottery noun (pl. **potteries**) **1** articles made of clay baked in a kiln. **2** the craft of making such articles. **3** a factory or workshop where such articles are made.

potting shed noun Brit. a shed used for potting plants and storing garden tools and supplies.

potty¹ adjective (**pottier**, **pottiest**) informal, chiefly Brit. **1** foolish; crazy. **2** extremely enthusiastic about someone or something.
– DERIVATIVES **pottiness** noun.
– ORIGIN unknown.

potty² noun (pl. **potties**) a container for a child to urinate or defecate into.

pouch noun **1** a small flexible bag, typically carried in a pocket or attached to a belt. **2** a pocket of skin in an animal's body, especially that in which marsupials carry their young.
– DERIVATIVES **pouched** adjective **pouchy** adjective.
– ORIGIN Old French *poche* 'bag'.

pouf¹ noun variant spelling of **POOF** or **POUFFE**.

pouf² /puuf/ noun **1** a part of a dress in which a large mass of material has been gathered so that it stands away from the body. **2** a bouffant hairstyle.

– ORIGIN French.

pouffe /poof/ (also **pouf**) noun a large, firm cushion used as a seat or stool.
– ORIGIN French.

poult /pohlt/ noun a young domestic fowl being raised for food.
– ORIGIN from **PULLET**.

poulterer noun Brit. a person who sells poultry.

poultice /pohl-tiss/ noun a soft moist mass, traditionally of flour, bran, and herbs, applied to the skin to reduce inflammation.
– ORIGIN from Latin *puls* 'pottage, pap'.

poultry /pohl-tri/ noun chickens, turkeys, ducks, and geese.
– ORIGIN Old French *pouletrie*.

pounce[1] verb **1** spring or swoop suddenly so as to seize or attack someone or something. **2** take swift advantage of a mistake or sign of weakness: *the press pounced on his words*. • noun an act of pouncing.
– ORIGIN uncertain.

pounce[2] noun a fine powder formerly used to prevent ink from spreading on paper or to prepare parchment for writing.
– ORIGIN French *poncer*.

pound[1] noun **1** a unit of weight equal to 16 oz avoirdupois (0.4536 kg), or 12 oz troy (0.3732 kg). **2** (also **pound sterling**) (pl. **pounds sterling**) the basic unit of money of the UK, equal to 100 pence. **3** another term for **PUNT**[4]. **4** the basic monetary unit of several Middle Eastern countries, equal to 100 piastres. **5** the basic monetary unit of Cyprus, equal to 100 cents.
– PHRASES **one's pound of flesh** something which one is owed but, if given, would cause suffering or trouble to the person who owes it. [with reference to Shakespeare's *Merchant of Venice*.]
– DERIVATIVES **pounder** noun.
– ORIGIN Old English, from Latin *libra pondo*, referring to a Roman 'pound weight' of 12 ounces.

pound[2] verb **1** strike or hit heavily and repeatedly: *the men pounded him with their fists*. **2** beat or throb with a strong regular rhythm. **3** walk or run with heavy steps. **4** (**pound something out**) produce a document or piece of music with heavy strokes on a keyboard or instrument. **5** crush or grind something into a powder or paste.
– ORIGIN Old English.

pound[3] noun a place where stray dogs or illegally parked vehicles may officially be taken and kept until claimed.
– ORIGIN uncertain.

poundage noun Brit. **1** a charge made for every pound weight of something, or for every pound sterling in value. **2** weight.

pound cake noun N. Amer. a rich cake originally made with a pound of each chief ingredient.

pour verb **1** flow or cause to flow in a steady stream. **2** (of rain) fall heavily. **3** prepare and serve a drink. **4** come or go in a steady stream: *people poured out of the train*. **5** (**pour something out**) express one's feelings freely.
– DERIVATIVES **pourer** noun.
– ORIGIN unknown.

USAGE: On the confusion of **pour** and **pore**, see the note at **PORE**[2].

poussin /poo-san/ noun a chicken killed young for eating.
– ORIGIN French.

pout verb push one's lips forward as an expression of sulky annoyance or in order to make oneself look sexually attractive. • noun a pouting expression.
– DERIVATIVES **pouty** adjective.
– ORIGIN perhaps related to Swedish dialect *puta* 'be inflated'.

pouter noun a kind of pigeon that is able to puff up its crop to a considerable extent.

poverty noun **1** the state of being extremely poor. **2** the state of being inadequate in quality or amount: *the poverty of her imagination*.
– ORIGIN Old French *poverte*.

poverty-stricken adjective extremely poor.

poverty trap noun Brit. a situation in which an increase in someone's income results in a loss of state benefits, leaving them no better off.

POW abbreviation prisoner of war.

powder noun **1** fine dry particles produced by the grinding, crushing, or disintegration of a solid substance. **2** a cosmetic in this form for use on the face. **3** dated a medicine in this form. **4** gunpowder. • verb **1** sprinkle or cover something with powder. **2** (often as adj. **powdered**) make something into a powder: *powdered milk*.
– PHRASES **keep one's powder dry** remain cautious and ready for a possible emergency.
– DERIVATIVES **powdery** adjective.
– ORIGIN Old French *poudre*.

powder blue noun a soft, pale blue.

powder keg noun **1** a situation that may suddenly become dangerous or violent. **2** a barrel of gunpowder.

powder puff noun a soft pad for applying powder to the face.

powder room noun euphemistic a women's toilet in a public building.

power noun **1** the ability to do something or act in a particular way: *the power of speech*. **2** the ability to control or influence people or events. **3** the right or authority to do something: *police have the power to seize equipment*. **4** political authority or control. **5** physical strength or force. **6** a country viewed in terms of its international influence and military strength: *a world power*. **7** capacity or performance of an engine or other device. **8** energy that is produced by mechanical, electrical, or other means. **9** Physics the rate of doing work, measured in watts or horse power. **10** Mathematics the product obtained when a number is multiplied by itself a certain number of times. • verb **1** supply a device with mechanical or electrical energy. **2** (**power something up/down**) switch a device on or off. **3** move with speed or force.
– PHRASES **the powers that be** the authorities.
– DERIVATIVES **powered** adjective.
– ORIGIN Old French *poeir*.

powerboat noun a fast motorboat.
– DERIVATIVES **powerboating** noun.

power broker noun a person who influences the balance of political or economic power.

power cut noun a temporary withdrawal or failure of an electrical power supply.

powerful adjective **1** having great power. **2** having a strong effect: *powerful anti-war images.*
– DERIVATIVES **powerfully** adverb.

powerhouse noun a person or thing having great energy or power.

powerless adjective without ability, influence, or power.
– DERIVATIVES **powerlessly** adverb **powerlessness** noun.

power line noun a cable carrying electrical power.

power of attorney noun the authority to act for another person in particular legal or financial matters.

power pack noun **1** a unit which stores and supplies electrical power. **2** a transformer for converting an alternating current (from the mains) to a direct current.

power plant noun a power station.

power station noun a building where electrical power is generated.

power steering noun steering aided by power from the vehicle's engine.

powwow noun **1** informal a meeting for discussion. **2** a North American Indian ceremony involving feasting and dancing. ⚫verb informal meet to discuss something.
– ORIGIN from a word in a North American Indian language meaning 'magician'.

pox noun **1** any disease caused by a virus and producing a rash of pus-filled pimples that leave pockmarks on healing. **2** (**the pox**) informal syphilis. **3** (**the pox**) historical smallpox.
– ORIGIN from *pocks*, plural of **POCK**.

poxy adjective (**poxier, poxiest**) informal, chiefly Brit. of poor quality; worthless.

pp abbreviation **1** (**pp.**) pages. **2** (also **p.p.**) per procurationem (used when signing a letter on someone else's behalf). [from Latin, 'through the agency of'.] **3** Music pianissimo.

PPE abbreviation philosophy, politics, and economics.

ppm abbreviation **1** part(s) per million. **2** page(s) per minute, a measure of the speed of a computer printer.

PPS abbreviation **1** post (additional) postscript. **2** Brit. Parliamentary Private Secretary.

PPV abbreviation pay-per-view.

PR abbreviation **1** proportional representation. **2** public relations.

Pr symbol the chemical element praseodymium.

practicable adjective able to be done or put into effect successfully: *it was not reasonably practicable to call her as a witness.*
– DERIVATIVES **practicability** noun **practicably** adverb.

practical adjective **1** relating to the actual doing or use of something rather than theory: *the candidate should have practical experience of agriculture.* **2** likely to be effective or successful: *practical solutions to transport problems.* **3** suitable for a particular purpose. **4** realistic or sensible in one's approach to a situation. **5** skilled at making or doing things.

6 almost complete; virtual: *it was a practical certainty that he would raise more money.* ⚫noun Brit. an exam or lesson in which theories and procedures are applied to making or doing something.
– ORIGIN from Greek *praktikos* 'concerned with action'.

practicality noun (pl. **practicalities**) **1** the quality or state of being practical. **2** (**practicalities**) the aspects of a situation that involve action or experience rather than theories or ideas.

practical joke noun a trick played on someone to make them look foolish.

practically adverb **1** virtually; almost. **2** in a practical way.

practice noun **1** the use or application of an idea or method, as opposed to the theories relating to it: *putting policy into practice.* **2** the usual way of doing something. **3** the work, business, or place of work of a doctor, dentist, or lawyer. **4** the action of doing something repeatedly so as to become more skilful in it: *maths improves with practice.* ⚫verb US spelling of **PRACTISE**.
– ORIGIN from **PRACTISE**.

USAGE: Practice is the correct spelling for the noun in both British and American English: *putting policy into practice.* Practice is also the spelling for the verb in American English, but in British English, the verb should be spelled practise: *I need to practise my French.*

practise (US **practice**) verb **1** do something repeatedly in order to become skilful in it: *I need to practise my French.* **2** carry out an activity or custom regularly. **3** work in a particular profession: *she began to practise law.* **4** observe the teaching and rules of a religion.
– ORIGIN Latin *practicare* 'perform, carry out'.

practised (US **practiced**) adjective expert in something as the result of much experience.

practitioner noun a person who practises a particular profession or activity.

praesidium noun variant spelling of **PRESIDIUM**.

praetor /pree-ter, pree-tor/ (US also **pretor**) noun each of two ancient Roman magistrates ranking below consul.
– DERIVATIVES **praetorian** adjective & noun.
– ORIGIN Latin.

praetorian guard noun (in ancient Rome) the bodyguard of the emperor.

pragmatic adjective **1** dealing with things in a realistic and practical way. **2** relating to philosophical pragmatism.
– DERIVATIVES **pragmatically** adverb.
– ORIGIN Greek *pragmatikos* 'relating to fact'.

pragmatism noun **1** a realistic and practical attitude or approach. **2** a philosophical approach that evaluates theories in terms of the success of their practical application.
– DERIVATIVES **pragmatist** noun.

prairie noun (in North America) a large open area of grassland.
– ORIGIN French.

prairie dog noun a type of rodent that lives in burrows in the grasslands of North America.

praise verb **1** express warm approval of or admiration for: *he praised the work being done*

by the security forces. **2** express respect and gratitude towards God or a god. •**noun 1** the expression of approval or admiration. **2** the expression of respect and gratitude as an act of worship.
– PHRASES **praise someone/thing to the skies** praise someone or something very highly or enthusiastically.
– ORIGIN Old French *preisier* 'to prize, praise'.

praiseworthy adjective deserving approval and admiration.
– DERIVATIVES **praiseworthily** adverb **praiseworthiness** noun.

praline /prah-leen, pray-leen/ noun a smooth substance made from nuts boiled in sugar, used as a filling for chocolates.
– ORIGIN named after Marshal de Plessis-*Praslin*, the French soldier whose cook invented it.

pram noun Brit. a four-wheeled vehicle for a baby, pushed by a person on foot.
– ORIGIN from **PERAMBULATOR**.

pranayama /prah-nuh-**yah**-muh/ noun (in yoga) the regulation of the breath through certain techniques and exercises.
– ORIGIN Sanskrit.

prance verb **1** move quickly with exaggerated steps. **2** (of a horse) move with high springy steps.
– ORIGIN unknown.

prandial /**pran**-di-uhl/ adjective formal during or relating to a meal.
– ORIGIN from Latin *prandium* 'meal'.

prang Brit. informal verb crash a motor vehicle or aircraft. •noun a collision or crash.
– ORIGIN imitating the sound.

prank noun a practical joke or mischievous act.
– DERIVATIVES **prankish** adjective.
– ORIGIN unknown.

prankster noun a person who is fond of playing pranks.

praseodymium /pray-zi-oh-**di**-mi-uhm/ noun a silvery-white metallic chemical element of the lanthanide series.
– ORIGIN Latin.

prat noun Brit. informal a stupid person.
– ORIGIN unknown.

prate verb talk too much in a foolish or boring way.
– ORIGIN from Dutch or German *praten*.

pratfall noun informal **1** a fall on to one's bottom. **2** an embarrassing mistake.

prattle verb talk too much in a foolish or trivial way. •noun foolish or trivial talk.
– ORIGIN German *pratelen*.

prawn noun an edible shellfish which resembles a large shrimp.
– ORIGIN unknown.

prawn cracker noun (in Chinese cooking) a light prawn-flavoured crisp.

praxis /**prak**-siss/ noun **1** practice, as distinguished from theory. **2** accepted practice or custom, especially in religion.
– ORIGIN Greek, 'doing'.

pray verb **1** say a prayer to God or a god. **2** wish or hope strongly for: *after days of rain, we were praying for sun*. •adverb formal or old use please: *pray continue*.
– ORIGIN Old French *preier*.

prayer noun **1** a request for help or expression of thanks addressed to God or a god. **2** (**prayers**) a religious service at which people gather to pray together. **3** an earnest hope or wish.

prayerful adjective **1** relating to praying or prayers. **2** tending to pray; devout.
– DERIVATIVES **prayerfully** adverb.

prayer wheel noun a small revolving cylinder inscribed with or containing prayers, used by Tibetan Buddhists.

praying mantis noun see **MANTIS**.

PRC abbreviation People's Republic of China.

pre- prefix before: *prearrange*.
– ORIGIN from Latin *prae-*.

preach verb **1** give a religious talk to a gathering of people. **2** strongly recommend a course of action: *my parents always preached tolerance*. **3** (**preach at**) give moral advice to someone in a pompous way.
– DERIVATIVES **preacher** noun.
– ORIGIN Old French *prechier*.

preachy adjective giving moral advice in a pompous or overbearing way.

preamble /pree-**am**-b'l, **pree**-am-b'l/ noun an opening statement; an introduction.
– ORIGIN from Latin *praeambulus* 'going before'.

prearrange verb arrange or agree something in advance.

prebendary /pre-**buhn**-duh-ri/ noun (pl. **prebendaries**) (in the Christian Church) an honorary canon.
– ORIGIN Latin *praebenda* 'pension'.

Precambrian /pree-**kam**-bri-uhn/ adjective Geology relating to the earliest period of the earth's history, ending about 570 million years ago, a time when living organisms first appeared.

precancerous adjective (of a cell or medical condition) likely to develop into cancer if untreated.

precarious adjective **1** likely to fall or to cause someone to fall. **2** not safe or stable; uncertain: *the country's precarious financial position*.
– DERIVATIVES **precariously** adverb **precariousness** noun.
– ORIGIN Latin *precarius* 'obtained by entreaty'.

precast adjective (especially of concrete) cast in its final shape before positioning.

precaution noun **1** something done in advance to avoid problems or danger: *the best ways to foil hackers is to take a few simple precautions*. **2** (**precautions**) informal contraception.
– DERIVATIVES **precautionary** adjective.
– ORIGIN Latin.

precede verb **1** come before in time, order, or position: *read the chapters that precede the recipes*. **2** go in front or ahead of someone.
– DERIVATIVES **preceding** adjective.
– ORIGIN Latin *praecedere*.

precedence /**press**-i-duhnss, pree-si-duhnss/ noun the state of coming before other people or things in order or importance: *his desire for power took precedence over everything*.

precedent noun /**press**-i-d'nt/ **1** an earlier event or action that acts as an example to be followed in a similar situation. **2** a previous

p

legal case or decision that may or must be followed in subsequent similar cases. • adjective /pri-**see**-d'nt, press-i-d'nt/ coming before in time, order, or importance.

precentor /pri-**sen**-ter/ noun a person who leads a congregation in its singing or (in a synagogue) prayers.
– ORIGIN from Latin *praecinere* 'sing before'.

precept /**pree**-sept/ noun **1** a general rule regulating behaviour or thought. **2** a writ or warrant.
– ORIGIN Latin *praeceptum* 'something advised'.

preceptor /pri-**sep**-ter/ noun (fem. **preceptress**) a teacher or instructor.

precession noun **1** the slow movement of the axis of a spinning body around another axis. **2** the earlier occurrence of the equinoxes each year.
– DERIVATIVES **precess** verb **precessional** adjective.
– ORIGIN from Latin *praecedere* 'go before'.

precinct /**pree**-singkt/ noun **1** the area within the walls or boundaries of a place. **2** Brit. an area in a town that is closed to traffic. **3** an enclosed area around a cathedral, church, or college. **4** N. Amer. one of the districts into which a city or town is divided for elections or policing purposes.
– ORIGIN Latin *praecinctum*.

preciosity /pre-shi-**oss**-i-ti/ noun affectation or pretentiousness in language or art.

precious adjective **1** very valuable. **2** greatly loved or treasured: *my daughter's very precious to me.* **3** ironic considerable: *a precious lot you know!* **4** sophisticated in an affected or exaggerated way.
– PHRASES **precious little** (or **few**) informal very little (or few).
– DERIVATIVES **preciously** adverb **preciousness** noun.
– ORIGIN Latin *pretiosus*.

precious metal noun a valuable metal such as gold, silver, or platinum.

precious stone noun a very attractive and valuable piece of mineral, used in jewellery.

precipice noun a tall and very steep rock face or cliff.
– ORIGIN Latin *praecipitium* 'abrupt descent'.

precipitant noun a cause of an action or event.

precipitate verb /pri-**sip**-i-tayt/ **1** cause something undesirable to happen suddenly or prematurely. **2** cause to move suddenly and with force: *the ladder broke, precipitating them down into a heap.* **3** Chemistry cause a substance to be deposited in solid form from a solution. **4** cause moisture in the atmosphere to condense and fall as rain, snow, sleet, or hail. • adjective /pri-**sip**-i-tuht/ done or occurring suddenly or without careful consideration. • noun /pri-**sip**-i-tayt, pri-**sip**-i-tuht/ Chemistry a substance precipitated from a solution.
– DERIVATIVES **precipitately** adverb **precipitator** noun.
– ORIGIN Latin *praecipitare* 'throw headlong'.

precipitation noun **1** rain, snow, sleet, or hail. **2** Chemistry the action of precipitating a substance from a solution. **3** old use sudden and unthinking action.

precipitous /pri-**sip**-i-tuhss/ adjective **1** dangerously high or steep. **2** (of a change to a worse situation) sudden and dramatic.

3 done suddenly and without consideration; precipitate.
– DERIVATIVES **precipitously** adverb.

precis /**pray**-si/ (also **précis**) noun (pl. same /**pray**-si, pray-seez/) a summary of a written work or speech. • verb (**precises** /**pray**-seez/, **precising** /**pray**-see-ing/, **precised** /**pray**-seed/) make a summary of a piece of writing or a speech.
– ORIGIN from French, 'precise'.

precise adjective **1** expressed in a detailed and accurate way: *precise directions.* **2** very attentive to detail. **3** exact; particular: *at that precise moment the car stopped.*
– DERIVATIVES **precisely** adverb **preciseness** noun.
– ORIGIN Old French *prescis*.

> **USAGE:** Precise does not mean the exactly the same as accurate. Accurate means 'correct in all details', while precise contains an idea of trying to specify details exactly: if you say 'It's 4.04 and 12 seconds' you are being *precise*, but not necessarily *accurate* (your watch might be slow).

precision noun the quality or fact of being precise. • adjective very accurate: *a precision instrument.*

preclude verb prevent something from happening or someone from doing something.
– DERIVATIVES **preclusion** noun.
– ORIGIN Latin *praecludere* 'shut off, impede'.

precocious /pri-**koh**-shuhss/ adjective (of a child) having developed certain abilities or ways of behaving at an earlier age than usual.
– DERIVATIVES **precociously** adverb **precociousness** noun **precocity** /pri-**koss**-i-ti/ noun.
– ORIGIN from Latin *praecox*, from *praecoquere* 'ripen fully'.

precognition /pree-kog-**ni**-sh'n/ noun knowledge of an event before it happens, especially through supposed paranormal means.
– DERIVATIVES **precognitive** adjective.

preconceived adjective (of an idea or opinion) formed before full knowledge or evidence is available.

preconception noun an idea or opinion that is formed before full knowledge or evidence is available.

precondition noun something that must exist or happen before other things can happen or be done.

precook verb cook something in advance.

precursor noun a person or thing that comes before another of the same kind: *the game was a precursor of cricket.*
– DERIVATIVES **precursory** adjective.
– ORIGIN Latin *praecursor*.

predacious /pri-**day**-shuhss/ (also **predaceous**) adjective (of an animal) predatory.

pre-date verb exist or occur at a date earlier than something.

predation /pri-**day**-sh'n/ noun the preying of one animal on others.
– ORIGIN Latin.

predator noun **1** an animal that hunts and kills other animals for food. **2** a person who exploits others: *a sexual predator.*

predatory adjective 1 (of an animal) hunting and killing other animals for food. 2 (of a person) exploiting other people.

predawn adjective relating to or taking place before dawn.

predecease verb formal die before another person.

predecessor noun 1 a person who held a job or office before the current holder. 2 a thing that has been followed or replaced by another: *the chapel was built on the site of its predecessor.*
– ORIGIN Latin *praedecessor.*

predestination noun the Christian belief that everything has been decided or planned in advance by God.

predestine verb (usu. as adj. **predestined**) (of God or fate) decide in advance that something will happen or that someone will have a particular fate.

predetermine verb establish or decide something in advance.
– DERIVATIVES **predetermination** noun.

predeterminer noun Grammar a word or phrase that occurs before a determiner, for example *both* or *a lot of.*

predicament /pri-**dik**-uh-m'nt/ noun a difficult or embarrassing situation.
– ORIGIN Latin *praedicamentum* 'something predicated'.

predicate noun /**pred**-i-kuht/ 1 Grammar the part of a sentence or clause containing a verb and stating something about the subject (e.g. *went home* in *John went home*). 2 Logic something which is declared or denied concerning an argument of a proposition. •verb /**pred**-i-kayt/ 1 (**predicate something on**) found or base something on: *the oil's low price is predicated on tax exemptions.* 2 declare or assert something as true or existing.
– DERIVATIVES **predication** noun.
– ORIGIN from Latin *praedicare* 'make known beforehand, declare'.

predicative /pri-**dik**-uh-tiv/ adjective Grammar (of an adjective or noun) forming part or the whole of the predicate and coming after a verb, for example, *old* in *the dog is old.* Contrasted with **ATTRIBUTIVE.**
– DERIVATIVES **predicatively** adverb.

predict verb state that an event will happen in the future.
– DERIVATIVES **predictive** adjective **predictor** noun.
– ORIGIN Latin *praedicere* 'make known beforehand, declare'.

predictable adjective 1 able to be predicted. 2 always behaving or occurring in the way expected and therefore boring.
– DERIVATIVES **predictability** noun **predictably** adverb.

prediction noun 1 a thing predicted; a forecast. 2 the action of predicting something.

predigest verb 1 (of an animal) treat food by a process similar to digestion to make it more easily digestible when subsequently eaten. 2 simplify information so that it is easier to absorb.

predilection /pree-di-**lek**-sh'n/ noun a preference or special liking for something.
– ORIGIN from Latin *praediligere* 'prefer'.

predispose verb make someone likely to do,

be, or think something: *certain people are predisposed to become drug abusers.*
– DERIVATIVES **predisposition** noun.

predominant adjective 1 present as the main element: *the bird's predominant colour was white.* 2 having the greatest control or power.
– DERIVATIVES **predominance** noun **predominantly** adverb.

predominate verb 1 be the main element in something: *small-scale producers predominate in the south.* 2 have control or power.

predominately adverb mainly; for the most part.

pre-eclampsia noun a condition in pregnancy characterized especially by high blood pressure.
– DERIVATIVES **pre-eclamptic** adjective & noun.

pre-eminent adjective better than all others; outstanding.
– DERIVATIVES **pre-eminence** noun **pre-eminently** adverb.

pre-empt verb 1 take action in order to prevent something happening. 2 prevent someone from saying something by speaking first.
– DERIVATIVES **pre-emptive** adjective **pre-emptor** noun.

pre-emption noun 1 the action of preventing something from happening. 2 the buying of goods or shares before the opportunity is offered to others.
– ORIGIN from Latin *praeemere* 'buy in advance'.

preen verb 1 (of a bird) tidy and clean its feathers with its beak. 2 make oneself look attractive and then admire one's appearance. 3 (**preen oneself**) congratulate or pride oneself: *he's preening himself on having such a pretty girlfriend.*
– ORIGIN probably from Latin *ungere* 'anoint'.

pre-exist verb (usu. as adj. **pre-existing**) exist before or from an earlier time.
– DERIVATIVES **pre-existence** noun **pre-existent** adjective.

prefab noun informal a prefabricated building.

prefabricated adjective (of a building) made in sections that can be easily assembled on site.
– DERIVATIVES **prefabrication** noun.

preface /**pref**-uhss/ noun 1 an introduction to a book, stating its subject, scope, or aims. 2 a preliminary explanation. •verb 1 (**preface something with/by**) begin a speech or event with or by doing something. 2 provide a book with a preface.
– DERIVATIVES **prefatory** /**pref**-uh-tuh-ri/ adjective.
– ORIGIN Old French.

prefect noun 1 chiefly Brit. a senior pupil who is appointed to enforce discipline in a school. 2 a chief officer, magistrate, or regional governor in certain countries.
– DERIVATIVES **prefectorial** adjective.
– ORIGIN Latin *praefectus.*

prefecture noun 1 a district governed by a prefect or governor. 2 the office or residence of a prefect of governor.
– DERIVATIVES **prefectural** adjective.

prefer verb (**prefers**, **preferring**, **preferred**)

p

1 like someone or something better than another or others: *I prefer Greece to Spain.* **2** put forward a formal accusation for consideration by a court of law. **3** old use promote someone to an important position.
– ORIGIN Latin *praeferre* 'bear or carry before'.

preferable adjective more desirable or suitable.
– DERIVATIVES **preferability** noun.

preferably adverb ideally; if possible.

preference noun **1** a greater liking for one alternative over another or others. **2** a thing preferred. **3** favour shown to one person over another or others: *preference is given to those who make a donation.*

preference share (N. Amer. **preferred share**) noun a share which entitles the holder to a fixed dividend whose payment takes priority over that of ordinary share dividends.

preferential adjective favouring a particular person or group: *he was giving his son-in-law preferential treatment.*
– DERIVATIVES **preferentially** adverb.

preferment noun promotion or appointment to a job or office.

prefigure verb be an early indication or version of: *the fall of Jericho was thought to prefigure the Last Judgement.*
– DERIVATIVES **prefiguration** noun.

prefix noun **1** a word, letter, or number placed before another. **2** a letter or group of letters placed at the beginning of a word to alter its meaning (e.g. *non-, re-*). **3** a title placed before a name (e.g. *Mr*). • verb add letters or numbers to the beginning of a word or number.

pregnancy noun (pl. **pregnancies**) the condition or period of being pregnant.

pregnant adjective **1** (of a woman or female animal) having a child or young developing in the womb. **2** full of meaning; significant: *a pregnant pause.*
– ORIGIN Latin *praegnans*.

preheat verb heat something beforehand.

prehensile /pri-hen-syl/ adjective (chiefly of an animal's limb or tail) capable of grasping things.
– ORIGIN from Latin *prehendere* 'to grasp'.

prehistoric adjective relating to the period before written records.

prehistory noun **1** the period of time before written records. **2** the early stages of the development of something: *the prehistory of capitalism.*
– DERIVATIVES **prehistorian** noun.

pre-industrial adjective before the development of industries on a large scale.

prejudge verb make a judgement about someone or something without having all the necessary information.

prejudice noun **1** an opinion that is not based on reason or actual experience: *English prejudice against foreigners.* **2** dislike or unjust behaviour based on this. **3** chiefly Law harm that may result from an action or judgement. • verb **1** influence someone so that they have a biased or unfair opinion: *the statement might prejudice the jury.* **2** have a harmful effect on a situation.
– PHRASES **without prejudice** Law without

adversely affecting any existing right or claim.
– DERIVATIVES **prejudiced** adjective.
– ORIGIN Latin *praejudicium.*

prejudicial adjective harmful to someone or something.

prelapsarian /pree-lap-**sair**-i-uhn/ adjective chiefly literary before the Fall of Man, when humans lapsed into a state of sin; innocent and unspoilt.
– ORIGIN from PRE- + Latin *lapsus* 'a fall'.

prelate /**prel**-uht/ noun formal a bishop or other high-ranking Christian priest.
– ORIGIN Latin *praelatus* 'civil dignitary'.

preliminary adjective happening before or done in preparation for a main action or event: *preliminary talks.* • noun (pl. **preliminaries**) **1** an action or event that comes before or is done in preparation for something. **2** a preliminary round in a sporting competition.
– ORIGIN from Latin *prae* 'before' + *limen* 'threshold'.

preliterate adjective relating to a society or culture that has not developed the use of writing.

prelude noun **1** an action or event acting as an introduction to something more important: *the talks should be the prelude to a final agreement.* **2** a piece of music acting as an introduction to a longer work. • verb act as an introduction to something.
– ORIGIN from Latin *praeludere* 'play beforehand'.

premarital adjective happening before marriage.

prematch adjective in or relating to the period before a sports match.

premature adjective **1** happening or done before the proper time: *the sun can cause premature ageing.* **2** (of a baby) born before the normal length of pregnancy is completed.
– DERIVATIVES **prematurely** adverb **prematurity** noun.
– ORIGIN Latin *praematurus* 'very early'.

premedication noun medication given in preparation for an operation or other treatment.

premeditated adjective (of an action, especially a crime) planned in advance.
– DERIVATIVES **premeditation** noun.

premenstrual adjective occurring or experienced before a menstrual period.

premenstrual syndrome noun a complex of symptoms (including emotional tension and fluid retention) experienced by some women before a menstrual period.

premier adjective first in importance, order, or position. • noun a Prime Minister or other head of government.
– ORIGIN Latin *primarius* 'principal'.

premiere noun the first performance of a play or musical work or the first showing of a film. • verb present the premiere of a play, film, ballet, or opera.
– ORIGIN French *première.*

premiership noun **1** the office or position of a Prime Minister or other head of government. **2** (**the Premiership**) the top division of professional football in England.

premise noun /**prem**-iss/ (Brit. also **premiss**) a

statement or idea that forms the basis for a theory, argument, or line of reasoning. •verb /pri-**myz**, prem-iss/ (**premise something on**) base an argument, theory, etc. on something.
– ORIGIN Old French *premisse*.

premises plural noun a building, together with its land and outbuildings, occupied by a business.

premium noun (pl. **premiums**) **1** an amount paid for an insurance policy. **2** a sum added to a basic price or other payment. •adjective (of a product) superior and more expensive: *premium lagers*.
– PHRASES **at a premium 1** scarce and in demand. **2** above the usual price. **put** (or **place**) **a premium on** regard something as particularly important.
– ORIGIN Latin *praemium* 'booty, reward'.

Premium Bond (also **Premium Savings Bond**) noun (in the UK) a government bond that is entered in regular draws for cash prizes rather than paying interest.

premolar (also **premolar tooth**) noun a tooth between the canines and molar teeth.

premonition /prem-uh-**ni**-sh'n, pree-muh-**ni**-sh'n/ noun a strong feeling that something is about to happen.
– DERIVATIVES **premonitory** adjective.
– ORIGIN from Latin *praemonere* 'forewarn'.

prenatal adjective N. Amer. before birth.
– DERIVATIVES **prenatally** adverb.

prenuptial adjective before marriage.

preoccupation noun **1** the state of thinking about something continuously and ignoring everything else. **2** a matter that fills someone's mind completely.

preoccupy verb (**preoccupies, preoccupying, preoccupied**) fill someone's mind completely, so that they ignore everything else: *her mother was preoccupied with paying the bills*.

preordain verb decide or determine something beforehand.

prep noun Brit. informal (especially in a private school) school work done outside lessons.
– ORIGIN abbreviation of PREPARATION.

pre-packed (also **pre-packaged**) adjective (of goods) packed or wrapped on before they are sold.

prepaid past and past participle of PREPAY.

preparation noun **1** the action of preparing or the state of being prepared: *the preparation of a draft contract*. **2** something done to get ready for something else. **3** a substance that has been prepared for use as a medicine, cosmetic, or food.

preparative adjective done in order to prepare for something; preparatory.

preparatory adjective done in order to prepare for something.

preparatory school noun **1** Brit. a private school for pupils between the ages of seven and thirteen. **2** N. Amer. a private school that prepares pupils for college or university.

prepare verb **1** make something ready for use. **2** make something from other parts, ingredients, or substances: *I had to prepare the evening meal*. **3** make or get ready to do or deal with something: *she took time off to prepare for her exams*. **4** (**be prepared to do**) be willing

to do.
– DERIVATIVES **preparer** noun.
– ORIGIN Latin *praeparare*.

preparedness noun a state of readiness, especially for war.

prepay verb (past and past part. **prepaid**) pay for something in advance.
– DERIVATIVES **prepayment** noun.

pre-plan verb plan something in advance.

preponderance noun the state of being greater in number: *the preponderance of women among older people*.

preponderant adjective greater in number or importance.
– DERIVATIVES **preponderantly** adverb.

preponderate verb be greater in number or importance: *the advantages preponderate over this apparent disadvantage*.
– ORIGIN Latin *praeponderare* 'weigh more'.

preposition /prep-uh-**zi**-sh'n/ noun Grammar a word used with a noun or pronoun to show place, position, time, or method.
– DERIVATIVES **prepositional** adjective.

> USAGE: A preposition (a word such as *from*, *to*, *on*, *after*, etc.) usually comes before a noun or pronoun and gives information about how, when, or where something has happened (*she arrived after dinner*). Some people believe that a preposition should never come at the end of a sentence, as in *where do you come from?*, and that you should say *from where do you come?* instead. However, this can result in English that sounds very awkward and unnatural, and is not a rule that has to be followed as long as the meaning of what you are saying is clear.

prepossessing adjective attractive or appealing in appearance: *he was not a prepossessing sight*.

preposterous adjective completely ridiculous or outrageous.
– DERIVATIVES **preposterously** adverb **preposterousness** noun.
– ORIGIN Latin *praeposterus* 'reversed, absurd'.

preppy (also **preppie**) N. Amer. informal adjective (**preppier, preppiest**) typical of a student at an expensive preparatory school, especially with reference to their neat style of dress. •noun (pl. **preppies**) a student attending an expensive preparatory school.

preprandial adjective formal or humorous done or taken before dinner.
– ORIGIN from Latin *prandium* 'a meal'.

pre-production noun work done on a product, film or broadcast programme before full-scale production begins.

preprogram verb (**preprograms, preprogramming, preprogrammed**) program a computer in advance for ease of use.

prep school noun a preparatory school.

prepubertal /pree-pyoo-buh-t'l/ adjective another term for PREPUBESCENT.
– DERIVATIVES **pre-puberty** noun

prepubescent adjective relating to or in the period before puberty.

prepuce /pree-pyooss/ noun **1** technical term for FORESKIN. **2** the fold of skin surrounding the clitoris.
– ORIGIN French *prépuce*.

prequel noun a story or film containing events which happen before those of an existing work.
– ORIGIN from PRE- + SEQUEL.

Pre-Raphaelite /pree-raf-uh-lyt/ noun a member of a group of English 19th-century artists who painted in the style of Italian artists from before the time of Raphael.
• adjective 1 relating to the Pre-Raphaelites. 2 (of a woman) resembling one depicted in a Pre-Raphaelite painting, typically in having long auburn hair and pale skin.
– DERIVATIVES **Pre-Raphaelitism** noun.

pre-record verb (often as adj. **pre-recorded**) record sound or film in advance.

prerequisite /pree-**rek**-wi-zit/ noun a thing that must exist or happen before something else can exist or happen: our solar system is a prerequisite for our existence. • adjective required before something else can exist or happen.

prerogative /pri-**rog**-uh-tiv/ noun a right or privilege belonging to a particular person or group: owning a car used to be the prerogative of the rich.
– ORIGIN Latin praerogativa 'verdict of the people chosen to vote first in the assembly'.

presage /**press**-ij/ verb /also pri-**sayj**/ be a sign or warning of an event that is about to happen. • noun a sign or warning of an event that is about to happen; an omen.
– ORIGIN Latin praesagire 'forebode'.

presbyter /**prez**-bi-ter/ noun historical 1 (in Presbyterian Churches) an elder. 2 an elder or minister of the Christian Church.
– DERIVATIVES **presbyteral** /prez-**bit**-uh-ruhl/ adjective **presbyterial** adjective.
– ORIGIN Greek presbuteros 'elder'.

Presbyterian /prez-bi-**teer**-i-uhn/ adjective relating to a Protestant Church or branch governed by elders all of equal rank. • noun a member of a Presbyterian Church.
– DERIVATIVES **Presbyterianism** noun.

presbytery /**prez**-bi-tuh-ri/ noun (pl. **presbyteries**) 1 (treated as sing. or pl.) a group of Church elders. 2 the house of a Roman Catholic parish priest. 3 the eastern part of a church near the altar.

preschool adjective relating to the time before a child is old enough to go to school.

prescient /**press**-i-uhnt/ adjective having knowledge of events before they take place.
– DERIVATIVES **prescience** noun **presciently** adverb.
– ORIGIN from Latin praescire 'know beforehand'.

prescribe verb 1 recommend and authorize the use of a medicine or treatment. 2 (often as adj. **prescribed**) state authoritatively that something should be done: doing things in the prescribed way.
– ORIGIN Latin praescribere 'direct in writing'.

USAGE: On the confusion between **prescribe** and **proscribe**, see the note at **PROSCRIBE**.

prescription noun 1 a doctor's written instruction authorizing a patient to be issued with a medicine or treatment. 2 the action of prescribing a medicine or treatment. 3 an authoritative recommendation.

prescriptive adjective 1 relating to the enforcement of a rule or method. 2 (of a right, title, etc.) legally established by long usage.
– DERIVATIVES **prescriptivism** noun **prescriptivist** noun & adjective.
– ORIGIN Latin praescriptivus 'relating to a legal exception'.

preseason adjective before the start of the season for a particular sport.

presence noun 1 the state or fact of being present: my presence in the flat made her happy. 2 a person's impressive manner or appearance. 3 a person or thing that is present but not seen. 4 a group of soldiers or police stationed in a particular place: the USA would maintain a presence in the region.
– PHRASES **presence of mind** the ability to remain calm and take quick, sensible action in a difficult situation.
– ORIGIN Latin praesentia 'being at hand'.

present[1] /**pre**-z'nt/ adjective 1 being or occurring in a particular place. 2 existing or occurring now. 3 Grammar (of a tense or participle) expressing an action now going on or a condition now existing. • noun 1 (**the present**) the period of time now occurring. 2 Grammar a present tense or form of a verb.
– PHRASES **at present** now. **for the present** for now; temporarily. **these presents** Law, formal this document.
– ORIGIN Latin praesens 'being at hand'.

present[2] /pri-**zent**/ verb 1 give something to someone formally or at a ceremony. 2 offer for acceptance or consideration: he stopped and presented his passport. 3 formally introduce someone to someone else. 4 put a show or exhibition before the public. 5 introduce and appear in a television or radio show. 6 be the cause of a problem. 7 give a particular impression to others: the EU presented a united front over the crisis. 8 (**present oneself**) appear at or attend a formal occasion.
– PHRASES **present arms** hold a rifle vertically in front of the body as a salute.
– ORIGIN Latin praesentare 'place before'.

present[3] /**pre**-z'nt/ noun a thing given to someone as a gift.
– ORIGIN Old French.

presentable adjective clean, smart, or decent enough to be seen in public.

presentation noun 1 the action of showing or giving something to someone. 2 the way in which something is presented: the presentation of food is designed to stimulate your appetite. 3 a talk or meeting at which a new product, idea, or piece of work is shown to an audience.
– DERIVATIVES **presentational** adjective **presentationally** adverb.

presenter noun Brit. a person who introduces and appears in a television or radio programme.

presentiment /pri-**zen**-ti-muhnt/ noun a feeling that something undesirable is going to happen.
– ORIGIN from former French présentiment.

presently adverb 1 after a short time; soon. 2 at the present time; now.

present participle noun Grammar the form of a verb, ending in -ing, which is used in forming tenses describing continuous action (e.g. *I'm thinking*), as a noun (e.g. *good thinking*), and as an adjective (e.g. *running water*).

preservation noun **1** the action of preserving something. **2** the degree to which something has been preserved: *the chapel is in a poor state of preservation.*

preservationist noun a person who supports the preservation of historic buildings or works of art.

preservative noun a substance used to prevent food or other materials from decaying. • adjective preventing something from decaying.

preserve verb **1** keep something in its original or existing state. **2** keep a quality, situation, memory, etc. in existence: *a fight to preserve local democracy.* **3** keep something safe from harm. **4** treat food or other material to prevent it from decaying. • noun **1** a type of jam made with fruit boiled in sugar. **2** something regarded as reserved for a particular person or group: *jobs that used to be the preserve of men.* **3** chiefly N. Amer. a place where game is protected and kept for private hunting.
– DERIVATIVES **preservable** adjective **preserver** noun.
– ORIGIN Latin *praeservare.*

preset verb (**presets**, **presetting**, **preset**) set the controls of a device at a certain level before using it.

pre-shrunk adjective (of a fabric or an item of clothing) shrunk during manufacture to prevent further shrinking when in use.

preside verb **1** be in charge of a meeting, court, etc. **2** (**preside over**) be in charge of a situation.
– ORIGIN Latin *praesidere.*

presidency noun (pl. **presidencies**) **1** the office or position of president. **2** the period of time that a president is in office.

president noun **1** the elected head of a republic. **2** the head of a society or similar organization. **3** N. Amer. the head of a bank or business.
– DERIVATIVES **presidential** adjective.
– ORIGIN from Latin *praesidere* 'preside'.

presidium /pri-si-di-uhm, pri-zi-di-uhm/ (also **praesidium**) noun a standing executive committee in a communist country.
– ORIGIN Russian *prezidium.*

press¹ verb **1** move into contact with something by using steady physical force: *he pressed his face to the glass.* **2** push something to operate a device. **3** apply pressure to something to flatten or shape it. **4** move along by pushing. **5** (**press on/ahead**) continue to do something. **6** forcefully put forward an opinion or claim. **7** make strong efforts to persuade someone to do something: *the directors were pressed to justify their expenditure.* **8** extract juice or oil by crushing or squeezing fruit, vegetables, etc. **9** (of time) be short. • noun **1** a device for crushing, flattening, or shaping something. **2** a printing press. **3** (**the press**) (treated as sing. or pl.) newspapers or journalists as a whole. **4** coverage in newspapers and magazines: *the government has had a bad press for years.* **5** a closely packed mass of people or things.
– PHRASES **be pressed for** have very little of

something, especially time. **go to press** go to be printed.
– DERIVATIVES **presser** noun.
– ORIGIN Latin *pressare* 'keep pressing'.

press² verb historical force someone to serve in the army or navy.
– PHRASES **press someone/thing into service** put someone or something to a specified use as a temporary measure.
– ORIGIN Latin *praestare* 'provide'.

press conference noun a meeting held with journalists in order to make an announcement or answer questions.

press gang noun historical a group of men employed to force other men to serve in the army or navy. • verb (**press-gang**) force someone to do something: *we press-ganged Simon into playing.*

pressing adjective **1** requiring urgent action. **2** expressing something strongly. • noun a record or other object made by moulding material under pressure.

pressman noun (pl. **pressmen**) chiefly Brit. a journalist.

press release noun an official statement issued to journalists.

press stud noun Brit. a small fastener with two parts that fit together when pressed.

press-up noun Brit. an exercise in which a person lies facing the floor and raises their body by pressing down on their hands.

pressure noun **1** the steady force brought to bear on an object by something in contact with it. **2** the use of persuasion or intimidation to make someone do something. **3** a feeling of stress caused by having many demands on one's time or resources: *she resigned due to pressure of work.* **4** the force per unit area applied by a fluid against a surface. • verb try to persuade or force someone to do something.
– ORIGIN Latin *pressura.*

pressure cooker noun an airtight pot in which food can be cooked quickly under steam pressure.

pressure group noun a group that tries to influence government policy and public opinion in the interest of a particular cause.

pressurize (or **pressurise**) verb **1** try to persuade or force someone to do something. **2** keep the air pressure in an aircraft cabin the same as it is at ground level.
– DERIVATIVES **pressurization** noun.

prestidigitation /press-ti-di-ji-tay-sh'n/ noun formal conjuring tricks performed as entertainment.
– DERIVATIVES **prestidigitator** noun.
– ORIGIN French.

prestige /pre-steezh/ noun respect and admiration resulting from achievements or high quality: *her prestige in Europe was tremendous.*
– ORIGIN French, 'illusion, glamour'.

prestigious /press-ti-juhss/ adjective having or bringing respect and admiration.

presto adverb & adjective Music in a quick tempo.
– ORIGIN Italian, 'quick, quickly'.

prestressed adjective (of concrete) strengthened by means of rods or wires inserted under tension before setting.

p

presumably adverb as may be supposed; probably.

presume verb 1 suppose that something is probably the case. 2 be bold enough to do something that one does not have the right to do: *don't presume to give me orders in my own house.* 3 (**presume on**) take advantage of someone's friendship or good nature.
– DERIVATIVES **presumable** adjective.
– ORIGIN Latin *praesumere* 'anticipate'.

presumption noun 1 an act of presuming something to be the case. 2 an idea that is presumed to be true. 3 disrespectful or excessively bold behaviour.

presumptive adjective 1 presumed in the absence of further information. 2 behaving with disrespectful boldness; presumptuous.
– DERIVATIVES **presumptively** adverb.

presumptuous adjective behaving with disrespectful boldness.
– DERIVATIVES **presumptuously** adverb **presumptuousness** noun.

presuppose verb 1 depend on something in order to exist or be true. 2 assume something to be the case.
– DERIVATIVES **presupposition** noun.

pretence (US **pretense**) noun 1 an attempt to make something that is not the case appear true: *his anger was masked by a pretence that all was well.* 2 affected and pretentious behaviour. 3 (**pretence to**) a claim to have or be something.

pretend verb 1 make it appear that something is the case when in fact it is not: *she turned the pages and pretended to read.* 2 (of a child) play an imaginative game. 3 give the appearance of feeling an emotion or having a quality. 4 (**pretend to**) claim to have a quality or title. •adjective informal imaginary; make-believe.
– ORIGIN Latin *praetendere* 'stretch forth, claim'.

pretender noun a person who claims to have a right to a title or position.

pretension noun 1 (often **pretensions**) a claim to a quality: *an ageing rocker with literary pretensions.* 2 the action of trying to appear more important or better than one actually is.

pretentious adjective attempting to impress others by pretending to be more important or better than one actually is.
– DERIVATIVES **pretentiously** adverb **pretentiousness** noun.

preterite /'pret-uh-rit/ (US also **preterit**) Grammar adjective expressing a past action or state. •noun a simple past tense or form.
– ORIGIN Latin *praeteritus.*

preternatural /pree-ter-**nach**-uh-ruhl/ adjective beyond what is normal or natural.
– DERIVATIVES **preternaturally** adverb.
– ORIGIN from Latin *praeter* 'past, beyond'.

pretext noun a false reason used to justify an action.
– ORIGIN Latin *praetextus* 'outward display'.

pretor noun US spelling of **PRAETOR**.

pretreat verb treat something with a chemical before use.
– DERIVATIVES **pretreatment** noun.

prettify verb (**prettifies, prettifying, prettified**) make something appear pretty.

– DERIVATIVES **prettification** noun.

pretty adjective (**prettier, prettiest**) 1 (of a woman or girl) attractive in a delicate way. 2 pleasant in appearance: *a pretty dress.* 3 informal used to express displeasure: *he led me a pretty dance.* •adverb informal to a certain extent; fairly. •noun (pl. **pretties**) informal a pretty object.
– PHRASES **be sitting pretty** informal be in a favourable position. **a pretty penny** informal a large sum of money.
– DERIVATIVES **prettily** adverb **prettiness** noun.
– ORIGIN Old English, 'cunning', later 'clever, pleasing'.

pretzel /'pret-z'l/ noun a crisp biscuit baked in the shape of a knot or stick and flavoured with salt.
– ORIGIN German.

prevail verb 1 be widespread or current: *a friendly atmosphere prevailed among the crowds.* 2 be more powerful: *it is hard for logic to prevail over emotion.* 3 (**prevail on**) persuade someone to do something.
– DERIVATIVES **prevailing** adjective.
– ORIGIN Latin *praevalere* 'have greater power'.

prevailing wind noun a wind from the predominant or most usual direction.

prevalent /**prev**-uh-luhnt/ adjective widespread in a particular area at a particular time.
– DERIVATIVES **prevalence** noun.
– ORIGIN from Latin *praevalere* (see **PREVAIL**).

prevaricate /pri-**va**-ri-kayt/ verb avoid giving a direct answer to a question.
– DERIVATIVES **prevarication** noun **prevaricator** noun.
– ORIGIN Latin *praevaricari* 'walk crookedly, deviate'.

prevent verb 1 stop something from happening or arising. 2 stop someone from doing something.
– DERIVATIVES **preventable** adjective **preventer** noun **prevention** noun.
– ORIGIN Latin *praevenire* 'precede, hinder'.

preventive (also **preventative**) adjective designed to prevent something from happening. •noun a medicine or other treatment intended to prevent disease or poor health.

preview noun 1 a viewing or display of something before it becomes generally available. 2 a publicity article or trailer of a forthcoming film, book, etc. •verb provide or have a preview of a product, film, etc.
– DERIVATIVES **previewer** noun.

previous adjective 1 coming before in time or order. 2 informal too hasty in acting.
– PHRASES **previous to** before.
– DERIVATIVES **previously** adverb.
– ORIGIN Latin *praevius* 'going before'.

pre-war adjective occurring or existing before a war.

prey noun 1 an animal hunted and killed by another for food. 2 a person who is easily exploited or harmed. 3 a person prone to experiencing distressing emotions. •verb (**prey on**) 1 hunt and kill another animal for food. 2 take advantage of someone. 3 cause constant distress to: *the problem had begun to prey on my mind.*
– ORIGIN Old French *preie.*

priapic /pry-**ap**-ik/ **adjective 1** relating to male
sexuality. **2** relating to an erect penis.
– DERIVATIVES **priapism** noun.
– ORIGIN from Greek *Priapos*, a god of fertility.

price noun **1** the amount of money for which
something is bought or sold. **2** something
unwelcome that has to be done or given in
order to achieve an aim: *some inequality would
be a fair price to pay for a society where there is
no poverty.* **3** the odds in betting. • **verb** decide
the price of something.
– PHRASES **at any price** no matter what is
involved. **at a price** at a high cost. **what price
something?** what has become of or what is the
chance of something?
– ORIGIN Old French *pris*.

priceless adjective **1** very valuable or precious.
2 informal very amusing.

price tag noun the cost of something.

pricey adjective (**pricier, priciest**) informal
expensive.

prick verb **1** make a small hole in something
with a sharp point. **2** feel as though a sharp
point or points were sticking into one. **3** (**prick
something out**) plant seedlings in small holes
made in the earth. • **noun 1** an act of pricking
someone or something. **2** a sharp pain, hole, or
mark caused by pricking. **3** vulgar slang a man's
penis. **4** vulgar slang a stupid or unpleasant man.
– PHRASES **kick against the pricks** hurt oneself
by continuing to resist something that cannot
be changed. [with reference to Acts of the
Apostles, chapter 9.] **prick up one's ears 1** (of a
horse or dog) make the ears stand erect when
alert. **2** (of a person) suddenly begin to pay
attention.
– DERIVATIVES **pricker** noun.
– ORIGIN Old English.

prickle noun **1** a small thorn on a plant or a
short spine on an animal. **2** a tingling or mildly
painful feeling on the skin. • **verb** have a
tingling feeling on the skin.
– ORIGIN Old English.

prickly adjective (**pricklier, prickliest**) **1** covered
in prickles. **2** having or causing a prickling
feeling. **3** easily offended.

prickly heat noun an itchy skin rash
experienced in hot moist weather.

prickly pear noun a cactus which produces
prickly, pear-shaped fruits.

pride noun **1** deep pleasure or satisfaction
gained from achievements, qualities, or
possessions. **2** a cause or source of deep
pleasure or satisfaction: *the swimming pool
was the pride of the village.* **3** a feeling of self-
respect. **4** an excessively high opinion of
oneself. **5** a group of lions forming a social
unit. • **verb** (**pride oneself on**) be especially
proud of a quality or skill.
– PHRASES **pride of place** the most noticeable
position.
– DERIVATIVES **prideful** adjective.
– ORIGIN Old English.

prie-dieu /pree-**dyer**/ noun (pl. **prie-dieux**
pronunc. same) a piece of furniture used for
prayer, consisting of a kneeling surface and a
narrow upright front with a rest for the
elbows or for books.
– ORIGIN French, 'pray God'.

priest noun **1** an ordained minister of the

Catholic, Orthodox, or Anglican Church,
authorized to perform certain ceremonies. **2** a
person who performs ceremonies in a non-
Christian religion.
– DERIVATIVES **priesthood** noun **priestly** adjective.
– ORIGIN Old English.

priestess noun a female priest of a non-
Christian religion.

prig noun a person who behaves as if they are
morally superior to others.
– DERIVATIVES **priggish** adjective.
– ORIGIN unknown.

prim adjective (**primmer, primmest**) very formal
and correct and disapproving of anything
improper or rude.
– DERIVATIVES **primly** adverb **primness** noun.
– ORIGIN probably from Old French *prin*,
'excellent, delicate'.

prima ballerina /pree-muh bal-luh-**ree**-nuh/
noun the chief female dancer in a ballet or
ballet company.
– ORIGIN Italian.

primacy /**pry**-muh-si/ noun the fact of being
primary or most important.
– ORIGIN Latin *primatia*.

prima donna /pree-muh **don**-uh/ noun **1** the
chief female singer in an opera or opera
company. **2** a very temperamental and self-
important person.
– ORIGIN Italian, 'first lady'.

primaeval adjective variant spelling of
PRIMEVAL.

prima facie /pry-muh **fay**-shi-ee/ adjective &
adverb Law accepted as correct until proved
otherwise.
– ORIGIN Latin.

primal adjective **1** at a very primitive or early
stage of development; primeval. **2** Psychology
relating to feelings or behaviour believed to
form the origins of emotional life: *primal fears.*
– ORIGIN Latin *primalis*.

primarily adverb for the most part; mainly.

primary adjective **1** of chief importance;
principal. **2** earliest in time or order. **3** chiefly Brit.
relating to education for children between the
ages of about five and eleven. • noun (pl.
primaries) (in the US) a preliminary election
to appoint delegates to a party conference or
to select candidates for an election.
– ORIGIN Latin *primarius*.

primary care noun health care provided in the
community by medical practitioners and
specialist clinics.

primary colour noun any of a group of
colours from which all others can be obtained
by mixing.

primary industry noun an industry
concerned with obtaining or providing raw
materials, such as mining or agriculture.

primate noun **1** a mammal of an order
including monkeys, apes, and humans. **2** (in
the Christian Church) an archbishop.
– ORIGIN from Latin *primas* 'of the first rank'.

primatology noun the branch of zoology
concerned with monkeys and other primates.
– DERIVATIVES **primatologist** noun.

prime[1] adjective **1** most important; main. **2** of
the highest quality; excellent. **3** (of a number)
that can be divided only by itself and one (e.g.
2, 3, 5, 7). • noun **1** a time of greatest vigour or

p

success in a person's life. **2** a prime number.
– ORIGIN from Latin *prima hora* 'first hour'.

prime² verb **1** prepare someone for a situation by giving them relevant information. **2** make something, especially a firearm or bomb, ready for use or action. **3** cover a surface with primer. **4** pour or spray liquid into a pump to make it operate more easily.
– PHRASES **prime the pump** stimulate the growth or success of something with funding.
– ORIGIN probably from Latin *primus* 'first'.

prime minister noun the head of an elected government.

prime mover noun a person who originates a plan or project.

primer¹ noun a substance painted on a surface as a base coat.

primer² noun a book providing a basic introduction to a subject or used for teaching reading.
– ORIGIN from Latin *primarius liber* 'primary book' and *primarium manuale* 'primary manual'.

prime time noun the time at which a radio or television audience is expected to be greatest.

primeval /pry-mee-v'l/ (also **primaeval**) adjective **1** relating to the earliest time in history. **2** (of behaviour or emotion) not based on reason; instinctive.
– ORIGIN Latin *primaevus*.

primitive adjective **1** relating to the earliest times in history or stages in development of something: *primitive mammals.* **2** referring to a simple form of society that has not yet developed writing or industry. **3** offering a very basic level of comfort or convenience. **4** (of behaviour or emotion) not based on reason; instinctive. •noun **1** a person belonging to a primitive society. **2** a painter who deliberately uses a simple, naive style that rejects conventional techniques.
– DERIVATIVES **primitively** adverb **primitiveness** noun.
– ORIGIN Latin *primitivus* 'first of its kind'.

primitivism noun **1** a belief in the value of what is simple and unsophisticated, expressed especially through art or literature. **2** instinctive and unreasoning behaviour.
– DERIVATIVES **primitivist** noun & adjective.

primogeniture /pry-moh-jen-i-cher/ noun **1** the state of being the firstborn child. **2** the system by which the firstborn child, especially the eldest son, inherits all his parents' property.
– ORIGIN Latin *primogenitura.*

primordial /pry-mor-di-uhl/ adjective existing at or from the beginning of time; primeval.
– ORIGIN Latin *primordialis* 'first of all'.

primordial soup noun a solution rich in organic compounds in which life on earth is supposed to have originated.

primp verb make minor adjustments to one's hair, clothes, or make-up.
– ORIGIN related to PRIM.

primrose noun **1** a plant of woods and hedgerows with pale yellow flowers. **2** a pale yellow colour.
– PHRASES **primrose path** the pursuit of pleasure, especially when bringing undesirable consequences. [with reference to

Shakespeare's *Hamlet* I. iii. 50.]
– ORIGIN probably related to Latin *prima rosa* 'first rose'.

primula /prim-yuu-luh/ noun a plant of a genus that includes primroses, cowslips, and polyanthus.
– ORIGIN from Latin *primula veris* 'little first thing'.

Primus /pry-muhss/ noun trademark a portable cooking stove that burns vaporized oil.

prince noun **1** a son or other close male relative of a monarch. **2** a king of a small state. **3** (in some European countries) a nobleman.
– DERIVATIVES **princedom** noun.
– ORIGIN from Latin *princeps* 'first, chief, sovereign'.

Prince Charming noun a handsome and honourable young male lover.
– ORIGIN from French *Roi Charmant*, 'King Charming', the title of a fairy tale.

prince consort noun the husband of a reigning queen who is himself a prince.

princeling noun **1** the ruler of a small or unimportant country. **2** a young prince.

princely adjective **1** relating to or suitable for a prince. **2** (of a sum of money) generous.

Prince of Darkness noun the Devil.

Prince of Wales noun a title granted to the heir apparent to the British throne (usually the eldest son of the monarch).

prince royal (or **princess royal**) noun the eldest son (or daughter) of a reigning monarch.

princess noun **1** a daughter or other close female relative of a monarch. **2** the wife or widow of a prince. **3** a female monarch of a small state.

principal adjective most important; main. •noun **1** the most important person in an organization or group. **2** the head of a school or college. **3** a sum of money lent or invested, on which interest is paid. **4** a person for whom another acts as a representative. **5** Law a person directly responsible for a crime.
– DERIVATIVES **principalship** noun.
– ORIGIN Latin *principalis* 'first, original'.

USAGE: Do not confuse **principal** and **principle**. Principal is usually an adjective meaning 'main or most important' (*the country's principal cities*), whereas **principle** is a noun that usually means 'a truth or general law used as the basis for something' (*the basic principles of democracy*).

principal boy noun Brit. a woman who takes the leading male role in a pantomime.

principality noun (pl. **principalities**) **1** a state ruled by a prince. **2** (**the Principality**) Brit. Wales.

principally adverb for the most part; chiefly.

principle noun **1** a truth or general law that is used as a basis for a theory or system of belief: *the basic principles of democracy.* **2** (usu. **principles**) a rule or belief governing a person's behaviour. **3** morally correct behaviour: *a man of principle.* **4** a general scientific theorem or natural law. **5** a fundamental quality or basis of something. **6** Chemistry an active or characteristic

constituent of a substance.
– PHRASES **in principle** in theory. **on principle** because of one's beliefs about what is right and wrong.
– ORIGIN Latin *principium* 'source'.

principled adjective (of actions or behaviour) based on one's beliefs about what is right and wrong.

prink verb (**prink oneself**) make minor improvements to one's appearance.
– ORIGIN probably related to former *prank* 'dress or adorn in a showy way'.

print verb **1** produce books, newspapers, etc. by a process involving the transfer of words or images to paper. **2** produce words or an image by printing. **3** produce a paper copy of information stored on a computer. **4** produce a photographic print from a negative. **5** write words clearly without joining the letters. **6** transfer a coloured design on to fabric or another surface. •noun **1** the printed words appearing in a book, newspaper, etc. **2** a mark where something has pressed or touched a surface: *paw prints*. **3** a printed picture or design. **4** a photograph printed on paper from a negative or transparency. **5** a copy of a motion picture on film. **6** a piece of fabric with a coloured design.
– PHRASES **in print 1** (of a book) available from the publisher. **2** in published form. **out of print** (of a book) no longer available from the publisher.
– DERIVATIVES **printable** adjective.
– ORIGIN Old French *preinte* 'pressed'.

printed circuit noun an electronic circuit based on thin strips of a conductor on an insulating board.

printer noun **1** a person or business involved in printing. **2** a machine for printing, especially one linked to a computer.

printing noun **1** the production of books, newspapers, etc. **2** all the copies of a book printed at one time. **3** handwriting in which the letters are written separately.

printing press noun a machine for printing from type or plates.

printmaker noun a person who creates and prints pictures or designs from plates or blocks.
– DERIVATIVES **printmaking** noun.

printout noun a page of printed material from a computer's printer.

print run noun the number of copies of a book, magazine, etc. printed at one time.

prion /pree-on/ noun a protein particle believed to be the cause of certain brain diseases such as BSE.
– ORIGIN by rearrangement of elements from *pro*(*teinaceous*) *in*(*fectious particle*).

prior[1] adjective coming before in time, order, or importance: *the government denied having any prior knowledge of the attack.*
– PHRASES **prior to** before.
– ORIGIN Latin, 'former, elder'.

prior[2] noun (fem. **prioress**) **1** (in an abbey) the person next in rank below an abbot (or abbess). **2** the head of a house of friars (or nuns).
– ORIGIN from Latin, 'former, elder'.

prioritize (or **prioritise**) verb **1** treat something

as most important. **2** decide the order of importance of items or tasks.
– DERIVATIVES **prioritization** noun.

priority noun (pl. **priorities**) **1** the condition of being treated as more important: *safety should take priority over any other matter.* **2** a thing regarded as more important than others. **3** Brit. the right to go before other traffic.

priory noun (pl. **priories**) a monastery or nunnery governed by a prior or prioress.

prise (US **prize**) verb **1** force something open or apart. **2** (**prise something out of/from**) obtain something from someone with difficulty.
– ORIGIN from Old French *prise* 'a grasp, taking hold'.

prism noun **1** a transparent object with triangular ends, that breaks light up into the colours of the rainbow. **2** a solid geometric figure whose two ends are parallel and of the same size and shape, and whose sides are parallelograms.
– ORIGIN Greek *prisma* 'thing sawn'.

prismatic adjective **1** relating to or in the shape of a prism. **2** (of colours) formed or distributed by a prism.

prison noun a building in which criminals or people awaiting trial are confined.
– ORIGIN Old French *prisun*.

prison camp noun a camp where prisoners of war or political prisoners are kept.

prisoner noun **1** a person found guilty of a crime and sent to prison. **2** a person captured and kept confined. **3** a person trapped by a situation: *he was a prisoner of his own fame.*
– PHRASES **take no prisoners** be ruthless in attempting to achieve one's objectives.

prisoner of conscience noun a person imprisoned for their political or religious views.

prisoner of war noun a person captured and imprisoned by the enemy in war.

prison officer noun Brit. a guard in a prison.

prissy adjective (**prissier**, **prissiest**) excessively concerned with behaving in a respectable way.
– DERIVATIVES **prissily** adverb **prissiness** noun.
– ORIGIN perhaps from PRIM and SISSY.

pristine /priss-teen/ adjective **1** in its original condition; unspoilt: *two miles of pristine beaches.* **2** clean and fresh as if new.
– DERIVATIVES **pristinely** adverb.
– ORIGIN Latin *pristinus* 'former'.

privacy /pri-vuh-si, pry-vuh-si/ noun a state in which one is not watched or disturbed by others.

private adjective **1** for or belonging to one particular person or group only: *his private plane.* **2** (of thoughts or feelings) not to be revealed to others. **3** not revealing thoughts and feelings to others. **4** (of a service or industry) provided by a person or commercial business rather than the state. **5** working for oneself rather than for the state or an organization. **6** not connected with one's work or official position: *the president visited the country in a private capacity.* **7** (of a place) free from people who may overhear or interrupt. •noun **1** (also **private soldier**) a soldier of the lowest rank in the army. **2** (**privates**) informal private parts; genitals.

p

- PHRASES **in private** with no one else present.
- DERIVATIVES **privately** adverb.
- ORIGIN Latin *privatus* 'withdrawn from public life'.

private company noun Brit. a company whose shares may not be offered to the public for sale.

private detective (also **private investigator**) noun a detective who is not a police officer and who carries out investigations for private clients.

private enterprise noun business or industry managed by independent companies rather than the state.

privateer /pry-vuh-teer/ noun historical a privately owned armed ship, authorized by a government for use in war.

private eye noun informal a private detective.

private life noun a person's personal relationships, interests, etc., as distinct from their work or public life.

private means plural noun Brit. income from investments, property, etc., rather than from employment.

private member noun (in the UK, Canada, Australia, and New Zealand) a member of a parliament who is not a minister or does not hold government office.

private parts plural noun euphemistic a person's genitals.

private school noun 1 Brit. an independent school that is wholly financed by fees paid by pupils. 2 N. Amer. a school supported by a private organization or individuals.

private secretary noun 1 a secretary who deals with the personal matters of their employer. 2 a civil servant acting as an assistant to a senior government official.

private sector noun the part of a country's economy not under direct state control.

privation /pry-vay-sh'n/ noun a state in which essentials such as food are lacking.
- ORIGIN Latin.

privatize (or **privatise**) verb transfer a business or industry from public to private ownership.
- DERIVATIVES **privatization** noun.

privet /pri-vit/ noun a shrub with small dark green leaves.
- ORIGIN unknown.

privilege noun 1 a special right or advantage granted or available to a particular person or group. 2 an opportunity to do something regarded as a special honour: *she had the privilege of giving the opening lecture.* 3 the rights and advantages of rich and powerful people: *a young man of wealth and privilege.*
- ORIGIN Latin *privilegium* 'bill or law affecting an individual'.

privileged adjective 1 having a special right or advantage. 2 (of information) legally protected from being made public.

privy adjective (**privy to**) sharing in the knowledge of something secret. ● noun (pl. **privies**) a toilet in a small shed outside a house.
- DERIVATIVES **privily** adverb.
- ORIGIN Old French *prive* 'private', also 'private place'.

Privy Council noun a group of advisers appointed by a sovereign or a Governor General.
- DERIVATIVES **privy counsellor** (also **privy councillor**) noun.

privy purse noun (in the UK) an allowance from the Duchy of Lancaster to meet some of the monarch's private and official costs.

privy seal noun (in the UK) a seal fixed to state documents.

prix fixe /pree feeks/ noun a meal of several courses costing a fixed price.
- ORIGIN French, 'fixed price'.

prize[1] noun 1 something given as a reward to a winner or in recognition of an outstanding achievement. 2 something of great value that is worth struggling to achieve: *the prize will be victory in the election.* ● adjective 1 having been or likely to be awarded a prize. 2 outstanding of its kind. ● verb value highly: *the berries were prized for their healing properties.*
- ORIGIN Old French *preisier* 'praise'.

prize[2] verb US spelling of PRISE.

prizefight noun a boxing match for prize money.
- DERIVATIVES **prizefighter** noun.

pro[1] noun (pl. **pros**) informal a professional. ● adjective professional.

pro[2] noun (pl. **pros**) (usu. in phrase **pros and cons**) an advantage or argument in favour of something. ● preposition & adverb in favour of.
- ORIGIN Latin, 'for, on behalf of'.

pro-[1] prefix 1 in favour of; supporting: *pro-choice.* 2 referring to movement forwards, out, or away: *propel.* 3 acting as a substitute for: *proconsul.*
- ORIGIN Latin *pro* 'in front of, instead of, because of'.

pro-[2] prefix before in time or order: *proactive.*
- ORIGIN Greek *pro.*

proactive adjective creating or controlling a situation rather than just responding to it.
- DERIVATIVES **proactively** adverb.

probabilistic adjective based on a theory of probability; involving chance.

probability noun (pl. **probabilities**) 1 the extent to which something is likely to happen or be the case: *rain will make the probability of postponement even greater.* 2 a probable or the most probable event.
- PHRASES **in all probability** most probably.

probable adjective likely to happen or be the case. ● noun Brit. a person likely to become or do something.
- ORIGIN Latin *probabilis.*

probably adverb almost certainly.

probate noun 1 the official process of proving that a will is valid. 2 a verified copy of a will with a certificate as handed to the executors.
- ORIGIN Latin *probatum* 'something proved'.

probation noun 1 the release of an offender from detention or prison on condition that they behave well and report regularly to a supervisor. 2 a period of training and testing a person in a new job or role.
- DERIVATIVES **probationary** adjective.

probationer noun 1 a person serving a period of probation in a job or role. 2 an offender on probation from detention or prison.

probation officer noun a person who supervises offenders on probation.

probe noun 1 a thorough investigation: *a probe into political corruption.* 2 a blunt-ended surgical instrument for exploring a wound or part of the body. 3 a small measuring or testing device, especially an electrode. 4 an unmanned exploratory spacecraft. • verb 1 investigate something thoroughly. 2 explore or examine something with the hands or an instrument.
– DERIVATIVES **prober** noun **probing** adjective.
– ORIGIN from Latin *proba* 'examination'.

probiotic /proh-by-ot-ik/ noun a substance which stimulates the growth of beneficial microorganisms, especially the natural bacteria in the intestines.

probity /proh-bi-ti/ noun the quality of having strong moral principles; honesty and good character.
– ORIGIN Latin *probitas.*

problem noun 1 a thing that is difficult to deal with or understand. 2 a question that can be resolved by using logical thought or mathematics.
– ORIGIN Greek *problēma.*

problematic adjective difficult to deal with or understand; presenting a problem.
– DERIVATIVES **problematical** adjective **problematically** adverb.

problematize (or **problematise**) verb make something into or regard something as a problem.

pro bono /proh bon-oh, proh boh-noh/ adverb & adjective chiefly N. Amer. referring to legal work undertaken without charge.
– ORIGIN Latin.

proboscis /pruh-boss-iss/ noun (pl. **probosces** /pruh-boss-eez/ or **proboscises**) 1 the long flexible nose of a mammal, such as an elephant's trunk. 2 an elongated sucking organ or mouthpart of an insect or worm.
– ORIGIN Greek *proboskis* 'means of obtaining food'.

proboscis monkey noun a monkey native to the forests of Borneo, the male of which has a large dangling nose.

procedure noun 1 an established or official way of doing something. 2 a series of actions carried out in a certain way. 3 a surgical operation.
– DERIVATIVES **procedural** adjective **procedurally** adverb.
– ORIGIN French *procédure.*

proceed /pruh-seed/ verb 1 begin a course of action. 2 do something after something else: *she got up and proceeded to cook us breakfast.* 3 (of an action) continue. 4 move forward. 5 start a lawsuit against someone.
– ORIGIN Latin *procedere.*

proceedings plural noun 1 an event or a series of activities with a set procedure. 2 action taken in a law court to settle a dispute. 3 a report of a set of meetings or a conference.

proceeds /proh-seedz/ plural noun money obtained from an event or activity.

process¹ /proh-sess/ noun 1 a series of actions or steps taken towards achieving a particular end. 2 a natural series of changes: *the ageing process.* 3 a summons to appear in a law court.

4 a natural projection or growth on the body or in an organism. • verb 1 treat raw material, food, etc. in order to change or preserve it. 2 deal with by means of an established procedure: *an administrator is needed to process applications.* 3 operate on data by means of a computer program.
– ORIGIN Latin *processus* 'progression, course'.

process² /pruh-sess/ verb (of people or vehicles) move forward in an orderly way.
– ORIGIN from **PROCESSION.**

procession noun 1 a number of people or vehicles moving forward in an orderly way. 2 the action of moving forward in an orderly way. 3 a large number of people or things coming one after the other.

processional adjective relating to a religious or ceremonial procession. • noun a book of litanies and hymns used in Christian religious processions.

processor noun 1 a machine that processes something. 2 a central processing unit in a computer.

pro-choice adjective supporting the right of a woman to choose to have an abortion.

proclaim verb 1 announce something officially or publicly. 2 declare someone officially or publicly to be: *he proclaimed James as King of England.* 3 show clearly; be a sign of: *his high forehead proclaimed his strength of mind.*
– DERIVATIVES **proclamation** noun.
– ORIGIN Latin *proclamare* 'cry out'.

proclivity /pruh-kliv-i-ti/ noun (pl. **proclivities**) a tendency to do something regularly; an inclination.
– ORIGIN Latin *proclivitas.*

proconsul /proh-kon-suhl/ noun 1 a governor or deputy consul of a colony. 2 a governor of a province in ancient Rome.

procrastinate /proh-krass-ti-nayt/ verb delay or postpone action.
– DERIVATIVES **procrastination** noun **procrastinator** noun.
– ORIGIN Latin *procrastinare* 'defer till the morning'.

procreate verb produce young; reproduce.
– DERIVATIVES **procreation** noun **procreative** adjective.
– ORIGIN Latin *procreare* 'generate, bring forth'.

Procrustean /proh-kruss-ti-uhn/ adjective literary enforcing uniformity regardless of natural variation or individuality.
– ORIGIN from *Procrustes,* a robber in Greek mythology who fitted victims to a bed by stretching or cutting off parts of them.

proctology /prok-tol-uh-ji/ noun the branch of medicine concerned with the anus and rectum.
– DERIVATIVES **proctological** adjective **proctologist** noun.
– ORIGIN from Greek *prōktos* 'anus'.

proctor noun Brit. an officer responsible for discipline at certain universities.
– ORIGIN contraction of **PROCURATOR.**

procurator /prok-yuu-ray-ter/ noun (in Scotland) a lawyer practising before the lower courts.
– ORIGIN Latin *procurator* 'administrator, finance agent'.

p

procurator fiscal noun (pl. **procurators fiscal** or **procurator fiscals**) (in Scotland) a local coroner and public prosecutor.

procure verb **1** get or obtain something. **2** Law persuade or cause someone to do something. **3** provide a prostitute for someone.
– DERIVATIVES **procurable** adjective **procurement** noun **procurer** noun.
– ORIGIN Latin *procurare* 'take care of, manage'.

prod verb (**prods, prodding, prodded**) **1** poke someone or something with a finger or pointed object. **2** persuade someone who is reluctant or slow to do something. ● noun **1** a poke. **2** a reminder to do something. **3** a pointed implement used to drive cattle.
– ORIGIN perhaps from **POKE**¹ and dialect *brod* 'to goad, prod'.

prodigal adjective **1** using money or resources in a wasteful way. **2** (**prodigal with**) having lavish amounts of something. ● noun **1** a wasteful and extravagant person. **2** (also **prodigal son**) a person who leaves home and lives a wasteful and extravagant life but returns repentant. [with reference to the Gospel of Luke, chapter 15.]
– DERIVATIVES **prodigality** noun **prodigally** adverb.
– ORIGIN Latin *prodigalis*.

prodigious /pruh-**dij**-uhss/ adjective impressively large.
– DERIVATIVES **prodigiously** adverb.
– ORIGIN Latin *prodigiosus*.

prodigy noun (pl. **prodigies**) **1** a young person with exceptional abilities. **2** an outstanding example of a quality: *his book is a prodigy of information gathering.*
– ORIGIN Latin *prodigium* 'portent'.

produce verb /pruh-**dyooss**/ **1** make, manufacture, or create something. **2** cause to happen or exist: *a report has concluded that richer colleges produce better results.* **3** show or provide something for inspection or use. **4** administer the financial and managerial aspects of a film or broadcast or the staging of a play. **5** supervise the making of a musical recording. ● noun /**prod**-yooss/ things that have been produced or grown: *dairy produce.*
– DERIVATIVES **producer** noun **producible** adjective.
– ORIGIN Latin *producere* 'bring forth, extend, produce'.

product noun **1** an article or substance manufactured for sale. **2** a result of an action or process: *the arrests were the product of a lengthy investigation.* **3** a substance produced during a natural, chemical, or manufacturing process. **4** Mathematics a quantity obtained by multiplying quantities together.
– ORIGIN Latin *productum* 'something produced'.

production noun **1** the action of producing something or the process of being produced. **2** the amount of something produced. **3** a film, record, or play viewed in terms of the way it is made or staged: *a new production of Hamlet.*

production line noun an assembly line in a factory.

productive adjective **1** producing or able to produce large amounts of goods or crops. **2** achieving or producing a significant amount or result: *a long and productive career.*
– DERIVATIVES **productively** adverb

productiveness noun.

productivity noun **1** the state of being able to produce something in large quantities. **2** the efficiency with which products are produced: *workers boosted productivity by 30 per cent.*

product placement noun a practice in which companies pay for their products to be featured in films and television programmes.

profane adjective **1** not holy or religious; secular. **2** not showing respect for God or holy things. **3** (of language) blasphemous or obscene. ● verb treat something holy with disrespect.
– DERIVATIVES **profanation** noun.
– ORIGIN Latin *profanus* 'outside the temple, not sacred'.

profanity noun (pl. **profanities**) **1** behaviour that shows a lack of respect for God or holy things. **2** a swear word.

profess verb **1** claim, often falsely, that something is true or the case: *she lied, cheated, and then professed her undying love.* **2** state openly that one has a particular feeling, opinion, etc. **3** belong to a particular religion.
– ORIGIN Latin *profiteri* 'declare publicly'.

professed adjective **1** (of a quality or feeling) claimed openly but often falsely. **2** openly declared to be: *a professed liberal.*
– DERIVATIVES **professedly** adverb.

profession noun **1** an occupation that involves training and a formal qualification. **2** (treated as sing. or pl.) a group of people working in a profession: *the legal profession.* **3** a claim that is often false. **4** a declaration of belief in a religion.

professional adjective **1** relating or belonging to a profession. **2** engaged in a sport or other activity as a paid occupation rather than as an amateur. **3** appropriate to a professional person; competent or skilful. ● noun **1** a person who is engaged or qualified in a profession. **2** a person who is very skilled in a particular activity.
– DERIVATIVES **professionalize** (or **professionalise**) verb **professionally** adverb.

professional foul noun Brit. (especially in football) a deliberate foul committed to prevent an opponent from scoring.

professionalism noun the competence or skill expected of a professional.

professor noun **1** a university academic of the highest rank. **2** N. Amer. a university teacher. **3** a person who openly declares their faith.
– DERIVATIVES **professorial** adjective **professorship** noun.
– ORIGIN Latin.

proffer verb offer something to someone for acceptance.
– ORIGIN Old French *proffrir*.

proficient adjective competent or skilled in doing or using something: *she's proficient in Urdu.*
– DERIVATIVES **proficiency** noun **proficiently** adverb.
– ORIGIN from Latin *proficere* 'to advance'.

profile noun **1** an outline of something, especially a face, as seen from one side. **2** a short descriptive article about someone. **3** the extent to which a person or organization attracts public notice: *her high profile as a pop*

star. • verb 1 describe someone in a short
article. 2 (be profiled) appear in outline.
– PHRASES in profile as seen from one side. keep
a low profile try not to attract attention.
– DERIVATIVES profiler noun.
– ORIGIN from former Italian *profilo* 'a drawing
or border'.

profiling noun the analysis of a person's
psychological and behavioural characteristics.

profit noun 1 a financial gain, especially the
difference between the amount earned and
the costs involved in producing, buying, or
operating something. 2 the advantage or
benefit gained from something. • verb (profits,
profiting, profited) benefit, especially
financially: *the only people to profit from the
episode were the lawyers.*
– DERIVATIVES profitless adjective.
– ORIGIN Latin *profectus* 'progress, profit'.

profitable adjective 1 (of a business or
activity) making a profit. 2 beneficial; useful:
he'd had a profitable day.
– DERIVATIVES profitability noun profitably
adverb.

profit and loss account noun an account to
which incomes and gains are added and
expenses and losses taken away, so as to show
the net profit or loss.

profiteering noun the making of an excessive
profit in an unfair or dishonest way.
– DERIVATIVES profiteer noun.

profiterole /pruh-fit-uh-rohl/ noun a small
ball of choux pastry filled with cream and
covered with chocolate sauce.
– ORIGIN French, 'small profit'.

profit margin noun the difference between
the cost of producing something and the price
for which it is sold.

profit-sharing noun a system in which the
people who work for a company receive a
direct share of its profits.

profligate /prof-li-guht/ adjective 1 recklessly
extravagant or wasteful. 2 indulging
excessively in physical pleasures; licentious.
• noun a licentious or wasteful person.
– DERIVATIVES profligacy noun.
– ORIGIN Latin *profligatus* 'dissolute'.

pro forma /proh for-muh/ adverb & adjective
as a matter of form or politeness. • noun a
standard document or form.
– ORIGIN Latin.

profound adjective (profounder, profoundest)
1 very great or intense: *profound feelings of
disquiet.* 2 showing great knowledge or
insight. 3 demanding deep study or thought.
4 old use very deep.
– DERIVATIVES profoundly adverb.
– ORIGIN Latin *profundus.*

profundity noun (pl. profundities) 1 great
depth of insight or knowledge. 2 intensity of a
state, quality, or emotion.

profuse adjective done or appearing in large
quantities; abundant: *I offered my profuse
apologies.*
– DERIVATIVES profusely adverb.
– ORIGIN Latin *profusus* 'lavish, spread out'.

profusion /pruh-fyoo-zh'n/ noun a large
quantity of something; an abundance.

progenitor /proh-jen-i-ter/ noun 1 an ancestor

or parent. 2 a person who originates a cultural
or intellectual movement.
– DERIVATIVES progenitorial adjective.
– ORIGIN Latin.

progeny /proj-uh-ni/ noun (treated as sing. or
pl.) the offspring of a person or animal.
– ORIGIN Old French *progenie.*

progesterone /pruh-jess-tuh-rohn/ noun a
hormone that stimulates the womb to prepare
for pregnancy.

progestogen /proh-jess-tuh-juhn/ noun a
hormone that maintains pregnancy and
prevents further ovulation, used in oral
contraceptives.

prognathous /prog-nay-thuss, prog-
nuh-thuss/ adjective (of a jaw or chin)
projecting.
– ORIGIN from PRO-² + Greek *gnathos* 'jaw'.

prognosis /prog-noh-siss/ noun (pl. prognoses
/prog-noh-seez/) a forecast, especially of the
likely course of a medical condition.
– ORIGIN Greek.

prognostic /prog-noss-tik/ adjective predicting
the likely course of a medical condition.
– DERIVATIVES prognostically adverb.

prognosticate verb make a forecast about a
future event.
– DERIVATIVES prognostication noun
prognosticator noun.

programmatic adjective relating to a
programme, schedule, or method.
– DERIVATIVES programmatically adverb.

programme (US program) noun 1 a planned
series of events. 2 a radio or television
broadcast. 3 a set of related measures or
activities with a long-term aim: *a programme
of reforms.* 4 a sheet or booklet giving details
of a performance or event. 5 (program) a
series of coded software instructions to
control the operation of a computer or other
machine. • verb (programmes, programming,
programmed; US programs, programing,
programed) 1 (program) provide a computer
with a program. 2 cause a person or animal to
behave in a predetermined way. 3 arrange
something according to a plan or schedule.
– DERIVATIVES programmable adjective
programmer noun.
– ORIGIN Greek *programma.*

progress noun /proh-gres/ 1 forward
movement towards a destination.
2 development towards an improved or more
advanced condition: *some states had made
significant progress in nuclear technology.* • verb
/pruh-gres/ 1 move towards a destination.
2 develop towards a more advanced condition.
– ORIGIN Latin *progressus* 'an advance'.

progression noun 1 a gradual movement or
development towards a destination or a more
advanced state. 2 a number of things in a
series. 3 a sequence of numbers following a
mathematical rule.
– DERIVATIVES progressional adjective.

progressive adjective 1 happening or
developing gradually: *a progressive decline in
popularity.* 2 favouring social reform or
original thinking. 3 (of tax) at a rate
increasing with the sum taxed. • noun a person
who favours social reform.

- DERIVATIVES **progressively** adverb **progressiveness** noun.

prohibit verb (**prohibits, prohibiting, prohibited**) **1** formally forbid someone from doing something by law or a rule. **2** make impossible; prevent: *the budget agreement had prohibited any tax cuts.*
- DERIVATIVES **prohibitory** adjective.
- ORIGIN Latin *prohibere* 'keep in check'.

prohibition /proh-hi-**bi**-sh'n, proh-i-**bi**-sh'n/ noun **1** the action of formally forbidding something. **2** an order that forbids something. **3** (**Prohibition**) the prevention by law of the manufacture and sale of alcohol in the US from 1920 to 1933.
- DERIVATIVES **Prohibitionist** noun.

prohibitive adjective **1** forbidding or preventing something. **2** (of a price) so high as to prevent something being done or bought.
- DERIVATIVES **prohibitively** adverb.

project noun /**pro**-jekt/ **1** an enterprise that is carefully planned to achieve a particular aim. **2** a piece of research work by a student. **3** N. Amer. a government-subsidized estate or block of homes. •verb /pruh-**jekt**/ **1** estimate or forecast something on the basis of present trends. **2** plan a scheme. **3** stick out beyond something else. **4** throw or send something forward or outward. **5** cause light, shadow, or an image to fall on a surface. **6** present a particular image or impression: *he strives to project an image of youth.* **7** (**project something on to**) think that another person has the same feelings or emotions as oneself, especially unconsciously.
- ORIGIN Latin *projectum* 'something prominent'.

projectile noun a missile fired or thrown at a target. •adjective **1** relating to a projectile. **2** propelled with great force.

projection noun **1** an estimate or forecast based on present trends. **2** a thing that sticks out from something. **3** the projecting of an image or sound. **4** the presentation of someone or something in a particular way: *the legal profession's projection of an image of altruism.* **5** a method for representing part of the surface of a solid object on a flat surface, used especially for making maps.
- DERIVATIVES **projective** adjective **projectionist** noun.

projector noun a device for projecting slides or film on to a screen.

prolapse /**proh**-laps/ noun **1** a condition in which a part or organ of the body has slipped forward or down. **2** a part or organ that has slipped forward or down.
- DERIVATIVES **prolapsed** adjective.
- ORIGIN from Latin *prolabi* 'slip forward'.

prole noun informal, derogatory a working-class person.
- ORIGIN from PROLETARIAT.

prolegomenon /proh-li-**gom**-i-nuhn/ noun (pl. **prolegomena** /proh-li-**gom**-i-nuh/) a critical or discursive introduction to a book.
- ORIGIN Greek.

proletarian /proh-li-**tair**-i-uhn/ adjective relating to workers or working-class people. •noun a working-class person.
- ORIGIN Latin *proletarius*, referring to a person

without wealth, who served the state only by producing offspring.

proletariat noun (treated as sing. or pl.) workers or working-class people.

pro-life adjective opposing abortion and euthanasia.
- DERIVATIVES **pro-lifer** noun.

proliferate /pruh-**lif**-uh-rayt/ verb **1** increase rapidly in number: *the rave clubs that proliferated in the late Eighties.* **2** (of a cell or organism) reproduce rapidly.
- DERIVATIVES **proliferation** noun **proliferative** adjective.
- ORIGIN from Latin *prolificus*.

prolific adjective **1** producing much fruit or foliage or many offspring. **2** (of an artist, author, or composer) producing many works. **3** present in large quantities; plentiful.
- DERIVATIVES **prolifically** adverb.
- ORIGIN Latin *prolificus*.

prolix /**proh**-liks, pruh-**liks**/ adjective (of speech or writing) long and boring.
- DERIVATIVES **prolixity** noun.
- ORIGIN Latin *prolixus* 'poured forth, extended'.

prologue noun **1** an introductory section or scene in a book, play, or musical work. **2** an event or action leading to another.
- ORIGIN Greek *prologos*.

prolong verb cause to last longer: *the council prolonged the deadline to March 9th.*
- DERIVATIVES **prolongation** noun.
- ORIGIN Latin *prolongare*.

prolonged adjective continuing for a long time; lengthy.

prom noun informal **1** Brit. a promenade along a seafront. **2** Brit. a promenade concert. **3** N. Amer. a formal dance at a high school or college.

promenade /prom-uh-**nahd**, prom-uh-nahd/ noun **1** a paved public walk along a seafront. **2** a leisurely walk taken for social reasons. •verb take a leisurely walk for social reasons.
- DERIVATIVES **promenader** noun.
- ORIGIN French.

promenade concert noun Brit. a concert of classical music at which part of the audience stands in an area without seating.

Promethean /pruh-**mee**-thi-uhn/ adjective daring or skilful like Prometheus, a minor god in Greek mythology who stole fire from the gods and gave it to the human race.

promethium /pruh-**mee**-thi-uhm/ noun an unstable radioactive metallic chemical element of the lanthanide series.
- ORIGIN named after *Prometheus* (see **PROMETHEAN**).

prominence noun **1** the state of being important, famous, or noticeable. **2** a thing that projects or sticks out.

prominent adjective **1** important; famous. **2** projecting or sticking out from something. **3** particularly noticeable: *the statue occupies a prominent position in the Sculpture Garden.*
- DERIVATIVES **prominently** adverb.
- ORIGIN from Latin *prominere* 'jut out'.

promiscuous /pruh-**miss**-kyuu-uhss/ adjective **1** having many sexual partners. **2** not selective in approach; indiscriminate: *a promiscuous mixing of styles.*

- DERIVATIVES **promiscuity** noun **promiscuously** adverb.
- ORIGIN Latin *promiscuus* 'indiscriminate'.

promise noun **1** an assurance that one will do something or that something will happen. **2** indications of future excellence or success: *he showed some promise as an actor.* **3** a sign that something is likely to happen. • verb **1** assure someone that one will do something or that something will happen. **2** make something seem likely: *it promised to be a night to remember.*
- ORIGIN Latin *promissum*.

Promised Land noun **1** the land of Canaan, promised to Abraham and his descendants in the Bible (Book of Genesis, chapter 12). **2** (**the promised land**) a place or situation where great happiness is expected.

promisee noun Law a person to whom a promise is made.

promising adjective showing signs of future excellence or success.
- DERIVATIVES **promisingly** adverb.

promisor noun Law a person who makes a promise.

promissory note /prom-i-suh-ri/ noun a signed document containing a written promise to pay a stated sum.

promo /proh-moh/ noun (pl. **promos**) informal a promotional film, video, etc.

promontory /prom-uhn-tuh-ri/ noun (pl. **promontories**) a point of high land jutting out into the sea or a lake.
- ORIGIN Latin *promontorium*.

promote verb **1** support or actively encourage a cause, venture, or aim. **2** publicize a product or celebrity. **3** appoint someone to a higher position or rank. **4** transfer a sports team to a higher division.
- ORIGIN Latin *promovere* 'move forward'.

promoter noun **1** the organizer of a sporting event or theatrical production. **2** a supporter of a cause or aim.

promotion noun **1** activity that supports or encourages something: *the promotion of human rights.* **2** the publicizing of a product or celebrity. **3** (**promotions**) the activity or business of publicizing a product or celebrity. **4** the action of promoting someone or something to a higher position or rank.
- DERIVATIVES **promotional** adjective.

prompt verb **1** cause something to happen. **2** (**prompt someone to/to do**) cause someone to do something. **3** encourage a hesitating speaker to say something. **4** supply a forgotten word or line to an actor. • noun **1** an act of prompting a speaker or actor. **2** a word or phrase used to prompt an actor. **3** a word or symbol that appears on a computer screen to show that input is required. • adjective done or acting without delay. • adverb Brit. exactly or punctually: *lunch is at 12 o'clock prompt.*
- DERIVATIVES **promptly** adverb **promptness** noun.
- ORIGIN Latin *promptus* 'brought to light', also 'ready'.

prompter noun a person who prompts the actors during a play.

promulgate /prom-uhl-gayt/ verb **1** make something widely known. **2** put a law or decree into effect by an official

announcement.
- DERIVATIVES **promulgation** noun **promulgator** noun.
- ORIGIN Latin *promulgare* 'expose to public view'.

prone adjective **1** (**prone to/to do**) likely or liable to suffer from, do, or experience something unpleasant or undesirable. **2** lying flat, especially face downwards.
- DERIVATIVES **proneness** noun.
- ORIGIN Latin *pronus* 'leaning forward'.

prong noun **1** each of two or more projecting pointed parts on a fork or other article. **2** each of the separate parts of an attack, argument, or scheme.
- DERIVATIVES **pronged** adjective.
- ORIGIN perhaps related to German *prange* 'pinching instrument'.

pronominal /proh-nom-i-n'l/ adjective relating to or acting as a pronoun.
- DERIVATIVES **pronominally** adverb.

pronoun noun a word used instead of a noun to indicate someone or something already mentioned or known, e.g. *I, she, this.*

pronounce /pruh-nownss/ verb **1** make the sound of a word or part of a word. **2** declare or announce something in a formal or solemn way. **3** (**pronounce on**) pass judgement or make a decision on.
- DERIVATIVES **pronounceable** adjective **pronouncer** noun.
- ORIGIN Latin *pronuntiare*.

pronounced adjective very noticeable.
- DERIVATIVES **pronouncedly** adverb.

pronouncement noun a formal public statement.

pronto adverb informal promptly; quickly.
- ORIGIN Spanish.

pronunciation /pruh-nun-si-ay-sh'n/ noun the way in which a word is pronounced.

USAGE: **Pronunciation** should be pronounced with **-nun-** as the second syllable (never as **-nownss-**).

proof noun **1** evidence that proves that a fact or statement is true. **2** the action of proving that something is true. **3** a series of stages in the solving of a mathematical or philosophical problem. **4** a copy of a printed page used for making corrections before final printing. **5** a trial photographic print. **6** a standard used to measure the strength of distilled alcoholic spirits. • adjective (in combination) able to resist: *bulletproof.* • verb **1** make a proof of a printed work. **2** make something waterproof.
- ORIGIN Old French *proeve*.

proof positive noun final or absolute proof of something.

proofread verb read printer's proofs and mark any errors.
- DERIVATIVES **proofreader** noun.

proof spirit noun a mixture of alcohol and water used as a standard of strength of distilled alcoholic spirits.

prop¹ noun **1** a pole or beam used as a temporary support. **2** a source of support or assistance. **3** (also **prop forward**) Rugby a forward at either end of the front row of a scrum. • verb (**props, propping, propped**) **1** support something with a prop. **2** lean

p

something against something else. **3 (prop someone/thing up)** support or help someone or something that would otherwise fail.
- ORIGIN probably from Dutch *proppe* 'support (for vines)'.

prop² noun a portable object used on the set of a play or film.
- ORIGIN abbreviation of **PROPERTY**.

prop³ noun informal an aircraft propeller.

propaganda noun information that is often biased or misleading, used to promote a political cause or point of view.
- ORIGIN from Latin *congregatio de propaganda fide* 'congregation for propagation of the faith'.

propagandist chiefly derogatory noun a person who spreads propaganda. ●adjective consisting of or spreading propaganda.
- DERIVATIVES **propagandize** (or **propagandise**) verb.

propagate verb **1** produce a new plant naturally from the parent stock. **2** promote an idea or knowledge widely. **3** transmit motion, light, sound, etc. in a particular direction.
- DERIVATIVES **propagation** noun.
- ORIGIN Latin *propagare* 'multiply from layers or shoots'.

propagator noun **1** a covered, heated container of earth or compost, used for germinating seedlings. **2** a person who spreads an idea or knowledge.

propane /proh-payn/ noun a flammable gas present in natural gas and used as bottled fuel.

propel verb (**propels**, **propelling**, **propelled**) **1** drive or push someone or something forwards. **2** send or force into a particular situation: *his doctorate propelled him into prominence.*
- ORIGIN Latin *propellere* 'to drive forward'.

propellant noun **1** a compressed gas that forces out the contents of an aerosol. **2** a substance used to provide thrust in a rocket engine. ●adjective capable of propelling something.

propeller (also **propellor**) noun a revolving shaft with two or more angled blades, for propelling a ship or aircraft.

propelling pencil noun a pencil with a thin lead that may be extended as the point is worn away.

propensity noun (pl. **propensities**) a tendency to behave in a particular way.
- ORIGIN from Latin *propensus* 'inclined'.

proper adjective **1** truly what something is said or regarded to be; genuine. **2** (after a noun) according to the precise meaning of the term: *the World Cup proper.* **3** suitable, right, or correct: *an artist needs the proper tools.* **4** respectable, especially excessively so. **5** (**proper to**) belonging particularly to: *the degree of certainty proper to mathematics.* ●adverb Brit. informal or dialect thoroughly.
- ORIGIN Latin *proprius* 'one's own, special'.

proper fraction noun a fraction that is less than one, with the numerator less than the denominator.

properly adverb **1** in a proper way. **2** in the precise sense. **3** informal, chiefly Brit. completely.

proper noun (also **proper name**) noun a name for a particular person, place, or organization,

having an initial capital letter. Often contrasted with **COMMON NOUN**.

propertied adjective owning property and land.

property noun (pl. **properties**) **1** a thing or things belonging to someone. **2** a building and the land belonging to it. **3** Law the right to possess, use, or dispose of something; ownership. **4** a characteristic or quality: *a perfumed oil with calming properties.*
- ORIGIN Latin *proprietas.*

prophecy /prof-i-si/ noun (pl. **prophecies**) **1** a prediction of a future event. **2** the power of prophesying the future.
- ORIGIN Greek *prophēteia.*

prophesy /prof-i-sy/ verb (**prophesies**, **prophesying**, **prophesied**) predict a future event.

USAGE: The words **prophesy** and **prophecy** are often confused. **Prophesy** is the spelling that should be used for the verb (*how can I prophesy the coming of a God in which I do not believe?*), whereas **prophecy** is the correct spelling for the noun (*a bleak prophecy of war*).

prophet noun (fem. **prophetess**) **1** (in some religions) a person believed to have been sent by God to teach people about his intentions. **2** a person who predicts the future. **3** a person who promotes a new belief or theory.
- ORIGIN Greek *prophētēs* 'spokesman'.

prophetic /pruh-fet-ik/ adjective **1** accurately predicting the future. **2** relating to a prophet or prophecy.
- DERIVATIVES **prophetical** adjective **prophetically** adverb.

prophylactic /prof-i-lak-tik/ adjective intended to prevent disease. ●noun **1** a medicine or course of action that is intended to prevent disease. **2** N. Amer. a condom.
- ORIGIN Greek *prophulaktikos.*

prophylaxis /pro-fi-lak-siss/ noun action taken to prevent disease.
- ORIGIN Greek *phulaxis* 'act of guarding'.

propinquity /pruh-ping-kwi-ti/ noun nearness in time or space; proximity.
- ORIGIN Latin *propinquitas.*

propitiate /pruh-pish-i-ayt/ verb win or regain the favour of a person, god, or spirit.
- DERIVATIVES **propitiation** noun **propitiatory** adjective.
- ORIGIN Latin *propitiare* 'make favourable'.

propitious /pruh-pish-uhss/ adjective giving or indicating a good chance of success; favourable: *it was a propitious moment for a global telephone network.*
- DERIVATIVES **propitiously** adverb **propitiousness** noun.

propolis /prop-uh-liss/ noun a substance collected by honeybees from tree buds for constructing and varnishing honeycombs.
- ORIGIN Greek, 'suburb', also 'bee glue'.

proponent /pruh-poh-nuhnt/ noun a person who supports a theory, proposal, or project.
- ORIGIN from Latin *proponere* 'put forward'.

proportion noun **1** a part, share, or number considered in relation to a whole. **2** the relationship of one thing to another in terms of size or quantity; a ratio. **3** the correct or

pleasing relationship of things or between the parts of a whole: *keep the size of the vase and the size of the flowers in your arrangement in proportion.* 4 (**proportions**) dimensions; size.
● **verb** formal adjust something so as to have a particular or suitable relationship to something else.
– PHRASES **in** (or **out of**) **proportion** regarded without (or with) exaggeration. **sense of proportion** the ability to judge the relative importance of things.
– DERIVATIVES **proportioned** adjective.
– ORIGIN Latin.

proportional adjective corresponding in size or amount to something else.
– DERIVATIVES **proportionality** noun **proportionally** adverb.

proportional representation noun an electoral system in which parties gain seats in proportion to the number of votes cast for them.

proportionate adjective another term for **PROPORTIONAL**.
– DERIVATIVES **proportionately** adverb.

proposal noun 1 a plan or suggestion put forward for consideration. 2 the action of proposing something. 3 an offer of marriage.

propose verb 1 put forward an idea or plan for consideration. 2 nominate someone for an office or position. 3 put forward a motion to a law-making body or committee. 4 plan or intend to do something. 5 make an offer of marriage to someone.
– DERIVATIVES **proposer** noun.
– ORIGIN Latin *proponere* 'put forward'.

proposition noun 1 a statement expressing a judgement or opinion. 2 a proposed scheme or plan. 3 a problem or task to be dealt with: *keeping weight off for life is a difficult proposition.* 4 Mathematics a formal statement of a theorem or problem. ● verb informal 1 make an offer or suggestion to someone. 2 ask someone to have sex.
– DERIVATIVES **propositional** adjective.

propound /pruh-**pownd**/ verb put forward an idea or theory for consideration.
– DERIVATIVES **propounder** noun.
– ORIGIN Latin *proponere* 'put forward'.

proprietary adjective 1 relating to an owner or ownership. 2 behaving as if one owned something or someone: *he looked around with a proprietary air.* 3 (of a product) marketed under a registered trade name.
– ORIGIN from Latin *proprietarius* 'proprietor'.

proprietary name (also **proprietary term**) noun a name of a product or service registered as a trademark.

proprietor noun (fem. **proprietress**) 1 the owner of a business. 2 a holder of property.

proprietorial /pruh-pry-uh-**tor**-i-uhl/ adjective behaving as if one owned someone or something; possessive: *he draped his arm across her shoulders in a proprietorial way.*
– DERIVATIVES **proprietorially** adverb.

propriety noun (pl. **proprieties**) 1 correctness of behaviour or morals. 2 (**proprieties**) the generally accepted details or rules of behaviour. 3 the quality of being appropriate or right: *they questioned the propriety of investments made by the council.*

– ORIGIN Latin *proprietas* 'property'.

propulsion noun the action of propelling or driving something forward.
– DERIVATIVES **propulsive** adjective.

propylene /**proh**-pi-leen/ noun a hydrocarbon gas obtained by cracking petroleum, used for making plastics and other chemicals.

pro rata /proh **rah**-tuh, proh **ray**-tuh/ adjective proportional. ● adverb proportionally.
– ORIGIN Latin, 'according to the rate'.

prorogue /pruh-**rohg**/ verb (**prorogues**, **proroguing**, **prorogued**) discontinue a session of a law-making assembly without dissolving it.
– DERIVATIVES **prorogation** /proh-ruh-**gay**-sh'n/ noun.
– ORIGIN Latin *prorogare* 'prolong, extend'.

prosaic /proh-**zay**-ik/ adjective 1 (of language) not imaginative or original. 2 ordinary, dull, or mundane: *a prosaic travel experience.*
– DERIVATIVES **prosaically** adverb.

proscenium /pruh-**see**-ni-uhm/ noun (pl. **prosceniums** or **proscenia** /pruh-**see**-ni-uh/) 1 the part of a stage in front of the curtain. 2 (also **proscenium arch**) an arch that frames the opening between the stage and the auditorium.
– ORIGIN Greek *proskēnion*.

prosciutto /pruh-**shoo**-toh/ noun raw cured Italian ham.
– ORIGIN Italian.

proscribe verb 1 officially forbid something. 2 criticize or condemn someone or something. 3 historical outlaw someone.
– DERIVATIVES **proscription** noun **proscriptive** adjective.
– ORIGIN Latin *proscribere* 'publish by writing'.

USAGE: The words **proscribe** and **prescribe** are often confused. **Proscribe** means 'officially forbid something' (*strikes remained proscribed in the armed forces*), whereas **prescribe** means either 'issue a medical prescription' or 'state authoritatively that something should be done' (*these rights can only be interfered with in circumstances prescribed by law*).

prose noun ordinary written or spoken language. ● verb talk in a boring way.
– ORIGIN from Latin *prosa oratio* 'straightforward discourse'.

Prosecco /proh-**sek**-oh/ noun (trademark in the UK) a sparkling white wine from NE Italy.
– ORIGIN Italian, probably from *Prosecco*, a town near Trieste.

prosecute verb 1 take legal proceedings against someone or with respect to an offence. 2 continue a course of action with a view to completing it.
– DERIVATIVES **prosecutable** adjective.
– ORIGIN Latin *prosequi* 'pursue, accompany'.

prosecution noun 1 the process of taking legal proceedings against someone. 2 (**the prosecution**) (treated as sing. or pl.) the party prosecuting someone in a lawsuit. 3 the continuation of a course of action.

prosecutor noun 1 a person, especially a public official, who takes legal proceedings against someone. 2 a lawyer who conducts the case against a person accused of a crime.
– DERIVATIVES **prosecutorial** adjective.

proselyte /**pross**-i-lyt/ noun a person who has

converted from one opinion, religion, or party to another.
- DERIVATIVES **proselytism** /pross-i-li-ti-z'm/ noun.
- ORIGIN Greek *prosēluthos* 'stranger, convert'.

proselytize (or **proselytise**) /pross-i-li-tyz/ verb convert someone from one religion, belief, or opinion to another.
- DERIVATIVES **proselytization** noun **proselytizer** noun.

prosody /pross-uh-di/ noun 1 the patterns of rhythm and sound used in poetry. 2 the theory or study of these patterns, or the rules governing them. 3 the patterns of stress and intonation in a language.
- DERIVATIVES **prosodic** adjective **prosodist** noun.
- ORIGIN Greek *prosōidia* 'song sung to music, tone of a syllable'.

prospect noun 1 the possibility or likelihood of a future event occurring: there was no prospect of a reconciliation. 2 a mental picture of a future or expected event. 3 (**prospects**) chances for success. 4 a person regarded as likely to be successful: he was seen as a leading medal prospect for the Olympics. 5 a wide view of landscape. • verb (**prospect for**) search for mineral deposits, especially by means of drilling and excavation.
- DERIVATIVES **prospector** noun.
- ORIGIN Latin *prospectus* 'view'.

prospective adjective likely to happen or be something in the future: a prospective buyer.
- DERIVATIVES **prospectively** adverb.

prospectus noun (pl. **prospectuses**) a printed booklet advertising a school or university or giving details of a share offer.
- ORIGIN Latin, 'view, prospect'.

prosper verb succeed or flourish, especially financially.
- ORIGIN Latin *prosperare*.

prosperous adjective rich and successful.
- DERIVATIVES **prosperity** noun **prosperously** adverb.

prostaglandin /pross-tuh-glan-din/ noun any of a group of compounds with various biological effects, such as causing contractions of the womb.

prostate noun a gland that surrounds the neck of the bladder in male mammals and produces a component of semen.
- DERIVATIVES **prostatic** adjective.
- ORIGIN Greek *prostatēs* 'one that stands before'.

prosthesis /pross-thee-siss/ noun (pl. **prostheses** /pross-thee-seez/) an artificial body part.
- ORIGIN Greek.

prosthetics /pross-thet-iks/ plural noun 1 artificial body parts. 2 pieces of flexible material applied to actors' faces to change their appearance. 3 (treated as sing.) the branch of surgery concerned with making and fitting artificial body parts.
- DERIVATIVES **prosthetic** adjective **prosthetist** /pross-thi-tist/ noun.

prostitute noun a person who has sex with people for money. • verb (often **prostitute oneself**) 1 do something unworthy or corrupt for the sake of money or personal advantage: he decided that he would no longer prostitute

his talent to win popularity. 2 offer someone or work as a prostitute.
- DERIVATIVES **prostitution** noun.
- ORIGIN Latin *prostituere* 'expose publicly, offer for sale'.

prostrate adjective /pross-trayt/ 1 lying stretched out on the ground with the face downwards. 2 completely overcome with distress or exhaustion. 3 (of a plant) growing along the ground. • verb /pross-trayt/ 1 (**prostrate oneself**) throw oneself flat on the ground, especially as an act of worship. 2 (**be prostrated**) be completely overcome with stress or exhaustion.
- DERIVATIVES **prostration** noun.
- ORIGIN Latin *prosternere* 'throw down'.

prosy /proh-zi/ adjective (of speech or writing) dull and unimaginative.

protactinium /proh-tak-tin-i-uhm/ noun a rare radioactive metallic chemical element.

protagonist noun 1 the leading character in a play, film, or novel. 2 an important person in a real situation. 3 an active supporter of a cause or idea.
- ORIGIN Greek *prōtagōnistēs*.

protea /proh-ti-uh/ noun a chiefly South African shrub with large cone-like flower heads surrounded by brightly coloured modified leaves (bracts).
- ORIGIN from *Proteus* (see PROTEAN), with reference to the many species of the genus.

protean /proh-ti-uhn, proh-tee-uhn/ adjective tending or able to change or adapt; variable or versatile.
- ORIGIN from the Greek sea god *Proteus*, who was able to change shape at will.

protect verb 1 keep safe from harm or injury: he tried to protect her from the attack. 2 shield a country's own industry from foreign competition by taxing imported goods. 3 (as adj. **protected**) (of a threatened plant or animal species) safeguarded through laws against collecting or hunting.
- ORIGIN Latin *protegere* 'cover in front'.

protectant noun a substance that provides protection, for example against ultraviolet radiation.

protection noun 1 the action of protecting or the state of being protected: the vehicle provides protection against anti-personnel mines. 2 a thing that protects someone or something . 3 the payment of money to criminals to prevent them from attacking oneself or one's property.

protectionism noun the theory or practice of shielding a country's own industries from foreign competition by taxing imports.
- DERIVATIVES **protectionist** noun & adjective.

protective adjective 1 intended to protect someone or something from harm or injury. 2 having a strong wish to protect someone from harm or injury.
- DERIVATIVES **protectively** adverb **protectiveness** noun.

protector noun 1 a person or thing that protects someone or something. 2 (**Protector**) historical a regent in charge of a kingdom when the monarch is away, ill, or too young to reign.
- DERIVATIVES **protectress** noun.

protectorate noun 1 a state that is controlled

and protected by another. **2** (**Protectorate**) historical the position or period of office of a Protector, in particular that of Oliver Cromwell and his son Richard as heads of state in England 1653–9.

protégé /prot-i-zhay, proh-ti-zhay/ **noun** (fem. **protégée**) a person who is guided and supported by an older and more experienced person.
– ORIGIN French, 'protected'.

protein noun any of a group of organic compounds forming part of body tissues and forming an important part of the diet.
– ORIGIN from Greek *prôteios* 'primary'.

pro tem /proh tem/ **adverb & adjective** for the time being.
– ORIGIN from Latin *pro tempore*.

Proterozoic /proh-tuh-ruh-**zoh**-ik/ **adjective** Geology relating to the later part of the Precambrian aeon (about 2,500 to 570 million years ago), in which the earliest forms of life evolved.
– ORIGIN from Greek *proteros* 'former' + *zōē* 'life'.

protest noun /**proh**-test/ **1** a statement or action expressing disapproval or objection. **2** an organized public demonstration objecting to an official policy or course of action. ●**verb** /pruh-**test**/ **1** express an objection to what someone has said or done. **2** take part in a public protest. **3** state strongly in response to an accusation or criticism: *she has always protested her innocence.*
– DERIVATIVES **protester** (also **protestor**) noun.
– ORIGIN Latin *protestari* 'assert formally'.

Protestant /**pro**-tiss-tuhnt/ **noun** a member or follower of any of the Western Christian Churches that are separate from the Roman Catholic Church. ●**adjective** relating or belonging to any of the Protestant Churches.
– DERIVATIVES **Protestantism** noun.
– ORIGIN Protestants are so called after the declaration (Latin *protestatio*) of Martin Luther and his supporters dissenting from the anti-Reformation decision of the Diet of Spires.

Protestant ethic (also **Protestant work ethic**) **noun** another term for **WORK ETHIC**.

protestation /prot-i-**stay**-sh'n/ **noun 1** a strong declaration that something is or is not the case. **2** an objection or protest.

protium /**proh**-ti-uhm/ **noun** Chemistry the common, stable isotope of hydrogen.
– ORIGIN Latin.

proto- **combining form 1** original; primitive: *prototype.* **2** first: *protozoan.*
– ORIGIN from Greek *prôtos.*

protocol noun 1 the official system of rules governing affairs of state or diplomatic occasions. **2** the accepted code of behaviour in a particular situation. **3** the original draft of a diplomatic document, especially of the terms of a treaty. **4** a formal record of scientific experimental observations. **5** Computing a set of rules governing the exchange or transmission of data between devices.
– ORIGIN Greek *prôtokollon* 'first page'.

proton /**proh**-ton/ **noun** Physics a subatomic particle with a positive electric charge, occurring in all atomic nuclei.

– ORIGIN Greek, 'first thing'.

protoplasm /proh-tuh-pla-z'm/ **noun** the material comprising the living part of a cell, including the cytoplasm and nucleus.
– DERIVATIVES **protoplasmic** adjective.
– ORIGIN Greek *prôtoplasma.*

prototype noun 1 a first or preliminary version of a device or vehicle from which other versions are developed or copied. **2** the first or typical form of something.
– DERIVATIVES **prototypical** adjective **prototypically** adverb.

protozoan /proh-tuh-**zoh**-uhn/ **noun** a single-celled microscopic animal such as an amoeba.
– ORIGIN from Greek *protos* 'first' + *zōion* 'animal'.

protract verb (often as adj. **protracted**) make something longer than expected or normal: *a protracted dispute.*
– ORIGIN Latin *protrahere.*

protraction noun the action of prolonging something or the state of being prolonged.

protractor noun an instrument for measuring angles, typically in the form of a flat semicircle marked with degrees along the curved edge.

protrude verb extend or stick out beyond or above a surface.
– ORIGIN Latin *protrudere* 'to thrust forward'.

protrusion noun 1 something that protrudes or sticks out. **2** the action of protruding.

protuberance /pruh-**tyoo**-buh-ruhnss/ **noun** a thing that protrudes or sticks out.

protuberant adjective sticking out or bulging.
– ORIGIN from Latin *protuberare* 'swell out'.

proud adjective 1 feeling pride or satisfaction in one's own achievements or those of someone close to one. **2** causing pride: *his proudest moment was when his son married Mandy.* **3** having or showing a high opinion of oneself. **4** having self-respect or dignity: *I was too proud to go home.* **5** (often **proud of**) slightly projecting from a surface.
– PHRASES **do someone proud** informal **1** make someone feel pleased or satisfied. **2** treat or entertain someone very well.
– DERIVATIVES **proudly** adverb.
– ORIGIN Old French *prud* 'valiant'.

prove /proov/ **verb** (past part. **proved** or **proven** /**proo**-v'n or proh-v'n/) **1** demonstrate by evidence or argument that something is true or exists. **2** show or be seen to be: *the scheme has proved a great success.* **3** (**prove oneself**) demonstrate one's abilities or courage. **4** Law establish the genuineness and validity of a will. **5** subject a gun to a testing process. **6** (of bread dough) rise through the action of yeast.
– DERIVATIVES **provable** adjective **prover** noun.
– ORIGIN Latin *probare* 'test, approve, demonstrate'.

USAGE: **Prove** has two past participles, **proved** and **proven**. You can correctly use either in sentences such as *this hasn't been proved yet* or *this hasn't been proven yet*. However, you should always use **proven** when the word is an adjective coming before the noun: *a proven talent* (not *a proved talent*).

provenance /**prov**-uh-nuhnss/ **noun 1** the

origin or earliest known history of something. **2** a record of ownership of a work of art or an antique.
– ORIGIN French.

Provençal /prov-on-**sahl**/ adjective relating to Provence in southern France. • noun **1** a person from Provence. **2** the language of Provence.

provençale /prov-on-**sahl**/ adjective (after a noun) cooked in a sauce made with tomatoes, garlic, and herbs.
– ORIGIN from French *à la provençale* 'in the Provençal style'.

provender /**prov**-in-der/ noun animal fodder.
– ORIGIN Old French *provendre*.

proverb noun a short saying that states a general truth or piece of advice.
– ORIGIN Latin *proverbium*.

proverbial adjective **1** referred to in a proverb or saying. **2** well known, especially so as to be stereotypical: *he was the proverbial, consummate showman.*
– DERIVATIVES **proverbially** adverb.

provide verb **1** make something available for use; supply something. **2** (**provide someone with**) equip or supply someone with something useful or necessary. **3** (**provide for**) make adequate preparation or arrangements for: *new qualifications must provide for changes in technology.* **4** state something in a will or other legal document.
– DERIVATIVES **provider** noun.
– ORIGIN Latin *providere* 'foresee, attend to'.

provided conjunction on the condition or understanding that.

providence noun the protective care of God or of nature as a spiritual power.

provident adjective careful in preparing for the future.
– DERIVATIVES **providently** adverb.

providential adjective **1** happening by chance at a favourable time; opportune: *it was providential that he was on call to provide free legal advice.* **2** involving the protective care of God or of nature.
– DERIVATIVES **providentially** adverb.

providing conjunction on the condition or understanding that.

province noun **1** a chief administrative division of a country or empire. **2** (**the provinces**) the whole of a country outside the capital, especially when regarded as unsophisticated or narrow-minded. **3** (**one's province**) one's particular area of knowledge, interest, or responsibility.
– ORIGIN Latin *provincia* 'charge, province'.

provincial adjective **1** relating to a province or the provinces. **2** unsophisticated or narrow-minded. • noun **1** an inhabitant of a province. **2** an inhabitant of the regions outside the capital city of a country.
– DERIVATIVES **provincialism** noun **provinciality** noun **provincially** adverb.

proving ground noun an area or situation in which a person or thing is tested or proved.

provision noun **1** the action of providing or supplying something. **2** something supplied or provided. **3** (**provision for/against**) arrangements for future events or requirements: *people must make provision for their retirement.* **4** (**provisions**) supplies of food, drink, or equipment, especially for a journey. **5** a condition or requirement in a legal document. • verb supply someone or something with provisions.

provisional adjective **1** arranged or existing for the present, possibly to be changed later. **2** (**Provisional**) relating to the unofficial wings of the IRA and Sinn Fein. • noun (**Provisional**) a member of the unofficial wing of the IRA or Sinn Fein.
– DERIVATIVES **provisionality** noun **provisionally** adverb.

proviso /pruh-**vy**-zoh/ noun (pl. **provisos**) a condition attached to an agreement.
– ORIGIN from Latin *proviso quod* 'it being provided that'.

provitamin noun a substance which is converted into a vitamin within an organism.

Provo /**proh**-voh/ noun (pl. **Provos**) informal a member of the Provisional IRA or Sinn Fein.

provocation noun **1** action or speech that makes someone angry or arouses a strong reaction. **2** the action of provoking someone.

provocative adjective **1** deliberately causing annoyance or anger. **2** intended to arouse sexual desire or interest.
– DERIVATIVES **provocatively** adverb **provocativeness** noun.

provoke verb **1** arouse a strong or unwelcome reaction or emotion in someone: *the decision provoked a storm of protest.* **2** deliberately make someone annoyed or angry. **3** make someone do or feel something, especially by arousing their anger.
– ORIGIN Latin *provocare* 'to challenge'.

provolone /pro-vuh-**loh**-nay, pro-vuh-**loh**-ni/ noun an Italian soft smoked cheese.
– ORIGIN Italian.

provost /**prov**-uhst/ noun **1** Brit. the head of certain university colleges and public schools. **2** Scottish a mayor. **3** N. Amer. a senior administrative officer in certain universities. **4** the head of a chapter in a cathedral.
– ORIGIN Old English.

provost marshal /pro-**voh**/ noun the officer in charge of military police in camp or on active service.

prow /prow/ noun the pointed front part of a ship; the bow.
– ORIGIN Old French *proue*.

prowess noun **1** skill or expertise in a particular activity or field. **2** bravery in battle.
– ORIGIN Old French *proesce*.

prowl verb move about in a stealthy or restless way, especially in search of prey.
– PHRASES **on the prowl** moving around in a stealthy way.
– DERIVATIVES **prowler** noun.
– ORIGIN unknown.

proximal adjective chiefly Anatomy situated nearer to the centre of the body or an area or the point of attachment. The opposite of **DISTAL**.
– DERIVATIVES **proximally** adverb.

proximate adjective closest in space, time, or relationship.
– ORIGIN Latin *proximatus* 'drawn near'.

proximity noun nearness in space, time, or

p

relationship.

proxy noun (pl. **proxies**) **1** the authority to represent someone else, especially in voting. **2** a person authorized to act on behalf of someone else.
– ORIGIN from former *procuracy*, 'the position or office of a procurator'.

Prozac /proh-zak/ noun trademark fluoxetine, a drug which is taken to treat depression.
– ORIGIN an invented name.

prude noun a person who is easily shocked by matters relating to sex or nudity.
– DERIVATIVES **prudish** adjective **prudery** noun.
– ORIGIN French *prudefemme* 'good woman and true'.

prudent adjective acting with or showing care and thought for the future.
– DERIVATIVES **prudence** noun **prudently** adverb.
– ORIGIN Latin *prudens*.

prudential adjective involving or showing care and forethought, especially in business.
– DERIVATIVES **prudentially** adverb.

prune¹ noun a dried plum with a black, wrinkled appearance.
– ORIGIN Greek *prounon* 'plum'.

prune² verb **1** trim a tree, shrub, or bush by cutting away dead or overgrown branches or stems. **2** make smaller by removing unwanted parts: *staff numbers have been pruned.* • noun an instance of pruning something.
– DERIVATIVES **pruner** noun.
– ORIGIN Old French *proignier*.

prurient /proor-i-uhnt/ adjective having or encouraging too great an interest in sexual matters.
– DERIVATIVES **prurience** noun **pruriently** adverb.
– ORIGIN from Latin *prurire* 'itch, long, be wanton'.

pruritus /pruu-ry-tuhss/ noun severe itching of the skin.
– DERIVATIVES **pruritic** adjective.
– ORIGIN Latin, 'itching'.

Prussian noun a person from the former German kingdom of Prussia. • adjective relating to Prussia.

Prussian blue noun a deep blue pigment.

prussic acid /pruss-ik/ noun old-fashioned term for HYDROCYANIC ACID.
– ORIGIN from French *prussique* 'relating to Prussian blue'.

pry¹ verb (**pries**, **prying**, **pried**) enquire too intrusively into a person's private affairs.
– DERIVATIVES **prying** adjective.
– ORIGIN unknown.

pry² verb (**pries**, **prying**, **pried**) chiefly N. Amer. another term for PRISE.
– ORIGIN from PRISE.

PS abbreviation **1** Police Sergeant. **2** postscript. **3** private secretary.

psalm /sahm/ noun a religious song or hymn, in particular any of those contained in the Book of Psalms in the Bible.
– DERIVATIVES **psalmist** noun.
– ORIGIN Greek *psalmos* 'song sung to harp music'.

psalmody /sah-muh-di, sal-muh-di/ noun the singing of psalms or similar religious verses.
– ORIGIN Greek *psalmōidia* 'singing to a harp'.

psalter /sawl-ter/ noun a copy of the Book of

Psalms in the Bible.
– ORIGIN Greek *psaltērion* 'stringed instrument'.

psaltery /sorl-tuh-ri, sol-tuh-ri/ noun (pl. **psalteries**) an ancient and medieval musical instrument like a dulcimer but played by plucking the strings.

PSBR abbreviation Brit. public-sector borrowing requirement.

psephology /se-fol-uh-ji/ noun the statistical study of elections and trends in voting.
– DERIVATIVES **psephologist** noun.
– ORIGIN from Greek *psēphos* 'pebble, vote'.

pseud /syood/ noun Brit. informal a person who tries to impress others by pretending to have knowledge, especially about art or literature.

pseudo /syoo-doh/ adjective informal not genuine; fake, pretentious, or insincere.

pseudo- (also **pseud-** before a vowel) combining form false; not genuine: *pseudonym.*
– ORIGIN from Greek *pseudēs* 'false'.

pseudonym /syoo-duh-nim/ noun a false name, especially one used by an author.
– ORIGIN from Greek *pseudēs* 'false' + *onoma* 'name'.

pseudonymous /syoo-don-i-muhss/ adjective writing or written under a false name.
– DERIVATIVES **pseudonymity** /syoo-duh-nim-i-ti/ noun **pseudonymously** adverb.

pseudoscience noun beliefs or practices mistakenly regarded as being based on scientific methods.
– DERIVATIVES **pseudoscientific** adjective.

p.s.i. abbreviation pounds per square inch.

psilocybin /sy-loh-sy-bin/ noun a substance that causes hallucinations, found in certain toadstools.
– ORIGIN from Greek *psilos* 'bald' + *kubē* 'head'.

psittacine /sit-tuh-kyn, sit-tuh-syn/ Ornithology adjective relating to birds of the parrot family. • noun a bird of the parrot family.
– ORIGIN from Greek *psittakos* 'parrot'.

psittacosis /sit-tuh-koh-siss/ noun a contagious disease of birds, which can be passed (especially from parrots) to human beings as a form of pneumonia.

PSNI abbreviation Police Service of Northern Ireland.

psoriasis /suh-ry-uh-siss/ noun a skin disease marked by red, itchy, scaly patches.
– DERIVATIVES **psoriatic** /sor-i-at-ik/ adjective.
– ORIGIN Greek, from *psōrian* 'to itch'.

PSV abbreviation Brit. public service vehicle.

psych /syk/ verb **1** (**psych someone up**) informal mentally prepare someone for a difficult task or occasion: *we had to psych ourselves up for the race.* **2** (**psych someone out**) intimidate an opponent or rival by appearing very confident or aggressive.

psyche /sy-ki/ noun the human soul, mind, or spirit.
– ORIGIN Greek *psukhē* 'breath, life, soul'.

psychedelia /sy-kuh-dee-li-uh/ noun music, culture, or art based on the experiences produced by psychedelic drugs.

psychedelic /sy-kuh-del-ik, sy-kuh-dee-lik/ adjective **1** (of drugs) producing hallucinations. **2** (of rock music) experimental and having drug-related lyrics. **3** having an intense, bright

colour or a swirling abstract pattern.
- DERIVATIVES **psychedelically** adverb.
- ORIGIN from Greek *psyche* 'soul' + *dēlos* 'clear, manifest'.

psychiatrist noun a doctor specializing in the diagnosis and treatment of mental illness.

psychiatry /sy-**ky**-uh-tri/ noun the branch of medicine concerned with the study and treatment of mental disorders.
- DERIVATIVES **psychiatric** /sy-ki-**at**-rik/ adjective **psychiatrically** adverb.
- ORIGIN from Greek *psukhē* 'soul, mind' + *iatreia* 'healing'.

psychic /sy-kik/ adjective **1** relating to abilities or phenomena that cannot be explained by natural laws, especially those involving telepathy or clairvoyance. **2** (of a person) appearing or considered to be telepathic or clairvoyant. **3** relating to the soul or mind.
•noun a person considered or claiming to have psychic powers; a medium.
- DERIVATIVES **psychical** adjective **psychically** adverb.

psycho noun (pl. **psychos**) informal a psychopath.

psycho- /sy-koh/ combining form relating to the mind or psychology: *psychometrics.*
- ORIGIN from Greek *psukhē* 'breath, soul, mind'.

psychoactive adjective affecting the mind.

psychoanalyse (US **psychoanalyze**) verb treat someone using psychoanalysis.

psychoanalysis noun a method of treating mental disorders by investigating the conscious and unconscious elements in the mind and bringing repressed fears and conflicts into the conscious mind.
- DERIVATIVES **psychoanalyst** noun **psychoanalytic** adjective.

psychobabble noun informal, derogatory jargon used in popular psychology.

psychodrama noun **1** a form of psycho-therapy in which patients act out events from their past. **2** a play, film, or novel in which psychological elements are the main interest.

psychokinesis /sy-koh-ki-**nee**-siss, sy-koh-ky-**nee**-siss/ noun the supposed ability to move objects by mental effort alone.
- DERIVATIVES **psychokinetic** adjective.

psychological adjective **1** relating to or affecting the mind. **2** relating to psychology.
- DERIVATIVES **psychologically** adverb.

psychological warfare noun actions intended to reduce an opponent's confidence.

psychology noun **1** the scientific study of the human mind and its functions. **2** the mental characteristics or attitude of a person.
- DERIVATIVES **psychologist** noun.

psychometrics plural noun (treated as sing.) the science of measuring mental abilities and processes.
- DERIVATIVES **psychometric** adjective.

psychopath noun a person suffering from a serious mental disorder that causes them to commit violent or antisocial acts.
- DERIVATIVES **psychopathic** adjective.

psychopathology noun **1** the scientific study of mental disorders. **2** mental or behavioural disorder.
- DERIVATIVES **psychopathological** adjective.

psychopathy /sy-**kop**-uh-thi/ noun mental illness or disorder.

psychosexual adjective relating to or involving the psychological aspects of a person's sexual feelings.
- DERIVATIVES **psychosexually** adverb.

psychosis /sy-koh-siss/ noun (pl. **psychoses** /sy-**koh**-seez/) a mental disorder in which a person's perception of reality is severely distorted.

psychosocial adjective relating to the way in which social factors and individual thought and behaviour are connected or linked.
- DERIVATIVES **psychosocially** adverb.

psychosomatic /sy-koh-suh-**mat**-ik/ adjective **1** (of a physical illness) caused or made worse by a mental factor such as stress. **2** relating to the way in which the mind and body affect each other.
- DERIVATIVES **psychosomatically** adverb.

psychosurgery noun brain surgery used to treat severe mental disorder.
- DERIVATIVES **psychosurgical** adjective.

psychotherapy noun the treatment of mental disorder by psychological rather than medical means.
- DERIVATIVES **psychotherapeutic** adjective **psychotherapist** noun.

psychotic /sy-**kot**-ik/ adjective relating to or having a mental disorder in which a person's perception of reality is severely distorted.
•noun a person with such a disorder.
- DERIVATIVES **psychotically** adverb.

psychotropic /sy-koh-**troh**-pik, sy-koh-**trop**-ik/ adjective (of drugs) affecting a person's mental state.

PT abbreviation Brit. physical training.

Pt abbreviation **1** Part. **2** (**pt**) pint. **3** (in scoring) point. **4** Printing point (as a unit of measurement). **5** (**Pt.**) Point (on maps). **6** (**pt**) port (a side of a ship or aircraft). •symbol the chemical element platinum.

PTA abbreviation parent–teacher association.

ptarmigan /**tar**-mi-guhn/ noun a grouse of northern mountains and the Arctic, whose grey and black plumage changes to white in winter.
- ORIGIN Scottish Gaelic *tàrmachan.*

Pte abbreviation Brit. Private (in the army).

pterodactyl /te-ruh-**dak**-til/ noun a pterosaur (fossil flying reptile) of the late Jurassic period, with a long slender head and neck.
- ORIGIN from Greek *pteron* 'wing' + *daktulos* 'finger'.

pterosaur /te-ruh-sor/ noun a fossil flying reptile of the Jurassic and Cretaceous periods.
- ORIGIN from Greek *pteron* 'wing' + *sauros* 'lizard'.

PTO abbreviation Brit. please turn over.

Ptolemaic /to-luh-**may**-ik/ adjective **1** relating to the 2nd-century Greek astronomer Ptolemy. **2** relating to the Ptolemies, rulers of Egypt 304–30 BC.

Ptolemaic system (also **Ptolemaic theory**) noun the former theory that the earth is the stationary centre of the universe. Compare with **COPERNICAN SYSTEM**.

ptomaine /**toh**-mayn/ noun any of a group of

organic compounds with an unpleasant taste and smell formed in decaying animal and vegetable matter.
– ORIGIN from Greek *ptōma* 'corpse'.

P2P abbreviation peer-to-peer, an Internet network that enables a group of users to access and copy files from each other's hard drives.

PTSD abbreviation post-traumatic stress disorder.

Pu symbol the chemical element plutonium.

pub noun 1 Brit. a building in which beer and other drinks may be bought and drunk. 2 Austral. a hotel.
– ORIGIN abbreviation of **PUBLIC HOUSE**.

pub crawl noun Brit. informal a tour of several pubs, with drinks at each.

pube /pyoob/ noun informal a pubic hair.

puberty noun the period during which adolescents reach sexual maturity and become able to have children.
– DERIVATIVES **pubertal** adjective.
– ORIGIN Latin *pubertas*, from *puber* 'adult'.

pubes noun 1 /pyoo-beez/ (pl. same) the lower part of the abdomen at the front of the pelvis, covered with hair from puberty. 2 /pyoo-beez/ plural of **PUBIS**. 3 /pyoobz/ informal plural of **PUBE**.
– ORIGIN Latin, 'pubic hair, genitals'.

pubescent /pyuu-bess-uhnt/ adjective 1 relating to a person at or approaching the age of puberty. 2 Botany & Zoology covered with short, soft hair; downy.
– DERIVATIVES **pubescence** noun.
– ORIGIN from Latin *pubescere* 'reach puberty'.

pubic adjective relating to the pubes or pubis.

pubis /pyoo-biss/ noun (pl. **pubes** /pyoo-beez/) either of a pair of bones forming the two sides of the pelvis.
– ORIGIN from Latin *os pubis* 'bone of the pubes'.

public adjective 1 relating to or available to the people as a whole: *a campaign to raise public awareness of the problem.* 2 relating to or involved in the affairs of the community, especially in government or entertainment: *a public figure.* 3 intended to be seen or heard by people in general: *a public apology.* 4 provided by the state rather than an independent commercial company. • noun 1 (**the public**) (treated as sing. or pl.) ordinary people in society in general. 2 a group of people with a shared interest or activity: *the cinema-going public.*
– PHRASES **go public** 1 reveal details about something that was previously secret or private. 2 become a public company. **in public** when other people are present. **the public eye** the state of being well known to people in general, especially through the media.
– DERIVATIVES **publicly** adverb.
– ORIGIN Latin *publicus.*

public address system noun a system of microphones, amplifiers, and loudspeakers used to amplify speech or music.

publican noun 1 Brit. a person who owns or manages a pub. 2 Austral. a person who owns or manages a hotel. 3 (in ancient Roman and biblical times) a tax collector.
– ORIGIN Latin *publicanus.*

publication noun 1 the action or process of publishing something. 2 a published book or journal.

public bar noun Brit. a bar in a pub or hotel that is more plainly furnished than the lounge bar.

public company (N. Amer. **public corporation**) noun a company whose shares are traded freely on a stock exchange.

public defender noun US Law a lawyer employed by the state in a criminal trial to represent a defendant who is unable to afford legal assistance.

public enemy noun a notorious wanted criminal.

public house noun formal term for **PUB**.

publicist noun a person responsible for publicizing a product or celebrity.

publicity noun 1 attention given to someone or something by the media. 2 information that is given out about a product, person, company, etc. in order to advertise or promote them.

publicize (or **publicise**) verb 1 make widely known: *their attempts to publicize the dangers of pesticides.* 2 advertise or promote something.

public lending right noun (in the UK) the right of authors to receive payment when their books are lent out by public libraries.

public limited company noun (in the UK) a company with shares offered to the public subject to conditions of limited legal responsibility for any company debts.

public nuisance noun Brit. 1 an act that is illegal because it interferes with the rights of the public generally. 2 informal an unpleasant or dangerous person or group.

public prosecutor noun Brit. a law officer who conducts criminal proceedings on behalf of the state or in the public interest.

public relations plural noun (treated as sing.) the business of creating and maintaining a good public image for an organization or well-known person.

public school noun 1 (in the UK) a private fee-paying secondary school. 2 (chiefly in North America) a school supported by public funds.

public sector noun the part of an economy that is controlled by the state.

public servant noun a person who works for the state or for local government.

public-spirited adjective showing a willingness to do things that will help other people in society.

public transport noun buses, trains, and other forms of transport that are available to the public, charge set fares, and run on fixed routes.

public utility noun an organization supplying the community with electricity, gas, water, or sewerage.

publish verb 1 prepare and issue and publish, newspaper, piece of music, etc. for public sale. 2 print something in a book, newspaper, or journal so as to make it generally known: *we pay £5 for every letter we publish.* 3 formally announce or read an edict or marriage banns.

– DERIVATIVES **publishable** adjective **publishing** noun.
– ORIGIN Latin *publicare* 'make public'.

publisher noun **1** a company or person that prepares and issues books, newspapers, journals, or music for sale. **2** chiefly N. Amer. a newspaper proprietor.

puce /pyooss/ noun a dark red or purple-brown colour.
– ORIGIN French, 'flea, flea-colour'.

puck[1] noun a black disc made of hard rubber, used in ice hockey.
– ORIGIN unknown.

puck[2] noun a mischievous or evil spirit.
– ORIGIN Old English.

pucker verb tightly gather or contract into wrinkles or small folds: *she puckered her lips.*
•noun a wrinkle or small fold.
– ORIGIN probably from POKE[2] and POCKET.

puckish adjective playful and mischievous.

pudding noun **1** chiefly Brit. a dessert, especially a cooked one. **2** chiefly Brit. the dessert course of a meal. **3** a baked or steamed savoury dish made with suet and flour or batter. **4** Brit. the intestines of a pig or sheep stuffed with oatmeal, spices, and meat and boiled.
– PHRASES **in the pudding club** Brit. informal pregnant.
– DERIVATIVES **puddingy** adjective.
– ORIGIN probably from Old French *boudin* 'black pudding'.

pudding basin noun Brit. a deep round bowl used for cooking steamed puddings.

puddle noun **1** a small pool of liquid, especially of rainwater on the ground. **2** clay and sand mixed with water and used as a watertight covering or lining for embankments or canals.
•verb **1** cover with or form puddles. **2** (usu. as noun **puddling**) historical stir molten iron with iron oxide in a furnace, to produce wrought iron.
– ORIGIN Old English, 'small ditch'.

pudendum /pyoo-**den**-duhm/ noun (pl. **pudenda** /pyoo-**den**-duh/) the external genitals, especially those of a woman.
– ORIGIN from Latin *pudenda membra* 'parts to be ashamed of'.

pudgy adjective (**pudgier, pudgiest**) informal fat or flabby.
– ORIGIN unknown.

pueblo /**pweb**-loh/ noun (pl. **pueblos**) **1** a town or village in Spain, Latin America, or the south-western US, especially an American Indian settlement. **2** (**Pueblo**) (pl. same or **Pueblos**) a member of any of various American Indian peoples living in pueblos, chiefly in New Mexico and Arizona.
– ORIGIN Spanish, 'people'.

puerile /**pyoor**-yl/ adjective childishly silly and trivial.
– DERIVATIVES **puerility** /pyoo-**ril**-i-ti/ noun (pl. **puerilities**).
– ORIGIN from Latin *puer* 'child, boy'.

puerperal fever /pyoo-**air**-puh-ruhl/ noun fever caused by infection of the womb after childbirth.
– ORIGIN from Latin *puer* 'child, boy' + *parus* 'bearing'.

Puerto Rican /pwair-toh **ree**-kuhn/ noun a person from Puerto Rico. •adjective relating to Puerto Rico.

puff noun **1** a small amount of air or smoke blown from somewhere. **2** an act of drawing quickly on a pipe, cigarette, or cigar. **3** a light pastry case, typically filled with cream or jam. **4** Brit. informal breath: *he had run out of puff.* **5** informal an over-complimentary review or advertisement. •verb **1** breathe in repeated short gasps. **2** move with short, noisy puffs of air or steam: *a train puffed steadily across the bridge.* **3** smoke a pipe, cigarette, or cigar. **4** (**be puffed/puffed out**) be out of breath. **5** (**puff out/up** or **puff something out/up**) swell or cause to swell: *he puffed his chest out.*
– DERIVATIVES **puffer** noun.
– ORIGIN imitating the sound.

puff adder noun a large African viper which inflates the upper part of its body and hisses loudly when under threat.

puffa jacket noun Brit. trademark a type of thick padded jacket.

puffball noun a fungus that produces a large round fruiting body which bursts when ripe to release a cloud of spores.

pufferfish noun (pl. same or **pufferfishes**) a fish with a spiny body which can inflate itself like a balloon when threatened.

puffery noun exaggerated or false praise.

puffin noun a seabird of the North Atlantic with a large head and a massive brightly coloured triangular bill.
– ORIGIN probably from PUFF.

puff pastry noun light flaky pastry.

puff sleeve noun a short sleeve gathered at the top and cuff and full in the middle.

puffy adjective (**puffier, puffiest**) **1** softly rounded: *puffy clouds.* **2** (of a part of the body) swollen and soft.
– DERIVATIVES **puffiness** noun.

pug noun a small dog with a broad flat nose and deeply wrinkled face.
– ORIGIN perhaps German.

pugilist /**pyoo**-ji-list/ noun chiefly humorous a boxer.
– DERIVATIVES **pugilism** noun **pugilistic** adjective.
– ORIGIN Latin *pugil* 'boxer'.

pugnacious /pug-**nay**-shuhss/ adjective eager or quick to argue, quarrel, or fight.
– DERIVATIVES **pugnacity** noun.
– ORIGIN from Latin *pugnare* 'to fight'.

pug nose noun a short nose with an upturned tip.

puissance /**pwee**-suhnss/ noun **1** /also pwee-sonss/ a showjumping competition that tests a horse's ability to jump large, high obstacles. **2** old use or literary great power or skill.
– DERIVATIVES **puissant** adjective (old use or literary).
– ORIGIN Old French, from Latin *posse* 'be able'.

puja /**poo**-jah/ noun a Hindu ceremonial offering.
– ORIGIN Sanskrit, 'worship'.

puke verb & noun informal vomit.
– DERIVATIVES **pukey** adjective.
– ORIGIN probably imitating the sound.

pukka /**puk**-kuh/ adjective informal **1** authentic or genuine. **2** socially acceptable. **3** Brit. excellent.
– ORIGIN Hindi, 'cooked, ripe, substantial'.

pula /**puu**-luh/ noun (pl. same) the basic unit of

money of Botswana.
– ORIGIN Setswana (a Bantu language), 'rain'.

pulao /puh-**low**/ noun variant spelling of PILAF.

pulchritude /pul-kri-tyood/ noun literary beauty.
– DERIVATIVES **pulchritudinous** adjective.
– ORIGIN from Latin *pulcher* 'beautiful'.

pule /pyool/ verb (often as adj. **puling**) literary cry feebly or in a complaining way.
– ORIGIN probably imitating the sound.

pull verb **1** apply force to someone or something so as to move them towards oneself or the origin of the force. **2** remove by pulling: *she pulled a handkerchief from her pocket.* **3** move steadily: *the bus pulled away.* **4** move oneself with effort or against resistance: *she tried to pull away from him.* **5** strain a muscle or ligament. **6** (**pull at/on**) inhale deeply while drawing on a cigarette. **7** attract as a customer: *a DJ who is expected to pull in the crowds.* **8** Brit. informal succeed in attracting someone sexually. **9** informal cancel an event or withdraw an advertisement. **10** informal bring out a weapon for use. **11** deliberately slow the speed of a horse to make it lose a race. •noun **1** an act of pulling. **2** a deep drink of something, or an act of taking a deep breath from a cigarette, pipe, etc. **3** a force, influence, or attraction: *the pull of her home town was a strong one.*
– PHRASES **on the pull** Brit. informal attempting to attract someone sexually. **pull back** retreat or withdraw. **pull something down** demolish a building. **pull someone/thing in 1** succeed in securing or obtaining something. **2** informal arrest someone. **pull someone's leg** deceive someone playfully. **pull something off** informal succeed in achieving or winning something difficult. **pull out** withdraw or retreat. **pull the plug on** informal prevent something from happening or continuing. **pull (one's) punches** be less forceful, severe, or critical than one could be. **pull strings** make use of one's influence to gain an advantage. **pull through** get through an illness or other difficult situation. **pull oneself together** regain one's self-control. **pull up** (of a vehicle) come to a halt. **pull someone up 1** make someone stop or pause. **2** Brit. reprimand someone. **pull one's weight** do one's fair share of work.
– DERIVATIVES **puller** noun.
– ORIGIN Old English, 'pluck, snatch'.

pullet noun a young hen, especially one less than one year old.
– ORIGIN Old French *poulet*.

pulley noun (pl. **pulleys**) a wheel with a grooved rim around which a rope, chain, or belt passes, used to raise heavy weights.
– ORIGIN Old French *polie*.

Pullman noun (pl. **Pullmans**) a luxurious railway carriage.
– ORIGIN named after its American designer George M. *Pullman*.

pullover noun a knitted garment put on over the head and covering the top half of the body.

pullulate /pul-yuu-layt/ verb **1** reproduce or spread so as to become very widespread. **2** be filled with life and activity.
– ORIGIN Latin *pullulare* 'to sprout'.

pulmonary /pul-muh-nuh-ri/ adjective relating to the lungs.
– ORIGIN from Latin *pulmo* 'lung'.

pulp noun **1** a soft, wet mass of crushed or pounded material. **2** the soft fleshy part of a fruit. **3** a soft, wet mass of fibres obtained from rags or wood, used in making paper. •verb **1** crush something into a pulp. **2** withdraw a publication from the market and recycle the paper. •adjective referring to popular or sensational books or magazines, often regarded as being badly written: *pulp fiction.*
– DERIVATIVES **pulpy** adjective.
– ORIGIN Latin *pulpa*.

pulpit /puul-pit/ noun a raised enclosed platform in a church or chapel from which the preacher gives a sermon.
– ORIGIN Latin *pulpitum* 'scaffold, platform'.

pulsar /pul-sar/ noun an object in outer space, thought to be a rapidly rotating neutron star, that gives off regular rapid pulses of radio waves.
– ORIGIN from *pulsating star*.

pulsate /pul-**sayt**/ verb **1** expand and contract with strong regular movements. **2** produce a regular throbbing sensation or sound. **3** (as adj. **pulsating**) very exciting: *a pulsating semi-final.*
– DERIVATIVES **pulsation** noun.
– ORIGIN Latin *pulsare* 'throb, pulse'.

pulse[1] noun **1** the regular throbbing of the arteries as blood is sent through them. **2** each successive throb of the arteries. **3** a single vibration or short burst of sound, electric current, or light. **4** a musical beat or other regular rhythm. **5** the centre of activity in a particular area or field: *those close to the economic pulse.* •verb **1** pulsate. **2** convert a wave or beam into a series of pulses.
– ORIGIN Latin *pulsus* 'beating'.

pulse[2] noun the edible seeds of certain plants of the pea family, e.g. lentils.
– ORIGIN Latin *puls* 'porridge of meal or pulse'.

pulverize (or **pulverise**) verb **1** crush something into fine particles. **2** informal defeat utterly: *he pulverized the opposition.*
– DERIVATIVES **pulverizer** noun.
– ORIGIN Latin *pulverizare*, from *pulvis* 'dust'.

puma noun a large American wild cat with a plain tawny to greyish coat.
– ORIGIN Quechua.

pumice /**pumm**-iss/ noun a light and porous form of solidified lava, used to remove hard skin.
– ORIGIN Old French *pomis*.

pummel verb (**pummels, pummelling, pummelled;** US **pummels, pummeling, pummeled**) strike someone or something repeatedly with the fists.
– ORIGIN variant of POMMEL.

pump[1] noun a mechanical device using suction or pressure to raise or move liquids, compress gases, or force air into inflatable objects. •verb **1** force liquid or gas to move by using a pump or by means of something that works like a pump: *the heart pumps blood round the body.* **2** (of liquid) flow as if being forced by a pump. **3** fill something with liquid or gas. **4** move or cause to move vigorously up and down: *we had to pump the handle like mad.* **5** (**pump something out**) produce something in large quantities or amounts: *carnival bands pumping out music.* **6** informal try to obtain information from someone by persistent questioning. **7** (as

adj. **pumped up**) informal very enthusiastic or excited
- PHRASES **pump iron** informal exercise with weights.
- ORIGIN related to Dutch *pomp* 'ship's pump'.

pump² noun **1** a plimsoll. **2** Brit. a light shoe for dancing. **3** N. Amer. a court shoe.
- ORIGIN unknown.

pump-action adjective referring to a firearm capable of firing several shots in succession without reloading, in which a new round is brought into the breech by a slide action in line with the barrel.

pumpernickel /pum-per-ni-k'l/ noun dark, dense German bread made from wholemeal rye.
- ORIGIN German, originally meaning 'lout, bumpkin'.

pumpkin noun **1** a large rounded orange-yellow fruit with a thick rind and edible flesh. **2** Brit. another term for SQUASH².
- ORIGIN former French *pompon*.

pun noun a joke playing on the different meanings of a word or exploiting the fact that there are words of the same sound and different meanings. •verb (**puns, punning, punned**) make a pun.
- DERIVATIVES **punster** noun.
- ORIGIN uncertain.

punch¹ verb **1** strike someone or something with the fist. **2** press a button or key on a machine. •noun **1** a blow with the fist. **2** informal effectiveness or impact: *photos give their argument an extra visual punch*.
- PHRASES **punch above one's weight** informal take part in an activity regarded as being beyond one's abilities.
- DERIVATIVES **puncher** noun.
- ORIGIN variant of POUNCE¹.

punch² noun **1** a device or machine for making holes in paper, leather, metal, etc. **2** a tool or machine for stamping a design on a material. •verb pierce a hole in paper, leather, metal, etc.
- ORIGIN perhaps an abbreviation of PUNCHEON, or from PUNCH¹.

punch³ noun a drink made from wine or spirits mixed with water, fruit juices, spices, etc.
- ORIGIN apparently from a Sanskrit word meaning 'five, five kinds of' (because the drink had five ingredients).

punch⁴ noun (also **Suffolk punch**) a short-legged thickset breed of draught horse.
- ORIGIN from a dialect term referring to a short, fat person.

punchbag noun Brit. a stuffed bag suspended from a rope, used for punching as exercise or training, especially by boxers.

punchball noun Brit. a stuffed ball mounted on a stand, used for punching as exercise or training, especially by boxers.

punchbowl noun **1** a deep bowl for mixing and serving punch. **2** chiefly Brit. a deep round hollow in a hilly area.

punch-drunk adjective confused or dazed as a result of a series of heavy blows to the head.

punched card (also **punchcard**) noun a card perforated according to a code, used to control the operation of a machine or (formerly) to program computers.

puncheon /pun-chuhn/ noun **1** a short post, especially one used for supporting the roof in a coal mine. **2** another term for PUNCH².
- ORIGIN Old French *poinchon*.

punchline noun the final part of a joke or story, providing the humour or climax.

punch-up noun informal, chiefly Brit. a brawl.

punchy adjective (**punchier, punchiest**) having an immediate impact; forceful.

punctilio /pungk-ti-li-oh/ noun (pl. **punctilios**) **1** a fine or trivial point of behaviour or procedure. **2** punctilious behaviour.
- ORIGIN Italian *puntiglio* and Spanish *puntillo* 'small point'.

punctilious /pungk-ti-li-uhss/ adjective showing great attention to detail or correct behaviour.
- DERIVATIVES **punctiliously** adverb **punctiliousness** noun.

punctual adjective happening at or keeping to the arranged time.
- DERIVATIVES **punctuality** noun **punctually** adverb.
- ORIGIN Latin *punctualis*, from *punctum* 'a point'.

punctuate /pungk-chuu-ayt, pungk-tyuu-ayt/ verb **1** occur or interrupt at intervals throughout: *the country's history has been punctuated by coups*. **2** put punctuation marks in a piece of writing.
- ORIGIN Latin *punctuare* 'bring to a point'.

punctuation noun the marks, such as full stop, comma, and brackets, used in writing to separate sentences and their parts and to make meaning clear.

puncture noun a small hole caused by a sharp object, especially one in a tyre. •verb **1** make a puncture in something. **2** destroy a mood, feeling, etc.
- ORIGIN Latin *punctura*.

pundit /pun-dit/ noun **1** an expert who frequently gives opinions about a subject in public. **2** variant spelling of PANDIT.
- DERIVATIVES **punditry** noun.
- ORIGIN from a Sanskrit word meaning 'learned'.

pungent adjective **1** having a sharply strong taste or smell. **2** (of remarks or humour) sharp and strongly worded.
- DERIVATIVES **pungency** noun **pungently** adverb.
- ORIGIN from Latin *pungere* 'to prick'.

Punic /pyoo-nik/ adjective relating to ancient Carthage. •noun the language of ancient Carthage.
- ORIGIN Latin *Punicus*, from Greek *Phoinix* 'Phoenician'.

punish verb **1** cause someone to experience something unpleasant as a result of a criminal or wrongful act. **2** treat harshly or unfairly: *a rise in prescription charges would punish the poor*.
- DERIVATIVES **punishable** adjective.
- ORIGIN Latin *punire*.

punishment noun **1** an unpleasant experience imposed on someone as a result of a criminal or wrongful act. **2** the action of punishing someone. **3** harsh or rough treatment.

punitive /pyoo-ni-tiv/ adjective **1** imposing or intended as punishment. **2** (of a tax or other

charge) extremely high.
- DERIVATIVES **punitively** adverb **punitiveness** noun.

Punjabi /pun-jah-bi, puun-jah-bi/ (also **Panjabi**) /pan-jah-bi/ noun (pl. **Punjabis**) **1** a person from Punjab, a region of NW India and Pakistan. **2** the language of Punjab. ●adjective relating to Punjab.

punk noun **1** (also **punk rock**) a loud, fast form of rock music characterized by aggressive lyrics and behaviour. **2** (also **punk rocker**) an admirer or player of punk music, typically having coloured spiked hair and clothing decorated with safety pins and zips. **3** informal, chiefly N. Amer. a worthless person; a thug or criminal. ●adjective relating to punk rock and its admirers.
- DERIVATIVES **punkish** adjective **punky** adjective.
- ORIGIN perhaps, in some senses, related to former *punk* 'prostitute', also to SPUNK.

punkah /pung-kuh/ noun chiefly historical (in India) a large cloth fan on a frame suspended from the ceiling, worked by a cord or electrically.
- ORIGIN Sanskrit, 'wing'.

punnet noun Brit. a small light basket or other container for fruit.
- ORIGIN perhaps from dialect *pun* 'a pound'.

punt¹ /punt/ noun a long, narrow, flat-bottomed boat, square at both ends and propelled with a long pole. ●verb travel in a punt.
- ORIGIN Latin *ponto*, referring to a flat-bottomed ferry boat.

punt² /punt/ verb **1** American Football & Rugby kick the ball after it has dropped from the hands and before it reaches the ground. **2** Football kick the ball a long distance upfield. ●noun a kick of this kind.
- ORIGIN probably from dialect *punt*, 'push forcibly'.

punt³ /punt/ verb **1** Brit. informal bet on or make a risky investment in something. **2** (in some gambling card games) lay a stake against the bank. ●noun Brit. informal a bet.
- ORIGIN French *ponte* 'player against the bank'.

punt⁴ /poont/ noun (until the introduction of the euro in 2002) the basic unit of money of the Republic of Ireland.
- ORIGIN Irish, 'a pound'.

punter noun informal **1** chiefly Brit. a person who gambles or places a bet. **2** Brit. a customer or client.

puny /pyoo-ni/ adjective (**punier, puniest**) **1** physically small and weak. **2** not impressive in quality, amount, or size: *their puny efforts*.
- DERIVATIVES **punily** adverb **puniness** noun.
- ORIGIN Old French *puisne* 'junior or inferior person'.

pup noun **1** a young dog. **2** a young wolf, seal, rat, or other mammal. **3** dated, chiefly Brit. a cheeky or arrogant boy or young man. ●verb (**pups, pupping, pupped**) give birth to a pup or pups.
- PHRASES **sell someone a pup** Brit. informal swindle someone by selling them something worthless.
- ORIGIN from PUPPY.

pupa /pyoo-puh/ noun (pl. **pupae** /pyoo-pee/) an insect in its inactive stage of development between larva and adult, e.g. a chrysalis.
- DERIVATIVES **pupal** adjective.
- ORIGIN Latin, 'girl, doll'.

pupate verb (of an insect) become a pupa.
- DERIVATIVES **pupation** noun.

pupil¹ noun **1** a person who is taught by someone, especially a schoolchild. **2** Brit. a trainee barrister.
- ORIGIN from Latin *pupillus* 'little boy' and *pupilla* 'little girl'.

pupil² noun the dark circular opening in the centre of the iris of the eye, which controls the amount of light reaching the retina.
- ORIGIN Latin *pupilla* 'little doll' (from the tiny reflected images visible in the eye).

pupillage noun **1** the state of being a pupil. **2** Law (in the UK) apprenticeship to a member of the Bar, which qualifies a barrister to practise independently.

puppet noun **1** a model of a person or animal which can be moved either by strings or by a hand inside it. **2** a person under someone else's control.
- DERIVATIVES **puppeteer** noun **puppetry** noun.
- ORIGIN later form of POPPET.

puppy noun (pl. **puppies**) **1** a young dog. **2** informal, dated a conceited or arrogant young man.
- DERIVATIVES **puppyish** adjective.
- ORIGIN perhaps from Old French *poupee* 'doll, toy'.

puppy fat noun Brit. fat on a child's body which disappears around adolescence.

puppy love noun intense but short-lived feelings of love for someone, associated with adolescents.

purblind /per-blynd/ adjective literary **1** lacking awareness or understanding. **2** partially sighted.
- ORIGIN from PURE 'utterly' + BLIND.

purchase verb buy something. ●noun **1** the action of buying something. **2** a thing bought. **3** firm contact or grip. **4** a pulley or similar device for moving heavy objects.
- DERIVATIVES **purchasable** adjective **purchaser** noun.
- ORIGIN Old French *pourchacier* 'seek to obtain or bring about'.

purdah /per-duh/ noun the practice in certain Muslim and Hindu societies of screening women from men or strangers by means of a curtain or clothes that completely conceal their bodies.
- ORIGIN from Urdu and Persian, 'veil, curtain'.

pure adjective **1** not mixed with any other substance or material: *the jacket was pure wool*. **2** free of contamination. **3** innocent or morally good. **4** complete; nothing but: *a shout of pure anger*. **5** theoretical rather than practical: *pure mathematics*. **6** (of a sound) perfectly in tune and with a clear tone.
- DERIVATIVES **purely** adverb.
- ORIGIN Latin *purus*.

pure-bred adjective (of an animal) bred from parents of the same breed or variety.

purée /pyoor-ay/ noun a thick smooth liquid made of crushed or sieved fruit or vegetables. ●verb (**purées, puréeing, puréed**) make a purée of fruit or vegetables.
- ORIGIN French, 'purified'.

p

purgation /per-gay-sh'n/ noun **1** purification. **2** emptying of the bowels brought about by laxatives.
– ORIGIN Latin, from *purgare* 'purify'.

purgative /per-guh-tiv/ adjective having a strong laxative effect. • noun a laxative.

purgatory /per-guh-tuh-ri/ noun (pl. **purgatories**) **1** (in Catholic belief) a place or state of suffering inhabited by the souls of sinners who are atoning for their sins before going to heaven. **2** extreme distress or mental pain.
– DERIVATIVES **purgatorial** adjective.
– ORIGIN Latin *purgatorium*.

purge verb **1** rid of unwanted or undesirable things: *years of analysis had purged him of anger.* **2** remove a group of people considered to be undesirable from an organization. **3** empty one's bowels, especially as a result of taking a laxative. **4** Law atone for or wipe out contempt of court. • noun **1** an act of removing of a group of people from an organization. **2** dated a laxative.
– ORIGIN Latin *purgare* 'purify'.

puri /poor-i/ noun (pl. **puris**) (in Indian cookery) a small, round piece of unleavened bread which puffs up when deep-fried.
– ORIGIN Sanskrit.

purify verb (**purifies**, **purifying**, **purified**) make something pure by removing harmful, dirty, or unwanted substances.
– DERIVATIVES **purification** noun **purifier** noun.

purist noun a person who insists on following traditional rules, especially in language or style.
– DERIVATIVES **purism** noun.

puritan noun **1** (**Puritan**) a member of a group of English Protestants in the 16th and 17th centuries who sought to simplify and regulate forms of worship. **2** a person with strict moral beliefs who is critical of self-indulgent behaviour. • adjective **1** (**Puritan**) relating to the Puritans. **2** characteristic of a puritan.
– DERIVATIVES **puritanism** (also **Puritanism**) noun.

puritanical adjective having a very strict or critical attitude towards self-indulgent behaviour.

purity noun the state of being pure.

purl¹ adjective (of a knitting stitch) made by putting the needle through the front of the stitch from right to left. Compare with **PLAIN** (in sense 8). • verb knit with a purl stitch.
– ORIGIN uncertain.

purl² verb literary (of a stream or river) flow with a swirling movement and a continuous murmuring sound.
– ORIGIN probably imitating the sound.

purler noun Brit. informal a headlong fall.
– ORIGIN from dialect *purl* 'upset, overturn'.

purlieu /pur-lyoo/ noun (pl. **purlieus** /pur-lyooz/) **1** (**purlieus**) the area near or surrounding a place. **2** Brit. historical an area of land on the border of a forest.
– ORIGIN probably from Old French *puralee* 'a walk round to settle boundaries'.

purlin /per-lin/ noun a horizontal beam along the length of a roof, supporting the rafters.
– ORIGIN perhaps French.

purloin /per-loyn/ verb formal or humorous steal something.
– ORIGIN Old French *purloigner* 'put away'.

purple noun **1** a colour between red and blue. **2** (**the purple**) the scarlet official dress of a cardinal. • adjective of a colour between red and blue.
– DERIVATIVES **purplish** adjective **purply** adjective.
– ORIGIN from Greek *porphura*, referring to molluscs from which a crimson dye was obtained, also to cloth dyed with this.

Purple Heart noun (in the US) a decoration for members or the armed forces wounded or killed in action.

purple passage noun an extremely ornate or elaborate passage in a literary work.

purple patch noun **1** Brit. informal a run of success or good luck. **2** a purple passage.

purple prose noun prose that is too ornate.

purport verb /per-port/ appear or claim to be someone or do something: *she is not the person she purports to be.* • noun /per-port/ **1** the meaning of something. **2** the purpose of something.
– DERIVATIVES **purported** adjective **purportedly** adverb.
– ORIGIN Latin *proportare*.

purpose noun **1** the reason for which something is done or for which something exists: *the purpose of the meeting is to appoint a trustee.* **2** determination: *there was a sense of purpose in her step as she set off.* • verb formal have something as one's aim or intention.
– PHRASES **on purpose** intentionally.
– ORIGIN Old French *porpos*.

purposeful adjective **1** having or showing determination. **2** having a useful purpose.
– DERIVATIVES **purposefully** adverb **purposefulness** noun.

purposeless adjective done with or having no purpose.
– DERIVATIVES **purposelessly** adverb **purposelessness** noun.

purposely adverb deliberately; on purpose.

purposive /per-puh-siv/ adjective having or done with a purpose.
– DERIVATIVES **purposively** adverb **purposiveness** noun.

purr verb **1** (of a cat) make a low continuous sound in the throat, especially when happy or contented. **2** (of a vehicle or engine) move or run smoothly while making a similar sound. • noun a purring sound.
– ORIGIN imitating the sound.

purse noun **1** chiefly Brit. a small pouch for carrying money. **2** N. Amer. a handbag. **3** money available for spending; funds. **4** a sum of money given as a prize in a sporting contest. • verb pucker one's lips into a tight, round shape.
– PHRASES **hold the purse strings** have control of expenditure.
– ORIGIN Latin *bursa*.

purser noun a ship's officer who keeps the accounts, especially on a passenger vessel.

purse seine noun a large seine (fishing net) which may be drawn into the shape of a bag, used for catching fish swimming in shoals.

purslane /pers-luhn/ noun a small plant with

fleshy leaves which grows in damp or marshy areas.
– ORIGIN Old French *porcelaine*.

pursuance noun formal the carrying out of a plan or action.

pursuant /per-syoo-uhnt/ adverb (**pursuant to**) formal in accordance with a law or legal resolution.
– ORIGIN Old French.

pursue verb (**pursues, pursuing, pursued**)
1 follow in order to catch or attack: *police officers pursued the car along the A34.* 2 try to achieve a goal. 3 engage in or continue with an activity or course of action: *he took a degree before pursuing his professional sports career.* 4 continue to investigate or discuss something.
– DERIVATIVES **pursuer** noun.
– ORIGIN Old French *pursuer*.

pursuit noun 1 the action of pursuing someone or something. 2 a leisure or sporting activity.

pursuivant /per-si-vuhnt/ noun Brit. an officer of the College of Arms ranking below a herald.
– ORIGIN Old French *pursivant* 'follower or attendant'.

purulent /pyoor-uu-luhnt/ adjective consisting of, containing, or discharging pus.
– ORIGIN Latin *purulentus*.

purvey verb formal provide or supply food or drink as one's business.
– DERIVATIVES **purveyor** noun.
– ORIGIN Old French *purveier* 'foresee'.

purview noun formal 1 the scope of the influence or concerns of something: *such crimes are not within the purview of the tribunal.* 2 a range of experience or thought.
– ORIGIN from Old French *purveu* 'foreseen'.

pus noun a thick yellowish or greenish liquid produced in infected tissue.
– ORIGIN Latin.

push verb 1 apply force to someone or something so as to move them away from oneself or from the source of the force. 2 move one's body or a part of it forcefully into a particular position: *she pushed her hands into her pockets.* 3 move forward by using force: *he pushed his way through the crowd.* 4 drive oneself or urge someone to greater effort. 5 (**push for**) make persistent demands for something: *some legislators are pushing for tighter border controls.* 6 informal promote the use, sale, or acceptance of something. 7 informal sell a drug illegally. 8 (**be pushed**) informal have very little of something, especially time. 9 (**be pushing**) informal be nearly a particular age: *she's pushing forty.* •noun 1 an act of pushing. 2 a great effort: *one last push for success.*
– PHRASES **at a push** Brit. informal only if necessary or with difficulty. **get** (or **give someone**) **the push** Brit. informal 1 be dismissed (or dismiss someone) from a job. 2 be rejected in (or end) a relationship. **push ahead** proceed with or continue a course of action. **push in** Brit. go in front of people who are already queuing. **push off** Brit. informal go away. **when push comes to shove** informal when one has no choice but to act or make a decision.
– DERIVATIVES **pusher** noun.
– ORIGIN Old French *pousser*.

pushbike noun Brit. informal a bicycle.

pushcart noun chiefly N. Amer. a small cart that is pushed or drawn by hand.

pushchair noun Brit. a folding chair on wheels, in which a young child can be pushed along.

pushover noun informal 1 a person who is easy to influence or defeat. 2 a thing that is easily done.

push-start verb start a motor vehicle by pushing it in order to make the engine turn.

pushy adjective (**pushier, pushiest**) too self-assertive or ambitious.
– DERIVATIVES **pushiness** noun.

pusillanimous /pyoo-si-lan-i-muhss/ adjective timid or cowardly.
– DERIVATIVES **pusillanimity** /pyoo-si-luh-nim-i-ti/ noun.
– ORIGIN from Latin *pusillus* 'very small' + *animus* 'mind'.

puss noun informal 1 a cat. 2 a girl or young woman: *a glamour puss.*
– ORIGIN probably from German *pūs* or Dutch *poes*.

pussy noun (pl. **pussies**) 1 informal a cat. 2 vulgar slang a woman's genitals. 3 vulgar slang women considered sexually.

pussycat noun informal 1 a cat. 2 a mild-tempered or easy-going person.

pussyfoot verb (**pussyfoots, pussyfooting, pussyfooted**) act very cautiously.

pussy willow noun a willow with soft fluffy catkins that appear before the leaves.

pustule /pus-tyool/ noun a small blister or pimple containing pus.
– DERIVATIVES **pustular** adjective.
– ORIGIN Latin *pustula*.

put verb (**puts, putting, put**) 1 move to or place in a particular position: *he put down his cup.* 2 bring into a particular state or condition: *she tried to put me at ease.* 3 (**put something on/on to**) make someone or something subject to something: *commentators put the blame on Congress.* 4 give a value, figure, or limit to something. 5 express something in a particular way: *to put it bluntly, we've been framed.* 6 (of a ship) proceed in a particular direction: *the boat put out to sea.* 7 throw a shot or weight as an athletic sport. •noun a throw of the shot or weight as a sport.
– PHRASES **be put upon** informal be taken advantage of as a result of one's good nature. **put about** (of a ship) turn on the opposite tack. **put something about** Brit. spread information or rumours. **put someone down** informal criticize someone. **put something down** 1 suppress a rebellion, coup, or riot by force. 2 kill a sick, old, or injured animal. 3 pay a sum as a deposit. **put something down to** attribute something to. **put one's hands together** applaud. **put someone off** 1 cause someone to feel dislike or lose enthusiasm. 2 distract someone. **put something off** postpone something. **put something on** 1 present or provide a play, service, etc. 2 become heavier by a particular amount. 3 adopt a particular expression, accent, etc. **put someone out** inconvenience, upset, or annoy someone. **put something out** dislocate a joint. **put one over on** informal deceive someone into accepting something that is not true. **put someone

through 1 subject someone to an unpleasant experience. **2** connect someone by telephone to another person or place. **put something to** offer or submit something to someone for consideration: *he put the proposal to his daughter.* **put someone up 1** give someone temporary accommodation. **2** propose someone for election or adoption. **put something up** present, provide, or offer something: *the sponsors are putting up £5,000.* **put someone up to** informal encourage someone to do something wrong or unwise. **put up with** tolerate or endure: *I'm too tired to put up with any nonsense.*
– ORIGIN Old English.

putative /pyoo-tuh-tiv/ adjective generally considered or believed to be: *the putative father of her children.*
– DERIVATIVES **putatively** adverb.
– ORIGIN from Latin *putare* 'think'.

put-down noun informal a humiliating or critical remark.

putrefy /pyoo-tri-fy/ verb (**putrefies, putrefying, putrefied**) decay or rot and produce a very unpleasant smell.
– DERIVATIVES **putrefaction** noun.
– ORIGIN Latin *putrefacere.*

putrescent /pyoo-tress-uhnt/ adjective becoming putrid; rotting.

putrid adjective **1** decaying or rotting and giving off a very unpleasant smell. **2** informal very unpleasant.
– ORIGIN from Latin *putrere* 'to rot'.

putsch /puuch/ noun a violent attempt to overthrow a government.
– ORIGIN Swiss German, 'thrust, blow'.

putt verb (**putts, putting, putted**) strike a golf ball gently so that it rolls into or near a hole.
•noun a stroke of this kind.
– ORIGIN Scots form of PUT.

puttanesca /puut-tuh-ness-kuh/ noun a pasta sauce made with tomatoes, garlic, olives, anchovies, etc.
– ORIGIN Italian, from *puttana* 'a prostitute' (the sauce is said to have been devised by prostitutes as one which could be cooked quickly between clients' visits).

puttee /put-tee/ noun a long strip of cloth wound round the leg from ankle to knee for protection and support.
– ORIGIN Hindi, 'band, bandage'.

putter[1] /put-ter/ noun a golf club designed for putting.

putter[2] /put-ter/ noun the rapid intermittent sound of a small petrol engine. •verb move with or make such a sound.
– ORIGIN imitating the sound.

putting green noun a smooth area of short grass surrounding a hole on a golf course.

putto /puut-toh/ noun (pl. **putti** /puut-ti/) a representation of a naked child, especially a cherub or a cupid in Renaissance art.
– ORIGIN Italian, 'boy'.

putty noun a paste that is easily pressed into shape and gradually hardens as it sets, used for sealing glass in window frames, filling holes in wood, etc.
– PHRASES **be (like) putty in someone's hands** be easily manipulated by someone.
– ORIGIN French *potée*, 'potful'.

put-up job noun informal something arranged beforehand in order to deceive someone.

putz /puuts, puts/ noun N. Amer. informal a stupid person.
– ORIGIN Yiddish, 'penis'.

puzzle verb **1** make someone feel confused as a result of being difficult to understand: *I was very puzzled by his reply.* **2** think hard about something that is difficult to understand: *he puzzled over this problem for years.* •noun **1** a game, toy, or problem designed to test mental skills or knowledge. **2** a person or thing that is difficult to understand.
– DERIVATIVES **puzzlement** noun **puzzler** noun.
– ORIGIN unknown.

PVA abbreviation polyvinyl acetate, a synthetic resin used in paints and glues.

PVC abbreviation polyvinyl chloride, a tough synthetic resin used for a wide variety of products including pipes and floor coverings.

PVS abbreviation Medicine persistent vegetative state.

PW abbreviation policewoman.

p.w. abbreviation per week.

PWR abbreviation pressurized-water reactor.

pye-dog noun (in Asia) a half-wild stray mongrel.
– ORIGIN from a Hindi word meaning 'outsider' + DOG.

pygmy (also **pigmy**) noun (pl. **pygmies**) **1 (Pygmy)** a member of certain peoples of very short stature in equatorial Africa. **2** chiefly derogatory a very small person or thing. **3** a person who is lacking in a particular respect: *intellectual pygmies.* •adjective very small; dwarf.
– ORIGIN Greek *pugmaios* 'dwarf'.

pyjamas (US **pajamas**) plural noun **1** a loose-fitting jacket and trousers worn in bed. **2** loose trousers with a drawstring waist, worn by both sexes in some Asian countries.
– ORIGIN from the Persian words for 'leg' + 'clothing'.

pylon noun (also **electricity pylon**) a tall tower-like metal structure for carrying electricity cables.
– ORIGIN Greek *pulōn* 'gateway' (first referring to the gateway of an ancient Egyptian temple).

pylorus /py-lor-uhss/ noun (pl. **pylori** /py-lor-I/) the opening from the stomach into the small intestine.
– DERIVATIVES **pyloric** adjective.
– ORIGIN Greek *pulouros* 'gatekeeper'.

pyracantha /py-ruh-kan-thuh/ noun a thorny evergreen shrub with white flowers and bright red or yellow berries.
– ORIGIN Latin, from Greek *pur* 'fire' + *akantha* 'thorn'.

pyramid noun **1** a huge stone structure with a square or triangular base and sloping sides that meet in a point at the top, especially one built as a royal tomb in ancient Egypt. **2** Geometry a polyhedron of which one face is a polygon and the other faces are triangles with a common vertex. **3** a pyramid-shaped thing or pile of things.
– DERIVATIVES **pyramidal** adjective.

– ORIGIN Greek *puramis*.

pyramid selling noun a system of selling goods in which agency rights are sold to an increasing number of distributors at successively lower levels.

pyre noun a large pile of wood on which a dead body is placed and burnt as part of a funeral ceremony.
– ORIGIN Greek *pur* 'fire'.

pyrethrum /py-ree-thruhm/ noun 1 a plant of the daisy family, typically with brightly coloured flowers. 2 an insecticide made from the dried flowers of these plants.
– ORIGIN Greek *purethron* 'feverfew'.

pyretic /py-ret-ik, pi-ret-ik/ adjective feverish or causing fever.
– ORIGIN from Greek *puretos* 'fever'.

Pyrex noun trademark a hard heat-resistant type of glass.

pyrexia /py-rek-si-uh, pi-rek-si-uh/ noun raised body temperature; fever.
– ORIGIN Greek *purexis*.

pyridoxine /pi-ri-dok-sin, pi-ri-dok-seen/ noun vitamin B$_6$, a compound present chiefly in cereals, liver oils, and yeast.
– ORIGIN from *pyrid(ine)* (a liquid chemical) + *oxy(gen)*.

pyrites /py-ry-teez/ (also **iron pyrites** or **pyrite**) noun a shiny yellow mineral that is a compound of iron and sulphur.
– ORIGIN from Greek *puritēs* 'of fire'.

pyro- combining form relating to fire: *pyromania*.
– ORIGIN from Greek *pur* 'fire'.

pyroclastic /py-roh-klass-tik/ adjective Geology relating to rock fragments or ash erupted by a volcano, especially as a hot, dense, destructive flow.

– ORIGIN from Greek *klastos* 'broken in pieces'.

pyrography /py-rog-ruh-fi/ noun another term for **POKERWORK**.

pyromania noun an obsessive desire to set fire to things.
– DERIVATIVES **pyromaniac** noun.

pyrotechnic /py-ruh-tek-nik/ adjective 1 relating to fireworks. 2 brilliant or spectacular.
– DERIVATIVES **pyrotechnical** adjective.

pyrotechnics plural noun 1 a firework display. 2 (treated as sing.) the art of making fireworks or staging firework displays. 3 a spectacular performance or display: *vocal pyrotechnics*.

pyrrhic /pir-rik/ adjective (of a victory) won at too great a cost to have been worthwhile for the victor.
– ORIGIN named after *Pyrrhus*, a king of Epirus whose victory over the Romans in 279 BC incurred heavy losses.

Pythagoras' theorem noun the theorem that the square on the hypotenuse of a right-angled triangle is equal in area to the sum of the squares on the other two sides.

Pythagorean /py-tha-guh-ree-uhn/ adjective relating to the Greek philosopher and mathematician Pythagoras (c.580–500 BC) or his philosophy.

python noun a large non-venomous snake which kills its prey by squeezing and crushing it.
– ORIGIN Greek *Puthōn*, a huge serpent killed by Apollo.

pyx /piks/ (also **pix**) noun Christian Church the container in which the consecrated bread used in the service of Holy Communion is kept.
– ORIGIN Greek *puxis* 'box'.

pzazz noun variant spelling of **PIZAZZ**.

p

Qq

Q[1] (also **q**) noun (pl. **Qs** or **Q's**) the seventeenth letter of the alphabet.

Q[2] abbreviation **1** queen (used especially in card games and chess). **2** question.

Qabalah noun variant spelling of **KABBALAH**.

Qatari /ka-**tah**-ri/ noun a person from Qatar, a country in the Persian Gulf. ▪ adjective relating to Qatar.

QC abbreviation **1** quality control. **2** Quebec. **3** Law Queen's Counsel.

QED abbreviation quod erat demonstrandum, used to state that something proves the truth of one's claim.
– ORIGIN Latin, 'which was to be demonstrated'.

qi /kee/ noun variant spelling of **CHI**[2].

qigong /chee-**gong**/ noun a Chinese system of physical exercises and breathing control related to t'ai chi.
– ORIGIN Chinese.

qt abbreviation quart(s).

q.t. noun (in phrase **on the q.t.**) informal secretly.
– ORIGIN abbreviation of *quiet*.

qua /kway, kwah/ conjunction formal in the capacity of; as being.
– ORIGIN Latin.

quack[1] noun the harsh sound made by a duck. ▪ verb make a quack.
– ORIGIN imitating the sound.

quack[2] noun **1** an unqualified person who dishonestly claims to have medical knowledge. **2** Brit. informal a doctor.
– DERIVATIVES **quackery** noun.
– ORIGIN abbreviation of earlier *quacksalver*, from Dutch, probably from former *quacken* 'prattle' + *salf* 'salve'.

quad noun **1** a quadrangle. **2** a quadruplet.

quad bike noun a motorcycle with four large tyres, for off-road use.

quadragenarian /kwod-ruh-ji-**nair**-i-uhn/ noun a person who is between 40 and 49 years old.
– ORIGIN Latin *quadragenarius*.

quadrangle noun **1** a square or rectangular courtyard enclosed by buildings. **2** a four-sided geometrical figure, especially a square or rectangle.
– DERIVATIVES **quadrangular** adjective.
– ORIGIN from Latin *quadri-* 'four' + *angulus* 'corner, angle'.

quadrant noun **1** each of four parts of a circle, plane, object, etc. divided by two lines or planes at right angles. **2** historical an instrument for measuring altitude in astronomy and navigation.
– ORIGIN Latin *quadrans* 'quarter'.

quadraphonic /kwod-ruh-**fon**-ik/ (also **quadrophonic**) adjective (of sound reproduction) transmitted through four channels.
– DERIVATIVES **quadraphony** noun.

quadrate /**kwod**-ruht/ adjective roughly square or rectangular.
– ORIGIN from Latin *quadrare* 'make square'.

quadratic /kwod-**rat**-ik/ adjective Mathematics involving the second and no higher power of an unknown quantity or variable.

quadrennial /kwod-**ren**-ni-uhl/ adjective lasting for or recurring every four years.
– ORIGIN from Latin *quadri-* 'four' + *annus* 'year'.

quadri- combining form four; having four: *quadriplegia*.
– ORIGIN Latin.

quadriceps /**kwod**-ri-seps/ noun (pl. same) a large muscle at the front of the thigh.
– ORIGIN from Latin, 'four-headed'.

quadrilateral noun a four-sided figure. ▪ adjective having four straight sides.

quadrille[1] /kwo-**dril**/ noun a square dance performed by four couples.
– ORIGIN Spanish *cuadrilla* or Italian *quadriglia* 'troop, company'.

quadrille[2] /kwo-**dril**/ noun a trick-taking card game for four players, fashionable in the 18th century.
– ORIGIN French.

quadrillion /kwod-**ril**-lyuhn/ cardinal number **1** a thousand million million; a thousand raised to the power of five (10^{15}). **2** (also **quadrillions**) informal a very large number or amount.
– DERIVATIVES **quadrillionth** ordinal number.

quadripartite /kwod-ri-**par**-tyt/ adjective **1** consisting of four parts. **2** shared by or involving four parties.

quadriplegia /kwod-ri-**plee**-juh/ noun paralysis of all four limbs.
– DERIVATIVES **quadriplegic** adjective & noun.

quadrophonic adjective variant spelling of **QUADRAPHONIC**.

quadruped /**kwod**-ruu-ped/ noun an animal which has four feet, especially a mammal.
– DERIVATIVES **quadrupedal** /kwod-ruu-**pee**-d'l, kwod-**roo**-pi-d'l/ adjective.
– ORIGIN from Latin *quadru-* 'four' + *pes* 'foot'.

quadruple adjective **1** consisting of four parts or elements. **2** four times as much or as many. **3** (of time in music) having four beats in a bar.

•**verb** multiply or be multiplied by four. •**noun** a quadruple number or amount.
- ORIGIN Latin *quadruplus*.

quadruplet noun each of four children born at one birth.

quadruplicate /kwod-**roo**-pli-kuht/ **adjective** consisting of four parts.
- PHRASES **in quadruplicate** in four copies.
- ORIGIN from Latin *quadruplicare* 'to quadruple'.

quaff /kwoff/ **verb** drink something heartily.
- DERIVATIVES **quaffable** adjective **quaffer** noun.
- ORIGIN probably imitating the sound.

quagga /**kwag**-guh/ **noun** an extinct South African zebra with a yellowish-brown coat with darker stripes.
- ORIGIN probably from Khoikhoi.

quagmire /**kwag**-my-er, **kwog**-my-er/ **noun** 1 a soft boggy area of land that gives way underfoot. 2 a complex or difficult situation: *a quagmire of unresolved issues.*
- ORIGIN from former *quag* 'a marshy place' + MIRE.

quail[1] **noun** (pl. same or **quails**) a small short-tailed game bird, typically with brown plumage.
- ORIGIN Old French *quaille*.

quail[2] **verb** feel or show fear or worry.
- ORIGIN unknown.

quaint adjective attractively unusual or old-fashioned.
- DERIVATIVES **quaintly** adverb **quaintness** noun.
- ORIGIN Old French *cointe* 'wise'.

quake noun informal an earthquake. •**verb** 1 shudder with fear. 2 (especially of the earth) shake or tremble.
- ORIGIN Old English.

Quaker noun a member of the Religious Society of Friends, a Christian movement that is strongly opposed to war and violence and that meets without any formal ceremony.
- DERIVATIVES **Quakerism** noun.
- ORIGIN from QUAKE, perhaps with reference to the founder's direction to his followers to 'tremble at the Word of the Lord'.

qualification noun 1 a pass of an exam or an official completion of a course. 2 the action of qualifying or the fact of becoming qualified: *England need to beat Poland to ensure qualification for the World Cup finals.* 3 a quality that makes someone suitable for a job or activity. 4 an official requirement. 5 a statement that restricts the meaning of another.

qualifier noun 1 a person or team that qualifies for a competition or its final rounds. 2 a match or contest to decide which people or teams qualify for a competition or its final rounds. 3 Grammar a word or phrase, especially an adjective, used to describe another word, especially a noun.

qualify verb (**qualifies**, **qualifying**, **qualified**) 1 meet the necessary standard or conditions to be entitled to do or receive something: *it's the best chance in years for the team to qualify for a major tournament.* 2 become officially recognized as able to practise a particular profession or activity. 3 make someone competent or knowledgeable enough to do something: *I'm not qualified to write on the subject.* 4 add restrictions to a statement to limit its meaning. 5 Grammar (of a word or phrase) describe another word in a particular way in order to restrict its meaning (e.g. in *the open door*, *open* is an adjective qualifying *door*).
- ORIGIN Latin *qualificare*.

qualitative /**kwol**-i-tuh-tiv/ **adjective** relating to or measured by quality.
- DERIVATIVES **qualitatively** adverb.

qualitative analysis noun Chemistry the identification of the constituents present in a substance.

quality noun (pl. **qualities**) 1 the standard of how good something is as measured against other similar things: *an improvement in product quality.* 2 general excellence. 3 a distinctive feature or characteristic: *strong leadership qualities.* 4 old use high social standing. •**adjective** informal of good quality; excellent: *he's a quality player.*
- ORIGIN Latin *qualitas*.

quality control noun a system of maintaining quality in manufactured products by testing a sample to see if it meets the required standard.

quality time noun time spent in giving one's full attention to one's child or partner, in order to strengthen the relationship.

qualm /kwahm/ **noun** 1 a feeling of doubt or unease, especially about one's behaviour: *he had no qualms about divorcing her.* 2 old use a brief faint or sick feeling.
- ORIGIN perhaps related to an Old English word meaning 'pain'.

quandary /**kwon**-duh-ri/ **noun** (pl. **quandaries**) a state of uncertainty over what to do in a difficult situation.
- ORIGIN perhaps partly from Latin *quando* 'when'.

quango /**kwang**-goh/ **noun** (pl. **quangos**) Brit., chiefly derogatory a semi-public administrative organization that receives financial support from the government, which makes senior appointments to it.
- ORIGIN from the initial letters of *quasi* (or *quasi-autonomous*) *non-governmental organization*.

quanta plural of QUANTUM.

quantify verb (**quantifies**, **quantifying**, **quantified**) express or measure the quantity of: *the method used to quantify how much acid rain it takes to damage ecosystems.*
- DERIVATIVES **quantifiable** adjective **quantification** noun **quantifier** noun.

quantitative /**kwon**-ti-tuh-tiv/ **adjective** relating to or measured by quantity.
- DERIVATIVES **quantitatively** adverb.

quantitative analysis noun Chemistry the measurement of the quantities of particular constituents present in a substance.

quantity noun (pl. **quantities**) 1 a certain amount or number of something. 2 the aspect of something that is measurable in number, amount, size, or weight: *wages depended on quantity of output.* 3 a considerable number or amount.
- ORIGIN Latin *quantitas*.

quantity surveyor noun Brit. a person who calculates the amount and cost of materials needed for building work.

quantum /kwon-tuhm/ noun (pl. **quanta**)
1 Physics a distinct quantity of energy corresponding to that involved in the absorption or emission of energy by an atom. **2** a share or portion.
– ORIGIN Latin.

quantum computer noun a hypothetical computer which makes use of the quantum states of subatomic particles to store information.

quantum leap (also **quantum jump**) noun a sudden large increase or advance.

quantum mechanics plural noun (treated as sing.) the branch of physics concerned with describing the behaviour of subatomic particles in terms of quanta.

quantum theory noun a theory of matter and energy based on the idea of quanta.

quarantine noun a state or period of isolation for people or animals that have or may have a disease. ● verb put a person or animal in quarantine.
– ORIGIN Italian *quarantina* 'forty days'.

quark¹ /kwawrk/ noun Physics any of a group of subatomic particles which carry a fractional electric charge and are believed to be building blocks of protons, neutrons, and other particles.
– ORIGIN invented by the American physicist Murray Gell-Mann.

quark² /kwaark/ noun a type of low-fat curd cheese.
– ORIGIN German, 'curd, curds'.

quarrel¹ noun **1** an angry argument or disagreement. **2** a reason for disagreement: *his quarrel is with those who exaggerate the benefits of the project.* ● verb (**quarrels, quarrelling, quarrelled;** US **quarrels, quarreling, quarreled**) **1** have a quarrel. **2** (**quarrel with**) disagree with.
– ORIGIN Latin *querella* 'complaint'.

quarrel² noun historical a short heavy square-headed arrow or bolt for a crossbow.
– ORIGIN Old French.

quarrelsome adjective tending or likely to quarrel.

quarry¹ noun (pl. **quarries**) an area of the earth's surface which has been dug open so that stone or other materials can be obtained. ● verb (**quarries, quarrying, quarried**) take stone or other materials from a quarry.
– DERIVATIVES **quarrier** noun.
– ORIGIN Old French *quarriere*.

quarry² noun (pl. **quarries**) **1** an animal being hunted. **2** a person or thing being chased or looked for.
– ORIGIN Old French *couree* 'parts of a deer given to the hounds'.

quarry³ noun (pl. **quarries**) **1** (also **quarry tile**) an unglazed floor tile. **2** a diamond-shaped pane in a lattice window.
– ORIGIN from **QUARREL**², which originally referred to a lattice windowpane.

quart noun a unit of liquid capacity equal to a quarter of a gallon or two pints, equivalent in Britain to approximately 1.13 litres and in the US to approximately 0.94 litre.
– ORIGIN from Latin *quarta pars* 'fourth part'.

quarter noun **1** each of four equal parts into which something is divided. **2** a period of three months, used especially in reference to financial transactions. **3** a quarter-hour. **4** one fourth of a pound weight, equal to 4 ounces avoirdupois. **5** a part of a town or city with a specific character or use: *the business quarter.* **6** (**quarters**) rooms or lodgings. **7** a US or Canadian coin worth 25 cents. **8** one fourth of a hundredweight (Brit. 28 lb or US 25 lb). **9** a person, group, or area regarded as the source of something: *help came from an unexpected quarter.* **10** mercy shown to an opponent: *they gave the enemy no quarter.* **11** (**quarters**) the haunches or hindquarters of a horse. **12** the direction of one of the points of the compass. ● verb **1** divide something into quarters. **2** (**be quartered**) be lodged somewhere. **3** historical cut the body of an executed person into four parts. **4** range over an area in all directions.
– ORIGIN Latin *quartarius* 'fourth part of a measure'.

quarterback noun American Football a player stationed behind the centre who directs a team's attacking play.

quarter day noun Brit. each of four days in the year on which some tenancies begin and end and quarterly payments fall due.

quarterdeck noun the part of a ship's upper deck near the stern, traditionally reserved for officers or for ceremonial use.

quarter-final noun a match of a knockout competition preceding the semi-final.
– DERIVATIVES **quarter-finalist** noun.

quarter-hour noun **1** (also **quarter of an hour**) a period of fifteen minutes. **2** a point of time fifteen minutes before or after a full hour of the clock.

quarter-light noun Brit. a window in the side of a car other than a main door window.

quarterly adjective & adverb produced or occurring once every quarter of a year. ● noun (pl. **quarterlies**) a publication produced four times a year.

quartermaster noun **1** a regimental officer in charge of providing accommodation and supplies. **2** a naval petty officer responsible for steering and signals.

quarter sessions plural noun historical (in England, Wales, and Northern Ireland) a court of limited powers, usually held quarterly.

quarterstaff noun a heavy pole 6–8 feet long, formerly used as a weapon.

quarter tone noun Music half a semitone.

quartet (also **quartette**) noun **1** a group of four people playing music or singing together. **2** a composition for a quartet. **3** a set of four people or things.
– ORIGIN Italian *quartetto.*

quartile /kwor-tyl/ noun Statistics each of four equal groups into which a population can be divided according to the distribution of values of a particular variable.
– ORIGIN Latin *quartilis.*

quarto /kwor-toh/ noun (pl. **quartos**) a page or paper size resulting from folding a sheet into four leaves, typically 10 inches × 8 inches (254 × 203 mm).
– ORIGIN from Latin *in quarto* 'in the fourth (of a sheet)'.

quartz noun a hard mineral consisting of silica, typically occurring as colourless or white hexagonal prisms.
– ORIGIN German *Quarz*.

quartz clock (or **watch**) noun a clock (or watch) regulated by vibrations of an electrically driven quartz crystal.

quartzite noun a compact, hard, granular rock consisting mainly of quartz.

quasar /kway-zar/ noun a massive and extremely remote object in space which emits huge amounts of energy.
– ORIGIN from *quasi-stellar radio source*.

quash verb 1 officially reject a legal decision as invalid. 2 put an end to; suppress: *rumours of job losses were quashed*.
– ORIGIN Old French *quasser* 'annul'.

quasi- /kway-zy/ combining form 1 seemingly: *quasi-scientific*. 2 being partly or almost: *quasicrystalline*.
– ORIGIN Latin, 'as if, almost'.

quassia /kwosh-uh, kwosh-i-uh, kwass-i-uh/ noun a South American shrub or small tree whose wood, bark, or root yields a bitter medicinal tonic and insecticide.
– ORIGIN named after Graman *Quassi*, the Surinamese slave who discovered its medicinal properties.

quaternary /kwuh-**ter**-nuh-ri/ adjective 1 fourth in order or rank. 2 (**Quaternary**) Geology relating to the most recent period in the Cenozoic era, from about 1.64 million years ago to the present.
– ORIGIN Latin *quaternarius*.

quatrain /kwot-rayn/ noun a verse of four lines, typically with alternate rhymes.
– ORIGIN French.

quatrefoil /kat-ruh-foyl/ noun an ornamental design of four lobes or leaves, resembling a clover leaf.
– ORIGIN from Old French *quatre* 'four' + *foil* 'leaf'.

quattrocento /kwa-troh-**chen**-toh/ noun the 15th century as a period of Italian art or architecture.
– ORIGIN Italian, '400' (shortened from *milquattrocento* '1400').

quaver verb (of a voice) tremble. •noun 1 a tremble in a voice. 2 chiefly Brit. a musical note having the value of half a crotchet, shown by a large dot with a hooked stem.
– DERIVATIVES **quavery** adjective.
– ORIGIN probably from an Old English word related to **QUAKE**.

quay /kee/ noun a platform lying alongside or projecting into water for loading and unloading ships.
– ORIGIN Old French *kay*.

quayside noun a quay and the area around it.

queasy adjective (**queasier**, **queasiest**) 1 feeling sick; nauseous. 2 slightly nervous or uneasy.
– DERIVATIVES **queasily** adverb **queasiness** noun.
– ORIGIN perhaps related to Old French *coisier* 'to hurt'.

Quechua /kech-wuh/ noun (pl. same or **Quechuas**) 1 a member of an American Indian people of Peru and neighbouring countries. 2 the language of the Quechua.
– DERIVATIVES **Quechuan** adjective & noun.

– ORIGIN Quechua, 'temperate valleys'.

queen noun 1 the female ruler of an independent state, especially one who inherits the position by birth. 2 (also **queen consort**) a king's wife. 3 the best or most important woman or thing in a field of activity or group. 4 a playing card bearing a picture of a queen, ranking next below a king. 5 the most powerful chess piece, able to move in any direction. 6 a reproductive female in a colony of ants, bees, wasps, or termites. 7 informal a very effeminate homosexual man. •verb 1 (**queen it**) (of a woman) act in an unpleasantly superior way. 2 Chess convert a pawn into a queen when it reaches the opponent's end of the board.
– DERIVATIVES **queendom** noun **queenly** adjective **queenship** noun.
– ORIGIN Old English.

Queen Anne adjective referring to a style of English furniture or architecture characteristic of the early 18th century.

queen bee noun 1 the single reproductive female in a colony of honeybees. 2 informal a dominant woman in a group.

queen mother noun the widow of a king and mother of the current sovereign.

queen post noun either of two upright timbers between the tie beam and main rafters of a roof truss.

Queen's Bench noun (in the UK) a division of the High Court of Justice.

Queensberry Rules plural noun the standard rules of boxing.
– ORIGIN named after the 9th Marquess of *Queensberry*, who supervised the preparation of the rules.

Queen's Counsel noun a senior barrister appointed on the recommendation of the Lord Chancellor.

Queen's English noun the English language as correctly written and spoken in Britain.

Queen's evidence noun English Law evidence for the prosecution given by a participant in the crime being tried.

Queen's Guide (or **Queen's Scout**) noun (in the UK) a Guide (or Scout) who has reached the highest rank of proficiency.

Queen's highway noun Brit. the public road network.

queen-sized (also **queen-size**) adjective of a larger size than the standard but smaller than king-sized.

Queen's Speech noun (in the UK) a statement read by the sovereign at the opening of parliament, detailing the government's proposed legislative programme.

queer adjective 1 strange; odd. 2 informal, derogatory (of a man) homosexual. 3 Brit. informal, dated slightly ill. •noun informal, derogatory a homosexual man. •verb informal spoil or ruin something.
– PHRASES **queer someone's pitch** Brit. informal spoil someone's plans or chances of doing something.
– DERIVATIVES **queerish** adjective **queerly** adverb **queerness** noun.
– ORIGIN perhaps from German *quer* 'oblique, perverse'.

q

quell verb **1** put an end to a rebellion or other disorder. **2** stop or reduce a strong or unpleasant feeling: *I hurried to quell her fears.*
– ORIGIN Old English, 'kill'.

quench verb **1** satisfy thirst by drinking. **2** satisfy a desire. **3** extinguish a fire. **4** stop or reduce a strong feeling. **5** rapidly cool hot metal.
– DERIVATIVES **quencher** noun.
– ORIGIN Old English.

quenelle /kuh-**nel**/ noun a small ball of minced fish or meat.
– ORIGIN French.

quern /kwern/ noun a simple hand mill for grinding grain, typically consisting of two circular stones.
– ORIGIN Old English.

querulous /kwe-ruu-luhss, kwe-ryuu-luhss/ adjective complaining in a petulant or irritable way.
– DERIVATIVES **querulously** adverb **querulousness** noun.
– ORIGIN Latin *querulus*.

query noun (pl. **queries**) **1** a question expressing doubt or asking for information. **2** chiefly Printing a question mark. • verb (**queries, querying, queried**) **1** ask a question to express doubt or obtain information. **2** N. Amer. put a query or queries to someone.
– ORIGIN from Latin *quaerere* 'ask, seek'.

quesadilla /kay-suh-**deel**-yuh, kay-suh-**dee**-yuh/ noun a hot tortilla with a spicy cheese filling.
– ORIGIN Spanish.

quest noun **1** a long or difficult search: *the quest for a better life.* **2** (in medieval romance) an expedition by a knight to accomplish a specific task. • verb search for something.
– DERIVATIVES **quester** (also **questor**) noun.
– ORIGIN Old French *queste*.

question noun **1** a sentence worded or expressed so as to obtain information. **2** a doubt as to whether something is true or valid. **3** the raising of a doubt or objection: *he obeyed without question.* **4** a problem that needs to be resolved. **5** a matter that depends on conditions: *it's only a question of time before something changes.* • verb **1** ask someone questions. **2** express doubt about or object to something.
– PHRASES **come** (or **bring**) **into question** become (or raise) an issue for further consideration or discussion. **in question 1** being considered. **2** in doubt. **no question of** no possibility of. **out of the question** not possible.
– DERIVATIVES **questioner** noun.
– ORIGIN Old French.

questionable adjective **1** open to doubt. **2** likely to be dishonest or morally wrong: *questionable financial deals.*
– DERIVATIVES **questionably** adverb.

question mark noun a punctuation mark (?) indicating a question.

question master noun Brit. the person who chairs a quiz or panel game.

questionnaire /kwess-chuh-**nair**/ noun a set of questions, usually with a choice of answers, written for a survey or statistical study.
– ORIGIN French.

question time noun (in the UK) a period during proceedings in the House of Commons when MPs may question ministers.

quetzal /ket-suhl, kwet-suhl/ noun a long-tailed tropical American bird with iridescent green plumage.
– ORIGIN from an Aztec word meaning 'brightly coloured tail feather'.

queue noun **1** chiefly Brit. a line of people or vehicles awaiting their turn for something or to continue. **2** Computing a list of data items, commands, etc., stored so as to be retrievable in a definite order. • verb (**queues, queuing** or **queueing, queued**) chiefly Brit. wait in a queue.
– ORIGIN French, 'tail'.

queue-jump verb Brit. move forward out of turn in a queue.

quibble noun **1** a minor objection or criticism. **2** old use a pun. • verb argue about a trivial matter.
– ORIGIN from former *quib* 'a petty objection'.

quiche /keesh/ noun a baked flan with a savoury filling thickened with eggs.
– ORIGIN French.

quick adjective **1** moving fast. **2** lasting or taking a short time: *a quick worker.* **3** with little or no delay; prompt. **4** able to think, learn, or notice things promptly; intelligent. **5** (of temper) easily roused. • noun **1** (**the quick**) the tender flesh below the growing part of a fingernail or toenail. **2** (as plural noun **the quick**) old use those who are living.
– PHRASES **a quick one** informal a rapidly consumed alcoholic drink. **cut someone to the quick** upset someone very much: *his laughter cut us to the quick.* **quick with child** old use at a stage of pregnancy when the fetus can be felt to move.
– DERIVATIVES **quickly** adverb **quickness** noun.
– ORIGIN Old English, 'alive, animated, alert'.

quicken verb **1** make or become quicker. **2** stimulate or be stimulated: *my interest quickened.* **3** old use reach a stage in pregnancy when the fetus can be felt to move.

quick-fire adjective **1** unhesitating and rapid. **2** (of a gun) firing shots in rapid succession.

quick fix noun a solution which is implemented quickly but which is not good enough for the long term.

quickie informal noun **1** a rapidly consumed alcoholic drink. **2** a brief act of sex. • adjective done or made quickly.

quicklime noun a white caustic alkaline substance consisting of calcium oxide, obtained by heating limestone.

quick march noun a brisk military march.

quicksand noun (also **quicksands**) loose wet sand that sucks in anything resting on it.

quickset noun Brit. hedging, especially of hawthorn, grown from cuttings.

quicksilver noun liquid mercury. • adjective moving or changing rapidly and unexpectedly.

quickstep noun a fast foxtrot (dance) in 4/4 time.

quick-tempered adjective easily angered.

quick-witted adjective able to think or respond quickly.

quid[1] noun (pl. same) Brit. informal one pound sterling.

- PHRASES **quids in** Brit. informal profiting or likely to profit from something.
- ORIGIN unknown.

quid[2] **noun** a lump of chewing tobacco.
- ORIGIN variant of **CUD**.

quiddity /kwid-i-ti/ **noun** (pl. **quiddities**) the essential nature of a person or thing.
- ORIGIN Latin *quidditas*.

quid pro quo /kwid proh kwoh/ **noun** (pl. **quid pro quos**) a favour given in return for something.
- ORIGIN Latin, 'something for something'.

quiescent /kwi-ess-uhnt/ **adjective** in a state or period of inactivity.
- DERIVATIVES **quiescence** noun **quiescently** adverb.
- ORIGIN from Latin *quiescere* 'be still'.

quiet adjective (**quieter**, **quietest**) **1** making little or no noise. **2** free from activity, disturbance, or excitement. **3** without being disturbed or interrupted: *a quiet drink*. **4** discreet, moderate, or restrained: *we wanted a quiet wedding*. **5** (of a person) calm and shy. •**noun** absence of noise or disturbance. •**verb** chiefly N. Amer. make or become quiet.
- PHRASES **keep quiet** say nothing or keep something secret. **on the quiet** informal secretly or without attracting attention.
- DERIVATIVES **quietly** adverb **quietness** noun.
- ORIGIN from Latin *quies* 'repose, quiet'.

> USAGE: Do not confuse **quiet** and **quite**. Quiet means 'making little or no noise' (*he spoke in a quiet voice*), whereas quite means 'moderately' or 'completely', as in *it's quite warm* or *I quite agree*.

quieten verb chiefly Brit. make or become quiet and calm.

quietism noun calm acceptance of things as they are.

quietude noun a state of calmness and quiet.

quietus /kwy-ee-tuhss/ **noun** (pl. **quietuses**) literary death or a cause of death, regarded as a release from life.
- ORIGIN from Latin *quietus est* 'he is quit'.

quiff noun chiefly Brit. a tuft of hair, brushed upwards and backwards from a man's forehead.
- ORIGIN unknown.

quill noun **1** a main wing or tail feather of a bird. **2** the hollow shaft of a feather. **3** a pen made from a main wing or tail feather of a bird. **4** a spine of a porcupine, hedgehog, etc.
- ORIGIN probably from German *quiele*.

quilling noun a type of ornamental craftwork in which paper or fabric is shaped into delicate pleats or folds.

quilt noun **1** a warm bed covering made of padding enclosed between layers of fabric and kept in place by lines of decorative stitching. **2** a bedspread with decorative stitching. •**verb** (usu. as adj. **quilted**) stitch padding between layers of fabric to form a quilt or item of clothing.
- DERIVATIVES **quilter** noun **quilting** noun.
- ORIGIN Old French *cuilte*.

quim noun Brit. vulgar slang a woman's genitals.
- ORIGIN unknown.

quin noun Brit. informal a quintuplet.

quince noun the hard, acid, pear-shaped fruit of an Asian shrub or small tree.
- ORIGIN Old French *cooin*.

quincentenary /kwin-sen-tee-nuh-ri, kwin-sen-ten-uh-ri/ **noun** (pl. **quincentenaries**) a five-hundredth anniversary.
- DERIVATIVES **quincentennial** noun & adjective.
- ORIGIN from Latin *quinque* 'five'.

quincunx /kwin-kungks/ **noun** (pl. **quincunxes**) an arrangement of five objects with four at the corners of a square or rectangle and the fifth at its centre.
- DERIVATIVES **quincuncial** /kwin-kung-sh'l/ adjective.
- ORIGIN Latin, 'five twelfths'.

quinine /kwi-neen, kwi-neen/ **noun** a bitter compound present in cinchona bark, formerly used to treat malaria.
- ORIGIN Quechua, 'bark'.

quinone /kwi-nohn/ **noun** any of a class of organic chemical compounds related to benzene but having two hydrogen atoms replaced by oxygen.
- ORIGIN from Spanish *quina* 'cinchona bark'.

quinquennial /kwing-kwen-ni-uhl/ adjective lasting for or recurring every five years.
- DERIVATIVES **quinquennially** adverb.
- ORIGIN from Latin *quinque* 'five' + *annus* 'year'.

quinquereme /kwing-kwi-reem/ **noun** an ancient Roman or Greek galley (ship) of a kind believed to have had five oarsman to a bank of oars.
- ORIGIN from Latin *quinque* 'five' + *remus* 'oar'.

quinsy /kwin-zi/ **noun** inflammation of the throat, especially an abscess near the tonsils.
- ORIGIN Greek *kunankhē* 'canine quinsy'.

quinta /kwin-tuh, kin-tuh/ **noun 1** (in Spain, Portugal, and Latin America) a large country house. **2** a wine-growing estate, especially in Portugal.
- ORIGIN Spanish and Portuguese.

quintal /kwin-t'l/ **noun 1** a unit of weight equal to a hundredweight (112 lb) or, formerly, 100 lb. **2** a unit of weight equal to 100 kg.
- ORIGIN Latin *quintale*.

quintessence /kwin-tess-uhnss/ **noun 1** the most perfect or typical example of a quality or type: *he's emerged as the quintessence of cool*. **2** a refined essence or extract of a substance.
- ORIGIN from Latin *quinta essentia* 'fifth essence', from the former belief that a fifth substance existed in addition to the four elements, which pervaded all things.

quintessential /kwin-ti-sen-sh'l/ adjective representing the most perfect or typical example of a quality or type.
- DERIVATIVES **quintessentially** adverb.

quintet noun **1** a group of five people playing music or singing together. **2** a composition for a quintet. **3** a set of five people or things.
- ORIGIN Italian *quintetto*.

quintillion /kwin-til-yuhn/ **cardinal number** a million million million; a thousand raised to the power of six (10^{18}).
- DERIVATIVES **quintillionth** ordinal number.

quintuple /kwin-tyuu-p'l, kwin-tyoo-p'l/ **adjective 1** consisting of five parts or elements. **2** five times as much or as many. **3** (of time in music) having five beats in a bar. •**verb**

q

multiply or be multiplied by five. •noun a quintuple number or amount.
– ORIGIN Latin *quintuplus*.

quintuplet /kwin-tyuu-plit, kwin-**tyoo**-plit/ noun each of five children born at one birth.

quip noun a witty remark. •verb (**quips, quipping, quipped**) make a witty remark.
– DERIVATIVES **quipster** noun.
– ORIGIN perhaps from Latin *quippe* 'indeed'.

quire /*rhymes with* squire/ noun 1 25 sheets of paper; one twentieth of a ream. 2 four sheets of paper folded to form eight leaves, as in medieval manuscripts.
– ORIGIN Old French *quaier*.

quirk noun 1 a peculiar aspect of a person's behaviour. 2 a strange thing that happens by chance: *a quirk of fate.* 3 a sudden twist or curve.
– ORIGIN unknown.

quirky adjective (**quirkier, quirkiest**) having peculiar or unexpected habits or qualities: *a quirky sense of humour.*
– DERIVATIVES **quirkily** adverb **quirkiness** noun.

quirt /kwert/ noun a short-handled riding whip with a braided leather lash.
– ORIGIN Spanish *cuerda* 'cord' or Mexican Spanish *cuarta* 'whip'.

quisling /kwiz-ling/ noun a traitor collaborating with an occupying enemy force.
– ORIGIN from Major Vidkun *Quisling*, who ruled Norway during the Second World War on behalf of the German occupying forces.

quit verb (**quits, quitting, quitted** or **quit**) 1 leave a place, especially permanently. 2 resign from a job. 3 informal, chiefly N. Amer. stop doing something.
– PHRASES **be quit of** be rid of someone or something.
– ORIGIN Old French *quiter*.

quite adverb 1 to a certain extent; moderately. 2 to the greatest extent or degree; completely: *I quite agree.* •exclamation (also **quite so**) expressing agreement.
– PHRASES **quite a** —— a remarkable or impressive person or thing.
– ORIGIN from **QUIT**.

> USAGE: For an explanation of the difference between **quite** and **quiet**, see the note at **QUIET**.

quits adjective on equal terms because a debt or score has been settled.
– PHRASES **call it quits 1** agree that terms are now equal. 2 decide to stop doing something.
– ORIGIN perhaps from Latin *quietus est* 'he is quit', used as a receipt.

quittance noun old use or literary a release from a debt or duty.

quitter noun informal a person who gives up easily.

quiver¹ verb shake or vibrate with a slight rapid movement. •noun a quivering movement or sound.
– DERIVATIVES **quivery** adjective.
– ORIGIN from an Old English word meaning 'nimble, quick'.

quiver² noun an archer's case for carrying arrows.
– ORIGIN Old French *quiveir*.

qui vive /kee veev/ noun (in phrase **on the qui vive**) on the alert or lookout.
– ORIGIN French, '(long) live who?', i.e. 'on whose side are you?', used as a sentry's challenge.

quixotic /kwik-**sot**-ik/ adjective unselfish and idealistic to an impractical extent: *the quixotic desire to do good.*
– DERIVATIVES **quixotically** adverb **quixotism** /**kwik**-suh-ti-z'm/ noun.
– ORIGIN from Don *Quixote*, hero of a book by the Spanish writer Cervantes.

quiz noun (pl. **quizzes**) 1 a game or competition involving a set of questions as a test of knowledge. 2 informal, chiefly Brit. a period of questioning. •verb (**quizzes, quizzing, quizzed**) question someone.
– ORIGIN uncertain.

quizmaster noun Brit. a person in charge of a quiz; a question master.

quizzical adjective showing mild or amused puzzlement.
– DERIVATIVES **quizzicality** noun **quizzically** adverb.

quoin /koyn, kwoyn/ noun 1 an external angle of a wall or building. 2 a cornerstone.
– DERIVATIVES **quoining** noun.
– ORIGIN from **COIN**, in the former senses 'cornerstone' and 'wedge'.

quoit /koyt, kwoyt/ noun 1 a ring thrown in a game with the aim of landing it over an upright peg. 2 (**quoits**) (treated as sing.) a game of throwing quoits.
– ORIGIN probably French.

quondam /kwon-dam/ adjective formal that once was; former.
– ORIGIN Latin, 'formerly'.

quorate /kwor-uht/ adjective Brit. (of a meeting) attended by the minimum number of members that must be present to make its business valid.

quorum /kwor-uhm/ noun (pl. **quorums**) the minimum number of members that must be present at a meeting to make its business valid.
– ORIGIN Latin, 'of whom'.

quota noun 1 a limited quantity of a product which may be produced, exported, or imported. 2 a share that a person or group is entitled to receive or has to contribute: *her weekly quota of articles is two for newspapers and one for a magazine.* 3 a fixed number of a group allowed to do something, e.g. immigrants entering a country.
– ORIGIN from Latin *quota pars* 'how great a part'.

quotable adjective suitable for or worth quoting.
– DERIVATIVES **quotability** noun.

quotation noun 1 a passage or remark repeated by someone other than the person who originally said or wrote it. 2 a short musical passage or visual image taken from one piece of music or work of art and used in another. 3 the action of quoting from a speech, artistic work, etc. 4 a formal statement of the estimated cost of a job or service. 5 a registration granted to a company enabling their shares to be officially listed and traded on a stock exchange.

quotation mark noun each of a set of

punctuation marks, single (' ') or double (" "), used to mark the beginning and end of a title or quotation.

quote verb **1** repeat or copy out a passage or remark by another person. **2** (**quote something as**) mention something as an example to support a point: *the figures were quoted as more evidence for the failure of our schools.* **3** give someone an estimate for a job or service. **4** (**quote someone/thing at/as**) name someone or something at specified odds. **5** give a company a listing on a stock exchange. •noun **1** a quotation. **2** (**quotes**) quotation marks.
– ORIGIN Latin *quotare* 'mark with numbers'.

quoth /*rhymes with* oath/ verb old use or humorous said (used only in first and third person singular before the subject).
– ORIGIN Germanic.

quotidian /kwuh-tid-i-uhn/ adjective **1** happening every day; daily. **2** ordinary or everyday.

– ORIGIN Latin *quotidianus*.

quotient /kwoh-shuhnt/ noun **1** Mathematics a result obtained by dividing one quantity by another. **2** a degree or amount of a specified quality: *my coolness quotient evaporated on the spot.*
– ORIGIN from Latin *quotiens* 'how many times'.

Qur'an /kuh-rahn/ (also **Quran**) noun Arabic spelling of **Koran**.

qursh /koorsh/ noun (pl. same) a unit of money of Saudi Arabia, equal to one twentieth of a rial.
– ORIGIN Arabic.

q.v. abbreviation used to direct a reader to another part of a written work for further information.
– ORIGIN from Latin *quod vide*, 'which see'.

qwerty /kwer-ti/ adjective referring to the standard layout on English-language typewriters and keyboards, having *q, w, e, r, t,* and *y* as the first keys on the top row of letters.

q

Rr

R¹ (also **r**) noun (pl. **Rs** or **R's**) the eighteenth letter of the alphabet.
– PHRASES **the three Rs** reading, writing, and arithmetic, regarded as the fundamentals of learning.

R² abbreviation **1** rand. **2** Regina or Rex. **3** (®) registered as a trademark. **4** (**R.**) River. **5** roentgen(s). **6** rook (in chess). **7** Cricket (on scorecards) run(s).

r abbreviation **1** radius. **2** right.

RA abbreviation **1** (in the UK) Royal Academician or Royal Academy. **2** (in the UK) Royal Artillery.

Ra symbol the chemical element radium.

RAAF abbreviation Royal Australian Air Force.

rabbi /rab-by/ noun (pl. **rabbis**) **1** a Jewish scholar or teacher, especially of Jewish law. **2** a Jewish religious leader.
– DERIVATIVES **rabbinate** /rab-bi-nuht/ noun.
– ORIGIN from a Hebrew word meaning 'my master'.

rabbinic /ruh-bin-ik/ adjective relating to rabbis or to Jewish law or teachings.
– DERIVATIVES **rabbinical** adjective.

rabbit noun **1** a burrowing mammal with long ears and a short tail. **2** N. Amer. a hare. **3** the fur of the rabbit. • verb (**rabbits, rabbiting, rabbited**) **1** (usu. as noun **rabbiting**) hunt rabbits. **2** Brit. informal talk a great deal; chatter. [from *rabbit and pork*, rhyming slang for 'talk'.]
– DERIVATIVES **rabbity** adjective.
– ORIGIN probably from Old French.

rabbit punch noun a sharp chop with the edge of the hand to the back of the neck.

rabble noun **1** a disorderly crowd. **2** (**the rabble**) ordinary people regarded as common or uncouth.
– ORIGIN perhaps related to dialect *rabble* 'to gabble'.

rabble-rouser noun a person who stirs up popular opinion, especially for political reasons.

Rabelaisian /rab-uh-lay-zi-uhn/ adjective relating to or like the French satirist François Rabelais or his writings, especially in being very imaginative and full of earthy humour.

rabid /rab-id, ray-bid/ adjective **1** extreme; fanatical: *rabid football fans.* **2** relating to or affected with rabies.
– DERIVATIVES **rabidly** adverb.

rabies /ray-beez, ray-biz/ noun a dangerous disease of dogs and other mammals, caused by a virus that can be transmitted through an animal's saliva to humans, causing madness and convulsions.
– ORIGIN Latin.

RAC abbreviation **1** (in the UK) Royal Armoured Corps. **2** (in the UK) Royal Automobile Club.

raccoon /ruh-koon/ (also **racoon**) noun a greyish-brown American mammal with a black face and a ringed tail.
– ORIGIN from an Algonquian dialect word.

race¹ noun **1** a competition between runners, horses, vehicles, etc. to see which is fastest over a set course. **2** a situation in which people compete to be first to achieve something: *the race for governor.* **3** a strong current flowing through a narrow channel. **4** a water channel, especially one in a mill or mine. **5** a smooth ring-shaped groove or guide for a ball bearing or roller bearing. • verb **1** compete in a race. **2** have a race with someone. **3** prepare and enter an animal or car for races. **4** move or progress swiftly: *I raced into the house.* **5** (of machinery) operate at excessive speed.
– DERIVATIVES **racer** noun.
– ORIGIN Old Norse, 'current'.

race² noun **1** each of the major divisions of humankind, having distinct physical characteristics. **2** racial origin or distinction. **3** a group of people sharing the same culture, language, etc.; an ethnic group. **4** a group of people or things with a shared feature: *a race of intelligent computers.* **5** Biology a subdivision of a species.
– ORIGIN French.

> **USAGE:** Some people think that the word **race** should be avoided, because of its associations with the now discredited theories of 19th-century anthropologists and physiologists about supposed racial superiority. Terms such as **people, community,** or **ethnic group** are less likely to cause offence.

racecard noun a programme giving information about the races at a race meeting.

racecourse noun a ground or track for horse or dog racing.

racehorse noun a horse bred and trained for racing.

raceme /ra-seem, ruh-seem/ noun a flower cluster with the separate flowers attached by short stalks along a central stem, the lower flowers developing first. Compare with **CYME**.
– ORIGIN Latin *racemus* 'bunch of grapes'.

race meeting noun Brit. a sporting event consisting of a series of horse races held at one course.

race relations plural noun relations between members of different races within a country.

racetrack noun **1** a racecourse. **2** a track for motor racing.

racial adjective **1** relating to race. **2** relating to differences or relations between races.
– DERIVATIVES **racially** adverb.

racialism noun racism.
– DERIVATIVES **racialist** noun & adjective

racialize (or **racialise**) verb make something racial or racist in nature or outlook.

racing noun a sport that involves competing in races. •adjective **1** moving swiftly. **2** interested in horse racing.

racing car noun a car built for racing.

racing driver noun a driver of racing cars.

racism noun **1** the belief that each race has certain qualities or abilities, giving rise to the view that some races are better than others. **2** discrimination against or hostility towards other races.
– DERIVATIVES **racist** noun & adjective.

rack¹ noun **1** a framework for holding or storing things. **2** a bar with cogs or teeth that fit into a wheel or pinion. **3** a triangular frame for positioning pool balls. **4** a single game of pool. **5** (**the rack**) historical an instrument of torture consisting of a frame on which the victim was tied by the wrists and ankles and stretched. •verb **1** (also **wrack**) cause great pain or distress to someone. **2** place something in or on a rack. **3** (**rack something up**) accumulate or achieve a score or amount.
– PHRASES **rack** (or **wrack**) **one's brains** think very hard.
– ORIGIN from Dutch *rec*, German *rek* 'horizontal bar or shelf'.

> **USAGE:** The words **rack** and **wrack** are often confused. The noun is always spelled **rack** (*a magazine rack*). The verb can be spelled **rack** or **wrack**, but only when it means 'cause great pain to someone' (*he was racked/wracked with guilt*) or in the phrase **rack** (or **wrack**) **one's brains**.

rack² noun a joint of meat, especially lamb, including the front ribs.
– ORIGIN unknown.

rack³ noun (in phrase **go to rack and ruin**) gradually fall into a bad condition.
– ORIGIN Old English, 'vengeance'.

rack⁴ verb draw off wine, beer, etc. from the sediment in the barrel.
– ORIGIN Provençal *arracar*.

rack-and-pinion adjective (of a mechanism) using a fixed bar with cogs or teeth that fit into a smaller cog.

racket¹ (also **racquet**) noun a bat consisting of an oval or round frame with strings stretched across it, used in tennis, badminton, and squash.
– ORIGIN French *raquette*.

racket² noun **1** a loud unpleasant noise. **2** informal a dishonest scheme for obtaining money: *a protection racket*. **3** informal a person's line of business. •verb (**rackets, racketing, racketed**) make a loud unpleasant noise.
– DERIVATIVES **rackety** adjective.

– ORIGIN perhaps imitating a loud noise.

racketeer noun a person who makes money from dishonest activities.
– DERIVATIVES **racketeering** noun.

rackets plural noun (treated as sing.) a ball game for two or four people played with rackets and a hard ball in a four-walled court.

raclette /ra-klet/ noun a Swiss dish of melted cheese, typically with potatoes.
– ORIGIN French, 'small scraper' (because the cheese is scraped on to a plate as it melts).

raconteur /ra-kon-ter/ noun a person who tells stories in an interesting way.
– ORIGIN French.

racoon noun variant spelling of RACCOON.

racquet noun variant spelling of RACKET¹.

racy adjective (**racier, raciest**) lively or exciting, especially in a sexual way.
– DERIVATIVES **racily** adverb **raciness** noun.

rad abbreviation radian(s).

RADA /rah-duh/ abbreviation (in the UK) Royal Academy of Dramatic Art.

radar noun a system for detecting the position and speed of aircraft, ships, etc., by sending out pulses of radio waves which are reflected off the object back to the source.
– ORIGIN from *radio detection and ranging*.

radar gun noun a hand-held radar device used by traffic police to estimate a vehicle's speed.

radar trap noun an area of road in which radar is used by the police to detect speeding vehicles.

raddled adjective showing signs of age or tiredness.
– ORIGIN related to RUDDY (originally in the sense 'coloured with rouge to conceal signs of ageing').

radial /ray-di-uhl/ adjective **1** relating to or arranged in lines coming out from a central point to the edge of a circle: *radial markings resembling spokes*. **2** (of a tyre) in which the layers of fabric have their cords running at right angles to the circumference of the tyre. •noun a radial tyre.
– DERIVATIVES **radially** adverb.
– ORIGIN from Latin *radius* 'spoke, ray'.

radial keratotomy /ker-uh-tot-uh-mi/ noun a surgical operation involving cutting into the cornea of the eye, performed to correct myopia (short-sightedness).

radial symmetry noun chiefly Biology symmetry about a central axis, as in a starfish.

radian /ray-di-uhn/ noun an angle of 57.3 degrees, equal to that at the centre of a circle formed by an arc equal in length to the radius.

radiant adjective **1** shining or glowing brightly. **2** showing great joy, love, or health: *a radiant smile*. **3** (of electromagnetic energy, especially heat) transmitted by radiation, rather than conduction or convection. **4** (of an appliance) emitting radiant energy for cooking or heating.
– DERIVATIVES **radiance** noun **radiantly** adverb.

radiate verb **1** (with reference to light, heat, or other energy) send out or be sent out in rays or waves. **2** show a strong feeling or quality: *she radiated an aura of ambition*. **3** spread out from a central point: *rows of cells radiated from a central hall*.

r

– DERIVATIVES **radiative** adjective.
– ORIGIN Latin *radiare*.

radiation noun **1** the action or process of radiating. **2** energy sent out as electromagnetic waves or subatomic particles.

radiation sickness noun illness caused when a person is exposed to X-rays, gamma rays, or other radiation.

radiation therapy noun radiotherapy.

radiator noun **1** a thing that radiates light, heat, or sound. **2** a heating device consisting of a metal case through which hot water circulates, or one heated by electricity or oil. **3** a cooling device in a vehicle or aircraft engine consisting of a bank of thin tubes in which circulating water is cooled by the surrounding air.

radical adjective **1** relating to the basic nature of something; fundamental: *she made radical changes in her life*. **2** supporting complete political or social reform. **3** departing from tradition; innovative or progressive. **4** Mathematics relating to the root of a number or quantity. **5** N. Amer. informal excellent. ● noun **1** a person who supports radical political or social reform. **2** Chemistry a group of atoms behaving as a unit in certain compounds.
– DERIVATIVES **radicalism** noun **radicalize** (or **radicalise**) verb **radically** adverb.
– ORIGIN Latin *radicalis*.

radical chic noun superficial and purely fashionable support for radical left-wing views.

radical sign noun Mathematics the sign √ which indicates the square root of the number following (or a higher root indicated by a raised numeral before the symbol).

radicchio /ra-dee-ki-oh/ noun (pl. **radicchios**) a variety of chicory with dark red leaves.
– ORIGIN Italian.

radicle /ra-di-k'l/ noun the part of a plant embryo that develops into the primary root.
– ORIGIN Latin *radicula* 'little root'.

radii plural of **RADIUS**.

radio noun (pl. **radios**) **1** the sending and receiving of electromagnetic waves carrying sound messages. **2** broadcasting in sound: *she's written plays for radio*. **3** a broadcasting station or channel. **4** a device for receiving radio programmes or for sending and receiving radio messages. ● verb (**radioes**, **radioing**, **radioed**) **1** send a message by radio. **2** communicate with a person or place by radio.
– ORIGIN abbreviation of **RADIO-TELEPHONE**.

radio- combining form **1** referring to radio waves or broadcasting: *radiogram*. **2** connected with rays, radiation, or radioactivity: *radiography*.

radioactive adjective emitting ionizing radiation or particles.
– DERIVATIVES **radioactively** adverb.

radioactivity noun **1** the emission of ionizing radiation or particles, caused when atomic nuclei disintegrate spontaneously. **2** radioactive particles.

radio astronomy noun the branch of astronomy concerned with radio emissions from stars and other celestial objects.

radiocarbon noun a radioactive isotope of carbon used in carbon dating.

radio-controlled adjective controllable from a distance by radio.

radiogram noun Brit. dated a combined radio and record player.
– ORIGIN from **RADIO-** + **GRAMOPHONE**.

radiograph noun an image produced on a sensitive plate or film by X-rays or other radiation.
– DERIVATIVES **radiographic** adjective

radiography /ray-di-og-ruh-fi/ noun the process of taking radiographs to assist in medical examinations.
– DERIVATIVES **radiographer** noun

radioisotope noun a radioactive isotope.

radiology noun the science of X-rays and similar radiation, especially as used in medicine.
– DERIVATIVES **radiologic** adjective **radiological** adjective **radiologist** noun.

radiometer /ray-di-om-i-ter/ noun an instrument for detecting or measuring radiation.
– DERIVATIVES **radiometry** noun.

radiometric adjective relating to the measurement of radioactivity.

radionics /ray-di-on-iks/ plural noun (treated as sing.) a system of alternative medicine based on the study of radiation supposedly emitted by living matter.
– ORIGIN from **RADIO-**, on the pattern of *electronics*.

radionuclide noun a radioactive isotope.

radiophonic adjective relating to sound that is produced electronically.

radio-telephone noun a telephone using radio transmission.

radio telescope noun an instrument used to detect radio emissions from space.

radiotherapy noun the treatment of cancer or other disease using X-rays or similar radiation.
– DERIVATIVES **radiotherapist** noun.

radio wave noun an electromagnetic wave having a frequency in the range 10^4 to 10^{11} or 10^{12} hertz.

radish noun the small, hot-tasting, red root of a plant that is eaten raw as a salad vegetable.
– ORIGIN Latin *radix* 'root'.

radium /ray-di-uhm/ noun a reactive, radioactive metallic chemical element.
– ORIGIN from Latin *radius* 'ray'.

radius /ray-di-uhss/ noun (pl. **radii** /ray-di-I/ or **radiuses**) **1** a straight line from the centre to the circumference of a circle or sphere. **2** a specified distance from a centre in all directions: *pubs within a two-mile radius*. **3** the thicker and shorter of the two bones in the human forearm.
– ORIGIN Latin, 'spoke, ray'.

radiused /ray-di-uhst/ adjective (of a corner or edge) rounded.

radome /ray-dohm/ noun a dome or other structure protecting radar equipment.
– ORIGIN blend of **RADAR** and **DOME**.

radon /ray-don/ noun a chemical element that is a rare radioactive gas.
– ORIGIN from **RADIUM**, on the pattern of *argon*.

RAF abbreviation (in the UK) Royal Air Force.

r

raffia noun fibre from the leaves of a tropical palm tree, used for making hats, baskets, etc.
– ORIGIN Malagasy.

raffish adjective slightly disreputable, but in an attractive way.
– ORIGIN from RIFF-RAFF.

raffle noun a lottery with goods rather than money as prizes. •verb offer something as a prize in a raffle.
– ORIGIN Old French.

raft¹ noun **1** a flat structure of pieces of timber fastened together, used as a boat or floating platform. **2** a small inflatable boat. •verb travel or transport on a raft.
– DERIVATIVES **rafting** noun.
– ORIGIN Old Norse, 'rafter'.

raft² noun a large amount: *she speaks a raft of languages.*
– ORIGIN perhaps Scandinavian.

rafter¹ noun a beam forming part of the internal framework of a roof.
– DERIVATIVES **raftered** adjective.
– ORIGIN Old English.

rafter² noun a person who travels by raft.

rag¹ noun **1** a piece of old cloth. **2** (**rags**) old or tattered clothes. **3** informal a low-quality newspaper. •verb (**rags, ragging, ragged**) give a decorative effect to a painted surface by applying paint with a rag.
– PHRASES **lose one's rag** Brit. informal lose one's temper.
– ORIGIN probably from RAGGED or RAGGY.

rag² noun Brit. a programme of entertainments organized by students to raise money for charity. •verb (**rags, ragging, ragged**) **1** tease or make fun of someone. **2** rebuke someone harshly.
– ORIGIN unknown.

rag³ noun a piece of ragtime music.

rag⁴ (also **ragstone**) noun Brit. a hard coarse rock that can be broken into thick slabs, used for walls or paving.
– ORIGIN unknown.

raga /rah-guh/ (also **rag**) noun (in Indian classical music) each of the six basic musical modes which express different moods in certain characteristic progressions.
– ORIGIN Sanskrit, 'colour, musical tone'.

ragamuffin noun **1** a person in ragged, dirty clothes. **2** (also **raggamuffin**) a person who performs or likes ragga dance music.
– ORIGIN probably from RAG¹.

rag-and-bone man noun Brit. a person who goes from door to door, collecting old clothes and other second-hand items to sell.

ragbag noun a collection of widely different things.

rage noun **1** violent uncontrollable anger. **2** (in combination) anger or aggression associated with conflict arising from a particular situation: *air rage.* **3** a strong desire: *a rage for order and purity.* •verb **1** feel or express violent anger. **2** continue with great force or intensity: *the battle raged for six hours.*
– PHRASES **all the rage** temporarily very popular or fashionable.
– DERIVATIVES **rager** noun.
– ORIGIN Old French.

ragga /rag-guh/ noun a style of dance music in

which a DJ improvises lyrics over a backing track.
– ORIGIN from RAGAMUFFIN, because of the scruffy clothing worn by its followers.

raggamuffin noun variant spelling of RAGAMUFFIN.

ragged /rag-gid/ adjective **1** (of cloth or clothes) old and torn. **2** wearing ragged clothes. **3** having a rough or irregular surface or edge. **4** not steady or uniform: *her breath came in ragged gasps.* **5** exhausted or stressed.
– PHRASES **run someone ragged** exhaust someone.
– DERIVATIVES **raggedly** adverb **raggedy** adjective (informal, chiefly N. Amer.).
– ORIGIN Scandinavian.

ragged robin noun a pink-flowered campion (plant) with divided petals.

raggle-taggle adjective untidy and scruffy.
– ORIGIN probably from RAGTAG.

raggy adjective informal ragged or shabby.
– ORIGIN Scandinavian.

raglan adjective having or referring to sleeves that continue in one piece up to the neck of a garment.
– ORIGIN named after Lord *Raglan*, a British commander in the Crimean War.

ragout /ra-goo/ noun a spicy stew of meat and vegetables.
– ORIGIN French.

rag paper noun paper made from cotton.

ragpicker noun chiefly historical a person who collects and sells rags.

rag-roll verb create a striped or marbled effect on a surface by painting it with a rag crumpled up into a roll.

rag rug noun a rug made from small strips of fabric hooked into or pushed through a material such as hessian.

ragstone noun another term for RAG⁴.

ragtag adjective untidy, disorganized, or very varied: *a ragtag group of idealists.*
– ORIGIN from RAG¹ + TAG¹.

ragtime noun an early form of jazz with a syncopated melody, played especially on the piano.
– ORIGIN probably referring to the 'ragged' rhythm.

rag trade noun informal the clothing or fashion industry.

ragwort noun a yellow-flowered plant with ragged leaves.

rai /rhymes with my/ noun a style of music blending Arabic and Algerian folk elements with Western rock.
– ORIGIN perhaps from an Arabic phrase found in the songs meaning 'that's the thinking, here is the view'.

raid noun **1** a sudden attack on an enemy or on a building to commit a crime. **2** a surprise visit by police to arrest suspects or seize illegal goods. •verb **1** make a raid on a place. **2** take something from a place in a secretive way: *she crept downstairs to raid the larder.*
– DERIVATIVES **raider** noun.
– ORIGIN Scots variant of ROAD in the early senses 'journey on horseback', 'attack'.

rail¹ noun **1** a bar or bars fixed on upright supports or attached to a wall or ceiling,

forming part of a fence or used to hang things on. **2** each of the two metal bars laid on the ground to form a railway track. **3** railways as a means of transport. • **verb 1** provide or enclose something with a rail or rails. **2** convey goods by rail.
- PHRASES **go off the rails** informal begin behaving in an odd or unacceptable way. **on the rails 1** informal functioning normally. **2** (of a racehorse or jockey) in a position on the racetrack nearest the inside fence.
- ORIGIN Old French *reille* 'iron rod'.

rail² verb (**rail against/at**) complain or protest strongly about something.
- ORIGIN French *railler*.

rail³ noun a secretive grey and brown waterside bird.
- ORIGIN Old French *raille*.

railcar noun **1** Brit. a powered railway passenger vehicle designed to operate singly or as part of a multiple unit. **2** (**rail car**) N. Amer. any railway carriage or wagon.

railcard noun Brit. a pass entitling the holder to reduced rail fares.

railhead noun a point at which a railway ends.

railing noun a fence made of rails.

raillery /rayl-luh-ri/ noun good-humoured teasing.
- ORIGIN from French *railler* 'complain strongly about'.

railroad noun N. Amer. a railway. • verb informal **1** rush or force someone into doing something. **2** cause a measure to be approved quickly by putting pressure on a group: *the Bill was railroaded through parliament.*

railway noun chiefly Brit. **1** a track made of rails along which trains run. **2** a system of such tracks with the trains, organization, and staff required to run it.

raiment /ray-muhnt/ noun old use or literary clothing.
- ORIGIN shortening of former *arrayment*, from ARRAY.

rain noun **1** the condensed moisture of the atmosphere falling in drops. **2** (**rains**) falls of rain. **3** a large quantity of things falling or descending: *a rain of blows.* • verb **1** (**it rains, it is raining, it rained**) rain falls. **2** (**be rained off** or N. Amer. **out**) (of an event) be cancelled or interrupted because of rain. **3** fall or cause to fall in large quantities.
- PHRASES **be as right as rain** be perfectly fit and well. **rain cats and dogs** rain heavily.
- ORIGIN Old English.

rainbow noun an arch of colours seen in the sky, caused by the refraction and dispersion of the sun's light by water droplets in the atmosphere.

rainbow coalition noun a political alliance of different groups, representing ethnic and other minorities.

rainbow trout noun a large trout with reddish sides, native to western North America and introduced elsewhere.

rain check noun N. Amer. a ticket given for later use when an outdoor event is rained off.
- PHRASES **take a rain check** refuse an offer but imply that one may take it up later.

raincoat noun a coat made from waterproofed

or water-resistant fabric.

raindrop noun a single drop of rain.

rainfall noun the quantity of rain falling within an area in a given time.

rainforest noun a dense forest found in tropical areas with consistently heavy rainfall.

rainmaker noun N. Amer. informal a person who generates income from a business by brokering deals or attracting clients or funds.

rainstorm noun a storm with heavy rain.

rainswept adjective frequently or recently exposed to rain and wind.

rainwater noun water that has fallen as rain.

rainwear noun waterproof or water-resistant clothes for wearing in the rain.

rainy adjective (**rainier, rainiest**) having a great deal of rain.
- PHRASES **a rainy day** a time in the future when money may be needed.

raise verb **1** lift or move someone or something upwards or into an upright position. **2** increase the amount, level, or strength of: *she had to raise her voice to be heard.* **3** cause to be heard, felt, or considered: *doubts have been raised.* **4** collect or bring together money or resources. **5** bring up a child. **6** breed or grow animals or plants. **7** abandon a blockade, embargo, etc. **8** generate an invoice or other document. **9** Brit. informal establish contact with someone, especially by telephone or radio. **10** bring someone back from death. **11** drive an animal from its lair. **12** (**raise something to**) Mathematics multiply a quantity to a specified power. • noun N. Amer. an increase in salary.
- PHRASES **raise hell** informal make a noisy disturbance. **raise the roof** make a great deal of noise, especially by cheering.
- DERIVATIVES **raiser** noun.
- ORIGIN Old Norse.

raisin noun a partially dried grape.
- DERIVATIVES **raisiny** adjective.
- ORIGIN Old French, 'grape'.

raison d'être /ray-zon de-truh/ noun (pl. **raisons d'être** /ray-zon de-truh/) the most important reason or purpose for someone's or something's existence.
- ORIGIN French, 'reason for being'.

raita /ry-tuh/ noun an Indian side dish of spiced yogurt containing chopped cucumber or other vegetables.
- ORIGIN Hindi.

Raj /rahj/ noun (**the Raj**) historical the period of British rule in India.
- ORIGIN Hindi, 'reign'.

raja /rah-juh/ (also **rajah**) noun historical an Indian king or prince.
- ORIGIN from Hindi or Sanskrit.

Rajput /rahj-puut/ noun a member of a Hindu military caste.
- ORIGIN from the Sanskrit words for 'king' + 'son'.

rake¹ noun a tool consisting of a pole with metal prongs at the end, used for drawing together leaves, cut grass, etc. or smoothing soil or gravel. • verb **1** draw together leaves or grass or smooth soil with a rake. **2** scratch something with a long sweeping movement. **3** pull or drag through something with a sweeping movement: *I raked a comb through my hair.*

4 sweep the air with gunfire or a beam of light. **5** (**rake through**) search through something.
- PHRASES **rake something in** informal make a lot of money. **rake over old coals** chiefly Brit. revive the memory of a past event. **rake something up/over** revive the memory of something best forgotten.
- DERIVATIVES **raker** noun.
- ORIGIN Old English or Old Norse.

rake² noun a fashionable or wealthy man who leads an immoral life.
- ORIGIN from former *rakehell* in the same sense.

rake³ verb set something at a sloping angle. ● noun the angle at which something slopes.
- ORIGIN probably from German *ragen* 'to project'.

rake-off noun informal a share of the profits from a deal, especially one that is underhand or illegal.

raki /ruh-kee, ra-ki/ noun a strong alcoholic spirit made in eastern Europe or the Middle East.
- ORIGIN Turkish.

rakish adjective **1** dashing, jaunty, or slightly disreputable: *a cap set at a rakish angle.* **2** (of a boat or car) smart and streamlined.
- DERIVATIVES **rakishly** adverb.

rallentando /ral-luhn-tan-doh/ adverb & adjective Music with a gradual decrease of speed.
- ORIGIN Italian, 'slowing down'.

rally¹ verb (**rallies, rallying, rallied**) **1** (with reference to troops) bring or come together again so as to continue fighting. **2** bring or come together as support or for united action: *my family rallied round.* **3** recover in health, spirits, or composure: *he floundered for a moment, then rallied again.* **4** (of share, currency, or commodity prices) increase after a fall. **5** drive in a motor rally. ● noun (pl. **rallies**) **1** a mass meeting held as a protest or in support of a cause. **2** a long-distance race for motor vehicles over roads or rough country. **3** an open-air event for people who own a particular kind of vehicle. **4** a quick or marked recovery: *the market staged a late rally.* **5** (in tennis and other racket sports) an exchange of several strokes between players.
- DERIVATIVES **rallyist** noun.
- ORIGIN French *rallier.*

rally² verb (**rallies, rallying, rallied**) dated tease someone.
- ORIGIN French *railler* 'complain strongly about'.

rallycross noun Brit. motor racing in which cars are driven in heats over rough country and private roads.

rallying noun the action or sport of participating in a motor rally. ● adjective having the effect of calling people to action: *a rallying cry.*

RAM abbreviation Computing random-access memory.

ram noun **1** an uncastrated adult male sheep. **2** a battering ram. **3** a striking or plunging device in some machines. ● verb (**rams, ramming, rammed**) **1** roughly force something into place. **2** strike or be struck with force.
- DERIVATIVES **rammer** noun.

- ORIGIN Old English.

Ramadan /ram-uh-dan/ (also **Ramadhan** /ram-uh-zan/) noun the ninth month of the Muslim year, during which Muslims fast from dawn to sunset.
- ORIGIN Arabic, 'be hot' (the fasting period was originally supposed to be in one of the hot months).

ramble verb **1** walk for pleasure in the countryside. **2** talk or write in an unfocused way for a long time: *he rambled on about Norman archways.* **3** (of a plant) grow over walls, fences, etc. ● noun a walk taken for pleasure in the countryside.
- DERIVATIVES **rambler** noun.
- ORIGIN probably related to Dutch *rammelen* 'wander about on heat' (referring to an animal), also to RAM.

Rambo /ram-boh/ noun an extremely tough and aggressive man.
- ORIGIN the hero of the novel *First Blood* (1972), and the films *First Blood* (1982) and *Rambo: First Blood Part II* (1985).

rambunctious /ram-bungk-shuhss/ adjective informal, chiefly N. Amer. uncontrollably exuberant.
- ORIGIN unknown.

rambutan /ram-byoo-tuhn/ noun the red, plum-sized fruit of a tropical tree, with soft spines and a slightly sour taste.
- ORIGIN Malay.

ramekin /ra-mi-kin/ noun a small dish for baking and serving an individual portion of food.
- ORIGIN French *ramequin.*

ramen /rah-men/ plural noun (in oriental cuisine) quick-cooking noodles.
- ORIGIN Japanese.

ramie /ra-mi/ noun a vegetable fibre from a tropical Asian plant, used in making textiles.
- ORIGIN Malay.

ramification noun **1** (**ramifications**) complex consequences of an action or event: *the ramifications of global environmental changes.* **2** a subdivision of a complex structure or process.

ramify /ra-mi-fy/ verb (**ramifies, ramifying, ramified**) chiefly technical form parts that branch out.
- ORIGIN Latin *ramificare.*

ramp noun **1** a sloping surface joining two different levels. **2** a movable set of steps for entering or leaving an aircraft. **3** Brit. a road hump. **4** N. Amer. an inclined slip road leading to or from a main road. ● verb **1** (**ramp something up**) increase the level or amount of something: *the company plans to ramp up production of TVs.* **2** (as adj. **ramped**) provided with a ramp.
- ORIGIN Old French *ramper* 'creep, crawl'.

rampage /ram-payj/ verb rush around in a wild and violent way. ● noun /ram-payj/ a period of wild and violent behaviour.
- ORIGIN perhaps from RAMP and RAGE.

rampant adjective **1** flourishing or spreading in an uncontrolled way: *rampant inflation.* **2** unrestrained or wild: *rampant sex.* **3** (after a noun) Heraldry (of an animal) shown standing on its left hind foot with its forefeet in the air.
- DERIVATIVES **rampantly** adverb.
- ORIGIN Old French, 'crawling'.

r

rampart noun a defensive wall of a castle or city, having a broad top with a walkway.
– ORIGIN French *rempart*.

ram raid noun Brit. a robbery in which a shop window is rammed with a vehicle and looted.

ramrod noun a rod for ramming down the charge of a muzzle-loading firearm. • adjective (of a person's posture) rigidly erect: *he stood ramrod straight.*

ramshackle adjective in a very bad condition.
– ORIGIN ultimately from RANSACK.

RAN abbreviation Royal Australian Navy.

ran past of RUN.

ranch noun 1 a large farm in America or Australia, where cattle or other animals are bred. 2 (also **ranch house**) N. Amer. a single-storey house. • verb run a ranch.
– DERIVATIVES **rancher** noun.
– ORIGIN Spanish *rancho* 'group of people eating together'.

rancid adjective 1 (of fatty or oily foods) stale and smelling or tasting unpleasant. 2 highly unpleasant.
– DERIVATIVES **rancidity** noun.
– ORIGIN Latin *rancidus* 'stinking'.

rancour (US **rancor**) noun bitter feeling or resentment.
– DERIVATIVES **rancorous** adjective.
– ORIGIN Latin *rancor* 'rankness', later 'bitter grudge'.

rand noun the basic unit of money of South Africa.
– ORIGIN from *the Rand*, a goldfield district near Johannesburg.

R & B abbreviation 1 rhythm and blues. 2 a kind of pop music with a vocal style derived from soul.

R & D abbreviation research and development.

random adjective done or happening without a deliberate order, purpose, or decision: *the trees had been planted in a random pattern.*
– PHRASES **at random** without thinking or planning in advance.
– DERIVATIVES **randomly** adverb **randomness** noun.
– ORIGIN Old French *randon* 'great speed'.

random access noun the process of storing or finding information on a computer without having to access items in a fixed sequence.

randomize (or **randomise**) verb (usu. as adj. **randomized**) technical make a random selection in an experiment, trial etc.

R & R abbreviation informal rest and recreation.

randy adjective (**randier**, **randiest**) informal sexually aroused or excited.
– ORIGIN perhaps from former Dutch *randen* 'to rant'.

rang past of RING².

range noun 1 the area of variation between limits on a particular scale: *the car's outside my price range.* 2 a set of different things of the same general type. 3 the scope or extent of a person's or thing's abilities or capacity: *he has shown his range in a number of roles.* 4 the distance within which something is able to operate or be effective. 5 a line of mountains or hills. 6 a large area of open land for grazing or hunting. 7 an area used as a testing ground for military equipment or for shooting

practice. 8 a large cooking stove with several burners or hotplates. • verb 1 vary between specified limits. 2 arrange people or things in a row or rows or in a particular way. 3 (**range someone against** or **be ranged against**) set oneself or be set in opposition to: *Japan ranged herself against the European nations.* 4 travel over a wide area. 5 cover a wide number of different topics.
– ORIGIN Old French, 'row, rank'.

rangefinder noun an instrument for estimating the distance of an object.

ranger noun 1 a keeper of a park, forest, or area of countryside. 2 a member of a body of armed men. 3 (**Ranger** or **Ranger Guide**) Brit. a senior Guide.

rangy /rayn-ji/ adjective (of a person) tall and slim with long limbs.

rank¹ noun 1 a position within the armed forces or an organization. 2 high social standing. 3 a line or row of people or things positioned side by side. 4 (**ranks**) the members of a group: *the ranks of the unemployed.* 5 (**the ranks**) (in the armed forces) those who are not commissioned officers. 6 each of the eight rows of eight squares running from side to side across a chessboard. Compare with FILE¹. • verb 1 give someone or something a rank within a grading system: *rank the samples in order of preference.* 2 hold a specified rank: *he now ranks third in the US.* 3 arrange things in a row or rows.
– PHRASES **break rank** (or **ranks**) fail to support a group to which you belong. **close ranks** unite so as to defend common interests. **pull rank** use your senior position to take advantage of someone. **rank and file** the ordinary members of an organization.
– ORIGIN Old French *ranc*.

rank² adjective 1 smelling very unpleasant. 2 complete and utter: *a rank amateur.* 3 (of vegetation) growing too thickly.
– ORIGIN Old English, 'proud, rebellious, sturdy'.

ranker noun chiefly Brit. 1 a private soldier. 2 a commissioned officer who has been in the ranks.

ranking noun a position on a scale of importance or achievement. • adjective having a specified rank: *high-ranking officers.*

rankle verb (of a comment or fact) cause continuing annoyance or resentment.
– ORIGIN Old French *rancler* 'fester'.

ransack verb 1 go hurriedly through a place stealing things and causing damage. 2 search something in a thorough and harmful way.
– ORIGIN Old Norse.

ransom noun a sum of money demanded or paid for the release of a captive. • verb 1 obtain the release of someone by paying a ransom. 2 hold a captive and demand payment for their release.
– PHRASES **hold someone to ransom** force someone to do something by threatening damaging action. **a king's ransom** a huge amount of money.
– ORIGIN Old French *ransoun*.

rant verb speak or shout in an angry or uncontrolled way. • noun a spell of ranting.
– DERIVATIVES **ranter** noun.

– ORIGIN Dutch *ranten* 'talk nonsense, rave'.

rap verb (**raps, rapping, rapped**) **1** hit a hard surface several times. **2** hit someone or something sharply. **3** informal criticize someone severely. **4** say sharply: *he rapped out an order.* **5** perform rap music. ●noun **1** a quick, sharp knock or blow. **2** a type of popular music of US black origin in which words are spoken rapidly and rhythmically over an instrumental backing. **3** N. Amer. informal a criminal charge: *a murder rap.*
– PHRASES **take the rap** informal be punished or blamed for something.
– DERIVATIVES **rapper** noun.
– ORIGIN probably Scandinavian.

rapacious /ruh-**pay**-shuhss/ adjective very greedy or grasping.
– DERIVATIVES **rapaciously** adverb **rapaciousness** noun **rapacity** /ruh-**pa**-si-ti/ noun.
– ORIGIN from Latin *rapere* 'seize'.

rape[1] verb (of a man) force someone to have sex with him against their will. ●noun **1** the crime of raping someone. **2** the spoiling or destruction of a place: *the rape of the countryside.*
– ORIGIN Latin *rapere* 'seize'.

rape[2] noun a plant with bright yellow flowers, especially a variety (**oilseed rape**) grown for its oil-rich seed.
– ORIGIN Latin *rapum, rapa* 'turnip'.

rapeseed noun seeds of the rape plant, used to make oil.

rapid adjective **1** happening in a short time: *several shots fired in rapid succession.* **2** (of an action) very fast. ●noun (usu. **rapids**) a part of a river where the water flows very fast, often over rocks.
– DERIVATIVES **rapidity** noun **rapidly** adverb.
– ORIGIN Latin *rapidus.*

rapier /**ray**-pee-er/ noun a thin, light sharp-pointed sword used for thrusting.
– ORIGIN French *rapière.*

rapine /**ra**-pyn, **ra**-pin/ noun literary the violent seizure of property.
– ORIGIN Old French.

rapist noun a man who commits rape.

rappel /ra-**pel**/ noun & verb (**rappels, rappelling, rappelled**) another term for ABSEIL.
– ORIGIN French.

rapport /rap-**por**/ noun a close relationship in which people understand each other and communicate well.
– ORIGIN French.

rapporteur /ra-por-**ter**/ noun a person appointed by an organization to report on its meetings.
– ORIGIN French.

rapprochement /ra-**prosh**-mon/ noun a renewal of friendly relations between countries or groups.
– ORIGIN French.

rapscallion /rap-**skal**-li-uhn/ noun old use a mischievous person.
– ORIGIN perhaps from RASCAL.

rapt adjective **1** completely fascinated and absorbed: *they listened with rapt attention.* **2** literary filled with an intense and pleasant emotion.
– DERIVATIVES **raptly** adverb.

– ORIGIN Latin *raptus* 'seized'.

raptor noun a bird of prey.
– DERIVATIVES **raptorial** adjective.
– ORIGIN Latin, 'plunderer'.

rapture noun **1** great pleasure or joy. **2** (**raptures**) expressions of great pleasure or enthusiasm.
– ORIGIN from Latin *raptura* 'seizing', influenced by RAPT.

rapturous adjective feeling or expressing great pleasure or enthusiasm.
– DERIVATIVES **rapturously** adverb.

rara avis /rair-uh ay-viss/ noun another term for RARE BIRD.
– ORIGIN Latin.

rare[1] adjective (**rarer, rarest**) **1** not occurring or found very often: *a rare genetic disorder.* **2** unusually good.
– ORIGIN Latin *rarus.*

rare[2] adjective (**rarer, rarest**) (of red meat) lightly cooked, so that the inside is still red.
– ORIGIN Old English, 'half-cooked'.

rare bird noun an exceptional or unusual person or thing.

rarebit (also **Welsh rarebit** or **Welsh rabbit**) noun a dish of melted cheese on toast.
– ORIGIN first recorded as *Welsh rabbit*; the term *rabbit* is unexplained.

rare earth noun any of a group of chemically similar metallic elements including the lanthanide elements together with (usually) scandium and yttrium.

rarefied /**rair**-i-fyd/ adjective **1** (of air) of lower pressure than usual; thin. **2** distant from the lives and concerns of ordinary people; esoteric: *rarefied scholarly pursuits.*
– ORIGIN from Latin *rareficare* 'make rare'.

rarely adverb not often; seldom.

raring adjective informal very eager to do something: *she was raring to go.*
– ORIGIN from *rare*, dialect variant of ROAR or REAR[2].

rarity noun (pl. **rarities**) **1** a rare or unusual thing. **2** the state or quality of being rare.

rascal noun **1** a mischievous or cheeky person. **2** a dishonest man.
– DERIVATIVES **rascality** noun **rascally** adjective.
– ORIGIN from Old French *rascaille* 'rabble'.

rash[1] adjective acting or done without careful consideration: *a rash decision.*
– DERIVATIVES **rashly** adverb **rashness** noun.
– ORIGIN Germanic.

rash[2] noun **1** an area of red spots or patches on a person's skin. **2** a series of unwelcome things happening within a short time: *a rash of strikes.*
– ORIGIN probably related to Old French *rasche* 'sores, scurf'.

rasher noun a thin slice of bacon.
– ORIGIN unknown.

rasp verb **1** make a harsh, grating sound: *cicadas rasped in the surrounding pines.* **2** say something in a harsh, grating tone. **3** (of a rough object) scrape something. **4** file something with a rasp. ●noun **1** a coarse file for use on metal or other hard material. **2** a harsh, grating noise.
– DERIVATIVES **raspy** adjective.
– ORIGIN Old French *rasper.*

raspberry noun (pl. **raspberries**) **1** an edible

reddish-pink soft fruit related to the blackberry. **2** informal a sound made with the tongue and lips, expressing scorn or contempt. [from *raspberry tart*, rhyming slang for 'fart'.]
– ORIGIN unknown.

Rasta /rass-tuh/ noun & adjective informal short for **RASTAFARIAN**.

Rastafarian /rass-tuh-**fair**-i-uhn, rass-tuh-**fah**-ri-uhn/ adjective relating to a religious movement of Jamaican origin believing that Haile Selassie (the former Emperor of Ethiopia) was the Messiah and that black people are the chosen people. • noun a member of the Rastafarian movement.
– DERIVATIVES **Rastafarianism** noun.
– ORIGIN from *Ras Tafari*, the name by which Haile Selassie was known.

Rastaman /rass-tuh-man/ noun (pl. **Rastamen**) informal a male Rastafarian.

raster /rass-ter/ noun a rectangular pattern of parallel scanning lines followed by the electron beam on a television screen or computer monitor.
– ORIGIN German, 'screen'.

rat noun **1** a long-tailed rodent resembling a large mouse, often considered a serious pest. **2** informal an unpleasant person. **3** N. Amer. informal a person who is associated with or often visits a particular place: *a mall rat*. • verb (**rats, ratting, ratted**) **1** (**rat on**) informal inform on someone. **2** (**rat on**) informal break an agreement or promise. **3** hunt or kill rats.
– ORIGIN Old English.

ratable adjective variant spelling of **RATEABLE**.

ratafia /ra-tuh-**fee**-uh/ noun **1** a liqueur flavoured with almonds or the kernels of peaches, apricots, or cherries. **2** an almond-flavoured biscuit like a small macaroon.
– ORIGIN French.

ratatouille /ra-tuh-**too**-i, ra-tuh-**twee**/ noun a dish consisting of onions, courgettes, tomatoes, aubergines, and peppers, stewed in oil.
– ORIGIN French.

ratbag noun Brit. informal an unpleasant or disliked person.

ratchet noun a device consisting of a bar or wheel with a set of angled teeth in which a cog, tooth, or pivoted bar fits, allowing motion in one direction only. • verb (**ratchets, ratcheting, ratcheted**) **1** (**ratchet something up/down**) make something rise (or fall) as a step in an inevitable process: *the Bank ratcheted up interest rates again.* **2** operate something by means of a ratchet.
– ORIGIN French *rochet*.

rate[1] noun **1** a measure, quantity, or frequency measured against another quantity or measure: *the island has the lowest crime rate in the world.* **2** the speed with which something moves or happens. **3** a fixed price paid or charged for something. **4** the amount of a charge or payment expressed as a percentage of another amount, or as a basis of calculation: *our current interest rates are very competitive.* **5** (**rates**) (in the UK) a tax on commercial land and buildings paid to a local authority. • verb **1** give a standard or value to something according to a particular scale. **2** consider to be of a certain quality or standard: *Atkinson rates*

him as England's top defender. **3** be worthy of or merit something. **4** informal have a high opinion of someone or something.
– PHRASES **at any rate** whatever happens or may have happened. **at this rate** if things continue in this way.
– ORIGIN Latin *rata*.

rate[2] verb old use scold someone angrily.
– ORIGIN unknown.

rateable (also **ratable**) adjective able to be rated or estimated.

rateable value noun (in the UK) a value given to a commercial property based on its size, location, etc., used to determine the rates payable by its owner.

rate of exchange noun another term for **EXCHANGE RATE**.

ratepayer noun (in the UK) a person liable to pay rates.

rather adverb **1** (**would rather**) would prefer: *I'd rather you didn't tell him.* **2** to a certain extent; quite. **3** used to correct something you have said or to be more precise: *I walked, or rather, limped home.* **4** instead of. • exclamation Brit. dated used to emphasize that you agree with or accept something.
– ORIGIN Old English, 'earlier, sooner'.

ratify verb (**ratifies, ratifying, ratified**) give formal consent to an agreement, making it officially valid.
– DERIVATIVES **ratification** noun.
– ORIGIN from Latin *ratus* 'fixed'.

rating noun **1** a classification or ranking based on quality, standard, or performance. **2** (**ratings**) the estimated audience size of a television or radio programme. **3** Brit. a non-commissioned sailor in the navy.

ratio noun (pl. **ratios**) the quantitative relationship between two amounts showing the number of times one value contains or is contained within the other.
– ORIGIN Latin, 'reckoning'.

ratiocination /ra-ti-oss-i-**nay**-sh'n, ra-shi-oss-i-**nay**-sh'n/ noun formal the formation of judgements by logic; reasoning.
– DERIVATIVES **ratiocinate** verb **ratiocinative** adjective.
– ORIGIN Latin *ratiocinari* 'deliberate, calculate'.

ration noun **1** a fixed amount of food, fuel, or a similar commodity, officially allowed to each person during a shortage. **2** (**rations**) a regular allowance of food supplied to members of the armed forces. • verb **1** limit the supply of a commodity to fixed rations. **2** (**ration someone to**) allow someone to have only a fixed amount of a commodity.
– ORIGIN Latin, 'reckoning, ratio'.

rational adjective **1** based on reason or logic: *a rational explanation.* **2** able to think sensibly or logically. **3** having the capacity to reason. **4** Mathematics (of a number or quantity) able to be expressed as a ratio of whole numbers.
– DERIVATIVES **rationality** noun **rationally** adverb.

rationale /ra-shuh-**nahl**/ noun a set of reasons for a course of action or a belief.

rationalism noun the belief that opinions and actions should be based on reason and knowledge rather than on religious belief or emotions.

– DERIVATIVES **rationalist** noun.

rationalize (or **rationalise**) verb **1** try to find a logical reason for an action or attitude: *rationalize your fear by thinking about it positively.* **2** Brit. reorganize a process or system so as to make it more logical. **3** Brit. make a company or industry more efficient by disposing of unwanted staff or equipment.

– DERIVATIVES **rationalization** noun **rationalizer** noun.

ratlines plural noun a series of small ropes fastened across the ropes supporting the mast of a sailing ship, used for climbing the rigging.

– ORIGIN unknown.

rat pack noun informal a group of journalists and photographers who pursue celebrities in an aggressive or relentless way.

rat race noun informal a way of life which is a fiercely competitive struggle for wealth or power.

rat run noun Brit. informal a minor street used by drivers to avoid congestion on main roads.

rat's tails plural noun Brit. informal hair hanging in damp or greasy strands.

rattan /ruh-**tan**/ noun the thin, pliable stems of a tropical climbing palm, used to make furniture.

– ORIGIN Malay.

rat-tat-tat noun a rapping sound.

– ORIGIN imitating the sound.

ratted adjective Brit. informal very drunk.

rattle verb **1** make or cause to make a rapid series of short, sharp knocking sounds. **2** move with a knocking sound. **3** informal make someone nervous or irritated. **4** (**rattle something off**) say or produce something quickly and easily: *he rattled off some safety tips.* **5** (**rattle on/away**) talk rapidly and at length. •noun **1** a rattling sound. **2** a device or toy that makes a rattling sound.

– DERIVATIVES **rattler** noun **rattly** adjective.

– ORIGIN related to Dutch and German *ratelen*.

rattlesnake noun an American viper with a series of horny rings on the tail that produce a rattling sound.

rattletrap noun informal an old or rickety vehicle.

rattling adjective informal, dated very: *a rattling good story.*

ratty adjective **1** resembling or like a rat. **2** informal in bad condition; shabby. **3** Brit. informal bad-tempered and irritable.

raucous /**raw**-kuhss/ adjective **1** (of a sound) loud and harsh. **2** noisy or rowdy: *a raucous late-night dinner.*

– DERIVATIVES **raucously** adverb **raucousness** noun.

– ORIGIN Latin *raucus* 'hoarse'.

raunch noun informal explicit earthiness or sexuality.

raunchy adjective (**raunchier, raunchiest**) informal earthy and sexually explicit.

– DERIVATIVES **raunchily** adverb **raunchiness** noun.

– ORIGIN unknown.

ravage verb cause severe damage to someone or something. •noun (**ravages**) the destructive effects of something.

– ORIGIN French *ravager*.

rave verb **1** talk in a wild or angry way. **2** speak or write very enthusiastically about: *critics raved about his technique.* •noun informal **1** a very large party or similar event with dancing to loud, fast electronic music. **2** a very popular person or thing. **3** chiefly N. Amer. a very enthusiastic review.

– ORIGIN probably from Old French *raver.*

ravel verb (**ravels, ravelling, ravelled**; US **ravels, raveling, raveled**) **1** (**ravel something out**) untangle something. **2** confuse or complicate a situation.

– ORIGIN probably from Dutch *ravelen* 'fray out, tangle'.

raven noun a large black crow. •adjective (of hair) black and glossy.

– ORIGIN Old English.

ravening /**rav**-uh-ning/ adjective (especially of a wild animal) very hungry and searching for food.

ravenous /**rav**-uh-nuhss/ adjective very hungry.

– DERIVATIVES **ravenously** adverb.

– ORIGIN from Old French *raviner* 'to ravage'.

raver noun informal **1** Brit. a person who has an exciting and uninhibited social life. **2** a person who regularly goes to raves.

rave-up noun Brit. informal a lively, noisy party.

ravine /ruh-**veen**/ noun a deep, narrow gorge with steep sides.

– ORIGIN French, 'violent rush'.

raving noun (**ravings**) wild talk that makes no sense. •adjective & adverb informal used for emphasis: *she was no raving beauty.*

ravioli /rav-i-**oh**-li/ plural noun small pasta cases filled with minced meat, fish, etc.

– ORIGIN Italian.

ravish verb **1** (**be ravished**) literary be filled with great pleasure: *ravished by a sunny afternoon, she had agreed without thinking.* **2** dated rape someone. **3** old use seize and carry off someone by force.

– ORIGIN Old French *ravir.*

ravishing adjective very beautiful or delightful: *a ravishing film star.*

– DERIVATIVES **ravishingly** adverb.

raw adjective **1** (of food) uncooked. **2** (of a material or substance) not processed or finished: *turn under the raw edges of the fabric.* **3** (of data) not organized or evaluated. **4** (of the skin) red and painful from being rubbed or scraped. **5** (of a person's nerves) very sensitive. **6** (of an emotion or quality) strong and undisguised: *raw masculinity.* **7** (of the weather) cold and damp. **8** new to an activity or job and therefore lacking experience.

– PHRASES **in the raw 1** in its true state. **2** informal naked. **a raw deal** informal unfair or harsh treatment.

– DERIVATIVES **rawly** adverb **rawness** noun.

– ORIGIN Old English.

raw-boned adjective having a bony or gaunt physique.

rawhide noun stiff leather that has not been tanned.

Rawlplug noun Brit. trademark a thin plastic or fibre sheath that is inserted into a hole in masonry to hold a screw.

– ORIGIN from *Rawlings* (the engineers who introduced it).

r

raw material noun a basic material from which a product is made.

ray[1] noun **1** a line of light coming from the sun or any luminous object. **2** the straight line in which radiation travels to a given point. **3** (**rays**) a specified form of non-luminous radiation: *ultraviolet rays.* **4** a slight indication of a welcome quality: *a ray of hope.*
– ORIGIN Old French *rai.*

ray[2] noun a broad flat fish with wing-like pectoral fins and a long thin tail.
– ORIGIN Latin *raia.*

ray[3] (also **re**) noun Music the second note of a major scale, coming after 'doh' and before 'me'.
– ORIGIN formerly spelled *re*, the first syllable of *resonare*, a word taken from a Latin hymn.

rayon noun a synthetic fibre or fabric made from viscose.
– ORIGIN invented name.

raze verb completely destroy a building, town, etc.
– ORIGIN Old French *raser* 'shave closely'.

razor noun an implement with a sharp blade, used to shave hair from the face or body. • verb cut hair with a razor.
– ORIGIN Old French *rasor.*

razorbill noun a black-and-white auk (seabird) with a deep bill.

razor shell noun a burrowing shellfish with a long straight shell.

razor wire noun metal wire with sharp edges or studded with small sharp blades, used as a barrier.

razz verb informal, chiefly N. Amer. tease someone playfully.
– ORIGIN from **RASPBERRY**.

razzle noun (in phrase **on the razzle**) Brit. informal out celebrating or enjoying oneself.
– ORIGIN from **RAZZLE-DAZZLE**.

razzle-dazzle noun another term for **RAZZMATAZZ**.
– ORIGIN from **DAZZLE**.

razzmatazz (also **razzamatazz**) noun informal exciting or noisy activity, intended to attract attention.
– ORIGIN probably from **RAZZLE-DAZZLE**.

Rb symbol the chemical element rubidium.

RC abbreviation **1** Red Cross. **2** Electronics resistance/capacitance (or resistor/capacitor). **3** Roman Catholic.

Rd abbreviation Road (used in street names).

RDA abbreviation recommended daily (or dietary) allowance.

RDS abbreviation radio data system.

RE abbreviation religious education (as a school subject).

Re symbol the chemical element rhenium.

re[1] /ree, ray/ preposition **1** in the matter of (used in headings or to introduce a reference). **2** about; concerning.
– ORIGIN Latin.

re[2] noun variant spelling of **RAY**[3].

re- prefix **1** once more; anew: *reactivate.* **2** with return to a previous state: *restore.*
– ORIGIN Latin.

USAGE: Words formed with the prefix (word beginning) re- are usually spelled without a hyphen (*react*). However, if the word to which re- is attached begins with e, then a hyphen is used to make it clear (*re-examine, re-enter*). You should also use a hyphen when the word formed with re- would be exactly the same as a word that already exists; use **re-cover** to mean 'cover again' and **recover** to mean 'get well again'.

're abbreviation informal are (usually after *you*, *we*, and *they*).

reach verb **1** stretch out an arm to touch or grasp something. **2** be able to touch something with an outstretched arm or leg. **3** arrive at a place. **4** achieve or extend to a specified point, level, or state: *unemployment reached a peak in 1933.* **5** succeed in achieving: *I hope we will be able to reach agreement.* **6** make contact with someone. • noun **1** an act of reaching. **2** the distance to which someone can stretch out their arm. **3** the extent to which someone or something has power, influence, or the ability to do something: *university was out of her reach.* **4** (often **reaches**) a continuous extent of water, especially a stretch of river between two bends.
– DERIVATIVES **reachable** adjective.
– ORIGIN Old English.

reacquaint verb (**reacquaint someone/oneself with**) make someone familiar or acquainted with again: *she came here to reacquaint herself with existing customers.*

react verb **1** respond to something in a particular way: *he reacted angrily to the news of his dismissal.* **2** suffer from harmful effects after eating, breathing, or touching a substance. **3** interact and undergo a chemical or physical change.

reactance noun Physics the non-resistive component of impedance in an alternating-current circuit, arising from inductance and/or capacitance.

reactant noun a substance that takes part in and undergoes change during a chemical reaction.

reaction noun **1** something done or experienced as a result of an event or situation: *her first reaction was one of relief.* **2** (**reactions**) a person's ability to respond to an event. **3** a response by the body to a drug or substance to which someone is allergic. **4** a way of thinking or behaving that is deliberately different from that of the past. **5** a process in which substances interact causing chemical or physical change. **6** Physics a force exerted in opposition to an applied force.

reactionary adjective opposing political or social progress or reform. • noun (pl. **reactionaries**) a person holding reactionary views.

reactivate verb bring something back into action.
– DERIVATIVES **reactivation** noun.

reactive adjective **1** showing a response to a stimulus. **2** acting in response to a situation rather than creating or controlling it. **3** having a tendency to react chemically.

r

– DERIVATIVES **reactivity** noun.

reactor noun 1 (also **nuclear reactor**) a structure or piece of equipment in which suitable material can be made to undergo a controlled nuclear reaction, so releasing nuclear energy. 2 a container or device in which substances are made to react chemically.

read /reed/ verb (past and past part. **read** /red/) 1 look at and understand the meaning of written or printed matter by interpreting its characters or symbols. 2 speak written or printed words aloud. 3 have a particular wording: *the placard read 'We want justice'*. 4 discover information by reading: *I read about the course in the paper.* 5 habitually read a particular newspaper or magazine. 6 understand or interpret the nature or significance of: *he didn't dare look away in case this was read as a sign of weakness.* 7 (**read something into**) think that something has a meaning or significance that it may not possess. 8 (**read up on**) gain information about a subject by reading. 9 chiefly Brit. study an academic subject at a university. 10 look at and record the figure indicated on a measuring instrument. 11 present a bill or other measure before a law-making body. 12 (of a computer) copy or transfer data. 13 hear and understand the words of someone speaking on a radio transmitter. •noun 1 chiefly Brit. a period or act of reading. 2 informal a book that is interesting or enjoyable to read.

– PHRASES **read between the lines** look for or find a meaning that not explicitly stated. **read someone's mind** know what someone else is thinking.

– DERIVATIVES **readable** adjective.

– ORIGIN Old English; early senses included 'advise' and 'interpret a riddle or dream'.

reader noun 1 a person who reads. 2 a person who assesses the quality of manuscripts submitted for publication. 3 (**Reader**) Brit. a university lecturer of the highest grade below professor. 4 a book containing extracts of another book or books for teaching purposes. 5 a device that produces a readable image from a microfiche or microfilm on a screen.

– DERIVATIVES **readerly** adjective.

readership noun 1 (treated as sing. or pl.) the readers of a publication as a group. 2 (**Readership**) Brit. the position of Reader at a university.

readily adverb 1 without hesitation; willingly. 2 without difficulty; easily.

reading noun 1 the action or skill of reading. 2 an instance of something being read to an audience. 3 a way of interpreting something: *his reading of the situation was justified.* 4 a figure recorded on a measuring instrument. 5 a stage of debate in parliament through which a bill must pass before it can become law.

reading age noun a child's reading ability, measured by comparing it with the average ability of children of a particular age.

readjust verb 1 set or adjust something again. 2 adjust or adapt to a changed situation or environment.

– DERIVATIVES **readjustment** noun.

read-only memory noun Computing memory read at high speed but not capable of being changed by program instructions.

read-out noun a visual record or display of the output from a computer or scientific instrument.

read-write adjective Computing capable of reading existing data and accepting alterations or further input.

ready adjective (**readier**, **readiest**) 1 prepared for an activity or situation. 2 made suitable and available for immediate use: *dinner's ready.* 3 easily available or obtained; within reach. 4 (**ready to/for**) willing to do or having a desire for. 5 immediate, quick, or prompt: *his ready wit.* •noun (**readies** or **the ready**) Brit. informal available money; cash. •verb (**readies**, **readying**, **readied**) prepare someone or something for an activity or purpose.

– PHRASES **at the ready** prepared or available for immediate use. **make ready** prepare.

– DERIVATIVES **readiness** noun.

– ORIGIN Old English.

ready-made adjective 1 made to a standard size or specification rather than to order. 2 easily available: *ready-made answers.*

ready-mixed adjective (of concrete, paint, food, etc.) having some or all of the constituents already mixed together.

ready money noun money in the form of cash that is immediately available.

ready reckoner noun a book, table, etc. listing standard numerical calculations or other kinds of information.

ready-to-wear adjective (of clothes) sold through shops rather than made to order for an individual customer.

reaffirm verb 1 state something again. 2 confirm the validity of something already established.

– DERIVATIVES **reaffirmation** noun.

reagent /ri-ay-juhnt/ noun a substance or mixture used to cause a chemical reaction, used especially to test for the presence of another substance.

real[1] /reel/ adjective 1 actually existing or occurring; not imagined or supposed. 2 not artificial; genuine: *real diamonds.* 3 worthy of the description; proper: *he's my idea of a real man.* 4 significant; serious: *a real danger of war.* 5 adjusted for changes in the value of money: *real incomes had fallen by 30 per cent.* 6 Mathematics (of a number or quantity) having no imaginary part. •adverb informal, chiefly N. Amer. really; very.

– DERIVATIVES **realness** noun.

– ORIGIN Latin *realis*.

real[2] /ray-ahl/ noun 1 the basic unit of money of Brazil since 1994, equal to 100 centavos. 2 a former coin and unit of money of various Spanish-speaking countries.

– ORIGIN Spanish and Portuguese, 'royal'.

real ale noun Brit. cask-conditioned beer that is served traditionally, without additional gas pressure.

real estate noun chiefly N. Amer. property in the form of land or buildings.

realign verb 1 change or restore something to a different or former position or state.

2 (**realign oneself with**) change one's opinions so as to share those of another person, group, etc.
– DERIVATIVES **realignment** noun.

realism noun **1** the practice of accepting a situation as it is and dealing with it accordingly. **2** (in art or literature) the representation of things in a way that is accurate and true to life. **3** Philosophy the theory that abstract ideas have their own existence, independent of the mind. Often contrasted with NOMINALISM.
– DERIVATIVES **realist** noun & adjective.

realistic adjective **1** having a sensible and practical idea of what can be achieved or expected. **2** representing things in a way that is accurate and true to life.
– DERIVATIVES **realistically** adverb.

reality noun (pl. **realities**) **1** the state of things as they actually exist, as opposed to how one might like them to be: *he refuses to face reality.* **2** a thing that is actually experienced or seen: *the harsh realities of life in a farming community.* **3** the state or quality of having existence or substance. • adjective referring to television programmes based on real people or situations, intended to be entertaining rather than informative: *reality TV.*

realize (or **realise**) verb **1** become fully aware of as a fact; understand clearly: *he realized his mistake at once.* **2** achieve something desired or anticipated: *he finally realized his lifelong ambition.* **3** (**be realized**) (of something one is afraid will happen) happen: *their worst fears were realized.* **4** give actual or physical form to something. **5** be sold for a particular amount. **6** convert property, shares, etc. into money by selling them.
– DERIVATIVES **realizable** adjective **realization** noun.

really adverb **1** in reality; in actual fact. **2** very; thoroughly. • exclamation expressing interest, surprise, or protest.

realm noun **1** literary or Law a kingdom. **2** a field of activity or interest: *the realm of chemistry.*
– ORIGIN Old French *reaume.*

realpolitik /ray-ahl-po-li-teek/ noun politics based on practical considerations rather than moral or ideological principles.
– ORIGIN German, 'practical politics'.

real property noun Law property consisting of land or buildings. Compare with PERSONAL PROPERTY.

real tennis noun the original form of tennis, played with a solid ball on an enclosed court.

real time noun the actual time during which something occurs. • adjective (**real-time**) (of a computer system) in which input data is processed extremely fast so that it is available virtually immediately as feedback to the process from which it is coming, e.g. in a missile guidance system.

realtor /ree-uhl-ter/ noun N. Amer. an estate agent.

realty /ree-uhl-ti/ noun Law a person's real property. Compare with PERSONALTY.

ream[1] noun **1** 500 (formerly 480) sheets of paper. **2** (**reams**) a large quantity of something, especially paper.
– ORIGIN Old French *raime.*

ream[2] verb widen a bore or hole with a special tool.
– DERIVATIVES **reamer** noun.
– ORIGIN unknown.

reanalyse verb carry out a further analysis of something.
– DERIVATIVES **reanalysis** noun.

reanimate verb bring someone back to life or consciousness.
– DERIVATIVES **reanimation** noun.

reap verb **1** cut or gather a crop or harvest. **2** receive something as a result of one's own or others' actions: *the company is poised to reap the benefits of this investment.*
– ORIGIN Old English.

reaper noun **1** a person or machine that harvests a crop. **2** (**the Reaper** or **the Grim Reaper**) a representation of death as a cloaked skeleton holding a large scythe.

reappear verb appear again.
– DERIVATIVES **reappearance** noun.

reappoint verb appoint someone again to a position they previously held.
– DERIVATIVES **reappointment** noun.

reappraise verb appraise something again or differently.
– DERIVATIVES **reappraisal** noun.

rear[1] noun **1** the back part of something. **2** (also **rear end**) informal a person's buttocks. • adjective at the back.
– PHRASES **bring up the rear 1** be at the very end of a queue. **2** come last in a race.
– ORIGIN Old French *rere.*

rear[2] verb **1** bring up and care for offspring. **2** breed or cultivate animals or plants. **3** (of an animal) raise itself upright on its hind legs. **4** (of a building, mountain, etc.) extend or appear to extend to a great height. **5** (**rear up**) show anger or irritation.
– ORIGIN Old English, 'set upright, construct'.

rear admiral noun a rank of naval officer, above commodore and below vice admiral.

rearguard noun **1** the soldiers at the rear of a body of troops, especially those protecting a retreating army. **2** a reactionary or conservative group in an organization.

rearguard action noun a defensive action carried out by a retreating army.

rearm verb provide with or obtain a new supply of weapons.
– DERIVATIVES **rearmament** noun.

rearmost adjective furthest back.

rearrange verb arrange something again in a different way.
– DERIVATIVES **rearrangement** noun.

rearrest verb arrest someone again.

rear-view mirror noun a mirror fixed inside the windscreen of a vehicle enabling the driver to see the vehicle or road behind.

rearward adjective directed towards the back. • adverb (also **rearwards**) towards the back.

rear-wheel drive noun a transmission system that provides power to the rear wheels of a motor vehicle.

reason noun **1** a cause, explanation, or justification. **2** good or obvious cause to do something: *we have reason to celebrate.* **3** the power to think, understand, and form judgements logically. **4** (**one's reason**) one's

sanity. **5** what is right, practical, or possible: *I'll answer anything, within reason.* • verb **1** think, understand, and form judgements logically. **2 (reason something out)** find a solution to a problem by considering possible options. **3 (reason with)** persuade someone by using logical argument.
– PHRASES **by reason of** formal because of. **listen to reason** be persuaded to act sensibly. **it stands to reason** it is obvious or logical.
– DERIVATIVES **reasoned** adjective.
– ORIGIN Old French *reisun*.

reasonable adjective **1** fair and sensible. **2** as much as is appropriate or fair in a particular situation: *they have had a reasonable time to reply* **3** fairly good; average. **4** not too expensive.
– DERIVATIVES **reasonableness** noun **reasonably** adverb.

reassemble verb put something back together.
– DERIVATIVES **reassembly** noun.

reassert verb state or declare something again.
– DERIVATIVES **reassertion** noun.

reassess verb consider or assess someone or something again, in the light of new or different factors.
– DERIVATIVES **reassessment** noun.

reassign verb assign someone or something again or differently.
– DERIVATIVES **reassignment** noun.

reassure verb make someone feel less worried or afraid.
– DERIVATIVES **reassurance** noun **reassuring** adjective.

reattach verb attach something again.
– DERIVATIVES **reattachment** noun.

reawaken verb awaken again.

rebalance verb restore the correct balance to someone or something.

rebar /ree-bar/ noun reinforcing steel, especially as rods in concrete.

rebarbative /ri-bar-buh-tiv/ adjective formal unattractive and unpleasant or offensive.
– ORIGIN French *rébarbatif*, from Old French *se rebarber* 'face each other aggressively' (literally 'beard to beard').

rebate[1] /ree-bayt/ noun **1** a partial refund to someone who has paid too much for tax, rent, etc. **2** a deduction or discount on a sum of money due. • verb pay money back as a rebate.
– ORIGIN from Old French *rebatre* 'beat back'.

rebate[2] /ree-bayt/ noun a step-shaped recess cut in a piece of wood, typically forming a match to the edge or tongue of another piece. • verb **(rebates, rebating, rebated) 1** make a rebate in a piece of wood. **2** join or fix something with a rebate.
– ORIGIN from Old French *rabbat* 'abatement, recess'.

rebec /ree-bek/ noun a medieval three-stringed instrument played with a bow.
– ORIGIN French.

rebel noun /reb-uhl/ a person who rebels. • verb /ri-bel/ **(rebels, rebelling, rebelled) 1** fight against or refuse to obey an established government or ruler. **2** resist authority, control, or accepted behaviour.
– ORIGIN Old French *rebelle*, from Latin *bellum*

'war'.

rebellion noun **1** an act of rebelling against an established government or ruler. **2** defiance of authority or control.

rebellious adjective rebelling or showing a desire to rebel.
– DERIVATIVES **rebelliously** adverb **rebelliousness** noun.

rebirth noun **1** the process of being reincarnated or born again. **2** a period of new life, growth, or activity: *the rebirth of a defeated nation.*

rebirthing noun a form of therapy involving controlled breathing intended to imitate the traumatic experience of being born.

reboot verb boot a computer system again.

reborn adjective **1** brought back to life or activity. **2** newly converted to a personal faith in Jesus; born-again.

rebound verb /ri-**bownd**/ **1** bounce back after hitting a hard surface. **2** recover in value, amount, or strength. **3 (rebound on)** have an unexpected and unpleasant consequence for: *his tricks are rebounding on him.* • noun /ree-bownd/ **1** a ball or shot that rebounds. **2** an instance of recovering in value, amount, or strength: *shares rose sharply in anticipation of an economic rebound.*
– PHRASES **on the rebound** while still distressed after the ending of a romantic relationship.
– ORIGIN Old French *rebondir*.

rebrand verb change the corporate image of a company or organization.

rebuff verb reject someone or something in an abrupt or ungracious way: *they rebuffed his attempt to negotiate a new deal.* • noun an abrupt or unkind rejection.
– ORIGIN former French *rebuffer*.

rebuild verb (past and past part. **rebuilt**) build something again.

rebuke verb criticize or reprimand someone sharply. • noun a sharp criticism.
– ORIGIN Old French *rebuker* 'beat down'.

rebus /ree-buhss/ noun (pl. **rebuses**) a puzzle in which words are represented by combinations of pictures and letters.
– ORIGIN Latin, 'by things'.

rebut /ri-but/ verb **(rebuts, rebutting, rebutted)** claim or prove that evidence or an accusation is false.
– ORIGIN Old French *rebuter*.

rebuttal noun an act of rebutting evidence or an accusation.

recalcitrant /ri-kal-si-truhnt/ adjective obstinately uncooperative or disobedient.
– DERIVATIVES **recalcitrance** noun **recalcitrantly** adverb.
– ORIGIN from Latin *recalcitrare* 'kick out with the heels'.

recalculate verb calculate something again.
– DERIVATIVES **recalculation** noun.

recall /ri-kawl/ verb **1** remember something. **2** cause one to remember or think of someone or something. **3** officially order to return: *the ambassador was recalled from Peru.* **4** (of a manufacturer) request all the purchasers of a product to return it, as a result of the discovery of a fault. **5** select a sports player as a member of a team from which they have

r

previously been dropped. **6** call up stored computer data. •**noun** /also **ree**-kawl/ **1** the action of remembering or the ability to remember. **2** an act of officially recalling someone or something.
– PHRASES **beyond recall** in such a way that restoration to the original state is impossible.

recant /ri-**kant**/ **verb** state that one no longer holds an opinion or belief.
– DERIVATIVES **recantation** /ree-kan-**tay**-sh'n/ noun.
– ORIGIN Latin *recantare* 'revoke', from *cantare* 'sing, chant'.

recap verb (**recaps, recapping, recapped**) recapitulate. •**noun** a recapitulation.

recapitulate /ree-kuh-**pit**-yuu-layt/ **verb** summarize and state again the main points of a speech, argument, etc.
– ORIGIN Latin *recapitulare* 'go through heading by heading', from *capitulum* 'chapter'.

recapitulation /ree-kuh-pit-yoo-**lay**-sh'n/ **noun 1** an act of recapitulating something. **2** Music a part of a movement in which themes from the exposition are repeated.

recapture verb 1 capture a person or animal that has escaped. **2** recover something taken or lost. **3** experience a past time, event, or feeling again: *the programmes give viewers a chance to recapture their own childhoods.* •**noun** an act of recapturing someone or something.

recast verb (past and past part. **recast**) **1** present something in a different form or style: *his thesis has been recast for the general reader.* **2** give roles in a play or film to different actors. **3** cast metal again or differently.

recce /**rek**-ki/ Brit. informal **noun** an act of reconnoitring a place or area. •**verb** (**recces, recceing, recced**) reconnoitre a place or area.

recede verb 1 move back or further away. **2** gradually diminish: *her panic receded.* **3** (of a man's hair) stop growing at the temples and above the forehead. **4** (as adj. **receding**) (of a facial feature) sloping backwards: *a receding chin.*
– ORIGIN Latin *recedere* 'go back'.

receipt noun 1 the action of receiving something or the fact of its being received. **2** a written statement confirming that something has been paid for or received. **3** (**receipts**) an amount of money received over a period by an organization.
– ORIGIN Old French *receite.*

receivable adjective able to be received. •**plural noun** (**receivables**) amounts owed to a business, regarded as assets.

receive verb 1 be given, presented with, or paid: *they received a £100,000 advance.* **2** accept or take delivery of something sent or offered. **3** form an idea or impression from an experience. **4** suffer, experience, or meet with: *the event received wide press coverage.* **5** (as adj. **received**) widely accepted as true or correct. **6** entertain someone as a guest. **7** admit someone as a member: *hundreds of converts were received into the Church.* **8** detect or pick up broadcast signals. **9** (in tennis and similar games) be the player to whom the server serves the ball. **10** chiefly Brit. buy or accept goods known to be stolen. **11** serve as a

container for something.
– PHRASES **be at** (or **on**) **the receiving end** informal be subjected to something unpleasant.
– ORIGIN Old French *receivre.*

received pronunciation noun the standard form of British English pronunciation, based on educated speech in southern England.

receiver noun 1 a person or thing that receives something. **2** a piece of radio or television equipment converting broadcast signals into sound or images. **3** a telephone handset, in particular the part that converts electrical signals into sounds. **4** (Brit. also **official receiver**) a person appointed to manage the financial affairs of a bankrupt business.

receivership noun the state of being managed by an official receiver.

recent adjective 1 having happened or been done lately; belonging to a period of time not long ago. **2** (**Recent**) Geology another term for HOLOCENE.
– DERIVATIVES **recently** adverb.
– ORIGIN Latin *recens.*

receptacle /ri-**sep**-tuh-k'l/ **noun 1** an object or space used to contain something. **2** Botany the base of a flower or flower head.
– ORIGIN Latin *receptaculum.*

reception noun 1 the action or process of receiving someone or something. **2** the way in which someone or something is received: *an enthusiastic reception.* **3** a formal social occasion held to welcome someone or celebrate an event. **4** chiefly Brit. the area in a hotel, office, etc. where visitors are greeted. **5** the quality with which broadcast signals are received.
– ORIGIN Latin, from *recipere* 'receive'.

receptionist noun a person who greets and deals with clients and visitors to an office, hotel, surgery, etc.

reception room noun 1 Brit. a room in a private house suitable for entertaining visitors. **2** a room in a hotel or other building used for functions such as parties and meetings.

receptive adjective 1 able or willing to receive something. **2** willing to consider new suggestions and ideas.
– DERIVATIVES **receptivity** noun.

receptor /ri-**sep**-ter/ **noun** an organ or cell in the body that responds to external stimuli such as light or heat and transmits signals to a sensory nerve.

recess /ri-**sess**, **ree**-sess/ **noun 1** a small space set back in a wall or into a surface. **2** a hollow space inside something. **3** (**recesses**) remote, secluded, or secret places. **4** a break between sessions of a parliament, law court, etc. **5** chiefly N. Amer. a break between school classes. •**verb** (often as adj. **recessed**) set a fitment back into a wall or surface.
– ORIGIN Latin *recessus.*

recession noun a temporary economic decline during which trade and industrial activity are reduced.
– DERIVATIVES **recessionary** adjective.

recessional noun a hymn sung while the clergy and choir withdraw after a service.

recessive adjective (of a gene) appearing in offspring only if a contrary gene is not also inherited. Compare with DOMINANT.

recharge verb charge a battery or a battery-operated device again.
– DERIVATIVES **rechargeable** adjective **recharger** noun.

recheck verb check something again.

recherché /ruh-**shair**-shay/ adjective too unusual or obscure to be easily understood.
– ORIGIN French, 'carefully sought out'.

rechristen verb give a new name to someone or something.

recidivist /ri-**sid**-i-vist/ noun a person who repeatedly commits crimes and is not discouraged by being punished.
– DERIVATIVES **recidivism** noun.
– ORIGIN French *récidiver*.

recipe /**res**-i-pee/ noun **1** a list of ingredients and instructions for preparing a dish. **2** something likely to lead to a particular outcome: *high interest rates are a recipe for disaster.*
– ORIGIN Latin, 'receive!' (originally used as an instruction in medical prescriptions).

recipient noun a person who receives something.

reciprocal /ri-**sip**-ruh-k'l/ adjective **1** given, felt, or done in return: *he showed no reciprocal interest.* **2** (of an agreement or arrangement) affecting two parties equally. **3** Grammar (of a pronoun or verb) expressing mutual action or relationship (e.g. *each other, they kissed*).
• noun Mathematics the quantity obtained by dividing the number one by a given quantity.
– DERIVATIVES **reciprocally** adverb.
– ORIGIN Latin *reciprocus*.

reciprocate /ri-**sip**-ruh-kayt/ verb respond to a gesture, action, or emotion with a corresponding one.
– DERIVATIVES **reciprocation** noun.

reciprocating engine noun a piston engine.

reciprocity /re-si-**pross**-i-ti/ noun the practice of exchanging things with other parties to the benefit or advantage of both.

recirculate verb circulate something again.
– DERIVATIVES **recirculation** noun.

recital noun **1** the performance of a programme of music by a soloist or small group. **2** a long account of a series of connected things: *a recital of Adam's failures.*
– DERIVATIVES **recitalist** noun.

recitative /re-si-tuh-**teev**/ noun the narrative and dialogue passages in an opera or oratorio, sung in a way that reflects the rhythms of ordinary speech.

recite verb **1** repeat a poem or passage aloud from memory in front of an audience. **2** state a series of names, facts, etc. in order.
– DERIVATIVES **recitation** noun **reciter** noun.
– ORIGIN Latin *recitare* 'read out'.

reck verb old use pay attention to something.
– ORIGIN Old English.

reckless adjective without thought or care for the consequences of an action.
– DERIVATIVES **recklessly** adverb **recklessness** noun.
– ORIGIN Old English.

reckon verb **1** be of the opinion; think: *I reckon he'll win.* **2** (be reckoned) be considered to be: *their goalkeeper was reckoned to be the best in*
the world. **3** calculate something. **4** (reckon on) rely on or expect: *no one had reckoned on a strike.* **5** (reckon with or without) take (or fail to take) something into account.
– PHRASES **to be reckoned with** not to be ignored or underestimated.
– ORIGIN Old English, 'recount, tell'.

reckoning noun **1** the action of calculating or estimating something. **2** an opinion or judgement. **3** punishment or retribution for one's actions.
– PHRASES **into** (or **out of**) **the reckoning** among (or not among) those who are likely to win or be successful.

reclaim verb **1** recover possession of something. **2** make waste land or land formerly under water usable for growing crops. • noun the action of reclaiming something.
– DERIVATIVES **reclamation** noun.

reclassify verb (**reclassifies**, **reclassifying**, **reclassified**) classify someone or something differently.
– DERIVATIVES **reclassification** noun.

recline verb **1** lean or lie back in a relaxed position. **2** (of a seat) have a back able to move into a sloping position.
– DERIVATIVES **reclinable** adjective **recliner** noun.
– ORIGIN Latin *reclinare*.

recluse /ri-**klooss**/ noun a person who avoids other people and lives a solitary life.
– ORIGIN from Old French *reclus* 'shut up'.

reclusive adjective tending to avoid the company of other people: *a reclusive former rock star.*

recognition noun **1** the action of recognizing or the process of being recognized. **2** appreciation or acknowledgement of something. **3** (also **diplomatic recognition**) formal acknowledgement by a country that another country or state has the status of an independent nation.

recognizance /ri-**kog**-ni-zuhnss/ (or **recognisance**) noun Law a bond by which a person undertakes before a court or magistrate to observe a particular condition, especially to appear when summoned.

recognize (or **recognise**) verb **1** identify or know someone or something from having come across them before. **2** accept or acknowledge the existence, validity, or legality of: *he was recognized as an international authority.* **3** show official appreciation of: *his work was recognized by an honorary degree from Glasgow University.*
– DERIVATIVES **recognizable** adjective.
– ORIGIN Latin *recognoscere*, from *cognoscere* 'to learn'.

recoil verb **1** suddenly spring back or flinch in fear, horror, or disgust. **2** spring back as a result of the force of impact or elasticity. **3** (of a gun) move abruptly backwards as a reaction on firing a bullet or shell. **4** (**recoil on**) (of an action) have an unwelcome result or effect on the person responsible. • noun the action of recoiling.
– ORIGIN Old French *reculer* 'move back'.

recollect /rek-uh-**lekt**/ verb **1** remember something. **2** (**recollect oneself**) manage to control one's feelings.

r

recollection noun 1 the action of remembering, or the ability to remember. 2 a memory.

recombinant /ri-kom-bi-nuhnt/ adjective relating to genetic material formed by recombination.

recombination noun 1 the process of recombining. 2 the rearrangement of genetic material, especially by exchange between chromosomes or by the artificial joining of DNA segments from different organisms.

recombine verb combine again or differently.

recommence verb begin again.

recommend verb 1 state that someone or something is good or would be suitable for a purpose or role. 2 advise as a course of action: *he recommended that I leave the country.* 3 make appealing or desirable: *the house had much to recommend it.*
– DERIVATIVES **recommendable** adjective.

recommendation noun 1 a suggestion or proposal as to the best course of action. 2 the action of recommending.

recommission verb commission something again.

recompense /rek-uhm-penss/ verb 1 compensate or make amends to someone for loss or harm suffered. 2 pay or reward someone for effort or work. •noun compensation or reward.
– ORIGIN Latin *recompensare.*

reconcile /rek-uhn-syl/ verb 1 restore friendly relations between people. 2 make apparently incompatible things able to exist together without problems or conflict: *an attempt to reconcile freedom with commitment.* 3 (reconcile someone to) make someone accept an unwelcome or unpleasant situation.
– DERIVATIVES **reconcilable** adjective.
– ORIGIN Latin *reconciliare.*

reconciliation noun 1 the end of a disagreement and the return to friendly relations. 2 the action of reconciling.

recondite /rek-uhn-dyt, ri-kon-dyt/ adjective not known about or understood by many people.
– ORIGIN Latin *reconditus* 'hidden, put away'.

recondition verb 1 condition something again. 2 Brit. overhaul or repair an engine or other piece of equipment.

reconfigure verb configure something differently.
– DERIVATIVES **reconfiguration** noun.

reconnaissance /ri-kon-ni-suhnss/ noun military observation of an area carried out to locate an enemy or gain information.
– ORIGIN French.

reconnect verb connect someone or something again.
– DERIVATIVES **reconnection** noun.

reconnoitre /rek-uh-noy-ter/ (US **reconnoiter**) verb make a military observation of an area. •noun an act of reconnoitring an area.
– ORIGIN former French.

reconsider verb consider something again, with a view to changing a decision that has been made.
– DERIVATIVES **reconsideration** noun.

reconstitute verb 1 change the form and organization of an institution. 2 restore dried food to its original state by adding water. 3 reconstruct something.
– DERIVATIVES **reconstitution** noun.

reconstruct verb 1 construct something again. 2 re-enact or form an impression of a past event from the evidence available.
– DERIVATIVES **reconstruction** noun **reconstructive** adjective.

reconvene verb come or bring together again for a meeting or activity.

reconvert verb change something back to a former state.
– DERIVATIVES **reconversion** noun.

record noun 1 a piece of evidence or information forming a permanent account of something that has happened, been said, etc. 2 a thin plastic disc carrying recorded sound in grooves on each surface, for reproduction by a record player. 3 the previous behaviour or performance of a person or thing: *the team preserved their unbeaten home record.* 4 the best performance or most remarkable event of its kind that has been officially recognized. 5 (also **criminal record**) a list of a person's previous criminal convictions. •verb 1 put in writing or some other permanent form for later reference: *they were asked to keep a diary and record everything they ate or drank.* 2 convert sound, a broadcast, etc. into permanent form to be reproduced later.
– PHRASES **for the record** so that the true facts are recorded or known. **on record** officially measured and noted. **on** (or **off**) **the record** made (or not made) as an official statement. **put** (or **set**) **the record straight** correct a mistaken belief.
– DERIVATIVES **recordable** adjective **recordist** noun.
– ORIGIN Latin *recordari* 'remember'.

record-breaking adjective beating a record or best-ever achievement.
– DERIVATIVES **record-breaker** noun.

recorded delivery noun Brit. a service in which the Post Office obtains a signature from the recipient of an item of post as a record that the item has been delivered.

recorder noun 1 a device for recording sound, pictures, or data. 2 a person who keeps records. 3 (**Recorder**) (in England and Wales) a barrister appointed to serve as a part-time judge. 4 a simple woodwind instrument without keys, played by blowing air through a shaped mouthpiece.

recording noun 1 a piece of music or film that has been recorded. 2 the process of recording something.

record player noun a device for playing records, with a turntable and a stylus that picks up sound from the groove.

recount[1] /ri-kownt/ verb tell someone about an event or experience.
– ORIGIN Old French *reconter* 'tell again'.

recount[2] verb /ree-kownt/ count something again. •noun /ree-kownt/ an act of counting something again.

recoup /ree-koop/ verb get back an amount of money that has been spent or lost.
– DERIVATIVES **recoupable** adjective **recoupment** noun.
– ORIGIN French *recouper* 'retrench, cut back'.

recourse noun 1 a source of help in a difficult situation. 2 (**recourse to**) the use of someone or something as a source of help.
– ORIGIN Latin *recursus*.

recover verb 1 return to a normal state of health, mind, or strength. 2 find or regain possession or control of: *he recovered his balance.* 3 regain or secure money by legal means or the making of profits. 4 remove or extract a substance from waste material for recycling or reuse.
– DERIVATIVES **recoverable** adjective.
– ORIGIN Old French *recoverer*, from Latin *recuperare* 'get again'.

re-cover verb put a new cover or covering on something.

recovery noun (pl. **recoveries**) 1 an act or the process of recovering. 2 the action of taking a vehicle that has broken down or crashed for repair.

recovery position noun Brit. a position used to prevent an unconscious person from choking, the body being placed face downwards and slightly to the side, supported by the bent limbs.

recreant /rek-ri-uhnt/ old use adjective 1 cowardly. 2 disloyal. • noun a recreant person.
– ORIGIN Old French, 'surrendering'.

recreate /ree-kri-ayt/ verb make or do something again.

recreation[1] /rek-ri-ay-sh'n/ noun enjoyable leisure activity.
– DERIVATIVES **recreational** adjective.
– ORIGIN Latin, from *recreare* 'create again'.

recreation[2] /ree-kri-ay-sh'n/ noun the action of recreating something.

recreation ground noun Brit. a piece of public land used for sports and games.

recrimination noun (usu. **recriminations**) an accusation made in response to one from someone else.
– ORIGIN Latin, from *recriminari* 'accuse in return'.

recrudescence /ree-kruu-dess-uhnss/ verb formal a renewed outbreak or occurrence of something.
– DERIVATIVES **recrudescent** adjective.
– ORIGIN from Latin *recrudescere* 'become raw again'.

recruit verb 1 enlist someone in the armed forces. 2 enrol someone as a member or worker in an organization. 3 informal persuade someone to do or help with something. • noun a newly recruited person.
– DERIVATIVES **recruiter** noun **recruitment** noun.
– ORIGIN former French *recrute*.

recta plural of RECTUM.

rectal adjective relating to the rectum.
– DERIVATIVES **rectally** adverb.

rectangle noun a plane figure with four straight sides and four right angles, and with unequal adjacent sides.
– DERIVATIVES **rectangular** adjective.
– ORIGIN Latin *rectangulum*, from *rectus* 'straight' + *angulus* 'an angle'.

rectifier noun an electrical device converting an alternating current into a direct one by allowing it to flow in one direction only.

rectify verb (**rectifies, rectifying, rectified**) 1 put something right. 2 convert alternating current to direct current.
– DERIVATIVES **rectifiable** adjective **rectification** noun.
– ORIGIN Latin *rectificare*, from *rectus* 'right'.

rectilinear /rek-ti-lin-i-er/ adjective contained by, consisting of, or moving in a straight line or lines.
– ORIGIN from Latin *rectus* 'straight' + *linea* 'line'.

rectitude noun morally correct behaviour.
– ORIGIN Old French, from Latin *rectus* 'right'.

recto noun (pl. **rectos**) a right-hand page of an open book, or the front of a loose document. Contrasted with VERSO.
– ORIGIN Latin, 'on the right'.

rector noun 1 (in an Anglican Church) a member of the clergy in charge of a parish. 2 (in the Roman Catholic Church) a priest in charge of a church or a religious institution. 3 the head of certain universities, colleges, and schools. 4 (in Scotland) a person elected to represent students on a university's governing body.
– DERIVATIVES **rectorial** adjective **rectorship** noun.
– ORIGIN Latin, 'ruler'.

rectory noun (pl. **rectories**) a rector's house.

rectum /rek-tuhm/ noun (pl. **rectums** or **recta** /rek-tuh/) the final section of the large intestine, ending at the anus.
– ORIGIN from Latin *rectum intestinum* 'straight intestine'.

recumbent /ri-kum-buhnt/ adjective 1 lying down. 2 (of a plant) growing close to the ground.
– DERIVATIVES **recumbency** noun.
– ORIGIN from Latin *recumbere* 'recline'.

recuperate /ri-koo-puh-rayt/ verb 1 recover from illness or physical exertion. 2 regain something lost.
– DERIVATIVES **recuperation** noun **recuperative** adjective.
– ORIGIN Latin *recuperare* 'regain'.

recur verb (**recurs, recurring, recurred**) 1 happen again or repeatedly. 2 (of a thought, image, etc.) come back to one's mind.
– DERIVATIVES **recurrence** noun.
– ORIGIN Latin *recurrere*, from *currere* 'run'.

recurrent adjective happening often or repeatedly.
– DERIVATIVES **recurrently** adverb.

recurring decimal noun a decimal fraction in which a figure or group of figures is repeated indefinitely, as in 0.666 ...

recursion /ri-ker-shuhn/ noun chiefly Mathematics & Linguistics the repeated application of a procedure or rule to successive results of the process.
– DERIVATIVES **recursive** adjective.

recusant /rek-yuu-zuhnt/ noun 1 a person who refuses to obey an authority or comply with a regulation. 2 historical a person who refused to attend services of the Church of England.
– DERIVATIVES **recusancy** noun.
– ORIGIN from Latin *recusare* 'refuse'.

recuse /ri-kyooz/ verb (**recuse oneself**) chiefly N. Amer. & S. African (of a judge) excuse oneself from a case because of a possible lack of impartiality.

recycle verb **1** convert waste into reusable material. **2** use something again.
– DERIVATIVES **recyclable** adjective **recycler** noun.

red adjective (**redder, reddest**) **1** of the colour of blood, fire, or rubies. **2** (of a person's face) red due to embarrassment, anger, or heat. **3** (of hair or fur) of a reddish-brown colour. **4** (of wine) made from dark grapes and coloured by their skins. **5** informal, chiefly derogatory communist or socialist. •noun **1** red colour or material. **2** informal, chiefly derogatory a communist or socialist.
– PHRASES **in the red** having spent more than is in one's bank account. **the red planet** Mars. **see red** informal suddenly become very angry.
– DERIVATIVES **reddish** adjective **reddy** adjective **redly** adverb **redness** noun.
– ORIGIN Old English.

redact /ri-dakt/ verb rare edit something for publication.
– DERIVATIVES **redaction** noun **redactor** noun.
– ORIGIN Latin *redigere* 'bring back'.

red admiral noun a butterfly having dark wings with red bands and white spots.

red blood cell noun less technical term for ERYTHROCYTE.

red-blooded adjective (of a man) full of strength and energy; virile.

redbreast noun informal, chiefly Brit. a robin.

red-brick adjective (of a British university) founded in the late 19th or early 20th century and often with buildings of red brick rather than stone, so being distinct from the older universities.

redcap noun **1** Brit. informal a member of the military police. **2** N. Amer. a railway porter.

red card noun (especially in football) a red card shown by the referee to a player being sent off the field.

red carpet noun a long, narrow red carpet for an important visitor to walk along.

red cell noun less technical term for ERYTHROCYTE.

redcoat noun **1** historical a British soldier. **2** (in the UK) an organizer and entertainer at a Butlin's holiday camp.

Red Crescent noun a national branch in Muslim countries of the International Movement of the Red Cross and the Red Crescent.

Red Cross noun the International Movement of the Red Cross and the Red Crescent, an organization bringing relief to victims of war or natural disaster.

redcurrant noun a small edible red berry.

red deer noun a deer with a rich red-brown summer coat that turns brownish-grey in winter, the male having large antlers.

redden verb **1** make or become red. **2** blush.

red dwarf noun Astronomy a small, old, relatively cool star.

redecorate verb decorate something again or differently.
– DERIVATIVES **redecoration** noun.

redeem verb **1** make up for the faults or bad aspects of: *a poor debate redeemed by an* outstanding speech. **2** (**redeem oneself**) make up for one's poor performance or behaviour in the past. **3** save someone from sin, error, or evil. **4** repay or clear a debt: *owners were unable to redeem their mortgages.* **5** exchange a coupon for goods or money. **6** gain or regain possession of something in exchange for payment. **7** fulfil a pledge or promise.
– DERIVATIVES **redeemable** adjective.
– ORIGIN Latin *redimere* 'buy back'.

redeemer noun **1** a person who redeems someone or something. **2** (**the Redeemer**) Jesus.

redefine verb define something again or differently.
– DERIVATIVES **redefinition** noun.

redemption noun **1** the action of redeeming or the process of being redeemed. **2** a thing that saves someone from error or evil.
– DERIVATIVES **redemptive** adjective.

red ensign noun a red flag with the Union Jack in the top corner next to the flagstaff, flown by British-registered ships.

redeploy verb move troops, employees, or resources to a new place or task.
– DERIVATIVES **redeployment** noun.

redesign verb design something again or differently. •noun the action or process of redesigning.

redevelop verb **1** develop something again or differently. **2** construct new buildings in an area, especially after demolishing the existing buildings.
– DERIVATIVES **redeveloper** noun **redevelopment** noun.

red-faced adjective embarrassed or ashamed.

red flag noun **1** a warning of danger. **2** the symbol of socialist revolution.

red giant noun a very large luminous star with a low surface temperature.

red grouse noun a British moorland grouse with reddish-brown plumage.

red-handed adjective in or just after the act of doing something wrong.

redhead noun a person, especially a woman, with red hair.
– DERIVATIVES **red-headed** adjective.

red heat noun the temperature or state of something so hot that it gives off red light.

red herring noun a clue or piece of information which is misleading or distracting.
– ORIGIN so named from the practice of using the scent of a dried smoked herring in training hounds.

red-hot adjective **1** so hot as to glow red. **2** extremely exciting or of great interest. **3** very passionate.

red-hot poker noun a plant with tall erect spikes of tubular flowers, the upper ones of which are red and the lower ones yellow.

redial verb (**redials, redialling, redialled;** US **redials, redialing, redialed**) dial a telephone number again.

redid past of REDO.

Red Indian noun old-fashioned term for AMERICAN INDIAN.

USAGE: The term **Red Indian** has largely fallen out of use, associated as it is with stereotypes of cowboys and Indians and the Wild West, and may cause offence. The normal terms in use today are **American Indian** and **Native American.**

redingote /red-ing-goht/ noun a woman's long coat with a cutaway or contrasting front.
– ORIGIN French, from English *riding coat*.

redirect verb direct something to a new or different place or purpose.
– DERIVATIVES **redirection** noun.

rediscover verb discover something forgotten or ignored again.
– DERIVATIVES **rediscovery** noun.

redistribute verb distribute something again or in a different way.
– DERIVATIVES **redistribution** noun **redistributive** adjective.

redivivus /re-di-vee-vuhss/ adjective (after a noun) literary having come back to life; reborn.
– ORIGIN Latin, from *re-* 'again' + *vivus* 'living'.

red lead noun a red form of lead oxide used as a pigment.

Red Leicester noun see LEICESTER.

red-letter day noun an important or memorable day.
– ORIGIN from the practice of highlighting a festival in red on a calendar.

red light noun a red light instructing moving vehicles to stop.

red-light district noun an area with many brothels, strip clubs, etc.
– ORIGIN from the use of a red light as the sign of a brothel.

redline verb N. Amer. informal **1** drive with a car's engine at its maximum rpm. **2** refuse a loan or insurance to someone because they live in an area considered to be a bad financial risk.
– ORIGIN from the use of *red* as a limit marker, in sense 2 a limit marked out by ringing part of a map.

red meat noun meat that is red when raw, e.g. beef or lamb.

red mullet noun a food fish with long, thin growths (barbels) on the chin, living in warmer seas.

redneck noun N. Amer. informal, derogatory a working-class white person from the southern US, especially one with politically conservative views.

redo verb (**redoes**, **redoing**; past **redid**; past part. **redone**) do something again or differently.

redolent /red-uh-luhnt/ adjective **1** (**redolent of/with**) strongly suggesting or making one think of something: *names redolent of history and tradition.* **2** (**redolent of/with**) literary strongly smelling of something. **3** old use or literary fragrant.
– DERIVATIVES **redolence** noun.
– ORIGIN from Latin *redolere* 'give out a strong smell'.

redouble verb make or become greater, more intense, or more numerous: *we will redouble our efforts.*

redoubt /ri-dowt/ noun a temporary or additional fortification.
– ORIGIN French *redoute.*

redoubtable adjective often humorous (of a person) worthy of respect or fear, especially as an opponent.
– DERIVATIVES **redoubtably** adverb.
– ORIGIN from Old French *redouter* 'to fear'.

redound /ri-downd/ verb (**redound to**) formal contribute greatly to a person's credit or honour.
– ORIGIN Latin *redundare* 'surge'.

redox /ree-doks, ri-doks/ adjective Chemistry involving the process of both oxidation and reduction.
– ORIGIN blend.

red pepper noun a ripe sweet pepper, red in colour and eaten as a vegetable.

redraft verb draft a document again in a different way.

redraw verb (past **redrew**; past part. **redrawn**) draw or draw up again or in a different way: *strategists will have to redraw their plans.*

redress /ri-dress/ verb put an undesirable or unfair situation right. •noun compensation for a grievance or an unjust act: *redress for victims of discrimination.*
– PHRASES **redress the balance** restore equality in a situation.
– ORIGIN Old French *redresser.*

red rose noun the emblem of Lancashire or the Lancastrians in the Wars of the Roses.

red salmon noun the sockeye salmon.

red setter noun less formal term for IRISH SETTER.

redshank noun a large sandpiper with long red legs.

redskin noun dated or offensive an American Indian.

red snapper noun a reddish edible marine fish.

red squirrel noun a small squirrel with a reddish coat.

redstart noun a small songbird of the thrush family with a reddish tail.
– ORIGIN from RED + START in the former sense 'tail'.

red tape noun time-consuming or complicated official rules and procedures.
– ORIGIN so named because of the red or pink tape used to tie up official documents.

red top noun Brit. a tabloid newspaper.
– ORIGIN from the red background on which the titles of certain British newspapers are printed.

reduce verb **1** make or become smaller or less in amount, degree, or size. **2** (**reduce someone/thing to**) bring someone or something to a particular state or action: *she had been reduced to near poverty.* **3** (**reduce something to**) change something to a simpler or more basic form. **4** boil a sauce or other liquid so that it becomes thicker and more concentrated. **5** Chemistry cause a substance to combine chemically with hydrogen. **6** Chemistry cause a substance to undergo a reaction in which electrons are gained from another substance or molecule. The opposite of OXIDIZE.
– PHRASES **reduced circumstances** a state of poverty after one has been relatively wealthy. **reduce someone to the ranks** demote a non-

commissioned officer to an ordinary soldier.
- DERIVATIVES **reducer** noun **reducible** adjective.
- ORIGIN Latin *reducere* 'bring or lead back'.

reductio ad absurdum /ri-duk-ti-oh ad ab-ser-duhm/ noun a method of proving that an argument or theory is false by showing that its logical consequence is absurd or contradictory.
- ORIGIN Latin, 'reduction to the absurd'.

reduction noun **1** the action of reducing something. **2** the amount by which something is reduced. **3** a smaller copy of a picture or photograph. **4** a thick and concentrated liquid or sauce.

reductionism noun often derogatory the analysis or explanation of something complex in terms of its simplest or most basic elements.
- DERIVATIVES **reductionist** noun & adjective.

reductive adjective **1** tending to present a subject or problem in an oversimplified form. **2** relating to chemical reduction.
- DERIVATIVES **reductively** adverb **reductiveness** noun.

redundant adjective **1** not or no longer needed or useful: *many of the old skills had become redundant.* **2** Brit. (of a person) no longer employed because there is no more work available.
- DERIVATIVES **redundancy** noun (pl. **redundancies**) **redundantly** adverb.
- ORIGIN first meaning 'abundant'; from Latin *redundare* 'surge'.

reduplicate verb repeat or copy something so as to form another of the same kind.
- DERIVATIVES **reduplication** noun.

redux /ree-duks/ adjective (after a noun) revived or restored.
- ORIGIN Latin, from *reducere* 'bring back'.

redwing noun a small thrush of northern Europe, having wings with red undersides.

redwood noun a giant coniferous tree with reddish wood, native to California and Oregon.

re-echo verb echo again or repeatedly.

reed noun **1** a tall, slender-leaved plant with a hollow stem, growing in water or on marshy ground. **2** a piece of thin cane or metal which vibrates in a current of air to produce the sound of various musical instruments, as in the mouthpiece of a clarinet or at the base of some organ pipes. **3** a wind instrument played with a reed.
- DERIVATIVES **reeded** adjective.
- ORIGIN Old English.

re-edit verb edit something again.

reed mace noun a tall reed-like water plant with a dark brown velvety cylindrical flower head.

reed organ noun a keyboard instrument similar to a harmonium, in which air is drawn upwards past metal reeds.

re-educate verb educate or train someone to behave or think differently.
- DERIVATIVES **re-education** noun.

reedy adjective (**reedier**, **reediest**) **1** (of a sound or voice) high and thin in tone. **2** full of or edged with reeds. **3** (of a person) tall and thin.

reef noun **1** a ridge of jagged rock or coral just above or below the surface of the sea. **2** a vein

of gold or other ore. **3** each of several strips across a sail which can be taken in or rolled up to reduce the area exposed to the wind. • verb take in one or more reefs of a sail.
- ORIGIN Old Norse, 'rib'.

reefer noun informal a cannabis cigarette.
- ORIGIN perhaps related to Mexican Spanish *grifo* 'smoker of cannabis'.

reefer jacket noun a thick, close-fitting double-breasted jacket.

reef knot noun chiefly Brit. a type of double knot that holds very securely but can be easily undone.

reek verb **1** have a very unpleasant smell. **2** (**reek of**) suggest something unpleasant or undesirable: *the whole thing reeks of hypocrisy.* • noun a very unpleasant smell.
- ORIGIN Old English.

reel noun **1** a cylinder on which film, wire, thread, etc. can be wound. **2** a part of a film. **3** a lively Scottish or Irish folk dance. • verb **1** (**reel something in**) bring something towards one by turning a reel. **2** (**reel something off**) say or recite something rapidly and with ease. **3** stagger or lurch violently. **4** feel shocked or bewildered: *workers are still reeling at the news that the factory is to close.*
- ORIGIN Old English.

re-elect verb elect someone to a further term of office.
- DERIVATIVES **re-election** noun.

reel-to-reel adjective (of a tape recorder) in which the tape passes between two reels mounted separately rather than within a cassette.

re-emerge verb emerge again; begin to exist or become prominent once more.
- DERIVATIVES **re-emergence** noun **re-emergent** adjective.

re-emphasize (or **re-emphasise**) verb emphasize something again.
- DERIVATIVES **re-emphasis** noun.

re-enact verb **1** act out a past event. **2** bring a law into effect again when the original statute has been repealed or has expired.
- DERIVATIVES **re-enactment** noun.

re-engineer verb **1** redesign a machine. **2** restructure a company or its operations.

re-enter verb enter again: *women who wish to re-enter the labour market.*
- DERIVATIVES **re-entrance** noun.

re-entrant adjective (of an angle) pointing inwards. The opposite of **SALIENT**.

re-entry noun (pl. **re-entries**) **1** the action or process of re-entering. **2** the return of a spacecraft or missile into the earth's atmosphere.

reeve[1] noun historical a local official, in particular the chief magistrate of a town or district in Anglo-Saxon England.
- ORIGIN Old English.

reeve[2] noun a female ruff (bird).
- ORIGIN unknown.

re-examine verb **1** examine something again or further. **2** Law examine one's own witness again, after cross-examination by the opposing counsel.
- DERIVATIVES **re-examination** noun.

r

re-export verb /ree-ik-**sport**/ export imported goods, typically after further processing or manufacture. • noun /**ree**-ek-sport/ the action of re-exporting goods.

ref noun informal (in sports) a referee.

ref. abbreviation **1** reference. **2** refer to.

reface verb put a new facing on a building.

refection noun literary or old use **1** the process of refreshing oneself by eating or drinking. **2** a light meal.
– ORIGIN Latin, from *reficere* 'refresh, renew'.

refectory noun (pl. **refectories**) a large room in an educational or religious institution in which people eat meals together.

refectory table noun a long, narrow table.

refer verb (**refers, referring, referred**) **1** (**refer to**) write or speak about; mention: *her mother never referred to him again.* **2** (**refer someone to**) direct the attention of someone to something. **3** (**refer to**) (of a word or phrase) describe someone or something. **4** (**refer someone/thing to**) pass a person or matter to an authority or specialist for a decision. **5** fail a candidate in an exam.
– DERIVATIVES **referable** adjective **referrer** noun.
– ORIGIN Latin *referre* 'carry back'.

referee noun **1** an official who supervises a game or match to ensure that players keep to the rules. **2** Brit. a person willing to provide a reference for someone applying for a job. **3** a person appointed to examine and assess an academic work submitted for publication. • verb (**referees, refereeing, refereed**) act as referee of something.

reference noun **1** the action of referring to something. **2** a note in book or article giving the source of a particular piece of information. **3** a letter from a previous employer giving information about someone's ability or reliability, used when applying for a new job. • verb **1** provide a book or article with references. **2** mention or refer to someone or something.
– PHRASES **with** (or **in**) **reference to** in relation to.

reference library noun a library in which the books are to be consulted in the building rather than borrowed.

reference point noun a basis or standard for assessment or comparison.

referendum /re-fuh-**ren**-duhm/ noun (pl. **referendums** or **referenda** /re-fuh-ren-duh/) a general vote by a country's electorate on a single political question which has been referred to them for a direct decision.
– ORIGIN Latin, 'something to be referred'.

referent noun Linguistics the thing in the world that a word or phrase refers to or stands for.

referential adjective containing or taking the form of a reference or references.

referral noun the action of referring someone or something to a specialist or higher authority.

referred pain noun pain felt in a part of the body other than its actual source.

refill verb /ree-**fil**/ fill a container again. • noun /**ree**-fil/ an act of refilling a container, or a glass that is refilled.
– DERIVATIVES **refillable** adjective.

refinance verb finance something again, typically with new loans at a lower rate of interest.

refine verb **1** remove impurities or unwanted elements from something. **2** make minor changes to something so as to improve it: *he gradually refined his technique.* **3** (as adj. **refined**) well educated, polite, and having good taste and manners.
– DERIVATIVES **refiner** noun.

refined adjective **1** with impurities or unwanted elements having been removed by processing. **2** elegant and cultured.

refinement noun **1** the process of refining. **2** an improvement brought about by the making of small changes. **3** the quality of being well educated, polite, and having good taste and manners.

refinery noun (pl. **refineries**) an industrial establishment where a substance is refined.

refinish verb apply a new finish to a surface or object.

refit verb (**refits, refitting, refitted**) replace or repair machinery, equipment, and fittings in a ship, building, etc. • noun an act of refitting something.

reflate verb (of a government) increase an economy's level of output.
– DERIVATIVES **reflation** noun **reflationary** noun.

reflect verb **1** throw back heat, light, or sound without absorbing it. **2** (of a mirror or shiny surface) show an image of: *he could see himself reflected in Keith's glasses.* **3** represent in a realistic or appropriate way: *the letters reflect all aspects of his life.* **4** (**reflect well/badly on**) bring about a good or bad impression of someone or something. **5** (**reflect on**) think deeply or carefully about.
– ORIGIN Latin *reflectere* 'bend back'.

reflectance noun Physics a property of a surface equal to the proportion of the light shining on it which it reflects or scatters.

reflecting telescope noun a telescope in which a mirror is used to collect and focus light.

reflection noun **1** the phenomenon of light, heat, sound, etc. being reflected. **2** an image formed by reflection. **3** a consequence or result of something: *healthy skin is a reflection of good health.* **4** a source of shame or blame: *his behaviour was no reflection on his wife.* **5** serious thought or consideration.

reflective adjective **1** providing or produced by reflection. **2** thoughtful.
– DERIVATIVES **reflectively** adverb **reflectivity** noun.

reflector noun **1** a piece of material that reflects light, e.g. a piece of red glass or plastic on the back of a motor vehicle or bicycle. **2** an object or device which reflects radio waves, sound, or other waves. **3** a reflecting telescope.

reflex noun **1** an action or movement performed without conscious thought as a response to something. **2** a thing that reproduces the essential features or qualities of something else: *politics was no more than a reflex of economics.* • adjective **1** performed as a reflex. **2** (of an angle) more than 180°.
– ORIGIN Latin *reflexus* 'a bending back'.

r

reflex camera noun a camera with a focusing screen on which the image given by the lens is reflected by an angled mirror, so that the scene viewed is the same as that photographed.

reflexion noun old-fashioned spelling of REFLECTION.

reflexive adjective **1** Grammar (of a pronoun) referring back to the subject of the clause in which it is used, e.g. *myself*. **2** Grammar (of a verb or clause) having a reflexive pronoun as its object (e.g. *wash oneself*). **3** performed without conscious thought; reflex.
– DERIVATIVES **reflexively** adverb **reflexivity** noun.

reflexology noun a system of massage used to relieve tension and treat illness, based on the theory that there are points on the feet, hands, and head linked to every part of the body.
– DERIVATIVES **reflexologist** noun.

reflux /ree-fluks/ noun **1** technical the flowing back of a liquid, especially that of a fluid in the body. **2** Chemistry the process of boiling a liquid so that any vapour is liquefied and returned to the stock of liquid.

refocus verb (**refocuses, refocusing** or **refocussing, refocused** or **refocussed**) **1** adjust the focus of a lens or one's eyes. **2** focus attention or resources on something new or different.

reforestation noun the process of planting new trees in an area of land that was formerly a forest.
– DERIVATIVES **reforest** verb.

reform verb **1** make changes in something in order to improve it: *a copyright law that needs to be reformed*. **2** abandon an immoral or criminal lifestyle, or make someone do this. •noun the action or process of reforming something: *a major reform of the tax system*.
– DERIVATIVES **reformer** noun.
– ORIGIN Latin *reformare* 'form or shape again'.

re-form verb form or cause to form again.
– DERIVATIVES **re-formation** noun.

reformat verb (**reformats, reformatting, reformatted**) chiefly Computing give a new format to something.

reformation noun **1** the action or process of reforming. **2** (**the Reformation**) a 16th-century movement for the reform of the Roman Catholic Church, ending in the establishment of the Reformed and Protestant Churches.

reformatory noun (pl. **reformatories**) N. Amer. dated an institution to which young offenders are sent as an alternative to prison.

Reformed Church noun a Church that has accepted the principles of the Reformation, especially a Calvinist Church (as distinct from a Lutheran one).

reformist adjective supporting or recommending gradual political or social reform. •noun a person who supports or recommends such a policy.
– DERIVATIVES **reformism** noun.

reform school noun historical an institution to which young offenders were sent as an alternative to prison.

reformulate verb formulate something again or differently.

– DERIVATIVES **reformulation** noun.

refract verb (of water, air, or glass) make a ray of light change direction when it enters at an angle.
– ORIGIN Latin *refringere* 'break up'.

refracting telescope noun a telescope which uses a lens to collect and focus the light.

refraction noun the fact or phenomenon of light changing direction when it enters water, air, or glass at an angle.

refractive adjective relating to or involving refraction.
– DERIVATIVES **refractively** adverb.

refractive index noun the ratio of the velocity of light in a vacuum to its velocity in a specified medium.

refractor noun **1** a lens or other object which causes refraction. **2** a refracting telescope.

refractory adjective **1** formal stubborn or difficult to control. **2** (of a disease or medical condition) not responding to treatment. **3** technical heat-resistant; hard to melt or fuse.
– DERIVATIVES **refractoriness** noun.
– ORIGIN Latin *refractarius* 'stubborn'.

refrain[1] verb (**refrain from**) stop oneself from doing something.
– ORIGIN Latin *refrenare*, from *frenum* 'bridle'.

refrain[2] noun a repeated line or section in a poem or song, typically at the end of each verse.
– ORIGIN from Latin *refringere* 'break up' (because the refrain 'broke' the sequence).

refresh verb **1** give new strength or energy to someone. **2** revise or update skills, knowledge, or information. **3** prompt someone's memory by going over previous information.

refresher adjective (of a course or activity) intended to update or improve one's skills or knowledge.

refreshing adjective **1** giving new energy or strength. **2** welcome because new or different: *a refreshing change of pace*.
– DERIVATIVES **refreshingly** adverb.

refreshment noun **1** a light snack or drink. **2** the giving of fresh strength or energy.

refrigerant noun a substance used for cooling things. •adjective causing cooling or refrigeration.

refrigerate verb chill food or drink in order to preserve it.
– DERIVATIVES **refrigeration** noun.
– ORIGIN Latin *refrigerare* 'make cool'.

refrigerator noun an appliance or compartment in which food and drink is stored at a low temperature.

refuel verb (**refuels, refuelling, refuelled**; US **refuels, refueling, refueled**) supply or be supplied with more fuel.

refuge noun **1** a place or state of safety from danger or trouble: *he took refuge in the French embassy*. **2** a place that provides a temporary home for those in need of protection or shelter.
– ORIGIN Latin *refugium*.

refugee noun a person who has been forced to leave their country in order to escape war, persecution, or natural disaster.

refulgent /ri-ful-juhnt/ adjective literary shining very brightly.

- DERIVATIVES **refulgence** noun **refulgently** adverb.
- ORIGIN from Latin *refulgere* 'shine out'.

refund verb /ri-**fund**/ pay a sum of money back to someone. • noun /**ree**-fund/ a repayment of a sum of money.
- DERIVATIVES **refundable** adjective.
- ORIGIN Latin *refundere* 'pour back'.

refurbish verb renovate and redecorate a building or room.
- DERIVATIVES **refurbishment** noun.

refusal noun **1** an act of refusing to do something. **2** an expression of unwillingness to accept or grant an offer or request.

refuse[1] /ri-**fyooz**/ verb **1** state that one is unwilling to do something. **2** state that one is unwilling to grant or accept something offered or requested. **3** (of a horse) be unwilling to jump a fence or other obstacle.
- DERIVATIVES **refuser** noun.
- ORIGIN Old French *refuser*.

refuse[2] /**ref**-yooss/ noun matter thrown away as worthless.
- ORIGIN perhaps from Old French *refusé* 'refused'.

refusenik /ri-**fyooz**-nik/ noun **1** a Jew in the former Soviet Union who was refused permission to emigrate to Israel. **2** a person who refuses to follow orders or obey the law as a protest.

refute /ri-**fyoot**/ verb **1** prove a statement, theory, or person to be wrong. **2** deny a statement or accusation.
- DERIVATIVES **refutable** adjective **refutation** noun.
- ORIGIN Latin *refutare* 'repel, rebut'.

USAGE: Strictly speaking, **refute** means 'prove a statement or theory to be wrong' (*attempts to refute Einstein's theory*). However, it is often now used to mean simply 'deny a statement or accusation' (*I absolutely refute the charges made against me*): although some people object to this use, it is widely accepted in standard English.

regain verb **1** get something back after losing control or possession of it. **2** get back to a place or position.

regal adjective relating to or fit for a monarch, especially in being magnificent or dignified.
- DERIVATIVES **regally** adverb.
- ORIGIN Latin *regalis*.

regale verb **1** entertain someone with conversation. **2** supply someone with generous amounts of food or drink.
- ORIGIN French *régaler*.

regalia /ri-**gay**-li-uh/ plural noun (treated as sing. or pl.) **1** objects such as the crown and sceptre, symbolizing royalty and used at coronations or other state occasions. **2** the distinctive clothing and objects of an office, activity, or group, worn at formal occasions: *full fox-hunting regalia*.
- ORIGIN Latin, 'royal privileges'.

regality noun (pl. **regalities**) **1** the state of being a monarch. **2** the dignified behaviour appropriate to a monarch.

regard verb **1** think of in a particular way: *he regarded London as his base.* **2** look at someone or something in a particular way. **3** old use pay attention to someone or something. • noun **1** care or concern: *she rescued him without regard for herself.* **2** high opinion; respect. **3** a steady look. **4** (**regards**) best wishes.
- PHRASES **as regards** concerning. **in this** (or **that**) **regard** in connection with the point previously mentioned. **with** (or **in**) **regard to** as concerns.
- ORIGIN Old French *regarder* 'to watch'.

regarding preposition about; concerning.

regardless adverb despite the current situation: *they were determined to carry on regardless.*
- PHRASES **regardless of** without care or concern for.

regatta noun a sporting event consisting of a series of boat or yacht races.
- ORIGIN Italian, 'a fight or contest'.

regency /**ree**-juhn-si/ noun (pl. **regencies**) **1** the office or period of government by a regent. **2** (**the Regency**) the period when George, Prince of Wales, acted as regent in Britain (1811–20). • adjective (**Regency**) relating to the neoclassical style of British architecture and furniture popular during the late 18th and early 19th centuries.

regenerate verb /ri-**jen**-uh-rayt/ **1** bring new and more vigorous life to an area, industry, or institution. **2** grow new tissue. • adjective /ri-**jen**-er-uht/ reborn, especially in a spiritual sense.
- DERIVATIVES **regeneration** noun **regenerative** adjective **regenerator** noun.

regent noun a person appointed to rule a state because the monarch is too young or unfit to rule, or is absent. • adjective (after a noun) acting as regent: *Prince Regent.*
- ORIGIN from Latin *regere* 'to rule'.

reggae /**reg**-gay/ noun a style of popular music with a strong beat, originating in Jamaica.
- ORIGIN perhaps from Jamaican English *regerege* 'quarrel, row'.

regicide /**rej**-i-syd/ noun **1** the killing of a king. **2** a person who kills a king.
- DERIVATIVES **regicidal** adjective.
- ORIGIN from Latin *rex* 'king'.

regime /ray-**zheem**/ noun **1** a government, especially one that strictly controls a state. **2** an ordered way of doing something; a system: *our approach is to simplify the licensing regime.* **3** a course of diet, exercise, or medical treatment; a regimen.
- ORIGIN French.

regimen /**rej**-i-muhn/ noun a course of diet, exercise, or medical treatment that is followed to improve one's health.
- ORIGIN Latin.

regiment noun /**rej**-i-muhnt/ **1** a permanent unit of an army, typically divided into several smaller units. **2** a large number of people or things. • verb /**rej**-i-ment/ organize according to a strict system: *every aspect of their life is strictly regimented.*
- DERIVATIVES **regimentation** noun.
- ORIGIN Latin *regimentum* 'rule'.

regimental adjective relating to an army regiment. • noun (**regimentals**) military uniform, especially that of a particular regiment.
- DERIVATIVES **regimentally** adverb.

Regina /ri-**jy**-nuh/ noun the reigning queen

r

(used following a name or in the titles of lawsuits, e.g. *Regina v. Jones*, the Crown versus Jones).

– ORIGIN Latin, 'queen'.

region noun 1 an area of a country or the world having particular characteristics: *the equatorial regions.* 2 an administrative district of a city or country. 3 (**the regions**) the parts of a country outside the capital or centre of government. 4 a part of the body.

– PHRASES **in the region of** approximately.

– ORIGIN Latin, 'direction, district'.

regional adjective 1 relating to or typical of a region. 2 Brit. relating to the regions of a country rather than the capital: *a regional accent.*

– DERIVATIVES **regionalize** (or **regionalise**) verb **regionally** adverb.

regionalism noun 1 loyalty to one's own region in cultural and political terms, rather than to central government. 2 a feature of language specific to a particular region.

– DERIVATIVES **regionalist** noun & adjective.

register noun 1 an official list or record. 2 a record of attendance, for example of pupils in a class. 3 the level and style of a piece of writing or speech, varying according to the situation in which it is used. 4 a particular part of the range of a voice or musical instrument: *boy trebles singing in a high register.* 5 a sliding device controlling a set of organ pipes, or a set of organ pipes controlled by such a device. 6 (in electronic devices) a location in a store of data. •verb 1 enter someone or something in a register. 2 put one's name on an official list. 3 officially report one's arrival as a guest at a hotel or a departing passenger at an airport. 4 express an opinion or emotion. 5 (of an emotion) show in a person's face or gestures. 6 become aware of: *he had not even registered her presence.* 7 (of an instrument) detect and show a reading automatically.

– DERIVATIVES **registrable** adjective.

– ORIGIN Latin *registrum.*

registered post noun Brit. a postal service in which the sender can claim compensation if the item sent is damaged, late, or lost.

register office noun (in the UK) a local government building where civil marriages are conducted and births, marriages, and deaths are recorded.

registrant noun a person who registers for something.

registrar /rej-i-strar, rej-i-**strar**/ noun 1 an official responsible for keeping official records. 2 the chief administrative officer in a university. 3 Brit. a middle-ranking hospital doctor undergoing training as a specialist. 4 (in the UK) the judicial and administrative officer of the High Court.

registration noun 1 the action of registering or recording someone or something. 2 (also **registration mark** or **registration number**) Brit. the series of letters and figures identifying a motor vehicle, displayed on a number plate.

registration document (also **vehicle registration document**) noun (in the UK) a document giving registered information about a vehicle, such as the owner's name and the date of its manufacture.

registry noun (pl. **registries**) 1 a place where official records are kept. 2 the registration of someone or something.

registry office noun (in informal and non-official use) a register office.

Regius professor /ree-juhss/ noun (in the UK) the holder of a university chair founded by a sovereign or filled by Crown appointment.

– ORIGIN from Latin *regius* 'royal'.

regnant /reg-nuhnt/ adjective 1 reigning; ruling. 2 formal currently having the greatest influence; dominant.

– ORIGIN from Latin *regnare* 'to reign'.

regrade verb grade someone or something again or differently.

regress verb /ri-gress/ 1 return to a former or less advanced state. 2 return mentally to a former stage of life or a supposed previous life. •noun /ri-gress/ a return to a former or less advanced state.

– ORIGIN Latin *regredi* 'go back, return'.

regression noun 1 a return to a former or less advanced state. 2 the action of returning mentally to an earlier stage of life or a supposed previous life.

regressive adjective 1 returning to a former or less advanced state. 2 (of a tax) taking a proportionally greater amount from people on lower incomes.

– DERIVATIVES **regressively** adverb **regressiveness** noun.

regret verb (**regrets, regretting, regretted**) feel or express sorrow or disappointment about something one has done or which one should have done. •noun 1 a feeling of such sorrow or disappointment: *she expressed her regret at Ann's death.* 2 (often **one's regrets**) used in polite expressions of apology or sadness.

– ORIGIN Old French *regreter* 'lament the dead'.

regretful adjective feeling or showing regret.

– DERIVATIVES **regretfulness** noun.

regretfully adverb 1 in a regretful way. 2 it is regrettable or undesirable that.

USAGE: The main sense of **regretfully** is 'in a regretful way' (*he sighed regretfully*). However, it is now also used to mean 'it is regrettable or undesirable that' (*regretfully, mounting costs forced the branch to close*), although some people object to this use.

regrettable adjective giving rise to regret; undesirable.

– DERIVATIVES **regrettably** adverb.

regroup verb gather into organized groups again, typically after being attacked or defeated.

– DERIVATIVES **regroupment** noun.

regrow verb (past **regrew**; past part. **regrown**) grow or cause to grow again.

– DERIVATIVES **regrowth** noun.

regular adjective 1 following or arranged in a pattern, especially with the same space between one thing and the next: *the association holds regular meetings.* 2 doing the same thing often: *regular worshippers.* 3 done or happening frequently. 4 following or controlled by an accepted standard: *the buying and selling of shares through regular channels.* 5 usual or customary. 6 Grammar (of a word)

r

following the normal pattern of inflection.
7 (of food or clothing) of average size.
8 belonging to the permanent professional
armed forces of a country. **9** chiefly N. Amer. of an
ordinary kind. **10** (of a geometrical figure)
having all sides and all angles equal. **11** (of a
member of the Christian clergy) belonging to
a religious or monastic order. **12** informal, dated
rightly so called; absolute: *this place is a regular
fisherman's paradise.* ●noun a regular customer,
member of a team, etc.
– DERIVATIVES **regularity** noun (pl. **regularities**)
regularly adverb.
– ORIGIN Latin *regularis*.

regular canon noun see CANON².

regularize (or **regularise**) verb **1** make
something regular. **2** place a temporary or
provisional arrangement on an official or
correct basis.
– DERIVATIVES **regularization** noun.

regulate verb **1** control or maintain the rate or
speed of a machine or process. **2** control
something, especially a business activity, by
means of rules.
– DERIVATIVES **regulative** adjective **regulator** noun
regulatory adjective.

regulation noun **1** a rule or order made and
enforced by an authority. **2** the action of
regulating something. ●adjective informal in
accordance with expectations or conventions:
regulation blonde hair.

regulo /reg-yuu-loh/ noun Brit. trademark used
before a number to indicate a temperature
setting in a gas oven.

regurgitate /ri-ger-ji-tayt/ verb **1** bring
swallowed food up again to the mouth.
2 repeat information without analysing or
understanding it.
– DERIVATIVES **regurgitation** noun.
– ORIGIN Latin *regurgitare.*

rehabilitate verb **1** prepare someone who has
been ill, in prison, or addicted to drugs to
resume normal life by training and therapy.
2 restore someone to their former status or
reputation after being out of favour. **3** restore
something to a former condition.
– DERIVATIVES **rehabilitation** noun **rehabilitative**
adjective.
– ORIGIN Latin *rehabilitare.*

rehash verb reuse old ideas or material without
significant change or improvement. ●noun a
reuse of old ideas or material.

rehearsal noun **1** a trial performance of a play
or other work for later public performance.
2 the action of rehearsing.

rehearse verb **1** practise a play, piece of music,
or other work for later public performance.
2 state a list of points that have been made
many times before.
– ORIGIN Old French *rehercier* 'repeat aloud'.

reheat verb heat something again.

rehouse verb provide someone with new
housing.

rehydrate verb absorb or cause to absorb
moisture after dehydration.
– DERIVATIVES **rehydration** noun.

reify /ree-i-fl, ray-i-fl/ verb (**reifies**, **reifying**,
reified) formal make something abstract more
real or physical.
– DERIVATIVES **reification** noun.

– ORIGIN from Latin *res* 'thing'.

reign verb **1** rule as monarch. **2** be the dominant
quality or aspect: *while the company remains
silent, confusion reigns supreme.* **3** (as adj.
reigning) (of a sports player or team)
currently holding a particular title. ●noun **1** the
period of rule of a monarch. **2** the period
during which someone or something is best or
most important.
– ORIGIN Old French *reignier.*

USAGE: On the confusion of **reign** and **rein**,
see the note at REIN.

reiki /ray-ki/ noun a healing technique based on
the belief that the therapist can channel
energy into the patient by means of touch, to
activate the natural healing processes of the
patient's body.
– ORIGIN Japanese, 'universal life energy'.

reimburse /ree-im-berss/ verb repay money to
a person who has spent or lost it.
– DERIVATIVES **reimbursable** adjective
reimbursement noun.
– ORIGIN Latin *imbursare* 'put in a purse'.

rein noun **1** a long, narrow strap attached at one
end to a horse's bit, used in pairs to control a
horse. **2** (**reins**) the power to direct and
control: *a new manager will soon take over the
reins.* ●verb **1** control a horse by pulling on its
reins. **2** keep under control; restrain: *he has
failed to rein in his own security forces.*
– PHRASES (**a**) **free rein** freedom of action. **keep
a tight rein on** exercise strict control over.
– ORIGIN Old French *rene.*

USAGE: The phrase **a free rein**, which comes
from the meaning of allowing a horse to move
freely without being controlled by reins, is
often misinterpreted and wrongly spelled as *a
free reign.*

reincarnate /ree-in-kar-nayt/ verb cause
someone to be born again in another body.

reincarnation noun **1** the rebirth of a soul in a
new body. **2** a person in whom a soul is
believed to have been reborn.

reindeer noun (pl. same or **reindeers**) a deer
with large branching antlers, native to the
northern tundra and subarctic regions.
– ORIGIN Old Norse.

reinfect verb infect someone or something
again.
– DERIVATIVES **reinfection** noun.

reinforce verb **1** strengthen or support an
object. **2** strengthen or intensify a feeling,
idea, etc. **3** strengthen a military force with
additional personnel or equipment.
– DERIVATIVES **reinforcer** noun.
– ORIGIN French *renforcer.*

reinforced concrete noun concrete in which
metal bars or wire are embedded to
strengthen it.

reinforcement noun **1** the action of
reinforcing something. **2** (**reinforcements**)
extra personnel sent to strengthen an army or
similar force.

reinstate verb restore someone or something
to a former position or state.
– DERIVATIVES **reinstatement** noun.

reinsure verb (of an insurer) transfer all or
part of a risk to another insurer to provide

protection against the risk of the first insurance.
– DERIVATIVES **reinsurance** noun **reinsurer** noun.

reintegrate verb **1** restore distinct elements into a whole. **2** integrate someone back into society.
– DERIVATIVES **reintegration** noun.

reinterpret verb (**reinterprets, reinterpreting, reinterpreted**) interpret something in a new or different light.
– DERIVATIVES **reinterpretation** noun.

reintroduce verb **1** bring something into effect again. **2** put a species of animal or plant back into a place where it once lived.
– DERIVATIVES **reintroduction** noun.

reinvent verb change something so much that it appears entirely new.
– PHRASES **reinvent the wheel** waste a great deal of time or effort in creating something that already exists.
– DERIVATIVES **reinvention** noun.

reinvest verb put the profit on a previous investment back into the same scheme.
– DERIVATIVES **reinvestment** noun.

reinvigorate verb give new energy or strength to someone or something.
– DERIVATIVES **reinvigoration** noun.

reissue verb (**reissues, reissuing, reissued**) make a new supply or different form of a book, record, or other product available for sale. •noun a new issue of a product.

reiterate verb say something again or repeatedly.
– DERIVATIVES **reiteration** noun.
– ORIGIN Latin *reiterare* 'go over again'.

reject verb /ri-**jekt**/ **1** dismiss as unsatisfactory or faulty: *union negotiators rejected a 1.5 per cent pay award.* **2** refuse to consider or agree to something. **3** fail to show proper affection or concern for someone. **4** (of the body) show a damaging immune response to a transplanted organ or tissue. •noun /**ree**-jekt/ a rejected person or thing.
– DERIVATIVES **rejection** noun.
– ORIGIN Latin *reicere* 'throw back'.

rejig verb (**rejigs, rejigging, rejigged**) Brit. rearrange something.

rejoice verb feel or show great joy.
– ORIGIN Old French *rejoir*.

rejoin[1] verb **1** join things together again. **2** return to a companion, organization, or route that one has left.

rejoin[2] verb say something in reply; retort.
– ORIGIN Old French *rejoindre*.

rejoinder noun a sharp or witty reply.

rejuvenate /ri-**joo**-vuh-nayt/ verb make someone or something appear younger, better, or more lively.
– DERIVATIVES **rejuvenation** noun **rejuvenator** noun.
– ORIGIN from Latin *juvenis* 'young'.

rekindle verb **1** revive a past feeling, relationship, or interest. **2** relight a fire.

relaid past and past participle of **RELAY**[2].

relapse verb /ri-**laps**/ **1** (of a sick or injured person) become ill again after a period of improvement. **2** (**relapse into**) return to a worse or less active state. •noun /**ree**-laps/ a return to poor health after a temporary

improvement.
– ORIGIN Latin *relabi* 'slip back'.

relate verb **1** make or show a connection between: *many drowning accidents are related to alcohol use.* **2** (**be related**) be connected by blood or marriage. **3** (**relate to**) have to do with; concern. **4** (**relate to**) feel sympathy for. **5** give an account of something.
– DERIVATIVES **relater** (also **relator**) noun.
– ORIGIN Latin *referre* 'bring back'.

related adjective belonging to the same family, group, or type; connected.
– DERIVATIVES **relatedness** noun.

relation noun **1** the way in which two or more people or things are connected or related. **2** (**relations**) the way in which two or more people or groups feel about and behave towards each other: *the meetings helped cement Anglo-American relations.* **3** a relative by blood or marriage. **4** (**relations**) formal sex or a sexual relationship. **5** the action of telling a story.
– PHRASES **in relation to** in connection with.
– DERIVATIVES **relational** adjective.

relationship noun **1** the way in which two or more people or things are connected, or the state of being connected: *the relationship between art and architecture.* **2** the way in which two or more people or groups feel about and behave towards each other. **3** a loving and sexual association between two people.

relative /**rel**-uh-tiv/ adjective **1** considered in relation or in proportion to something else. **2** existing only in comparison to something else: *months of relative calm ended in April.* **3** Grammar (of a pronoun, determiner, or adverb) referring to an earlier noun, sentence, or clause (e.g. *which* in *a conference in Paris which ended on Friday*). **4** Grammar (of a clause) connected to a main clause by a relative pronoun, determiner, or adverb. •noun **1** a person connected by blood or marriage. **2** a species related to another.
– PHRASES **relative to 1** compared with or in relation to. **2** about; concerning.

relative atomic mass noun the ratio of the average mass of one atom of an element to one twelfth of the mass of an atom of carbon-12.

relatively adverb in relation, comparison, or proportion to something else: *the room was relatively clean.*

relative molecular mass noun the ratio of the average mass of one molecule of an element or compound to one twelfth of the mass of an atom of carbon-12.

relativism noun the belief that knowledge, truth, and morality exist in relation to culture, society, or historical context, and are not always the same.
– DERIVATIVES **relativist** noun.

relativity noun **1** the state of being relative in comparison to something else. **2** Physics a description of matter, energy, space, and time according to Einstein's theories based on the importance of relative motion and the principle that the speed of light is constant for all observers.

relativize (or **relativise**) verb make or treat something as relative to or dependent on something else.

r

– DERIVATIVES **relativization** noun.

relaunch verb launch a product again or in a different form. ● noun an instance of relaunching a product.

relax verb **1** make or become less tense, anxious, or rigid. **2** rest from work or engage in a leisure activity. **3** make a rule or restriction less strict.
– ORIGIN Latin *relaxare*.

relaxant noun a drug that causes relaxation or reduces tension. ● adjective causing relaxation.

relaxation noun **1** the state of being free from tension and worry. **2** the action of making something less strict.

relay[1] /ree-lay/ noun **1** a group of people or animals performing a task for a period of time and then replaced by a similar group. **2** a race between teams of runners, each team member in turn covering part of the total distance. **3** an electrical device which opens or closes a circuit in response to a current in another circuit. **4** a device to receive, reinforce, and transmit a signal again. ● verb /also ri-**lay**/ **1** receive and pass on information or a message. **2** broadcast something by means of a relay.
– ORIGIN Old French *relayer*.

relay[2] /ree-lay/ verb (past and past part. **relaid**) lay something again or differently.

release verb **1** set someone free from imprisonment or confinement. **2** free someone from a duty. **3** allow to move freely: *she released his arm and pushed him aside.* **4** allow information to be generally available. **5** make a film or recording available to the public. **6** make property, money, or a right available to someone else. ● noun **1** the action of releasing or freeing someone or something. **2** a film or recording released to the public. **3** a handle or catch that releases part of a mechanism.
– DERIVATIVES **releasable** adjective **releaser** noun.
– ORIGIN Old French *relesser*.

relegate verb **1** place someone or something in a less important rank or position. **2** Brit. transfer a sports team to a lower division of a league.
– DERIVATIVES **relegation** noun.
– ORIGIN Latin *relegare* 'send away'.

relent verb **1** finally agree to something after first refusing it. **2** become less severe or intense.
– ORIGIN from Latin *re-* 'back' + *lentare* 'to bend'.

relentless adjective **1** never stopping or becoming weaker: *the relentless pursuit of wealth.* **2** refusing to give up; determined or strict.
– DERIVATIVES **relentlessly** adverb **relentlessness** noun.

relevant adjective closely connected or appropriate to the current matter.
– DERIVATIVES **relevance** noun **relevancy** noun **relevantly** adverb.
– ORIGIN from Latin *relevare* 'raise up'.

reliable adjective able to be depended on or trusted.
– DERIVATIVES **reliability** noun **reliably** adverb.

reliance noun dependence on or trust in someone or something.
– DERIVATIVES **reliant** adjective.

relic noun **1** an interesting object that has survived from the past. **2** a person or thing that has survived from the past but is now outdated. **3** a part of a holy person's body or belongings kept and treated as holy after their death.
– ORIGIN from Latin *reliquiae* 'remains'.

relict /rel-ikt/ noun **1** an organism or other thing which has survived from an earlier period. **2** old use a widow.
– ORIGIN from Latin *relictus* 'left behind'.

relief noun **1** a feeling of reassurance and relaxation following release from anxiety or distress: *the mixed US economic data was greeted with relief.* **2** a cause of relief. **3** the action of removing or reducing pain, distress, or discomfort. **4** (usu. **light relief**) a temporary break in a tense or boring situation. **5** financial or practical assistance given to those in need or difficulty: *famine relief.* **6** a person or group replacing others who have been on duty. **7** the action of lifting a siege on a town. **8** the quality of being more noticeable than surrounding objects: *the sun threw the peaks into relief.* **9** a way of cutting a design into wood, stone, etc. so that parts of it stand out from the surface.
– ORIGIN from Latin *relevare* 'raise again, alleviate'.

relief map noun a map that shows hills and valleys by shading rather than by contour lines alone.

relief road noun Brit. a road taking traffic around a congested urban area.

relieve verb **1** reduce or remove pain, distress, or difficulty. **2** cause someone to stop feeling distressed or anxious. **3** take over from someone who is on duty. **4** (**relieve someone of**) take a responsibility from someone. **5** make less boring or monotonous: *the bird's body is black, relieved only by white under the tail.* **6** bring military support for a besieged place. **7** (**relieve oneself**) formal or euphemistic urinate or defecate.
– DERIVATIVES **reliever** noun.
– ORIGIN Old French *relever*.

relight verb (past and past part. **relighted** or **relit**) light something again.

religion noun **1** the belief in and worship of a God or gods. **2** a particular system of faith and worship. **3** a pursuit or interest that is very important to someone.
– ORIGIN Latin *religio* 'obligation, reverence'.

religiosity /ri-lij-i-oss-i-ti/ noun the state of being excessively religious.
– DERIVATIVES **religiose** adjective.

religious adjective **1** relating to or believing in a religion. **2** treated as very important or done with great care: *a boy with an almost religious devotion to fishing.* ● noun (pl. same) a monk or nun.
– DERIVATIVES **religiously** adverb **religiousness** noun.

relinquish verb willingly give something up.
– DERIVATIVES **relinquishment** noun.
– ORIGIN Latin *relinquere*.

reliquary /rel-i-kwuh-ri/ noun (pl. **reliquaries**) a container for holy relics.

relish noun **1** great enjoyment. **2** a pleasant feeling of looking forward to something: *he*

r

was waiting with relish for her promised visit. **3** a tangy or spicy sauce or pickle. • verb **1** enjoy something greatly. **2** look forward to something with pleasure.
– ORIGIN Old French *reles* 'remainder'.

relive verb live through an experience or feeling again in one's imagination.

reload verb load something, especially a gun again.

relocate verb move to a new place and establish one's home or business there.
– DERIVATIVES **relocation** noun.

reluctance noun unwillingness to do something.

reluctant adjective unwilling and hesitant.
– DERIVATIVES **reluctantly** adverb.
– ORIGIN from Latin *reluctari* 'struggle against'.

rely verb (**relies, relying, relied**) (**rely on**) **1** have complete trust or confidence in someone or something. **2** be dependent on: *the charity has to rely on public donations.*
– ORIGIN Old French *relier* 'bind together'.

REM abbreviation rapid eye movement, referring to a kind of sleep that occurs at intervals during the night and is characterized by rapid eye movement and more dreaming.

remade past and past participle of REMAKE.

remain verb **1** stay in the same place or condition during further time. **2** continue to have a particular quality or fill a particular role. **3** be left over or outstanding after others or other parts have been dealt with or used: *a more difficult problem remains.*
– ORIGIN Latin *remanere*.

remainder noun **1** a part, number, or quantity that is left over. **2** a part that is still to come: *the remainder of the year.* **3** the number which is left over when one quantity does not exactly divide another. **4** a copy of a book left unsold when demand has fallen. • verb put an unsold book on sale at a reduced price.

remains plural noun **1** things remaining. **2** historical or archaeological relics. **3** a person's body after death.

remake verb /ree-**mayk**/ (past and past part. **remade**) make something again or differently. • noun /**ree**-mayk/ a film or piece of music that has been filmed or recorded again and re-released.

remand Law verb place a person charged with a crime on bail or in custody to await their trial. • noun the process of remanding someone to await trial.
– ORIGIN Latin *remandare* 'commit again'.

remark verb **1** say something as a comment; mention something. **2** notice someone or something. • noun **1** a comment. **2** the fact of being noticed or commented on: *the landscape was not worthy of remark.*
– ORIGIN French *remarquer* 'note again'.

remarkable adjective worthy of attention; extraordinary or striking.
– DERIVATIVES **remarkably** adverb.

remarry verb (**remarries, remarrying, remarried**) marry again.
– DERIVATIVES **remarriage** noun.

remaster verb make a new or improved master of a sound recording.

rematch noun a second match or game

between two sports teams or players.

remedial /ri-**mee**-di-uhl/ adjective **1** intended to set right or cure something: *an obligation to take remedial action in case animals are suffering.* **2** provided or intended for children with learning difficulties.

remediation /ri-mee-di-ay-sh'n/ noun **1** the action of setting something right, in particular environmental damage. **2** the giving of remedial teaching or therapy to children with learning difficulties.
– DERIVATIVES **remediate** verb.

remedy noun (pl. **remedies**) **1** a medicine or treatment for a disease or injury. **2** a way of setting right or improving an undesirable situation. **3** a means of gaining legal amends for a wrong. • verb (**remedies, remedying, remedied**) set right an undesirable situation.
– DERIVATIVES **remediable** adjective.
– ORIGIN Latin *remedium.*

remember verb **1** have in or bring to one's mind someone or something from the past. **2** keep something necessary in mind: *remember to post the letters.* **3** bear someone in mind by making them a gift or by mentioning them in prayer: *he remembered the boy in his will.* **4** (**remember someone to**) pass on greetings from one person to another.
– ORIGIN Latin *rememorari* 'call to mind'.

remembrance noun **1** the action of remembering. **2** a memory. **3** a thing kept or given as a reminder of someone.

Remembrance Sunday (also **Remembrance Day**) noun (in the UK) the Sunday nearest 11 November, when those who were killed in the First and Second World Wars and later conflicts are commemorated.

remind verb **1** cause someone to remember something. **2** (**remind someone of**) cause someone to think of someone or something because they are similar in some way.

reminder noun **1** a thing that causes someone to remember something. **2** a letter sent to remind someone to pay a bill.

reminisce /re-mi-**niss**/ verb think or talk contentedly about the past.

reminiscence /re-mi-**niss**-uhnss/ noun **1** a story told by a person about a past event that they remember. **2** the enjoyable recollection of past events.
– ORIGIN from Latin *reminisci* 'remember'.

reminiscent adjective **1** tending to remind one of someone or something; similar: *the leaves have a fresh taste reminiscent of cucumber.* **2** with one's mind full of memories.
– DERIVATIVES **reminiscently** adverb.

remiss /ri-**miss**/ adjective lacking care or attention to duty.
– ORIGIN from Latin *remittere* 'slacken'.

remission noun **1** the cancellation of a debt, charge, or penalty. **2** Brit. the reduction of a prison sentence, especially as a reward for good behaviour. **3** a temporary period during which a serious illness becomes less severe. **4** formal forgiveness of sins.

remit noun /**ree**-mit/ chiefly Brit. the area of activity that a person or organization controls or is officially responsible for: *food labelling falls within the remit of the Food Standards Agency.* • verb /ri-**mit**/ (**remits, remitting,**

remitted) **1** send money in payment. **2** cancel a debt or punishment. **3** refer a matter for decision to an authority. **4** forgive a sin.
– ORIGIN Latin *remittere* 'send back, restore'.

remittance noun **1** a sum of money sent in payment. **2** the action of sending payment.

remix verb /ree-**miks**/ **1** mix something again. **2** produce a different version of a musical recording by altering the balance of the separate tracks. •noun /**ree**-miks/ a remixed musical recording.
– DERIVATIVES **remixer** noun.

remnant noun **1** a small remaining part or quantity. **2** a piece of cloth left when the greater part has been used or sold.
– ORIGIN Old French *remenant*.

remodel verb (**remodels, remodelling, remodelled**; US **remodels, remodeling, remodeled**) **1** change the structure or form of something. **2** shape an object again or differently.

remold verb US spelling of **REMOULD**.

remonstrance /ri-**mon**-struhnss/ noun a strongly critical protest.

remonstrate /**rem**-uhn-strayt/ verb make a strongly critical protest.
– DERIVATIVES **remonstration** noun.
– ORIGIN Latin *remonstrare* 'demonstrate'.

remora /**rem**-uh-ruh/ noun a slender sea fish which attaches itself to large fish by means of a sucker on top of the head.
– ORIGIN Latin, 'hindrance' (because of the former belief that the fish slowed down ships).

remorse noun deep regret or guilt for a wrong that one has done.
– ORIGIN Latin *remorsus*.

remorseful adjective filled with deep regret or guilt.
– DERIVATIVES **remorsefully** adverb.

remorseless adjective **1** (of something unpleasant) never ending or improving; relentless. **2** without regret or guilt.
– DERIVATIVES **remorselessly** adverb **remorselessness** noun.

remortgage verb take out another or a different mortgage on a property. •noun a different or additional mortgage.

remote adjective (**remoter, remotest**) **1** far away in space or time. **2** situated far from the main cities or towns. **3** distantly related. **4** having very little connection: *the theory seems rather remote from everyday experience.* **5** (of a chance or possibility) unlikely to occur. **6** aloof and unfriendly. **7** (of an electronic device) operating or operated by means of radio or infrared signals. **8** Computing (of a device) that can only be accessed by means of a network. •noun a remote control device.
– DERIVATIVES **remotely** adverb **remoteness** noun.
– ORIGIN Latin *remotus* 'removed'.

remote control noun **1** control of a device from a distance by means of signals transmitted from a radio or electronic device. **2** (also **remote controller**) a device that controls another device in this way.
– DERIVATIVES **remote-controlled** adjective.

remoulade /**rem**-uu-lahd/ noun salad or seafood dressing made with hard-boiled egg yolks, oil, vinegar, and seasoning.
– ORIGIN French.

remould (US **remold**) verb /ree-**mohld**/ **1** change the appearance or structure of something. **2** Brit. put a new tread on a worn tyre. •noun /**ree**-mohld/ Brit. a tyre that has been given a new tread.

remount verb /ree-**mownt**/ **1** get on a horse or vehicle again. **2** attach something to a new frame or setting. **3** organize or begin a course of action again. •noun /**ree**-mownt/ a fresh horse for a rider.

removal noun **1** the action of removing someone or something. **2** Brit. the transfer of furniture and other contents when moving house.

remove verb **1** take something off or away from the position occupied. **2** abolish or get rid of something. **3** dismiss someone from a job. **4** (**be removed from**) be very different from. **5** (as adj. **removed**) separated by a particular number of steps of descent: *his second cousin once removed.* •noun the extent to which people or things are separated or remote from each other: *he kept himself at a certain remove from the confrontations.*
– DERIVATIVES **removable** adjective **remover** noun.
– ORIGIN Latin *removere*.

remunerate /ri-**myoo**-nuh-rayt/ verb pay someone for services rendered or work done.
– DERIVATIVES **remunerative** adjective.
– ORIGIN Latin *remunerari* 'reward, recompense'.

remuneration noun money paid for work or a service.

Renaissance /ri-**nay**-suhnss, ri-**nay**-sonss/ noun **1** the revival of European art and literature under the influence of classical styles in the 14th–16th centuries. **2** (**renaissance**) a revival of or renewed interest in something.
– ORIGIN French, 'rebirth'.

Renaissance man noun a person with a wide range of talents or interests.

renal /**ree**-n'l/ adjective relating to the kidneys.
– ORIGIN Latin *renalis*.

rename verb give a new name to someone or something.

renascent /ri-**nay**-s'nt/ adjective becoming active again.
– DERIVATIVES **renascence** noun.
– ORIGIN from Latin *renasci* 'be born again'.

rend verb (past and past part. **rent**) literary **1** tear something to pieces. **2** cause great distress to someone.
– ORIGIN Old English.

render verb **1** provide a service, help, etc. **2** present something for inspection, consideration, or payment. **3** cause to be or become: *I was rendered speechless.* **4** perform or represent musically or artistically: *the children are very sensitively rendered.* **5** translate something into another language. **6** literary hand something over. **7** melt down fat so as to separate out its impurities. **8** cover stone or brick with a coat of plaster. •noun a first coat of plaster applied to a brick or stone surface.
– DERIVATIVES **renderer** noun.
– ORIGIN Old French *rendre*.

r

rendering noun **1** a performance of a piece of music or a role in a play. **2** a translation. **3** a first coat of plaster.

rendezvous /ron-day-voo/ noun (pl. same /ron-day-vooz/) **1** a meeting at an agreed time and place. **2** a meeting place. •verb (**rendezvouses** /ron-day-vooz/, **rendezvousing** /ron-day-voo-ing/, **rendezvoused** /ron-day-vood/) meet at an agreed time and place.
– ORIGIN French *rendez-vous!* 'present yourselves!'.

rendition noun **1** a way that something is rendered, performed, or represented, especially a performance of a dramatic role or a musical work: *a quick rendition of 'Happy Birthday to You'.* **2** a translation.

renegade /ren-i-gayd/ noun a person who deserts and betrays an organization, country, or set of principles. •adjective having treacherously changed allegiance.
– ORIGIN Spanish *renegado*.

renege /ri-nayg, ri-neeg/ verb go back on a promise or contract.
– ORIGIN Latin *renegare*.

renegotiate verb negotiate something again in order to change the original agreed terms.
– DERIVATIVES **renegotiable** adjective **renegotiation** noun.

renew verb **1** begin something again after an interruption. **2** (usu. as adj. **renewed**) give fresh life or intensity to: *a renewed interest in exercise.* **3** extend the period for which a licence, subscription, or contract is valid. **4** replace something broken or worn out.
– DERIVATIVES **renewal** noun **renewer** noun.

renewable adjective **1** capable of being renewed. **2** (of energy or its source) not exhausted when used.
– DERIVATIVES **renewability** noun.

renminbi /ren-min-bi/ noun (pl. same) **1** the system of currency of China. **2** a yuan.
– ORIGIN Chinese.

rennet /ren-nit/ noun a substance made from curdled milk from the stomach of a calf, used in curdling milk for cheese.
– ORIGIN probably related to **RUN**.

renounce verb **1** formally state that one has given up a claim, right, or possession. **2** state publicly that one no longer has a particular belief or supports a particular cause. **3** abandon a bad habit or way of life.
– DERIVATIVES **renounceable** adjective **renouncement** noun **renouncer** noun.
– ORIGIN Old French *renoncer*.

renovate /ren-uh-vayt/ verb restore something old to a good state of repair.
– DERIVATIVES **renovation** noun **renovator** noun.
– ORIGIN Latin *renovare* 'make new again'.

renown noun the state of being famous and respected.
– DERIVATIVES **renowned** adjective.
– ORIGIN from Old French *renomer* 'make famous'.

rent[1] noun **1** a tenant's regular payment to a landlord for the use of property or land. **2** a payment for the hire of equipment. •verb **1** pay someone for the use of something. **2** let someone use something in return for payment.
– DERIVATIVES **rentable** adjective **renter** noun.

– ORIGIN Old French *rente*.

rent[2] noun a large tear in a piece of fabric.
– ORIGIN from **REND**.

rent[3] past and past participle of **REND**.

rental noun **1** an amount paid or received as rent. **2** the action of renting something. **3** N. Amer. a rented house or car. •adjective relating to or available for rent.

rent boy noun Brit. informal a young male prostitute.

rentier /ron-ti-ay/ noun a person living on income from property or investments.
– ORIGIN French.

renumber verb change the number or numbers given to something.

renunciation noun the formal giving up of a claim, belief, or course or action.

reoccupy verb (**reoccupies, reoccupying, reoccupied**) occupy a place or position again.
– DERIVATIVES **reoccupation** noun.

reoccur verb (**reoccurs, reoccurring, reoccurred**) occur again or repeatedly.
– DERIVATIVES **reoccurrence** noun.

reoffend verb commit a further offence.
– DERIVATIVES **reoffender** noun.

reopen verb open again: *the house was reopened to the public.*

reorder verb **1** order goods again. **2** arrange something again or differently. •noun a repeated order for goods.

reorganize (or **reorganise**) verb change the way in which something is organized.
– DERIVATIVES **reorganization** noun **reorganizer** noun.

reorient /ree-or-i-ent, ree-o-ri-ent/ verb **1** change the focus or direction of something. **2** (**reorient oneself**) find one's position again in relation to one's surroundings.
– DERIVATIVES **reorientate** verb **reorientation** noun.

Rep. abbreviation **1** (in the US Congress) Representative. **2** Republic. **3** US a Republican.

rep[1] informal noun a representative.

rep[2] noun informal **1** repertory. **2** a repertory theatre or company.

rep[3] (also **repp**) noun a fabric with a ribbed surface, used in curtains and upholstery.
– ORIGIN French *reps*.

rep[4] noun (in weight training) a repetition of a set of exercises.

repackage verb package or present something again or differently.

repaid past and past participle of **REPAY**.

repaint verb cover something with a new coat of paint.

repair[1] verb **1** restore something damaged, worn, or faulty to a good condition. **2** set right a breakdown in relations. •noun **1** the action of repairing something. **2** a part that has been repaired. **3** the relative condition of something: *the cottages were in good repair.*
– DERIVATIVES **repairable** adjective **repairer** noun.
– ORIGIN Latin *reparare*.

repair[2] verb (**repair to**) formal or humorous go to a place.
– ORIGIN Old French *repairer*.

repairman noun (pl. **repairmen**) a person who repairs vehicles, machinery, or appliances.

r

reparable /rep-uh-ruh-b'l/ adjective able to be repaired or rectified.

reparation /rep-uh-ray-sh'n/ noun **1** the making of amends for a wrong: *sinners who make reparation for their sins.* **2** (**reparations**) compensation for war damage paid by a defeated state.
– DERIVATIVES **reparative** /rep-uh-ruh-tiv, ri-pa-ruh-tiv/ adjective.
– ORIGIN Latin.

repartee /rep-ar-tee/ noun conversation characterized by quick, witty comments or replies.
– ORIGIN from French *repartie* 'replied promptly'.

repast /ri-pahst/ noun formal a meal.
– ORIGIN Old French.

repatriate /ree-pat-ri-ayt, ree-pay-tri-ayt/ verb send someone back to their own country.
– DERIVATIVES **repatriation** noun.
– ORIGIN Latin *repatriare* 'return to one's country'.

repay verb (past and past part. **repaid**) **1** pay back a loan that is owed to someone. **2** do or give something as reward for a favour or kindness received. **3** Brit. be worth spending time on: *these sites would repay more detailed investigation.*
– DERIVATIVES **repayable** adjective **repayment** noun.

repayment mortgage noun Brit. a mortgage in which the borrower repays the money borrowed and interest together in fixed instalments over a fixed period.

repeal verb officially cancel a law or act of parliament. • noun the action of repealing a law or act of parliament.
– ORIGIN Old French *repeler*.

repeat verb **1** say something again. **2** do something again or more than once. **3** (**repeat itself**) occur again in the same way: *I don't intend to let history repeat itself.* **4** chiefly Brit. (of food) be tasted again after being swallowed, as a result of indigestion. • noun **1** something that occurs or is done again. **2** a repeated broadcast of a television or radio programme. **3** a musical passage that is to be repeated. • adjective happening, done, or used more than once: *a repeat prescription.*
– DERIVATIVES **repeatable** adjective **repeatedly** adverb **repeater** noun.
– ORIGIN Latin *repetere*.

repel verb (**repels, repelling, repelled**) **1** drive or force an attack or attacker back or away. **2** make someone feel disgust or horror. **3** (of a substance) be able to keep something out or be unable to mix with something: *boots with leather uppers to repel moisture.* **4** (of a magnetic pole or electric field) force away something similarly magnetized or charged.
– DERIVATIVES **repeller** noun.
– ORIGIN Latin *repellere*.

repellent (also **repellant**) adjective **1** able to repel a particular thing: *water-repellent nylon.* **2** disgusting or distasteful. • noun **1** a substance that deters insects or other pests. **2** a substance used to treat something to make it repel water.
– DERIVATIVES **repellence** noun **repellency** noun **repellently** adverb.

repent verb feel or express sincere regret or remorse about something bad or wrong that one has done.
– DERIVATIVES **repentance** noun **repentant** adjective **repenter** noun.
– ORIGIN Old French *repentir*.

repercussions plural noun the consequences of an event or action.
– ORIGIN from Latin *repercutere* 'cause to rebound, push back'.

repertoire /rep-er-twar/ noun the plays, operas, or other items known or regularly performed by a performer or company.
– ORIGIN French.

repertory /rep-er-tuh-ri/ noun (pl. **repertories**) **1** the performance by a company of the plays, operas, or ballets in its repertoire at regular short intervals. **2** another term for **REPERTOIRE**.
– ORIGIN Latin *repertorium* 'catalogue, storehouse'.

repertory company noun a theatrical company that performs plays from its repertoire for regular, short periods of time, moving on from one play to another.

repetition noun **1** the action of repeating something. **2** a thing that has been said or done before.

repetitious /re-pi-tish-uhss/ adjective having too much repetition; repetitive.
– DERIVATIVES **repetitiously** adverb **repetitiousness** noun.

repetitive /ri-pet-it-iv/ adjective repeated many times or too much.
– DERIVATIVES **repetitively** adverb **repetitiveness** noun.

repetitive strain injury noun a condition in which prolonged repetitive action causes pain or weakening in the tendons and muscles involved.

rephrase verb express something in an alternative way.

repine verb literary be discontented; fret.

replace verb **1** take the place of someone or something. **2** provide a substitute for something that is faulty, old, or damaged. **3** remove from a role and substitute with someone or something different: *he was replaced by a lightweight who knew nothing about the case.* **4** put something back in the place it occupied before.
– DERIVATIVES **replaceable** adjective **replacer** noun.

replacement noun **1** the action of replacing someone or something. **2** a person or thing that takes the place of another.

replant verb **1** plant a tree or other plant in a new pot or site. **2** provide an area with new plants.

replay noun **1** a match that is played again because the previous game was a draw. **2** an instance of playing a recording again. **3** an event which closely follows the pattern of a previous event. • verb **1** play back a recording. **2** play a match again.

replenish verb **1** fill something up again. **2** restore a stock or supply to a former level.
– DERIVATIVES **replenisher** noun **replenishment** noun.
– ORIGIN Old French *replenir*.

replete /ri-pleet/ adjective **1** (**replete with**)

r

filled or well supplied with: *a courtyard replete with cacti.* **2** very full with food.
- DERIVATIVES **repletion** noun.
- ORIGIN from Latin *replere* 'fill up'.

replica /rep-li-kuh/ noun an exact copy or model of something, especially one on a smaller scale.
- ORIGIN Italian.

replicate verb /rep-li-kayt/ **1** make an exact copy of something. **2** (**replicate itself**) (of genetic material or a living organism) reproduce or give rise to a copy of itself. **3** repeat an experiment to obtain a consistent result. •noun /rep-li-kuht/ a close or exact copy; a replica.
- DERIVATIVES **replicable** /rep-li-kuh-b'l/ adjective **replication** noun **replicator** noun.
- ORIGIN Latin *replicare*.

reply verb (**replies, replying, replied**) **1** say or write something as an answer to something. **2** respond with a similar action: *they replied to the shelling with a mortar attack.* •noun (pl. **replies**) **1** a spoken or written answer. **2** the action of answering or responding to someone or something.
- DERIVATIVES **replier** noun.
- ORIGIN Old French *replier*.

repopulate verb **1** introduce a population into an area previously deserted. **2** populate or fill again: *probiotics repopulate your gut with healthy bacteria.*
- DERIVATIVES **repopulation** noun.

report verb **1** give a spoken or written account of something. **2** cover an event or situation as a journalist. **3** (**be reported**) be said or rumoured. **4** make a formal complaint about someone or something. **5** present oneself as having arrived somewhere or as ready to do something: *he had to report to the boss at 9 a.m.* **6** (**report to**) be responsible to a supervisor or manager. •noun **1** an account given of a matter after investigation or consideration. **2** a description of an event or situation. **3** Brit. a teacher's written assessment of a pupil's work and progress. **4** a sudden loud noise, especially of gunfire.
- DERIVATIVES **reportable** adjective.
- ORIGIN Latin *reportare* 'bring back'.

reportage /rep-or-**tahzh**, ri-**por**-tij/ noun **1** the reporting of news by the media. **2** factual, journalistic writing in a book.

reported speech noun a speaker's words reported with the required changes of person and tense (e.g. *he said that he would go*, based on *I will go*). Contrasted with **DIRECT SPEECH**.

reporter noun a person who reports news for a newspaper or broadcasting company.

repose[1] /ri-**pohz**/ noun **1** a state of rest or tranquillity. **2** the state of being calm and composed. •verb formal **1** lie down and rest. **2** be situated or kept in a particular place.
- ORIGIN Old French *reposer*.

repose[2] /ri-**pohz**/ verb (**repose something in**) place one's confidence or trust in.
- ORIGIN from **POSE**.

reposition verb **1** alter the position of someone or something. **2** change the image of a company, product, etc. to target a different market.

repository /ri-**poz**-i-tuh-ri/ noun (pl. **repositories**) **1** a place or container for storage. **2** a person or thing that is full of information or a particular quality: *the lighthouse keeper is a repository of local history.*
- ORIGIN Latin *repositorium*.

repossess verb retake possession of something when a buyer fails to make the required payments.
- DERIVATIVES **repossession** noun **repossessor** noun.

repot verb (**repots, repotting, repotted**) put a plant in another pot.

repoussé /ruh-**poo**-say/ adjective (of metalwork) hammered into relief from the reverse side.
- ORIGIN French, 'pushed back'.

repp noun variant spelling of **REP**[3].

reprehend /rep-ri-**hend**/ verb reprimand someone.
- DERIVATIVES **reprehension** noun.
- ORIGIN Latin *reprehendere* 'seize, check, rebuke'.

reprehensible adjective wrong or bad and deserving condemnation.
- DERIVATIVES **reprehensibility** noun **reprehensibly** adverb.

represent verb **1** be entitled or appointed to act and speak on behalf of someone. **2** be an elected member of a law-making body for a constituency or party. **3** constitute; amount to: *this figure represents eleven per cent of total sales.* **4** be a specimen or typical example of something. **5** (**be represented**) be present to a particular degree: *abstract art is well represented in this exhibition.* **6** portray in a particular way: *they were represented as being in need of protection.* **7** depict a subject in a work of art. **8** be a symbol of something.
- ORIGIN Latin *repraesentare*.

re-present verb present something again.
- DERIVATIVES **re-presentation** noun.

representation noun **1** the action or an instance of representing someone or something. **2** an image, model, or other depiction of something. **3** (**representations**) statements made to an authority to express an opinion or register a protest.

representational adjective **1** relating to representation. **2** relating to art which shows the physical appearance of things.
- DERIVATIVES **representationally** adverb.

representative adjective **1** typical of a class or group. **2** containing typical examples of many or all types: *a representative sample.* **3** (of a law-making body) consisting of people chosen to act and speak on behalf of a wider group. **4** serving as a portrayal or symbol of something. •noun **1** a person chosen to act and speak on behalf of another or others. **2** an agent of a firm who visits potential clients to sell its products. **3** an example of a class or group.
- DERIVATIVES **representatively** adverb **representativeness** noun.

repress verb **1** use force to control or stop : *the regime continues to repress political parties.* **2** prevent or restrict the expression or development of something. **3** try not to allow a thought or feeling to enter one's conscious mind.

- DERIVATIVES **represser** noun **repressible** adjective **repression** noun.
- ORIGIN Latin *reprimere* 'press back, check'.

repressed adjective **1** (of a thought or feeling) not acknowledged; kept unconscious in one's mind. **2** tending to suppress one's feelings and desires.

repressive adjective severely restricting personal freedom; oppressive.
- DERIVATIVES **repressively** adverb **repressiveness** noun.

reprieve verb **1** cancel the punishment of someone. **2** abandon or postpone plans to close: *the threatened pits could be reprieved.* •noun **1** the cancellation of a punishment. **2** a brief delay before something undesirable happens.
- ORIGIN Old French *reprendre*.

reprimand /rep-ri-mahnd/ noun a formal expression of disapproval; a rebuke. •verb formally tell someone that they have done something wrong.
- ORIGIN French *réprimande*.

reprint verb /ree-print/ print something again or in a revised form. •noun /ree-print/ **1** an act of reprinting. **2** a copy of a book or other material that has been reprinted.

reprisal /ri-pry-z'l/ noun a violent or aggressive act done in return for a similar act.
- ORIGIN Old French *reprisaille*.

reprise /ri-preez/ noun **1** a repeated passage in music. **2** a repeat of something: *Everton visit Watford in a reprise of the 1984 final.* •verb repeat a piece of music or a performance.
- ORIGIN French, 'taken up again'.

reproach verb **1** express one's disapproval of or disappointment with someone. **2** (reproach someone with) accuse someone of. •noun an expression of disapproval or disappointment.
- PHRASES **above** (or **beyond**) **reproach** so perfect as to be beyond criticism.
- DERIVATIVES **reproachable** adjective.
- ORIGIN Old French *reprochier*.

reproachful adjective expressing disapproval or disappointment.
- DERIVATIVES **reproachfully** adverb.

reprobate /rep-ruh-bayt/ noun a person who behaves in an immoral way.
- DERIVATIVES **reprobation** noun.
- ORIGIN from Latin *reprobare* 'disapprove'.

reprocess verb process something again or differently in order to reuse it.

reproduce verb **1** produce a copy of something. **2** produce something similar to something else in a different situation. **3** (of an organism) produce offspring.
- DERIVATIVES **reproducer** noun **reproducible** adjective.

reproduction noun **1** the action of reproducing. **2** a copy of a work of art, especially a print made of a painting. •adjective made to imitate the style of an earlier period or particular craftsman: *reproduction furniture.*
- DERIVATIVES **reproductive** adjective.

reproof /ri-proof/ noun a criticism or rebuke.
- ORIGIN from Old French *reprover* 'reprove'.

reprove verb rebuke or reprimand someone.
- ORIGIN Old French *reprover*.

reptile noun a cold-blooded vertebrate animal of a class that includes snakes, lizards, crocodiles, turtles, and tortoises, typically having a dry scaly skin and laying soft-shelled eggs.
- DERIVATIVES **reptilian** adjective & noun.
- ORIGIN from Latin *reptilis* 'crawling'.

republic noun a state in which power is held by the people and their elected representatives, and which has a president rather than a monarch.
- ORIGIN Latin *respublica*.

republican adjective **1** belonging to or typical of a republic. **2** supporting the principles of a republic. **3** (Republican) (in the US) supporting the Republican Party. •noun **1** a person in favour of republican government. **2** (Republican) (in the US) a member or supporter of the Republican Party. **3** (Republican) an advocate of a united Ireland.
- DERIVATIVES **republicanism** noun.

repudiate /ri-pyoo-di-ayt/ verb **1** refuse to accept something. **2** deny the truth or validity of: *he repudiated allegations that he was a shirker.* **3** chiefly Law refuse to fulfil an agreement, obligation, or debt. **4** old use disown or divorce one's wife.
- DERIVATIVES **repudiation** noun **repudiator** noun.
- ORIGIN from Latin *repudiatus* 'divorced, cast off'.

repugnance /ri-pug-nuhnss/ noun intense disgust.
- DERIVATIVES **repugnancy** noun.
- ORIGIN from Latin *repugnare* 'oppose'.

repugnant adjective unpleasant and completely unacceptable.

repulse verb **1** drive back an attacking enemy by force. **2** reject or refuse to accept an offer or the person making it. **3** cause someone to feel intense distaste or disgust. •noun **1** the action of driving back an attack. **2** a rejection or refusal of an offer or approach.
- ORIGIN Latin *repellere*.

repulsion noun **1** a feeling of intense distaste or disgust. **2** Physics a force under the influence of which objects tend to move away from each other, e.g. through having the same magnetic polarity.

repulsive adjective **1** arousing intense distaste or disgust. **2** Physics relating to repulsion between objects.
- DERIVATIVES **repulsively** adverb **repulsiveness** noun.

repurpose verb adapt something for use in a different purpose.

reputable /rep-yoo-tuh-b'l/ adjective having a good reputation.
- DERIVATIVES **reputably** adverb.

reputation noun **1** the beliefs or opinions that are generally held about someone or something. **2** a high public opinion of someone or something: *they have damaged the reputation of public service broadcasting.*

repute noun **1** the opinion generally held of someone or something. **2** the state of being highly regarded. •verb **1** (be reputed) be generally regarded as having done something or as having particular characteristics. **2** (as adj. reputed) generally believed to exist: *the reputed flatness of the country.*

- DERIVATIVES **reputedly** adverb.
- ORIGIN from Latin *reputare* 'think over'.

request noun **1** an act of asking politely or formally for something. **2** a thing that is asked for politely or formally. •verb politely or formally ask for something or ask someone to do something.
- DERIVATIVES **requester** noun.
- ORIGIN from Latin *requirere* 'require'.

request stop noun Brit. a bus stop at which the bus halts only if requested by a passenger or if signalled.

requiem /rek-wi-uhm, rek-wi-em/ noun **1** (especially in the Roman Catholic Church) a Mass for the souls of the dead. **2** a musical composition setting parts of such a Mass.
- ORIGIN Latin.

require verb **1** need something for a purpose. **2** instruct or expect someone to do something. **3** specify as compulsory: *the minimum car insurance required by law.* **4** (**require something of**) regard an action or quality as due from someone because of the position they hold.
- ORIGIN Latin *requirere*.

requirement noun **1** something required; a need. **2** something that is compulsory.

requisite /rek-wi-zit/ adjective made necessary by particular circumstances or regulations: *some lack the requisite skills to succeed.* •noun a thing that is necessary for a purpose.
- ORIGIN Latin *requisitus* 'searched for, deemed necessary'.

requisition /rek-wi-zish'n/ noun **1** an official order enabling property or materials to be taken and used. **2** the taking of goods for military or public use. **3** a formal written demand that something should be done or put into operation. •verb demand the use or supply of something by an official order.

requite /ri-kwyt/ verb formal give or do something suitable in return for a favour, love, kindness, etc.
- DERIVATIVES **requital** noun.
- ORIGIN from RE- + former *quite* 'behave'.

reran past of RERUN.

reread verb (past and past part. **reread**) read a written work or passage again.

reredos /reer-doss/ noun (pl. same) an ornamental screen at the back of an altar in a church.
- ORIGIN Old French *areredos*.

re-release verb release a recording or film again. •noun a re-released recording or film.

re-route verb send someone or something by or along a different route.

rerun verb (**reruns, rerunning, reran;** past part. **rerun**) show, stage, or perform something again. •noun an event or programme that is run again.

resale noun the sale of a thing previously bought.
- DERIVATIVES **resaleable** (also **resalable**) adjective.

resat past and past participle of RESIT.

reschedule verb **1** change the time of a planned event. **2** arrange a new scheme of repayments of a debt.

rescind /ri-sind/ verb formally cancel a law, order, or agreement.

- DERIVATIVES **rescindable** adjective.
- ORIGIN Latin *rescindere*.

rescission /ri-si-zh'n/ noun formal the official cancelling of a law, order, or agreement.

rescue verb (**rescues, rescuing, rescued**) save someone or something from a dangerous or difficult situation. •noun an act of rescuing someone or something.
- DERIVATIVES **rescuable** adjective **rescuer** noun.
- ORIGIN Old French *rescoure*.

reseal verb seal something again.
- DERIVATIVES **resealable** adjective.

research /ri-serch, ree-serch/ noun the systematic study of materials and sources in order to establish facts and reach new conclusions. •verb /ri-serch/ **1** carry out research into a subject. **2** discover or check information for a book, programme, etc.
- DERIVATIVES **researcher** noun.
- ORIGIN from former French *recercher*.

research and development noun (in industry) work directed towards new ideas and improvement of products and processes.

reselect verb select someone or something again or differently.
- DERIVATIVES **reselection** noun.

resell verb (past and past part. **resold**) sell something one has bought to someone else.
- DERIVATIVES **reseller** noun.

resemblance noun **1** the fact of looking like or being similar to someone or something: *he bears a strong resemblance to his mother.* **2** a way in which things are alike.

resemble verb be similar to someone or something in appearance or qualities.
- ORIGIN Old French *resembler*.

resent verb feel bitter or angry towards someone or something.
- ORIGIN from former French *resentir*.

resentful adjective feeling bitter or angry about something, especially unfair treatment.
- DERIVATIVES **resentfully** adverb **resentfulness** noun.

resentment noun bitterness or anger at unfair treatment.

reservation noun **1** the action of reserving something. **2** an arrangement in which something is reserved. **3** an area of land set aside for occupation by North American Indians or Australian Aboriginals. **4** an expression of doubt qualifying overall approval of a plan or statement: *some generals voiced reservations about making air strikes.*

reserve verb **1** keep something for future use. **2** arrange for a seat, ticket, etc. to be kept for a particular person. **3** retain or hold a right or entitlement. **4** hold back from delivering a decision without proper consideration or evidence: *I'll reserve my views on his ability until he's played again.* •noun **1** a supply of something available for use if required. **2** funds kept available by a bank, company, or government. **3** a military force withheld from action to protect others, or additional to the regular forces and available in an emergency. **4** an extra player in a team, serving as a possible substitute. **5** (**the reserves**) the second-choice team. **6** an area of land set aside for occupation by a native people. **7** a protected area for wildlife. **8** a lack of warmth

or openness: *he smiled and some of her natural reserve melted.*
– DERIVATIVES **reservable** adjective.
– ORIGIN Latin *reservare* 'keep back'.

reserve bank noun (in the US) a regional bank operating under and implementing the policies of the Federal Reserve.

reserve currency noun a strong currency widely used in international trade that a central bank is prepared to hold as part of its foreign exchange reserves.

reserved adjective slow to reveal emotion or opinions.
– DERIVATIVES **reservedly** adverb **reservedness** noun.

reserve price noun the price set as the lowest acceptable by the seller for an item sold at auction.

reservist noun a member of a military reserve force.

reservoir noun 1 a large lake used as a source of water supply. 2 a place where fluid collects, especially in rock strata or in the body. 3 a container or part of a machine designed to hold fluid. 4 a supply or source of something: *the country's vast reservoir of computer scientists.*
– ORIGIN French.

reset verb (**resets, resetting, reset**) 1 set something again or differently. 2 set a counter, clock, etc. to zero.
– DERIVATIVES **resettable** adjective.

resettle verb settle or cause to settle in a different place.
– DERIVATIVES **resettlement** noun.

reshape verb shape or form something differently or again.

reshuffle verb 1 change around the positions of members of a team, especially government ministers. 2 rearrange something. •noun an act of reshuffling.

reside verb 1 live in a particular place. 2 (of a right or legal power) belong to a person or body. 3 (**reside in**) (of a quality) be present in: *intelligence and judgement reside in old men.*

residence noun 1 the fact of living somewhere. 2 a person's home. 3 the official house of a government minister or other official.
– PHRASES **artist** (or **writer**) **in residence** an artist or writer who is based for a set period within a college or other institution and is available for teaching purposes.

residency noun (pl. **residencies**) 1 the fact of living in a place. 2 a residential post held by an artist or writer. 3 Brit. a musician's regular engagement at a club or other venue. 4 N. Amer. a period of specialized medical training in a hospital.

resident noun 1 a person who lives somewhere on a long-term basis. 2 Brit. a guest in a hotel. 3 N. Amer. a medical graduate engaged in specialized practice under supervision in a hospital. 4 a bird, butterfly, or other animal of a species that does not migrate. •adjective 1 living somewhere on a long-term basis. 2 having living quarters at one's place of work. 3 attached to and working regularly for a particular institution.
– ORIGIN from Latin *residere* 'remain'.

residential adjective 1 designed for people to live in. 2 (of a job, course, etc.) requiring someone to live in a particular place. 3 (of an area) occupied by private houses.
– DERIVATIVES **residentially** adverb.

residua plural of RESIDUUM.

residual adjective remaining after the greater part or quantity has gone or been removed. •noun a quantity remaining after the greater part has gone or been removed.
– DERIVATIVES **residually** adverb.

residue /rez-i-dyoo/ noun 1 a small amount of something that remains after the main part has gone or been taken or used. 2 Law the part of an estate that is left after the payment of charges, debts, and bequests. 3 a substance that remains after a process such as combustion or evaporation.
– ORIGIN Latin *residuum.*

residuum /ri-zi-dyoo-uhm/ noun (pl. **residua** /ri-zi-dyoo-uh/) technical a chemical residue.
– ORIGIN Latin.

resign verb 1 voluntarily leave a job or position of office. 2 (**be resigned**) accept that something undesirable cannot be avoided.
– ORIGIN Latin *resignare* 'unseal, cancel'.

re-sign verb sign a document or contract again.

resignation noun 1 an act of resigning from a job. 2 a letter stating one's intention to resign. 3 acceptance of something undesirable that cannot be avoided: *he confronted old age with his usual resignation.*

resilient adjective 1 able to recoil or spring back into shape after bending, stretching, or being compressed. 2 (of a person) able to recover quickly from difficult conditions.
– DERIVATIVES **resilience** noun **resiliently** adverb.
– ORIGIN from Latin *resilire* 'leap back'.

resin /rez-in/ noun 1 a sticky substance produced by some trees. 2 a synthetic polymer used as the basis of plastics, adhesives, varnishes, etc.
– DERIVATIVES **resinous** adjective.
– ORIGIN Latin *resina.*

resist verb 1 withstand the action or effect of something. 2 try to prevent something by action or argument. 3 stop oneself from having or doing something tempting: *I couldn't resist taking a peek.* 4 struggle or fight back when attacked.
– DERIVATIVES **resister** noun **resistible** adjective.
– ORIGIN Latin *resistere.*

resistance noun 1 the action of resisting. 2 the ability not to be affected by something undesirable. 3 the impeding or stopping effect that one material thing has on another: *air resistance was reduced by streamlining.* 4 the degree to which a material or device opposes the passage of an electric current. 5 (also **resistance movement**) a secret organization that fights against authority in an occupied country.
– PHRASES **the line** (or **path**) **of least resistance** the easiest course of action.
– DERIVATIVES **resistant** adjective.

resistive adjective 1 technical able to resist something. 2 relating to electrical resistance.
– DERIVATIVES **resistivity** noun.

resistor noun a device that resists the passage of an electric current.

r

resit Brit. verb (**resits, resitting, resat**) take an exam again after failing. •noun an exam that is taken again for this reason.

resize verb alter the size of something, especially a computer window or image.

reskill verb teach someone new skills.

resold past and past participle of RESELL.

resolute /rez-uh-loot/ adjective admirably purposeful and determined.
– DERIVATIVES **resolutely** adverb **resoluteness** noun.
– ORIGIN Latin *resolutus* 'loosened, paid'.

resolution noun **1** a firm decision. **2** a formal expression of opinion or intention agreed on by a law-making body. **3** the quality of being resolute or determined. **4** the resolving of a problem or dispute. **5** the process of separating something into its component parts. **6** the degree of detail visible in a photographic or television image. **7** the smallest interval between adjacent objects that is measurable by a telescope or other scientific instrument.

resolve verb **1** settle or find a solution to a problem. **2** decide firmly on a course of action. **3** (of a law-making body) take a decision by a formal vote. **4** (**resolve something into**) separate something into its component parts. **5** (of something seen at a distance) turn into a different form when seen more clearly. **6** (of optical or photographic equipment) separate or distinguish between objects that are close together. •noun firm determination to do something.
– DERIVATIVES **resolvable** adjective **resolver** noun.
– ORIGIN Latin *resolvere*.

resolving power noun the ability of an optical instrument or type of film to distinguish small or closely adjacent images.

resonance noun **1** the quality in a sound of being deep, clear, and reverberating. **2** the power to suggest images, emotions, or a quality. **3** Physics the reinforcement or prolongation of sound by reflection from a surface or by the vibration of an adjacent object at the same time.

resonant adjective **1** (of sound) deep, clear, and continuing to reverberate. **2** (of a room, musical instrument, or hollow body) tending to reinforce or prolong sounds. **3** (**resonant with**) filled or resounding with a sound. **4** suggesting images, emotions, or a quality: *a name resonant with Hollywood glamour.*
– DERIVATIVES **resonantly** adverb.
– ORIGIN from Latin *resonare* 'sound again, resound'.

resonate verb produce or be filled with a deep, clear reverberating sound.
– DERIVATIVES **resonator** noun.

resort noun **1** a place visited for holidays or recreation. **2** the adoption of a course of action in a difficult situation: *achieving desired outcomes without resort to war.* **3** a strategy or course of action. •verb (**resort to**) adopt a course of action, especially an undesirable one, so as to resolve a difficult situation.
– PHRASES **as a first** (or **last** or **final**) **resort** before anything else is attempted (or when all else has failed).
– ORIGIN Old French *resortir* 'come or go out

again'.

resound /ri-zownd/ verb **1** fill or be filled with a ringing, booming, or echoing sound. **2** (of fame, success, etc.) be much talked about. **3** (as adj. **resounding**) emphatic; definite: *a resounding success.*

resource /ri-zorss, ri-sorss/ noun **1** (**resources**) a stock or supply of materials or assets that can be drawn on when required. **2** (**resources**) a country's means of supporting itself or becoming wealthier, as represented by its minerals, land, and other assets. **3** a source of help or information: *the database could be used as a teaching resource.* **4** a strategy adopted in a difficult situation. **5** (**resources**) personal qualities that help one to cope in a difficult situation. •verb provide someone or something with resources.
– ORIGIN from Old French dialect *resourdre* 'rise again, recover'.

resourceful adjective able to find quick and clever ways to overcome difficulties.
– DERIVATIVES **resourcefully** adverb **resourcefulness** noun.

respect noun **1** a feeling of admiration for someone or something because of their qualities or achievements. **2** consideration for the feelings or rights of others. **3** (**respects**) polite greetings. **4** a particular aspect or point: *the government's record in this respect is a mixed one.* •verb **1** feel or have respect for someone or something. **2** avoid harming or interfering with something. **3** agree to recognize and observe a law or rule.
– PHRASES **in respect of** (or **with respect to**) as regards; with reference to.
– DERIVATIVES **respecter** noun.
– ORIGIN Latin *respectus*.

respectable adjective **1** regarded by society to be proper, correct, and good. **2** adequate or acceptable; fairly good.
– DERIVATIVES **respectability** noun **respectably** adverb.

respectful adjective feeling or showing respect or consideration.
– DERIVATIVES **respectfully** adverb **respectfulness** noun.

respecting preposition with reference to.

respective adjective belonging or relating separately to each of two or more people or things: *they chatted about their respective lives.*

respectively adverb separately and in the order already mentioned.

respell verb (**respells, respelling, respelled** or chiefly Brit. **respelt**) spell a word differently, especially to show how to pronounce it.

respiration /ress-pi-ray-sh'n/ noun **1** the action of breathing. **2** a single breath. **3** the processes in living organisms involving the production of energy, typically with the intake of oxygen and the release of carbon dioxide.

respirator noun **1** a device worn over the face to prevent the inhalation of smoke or other harmful substances. **2** a device that enables someone to breathe artificially.

respiratory /ri-spi-ruh-tuh-ri, ress-pi-ruh-tuh-ri/ adjective relating to breathing.

respiratory tract noun the passage formed by the mouth, nose, throat, and lungs, through which air passes during breathing.

respire verb **1** breathe. **2** (of a plant) carry out the process of respiration.
– DERIVATIVES **respirable** adjective.
– ORIGIN Latin *respirare* 'breathe out'.

respite /ress-pyt, ress-pit/ noun a short period of rest or relief from something difficult or unpleasant.
– ORIGIN Old French *respit*.

respite care noun temporary care of a sick, elderly, or disabled person, providing relief for their usual carer.

resplendent /ri-splen-duhnt/ adjective attractive and colourful in an impressive way.
– DERIVATIVES **resplendence** noun **resplendently** adverb.
– ORIGIN from Latin *resplendere* 'shine out'.

respond verb **1** say something in reply. **2** do something as a reaction to someone or something.
– DERIVATIVES **responder** noun.
– ORIGIN Latin *respondere* 'answer, offer in return'.

respondent noun **1** Law a person against whom a petition is filed, especially one in an appeal or a divorce case. **2** a person who responds to a questionnaire or an advertisement.

response noun **1** a spoken or written answer. **2** a reaction to something. **3** technical a physical reaction to a stimulus or situation.

responsibility noun (pl. **responsibilities**) **1** the state of being responsible for someone or something. **2** the opportunity or ability to act independently and take decisions without authorization. **3** a thing which one is required to do as part of a job or legal obligation.

responsible adjective **1** having a duty to do something, or having control over or care for someone. **2** being the cause of something and so able to be blamed or credited for it: *the prime minister is ultimately responsible for this situation.* **3** capable of being trusted. **4** (of a job or position) involving important duties or decisions or control over others.
5 (**responsible to**) having to report to a senior person.
– DERIVATIVES **responsibleness** noun **responsibly** adverb.
– ORIGIN from Latin *respondere* 'answer, offer in return'.

responsive adjective **1** responding readily and with interest. **2** in response; answering.
– DERIVATIVES **responsively** adverb **responsiveness** noun.

respray verb /ree-spray/ spray something with a new coat of paint. • noun /ree-spray/ an instance of respraying.

rest¹ verb **1** stop work or activity in order to relax or recover strength. **2** place or be placed so as to stay in a specified position. **3** (**rest on**) depend or be based on. **4** (**rest something in/on**) place trust, hope, or confidence in or on. **5** (**rest with**) be the responsibility of or belong to: *the final say rests with the regional assemblies.* **6** (of an issue) be left without further investigation or discussion. • noun **1** the state or a period of resting. **2** an object that is used to hold or support something. **3** Music an interval of silence of a specified duration.
– PHRASES **rest one's case** conclude one's

presentation of evidence and arguments in a lawsuit.
– ORIGIN Old English.

rest² noun **1** the remaining part of something. **2** (treated as pl.) the remaining people or things; the others. • verb remain or be left in a specified condition: *rest assured we will do everything we can.*
– ORIGIN from Latin *restare* 'remain'.

restart verb /ree-start/ start again. • noun /ree-start/ a new start or beginning.

restate verb state something again or differently.

restaurant /ress-tuh-ront, ress-tront/ noun a place where people pay to sit and eat meals that are cooked on the premises.
– ORIGIN French.

restaurateur /ress-tuh-ruh-ter/ noun a person who owns and manages a restaurant.
– ORIGIN French.

USAGE: Although **restaurateur** is related to *restaurant*, it is not spelled with an *n*.

restful adjective having a quiet and soothing quality.
– DERIVATIVES **restfully** adverb.

rest home noun an institution where old or frail people live and are cared for.

restitution noun **1** the restoration of something lost or stolen to its proper owner. **2** payment to compensate for injury or loss. **3** the restoration of something to its original state.
– DERIVATIVES **restitutive** adjective.
– ORIGIN Latin.

restive adjective unable to keep still or unwilling to submit to control: *the republic's restive minorities.*
– DERIVATIVES **restively** adverb **restiveness** noun.
– ORIGIN Old French.

restless adjective **1** unable to rest or relax as a result of anxiety or boredom. **2** offering no physical or emotional rest: *a restless night.*
– DERIVATIVES **restlessly** adverb **restlessness** noun.

restock verb replenish a store with fresh stock or supplies.

restoration noun **1** the action of returning something to a former condition, place, or owner. **2** the process of repairing or renovating a building, work of art, etc. **3** the reinstatement of a previous practice, right, or situation. **4** the return of a monarch to a throne, a head of state to government, or a regime to power. **5** (**the Restoration**) the re-establishment of Charles II as King of England in 1660, or the period following this.

restorative /ri-sto-ruh-tiv/ adjective having the ability to restore health, strength, or well-being. • noun a medicine or drink that restores health, strength, or well-being.
– DERIVATIVES **restoratively** adverb.

restore verb **1** bring back a previous practice, right, or situation. **2** return to a former condition, place, or owner: *he was restored to full favour.* **3** repair or renovate a building, work of art, etc.
– DERIVATIVES **restorable** adjective **restorer** noun.
– ORIGIN Latin *restaurare* 'rebuild, restore'.

restrain verb **1** keep someone or something

under control or within limits. **2** prevent someone from moving or acting as they wish. **3** control a strong emotion.
– DERIVATIVES **restrainable** adjective **restrainer** noun.
– ORIGIN Latin *restringere* 'tie back'.

restrained adjective **1** reserved or unemotional. **2** not highly decorated or brightly coloured.

restraint noun **1** a rule, measure, or fact that limits or controls: *the financial restraints of the budget*. **2** the action of restraining someone or something. **3** a device which limits or prevents freedom of movement. **4** unemotional or controlled behaviour.

restrict verb **1** put a limit on something; keep something under control. **2** prevent someone from moving or acting as they wish.
– ORIGIN Latin *restringere* 'tie back'.

restricted adjective **1** limited in extent, number, or scope. **2** Brit. not revealed or made public for reasons of national security.

restriction noun **1** a limiting rule, measure, or condition. **2** the limitation or control of someone or something, or the state of being restricted.

restrictive adjective limiting or controlling freedom of action or movement.
– DERIVATIVES **restrictively** adverb **restrictiveness** noun.

restrictive practice noun Brit. **1** an arrangement by a group of workers to limit output or restrict the entry of new workers in order to protect their own interests. **2** an arrangement in industry or trade that restricts or controls competition between companies.

restring verb (past and past part. **restrung**) fit new strings to a musical instrument or sports racket.

restroom noun N. Amer. a toilet in a public building.

restructure verb **1** organize something differently. **2** convert a debt into another debt that is repayable at a later time.

restyle verb /ree-**styl**/ **1** give something a new shape or layout. **2** give a new description or name to someone or something. •noun /ree-styl/ an instance of restyling something.

result noun **1** a thing that is caused or produced by something else; an outcome. **2** a quantity or another item of information obtained by experiment or calculation. **3** a final score, mark, or placing in a sporting event or exam. **4** a satisfactory or favourable outcome: *determination and persistence guarantee results*. **5** the outcome of a business's trading over a particular period, expressed as a statement of profit or loss. •verb **1** happen because of something else. **2** (**result in**) have a specified outcome.
– ORIGIN Latin *resultare* 'spring back, result'.

resultant adjective happening or produced as a result.

resume verb **1** begin again or continue after a pause or interruption. **2** return to a seat or place.
– ORIGIN Latin *resumere* 'take back'.

résumé /rez-yuu-may/ noun **1** a summary of something. **2** N. Amer. a curriculum vitae.

– ORIGIN from French, 'resumed'.

resumption noun the action of beginning something again after an interruption.

resupply verb (**resupplies**, **resupplying**, **resupplied**) provide with or obtain a fresh supply.

resurface verb **1** put a new coating on a surface. **2** come back up to the surface of deep water. **3** arise or become evident again: *the old animosities have resurfaced*.

resurgent adjective becoming stronger, or more active or popular again.
– DERIVATIVES **resurgence** noun.
– ORIGIN from Latin *resurgere* 'rise again'.

resurrect verb **1** restore a dead person to life. **2** revive something inactive, disused, or forgotten.

resurrection noun **1** the action of resurrecting or reviving someone or something. **2** (**the Resurrection**) (in Christian belief) the time when Jesus rose from the dead.
– ORIGIN Latin.

resuscitate /ri-**suss**-i-tayt/ verb **1** revive someone from unconsciousness. **2** make something active again.
– DERIVATIVES **resuscitation** noun **resuscitative** adjective **resuscitator** noun.
– ORIGIN Latin *resuscitare* 'raise again'.

retail noun the sale of goods to the general public (rather than to a wholesaler). •verb **1** sell goods to the public. **2** (**retail at/for**) be sold by retail for a specified price. **3** describe the details of an incident to others.
– DERIVATIVES **retailer** noun.
– ORIGIN Old French *retaillier*.

retail price index noun (in the UK) an index of the variation in the prices of retail goods and other items.

retain verb **1** continue to have or own something. **2** absorb and continue to hold a substance. **3** keep something in place. **4** keep someone as an employee. **5** obtain the services of a barrister with a preliminary payment.
– DERIVATIVES **retainable** adjective.
– ORIGIN Latin *retinere* 'hold back'.

retainer noun **1** a thing that holds something in place. **2** a fee paid in advance to a barrister to obtain their services. **3** Brit. a reduced rent paid to reserve accommodation when one is not occupying it. **4** a servant who has worked for someone for a long time.

retaining wall noun a wall that holds back earth or water on one side of it.

retake verb (past **retook**; past part. **retaken**) **1** take a test or exam again. **2** regain possession or control of something. •noun **1** a test or exam that is retaken. **2** an instance of filming a scene or recording a piece of music again.

retaliate /ri-**tal**-i-ayt/ verb make an attack in return for a similar attack.
– DERIVATIVES **retaliation** noun **retaliative** adjective **retaliator** noun **retaliatory** adjective.
– ORIGIN Latin *retaliare* 'return in kind'.

retard verb /ri-**tard**/ hold back the development or progress of someone or something. •noun /ree-tard/ offensive a person who has a mental disability.
– DERIVATIVES **retardation** noun **retarder** noun.
– ORIGIN Latin *retardare*.

r

retardant adjective preventing or inhibiting: *fire-retardant polymers.* •noun a fabric or substance that prevents or inhibits the outbreak of fire.

retarded adjective chiefly offensive less advanced in mental, physical, or social development than is usual for one's age.

retch verb make the sound and movement of vomiting. •noun an instance of retching.
– ORIGIN from a Germanic word meaning 'spittle'.

retell verb (past and past part. **retold**) tell a story again or differently.

retention noun 1 the action of keeping or holding something or the fact of being retained. 2 failure to remove a substance from the body.

retentive adjective 1 (of a person's memory) good at storing facts and impressions. 2 (of a substance) able to absorb and hold moisture.
– DERIVATIVES **retentively** adverb **retentiveness** noun **retentivity** noun.

rethink verb (past and past part. **rethought**) consider a policy or course of action again. •noun an instance of rethinking.

reticent /ret-i-suhnt/ adjective not revealing one's thoughts or feelings readily.
– DERIVATIVES **reticence** noun **reticently** adverb.
– ORIGIN from Latin *reticere* 'remain silent'.

reticulated adjective arranged or marked like a net or network.
– ORIGIN Latin *reticulatus.*

reticulation /ri-tik-yuu-**lay**-sh'n/ noun a pattern or arrangement of interlacing lines resembling a net.

reticule /**re**-ti-kyool/ noun chiefly historical a woman's small handbag, closed with a drawstring.
– ORIGIN French.

retie verb (**reties, retying, retied**) tie something again.

retina /**ret**-i-nuh/ noun (pl. **retinas** or **retinae** /**ret**-i-nee/) a layer at the back of the eyeball containing cells that are sensitive to light and from which impulses are sent to the brain.
– DERIVATIVES **retinal** adjective.
– ORIGIN Latin.

retinitis /re-ti-**ny**-tiss/ noun inflammation of the retina.

retinol /**ret**-i-nol/ noun vitamin A.

retinopathy /re-ti-**nop**-uh-thi/ noun disease of the retina of the eye which results in impairment or loss of vision.

retinue /**ret**-i-nyoo/ noun a group of advisers or assistants accompanying an important person.
– ORIGIN from Old French *retenir* 'keep back, retain'.

retire verb 1 leave one's job and stop working, especially because one has reached a particular age. 2 (of a player) withdraw from a race or match because of injury. 3 leave a place, especially so as to go somewhere more private: *it was Mr Theil's habit to retire to his sitting room and stay there.* 4 go to bed. 5 (of a jury) leave the courtroom to decide the verdict of a trial.
– DERIVATIVES **retired** adjective **retiree** noun.
– ORIGIN French *retirer* 'draw back'.

retirement noun 1 the action or fact of retiring. 2 the period of one's life after retiring from work. 3 the state of being private; seclusion.

retirement pension noun Brit. a pension paid by the state to retired people above a certain age.

retiring adjective tending to avoid other people; shy.

retitle verb give a different title to a book, play, film, etc.

retold past and past participle of **RETELL**.

retook past of **RETAKE**.

retort[1] verb say something sharp or witty in answer to a remark or accusation. •noun a sharp or witty reply.
– ORIGIN Latin *retorquere* 'twist back'.

retort[2] noun 1 a container or furnace for carrying out a chemical process on a large or industrial scale. 2 historical a glass container with a long neck, used in distilling liquids and other chemical operations.
– ORIGIN Latin *retorta.*

retouch verb improve a painting, photograph, or other image by making slight additions or alterations.
– DERIVATIVES **retoucher** noun.

retrace verb 1 go back over the same route that one has just taken. 2 discover and follow a route taken by someone else. 3 trace something back to its source or beginning.

retract verb 1 withdraw a statement or accusation because it is not supported by evidence. 2 go back on an agreement or promise. 3 draw or be drawn back.
– DERIVATIVES **retractable** adjective **retraction** noun **retractor** noun.
– ORIGIN Latin *retrahere* 'draw back'.

retractile /ri-**trak**-tyl/ adjective capable of being retracted or drawn back: *retractile claws.*

retrain verb teach or learn new skills.

retransmit verb (**retransmits, retransmitting, retransmitted**) transmit data, a radio signal, or a broadcast again or on to another receiver.
– DERIVATIVES **retransmission** noun.

retread verb 1 (past **retrod**; past part. **retrodden**) go back over a path or one's steps. 2 (past and past part. **retreaded**) put a new tread on a worn tyre. •noun a tyre that has been given a new tread; a remould.

retreat verb 1 (of an army) withdraw from an attack on enemy forces. 2 move away or back. 3 go to a quiet or secluded place. 4 change one's mind as a result of criticism or difficulty. •noun 1 an act of retreating. 2 a quiet or secluded place. 3 a place where a person goes for a time in order to be quiet and pray or meditate. 4 a military musical ceremony carried out at sunset.
– ORIGIN Latin *retrahere* 'draw back'.

retrench verb reduce costs or spending in response to economic difficulty.
– DERIVATIVES **retrenchment** noun.
– ORIGIN French *retrancher* 'cut out'.

retrial noun a second or further trial on the same issues and with the same parties.

retribution /ret-ri-**byoo**-sh'n/ noun severe punishment in revenge for a wrong or criminal act.
– DERIVATIVES **retributive** /ri-**trib**-yuu-tiv/

adjective **retributory** /ri-trib-yuu-tuh-ri/ adjective.
– ORIGIN Latin.

retrieve verb **1** get or bring something back.
2 (of a dog) find and bring back game that has been shot. **3** find or extract information stored in a computer. **4** make a difficult situation better.
– DERIVATIVES **retrievable** adjective **retrieval** noun.
– ORIGIN Old French *retrover* 'find again'.

retriever noun a dog of a breed used for finding and bringing back game that has been shot.

retro adjective imitative of a style from the recent past. ●noun retro clothes, music, or style.
– ORIGIN French.

retro- combining form **1** back or backwards: *retrogression.* **2** behind: *retrorocket.*
– ORIGIN Latin *retro* 'backwards'.

retroactive adjective (especially of a law) taking effect from a date in the past.
– DERIVATIVES **retroactively** adverb.

retrod past of RETREAD (in sense 1).

retrodden past participle of RETREAD (in sense 1).

retrofit verb (retrofits, retrofitting, retrofitted) fit something with a component or accessory not fitted during manufacture. ●noun an act of fitting a component or accessory to something after manufacture.
– ORIGIN from RETROACTIVE and REFIT.

retrograde adjective **1** directed or moving backwards. **2** going back to an earlier and worse situation: *reconsidering these concepts would be a retrograde step.* **3** (of the order of something) reversed. **4** chiefly Astronomy (of the apparent motion of a planet) in a reverse direction from normal (from east to west). ●verb go back in position or time.
– DERIVATIVES **retrogradation** noun.
– ORIGIN Latin *retrogradus.*

retrogression noun the process of returning to an earlier state, especially a worse one.
– DERIVATIVES **retrogressive** adjective.

retrorocket noun a small auxiliary rocket on a spacecraft or missile, fired in the direction of travel to slow it down.

retrospect noun (in phrase **in retrospect**) when looking back on a past event; with hindsight.
– DERIVATIVES **retrospection** noun.

retrospective adjective **1** looking back on or dealing with past events. **2** (of an exhibition) showing the development of an artist's work over a period of time. **3** (of a statute or legal decision) taking effect from a date in the past. ●noun an exhibition showing the development of an artist's work over time.
– DERIVATIVES **retrospectively** adverb.

retroussé /ruh-troo-say/ adjective (of a person's nose) turned up at the tip.
– ORIGIN French, 'tucked up'.

retrovirus /re-troh-vy-ruhss/ noun any of a group of RNA viruses which insert a DNA copy of their genetic material into the host cell in order to replicate, e.g. HIV.
– DERIVATIVES **retroviral** adjective.
– ORIGIN from the initial letters of *reverse transcriptase* + VIRUS.

retsina /ret-see-nuh/ noun a Greek white wine flavoured with resin.
– ORIGIN modern Greek.

retune verb tune a radio, musical instrument, etc. again or differently.

return verb **1** come or go back to a place. **2** (**return to**) go back to a particular state or activity. **3** give, send, or put back: *she returned the spider to the garden.* **4** feel, say, or do the same feeling, action, etc. in response: *she didn't return my phone calls.* **5** (in tennis) hit or send the ball back to an opponent. **6** (of a judge or jury) state a verdict in response to a formal request. **7** yield or make a profit. **8** (of voters) elect a person or party to office. ●noun **1** an act or the action of returning. **2** a profit from an investment. **3** Brit. a ticket allowing travel to a place and back again. **4** (also **return match** or **game**) a second sporting contest between the same opponents. **5** a ticket for an event that has been returned because no longer wanted. **6** an official report in response to a formal demand: *census returns.*
– PHRASES **by return of post** Brit. in the next available mail delivery to the sender. **many happy returns of the day** a greeting to someone on their birthday.
– DERIVATIVES **returnable** adjective **returner** noun.
– ORIGIN Old French *returner.*

returnee noun **1** a person who returns to their own country from abroad. **2** a person who returns to work after a long absence.

returning officer noun Brit. the official in each constituency who conducts an election and announces the result.

retying present participle of RETIE.

retype verb type words again, especially to correct a mistake.

reunify verb (reunifies, reunifying, reunified) restore political unity to a place or group.
– DERIVATIVES **reunification** noun.

reunion noun **1** the action of coming or bringing together again after a period of separation. **2** a social gathering of people who have not seen each other for some time.

reunite verb bring or come together again after a period of separation.

reuse verb /ree-yooz/ use something again or more than once. ●noun /ree-yooss/ the action of using something again.
– DERIVATIVES **reusable** adjective.

Rev. abbreviation Reverend.

rev informal noun (**revs**) the number of revolutions of an engine per minute. ●verb (**revs, revving, revved**) increase the running speed of an engine by pressing the accelerator.

revalue verb (revalues, revaluing, revalued) **1** assess the value of something again. **2** adjust the official value of a currency in relation to other currencies.
– DERIVATIVES **revaluation** noun.

revamp verb /ree-vamp/ alter something so as to improve its appearance. ●noun /ree-vamp/ an act of improving the appearance of something.

revanchism /ri-vanch-i-z'm/ noun a policy of retaliation, especially to recover lost territory.
– DERIVATIVES **revanchist** adjective & noun.
– ORIGIN from French *revanche* 'revenge'.

r

Revd abbreviation Brit. Reverend.

reveal[1] verb **1** make information that was previously unknown or secret known to others. **2** cause or allow to be seen: *the clouds were breaking up to reveal a clear blue sky.*
– DERIVATIVES **revealer** noun.
– ORIGIN Latin *revelare.*

reveal[2] noun either side surface of an opening in a wall for a door or window.
– ORIGIN from Old French *revaler* 'to lower'.

revealing adjective **1** making interesting information known to others. **2** (of an item of clothing) allowing much of the wearer's body to be seen.
– DERIVATIVES **revealingly** adverb.

reveille /ri-val-li/ noun a signal sounded on a bugle or drum to wake personnel in the armed forces.
– ORIGIN from French *réveillez!* 'wake up!'

revel verb (**revels, revelling, revelled;** US **revels, reveling, reveled**) **1** enjoy oneself with others in a lively and noisy way. **2** (**revel in**) gain great pleasure from. •noun (**revels**) lively and noisy celebrations.
– DERIVATIVES **reveller** noun **revelry** noun (pl. **revelries**).
– ORIGIN Old French *reveler* 'rise up in rebellion'.

revelation noun **1** the revealing of something previously secret or unknown. **2** a surprising and previously unknown fact: *revelations about his personal life.* **3** the revealing of knowledge to humans by God. **4** (**Revelation** or informal **Revelations**) the last book of the New Testament, describing God's revelation of the future to St John.
– DERIVATIVES **revelational** adjective.

revelatory /rev-uh-lay-tuh-ri, rev-uh-luh-tuh-ri/ adjective revealing something previously unknown.

revenant /rev-uh-nuhnt/ noun a person who has returned, especially supposedly from the dead.
– ORIGIN from French, 'coming back'.

revenge noun harmful action taken in return for an injury or wrong: *he would some day take his revenge on reporters.* •verb **1** (**revenge oneself** or **be revenged**) take harmful action against someone for an injury or wrong done to oneself. **2** take revenge on behalf of someone else for a wrong or injury.
– ORIGIN Old French *revencher.*

revengeful adjective eager for revenge.

revenue noun **1** the income received by an organization. **2** a state's annual income, received especially from taxes, from which public expenses are met.
– ORIGIN from Latin *revenire* 'return'.

reverberate verb **1** (of a loud noise) be repeated as an echo. **2** have continuing serious effects: *the effects of his suicide reverberated around the globe*
– DERIVATIVES **reverberant** adjective **reverberation** noun.
– ORIGIN Latin *reverberare* 'strike again'.

revere /ri-veer/ verb respect or admire someone or something deeply.
– ORIGIN Latin *revereri.*

reverence noun **1** deep respect or admiration for someone or something. **2** (**His/Your**

Reverence) a title given to a member of the clergy, especially a priest in Ireland. •verb respect or admire someone or something deeply.

reverend adjective a title or form of address to members of the Christian clergy. •noun informal a clergyman.

reverent adjective showing deep respect.
– DERIVATIVES **reverential** adjective **reverently** adverb.

reverie /rev-uh-ri/ noun a daydream.
– ORIGIN Old French, 'rejoicing, revelry'.

revers /ri-veer/ noun (pl. same /ri-veerz/) the turned-back edge of a garment revealing the underside, especially at the lapel.
– ORIGIN French, 'reverse'.

reversal noun **1** a change to an opposite direction, position, or course of action. **2** an adverse change of fortune.

reverse verb **1** move backwards. **2** make something the opposite of what it was: *the damage done to the ozone layer may be reversed.* **3** turn something the other way round or up or inside out. **4** cancel or annul a judgement by a lower court or authority. **5** (of an engine) work in an opposite direction from normal. •adjective **1** going in or turned towards the opposite direction. **2** operating or behaving in a way opposite to that which is usual or expected. •noun **1** a complete change of direction or action. **2** (**the reverse**) the opposite to that previously stated. **3** a setback or defeat. **4** the opposite side or face to the observer. **5** the side of a coin or medal bearing the value or secondary design. **6** reverse gear.
– PHRASES **reverse the charges** chiefly Brit. make the person who receives a telephone call responsible for paying for it.
– ORIGIN Latin *revertere* 'turn back'.

reverse engineering noun the reproduction of another manufacturer's product after detailed examination of how it is made.

reverse gear noun a gear making a vehicle or piece of machinery move or work backwards.

reversible adjective **1** able to be returned to an original state or position: *the rise in crime is reversible.* **2** (of a garment or fabric) able to be turned inside out and worn or used with either side visible.
– DERIVATIVES **reversibility** noun **reversibly** adverb.

reversion /ri-ver-sh'n/ noun **1** a return to a previous state, practice, or belief. **2** Biology the action of an organism returning to a former or ancestral type. **3** the legal right, especially of the original owner, to possess or succeed to property when the present possessor dies or a lease ends.
– DERIVATIVES **reversionary** adjective.

revert verb (**revert to**) **1** return to a previous state, condition, or subject. **2** Biology (of an organism) return to a former or ancestral type. **3** (of property) legally return to the original owner.
– ORIGIN Latin *revertere* 'turn back'.

revetment /ri-vet-muhnt/ noun **1** a retaining wall of masonry that supports or protects a rampart, wall, etc. **2** a barricade of earth or sandbags providing protection from blast or to

r

prevent aircraft from overrunning when landing.
– ORIGIN French *revêtement*.

review noun **1** a formal assessment of something with the intention of making changes if necessary. **2** a critical assessment of a book, play, or other work. **3** a report on a past event. **4** Law a reconsideration of a judgement, sentence, etc. by a higher court or authority. **5** a ceremonial display and formal inspection of military or naval forces. •verb **1** assess something formally with the intention of making changes if necessary. **2** write a review of a play, book, or other work. **3** Law submit a sentence, case, etc. for reconsideration by a higher court or authority. **4** view something again.
– DERIVATIVES **reviewable** adjective **reviewer** noun.
– ORIGIN from former French *reveue*.

revile verb criticize someone in an abusive or scornful way.
– ORIGIN Old French *reviler*.

revise verb **1** reconsider and alter an opinion or judgement in the light of further evidence. **2** examine and amend a piece of writing. **3** Brit. reread work done previously in order to prepare for an exam. •noun Printing a proof including corrections made in an earlier proof.
– DERIVATIVES **reviser** noun.
– ORIGIN Latin *revisere* 'look at again'.

revision noun **1** the action of revising something. **2** a revised edition or form of something.
– DERIVATIVES **revisionary** adjective.

revisionism noun often derogatory the reconsideration or modification of accepted theories or principles.
– DERIVATIVES **revisionist** noun & adjective.

revisit verb (**revisits, revisiting, revisited**) **1** come back to or visit a place again. **2** consider a situation again or from a different perspective.

revitalize (or **revitalise**) verb give new life and vitality to someone or something.
– DERIVATIVES **revitalization** noun.

revival noun **1** an improvement in the condition, strength, or popularity of something: *an economic revival.* **2** a new production of a play that has not been performed for some time. **3** a reawakening of religious faith brought about by evangelistic meetings.

revivalism noun **1** the promotion of a revival of religious faith. **2** a tendency or desire to revive a former custom or practice.
– DERIVATIVES **revivalist** noun & adjective.

revive verb **1** make someone conscious, healthy, or strong again. **2** restore interest in or the popularity of: *this style was revived in the 1970s.* **3** improve the condition of something.
– DERIVATIVES **revivable** adjective **reviver** noun.
– ORIGIN Latin *revivere*.

revivify /ree-viv-i-fy/ verb (**revivifies, revivifying, revivified**) give new life or strength to someone or something.
– DERIVATIVES **revivification** noun.

revoke verb officially cancel a decree or decision.
– DERIVATIVES **revocable** adjective **revocation** noun.

– ORIGIN Latin *revocare* 'call back'.

revolt verb **1** take violent action against a government or ruler. **2** refuse to acknowledge someone or something as having authority: *the new chefs began to revolt against classic haute cuisine.* **3** make someone feel disgust. •noun **1** an attempt to overthrow a government or ruler by violent action. **2** a refusal to continue to obey something: *a revolt over tax increases.*
– DERIVATIVES **revolting** adjective.
– ORIGIN French *révolter*.

revolution noun **1** a forcible overthrow of a government or social order, in favour of a new system. **2** a great and far-reaching change: *marketing underwent a revolution.* **3** movement in orbit or in a circular course around a central point. **4** a complete circular movement around a central point.
– DERIVATIVES **revolutionist** noun.
– ORIGIN Latin.

revolutionary adjective **1** involving or causing great change: *a revolutionary new drug.* **2** engaged in or relating to political revolution. •noun (pl. **revolutionaries**) a person who starts or supports a political revolution.

revolutionize (or **revolutionise**) verb change something greatly or completely.

revolve verb **1** move in a circle around a central point. **2** (**revolve about/around**) move in a circular orbit around. **3** (**revolve around**) treat as the most important aspect: *her life revolved around her husband.*
– ORIGIN Latin *revolvere* 'roll back'.

revolver noun a pistol with revolving chambers enabling several shots to be fired without reloading.

revolving door noun an entrance to a large building in which four partitions turn about a central point.

revue noun a theatrical show with short sketches, songs, and dances, typically dealing satirically with topical issues.
– ORIGIN French, 'review'.

revulsion noun a feeling of disgust and horror.
– ORIGIN Latin.

reward noun **1** a thing given in recognition of service, effort, or achievement. **2** a fair return for good or bad behaviour: *a slap in the face was his reward for his cheek.* **3** a sum of money offered for helping to find a criminal or handing in lost property. •verb **1** give a reward to someone to show appreciation of their service, qualities, or achievements. **2** (**be rewarded**) receive what one deserves.
– ORIGIN Old French *reguard* 'regard, heed'.

rewarding adjective providing satisfaction.
– DERIVATIVES **rewardingly** adverb.

rewind verb (past and past part. **rewound**) wind a film or tape back to the beginning. •noun a mechanism for rewinding a film or tape.
– DERIVATIVES **rewinder** noun.

rewire verb provide a building, device, or vehicle with new electric wiring.
– DERIVATIVES **rewirable** adjective.

reword verb put something into different words.

rework verb change something in order to improve or update it.

r

rewound past and past participle of REWIND.

rewritable adjective Computing (of a storage device) enabling previously recorded data to be overwritten.

rewrite verb (past **rewrote**; past part. **rewritten**) write something again so as to change or improve it. •noun an instance of rewriting.

Rex noun the reigning king (following a name or in the titles of lawsuits, e.g. *Rex v. Jones*: the Crown versus Jones).
– ORIGIN Latin, 'king'.

Rf symbol the chemical element rutherfordium.

RFC abbreviation Rugby Football Club.

Rg symbol the chemical element roentgenium.

RGN abbreviation Registered General Nurse.

Rh abbreviation rhesus (factor).

rhapsodize (or **rhapsodise**) verb express great enthusiasm about someone or something.

rhapsody noun (pl. **rhapsodies**) **1** an expression of great joy or enthusiasm: *rhapsodies of praise*. **2** a musical composition that is full of feeling and is not regular in form. **3** (in ancient Greece) an epic poem of a suitable length for recitation at one time.
– DERIVATIVES **rhapsodic** adjective.
– ORIGIN Greek *rhapsōidia*.

rhea /ree-uh/ noun a large flightless bird of South American grasslands, resembling a small ostrich with greyish-brown plumage.
– ORIGIN from *Rhea*, the mother of Zeus in Greek mythology.

Rhenish /ren-ish/ adjective relating to the River Rhine and the regions adjoining it.
– ORIGIN from Latin *Rhenus* 'Rhine'.

rhenium /ree-ni-uhm/ noun a rare silvery-white metallic element.
– ORIGIN from Latin *Rhenus* 'Rhine'.

rheology /ri-ol-uh-ji/ noun the branch of physics concerned with the deformation and flow of matter.
– DERIVATIVES **rheological** adjective **rheologist** noun.
– ORIGIN from Greek *rheos* 'stream'.

rheostat /ree-uh-stat/ noun an instrument used to control the current in an electrical circuit by varying the amount of resistance in it.
– DERIVATIVES **rheostatic** adjective.
– ORIGIN from Greek *rheos* 'stream'.

rhesus factor /ree-suhss/ noun a substance in red blood cells which can cause disease in a newborn baby whose blood contains the factor (i.e. is **rhesus positive**) while the mother's blood does not (i.e. is **rhesus negative**).
– ORIGIN from RHESUS MONKEY, in which the substance was first observed.

rhesus monkey noun a small brown macaque with red skin on the face and rump, native to southern Asia.
– ORIGIN Greek *Rhēsos*, a mythical king of Thrace.

rhetoric /ret-uh-rik/ noun **1** the art of effective or persuasive speaking or writing. **2** persuasive or impressive language that is insincere or meaningless: *I was sick of empty nationalist rhetoric*.
– ORIGIN from Greek *rhētorikē tekhnē* 'art of rhetoric'.

rhetorical /ri-tor-i-k'l/ adjective **1** relating to rhetoric. **2** (of a statement) intended to persuade or impress. **3** (of a question) asked for effect or to make a statement rather than to obtain an answer.
– DERIVATIVES **rhetorically** adverb.

rhetorician /ret-uh-ri-sh'n/ noun **1** an expert in the art of effective or persuasive speaking or writing. **2** a speaker whose words are intended to impress or persuade.

rheum /rhymes with room/ noun chiefly literary a watery fluid that collects in or drips from the nose or eyes.
– DERIVATIVES **rheumy** adjective.
– ORIGIN Greek *rheuma* 'stream'.

rheumatic /roo-mat-ik/ adjective relating to or having rheumatism. •noun a person with rheumatism.
– DERIVATIVES **rheumaticky** adjective (informal).
– ORIGIN first referring to infection characterized by a watery fluid (see RHEUM).

rheumatic fever noun an acute fever marked by inflammation and pain in the joints, caused by a bacterial infection.

rheumatics plural noun (usu. treated as sing.) informal rheumatism.

rheumatism noun any disease marked by inflammation and pain in the joints, muscles, or fibrous tissue.
– ORIGIN from Greek *rheuma* 'stream' (the disease was believed to be caused by the internal flow of 'watery' humours).

rheumatoid /roo-muh-toyd/ adjective relating to or resembling rheumatism.

rheumatoid arthritis noun a disease that gradually worsens, causing inflammation in the joints and painful swelling and immobility.

rheumatology /roo-muh-tol-uh-ji/ noun the study of rheumatism, arthritis, and other disorders of the joints, muscles, and ligaments.
– DERIVATIVES **rheumatological** adjective **rheumatologist** noun.

rhinestone noun an imitation diamond.
– ORIGIN translating French *caillou du Rhin* 'pebble of the Rhine'.

rhinitis /ry-ny-tiss, ri-ny-tiss/ noun inflammation of the mucous membrane of the nose, caused by infection with a virus or an allergic reaction.
– ORIGIN from Greek *rhis* 'nose'.

rhino noun (pl. same or **rhinos**) informal a rhinoceros.

rhinoceros /ry-noss-uh-ruhss/ noun (pl. same or **rhinoceroses**) a large plant-eating mammal with one or two horns on the nose and thick folded skin, native to Africa and South Asia.
– ORIGIN from Greek *rhis* 'nose' + *keras* 'horn'.

rhinoplasty /ry-noh-plass-ti/ noun (pl. **rhinoplasties**) plastic surgery performed on the nose.

rhizome /ry-zohm/ noun a horizontal underground plant stem bearing both roots and shoots.
– ORIGIN Greek *rhizōma*.

Rhodesian /roh-dee-sh'n, roh-dee-zh'n/ noun a person from Rhodesia (now Zimbabwe). •adjective relating to Rhodesia.

r

Rhodes Scholarship noun any of several scholarships awarded annually for study at Oxford University by students from certain Commonwealth countries, the US, and Germany.
– DERIVATIVES **Rhodes scholar** noun.
– ORIGIN named after the South African statesman and founder of the scholarships Cecil *Rhodes*.

rhodium /roh-di-uhm/ noun a hard, dense silvery-white metallic element.
– ORIGIN from Greek *rhodon* 'rose'.

rhododendron /roh-duh-**den**-druhn/ noun a shrub with large clusters of colourful trumpet-shaped flowers and large evergreen leaves.
– ORIGIN from Greek *rhodon* 'rose' + *dendron* 'tree'.

rhombi plural of RHOMBUS.

rhombohedron /rom-buh-**hee**-druhn/ noun (pl. **rhombohedra** /rom-buh-**hee**-druh/ or **rhombohedrons**) a solid figure whose faces are six equal rhombuses.
– DERIVATIVES **rhombohedral** adjective.

rhomboid /**rom**-boyd/ adjective having or resembling the shape of a rhombus. • noun a parallelogram in which adjacent sides are unequal.
– DERIVATIVES **rhomboidal** adjective.

rhombus /**rom**-buhss/ noun (pl. **rhombuses** or **rhombi** /**rom**-by/) a quadrilateral whose sides all have the same length.
– ORIGIN Greek *rhombos* 'thing that can be spun round, a rhombus'.

rhubarb noun 1 the thick reddish or green leaf stalks of a plant, which are cooked and eaten as a fruit. 2 Brit. informal noise made by a group of actors to give the impression of indistinct background conversation.
– ORIGIN Latin *rheubarbarum, rhabarbarum* 'foreign rhubarb'.

rhumba noun variant spelling of RUMBA.

rhyme noun 1 a word that has the same sound or ends with the same sound as another. 2 similarity of sound between words or the endings of words. 3 a short poem with rhyming lines. • verb 1 (of a word, syllable, or line) have or end with the same sound as another. 2 (**rhyme something with**) put a word together with another word that has a similar sound. 3 literary compose poetry.
– PHRASES **rhyme or reason** logical explanation: *there's no rhyme or reason to it.*
– DERIVATIVES **rhymer** noun.
– ORIGIN Greek *rhuthmos* 'rhythm'.

rhymester noun a person who composes simple or inferior rhymes.

rhyming slang noun a type of slang that replaces words with rhyming words or phrases, typically with the rhyming element omitted (e.g. *butcher's*, short for *butcher's hook*, meaning 'look').

rhyolite /**ry**-uh-lyt/ noun a pale, fine-grained volcanic rock similar to granite in composition.
– ORIGIN German *Rhyolit*.

rhythm /**ri**-thuhm/ noun 1 a strong, regular repeated pattern of music, sound, or movement. 2 a particular pattern formed by musical rhythm: *a slow waltz rhythm.* 3 the measured flow of words and phrases in verse or prose as determined by the length of and stress on syllables. 4 a regularly recurring sequence of events or processes: *the twice daily rhythms of the tides.*
– DERIVATIVES **rhythmless** adjective.
– ORIGIN Greek *rhuthmos*.

rhythm and blues noun popular music of US black origin, arising from a combination of blues with jazz rhythms.

rhythmic adjective 1 having or relating to rhythm. 2 occurring regularly.
– DERIVATIVES **rhythmical** adjective **rhythmically** adverb **rhythmicity** noun.

rhythm method noun a method of birth control in which sex is restricted to the times of a woman's menstrual cycle when ovulation is likely to occur.

rhythm section noun the part of a pop or jazz group supplying the rhythm, in particular the bass and drums.

RI abbreviation Rhode Island.

ria /**ree**-uh/ noun a long narrow inlet formed by the partial submerging of a river valley by the sea.
– ORIGIN Spanish, 'estuary'.

rial /ree-**ahl**, ree-ahl/ (also **riyal**) noun 1 the basic unit of money of Iran and Oman. 2 (usu. **riyal**) the basic unit of money of Saudi Arabia, Qatar, and Yemen.
– ORIGIN Arabic.

rib noun 1 each of a series of thin bones attached in pairs to the spine and curving round to protect the chest and its organs. 2 a curved structure that supports a vault. 3 a curved strut forming part of the framework of a ship's hull. 4 a vein of a leaf or an insect's wing. 5 a combination of alternate plain and purl knitting stitches producing a ridged, slightly elastic fabric. • verb (**ribs, ribbing, ribbed**) 1 mark with or form into ridges: *the road was ribbed with furrows of slush.* 2 informal tease someone good-naturedly.
– ORIGIN Old English.

RIBA abbreviation Royal Institute of British Architects.

ribald /**ri**-buhld, ry-bawld/ adjective referring to sex in an amusingly coarse way.
– ORIGIN from Old French *riber* 'indulge in licentious pleasures'.

ribaldry noun coarse humorous talk or behaviour.

riband /**ri**-buhnd/ noun old use a ribbon.
– ORIGIN Old French *riban*.

ribbed adjective 1 having a pattern of raised bands. 2 (of a vault or other structure) strengthened with ribs.

ribbing noun 1 a rib-like structure or pattern. 2 informal good-natured teasing.

ribbon noun 1 a long, narrow strip of fabric, used for tying something or for decoration. 2 a ribbon of a special colour or design awarded as a prize or worn to indicate the holding of an honour. 3 something that is long and narrow in shape. 4 a narrow band of inked material on a spool, used to produce the characters in some typewriters and computer printers.
– PHRASES **cut** (or **tear**) **something to ribbons** severely damage something.

r

– DERIVATIVES **ribboned** adjective.
– ORIGIN from RIBAND.

ribbon development noun Brit. the development of a settlement along a main road.

ribby adjective having prominent ribs.

ribcage noun the bony frame formed by the ribs.

riboflavin /ry-boh-**flay**-vin/ noun vitamin B₂, a compound essential for energy production and present in milk, liver, and green vegetables.
– ORIGIN from *ribose* (a sugar found in DNA) + Latin *flavus* 'yellow'.

ribonucleic acid /ry-boh-nyoo-**klay**-ik, ry-boh-nyoo-**klee**-ik/ noun see **RNA**.
– ORIGIN from *ribose* (a sugar found in DNA) + NUCLEIC ACID.

rib-tickler noun informal a very amusing joke or story.

rice noun the grains of a cereal plant which is grown for food on wet land in warm countries. • verb N. Amer. force cooked potatoes or other vegetables through a sieve or similar utensil.
– DERIVATIVES **ricer** noun (N. Amer.).
– ORIGIN Old French *ris*.

ricepaper noun thin edible paper made from the flattened and dried pith of a shrub, used in oriental painting and in baking biscuits and cakes.

rich adjective 1 having a great deal of money or assets. 2 (of a country or region) having valuable natural resources or a successful economy. 3 made of expensive materials: *rich mahogany furniture.* 4 existing in plentiful quantities; abundant. 5 having or producing something in large amounts: *fruits rich in vitamins.* 6 (of food) containing much fat, sugar, etc. 7 (of a colour, sound, or smell) pleasantly deep and strong. 8 (of soil or land) fertile. 9 (of the mixture in an internal-combustion engine) containing a high proportion of fuel. 10 informal (of a remark) causing ironic amusement or indignation.
– DERIVATIVES **richness** noun.
– ORIGIN Old English, 'powerful, wealthy'.

riches plural noun 1 material wealth. 2 valuable natural resources.

richly adverb 1 in a rich way. 2 fully: *a richly deserved holiday.*

Richter scale /**rik**-ter/ noun a scale for expressing the magnitude of an earthquake.
– ORIGIN named after the American geologist Charles F. *Richter.*

ricin /**ry**-sin, **ri**-sin/ noun a highly toxic protein obtained from the seeds of the castor oil plant.
– ORIGIN from Latin *Ricinus communis* (referring to the castor oil plant).

rick¹ noun a stack of hay, corn, or straw, especially one built into a regular shape.
– ORIGIN Old English.

rick² Brit. noun a slight sprain or strain in the neck or back. • verb strain one's neck or back slightly.
– ORIGIN dialect.

rickets /**ri**-kits/ noun (treated as sing. or pl.) a disease of children caused by a lack of vitamin D, in which the bones become softened and distorted.
– ORIGIN perhaps from Greek *rhakhitis*, from

rhakhis 'spine'.

rickety adjective poorly made and likely to collapse.
– DERIVATIVES **ricketiness** noun.

rickrack noun braided trimming in a zigzag pattern, used on clothes.
– ORIGIN unknown.

rickshaw noun a light two-wheeled hooded vehicle drawn by one or more people, used in Asian countries.
– ORIGIN Japanese, 'person-strength-vehicle'.

ricochet verb (ricochets /**ri**-kuh-shayz/, ricocheting /**ri**-kuh-shay-ing/, ricocheted /ri-kuh-shayd/) (of a bullet or other fast moving object) rebound off a surface. • noun /**ri**-kuh-shay/ 1 a shot or hit that rebounds off a surface. 2 the action of rebounding off a surface.
– ORIGIN French.

ricotta /ri-**kot**-tuh/ noun a soft white unsalted Italian cheese.
– ORIGIN Italian, 'cooked again'.

rictus /**rik**-tuhss/ noun a fixed grimace or grin.
– DERIVATIVES **rictal** adjective.
– ORIGIN Latin, 'open mouth'.

rid verb (rids, ridding, rid) 1 (rid someone/thing of) make someone or something free of an unwanted person or thing. 2 (be (or get) rid of) be or make oneself free of someone or something that is unwanted or annoying.
– ORIGIN Old Norse.

riddance noun (in phrase good riddance) said to express relief at being rid of someone or something.

ridden past participle of RIDE. adjective (in combination) full of a particular thing: *guilt-ridden.*

riddle¹ noun 1 a question or statement that is worded in such a way that one needs to think hard to find its answer or meaning. 2 a puzzling person or thing.
– DERIVATIVES **riddler** noun.
– ORIGIN Old English.

riddle² verb 1 make many holes in someone or something. 2 fill with something undesirable: *my foot is now riddled with arthritis.* 3 pass a substance through a large coarse sieve. • noun a large coarse sieve.
– ORIGIN Old English.

ride verb (past rode; past part. **ridden**) 1 sit on and control the movement of a horse, bicycle, or motorcycle. 2 (usu. ride in/on) travel in a vehicle or on a horse. 3 travel over an area on horseback or on a bicycle or motorcycle. 4 be carried or supported by: *surfers rode the waves.* 5 sail or float: *a ship rode at anchor in the dock.* 6 (ride on) depend on. 7 (ride something out) come safely through a difficult situation. 8 (ride up) (of an item of clothing) gradually move upwards out of its proper position. 9 yield to a blow so as to reduce its impact. 10 (be ridden) be full of or dominated by: *people ridden by ill health.* • noun 1 an act of riding. 2 a roller coaster, roundabout, etc. ridden at a fair or amusement park. 3 a path for horse riding.
– PHRASES **be riding for a fall** informal be acting in a reckless way that invites failure. **let something ride** take no immediate action over something. **ride high** be successful. **ride to**

r

hounds chiefly Brit. go fox-hunting on horseback. **a rough** (or **easy**) **ride** a difficult (or easy) time. **take someone for a ride** informal deceive someone.
– DERIVATIVES **rideable** (also **ridable**) adjective.
– ORIGIN Old English.

rider noun **1** a person who rides a horse, bicycle, motorcycle, etc. **2** a condition added to something already agreed.
– DERIVATIVES **riderless** adjective.

ridge noun **1** a long narrow hilltop or mountain range. **2** a narrow raised strip on a surface. **3** Meteorology a long, narrow region of high pressure. **4** the edge formed where the two sloping sides of a roof meet at the top. •**verb** (often as adj. **ridged**) form something into ridges.
– DERIVATIVES **ridgy** adjective.
– ORIGIN Old English, 'spine, crest'.

ridge tent noun a tent with a central ridge supported by a pole or frame at each end.

ridicule noun the use of language to make fun of someone or something in an unkind way: *he became an object of ridicule among his own aides.* •**verb** mock or make fun of someone or something.

ridiculous adjective very silly or unreasonable; absurd.
– DERIVATIVES **ridiculously** adverb **ridiculousness** noun.
– ORIGIN Latin *ridiculus* 'laughable'.

riding[1] noun the sport or activity of riding horses.

riding[2] noun **1** (usu. **the East/North/West Riding**) one of three former administrative divisions of Yorkshire. **2** an electoral district of Canada.
– ORIGIN Old Norse, 'third part'.

riding crop noun a short flexible whip with a loop for the hand, used when riding horses.

riding habit noun a woman's riding dress, consisting of a skirt and a double-breasted jacket.

riel /*rhymes with* reel/ noun the basic unit of money of Cambodia.
– ORIGIN Khmer.

Riesling /**reez**-ling, **reess**-ling/ noun a dry white wine made from a variety of grape grown especially in Germany and Austria.
– ORIGIN German.

rife adjective **1** (especially of something undesirable) widespread: *drug addiction is rife.* **2** (**rife with**) full of something, especially something undesirable.
– ORIGIN Old English.

riff noun a short repeated phrase in popular music or jazz. •**verb** play riffs.
– ORIGIN from **RIFFLE**.

riffle verb **1** turn over the pages of a book or document quickly and casually. **2** (**riffle through**) search quickly through. •**noun** an act of turning over pages or searching through something.
– ORIGIN perhaps from **RUFFLE**, influenced by **RIPPLE**.

riff-raff noun people who are considered disreputable or socially unacceptable.
– ORIGIN from Old French *rif et raf* 'one and all, every bit'.

rifle[1] noun **1** a gun having a long spirally grooved barrel to make a bullet spin and thereby increase accuracy over a long distance. **2** (**rifles**) troops armed with rifles. •**verb** **1** (usu. as adj. **rifled**) make spiral grooves in a gun or its barrel or bore. **2** hit or kick a ball hard and straight.
– ORIGIN from French *rifler* 'graze, scratch'.

rifle[2] verb **1** search through something hurriedly to find or steal something. **2** steal something.
– ORIGIN Old French *rifler* 'graze, plunder'.

rifleman noun (pl. **riflemen**) a soldier armed with a rifle.

rifling noun spiral grooves on the inside of a rifle barrel.

rift noun **1** a crack, split, or break. **2** a serious break in friendly relations.
– ORIGIN Scandinavian.

rift valley noun a steep-sided valley formed by subsidence of the earth's surface between nearly parallel faults.

rig[1] verb (**rigs**, **rigging**, **rigged**) **1** provide a boat with sails and rigging. **2** assemble and adjust the equipment of a sailing boat, aircraft, etc. in readiness for operation. **3** set up a device or structure, often in a makeshift way: *he'd rigged up a sort of tent.* **4** (**rig someone out**) dress someone in a particular outfit. •**noun** **1** the arrangement of a boat's sails and rigging. **2** equipment or a device for a particular purpose: *a lighting rig.* **3** an oil rig or drilling rig. **4** a person's costume or outfit. **5** chiefly N. Amer. & Austral./NZ a lorry.
– DERIVATIVES **rigged** adjective.
– ORIGIN perhaps Scandinavian.

rig[2] verb (**rigs**, **rigging**, **rigged**) manage or arrange in a dishonest way so as to gain an advantage: *the results of the elections had been rigged.*
– ORIGIN unknown.

rigatoni /ri-guh-**toh**-ni/ plural noun pasta in the form of short hollow fluted tubes.
– ORIGIN Italian.

rigger[1] noun **1** (in combination) a ship rigged in a particular way: *a square-rigger.* **2** a person who erects and maintains scaffolding or cranes. **3** a person who works on or helps to build an oil rig.

rigger[2] noun a person who dishonestly manages something to their advantage.

rigging noun **1** the system of ropes or chains supporting a ship's masts and controlling or setting the yards and sails. **2** the ropes and wires supporting the structure of a hang-glider or parachute.

right adjective **1** on, towards, or relating to the side of a person or thing which is to the east when the person or thing is facing north. **2** morally good, justified, or acceptable: *I hope we're doing the right thing.* **3** factually correct. **4** most appropriate: *the right man for the job.* **5** in a satisfactory, sound, or normal condition. **6** relating to a right-wing person or group. **7** Brit. informal complete; absolute: *I felt a right idiot.* •**adverb** **1** on or to the right side. **2** to the furthest extent or degree; completely: *the car spun right off the track.* **3** exactly; directly. **4** in a correct or satisfactory way. **5** informal without delay; immediately. •**noun** **1** that which is

morally right. **2** a moral or legal entitlement to have or do something: *you have every right to be angry.* **3** (**rights**) the authority to perform, publish, or film a particular work or event. **4** (**the right**) the right-hand part, side, or direction. **5** a right turn. **6** a person's right fist, or a blow given with it. **7** (often **the Right**) (treated as sing. or pl.) a group or political party favouring conservative views. •verb **1** return someone or something to a normal or upright position. **2** return to a normal or correct condition: *righting the economy demanded cuts in defence spending.* **3** make amends for a wrong.
– PHRASES **bang to rights** Brit. informal (of a criminal) with positive proof of guilt. **by rights** if things were fair or correct. **in one's own right** as a result of one's own qualifications or efforts. **put** (or **set**) **someone right** tell someone the true facts of a situation. **put** (or **set**) **something to rights** return something to its correct or normal state. **right** (or **straight**) **away** immediately. **right on** informal **1** expressing support, approval, or encouragement. **2** (**right-on**) informal, often derogatory in keeping with fashionable liberal or left-wing opinions and values. **a right one** Brit. informal a silly person.
– DERIVATIVES **righter** noun **rightish** adjective **rightmost** adjective **rightness** noun **rightward** adjective & adverb **rightwards** adverb.
– ORIGIN Old English.

right angle noun an angle of 90°, as in a corner of a square.
– PHRASES **at right angles to** forming an angle of 90° with.
– DERIVATIVES **right-angled** adjective.

right back noun a defender in football or field hockey who plays mainly on the right of the field.

righteous /ry-chuhss/ adjective **1** morally right or justifiable: *righteous indignation about pay and conditions.* **2** (of a person) morally good; virtuous.
– DERIVATIVES **righteously** adverb **righteousness** noun.

rightful adjective **1** having a legal or moral right to something. **2** rightly claimed; appropriate: *helping the sport reach its rightful place in the Olympics.*
– DERIVATIVES **rightfully** adverb **rightfulness** noun.

right hand noun **1** the region or direction on the right side of someone or something. **2** the most important position next to someone. •adjective **1** on or towards the right side. **2** done with or using the right hand.

right-hand drive noun a motor-vehicle steering system with the steering wheel and other controls fitted on the right side, for use in countries where vehicles drive on the left.

right-handed adjective **1** using or done with the right hand. **2** turning to the right; towards the right. **3** (of a screw) that is to be turned clockwise.

right-hander noun **1** a right-handed person. **2** a blow struck with a person's right hand.

right-hand man noun a person's chief assistant.

Right Honourable adjective Brit. a title given to certain high officials such as government

ministers.

rightism noun the political views or policies of the right.
– DERIVATIVES **rightist** noun & adjective.

rightly adverb **1** in accordance with what is true, morally right, or just. **2** with good reason.

right-minded (also **right-thinking**) adjective having views and principles that most people approve of.

right of abode noun chiefly Brit. a person's right to live in a country.

right of way noun **1** the legal right to pass along a specific route through another's property. **2** a public path through another's property. **3** the right of a vehicle or ship to go before another.

Right Reverend adjective a title given to a bishop, especially in the Anglican Church.

right side noun the side of something intended to be at the top or front.
– PHRASES **on the right side of 1** in favour with. **2** rather less than a specified age.

rights issue noun an issue of shares offered at a special price by a company to its existing shareholders.

rightsize verb chiefly US convert something to an appropriate size, especially by reducing staff levels in an organization.

right-to-life adjective another term for PRO-LIFE.

right whale noun a whale with a large head and a deeply curved jaw, of Arctic and temperate waters.

right wing noun **1** the conservative or reactionary section of a political party or system. [see LEFT WING.] **2** the right side of a sports team on the field or of an army.
– DERIVATIVES **right-winger** noun.

rigid adjective **1** unable to bend or be forced out of shape. **2** not able to be changed or adapted: *rigid rules governing the production of certain wines.* **3** stiff and unmoving, especially with fear.
– DERIVATIVES **rigidify** verb (**rigidifies, rigidifying, rigidified**). **rigidity** noun **rigidly** adverb.
– ORIGIN Latin *rigidus*.

rigmarole /rig-muh-rohl/ noun **1** a lengthy and complicated procedure. **2** a long, rambling story.
– ORIGIN probably from former *ragman roll*, referring to a legal document recording a list of offences.

rigor mortis /ri-ger mor-tiss/ noun stiffening of the joints and muscles a few hours after death, lasting from one to four days.
– ORIGIN Latin, 'stiffness of death'.

rigorous adjective **1** very thorough or accurate. **2** (of a rule or system) strictly applied or followed. **3** strictly following a belief or system. **4** harsh and demanding: *rigorous military training.*
– DERIVATIVES **rigorously** adverb **rigorousness** noun.

rigour (US **rigor**) noun **1** the quality of being thorough or severe: *his analysis is lacking in rigour.* **2** (**rigours**) demanding or extreme conditions.

r

– ORIGIN Latin *rigor* 'stiffness'.

rig-out noun informal, chiefly Brit. an outfit of clothes.

rijsttafel /ryst-tah-f'l/ noun a meal of SE Asian food consisting of a selection of spiced rice dishes.
– ORIGIN Dutch.

rile verb informal annoy or irritate someone.
– ORIGIN from **ROIL**.

Riley noun (in phrase **the life of Riley**) informal a luxurious or carefree existence.
– ORIGIN unknown.

rill noun a small stream.
– ORIGIN probably German.

rillettes /ree-yet/ plural noun (treated as sing. or pl.) pâté of minced pork or other light meat combined with fat.
– ORIGIN French.

rim noun 1 the upper or outer edge of something circular. 2 (also **wheel rim**) the outer edge of a wheel, on which the tyre is fitted. 3 a stain or deposit left on a surface by dirty water. ● verb (**rims, rimming, rimmed**) provide or mark with a rim: *a lake rimmed by glaciers.*
– DERIVATIVES **rimless** adjective **rimmed** adjective.
– ORIGIN Old English, 'a border, coast'.

rime¹ /rhymes with time/ noun technical & literary hoar frost. ● verb literary cover something with hoar frost.
– DERIVATIVES **rimy** adjective.
– ORIGIN Old English.

rime² noun & verb old-fashioned spelling of **RHYME**.

rimu /ree-moo/ noun a tall conifer which is the chief native softwood tree of New Zealand.
– ORIGIN Maori.

rind noun the tough skin of some fruit, or the hard outer edge of cheese or bacon.
– DERIVATIVES **rinded** adjective **rindless** adjective.
– ORIGIN Old English.

ring¹ noun 1 a small circular metal band worn on a finger. 2 a circular band, object, or mark. 3 an enclosed space in which a sport, performance, or show takes place. 4 a group of people or things arranged in a circle. 5 a group of people involved in a shared activity, especially one that is illegal or secret: *a drug ring.* 6 chiefly Brit. a flat circular heating device forming part of a gas or electric hob. 7 a number of atoms bonded together to form a closed loop in a molecule. ● verb 1 surround someone or something. 2 chiefly Brit. draw a circle round something.
– PHRASES **run** (or **make**) **rings round** (or **around**) informal outclass or outwit easily.
– DERIVATIVES **ringed** adjective.
– ORIGIN Old English.

ring² verb (past **rang**; past part. **rung**) 1 make or cause to make a clear resounding sound. 2 (**ring with**) be filled or resound with a sound. 3 Brit. telephone someone. 4 (**ring off**) Brit. end a telephone call by replacing the receiver. 5 call for attention by sounding a bell. 6 sound the hour or a peal on a bell or bells. 7 (of the ears) be filled with a buzzing or humming sound due to a blow or loud noise. 8 convey a specified impression or quality: *her honesty rings true.* 9 (**ring something up**) record an amount on a cash register. ● noun

1 an act of ringing. 2 a resounding sound or tone. 3 Brit. informal a telephone call. 4 a quality conveyed by something heard: *the tale had a ring of truth.* 5 a set of bells, especially church bells.
– PHRASES **ring down** (or **up**) **the curtain** 1 lower (or raise) a theatre curtain. 2 mark the end (or beginning) of something.
– ORIGIN Old English.

ring binder noun a loose-leaf binder with ring-shaped clasps that can be opened to pass through holes in the paper.

ringdove noun Brit. a wood pigeon.

ringer noun 1 a person or device that rings. 2 informal another term for **DEAD RINGER**. 3 informal an athlete or horse fraudulently substituted for another in a competition.

ring-fence verb 1 Brit. guarantee that funds intended for a particular purpose will not be spent on anything else. 2 enclose land completely with a fence. ● noun (**ring fence**) 1 a fence completely enclosing a piece of land. 2 a set of measures intended to ensure that funds are used only for a specific purpose.

ring finger noun the finger next to the little finger of the left hand, on which the wedding ring is worn.

ringgit /ring-git/ noun (pl. same or **ringgits**) the basic unit of money of Malaysia.
– ORIGIN Malay.

ringing adjective 1 having a clear resounding tone or sound. 2 (of a statement) forceful and completely clear.
– DERIVATIVES **ringingly** adverb.

ringleader noun a person who leads others in crime or causing trouble.

ringlet noun a corkscrew-shaped curl of hair.
– DERIVATIVES **ringletted** (also **ringleted**) adjective.

ring main noun Brit. 1 an electrical supply serving a series of consumers and returning to the original source. 2 an electric circuit serving a number of power points, with one fuse in the supply.

ringmaster noun the person who directs a circus performance.

ring ouzel noun a bird resembling a blackbird with a white crescent across the breast, native to high moors and mountainous country.

ring pull noun Brit. a ring on a can that is pulled to open it.

ring road noun Brit. a bypass encircling a town.

ringside noun the area beside a boxing ring or circus ring.
– DERIVATIVES **ringsider** noun.

ringside seat noun a very good position from which to observe something.

ringtone noun a sound made by a mobile phone when an incoming call is received.

ringworm noun a skin disease occurring in small circular itchy patches, caused by various fungi and affecting chiefly the scalp or feet.

rink noun 1 (also **ice rink**) an enclosed area of ice for skating, ice hockey, or curling. 2 (also **roller rink**) a smooth enclosed floor for roller skating. 3 (also **bowling rink**) the strip of a bowling green used for a match. 4 a team in curling or bowls.
– ORIGIN perhaps from Old French *renc* 'rank'.

rinse verb **1** wash something with clean water to remove soap or dirt. **2** (often **rinse something off/out**) remove soap or dirt by rinsing. •noun **1** an act of rinsing. **2** a liquid for conditioning or colouring the hair. **3** an antiseptic liquid for cleaning the mouth.
– DERIVATIVES **rinser** noun.
– ORIGIN Old French *rincer*.

Rioja /ri-o-khuh, ri-o-kuh/ noun a wine produced in La Rioja, Spain.

riot noun **1** a violent public disturbance by a crowd of people. **2** a large or varied display or combination: *the garden was a riot of colour.* **3** (**a riot**) informal a highly amusing or entertaining person or thing. •verb take part in a riot.
– PHRASES **read someone the Riot Act** Brit. give someone a severe warning or reprimand. [from the name of a former act partly read out to disperse rioters.] **run riot 1** behave in a violent and uncontrolled way. **2** spread uncontrollably.
– DERIVATIVES **rioter** noun.
– ORIGIN Old French *riote* 'debate'.

riotous /ry-uh-tuhss/ adjective **1** involving uncontrolled behaviour, especially in celebration of something: *a riotous party.* **2** having a vivid, varied appearance. **3** involving public disorder.
– DERIVATIVES **riotously** adverb **riotousness** noun.

RIP abbreviation rest in peace (used on graves).
– ORIGIN from Latin *requiescat* (or (plural) *requiescant*) *in pace*.

rip[1] verb (**rips, ripping, ripped**) **1** tear or pull something forcibly away from something or someone. **2** make a tear or hole in something. **3** move forcefully and rapidly: *a fire ripped through the building.* **4** (**rip someone off**) informal cheat someone. **5** (**rip something off**) informal steal or copy something. •noun a long tear or cut.
– PHRASES **let rip** informal **1** do something without restraint. **2** express oneself forcefully or angrily.
– DERIVATIVES **ripper** noun.
– ORIGIN unknown.

rip[2] (also **rip tide**) noun a stretch of fast-flowing and rough water caused by the meeting of currents.
– ORIGIN perhaps from **RIP**[1].

riparian /ri-pair-i-uhn, ry-pair-i-uhn/ adjective relating to or situated on the banks of a river.
– ORIGIN from Latin *riparius*.

ripcord noun a cord that is pulled to open a parachute.

ripe adjective **1** (of fruit or grain) ready for harvesting and eating. **2** (of a cheese or wine) full-flavoured and mature. **3** (**ripe for**) having reached a fitting time for: *land ripe for development.* **4** (**ripe with**) full of something.
– PHRASES **ripe old age** a person's age that is very old.
– DERIVATIVES **ripely** adverb **ripeness** noun.
– ORIGIN Old English.

ripen verb become or make ripe or ready for eating.

rip-off noun informal **1** an article that is greatly overpriced. **2** a poor-quality copy of something.

riposte /ri-posst/ noun **1** a quick clever reply to a critical or insulting remark. **2** a quick return thrust in fencing. •verb make a quick clever reply to an insult or criticism.
– ORIGIN French.

ripping adjective Brit. informal, dated splendid; excellent.

ripple noun **1** a small wave or series of waves. **2** a sound or feeling that spreads through a person, group, or place: *a ripple of laughter went round the hall.* **3** a type of ice cream with wavy lines of coloured flavoured syrup running through it. **4** a small periodic variation in voltage. •verb **1** form or move with a series of small waves. **2** (of a sound or feeling) spread through a person, group, or place.
– DERIVATIVES **ripply** adjective.
– ORIGIN unknown.

rip-roaring adjective full of energy and excitement.

ripsaw noun a coarse saw for cutting wood along the grain.

ripstop noun nylon fabric that is woven so that a tear will not spread.

RISC noun computers or computing based on a form of microprocessor designed to perform a limited set of operations very quickly.
– ORIGIN from *reduced instruction set computer* (or *computing*).

rise verb (past **rose**; past part. **risen**) **1** come or go up. **2** get up from lying, sitting, or kneeling. **3** increase in number, size, intensity, or quality: *house prices had risen.* **4** (of land) slope upwards. **5** (of the sun, moon, or stars) appear above the horizon. **6** reach a higher social or professional position. **7** (**rise above**) succeed in not being restricted by: *try to rise above prejudice.* **8** (**rise to**) respond well to a challenging situation. **9** (often **rise up**) rebel against authority. **10** (of a river) have its source in a particular place. **11** chiefly Brit. (of a meeting or a session of a court) break off with the intention of resuming later; adjourn. •noun **1** an act of rising. **2** an increase in number, size, amount, or degree. **3** Brit. an increase in salary or wages. **4** an upward slope or hill. **5** the vertical height of a step or slope.
– PHRASES **get** (or **take**) **a rise out of** informal provoke an angry or irritated response from. **on the rise 1** increasing. **2** becoming more successful. **rise and shine** informal wake up and get out of bed promptly. **rise from the dead** come to life again.
– ORIGIN Old English, 'make an attack', 'get out of bed'.

riser noun **1** a person who usually gets out of bed at a particular time of the morning: *an early riser.* **2** a vertical section between the treads of a staircase. **3** a vertical pipe for the upward flow of liquid or gas.

risible /ri-zi-b'l/ adjective causing laughter; ridiculous.
– DERIVATIVES **risibility** noun **risibly** adverb.
– ORIGIN Latin *risibilis*.

rising noun a rebellion or revolt. •adjective approaching a specified age.

rising damp noun Brit. moisture absorbed from the ground into a wall.

risk noun **1** a situation that could be dangerous or have an undesirable outcome: *outdoor*

activities carry an element of risk. **2** the possibility that something unpleasant will happen. **3** a person or thing regarded as a likely source of danger or harm: *gloss paint can pose a fire risk.* • verb **1** expose someone or something to danger, harm, or loss. **2** act in such a way as to make an undesirable outcome possible: *children risk serious injury as a result of strenuous gymnastics training.* **3** take a risk by engaging in a particular activity.
– PHRASES **at one's (own) risk** taking responsibility for one's own safety or possessions. **run (or take) a risk (or risks)** act in such a way as to make an undesirable outcome possible.
– ORIGIN Italian *risco* 'danger'.

risk capital noun another term for VENTURE CAPITAL.

risky adjective (**riskier, riskiest**) involving the possibility of danger, failure, or loss.
– DERIVATIVES **riskily** adverb **riskiness** noun.

risotto /ri-**zot**-toh/ noun (pl. **risottos**) an Italian dish of rice cooked in stock with ingredients such as meat or seafood.
– ORIGIN Italian.

risqué /**riss**-kay, riss-**kay**/ adjective referring to sex in an indecent or slightly shocking way.
– ORIGIN French.

rissole noun Brit. a small cake or ball of meat and spices, coated in breadcrumbs and fried.
– ORIGIN French.

ritardando /ri-tar-**dan**-doh/ adverb & adjective Music another term for RALLENTANDO.
– ORIGIN Italian.

rite noun **1** a religious or other solemn ceremony or act. **2** a set of customary practices typical of a Church or a part of it: *the celebration of the full Roman rite.*
– PHRASES **rite of passage** a ceremony or event, e.g. marriage, marking an important stage in someone's life.
– ORIGIN Latin *ritus* '(religious) usage'.

ritual noun **1** a religious or solemn ceremony involving a series of actions performed according to a set order. **2** a set order of performing such a ceremony. **3** a series of actions done regularly and without variation: *it became a ritual to take her out every week to the hairdresser.* • adjective relating to or done as a ritual.
– DERIVATIVES **ritually** adverb.

ritualistic adjective relating to or followed as part of a religious or other ritual: *a ritualistic act of worship.*
– DERIVATIVES **ritualistically** adverb **ritualism** noun.

ritualize (or **ritualise**) verb make something into a ritual by following a pattern of actions or behaviour.
– DERIVATIVES **ritualization** noun.

ritzy adjective (**ritzier, ritziest**) informal expensively stylish.
– ORIGIN from *Ritz*, a proprietary name of luxury hotels.

rival noun **1** a person or thing competing with another for the same objective or to be better than the other. **2** a person or thing equal to another in quality: *she has no rivals as a female rock singer.* • verb (**rivals, rivalling, rivalled**; US **rivals, rivaling, rivaled**) be equal or

comparable to: *a weekly TV ad budget that rivals any Broadway musical.*
– DERIVATIVES **rivalrous** adjective.
– ORIGIN Latin *rivalis*, first meaning 'person using the same stream as another'.

rivalry noun (pl. **rivalries**) a situation in which two people or groups are competing for the same thing.

rive /*rhymes with* dive/ verb (past **rived**; past part. **riven** /**ri**-vuhn/) (usu. **be riven**) literary tear apart or split.
– ORIGIN Old Norse.

river noun **1** a large natural flow of water travelling along a channel to the sea, a lake, or another river. **2** a large quantity of a flowing liquid.
– PHRASES **sell someone down the river** informal betray someone. [with reference to the sale of a troublesome slave to a plantation owner on the lower Mississippi, where conditions were worse.]
– ORIGIN Old French.

riverbank noun the bank of a river.

riverbed noun the bed or channel in which a river flows.

riverboat noun a boat designed for use on rivers.

riverine /**ri**-vuh-ryn/ adjective technical or literary relating to or situated on a river or riverbank.

riverside noun the ground along a riverbank.

rivet /**ri**-vit/ noun a short metal pin or bolt for holding together two metal plates, its headless end being beaten out or pressed down when in place. • verb (**rivets, riveting, riveted**) **1** join metal plates with a rivet or rivets. **2** hold someone's interest or attention completely: *cinema-goers have been riveted by great car chases for years.*
– DERIVATIVES **riveter** noun **riveting** adjective.
– ORIGIN Old French.

riviera /ri-vi-**air**-uh/ noun a coastal region with a subtropical climate and vegetation, especially that of southern France and northern Italy.
– ORIGIN Italian, 'seashore'.

rivulet /**riv**-yuu-lit/ noun a very small stream.
– ORIGIN from former French *riveret* 'small river'.

riyal noun variant spelling of RIAL.

RL abbreviation rugby league.

RM abbreviation (in the UK) Royal Marines.

RN abbreviation (in the UK) Royal Navy.

Rn symbol the chemical element radon.

RNA noun ribonucleic acid, a substance in living cells which carries instructions from DNA for controlling the synthesis of proteins.

RNLI abbreviation (in the UK) Royal National Lifeboat Institution.

roach[1] noun (pl. same) a common freshwater fish of the carp family.
– ORIGIN Old French *roche.*

roach[2] noun informal **1** N. Amer. a cockroach. **2** a roll of card or paper that forms the butt of a cannabis cigarette.

road noun **1** a wide way between places, especially one with a hard surface for vehicles to travel on. **2** a way to achieving a particular outcome: *he's well on the road to recovery.* **3** (usu. **roads**) a partly sheltered stretch of

water near the shore in which ships can ride at anchor.
– PHRASES **one for the road** informal a final alcoholic drink before leaving. **on the road 1** on a long journey or series of journeys. **2** (of a car) able to be driven.
– DERIVATIVES **roadless** adjective.
– ORIGIN Old English, 'journey on horseback, foray'.

roadblock noun a barrier put across a road by the police or army to stop and examine traffic.

road fund licence noun Brit. a disc displayed on a vehicle certifying payment of road tax.

road hog noun informal a motorist who makes it difficult for others to overtake.

roadholding noun the ability of a moving vehicle to remain stable, especially when cornering at high speeds.

roadhouse noun a pub or restaurant on a country road.

road hump noun a hump in the road intended to make traffic slow down.

roadie noun informal a person employed by a touring pop or rock group to set up and maintain equipment.

roadkill noun chiefly N. Amer. animals killed on the road by a vehicle.

road map noun **1** a map showing the roads of a country or area. **2** a document setting out the procedure for achieving a goal: *a road map for peace.*

road pricing noun the practice of charging motorists to use busy roads at certain times, especially to relieve congestion.

road rage noun violent anger arising from conflict with the driver of another motor vehicle.

roadshow noun **1** a touring show of pop musicians. **2** each of a series of radio or television programmes broadcast on location from different places. **3** a touring political or promotional campaign.

roadside noun the strip of land beside a road.

roadstead noun another term for ROAD (in sense 3).

roadster noun **1** an open-top car with two seats. **2** a bicycle for use on the road.

road tax noun Brit. a tax to be paid on motor vehicles using public roads.

road test noun **1** a test of the performance of a vehicle or engine on the road. **2** a test of equipment carried out in working conditions. •verb (**road-test**) **1** test a vehicle or engine on the road. **2** try out something under working conditions, especially before it is made generally available: *we road-tested a new laptop computer.*

roadway noun **1** a road. **2** the part of a road intended for vehicles, in contrast to the pavement or verge.

roadworks plural noun Brit. repairs to roads or to pipes or cables under roads.

roadworthy adjective (of a vehicle) fit to be used on the road.
– DERIVATIVES **roadworthiness** noun.

roam verb **1** travel aimlessly over a wide area. **2** (of the eyes or hands) pass lightly over something without stopping.
– DERIVATIVES **roamer** noun.

– ORIGIN unknown.

roaming noun the use of or ability to use a mobile phone on another operator's network, typically while abroad.

roan adjective (of a horse or cow) having a coat that is mainly bay, chestnut, or black mixed with another colour, typically white. •noun a roan animal.
– ORIGIN Old French.

roar noun **1** a long, deep sound such as that made by a lion, natural force, or engine. **2** a loud, deep sound uttered by a person, especially as an expression of pain, anger, or amusement. •verb **1** make a roar. **2** laugh loudly. **3** move, act, or happen fast or decisively: *Korean stocks roared back, closing with a gain of almost five per cent.*
– ORIGIN Old English.

roaring adjective informal complete: *a roaring success.*
– PHRASES **do a roaring trade** informal do very good business. **the roaring forties** stormy ocean areas between latitudes 40° and 50° south. **the roaring twenties** the prosperous years of the 1920s.
– DERIVATIVES **roaringly** adverb.

roast verb **1** cook meat or vegetables in an oven or over a fire. **2** process coffee beans, nuts, etc. in intense heat. **3** make or become very warm. **4** informal criticize or reprimand someone severely. •adjective (of food) having been roasted. •noun **1** a joint of meat that has been roasted. **2** the process of roasting something, especially coffee. **3** an outdoor party at which meat is roasted: *a pig roast.*
– DERIVATIVES **roaster** noun.
– ORIGIN Old French *rostir.*

roasting informal adjective very hot and dry. •noun a severe criticism or reprimand.

rob verb (**robs, robbing, robbed**) **1** take property unlawfully from a person or place by force or threat of force. **2** (**rob someone of**) deprive someone of something needed, deserved, or important. **3** informal overcharge someone.
– PHRASES **rob Peter to pay Paul** deprive one person of something in order to pay another. [probably with reference to the saints *Peter* and *Paul.*]
– DERIVATIVES **robber** noun.
– ORIGIN Old French *rober.*

robbery noun (pl. **robberies**) **1** the action of robbing a person or place. **2** informal blatant overcharging.

robe noun **1** a loose outer garment reaching to the ankles, often worn on formal or ceremonial occasions as an indication of the wearer's rank, office, or profession. **2** a bathrobe or dressing gown. •verb dress someone or oneself in a robe.
– ORIGIN Old French, 'garment, booty'.

robin noun **1** a small European songbird of the thrush family, with a red breast and brown back and wings. **2** (also **American robin**) a large North American thrush with an orange-red breast.
– ORIGIN Old French, familiar form of the man's name *Robert.*

robot /roh-bot/ noun a machine capable of carrying out a complex series of actions

automatically, especially one programmable by a computer.
- DERIVATIVES **robotize** (or **robotise**) verb.
- ORIGIN Czech *robota* 'forced labour'; the term was coined in K. Čapek's play *R.U.R.* 'Rossum's Universal Robots'.

robotic /roh-bot-ik/ **adjective 1** relating to robots. **2** mechanical, stiff, or unemotional.
- DERIVATIVES **robotically** adverb.

robotics plural noun (treated as sing.) the branch of technology concerned with the design, construction, and use of robots.

robust adjective 1 able to withstand heavy use; sturdy. **2** strong and healthy. **3** determined and forceful: *a robust approach to reform.* **4** (of wine or food) strong and rich in flavour or smell.
- DERIVATIVES **robustly** adverb **robustness** noun.
- ORIGIN Latin *robustus* 'firm and hard'.

robusta noun a type of coffee bean from a West African species of coffee plant, used especially in making instant coffee.
- ORIGIN Latin.

rock¹ noun 1 the hard mineral material of the earth's crust. **2** a mass of rock projecting out of the ground or water. **3** a boulder. **4** Geology any natural material with a distinctive composition of minerals. **5** Brit. a kind of hard sweet in the form of a cylindrical stick. **6** informal a diamond or other precious stone.
- PHRASES **on the rocks** informal **1** in difficulties and likely to fail. **2** (of a drink) served undiluted and with ice cubes.
- ORIGIN Latin *rocca*.

rock² verb 1 move gently to and fro or from side to side. **2** shake violently, especially because of an earthquake or explosion. **3** shock or distress greatly: *the company was rocked by the resignation of its chairman.* **4** informal dance to or play rock music. **5** (often as adj. **rocking**) informal (of a place) be exciting or full of social activity. • **noun 1** (also **rock music**) a form of popular music with a strong beat, played on electric guitars, drums, etc. **2** rock and roll music. **3** a rocking movement.
- ORIGIN Old English.

rockabilly noun a type of popular music combining rock and roll and country music.
- ORIGIN from **ROCK AND ROLL** and **HILLBILLY**.

rock and roll (also **rock 'n' roll**) **noun** a type of popular dance music originating in the 1950s, having a heavy beat and simple melodies.

rock-bottom adjective at the lowest possible level.

rock cake noun chiefly Brit. a small currant cake with a hard rough surface.

rock climbing noun the sport or pastime of climbing rock faces, especially with ropes and special equipment.

rock crystal noun transparent quartz, typically in the form of colourless hexagonal crystals.

rock dove noun a mainly blue-grey pigeon found on cliffs, the ancestor of domestic and wild pigeons.

rocker noun 1 a person who performs or enjoys rock music. **2** Brit. (especially in the 1960s) a young person of a group who wore leather clothing, rode motorcycles, and liked rock music. **3** a rocking chair. **4** a curved bar or similar support on which something such as a

chair can rock. **5** a rocking device forming part of a mechanism.
- PHRASES **off one's rocker** informal mad.

rockery noun (pl. **rockeries**) a heaped arrangement of rocks with soil between them, planted with rock plants.

rocket¹ noun 1 a cylindrical missile or spacecraft propelled to a great height or distance by a stream of burning gases. **2** a firework or signal propelled in this way. **3** Brit. informal a severe reprimand. • **verb** (**rockets, rocketing, rocketed**) **1** increase very rapidly and suddenly. **2** move or progress very rapidly: *he rocketed to national stardom.* **3** attack something with rocket-propelled missiles.
- ORIGIN Italian *rocchetto* 'small distaff (for spinning)'.

rocket² noun Brit. an edible Mediterranean plant eaten in salads.
- ORIGIN French *roquette*.

rocketeer noun a person who designs or operates space rockets.

rocketry noun the branch of science and technology concerned with rockets.

rocket science noun humorous something very difficult to understand.
- DERIVATIVES **rocket scientist** noun.

rock face noun a vertical surface of bare rock.

rock garden noun a rockery.

rocking chair noun a chair mounted on rockers or springs.

rocking horse noun a model of a horse mounted on rockers or springs for a child to ride on.

rock plant noun a plant that grows on or among rocks.

rock pool noun a pool of water among rocks along a shoreline.

rock rose noun a herbaceous or shrubby plant with rose-like flowers, native to temperate and warm regions.

rock salmon noun Brit. dogfish as food.

rock salt noun common salt occurring naturally as a mineral.

rock solid adjective completely firm or stable.

rock wool noun inorganic material made into matted fibre, used especially for insulation or soundproofing.

rocky¹ adjective (**rockier, rockiest**) **1** consisting of rock. **2** full of rocks.

rocky² adjective (**rockier, rockiest**) **1** unsteady or unstable. **2** relating to rock music.

rococo /ruh-koh-koh/ **adjective 1** relating to an elaborately ornate style of European furniture or architecture of the 18th century. **2** (of music or literature) highly or excessively ornate. • **noun** the rococo style of architecture, furniture, etc.
- ORIGIN French.

rod noun 1 a thin straight bar, especially of wood or metal. **2** a fishing rod. **3** (**the rod**) the use of a stick for caning or flogging someone. **4** one of two types of light-sensitive cell in the retina of the eye, responsible mainly for monochrome vision in poor light. Compare with **CONE**. **5** historical another term for **PERCH³**.
- PHRASES **make a rod for one's own back** do something likely to cause difficulties for oneself later.
- ORIGIN Old English.

r

rode past of **RIDE**.

rodent noun a mammal of a large group including rats, mice, and squirrels and distinguished by strong constantly growing incisors.
– ORIGIN from Latin *rodere* 'gnaw'.

rodenticide /roh-**den**-ti-syd/ noun a poison used to kill rodents.

rodent ulcer noun a slow-growing cancerous tumour of the face.

rodeo /**roh**-di-oh, roh-**day**-oh/ noun (pl. **rodeos**) **1** a contest or entertainment in which cowboys show their skill at riding broncos, roping calves, etc. **2** a competitive display of other skills, such as motorcycle riding.
– ORIGIN Spanish.

rodomontade /ro-duh-mon-**tayd**/ noun literary boastful talk or behaviour.
– ORIGIN from Italian *rodomonte* 'boaster'.

roe¹ noun **1** (also **hard roe**) the mass of eggs contained in the ovaries of a female fish or shellfish, especially when ripe and used as food. **2** (**soft roe**) the ripe testes of a male fish, especially when used as food.
– ORIGIN related to German, Dutch *roge*.

roe² (also **roe deer**) noun (pl. same or **roes**) a small deer with a reddish summer coat that turns greyish in winter.
– ORIGIN Old English.

roebuck noun a male roe deer.

roentgen /**runt**-yuhn, **rernt**-yuhn, **ront**-yuhn/ noun a unit of quantity of ionizing radiation.
– ORIGIN named after the German physicist Wilhelm Conrad *Röntgen*.

roentgenium /runt-yuh-ni-uhm/ noun a radioactive chemical element produced artificially.
– ORIGIN named after Wilhelm Conrad *Röntgen* (see **ROENTGEN**).

rogan josh /roh-guhn **johsh**/ noun an Indian dish of curried meat in a rich tomato-based sauce.
– ORIGIN Urdu.

roger exclamation your message has been received (used in radio communication). • verb Brit. vulgar slang (of a man) have sex with someone.
– ORIGIN from the man's name *Roger*; the verb is from the former noun sense 'penis'.

rogue noun **1** a dishonest or immoral man. **2** a mischievous but likeable person. • adjective **1** (of an elephant or other large wild animal) destructive and living apart from the herd. **2** behaving in a faulty, unpredictable, or dangerous way: *a rogue state*.
– ORIGIN probably from Latin *rogare* 'beg, ask'.

roguery noun (pl. **rogueries**) dishonest, immoral, or mischievous behaviour.

rogues' gallery noun informal a collection of photographs of known criminals, used by police to identify suspects.

roguish adjective playfully mischievous: *a roguish smile*.
– DERIVATIVES **roguishly** adverb **roguishness** noun.

roil /royl/ verb **1** make a liquid muddy by disturbing the sediment. **2** (of a liquid) move in a turbulent way.
– ORIGIN perhaps from Old French *ruiler* 'mix mortar'.

roister /**roy**-ster/ verb enjoy oneself or celebrate in a noisy or boisterous way.
– DERIVATIVES **roisterer** noun **roisterous** adjective.
– ORIGIN from French *rustre* 'ruffian'.

role noun **1** an actor's part in a play, film, etc. **2** a person's or thing's function in a particular situation: *religion plays a vital role in society*.
– ORIGIN from former French *roule* 'roll', first referring to the roll of paper on which an actor's part was written.

USAGE: Do not confuse **role** with **roll**. **Role** means 'a part played by an actor', whereas **roll** mainly means 'move by turning over and over' or 'a rolling movement' (*a roll of the dice*).

role model noun a person who others look to as an example to be imitated.

role playing (also **role play**) noun the acting out of a particular role, either consciously (as a technique in psychotherapy or training) or unconsciously (in accordance with the expectations of society).

Rolfing noun a deep massage technique aimed at releasing muscular tension by manipulating connective tissue.
– ORIGIN named after the American physiotherapist Ida P. *Rolf*.

roll verb **1** move by turning over and over on an axis. **2** move forward on wheels or with a smooth, wave-like motion: *the fog rolled across the fields*. **3** (of a moving ship, aircraft, or vehicle) sway from side to side. **4** (of a machine or device) begin operating. **5** (often **roll something up**) turn something flexible over and over on itself to form a cylindrical or round shape. **6** (**roll up**) curl up tightly. **7** flatten something by passing a roller over it or by passing it between rollers. **8** (of a loud, deep sound) resound or reverberate. **9** pronounce a consonant, typically an *r*, with a trill. • noun **1** a cylinder formed by rolling flexible material. **2** a rolling movement. **3** a gymnastic exercise in which the body is rolled into a tucked position and turned in a forward or backward circle. **4** a long, deep, reverberating sound. **5** (in drumming) a sustained, rapid alternation of single or double strokes of each stick. **6** a very small loaf of bread. **7** an official list of names.
– PHRASES **a roll in the hay** informal an act of sex. **be rolling in it** (or **money**) informal be very rich. **on a roll** informal experiencing a prolonged spell of success or good luck. **roll in** informal **1** be received in large amounts. **2** arrive in a casual way in spite of being late. **roll of honour** a list of people whose deeds are honoured, especially a list of those who have died in battle. **roll on** Brit. informal used to indicate that one wants a time or event to come quickly. **roll something out** officially launch a new product. **roll something over** extend a financial arrangement. **roll up** informal arrive. **roll up one's sleeves** prepare to work or fight.
– ORIGIN Old French *roller*.

roll bar noun a metal bar running up the sides and across the top of a sports car, protecting the occupants if the car overturns.

roll call noun the reading aloud of a list of names to establish who is present.

rolled gold noun gold in the form of a thin coating applied to a non-precious metal by rolling.

rolled oats plural noun oats that have had the husks removed and been crushed.

roller noun **1** a rotating cylinder used to move, flatten, or spread something. **2** a small cylinder on which hair is rolled to produce curls. **3** a long swelling wave that appears to roll steadily towards the shore.

rollerball noun **1** a ballpoint pen using thinner ink than other such pens. **2** Computing an input device containing a ball which is moved with the fingers to control the cursor.

roller bearing noun a bearing similar to a ball bearing but using small rollers instead of balls.

Rollerblade noun trademark a skate with wheels fixed in a single line. •verb skate using Rollerblades.
– DERIVATIVES **rollerblader** noun **rollerblading** noun.

roller blind noun a window blind fitted on a roller.

roller coaster noun a fairground attraction consisting of a light railway track with many tight turns and steep slopes, on which people ride in small open carriages.

roller skate noun each of a pair of boots having four or more small wheels and used for gliding across a hard surface.
– DERIVATIVES **roller skater** noun **roller skating** noun.

roller towel noun a long towel with the ends joined and hung on a roller.

rollicking[1] adjective lively and amusing in a high-spirited way.
– ORIGIN perhaps from **ROMP** and **FROLIC**.

rollicking[2] (also **rollocking**) noun Brit. informal a severe reprimand.
– ORIGIN from **BOLLOCKING**.

rolling adjective **1** (of land) extending in a series of gently rounded hills. **2** done in regular stages over a period of time: *a rolling programme of reforms.*

rolling mill noun a factory or machine for rolling steel or other metal into sheets.

rolling pin noun a cylinder for rolling out dough.

rolling stock noun locomotives, carriages, or other vehicles used on a railway.

rollmop noun a rolled uncooked pickled herring fillet.
– ORIGIN German *Rollmops.*

roll neck noun a high loosely turned-over collar.

rollocking noun variant spelling of **ROLLICKING**[2].

roll-on adjective (of a deodorant or cosmetic) applied by means of a rotating ball in the neck of the container.

roll-on roll-off adjective Brit. (of a ferry) in which vehicles are driven directly on at the start of the voyage and driven off at the end of it.

roll-out noun the launch of a new aircraft, spacecraft, or product.

rollover noun Brit. (in a lottery) the carry-over of prize money that is not won in a particular draw to the next draw.

roll-top desk noun a writing desk with a semicircular flexible cover sliding in curved grooves.

roll-up noun Brit. informal a hand-rolled cigarette.

roly-poly adjective informal round and plump. •noun (also **roly-poly pudding**) Brit. a pudding made of a sheet of suet pastry covered with jam or fruit, formed into a roll, and steamed or baked.
– ORIGIN from **ROLL**.

ROM abbreviation Computing read-only memory.

romaine /roh-**mayn**/ noun a cos lettuce.
– ORIGIN French.

Roman adjective **1** relating to the ancient city of Rome or its empire or people. **2** relating to the modern city of Rome. **3** referring to the alphabet used for writing Latin, English, and most European languages. **4** (**roman**) (of type) of a plain upright kind used in ordinary print. •noun **1** an inhabitant of Rome. **2** (**roman**) roman type.

roman-à-clef /roh-mon-ah-**klay**/ noun (pl. **romans-à-clef** pronunc. same) a novel in which real people or events appear with invented names.
– ORIGIN French, 'novel with a key'.

Roman candle noun a firework giving off flaming coloured balls and sparks.

Roman Catholic adjective relating to the Roman Catholic Church. •noun a member of the Roman Catholic Church.
– DERIVATIVES **Roman Catholicism** noun.

Roman Catholic Church noun the part of the Christian Church which has the Pope as its head.

Romance /roh-**manss**, **roh**-manss/ noun the group of languages descended from Latin, such as French, Spanish, Portuguese, and Italian.
– ORIGIN from Latin *Romanicus* 'Roman'.

romance /roh-**manss**, **roh**-manss/ noun **1** a pleasurable feeling of excitement and wonder associated with love. **2** a love affair. **3** a book or film dealing with love in a sentimental or idealized way. **4** a quality or feeling of mystery, excitement, and remoteness from everyday life: *the romance of the past.* **5** a medieval story dealing with the adventures of knights. •verb **1** try to win someone's love. **2** informal seek someone's custom or attention: *he's being romanced by the big boys in New York.* **3** deal with something in an idealized way.
– DERIVATIVES **romancer** noun.
– ORIGIN from **ROMANCE**.

Roman Empire noun the empire under Roman rule established in 27 BC and divided into two parts in AD 395.

Romanesque /roh-muh-**nesk**/ adjective relating to a style of architecture prevalent in Europe *c.*900–1200, with massive vaulting and round arches.
– ORIGIN French.

Romanian (also **Rumanian**) noun **1** a person from Romania. **2** the language of Romania. •adjective relating to Romania.

romanize (or **romanise**) /roh-muh-nyz/ verb put written words into the Roman alphabet or into roman type.
– DERIVATIVES **romanization** noun.

Roman law noun the law code of the ancient Romans forming the basis of civil law in many

r

countries today.

Roman nose noun a nose with a high bridge.

Roman numeral noun any of the letters representing numbers in the ancient Roman system: I = 1, V = 5, X = 10, L = 50, C = 100, D = 500, M = 1,000.

romantic adjective **1** relating to or likely to lead to love or romance: *a romantic dinner for two*. **2** showing or regarding life in an idealized and unrealistic way: *Buffalo Bill is largely responsible for our romantic view of the Old West*. **3** (**Romantic**) relating to the artistic and literary movement of romanticism. • noun **1** a person who is emotional and has an unrealistic view of life or love. **2** (**Romantic**) a writer or artist of the Romantic movement.
– DERIVATIVES **romantically** adverb.

romanticism noun a literary and artistic movement which began in the late 18th century and emphasized creative inspiration and individual feeling.
– DERIVATIVES **romanticist** noun.

romanticize (or **romanticise**) verb deal with or describe in an idealized or unrealistic way: *folklore romanticizes pirates, who made their living by murder and robbery*.
– DERIVATIVES **romanticization** noun.

Romany /roh-muh-ni, ro-muh-ni/ noun (pl. **Romanies**) **1** the language of the Gypsies. **2** a Gypsy.
– ORIGIN from Romany *Rom* 'man, husband'.

romcom noun informal (in film or television) a romantic comedy.

Romeo /roh-mi-oh/ noun (pl. **Romeos**) an attractive, passionate male lover.
– ORIGIN the hero of Shakespeare's *Romeo and Juliet*.

Romish /roh-mish/ adjective chiefly derogatory Roman Catholic.

romp verb **1** play about roughly and energetically. **2** informal achieve or win something easily: *India romped home with three balls to spare*. **3** informal engage in sexual activity. • noun **1** a spell of romping. **2** a light-hearted film or other work. **3** informal an easy victory.
– ORIGIN perhaps from RAMP.

rompers (also **romper suit**) plural noun a young child's one-piece outer garment.

rondavel /ron-dah-v'l/ noun a traditional circular African house with a conical thatched roof.
– ORIGIN from Afrikaans *rondawel*.

rondeau /ron-doh/ noun (pl. **rondeaux** pronunc. same or /ron-dohz/) a poem of ten or thirteen lines with only two rhymes throughout and with the opening words used twice as a refrain.
– ORIGIN French.

rondo /ron-doh/ noun (pl. **rondos**) a musical form with a recurring leading theme, often found in the final movement of a sonata or concerto.
– ORIGIN Italian.

röntgen noun variant spelling of ROENTGEN.

roo noun Austral. informal a kangaroo.

rood /rood/ noun **1** a crucifix, especially one in a church. **2** chiefly Brit. a former measure of land area equal to a quarter of an acre.
– ORIGIN Old English.

rood screen noun a screen of wood or stone separating the nave from the chancel of a church.

roof noun (pl. **roofs**) **1** the structure forming the upper covering of a building or vehicle. **2** the top inner surface of a covered area or space. **3** the upper limit or level of prices or wages. • verb cover a building with a roof.
– PHRASES **go through the roof** informal (of prices or figures) reach very high levels. **hit** (or **go through**) **the roof** informal suddenly become very angry. **the roof of the mouth** the palate.
– DERIVATIVES **roofer** noun **roofless** adjective.
– ORIGIN Old English.

roofing noun material for constructing the roof of a building.

roof rack noun a framework for carrying luggage or equipment on the roof of a vehicle.

rooftop noun the outer surface of a building's roof.

rook¹ noun a crow with black plumage and a bare face, nesting in colonies in treetops. • verb informal swindle or overcharge someone.
– ORIGIN Old English.

rook² noun a chess piece, typically with its top in the shape of a battlement, that can move in any direction along a rank or file on which it stands.
– ORIGIN Arabic.

rookery noun (pl. **rookeries**) **1** a collection of rooks' nests high in a clump of trees. **2** a breeding colony of seabirds (especially penguins), seals, or turtles.

rookie noun informal a new recruit or member, especially in the army or police or a sports team.
– ORIGIN perhaps from RECRUIT.

room /room, ruum/ noun **1** a part of a building enclosed by walls, floor, and ceiling. **2** empty space that can be occupied or where something can be done: *there was no room to move*. **3** opportunity or scope: *there's room for improvement in kayak design*. **4** (**rooms**) Brit. a set of rooms rented out to lodgers. • verb N. Amer. share lodgings, especially at a college or similar institution.
– DERIVATIVES **roomed** adjective.
– ORIGIN Old English.

rooming house noun chiefly N. Amer. a lodging house.

room-mate noun **1** a person occupying the same room as another. **2** N. Amer. a person occupying the same flat or house as another.

room service noun provision of food and drink to hotel guests in their rooms.

room temperature noun a comfortable indoor temperature, generally taken as about 20°C.

roomy adjective (**roomier**, **roomiest**) having plenty of room; spacious.
– DERIVATIVES **roominess** noun.

roost noun a place where birds or bats regularly settle to rest. • verb (of a bird or bat) settle or gather for rest.
– ORIGIN Old English.

rooster noun chiefly N. Amer. a male domestic fowl.

root¹ noun **1** a part of a plant normally below ground, which acts as a support and collects

water and nutrients. **2** the part of a bodily organ or structure such as a hair that is embedded in tissue. **3** the basic cause, source, or origin: *money is the root of all evil.* **4** (**roots**) a person's family, ethnic, or cultural origins. **5** a form from which words have been made by adding prefixes or suffixes or by other modification. **6** Mathematics a number or quantity that when multiplied by itself one or more times gives a specified number or quantity. ● **verb 1** (of a plant or cutting) establish roots. **2** establish deeply and firmly: *vegetarianism is rooted in Indian culture.* **3** (**be rooted**) stand completely still through fear or amazement. **4** (**root something out/up**) find and get rid of something.
– PHRASES **at root** basically; fundamentally. **put down roots** begin to have a settled life in a place. **root and branch** (of a process or operation) thorough or radical. **take root** become established.
– DERIVATIVES **rootless** adjective.
– ORIGIN Old English.

root² verb **1** (of an animal) turn up the ground with its snout in search of food. **2** search through something; rummage. **3** (**root for**) informal support a person or team enthusiastically.
– ORIGIN Old English.

root beer noun N. Amer. a fizzy drink made from an extract of the roots and bark of certain plants.

root canal noun the pulp-filled cavity in the root of a tooth.

rootle verb Brit. informal search or rummage.
– ORIGIN from **ROOT²**.

root mean square noun Mathematics the square root of the arithmetic mean of the squares of a set of values.

root sign noun Mathematics the radical sign.

rootstock noun **1** a rhizome. **2** a plant on to which another variety is grafted.

rootsy adjective informal (of music) not commercialized and emphasizing its traditional or ethnic origins.

root vegetable noun a carrot or other vegetable which grows as the root of a plant.

rope noun **1** a length of thick cord made by twisting together strands of hemp, nylon, etc. **2** a quantity of objects strung together: *a rope of pearls.* **3** (**the ropes**) the ropes enclosing a boxing or wrestling ring. **4** (**the ropes**) informal the established way of doing something: *I showed her the ropes.* ● verb **1** catch or tie someone or something with rope. **2** (**rope someone in/into**) persuade someone to take part in something.
– PHRASES **on the ropes 1** Boxing forced against the ropes by the opponent's attack. **2** in state of near collapse.
– ORIGIN Old English.

rope ladder noun two long ropes connected by short crosspieces, used as a ladder.

ropy (also **ropey**) adjective (**ropier, ropiest**) **1** Brit. informal poor in quality or health. **2** resembling a rope.
– DERIVATIVES **ropily** adverb **ropiness** noun.

Roquefort /rok-for/ noun trademark a soft blue cheese made from ewes' milk.
– ORIGIN from *Roquefort*-sur-Soulzon, a village

in southern France.

ro-ro abbreviation Brit. (of a ferry) roll-on roll-off.

rorqual /ror-kwuhl/ noun a whale of a small group with pleated skin on the underside, e.g. the blue whale.
– ORIGIN Norwegian *røyrkval* 'fin whale'.

Rorschach test /ror-shahk/ noun a test used in psychoanalysis, in which a standard set of symmetrical ink blots is presented to a person, who is asked to describe what they suggest or resemble.
– ORIGIN named after the Swiss psychiatrist Hermann *Rorschach.*

rosacea /roh-zay-shi-uh/ noun a condition in which some facial blood vessels enlarge, giving the cheeks and nose a flushed appearance.
– ORIGIN short for Latin *acne rosacea* 'rose-coloured acne'.

rosaceous /roh-zay-shuhss/ adjective relating to plants of the rose family.

rosary /roh-zuh-ri/ noun (pl. **rosaries**) **1** (in the Roman Catholic Church) a form of devotion in which five (or fifteen) sets of ten Hail Marys are repeated. **2** a string of beads for keeping count of prayers said.
– ORIGIN Latin *rosarium* 'rose garden'.

rose¹ noun **1** a sweet-smelling flower that grows on a prickly bush. **2** a perforated cap attached to a shower, the spout of a watering can, or the end of a hose to produce a spray. **3** a warm pink or light crimson colour.
– PHRASES **come up roses** (of a situation) develop in a very favourable way. **come up** (or **out**) **smelling of roses** keep one's good reputation after involvement in a difficult situation.
– ORIGIN Latin *rosa.*

rose² past of **RISE**.

rosé /roh-zay/ noun deep pink wine coloured by only brief contact with red grape skins.
– ORIGIN French, 'pink'.

roseate /roh-zi-uht/ adjective literary rose-coloured.

rosebay willowherb noun a tall willowherb with pink flowers.

rosebud noun the bud of a rose.

rose-coloured (also **rose-tinted**) adjective (of a person's viewpoint) unrealistic and naive: *you look at the world through rose-coloured spectacles.*

rose hip noun fuller form of **HIP²**.

rosemary noun an evergreen shrub of southern Europe, the leaves of which are used as a herb in cooking.
– ORIGIN from Latin *ros* 'dew' + *marinus* 'of the sea'.

rose of Sharon noun a low shrub with dense foliage and large golden-yellow flowers.
– ORIGIN from *Sharon*, a fertile coastal plain in Israel.

rosette noun **1** a rose-shaped decoration made of ribbon, worn by supporters of a team or political party or awarded as a prize. **2** a design or object resembling a rose.
– ORIGIN French, 'little rose'.

rose water noun scented water made with rose petals.

rose window noun a circular window in a

church with tracery radiating in a rose-like pattern.

rosewood noun a close-grained timber of a tropical tree, used for making furniture and musical instruments.

Rosh Hashana /rosh huh-**shah**-nuh/ (also **Rosh Hashanah**) noun the Jewish New Year festival.
– ORIGIN Hebrew, 'head of the year'.

Rosicrucian /roh-zi-**kroo**-sh'n/ noun a member of a secretive 17th- and 18th-century society devoted to the study of alchemy and the occult. ●adjective relating to the Rosicrucians.
– DERIVATIVES **Rosicrucianism** noun.
– ORIGIN from the Latin form of the name of Christian *Rosenkreuz*, legendary founder of the movement.

rosin /ro-zin/ noun a kind of resin produced by distilling oil of turpentine, used for treating the bows of stringed instruments. ●verb (**rosins**, **rosining**, **rosined**) rub or treat something with rosin.
– ORIGIN Latin *rosina*.

RoSPA /ross-puh/ abbreviation (in the UK) Royal Society for the Prevention of Accidents.

roster /ross-ter/ noun 1 a list of people's names together with the jobs they have to do at a particular time. 2 a list of sports players available for team selection. ●verb put a person's name on a roster.
– ORIGIN Dutch *rooster* 'list'.

rösti /rer-sti/ noun a Swiss dish of grated potatoes formed into a small flat cake and fried.
– ORIGIN Swiss German.

rostrum /ross-truhm/ noun (pl. rostra /ross-truh/ or **rostrums**) 1 a raised platform on which a person stands to make a public speech, play music, or conduct an orchestra. 2 a platform for supporting a film or television camera.
– ORIGIN Latin, 'beak'; the word first referred to an orator's platform in ancient Rome, which was decorated with the beak-like projections from captured warships.

rosy adjective (**rosier**, **rosiest**) 1 (especially of a person's skin) pink. 2 promising or hopeful: *he painted a rosy picture of the future.*
– DERIVATIVES **rosily** adverb **rosiness** noun.

rot verb (**rots**, **rotting**, **rotted**) 1 (of organic matter) decompose by the action of bacteria and fungi; decay. 2 gradually get worse: *the education system has been allowed to rot.* ●noun 1 the process of decaying. 2 rotten or decayed matter. 3 (**the rot**) Brit. a decline in quality or standards: *there is enough talent to stop the rot.* 4 a disease that causes tissue decay, especially in plants. 5 informal, chiefly Brit. nonsense; rubbish: *don't talk rot.*
– ORIGIN Old English.

rota noun Brit. a list showing when each of a number of people has to do a particular job.
– ORIGIN Latin, 'wheel'.

Rotary noun a worldwide charitable society of business and professional people organized into local Rotary clubs.
– DERIVATIVES **Rotarian** noun & adjective.

rotary adjective 1 revolving around a centre or axis. 2 having a rotating part or parts: *a rotary mower.*

rotate verb 1 move in a circle round a central point or axis. 2 pass to each member of a group in a regularly recurring order: *the job of chairing the meeting rotates.* 3 grow different crops one after the other on the same area of land.
– DERIVATIVES **rotatable** adjective **rotator** noun **rotatory** /roh-**tay**-tuh-ri/ adjective.
– ORIGIN Latin *rotare* 'turn in a circle'.

rotation noun 1 the action of rotating around a central point. 2 the action or system of changing people or things in a repeated sequence: *crop rotation.* 3 a complete circular movement around a central point.
– DERIVATIVES **rotational** adjective **rotationally** adverb.

rotavator /roh-tuh-vay-ter/ noun trademark a machine with rotating blades for breaking up or tilling the soil.
– DERIVATIVES **rotavate** verb.
– ORIGIN from ROTARY + CULTIVATOR.

rote noun regular repetition of something to be learned: *a poem learnt by rote.*
– ORIGIN unknown.

rotgut noun informal poor-quality alcoholic drink.

roti /roh-ti/ noun (pl. **rotis**) (in Indian cooking) bread, especially a flat round bread cooked on a griddle.
– ORIGIN Hindi.

rotisserie /roh-**tiss**-uh-ri/ noun 1 a rotating spit for roasting and barbecuing meat. 2 a restaurant specializing in roasted or barbecued meat.
– ORIGIN French.

rotor noun 1 the rotating part of a turbine, electric motor, or other device. 2 a hub with a number of blades spreading out from it that is rotated to provide the lift for a helicopter.

rotten adjective 1 rotting or decaying. 2 morally or politically corrupt. 3 informal very bad or unpleasant. ●adverb informal very much: *your mother spoiled you rotten.*
– DERIVATIVES **rottenness** noun.
– ORIGIN Old Norse.

rotten borough noun Brit. (before the Reform Act of 1832) a borough that was able to elect an MP though having very few voters.

rotter noun informal, dated a cruel or unpleasant person.

Rottweiler /rot-vy-ler, rot-wy-ler/ noun a large powerful black-and-tan breed of dog.
– ORIGIN from *Rottweil*, a town in SW Germany.

rotund /roh-**tund**/ adjective having a large and rounded body or shape.
– DERIVATIVES **rotundity** noun **rotundly** adverb.
– ORIGIN Latin *rotundus.*

rotunda noun a round building or room, especially one with a dome.
– ORIGIN from Italian *rotonda camera* 'round chamber'.

rouble /roo-b'l/ (also chiefly N. Amer. **ruble**) noun the basic unit of money of Russia and some other former republics of the Soviet Union.
– ORIGIN Russian.

roué /roo-ay/ noun a man who leads an immoral life.
– ORIGIN French, 'broken on a wheel', referring to the instrument of torture thought to be deserved by such a person.

rouge /roozh/ noun a red powder or cream used as a cosmetic for colouring the cheeks. • verb colour the cheeks with rouge. • adjective (of wine) red.
– ORIGIN French, 'red'.

rough adjective 1 having an uneven or irregular surface; not smooth or level. 2 not gentle or careful; violent: *rough treatment*. 3 (of weather or the sea) wild and stormy. 4 not finished tidily; plain and basic: *rough wooden tables*. 5 not worked out or correct in every detail; approximate: *a rough guess*. 6 harsh in sound or taste. 7 not sophisticated or cultured. 8 informal difficult and unpleasant. • noun 1 a basic, preliminary state: *jot things down in rough first*. 2 chiefly Brit. a violent person. 3 (on a golf course) the area of longer grass around the fairway and the green. • verb 1 (**rough something out**) make a basic, preliminary version of something. 2 make something uneven. 3 (**rough it**) informal live in discomfort with only basic necessities. 4 (**rough someone up**) informal beat someone up.
– PHRASES **in the rough** in a natural state. **rough and ready** 1 basic but effective. 2 not sophisticated or refined. **rough edges** small flaws in something that is otherwise satisfactory. **rough justice** treatment that is not fair or in accordance with the law. **sleep rough** Brit. sleep outside in uncomfortable conditions. **take the rough with the smooth** accept the unpleasant aspects of life as well as the good.
– DERIVATIVES **roughness** noun.
– ORIGIN Old English.

roughage noun fibre in vegetables, cereals, and fruit that cannot be digested and which helps food and waste products to pass through the gut.

rough and tumble noun a situation without rules or organization.
– ORIGIN boxing slang.

roughcast noun plaster of lime, cement, and gravel, used on outside walls. • adjective coated with roughcast. • verb coat a wall with roughcast.

rough diamond noun 1 an uncut diamond. 2 Brit. a good or kind person who is not very polite or well educated.

roughen verb make or become rough.

rough-hewn adjective (of a person) unsophisticated or uncouth.

roughhouse informal, chiefly N. Amer. noun a violent disturbance. • verb act or treat in a rough, violent way.

roughly adverb 1 in a rough or harsh way. 2 not exactly; approximately.

roughneck noun informal 1 a rough, uncouth person. 2 an oil-rig worker.

roughshod adjective (in phrase **ride roughshod over**) fail to consider a person's wishes or feelings.
– ORIGIN first referring to a horse having shoes with nail heads projecting to prevent slipping.

rough trade noun informal male homosexual prostitution, especially when involving brutality or sadism.

roulade /roo-**lahd**/ noun a piece of meat, sponge cake, or other food, spread with a filling and rolled up.

– ORIGIN French.

roulette noun a gambling game in which a ball is dropped on to a revolving wheel with numbered compartments, the players betting on the number at which the ball comes to rest.
– ORIGIN French, 'small wheel'.

round adjective 1 shaped like a circle, cylinder, or sphere. 2 having a curved shape: *round red cheeks*. 3 (of a person's shoulders) bent forward. 4 (of a voice or musical tone) rich and mellow. 5 (of a number) expressed in convenient units rather than exactly, for example to the nearest whole number. 6 frank and truthful: *she berated him in round terms*. • noun 1 a circular piece or shape. 2 a route by which a number of people or places are visited or inspected in turn: *a newspaper round*. 3 a regularly recurring sequence of activities: *their lives were a daily round of housework and laundry*. 4 each of a sequence of sessions in a process, especially in a sports contest. 5 a single division of a boxing or wrestling match. 6 a set of drinks bought for all the members of a group. 7 the amount of ammunition needed to fire one shot. 8 Brit. a slice of bread. 9 Brit. the quantity of sandwiches made from two slices of bread. 10 a song for three or more unaccompanied voices or parts, each singing the same theme but starting one after another. • adverb chiefly Brit. 1 with circular movement; so as to rotate. 2 so as to cover the whole area surrounding a particular centre: *she glanced round admiringly at the decor.* 3 so as to turn and face in the opposite direction. 4 used in describing the relative position of something: *the pieces are the wrong way round*. 5 so as to surround or give support. 6 so as to reach a new place or position. • preposition chiefly Brit. 1 on every side of a central point. 2 so as to encircle or surround. 3 from or on the other side of. 4 so as to cover the whole area of. • verb 1 pass and go round something. 2 make a figure less exact but more convenient for calculations: *round the weight up to the nearest kilo*. 3 make or become round in shape.
– PHRASES **in the round** 1 (of sculpture) standing free, rather than carved in relief. 2 fully and thoroughly. 3 (of theatre) with the audience placed on at least three sides of the stage. **round something off** 1 smooth the edges of something. 2 complete something in a satisfying or suitable way. **round on** make a sudden attack on. **round someone/thing up** drive or collect people or animals together.
– DERIVATIVES **roundish** adjective **roundness** noun.
– ORIGIN Old French.

roundabout noun Brit. 1 a road junction at which traffic moves in one direction round a central island to reach one of the roads converging on it. 2 a large revolving device in a playground, for children to ride on. 3 a merry-go-round. • adjective not following a direct route; circuitous.

round dance noun 1 a folk dance in which the dancers form one large circle. 2 a ballroom dance such as a waltz or polka in which couples move in circles round the ballroom.

rounded adjective 1 round or curved. 2 well developed in all aspects; balanced: *a rounded human being*.

roundel /rown-d'l/ noun 1 a small disc, especially a decorative medallion. 2 a circular identifying mark painted on military aircraft.
– ORIGIN Old French *rondel*.

roundelay /rown-duh-lay/ noun literary 1 a short simple song with a refrain. 2 a circle dance.
– ORIGIN Old French *rondelet*.

rounders plural noun (treated as sing.) a ball game in which players run round a circuit of bases after hitting the ball with a cylindrical wooden bat, scoring a **rounder** if all four bases are reached before the ball is fielded.

Roundhead noun historical a member or supporter of the Parliamentary party in the English Civil War.
– ORIGIN with reference to their short-cropped hair.

roundhouse noun 1 a railway locomotive maintenance shed built around a turntable. 2 informal a blow given with a wide sweep of the arm.

roundly adverb 1 in an emphatic or blunt way. 2 so as to form a circular shape.

round robin noun 1 a tournament in which each competitor plays in turn against every other. 2 a petition, especially one with signatures written in a circle to conceal the order of writing.

roundsman noun (pl. **roundsmen**) 1 Brit. a trader's employee who goes round delivering and taking orders. 2 US a police officer in charge of a patrol.

round table noun (usu. before another noun) a meeting at which parties meet on equal terms for discussion.

round trip noun a journey to a place and back again.

round-up noun 1 a gathering together of people or things. 2 a summary of facts or events.

roundworm noun a parasitic worm found in the intestines of some mammals.

rouse /rowz/ verb 1 bring or come out of sleep. 2 cause someone to move or take interest after being inactive. 3 stir up or arouse: *his evasiveness roused my curiosity.*
– ORIGIN probably from Old French.

rousing adjective exciting; stirring: *a rousing speech.*
– DERIVATIVES **rousingly** adverb.

roust /rowsst/ verb N. Amer. informal make someone get up or start moving.
– ORIGIN perhaps from ROUSE.

roustabout /rowsst-uh-bowt/ noun an unskilled or casual worker, especially a labourer on an oil rig.
– ORIGIN from ROUST.

rout¹ /rowt/ noun 1 a disorderly retreat of defeated troops. 2 a decisive defeat. •verb defeat someone decisively and force them to retreat.
– ORIGIN Old French *rute*.

rout² /rowt/ verb 1 cut a groove in a hard surface. 2 search around for someone or something.
– DERIVATIVES **router** noun.
– ORIGIN from ROOT².

route /root/ noun 1 a way taken in getting from a starting point to a destination. 2 a method or

process that leads to a particular result: *a fast-track route to a coaching career.* •verb (**routes, routeing** or **routing, routed**) send someone or something along a particular course.
– ORIGIN Old French *rute* 'road'.

routine noun 1 a sequence of actions regularly followed. 2 a set sequence in a dance or comedy act. •adjective 1 performed as part of a regular procedure: *a routine inspection.* 2 without variety; dull.
– DERIVATIVES **routinely** adverb.
– ORIGIN French.

roux /roo/ noun (pl. same) Cookery a mixture of fat (especially butter) and flour used in making sauces.
– ORIGIN from French *beurre roux* 'browned butter'.

rove verb 1 travel constantly without a fixed destination; wander. 2 (of a person's eyes) look around in all directions.
– DERIVATIVES **rover** noun.
– ORIGIN perhaps from dialect *rave* 'to stray'.

row¹ /roh/ noun a number of people or things in a line.
– PHRASES **in a row** informal one after the other; in succession.
– ORIGIN Old English.

row² /roh/ verb 1 propel a boat with oars. 2 row a boat as a sport. •noun a spell of rowing.
– DERIVATIVES **rower** noun.
– ORIGIN Old English.

row³ /row/ chiefly Brit. noun 1 an angry quarrel. 2 a serious dispute. 3 a loud noise or uproar. •verb have an angry quarrel.
– ORIGIN unknown.

rowan /roh-uhn, row-uhn/ noun a small tree with white flowers and red berries.
– ORIGIN Scandinavian.

rowdy adjective (**rowdier, rowdiest**) noisy and disorderly. •noun (pl. **rowdies**) a rowdy person.
– DERIVATIVES **rowdily** adverb **rowdiness** noun **rowdyism** noun.
– ORIGIN unknown.

rowel /row-uhl/ noun a spiked revolving disc at the end of a spur.
– ORIGIN Old French *roele*.

row house noun N. Amer. a terrace house.

rowing boat (N. Amer. **rowboat**) noun a small boat propelled by oars.

rowing machine noun an exercise machine with oars and a sliding seat.

rowlock /rol-luhk/ noun Brit. a fitting on the side of a boat for holding an oar.

royal adjective 1 relating to or having the status of a king or queen or a member of their family. 2 of a quality or size suitable for a king or queen; splendid. 3 Brit. informal real; complete: *she's a right royal pain in the behind.* •noun informal a member of the royal family.
– DERIVATIVES **royally** adverb.
– ORIGIN Old French *roial*.

royal blue noun a deep, vivid blue.

Royal Commission noun (in the UK) a commission of inquiry appointed by the Crown on the recommendation of the government.

royal icing noun chiefly Brit. hard white icing, typically used to decorate fruit cakes.

royalist noun 1 a person who supports the

principle of rule by a king or queen.
2 (Royalist) a supporter of the King against
Parliament in the English Civil War.
– DERIVATIVES **royalism** noun.

royal jelly noun a substance produced by
honeybee workers and fed by them to larvae
which are being raised as potential queen
bees.

royalty noun (pl. **royalties**) **1** people of royal
blood or status. **2** the status or power of a king
or queen: *the insignia of royalty.* **3** a sum paid
for the use of a patent or to an author or
composer for each copy of a work sold or for
each public performance.

royal warrant noun a warrant issued by the
sovereign and authorizing a company to
display the royal arms, indicating that goods
or services are supplied to the royal family.

rozzer noun Brit. informal a police officer.
– ORIGIN unknown.

RP abbreviation received pronunciation.

RPI abbreviation retail price index.

rpm abbreviation revolutions per minute.

RRP abbreviation Brit. recommended retail price.

Rs abbreviation rupee(s).

RSA abbreviation **1** Republic of South Africa.
2 Royal Scottish Academy; Royal Scottish
Academician. **3** Royal Society of Arts.

RSC abbreviation Royal Shakespeare Company.

RSI abbreviation repetitive strain injury.

RSJ abbreviation rolled steel joist.

RSM abbreviation (in the British army)
Regimental Sergeant Major.

RSPB abbreviation (in the UK) Royal Society for
the Protection of Birds.

RSPCA abbreviation (in the UK) Royal Society
for the Prevention of Cruelty to Animals.

RSVP abbreviation répondez s'il vous plaît;
please reply (used at the end of invitations).
– ORIGIN French.

RTF abbreviation Computing rich text format.

Rt Hon. abbreviation Brit. Right Honourable.

Rt Revd (also **Rt Rev.**) abbreviation Brit. Right
Reverend.

RU abbreviation rugby union.

Ru symbol the chemical element ruthenium.

rub verb (**rubs, rubbing, rubbed**) **1** move back
and forth over a surface while pressing
against it. **2** apply with a rubbing action: *she
rubbed some cream on her nose.* **3** (**rub
something down**) dry, smooth, or clean
something by rubbing. **4** (**rub something
in/into**) work fat into a mixture by breaking
and blending it with the fingertips. ● noun **1** an
act of rubbing. **2** an ointment for rubbing into
the skin. **3** (**the rub**) the central or most
important difficulty. [from Shakespeare's
Hamlet (III. i. 65).]
– PHRASES **rub along** Brit. informal cope or get
along without much difficulty. **rub one's
hands** show satisfaction. **rub it in** (or **rub
someone's nose in something**) informal
forcefully draw someone's attention to an
embarrassing fact. **rub off** be transferred: *she
hoped that some of his confidence would rub off
on her.* **rub something out** chiefly Brit. erase
pencil marks with a rubber. **rub shoulders
with** associate or come into contact with
someone. **rub someone (up) the wrong way**

irritate someone.
– ORIGIN perhaps from German *rubben.*

rubato /ruu-bah-toh/ noun (pl. **rubatos** or **rubati**
/ruu-bah-ti/) Music temporary disregard for
strict tempo to allow an expressive quickening
or slackening.
– ORIGIN Italian, 'robbed'.

rubber[1] noun **1** a tough elastic substance made
from the latex of a tropical tree or
synthetically. **2** Brit. a piece of rubber for
erasing pencil marks. **3** N. Amer. informal a
condom.
– DERIVATIVES **rubberize** (or **rubberise**) verb
rubbery adjective.
– ORIGIN from **RUB**.

rubber[2] noun **1** a contest consisting of a series
of matches between the same sides in cricket,
tennis, and other games. **2** Bridge a unit of play
in which one side scores bonus points for
winning the best of three games.
– ORIGIN unknown.

rubber band noun a loop of rubber for
holding things together.

rubber bullet noun a bullet made of rubber,
used in riot control.

rubberneck informal verb turn one's head to
stare at something in a foolish way. ● noun a
person who stares in a foolish way.
– DERIVATIVES **rubbernecker** noun.

rubber plant noun an evergreen tree with
large dark green shiny leaves, native to SE
Asia and formerly grown as a source of
rubber.

rubber stamp noun **1** a hand-held device for
stamping dates, addresses, etc. on a surface.
2 an instance of automatic approval given
without proper consideration. ● verb (**rubber-
stamp**) approve something automatically
without proper consideration.

rubber tree noun a tree that produces the
latex from which rubber is manufactured,
native to the Amazonian rainforest.

rubbing noun an impression of a design on
brass or stone, made by placing a sheet of
paper over it and rubbing it with chalk, wax,
or a pencil.

rubbish noun chiefly Brit. **1** waste material; refuse
or litter. **2** unimportant or inferior material:
wasn't their last album rubbish? **3** ridiculous or
foolish talk or ideas; nonsense. ● verb Brit. informal
criticize and reject something as worthless.
● adjective Brit. informal very bad.
– DERIVATIVES **rubbishy** adjective.
– ORIGIN Old French *rubbous.*

rubble noun rough fragments of stone, brick,
concrete, etc., especially as the debris from
the demolition of buildings.
– DERIVATIVES **rubbly** adjective.
– ORIGIN perhaps from Old French *robe* 'spoils'.

rube /roob/ noun N. Amer. informal a country
bumpkin.
– ORIGIN abbreviation of the man's name
Reuben.

rubella /roo-bel-luh/ noun a disease
transmitted by a virus and with symptoms like
mild measles; German measles.
– ORIGIN Latin, 'reddish things'.

Rubicon /roo-bi-k'n, roo-bi-kon/ noun a point
of no return.

r

- ORIGIN a stream in NE Italy marking the ancient boundary between Italy and Gaul; by leading his army across it, Julius Caesar caused a civil war.

rubicund /roo-bi-kuhnd/ adjective having a reddish complexion.
- ORIGIN Latin *rubicundus*.

rubidium /ruu-bid-i-uhm/ noun a rare soft silvery reactive metallic element.
- ORIGIN from Latin *rubidus* 'red'.

ruble noun variant spelling of ROUBLE.

rubric /roo-brik/ noun 1 a heading on a document. 2 a set of instructions or rules. 3 a direction as to how a church service should be conducted.
- ORIGIN first referring to material written in red for emphasis: from Latin *rubrica terra* 'red earth or ochre as writing material'.

ruby noun (pl. **rubies**) 1 a precious stone that is typically deep crimson in colour. 2 a deep red colour.
- ORIGIN Latin *rubinus*.

ruby wedding noun Brit. the fortieth anniversary of a wedding.

RUC abbreviation historical Royal Ulster Constabulary.

ruche /roosh/ noun a frill or pleat of fabric.
- DERIVATIVES **ruched** adjective **ruching** noun.
- ORIGIN French.

ruck¹ noun 1 Rugby a loose scrum formed around a player with the ball on the ground. 2 a tightly packed crowd of people. • verb Rugby take part in a ruck.
- ORIGIN probably of Scandinavian origin.

ruck² verb make or form creases or folds: *her skirt was rucked up.* • noun a crease or wrinkle.
- ORIGIN Old Norse.

ruck³ noun Brit. informal a brawl.
- ORIGIN perhaps from RUCTION or RUCKUS.

rucksack /ruk-sak/ noun a bag with two shoulder straps which allow it to be carried on the back.
- ORIGIN German.

ruckus /ruk-uhss/ noun a row or commotion.
- ORIGIN perhaps related to RUCTION and RUMPUS.

ruction noun informal 1 (**ructions**) Brit. angry reactions; trouble. 2 a disturbance or quarrel.
- ORIGIN perhaps from INSURRECTION.

rudbeckia /rood-bek-i-uh, rud-bek-i-uh/ noun a North American plant of the daisy family, with yellow or orange flowers and a dark cone-shaped centre.
- ORIGIN named after the Swedish botanist Olaf Rudbeck.

rudd noun (pl. same) a freshwater fish of the carp family with a silvery body and red fins.
- ORIGIN probably from former *rud* 'red colour'.

rudder noun 1 a flat hinged upright piece at the back of a boat, used for steering. 2 an upright aerofoil pivoted from the tailplane of an aircraft, used for steering.
- ORIGIN Old English, 'paddle, oar'.

rudderless adjective lacking a clear sense of one's aims or direction.

ruddy adjective (**ruddier, ruddiest**) 1 (of a person's face) having a healthy red colour. 2 reddish in colour. 3 Brit. informal used as a euphemism for 'bloody'.
- DERIVATIVES **ruddiness** noun.

- ORIGIN Old English.

rude adjective 1 offensively impolite or bad-mannered. 2 referring to sex or bodily functions in an offensive way. 3 very abrupt: *the war came as a rude awakening.* 4 chiefly Brit. vigorous or hearty: *she'd always been in rude health.* 5 dated roughly made or done. 6 old use ignorant and uneducated.
- DERIVATIVES **rudely** adverb **rudeness** noun **rudery** noun.
- ORIGIN Latin *rudis* 'not wrought or cultivated'.

rude boy noun (in Jamaica) a lawless urban youth who likes ska or reggae.

rudiment /roo-di-muhnt/ noun 1 (**rudiments**) the basic facts of a subject. 2 (**rudiments**) a basic or primitive form of something. 3 Biology an undeveloped or immature part or organ.
- ORIGIN Latin *rudimentum*.

rudimentary /roo-di-men-tuh-ri/ adjective 1 involving only the basic facts or elements: *a rudimentary education.* 2 not highly or fully developed: *a rudimentary stage of evolution.*
- DERIVATIVES **rudimentarily** adverb.

rue¹ verb (**rues, rueing** or **ruing, rued**) bitterly regret a past event or action.
- ORIGIN Old English.

rue² noun an evergreen shrub with bitter strong-scented leaves which are used in herbal medicine.
- ORIGIN Greek *rhutē*.

rueful adjective expressing regret: *a rueful smile.*
- DERIVATIVES **ruefully** adverb **ruefulness** noun.

ruff¹ noun 1 a projecting starched frill worn round the neck, especially in Elizabethan and Jacobean times. 2 a ring of feathers or hair round the neck of a bird or mammal. 3 (pl. same or **ruffs**) a wading bird, the male of which has a large ruff and ear tufts in the breeding season.
- ORIGIN probably from ROUGH.

ruff² verb (in bridge and whist) play a trump in a trick which was led in a different suit. • noun an act of playing such a trump.
- ORIGIN Old French *rouffle*.

ruffian noun a violent or lawless person.
- DERIVATIVES **ruffianism** noun **ruffianly** adjective.
- ORIGIN Old French.

ruffle verb 1 disrupt the smooth surface of something. 2 irritate or upset someone. 3 (as adj. **ruffled**) gathered into a frill. • noun a gathered frill on a garment.
- ORIGIN unknown.

rufiyaa /roo-fee-yah/ noun (pl. same) the basic unit of money of the Maldives.
- ORIGIN Maldivian.

rufous /roo-fuhss/ adjective (especially of an animal or bird) reddish brown in colour.
- ORIGIN Latin *rufus* 'red, reddish'.

rug noun 1 a small carpet. 2 Brit. a thick woollen blanket.
- PHRASES **pull the rug out from under someone** abruptly withdraw support from someone.
- ORIGIN probably Scandinavian.

rugby (also **rugby football**) noun a team game played with an oval ball that may be kicked, carried, and passed by hand, in which points are won by scoring a try or by kicking the ball

over the crossbar of the opponents' goal.
– ORIGIN named after *Rugby* School in England, where it was first played.

rugby league noun a form of rugby played in teams of thirteen.

rugby union noun a form of rugby played in teams of fifteen.

rugged /rug-gid/ **adjective 1** having a rocky and uneven surface. **2** (of clothing or equipment) strong and capable of withstanding rough handling. **3** having or requiring toughness and determination: *a stubborn, rugged individualist.* **4** (of a man) having attractively strong features.
– DERIVATIVES **ruggedly** adverb **ruggedness** noun.
– ORIGIN probably of Scandinavian origin.

rugger noun Brit. informal rugby.

ruin noun 1 the physical destruction or collapse of something. **2** the remains of a building that has decayed or suffered much damage. **3** a severe downfall or decline: *such action can only result in the utter ruin of our nation.* **4** the complete loss of a person's money and other assets. •**verb 1** destroy or severely damage a building or other structure. **2** have a very damaging effect on: *the motorway has ruined village life.* **3** make someone very poor or bankrupt.
– ORIGIN Latin *ruina.*

ruination noun the action of ruining someone or something or the state of being ruined.

ruinous adjective 1 disastrous or destructive. **2** costing far more than a person can afford. **3** (of a building) in ruins.
– DERIVATIVES **ruinously** adverb.

rule noun 1 a regulation or statement controlling behaviour or procedure within a particular area of activity. **2** control of a country or people: *British rule.* **3** a code of practice and discipline for a religious community. **4** (**the rule**) the normal or usual state of things. **5** a ruler for measuring things. **6** a thin printed line or dash. •**verb 1** control or govern a people or country. **2** have a powerful and restricting influence on: *her whole life was ruled by fear.* **3** state with legal authority that something is the case. **4** informal be very good or the best. **5** make parallel lines on paper.
– PHRASES **as a rule** usually, but not always. **rule of thumb** a broadly accurate guide or principle, based on practice rather than theory. **rule something out/in** exclude (or include) something as a possibility. **rule the roost** be in complete control.
– ORIGIN Old French *reule.*

ruler noun 1 a person who rules a people or country. **2** a straight strip of rigid material, marked at regular intervals and used to draw straight lines or measure distances.

ruling noun a decision or statement made by someone in authority. •**adjective** in control; governing.

rum¹ noun an alcoholic spirit distilled from sugar-cane residues or molasses.
– ORIGIN perhaps from former *rumbullion.*

rum² adjective (**rummer, rummest**) Brit. informal, dated odd; peculiar.
– ORIGIN unknown.

Rumanian adjective & noun variant spelling of ROMANIAN.

rumba /rum-buh/ (also **rhumba**) **noun 1** a rhythmic dance with Spanish and African elements, originating in Cuba. **2** a ballroom dance based on the Cuban rumba.
– ORIGIN Latin American Spanish.

rum baba /bah-bah/ **noun** a rich sponge cake, soaked in rum-flavoured syrup.
– ORIGIN Polish, 'married peasant woman'.

rumble verb 1 make or move with a continuous deep sound. **2** (**rumble on**) (of a dispute) continue in a low-key way. **3** Brit. informal discover an underhand activity or the person involved in it. •**noun 1** a continuous deep sound like distant thunder. **2** N. Amer. informal a street fight between rival gangs.
– DERIVATIVES **rumbler** noun.
– ORIGIN probably from Dutch *rommelen, rummelen.*

rumble strip noun one of a series of raised strips set in a road to warn drivers to slow down.

rumbustious /rum-buss-chuhss, rum-buss-ti-uhss/ **adjective** informal, chiefly Brit. high-spirited or difficult to control.
– ORIGIN probably from former *robustious* 'boisterous, robust'.

ruminant noun a mammal of a type that chews the cud, such as cattle, sheep, or deer. •**adjective** relating to mammals that chew the cud.
– ORIGIN from Latin *ruminari* 'chew over again'.

ruminate /roo-mi-nayt/ **verb 1** think deeply about something. **2** (of a cow, sheep, etc.) chew the cud.
– DERIVATIVES **rumination** noun **ruminative** adjective.

rummage verb search for something in an unmethodical way. •**noun** an act of rummaging.
– ORIGIN from Old French *arrumer* 'stow in a hold (of a ship)'.

rummage sale noun chiefly N. Amer. a jumble sale.

rummy noun a card game in which the players try to form sets and sequences of cards.
– ORIGIN unknown.

rumour (US **rumor**) **noun** a story spread among a number of people which is unconfirmed and may be false. •**verb** (**be rumoured**) be spread as a rumour.
– ORIGIN Latin *rumor* 'noise'.

rump noun 1 the hind part of the body of a mammal or the lower back of a bird. **2** a small or unimportant part left over from something larger.
– ORIGIN probably Scandinavian.

rumple verb make something untidy or dishevelled.
– DERIVATIVES **rumpled** adjective.
– ORIGIN Dutch *rompel* 'wrinkle'.

rumpus noun (pl. **rumpuses**) a noisy disturbance.
– ORIGIN uncertain.

rumpy pumpy noun informal, humorous sexual activity.
– ORIGIN from RUMP.

run verb (**runs, running, ran**; past part. **run**) **1** move fast using the legs. **2** move or pass something in a particular direction: *Helen ran*

r

her fingers through her hair. **3** move forcefully or fast: *the tanker ran aground.* **4** be in charge of people or an organization. **5** continue, operate, or proceed: *everything's running according to plan.* **6** function or cause to function. **7** pass into or reach a specified state or level: *inflation is running at 11 per cent.* **8** (of a liquid) flow. **9** send out a liquid. **10** (**run in**) (of a quality) be common in members of a family. **11** stand as a candidate in an election. **12** enter or be entered in a race. **13** (of dye or colour) dissolve and spread when wet. **14** (of a bus, train, etc.) make a regular journey on a particular route. **15** transport someone in a car. **16** publish or be published in a newspaper or magazine. **17** smuggle goods. **18** chiefly N. Amer. (of a stocking or pair of tights) develop a ladder. • **noun 1** an act or spell of running. **2** a running pace. **3** a journey or route. **4** a short trip in a car. **5** a course or track made or regularly used: *a ski run.* **6** a spell or stretch of something: *a run of bad luck.* **7** an enclosed area in which animals or birds may run freely in the open. **8** (**the run of**) free and unrestricted use of or access to somewhere. **9** (**the run**) the average or usual type: *she stood out from the general run of Tory women.* **10** a rapid series of musical notes. **11** a sequence of cards of the same suit. **12** Cricket a unit of scoring achieved by hitting the ball so that both batsmen are able to run between the wickets. **13** Baseball a point scored by the batter returning to the home plate after touching the bases. **14** a ladder in stockings or tights. **15** (**the runs**) informal diarrhoea.
– PHRASES **be run off one's feet** be very busy. **give someone/thing a (good) run for their money** provide someone or something with challenging competition. **have a (good) run for one's money** receive reward or enjoyment in return for one's efforts. **on the run 1** escaping from arrest. **2** while running or moving. **run across** meet or find by chance. **run after** informal pursue persistently. **run along** informal go away. **run away 1** escape from a person, place, or situation. **2** try to avoid facing up to danger or difficulty. **run away with 1** be out of the control of: *her imagination was running away with her.* **2** win a competition or prize easily. **run before one can walk** attempt something difficult before one has grasped the basic skills. **run something by** (or **past**) tell someone about something to find out their opinion. **run something down** (or **run down**) **1** gradually lose or cause to lose power. **2** reduce or be reduced in size or resources. **3** get worse or cause to get worse in quality. **run someone/thing down 1** knock someone or something down with a vehicle. **2** criticize someone or something. **run someone in** informal arrest someone. **run something in** Brit. use something new in such a way as not to make heavy demands on it. **run into 1** collide with. **2** meet someone by chance. **3** experience a problem. **run something off 1** produce a copy on a machine. **2** write or recite something quickly and with little effort. **run on** continue without stopping. **run out 1** use up or be used up. **2** become no longer valid. **run someone out** Cricket dismiss a batsman by dislodging the bails with the ball

while the batsman is still running. **run over** (of a container or its contents) overflow. **run someone/thing over** knock someone or something down with a vehicle. **run through** (or **over**) go over quickly or briefly as a rehearsal or reminder. **run to 1** extend to or reach an amount or size. **2** show a tendency towards. **run something up 1** allow a bill, score, etc. to build up. **2** make something quickly or hurriedly. **3** raise a flag. **run up against** experience or meet a problem.
– DERIVATIVES **runnable** adjective.
– ORIGIN Old English.

runabout noun a small car or light aircraft, especially one used for short journeys.

runaround noun informal (in phrase **give someone the runaround**) treat someone badly by misleading them or failing to do or provide something.

runaway noun a person who has run away from their home or an institution. • **adjective 1** (of an animal or vehicle) running out of control. **2** happening or done quickly or uncontrollably: *the runaway success of his first novel.*

rundown noun a brief analysis or summary. • **adjective** (**run-down**) **1** in a poor or neglected state. **2** tired and rather unwell, especially through overwork.

rune /roon/ noun **1** a letter of an ancient Germanic alphabet used especially in Scandinavia. **2** a symbol with mysterious or magical significance.
– DERIVATIVES **runic** adjective.
– ORIGIN Old English, 'secret, mystery'.

rung¹ noun **1** a horizontal bar on a ladder to stand on. **2** a level or rank in society, a profession, etc.: *a youth on a low rung at the Foreign Office.* **3** a strengthening crosspiece in the structure of a chair.
– ORIGIN Old English.

rung² past participle of RING².

run-in noun **1** Brit. the approach to an action or event. **2** informal a disagreement or fight.

runnel noun **1** a gutter. **2** a brook or stream.
– ORIGIN dialect *rindle*.

runner noun **1** a person or animal that runs. **2** a rod, groove, blade, or roller on which something slides. **3** a messenger or collector, especially for a bookmaker. **4** a shoot of a plant which grows along the ground and can take root at points along its length. **5** a long, narrow rug.
– PHRASES **do a runner** Brit. informal leave hastily to escape something.

runner bean noun a climbing bean plant with scarlet flowers and long green edible pods.

runner-up noun (pl. **runners-up**) a competitor or team taking second place in a contest.

running adjective **1** (of water) flowing naturally or supplied through pipes and taps. **2** producing liquid or pus. **3** continuous or recurring: *a running joke.* **4** done while running. **5** (after a noun) in succession: *the third week running.*
– PHRASES **in** (or **out of**) **the running** in (or no longer in) with a chance of success. **make the running** Brit. set the pace.

running battle noun a battle which does not occur at a fixed location.

running board noun a footboard extending along the side of a vehicle.

running commentary noun a spoken description of events, given as they occur.

running head noun a heading printed at the top of each page of a book or chapter.

running mate noun chiefly N. Amer. an election candidate for the lesser of two linked political offices.

running repairs plural noun minor or temporary repairs carried out on machinery while it is in use.

running stitch noun a simple needlework stitch consisting of a line of small even stitches which run back and forth through the cloth.

running total noun a total that is continually adjusted to take account of further items.

runny adjective (**runnier**, **runniest**) 1 more liquid in consistency than is usual or expected. 2 (of a person's nose) producing mucus.

run-off noun 1 a further contest after a clear winner has not emerged in a previous one. 2 rainfall or other liquid that drains away from the surface of an area.

run-of-the-mill adjective lacking unusual or special aspects; ordinary.

runt noun a small pig or other animal, especially the smallest in a litter.
– DERIVATIVES **runtish** adjective **runty** adjective.
– ORIGIN unknown.

run-through noun 1 a rehearsal. 2 a brief summary.

run-up noun 1 a period of preparation before an important event. 2 an act of running briefly to gain momentum before bowling, performing a jump, etc.

runway noun 1 a strip of hard ground along which aircraft take off and land. 2 N. Amer. a catwalk in a fashion show.

rupee /roo-pee, ruu-pee/ noun the basic unit of money of India, Pakistan, Sri Lanka, and some other countries.
– ORIGIN Sanskrit, 'wrought silver'.

rupiah /roo-pee-uh/ noun the basic unit of money of Indonesia.
– ORIGIN Indonesian.

rupture verb 1 break or burst suddenly. 2 (**be ruptured** or **rupture oneself**) suffer a hernia in the abdomen. 3 disturb good relations. •noun 1 a sudden breaking or bursting of something. 2 a hernia in the abdomen.
– ORIGIN Latin *ruptura*.

rural adjective relating to or typical of the countryside rather than the town.
– DERIVATIVES **rurality** noun **ruralize** (or **ruralise**) verb **rurally** adverb.
– ORIGIN Latin *ruralis*.

Ruritanian /roo-ri-tay-ni-uhn/ adjective relating to or typical of romantic adventure or its setting.
– ORIGIN from *Ruritania*, the imaginary setting for the novels written by the English novelist Anthony Hope.

ruse /rooz/ noun an action intended to deceive someone; a trick.
– ORIGIN from Old French *ruser* 'use trickery'.

rush[1] verb 1 move or act with urgent haste. 2 deliver or produce something with urgent haste. 3 deal with hurriedly: *panic measures were rushed through parliament.* 4 (of air or a liquid) flow strongly. 5 try to attack or capture a person or place suddenly. •noun 1 a sudden quick movement or flow: *there was a rush for the door.* 2 a flurry of hasty activity. 3 a sudden strong demand for a product. 4 a sudden intense feeling. 5 informal a sudden thrill experienced after taking certain drugs. 6 (**rushes**) the first prints made of a film after a period of shooting.
– ORIGIN Old French *ruser* 'drive back'.

rush[2] noun a marsh or waterside plant with slender pith-filled leaves, some kinds of which are used for matting, baskets, etc.
– DERIVATIVES **rushy** adjective.
– ORIGIN Old English.

rush hour noun a time at the start and end of the working day when traffic is at its heaviest.

rushlight noun historical a candle made by dipping the pith of a rush in tallow.

rusk noun chiefly Brit. a dry biscuit, especially one eaten by babies.
– ORIGIN Spanish or Portuguese *rosca* 'twist, coil, roll of bread'.

russet adjective reddish brown. •noun 1 a reddish-brown colour. 2 a variety of dessert apple with a slightly rough greenish-brown skin.
– DERIVATIVES **russety** adjective.
– ORIGIN Old French *rousset*.

Russian noun 1 a person from Russia. 2 the language of Russia. •adjective relating to Russia.

Russian doll noun each of a set of brightly painted hollow wooden dolls that fit inside each other.

Russian Orthodox Church noun the national Church of Russia.

Russian roulette noun a dangerous game of chance in which a person loads a bullet into one chamber of a revolver, spins the cylinder, and then pulls the trigger while pointing the gun at their own head.

Russki /russ-ki/ (also **Russky**) noun (pl. **Russkis** or **Russkies**) informal, chiefly derogatory a Russian.

rust noun 1 a reddish-brown flaky coating of iron oxide that is formed on iron or steel by the action of water and oxygen. 2 a disease of plants caused by a fungus, which results in reddish or brownish patches. 3 a reddish-brown colour. •verb be affected with rust.
– DERIVATIVES **rustless** adjective.
– ORIGIN Old English.

rust belt noun informal (especially in the American Midwest and NE states) a region where heavy industry is in decline and the population is falling.

rust bucket noun informal a vehicle or ship which is old and badly rusted.

rustic adjective 1 relating to or typical of the country, especially in being attractively simple or unsophisticated: *hearty rustic dishes.* 2 (of furniture) made of rough branches or timber. •noun often derogatory an unsophisticated country person.
– DERIVATIVES **rustically** adverb **rusticity** noun.
– ORIGIN Latin *rusticus*.

rusticate /russ-ti-kayt/ verb 1 Brit. (chiefly at

r

Oxford and Cambridge) suspend a student
from a university as a punishment. **2** (usu. as
adj. **rusticated**) shape masonry in large blocks
with sunken joints and a roughened surface.
– DERIVATIVES **rustication** noun.
– ORIGIN from Latin *rusticus* 'rustic'.

rustle verb **1** make or move with a soft
crackling sound like that caused by the
movement of dry leaves. **2** round up and steal
cattle, horses, or sheep. **3** (**rustle something
up**) informal produce food or a drink quickly.
●noun a rustling sound.
– DERIVATIVES **rustler** noun.
– ORIGIN imitating the sound.

rustproof adjective not able to be corroded by
rust. ●verb make something rustproof.

rusty adjective (**rustier, rustiest**) **1** affected by
rust. **2** (of knowledge or a skill) less good than
it used to be because of lack of practice. **3** rust-
coloured; reddish-brown.
– DERIVATIVES **rustily** adverb **rustiness** noun.

rut[1] noun **1** a long deep track made by the
repeated passage of the wheels of vehicles. **2** a
pattern of behaviour that has become dull but
is hard to change: *here's me, stuck in a rut with
Roger after all these years.*
– DERIVATIVES **rutted** adjective **rutty** adjective.
– ORIGIN probably from Old French *rute* 'road'.

rut[2] noun an annual period of sexual activity in
deer and some other mammals, during which
the males fight each other for access to the
females. ●verb (**ruts, rutting, rutted**) be in such
a period of activity.

– ORIGIN Old French.

ruthenium /ruu-**thee**-ni-uhm/ noun a hard
silvery-white metallic chemical element.
– ORIGIN from *Ruthenia*, a region of central
Europe.

rutherfordium /ru-*ther*-for-di-uhm/ noun a
very unstable chemical element made by high-
energy atomic collisions.
– ORIGIN named after the New Zealand
physicist Ernest *Rutherford*.

ruthless adjective having or showing no pity or
sympathy; hard and selfish.
– DERIVATIVES **ruthlessly** adverb **ruthlessness**
noun.
– ORIGIN from the old-fashioned word *ruth*
'pity'.

RV abbreviation N. Amer. recreational vehicle
(especially a motorized caravan).

Rwandan /ruu-an-duhn/ (also **Rwandese**
/ruu-an-deez/) noun a person from Rwanda, a
country in central Africa. ●adjective relating to
Rwanda.

rye noun **1** a cereal plant resembling wheat,
which grows in poor soils. **2** whisky in which
much of the grain used in distilling it is
fermented rye.
– ORIGIN Old English.

rye bread noun a dense, chewy bread made
with rye flour.

ryegrass noun a grass used for fodder and
lawns.
– ORIGIN unknown.

r

Ss

S[1] (also **s**) noun (pl. **Ss** or **S's**) the nineteenth letter of the alphabet.

S[2] abbreviation **1** (chiefly in Catholic use) Saint. **2** siemens. **3** small (as a clothes size). **4** South or Southern. ● symbol the chemical element sulphur.

s abbreviation **1** second or seconds. **2** shilling or shillings.

's contraction informal **1** is: *she's an editor.* **2** has: *he's just gone.* **3** us: *let's be honest.* **4** does.

-'s suffix **1** showing possession in singular nouns, also in plural nouns not ending in -s: *John's car | the children's school.* **2** forming the plural of a letter or symbol: *9's.*

SA abbreviation **1** Salvation Army. **2** South Africa. **3** South America. **4** South Australia.

sabbatarian /sab-uh-**tair**-i-uhn/ noun a person who strictly observes Sunday as the sabbath.
– DERIVATIVES **sabbatarianism** noun.

sabbath noun (often **the Sabbath**) a day intended for religious worship and rest from work, kept by Jews from Friday evening to Saturday evening, and by most Christians on Sunday.
– ORIGIN from Hebrew, 'to rest'.

sabbatical /suh-**bat**-i-k'l/ noun a period of paid leave granted to a university teacher for study or travel. ● adjective relating to a sabbatical.
– ORIGIN from Greek *sabbatikos* 'of the sabbath'.

saber noun US spelling of **SABRE**.

sable /rhymes with table/ noun **1** a marten with a short tail and dark brown fur, native to Japan and Siberia. **2** the fur of the sable. ● adjective literary or Heraldry black.
– ORIGIN Old French.

sabot /**sab**-oh/ noun a kind of simple wooden shoe resembling a clog.
– ORIGIN French.

sabotage /**sab**-uh-tah*zh*/ verb deliberately destroy, damage, or hinder: *they might try and sabotage the deal.* ● noun the action of sabotaging something.
– ORIGIN from French *saboter* 'kick with sabots, destroy'.

saboteur /sab-uh-**ter**/ noun a person who sabotages something.
– ORIGIN French.

sabra /**sab**-ruh/ noun a Jew born in Israel (or before 1948 in Palestine).
– ORIGIN Hebrew, 'opuntia fruit' (opuntias being common in parts of Israel).

sabre /**say**-ber/ (US **saber**) noun **1** a heavy cavalry sword with a curved blade and a single cutting edge. **2** a light fencing sword with a tapering, typically curved blade.
– ORIGIN French.

sabre-rattling noun the display or threat of military force.

sabretooth (also **sabre-toothed tiger**) noun a large extinct member of the cat family with huge curved upper canine teeth.

sac noun a hollow, flexible structure in the body or a plant, resembling a bag or pouch and containing air or liquid.
– ORIGIN Latin *saccus* 'sack, bag'.

saccharin /sak-kuh-rin/ noun a synthetic substance used as a low-calorie sweetener.
– ORIGIN Greek *sakkharon* 'sugar'.

saccharine /sak-kuh-rin, sak-kuh-reen/ adjective very sweet or sentimental: *horribly saccharine sitcoms.* ● noun saccharin.

sacerdotal /sak-er-**doh**-t'l/ adjective relating to priests or the priesthood.
– ORIGIN Latin *sacerdotalis.*

sachem /**say**-chuhm, **sach**-uhm/ noun **1** (among some American Indian peoples) a chief. **2** N. Amer. informal a boss or leader.
– ORIGIN Narragansett, a North American Indian language.

sachet /sa-**shay**/ noun Brit. a small sealed bag or packet containing a small quantity of something.
– ORIGIN French, 'little bag'.

sack[1] noun **1** a large bag made of strong fabric, paper, or plastic, used for storing and carrying goods. **2** (**the sack**) informal dismissal from employment: *he got the sack for swearing.* **3** (**the sack**) informal bed. ● verb informal dismiss someone from employment.
– PHRASES **hit the sack** informal go to bed.
– DERIVATIVES **sackable** adjective **sackful** noun.
– ORIGIN Greek *sakkos* 'sack, sackcloth'.

sack[2] verb (in historical contexts) plunder and destroy a town or building. ● noun the plundering and destruction of a place.
– ORIGIN from French *mettre à sac* 'put to sack' which perhaps first referred to filling a sack with plunder.

sack[3] noun historical a dry white wine formerly imported into Britain from Spain.
– ORIGIN from French *vin sec* 'dry wine'.

sackbut /**sak**-but/ noun an early form of trombone used in Renaissance music.
– ORIGIN French *saquebute.*

sackcloth noun a coarse fabric woven from flax or hemp.
– PHRASES **sackcloth and ashes** an expression of

extreme sorrow or remorse. [with reference to the wearing of sackcloth and having ashes sprinkled on the head as a sign of deep regret for having done wrong.]

sacking noun coarse material for making sacks; sackcloth.

sacra plural of SACRUM.

sacral /**say**-kruhl, sak-ruhl/ adjective 1 Anatomy relating to the sacrum in the lower back. 2 relating to sacred rites or symbols.

sacrament /sak-ruh-muhnt/ noun 1 (in the Christian Church) a religious ceremony in which the participants receive the grace of God, such as Holy Communion. 2 (also **the Blessed Sacrament** or **the Holy Sacrament**) (in Roman Catholic use) the consecrated bread and wine used in Holy Communion.
– DERIVATIVES **sacramental** adjective.
– ORIGIN Latin *sacramentum* 'solemn oath'.

sacred /**say**-krid/ adjective 1 connected with God or a god and treated as holy. 2 (of a text) containing the doctrines of a religion. 3 religious rather than secular: *sacred music.* 4 regarded as too valuable to be interfered with: *nothing is sacred, no name is beyond reach.*
– DERIVATIVES **sacredly** adverb **sacredness** noun.
– ORIGIN from Latin *sacer* 'holy'.

sacred cow noun an idea, custom, or institution regarded as being above criticism (with reference to the Hindu belief that the cow is a sacred animal).

sacrifice noun 1 an act of killing an animal or person or giving up a possession as an offering to a god or goddess. 2 an animal, person, or object offered to a god or goddess. 3 an act of giving up something you value for the sake of something more important: *parents make sacrifices to give their children an education.*
● verb offer or give up someone or something as a sacrifice.
– DERIVATIVES **sacrificial** adjective.
– ORIGIN Latin *sacrificium.*

sacrilege /sak-ri-lij/ noun the treating of something sacred or highly valued with great disrespect.
– DERIVATIVES **sacrilegious** adjective.
– ORIGIN Latin *sacrilegium.*

sacristan /sak-ri-stuhn/ noun a person in charge of a church sacristy.

sacristy /sak-ri-sti/ noun (pl. **sacristies**) a room in a church where a priest prepares for a service, and where things used in worship are kept.
– ORIGIN Latin *sacristia.*

sacrosanct /sak-ruh-sangkt/ adjective regarded as too important or valuable to be changed or questioned: *the protection of free speech by the constitution is sacrosanct.*
– DERIVATIVES **sacrosanctity** noun.
– ORIGIN Latin *sacrosanctus.*

sacrum /**say**-kruhm/ noun (pl. **sacra** /**say**-kruh/ or **sacrums**) Anatomy a triangular bone in the lower back situated between the two hip bones of the pelvis.
– ORIGIN from Latin *os sacrum* 'sacred bone'.

SAD abbreviation seasonal affective disorder, depression that is associated with late autumn and winter and thought to be caused by a lack of light.

sad adjective (**sadder**, **saddest**) 1 feeling sorrow; unhappy. 2 causing or characterized by sorrow or regret: *the sad story of his life.* 3 informal very inadequate or unfashionable; pathetic.
– DERIVATIVES **sadness** noun.
– ORIGIN Old English 'sated, weary'.

sadden verb make someone unhappy.

saddle noun 1 a seat with a raised ridge at the front and back, fastened on the back of a horse for riding. 2 a seat on a bicycle or motorcycle. 3 a low part of a hill or mountain ridge between two higher points. 4 a joint of meat consisting of the two loins. ● verb 1 put a saddle on a horse. 2 (**be saddled with**) be burdened with: *he's saddled with debts of £2 million.*
– PHRASES **in the saddle** 1 on horseback. 2 in a position of control or responsibility.
– ORIGIN Old English.

saddleback noun 1 a hill with a ridge along the top that dips in the middle. 2 a pig of a black breed with a white stripe across the back.

saddlebag noun a bag attached to a saddle.

saddle horse noun chiefly N. Amer. a horse kept for riding only.

saddler noun a person who makes, repairs, or deals in equipment for horses.

saddlery noun (pl. **saddleries**) 1 saddles, bridles, and other equipment for horses. 2 the making or repairing of such equipment. 3 a saddler's premises.

saddle soap noun a kind of soft soap used for cleaning leather.

saddle-sore adjective chafed by riding on a saddle.

saddle stitch noun 1 a stitch of thread or a wire staple passed through the fold of a magazine or booklet. 2 (in needlework) a decorative stitch made with long stitches on the upper side of the cloth alternated with short stitches on the underside.

Sadducee /sad-yoo-see/ noun a member of an ancient Jewish sect that denied the resurrection of the dead and the existence of spirits, and that emphasized acceptance of the written Law rather than oral tradition.
– ORIGIN Hebrew, 'descendant of Zadok' (high priest in the time of kings David and Solomon).

sadhu /**sah**-doo/ noun Indian a holy man or wise man.
– ORIGIN Sanskrit.

sadism /**say**-diz'm/ noun the desire to gain sexual or other pleasure from hurting or humiliating other people.
– DERIVATIVES **sadist** noun **sadistic** adjective **sadistically** adverb.
– ORIGIN French *sadisme*, from the name of the French writer the Marquis de *Sade.*

sadly adverb 1 in a sad way. 2 it is sad or regrettable that: *sadly, I never spoke to Jenny again.*

sadomasochism /say-doh-**mass**-uh-ki-z'm/ noun sexual activity or psychological tendency which combines sadism and masochism.
– DERIVATIVES **sadomasochist** noun **sadomasochistic** adjective.

S

sae abbreviation Brit. stamped addressed envelope.

safari noun (pl. **safaris**) an expedition to observe or hunt animals in their natural habitat.
– ORIGIN Kiswahili.

safari park noun an area of parkland where wild animals can move freely and can be observed by visitors driving through.

safari suit noun a lightweight suit consisting of a belted jacket with patch pockets and matching trousers, shorts, or skirt.

safe adjective **1** protected from danger or risk. **2** not leading to harm; not risky: *a safe investment providing regular income.* **3** providing security or protection: *keep your valuables in a safe place.* **4** (of a statement, verdict, etc.) based on good reasons or evidence and not likely to be wrong. ● noun a strong fireproof cabinet with a complex lock, used for storing valuables.
– PHRASES **safe and sound** with no harm done; uninjured. **to be on the safe side** so as to avoid the risk of something happening.
– DERIVATIVES **safely** adverb.
– ORIGIN Old French *sauf.*

safe conduct noun the official protection of someone from arrest or harm when passing through an area.

safe deposit box (also **safety deposit box**) noun a metal box for valuables in a bank or hotel.

safeguard noun a measure taken to protect or prevent something. ● verb protect against something undesirable: *a programme to safeguard the future of endangered species.*

safe house noun a house in a secret location, used by spies or criminals in hiding.

safekeeping noun the keeping of something in a safe place.

safe period noun the time during and near a woman's menstrual period when conception is least likely.

safe seat noun Brit. a parliamentary seat that is likely to be held by the same party in an election.

safe sex noun sexual activity in which people take precautions to protect themselves against sexually transmitted diseases.

safety noun the condition of being safe: *the survivors were airlifted to safety.* ● adjective designed to prevent injury or damage: *a safety barrier.*

safety belt noun a belt or strap securing a person to their seat in a vehicle or aircraft.

safety catch noun a device that prevents a gun being fired or a machine being operated accidentally.

safety curtain noun a fireproof curtain that can be lowered between the stage and the main part of a theatre to prevent the spread of fire.

safety deposit box noun a safe deposit box.

safety glass noun glass that has been toughened or laminated so that it is less likely to splinter when broken.

safety match noun a match that can be lit only by striking it on a special surface, such as that on the side of a matchbox.

safety net noun **1** a net placed to catch an acrobat in case of a fall. **2** a safeguard against hardship or risk: *a safety net of measures to protect vulnerable children.*

safety pin noun a pin with a point that is bent back to the head and is held in a guard when closed.

safety razor noun a razor with a guard to reduce the risk of cutting the skin.

safety valve noun **1** a valve that opens automatically to relieve excessive pressure. **2** a means of releasing feelings of tension or stress in a harmless way.

safflower noun an orange-flowered plant resembling a thistle, with seeds that are used to produce an edible oil.
– ORIGIN from Arabic, 'yellow'.

saffron noun an orange-yellow spice and food colouring made from the dried stigmas of a crocus.
– ORIGIN Arabic.

sag verb (**sags**, **sagging**, **sagged**) **1** sink downwards gradually under weight or pressure. **2** hang down loosely or unevenly. **3** (often as adj. **sagging**) weaken or decline: *the company is trying to boost sagging sales.* ● noun an instance of sagging.
– DERIVATIVES **saggy** adjective.
– ORIGIN probably related to German *sacken,* Dutch *zakken* 'subside'.

saga noun **1** a long story describing heroic adventures, especially a medieval Norse or Icelandic one. **2** a long, involved story or series of incidents.
– ORIGIN Old Norse, 'narrative'.

sagacious /suh-**gay**-shuhss/ adjective having or showing good judgement; wise.
– DERIVATIVES **sagaciously** adverb **sagacity** /suh-**ga**-si-ti/ noun.
– ORIGIN from Latin *sagax* 'wise'.

sage[1] noun a Mediterranean plant with greyish-green leaves that are used as a herb in cookery.
– ORIGIN Latin *salvia* 'healing plant'.

sage[2] noun a very wise man. ● adjective very wise.
– DERIVATIVES **sagely** adverb.
– ORIGIN Old French.

sagebrush noun **1** a shrubby aromatic North American plant of the daisy family. **2** semi-arid country dominated by sagebrush.

sage green noun a greyish-green colour.

Sagittarius /saj-i-**tair**-i-uhss/ noun a constellation (the Archer) and sign of the zodiac, which the sun enters about 22 November.
– DERIVATIVES **Sagittarian** noun & adjective.
– ORIGIN Latin, 'archer'.

sago /**say**-goh/ noun flour or starchy granules obtained from a palm tree, often cooked with milk to make a pudding.
– ORIGIN Malay.

Saharan /suh-**hah**-ruhn/ adjective relating to the Sahara Desert in North Africa.

Sahelian /suh-**hee**-li-uhn/ adjective relating to the Sahel, a semi-arid region bordering the southern Sahara Desert in North Africa.

sahib /sahb, suh-**heeb**/ noun Indian a polite way of addressing a man.
– ORIGIN Arabic, 'friend, lord'.

said past and past participle of SAY. adjective

referring to someone or something already mentioned: *the said agreement.*

sail noun **1** a piece of material spread on a mast to catch the wind and propel a boat or ship. **2** a trip in a sailing boat or ship. **3** a wind-catching structure attached to the arm of a windmill. ●verb **1** travel in a sailing boat as a sport or pastime. **2** travel in any ship or boat. **3** begin a voyage. **4** navigate or control a boat or ship. **5** move smoothly or confidently: *she sailed into the room.* **6** (**sail through**) informal achieve something easily.
– PHRASES **sail close to the wind 1** behave or operate in a risky way. **2** sail as nearly against the wind as possible. **under sail** with the sails hoisted.
– ORIGIN Old English.

sailboard noun a board with a mast and a sail, used in windsurfing.
– DERIVATIVES **sailboarder** noun **sailboarding** noun.

sailcloth noun **1** canvas or other strong fabric used for making sails. **2** a similar strong fabric used for making clothes.

sailfish noun (pl. same or **sailfishes**) an edible marine fish with a high sail-like fin on its back.

sailing boat (N. Amer. **sailboat**) noun a boat propelled by sails.

sailor noun **1** a person who works as a member of the crew of a ship or boat. **2** a person who sails as a sport or pastime. **3** (**a good/bad sailor**) a person who rarely (or often) becomes seasick.

sailor suit noun a boy's blue and white suit resembling the traditional uniform of a sailor.

sailplane noun a glider designed to fly for long distances.

sainfoin /sayn-foyn, san-foyn/ noun a pink-flowered Asian plant, grown for fodder.
– ORIGIN from Latin *sanum foenum* 'wholesome hay'.

saint noun **1** a very good or holy person whom Christians believe will go to heaven after they die. **2** a very good or holy person who is officially declared to be a saint by the Christian Church after they die. **3** informal a very kind or patient person.
– DERIVATIVES **sainthood** noun
– ORIGIN from Latin *sanctus* 'holy'.

St Bernard noun a breed of very large dog originally kept to rescue travellers by the monks of the hospice on the Great St Bernard, a pass across the Alps.

sainted adjective very good or kind, like a saint.

St Elmo's fire /suhnt el-mohz/ noun a luminous electrical discharge sometimes seen on a ship or aircraft during a storm.
– ORIGIN regarded as a sign of protection given by *St Elmo*, the patron saint of sailors.

St George's cross noun a red cross (+) on a white background (especially as a national emblem of England).

St John's wort noun a herbaceous plant or shrub with yellow flowers.
– ORIGIN because some species come into flower near the feast day of St John the Baptist (24 June).

saintly adjective very holy or good.
– DERIVATIVES **saintliness** noun.

saintpaulia /suhnt-por-li-uh/ noun an African violet.
– ORIGIN from the name of the German explorer Baron W. von *Saint Paul.*

saint's day noun (in the Christian Church) a day on which a saint is particularly commemorated.

St Swithin's day noun 15 July, a Church festival commemorating St Swithin; there is a superstition that if it rains on this day it will continue raining for the next forty days.

St Vitus's dance /vy-tuh-siz/ noun old-fashioned term for **SYDENHAM'S CHOREA**.
– ORIGIN because a visit to the shrine of *St Vitus* was believed to alleviate the disease.

saith /seth/ old-fashioned third person singular present of **SAY**.

saithe /sayth/ noun a North Atlantic food fish of the cod family.
– ORIGIN Old Norse.

sake¹ /sayk/ noun (**for the sake of**) **1** so as to achieve (something); in the interest of: *they moved to the coast for the sake of her health.* **2** out of consideration for or to help (someone).
– PHRASES **for old times' sake** in memory of former times. **for God's/goodness sake** expressing impatience or desperation.
– ORIGIN Old English, 'contention, crime'.

sake² /sah-ki, sa-kay/ noun a Japanese alcoholic drink made from fermented rice.
– ORIGIN Japanese.

salaam /suh-lahm/ noun a gesture of greeting or respect in Arabic-speaking and Muslim countries, consisting of a low bow with the hand or fingers touching the forehead. ●verb make a gesture of salaam.
– ORIGIN from Arabic, 'peace be upon you'.

salable adjective variant spelling of **SALEABLE**.

salacious /suh-lay-shuhss/ adjective having or showing too much interest in sexual matters.
– DERIVATIVES **salaciously** adverb.
– ORIGIN from Latin *salax.*

salad noun a cold dish of mixed raw vegetables.
– PHRASES **one's salad days** the period when one is young and inexperienced. [from Shakespeare's *Antony and Cleopatra.*]
– ORIGIN Old French *salade.*

salad cream noun Brit. a creamy dressing resembling mayonnaise.

salade niçoise /sal-ahd nee-swahz/ noun (pl. **salades niçoises** /sal-ahd nee-swahz/) a salad made typically from hard-boiled eggs, tuna, black olives, and tomatoes.
– ORIGIN French, 'salad from Nice'.

salamander /sal-uh-man-der/ noun **1** a long-tailed amphibian resembling a newt, typically with bright markings. **2** a mythical lizard-like creature said to live in fire.
– ORIGIN Greek *salamandra.*

salami /suh-lah-mi/ noun (pl. same or **salamis**) a type of spicy preserved sausage.
– ORIGIN Italian.

salaried adjective earning or offering a salary: *a salaried job.*

salary noun (pl. **salaries**) a fixed regular payment made by an employer to an employee, especially a professional or white-collar worker.

– ORIGIN Latin *salarium*, first meaning a Roman soldier's allowance to buy salt.

sale noun **1** the exchange of something for money: *cars for sale at reasonable prices.* **2** (**sales**) the activity or profession of selling. **3** a period in which goods are sold at reduced prices. **4** a public event at which goods are sold or auctioned.
– PHRASES **sale or return** Brit. an arrangement by which a retailer takes a quantity of goods with the right to return unsold items.
– ORIGIN Old English.

saleable (also **salable**) adjective fit or able to be sold.
– DERIVATIVES **saleability** noun.

saleroom noun Brit. a room in which auctions are held.

sales clerk noun N. Amer. a shop assistant.

salesgirl noun a female shop assistant.

salesman (or **saleswoman**) noun (pl. **salesmen** or **saleswomen**) a person whose job involves selling or promoting goods.
– DERIVATIVES **salesmanship** noun.

salesperson noun (pl. **salespeople** or **salespersons**) a salesman or saleswoman.

salicylic acid /sali-sill-ik/ noun a bitter substance present in certain plants, used in making aspirin and dyes.
– ORIGIN from Latin *salix* 'willow' (because originally derived from willow bark).

salient /say-li-uhnt/ adjective **1** most important: *the salient points of the case.* **2** (of an angle) pointing outwards. The opposite of **RE-ENTRANT**.
• noun **1** a piece of land or section of fortification that juts out to form an angle. **2** an outward bulge in a military line.
– DERIVATIVES **salience** noun **saliency** noun.
– ORIGIN from Latin *salire* 'to leap'.

saline /say-lyn/ adjective **1** containing salt. **2** chiefly Medicine (of a solution) containing sodium chloride and/or other salts, especially in the same concentration as in the body.
• noun a saline solution.
– DERIVATIVES **salinity** noun **salinization** (or **salinisation**) noun.
– ORIGIN from Latin *sal* 'salt'.

Salish /say-lish/ noun (pl. same) a member of a group of American Indian peoples of the north-western US and the west coast of Canada.
– DERIVATIVES **Salishan** adjective.
– ORIGIN a local name, literally 'Flatheads'.

saliva /suh-ly-vuh/ noun a watery liquid produced by glands in the mouth, helping chewing, swallowing, and digestion.
– DERIVATIVES **salivary** /suh-ly-vuh-ri/ adjective.
– ORIGIN Latin.

salivate /sal-i-vayt/ verb **1** produce saliva. **2** show great delight at the sight or prospect of something: *companies are salivating over the promise of the new technology.*
– DERIVATIVES **salivation** noun.
– ORIGIN Latin *salivare*.

sallow adjective (of a person's face or complexion) yellowish or pale brown in colour.
– ORIGIN Old English, 'dusky'.

sally noun (pl. **sallies**) **1** a sudden charge out of a place surrounded by an enemy. **2** a witty or

lively reply. • verb (**sallies**, **sallying**, **sallied**) set out: *they sallied forth to battle with disease.*
– ORIGIN French *saillie*.

salmon /rhymes with gammon/ noun (pl. same or **salmons**) a large fish with edible pink flesh, that matures in the sea and migrates to freshwater streams to spawn.
– ORIGIN Latin *salmo*.

salmonella /sal-muh-nel-luh/ noun **1** a bacterium that occurs mainly in the gut and can cause food poisoning. **2** food poisoning caused by this bacterium.
– ORIGIN named after the American veterinary surgeon Daniel E. *Salmon*.

salmon pink noun a pale orange-pink colour.

salmon trout noun a sea trout or other fish resembling a small salmon.

salon noun **1** a place where a hairdresser, beautician, or fashion designer carries out their work. **2** a reception room in a large house. **3** chiefly historical a regular gathering of writers, artists, etc., held in a fashionable household.
– ORIGIN French.

saloon noun **1** Brit. a car with a closed body and separate boot. **2** Brit. a lounge bar in a pub. **3** a large public lounge on a ship. **4** N. Amer. dated a bar.
– ORIGIN French *salon*.

salopettes /sal-uh-pets/ plural noun padded trousers with a high waist and shoulder straps, worn for skiing.
– ORIGIN French *salopette*.

salsa /sal-suh/ noun **1** a type of Latin American dance music incorporating elements of jazz and rock. **2** a dance performed to this music. **3** a spicy tomato sauce.
– ORIGIN Spanish, 'sauce'.

salsify /sal-si-fi/ noun a plant with a long edible root like that of a parsnip.
– ORIGIN French *salsifis*.

SALT /sorlt, solt/ abbreviation Strategic Arms Limitation Talks.

salt noun **1** (also **common salt**) sodium chloride, a white substance in the form of crystals used for seasoning or preserving food. **2** any chemical compound formed by the reaction of an acid with a base, with the hydrogen of the acid replaced by a metal or equivalent group.
• adjective containing or treated with salt: *salt water.* • verb **1** season or preserve something with salt. **2** sprinkle a road or path with salt to melt snow or ice. **3** (**salt something away**) informal secretly put money away for future use.
– PHRASES **rub salt into the wound** make a painful experience even more distressing. **the salt of the earth** a very kind, honest, or reliable person. [with reference to the Gospel of Matthew, chapter 5.] **take something with a pinch (or grain) of salt** be aware that something may be exaggerated. **worth one's salt** good or competent at one's job.
– DERIVATIVES **saltless** adjective **saltness** noun.
– ORIGIN Old English.

saltbush noun a salt-tolerant plant, sometimes planted on saline soils to provide grazing.

salt cellar noun a container for salt, typically with perforations in the lid.
– ORIGIN *cellar* is from Old French *salier* 'salt box'.

salt flats plural noun areas of flat land covered with a layer of salt.

salt-glazed adjective (of pottery, especially stoneware) covered with a hard glaze with a pitted surface, produced by adding salt to the kiln during firing.

saltings plural noun Brit. an area of coastal land that is regularly covered by the tide.

saltire /**sawl**-ty-er, **sol**-ty-er/ noun Heraldry an X-shaped cross.
– ORIGIN Old French *saultoir* 'stirrup cord, stile, saltire'.

salt lick noun **1** a place where animals go to lick salt from the ground. **2** a block of salt provided for animals to lick.

salt marsh noun an area of coastal grassland that is regularly flooded by seawater.

salt pan noun a shallow container or hollow in the ground in which salt water evaporates to leave a deposit of salt.

saltpetre /**sawlt-pee**-ter, **solt-pee**-ter/ (US **saltpeter**) noun potassium nitrate or (**Chile saltpetre**) sodium nitrate.
– ORIGIN Latin *salpetra*.

saltwater adjective relating to or found in salt water; living in the sea.

salty adjective (**saltier**, **saltiest**) **1** tasting of or containing salt. **2** (of language or humour) racy or coarse: *recounting salty anecdotes*.
– DERIVATIVES **saltily** adverb **saltiness** noun.

salubrious /suh-**loo**-bri-uhss/ adjective **1** good for the health; healthy. **2** (of a place) clean, well kept and pleasant.
– DERIVATIVES **salubriously** adverb **salubrity** noun.
– ORIGIN from Latin *salus* 'health'.

saluki /suh-**loo**-ki/ noun (pl. **salukis**) a tall, slender breed of dog with a silky coat and large drooping ears.
– ORIGIN Arabic.

salutary /**sal**-yuu-tuh-ri/ adjective **1** (of something unpleasant) beneficial because providing an opportunity to learn from experience: *the cut and thrust over pricing proved a salutary experience for the company.* **2** dated health-giving.
– ORIGIN from Latin *salus* 'health'.

salutation noun formal a greeting.

salute noun **1** a gesture of respect or acknow- ledgement. **2** a movement, typically a raising of a hand to the head, made as a formal gesture of respect by a member of a military or similar force. **3** the firing of a gun or guns as a formal or ceremonial sign of respect or celebration. • verb **1** make a formal salute to a member of a military or similar force. **2** greet someone with a gesture. **3** express admiration and respect for: *we salute his genius.*
– ORIGIN from Latin *salutare* 'greet, pay one's respects to'.

Salvadorean /sal-vuh-**dori**-uhn/ noun a person from El Salvador, a country in Central America. • adjective relating to El Salvador.

salvage verb **1** rescue a ship or its cargo from loss at sea. **2** save from possible loss, harm, or failure: *his latest stunt will do nothing to salvage his reputation.* • noun **1** the rescue of a ship or its cargo from loss at sea. **2** cargo, property, or other items that have been saved from loss or harm. **3** Law payment made or due to a person who has salvaged a ship or its cargo.
– DERIVATIVES **salvageable** adjective **salvager** noun.
– ORIGIN from Latin *salvare* 'to save'.

salvation noun **1** the saving or protection of someone or something from harm or ruin. **2** (**one's salvation**) a means of being saved from harm or ruin: *his only salvation was to outwit the enemy.* **3** (in Christian belief) deliverance from sin and its consequences, believed to be brought about by faith in Jesus.
– ORIGIN from Latin *salvare* 'to save'.

salvationist noun (**Salvationist**) a member of the Salvation Army, a Christian evangelical organization. • adjective **1** relating to salvation in Christian belief. **2** (**Salvationist**) relating to the Salvation Army.

salve noun **1** an ointment used to help the skin to heal. **2** something that helps to reduce distress, guilt, etc.: *shopping is the perfect salve for my wounded ego.* • verb do something to feel less guilty: *charity salves our conscience.*
– ORIGIN Old English.

salver noun a tray, typically one made of silver and used on formal occasions.
– ORIGIN French *salve* 'tray for presenting food to the king'.

salvia noun a plant of a large group that includes sage, especially one grown for its bright scarlet flowers.
– ORIGIN Latin, 'sage'.

salvo noun (pl. **salvos** or **salvoes**) **1** a simultaneous firing of artillery or other guns in a battle. **2** a sudden vigorous or aggressive series of acts: *a salvo of accusations.*
– ORIGIN Italian *salva* 'salutation'.

sal volatile /sal vuh-**lat**-i-li/ noun a scented solution of ammonium carbonate in alcohol, used as smelling salts.
– ORIGIN Latin, 'volatile salt'.

salwar /**sul-wah**/ noun variant spelling of **SHALWAR**.

SAM abbreviation surface-to-air missile.

Samaritan noun **1** (**good Samaritan**) a charitable or helpful person. [with reference to the story of the man from ancient Samaria who helped a man in need whom others had passed by, in the Gospel of Luke.] **2** (**the Samaritans**) (in the UK) an organization which counsels those in distress, mainly through a telephone service. **3** a member of a people inhabiting Samaria, an ancient city and region of Palestine, in biblical times.

samarium /suh-**mair**-i-uhm/ noun a hard silvery-white metallic chemical element of the lanthanide series.
– ORIGIN named after a Russian official called *Samarsky*).

samba /**sam-buh**/ noun a Brazilian dance of African origin. • verb (**sambas**, **sambaing** /**sam**-buh-(r)ing/, **sambaed** /**sam**-buhd/) dance the samba.
– ORIGIN Portuguese.

sambal /**sam-bal**/ noun (in oriental cookery) a spicy vegetable or fruit relish.
– ORIGIN Malay.

Sam Browne noun a leather belt with a supporting strap that passes over the right shoulder, worn by army and police officers.

S

– ORIGIN named after the British military commander Sir *Sam*uel J. *Brown(e)*.

sambuca /sam-**buu**-kuh/ noun an Italian aniseed-flavoured liqueur.
– ORIGIN Italian.

same adjective 1 (**the same**) exactly alike; not different or changed. 2 (**this/that same**) referring to a person or thing just mentioned: *that same year I went to Boston*. •pronoun (**the same**) 1 the same thing as previously mentioned. 2 identical people or things. •adverb in the same way.
– PHRASES all (or just) the same in spite of this; even so.
– DERIVATIVES **sameness** noun.
– ORIGIN Old Norse.

samey adjective Brit. informal lacking in variety.

Sami /**sah**-mi, sahm/ plural noun the people of Lapland in northern Scandinavia.
– ORIGIN Lappish (the language of the Lapps).

USAGE: Sami is the term by which the Lapps themselves prefer to be known.

samite /**sa**-myt, **say**-myt/ noun historical a rich silk fabric interwoven with gold and silver threads.
– ORIGIN Old French *samit*.

samizdat /sam-iz-dat/ noun (especially in the former Soviet Union) the secret copying and distribution of literature banned by the state.
– ORIGIN Russian, 'self-publishing house'.

Samoan /suh-**moh**-uhn/ noun 1 a person from Samoa. 2 the Polynesian language of Samoa. •adjective relating to Samoa.

samosa /suh-**moh**-suh/ noun a triangular fried Indian pastry containing spiced vegetables or meat.
– ORIGIN Persian and Urdu.

samovar /**sam**-uh-var/ noun a decorated Russian tea urn.
– ORIGIN Russian, 'self-boiler'.

Samoyed /**sam**-uh-yed, sam-oy-**yed**/ noun 1 a white Arctic breed of dog. 2 a member of a group of mainly nomadic peoples of northern Siberia.
– ORIGIN Russian *samoed*.

sampan /**sam**-pan/ noun a small boat propelled with an oar at the stern, used in the Far East.
– ORIGIN from Chinese words meaning 'three' and 'board'.

samphire /**sam**-fy-er/ noun an edible fleshy-leaved plant which grows on rocks near the sea.
– ORIGIN from French *herbe de Saint Pierre* 'St Peter's herb'.

sample noun 1 a small part or quantity intended to show what the whole is like. 2 a specimen of a substance taken for scientific testing or analysis. 3 a sound created by sampling. •verb 1 take a sample or samples of something. 2 experience something briefly to see what it is like: *our children sampled the hotel's disco*. 3 (often as noun **sampling**) record or extract a small piece of music or sound digitally for use in a different piece of music.
– ORIGIN Old French *essample* 'example'.

sampler noun 1 a piece of embroidery worked in various stitches to demonstrate a person's skill. 2 a representative collection or example of something. 3 an electronic device for

sampling music and sound.

samurai /**sam**-uh-ry/ noun (pl. same) historical a member of a powerful military class in Japan.
– ORIGIN Japanese.

San /sahn/ noun (pl. same) 1 a member of the Bushmen (a number of aboriginal peoples) of southern Africa. 2 the languages spoken by the San.
– ORIGIN Nama, 'aboriginals, settlers'.

sanatorium /san-uh-**tor**-i-uhm/ noun (pl. **sanatoriums** or **sanatoria** /san-uh-**tor**-i-uh/) 1 a place for the care of people who are recovering from an illness or who are chronically ill. 2 Brit. a place in a boarding school for children who are unwell.
– ORIGIN Latin.

Sancerre /son-**sair**/ noun a light white wine produced in Sancerre, in the Loire region of France.

sanctify /**sangk**-ti-fy/ verb (**sanctifies, sanctifying, sanctified**) 1 make or declare something holy; consecrate. 2 make official or binding by a religious ceremony: *their love is sanctified by the sacrament of marriage*. 3 free someone or something from sin.
– DERIVATIVES **sanctification** noun.
– ORIGIN Latin *sanctificare*.

sanctimonious /sangk-ti-**moh**-ni-uhss/ adjective derogatory making a show of being morally better than other people.
– DERIVATIVES **sanctimoniously** adverb **sanctimoniousness** noun **sanctimony** /**sangk**-ti-muh-ni/ noun.
– ORIGIN from Latin *sanctimonia* 'sanctity'.

sanction noun 1 a threatened penalty or punishment for disobeying a law or rule. 2 (**sanctions**) measures taken by a state to try to force another to do or obey something. 3 official permission or approval. •verb 1 give official permission for: *the scheme was sanctioned by the court*. 2 impose a penalty on someone or something.
– DERIVATIVES **sanctionable** adjective.
– ORIGIN from Latin *sancire* 'ratify'.

sanctity noun 1 the state or quality of being holy. 2 the state of being highly valued and worthy of great respect: *the sanctity of human life*.
– ORIGIN from Latin *sanctus* 'holy'.

sanctuary noun (pl. **sanctuaries**) 1 a place or state of safety or protection: *they fled to Kabul where they were offered sanctuary*. 2 a nature reserve. 3 a place where injured or unwanted animals are cared for. 4 a holy place. 5 the part of the chancel of a church containing the high altar.
– ORIGIN Latin *sanctuarium*.

sanctum /**sangk**-tuhm/ noun (pl. **sanctums**) 1 a sacred or holy place. 2 a room to which a person can go for privacy and quiet: *the inner sanctum of the England team*.
– ORIGIN Latin.

Sanctus /**sangk**-tuhss/ noun (in the Christian Church) a hymn beginning *Sanctus, sanctus, sanctus* (Holy, holy, holy) forming a set part of the Mass.
– ORIGIN Latin.

sand noun 1 a substance consisting of very fine particles resulting from the erosion of rocks, found on beaches, river beds, the seabed, and

deserts. **2** (**sands**) a wide area of sand. •**verb 1** smooth something with sandpaper or a sander. **2** sprinkle something with sand.
– ORIGIN Old English.

sandal noun a shoe with a partly open upper or straps attaching the sole to the foot.
– DERIVATIVES **sandalled** (US **sandaled**) adjective.
– ORIGIN Greek *sandalon* 'wooden shoe'.

sandalwood noun the sweet-smelling wood of an Indian or SE Asian tree.
– ORIGIN Latin *sandalum*.

sandbag noun a bag of sand, used for protection against floods or explosions. •**verb** (**sandbags**, **sandbagging**, **sandbagged**) **1** protect or reinforce something with sandbags. **2** informal cause severe harm or damage to: *they saw their marriage sandbagged by problems.*
– DERIVATIVES **sandbagger** noun.

sandbank noun a build-up of sand forming a raised bank in the sea or a river.

sandbar noun a long, narrow sandbank.

sandblast verb roughen or clean something with a jet of sand driven by compressed air or steam.
– DERIVATIVES **sandblaster** noun.

sandboard noun a long, narrow board, often a modified snowboard, used for sliding down sand dunes.
– DERIVATIVES **sandboarder** noun **sandboarding** noun.

sandboy noun (in phrase **as happy as a sandboy**) very happy or carefree.
– ORIGIN probably first referring to a boy going around selling sand.

sandcastle noun a model of a castle built out of sand.

sander noun a power tool used for smoothing a surface.

sanderling noun a small sandpiper, typically seen running after waves on the beach.
– ORIGIN unknown.

sandfly noun (pl. **sandflies**) a small biting fly of tropical and subtropical regions, which transmits a number of diseases.

sandglass noun an hourglass.

Sandinista /san-di-nee-stuh/ noun a member of a left-wing Nicaraguan political organization, in power from 1979 until 1990.
– ORIGIN named after a similar organization founded by the nationalist leader Augusto César *Sandino.*

sandman noun (**the sandman**) (in stories) a man supposed to make children sleep by sprinkling sand in their eyes.

sand martin noun a small swallow with dark brown and white plumage, which digs nest holes in sandy banks near water.

sandpaper noun paper with sand or another rough substance stuck to it, used for smoothing surfaces. •**verb** smooth something with sandpaper.
– DERIVATIVES **sandpapery** adjective.

sandpiper noun a wading bird with a long bill and long legs, found in coastal areas.

sandpit noun **1** Brit. a shallow box or hollow containing sand for children to play in. **2** a quarry from which sand is excavated.

sandshoe noun chiefly Scottish & Austral./NZ a plimsoll.

sandstone noun red, yellow, or brown rock consisting of sand or quartz grains cemented together.

sandstorm noun a strong wind in a desert carrying clouds of sand.

sandwich noun **1** two pieces of bread with a filling between them. **2** Brit. a sponge cake of two or more layers with jam or cream between them. •**verb 1** place in a restricted space between two other people or things: *the house was sandwiched between a shop and a clinic.* **2** (**sandwich things together**) squeeze two things together.
– ORIGIN named after the English nobleman the 4th Earl of *Sandwich*, said to have eaten sandwiches so as to stay at the gambling table.

sandwich board noun a pair of advertisement boards connected by straps by which they are hung over a person's shoulders.

sandwich course noun Brit. a training course with alternate periods of study and practical experience.

sandy adjective (**sandier**, **sandiest**) **1** covered in or consisting of sand. **2** light yellowish brown.

sane adjective **1** having a normal mind; not mad. **2** reasonable or sensible: *a sane discussion of important issues.*
– DERIVATIVES **sanely** adverb.
– ORIGIN Latin *sanus* 'healthy'.

sang past of SING.

sangfroid /song-frwah/ noun the ability to stay calm in difficult circumstances.
– ORIGIN French, 'cold blood'.

Sangiovese /san-ji-oh-vay-zi/ noun an Italian red wine made from a variety of black wine grape.
– ORIGIN Italian.

sangria /sang-gree-uh/ noun a Spanish drink of red wine, lemonade, fruit, and spices.
– ORIGIN Spanish, 'bleeding'.

sanguinary /sang-gwi-nuh-ri/ adjective chiefly literary involving or causing much bloodshed.

sanguine /sang-gwin/ adjective **1** cheerfully confident about the future. **2** (in medieval medicine) having a predominance of blood among the bodily humours, supposedly marked by a ruddy complexion and an optimistic disposition.
– ORIGIN from Latin *sanguis* 'blood'.

Sanhedrin /san-hed-rin, san-hee-drin/ noun the highest court of justice and the supreme council in ancient Jerusalem.
– ORIGIN Hebrew.

sanitarium /san-i-tair-i-uhm/ noun (pl. **sanitariums** or **sanitaria** /san-i-tair-i-uh/) North American term for SANATORIUM.

sanitary adjective **1** relating to sanitation: *a sanitary engineer.* **2** hygienic and clean. **3** referring to sanitary towels and tampons.
– ORIGIN from Latin *sanitas* 'health'.

sanitary towel (N. Amer. **sanitary napkin**) noun a pad worn by women to absorb blood during a menstrual period.

sanitaryware noun toilet bowls, cisterns, and other fittings.

sanitation noun arrangements to protect public health, especially the provision of clean

S

drinking water and the disposal of sewage.

sanitize (or **sanitise**) verb **1** make something hygienic. **2** (often as adj. **sanitized**) derogatory make more acceptable by removing inappropriate or unpleasant material: *sanitized versions of raunchy CDs.*
– DERIVATIVES **sanitizer** noun.

sanity noun **1** the condition of being mentally healthy. **2** reasonable and rational behaviour.

sank past of SINK¹.

sans /sanz/ preposition literary without: *she plays her role sans accent.*
– ORIGIN Old French *sanz.*

sans-culotte /sanz-kyuu-**lot**/ noun an extreme republican or revolutionary.
– ORIGIN French, 'without knee breeches' (first referring to a lower-class Parisian republican in the French Revolution).

Sanskrit /**san**-skrit/ noun an ancient language of India, still used as a language of religion and scholarship.
– ORIGIN from Sanskrit, 'composed, elaborated'.

sans serif /san se-**rif**/ noun a style of type without serifs (small projections on the letters).

Santa Claus (also informal **Santa**) noun Father Christmas.
– ORIGIN Dutch *Sante Klaas* 'St Nicholas'.

santim /**san**-teem/ noun a unit of money of Latvia, equal to one hundredth of a lat.
– ORIGIN Latvian.

sap¹ noun the fluid which circulates in plants, consisting chiefly of water with nutrients.
●verb (**saps**, **sapping**, **sapped**) **1** gradually weaken a person's strength or power. **2** (**sap someone of**) drain someone of strength or power: *they were sapped of stamina and their self-belief.*
– ORIGIN Old English.

sap² noun historical a tunnel or trench dug to conceal the approach of an attacker to a fortified place.
– ORIGIN from Italian *zappa* 'spade, spadework'.

sap³ noun informal, chiefly N. Amer. a foolish person.
– ORIGIN abbreviation of *sapskull* 'person with a head like sapwood' (soft layers of new wood in a tree).

sapele /suh-**pee**-li/ noun a large tropical African hardwood tree, with reddish-brown wood.
– ORIGIN named after a port in Nigeria.

sapid /**sa**-pid/ adjective chiefly N. Amer. having a strong and pleasant taste.
– ORIGIN Latin *sapidus.*

sapient /**say**-pi-uhnt/ adjective formal wise or intelligent.
– ORIGIN from Latin *sapere* 'be wise'.

sapling noun a young, slender tree.

sapodilla /sap-uh-**dil**-uh/ noun **1** a large evergreen tropical American tree with hard wood and a milky latex which is used to make chewing gum. **2** the sweet brownish bristly fruit of the sapodilla.
– ORIGIN Spanish *zapotillo.*

saponify /suh-**pon**-i-fy/ verb (**saponifies**, **saponifying**, **saponified**) turn fat or oil into soap by reaction with an alkali.
– DERIVATIVES **saponification** noun.
– ORIGIN from Latin *sapo* 'soap'.

sapper noun **1** a military engineer who lays or detects and disarms mines. **2** Brit. a soldier in the Corps of Royal Engineers.
– ORIGIN from SAP².

sapphic /**saf**-fik/ adjective **1** (**Sapphic**) relating to the ancient Greek poet Sappho, or her poetry expressing love and affection for women. **2** formal or humorous relating to lesbians.

sapphire /**saf**-fy-er/ noun **1** a transparent blue precious stone. **2** a bright blue colour.
– ORIGIN Greek *sappheiros,* probably referring to lapis lazuli.

sappy adjective (**sappier**, **sappiest**) **1** informal, chiefly N. Amer. excessively sentimental. **2** (of a plant) containing a lot of sap.

saprophyte /**sap**-ruh-fyt/ noun a plant, fungus, or microorganism that lives on decaying matter.
– DERIVATIVES **saprophytic** adjective.
– ORIGIN from Greek *sapros* 'putrid' + *phuton* 'plant'.

sapwood noun the soft outer layers of new wood between the heartwood and the bark of a tree.

saraband /**sa**-ruh-band/ (also **sarabande**) noun a slow, stately Spanish dance in triple time.
– ORIGIN Spanish and Italian *zarabanda.*

Saracen /**sa**-ruh-suhn/ noun an Arab or Muslim at the time of the Crusades.
– ORIGIN Greek *Sarakēnos.*

sarape /se-**rah**-pay/ noun variant of SERAPE.

sarcasm noun a way of using words which say the opposite of what one means, in order to mock someone.
– ORIGIN Greek *sarkasmos.*

sarcastic adjective using words which say the opposite of what one means, in order to mock someone.
– DERIVATIVES **sarcastically** adverb.

sarcoma /sar-**koh**-muh/ noun (pl. **sarcomas** or **sarcomata** /sar-**koh**-muh-tuh/) a cancerous tumour of a kind found chiefly in connective tissue.
– ORIGIN Greek *sarkōma.*

sarcophagus /sar-**kof**-fuh-guhss/ noun (pl. **sarcophagi** /sar-**kof**-fuh-gy/) a stone coffin.
– ORIGIN from Greek *sarkophagos* 'flesh-consuming'.

sardine noun a young pilchard or other young or small herring-like fish.
– ORIGIN Latin *sardina.*

Sardinian noun **1** a person from Sardinia. **2** the language of Sardinia. ●adjective relating to Sardinia.

sardonic /sar-**don**-ik/ adjective showing a mocking or cynical attitude.
– DERIVATIVES **sardonically** adverb **sardonicism** noun.
– ORIGIN French *sardonique.*

sardonyx /**sar**-duh-niks/ noun onyx (a semi-precious stone) in which white layers alternate with yellow or reddish ones.
– ORIGIN Greek *sardonux.*

sargasso /sar-**gass**-oh/ (also **sargassum**) noun a brown seaweed with fronds that contain sacs filled with air, typically floating in large masses.
– ORIGIN Portuguese *sargaço.*

sarge noun informal sergeant.

sari /**sah**-ri/ (also **saree**) noun (pl. **saris** or **sarees**) an item of clothing consisting of a length of cotton or silk draped around the body, worn by women from the Indian subcontinent.
– ORIGIN Hindi.

sarin /**sah**-rin/ noun a nerve gas developed during the Second World War.
– ORIGIN German.

sarky adjective Brit. informal sarcastic.
– DERIVATIVES **sarkily** adverb **sarkiness** noun.

sarnie noun Brit. informal a sandwich.

sarong /suh-**rong**/ noun an item of clothing consisting of a long piece of cloth wrapped round the body and tucked at the waist or under the armpits.
– ORIGIN Malay, 'sheath'.

SARS (also **Sars**) abbreviation severe acute respiratory syndrome.

sarsaparilla /sar-suh-puh-**ril**-luh/ noun **1** a preparation of the dried roots of a tropical plant, used as a flavouring. **2** a sweet drink flavoured with sarsaparilla.
– ORIGIN Spanish *zarzaparilla*.

sarsen /**sar**-suhn/ noun a sandstone boulder of a kind used to construct Stonehenge and other prehistoric monuments in southern England.
– ORIGIN probably from **SARACEN**.

sartorial /sah-**tor**-i-uhl/ adjective relating to clothes or a person's style of dress: *their sartorial splendour has been emulated around the world.*
– DERIVATIVES **sartorially** adverb.
– ORIGIN from Latin *sartor* 'tailor'.

SAS abbreviation Special Air Service.

sash[1] noun a long strip of cloth worn over one shoulder or round the waist.
– ORIGIN Arabic, 'muslin, turban'.

sash[2] noun a frame holding the glass in a window.
– ORIGIN from **CHASSIS**.

sashay /sa-**shay**/ verb informal walk in a confident way, swinging the hips from side to side.
– ORIGIN from French *chassé* 'chased'.

sash cord noun a strong cord attaching either of the weights of a sash window to a sash (frame of glass).

sashimi /**sah**-shee-mi, sash-i-mi/ noun a Japanese dish of small pieces of raw fish eaten with soy sauce and horseradish paste.
– ORIGIN Japanese.

sash window noun a window with one or two sashes (frames of glass) which can be slid up or down to open it.

Sasquatch /**sask**-wach/ noun another name for **BIGFOOT**.
– ORIGIN Salish.

sassafras /**sass**-uh-frass/ noun an extract of the aromatic leaves or bark of a North American tree, used in medicines and perfumes.
– ORIGIN Spanish *sasafrás*.

Sassenach /**sass**-uh-nakh, sass-uh-nak/ Scottish & Irish derogatory noun an English person. •adjective English.
– ORIGIN Scottish Gaelic *Sasunnoch* or Irish *Sasanach*.

sassy adjective (**sassier**, **sassiest**) informal, chiefly N. Amer. lively, confident, or cheeky.
– DERIVATIVES **sassiness** noun.

– ORIGIN from **SAUCY**.

SAT abbreviation (in the UK) standard assessment task, a standard test given to schoolchildren to assess their progress.

sat past and past participle of **SIT**.

Satan noun the Devil.
– ORIGIN Hebrew, 'adversary'.

satang /**sat**-ang/ noun (pl. same or **satangs**) a unit of money of Thailand, equal to one hundredth of a baht.
– ORIGIN Thai.

satanic adjective **1** relating to or typical of Satan, especially in being evil. **2** connected with satanism.

satanism noun the worship of Satan.
– DERIVATIVES **satanist** noun & adjective.

satay /**sat**-ay/ (also **saté**) noun a SE Asian dish consisting of small pieces of meat grilled on a skewer and served with spiced peanut sauce.
– ORIGIN Malay and Indonesian.

satchel noun a shoulder bag with a long strap, used especially for school books.
– ORIGIN Old French *sachel*.

sate verb **1** satisfy a desire fully. **2** supply with as much as or more than is desired: *the child slept, sated with food.*
– ORIGIN Old English, 'become sated or weary'.

sateen /sa-**teen**/ noun a cotton fabric with a glossy surface.
– ORIGIN from **SATIN**.

satellite noun **1** an artificial object placed in orbit round the earth or another planet to collect information or for communication. **2** a natural object orbiting a planet. **3** (usu. before another noun) a country, community, or organization dependent on or controlled by a larger or more powerful one: *satellite offices in London and New York.*
– ORIGIN Latin *satelles* 'attendant'.

satellite dish noun a bowl-shaped aerial with which signals are transmitted to or received from a communications satellite.

satellite television noun television in which the signals are broadcast via satellite.

sati /su-**tee**/ (also **suttee** /su-**tee**/) noun the former Hindu practice of a widow throwing herself on to her husband's funeral pyre.
– ORIGIN Sanskrit, 'faithful wife'.

satiate /**say**-shi-ayt/ verb give someone as much or more than they want.
– DERIVATIVES **satiation** noun.
– ORIGIN Latin *satiare*.

satiety /suh-**ty**-i-ti/ noun the feeling or state of being fully satisfied.

satin noun a smooth, glossy fabric, usually of silk. •adjective having a smooth, glossy surface or finish.
– DERIVATIVES **satiny** adjective.
– ORIGIN from an Arabic word meaning 'of *Tsinkiang*', a town in China.

satin stitch noun a long straight embroidery stitch, giving the appearance of satin.

satinwood noun the glossy yellowish wood of a tropical tree, used in making furniture.

satire /**sa**-ty-er/ noun **1** the use of humour, irony, or exaggeration as a form of mockery or criticism. **2** a play, novel, etc. using satire.
– DERIVATIVES **satirist** noun.

S

– ORIGIN Latin *satira* 'poetic medley'.

satirical /suh-ti-ri-k'l/ (also **satiric**) adjective using humour, irony, or exaggeration to mock or criticize.
– DERIVATIVES **satirically** adverb.

satirize (or **satirise**) /sat-i-ryz/ verb mock or criticize by using humour, irony, or exaggeration: *the movie satirized the idea of national superiority.*

satisfaction noun **1** the state of being pleased because one's needs have been met or one has achieved something. **2** Law the payment of a debt or fulfilment of a duty or claim. **3** something due to one to make up for an injustice: *the work will stop if they don't get satisfaction.*

satisfactory adjective acceptable, but not outstanding or perfect.
– DERIVATIVES **satisfactorily** adverb.

satisfied adjective contented; pleased: *satisfied customers.*

satisfy verb (**satisfies, satisfying, satisfied**) **1** please someone by meeting their expectations, needs, or desires: *I've never been satisfied with my job.* **2** fulfil a desire, demand, or need. **3** provide someone with adequate information about or proof of something. **4** meet or comply with a condition or duty: *he had ceased to satisfy the conditions for residence.*
– ORIGIN Latin *satisfacere* 'to content'.

satphone noun a telephone that transmits its signal via a communications satellite.

satrap /sat-rap/ noun **1** a subordinate or local ruler. **2** a provincial governor in the ancient Persian empire.
– ORIGIN Latin *satrapa.*

satsuma /sat-soo-muh/ noun a variety of tangerine with a loose skin.
– ORIGIN named after the former Japanese province of *Satsuma.*

saturate verb /sach-uh-rayt/ **1** soak someone or something thoroughly with water or other liquid. **2** fill a market with so many products that demand is fully satisfied and no more products can be sold. **3** Chemistry cause a substance to combine with, dissolve, or hold the greatest possible quantity of another substance. • noun /sach-uh-ruht/ a saturated fat.
– ORIGIN Latin *saturare* 'fill, glut'.

saturated adjective **1** (of fats) having only single bonds between carbon atoms in their molecules and as a result being less easily processed by the body. **2** Chemistry (of a solution) containing the largest possible amount of the substance dissolved in it. **3** (of colour) bright and rich.

saturation noun the state of being so full that nothing else can be added: *a bid for market saturation.* • adjective to the fullest extent: *saturation coverage by the press of police shootings.*

saturation point noun the stage beyond which no more can be absorbed or accepted.

Saturday noun the day of the week before Sunday and following Friday.
– ORIGIN from Latin *Saturni dies* 'day of Saturn'.

Saturn noun a planet of the solar system, sixth in order from the sun and circled by broad flat rings.
– DERIVATIVES **Saturnian** adjective.

Saturnalia /sat-uh-nay-li-uh/ noun (treated as sing. or pl.) **1** the ancient Roman festival of the god Saturn in December, a period of wild celebration. **2** (**saturnalia**) literary a period or spell of wild celebration or self-indulgence.
– DERIVATIVES **saturnalian** adjective.
– ORIGIN Latin, 'matters relating to Saturn'.

saturnine /sat-er-nyn/ adjective **1** gloomy or serious. **2** (of looks) dark and moody.
– ORIGIN from Latin *Saturninus* 'of Saturn' (associated with slowness and gloom by astrologers).

satyr /sat-er/ noun **1** (in Greek Mythology) a lustful, drunken woodland god, represented as a man with a horse's ears and tail or (in Roman myth) with a goat's ears, tail, legs, and horns. **2** a man with strong sexual desires.
– DERIVATIVES **satyric** adjective.
– ORIGIN Greek *saturos.*

sauce noun **1** a liquid substance served with food to add moistness and flavour. **2** informal, chiefly Brit. cheeky language or behaviour; impudence. • verb **1** provide with a sauce: *the noodles are sauced with a fish curry.* **2** informal be cheeky or impudent to someone.
– ORIGIN Old French.

sauce boat noun a long, narrow jug for serving sauce.

saucepan noun a deep cooking pan with a long handle and a lid.

saucer noun a shallow dish with a central circular hollow, on which a cup is placed.
– ORIGIN Old French *saussier* 'sauce boat'.

saucy adjective (**saucier, sauciest**) informal **1** sexually suggestive in a light-hearted way: *saucy postcards.* **2** cheeky or impudent.
– DERIVATIVES **saucily** adverb **sauciness** noun.

Saudi /sow-di, saw-di/ noun (pl. **Saudis**) a person from Saudi Arabia, or a member of its ruling dynasty. • adjective relating to Saudi Arabia or its ruling dynasty.
– DERIVATIVES **Saudi Arabian** noun & adjective.

sauerkraut /sow-er-krowt/ noun a German dish of chopped pickled cabbage.
– ORIGIN German.

sauna /saw-nuh/ noun **1** a small room used as a hot-air or steam bath for cleaning and refreshing the body. **2** a session in a sauna.
– ORIGIN Finnish.

saunter verb walk in a slow, relaxed way. • noun a leisurely stroll.
– ORIGIN unknown.

saurian /saw-ri-uhn/ adjective relating to or like a lizard.
– ORIGIN from Greek *sauros* 'lizard'.

sausage noun **1** a short tube of raw minced meat encased in a skin, that is grilled or fried before eating. **2** a tube of spicy minced meat that is cooked or preserved and eaten cold in slices. **3** a cylindrical object.
– PHRASES **not a sausage** Brit. informal nothing at all.
– ORIGIN Old French *saussiche.*

sausage dog noun Brit. informal a dachshund.

sausage meat noun minced meat with spices

and cereal, used in sausages or as a stuffing.

sausage roll noun a piece of sausage meat baked in a roll of pastry.

sauté /soh-tay/ (also **saute**) adjective fried quickly in a little hot fat. • noun a dish of sautéed food. • verb (**sautés, sautéing, sautéed** or **sautéd**) fry food quickly in a little hot fat.
– ORIGIN French, 'jumped'.

Sauternes /soh-tern/ noun a sweet white wine from Sauternes in the Bordeaux region of France.

Sauvignon /soh-vin-yon/ (also **Sauvignon Blanc**) noun a white wine made from the Sauvignon variety of grape.
– ORIGIN French.

savage adjective 1 fierce and violent. 2 cruel or highly damaging: *a savage attack on the President.* 3 primitive; uncivilized. • noun 1 a member of a people regarded as primitive and uncivilized. 2 a brutal or vicious person. • verb 1 (especially of a dog) attack someone or something ferociously. 2 criticize someone or something harshly.
– DERIVATIVES **savagely** adverb **savagery** noun.
– ORIGIN Old French *sauvage* 'wild'.

savannah (also **savanna**) noun a grassy plain in tropical and subtropical regions, with few trees.
– ORIGIN Spanish *sabana*.

savant /sav-uhnt/ noun a very knowledgeable person.
– ORIGIN French, 'knowing'.

save¹ verb 1 rescue someone or something from harm or danger. 2 prevent someone from dying. 3 store or keep something for future use. 4 keep data in a computer. 5 avoid the need to use up or spend: *computers save time.* 6 avoid something or prevent someone from doing or experiencing something: *this approach saves wear and tear on the books.* 7 prevent an opponent from scoring a goal or point. 8 (in Christian use) protect a person's soul from damnation. • noun chiefly Football an act of preventing an opponent from scoring.
– PHRASES **save one's breath** not bother to say something pointless. **save someone's skin** (or **neck** or **bacon**) rescue someone from difficulty.
– ORIGIN Latin *salvare*.

save² preposition & conjunction formal or literary except; other than.
– ORIGIN from Latin *salvus* 'safe'.

saveloy /sav-uh-loy/ noun Brit. a spicy smoked pork sausage.
– ORIGIN Italian *cervellata*.

saver noun 1 a person who regularly saves money through a bank or recognized scheme. 2 something that prevents a resource from being used up: *a space-saver.*

saving noun 1 a reduction in a resource such as money or time. 2 (**savings**) money saved. • adjective (in combination) preventing waste of a resource: *energy-saving.* • preposition not including; except.

saving grace noun a good quality that makes up for the faults of someone or something.

savings account noun a deposit account.

savings and loan (also **savings and loan association**) noun (in the US) an institution which pays interest on money deposited and lends money to savers.

savings bank noun a non-profit-making bank that pays interests on small deposits of money.

Savings Bond noun a Premium Bond.

saviour (US **savior**) noun 1 a person who saves someone or something from danger or harm. 2 (**the/our Saviour**) (in Christianity) God or Jesus.
– ORIGIN Old French *sauveour*.

savoir faire /sav-war fair/ noun the ability to act appropriately in social situations.
– ORIGIN French, 'know how to do'.

savory noun a plant of the mint family, used as a herb in cookery.
– ORIGIN Latin *satureia*.

savour (US **savor**) verb 1 taste food or drink and enjoy it to the full. 2 enjoy or appreciate to the full: *I wanted to savour every moment.* 3 (**savour of**) have a suggestion or trace of an undesirable quality. • noun 1 a characteristic taste or smell. 2 a trace, especially of something undesirable.
– ORIGIN Old French.

savoury (US **savory**) adjective 1 (of food) salty or spicy rather than sweet. 2 morally wholesome or acceptable: *the less savoury aspects of the story.* • noun (pl. **savouries**) chiefly Brit. a savoury snack.

savoy noun a cabbage of a variety with wrinkled leaves.
– ORIGIN from *Savoy*, an area of SE France.

savvy informal noun common sense or shrewdness. • adjective (**savvier, savviest**) having common sense; shrewd. • verb (**savvies, savvying, savvied**) know or understand something.
– ORIGIN black and pidgin English imitating Spanish *sabe usted* 'you know'.

saw¹ noun 1 a hand tool for cutting wood or other hard materials, having a long, thin toothed blade. 2 a mechanical power-driven cutting tool with a toothed rotating disc or moving band. • verb (past part. chiefly Brit. **sawn** or chiefly N. Amer. **sawed**) 1 cut or make something with a saw. 2 cut something roughly. 3 make rapid movements like those of a saw.
– ORIGIN Old English.

saw² past of SEE¹.

saw³ noun a proverb or wise saying.
– ORIGIN Old English.

sawdust noun powdery particles of wood produced by sawing.

sawfish noun (pl. same or **sawfishes**) a large tropical fish with a long flattened snout bearing large blunt teeth along each side.

sawfly noun (pl. **sawflies**) an insect related to the wasps, with a saw-like tube used in laying eggs in plant tissue.

sawmill noun a factory in which logs are sawn by machine.

sawn past participle of SAW¹.

sawn-off (N. Amer. **sawed-off**) adjective 1 (of a gun) having had the barrel shortened for ease of handling and a wider field of fire. 2 informal (of an item of clothing) having been cut short.

sawtooth (also **sawtoothed**) adjective shaped like the teeth of a saw.

sawyer noun a person who saws timber.

sax noun informal a saxophone.
– DERIVATIVES **saxist** noun.

saxifrage /saks-i-frayj/ noun a low-growing plant of rocky or stony ground, bearing small white, yellow, or red flowers.
– ORIGIN Latin *saxifraga*.

Saxon noun **1** a member of a Germanic people that conquered and settled in much of southern England in the 5th–6th centuries. **2** a person from modern Saxony in Germany. **3** (**Old Saxon**) the language of the ancient Saxons. •adjective **1** relating to the Anglo-Saxons or their period of dominance in England (5th–11th centuries). **2** relating to modern Saxony.
– ORIGIN Greek *Saxones*.

saxophone /saks-uh-fohn/ noun a member of a family of metal wind instruments with a reed like a clarinet, used especially in jazz.
– DERIVATIVES **saxophonic** /saks-uh-**fon**-ik/ adjective **saxophonist** /saks-**off**-uh-nist/ noun.
– ORIGIN named after the Belgian instrument-maker Adolphe *Sax*.

say verb (**says**, **saying**, **said**) **1** speak words so as to convey information, an opinion, an instruction, etc. **2** (of a piece of writing or a symbol) convey information or instructions. **3** (of a clock or watch) indicate a time. **4** (**be said**) be claimed or reported. **5** (**say something for**) present a consideration in favour of or excusing: *he had nothing to say for himself.* **6** suggest as an example, possibility, or a basis for a theory: *let's say the fine is $79.* •noun an opportunity to state one's opinion or to influence events.
– PHRASES **go without saying** be obvious. **say the word** give permission or instructions. **there is no saying** it is impossible to know. **when all is said and done** when everything is taken into account.
– DERIVATIVES **sayable** adjective **sayer** noun.
– ORIGIN Old English.

saying noun a short, well-known expression containing advice or wisdom.

say-so noun informal the power to decide or allow something: *an owner can only close an area with the say-so of the council.*

Sb symbol the chemical element antimony.
– ORIGIN from Latin *stibium*.

SBS abbreviation **1** sick building syndrome. **2** Special Boat Service.

SC abbreviation South Carolina.

Sc symbol the chemical element scandium.

scab noun **1** a dry protective crust that forms over a cut or wound during healing. **2** mange or a similar skin disease in animals. **3** a plant disease caused by a fungus, in which rough patches develop. **4** informal, derogatory a person who refuses to take part in a strike.
– DERIVATIVES **scabbed** adjective **scabby** adjective.
– ORIGIN Old Norse.

scabbard /skab-berd/ noun **1** a sheath for the blade of a sword or dagger. **2** a sheath for a gun or tool.
– ORIGIN Old French *escalberc*.

scabies /skay-beez/ noun a contagious skin disease marked by itching and small raised red spots, caused by a mite.
– ORIGIN Latin, from *scabere* 'to scratch'.

scabious /skay-bi-uhss/ noun a plant with blue, pink, or white pincushion-shaped flowers.
– ORIGIN from Latin *scabiosa herba* 'rough, scabby plant'.

scabrous /skay-bruhss, skab-ruhss/ adjective **1** indecent or sordid: *scabrous Hollywood gossip.* **2** rough and covered with scabs.
– ORIGIN Latin *scabrosus*.

scads plural noun informal, chiefly N. Amer. a large number or quantity.
– ORIGIN unknown.

scaffold noun **1** a raised wooden platform formerly used for public executions. **2** a structure made using scaffolding. •verb attach scaffolding to a building.
– DERIVATIVES **scaffolder** noun.
– ORIGIN Old French *eschaffaut*.

scaffolding noun **1** a temporary structure made of wooden planks and metal poles, used while building, repairing, or cleaning a building. **2** the materials used in scaffolding.

scalable (also **scaleable**) adjective **1** able to be climbed. **2** able to be changed in size or scale. **3** technical able to be graded according to a scale.
– DERIVATIVES **scalability** noun.

scalar /skay-ler/ Mathematics & Physics adjective having only magnitude, not direction. •noun a quantity having only magnitude, not direction.
– ORIGIN Latin *scalaris*.

scalawag noun N. Amer. variant spelling of SCALLYWAG.

scald verb **1** burn someone or something with very hot liquid or steam. **2** heat a liquid to near boiling point. **3** dip something briefly in boiling water. •noun a burn caused by hot liquid or steam.
– ORIGIN Latin *excaldare*.

scale[1] noun **1** each of the small overlapping plates protecting the skin of fish and reptiles. **2** a thick dry flake of skin. **3** limescale in a kettle, boiler, etc. **4** tartar formed on teeth. •verb **1** remove scale or scales from something. **2** (often as noun **scaling**) (especially of the skin) form or flake off in scales.
– ORIGIN Old French *escale*.

scale[2] noun **1** (usu. **scales**) an instrument or device for weighing. **2** either of the dishes on a simple scale balance.
– PHRASES **tip the scales** (or **balance**) be the deciding factor.
– ORIGIN Old Norse, 'bowl'.

scale[3] noun **1** a range of values forming a standard system for measuring or grading something: *a pay scale.* **2** a measuring instrument with a series of marks at regular intervals. **3** relative size or extent: *he operated on a grand scale.* **4** a ratio of size in a map, model, drawing, or plan. **5** an arrangement of the notes in a system of music in ascending or descending order of pitch. •verb **1** climb up or over something high and steep. **2** (**scale something back/down** or **up**) reduce (or increase) something in size, number, or extent. **3** (usu. as adj. **scaled**) represent in measurements that are in proportion to the size of the original: *a strictly scaled depiction of Scotland's regions.*
– PHRASES **to scale** reduced or enlarged in proportion to something.
– ORIGIN Latin *scala* 'ladder'.

scale insect noun a small bug which produces a shield-like scale and spends its life attached to a single plant.

scalene /skay-leen/ adjective (of a triangle) having sides unequal in length.
– ORIGIN Greek *skalēnos* 'unequal'.

scallion /skal-li-uhn/ noun chiefly N. Amer. a spring onion.
– ORIGIN Old French *scaloun*.

scallop /skol-luhp, skal-luhp/ noun 1 an edible shellfish with two hinged fan-shaped shells. 2 each of a series of small curves resembling the edge of a scallop shell, forming a decorative edging. •verb (**scallops, scalloping, scalloped**) (usu. as adj. **scalloped**) decorate something with a series of small curves.
– ORIGIN Old French *escalope*.

scally noun (pl. **scallies**) informal (especially in Liverpool) a rascally young working-class man.
– ORIGIN from **SCALLYWAG**.

scallywag (US also **scalawag**) noun informal a mischievous person; a rascal.
– ORIGIN unknown.

scalp noun 1 the skin covering the top and back of the head. 2 historical the scalp with the hair cut away from an enemy's head as a battle trophy, a former practice among American Indians. •verb historical (of an American Indian) take the scalp of an enemy.
– DERIVATIVES **scalper** noun.
– ORIGIN probably Scandinavian.

scalpel noun a knife with a small sharp blade, used by a surgeon.
– ORIGIN Latin *scalpellum* 'small chisel'.

scaly adjective 1 covered in scales. 2 (of skin) dry and flaking.

scam informal noun a dishonest scheme; a fraud. •verb (**scams, scamming, scammed**) swindle someone.
– DERIVATIVES **scammer** noun.
– ORIGIN unknown.

scamp noun informal a mischievous person, especially a child.
– DERIVATIVES **scampish** adjective.
– ORIGIN probably from Dutch *schampen* 'slip away'.

scamper verb run with quick light steps, especially through fear or excitement. •noun an act of scampering.
– ORIGIN probably from **SCAMP**.

scampi noun (treated as sing. or pl.) a dish consisting of the tails of a kind of large prawn, typically fried in breadcrumbs.
– ORIGIN Italian.

scan verb (**scans, scanning, scanned**) 1 look over something quickly in order to find relevant features or information. 2 move a detector or electromagnetic beam across someone or something, especially to obtain an image. 3 convert a document or picture into digital form for storage or processing on a computer. 4 analyse the metre of a line of verse. 5 (of verse) follow metrical principles. •noun 1 an act of scanning. 2 a medical examination using a scanner. 3 an image obtained by scanning.
– DERIVATIVES **scannable** adjective.
– ORIGIN Latin *scandere* 'climb' (later 'scan verses').

scandal noun 1 behaviour or a situation regarded as wrong or unacceptable and causing general outrage. 2 outrage or gossip arising from such behaviour: *the media's craving for scandal*.
– ORIGIN Latin *scandalum* 'cause of offence'.

scandalize (or **scandalise**) verb shock or horrify someone by acting in an immoral or unacceptable way.

scandalmonger noun a person who spreads rumours or spiteful gossip.

scandalous adjective 1 causing general outrage by being wrong or unacceptable. 2 (of a situation) disgracefully bad.
– DERIVATIVES **scandalously** adverb.

Scandinavian adjective relating to Scandinavia. •noun 1 a person from Scandinavia. 2 the northern branch of the Germanic languages, comprising Danish, Norwegian, Swedish, Icelandic, and Faroese.

scandium /skan-di-uhm/ noun a soft silvery-white metallic chemical element.
– ORIGIN Latin.

scanner noun 1 a machine that examines the body through the use of radiation, ultrasound etc., used to aid diagnosis. 2 a device that scans documents and converts them into digital data.

scansion /skan-sh'n/ noun 1 the action of scanning a line of verse to determine its rhythm. 2 the rhythm of a line of verse.

scant adjective 1 not enough; hardly any: *he paid scant attention to the needs of his wife*. 2 only just reaching the amount specified: *she weighed a scant two pounds*.
– DERIVATIVES **scantly** adverb.
– ORIGIN Old Norse, 'short'.

scanty adjective (**scantier, scantiest**) too little in quantity or amount. •plural noun (**scanties**) informal women's skimpy knickers.
– DERIVATIVES **scantily** adverb.

scapegoat noun 1 a person who is blamed for the wrongdoings or mistakes of others. 2 (in the Bible) a goat sent into the wilderness after the Jewish chief priest had symbolically laid the sins of the people on it. •verb blame someone for the wrongdoings or mistakes of others.
– ORIGIN from former *scape* 'escape' + **GOAT**.

scapula /skap-yuu-luh/ noun (pl. **scapulae** /skap-yuu-lee/ or **scapulas**) technical term for **SHOULDER BLADE**.
– ORIGIN Latin.

scapular adjective relating to the shoulder or shoulder blade. •noun a short cloak worn by monks, covering the shoulders.

scar¹ noun 1 a mark left on the skin or within body tissue after a wound or burn has healed. 2 a lasting effect left following an unpleasant experience. 3 a mark left at the point where a leaf or other part has separated from a plant. •verb (**scars, scarring, scarred**) 1 mark someone or something with a scar or scars. 2 have a lasting and unpleasant effect on: *he was so traumatized by his childhood that he was scarred for life*.
– ORIGIN Greek *eskhara* 'scab'.

scar² noun a steep high cliff or rock outcrop.
– ORIGIN Old Norse, 'low reef'.

scarab /ska-ruhb/ noun 1 a large dung beetle,

S

treated as sacred in ancient Egypt. **2** an ancient Egyptian gem in the form of a scarab.
– ORIGIN Greek *skarabeios*.

scarce adjective **1** (of a resource) available in quantities that are too small to meet the demand for it. **2** occurring in small numbers or quantities; rare.
– PHRASES **make oneself scarce** informal leave a place, especially so as to avoid a difficult situation.
– DERIVATIVES **scarcity** noun.
– ORIGIN Old French *escars*.

scarcely adverb **1** only just. **2** only a very short time before. **3** used to suggest that something is unlikely: *they could scarcely all be wrong.*

scare verb **1** frighten or become frightened: *just seeing those needles scared me to death.* **2** (**scare someone away/off**) drive or keep someone away by fear. •**noun 1** a sudden attack of fright. **2** a period of general anxiety or alarm: *a bomb scare.*
– ORIGIN Old Norse.

scarecrow noun an object made to resemble a person, set up to scare birds away from a field where crops are growing.

scared adjective feeling or showing fear or nervousness.

scaremonger noun a person who spreads frightening rumours.
– DERIVATIVES **scaremongering** noun.

scarf[1] noun (pl. **scarves** or **scarfs**) a length or square of fabric worn around the neck or head.
– DERIVATIVES **scarfed** (also **scarved**) adjective.
– ORIGIN probably from Old French *escarpe* 'pilgrim's pouch'.

scarf[2] verb join the ends of two pieces of timber or metal by bevelling or notching them so that they fit together. •**noun** a joint made by scarfing.
– ORIGIN Old Norse.

scarify /ska-ri-fy/ verb (**scarifies, scarifying, scarified**) **1** make shallow cuts in the skin. **2** break up the surface of soil or a road or pavement. **3** break up and remove matted vegetation from a lawn. **4** criticize someone harshly.
– DERIVATIVES **scarification** noun **scarifier** noun.
– ORIGIN Old French *scarifier*.

scarlatina /skar-luh-tee-nuh/ noun another term for SCARLET FEVER.
– ORIGIN Latin.

scarlet noun a bright red colour.
– ORIGIN Latin *scarlata* 'brightly coloured cloth'.

scarlet fever an infectious disease that particularly affects children, caused by a bacteria and marked by fever and a scarlet rash.

scarlet woman noun chiefly humorous a woman known for having many sexual relationships.

scarp noun a very steep bank or slope; an escarpment.
– ORIGIN Italian *scarpa.*

scarper verb Brit. informal run away.
– ORIGIN probably from Italian *scappare* 'to escape'.

Scart (also **SCART**) noun a 21-pin socket used to connect video equipment.

– ORIGIN from French *Syndicat des Constructeurs des Appareils Radiorécepteurs et Téléviseurs*, the committee which designed the connector.

scarves plural of SCARF[1].

scary adjective (**scarier, scariest**) informal causing fear; frightening.
– DERIVATIVES **scarily** adverb.

scat[1] verb (**scats, scatting, scatted**) informal go away; leave.
– ORIGIN perhaps from SCATTER.

scat[2] noun improvised jazz singing in which the voice is used to imitate an instrument. •**verb** (**scats, scatting, scatted**) sing using the voice to imitate an instrument.
– ORIGIN probably imitating the sound.

scathing /skay-*th*ing/ adjective harshly critical or scornful.
– DERIVATIVES **scathingly** adverb.
– ORIGIN from Old Norse, 'harm, injure'.

scatological /skat-uh-**loj**-i-k'l/ adjective obsessed with excrement and excretion.
– DERIVATIVES **scatology** noun.
– ORIGIN from Greek *skōr* 'dung'.

scatter verb **1** throw a number of things in various random directions. **2** (of a group of people or animals) separate and move off in different directions. **3** (**be scattered**) occur or be found at various places rather than all together: *more than 73,000 mobile phone masts are scattered across the landscape.*
– ORIGIN probably from SHATTER.

scatterbrained adjective disorganized and unable to concentrate on things.

scatter cushion noun a small cushion placed randomly so as to create a casual effect.

scattergun adjective (also **scattershot**) covering a broad range in an unsystematic way: *the scattergun approach to selecting material.* •**noun** chiefly N. Amer. a shotgun.

scattering (also **scatter**) noun a small amount or number of things spread over an area: *a scattering of chairs and tables on the pavement.*

scatty adjective (**scattier, scattiest**) Brit. informal absent-minded and disorganized.
– ORIGIN from *scatterbrained.*

scavenge /ska-vinj/ verb **1** search for and collect anything usable from rubbish. **2** (of an animal or bird) search for and eat dead animals.
– ORIGIN from SCAVENGER.

scavenger noun **1** an animal that feeds on dead animals or waste material. **2** a person who searches for and collects usable items from rubbish.
– ORIGIN first referring to an official who collected *scavage*, a toll on foreign merchants' goods, later a person who kept the streets clean: from Old French *escauwer* 'inspect'.

SCE abbreviation Scottish Certificate of Education.

scenario /si-**nah**-ri-oh/ noun (pl. **scenarios**) **1** a suggested sequence of events: *in the worst-case scenario, he could be looking at assault charges.* **2** a written outline of a film, novel, or stage work giving details of the plot and individual scenes.
– ORIGIN Italian.

scene noun **1** the place where an incident

occurs or occurred. **2** a view or landscape as seen by a spectator. **3** an incident or situation of a particular kind: *scenes of violence.* **4** a sequence of continuous action in a play, film, opera, or book. **5** a public display of emotion or anger: *she was loath to make a scene in the office.* **6** a specified area of activity or interest: *the literary scene.* **7** the scenery used in a play or opera.
– PHRASES **behind the scenes** out of public view. **come** (or **appear** or **arrive**) **on the scene** arrive; appear.
– ORIGIN Greek *skēnē* 'tent, stage'.

scenery noun **1** the natural features of a landscape considered in terms of their appearance. **2** the painted background used to represent a place on a stage or film set.

scenic adjective **1** relating to impressive or beautiful natural scenery: *the scenic route.* **2** relating to theatrical scenery.
– DERIVATIVES **scenically** adverb.

scent noun **1** a distinctive smell, especially one that is pleasant. **2** pleasant-smelling liquid worn on the skin; perfume. **3** a trail indicated by the smell of an animal. •verb **1** give a pleasant scent to something. **2** find or recognize something by the sense of smell. **3** sense that something exists or is about to happen: *the Premier scented victory last night.*
– DERIVATIVES **scented** adjective.
– ORIGIN from Latin *sentire* 'perceive, smell'.

sceptic /skep-tik/ (old use & N. Amer. **skeptic**) noun **1** a person who tends to question or doubt accepted opinions. **2** a person who doubts the truth of Christianity and other religions; an atheist.
– DERIVATIVES **scepticism** noun.
– ORIGIN Greek *skeptikos.*

USAGE: Do not confuse **sceptic** with **septic**. See the note at **SEPTIC**.

sceptical adjective not easily convinced; having doubts.

sceptre /sep-ter/ (US **scepter**) noun a staff carried by a king or queen on ceremonial occasions.
– ORIGIN Greek *skēptron.*

Schadenfreude /shah-d'n-froy-duh/ noun pleasure that someone gains from another person's misfortune.
– ORIGIN German.

schedule /shed-yool, sked-yool/ noun **1** a plan that lists the intended tasks, events, and times needed to achieve something. **2** a timetable. **3** chiefly Law an appendix to a formal document or statute. •verb **1** arrange or plan for something to happen or for someone to do something. **2** Brit. include a building in a list for legal preservation or protection.
– PHRASES **to** (or **on** or **according to**) **schedule** on time; as planned.
– DERIVATIVES **scheduler** noun.
– ORIGIN Latin *schedula* 'slip of paper'.

scheduled adjective **1** forming part of or included on a schedule. **2** (of an airline or flight) forming part of a regular service rather than specially chartered.

scheduled caste noun the official name given in India to the caste considered 'untouchable' in orthodox Hindu scriptures and practice,

officially regarded as socially disadvantaged.

schema /skee-muh/ noun (pl. **schemata** /skee-muh-tuh/ or **schemas**) technical an outline of a plan or theory.
– ORIGIN Greek *skhēma* 'form, figure'.

schematic adjective **1** (of a diagram) outlining the main features of something; simplified. **2** following a fixed pattern or plan: *the plot feels manipulative and schematic.*
– DERIVATIVES **schematically** adverb.

schematize (or **schematise**) verb arrange or represent something in a schematic or simplified form.

scheme noun **1** a systematic plan for achieving a particular aim. **2** a secret or underhand plan; a plot. **3** an ordered system or pattern: *a classical rhyme scheme.* •verb make plans in an underhand way; plot.
– DERIVATIVES **schemer** noun.
– ORIGIN Greek *skhēma* 'form, figure'.

scherzo /skair-tsoh/ noun (pl. **scherzos** or **scherzi** /skair-tsi/) a lively, light, or playful musical composition, typically comprising a movement in a symphony or sonata.
– ORIGIN Italian, 'jest'.

schilling /shil-ing/ noun (until the introduction of the euro in 2002) the basic unit of money of Austria.
– ORIGIN German *Schilling.*

schism /si-z'm, ski-z'm/ noun **1** a split between strongly opposed groups within an organization, caused by differences of opinion or belief. **2** the formal separation of a Church into two Churches owing to differences in belief.
– DERIVATIVES **schismatic** adjective & noun.
– ORIGIN Greek *skhisma* 'cleft'.

schist /shist/ noun a coarse-grained metamorphic rock which consists of layers of different minerals.
– ORIGIN from Greek *skhistos* 'split'.

schistosomiasis /shis-toh-suh-my-uh-sis/ noun another term for BILHARZIA.
– ORIGIN from *schistosome*, referring to the worm that causes bilharzia, from Greek *skhistos* 'divided' + *sōma* 'body'.

schizoid /skit-soyd/ adjective **1** referring to a personality type characterized by emotional coldness, eccentric behaviour, and withdrawal into a fantasy world. **2** informal mad or crazy. •noun a person with a schizoid personality.

schizophrenia /skit-suh-free-ni-uh/ noun a long-term mental disorder whose symptoms include a disintegration in the process of thinking and withdrawal from reality into fantasy.
– ORIGIN from Greek *skhizein* 'to split' + *phrēn* 'mind'.

schizophrenic /skits-uh-fren-ik/ adjective **1** having schizophrenia. **2** informal having inconsistent or contradictory elements. •noun a person with schizophrenia.

schlep /shlep/ (also **schlepp**) informal, chiefly N. Amer. verb (**schleps, schlepping. schlepped**) **1** haul or carry something heavy or awkward. **2** go or move reluctantly or with effort. •noun a boring or difficult journey.
– ORIGIN Yiddish, 'drag'.

schlock /shlok/ noun informal, chiefly N. Amer. cheap or inferior goods or material; rubbish.

S

- DERIVATIVES **schlocky** adjective.
- ORIGIN probably from Yiddish words meaning 'an apoplectic stroke' and 'wretch, untidy person'.

schloss /shlos/ noun (in Germany and Austria) a castle.
- ORIGIN German.

schmaltz /shmawlts/ noun informal excessive sentimentality.
- DERIVATIVES **schmaltzy** adjective.
- ORIGIN German *Schmalz* 'dripping, lard'.

schmooze /shmooz/ informal, chiefly N. Amer. verb 1 chat, especially at a social event. 2 talk in a friendly way to someone in order to gain an advantage.
- DERIVATIVES **schmoozer** noun **schmoozy** adjective.
- ORIGIN Yiddish.

schmuck /shmuk/ noun N. Amer. informal a stupid or worthless person.
- ORIGIN Yiddish, 'penis'.

schnapps /shnaps/ noun a strong alcoholic drink resembling gin.
- ORIGIN German *Schnaps* 'dram of liquor'.

schnauzer /shnow-zuh/ noun a German breed of dog with a close wiry coat and heavy whiskers round the muzzle.
- ORIGIN German.

schnitzel /shnit-z'l/ noun a thin slice of veal or other pale meat, coated in breadcrumbs and fried.
- ORIGIN German, 'slice'.

scholar noun 1 a person who studies a particular subject in detail; an academic. 2 a university student holding a scholarship.
- ORIGIN Latin *scholaris*.

scholarly adjective 1 relating to serious academic study. 2 devoted to academic studies; learned.

scholarship noun 1 serious academic study. 2 a grant made to support a student's education, awarded on the basis of achievement.

scholastic adjective 1 relating to schools and education. 2 relating to medieval scholasticism. •noun a follower of medieval scholasticism.

scholasticism noun the system of theology and philosophy taught in medieval European universities, based mainly on Aristotle's philosophy and logic and the works of early Christian religious writers.

school¹ noun 1 an institution for educating children. 2 a day's work at school. 3 any institution at which instruction is given in a particular subject. 4 a department or faculty of a university. 5 N. Amer. informal a college or university. 6 a group of artists, writers, or philosophers who share similar ideas or methods. 7 Brit. a group of people gambling together. •verb 1 formal or N. Amer. send someone to school. 2 train in a particular skill or activity: *he schooled her in horsemanship.*
- PHRASES **school of thought** a particular way of thinking.
- ORIGIN Greek *skholē* 'leisure, philosophy, lecture-place'.

school² noun a large group of fish or sea mammals.
- ORIGIN German or Dutch *schōle*.

schoolboy (or **schoolgirl**) noun a boy (or girl) attending school.

schoolchild noun (pl. **schoolchildren**) a child attending school.

schoolhouse noun a building used as a school, especially in a village.

schooling noun education received at school.

schoolmarm noun chiefly N. Amer. a schoolmistress, especially one who is prim and strict.

schoolmaster (or **schoolmistress**) noun chiefly Brit. a teacher in a school.

schoolmate noun informal a fellow pupil.

schoolteacher noun a person who teaches in a school.

schooner /skoo-ner/ noun 1 a sailing ship with two or more masts, typically with a mainmast that is larger than the the mast nearer the front. 2 Brit. a large glass for sherry.
- ORIGIN perhaps from dialect *scun* 'skim along'.

schottische /sho-teesh, shot-ish/ noun a dance resembling a slow polka.
- ORIGIN from German *der schottische Tanz* 'the Scottish dance'.

schtum /shtuum/ adjective variant spelling of **SHTUM**.

schuss /shuus/ noun a straight downhill run on skis. •verb make a straight downhill run on skis.
- ORIGIN German, 'shot'.

sciatic /sy-at-ik/ adjective 1 relating to the hip. 2 affecting the sciatic nerve. 3 suffering from sciatica.
- ORIGIN Greek *iskhiadikos* 'relating to the hips'.

sciatica noun pain affecting the back, hip, and outer side of the leg, caused by pressure on the sciatic nerve root in the lower back.

sciatic nerve noun a major nerve extending from the lower end of the spinal cord down the back of the thigh.

science noun 1 the systematic study of the structure and behaviour of the physical and natural world through observation and experiment. 2 an organized body of knowledge on any subject.
- ORIGIN Latin *scientia*.

science fiction noun fiction set in the future and dealing with imagined scientific, technological, or social developments.

science park noun an area devoted to scientific research or the development of science-based industries.

scientific adjective 1 relating to or based on science. 2 done in a methodical or organized way.
- DERIVATIVES **scientifically** adverb.

scientist noun a person who has expert knowledge of one or more of the natural or physical sciences.

Scientology noun trademark a religious system based on the seeking of self-knowledge and spiritual fulfilment through courses of study and training.
- DERIVATIVES **Scientologist** noun.
- ORIGIN from Latin *scientia* 'knowledge'.

sci-fi noun informal short for **SCIENCE FICTION**.

scilla /sil-uh/ noun a plant with small blue star-

or bell-shaped flowers and glossy leaves.
– ORIGIN Greek *skilla* 'sea onion'.

scimitar /sim-i-ter/ **noun** a short sword with a curved blade that broadens towards the point, first used in Eastern countries.
– ORIGIN French *cimeterre* or Italian *scimitarra*.

scintilla /sin-til-luh/ **noun** a tiny trace or amount: *not a scintilla of doubt.*
– ORIGIN Latin, 'spark'.

scintillate /sin-ti-layt/ **verb** give off flashes of light; sparkle.
– DERIVATIVES **scintillant** adjective & noun **scintillation** noun.
– ORIGIN Latin *scintillare* 'to sparkle'.

scintillating adjective **1** very clever, skilful, or exciting: *a scintillating performance.* **2** sparkling brightly.

scion /sy-uhn/ **noun 1** a young shoot or twig of a plant that is cut off to create a new plant. **2** a descendant of an important or famous family.
– ORIGIN Old French *ciun* 'shoot, twig'.

scissor verb **1** cut something with scissors. **2** move the legs back and forwards in a way that resembles the action of scissors.

scissors plural noun (also **a pair of scissors**) a tool for cutting cloth and paper, consisting of two crossing blades pivoted in the middle.
•adjective (also **scissor**) (of an action) in which two things cross each other or open and close like a pair of scissors: *a scissor kick.*
– ORIGIN Latin *cisorium* 'cutting instrument'.

sclera /skleer-uh/ noun the white outer layer of the eyeball.
– ORIGIN Latin.

scleroderma /skleer-uh-der-muh/ noun a medical condition in which the skin and connective tissue hardens and contracts.

sclerosis /skluh-roh-siss, skleer-oh-siss/ noun **1** abnormal hardening of body tissue. **2** (in full **multiple sclerosis**) a disease involving damage to the sheaths of nerve cells in the brain and spinal cord, leading to partial or complete paralysis.
– ORIGIN Greek *sklērōsis*.

sclerotic /skluh-rot-ik/ adjective **1** Medicine relating to or having sclerosis. **2** unable to adapt; rigid: *sclerotic management.*

scoff[1] verb speak about someone or something in a scornful way.
– DERIVATIVES **scoffer** noun.
– ORIGIN perhaps Scandinavian.

scoff[2] verb informal eat something quickly and greedily.
– ORIGIN from Dutch *schoft* 'quarter of a day, meal'.

scold verb angrily tell someone that they have done something wrong. •noun old use a woman who nags or grumbles constantly.
– ORIGIN probably from Old Norse, 'person who writes and recites epic poems'.

sconce noun a candle holder attached to a wall with an ornamental bracket.
– ORIGIN Old French *esconse* 'lantern'.

scone /skon, skohn/ noun a small plain cake made from flour, fat, and milk.
– ORIGIN perhaps from Dutch *schoonbroot* 'fine bread'.

scoop noun **1** a utensil resembling a spoon, having a short handle and a deep bowl. **2** the

bowl-shaped part of a digging machine or dredger. **3** informal a piece of news published by a newspaper or broadcast by a television or radio station before its rivals know about it.
•verb **1** pick something up with a scoop. **2** create a hollow in something. **3** pick up in a swift, smooth movement: *he scooped her up in his arms.* **4** informal publish a news story before a rival. **5** informal win a prize.
– ORIGIN German *schōpe* 'waterwheel bucket'.

scoop neck noun a deeply curved wide neckline on a woman's garment.

scoot verb informal go or leave somewhere quickly.
– ORIGIN unknown.

scooter noun **1** (also **motor scooter**) a light two-wheeled motorcycle. **2** a child's toy consisting of a footboard mounted on two wheels and a long steering handle, moved by pushing one foot against the ground. •verb travel or ride on a scooter.

scope[1] noun **1** the opportunity or possibility for doing something: *there is clearly scope for development in the future.* **2** the range of the area or subject matter that something deals with: *these matters are beyond the scope of this book.*
– ORIGIN Greek *skopos* 'target'.

scope[2] noun informal a telescope, microscope, or other device having a name ending in *-scope.*

-scope combining form referring to an instrument for observing or examining: *telescope.*
– ORIGIN from Greek *skopein* 'look at'.

scorbutic /skor-byoo-tik/ adjective relating to or affected with scurvy.
– ORIGIN from Latin *scorbutus* 'scurvy'.

scorch verb **1** burn or become burnt on the surface or edges. **2** (as adj. **scorched**) dried out and withered as a result of extreme heat. **3** informal move very fast: *a car scorching along the motorway.* •noun the burning of the surface of something.
– ORIGIN perhaps related to Old Norse, 'be shrivelled'.

scorched earth policy noun a military strategy of burning or destroying all crops and other resources that might be of use to an invading enemy force.

scorcher noun informal **1** a day or period of very hot weather. **2** Brit. an impressive or powerful example of something.

score noun **1** the number of points, goals, runs, etc. achieved by a person or side in a game. **2** (pl. same) a group or set of twenty. **3** (**scores of**) a large number of. **4** the written music for a composition, showing all the vocal and instrumental parts. **5** (**the score**) informal the real situation or facts: *I'm not thick, I know the score.* **6** a notch or line cut into a surface. •verb **1** gain a point, goal, run, etc. in a game. **2** be worth a number of points. **3** record the score during a game. **4** cut or scratch a mark on a surface. **5** (**score something out/through**) delete part of a piece of writing by drawing a line through it. **6** orchestrate or arrange a piece of music. **7** informal succeed in obtaining illegal drugs. **8** informal succeed in attracting a sexual partner.

S

– PHRASES **settle a score** take revenge on someone.
– DERIVATIVES **scoreless** adjective **scorer** noun.
– ORIGIN Old Norse, 'notch, tally, twenty'.

scoreboard noun a large board on which the score in a game or match is displayed.

scorecard noun 1 (also **scoresheet**) a card or sheet or paper in which scores are recorded. 2 a card listing the names and positions of players in a team.

scoreline noun Brit. the score in a game or match.

scorn noun a strong feeling that someone or something is worthless; contempt. • verb 1 express contempt for someone or something. 2 reject in a scornful way: *I have never scorned newspapers as many people do.*
– ORIGIN Old French *escarn*.

scornful adjective showing that one feels someone or something is worthless; contemptuous.
– DERIVATIVES **scornfully** adverb.

Scorpio noun the eighth sign of the zodiac (the Scorpion), which the sun enters about 23 October.
– DERIVATIVES **Scorpian** noun & adjective.
– ORIGIN Latin.

scorpion noun a creature related to spiders, with pincers and a poisonous sting at the end of its tail.
– ORIGIN Greek *skorpios*.

scorzonera /skor-zoh-**neer**-uh/ noun the purple-brown root of a plant of the daisy family, eaten as a vegetable.
– ORIGIN Italian.

Scot noun 1 a person from Scotland. 2 a member of a Gaelic people that migrated from Ireland to Scotland around the late 5th century.
– ORIGIN Latin *Scottus*.

Scotch noun (also **Scotch whisky**) whisky made in Scotland. • adjective old-fashioned term for **Scottish**.
– ORIGIN from **Scottish**.

scotch verb decisively put an end to: *they were quick to scotch talk of a disagreement.*
– ORIGIN perhaps related to **skate**¹.

Scotch broth noun a traditional Scottish soup made from meat stock with pearl barley and vegetables.

Scotch egg noun Brit. a hard-boiled egg coated in sausage meat, rolled in breadcrumbs, and fried.

Scotch whisky noun another term for **Scotch**.

scot-free adverb without suffering any punishment or injury: *the people who kidnapped her will get off scot-free.*
– ORIGIN from former *scot* 'a tax'.

Scots adjective another term for **Scottish**. • noun the form of English used in Scotland.

Scotsman (or **Scotswoman**) noun (pl. **Scotsmen** or **Scotswomen**) a person from Scotland.

Scots pine noun a pine tree widely grown for timber and other products.

Scotticism /skot-i-siz-uhm/ noun a characteristically Scottish word or phrase.

Scottie noun informal a Scottish terrier.

Scottish adjective relating to Scotland or its people. • noun (as plural noun **the Scottish**) the people of Scotland.

– DERIVATIVES **Scottishness** noun.

Scottish terrier noun a small rough-haired breed of terrier.

scoundrel noun a person who takes advantage or deceives others; a rogue.
– DERIVATIVES **scoundrelly** adjective.
– ORIGIN unknown.

scour¹ verb 1 clean something by rubbing it with a detergent or something rough. 2 (of running water) wear away rock to form a channel or pool.
– DERIVATIVES **scourer** noun.
– ORIGIN Old French *escurer*.

scour² verb search a place thoroughly.
– ORIGIN unknown.

scourge /rhymes with urge/ noun 1 a cause of great trouble or suffering: *the plague was the scourge of the Middle Ages.* 2 historical a whip used to punish people. • verb 1 cause great suffering to someone or something. 2 historical whip someone as a punishment.
– ORIGIN Old French *escorge*.

Scouse Brit. informal noun 1 the dialect or accent of people from Liverpool. 2 (also **Scouser**) a person from Liverpool. • adjective relating to Liverpool.
– ORIGIN from *lobscouse*, a stew formerly eaten by sailors.

scout noun 1 a person sent ahead of a main force to gather information about the enemy. 2 (also **Scout**) a member of the Scout Association, a boys' organization which aims to develop their character through outdoor and other activities. 3 a talent scout. 4 an instance of searching somewhere to gather information. • verb 1 search a place in order to discover something. 2 explore or examine so as to gather information: *they are keen to scout out business opportunities.* 3 act as a talent scout.
– DERIVATIVES **scouting** noun.
– ORIGIN Old French *escouter* 'listen'.

scow /skow/ noun N. Amer. a flat-bottomed boat for transporting cargo to and from ships in harbour.
– ORIGIN Dutch *schouw* 'ferry boat'.

scowl noun an angry or bad-tempered expression. • verb frown in an angry or bad-tempered way.
– ORIGIN probably Scandinavian.

scrabble verb 1 grope around with the fingers to find or hold on to something. 2 move quickly and awkwardly; scramble. • noun (**Scrabble**) trademark a board game in which players build up words from small lettered squares or tiles.
– ORIGIN Dutch *schrabbelen*.

scrag verb (**scrags, scragging, scragged**) informal, chiefly Brit. beat someone up. • noun an unattractively thin person or animal.
– ORIGIN perhaps from Scots and northern English *crag* 'neck'.

scrag-end noun Brit. the poor-quality end of a neck of mutton.

scraggy adjective 1 thin and bony. 2 (also chiefly N. Amer. **scraggly**) ragged or untidy in appearance.

scram verb (**scrams, scramming, scrammed**) informal go away or leave quickly.
– ORIGIN probably from **scramble**.

scramble verb 1 move or make one's way quickly and awkwardly, using the hands as well as the feet. 2 make or become jumbled or confused. 3 put a broadcast transmission or telephone conversation into a form that can only be understood if received by a decoding device. 4 cook beaten eggs with a little liquid in a pan. 5 informal act in a hurried or undignified way: *firms scrambled to win contracts.* 6 (of fighter aircraft) take off immediately in an emergency or for action. • noun 1 an act of scrambling up or over something. 2 Brit. a motorcycle race over rough and hilly ground. 3 a hasty or undignified struggle to achieve or get something. – ORIGIN imitating the sound.

scrambler noun 1 a device for scrambling a broadcast transmission or telephone conversation. 2 Brit. a motorcycle for racing over rough and hilly ground. – DERIVATIVES **scrambling** noun.

scrap[1] noun 1 a small piece or amount of something, especially one that is left over after the rest has been used. 2 (**scraps**) bits of uneaten food left after a meal. 3 waste metal and other material that can be reprocessed. • verb (**scraps, scrapping, scrapped**) 1 abolish or cancel a plan, policy, or law. 2 remove something from use so as to convert it to scrap metal. – ORIGIN Old Norse.

scrap[2] informal noun a brief or minor fight or quarrel. • verb (**scraps, scrapping, scrapped**) have a brief or minor fight or quarrel. – DERIVATIVES **scrapper** noun. – ORIGIN perhaps from **SCRAPE**.

scrapbook noun a book of blank pages for sticking cuttings, drawings, or pictures in.

scrape verb 1 drag or pull a hard or sharp implement across a surface or object to remove dirt or waste matter. 2 damage something by rubbing against a rough or hard surface. 3 just manage to achieve, succeed, or pass: *he now scrapes a living from a roadside stall.* 4 (**scrape something together/up**) collect or accumulate something with difficulty. 5 (**scrape by/along**) manage to live with difficulty. • noun 1 an act or sound of scraping. 2 an injury or mark caused by scraping. 3 informal an embarrassing or difficult situation that one has caused oneself. – PHRASES **scrape the barrel** (or **the bottom of the barrel**) informal be forced to use the last and poorest resources because nothing else is available. – DERIVATIVES **scraper** noun. – ORIGIN Old English, 'scratch with the fingernails'.

scrapheap noun a pile of things that have been thrown away as rubbish. – PHRASES **on the scrapheap** rejected as no longer wanted or useful.

scrapie /skray-pi/ noun a disease of sheep involving the central nervous system, in which the animals suffer from a lack of coordination. – ORIGIN from **SCRAPE**.

scrappy adjective (**scrappier, scrappiest**) disorganized, untidy, or incomplete. – DERIVATIVES **scrappily** adverb **scrappiness** noun.

scrapyard noun a place where waste metal and other material is collected before being discarded or recycled.

scratch verb 1 make a long mark or wound on a surface with something sharp. 2 rub a part of one's body with one's fingernails to relieve itching. 3 cross out writing. 4 cancel or abandon a plan or project. 5 withdraw from a competition. 6 make a living or achieve something with difficulty: *he was just scratching a living from the black market.* 7 (as noun **scratching**) the technique, used in rap music, of stopping a record by hand and moving it back and forwards to give a rhythmic scratching effect. 8 (of a bird or mammal) rake the ground with the beak or claws in search of food. • noun 1 a mark or wound made by scratching. 2 an act or spell of scratching. 3 informal a slight wound or injury. • adjective put together from whatever is available: *United were fielding a scratch squad.* – PHRASES **from scratch** from the very beginning. **scratch the surface** deal with a matter only in the most superficial way. **up to scratch** up to the required standard; satisfactory. – DERIVATIVES **scratcher** noun. – ORIGIN uncertain.

scratch card noun a card with a section or sections coated in a waxy substance which may be scraped away to reveal whether a prize has been won.

scratchy adjective (**scratchier, scratchiest**) 1 rough in texture and causing scratching. 2 (of a voice or sound) rough; grating.

scrawl verb write in a hurried, careless way. • noun hurried, careless handwriting. – ORIGIN probably from **CRAWL**.

scrawny adjective (**scrawnier, scrawniest**) unattractively thin and bony. – ORIGIN from dialect *scranny.*

scream verb 1 make a long, loud, piercing cry or sound expressing strong emotion or pain. 2 move very rapidly, especially with a loud, high-pitched sound. 3 present in an urgent or obvious way: *the headlines screamed 'he offered me sex'.* • noun 1 a long, loud, piercing cry or sound. 2 (**a scream**) informal a very funny person or thing. – DERIVATIVES **screamer** noun. – ORIGIN perhaps Dutch.

screamingly adverb to a very great extent; extremely: *screamingly funny television.*

scree noun a mass of small loose stones that form or cover a slope on a mountain. – ORIGIN probably from Old Norse, 'landslip'.

screech verb 1 make a loud, harsh cry. 2 move fast with a loud, harsh sound. • noun a loud, harsh cry or sound. – DERIVATIVES **screecher** noun **screechy** adjective. – ORIGIN imitating the sound.

screech owl noun Brit. another term for **BARN OWL**.

screed noun 1 a long speech or piece of writing. 2 a layer of material applied to level a floor or other surface. – ORIGIN probably from **SHRED**.

screen noun 1 an upright partition used to divide a room, give shelter, or conceal something. 2 a thing that shelters or conceals:

S

his jeep was parked behind a screen of trees.
3 the flat front surface of a television, VDU, or monitor, on which images and data are displayed. **4** a blank surface on which films are projected. **5 (the screen)** films or television. •**verb 1** conceal, protect, or shelter with a screen: *her hair swung across to screen her face.* **2** show a film or video or broadcast a television programme. **3** protect someone from something dangerous or unpleasant. **4** test someone to find out whether or not they have a disease. **5** investigate someone to assess their suitability for a job.
– DERIVATIVES **screener** noun **screenful** noun.
– ORIGIN Old French *escren.*

screenplay noun the script of a film, including acting instructions and scene directions.

screen-print verb force ink on to a surface through a prepared piece of fine material such as silk or nylon so as to create a picture or pattern. •**noun** (**screen print**) a picture or design produced by screen-printing.

screen saver noun a computer program which replaces an unchanging screen display with a moving image to prevent damage to the phosphor.

screen test noun a filmed test to assess whether an actor is suitable for a film role. •**verb** (**screen-test**) give a screen test to an actor.

screenwriter noun a person who writes a screenplay for a film.
– DERIVATIVES **screenwriting** noun.

screw noun **1** a metal pin with a spiral thread running around it and a slotted head, used to join things together by being turned and pressed in. **2** a cylinder with a spiral ridge or thread running round the outside that can be turned to seal an opening, apply pressure, adjust position, etc. **3** (also **screw propeller**) a ship's or aircraft's propeller. **4** informal, derogatory a prison warder. **5** vulgar slang an act of having sex. •**verb 1** fasten or tighten something with a screw or screws. **2** turn something so as to attach or remove it by means of a spiral thread. **3** informal cheat or swindle someone. **4** vulgar slang have sex with someone.
– PHRASES **have one's head screwed on (the right way)** informal have common sense. **have a screw loose** informal be slightly eccentric or mentally disturbed. **screw someone up** informal make someone emotionally disturbed. **screw something up 1** crush something into a tight mass. **2** informal make something go wrong.
– ORIGIN Old French *escroue* 'female screw, nut'.

screwball informal, chiefly N. Amer. noun a mad or eccentric person. •**adjective 1** crazy; absurd. **2** referring to a style of fast-moving comedy film involving eccentric characters or ridiculous situations.

screwdriver noun **1** a tool with a shaped tip that fits into the head of a screw to turn it. **2** a cocktail made from vodka and orange juice.

screwy adjective (**screwier, screwiest**) informal, chiefly N. Amer. rather odd or eccentric.

scribble verb **1** write or draw something carelessly or hurriedly. **2** informal write for a living or as a hobby. •**noun** a piece of writing or a picture produced carelessly or hurriedly.
– DERIVATIVES **scribbler** noun.
– ORIGIN Latin *scribillare.*

scribe noun **1** historical a person who copied out documents. **2** informal, often humorous a writer, especially a journalist. **3** historical a Jewish record-keeper or, later, a professional religious and legal expert. **4** (also **scriber**) a pointed instrument used for making marks to guide a saw or in signwriting. •**verb 1** literary write something. **2** mark something with a pointed instrument.
– DERIVATIVES **scribal** adjective.
– ORIGIN Latin *scriba.*

scrim noun strong, coarse fabric used for heavy-duty lining or upholstery.
– ORIGIN unknown.

scrimmage noun a confused struggle or fight.
– ORIGIN from SKIRMISH.

scrimp verb be very careful with money; economize.
– ORIGIN Scots, 'meagre'.

scrimshaw /skrim-shaw/ noun decorative work consisting of shells or ivory with carved designs.
– ORIGIN unknown.

scrip noun **1** a certificate that demonstrates ownership of stocks, shares, and bonds, especially a certificate relating to an issue of additional shares to shareholders in proportion to the shares they already hold. **2** such certificates as a whole.
– ORIGIN short for *subscription receipt.*

script noun **1** the written part of a play, film, or broadcast. **2** handwriting as distinct from print. **3** writing using a particular alphabet: *Russian script.* **4** Brit. a candidate's written answers in an exam. •**verb** write a script for a play, film, or broadcast.
– ORIGIN Latin *scriptum.*

scriptural adjective relating to the Bible.

scripture (also **scriptures**) noun **1** the sacred writings of Christianity contained in the Bible. **2** the sacred writings of a religion other than Christianity.
– ORIGIN Latin *scriptura* 'writings'.

scriptwriter noun a person who writes a script for a play, film, or broadcast.
– DERIVATIVES **scriptwriting** noun.

scrivener /skriv-uh-ner/ noun historical a person who made a living by writing out documents; a clerk or scribe.
– ORIGIN Old French *escrivein.*

scrofula /skrof-yuu-luh/ noun historical a disease characterized by swollen glands, probably a form of tuberculosis.
– DERIVATIVES **scrofulous** adjective.
– ORIGIN from Latin *scrofa* 'breeding sow' (said to be subject to the disease).

scroll noun **1** a roll of parchment or paper for writing or painting on. **2** an ornamental design or carving resembling a partly unrolled scroll of parchment. •**verb** move displayed writing or graphics on a computer screen in order to view different parts of them.
– DERIVATIVES **scrollable** adjective **scroller** noun.
– ORIGIN from former *scrow* 'roll'.

scroll bar noun a long, thin section at the edge of a computer display by which material can be scrolled using a mouse.

scrolled adjective having an ornamental design or carving resembling a scroll.

scrollwork noun decoration consisting of spiral lines or patterns.

Scrooge noun a person who is mean with money.
– ORIGIN from Ebenezer *Scrooge* in Charles Dickens's story *A Christmas Carol*.

scrotum /skroh-tuhm/ noun (pl. **scrota** /skroh-tuh/ or **scrotums**) the pouch of skin containing the testicles.
– DERIVATIVES **scrotal** adjective.
– ORIGIN Latin.

scrounge verb informal try to get something from someone without having to pay or work for it.
– PHRASES **on the scrounge** trying to get something from someone without paying or working for it.
– DERIVATIVES **scrounger** noun.
– ORIGIN from dialect *scrunge* 'steal'.

scrub¹ verb (**scrubs, scrubbing, scrubbed**) **1** rub someone or something hard so as to clean them. **2** (**scrub up**) thoroughly clean one's hands and arms before performing surgery. **3** informal cancel or abandon something. • noun **1** an act of scrubbing. **2** a cosmetic lotion used to remove dead cells and cleanse the skin. **3** (**scrubs**) hygienic clothing worn by surgeons during operations.
– ORIGIN probably from German or Dutch *schrobben, schrubben*.

scrub² noun **1** vegetation consisting mainly of brushwood or stunted trees. **2** land covered with brushwood or stunted trees. • adjective referring to a shrubby or small form of a plant: *scrub oak*.
– DERIVATIVES **scrubby** adjective.
– ORIGIN from SHRUB.

scrubber noun **1** a brush for scrubbing. **2** a device that uses water or a solution for purifying gases. **3** Brit. informal, derogatory a woman who has many brief sexual relationships.

scrubland noun (also **scrublands**) land consisting of brushwood or stunted trees.

scruff¹ noun the back of a person's or animal's neck.
– ORIGIN from dialect *scuff*.

scruff² noun Brit. informal a scruffy person.
– ORIGIN from SCURF.

scruffy adjective (**scruffier, scruffiest**) shabby and untidy or dirty.
– DERIVATIVES **scruffily** adverb **scruffiness** noun.

scrum noun **1** Rugby an ordered formation of players in which the forwards of each team push against each other with heads down and the ball is thrown in. **2** Brit. informal a disorderly crowd. • verb (**scrums, scrumming, scrummed**) Rugby form or take part in a scrum.
– ORIGIN from SCRUMMAGE.

scrum half noun Rugby a halfback who puts the ball into the scrum and stands ready to receive it again.

scrummage noun & verb fuller form of SCRUM.
– ORIGIN from SCRIMMAGE.

scrummy adjective informal very pleasant to eat; delicious.
– ORIGIN from SCRUMPTIOUS.

scrump verb Brit. informal steal fruit from an orchard or garden.
– ORIGIN from dialect, 'withered apple'.

scrumptious adjective informal very delicious or attractive.
– ORIGIN unknown.

scrumpy noun Brit. rough strong cider, especially as made in Somerset, Cornwall, and Devon.

scrunch verb **1** make a loud crunching noise. **2** crush or squeeze something into a tight mass. • noun a loud crunching noise.
– ORIGIN probably imitating the sound.

scrunchy adjective making a loud crunching noise when crushed. • noun (also **scrunchie**) (pl. **scrunchies**) chiefly Brit. a circular band of fabric-covered elastic used for fastening the hair.

scruple noun **1** a feeling of doubt as to whether an action is morally right: *I had no scruples about eavesdropping.* **2** historical a unit of weight equal to 20 grains. • verb hesitate to do something that one thinks may be wrong: *she doesn't scruple to ask her parents for money.*
– ORIGIN from Latin *scrupus* 'anxiety, rough pebble'.

scrupulous adjective **1** very careful and thorough. **2** very concerned to avoid doing wrong.
– DERIVATIVES **scrupulosity** noun **scrupulously** adverb **scrupulousness** noun.

scrutineer noun **1** a person who examines something closely and thoroughly. **2** chiefly Brit. a person who supervises the way in which an election or competition is run.

scrutinize (or **scrutinise**) verb examine someone or something closely and thoroughly.

scrutiny noun (pl. **scrutinies**) close and critical observation or examination.
– ORIGIN Latin *scrutinium*.

scry verb (**scries, scrying, scried**) foretell the future with a crystal ball.
– ORIGIN from DESCRY.

SCSI abbreviation small computer system interface.

scuba /skoo-buh/ noun a portable breathing apparatus for divers, consisting of cylinders of compressed air attached to a mouthpiece or mask.
– ORIGIN from the initial letters of *self-contained underwater breathing apparatus*.

scuba-diving noun the sport or pastime of swimming underwater using a scuba.

scud verb (**scuds, scudding, scudded**) move fast because driven by the wind: *clouds scudded across the sky.* • noun literary clouds or spray driven by the wind.
– ORIGIN perhaps from SCUT, reflecting the sense 'race like a hare'.

scuff verb **1** scrape a shoe or other object against something. **2** mark a surface by scraping it. **3** drag one's feet when walking. • noun a mark made by scraping a surface or object.
– ORIGIN perhaps imitating the sound.

scuffle noun a short, confused fight or struggle. • verb **1** take part in a scuffle. **2** move in a hurried way, making a rustling or shuffling sound.
– ORIGIN probably Scandinavian.

S

scull noun 1 each of a pair of small oars used by a single rower. 2 an oar placed over the back of a boat and moved from side to side to propel it. 3 a light, narrow boat propelled with a scull or a pair of sculls. •verb propel a boat with sculls.
– DERIVATIVES **sculler** noun.
– ORIGIN unknown.

scullery noun (pl. **sculleries**) a small kitchen or room at the back of a house used for washing dishes and other dirty household work.
– ORIGIN Old French escuelerie.

scullion noun old use a servant given the most menial tasks in a kitchen.
– ORIGIN perhaps influenced by **SCULLERY**.

sculpt verb make a sculpture of someone or something.

sculptor noun (fem. **sculptress**) an artist who makes sculptures.

sculpture noun 1 the art of making three-dimensional figures and shapes by carving stone or wood or casting metal. 2 a work made by carving stone or wood or casting metal. •verb 1 make something by carving stone or wood or casting metal. 2 (as adj. **sculptured**) having strong, smooth curves: sculptured bodies doing press-ups.
– DERIVATIVES **sculptural** adjective.
– ORIGIN from Latin sculpere 'carve'.

scum noun 1 a layer of dirt or froth on the surface of a liquid. 2 informal a worthless or hated person or group of people. •verb (**scums, scumming, scummed**) cover the surface of a liquid with a layer of dirt or froth.
– DERIVATIVES **scummy** adjective.
– ORIGIN German or Dutch schüm.

scumbag noun informal a hated or unpleasant person.

scumble Art verb give a softer or duller effect to a painting or colour by applying a very thin coat of paint. •noun a very thin coat of paint applied to a painting or colour.
– ORIGIN perhaps from **SCUM**.

scupper[1] noun a hole in a ship's side to allow water to run away from the deck.
– ORIGIN perhaps from Old French escopir 'to spit'.

scupper[2] verb chiefly Brit. 1 informal prevent from working or succeeding; thwart: the unions scuppered the plan. 2 sink a ship deliberately.
– ORIGIN unknown.

scurf noun flakes on the surface of the skin, occurring especially as dandruff.
– DERIVATIVES **scurfy** adjective.
– ORIGIN from Old English, 'cut to shreds'.

scurrilous /skur-ri-luhss/ adjective rude and insulting, and intended to damage someone's reputation: a scurrilous attack.
– DERIVATIVES **scurrility** noun (pl. **scurrilities**).
– ORIGIN Latin scurrilus.

scurry verb (**scurries, scurrying, scurried**) move hurriedly with short, quick steps. •noun a situation of hurried and confused movement.
– ORIGIN from **HURRY**.

scurvy noun a disease caused by a lack of vitamin C, characterized by bleeding gums and the opening of previously healed wounds. •adjective (**scurvier, scurviest**) old use worthless or contemptible.
– ORIGIN from **SCURF**.

scut noun the short tail of a hare, rabbit, or deer.
– ORIGIN unknown.

scutter chiefly Brit. verb move hurriedly with short steps. •noun an act or sound of scuttering.
– ORIGIN perhaps from **SCUTTLE**[2].

scuttle[1] noun a metal container with a lid and a handle, used to store coal for a domestic fire.
– ORIGIN Latin scutella 'dish'.

scuttle[2] verb run with short, quick steps. •noun an act or sound of scuttling.
– ORIGIN probably from **SCUD**.

scuttle[3] verb 1 deliberately cause a scheme to fail. 2 sink one's own ship deliberately. •noun an opening with a lid in a ship's deck or side.
– ORIGIN perhaps from Spanish escotilla 'hatchway'.

scuzzy adjective (**scuzzier, scuzziest**) informal disgustingly dirty or unpleasant.
– DERIVATIVES **scuzz** noun.
– ORIGIN probably from disgusting.

scythe noun a tool used for cutting crops such as grass or corn, with a long curved blade at the end of a long pole. •verb 1 cut crops with a scythe. 2 move through something rapidly and forcefully. 3 (**scythe someone down**) (in sport) knock an opposing player down.
– ORIGIN Old English.

Scythian /sith-i-uhn/ noun a person from Scythia, an ancient region of SE Europe and Asia. •adjective relating to Scythia.

SD abbreviation South Dakota.

SDI abbreviation Strategic Defense Initiative.

SDLP abbreviation (in Northern Ireland) Social Democratic and Labour Party.

SE abbreviation 1 south-east. 2 south-eastern.

Se symbol the chemical element selenium.

sea noun 1 the large continuous area of salt water that covers most of the earth's surface and surrounds its land masses. 2 a particular area of sea: the Black Sea. 3 a vast expanse or quantity: a sea of faces.
– PHRASES **at sea** 1 sailing on the sea. 2 confused; uncertain. **one's sea legs** one's ability to keep one's balance and not feel seasick on board a ship.
– DERIVATIVES **seaward** adjective & adverb **seawards** adverb.
– ORIGIN Old English.

sea anchor noun an object dragged in the water behind a boat in order to keep its front pointing into the waves or to reduce sideways drift.

sea anemone noun a sea creature with a tube-shaped body which bears a ring of stinging tentacles around the mouth.

sea bass noun a sea fish with a spiny fin on its back, resembling the freshwater perch.

seabed noun the ground under the sea; the ocean floor.

seabird noun a bird that lives near to the sea or coast.

seaboard noun a region bordering the sea; the coastline.

seaborgium /see-borg-i-uhm/ noun a very unstable chemical element made by high-energy atomic collisions.
– ORIGIN named after the American nuclear chemist Glenn Seaborg.

S

seaborne adjective transported or travelling by sea.

sea bream noun a sea fish that resembles the freshwater bream.

sea breeze noun **1** a breeze blowing towards the land from the sea. **2** a cocktail consisting of vodka, grapefruit juice, and cranberry juice.

sea change noun a great and very noticeable change in a situation.
– ORIGIN from Shakespeare's *The Tempest*.

sea cow noun a manatee or similar mammal that lives in the sea.

sea cucumber noun a sea creature having a thick worm-like body with tentacles around the mouth.

sea dog noun informal an old or experienced sailor.

seafaring adjective (of a person) regularly travelling by sea. •noun travel by sea.
– DERIVATIVES seafarer noun.

seafood noun shellfish and sea fish as food.

seafront noun the part of a coastal town next to and facing the sea.

seagoing adjective **1** (of a ship) suitable for voyages on the sea. **2** relating to travel by sea.

sea green noun a pale bluish-green colour.

seagull noun a gull.

sea horse noun a small sea fish that swims upright and has a head that resembles that of a horse.

seakale noun a coastal plant of the cabbage family, grown for its edible shoots.

SEAL (also **Seal**) noun a member of an elite force within the US Navy.
– ORIGIN abbreviation of 'sea, air, land'.

seal[1] noun **1** a device or substance used to join two things together or to prevent anything from passing between them. **2** a piece of wax or lead with a design stamped into it, attached to a document as a guarantee that it is genuine. **3** a confirmation or guarantee: *the scheme has the government's seal of approval.*
•verb **1** fasten or close something securely. **2** (**seal something off**) isolate an area by preventing people from entering or leaving it. **3** apply a coating to a surface to prevent something from passing through it. **4** make definite; finalize: *the consortium said they hoped to seal a deal within two weeks.* **5** fix a seal to a document to show that it is genuine.
– PHRASES **my lips are sealed** I will not discuss or reveal something. **put** (or **set**) **the seal on** finally confirm or complete something.
– DERIVATIVES sealable adjective.
– ORIGIN Old French *seel*.

seal[2] noun a fish-eating mammal that lives in the sea, with flippers and a streamlined body. •verb (usu. as noun **sealing**) hunt for seals.
– ORIGIN Old English.

sealant noun material used to make something airtight or watertight.

sea lavender noun another name for **STATICE**.

sealer[1] noun a device or substance used to make something airtight or watertight.

sealer[2] noun a ship or person engaged in hunting seals.

sea level noun the level of the sea's surface, used in calculating the height of geographical features such as hills.

sealing wax noun a mixture of shellac and rosin with turpentine, used to make seals.

sea lion noun a large seal of the Pacific Ocean, the male of which has a mane on the neck and shoulders.

Sea Lord noun either of two senior officers in the Royal Navy (**First Sea Lord, Second Sea Lord**) serving originally as members of the Admiralty Board (now of the Ministry of Defence).

sealskin noun the skin or prepared fur of a seal, used for making clothes.

Sealyham /see-li-uhm/ noun a terrier of a wire-haired short-legged breed.
– ORIGIN from the Welsh village of *Sealyham*, where the dog was first bred.

seam noun **1** a line where two pieces of fabric are sewn together. **2** a line where the edges of two pieces of wood or other material touch each other. **3** an underground layer of a mineral such as coal or gold. **4** a supply of something valuable: *City have a rich seam of experienced players.* •verb join things with a seam.
– ORIGIN Old English.

seaman noun (pl. **seamen**) a sailor, especially one below the rank of officer.
– DERIVATIVES seamanlike adjective seamanship noun.

seam bowler (also **seamer**) noun Cricket a bowler who makes the ball change direction by causing it to bounce on its seam.

seamless adjective smooth and without seams or obvious joins.
– DERIVATIVES seamlessly adverb.

seamstress noun a woman who sews, especially as a job.
– ORIGIN from old-fashioned *seamster* 'tailor, seamstress'.

seamy adjective (**seamier, seamiest**) immoral and unpleasant; sordid.

seance /say-onss/ noun a meeting at which people attempt to make contact with the spirits of people who are dead.
– ORIGIN French.

seaplane noun an aircraft with floats or skis instead of wheels, designed to land on and take off from water.

seaport noun a town or city with a harbour for seagoing ships.

sear verb **1** burn or scorch something with a sudden intense heat. **2** (of pain) be experienced as a sudden burning sensation. **3** brown food quickly at a high temperature. •adjective (also **sere**) literary (of a plant) withered.
– ORIGIN Old English.

search verb **1** try to find someone or something by looking carefully and thoroughly. **2** examine thoroughly in order to find something or someone: *she searched the house from top to bottom.* **3** look for information in a computer network or database by using a search engine. **4** (as adj. **searching**) investigating very thoroughly: *searching questions.* •noun an act of searching.
– PHRASES **search me!** informal I do not know.
– DERIVATIVES searchable adjective searcher noun.
– ORIGIN Old French *cerchier*.

S

search engine noun a computer program that searches for and identifies specified items in a database, used especially for searching the Internet.

searchlight noun a powerful outdoor electric light with a beam that can be turned in the required direction.

search party noun a group of people organized to look for someone or something.

search warrant noun a legal document authorizing a police officer or other official to enter and search a place.

sea salt noun salt produced by the evaporation of seawater.

seascape noun a view or picture of an area of sea.

seashell noun the shell of a marine shellfish.

seashore noun an area of sandy or rocky land next to the sea.

seasick adjective suffering from nausea caused by the motion of a ship at sea.
– DERIVATIVES **seasickness** noun.

seaside noun a beach area or holiday resort.

season noun 1 each of the four divisions of the year (spring, summer, autumn, and winter) marked by particular weather patterns and daylight hours. 2 a period of the year with particular weather or when a particular activity is done: *the football season.* 3 (**the season**) the time of year traditionally marked by fashionable upper-class social events. • verb 1 add salt, herbs, or spices to food. 2 make more lively or interesting: *his conversation is seasoned with punchlines.* 3 keep wood so as to dry it for use as timber. 4 (as adj. **seasoned**) used to particular conditions; experienced: *a seasoned traveller.*
– PHRASES **in season** 1 (of a fruit, vegetable, or other food) ready to eat and in good condition at a particular time of year. 2 (of a female mammal) ready to mate.
– ORIGIN Old French *seson.*

seasonable adjective usual for or appropriate to a particular season of the year.

seasonal adjective 1 relating to or typical of a particular season of the year. 2 changing according to the season.
– DERIVATIVES **seasonality** noun **seasonally** adverb.

seasonal affective disorder noun full form of **SAD**.

seasoning noun salt, herbs, or spices added to food to improve the flavour.

season ticket noun a ticket allowing travel within a particular period or admission to a series of events.

sea squirt noun a sea animal which has a bag-like body with openings through which water flows in and out.

seat noun 1 a thing made or used for sitting on. 2 the part of a chair for sitting on. 3 a sitting place for a passenger in a vehicle or for a member of an audience. 4 a person's buttocks. 5 a place in an elected parliament or council. 6 Brit. a parliamentary constituency. 7 a place where someone or something is based or something is carried out: *the town is the island's seat of government.* 8 Brit. a large country house belonging to an aristocratic family. 9 the way in

which a person sits on a horse. 10 a part of a machine that supports or guides another part.
• verb 1 arrange for someone to sit somewhere. 2 (**seat oneself** or **be seated**) sit down. 3 (of a place) have sufficient seats for a specified number of people.
– DERIVATIVES **seating** noun **seatless** adjective.
– ORIGIN Old Norse.

seat belt noun a belt used to secure someone in the seat of a motor vehicle or aircraft.

sea trout noun Brit. a brown trout of a salmon-like race.

sea urchin noun a sea animal which has a shell covered in spines.

sea wall noun a wall built to prevent the sea from flowing over an area of land.

seawater noun water in or taken from the sea.

seaway noun a waterway or channel used by seagoing ships.

seaweed noun large algae growing in the sea or on rocks at the edge of the sea.

seaworthy adjective (of a boat) in a good enough condition to sail on the sea.
– DERIVATIVES **seaworthiness** noun.

sebaceous /si-bay-shuhss/ adjective technical 1 relating to a sebaceous gland. 2 relating to oil or fat.
– ORIGIN Latin *sebaceus.*

sebaceous gland noun a gland in the skin which produces an oily substance to lubricate the skin and hair.

sebum /see-buhm/ noun an oily substance produced by the sebaceous glands.
– ORIGIN Latin, 'grease'.

sec[1] abbreviation secant.

sec[2] noun informal a second or a very short space of time.

sec[3] adjective (of wine) dry.
– ORIGIN French, from Latin *siccus.*

secant /see-kuhnt, sek-uhnt/ noun 1 Mathematics (in a right-angled triangle) the ratio of the hypotenuse to the shorter side adjacent to an acute angle. 2 Geometry a straight line that cuts a curve in two or more parts.
– ORIGIN from Latin *secare* 'to cut'.

secateurs /sek-uh-terz, sek-uh-terz/ plural noun Brit. a pair of pruning clippers for use with one hand.
– ORIGIN French, 'cutters'.

secede /si-seed/ verb withdraw formally from membership of a federation of states or other alliance.
– DERIVATIVES **seceder** noun.
– ORIGIN Latin *secedere* 'withdraw'.

secession /si-sesh-uhn/ noun the action of withdrawing from a federation or other alliance.

seclude verb keep someone or oneself away from other people.
– ORIGIN Latin *secludere.*

secluded adjective 1 (of a place) not seen or visited by many people; sheltered and private. 2 (of a person's life) having little contact with other people.

seclusion noun the state of being private and away from other people.

second[1] /sek-uhnd/ ordinal number 1 that is number two in a sequence; 2nd. 2 lower in position, rank, or importance: *New York is*

second only to Los Angeles for air pollution.
3 (**seconds**) goods of less than perfect quality.
4 (**seconds**) informal a second helping of food at
a meal. **5** secondly (used to introduce a second
point). **6** Brit. a place in the second highest
grade in an exam for a degree. **7** a person who
assists a contestant in a boxing match or duel.
• verb **1** formally support a proposal, nomination, etc. before it is voted on or discussed
further. **2** express agreement with someone
or something.
– DERIVATIVES **seconder** noun.
– ORIGIN Latin *secundus* 'following, second'.

second² /sek-uhnd/ noun **1** the unit of time in
the SI system, equal to one-sixtieth of a
minute. **2** informal a very short time. **3** (also **arc
second** or **second of arc**) a measurement of an
angle equal to one sixtieth of a minute.
– ORIGIN from Latin *secunda minuta* 'second
minute'.

second³ /si-kond/ verb Brit. temporarily
transfer an employee to another position or
role.
– DERIVATIVES **secondee** noun **secondment** noun.
– ORIGIN from French *en second* 'in the second
rank (of officers)'.

secondary adjective **1** coming after, less
important than, or resulting from someone or
something that is first or most important: *a
secondary road*. **2** relating to education for
children from the age of eleven to sixteen or
eighteen.
– DERIVATIVES **secondarily** adverb.

secondary colour noun a colour that is a
result of mixing two primary colours.

secondary industry noun industry that
converts raw materials into commodities and
products; manufacturing industry.

secondary modern school noun historical (in
the UK) a secondary school for children not
selected for grammar or technical schools.

secondary picketing noun Brit. picketing of a
company not directly involved in a particular
industrial dispute.

secondary sexual characteristics plural
noun physical characteristics developed at
puberty which distinguish between the sexes
but are not involved in reproduction.

second best adjective next after the best.
• noun a less adequate or less desirable
alternative.

second class noun **1** a set of people or things
grouped together as the second best. **2** the
second-best accommodation in an aircraft,
train, or ship. **3** Brit. the second-highest
division in the results of the exams for a
university degree. • adjective & adverb relating
to the second class.

Second Coming noun (in Christian belief)
the prophesied return of Jesus to Earth at the
Last Judgement.

second-degree adjective **1** (of burns) that
cause blistering but not permanent scars.
2 Law, chiefly N. Amer. (of a crime, especially a
murder) less serious than a first-degree crime.

second-generation adjective **1** referring to
the children of parents who have emigrated
from one country to another. **2** of a more
advanced stage of technology than previous
models or systems.

second-guess verb predict someone's actions
or thoughts by guessing.

second-hand adjective & adverb **1** (of goods)
having had a previous owner; not new.
2 accepted on another person's authority and
not from original investigation: *authors have
had to make do with second-hand information
from 'royal sources'.*
– PHRASES **at second hand** on the basis of what
others have said rather than direct observation or experience.

second hand noun an extra hand in some
watches and clocks which moves round to
indicate the seconds.

second in command noun the officer next in
authority to the commanding or chief officer.

secondly adverb in the second place; second.

second name noun Brit. a surname.

second nature noun something that one does
very easily or naturally because one has done
it so often or is particularly suited to it.

second person noun see PERSON (sense 3).

second-rate adjective poor in quality.
– DERIVATIVES **second-rater** noun.

second reading noun a second presentation
of a bill to a law-making assembly.

second sight noun the supposed ability to
predict future events or to know what is
happening in a different place.

second string noun (often in phrase **a second
string to one's bow**) an alternative resource or
course of action in case another one fails.

second thoughts plural noun a change of
opinion or decision after considering
something again.

second wind noun fresh energy that enables
one to continue with an activity after being
tired.

secret adjective **1** kept from or not known or
seen by others. **2** fond of keeping secrets;
secretive. • noun **1** something that others do
not know about. **2** a method of achieving
something that is not generally known: *the
secret of a happy marriage is compromise.*
3 something that is not fully understood; a
mystery: *the secrets of the universe.*
– DERIVATIVES **secrecy** noun **secretly** adverb.
– ORIGIN Latin *secretus* 'separate, set apart'.

secret agent noun a spy acting for a country.

secretaire /sek-ri-tair/ noun a small writing
desk.
– ORIGIN French, 'secretary'.

secretariat /sek-ri-tair-i-uht/ noun a
governmental administrative office or
department.

secretary noun (pl. **secretaries**) **1** a person
employed to deal with letters and telephone
calls, make arrangements, and keep records.
2 an official of a society or other organization
who deals with its correspondence and keeps
its records. **3** the chief assistant of a UK
government minister or ambassador.
– DERIVATIVES **secretarial** adjective.
– ORIGIN Latin *secretarius* 'confidential officer'.

secretary bird noun a slender long-legged
African bird of prey, having a crest resembling
a quill pen stuck behind the ear.

Secretary General noun (pl. **Secretaries**

S

General) the chief administrator of some organizations.

Secretary of State noun **1** (in the UK) the head of a major government department. **2** (in the US) the head of the State Department, responsible for foreign affairs.

secrete[1] /si-**kreet**/ verb (of a cell, gland, or organ) produce and discharge a substance.
– DERIVATIVES **secretor** noun **secretory** adjective.

secrete[2] /si-**kreet**/ verb conceal or hide something.
– ORIGIN from the former verb *secret* 'keep secret'.

secretion /si-**kree**-sh'n/ noun **1** a process by which substances are produced and discharged from a cell, gland, or organ for a particular function in the organism or for excretion. **2** a substance discharged by this process.
– ORIGIN Latin, 'separation'.

secretive adjective inclined to keep information secret or to hide one's feelings and intentions.
– DERIVATIVES **secretively** adverb **secretiveness** noun.

secret police noun (treated as pl.) a police force working in secret against a government's political opponents.

secret service noun **1** a government department concerned with spying. **2** (**Secret Service**) (in the US) a branch of the Treasury Department dealing with counterfeiting and providing protection for the President.

secret society noun an organization whose members are sworn to secrecy about its activities.

sect noun a group of people with different religious beliefs from those of a larger group to which they belong.
– ORIGIN Latin *secta* 'following, faction'.

sectarian adjective **1** relating to a religious sect or sects. **2** resulting from the differences that exist between members of different sects: *sectarian killings.* • noun a member of a sect.
– DERIVATIVES **sectarianism** noun.

section noun **1** any of the parts into which something is divided or from which it is made up. **2** a distinct group within a larger body of people or things: *eco-warriors enjoyed widespread support from large sections of the population.* **3** the shape resulting from cutting a solid by or along a plane. **4** a representation of the internal structure of something as if it has been cut through. **5** a thin slice of plant or animal tissue prepared for examination with a microscope. **6** a separation by surgical cutting. • verb **1** divide something into sections. **2** divide something by surgical cutting. **3** Brit. commit someone compulsorily to a psychiatric hospital in accordance with a section of the Mental Health Act.
– DERIVATIVES **sectional** adjective.
– ORIGIN Latin.

sector noun **1** an area or part that is distinct from others. **2** a distinct part of an economy, society, or field of activity: *the government aimed to reassure the commercial sector.* **3** a subdivision of an area for military operations. **4** a part of a circle between two lines drawn from its centre to its circumference.

– DERIVATIVES **sectoral** adjective.
– ORIGIN Latin, 'cutter'.

secular /**sek**-yuu-ler/ adjective **1** not religious or spiritual. **2** (of Christian clergy) not belonging to or living in a monastic or other order.
– DERIVATIVES **secularism** noun **secularist** noun **secularize** (or **secularise**) verb **secularly** adverb.
– ORIGIN Latin *saecularis* 'relating to an age or period'.

secure adjective **1** likely to continue or to remain safe: *the days of secure staff jobs are over.* **2** fixed or fastened so as not to give way, become loose, or be lost. **3** feeling confident and free from fear or anxiety. **4** protected against attack or other criminal activity. **5** (of a prison or similar establishment) having measures in place to prevent the escape of inmates. • verb **1** protect someone or something from danger or threat. **2** fix or fasten something securely. **3** succeed in obtaining: *the side were determined to secure a place in the UEFA Cup.* **4** guarantee a loan by having the right to take possession of property or goods if the borrower is unable to repay the money.
– DERIVATIVES **securely** adverb.
– ORIGIN Latin *securus*.

security noun (pl. **securities**) **1** the state of being or feeling secure: *long-term job security.* **2** the safety of a state or organization against criminal activity such as terrorism. **3** something that is promised as a guarantee that a loan will be repaid. **4** a certificate proving ownership of stocks or bonds.

sedan /si-**dan**/ noun **1** an enclosed chair carried between two horizontal poles, used especially in the 17th and 18th centuries. **2** chiefly N. Amer. a car for four or more people.
– ORIGIN perhaps from Latin *sella* 'saddle'.

sedate[1] adjective **1** slow, calm, and relaxed. **2** serious, quiet, and rather dull: *sedate small-town life.*
– DERIVATIVES **sedately** adverb **sedateness** noun.
– ORIGIN from Latin *sedare* 'settle'.

sedate[2] verb give someone a drug to make them calm or fall asleep.

sedation noun the giving of a sedative drug to someone to calm them or make them sleep.
– ORIGIN Latin.

sedative noun a drug that makes someone calm or sleepy. • adjective making someone calm or sleepy.

sedentary /**sed**-uhn-tri/ adjective **1** (of work or a way of life) involving much sitting and little exercise. **2** tending to sit down a lot; taking little exercise: *healthy but sedentary young men.* **3** (of an animal or people) tending to stay in the same place for much of the time.
– ORIGIN Latin *sedentarius*.

sedge noun a grass-like plant with triangular stems and small flowers, growing in wet ground.
– ORIGIN Old English.

sedge warbler noun a common songbird with streaky brown plumage, found in marshes and reed beds.

sediment noun **1** matter that settles to the bottom of a liquid. **2** material carried in particles by water or wind and deposited on

the land surface or seabed. • verb settle or deposit as sediment.
- DERIVATIVES **sedimentation** noun.
- ORIGIN Latin *sedimentum* 'settling'.

sedimentary adjective Geology (of rock) formed from sediment deposited by water or wind.

sedition /si-**di**-sh'n/ noun actions or speech which encourage rebellion against the authority of a state or ruler.
- DERIVATIVES **seditious** adjective.
- ORIGIN Latin, from *sed-* 'apart' + *itio* 'going'.

seduce verb 1 tempt someone into sexual activity. 2 persuade someone to do something unwise: *she was almost seduced into believing him.*
- DERIVATIVES **seducer** noun **seduction** noun **seductress** noun.
- ORIGIN Latin *seducere* 'lead aside or away'.

seductive adjective tempting and attractive.
- DERIVATIVES **seductively** adverb **seductiveness** noun.

sedulous /**sed**-yuu-luhss/ adjective showing dedication and great care or effort.
- DERIVATIVES **sedulously** adverb.
- ORIGIN Latin *sedulus* 'zealous'.

sedum /**see**-duhm/ noun a plant of a large group having fleshy leaves and small star-shaped flowers.
- ORIGIN Latin.

see¹ verb (**sees**, **seeing**; past **saw**; past part. **seen**) 1 become aware of someone or something with the eyes. 2 experience or witness an event or situation. 3 meet someone one knows socially or by chance. 4 form an opinion or conclusion after thinking or from information: *I saw that he was right.* 5 regard in a particular way: *he saw himself as a good teacher.* 6 view as a possibility: *I can't see him earning any more anywhere else.* 7 meet someone regularly as a boyfriend or girlfriend. 8 consult a specialist or professional. 9 give someone an interview or consultation. 10 guide or take someone somewhere: *don't bother seeing me out.* 11 (**see to**) deal with something. 12 (**see that**) ensure that.
- PHRASES **see about** deal with something. **see someone off** 1 accompany a person who is leaving to their point of departure. 2 Brit. force an intruder or attacker to leave. **see someone out** Brit. last longer than someone will live. **see something out** come to the end of a period of time or undertaking. **see through** realize someone's or something's true nature. **see someone through** support someone during a difficult period. **see something through** carry on with an undertaking until it is completed.
- ORIGIN Old English.

see² noun the district or position of a bishop or archbishop, centred on a cathedral church.
- ORIGIN Latin *sedes* 'seat'.

seed noun 1 a flowering plant's unit of reproduction, capable of developing into another such plant. 2 the beginning of a feeling, process, or condition: *the conversation sowed a seed of doubt in his mind.* 3 any of a number of stronger competitors in a sports tournament who have been given a position in an ordered list to ensure that they do not play each other in the early rounds. 4 old use a man's

semen. 5 old use (chiefly in the Bible) a person's offspring or descendants. • verb 1 sow land with seeds. 2 produce or drop seeds. 3 remove the seeds from vegetables or fruit. 4 make a competitor a seed in a sports tournament.
- PHRASES **go** (or **run**) **to seed** 1 (of a plant) stop flowering as the seeds develop. 2 deteriorate, especially as a result of neglect: *he had gone to seed after his wife left him.*
- DERIVATIVES **seedless** adjective.
- ORIGIN Old English, related to **sow**¹.

seedbed noun a bed of fine soil in which seedlings are germinated.

seedcorn noun 1 good-quality corn kept for seed. 2 Brit. assets set aside in order to be profitable or useful in the future.

seed head noun a flower head when it is producing seeds.

seed leaf noun a cotyledon.

seedling noun a young plant raised from seed.

seed money (also **seed capital**) noun money provided to start up a project.

seed pearl noun a very small pearl.

seed potato noun a potato intended for replanting to produce a new plant.

seedsman noun (pl. **seedsmen**) a person who buys and sells seeds as a profession.

seedy adjective (**seedier**, **seediest**) 1 sordid or immoral: *his seedy affair with a soft-porn starlet.* 2 shabby, dirty, and unpleasant: *a seedy bar.* 3 dated unwell.
- DERIVATIVES **seedily** adverb **seediness** noun.

seeing conjunction because; since.

seek verb (past and past part. **sought**) 1 try to find or obtain: *she may decide to seek alternative employment.* 2 (**seek someone/thing out**) search for and find someone or something. 3 ask for: *we are seeking legal advice.* 4 (**seek to do**) try or want to do: *they had never sought to interfere with her freedom.*
- DERIVATIVES **seeker** noun.
- ORIGIN Old English.

seem verb 1 give the impression of being: *she seemed annoyed.* 2 (**cannot seem to do**) appear to be unable to do something, despite having tried.
- ORIGIN from an Old Norse word meaning 'appropriate, fitting'.

seeming adjective appearing to be real or true; apparent.
- DERIVATIVES **seemingly** adverb.

seemly adjective in keeping with good taste or correct behaviour.
- DERIVATIVES **seemliness** noun.
- ORIGIN Old Norse, 'fitting'.

seen past participle of **see**¹.

seep verb (of a liquid) flow or leak slowly through or into something.
- DERIVATIVES **seepage** noun.
- ORIGIN perhaps a dialect form of an Old English word meaning 'to soak'.

seer /rhymes with beer/ noun a person who is supposedly able to see visions of the future.

seersucker noun a fabric with a puckered surface.
- ORIGIN from a Persian phrase meaning 'milk and sugar' (with reference to the alternating stripes in which the fabric was originally woven).

S

see-saw noun **1** a long plank balanced on a fixed support, on each end of which children sit and move up and down by pushing the ground with their feet. **2** a situation characterized by repeated changes from one state or condition to another: *the emotional see-saw of a first love affair.* •verb repeatedly change from one state or condition to another and back again.
– ORIGIN from SAW¹.

seethe verb **1** be filled with strong but unexpressed anger. **2** be crowded with people or things. **3** (of a liquid) boil or churn as if boiling.
– ORIGIN Old English.

see-through adjective transparent or translucent.

segment /seg-muhnt/ noun **1** each of the parts into which something is divided. **2** Geometry a part of a circle cut off by a chord, or a part of a sphere cut off by a plane not passing through the centre. •verb /seg-ment/ divide something into segments.
– DERIVATIVES **segmental** adjective **segmentation** noun.
– ORIGIN Latin *segmentum*.

segregate /seg-ri-gayt/ verb **1** set apart from the rest or from each other: *disabled people should not be segregated from the rest of society.* **2** separate people along racial, sexual, or religious lines.
– ORIGIN Latin *segregare* 'separate from the flock'.

segregation noun **1** the action of segregating or the state of being segregated. **2** the enforced separation of different racial groups in a country, community, or place.
– DERIVATIVES **segregational** adjective **segregationist** adjective & noun.

segue /seg-way/ verb (**segues, segueing** or **seguing, segued**) (in music and film) move without interruption from one song, melody, or scene to another. •noun an instance of this.
– ORIGIN Italian, 'follows'.

seicento /say-chen-toh/ noun the style of Italian art and literature of the 17th century.
– ORIGIN Italian, '600' (shortened from *mille seicento* '1600').

seigneur /say-nyer/ noun a feudal lord; a lord of a medieval manor.
– DERIVATIVES **seigneurial** adjective.
– ORIGIN Old French.

seine /rhymes with rain/ noun a fishing net which hangs vertically in the water with floats at the top and weights at the bottom edge, the ends being drawn together to encircle the fish.
– ORIGIN Greek *sagēnē*.

seismic /syz-mik/ adjective **1** relating to earthquakes or other vibrations of the earth and its crust. **2** very great in size or effect: *seismic shifts in the global economy.*
– DERIVATIVES **seismically** adverb.
– ORIGIN from Greek *seismos* 'earthquake'.

seismicity /syz-mi-si-ti/ noun the occurrence or frequency of earthquakes in a region.

seismograph /syz-muh-grahf/ noun an instrument that measures and records details of earthquakes, such as force and duration.

seismology /syz-mol-uh-ji/ noun the branch of science concerned with earthquakes.

– DERIVATIVES **seismological** adjective **seismologist** noun.

seismometer /syz-mom-i-ter/ noun another term for SEISMOGRAPH.

seize verb **1** take hold of someone or something suddenly and forcibly. **2** take possession of something by force. **3** (of the police or another authority) officially take possession of: *customs officers seized drugs with a street value of over £300 million.* **4** take an opportunity eagerly and decisively. **5** (**seize on**) take eager advantage of. **6** (often **seize up**) (of a machine or part in a machine) become jammed.
– ORIGIN Latin *sacire*, in the phrase *ad proprium sacire* 'claim as one's own'.

seizure noun **1** the action of seizing. **2** a sudden attack of illness, especially a stroke or an epileptic fit.

seldom adverb not often; rarely.
– ORIGIN Old English.

select verb carefully choose someone or something as being the best or most suitable. •adjective **1** carefully chosen as being among the best. **2** used by or consisting of wealthy or sophisticated people: *a select area of London.*
– DERIVATIVES **selectable** adjective.
– ORIGIN Latin *seligere* 'choose'.

select committee noun a small parliamentary committee appointed for a special purpose.

selection noun **1** the action of selecting. **2** a thing or number of things that have been chosen from a wider group. **3** a range of things from which a choice may be made: *a wide selection of hot and cold dishes.*

selective adjective **1** relating to or involving selection. **2** tending to choose carefully: *he's very selective in his reading.* **3** affecting some things and not others: *modern pesticides are selective in effect.*
– DERIVATIVES **selectively** adverb **selectivity** noun.

selector noun **1** Brit. a person appointed to select a team in a sport. **2** a device for selecting a particular gear or other setting of a machine or device.

selenium /si-lee-ni-uhm/ noun a grey crystalline non-metallic chemical element with semiconducting properties.
– ORIGIN Greek *selēnē* 'moon'.

self noun (pl. **selves**) **1** a person's essential being that distinguishes them from other people. **2** a person's particular nature or personality: *he was back to his old self.* •pronoun (pl. **selves**) oneself. •adjective (of a trimming, woven design, etc.) of the same material or colour as the rest of the item.
– ORIGIN Old English.

self- combining form **1** relating to or directed towards oneself or itself: *self-hatred.* **2** by one's own efforts; by its own action: *self-adjusting.* **3** on, in, for, or relating to oneself or itself: *self-adhesive.*

self-absorbed adjective preoccupied with one's own emotions, interests, or situation.
– DERIVATIVES **self-absorption** noun.

self-abuse noun **1** behaviour which causes damage or harm to oneself. **2** dated masturbation.

self-addressed adjective (of an envelope) addressed to oneself.

self-adhesive adjective sticking without needing to be moistened.

self-adjusting adjective (chiefly of machinery) adjusting itself to meet changing requirements.

self-aggrandizement (or self-aggrandisement) noun the action of increasing one's own power or importance.
– DERIVATIVES **self-aggrandizing** adjective.

self-appointed adjective having taken on a position or role without the agreement of other people.

self-assembly noun the construction of a piece of furniture from materials sold in kit form.
– DERIVATIVES **self-assemble** verb.

self-assertion noun the quality of being confident or forceful in the expression of one's opinions.
– DERIVATIVES **self-assertive** adjective **self-assertiveness** noun.

self-assessment noun 1 the process of judging oneself or one's actions or performance. 2 Brit. a system whereby a person is responsible for calculating themselves how much income tax they should pay.

self-assurance noun confidence in one's own abilities or character.
– DERIVATIVES **self-assured** adjective.

self-awareness noun conscious knowledge and understanding of one's own character, feelings, and motives.
– DERIVATIVES **self-aware** adjective.

self-catering adjective Brit. (of a holiday or accommodation) offering facilities for people to cook their own meals.

self-censorship noun the exercising of control over what one says and does.

self-centred adjective preoccupied with oneself and one's own feelings or needs.
– DERIVATIVES **self-centredness** noun.

self-certification noun 1 the practice, for the purpose of claiming sick pay, by which an employee rather than a doctor declares in writing that an absence was due to illness. 2 the practice of giving information about oneself or one's company in a formal statement rather than being obliged to ask a third party to do so.

self-coloured adjective 1 of a single uniform colour. 2 (of a trimming or accessory) of the same colour as the rest of the item.

self-confessed adjective openly admitting to having certain characteristics: *a self-confessed alcoholic.*

self-confidence noun a feeling of trust in one's abilities, qualities, and judgement.
– DERIVATIVES **self-confident** adjective **self-confidently** adverb.

self-congratulation noun too much pride in one's achievements or qualities.
– DERIVATIVES **self-congratulatory** adjective.

self-conscious adjective 1 nervous, awkward, or embarrassed as a result of being worried about how one appears to other people. 2 done deliberately and with full awareness of the effect produced.

– DERIVATIVES **self-consciously** adverb **self-consciousness** noun.

self-consistent adjective not having conflicting parts or aspects; consistent.
– DERIVATIVES **self-consistency** noun.

self-contained adjective 1 complete, or having all that is needed, in itself. 2 chiefly Brit. (of accommodation) having its own kitchen and bathroom, and typically its own private entrance. 3 not depending on or influenced by other people.

self-contradiction noun inconsistency between aspects or parts of a whole.

self-control noun the ability to control one's emotions or behaviour in difficult situations.
– DERIVATIVES **self-controlled** adjective.

self-deception noun the tendency to deceive oneself into believing that a false or unfounded feeling, idea, or situation is true.

self-defeating adjective (of an action or policy) preventing rather than achieving a desired result.

self-defence noun the defending of oneself or one's interests, especially through the use of physical force, which is permitted in certain cases as an answer to a charge of violent crime.
– DERIVATIVES **self-defensive** adjective.

self-denial noun the action of going without or not doing something that one desires to have or do.
– DERIVATIVES **self-denying** adjective.

self-deprecating adjective modest about or critical of oneself.
– DERIVATIVES **self-deprecation** noun **self-deprecatory** adjective.

self-destruct verb (of a device) destroy itself by exploding or disintegrating automatically, having been preset to do so.

self-destructive adjective causing harm to oneself.
– DERIVATIVES **self-destruction** noun **self-destructively** adverb.

self-determination noun 1 the process by which a country gains independence and forms its own government and political system. 2 the right or ability of a person to control their own life.

self-directed adjective 1 (of an emotion, statement, or activity) directed at oneself. 2 (of an activity) under one's own control.
– DERIVATIVES **self-direction** noun.

self-discipline noun the ability to control one's feelings and overcome one's weaknesses.
– DERIVATIVES **self-disciplined** adjective.

self-doubt noun lack of confidence in oneself and one's abilities.

self-drive adjective 1 Brit. (of a hired vehicle) driven by the hirer. 2 (of a holiday) involving use of one's own car rather than transport arranged by the operator.

self-educated adjective educated largely through one's own efforts, rather than by formal instruction.
– DERIVATIVES **self-education** noun.

self-effacing adjective not seeking to attract attention to oneself or one's abilities or achievements.

S

– DERIVATIVES **self-effacement** noun.

self-employed adjective working for oneself as a freelance or the owner of a business rather than for an employer.

– DERIVATIVES **self-employment** noun.

self-esteem noun confidence in one's own worth or abilities.

self-evaluation noun another term for SELF-ASSESSMENT.

self-evident adjective not needing to be demonstrated or explained; obvious.

self-examination noun 1 the study of one's behaviour and motivations. 2 the examination of one's body for any signs of illness.

self-explanatory adjective not needing explanation; clearly understood.

self-expression noun the expression of one's feelings or thoughts, especially in writing, art, music, or dance.

self-fertile adjective (of a plant) capable of self-fertilization.

self-fertilization (or **self-fertilisation**) noun the fertilization of plants and some invertebrate animals by their own pollen or sperm.

– DERIVATIVES **self-fertilize** verb.

self-financing adjective (of an organization or enterprise) having or generating enough income to finance itself.

– DERIVATIVES **self-financed** adjective.

self-fulfilling adjective (of a prediction) bound to become true because people expect it to and so act in a way that will make it happen.

self-governing adjective 1 (of a British hospital or school) having opted out of local authority control. 2 (of a former colony or dependency) administering its own affairs.

– DERIVATIVES **self-government** noun.

self-harm noun deliberate injury to oneself, typically as a sign of psychological or psychiatric disorder. ◆verb commit self-harm.

– DERIVATIVES **self-harmer** noun.

self-help noun the use of one's own efforts and resources to achieve things without relying on other people.

selfhood noun the quality that forms a person's individual character.

self-image noun the idea one has of one's abilities, appearance, and personality.

self-importance noun an exaggerated sense of one's own value or importance.

– DERIVATIVES **self-important** adjective.

self-improvement noun the improvement of one's knowledge, status, or character by one's own efforts.

self-induced adjective brought about by oneself.

self-indulgent adjective allowing oneself to do or have what one wants, especially to an excessive extent.

– DERIVATIVES **self-indulgence** noun.

self-inflicted adjective (of a wound or other harm) caused by oneself.

self-interest noun one's personal interest or advantage, especially when pursued without concern for other people.

– DERIVATIVES **self-interested** adjective.

self-involved adjective wrapped up in oneself

or one's own thoughts.

selfish adjective concerned mainly with one's own needs or wishes at the expense of consideration for other people.

– DERIVATIVES **selfishly** adverb **selfishness** noun.

selfless adjective concerned more with the needs and wishes of other people than with one's own.

– DERIVATIVES **selflessly** adverb **selflessness** noun.

self-limiting adjective (of a disease or condition) ultimately resolving itself without medical treatment.

self-love noun care or concern for one's own well-being and happiness.

self-made adjective having become successful or rich by one's own efforts.

self-medicate verb treat oneself with medicine without seeking any medical supervision.

– DERIVATIVES **self-medication** noun.

self-motivated adjective motivated to do something because of one's own enthusiasm or interest, without needing pressure from others.

– DERIVATIVES **self-motivation** noun.

self-mutilation noun deliberate injury to one's own body.

self-opinionated adjective having too high a regard for one's own opinions and unwilling to listen to those of other people.

self-perpetuating adjective able to continue indefinitely without the assistance of anything or anyone else.

self-pity noun excessive concern with and unhappiness over one's own troubles.

– DERIVATIVES **self-pitying** adjective.

self-policing noun the process of keeping order or maintaining control within a community without being accountable to an outside authority.

self-pollination noun the pollination of a flower by pollen from the same plant.

– DERIVATIVES **self-pollinate** verb.

self-portrait noun a portrait by an artist of himself or herself.

self-possessed adjective calm, confident, and in control of one's feelings.

– DERIVATIVES **self-possession** noun.

self-preservation noun the protection of oneself from harm or death, regarded as a basic instinct in human beings and animals.

self-proclaimed adjective describing oneself as something, without the agreement or approval of other people: *self-proclaimed experts.*

self-propelled adjective moving or able to move without external propulsion.

– DERIVATIVES **self-propelling** adjective.

self-raising flour noun Brit. flour that contains baking powder.

self-realization (or **self-realisation**) noun fulfilment of one's own potential.

self-referential adjective (especially of a literary or other creative work) making references to itself, its author or creator, or their other work.

self-regard noun 1 consideration for oneself. 2 too much pride in oneself; vanity.

– DERIVATIVES **self-regarding** adjective.

S

self-regulating adjective regulating itself without intervention from external organizations, systems, etc.
 – DERIVATIVES **self-regulation** noun **self-regulatory** adjective.

self-reliance noun reliance on one's own powers and resources rather than those of other people.
 – DERIVATIVES **self-reliant** adjective.

self-respect noun pride and confidence in oneself.
 – DERIVATIVES **self-respecting** adjective.

self-restraint noun self-control.

self-righteous adjective certain that one is totally correct or morally superior to other people.
 – DERIVATIVES **self-righteously** adverb **self-righteousness** noun.

self-rule noun government of a state or area by its own people.

self-sacrifice noun the giving up of one's own interests or wishes in order to help other people.
 – DERIVATIVES **self-sacrificing** adjective.

selfsame adjective (**the selfsame**) the very same.

self-satisfied adjective smugly pleased with oneself.
 – DERIVATIVES **self-satisfaction** noun.

self-seed verb (of a plant) propagate itself by the seed it produces, without human intervention.
 – DERIVATIVES **self-seeder** noun.

self-seeking adjective concerned with one's own welfare and interests rather than those of other people.
 – DERIVATIVES **self-seeker** noun.

self-service adjective (of a shop or restaurant) in which customers choose goods for themselves and pay at a checkout.

self-serving adjective another term for SELF-SEEKING.

self-starter noun an ambitious person who acts on their own initiative.

self-styled adjective using a description or title that one has given oneself: *self-styled experts.*

self-sufficient adjective **1** able to support oneself or produce what one needs without outside help. **2** emotionally and intellectually independent.
 – DERIVATIVES **self-sufficiency** noun.

self-supporting adjective **1** having the resources to be able to survive without outside help. **2** staying up or upright without being supported by something else.

self-sustaining adjective able to continue in a healthy state without outside help.
 – DERIVATIVES **self-sustained** adjective.

self-tanner noun a lotion containing ingredients that react with the skin to produce an artificial tan.
 – DERIVATIVES **self-tanning** adjective.

self-tapping adjective (of a screw) able to cut a thread in the material into which it is inserted.

self-taught adjective having gained knowledge or skill by reading or experience rather than through formal teaching or training.

self-timer noun a mechanism in a camera that introduces a delay between the operation of the shutter release and the opening of the shutter, enabling the photographer to be included in the photograph.

self-willed adjective determined to have one's own way, without concern for the wishes of other people.

self-worth noun self-esteem.

sell verb (past and past part. **sold**) **1** hand over something in exchange for money. **2** offer goods or property for sale. **3** (of goods) be bought in particular amounts or for a particular price: *the book didn't sell well.* **4** (**sell out**) sell all of one's stock of something. **5** (**sell up**) sell all of one's property or assets. **6** persuade someone that something has particular good qualities. **7** (**sell out**) abandon one's principles because it is expedient to do so. **8** (**sell someone out**) betray someone for one's own financial or material benefit.
 – PHRASES **sell someone/thing short** fail to recognize or describe the true value of someone or something.
 – DERIVATIVES **sellable** adjective.
 – ORIGIN Old English.

sell-by date noun **1** a date marked on packaged food indicating the recommended time by which it should be sold. **2** informal a time after which something or someone is no longer considered desirable or effective.

seller noun **1** a person who sells something. **2** a product that sells in a particular way.

selling point noun a feature of a product for sale that makes it attractive to customers.

sell-off noun a sale of business assets at a low price, carried out in order to dispose of them rather than as part of normal trading.

Sellotape Brit. noun trademark transparent adhesive tape. •verb fasten or stick something with Sellotape.
 – ORIGIN from an alteration of CELLULOSE + TAPE.

sell-out noun **1** the selling of the whole stock of something. **2** an event for which all tickets are sold. **3** a sale of a business or company. **4** a betrayal.

seltzer /ˈselt-zer/ noun dated carbonated mineral water.
 – ORIGIN from German *Selterser.*

selvedge /ˈsel-vij/ (chiefly N. Amer. also **selvage**) noun an edge produced on woven fabric during manufacture that prevents it from unravelling.
 – ORIGIN from SELF + EDGE.

selves plural of SELF.

semantic /si-ˈman-tik/ adjective relating to the meaning of words and sentences.
 – DERIVATIVES **semantically** adverb.
 – ORIGIN Greek *sēmantikos* 'significant'.

semantics plural noun (usu. treated as sing.) **1** the branch of linguistics concerned with meaning. **2** the meaning of a word, phrase, sentence, or piece of writing.

semaphore noun **1** a system of sending messages by holding the arms or two flags or poles in certain positions that represent letters of the alphabet. **2** a device for sending messages in this way, consisting of an upright with movable parts. •verb send a message by

semaphore or by signals resembling semaphore.
- ORIGIN French *sémaphore*.

semblance noun the outward appearance or apparent form of something.
- ORIGIN from Old French *sembler* 'seem'.

semen /see-muhn/ noun the fluid containing spermatozoa that is produced by men and male animals.
- ORIGIN Latin, 'seed'.

semester /si-mess-ter/ noun a half-year term in a school or university, especially in North America.
- ORIGIN from Latin *semestris* 'six-monthly'.

semi noun (pl. semis) informal 1 Brit. a semi-detached house. 2 a semi-final.

semi- prefix 1 half: *semicircular.* 2 partly; in some degree: *semi-conscious.*
- ORIGIN Latin.

semi-automatic adjective 1 partially automatic. 2 (of a firearm) able to load bullets automatically but not fire continuously.

semibreve /sem-i-breev/ noun Brit. a musical note having the time value of two minims or four crotchets, represented by a ring with no stem.

semicircle noun a half of a circle or of its circumference.
- DERIVATIVES semicircular adjective.

semicircular canals plural noun a system of three fluid-filled bony channels in the inner ear, involved in sensing and maintaining balance.

semicolon /sem-i-koh-luhn, sem-i-koh-lon/ noun a punctuation mark (;) indicating a longer pause than that indicated by a comma.

semiconductor noun a solid, e.g. silicon, whose capacity to conduct electricity is limited but increases with temperature.
- DERIVATIVES semiconducting adjective.

semi-conscious adjective partially conscious.

semi-detached adjective Brit. (of a house) joined to another house on one side by a common wall.

semi-double adjective (of a flower) intermediate between single and double, with the additional petals not completely concealing the centre of the flower.

semi-final noun (in sport) a match or round immediately preceding the final.
- DERIVATIVES semi-finalist noun.

semi-fluid adjective having a thick consistency between solid and liquid.

semi-liquid adjective another term for SEMI-FLUID.

Semillon /sem-i-yon/ noun a variety of white wine grape grown in France, Australia, and South America.
- ORIGIN French, from Latin *semen* 'seed'.

seminal adjective 1 (of a work, event, or idea) strongly influencing later developments. 2 referring to semen. 3 relating to the seed of a plant.
- DERIVATIVES seminally adverb.
- ORIGIN Latin *seminalis*, from *semen* 'seed'.

seminar /sem-i-nar/ noun 1 a conference or other meeting for discussion or training. 2 a small group of students at university, meeting to discuss topics with a teacher.

- ORIGIN German, from Latin *seminarium* 'seed plot'.

seminary /sem-i-nuh-ri/ noun (pl. seminaries) a training college for priests or rabbis.
- DERIVATIVES seminarian /sem-i-nair-i-uhn/ noun.
- ORIGIN Latin *seminarium* 'seed plot', from *semen* 'seed'.

semiology /sem-i-ol-uh-ji/ noun another term for SEMIOTICS.
- DERIVATIVES semiological adjective semiologist noun.
- ORIGIN from Greek *sēmeion* 'sign'.

semiotics /sem-i-ot-iks/ plural noun (treated as sing.) the study of signs and symbols and their use or interpretation.
- DERIVATIVES semiotic adjective semiotician /sem-i-uh-ti-sh'n/ noun.
- ORIGIN from Greek *sēmeiotikos* 'of signs'.

semipermeable adjective (of a cell membrane) allowing small molecules to pass through but not large ones.

semi-precious adjective referring to minerals which can be used as gems but are considered to be less valuable than precious stones.

semiquaver /sem-i-kway-ver/ noun Brit. a musical note having the time value of a sixteenth of a semibreve or half a quaver, represented by a large dot with a two-hooked stem.

semi-retired adjective having retired from employment but continuing to work part-time or occasionally.
- DERIVATIVES semi-retirement noun.

semi-skilled adjective (of work or a worker) needing or having some, but not extensive, training.

semi-skimmed adjective Brit. (of milk) having had some of the cream removed.

semi-solid adjective having a very thick, sticky consistency; slightly thicker than semi-fluid.

Semite /see-myt/ noun a member of a people speaking a Semitic language, in particular the Jews and Arabs.
- ORIGIN from Greek *Sēm* 'Shem', son of Noah in the Bible, from whom these people are traditionally descended.

Semitic /si-mit-ik/ noun a family of languages that includes Hebrew, Arabic, and Aramaic.
• adjective relating to these languages or their speakers.

semitone noun Brit. the smallest interval used in classical Western music, equal to a twelfth of an octave or half a tone.

semolina noun the hard grains left after the milling of flour, used in puddings and in pasta.
- ORIGIN Italian *semolino.*

sempiternal /sem-pi-ter-nuhl/ adjective literary eternal and unchanging; everlasting.
- ORIGIN Latin *sempiternus.*

Semtex noun a type of plastic explosive.
- ORIGIN probably a blend of *Semtin* (a village in the Czech Republic near the place of production) and EXPLOSIVE.

SEN abbreviation (in the UK) State Enrolled Nurse.

senate noun 1 a law-making or governing body, especially the smaller upper assembly in the US, US states, France, and other countries.

2 the governing body of a university or college. **3** the state council of the ancient Roman republic and empire.
– ORIGIN Latin *senatus*, from *senex* 'old man'.

senator noun a member of a senate.
– DERIVATIVES **senatorial** adjective **senatorship** noun.

send verb (past and past part. **sent**) **1** cause something to go or be taken to a destination. **2** order or instruct someone to go somewhere. **3** move something sharply or quickly. **4** cause to be in a particular state: *the traffic nearly sent me crazy.*
– PHRASES **send someone down** Brit. **1** expel a student from a university. **2** informal sentence someone to imprisonment. **send for 1** order someone to come. **2** order something by post. **send someone off** (of a football or rugby referee) order a player to leave the field and take no further part in the game. **send someone to Coventry** chiefly Brit. refuse to associate with or speak to someone. [perhaps from the unpopularity of royalist soldiers or prisoners quartered in *Coventry* (sympathetic to parliament) during the English Civil War.] **send someone up** informal, chiefly Brit. make fun of someone by imitating them in an exaggerated way. **send word** send a message to someone.
– DERIVATIVES **sender** noun.
– ORIGIN Old English.

send-off noun a gathering of people to wish good luck to someone who is leaving.

send-up noun informal an exaggerated imitation of someone or something, done in order to make fun of them.

Senegalese /sen-i-guh-**leez**/ noun (pl. **Senegalese**) a person from Senegal, a country on the coast of West Africa. •adjective relating to Senegal.

senescence /si-**ness**-uhnss/ noun the process by which a living thing gradually deteriorates with age.
– DERIVATIVES **senescent** adjective.
– ORIGIN Latin *senescere*, from *senex* 'old'.

seneschal /**sen**-i-shuhl/ noun **1** the steward of a noble's or monarch's house in medieval times. **2** chiefly historical a governor or other administrative or judicial officer.
– ORIGIN Latin *seniscalus*.

senile /**see**-nyl/ adjective having the weaknesses or diseases of old age, especially a loss of mental abilities.
– DERIVATIVES **senility** noun.
– ORIGIN Latin *senilis*, from *senex* 'old man'.

senile dementia noun severe mental deterioration in old age, with loss of memory and lack of control of bodily functions.

senior adjective **1** relating to older people. **2** high or higher in rank or status. **3** Brit. relating to schoolchildren above the age of about eleven. **4** US relating to the final year at a university or high school. **5** (after a name) referring to the the elder of two with the same name in a family. •noun **1** a person who is a specified number of years older than someone else: *she was two years his senior.* **2** a student at a senior school, or a student in one of the older classes in a school. **3** (in sport) a competitor of above a certain age or of the highest status. **4** an elderly person, especially

an old-age pensioner.
– DERIVATIVES **seniority** noun.
– ORIGIN Latin, from *senex* 'old'.

senior aircraftman (or **senior aircraftwoman**) noun a rank in the RAF, above leading aircraftman (or leading aircraftwoman).

senior citizen noun an elderly person, especially an old-age pensioner.

senior common room noun Brit. a room used for social purposes by fellows, lecturers, and other senior members of a college.

senior nursing officer noun Brit. the person in charge of nursing services in a hospital.

senior registrar noun Brit. a hospital doctor undergoing specialist training, one grade below that of consultant.

Senior Service noun Brit. the Royal Navy.

senna noun a laxative prepared from the dried pods of the cassia tree.
– ORIGIN Arabic.

señor /sen-**yor**/ noun a title or form of address for a Spanish-speaking man, corresponding to *Mr* or *sir*.

señora /sen-**yor**-uh/ noun a title of form of address for a Spanish-speaking woman, corresponding to *Mrs* or *madam*.

señorita /sen-yuh-**ree**-tuh/ noun a title or form of address for a Spanish-speaking unmarried woman, corresponding to *Miss*.

sensate /**sen**-sayt/ adjective becoming aware of things through the senses.

sensation noun **1** a physical feeling resulting from something that happens to or comes into contact with the body. **2** the ability to have such feelings. **3** a general awareness or impression not caused by anything that can be seen or defined: *the eerie sensation that she was being watched.* **4** a widespread reaction of interest and excitement, or a person or thing causing it.

sensational adjective **1** causing or intending to cause great public interest and excitement. **2** informal very impressive or attractive.
– DERIVATIVES **sensationally** adverb.

sensationalism noun (in the media) the use of exciting or shocking stories or language at the expense of accuracy, in order to arouse public interest or excitement.
– DERIVATIVES **sensationalist** noun & adjective **sensationalistic** adjective.

sensationalize (or **sensationalise**) verb present information in an exaggerated way in order to make it seem more interesting or exciting.

sense noun **1** any of the faculties of sight, smell, taste, and touch, by which the body becomes aware of external things. **2** a feeling that something is the case. **3** (**sense of**) awareness or sensitivity to: *a sense of direction.* **4** a sensible and practical attitude to situations or problems. **5** reason or purpose; good judgement: *there's no sense in standing in the rain.* **6** a meaning of a word or expression or the way in which a word or expression can be interpreted. •verb **1** become aware of something by a sense or senses. **2** be vaguely aware of something. **3** (of a machine or similar device) detect something.

S

- PHRASES **come to one's senses 1** regain consciousness. **2** think and behave reasonably or sensibly again. **make sense** be understandable, justifiable, or sensible. **make sense of** manage to understand something.
- ORIGIN Latin *sensus* 'faculty of feeling, thought, meaning', from *sentire* 'feel'.

sensei /sen-**say**/ noun (pl. same) (in martial arts) a teacher.
- ORIGIN Japanese, from *sen* 'previous' + *sei* 'birth'.

senseless adjective **1** lacking meaning, purpose, or common sense. **2** unconscious.
- DERIVATIVES **senselessly** adverb **senselessness** noun.

sense organ noun an organ of the body which responds to external stimuli by sending impulses to the brain.

sensibility noun (pl. **sensibilities**) **1** the ability to appreciate and respond to complex emotions, especially as expressed in art and literature. **2** (**sensibilities**) a person's feelings which are liable to be easily shocked or offended.

sensible adjective **1** having or showing common sense. **2** practical and functional rather than decorative. **3** (**sensible of/to**) formal or dated aware of: *I am very sensible to your concerns.*
- DERIVATIVES **sensibly** adverb.

sensitive adjective **1** quick to detect, respond to, or be affected by slight changes or influences. **2** appreciating the feelings of other people. **3** easily offended or upset. **4** (of a subject or issue) needing careful handling because likely to cause offence or controversy. **5** (of information) kept secret to avoid endangering national security.
- DERIVATIVES **sensitively** adverb **sensitiveness** noun.
- ORIGIN Latin *sensitivus*, from *sentire* 'feel'.

sensitive plant noun a tropical American plant of the pea family, whose leaves bend down when touched.

sensitivity noun (pl. **sensitivities**) **1** the quality or condition of being sensitive. **2** (**sensitivities**) a person's feelings which might be easily offended or hurt.

sensitize (or **sensitise**) verb make someone or something sensitive to or aware of something.
- DERIVATIVES **sensitization** noun **sensitizer** noun.

sensor noun a device which detects or measures a physical property.

sensory adjective relating to sensation or the senses.
- DERIVATIVES **sensorily** adverb.

sensual /sen-**shuu**-uhl/ adjective relating to the physical senses as a source of pleasure, especially sexual pleasure.
- DERIVATIVES **sensualist** noun **sensuality** noun **sensually** adverb.

USAGE: Strictly speaking there is a difference between **sensual** and **sensuous**. Sensual is used in relation to pleasure experienced through the senses, especially sexual pleasure, while **sensuous** is a more neutral term, meaning 'relating to the senses rather than the intellect'.

sensuous /sen-**shuu**-uhss/ adjective **1** relating

to or affecting the senses rather than the intellect. **2** attractive or pleasing physically, especially sexually.
- DERIVATIVES **sensuously** adverb **sensuousness** noun.
- ORIGIN from Latin *sensus* 'sense'.

sent[1] past and past participle of **SEND**.

sent[2] noun a unit of money of Estonia, equal to one hundredth of a kroon.
- ORIGIN respelling of **CENT**.

sentence noun **1** a set of words that is complete in itself, conveying a statement, question, exclamation, or command. **2** the punishment given to someone found guilty by a court. • verb declare in a court that a person found guilty is to receive a particular punishment.
- ORIGIN from Latin *sententia* 'opinion'.

sententious /sen-**ten**-shuhss/ adjective given to making pompous comments on moral issues.
- DERIVATIVES **sententiously** adverb **sententiousness** noun.
- ORIGIN from Latin *sententia* 'opinion'.

sentient /sen-ti-uhnt, sen-shuhnt/ adjective able to perceive or feel things.
- DERIVATIVES **sentience** noun.
- ORIGIN from Latin *sentire* 'to feel'.

sentiment noun **1** a view, opinion, or feeling. **2** exaggerated and self-indulgent feelings of tenderness, sadness, or nostalgia.
- ORIGIN Latin *sentimentum*, from *sentire* 'feel'.

sentimental adjective **1** connected with or caused by feelings of tenderness, sadness, or nostalgia: *he had a sentimental attachment to the place.* **2** having or causing such feelings in a way that is exaggerated or self-indulgent: *a sentimental love song.*
- DERIVATIVES **sentimentalism** noun **sentimentalist** noun **sentimentality** noun **sentimentally** adverb.

sentimentalize (or **sentimentalise**) verb present or treat something in a sentimental way.

sentimental value noun the value of an object which comes from its personal or emotional associations rather than its material worth.

sentinel /sen-ti-nuhl/ noun a soldier or guard whose job is to stand and keep watch.
- ORIGIN Italian *sentinella*.

sentry noun (pl. **sentries**) a soldier stationed to keep guard or to control access to a place.
- ORIGIN perhaps from former *centrinel*, from **SENTINEL**.

sentry box noun a structure with an open front, providing shelter for a standing sentry.

sepal /sep-uhl, see-puhl/ noun each of the leaf-like parts of a flower that surround the petals, enclosing them when the flower is in bud.
- ORIGIN from Greek *skepē* 'covering'.

separable adjective able to be separated or treated separately.
- DERIVATIVES **separability** noun.

separate adjective /sep-uh-ruht, sep-ruht/ **1** forming or seen as a unit apart or by itself; not joined or united with others. **2** different; distinct. • verb /sep-uh-rayt/ **1** move or come apart. **2** form a distinction or boundary

S

between: *a footpath separated their garden from the shore.* **3** stop living together as a couple. **4** divide into component parts: *the milk had separated into curds and whey.* **5** extract or remove something for use or because it is unwanted. **6** distinguish between or from others; consider individually: *it is impossible to separate belief from emotion.* • noun /sep-uh-ruht/ (**separates**) individual items of clothing designed to be worn in different combinations.
– DERIVATIVES **separately** adverb **separateness** noun **separator** noun.
– ORIGIN from Latin *separare*.

separation noun **1** the action of separating or the state of being separated. **2** the state in which a husband and wife remain married but live apart.

separatist noun a person who supports the separation of a particular group from a larger body on the basis of ethnic origin, religion, etc. • adjective relating to such separation or those who support it.
– DERIVATIVES **separatism** noun.

Sephardi /si-**far**-di/ noun (pl. **Sephardim** /si-**far**-dim/) a Jew of Spanish or Portuguese descent. Compare with **ASHKENAZI**.
– DERIVATIVES **Sephardic** adjective.
– ORIGIN Hebrew, from the name of a country mentioned in the Bible (Obadiah 20) and taken to be Spain.

sepia /**see**-pi-uh/ noun **1** a reddish-brown colour, associated particularly with early photographs. **2** a brown pigment prepared from cuttlefish ink, used in drawing and in watercolours.
– ORIGIN Greek, 'cuttlefish'.

sepoy /**see**-poy, si-**poy**/ noun historical an Indian soldier serving under British or other European orders.
– ORIGIN Urdu and Persian, 'soldier'.

seppuku /sep-**poo**-koo/ noun another term for **HARA-KIRI**.
– ORIGIN Japanese, from words meaning 'to cut' and 'abdomen'.

sepsis /**sep**-siss/ noun the presence in tissues of harmful bacteria, typically through infection of a wound.
– ORIGIN Greek, from *sēpein* 'make rotten'.

Sept. abbreviation September.

septa plural of **SEPTUM**.

septal adjective relating to a septum or septa.

September noun the ninth month of the year.
– ORIGIN from Latin *septem* 'seven' (being originally the seventh month of the Roman year).

septet /sep-**tet**/ noun a group of seven people playing music or singing together.
– ORIGIN from Latin *septem* 'seven'.

septic /**sep**-tik/ adjective (of a wound or a part of the body) infected with bacteria.
– ORIGIN Greek *sēptikos*, from *sēpein* 'make rotten'.

USAGE: Do not confuse **septic** with **sceptic**. **Septic** means 'infected with bacteria' (*a septic finger*), whereas **sceptic** means 'a person who tends to question or doubt accepted opinions' (*numerous sceptics poured scorn on his claim*).

septicaemia /sep-ti-**see**-mi-uh/ (US

septicemia) noun blood poisoning caused by bacteria.

septic tank noun a underground tank in which sewage is allowed to decompose through the action of bacteria before draining away into the ground.

septuagenarian /sep-tyuu-uh-ji-**nair**-i-uhn/ noun a person who is between 70 and 79 years old.
– ORIGIN Latin *septuagenarius*.

Septuagint /sep-tyuu-uh-jint/ noun a Greek version of the Hebrew Bible (or Old Testament), including the Apocrypha, produced in the 3rd and 2nd centuries BC.
– ORIGIN from Latin *septuaginta* 'seventy', because of the tradition that it was produced by seventy-two translators working independently.

septum /**sep**-tuhm/ noun (pl. **septa** /**sep**-tuh/) a partition separating two cavities in the body, such as that between the nostrils.
– ORIGIN Latin.

septuple /sep-**tyuu**-p'l, sep-**tyoo**-p'l/ adjective **1** consisting of seven parts. **2** (of time in music) having seven beats in a bar. **3** seven times as much or as many.
– ORIGIN from Latin *septem* 'seven'.

septuplet /**sep**-tyuu-plit, sep-**tyoo**-plit/ noun each of seven children born at one birth.

sepulchral /si-**pul**-kruhl/ adjective **1** gloomy and solemn: *a speech delivered in sepulchral tones.* **2** relating to a tomb or burial.
– DERIVATIVES **sepulchrally** adverb.

sepulchre /**sep**-uhl-ker/ (US **sepulcher**) noun a stone tomb or monument in which a dead person is laid or buried.
– ORIGIN Latin *sepulcrum* 'burial place'.

seq. (also **seqq.**) adverb short for **ET SEQ.**

sequel noun **1** a book, film, or programme that continues the story or develops the theme of an earlier one. **2** something that takes place after or as a result of an earlier event.
– ORIGIN Latin *sequella*, from *sequi* 'follow'.

sequela /si-**kway**-luh/ noun (pl. **sequelae** /si-**kway**-lee/) a medical condition which is the consequence of a previous disease or injury.
– ORIGIN Latin, from *sequi* 'follow'.

sequence noun **1** a particular order in which related things follow each other. **2** a set of related things that follow each other in a particular order. **3** a part of a film dealing with one particular event or topic. **4** Music a repetition of a phrase or melody at a higher or lower pitch. • verb **1** arrange something in a sequence. **2** play or record music with a sequencer.
– ORIGIN Latin *sequentia*, from *sequi* 'follow'.

sequencer noun an electronic device for storing sequences of musical notes, chords, or rhythms and transmitting them to an electronic musical instrument.

sequential adjective forming or following in a logical order or sequence.
– DERIVATIVES **sequentially** adverb.

sequester /si-**kwess**-ter/ verb **1** isolate or hide away: *he sequestered himself in his studio.* **2** another term for **SEQUESTRATE**.

S

- ORIGIN Latin *sequestrare* 'commit for safekeeping'.

sequestrate /si-**kwess**-trayt, see-kwi-strayt/ **verb 1** take legal possession of assets until a debt has been paid or other claims have been met. **2** take forcible possession of something.
- DERIVATIVES **sequestration** noun **sequestrator** noun.

sequin noun a small shiny disc sewn on to clothing for decoration.
- DERIVATIVES **sequinned** (also **sequined**) adjective.
- ORIGIN from Italian *zecchino*, first referring to a former Venetian gold coin.

sequoia /si-**kwoy**-uh/ noun a redwood tree, especially the California redwood.
- ORIGIN named after *Sequoya*, a Cherokee Indian scholar.

sera plural of SERUM.

seraglio /si-**rah**-li-oh/ noun (pl. **seraglios**) **1** the women's rooms in a Muslim house or palace. **2** a harem.
- ORIGIN Italian *serraglio*.

serape /se-**rah**-pay/ (also **sarape**) noun a shawl or blanket worn as a cloak by people from Latin America.
- ORIGIN Mexican Spanish.

seraph /se-**ruhf**/ noun (pl. **seraphim** /se-ruh-fim/ or **seraphs**) a type of angel associated with light and purity.
- DERIVATIVES **seraphic** adjective **seraphically** adverb.
- ORIGIN Hebrew.

Serb noun a person from Serbia.

Serbian noun **1** the language of the Serbs. **2** a Serb. ●adjective relating to Serbia.

Serbo-Croat /ser-boh-**kroh**-at/ (also **Serbo-Croatian** /ser-boh-kroh-**ay**-sh'n/) noun the language spoken in Serbia, Croatia, and elsewhere in the former Yugoslavia.

sere adjective variant spelling of SEAR.

serenade noun a piece of music sung or played in the open air at night, especially by a man under the window of the woman he loves. ●verb entertain someone with a serenade.
- DERIVATIVES **serenader** noun.
- ORIGIN Italian *serenata*.

serendipity /se-ruhn-**dip**-i-ti/ noun the occurrence of events by chance in a beneficial or lucky way: *many cancer drugs have been discovered through serendipity*.
- DERIVATIVES **serendipitous** adjective **serendipitously** adverb.
- ORIGIN coined by the English politician Horace Walpole from *The Three Princes of Serendip*, a fairy tale in which the heroes were always making fortunate discoveries (*Serendip* was a former name for Sri Lanka).

serene adjective calm, peaceful, and untroubled; tranquil.
- DERIVATIVES **serenely** adverb **serenity** noun.
- ORIGIN Latin *serenus*.

serf noun (in the feudal system) an agricultural labourer who was tied to working on a particular estate.
- DERIVATIVES **serfdom** noun.
- ORIGIN Latin *servus* 'slave'.

serge /*rhymes with* urge/ noun a hard-wearing woollen or worsted fabric.

- ORIGIN Old French *sarge*.

sergeant /**sar**-juhnt/ noun **1** a rank of non-commissioned officer in the army or air force, above corporal. **2** Brit. a police officer ranking below an inspector.
- ORIGIN Old French *sergent*.

sergeant-at-arms noun N. Amer. variant spelling of SERJEANT-AT-ARMS.

sergeant major noun a warrant officer in the British army who assists with administrative duties.

serial adjective **1** consisting of or taking place in a series. **2** repeatedly committing the same offence or following a characteristic behaviour pattern: *a serial killer*. **3** Computing (of a device) involving the transfer of data as a single sequence of bits. ●noun a story or play published or broadcast in regular instalments.
- DERIVATIVES **seriality** noun **serially** adverb.

serialism noun a technique of musical composition using the twelve notes of the chromatic scale (one that rises or falls by semitones) in a fixed order which is subject to change only in specific ways.
- DERIVATIVES **serialist** adjective & noun.

serialize (or **serialise**) verb **1** publish or broadcast a story or play in regular instalments. **2** arrange something in a series.
- DERIVATIVES **serialization** noun.

serial number noun an identification number showing the position of a manufactured item in a series.

series noun (pl. same) **1** a number of similar or related things coming one after another. **2** a sequence of related television or radio programmes. **3** Geology a range of rock strata corresponding to an epoch in time: *the Pliocene series*. **4** Mathematics a set of quantities constituting a progression or having values determined by a common relation.
- PHRASES **in series** (of electrical components or circuits) arranged so that the current passes through each in turn.
- ORIGIN Latin, 'row, chain'.

serif /**se**-rif/ noun a slight projection finishing off a stroke of a letter, as in T contrasted with T.
- ORIGIN perhaps from Dutch *schreef* 'dash, line'.

serio-comic /seer-i-oh-**kom**-ik/ adjective combining serious and comic elements.

serious adjective **1** dangerous or very bad: *serious injury*. **2** needing or showing careful consideration or action: *marriage is a serious matter*. **3** solemn or sensible. **4** sincere and in earnest. **5** informal substantial in size, number, or quality: *every minute is costing you serious money*.
- DERIVATIVES **seriousness** noun.
- ORIGIN Latin *serius*.

seriously adverb **1** in a serious way. **2** very; extremely: *he's seriously rich*.

serjeant-at-arms (also N. Amer. **sergeant-at-arms**) noun (pl. **serjeants-at-arms**) an official of a law-making body whose duties include maintaining order and security.

sermon noun **1** a talk on a religious or moral subject, especially one given during a church service. **2** informal a long or boring reprimand.
- DERIVATIVES **sermonic** adjective.

– ORIGIN Latin, 'discourse, talk'.

sermonize (or **sermonise**) verb give a long talk about morals to someone.

serology /si-uh-**rol**-uh-ji/ noun the scientific study or examination of blood serum.
– DERIVATIVES **serologic** adjective **serological** adjective **serologist** noun.

seropositive /si-uh-roh-**pos**-i-tiv/ (or **seronegative** /si-uh-roh-**neg**-uh-tiv/) adjective giving a positive (or negative) result in a test of blood serum, especially for the presence of a virus.

serotonin /se-ruh-**toh**-nin/ noun a compound in blood which constricts the blood vessels and brings about the transfer of impulses from one nerve to another.
– ORIGIN from **SERUM** + **TONIC**.

serous /**see**-ruhss/ adjective relating to, resembling, or producing serum.

serpent noun literary a large snake.
– ORIGIN from Latin *serpere* 'to creep'.

serpentine /**ser**-puhn-tyn/ adjective like a serpent or snake, especially in being winding or twisting. •noun a dark green mineral that is often mottled or spotted like a snake's skin.

SERPS /serps/ abbreviation (in the UK) state earnings-related pension scheme.

serrated adjective having a jagged edge like the teeth of a saw.
– ORIGIN Latin *serratus*.

serration noun a tooth or point of a jagged edge.

serried adjective (of rows of people or things) standing close together.
– ORIGIN probably from French *serré* 'close together'.

serum /**seer**-uhm/ noun (pl. **sera** /**seer**-uh/ or **serums**) the thin amber-coloured liquid which separates out when blood has clotted.
– ORIGIN Latin, 'whey'.

servant noun 1 a person employed to perform domestic duties in a household or for a person. 2 a person providing support or service for an organization or person: *he was a great servant of the Labour Party.*
– ORIGIN Old French, 'person serving'.

serve verb 1 perform duties or provide a service for: *the hospital serves a large area of Wales.* 2 be employed as a member of the armed forces. 3 spend a period in office, in an apprenticeship, or in prison. 4 present someone with food or drink. 5 attend to a customer in a shop. 6 fulfil a purpose. 7 treat in a specified way: *homeowners wonder if they are being fairly served.* 8 (of food or drink) be enough for a specified number of people. 9 Law formally deliver a summons or writ to the person to whom it is addressed. 10 (in tennis and other racket sports) hit the ball or shuttlecock to begin play for each point of a game. 11 (of a male breeding animal) mate with a female. •noun an act of serving in tennis, badminton, etc.
– PHRASES **serve someone right** be someone's deserved punishment or bad luck. **serve one's** (or **its**) **turn** be useful.
– ORIGIN Latin *servire*.

server noun 1 a person or thing that serves. 2 a computer or program which controls or

supplies information to a computer network.

servery noun (pl. **serveries**) Brit. a counter, hatch, or room from which meals are served.

service noun 1 the action of serving, helping, or providing: *he complained about the poor service in the hotel.* 2 a period of employment with an organization. 3 assistance or advice given to customers. 4 a ceremony of religious worship that follows a set form. 5 a system supplying a public need such as transport, or utilities such as water. 6 a department or organization run by the state: *the probation service.* 7 (**the services**) the armed forces. 8 (often in phrase **in service**) employment as a servant. 9 a set of matching crockery used for serving a particular meal. 10 (in tennis, badminton, etc.) a serve. 11 a regular inspection and maintenance of a vehicle or other machine. •verb 1 perform regular maintenance or repair work on a vehicle or machine. 2 provide a service or services for someone. 3 pay interest on a debt. 4 (of a male animal) mate with a female animal.
– PHRASES **in** (or **out of**) **service** available (or not available) for use.
– ORIGIN Latin *servitium* 'slavery'.

serviceable adjective 1 usable or in working order. 2 useful and hard-wearing rather than attractive.
– DERIVATIVES **serviceability** noun.

service area noun Brit. a roadside area where services are available to motorists.

service charge noun 1 a charge added to a bill for service in a restaurant. 2 a charge made for other services, such as maintenance on a leased property.

service flat noun Brit. a rented flat in which cleaning and similar domestic tasks are provided by the management.

service industry noun a business that provides a service for a customer rather than manufacturing goods.

serviceman (or **servicewoman**) noun (pl. **servicemen** or **servicewomen**) 1 a person serving in the armed forces. 2 a person providing maintenance for machinery.

service provider noun a company which provides access to the Internet for its subscribers.

service road noun a minor road running parallel to a main road and giving access to houses, shops, or businesses.

service station noun a garage selling petrol and oil and sometimes offering vehicle maintenance.

serviette noun Brit. a table napkin.
– ORIGIN Old French.

servile adjective 1 excessively willing to serve or please others. 2 relating to a slave or slaves.
– DERIVATIVES **servilely** adverb **servility** noun.
– ORIGIN Latin *servilis.*

serving noun a quantity of food suitable for or served to one person.

servitor noun old use a servant or attendant.

servitude /**ser**-vi-tyood/ noun the state of being a slave or of being under the complete control of someone more powerful.
– ORIGIN Latin *servitudo.*

servomechanism noun a powered

mechanism producing motion or forces at a higher level of energy than the input level, e.g. in the brakes and steering of large motor vehicles.

servomotor noun the element in a servomechanism that provides mechanical motion.

sesame /sess-uh-mi/ noun a tall plant of tropical and subtropical areas, grown for its oil-rich seeds.
– PHRASES **open sesame** a free or unrestricted means of entering or accessing something. [from the magic words spoken in the tale of Ali Baba and the Forty Thieves.]
– ORIGIN Greek *sēsamon, sēsamē*.

sesquipedalian /ses-kwi-pi-**day**-li-uhn/ adjective formal **1** (of a word) having many syllables; long. **2** full of long words; long-winded.
– ORIGIN from Latin *sesquipedalis* 'a foot and a half long'.

sessile /**ses**-yl, ses-il/ adjective technical **1** (of an organism, e.g. a barnacle) fixed in one place; immobile. **2** (of a plant or animal structure) attached directly by its base without a stalk or similar structure.
– ORIGIN Latin *sessilis*.

session noun **1** a period devoted to a particular activity: *a training session.* **2** a meeting of a council, court, or law-making body to carry out its business. **3** a period during which council and other meetings are regularly held. **4** an academic year.
– DERIVATIVES **sessional** adjective.
– ORIGIN Latin.

session musician noun a freelance musician hired to play on recording sessions.

sestet /ses-**tet**/ noun the last six lines of a sonnet.
– ORIGIN Italian *sestetto.*

set¹ verb (**sets, setting, set**) **1** put, lay, or stand something in a specified place or position. **2** put or bring into a specified state: *the hostages were set free.* **3** cause to start doing something: *the incident set me thinking.* **4** give someone a task. **5** decide on or fix a time, value, or limit. **6** establish something as an example or record. **7** adjust a device as required: *don't set the volume too loud.* **8** prepare a table for a meal by placing cutlery, crockery, etc. on it. **9** harden into a solid, semi-solid, or fixed state. **10** arrange damp hair into the required style. **11** put a broken or dislocated bone or limb into the correct position for healing. **12** (of the sun or moon) appear to move towards and below the earth's horizon. **13** arrange type or written material for printing as required. **14** (of blossom or a tree) form into or produce fruit.
– PHRASES **set about 1** start doing something in an energetic or determined way. **2** Brit. informal attack someone. **set someone apart** make someone seem superior to others. **set something aside 1** keep something for a particular purpose. **2** formally cancel a legal decision or order. **set someone back** informal cost someone a particular amount of money. **set something down** record something in writing. **set forth** dated begin a journey. **set something forth** state something in writing or

speech. **set in** (of something unwelcome) begin and seem likely to continue. **set off** begin a journey. **set something off 1** cause a bomb or alarm to go off. **2** make something more attractive by being placed near to something else. **set on** attack someone violently. **set out 1** begin a journey. **2** intend to do something. **set something out** arrange or display something. **set sail 1** begin a voyage. **2** hoist the sails of a boat. **set to** begin doing something in an energetic way. **set something to music** provide music for a written work. **set something up 1** place or erect something in position. **2** establish a business or other organization. **set someone up 1** establish someone in a particular enterprise or role. **2** informal make an innocent person appear guilty.
– ORIGIN Old English.

set² noun **1** a number of things or people grouped together as similar or forming a unit. **2** a group of people with shared interests or occupations: *the literary set.* **3** the way in which something is set or positioned: *that cold set of his jaw.* **4** a radio or television receiver. **5** (in tennis and other games) a group of games counting as a unit towards a match. **6** a collection of scenery, stage furniture, etc. used for a scene in a play or film. **7** (in jazz or popular music) a sequence of songs or pieces forming part of all of a live show or recording. **8** Mathematics a collection of distinct entities satisfying specified conditions and regarded as a unit. **9** a cutting, young plant, or bulb used to produce new plants: *an onion set.* **10** variant spelling of **SETT**.
– ORIGIN partly from Old French *sette*, partly from **SET¹**.

set³ adjective **1** fixed or arranged in advance. **2** firmly fixed and unchanging: *set ideas about race and culture.* **3** having a fixed wording. **4** ready or likely to do something: *we're all set for tonight!* **5** (**set on**) determined to do something.

set-aside noun the policy of reducing surpluses by paying farmers not to use some of their land for growing crops.

setback noun a problem that prevents or holds up progress.

set piece noun **1** a part of a novel, film, play, or piece of music that is arranged in a recognized or elaborate way to create a particular effect. **2** Brit. a carefully organized move in a team game.

set play noun Sport a prearranged manoeuvre carried out from a restart by the team who have the advantage.

set point noun (in tennis and other sports) a point which if won by one of the players will also win them a set.

set square noun a right-angled triangular plate for drawing lines, especially at 90°, 45°, 60°, or 30°.

sett (also **set**) noun **1** the earth or burrow of a badger. **2** a granite paving block.
– ORIGIN from **SET²**.

settee noun Brit. a long upholstered seat for more than one person, typically with a back and arms.
– ORIGIN perhaps from **SETTLE²**.

setter noun a breed of large dog with long hair, trained to stand rigid when scenting game.

set theory noun the branch of mathematics concerned with the properties and applications of sets.

setting noun 1 the way or place in which something is set: *the islands offer a perfect setting for a family holiday.* 2 a piece of metal in which a precious stone or gem is fixed to form a piece of jewellery. 3 a piece of vocal or choral music composed for particular words. 4 (also **place setting**) a complete set of crockery and cutlery for one person at a meal.

settle[1] verb 1 reach agreement on something disputed. 2 decide or arrange something finally: *they hadn't settled on a date for the wedding.* 3 make one's home in a new place. 4 (often **settle down**) adopt a more steady or secure life. 5 become or make calmer or quieter. 6 sit or place so as to be comfortable or secure: *she settled her bag on her shoulder.* 7 sink or fall slowly downwards: *dust from the mill had settled on the roof.* 8 (often **settle in**) begin to feel comfortable in a new situation. 9 pay a debt or bill. 10 (**settle for**) accept something less than satisfactory. 11 (**settle down to**) begin to concentrate on an activity. 12 (**settle something on**) give money or property to someone through a legal document such as a will.
– ORIGIN Old English, 'to seat, place'.

settle[2] noun a wooden bench with a high back and arms.
– ORIGIN Old English.

settlement noun 1 the action of settling. 2 an official agreement intended to settle a dispute or conflict. 3 a place where people establish a community. 4 a legal arrangement by which a person gives money or property to someone else: *a divorce settlement.*

settler noun a person who establishes a community in a new area.

settlor noun a person who makes a legal arrangement to transfer property to establish a trust.

set-to noun (pl. **set-tos**) informal a fight or argument.

set-top box noun a device which converts a digital television signal to an analogue one, so that it can be seen on a conventional set.

set-up noun informal 1 the way in which something is organized. 2 an organization. 3 a scheme intended to trick someone or make it appear that they have done something wrong.

seven cardinal number one more than six; 7. (Roman numeral: **vii** or **VII**.)
– PHRASES **the seven deadly sins** (in Christian tradition) the sins of pride, covetousness, lust, anger, gluttony, envy, and sloth. **the seven seas** all the oceans of the world (the Arctic, Antarctic, North Pacific, South Pacific, North Atlantic, South Atlantic, and Indian Oceans). **the seven-year itch** a tendency to be unfaithful, supposed to arise after seven years of marriage.
– DERIVATIVES **sevenfold** adjective & adverb.
– ORIGIN Old English.

seventeen cardinal number one more than sixteen; 17. (Roman numeral: **xvii** or **XVII**.)
– DERIVATIVES **seventeenth** adjective & noun.

seventh ordinal number 1 that is number seven in a sequence; 7th. 2 (**a seventh/one seventh**) each of seven equal parts into which something is divided. 3 a musical interval spanning seven consecutive notes in a scale.

Seventh-Day Adventist noun a member of a strict Protestant sect which preaches that Jesus is about to return to earth and observes Saturday as the sabbath.

seventy cardinal number (pl. **seventies**) ten less than eighty; 70. (Roman numeral: **lxx** or **LXX**.)
– DERIVATIVES **seventieth** ordinal number.

seventy-eight noun an old gramophone record designed to be played at 78 rpm.

sever verb 1 cut something off or into pieces. 2 put an end to a connection or relationship.
– ORIGIN Old French *severer.*

several determiner & pronoun more than two but not many. •adjective separate or respective: *the two levels of government sorted out their several responsibilities.*
– DERIVATIVES **severally** adverb.
– ORIGIN Old French.

severance noun 1 the ending of a connection or relationship. 2 the state of being separated or cut off.

severance pay noun money paid to an employee on the early ending of a contract.

severe adjective 1 (of something bad or difficult) very great; intense. 2 strict or harsh: *severe penalties for hackers.* 3 very plain in style or appearance.
– DERIVATIVES **severely** adverb **severity** noun.
– ORIGIN Latin *severus.*

seviche /se-**veet**-shay/ noun variant spelling of **CEVICHE.**

Seville orange /suh-**vil**/ noun a bitter orange used for marmalade.
– ORIGIN from the Spanish city of *Seville.*

Sèvres /**sev**-ruh/ noun a type of elaborately decorated fine porcelain.
– ORIGIN from *Sèvres* in Paris.

sew verb (past part. **sewn** or **sewed**) 1 join or repair something by making stitches with a needle and thread or a sewing machine. 2 (**sew something up**) informal bring something to a favourable conclusion.
– ORIGIN Old English.

sewage /**soo**-ij/ noun waste water and excrement that is carried away in sewers.
– ORIGIN from **SEWER**[1].

sewage farm (also **sewage works**) noun Brit. a place where sewage is treated.

sewer[1] /**soo**-er/ noun an underground pipe for carrying off drainage water and waste matter.
– ORIGIN Old French *seuwiere* 'channel to drain the overflow from a fish pond'.

sewer[2] /**soh**-er/ noun a person who sews.

sewerage noun 1 the provision of drainage by sewers. 2 US term for **SEWAGE.**

sewing machine noun a machine with a mechanically driven needle for sewing cloth.

sewn past participle of **SEW.**

sex noun 1 either of the two main categories (male and female) into which humans and most other living things are divided on the basis of their reproductive functions. 2 sexual intercourse. 3 the fact of being male or female. 4 the group of all members of either sex: *her efforts to improve the condition of her sex.* •verb 1 (**sex something up**) informal present something in a more interesting or lively way.

S

2 determine the sex of an animal.
- DERIVATIVES **sexer** noun.
- ORIGIN Latin *sexus*.

USAGE: On the difference between the words sex and gender, see the note at GENDER.

sexagenarian /seks-uh-ji-**nair**-i-uhn/ noun a person between 60 and 69 years old.
- ORIGIN Latin *sexagenarius*.

sex appeal noun the quality of being attractive in a sexual way.

sex bomb noun informal a woman who is very sexually attractive.

sex change noun a change in a person's physical sexual characteristics by surgery and hormone treatment.

sex chromosome noun a chromosome concerned in determining the sex of an organism (in mammals the X and Y chromosomes).

sexed adjective having specified sexual appetites: *highly sexed men.*

sex hormone noun a hormone affecting sexual development or reproduction, such as oestrogen or testosterone.

sexism noun prejudice or discrimination, typically against women, on the basis of a person's sex.
- DERIVATIVES **sexist** adjective & noun.

sex kitten noun informal a young woman who is very sexually attractive.

sexless adjective **1** not sexually attractive or active. **2** neither male nor female.

sex life noun a person's sexual activity and relationships considered as a whole.

sex object noun a person regarded purely in terms of their sexual attractiveness or availability.

sexology noun the study of people's sexual behaviour.
- DERIVATIVES **sexological** adjective **sexologist** noun.

sexpot noun informal a sexy person.

sex symbol noun a person famous for their sexual attractiveness.

sextant /seks-tuhnt/ noun an instrument for measuring the angular distances between objects, used for navigation and surveying.
- ORIGIN first referring to the sixth part of a circle: from Latin *sextans* 'sixth part'.

sextet noun **1** a group of six people playing music or singing together. **2** a composition for a sextet. **3** a set of six.
- ORIGIN from Latin *sex* 'six'.

sexton noun a person who looks after a church and churchyard, typically acting as bell-ringer and gravedigger.
- ORIGIN Old French *segrestein*.

sex tourism noun the organization of holidays abroad with the aim of taking advantage of the lack of restrictions on sexual activity and prostitution in some countries.

sextuple /seks-tyuu-p'l, seks-tyoo-p'l/ adjective **1** consisting of six parts. **2** six times as much or as many.
- ORIGIN Latin *sextuplus*.

sextuplet /seks-tyuu-plit, seks-tyoo-plit/ noun each of six children born at one birth.

sexual adjective **1** relating to sex or to physical attraction or intimate contact between people or animals. **2** relating to the two sexes or to gender. **3** (of reproduction) involving the fusion of male and female cells.
- DERIVATIVES **sexualize** (or **sexualise**) verb **sexually** adverb.

sexual harassment noun the making of unwanted sexual advances or obscene remarks to a person, especially at work.

sexual intercourse noun sexual contact in which a man puts his erect penis into a woman's vagina.

sexuality noun (pl. **sexualities**) **1** a person's capacity for sexual feelings. **2** a person's sexual preference.

sexual politics plural noun (treated as sing.) relations between the sexes regarded in terms of power.

sex worker noun euphemistic a prostitute.

sexy adjective (**sexier**, **sexiest**) **1** sexually attractive or exciting. **2** sexually aroused. **3** informal exciting or appealing: *a sexy marketing buzzword.*
- DERIVATIVES **sexily** adverb **sexiness** noun.

Seychellois /say-shel-**wah**/ noun a person from the Seychelles. • adjective relating to the Seychelles.

SF abbreviation science fiction.

SFX abbreviation special effects.
- ORIGIN *FX* representing a pronunciation of *effects*.

SG abbreviation Physics specific gravity.

Sg symbol the chemical element seaborgium.

SGML abbreviation Computing Standard Generalized Markup Language, a system for encoding electronic texts so that they can be displayed in any format.

shabby adjective (**shabbier**, **shabbiest**) **1** in poor condition because of long use or neglect. **2** dressed in old or worn clothes. **3** mean and unfair: *a shabby trick.*
- DERIVATIVES **shabbily** adverb **shabbiness** noun.
- ORIGIN from Germanic.

shack noun a roughly built hut or cabin. • verb (**shack up with**) informal live with someone as a lover.
- ORIGIN perhaps from Mexican or Nahuatl.

shackle noun **1** (**shackles**) a pair of metal rings connected by a chain, used to fasten a prisoner's wrists or ankles together.
2 (**shackles**) something that restricts freedom: *the human need to be free of the shackles of oppression.* **3** a metal link closed by a bolt, used to secure a chain or rope to something. • verb **1** chain someone with shackles. **2** restrain or limit someone or something.
- ORIGIN Old English.

shad noun (pl. same or **shads**) an edible herring-like sea fish.
- ORIGIN Old English.

shaddock /shad-uhk/ noun another term for POMELO.
- ORIGIN named after Captain *Shaddock*, who introduced it to the West Indies.

shade noun **1** an area that is dark and cool because it is sheltered from direct sunlight. **2** a form of a colour with regard to how light or dark it is: *various shades of blue.* **3** a slightly different variety of something: **4** a lampshade.

5 (shades) informal sunglasses. **6** literary a ghost.
•**verb 1** screen someone or something from
direct light. **2** block all or some of the light
coming from something. **3** represent a darker
area in a picture with pencil or a block of
colour. **4** pass or change gradually: *outrage
began to shade into dismay.*
– PHRASES **a shade** a slight amount: *I felt a shade
anxious.* **shades of —— ** similar to or
reminiscent of. **put someone/thing in the
shade** be much better or more impressive than
someone or something.
– DERIVATIVES **shadeless** adjective **shader** noun.
– ORIGIN Old English.

shading noun **1** the representation of light and
shade on a drawing or map. **2** a very slight
variation in something.

shadow noun **1** a dark area or shape produced
by an object coming between light rays and a
surface. **2** partial or complete darkness. **3** a
feeling of sadness or gloom. **4** the slightest
trace: *without a shadow of a doubt.* **5** a weak or
less good version: *she was a shadow of her
former self.* **6** a position of less importance: *he
lived in the shadow of his father.* **7** a person who
constantly accompanies or secretly follows
another. •**verb 1** cast a shadow over someone
or something. **2** follow and observe someone
secretly. **3** accompany an employee in their
daily activities to gain experience of a job.
•**adjective** Brit. referring to a government
minister's counterpart in the opposition party.
– DERIVATIVES **shadower** noun **shadowless**
adjective.
– ORIGIN Old English.

shadow-box verb box against an imaginary
opponent as a form of training.

shadow economy noun illicit economic
activity existing alongside a country's official
economy.

shadowland (also **shadowlands**) noun literary a
place or situation that is vague or that exists
on the boundaries of other places or states.

shadowy adjective (**shadowier, shadowiest**)
1 full of shadows. **2** not well known; full of
mystery: *the shadowy world of computer
hacking.*
– DERIVATIVES **shadowiness** noun.

shady adjective (**shadier, shadiest**) **1** situated in
or full of shade. **2** giving shade from the sun.
3 informal seeming to be dishonest or illegal.
– DERIVATIVES **shadiness** noun.

shaft noun **1** a long, narrow part forming the
handle of a tool or club, the body of a spear or
arrow, or similar object. **2** a ray of light or bolt
of lightning. **3** a long, narrow, passage giving
access to a mine, accommodating a lift, or
providing ventilation. **4** each of the pair of
poles between which a horse is harnessed to a
vehicle. **5** a cylindrical rotating rod for the
transmission of mechanical power in a
machine. **6** the part of a column between the
base and capital. **7** a sudden flash of a quality
or feeling: *a shaft of inspiration.* **8** a witty or
hurtful remark. •**verb 1** (of light) shine in
beams. **2** informal treat someone harshly or
unfairly.
– DERIVATIVES **shafted** adjective.
– ORIGIN Old English.

shag[1] noun **1** a thick, tangled hairstyle. **2** coarse
cut tobacco. •**adjective 1** (of a carpet or rug)
having a long, rough pile. **2** (of pile on a
carpet) long and rough.
– ORIGIN Old English.

shag[2] noun a cormorant (seabird) with
greenish-black plumage and a long curly crest.
– ORIGIN perhaps from **SHAG**[1], with reference to
the bird's 'shaggy' crest.

shag[3] Brit. vulgar slang verb (**shags, shagging,
shagged**) have sex with someone. •**noun** an act
of sex.
– DERIVATIVES **shagger** noun.
– ORIGIN unknown.

shagged (also **shagged out**) adjective Brit. vulgar
slang very tired; exhausted.

shaggy adjective (**shaggier, shaggiest**) **1** (of
hair or fur) long, thick, and untidy. **2** having
shaggy hair or fur.
– PHRASES **shaggy-dog story** a long, rambling
story or joke, amusing only because it is
pointless.
– DERIVATIVES **shaggily** adverb **shagginess** noun.

shagreen /sha-**green**/ noun **1** sharkskin used
for decoration or for cleaning or polishing
hard surfaces. **2** a kind of leather that has not
been tanned, with a rough surface.
– ORIGIN from **CHAGRIN** in the sense 'rough skin'.

shah /rhymes with lah/ noun historical a title of
the former king of Iran.
– ORIGIN Persian, 'king'.

shake verb (past **shook**; past part. **shaken**) **1** move
quickly and jerkily up and down or to and fro.
2 tremble uncontrollably with strong
emotion. **3** make a threatening gesture with:
he shook his fist. **4** remove something by
shaking. **5** shock or astonish someone. **6** get
rid of or put an end to: *old habits he couldn't
shake off.* •**noun 1** an act of shaking. **2** an
amount sprinkled from a container. **3** informal a
milkshake. **4** (**the shakes**) informal a fit of
trembling.
– PHRASES **in two shakes (of a lamb's tail)**
informal very quickly. **no great shakes** informal not
very good. **shake down** settle down. **shake
hands (with someone)** hold someone's right
hand in one's own when meeting or leaving
them, to congratulate them, or to show
agreement. **shake on it** informal confirm an
agreement by shaking hands. **shake someone
up** stir someone into action. **shake something
up** make major changes to an organization or
system.
– ORIGIN Old English.

shakedown noun informal, chiefly N. Amer. **1** a
thorough search. **2** a major change or
restructuring. **3** an act of swindling someone.
4 a makeshift bed.

shaker noun **1** a container for mixing
ingredients by shaking them. **2** a container
with a pierced top from which a powdered
substance such as flour is poured by shaking.
3 (**Shaker**) a member of an American
Christian sect living simply in celibate mixed
communities. [so named from the wild
movements they engaged in during worship.]
•**adjective** (**Shaker**) referring to a style of
elegant but functional furniture traditionally
produced by Shakers.

Shakespearean /shayk-**speer**-i-uhn/ (also
Shakespearian) adjective relating to the

S

English dramatist William Shakespeare. • **noun** an expert in or student of Shakespeare's works.

shake-up (also **shake-out**) **noun** informal a major reorganization.

shako /shay-koh, sha-koh/ **noun** (pl. **shakos**) a cylindrical military hat with a peak and a plume or pompom.
– ORIGIN Hungarian *csákó süveg* 'peaked cap'.

Shakti /shuk-tee/ **noun** Hinduism female creative power or divine energy.
– ORIGIN Sanskrit.

shaky adjective (**shakier**, **shakiest**) **1** shaking or trembling. **2** not steady or stable. **3** likely to fail or falter: *after a shaky start the team made superb efforts.*
– DERIVATIVES **shakily** adverb **shakiness** noun.

shale noun soft rock formed from compressed mud or clay, that can be split into thin layers.
– DERIVATIVES **shaly** (also **shaley**) adjective.
– ORIGIN probably from German *Schale.*

shall modal verb (3rd sing. present **shall**) **1** used with *I* and *we* to express the future tense.
2 expressing a strong statement, intention, or order. **3** used in questions to make offers or suggestions.
– ORIGIN Old English.

> **USAGE:** The traditional rule is that when forming the future tense, **shall** should be used with **I** and **we** (*I shall be late*), while **will** should be used with **you, he, she, it**, and **they** (*he will not be there*). However, when telling someone what to do or showing determination, this rule is reversed: **will** is used with **I** and **we** (*I will not tolerate this*), and **shall** is used with **you, he, she, it**, and **they** (*you shall go to school*). Nowadays, people do not follow these rules so strictly and are more likely to use the shortened forms **I'll, she'll**, etc., especially when speaking.

shallot /shuh-lot/ noun a small vegetable of the onion family.
– ORIGIN Old French *eschaloigne, scaloun* 'scallion'.

shallow adjective **1** having a short distance between the top and the bottom; not deep.
2 not thinking or thought out seriously or in detail: *a shallow analysis of society.* • **noun** (**shallows**) a shallow area of water.
– DERIVATIVES **shallowly** adverb **shallowness** noun.
– ORIGIN related to **SHOAL**².

shalom /shuh-lom/ exclamation said by Jews at meeting or parting.
– ORIGIN Hebrew, 'peace'.

shalt old-fashioned second person singular of **SHALL**.

shalwar /shul-wah/ (also **salwar**) noun a pair of loose trousers tapering to a tight fit around the ankles, worn by women from the Indian subcontinent, typically with a kameez.
– ORIGIN Persian and Urdu.

sham noun **1** a thing that is not as good or as genuine as it seems to be: *our current free health service is a sham.* **2** a person who pretends to be something that they are not.
• **adjective** not genuine; false. • **verb** (**shams, shamming, shammed**) pretend or pretend to be: *people who are shamming insanity.*

– ORIGIN perhaps from **SHAME**.

shaman /shay-muhn, sha-muhn/ noun (pl. **shamans**) (especially among some peoples of northern Asia and North America) a person who is believed to be able to contact good and evil spirits.
– DERIVATIVES **shamanic** /shuh-man-ik/ adjective **shamanism** noun **shamanistic** adjective.
– ORIGIN Tungus (a language of Siberia).

shamateur noun derogatory a sports player who makes money from sporting activities though classified as amateur.
– ORIGIN blend of **SHAM** and **AMATEUR**.

shamble verb walk in a slow, shuffling, awkward way. • **noun** a slow, shuffling walk.
– ORIGIN probably from dialect *shamble* 'ungainly'.

shambles plural noun **1** informal a state of complete disorder. **2** old use a butcher's slaughterhouse.
– ORIGIN first meaning 'meat market': from Latin *scamellum* 'little bench'.

shambolic adjective informal, chiefly Brit. chaotic or disorganized.
– DERIVATIVES **shambolically** adverb.
– ORIGIN from **SHAMBLES**.

shame noun **1** a feeling of humiliation or distress arising from one's awareness that one has done something wrong or foolish. **2** loss of respect; dishonour: *the incident had brought shame on his family.* **3** a cause of shame or dishonour. **4** a cause for regret or disappointment: *what a shame Ellie won't be here.* • **verb** make someone feel ashamed.
– PHRASES **put someone to shame** make someone feel ashamed by being much better than them.
– ORIGIN Old English.

shamefaced adjective showing shame.
– DERIVATIVES **shamefacedly** adverb **shamefacedness** noun.

shameful adjective causing or worthy of shame or disgrace: *a shameful secret.*
– DERIVATIVES **shamefully** adverb **shamefulness** noun.

shameless adjective not feeling ashamed, even though one has done something wrong or foolish.
– DERIVATIVES **shamelessly** adverb **shamelessness** noun.

shammy noun (pl. **shammies**) informal a chamois leather.

shampoo noun **1** a liquid soap for washing the hair. **2** a similar liquid for cleaning a carpet, car, etc. **3** an act of washing with shampoo.
• **verb** (**shampoos, shampooing, shampooed**) wash or clean something with shampoo.
– ORIGIN Hindi, 'to press'.

shamrock noun a clover-like plant with three rounded leaves on each stem, the national emblem of Ireland.
– ORIGIN Irish *seamróg.*

shandy noun (pl. **shandies**) beer mixed with lemonade or ginger beer.
– ORIGIN unknown.

shanghai /shang-hy/ verb (**shanghais, shanghaiing, shanghaied**) **1** informal force or trick someone into doing something. **2** historical force someone to join a ship's crew.
– ORIGIN from *Shanghai*, a Chinese seaport.

S

Shangri-La /shang-gri-**lah**/ noun a very pleasant or unspoilt place.
– ORIGIN named after a Tibetan Utopia in James Hilton's novel *Lost Horizon*.

shank noun 1 the lower part of a person's leg. 2 the lower part of an animal's foreleg, especially as a cut of meat. 3 the shaft or stem of a tool, spoon, etc. 4 the band of a ring rather than the setting.
– PHRASES **Shanks's pony** one's own legs as a means of transport.
– DERIVATIVES **shanked** adjective.
– ORIGIN Old English.

shan't contraction shall not.

shantung /shan-**tung**/ noun a type of soft silk with a coarse surface.
– ORIGIN from *Shantung* in China, where it was first made.

shanty[1] noun (pl. **shanties**) a small roughly built shack.
– ORIGIN perhaps from Canadian French *chantier* 'lumberjack's cabin'.

shanty[2] (Brit. also **sea shanty**; US **chanty**) noun (pl. **shanties**) a song in which a solo part alternates with a chorus, sung by sailors when working together.
– ORIGIN probably from French *chantez!* 'sing!'.

shanty town noun a settlement in or near a city where poor people live in makeshift houses or shacks.

shape noun 1 the outward form of someone or something as produced by their outline. 2 a geometric figure such as a rectangle. 3 a piece of material or paper made or cut in a particular form. 4 the correct or original form of something: *the wheels are out of shape and not perfectly circular.* 5 organized or well-defined structure or arrangement. 6 a particular condition or state: *the house was in poor shape.* 7 good physical condition. • verb 1 give a shape to something. 2 determine the nature of. 3 develop in a particular way: *it was shaping up to be another bleak year.* 4 (**shape up**) improve one's fitness, performance, or behaviour.
– PHRASES **lick** (or **knock**) **someone/thing into shape** take forceful action to improve someone or something. **take shape** develop into something more definite or organized.
– DERIVATIVES **shaped** adjective **shaper** noun.
– ORIGIN Old English.

shapeless adjective lacking a definite or attractive shape.
– DERIVATIVES **shapelessly** adverb **shapelessness** noun.

shapely adjective (**shapelier**, **shapeliest**) having an attractive or well-proportioned shape: *shapely legs.*
– DERIVATIVES **shapeliness** noun.

shape-shifter noun an imaginary being who is able to change their physical form when they want to.
– DERIVATIVES **shape-shifting** noun & adjective.

shard noun a sharp piece of broken pottery, metal, glass, etc.
– ORIGIN Old English, 'gap, notch, shard'.

share[1] noun 1 a part of a larger amount which is divided among or contributed by a number of people. 2 any of the equal parts into which a company's capital is divided, which can be bought by people in return for a proportion of the profits. 3 an amount regarded as normal or acceptable: *the new system had more than its fair share of problems.* 4 a person's contribution to an activity. • verb 1 have or give a share of something. 2 possess or use jointly with others: *they shared a flat.* 3 (**share in**) participate in an activity. 4 tell someone about something.
– DERIVATIVES **shareable** (also **sharable**) adjective **sharer** noun.
– ORIGIN Old English.

share[2] noun a ploughshare.

sharecropper noun chiefly N. Amer. a tenant farmer who gives a part of each crop as rent.

shareholder noun an owner of shares in a company.
– DERIVATIVES **shareholding** noun.

share option noun an option for an employee to buy shares in their company at a discount or at a stated fixed price.

shareware noun computer software that is available free of charge and often distributed informally for users to evaluate.

sharia /shuh-**ree**-uh/ noun Islamic law, based on the teachings of the Koran and the traditions of Muhammad.
– ORIGIN Arabic.

shark[1] noun a large sea fish with a triangular fin on its back, many kinds of which prey on other animals.
– ORIGIN unknown.

shark[2] noun informal a person who exploits or swindles others.
– ORIGIN perhaps from German *Schurke* 'worthless rogue'.

sharkskin noun a stiff, slightly shiny synthetic fabric.

sharp adjective 1 having a cutting or piercing edge or point. 2 tapering to a point or edge. 3 sudden and rapid: *a sharp increase in interest rates.* 4 clear and definite: *the mood is in sharp contrast to last year's summit.* 5 (of a feeling or emotion) sudden and intense. 6 quick to understand, notice, or respond. 7 (of a food, taste, or smell) strong and slightly bitter. 8 (of a sound) sudden and penetrating. 9 (of a person or remark) critical or hurtful. 10 quick to take advantage, especially in a dishonest way. 11 making a sudden change of direction. 12 informal smart and stylish. 13 (after a noun) (of a note or key) higher by a semitone than a specified note or key: *F sharp.* • adverb 1 precisely: *the meeting starts at 7.30 sharp.* 2 suddenly or abruptly. • noun 1 a musical note raised a semitone above natural pitch, shown by the sign ♯. 2 an object with a sharp point.
– DERIVATIVES **sharply** adverb **sharpness** noun.
– ORIGIN Old English.

sharpen verb make or become sharp.
– DERIVATIVES **sharpener** noun.

sharper noun informal a swindler, especially at cards.

sharpish adjective fairly sharp. • adverb Brit. informal quickly; soon.

sharp practice noun dishonest business dealings.

sharpshooter noun a person skilled in shooting.

S

sharp-tongued adjective using harsh or critical language.

sharp-witted adjective intelligent and quick to notice things.

shashlik /shash-lik/ noun (pl. same or **shashliks**) (in Asia and eastern Europe) a mutton kebab.
– ORIGIN Russian *shashlyk*.

shat past and past participle of **SHIT**.

shatter verb **1** break suddenly and violently into pieces. **2** damage or destroy: *he broke her heart and shattered her dreams.* **3** upset someone greatly. **4** (as adj. **shattered**) Brit. informal completely exhausted.
– DERIVATIVES **shatterer** noun.
– ORIGIN uncertain.

shave verb **1** remove hair from the face or body by cutting it off close to the skin with a razor. **2** cut a thin slice or slices from something. **3** reduce by a small amount: *21 per cent was shaved off the research budget.* **4** pass very close to something. •noun an act of shaving.
– ORIGIN Old English.

shaven adjective (of a part of the body) shaved.

shaver noun **1** an electric razor. **2** informal, dated a young lad.

Shavian /shay-vi-uhn/ adjective relating to or in the style of the Irish dramatist George Bernard Shaw. •noun an admirer of Shaw or his work.
– ORIGIN from *Shavius*, the Latin form of *Shaw*.

shaving noun a thin strip cut off a surface.

Shavuot /shuh-voo-uhs, shah-vuu-ot/ noun a major Jewish festival held fifty days after the second day of Passover.
– ORIGIN from Hebrew *šāḇŭ'ōṯ* 'weeks'.

shawl noun a large piece of fabric worn by women over the shoulders or head or wrapped round a baby.
– DERIVATIVES **shawled** adjective.
– ORIGIN Urdu and Persian.

shawl collar noun a rounded collar without lapel notches that extends down the front of a garment.

shawm /shorm/ noun a medieval and Renaissance wind instrument, forerunner of the oboe, with a double reed in a wooden mouthpiece.
– ORIGIN Old French *chalemel*.

Shawnee /shor-nee/ noun (pl. same or **Shawnees**) a member of an American Indian people now living chiefly in Oklahoma.
– ORIGIN the name in Delaware (an American Indian language).

shaykh noun variant spelling of **SHEIKH**.

she pronoun (third person sing.) **1** used to refer to a woman, girl, or female animal previously mentioned or easily identified. **2** used to refer to a ship, country, or other thing regarded as female. •noun a female; a woman.
– ORIGIN Old English.

sheaf noun (pl. **sheaves**) **1** a bundle of papers. **2** a bundle of grain stalks tied together after reaping. •verb tie grain stalks into bundles.
– ORIGIN Old English.

shear verb (past part. **shorn** or **sheared**) **1** cut the wool off a sheep or other animal. **2** cut off hair or wool with scissors or shears. **3** (**be shorn of**) have something taken away: *he was shorn*

of nearly $2 billion. **4** break off because of a structural strain. •noun a strain produced by pressure in the structure of a substance, so that each layer slides over the next.
– DERIVATIVES **shearer** noun.
– ORIGIN Old English.

USAGE: Do not confuse **shear** and **sheer**. **Shear** means 'cut the wool off a sheep'. As a verb, **sheer** means 'change course quickly' (*the boat sheered off*); **sheer** is also an adjective meaning 'nothing but; absolute' (*sheer hard work*).

shears (also **a pair of shears**) plural noun a cutting instrument resembling a very large pair of scissors.

shearwater noun a long-winged seabird related to the petrels.

sheath /sheeth/ noun (pl. **sheaths** /sheethz, sheeths/) **1** a cover for the blade of a knife or sword. **2** chiefly Brit. a condom. **3** a close-fitting covering or protective structure. **4** (also **sheath dress**) a close-fitting dress.
– ORIGIN Old English.

sheathe /sheeth/ verb **1** put a knife or sword into a sheath. **2** cover in a close-fitting or protective covering: *her legs were sheathed in black stockings.*

sheathing /shee-thing/ noun a protective casing or covering.

sheath knife noun a short knife similar to a dagger, carried in a sheath.

sheaves plural of **SHEAF**.

shebang /shi-bang/ noun (in phrase **the whole shebang**) informal the whole thing; everything.
– ORIGIN unknown.

shebeen /shi-been/ noun (especially in Ireland, Scotland, and South Africa) a place that sells alcoholic drink illegally.
– ORIGIN Anglo-Irish *síbín*.

shed[1] noun **1** a simple building used for storage or to shelter animals. **2** a larger structure, typically with one or more sides open, for storing vehicles or machinery.
– ORIGIN probably from **SHADE**.

shed[2] verb (**sheds**, **shedding**, **shed**) **1** get rid of: *exercise helps you shed pounds.* **2** cast or give off light. **3** allow leaves, hair, skin, etc. to fall off naturally. **4** take off clothes. **5** Brit. accidentally drop or spill something. **6** be able to repel water.
– PHRASES **shed tears** cry.
– DERIVATIVES **shedder** noun.
– ORIGIN Old English, 'divide, scatter'.

she'd contraction she had; she would.

shedload noun Brit. informal a large amount or number.

sheen noun a soft shine on a surface.
– DERIVATIVES **sheeny** adjective.
– ORIGIN probably from **SHINE**.

sheep noun (pl. same) a grass-eating mammal with a thick woolly coat, kept in flocks for its wool or meat.
– PHRASES **like sheep** (of people) easily led or influenced.
– DERIVATIVES **sheeplike** adjective.
– ORIGIN Old English.

sheep dip noun **1** a liquid in which sheep are dipped to clean and disinfect their wool. **2** a place where sheep are dipped in this liquid.

sheepdog noun **1** a dog trained to guard and herd sheep. **2** a breed of dog suitable for guarding and herding sheep.

sheepish adjective embarrassed as a result of having done something foolish.
– DERIVATIVES **sheepishly** adverb **sheepishness** noun.

sheepshank noun a knot made in a rope to shorten it temporarily.

sheepskin noun a sheep's skin with the wool on, made into a garment or rug.

sheer[1] adjective **1** nothing but; absolute: *sheer hard work.* **2** (of a cliff, wall, etc.) vertical or almost vertical. **3** (of a fabric) very thin and almost transparent. • adverb vertically; perpendicularly.
– DERIVATIVES **sheerly** adverb **sheerness** noun.
– ORIGIN probably from **SHINE**.

> USAGE: On the confusion of **sheer** and **shear**, see the note at **SHEAR**.

sheer[2] verb **1** (especially of a boat) swerve or change course quickly. **2** avoid or move away from an unpleasant topic.
– ORIGIN perhaps from German *scheren* 'to shear'.

sheet[1] noun **1** a large rectangular piece of cotton or other fabric, used on a bed to lie on or under. **2** a broad flat piece of metal or glass. **3** a rectangular piece of paper. **4** a wide expanse or moving mass of water, ice, flame, etc. • verb **1** cover something with a sheet of cloth. **2** (of rain) fall heavily.
– ORIGIN Old English.

sheet[2] noun a rope attached to the lower corner of a sail, to hold and adjust it.
– PHRASES **two** (or **three**) **sheets to the wind** informal drunk.
– ORIGIN Old English, 'lower corner of a sail'.

sheeting noun material formed into or used as a sheet.

sheet lightning noun lightning seen as a broad area of light in the sky.

sheet metal noun metal formed into thin sheets.

sheet music noun music published on loose sheets of paper and not bound into a book.

sheikh /shayk, sheek/ (also **shaykh** or **sheik**) noun **1** the leader of an Arab tribe, family, or village. **2** a leader in a Muslim community or organization.
– DERIVATIVES **sheikhdom** noun.
– ORIGIN Arabic, 'old man, sheikh'.

sheila noun Austral./NZ informal a girl or woman.
– ORIGIN unknown.

shekel /rhymes with heckle/ noun **1** the basic unit of money of modern Israel. **2** (**shekels**) informal money; wealth.
– ORIGIN Hebrew.

shelduck noun (pl. same or **shelducks**) a large goose-like duck with brightly coloured plumage.
– ORIGIN probably from dialect *sheld* 'black and white' + **DUCK**[1].

shelf noun (pl. **shelves**) **1** a flat length of wood or other rigid material fixed horizontally to a wall or forming part of a piece of furniture and used to display or store things. **2** a ledge

of rock or protruding strip of land.
– PHRASES **off the shelf** taken from existing stock, not made to order. **on the shelf** (of a woman) past an age when she might expect to be married.
– ORIGIN German *schelf*.

shelf life noun the length of time for which an item remains able to be eaten, used, or sold.

shell noun **1** the hard protective outer case of an animal such as a snail, shellfish, or turtle. **2** the outer covering of an egg, nut kernel, or seed. **3** a metal case filled with explosive, to be fired from a large gun. **4** a hollow case, especially one used as a container for fireworks, cartridges, etc. **5** an outer structure or framework of a building or vehicle. **6** a light racing boat. • verb **1** fire explosive shells at something. **2** remove the shell or pod from a nut or seed. **3** (**shell something out**) informal pay an amount of money.
– PHRASES **come out of one's shell** stop being shy.
– DERIVATIVES **shelled** adjective **shell-less** adjective **shell-like** adjective **shelly** adjective.
– ORIGIN Old English.

she'll contraction she shall; she will.

shellac /shuh-**lak**/ noun lac resin melted into thin flakes, used for making varnish. • verb (**shellacs**, **shellacking**, **shellacked**) varnish something with shellac.
– ORIGIN from **SHELL** + **LAC**.

shellfire noun bombardment by explosive shells.

shellfish noun a creature such as a crab or oyster that has a shell and lives in water, especially an edible one.

shell pink noun a delicate pale pink.

shell shock noun a mental disorder that can affect soldiers who have been in battle for a long time.
– DERIVATIVES **shell-shocked** adjective.

shell suit noun Brit. a casual outfit consisting of a loose top and trousers with a soft lining and a shiny outer layer.

Shelta /**shel**-tuh/ noun an ancient secret language used by Irish and Welsh tinkers and Gypsies, based on altered Irish or Gaelic words.
– ORIGIN unknown.

shelter noun **1** a place giving protection from bad weather or danger. **2** a place providing food and accommodation for homeless people. **3** protection from something unpleasant or dangerous: *he waited in the shelter of a rock.* • verb **1** provide someone or something with shelter. **2** take cover from bad weather or danger. **3** (as adj. **sheltered**) protected from the more unpleasant aspects of life.
– ORIGIN perhaps from a former spelling of **SHIELD**.

sheltered housing (also **sheltered accommodation**) noun Brit. accommodation for elderly or disabled people, staffed by a warden and consisting of private units with some shared facilities.

shelve[1] verb **1** place something on a shelf. **2** decide not to continue with; cancel or postpone: *the company shelved plans for a big pay rise for its Chief Executive.* **3** fit something with shelves.

S

– DERIVATIVES **shelver** noun.
– ORIGIN from *shelves*, plural of SHELF.

shelve² verb (of ground) slope downwards.
– ORIGIN perhaps from SHELF.

shelves plural of SHELF.

shelving noun shelves as a whole.

shenanigans /shi-nan-i-guhnz/ plural noun informal **1** secret or dishonest activity. **2** high-spirited or mischievous behaviour.
– ORIGIN unknown.

shepherd noun **1** a person who looks after sheep. **2** a member of the clergy regarded as providing spiritual care and guidance for a congregation. •verb **1** guide or direct somewhere: *she shepherded them through the door.* **2** look after sheep.
– DERIVATIVES **shepherdess** noun.
– ORIGIN Old English.

shepherd's pie noun Brit. a dish of minced meat under a layer of mashed potato.

Sheraton /she-ruh-tuhn/ adjective (of furniture) designed by or in the simple, graceful style of the English furniture-maker Thomas Sheraton.

sherbet noun **1** Brit. a flavoured sweet fizzing powder eaten alone or made into a drink. **2** N. Amer. water ice; sorbet. **3** (in Arab countries) a drink of sweet diluted fruit juices.
– ORIGIN Arabic, 'drink'.

sherd noun another term for POTSHERD.
– ORIGIN from SHARD.

sheriff noun **1** (also **high sheriff**) (in England and Wales) the chief executive officer representing the monarch in a county. **2** (in Scotland) a judge. **3** US an elected officer in a county, responsible for keeping the peace.
– ORIGIN Old English, 'shire reeve'.

sheriff court noun (in Scotland) a court for civil cases, equivalent to a county court.

Sherpa /sher-puh/ noun (pl. same or **Sherpas**) a member of a Himalayan people living on the borders of Nepal and Tibet.
– ORIGIN Tibetan, 'inhabitant of an Eastern country'.

sherry noun (pl. **sherries**) a fortified wine originally from southern Spain.
– ORIGIN from Spanish *vino de Xeres* 'Xeres wine' (Xeres being the former name of the city of *Jerez de la Frontera*).

she's contraction she is; she has.

Shetlander noun a person from the Shetland Islands.

Shetland pony noun a small breed of pony with a rough coat.

shew verb old-fashioned variant of SHOW.

Shia /shi-uh/ (also **Shi'a**) noun (pl. same or **Shias**) **1** one of the two main branches of Islam, the other being Sunni. **2** a Muslim who follows the Shia branch of Islam.
– ORIGIN Arabic, 'party (of Ali)'.

shiatsu /shi-at-soo/ noun a Japanese therapy in which pressure is applied with the hands to points on the body.
– ORIGIN Japanese, 'finger pressure'.

shibboleth /shib-buh-leth/ noun a long-standing belief or principle that many people regard as outdated or no longer important: *the conflict challenged a series of military shibboleths.*

– ORIGIN Hebrew, 'ear of corn'; first meaning in English 'a word which a foreigner is unable to pronounce' (according to the Book of Judges, the word was used as a test of nationality because it was difficult to pronounce).

shied past and past participle of SHY².

shield noun **1** a broad piece of armour held for protection against blows or missiles. **2** a person or thing that provides protection. **3** a sporting trophy consisting of an engraved metal plate mounted on a piece of wood. **4** a drawing or model of a shield used for displaying a coat of arms. **5** a US police officer's badge. •verb **1** protect someone or something from something dangerous, unpleasant, or risky. **2** prevent from being seen: *the runners were shielded from view by the tunnel.* **3** enclose machinery or a source of sound, light, or radiation to protect the user.
– ORIGIN Old English.

shift verb **1** move or change from one position or direction to another: *the warming Gulf Stream could shift away from the UK.* **2** transfer responsibility, blame, or power to someone else. **3** Brit. informal move quickly. **4** Brit. informal remove a stain. **5** informal sell goods quickly or in large quantities. **6** chiefly N. Amer. change gear in a vehicle. •noun **1** a slight change in position, direction, or tendency: *a shift in public opinion.* **2** a period of time worked by a group of workers who start work as another group finishes. **3** a straight dress without a waist. **4** a key used to switch between two sets of characters or functions on a keyboard. **5** N. Amer. a gear lever or gear-changing mechanism. **6** old use a clever or crafty plan.
– PHRASES **shift for oneself** manage without help from others.
– DERIVATIVES **shifter** noun.
– ORIGIN Old English, 'arrange, divide'.

shiftless adjective lazy and lacking ambition.
– DERIVATIVES **shiftlessness** noun.

shifty adjective (**shiftier, shiftiest**) informal appearing untrustworthy or dishonest.
– DERIVATIVES **shiftily** adverb **shiftiness** noun.

shih-tzu /shee-tsoo/ noun a breed of dog with long, silky erect hair and short legs.
– ORIGIN Chinese, 'lion'.

shiitake /shi-tah-kay/ noun an edible mushroom grown in Japan and China.
– ORIGIN Japanese.

Shiite /shee-It/ (also **Shi'ite**) noun a follower of the Shia branch of Islam. •adjective relating to the Shia branch of Islam.
– DERIVATIVES **Shiism** /shee-i-z'm/ noun.

shiksa /shik-suh/ noun derogatory (in Jewish use) a non-Jewish girl or woman.
– ORIGIN Hebrew, 'detested thing'.

shillelagh /shi-lay-luh, shi-lay-li/ noun (in Ireland) a wooden cudgel.
– ORIGIN named after the Irish town of *Shillelagh.*

shilling noun **1** a former British coin and unit of money equal to one twentieth of a pound or twelve pence. **2** the basic unit of money of Kenya, Tanzania, and Uganda.
– PHRASES **not the full shilling** Brit. informal not very clever.
– ORIGIN Old English.

shilly-shally verb (**shilly-shallies, shilly-**

shallying, shilly-shallied) be unable to make up one's mind.
– ORIGIN from *shill I, shall I?*

shim noun a washer or thin strip of material used in machinery to fill a space between parts or reduce wear. • verb (**shimms, shimming, shimmed**) fill up a space with a shim.
– ORIGIN unknown.

shimmer verb shine with a soft wavering light. • noun a soft wavering light or reflected light.
– DERIVATIVES **shimmery** adjective.
– ORIGIN Old English.

shimmy verb (**shimmies, shimmying, shimmied**) 1 walk or move with a smooth swaying motion. 2 shake or vibrate abnormally. 3 dance the shimmy. • noun (pl. **shimmies**) a kind of ragtime dance in which the dancer shakes or sways the whole body.
– ORIGIN unknown.

shin noun 1 the front of the leg below the knee. 2 a cut of beef from the lower part of a cow's leg. • verb (**shins, shinning, shinned**) (**shin up/down**) climb quickly up or down by gripping with the arms and legs.
– ORIGIN Old English.

shin bone noun the tibia.

shindig noun informal 1 a large, lively party. 2 a noisy disturbance or quarrel.
– ORIGIN probably from **shin** and **dig**.

shindy noun (pl. **shindies**) informal a noisy disturbance or quarrel.
– ORIGIN perhaps from **shinty**.

shine verb (past and past part. **shone** or **shined**) 1 give out or reflect light. 2 point a torch or other light in a particular direction. 3 (of a person's eyes) be bright with an emotion. 4 be very good at something: *she shines at comedy.* 5 (**shine through**) (of a quality or skill) be clearly evident. 6 (past and past part. **shined**) polish something. • noun 1 a quality of brightness produced by reflected light. 2 an act of polishing.
– PHRASES **take the shine off** make something seem less good or exciting. **take a shine to** informal develop a liking for someone.
– ORIGIN Old English.

shiner noun informal a black eye.

shingle¹ noun a mass of small rounded pebbles, especially on a seashore.
– DERIVATIVES **shingly** adjective.
– ORIGIN unknown.

shingle² noun 1 a rectangular wooden tile used on walls or roofs. 2 dated a woman's short haircut, tapering from the back of the head to the nape of the neck. • verb 1 roof or clad something with wooden tiles. 2 dated cut hair in a shingle.
– ORIGIN probably from Latin *scindula* 'a split piece of wood'.

shingles plural noun (treated as sing.) a disease caused by a virus, in which painful blisters form along the path of a nerve or nerves.
– ORIGIN from Latin *cingulum* 'girdle'.

shin splints plural noun (treated as sing. or pl.) pain in the shin and lower leg caused by prolonged running on hard surfaces.

Shinto /shin-toh/ noun a Japanese religion involving the worship of ancestors and nature spirits.
– DERIVATIVES **Shintoism** noun **Shintoist** noun.

– ORIGIN Chinese, 'way of the gods'.

shinty noun a Scottish game resembling hockey, played with curved sticks and taller goalposts.
– ORIGIN unknown.

shiny adjective (**shinier, shiniest**) reflecting light because very smooth, clean, or polished.
– DERIVATIVES **shinily** adverb **shininess** noun.

ship noun 1 a large boat for transporting people or goods by sea. 2 a sailing boat with a bowsprit and three or more square-rigged masts. • verb (**ships, shipping, shipped**) 1 transport people or goods on a ship or by other means. 2 make a product available for sale. 3 (of a boat) take in water over the side. 4 take oars from the rowlocks and lay them inside a boat. 5 (of a sailor) be employed on a ship.
– PHRASES **when someone's ship comes in** when someone's fortune is made.
– DERIVATIVES **shipload** noun **shipper** noun.
– ORIGIN Old English.

-ship suffix forming nouns referring to: 1 a quality or condition: *companionship.* 2 status or office: *citizenship.* 3 a skill: *workmanship.* 4 the members of a group: *membership.*
– ORIGIN Old English.

shipboard adjective used or occurring on board a ship.

shipbuilder noun a person or company that designs and builds ships.
– DERIVATIVES **shipbuilding** noun.

shiplap noun boards that are fitted together so that each overlaps the one below, used for cladding.

shipmate noun a fellow member of a ship's crew.

shipment noun 1 the action of transporting goods. 2 a quantity of goods shipped.

ship of the line noun historical a warship of the largest size.

shipping noun 1 ships as a whole. 2 the transport of goods.

shipshape adjective in good order; neat and clean.

shipwreck noun 1 the sinking or breaking up of a ship at sea. 2 a ship that has sunk or been destroyed at sea. • verb (**be shipwrecked**) 1 be left somewhere after one's ship has sunk or been destroyed. 2 (of a ship) suffer a shipwreck.

shipwright noun a shipbuilder.

shipyard noun a place where ships are built and repaired.

Shiraz /shi-raz, sheer-az/ noun a red wine made from a variety of black wine grape.
– ORIGIN from the city of *Shiraz* in Iran.

shire noun 1 Brit. a county in England. 2 (**the Shires**) the rural areas of the English Midlands, regarded as strongholds of traditional country life. 3 Austral. a rural area with its own elected council.
– ORIGIN Old English, 'care, official charge, county'.

shire horse noun a heavy powerful breed of horse, used for pulling loads.

shirk verb avoid or neglect work or a duty.
– DERIVATIVES **shirker** noun.

S

– ORIGIN perhaps from German *Schurke* 'scoundrel'.

shirr /shur/ verb (usu. as adj. **shirred**) gather fabric by means of drawn or elastic threads in parallel rows.
– ORIGIN unknown.

shirt noun **1** an item of clothing for the upper body, with a collar and sleeves and buttons down the front. **2** a similar top of light material without full fastenings, worn for sports and leisure: *a football shirt.*
– PHRASES **keep your shirt on** informal stay calm. **lose one's shirt** informal lose all one's money.
– DERIVATIVES **shirted** adjective.
– ORIGIN Old English.

shirt dress noun a dress with a collar and button fastening in the style of a shirt, without a seam at the waist.

shirtsleeve noun the sleeve of a shirt.
– PHRASES **in (one's) shirtsleeves** wearing a shirt without a jacket over it.
– DERIVATIVES **shirtsleeved** adjective.

shirt tail noun the curved part of a shirt which comes below the waist.

shirtwaister (N. Amer. **shirtwaist**) noun a shirt dress with a seam at the waist.

shirty adjective (**shirtier, shirtiest**) Brit. informal bad-tempered or annoyed.
– DERIVATIVES **shirtily** adverb **shirtiness** noun.

shish kebab /shish ki-bab/ noun a dish of pieces of meat and vegetables cooked and served on skewers.
– ORIGIN Turkish *şiş kebap.*

shit vulgar slang verb (**shits, shitting, shitted** or **shit** or **shat**) **1** pass faeces from the body. **2** (**shit oneself**) be very frightened. ▪ noun **1** faeces. **2** something worthless; rubbish. **3** an unpleasant or disliked person. ▪ exclamation expressing disgust or annoyance.
– DERIVATIVES **shitty** adjective.
– ORIGIN Old English, 'diarrhoea'.

shite noun & exclamation Brit. vulgar slang another term for **SHIT**.

shiver¹ verb shake slightly and uncontrollably from cold, fear, or excitement. ▪ noun **1** a brief trembling movement. **2** (**the shivers**) a spell of shivering from fear or cold.
– DERIVATIVES **shivery** adjective.
– ORIGIN perhaps from an Old English word meaning 'jaw'.

shiver² noun a splinter or fragment of a material such as glass. ▪ verb break into splinters or fragments.
– ORIGIN from a Germanic word meaning 'to split'.

Shoah /shoh-uh/ noun (in Jewish use) the Holocaust.
– ORIGIN modern Hebrew, 'catastrophe'.

shoal¹ noun **1** a large number of fish swimming together. **2** informal, chiefly Brit. a large number of people or things. ▪ verb (of fish) swim together in a shoal.
– ORIGIN probably from Dutch *schôle* 'troop'.

shoal² noun **1** an area of shallow water. **2** a submerged sandbank that is visible at low tide. ▪ verb (of water) become shallower.
– ORIGIN Old English.

shock¹ noun **1** a sudden upsetting or surprising event or experience: *her illness has come as a*

great shock to all of us. **2** an unpleasant feeling of surprise and distress. **3** a serious medical condition associated with a fall in blood pressure, caused by loss of blood, severe injury, or sudden emotional stress. **4** a violent shaking movement caused by an impact, explosion, or earthquake. **5** an electric shock. ▪ verb **1** make someone feel very surprised and upset. **2** make someone feel outraged or disgusted. **3** cause someone to be in a state of medical shock.
– DERIVATIVES **shockable** adjective **shockproof** adjective.
– ORIGIN French *choc.*

shock² noun an untidy or thick mass of hair.
– ORIGIN uncertain.

shock³ noun a group of twelve sheaves of grain placed upright and supporting each other to allow the grain to dry and ripen.
– ORIGIN perhaps from Dutch, German *schok.*

shock absorber noun a device for absorbing jolts and vibrations, especially on a vehicle.

shocker noun informal a thing that shocks, especially through being unacceptable or sensational.

shocking adjective **1** causing great surprise or disgust. **2** Brit. informal very bad.
– DERIVATIVES **shockingly** adverb.

shocking pink noun a very bright shade of pink.

shock tactics plural noun the use of sudden violent or extreme action to shock someone into doing something.

shock therapy (also **shock treatment**) noun treatment of certain mental illnesses by giving controlled electric shocks to the brain.

shock troops plural noun troops trained to carry out sudden attacks.

shock wave noun a moving wave of very high pressure caused by an explosion or by something travelling faster than sound.

shod past and past participle of **SHOE**.

shoddy adjective (**shoddier, shoddiest**) **1** badly made or done. **2** dishonest or underhand: *a shoddy political deal.*
– DERIVATIVES **shoddily** adverb **shoddiness** noun.
– ORIGIN unknown.

shoe noun **1** a covering for the foot with a stiff sole, ending just below the ankle. **2** a horseshoe. **3** a socket on a camera for fitting a flash unit. **4** a brake shoe. ▪ verb (**shoes, shoeing, shod**) **1** fit a horse with a shoe or shoes. **2** (**be shod**) be wearing shoes of a specified kind: *his large feet were shod in trainers.*
– PHRASES **be (or put oneself) in someone else's shoes** imagine oneself in another person's situation.
– ORIGIN Old English.

shoebox noun informal a very small room or space.

shoehorn noun a curved piece of metal or plastic, used for easing one's heel into a shoe. ▪ verb force into a space that is too small: *seven lecturers shoehorned into an office designed for one person.*

shoelace noun a cord or leather strip passed through holes or hooks on opposite sides of a shoe and pulled tight to fasten it.

shoemaker noun a person who makes footwear as a profession.

shoestring noun **1** informal a small or inadequate amount of money: *living on a shoestring.* **2** N. Amer. a shoelace.

shoe tree noun a shaped block put into a shoe when it is not being worn to keep it in shape.

shogun /shoh-guhn/ noun (formerly, in Japan) a hereditary commander-in-chief of the army.
– DERIVATIVES **shogunate** /shoh-guh-nuht/ noun.
– ORIGIN Japanese.

Shona /shoh-nuh/ noun (pl. same or **Shonas**) **1** a member of a group of peoples inhabiting parts of southern Africa, particularly Zimbabwe. **2** any of the related languages spoken by the Shona.
– ORIGIN the name in Shona.

shone past and past participle of **SHINE**.

shoo exclamation used to drive away an animal or person. • verb (**shoos, shooing, shooed**) drive a person or animal away by saying 'shoo' or otherwise acting in a discouraging way.

shoo-in noun informal, chiefly N. Amer. a person or thing that is certain to succeed or win.

shook past of **SHAKE**.

shoot verb (past and past part. **shot**) **1** kill or wound a person or animal with a bullet or arrow. **2** fire a missile from a weapon. **3** move suddenly and rapidly: *the car shot forward.* **4** glance at or say something to someone quickly or abruptly. **5** film or photograph a scene, film, etc. **6** (in sport) kick, hit, or throw the ball or puck in an attempt to score a goal. **7** (as adj. **shooting**) (of a pain) sudden and piercing. **8** (of a boat) sweep swiftly down or under rapids, a waterfall, or a bridge. **9** move a door bolt to fasten or unfasten a door. **10** (of a plant) send out buds or shoots. **11** informal drive past a traffic light that is at red. • noun **1** a new part growing from the main trunk or stem of a tree or other plant. **2** an occasion of taking photographs professionally or making a film or video: *a fashion shoot.* **3** an occasion when a group of people hunt and shoot game for sport. **4** Brit. land used for shooting game. **5** variant spelling of **CHUTE¹**.
– PHRASES **shoot the breeze** N. Amer. informal have a casual conversation. **shoot oneself in the foot** informal accidentally make a situation worse for oneself. **shoot one's mouth off** informal talk boastfully or too freely. **the whole shooting match** informal everything. **shoot up** informal inject oneself with a narcotic drug.
– ORIGIN Old English.

shooter noun **1** a person who uses a gun. **2** informal a gun. **3** (in netball or basketball) a player whose role is to attempt to score goals.

shooting gallery noun a room or fairground booth for shooting at targets.

shooting star noun a small, rapidly moving meteor that burns up on entering the earth's atmosphere.

shooting stick noun a walking stick with a handle that unfolds to form a seat and a pointed end which can be stuck in the ground.

shoot-out noun **1** a gun battle that continues until one side is killed or defeated. **2** Football a tiebreaker decided by each side taking a specified number of penalty kicks.

shop noun **1** a building or part of a building where goods or services are sold. **2** a place where things are manufactured or repaired; a workshop. **3** informal an act of going shopping. • verb (**shops, shopping, shopped**) **1** go to a shop or shops to buy goods. **2** (**shop around**) look for the best available price or rate for something. **3** Brit. informal inform on someone.
– PHRASES **talk shop** discuss work matters with a colleague when one is not at work.
– ORIGIN Old French *eschoppe* 'lean-to booth'.

shopaholic noun informal a person with an uncontrollable urge to go shopping.

shop assistant noun Brit. a person who serves customers in a shop.

shopfitter noun a person whose job it is to fit the counters, shelves, etc. with which a shop is equipped.

shop floor noun Brit. the part of a factory where things are made or assembled.

shopfront noun Brit. the part of a shop that faces the street.

shopkeeper noun the owner and manager of a shop.

shoplifting noun the theft of goods from a shop by someone pretending to be a customer.
– DERIVATIVES **shoplift** verb **shoplifter** noun.

shopper noun **1** a person who is shopping. **2** Brit. a wheeled carrier for shopping.

shopping noun **1** the buying of goods from shops. **2** goods bought from shops.

shopping centre noun a group of shops situated together, sometimes under one roof.

shop-soiled (N. Amer. **shopworn**) adjective (of an article) dirty or damaged from being displayed or handled in a shop.

shop steward noun a person elected by workers in a factory to represent them in dealings with management.

shore¹ noun **1** the land along the edge of a sea, lake, or large river. **2** (also **shores**) literary a foreign country: *distant shores.*
– PHRASES **on shore** ashore; on land.
– DERIVATIVES **shoreward** adjective & adverb **shorewards** adverb.
– ORIGIN Dutch, German *schôre*.

shore² verb (**shore something up**) **1** support or strengthen something weak or in difficulties: *the company will cut its investment programme to shore up its shaky finances.* **2** support something with a prop or beam. • noun a prop or beam set up against something to support it.
– DERIVATIVES **shoring** noun.
– ORIGIN Dutch, German *schore* 'prop'.

shore leave noun leisure time spent ashore by a sailor.

shoreline noun the line along which the sea or other large body of water meets the land.

shorn past participle of **SHEAR**.

short adjective **1** of a small length in space or time. **2** (of a person) small in height. **3** smaller than is usual or expected: *a short speech.* **4** (**short of/on**) not having enough of something. **5** not available in sufficient quantities; scarce. **6** rude and abrupt. **7** (of a ball in sport) travelling a small distance, or not far enough. **8** (of odds in betting) reflecting a high level of probability. **9** (of a vowel)

S

pronounced in a way that takes a shorter time than a long vowel in the same position (e.g. in standard British English the vowel sound in *good*). **10** (of pastry) containing a high proportion of fat to flour and therefore crumbly. • **adverb** not as far as the point aimed at: *all too often you pitch the ball short.* • **noun 1** Brit. a drink of spirits served in small measures. **2** a short film as opposed to a feature film. • **verb** experience a short-circuit. – PHRASES **be caught short 1** be put at a disadvantage. **2** Brit. informal urgently need to go to the toilet. **bring** (or **pull**) **someone up short** make someone stop or pause abruptly. **for short** as an abbreviation or nickname. **go short** not have enough of something. **in short** to sum up; briefly. **in the short run** (or **term**) in the near future. **in short supply** (of a commodity) scarce. **make short work of** achieve, eat, or drink something quickly. **short for** an abbreviation or nickname for. **short of 1** less than. **2** not reaching as far as. **3** without going so far as doing something extreme. **stop short** stop suddenly. – DERIVATIVES **shortish** adjective **shortness** noun. – ORIGIN Old English.

shortage noun a situation in which there is not enough of something needed.

shortbread (Brit. also **shortcake**) noun a crisp, rich, crumbly type of biscuit made with butter, flour, and sugar.

short change verb (**short-change**) **1** cheat someone by giving them less than the correct change. **2** treat unfairly by withholding something deserved: *women have been short-changed by our education system.*

short circuit noun a faulty connection in an electrical circuit in which the current flows along a shorter route than it should do. • **verb** (**short-circuit**) **1** cause or suffer a short circuit. **2** shorten a process by using a more direct but irregular method.

shortcoming noun a failure to meet a certain standard; a fault or weakness: *the shortcomings of the legal system.*

shortcrust pastry noun Brit. crumbly pastry made with flour, fat, and a little water.

short cut noun **1** an alternative route that is shorter than the one usually taken. **2** a way of achieving something that is quicker than usual.

short division noun the process of dividing one number by another without writing down the calculations.

shorten verb make or become shorter.

shortening noun fat used for making pastry.

shortfall noun a situation in which there is less of something than is required or expected.

short fuse noun informal a quick temper.

shorthand noun **1** a method of rapid writing by means of abbreviations and symbols, used for recording what someone is saying. **2** a short and simple way of expressing or referring to something: *she learned that 'HS' is military shorthand for mustard gas.*

short-handed adjective not having enough or the usual number of staff.

short haul noun a relatively short distance in terms of travel or the transport of goods.

short head noun Brit. Horse Racing a distance less than the length of a horse's head.

shorthold adjective English Law (of a tenancy) in which the tenant agrees to rent a property for a stated period, at the end of which the landlord may recover it.

shorthorn noun a breed of cattle with short horns.

shortlist noun a list of selected candidates from which a final choice is made. • **verb** put someone or something on a shortlist.

short-lived adjective lasting only a short time.

shortly adverb **1** in a short time; soon. **2** abruptly or sharply.

short-range adjective **1** able to be used or be effective only over short distances. **2** relating to a period of future time that is near to the present: *a short-range weather forecast.*

shorts plural noun **1** short trousers that reach to the knees or thighs. **2** N. Amer. men's underpants.

short shrift noun abrupt and unsympathetic treatment: *he gave short shrift to admirers who praised his courage.* – ORIGIN first meaning 'little time allowed for making confession between being condemned and punished'; from **SHRIVE**.

short-sighted adjective Brit. **1** unable to see things clearly unless they are close to the eyes. **2** not thinking carefully about the consequences of something. – DERIVATIVES **short-sightedly** adverb **short-sightedness** noun.

short-staffed adjective not having enough or the usual number of staff.

shortstop noun Baseball a fielder positioned between second and third base.

short-tempered adjective having a tendency to lose one's temper quickly.

short-termism noun a policy of achieving profit or benefit in the near future without concern for more far-reaching effects.

short wave noun **1** a radio wave of a wavelength between about 10 and 100 metres (and a frequency of about 3 to 30 megahertz). **2** broadcasting using a wavelength between about 10 and 100 metres.

short-winded adjective out of breath, or tending to run out of breath quickly.

shorty (also **shortie**) noun (pl. **shorties**) informal **1** a short person. **2** a short dress, nightdress, or raincoat.

Shoshone /shuh-**shoh**-ni/ noun (pl. same or **Shoshones**) a member of an American Indian people living chiefly in Wyoming, Idaho, and Nevada. – ORIGIN unknown.

shot¹ noun **1** the firing of a gun or cannon. **2** a hit, stroke, or kick of the ball in sport, especially as an attempt to score. **3** informal an attempt to do something. **4** a photograph. **5** a film sequence photographed continuously by one camera. **6** a person with a specified level of ability in shooting: *he was an excellent shot.* **7** (also **lead shot**) tiny lead pellets used in a single charge or cartridge in a shotgun. **8** (pl. same) a ball of stone or metal fired from a large gun or cannon. **9** a heavy ball thrown by a shot-putter. **10** the launch of a rocket: *a*

moon shot. **11** informal a small drink of spirits. **12** informal an injection of a drug or vaccine.
– PHRASES **give it one's best shot** informal do the best that one can. **like a shot** informal without hesitation. **a shot in the arm** informal a source of encouragement.
– ORIGIN Old English.

shot² past and past participle of **SHOOT**. adjective **1** (of cloth) woven with a warp and weft of different colours, giving a contrasting effect when looked at from different angles. **2** interspersed with a different colour: *dark hair shot with silver*. **3** informal ruined or worn out.
– PHRASES **get** (or **be**) **shot of** Brit. informal get (or be) rid of. **shot through with** filled with a quality or feature.

shot glass noun a small glass for serving spirits.

shotgun noun a gun for firing small shot at short range.

shotgun marriage (also **shotgun wedding**) noun informal an enforced or hurried wedding, especially because the bride is pregnant.

shot put noun an athletic contest in which a very heavy round ball is thrown as far as possible.
– DERIVATIVES **shot-putter** noun **shot-putting** noun.

should modal verb (3rd sing. **should**) **1** used to indicate what is right or ought to be done. **2** used to indicate what is probable. **3** formal used to state what would happen if something else was the case: *if you should change your mind, I'll be at the hotel*. **4** used with *I* and *we* to express a polite request, opinion, or hope.
– ORIGIN past of **SHALL**.

> USAGE: As with **shall** and **will**, there are traditional rules as to when to use **should** and when to use **would**. These say that **should** is used with I and we (*I said I should be late*), while **would** is used with **you, he, she, it,** and **they** (*you didn't say you would be late*). Nowadays, people do not follow these rules so strictly and are in any case more likely to use the shortened forms **I'd, we'd,** etc., especially when speaking.

shoulder noun **1** the joint between the upper arm or forelimb and the main part of the body. **2** a joint of meat from the upper foreleg and shoulder blade of an animal. **3** a steep sloping side of a mountain. • verb **1** put something heavy over one's shoulder or shoulders to carry it. **2** take on a responsibility. **3** push someone or something out of one's way with one's shoulder.
– PHRASES **put one's shoulder to the wheel** set to work in a determined way. **shoulder arms** hold a rifle against the right side of the body, barrel upwards. **shoulder to shoulder** side by side or acting together.
– DERIVATIVES **shouldered** adjective.
– ORIGIN Old English.

shoulder bag noun a bag with a long strap that is hung over the shoulder.

shoulder blade noun either of the large, flat triangular bones at the top of the back; the scapula.

shoulder pad noun a pad sewn into the shoulder of a jacket, dress, etc. to provide shape or give protection.

shoulder strap noun **1** a narrow strip of material going over the shoulder from front to back of a dress or top. **2** a long strap attached to a bag for carrying it over the shoulder.

shouldn't contraction should not.

shout verb **1** speak or call out very loudly. **2** (**shout at**) speak angrily and loudly to someone. **3** (**shout someone down**) prevent someone from speaking or being heard by shouting. • noun **1** a loud cry or call. **2** (**one's shout**) Brit. informal one's turn to buy a round of drinks.
– PHRASES **in with a shout** Brit. informal having a good chance.
– ORIGIN perhaps from **SHOOT**.

shove verb **1** push someone or something roughly. **2** put something somewhere carelessly or roughly. **3** (**shove off**) informal go away. **4** (**shove off**) push away from the shore in a boat. • noun a strong push.
– ORIGIN Old English.

shovel noun a tool resembling a spade with a broad blade and upturned sides, used for moving earth, snow, etc. • verb (**shovels, shovelling, shovelled;** US **shovels, shoveling, shoveled**) **1** move earth, snow, etc. with a shovel. **2** (**shovel something down/in**) informal eat food quickly and in large quantities.
– ORIGIN Old English.

shoveler (also **shoveller**) noun a duck with a long, broad bill.

show verb (past part. **shown** or **showed**) **1** be or make visible: *wrinkles were starting to show on her face*. **2** offer something to be inspected or viewed. **3** present an image of: *a postcard showing Mount Etna*. **4** display a quality, emotion, or characteristic. **5** be evidence of or prove something. **6** treat someone in a particular way. **7** make someone understand something by explaining it or doing it oneself. **8** lead or guide: *show them in, please*. **9** (also **show up**) informal arrive for an appointment. • noun **1** a theatrical performance, especially a musical. **2** a light entertainment programme on television or radio. **3** an event or competition involving the public display of animals, plants, or products. **4** an impressive or attractive sight or display. **5** a display of a quality or feeling. **6** an outward display intended to give a false impression. **7** a ridiculous display: *don't make a show of yourself*. **8** informal a project or organization: *I run the show*.
– PHRASES **for show** for the sake of appearance rather than use. **get the show on the road** informal begin a project or enterprise. **good** (or **bad** or **poor**) **show!** Brit. informal, dated used to express approval (or disapproval or dissatisfaction). **show one's hand** reveal one's plans. **show off** try to impress others by talking about one's abilities or possessions. **show something off** display something that one is proud of. **show of hands** a vote carried out by the raising of hands. **show oneself** (or **one's face**) appear in public. **show someone round** point out interesting features in a place or building to someone. **show someone/thing up 1** reveal someone or something as being

bad or at fault. **2** informal embarrass or humiliate someone.

– ORIGIN Old English, 'look at, inspect'.

showbiz noun informal show business.

– DERIVATIVES **showbizzy** adjective.

show business noun the world of films, television, pop music, and the theatre as a profession or industry.

showcase noun **1** an occasion for presenting someone or something favourably to the public. **2** a glass case for displaying articles in a shop or museum. •**verb** put on display: *he made a short film to showcase his directing talents.*

showdown noun a final test or confrontation intended to settle a dispute.

shower /rhymes with flower/ noun **1** a brief fall of rain or snow. **2** a mass of small things falling at once. **3** a large number of things arriving at the same time: *a shower of awards.* **4** a piece of equipment that creates a spray of water under which a person stands to wash themselves. **5** an act of washing in a shower. **6** Brit. informal an incompetent or worthless group of people. **7** N. Amer. a party at which presents are given to a woman who is about to get married or have a baby. •**verb 1** fall or cause to fall in a shower. **2** (**shower someone with** or **shower something on**) give a large number of things to someone. **3** wash oneself in a shower.

– ORIGIN Old English.

showerproof adjective (of a raincoat or jacket) able to keep out light rain.

showery adjective with frequent showers of rain.

showgirl noun an actress who sings and dances in a musical or variety show.

showground noun an area of land on which a show takes place.

show house (also **show home**) noun Brit. a house on a newly built estate which is furnished and decorated to be shown to possible buyers.

showing noun **1** a presentation of a cinema film or television programme. **2** a performance of a particular quality: *poor opinion poll showings.*

showjumping noun the competitive sport of riding horses over a course of fences and other obstacles in an arena.

– DERIVATIVES **showjumper** noun.

showman noun (pl. **showmen**) **1** the manager or presenter of a circus, fair, etc. **2** a person who is skilled at entertaining people or gaining their attention.

– DERIVATIVES **showmanship** noun.

shown past participle of **SHOW**.

show-off noun informal a person who tries to impress others by talking about their own abilities or possessions.

showpiece noun **1** an outstanding example of something: *the harbour is one of the showpieces of the city.* **2** an item of work put on exhibition or display.

showplace noun a beautiful or interesting place that attracts many visitors.

showroom noun a room used to display cars, furniture, or other goods for sale.

show-stopper noun informal something that is very impressive, striking, or appealing.

– DERIVATIVES **show-stopping** adjective.

show trial noun a trial that is held in public to influence or satisfy public opinion, rather than to ensure that justice is done.

showy adjective (**showier, showiest**) very bright or colourful and attracting much attention.

– DERIVATIVES **showily** adverb **showiness** noun.

shrank past of **SHRINK**.

shrapnel /shrap-n'l/ noun small metal fragments thrown out by the explosion of a shell, bomb, etc.

– ORIGIN named after the British soldier General Henry *Shrapnel*, inventor of shells that explode with a shower of shrapnel.

shred noun **1** a strip of material that has been torn, cut, or scraped from something larger. **2** a very small amount: *not a shred of evidence.* •**verb** (**shreds, shredding, shredded**) tear or cut something into shreds.

– DERIVATIVES **shredder** noun.

– ORIGIN Old English.

shrew noun **1** a small mammal resembling a mouse, with a long pointed snout and tiny eyes. **2** a bad-tempered woman.

– ORIGIN Old English.

shrewd adjective having or showing sharp powers of judgement; astute: *he's a shrewd businessman who knows how to make money.*

– DERIVATIVES **shrewdly** adverb **shrewdness** noun.

– ORIGIN from **SHREW** in the former sense 'evil person or thing'.

shrewish adjective (of a woman) bad-tempered or nagging.

– DERIVATIVES **shrewishly** adverb **shrewishness** noun.

shriek verb make a high-pitched piercing cry or sound. •**noun** a high-pitched piercing cry or sound.

– DERIVATIVES **shrieker** noun.

– ORIGIN imitating the sound.

shrike noun a songbird with a hooked bill that often impales its prey on thorns.

– ORIGIN imitating its call.

shrill adjective **1** (of a voice or sound) high-pitched and piercing. **2** (of a complaint or demand) loud and forceful. •**verb** make a high-pitched piercing noise.

– DERIVATIVES **shrillness** noun **shrilly** adverb.

– ORIGIN Germanic.

shrimp noun **1** (pl. same or **shrimps**) a small edible shellfish with ten legs. **2** informal, derogatory a small weak person. •**verb** (often as noun **shrimping**) fish for shrimps.

– DERIVATIVES **shrimper** noun.

– ORIGIN probably from German *schrempen* 'to wrinkle'.

shrine noun **1** a place regarded as holy because it is connected to a holy person or event. **2** a place or receptacle containing a religious statue or holy object. **3** a place regarded as important because it is associated with a particular person or thing: *the room was a shrine to middle-class taste.*

– ORIGIN Old English, 'cabinet, chest'.

shrink verb (past **shrank**; past part. **shrunk** or (especially as adj.) **shrunken**) **1** become or make smaller in size or amount. **2** (of clothes

or material) become smaller as a result of being washed in water that is too hot. **3** move back or away in fear or disgust. **4 (shrink from)** be unwilling to do: *I don't shrink from my responsibilities.* • **noun** informal a psychiatrist.
– DERIVATIVES **shrinkable** adjective.
– ORIGIN Old English; the noun is from *headshrinker.*

shrinkage noun **1** the process of shrinking or the amount by which something has shrunk. **2** an allowance made for reduction in the takings of a business due to theft or wastage.

shrinking violet noun informal a very shy person.

shrink-wrap verb package an object in clinging plastic film. • **noun (shrink wrap)** clinging plastic film used to package an object.

shrive /rhymes with drive/ verb (past **shrove**; past part. **shriven**) old use (of a priest) hear a person's confession, give them a religious duty, and declare them free from sin.
– ORIGIN Old English.

shrivel verb (**shrivels, shrivelling, shrivelled**; US **shrivels, shriveling, shriveled**) wrinkle and shrink through loss of moisture.
– ORIGIN perhaps Scandinavian.

shroud noun **1** a length of cloth in which a dead person is wrapped for burial. **2** a thing that surrounds or hides someone or something: *a shroud of mist often envelops the island.* **3** (**shrouds**) a set of ropes supporting the mast or topmast of a sailing boat. • **verb** surround so as to cover or hide: *his early life is shrouded in mystery.*
– ORIGIN Old English, 'garment, clothing'.

shrove past of SHRIVE.

Shrove Tuesday noun the day before Ash Wednesday.

shrub noun a woody plant which is smaller than a tree and divided into separate stems at or near the ground.
– DERIVATIVES **shrubby** adjective.
– ORIGIN Old English.

shrubbery noun (pl. **shrubberies**) an area in a garden planted with shrubs.

shrug verb (**shrugs, shrugging, shrugged**) **1** raise one's shoulders slightly and briefly as a sign that one does not know or care about something. **2** (**shrug something off**) dismiss something as unimportant. • **noun 1** an act of shrugging one's shoulders. **2** a woman's close-fitting cardigan or jacket, cut short at the front and back so that only the arms and shoulders are covered.
– ORIGIN unknown.

shrunk (also **shrunken**) past participle of SHRINK.

shtick /shtik/ noun informal **1** a performer's routine or gimmick. **2** a person's talent or typical behaviour: *he has developed a distinctive courtroom shtick.*
– ORIGIN German *Stück* 'piece'.

shtum /shtuum/ (also **schtum**) adjective (in phrase **keep/stay shtum**) Brit. informal stay silent.
– ORIGIN German *stumm.*

shuck /shuk/ chiefly N. Amer. verb **1** remove the husks or shells from maize or shellfish. **2** informal get rid of something. **3** informal take off an item of clothing. • **noun 1** the husk of an ear

of maize. **2** the shell of an oyster or clam.
– ORIGIN unknown.

shucks exclamation informal, chiefly N. Amer. used to express surprise, regret, etc.

shudder verb tremble or shake violently, especially as a result of fear or disgust. • **noun** an act of shuddering.
– DERIVATIVES **shuddery** adjective.
– ORIGIN Dutch *schüderen.*

shuffle verb **1** walk without lifting the feet completely from the ground. **2** move restlessly while sitting or standing. **3** rearrange a pack of cards by sliding them over each other quickly. **4** rearrange people or things. **5 (shuffle through)** look through a number of things hurriedly. **6 (shuffle something off)** get out of or avoid a responsibility. • **noun 1** a shuffling walk or sound. **2** an act of shuffling a pack of cards. **3** a rearrangement of people or things; a reshuffle. **4** a dance performed with a quick dragging movement of the feet.
– DERIVATIVES **shuffler** noun.
– ORIGIN perhaps from German *schuffeln* 'walk clumsily', also 'deal dishonestly, shuffle cards'.

shufti /shuuf-ti/ noun (pl. **shuftis**) Brit. informal a quick look.
– ORIGIN from an Arabic word meaning 'try to see'.

shun verb (**shuns, shunning, shunned**) avoid, ignore, or reject: *he shunned fashionable society.*
– ORIGIN Old English, 'hate, shrink back in fear'.

shunt verb **1** slowly push or pull a railway vehicle or vehicles from one set of tracks to another. **2** push or shove someone or something. **3** divert to a less important place or position: *amateurs were gradually being shunted to filing jobs.* • **noun 1** an act of shunting. **2** Brit. informal an accident in which a vehicle runs into the back of another that is travelling in front of it. **3** an electrical conductor joining two points of a circuit.
– DERIVATIVES **shunter** noun.
– ORIGIN perhaps from SHUN.

shush exclamation be quiet. • **noun 1** an utterance of 'shush'. **2** a soft swishing or rustling sound. • **verb 1** tell or signal someone to be silent. **2** move with a soft swishing or rustling sound.
– ORIGIN imitating the sound.

shut verb (**shuts, shutting, shut**) **1** move something into position to block an opening. **2** (**shut someone/thing in/out**) keep someone or something in or out by closing a door, gate, etc. **3** prevent access to a place or along a route. **4** stop operating for business: *we shut the shop for lunch.* **5** close a book, curtains, etc.
– PHRASES **be** (or **get) shut of** informal be (or get) rid of. **shut down** stop operating or opening for business. **shut something off** stop something from flowing or working. **shut something out** prevent oneself from thinking about something. **shut up** informal stop talking.
– ORIGIN Old English, 'put a bolt in position to hold fast'.

shutdown noun an act of closing a factory or of turning off a machine.

shut-eye noun informal sleep.

shutter noun **1** each of a pair of hinged panels fixed inside or outside a window that can be closed for security or to keep out the light. **2** a device that opens and closes to expose the film in a camera. •**verb** close the shutters of a window or building.

shuttle noun 1 a form of transport that travels regularly between two places. **2** (in weaving) a bobbin used for carrying the weft thread across the cloth between the warp threads. **3** a bobbin carrying the lower thread in a sewing machine. •**verb** travel or transport someone or something regularly between places.
– ORIGIN Old English, 'dart, missile'.

shuttlecock noun a light cone-shaped object consisting of a rounded piece of cork or plastic with feathers attached, struck with rackets in badminton.

shuttle diplomacy noun negotiations conducted by a person who travels between two or more countries that are reluctant to hold direct discussions.

shy¹ adjective (shyer, shyest) 1 nervous or timid in the company of other people. **2** (**shy of/about**) slow or reluctant to do something. **3** (in combination) having a specified dislike: *camera-shy.* **4** (**shy of**) informal less than; short of: *the car weighs just shy of 3,000 pounds.* •**verb** (**shies, shying, shied**) **1** (of a horse) suddenly turn aside in fright. **2** (usu. **shy away from**) avoid something through nervousness or lack of confidence.
– DERIVATIVES **shyly** adverb **shyness** noun.
– ORIGIN Old English.

shy² verb (shies, shying, shied) throw something at a target.
– ORIGIN unknown.

shyster noun informal a dishonest or deceitful person, especially a lawyer.
– ORIGIN said to be from *Scheuster,* the name of a lawyer.

SI abbreviation Système International, the international system of units of measurement based on the metre, kilogram, second, ampere, kelvin, candela, and mole.

Si symbol the chemical element silicon.

Siamese noun (pl. same) **1** (also **Siamese cat**) a breed of cat that has short pale fur with a darker face, ears, feet, and tail. **2** dated a person from Siam (now Thailand) in SE Asia. •**adjective** dated relating to Thailand.

Siamese twins plural noun twins whose bodies are joined at birth.
– ORIGIN with reference to the *Siamese* men Chang and Eng, who were joined in this way.

> **USAGE:** The technical term is *conjoined twins.*

sib noun a brother or sister; a sibling.
– ORIGIN from Old English, 'related by birth or descent'.

Siberian /sy-**beer**-i-uhn/ **noun** a person from Siberia. •**adjective** relating to Siberia.

sibilant adjective making a soft hissing sound. •**noun** a speech sound made with a hissing effect, for example *s, sh.*
– DERIVATIVES **sibilance** noun.
– ORIGIN from Latin *sibilare* 'hiss'.

sibling noun a brother or sister.
– ORIGIN Old English, 'relative'.

sibyl noun (in ancient Greece and Rome) a woman supposedly able to pass on the messages and prophecies of a god.

– DERIVATIVES **sibylline** adjective.
– ORIGIN Greek *Sibulla.*

sic /sik/ **adverb** (after a copied or quoted word that appears odd or wrong) written exactly as it stands in the original.
– ORIGIN Latin, 'so, thus'.

Sicilian noun a person from Sicily. •**adjective** relating to Sicily.

sick¹ adjective 1 affected by physical or mental illness. **2** feeling nauseous and wanting to vomit. **3** (**sick of**) bored by or annoyed with someone or something because one has had too much of them. **4** informal behaving in an abnormal or cruel way. **5** informal (of humour) dealing with unpleasant subjects in a cruel or upsetting way. •**noun** Brit. informal vomit. •**verb** (**sick something up**) Brit. informal bring something up by vomiting.
– PHRASES **be sick 1** be ill. **2** Brit. vomit.
– ORIGIN Old English.

sick² verb (**sick something on**) set a dog on someone or something.
– ORIGIN dialect variant of SEEK.

sickbay noun a room or building in a school or on a ship that is set aside for sick people.

sickbed noun the bed of a person who is ill.

sick building syndrome noun a condition affecting office workers, including headaches and breathing problems, which is said to be caused by factors such as poor ventilation.

sicken verb 1 make someone feel disgusted or appalled. **2** become ill. **3** (**be sickening for**) be showing the first symptoms of an illness. **4** (as adj. **sickening**) informal very annoying.
– DERIVATIVES **sickeningly** adverb.

sickener noun informal something which causes disgust or great disappointment.

sickie noun Brit. informal a period of sick leave taken when a person is not actually ill.

sickle noun a farming tool with a short handle and a semicircular blade, used for cutting corn or grass.
– ORIGIN Latin *secula.*

sick leave noun permission to be absent from work because of illness.

sickle-cell anaemia (also **sickle-cell disease**) **noun** a severe hereditary form of anaemia in which the red blood cells are distorted into a crescent shape at low oxygen levels.

sickly adjective (**sicklier, sickliest**) **1** often ill; in poor health. **2** showing or causing poor health. **3** (of flavour, colour, etc.) so bright or sweet as to be unpleasant or make one feel sick. **4** excessively sentimental.
– DERIVATIVES **sickliness** noun.

sickness noun 1 the state of being ill. **2** a particular type of illness or disease. **3** nausea or vomiting.

sickness benefit noun (in the UK) benefit paid weekly by the state to a person for sickness which interrupts paid employment.

sicko noun (pl. **sickos**) informal a perverted person.

sickroom noun a room occupied by or set apart for people who are unwell.

side noun 1 a position to the left or right of an object, place, or central point. **2** either of the two halves into which something can be divided: *she lay on her side of the bed.* **3** an upright or sloping surface of a structure or

object that is not the top, bottom, front, or back. **4** each of the flat surfaces of a solid object. **5** either of the two surfaces of something flat and thin, e.g. paper. **6** a part or area near the edge of something. **7** a person or group opposing another or others in a dispute or contest. **8** a sports team. **9** a particular aspect: *he had a disagreeable side.* **10** either of the two faces of a record or of the corresponding parts of a cassette tape. **11** Geometry each of the lines forming the boundary of a plane rectilinear figure. **12** a person's line of descent as traced through either their father or mother. **13** Brit. informal a television channel. **14** Brit. informal a superior attitude towards others. •**adjective** additional or less important: *a side dish.* •**verb** (**side with/against**) support or oppose one person or group in a conflict or dispute.
- PHRASES **on the side 1** informal in addition to one's regular job. **2** informal as a secret additional sexual relationship. **3** (of food) served separately from the main dish. **side by side** close together and facing the same way. **side on** on, from, or towards the side. **take sides** support one person or cause against another.
- DERIVATIVES **sided** adjective **sideward** adjective & adverb **sidewards** adverb.
- ORIGIN Old English.

sidebar noun a short piece of additional information placed alongside a main article in a newspaper or magazine.

sideboard noun **1** a flat-topped piece of furniture with cupboards and drawers, used for storing crockery, glasses, etc. **2** (**sideboards**) Brit. sideburns.

sideburns plural noun a strip of hair growing down each side of a man's face in front of his ears.
- ORIGIN reversal of the name of the American General Ambrose *Burnside*, who had sideburns.

sidecar noun a small, low vehicle attached to the side of a motorcycle for carrying passengers.

side effect noun a secondary, typically undesirable effect of a drug or medical treatment.

sidekick noun informal a person's assistant.

sidelight noun **1** Brit. a small additional light on either side of a motor vehicle's headlights. **2** (**sidelights**) a ship's navigation lights. **3** a narrow pane of glass alongside a door or larger window.

sideline noun **1** an activity done in addition to a person's main job. **2** either of the two lines forming the boundaries of the longer sides of a football field, basketball court, etc. **3** (**the sidelines**) a position of observing a situation rather than being directly involved in it. •**verb 1** prevent a player from playing in a team or game. **2** remove from an influential position: *backbench MPs have been sidelined and excluded from decision-making.*

sidelong adjective & adverb (especially of a look) to or from one side; sideways.

sideman noun (pl. **sidemen**) a supporting musician in a jazz band or rock group.

sidereal /sy-**deer**-i-uhl/ adjective relating to the distant stars or their apparent positions in the sky.
- ORIGIN from Latin *sidus* 'star'.

sidereal time noun Astronomy time reckoned from the motion of the earth (or a planet) relative to the distant stars (rather than with respect to the sun).

side road noun a minor road joining or branching from a main road.

side-saddle adverb (of a woman rider) sitting with both feet on the same side of the horse.

sideshow noun **1** a small show or stall at an exhibition, fair, or circus. **2** a minor incident or issue that diverts attention from the main subject.

side-splitting adjective informal very amusing.

sidestep verb (**sidesteps, sidestepping, sidestepped**) **1** avoid someone or something by stepping sideways. **2** avoid dealing with or discussing: *he neatly sidestepped the questions about riots.* •**noun** a step to one side to avoid someone or something.

side street noun a minor street.

sideswipe noun a critical remark made while discussing another matter. •**verb** chiefly N. Amer. strike something, especially a motor vehicle, with a glancing blow.

sidetrack verb distract someone from an urgent or important issue.

sidewalk noun N. Amer. a pavement.

sideways adverb & adjective **1** to, towards, or from the side. **2** not conventional; alternative: *a sideways look at life.*
- DERIVATIVES **sidewise** adverb & adjective (US).

side whiskers plural noun sideburns on a man's cheeks.

side wind noun a wind blowing mainly from one side.

sidewinder /syd-**wyn**-der/ noun a burrowing rattlesnake of North American deserts that moves sideways by throwing its body into S-shaped curves.

siding noun **1** a short track beside and opening on to a main railway line, where trains are shunted or left. **2** N. Amer. cladding material for the outside of a building.

sidle verb walk in a stealthy or uncertain way.
- ORIGIN from former *sideling* 'sidelong'.

SIDS abbreviation sudden infant death syndrome (technical term for COT DEATH).

siege noun **1** a military operation in which enemy forces try to capture a town or building by surrounding it and cutting off essential supplies. **2** a similar operation by a police team to force an armed person to surrender.
- PHRASES **lay siege to** begin a siege of a place. **under siege** under constant pressure or attack: *Scotland's farmed salmon industry is under siege.*
- ORIGIN Old French *sege* 'seat'.

siege mentality noun a defensive or paranoid attitude based on the belief that others are hostile towards one.

siemens /**see**-muhnz/ noun Physics the SI unit of conductance.
- ORIGIN named after the German-born British engineer Sir Charles William *Siemens*.

sienna noun a kind of earth used as a pigment in painting, normally yellowish-brown (**raw**

S

sienna) or deep reddish-brown when roasted (**burnt sienna**).
– ORIGIN from Italian *terra di Sienna* 'earth of *Siena*' (an Italian city).

sierra /si-**air**-uh/ noun (in Spanish-speaking countries or the western US) a long jagged mountain chain.
– ORIGIN Spanish.

Sierra Leonean /si-air-uh li-**oh**-ni-uhn/ noun a person from Sierra Leone, a country in West Africa. • adjective relating to Sierra Leone.

siesta /si-**ess**-tuh/ noun an afternoon rest or nap, especially one taken regularly in hot countries.
– ORIGIN Spanish.

sieve /siv/ noun a utensil consisting of a wire or plastic mesh held in a frame, used for straining solids from liquids or separating coarser particles from finer ones. • verb put a substance through a sieve.
– ORIGIN Old English.

sievert /**see**vuht/ noun Physics the SI unit of dose equivalent, defined as a dose which delivers a joule of energy per kilogram of recipient mass.
– ORIGIN named after the Swedish physicist Rolf M. *Sievert* (1896–1966).

sift verb 1 put a fine or loose substance through a sieve so as to remove lumps or large particles. 2 examine something thoroughly to sort out what is important or useful.
– DERIVATIVES **sifter** noun.
– ORIGIN Old English.

sigh verb 1 let out a long, deep breath expressing sadness, relief, tiredness, etc. 2 (**sigh for**) literary long for someone or something. • noun an act of sighing.
– ORIGIN Old English.

sight noun 1 the faculty of seeing. 2 the action of seeing: *I hate the sight of blood.* 3 the area or distance within which someone can see or something can be seen. 4 a thing that is seen. 5 (**sights**) places of interest to tourists and other visitors. 6 (**a sight**) informal a ridiculous or unattractive person or thing. 7 (also **sights**) a device that one looks through to aim a gun or to see with a telescope or similar instrument. • verb 1 manage to see or glimpse: *two suspicious men had been sighted in the area.* 2 take aim by looking through the sights of a gun.
– PHRASES **at first sight** on the first impression. **catch sight of** manage to glimpse. **in sight** close to being achieved. **in** (or **within**) **sight of** 1 so as to see or be seen from. 2 close to achieving. **in** (or **within**) **one's sights** within the scope of one's ambitions or expectations. **lose sight of** fail to consider, be aware of, or remember. **on** (or **at**) **sight** as soon as someone or something has been seen. **raise** (or **lower**) **one's sights** increase (or lower) one's expectations. **set one's sights on** hope strongly to achieve. **a sight —** informal considerably: *she is a sight cleverer than Sarah.* **a sight for sore eyes** informal a person or thing that one is very pleased or relieved to see.
– DERIVATIVES **sighter** noun **sighting** noun.
– ORIGIN Old English.

USAGE: For an explanation of the difference between **sight** and **site**, see the note at **SITE**.

sighted adjective 1 having the ability to see; not blind. 2 having a specified kind of sight: *keen-sighted.*

sightless adjective unable to see; blind.

sight line noun an imaginary line from someone's eye to what is seen.

sight-read verb read a musical score and perform it without preparation.

sight screen noun Cricket a large white screen placed near the boundary in line with the wicket to help the batsman see the ball.

sightseeing noun the activity of visiting places of interest.
– DERIVATIVES **sightseer** noun.

sigil /**sij**-il/ noun literary a sign or symbol.
– ORIGIN Latin *sigillum* 'sign'.

sign noun 1 a thing whose presence or occurrence indicates that something exists, is happening, or may happen: *dark circles under the eyes are a sign of stress.* 2 a signal, gesture, or notice giving information or an instruction. 3 a symbol or word used to represent something in algebra, music, or other subjects. 4 each of the twelve equal sections into which the zodiac is divided. • verb 1 write one's name on a letter, document, etc. in order to show that one has written it or that one authorizes its contents. 2 recruit a sports player, musician, etc. by signing a contract with them. 3 use gestures to give information or instructions.
– PHRASES **sign off** conclude a letter, broadcast, or other message. **sign someone off** authorize someone to be absent from work. **sign on** 1 commit oneself to a job or other undertaking. 2 Brit. register as unemployed. **sign someone on** employ someone. **sign up** commit oneself to a job, course of study, etc.
– DERIVATIVES **signer** noun.
– ORIGIN Latin *signum* 'mark, token'.

signage noun chiefly N. Amer. commercial or public display signs.

signal[1] noun 1 a gesture, action, or sound giving information or an instruction. 2 a sign of a particular situation: *pain is a warning signal, telling you that something is wrong.* 3 an electrical impulse or radio wave transmitted or received. 4 a device that uses lights or a movable arm, used to tell drivers to stop or beware on a road or railway. • verb (**signals, signalling, signalled**; US **signals, signaling, signaled**) give information or an instruction to someone by means of a signal.
– DERIVATIVES **signaller** noun.
– ORIGIN Latin *signum* 'mark, token'.

signal[2] adjective striking in extent, seriousness, or importance.
– DERIVATIVES **signally** adverb.
– ORIGIN Italian *segnalato* 'distinguished'.

signal box noun Brit. a building next to a railway track from which signals, points, and other equipment are controlled.

signalman noun (pl. **signalmen**) 1 a railway worker responsible for operating signals and points. 2 a person responsible for sending and receiving naval or military signals.

signal-to-noise ratio noun the ratio of the strength of an electrical or other signal carrying information to that of unwanted interference, generally given in decibels.

signatory /sig-nuh-tuh-ri/ noun (pl. **signatories**) a person, organization, or state that has signed an agreement.
– ORIGIN from Latin *signare* 'to sign'.

signature noun **1** a person's name written in a distinctive way, used in signing a document, letter, etc. **2** the action of signing something. **3** a distinctive product or quality by which someone or something can be recognized: *the chef produced the pâté that was his signature.* **4** Music a key signature or time signature.
– ORIGIN from Latin *signare* 'to sign'.

signature tune noun chiefly Brit. a piece of music used to introduce a particular television or radio programme.

signboard noun a board displaying the name or logo of a business or product.

signet noun historical a small seal, especially one set in a ring, used to authorize an official document.
– ORIGIN Latin *signetum.*

signet ring noun a ring with letters or a design set into it.

significance noun **1** the quality of being significant; importance. **2** the meaning of something: *he took in the full significance of Peter's remarks.*
– ORIGIN Latin *significantia*, from *significare* 'indicate'.

significant adjective **1** important or large enough to be noticed. **2** having a particular meaning: *it's significant that he set the story in Italy.* **3** having a meaning that is not stated directly: *a significant look.*
– DERIVATIVES **significantly** adverb.

significant figure noun Mathematics each of the digits of a number that are used to express it to the required degree of accuracy.

signify verb (**signifies, signifying, signified**) **1** be an indication of something. **2** be a symbol of something. **3** make a feeling or intention known. **4** be of importance: *the locked door doesn't necessarily signify.*
– DERIVATIVES **signification** noun.
– ORIGIN Latin *significare.*

signing noun **1** Brit. a person who has recently been recruited to a sports team, record company, etc. **2** an event at which an author signs copies of their book to gain publicity and sales. **3** sign language.

sign language noun a system of communication used among and with deaf people, consisting of gestures and signs made by the hands and face.

signor /see-**nyor**/ noun a title or form of address for an Italian-speaking man, corresponding to *Mr* or *sir.*

signora /see-**nyor**-uh/ noun a title or form of address for an Italian-speaking married woman, corresponding to *Mrs* or *madam.*

signorina /see-nyuh-**ree**-nuh/ noun a title or form of address for an Italian-speaking unmarried woman, corresponding to *Miss.*

signpost noun a sign on a post, giving information such as the direction and distance to a nearby town. •verb chiefly Brit. mark a place or a feature with a signpost or signposts.

signwriter noun a person who paints commercial signs and advertisements.

– DERIVATIVES **signwriting** noun.

sika /**see**-kuh/ noun a deer with a greyish coat that turns yellowish-brown with white spots in summer, native to Japan and SE Asia.
– ORIGIN Japanese.

Sikh /seek/ noun a member of a religion (**Sikhism**) that was founded in the Punjab in the 15th century by Guru Nanak and is based on the belief that there is only one God. •adjective relating to Sikhs or Sikhism.
– ORIGIN Punjabi, 'disciple'.

silage /**sy**-lij/ noun grass or other green crops that are stored in airtight conditions without first being dried, used as animal feed in the winter.
– ORIGIN from Spanish *ensilar* 'put into a silo'.

silence noun **1** complete lack of sound. **2** a situation in which someone refuses or fails to speak: *he withdrew into sullen silence.* •verb **1** prevent someone from speaking. **2** make something silent.
– ORIGIN Latin *silentium.*

silencer noun a device for reducing the noise made by a mechanism, especially a gun or (Brit.) a vehicle's exhaust system.

silent adjective **1** not making or accompanied by any sound. **2** not speaking or not spoken aloud: *a silent prayer.* **3** (of a film) without an accompanying soundtrack. **4** (of a letter) written but not pronounced, e.g. *b* in *doubt.*
– DERIVATIVES **silently** adverb.

silent partner noun North American term for SLEEPING PARTNER.

silhouette /si-luu-et/ noun **1** the dark shape and outline of someone or something visible against a lighter background. **2** a representation of someone or something which shows them as a black shape on a light background. •verb show as a silhouette: *the castle was silhouetted against the sky.*
– ORIGIN named after the French author and politician Étienne de *Silhouette.*

silica /si-li-kuh/ noun silicon dioxide, a hard colourless compound which occurs as quartz and in sandstone and many other rocks.
– DERIVATIVES **siliceous** /si-**lish**-uhss/ adjective.
– ORIGIN from Latin *silex* 'flint'.

silica gel noun hydrated silica in a hard granular form which absorbs moisture from the air.

silicate /si-li-kayt, si-li-kuht/ noun a compound of silica combined with a metal oxide.

silicon /sil-i-k'n/ noun a grey non-metallic chemical element with semiconducting properties, used in making electronic circuits.
– ORIGIN from Latin *silex* 'flint'.

USAGE: Do not confuse **silicon** with **silicone**. **Silicon** is a chemical element used in electronic circuits and microchips, while **silicone** is the material used in cosmetic implants.

silicon chip noun a microchip.

silicone /sil-i-kohn/ noun a synthetic resin made from silicon, used to make cosmetic implants, plastic, paints, etc.

silicosis /si-li-koh-siss/ noun a lung disease caused by breathing dust containing silica.

silk noun **1** a fine, soft fibre produced by silkworms. **2** thread or fabric made from silk.

S

3 (silks) clothes made from silk, worn by a jockey. **4** Brit. informal a Queen's (or King's) Counsel. [so named because entitled to wear a gown made of silk.]
– PHRASES **take silk** Brit. become a Queen's (or King's) Counsel.
– ORIGIN Latin *sericus*, from Greek *Sēres*, the name given to the inhabitants of the Far Eastern countries from which silk first came overland to Europe.

silken adjective **1** smooth, soft, and shiny like silk: *her silken hair.* **2** made of silk.

silk screen noun a piece of fine material used in screen printing. • verb **(silk-screen)** print, decorate, or reproduce something using a silk screen.

silkworm noun a caterpillar which spins a silk cocoon from which silk fibre is obtained.

silky adjective **(silkier, silkiest) 1** smooth, soft, and shiny like silk. **2** (of a person's voice) smooth and gentle or persuasive.
– DERIVATIVES **silkily** adverb **silkiness** noun.

sill noun **1** a shelf or slab of stone, wood, or metal at the foot of a window or doorway. **2** a horizontal piece of metal that forms part of the frame of a vehicle. **3** Geology a sheet of igneous rock intruded between and parallel with existing strata. Compare with **DYKE**[1].
– ORIGIN Old English.

silly adjective **(sillier, silliest) 1** showing a lack of common sense or judgement; foolish. **2** Cricket referring to fielding positions very close to the batsman: *silly mid-on.* • noun (pl. **sillies**) informal a silly person.
– DERIVATIVES **silliness** noun.
– ORIGIN first in the sense 'happy', later 'innocent, feeble, ignorant': from dialect *seely*, from Germanic.

silo /sy-loh/ noun (pl. **silos**) **1** a tall tower on a farm, used to store grain. **2** a pit or other airtight structure in which green crops are stored as silage. **3** an underground chamber in which a guided missile is kept ready for firing.
– ORIGIN Spanish.

silt noun fine sand, clay, or other material carried by running water and deposited as a sediment. • verb (usu. **silt up** or **silt something up**) fill or block something with silt.
– DERIVATIVES **siltation** noun **silty** adjective.
– ORIGIN probably Scandinavian; related to **SALT**.

Silurian /sy-**lyoor**-i-uhn/ adjective Geology referring to the third period of the Palaeozoic era (about 439 to 409 million years ago), when the first fish and land plants appeared.
– ORIGIN from *Silures*, the Latin name of a people of ancient Wales.

silver noun **1** a precious greyish-white metallic chemical element. **2** a shiny grey-white colour like that of silver. **3** coins made from silver or from a metal that resembles silver. **4** silver dishes, containers, or cutlery. • verb **1** coat or plate something with silver. **2** literary give a silvery appearance to: *the dome was silvered with frost.* **3** (of a person's hair) turn grey or white.
– PHRASES **be born with a silver spoon in one's mouth** be born into a wealthy upper-class family. **the silver screen** the cinema industry.
– DERIVATIVES **silveriness** noun **silvery** adjective.
– ORIGIN Old English.

silver birch noun a birch tree with silver-grey bark.

silverfish noun (pl. same or **silverfishes**) a small silvery wingless insect that lives in buildings.

silver jubilee noun the twenty-fifth anniversary of an important event.

silver medal noun a medal made of or coloured silver, awarded for second place in a race or competition.

silver plate noun **1** a thin layer of silver applied as a coating to another metal. **2** plates, dishes, etc. made of or plated with silver.

silver service noun a style of serving food at formal meals in which the server places food on the diner's plate using a spoon and fork held in one hand.

silverside noun Brit. the upper side of a round of beef from the outside of the leg.

silversmith noun a person who makes silver articles.
– DERIVATIVES **silversmithing** noun.

silver tongue noun an ability to be eloquent and persuasive in speaking.
– DERIVATIVES **silver-tongued** adjective.

silver wedding noun Brit. the twenty-fifth anniversary of a wedding.

silviculture /**sil**-vi-kul-cher/ noun the growing and cultivation of trees.
– DERIVATIVES **silvicultural** adjective.
– ORIGIN from Latin *silva* 'wood'.

SIM (also **SIM card**) noun a smart card inside a mobile phone, carrying an identification number unique to the user, storing personal data, and preventing operation of the phone if removed.
– ORIGIN from the initial letters of *subscriber identification module*.

simian /**sim**-i-uhn/ adjective relating to or resembling apes or monkeys. • noun an ape or monkey.
– ORIGIN from Latin *simia* 'ape'.

similar adjective **1** like something else in appearance, character, etc., but not exactly the same: *a soft cheese similar to Brie.* **2** (of geometrical figures) having the same angles and proportions, though of different sizes.
– DERIVATIVES **similarity** noun (pl. **similarities**) **similarly** adverb.
– ORIGIN Latin *similaris*, from *similis* 'like'.

> USAGE: It is not good English to say **similar as** (*I've had similar problems as yourself*); use **similar to** instead (*I've had problems similar to yours*).

simile /**sim**-i-li/ noun a figure of speech in which one thing is compared to another of a different kind (e.g. *our team was solid as a rock*).
– ORIGIN Latin, from *similis* 'like'.

similitude /si-**mil**-i-tyood/ noun the quality or state of being similar.

SIMM abbreviation Computing single in-line memory module.

simmer verb **1** stay or keep just below boiling point while bubbling gently. **2** be filled with anger or another strong emotion which is only just kept under control. **3** (**simmer down**) become calmer and quieter. • noun a state or temperature just below boiling point.

- ORIGIN from dialect *simper* in the same sense.

simnel cake noun chiefly Brit. a rich fruit cake with a layer of marzipan on top, eaten especially at Easter or during Lent.
- ORIGIN from Latin *simila* or Greek *semidalis* 'fine flour'.

simony /sy-muh-ni, sim-uh-ni/ noun chiefly historical the buying or selling of pardons and other Church privileges.
- ORIGIN from *Simon* Magus in the Bible, who offered money to the Apostles.

simoom /si-moom/ (also **simoon** /si-moon/) noun a hot, dry, dusty wind blowing in the desert.
- ORIGIN from an Arabic word meaning 'to poison'.

simper verb smile in a coy or affected way. • noun a coy or affected smile.
- DERIVATIVES **simpering** adjective.
- ORIGIN unknown.

simple adjective (**simpler, simplest**) **1** easily understood or done. **2** plain and basic or uncomplicated in form, nature, or design: *a simple white blouse.* **3** of low or ordinary status: *she's a simple country girl.* **4** of very low intelligence. **5** consisting of a single element; not compound. **6** (of interest) payable on the sum loaned only. Compare with **COMPOUND¹**. **7** (of a leaf or stem) not divided. • noun chiefly historical a herb with healing properties, or a medicine made from one.
- DERIVATIVES **simpleness** noun.
- ORIGIN Latin *simplus.*

simple fracture noun an injury in which a broken bone does not pierce the skin.

simple-minded adjective having or showing very little intelligence or judgement.

simple time noun musical rhythm or metre in which each beat in a bar may be subdivided simply into halves or quarters.

simpleton noun a foolish or unintelligent person.

simplex adjective technical made up of a single part or structure.
- ORIGIN Latin, 'single'.

simplicity noun the quality or condition of being simple.

simplify verb (**simplifies, simplifying, simplified**) make something easier to do or understand.
- DERIVATIVES **simplification** noun.

simplistic adjective treating complex issues and problems as simpler than they really are.
- DERIVATIVES **simplistically** adverb.

simply adverb **1** in a simple way. **2** merely; just. **3** absolutely; completely.

simulacrum /sim-yuu-lay-kruhm/ noun (pl. **simulacra** /sim-yuu-lay-kruh/ or **simulacrums**) **1** an image or representation of someone or something. **2** an unsatisfactory copy or substitute.
- ORIGIN Latin.

simulate verb **1** imitate the appearance or nature of: *red ochre intended to simulate blood.* **2** use a computer to create conditions resembling those in real life. **3** pretend to feel an emotion.
- DERIVATIVES **simulation** noun.
- ORIGIN Latin *simulare* 'copy, represent'.

simulator noun a machine that imitates the controls and conditions of a real vehicle, process, etc., used for training or testing.

simulcast /sim-uhl-kahst/ noun a broadcast of the same programme on radio and television at the same time, or on two or more channels at the same time. • verb broadcast a programme in this way.
- ORIGIN blend of **SIMULTANEOUS** and **BROADCAST**.

simultaneous /sim-uhl-tay-ni-uhss/ adjective happening, operating, or done at the same time.
- DERIVATIVES **simultaneity** /sim-uhl-tuh-nay-i-ti/ noun **simultaneously** adverb.
- ORIGIN from Latin *simul* 'at the same time'.

simultaneous equations plural noun equations involving two or more unknowns that are to have the same values in each equation.

sin¹ /*rhymes with* tin/ noun **1** an act considered to break a religious or moral law. **2** an act regarded as a serious offence. • verb (**sins, sinning, sinned**) commit a sin.
- PHRASES **live in sin** informal, dated (of an unmarried couple) live together.
- ORIGIN Old English.

sin² /*rhymes with* line/ abbreviation sine.

sin bin noun informal (in sport) a box or bench to which offending players can be sent as a penalty during a game.

since preposition in the period between a time in the past and the present. • conjunction **1** during or in the time after. **2** for the reason that; because. • adverb **1** from the time mentioned until the present. **2** ago.
- ORIGIN Old English.

sincere adjective (**sincerer, sincerest**) showing genuine feelings; free from deceit or pretence.
- DERIVATIVES **sincerely** adverb **sincerity** noun.
- ORIGIN Latin *sincerus* 'clean, pure'.

sine /*rhymes with* line/ noun (in a right-angled triangle) the ratio of the side opposite a particular acute angle to the hypotenuse.
- ORIGIN Latin *sinus* 'curve'.

sinecure /syn-i-kyoor, sin-i-kyoor/ noun a position for which the holder is paid but which involves little or no work.
- ORIGIN from Latin *sine cura* 'without care'.

sine die /see-nay dee-ay/ adverb (with reference to something that has been adjourned) with no date fixed for resuming the proceedings.
- ORIGIN Latin, 'without a day'.

sine qua non /si-ni kwah nohn/ noun a thing that is absolutely essential.
- ORIGIN Latin, 'without which not'.

sinew noun a piece of tough fibrous tissue that joins muscle to bone; a tendon or ligament.
- DERIVATIVES **sinewy** adjective.
- ORIGIN Old English.

sinfonia /sin-foh-ni-uh, sin-fuh-nee-uh/ noun **1** a symphony. **2** (in baroque music) an orchestral piece used as an introduction to an opera, cantata, or suite. **3** a small symphony orchestra.
- ORIGIN Italian.

sinful adjective **1** wicked and immoral. **2** disgraceful: *a sinful waste.*
- DERIVATIVES **sinfully** adverb **sinfulness** noun.

S

sing verb (past **sang**; past part. **sung**) **1** make musical sounds with the voice in the form of a song or tune. **2** (of a bird) make characteristic tuneful whistling and twittering sounds. **3** make a high-pitched whistling sound.
– PHRASES **sing the praises of** express enthusiastic approval or admiration of.
– DERIVATIVES **singable** adjective **singer** noun.
– ORIGIN Old English.

singalong noun an informal occasion when people sing together in a group.

Singaporean /sing-uh-**por**-i-uhn/ noun a person from Singapore. ●adjective relating to Singapore.

singe verb (**singes, singeing, singed**) burn the surface of something lightly. ●noun a slight burn.
– ORIGIN Old English.

Singhalese /sing-guh-**leez**/ noun & adjective variant spelling of **SINHALESE**.

single adjective **1** only one; not one of several. **2** designed or suitable for one person. **3** consisting of one part. **4** not involved in an established romantic or sexual relationship. **5** regarded as distinct or separate from others in a group: *alcohol is the single most important cause of violence.* **6** even one: *they didn't receive a single reply.* **7** Brit. (of a ticket) valid for an outward journey only. ●noun **1** a single person or thing. **2** a short record or CD featuring one main song. **3** (**singles**) a game or competition for individual players. **4** Cricket one run. ●verb (**single someone/thing out**) choose someone or something from a group for special treatment.
– DERIVATIVES **singleness** noun **singly** adverb.
– ORIGIN Latin *singulus*.

single bond noun a chemical bond in which one pair of electrons is shared between two atoms.

single-breasted adjective (of a jacket or coat) fastened by one row of buttons at the centre of the front.

single combat noun fighting between two people.

single cream noun Brit. thin cream with a relatively low fat content.

single currency noun **1** a currency used by all the members of an economic federation. **2** (also **single European currency**) the currency (the euro) which replaced the national currencies of twelve member states of the European Union in 2002.

single file noun a line of people or things arranged one behind another.

single-handed adverb & adjective done without help from other people.
– DERIVATIVES **single-handedly** adverb.

single-lens reflex adjective referring to a reflex camera in which the lens that forms the image on the film also provides the image in the viewfinder.

single malt noun malt whisky that been produced by one distillery and is not blended with any other malt whisky.

single market noun an association of countries that have few or no restrictions on the movement of goods, money, or people within the association.

single-minded adjective concentrating with determination on one particular aim.
– DERIVATIVES **single-mindedly** adverb **single-mindedness** noun.

single parent noun a person bringing up a child or children without a partner.

singlet noun chiefly Brit. a vest or similar sleeveless garment.
– ORIGIN first referring to a man's short jacket: from **SINGLE** (because the jacket was not lined).

singleton noun **1** a single person or thing of the kind under consideration. **2** informal a person who is not in a long-term relationship. **3** (in card games) a card that is the only one of its suit in a hand.

single transferable vote noun an electoral system of proportional representation in which a person's vote can be transferred to a further choice of candidate.

sing-song adjective (of a person's voice) having a repeated rising and falling rhythm. ●noun Brit. informal an informal occasion when people sing together in a group.

singular adjective **1** Grammar (of a word or form) referring to just one person or thing. **2** very good or great; remarkable. **3** strange or eccentric. ●noun Grammar the singular form of a word.
– DERIVATIVES **singularity** noun (pl. **singularities**) **singularly** adverb.
– ORIGIN Latin *singularis*.

Sinhalese /sin-huh-**leez**, sin-uh-**leez**/ (also **Singhalese, Sinhala** /sin-**hah**-luh/) noun (pl. same) **1** a member of an Indian people now forming the majority of the population of Sri Lanka. **2** the language spoken by the Sinhalese. ●adjective relating to the Sinhalese.
– ORIGIN from Sanskrit, 'Sri Lanka'.

sinister adjective **1** giving the impression that something harmful or evil will happen or is happening: *a dark building with a sinister air.* **2** old use & Heraldry on or towards the bearer's left-hand side of a coat of arms. The opposite of **DEXTER**.
– DERIVATIVES **sinisterly** adverb.
– ORIGIN Latin, 'left'.

sink¹ verb (past **sank**; past part. **sunk**) **1** go down below the surface of liquid. **2** (with reference to a ship) go or cause to go to the bottom of the sea. **3** drop downwards. **4** lower oneself or drop down gently: *she sank back on to her pillow.* **5** gradually decrease in amount or intensity. **6** (**sink in**) (of words or facts) become fully understood or realized. **7** (**sink something into**) force something sharp through a surface: *the dog sank its teeth into her arm.* **8** insert something beneath a surface. **9** pass into a particular state or condition: *she sank into sleep.* **10** (**sink something in/into**) put money or resources into.
– PHRASES **a sinking feeling** an unpleasant feeling caused by the realization that something unpleasant or undesirable has happened or will happen. **sink or swim** fail or succeed by one's own efforts.
– ORIGIN Old English.

sink² noun **1** a fixed basin with a water supply and outflow pipe. **2** a sinkhole. ●adjective Brit. (of a school or housing estate) in a socially deprived area.

– ORIGIN from **sink¹**.

sinker noun a weight used to keep a fishing line beneath the water.

sinkhole noun a cavity in the ground caused by water erosion and providing a route for surface water to disappear underground.

sinking fund noun a fund formed by regularly setting aside money in order to pay off a particular debt.

sinner noun a person who sins.

Sino- /sy-noh/ combining form Chinese; Chinese and ...: *Sino-American.*

– ORIGIN from Latin *Sinae.*

sinology /sy-**nol**-uh-ji, si-**nol**-uh-ji/ noun the study of Chinese language, history, and culture.

– DERIVATIVES **sinologist** noun.

sinter noun a hard substance that is deposited from mineral springs. • verb make a powdered material form a solid mass by heating and compressing it.

– ORIGIN German, 'cinder'.

sinuous /sin-yuu-uhss/ adjective **1** having many curves and turns. **2** lithe and supple.

– DERIVATIVES **sinuosity** noun **sinuously** adverb.

– ORIGIN Latin *sinuosus*, from *sinus* 'a bend'.

sinus /sy-nuhss/ noun a hollow space within a bone or other tissue, especially one in the bones of the face or skull that connects with the inside of the nose.

– ORIGIN Latin, 'a recess, bend'.

sinusitis /si-nuh-sy-tiss/ noun inflammation of a sinus that connects with the inside of the nose.

Sioux /soo/ noun (pl. same) a member of a North American Indian people of the northern Mississippi valley area.

– ORIGIN from Ojibwa (an American Indian language).

sip verb (**sips, sipping, sipped**) drink something by taking small mouthfuls. • noun a small mouthful of liquid.

– DERIVATIVES **sipper** noun.

– ORIGIN perhaps from **sup¹**.

siphon (also **syphon**) noun a tube used to convey liquid upwards from a container and then down to a lower level, using the different fluid pressures at the tube openings to maintain the flow. • verb **1** draw off or convey liquid by means of a siphon. **2** take small amounts of money from a source over a period of time, especially illicitly.

– DERIVATIVES **siphonage** noun **siphonic** adjective.

– ORIGIN Greek, 'pipe'.

SIPP noun (in the UK) a self-invested personal pension, a pension plan that enables the holder to choose and manage the investments made.

sir (also **Sir**) noun **1** a polite form of address to a man. **2** used to address a man at the beginning of a formal letter. **3** used as a title before the first name of a knight or baronet.

– ORIGIN from **sire**.

sire /rhymes with fire/ noun **1** the male parent of an animal. **2** literary a father or other male ancestor. **3** old use a respectful form of address to someone of high social status, especially a king. • verb **1** be the male parent of an animal. **2** literary be the father of a child.

– ORIGIN Old French.

siren noun **1** a device that makes a long, loud signal or warning sound. **2** Greek Mythology each of a group of female creatures whose singing lured unwary sailors on to rocks. **3** a woman whose sexual attractiveness is regarded as dangerous to men.

– ORIGIN Greek *Seirēn*, first referring to an imaginary type of snake.

sirenian /sy-ree-ni-uhn/ noun a large plant-eating sea mammal of a group that includes the dugong and manatee.

– ORIGIN Latin, from **siren**.

sirloin noun good-quality beef cut from the loin.

– ORIGIN Old French, 'above the loin'.

sirocco /si-rok-koh/ noun (pl. **siroccos**) a hot wind blowing from North Africa to southern Europe.

– ORIGIN Arabic, 'east wind'.

SIS abbreviation (in the UK) Secret Intelligence Service.

sis noun informal sister.

sisal /sy-z'l/ noun fibre from the leaves of a tropical Mexican plant, used for ropes or matting.

– ORIGIN named after the Mexican port of *Sisal*.

siskin noun a small yellowish-green finch.

– ORIGIN Dutch *siseken*.

sissy (also **cissy**) informal noun (pl. **sissies**) a weak or effeminate person. • adjective (**sissier, sissiest**) weak or effeminate.

– DERIVATIVES **sissified** adjective.

– ORIGIN from **sis**.

sister noun **1** a woman or girl in relation to other children of her parents. **2** a female friend or fellow member of a group or organization. **3** (often **Sister**) a member of a religious order of women. **4** (often **Sister**) Brit. a senior female nurse. • adjective belonging to the same group or type as something else: *a sister company.*

– DERIVATIVES **sisterly** adjective.

– ORIGIN Old English.

sisterhood noun **1** the relationship between sisters. **2** a feeling of closeness and loyalty to a group of women or all women. **3** a group of women linked by a shared interest, belief, trade, etc.

sister-in-law noun (pl. **sisters-in-law**) **1** the sister of one's wife or husband. **2** the wife of one's brother or brother-in-law.

Sisyphean /siss-i-fee-uhn/ adjective (of a task) unending.

– ORIGIN from *Sisyphus* in Greek mythology who was condemned to the never-ending task of rolling a large stone to the top of a hill, from which it always rolled down again.

sit verb (**sits, sitting;** past and past part. **sat**) **1** be or put in a position in which one's weight is supported by one's buttocks and one's back is upright. **2** be or remain in a particular position or state: *the fridge was sitting in a pool of water.* **3** (of an animal) rest with the hind legs bent and the body close to the ground. **4** (of a parliament, committee, or court of law) be carrying on its business. **5** serve as a member of a council, jury, or other official body. **6** Brit. take an exam. **7** (of a table or room) have enough seats for: *the dining room sat 200 people.* **8** (**sit for**) pose for an artist or photographer. • noun a period of sitting.

– PHRASES **sit in for** temporarily carry out someone else's duties. **sit something out** not

S

take part in something. **sit tight** informal **1** remain firmly in one's place. **2** hold back from taking action. **sit up** go to bed later than usual.
– ORIGIN Old English.

> USAGE: It is good English to use the present participle **sitting** rather than the past participle **sat** with the verb 'to be': *we were sitting there for hours* rather than *we were sat there for hours.*

sitar /si-tar/ noun a large Indian lute with a long neck.
– DERIVATIVES **sitarist** noun.
– ORIGIN from the Persian words for 'three' and 'string'.

sitcom noun a television or radio series in which the same set of characters are involved in amusing situations.
– ORIGIN abbreviation of **SITUATION COMEDY**.

sit-down adjective **1** (of a meal) eaten sitting at a table. **2** (of a protest) in which demonstrators occupy their workplace or sit down on the ground in a public place. • noun a period of sitting down.

site noun **1** an area of ground on which something is or will be located. **2** a place where a particular event or activity is happening or has happened. **3** a website. • verb build or locate something in a particular place.
– ORIGIN Latin *situs* 'local position'.

> USAGE: Do not confuse **site** and **sight**. As a noun, **site** means 'a place where something is located or has happened' (*the site of the battle*), while **sight** chiefly means 'the ability to see' (*he lost his sight as a baby*).

sit-in noun a form of protest in which demonstrators occupy a place until their demands are met.

Sitka /sit-kuh/ noun a fast-growing North American spruce tree, grown for its strong lightweight wood.
– ORIGIN named after the town of *Sitka* in Alaska.

sitter noun **1** a person who poses for an artist or photographer. **2** a person who looks after children, pets, or a house while the parents or owners are away. **3** Brit. informal (in sport) an easy catch or shot.

sitting noun **1** a period of being seated. **2** a period of time when a group of people are served a meal. **3** a period of time during which a committee, parliament, or court of law is carrying out its normal business. • adjective **1** in a seated position. **2** (of an elected representative) currently present or in office.

sitting duck noun informal a person or thing with no protection against attack.

sitting room noun chiefly Brit. a room that for sitting and relaxing in.

sitting tenant noun Brit. a tenant already occupying rented accommodation or premises.

situate verb **1** put in a particular place or context. **2** (**be situated**) be in a particular situation or set of circumstances: *she is now comfortably situated.*
– ORIGIN Latin *situare* 'place', from *situs* 'site'.

situation noun **1** a set of circumstances which exist at a particular time and in a particular place: *the political situation in Russia.* **2** the location and surroundings of a place. **3** formal a job.
– DERIVATIVES **situational** adjective.

situation comedy noun full form of **SITCOM**.

situationism noun a radical cultural and political movement of the mid 20th century which rejected conventional politics and aimed to transform attitudes to all aspects of everyday life.
– DERIVATIVES **situationist** noun & adjective.

sit-up noun an exercise designed to strengthen the abdominal muscles, in which a person sits up from a horizontal position without using the arms.

sitz bath /sits/ noun a bath in which only the buttocks and hips are immersed in water.
– ORIGIN partial translation of German *Sitzbad,* from *sitzen* 'sit' + *Bad* 'bath'.

six cardinal number **1** one more than five; 6. (Roman numeral: **vi** or **VI**.) **2** Cricket a hit that reaches the boundary without first striking the ground, scoring six runs.
– PHRASES **at sixes and sevens** in a state of confusion or disorganization. **knock someone for six** Brit. informal greatly surprise someone. **six of one and half a dozen of the other** a situation in which there is not much difference between two alternatives.
– DERIVATIVES **sixfold** adjective & adverb.
– ORIGIN Old English.

six-pack noun **1** a pack of six cans of beer. **2** informal a man's set of well-developed abdominal muscles.

sixpence noun Brit. a small coin worth six old pence (2½ p), withdrawn in 1980.

sixpenny adjective Brit. costing or worth six pence, especially before decimalization (1971).

six-shooter noun a revolver with six chambers.

sixteen cardinal number one more than fifteen; 16. (Roman numeral: **xvi** or **XVI**.)
– DERIVATIVES **sixteenth** ordinal number.

sixth ordinal number **1** that is number six in a sequence; 6th. **2** (**a sixth/one sixth**) each of six equal parts into which something is divided. **3** a musical interval spanning six consecutive notes in a scale.

sixth-form college noun Brit. a college for students aged 16–18.

sixth sense noun a supposed ability to know things by intuition or instinct rather than by sight, smell, hearing, etc.

sixty cardinal number (pl. **sixties**) ten more than fifty; 60. (Roman numeral: **lx** or **LX**.)
– DERIVATIVES **sixtieth** ordinal number.

sixty-four thousand dollar question noun informal something that is not known and on which a great deal depends.
– ORIGIN first as *sixty-four dollar question,* from a question posed for the top prize in a broadcast quiz show.

size¹ noun **1** the overall measurements or extent of something. **2** each of a series of standard measurements in which articles are made or sold. • verb **1** group or sort items according to their size. **2** (**size someone/thing up**) form a judgement of someone or something.

– DERIVATIVES **sized** adjective.
– ORIGIN Old French *sise*.

size² noun a sticky solution used to glaze paper, stiffen textiles, and prepare plastered walls for decoration. •verb treat something with size.
– ORIGIN perhaps the same word as **size¹**.

sizeable (also **sizable**) adjective fairly large.

sizeism noun prejudice or discrimination against people on the grounds of their size.
– DERIVATIVES **sizeist** adjective.

sizzle verb 1 (of food) make a hissing sound when frying or roasting. 2 (as adj. **sizzling**) informal very hot or exciting. •noun the sound of food sizzling.
– DERIVATIVES **sizzler** noun.
– ORIGIN imitating the sound.

sjambok /sham-bok/ noun (in South Africa) a long, stiff whip, originally made of rhinoceros hide.
– ORIGIN South African Dutch *tjambok*.

SK abbreviation Saskatchewan.

ska /skah/ noun a style of fast popular music originating in Jamaica in the 1960s.
– ORIGIN unknown.

skank /skangk/ noun a dance performed to reggae music, characterized by rhythmically bending forward, raising the knees, and extending the hands palms-downwards. •verb play reggae music or dance in this style.
– ORIGIN unknown.

skanky adjective informal, chiefly N. Amer. very unpleasant.

skate¹ noun an ice skate or roller skate. •verb 1 glide on ice skates or roller skates. 2 ride on a skateboard. 3 (**skate over/round/around**) pass over or refer only briefly to a subject or problem.
– PHRASES **get one's skates on** Brit. informal hurry up.
– DERIVATIVES **skater** noun **skating** noun.
– ORIGIN Dutch *schaats*.

skate² noun (pl. same or **skates**) an edible sea fish with a flattened diamond-shaped body.
– ORIGIN Old Norse.

skateboard noun a short, narrow board with two small wheels fixed to the bottom of either end, on which a person can ride. •verb ride on a skateboard.
– DERIVATIVES **skateboarder** noun **skateboarding** noun.

skatepark noun an area set aside and equipped for skateboarding.

skean dhu /skeen doo/ noun a dagger worn in the stocking as part of Highland dress.
– ORIGIN from Irish and Scottish Gaelic *sgian* 'knife' + Scottish Gaelic *dubh* 'black'.

skedaddle verb informal leave hurriedly.
– ORIGIN unknown.

skeet (also **skeet shooting**) noun a shooting sport in which a clay target is thrown from a trap.
– ORIGIN apparently an alteration of **shoot**.

skein /skayn/ noun 1 a length of thread or yarn, loosely coiled and knotted. 2 a flock of wild geese or swans in flight.
– ORIGIN Old French *escaigne*.

skeletal /skel-i-t'l, skuh-**lee**-t'l/ adjective 1 relating to a skeleton. 2 extremely thin.

3 existing only in outline or as a framework: *a skeletal plot for a novel.*
– DERIVATIVES **skeletally** adverb.

skeleton noun 1 a framework of bone, cartilage, or other rigid material supporting or containing the body of an animal. 2 a supporting framework or basic structure: *the concrete skeleton of an unfinished building.* •adjective referring to an essential or minimum number of people or things: *a skeleton staff.*
– PHRASES **skeleton in the cupboard** an embarrassing or shocking fact that someone wishes to keep secret.
– DERIVATIVES **skeletonize** (or **skeletonise**) verb.
– ORIGIN Greek, from *skeletos* 'dried up'.

skeleton key noun a key designed to fit many locks.

skep (also **skip**) noun a straw or wicker beehive.
– ORIGIN Old Norse, 'basket, bushel'.

skeptic noun US spelling of **sceptic**.

skerry noun (pl. **skerries**) Scottish a reef or rocky island.
– ORIGIN Old Norse.

sketch noun 1 a rough or unfinished drawing or painting. 2 a short, funny, self-contained scene in a comedy show. 3 a brief written or spoken account or description of something. •verb 1 make a sketch of someone or something. 2 give a brief account or description of: *he sketched out his business plan.*
– DERIVATIVES **sketcher** noun.
– ORIGIN Italian *schizzo*.

sketchbook (also **sketch pad**) noun a pad of drawing paper for sketching on.

sketchy adjective (**sketchier**, **sketchiest**) not thorough or detailed.
– DERIVATIVES **sketchily** adverb **sketchiness** noun.

skew verb 1 suddenly change direction or move at an angle. 2 change or influence something so that it is not accurate, normal, or fair. •noun 1 a slant. 2 a bias towards one particular group or subject: *the paper had a working-class skew.*
– DERIVATIVES **skewness** noun.
– ORIGIN from Old French *eschiver* 'eschew'.

skewbald adjective (of a horse) with irregular patches of white and another colour, typically a shade of brown. •noun a skewbald horse.
– ORIGIN from former *skewed* 'skewbald', on the pattern of *piebald*.

skewer noun a long piece of wood or metal used for holding pieces of food together during cooking. •verb hold something in place or pierce something with a skewer or other pointed object.
– ORIGIN unknown.

skew-whiff adverb & adjective Brit. informal not straight; askew.

ski noun (pl. **skis**) 1 each of a pair of long, narrow pieces of wood, metal, or plastic attached to boots for travelling over snow. 2 a similar device attached beneath a vehicle or aircraft. •verb (**skis**, **skiing**, **skied**) travel over snow on skis.
– DERIVATIVES **skiable** adjective **skier** noun **skiing** noun.
– ORIGIN Norwegian.

skid verb (**skids**, **skidding**, **skidded**) 1 (of a vehicle) slide sideways on slippery ground or as a result of stopping or turning too quickly. 2 slip or slide. •noun 1 an act of skidding. 2 a runner attached to the underside of an aircraft for use when landing on snow or grass. **3** a braking device consisting of a wooden or metal shoe that prevents a wheel from revolving.

– PHRASES **hit the skids** informal begin a rapid decline. **on the skids** informal in a bad state; failing.

– ORIGIN perhaps related to SKI.

skidoo /ski-**doo**/ noun trademark, chiefly N. Amer. a motorized toboggan.

– ORIGIN from SKI.

skidpan noun a slippery road surface prepared for drivers to practise control of skidding.

skid row noun informal, chiefly N. Amer. a run-down part of a town inhabited by homeless people and alcoholics.

skiff noun a light rowing boat, usually for one person.

– ORIGIN Italian *schifo*.

skiffle noun Brit. a kind of folk music popular in the 1950s, often featuring improvised instruments such as washboards.

– ORIGIN perhaps imitating the sound.

ski jump noun a steep slope levelling off before a sharp drop to allow a skier to leap through the air.

skilful (also chiefly N. Amer. **skillful**) adjective having or showing skill.

– DERIVATIVES **skilfully** adverb **skilfulness** noun.

ski lift noun a system used to carry skiers up a slope to the top of a run, consisting of moving seats attached to an overhead cable.

skill noun **1** the ability to do something well. **2** a particular ability: *practical skills such as cooking.*

– ORIGIN Old Norse, 'knowledge'.

skilled adjective **1** having or showing skill. **2** (of work) requiring special skills.

skillet noun **1** N. Amer. a frying pan. **2** historical a small metal cooking pot with a long handle.

– ORIGIN perhaps from Latin *scutella* 'dish, platter'.

skim verb (**skims, skimming, skimmed**) **1** remove a substance from the surface of a liquid. **2** move quickly and lightly over or on a surface or through the air. **3** read through something quickly, noting only the important points. **4** (**skim over**) deal with a subject briefly or superficially. **5** throw a flat stone so that it bounces several times on the surface of water. **6** (usu. as noun **skimming**) fraudulently copy credit or debit card details with an electronic device.

– DERIVATIVES **skimmer** noun.

– ORIGIN Old French *escumer*.

ski mask noun a protective covering for the head and face, with holes for the eyes, nose, and mouth.

skimmed milk (N. Amer. also **skim milk**) noun milk from which the cream has been removed.

skimp verb spend less money or use less of something than is really necessary in an attempt to economize: *don't skimp on holiday insurance.*

– ORIGIN unknown.

skimpy adjective (**skimpier, skimpiest**) **1** providing or consisting of less than is necessary; meagre. **2** (of clothes) small and

not covering much of the body.

skin noun **1** the thin layer of tissue forming the natural outer covering of the body of a person or animal. **2** the skin of a dead animal used as material for clothing or other items. **3** the peel or outer layer of a fruit or vegetable. **4** an outer layer. **5** Brit. informal a skinhead. ● adjective informal referring to pornography: *the skin trade.* ● verb (**skins, skinning, skinned**) **1** remove the skin from something. **2** graze a part of one's body.

– PHRASES **by the skin of one's teeth** by a very narrow margin; only just. **get under someone's skin** informal annoy someone greatly. **have a thick** (or **thin**) **skin** be insensitive (or oversensitive) to criticism or insults. **it's no skin off my** (or **his** etc.) **nose** informal someone is not annoyed or upset about something.

– DERIVATIVES **skinless** adjective.

– ORIGIN Old English.

skincare noun the use of cosmetics to care for the skin.

skin-deep adjective not deep or lasting; superficial.

skin-diving noun the activity of swimming under water without a diving suit, typically using an aqualung and flippers.

– DERIVATIVES **skin-diver** noun.

skinflint noun informal a very mean person.

skinful noun Brit. informal enough alcoholic drink to make one drunk.

skinhead noun a young man of a group with close-cropped hair, especially one who is aggressive and openly racist.

skink noun a smooth-bodied lizard with short or absent limbs.

– ORIGIN Greek *skinkos*.

skinny adjective (**skinnier, skinniest**) **1** very thin. **2** (of a piece of clothing) tight-fitting.

– DERIVATIVES **skinniness** noun.

skinny-dip verb informal swim naked.

skinny-rib noun a tightly fitting sweater or top.

skint adjective Brit. informal having little or no money.

– ORIGIN variant of informal *skinned*, in the same sense.

skin test noun a test to discover whether an immune reaction occurs when a substance is applied to or injected into the skin.

skintight adjective (of a piece of clothing) very close-fitting.

skip[1] verb (**skips, skipping, skipped**) **1** move along lightly, stepping from one foot to the other with a little jump. **2** Brit. jump repeatedly over a rope which is held at both ends and turned over the head and under the feet. **3** leave out or move quickly over a section of something being read or watched. **4** not have or do something that one should have or do: *try not to skip breakfast.* ● noun a skipping movement.

– ORIGIN probably Scandinavian.

skip[2] noun Brit. **1** a large open-topped container for holding and transporting bulky waste items. **2** a cage or bucket in which workers or materials are lowered and raised in mines and quarries.

– ORIGIN variant of SKEP.

S

ski pants plural noun women's stretchy trousers with tapering legs and an elastic stirrup under each foot.

skipjack noun (also **skipjack tuna**) a small tuna with dark horizontal stripes.
– ORIGIN from **SKIP**[1] + **JACK** (with reference to the fish's habit of jumping out of the water).

skipper informal noun **1** the captain of a ship, boat, or aircraft. **2** the captain of a sports team. ●verb be the captain of a ship, boat, aircraft, or sports team.
– ORIGIN Dutch or German *schipper*, from *schip* 'ship'.

skipping rope noun Brit. a length of rope used for skipping.

skirl noun a shrill sound, especially that made by bagpipes. ●verb (of bagpipes) make a shrill sound.
– ORIGIN probably Scandinavian.

skirmish noun a brief period of unplanned fighting. ●verb take part in a skirmish.
– DERIVATIVES **skirmisher** noun.
– ORIGIN Old French *eskirmir*.

skirt noun **1** a woman's outer garment that hangs from the waist and covers part or all of the legs. **2** the part of a coat or dress that hangs below the waist. **3** a surface that conceals or protects the wheels or underside of a vehicle or aircraft. **4** Brit. a cut of meat from the lower flank of an animal. **5** informal women regarded as sexually desirable. ●verb (also **skirt along/around**) **1** go round or past the edge of something. **2** avoid dealing with: *they are both skirting the issue.*
– ORIGIN Old Norse, 'shirt'.

skirting (also **skirting board**) noun Brit. a wooden board running along the base of the inside wall of a room.

skit noun a short comedy sketch or piece of humorous writing, especially one that makes fun of someone or something by imitating them.
– ORIGIN related to former *skit* 'move lightly and quickly'.

skitter verb move lightly and quickly.
– ORIGIN perhaps from dialect *skite* 'move quickly'.

skittery adjective restless; skittish.

skittish adjective **1** (of a horse) excitable or easily frightened and therefore difficult to control. **2** playful and unpredictable.
– DERIVATIVES **skittishly** adverb **skittishness** noun.
– ORIGIN perhaps related to **SKIT**.

skittle noun **1** (**skittles**) (treated as sing.) a game played with wooden pins set up at the end of an alley to be bowled down with a wooden ball. **2** a pin used in the game of skittles. **3** (also **table skittles**) a game played with similar pins set up on a board to be knocked down by swinging a suspended ball.
– ORIGIN unknown.

skive /rhymes with dive/ verb Brit. informal avoid work or a duty by staying away or leaving early.
– DERIVATIVES **skiver** noun.
– ORIGIN perhaps from French *esquiver* 'slink away'.

skivvy Brit. informal noun (pl. **skivvies**) a female servant who does the boring or unpleasant tasks in a house. ●verb (**skivvies, skivvying,**

skivvied) do boring or unpleasant household tasks.
– ORIGIN unknown.

skua /skyoo-uh/ noun a large predatory seabird which pursues other birds to make them regurgitate fish.
– ORIGIN Faroese.

skulduggery (also **skullduggery**) noun underhand or dishonest behaviour.
– ORIGIN alteration of Scots *sculduddery*.

skulk verb hide or move around in a stealthy or furtive way.
– DERIVATIVES **skulker** noun.
– ORIGIN Scandinavian.

skull noun **1** the bone framework that surrounds and protects the brain of a person or animal. **2** informal a person's head or brain.
– PHRASES **skull and crossbones** a representation of a skull with two thigh bones crossed below it, used formerly by pirates and now as a warning symbol.
– ORIGIN unknown.

skullcap noun a small close-fitting cap without a peak.

skunk noun a black-and-white striped American mammal able to spray foul-smelling liquid at attackers.
– ORIGIN Abnaki (an American Indian language).

sky noun (pl. **skies**) **1** the region of the upper atmosphere seen from the earth. **2** literary heaven. ●verb (**skies, skying, skied**) informal hit a ball high into the air.
– PHRASES **the sky is the limit** there is practically no limit.
– DERIVATIVES **skyward** adjective & adverb **skywards** adverb.
– ORIGIN Old Norse, 'cloud'.

sky blue noun a bright, clear blue.

skydiving noun the sport of jumping from an aircraft and performing acrobatic manoeuvres in the air before landing by parachute.
– DERIVATIVES **skydiver** noun.

sky-high adverb & adjective very high.

skylark noun a lark that sings while flying high up in the sky. ●verb behave in a playful or mischievous way.

skylight noun a window set in a roof or ceiling.

skyline noun an outline of land and buildings seen against the sky.

skyrocket verb (**skyrockets, skyrocketing, skyrocketed**) informal (of a price or amount) increase very quickly.

skyscape noun a view or picture of an expanse of sky.

skyscraper noun a very tall building.

skyway noun chiefly N. Amer. **1** a route used by aircraft. **2** (also **skywalk**) a covered overhead walkway between buildings.

slab noun **1** a large, thick, flat piece of stone, concrete, or other hard material. **2** a thick slice or piece of food.
– ORIGIN unknown.

slack[1] adjective **1** not taut or held tightly in position; loose. **2** (of business or trade) not busy; quiet. **3** careless or lazy: *slack accounting procedures.* **4** (of a tide) neither ebbing nor flowing. ●noun **1** the part of a rope or line which is not held taut. **2** (**slacks**) casual

S

trousers. ● **verb 1** make slower or less intense: *the horse slacked his pace.* **2** (**slack off/up**) become slower or less intense. **3** Brit. informal work slowly or lazily.
– PHRASES **take** (or **pick**) **up the slack 1** improve the use of resources in a business. **2** pull on the loose part of a rope to make it taut.
– DERIVATIVES **slacken** verb **slackly** adverb **slackness** noun.
– ORIGIN Old English, 'inclined to be lazy, unhurried'.

slack² noun coal dust or small pieces of coal.
– ORIGIN probably German or Dutch.

slacker noun informal a person who is lazy and avoids work.

slack water noun the state of the tide when it is turning.

slag noun **1** stony waste matter that is left when metal has been separated from ore by smelting or refining. **2** Brit. informal, derogatory a woman who has had many sexual partners. ● verb (**slags, slagging, slagged**) (usu. **slag someone off**) Brit. informal criticize someone in a rude or unpleasant way.
– ORIGIN German *slagge.*

slag heap noun a large pile of waste material from a mine or industrial site.

slain past participle of SLAY.

slake verb satisfy a desire, one's thirst, etc.
– ORIGIN Old English, 'become less eager'.

slaked lime noun calcium hydroxide, a soluble substance produced by combining quicklime with water.

slalom /slah-luhm/ noun a skiing, canoeing, or sailing race following a winding course marked out by poles. ● verb move or race in a winding path, avoiding obstacles.
– ORIGIN Norwegian, 'sloping track'.

slam¹ verb (**slams, slamming, slammed**) **1** shut something forcefully and loudly. **2** push, put, or hit with great force: *she slammed down the phone.* **3** put into action suddenly or forcefully: *I slammed on the brakes.* **4** informal criticize someone or something severely. ● noun a loud bang caused by the forceful shutting of something.
– ORIGIN probably Scandinavian.

slam² noun Bridge the bidding and winning of a grand slam (all thirteen tricks) or a small slam (twelve tricks).
– ORIGIN perhaps from former *slampant* 'trickery'.

slam-dance verb chiefly N. Amer. a form of dancing to rock music in which the dancers deliberately collide with one another.

slam dunk noun **1** Basketball a shot thrust down through the basket. **2** N. Amer. informal a foregone conclusion or certainty. ● verb (**slam-dunk**) Basketball thrust the ball down through the basket.

slammer noun **1** informal prison. **2** (also **tequila slammer**) a cocktail made with tequila and champagne or another fizzy drink, which is covered, slammed on the table, and then drunk in one swallow.

slander noun **1** the action or crime of making untrue statements that damage a person's reputation. Compare with LIBEL. **2** a statement of this kind. ● verb make untrue and damaging

statements about someone.
– DERIVATIVES **slanderer** noun **slanderous** adjective.
– ORIGIN Old French *esclandre.*

slang noun very informal words and phrases that are more common in speech than in writing and are used by a particular group of people.
– DERIVATIVES **slangy** adjective.
– ORIGIN unknown.

slanging match noun Brit. informal a prolonged exchange of insults.

slant verb **1** slope or lean in a particular direction. **2** present information from a particular angle, especially in an unfair way. ● noun **1** a sloping position. **2** a point of view: *a new slant on science.* ● adjective at an angle; sloping.
– DERIVATIVES **slantwise** adjective & adverb.
– ORIGIN Scandinavian.

slap verb (**slaps, slapping, slapped**) **1** hit someone or something with the palm of the hand or a flat object. **2** hit against something with a slapping sound. **3** (**slap someone down**) informal reprimand someone forcefully. **4** (**slap something on**) put something on a surface quickly, carelessly, or forcefully. **5** (**slap something on**) informal impose a fine or other penalty on. ● noun **1** a blow with the palm of the hand. **2** informal make-up. ● adverb (also **slap bang**) informal suddenly and forcefully.
– PHRASES **slap and tickle** Brit. informal playful sexual activity. **slap in the face** an unexpected rejection. **slap on the back** an instance of congratulating or praising someone. **slap on the wrist** a mild reprimand.
– ORIGIN probably imitating the sound.

slapdash adjective & adverb done too hurriedly and carelessly.

slaphead noun Brit. informal, derogatory a bald or balding man.

slapper noun Brit. informal, derogatory a woman who has many sexual partners.

slapstick noun comedy based on deliberately clumsy actions and embarrassing events.
– ORIGIN first referring to a device consisting of two pieces of wood joined at one end, used by clowns to make a loud slapping sound.

slap-up adjective Brit. informal (of a meal) large and extravagant.

slash verb **1** cut someone or something with a forceful sweeping movement. **2** informal reduce a price, quantity, or amount greatly. ● noun **1** a cut made with a sweeping stroke. **2** a bright patch or flash of colour or light. **3** a slanting stroke (/) used chiefly between alternatives and in fractions and ratios. **4** Brit. informal an act of urinating.
– DERIVATIVES **slasher** noun.
– ORIGIN Old French *esclachier* 'break in pieces'.

slash-and-burn adjective (of agriculture) in which vegetation is cut down and burned off before new seeds are sown.

slashed adjective (of a garment) having slits to show the lining material or skin beneath.

slat noun each of a series of thin, narrow pieces of wood or other material, arranged so as to overlap or fit into each other.
– DERIVATIVES **slatted** adjective.
– ORIGIN Old French *esclat* 'splinter'.

S

slate noun **1** a grey, green, or bluish-purple rock easily split into smooth, flat plates, used as roofing material. **2** a plate of slate formerly used in schools for writing on. **3** a bluish-grey colour. **4** a list of candidates for election to a post or office. **5** Brit. a record of what a person owes, especially in pub or bar. • verb **1** Brit. informal criticize severely: *his work was slated by the critics.* **2** schedule or plan something. **3** cover a roof with slates.
– DERIVATIVES **slater** noun.
– ORIGIN Old French *esclate* 'splinter'.

slather /sla-*th*er/ verb informal spread or smear a substance thickly or liberally.
– ORIGIN unknown.

slattern /slat-tern/ noun dated a dirty, untidy woman.
– DERIVATIVES **slatternly** adjective.
– ORIGIN unknown.

slaughter /slaw-ter/ noun **1** the killing of farm animals for food. **2** the killing of a large number of people in a cruel or violent way. • verb **1** kill animals for food. **2** kill many people in a cruel or violent way. **3** informal defeat an opponent thoroughly.
– DERIVATIVES **slaughterer** noun.
– ORIGIN Old Norse, 'butcher's meat'.

slaughterhouse noun a place where animals are killed for food.

Slav /slahv/ noun a member of a group of peoples in central and eastern Europe who speak Slavic languages.
– ORIGIN Greek *Sklabos*.

slave noun **1** historical a person who was the legal property of another and was forced to obey them. **2** a person who is strongly influenced by or controlled by something: *she was no slave to fashion.* • verb work excessively hard.
– ORIGIN Latin *sclava* 'Slavonic captive'.

slave-driver noun informal a person who makes others work very hard.

slave labour noun work that is demanding and very poorly paid.

slaver[1] /slay-ver/ noun historical **1** a person dealing in or owning slaves. **2** a ship used for transporting slaves.

slaver[2] /sla-ver, slay-ver/ verb **1** let saliva run from the mouth. **2** show excessive desire or admiration: *the critics were slavering over his every move on court.* • noun saliva running from the mouth.
– ORIGIN probably from German.

slavery noun **1** the state of being a slave. **2** the practice or system of owning slaves.

slave trade noun historical the buying, trans-porting, and selling of people, especially black Africans, as slaves.

Slavic /slah-vik/ noun the group of languages that includes Russian, Polish, Czech, Bulgarian, and Serbo-Croat. • adjective relating to Slavic or the Slavs.

slavish adjective **1** following or copying something without trying to be original: *he's a slavish follower of White House policy.* **2** obeying someone in a servile way.
– DERIVATIVES **slavishly** adverb.

Slavonic /sluh-von-ik/ noun & adjective another term for SLAVIC.

slaw noun N. Amer. coleslaw.

– ORIGIN Dutch *sla*.

slay verb (past **slew**; past part. **slain**) **1** old use or literary kill a person or animal in a violent way. **2** N. Amer. murder someone.
– DERIVATIVES **slayer** noun.
– ORIGIN Old English.

sleaze noun informal **1** immoral or dishonest behaviour or activities, especially in politics or business: *the Chancellor has dissociated himself from the rows over spin and sleaze.* **2** chiefly N. Amer. a dishonest or immoral person.
– ORIGIN from SLEAZY.

sleazy adjective (**sleazier, sleaziest**) **1** dishonest or immoral: *a sleazy vice lord.* **2** (of a place) dirty and seedy.
– DERIVATIVES **sleazily** adverb **sleaziness** noun.
– ORIGIN unknown.

sled noun & verb (**sleds, sledding, sledded**) North American term for SLEDGE.
– ORIGIN German *sledde*.

sledge[1] chiefly Brit. noun **1** a vehicle on runners for travelling over snow or ice, either pushed, pulled, or allowed to slide downhill. **2** a toboggan. • verb ride on a sledge.
– ORIGIN Dutch *sleedse*.

sledge[2] noun a sledgehammer. • verb (as noun **sledging**) Cricket offensive remarks made by a fielder to a batsman in order to break their concentration.
– ORIGIN Old English.

sledgehammer noun a large, heavy hammer used for breaking rocks, driving in posts, etc. • adjective very powerful, forceful, or unsubtle: *sledgehammer blows.*

sleek adjective **1** (of hair or fur) smooth and glossy. **2** wealthy and smart in appearance. **3** elegant and streamlined: *a sleek black car.* • verb make hair smooth and glossy.
– DERIVATIVES **sleekly** adverb **sleekness** noun.
– ORIGIN from SLICK.

sleep noun **1** a state of rest in which the eyes are closed, the muscles are relaxed, the nervous system is inactive, and the mind is unconscious. **2** a gummy substance found in the corners of the eyes after sleep. • verb (past and past part. **slept**) **1** be asleep. **2** (**sleep something off**) recover from something by going to sleep. **3** (**sleep in**) remain asleep or in bed later than usual in the morning. **4** provide a specified number of people with beds or bedrooms. **5** (**sleep with**) have sex or be in a sexual relationship with someone. **6** (**sleep around**) have many casual sexual partners.
– PHRASES **put something to sleep** kill an animal painlessly.
– DERIVATIVES **sleepless** adjective.
– ORIGIN Old English.

sleeper noun **1** Brit. each of the wooden or concrete beams on which a railway track rests. **2** Brit. a ring or bar worn in a pierced ear to keep the hole from closing. **3** a sleeping car or a train carrying sleeping cars. **4** a film, book, or play that suddenly achieves success after first attracting little attention.

sleeping bag noun a warm padded bag to sleep in, especially when camping.

sleeping car noun a railway carriage provided with beds or berths.

sleeping partner noun Brit. a partner who

invests money in a business but is not involved in running it.

sleeping pill noun a tablet of a drug that helps a person to sleep.

sleeping policeman noun Brit. a hump in the road for slowing down traffic.

sleeping sickness noun a tropical disease transmitted by the bite of the tsetse fly, causing extreme tiredness.

sleepover noun a night spent by children or young people at a friend's house.

sleepwalk verb walk around while asleep.
– DERIVATIVES **sleepwalker** noun.

sleepy adjective (**sleepier, sleepiest**) 1 needing or ready for sleep. 2 (of a place) without much activity.
– DERIVATIVES **sleepily** adverb **sleepiness** noun.

sleet noun rain containing some ice, or snow melting as it falls. •verb (**it sleets, it is sleeting, it sleeted**) sleet falls.
– DERIVATIVES **sleety** adjective.
– ORIGIN Germanic.

sleeve noun 1 the part of a piece of clothing that wholly or partly covers the arm. 2 a protective cover for a record. 3 a protective or connecting tube fitting over a rod, spindle, or smaller tube.
– PHRASES **up one's sleeve** kept secret and ready for use when needed.
– DERIVATIVES **sleeved** adjective **sleeveless** adjective.
– ORIGIN Old English.

sleigh /slay/ noun a sledge drawn by horses or reindeer.
– DERIVATIVES **sleighing** noun.
– ORIGIN Dutch *slee*.

sleight /rhymes with slight/ noun (in phrase **sleight of hand**) 1 skilful use of the hands, typically in performing conjuring tricks. 2 the use of cunning to deceive people.
– ORIGIN from Old Norse, 'sly'.

slender adjective (**slenderer, slenderest**) 1 thin in a graceful and attractive way. 2 barely enough: *a slender majority.*
– DERIVATIVES **slenderly** adverb **slenderness** noun.
– ORIGIN unknown.

slept past and past participle of SLEEP.

sleuth /rhymes with truth/ informal noun a detective. •verb (usu. as noun **sleuthing**) carry out a search or investigation.
– ORIGIN from Old Norse, 'track'.

slew[1] verb turn or slide violently or uncontrollably. •noun a violent or uncontrollable turn or slide.
– ORIGIN unknown.

slew[2] past of SLAY.

slew[3] noun informal a large number or quantity: *he won a slew of awards for his film.*
– ORIGIN Irish *sluagh*.

slice noun 1 a thin, broad piece of food cut from a larger portion. 2 a portion or share. 3 a utensil with a broad, flat blade for lifting foods such as cake and fish. 4 (in sports) a stroke or shot that makes the ball spin to one side. •verb 1 cut something into slices. 2 cut something with a sharp implement. 3 move easily and quickly: *a missile sliced through the air.* 4 (in sport) hit the ball at a slight angle so that it spins and curves as it travels.

– DERIVATIVES **slicer** noun.
– ORIGIN Old French *esclice* 'splinter'.

slick adjective 1 done or operating in an impressively smooth and efficient way: *a slick piece of software.* 2 self-confident but shallow or insincere. 3 smooth, wet, and slippery or glossy: *his face was slick with sweat.* •noun 1 an oil slick. 2 an application or amount of a glossy or oily substance. •verb make hair smooth and glossy with water, oil, or cream.
– DERIVATIVES **slickly** adverb **slickness** noun.
– ORIGIN probably from an Old Norse word meaning 'smooth'.

slicker noun N. Amer. 1 a raincoat. 2 informal a cheat or swindler.

slide verb (past and past part. **slid**) 1 move along a smooth surface while remaining in contact with it. 2 move smoothly, quickly, or without being noticed. 3 change gradually to a worse condition or lower level: *shares in the company slid to a ten-year low.* •noun 1 a structure with a smooth sloping surface for children to slide down. 2 a smooth stretch of ice or packed snow for sliding on. 3 an act of sliding. 4 a rectangular piece of glass on which an object is placed to be viewed under a microscope. 5 a small piece of photographic film set in a frame and viewed with a projector. 6 Brit. a hairslide.
– DERIVATIVES **slider** noun.
– ORIGIN Old English.

slide rule noun a ruler with a sliding central strip, marked with logarithmic scales and used for making calculations.

sliding scale noun a scale of fees, wages, etc. that varies according to particular conditions.

slight adjective 1 small in degree: *a slight increase in inflation.* 2 not sturdy and strongly built. 3 rather trivial or superficial. •verb insult someone by treating them without proper respect. •noun an insult.
– DERIVATIVES **slightly** adverb **slightness** noun.
– ORIGIN Old Norse, 'smooth'.

slim adjective (**slimmer, slimmest**) 1 thin in a graceful way; slender. 2 small in width and long and narrow in shape. 3 very small: *a slim chance of success.* •verb (**slims, slimming, slimmed**) Brit. 1 make or become thinner, especially by dieting. 2 (usu. **slim down**) reduce a business to a smaller size to make it more efficient.
– DERIVATIVES **slimmer** noun **slimness** noun.
– ORIGIN German or Dutch.

slime noun an unpleasant moist, soft, and slippery substance. •verb cover something with slime.
– ORIGIN Old English.

slimline adjective 1 slender in design. 2 Brit. (of food or drink) low in calories.

slimy adjective (**slimier, slimiest**) 1 covered by or resembling slime. 2 informal flattering in an unpleasantly insincere way.

sling[1] verb (past and past part. **slung**) 1 Brit. informal throw something casually. 2 hang or carry loosely: *he had a huge bag slung over his shoulder.* 3 hurl something from a sling or similar weapon. •noun 1 a flexible loop of fabric used to support or raise a hanging weight. 2 a weapon in the form of a strap or loop, used to hurl stones or other small missiles.

– DERIVATIVES **slinger** noun.
– ORIGIN probably from German.

sling² noun a sweetened drink of spirits, especially gin, and water.
– ORIGIN unknown.

slingback noun a shoe held in place by a strap around the ankle above the heel.

slingshot noun chiefly N. Amer. a hand-held catapult.

slink verb (past and past part. **slunk**) move smoothly and quietly in a stealthy way. •noun an act of slinking.
– ORIGIN Old English, 'crawl, creep'.

slinky adjective (**slinkier, slinkiest**) informal 1 (of an item of clothing) fitting closely to the curves of the body. 2 moving in a graceful and sensuous way: *slinky models sashayed down the catwalk.*

slip¹ verb (**slips, slipping, slipped**) 1 lose one's balance or footing and slide for a short distance. 2 accidentally slide or move out of position or from someone's grasp: *the paper slipped from his fingers.* 3 fail to grip or make proper contact with a surface. 4 move or place quietly, quickly, or stealthily: *we slipped out by the back door.* 5 gradually become worse. 6 (usu. **slip up**) make a careless error. 7 escape or get free from something. 8 fail to be remembered by someone's mind. 9 release the clutch of a motor vehicle slightly or for a moment. 10 Knitting move a stitch to the other needle without knitting it. •noun 1 an act of slipping. 2 a minor or careless mistake. 3 a loose-fitting short petticoat. 4 Cricket a fielding position close behind the batsman on the off side.
– PHRASES **give someone the slip** informal avoid or escape from someone. **let something slip** reveal something accidentally in conversation. **slip of the pen** (or **the tongue**) a minor mistake in writing (or speech).
– DERIVATIVES **slippage** noun.
– ORIGIN probably from German *slippen*.

slip² noun 1 a small piece of paper for writing on or that gives printed information. 2 a cutting taken from a plant for grafting or planting.
– PHRASES **a slip of a boy/girl/thing** a small, slim young person.
– ORIGIN probably from Dutch or German *slippe* 'cut, strip'.

slip³ noun a creamy mixture of clay, water, and typically a pigment, used for decorating earthenware.
– ORIGIN uncertain.

slip cover noun chiefly N. Amer. 1 a detachable cover for a chair or sofa. 2 a jacket for a book.

slip knot noun a knot that can be undone by a pull, or that can slide along the rope on which it is tied.

slip-on adjective (of shoes or clothes) having no fastenings and able to be put on and taken off quickly.

slipped disc noun an instance of the inner material of a disc between the bones of the spine protruding through the outer coat, pressing on nearby nerves and causing pain.

slipper noun a comfortable slip-on shoe that is worn indoors.
– DERIVATIVES **slippered** adjective.

slippery adjective 1 difficult to hold firmly or

stand on through being smooth, wet, or slimy. 2 (of a person) not able to be relied on or trusted.
– PHRASES **slippery slope** a course of action very likely to lead to something undesirable: *she was on the slippery slope to alcoholism.*
– DERIVATIVES **slipperiness** noun.

slippery elm noun a North American elm tree with a slimy inner bark that is used in herbal medicine.

slippy adjective (**slippier, slippiest**) informal difficult to hold or stand on through being smooth or wet; slippery.

slip road noun Brit. a road entering or leaving a motorway or dual carriageway.

slipshod adjective careless, thoughtless, or disorganized.
– ORIGIN first meaning 'wearing loose shoes or slippers'.

slip stitch noun (in sewing) a loose stitch used to join layers of fabric, invisible from the outside of the garment.

slipstream noun 1 a current of air or water driven back by a revolving propeller or jet engine. 2 the partial vacuum created behind a moving vehicle. •verb (especially in motor racing) follow in the slipstream of a vehicle to assist in overtaking it.

slip-up noun informal a mistake.

slipway noun a slope leading into water, used for launching and landing boats and ships or for building and repairing them.

slit noun a long, narrow cut or opening. •verb (**slits, slitting, slit**) 1 make a slit in something. 2 (past and past part. **slitted**) narrow one's eyes into slits; squint.
– ORIGIN Old English.

slither verb 1 move smoothly over a surface with a twisting motion. 2 slide unsteadily on a loose or slippery surface. •noun 1 a sliding or twisting movement. 2 a small, narrow piece of something; a sliver.
– DERIVATIVES **slithery** adjective.
– ORIGIN from **SLIDE**.

slitty adjective (**slittier, slittiest**) chiefly derogatory (of the eyes) long and narrow.

sliver /rhymes with river/ noun a small, narrow piece cut or split off a larger piece. •verb cut or break something into slivers.
– ORIGIN from dialect *slive* 'cleave'.

slivovitz /sliv-uh-vits/ noun a type of plum brandy made chiefly in the former Yugoslavia and in Romania.
– ORIGIN Serbo-Croat.

Sloane (also **Sloane Ranger**) noun Brit. informal a fashionable upper-class young woman.
– DERIVATIVES **Sloaney** adjective.
– ORIGIN from *Sloane* Square, London + *Lone Ranger*, a fictional cowboy hero.

slob Brit. informal noun a lazy and untidy person. •verb behave in a lazy and untidy way.
– DERIVATIVES **slobbish** adjective **slobby** adjective.
– ORIGIN Irish *slab* 'mud'.

slobber verb 1 have saliva dripping from the mouth. 2 (**slobber over**) show excessive enthusiasm for someone or something. •noun excessive saliva dripping from the mouth.
– DERIVATIVES **slobbery** adjective.
– ORIGIN probably from Dutch *slobberen* 'walk

S

through mud, feed noisily'.

sloe noun **1** the small bluish-black fruit of the blackthorn, with a sharp sour taste. **2** another term for **BLACKTHORN**.
– ORIGIN Old English.

sloe-eyed adjective having attractive dark almond-shaped eyes.

slog informal verb (**slogs, slogging, slogged**) **1** work hard over a period of time. **2** walk or move with difficulty or effort. **3** hit something forcefully but wildly. **4** (**slog it out**) Brit. fight or compete fiercely. ●noun a spell of difficult, tiring work or travelling.
– DERIVATIVES **slogger** noun.
– ORIGIN unknown.

slogan noun a short, memorable phrase used in advertising or associated with a political party or other group.
– ORIGIN from Scottish Gaelic *sluagh* 'army' + *gairm* 'shout'.

sloganeer verb (usu. as noun **sloganeering**) use slogans, especially in politics.

slo-mo noun short for **SLOW MOTION**.

sloop noun a type of sailing boat with one mast.
– ORIGIN Dutch *sloep*.

sloosh verb Brit. informal flow, pour, or rinse with a rush of water.
– ORIGIN imitating the sound.

slop verb (**slops, slopping, slopped**) **1** (of a liquid) spill over the edge of a container. **2** apply something casually or carelessly. **3** (**slop out**) Brit. (in prison) empty the contents of a chamber pot. **4** (**slop about/around**) chiefly Brit. relax while dressed in a casual or untidy way. ●noun (**slops**) **1** waste water that has to be emptied by hand. **2** unappetizing semi-liquid food.
– ORIGIN probably from **SLIP³**.

slope noun **1** a surface with one end or side at a higher level than another. **2** a part of the side of a hill or mountain. ●verb **1** (of a surface) be at an angle so that one end is higher than another. **2** Brit. informal move in an aimless way. **3** (**slope off**) informal leave without attracting attention, typically to avoid work.
– ORIGIN uncertain.

sloppy adjective (**sloppier, sloppiest**) **1** careless and disorganized: *the organization's sloppy management is hindering its work.* **2** (of a substance) containing too much liquid; watery. **3** (of a piece of clothing) casual and loose-fitting. **4** informal excessively sentimental.
– DERIVATIVES **sloppily** adverb **sloppiness** noun.

slosh verb **1** (of liquid in a container) move around with a splashing sound. **2** move through liquid with a splashing sound. **3** pour liquid clumsily. **4** Brit. informal hit someone hard. ●noun an act or sound of splashing.
– DERIVATIVES **sloshy** adjective.
– ORIGIN from **SLUSH**.

sloshed adjective informal drunk.

slot noun **1** a long, narrow opening into which something may be placed or fitted. **2** a place given to someone or something in an arrangement or scheme: *her show is taking its rightful place in the Saturday evening slot.* ●verb (**slots, slotting, slotted**) **1** place or be placed into a slot. **2** (**slot in/into**) fit easily into a new role or situation.
– DERIVATIVES **slotted** adjective.

– ORIGIN Old French *esclot*.

sloth /slohth/ noun **1** reluctance to work or make an effort; laziness. **2** a slow-moving tropical American mammal that hangs upside down from branches.
– DERIVATIVES **slothful** adjective.
– ORIGIN Old English.

slot machine noun a fruit machine or (Brit.) vending machine.

slouch verb stand, move, or sit in a lazy, drooping way. ●noun a lazy, drooping way of standing or sitting.
– PHRASES **be no slouch** informal be good or fast at something.
– DERIVATIVES **slouchy** adjective.
– ORIGIN unknown.

slouch hat noun a hat with a wide, flexible brim.

slough¹ /rhymes with plough/ noun **1** a swamp. **2** a situation in which there is no progress or activity.
– ORIGIN Old English.

slough² /rhymes with rough/ verb **1** (of an animal, especially a snake) shed an old skin. **2** (**slough something off**) get rid of something that is unwanted.
– ORIGIN perhaps from German *sluwe* 'husk, peel'.

Slovak /sloh-vak/ noun **1** a person from Slovakia. **2** the language of Slovakia.

Slovakian /sluh-vak-i-uhn/ noun a person from Slovakia. ●adjective relating to Slovakia.

sloven /slu-vuhn/ noun dated a person who is always untidy or careless.
– ORIGIN perhaps from Flemish *sloef* 'dirty' or Dutch *slof* 'careless'.

Slovene /sloh-veen/ noun **1** a person from Slovenia. **2** the language of Slovenia.
– DERIVATIVES **Slovenian** noun & adjective.

slovenly adjective **1** untidy and dirty. **2** excessively casual; careless.
– DERIVATIVES **slovenliness** noun.

slow adjective **1** moving or capable of moving only at a low speed. **2** taking a long time. **3** (of a clock or watch) showing a time earlier than the correct time. **4** not quick to understand, think, or learn. **5** showing little activity: *sales were slow.* **6** (of photographic film) needing long exposure. **7** (of an oven) giving off heat gently. ●verb (often **slow down/up**) **1** reduce one's speed or the speed of a vehicle or process. **2** work or live less actively or intensely.
– DERIVATIVES **slowly** noun **slowness** noun.
– ORIGIN Old English.

USAGE: Slow is normally used as an adjective (*a slow learner*). It is also used as an adverb in certain situations, including compounds such as **slow-acting** and in the expression **go slow**. However, it is not acceptable to use **slow** as an adverb in other ways (e.g. *he drives too slow*): in these cases, you should use **slowly** instead.

slowcoach noun Brit. informal a person who acts or moves slowly.

slow cooker noun a large electric pot used for cooking food very slowly.

slowdown noun a reduction in speed or activity, especially economic activity.

slow motion noun the action of showing film or video more slowly than it was made or recorded, so that the action appears much slower than in real life.

slow-worm noun a small snake-like lizard without legs.
– ORIGIN Old English.

SLR abbreviation **1** self-loading rifle. **2** single-lens reflex.

slub noun fabric woven from yarn containing lumps.
– DERIVATIVES **slubbed** adjective.
– ORIGIN unknown.

sludge noun **1** thick, soft, wet mud. **2** semi-solid industrial waste.
– DERIVATIVES **sludgy** adjective.
– ORIGIN uncertain.

slug¹ noun **1** a small mollusc which resembles a snail without a shell. **2** a small amount of an alcoholic drink. **3** chiefly N. Amer. a bullet. •verb (**slugs, slugging, slugged**) gulp a drink, especially an alcoholic one.
– ORIGIN probably Scandinavian.

slug² informal, chiefly N. Amer. verb (**slugs, slugging, slugged**) **1** hit someone hard. **2** (**slug it out**) settle a dispute or contest by fighting or competing fiercely. •noun a hard blow.
– DERIVATIVES **slugger** noun.
– ORIGIN unknown.

sluggard noun a lazy, inactive person.
– DERIVATIVES **sluggardly** adjective.
– ORIGIN from former *slug* 'be lazy or slow'.

sluggish adjective **1** slow-moving or inactive. **2** lacking energy or alertness.
– DERIVATIVES **sluggishly** adverb **sluggishness** noun.

slug pellet noun a pellet containing a substance poisonous to slugs, placed among plants to prevent them being damaged.

sluice /slooss/ noun **1** (also **sluice gate**) a sliding gate or other device for controlling the flow of water. **2** (also **sluiceway**) an artificial channel for carrying off surplus water. **3** an act of rinsing with water. •verb wash or rinse someone or something with water.
– ORIGIN Old French *escluse*.

slum noun **1** a run-down and overcrowded area of a city or town inhabited by very poor people. **2** a house or building that is unfit to be lived in. •verb (**slums, slumming, slummed**) (**slum it**) informal accept conditions that are worse than those one is used to.
– DERIVATIVES **slummer** noun **slummy** adjective.
– ORIGIN unknown.

slumber literary verb be asleep. •noun a sleep.
– DERIVATIVES **slumberous** (also **slumbrous**) adjective.
– ORIGIN from Scots and northern English *sloom*.

slump verb **1** sit, lean, or fall heavily and limply. **2** decline greatly or over a prolonged period: *prices slumped due to sluggish demand.* •noun **1** a sudden or severe drop in the price or value of something. **2** a prolonged period of abnormally low economic activity.
– ORIGIN probably from Norwegian *slumpe* 'to fall'.

slung past and past participle of **SLING**¹.

slunk past and past participle of **SLINK**.

slur verb (**slurs, slurring, slurred**) **1** speak words in an unclear way, with the sounds running into one another. **2** perform a group of musical notes so that each runs smoothly into the next. **3** make damaging or false statements about someone. •noun **1** an insult or accusation intended to damage someone's reputation. **2** an act of speaking indistinctly. **3** a curved line indicating that musical notes are to be performed so that each runs into the next.
– ORIGIN unknown.

slurp verb eat or drink something with a loud sucking sound. •noun an act or sound of slurping.
– ORIGIN Dutch *slurpen*.

slurry /rhymes with hurry/ noun (pl. **slurries**) a semi-liquid mixture of manure, cement, or coal and water.
– ORIGIN unknown.

slush noun **1** partially melted snow or ice. **2** informal excessive sentiment in novels, films, etc. •verb make a soft splashing sound.
– DERIVATIVES **slushy** adjective.
– ORIGIN uncertain.

slush fund noun a reserve of money used for underhand or dishonest purposes, especially political bribery.
– ORIGIN from nautical slang, referring to money collected to buy luxuries, from the sale of watery food known as *slush*.

slut noun **1** a woman who has many sexual partners. **2** a woman who is untidy or lazy.
– DERIVATIVES **sluttish** adjective **slutty** adjective.
– ORIGIN unknown.

sly adjective (**slyer, slyest**) **1** having a cunning and deceitful nature. **2** (of a remark, glance, or expression) suggesting that one has secret knowledge that may be damaging or embarrassing: *slip the doorman a note with a sly grin.* **3** (of an action) done secretly.
– PHRASES **on the sly** in a secret way.
– DERIVATIVES **slyly** adverb **slyness** noun.
– ORIGIN Old Norse, 'cunning'.

SM abbreviation **1** sadomasochism. **2** Sergeant Major.

Sm symbol the chemical element samarium.

smack¹ noun **1** a sharp blow given with the palm of the hand. **2** a loud, sharp sound. **3** a loud kiss. •verb **1** hit someone or something sharply with the palm of the hand. **2** hit or smash something into something else. **3** part the lips noisily. •adverb (Brit. also **smack bang**) informal **1** in a sudden and violent way. **2** exactly; precisely.
– ORIGIN Dutch *smacken*.

smack² verb (**smack of**) **1** seem to contain or involve something wrong or undesirable: *such writing smacks of racism.* **2** taste of something. •noun (**a smack of**) a taste or suggestion of something.
– ORIGIN Old English.

smack³ noun Brit. a sailing boat with one mast, used for fishing.
– ORIGIN Dutch *smak*.

smack⁴ noun informal heroin.
– ORIGIN probably from a Yiddish word meaning 'a sniff'.

smacker (also **smackeroo**) noun informal **1** a loud kiss. **2** Brit. one pound sterling. **3** N. Amer. one dollar.

S

small adjective **1** not large in size, amount, or number. **2** not great in strength, importance, or power: *a small voice.* **3** not fully grown or developed; young. **4** (of a business or its owner) operating on a modest scale: *a small farmer.* •noun (**smalls**) Brit. informal underwear. •adverb into small pieces.
– PHRASES **feel** (or **look**) **small** feel (or look) foolish or unimportant. **small beer** Brit. something unimportant. **the small of the back** the part of a person's back where the spine curves in at the level of the waist. **the small screen** television.
– DERIVATIVES **smallness** noun.
– ORIGIN Old English.

small arms plural noun portable firearms.

small change noun **1** coins of low value. **2** something trivial.

small claims court noun a local court in which claims for small sums of money can be heard and decided quickly and cheaply, without using a lawyer.

small end noun (in a piston engine) the end of the connecting rod connected to the piston.

small fry plural noun **1** unimportant people or things. **2** young or small fish.

smallholding noun Brit. a piece of leased agricultural land that is smaller than a farm.
– DERIVATIVES **smallholder** noun.

small hours plural noun (**the small hours**) the early hours of the morning after midnight.

small intestine noun the part of the intestine that runs between the stomach and the large intestine.

small-minded adjective having a narrow outlook; petty.

smallpox noun a serious disease spread by a virus, with fever and blisters that leave permanent scars.

small print noun important details or conditions in an agreement or contract that are printed in small type so that they are not easily noticed.

small-scale adjective of limited size or extent.

small talk noun polite conversation about unimportant matters.

small-time adjective informal unimportant; minor.

smarm verb informal, chiefly Brit. try to gain favour with someone by flattering or trying to please them.
– ORIGIN unknown.

smarmy adjective (**smarmier, smarmiest**) Brit. informal friendly or flattering in an insincere or excessive way.
– DERIVATIVES **smarmily** adverb **smarminess** noun.

smart adjective **1** clean, tidy, and stylish. **2** (of a place) fashionable and upmarket. **3** attractive and new in appearance: *smart bathroom furniture.* **4** informal quick-witted and clever. **5** chiefly N. Amer. clever in a cheeky or sarcastic way. **6** quick; brisk: *I set off at a smart pace.* •verb **1** feel a sharp, stinging pain. **2** feel upset and annoyed. •noun **1** a sharp, stinging pain. **2** (**smarts**) N. Amer. informal intelligence or shrewdness.
– PHRASES **look smart** chiefly Brit. be quick.
– DERIVATIVES **smartly** adverb **smartness** noun.
– ORIGIN Old English.

smart alec (chiefly N. Amer. also **smart aleck**) noun informal a person who is irritating because they behave as if they know everything.

smart card noun a plastic card on which information is stored in electronic form, used for financial transactions.

smarten verb (**smarten up**) make or become smarter.

smartish adverb informal, chiefly Brit. quickly; briskly.

smartphone noun a mobile phone which incorporates a palmtop computer.

smash verb **1** break violently into pieces. **2** hit or collide forcefully. **3** crash and severely damage a vehicle. **4** (in sport) hit the ball very hard. **5** completely defeat, destroy, or put an end to: *police smashed a major crime network.* •noun **1** an act or sound of smashing. **2** (also **smash hit**) informal a very successful song, film, or show.
– ORIGIN probably imitating the sound.

smash-and-grab adjective Brit. (of a robbery) in which the thief smashes a shop window and seizes goods.

smashed adjective informal very drunk.

smasher noun Brit. informal a very attractive or impressive person or thing.

smashing adjective Brit. informal excellent; wonderful.

smattering noun **1** a small amount. **2** a slight knowledge of a language or subject.
– ORIGIN unknown.

smear verb **1** coat or mark someone or something with a greasy or sticky substance. **2** blur or smudge something. **3** damage a person's reputation by false accusations. •noun **1** a greasy or sticky mark. **2** a false accusation. **3** a sample thinly spread on a slide for examination under a microscope.
– DERIVATIVES **smeary** adjective.
– ORIGIN Old English.

smear test noun Brit. a test to detect signs of cancer in the neck of the womb.

smell noun **1** the faculty of sensing things by means of the organs in the nose. **2** something sensed by the nose; a scent or odour. **3** an act of smelling. •verb (past and past part. **smelt** or **smelled**) **1** sense the scent or odour of someone or something. **2** sniff at something in order to find out its smell. **3** have a particular scent or odour: *the room smelled of damp.* **4** have a strong or unpleasant odour. **5** sense or suspect that something exists or is about to happen: *I can smell trouble.*
– PHRASES **smell a rat** informal suspect a trick.
– DERIVATIVES **smeller** noun.
– ORIGIN unknown.

smelling salts plural noun chiefly historical a chemical mixed with perfume, sniffed by someone who feels faint.

smelly adjective (**smellier, smelliest**) having a strong or unpleasant smell.
– DERIVATIVES **smelliness** noun.

smelt[1] verb extract metal from its ore by a process involving heating and melting.
– DERIVATIVES **smelter** noun.
– ORIGIN Dutch, German *smelten.*

smelt[2] past and past participle of SMELL.

smelt[3] noun (pl. same or **smelts**) a small silvery

fish that lives both in fresh water and the sea.
– ORIGIN Old English.

smidgen (also **smidgeon** or **smidgin**) noun informal a tiny amount of something.
– ORIGIN perhaps from Scots *smitch* in the same sense.

smile verb **1** form the features of the face into a pleased, friendly, or amused expression, with the corners of the mouth turned up. **2** (**smile at/on**) be favourable to: *luck was smiling on them as they carried out their plan.* •noun an act of smiling.
– ORIGIN perhaps Scandinavian.

smiley adjective informal smiling; cheerful. •noun (pl. **smileys**) a symbol which represents a smiling face, formed by the characters :-) and used in emails and similar electronic communications.

smirch /smerch/ verb **1** make someone or something dirty. **2** damage a person's reputation.
– ORIGIN uncertain.

smirk verb smile in a smug or silly way. •noun a smug or silly smile.
– DERIVATIVES **smirker** noun **smirky** adjective.
– ORIGIN Old English.

smite verb (past **smote**; past part. **smitten**) **1** (**be smitten**) be affected severely by a disease or feeling. **2** (**be smitten**) be strongly attracted to someone or something: *Vince had been smitten with Tess for years.* **3** literary hit someone or something with a hard blow. **4** old use defeat or conquer an opponent.
– ORIGIN Old English, 'to smear, blemish'.

smith noun **1** a person who works in metal. **2** a blacksmith. •verb treat metal by heating, hammering, and forging it.
– ORIGIN Old English.

smithereens /smi-*th*uh-reenz/ plural noun informal small pieces.
– ORIGIN probably from Irish *smidirín*.

smithy /smi-*th*i/ noun (pl. **smithies**) a blacksmith's workshop.
– ORIGIN Old Norse.

smitten past participle of SMITE.

smock noun **1** a loose dress or blouse with the upper part closely gathered in smocking. **2** a loose overall worn to protect one's clothes. •verb decorate a dress or blouse with smocking.
– ORIGIN Old English.

smocking noun decoration on a garment created by gathering a section of the material into tight pleats and holding them together with a pattern of parallel stitches.

smog noun fog or haze intensified by smoke or other pollution in the atmosphere.
– DERIVATIVES **smoggy** adjective.
– ORIGIN blend of SMOKE and FOG.

smoke noun **1** a visible vapour in the air, produced by a burning substance. **2** an act of smoking tobacco. **3** informal a cigarette or cigar. **4** (**the Smoke** or **the Big Smoke**) Brit. a big city, especially London. •verb **1** give out smoke. **2** breathe the smoke of a cigarette, pipe, etc. in and out. **3** cure or preserve meat or fish by hanging it in smoke. **4** (**smoke someone/thing out**) drive someone or something out of a place by using smoke. **5** (as adj. **smoked**) (of glass) treated so as to darken it.

– PHRASES **go up in smoke** informal **1** be destroyed by fire. **2** (of a plan) come to nothing. **there's no smoke without fire** there is always a reason for a rumour.
– DERIVATIVES **smokable** adjective **smokeless** adjective **smoker** noun.
– ORIGIN Old English.

smoke alarm noun a device that detects and gives a warning of the presence of smoke.

smokeless zone noun Brit. a district in which it is illegal to create smoke and where only smokeless fuel may be used.

smokescreen noun **1** something intended to disguise someone's real intentions or activities. **2** a cloud of smoke created to conceal military operations.

smokestack noun a chimney or funnel for discharging smoke from a locomotive, ship, or factory.

smoking gun noun a piece of evidence that proves without doubt that someone is guilty of wrongdoing.

smoking jacket noun a man's comfortable jacket, formerly worn while smoking after dinner.

smoky (also **smokey**) adjective (**smokier**, **smokiest**) **1** producing or filled with smoke. **2** having the taste or smell of smoked food. **3** resembling smoke in colour or appearance: *smoky grey eyeshadows.*
– DERIVATIVES **smokily** adverb **smokiness** noun.

smolder verb US spelling of SMOULDER.

smolt /smohlt/ noun a young salmon or trout after the parr stage (two years old), when it migrates to the sea for the first time.
– ORIGIN unknown.

smooch informal verb **1** kiss and cuddle amorously. **2** Brit. dance slowly in a close embrace. •noun a spell of kissing and cuddling.
– DERIVATIVES **smoocher** noun **smoochy** adjective.
– ORIGIN imitating the sound.

smooth adjective **1** having an even and regular surface. **2** (of a liquid) without lumps. **3** (of movement) without jerks. **4** happening without problems: *the organizers deserve thanks for the smooth running of the festival.* **5** charming in very confident or flattering way. **6** (of a flavour) not harsh or bitter. •verb (also **smoothe**) **1** make something smooth. **2** deal successfully with a problem: *these disputes were smoothed over.*
– DERIVATIVES **smoothly** adverb **smoothness** noun.
– ORIGIN Old English.

smoothie noun **1** a thick, smooth drink of fresh fruit puréed with milk, yogurt, or ice cream. **2** informal a charming and confident man who is often not sincere.

smooth snake noun a harmless snake which is grey to reddish in colour, typically living in heathland.

smooth-talking adjective informal using very persuasive or flattering language.
– DERIVATIVES **smooth-talker** noun.

smorgasbord /smor-guhz-bord/ noun a selection of open sandwiches and savoury items served as hors d'oeuvres or a buffet.
– ORIGIN Swedish.

smote past of SMITE.

smother verb **1** suffocate someone by covering

S

the nose and mouth. **2 (smother someone/ thing in/with)** cover someone or something entirely with something. **3** prevent from developing or being expressed: *she smothered a sigh.* **4** make someone feel overwhelmed by treating them too protectively. **5** put out a fire by covering it.
– ORIGIN Old English.

smoulder (US also **smolder**) verb **1** burn slowly with smoke but no flame. **2** feel intense and barely concealed anger, hatred, lust, etc.
– ORIGIN Dutch *smeulen.*

SMS abbreviation Short Message (or Messaging) Service, a system that enables mobile phone users to send and receive text messages. noun a message sent or received using SMS. verb (**SMSs, SMSing, SMSed**) send a message by SMS.

SMTP abbreviation Simple Mail Transfer (or Transport) Protocol, a standard for the transmission of email on a computer network.

smudge verb make or become blurred or smeared. • noun a blurred or smeared mark.
– DERIVATIVES **smudgy** adjective.
– ORIGIN unknown.

smug adjective (**smugger, smuggest**) pleased with oneself in an irritating way; self-satisfied.
– DERIVATIVES **smugly** adverb **smugness** noun.
– ORIGIN German *smuk* 'pretty'.

smuggle verb **1** move goods illegally into or out of a country. **2** take someone or something secretly to or from a place.
– DERIVATIVES **smuggler** noun **smuggling** noun.
– ORIGIN German *smuggelen.*

smut noun **1** a small flake of soot or dirt. **2** indecent or obscene talk, writing, or pictures. **3** a disease of cereal crops caused by a fungus, in which parts of the ear change to black powder.
– ORIGIN from German *schmutzen* 'make dirty or corrupt'.

smutty adjective (**smuttier, smuttiest**) **1** indecent or obscene. **2** dirty or sooty.

Sn symbol the chemical element tin.
– ORIGIN from Latin *stannum* 'tin'.

snack noun a small quantity of food eaten between meals or instead of a meal. • verb eat a snack.
– ORIGIN Dutch.

snaffle verb Brit. informal take something quickly or secretly for oneself. • noun a simple bit on a horse's bridle, used with a single set of reins.
– ORIGIN probably German or Dutch.

snafu /sna-foo, sna-foo/ noun informal a situation that is confused or that has gone wrong.
– ORIGIN from the initial letters of *situation normal: all fouled* (or *fucked*) *up.*

snag noun **1** an unexpected difficulty or drawback. **2** a sharp or jagged projection. **3** a small tear in fabric. • verb (**snags, snagging, snagged**) **1** catch or tear something on a sharp projection. **2** N. Amer. informal manage to get or obtain something.
– DERIVATIVES **snaggy** adjective.
– ORIGIN probably Scandinavian.

snaggle-toothed adjective having irregular or projecting teeth.
– ORIGIN from **SNAG**.

snail noun a slow-moving mollusc with a spiral shell into which it can withdraw its whole body.
– PHRASES **snail's pace** a very slow speed or rate of progress.
– ORIGIN Old English.

snail mail noun informal the ordinary post as opposed to email.

snake noun a reptile with a long, slender limbless body, many kinds of which have a venomous bite. • verb move or extend with the twisting motion of a snake: *the road snakes inland.*
– PHRASES **snake in the grass** a person who pretends to be friendly but is secretly working against someone.
– ORIGIN Old English.

snakebite noun Brit. a drink consisting of draught cider and lager in equal proportions.

snake charmer noun an entertainer who appears to make snakes move by playing music.

snakehead noun a member of a Chinese criminal network chiefly involved in smuggling illegal immigrants.
– ORIGIN translation of Chinese *shetou.*

snakes and ladders plural noun (treated as sing.) Brit. a board game in which players proceed up ladders or fall back down snakes depicted on the board.

snakeskin noun the skin of a snake.

snaky (also **snakey**) adjective (**snakier, snakiest**) **1** long and winding. **2** cold and cunning.

snap verb (**snaps, snapping, snapped**) **1** break with a sharp cracking sound. **2** open or close with a brisk movement or sharp sound. **3** (of an animal) make a sudden bite. **4 (snap someone/thing up)** quickly obtain someone or something that is desirable or in short supply. **5** suddenly lose one's self-control. **6** say something quickly and irritably. **7 (snap out of)** informal get out of a bad mood by a sudden effort. **8** take a snapshot of someone or something. • noun **1** an act or sound of snapping. **2** a snapshot. **3** a crisp, brittle biscuit. **4** Brit. a card game in which players compete to call 'snap' as soon as two cards of the same type are exposed. • adjective done or taken on the spur of the moment: *a snap decision.*
– ORIGIN probably from Dutch or German *snappen* 'seize'.

snapdragon noun a plant with brightly coloured flowers which have a mouth-like opening.

snap-lock adjective (of a device or part) that fastens automatically when pushed into position.

snapper noun an edible sea fish noted for snapping its toothed jaws.

snappish adjective informal irritable; snappy.
– DERIVATIVES **snappishly** adverb **snappishness** noun.

snappy adjective (**snappier, snappiest**) informal **1** irritable and sharp. **2** cleverly brief and to the point: *a comedy loaded with snappy dialogue.* **3** neat and stylish: *a snappy dresser.*
– PHRASES **make it snappy** do it quickly.
– DERIVATIVES **snappily** adverb.

snapshot noun an informal photograph, taken quickly.

snare noun 1 a trap for catching small animals, consisting of a loop of wire or cord that pulls tight. 2 something likely to lure someone into harm or trouble. 3 (also **snare drum**) a drum with a length of wire, gut, or hide stretched across the head to make a rattling sound. • verb catch someone or something in a snare or trap.
– ORIGIN Old Norse; sense 3 is probably from German or Dutch, 'harp string'.

snarl¹ verb 1 growl with bared teeth. 2 say something aggressively. • noun an act or sound of snarling.
– DERIVATIVES **snarly** adjective.
– ORIGIN Germanic.

snarl² verb (**snarl something up**) 1 tangle something up. 2 hinder something. • noun a knot or tangle.
– ORIGIN from SNARE.

snarl-up noun Brit. informal 1 a traffic jam. 2 a muddle.

snatch verb 1 grab something in a rude or eager way. 2 informal steal something or kidnap someone suddenly. 3 quickly take when the chance presents itself: *I snatched a few hours' sleep.* • noun 1 an act of snatching. 2 a fragment of music or talk.
– DERIVATIVES **snatcher** noun.
– ORIGIN perhaps from SNACK.

snazzy adjective (**snazzier, snazziest**) informal smart and stylish.
– ORIGIN unknown.

sneak verb (past and past part. **sneaked** or informal, chiefly N. Amer. **snuck**) 1 move or take in a stealthy or secretive way. 2 do or achieve in a stealthy way: *she sneaked a glance at her watch.* 3 Brit. informal inform someone in authority of a person's wrongdoings. • noun Brit. informal a person who behaves in an underhand way, especially by informing someone in authority of a person's wrongdoings. • adjective acting or done secretly or unofficially: *a sneak preview.*
– ORIGIN perhaps from former *snike* 'to creep'.

sneaker noun chiefly N. Amer. a soft shoe worn for sports or casual occasions.

sneaking adjective (of a feeling) remaining in one's mind.

sneaky adjective (**sneakier, sneakiest**) secretive in a sly or guilty way.
– DERIVATIVES **sneakily** adverb **sneakiness** noun.

sneer noun a scornful or mocking smile, remark, or tone. • verb smile or speak in a scornful or mocking way.
– ORIGIN uncertain.

sneeze verb suddenly expel air from the nose and mouth due to irritation of the nostrils. • noun an act or the sound of sneezing.
– PHRASES **not to be sneezed at** informal not to be rejected without careful consideration.
– DERIVATIVES **sneezer** noun **sneezy** adjective.
– ORIGIN Old English.

snick verb 1 cut a small notch in something. 2 make a clicking sound. • noun 1 a small notch or cut. 2 a sharp click.
– ORIGIN probably from former *snick or snee* 'fight with knives'.

snicker verb 1 chiefly N. Amer. give a smothered scornful laugh; snigger. 2 (of a horse) make a gentle high-pitched neigh. • noun an act of snickering; a snigger or gentle high-pitched neigh.

– ORIGIN imitating the sound.

snide adjective disrespectful or mocking in an indirect way.
– DERIVATIVES **snidely** adverb **snidey** adjective.
– ORIGIN unknown.

sniff verb 1 draw in air audibly through the nose. 2 (**sniff around/round**) informal investigate something secretly. 3 (**sniff something out**) informal discover something by investigation. • noun 1 an act or sound of sniffing. 2 informal a hint or sign: *they're off at the first sniff of trouble.* 3 informal a slight chance.
– PHRASES **not to be sniffed at** informal worth having or considering.
– DERIVATIVES **sniffer** noun.
– ORIGIN imitating the sound.

sniffer dog noun a dog trained to find drugs or explosives by smell.

sniffle verb sniff slightly or repeatedly, typically because of a cold or fit of crying. • noun 1 an act of sniffling. 2 a slight head cold.
– DERIVATIVES **sniffly** adjective.
– ORIGIN imitating the sound.

sniffy adjective (**sniffier, sniffiest**) informal scornful; contemptuous.
– DERIVATIVES **sniffily** adverb.

snifter noun Brit. informal a small quantity of an alcoholic drink.
– ORIGIN uncertain.

snigger chiefly Brit. verb give a smothered and scornful laugh. • noun a smothered and scornful laugh.
– ORIGIN from SNICKER.

snip verb (**snips, snipping, snipped**) cut something with scissors using small, quick strokes. • noun 1 an act of snipping. 2 a small piece that has been cut off. 3 Brit. informal a bargain. 4 (**snips**) hand shears for cutting metal.
– ORIGIN from German, 'small piece'.

snipe /rhymes with pipe/ verb (usu. **snipe at**) 1 shoot at someone from a hiding place at long range. 2 criticize someone or something in a sly or petty way. • noun (pl. same or **snipes**) a wading bird with brown plumage and a long straight bill.
– DERIVATIVES **sniper** noun.
– ORIGIN probably Scandinavian.

snippet noun a small piece or brief extract.

snippy adjective informal curt or sharp.

snitch informal verb 1 steal something. 2 inform on someone. • noun an informer.
– ORIGIN unknown.

snivel verb (**snivels, snivelling, snivelled;** US **snivels, sniveling, sniveled**) 1 cry and sniffle. 2 complain in a whining or tearful way. • noun a spell of snivelling.
– DERIVATIVES **sniveller** noun.
– ORIGIN from Old English, 'mucus'.

snob noun 1 a person who greatly respects upper-class or rich people and who looks down on people of a lower class. 2 a person who believes that their tastes in a particular area are superior to others: *a wine snob.*
– DERIVATIVES **snobbery** noun (pl. **snobberies**) **snobbism** noun **snobby** adjective (**snobbier, snobbiest**).
– ORIGIN uncertain.

snobbish adjective relating to or typical of a snob: *his snobbish contempt for the lower classes.*
– DERIVATIVES **snobbishly** adverb.

snog Brit. informal verb (**snogs, snogging, snogged**) kiss amorously. ●noun an act or spell of amorous kissing.
– ORIGIN unknown.

snood /snood/ noun 1 an ornamental hairnet or pouch worn over the hair at the back of a woman's head. 2 a wide ring of knitted material worn as a hood or scarf.
– ORIGIN Old English.

snook /snook/ noun (in phrase **cock a snook at**) informal, chiefly Brit. 1 openly show contempt or a lack of respect for someone or something. 2 place one's hand so that the thumb touches one's nose and the fingers are spread out, as a gesture of contempt.
– ORIGIN unknown.

snooker noun 1 a game played with cues on a billiard table, in which the players use a white cue ball to pocket the other balls in a set order. 2 a position in a game of snooker or pool in which a player cannot make a direct shot at any permitted ball. ●verb 1 (in snooker and pool) put an opponent in a position in which they cannot make a direct shot at any permitted ball. 2 (**be snookered**) Brit. informal be placed in an impossible position.
– ORIGIN unknown.

snoop informal verb look around or investigate secretly to try to find out private information. ●noun an act of snooping.
– DERIVATIVES **snooper** noun.
– ORIGIN Dutch *snoepen* 'eat on the sly'.

snooty adjective (**snootier, snootiest**) informal treating people as if they are socially inferior; snobbish.
– DERIVATIVES **snootily** adverb **snootiness** noun.
– ORIGIN from **SNOUT**.

snooze informal noun a short, light sleep. ●verb sleep lightly and briefly.
– DERIVATIVES **snoozer** noun **snoozy** adjective.
– ORIGIN unknown.

snooze button noun a control on a clock which sets an alarm to repeat after a short interval.

snore noun a snorting sound in a person's breathing while they are asleep. ●verb make a snorting sound while asleep.
– DERIVATIVES **snorer** noun.
– ORIGIN probably imitating the sound.

snorkel /snor-k'l/ noun a tube for a swimmer to breathe through while under water. ●verb (**snorkels, snorkelling, snorkelled**; US **snorkels, snorkeling, snorkeled**) (often as noun **snorkelling**) swim using a snorkel.
– DERIVATIVES **snorkeller** noun.
– ORIGIN German *Schnorchel*.

snort noun 1 an explosive sound made by the sudden forcing of breath through the nose. 2 informal an amount of cocaine that is breathed in through the nose. 3 informal a measure of an alcoholic drink. ●verb 1 make a snort, especially to express anger or mockery. 2 informal inhale cocaine.
– DERIVATIVES **snorter** noun.
– ORIGIN probably imitating the sound.

snot noun informal 1 mucus in the nose. 2 an unpleasant person.
– ORIGIN probably from Dutch, German.

snotty adjective (**snottier, snottiest**) informal 1 full of or covered with mucus from the nose. 2 having a superior or arrogant attitude.
– DERIVATIVES **snottily** adverb **snottiness** noun.

snout noun 1 the projecting nose and mouth of an animal. 2 the projecting front or end of something such as a pistol. 3 Brit. informal a police informer.
– DERIVATIVES **snouted** adjective.
– ORIGIN Dutch, German *snût*.

snow noun 1 frozen water vapour in the atmosphere that falls in light white flakes. 2 (**snows**) falls of snow. 3 a mass of flickering white spots on a television or radar screen, caused by interference or a poor signal. ●verb 1 (**it snows, it is snowing, it snowed**) snow falls. 2 (**be snowed in/up**) be unable to leave somewhere due to heavy snow. 3 (**be snowed under**) be overwhelmed with a large quantity of something, especially work.
– DERIVATIVES **snowless** adjective.
– ORIGIN Old English.

snowball noun 1 a ball of packed snow. 2 a cocktail containing advocaat and lemonade. ●verb 1 increase rapidly in size, intensity, or importance: *my enthusiasm quickly snowballed.* 2 throw snowballs at someone.

snow-blindness noun temporary blindness caused by the glare of light reflected by a large expanse of snow.

snowboard noun a board resembling a short, broad ski, used for sliding downhill on snow.
– DERIVATIVES **snowboarder** noun **snowboarding** noun.

snowbound adjective 1 prevented from travelling or going out by snow. 2 (of a place) cut off because of snow.

snowdrift noun a bank of deep snow heaped up by the wind.

snowdrop noun a plant which bears drooping white flowers during late winter.

snowfall noun 1 a fall of snow. 2 the quantity of snow falling within a particular area in a given time.

snowfield noun a permanent wide expanse of snow in mountainous or polar regions.

snowflake noun each of the many feathery ice crystals that fall as snow.

snow goose noun a goose that breeds in Arctic Canada and Greenland, having white plumage with black wing tips.

snow leopard noun a rare large cat which has pale grey fur patterned with dark blotches and rings, living in mountainous parts of central Asia.

snowline noun the altitude above which some snow remains on the ground throughout the year.

snowman noun (pl. **snowmen**) a model of a human figure created with compressed snow.

snowmobile noun a motor vehicle with runners or caterpillar tracks for travelling over snow.

snowplough (US **snowplow**) noun 1 a device or vehicle for clearing roads of snow. 2 an act of turning the points of one's skis inwards in order to slow down or turn.

S

snowshoe noun a flat device resembling a tennis racket, which is attached to the sole of a boot and used for walking on snow.

snowstorm noun a heavy fall of snow accompanied by a high wind.

snowy adjective (**snowier**, **snowiest**) **1** covered with snow. **2** (of weather or a period of time) characterized by snowfall. **3** like snow, especially in being pure white.

snowy owl noun a large northern owl, the male being entirely white.

snub verb (**snubs**, **snubbing**, **snubbed**) ignore or reject someone or something scornfully. •noun an act of snubbing someone or something. •adjective (of a person's nose) short and turned up at the end.
– ORIGIN Old Norse, 'chide'.

snuck informal, chiefly N. Amer. past and past participle of **SNEAK**.

snuff¹ verb **1** put out a candle. **2** (**snuff something out**) abruptly put an end to something. **3** (**snuff it**) Brit. informal die. •noun the charred part of a candle wick.
– ORIGIN unknown.

snuff² noun powdered tobacco that is sniffed up the nostril. •verb inhale or sniff at something.
– PHRASES **up to snuff** informal **1** up to the required standard. **2** in good health.
– ORIGIN probably an abbreviation of Dutch *snuftabak*; the verb is from Dutch *snuffen* 'to snuffle'.

snuffer noun a small hollow metal cone on the end of a handle, used to put out a candle by smothering the flame.

snuffle verb **1** breathe noisily through a partially blocked nose. **2** (of an animal) make repeated sniffing sounds. •noun **1** a snuffling sound. **2** (**the snuffles**) informal a cold.
– DERIVATIVES **snuffly** adjective.
– ORIGIN probably from German and Dutch *snuffelen*.

snuff movie noun informal a pornographic film or video recording of an actual murder.

snug adjective (**snugger**, **snuggest**) **1** warm and cosy. **2** close-fitting. •noun Brit. a small, cosy bar in a pub or small hotel.
– DERIVATIVES **snugly** adverb **snugness** noun.
– ORIGIN probably from German or Dutch.

snuggery noun (pl. **snuggeries**) a cosy place, especially someone's private room.

snuggle verb settle into a warm, comfortable position.
– ORIGIN from **SNUG**.

so¹ adverb **1** to such a great extent. **2** extremely; very much. **3** to the same extent: *he isn't so bad as you'd think.* **4** referring back to something previously mentioned. **5** similarly: *times have changed and so have I.* **6** in the way described or demonstrated; thus. •conjunction **1** therefore. **2** (**so that**) with the result or aim that. **3** and then. **4** introducing a question or concluding statement. **5** in the same way.
– PHRASES **and so on** (or **forth**) and similar things; et cetera. **or so** approximately. **so long!** informal goodbye. **so much as** even: *without so much as a word.*
– ORIGIN Old English.

so² noun variant spelling of **SOH**.

soak verb **1** make or become thoroughly wet by leaving or remaining in liquid. **2** (of a liquid) penetrate or spread through completely: *the rain soaked their hair.* **3** (**soak something up**) absorb a liquid. **4** (**soak something up**) expose oneself to something beneficial or enjoyable: *soak up the Mediterranean sun.* **5** (**soak oneself in**) involve oneself deeply in a particular experience. •noun **1** an act or period of soaking. **2** informal a heavy drinker.
– ORIGIN Old English.

soakaway noun Brit. a pit through which waste water drains slowly out into the surrounding soil.

soaking (also **soaking wet**) adjective very wet.

so-and-so noun (pl. **so-and-sos**) informal **1** a person or thing whose name the speaker does not know or need to specify. **2** an unpleasant or disliked person (used instead of an offensive word): *a nosy so-and-so.*

soap noun **1** a substance used with water for washing and cleaning, made of natural oils or fats combined with an alkali, and typically perfumed. **2** informal a soap opera. •verb wash someone or something with soap.
– ORIGIN Old English.

soapbox noun **1** a box or crate used as a stand when making a speech in public. **2** an opportunity for someone to express their views publicly: *I tend to get up on my soapbox about this issue.*

soap opera noun a television or radio drama serial dealing with daily events in the lives of the same group of characters.
– ORIGIN so named because such serials were originally sponsored in the US by soap manufacturers.

soapstone noun a soft rock consisting largely of the mineral talc.

soapsuds plural noun another term for **SUDS**.

soapy adjective (**soapier**, **soapiest**) **1** containing or covered with soap. **2** like soap.

soar verb **1** fly or rise high into the air. **2** maintain height in the air by gliding. **3** increase rapidly above the usual level.
– ORIGIN Old French *essorer*.

Soave /swah-vay, soh-ah-vay/ noun a dry white Italian wine.
– ORIGIN named after the village of *Soave* in northern Italy.

sob verb (**sobs**, **sobbing**, **sobbed**) **1** cry making loud gasping noises. **2** say something while sobbing. •noun an act or sound of sobbing.
– ORIGIN perhaps Dutch or German.

sober adjective (**soberer**, **soberest**) **1** not affected by alcohol; not drunk. **2** serious and sensible or thoughtful. **3** (of a colour) not bright or conspicuous. •verb **1** (usu. **sober up** or **sober someone up**) become or make sober after being drunk. **2** (often as adj. **sobering**) make or become serious: *a sobering thought.*
– DERIVATIVES **soberly** adverb.
– ORIGIN Latin *sobrius*.

sobriety /suh-bry-uh-ti/ noun the state of being sober.

sobriquet /soh-bri-kay/ (also **soubriquet**) noun a person's nickname.
– ORIGIN French.

sob story noun informal a story intended to arouse sympathy.

soca /soh-kuh/ noun calypso music with elements of soul, originally from Trinidad.
– ORIGIN blend of SOUL and CALYPSO.

so-called adjective called by the name or term specified (often in the speaker's view, inappropriately): *her so-called friends.*

soccer noun a form of football played with a round ball which may not be handled during play except by the goalkeepers, the object being to score goals by kicking or heading the ball into the opponents' goal.
– ORIGIN shortening of *Assoc.* from **ASSOCIATION FOOTBALL**.

sociable adjective 1 liking to talk to and join in activities with other people. 2 friendly and welcoming: *a very sociable little village.*
– DERIVATIVES **sociability** noun **sociably** adverb.
– ORIGIN Latin *sociabilis*, from *sociare* 'unite'.

social adjective 1 relating to society and its organization. 2 needing the company of other people; suited to living in communities. 3 relating to or designed for activities in which people meet each other for pleasure. 4 (of birds, insects, or mammals) breeding or living in colonies or organized communities.
• noun an informal social gathering organized by the members of a club or group.
– DERIVATIVES **sociality** noun **socially** adverb.
– ORIGIN Latin *socialis* 'allied', from *socius* 'friend'.

social climber noun derogatory a person who is anxious to gain a higher social status.

social contract (also **social compact**) noun an unspoken agreement among the members of a society to cooperate for the benefit of everyone, for example by sacrificing some individual freedom in return for state protection.

social democracy noun a socialist system of government achieved by democratic means.

social fund noun (in the UK) a social security fund from which loans or grants are made to people in need.

socialism noun a political and economic theory of social organization which holds that a country's land, transport, natural resources, and chief industries should be owned or controlled by the community as a whole.
– DERIVATIVES **socialist** noun & adjective **socialistic** adjective.

socialite noun a person who mixes in fashionable society.

socialize (or **socialise**) verb 1 mix socially with other people. 2 make someone behave in a way that is acceptable to society.
– DERIVATIVES **socialization** noun.

social market economy (also **social market**) noun an economic system based on a free market operating together with a welfare state to protect those who are unable to sell their labour, such as the elderly or unemployed.

social realism noun the realistic portrayal in art of contemporary life, as a means of commenting on the social or political situation.

social science noun 1 the scientific study of human society and social relationships. 2 a subject within this field, such as economics.

social security noun (in the UK) money provided by the state for people who are poor, unemployed, ill, etc.

social services plural noun services provided by the state for the community, such as education and medical care.

social studies plural noun (treated as sing.) the study of human society.

social work noun work carried out by people trained to help improve the conditions of people who are poor, old, or socially deprived.
– DERIVATIVES **social worker** noun.

society noun (pl. **societies**) 1 all the people living together in a more or less ordered community. 2 a particular community of people living in a country or region, and having shared customs, laws, and organizations. 3 (also **high society**) people who are fashionable, wealthy, and influential, viewed as a distinct social group. 4 an organization or club formed for a particular purpose or activity. 5 the situation of being in the company of other people: *she shunned the society of others.*
– DERIVATIVES **societal** adjective.
– ORIGIN Latin *societas*, from *socius* 'companion'.

sociobiology noun the scientific study of the biological aspects of social behaviour in animals and humans.
– DERIVATIVES **sociobiological** adjective **sociobiologist** noun.

sociocultural adjective combining social and cultural factors.

socio-economic adjective relating to the interaction of social and economic factors.

sociology noun the study of the structure and functioning of human society.
– DERIVATIVES **sociological** adjective **sociologist** noun.

sociopath /soh-si-oh-path, soh-shi-oh-path/ noun a person with a personality disorder showing itself in extreme antisocial attitudes and behaviour.
– DERIVATIVES **sociopathic** adjective.

sociopolitical adjective combining social and political factors.

sock noun 1 a knitted garment for the foot and lower part of the leg. 2 informal a hard blow.
• verb informal hit someone or something hard.
– PHRASES **pull one's socks up** informal make an effort to improve. **put a sock in it** Brit. informal stop talking. **sock it to** informal make a forceful impression on someone.
– ORIGIN Greek *sukkhos* 'comic actor's shoe'.

socket noun 1 a hollow in which something fits or revolves. 2 an electrical device into which a plug or light bulb is fitted.
– ORIGIN Old French *soket* 'small ploughshare'.

sockeye noun a North Pacific salmon which is an important food fish.
– ORIGIN Salish, 'fish of fishes'.

socking adverb Brit. informal very: *a socking great diamond.*

Socratic /suh-krat-ik/ adjective relating to the ancient Greek philosopher Socrates or his ideas.

S

sod[1] noun **1** grass-covered ground; turf. **2** a piece of turf.
– ORIGIN Dutch or German *sode*.

sod[2] vulgar slang, chiefly Brit. noun **1** an unpleasant person. **2** a person of a specified kind. **3** a difficult or problematic thing.
– PHRASES **sod all** absolutely nothing. **sod off** go away.
– ORIGIN abbreviation of SODOMITE.

soda noun **1** (also **soda water**) fizzy water (originally made with sodium bicarbonate). **2** N. Amer. a sweet fizzy drink. **3** sodium carbonate.
– ORIGIN Latin.

soda bread noun bread in which baking soda is used as the raising agent.

soda fountain noun N. Amer. **1** a device dispensing soda water or soft drinks. **2** a cafe or counter selling soft drinks, ice creams, etc.

sodality /soh-**dal**-i-ti/ noun (pl. **sodalities**) a group or association, especially a Roman Catholic religious guild or brotherhood.
– ORIGIN from Latin *sodalis* 'comrade'.

sodden adjective **1** soaked through. **2** (in combination) having drunk too much of an alcoholic drink: *whisky-sodden*.
– ORIGIN from SEETHE, first meaning 'boiled'.

sodium /soh-di-uhm/ noun a soft silver-white metallic chemical element of which common salt and soda are compounds.
– ORIGIN from SODA.

sodium bicarbonate noun a soluble white powder used chiefly in fizzy drinks and as a raising agent in baking.

sodium chloride noun the chemical name for common salt.

sodium hydroxide noun a strongly alkaline white compound used in many industrial processes; caustic soda.

sodium-vapour lamp (also **sodium lamp**) noun a lamp in which an electrical discharge in sodium vapour gives a yellow light.

sodomite /sod-uh-myt/ noun a person who engages in sodomy.

sodomy noun anal intercourse.
– DERIVATIVES **sodomize** (or **sodomise**) verb.
– ORIGIN from Latin *peccatum Sodomiticum* 'sin of Sodom' (after the Book of Genesis chapter 19, which implies that the men of the town of Sodom in ancient Palestine practised homosexual rape).

Sod's Law noun Brit. another name for MURPHY'S LAW.

sofa noun a long upholstered seat with a back and arms, for two or more people.
– ORIGIN French.

sofa bed noun a sofa that can be converted into a bed.

soffit /sof-fit/ noun the underside of an arch, a balcony, overhanging eaves, etc.
– ORIGIN Italian *soffitto*.

soft adjective **1** easy to mould, cut, compress, or fold. **2** not rough or coarse in texture. **3** quiet and gentle. **4** (of light or colour) not harsh. **5** sympathetic or lenient; not strict or strict enough. **6** informal (of a job or way of life) needing little effort. **7** informal foolish. **8** (**soft on**) informal having romantic feelings for someone. **9** (of a drink) not alcoholic. **10** (of a

drug) not likely to cause addiction. **11** (of water) free from mineral salts. **12** (of a group within a political party) willing to compromise. **13** (also **soft-core**) (of pornography) suggestive but not explicit.
– PHRASES **have a soft spot for** be fond of. **a soft** (or **easy**) **touch** informal a person who is easily persuaded or imposed on.
– DERIVATIVES **softish** adjective **softly** adverb **softness** noun.
– ORIGIN Old English.

softback adjective & noun another term for PAPERBACK.

softball noun a form of baseball played on a smaller field with a larger, softer ball.

soft-boiled adjective (of an egg) lightly boiled, leaving the yolk soft or liquid.

soften verb **1** make or become soft or softer. **2** (often **soften someone up**) make someone more likely to do something.
– DERIVATIVES **softener** noun.

soft focus noun deliberate slight blurring or lack of definition in a photograph or film.

soft fruit noun Brit. a small fruit without a stone, e.g. a strawberry.

soft furnishings plural noun Brit. curtains, chair coverings, and other cloth items used to decorate a room.

soft-hearted adjective kind, caring and sympathetic.

softie (also **softy**) noun (pl. **softies**) informal a weak or soft-hearted person.

softly-softly adjective Brit. cautious and patient.

soft palate noun the fleshy, flexible part towards the back of the roof of the mouth.

soft-pedal verb play down the unpleasant aspects of something. •noun (**soft pedal**) a pedal on a piano that can be pressed to soften the tone.

soft sell noun the selling of something in a gentle and persuasive way.

soft-soap verb informal use flattery to persuade someone to do something.

soft target noun a person or thing that is relatively unprotected or vulnerable.

soft top noun a motor vehicle with a roof that can be folded back.

software noun programs and other operating information used by a computer.

softwood noun the wood from conifers as opposed to that of broadleaved trees.

softy noun variant spelling of SOFTIE.

soggy adjective (**soggier**, **soggiest**) very wet and soft.
– DERIVATIVES **soggily** adverb **sogginess** noun.
– ORIGIN from dialect *sog* 'a swamp'.

soh /soh/ (also **so** or **sol**) noun Music the fifth note of a major scale, coming after 'fah' and before 'lah'.
– ORIGIN the first syllable of *solve*, taken from a Latin hymn.

soi-disant /swah-dee-zon/ adjective using a description or title that one has given oneself; self-styled: *a soi-disant novelist*.
– ORIGIN French, from *soi* 'oneself' + *disant* 'saying'.

soigné /swun-yay/ adjective (fem. **soignée** pronunc. same) elegant and well groomed.

S

- ORIGIN French, from *soigner* 'take care of'.

soil[1] noun 1 the upper layer of earth in which plants grow. 2 the territory of a particular nation.
- ORIGIN Old French.

soil[2] verb 1 make something dirty. 2 damage someone's reputation. • noun waste matter, especially sewage.
- ORIGIN Old French *soiller*.

soirée /swah-ray/ noun an evening social gathering, typically in a private house, for conversation or music.
- ORIGIN French, from *soir* 'evening'.

sojourn /so-juhn, so-jern/ literary noun a temporary stay. • verb stay somewhere temporarily.
- DERIVATIVES **sojourner** noun.
- ORIGIN from Old French *sojourner*.

sol[1] noun variant of SOH.

sol[2] noun Chemistry a liquid containing a colloid in suspension.
- ORIGIN abbreviation of SOLUTION.

sol[3] noun (pl. **soles**) the basic unit of money of Peru.
- ORIGIN Spanish, 'sun'.

solace /sol-iss/ noun comfort or consolation given in a time of difficulty or sadness. • verb give solace to someone.
- ORIGIN Old French *solas*.

solar /soh-ler/ adjective relating to the sun or its rays, or using the sun's energy.
- ORIGIN from Latin *sol* 'sun'.

solar battery (also **solar cell**) noun a device which converts the sun's radiation into electricity.

solar eclipse noun an eclipse in which the sun is hidden by the moon.

solar energy noun energy in the form of radiation given off by the sun.

solar flare noun a brief eruption of intense high-energy radiation from the sun's surface.

solarium /suh-lair-i-uhm/ noun (pl. **solariums** or **solaria** /suh-lair-i-uh/) 1 a room equipped with sunlamps or sunbeds. 2 a room with large areas of glass to let in sunlight.
- ORIGIN Latin, 'sundial, place for sunning oneself'.

solar panel noun a panel designed to absorb the sun's rays as a source of energy for generating electricity or heating.

solar plexus noun a network of nerves at the pit of the stomach.

solar power noun power obtained by controlling and using the energy of the sun's rays.

solar system noun the sun together with the planets, asteroids, comets, etc. in orbit around it.

solar wind noun a continuous flow of charged particles from the sun, spreading throughout the solar system.

solar year noun the time between one spring or autumn equinox and the next, or between one winter or summer solstice and the next (365 days, 5 hours, 48 minutes, and 46 seconds).

sola topi /soh-luh toh-pi/ noun a sun hat made from the pith of a type of plant, formerly worn in India.

- ORIGIN Hindi.

sold past and past participle of SELL.

solder /sohl-der/ noun an alloy, especially one based on lead and tin, that is heated and melted and used to join pieces of metal together. • verb join pieces of metal with solder.
- ORIGIN Old French *soudure*.

soldering iron noun an electrical tool for melting and applying solder.

soldier noun 1 a person who serves in an army. 2 (also **common soldier** or **private soldier**) a private in an army. 3 Brit. informal a strip of bread or toast, dipped into a soft-boiled egg. • verb 1 serve as a soldier. 2 (**soldier on**) informal continue doing something in spite of difficulty.
- PHRASES **soldier of fortune** a professional soldier hired to serve in a foreign army.
- DERIVATIVES **soldierly** adjective.
- ORIGIN Old French.

soldiery noun 1 soldiers as a group. 2 military training or knowledge.

sole[1] noun 1 the underside of a person's foot. 2 the section forming the underside of a piece of footwear. 3 the underside of a tool or implement such as a plane. • verb replace the sole on a shoe.
- ORIGIN Latin *solea* 'sandal, sill'.

sole[2] noun (pl. same) an edible flatfish.
- ORIGIN Latin *solea* (see SOLE[1]), named from its shape.

sole[3] adjective 1 one and only. 2 belonging or restricted to one person or group.
- ORIGIN Latin *sola*, feminine of *solus* 'alone'.

solecism /sol-i-si-z'm/ noun 1 a grammatical mistake. 2 an instance of bad manners or incorrect behaviour.
- ORIGIN Greek *soloikismos*.

solely adverb not involving anyone or anything else; only.

solemn adjective 1 formal and dignified. 2 not cheerful; serious. 3 deeply sincere: *a solemn oath*.
- DERIVATIVES **solemnly** adverb.
- ORIGIN Latin *sollemnis* 'customary'.

solemnity /suh-lem-ni-ti/ noun (pl. **solemnities**) 1 the state or quality of being solemn. 2 (**solemnities**) formal, dignified rites or ceremonies.

solemnize (or **solemnise**) /sol-uhm-nyz/ verb 1 perform a ceremony, especially that of marriage. 2 mark an occasion with a formal ceremony.
- DERIVATIVES **solemnization** noun.

solenoid /sol-uh-noyd, soh-luh-noyd/ noun a cylindrical coil of wire which becomes magnetic when an electric current is passed through it.
- ORIGIN from Greek *sōlēn* 'channel, pipe'.

soleplate noun 1 a metal plate forming the base of an electric iron, machine saw, or other machine. 2 a horizontal timber at the base of a wall frame.

sol-fa /sol-fah/ noun short for TONIC SOL-FA.

solicit verb (**solicits**, **soliciting**, **solicited**) 1 ask for or try to obtain something from someone: *he called a meeting to solicit their views*. 2 (of a prostitute) approach someone and offer sex

for money.
- DERIVATIVES **solicitation** noun.
- ORIGIN Latin *sollicitare* 'agitate'.

solicitor noun **1** Brit. a lawyer qualified to deal with conveyancing, draw up wills, advise clients and instruct barristers, and represent clients in lower courts. Compare with **BARRISTER**. **2** N. Amer. the chief law officer of a city, town, or government department.

Solicitor General noun (pl. **Solicitors General**) (in the UK) the Law Officer of the Crown below the Attorney General or (in Scotland) below the Lord Advocate.

solicitous /suh-liss-i-tuhss/ adjective showing interest or concern about a person's well-being.
- DERIVATIVES **solicitously** adverb **solicitousness** noun.

solicitude /suh-liss-i-tyood/ noun care or concern for someone or something.

solid adjective (**solider**, **solidest**) **1** firm and stable in shape; not liquid or fluid. **2** strongly built or made. **3** not hollow or having spaces or gaps. **4** consisting of the same substance throughout. **5** (of time) continuous: *two solid hours of entertainment*. **6** able to be relied on: *solid evidence*. **7** Geometry three-dimensional. •noun **1** a solid substance or object. **2** (**solids**) food that is not liquid. **3** a three-dimensional body or geometric figure.
- DERIVATIVES **solidity** noun **solidly** adverb **solidness** noun.
- ORIGIN Latin *solidus*.

solidarity noun unity and mutual support resulting from shared interests, feelings, or opinions.

solidi plural of **SOLIDUS**.

solidify verb (**solidifies**, **solidifying**, **solidified**) make or become hard or solid.
- DERIVATIVES **solidification** noun.

solid-state adjective (of an electronic device) using solid semiconductors, e.g. transistors, as opposed to valves.

solidus /sol-i-duhss/ noun (pl. **solidi** /sol-i-dy/) chiefly Brit. another term for **SLASH** (in sense 3).
- ORIGIN Latin, 'solid'.

soliloquy /suh-lil-uh-kwi/ noun (pl. **soliloquies**) a speech in a play in which a character speaks their thoughts aloud when alone on stage.
- DERIVATIVES **soliloquize** (or **soliloquise**) verb.
- ORIGIN from Latin *solus* 'alone' + *loqui* 'speak'.

solipsism /sol-ip-siz-uhm/ noun **1** the view that the self is all that can be known to exist. **2** the quality of being selfish.
- DERIVATIVES **solipsist** noun **solipsistic** adjective.
- ORIGIN from Latin *solus* 'alone' + *ipse* 'self'.

solitaire /sol-i-tair, sol-i-**tair**/ noun **1** Brit. a game for one player played by removing pegs from a board one at a time by jumping others over them from adjacent holes, the object being to be left with only one peg. **2** N. Amer. the card game patience. **3** a single diamond or other gem in a piece of jewellery.
- ORIGIN French.

solitary adjective **1** done or existing alone. **2** (of a place) secluded or isolated. **3** single: *not a solitary shred of evidence*. •noun (pl. **solitaries**) **1** a person who lives alone for personal or religious reasons. **2** informal solitary confinement.

- DERIVATIVES **solitariness** noun.
- ORIGIN Latin *solitarius*, from *solus* 'alone'.

solitary confinement noun the isolating of a prisoner in a separate cell as a punishment.

solitude noun **1** the state of being alone. **2** a lonely or uninhabited place.

solmization /sol-mi-**zay**-sh'n/ (or **solmisation**) noun a system of associating each note of a musical scale with a particular syllable (typically the sequence doh, ray, me, fah, soh, lah, te), especially to teach singing.
- ORIGIN French, from *sol* 'soh' + *mi* (see **ME**²).

solo noun (pl. **solos**) **1** a song, dance, or piece of music for one performer. **2** a flight undertaken by a single pilot. **3** (also **solo whist**) a card game resembling whist in which the players make bids and the highest bidder plays against the others. •adjective & adverb for or done by one person. •verb (**soloes**, **soloing**, **soloed**) perform a solo.
- ORIGIN Latin *solus* 'alone'.

soloist noun a musician or singer who performs a solo.

Solomon /sol-uh-muhn/ noun a very wise person.
- ORIGIN the name of a king of ancient Israel who was famed for his wisdom.

Solomon's seal noun a plant with arching stems bearing a double row of broad leaves and drooping green and white flowers.

solstice /sol-stiss/ noun each of the two times in the year, respectively at midsummer and midwinter, when the sun reaches its highest or lowest point in the sky at noon, marked by the longest and shortest days.
- ORIGIN Latin *solstitium*, from *sol* 'sun' + *sistere* 'stop'.

soluble adjective **1** (of a substance) able to be dissolved, especially in water. **2** (of a problem) able to be solved.
- DERIVATIVES **solubility** noun.
- ORIGIN Latin *solubilis*.

solute /sol-yoot/ noun the minor component in a solution, dissolved in the solvent.

solution noun **1** a means of solving a problem. **2** the correct answer to a puzzle. **3** a mixture formed when a substance (the solute) is dissolved in a liquid (the solvent). **4** the process of dissolving or the state of being dissolved.
- ORIGIN Latin, from *solvere* 'loosen'.

solve verb find an answer to, explanation for, or way of dealing with a problem or mystery.
- DERIVATIVES **solvable** adjective **solver** noun.
- ORIGIN Latin *solvere* 'loosen, unfasten'.

solvent adjective **1** having more money than one owes. **2** able to dissolve other substances. •noun **1** a liquid that can dissolve other substances. **2** the liquid in which another substance is dissolved to form a solution.
- DERIVATIVES **solvency** noun.

solvent abuse noun the deliberate inhalation of the intoxicating fumes of certain solvents such as glue.

Som. abbreviation Somerset.

soma /soh-muh/ noun **1** Biology the parts of an organism other than the reproductive cells. **2** the body as distinct from the soul or mind.
- ORIGIN Greek, 'body'.

S

Somali /suh-**mah**-li/ noun (pl. same or **Somalis**) **1** a person from Somalia. **2** a member of a mainly Muslim people of Somalia. **3** the language of the Somali. • adjective relating to Somalia.
– DERIVATIVES **Somalian** adjective & noun.

somatic /suh-**mat**-ik/ adjective relating to the body, especially as distinct from the mind.
– ORIGIN Greek *sōmatikos*.

sombre (US also **somber**) adjective **1** dark or dull. **2** serious and sad.
– DERIVATIVES **sombrely** adverb **sombreness** noun.
– ORIGIN French, from Latin *sub* 'under' + *umbra* 'shade'.

sombrero /som-**brair**-oh/ noun (pl. **sombreros**) a broad-brimmed hat, typically worn in Mexico and the south-western US.
– ORIGIN Spanish.

some determiner **1** an unspecified amount or number of. **2** referring to an unknown or unspecified person or thing. **3** (used with a number) approximately. **4** a considerable amount or number of. **5** a certain small amount or number of. **6** expressing admiration: *that was some goal.* • pronoun **1** an unspecified number or amount of people or things. **2** a certain small number or amount of people or things.
– ORIGIN Old English.

somebody pronoun someone.

some day (also **someday**) adverb at some time in the future.

somehow adverb **1** by one means or another. **2** for an unknown or unspecified reason.

someone pronoun **1** an unknown or unspecified person. **2** an important or famous person.

someplace adverb & pronoun N. Amer. informal somewhere.

somersault noun an acrobatic movement in which a person turns head over heels in the air or on the ground and finishes on their feet. • verb perform a somersault.
– ORIGIN Old French *sombresault*.

something pronoun **1** an unspecified or unknown thing. **2** an unspecified or unknown amount or degree. • adverb informal used for emphasis: *my back hurts something terrible.*

sometime adverb at some unspecified or unknown time. • adjective former: *the sometime editor of the paper.*

sometimes adverb occasionally.

somewhat adverb to some extent; rather.

somewhere adverb **1** in or to an unspecified or unknown place. **2** used to indicate an approximate amount. • pronoun some unspecified place.
– PHRASES **get somewhere** informal make progress.

sommelier /suh-**mel**-yay/ noun a waiter who serves wine.
– ORIGIN French, 'butler'.

somnambulism /som-**nam**-byuu-li-z'm/ noun sleepwalking.
– DERIVATIVES **somnambulant** adjective **somnambulist** noun **somnambulistic** adjective.
– ORIGIN from Latin *somnus* 'sleep' + *ambulare* 'to walk'.

somnolent /som-nuh-luhnt/ adjective **1** sleepy.

2 causing sleepiness.
– DERIVATIVES **somnolence** noun **somnolently** adverb.
– ORIGIN from Latin *somnus* 'sleep'.

son noun **1** a boy or man in relation to his parents. **2** a male descendant. **3** (**the Son** or **the Son of Man**) Jesus. **4** (also **my son**) a form of address for a boy or younger man.
– ORIGIN Old English.

sonar /**soh**-nar/ noun **1** a system for detecting objects under water based on the emission and reflection of sound pulses. **2** a device used in this system.
– ORIGIN from *so(und)* *na(vigation and)* *r(anging)*, on the pattern of *radar*.

sonata /suh-**nah**-tuh/ noun a piece of classical music for a solo instrument, often with a piano accompaniment.
– ORIGIN Italian, 'sounded'.

son et lumière /son ay **loo**-mi-air/ noun an entertainment held by night at a historic monument or building, telling its history by the use of lighting effects and recorded sound.
– ORIGIN French, 'sound and light'.

song noun **1** a poem or other set of words set to music. **2** singing: *they broke into song.* **3** the musical sounds made by some birds, whales, and insects. **4** literary a poem.
– PHRASES **for a song** informal very cheaply. **on song** Brit. informal performing well. **a song and dance** informal, chiefly Brit. a fuss.
– ORIGIN Old English.

songbird noun a bird with a musical song.

song cycle noun a set of related songs forming a single musical work.

songsmith noun informal a writer of popular songs.

songster noun (fem. **songstress**) a person who sings.

song thrush noun a thrush with a song in which phrases are repeated two or three times.

songwriter noun a writer of songs or the music for them.

sonic adjective relating to or using sound waves.
– DERIVATIVES **sonically** adverb.
– ORIGIN from Latin *sonus* 'sound'.

sonic boom noun an explosive noise caused by the shock wave from an aircraft or other object travelling faster than the speed of sound.

sonics plural noun musical sounds artificially produced or reproduced.

son-in-law noun (pl. **sons-in-law**) the husband of one's daughter.

sonnet noun a poem of fourteen lines using any of a number of fixed rhyme schemes.
– ORIGIN Italian *sonetto* 'little sound'.

sonneteer /so-ni-**ti**-er/ noun a writer of sonnets.

sonny noun informal a familiar form of address to a boy or young man.

sonogram /**soh**-nuh-gram/ noun **1** a graph showing the distribution of energy at different frequencies in a sound. **2** a visual image produced from an ultrasound examination.
– DERIVATIVES **sonographic** adjective **sonography** noun.

S

– ORIGIN from Latin *sonus* 'sound'.

sonorous /son-uh-ruhss/ adjective 1 (of a sound) deep and full. 2 (of speech) using grand or impressive language.
– DERIVATIVES **sonority** noun **sonorously** adverb.
– ORIGIN from Latin *sonor* 'sound'.

soon adverb 1 in or after a short time. 2 early. 3 used to indicate a preference: *I'd just as soon Tim did it.*
– PHRASES **no sooner than** at the very moment that. **sooner or later** eventually.
– DERIVATIVES **soonish** adverb.
– ORIGIN Old English.

> USAGE: The phrase **no sooner** should be followed by **than** rather than **when** in standard English: *we had no sooner arrived than we had to leave*, not *we had no sooner arrived when we had to leave*. This is because **sooner** is a comparative form, and comparative forms should be followed by **than**.

soot noun a black powdery or flaky substance produced when an organic substance such as coal is burnt.
– ORIGIN Old English.

sooth /rhymes with truth/ noun old use truth.
– PHRASES **in sooth** truly.
– ORIGIN Old English.

soothe verb 1 gently calm a person or their fears. 2 relieve pain or discomfort.
– DERIVATIVES **soother** noun **soothing** adjective.
– ORIGIN Old English, 'verify', from SOOTH.

soothsayer noun a person supposed to be able to foresee the future.
– DERIVATIVES **soothsaying** noun.

sooty adjective (**sootier, sootiest**) covered with or coloured like soot.

sop noun a thing of no great value given or done in an attempt to appease someone who is angry or disappointed. • verb (**sops, sopping, sopped**) (**sop something up**) soak up liquid.
– ORIGIN Old English.

sophism /soff-i-z'm/ noun a clever but false argument, especially one used to deceive other people.
– ORIGIN Greek *sophisma* 'clever device'.

sophist /soff-ist/ noun a person who uses clever but false arguments.
– DERIVATIVES **sophistic** /suh-fiss-tik/ adjective **sophistical** /suh-fiss-ti-k'l/ adjective.

sophisticate noun /suh-fiss-ti-kuht/ a person having experience and taste in matters of fashion and culture. • verb /suh-fiss-ti-kayt/ make someone or something more sophisticated.
– DERIVATIVES **sophistication** noun.
– ORIGIN Latin *sophisticare* 'tamper with'.

sophisticated adjective 1 having or showing experience and taste in matters of culture or fashion. 2 appealing to sophisticated people. 3 (of a machine, system, or technique) highly developed and complex.

sophistry /soff-iss-tri/ noun (pl. **sophistries**) 1 the use of clever false arguments, especially to deceive other people. 2 a clever but false argument.

sophomore /soff-uh-mor/ noun N. Amer. a second-year university or high-school student.
– DERIVATIVES **sophomoric** adjective.
– ORIGIN probably from *sophum, sophom*

(former variants of SOPHISM).

soporific /sop-uh-ri-fik/ adjective causing drowsiness or sleep. • noun a drug or other substance that causes drowsiness or sleep.
– ORIGIN from Latin *sopor* 'sleep'.

sopping (also **sopping wet**) adjective wet through.

soppy adjective (**soppier, soppiest**) Brit. informal 1 sentimental in a silly or self-indulgent way. 2 rather weak and feeble.
– DERIVATIVES **soppily** adverb **soppiness** noun.
– ORIGIN first meaning 'soaked with water': from SOP.

soprano /suh-prah-noh/ noun (pl. **sopranos**) the highest singing voice. • adjective (of an instrument) of a high or the highest pitch in its family: *a soprano saxophone.*
– ORIGIN Italian, from *sopra* 'above'.

sorbet /sor-bay/ noun a frozen dessert consisting of fruit juice or purée in a sugar syrup.
– ORIGIN French, from an Arabic word meaning 'to drink'.

sorcerer noun (fem. **sorceress**) a person believed to practise magic; a wizard.
– DERIVATIVES **sorcery** noun.
– ORIGIN Old French *sorcier*.

sordid adjective 1 dishonest or immoral; morally distasteful: *the truth about his sordid past.* 2 dirty or squalid.
– DERIVATIVES **sordidly** adverb **sordidness** noun.
– ORIGIN Latin *sordidus*.

sore adjective 1 painful or aching. 2 great; urgent: *we're in sore need of him.* 3 informal, chiefly N. Amer. upset and angry. • noun a raw or painful place on the body. • adverb old use extremely: *sore afraid.*
– PHRASES **sore point** an issue about which someone feels distressed or annoyed. **stand** (or **stick**) **out like a sore thumb** be quite obviously different.
– DERIVATIVES **soreness** noun.
– ORIGIN Old English.

sorely adverb extremely; greatly.

sorghum /sor-guhm/ noun a cereal native to warm regions, grown for grain and animal feed.
– ORIGIN Italian *sorgo*.

sorority /suh-ro-ri-ti/ noun (pl. **sororities**) N. Amer. a society for female students in a university or college.
– ORIGIN from Latin *soror* 'sister'.

sorrel[1] noun an edible plant of the dock family with arrow-shaped leaves and a bitter flavour.
– ORIGIN Old French *sorele*.

sorrel[2] noun 1 a light reddish-brown colour. 2 a horse with a sorrel coat.
– ORIGIN Old French *sorel*.

sorrow noun 1 deep distress caused by loss or disappointment. 2 a cause of sorrow. • verb feel sorrow.
– ORIGIN Old English.

sorrowful adjective 1 feeling or showing sorrow. 2 causing sorrow.
– DERIVATIVES **sorrowfully** adverb.

sorry adjective (**sorrier, sorriest**) 1 feeling distress or pity through sympathy with someone else's misfortune. 2 feeling or expressing regret. 3 in a poor or pitiful state.

S

4 unpleasant and regrettable: *a sorry business.*
- DERIVATIVES **sorriness** noun.
- ORIGIN Old English, 'pained, distressed'.

sort noun **1** a category of people or things with a common feature or features. **2** informal a person with a particular nature: *he was a friendly sort.*
•verb **1** arrange systematically in groups: *he sorted the contents of the desk into two piles.* **2** (often **sort something out**) separate something from a mixed group. **3** (**sort something out**) resolve a problem or difficulty. **4** (**sort someone out**) informal deal with a troublesome person.
- PHRASES **of a sort** (or **of sorts**) of a somewhat unusual or inferior kind. **out of sorts** slightly unwell or unhappy. **sort of** informal to some extent.
- DERIVATIVES **sorter** noun.
- ORIGIN Old French *sorte.*

> USAGE: The expression **these sort of**, as in *I don't want to answer these sort of questions*, is not grammatical and should be avoided in formal writing. This is because **these** is plural and needs to agree with a plural noun; the correct usage is *these sorts of questions*. See also the note at **KIND**[1].

sorted adjective Brit. informal **1** organized; arranged. **2** emotionally well balanced.

sortie noun **1** an attack made by troops coming out from a position of defence. **2** a flight by a single aircraft on a military operation. **3** a short trip.
- ORIGIN French, from *sortir* 'go out'.

SOS noun **1** an international signal of extreme distress, used especially by ships at sea. **2** an urgent appeal for help.
- ORIGIN letters chosen as being easily transmitted and recognized in Morse code; popularly taken as an abbreviation of *save our souls.*

so-so adjective neither very good nor very bad.

sot noun a person who is regularly drunk.
- DERIVATIVES **sottish** adjective.
- ORIGIN Latin *sottus* 'foolish person'.

sotto voce /sot-toh **voh**-chay/ adverb & adjective in a quiet voice.
- ORIGIN from Italian *sotto* 'under' + *voce* 'voice'.

sou /soo/ noun informal a very small amount of money.
- ORIGIN French, first referring to a former French coin of low value.

soubrette /soo-**bret**/ noun a pert maidservant or similar minor female role in a comedy.
- ORIGIN Provençal *soubret* 'coy'.

soubriquet /soo-bri-kay/ noun variant spelling of **SOBRIQUET**.

soufflé /soo-flay/ noun a light, spongy baked dish made by mixing egg yolks and another ingredient such as cheese or fruit with stiffly beaten egg whites.
- ORIGIN French, 'blown'.

sough /sow, suf/ verb literary (of the wind, sea, etc.) make a moaning, whistling, or rushing sound.
- ORIGIN Old English.

sought past and past participle of **SEEK**.
- PHRASES **sought after** in great demand.

souk /sook/ noun an Arab market.

- ORIGIN Arabic.

soukous /soo-koos/ noun a style of African popular music with syncopated rhythms and contrasting guitar melodies.
- ORIGIN perhaps from French *secouer* 'to shake'.

soul noun **1** the spiritual element of a person, believed to be immortal. **2** a person's moral or emotional nature. **3** emotional or intellectual energy or power: *their performance lacked soul.* **4** a person regarded as a perfect example of a particular quality: *she's the soul of discretion.* **5** an individual person: *I'll never tell a soul.* **6** (also **soul music**) a kind of music which incorporates elements of gospel music and rhythm and blues, popularized by black Americans.
- ORIGIN Old English.

soul-destroying adjective unbearably dull and repetitive.

soul food noun food traditionally associated with black people of the southern US.

soulful adjective expressing deep and usually sorrowful feeling.
- DERIVATIVES **soulfully** adverb **soulfulness** noun.

soulless adjective **1** lacking character and individuality: *soulless post-war apartment blocks.* **2** (of an activity) dull and uninspiring. **3** lacking human feelings.

soulmate noun a person ideally suited to another.

soul-searching noun close examination of one's emotions and motives.

sound[1] noun **1** vibrations which travel through air or water and are sensed by the ear. **2** a thing that can be heard. **3** music, speech, and sound effects accompanying a film or broadcast. **4** an idea or impression given by words: *you've had a hard day, by the sound of it.*
•verb **1** make a sound. **2** make a sound to show or warn of something. **3** give a particular impression: *the job sounds great.* **4** (**sound off**) express one's opinions loudly or forcefully.
- DERIVATIVES **soundless** adjective.
- ORIGIN Latin *sonus.*

sound[2] adjective **1** in good condition. **2** based on reason or good judgement. **3** financially secure. **4** competent or reliable. **5** (of sleep) deep and unbroken. **6** severe or thorough: *a sound thrashing.* •adverb in a sound way.
- DERIVATIVES **soundly** adverb **soundness** noun.
- ORIGIN Old English.

sound[3] verb **1** find out the depth of water in the sea, a lake, etc. by means of a line or pole or using sound echoes. **2** (**sound someone out**) question someone discreetly or cautiously about their opinions or feelings. **3** examine the bladder or another part of the body with a long surgical probe.
- DERIVATIVES **sounder** noun.
- ORIGIN Old French *sonder.*

sound[4] noun a narrow stretch of water forming an inlet or connecting two larger areas of water.
- ORIGIN Old Norse, 'swimming, strait'.

sound barrier noun the point at which an aircraft reaches the speed of sound, causing reduced control, an explosive noise, and various other effects.

sound bite noun a short, memorable extract

from a speech or interview.

soundboard (also **sounding board**) noun a thin board over which the strings of a piano or similar instrument are positioned to increase the sound produced.

soundbox noun the hollow chamber which forms the body of a stringed instrument and makes the sound resonate.

soundcheck noun a test of sound equipment before a musical performance or recording.

sound effect noun a sound other than speech or music made artificially for use in a play, film, etc.

sounding noun 1 the action of sounding the depth of water. 2 a measurement taken by sounding. 3 (**soundings**) information or evidence found out before taking action.

sounding board noun 1 a person or group with whom new ideas or opinions are discussed to test their validity or likelihood of success. 2 a board over or behind a pulpit or stage to reflect a speaker's voice forward. 3 a soundboard.

sounding line noun a weighted line used to measure the depth of water under a boat.

soundproof adjective preventing sound getting in or out. • verb make something soundproof.

soundscape noun a piece of music considered in terms of the different sounds of which it is composed.

sound system noun a set of equipment for reproducing and amplifying sound.

soundtrack noun the sound accompaniment to a film.

sound wave noun a wave of alternate compression and reduction in density by which sound travels through air or water.

soup noun a savoury liquid dish made by boiling meat, fish, or vegetables in stock or water. • verb (**soup something up**) informal 1 increase the power and efficiency of an engine or other machine. 2 make something more elaborate or impressive.
– PHRASES **in the soup** informal in trouble.
– ORIGIN Old French *soupe* 'broth (poured on slices of bread)'.

soupçon /soop-son/ noun a very small amount of something.
– ORIGIN French, from Latin *suspectio* 'suspicion'.

soup kitchen noun a place where free food is served to homeless or destitute people.

soupy adjective (**soupier**, **soupiest**) 1 having the appearance or consistency of soup. 2 informal foolishly sentimental.

sour adjective 1 having a sharp taste like lemon or vinegar. 2 tasting or smelling unpleasant as a result of fermentation or staleness. 3 resentful, bitter, or angry. • verb make or become sour. • noun a cocktail made by mixing a spirit with lemon or lime juice.
– PHRASES **go** (or **turn**) **sour** become less pleasant; turn out badly. **sour grapes** an attitude in which someone pretends to hate or dislike something because they cannot have it themselves. [with allusion to Aesop's fable *The Fox and the Grapes*.]
– DERIVATIVES **sourly** adverb **sourness** noun.

– ORIGIN Old English.

source noun 1 a place, person, or thing from which something originates. 2 a person, book, or document that provides information or evidence. 3 the spring or other place from which a river or stream begins. • verb get something from a particular place: *the milk is sourced from local farms.*
– ORIGIN Old French *sourse.*

sour cream noun cream deliberately made sour by the addition of certain bacteria.

sourdough noun bread made from fermenting dough, originally that left over from a previous baking.

sourpuss noun informal a bad-tempered or grumpy person.

soursop noun a large acidic custard apple with white fibrous flesh.

sousaphone /soo-zuh-fohn/ noun an American form of tuba with a wide end which points forward above the player's head.
– ORIGIN named after the American composer J. P. *Sousa.*

souse /sowss/ verb 1 soak or drench something with liquid. 2 (as adj. **soused**) (of gherkins, fish, etc.) pickled or marinaded: *soused herring.* 3 (as adj. **soused**) informal drunk. • noun liquid used for pickling.
– ORIGIN Old French *sous* 'pickle'.

soutane /soo-tahn/ noun a type of cassock worn by Roman Catholic priests.
– ORIGIN Italian *sottana.*

south noun 1 the direction towards the point of the horizon 90° clockwise from east. 2 the southern part of a place. • adjective 1 lying towards, near, or facing the south. 2 (of a wind) blowing from the south. • adverb to or towards the south.
– DERIVATIVES **southbound** adjective & adverb.
– ORIGIN Old English.

South African noun a person from South Africa. • adjective relating to South Africa.

South American noun a person from South America. • adjective relating to South America.

south-east noun the direction or region halfway between south and east. • adjective 1 lying towards, near, or facing the south-east. 2 (of a wind) from the south-east. • adverb to or towards the south-east.
– DERIVATIVES **south-eastern** adjective.

south-easterly adjective & adverb in a south-eastward position or direction. • noun a wind blowing from the south-east.

south-eastward adverb (also **south-eastwards**) towards the south-east. • adjective in, towards, or facing the south-east.

southerly adjective & adverb 1 facing or moving towards the south. 2 (of a wind) blowing from the south. • noun (pl. **southerlies**) a south wind.

southern adjective 1 situated in, directed towards, or facing the south. 2 (usu. **Southern**) relating to or typical of the south.
– DERIVATIVES **southernmost** adjective.

southerner noun a person from the south of a region or country.

Southern Lights plural noun the aurora australis.

southing noun 1 distance travelled or measured southward, especially at sea. 2 a figure or line representing southward distance on a map.

southpaw noun 1 a left-handed boxer who leads with the right hand. 2 informal, chiefly N. Amer. a left-handed person.

south-south-east noun the direction halfway between south and south-east.

south-south-west noun the direction halfway between south and south-west.

southward adjective in a southerly direction. ● adverb (also **southwards**) towards the south.

south-west noun the direction or region halfway between south and west. ● adjective 1 lying towards or facing the south-west. 2 (of a wind) from the south-west. ● adverb to or towards the south-west.
– DERIVATIVES **south-western** adjective.

south-westerly adjective & adverb in a south-westward position or direction. ● noun (pl. **south-westerlies**) a wind blowing from the south-west.

south-westward adverb (also **south-westwards**) towards the south-west. ● adjective in, towards, or facing the south-west.

souvenir /soo-vuh-**neer**/ noun a thing that is kept as a reminder of a person, place, or event.
– ORIGIN French.

sou'wester /sow-**wess**-ter/ noun a waterproof hat with a broad brim or flap covering the back of the neck.

sovereign /**sov**-rin/ noun 1 a king or queen who is the supreme ruler of a country. 2 a former British gold coin worth one pound sterling. ● adjective 1 possessing supreme power. 2 (of a nation or its affairs) acting or done independently.
– ORIGIN Old French *soverain*.

sovereignty /**sov**-rin-ti/ noun (pl. **sovereignties**) 1 supreme power or authority. 2 a self-governing state.

soviet /**soh**-vi-uht, **sov**-i-uht/ noun 1 (Soviet) a citizen of the former Soviet Union. 2 an elected council in the former Soviet Union. ● adjective (Soviet) relating to the former Soviet Union.
– DERIVATIVES **Sovietism** noun **Sovietize** (or **Sovietise**) verb.
– ORIGIN Russian *sovet* 'council'.

Sovietologist /soh-vi-uh-**tol**-uh-jist, sov-i-uh-**tol**-uh-jist/ noun an expert on the former Soviet Union.

sow[1] /*rhymes with* toe/ verb (past **sowed**; past part. **sown** or **sowed**) 1 plant seed by scattering it on or in the earth. 2 spread or introduce something unwelcome: *the new policy has sown confusion and doubt.*
– DERIVATIVES **sower** noun.
– ORIGIN Old English.

sow[2] /*rhymes with* cow/ noun an adult female pig.
– ORIGIN Old English.

soya bean (also **soybean**) noun an edible bean that is high in protein.
– ORIGIN Malay.

soya milk noun a liquid made from soya bean flour in water, used as a substitute for milk.

soy sauce (also **soy**) noun a sauce made with fermented soya beans, used in Chinese and Japanese cooking.

– ORIGIN Chinese.

sozzled adjective informal very drunk.
– ORIGIN from dialect *sozzle* 'mix sloppily'.

SP abbreviation starting price.

spa noun 1 a place or resort with a mineral spring that is considered to have health-giving properties. 2 a place offering a range of health and beauty treatments. 3 (also **spa bath** or **pool**) a bath containing hot aerated water.
– ORIGIN from *Spa*, a town in Belgium noted for its mineral springs.

space noun 1 a continuous area or expanse that is free or unoccupied. 2 the dimensions of height, depth, and width within which all things exist and move. 3 (also **outer space**) the physical universe beyond the earth's atmosphere. 4 an interval of time (indicating that it is short): *forty men died in the space of two days.* 5 a blank between typed or written words or characters. 6 the freedom to live and develop as one wishes. ● verb 1 position things at a distance from one another. 2 (**be spaced out**) informal be in a state of great happiness or confusion, especially from taking drugs.
– DERIVATIVES **spacer** noun **spacing** noun.
– ORIGIN Latin *spatium*.

space age noun (**the space age**) the era that started when the exploration of space became possible. ● adjective (**space-age**) very modern; technologically advanced.

space bar noun a long key on a typewriter or computer keyboard for making a space.

space cadet noun informal a person regarded as being out of touch with reality.

space capsule noun a small spacecraft or the part of a larger one that contains the instruments or crew, designed to be returned to earth.

spacecraft noun (pl. same or **spacecrafts**) a vehicle used for travelling in space.

spaceman noun (pl. **spacemen**) a male astronaut.

space probe noun an unmanned spacecraft used for exploration.

spaceship noun a manned spacecraft.

space shuttle noun a rocket-launched spacecraft able to land like an unpowered aircraft, used to make repeated journeys between earth and craft orbiting the earth.

space station noun a large artificial satellite used as a long-term base for manned operations in space.

spacesuit noun a sealed and pressurized suit designed to allow an astronaut to survive in space.

space-time noun Physics the concepts of time and three-dimensional space regarded as forming a four-dimensional continuum.

spacewalk noun a period of activity by an astronaut outside a spacecraft.
– DERIVATIVES **spacewalker** noun

spacey (also **spacy**) adjective (**spacier**, **spaciest**) informal 1 out of touch with reality. 2 (of popular music) drifting and unworldly.

spacial adjective variant spelling of SPATIAL.

spacious adjective (of a room or building) having plenty of space.
– DERIVATIVES **spaciously** adverb **spaciousness** noun.

spade noun a tool with a rectangular metal blade and a long handle, used for digging. •verb dig or move earth with a spade.
– PHRASES **call a spade a spade** speak plainly and frankly.
– ORIGIN Old English.

spades noun one of the four suits in a pack of playing cards, represented by an upside-down black heart shape with a small stalk.
– PHRASES **in spades** informal in large amounts or to a high degree.
– ORIGIN Italian *spade* 'swords'.

spadework noun hard or routine work done to prepare for something.

spadix /spay-diks/ noun (pl. **spadices** /spay-di-seez/) Botany a spike of tiny flowers closely arranged round a fleshy stem and typically enclosed in a spathe (large modified leaf).
– ORIGIN Greek, 'palm branch'.

spaghetti /spuh-get-ti/ plural noun pasta made in long strands.
– ORIGIN Italian, 'little strings'.

spaghetti bolognese /bol-uh-nayz/ noun a dish of spaghetti with a sauce of minced beef, tomato, onion, and herbs.
– ORIGIN Italian, 'spaghetti of Bologna'.

spaghetti western noun informal a western film made in Europe by an Italian director.

spake old use past of SPEAK.

spam noun 1 email that has not been requested, sent to large numbers of Internet users. 2 (**Spam**) trademark a canned meat product made mainly from ham. •verb (**spams, spamming, spammed**) send email that has not been requested to large numbers of Internet users.
– DERIVATIVES **spammer** noun.
– ORIGIN probably from *spiced ham*; the Internet sense probably derives from a sketch in the British 'Monty Python' comedy show, in which every item on a cafe's menu includes spam.

span noun 1 the length of time for which something lasts: *he scored twice within a span of four minutes.* 2 the full extent of something from end to end. 3 a part of a bridge between the uprights supporting it. 4 a wingspan of a bird or aircraft. 5 (also **handspan**) the maximum distance between the tips of the thumb and little finger. •verb (**spans, spanning, spanned**) 1 extend from side to side of something. 2 extend across a period of time or a range of subjects: *their interests span almost all the conventional disciplines.*
– ORIGIN Old English.

spandex noun a type of stretchy synthetic fabric.
– ORIGIN from EXPAND.

spandrel /span-druhl/ noun Architecture the roughly triangular space between the curve of an arch and the ceiling or framework above.
– ORIGIN perhaps from Old French *espaundre* 'expand'.

spangle noun 1 a small thin piece of glittering material, used to decorate an item of clothing; a sequin. 2 a spot of bright colour or light. •verb (usu. as adj. **spangled**) cover an item of clothing with spangles.
– DERIVATIVES **spangly** adjective.
– ORIGIN Dutch *spange* 'buckle'.

Spaniard /span-yerd/ noun a person from Spain.

spaniel noun a breed of dog with a long, silky coat and drooping ears.
– ORIGIN Old French *espaigneul* 'Spanish (dog)'.

Spanish noun the main language of Spain and of much of Central and South America. •adjective relating to Spain or Spanish.
– DERIVATIVES **Spanishness** noun.

Spanish fly noun a toxic preparation of the dried bodies of a kind of beetle, sometimes taken as an aphrodisiac.

Spanish guitar noun the standard six-stringed acoustic guitar, used especially for classical and folk music.

Spanish omelette noun an omelette containing chopped vegetables, served open rather than folded.

Spanish onion noun a large onion with a mild flavour.

spank verb slap someone on the buttocks with the open hand or a flat object, especially as a punishment. •noun a slap or series of slaps on the buttocks.
– ORIGIN uncertain.

spanking adjective 1 lively; brisk: *a spanking pace.* 2 informal impressive or pleasing. •noun a series of spanks on the buttocks.

spanner noun chiefly Brit. a tool with a shaped opening or jaws for gripping and turning a nut or bolt.
– PHRASES **a spanner in the works** a thing that prevents a plan from being carried out successfully.
– ORIGIN from German *spannen* 'draw tight'.

spar¹ noun a thick, strong pole used as a mast or yard on a ship.
– ORIGIN from Old French *esparre* or Old Norse.

spar² verb (**spars, sparring, sparred**) 1 make the motions of boxing without landing heavy blows, as a form of training. 2 argue with someone without hostility. •noun a period of sparring.
– ORIGIN Old English, 'strike out'.

spar³ noun a crystalline transparent or semi-transparent mineral that is easily split.
– ORIGIN German.

spare adjective 1 not currently being used or needed: *the spare bedroom was filled with boxes.* 2 (of time) not taken up by one's usual work or activities. 3 with no excess fat; thin. 4 elegantly simple: *her clothes are smart and spare in style.* •noun an item kept in case another of the same type is lost, broken, or worn out. •verb 1 give something which one has enough of to someone. 2 make free or available: *can you spare me a moment?* 3 hold back from killing or harming someone. 4 protect someone from something unpleasant.
– PHRASES **go spare** Brit. informal become very angry or upset. **spare no expense** (or **no expense spared**) be prepared to pay any amount. **to spare** left over.
– DERIVATIVES **sparely** adverb **spareness** noun.
– ORIGIN Old English, 'not plentiful, meagre'.

spare ribs plural noun trimmed ribs of pork.
– ORIGIN probably from German *ribbesper*.

spare tyre noun 1 an extra tyre carried in a motor vehicle in case of a puncture. 2 informal a roll of fat round a person's waist.

sparing adjective using or giving only a little of something: *sparing use of hair sprays.*
– DERIVATIVES **sparingly** adverb.

spark noun **1** a small fiery particle produced by burning or caused by friction. **2** a flash of light produced by an electrical discharge. **3** an electrical discharge which ignites the explosive mixture in an internal-combustion engine. **4** a small amount of an intense feeling: *a tiny spark of anger.* **5** a sense of liveliness and excitement. • verb **1** produce sparks. **2** ignite a fire. **3** (also **spark off**) cause to happen: *the announcement sparked off protests.*
– PHRASES **spark out** Brit. informal unconscious.
– DERIVATIVES **sparky** adjective.
– ORIGIN Old English.

sparkle verb **1** shine brightly with flashes of light. **2** be lively and witty. **3** (as adj. **sparkling**) (of drink) fizzy. • noun **1** a glittering flash of light. **2** liveliness and wit.
– DERIVATIVES **sparkly** adjective.

sparkler noun a hand-held firework that gives out sparks.

spark plug noun a device for firing the explosive mixture in an internal-combustion engine.

sparrow noun a small bird with brown and grey plumage.
– ORIGIN Old English.

sparrowhawk noun a small hawk that preys on small birds.

sparse adjective present in small amounts or numbers and often thinly scattered: *Australia's relatively sparse rural population.*
– DERIVATIVES **sparsely** adverb **sparseness** noun **sparsity** noun.
– ORIGIN Latin *sparsus.*

Spartan adjective **1** relating to Sparta, a city state in ancient Greece. **2** (**spartan**) not comfortable or luxurious; basic: *spartan barrack-like hotels.* • noun a citizen of Sparta.

spasm noun **1** a sudden and uncontrollable tightening of a muscle. **2** a sudden brief spell of an activity or feeling.
– ORIGIN Greek *spasmos.*

spasmodic /spaz-mod-ik/ adjective occurring or done in brief, irregular bursts: *spasmodic fighting.*
– DERIVATIVES **spasmodically** adverb.

spastic adjective **1** relating to or affected by muscle spasm. **2** relating to cerebral palsy, which makes it difficult for a person to control their muscles and movements. • noun offensive **1** a person with cerebral palsy. **2** informal an incompetent person.
– DERIVATIVES **spastically** adverb **spasticity** noun.
– ORIGIN Greek *spastikos* 'pulling'.

> USAGE: You should not use the word **spastic** as a noun because many people think it is offensive; say *person with cerebral palsy* instead.

spat¹ past and past participle of SPIT¹.

spat² noun a cloth covering formerly worn by men over the ankles and shoes.
– ORIGIN from *spatterdash*, a long legging formerly worn when riding.

spat³ noun informal a petty quarrel.

– ORIGIN uncertain.

spatchcock verb split open a chicken or game bird and grill or roast it.
– ORIGIN perhaps from DISPATCH + COCK.

spate noun **1** a large number of similar things coming quickly one after the other. **2** chiefly Brit. a sudden flood in a river.
– ORIGIN unknown.

spathe /spayth/ noun Botany a large bract (modified leaf) enclosing the flower cluster of certain plants.
– ORIGIN Greek, 'broad blade'.

spatial /spay-sh'l/ (also **spacial**) adjective relating to space: *a map showing spatial distribution of species of birds.*
– DERIVATIVES **spatiality** noun **spatially** adverb.
– ORIGIN from Latin *spatium* 'space'.

spatter verb cover someone or something with drops or spots of a liquid or substance. • noun a spray or splash of a liquid or substance.
– ORIGIN from Dutch, German *spatten* 'burst, spout'.

spatula /spat-yuu-luh/ noun an implement with a broad flat blunt blade, used for mixing or spreading.
– ORIGIN Latin.

spatulate /spat-yuu-luht/ adjective having a broad rounded end.

spawn verb **1** (of a fish, frog, etc.) release or deposit eggs. **2** give rise to: *overeating has spawned a weight-loss industry that reaps $40 billion per year.* • noun the eggs of fish, frogs, etc.
– DERIVATIVES **spawner** noun.
– ORIGIN Old French *espaundre* 'to shed roe'.

spay verb sterilize a female animal by removing the ovaries.
– ORIGIN Old French *espeer* 'cut with a sword'.

speak verb (**speaks, speaking, spoke**; past part. **spoken**) **1** say something. **2** (**speak to**) talk to someone in order to pass on information, advise them, etc. **3** communicate in or be able to communicate in a specified language: *my mother spoke Russian.* **4** (**speak up**) speak more loudly. **5** (**speak out/up**) express one's opinions frankly and publicly. **6** (**speak for**) express the views or position of another person. **7** be evidence of: *the islands speak of history.* **8** (**speak to**) appeal or relate to someone. **9** make a speech.
– PHRASES **speak in tongues** speak in an unknown language during religious worship, regarded as one of the gifts of the Holy Spirit (Acts 2). **speak one's mind** express one's opinions frankly. **speak volumes** express a great deal without using words.
– ORIGIN Old English.

speakeasy noun (pl. **speakeasies**) informal (in the US during Prohibition) a secret illegal drinking club.

speaker noun **1** a person who speaks. **2** a person who speaks a particular language. **3** a person who makes a speech. **4** (**Speaker**) the officer in charge of proceedings in a law-making assembly. **5** a loudspeaker.

speaking adjective **1** used for or engaged in speech. **2** able to speak a particular language.
– PHRASES **on speaking terms** polite or friendly towards someone, especially after an argument.

spear noun **1** a weapon with a pointed metal tip set on a long shaft. **2** a pointed stem of asparagus or broccoli. •verb pierce or hit someone or something with a spear or other pointed object.
– PHRASES **the spear side** the male side of a family.
– ORIGIN Old English.

spearhead verb lead a campaign, activity, or attack. •noun a person or group that leads a campaign, activity, or attack.

spearmint noun the common garden mint, used in cooking as a herb and as a flavouring.

spec¹ noun (in phrase **on spec**) informal in the hope of success but without any specific preparation or plan.
– ORIGIN short for *speculation*.

spec² informal noun a detailed working description; a specification. •verb (**specs, speccing, specced**) construct something to a specified standard.

special adjective **1** better, greater, or otherwise different from what is usual: *they make a special effort at Christmas.* **2** organized or intended for a particular purpose. **3** belonging or particular to a specific person or thing: *we want to preserve the town's special character.* **4** (of education) for children with particular needs, especially those with learning difficulties. •noun **1** something designed or organized for a particular occasion or purpose. **2** a dish not on a restaurant's regular menu but served on a particular day.
– DERIVATIVES **specialness** noun.
– ORIGIN Latin *specialis*.

special constable noun (in the UK) a person who is trained to act as a police officer on particular occasions, especially in times of emergency.

special effects plural noun illusions created for films and television by camerawork, computer graphics, etc.

special forces plural noun the units of a country's armed forces that undertake counterterrorist and other specialized operations.

specialist noun a person who is highly skilled or knowledgeable in a particular field. •adjective relating to or involving detailed knowledge within a field.
– DERIVATIVES **specialism** noun.

speciality /spesh-i-al-i-ti/ (chiefly N. Amer. & Medicine also **specialty**) noun (pl. **specialities**) **1** a pursuit, area of study, or skill to which someone has devoted themselves and in which they are expert. **2** a product for which a person or region is famous. **3** (usu. **specialty**) a branch of medicine or surgery.

specialize (or **specialise**) verb **1** concentrate on and become expert in a particular skill or area: *he could specialize in neurosurgery.* **2** focus on providing a particular product or service. **3** (**be specialized**) (of an organ or part) be adapted or set apart to serve a special function.
– DERIVATIVES **specialization** noun.

specially adverb **1** for a special purpose. **2** informal in particular; chiefly.

> USAGE: For an explanation of the difference between **specially** and **especially**, see the note at ESPECIALLY.

special needs plural noun particular educational requirements of children with learning difficulties, a physical disability, or emotional and behavioural difficulties.

special pleading noun argument in which the speaker deliberately ignores aspects that are unfavourable to their point of view.

specialty /spesh-uhl-ti/ noun (pl. **specialties**) chiefly N. Amer. & Medicine another term for SPECIALITY.

speciation /spee-shi-ay-sh'n, spee-si-ay-sh'n/ noun Biology the formation of new and distinct species in the course of evolution.

specie /spee-shee/ noun money in the form of coins rather than notes.
– ORIGIN from Latin *in specie* 'in kind', from *species* 'form, kind'.

species /spee-shiz, spee-sheez, spee-siz/ noun (pl. same) **1** a group of living organisms consisting of similar individuals capable of breeding with each other. **2** a kind or sort: *they reject this species of feminism.*
– ORIGIN Latin, 'appearance, form'.

specific /spuh-si-fik/ adjective **1** clearly defined or identified. **2** precise and clear. **3** (**specific to**) belonging or relating only to: *the term is specific to Canada.* **4** relating to species or a species. •noun (**specifics**) precise details.
– DERIVATIVES **specifically** adverb **specificity** /spe-si-fis-i-ti/ noun.
– ORIGIN Latin *specificus*.

specification noun **1** the action of identifying something precisely or of stating a precise requirement. **2** (usu. **specifications**) a detailed description of the design and materials used to make something. **3** a standard of workmanship and materials required to be met in a piece of work.

specific gravity noun technical the ratio of the density of a substance to a standard density, usually that of water or air.

specify verb (**specifies, specifying, specified**) state or identify clearly and definitely: *the company can't specify a delivery date.*
– DERIVATIVES **specifiable** adjective **specifier** noun.

specimen noun **1** an animal, plant, object, etc. used as an example of its species or type for scientific study or display. **2** a sample for medical testing, especially of urine. **3** a typical example of something. **4** informal a person or animal of a specific type: *this odd female specimen.*
– ORIGIN Latin, 'pattern, model'.

specious /spee-shuhss/ adjective **1** seeming reasonable or plausible, but actually wrong: *a specious argument.* **2** misleading in appearance.
– DERIVATIVES **speciously** adverb **speciousness** noun.
– ORIGIN Latin *speciosus* 'fair, plausible'.

speck noun a tiny spot or particle. •verb mark something with small spots.
– ORIGIN Old English.

speckle noun a small spot or patch of colour. •verb (often as adj. **speckled**) mark with speckles: *a speckled brown egg.*

S

- ORIGIN Dutch *spekkel*.

specs plural noun informal a pair of spectacles.

spectacle noun a visually impressive performance or display.
- PHRASES **make a spectacle of oneself** draw attention to oneself by behaving in a ridiculous way in public.
- ORIGIN Latin *spectaculum* 'public show'.

spectacles plural noun Brit. a pair of glasses.
- DERIVATIVES **spectacled** adjective.

spectacular adjective very impressive, striking, or dramatic. • noun a large-scale and impressive performance or event.
- DERIVATIVES **spectacularly** adverb.

spectate verb watch an event; be a spectator.

spectator noun a person who watches at a show, game, or other event.
- ORIGIN Latin.

specter noun US spelling of SPECTRE.

spectra plural of SPECTRUM.

spectral¹ adjective relating to or like a spectre or ghost.
- DERIVATIVES **spectrally** adverb.

spectral² adjective relating to spectra or the spectrum.
- DERIVATIVES **spectrally** adverb.

spectre (US **specter**) noun 1 a ghost. 2 a possible unpleasant or dangerous situation:
- ORIGIN French.

spectrograph noun a device for photographing or otherwise recording spectra.
- DERIVATIVES **spectrographic** adjective.

spectrometer /spek-**trom**-i-ter/ noun a device used for recording and measuring spectra, especially as a method of analysis.
- DERIVATIVES **spectrometric** adjective **spectrometry** noun.

spectroscope noun a device for producing and recording spectra for examination.

spectroscopy /spek-**tross**-kuh-pi/ noun the branch of science concerned with the investigation and measurement of spectra produced when matter interacts with or emits electromagnetic radiation.
- DERIVATIVES **spectroscopic** adjective **spectroscopist** noun.

spectrum /spek-truhm/ noun (pl. **spectra** /spek-truh/) 1 a band of colours produced by separating light into elements with different wavelengths, e.g. in a rainbow. 2 the entire range of wavelengths of electromagnetic radiation (such as light and radio waves). 3 the components of a sound or other phenomenon arranged according to frequency, energy, etc. 4 a range of beliefs, ideas, qualities, etc.: *the idea could gain support across the political spectrum.*
- ORIGIN Latin, 'image, apparition'.

specula plural of SPECULUM.

speculate /spek-yuu-layt/ verb 1 form a theory or opinion without firm evidence. 2 invest in stocks, property, or other ventures in the hope of making a profit but with the risk of loss.
- DERIVATIVES **speculation** noun **speculator** noun.
- ORIGIN Latin *speculari* 'observe'.

speculative adjective 1 based on theory or guesswork rather than knowledge. 2 (of an investment) involving a high risk of loss.
- DERIVATIVES **speculatively** adverb

speculativeness noun.

speculum /spek-yuu-luhm/ noun (pl. **specula** /spek-yuu-luh/) Medicine a metal instrument that is used to widen an opening or passage in the body to allow inspection.
- ORIGIN Latin, 'mirror'.

sped past and past participle of SPEED.

speech noun 1 the expression of thoughts and feelings using spoken language. 2 a formal talk delivered to an audience. 3 a sequence of lines written for one character in a play.
- ORIGIN Old English.

speech day noun Brit. an annual event held at some schools, at which speeches are made and prizes are presented.

speechify verb (**speechifies, speechifying, speechified**) deliver a speech in a boring or pompous way.
- DERIVATIVES **speechifier** noun.

speechless adjective unable to speak, especially as a result of shock or strong emotion.
- DERIVATIVES **speechlessly** adverb **speechlessness** noun.

speech recognition noun the process of enabling a computer to identify and respond to the sounds produced in human speech.

speech therapy noun treatment to help people with speech and language problems.
- DERIVATIVES **speech therapist** noun.

speed noun 1 the rate at which someone or something moves or operates: *the car has a top speed of 147 mph.* 2 a fast rate of movement or action. 3 each of the possible gear ratios of a bicycle. 4 the light-gathering power of a camera lens. 5 the sensitivity of photographic film to light. 6 informal an amphetamine drug. • verb (past and past part. **sped** or **speeded**) 1 move quickly. 2 (**speed up**) move or work more quickly. 3 (usu. **speed something up**) cause something to happen more quickly. 4 (of a motorist) travel at a speed greater than the legal limit. 5 old use make prosperous or successful: *may God speed you.*
- PHRASES **at speed** quickly. **up to speed** informal fully informed or up to date.
- DERIVATIVES **speeder** noun.
- ORIGIN Old English.

speedboat noun a motorboat designed for high speed.

speed bump (Brit. also **speed hump**) noun a ridge set in a road to control the speed of vehicles.

speed camera noun a roadside camera designed to catch speeding vehicles.

speed dating (US trademark **SpeedDating**) noun an organized activity in which a person has short conversations with a series of people to see if they like each other enough to begin a relationship.

speed dial noun a function on some telephones which allows numbers to be entered into a memory and dialled with the push of a single button. • verb (**speed-dial**) dial a telephone number by using a speed dial function.

speed limit noun the maximum speed at which a vehicle may legally travel on a particular stretch of road.

speedo noun (pl. **speedos**) informal a speedometer.

speedometer /spee-dom-i-ter/ noun an instrument on a vehicle's dashboard that indicates its speed.

speedster noun informal a person or thing that operates well at high speed.

speedway noun Brit. a form of motorcycle racing in which the riders race laps around an oval dirt track.

speedwell noun a small creeping plant with blue or pink flowers.

speedy adjective (**speedier**, **speediest**) **1** done or occurring quickly. **2** moving or able to move quickly.
– DERIVATIVES **speedily** adverb **speediness** noun.

speleology /spee-li-ol-uh-ji/ noun the study or exploration of caves.
– DERIVATIVES **speleological** adjective **speleologist** noun.
– ORIGIN from Greek *spēlaion* 'cave'.

spell[1] verb (past and past part. **spelled** or chiefly Brit. **spelt**) **1** write or name the letters that form a word in the correct order. **2** (of letters) form a word. **3** be a sign of; lead to: *the plans would spell disaster.* **4** (**spell something out**) explain something clearly.
– DERIVATIVES **speller** noun.
– ORIGIN Old French *espeller*.

spell[2] noun **1** a form of words thought to have magical power. **2** a very attractive or fascinating quality: *those who fell under the spell of his undeniable charm.*
– ORIGIN Old English, 'narration'.

spell[3] noun a short period of time. • verb chiefly N. Amer. allow someone to rest briefly by taking over from them in an activity.
– ORIGIN unknown.

spellbind verb (past and past part. **spellbound**) hold someone's complete attention: *the singer held the audience spellbound.*
– DERIVATIVES **spellbinder** noun.

spellchecker noun a computer program which checks the spelling of words in a computer document.
– DERIVATIVES **spellcheck** verb & noun.

spelling noun **1** the way in which a word is spelled. **2** a person's ability to spell.

spelt past and past participle of **SPELL**[1].

spend verb (past and past part. **spent**) **1** pay out money to buy or hire goods or services. **2** use or use up energy or resources. **3** pass time in a specified way: *she spent a lot of time travelling.* • noun informal an amount of money paid out.
– PHRASES **spend a penny** Brit. informal, euphemistic urinate. [with reference to the coin-operated locks of public toilets.]
– DERIVATIVES **spendable** adjective **spender** noun.
– ORIGIN Latin *expendere* 'pay out'.

spendthrift noun a person who spends money in an extravagant and irresponsible way.

spent past and past participle of **SPEND**. adjective used up; exhausted.

sperm noun (pl. same or **sperms**) **1** semen. **2** a spermatozoon (male sex cell).
– ORIGIN Greek *sperma* 'seed'.

spermaceti /sper-muh-see-ti, sper-muh-set-i/ noun a white waxy substance obtained from an organ in the head of the sperm whale, formerly used in candles and ointments.
– ORIGIN from Latin *sperma* 'sperm' + *ceti* 'of a whale', from the belief that it was whale spawn.

spermatozoon /sper-muh-tuh-zoh-on/ noun (pl. **spermatozoa** /sper-muh-tuh-zoh-uh/) the male sex cell of an animal, which fertilizes the ovum (female reproductive cell).
– ORIGIN from Greek *sperma* 'seed' + *zōion* 'animal'.

sperm count noun the number of spermatozoa in a measured amount of semen, used as an indication of a man's fertility.

spermicide noun a substance that kills sperm, used as a contraceptive.
– DERIVATIVES **spermicidal** adjective.

sperm whale noun a toothed whale with a massive head, feeding largely on squid.
– ORIGIN from **SPERMACETI**.

spew verb **1** pour out or discharge rapidly and in large quantities: *a fax machine spewed out information.* **2** informal vomit. • noun informal vomit.
– DERIVATIVES **spewer** noun.
– ORIGIN Old English.

SPF abbreviation sun protection factor.

sphagnum /sfag-nuhm/ noun a type of moss that grows on bogs.
– ORIGIN Latin.

sphere /sfeer/ noun **1** a round solid figure in which every point on the surface is at an equal distance from the centre. **2** an area of activity, interest, or expertise: *political reforms to match those in the economic sphere.* **3** a particular section of society.
– ORIGIN Greek *sphaira* 'ball'.

spherical /sfer-i-k'l/ adjective shaped like a sphere.
– DERIVATIVES **spherically** adverb.

spheroid /sfeer-oyd/ noun an object that is roughly the same shape as a sphere.
– DERIVATIVES **spheroidal** adjective.

sphincter /sfingk-ter/ noun a ring of muscle that surrounds an opening such as the anus, and can be tightened to close it.
– ORIGIN Greek *sphinktēr*.

sphinx noun an ancient Egyptian stone figure with a lion's body and a human or animal head.
– ORIGIN Greek, first referring to a winged monster in Greek mythology with a woman's head and a lion's body, who set a riddle and killed those who could not solve it.

sphygmomanometer /sfig-moh-muh-nom-i-ter/ noun an instrument for measuring blood pressure, consisting of an inflatable rubber cuff which is fitted around the arm and connected to a column of mercury next to a graduated scale.
– ORIGIN from Greek *sphugmos* 'pulse'.

spic noun US informal, offensive a Spanish-speaking person from Central or South America or the Caribbean.
– ORIGIN perhaps from *speak the* in 'no speak the English'.

spice noun **1** a strong-tasting vegetable substance used to flavour food. **2** something that adds interest and excitement: *shared highs*

S

and lows can add spice to your relationship.
●verb **1** flavour something with spice. **2** (**spice something up**) make something more exciting or interesting.
– ORIGIN Old French *espice*.

spick and span adjective neat, clean, and well looked after.
– ORIGIN from Old Norse words meaning 'chip' and 'new'.

spicule /spik-yool/ noun chiefly Zoology a small needle-like object or structure.
– ORIGIN Latin *spicula* 'little ear of grain'.

spicy adjective (**spicier**, **spiciest**) **1** strongly flavoured with spice. **2** mildly indecent: *spicy jokes.*
– DERIVATIVES **spicily** adverb **spiciness** noun.

spider noun **1** an eight-legged arachnid (insect-like creature), most kinds of which spin webs in which to capture insects. **2** Billiards & Snooker a long-legged rest for a cue that can be placed over a ball without touching it.
– ORIGIN Old English.

spider crab noun a crab with long, thin legs and a compact pear-shaped body.

spider mite noun a plant-feeding mite resembling a tiny spider.

spider monkey noun a South American monkey with very long limbs and a long tail which it can use for grasping.

spider plant noun a plant having long, narrow leaves with a central yellow stripe, popular as a house plant.

spidery adjective long and thin, like a spider's legs: *spidery writing.*

spiel /shpeel, speel/ noun informal an elaborate and insincere speech made to persuade someone to buy or believe something.
– ORIGIN German, 'a game'.

spiffing adjective Brit. informal, dated excellent; splendid.
– ORIGIN unknown.

spiffy adjective (**spiffier**, **spiffiest**) N. Amer. informal smart or stylish.
– DERIVATIVES **spiffily** adverb.
– ORIGIN unknown.

spigot /spi-guht/ noun **1** a small peg or plug, especially for putting into the vent of a cask. **2** US a tap. **3** the plain end of a section of a pipe fitting into the socket of the next one.
– ORIGIN perhaps from Provençal *espigou*.

spike[1] noun **1** a thin pointed piece of metal or wood. **2** each of several metal points set into the sole of a sports shoe to prevent slipping. **3** a sharp increase: *a spike in demand.* ●verb **1** impale on or pierce with something sharp: *she spiked another oyster.* **2** form something into or cover something with sharp points. **3** informal secretly add alcohol or a drug to drink or food. **4** put an end to a plan or undertaking. **5** increase and then decrease sharply: *oil prices would spike and then fall again.*
– ORIGIN perhaps from German, Dutch *spiker*; sense 4 of the verb comes from the editorial practice of rejecting submitted news stories by filing them on a metal spike.

spike[2] noun Botany a flower cluster formed of many flower heads attached directly to a long stem.
– ORIGIN Latin *spica* 'ear of corn'.

spikenard /spyk-nahd/ noun historical an expensive perfumed ointment made from the rhizome (underground stem) of a Himalayan plant.
– ORIGIN from Latin *spica* 'spike' + Greek *nardos* 'spikenard'.

spiky adjective (**spikier**, **spikiest**) **1** like a spike or spikes or having many spikes: *short spiky hair.* **2** informal easily annoyed; irritable.
– DERIVATIVES **spikily** adverb **spikiness** noun.

spill[1] verb (past and past part. **spilt** or **spilled**) **1** flow or cause to flow over the edge of a container. **2** move or empty out from a place: *students began to spill out of the building.* **3** reveal private or personal information. ●noun **1** an instance of a liquid spilling or the quantity spilt. **2** a fall from a horse or bicycle.
– PHRASES **spill the beans** informal reveal secret information. **spill blood** kill or wound people.
– DERIVATIVES **spillage** noun **spiller** noun.
– ORIGIN Old English, 'kill, waste, shed blood'.

spill[2] noun a thin strip of wood or paper used for lighting a fire.
– ORIGIN probably from Dutch or German.

spillover noun **1** a thing that overflows or has spread into another area. **2** (usu. before another noun) an unexpected result or effect of something.

spilt past and past participle of **SPILL**[1].

spin verb (**spins**, **spinning**, **spun**) **1** turn round quickly. **2** (of a person's head) have a feeling of dizziness. **3** (of a ball) move through the air with a revolving motion. **4** draw out and twist the fibres of wool, cotton, etc. to convert them into yarn. **5** (of a spider or a silkworm or other insect) produce a web, silk, or cocoon by forcing out a fine thread from a special gland. **6** (**spin something out**) make something last as long as possible. ●noun **1** a spinning motion. **2** informal a brief trip in a vehicle for pleasure. **3** a favourable slant given to a news story.
– PHRASES **flat spin** Brit. informal a state of agitation. **spin a yarn** tell a far-fetched story.
– DERIVATIVES **spinner** noun.
– ORIGIN Old English.

spina bifida /spy-nuh bi-fi-duh/ noun a condition present from birth in which part of the spinal cord is exposed through a gap in the backbone, and which can cause paralysis and other problems.
– ORIGIN from Latin *spina* 'backbone, thorn' + *bifidus* 'doubly split'.

spinach noun a vegetable with large dark green leaves.
– ORIGIN probably from Old French *espinache*.

spinal adjective relating to the spine.
– DERIVATIVES **spinally** adverb.

spinal column noun the spine.

spinal cord noun the cylindrical bundle of nerve fibres in the spine that connects all parts of the body to the brain.

spindle noun **1** a slender rounded rod with tapered ends, used in spinning wool, flax, etc. by hand. **2** a rod serving as an axis that revolves or on which something revolves.
– ORIGIN Old English.

spindly adjective long or tall and thin.

spin doctor noun informal a spokesperson for a political party or politician employed to present events in a favourable way to the media.

spindrift noun 1 spray blown from the crests of waves by the wind. 2 driving snow.
– ORIGIN from former *spoon* 'run before wind or sea' + DRIFT.

spin dryer noun Brit. a machine for drying wet clothes by spinning them in a revolving perforated drum.

spine noun 1 a series of vertebrae (bones) extending from the skull to the small of the back, enclosing the spinal cord; the backbone. 2 the part of a book that encloses the inner edges of the pages. 3 a central or strengthening feature: *Norway's mountainous spine.* 4 a hard pointed projection found on certain plants (e.g. cacti) and animals (e.g. hedgehogs).
– ORIGIN Latin *spina* 'thorn, backbone'.

spine-chiller noun a story or film that causes terror and excitement.
– DERIVATIVES **spine-chilling** adjective.

spinel /spi-nel, spin-uhl/ noun a hard glassy mineral consisting chiefly of magnesium and aluminium oxides.
– ORIGIN Italian *spinella* 'little thorn'.

spineless adjective 1 lacking courage and determination. 2 (of an animal) having no backbone; invertebrate. 3 (of an animal or plant) lacking spines.
– DERIVATIVES **spinelessly** adverb **spinelessness** noun.

spinet /spi-net, spin-it/ noun a type of small harpsichord popular in the 18th century.
– ORIGIN Italian *spinetta* 'virginal, spinet'.

spine-tingling adjective informal thrilling or pleasurably frightening.

spinifex /spin-i-feks/ noun a grass with spiny flower heads which break off and are blown about, occurring from east Asia to Australia.
– ORIGIN Latin.

spinnaker /spin-nuh-ker/ noun a large three-cornered sail set in front of the mainsail of a racing yacht when the wind is coming from behind.
– ORIGIN probably from *Sphinx*, the yacht first using such a sail.

spinneret /spin-uh-ret/ noun an organ through which the silk, gossamer, or thread of spiders, silkworms, and certain other insects is produced.

spinney noun (pl. **spinneys**) Brit. a small area of trees and bushes.
– ORIGIN Old French *espinei*.

spinning jenny noun historical a machine for spinning with more than one spindle at a time.

spinning wheel noun a machine for spinning yarn or thread with a spindle driven by a wheel attached to a crank or treadle.

spin-off noun 1 a product or benefit produced during or after the main activity. 2 a book, film, television programme, etc. based on another book, film, programme, etc.

spinster noun chiefly derogatory a single woman beyond the usual age for marriage.
– DERIVATIVES **spinsterhood** noun **spinsterish** adjective.
– ORIGIN first meaning 'woman who spins'.

spiny adjective (**spinier, spiniest**) full of or covered with prickles.
– DERIVATIVES **spininess** noun.

spiny anteater noun another term for ECHIDNA.

spiracle /spy-ruh-k'l/ noun an external opening used for breathing in certain insects, fish, and other animals.
– DERIVATIVES **spiracular** adjective.
– ORIGIN Latin *spiraculum*.

spiraea /spy-ree-uh/ (chiefly US also **spirea**) noun a shrub with clusters of small white or pink flowers.
– ORIGIN Greek *speiraia*.

spiral adjective winding in a continuous curve around a central point or axis. • noun 1 a spiral curve, shape, or pattern. 2 a continuous increase or decrease in prices, wages, etc. that gradually gets faster: *a downward spiral of crippling debt.* • verb (**spirals, spiralling, spiralled;** US **spirals, spiraling, spiraled**) 1 move in a spiral course. 2 show a continuous and rapid increase or decrease.
– DERIVATIVES **spirally** adverb.
– ORIGIN Latin *spiralis*.

spiral-bound adjective (of a book or notepad) bound with a spiral wire threaded through a row of holes along one edge.

spire noun a tall pointed structure on the top of a church tower or other building.
– ORIGIN Old English, 'tall plant stem'.

spirea noun chiefly US variant spelling of SPIRAEA.

spirit noun 1 the part of a person that consists of their character and feelings rather than their body, often believed to survive after their body is dead. 2 a ghost or other supernatural being. 3 the typical or dominant character, quality, or mood: *they shared her spirit of adventure.* 4 (**spirits**) a person's mood. 5 courage, energy, and determination. 6 the real meaning of something as opposed to its strict interpretation: *the rule had been broken in spirit if not in letter.* 7 chiefly Brit. strong distilled alcoholic drink, such as rum. 8 purified distilled alcohol, such as methylated spirit. • verb (**spirits, spiriting, spirited**) (**spirit someone/thing away**) take someone or something away rapidly and secretly.
– PHRASES **when the spirit moves someone** when someone feels inclined to do something.
– ORIGIN Latin *spiritus* 'breath, spirit'.

spirited adjective 1 full of energy, enthusiasm, and determination. 2 having a specified character: *a generous-spirited man.*
– DERIVATIVES **spiritedly** adverb **spiritedness** noun.

spirit gum noun a quick-drying solution of gum, used by actors to attach false hair to their faces.

spirit lamp noun a lamp that burns methylated or other volatile spirits rather than oil.

spiritless adjective lacking courage, energy, or determination.
– DERIVATIVES **spiritlessly** adverb **spiritlessness** noun.

spirit level noun a device consisting of a sealed glass tube partially filled with a liquid, containing an air bubble whose position reveals whether a surface is perfectly level.

spiritual adjective 1 relating to the human

S

spirit as opposed to material or physical things: *I'm responsible for his spiritual welfare.* **2** relating to religion or religious belief. •**noun** a religious song of a kind associated with black Christians of the southern US.
– DERIVATIVES **spirituality** noun **spiritualize** (or **spiritualise**) verb **spiritually** adverb.

spiritualism noun the belief that it is possible to communicate with the spirits of the dead, especially through mediums.
– DERIVATIVES **spiritualist** noun **spiritualistic** adjective.

spirituous /spir-it-yoo-uhss/ adjective old use containing much alcohol.

spirogyra /spy-ruh-jy-ruh/ noun a type of algae consisting of long green threads.
– ORIGIN from Greek *speira* 'coil' + *guros* 'round'.

spirometer /spy-rom-i-ter/ noun an instrument for measuring the air capacity of the lungs.
– DERIVATIVES **spirometry** noun.

spit[1] verb (**spits, spitting, spat** or **spit**) **1** force saliva, food, or liquid from the mouth. **2** say something in a hostile way. **3** (of a fire or food being cooked) give out small bursts of sparks or hot fat. **4** (**it spits, it is spitting**) Brit. light rain falls. •**noun 1** saliva. **2** an act of spitting.
– PHRASES **be the spitting image of** (or **be the spit of**) informal look exactly like. [perhaps from the idea of a person apparently being formed from the spit of another, so similar are they.] **spit and polish** thorough cleaning and polishing. **spit blood** feel or express strong anger. **spit it out** informal say it quickly; stop hesitating.
– DERIVATIVES **spitter** noun.
– ORIGIN Old English.

spit[2] noun **1** a thin metal rod pushed through meat in order to hold and turn it while it is roasted. **2** a narrow point of land projecting into the sea.
– ORIGIN Old English.

spite noun a desire to hurt, annoy, or offend someone. •**verb** deliberately hurt, annoy, or offend someone.
– PHRASES **in spite of** without being affected by. **in spite of oneself** although one did not want or expect to do so.
– ORIGIN Old French *despit* 'contempt'.

spiteful adjective deliberately hurtful; malicious.
– DERIVATIVES **spitefully** adverb **spitefulness** noun.

spitfire noun a person with a fierce temper.

spit-roasted adjective (of meat) cooked on a spit.

spittle noun saliva; spit.
– ORIGIN from dialect *spattle*.

spittoon /spit-toon/ noun a container for spitting into.

spiv noun Brit. informal a flashily dressed man who makes a living by dishonest dealings.
– DERIVATIVES **spivvy** adjective.
– ORIGIN perhaps from SPIFFY.

splash verb **1** (with reference to a liquid) fall or cause to fall in scattered drops: *wine splashed on to the bed.* **2** make someone or something wet with scattered drops. **3** move around in water, causing it to fly about. **4** (**splash down**) (of a spacecraft) land on water. **5** display a

story or photograph very noticeably in a newspaper or magazine. **6** (**splash out**) Brit. informal spend money freely. •**noun 1** an instance or sound of splashing. **2** a small quantity of liquid that has splashed on to a surface. **3** a small quantity of liquid added to a drink. **4** a bright patch of colour. **5** informal a noticeable or sensational news story.
– PHRASES **make a splash** informal attract a great deal of attention.
– DERIVATIVES **splashy** adjective (**splashier, splashiest**).
– ORIGIN from PLASH.

splashback noun Brit. a panel behind a sink or cooker that protects the wall from splashes.

splat informal noun a sound of something soft and wet or heavy striking a surface. •**verb** (**splats, splatting, splatted**) hit or land with a splat.
– ORIGIN from SPLATTER.

splatter verb splash someone or something with a sticky or thick liquid. •**noun** a splash of a sticky or thick liquid. •**adjective** informal (of a film) featuring many violent and gruesome deaths.
– ORIGIN imitating the sound.

splay verb spread or be spread out or further apart: *he stood with his legs splayed out.* •**adjective** turned outward or widened: *she sat splay-legged.*
– ORIGIN from DISPLAY.

splay-footed adjective having a broad flat foot turned outward.

spleen noun **1** an organ in the abdomen that is involved in the production and removal of blood cells and forms part of the immune system. **2** bad temper; spite.
– ORIGIN Greek *splēn*; sense 2 comes from the former belief that bad temper originated in the spleen.

splendid adjective **1** magnificent; very impressive. **2** informal excellent; very good.
– DERIVATIVES **splendidly** adverb.
– ORIGIN Latin *splendidus*.

splendiferous adjective informal, humorous very good; splendid.

splendour (US **splendor**) noun magnificent and impressive quality or appearance: *the splendour of Mount Everest.*

splenetic /spli-net-ik/ adjective bad-tempered or spiteful.
– ORIGIN Latin *spleneticus*.

splenic /sple-nik, splee-nik/ adjective relating to the spleen.

splice verb **1** join a rope or ropes by the strands together at the ends. **2** join pieces of timber, film, or tape at the ends. •**noun** a place where film, rope, etc. has been spliced together.
– PHRASES **get spliced** Brit. informal get married.
– DERIVATIVES **splicer** noun.
– ORIGIN probably from Dutch *splissen*.

spliff noun informal a cannabis cigarette.
– ORIGIN unknown.

spline noun a rectangular key fitting into grooves in the hub and shaft of a wheel. •**verb** secure a part with a spline.
– ORIGIN perhaps from SPLINTER.

splint noun a strip of rigid material for supporting a broken bone when it has been set. •**verb** secure a broken limb with a splint or

splints.
- ORIGIN Dutch, German *splinte* 'metal plate or pin'.

splinter noun a small, thin sharp piece of wood, glass, etc. broken off from a larger piece. •verb 1 break into splinters. 2 (of a group) divide into smaller separate groups: *the company splintered into seven regional operating companies.*
- DERIVATIVES **splintery** adjective.
- ORIGIN Dutch.

splinter group noun a small organization that has broken away from a larger one.

split verb (**splits, splitting, split**) 1 break into parts by force. 2 divide into parts or groups: *once again the family was split up.* 3 (often **split up**) end a marriage or other relationship. 4 (**be splitting**) informal (of a person's head) be suffering from a bad headache. 5 (**split on**) Brit. informal betray the secrets of or inform on someone. •noun 1 a tear or crack. 2 an instance of splitting or dividing: *a 72–25 split of the proceeds.* 3 a division between members of a group or an end of a relationship: *a split in the ruling party.* 4 (**the splits**) (in gymnastics and dance) an act of leaping in the air or sitting down with the legs straight and at right angles to the body.
- PHRASES **split the difference** take the average of two proposed amounts. **split one's sides** informal laugh heartily or uncontrollably.
- DERIVATIVES **splitter** noun.
- ORIGIN Dutch *splitten* '(of a storm or rock) break up a ship'.

split end noun a tip of a person's hair which has split from dryness or ill-treatment.

split infinitive noun a sentence consisting of the infinitive of a verb with an adverb or other word placed between *to* and the verb, e.g. *she seems to really like it.*

USAGE: Many people still think that splitting infinitives (putting a word between *to* and the verb) is wrong. They think that it is better to say *she used secretly to admire him* rather than *she used to secretly admire him,* although this sometimes sounds awkward or gives a different emphasis to what is being said. For this reason, the rule about not splitting infinitives is not followed so strictly today, although it is best not to split them in formal writing.

split-level adjective 1 (of a room or building) having the floor divided into different levels. 2 (of a cooker) having the oven and hob in separate units.

split pea noun a pea dried and split in half for cooking.

split pin noun a metal cotter pin with two arms passed through a hole, held in place by the springing apart of the arms.

split screen noun a cinema, television, or computer screen on which two or more separate images are displayed.

split second noun a very brief moment of time. •adjective (**split-second**) very rapid or accurate: *split-second timing.*

splodge noun & verb Brit. another term for SPLOTCH.

splosh informal verb move with a soft splashing

sound. •noun a splash.
- ORIGIN imitating the sound.

splotch informal noun a spot, splash, or smear of something. •verb mark something with a spot, splash or smear.
- DERIVATIVES **splotchy** adjective.
- ORIGIN perhaps from SPOT and former *plotch* 'blotch'.

splurge informal verb spend extravagantly: *this is a good place to splurge on extravagant materials.* •noun a sudden spell of spending money extravagantly.
- ORIGIN uncertain.

splutter verb 1 make a series of short explosive spitting or choking sounds. 2 say something in a rapid and unclear way. •noun a spluttering sound.
- DERIVATIVES **splutterer** noun.
- ORIGIN imitating the sound.

Spode noun trademark fine decorated pottery or porcelain made by the English potter Josiah Spode or his successors.

spoil verb (past and past part. **spoilt** (chiefly Brit.) or **spoiled**) 1 make less good or enjoyable: *I am not going to let her spoil my day.* 2 harm a child's character by not treating them strictly enough. 3 treat someone with great or excessive kindness. 4 (of food) become unfit for eating. 5 (**be spoiling for**) be very eager for: *Cooper was spoiling for a fight.* •noun (**spoils**) stolen goods.
- PHRASES **be spoilt for choice** Brit. have so many options that it is difficult to make a choice.
- ORIGIN Latin *spoliare.*

spoilage noun the decay of food and other perishable goods.

spoiler noun 1 a part fitted to a car in order to improve roadholding at high speeds. 2 a flap on an aircraft wing which can be raised to create drag and so reduce speed. 3 a news story published with the intention of reducing the impact of a similar item published in a rival paper.

spoilsport noun a person who spoils the pleasure of others.

spoilt chiefly Brit. past and past participle of SPOIL.

spoke[1] noun 1 each of the bars or wire rods connecting the centre of a wheel to its rim. 2 each of the metal rods in an umbrella to which the material is attached.
- PHRASES **put a spoke in someone's wheel** Brit. prevent someone from carrying out a plan.
- ORIGIN Old English.

spoke[2] past of SPEAK.

spoken past participle of SPEAK. adjective (in combination) speaking in a specified way: *a soft-spoken man.*
- PHRASES **be spoken for** 1 be already claimed or reserved. 2 already have a romantic relationship.

spokeshave noun a small plane with a handle on each side of its blade, used for shaping curved surfaces.

spokesman (or **spokeswoman**) noun (pl. **spokesmen** or **spokeswomen**) a person who makes statements on behalf of a group.

spokesperson noun (pl. **spokespersons** or **spokespeople**) a spokesman or spokeswoman.

spoliation /spoh-li-ay-shuhn/ noun 1 the

action of destroying or ruining something. **2** the action of plundering a place.

spondee /spon-dee/ noun a foot (unit of poetic metre) consisting of two long (or stressed) syllables.
– ORIGIN from Greek *spondeios pous* 'metrical foot relating to a ritual offering of drink'.

spondulicks /spon-**dyoo**-liks/ plural noun Brit. informal money.
– ORIGIN unknown.

spondylitis /spon-di-**ly**-tis/ noun arthritis in the backbone, especially (**ankylosing spondylitis**) a form in which the vertebrae (bones) become fused.
– ORIGIN from Latin *spondylus* 'vertebra'.

sponge noun **1** an invertebrate sea creature with a soft porous body. **2** a piece of a light absorbent substance used for washing, as padding, etc. **3** Brit. a very light cake made with eggs, sugar, and flour but little or no fat. ● verb (**sponges, sponging** or **spongeing, sponged**) **1** wipe or clean someone or something with a wet sponge or cloth. **2** (usu. **sponge off**) informal obtain money or food from others without giving anything in return.
– DERIVATIVES **sponge-like** adjective.
– ORIGIN Greek *spongos*.

sponge bag noun Brit. a toilet bag.

sponge pudding noun Brit. a steamed or baked pudding of fat, flour, and eggs.

sponger noun informal a person who lives by obtaining money or food from others.

spongiform /spun-ji-form/ adjective technical having a porous structure or consistency like that of a sponge.

spongy adjective (**spongier, spongiest**) like a sponge in being porous, absorbent, or compressible.
– DERIVATIVES **sponginess** noun.

sponsor noun **1** a person or organization that pays for or contributes to the costs of an event or a radio or television programme in return for advertising. **2** a person who promises to give money to a charity after another person has participated in a fund-raising activity. **3** a person who introduces and supports a proposal for a new law. **4** a person taking official responsibility for the actions of another. **5** a godparent at a child's baptism. ● verb be a sponsor for a person, event, or fund-raising activity.
– DERIVATIVES **sponsorship** noun.
– ORIGIN Latin.

spontaneous /spon-**tay**-ni-uhss/ adjective **1** done or occurring as a result of an unplanned impulse: *the crowd broke into spontaneous applause.* **2** open, natural, and uninhibited. **3** (of a process or event) happening naturally, without being made to do so.
– DERIVATIVES **spontaneity** /spon-tuh-**nay**-i-ti/ noun **spontaneously** adverb.
– ORIGIN Latin *spontaneus*.

spontaneous combustion noun the burning of organic matter caused by chemical changes within the substance itself.

spoof informal noun **1** a humorous imitation of something in which its typical features are exaggerated: *a spoof of Bond films.* **2** a trick played on someone as a joke. ● verb **1** imitate

something while exaggerating its typical features. **2** trick someone.
– DERIVATIVES **spoofer** noun **spoofery** noun.
– ORIGIN coined by the English comedian Arthur Roberts.

spook informal noun **1** a ghost. **2** chiefly N. Amer. a spy. ● verb frighten someone or something.
– ORIGIN Dutch.

spooky adjective (**spookier, spookiest**) informal sinister or ghostly.
– DERIVATIVES **spookily** adverb **spookiness** noun.

spool noun a cylindrical device on which thread, film, etc. can be wound. ● verb **1** wind or be wound on to a spool. **2** Computing send data for printing or processing on a peripheral device to an intermediate store.
– ORIGIN Old French *espole* or German *spôle*; sense 2 of the verb is from the initial letters of *simultaneous peripheral operation online.*

spoon noun an implement consisting of a small shallow bowl on a long handle, used for eating, stirring, and serving food. ● verb **1** transfer food with a spoon. **2** informal, dated (of a couple) kiss and cuddle amorously.
– DERIVATIVES **spoonful** noun.
– ORIGIN Old English, 'chip of wood'.

spoonbill noun a tall wading bird having a long bill with a very broad flat tip.

spoonerism noun an error in speech in which the initial sounds or letters of two or more words are accidentally swapped around, as in *you have hissed the mystery lectures.*
– ORIGIN named after the English scholar Revd W. A. *Spooner*, who was said to have made such errors.

spoon-feed verb **1** provide someone with so much help or information that they do not need to think for themselves. **2** feed a baby with a spoon.

spoor noun the track or scent of an animal.
– ORIGIN Dutch *spor.*

sporadic /spuh-**rad**-ik/ adjective occurring at irregular intervals or only in a few places: *sporadic fighting broke out.*
– DERIVATIVES **sporadically** adverb.
– ORIGIN Greek *sporadikos.*

spore noun a tiny reproductive cell produced by plants without vascular systems (such as mosses and algae), fungi, etc.
– ORIGIN Greek *spora* 'sowing, seed'.

sporran /spo-ruhn/ noun a small pouch worn around the waist so as to hang in front of the kilt as part of men's Scottish Highland dress.
– ORIGIN Scottish Gaelic *sporan.*

sport noun **1** an activity involving physical effort and skill in which a person or team competes against another or others. **2** informal a person who behaves in a good or specified way when teased or defeated: *go on, be a sport!* **3** success or pleasure derived from an activity such as hunting. **4** dated entertainment; fun. **5** chiefly Austral./NZ a friendly form of address, especially between men. **6** Biology an animal or plant that is markedly different from the parent type as a result of mutation. ● verb **1** wear or display a distinctive item. **2** literary play in a lively way.
– PHRASES **the sport of kings** horse racing.
– DERIVATIVES **sporter** noun.
– ORIGIN from DISPORT.

S

sporting adjective **1** connected with or interested in sport. **2** fair and generous towards others.
– DERIVATIVES **sportingly** adverb.

sporting chance noun a reasonable chance of winning or succeeding.

sportive adjective playful; light-hearted.

sports car noun a low-built fast car.

sports jacket noun a man's informal jacket resembling a suit jacket.

sportsman (or **sportswoman**) noun (pl. sportsmen or sportswomen) **1** a person who takes part in a sport, especially as a professional. **2** a person who behaves in a fair and generous way towards others.
– DERIVATIVES **sportsmanlike** adjective **sportsmanship** noun.

sportsperson noun (pl. sportspersons or sportspeople) a sportsman or sportswoman.

sportster noun a sports car.

sportswear noun clothes worn for sport or for casual use.

sport utility (also **sport utility vehicle**) noun chiefly N. Amer. a high-performance four-wheel-drive vehicle.

sporty adjective (sportier, sportiest) informal **1** fond of or good at sport. **2** (of clothing) suitable for sport or casual wear. **3** (of a car) compact and with fast acceleration.
– DERIVATIVES **sportiness** noun.

spot noun **1** a small round mark on a surface. **2** a pimple. **3** a particular place, point, or position: an ideal picnic spot. **4** a place for an individual item in a show. **5** informal, chiefly Brit. a small amount: he was having a spot of bother. •verb (spots, spotting, spotted) **1** notice or recognize someone or something that is difficult to find or that one is searching for. **2** mark something with spots. **3** (it spots, it is spotting, it spotted) light rain falls.
– PHRASES **on the spot 1** immediately. **2** at the scene of an event. **3** Brit. (of an action) performed without moving from one's original position. **put someone on the spot** informal force someone into a situation in which they must respond or act. **spot on** Brit. informal completely accurate or accurately.
– DERIVATIVES **spotted** adjective.
– ORIGIN perhaps from Dutch spotte.

spot check noun a test made without warning on a person or thing selected at random. •verb (spot-check) make a random check on someone or something without warning.

spotless adjective **1** absolutely clean. **2** without any mistakes or moral faults; perfect: the defendant has a spotless record.
– DERIVATIVES **spotlessly** adverb **spotlessness** noun.

spotlight noun **1** a lamp projecting a narrow, intense beam of light directly on to a place or person. **2** (the spotlight) intense public attention. •verb (past and past part. spotlighted or spotlit) **1** light up someone or something with a spotlight. **2** direct attention to a problem or situation.

spotted dick noun Brit. a suet pudding containing currants.

spotter noun **1** (usu. in combination) a person who observes or looks for a particular thing as a hobby or job: a talent spotter. **2** a pilot or aircraft employed in spotting enemy positions.

spotty adjective (spottier, spottiest) **1** marked with or having spots. **2** N. Amer. of uneven quality.

spot-weld verb join things by welding them at a number of separate points.

spousal /spow-zuhl/ adjective Law, chiefly N. Amer. relating to marriage or to a husband or wife.

spouse noun a husband or wife.
– ORIGIN Latin sponsus.

spout noun **1** a projecting tube or lip through or over which liquid can be poured from a container. **2** a stream of liquid flowing out with great force. •verb **1** send out or flow forcibly in a stream: water spouted from a pipe. **2** express one's views in a lengthy or emphatic way.
– PHRASES **up the spout** Brit. informal **1** useless or ruined. **2** (of a woman) pregnant.
– DERIVATIVES **spouted** adjective **spouter** noun.
– ORIGIN from an Old Norse word meaning 'to spit'.

sprain verb wrench the ligaments of a joint so as to cause pain and swelling. •noun the result of wrenching a joint.
– ORIGIN unknown.

sprang past of SPRING.

sprat noun a small edible sea fish of the herring family.
– ORIGIN Old English.

sprawl verb **1** sit, lie, or fall with the limbs spread out in an awkward way. **2** (often as adj. sprawling) spread out irregularly over a large area: a sprawling city. •noun **1** the disorganized expansion of an urban or industrial area into the nearby countryside. **2** a relaxed or awkward position with the limbs spread out.
– ORIGIN Old English, 'move the limbs convulsively'.

spray[1] noun **1** liquid sent through the air in tiny drops. **2** a liquid which can be forced out of an aerosol or other container in a spray. •verb **1** apply liquid in a spray. **2** cover or treat someone or something with a spray. **3** (of liquid) be sent through the air in a spray. **4** scatter over an area or object with force: the gunmen sprayed bullets at all three cars.
– DERIVATIVES **sprayer** noun.
– ORIGIN from Dutch spraeyen 'sprinkle'.

spray[2] noun **1** a stem or small branch of a tree or plant, bearing flowers and leaves. **2** a bunch of cut flowers arranged in an attractive way.
– ORIGIN Old English.

spray gun noun a device resembling a gun which is used to spray a liquid such as paint under pressure.

spread verb (past and past part. spread) **1** open something out so as to increase its surface area, width, or length. **2** stretch out limbs, hands, fingers, or wings so that they are far apart. **3** extend or distribute over a large or increasing area: rain will spread south-east during the day. **4** reach or cause to reach more and more people: panic spread among the crowd. **5** apply a substance in an even layer. •noun **1** the action of spreading over an area. **2** the extent, width, or area covered by something. **3** the range of something: a wide

S

spread of ages. **4** a soft paste that can be spread on bread. **5** an article or advertisement covering several columns or pages of a newspaper or magazine. **6** informal a large and impressive meal. **7** N. Amer. a large farm or ranch.
– DERIVATIVES **spreadable** adjective **spreader** noun.
– ORIGIN Old English.

spread betting noun a form of betting in which money is won or lost according to the degree by which the score or result of a sporting fixture varies from the spread of expected values quoted by the bookmaker.

spreadeagle verb (**be spreadeagled**) be stretched out with the arms and legs spread wide.

spreadsheet noun a computer program in which figures arranged in a grid can be manipulated and used in calculations.

spree noun a spell of unrestrained activity: *a shopping spree.*
– ORIGIN unknown.

sprig noun **1** a small stem bearing leaves or flowers, taken from a bush or plant. **2** a descendant or younger member of a family or social class. **3** a small moulded decoration applied to a piece of pottery before firing.
– DERIVATIVES **sprigged** adjective.
– ORIGIN German *sprick.*

sprightly adjective (**sprightlier, sprightliest**) (especially of an old person) lively; energetic.
– DERIVATIVES **sprightliness** noun.
– ORIGIN from **SPRITE**.

spring verb (past **sprang** or chiefly N. Amer. **sprung**; past part. **sprung**) **1** move suddenly or rapidly upwards or forwards. **2** move or do suddenly: *the door sprang open.* **3** (**spring from**) originate or arise from: *his short film sprang from a midlife crisis.* **4** (**spring up**) suddenly develop or appear. **5** (as adj. **sprung**) (of a vehicle or item of furniture) having springs. **6** (**spring something on**) present something suddenly or unexpectedly to someone. **7** informal bring about the escape or release of a prisoner. • noun **1** the season after winter and before summer. **2** a spiral metal coil that can be pressed or pulled but returns to its former shape when released. **3** a sudden jump upwards or forwards. **4** a place where water wells up from an underground source. **5** the ability to spring back strongly; elastic quality.
– PHRASES **spring a leak** (of a boat or container) develop a leak.
– DERIVATIVES **springless** adjective **springlike** adjective.
– ORIGIN Old English.

spring balance noun a balance that measures weight by the tension of a spring.

springboard noun **1** a flexible board from which a diver or gymnast may jump in order to push off more strongly. **2** a thing that starts off an activity or enterprise: *a book can be a springboard for discussions with children about their own lives.*

springbok noun **1** a southern African gazelle that leaps when disturbed. **2** (**the Springboks**) the South African international rugby union team.
– ORIGIN Afrikaans.

spring chicken noun **1** informal a young person:

I'm no spring chicken. **2** a young chicken for eating (originally available only in spring).

spring clean noun Brit. a thorough cleaning of a house or room. • verb (**spring-clean**) clean a house or room thoroughly.

springer (also **springer spaniel**) noun a small spaniel of a breed originally used to drive game birds out of cover.

spring greens plural noun the leaves of young cabbage plants of a variety that does not develop a heart.

spring-loaded adjective containing a compressed or stretched spring pressing one part against another.

spring onion noun Brit. a small onion with a long green stem, eaten chiefly in salads.

spring roll noun a Chinese snack consisting of a pancake filled with vegetables and sometimes meat, rolled into a cylinder and deep-fried.

spring tide noun a tide just after a new or full moon, when there is the greatest difference between high and low water.

springtime noun the season of spring.

springy adjective (**springier, springiest**) **1** springing back quickly when squeezed or stretched. **2** (of movements) light and confident.
– DERIVATIVES **springily** adverb **springiness** noun.

sprinkle verb **1** scatter or pour small drops or particles over an object or surface. **2** distribute something randomly throughout: *the city is sprinkled with factories producing computers.* • noun a small amount that is sprinkled over something.
– ORIGIN perhaps from Dutch *sprenkelen.*

sprinkler noun **1** a device for watering lawns. **2** an automatic fire extinguisher installed in a ceiling.

sprinkling noun a small, thinly distributed amount of something.

sprint verb run at full speed over a short distance. • noun **1** an act of sprinting. **2** a short, fast race.
– DERIVATIVES **sprinter** noun.
– ORIGIN from Swedish *spritta.*

sprit noun a small pole reaching diagonally from a mast to the upper outer corner of a sail.
– ORIGIN Old English, 'punting pole'.

sprite noun **1** an elf or fairy. **2** a computer graphic which can be moved on-screen and otherwise manipulated as a single entity.
– ORIGIN a shortening of **SPIRIT**.

spritsail /sprit-sayl, sprit-s'l/ noun a sail that is extended diagonally from the mast by a small pole reaching to the upper outer corner.

spritz verb spray liquid in quick short bursts at or on to something. • noun an act of spraying a short burst of liquid.
– ORIGIN German *spritzen* 'to squirt'.

spritzer noun a mixture of wine and soda water.
– ORIGIN German, 'a splash'.

sprocket noun **1** each of several projections on the rim of a wheel that fit into the links of a chain or holes in film, tape, or paper. **2** (also **sprocket wheel**) a wheel with sprockets.
– ORIGIN unknown.

sprog noun Brit. informal, humorous a child.

– ORIGIN unknown.

sprout verb 1 (of a plant) produce shoots. 2 start to grow something, especially hair. 3 appear or develop in large numbers: *multiplexes are sprouting up around the country.* • noun 1 a shoot of a plant. 2 a Brussels sprout.
– ORIGIN Germanic.

spruce¹ adjective neat and smart. • verb (spruce someone/thing up) make someone or something smarter.
– ORIGIN perhaps from SPRUCE² in the former sense 'Prussian'.

spruce² noun a conical coniferous tree which has hanging cones.
– ORIGIN from former *Pruce* 'Prussia'.

sprue noun 1 a channel through which metal or plastic is poured into a mould. 2 a piece of metal or plastic which has solidified in a sprue.
– ORIGIN unknown.

sprung past participle and (especially in North America) past of SPRING.

spry adjective (spryer, spryest) (especially of an old person) lively.
– ORIGIN unknown.

spud noun informal a potato.
– ORIGIN unknown.

spumante /spoo-man-tay, spoo-man-ti/ noun an Italian sparkling white wine.
– ORIGIN Italian, 'sparkling'.

spume /spyoom/ literary noun froth or foam that is found on waves. • verb form froth or foam.
– ORIGIN Latin *spuma*.

spun past and past participle of SPIN.

spunk noun 1 informal courage and determination. 2 Brit. vulgar slang semen.
– DERIVATIVES spunky adjective (spunkier, spunkiest).
– ORIGIN perhaps from SPARK and former *funk* 'spark'.

spur noun 1 a device with a small spike or a spiked wheel, worn on a rider's heel for urging a horse forward. 2 a thing that encourages an act or activity: *wars act as a spur to invention.* 3 a projection from a mountain. 4 a short branch road or railway line. 5 Botany a slender tubular projection from the base of a flower. • verb (spurs, spurring, spurred) 1 encourage someone to do something or cause something to speed up: *governments should be providing incentives to spur economic growth.* 2 urge a horse forward with spurs.
– PHRASES on the spur of the moment on an impulse; without thinking.
– ORIGIN Old English.

spurge noun a plant or shrub with milky latex and small greenish flowers.
– ORIGIN Old French *espurge*.

spur gear noun a gearwheel with teeth projecting parallel to the wheel's axis.

spurious /rhymes with curious/ adjective 1 not being what it seems to be; false. 2 (of reasoning) apparently but not actually correct.
– DERIVATIVES spuriously adverb spuriousness noun.
– ORIGIN Latin *spurius* 'false'.

spurn verb reject someone or something with contempt.

– ORIGIN Old English.

spurt verb 1 gush out in a sudden stream. 2 move with a sudden burst of speed. • noun 1 a sudden gushing stream. 2 a sudden burst of activity or speed.
– ORIGIN unknown.

sputnik noun each of a series of Soviet artificial satellites, the first of which was the first to be placed in orbit.
– ORIGIN Russian, 'fellow traveller'.

sputter verb 1 make a series of soft explosive sounds. 2 say something in a rapid and unclear way; splutter. • noun a sputtering sound.
– ORIGIN Dutch *sputteren*.

sputum /spyoo-tuhm/ noun a mixture of saliva and mucus coughed up from the throat or lungs.
– ORIGIN Latin.

spy noun (pl. spies) 1 a person employed to collect and report secret information on an enemy or competitor. 2 a person or device that observes people secretly. • verb (spies, spying, spied) 1 work as a spy. 2 (spy on) watch someone secretly. 3 be able to see; notice: *he could spy a figure in the distance.* 4 (spy something out) collect information about something before deciding how to act.
– ORIGIN from Old French *espier* 'espy'.

spyglass noun a small telescope.

spyhole noun Brit. a peephole.

spyware noun software that enables someone to gather information about another's computer activities by transmitting data secretly from their hard drive.

sq. abbreviation square.

SQL abbreviation Structured Query Language, a computer language used for database manipulation.

squab /skwob/ noun a young pigeon that is yet to leave the nest.
– ORIGIN unknown.

squabble noun a quarrel about an unimportant matter. • verb quarrel about an unimportant matter.
– ORIGIN uncertain.

squad noun (treated as sing. or pl.) 1 a division of a police force dealing with a particular type of crime: *the vice squad.* 2 a group of sports players from which a team is chosen. 3 a small number of soldiers assembled for drill or given a particular task.
– ORIGIN Italian *squadra* 'square'.

squad car noun a police patrol car.

squaddie noun (pl. squaddies) Brit. informal a private soldier.

squadron noun 1 an operational unit in an air force. 2 a main division of an armoured or cavalry regiment. 3 a group of warships on a particular duty.
– ORIGIN Italian *squadra* 'square'.

squadron leader noun a rank of officer in the RAF, above flight lieutenant and below wing commander.

squalid adjective 1 very dirty and unpleasant. 2 highly immoral or dishonest: *a squalid attempt to buy votes.*
– ORIGIN Latin *squalidus*.

squall noun 1 a sudden violent gust of wind or localized storm. 2 a loud cry. • verb (of a baby

or small child) cry noisily and continuously.
– DERIVATIVES **squally** adjective.
– ORIGIN probably from SQUEAL.
squalor /rhymes with collar/ noun the state of being dirty and unpleasant.
squander verb waste money, time, or an opportunity in a reckless or foolish way.
– ORIGIN unknown.
square noun **1** a plane figure with four equal straight sides and four right angles. **2** an open four-sided area surrounded by buildings. **3** an area within a military barracks or camp that is used for drill. **4** the product of a number multiplied by itself. **5** an L-shaped or T-shaped instrument used for obtaining or testing right angles. **6** informal an old-fashioned or boringly conventional person. •adjective **1** having the shape of a square. **2** having or forming a right angle. **3** (of a unit of measurement) equal to the area of a square whose side is of the unit specified: *1,500 square metres of land.* **4** (after a noun) referring to the length of each side of a square shape or object: *the room was ten metres square.* **5** at right angles. **6** (of two or more things) level or parallel. **7** broad and solid in shape. **8** fair and honest: *she'd been as square with him as anybody could be.* **9** informal old-fashioned or boringly conventional. •adverb directly; straight. •verb **1** make something square or rectangular. **2** (as adj. **squared**) marked out in squares. **3** multiply a number by itself. **4** (**square with**) agree or be consistent with: *do those claims square with the facts?* **5** settle a bill or debt. **6** make the score of a match or game even. **7** informal pay someone money in order to obtain their cooperation. **8** bring the shoulders into a position in which they appear square and broad.
– PHRASES **back to square one** informal back to where one started. **a square deal** see DEAL¹. **a square peg in a round hole** see PEG. **square up 1** take up the position of a person about to fight. **2** (**square up to**) tackle a difficulty with determination.
– DERIVATIVES **squareness** noun **squarer** noun **squarish** adjective.
– ORIGIN Old French *esquare.*
square-bashing noun Brit. informal military drill performed repeatedly on a barrack square.
square dance noun a country dance that starts with four couples facing one another in a square.
square leg noun Cricket a fielding position level with the batsman approximately halfway towards the boundary on the leg side.
squarely adverb **1** not at an angle; directly. **2** without any doubt; firmly: *he put the blame squarely on your shoulders.*
square meal noun a large and satisfying meal.
square measure noun a unit of measurement relating to area.
square number noun the product of a number multiplied by itself, e.g. 1, 4, 9, 16.
square-rigged adjective (of a sailing ship) having the main sails at right angles to the length of the ship.
square root noun a number which produces a specified quantity when multiplied by itself.
squash¹ verb **1** crush or squeeze something so that it becomes flat, soft, or out of shape.

2 force someone or something into a restricted space. **3** put an end to: *he squashed reports that the firm had changed its mind.* •noun **1** a state of being squashed. **2** Brit. a concentrated liquid made from fruit juice and sugar, to which water is added to make a drink. **3** (also **squash rackets**) a game in which two players use rackets to hit a small rubber ball against the walls of a closed court.
– DERIVATIVES **squashy** adjective.
– ORIGIN from QUASH.
squash² noun (pl. same or **squashes**) a gourd with flesh that can be cooked and eaten as a vegetable.
– ORIGIN from a North American Indian language.
squat verb (**squats, squatting, squatted**) **1** crouch or sit with the knees bent and the heels close to the bottom or thighs. **2** unlawfully occupy an uninhabited building or area of land. •adjective (**squatter, squattest**) short and wide or broad. •noun **1** a squatting position. **2** a building occupied unlawfully.
– DERIVATIVES **squatter** noun.
– ORIGIN Old French *esquatir* 'flatten'.
squat thrust noun an exercise in which the legs are thrust backwards to their full extent from a squatting position with the hands on the floor.
squaw /skwaw/ noun offensive an American Indian woman or wife.
– ORIGIN from a North American Indian language.
squawk verb **1** (of a bird) make a loud, harsh noise. **2** say something in a loud, shrill tone. •noun an act of squawking.
– DERIVATIVES **squawker** noun.
– ORIGIN imitating the sound.
squeak noun **1** a short, high-pitched sound or cry. **2** a single communication or sound: *I didn't hear a squeak from him.* •verb **1** make a squeak. **2** say something in a high-pitched tone. **3** informal only just manage to succeed or to achieve something: *the bill squeaked through with just six votes to spare.*
– PHRASES **a narrow squeak** Brit. informal something that is only just achieved.
– DERIVATIVES **squeaker** noun **squeaky** adjective (**squeakier, squeakiest**).
– ORIGIN imitating the sound.
squeaky clean adjective informal **1** completely clean. **2** morally correct; very virtuous.
squeal verb **1** make a long, high-pitched cry or noise. **2** say something in a high-pitched tone. **3** (often **squeal on**) informal inform on someone. **4** informal complain about something. •noun a long, high-pitched cry or noise.
– DERIVATIVES **squealer** noun.
– ORIGIN imitating the sound.
squeamish adjective **1** easily disgusted or made to feel sick. **2** having very firm moral views.
– DERIVATIVES **squeamishly** adverb **squeamishness** noun.
– ORIGIN Old French *escoymos.*
squeegee /skwee-jee/ noun a scraping tool with a rubber-edged blade, used for cleaning windows. •verb (**squeegees, squeegeeing, squeegeed**) clean something with a squeegee.
– ORIGIN from SQUEEZE.

S

squeeze verb 1 firmly press something from opposite or all sides. 2 extract liquid or a soft substance from something by squeezing. 3 (**squeeze in/into/through**) manage to get into or through a restricted space. 4 (**squeeze someone/thing in**) manage to find time for someone or something. 5 obtain by pressure, force, etc.: *a series of confidence tricks designed to squeeze money out of the government.* • noun 1 an act of squeezing or the state of being squeezed. 2 a hug. 3 a small amount of liquid that is squeezed out. 4 a strong financial demand or pressure: *a squeeze on profits.* 5 (usu. **main squeeze**) N. Amer. informal a person's girlfriend or boyfriend.
- PHRASES **put the squeeze on** informal pressurize someone into doing something.
- DERIVATIVES **squeezable** adjective **squeezer** noun.
- ORIGIN unknown.

squeeze box noun informal an accordion or concertina.

squeezy adjective (especially of a container) able to be squeezed to force out the contents.

squelch verb 1 make a soft sucking sound such as that made by treading in thick mud. 2 informal forcefully silence someone or put an end to something. • noun a squelching sound.
- DERIVATIVES **squelchy** adjective.
- ORIGIN imitating the sound.

squib noun 1 a small firework that hisses before exploding. 2 a short piece of satirical writing.
- ORIGIN unknown.

squid noun (pl. same or **squids**) a mollusc that lives in the sea, with a long body, eight arms, and two long tentacles.
- ORIGIN unknown.

squidge verb informal squash or crush something.
- ORIGIN uncertain.

squidgy adjective informal, chiefly Brit. soft and moist.

squiffy adjective (**squiffier, squiffiest**) Brit. informal slightly drunk.
- ORIGIN unknown.

squiggle noun a short line that curls and loops irregularly.
- DERIVATIVES **squiggly** adjective.
- ORIGIN perhaps from **SQUIRM** and **WIGGLE** or **WRIGGLE**.

squill noun 1 (also **sea squill**) a Mediterranean plant with broad leaves and white flowers. 2 a small plant resembling a hyacinth, with clusters of violet-blue or blue-striped flowers.
- ORIGIN Greek *skilla*.

squillion cardinal number informal an indefinite very large number.
- DERIVATIVES **squillionth** ordinal number.
- ORIGIN humorous formation on the pattern of *billion.*

squint verb 1 look at someone or something with partly closed eyes. 2 partly close the eyes. 3 have an eye that looks in a different direction to the other eye. • noun 1 a permanent condition in which one eye does not look in the same direction as the other. 2 informal a quick look.
- DERIVATIVES **squinty** adjective.
- ORIGIN perhaps from Dutch *schuinte* 'slant'.

squire noun 1 a country gentleman, especially the chief landowner in an area. 2 Brit. informal used as a friendly form of address by one man to another. 3 historical a young nobleman acting as an attendant to a knight before becoming a knight himself. • verb (of a man) accompany or escort a woman.
- ORIGIN Old French *esquier* 'esquire'.

squirearchy noun (pl. **squirearchies**) country landowners as a group.
- ORIGIN from **SQUIRE**, on the pattern of words such as *hierarchy.*

squirm verb 1 wriggle or twist the body from side to side, especially from nervousness or discomfort. 2 be embarrassed or ashamed. • noun a wriggling movement.
- DERIVATIVES **squirmy** adjective.
- ORIGIN probably from **WORM**.

squirrel noun an agile rodent with a bushy tail that lives in trees. • verb (**squirrels, squirrelling, squirrelled**; US also **squirrels, squirreling, squirreled**) (**squirrel something away**) hide or keep money or valuables in a safe place.
- ORIGIN Old French *esquireul.*

squirrelly adjective 1 relating to or resembling a squirrel. 2 N. Amer. informal restless or nervous.

squirt verb 1 force out liquid in a thin jet from a small opening. 2 wet someone or something with a jet of liquid. • noun 1 a thin jet of liquid. 2 informal a weak or insignificant person.
- ORIGIN imitating the sound.

squish verb 1 make a soft squelching sound. 2 informal squash something. • noun a soft squelching sound.
- DERIVATIVES **squishy** adjective.
- ORIGIN imitating the sound.

Sr symbol the chemical element strontium.

SRAM abbreviation Electronics static random-access memory.

Sri Lankan /sri lang-kuhn, shri lang-kuhn/ noun a person from Sri Lanka. • adjective relating to Sri Lanka.

SRN abbreviation State Registered Nurse.

SS¹ abbreviation 1 Saints. 2 steamship.

SS² noun the Nazi special police force.
- ORIGIN short for German *Schutzstaffel* 'defence squadron'.

SSE abbreviation south-south-east.

SSP abbreviation (in the UK) statutory sick pay.

SSRI abbreviation selective serotonin reuptake inhibitor, any of a group of antidepressant drugs which prevent the uptake of serotonin in the brain.

SSSI abbreviation (in the UK) Site of Special Scientific Interest.

SSW abbreviation south-south-west.

St abbreviation 1 Saint. 2 (usu. **St.**) Street.

st abbreviation stone (in weight).

stab verb (**stabs, stabbing, stabbed**) 1 thrust a knife or other pointed weapon into someone. 2 make a short, forceful movement with a pointed object: *I stabbed at my salad in irritation.* 3 (of a pain) cause a sudden sharp feeling. • noun 1 an act of stabbing. 2 a sudden sharp feeling or pain. 3 (**a stab at**) informal an attempt to do something.
- PHRASES **stab someone in the back** betray someone.
- DERIVATIVES **stabber** noun.
- ORIGIN unknown.

S

stability noun the state of being stable, steady, or unchanging.

stabilize (or **stabilise**) verb make or become stable, steady, or unchanging.
– DERIVATIVES **stabilization** noun.

stabilizer (or **stabiliser**) noun 1 (**stabilizers**) Brit. a pair of small supporting wheels fitted on a child's bicycle. 2 a device used to stabilize a ship or aircraft. 3 a substance preventing the breakdown of emulsions in food or paint.

stable¹ adjective (**stabler**, **stablest**) 1 not likely to give way or overturn; firmly fixed. 2 not likely to change or fail: *a stable relationship.* 3 not worsening in health after an injury or operation. 4 not easily upset or disturbed; sane and sensible. 5 not liable to undergo chemical decomposition or radioactive decay.
– DERIVATIVES **stably** adverb.
– ORIGIN Latin *stabilis.*

stable² noun 1 a building for housing horses. 2 a place where racehorses are kept and trained. 3 an organization or place that produces particular types of people or things: *the magazine is from the same stable as* Vogue. •verb put or keep a horse in a stable.
– ORIGIN Old French *estable* 'stable, pigsty'.

stablemate noun 1 a horse from the same stable as another. 2 a person or product from the same organization or background as another.

stabling noun accommodation for horses.

staccato /stuh-**kah**-toh/ adverb & adjective Music with each sound or note sharply separated from the others. •noun (pl. **staccatos**) 1 Music a staccato passage or performance. 2 a series of short detached sounds or words.
– ORIGIN Italian, 'detached'.

stack noun 1 a neat pile of objects. 2 a rectangular or cylindrical pile of hay, straw, etc. 3 informal a large quantity of something. 4 a chimney. 5 (also **sea stack**) Brit. a column of rock standing in the sea. •verb 1 arrange things in a stack. 2 fill or cover a place with stacks of things. 3 cause aircraft to fly at different altitudes while waiting to land. 4 shuffle or arrange a pack of cards dishonestly. 5 (**be stacked against/in favour of**) (of a situation) be very likely to produce an unfavourable or favourable outcome for: *the odds were stacked against Fiji in the World Cup.*
– DERIVATIVES **stackable** adjective **stacker** noun.
– ORIGIN Old Norse, 'haystack'.

stadium /**stay**-di-uhm/ noun (pl. **stadiums** or **stadia** /**stay**-di-uh/) an athletic or sports ground with tiers of seats for spectators.
– ORIGIN Greek *stadion* 'racing track'.

staff noun 1 (treated as sing. or pl.) the employees of an organization. 2 (treated as sing. or pl.) a group of officers assisting a commanding officer. 3 a long stick used as a support or weapon. 4 a rod or sceptre held as a sign of office or authority. 5 Music a stave. •verb provide an organization with staff.
– PHRASES **the staff of life** a basic food, especially bread.
– ORIGIN Old English.

staffer noun chiefly N. Amer. a member of a staff, especially of a newspaper.

staff nurse noun Brit. an experienced hospital nurse less senior than a sister or charge nurse.

staff officer noun a military officer serving on the staff of a headquarters or government department.

Staffordshire bull terrier noun a small, stocky breed of terrier with a short, broad head.

staffroom noun chiefly Brit. a common room for teachers in a school or college.

Staffs. abbreviation Staffordshire.

staff sergeant noun a rank of non-commissioned officer in the army, above sergeant and below warrant officer.

stag noun 1 a fully adult male deer. 2 Brit. Stock Exchange a person who applies for shares in a new issue with a view to selling them at once for a profit.
– ORIGIN from an Old Norse word meaning 'male bird'.

stag beetle noun a large dark beetle, the male of which has large branched jaws resembling antlers.

stage noun 1 a part, period, or point in a process: *she was in the early stages of pregnancy.* 2 a raised floor or platform on which actors, entertainers, or speakers perform. 3 (**the stage**) the theatre as a profession or form of entertainment. 4 a part of a journey. 5 an area of public activity: *his aim is to put Latin American art back on the world stage.* 6 a floor or level of a structure. 7 each of two or more sections of a rocket or spacecraft that are jettisoned in turn when their fuel is exhausted. 8 Electronics a part of a circuit containing a single amplifying transistor or valve. •verb 1 present a performance of a play or other show. 2 organize and participate in a public event. 3 cause something dramatic or unexpected to happen.
– PHRASES **set the stage for** prepare the conditions for something to happen.
– DERIVATIVES **stageable** adjective.
– ORIGIN Old French *estage* 'dwelling'.

stagecoach noun a closed horse-drawn vehicle formerly used to carry passengers and often mail along a regular route.

stagecraft noun skill in writing or staging plays.

stage direction noun an instruction in a play script indicating the position or tone of an actor, or specifying sound effects, lighting, etc.

stage door noun an actors' and workmen's entrance from the street to the backstage area of a theatre.

stage fright noun nervousness before or during a performance.

stagehand noun a person dealing with scenery or props during a play.

stage-manage verb 1 arrange and control carefully to produce a particular effect: *he stage-managed his image with astounding success.* 2 be the stage manager of a play or other production.
– DERIVATIVES **stage management** noun.

stage manager noun the person responsible for lighting and other technical arrangements for a stage play.

stage name noun a name used by an actor for

professional purposes.

stage-struck adjective having a passionate wish to become an actor.

stage whisper noun a loud whisper by an actor on stage, intended to be heard by the audience.

stagey adjective variant spelling of **STAGY**.

stagflation noun high inflation combined with high unemployment and stagnant demand in a country's economy.
- ORIGIN from *stagnation* and *inflation*.

stagger verb 1 walk or move unsteadily, as if about to fall. 2 astonish someone greatly. 3 spread payments, events, etc. over a period of time. 4 arrange objects or parts so that they are not in line. •noun an act of staggering.
- ORIGIN Old Norse.

staging noun 1 a way of staging a play or similar production. 2 a temporary platform for working or standing on.

staging post noun a place at which people or vehicles regularly stop during a journey.

stagnant adjective 1 (of water or air) completely still and often having an unpleasant smell. 2 showing little activity: *a stagnant economy.*
- ORIGIN from Latin *stagnare* 'form a pool of standing water'.

stagnate verb 1 stop developing; become inactive: *while the economy has stagnated, individual savings have increased.* 2 (of water or air) become still or stagnant.
- DERIVATIVES **stagnation** noun.

stag night (also N. Amer. **stag party**) noun an all-male celebration, especially one held for a man about to be married.

stagy (also **stagey**) adjective excessively theatrical or exaggerated.
- DERIVATIVES **stagily** adverb **staginess** noun.

staid adjective respectable, serious, and unadventurous.
- ORIGIN former past participle of **STAY¹**.

stain verb 1 mark or discolour something with something that is difficult to remove. 2 damage the reputation of someone or something. 3 colour something with a dye or chemical. •noun 1 a discoloured patch or dirty mark that is difficult to remove. 2 a thing that damages a person's reputation: *I left the court without a stain on my character.* 3 a dye or chemical used to colour materials.
- DERIVATIVES **stainable** adjective **stainer** noun.
- ORIGIN from Old French *desteindre* 'tinge with a different colour'.

stained glass noun coloured glass used to form pictures or designs, typically used for church windows.

stainless adjective unmarked by or resistant to stains.

stainless steel noun a form of steel containing chromium, resistant to tarnishing and rust.

stair noun 1 each of a set of fixed steps. 2 (**stairs**) a set of fixed steps leading from one floor of a building to another.
- ORIGIN from a Germanic word meaning 'climb'.

staircase (also **stairway**) noun a set of stairs and its surrounding structure.

stairclimber noun an exercise machine on which the user simulates the action of climbing a staircase.

stairlift noun a lift in the form of a chair that can be raised or lowered at the edge of a staircase.

stairwell noun a shaft in which a staircase is built.

stake¹ noun 1 a strong post with a point at one end, driven into the ground to support a tree, form part of a fence, etc. 2 (**the stake**) historical a wooden post to which a person was tied before being burned alive. •verb 1 support a plant with a stake. 2 (**stake something out**) state one's position or assert one's rights forcefully. 3 (**stake someone/thing out**) informal keep a place or person under secret observation.
- PHRASES **stake a claim** assert one's right to something.
- ORIGIN Old English.

stake² noun 1 a sum of money gambled. 2 a share or interest in a business or situation. 3 (**stakes**) prize money. 4 (**stakes**) a competitive situation: *one step ahead in the fashion stakes.* •verb gamble money or something of value.
- PHRASES **at stake** 1 at risk. 2 in question.
- ORIGIN perhaps from **STAKE¹**.

stakeholder noun a person with an interest or concern in a business or similar venture. •adjective (of an organization or system) in which all those involved are seen as having an interest in its success: *a stakeholder economy.*
- DERIVATIVES **stakeholding** noun & adjective.

stakeholder pension noun (in the UK) a pension plan which invests the money a person saves and uses the fund to buy a pension from a pension provider when the person retires.

stake-out noun informal a period of secret observation.

Stakhanovite /stuh-**kahn**-uh-vyt/ noun a person who is exceptionally hard-working and enthusiastic.
- ORIGIN from the Russian coal miner Aleksei *Stakhanov.*

stalactite /sta-**luhk**-tyt/ noun a tapering structure hanging from the roof of a cave, formed of calcium salts deposited by dripping water.
- ORIGIN from Greek *stalaktos* 'dripping'.

stalagmite /sta-**luhg**-myt/ noun a tapering column rising from the floor of a cave, formed of calcium salts deposited by dripping water.
- ORIGIN from Greek *stalagma* 'a drop'.

stale adjective (**staler**, **stalest**) 1 (of food) no longer fresh or pleasant to eat. 2 no longer new and interesting: *their marriage had gone stale.* 3 (of a person) no longer performing well because of having done something for too long. •verb make or become stale.
- DERIVATIVES **stalely** adverb **staleness** noun.
- ORIGIN probably from Old French *estaler* 'to halt'.

stalemate noun 1 a situation in which further progress by opposing sides seems impossible. 2 Chess a position counting as a draw, in which a player is not in check but can only move into check. •verb cause a situation to reach stalemate.

S

- ORIGIN from Old French *estale* 'position' + MATE².

Stalinism noun the ideology and policies adopted by the Soviet Communist Party leader and head of state Joseph Stalin, based on dictatorial state control and the pursuit of communism.
- DERIVATIVES **Stalinist** noun & adjective.

stalk¹ noun 1 the main stem of a plant. 2 the attachment or support of a leaf, flower, or fruit. 3 a slender support or stem of an object.
- DERIVATIVES **stalk-like** adjective **stalky** adjective.
- ORIGIN probably from an Old English word meaning 'rung of a ladder, long handle'.

stalk² verb 1 follow someone or something stealthily. 2 harass someone with unwanted and obsessive attention. 3 stride in a proud, stiff, or angry way. 4 chiefly literary move silently or threateningly through a place: *fear stalks the streets.*
- DERIVATIVES **stalker** noun.
- ORIGIN Old English.

stalking horse noun a person or thing that is used to disguise a person's real intentions.
- ORIGIN first referring to a horse used by a hunter to hide behind until within easy range of wildfowl.

stall noun 1 a stand, booth, or compartment for the sale of goods in a market. 2 an individual compartment for an animal in a stable or cowshed. 3 a stable or cowshed. 4 (also **starting stall**) a compartment in which a horse is held before the start of a race. 5 a compartment for one person in a set of toilets or shower cubicles. 6 (**stalls**) Brit. the ground-floor seats in a theatre. 7 a seat in the choir or chancel of a church, enclosed at the back and sides. •verb 1 (of a motor vehicle or its engine) stop running. 2 stop making progress. 3 be vague or indecisive in order to gain time to deal with something: *she was stalling for time.* 4 (of an aircraft) be moving too slowly to allow it to be controlled effectively.
- ORIGIN Old English.

stallholder noun Brit. a person in charge of a market stall.

stallion noun an adult male horse that has not been castrated.
- ORIGIN Old French *estalon.*

stalwart /stawl-wert, stol-wert/ adjective 1 loyal, reliable, and hard-working. 2 dated sturdy and strongly built. •noun a loyal and reliable supporter or member of an organization.
- ORIGIN from Old English words meaning 'place' and 'worth'.

stamen /stay-muhn/ noun the male fertilizing organ of a flower, typically consisting of a pollen-containing anther on a very thin stalk.
- ORIGIN Latin, 'warp in an upright loom, thread'.

stamina noun the ability to keep up physical or mental effort over a long period.
- ORIGIN from Latin, plural of STAMEN in the sense 'threads spun by the Fates'.

stammer verb speak or say something with difficulty, repeating the first letters of words and often pausing. •noun a tendency to stammer.
- DERIVATIVES **stammerer** noun.

- ORIGIN Old English, related to STUMBLE.

stamp verb 1 bring the foot down heavily on the ground or an object. 2 walk with heavy, forceful steps. 3 (**stamp something out**) put an end to something by taking decisive action. 4 press a device against something in order to leave a mark or pattern. 5 (**stamp something on**) fix something in the mind: *the date was stamped on his memory.* 6 stick a postage stamp on a letter or parcel. •noun 1 a small piece of paper that is stuck to a letter or parcel to show that postage has been paid. 2 an instrument for stamping a pattern or mark. 3 a mark or pattern made by a stamp. 4 a distinctive impression or quality: *the whole project has the stamp of authority.* 5 a particular class or type: *he went around with men of his own stamp.* 6 an act of stamping the foot.
- DERIVATIVES **stamper** noun.
- ORIGIN Germanic.

stamp duty noun a duty which must be paid in order for certain documents to be legally recognized.

stampede noun 1 a sudden panicked or excited rush of a group of people or animals. 2 a situation in which a large number of people are trying to respond to something at once: *he tried in vain to stem the stampede towards modernism.* •verb 1 (of animals or people) rush in a sudden mass panic. 2 rush someone into doing something: *she claimed to have been stampeded into making wrong decisions.*
- DERIVATIVES **stampeder** noun.
- ORIGIN Spanish *estampida* 'crash, uproar'.

stamping ground (N. Amer. also **stomping ground**) noun a place that a person regularly visits or spends time at.

stance /stahnss, stanss/ noun 1 the way in which someone stands. 2 an attitude towards something; a standpoint.
- ORIGIN French.

stanch /stawnch/ verb chiefly US variant spelling of STAUNCH².

stanchion /stan-shuhn/ noun an upright bar, post, or frame forming a support or barrier.
- ORIGIN Old French *stanchon.*

stand verb (past and past part. **stood**) 1 be in or rise to an upright position, supported by the feet. 2 place or be situated in a particular position. 3 move in a standing position to a specified place: *I stood aside to let him enter.* 4 be in a particular state or condition: *since gran's death the house had stood empty.* 5 remain motionless or unchanged. 6 remain valid: *my decision stands.* 7 withstand an experience without being damaged. 8 tolerate or like: *I can't stand brandy.* 9 be likely to do something: *investors stood to lose heavily.* 10 adopt a particular attitude towards an issue. 11 Brit. be a candidate in an election. 12 take a particular role: *he stood security for the government's borrowings.* 13 buy a meal or drink for someone. •noun 1 an attitude towards a particular issue: *the party's tough stand on immigration.* 2 a determined effort to hold one's ground or resist something. 3 a rack, base, or item of furniture for holding or displaying something. 4 a large structure for spectators to sit or stand in at different levels. 5 a small stall from which goods are sold or

displayed. **6** a raised platform for a band, orchestra, or speaker. **7 (the stand)** a witness box in a law court. **8** a stopping of movement or progress. **9** a place where vehicles wait for passengers. **10** a group of trees of the same kind.
– PHRASES **stand by 1** watch something bad without becoming involved. **2** support someone or keep a promise. **3** be ready to take action if required. **stand down 1** (also **stand aside**) resign from or leave a job or office. **2** relax after a state of readiness. **stand for 1** be an abbreviation of or symbol for. **2** put up with; tolerate. **stand in** take someone's place; deputize. **stand on** be very concerned to follow correct behaviour: *one doesn't stand on rights when driving in Japan.* **stand on one's own (two) feet** be or become independent. **stand out 1** project or be easily noticeable. **2** be clearly better. **stand to** Military stand ready for an attack. **stand trial** be tried in a court of law. **stand someone up** informal fail to keep a date with someone. **stand up for** speak or act in support of. **stand up to 1** resist someone in a spirited way. **2** resist the harmful effects of.
– ORIGIN Old English.

> USAGE: It is good English to use the present participle **standing** rather than the past participle **stood** with the verb 'to be'; say *we were standing in a line for hours*, not *we were stood in a line for hours.*

stand-alone adjective (of computer hardware or software) able to operate independently of other hardware or software.
standard noun 1 a level of quality or achievement: *the restaurant offers a high standard of service.* **2** a required or accepted level of quality or achievement. **3** something used as a measure in order to make comparisons. **4 (standards)** principles of morally acceptable behaviour. **5** a military or ceremonial flag. **6** a popular tune or song that has become well established. **7** (usu. before another noun) a shrub grafted on an upright stem and trained to grow in the shape of a tree: *a standard rose.* •**adjective 1** used or accepted as normal or average. **2** (of a size, measure, etc.) regularly used or produced. **3** (of a work, writer, etc.) viewed as authoritative and so widely read.
– DERIVATIVES **standardly** adverb.
– ORIGIN Old French *estendart.*
standard-bearer noun 1 a leading figure in a cause or movement. **2** a soldier carrying the flag of a unit, regiment, or army.
Standard Grade noun (in Scotland) an exam equivalent to the GCSE.
standardize (or **standardise**) **verb** make things of the same type have the same features or qualities.
– DERIVATIVES **standardization** noun.
standard lamp noun a lamp with a tall stem whose base stands on the floor.
standard of living noun the amount of money and level of comfort available to a person or community.
standard time noun a uniform time for places in approximately the same longitude.
standby noun (pl. **standbys**) **1** readiness for

duty or immediate action. **2** a person or thing ready to be used in an emergency. •**adjective** (of tickets for a journey or performance) sold only at the last minute if still available.
standee /stan-**dee**/ **noun** a person who is standing rather than seated.
stand-in noun a person who stands in or deputizes for another.
standing noun 1 the position, status, or reputation of someone or something. **2** the length of time that something has existed: *a problem of long standing.* •**adjective 1** remaining in force or use: *a standing invitation.* **2** (of a jump or start of a race) performed from rest or an upright position. **3** (of water) stagnant or still.
– PHRASES **leave someone/thing standing** informal be much better or faster than someone or something.
standing joke noun something that regularly causes amusement.
standing order noun Brit. **1** an instruction to a bank to make regular fixed payments to someone. **2** an order placed on a regular basis with a retailer.
standing ovation noun a period of prolonged applause during which the audience rise to their feet.
standing stone noun another term for **MENHIR**.
stand-off noun a situation in a dispute in which no agreement can be reached.
stand-off half noun Rugby a halfback who forms a link between the scrum half and the three-quarters.
stand-offish adjective informal cold and unfriendly.
standout noun informal, chiefly N. Amer. an outstanding person or thing.
standpipe noun a vertical pipe extending from a water supply, connecting a temporary tap to the mains.
standpoint noun 1 an attitude towards a particular issue. **2** the position from which a person can view a scene or an object.
standstill noun a situation without movement or activity.
stand-up adjective 1 (of comedy or a comedian) performed or performing by telling jokes to an audience. **2** (of a fight or argument) loud or violent. **3** designed to stay upright or erect: *a stand-up collar.* **4** involving or used by people standing up.
stank past of **STINK**.
Stanley knife noun Brit. trademark a utility knife with a short, strong replaceable blade.
– ORIGIN named after the manufacturer, The *Stanley* Rule and Level Company.
stanza /stan-zuh/ **noun** a group of lines forming the basic recurring unit in a poem; a verse.
– ORIGIN Italian, 'standing place, stanza'.
staphylococcus /staf-fi-luh-**kok**-kuhss/ **noun** (pl. **staphylococci** /staf-fi-luh-**kok**-ky/) a bacterium of a group including many kinds that cause pus to be formed.
– ORIGIN from Greek *staphulē* 'bunch of grapes' + *kokkos* 'berry'.
staple¹ noun 1 a small U-shaped piece of wire

S

used to fasten papers together. **2** a small U-shaped metal bar with pointed ends, driven into wood to hold things such as wires in place. • verb secure something with a staple or staples.
– ORIGIN Old English, 'pillar'.

staple[2] noun **1** a main item of trade or production. **2** a main or important element of something. **3** the fibre of cotton or wool considered in terms of its length and fineness. • adjective main or important: *a staple food.*
– ORIGIN from German or Dutch *stapel* 'pillar, emporium'.

stapler noun a device for fastening papers together with staples.

star noun **1** a huge mass of burning gas which is visible as a glowing point in the night sky. **2** a shape with five or six points representing a star, often used to indicate a category of excellence. **3** a famous or talented entertainer or sports player. **4** an outstanding person or thing in a group. **5** Astrology a planet, constellation, etc. considered to influence one's fortunes or personality: *his destiny was written in the stars.* • verb (**stars**, **starring**, **starred**) **1** (of a film, play, etc.) have someone as a leading performer. **2** (of a performer) have a leading role in a film, play, etc. **3** mark, decorate, or cover something with star-shaped marks or objects.
– PHRASES **see stars** seem to see flashes of light as a result of a blow on the head.
– ORIGIN Old English.

star anise noun a small star-shaped fruit with an aniseed flavour, used in Asian cookery.

starboard /star-bord, star-berd/ noun the side of a ship or aircraft on the right when one is facing forward. The opposite of PORT[3].
– ORIGIN Old English, 'rudder side', because early sailing vessels were steered with a paddle on the right side.

starburst noun **1** a pattern of lines or rays radiating from a central point. **2** a period of intense activity in a galaxy involving the formation of stars.

starch noun **1** a carbohydrate which is obtained chiefly from cereals and potatoes and is an important constituent of the human diet. **2** powder or spray made from starch, used to stiffen fabric. • verb stiffen fabric with starch.
– ORIGIN from Old English, 'stiffened'.

starchy adjective (**starchier**, **starchiest**) **1** (of food) containing a lot of starch. **2** informal (of a person) stiff and formal in manner or behaviour.
– DERIVATIVES **starchily** adverb **starchiness** noun.

star-crossed adjective literary fated to be unlucky.

stardom noun the state or status of being a famous or talented entertainer or sports player.

stare verb **1** look fixedly at someone or something with the eyes wide open. **2** (**stare someone out**) look fixedly at someone until they feel forced to look away. • noun an act of staring.
– PHRASES **be staring someone in the face** be obvious.
– DERIVATIVES **starer** noun.
– ORIGIN Old English.

starfish noun (pl. same or **starfishes**) a sea creature having a flattened body with five or more arms.

starfruit noun another term for CARAMBOLA.

stargazer noun informal an astronomer or astrologer.

stark adjective **1** severe or bare in appearance. **2** unpleasantly or sharply clear. **3** complete; sheer: *stark terror.*
– PHRASES **stark naked** completely naked. **stark raving** (or **staring**) **mad** informal completely mad.
– DERIVATIVES **starkly** adverb **starkness** noun.
– ORIGIN Old English, 'unyielding, severe'.

starkers adjective Brit. informal completely naked.

starlet noun informal a promising young actress or performer.

starlight noun light coming from the stars.
– DERIVATIVES **starlit** adjective.

starling noun a songbird with dark shiny plumage.
– ORIGIN Old English.

Star of David noun a six-pointed figure consisting of two interlaced equilateral triangles, used as a Jewish and Israeli symbol.

starry adjective (**starrier**, **starriest**) **1** full of or lit by stars. **2** informal relating to stars in entertainment.

starry-eyed adjective full of unrealistic hopes and dreams about someone or something.

Stars and Bars plural noun (treated as sing.) historical the flag of the Confederate States of America.

Stars and Stripes plural noun (treated as sing.) the national flag of the US.

starship noun (in science fiction) a large manned spaceship for travel between the stars.

star sign noun a sign of the zodiac.

star-spangled adjective informal impressively successful.

star-struck adjective fascinated and very impressed by famous people.

star-studded adjective featuring a number of famous people.

START abbreviation Strategic Arms Reduction Talks.

start verb **1** begin to do, be, happen, or engage in: *she started talking to him.* **2** begin to operate or work. **3** make something happen or operate. **4** begin to move or travel. **5** jump or jerk from surprise. • noun **1** the point at which something begins. **2** an act of beginning. **3** an advantage consisting in having set out in a race or on a journey before one's rivals or opponents. **4** a sudden movement of surprise.
– PHRASES **for a start** in the first place. **start at** cost at least a specified amount. **start out** (or **up**) begin a venture or undertaking. **to start with** as the first thing to be taken into account.
– ORIGIN Old English, 'to caper, leap'.

starter noun **1** a person or thing that starts. **2** chiefly Brit. the first course of a meal. **3** an automatic device for starting a machine. **4** a competitor taking part in a race or game at the start. **5** a topic or question with which to start a discussion or course of study.

S

- PHRASES **for starters** informal first of all. **under starter's orders** waiting for the signal to start a race.

starter home noun a small house or flat designed for people buying their first home.

starting block noun a block against which a runner braces their feet at the start of a race.

starting gate noun a barrier raised at the start of a horse race to ensure that all the competitors start at the same time.

starting price noun the final odds at the start of a horse race.

startle verb make someone feel sudden shock or alarm.
- DERIVATIVES **startled** adjective.
- ORIGIN Old English, 'kick, struggle'.

startling adjective very surprising or remarkable.
- DERIVATIVES **startlingly** adverb.

start-up noun 1 the action of starting something. 2 a newly established business.

star turn noun the main act or performer in a programme.

starve verb 1 suffer or die from hunger. 2 make someone starve by preventing them from eating. 3 (**be starving** or **starved**) informal feel very hungry. 4 (**be starved of**) be deprived of: *the arts are being starved of funds.*
- DERIVATIVES **starvation** noun.
- ORIGIN Old English, 'to die'.

starveling /stah-vling/ adjective old use starving or extremely thin.

stash informal verb store something safely in a secret place. • noun a secret store of something.
- ORIGIN unknown.

stasis /stay-sis/ noun 1 formal or technical a period or state when there is no change or development. 2 Medicine a stopping of the normal flow of a body fluid.
- ORIGIN Greek, 'standing, stoppage'.

state noun 1 the condition of someone or something at a particular time. 2 a nation or territory considered as an organized political community under one government. 3 a community or area forming part of a federal republic. 4 (**the States**) the United States of America. 5 the government of a country. 6 the grand ceremonial procedures associated with monarchy or government: *he was buried in state.* 7 (**a state**) informal an agitated, untidy, or dirty condition. • verb express something definitely or clearly in speech or writing.
- PHRASES **state of affairs** a situation. **state-of-the-art** using the newest ideas and most up-to-date features. **state of emergency** a situation of national danger or disaster in which a government suspends normal constitutional procedures. **state of grace** a state of being free from sin.
- DERIVATIVES **statehood** noun.
- ORIGIN partly a shortening of ESTATE, partly from Latin *status* 'standing'.

statecraft noun the skilful management of state affairs.

State Department noun (in the US) the department of foreign affairs.

state house noun 1 (in the US) the building where the law-making body of a state meets.

2 NZ a private house owned and let by the government.

stateless adjective not recognized as a citizen of any country.

stately adjective (**statelier, stateliest**) dignified, grand, or impressive.
- DERIVATIVES **stateliness** noun.

stately home noun Brit. a large, impressive house occupied or formerly occupied by an aristocratic family.

statement noun 1 a definite or clear expression of something in speech or writing. 2 a formal account of facts or events, especially one given to the police or in court. 3 a document setting out items of debit and credit between a bank or other organization and a customer.

stateroom noun 1 a large room in a palace or public building, for use on formal occasions. 2 a private room on a ship.

state school noun Brit. a school funded and controlled by the state.

state's evidence noun US Law evidence for the prosecution given by a participant in or accomplice to the crime being tried.

stateside adjective & adverb informal relating to, in, or towards the US.

statesman (or **stateswoman**) noun (pl. **statesmen** or **stateswomen**) an experienced and respected political leader.
- DERIVATIVES **statesmanlike** adjective **statesmanship** noun.

static /sta-tik/ adjective 1 not moving, changing, or active: *they believed in a static social order.* 2 Physics concerned with bodies at rest or forces in equilibrium. Often contrasted with DYNAMIC. 3 (of an electric charge) acquired by objects that cannot conduct a current. • noun 1 static electricity. 2 crackling or hissing on a telephone, radio, etc.
- DERIVATIVES **statically** adverb.
- ORIGIN Greek *statikos* 'causing to stand'.

statice /sta-ti-si/ noun a plant with small pink or lilac funnel-shaped flowers, growing mainly in coastal areas.
- ORIGIN Latin.

static electricity noun stationary electric charge produced by friction, causing sparks or crackling or the attraction of dust or hair.

statics plural noun (usu. treated as sing.) the branch of mechanics concerned with bodies at rest and forces in equilibrium.

statin /sta-tin/ noun any of a group of drugs which act to reduce levels of cholesterol in the blood.

station noun 1 a place where passenger trains stop on a railway line, typically with platforms and buildings. 2 a place where a particular activity or service is based: *a radar station.* 3 a broadcasting company. 4 the place where someone or something stands or is placed for a particular purpose or duty. 5 a person's social rank or position. 6 Austral./NZ a large sheep or cattle farm. • verb put in or send to a particular place: *troops were stationed in the town.*
- ORIGIN Latin.

S

stationary adjective **1** not moving. **2** not changing in quantity or condition.

USAGE: Do not confuse **stationary** and **stationery**: **stationary** is an adjective meaning 'not moving or changing' (*the lorry crashed into a stationary car*), while **stationery** is a noun meaning 'paper and other writing materials'.

stationer noun a person who sells stationery.
– ORIGIN Latin *stationarius* 'tradesman at a fixed location'.

stationery noun paper and other materials needed for writing.

stationmaster noun a person in charge of a railway station.

Station of the Cross noun each of a series of fourteen pictures representing incidents during Jesus's progress from Pilate's house to his crucifixion at Calvary.

station wagon noun N. Amer. & Austral./NZ an estate car.

statism /stay-ti-zuhm/ noun a political system in which the state has a great deal of central control over social and economic affairs.
– DERIVATIVES **statist** noun & adjective.

statistic noun a fact or piece of data obtained from a study of a large quantity of numerical information.
– ORIGIN German *Statistik*.

statistical adjective relating to statistics.
– DERIVATIVES **statistically** adverb.

statistics plural noun (treated as sing.) the collection and analysis of large quantities of numerical information.
– DERIVATIVES **statistician** noun.

stats plural noun informal statistics.

statuary /stat-yoo-ri/ noun statues considered as a group.

statue noun a carved or cast figure of a person or animal, especially one that is life-size or larger.
– ORIGIN Latin *statua*.

statuesque /sta-tyuu-esk, sta-chuu-esk/ adjective (of a woman) attractively tall, graceful, and dignified.

statuette noun a small statue.

stature noun **1** a person's natural height when standing. **2** the importance or reputation gained by a person as a result of their ability or achievements: *an architect of international stature*.
– ORIGIN Latin *statura*.

status noun **1** a person's social or professional standing in relation to other people. **2** high rank or social standing. **3** the situation at a particular time during a process. **4** the official classification given to someone or something.
– ORIGIN Latin, 'standing'.

status quo /stay-tuhss kwoh/ noun the existing situation.
– ORIGIN Latin, 'the state in which'.

status symbol noun a possession seen as an indication of a person's wealth or high social or professional status.

statute /sta-tyoot/ noun **1** a written law passed by a parliament or other legislative assembly. **2** a rule of an organization or institution.
– ORIGIN Latin *statutum* 'thing set up'.

statute book noun (the statute book) the whole of a nation's laws.

statute law noun all the written laws of a parliament, country, etc. considered as a group.

statute of limitations noun a law which limits the period in which certain kinds of actions can be brought.

statutory adjective **1** required, permitted, or enacted by law. **2** having come to be required or expected as a result of being done regularly: *the statutory Christmas phone call to his mother.*
– DERIVATIVES **statutorily** adverb.

staunch¹ /stawnch/ adjective very loyal and committed.
– DERIVATIVES **staunchly** adverb.
– ORIGIN Old French *estanche* 'watertight'.

staunch² /stawnch, staanch/ (US also **stanch**) verb stop or restrict the flow of something, especially blood from a wound.
– ORIGIN Old French *estanchier*.

stave noun **1** any of the lengths of wood fixed side by side to make a barrel, bucket, etc. **2** a strong stick, post, or pole. **3** (also **staff**) Music a set of five parallel lines on or between any of which a note is written to indicate its pitch. **4** a verse or stanza of a poem. •verb **1** (past and past part. **staved** or **stove**) (**stave something in**) break something by forcing it inwards or piercing it roughly. **2** (past and past part. **staved**) (**stave something off**) prevent or delay something undesirable: *emergency measures were introduced to stave off a crisis.*
– ORIGIN from *staves*, former plural of **STAFF**.

stay¹ verb **1** remain in the same place. **2** remain in a particular state or position: *inflation will stay down.* **3** live somewhere temporarily as a visitor or guest. **4** Scottish & S. African live somewhere permanently. **5** stop, delay, or prevent something. •noun **1** a period of staying somewhere. **2** a suspension or postponement of judicial or legal proceedings: *a stay of execution.* **3** (**stays**) historical a corset made of two pieces laced together and stiffened by strips of whalebone.
– PHRASES **stay the course** (or **distance**) **1** keep going to the end of a race or contest. **2** continue with a difficult task or activity to the end. **stay on** continue to study, work, or be somewhere after others have left. **stay over** stay for the night as a visitor or guest. **stay put** remain somewhere without moving.
– DERIVATIVES **stayer** noun.
– ORIGIN Old French *ester*.

stay² noun **1** a large rope, wire, or rod used to support a ship's mast or other upright pole. **2** a supporting wire or cable on an aircraft.
– ORIGIN Old English.

staying power noun endurance or stamina.

staysail /stay-sayl, stay-suhl/ noun a triangular sail fastened on a stay.

STD abbreviation **1** sexually transmitted disease. **2** Brit. subscriber trunk dialling, the automatic connection of trunk (long-distance) calls by dialling without the help of an operator.

stead noun (in phrase **in someone's**/**something's stead**) instead of someone or something: *she was appointed in his stead.*
– PHRASES **stand someone in good stead** be useful to someone over time or in the future.

– ORIGIN Old English.

steadfast adjective completely unwavering in one's attitudes or aims.
– DERIVATIVES **steadfastly** adverb **steadfastness** noun.
– ORIGIN Old English, 'standing firm'.

steading noun Scottish & N. English a farmstead.

steady adjective (**steadier, steadiest**) **1** firmly fixed, supported, or balanced. **2** not faltering or wavering: *a steady gaze*. **3** sensible and reliable. **4** regular, even, and continuous in development, frequency, or strength: *a steady decline in the national birth rate*. • verb (**steadies, steadying, steadied**) make or become steady. • exclamation (also **steady on!**) a warning to keep calm or take care.
– PHRASES **go steady** informal have a regular romantic or sexual relationship with someone.
– DERIVATIVES **steadily** adverb **steadiness** noun.
– ORIGIN from STEAD.

steak noun **1** high-quality beef from the hindquarters of the animal, cut into thick slices for grilling or frying. **2** a thick slice of other meat or fish. **3** poorer-quality beef for braising or stewing.
– ORIGIN Old Norse.

steak tartare noun a dish consisting of raw minced steak mixed with raw egg.

steal verb (past **stole**; past part. **stolen**) **1** take something without permission or legal right and without intending to return it. **2** move somewhere quietly or surreptitiously. • noun informal a bargain.
– PHRASES **steal a look** (or **glance**) take a quick and surreptitious look at someone or something. **steal a march on** gain an advantage over someone by acting before they do. **steal the show** attract the most attention and praise. **steal someone's thunder** win the praise or attention expected by someone else by acting or speaking before them.
– DERIVATIVES **stealer** noun.
– ORIGIN Old English.

stealth noun cautious and surreptitious action or movement. • adjective (of aircraft) designed to be difficult to detect by radar or sonar: *a stealth bomber*.
– ORIGIN first in the sense 'theft': probably related to STEAL.

stealth tax noun a tax charged in such a way that it is not noticed as a tax.

stealthy adjective (**stealthier, stealthiest**) cautious and surreptitious.
– DERIVATIVES **stealthily** adverb **stealthiness** noun.

steam noun **1** the hot vapour into which water is converted when heated, which condenses in the air into a mist of minute water droplets. **2** power for machines produced by steam under pressure. **3** energy or force of movement; momentum: *the dispute gathered steam*. • verb **1** give off or produce steam. **2** (**steam up**) mist over with steam. **3** cook food by heating it in steam from boiling water. **4** clean or treat something with steam. **5** (of a ship or train) travel somewhere under steam power. **6** informal move somewhere rapidly or forcefully. **7** (**be/get steamed up**) informal be or become very agitated or angry.
– PHRASES **get up** (or **pick up**) **steam 1** generate enough pressure to drive a steam engine. **2** (of

an activity, project, etc.) gradually gain momentum. **let off steam** informal get rid of pent-up energy or strong emotion. **run out of steam** informal lose momentum or enthusiasm. **under one's own steam** without help from other people.
– ORIGIN Old English.

steam bath noun a room filled with hot steam for cleaning and refreshing the body.

steamboat noun a boat propelled by a steam engine, especially (in the US) a paddle-wheel craft of a type used on rivers in the 19th century.

steam engine noun **1** an engine that uses the expansion or rapid condensation of steam to generate power. **2** a steam locomotive.

steamer noun **1** a ship or boat powered by steam. **2** a type of saucepan in which food can be steamed.

steam iron noun an electric iron that gives off steam from holes in its flat surface.

steamroller noun a heavy, slow-moving vehicle with a roller, used to flatten the surfaces of roads during construction. • verb (also **steamroll**) **1** force someone into doing or accepting something. **2** (of a government or other authority) forcibly pass a law by limiting debate or overriding opposition.

steamship noun a ship that is powered by a steam engine.

steamy adjective (**steamier, steamiest**) **1** producing, filled with, or clouded with steam. **2** hot and humid. **3** informal involving passionate sexual activity.
– DERIVATIVES **steamily** adverb **steaminess** noun.

stearic acid /stee-uh-rik/ noun a solid saturated fatty acid obtained from animal or vegetable fats.
– ORIGIN from Greek *stear* 'tallow'.

steatite /stee-uh-tyt/ noun the mineral talc occurring especially as soapstone.
– ORIGIN Greek *steatitēs*.

steed noun old use or literary a horse.
– ORIGIN Old English.

steel noun **1** a hard, strong grey or bluish-grey alloy of iron with carbon and usually other elements, used as a structural material and in manufacturing. **2** strength and determination: *nerves of steel*. • verb mentally prepare oneself to do or face something difficult.
– ORIGIN Old English.

steel band noun a band that plays music on steel drums.

steel drum (also **steel pan**) noun a percussion instrument made out of an oil drum with one end beaten down and divided into sections to give different notes.

steel wool noun fine strands of steel matted together into a mass, used for polishing or cleaning hard surfaces.

steelwork noun articles made of steel.

steelworks plural noun (usu. treated as sing.) a factory where steel is manufactured.

steely adjective (**steelier, steeliest**) **1** resembling steel in colour, brightness, or strength. **2** coldly determined.
– DERIVATIVES **steeliness** noun.

steelyard noun a weighing device that has a short arm taking the item to be weighed and a

S

long graduated arm along which a weight is moved until it balances.
– ORIGIN from STEEL + YARD¹ in the former sense 'rod, measuring stick'.

steep¹ adjective **1** rising or falling sharply; almost perpendicular. **2** (of a rise or fall in an amount) very large or rapid. **3** informal (of a price or demand) not reasonable; excessive. •noun chiefly literary a steep mountain slope.
– DERIVATIVES **steeply** adverb **steepness** noun.
– ORIGIN Old English, 'extending to a great height'.

steep² verb **1** soak something in water or other liquid. **2** (be steeped in) be filled with a particular quality: a castle steeped in history.
– ORIGIN Germanic.

steepen verb become or make steeper.

steeple noun **1** a church tower and spire. **2** a spire on the top of a church tower or roof. •verb place the fingers or hands together so that they form an upward-pointing V-shape.
– ORIGIN Old English.

steeplechase noun **1** a horse race run on a racecourse which has ditches and hedges as jumps. **2** a running race in which runners must clear hurdles and water jumps.
– DERIVATIVES **steeplechaser** noun **steeplechasing** noun.
– ORIGIN so named because the race was originally run across country, with a steeple marking the finishing point.

steeplejack noun a person who climbs tall structures such as chimneys and steeples in order to carry out repairs.

steer¹ verb **1** guide or control the movement of a vehicle, ship, or aircraft. **2** direct or guide: he steered her to a chair. •noun informal a piece of advice or information.
– PHRASES **steer clear of** take care to avoid.
– DERIVATIVES **steerable** adjective **steerer** noun.
– ORIGIN Old English.

steer² noun a bullock.
– ORIGIN Old English.

steerage noun **1** historical the cheapest accommodation in a ship. **2** old use or literary the action of steering a boat.

steering noun the mechanism in a vehicle, ship, or aircraft which allows it to be steered.

steering column noun a shaft that connects the steering wheel of a vehicle to the rest of the steering mechanism.

steering committee (also **steering group**) noun a committee that decides on the priorities or order of business of an organization.

steering wheel noun a wheel that a driver turns in order to steer a vehicle.

steersman noun (pl. **steersmen**) a person who steers a boat or ship.

stegosaur /steg-uh-sor/ (also **stegosaurus** /steg-uh-sor-ruhss/) noun a plant-eating dinosaur with a double row of large bony plates along the back.
– ORIGIN from Greek stegē 'covering' + sauros 'lizard'.

stein /styn/ noun a large earthenware beer mug.
– ORIGIN German, 'stone'.

stela /stee-luh/ (also **stele** /steel, stee-lee/) noun (pl. **stelae** /stee-lee/) Archaeology an upright stone slab or column with an inscription or design.
– ORIGIN Greek.

stellar /stel-ler/ adjective **1** relating to a star or stars. **2** informal featuring or having the quality of a star performer. **3** informal excellent; outstanding.
– ORIGIN from Latin stella 'star'.

stem¹ noun **1** the main body or stalk of a plant or shrub. **2** the stalk supporting a fruit, flower, or leaf. **3** a long, thin supporting or main section of something, such as that of a wine glass or tobacco pipe. **4** a vertical stroke in a letter or musical note. **5** Grammar the root or main part of a word, to which other elements are added. **6** the main upright timber or metal piece at the bow of a ship. •verb (**stems, stemming, stemmed**) (**stem from**) come from or be caused by: depression stemming from domestic difficulties.
– PHRASES **from stem to stern** from one end to the other, especially of a ship.
– ORIGIN Old English.

stem² verb (**stems, stemming, stemmed**) stop or restrict the flow or progress of something.
– ORIGIN Old Norse.

stem cell noun an undifferentiated cell within an organism that can divide to produce more cells of the same kind or develop into a specialized cell.

stem ginger noun pieces of crystallized or preserved ginger.

stem stitch noun an embroidery stitch forming a continuous line of long, overlapping stitches.

stench noun a strong and very unpleasant smell.
– ORIGIN Old English.

stencil noun a thin sheet of card, plastic, or metal with a pattern or letters cut out of it, used to produce a design on the surface below by applying ink or paint through the holes. •verb (**stencils, stencilling, stencilled**; US **stencils, stenciling, stenciled**) decorate something with a stencil.
– ORIGIN from Old French estanceler 'decorate brightly'.

Sten gun noun a type of lightweight British sub-machine gun.
– ORIGIN from the initials of the inventors' surnames, Shepherd and Turpin, suggested by BREN GUN.

stenographer /sti-nog-ruh-fer/ noun N. Amer. a shorthand typist.
– ORIGIN from Greek stenos 'narrow'.

stentorian /sten-tor-i-uhn/ adjective (of a person's voice) loud and powerful.
– ORIGIN from Stentor, a herald in the Trojan War.

step noun **1** an act of lifting and putting down the foot or alternate feet, as in walking. **2** the distance covered by a step. **3** a flat surface on which to place one's foot when moving from one level to another. **4** a measure or action taken to deal with or achieve something: the local authority must take steps to protect the children. **5** a position or grade in a scale or series. **6** (**steps** or **a pair of steps**) Brit. a stepladder. **7** a block fixed to a boat's keel to take the base of a mast or other fitting. •verb (**steps, stepping, stepped**) lift and put down

one's foot or alternate feet.
– PHRASES **in** (or **out of**) **step** 1 walking, marching, or dancing in the same (or a different) rhythm and pace as other people. 2 conforming (or not conforming) to what other people are doing or thinking. **mind** (or **watch**) **one's step** walk or act carefully. **step down** (or **aside**) withdraw or resign from a position or job. **step forward** offer one's help or services. **step in** 1 become involved in a difficult situation, especially in order to help. 2 act as a substitute for someone. **step on it** informal go faster. **step out of line** behave inappropriately or disobediently. **step something up** increase the amount, speed, or strength of something.
– ORIGIN Old English.

step- combining form referring to a relationship resulting from a remarriage: *stepmother.*
– ORIGIN Old English.

step aerobics plural noun a type of aerobics that involves stepping up on to and down from a portable block.

stepbrother noun a son of one's step-parent by a marriage other than that with one's own father or mother.

step change noun (in business or politics) a significant change in policy or attitude, especially one that results in an improvement or increase.

stepchild noun (pl. **stepchildren**) a child of one's husband or wife by a previous marriage.

stepdaughter noun a daughter of one's husband or wife by a previous marriage.

stepfather noun a man who is married to one's mother after the divorce of one's parents or the death of one's father.

stephanotis /stef-fuh-**noh**-tiss/ noun a climbing plant with fragrant waxy white flowers.
– ORIGIN Greek, 'fit for a wreath'.

stepladder noun a short folding ladder with flat steps and a small platform.

stepmother noun a woman who is married to one's father after the divorce of one's parents or the death of one's mother.

steppe /step/ noun a large area of flat grassland without trees in SE Europe or Siberia.
– ORIGIN Russian *step'*.

stepping stone noun 1 a raised stone on which to step when crossing a stream or muddy area. 2 an action that helps someone make progress towards a goal.

stepsister noun a daughter of one's step-parent by a marriage other than that with one's own father or mother.

stepson noun a son of one's husband or wife by a previous marriage.

stereo /ste-ri-oh/ noun (pl. **stereos**) 1 sound that is directed through two or more speakers so that it seems to surround the listener and come from more than one source. 2 a CD player, record player, etc. that has two or more speakers and produces this type of sound.
•adjective relating to or producing this type of sound.

stereophonic adjective full form of **STEREO**.
– ORIGIN from Greek *stereos* 'solid'.

stereoscope noun a device by which two

photographs of the same object taken at slightly different angles are viewed together, creating a three-dimensional impression.

stereoscopic noun 1 able to see objects as three-dimensional forms. 2 relating to a stereoscope.

stereotype noun a widely held but oversimplified idea of the typical characteristics of a person or thing. •verb view or represent someone or something as a stereotype.

stereotypical adjective relating to or resembling a stereotype: *stereotypical images of femininity.*
– DERIVATIVES **stereotypically** adverb.

sterile adjective 1 not able to produce children, young, crops, or fruit. 2 free from bacteria or other living microorganisms. 3 lacking imagination, creativity, or excitement.
– DERIVATIVES **sterility** noun.
– ORIGIN Latin *sterilis.*

sterilize (or **sterilise**) verb 1 make something free from bacteria. 2 make a person or animal unable to produce offspring by removing or blocking the sex organs.
– DERIVATIVES **sterilization** noun.

sterling noun British money. •adjective excellent; of great value: *they do sterling work for charity.*
– ORIGIN probably from Old English *steorra* 'star' (because some early Norman pennies bore a small star).

sterling silver noun silver of at least 92¼ per cent purity.

stern¹ adjective 1 serious and strict. 2 severe; demanding: *the team are facing a stern test.*
– DERIVATIVES **sternly** adverb **sternness** noun.
– ORIGIN Old English.

stern² noun the rearmost part of a ship or boat.
– ORIGIN probably from an Old Norse word meaning 'steering'.

sternum /ster-nuhm/ noun (pl. **sternums** or **sterna** /ster-nuh/) the breastbone.
– ORIGIN Greek *sternon* 'chest'.

steroid /ste-royd, steer-oyd/ noun 1 any of a large class of organic compounds that includes certain hormones and vitamins. 2 an anabolic steroid.
– DERIVATIVES **steroidal** adjective.
– ORIGIN from **STEROL**.

sterol /steer-ol, ste-rol/ noun Biochemistry any of a group of naturally occurring unsaturated steroid alcohols, such as cholesterol.
– ORIGIN from the ending of words such as CHOLESTEROL.

stertorous /ster-tuh-ruhss/ adjective (of breathing) noisy and laboured.
– DERIVATIVES **stertorously** adverb.
– ORIGIN from Latin *stertere* 'to snore'.

stet verb let it stand (used as an instruction on a printed proof to ignore a correction).
– ORIGIN Latin.

stethoscope /steth-uh-skohp/ noun a medical instrument for listening to the action of someone's heart or breathing, having a small disc that is placed against the chest and two tubes connected to earpieces.
– ORIGIN from Greek *stēthos* 'breast' + *skopein* 'look at'.

S

Stetson /stet-suhn/ noun (trademark in the US) a hat with a high crown and a very wide brim, traditionally worn by cowboys in the US.
– ORIGIN named after the American hat manufacturer John B. *Stetson*.

stevedore /stee-vuh-dor/ noun a person employed at a dock to load and unload ships.
– ORIGIN Spanish *estivador*.

stew noun **1** a dish of meat and vegetables cooked slowly in liquid in a closed dish. **2** informal a state of anxiety or agitation. **3** old use a brothel. •verb **1** cook food slowly in liquid in a closed dish. **2** Brit. (of tea) become strong and bitter with prolonged brewing. **3** informal be in a heated or stuffy atmosphere. **4** informal be in anxious or agitated.
– PHRASES **stew in one's own juice** informal be left to suffer the consequences of one's own actions.
– ORIGIN Old French *estuve*.

steward noun **1** a person who looks after the passengers on a ship or aircraft. **2** an official who supervises arrangements at a large public event. **3** a person employed to manage a large house or estate. **4** a person responsible for supplies of food to a college, club, etc. **5** chiefly historical an officer of the British royal household, especially an administrator of Crown estates. •verb act as a steward of something.
– DERIVATIVES **stewardship** noun.
– ORIGIN Old English.

stewardess noun a woman who looks after the passengers on a ship or aircraft.

stick¹ noun **1** a thin piece of wood that has fallen or been cut off a tree. **2** a piece of trimmed wood used for support in walking or as a weapon. **3** (in hockey, polo, etc.) a long, thin implement used to hit or direct the ball or puck. **4** a long, thin object or piece: *a stick of dynamite.* **5** Brit. informal harsh criticism. **6** (**the sticks**) informal, derogatory country areas far from towns or cities. **7** informal, dated a person of a particular kind: *Janet's not a bad old stick.*
– PHRASES **up sticks** Brit. informal go to live elsewhere. [from nautical slang *to up sticks* 'to set up a boat's mast' (ready for departure).]
– ORIGIN Old English.

stick² verb (past and past part. **stuck**) **1** (**stick something in/into/through**) insert or push a pointed object into or through something. **2** (**stick in/into/through**) (of a pointed object) be or remain fixed with its point embedded in something. **3** protrude or extend in a particular direction: *his front teeth stick out.* **4** fasten or become fastened to something: *she stuck the stamp on the envelope.* **5** informal put something somewhere in a quick or careless way. **6** (**be stuck**) be fixed in a particular position or unable to move or be moved. **7** (**be stuck**) be unable to continue with a task or find the answer or solution. **8** Brit. informal accept or tolerate: *I can't stick him.*
– PHRASES **be stuck for** be at a loss for or in need of something. **be stuck on** informal be infatuated with. **be stuck with** informal be unable to get rid of or escape from. **get stuck in** (or **into**) Brit. informal start doing something with determination. **stick around** informal remain in or near a place. **stick at** informal

persevere with something. **stick by** continue to support or be loyal to someone. **stick in one's throat** (or **craw**) be difficult or impossible to accept. **stick it out** informal put up with or persevere with something difficult or unpleasant. **stick one's neck out** informal risk criticism or anger by acting or speaking boldly. **stick out** be extremely noticeable. **stick to** continue doing or using something rather than changing to something else: *I'll stick to bitter lemon.* **stick together** informal (of two or more people) support and remain loyal to each other. **stick up for** support or defend a person or cause.
– ORIGIN Old English.

sticker noun a sticky label or notice.

sticking point noun an obstacle which prevents progress towards an agreement or goal.

stick insect noun a long, thin, slow-moving insect that resembles a twig.

stick-in-the-mud noun informal a person who is unwilling to try anything new or exciting.

stickleback noun a small freshwater or coastal fish with sharp spines along its back.
– ORIGIN from Old English words meaning 'thorn, sting' + 'back'.

stickler noun a person who insists on a certain quality or type of behaviour: *Susan was a stickler for punctuality.*
– ORIGIN from Old English, 'set in order'.

stick shift noun N. Amer. a gear lever or manual gearbox.

stick-up noun informal an armed robbery in which a gun is used to threaten people.

sticky adjective (**stickier, stickiest**) **1** tending or designed to stick to things on contact; adhesive. **2** (of a substance) like glue in texture. **3** (of the weather) hot and humid; muggy. **4** informal difficult or awkward: *the relationship is going through a sticky patch.* •noun (pl. **stickies**) a piece of paper with an adhesive strip on one side, used for leaving notes.
– PHRASES **come to a sticky end** informal be led by one's own actions to disaster or an unpleasant death.
– DERIVATIVES **stickily** adverb **stickiness** noun.

stiff adjective **1** not easily bent; rigid. **2** not moving freely; difficult to turn or operate. **3** unable to move easily and without pain. **4** (of a person or their manner) not relaxed or friendly. **5** severe or difficult: *the company faces stiff competition for the contracts.* **6** (of an alcoholic drink) strong. **7** (—— **stiff**) informal having a particular unpleasant feeling to an extreme extent: *scared stiff.* •noun informal a dead body.
– PHRASES **stiff upper lip** the tendency to endure difficulty without complaining or showing one's feelings.
– DERIVATIVES **stiffly** adverb **stiffness** noun.
– ORIGIN Old English.

stiffen verb **1** make or become stiff. **2** make or become stronger.
– DERIVATIVES **stiffener** noun.

stiff-necked adjective proud and stubborn.

stifle¹ verb **1** prevent someone from breathing freely. **2** smother or suppress: *she stifled a giggle.*

stoned adjective informal strongly affected by drugs or alcohol.

stone-faced adjective informal revealing no emotions through the expressions of the face.

stoneground adjective (of flour) ground with millstones.

stonemason noun a person who cuts, prepares, and builds with stone.

stoner noun informal a person who regularly takes drugs, especially cannabis.

stonewall verb 1 delay or block a person or process by refusing to answer questions or by giving evasive replies. 2 Cricket bat very defensively.

stoneware noun a type of hard and impermeable pottery.

stonewashed (also **stonewash**) adjective (of a garment or fabric) washed with small stones to produce a worn or faded appearance.

stonework noun the parts of a building that are made of stone.

stonker noun Brit. informal something very large or impressive of its kind.

– DERIVATIVES **stonking** adjective.
– ORIGIN from military slang *stonk* 'a concentrated artillery bombardment'.

stony adjective (**stonier**, **stoniest**) 1 full of stones. 2 made of or resembling stone. 3 cold and unfeeling: *a stony glare*.

– PHRASES **fall on stony ground** (of words or a suggestion) be ignored or badly received. [with reference to the parable of the sower in the Gospel of Matthew.]
– DERIVATIVES **stonily** adverb.

stony broke adjective Brit. informal having no money at all.

stood past and past participle of **STAND**.

stooge noun informal 1 derogatory a less important person used by another to do routine or unpleasant work. 2 a performer whose act involves being the butt of a comedian's jokes.

– ORIGIN unknown.

stook /stuuk, stook/ noun Brit. a group of sheaves of grain stood on end in a field.

– ORIGIN German *stūke*.

stool noun 1 a seat without a back or arms. 2 chiefly Medicine a piece of faeces.

– PHRASES **fall between two stools** Brit. fail to be either of two satisfactory alternatives.
– ORIGIN Old English.

stool pigeon noun informal a police informer.

– ORIGIN from the former use of a pigeon fixed to a stool as a decoy.

stoop[1] verb 1 bend the head or body forwards and downwards. 2 have the head and shoulders permanently bent forwards. 3 lower one's moral standards to do something wrong: *Craig wouldn't stoop to thieving*. •noun a stooping posture.

– ORIGIN Old English.

stoop[2] noun N. Amer. a porch with steps in front of a building.

– ORIGIN Dutch *stoep*.

stooshie /stoo-shi/ (also **stushie**) noun Scottish informal a row or fracas.

– ORIGIN uncertain.

stop verb (**stops**, **stopping**, **stopped**) 1 come or bring to an end. 2 prevent something from happening, moving, or operating. 3 prevent

someone from doing something. 4 no longer move or operate: *my watch has stopped*. 5 (of a bus or train) call at a particular place to pick up or set down passengers. 6 Brit. informal stay somewhere for a short time. 7 block or close up a hole or leak. 8 withhold or deduct: *they stopped the strikers' wages*. 9 ask a bank to withhold payment on a cheque. 10 obtain the required pitch from the string of a musical instrument by pressing at the appropriate point with the finger. •noun 1 an act of stopping. 2 a place where a bus or train regularly stops. 3 an object or part of a mechanism which prevents movement. 4 a set of organ pipes of a particular tone and range of pitch. 5 a knob which controls such a set of organ pipes.

– PHRASES **pull out all the stops** make a very great effort to achieve something. [with reference to the stops of an organ.] **stop off** (or **over**) pay a short visit to a place on the way to somewhere else.
– ORIGIN Old English.

stopcock noun an externally operated valve regulating the flow of a liquid or gas through a pipe.

stopgap noun a temporary solution or substitute.

stop-motion noun a technique of film animation in which the camera is repeatedly stopped and started to give the impression of movement.

stopover noun a break in a journey.

stoppage noun 1 an instance of stopping. 2 an instance of industrial action. 3 a blockage. 4 (**stoppages**) Brit. deductions from wages by an employer for tax, National Insurance, etc.

stoppage time noun another term for **INJURY TIME**.

stopper noun 1 a plug for sealing a container. 2 a person or thing that stops something: *a conversation stopper*. •verb seal a container with a stopper.

stop press noun Brit. late news added to a newspaper or magazine either just before printing or during printing.

stopwatch noun a special watch with buttons that start and stop the display, used to time races.

storage noun 1 the action of storing something. 2 space available for storing: *w... put most of the furniture into storage*.

storage heater noun Brit. an electric heat... that stores up heat during the night an... releases it during the day.

store noun 1 a quantity or supply of s... kept for use as needed. 2 Brit. a large... selling different types of goods. 3 ... a shop. 4 a place where things are... future use or sale: *a grain store*. ... supplies of equipment and food... by members of an army, navy,... institution. 6 Brit. a computer... 1 keep for future use: *a sma*... storing furniture. 2 enter or... in the memory of a comp... **something up**) fail to d... especially when this re...problems.

– PHRASES **in store** ab...

– ORIGIN perhaps from Old French *estouffer*.

stifle[2] noun a joint in the legs of horses and other animals, equivalent to the knee in humans.

– ORIGIN unknown.

stifling adjective unpleasantly hot and stuffy.
– DERIVATIVES **stiflingly** adverb.

stigma /stig-muh/ noun (pl. **stigmas** or in sense 2 **stigmata** /stig-mah-tuh, stig-muh-tuh/) 1 a mark or sign of disgrace. 2 (**stigmata**) (in Christian tradition) marks on a person's body corresponding to those left on Jesus's body by the Crucifixion. 3 the part of a plant's pistil that receives the pollen during pollination.

– ORIGIN Greek, 'a mark made by a pointed instrument, a dot'.

stigmatic adjective relating to a stigma or stigmas. •noun a person with stigmata.

stigmatize (or **stigmatise**) verb regard or treat someone or something as worthy of disgrace or great disapproval.

– DERIVATIVES **stigmatization** noun.

stile noun an arrangement of steps set into a fence or wall that allows people to climb over.

– ORIGIN Old English.

stiletto noun (pl. **stilettos**) 1 chiefly Brit. a thin, high tapering heel on a woman's shoe. 2 a short dagger with a tapering blade.

– ORIGIN Italian, 'little dagger'.

still[1] adjective 1 not moving. 2 (of air or water) not disturbed by wind, sound, or currents. 3 Brit. (of a drink) not fizzy. •noun 1 a state of deep and quiet calm. 2 a photograph or a single shot from a cinema film. •adverb 1 even now or at a particular time. 2 nevertheless. 3 even: *better still*. •verb make or become still.

– DERIVATIVES **stillness** noun.
– ORIGIN Old English.

still[2] noun a piece of equipment for distilling alcoholic drinks such as whisky.

– ORIGIN from **DISTIL**.

stillbirth noun the birth of a baby that has died in the womb.

stillborn adjective 1 (of a baby) born dead. 2 (of a proposal or plan) having failed to develop or succeed.

still life noun (pl. **still lifes**) a painting or drawing of an arrangement of objects such as flowers or fruit.

stilt noun 1 either of a pair of upright poles with supports for the feet enabling the user to walk raised above the ground. 2 each of a set of posts supporting a building. 3 a wading bird with very long, slender legs.

– ORIGIN Germanic.

stilted adjective (of speech or writing) not natural, relaxed, or flowing easily.

– DERIVATIVES **stiltedly** adverb **stiltedness** noun.

Stilton noun trademark a kind of strong, rich blue cheese.

– ORIGIN so named because it was formerly sold in *Stilton*, Cambridgeshire.

stimulant noun 1 a substance that acts to increase levels of physiological or nervous activity in the body. 2 something that increases activity, interest, or enthusiasm. •adjective acting as a stimulant.

stimulate verb 1 help something to develop or become more active: *policies designed to*

stimulate economic growth. 2 encourage or arouse interest or enthusiasm in someone. 3 raise levels of physiological or nervous activity in the body.

– DERIVATIVES **stimulation** noun **stimulator** noun **stimulatory** adjective.
– ORIGIN Latin *stimulare* 'urge, goad'.

stimulus /stim-yuu-luhss/ noun (pl. **stimuli** /stim-yuu-ly, stim-yuu-lee/) 1 something that causes a specific reaction in an organ or tissue of the body. 2 something that encourages activity, interest, or enthusiasm.

– ORIGIN Latin, 'goad, incentive'.

sting noun 1 a small sharp-pointed organ of an insect, capable of inflicting a painful wound by injecting poison. 2 any of a number of minute hairs on certain plants, causing inflammation if touched. 3 a wound from a sting. 4 a sharp tingling sensation or hurtful effect. 5 informal a carefully planned undercover operation. •verb (past and past part. **stung**) 1 wound someone or something with a sting. 2 produce a stinging sensation. 3 make someone feel angry or upset. 4 (**sting someone into**) provoke someone to do something by causing annoyance or offence. 5 informal swindle or overcharge someone.

– PHRASES **sting in the tail** an unexpected and unpleasant end to something.
– DERIVATIVES **stinger** noun.
– ORIGIN Old English.

stinging nettle noun a nettle covered in stinging hairs.

stingray noun a ray (fish) with a long poisonous serrated spine at the base of the tail.

stingy /stin-ji/ adjective (**stingier**, **stingiest**) informal not generous; mean.

– DERIVATIVES **stingily** adverb **stinginess** noun.
– ORIGIN perhaps a dialect variant of **STING**.

stink verb (past **stank** or **stunk**; past part. **stunk**) 1 have a strong, unpleasant smell. 2 informal seem very bad, unpleasant, or dishonest. •noun 1 a strong, unpleasant smell. 2 informal a row or fuss.

– ORIGIN Old English.

stink bomb noun a small container that when broken releases a substance with a very unpleasant smell.

stinker noun informal a very unpleasant person or thing.

stinkhorn noun a fungus with a rounded head that turns into a foul-smelling slimy substance containing the spores.

stinking adjective 1 smelling very unpleasant. 2 informal very bad or unpleasant. •adverb informal extremely: *stinking rich*.

stinky adjective (**stinkier**, **stinkiest**) informal having a strong, unpleasant smell.

stint verb (also **stint on**) be very economical or mean about spending or providing something: *he doesn't stint on wining and dining*. •noun 1 a period of work: *his career included a stint as a musician*. 2 limited supply or effort.

– ORIGIN Old English, 'make blunt'.

stipend /sty-pend/ noun a fixed regular sum paid as a salary or allowance to a clergyman, teacher, or public official.

– ORIGIN Latin *stipendium*.

stipendiary /sty-**pen**-di-uh-ri/ adjective

S

1 receiving a stipend; working for pay rather than voluntarily. **2** relating to a stipend.

stipple verb **1** mark a surface with numerous small dots or specks. **2** produce a decorative effect on paint or other material by roughening its surface when wet.
– ORIGIN Dutch *stippelen* 'to prick'.

stipulate /stip-yuu-layt/ verb demand or specify something as part of a bargain or agreement.
– DERIVATIVES **stipulation** noun.
– ORIGIN Latin *stipulari* 'demand as a formal promise'.

stir[1] verb (**stirs, stirring, stirred**) **1** move an implement round and round in a liquid or soft substance to mix it thoroughly. **2** move slightly or begin to be active. **3** wake up or get out of bed. **4** (often **stir someone up**) arouse a strong feeling in someone. **5** Brit. informal deliberately cause trouble by spreading rumours or gossip. • noun **1** an act of stirring. **2** a disturbance or commotion: *the event caused quite a stir.*
– DERIVATIVES **stirrer** noun.
– ORIGIN Old English.

stir[2] noun informal prison.
– ORIGIN perhaps from Romany *sturbin* 'jail'.

stir-crazy adjective informal psychologically disturbed as a result of being imprisoned.

stir-fry verb fry food rapidly over a high heat while stirring it briskly.

stirring adjective causing great excitement or strong emotion. • noun a first sign of activity, movement, or emotion.

stirrup noun **1** each of a pair of metal loops attached at either side of a horse's saddle to support the rider's foot. **2** a pair of metal supports for the ankles used during gynaecological examinations.
– ORIGIN Old English.

stirrup pump noun a hand-operated water pump with a footrest resembling a stirrup, used to put out small fires.

stitch noun **1** a loop of thread or yarn made by a single pass of the needle in sewing, knitting, or crocheting. **2** a method of sewing, knitting, or crocheting producing a particular pattern. **3** informal the smallest item of clothing: *a voluptuous woman without a stitch on.* **4** a sudden sharp pain in the side of the body, caused by vigorous exercise. • verb make or mend something with stitches.
– PHRASES **in stitches** informal laughing uncontrollably. **stitch someone/thing up** Brit. informal **1** manipulate a situation so that someone is at a disadvantage or wrongly blamed for something. **2** arrange or complete a deal or agreement.
– DERIVATIVES **stitcher** noun **stitching** noun.
– ORIGIN Old English.

stoat noun a small mammal of the weasel family, with chestnut fur (white in northern animals in winter), white underparts, and a black-tipped tail.
– ORIGIN unknown.

stochastic /stuh-kas-tik/ adjective technical not precisely predictable; random or affected by chance.
– ORIGIN Greek *stokhastikos*.

stock noun **1** a supply of goods or materials

available for sale or use. **2** farm animals bred and kept for their meat or milk; livestock. **3** the capital of a company raised through the selling of shares. **4** (**stocks**) a portion of a company's stock held by an individual or group as an investment. **5** (in the UK) securities issued by the government in fixed units with a fixed rate of interest. **6** water in which bones, meat, fish, or vegetables have been slowly simmered. **7** a person's ancestry. **8** a breed, variety, or population of an animal or plant. **9** the trunk or woody stem of a tree or shrub. **10** a plant with sweet-smelling white, pink, or lilac flowers. **11** (**the stocks**) (treated as sing. or pl.) historical a wooden structure with holes for securing a person's feet and hands, in which criminals were locked as a public punishment. **12** the part of a rifle or other gun to which the barrel and firing mechanism are attached, held against the shoulder when firing. **13** a band of material worn round the neck. • adjective **1** (of a product) usually kept in stock and so regularly available for sale. **2** (of a phrase or expression) used too regularly: *a stock response.* **3** referring to a conventional character type that recurs in a particular genre of literature, theatre, or film. • verb **1** have or keep a supply of a product. **2** (also **stock something up**) fill something with a supply of goods. **3** (**stock up**) obtain supplies of something for future use.
– PHRASES **in** (or **out of**) **stock** available (or unavailable) for immediate sale or use. **take stock** make an overall assessment of a particular situation.
– ORIGIN Old English, 'trunk, post'.

stockade noun **1** a barrier or enclosure formed from upright wooden posts. **2** chiefly N. Amer. a military prison.
– ORIGIN former French *estocade.*

stockbreeder noun a farmer who breeds livestock.

stockbroker noun a person who buys and sells stocks and shares on behalf of clients.
– DERIVATIVES **stockbroking** noun.

stock car noun an ordinary car that has been strengthened for use in a race in which the competing cars collide with each other.

stock cube noun a cube of dried meat, vegetable, or fish stock for use in cooking.

stock exchange noun a market in which stocks and shares are bought and sold.

stockholder noun chiefly N. Amer. a shareholder.

stockinette noun a soft, loosely knitted stretchy fabric.
– ORIGIN probably an alteration of *stocking-net.*

stocking noun **1** either of a pair of separate close-fitting nylon garments covering the foot and leg, worn by women. **2** US or old use a long sock worn by men. **3** a long sock or sock-shaped receptacle hung up by children on Christmas Eve to be filled with presents. **4** a white marking of the lower part of a horse's leg.
– PHRASES **in one's stockinged** (or **stocking**) **feet** without shoes.
– DERIVATIVES **stockinged** adjective.
– ORIGIN from *stock* in the dialect sense 'stocking'.

stocking cap noun a knitted hat with a long tapered end that hangs down.

stocking stitch noun a knitting stitch consisting of alternate rows of plain and purl stitch.

stock-in-trade noun the typical subject or item a person, company, or profession uses or deals in.

stockist noun Brit. a retailer selling a particular type of goods.

stockman noun (pl. **stockmen**) **1** a person who looks after livestock. **2** US an owner of livestock.

stock market noun a stock exchange.

stockpile noun a large supply of goods or materials that has been gathered together. • verb gather together and keep a large supply of goods or materials.

stockpot noun a pot in which stock is prepared by long, slow cooking.

stockroom noun a room in which stocks of goods or materials are stored.

stock-still adverb without any movement; completely still.

stocktaking noun the action or process of recording the amount of stock held by a business.
– DERIVATIVES **stocktake** noun & verb.

stocky adjective (**stockier, stockiest**) (especially of a person) short and sturdy.
– DERIVATIVES **stockily** adverb **stockiness** noun.

stockyard noun N. Amer. a large yard containing pens and sheds in which livestock is kept.

stodge noun Brit. informal food that is heavy, filling, and high in carbohydrates.
– ORIGIN first a verb meaning 'stuff to stretching point': suggested by **stuff** and *podge* 'fat'.

stodgy adjective **1** (of food) heavy and filling. **2** rather serious and dull.
– DERIVATIVES **stodginess** noun.

stoep /stoop/ noun S. African a veranda in front of a house.
– ORIGIN Afrikaans.

stoic /stoh-ik/ noun **1** a stoical person. **2** (**Stoic**) a member of the ancient philosophical school of Stoicism. • adjective **1** stoical. **2** (**Stoic**) relating to the Stoics or Stoicism.
– ORIGIN Greek *stōikos.*

stoical /stoh-i-k'l/ adjective enduring pain and hardship without showing one's feelings or complaining.
– DERIVATIVES **stoically** adverb.

stoicism /stoh-i-si-z'm/ noun **1** stoical behaviour. **2** (**Stoicism**) an ancient Greek school of philosophy which taught that it is wise to remain indifferent to changes of fortune and to pleasure and pain.

stoke verb **1** add coal to a fire, furnace, etc. **2** encourage or stir up a strong emotion. **3** (**stoke up**) informal eat a large quantity of food to give oneself energy.

stoker noun a person who tends the furnace on a steamship or steam train.
– ORIGIN Dutch.

stole[1] noun **1** a woman's long scarf or shawl, worn loosely over the shoulders. **2** a priest's vestment worn over the shoulders.
– ORIGIN Greek, 'clothing'.

stole[2] past of STEAL.

stolen past participle of STEAL.

stolid adjective calm, dependable, and showing little emotion or reaction.
– DERIVATIVES **stolidity** noun **stolidly** adv
– ORIGIN Latin *stolidus,* perhaps related *stultus* 'foolish'.

stollen /sto-luhn, shto-luhn/ noun a rich German fruit and nut cake.
– ORIGIN German.

stoma /stoh-muh/ noun (pl. **stomas** or **stom** /stoh-muh-tuh/) technical **1** a minute pore i leaf or stem of a plant, allowing gases to m in and out. **2** a small mouth-like opening in some invertebrate animals. **3** an artificial opening made into a hollow organ, especial the gut.
– ORIGIN Greek, 'mouth'.

stomach noun **1** the organ of the body in whic the first part of digestion occurs. **2** the abdominal area of the body; the belly. **3** an appetite or desire for something: *they had no stomach for a fight.* • verb **1** consume food or drink without feeling or being sick: *he cannot stomach milk.* **2** endure or accept: *what I won't stomach is thieving.*
– PHRASES **a strong stomach** an ability to see or do unpleasant things without feeling sick or squeamish.
– ORIGIN Greek *stomakhos* 'gullet'.

stomacher noun historical a V-shaped ornamental panel worn over the chest and stomach by men and women in the 16th century, later only by women.

stomach pump noun a syringe attached to a long tube, used for extracting the contents of a person's stomach (for example, if they have swallowed poison).

stomata plural of STOMA.

stomp verb tread or stamp heavily and noisily.
– ORIGIN variant of STAMP.

stomping ground noun N. Amer. another term for STAMPING GROUND.

stone noun **1** the hard, solid non-metallic mineral matter which rock is made of. **2** a small piece of stone found on the ground. **3** a piece of stone shaped as a memorial or to mark out a boundary. **4** a gem or jewel. **5** a hard seed in certain fruits. **6** (pl. same) Brit. a unit of weight equal to 14 lb (6.35 kg). **7** a whitish or brownish-grey colour. • verb **1** throw stones at someone. **2** remove the stone from a fruit. • adverb extremely or totally: *stone cold.*
– PHRASES **leave no stone unturned** try everything possible in order to achieve something. **a stone's throw** a short distance.
– ORIGIN Old English.

Stone Age noun a prehistoric period that came before the Bronze Age, when weapons and tools were made of stone.

stonechat noun a small heathland bird with a call resembling two stones being knocked together.

stone circle noun a prehistoric monument consisting of stones arranged in a circle.

stonecrop noun a plant with star-shaped yellow or white flowers which grows among rocks or on walls.

consider to be of a particular level of importance: *he set great store by teamwork.*
– ORIGIN Old French *estore.*

storefront noun N. Amer. **1** another term for **SHOPFRONT**. **2** a room or rooms facing the street on the ground floor of a commercial building, used as a shop, small business, etc.

storehouse noun **1** a building used for storing goods. **2** a thing that contains a large store of something: *the CD is an interactive storehouse of garden information.*

storeroom noun a room in which items are stored.

storey (N. Amer. also **story**) noun (pl. **storeys** or **stories**) a floor or level of a building.
– ORIGIN from Latin *historia* 'history': perhaps first referring to a row of painted windows or sculptures on a building, representing a historical subject.

USAGE: Do not confuse **storey** with **story**. **Storey** means 'a floor of a building' (*a three-storey house*), while **story** means 'an account told for entertainment' (*an adventure story*). In American English, the spelling **story** is used for both senses.

storied adjective literary celebrated in or associated with stories or legends.

stork noun a tall long-legged bird with a long heavy bill and white and black plumage.
– ORIGIN Old English.

storm noun **1** a violent disturbance of the atmosphere with strong winds and rain, and often thunder, lightning, or snow. **2** an uproar or controversy. **3** an intense outburst of a specified feeling or reaction: *the comedy attracted a storm of criticism.* ●verb **1** move angrily or forcefully: *he stormed out of the house.* **2** (of troops) suddenly attack and capture a place. **3** shout something angrily.
– PHRASES **go down a storm** be received very enthusiastically. **a storm in a teacup** Brit. great anger or excitement about a trivial matter. **take something by storm 1** capture a place by a sudden attack. **2** have great and rapid success in a place.
– ORIGIN Old English.

storm cloud noun **1** a large dark rain cloud. **2** (**storm clouds**) a sign of problems or trouble to come: *storm clouds are looming over the PC market.*

storm door (or **storm window**) noun chiefly N. Amer. an additional outer door or window for protection in bad weather.

storm drain (N. Amer. **storm sewer**) noun a drain built to carry away excess water in times of heavy rain.

stormer noun Brit. informal a thing which is particularly impressive of its kind.
– DERIVATIVES **storming** adjective.

storm petrel noun a small petrel (bird) with blackish plumage, formerly believed to be a sign of bad weather to come.

storm trooper noun a member of a Nazi military force.

stormy adjective (**stormier**, **stormiest**) **1** affected by a storm. **2** full of angry or violent outbursts of feeling.
– DERIVATIVES **stormily** adverb **storminess** noun.

story[1] noun (pl. **stories**) **1** an account of imaginary or real people and events told for entertainment. **2** a description of past events, experiences, etc.: *he issued a dossier giving his side of the story.* **3** an item of news. **4** a plot or storyline. **5** informal a lie.
– ORIGIN Old French *estorie.*

USAGE: For an explanation of the difference between **story** and **storey**, see the note at **STOREY**.

story[2] noun N. Amer. variant spelling of **STOREY**.

storyboard noun a sequence of drawings representing the shots planned for a film or television production.

storybook noun a book containing a story or stories for children. ●adjective perfect, as things typically are in children's stories: *a storybook romance.*

storyline noun the plot of a novel, play, film, etc.

storyteller noun a person who tells stories.
– DERIVATIVES **storytelling** noun.

stotin /sto-teen/ noun a unit of money of Slovenia, equal to one hundredth of a tolar.
– ORIGIN Slovene.

stotinka /sto-ting-kuh/ noun (pl. **stotinki** /sto-ting-ki/) a unit of money of Bulgaria, equal to one hundredth of a lev.
– ORIGIN Bulgarian, 'one hundredth'.

stoup /stoop/ noun a basin for holy water in a church.
– ORIGIN Old Norse.

stout adjective **1** rather fat or heavily built. **2** (of an object) sturdy and thick. **3** brave and determined: *he put up a stout defence.* ●noun a kind of strong, dark beer brewed with roasted malt or barley.
– DERIVATIVES **stoutly** adverb **stoutness** noun.
– ORIGIN Old French.

stove[1] noun a piece of equipment for cooking or heating that operates by burning fuel or using electricity.
– ORIGIN Dutch or German.

stove[2] past and past participle of **STAVE**.

stovepipe noun a pipe taking the smoke and gases from a stove up through a roof or to a chimney.

stovepipe hat noun a type of tall top hat.

stow verb **1** pack or store an object tidily in a particular place. **2** (**stow away**) hide oneself on a ship, aircraft, etc. so as to travel secretly or without paying.
– DERIVATIVES **stowage** noun.
– ORIGIN from **BESTOW**.

stowaway noun a person who stows away on a ship, aircraft, etc.

strabismus /struh-biz-muhss/ noun Medicine the condition of having a squint.
– ORIGIN Greek *strabismos.*

straddle verb **1** sit or stand with one leg on either side of something or someone. **2** extend across both sides of: *the plain straddles the border between Alaska and the Yukon.*
– ORIGIN from dialect *striddling* 'astride'.

Stradivarius /strad-i-vair-i-uhss/ noun a violin or other stringed instrument made by the Italian violin-maker Antonio Stradivari or his followers.

S

strafe /strahf, strayf/ **verb** attack something with machine-gun fire or bombs from low-flying aircraft.
– ORIGIN from the German First World War catchphrase *Gott strafe England* 'may God punish England'.

straggle verb 1 trail slowly behind the person or people in front. **2** grow or spread out in an irregular, untidy way. •**noun** an irregular and untidy group.
– DERIVATIVES **straggler** noun **straggly** adjective.
– ORIGIN perhaps from dialect *strake* 'go'.

straight adjective 1 extending uniformly in one direction only; without a curve or bend. **2** properly positioned so as to be level, upright, or symmetrical. **3** in proper order or condition: *it'll take a long time to get the place straight.* **4** honest and direct. **5** in continuous succession: *his fourth straight win.* **6** (of an alcoholic drink) undiluted. **7** informal conventional or respectable. **8** informal heterosexual. **9** (of drama) serious as opposed to comic or musical. •**adverb 1** in a straight line or in a straight way. **2** without delay or diversion. **3** clearly and logically: *I'm so tired I can't think straight.* •**noun 1** the straight part of something. **2** informal a conventional person. **3** informal a heterosexual person.
– PHRASES **go straight** live an honest life after being a criminal. **the straight and narrow** the honest and morally acceptable way of living. **straight away** immediately. **straight off** (or **out**) informal without hesitating. **straight up** Brit. informal honestly.
– DERIVATIVES **straightly** adverb **straightness** noun.
– ORIGIN former past participle of STRETCH.

USAGE: Do not confuse **straight** with **strait**. **Straight** means 'without a curve or bend' (*a long, straight road*), whereas **strait** means 'a narrow passage of water' (*the Straits of Gibraltar*) or 'trouble or difficulty' (*the economy is in dire straits*).

straight angle noun Mathematics an angle of 180°.

straight edge noun a bar with one edge accurately straight, used for testing straightness.

straighten verb 1 make or become straight. **2** stand or sit up straight after bending.

straight-faced adjective having a blank or serious facial expression.
– DERIVATIVES **straight face** noun.

straightforward adjective 1 easy to do or understand. **2** honest and open.
– DERIVATIVES **straightforwardly** adverb **straightforwardness** noun.

straightjacket noun variant spelling of STRAITJACKET.

straight-laced adjective variant spelling of STRAIT-LACED.

straight man noun a person in a show whose role is to provide a comedian with opportunities to make jokes.

strain¹ verb 1 force a part of one's body or oneself to make an unusually great effort. **2** injure a limb, muscle, or organ by making it work too hard. **3** make severe or excessive demands on: *he strained her tolerance to the*

limit. **4** pull or push forcibly at something. **5** pour a mainly liquid substance through a sieve or similar device to separate out any solid matter. •**noun 1** a force tending to pull or stretch something to an extreme degree. **2** an injury caused by straining a muscle, limb, etc. **3** a severe demand on strength or resources: *the large order is already putting a strain on the airline.* **4** a state of tension or exhaustion caused by severe demands on a person's strength or resources. **5** the sound of a piece of music as it is played.
– ORIGIN Old French *estreindre.*

strain² noun 1 a distinct breed or variety of an animal, plant, or other organism. **2** a tendency in a person's character. **3** a type or kind of something: *the Tibetan strain of Buddhism.*
– ORIGIN Old English, 'acquisition, gain'.

strained adjective 1 tense, tired, or uneasy. **2** produced by deliberate effort; artificial or forced: *a strained conversation.*

strainer noun a device for straining liquids, having holes punched in it or made of wire mesh.

strait noun 1 (also **straits**) a narrow passage of water connecting two seas or other large areas of water. **2** (**straits**) a situation of trouble or difficulty: *the economy is in dire straits.*
– ORIGIN Old French *estreit* 'tight, narrow'.

USAGE: On the confusion of **strait** and **straight**, see the note at STRAIGHT.

straitened adjective restricted because of poverty: *they lived in straitened circumstances.*

straitjacket (also **straightjacket**) **noun 1** a strong garment with long sleeves which can be tied together to confine the arms of a violent prisoner or mental patient. **2** something which severely restricts freedom of action or development.

strait-laced (also **straight-laced**) **adjective** having very strict moral attitudes.

stramash /struh-mash/ **noun** Scottish & N. English an uproar; a row.
– ORIGIN uncertain.

strand¹ verb 1 drive or leave a boat, person, or sea creature aground on a shore. **2** leave without the means to move from a place: *the lorries are stranded in France.* •**noun** literary or Irish the shore of a sea, lake, or large river.
– ORIGIN Old English.

strand² noun 1 a single thin length of thread, wire, etc. **2** a single hair or thin lock of hair. **3** a part of a complex whole: *the two main strands of feminism.*
– ORIGIN unknown.

strange adjective 1 unusual or surprising and often difficult to understand. **2** not previously visited, seen, or encountered; unfamiliar: *finding ATM machines in a strange city can be a problem.*
– DERIVATIVES **strangely** adverb **strangeness** noun.
– ORIGIN Old French *estrange.*

stranger noun 1 a person one does not know. **2** a person who does not know, or is not known in, a particular place.
– PHRASES **be no** (or **a**) **stranger to** be familiar (or not familiar) with a feeling or situation.

strangle verb 1 kill or injure someone by squeezing their neck. **2** prevent from

S

happening or developing: *industry is being strangled by high diesel taxes.*
– DERIVATIVES **strangler** noun.
– ORIGIN Old French *estrangler*.

stranglehold noun 1 a grip around a person's neck that deprives them of oxygen and so can kill them. 2 complete control over something.

strangulate /strang-gyuu-layt/ verb (usu. as adj. **strangulated**) Medicine squeeze a part of the body so tightly that blood cannot circulate through it.
– ORIGIN Latin *strangulare* 'choke'.

strangulation noun 1 the action of strangling someone or the state of being strangled. 2 a medical condition in which a part of the body is squeezed so tightly that blood cannot circulate through it.

strap noun 1 a strip of flexible material used for fastening, securing, carrying, or holding on to someone or something. 2 (**the strap**) punishment by beating with a leather strap. •verb (**strapped**, **strapping**, **strapped**) 1 fasten or secure someone or something with a strap. 2 Brit. wrap adhesive plaster round an injured part of the body. 3 beat someone with a leather strap. 4 (as adj. **strapped**) informal short of money: *I'm constantly strapped for cash.*
– DERIVATIVES **strapless** adjective **strappy** adjective.
– ORIGIN dialect form of **STROP**[1].

strapline noun a subheading or caption in a newspaper or magazine.

strapping[1] adjective (of a person) big and strong.

strapping[2] noun 1 adhesive plaster for strapping injuries. 2 strips of flexible material or metal used to fasten or strengthen something.

strata plural of **STRATUM**.

stratagem /stra-tuh-juhm/ noun a plan or scheme intended to outwit an opponent.
– ORIGIN Greek *stratēgēma*.

strategic /struh-tee-jik/ adjective 1 forming part of a long-term plan to achieve a specific purpose. 2 relating to the gaining of long-term military advantage. 3 (of weapons) intended to be fired at enemy industrial areas and communication centres rather than used in a battle. Often contrasted with **TACTICAL**.
– DERIVATIVES **strategically** adverb.

strategy /stra-ti-ji/ noun (pl. **strategies**) 1 a plan designed to achieve a particular long-term aim. 2 the art of planning and directing military activity in a war or battle. Often contrasted with tactics (see **TACTIC**).
– DERIVATIVES **strategist** noun.
– ORIGIN Greek *stratēgia* 'generalship'.

strath /strath/ noun Scottish a broad river valley.
– ORIGIN Scottish Gaelic *srath*.

strathspey /strath-spay/ noun a slow Scottish dance.
– ORIGIN named after *Strathspey* in Scotland.

stratify /stra-ti-fy/ verb (**stratifies, stratifying, stratified**) (usu. as adj. **stratified**) 1 form or arrange something into strata, layers, or levels. 2 arrange or classify someone or something.
– DERIVATIVES **stratification** noun.

stratigraphy /struh-tig-ruh-fi/ noun the branch of geology concerned with the order

and relative dating of rock strata.
– DERIVATIVES **stratigraphic** adjective **stratigraphical** adjective.

stratocumulus /stra-toh-kyoo-myuu-luhss/ noun cloud forming a low layer of clumped or broken grey masses.

stratosphere /stra-tuh-sfeer/ noun 1 the layer of the earth's atmosphere above the troposphere and below the mesosphere. 2 informal the very highest levels of something.
– DERIVATIVES **stratospheric** /stra-tuhss-fer-ik/ adjective.

stratum /strah-tuhm/ noun (pl. **strata** /strah-tuh/) 1 a layer or a series of layers of rock. 2 a thin layer within any structure. 3 a level or class of society.
– DERIVATIVES **stratal** adjective.
– ORIGIN Latin, 'something spread or laid down'.

USAGE: Remember that, as in Latin, the singular form in English is **stratum** and the plural is **strata**: it is incorrect to create the form **stratas** as the plural.

stratus /strah-tuhss, stray-tuhss/ noun cloud forming a continuous horizontal grey sheet, often with rain or snow.
– ORIGIN Latin, 'strewn'.

straw noun 1 dried stalks of grain, used as fodder or bedding for animals and for thatching, packing, or weaving. 2 a single dried stalk of grain. 3 a thin hollow tube of paper or plastic for sucking drink from a container. 4 a pale yellow colour.
– PHRASES **clutch at straws** turn in desperation to something which is unlikely to be helpful. [from the proverb *a drowning man will clutch at a straw*.] **draw the short straw** be chosen to perform an unpleasant task. **the last** (or **final**) **straw** a further minor difficulty that comes after a series of difficulties and makes a situation unbearable. [from the proverb *the last straw breaks the* (*laden*) *camel's back*.]
– ORIGIN Old English.

strawberry noun (pl. **strawberries**) a sweet soft red fruit with many seeds on the surface.

strawberry blonde adjective (of hair) light reddish-blonde in colour.

straw poll (N. Amer. also **straw vote**) noun an unofficial test of opinion.

stray verb 1 move away aimlessly from a group or from the right course or place: *the child had strayed from home and was lost in the desert.* 2 (of the eyes or a hand) move idly in a particular direction. 3 informal be unfaithful to a husband, wife, or lover. •adjective 1 not in the right place; separated from a group. 2 (of a domestic animal) having no home or having wandered away from home. •noun a stray person or thing, especially a domestic animal.
– ORIGIN Old French *estrayer*.

streak noun 1 a long, thin mark. 2 an element of a particular kind in someone's character: *Lucy had a ruthless streak.* 3 a spell of successes or failures: *he hit a winning streak.* •verb 1 mark something with streaks. 2 move very fast. 3 informal run naked in a public place so as to cause shock or amusement.
– DERIVATIVES **streaker** noun **streaking** noun.

S

– ORIGIN Old English.

streaky adjective (**streakier, streakiest**)
1 having streaks. **2** Brit. (of bacon) from a pig's belly, so having alternate strips of fat and lean.
– DERIVATIVES **streakily** adverb **streakiness** noun.

stream noun **1** a small, narrow river. **2** a continuous flow of liquid, air, gas, people, etc. **3** Brit. a group in which schoolchildren of the same age and ability are taught. •verb **1** run or move in a continuous flow. **2** run with tears, sweat, or other liquid: *I woke up in the night, streaming with sweat.* **3** float at full extent in the wind. **4** Brit. put schoolchildren in groups of the same age and ability to be taught together.
– PHRASES **on stream** in or into production or operation.
– ORIGIN Old English.

streamer noun a long, narrow strip of material used as a decoration or flag.

streaming adjective (of a cold) accompanied by running of the nose and eyes. •noun a method of relaying data (especially video and audio material) over a computer network as a steady continuous stream.

streamline verb **1** (usu. as adj. **streamlined**) design or form in a way that presents very little resistance to a flow of air or water: *a streamlined train.* **2** make an organization or system more efficient by employing faster or simpler working methods.

stream of consciousness noun a literary style which records the continuous flow of thoughts and reactions in the mind of a character.

street noun a public road in a city, town, or village. •adjective **1** relating to fashionable young people living in cities and towns: *street style.* **2** homeless: *street children.*
– PHRASES **on the streets 1** homeless. **2** working as a prostitute. **streets ahead** Brit. informal very much better. **up** (or **right up**) **one's street** informal well suited to one's interests or abilities.
– ORIGIN from Latin *strāta via* 'paved way'.

streetcar noun N. Amer. a tram.

street-smart adjective N. Amer. another term for **STREETWISE**.

street value noun the price for which something that is illegal or has been illegally obtained, especially drugs, can be sold.

streetwalker noun a prostitute who seeks clients in the street.

streetwise adjective informal having the skills and knowledge necessary for dealing with the difficulties of modern city life.

strength /strength, strengkth/ noun **1** the quality or state of being strong or powerful. **2** a good or valuable quality. **3** the number of people making up a group. **4** the number of people that makes a group complete: *we are now 30 staff below strength.*
– PHRASES **go from strength to strength** progress with increasing success. **in strength** in large numbers. **on the strength of** on the basis of. **tower** (or **pillar**) **of strength** a person who can be relied on to support and comfort others.
– ORIGIN Old English.

strengthen verb make or become stronger.
– DERIVATIVES **strengthener** noun.

strenuous /stren-yuu-uhss/ adjective requiring or using great effort or exertion.
– DERIVATIVES **strenuously** adverb **strenuousness** noun.
– ORIGIN Latin *strenuus* 'brisk'.

streptococcus /strep-tuh-kok-kuhss/ noun (pl. **streptococci** /strep-tuh-kok-ky/) a bacterium of a large genus including those causing scarlet fever, pneumonia, and tooth decay.
– DERIVATIVES **streptococcal** adjective.
– ORIGIN from Greek *streptos* 'twisted'.

streptomycin /strep-tuh-my-sin/ noun an antibiotic used against tuberculosis.
– ORIGIN from Greek *streptos* 'twisted' + *mukēs* 'fungus'.

stress noun **1** pressure or tension exerted on an object. **2** a state of mental or emotional strain. **3** particular emphasis or importance. **4** emphasis given to a syllable or word in speech. •verb **1** emphasize a point, statement, etc. when speaking or writing. **2** give emphasis to a syllable or word when pronouncing it. **3** subject to strain, tension, or pressure: *this type of workout does stress the knee joints.*
– ORIGIN from **DISTRESS**, or partly from Old French *estresse* 'narrowness, oppression'.

stressful adjective causing mental or emotional stress.

stretch verb **1** (of something soft or elastic) be made or be able to be made longer or wider without tearing or breaking. **2** pull something tightly from one point to another. **3** extend the body or a part of the body to its full length. **4** extend over an area or period of time: *the beach stretches for over four miles.* **5** last longer than expected. **6** (of finances or resources) be enough for a particular purpose. **7** make demands on: *directors churned out pictures that failed to stretch the imagination.* •noun **1** a continuous area or period of time: *a treacherous stretch of road.* **2** an act of stretching. **3** the capacity to stretch or be stretched; elasticity. **4** the fact or state of being stretched. **5** informal a period of time spent in prison. •adjective informal (of a car) much longer than usual and seating more people: *a stretch limo.*
– PHRASES **at full stretch** using the maximum amount of one's resources or energy. **at a stretch 1** in one continuous period. **2** just possible but with difficulty. **stretch one's legs** go for a short walk. **stretch a point** allow or do something not usually acceptable.
– DERIVATIVES **stretchy** adjective (**stretchier, stretchiest**).
– ORIGIN Old English.

stretcher noun **1** a framework of two poles with a long piece of canvas slung between them, used for carrying sick, injured, or dead people. **2** a brick or stone laid with its long side along the face of a wall. •verb carry someone on a stretcher.

stretch marks plural noun marks on the skin, especially on the abdomen, caused by stretching of the skin from obesity or during pregnancy.

strew verb (past part. **strewn** or **strewed**)
1 scatter things untidily over a surface or area. **2** (**be strewn with**) be covered with untidily scattered things.

– ORIGIN Old English.

strewth exclamation informal used to express surprise or dismay.
– ORIGIN shortening of *God's truth.*

stria /stry-uh/ noun (pl. **striae** /stry-ee/) technical a line, ridge, or groove, especially one of a number of similar parallel features.
– ORIGIN Latin, 'furrow'.

striated /stry-ayt-id/ adjective technical **1** marked with a series of ridges or grooves. **2** striped or streaked.
– DERIVATIVES **striation** noun.

stricken North American or old-fashioned past participle of STRIKE. adjective **1** seriously affected by something unpleasant. **2** (of a face or look) showing great distress.

strict adjective **1** demanding that rules about behaviour are obeyed. **2** (of a rule) that must be obeyed exactly. **3** (of a person) following rules or beliefs exactly. **4** very exact and clearly defined: *the characters are not soldiers in the strict sense of the word.*
– DERIVATIVES **strictly** adverb **strictness** noun.
– ORIGIN Latin *strictus* 'tightened'.

stricture /strik-cher/ noun **1** a rule restricting behaviour or action. **2** a sternly critical remark. **3** Medicine abnormal narrowing of a passage or duct in the body: *a colonic stricture.*

stride verb (past **strode**; past part. **stridden**) walk with long, decisive steps. •noun **1** a long, decisive step. **2** the length of a step in running or walking. **3** a step made towards an aim: *the company has made huge strides in product quality.* **4** (one's stride) a good or regular rate of progress, especially after a slow start.
– PHRASES **take something in one's stride** deal calmly with something difficult.
– ORIGIN Old English.

strident adjective **1** loud and harsh. **2** presenting a point of view in an excessively forceful way.
– DERIVATIVES **stridency** noun **stridently** adverb.
– ORIGIN from Latin *stridere* 'creak'.

stridulate /strid-yuu-layt/ verb (of a grasshopper or similar insect) make a shrill sound by rubbing the legs, wings, or other parts of the body together.
– DERIVATIVES **stridulation** noun.
– ORIGIN from Latin *stridulus* 'creaking'.

strife noun angry or bitter disagreement; conflict.
– ORIGIN Old French *estrif.*

strike verb (past and past part. **struck**) **1** deliver a hard blow to someone or something. **2** come forcefully into contact with someone or something. **3** (in sport) hit or kick a ball. **4** (of a disaster, disease, etc.) occur suddenly and have harmful effects on: *a major earthquake struck the island.* **5** attack someone or something suddenly. **6** (strike something into) cause a strong emotion in someone. **7** cause to become suddenly: *he was struck dumb.* **8** suddenly come into the mind of someone. **9** (be struck by/with) find particularly interesting or impressive: *she was struck by the beauty of the scene.* **10** light a match by rubbing it against a rough surface. **11** (of employees) refuse to work as a form of organized protest. **12** go somewhere vigorously or purposefully: *those who could*

swim struck out for the bank. **13** (strike out) start out on a new or independent course. **14** reach an agreement or compromise. **15** cross something out with a pen. **16** (strike someone off) officially remove someone from membership of a professional group. **17** (of a clock) indicate the time by sounding a chime or stroke. **18** make a coin or medal by stamping metal. **19** discover gold, minerals, or oil by drilling or mining. **20** take down a tent or camp. •noun **1** an act of striking by employees. **2** a refusal to do something, as a form of organized protest: *a rent strike.* **3** a sudden attack. **4** (in sport) an act of striking a ball. **5** an act of striking gold, minerals, or oil.
– PHRASES **strike an attitude** (or **pose**) hold one's body in a particular position to create an impression. **strike up** begin to play a piece of music. **strike something up** begin a friendship or conversation with someone. **strike while the iron is hot** make use of an opportunity immediately.
– ORIGIN Old English, 'go, flow' and 'rub lightly'.

strike-breaker noun a person who works or is employed in place of others who are on strike.

striker noun **1** an employee on strike. **2** (chiefly in football) a forward or attacker.

strike rate noun the success rate of a sports team in scoring goals or runs.

striking adjective **1** attracting attention; noticeable. **2** very attractive.
– DERIVATIVES **strikingly** adverb.

strimmer noun Brit. trademark an electrically powered grass trimmer with a cutting cord which rotates rapidly on a spindle.
– DERIVATIVES **strim** verb (**strims, strimming, strimmed**).

Strine /rhymes with fine/ noun informal Australian English or the Australian accent.
– ORIGIN representing *Australian* in Strine.

string noun **1** material consisting of threads twisted together to form a thin length. **2** a piece of string. **3** a length of catgut or wire on a musical instrument, producing a note by vibration. **4** (strings) the stringed instruments in an orchestra. **5** a piece of nylon or similar material interwoven with others to form the head of a sports racket. **6** a set of things tied or threaded together on a thin cord. **7** a sequence of similar items or events: *a string of burglaries.* **8** Computing a sequence of characters or other data. **9** a G-string or thong. •verb (past and past part. **strung**) **1** hang or thread things on a string. **2** (be strung or be strung out) be arranged in a long line. **3** fit a string or strings to a musical instrument, a racket, or a bow.
– PHRASES **be strung out** (or Brit. **up**) informal be tense or nervous. **no strings attached** informal there are no special conditions. **string along** informal stay with a person or group. **string someone along** informal mislead someone deliberately. **string something out** prolong something. **string someone up** kill someone by hanging.
– DERIVATIVES **stringed** adjective.
– ORIGIN Old English.

string bass noun (especially among jazz musicians) a double bass.

string bean noun a runner bean.

string course noun a raised horizontal band or course of bricks on a building.

stringent /strin-juhnt/ adjective (of regulations or requirements) very strict; that must be obeyed.
– DERIVATIVES **stringency** noun **stringently** adverb.
– ORIGIN from Latin *stringere* 'draw tight'.

stringer noun 1 informal a journalist who is not on the regular staff of a newspaper, but who reports part-time on a particular place. 2 a structural piece running lengthwise in a framework, especially that of a ship or aircraft.

string quartet noun a chamber music group consisting of a first and second violin, viola, and cello.

string vest noun a man's vest made of a meshed fabric.

stringy adjective (stringier, stringiest) 1 long and thin. 2 (of food) containing chewy fibres.

strip¹ verb (strips, stripping, stripped) 1 remove all coverings or clothes from someone or something. 2 take off one's clothes. 3 remove all the contents from a room, vehicle, etc. 4 (strip someone of) deprive someone of rank, power, or property. 5 remove paint or varnish from a surface. 6 sell off a company's assets for profit. • noun 1 an act of undressing. 2 Brit. the identifying outfit worn by the members of a sports team while playing.
– ORIGIN Germanic.

strip² noun 1 a long, narrow piece of cloth, paper, or other material. 2 a long, narrow area of land. 3 chiefly N. Amer. a main road lined with shops and other facilities.
– ORIGIN German *strippe* 'strap, thong'.

stripe noun 1 a long narrow band of a different colour or texture from its surroundings. 2 a chevron on a uniform, showing military rank. 3 chiefly N. Amer. a type or category. • verb mark someone or something with stripes.
– DERIVATIVES **striped** adjective **stripy** (also **stripey**) adjective.
– ORIGIN perhaps from Dutch or German.

strip light noun Brit. a tubular fluorescent lamp.

stripling noun old use or humorous a young man.
– ORIGIN probably from **STRIP**² (from the idea of 'narrowness', i.e. slimness).

strip mine chiefly N. Amer. noun an opencast mine. • verb (strip-mine) obtain ore or coal by opencast mining.

stripper noun 1 a striptease performer. 2 a device or substance for stripping paint, varnish, etc.

strip-search verb search someone for concealed drugs, weapons, or other items, by stripping off their clothes.

striptease noun a form of entertainment in which a performer gradually undresses to music in a sexually exciting way.

strive verb (past strove or strived; past part. striven or strived) make great efforts, especially to achieve or prevent something: *the charity strives to keep costs low.*
– DERIVATIVES **striver** noun.
– ORIGIN Old French *estriver*.

strobe noun a stroboscope. • verb flash at rapid intervals.

stroboscope /stroh-buh-skohp/ noun an instrument which shines a bright light at rapid intervals so that a moving person or object appears stationary.
– DERIVATIVES **stroboscopic** adjective.
– ORIGIN from Greek *strobos* 'whirling'.

strode past of **STRIDE**.

stroganoff /strog-uh-nof/ noun a dish in which the main ingredient, typically beef, is cooked in a sour cream sauce.
– ORIGIN named after the Russian diplomat Count Pavel *Stroganov*.

stroke noun 1 an act of hitting. 2 a mark made by drawing a pen, pencil, or paintbrush once across paper or canvas. 3 a line forming part of a written or printed character. 4 a short diagonal line separating characters or figures. 5 a sudden disabling attack or loss of consciousness caused by an interruption in the flow of blood to the brain. 6 a sound made by a striking clock. 7 an act of stroking with the hand. 8 one of a series of repeated movements, especially in swimming or rowing. 9 a style of moving the arms and legs in swimming. 10 the way in which the oar is moved in rowing. 11 Golf an act of hitting the ball with a club, as a unit of scoring. • verb gently move one's hand over someone or something.
– PHRASES **at a stroke** by a single action which has immediate effect. **not do a stroke of work** do no work at all. **put someone off their stroke** put someone off so that they make a mistake or hesitate. **stroke of genius** an outstandingly original idea. **stroke of luck** a lucky and unexpected event.
– DERIVATIVES **stroker** noun.
– ORIGIN Old English.

stroke play noun golf in which the score is reckoned by counting the number of strokes taken overall. Compare with **MATCH PLAY**.

stroll verb 1 walk in a leisurely way. 2 informal achieve a sporting victory easily. • noun 1 a short leisurely walk. 2 informal a victory that is easily achieved.
– ORIGIN probably from German *strollen*.

stroller noun N. Amer. a pushchair.

strong adjective (stronger, strongest) 1 physically powerful. 2 done with or exerting great force: *a strong current.* 3 able to withstand great force or pressure. 4 secure, stable, or firmly established. 5 great in power, influence, or ability: *a strong leader.* 6 (of something smelt, tasted, etc.) very intense. 7 (of language) forceful and using swear words. 8 (of a solution or drink) containing a large proportion of a substance. 9 used after a number to indicate the size of a group: *a crowd several thousands strong.* 10 (of verbs) forming the past tense and past participle by a change of vowel within the stem rather than by adding an ending or suffix (e.g. *swim, swam, swum*).
– PHRASES **going strong** informal continuing to be healthy, vigorous, or successful. **strong on** 1 good at. 2 possessing large quantities of. **one's strong point** (or **suit**) something one is very good at.
– DERIVATIVES **strongly** adverb.
– ORIGIN Old English, related to **STRING**.

strong-arm adjective using force or violence.

● **verb** use force or violence against someone.

strongbox noun a small lockable metal box in which valuables may be kept.

stronghold noun 1 a place of strong support for a cause or political party. 2 a place that has been fortified against attack.

strongman noun (pl. **strongmen**) 1 a very strong man, especially one who performs feats of strength for entertainment. 2 a leader who rules by force or violence.

strongroom noun a room, typically one in a bank, designed to protect valuable items against fire and theft.

strontium /stron-ti-uhm/ noun a soft silver-white metallic chemical element.
– ORIGIN from *Strontian* in Scotland.

strop[1] noun a strip of leather for sharpening razors. ● **verb** (**strops**, **stropping**, **stropped**) sharpen a razor on or with a strop.
– ORIGIN probably from Latin *stroppus* 'thong'.

strop[2] noun Brit. informal a bad mood; a temper.

stroppy adjective (**stroppier**, **stroppiest**) Brit. informal bad-tempered; argumentative.
– ORIGIN perhaps from **OBSTREPEROUS**.

strove past of **STRIVE**.

struck past and past participle of **STRIKE**.

structural adjective relating to or forming part of a structure.
– DERIVATIVES **structurally** adverb.

structuralism noun a theory that pieces of writing, languages, and social systems should be seen as a structure whose various parts have meaning only when considered in relation to each other.
– DERIVATIVES **structuralist** noun & adjective.

structure noun 1 the arrangement of and relations between the parts of something complex: *changes to the company's organizational structure.* 2 a building or other object constructed from several parts. 3 the quality of being well organized. ● **verb** organize or arrange something according to a plan or system.
– ORIGIN Latin *structura*.

strudel /stroo-duhl/ noun a dessert of thin pastry rolled up round a fruit filling and baked.
– ORIGIN German, 'whirlpool'.

struggle verb 1 make forceful efforts to get free. 2 try hard to do something under difficult circumstances. 3 make one's way with difficulty. ● **noun** 1 an act of struggling. 2 a conflict or contest: *a power struggle for the leadership.* 3 a very difficult task.
– DERIVATIVES **struggler** noun.
– ORIGIN uncertain.

strum verb (**strums**, **strumming**, **strummed**) play a guitar or similar instrument by sweeping the thumb or a plectrum up or down the strings.
– ORIGIN imitating the sound.

strumpet noun old use or humorous a woman who has many sexual partners.
– ORIGIN unknown.

strung past and past participle of **STRING**.

strut noun 1 a bar used to support or strengthen a structure. 2 an arrogant or very confident walk. ● **verb** (**struts**, **strutting**, **strutted**) 1 walk in an arrogant or very confident way, with

one's back straight and head up. 2 brace something with a strut or struts.
– ORIGIN from Old English, 'protrude stiffly'.

strychnine /strik-neen/ noun a bitter and highly poisonous substance obtained from the seeds of nux vomica (an Asian tree).
– ORIGIN from Greek *strukhnos*, referring to a kind of nightshade.

Stuart (also **Stewart**) adjective belonging or relating to the royal family ruling Scotland 1371–1714 and Britain 1603–1714 (interrupted by the Commonwealth 1649–60). ● **noun** a member of the Stuart family.

stub noun 1 the remnant of a pencil, cigarette, or similar-shaped object after use. 2 a shortened or unusually short thing. 3 the counterfoil of a cheque, ticket, or other document. ● **verb** (**stubs**, **stubbing**, **stubbed**) 1 accidentally hit one's toe against something. 2 (often **stub something out**) put a cigarette out by pressing the lighted end against something.
– ORIGIN Old English, 'stump of a tree'.

stubble noun 1 short, stiff hairs growing on a man's face when he has not shaved for a while. 2 the cut stalks of cereal plants left in the ground after harvesting.
– DERIVATIVES **stubbly** adjective.
– ORIGIN Old French *stuble*.

stubborn adjective 1 determined not to change one's attitude or position. 2 difficult to move, remove, or cure: *a stubborn stain.*
– DERIVATIVES **stubbornly** adverb **stubbornness** noun.
– ORIGIN unknown.

stubby adjective (**stubbier**, **stubbiest**) short and thick.

stucco noun fine plaster used for coating wall surfaces or moulding into architectural decorations.
– DERIVATIVES **stuccoed** adjective.
– ORIGIN Italian.

stuck past participle of **STICK**[2].

stuck-up adjective informal unfriendly towards others because one believes that one is superior to them.

stud[1] noun 1 a large-headed piece of metal that pierces and projects from a surface, especially for decoration. 2 Brit. a small projection fixed to the base of a shoe or boot to provide better grip. 3 a small piece of jewellery which is pushed through a pierced ear or nostril. 4 a device consisting of two buttons joined with a bar, used to fasten a collar to a shirt. ● **verb** (**studs**, **studding**, **studded**) 1 decorate something with studs or similar small objects. 2 cover or scatter with many small things: *the sky was studded with stars.*
– DERIVATIVES **studding** noun.
– ORIGIN Old English, 'post, upright prop'.

stud[2] noun 1 an establishment where horses or other domesticated animals are kept for breeding. 2 (also **stud horse**) a stallion. 3 informal a man who has many sexual partners or is considered sexually desirable.
– ORIGIN Old English.

student noun 1 a person studying at a university or college. 2 a school pupil. 3 a person who takes a particular interest in a subject. ● **adjective** referring to a person who is

studying to enter a particular profession: *a student nurse.*
- DERIVATIVES **studentship** noun (Brit.) **studenty** adjective (Brit. informal).
- ORIGIN from Latin *studere* 'apply oneself to'.

studio noun (pl. **studios**) 1 a room from which television or radio programmes are broadcast, or in which they are recorded. 2 a place where film or sound recordings are made. 3 a room where an artist works or where dancers practise.
- ORIGIN Italian.

studio flat noun Brit. a flat containing one main room.

studious adjective 1 spending a lot of time studying or reading. 2 done deliberately or with great care.
- DERIVATIVES **studiously** adverb **studiousness** noun.

studly adjective (**studlier, studliest**) informal (of a man) sexually attractive in a strongly masculine way.
- ORIGIN from **STUD**².

study noun (pl. **studies**) 1 the activity of learning or gaining knowledge, typically by reading or research. 2 a detailed investigation and analysis of a subject or situation: *a recent study of army recruits.* 3 a room for reading, writing, or academic work. 4 a drawing or painting done for practice or before creating a larger picture. 5 a piece of music designed to develop a player's technical skill. •verb (**studies, studying, studied**) 1 gain knowledge of a subject. 2 investigate and analyse a subject or situation in detail. 3 concentrate on gaining knowledge. 4 look at closely: *she bent her head to study the plans.* 5 (as adj. **studied**) done deliberately and carefully: *she takes a studied approach to her work.*
- PHRASES **a study in** a good example of a quality or emotion.
- ORIGIN Latin *studium* 'zeal, painstaking application'.

stuff noun 1 substance, things, or activities that one does not know the name of or that one does not need to specify. 2 basic characteristics: *Helen was made of sterner stuff.* 3 (**one's stuff**) informal the things that one has knowledge of or experience in. 4 Brit. dated woollen fabric. •verb 1 fill a container or space tightly or hastily with something. 2 fill out the skin of a dead animal or bird with material to restore its original shape and appearance. 3 fill the inside of an item of food with a savoury or sweet mixture. 4 (**be stuffed up**) informal have one's nose blocked up with catarrh. 5 (**stuff oneself**) informal eat greedily.
- PHRASES **get stuffed** Brit. informal said in anger to tell someone to go away.
- ORIGIN Old French *estoffe* 'material, furniture'.

stuffed shirt noun informal a pompous or conventional person.

stuffing noun 1 a mixture used to stuff poultry or meat before cooking. 2 padding used to stuff cushions, furniture, or soft toys.
- PHRASES **knock the stuffing out of** informal severely damage someone's confidence or strength.

stuffy adjective (**stuffier, stuffiest**) 1 lacking fresh air or ventilation. 2 conventional and narrow-minded. 3 (of a person's nose) blocked up.
- DERIVATIVES **stuffily** adverb **stuffiness** noun.

stultify /stul-ti-fy/ verb (**stultifies, stultifying, stultified**) (usu. as adj. **stultifying**) make someone feel bored or drained of energy.
- DERIVATIVES **stultification** noun **stultifyingly** adverb.
- ORIGIN Latin *stultificare*.

stumble verb 1 trip and briefly lose one's balance. 2 walk unsteadily. 3 make a mistake or mistakes in speaking. 4 (**stumble across/ on/upon**) find someone or something by chance. •noun an act of stumbling.
- ORIGIN Old Norse.

stumbling block noun an obstacle.

stump noun 1 the part of a tree trunk left projecting from the ground after the rest has fallen or been cut down. 2 a part of something that remains after the rest has been cut off or worn away. 3 Cricket each of the three upright pieces of wood which form a wicket. •verb 1 informal baffle someone. 2 Cricket dismiss a batsman by dislodging the bails with the ball while the batsman is out of the crease but not running. 3 walk stiffly and noisily. 4 (**stump something up**) Brit. informal pay a sum of money.
- ORIGIN German *stumpe* or Dutch *stomp*.

stumpy adjective short and thick; squat.

stun verb (**stuns, stunning, stunned**) 1 make a person or animal unconscious or dazed by hitting them on the head. 2 astonish or shock someone so that they are temporarily unable to react.
- ORIGIN Old French *estoner* 'astonish'.

stung past and past participle of **STING**.

stun gun noun a device that makes an attacker unable to move, typically by giving them a small electric shock.

stunk past and past participle of **STINK**.

stunner noun informal a strikingly beautiful or impressive person or thing.

stunning adjective very impressive or attractive.
- DERIVATIVES **stunningly** adverb.

stunt¹ verb slow down the growth or development of someone or something.
- ORIGIN Germanic.

stunt² noun 1 an action displaying spectacular skill and daring. 2 something unusual done to attract attention: *a publicity stunt.*
- ORIGIN unknown.

stuntman (or **stuntwoman**) noun (pl. **stuntmen** or **stuntwomen**) a person who takes an actor's place in performing dangerous stunts.

stupa /stoo-puh/ noun a Buddhist shrine in the form of a dome-shaped building.
- ORIGIN Sanskrit.

stupefy /styoo-pi-fy/ verb (**stupefies, stupefying, stupefied**) 1 make someone unable to think or feel properly. 2 astonish and shock someone.
- DERIVATIVES **stupefaction** noun.
- ORIGIN Latin *stupefacere*.

stupendous /styoo-pen-duhss/ adjective very impressive.
- DERIVATIVES **stupendously** adverb.
- ORIGIN Latin *stupendus* 'to be wondered at'.

S

stupid adjective (**stupider**, **stupidest**) **1** lacking intelligence or common sense. **2** informal used to express annoyance or boredom: *your stupid paintings!* **3** dazed and unable to think clearly.
– DERIVATIVES **stupidity** noun **stupidly** adverb.
– ORIGIN Latin *stupidus*.

stupor /styoo-per/ noun a state of being dazed or nearly unconscious.
– DERIVATIVES **stuporous** adjective.
– ORIGIN Latin.

sturdy adjective (**sturdier**, **sturdiest**) **1** strongly and solidly built or made. **2** confident and determined: *the townspeople have a sturdy independence.*
– DERIVATIVES **sturdily** adverb **sturdiness** noun.
– ORIGIN Old French *esturdi* 'stunned, dazed'.

sturgeon /ster-juhn/ noun a very large river or sea fish with bony plates on the body, from whose roe caviar is made.
– ORIGIN Old French.

Sturm und Drang /shtoorm uunt drang/ noun **1** an 18th-century German literary and artistic movement characterized by the expression of emotional unrest. **2** a state or situation of emotional upheaval or stress: *the Sturm und Drang of adolescence.*
– ORIGIN German, 'storm and stress'.

stushie noun variant spelling of **STOOSHIE**.

stutter verb **1** have difficulty speaking as a result of the involuntary repetition of the first sounds of a word. **2** (of a machine or gun) produce a series of short, sharp sounds. •noun a tendency to stutter while speaking.
– DERIVATIVES **stutterer** noun.
– ORIGIN Germanic.

sty¹ noun (pl. **sties**) a pigsty.
– ORIGIN Old English.

sty² (also **stye**) noun (pl. **sties** or **styes**) an inflamed swelling on the edge of an eyelid.
– ORIGIN from an Old English word meaning 'riser' + EYE.

Stygian /sti-ji-uhn/ adjective literary very dark.
– ORIGIN from the *Styx*, an underworld river in Greek mythology.

style noun **1** a way of doing something. **2** a distinctive appearance, design, or arrangement: *new styles in jewellery.* **3** a way of painting, writing, etc., characteristic of a particular period, person, or movement. **4** elegance and sophistication. **5** an official or legal title. **6** a narrow extension of a plant's ovary, bearing the stigma. •verb **1** design, make, or arrange in a particular form: *he styled my hair differently this time.* **2** give a particular name, description, or title to someone or something.
– DERIVATIVES **styleless** adjective **styler** noun.
– ORIGIN Latin *stilus* 'stylus, stake, style'.

styli plural of **STYLUS**.

stylish adjective **1** having or showing a good sense of style. **2** fashionably elegant.
– DERIVATIVES **stylishly** adverb **stylishness** noun.

stylist noun **1** a person who cuts hair or designs fashionable clothes. **2** a person whose job is to arrange and coordinate food, clothes, etc. in an attractive way in photographs or films.

stylistic adjective relating to style, especially literary style.
– DERIVATIVES **stylistically** adverb.

stylistics plural noun (treated as sing.) the study

of the literary styles of particular writers or types of literature.

stylized (or **stylised**) adjective represented or treated in a non-realistic style.
– DERIVATIVES **stylization** noun.

stylus /sty-luhss/ noun (pl. **styli** /sty-ly/) **1** a hard point following a groove in a gramophone record and transmitting the recorded sound for reproduction. **2** a pointed implement used for scratching or tracing letters or engraving. **3** a pen-like device used to input handwriting directly into a computer.
– ORIGIN Latin *stilus*.

stymie /sty-mi/ verb (**stymies**, **stymying** or **stymieing**, **stymied**) informal prevent or hinder the progress of someone or something.
– ORIGIN unknown.

styptic /stip-tik/ adjective able to stop bleeding. •noun a substance that stops bleeding.
– ORIGIN Greek *stuptikos*.

styrene /sty-reen/ noun Chemistry an unsaturated liquid hydrocarbon obtained as a petroleum by-product and used to make plastics.
– ORIGIN from *styrax*, a resin obtained from a tree.

styrofoam noun (trademark in the US) a kind of expanded polystyrene, used for making food containers.
– ORIGIN from POLYSTYRENE + FOAM.

suasion /sway-zhuhn/ noun formal persuasion as opposed to force.
– ORIGIN Latin.

suave /swahv/ adjective (**suaver**, **suavest**) (of a man) charming, confident, and elegant.
– DERIVATIVES **suavely** adverb **suaveness** noun **suavity** noun (pl. **suavities**).
– ORIGIN Latin *suavis* 'agreeable'.

sub informal noun **1** a submarine. **2** a substitute, especially in a sports team. **3** Brit. a subscription. **4** Brit. a subeditor. **5** Brit. an advance payment of money. •verb (**subs**, **subbing**, **subbed**) **1** act as a substitute. **2** Brit. advance a sum of money to someone.

sub- prefix **1** under: *submarine.* **2** lower in rank or importance: *subaltern.* **3** below; less than: *sub-zero.* **4** subsequent or secondary: *subdivision.*
– ORIGIN from Latin *sub* 'under, close to'.

> USAGE: Sub- changes to suc- before *c*; suf- before *f*; sug- before *g*; sup- before *p*; sur- before *r*; sus- before *c*, *p*, and *t*.

subaltern /sub-uhl-tern/ noun an officer in the British army below the rank of captain.
– ORIGIN from Latin *sub-* 'next below' + *alternus* 'every other'.

sub-aqua adjective relating to swimming or exploring under water, especially with an aqualung.

subaqueous /sub-ayk-wi-uhss/ adjective existing, formed, or taking place under water.

subarctic adjective relating to the region immediately south of the Arctic Circle.

sub-assembly noun (pl. **sub-assemblies**) a unit assembled separately but designed to be incorporated with other units into a larger manufactured product.

subatomic adjective smaller than or occurring within an atom.

subcategory noun (pl. **subcategories**) a secondary or less important category.

subcommittee noun a committee consisting of some members of a larger committee, formed in order to study a subject in more detail.

subconscious adjective relating to the part of the mind of which one is not fully aware but which influences one's actions and feelings. ●noun (**one's/the subconscious**) this part of the mind.
– DERIVATIVES **subconsciously** adverb **subconsciousness** noun.

subcontinent noun a large part of a continent considered as a particular area, such as North America.
– DERIVATIVES **subcontinental** adjective.

subcontract verb /sub-kuhn-**trakt**/ employ a firm or person outside one's company to do work as part of a larger project. ●noun /sub-**kon**-trakt/ a contract to do work for another company as part of a larger project.
– DERIVATIVES **subcontractor** noun.

subculture noun a distinct group within a society or class, having beliefs or interests that are different from those of the larger group.
– DERIVATIVES **subcultural** adjective.

subcutaneous /sub-kyoo-**tay**-ni-uhss/ adjective situated or applied under the skin.
– DERIVATIVES **subcutaneously** adverb.

subdivide verb divide something that has already been divided into smaller parts.

subdivision noun **1** the action of subdividing something. **2** a secondary or less important division.

subdue verb (**subdues, subduing, subdued**) **1** overcome, quieten, or bring under control: *she managed to subdue an instinct to applaud.* **2** bring a country under control by force.
– ORIGIN Latin *subducere* 'draw from below'.

subdued adjective **1** quiet and rather thoughtful or depressed. **2** (of colour or lighting) soft; muted.

subedit verb (**subedits, subediting, subedited**) chiefly Brit. check and correct the written part of a newspaper or magazine before printing.
– DERIVATIVES **subeditor** noun.

subframe noun a supporting frame.

subfusc /sub-fusk, sub-**fusk**/ adjective literary dull or gloomy. ●noun Brit. the formal clothing worn for exams and formal occasions at some universities.
– ORIGIN from Latin *sub-* 'somewhat' + *fuscus* 'dark brown'.

subgroup noun a small group that is part of a larger one.

subheading (also **subhead**) noun a heading given to a section within a larger piece of writing.

subhuman adjective not having the normal qualities of a human being, especially so as to be lacking in intelligence. ●noun a subhuman creature or person.

subject noun /sub-jikt, sub-jekt/ **1** a person or thing that is being discussed, studied, or dealt with. **2** a branch of knowledge studied or taught in a school, college, etc. **3** Grammar the word or words in a sentence that name who or what performs the action of the verb. **4** a member of a country or state other than its ruler. ●adjective /sub-jikt, sub-jekt/ (**subject to**) **1** likely or having a tendency to be affected by something unpleasant or unwelcome: *he was subject to bouts of depression.* **2** dependent or conditional on: *the merger is subject to shareholders' approval.* **3** under someone's or something's control or authority. ●adverb /sub-jikt, sub-jekt/ (**subject to**) if certain conditions are fulfilled. ●verb /suhb-**jekt**/ (usu. **subject someone/thing to**) **1** make someone's or something undergo an unpleasant experience. **2** bring a person or country under one's control or authority.
– DERIVATIVES **subjection** noun.
– ORIGIN from Latin *subicere* 'bring under'.

subjective adjective **1** based on or influenced by personal feelings, tastes, or opinions. **2** Grammar relating to a case of nouns and pronouns used for the subject of a sentence.
– DERIVATIVES **subjectively** adverb **subjectivity** noun.

subject matter noun the thing dealt with or represented in a book, speech, work of art, etc.

sub judice /sub joo-di-si/ adjective being considered by a court of law and therefore not permitted to be publicly discussed elsewhere.
– ORIGIN Latin, 'under a judge'.

subjugate /sub-juu-gayt/ verb conquer or gain control of someone or something.
– DERIVATIVES **subjugation** noun.
– ORIGIN Latin *subjugare* 'bring under a yoke'.

subjunctive Grammar adjective (of a form of a verb) expressing what is imagined or wished or possible. ●noun a subjunctive form of a verb.
– ORIGIN Latin *subjunctivus*.

USAGE: The **subjunctive** form of a verb is used to express what is imagined, wished, or possible. It is usually the same as the ordinary (**indicative**) form of the verb except in the third person singular (*he, she,* or *it*), where the normal **-s** ending is omitted. For example, you should say *face* rather than *faces* in the sentence *the report recommends that he face the tribunal.* The subjunctive is also different from the indicative when using the verb 'to be'; for example, you should say *I were* rather than *I was* in the sentence *I wouldn't try it if I were you.*

sublet verb (**sublets, subletting, sublet**) let a property or part of a property that one is already renting to someone else.

sub lieutenant noun a rank of officer in the Royal Navy, above midshipman and below lieutenant.

sublimate /sub-li-mayt/ verb **1** direct an instinctive impulse, especially sexual energy, into a more socially acceptable activity. **2** transform something into a purer or idealized form. **3** Chemistry another term for SUBLIME.
– DERIVATIVES **sublimation** noun.
– ORIGIN Latin *sublimare* 'raise up'.

sublime adjective (**sublimer, sublimest**) **1** of such excellence or beauty as to inspire great admiration or awe. **2** extreme: *the sublime confidence of youth.* ●verb Chemistry (with reference to a solid substance) change directly into vapour when heated, typically forming a

solid deposit again on cooling.
- DERIVATIVES **sublimely** adverb **sublimity** noun.
- ORIGIN Latin *sublimis*.

subliminal /suhb-**lim**-i-n'l/ adjective (of a stimulus or mental process) affecting someone's mind without their being aware of it.
- DERIVATIVES **subliminally** adverb.
- ORIGIN from **sub-** + Latin *limen* 'threshold'.

sublunary /sub-**loo**-nuh-ri/ adjective literary belonging to this world rather than a better or more spiritual one.
- ORIGIN Latin *sublunaris*, from *luna* 'moon'.

sub-machine gun noun a hand-held lightweight machine gun.

submarine noun a streamlined warship designed to operate under the surface of the sea for long periods. •adjective existing, happening, done, or used under the surface of the sea.
- DERIVATIVES **submariner** /sub-**ma**-ri-ner/ noun.

submerge verb **1** push or hold someone or something under water. **2** go down below the surface of water. **3** completely cover or hide something.
- DERIVATIVES **submergence** noun.
- ORIGIN Latin *submergere*.

submerse verb technical submerge something.

submersible adjective designed to operate under water. •noun a small boat or craft that is submersible.

submersion noun the action of submerging or the state of being submerged.

submicroscopic adjective too small to be seen by an ordinary microscope.

submission noun **1** the action of submitting something. **2** a proposal or application submitted for consideration.

submissive adjective meekly obedient or passive.
- DERIVATIVES **submissively** adverb **submissiveness** noun.

submit verb (**submits, submitting, submitted**) **1** accept or give in to someone's or something's authority, control, or greater strength. **2** present a proposal or application to a person or group of people for consideration or assessment. **3** subject someone or something to a particular process or treatment. **4** (especially in the context of a court of law) suggest or argue.
- ORIGIN Latin *submittere*.

subnormal adjective not meeting standards or reaching a level regarded as normal or usual.
- DERIVATIVES **subnormality** noun.

suboptimal adjective technical of less than the highest standard or quality.

subordinate adjective /suh-**bor**-di-nuht/ **1** lower in rank or position. **2** less important. •noun /suh-**bor**-di-nuht/ a person under the authority or control of someone else. •verb /suh-**bor**-di-nayt/ treat or regard as less important: *economic reforms should be subordinated to financial constraints*.
- DERIVATIVES **subordination** noun.
- ORIGIN Latin *subordinatus* 'placed in a lower rank'.

subordinate clause noun a clause that forms part of and is dependent on a main clause (e.g.

when it rang in *she answered the phone when it rang*).

suborn /suh-**born**/ verb persuade or bribe someone to commit an unlawful act such as perjury.
- ORIGIN Latin *subornare* 'incite secretly'.

subplot noun a plot in a play, novel, etc. that is secondary to the main plot.

subpoena /suh-**pee**-nuh/ noun a written order instructing a person to attend a court of law. •verb (**subpoenas, subpoenaing, subpoenaed** or **subpoena'd**) summon someone with a subpoena.
- ORIGIN from Latin *sub poena* 'under penalty' (the first words of the order).

sub-post office noun (in the UK) a small local post office offering fewer services than a main post office.

sub rosa /sub **roh**-zuh/ adjective & adverb formal happening or done in secret.
- ORIGIN Latin, 'under the rose' (the rose being an emblem of secrecy).

subroutine noun Computing a set of instructions designed to perform a frequently used operation within a program.

sub-Saharan adjective from or forming part of the African regions south of the Sahara Desert.

subscribe verb **1** (often **subscribe to**) arrange to receive something, especially a magazine, on a regular basis by paying in advance. **2** (**subscribe to**) contribute a sum of money to a project or cause on a regular basis. **3** apply to take part in: *the course is fully subscribed*. **4** apply to buy shares in a company. **5** (**subscribe to**) express agreement with an idea or proposal.
- DERIVATIVES **subscriber** noun.
- ORIGIN Latin *subscribere* 'write below'.

subscript adjective (of a letter, figure, or symbol) written or printed below the line.

subscription noun **1** an advance payment made in order to receive or take part in something, or as a donation. **2** the action or fact of subscribing.

subsection noun a division of a section.

subsense noun a related but less important sense of a word defined in a dictionary.

subsequent adjective coming after something in time.
- DERIVATIVES **subsequently** adverb.
- ORIGIN from Latin *subsequi* 'follow after'.

subservient adjective **1** too willing to obey other people. **2** less important.
- DERIVATIVES **subservience** noun.
- ORIGIN Latin, 'complying with'.

subset noun **1** a part of a larger group of related things. **2** Mathematics a set of which all the elements are contained in another set.

subside verb **1** become less intense, violent, or severe. **2** (of water) go down to a lower or the normal level. **3** (of a building) sink lower into the ground. **4** (of the ground) cave in; sink. **5** (**subside into**) give way to a strong feeling.
- ORIGIN Latin *subsidere*.

subsidence /suhb-**sy**-duhnss, **sub**-si-duhnss/ noun the gradual caving in or sinking of an area of land.

subsidiarity /suhb-si-di-**ar**-it-i/ noun (in

S

politics) the principle that a central authority should carry out only those tasks which cannot be carried out at a more local level.

subsidiary adjective 1 related but less important. 2 (of a company) controlled by a holding or parent company. •noun (pl. subsidiaries) a subsidiary company.
– ORIGIN Latin *subsidiarius*.

subsidize (or subsidise) verb 1 support an organization or activity financially. 2 pay part of the cost of producing something to help keep the price low.
– DERIVATIVES **subsidization** noun.

subsidy noun (pl. subsidies) 1 a sum of money given to an industry or business from public funds to help keep the price of a product or service low. 2 a sum of money granted to support an activity or undertaking that is held to be in the public interest. 3 a grant or contribution of money.
– ORIGIN Latin *subsidium* 'assistance'.

subsist verb 1 manage to stay alive, especially with limited resources. 2 chiefly Law remain in force or effect.
– ORIGIN Latin *subsistere* 'stand firm'.

subsistence noun the action or fact of subsisting. •adjective referring to production at a level which is only enough for one's own use, without any surplus for trade: *subsistence agriculture*.

subsistence level (also subsistence wage) noun a standard of living (or wage) that provides only the basic necessities of life.

subsoil noun the soil lying immediately under the surface soil.

subsonic adjective relating to or flying at a speed or speeds less than that of sound.

subspecies noun (pl. same) Biology a subdivision of a species.

substance noun 1 a type of solid, liquid, or gas that has particular properties. 2 the real physical matter of which a person or thing consists. 3 solid basis in reality or fact: *the claim has no substance*. 4 the most important or essential part or meaning. 5 the quality of being important or significant: *nothing of substance was achieved*. 6 the subject matter of a piece of writing or work of art. 7 an intoxicating or narcotic drug, especially an illegal one.
– PHRASES **in substance** with regard to the fundamental points; essentially.
– ORIGIN Latin *substantia* 'being, essence'.

substandard adjective below the usual or required standard.

substantial adjective 1 of great importance, size, or value. 2 strongly built or made. 3 concerning the essential points of something: *there was substantial agreement on changing policies*. 4 real and tangible rather than imaginary.
– DERIVATIVES **substantiality** noun.

substantially adverb 1 to a great extent. 2 for the most part; mainly: *things will remain substantially the same*.

substantiate /suhb-stan-shi-ayt/ verb provide evidence to prove that something is true.
– DERIVATIVES **substantiation** noun.
– ORIGIN Latin *substantiare* 'give substance'.

substantive /sub-stuhn-tiv, suhb-stan-tiv/ adjective important or meaningful. •noun Grammar, dated a noun.
– DERIVATIVES **substantively** adverb.

substation noun 1 a set of equipment reducing the high voltage of electrical power transmission to that suitable for supply to consumers. 2 a small police station or fire station.

substitute noun 1 a person or thing acting or used in place of another. 2 a sports player who may replace another after a match has begun. •verb 1 use one person or thing instead of another. 2 replace one person or thing with another. 3 replace a sports player with a substitute during a match.
– DERIVATIVES **substitutable** adjective **substitution** noun.
– ORIGIN Latin *substituere* 'put in place of'.

USAGE: Traditionally, **substitute** is followed by **for** and means 'use one person or thing instead of another', as in *she substituted the fake vase for the real one*. It may also be used with **with** or **by** to mean 'replace something with something else', as in *she substituted the real vase with the fake one*. This can be confusing, since the two sentences shown above mean the same thing, yet the object of the verb and the object of the preposition have swapped positions. Despite the potential confusion, the second, newer use is acceptable, although still disapproved of by some people.

substrate /sub-strayt/ noun 1 the surface or material on which an organism lives, grows, or feeds. 2 the substance on which an enzyme acts.
– ORIGIN from **SUBSTRATUM**.

substratum noun (pl. substrata) 1 an underlying layer or substance, in particular a layer of rock or soil beneath the surface of the ground. 2 a foundation or basis.

substructure noun an underlying or supporting structure.

subsume verb include something in a larger category or group.
– ORIGIN Latin *subsumere*.

subtenant noun a person who rents property from a tenant.

subtend verb Geometry (of a line, arc, etc.) form an angle at a particular point when straight lines from its extremities meet.
– ORIGIN Latin *subtendere*.

subterfuge /sub-ter-fyooj/ noun secret or dishonest actions used in order to achieve an aim.
– ORIGIN from Latin *subterfugere* 'escape secretly'.

subterranean /sub-tuh-ray-ni-uhn/ adjective existing or happening under the earth's surface.
– DERIVATIVES **subterraneous** adjective.
– ORIGIN Latin *subterraneus*, from *terra* 'earth'.

subtext noun an underlying theme in a speech or piece of writing.

subtitle noun 1 (subtitles) captions displayed at the bottom of a cinema or television screen that translate the dialogue. 2 a secondary title of a published work. •verb provide something with a subtitle or subtitles.

subtle /sut-uhl/ adjective (**subtler**, **subtlest**) **1** so delicate or precise that it is difficult to analyse or describe: *a subtle distinction*. **2** cleverly achieving an effect in a way that is not immediately obvious: *subtle lighting*. **3** making use of clever and indirect methods to achieve something. **4** able to make fine distinctions: *a subtle mind*.
– DERIVATIVES **subtlety** noun (pl. **subtleties**) **subtly** adverb.
– ORIGIN Latin *subtilis*.

subtotal noun the total of one set within a larger group of figures to be added.

subtract verb take one number or amount away from another to calculate the difference between them.
– DERIVATIVES **subtraction** noun **subtractive** adjective.
– ORIGIN Latin *subtrahere* 'draw away'.

subtropical adjective relating to the regions of the world that are near or next to the tropics.
– DERIVATIVES **subtropics** plural noun.

subunit noun a distinct component of something.

suburb noun a residential district on the outskirts of a city.
– DERIVATIVES **suburbanize** (or **suburbanise**) verb.
– ORIGIN from Latin *sub-* 'near to' + *urbs* 'city'.

suburban adjective **1** relating to or like a suburb. **2** boringly conventional.

suburbanite noun a person who lives in a suburb.

suburbia noun suburbs and the way of life of the people who live in them.

subvention noun a grant of money, especially from a government.
– ORIGIN Latin, from *subvenire* 'assist'.

subversive adjective trying or intended to damage or weaken the power of an established system or institution. •noun a subversive person.
– DERIVATIVES **subversively** adverb **subversiveness** noun.

subvert verb damage or weaken the power of an established system or institution.
– DERIVATIVES **subversion** noun **subverter** noun.
– ORIGIN Latin *subvertere*.

subway noun **1** Brit. a tunnel under a road for pedestrians to use. **2** N. Amer. an underground railway.

subwoofer noun a part of a loudspeaker designed to reproduce very low bass frequencies.

sub-zero adjective (of temperature) lower than zero; below freezing.

succeed verb **1** achieve an aim or purpose. **2** gain fame, wealth, or social status. **3** take over a position or title from someone else. **4** become the new rightful holder of a position or title: *James I succeeded to the throne in 1603*. **5** come after and take the place of: *her embarrassment was succeeded by fear*.
– ORIGIN Latin *succedere* 'come close after'.

success noun **1** the achievement of an aim or purpose. **2** the gaining of fame, wealth, or social status. **3** a person or thing that achieves success.
– ORIGIN Latin *successus*.

successful adjective **1** having achieved an aim or purpose. **2** having achieved fame, wealth, or social status.
– DERIVATIVES **successfully** adverb.

succession noun **1** a number of people or things following one after the other. **2** the action or right of inheriting a position or title.
– PHRASES **in quick succession** following one another at short intervals. **in succession** following one after the other without interruption.

successive adjective following one another or following others.
– DERIVATIVES **successively** adverb.

successor noun a person or thing that succeeds another.

success story noun informal a successful person or thing.

succinct /suhk-**singkt**/ adjective expressed clearly and in few words.
– DERIVATIVES **succinctly** adverb **succinctness** noun.
– ORIGIN from Latin *succingere* 'tuck up'.

succour /**suk**-ker/ (US **succor**) noun help given to someone who is suffering or in difficulty. •verb help someone who is suffering or in difficulty.
– ORIGIN Latin *succursus*, from *succurrere* 'run to the help of'.

succubus /**suk**-kyuu-buhss/ noun (pl. **succubi** /**suk**-kyuu-by/) a female demon believed to have sex with sleeping men.
– ORIGIN Latin, 'prostitute'.

succulent adjective **1** (of food) tender, juicy, and tasty. **2** (of a plant) having thick fleshy leaves or stems adapted to storing water. •noun a succulent plant.
– DERIVATIVES **succulence** noun **succulently** adverb.
– ORIGIN Latin *succulentus*, from *succus* 'juice'.

succumb verb **1** give in to pressure, temptation, etc. **2** die from the effect of a disease or injury.
– ORIGIN Latin *succumbere*.

such determiner, predeterminer, & pronoun **1** of the type previously mentioned. **2** (**such** —— **as/that**) of the type about to be mentioned: *there's no such thing as a free lunch*. **3** to so high a degree; so great.
– PHRASES **as such** in the exact sense of the word. **such-and-such** an unspecified person or thing. **such as 1** for example. **2** of a kind that; like.
– ORIGIN Old English, related to **so**¹ and **ALIKE**.

suchlike pronoun things of the type mentioned. •determiner of the type mentioned.

suck verb **1** draw liquid or air into the mouth by tightening the lip muscles and breathing in. **2** hold something in the mouth and draw at it by tightening the lip and cheek muscles. **3** pull forcefully: *he was sucked under the surface of the river*. **4** (**suck someone in/into**) involve someone in a situation or activity, especially against their will. **5** (**suck up to**) informal try to please someone in authority in order to gain advantage for oneself. **6** N. Amer. informal be very bad or unpleasant. •noun an act or sound of sucking.
– ORIGIN Old English, related to **SOAK**.

sucker noun **1** a rubber cup that sticks to a

S

surface by suction. **2** a flat or concave organ that enables an animal to cling to a surface by suction. **3** informal a gullible person. **4** (**a sucker for**) informal a person who is especially influenced by or fond of a particular thing: *I was a sucker for flattery.* **5** a shoot springing from the base of a tree or other plant, especially one coming from the root at some distance from the trunk.

sucker punch informal noun an unexpected punch or blow. • verb (**sucker-punch**) punch or hit someone unexpectedly.

suckle verb (with reference to a baby or young animal) feed from the breast or udder.

suckling noun a baby or young animal that is still feeding on its mother's milk.

sucre /soo-kray/ noun the basic unit of money of Ecuador.
– ORIGIN named after the Venezuelan revolutionary Antonio José de *Sucre.*

sucrose /soo-krohz/ noun a compound which is the chief component of cane or beet sugar.
– ORIGIN from French *sucre* 'sugar'.

suction noun the process of removing air or liquid from a space or container, creating a partial vacuum that causes something else to be sucked in or surfaces to stick together.
• verb remove something using suction.
– ORIGIN Latin, from *sugere* 'to suck'.

Sudanese /soo-duh-neez/ noun a person from Sudan. • adjective relating to Sudan.

sudden adjective happening or done quickly and unexpectedly.
– PHRASES (**all**) **of a sudden** suddenly.
– DERIVATIVES **suddenly** adverb **suddenness** noun.
– ORIGIN Old French *sudein.*

sudden death noun a means of deciding the winner in a tied match, in which play continues and the winner is the first side or player to score.

sudden infant death syndrome noun technical term for COT DEATH.

sudoku /soo-dok-oo, soo-doh-koo/ noun a number puzzle in which players insert numbers into a grid consisting of nine squares subdivided into a further nine squares.
– ORIGIN from Japanese *su doku*, from *su* 'number' + *doku* 'place'.

sudorific /syoo-duh-rif-ik/ adjective relating to or causing sweating. • noun a drug which causes sweating.
– ORIGIN from Latin *sudor* 'sweat'.

Sudra /soo-druh, shoo-druh/ noun a member of the worker caste, lowest of the four Hindu castes.
– ORIGIN Sanskrit.

suds plural noun froth made from soap and water.
– DERIVATIVES **sudsy** adjective.
– ORIGIN probably related to SEETHE.

sue verb (**sues, suing, sued**) **1** take legal action against a person, institution, etc. typically in order to get compensation for something. **2** (**sue for**) formal appeal formally to a person for: *the rebels were forced to sue for peace.*
– ORIGIN Old French *suer.*

suede noun leather with the flesh side rubbed to make a velvety nap.
– ORIGIN from French *gants de Suède* 'gloves of Sweden'.

suet /soo-it/ noun the hard white fat on the kidneys of cattle, sheep, and other animals, used in making puddings, pastry, etc.
– DERIVATIVES **suety** adjective.
– ORIGIN Old French.

suffer verb **1** experience or be subjected to something bad or unpleasant. **2** (**suffer from**) be affected by or subject to an illness or condition. **3** become or appear worse in quality: *his relationship with her did suffer.* **4** old use tolerate someone or something. **5** old use allow someone to do something.
– DERIVATIVES **sufferer** noun.
– ORIGIN Latin *sufferre.*

sufferance noun lack of objection rather than genuine approval; toleration.

suffice /suh-fyss/ verb be enough or adequate.
– PHRASES **suffice** (**it**) **to say** used to indicate that one is withholding details in order to be brief or discreet.
– ORIGIN Latin *sufficere.*

sufficiency noun (pl. **sufficiencies**) **1** the condition or quality of being sufficient. **2** an adequate amount.

sufficient adjective & determiner enough; adequate.
– DERIVATIVES **sufficiently** adverb.

suffix /suf-fiks/ noun a letter or group of letters added at the end of a word to form another word (e.g. *-ation*).

suffocate verb **1** die or cause to die from lack of air or inability to breathe. **2** have or cause to have difficulty in breathing.
– DERIVATIVES **suffocation** noun.
– ORIGIN Latin *suffocare* 'stifle'.

suffragan /suf-ruh-guhn/ (also **suffragan bishop**) noun a bishop appointed to help the bishop in charge of a diocese.
– ORIGIN Latin *suffraganeus* 'assistant'.

suffrage /suf-frij/ noun the right to vote in political elections.
– ORIGIN Latin *suffragium.*

suffragette /suf-fruh-jet/ noun historical a woman who campaigned for women to be given the right to vote in political elections.

suffragist noun historical a person in favour of women being given the right to vote in political elections.

suffuse /suh-fyooz/ verb gradually spread through or over: *her cheeks were suffused with colour.*
– DERIVATIVES **suffusion** noun.
– ORIGIN Latin *suffundere* 'pour into'.

Sufi /soo-fi/ noun (pl. **Sufis**) a member of a Muslim group devoting themselves to prayer and meditation and leading a very strict, simple life.
– DERIVATIVES **Sufism** noun.
– ORIGIN Arabic.

sugar noun **1** a sweet crystalline substance obtained especially from sugar cane and sugar beet. **2** any of the class of soluble crystalline sweet-tasting carbohydrates found in plant and animal tissue, including sucrose and glucose. • verb sweeten, sprinkle, or coat something with sugar.
– PHRASES **sugar the pill** see PILL.
– DERIVATIVES **sugarless** adjective.
– ORIGIN Old French *sukere*, from Arabic.

sugar beet noun a type of beet (plant) from

which sugar is extracted.

sugar cane noun a tropical grass with tall thick stems from which sugar is extracted.

sugar-coated adjective superficially attractive or acceptable.

sugar daddy noun informal a rich older man who lavishes gifts on a much younger woman.

sugar snap (also **sugar snap pea**) noun a type of mangetout pea with thick, rounded pods.

sugar soap noun Brit. an alkaline preparation containing washing soda and soap, used for cleaning or removing paint.

sugary adjective 1 containing much sugar. 2 coated in sugar. 3 too sentimental.

suggest verb 1 put an idea or plan forward for consideration. 2 make someone think that something exists or is the case: *evidence suggests that he died soon after 1190.* 3 say or express indirectly: *are you suggesting that I should ignore her?* 4 (**suggest itself**) (of an idea) come into one's mind.
– ORIGIN Latin *suggerere* 'suggest, prompt'.

suggestible adjective quick to accept other people's ideas or suggestions; easily influenced.
– DERIVATIVES **suggestibility** noun.

suggestion noun 1 an idea or plan put forward for consideration. 2 something that implies or indicates a certain fact or situation: *there is no suggestion that she was involved in wrongdoing.* 3 a slight trace or indication: *a suggestion of a smile.* 4 Psychology the process by which a person is led to accept an idea or belief uncritically, especially as a technique in hypnosis.

suggestive adjective 1 bringing ideas, images, etc. to mind: *flavours suggestive of coffee and blackberry.* 2 (of a remark, joke, etc.) hinting at sexual matters; mildly indecent.
– DERIVATIVES **suggestively** adverb **suggestiveness** noun.

suicide noun 1 the action of killing oneself deliberately. 2 a person who commits suicide. 3 a course of action which is likely to be very damaging to one's career, position in society, etc. • adjective referring to a military operation carried out by people who do not expect to survive it: *a suicide bomber.*
– DERIVATIVES **suicidal** adjective **suicidally** adverb.
– ORIGIN from Latin *sui* 'of oneself' + *caedere* 'kill'.

suicide pact noun an agreement between two or more people to commit suicide together.

sui generis /soo-i **jen**-uh-riss/ adjective unique.
– ORIGIN Latin, 'of its own kind'.

suit /rhymes with boot/ noun 1 a set of outer clothes made of the same fabric and designed to be worn together, consisting of a jacket and trousers or a skirt. 2 a set of clothes for a particular activity. 3 any of the sets into which a pack of playing cards is divided (spades, hearts, diamonds, and clubs). 4 a lawsuit. 5 informal a high-ranking business executive. 6 the process of trying to win a woman's affection with a view to marriage. • verb 1 be convenient for or acceptable to: *what time would suit you?* 2 (of clothes, colours, etc.) go well with or be right for someone's features or figure. 3 (**suit oneself**) do exactly as one wants. 4 (as adj. **suited**) right or appropriate for a particular person,

purpose, or situation: *washable wallpaper ideally suited to bathrooms and kitchens.*
– PHRASES **suit someone down to the ground** Brit. be extremely convenient or appropriate for someone.
– ORIGIN Old French *siwte*.

suitable adjective right or appropriate for a particular person, purpose, or situation.
– DERIVATIVES **suitability** noun **suitably** adverb.

suitcase noun a case with a handle and a hinged lid, used for carrying clothes and other personal possessions.

suite /sweet/ noun 1 a set of rooms for one person's or family's use or for a particular purpose. 2 a set of furniture of the same design. 3 a set of pieces of instrumental music to be played in succession. 4 a set of pieces from an opera or musical arranged as one instrumental work.
– ORIGIN French.

suitor /soo-ter/ noun a man who wishes to marry a particular woman.

sulfur etc. noun US spelling of **SULPHUR** etc.

sulk verb be silent, bad-tempered, and resentful as a result of annoyance or disappointment. • noun a period of sulking.

sulky adjective (**sulkier, sulkiest**) silent, bad-tempered, and resentful.
– DERIVATIVES **sulkily** adverb **sulkiness** noun.
– ORIGIN perhaps from former *sulke* 'hard to dispose of'.

sullen adjective bad-tempered and sulky.
– DERIVATIVES **sullenly** adverb **sullenness** noun.
– ORIGIN Old French *sulein*.

sully verb (**sullies, sullying, sullied**) literary 1 damage someone's or something's purity or reputation. 2 make something dirty.
– ORIGIN perhaps from French *souiller* 'to soil'.

sulphate (US **sulfate**) noun Chemistry a salt or ester of sulphuric acid.

sulphide /sul-fyd/ (US **sulfide**) noun a compound of sulphur with another element or group.

sulphonamide /sul-fo-nuh-myd/ (US **sulfonamide**) noun any of a class of sulphur-containing drugs which are able to prevent the multiplication of certain bacteria.

sulphur (US & Chemistry **sulfur**) noun a non-metallic chemical element which easily catches fire, typically occurring as yellow crystals.
– ORIGIN Latin *sulfur, sulphur*.

sulphur dioxide noun a colourless strong-smelling poisonous gas formed by burning sulphur.

sulphuric /sul-**fyoor**-ik/ (US **sulfuric**) adjective containing sulphur or sulphuric acid.

sulphuric acid noun a strong corrosive acid made by oxidizing solutions of sulphur dioxide.

sulphurous (US **sulfurous**) adjective containing or obtained from sulphur.

sultan noun the title given to a ruler in some Muslim countries.
– ORIGIN Arabic, 'power, ruler'.

sultana noun 1 Brit. a small light brown seedless raisin. 2 a wife of a sultan.
– ORIGIN Italian, feminine of *sultano* 'sultan'.

sultanate noun 1 the rank or position of a sultan. 2 the territory ruled by a sultan.

sultry adjective (**sultrier, sultriest**) 1 (of the

S

weather) hot and humid. 2 displaying or suggesting sexual passion.
– ORIGIN from former *sulter* 'swelter'.

sum noun 1 a particular amount of money. 2 (also **sum total**) the total amount resulting from the addition of two or more numbers or amounts. 3 an arithmetical calculation. •verb (**sums, summing, summed**) (**sum someone/ thing up**) 1 concisely describe someone's or something's nature or character. 2 (**sum something up** or **sum up**) summarize something briefly. 3 Law (of a judge) review the evidence at the end of a case, and direct the jury about points of law.
– PHRASES **in sum** to sum up.
– ORIGIN Latin *summa* 'main part, sum total'.

sumac /soo-mak, shoo--mak/ (also **sumach**) noun a shrub or small tree with clusters of fruits which are ground and used as a spice in Middle Eastern cooking.
– ORIGIN Arabic.

Sumatran /suu-mah-truhn/ noun a person from the Indonesian island of Sumatra. •adjective relating to Sumatra.

Sumerian /soo-meer-i-uhn/ adjective relating to Sumer, an ancient region of what is now Iraq. •noun a person from Sumer.

summarize (or **summarise**) verb give a brief statement of the main points of something.

summary noun (pl. **summaries**) a brief statement of the main points of something. •adjective 1 not including unnecessary details or formalities. 2 (of a legal process or judgement) done or made without the normal legal formalities.
– DERIVATIVES **summarily** adverb.
– ORIGIN Latin *summarius*.

> **USAGE:** Do not confuse **summary** and **summery**. A **summary** is a brief statement of the main points of something (*a summary of today's news*), whereas **summery** is an adjective meaning 'typical of or suitable for summer' (*summery weather*).

summation /sum-may-sh'n/ noun 1 the process of adding things together. 2 the action of summing something up. 3 a summary.

summer noun the season after spring and before autumn, when the weather is warmest. •verb spend the summer in a particular place.
– DERIVATIVES **summery** adjective.
– ORIGIN Old English.

summer house noun a small building in a garden, used for relaxing in during fine weather.

summer pudding noun Brit. a pudding of soft summer fruit encased in bread or sponge.

summer school noun a course of lectures held during school and university summer vacations.

summertime noun 1 the season or period of summer. 2 (**summer time**) Brit. time as advanced one hour ahead of standard time so that it is light for an extra hour in the evening.

summing-up noun 1 a summary. 2 a judge's review of evidence at the end of a case, with a direction to the jury about points of law.

summit noun 1 the highest point of a hill or mountain. 2 the highest possible level of achievement. 3 a meeting between heads of government.
– ORIGIN Old French *somete*.

summiteer noun a person taking part in a government summit.

summon verb 1 instruct someone to be present. 2 order someone to appear in a court of law. 3 urgently ask for help. 4 call people to attend a meeting. 5 make an effort to produce a quality or reaction from within oneself: *she managed to summon up a smile.*
– ORIGIN Latin *summonere* 'give a hint'.

summons noun (pl. **summonses**) 1 an order to appear in a court of law. 2 an act of instructing someone to be present. •verb chiefly Law serve someone with a summons.

sumo /soo-moh/ noun Japanese wrestling in which a wrestler must not go outside a circle or touch the ground with any part of his body except the soles of his feet.
– ORIGIN Japanese.

sump noun 1 the base of an internal-combustion engine, which serves as a reservoir of oil for the lubrication system. 2 a hollow in the floor of a mine or cave in which water collects. 3 a cesspool.
– ORIGIN from Dutch or German *sump* 'marsh'.

sumptuary /sumpt-yoo-ri/ adjective chiefly historical referring to laws that limit private spending on food and personal items.
– ORIGIN Latin *sumptuarius*.

sumptuous adjective splendid and expensive-looking.
– DERIVATIVES **sumptuously** adverb **sumptuousness** noun.
– ORIGIN Latin *sumptuosus*, from *sumptus* 'cost'.

sum total noun another term for **sum** (in sense 2).

sun noun 1 (also **Sun**) the star round which the earth orbits. 2 any similar star, with or without planets. 3 the light or warmth received from the sun. •verb (**suns, sunning, sunned**) (**sun oneself**) sit or lie in the sun.
– PHRASES **under the sun** in existence.
– DERIVATIVES **sunless** adjective.
– ORIGIN Old English.

sun-baked adjective exposed to the heat of the sun.

sunbathe verb sit or lie in the sun to get a suntan.
– DERIVATIVES **sunbather** noun.

sunbeam noun a ray of sunlight.

sunbed noun Brit. 1 a long chair used for sunbathing. 2 a piece of equipment for acquiring an artificial tan, consisting of two banks of sunlamps between which a person lies or stands.

sunbelt noun a strip of territory receiving a high amount of sunshine, especially the southern US from California to Florida.

sunblock noun a cream or lotion for protecting the skin from sunburn.

sunburn noun inflammation of the skin caused by too much exposure to the ultraviolet rays of the sun.
– DERIVATIVES **sunburned** (or **sunburnt**) adjective.

sunburst noun 1 a design or ornament representing the sun and its rays. 2 a sudden brief appearance of the full sun from behind clouds.

suncream noun a cream rubbed on to the skin to protect it from sunburn.

sundae noun a dish of ice cream with added ingredients such as fruit, nuts, and syrup.
– ORIGIN perhaps from **SUNDAY**, either because the dish was made with ice cream left over from Sunday, or because it was sold only on Sundays.

Sunday noun the day of the week before Monday and following Saturday, observed by Christians as a day of religious worship.
– ORIGIN Old English, 'day of the sun'.

Sunday best noun a person's best clothes.

Sunday school noun a class held on Sundays to teach children about Christianity or Judaism.

sun deck noun the deck of a yacht or cruise ship that is open to the sky.

sunder verb literary **1** split something apart. **2** break the connection or relationship between two or more people or things.
– ORIGIN Old English.

sundew noun a small carnivorous plant found in boggy places, with leaves bearing sticky hairs for trapping insects.

sundial noun a device used for telling the time, consisting of a pointer that casts a shadow on a surface marked with hours like a clock.

sundown noun sunset.

sundress noun a light, loose sleeveless dress.

sun-dried adjective dried in the sun, as opposed to by artificial heat.

sundry adjective of various kinds. ● plural noun (**sundries**) various items not important enough to be mentioned individually.
– ORIGIN Old English, 'distinct, separate'.

sunfish noun (pl. same or **sunfishes**) a large sea fish with tall fins near the rear of the body.

sunflower noun a tall plant bearing very large yellow flowers with edible seeds from which an oil used in cooking, margarine, etc. is extracted.

sung past participle of **SING**.

sunglasses plural noun glasses tinted to protect the eyes from sunlight or glare.

sunk past participle of **SINK**[1].

sunken adjective **1** having sunk. **2** at a lower level than the surrounding area. **3** (of a person's cheeks or eyes) hollow or appearing set back into the face as a result of age, disease, etc.
– ORIGIN past participle of **SINK**[1].

sun-kissed adjective made warm or brown by the sun.

sunlamp noun a lamp giving off ultraviolet rays, used chiefly to produce an artificial suntan.

sunlight noun light from the sun.
– DERIVATIVES **sunlit** adjective.

Sunna /suu-nuh, sun-nuh/ noun the traditional part of Muslim law based on Muhammad's words or acts, accepted as authoritative by Muslims.
– ORIGIN Arabic, 'form, way, rule'.

Sunni /suu-ni, sun-ni/ noun (pl. same or **Sunnis**) **1** one of the two main branches of Islam, the other being Shia. **2** a Muslim who follows the

Sunni branch of Islam.
– ORIGIN Arabic, 'custom, standard rule'.

sunny adjective (**sunnier**, **sunniest**) **1** bright with or receiving much sunlight. **2** cheerful.

sunrise noun **1** the time in the morning when the sun rises. **2** the colours and light visible in the sky at sunrise.

sunroof noun a panel in the roof of a car that can be opened for extra ventilation.

sunscreen noun a cream or lotion rubbed on to the skin to protect it from the sun.

sunset noun **1** the time in the evening when the sun sets. **2** the colours and light visible in the sky at sunset.

sunshade noun a parasol, awning, or other device giving protection from the sun.

sunshine noun sunlight unbroken by cloud.
– DERIVATIVES **sunshiny** adjective.

sunspot noun a temporary darker and cooler patch on the sun's surface.

sunstroke noun heatstroke caused by spending too much time exposed to hot sunlight.

suntan noun a golden-brown colouring of the skin caused by spending time in the sun.
– DERIVATIVES **suntanned** adjective.

sunup noun chiefly N. Amer. sunrise.

sup[1] verb (**sups**, **supping**, **supped**) dated or N. English take drink or liquid food by sips or spoonfuls. ● noun a sip.
– ORIGIN Old English.

sup[2] verb (**sups**, **supping**, **supped**) dated eat supper.
– ORIGIN Old French *super*.

super adjective informal excellent.

super- combining form **1** above; over; beyond: *superstructure*. **2** to a great or extreme degree: *superabundant*. **3** extra large of its kind: *superpower*.
– ORIGIN from Latin *super* 'above, beyond'.

superabundant adjective formal occurring in very large quantities.
– DERIVATIVES **superabundance** noun.

superannuated adjective **1** (of an employee) discharged from a job with a pension. **2** too old to be effective or useful.
– ORIGIN from Latin *super-* 'over' + *annus* 'year'.

superannuation noun regular payment made into a fund by an employee towards a future pension.

superb adjective extremely good or impressive.
– DERIVATIVES **superbly** adverb.
– ORIGIN Latin *superbus* 'proud, magnificent'.

superbike noun a high-performance motorcycle.

superbug noun informal a bacterium, insect, etc. which has become resistant to antibiotics or pesticides.

supercar noun a high-performance sports car.

supercharge verb (usu. as adj. **supercharged**) **1** provide an engine with a supercharger. **2** give extra power, energy, or intensity to: *a supercharged collection of dance tracks*.

supercharger noun a device that increases the efficiency of an internal-combustion engine by raising the pressure of the fuel-air mixture supplied to it.

S

supercilious /soo-per-sil-i-uhss/ adjective behaving as though one thinks one is superior to other people.
– DERIVATIVES **superciliously** adverb **superciliousness** noun.
– ORIGIN Latin *superciliosus* 'haughty'.

supercomputer noun a particularly powerful mainframe computer.

superconductivity noun Physics the property of zero electrical resistance in some substances at very low temperatures.
– DERIVATIVES **superconducting** adjective **superconductor** noun.

supercontinent noun a huge land mass believed to have divided in the geological past to form some of the present continents.

supercool verb Chemistry cool a liquid below its freezing point without solidification or crystallization.

superego noun (pl. **superegos**) the part of the mind that acts as a conscience, reflecting social standards that have been learned. Compare with **EGO** and **ID**.

supererogatory /soo-puh-ri-rog-uh-tuh-ri/ adjective more than what is needed or required; superfluous.
– ORIGIN Latin, from *supererogare* 'pay in addition'.

superficial adjective 1 existing or happening at or on the surface. 2 appearing to exist or be true until examined more closely: *the resemblance is superficial*. 3 not thorough: *a superficial knowledge of the system*. 4 lacking depth of character or understanding; not concerned with serious matters.
– DERIVATIVES **superficiality** noun (pl. **superficialities**) **superficially** adverb.
– ORIGIN Latin *superficialis*.

superfluous /soo-per-floo-uhss/ adjective more than is needed; unnecessary.
– DERIVATIVES **superfluity** noun (pl. **superfluities**) **superfluously** adverb.
– ORIGIN Latin *superfluus*.

supergiant noun a star that is larger and more luminous than a giant.

superglue noun a very strong quick-setting glue.

supergrass noun Brit. informal a police informer who gives information about the criminal activities of a large number of people.

superheat verb Physics 1 heat a liquid under pressure above its boiling point without vaporization. 2 heat steam or other vapour above the temperature of the liquid from which it was formed.

superhero noun (pl. **superheroes**) a fictional hero with superhuman powers.

superhighway noun N. Amer. a dual carriageway.

superhuman adjective having or showing exceptional ability or powers.
– DERIVATIVES **superhumanly** adverb.

superimpose verb place or lay one thing over another.
– DERIVATIVES **superimposition** noun.

superintend verb manage or oversee an activity, organization, etc.
– DERIVATIVES **superintendence** noun.

superintendent noun 1 a person who supervises or is in charge of an activity, organization, etc. 2 (in the UK) a police officer ranking above chief inspector. 3 (in the US) the chief of a police department. 4 N. Amer. the caretaker of a building.
– ORIGIN from Latin *superintendere*.

superior adjective 1 higher in status, quality, or power. 2 of a high standard or quality. 3 having or showing a belief that one is better than other people: *he had a rather superior manner*. 4 (of a letter, figure, or symbol) written or printed above the line. 5 chiefly Anatomy higher in position. •noun 1 a person of higher rank. 2 the head of a monastery or other religious institution.
– ORIGIN Latin, 'higher'.

superiority noun the state of being superior.

superlative /soo-per-luh-tiv/ adjective 1 of the highest quality or degree. 2 Grammar (of an adjective or adverb) expressing the highest degree of a quality (e.g. *bravest*, *most fiercely*). Contrasted with **POSITIVE** and **COMPARATIVE**. •noun an exaggerated expression of praise.
– DERIVATIVES **superlatively** adverb.
– ORIGIN Latin *superlativus*.

superman (or **superwoman**) noun (pl. **supermen** or **superwomen**) informal a person with exceptional physical or mental abilities.

supermarket noun a large self-service shop selling foods and household goods.

supermodel noun a very successful and famous fashion model.

supernal /soo-per-nuhl/ adjective literary 1 relating to the sky or the heavens. 2 of supreme excellence.
– ORIGIN Latin *supernalis*.

supernatural adjective referring or relating to events, forces, or powers that cannot be explained by science or the laws of nature. •noun (**the supernatural**) supernatural events, forces, or powers.
– DERIVATIVES **supernaturally** adverb.

supernova /soo-per-noh-vuh/ noun (pl. **supernovae** /soo-per-noh-vee/ or **supernovas**) a star that undergoes an explosion, becoming suddenly very much brighter.

supernumerary /soo-per-nyoo-muh-ruh-ri/ adjective 1 more than is normally needed; extra. 2 not belonging to a regular staff but employed for extra work. •noun (pl. **supernumeraries**) an extra person or thing.
– ORIGIN Latin *supernumerarius* 'soldier added to a legion after it is complete'.

superordinate /soo-per-or-di-nuht/ noun a thing that represents a higher order or category within a system of classification.

superpose verb place something on or above something else.
– DERIVATIVES **superposition** noun.
– ORIGIN French *superposer*.

superpower noun a very powerful and influential nation.

superscript adjective (of a letter, figure, or symbol) written or printed above the line.

supersede /soo-per-seed/ verb take the place of someone or something previously in authority or use.
– ORIGIN Latin *supersedere* 'be superior to'.

supersonic adjective involving or referring to a speed greater than that of sound.
– DERIVATIVES **supersonically** adverb.

superstar noun an extremely famous and successful performer or sports player.
– DERIVATIVES **superstardom** noun.

superstate noun a large and powerful state formed from a federation or union of several nations.

superstition noun 1 irrational belief in supernatural events. 2 a widely held but irrational belief that certain objects, actions, or events bring good or bad luck.
– ORIGIN Latin.

superstitious adjective believing in the supernatural and its influence in bringing good or bad luck.
– DERIVATIVES **superstitiously** adverb.

superstore noun a very large out-of-town supermarket.

superstructure noun 1 a structure built on top of something else. 2 the part of a building above its foundations. 3 the parts of a ship, other than masts and rigging, above its hull and main deck.

supertanker noun a very large oil tanker.

supervene /soo-per-veen/ verb happen so as to interrupt or change an existing situation.
– DERIVATIVES **supervenient** adjective **supervention** noun.
– ORIGIN Latin *supervenire* 'come in addition'.

supervise verb observe and direct the performance of a task or the work of a person.
– DERIVATIVES **supervision** noun **supervisor** noun **supervisory** adjective.
– ORIGIN Latin *supervidere* 'survey, supervise'.

supine /soo-pyn/ adjective 1 lying face upwards. 2 failing to act as a result of laziness or weakness.
– DERIVATIVES **supinely** adverb **supineness** noun.
– ORIGIN Latin *supinus* 'bent backwards'.

supper noun a light or informal evening meal.
– PHRASES **sing for one's supper** provide a service in return for a benefit.
– ORIGIN from Old French *super* 'to sup'.

supplant verb take the place of: *another technology might supplant the CD.*
– DERIVATIVES **supplanter** noun.
– ORIGIN Latin *supplantare* 'trip up'.

supple adjective (**suppler**, **supplest**) able to bend or move easily; flexible.
– DERIVATIVES **suppleness** noun.
– ORIGIN Latin *supplex* 'submissive'.

supplement noun 1 a thing added to something else to improve or complete it. 2 a separate section added to a newspaper or magazine. 3 an additional charge payable for an extra service or facility. •verb add an extra element or amount to something.
– DERIVATIVES **supplemental** adjective **supplementation** noun.
– ORIGIN Latin *supplementum*.

supplementary adjective provided in addition to something so as to complete or improve it: *supplementary information.*

suppliant /sup-pli-uhnt/ noun a person who makes a humble request.

supplicate /sup-pli-kayt/ verb humbly ask or beg for something.
– DERIVATIVES **supplicant** noun **supplication** noun **supplicatory** adjective.
– ORIGIN Latin *supplicare* 'implore'.

supply verb (**supplies**, **supplying**, **supplied**) make something needed available to someone; provide someone with something. •noun (pl. **supplies**) 1 a stock or amount of something supplied or available. 2 the action of supplying something. 3 (**supplies**) provisions and equipment necessary for an army or expedition. •adjective acting as a temporary substitute for another: *a supply teacher.*
– PHRASES **supply and demand** the amount of goods or services available and the desire of buyers for them, considered as factors deciding their price.
– DERIVATIVES **supplier** noun.
– ORIGIN Latin *supplere* 'fill up'.

supply-side adjective Economics (of a policy) designed to increase output and employment by reducing taxation.

support verb 1 bear all or part of the weight of someone or something. 2 give help, encouragement, or approval to: *many famous women have supported her cause.* 3 be actively interested in a sports team. 4 provide someone with a home and the necessities of life. 5 provide enough food and water for life to exist. 6 confirm the truth of; back up: *the studies support our findings.* 7 (of a pop or rock group or performer) appear before the main act at a concert. 8 (as adj. **supporting**) of secondary importance to the leading roles in a play or film. •noun 1 a person or thing that supports someone or something. 2 the action of supporting or the state of being supported. 3 help, encouragement, or approval: *her loyal support of her husband.*
– DERIVATIVES **supportable** adjective.
– ORIGIN Latin *supportare*.

supporter noun a person who supports a sports team, political party, etc.

supportive adjective providing encouragement or emotional help.
– DERIVATIVES **supportively** adverb **supportiveness** noun.

suppose verb 1 think that something is true or probable, but without proof. 2 (of a theory or argument) assume or require that something is the case as a necessary condition: *the procedure supposes that a will has already been proved.* 3 (**be supposed to do**) be required or expected to do something.
– ORIGIN Latin *supponere*.

supposedly adverb according to what is generally believed.

supposition noun a belief held without proof or certain knowledge; an assumption or hypothesis.

suppository noun (pl. **suppositories**) a small piece of a medicinal substance that dissolves after being placed in the rectum or vagina.
– ORIGIN Latin *suppositorium* 'thing placed underneath'.

suppress verb 1 forcibly put an end to an activity that threatens an established authority. 2 prevent from acting or

S

developing: *the immune system is suppressed with powerful drugs.* **3** prevent something from being published. **4** consciously avoid thinking of an unpleasant idea or memory.
– DERIVATIVES **suppression** noun **suppressive** adjective **suppressor** noun.
– ORIGIN Latin *supprimere* 'press down'.

suppressant noun a drug or other substance which prevents a bodily function from working.

suppurate /sup-pyuh-rayt/ verb (of a wound, ulcer, etc.) form or discharge pus.
– DERIVATIVES **suppuration** noun **suppurative** /sup-pyuhr-uh-tiv/ adjective.
– ORIGIN from Latin *sub-* 'below' + *pus* 'pus'.

supranational adjective having power or influence that goes beyond national boundaries or governments.
– ORIGIN from Latin *supra* 'above, beyond'.

supremacist noun a person who believes that a particular group, especially a racial group, is superior to all others. • adjective relating to the belief that a particular group is superior to all others.
– DERIVATIVES **supremacism** noun.

supremacy /soo-prem-uh-si/ noun the state of being superior to all others in authority, power, or status.

supreme adjective **1** highest in authority, rank, or importance. **2** very great or greatest: *the chapel is a supreme example of medieval architecture.* • noun (also **suprême** /soo-prem/) a rich cream sauce or a dish served in a cream sauce.
– DERIVATIVES **supremely** adverb
– ORIGIN Latin *supremus* 'highest'.

supreme court noun the highest court of law in a country or state.

supremo /soo-pree-moh/ noun (pl. **supremos**) Brit. informal **1** a person in charge of an organization. **2** a person with great skill in a particular area: *a marketing supremo.*
– ORIGIN Spanish, 'supreme'.

sur- prefix equivalent to SUPER-.
– ORIGIN French.

surcease /ser-sees/ noun old use or N. Amer. **1** the ending or stopping of something. **2** relief from something unpleasant.
– ORIGIN from Old French *surseoir* 'refrain, delay'.

surcharge noun an additional charge or payment. • verb make someone pay an additional charge.

surcoat /ser-koht/ noun historical a loose sleeveless robe worn over armour.

surd /rhymes with curd/ noun Mathematics a number which cannot be expressed as a ratio of two whole numbers.
– ORIGIN from Latin *surdus* 'deaf, mute'.

sure adjective **1** completely confident that one is right. **2** (**sure of/to do**) certain to receive, get, or do: *the menu is sure to please everyone.* **3** undoubtedly true; completely reliable. **4** steady and confident. • adverb informal, chiefly N. Amer. certainly.
– PHRASES **be sure to do** do not fail to do. **for sure** informal without doubt. **make sure** confirm or ensure that something is the case or is done. **to be sure** certainly; it must be admitted.
– DERIVATIVES **sureness** noun.

– ORIGIN Old French *sur*.

sure-fire adjective informal certain to succeed.

sure-footed adjective **1** unlikely to stumble or slip. **2** confident and competent.

surely adverb **1** it must be true that. **2** without doubt; certainly. **3** in a confident way. **4** N. Amer. informal of course.

surety /shoor-i-ti, shoor-ti/ noun (pl. **sureties**) **1** a person who accepts responsibility if another person fails to pay a debt, appear in court, etc. **2** money given as a guarantee that someone will do something. **3** the state of being sure or certain of something.

surf noun waves that break and form foam on a seashore or reef. • verb **1** stand or lie on a surfboard and ride on the crest of a wave towards the shore. **2** move from site to site on the Internet.
– DERIVATIVES **surfer** noun **surfing** noun.
– ORIGIN unknown.

surface noun **1** the outside part or uppermost layer of something. **2** the upper limit of a body of liquid. **3** the outward appearance of someone or something as distinct from less obvious aspects: *Tom was a womanizer, but on the surface he remained respectable.* • adjective **1** relating to or occurring on the surface. **2** (of transportation) by sea or overland rather than by air. **3** outward or superficial: *surface politeness.* • verb **1** rise or come up to the surface. **2** become apparent: *the row first surfaced two years ago.* **3** provide something, especially a road, with a particular surface. **4** informal appear after having been asleep.
– ORIGIN French.

surface tension noun the tension of the surface film of a liquid, which tends to minimize surface area.

surfactant /ser-fak-tuhnt/ noun a substance, such as a detergent, that is added to a liquid to increase its spreading or wetting properties by reducing its surface tension.
– ORIGIN from *surface-active.*

surfboard noun a long, narrow board used in surfing.

surfeit /ser-fit/ noun **1** an excessive amount of something. **2** old use an illness caused by excessive eating or drinking. • verb (**surfeits, surfeiting, surfeited**) make someone want no more of something as a result of having consumed or done it to excess: *I am surfeited with shopping.*
– ORIGIN Old French.

surge noun **1** a sudden powerful forward or upward movement. **2** a sudden large temporary increase. **3** a powerful rush of an emotion. • verb **1** move suddenly and powerfully forward or upward. **2** increase suddenly and powerfully: *shares surged to a record high.*
– ORIGIN from Latin *surgere* 'to rise'.

surgeon noun **1** a medical practitioner qualified to practise surgery. **2** a doctor in the navy.
– ORIGIN Old French *serurgien.*

surgery noun (pl. **surgeries**) **1** the medical treatment of injuries or disorders by cutting open the body and removing or repairing parts. **2** Brit. a place where a doctor or nurse treats or advises patients. **3** Brit. an occasion on which an MP, lawyer, or other professional person gives advice.

surgical adjective **1** relating to or used in surgery. **2** worn to correct or relieve an injury, illness, or deformity. **3** done with great precision: *surgical bombing.*
– DERIVATIVES **surgically** adverb.

surgical spirit noun Brit. methylated spirit used for cleaning the skin before injections or surgery.

Surinamese /syoor-i-nuh-**meez**/ adjective relating to Surinam, a country on the NE coast of South America.

surly adjective (**surlier, surliest**) bad-tempered and unfriendly.
– DERIVATIVES **surlily** adverb **surliness** noun.
– ORIGIN from former *sirly* 'haughty', from SIR.

surmise /ser-**myz**/ verb believe something to be true without having evidence. •noun a belief that something is true without having evidence to confirm it.
– ORIGIN from Old French, 'accused'.

surmount verb **1** overcome a difficulty or obstacle. **2** stand or be placed on top of something.
– DERIVATIVES **surmountable** adjective.

surname noun an inherited name shared by all members of a family, as distinct from a personal name.

surpass verb **1** be greater or better than: *demand for the college's Latin courses has surpassed expectations.* **2** (as adj. **surpassing**) old use or literary outstanding; very great.
– DERIVATIVES **surpassable** adjective.

surplice /ser-pliss/ noun a loose white garment worn over a cassock by Christian clergy and members of church choirs.
– ORIGIN Old French *sourpelis.*

surplus noun **1** an amount left over when requirements have been met. **2** the amount by which the amount of money received is greater than the amount of money spent over a specific period. •adjective more than what is needed or used; extra.
– ORIGIN from Latin *super-* 'in addition' + *plus* 'more'.

surprise noun **1** a feeling of mild astonishment or shock caused by something unexpected. **2** an unexpected or astonishing thing. •verb **1** make someone feel mild astonishment or shock. **2** capture, attack, or discover suddenly and unexpectedly: *he surprised a gang stealing scrap metal.*
– PHRASES **take someone by surprise** happen when someone is not prepared. **take someone/ thing by surprise** attack or capture someone or something unexpectedly.
– DERIVATIVES **surprised** adjective **surprising** adjective **surprisingly** adverb.
– ORIGIN Old French.

surreal adjective having ideas or images mixed together in a strange way; like a dream: *a surreal road movie.*
– DERIVATIVES **surreally** adverb.

surrealism noun a 20th-century movement in art and literature in which unrelated images or events are combined in a strange or irrational way.
– DERIVATIVES **surrealist** noun & adjective **surrealistic** adjective.

surrender verb **1** stop resisting an opponent and put oneself under their control. **2** give up a person, right, or possession when demanded to do so. **3** (**surrender to**) give in completely to a powerful emotion or influence. **4** cancel a life insurance policy and receive back a proportion of the premiums paid. •noun the action or an act of surrendering: *the final surrender of Germany on 8 May 1945.*
– ORIGIN Old French *surrendre.*

surreptitious /sur-ruhp-**ti**-shuhss/ adjective done secretly.
– DERIVATIVES **surreptitiously** adverb.
– ORIGIN Latin *surreptitius* 'obtained secretly'.

surrogate /**sur**-ruh-guht/ noun **1** a substitute, especially a person who stands in for another in a role or office. **2** (in the Christian Church) a bishop's deputy who grants marriage licences.
– DERIVATIVES **surrogacy** noun.
– ORIGIN from Latin *surrogare* 'elect as a substitute'.

surrogate mother noun a woman who bears a child on behalf of another woman, either from her own egg or from having a fertilized egg from the other woman implanted in her womb.

surround verb **1** be all round or encircle someone or something. **2** be associated with: *the killings were surrounded by controversy.* •noun **1** a border or edging. **2** (**surrounds**) the area around something; surroundings.
– ORIGIN Latin *superundare* 'to overflow'.

surroundings plural noun the area or conditions around a person or thing: *a school in rural surroundings.*

surtax noun an additional tax on something already taxed, especially a higher rate of tax on incomes above a certain level.

surtitle noun a caption projected on a screen above the stage in an opera, translating the words being sung. •verb provide with surtitles.

surveillance /ser-**vay**-luhnss/ noun close observation, especially of a suspected spy or criminal.
– ORIGIN French.

survey verb /ser-**vay**/ **1** look carefully and thoroughly at someone or something. **2** examine and record the features of an area of land to produce a map or description. **3** Brit. examine and report on the condition of a building, especially for a prospective buyer. **4** question a group of people to investigate their opinions. •noun /**ser**-vay/ **1** a general view, examination, or description. **2** an investigation of the opinions or experience of a group of people, based on a series of questions. **3** an act of surveying a building or area of land. **4** a map or report obtained by surveying.
– ORIGIN Old French *surveier.*

surveyor noun a person who surveys land, buildings, etc. as a profession.

survival noun **1** the state or fact of surviving: *the animal's chances of survival were low.* **2** an object or practice that has survived from an earlier time.
– PHRASES **survival of the fittest** the principle that only the people or things that are best

S

adapted to their situation or environment will continue to exist.

survivalist noun a person who practises outdoor survival skills as a sport or hobby.
– DERIVATIVES **survivalism** noun.

survive verb 1 continue to live or exist. 2 continue to live in spite of an accident or ordeal. 3 remain alive after the death of someone.
– DERIVATIVES **survivability** noun **survivable** adjective.
– ORIGIN Old French *sourvivre*.

survivor noun a person who survives, especially one who remains alive after an accident or ordeal.

susceptibility noun (pl. **susceptibilities**) 1 the state of being easily harmed or influenced. 2 (**susceptibilities**) a person's sensitive feelings.

susceptible /suh-**sep**-ti-b'l/ adjective 1 likely to be influenced or harmed by a particular thing: *patients with liver disease may be susceptible to infection.* 2 easily influenced by feelings or emotions. 3 (**susceptible of**) capable of something.
– DERIVATIVES **susceptibly** adverb.
– ORIGIN Latin *susceptibilis.*

sushi /**soo**-shi/ noun a Japanese dish consisting of small balls or rolls of cold rice with vegetables, egg, or raw seafood.
– ORIGIN Japanese.

suspect verb /suh-**spekt**/ 1 believe to be probable or possible: *if you suspect a problem with the thermostat, call a repair technician.* 2 believe that someone is guilty of a crime or offence, without definite proof. 3 doubt that something is genuine or true. • noun /**suss**-pekt/ a person suspected of a crime or offence. • adjective /**suss**-pekt/ possibly dangerous or false.
– ORIGIN Latin *suspicere* 'mistrust'.

suspend verb 1 stop something temporarily. 2 temporarily bar someone from a job or from attending school, as a punishment or during investigation. 3 postpone or delay an action, event, or judgement. 4 (as adj. **suspended**) Law (of a sentence) not enforced as long as no further offence is committed within a specified period. 5 hang from somewhere. 6 (**be suspended**) technical (of particles) be dispersed throughout a fluid.
– ORIGIN Latin *suspendere.*

suspended animation noun a state in which most of the functions of an animal or plant stop for a time, without death.

suspended ceiling noun a ceiling with a space between it and the floor above from which it hangs.

suspender noun 1 Brit. an elastic strap attached to a belt or garter, fastened to the top of a stocking to hold it up. 2 (**suspenders**) N. Amer. braces for holding up trousers.

suspender belt noun Brit. a woman's undergarment consisting of a decorative belt and suspenders.

suspense noun a state or feeling of excited or anxious uncertainty about what may happen.
– DERIVATIVES **suspenseful** adjective.
– ORIGIN Old French *suspens* 'abeyance'.

suspension noun 1 the action of suspending

or the state of being suspended. 2 the temporary barring of someone from a job or from school, especially as a punishment. 3 the system of springs and shock absorbers which supports a vehicle on its wheels. 4 technical a mixture in which particles are dispersed throughout a fluid.

suspension bridge noun a bridge in which the deck is suspended from cables running between towers.

suspicion noun 1 a feeling or thought that something is true or probable: *she had a suspicion that he was laughing at her.* 2 a feeling or belief that someone has done something wrong. 3 distrust of someone or something. 4 a very slight trace: *a suspicion of a smile.*
– PHRASES **above suspicion** too good or honest to be thought capable of wrongdoing. **under suspicion** suspected of wrongdoing.
– ORIGIN Old French *suspeciun.*

suspicious adjective 1 having a feeling that someone has done something wrong. 2 (also **suspicious of**) not able to trust someone or something. 3 seeming to be dishonest or dangerous: *a suspicious package.*
– DERIVATIVES **suspiciously** adverb **suspiciousness** noun.

suss verb (**susses, sussing, sussed**) Brit. informal 1 (often **suss someone/thing out**) realize or understand the true nature of someone or something. 2 (as adj. **sussed**) clever and well informed.
– ORIGIN from **SUSPECT**.

sustain verb 1 support someone physically or mentally. 2 cause to continue for some time: *he cannot sustain a normal conversation.* 3 suffer something unpleasant. 4 decide that a claim is valid. 5 bear the weight of an object.
– DERIVATIVES **sustainer** noun **sustainment** noun.
– ORIGIN Latin *sustinere.*

sustainable adjective 1 able to be sustained or continued. 2 (of industry, development, or agriculture) not making excessive use of natural resources.
– DERIVATIVES **sustainability** noun **sustainably** adverb.

sustenance noun 1 food and drink as needed to keep someone alive. 2 the process of making something continue.

susurration /soo-suh-**ray**-sh'n/ (also **susurrus** /soo-**surr**-uhss/) noun literary whispering or rustling: *the susurration of sleet on windows.*
– ORIGIN Latin.

sutra /**soo**-truh/ noun 1 a rule or saying in Sanskrit literature, or a set of these on grammar or Hindu law or philosophy. 2 a Buddhist or Jainist scripture.
– ORIGIN Sanskrit, 'thread, rule'.

suttee noun variant spelling of **SATI**.

suture /**soo**-cher/ noun 1 a stitch or stitches holding together the edges of a wound or surgical cut. 2 a thread or wire used for stitching a wound or cut. • verb stitch up a wound or cut with a suture.
– ORIGIN Latin *sutura.*

SUV abbreviation sport utility vehicle.

suzerainty /**soo**-zuh-ruhn-ti/ noun the right of one country to rule over another country that has its own ruler but is not fully independent.
– DERIVATIVES **suzerain** noun.

S

– ORIGIN French.

Sv abbreviation sievert(s).

s.v. abbreviation (in references in written works) under the word or heading given.
– ORIGIN from Latin *sub voce* or *sub verbo* 'under the word or voice'.

svelte adjective slender and elegant.
– ORIGIN Italian *svelto*.

Svengali /sven-**gah**-li/ noun a person who exercises a controlling influence on another, especially for a sinister purpose.
– ORIGIN from *Svengali*, a musician in George Du Maurier's novel *Trilby*.

S-VHS abbreviation super video home system, an improved version of VHS.

SW abbreviation **1** south-west. **2** south-western.

swab noun **1** an absorbent pad used for cleaning wounds or taking a sample from the body for testing. **2** a sample taken with a swab. • verb (**swabs**, **swabbing**, **swabbed**) **1** clean a wound with an absorbent pad. **2** wash a floor or ship's deck with a mop or cloth.
– ORIGIN Dutch *zwabber* 'sailor who cleans a ship's deck'.

swaddle verb wrap someone in clothes or cloth.
– ORIGIN from **SWATHE²**.

swaddling clothes plural noun strips of cloth formerly wrapped round a newborn baby to calm it.

swag noun **1** a decorative garland of flowers, fruit, and greenery. **2** a curtain or piece of fabric fastened to hang in a drooping curve. **3** informal money or goods taken by a thief or burglar. **4** Austral./NZ a traveller's or miner's bundle of personal belongings. • verb (**swags**, **swagging**, **swagged**) arrange fabric so as to hang in a drooping curve.
– ORIGIN probably Scandinavian.

swagger verb walk or behave in a very confident or arrogant way. • noun a very confident or arrogant way of walking. • adjective (of a coat or jacket) cut with a loose flare from the shoulders.
– ORIGIN probably from **SWAG**.

swagger stick noun a short cane carried by a military officer.

swagman noun (pl. **swagmen**) Austral./NZ a tramp or travelling worker carrying a bundle of belongings.

Swahili /swuh-**hee**-li, swah-**hee**-li/ noun (pl. same) **1** a Bantu language widely spoken in East Africa. **2** a member of a people of Zanzibar and nearby coastal regions.
– ORIGIN from an Arabic word meaning 'coasts'.

swain noun **1** literary a young male lover. **2** old use a country youth.
– ORIGIN Old Norse, 'lad'.

swallow¹ verb **1** pass food, drink, or saliva down the throat. **2** take in or cover completely: *the dark mist swallowed her up.* **3** use the throat muscles as if swallowing, especially because of nervousness. **4** completely use up money or resources. **5** put up with unfair treatment. **6** believe something untrue without question. **7** hide a feeling: *he swallowed his pride.* • noun an act of swallowing.
– DERIVATIVES **swallower** noun.

– ORIGIN Old English.

swallow² noun a swift-flying migratory songbird with a forked tail.
– ORIGIN Old English.

swallow dive noun Brit. a dive performed with the arms spread out until close to the water.

swallowtail noun a large brightly coloured butterfly with tail-like projections on the hind wings.

swam past of **SWIM**.

swami /**swah**-mi/ noun (pl. **swamis**) a male Hindu religious teacher.
– ORIGIN Hindi, 'master, prince'.

swamp noun a bog or marsh. • verb **1** overwhelm or flood something with water. **2** overwhelm with too much of something; inundate: *the country was swamped with goods from abroad.*
– DERIVATIVES **swampy** adjective.
– ORIGIN probably from a Germanic word meaning 'sponge' or 'fungus'.

swampland noun (also **swamplands**) land consisting of swamps.

swan noun a large white waterbird with a long flexible neck and webbed feet. • verb (**swans**, **swanning**, **swanned**) Brit. informal go around enjoying yourself in a way that makes other people jealous or annoyed.
– ORIGIN Old English.

swank informal verb try to impress others with one's wealth, knowledge, or achievements. • noun behaviour or talk intended to impress others.
– ORIGIN unknown.

swanky adjective (**swankier**, **swankiest**) informal **1** stylishly luxurious and expensive. **2** inclined to show off.

swannery noun (pl. **swanneries**) Brit. a place where swans are kept or bred.

swansdown noun the fine soft feathers of a swan, used for trimmings and powder puffs.

swansong noun the final performance or activity of a person's career.
– ORIGIN suggested by German *Schwanengesang*, referring to a mythical song sung by a dying swan.

swap (also **swop**) verb (**swaps**, **swapping**, **swapped**) exchange or substitute one thing or person for another. • noun an act of exchanging one thing or person for another.
– ORIGIN uncertain.

SWAPO /**swah**-poh/ abbreviation South West Africa People's Organization.

sward /sword/ noun literary an expanse of short grass.
– ORIGIN Old English, 'skin'.

swarf /swahf/ noun fine chips or filings produced by machining.
– ORIGIN Old English or Old Norse.

swarm noun **1** a large group of insects flying closely together. **2** a large number of honeybees that leave a hive with a queen in order to establish a new colony. **3** a large group of people or things. • verb **1** move in or form a swarm. **2** (**swarm with**) be crowded or overrun with: *the place was swarming with police.* **3** (**swarm up**) climb rapidly by gripping something with one's hands and feet.
– ORIGIN Old English.

swarthy adjective (**swarthier, swarthiest**) having a dark complexion.
- DERIVATIVES **swarthiness** noun.
- ORIGIN Old English.

swash verb **1** (of water) move with a splashing sound. **2** old use swagger about or wield a sword. •noun the rush of seawater up the beach after the breaking of a wave.
- ORIGIN imitating the sound.

swashbuckling adjective engaging in or showing daring and romantic adventures: *he made eight swashbuckling films.*
- DERIVATIVES **swashbuckler** noun.

swastika /swoss-ti-kuh/ noun an ancient symbol in the form of an equal-armed cross with each arm continued at a right angle, used (in clockwise form) as the emblem of the German Nazi party.
- ORIGIN from a Sanskrit word meaning 'well-being'.

swat verb (**swats, swatting, swatted**) hit someone or something with a sharp blow from a flat object.
- ORIGIN northern English and US form of SQUAT.

swatch noun **1** a piece of fabric used as a sample. **2** a number of fabric samples bound together.
- ORIGIN unknown.

swathe¹ /swayth/ (chiefly N. Amer. also **swath** /swawth/) noun (pl. **swathes** or **swaths** /swaythz, swawths/) **1** a broad strip or area: *vast swathes of countryside.* **2** a row or line of grass, corn, etc. as it falls when mown or reaped.
- ORIGIN Old English, 'track, trace'.

swathe² /swayth/ verb wrap someone or something in several layers of fabric. •noun a strip of material in which something is wrapped.
- ORIGIN Old English.

SWAT team noun (in the US) a group of police marksmen who specialize in high-risk tasks such as hostage rescue.
- ORIGIN from the initial letters of *Special Weapons and Tactics.*

sway verb **1** move slowly and rhythmically backwards and forwards or from side to side. **2** make someone change their opinion. •noun **1** a swaying movement. **2** power, influence, or control: *he fell under the sway of a revolutionary scientist.*
- PHRASES **hold sway** have great power or influence.
- ORIGIN perhaps from German *swājen* 'be blown to and fro'.

Swazi /swah-zi/ noun (pl. same or **Swazis**) a member of a people traditionally inhabiting Swaziland and Mpumalanga province in South Africa.

swear verb (past **swore**; past part. **sworn**) **1** state or promise something solemnly or on oath. **2** make someone promise to do something: *I am sworn to secrecy.* **3** use offensive or obscene language.
- PHRASES **swear by** informal be certain that something is very good or useful. **swear someone in** admit someone to a new post or job by making them take a formal oath. **swear off** informal promise to stop doing or to give up

something. **swear to** say that something is definitely the case.
- DERIVATIVES **swearer** noun.
- ORIGIN Old English.

swear word noun an offensive or obscene word.

sweat noun **1** moisture given out through the pores of the skin, especially in reaction to heat, physical effort, or anxiety. **2** informal hard work. **3** informal a state of anxiety or distress. •verb (past and past part. **sweated** or N. Amer. **sweat**) **1** produce sweat. **2** make a great deal of effort: *I've sweated over this for six months.* **3** be very anxious. **4** (of a substance) give off moisture. **5** cook chopped vegetables slowly in a pan with a small amount of fat.
- PHRASES **break sweat** informal make a great physical effort. **no sweat** informal all right; no problem. **sweat blood** informal make a very great effort.
- ORIGIN Old English.

sweatband noun a band of absorbent material worn to soak up sweat.

sweated adjective (of work or workers) done or employed at very low wages for long hours and under poor conditions: *sweated labour.*

sweater noun a pullover with long sleeves.

sweatpants plural noun loose, warm trousers with an elasticated or drawstring waist, worn for exercise or leisure.

sweatshirt noun a loose knitted cotton sweater worn for exercise or leisure.

sweatshop noun a factory or workshop employing workers for long hours in poor conditions.

sweaty adjective (**sweatier, sweatiest**) soaked in or causing sweat.
- DERIVATIVES **sweatily** adverb **sweatiness** noun.

Swede noun a person from Sweden.

swede noun Brit. a round yellow root vegetable.
- ORIGIN the vegetable was introduced into Scotland from Sweden.

Swedish noun the Scandinavian language of Sweden. •adjective relating to Sweden.

sweep verb (past and past part. **swept**) **1** clean an area by brushing away dirt or litter. **2** move forcefully: *I was swept along by the crowd.* **3** move swiftly and smoothly. **4** affect swiftly and widely: *violence swept the country.* **5** (**sweep something away/aside**) remove or abolish something quickly and suddenly. **6** search an area. **7** extend continuously in an arc or curve: *forests swept down the hillsides.* •noun **1** an act of sweeping. **2** a long, slow curving movement. **3** a long curved stretch of road, river, etc. **4** the range or scope of something: *the whole sweep of the history of the USA.* **5** a chimney sweep. **6** informal a sweepstake.
- PHRASES **sweep the board** win every event or prize in a contest.
- ORIGIN Old English.

sweeper noun **1** a person or device that cleans by sweeping. **2** Football a player stationed behind the other defenders, free to defend at any point across the field.

sweeping adjective **1** extending or performed in a long, continuous curve. **2** wide in range or effect. **3** (of a statement) too general. •noun

(**sweepings**) dirt or refuse collected by sweeping.
– DERIVATIVES **sweepingly** adverb.

sweepstake (also **sweepstakes**) noun a form of gambling in which the winner receives all the money bet by the other participants.

sweet adjective **1** having the pleasant taste of sugar or honey. **2** having a pleasant smell; fragrant. **3** pleasant or satisfying: *the sweet life.* **4** kind or thoughtful. **5** charming and endearing. **6** working or done smoothly or easily: *the sweet handling of this motorcycle.* **7** (of air, water, etc.) fresh and pure. **8** (**sweet on**) informal, dated in love with someone. •noun **1** Brit. a small shaped piece of confectionery made with sugar. **2** Brit. a sweet dish forming a course of a meal; a dessert.
– DERIVATIVES **sweetish** adjective **sweetly** adverb.
– ORIGIN Old English.

sweet-and-sour adjective cooked with sugar and either vinegar or lemon.

sweetbread noun the thymus gland or pancreas of an animal, used for food.

sweetcorn noun a variety of maize with sweet kernels that are eaten as a vegetable.

sweeten verb **1** make or become sweet or sweeter. **2** make something more acceptable. **3** (**sweeten someone up**) informal be pleasant to someone in order to make them agree to something, help, etc.

sweetener noun **1** a substance used to sweeten food or drink. **2** informal, chiefly Brit. a bribe.

sweetheart noun a person who is in love with someone. •adjective informal agreed privately by two sides in their own interests: *a sweetheart deal.*

sweetheart neckline noun a low neckline shaped like the top of a heart.

sweetie noun informal **1** Brit. a sweet. **2** used as a term of affection.

sweetmeat noun old use a sweet or item of sweet food.

sweetness noun the quality of being sweet.
– PHRASES **sweetness and light** pleasantness or harmony.

sweet pea noun a climbing plant of the pea family with colourful fragrant flowers.

sweet pepper noun a variety of pepper with a mild or sweet flavour.

sweet potato noun the edible tuber of a tropical climbing plant, with pinkish-orange flesh.

sweet-talk verb informal use charm or flattery to persuade someone to do something.

sweet tooth noun (pl. **sweet tooths**) a great liking for sweet foods.

sweet william noun a fragrant plant with clusters of vivid red, pink, or white flowers.

swell verb (past part. **swollen** or **swelled**) **1** become larger or rounder in size. **2** increase in intensity, amount, or volume: *the low murmur swelled to a roar.* •noun **1** a full or gently rounded form. **2** a gradual increase in sound, amount, or intensity. **3** a slow, regular movement of the sea in rolling waves that do not break. **4** informal, dated a fashionable upper-class person. •adjective N. Amer. informal, dated excellent; very good.

– ORIGIN Old English.

swelling noun a place on the body that has swollen as a result of illness or an injury.

swelter verb be uncomfortably hot.
– ORIGIN Germanic.

swept past and past participle of **SWEEP**. adjective (also **swept back**) (of an aircraft's wings) directed backwards from the fuselage.

swerve verb abruptly depart from a straight course. •noun an abrupt change of course.
– ORIGIN Old English, 'leave, turn aside'.

swift adjective **1** happening quickly or promptly. **2** moving or capable of moving at high speed. •noun a fast-flying bird with long, slender wings, spending most of its life on the wing.
– DERIVATIVES **swiftly** adverb **swiftness** noun.
– ORIGIN from an Old English word meaning 'move in a course, sweep'.

swig informal verb (**swigs, swigging, swigged**) drink something in large gulps. •noun a large gulp of a drink.
– ORIGIN unknown.

swill verb **1** Brit. rinse something out with large amounts of water. **2** Brit. (of liquid) swirl round in a container or cavity. **3** informal drink something in large quantities. •noun waste food mixed with water for feeding to pigs.
– ORIGIN Old English.

swim verb (**swims, swimming, swam**; past part. **swum**) **1** propel oneself through water by moving the arms and legs. **2** be immersed in or covered with liquid. **3** experience a dizzily confusing feeling. •noun an act or period of swimming.
– PHRASES **in the swim** involved in or aware of current events.
– DERIVATIVES **swimmer** noun.
– ORIGIN Old English.

swimming costume noun Brit. a woman's one-piece swimsuit.

swimmingly adverb informal smoothly and satisfactorily.

swimming pool noun an artificial pool for swimming in.

swimming trunks plural noun shorts worn by men for swimming.

swimsuit noun a woman's one-piece swimming costume.

swimwear noun clothing worn for swimming.

swindle verb use deception to obtain money or possessions from someone. •noun a scheme or act designed to obtain money dishonestly.
– DERIVATIVES **swindler** noun.
– ORIGIN German *schwindeln* 'be giddy, tell lies'.

swine noun **1** (pl. same) chiefly formal or N. Amer. a pig. **2** (pl. same or **swines**) informal an unpleasant person.
– DERIVATIVES **swinish** adjective.
– ORIGIN Old English.

swine fever noun an intestinal disease of pigs, caused by a virus.

swineherd noun chiefly historical a person who tends pigs.

swing verb (past and past part. **swung**) **1** move back and forth or from side to side while hanging from a fixed point. **2** move by grasping a support and leaping. **3** move in a smooth, curving line: *the cab swung into the car park.* **4** (**swing at**) attempt to punch

S

someone. **5** shift from one opinion, mood, or situation to another: *opinion swung in the Chancellor's favour.* **6** have a decisive influence on a vote or decision. **7** informal succeed in bringing something about. **8** informal swap sexual partners or engage in group sex. **9** informal be lively, exciting, or fashionable. ●noun **1** a seat hanging from ropes or chains, on which someone can sit and swing. **2** an act of swinging. **3** a clear change in public opinion, especially in an election. **4** a style of jazz or dance music with an easy flowing rhythm.
– PHRASES **get into the swing of things** Brit. informal become used to an activity. **go with a swing** informal be lively and enjoyable. **in full swing** at the height of activity. **swings and roundabouts** Brit. a situation in which different actions result in no eventual gain or loss.
– DERIVATIVES **swinger** noun **swingy** adjective.
– ORIGIN Old English, 'beat, whip, rush'.

swingboat noun chiefly Brit. a boat-shaped swing seating several people, found at fairs.

swing bridge noun a bridge that can be swung to one side to allow ships to pass.

swing door noun a door that can be opened in either direction and swings back when released.

swingeing /swin-jing/ adjective Brit. severe or otherwise extreme: *swingeing cuts in expenditure.*
– ORIGIN from Old English, 'shake, shatter'.

swinging adjective informal **1** lively, exciting, and fashionable. **2** sexually liberated.

swipe informal verb **1** hit or try to hit someone or something with a swinging blow. **2** steal something. **3** pass a swipe card through an electronic reader. ●noun **1** a sweeping blow. **2** an act of criticizing someone or something.
– ORIGIN perhaps from SWEEP.

swipe card noun a plastic card carrying coded information which is read when the card is slid through an electronic device.

swirl verb move in a twisting or spiralling pattern. ●noun a swirling movement or pattern.
– DERIVATIVES **swirly** adjective.
– ORIGIN perhaps German or Dutch.

swish verb move with a soft rushing sound. ●noun a soft rushing sound or movement. ●adjective Brit. informal impressively smart and fashionable.
– DERIVATIVES **swishy** adjective.
– ORIGIN imitating the sound.

Swiss adjective relating to Switzerland or its people. ●noun (pl. same) a person from Switzerland.

Swiss roll noun Brit. a flat thin rectangular sponge cake spread with jam or cream and rolled up.

switch noun **1** a device for making and breaking an electrical connection. **2** a change from one thing to another. **3** a slender, flexible shoot cut from a tree. **4** N. Amer. a set of points on a railway track. ●verb **1** change from one thing to another: *she worked as a librarian and then switched to teaching.* **2** exchange one thing for another. **3** (**switch something off/on**) turn an electrical device off or on.
4 (**switch off**) informal cease to pay attention.

– DERIVATIVES **switchable** adjective **switcher** noun.
– ORIGIN probably German.

switchback noun **1** Brit. a road with alternate sharp ascents and descents. **2** a roller coaster.

switchblade noun chiefly N. Amer. a flick knife.

switchboard noun a device for routing telephone calls within an organization.

switched-on adjective Brit. informal aware of what is going on or what is up to date.

switchgear noun electrical switching equipment.

swivel verb (**swivels, swivelling, swivelled;** US **swivels, swiveling, swiveled**) turn round, or around a central point. ●noun a connecting device between two parts enabling one to revolve without turning the other.
– ORIGIN Old English, 'move along a course, sweep'.

swizz noun Brit. informal a disappointment or minor swindle.
– ORIGIN probably from SWINDLE.

swizzle stick noun a stick used for frothing up or taking the fizz out of drinks.
– ORIGIN unknown.

swollen past participle of SWELL.

swoon literary verb faint, especially from extreme emotion. ●noun an instance of fainting.
– ORIGIN Old English, 'overcome'.

swoop verb **1** move rapidly downwards through the air. **2** carry out a sudden raid. ●noun a swooping or snatching movement or action.
– PHRASES **at** (or **in**) **one fell swoop** see FELL⁴.
– ORIGIN perhaps from SWEEP.

swoosh noun **1** the sound produced by a sudden rush of air or liquid. **2** an emblem or design representing a flash or stripe of colour. ●verb move with a rushing sound.
– ORIGIN imitating the sound.

swop verb & noun variant spelling of SWAP.

sword noun **1** a weapon with a long metal blade and a handle, used for thrusting or striking. **2** (**the sword**) literary military power; violence.
– PHRASES **put someone to the sword** kill someone, especially in war.
– ORIGIN Old English.

swordfish noun (pl. same or **swordfishes**) a large sea fish with a long sword-like snout.

sword of Damocles /dam-uh-kleez/ noun something bad that threatens to happen at any time.
– ORIGIN with reference to *Damocles*, a courtier who praised the happiness of the ancient Greek ruler Dionysius I so much that the king made him sit under a sword suspended by a single hair, to show him how insecure this happiness was.

swordplay noun fencing with swords or foils.

swordsman noun (pl. **swordsmen**) a man who fights with a sword.
– DERIVATIVES **swordsmanship** noun.

swordstick noun a hollow walking stick containing a blade that can be used as a sword.

swore past of SWEAR.

sworn past participle of SWEAR. adjective **1** given under oath. **2** determined to remain in the specified thing: *sworn enemies.*

swot Brit. informal verb (**swots, swotting,**

swotted) (also **swot up**) study very hard.
• **noun** derogatory a person who spends a lot of time studying.
– DERIVATIVES **swotty** adjective.
– ORIGIN from SWEAT.

swum past participle of SWIM.

swung past and past participle of SWING.

sybarite /si-buh-ryt/ **noun** a person who is very fond of luxury and pleasure.
– DERIVATIVES **sybaritic** /sib-uh-**rit**-ik/ adjective.
– ORIGIN first referring to an inhabitant of *Sybaris*, an ancient Greek city in Italy.

sycamore **noun** 1 a large maple tree native to central and southern Europe. 2 N. Amer. a plane tree.
– ORIGIN Greek *sukomoros*.

sycophant /si-kuh-fant/ **noun** a person who flatters someone important in order to try to gain favour with them.
– DERIVATIVES **sycophancy** noun **sycophantic** adjective.
– ORIGIN Greek *sukophantēs* 'informer'.

Sydenham's chorea **noun** a form of chorea (disorder of the nervous system) chiefly affecting children and associated with rheumatic fever.
– ORIGIN named after the English physician Thomas *Sydenham*.

syllabic /sil-**lab**-ik/ adjective 1 relating to or based on syllables. 2 (of a consonant) that forms a whole syllable, such as the *l* in *bottle*.
– DERIVATIVES **syllabically** adverb.

syllabify /sil-**lab**-i-fy/ **verb** (**syllabifies**, **syllabifying**, **syllabified**) divide words into syllables.
– DERIVATIVES **syllabification** noun.

syllable /**sil**-luh-b'l/ **noun** a unit of pronunciation having one vowel sound and forming all or part of a word (e.g. *butter* has two syllables).
– ORIGIN Greek *sullabē*.

syllabub /**sil**-luh-bub/ **noun** a whipped cream dessert, typically flavoured with white wine or sherry.
– ORIGIN unknown.

syllabus /**sil**-luh-buhss/ **noun** (pl. **syllabuses** or **syllabi** /**sil**-luh-by/) the subjects covered in a course of study or teaching.
– ORIGIN Latin.

syllogism /**sil**-luh-ji-z'm/ **noun** a form of reasoning in which a conclusion is drawn from two propositions (premises) (e.g. *all dogs are animals; all animals have four legs; therefore all dogs have four legs*).
– DERIVATIVES **syllogistic** adjective.
– ORIGIN Greek *sullogismos*.

sylph /silf/ **noun** 1 an imaginary spirit of the air. 2 a slender woman or girl.
– DERIVATIVES **sylphlike** adjective.
– ORIGIN Latin *sylphes* (plural).

sylvan adjective chiefly literary consisting of or relating to woods; wooded.
– ORIGIN from Latin *silva* 'a wood'.

symbiosis /sim-by-**oh**-siss/ **noun** (pl. **symbioses** /sim-by-**oh**-seez/) 1 Biology a situation in which two different organisms live with and are dependent on each other, to the advantage of both. 2 a relationship between different people or groups that is beneficial to both: *his dances celebrate the symbiosis of music and dance.*
– DERIVATIVES **symbiotic** /sim-by-**ot**-ik/ adjective.
– ORIGIN Greek *sumbiōsis.*

symbol **noun** 1 a thing or person that represents or stands for something else: *the limousine was a symbol of his wealth.* 2 a sign, letter, or mark that has a fixed meaning, especially in music, science, or mathematics.
– ORIGIN Greek *sumbolon* 'mark, token'.

symbolic adjective 1 acting as a symbol: *a repeating design symbolic of eternity.*
2 involving the use of symbols or symbolism.
– DERIVATIVES **symbolically** adverb.

symbolism **noun** 1 the use of symbols to represent ideas or qualities. 2 (**Symbolism**) an artistic and poetic movement or style using symbolic images and indirect suggestion to express mystical ideas, emotions, and states of mind.
– DERIVATIVES **symbolist** noun & adjective.

symbolize (or **symbolise**) **verb** 1 be a symbol of: *the ceremonial dagger symbolizes justice.*
2 represent something by means of symbols.
– DERIVATIVES **symbolization** noun.

symbology **noun** 1 the study or use of symbols. 2 symbols as a whole.

symmetrical adjective made up of exactly similar parts facing each other or around an axis; showing symmetry.
– DERIVATIVES **symmetric** adjective **symmetrically** adverb.

symmetry /**sim**-mi-tri/ **noun** (pl. **symmetries**)
1 the quality of being made up of exactly similar parts facing each other or around an axis. 2 the quality of being the same or very similar: *the political symmetry between the two debates.* 3 correct or pleasing proportion of the parts of something.
– ORIGIN Latin *symmetria.*

sympathetic adjective 1 feeling or expressing kindness or understanding towards someone. 2 showing that one approves of an idea or action: *many people are sympathetic to the idea of globalization.* 3 pleasing or likeable. 4 referring to the part of the nervous system supplying the internal organs, blood vessels, and glands.
– DERIVATIVES **sympathetically** adverb.

sympathize (or **sympathise**) **verb** 1 feel or express sympathy. 2 support an opinion or political movement.
– DERIVATIVES **sympathizer** noun.

sympathy **noun** (pl. **sympathies**) 1 the feeling of being sorry for someone who is unhappy or in difficulty: *they had great sympathy for the flood victims.* 2 support for or approval of an idea, cause, etc. 3 understanding between people who have similar views or interests.
– PHRASES **in sympathy** 1 relating harmoniously to something else; in keeping. 2 happening in a way that corresponds to something else.
– ORIGIN Greek *sumpatheia.*

USAGE: On the difference between **sympathy** and **empathy**, see the note at EMPATHY.

symphonic adjective relating to or having the form of a symphony.

symphonist **noun** a composer of symphonies.

symphony **noun** (pl. **symphonies**) an elaborate

S

musical composition for full orchestra, typically in four movements.
– ORIGIN Greek *sumphōnia*.

symphony orchestra noun a large classical orchestra, including string, woodwind, brass, and percussion instruments.

symposium /sim-poh-zi-uhm/ noun (pl. **symposia** /sim-poh-zi-uh/ or **symposiums**) 1 a conference to discuss a particular academic or specialist subject. 2 a collection of related papers by a number of contributors.
– ORIGIN Greek *sumposion*.

symptom noun 1 a change in the body or mind which is the sign of a disease. 2 an indication of an undesirable situation.
– ORIGIN Greek *sumptōma* 'chance, symptom'.

symptomatic adjective acting as a symptom or sign of something: *these difficulties are symptomatic of fundamental problems.*
– DERIVATIVES **symptomatically** adverb.

synagogue /sin-uh-gog/ noun a building where Jewish people meet for religious worship and instruction.
– ORIGIN Greek *sunagōgē* 'meeting'.

synapse /sy-naps, si-naps/ noun a gap between two nerve cells, across which impulses are conducted.
– DERIVATIVES **synaptic** adjective.
– ORIGIN Greek *sunapsis*.

sync (also **synch**) informal noun synchronization. • verb synchronize something with something else.
– PHRASES **in** (or **out of**) **sync** working well (or badly) together.

synchromesh noun a system of gear changing in which the gearwheels are made to revolve at the same speed during engagement.
– ORIGIN from *synchronized mesh*.

synchronicity /sing-kruh-**niss**-it-i/ noun the occurrence of events at the same time, which appear to be related but have no obvious connection.

synchronism noun another term for **SYNCHRONY**.

synchronize (or **synchronise**) verb cause to occur or operate at the same time or rate: *synchronize your hand gestures with your main points.*
– DERIVATIVES **synchronization** noun **synchronizer** noun.

synchronized swimming noun a sport in which teams of swimmers perform coordinated movements in time to music.

synchronous /sing-kruh-nuhss/ adjective existing or occurring at the same time.
– DERIVATIVES **synchronously** adverb.
– ORIGIN Greek *sunkhronos*.

synchrony /sing-kruh-ni/ noun the state of operating or developing at the same time or rate as something else.

syncline noun a ridge or fold of rock in which the strata slope upwards from the axis. Compare with **ANTICLINE**.
– ORIGIN from Greek *sun* 'with' + *klinein* 'to lean'.

syncopated /sing-kuh-payt-id/ adjective (of music or a rhythm) having the beats or accents altered so that strong beats become weak and vice versa.

– DERIVATIVES **syncopation** noun.
– ORIGIN from **SYNCOPE**.

syncope /sing-kuh-pi/ noun 1 Medicine fainting caused by low blood pressure. 2 Grammar the omission of sounds or letters from within a word, for example when *library* is pronounced /ly-bri/.
– ORIGIN Greek *sunkopē*.

syncretism /sing-kri-ti-z'm/ noun the combining of different religions, cultures, or schools of thought.
– DERIVATIVES **syncretic** adjective **syncretist** noun & adjective **syncretistic** adjective.
– ORIGIN from Greek *sunkrētizein* 'unite against a third party'.

syncretize (or **syncretise**) /sin-kri-tyz/ verb attempt to combine differing religious beliefs, cultures, or schools of thought.
– DERIVATIVES **syncretization** noun.

syndic noun 1 (in the UK) a business agent of certain universities and corporations. 2 a government official in various countries.
– ORIGIN Greek *sundikos*.

syndicalism noun historical a movement that believed in transferring the ownership and control of industry and business to workers' unions.
– DERIVATIVES **syndicalist** noun & adjective.

syndicate noun /sin-di-kuht/ 1 a group of people or organizations that combine to promote a common interest. 2 an agency that supplies items to a number of news media at the same time. • verb /sin-di-kayt/ 1 publish or broadcast material in a number of news media at the same time. 2 control or manage something by a syndicate.
– DERIVATIVES **syndication** noun.

syndrome noun 1 a group of medical symptoms which consistently occur together. 2 a set of opinions or behaviour that is typical of a particular group of people.
– ORIGIN Greek *sundromē*.

synecdoche /si-nek-duh-ki/ noun a figure of speech in which a part is made to represent the whole or vice versa, as in *England lost by six wickets* (meaning 'the English cricket team').
– ORIGIN Greek *sunekdokhē*.

synergy /sin-er-ji/ (also **synergism**) noun cooperation of two or more people or things to produce a combined effect that is greater than the sum of their separate effects: *the synergy between artist and record company.*
– DERIVATIVES **synergetic** adjective.
– ORIGIN from Greek *sunergos* 'working together'.

synod /si-nod/ noun an official meeting of the ministers and other members of a Christian Church.
– DERIVATIVES **synodal** adjective **synodical** adjective.
– ORIGIN Greek *sunodos* 'meeting'.

synonym /sin-uh-nim/ noun a word or phrase that means the same as another word or phrase in the same language.
– DERIVATIVES **synonymy** /si-non-i-mi/ noun.
– ORIGIN Greek *sunōnumon*.

synonymous /si-non-i-muhss/ adjective 1 (of a word or phrase) having the same meaning as another word or phrase in the same language. 2 closely associated with something: *his name*

was synonymous with victory.
– DERIVATIVES **synonymously** adverb.

synopsis /si-**nop**-siss/ noun (pl. **synopses** /si-**nop**-seez/) a brief summary or outline.
– ORIGIN from Greek *sun-* 'together' + *opsis* 'seeing'.

synoptic adjective **1** relating to a synopsis. **2 (Synoptic)** referring to the Gospels of Matthew, Mark, and Luke, which describe events from a similar point of view, as contrasted with that of John.

synovial /sy-**noh**-vi-uhl/ adjective relating to a type of joint in the body that is enclosed in a flexible membrane containing a lubricating fluid.
– ORIGIN from Latin *synovia.*

syntax noun **1** the arrangement of words and phrases to create well-formed sentences. **2** a set of rules for the formation of sentences.
– DERIVATIVES **syntactic** adjective **syntactical** adjective **syntactically** adverb.
– ORIGIN Greek *suntaxis.*

synth noun informal a synthesizer.
– DERIVATIVES **synthy** adjective.

synthesis /sin-**thuh**-siss/ noun (pl. **syntheses** /sin-**thuh**-seez/) **1** the combination of parts to form a connected whole. **2** the production of chemical compounds by reaction from simpler materials.
– DERIVATIVES **synthesist** noun.
– ORIGIN Greek *sunthesis.*

synthesize /sin-**thuh**-syz/ (or **synthesise**) verb **1** combine things into a connected whole. **2** make something by chemical synthesis. **3** produce sound electronically.

synthesizer (or **synthesiser**) noun an electronic musical instrument that produces sounds by generating and combining signals of different frequencies.

synthetic /sin-**thet**-ik/ adjective **1** made by chemical synthesis, especially to imitate a natural product: *synthetic rubber.* **2** not genuine; insincere. •noun a synthetic substance.
– DERIVATIVES **synthetically** adverb.

syphilis noun a serious sexually transmitted disease spread by bacteria.
– DERIVATIVES **syphilitic** adjective & noun.
– ORIGIN from *Syphilus*, the subject of a Latin poem who was the supposed first sufferer of the disease.

syphon noun & verb variant spelling of **SIPHON.**

Syrah /**see**-ruh/ noun another term for **SHIRAZ.**

Syrian noun a person from Syria. •adjective relating to Syria.

syringe /si-**rinj**/ noun a tube with a nozzle and piston for sucking in and forcing out liquid in a thin stream, often one fitted with a hollow needle for injecting drugs or withdrawing bodily fluids. •verb (**syringes, syringing, syringed**) spray liquid into or over something with a syringe.
– ORIGIN Latin *syringa.*

syrup noun **1** a thick sweet liquid made by dissolving sugar in boiling water. **2** a thick sweet liquid containing medicine or used as a drink.
– ORIGIN Arabic, 'beverage'.

syrupy adjective **1** thick or sweet, like syrup. **2** excessively sentimental.

system noun **1** a set of things working together as a mechanism or network: *the railway system.* **2** an organized scheme or method by which something is done. **3** a person's body. **4** the state of being well organized. **5 (the system)** the rules or people that control a country or society, especially when regarded as restrictive or unfair. **6** Computing a group of related hardware units or programs or both. **7** Geology a major range of rock strata that corresponds to a period in time: *the Devonian system.*
– ORIGIN Greek *sustēma.*

systematic adjective done or acting according to a system; methodical.
– DERIVATIVES **systematically** adverb **systematist** noun.

systematize (or **systematise**) verb arrange things according to an organized system.
– DERIVATIVES **systematization** noun.

systemic /si-**stem**-ik, si-**steem**-ik/ adjective **1** relating to a system as a whole. **2** (of an insecticide or fungicide) entering the plant via the roots or shoots and passing through the tissues.
– DERIVATIVES **systemically** adverb.

systems analyst noun a person who analyses a complex process or operation in order to improve its efficiency.
– DERIVATIVES **systems analysis** noun.

systole /**siss**-tuh-li/ noun the phase of the heartbeat when the heart muscle contracts and pumps blood into the arteries. Often contrasted with **DIASTOLE.**
– DERIVATIVES **systolic** /si-**stol**-lik/ adjective.
– ORIGIN Greek *sustolē.*

S

Tt

T¹ (also **t**) noun (pl. **Ts** or **T's**) the twentieth letter of the alphabet.
– PHRASES **to a T** informal to perfection; exactly.

T² abbreviation 1 tera- (10¹²). 2 tesla.

t abbreviation ton(s).

TA abbreviation (in the UK) Territorial Army.

Ta symbol the chemical element tantalum.

ta exclamation Brit. informal thank you.
– ORIGIN a child's word.

tab¹ noun 1 a small flap or strip of material attached to something, used to give information or to hold it, fasten it, etc. 2 informal a tally of items ordered in a bar or restaurant. 3 informal, chiefly N. Amer. a restaurant bill. 4 N. Amer. a ring pull. • verb (**tabs, tabbing, tabbed**) mark something with a tab.
– PHRASES **keep tabs on someone** informal monitor someone's activities. **pick up the tab** informal pay for something.
– ORIGIN perhaps from TAG¹.

tab² noun short for TABULATOR. • verb (**tabs, tabbing, tabbed**) short for TABULATE.

tab³ noun informal a tablet, especially one containing an illegal drug.

tabard /**tab**-erd, tab-ard/ noun 1 a sleeveless jacket consisting only of front and back pieces with a hole for the head. 2 a herald's official coat depicting the arms of the sovereign.
– ORIGIN Old French *tabart*.

Tabasco /tuh-**bas**-koh/ noun trademark a very hot sauce made from a type of pepper.
– ORIGIN named after the state of *Tabasco* in Mexico.

tabbouleh /tuh-**boo**-lay, tab-oo-lay/ noun a Middle Eastern salad of cracked wheat mixed with finely chopped tomatoes, onions, parsley, etc.
– ORIGIN Arabic.

tabby noun (pl. **tabbies**) a grey or brownish cat with dark stripes.
– ORIGIN French *tabis* 'striped silk taffeta'.

tabernacle /**tab**-er-na-k'l/ noun 1 a place of worship used by Nonconformists or Mormons. 2 (in a Roman Catholic church) a box or cabinet in which the bread consecrated for Holy Communion may be placed. 3 (in the Bible) a tent used by the Israelites to house the Ark of the Covenant during the Exodus.
– ORIGIN Latin *tabernaculum* 'tent'.

tabla /**tab**-luh, tub-luh/ noun a pair of small hand drums fixed together, used in Indian music.
– ORIGIN Arabic.

tablature /**tab**-luh-cher/ noun a form of musical notation indicating fingering rather than the pitch of notes.
– ORIGIN French.

table noun 1 a piece of furniture with a flat top supported by legs, for eating, writing, or working at. 2 a set of facts or figures displayed in rows or columns. 3 (**tables**) multiplication tables. 4 food provided in a restaurant or household: *food includes a lunchtime buffet table*. • verb Brit. formally present something for discussion at a meeting.
– PHRASES **on the table** available for discussion. **turn the tables** turn a situation of disadvantage to oneself into one of advantage.
– ORIGIN Latin *tabula* 'plank, tablet, list'.

tableau /**tab**-loh/ noun (pl. **tableaux** or **tableaus** /**tab**-lohz/) a group of models or motionless figures representing a scene from a story or from history.
– ORIGIN French, 'picture'.

tableau vivant /**tab**-loh vee-von/ noun (pl. **tableaux vivants** pronunc. same) a silent and motionless group of people arranged to represent a scene.
– ORIGIN French, 'living picture'.

tablecloth noun a cloth spread over a table, especially during meals.

table d'hôte /tah-bluh **doht**/ noun a restaurant menu or meal offered at a fixed price and with limited choices.
– ORIGIN French, 'host's table'.

tableland noun a broad, high, level region; a plateau.

table manners plural noun behaviour that is considered polite while eating at a table.

tablespoon noun 1 a large spoon for serving food. 2 the amount held by a tablespoon, in the UK considered to be 15 millilitres.
– DERIVATIVES **tablespoonful** noun.

tablet noun 1 chiefly Brit. a pill. 2 a slab of stone, clay, or wood on which an inscription is written. 3 Brit. a small flat piece of soap.
– ORIGIN Latin *tabula* 'plank, tablet, list'.

table tennis noun an indoor game played with small bats and a small hollow ball hit across a table divided by a net.

tableware noun crockery, cutlery, and glassware used for serving and eating meals.

table wine noun wine of moderate quality considered suitable for drinking with a meal.

tabloid noun a newspaper having pages half the size of those of a broadsheet, written in a popular style.
– DERIVATIVES **tabloidization** (or

tabloidisation) noun.
– ORIGIN first referring to a tablet of medicine: the current sense reflects the idea of information being presented in a form that is concentrated and easily digested.

taboo noun (pl. **taboos**) a social or religious custom placing a ban or restriction on a particular thing or person. •**adjective** banned or restricted by social custom: *sex was a taboo subject*. •**verb** (**taboos, tabooing, tabooed**) put a ban or taboo on someone or something.
– ORIGIN from Tongan, 'set apart, forbidden'.

tabor /**tay**-bor/ noun historical a small drum, especially one played at the same time as a simple pipe.
– ORIGIN Old French *tabour*.

tabular /**tab**-yoo-ler/ adjective 1 (of data) consisting of or presented in columns or tables. 2 broad and flat like the top of a table.
– ORIGIN Latin *tabularis*.

tabula rasa /tab-yoo-luh **rah**-zuh/ noun 1 an absence of preconceived ideas. 2 a person's mind, especially at birth, regarded as being empty of ideas.
– ORIGIN Latin, 'scraped tablet', i.e. a tablet with the writing erased.

tabulate /**tab**-yoo-layt/ verb arrange data in columns or tables.
– DERIVATIVES **tabulation** noun.

tabulator noun a facility in a word-processing program, or a device on a typewriter, for advancing to set positions when producing tables of data.

tache noun variant spelling of **TASH**.

tachograph /**tak**-uh-grahf/ noun a tachometer used in commercial road vehicles to provide a record of vehicle speed over a period.
– ORIGIN from Greek *takhos* 'speed'.

tachometer /ta-**kom**-i-ter/ noun an instrument which measures the working speed of an engine, typically in revolutions per minute.

tachycardia /ta-ki-**kah**-di-uh/ noun an abnormally rapid heart rate.
– ORIGIN from Greek *takhus* 'swift' + *kardia* 'heart'.

tacit /**ta**-sit/ adjective understood or suggested without being stated: *your silence may be taken to mean tacit agreement*.
– DERIVATIVES **tacitly** adverb.
– ORIGIN Latin *tacitus* 'silent'.

taciturn /**ta**-si-tern/ adjective saying little; uncommunicative.
– DERIVATIVES **taciturnity** noun **taciturnly** adverb.
– ORIGIN Latin *taciturnus*.

tack¹ noun 1 a course of action: *the board changed tack and recommended that shareholders accept a takeover*. 2 a small broad-headed nail. 3 N. Amer. a drawing pin. 4 a long stitch used to fasten fabrics together temporarily. 5 a sailing boat's course relative to the direction of the wind: *the ketch swung to the opposite tack*. •**verb** 1 fasten or fix something with tacks. 2 (**tack something on**) add something to something that already exists. 3 change the direction of a sailing boat so that the wind blows into the sails from the opposite side.
– ORIGIN probably from Old French *tache* 'clasp, large nail'.

tack² noun equipment used in horse riding, including the saddle and bridle.
– ORIGIN from **TACKLE**.

tack³ noun informal cheap, shoddy, or tasteless material.
– ORIGIN from **TACKY**².

tackle verb 1 make a determined effort to deal with a problem or difficult task: *police launched an initiative to tackle rising crime*. 2 begin to discuss a difficult issue with someone. 3 (in football, hockey, rugby, etc.) try to take the ball from or prevent the movement of an opponent. •**noun** 1 the equipment required for a task or sport. 2 a mechanism consisting of ropes, pulley blocks, and hooks for lifting heavy objects. 3 (in sport) an act of tackling an opponent. 4 the rigging and pulleys used to work a boat's sails. 5 Brit. vulgar slang a man's genitals.
– DERIVATIVES **tackler** noun.
– ORIGIN probably from German *taken* 'lay hold of'.

tacky¹ adjective (**tackier, tackiest**) (of glue, paint, etc.) slightly sticky because not fully dry.
– DERIVATIVES **tackiness** noun.

tacky² adjective (**tackier, tackiest**) informal showing poor taste and quality.
– DERIVATIVES **tackiness** noun.
– ORIGIN unknown.

taco /**ta**-koh, **tah**-koh/ noun (pl. **tacos**) a Mexican dish consisting of a folded tortilla filled with spicy meat or beans.
– ORIGIN Spanish, 'plug, wad'.

tact noun sensitivity and skill in dealing with others or with difficult issues.
– ORIGIN Latin *tactus* 'touch, sense of touch'.

tactful adjective having or showing skill and sensitivity in dealing with others or with difficult issues.
– DERIVATIVES **tactfully** adverb **tactfulness** noun.

tactic noun 1 an action or plan that is intended to achieve a specific result. 2 (**tactics**) the art of directing and organizing the movement of armed forces and equipment during a war. Often contrasted with **STRATEGY**.
– DERIVATIVES **tactician** noun.
– ORIGIN from Greek *taktikē tekhnē* 'art of tactics'.

tactical adjective 1 done or planned to achieve a particular result. 2 (of weapons) for use in direct support of military or naval operations. Often contrasted with **STRATEGIC**. 3 relating to military tactics. 4 Brit. (of voting) aimed at preventing the strongest candidate from winning by supporting the next strongest, regardless of one's true political loyalty.
– DERIVATIVES **tactically** adverb.

tactile adjective 1 relating to the sense of touch. 2 liking to touch others in a friendly or sympathetic way.
– DERIVATIVES **tactility** noun.
– ORIGIN Latin *tactilis*.

tactless adjective thoughtless and insensitive.
– DERIVATIVES **tactlessly** adverb **tactlessness** noun.

tad informal adverb (**a tad**) to a minor extent; rather. •**noun** a small amount of something.
– ORIGIN perhaps from **TADPOLE**.

tadpole noun the larva of an amphibian such as a frog or toad, at the stage when it lives in

water and has gills and a tail.
– ORIGIN from an Old English word meaning 'toad' + POLL.

Tadzhik noun variant spelling of **TAJIK**.

tae-bo /ty-boh/ noun trademark an exercise system combining elements of aerobics and kick-boxing.
– ORIGIN from Korean *tae* 'leg' + *bo*, short for *boxing*.

tae kwon do /ty kwon doh/ noun a modern Korean martial art similar to karate.
– ORIGIN Korean, 'art of hand and foot fighting'.

taffeta noun a fine shiny silk or similar synthetic fabric.
– ORIGIN Latin.

taffrail noun a rail round a ship's stern.
– ORIGIN Dutch *tafereel* 'panel'.

Taffy (also **Taff**) noun (pl. **Taffies**) Brit. informal, often offensive a Welshman.
– ORIGIN representing a supposed Welsh pronunciation of the man's name *Davy* or *David* (Welsh *Dafydd*).

tag[1] noun **1** a label used to identify something or to give other information about it. **2** an electronic device attached to someone to monitor their movements. **3** a nickname or description by which someone or something is widely known. **4** a nickname or other identifying mark written as the signature of a graffiti artist. **5** a frequently repeated quotation or phrase. **6** a metal or plastic point at the end of a shoelace. **7** Computing a character or set of characters attached to an item of data in order to identify it. •verb (**tags, tagging, tagged**) **1** attach a tag or label to someone or something. **2** (**tag something on/to**) add something to the end of something else as an afterthought. **3** (**tag along/on**) accompany someone without being invited. **4** (of a graffiti artist) write a tag or nickname on a surface.
– ORIGIN unknown.

tag[2] noun a children's game in which one player chases the rest, and anyone who is caught then becomes the person doing the chasing.
– ORIGIN perhaps from TIG.

Tagalog /tuh-**gah**-log/ noun **1** a member of a people from the Philippine Islands. **2** the language of the Tagalogs, the basis of Filipino.
– ORIGIN from the Tagalog words for 'native' + 'river'.

tag end noun chiefly N. Amer. the last remaining part of something.

tagine /tuh-**zheen**, tuh-**jeen**/ (also **tajine**) noun a North African stew of spiced meat and vegetables.
– ORIGIN Arabic, 'frying pan'.

tagliatelle /tal-yuh-**tel**-li/ plural noun pasta in narrow ribbons.
– ORIGIN Italian.

tag wrestling noun a form of wrestling involving pairs of wrestlers who fight as a team, each taking turns in the ring.

tahini /tah-**hee**-ni/ noun a Middle Eastern paste or spread made from ground sesame seeds.
– ORIGIN modern Greek *takhini*.

Tahitian /tah-**hee**-shuhn/ noun **1** a person from Tahiti. **2** the language of Tahiti. •adjective relating to Tahiti.

t'ai chi /ty **chee**/ (also **t'ai chi ch'uan** /ty chee

chwahn/) noun a Chinese martial art and system of exercises, consisting of sequences of very slow controlled movements.
– ORIGIN Chinese, 'great ultimate boxing'.

taiga /ty-guh/ noun swampy coniferous forest of high northern latitudes, especially that between the tundra and steppes of Siberia.
– ORIGIN Mongolian.

tail[1] noun **1** the part at the rear of an animal that sticks out from the rest of the body. **2** something that resembles an animal's tail in shape or position. **3** the rear part of an aircraft, with the tailplane and rudder. **4** the final, more distant, or weaker part: *the tail of a hurricane*. **5** (**tails**) the side of a coin without the image of a head on it. **6** (**tails**) informal a tailcoat, or a man's formal evening suit with such a coat. **7** informal a person secretly following another to observe their movements. •verb **1** informal secretly follow and observe someone. **2** (**tail off/away**) gradually become smaller or weaker. **3** (**tail back**) Brit. (of traffic) become congested and form a tailback.
– PHRASES **on someone's tail** informal following someone closely. **with one's tail between one's legs** informal feeling dejected or humiliated.
– DERIVATIVES **tailed** adjective **tailless** adjective.
– ORIGIN Old English.

USAGE: Do not confuse **tail** with **tale**. **Tail** means 'the rear or end part of an animal or thing' (*the dog wagged its tail*), whereas **tale** means 'a story' (*a fairy tale*).

tail[2] noun Law, chiefly historical limitation of ownership of an estate or title to a person and their direct descendants.
– ORIGIN Old French *taille* 'notch, tax'.

tailback noun Brit. a long queue of traffic extending back from a junction or obstruction.

tailboard noun Brit. a tailgate.

tailcoat noun Brit. a man's formal coat, with a long skirt divided at the back into tails and cut away in front.

tail end noun the last or rear part of something.

tail fin noun **1** a fin at the rear of a fish's body. **2** a projecting vertical surface on the tail of an aircraft, providing stability. **3** an upswept projection on each rear corner of a car, popular in the 1950s.

tailgate noun **1** a hinged flap at the back of a lorry. **2** the door at the back of an estate or hatchback car. •verb informal drive too closely behind another vehicle.
– DERIVATIVES **tailgater** noun.

tail light noun a red light at the rear of a vehicle.

tailor noun a person whose occupation is making men's clothing for individual customers. •verb **1** make clothes to fit individual customers. **2** make or adapt for a particular purpose or person: *the database has been tailored to meet the needs of the restaurant industry*.
– ORIGIN Old French *taillour* 'cutter'.

tailored adjective (of clothes) smart, fitted, and well cut.

tailoring noun **1** the activity or occupation of a tailor. **2** the style or cut of an item of clothing.

tailor-made adjective **1** made or adapted for a

particular purpose or person. **2** (of clothes) made by a tailor for a particular customer.

tailpiece noun **1** the final or end part of something. **2** a part added to the end of a piece of writing. **3** a small decorative design at the foot of a page or the end of a chapter or book.

tailpipe noun chiefly N. Amer. the rear section of the exhaust pipe of a motor vehicle.

tailplane noun Brit. a horizontal aerofoil at the tail of an aircraft.

tailspin noun a fast revolving motion made by a rapidly descending aircraft.

tailwind noun a wind blowing in the direction that a vehicle or aircraft is travelling in.

taint verb **1** affect with an undesirable quality: *his reputation was tainted by scandal.* **2** contaminate or pollute something. •noun a trace of an undesirable quality or substance.
– ORIGIN from Old French *teint* 'tinged'.

taipan /ty-pan/ noun a foreigner who is head of a business in China.
– ORIGIN Chinese.

Taiwanese /ty-wuh-**neez**/ noun (pl. same) a person from Taiwan. •adjective relating to Taiwan.

Tajik /tah-**jeek**/ (also **Tadzhik**) noun **1** a member of a mainly Muslim people inhabiting Tajikistan and parts of neighbouring countries. **2** a person from the republic of Tajikistan.

tajine noun variant spelling of **TAGINE**.

taka /**tah**-kah/ noun (pl. same) the basic unit of money of Bangladesh.
– ORIGIN Bengali.

takahe /**tah**-kuh-hi/ noun a large, rare flightless rail (bird) found in New Zealand.
– ORIGIN Maori.

take verb (past **took**; past part. **taken**) **1** reach for and hold something. **2** occupy a place or position. **3** carry or bring someone or something with one. **4** remove someone or something from a place. **5** bring into a particular state: *the invasion took Europe to the brink of war.* **6** perform an action or undertake a task. **7** accept or receive someone or something. **8** require or use up: *the journey took four hours in all.* **9** experience or be affected by something. **10** consume something as food, drink, medicine, or drugs. **11** acquire or assume a position, state, or form. **12** act on an opportunity. **13** use something as a route or a means of transport. **14** hold or accommodate: *the hotel takes just twenty guests.* **15** view or deal with in a specified way: *he took it as an insult.* **16** subtract something from something else. **17** tolerate or endure: *I can't take it any more.* **18** gain possession of something by force. **19** study a subject. **20** do an exam or test. **21** make a photograph with a camera. •noun **1** a sequence of sound or part of a film photographed or recorded continuously. **2** a particular version of or approach to something: *his whimsical take on life.* **3** an amount gained or acquired from one source or in one session.
– PHRASES **be on the take** informal take bribes. **take after** resemble a parent or ancestor. **take something as read** Brit. assume something without the need for further discussion. **take something back** withdraw a statement. **take**

five informal, chiefly N. Amer. have a short break. **take someone in** cheat or deceive someone. **take something in 1** make an item of clothing tighter by altering its seams. **2** include or understand something. **take someone in hand** undertake to control or reform someone. **take something in hand** start dealing with a task. **take it out of** exhaust someone. **take off 1** become airborne. **2** leave hastily. **take someone off** imitate someone. **take something off** remove clothing. **take someone on** engage an employee. **take something on 1** undertake a task. **2** begin to have a particular meaning or quality. **take something out on** relieve one's frustration or anger by mistreating someone. **take over** assume control of or responsibility for something. **take one's time** not hurry. **take to 1** get into the habit of. **2** form a liking or develop an ability for. **3** go to a place to escape danger. **take something up 1** become interested in a pursuit. **2** occupy time, space, or attention. **3** pursue a matter further. **take someone up on** accept an offer or challenge from someone. **take up with** begin to associate with someone.
– DERIVATIVES **taker** noun.
– ORIGIN Old Norse.

takeaway noun Brit. **1** a restaurant or shop selling cooked food to be eaten elsewhere. **2** a meal of such food.

take-home pay noun the pay received by an employee after tax and insurance have been deducted.

take-off noun **1** an act of becoming airborne. **2** informal an act of imitating someone or something.

takeout noun N. Amer. a takeaway.

takeover noun an act of taking control of something such as a company from someone else.

take-up noun the acceptance of something offered.

taking noun (**takings**) the amount of money earned by a business from the sale of goods or services. •adjective dated pleasant and charming.
– PHRASES **for the taking** available to take advantage of.

talc noun **1** talcum powder. **2** a soft mineral that is a form of magnesium silicate.

talcum powder noun the mineral talc in powdered form used on the skin to make it feel smooth and dry.
– ORIGIN Latin, from Persian.

tale noun **1** a fictional or true story. **2** a lie.
– ORIGIN Old English, 'telling, something told'.

> USAGE: On the confusion of **tale** and **tail**, see the note at **TAIL**[1].

taleggio /ta-**lej**-i-oh/ noun a soft Italian cheese made from cow's milk.
– ORIGIN named after the *Taleggio* valley in Lombardy.

talent noun **1** natural ability or skill. **2** people possessing natural ability or skill. **3** Brit. informal people regarded in terms of their sexual attractiveness or availability. **4** an ancient weight and unit of currency.
– DERIVATIVES **talented** adjective **talentless** adjective.
– ORIGIN Greek *talanton* 'weight, sum of

t

money': sense 1 derives from the parable of the talents (Gospel of Matthew, chapter 25).

talent scout noun a person whose job is searching for talented performers, especially in sport and entertainment.

talisman /tal-iz-muhn/ noun (pl. **talismans**) an object thought to have magic powers and to bring good luck.
- DERIVATIVES **talismanic** /tal-iz-**man**-ik/ adjective.
- ORIGIN Arabic.

talk verb **1** speak in order to give information or express ideas or feelings. **2** be able to speak. **3** (**talk something over/through**) discuss something thoroughly. **4** (**talk back**) reply in a defiant or cheeky way. **5** (**talk down to**) speak to someone in a way that suggests one feels superior to them. **6** (**talk someone round**) persuade someone to accept or agree to something. **7** (**talk someone into/out of**) convince someone to do or not to do something. **8** reveal secret or private information. •noun **1** conversation or discussion. **2** a speech or lecture. **3** (**talks**) formal discussions or negotiations. **4** rumour, gossip, or speculation: *there's talk of a conspiracy.*
- PHRASES **you can't** (or **can**) **talk** informal used to tell someone that the criticism they are making applies equally well to them. **now you're talking** informal expressing enthusiastic agreement or approval. **talk the talk** informal speak in a way intended to convince or impress someone.
- DERIVATIVES **talker** noun.
- ORIGIN from TALE or TELL.

talkative adjective fond of talking.
- DERIVATIVES **talkatively** adverb **talkativeness** noun.

talkboard noun an Internet bulletin board or chat room.

talkie noun informal a film with a soundtrack, as distinct from a silent film.

talking book noun a recorded reading of a book.

talking head noun informal a presenter or reporter on television who speaks to the camera and is viewed in close-up.

talking point noun a topic that causes discussion or argument.

talking shop noun Brit. a place or group regarded as a centre for unproductive talk rather than action.

talking-to noun informal a sharp reprimand.

talk radio noun a type of radio programme in which topical issues are discussed by the presenter and by listeners who phone in.

talk show noun a chat show.

talktime noun the time during which a mobile telephone is in use to handle calls, especially as a measure of the duration of the battery.

tall adjective **1** of great or more than average height. **2** measuring a specified distance from top to bottom.
- PHRASES **a tall order** an unreasonable or difficult demand. **a tall story** (or **tale**) an account that is difficult to believe and seems unlikely to be true.
- DERIVATIVES **tallish** adjective **tallness** noun.

- ORIGIN probably from Old English, 'swift, prompt'.

tallboy noun Brit. a tall chest of drawers in two sections, one standing on the other.

tallow /tal-loh/ noun a hard substance made from animal fat, used (especially in the past) in making candles and soap.
- DERIVATIVES **tallowy** adjective.
- ORIGIN perhaps from German.

tall ship noun a sailing ship with a high mast or masts.

tally noun (pl. **tallies**) **1** a current score or amount. **2** a record of a score or amount. **3** (also **tally stick**) historical a piece of wood marked with notches as a record of the items in an account. •verb (**tallies, tallying, tallied**) **1** agree or correspond: *this account does not tally with accounts from local people.* **2** calculate the total number of something.
- ORIGIN Old French *tallie*.

tally-ho exclamation a huntsman's cry to the hounds on sighting a fox.
- ORIGIN probably from French *taïaut*.

Talmud /tal-muud/ noun a collection of ancient writings on Jewish civil and ceremonial law and legend.
- DERIVATIVES **Talmudic** adjective **Talmudist** noun.
- ORIGIN Hebrew, 'instruction'.

talon noun a claw of a bird of prey.
- DERIVATIVES **taloned** adjective.
- ORIGIN Old French, 'heel'.

talus[1] /tay-luhss/ noun (pl. **tali** /tay-ly/) the bone in the ankle that forms a movable joint with the shin bone.
- ORIGIN Latin, 'ankle, heel'.

talus[2] /tay-luhss/ noun (pl. **taluses**) a sloping mass of rock fragments at the foot of a cliff.
- ORIGIN French.

tam noun a tam-o'-shanter.

tamale /tuh-**mah**-lay, tuh-**mah**-li/ noun a Mexican dish of spicy meat and maize flour steamed or baked in maize husks.
- ORIGIN Mexican Spanish *tamal*, from Nahuatl.

tamarillo /ta-muh-**ril**-loh/ noun (pl. **tamarillos**) the red egg-shaped fruit of a tropical South American plant.
- ORIGIN an invented name.

tamarin /tam-uh-rin/ noun a small monkey native to forests in South America.
- ORIGIN Carib.

tamarind /tam-uh-rind/ noun sticky brown acidic pulp from the pod of a tropical African tree, used in Asian cookery.
- ORIGIN Arabic, 'Indian date'.

tamarisk /tam-uh-risk/ noun a shrub or small tree with tiny scale-like leaves on slender branches.
- ORIGIN Latin *tamarix*.

tambour /tam-boor/ noun **1** historical a small drum. **2** a circular frame for holding fabric taut while it is being embroidered.
- ORIGIN French, 'drum'.

tambourine /tam-buh-**reen**/ noun a percussion instrument resembling a shallow drum with metal discs around the edge, played by being shaken or hit with the hand.
- ORIGIN French *tambourin* 'small tambour'.

tame adjective **1** (of an animal) not dangerous or frightened of people. **2** not exciting or

adventurous: *Saturday night TV is a pretty tame affair.* **3** informal (of a person) willing to cooperate. •**verb 1** make an animal tame. **2** control or make less powerful: *the battle to tame inflation.*
– DERIVATIVES **tamely** adverb **tameness** noun **tamer** noun.
– ORIGIN Old English.

Tamil noun **1** a member of a people living in parts of South India and Sri Lanka. **2** the language of the Tamils.
– ORIGIN Tamil.

tam-o'-shanter /tam-uh-**shan**-ter/ noun a round Scottish cap with a bobble in the centre.
– ORIGIN named after the hero of Robert Burns's poem *Tam o' Shanter.*

tamoxifen /tuh-**mok**-si-fen/ noun a synthetic drug used to treat breast cancer and infertility in women.
– ORIGIN from the drug's chemical name.

tamp verb firmly ram or pack a substance down or into something.
– ORIGIN probably from French *tampon* 'tampon, plug'.

tamper verb (**tamper with**) interfere with something without permission or so as to cause damage.
– DERIVATIVES **tamperer** noun.
– ORIGIN from TEMPER.

tampon noun a plug of soft material put into the vagina to absorb blood during a woman's period.
– ORIGIN French.

tan¹ noun **1** a golden-brown shade of skin developed by pale-skinned people after being in the sun. **2** a yellowish-brown colour. •verb (**tans, tanning, tanned**) **1** become golden brown after being in the sun. **2** convert animal skin into leather. **3** informal, dated beat someone as a punishment.
– ORIGIN Old English.

tan² abbreviation tangent.

tanager /tan-uh-jer/ noun a brightly coloured American songbird.
– ORIGIN Tupi.

tandem noun a bicycle with seats and pedals for two riders, one behind the other.
– PHRASES **in tandem** together or at the same time.
– ORIGIN from Latin, 'at length'.

tandoor /tan-door, tan-**door**/ noun a clay oven of a type used originally in northern India and Pakistan.
– ORIGIN Arabic.

tandoori /tan-**door**-i/ adjective (of Indian food) cooked in a tandoor (clay oven).

tang noun **1** a strong taste, flavour, or smell. **2** the projection on the blade of a knife or other tool by which the blade is held firmly in the handle.
– ORIGIN Old Norse, 'point, tang of a knife'.

tanga /tang-uh/ noun Brit. a pair of briefs consisting of small triangles connected by strings at the sides.
– ORIGIN Bantu, 'loincloth'.

tangent /tan-juhnt/ noun **1** a straight line or plane that touches a curve or curved surface at a point, but if extended does not cross it at that point. **2** Mathematics the ratio of the sides

(other than the hypotenuse) opposite and adjacent to an angle in a right-angled triangle. **3** a completely different line of thought or action: *her mind went off at a tangent.*
– DERIVATIVES **tangency** noun.
– ORIGIN from Latin *tangere* 'to touch'.

tangential /tan-jen-sh'l/ adjective **1** only slightly connected or relevant: *such concoctions have only a tangential relationship with food as eaten in India.* **2** relating to or along a tangent.
– DERIVATIVES **tangentially** adverb.

tangerine noun **1** a small citrus fruit with a loose orange-red skin. **2** a deep orange-red colour.
– ORIGIN from *Tanger*, the former name of *Tangier* in Morocco.

tangible /tan-ji-b'l/ adjective **1** able to be perceived by touch. **2** clear and definite; real: *I was seeing tangible benefits from working out.*
– DERIVATIVES **tangibility** noun **tangibly** adverb.
– ORIGIN Latin *tangibilis.*

tangle verb **1** twist strands together into a confused mass. **2** (**tangle with**) informal become involved in a conflict with. •noun **1** a confused mass of something twisted together. **2** a confused or complicated state.
– DERIVATIVES **tangly** adjective.
– ORIGIN probably Scandinavian.

tango noun (pl. **tangos**) **1** a Latin American ballroom dance characterized by marked rhythms and postures and abrupt pauses. **2** a piece of music in the style of a tango. •verb (**tangoes, tangoing, tangoed**) dance the tango.
– ORIGIN Latin American Spanish.

tangy adjective (**tangier, tangiest**) having a strong, sharp flavour or smell.
– DERIVATIVES **tanginess** noun.

tank noun **1** a large container or storage chamber for holding liquid or gas. **2** the container holding the fuel supply in a motor vehicle. **3** a container with transparent sides in which to keep fish. **4** a heavy armoured fighting vehicle carrying guns and moving on a continuous metal track. •verb (**be/get tanked up**) informal drink heavily or become drunk.
– DERIVATIVES **tankful** noun **tankless** adjective.
– ORIGIN perhaps from a word in Gujarati or Marathi (an Indian language) meaning 'underground cistern'.

tankard noun a tall beer mug with a handle and sometimes a hinged lid.
– ORIGIN perhaps from Dutch *tanckaert.*

tank engine noun a steam locomotive carrying fuel and water holders in its own frame rather than in a separate wagon.

tanker noun a ship, road vehicle, or aircraft for carrying liquids in bulk.

tankini /tan-kee-ni/ noun a women's two-piece swimsuit combining a top half like a tank top with a bikini bottom.

tank top noun a close-fitting sleeveless top worn over a shirt or blouse.

tanner¹ noun Brit. informal, historical a sixpence.
– ORIGIN unknown.

tanner² noun a person employed to tan animal hides.

tannery noun (pl. **tanneries**) a place where

animal hides are tanned.

tannic acid noun another term for TANNIN.

tannin noun a bitter yellowish or brownish substance present in tea, grapes, and the bark of some trees.
- DERIVATIVES **tannic** adjective.
- ORIGIN French *tanin*.

tannoy noun Brit. trademark a type of public address system.
- ORIGIN from *tantalum alloy*, a substance used in the system.

tansy noun a plant with yellow flat-topped button-like flower heads.
- ORIGIN Old French *tanesie*.

tantalize (or **tantalise**) verb torment or tease someone by showing or promising them something that they cannot have.
- DERIVATIVES **tantalization** noun **tantalizing** adjective.
- ORIGIN from *Tantalus* in Greek mythology, who was punished by being provided with fruit and water which moved away when he reached for them.

tantalum /tan-tuh-luhm/ noun a hard silver-grey metallic chemical element.
- ORIGIN from *Tantalus* (see TANTALIZE), with reference to its frustrating insolubility in acids.

tantalus /tan-tuh-luhss/ noun Brit. a stand in which decanters of spirits may be locked up though still visible.
- ORIGIN from *Tantalus* (see TANTALIZE).

tantamount adjective (**tantamount to**) equivalent in seriousness to: *the resignations were tantamount to an admission of guilt.*
- ORIGIN from Italian *tanto montare* 'amount to as much'.

tantra /tan-truh/ noun 1 a Hindu or Buddhist written work dealing with mystical or magical practices. 2 the fact of following the principles of these works, involving mantras, meditation, yoga, and ritual.
- DERIVATIVES **tantric** adjective **tantrism** noun.
- ORIGIN Sanskrit, 'loom, groundwork, doctrine'.

tantrum noun an uncontrolled outburst of anger and frustration.
- ORIGIN unknown.

Tanzanian /tan-zuh-nee-uhn/ noun a person from Tanzania, a country in East Africa.
- adjective relating to Tanzania.

Taoiseach /tee-shuhkh/ noun the Prime Minister of the Irish Republic.
- ORIGIN Irish, 'chief, leader'.

Taoism /tow-i-z'm/ noun a Chinese philosophy based on the belief that everything in the universe is connected and that a person should try to balance the opposing principles of yin and yang to reach a calm acceptance of life.
- DERIVATIVES **Taoist** noun & adjective.
- ORIGIN from Chinese, 'the right way'.

tap¹ noun 1 a device for controlling a flow of liquid or gas from a pipe or container. 2 a device connected to a telephone for listening secretly to conversations. • verb (**taps, tapping, tapped**) 1 make use of a resource or supply: *clients seeking to tap Edinburgh's resources of expertise.* 2 connect a device to a telephone in order to listen to conversations secretly.

3 draw liquid through the tap or spout of a cask, barrel, etc. 4 draw sap from a tree by cutting into it. 5 informal obtain money or information from someone.
- PHRASES **on tap** informal freely available whenever needed.
- DERIVATIVES **tappable** adjective.
- ORIGIN Old English, 'stopper for a cask'.

tap² verb (**taps, tapping, tapped**) 1 hit someone or something with a quick, light blow or blows. 2 strike something lightly and repeatedly against something else. • noun 1 a quick, light blow. 2 a piece of metal attached to the toe and heel of a tap dancer's shoe. 3 tap dancing.
- DERIVATIVES **tapper** noun.
- ORIGIN Old French *taper*.

tapas /tap-uhss/ plural noun small Spanish savoury dishes, typically served with drinks at a bar.
- ORIGIN Spanish *tapa* 'cover, lid' (because the dishes were served on a dish balanced on the glass of a drink).

tap dance noun a dance performed wearing shoes fitted with metal taps, characterized by rhythmical tapping of the toes and heels.
- DERIVATIVES **tap dancer** noun **tap-dancing** noun.

tape noun 1 light, flexible material in a narrow strip, used to hold, fasten, or mark off something. 2 (also **adhesive tape**) a strip of paper or plastic coated with adhesive, used to stick things together. 3 a kind of tape with magnetic properties, used for recording sound, pictures, or computer data. 4 a cassette or reel containing magnetic tape. • verb 1 record sound or pictures on magnetic tape. 2 fasten, attach, or mark off something with tape.
- ORIGIN Old English.

tape measure noun a strip of tape marked at regular intervals for measuring something.

tapenade /tap-uh-nahd/ noun a Provençal savoury paste or dip, made from black olives, capers, and anchovies.
- ORIGIN Provençal.

taper verb 1 reduce in thickness towards one end. 2 (**taper off**) gradually lessen. • noun 1 a long, thin candle. 2 a wick coated with wax, or a long piece of paper or wood, used for lighting a lamp, candle, etc.
- ORIGIN Old English.

tape recorder noun a device for recording sounds on magnetic tape and then reproducing them.
- DERIVATIVES **tape-record** verb **tape recording** noun.

tapestry noun (pl. **tapestries**) a piece of thick fabric with pictures or designs woven or embroidered on it.
- DERIVATIVES **tapestried** adjective.
- ORIGIN Old French *tapisserie*.

tapeworm noun a flatworm with a long ribbon-like body, the adult of which lives as a parasite in the intestines.

tapioca /ta-pi-oh-kuh/ noun a starchy substance in the form of hard white grains, obtained from cassava and used for puddings and other dishes.
- ORIGIN Tupi-Guarani, 'squeezed-out dregs'.

tapir /tay-peer/ noun a pig-like mammal with a long flexible snout, native to tropical America

and Malaysia.
– ORIGIN Tupi.

tappet noun a moving part in a machine which transmits motion in a straight line between a cam and another part.
– ORIGIN from **TAP²**.

taproom noun a room in a pub in which beer is served from barrels.

taproot noun a tapering root growing straight downwards and forming the centre from which smaller roots spring.

tar¹ noun **1** a dark, thick flammable liquid distilled from wood or coal, used in road-making and for preserving timber. **2** a similar substance formed by burning tobacco or other material. •verb (**tars, tarring, tarred**) cover something with tar.
– PHRASES **tar and feather someone** smear someone with tar and then cover them with feathers as a punishment. **tar people with the same brush** consider certain people to have the same faults.
– ORIGIN Old English.

tar² noun informal, dated a sailor.
– ORIGIN perhaps short for **TARPAULIN**, formerly used as a nickname for a sailor.

taramasalata /ta-ruh-muh-suh-**lah**-tuh/ noun a dip made from the roe of cod or other fish, olive oil, and seasoning.
– ORIGIN from modern Greek *taramas* 'roe' + *salata* 'salad'.

tarantella /ta-ruhn-**tel**-luh/ noun a rapid whirling dance originating in southern Italy.
– ORIGIN Italian.

tarantula /tuh-**ran**-tyuu-luh/ noun a very large hairy spider found chiefly in tropical and subtropical America. **2** a large black spider of southern Europe.
– ORIGIN Italian *tarantola*.

tarboosh /tah-**boosh**/ noun a hat similar to a fez worn by Muslim men in some countries.
– ORIGIN Egyptian Arabic.

tardy adjective (**tardier, tardiest**) **1** late in happening. **2** slow to act or respond: *the law may be tardy in reacting to changing attitudes.*
– DERIVATIVES **tardily** adverb **tardiness** noun.
– ORIGIN Latin *tardus* 'slow'.

tare¹ /tair/ noun **1** a vetch (plant). **2** (in the Bible) a type of weed.
– ORIGIN unknown.

tare² /tair/ noun **1** the weight of a vehicle without its fuel or load. **2** an allowance made for the weight of the packaging in determining the net weight of goods.
– ORIGIN French, 'deficiency, tare'.

target noun **1** a person, object, or place selected as the aim of an attack. **2** a board marked with a series of circles sharing the same centre, aimed at in archery or shooting. **3** a goal or result which one aims to achieve: *a sales target.* •verb (**targets, targeting, targeted**) **1** select someone or something as an object of attention or attack. **2** aim or direct something.
– PHRASES **on** (or **off**) **target** succeeding (or not succeeding) in hitting or achieving the thing aimed at.
– DERIVATIVES **targetable** adjective.
– ORIGIN Old English, 'small round shield'.

tariff noun **1** a tax or duty to be paid on a particular class of imports or exports. **2** a list

of the fixed prices charged by a business such as a hotel or restaurant. **3** Law a scale of sentences and damages for crimes and injuries of varying degrees of seriousness. •verb fix the price of something according to a tariff.
– ORIGIN Italian *tariffa*.

tarmac noun **1** (trademark in the UK) material used for surfacing roads or other outdoor areas, consisting of broken stone mixed with tar. **2** (**the tarmac**) a runway or other area surfaced with tarmac. •verb (**tarmacs, tarmacking, tarmacked**) surface an area with tarmac.
– ORIGIN from **TAR¹** + **MACADAM**.

tarn noun a small mountain lake.
– ORIGIN Old Norse.

tarnation noun & exclamation chiefly N. Amer. used as a euphemism for 'damnation'.

tarnish verb **1** (of metal) become dull as a result of exposure to air or moisture. **2** cause harm or a loss of respect to: *they will make up negative stories to tarnish my image.* •noun a film or stain formed on an exposed surface of a mineral or metal.
– DERIVATIVES **tarnishable** adjective.
– ORIGIN French *ternir*.

taro /**tah**-roh, ta-roh/ noun the starchy corm (underground storage organ) of a tropical Asian plant, eaten as a vegetable.
– ORIGIN Polynesian.

tarot /**ta**-roh/ noun a set of special playing cards used for fortune telling.
– ORIGIN French.

tarpaulin /tar-**por**-lin/ noun **1** heavy-duty waterproof cloth. **2** a sheet of tarpaulin used as a covering.
– ORIGIN probably from **TAR¹** + **PALL¹** (the cloth was originally made of tarred canvas).

tarpon noun a large tropical sea fish resembling a herring in appearance.
– ORIGIN probably from Dutch *tarpoen*.

tarragon /**ta**-ruh-guhn/ noun a plant with narrow strong-tasting leaves, used as a herb in cooking.
– ORIGIN from Latin *tragonia* and *tarchon*.

tarry¹ /rhymes with starry/ adjective relating to or covered with tar.
– DERIVATIVES **tarriness** noun.

tarry² /rhymes with marry/ verb (**tarries, tarrying, tarried**) literary stay longer than intended.
– ORIGIN unknown.

tarsal /**tar**-s'l/ adjective relating to the tarsus (group of bones in the ankle and upper foot). •noun a bone of the tarsus.

tarsier /**tar**-si-uh/ noun a small tree-dwelling primate (mammal) with very large eyes, native to the islands of SE Asia.
– ORIGIN French.

tarsus /**tar**-suhss/ noun (pl. **tarsi** /**tar**-sy/) the group of small bones in the ankle and upper foot.
– ORIGIN Greek *tarsos* 'flat of the foot, the eyelid'.

tart¹ noun an open pastry case containing a sweet or savoury filling.
– DERIVATIVES **tartlet** noun.
– ORIGIN Old French *tarte*.

tart² informal noun **1** derogatory a woman who has

many sexual partners. **2** a prostitute. ● **verb 1 (tart oneself up)** informal, chiefly Brit. make oneself look attractive with clothes or make-up. **2 (tart something up)** improve the appearance of something.
– DERIVATIVES **tarty** adjective **(tartier, tartiest)**.
– ORIGIN probably from **SWEETHEART**.

tart³ adjective **1** sharp or acid in taste. **2** (of a remark or tone of voice) sharp or sarcastic.
– DERIVATIVES **tartly** adverb **tartness** noun.
– ORIGIN Old English, 'harsh, severe'.

tartan noun **1** a pattern of coloured checks and intersecting lines, especially one associated with a particular Scottish clan. **2** a woollen cloth with a tartan pattern.
– ORIGIN perhaps from Old French *tertaine*, referring to a kind of cloth.

Tartar /**tar**-ter/ noun **1** historical a member of a group of central Asian peoples who conquered much of Asia and eastern Europe in the early 13th century. **2 (tartar)** a person who is fierce or difficult to deal with.
– ORIGIN from *Tatar*, the name of a tribe formerly living in parts of Russia and Ukraine.

tartar /**tar**-ter/ noun **1** a hard deposit that forms on the teeth and contributes to their decay. **2** a deposit of impure cream of tartar formed during the fermentation of wine.
– ORIGIN Greek *tartaron*.

tartare /tah-**tah**/ adjective (of fish or meat) served raw, seasoned and shaped into small cakes: *steak tartare*.
– ORIGIN French, 'Tartar'.

tartare sauce (also **tartar sauce**) noun mayonnaise mixed with chopped onions, gherkins, and capers, typically eaten with fish.

tartaric acid noun an organic acid found especially in unripe grapes and used in baking powders and as a food additive.
– ORIGIN from **TARTAR**.

tartrazine /**tah**-truh-zeen/ noun a bright yellow synthetic dye made from tartaric acid and used to colour food, drugs, and cosmetics.

Tarzan noun a very strong and agile man.
– ORIGIN named after a fictional character created by the American writer Edgar Rice Burroughs.

tash (also **tache**) noun informal a moustache.

task noun a piece of work to be done. ● verb **(task someone with)** give a task to someone.
– PHRASES **take someone to task** reprimand or criticize someone.
– ORIGIN Old French *tasche*.

task force noun **1** an armed force organized for a special operation. **2** a group of people specially organized for a task.

taskmaster noun (fem. **taskmistress**) a person who makes someone work very hard.

Tasmanian devil noun a heavily built aggressive marsupial with a large head, powerful jaws, and mainly black fur, found only on the Australian island of Tasmania.

tassel noun **1** a tuft of hanging threads, knotted together at one end and used for decoration in soft furnishing and clothing. **2** the tufted head of some plants.
– DERIVATIVES **tasselled** (US **tasseled**) adjective.
– ORIGIN Old French, 'clasp'.

taste noun **1** the sensation of flavour perceived in the mouth on contact with a substance. **2** the sense by which taste is perceived. **3** a small amount of food or drink taken as a sample. **4** a brief experience of something: *it was his first taste of artistic success.* **5** a person's liking for something. **6** the ability to judge what is of good quality or of a high artistic standard. **7** (often **in good** (or **bad**) **taste**) the quality of being (or not being) acceptable: *a joke in bad taste.* ● verb **1** perceive the flavour of something. **2** have a specified flavour. **3** test the flavour of something by eating or drinking a small amount of it. **4** have a brief experience of: *the team has not yet tasted victory.*
– PHRASES **to taste** according to one's personal liking.
– ORIGIN Old French *taster* 'touch, try, taste'.

taste bud noun any of the clusters of nerve endings on the tongue and in the lining of the mouth which provide the sense of taste.

tasteful adjective showing good judgement as to quality, appearance, or appropriate behaviour.
– DERIVATIVES **tastefully** adverb **tastefulness** noun.

tasteless adjective **1** lacking flavour. **2** lacking in judgement as to quality, appearance, or appropriate behaviour.
– DERIVATIVES **tastelessly** adverb **tastelessness** noun.

tastemaker noun a person who decides or influences what is or will become fashionable.

taster noun **1** a person who tests food or drink by tasting it. **2** Brit. a sample or brief experience of something.

-tastic combining form informal forming adjectives referring to someone or something that is excellent in a particular respect: *poptastic.*
– ORIGIN from **FANTASTIC**.

tasty adjective **(tastier, tastiest) 1** (of food) having a pleasant, distinct flavour. **2** informal, chiefly Brit. attractive or appealing.
– DERIVATIVES **tastily** adverb **tastiness** noun.

tat noun Brit. informal tasteless or shoddy articles.
– ORIGIN probably from **TATTY**.

tatami /tuh-**tah**-mi/ noun (pl. same or **tatamis**) a rush-covered straw mat forming a traditional Japanese floor covering.
– ORIGIN Japanese.

tater /**tay**-ter/ noun informal a potato.
– ORIGIN from **POTATO**.

tatterdemalion /tat-uh-di-**may**-li-uhn/ adjective tattered or in poor condition.
– ORIGIN from **TATTERS** or **TATTERED**.

tattered adjective **1** old and torn. **2** ruined; in tatters.

tatters plural noun irregularly torn pieces of cloth, paper, etc.
– PHRASES **in tatters** destroyed; ruined.
– ORIGIN Old Norse, 'rags'.

tattersall /**tat**-uh-suhl/ noun a woollen fabric with a pattern resembling a tartan.
– ORIGIN named after *Tattersalls*, a firm of horse auctioneers (with reference to the traditional design of horse blankets).

tatting noun **1** a kind of knotted lace made by hand with a small shuttle. **2** the process of making such lace.
– ORIGIN unknown.

tattle noun gossip; casual talk. •verb gossip about someone or something.
– DERIVATIVES **tattler** noun.
– ORIGIN Flemish *tatelen, tateren*.

tattletale noun N. Amer. a person who tells tales; a telltale.

tattoo[1] noun (pl. **tattoos**) a permanent design made on the skin by making small holes in it with a needle and filling them with coloured ink. •verb (**tattoos, tattooing, tattooed**) mark a person's skin in this way.
– DERIVATIVES **tattooer** noun **tattooist** noun.
– ORIGIN Polynesian.

tattoo[2] noun (pl. **tattoos**) 1 Brit. a military display consisting of music, marching, and exercises. 2 a rhythmic tapping or drumming. 3 an evening drum or bugle signal recalling soldiers to their quarters.
– ORIGIN from Dutch *taptoe!* 'close the tap of the cask!'

tatty adjective (**tattier, tattiest**) informal worn and shabby.
– DERIVATIVES **tattily** adverb **tattiness** noun.
– ORIGIN from Old English, 'rag'.

taught past and past participle of TEACH.

taunt noun a remark made in order to anger, upset, or provoke someone. •verb provoke or upset someone with taunts.
– DERIVATIVES **taunter** noun.
– ORIGIN from French *tant pour tant* 'like for like, tit for tat'.

taupe /rhymes with rope/ noun a grey colour tinged with brown.
– ORIGIN French, 'mole, moleskin'.

Taurus /taw-ruhss/ noun a constellation (the Bull) and sign of the zodiac, which the sun enters about 21 April.
– DERIVATIVES **Taurean** /taw-ree-uhn/ noun & adjective.
– ORIGIN Latin.

taut adjective 1 stretched or pulled tight. 2 (of muscles or nerves) tense. 3 (of writing, music, etc.) concise and controlled.
– DERIVATIVES **tauten** verb **tautly** adverb **tautness** noun.
– ORIGIN perhaps from TOUGH.

tautology /taw-tol-uh-ji/ noun (pl. **tautologies**) the saying of the same thing over again in different words, considered as a fault of style (e.g. *they arrived one after the other in succession*).
– DERIVATIVES **tautological** adjective **tautologous** adjective.
– ORIGIN from Greek *tauto-* 'same' + *logos* 'word, telling'.

tavern noun chiefly old use or N. Amer. an inn or pub.
– ORIGIN Latin *taberna* 'hut, tavern'.

taverna /tuh-ver-nuh/ noun a small Greek restaurant.
– ORIGIN modern Greek.

tawdry adjective (**tawdrier, tawdriest**) 1 showy but cheap and of poor quality. 2 sleazy or unpleasant: *the tawdry business of politics*.
– DERIVATIVES **tawdriness** noun.
– ORIGIN short for *tawdry lace*, from *St Audrey's lace*, a fine silk lace or ribbon.

tawny adjective (**tawnier, tawniest**) orange-brown or yellowish-brown in colour.
– DERIVATIVES **tawniness** noun.
– ORIGIN Old French *tane*.

tawny owl noun a common owl with either reddish-brown or grey plumage, and a quavering hoot.

tax noun money that must be paid to the state, charged by the government as a proportion of personal income and business profits or added to the cost of some goods, services, and transactions. •verb 1 put a tax on something, or make someone pay a tax. 2 pay tax on a vehicle. 3 make heavy demands on: *the ordeal would tax her strength.* 4 accuse someone of wrongdoing.
– DERIVATIVES **taxable** adjective.
– ORIGIN from Latin *taxare* 'to censure, charge'.

taxation noun 1 the imposing of tax on someone or something. 2 money paid as tax.

tax avoidance noun the arrangement of one's financial affairs so as to pay only the minimum of tax that is legally required.

tax break noun informal a tax reduction or advantage allowed by the government.

tax-deductible adjective permitted to be deducted from income before the amount of tax to be paid is calculated.

tax disc noun Brit. a circular label displayed on the windscreen of a vehicle, showing that road tax has been paid.

tax evasion noun the illegal non-payment or underpayment of tax.

tax exile noun a person with a high taxable income who chooses to live in a country with low rates of taxation.

tax haven noun a country or independent area where taxes are low.

taxi noun (pl. **taxis**) a motor vehicle licensed to carry passengers to the place of their choice in return for payment of a fare. •verb (**taxies, taxiing** or **taxying, taxied**) (of an aircraft) move slowly along the ground before take-off or after landing.
– ORIGIN abbreviation of *taxicab* or *taximeter cab* (see TAXIMETER).

taxicab noun a taxi.

taxidermy /tak-si-der-mi/ noun the art of preparing, stuffing, and mounting the skins of animals so that they appear lifelike.
– DERIVATIVES **taxidermic** adjective **taxidermist** noun.
– ORIGIN from Greek *taxis* 'arrangement' + *derma* 'skin'.

taximeter noun a device used in taxis that automatically records the distance travelled and the fare to be paid.
– ORIGIN French *taximètre*, from *taxe* 'tariff' + *mètre* 'meter'.

taxing adjective physically or mentally demanding.

taxi rank (N. Amer. **taxi stand**) noun a place where taxis park while waiting to be hired.

taxiway noun a route along which an aircraft taxies when moving to or from a runway.

taxman noun (pl. **taxmen**) informal an inspector or collector of taxes.

taxonomy /tak-son-uh-mi/ noun 1 the branch of science concerned with the classification of things, especially plants and animals. 2 a particular scheme of classification.
– DERIVATIVES **taxonomic** adjective **taxonomist** noun.

– ORIGIN from Greek *taxis* 'arrangement' + *-nomia* 'distribution'.

taxpayer noun a person who pays taxes.

tax return noun a form on which a taxpayer makes a statement of their income and personal circumstances, used to assess how much tax they should pay.

tax year noun a period of twelve months used for calculating taxes (in Britain from 6 April).

TB abbreviation tubercle bacillus; tuberculosis.

Tb symbol the chemical element terbium.

TBA abbreviation to be arranged (or announced).

TBC abbreviation to be confirmed.

T-bone noun a large choice piece of loin steak containing a T-shaped bone.

tbsp (also **tbs**) (pl. same or **tbsps**) abbreviation tablespoonful.

Tc symbol the chemical element technetium.

TCP/IP abbreviation trademark transmission control protocol/Internet protocol, used to govern the connection of computer systems to the Internet.

TD abbreviation (in the Republic of Ireland) Teachta Dála, Member of the Dáil.

Te symbol the chemical element tellurium.

te (N. Amer. **ti**) noun Music the seventh note of a major scale, coming after 'lah'.
– ORIGIN alteration of former *si*, adopted to avoid having two notes (*soh* and *si*) beginning with the same letter.

tea noun **1** a hot drink made by infusing the dried, crushed leaves of an evergreen Asian shrub (the tea plant) in boiling water. **2** the dried leaves used to make tea. **3** a drink made from the leaves, fruits, or flowers of other plants. **4** chiefly Brit. a light afternoon meal consisting of sandwiches, cakes, etc., with tea to drink. **5** Brit. a cooked evening meal.
– ORIGIN Chinese.

tea bag noun a small sachet containing tea leaves, on to which boiling water is poured to make tea.

tea break noun Brit. a short rest period during the working day.

teacake noun Brit. a light sweet bun containing dried fruit, usually served toasted and buttered.

teach verb (past and past part. **taught**) **1** give information about a particular subject to a class or pupil. **2** show someone how to do something. **3** make someone realize or understand something: *the experience taught me the real value of money.*
– DERIVATIVES **teachable** adjective **teaching** noun.
– ORIGIN Old English, 'show, present, point out'.

teacher noun a person who teaches in a school.
– DERIVATIVES **teacherly** adjective.

tea chest noun a light metal-lined wooden box in which tea is transported.

teaching hospital noun a hospital officially linked to a medical school, in which medical students receive training.

Teachta Dála /tyokh-tuh daw-luh/ noun (pl. **Teachti** /tyokh-ti/) (in the Republic of Ireland) a member of the Dáil or lower house of Parliament.
– ORIGIN Irish.

tea cloth noun a tea towel.

tea cosy noun a thick or padded cover placed over a teapot to keep the tea hot.

teacup noun a cup from which tea is drunk.

tea dance noun a social occasion consisting of afternoon tea and dancing.

teak noun hard wood used in shipbuilding and for making furniture, obtained from a tree native to India and SE Asia.
– ORIGIN Portuguese *teca*.

teal noun (pl. same or **teals**) **1** a small freshwater duck, typically with a bright blue-green patch on the wing plumage. **2** (also **teal blue**) a dark greenish-blue colour.
– ORIGIN unknown.

team noun **1** a group of players forming one side in a competitive game or sport. **2** two or more people working together. **3** two or more horses harnessed together to pull a vehicle.
• verb **1** (**team up**) join with another person or group to do or achieve something. **2** (**team something with**) wear an item of clothing with another: *a pinstripe suit teamed with a white shirt.*
– ORIGIN Old English.

USAGE: Do not confuse **team** with **teem**. Team means 'a group of people playing or working together' or 'join with another person or group to achieve something' (*she teamed up with other singers to form the group*), while teem means 'be full of something' (*every garden is teeming with wildlife*) or 'pour down' (*rain teemed down all morning*).

teammate noun a fellow member of a team.

team player noun a person who plays or works well as a member of a team.

team spirit noun feelings of trust and cooperation among the members of a team.

teamster noun **1** N. Amer. a lorry driver. **2** a driver of a team of animals.

teamwork noun the effective action of a team of people working together.

teapot noun a pot with a handle, spout, and lid, in which tea is prepared.

tear¹ /tair/ verb (past **tore**; past part. **torn**) **1** (often **tear something up**) pull something apart or into pieces: *I tore up the letter.* **2** rip a hole or split in something. **3** remove something by pulling it roughly or forcefully: *he tore a page from his notebook.* **4** damage a muscle or ligament by overstretching it. **5** (**tear something down**) demolish or destroy something. **6** (**tear something apart**) destroy good relations between people. **7** (**tear oneself away**) leave despite a strong desire to stay. **8** (**be torn**) be unable to choose between two options. **9** informal move very quickly and in a reckless or excited way. **10** (**tear into**) attack someone verbally. • noun a hole or split caused by tearing.
– DERIVATIVES **tearable** adjective.
– ORIGIN Old English.

tear² /teer/ noun a drop of clear salty liquid produced by glands in a person's eye when they are crying or when the eye is irritated.
– PHRASES **in tears** crying.
– DERIVATIVES **teary** adjective.
– ORIGIN Old English.

tearaway noun Brit. a young person who behaves in a wild or reckless way.

teardrop noun a single tear. •adjective shaped like a tear.

tear duct noun a passage through which tears pass from the glands which produce them to the eye or from the eye to the nose.

tearful adjective 1 crying or about to cry. 2 causing tears; sad: *a tearful farewell*.
– DERIVATIVES **tearfully** adverb **tearfulness** noun.

tear gas noun gas that causes severe irritation to the eyes, used in warfare and riot control.

tearing /tair-ing/ adjective great; extreme: *a tearing hurry*.

tear-jerker noun informal a story or film intended to arouse feelings of sadness in an audience.

tea room noun a small restaurant or cafe where tea and other light refreshments are served.

tea rose noun a garden rose having flowers that are pale yellow tinged with pink, and a delicate scent resembling that of tea.

tease verb 1 make fun of someone in a playful way or in order to annoy or embarrass them. 2 tempt someone sexually, without intending to have sex with them. 3 (**tease something out**) find out something by searching through a mass of information. 4 gently pull or comb tangled wool, hair, etc. into separate strands. •noun informal 1 a person who teases. 2 an act of teasing someone.
– ORIGIN Old English, related to **TEASEL**.

teasel (also **teazle** or **teazel**) noun a tall prickly plant with spiny purple flower heads.
– ORIGIN Old English.

teaser noun informal a tricky question or task.

tea set noun a set of crockery for serving tea.

teaspoon noun 1 a small spoon used for adding sugar to and stirring hot drinks. 2 the amount held by a teaspoon, in the UK considered to be 5 millilitres.

teat noun 1 one of the parts of a female animal's body from which milk is sucked by the young. 2 Brit. a perforated plastic nipple-shaped device by which a baby or young animal can suck milk from a bottle.
– ORIGIN Old French *tete*.

teatime noun chiefly Brit. the time in the afternoon when tea is served.

tea towel noun chiefly Brit. a cloth for drying washed crockery, cutlery, and glasses.

tea tree noun an Australasian flowering shrub or small tree with leaves that are sometimes used for tea.

tea-tree oil noun an oil obtained from a species of tea tree, used in soaps and other products for its refreshing fragrance and antiseptic properties.

teazle (also **teazel**) noun variant spelling of **TEASEL**.

tech (also **tec**) noun Brit. informal a technical college.

techie /tek-i/ noun (pl. **techies**) informal a person who is an expert in technology, especially computing.

technetium /tek-nee-shi-uhm/ noun an unstable radioactive metallic element made by high-energy collisions.
– ORIGIN from Greek *tekhnētos* 'artificial'.

technic /tek-nik/ noun 1 /also tek-**neek**/ chiefly US

technique. 2 (**technics**) (treated as sing. or pl.) technical terms, details, and methods.
– DERIVATIVES **technicist** noun.
– ORIGIN from Greek *tekhnē* 'art'.

technical adjective 1 relating to a particular subject, art, or craft, or its practical skills and techniques. 2 relating to the practical use of machinery and methods in science and industry. 3 requiring specialized knowledge in order to be understood. 4 according to a strict application or interpretation of the law or rules: *a technical violation of the treaty*.
– DERIVATIVES **technically** adverb.

technical college noun a college of further education providing courses in applied sciences and other practical subjects.

technicality noun (pl. **technicalities**) 1 a small formal detail within a set of rules, as contrasted with the intent or purpose of the rules. 2 (**technicalities**) the details of how something works or is done: *the technicalities of police procedure*. 3 the use of technical terms or methods.

technical knockout noun Boxing the ending of a fight by the referee because a contestant is judged to be unable to continue, the opponent being declared the winner.

technician noun 1 a person employed to look after technical equipment or do practical work in a laboratory. 2 a person skilled in the technique of an art, science, craft, or sport.

Technicolor noun 1 trademark a process of producing cinema films in colour by using synchronized monochrome films, each of a different colour, to produce a colour print. 2 (**technicolor** or Brit. also **technicolour**) informal vivid colour.

technique noun 1 a method or skill used for carrying out a particular task. 2 a person's level of skill in a particular field. 3 a skilful or efficient way of doing or achieving something.
– ORIGIN French, from Greek *tekhnē* 'art'.

techno noun a style of fast electronic dance music, with a strong beat and few or no vocals.
– ORIGIN abbreviation of technological (see **TECHNOLOGY**).

technobabble noun informal incomprehensible technical jargon.

technocracy /tek-nok-ruh-si/ noun (pl. **technocracies**) a social or political system in which scientific or technical experts hold a great deal of power.
– DERIVATIVES **technocrat** noun **technocratic** adjective.

technology noun (pl. **technologies**) 1 the application of scientific knowledge for practical purposes. 2 machinery and equipment developed from such scientific knowledge. 3 the branch of knowledge concerned with applied sciences.
– DERIVATIVES **technological** adjective **technologically** adverb **technologist** noun.
– ORIGIN Greek *tekhnologia* 'systematic treatment'.

technology transfer noun the transfer of new technology from the originator to a secondary user, especially from developed to underdeveloped countries.

technophile noun a person who is enthusiastic about new technology.

t

– DERIVATIVES **technophilia** noun **technophilic** adjective.

technophobe noun a person who dislikes or fears new technology.
– DERIVATIVES **technophobia** noun **technophobic** adjective.

technospeak noun another term for TECHNOBABBLE.

tectonic /tek-ton-ik/ adjective **1** Geology relating to the structure of the earth's crust and the large-scale processes which take place within it. **2** relating to building or construction. **3** (of a change or development) very significant or considerable: *a tectonic shift in public attitudes.*
– DERIVATIVES **tectonically** adverb.
– ORIGIN from Greek *tektōn* 'carpenter, builder'.

tectonics plural noun (treated as sing. or pl.) Geology large-scale processes affecting the structure of the earth's crust.

teddy noun (pl. **teddies**) **1** (also **teddy bear**) a soft toy bear. **2** a woman's all-in-one undergarment.
– ORIGIN from *Teddy*, informal form of the man's name *Theodore*: in sense 1 referring to the US President *Theodore* Roosevelt, an enthusiastic bear hunter.

Teddy boy noun (in Britain during the 1950s) a young man of a group who wore clothes based on Edwardian fashions, had their hair slicked up in a quiff, and listened to rock-and-roll music.
– ORIGIN from *Teddy*, informal form of the man's name *Edward* (with reference to the Edwardian style of dress).

Te Deum /tee dee-uhm, tay day-uhm/ noun a Christian hymn beginning *Te Deum laudamus*, 'We praise Thee, O God', sung at matins or on special occasions such as a thanksgiving.
– ORIGIN Latin.

tedious adjective too long or slow; dull.
– DERIVATIVES **tediously** adverb **tediousness** noun.
– ORIGIN from Latin *taedium* 'tedium'.

tedium noun the state of being tedious.

tee¹ noun **1** a cleared space on a golf course, from which the ball is struck at the beginning of play for each hole. **2** a small peg placed in the ground to support a golf ball before it is struck from a tee. **3** a mark aimed at in bowls, quoits, curling, and other similar games. •verb (**tees, teeing, teed**) Golf **1** (**tee up**) place the ball on a tee ready to make the first stroke of the round or hole. **2** (**tee off**) begin a round or hole by playing the ball from a tee.
– ORIGIN unknown.

tee² noun informal a T-shirt.

tee-hee noun a giggle or laugh.
– ORIGIN imitating the sound.

teem¹ verb (**teem with**) be full of or swarming with.
– ORIGIN Old English, 'give birth to'.

> USAGE: On the confusion of **teem** and **team**, see the note at TEAM.

teem² verb (of rain) pour down; fall heavily.
– ORIGIN Old Norse, 'to empty'.

teen informal adjective relating to teenagers. •noun a teenager.

-teen suffix forming the names of numerals from 13 to 19.
– ORIGIN Old English.

teenage adjective relating to a teenager or teenagers.
– DERIVATIVES **teenaged** adjective.

teenager noun a person aged between 13 and 19 years.

teens plural noun the years of a person's age from 13 to 19.

teensy adjective (**teensier, teensiest**) informal very tiny.
– ORIGIN probably from TEENY.

teeny adjective (**teenier, teeniest**) informal tiny.
– ORIGIN variant of TINY.

teeny-bopper noun informal a young teenager who follows the latest fashions in clothes and pop music.

teeny-weeny (also **teensy-weensy**) adjective informal very tiny.

teepee noun variant spelling of TEPEE.

tee shirt noun variant spelling of T-SHIRT.

teeter verb **1** move or balance unsteadily. **2** be unable to decide between different options.
– ORIGIN Old Norse, 'shake, shiver'.

teeth plural of TOOTH.

teethe verb (of a baby) develop its first teeth.

teething ring noun a small ring for a baby to bite on while teething.

teething troubles (also **teething problems**) plural noun short-term problems that occur in the early stages of a new project.

teetotal adjective choosing never to drink alcohol.
– DERIVATIVES **teetotalism** noun **teetotaller** noun.
– ORIGIN from TOTAL (referring to total abstinence from all alcohol).

TEFL /tef-uhl/ abbreviation teaching of English as a foreign language.

Teflon /tef-lon/ noun trademark a tough synthetic resin used to make seals and bearings and to coat non-stick cooking utensils.

tele- /tel-i/ combining form **1** to or at a distance: *telecommunication.* **2** relating to television: *telegenic.* **3** done by means of the telephone: *telemarketing.*
– ORIGIN Greek, 'far off'. Senses 2 and 3 are abbreviations.

telecast noun a television broadcast. •verb broadcast a programme by television.
– DERIVATIVES **telecaster** noun.

telecommunication noun **1** long-distance communication by means of cable, telephone, broadcasting, satellite, etc. **2** (**telecommunications**) (treated as sing.) the technology concerned with this.

telecommuting noun the practice of working from home, communicating with a central workplace by telephone, email, and fax.
– DERIVATIVES **telecommute** verb **telecommuter** noun.

telecoms (also **telecomms**) plural noun (treated as sing.) telecommunications.

teleconference noun a conference in which participants in different locations are linked by telecommunication devices.
– DERIVATIVES **teleconferencing** noun.

tele-evangelist noun variant of TELEVANGELIST.

telegenic /te-li-jen-ik/ adjective having an appearance or manner that is attractive on television.

telegram noun a message sent by telegraph

and delivered in written or printed form, used in the UK only for international messages since 1981.

telegraph noun a system or device for transmitting messages from a distance along a wire, especially one creating signals by making and breaking an electrical connection. •**verb 1** send a message to someone by telegraph. **2** convey a message by one's facial expression or body language.
– DERIVATIVES **telegrapher** noun **telegraphic** adjective **telegraphist** noun **telegraphy** noun.

telegraph pole noun a tall pole used to carry telegraph or telephone wires above the ground.

telekinesis /te-li-ki-**nee**-siss/ noun the supposed ability to move objects at a distance by mental power or other non-physical means.
– DERIVATIVES **telekinetic** adjective.
– ORIGIN from Greek *kinēsis* 'motion'.

telemarketing noun the marketing of goods or services by telephoning potential customers.
– DERIVATIVES **telemarketer** noun.

telematics plural noun (treated as sing.) the branch of information technology which deals with the long-distance transmission of computerized information.
– DERIVATIVES **telematic** adjective.
– ORIGIN blend of **TELECOMMUNICATION** and **INFORMATICS**.

telemedicine noun the diagnosis and treatment of patients at a distance by means of telecommunications technology.

telemessage noun trademark a message sent by telephone or telex and delivered in written form, which replaced the telegram for inland messages in the UK in 1981.

telemeter /**tel**-i-mee-ter, ti-**lem**-i-ter/ noun a piece of equipment for recording the readings of an instrument and transmitting them by radio.
– DERIVATIVES **telemetric** adjective **telemetry** noun.

teleology /te-li-**ol**-uh-ji, tee-li-**ol**-uh-ji/ noun (pl. **teleologies**) **1** the philosophical theory that all natural phenomena can be explained with reference to their purpose. **2** the theological doctrine that there is evidence of design and purpose in the natural world.
– DERIVATIVES **teleological** adjective.
– ORIGIN from Greek *telos* 'end' + *logos* 'account, reason'.

telepathy /ti-**lep**-uh-thi/ noun the supposed communication of thoughts or ideas without using speech, writing, or any other normal method.
– DERIVATIVES **telepath** noun **telepathic** /tel-i-**path**-ik/ adjective.

telephone noun **1** a system for transmitting voices over a distance using wire or radio, by converting sound vibrations to electrical signals. **2** a piece of equipment used as part of such a system, typically having a handset with a transmitting microphone and a set of numbered buttons by which a connection can be made to another such piece of equipment. •**verb** contact someone by telephone.
– DERIVATIVES **telephonic** adjective **telephonically** adverb.

telephone box noun Brit. a public booth or

enclosure in which a payphone is situated.

telephone directory noun a book listing the names, addresses, and telephone numbers of the people in a particular area.

telephone exchange noun a set of equipment that connects telephone lines during a call.

telephone number noun a number given to a particular telephone and used in making connections to it.

telephonist noun Brit. a person who operates a telephone switchboard.

telephony /ti-**lef**-uh-ni/ noun the working or use of telephones.

telephoto lens noun a lens with a longer focal length than standard, producing a magnified image of a distant object.

teleport noun a centre providing connections between different forms of telecommunications, especially one which links satellites to ground-based communications. •**verb** (especially in science fiction) transport or be transported across space and distance instantly.
– DERIVATIVES **teleportation** noun.
– ORIGIN from **TELE-** + a shortened form of *transportation*.

telepresence noun the use of virtual reality technology, especially for the remote control of machinery or to produce the impression of being in another location.

teleprinter noun Brit. a device for transmitting telegraph messages as they are keyed, and for printing messages received.

teleprompter noun North American term for **AUTOCUE**.

telesales plural noun chiefly Brit. the selling of goods or services over the telephone.

telescope noun an optical instrument designed to make distant objects appear nearer, containing an arrangement of lenses, or of curved mirrors and lenses, by which rays of light are collected and focused and the resulting image magnified. •**verb 1** (of an object made of several tubular parts fitting into each other) slide into itself so as to become smaller. **2** condense or combine so as to occupy less space or time: *at sea the years are telescoped into hours.*
– DERIVATIVES **telescopic** adjective **telescopically** adverb.

teletext noun a news and information service transmitted to televisions with appropriate receivers.

telethon noun a long television programme broadcast to raise money for a charity.
– ORIGIN from **TELE-** + -*thon* on the pattern of *marathon*.

teletype noun trademark a kind of teleprinter.

televangelist (also **tele-evangelist**) noun chiefly N. Amer. an evangelical preacher who appears regularly on television.

televise verb broadcast something on television.

television noun **1** a system for converting visual images (with sound) into electrical signals, transmitting them by radio or other means, and displaying them electronically on a screen. **2** (also **television set**) a device with a screen for receiving television signals. **3** the process or business of broadcasting programmes on television.

televisual adjective relating to or suitable for television.
– DERIVATIVES **televisually** adverb.

teleworking noun another term for TELECOMMUTING.
– DERIVATIVES **teleworker** noun.

telex noun **1** an international system of telegraphy in which printed messages are transmitted and received by teleprinters. **2** a machine used for this. **3** a message sent by telex. • verb send a message to someone by telex.
– ORIGIN blend of TELEPRINTER and EXCHANGE.

tell verb (past and past part. **told**) **1** communicate information to someone. **2** order or advise someone to do something. **3** express something in words: *tell me the story again.* **4** (**tell someone off**) informal reprimand someone. **5** establish that something is the case: *you can tell they're in love.* **6** be able to recognize a difference. **7** (of an experience or period of time) have a noticeable effect on someone. **8** (**tell on**) informal inform someone about a person's wrongdoings.
– PHRASES **tell tales** gossip about another person's secrets or wrongdoings. **tell the time** (or N. Amer. **tell time**) be able to read the time from the face of a clock or watch.
– ORIGIN Old English, 'relate, count'.

teller noun **1** chiefly N. Amer. a person who deals with customers' transactions in a bank. **2** a person appointed to count votes. **3** a person who tells something.

telling adjective having a striking or revealing effect; significant.
– DERIVATIVES **tellingly** adverb.

telling-off noun (pl. **tellings-off**) Brit. informal a reprimand.

telltale adjective revealing something: *the telltale signs of a woman in love.* • noun Brit. a person who reports other people's wrongdoings or reveals their secrets.

telluric /tel-**yoor**-ik/ adjective **1** relating to the earth as a planet. **2** relating to the soil.
– ORIGIN from Latin *tellus* 'earth'.

tellurium /tel-**yoor**-i-uhm/ noun a silvery-white crystalline non-metallic element with semiconducting properties.
– ORIGIN from Latin *tellus* 'earth'.

telly noun (pl. **tellies**) Brit. informal term for TELEVISION.

telnet noun Computing a network protocol or program that allows a user on one computer to log in to another computer that is part of the same network.

temazepam /tuh-**maz**-i-pam/ noun a sedative drug.

temerity /ti-**me**-ri-ti/ noun excessively confident or bold behaviour.
– ORIGIN Latin *temeritas.*

temp informal noun a person working in an office who is employed on a temporary basis. • verb work as a temp.

tempeh /**tem**-pay/ noun an Indonesian dish consisting of deep-fried fermented soya beans.

– ORIGIN Indonesian.

temper noun **1** a person's state of mind in terms of their being angry or calm: *she regained her temper.* **2** a tendency to become angry easily. **3** an angry state of mind. **4** the degree of hardness and elasticity in steel or another metal. • verb **1** balance or modify something so as to make it less extreme: *their idealism is tempered with realism.* **2** improve the hardness and elasticity of a metal by reheating and then cooling it.
– PHRASES **keep** (or **lose**) **one's temper** manage (or fail to manage) to control one's anger.
– ORIGIN Latin *temperare* 'mingle, restrain oneself'.

tempera /**tem**-puh-ruh/ noun a method of painting which uses powdered colours mixed with egg yolk.
– ORIGIN from Italian *pingere a tempera* 'paint in distemper'.

temperament noun a person's nature in terms of the effect it has on their behaviour.
– ORIGIN Latin *temperamentum* 'correct mixture'.

temperamental adjective **1** liable to unreasonable changes of mood. **2** relating to or caused by a person's temperament.
– DERIVATIVES **temperamentally** adverb.

temperance noun the practice of never drinking alcohol.
– ORIGIN Old French *temperaunce.*

temperate adjective **1** (of a region or climate) having mild temperatures. **2** showing moderation or self-restraint.
– ORIGIN Latin *temperatus.*

temperate zone noun each of the two regions of the earth between the Arctic Circle and the Tropic of Cancer and the Antarctic Circle and the Tropic of Capricorn.

temperature noun **1** the degree or intensity of heat present in a place, substance, or object. **2** a body temperature above normal. **3** the degree of excitement or tension in a situation or discussion: *the temperature of the debate lowered.*
– ORIGIN Latin *temperatura* 'the state of being mixed'.

tempest noun a violent windy storm.
– ORIGIN Latin *tempestas* 'season, weather, storm'.

tempestuous /tem-**pess**-tyoo-uhss/ adjective **1** very stormy. **2** full of strong and changeable emotions: *a tempestuous relationship.*
– DERIVATIVES **tempestuously** adverb **tempestuousness** noun.

tempi plural of TEMPO.

Templar /**tem**-pler/ noun historical a member of the Knights Templar, a powerful religious and military order.
– ORIGIN Latin *templarius*, from *templum* (see TEMPLE¹).

template /**tem**-playt/ noun **1** a shaped piece of rigid material used as a pattern for processes such as cutting out, shaping, or drilling. **2** something which acts as a model or example for others to copy.
– ORIGIN probably from *temple* 'a device in a loom for keeping the cloth stretched'.

temple¹ noun **1** a building used for the worship of a god or gods. **2** (**the Temple**) either of two

ancient religious buildings of the Jews in Jerusalem.
– ORIGIN Latin *templum* 'open or consecrated space'.

temple² noun the flat part either side of the head between the forehead and the ear.
– ORIGIN Old French.

tempo /tem-poh/ noun (pl. **tempos** or **tempi** /tem-pi/) 1 the speed at which a passage of music is played. 2 the pace of an activity or process.
– ORIGIN Italian, from Latin *tempus* 'time'.

temporal¹ /tem-puh-ruhl/ adjective 1 relating to time. 2 relating to the physical world rather than to spiritual matters.
– DERIVATIVES **temporally** adverb.
– ORIGIN Latin *temporalis*, from *tempus* 'time'.

temporal² /tem-puh-ruhl/ adjective relating to or situated in the temples of the head.

temporal bone noun either of a pair of bones which form part of the side of the skull on each side and enclose the middle and inner ear.

temporal lobe noun each of the paired lobes of the brain lying beneath the temples, including areas concerned with the understanding of speech.

temporary adjective lasting for only a short or limited time.
– DERIVATIVES **temporarily** adverb **temporariness** noun.
– ORIGIN Latin *temporarius*, from *tempus* 'time'.

temporize (or **temporise**) verb be evasive or delay making a decision in order to gain time.
– ORIGIN French *temporiser* 'bide one's time'.

tempt verb 1 try to persuade someone to do something appealing but wrong or unwise. 2 (**be tempted to do**) have an urge or inclination to do something: *I was tempted to look at my watch*. 3 entice or attract: *programmes designed to tempt young people into engineering*.
– PHRASES **tempt fate** (or **providence**) do something risky or dangerous.
– DERIVATIVES **tempter** noun **tempting** adjective.
– ORIGIN Latin *temptare* 'to handle, test, try'.

temptation noun 1 the action of tempting or the state of being tempted. 2 a tempting thing.

temptress noun a sexually attractive woman who sets out to make a man desire her.

tempura /tem-puu-ruh/ noun a Japanese dish of fish, shellfish, or vegetables, fried in batter.
– ORIGIN Japanese.

ten cardinal number one more than nine; 10. (Roman numeral: **x** or **X**.)
– PHRASES **ten out of ten** referring to an excellent performance. **ten to one** very probably.
– DERIVATIVES **tenfold** adjective & adverb.
– ORIGIN Old English.

tenable adjective 1 able to be defended against attack or objection. 2 (of a post, grant, etc.) able to be held or used for a particular period: *a scholarship tenable for three years*.
– ORIGIN French, from Latin *tenere* 'to hold'.

tenacious /ti-nay-shuhss/ adjective 1 holding firmly to something. 2 continuing to exist or do something for longer than might be expected: *a tenacious belief*.

– DERIVATIVES **tenaciously** adverb **tenacity** /ti-nass-i-ti/ noun.
– ORIGIN from Latin *tenere* 'to hold'.

tenancy noun (pl. **tenancies**) the possession or occupation of land or property as a tenant.

tenant noun 1 a person who rents land or property from a landlord. 2 Law a person privately owning land or property. •verb occupy property as a tenant.
– ORIGIN Old French, 'holding'.

tenant farmer noun a person who farms rented land.

tench noun (pl. same) a freshwater fish of the carp family.
– ORIGIN Old French *tenche*.

Ten Commandments plural noun (in the Bible) the rules of conduct given by God to Moses on Mount Sinai.

tend¹ verb 1 frequently behave in a particular way or have a certain characteristic: *men tend to marry younger women*. 2 go or move in a particular direction.
– ORIGIN Latin *tendere* 'stretch, tend'.

tend² verb care for or look after: *ambulance crews were tending to the injured*.
– ORIGIN from ATTEND.

tendency noun (pl. **tendencies**) 1 an inclination towards a particular characteristic or type of behaviour. 2 a group within a larger political party or movement.

tendentious /ten-den-shuhss/ adjective expressing a strong opinion, especially a controversial one.
– DERIVATIVES **tendentiously** adverb **tendentiousness** noun.
– ORIGIN suggested by German *tendenziös*.

tender¹ adjective (**tenderer**, **tenderest**) 1 gentle and kind. 2 (of food) easy to cut or chew. 3 (of a part of the body) painful to the touch. 4 young and vulnerable: *he started sailing at the tender age of ten*. 5 (of a plant) easily damaged by severe weather.
– DERIVATIVES **tenderly** adverb **tenderness** noun.
– ORIGIN Old French *tendre*.

tender² verb 1 offer or present something formally: *he tendered his resignation*. 2 make a formal written offer to carry out work, supply goods, etc. for a stated fixed price. 3 give money as payment for something. •noun a formal offer to carry out work, supply goods, etc. for a stated fixed price.
– PHRASES **put something out to tender** ask for offers to carry out work, supply goods, etc. to be submitted.
– DERIVATIVES **tenderer** noun.
– ORIGIN Latin *tendere* 'stretch, hold out'.

tender³ noun 1 a vehicle used by a fire service or the armed forces for carrying supplies or fulfilling a particular role. 2 a wagon attached to a steam locomotive, carrying fuel and water. 3 a boat used to ferry people and supplies to and from a ship.
– ORIGIN from TEND² or ATTEND.

tenderfoot noun (pl. **tenderfoots** or **tenderfeet**) chiefly N. Amer. a person who is new to and lacks experience in an activity or situation.

tender-hearted adjective having a kind, gentle, or sentimental nature.

tenderize (or **tenderise**) **verb** make meat more tender by beating it or cooking it slowly.
– DERIVATIVES **tenderizer** noun.

tenderloin noun the tenderest part of a loin of beef, pork, etc., taken from under the short ribs in the hindquarters.

tendinitis /ten-di-**ny**-tiss/ (also **tendonitis** /ten-duh-**ny**-tiss/) **noun** inflammation of a tendon.

tendon /**ten**-duhn/ **noun 1** a band of strong fibrous tissue which attaches a muscle to a bone. **2** the hamstring of a four-legged mammal.
– ORIGIN Greek *tenōn* 'sinew'.

tendril noun **1** a slender thread-like part of a climbing plant, which stretches out and twines round any suitable support. **2** a slender ringlet of hair.
– ORIGIN probably from Old French *tendron* 'young shoot'.

tenebrous /**ten**-i-bruhss/ **adjective** literary dark; shadowy.
– ORIGIN Latin *tenebrosus*.

tenement /**ten**-uh-muhnt/ **noun 1** (also **tenement house**) a large house divided into several separate flats. **2** (especially in Scotland or the US) a room or set of rooms forming a separate home within a house or block of flats.
– ORIGIN Latin *tenementum*.

tenet /**ten**-it/ **noun** one of the main principles or beliefs of a religion, philosophy, etc.
– ORIGIN Latin, 'he holds'.

ten-gallon hat noun a large, broad-brimmed hat, traditionally worn by cowboys.

tenner noun Brit. informal a ten-pound note.

tennis noun a game for two or four players, who use rackets to strike a ball over a net stretched across a grass or clay court. See also **REAL TENNIS**.
– ORIGIN apparently from Old French *tenez* 'take, receive' (called by the server in the game of real tennis).

tennis elbow noun inflammation of the tendons of the elbow caused by overuse of the forearm muscles.

tenon noun a projecting piece of wood made to fit into a mortise in another piece of wood.
– ORIGIN French.

tenon saw noun a small saw with a strong brass or steel back.

tenor[1] noun a singing voice between baritone and alto or countertenor, the highest of the ordinary adult male range. • **adjective** referring to an instrument of the second or third lowest pitch in its family: *a tenor sax*.
– ORIGIN from Latin *tenere* 'to hold' (because the tenor part 'held' the melody).

tenor[2] noun the general meaning or nature of something: *the even tenor of life in the village*.
– ORIGIN Latin *tenor* 'course'.

tenosynovitis /te-noh-sy-noh-**vy**-tiss/ **noun** inflammation and swelling of a tendon, especially in the wrist, often caused by repetitive movements such as those made when typing.
– ORIGIN from Greek *tenōn* 'tendon' + *synovitis* 'inflammation of a synovial membrane'.

tenpin noun a skittle used in tenpin bowling.

tenpin bowling noun a game in which ten skittles are set up at the end of a track and knocked down by rolling a hard, heavy ball at them.

TENS abbreviation transcutaneous electrical nerve stimulation, a technique for relieving pain by applying electrodes to the skin.

tense[1] adjective **1** feeling, causing, or showing anxiety and nervousness. **2** (especially of a muscle) stretched tight or rigid. • **verb** make or become tense.
– DERIVATIVES **tensely** adverb **tenseness** noun.
– ORIGIN Latin *tensus*, from *tendere* 'stretch'.

tense[2] noun Grammar a set of forms taken by a verb to indicate the time or completeness of the action.
– ORIGIN Latin *tempus* 'time'.

tensile /**ten**-syl/ **adjective 1** relating to tension or being stretched. **2** capable of being drawn out or stretched.

tensile strength noun the resistance of a material to breaking when being stretched.

tension noun **1** a situation in which there is conflict or distrust because of differing views, aims, or needs: *months of tension between the military and the government.* **2** a feeling of anxiety and mental pressure. **3** the state of being stretched tight. **4** the degree of stitch tightness in knitting and machine sewing. **5** voltage of a particular magnitude: *high tension.*
– DERIVATIVES **tensional** adjective.

tent noun a portable shelter made of cloth, supported by one or more poles and stretched tight by cords attached to pegs driven into the ground.
– ORIGIN Old French *tente*.

tentacle noun a long, thin flexible part extending from the body of an animal, used for feeling or holding things, or for moving about.
– DERIVATIVES **tentacled** adjective **tentacular** adjective.
– ORIGIN Latin *tentaculum*.

tentative adjective **1** done without confidence; hesitant: *a few tentative steps.* **2** not certain or fixed; provisional: *a tentative arrangement.*
– DERIVATIVES **tentatively** adverb **tentativeness** noun.
– ORIGIN Latin *tentativus*.

tenterhook noun (in phrase **on tenterhooks**) in a state of nervous suspense.
– ORIGIN first meaning a hook used to fasten cloth on a *tenter*, a framework on which fabric was held taut during manufacture.

tenth ordinal number **1** that is number ten in a sequence; 10th. **2** (**a tenth**/**one tenth**) each of ten equal parts into which something is divided. **3** a musical interval spanning an octave and a third in a scale.
– DERIVATIVES **tenthly** adverb.

tent stitch noun a series of parallel diagonal stitches.

tenuous adjective **1** very slight or weak: *a sick woman with only a tenuous grasp of reality.* **2** very slender or fine.
– DERIVATIVES **tenuously** adverb **tenuousness** noun.
– ORIGIN Latin *tenuis* 'thin'.

tenure /**ten**-yer/ **noun 1** the conditions under which land or buildings are held or occupied.

2 the holding of a job or position. **3** guaranteed permanent employment, especially in a teaching post at a university.
- PHRASES **security of tenure** the right of a tenant of property to occupy it after the lease expires (unless a court should order otherwise).
- ORIGIN Old French, from Latin *tenere* 'to hold'.

tenured adjective (especially of a university lecturer) having a permanent post.

tepee /tee-pee/ (also **teepee** or **tipi**) noun a cone-shaped tent made of skins or cloth on a frame of poles, as used by American Indians.
- ORIGIN Sioux, 'dwelling'.

tepid adjective **1** (especially of a liquid) lukewarm. **2** unenthusiastic: *a tepid response*.
- DERIVATIVES **tepidity** noun **tepidly** adverb.
- ORIGIN Latin *tepidus*, from *tepere* 'be warm'.

tequila /ti-kee-luh/ noun a Mexican alcoholic spirit made from the agave plant.
- ORIGIN named after the town of *Tequila* in Mexico.

tequila sunrise noun a cocktail of tequila, orange juice, and grenadine.

ter- combining form three; having three: *tercentenary*.
- ORIGIN Latin *ter* 'thrice'.

tera- /te-ruh/ combining form **1** referring to a factor of one million million (10^{12}): *terawatt*. **2** Computing referring to a factor of 2^{40}: *terabyte*.
- ORIGIN from Greek *teras* 'monster'.

terabyte noun a unit of information stored in a computer equal to one million million (10^{12}) or (strictly) 2^{40} bytes.

teraflop noun a unit of computing speed equal to one million million floating-point operations per second.

teratogen /te-rat-uh-juhn, te-ruh-tuh-juhn/ noun a substance or factor which causes abnormalities to develop in an embryo.
- DERIVATIVES **teratogenic** adjective.
- ORIGIN from Greek *teras* 'monster'.

terbium /ter-bi-uhm/ noun a silvery-white metallic chemical element.
- ORIGIN from *Ytterby*, a Swedish quarry where it was first found.

tercentenary noun (pl. **tercentenaries**) a three-hundredth anniversary.

tergiversation /ter-ji-ver-say-sh'n/ noun the use of language that is evasive or ambiguous.
- DERIVATIVES **tergiversate** verb.
- ORIGIN from Latin *tergiversari* 'turn one's back'.

teriyaki /te-ri-yah-ki/ noun a Japanese dish of fish or meat marinated in soy sauce and grilled.
- ORIGIN Japanese.

term noun **1** a word or phrase used to describe a thing or to express an idea. **2** (**terms**) language used on a particular occasion: *a protest in the strongest possible terms*. **3** (**terms**) requirements or conditions laid down or agreed. **4** (**terms**) relations between people: *we're on good terms*. **5** each of the periods in the year during which teaching is given in a school or college or during which a law court holds sessions. **6** a period for which something lasts or is intended to last. **7** (also **full term**) the completion of a normal length of

pregnancy. **8** Mathematics each of the quantities in a ratio, series, or mathematical expression. **9** Logic a word or words that may be the subject or predicate of a proposition. •verb call by a particular word or phrase: *a period termed as the dawn of civilization*.
- PHRASES **come to terms with** become able to accept or deal with something. **in terms of** (or **in —— terms**) with regard to a particular aspect of something: *there are benefits to be gained in terms of cost*. **the —— term** a period that is a specified way into the future: *in the long term*. **on terms 1** in a state of friendship or equality. **2** (in sport) level in score. **terms of reference** Brit. the scope and limitations of an inquiry, discussion, etc.
- DERIVATIVES **termly** adjective & adverb.
- ORIGIN Latin *terminus* 'end, limit'.

termagant /ter-muh-guhnt/ noun a bad-tempered or overbearing woman.
- ORIGIN Italian *Trivagante* 'thrice-wandering', referring to a violent imaginary god or goddess often appearing in medieval morality plays.

terminable adjective **1** able to be terminated. **2** coming to an end after a certain time.

terminal adjective **1** relating to, forming, or situated at the end. **2** (of a disease) predicted to lead to a person's death. **3** informal extreme and usually beyond cure or alteration: *an industry in terminal decline*. •noun **1** the station at the end of a railway or other transport route. **2** a departure and arrival building for passengers at an airport. **3** a point of connection for closing an electric circuit. **4** a piece of equipment, usually consisting of a keyboard and a screen, which is connected to a central computer system. **5** a place where oil or gas is stored at the end of a pipeline or at a port.
- DERIVATIVES **terminally** adverb.
- ORIGIN from Latin *terminus* 'end, boundary'.

terminal velocity noun Physics the constant speed that a freely falling object reaches when the resistance of the medium through which it is falling prevents it from moving any faster.

terminate verb **1** bring something to an end. **2** end a pregnancy at an early stage by a medical procedure. **3** (of a train or bus service) end its journey. **4** (**terminate in**) (of a thing) have its end at a particular place or in a particular form: *the cord terminates in a five-pin plug*.
- DERIVATIVES **termination** noun **terminator** noun.

terminology noun (pl. **terminologies**) the set of terms used in a particular subject, profession, etc.
- DERIVATIVES **terminological** adjective.

terminus noun (pl. **termini** /ter-mi-ny/ or **terminuses**) chiefly Brit. a railway or bus terminal.
- ORIGIN Latin, 'end, limit, boundary'.

termite /ter-myt/ noun a small, soft-bodied insect which feeds on wood and lives in colonies in large nests of earth.
- ORIGIN Latin *termes* 'woodworm'.

tern /rhymes with fern/ noun a seabird resembling a gull, with long pointed wings and a forked tail.
- ORIGIN Scandinavian.

ternary /ter-nuh-ri/ adjective 1 composed of three parts. 2 Mathematics using three as a base.
– ORIGIN Latin *ternarius*, from *terni* 'three at once'.

terpene /ter-peen/ noun Chemistry any of a large group of unsaturated hydrocarbons found in the essential oils of conifers and other plants.
– ORIGIN from German *Terpentin* 'turpentine'.

terpsichorean /terp-si-kuh-ree-uhn/ adjective formal or humorous relating to dancing.
– ORIGIN from *Terpsichore*, the ancient Greek and Roman Muse of dance.

terrace noun 1 a level paved area next to a building; a patio. 2 Brit. a row of houses in the same style built in one block. 3 each of a series of flat areas on a slope, used for growing crops. 4 Brit. a flight of wide, shallow steps providing standing room for spectators in a stadium. •verb make sloping land into terraces.
– DERIVATIVES **terracing** noun.
– ORIGIN Old French, 'rubble, platform', from Latin *terra* 'earth'.

terraced adjective 1 Brit. (of a house) forming part of a terrace. 2 (of land) having been formed into terraces.

terracotta /te-ruh-kot-tuh/ noun 1 brownish-red earthenware that has not been glazed, used as a decorative building material and in modelling. 2 a strong brownish-red colour.
– ORIGIN from Italian *terra cotta* 'baked earth'.

terra firma /te-ruh fer-muh/ noun dry land; the ground.
– ORIGIN Latin, 'firm land'.

terraform verb (especially in science fiction) transform a planet to make it resemble the earth.
– ORIGIN from Latin *terra* 'earth'.

terrain /te-rayn/ noun a stretch of land, especially seen in terms of its physical features: *mountainous terrain*.
– ORIGIN French.

terra incognita /te-ruh in-kog-ni-tuh/ noun unknown territory.
– ORIGIN Latin, 'unknown land'.

terrapin noun a small freshwater turtle.
– ORIGIN Algonquian.

terrarium /ter-rair-i-uhm/ noun (pl. **terrariums** or **terraria** /ter-rair-i-uh/) 1 a glass-fronted case in which to keep small reptiles or amphibians. 2 a sealed transparent globe or similar container in which plants are grown.
– ORIGIN from Latin *terra* 'earth', on the pattern of *aquarium*.

terrazzo /te-rat-zoh/ noun flooring material consisting of chips of marble or granite set in concrete and polished smooth.
– ORIGIN Italian, 'terrace'.

terrestrial /tuh-ress-tri-uhl/ adjective 1 relating to the earth or dry land. 2 (of an animal or plant) living on or in the ground. 3 (of television broadcasting) using ground-based equipment rather than a satellite.
– DERIVATIVES **terrestrially** adverb.
– ORIGIN from Latin *terra* 'earth'.

terrible adjective 1 extremely bad, serious, or unpleasant. 2 troubled, guilty, or unwell: *I felt terrible about forgetting her name.* 3 causing terror.
– ORIGIN Latin *terribilis*, from *terrere* 'frighten'.

terribly adverb 1 extremely. 2 very badly.

terrier noun a small breed of dog originally used for hunting animals that live underground.
– ORIGIN from Old French *chien terrier* 'earth dog'.

terrific adjective 1 of great size, amount, or strength. 2 informal excellent.
– DERIVATIVES **terrifically** adverb.
– ORIGIN Latin *terrificus*, from *terrere* 'frighten'.

terrify verb (**terrifies, terrifying, terrified**) make someone feel terror.
– DERIVATIVES **terrifying** adjective.

terrine /tuh-reen/ noun 1 a mixture of chopped meat, fish, or vegetables pressed into a container and served cold. 2 an earthenware container for such a dish.
– ORIGIN French, 'large earthenware pot'.

territorial adjective 1 relating to the ownership of an area of land or sea: *a territorial dispute.* 2 (of an animal) having and defending a territory. •noun (**Territorial**) (in the UK) a member of the Territorial Army.
– DERIVATIVES **territoriality** noun **territorially** adverb.

Territorial Army noun (in the UK) a reserve force of people who volunteer to undergo military training in their spare time, able to be called on in an emergency.

territorial waters plural noun the part of the sea legally under the control of a state, especially those within a stated distance from its coast.

territory noun (pl. **territories**) 1 an area under the control of a ruler or state. 2 (**Territory**) an organized division of a country not having the full rights of a state. 3 an area defended by an animal against others of the same sex or species. 4 an area of land of a particular type: *a campaign in mountainous territory.* 5 an area in which a person has particular rights, responsibilities, experience, or knowledge: *the Oscars are familiar territory for this actor.*
– ORIGIN Latin *territorium*.

terroir /ter-wah/ noun the complete natural environment in which a particular wine is produced, including factors such as the soil and climate.
– ORIGIN French.

terror noun 1 extreme fear. 2 a cause of terror. 3 the use or threat of violence to cause extreme fear: *a campaign of terror.* 4 informal a person who is annoying or difficult to control.
– ORIGIN Latin, from *terrere* 'frighten'.

terrorism noun the unofficial or unauthorized use of violence and intimidation in the attempt to achieve political aims.
– DERIVATIVES **terrorist** noun & adjective.

terrorize (or **terrorise**) verb threaten and frighten someone over a period of time.

terry noun (pl. **terries**) fabric with raised loops of thread on both sides, used for towels.
– ORIGIN unknown.

terse adjective (**terser, tersest**) using few words; abrupt.
– DERIVATIVES **tersely** adverb **terseness** noun.

– ORIGIN Latin *tersus* 'wiped, polished'.

tertiary /ter-shuh-ri/ **adjective 1** third in order or level. **2** chiefly Brit. (of education) at a level beyond that provided by schools. **3** (of medical treatment) provided at a specialist institution. **4 (Tertiary)** Geology relating to the first period of the Cenozoic era, about 65 to 1.64 million years ago.
– ORIGIN Latin *tertiarius* 'of the third part'.

tertiary industry noun the service industry of a country.

terylene noun Brit. trademark a polyester fibre used to make clothing, bed linen, etc.

TESL abbreviation teaching of English as a second language.

tesla /tess-luh, tez-luh/ noun Physics the SI unit of magnetic flux density.
– ORIGIN named after the American electrical engineer Nikola *Tesla*.

TESOL /tee-sol/ abbreviation teaching of English to speakers of other languages.

tessellated /tess-uh-lay-tid/ adjective (of a floor) decorated with mosaics.
– DERIVATIVES **tessellation** noun.
– ORIGIN from Latin *tessellare* 'decorate with mosaics'.

tessera /tess-uh-ruh/ noun (pl. **tesserae** /tess-uh-ree/) a small tile or block of stone used in a mosaic.
– ORIGIN Greek.

tessitura /tess-i-tyoor-uh/ noun the range within which most musical notes of a vocal part fall.
– ORIGIN Italian, 'texture'.

test¹ noun **1** a procedure intended to establish the quality, performance, or reliability of something. **2** a short examination of a person's skill or knowledge. **3** a means of testing something. **4** a difficult situation that reveals the strength or quality of someone or something: *this is the first serious test of the peace agreement.* **5** an examination of part of the body or a body fluid for medical purposes. **6** Chemistry a procedure for identifying a substance or revealing whether it is present. **7 (Test)** a Test match. •verb **1** make someone or something undergo a test. **2** touch or taste something before taking further action. **3** severely try a person's endurance or patience.
– PHRASES **test the water** find out people's feelings or opinions before taking further action.
– DERIVATIVES **testable** adjective.
– ORIGIN Latin *testum* 'earthen pot'.

test² noun Zoology the shell or tough outer covering of some invertebrates and protozoans.
– ORIGIN Latin *testa* 'tile, jug, shell'.

testa /tess-tuh/ noun (pl. **testae** /tess-tee/) Botany the protective outer covering of a seed.
– ORIGIN Latin, 'tile, shell'.

testament noun **1** a person's will. **2** evidence of a fact, event, or quality: *the show's success is a testament to her talent.* **3 (Testament)** a division of the Bible (see OLD TESTAMENT, NEW TESTAMENT).
– ORIGIN Latin *testamentum* 'a will'.

testamentary adjective relating to a will.

testate /tess-tayt/ adjective having made a valid will before dying.
– ORIGIN Latin *testatus* 'testified, witnessed'.

testator /tess-tay-ter/ noun (fem. **testatrix** /tess-tay-triks/) a person who has made a will or given a legacy.
– ORIGIN Latin.

test bed noun a piece of equipment for testing new devices.

test card noun Brit. a still television picture transmitted outside normal programme hours to aid in judging the quality of the image.

test case noun a legal case whose result is used as an example when decisions are being made on similar cases in the future.

test-drive verb drive a motor vehicle to judge its performance and other qualities.

tester¹ noun **1** a person or device that tests something. **2** a sample of a product allowing customers to try it before buying.

tester² noun a canopy over a four-poster bed.
– ORIGIN Latin *testerium*.

testicle noun either of the two oval organs that produce sperm in male mammals, enclosed in the scrotum behind the penis.
– DERIVATIVES **testicular** adjective.
– ORIGIN Latin *testiculus*.

testify verb (**testifies**, **testifying**, **testified**) **1** give evidence as a witness in a law court. **2 (testify to)** be evidence or proof of: *luxurious villas testify to the wealth here.*
– ORIGIN Latin *testificari*.

testimonial /tess-ti-moh-ni-uhl/ noun **1** a formal statement of a person's character and qualifications. **2** a public tribute to someone. **3** (in sport) a game or event held in honour of a player, who receives part of the income generated.

testimony noun (pl. **testimonies**) **1** a formal statement, especially one given in a court of law. **2 (testimony to)** evidence or proof of something.
– ORIGIN Latin *testimonium*.

testis /tess-tiss/ noun (pl. **testes** /tess-teez/) an organ which produces sperm.
– ORIGIN Latin, 'witness'.

Test match noun an international cricket or rugby match played between teams representing two different countries.

testosterone /tess-toss-tuh-rohn/ noun a steroid hormone that stimulates the development of male secondary sexual characteristics.
– ORIGIN from TESTIS.

test pilot noun a pilot who flies new or modified aircraft to test their performance.

test tube noun a thin glass tube closed at one end, used to hold material for laboratory testing or experiments.

test-tube baby noun informal a baby conceived by in vitro fertilization.

testy adjective (**testier**, **testiest**) easily irritated; irritable.
– DERIVATIVES **testily** adverb **testiness** noun.
– ORIGIN first meaning 'headstrong': from Old French *teste* 'head'.

tetanus /tet-uh-nuhss/ noun a disease causing the muscles to stiffen and go into spasms, spread by bacteria.

– DERIVATIVES **tetanic** /ti-**tan**-ik/ adjective.
– ORIGIN Greek *tetanos* 'muscular spasm'.

tetchy adjective (**tetchier**, **tetchiest**) bad-tempered and irritable.
– DERIVATIVES **tetchily** adverb **tetchiness** noun.
– ORIGIN probably from Old French *teche* 'blotch, fault'.

tête-à-tête /tayt-ah-**tayt**/ noun (pl. same or **tête-à-têtes** pronunc. same) a private conversation between two people.
– ORIGIN French, 'head-to-head'.

tether verb tie an animal with a rope or chain so as to restrict its movement. •noun a rope or chain used to tether an animal.
– ORIGIN Old Norse.

tetra- (also **tetr-** before a vowel) combining form four; having four: *tetrahedron*.
– ORIGIN from Greek *tettares* 'four'.

tetrad /**tet**-rad/ noun technical a group or set of four.
– ORIGIN Greek *tetras*.

tetrahedron /tet-ruh-**hee**-druhn/ noun (pl. **tetrahedra** /tet-ruh-**hee**-druh/ or **tetrahedrons**) a solid having four plane triangular faces.
– DERIVATIVES **tetrahedral** adjective.

tetralogy /ti-**tral**-uh-ji/ noun (pl. **tetralogies**) a group of four related books, operas, plays, etc.

tetrameter /ti-**tram**-i-ter/ noun a line of verse made up of four metrical feet.

tetrapod /**tet**-ruh-pod/ noun an animal of a group which includes all vertebrates apart from fish.
– ORIGIN from Greek *tetrapous* 'four-footed'.

Teuton /**tyoo**-tuhn/ noun **1** a member of an ancient Germanic people who lived in Jutland. **2** often derogatory a German.
– ORIGIN from Latin *Teutones* (plural).

Teutonic /tyoo-**ton**-ik/ adjective **1** informal, often derogatory displaying qualities regarded as typical of Germans. **2** relating to the Teutons.

Texan noun a person from the US state of Texas. •adjective relating to Texas.

Tex-Mex adjective (especially of food or music) having a blend of Mexican and southern American features. •noun Tex-Mex music or food.

text noun **1** a book or other written or printed work. **2** the main body of a written work as distinct from appendices, illustrations, etc. **3** written or printed words or computer data. **4** a written work chosen as a subject of study. **5** a passage from the Bible, especially as the subject of a sermon. **6** a text message. •verb send a text message to someone.
– DERIVATIVES **texter** noun **texting** noun.
– ORIGIN Latin *textus* 'tissue, literary style'.

textbook noun a book used as a standard work for the study of a subject. •adjective done in exactly the recommended way: *a textbook example of damage control*.

textile noun a type of cloth or woven fabric. •adjective relating to fabric or weaving.
– ORIGIN Latin *textilis*.

text message noun an electronic message sent and received by mobile phone.
– DERIVATIVES **text messaging** noun.

textual adjective relating to a text or texts.
– DERIVATIVES **textually** adverb.

textuality noun the quality or use of language that is typical of written works as distinct from spoken usage.

texture noun **1** the feel, appearance, or consistency of a surface, substance, or fabric. **2** the quality created by the combination of elements in a work of music or literature: *a closely knit symphonic texture.* •verb give a rough or raised texture to a surface.
– DERIVATIVES **textural** adjective.
– ORIGIN Latin *textura* 'weaving'.

texturize (or **texturise**) verb give a particular texture to something.

TFT abbreviation thin-film transistor, used to make flat colour display screens.

TGV noun a French high-speed passenger train.
– ORIGIN abbreviation of French *train à grande vitesse*.

Th symbol the chemical element thorium.

Thai /ty/ noun (pl. same or **Thais**) **1** a person from Thailand. **2** the official language of Thailand.
– ORIGIN Thai, 'free'.

thalamus /**thal**-uh-muhss/ noun (pl. **thalami** /**thal**-uh-my/) each of two masses of grey matter in the front part of the brain, relaying sensory information to other parts of the brain.
– ORIGIN Greek *thalamos*.

thalassotherapy /thuh-la-soh-**the**-ruh-pi/ noun the use of seawater in cosmetic and health treatment.
– ORIGIN from Greek *thalassa* 'sea'.

thali /**tah**-li/ noun (pl. **thalis**) a set meal at an Indian restaurant consisting of a variety of dishes and accompaniments.
– ORIGIN Sanskrit.

thalidomide /thuh-**lid**-uh-myd/ noun a drug formerly used as a sedative, but found to cause malformation of the fetus when taken in early pregnancy.

thallium /**thal**-li-uhm/ noun a soft silvery-white metallic chemical element whose compounds are very poisonous.
– ORIGIN from Greek *thallos* 'green shoot'.

than conjunction & preposition **1** used to introduce the second part of a comparison. **2** used to introduce an exception or contrast. **3** used in expressions indicating one thing happening immediately after another.
– ORIGIN Old English.

> **USAGE:** For an explanation of whether to use **I** and **we** or **me** and **us** after **than**, see the note at **PERSONAL PRONOUN**.

thanatology /than-uh-**tol**-uh-ji/ noun the scientific study of death and practices associated with it.
– ORIGIN from Greek *thanatos* 'death'.

thane /thayn/ noun **1** (in Anglo-Saxon England) a nobleman granted land by the king or a higher-ranking nobleman. **2** (in Scotland) a nobleman who held land from a Scottish king.
– ORIGIN Old English, 'servant, soldier'.

thank verb **1** express gratitude to someone. **2** ironic blame or hold responsible: *you have only yourself to thank.*
– PHRASES **thank goodness** (or **God** or **heavens**) an expression of relief. **thank you** a polite expression of gratitude.

– ORIGIN Old English.

thankful adjective **1** pleased and relieved.
2 expressing gratitude.
– DERIVATIVES **thankfulness** noun.

thankfully adverb **1** in a thankful way.
2 luckily; fortunately.

> USAGE: The traditional sense of **thankfully** is
> 'in a thankful way' (*she accepted the offer
> thankfully*). The newer use, meaning 'luckily;
> fortunately' (*thankfully, we didn't have to
> wait*) is now by far the most common,
> although some people think that it is incorrect.

thankless adjective **1** (of a job or task)
unpleasant and unlikely to be appreciated by
others. **2** not showing or feeling gratitude.

thanks plural noun **1** an expression of gratitude.
2 thank you.
– PHRASES **no thanks to** despite the
unhelpfulness of. **thanks to** due to.
– ORIGIN Old English.

thanksgiving noun **1** the expression of
gratitude to God. **2** (**Thanksgiving**) (in North
America) an annual national holiday
commemorating a harvest festival celebrated
by the Pilgrim Fathers in 1621, held in the US
on the fourth Thursday in November and in
Canada usually on the second Monday in
October.

that pronoun & determiner **1** (pl. **those**) used to
refer to a person or thing seen or heard by the
speaker or already mentioned or known. **2** (pl.
those) referring to the more distant of two
things near to the speaker. **3** (pl. **those**) used in
singling out someone or something with a
particular feature. **4** (as pronoun) (pl. **that**) used
instead of which, who, when, etc. to introduce
a clause that defines or identifies something:
the woman that owns the place. •adverb **1** to
such a degree. **2** informal very: *he wasn't that far
away.* •conjunction **1** introducing a subordinate
clause (one that depends on a main clause):
she said that she'd be late. **2** literary expressing a
wish or regret.
– PHRASES **that is** (or **that is to say**) a set
expression introducing or following an
explanation. **that said** even so. **that's that**
there is nothing more to do or say about the
matter.
– ORIGIN Old English.

> USAGE: When is it right to use **that** and when
> should you use **which**? The general rule is that,
> when introducing clauses that define or
> identify something, it is acceptable to use **that**
> or **which**: *a book which aims to simplify
> scientific language* or *a book that aims to
> simplify scientific language.* You should use
> **which**, but never **that**, to introduce a clause
> giving additional information: *the book, which
> costs £15, has sold over a million copies* (not
> *the book, that costs £15, has sold over a million
> copies*).

thatch noun **1** a roof covering of straw, reeds, or
similar material. **2** informal a person's hair. •verb
cover a roof or building with thatch.
– DERIVATIVES **thatcher** noun.
– ORIGIN Old English, 'cover'.

Thatcherism noun the political and economic

policies that characterized the government of
the British Conservative politician Margaret
Thatcher, Prime Minister 1979–90.
– DERIVATIVES **Thatcherite** noun & adjective.

thaw verb **1** become or make liquid or soft after
being frozen. **2** (**it thaws, it is thawing, it
thawed**) the weather becomes warmer and
causes snow and ice to melt. **3** (of a part of the
body) become warm enough to stop feeling
numb. **4** make or become friendlier. •noun **1** a
period of warmer weather that thaws ice and
snow. **2** an improvement in relations or an
increase in friendliness.
– ORIGIN Old English.

the determiner **1** used to refer to one or more
people or things already mentioned or easily
understood; the definite article. **2** used to
refer to someone or something that is unique:
the sun. **3** used to refer to something in a
general rather than a specific way. **4** used to
explain which person or thing is being
referred to: *the house at the end of the street.*
5 enough of: *I don't have the money to buy a
house.*
– ORIGIN Old English.

theatre (US **theater**) noun **1** a building in which
plays and other dramatic performances are
given. **2** the writing and production of plays.
3 a play considered in terms of its dramatic
quality: *this is intense, moving theatre.* **4** (also
lecture theatre) a room for lectures with seats
in tiers. **5** Brit. an operating theatre. **6** the area
in which something happens: *a new theatre of
war has opened up.*
– ORIGIN Greek *theatron*.

theatrical adjective **1** relating to acting, actors,
or the theatre. **2** exaggerated and excessively
dramatic: *he looked over his shoulder with
theatrical caution.* •noun **1** (**theatricals**)
theatrical performances or behaviour. **2** a
professional actor or actress.
– DERIVATIVES **theatricality** noun **theatrically**
adverb.

theatrics plural noun theatrical performances
or behaviour; theatricals.

thee pronoun old use or dialect you (as the singular
object of a verb or preposition).
– ORIGIN Old English.

theft noun the action or crime of stealing.
– ORIGIN Old English.

their possessive determiner **1** belonging to or
associated with the people or things
previously mentioned or easily identified.
2 belonging to or associated with a person
whose sex is not specified (used in place of
either 'his' or 'his or her'). **3** (**Their**) used in
titles.
– ORIGIN Old Norse.

> USAGE: Do not confuse **their**, **there**, and
> **they're**. **Their** means 'belonging to them' (*I
> went round to their house*), while **there** means
> 'in, at, or to that place' (*it will take an hour to
> get there*), and **they're** is short for 'they are'
> (*they're going to be late*).
>   On the use of **their** in the singular to mean
> 'his or her', see the note at THEY.

theirs possessive pronoun used to refer to
something belonging to or associated with

t

two or more people or things previously mentioned.

> **USAGE:** There is no apostrophe: the spelling should be **theirs** not *their's*.

theism /thee-i-z'm/ noun belief in the existence of a god or gods, specifically of a creator who intervenes in the universe. Compare with **DEISM.**
– DERIVATIVES **theist** noun **theistic** adjective.
– ORIGIN from Greek *theos* 'god'.

them pronoun (third person pl.) **1** used as the object of a verb or preposition to refer to two or more people or things previously mentioned or easily identified. **2** referring to a person whose sex is not specified (used in place of either 'him' or 'him or her').
– ORIGIN Old Norse.

> **USAGE:** For an explanation of the use of **them** in the singular to mean 'his or her', see the note at **THEY.**

thematic adjective arranged according to subject or relating to a subject.
– DERIVATIVES **thematically** adverb.

theme noun **1** the subject of a talk, piece of writing, etc. **2** a prominent or frequently recurring melody or group of notes in a musical composition. **3** an idea that often recurs in a work of art or literature: *the theme of journeys is apparent throughout the book.* **4** (also **theme tune** or **music**) a piece of music played at the beginning and end of a film or programme. ●adjective (of a restaurant, pub, or leisure venue) designed in the style of a particular country, historical period, etc. ●verb (often as adj. **themed**) give a particular setting or style to: *an American themed restaurant.*
– ORIGIN Greek *thema* 'proposition'.

theme park noun a large amusement park based around a particular idea.

themself pronoun (third person sing.) informal used instead of 'himself' or 'herself' to refer to a person whose sex is not specified.

> **USAGE:** The standard reflexive pronoun (a word such as *myself* or *herself*) corresponding to **they** and **them** is **themselves**, as in *they can do it themselves.* The singular form **themself** has been used recently to correspond to the singular use of **they** when referring to a person whose sex is not specified (*helping someone to help themself*). However, **themself** is not good English, and you should use **themselves** instead.

themselves pronoun (third person pl.) **1** used as the object of a verb or preposition to refer to a group of people or things previously mentioned as the subject of the clause. **2** they or them personally. **3** used instead of 'himself' or 'herself' to refer to a person whose sex is not specified.

then adverb **1** at that time. **2** after that; next. **3** also; in addition. **4** in that case; therefore.
– PHRASES **but then** (**again**) on the other hand. **then and there** immediately.
– ORIGIN Old English.

thence (also **from thence**) adverb formal **1** from a place or source previously mentioned. **2** as a consequence.

> **USAGE:** **Thence** means 'from that place', as in *he travelled across France and thence to England.* Strictly speaking, the preposition **from**, as in *they proceeded from thence to Sunderland,* is unnecessary, but nevertheless **from thence** is usually accepted as good English.

thenceforth (also **thenceforward**) adverb old use or literary from that time, place, or point onward.

theocracy /thi-ok-ruh-si/ noun (pl. **theocracies**) a system of government in which priests rule in the name of God or a god.
– DERIVATIVES **theocratic** adjective.
– ORIGIN from Greek *theos* 'god'.

theodolite /thi-od-uh-lyt/ noun a surveying instrument with a rotating telescope for measuring horizontal and vertical angles.
– ORIGIN Latin *theodelitus.*

theologian /thi-uh-loh-juhn/ noun a person expert in or studying theology.

theology /thi-ol-uh-ji/ noun (pl. **theologies**) **1** the study of God and religious belief. **2** a system of religious beliefs and theory.
– DERIVATIVES **theological** adjective **theologically** adverb **theologist** noun.

theorem /theer-uhm/ noun **1** Physics & Mathematics a general proposition or rules that can be proved by reasoning. **2** Mathematics a rule expressed by symbols or formulae.
– ORIGIN Greek *theōrēma* 'speculation, proposition'.

theoretical (also **theoretic**) adjective **1** concerned with the theory of a subject rather than its practical application. **2** based on theory rather than experience or practice: *the theoretical possibility of a chain reaction.*
– DERIVATIVES **theoretically** adverb.

theoretician /theer-uh-**ti**-sh'hn/ noun a person who develops or studies the theory of a subject.

theorize (or **theorise**) verb form a theory or theories about something.
– DERIVATIVES **theorist** noun **theorization** noun.

theory noun (pl. **theories**) **1** a reasoned set of ideas that is intended to explain why something happens or exists. **2** an idea that explains or justifies something: *I have this theory that these guys were mean because they had silly names.* **3** a set of principles on which an activity is based: *a theory of education.*
– PHRASES **in theory** in a possible situation, but probably not in reality.
– ORIGIN Greek *theōria* 'contemplation, speculation'.

theosophy /thi-oss-uh-fi/ noun a philosophy which believes that a person may achieve knowledge of God through such things as intuition, meditation, and prayer.
– DERIVATIVES **theosophical** adjective **theosophist** noun.
– ORIGIN from Greek *theosophos* 'wise concerning God'.

therapeutic /the-ruh-**pyoo**-tik/ adjective **1** relating to the healing of disease. **2** having a good effect on the body or mind.
– DERIVATIVES **therapeutically** adverb **therapeutics** plural noun.

therapy noun (pl. **therapies**) **1** treatment intended to relieve or heal a physical disorder. **2** the treatment of mental or emotional problems by psychological means.
– DERIVATIVES **therapist** noun.
– ORIGIN Greek *therapeia* 'healing'.

Theravada /the-ruh-vah-duh/ noun the more conservative of the two major traditions of Buddhism (the other being Mahayana), practised mainly in Sri Lanka, Burma (Myanmar), Thailand, Cambodia, and Laos.
– ORIGIN Pali (an ancient language related to Sanskrit), 'doctrine of the elders'.

there adverb **1** in, at, or to that place or position. **2** on that issue. **3** used in attracting attention to someone or something. **4** (usu. **there is/are**) used to indicate the fact or existence of something. •exclamation **1** used to focus attention. **2** used to comfort someone.
– PHRASES **so there** informal used to express defiance. **there and then** immediately.
– ORIGIN Old English.

USAGE: For an explanation of the difference between **there**, **their**, and **they're**, see the note at **THEIR**.

thereabouts (also **thereabout**) adverb near that place, time, or figure.

thereafter adverb formal after that time.

thereat adverb old use or formal **1** at that place. **2** on account of or after that.

thereby adverb by that means; as a result of that.

therefore adverb for that reason; consequently.

therefrom adverb old use or formal from that or that place.

therein adverb formal in that place, document, or respect.

theremin /the-ruh-min/ noun an electronic musical instrument in which the tone is generated by two high-frequency oscillators and the pitch controlled by the movement of the performer's hand towards and away from the circuit.
– ORIGIN named after its Russian inventor Lev *Theremin*.

thereof adverb formal of the thing just mentioned; of that.

thereon adverb formal on or following from the thing just mentioned.

there's contraction **1** there is. **2** there has.

thereto adverb formal to that or that place.

thereunder adverb chiefly formal in accordance with the thing mentioned.

thereunto adverb old use or formal to that.

thereupon adverb formal immediately or shortly after that.

therewith adverb old use or formal **1** with or in the thing mentioned. **2** soon or immediately after that.

therm noun a unit of heat, especially as the former statutory unit of gas supplied in the UK equivalent to 1.055×10^8 joules.
– ORIGIN from Greek *thermē* 'heat'.

thermal adjective **1** relating to heat. **2** (of an item of clothing) made of a fabric that provides good insulation to keep the body warm. •noun **1** an upward current of warm air,

used by birds, gliders, and balloonists to gain height. **2** (**thermals**) thermal underwear.
– DERIVATIVES **thermally** adverb.

thermal imaging noun the technique of using the heat given off by an object to produce an image of it or locate it.

thermal spring noun a spring of naturally hot water.

thermic adjective relating to heat.

thermionic /ther-mi-on-ik/ adjective relating to the emission of electrons from substances heated to very high temperatures.

thermionic valve noun Electronics a vacuum tube giving a flow of thermionic electrons in one direction, used in rectifying a current and in radio reception.

thermistor /ther-miss-ter/ noun an electrical resistor whose resistance is greatly reduced by heating, used for measurement and control.
– ORIGIN from *thermal resistor*.

thermocouple noun a device for measuring or sensing a temperature difference, consisting of two wires of different metals connected at two points, between which a voltage is developed in proportion to any temperature difference.

thermodynamics plural noun (treated as sing.) the branch of science concerned with the relations between heat and other forms of energy involved in physical and chemical processes.
– DERIVATIVES **thermodynamic** adjective **thermodynamically** adverb.

thermoelectric adjective producing electricity by a difference of temperatures.

thermogenesis /ther-moh-jen-i-sis/ noun technical the production of bodily heat.
– DERIVATIVES **thermogenic** adjective.

thermography /ther-mog-ruh-fi/ noun a printing technique in which a resinous powder is dusted on to wet ink and fused by heating to produce a raised impression.
– DERIVATIVES **thermographic** adjective.

thermometer noun an instrument for measuring temperature, typically consisting of a glass tube marked with a temperature scale and containing mercury or alcohol which expands when heated.

thermonuclear adjective relating to or using nuclear fusion reactions that occur at very high temperatures.

thermoplastic adjective (of a substance) becoming plastic when heated.

thermoregulation noun technical the regulation of bodily temperature.

Thermos noun trademark a vacuum flask.
– ORIGIN from Greek, 'hot'.

thermosetting adjective (of a substance) setting permanently when heated.

thermosphere noun the upper region of the atmosphere above the mesosphere.

thermostat /ther-muh-stat/ noun a device that automatically regulates temperature or activates a device at a set temperature.
– DERIVATIVES **thermostatic** adjective **thermostatically** adverb.

thesaurus /thi-saw-ruhss/ noun (pl. **thesauri** /thi-saw-ry/ or **thesauruses**) a book containing

lists of words which have the same, similar, or a related meaning.
– ORIGIN Greek *thēsauros* 'storehouse, treasure'.

these plural of **THIS**.

thesis /thee-siss/ noun (pl. **theses** /thee-seez/) **1** a statement or theory put forward to be supported or proved. **2** a long essay involving personal research, written as part of a university degree.
– ORIGIN Greek, 'placing, a proposition'.

thespian /thess-pi-uhn/ adjective relating to drama and the theatre. • noun an actor or actress.
– ORIGIN from the ancient Greek dramatic poet *Thespis*).

thew /thyoo/ (also **thews**) noun literary muscle or muscular strength.
– ORIGIN Old English, 'usage, custom', later 'good quality'.

they pronoun (third person pl.) **1** used to refer to two or more people or things previously mentioned or easily identified. **2** people in general. **3** informal people in authority regarded as a whole. **4** used to refer to a person whose sex is not specified (in place of either 'he' or 'he or she').
– ORIGIN Old Norse.

> USAGE: Many people now think that the traditional use of **he** to refer to a person of either sex is old-fashioned and sexist; the alternative, **he or she**, is rather clumsy. For this reason, **they** (with its counterparts **them** or **their**) have become acceptable instead, as in *anyone can join if they are a resident* and *each to their own*.

they'd contraction **1** they had. **2** they would.
they'll contraction **1** they shall. **2** they will.
they're contraction they are.

> USAGE: For an explanation of the difference between **they're**, **their**, and **there**, see the note at **THEIR**.

they've contraction they have.

thiamine /thy-uh-meen/ (also **thiamin**) /thy-uh-min/ noun vitamin B₁, found in unrefined cereals, beans, and liver, a deficiency of which causes beriberi.
– ORIGIN from Greek *theion* 'sulphur'.

thick adjective **1** with opposite sides or surfaces relatively far apart. **2** (of a garment or fabric) made of heavy material. **3** made up of a large number of things or people close together: *thick forest*. **4** (**thick with**) densely filled or covered with something. **5** (of the air or atmosphere) heavy, or difficult to see through. **6** (of a liquid or a semi-liquid substance) relatively firm in consistency; not flowing freely. **7** informal of low intelligence; stupid. **8** (of a voice) hoarse or husky. **9** (of an accent) very marked and difficult to understand. **10** informal having a very close, friendly relationship. • noun (**the thick**) the middle or the busiest part: *in the thick of battle*.
– PHRASES **a bit thick** Brit. informal unfair or unreasonable. **thick and fast** rapidly and in great numbers. (**as**) **thick as thieves** informal very close or friendly. **through thick and thin** under all circumstances, no matter how

difficult.
– DERIVATIVES **thickly** adverb.
– ORIGIN Old English.

thicken verb make or become thick or thicker.
– PHRASES **the plot thickens** the situation is becoming more complicated and puzzling.
– DERIVATIVES **thickener** noun.

thickening noun **1** a thicker area or part. **2** a substance added to a liquid to make it thicker.

thicket noun a dense group of bushes or trees.
– ORIGIN Old English.

thickheaded noun informal dull and stupid.

thickness noun **1** the distance through an object, as distinct from width or height. **2** the state or quality of being thick. **3** a layer of material. **4** a thicker part of something: *beams set into the thickness of the wall*.

thickset adjective heavily or solidly built; stocky.

thief noun (pl. **thieves**) a person who steals another person's property.
– ORIGIN Old English.

thieve verb be a thief; steal things.
– DERIVATIVES **thievery** noun **thievish** adjective.

thigh noun the part of the leg between the hip and the knee.
– ORIGIN Old English.

thigh bone noun the femur.

thimble noun a small metal or plastic cap, worn to protect the finger and push the needle in sewing.
– ORIGIN Old English.

thimbleful noun a small quantity of something.

thin adjective (**thinner, thinnest**) **1** having opposite surfaces or sides close together. **2** (of a garment or fabric) made of light material. **3** having little flesh or fat on the body. **4** having few parts or members in relation to the area covered or filled: *a thin crowd*. **5** (especially of the air) not dense or heavy. **6** containing much liquid and not much solid substance. **7** (of a sound) faint and high-pitched. **8** lacking substance; weak and inadequate: *the evidence is rather thin*. • verb (**thins, thinning, thinned**) **1** make or become less thick. **2** (often **thin something out**) remove some plants from a row or area to allow the others more room to grow.
– PHRASES **into thin air** so as to become invisible or non-existent.
– DERIVATIVES **thinly** adverb **thinness** noun.
– ORIGIN Old English.

thine old use possessive pronoun yours. • possessive determiner (before a vowel) your.
– ORIGIN Old English.

thing noun **1** an unspecified object, action, creature, etc. **2** an object as distinct from a living creature. **3** (**one's things**) a person's belongings or clothing. **4** (**things**) unspecified circumstances or matters: *how are things?* **5** (**the thing**) informal what is needed, acceptable, or fashionable. **6** (**one's thing**) informal one's special interest.
– ORIGIN Old English (also in the senses 'meeting' and 'matter, concern').

thingamabob /thing-uh-muh-bob/ (also **thingamajig** /thing-uh-muh-jig/) noun another term for **THINGUMMY**.

thingummy /thing-uh-mi/ noun (pl. **thingummies**) informal a person or thing whose name one has forgotten, does not know, or does not wish to mention.

thingy noun (pl. **thingies**) another term for THINGUMMY.

think verb (past and past part. **thought**) **1** have a particular opinion, belief, or idea about someone or something. **2** use the mind to form connected ideas about someone or something. **3** (**think of/about**) take someone or something into account or consideration. **4** (**think of/about**) consider the possibility or advantages of: *I was thinking of going home.* **5** (**think of**) have a particular opinion of: *she thought of him as a friend.* **6** (**think of**) call something to mind. •noun an act of thinking.
– PHRASES **think better of** decide not to do something after reconsideration. **think nothing of** consider an activity others regard as odd, wrong, or difficult as easy or normal. **think something over** consider something carefully. **think something through** consider every aspect of something before acting. **think twice** consider a course of action carefully before going ahead with it. **think something up** informal invent something.
– DERIVATIVES **thinkable** adjective **thinker** noun.
– ORIGIN Old English.

thinking noun a person's ideas or opinions. •adjective using thought or rational judgement; intelligent.
– PHRASES **put on one's thinking cap** informal think carefully about a problem.

think tank noun a group of experts providing advice and ideas on specific political or economic problems.

thinner (also **thinners**) noun a solvent used to thin paint or other solutions.

thinnings plural noun seedlings, trees, or fruit which have been thinned out to improve the growth of those remaining.

third ordinal number **1** that is number three in a sequence; 3rd. **2** (**a third/one third**) each of three equal parts into which something is divided. **3** a musical interval spanning three consecutive notes in a scale. **4** Brit. a place in the third grade in the exams for a university degree.
– DERIVATIVES **thirdly** adverb.
– ORIGIN Old English.

third age noun Brit. the period in life of active retirement, following middle age.

third class noun **1** a set of people or things grouped together as the third best. **2** Brit. the third-highest division in the results of the exams for a university degree. **3** chiefly historical the cheapest and least comfortable accommodation in a train or ship. •adjective & adverb relating to the third class.

third-degree adjective **1** (of burns) being of the most severe kind, affecting tissue below the skin. **2** Law, N. Amer. (of a crime, especially murder) in the least serious category. •noun (**the third degree**) long and harsh questioning to obtain information or a confession.

third-generation adjective (of a broadband digital telephone technology) that supports Internet connection and multimedia services.

third man noun Cricket a fielding position near the boundary behind the slips.

third party noun a person or group besides the two main ones involved in a situation or dispute. •adjective Brit. (of insurance) covering damage or injury suffered by a person other than the person who is insured.

third person noun **1** a third party. **2** see PERSON (sense 3).

third-rate adjective of very poor quality; inferior.

third reading noun a third presentation of a bill to a law-making assembly, in the UK to debate committee reports and in the US to consider it for the last time.

Third Reich /rykh, ryk/ noun the Nazi regime in Germany, 1933–45.
– ORIGIN German *Reich* 'empire'.

third way noun a political agenda which is moderate and based on general agreement rather than left- or right-wing.

Third World noun the developing countries of Asia, Africa, and Latin America.
– ORIGIN first used to distinguish the developing countries from the capitalist and Communist blocs.

thirst noun **1** a feeling of needing or wanting to drink. **2** the state of not having enough water to stay alive. **3** (**thirst for**) a strong desire for something. •verb **1** (**thirst for/after**) have a strong desire for: *an opponent thirsting for revenge.* **2** old use feel a need to drink.
– ORIGIN Old English.

thirsty adjective (**thirstier**, **thirstiest**) **1** feeling or causing a need to drink: *modelling is thirsty work.* **2** (**thirsty for**) having or showing a strong desire for something. **3** (of an engine or plant) consuming a lot of fuel or water.
– DERIVATIVES **thirstily** adverb **thirstiness** noun.

thirteen cardinal number one more than twelve; 13. (Roman numeral: **xiii** or **XIII**.)
– DERIVATIVES **thirteenth** ordinal number.
– ORIGIN Old English.

thirty cardinal number (pl. **thirties**) ten less than forty; 30. (Roman numeral: **xxx** or **XXX**.)
– DERIVATIVES **thirtieth** ordinal number.
– ORIGIN Old English.

this pronoun & determiner (pl. **these**) **1** used to identify a specific person or thing close at hand, just mentioned, or being indicated or experienced. **2** referring to the nearer of two things close to the speaker. **3** (as determiner) used with periods of time related to the present. •adverb to the degree or extent indicated: *they can't handle a job this big.*
– ORIGIN Old English.

thistle noun a plant with a prickly stem and leaves and rounded heads of purple flowers.
– ORIGIN Old English.

thistledown noun the light fluffy down of thistle seeds, which enables them to be blown about in the wind.

thither adverb old use or literary to or towards that place.
– ORIGIN Old English.

tho' (also **tho**) conjunction & adverb informal spelling of THOUGH.

thole[1] /thohl/ (also **thole pin**) noun a pin fitted to the gunwale of a rowing boat, on which an oar turns.

t

– ORIGIN Old English.

thole[2] /thohl/ **verb** Scottish or old use endure something without complaining.
– ORIGIN Old English.

thong noun 1 a narrow strip of leather or other material, used as a fastening or as the lash of a whip. **2** a pair of knickers or skimpy bathing garment like a G-string. **3** N. Amer. & Austral. a light sandal or flip-flop.
– ORIGIN Old English.

thoracic /thuh-rass-ik/ **adjective** relating to the thorax.

thorax /thor-aks/ **noun** (pl. **thoraces** /thor-uh-seez/ or **thoraxes**) **1** the part of the body between the neck and the abdomen. **2** the middle section of the body of an insect, bearing the legs and wings.
– ORIGIN Greek.

thorium /thor-i-uhm/ **noun** a white radioactive metallic chemical element.
– ORIGIN named after *Thor*, the Scandinavian god of thunder.

thorn noun 1 a stiff, sharp-pointed woody projection on the stem or other part of a plant. **2** a thorny bush, shrub, or tree.
– PHRASES **a thorn in someone's side** (or **flesh**) a source of continual annoyance or trouble.
– ORIGIN Old English.

thorny adjective (**thornier**, **thorniest**) **1** having many thorns or thorn bushes. **2** causing difficulty or trouble: *the thorny issue of censorship.*

thorough adjective 1 complete with regard to every detail. **2** done with or showing great care and completeness. **3** absolute; utter: *he is a thorough nuisance.*
– DERIVATIVES **thoroughly** adverb **thoroughness** noun.
– ORIGIN Old English, 'through'.

thoroughbred adjective 1 (especially of a horse) of pure breed. **2** informal of outstanding quality. •**noun** a thoroughbred animal.

thoroughfare noun a road or path forming a route between two places.

thoroughgoing adjective 1 involving or dealing with every detail or aspect. **2** complete; absolute.

those plural of **THAT**.

thou[1] /thow/ **pronoun** old use or dialect you (as the singular subject of a verb).
– ORIGIN Old English.

thou[2] /thow/ **noun** (pl. same or **thous**) **1** informal a thousand. **2** one thousandth of an inch.

though conjunction 1 despite the fact that; although. **2** however; but. •**adverb** however: *he was able to write, though.*
– ORIGIN Old English.

thought[1] **noun 1** an idea or opinion produced by thinking, or that suddenly comes into the mind. **2** the process of thinking. **3** (one's **thoughts**) one's mind or attention. **4** careful consideration: *I haven't given much thought to sexism.* **5** (**thought of**) an intention, hope, or idea of: *they had no thought of surrender.* **6** the formation of opinions, especially as a system of ideas, or the opinions so formed: *traditions of Western thought.*
– ORIGIN Old English.

thought[2] past and past participle of **THINK**.

thoughtful adjective 1 thinking deeply. **2** showing careful consideration. **3** considerate towards other people.
– DERIVATIVES **thoughtfully** adverb **thoughtfulness** noun.

thoughtless adjective 1 not considerate towards other people. **2** without considering the consequences: *to think a few minutes of thoughtless pleasure could end in this.*
– DERIVATIVES **thoughtlessly** adverb **thoughtlessness** noun.

thought police noun (treated as pl.) a group of people who aim to suppress ideas that depart from the way of thinking that they believe to be correct.

thousand cardinal number 1 (a/one thousand) the number equivalent to the product of a hundred and ten; 1,000. (Roman numeral: **m** or **M**.) **2** (**thousands**) informal an unspecified large number.
– DERIVATIVES **thousandfold** adjective & adverb **thousandth** ordinal number.
– ORIGIN Old English.

Thousand Island dressing noun a dressing for salad or seafood consisting of mayonnaise with ketchup and chopped pickles.
– ORIGIN named after a large group of islands in the St Lawrence River between the US and Canada.

thrall /thrawl/ **noun** the state of being in another's power: *she was in thrall to her husband.*
– DERIVATIVES **thraldom** (also **thralldom**) noun.
– ORIGIN Old Norse, 'slave'.

thrash verb 1 beat someone or something repeatedly and violently with a stick or whip. **2** move in a violent or uncontrolled way: *he lay thrashing around in pain.* **3** informal defeat someone heavily. **4** (**thrash something out**) discuss an issue frankly and thoroughly so as to reach a decision. •**noun 1** Brit. informal a loud or lively party. **2** a violent or noisy movement. **3** (also **thrash metal**) a style of fast, loud, harsh-sounding rock music.
– DERIVATIVES **thrasher** noun.
– ORIGIN Old English.

thread noun 1 a long, thin strand of cotton, nylon, or other fibres used in sewing or weaving. **2** a long, thin line or piece of something. **3** (also **screw thread**) a spiral ridge on the outside of a screw, bolt, etc. or on the inside of a cylindrical hole, to allow two parts to be screwed together. **4** a theme running through a situation or piece of writing. **5** (**threads**) informal, chiefly N. Amer. clothes. •**verb 1** pass a thread through the eye of a needle. **2** move or weave in and out of obstacles: *I threaded my way through the tables.* **3** (as adj. **threaded**) (of a hole, screw, etc.) having a screw thread.
– DERIVATIVES **threader** noun **thready** adjective.
– ORIGIN Old English.

threadbare adjective 1 (of cloth, clothing, etc.) old, thin, and shabby. **2** lacking originality or freshness: *threadbare clichés.*

threadworm noun a very thin worm that lives as a parasite in the intestines of humans and animals.

threat noun 1 a stated intention to harm someone, especially if they do not do what one

wants. **2** a likely cause of damage or danger. **3** the possibility of trouble or danger: *their culture is under threat from logging and dams.*
– ORIGIN Old English, 'oppression'.

threaten verb **1** state that one intends to harm someone or cause trouble if one does not get what one wants. **2** put at risk: *a broken finger threatened his career.* **3** (of a situation or the weather) seem likely to produce an unwelcome result.
– DERIVATIVES **threatening** adjective.

three cardinal number one more than two; 3. (Roman numeral: **iii** or **III**.)
– DERIVATIVES **threefold** adjective & adverb.
– ORIGIN Old English.

three-dimensional adjective **1** having or appearing to have length, breadth, and depth. **2** lifelike or real.

3G adjective (of telephone technology) third-generation.

three-legged race noun a race run by pairs of people, one member of each pair having their left leg tied to the right leg of the other.

three-line whip noun (in the UK) a written notice, underlined three times to stress its urgency, requiring members of a political party to attend a vote in parliament.

threepence /thrup-uhnss/ noun Brit. the sum of three pence before decimalization (1971).

threepenny bit /thru-puh-ni/ noun Brit. historical a coin worth three old pence (1¼ p).

three-piece adjective **1** (of a set of furniture) consisting of a sofa and two armchairs. **2** (of a set of clothes) consisting of trousers or a skirt with a waistcoat and jacket.

three-point turn noun a method of turning a vehicle round in a narrow space by moving forwards, backwards, and forwards again in a sequence of arcs.

three-quarter noun Rugby each of four players in a team positioned across the field behind the halfbacks.

three-ring circus noun informal a confused or disorganized situation.

threescore cardinal number literary sixty.

threesome noun a group of three people.

threnody /thren-uh-di/ noun (pl. **threnodies**) a song, piece of music, or poem expressing grief or regret.
– ORIGIN Greek *thrēnōidia.*

thresh verb **1** separate grains of corn from the rest of the plant. **2** move violently; thrash.
– DERIVATIVES **thresher** noun.
– ORIGIN Old English.

threshold /thresh-ohld, thresh-hohld/ noun **1** a strip of wood or stone forming the bottom of a doorway. **2** a level or point at which something would begin or come into effect: *he was on the threshold of a dazzling career.*
– ORIGIN Old English.

threw past of **THROW**.

thrice /thryss/ adverb old use or literary **1** three times. **2** extremely; very: *I was thrice blessed.*
– ORIGIN Old English.

thrift noun **1** carefulness and economy in the use of money and other resources. **2** a plant which forms low-growing tufts of slender leaves with rounded pink flower heads, found on sea cliffs and mountains.
– ORIGIN from Old Norse, 'grasp'.

thriftless adjective spending money in an extravagant and wasteful way.

thrift shop (also **thrift store**) noun N. Amer. a shop selling second-hand clothes and other household goods.

thrifty adjective (**thriftier, thriftiest**) careful with money; economical.
– DERIVATIVES **thriftily** adverb.

thrill noun **1** a sudden feeling of excitement and pleasure. **2** an exciting or pleasurable experience. **3** a wave of emotion or sensation: *a thrill of excitement ran through her.* •verb **1** give someone a sudden feeling of excitement and pleasure. **2** (**thrill to**) experience something exciting.
– DERIVATIVES **thrilling** adjective.
– ORIGIN from dialect *thirl* 'pierce, bore'.

thriller noun a novel, play, or film with an exciting plot that involves crime or spying.

thrips /thrips/ (also **thrip**) noun (pl. same) a minute black insect which sucks plant sap, noted for swarming on warm still summer days.
– ORIGIN Greek, 'woodworm'.

thrive verb (past **thrived** or **throve**; past part. **thrived** or **thriven**) **1** grow or develop well or vigorously. **2** be successful; flourish: *she has managed to thrive in a fickle sport.*
– ORIGIN Old Norse, 'grasp'.

thro' preposition, adverb, & adjective literary or informal spelling of **THROUGH**.

throat noun **1** the passage which leads from the back of the mouth, through which food passes to the oesophagus and air passes to the lungs. **2** the front part of the neck.
– PHRASES **be at each other's throats** quarrel or fight persistently. **force something down someone's throat** force something on a person's attention. **stick in one's throat** be unwelcome or difficult to accept.
– ORIGIN Old English.

throaty adjective (**throatier, throatiest**) (of a voice or other sound) deep and husky.
– DERIVATIVES **throatily** adverb **throatiness** noun.

throb verb (**throbs, throbbing, throbbed**) **1** beat or sound with a strong, regular rhythm. **2** feel pain in a series of regular beats. •noun a strong, regular beat or sound.
– ORIGIN probably imitating the sound.

throes /throhz/ plural noun intense or violent pain and struggle.
– PHRASES **in the throes of** in the middle of experiencing or doing something difficult.
– ORIGIN perhaps from an Old English word meaning 'calamity'.

thrombosis /throm-boh-siss/ noun (pl. **thromboses** /throm-boh-seez/) the formation of a blood clot in a blood vessel or the heart.
– DERIVATIVES **thrombotic** adjective.
– ORIGIN Greek, 'curdling'.

throne noun **1** a ceremonial chair for a sovereign or bishop. **2** (**the throne**) the power or rank of a sovereign.
– ORIGIN Greek *thronos* 'elevated seat'.

throng noun a large, densely packed crowd. •verb gather somewhere in large numbers.
– ORIGIN Old English.

t

throstle /thro-s'l/ noun Brit. old-fashioned term for SONG THRUSH.
– ORIGIN Old English.

throttle noun a device controlling the flow of fuel or power to an engine. •verb 1 attack or kill someone by choking or strangling them. 2 control an engine or vehicle with a throttle.
– ORIGIN perhaps from THROAT.

through preposition & adverb 1 moving in one side and out of the other side of an opening or location. 2 so as to make a hole or passage in. 3 (preposition) expressing the location of something beyond an opening or an obstacle. 4 continuing in time towards: *she struggled through until pay day.* 5 from beginning to end of an experience or activity. 6 so as to inspect all or part of: *he read the letter through carefully.* 7 by means of. 8 (adverb) so as to be connected by telephone. 9 expressing the extent of turning from one direction to another. •adjective 1 (of public transport or a ticket) continuing or valid to the final destination. 2 (of traffic, roads, etc.) passing straight through a place. 3 having successfully passed to the next stage of a competition. 4 informal having finished an activity, relationship, etc.
– PHRASES **through and through** thoroughly or completely.
– ORIGIN Old English.

throughout preposition & adverb all the way through.

throughput noun the amount of material or items passing through a system or process.

throve past of THRIVE.

throw verb (past **threw**; past part. **thrown**) 1 send something from one's hand through the air by a rapid movement of the arm and hand. 2 move or place quickly, hurriedly, or forcefully: *the door was thrown open.* 3 direct, or cast light, an expression, etc. in a particular direction. 4 send suddenly into a particular state: *the country was thrown into chaos.* 5 disconcert or confuse someone. 6 have a fit or tantrum. 7 hold a party. 8 make a clay pot, dish, etc. on a potter's wheel. 9 (of a horse) cause its rider to fall off. 10 project one's voice so that it appears to come from somewhere else. 11 informal lose a race or contest on purpose. •noun 1 an act of throwing. 2 a light cover for furniture. 3 (a throw) informal a single turn, round, or item: *on-the-spot portraits at £25 a throw.*
– PHRASES **throw something away** 1 get rid of something useless or unwanted. 2 fail to make use of an opportunity or advantage. **throw one's hand in** withdraw; give up. **throw something in** 1 include something extra with something that is being sold or offered. 2 interrupt a conversation with a casual remark. **throw in the towel** 1 (in boxing) throw a towel into the ring as a sign of defeat. 2 admit defeat. **throw oneself into** start to do something in an enthusiastic way. **throw something open** make something generally accessible. **throw someone out** force someone to leave. **throw somthing out** 1 get rid of something useless or unwanted. 2 (of a court, law-making body, etc.) dismiss or reject something. **throw someone over** abandon or reject a lover. **throw up** informal vomit.
– DERIVATIVES **thrower** noun.
– ORIGIN Old English, 'to twist, turn'.

throwaway adjective 1 intended to be thrown away after being used once or a few times. 2 (of a remark) said in a casual way.

throwback noun a person or thing that resembles someone or something that existed in the past.

throw-in noun Football & Rugby the act of throwing the ball from the sideline to restart the game after the ball has gone out of play.

thru preposition, adverb, & adjective informal spelling of THROUGH.

thrum verb (**thrums, thrumming, thrummed**) 1 make a continuous rhythmic humming sound. 2 strum the strings of a musical instrument in a rhythmic way. •noun a continuous rhythmic humming sound.
– ORIGIN imitating the sound.

thrush[1] noun a small or medium-sized songbird with a brown back and spotted breast.
– ORIGIN Old English.

thrush[2] noun infection of the mouth and throat or the genitals by a yeast-like fungus.
– ORIGIN uncertain.

thrust verb (past and past part. **thrust**) 1 push suddenly or forcibly: *she thrust her hands into her pockets.* 2 make one's way forcibly. 3 (**thrust something on**) force someone to accept or deal with something. 4 extend or project: *the jetty thrust out into the water.* •noun 1 a sudden or violent lunge or attack. 2 the main theme of a course of action or argument: *the thrust of the book is to guard young men from folly.* 3 the force produced by an engine to propel a jet or rocket.
– DERIVATIVES **thruster** noun.
– ORIGIN Old Norse.

thrusting adjective ambitious in an aggressive way.

thud noun a dull, heavy sound. •verb (**thuds, thudding, thudded**) move, fall, or hit something with a thud.
– ORIGIN probably from Old English, 'to thrust, push'.

thug noun 1 a violent and aggressive man. 2 (**Thug**) historical a member of an organization of robbers and assassins in India.
– DERIVATIVES **thuggery** noun **thuggish** adjective.
– ORIGIN Hindi, 'swindler, thief'.

thulium /thyoo-li-uhm/ noun a soft silvery-white metallic chemical element.
– ORIGIN Latin, from *Thule*, a country said in ancient times to be the northernmost part of the world.

thumb noun the short, thick first digit of the hand, set lower and apart from the other four. •verb 1 press, touch, or indicate something with the thumb. 2 turn over pages with the thumb. 3 (as adj. **thumbed**) (of a book's pages) worn or dirty by repeated handling. 4 request a free ride in a passing vehicle by signalling with the thumb.
– PHRASES **thumb one's nose at** informal show contempt for. **thumbs up** (or **down**) informal an indication of satisfaction or approval (or of rejection or failure). [with reference to the signal of approval or disapproval used by spectators at a Roman amphitheatre

(although the Romans used the symbols in reverse).] **under someone's thumb** completely under someone's influence.
– ORIGIN Old English.

thumb index noun a set of lettered notches cut down the side of a book to make it easier to find the required section.

thumbnail noun the nail of the thumb. •adjective brief or concise: *a thumbnail sketch*.

thumbprint noun 1 a mark made by the inner part of the top joint of the thumb. 2 an identifying characteristic.

thumbscrew noun an instrument of torture that crushes the thumbs.

thumbtack noun N. Amer. a drawing pin.

thump verb 1 hit someone or something heavily with the fist or a blunt object. 2 put down or move forcefully or noisily: *he thumped the gun down on the counter.* 3 (of a person's heart or pulse) beat strongly. 4 informal defeat someone heavily. •noun a heavy, dull blow or noise.
– DERIVATIVES **thumper** noun.
– ORIGIN imitating the sound.

thumping adjective informal impressively large: *a thumping 64 per cent majority.*

thunder noun 1 a loud rumbling or crashing noise heard after a lightning flash due to the expansion of rapidly heated air. 2 a loud deep resounding noise. •verb 1 (it thunders, it is thundering, it thundered) thunder sounds. 2 make or move with a loud deep noise. 3 speak loudly and angrily.
– DERIVATIVES **thundery** adjective.
– ORIGIN Old English.

thunderbolt noun a flash of lightning with a crash of thunder at the same time.

thunderclap noun a crash of thunder.

thundercloud noun a cumulus cloud with a towering or spreading top, charged with electricity and producing thunder and lightning.

thunderhead noun a rounded, projecting head of a cumulus cloud, which is a sign of a thunderstorm.

thundering adjective informal very great or impressive: *he's a thundering bore.*

thunderous adjective 1 relating to or resembling thunder. 2 (of a person's expression or mood) very angry or menacing.
– DERIVATIVES **thunderously** adverb.

thunderstorm noun a storm with thunder and lightning.

thunderstruck adjective very surprised or shocked.

thurible /thyoor-ib-uhl/ noun a container in which incense is burnt; a censer.
– ORIGIN Latin *thuribulum*.

Thursday noun the day of the week before Friday and following Wednesday.
– ORIGIN Old English, 'day of thunder' (named after *Thor*, the Germanic god of thunder).

thus adverb literary or formal 1 as a result of this; therefore. 2 in this way. 3 to this point; so.
– ORIGIN Old English.

thwack verb hit someone or something with a sharp blow. •noun a sharp blow.
– ORIGIN imitating the sound.

thwart /thwort/ verb 1 prevent someone from accomplishing something. 2 prevent something from succeeding. •noun a crosspiece forming a seat for a rower in a boat.
– ORIGIN from Old Norse, 'transverse'.

thy (also **thine** before a vowel) possessive determiner old use or dialect belonging to you; your.
– ORIGIN Old English.

thyme /rhymes with time/ noun a low-growing plant of the mint family, used as a herb in cooking.
– ORIGIN Greek *thumon*.

thymol /thy-mol/ noun a white crystalline compound present in oil of thyme and used as a flavouring and preservative.
– ORIGIN from Greek *thumon* 'thyme'.

thymus /thy-muhss/ noun (pl. **thymi** /thy-my/) a gland in the neck which produces white blood cells for the immune system.
– DERIVATIVES **thymic** adjective.
– ORIGIN Greek *thumos*.

thyroid /thy-royd/ (also **thyroid gland**) noun a large gland in the neck which produces hormones regulating growth and development through the rate of metabolism.
– ORIGIN from Greek *khondros thureoeidēs* 'shield-shaped cartilage'.

thyrotoxicosis /thy-roh-tok-si-koh-sis/ noun another term for HYPERTHYROIDISM.

thyself pronoun (second person sing.) old use or dialect yourself.

Ti symbol the chemical element titanium.

ti noun North American form of TE.

tiara noun 1 a semicircular jewelled ornamental band worn on the front of a woman's hair. 2 a crown with three tiers worn by a pope.
– ORIGIN Greek.

Tibetan noun 1 a person from Tibet. 2 the language of Tibet. •adjective relating to Tibet.

tibia /ti-bi-uh/ noun (pl. **tibiae** /ti-bi-ee/ or **tibias**) the inner and typically larger of the two bones between the knee and the ankle, parallel with the fibula.
– DERIVATIVES **tibial** adjective.
– ORIGIN Latin, 'shin bone'.

tic noun a recurring spasm of the muscles, most often in the face.
– ORIGIN Italian *ticchio*.

tick¹ noun 1 Brit. a mark (✓) used to show that something is correct or has been chosen or checked. 2 a regular short, sharp sound. 3 Brit. informal a moment. •verb 1 chiefly Brit. mark something with a tick. 2 make regular short, sharp sounds. 3 (**tick away/by/past**) (of time) pass. 4 (**tick over**) (of an engine) run slowly while the vehicle is not moving. 5 (**tick over**) work or operate slowly or at a minimum level. 6 (**tick someone off**) Brit. informal reprimand someone.
– PHRASES **what makes someone tick** informal what motivates someone.
– ORIGIN probably Germanic.

tick² noun a tiny creature related to the spiders, which attaches itself to the skin and sucks blood.
– ORIGIN Old English.

tick³ noun (in phrase **on tick**) on credit.
– ORIGIN probably from the phrase *on the ticket*, referring to a promise to pay.

t

ticker noun informal **1** a person's heart. **2** a watch.

ticker tape noun a paper strip on which messages are recorded in an electronic or telegraphic machine.

ticket noun **1** a piece of paper or card giving the holder a right to be admitted to a place or event or to travel on public transport. **2** an official notice of a parking or driving offence. **3** a label attached to an item in a shop, giving its price, size, etc. **4** chiefly N. Amer. a set of policies supported by a party in an election: *he stood for office on a right-wing ticket.* **5** (**the ticket**) informal the desirable thing. • verb (**tickets, ticketing, ticketed**) issue someone with a ticket.
– ORIGIN Old French *estiquet.*

tickety-boo adjective Brit. informal, dated in good order.
– ORIGIN perhaps from a Hindi phrase meaning 'all right'.

ticking noun a hard-wearing material used to cover mattresses.
– ORIGIN probably from Greek *thēkē* 'case'.

tickle verb **1** lightly touch someone in a way that causes them to itch, twitch, or laugh. **2** be appealing or amusing to: *I was tickled by the idea.* • noun an act of tickling or the feeling of being tickled.
– PHRASES **be tickled pink** informal be very amused or pleased.
– DERIVATIVES **tickler** noun **tickly** adjective.
– ORIGIN perhaps from TICK¹, or from Scots and dialect *kittle* 'to tickle'.

ticklish adjective **1** sensitive to being tickled. **2** (of a situation or problem) needing careful handling; tricky.

tic-tac (also **tic-tack**) noun (in the UK) a system of hand signals used by racecourse bookmakers to exchange information.
– ORIGIN imitating the sound.

tic-tac-toe (also **tick-tack-toe**) noun N. Amer. noughts and crosses.
– ORIGIN from *tick-tack*, used earlier to refer to games in which the pieces made clicking sounds.

tidal adjective relating to or affected by tides.
– DERIVATIVES **tidally** adverb.

tidal bore noun another term for BORE³.

tidal wave noun **1** an exceptionally large ocean wave, especially one caused by an underwater earthquake or volcanic eruption. **2** an overwhelming or widespread occurrence of an activity, emotion, or reaction: *a tidal wave of patriotism swept the nation.*

tidbit noun N. Amer. variant spelling of TITBIT.

tiddler noun Brit. informal **1** a small fish. **2** a young or unusually small person or thing.
– ORIGIN perhaps from TIDDLY² or *tittlebat*, a child's word for *stickleback.*

tiddly¹ adjective (**tiddlier, tiddliest**) Brit. informal slightly drunk.
– ORIGIN perhaps from former slang *tiddlywink*, referring to an unlicensed pub.

tiddly² adjective (**tiddlier, tiddliest**) Brit. informal little; tiny.
– ORIGIN unknown.

tiddlywinks plural noun (treated as sing.) a game in which small plastic counters are flicked into a central container, using a larger

counter.
– ORIGIN unknown.

tide noun **1** the alternate rising and falling of the sea due to the attraction of the moon and sun. **2** a powerful surge of feeling or trend of events: *the rising tide of urban violence.* • verb (**tide someone over**) help someone through a difficult period.
– ORIGIN Old English, 'time, period, era'.

tideline noun a line left or reached by the sea on a shore at the highest point of a tide.

tidemark noun **1** Brit. informal a dirty mark left around the inside of a bath or washbasin at the level reached by the water. **2** a tideline.

tidewater noun water brought or affected by tides.

tidings plural noun literary news; information.
– ORIGIN Old English.

tidy adjective (**tidier, tidiest**) **1** arranged neatly and in order. **2** liking to keep oneself and one's possessions neat and in order. **3** informal (of a sum of money) considerable. • verb (**tidies, tidying, tidied**) **1** (often **tidy someone/thing up**) make someone or something tidy. **2** (**tidy something away**) put away for the sake of tidiness. • noun (pl. **tidies**) **1** (also **tidy-up**) Brit. an act of tidying. **2** a container for holding small objects.
– DERIVATIVES **tidily** adverb **tidiness** noun.
– ORIGIN first meaning 'timely': from TIDE.

tie verb (**ties, tying, tied**) **1** attach or fasten someone or something with string, cord, etc. **2** form a string, lace, etc. into a knot or bow. **3** restrict or limit to a particular situation or place: *he didn't want to be tied down by a full-time job.* **4** connect or link: *Canada's economy is closely tied to that of the US.* **5** achieve the same score or ranking as another competitor. **6** hold things together by a crosspiece or tie. • noun (pl. **ties**) **1** a thing that ties. **2** a strip of material worn beneath a collar, tied in a knot at the front. **3** a result in a game or match in which two or more competitors are equal. **4** Brit. a sports match in which the winners proceed to the next round of the competition. **5** Cricket a game in which the scores are level and both sides have completed their innings. Compare with DRAW. **6** a rod or beam holding parts of a structure together. **7** Music a curved line above or below two notes of the same pitch indicating that they are to be played as one note.
– PHRASES **tie in** fit or be in harmony: *her ideas don't tie in with mine.* **tie someone up 1** restrict someone's movement by binding their limbs or tying them to something. **2** informal occupy someone so that they have no time for any other activity. **tie something up 1** settle something in a satisfactory way. **2** invest capital so that it is not immediately available for use.
– ORIGIN Old English.

tie-back noun a decorative strip of fabric or cord used for holding an open curtain back from the window.

tiebreaker (also **tiebreak**) noun a means of deciding a winner from competitors who are equal at the end of a game or match.

tied adjective Brit. **1** (of accommodation) rented

by someone on the condition that they work for the owner. **2** (of a pub) owned and controlled by a brewery.

tie-dye verb produce patterns on fabric by tying knots in it before it is dyed.

tie-in noun **1** a connection or association. **2** a product produced to take commercial advantage of a related film, book, etc.

tiepin noun an ornamental pin for holding a tie in place.

tier noun **1** one of a series of rows or levels placed one above and behind the other. **2** a level or grade within an organization or system.
– DERIVATIVES **tiered** adjective.
– ORIGIN French *tire* 'sequence, order'.

tie-up noun a link or connection.

TIFF abbreviation Computing tagged image file format.

tiff noun informal a trivial quarrel.
– ORIGIN probably dialect.

tiffin noun dated or Indian a snack or light meal.
– ORIGIN unknown.

tig noun & verb chiefly Brit. another term for **TAG²**.
– ORIGIN perhaps from **TICK¹**.

tiger noun **1** a large member of the cat family with a yellow-brown coat striped with black, native to the forests of Asia. **2** (also **tiger economy**) a dynamic economy of an East Asian country such as Taiwan or South Korea.
– ORIGIN Greek *tigris*.

tigerish adjective resembling a tiger, especially in being fierce.

tiger lily noun a tall Asian lily which has orange flowers spotted with black or purple.

tiger moth noun a moth with boldly spotted and streaked wings.

tiger prawn (also **tiger shrimp**) noun a large edible prawn marked with dark bands.

tight adjective **1** fixed, closed, or fastened firmly. **2** (of clothes) close-fitting. **3** well sealed against something such as water or air. **4** (of a rope, fabric, or surface) stretched so as to leave no slack. **5** (of an area or space) allowing little room for manoeuvre: *a tight parking spot.* **6** (of people or things) closely packed together. **7** (of a community or other group) having a close relationship between its members. **8** (of a form of control) strictly imposed: *security was tight.* **9** (of money or time) limited. **10** (of a bend, turn, or angle) changing direction sharply. **11** Brit. informal not generous; mean. **12** informal drunk. ●adverb very firmly, closely, or tensely.
– PHRASES **a tight ship** a strictly controlled organization or operation. **a tight corner** (or **spot**) a difficult situation.
– DERIVATIVES **tightly** adverb **tightness** noun.
– ORIGIN probably from Germanic.

tighten verb make or become tight or tighter.

tight-fisted adjective informal not willing to spend or give much money; mean.

tight-knit (also **tightly knit**) adjective (of a group of people) closely linked by strong relationships and shared interests.

tight-lipped adjective unwilling to reveal information or express emotion.

tightrope noun a rope or wire stretched high above the ground, on which acrobats balance.

tights plural noun a close-fitting garment made of stretchy material, covering the hips, legs, and feet.

tigress noun a female tiger.

tike noun variant spelling of **TYKE**.

tikka /tik-uh, tee-kuh/ noun an Indian dish of pieces of meat or vegetables marinated in a spice mixture.
– ORIGIN Punjabi.

tilapia /ti-lay-pi-uh, ti-lap-i-uh/ noun an African freshwater fish, introduced in other parts of the world for food.
– ORIGIN Latin.

tilde /til-duh/ noun an accent (˜) placed over Spanish *n* or Portuguese *a* or *o* to show that they should be pronounced in a particular way.
– ORIGIN Spanish.

tile noun **1** a thin square or rectangular piece of baked clay, concrete, cork, etc., used for covering roofs, floors, or walls. **2** a thin, flat piece used in Scrabble, mah-jong, and other games. ●verb cover a surface with tiles.
– PHRASES **on the tiles** informal, chiefly Brit. having a lively night out.
– DERIVATIVES **tiler** noun.
– ORIGIN Latin *tegula*.

tiling noun a surface covered by tiles.

till¹ preposition & conjunction less formal way of saying **UNTIL**.
– ORIGIN Old English (not a shortened form of *until*).

> USAGE: Although **till** and **until** have the same meaning, **till** is more informal and is used more often in speech than in writing. It is also more usual to use **until** at the beginning of a sentence.

till² noun a cash register or drawer for money in a shop, bank, or restaurant.
– ORIGIN unknown.

till³ verb prepare and cultivate land for crops.
– DERIVATIVES **tillable** adjective **tillage** noun.
– ORIGIN Old English, 'strive for, obtain by effort'.

tiller¹ noun a horizontal bar fitted to the head of a boat's rudder post and used for steering.
– ORIGIN Old French *telier* 'weaver's beam, stock of a crossbow'.

tiller² noun an implement or machine for breaking up soil, such as a plough.

tilt verb **1** move into a sloping position. **2** change in attitude or tendency: *the balance of power tilted towards the workers.* **3** (**tilt at**) historical (in jousting) thrust at someone with a lance or other weapon. ●noun **1** a sloping position or movement. **2** (**tilt at**) an attempt to win something. **3** a bias or tendency. **4** historical a joust.
– PHRASES (**at**) **full tilt** with maximum speed or force. **tilt at windmills** attack imaginary enemies. [with reference to the story of Don Quixote, who tilted at windmills believing they were giants.]
– DERIVATIVES **tilter** noun.
– ORIGIN perhaps from an Old English word meaning 'unsteady'.

tilth noun the condition of soil that has been prepared for growing crops.
– ORIGIN Old English.

t

timbale /tam-bahl/ noun a dish of finely minced meat or fish cooked with other ingredients in a mould or a pastry shell.
– ORIGIN French, 'drum'.

timber noun **1** wood prepared for use in building and carpentry. **2** a wooden beam used in building.
– DERIVATIVES **timbered** adjective **timbering** noun.
– ORIGIN Old English, 'a building', also 'building material'.

timberline noun chiefly N. Amer. another term for **TREELINE**.

timber wolf noun a wolf of a large variety found mainly in northern North America, with tawny-grey fur.

timbre /tam-ber/ noun **1** the quality of a musical sound or voice as distinct from its pitch and intensity. **2** distinctive quality or character: *the phrase had the right bureaucratic timbre.*
– ORIGIN French.

timbrel /tim-bruhl/ noun old use a tambourine or similar instrument.
– ORIGIN perhaps from Old French and related to **TIMBRE**.

time noun **1** the unlimited continued progress of existence and events in the past, present, and future, regarded as a whole. **2** (also **times**) a particular point or period of time: *Victorian times.* **3** a point of time as measured in hours and minutes past midnight or noon. **4** the right or appropriate moment to do something: *it was time to go.* **5** (**a time**) an indefinite period. **6** the length of time taken to complete an activity. **7** time as available or used: *a waste of time.* **8** (**one's time**) a period regarded as characteristic of a stage of one's life. **9** an instance of something happening or being done: *the nurse came in four times a day.* **10** (**times**) (following a number) expressing multiplication. **11** the rhythmic pattern or tempo of a piece of music. **12** Brit. the moment at which the opening hours of a pub end. **13** the normal rate of pay for time spent working. **14** informal a prison sentence. • verb **1** arrange a time for: *the first race is timed for 11.15.* **2** perform an action at a particular time. **3** measure the time taken by someone or something. **4** (**time something out**) (of a computer or a program) cancel an operation automatically because a set interval of time has passed.
– PHRASES **about time** used to say that something should have happened earlier. **at the same time** nevertheless. **at a time** separately in the specified groups or numbers: *he took the stairs two at a time.* **behind the times** not aware of or using the latest ideas or techniques. **for the time being** until some other arrangement is made. **have no time for** dislike or disapprove of someone or something. **in time 1** not late. **2** eventually. **3** in accordance with the appropriate musical rhythm or tempo. **keep good time 1** (of a clock or watch) record time accurately. **2** be punctual. **keep time** play or accompany music in time. **on time** punctual; punctually. **pass the time of day** exchange greetings or casual remarks. **time immemorial** a time in the past that is so long ago that people cannot remember it. **the time of one's life** a very enjoyable period or occasion. **time will tell** the truth about something will be established in the future.
– ORIGIN Old English.

time-and-motion study noun a study of the efficiency of a company's working methods.

time bomb noun **1** a bomb designed to explode at a set time. **2** a situation that is likely to cause serious problems if action is not taken: *the treatment of refugees had become a political time bomb.*

time capsule noun a container holding a selection of objects chosen as being typical of the present time, buried for discovery in the future.

time-consuming adjective taking a lot of or too much time.

time frame noun a specified period of time.

time-honoured adjective (of a custom or tradition) respected or valued because it has existed for a long time.

timekeeper noun **1** a person who records the amount of time taken by a process or activity. **2** a person regarded in terms of how punctual they are. **3** a watch or clock regarded in terms of how accurate it is.
– DERIVATIVES **timekeeping** noun.

time-lapse adjective (of a photographic technique) taking a sequence of frames at set intervals to record changes that take place slowly over time.

timeless adjective not affected by the passage of time or changes in fashion.
– DERIVATIVES **timelessly** adverb **timelessness** noun.

timely adjective done or occurring at a favourable or appropriate time.
– DERIVATIVES **timeliness** noun.

time machine noun (in science fiction) a machine capable of taking a person to the past or future.

time off noun time that is not occupied with one's usual work or studies.

time out noun chiefly N. Amer. **1** time for rest or leisure. **2** (**timeout**) a brief break from play in a game or sport.

timepiece noun an instrument for measuring time; a clock or watch.

timer noun **1** an automatic device for stopping or starting a machine at a preset time. **2** a person or device that records the amount of time taken by something. **3** indicating how many times someone has done something: *a first-timer.*

timescale noun the time allowed for or taken by a process or sequence of events.

time-server noun a person who makes very little effort at work because they are waiting to leave or retire.

timeshare noun an arrangement in which joint owners use a property as a holiday home at different specified times.

time sheet noun a piece of paper for recording the number of hours worked.

time signature noun a sign in the form of two numbers at the start of a piece of music showing the number of beats in a bar.

time switch noun a switch that is

automatically activated at a set time.

timetable noun a list or plan of times at which events are scheduled to take place. • verb schedule something to happen at a particular time.

time trial noun (in various sports) a test of a competitor's individual speed over a set distance.

time warp noun (especially in science fiction) a situation in which it is possible for people or things belonging to one period to move to another.

time-worn adjective damaged or made less interesting as a result of age or a great deal of use.

timid adjective (**timider**, **timidest**) not brave or confident.
– DERIVATIVES **timidity** noun **timidly** adverb **timidness** noun.
– ORIGIN Latin *timidus*.

timing noun 1 the quality of being able to judge the right time to do something: *a politician with an unerring sense of timing.* 2 a particular time when something happens.

timorous /tim-uh-ruhss/ adjective lacking in courage or confidence; nervous.
– DERIVATIVES **timorously** adverb **timorousness** noun.
– ORIGIN Latin *timorosus*.

timpani /tim-puh-ni/ (also **tympani**) plural noun kettledrums.
– DERIVATIVES **timpanist** noun.
– ORIGIN Italian.

tin noun 1 a silvery-white metallic chemical element. 2 an airtight container with a lid, made of tinplate or aluminium. 3 Brit. a sealed tinplate or aluminium container for preserving food; a can. 4 Brit. an open metal container for baking food. • verb (**tins**, **tinning**, **tinned**) 1 cover something with a thin layer of tin. 2 (as adj. **tinned**) Brit. preserved in a tin.
– ORIGIN Old English.

tincture /tingk-cher/ noun 1 a medicine made by dissolving a drug in alcohol. 2 a slight trace of something. • verb (**be tinctured**) be tinged with a slight trace of: *his affability was tinctured with faint sarcasm.*
– ORIGIN Latin *tinctura* 'dyeing'.

tinder noun dry, flammable material used for lighting a fire.
– ORIGIN Old English.

tinderbox noun 1 a situation that is likely to become dangerous: *some prisons are tinderboxes of violence.* 2 historical a box containing tinder, flint, a steel, and other items for lighting a fire.

tine /rhymes with line/ noun a prong or sharp point, especially of a fork.
– DERIVATIVES **tined** adjective.
– ORIGIN Old English.

tinea /tin-i-uh/ noun technical term for RINGWORM.
– ORIGIN Latin, 'worm'.

tinfoil noun metal foil used for covering or wrapping food.

ting noun a sharp, clear ringing sound. • verb make a sharp, clear ringing sound.
– ORIGIN imitating the sound.

tinge verb (**tinges**, **tinging** or **tingeing**, **tinged**) 1 colour something slightly. 2 affect with a small amount of a quality: *a visit tinged with sadness.* • noun a slight trace of a colour, feeling, or quality.
– ORIGIN Latin *tingere* 'to dip or colour'.

tingle verb experience a slight prickling or stinging sensation. • noun a slight prickling or stinging sensation.
– DERIVATIVES **tingly** adjective.
– ORIGIN perhaps from TINKLE.

tinker noun 1 a travelling mender of pots, kettles, etc. 2 Brit., chiefly derogatory a Gypsy or other person living in a travelling community. 3 an act of tinkering with something. • verb (**tinker with**) try to repair or improve something by making many small changes.
– DERIVATIVES **tinkerer** noun.
– ORIGIN unknown.

tinkle verb make a light, clear ringing sound. • noun a light, clear ringing sound.
– DERIVATIVES **tinkly** adjective.
– ORIGIN imitating the sound.

tinnitus /tin-ni-tuhss, ti-ny-tuhss/ noun Medicine ringing or buzzing in the ears.
– ORIGIN Latin.

tinny adjective 1 having a thin, metallic sound. 2 made of thin or poor-quality metal. 3 having an unpleasantly metallic taste.
– DERIVATIVES **tinnily** adverb **tinniness** noun.

tinplate noun sheet steel or iron coated with tin.
– DERIVATIVES **tinplated** adjective.

tinpot adjective informal not significant or effective: *a tinpot dictator.*

tinsel noun 1 a form of decoration consisting of thin strips of shiny metal foil attached to a length of thread. 2 superficial attractiveness or glamour: *the phoney tinsel of Hollywood.*
– DERIVATIVES **tinselled** adjective **tinsely** adjective.
– ORIGIN Old French *estincele* 'spark'.

Tinseltown noun the glamorous but artificial world of Hollywood and its film industry.

tinsmith noun a person who makes or repairs articles made of tin or tinplate.

tinsnips plural noun a pair of clippers for cutting sheet metal.

tint noun 1 a shade of a colour. 2 a dye for colouring the hair. • verb 1 colour slightly: *the clouds were tinted with crimson.* 2 dye the hair.
– ORIGIN Latin *tinctus* 'dyeing'.

tintinnabulation /tin-tin-nab-yuu-lay-sh'n/ noun a ringing or tinkling sound.
– ORIGIN from Latin *tintinnabulum* 'tinkling bell'.

tin whistle noun a metal musical instrument resembling a small flute.

tiny adjective (**tinier**, **tiniest**) very small. • noun (pl. **tinies**) informal a very young child.
– DERIVATIVES **tinily** adverb **tininess** noun.
– ORIGIN unknown.

tip¹ noun 1 the pointed or rounded end of something thin or tapering. 2 a small part fitted to the end of an object. • verb (**tips**, **tipping**, **tipped**) (usu. as adj. **tipped**) attach to or cover the tip of: *a tipped cigarette.*
– PHRASES **on the tip of one's tongue** almost but not quite spoken or coming to mind.
– ORIGIN Old Norse.

tip² verb (**tips**, **tipping**, **tipped**) 1 overbalance so

t

as to fall or turn over. **2** be or put in a sloping position. **3** empty out the contents of a container by holding it at an angle. **4** (**it tips down, it is tipping down, it tipped down**) Brit. informal rain heavily. **5** hit or touch lightly: *his shot was tipped over the bar by Nixon.* •**noun** **1** Brit. a place where rubbish is left. **2** informal a dirty or untidy place.
– PHRASES **tip one's hat** raise or touch one's hat as a greeting or mark of respect.
– ORIGIN perhaps Scandinavian.

tip³ noun **1** a small extra sum of money given to someone to reward good service. **2** a piece of practical advice. **3** a piece of expert information about the likely winner of a race or contest. •**verb** (**tips, tipping, tipped**) **1** give a tip to someone as a reward for good service. **2** Brit. predict as likely to win or achieve something: *he was widely tipped to get the job.* **3** (**tip someone off**) informal give someone secret information.
– PHRASES **tip someone the wink** Brit. informal give someone secret information.
– ORIGIN probably from TIP¹.

tipi noun variant spelling of TEPEE.

tip-off noun informal a piece of secret information.

tipper noun **1** a lorry with a rear platform which can be raised at its front end, thus enabling goods to be unloaded. **2** a person who leaves a tip of a specified amount: *a good tipper.*

tippet noun a long piece of fur worn around the neck, or the neck and shoulders, by women.
– ORIGIN probably from TIP¹.

Tippex (also **Tipp-Ex**) noun Brit. trademark a type of correction fluid. •**verb** delete something with correction fluid.
– ORIGIN from German *tippen* 'to type' and Latin *ex* 'out'.

tipple verb drink alcohol regularly. •**noun** informal an alcoholic drink.
– DERIVATIVES **tippler** noun.
– ORIGIN unknown.

tippy-toe verb informal, chiefly N. Amer. tiptoe.

tipstaff noun a sheriff's officer; a bailiff.
– ORIGIN from *tipped staff*, a metal-tipped staff carried by a bailiff.

tipster noun a person who gives tips as to the likely winner of a race or contest.

tipsy adjective (**tipsier, tipsiest**) slightly drunk.
– DERIVATIVES **tipsily** adverb **tipsiness** noun.
– ORIGIN from TIP².

tiptoe verb (**tiptoes, tiptoeing, tiptoed**) walk quietly and carefully with the heels raised and the weight on the balls of the feet.
– PHRASES **on tiptoe** (or **tiptoes**) with the heels raised and the weight on the balls of the feet.

tip-top adjective of the very best quality; excellent.

tirade /ty-**rayd**, ti-**rayd**/ noun a long angry speech criticizing someone or something.
– ORIGIN French.

tiramisu /tir-uh-mi-**soo**/ noun an Italian dessert consisting of layers of sponge cake soaked in coffee and brandy, with powdered chocolate and mascarpone cheese.
– ORIGIN from Italian *tira mi sù* 'pick me up'.

tire¹ verb **1** make or become in need of rest or

sleep. **2** make someone feel impatient or bored. **3** (**tire of**) become impatient or bored with: *she will stay with him until she tires of her.*
– ORIGIN Old English.

tire² noun US spelling of TYRE.

tired adjective **1** in need of sleep or rest; weary. **2** (**tired of**) bored with someone or something. **3** (of a statement or idea) boring or uninteresting because used too often..
– DERIVATIVES **tiredly** adverb **tiredness** noun.

tireless adjective having or showing great effort or energy.
– DERIVATIVES **tirelessly** adverb **tirelessness** noun.

tiresome adjective annoying or boring.
– DERIVATIVES **tiresomely** adverb **tiresomeness** noun.

'tis contraction chiefly literary it is.

tisane /ti-**zan**/ noun a herb tea.
– ORIGIN French.

tissue /ti-**shoo**/ noun **1** any of the distinct types of material of which animals or plants are made, consisting of specialized cells. **2** tissue paper. **3** a paper handkerchief. **4** delicate gauzy fabric.
– PHRASES **a tissue of lies** a story that is full of lies.
– DERIVATIVES **tissuey** adjective.
– ORIGIN from Old French *tissu* 'woven'.

tissue culture noun Biology & Medicine the growing of cells from a living organism in an artificial medium outside the organism.

tissue paper noun very thin, soft paper.

tit¹ noun a small insect-eating songbird; a titmouse.
– ORIGIN probably Scandinavian.

tit² noun vulgar slang a woman's breast.
– ORIGIN Old English, 'teat, nipple'.

tit³ noun (in phrase **tit for tat**) a situation in which a person insults or hurts someone to retaliate for something they have done.
– ORIGIN from former *tip for tap*, from TIP².

Titan /**ty**-tuhn/ noun **1** any of a family of giant gods in Greek mythology. **2** (**titan**) a very strong, intelligent, or important person.

titanic adjective very strong, large, or powerful: *a titanic struggle for survival.*
– DERIVATIVES **titanically** adverb.

titanium /ti-**tay**-ni-uhm, ty-**tay**-ni-uhm/ noun a hard silver-grey metal used in strong corrosion-resistant alloys.
– ORIGIN from TITAN.

titbit (N. Amer. **tidbit**) noun **1** a small piece of tasty food. **2** a small item of very interesting information.
– ORIGIN from dialect *tid* 'tender' + BIT¹.

titch noun Brit. informal a small person.
– ORIGIN from *Little Tich*, stage name of Harry Relph, an English music-hall comedian who was given the nickname because he resembled Arthur Orton, the unsuccessful claimant to the valuable Tichborne estate.

titchy adjective Brit. informal very small.

titfer noun Brit. informal a hat.
– ORIGIN from rhyming slang *tit for tat*.

tithe /tyth/ noun **1** one tenth of the amount people produced or earned in a year, formerly taken as a tax to support the Church. **2** (in certain religious denominations) a tenth of a person's income pledged to the Church. •**verb** pay a tenth of one's income as a tithe.

– ORIGIN Old English, 'tenth'.

tithe barn noun a barn built to hold produce given as tithes to the Church.

Titian /ti-shuhn/ adjective (of hair) bright golden auburn.
– ORIGIN from the Italian painter *Titian*, with reference to the bright auburn hair portrayed in many of his works.

titillate /ti-til-layt/ verb interest or excite someone, especially in a sexual way.
– DERIVATIVES **titillation** noun.
– ORIGIN Latin *titillare* 'to tickle'.

> USAGE: Do not confuse **titillate** with **titivate**. Titillate means 'interest or excite someone, especially sexually' (*the press are paid to titillate the public*), whereas **titivate** means 'make smarter or more attractive' (*she slapped on her make-up and titivated her hair*).

titivate /ti-ti-vayt/ verb informal make someone or something smarter or more attractive.
– DERIVATIVES **titivation** noun.
– ORIGIN perhaps from TIDY.

title noun 1 the name of a book, musical composition, or other work. 2 a name that describes someone's position or job. 3 a word, such as *Dr*, *Mrs*, or *Lord*, used before or instead of someone's name to indicate their rank, profession, or status. 4 the position of being the winner of a competition, especially of being the champion of a sports competition: *he won the world title*. 5 a caption or credit in a film or broadcast. 6 the legal right to own something, especially land or property. ●verb give a title to someone or something.
– ORIGIN Latin *titulus* 'inscription, title'.

titled adjective having a title indicating nobility or rank.

title deed noun a legal document providing evidence of a person's right to own a property.

title role noun the role in a play or film from which the work's title is taken.

titmouse noun (pl. **titmice**) another term for TIT¹.
– ORIGIN from TIT¹ + the former word *mose* 'titmouse'.

titrate /ty-trayt/ verb Chemistry calculate the amount of a substance in a solution by measuring the volume of a standard reagent required to react with it.
– DERIVATIVES **titration** noun.
– ORIGIN from French *titre* 'fineness of alloyed gold or silver'.

titter verb laugh quietly. ●noun a short, quiet laugh.
– ORIGIN imitating the sound.

tittle noun a tiny amount or part of something.
– ORIGIN Latin *titulus* 'title', later 'small stroke, accent'.

tittle-tattle noun trivial talk; gossip. ●verb engage in gossip.
– ORIGIN from TATTLE.

titular /tit-yuu-ler/ adjective 1 holding a formal position or title without any real authority: *the queen is titular head of the Church of England*. 2 relating to a title.
– DERIVATIVES **titularly** adverb.

tizzy (also **tizz**) noun (pl. **tizzies**) informal a state of nervous excitement or agitation.

– ORIGIN unknown.

T-junction noun Brit. a road junction at which one road joins another at right angles without crossing it.

Tl symbol the chemical element thallium.

TLC abbreviation informal tender loving care.

TM abbreviation (trademark in the US) Transcendental Meditation.

Tm symbol the chemical element thulium.

TN abbreviation Tennessee.

TNC abbreviation transnational corporation.

TNT abbreviation trinitrotoluene, a high explosive.

to preposition 1 in the direction of. 2 situated in the direction mentioned from: *there are mountains to the north*. 3 so as to reach a particular state. 4 identifying the person or thing affected by an action: *you were unkind to her*. 5 indicating that people or things are related, linked, or attached. 6 chiefly Brit. (in telling the time) before the hour specified. 7 indicating a rate of return: *the car only does ten miles to the gallon*. 8 introducing the second part of a comparison: *the club's nothing to what it once was*. ●infinitive marker used with the base form of a verb to indicate that the verb is in the infinitive. ●adverb so as to be closed or nearly closed: *he pulled the door to*.
– PHRASES **to and fro** in a constant movement backwards and forwards or from side to side.
– ORIGIN Old English.

> USAGE: Do not confuse **to** with **too** or **two**. To mainly means 'in the direction of' (*the next train to London*), while **too** means 'excessively' (*she was driving too fast*) or 'in addition' (*is he coming too?*). **Two** is a number meaning 'one less than three' (*we met two years ago*).

toad noun a tailless amphibian with a short stout body and short legs. 2 a very unpleasant or disliked person.
– ORIGIN Old English.

toadflax noun a plant with yellow or purplish flowers that resemble those of the snapdragon.

toad-in-the-hole noun Brit. a dish consisting of sausages baked in batter.

toadstool noun a fungus, typically in the form of a rounded cap on a stalk.

toady noun (pl. **toadies**) a person who behaves in an excessively respectful way towards another in order to gain their favour. ●verb (**toadies**, **toadying**, **toadied**) act in an excessively respectful way to gain someone's favour.
– ORIGIN probably from *toad-eater*, a charlatan's assistant who ate toads (regarded as poisonous) as a demonstration of the power of the charlatan's remedy.

toast noun 1 sliced bread that has been browned by putting it close to a source of heat, such as a grill or fire. 2 an act of raising glasses at a gathering and drinking together in honour of a person or thing. 3 a person who is respected or admired: *he was the toast of the baseball world*. ●verb 1 make bread or other food brown by putting it under a grill or close to another source of heat. 2 drink a toast to someone. 3 (of a DJ) accompany reggae music

with improvised rhythmic speech.
- PHRASES **be toast** informal, chiefly N. Amer. be finished, defunct, or dead.
- ORIGIN from Old French *toster* 'to roast'; sense 2 came from the idea that the name of the lady whose health was being drunk flavoured the drink like the pieces of spiced toast formerly placed in wine.

toaster noun an electrical device for making toast.

toastie noun Brit. informal a toasted sandwich or snack.

toasting fork noun a long-handled fork for making toast in front of a fire.

toastmaster (or **toastmistress**) noun an official responsible for proposing toasts and making other formal announcements at a large social event.

tobacco noun (pl. **tobaccos**) the dried nicotine-rich leaves of an American plant, used for smoking or chewing.
- ORIGIN Spanish *tabaco*.

tobacconist noun chiefly Brit. a shopkeeper who sells cigarettes and tobacco.

toboggan noun a light, narrow vehicle on runners, used for sliding downhill over snow or ice. •verb ride on a toboggan.
- ORIGIN Micmac.

toby jug noun a beer jug or mug in the form of a seated old man wearing a three-cornered hat.
- ORIGIN probably from a poem about *Toby Philpot* (with a pun on *fill pot*), a soldier who liked to drink.

toccata /tuh-**kah**-tuh/ noun a musical composition for a keyboard instrument designed to display the performer's touch and technique.
- ORIGIN Italian, 'touched'.

tocopherol /to-**kof**-uh-rol/ noun vitamin E.
- ORIGIN from Greek *tokos* 'offspring' + *pherein* 'to bear'.

tocsin /**tok**-sin/ noun old use an alarm bell or signal.
- ORIGIN Provençal *tocasenh*.

tod noun (in phrase **on one's tod**) Brit. informal on one's own.
- ORIGIN from rhyming slang *Tod Sloan*, an American jockey.

today adverb 1 on or during this present day. 2 at the present period of time; nowadays. •noun 1 this present day. 2 the present period of time.
- ORIGIN Old English, 'on this day'.

toddle verb 1 (of a young child) move with short unsteady steps while learning to walk. 2 informal go somewhere in a casual or leisurely way. •noun an act of toddling.
- ORIGIN unknown.

toddler noun a young child who is just beginning to walk.

toddy noun (pl. **toddies**) a drink made of spirits with hot water and sugar.
- ORIGIN Sanskrit, 'palmyra' (referring to a palm tree with a naturally alcoholic sap).

to-do noun informal a commotion or fuss.
- ORIGIN from *much to do*, first meaning 'much needing to be done'.

toe noun 1 any of the five digits at the end of

the foot. 2 the lower end or tip of something. •verb (**toes, toeing, toed**) push or touch someone or something with the toes.
- PHRASES **make someone's toes curl** informal make someone feel very embarrassed. **on one's toes** ready and alert. **toe the line** obey authority.
- DERIVATIVES **toed** adjective **toeless** adjective.
- ORIGIN Old English.

USAGE: The phrase **toe the line**, which comes from the meaning 'stand with the tips of the toes exactly touching a line', is often misinterpreted and wrongly spelled as *tow the line*.

toecap noun a piece of steel or leather on the front part of a boot or shoe.

toehold noun 1 a relatively minor position from which further progress may be made: *the initiative is helping companies to gain a toehold in the Gulf.* 2 (in climbing) a small foothold.

toenail noun a nail on the upper surface of the tip of each toe.

toerag noun Brit. informal an unpleasant or disliked person.
- ORIGIN first referring to a rag wrapped round the foot as a sock, such as might be worn by a homeless person.

toe-tapping adjective informal (of music) lively.

toff noun Brit. informal, derogatory a rich upper-class person.
- ORIGIN perhaps from TUFT, referring to a gold tassel worn on the cap by titled undergraduates at Oxford and Cambridge.

toffee noun a kind of firm sweet which softens when sucked or chewed, made by boiling together sugar and butter.
- ORIGIN unknown.

toffee apple noun Brit. an apple coated with a thin layer of toffee and fixed on a stick.

toffee-nosed adjective Brit. informal acting as if one is superior to others; snobbish.

tofu /**toh**-foo/ noun a soft white substance made from mashed soya beans, used in Asian and vegetarian cookery.
- ORIGIN Chinese, 'rotten beans'.

tog[1] informal noun (**togs**) clothes. •verb (**be togged up/out**) be fully dressed for a particular occasion or activity.
- ORIGIN probably from former criminals' slang *togeman* 'light cloak', from Latin *toga* 'toga'.

tog[2] noun Brit. a unit for measuring the insulating properties of clothes and quilts.
- ORIGIN from TOG[1], on the pattern of an earlier unit called the *clo* (first part of *clothes*).

toga /**toh**-guh/ noun a loose outer garment made of a single piece of cloth, worn by the citizens of ancient Rome.
- ORIGIN Latin.

together adverb 1 with or near to another person or people. 2 so as to touch, combine, or be united. 3 regarded as a whole. 4 (of two people) married or in a sexual relationship. 5 at the same time. 6 without interruption. •adjective informal sensible, calm, or well organized.
- PHRASES **together with** as well as.
- DERIVATIVES **togetherness** noun.
- ORIGIN Old English.

toggle noun **1** a narrow piece of wood or plastic attached to a coat or jacket, pushed through a loop to act as a fastener. **2** Computing a key or command that is used to alternate between one effect, feature, or state and another. •verb Computing switch from one effect, feature, or state to another by using a toggle.
– ORIGIN unknown.

toggle switch noun an electric switch operated by means of a projecting lever that is moved up and down.

Togolese /toh-guh-**leez**/ noun (pl. same) a person from Togo, a country in West Africa. •adjective relating to Togo.

toil verb **1** work very hard. **2** move along slowly and with difficulty. •noun exhausting work.
– DERIVATIVES **toiler** noun.
– ORIGIN Old French *toiler* 'strive, dispute'.

toile /twahl/ noun **1** an early version of a finished garment made up in cheap material so that the design can be tested. **2** a semi-transparent fabric.
– ORIGIN French, 'cloth, web'.

toilet noun **1** a large bowl for urinating or defecating into. **2** the process of washing oneself, dressing, and attending to one's appearance.
– ORIGIN first referring to a cloth cover for a dressing table: from French *toilette* 'cloth, wrapper'.

toilet bag noun Brit. a waterproof bag for holding toothpaste, soap, etc. when travelling.

toiletries plural noun articles used in washing and taking care of the body, such as soap and shampoo.

toilette /twah-**let**/ noun old-fashioned term for TOILET (in sense 2).
– ORIGIN French (see TOILET).

toilet-train verb teach a young child to use the toilet.

toilet water noun a diluted form of perfume.

toils plural noun literary a situation regarded as a trap: *some episodes involved the hero in the toils of drugs.*
– ORIGIN first referring to a net into which a hunted animal is driven: from Old French *toile* 'net, trap'.

toilsome adjective old use or literary involving hard work or effort.

Tokay /toh-**kay**/ noun a sweet aromatic wine, originally made near Tokaj in Hungary.

toke informal noun a pull on a cigarette or pipe, especially one containing cannabis. •verb smoke cannabis or tobacco.
– ORIGIN unknown.

token noun **1** a thing that represents a fact, quality, or feeling: *the gift of a plant is a token of love.* **2** a voucher that can be exchanged for goods or services. **3** a disc used to operate a machine or in exchange for certain goods or services. •adjective **1** done for the sake of appearances: *cases like this often bring token fines.* **2** chosen by way of tokenism to represent a particular group.
– PHRASES **by the same token** in the same way or for the same reason.
– ORIGIN Old English.

tokenism noun the practice of doing something in a superficial way, so as to be seen to be obeying the law or satisfying a particular group of people.
– DERIVATIVES **tokenistic** adjective.

tolar /**to**-lah/ noun the basic unit of money of Slovenia.
– ORIGIN Slovene.

told past and past participle of TELL.

tolerable adjective **1** able to be tolerated or endured. **2** fairly good.
– DERIVATIVES **tolerability** noun **tolerably** adverb.

tolerance noun **1** the ability to accept things that one dislikes or disagrees with. **2** the ability to endure specified conditions or treatment: *the plant's tolerance to pests and herbicides.* **3** an allowable amount of variation of a measurement, especially in the dimensions of a machine or part.

tolerant adjective **1** able to accept things that one dislikes or disagrees with. **2** able to endure specified conditions or treatment.
– DERIVATIVES **tolerantly** adverb.

tolerate verb **1** allow something that one dislikes or disagrees with to exist or continue: *the organization will not tolerate racism.* **2** patiently endure someone or something that is unpleasant or annoying. **3** be able to be exposed to a drug, toxin, etc. without a bad reaction.
– DERIVATIVES **toleration** noun.
– ORIGIN Latin *tolerare* 'endure'.

toll[1] /tohl/ noun **1** a charge payable to use a bridge or road or (N. Amer.) for a long-distance telephone call. **2** the number of deaths or casualties arising from an accident, disaster, etc. **3** the cost or damage resulting from something: *the policy's environmental toll has been high.*
– PHRASES **take its toll** (or **take a heavy toll**) have a very harmful effect.
– ORIGIN Greek *telōnion* 'toll house'.

toll[2] /tohl/ verb **1** (of a bell) sound with slow, even strokes. **2** (of a bell) ring to announce the time, a service, or a person's death. •noun a single ring of a bell.
– ORIGIN probably from dialect *toll* 'drag, pull'.

tollbooth noun a roadside kiosk where tolls are paid.

toll gate noun a barrier across a road where a toll must be paid to pass through.

Toltec /**tol**-tek/ noun a member of an American Indian people that flourished in Mexico before the Aztecs.
– DERIVATIVES **Toltecan** adjective.
– ORIGIN Nahuatl, 'person from *Tula*' (a town and former Toltec site in Mexico).

toluene /**tol**-yuu-een/ noun a liquid hydrocarbon resembling benzene, present in coal tar and petroleum.
– ORIGIN from *tolu*, a substance obtained from a South American tree.

tom noun the male of various animals, especially a domestic cat.
– ORIGIN from the man's name *Thomas*.

tomahawk /**tom**-uh-hawk/ noun a light axe formerly used as a tool or weapon by American Indians.
– ORIGIN from an Algonquian language.

tomato noun (pl. **tomatoes**) a glossy red or

yellow edible fruit, eaten as a vegetable or in salads.
– ORIGIN Nahuatl.

tomb noun **1** a burial place consisting of a stone structure above ground or a large underground vault. **2** a monument to a dead person, erected over their burial place. **3** (**the tomb**) literary death.
– ORIGIN Greek *tumbos*.

tombola /tom-boh-luh/ noun Brit. a game in which tickets are drawn from a revolving drum to win prizes.
– ORIGIN Italian.

tomboy noun a girl who enjoys rough, noisy activities traditionally associated with boys.
– DERIVATIVES **tomboyish** adjective.

tombstone noun a large, flat inscribed stone standing or laid over a grave.

tomcat noun a male domestic cat.

Tom Collins noun a cocktail made from gin mixed with soda, sugar, and lemon or lime juice.
– ORIGIN probably named after a London bartender.

Tom, Dick, and Harry noun ordinary people in general.

tome noun chiefly humorous a book, especially a large, serious one.
– ORIGIN Greek *tomos* 'roll of papyrus, volume'.

tomfoolery noun silly behaviour.

Tommy noun (pl. **Tommies**) informal a British private soldier.
– ORIGIN from a use of the name *Thomas Atkins* in examples of completed forms in the British army.

tommy gun noun informal a type of sub-machine gun.
– ORIGIN from *Thompson gun*, named after John T. *Thompson*, the American army officer who conceived it.

tommyrot noun informal, dated nonsense; rubbish.

tomography /tuh-mog-ruh-fi/ noun a technique for displaying a cross section through a human body or other solid object using X-rays or ultrasound.
– DERIVATIVES **tomogram** noun **tomographic** adjective.
– ORIGIN from Greek *tomos* 'slice, section'.

tomorrow adverb **1** on the day after today. **2** in the near future. • noun **1** the day after today. **2** the near future.

tomtit noun a small tit or similar bird, especially (Brit.) the blue tit.

tom-tom noun a drum beaten with the hands, associated with North American Indian, African, or Eastern cultures.
– ORIGIN Hindi.

ton /tun/ noun **1** (also **long ton**) a unit of weight equal to 2,240 lb avoirdupois (1016.05 kg). **2** (also **short ton**) chiefly N. Amer. a unit of weight equal to 2,000 lb avoirdupois (907.19 kg). **3** a metric ton. **4** (also **displacement ton**) a unit of measurement of a ship's weight equal to 2,240 lb or 35 cu. ft (0.99 cubic metres). **5** (also **tons**) informal a large number or amount of something. **6** Brit. informal a hundred, in particular a speed of 100 mph. • adverb (**tons**) Brit. informal much; a great deal.

– ORIGIN variant of **TUN**.

tonal /toh-n'l/ adjective **1** relating to tone. **2** (of music) written using conventional keys and harmony.
– DERIVATIVES **tonally** adverb.

tonality noun (pl. **tonalities**) **1** the character of a piece of music as determined by the key in which it is played or the relationships between the notes of a scale or key. **2** the use of conventional keys and harmony as the basis of musical composition.

tondo /ton-doh/ noun (pl. **tondi** /ton-di/) a circular painting.
– ORIGIN Italian, 'round object'.

tone noun **1** a musical or vocal sound with reference to its pitch, quality, and strength: *they spoke in hushed tones.* **2** the sound of a person's voice, expressing a feeling or mood. **3** the general character of something: *trust her to lower the tone of the conversation.* **4** (also **whole tone**) a basic interval in classical Western music, equal to two semitones. **5** the particular quality of brightness or deepness of a shade of a colour. **6** the normal level of firmness in a resting muscle. • verb **1** (often **tone something up**) make the body or a muscle stronger or firmer. **2** (**tone something down**) make something less harsh, extreme, or intense: *he toned down his criticisms.* **3** (**tone with**) match the colour of something.
– DERIVATIVES **toned** adjective **toneless** adjective.
– ORIGIN Greek *tonos* 'tension, tone'.

tone arm noun the movable arm supporting the pickup of a record player.

tone-deaf adjective unable to recognize differences in musical pitch accurately.

tone poem noun a piece of orchestral music, typically in one movement, describing a subject taken from mythology, literature, history, etc.

toner noun **1** a liquid applied to the skin to reduce oiliness and improve its condition. **2** a powder used in photocopiers. **3** a chemical solution used to change the tone of a photographic print.

tong noun a Chinese association or secret society associated with organized crime.
– ORIGIN Chinese, 'meeting place'.

Tongan /tong-uhn/ noun **1** a person from Tonga, a group of islands in the South Pacific. **2** the Polynesian language spoken in Tonga. • adjective relating to Tonga.

tongs plural noun **1** a tool with two movable arms that are joined at one end, used for picking up and holding things. **2** curling tongs.
– ORIGIN Old English.

tongue noun **1** the fleshy muscular organ in the mouth, used for tasting, licking, swallowing, and (in humans) producing speech. **2** the tongue of an ox or lamb as food. **3** a person's style or way of speaking: *his sharp tongue.* **4** a particular language. **5** a strip of leather or fabric under the laces in a shoe. **6** the clapper of a bell. **7** a long, low promontory of land. **8** a projecting strip on a wooden board which fits into a groove on another. **9** the vibrating reed of a musical instrument or organ pipe. • verb (**tongues, tonguing, tongued**) **1** sound a note distinctly on a wind instrument by interrupting the air flow with the tongue.

2 lick something with the tongue.
- PHRASES **the gift of tongues** the power of speaking in unknown languages, believed to be one of the gifts of the Holy Spirit. **have lost one's tongue** be silent, especially as a result of shock, shyness, etc. **hold one's tongue** informal remain silent. **(with) tongue in cheek** not seriously meaning what one is saying.
- ORIGIN Old English.

tongue and groove noun wooden planking in which adjacent boards are joined by means of interlocking ridges and grooves down their sides.

tongue-lashing noun a severe scolding.

tongue-tied adjective too shy or embarrassed to speak.

tongue-twister noun a sequence of words that are difficult to pronounce quickly and correctly.

tonic noun **1** a medicinal drink taken to make a person feel healthier or more energetic. **2** anything that makes a person feel better: *a holiday is just the tonic you need to shake off those midwinter blues.* **3** (also **tonic water**) a fizzy soft drink with a bitter flavour, used as a mixer with gin or spirits. **4** the first note in a musical scale which, in conventional harmony, provides the keynote of a piece of music.
- ORIGIN Greek *tonikos* 'for stretching'.

tonic sol-fa noun a system of naming the notes of the scale used to teach singing, with doh as the keynote of all major keys and lah as the keynote of all minor keys.

tonight adverb on the evening or night of the present day. •noun the evening or night of the present day.

tonnage noun **1** weight in tons. **2** the size or carrying capacity of a ship measured in tons.

tonne /tun/ noun another term for **METRIC TON**.
- ORIGIN French.

tonneau /ton-noh/ noun **1** the part of an open car taken up by the back seats. **2** a protective cover for the seats in an open car or cabin cruiser when they are not in use.
- ORIGIN French, 'cask, tun'.

tonsil noun either of two small masses of tissue in the throat, one on each side of the root of the tongue.
- ORIGIN Latin *tonsillae* (plural).

tonsillectomy /ton-sil-**lek**-tuh-mi/ noun (pl. **tonsillectomies**) a surgical operation to remove the tonsils.

tonsillitis noun inflammation of the tonsils.

tonsorial /ton-**sor**-i-uhl/ adjective chiefly humorous relating to hairdressing.
- ORIGIN Latin *tonsor* 'barber'.

tonsure /ton-syer, ton-sher/ noun a circular area on a monk's or priest's head where the hair is shaved off.
- DERIVATIVES **tonsured** adjective.
- ORIGIN Latin *tonsura*.

tony adjective (**tonier**, **toniest**) N. Amer. informal fashionable, stylish, or high-class.
- ORIGIN from **TONE**.

too adverb **1** to a higher degree than is desirable, allowed, or possible. **2** in addition; also: *is he coming too?* **3** informal very: *you're too kind.*
- PHRASES **none too** —— not very: *she was none*

too pleased.
- ORIGIN Old English.

> USAGE: On the confusion of **too** with **to** or **two**, see the note at **TO**.

took past of **TAKE**.

tool noun **1** a piece of equipment, especially a hand-held one, used to carry out a particular function. **2** a thing used to help achieve something or perform a job: *a dictionary is an invaluable tool while you are learning a language.* **3** a person used or controlled by another. •verb **1** make a decorative design on a leather book cover by using a heated tool. **2** provide a factory with the equipment needed to do or make something. **3** (**tool up** or **be tooled up**) Brit. informal be or become armed. **4** informal, chiefly N. Amer. drive around in a casual or leisurely way.
- ORIGIN Old English.

toolbar noun Computing a strip of icons used to perform certain functions.

toolbox noun **1** a box or container for tools. **2** Computing the set of programs or functions accessible from a single menu.

toolmaker noun a person who makes and repairs tools for use in a manufacturing process.

toot noun a short, sharp sound made by a horn, trumpet, or similar instrument. •verb make a toot.
- ORIGIN perhaps from German *tüten*.

tooth noun (pl. **teeth**) **1** each of a set of hard enamel-coated structures in the jaws, used for biting and chewing. **2** a projecting part, especially a cog on a gearwheel or a point on a saw or comb. **3** (**teeth**) genuine power or effectiveness: *the Charter would be fine if it had teeth.*
- PHRASES **armed to the teeth** having many weapons. **fight tooth and nail** fight very fiercely. **get one's teeth into** work energetically and enthusiastically on a particular task. **in the teeth of 1** directly against the wind. **2** in spite of opposition or difficulty.
- DERIVATIVES **toothed** adjective.
- ORIGIN Old English.

toothache noun pain in a tooth or teeth.

toothbrush noun a small brush with a long handle, used for cleaning the teeth.

toothed whale noun any of the large group of predatory whales with teeth, including sperm whales, killer whales, and dolphins.

tooth fairy noun a fairy said to take children's milk teeth after they fall out and leave a coin under their pillow.

toothless adjective **1** having no teeth. **2** lacking genuine power or effectiveness: *laws that are well intentioned but toothless.*

toothpaste noun a paste used on a brush for cleaning the teeth.

toothpick noun a short pointed piece of wood or plastic used for removing bits of food stuck between the teeth.

toothsome adjective **1** (of food) appetizing or tasty. **2** informal attractive; appealing.

toothy adjective (**toothier**, **toothiest**) having or

showing numerous, large, or prominent teeth.
– DERIVATIVES **toothily** adverb.

tootle verb **1** casually make a series of sounds on a horn, trumpet, etc. **2** informal go or travel in a leisurely way. • noun **1** an act or sound of tootling. **2** informal a leisurely journey.
– ORIGIN from **TOOT**.

tootsie (also **tootsy**) noun (pl. **tootsies**) informal **1** a person's foot. **2** a young woman.
– ORIGIN from **FOOT**.

top[1] noun **1** the highest or uppermost point, part, or surface. **2** a thing placed on, fitted to, or covering the upper part of something. **3** (**the top**) the highest or most important rank, level, or position. **4** the utmost degree: *she shouted at the top of her voice.* **5** chiefly Brit. the end that is furthest from the speaker or a point of reference. **6** an item of clothing covering the upper part of the body. **7** (**tops**) informal a particularly good person or thing. • adjective **1** highest in position, rank, or degree: *the top floor.* **2** chiefly Brit. furthest away from the speaker or a point of reference. • verb (**tops, topping, topped**) **1** be more, better, or taller than: *sales topped £500,000 last year.* **2** be at the highest place or rank in: *the album topped the charts for five weeks.* **3** provide something with a top or topping. **4** reach the top of a hill, slope, etc. **5** Brit. informal kill someone. • adverb (**tops**) informal at the most.
– PHRASES **get on top of** be more than someone can bear or cope with. **on top** in addition. **on top of 1** so as to cover. **2** very near to. **3** in command or control of. **4** in addition to. **on top of the world** informal very happy. **over the top 1** informal, chiefly Brit. to an excessive or exaggerated degree. **2** chiefly historical over the parapet of a trench and into battle. **top and tail** Brit. remove the top and bottom of a fruit or vegetable while preparing it as food. **top something off** finish something in a memorable way. **top something out** put the highest structural feature on a building. **top something up** chiefly Brit. **1** add to a number or amount to bring it up to a certain level. **2** fill up a partly full container.
– DERIVATIVES **topmost** adjective.
– ORIGIN Old English.

top[2] noun a toy with a rounded top and pointed base, that can be made to spin when turned round very quickly.
– ORIGIN Old English.

topaz noun **1** a colourless, yellow, or pale blue precious stone. **2** a dark yellow colour.
– ORIGIN Greek *topazos.*

top brass noun see **BRASS** (sense 5).

topcoat noun **1** an overcoat. **2** an outer coat of paint.

top dog noun informal a person who is successful or dominant in their field.

top drawer adjective informal of the highest quality or social class.

top dressing noun a layer of manure or fertilizer spread on the surface of soil or a lawn.

tope[1] verb old use or literary regularly drink too much alcohol.
– DERIVATIVES **toper** noun.
– ORIGIN perhaps from former *top* 'overbalance'.

tope[2] noun a small shark found chiefly in coastal waters.
– ORIGIN perhaps Cornish.

top flight noun the highest rank or level.

topgallant /top-gal-luhnt, tuh-gal-luhnt/ noun **1** the section of a square-rigged sailing ship's mast immediately above the topmast. **2** a sail set on a topgallant mast.

top hat noun a man's formal black hat with a high cylindrical crown.

top-heavy adjective **1** too heavy at the top and therefore likely to fall over or be unstable. **2** (of an organization) having too many senior executives compared to the number of ordinary workers.

top-hole adjective Brit. informal, dated excellent.

topiary /toh-pi-uh-ri/ noun (pl. **topiaries**) **1** the art of clipping bushes or trees into decorative shapes. **2** bushes or trees clipped into decorative shapes.
– ORIGIN Latin *topiarius* 'ornamental gardener'.

topic noun a subject of a piece of writing, speech, conversation, etc.
– ORIGIN from Greek *ta topika* 'matters concerning commonplaces' (the title of a work by Aristotle).

topical adjective **1** relating to or dealing with current affairs. **2** relating to a particular subject.
– DERIVATIVES **topicality** noun **topically** adverb.

topknot noun **1** a section of hair tied up on the top of the head. **2** a tuft or crest of hair or feathers on the head of an animal or bird.

topless adjective having the breasts uncovered.

top-level adjective of the highest level of importance.

topmast /top-mahst, top-muhst/ noun the second section of a square-rigged sailing ship's mast, immediately above the lower mast.

top-notch adjective informal of the highest quality.

topography /tuh-pog-ruh-fi/ noun (pl. **topographies**) **1** the arrangement of the physical features of an area. **2** a detailed representation of the physical features of an area on a map.
– DERIVATIVES **topographer** noun **topographic** adjective **topographical** adjective.
– ORIGIN from Greek *topos* 'place'.

topoi plural of **TOPOS**.

topology /tuh-pol-uh-ji/ noun (pl. **topologies**) **1** Mathematics the study of geometrical properties and spatial relations which remain unaffected by smooth changes in shape or size of figures. **2** the way in which the parts of something are interrelated or arranged.
– DERIVATIVES **topological** adjective.

toponym /top-uh-nim/ noun a place name, especially one derived from a physical feature of the area.

topos /top-oss/ noun (pl. **topoi** /top-oy/) a traditional theme in literature.
– ORIGIN Greek, 'place'.

topper noun informal a top hat.

topping noun a layer of food poured or spread over another food. • adjective Brit. informal, dated excellent.

topple verb **1** overbalance and fall over.

t

2 remove a government or leader from power.
– ORIGIN from TOP¹.

topsail /top-sayl, top-s'l/ **noun 1** a sail set on a ship's topmast. **2** a sail set lengthwise, above the gaff.

top secret adjective of the highest secrecy.

top-shelf adjective **1** Brit. (of a magazine or other publication) pornographic. **2** chiefly N. Amer. of a high quality; excellent.

topside noun **1** Brit. the outer side of a round of beef. **2** the upper part of a ship's side, above the waterline.

topsoil noun the top layer of soil.

topspin noun a fast forward spin given to a moving ball, often resulting in a curved path or a strong forward motion on rebounding.

topsy-turvy adjective & adverb **1** upside down. **2** in a state of confusion.
– ORIGIN apparently from TOP¹ and former *terve* 'overturn'.

top-up noun Brit. an additional amount or portion that restores something to a former level.

toque /tohk/ noun **1** a woman's small hat with a narrow, closely turned-up brim. **2** a tall white hat with a full crown, worn by chefs.
– ORIGIN French.

tor noun a steep hill or rocky peak.
– ORIGIN perhaps Celtic.

Torah /tor-uh, tor-ah/ noun (in Judaism) the law of God as revealed to Moses and recorded in the Pentateuch.
– ORIGIN Hebrew, 'instruction, doctrine, law'.

torc /tork/ (also **torque**) noun a neck ornament consisting of a band of twisted metal, worn by the ancient Gauls and Britons.
– ORIGIN Latin *torques* 'necklace, wreath'.

torch noun **1** Brit. a portable battery-powered electric lamp. **2** chiefly historical a piece of wood or cloth soaked in tallow and ignited. **3** a valuable quality, principle, or cause which needs to be protected and maintained: *the torch of freedom*. • verb informal set fire to something.
– PHRASES **carry a torch for** be in love with someone who does not return one's love.
– ORIGIN Latin *torqua, torques* 'necklace, wreath', from *torquere* 'to twist'.

torchlight noun the light of a torch or torches.
– DERIVATIVES **torchlit** adjective.

torch song noun a sad or sentimental romantic song.

tore past of TEAR¹.

toreador /to-ri-uh-dor/ noun a bullfighter, especially one on horseback.
– ORIGIN Spanish, from *toro* 'bull'.

torero /tuh-rair-oh/ noun (pl. **toreros**) a bullfighter, especially one on foot.
– ORIGIN Spanish.

tori plural of TORUS.

torment noun **1** great physical or mental suffering. **2** a cause of great suffering. • verb **1** make someone suffer greatly. **2** annoy or tease a person or animal in a cruel or unkind way.
– DERIVATIVES **tormentor** noun.
– ORIGIN Latin *tormentum* 'instrument of torture'.

torn past participle of TEAR¹.

tornado /tor-nay-doh/ noun (pl. **tornadoes** or

tornados) a storm with violently rotating winds having the appearance of a funnel-shaped cloud.
– ORIGIN perhaps from Spanish *tronada* 'thunderstorm'.

torpedo noun (pl. **torpedoes**) a long, narrow self-propelled underwater missile designed to be fired from a ship, submarine, or an aircraft. • verb (**torpedoes, torpedoing, torpedoed**) **1** attack a ship with a torpedo or torpedoes. **2** ruin a plan or project.
– ORIGIN first meaning an electric ray (fish): from Latin, 'numbness'.

torpedo boat noun a small, fast, light warship armed with torpedoes.

torpid adjective **1** mentally or physically inactive; lacking energy. **2** (of an animal) dormant, especially during hibernation.
– DERIVATIVES **torpidity** noun **torpidly** adverb.
– ORIGIN Latin *torpidus*.

torpor /tor-per/ noun the state of being inactive and lacking in energy.
– ORIGIN Latin.

torque /tork/ noun **1** a force that tends to cause rotation. **2** variant spelling of TORC.
– ORIGIN from Latin *torquere* 'to twist'.

torrent noun **1** a strong and fast-moving stream of water or other liquid. **2** an overwhelming outpouring of something: *a torrent of abuse*.
– ORIGIN French.

torrential adjective (of rain) falling rapidly and heavily.
– DERIVATIVES **torrentially** adverb.

torrid adjective **1** very hot and dry. **2** full of sexual passion. **3** Brit. full of difficulty: *he had a torrid time when he first joined the team*.
– DERIVATIVES **torridly** adverb.
– ORIGIN Latin *torridus*, from *torrere* 'scorch'.

torrid zone noun the hot central region of the earth bounded by the tropics of Cancer and Capricorn.

torsion /tor-sh'n/ noun the action of twisting or the state of being twisted, especially of one end of an object in relation to the other.
– DERIVATIVES **torsional** adjective.
– ORIGIN Latin, from *torquere* 'to twist'.

torsion bar noun a bar forming part of a vehicle suspension, twisting in response to the motion of the wheels and absorbing their vertical movement.

torso noun (pl. **torsos**) **1** the trunk of the human body. **2** a statue of a torso.
– ORIGIN Italian, 'stalk, stump'.

tort noun Law a wrongful act or a violation of a right (other than under contract) leading to legal liability.
– ORIGIN Latin *tortum* 'wrong, injustice'.

torte /tor-tuh, tort/ noun a sweet cake or tart.
– ORIGIN German.

tortellini /tor-tuhl-lee-ni/ plural noun small pieces of pasta stuffed with meat, cheese, vegetables, etc. and then rolled and formed into the shape of rings.
– ORIGIN Italian, from *tortello* 'small cake, fritter'.

tortilla /tor-tee-yuh/ noun **1** (in Mexican cookery) a thin, flat maize pancake. **2** (in Spanish cookery) an omelette.
– ORIGIN Spanish, 'little cake'.

tortoise /tor-tuhss/ noun a slow-moving land

t

reptile with a scaly or leathery domed shell into which it can draw its head and legs.
– ORIGIN Latin *tortuca*.

tortoiseshell noun **1** the semi-transparent mottled yellow and brown shell of certain turtles, used to make jewellery or ornaments. **2** a domestic cat with markings resembling tortoiseshell. **3** a butterfly with mottled orange, yellow, and black markings.

tortuous /tor-chuu-uhss, tor-tyuu-uhss/ adjective **1** full of twists and turns. **2** extremely long and complicated: *a tortuous legal battle*.
– DERIVATIVES **tortuosity** noun **tortuously** adverb **tortuousness** noun.
– ORIGIN Latin *tortuosus*, from *torquere* 'to twist'.

torture noun **1** the action of causing someone severe pain as a punishment or a means of persuasion. **2** great suffering or anxiety. •verb subject someone to torture.
– DERIVATIVES **torturer** noun.
– ORIGIN Latin *tortura* 'torment'.

torturous adjective involving or causing pain or suffering.

torus /tor-uhss/ noun (pl. **tori** /tor-y/ or **toruses**) **1** Geometry a surface or solid resembling a ring doughnut, formed by rotating a closed curve about a line which lies in the same plane but does not intersect it. **2** a ring-shaped object or chamber. **3** Architecture a large convex moulding with a semicircular cross section.
– ORIGIN Latin, 'swelling, round moulding'.

Tory noun (pl. **Tories**) **1** a member or supporter of the British Conservative Party. **2** a member of the English political party that opposed the exclusion of James II from the succession and later gave rise to the Conservative Party.
– DERIVATIVES **Toryism** noun.
– ORIGIN first referring to Irish peasants dispossessed by English settlers and living as robbers: probably from Irish *toraidhe* 'outlaw, highwayman'.

tosh noun Brit. informal rubbish; nonsense.
– ORIGIN unknown.

toss verb **1** throw something lightly or casually. **2** move from side to side or back and forth. **3** jerk one's head or hair sharply backwards. **4** throw a coin into the air so as to make a decision, based on which side of the coin faces uppermost when it lands. **5** shake or turn food in a liquid to coat it lightly. •noun an act of tossing something.
– PHRASES **not give** (or **care**) **a toss** Brit. informal not care at all. **toss something off 1** drink something rapidly or all at once. **2** produce something rapidly or without thought or effort.
– ORIGIN unknown.

tosser noun Brit. vulgar slang a stupid or disliked person.

toss-up noun informal **1** a situation in which any of two or more outcomes is equally possible. **2** the tossing of a coin to make a decision.

tot[1] noun **1** a very young child. **2** chiefly Brit. a small drink of spirits.
– ORIGIN unknown.

tot[2] verb (**tots, totting, totted**) (**tot something up**) chiefly Brit. **1** add up numbers or amounts. **2** accumulate something over time: *he totted up 180 League appearances*.

– ORIGIN from **TOTAL** or Latin *totum* 'the whole'.

total adjective **1** being the whole number or amount. **2** complete; absolute: *a total stranger*. •noun the whole number or amount of something. •verb (**totals, totalling, totalled**; US **totals, totaling, totaled**) **1** amount to a total number: *debts totalling £6,000*. **2** find the total of: *the scores were totalled*. **3** informal, chiefly N. Amer. damage something beyond repair.
– DERIVATIVES **totally** adverb.
– ORIGIN Latin *totalis*, from *totum* 'the whole'.

total eclipse noun an eclipse in which the whole of the disc of the sun or moon is obscured.

totalitarian /toh-tal-i-tair-i-uhn/ adjective (of a system of government) consisting of only one leader or party that has complete power and control and permits no opposition. •noun a person in favour of a totalitarian system of government.
– DERIVATIVES **totalitarianism** noun.

totality noun **1** the whole of something. **2** the time during which the sun or moon is totally obscured during an eclipse.

totalizator (or **totalisator** or **totalizer**) noun **1** a device showing the number and amount of bets staked on a race. **2** another term for **TOTE**[1].

totalize (or **totalise**) verb combine things into a total.

total war noun a war which is unrestricted in terms of the weapons used, the territory or combatants involved, or the objectives pursued.

tote[1] noun (**the tote**) informal a system of betting based on the use of the totalizator, in which winnings are calculated according to the amount staked rather than odds offered.

tote[2] verb informal carry something.
– ORIGIN probably dialect.

tote bag noun a large bag for carrying a number of items.

totem /toh-tuhm/ noun a natural object or animal believed by a particular society to have spiritual significance and adopted by it as an emblem.
– DERIVATIVES **totemic** /toh-tem-ik/ adjective.
– ORIGIN Ojibwa, a North American Indian language.

totem pole noun a pole on which totems are hung or on which the images of totems are carved.

totter verb **1** move in an unsteady way. **2** shake or rock as if about to collapse. **3** be insecure or on the point of failure. •noun an unsteady walk.
– DERIVATIVES **tottery** adjective.
– ORIGIN Dutch *touteren* 'to swing'.

totty noun Brit. informal sexually desirable girls or women.
– ORIGIN from **TOT**[1].

toucan /too-kuhn/ noun a tropical American fruit-eating bird with a massive bill and brightly coloured plumage.
– ORIGIN Tupi.

touch verb **1** come into or be in contact with someone or something. **2** bring one's hand or another part of one's body into contact with someone or something. **3** handle in order to harm or interfere with: *I didn't touch any of her*

stuff. **4** use or consume: *he barely touched the food on his plate.* **5** have an effect on someone or something. **6** produce feelings of affection, gratitude, or sympathy in: *she was touched by his loyalty.* **7** have any dealings with. **8** informal be comparable to in quality, skill, etc.: *no one can touch him at judo.* **9** (as adj. **touched**) informal slightly mad. • **noun 1** an act or way of touching. **2** the ability to be aware of something through physical contact, especially with the fingers. **3** a small amount. **4** a distinctive detail or feature. **5** a distinctive or skilful way of dealing with something: *a sure political touch.* **6** Rugby & Football the area beyond the sidelines, out of play.
– PHRASES **in touch 1** in or into communication. **2** having up-to-date knowledge about a particular subject, situation, etc. **lose touch 1** no longer be in communication. **2** stop being aware of or informed about a particular subject, situation, etc. **out of touch** lacking awareness of or up-to-date knowledge about a particular subject, situation, etc. **touch down 1** (of an aircraft or spacecraft) land. **2** Rugby touch the ground with the ball behind the opponents' goal line, scoring a try. **3** American Football score six points by being in possession of the ball behind the opponents' goal line. **touch someone for** informal ask someone for money as a loan or gift. **touch something off 1** cause something to ignite or explode by touching it with a match. **2** make something happen suddenly: *the incident touched off a global banking crisis.* **touch on** deal briefly with a subject. **touch someone up** Brit. informal caress someone sexually in a way that is not expected or welcome. **touch something up** make small improvements to something.
– DERIVATIVES **touchable** adjective.
– ORIGIN Old French *tochier.*

touch-and-go adjective (of an outcome) possible but very uncertain.

touchdown noun **1** the moment at which an aircraft touches down. **2** Rugby & American Football an act of scoring by touching the ball down behind the opponents' goal line.

touché /too-**shay**/ exclamation **1** used to acknowledge a good or clever point made at one's expense. **2** (in fencing) used to acknowledge a hit by one's opponent.
– ORIGIN French, 'touched'.

touching adjective arousing gratitude or sympathy; moving. • preposition concerning.
– DERIVATIVES **touchingly** adverb.

touch judge noun Rugby a linesman.

touchline noun Rugby & Football the boundary line on each side of the field.

touchpaper noun a strip of paper treated with nitre, for setting light to fireworks or gunpowder.

touch screen noun a display device which allows the user to interact with a computer by touching areas on the screen.

touchstone noun **1** a standard or criterion by which something may be judged. **2** a piece of stone formerly used for testing alloys of gold by observing the colour of the mark which they made on it.

touch-tone adjective (of a telephone) having buttons which produce different sounds when

pushed, rather than a dial.

touch-type verb type using all of one's fingers and without looking at the keys.

touchy adjective (**touchier, touchiest**) **1** quick to take offence; oversensitive. **2** (of a situation or issue) requiring careful handling.
– DERIVATIVES **touchily** adverb **touchiness** noun.
– ORIGIN perhaps an alteration of TETCHY, influenced by TOUCH.

touchy-feely adjective informal, often derogatory openly expressing affection or other emotions, especially through physical contact.

tough adjective **1** strong enough to withstand wear and tear. **2** able to endure hardship, difficulty, or pain. **3** involving difficulty or hardship: *the training has been quite tough.* **4** strict and uncompromising: *tough anti-smoking laws.* **5** (of a person) rough or violent. **6** used to express a lack of sympathy. • noun informal a rough and violent man.
– PHRASES **tough it out** informal endure a period of hardship or difficulty.
– DERIVATIVES **toughness** noun.
– ORIGIN Old English.

toughen verb make or become tough.

tough love noun the practice of helping a person by adopting a strict attitude towards them or requiring them to take responsibility for their actions.

tough-minded adjective realistic and unsentimental.

toupee /**too**-pay/ noun a small wig or artificial hairpiece worn to cover a bald spot.
– ORIGIN French, from Old French *toup* 'tuft'.

tour noun **1** a journey for pleasure in which several different places are visited. **2** a short trip made to view or inspect something. **3** a journey made by performers or a sports team, in which they perform or play in several different places. **4** (also **tour of duty**) a period of duty on military or diplomatic service. • verb make a tour of an area.
– ORIGIN Old French, 'turn'.

tour de force /toor duh **forss**/ noun (pl. **tours de force** pronunc. same) a performance or achievement that has been accomplished with great skill.
– ORIGIN French, 'feat of strength'.

tourer noun a car, caravan, or bicycle designed for touring.

Tourette's syndrome /tuu-**rets**/ noun a disorder of the nervous system characterized by involuntary muscle spasms and often the compulsive utterance of obscene words.
– ORIGIN named after the French neurologist Gilles de la *Tourette.*

tourism noun the business of organizing and running holidays and visits to places of interest.

tourist noun **1** a person who travels for pleasure. **2** Brit. a member of a touring sports team.
– DERIVATIVES **touristic** adjective.

tourist class noun the cheapest accommodation or seating in a ship, aircraft, or hotel.

touristy adjective informal, often derogatory appealing to or visited by many tourists.

tourmaline /**toor**-muh-lin, **toor**-muh-leen/

t

noun a brittle grey or black mineral used as a gemstone and in electrical devices.
– ORIGIN Sinhalese, 'carnelian'.

tournament noun 1 a series of contests between a number of competitors, competing for an overall prize. **2** a medieval sporting event in which knights jousted with blunted weapons for a prize.
– ORIGIN Old French *torneiement*.

tournedos /toor-nuh-doh/ **noun** (pl. same /toor-nuh-dohz/) a small, round, thick piece of meat cut from a fillet of beef.
– ORIGIN French, from *tourner* 'to turn' + *dos* 'back'.

tourney /toor-ni, ter-ni/ **noun** (pl. **tourneys**) a medieval joust.
– ORIGIN Old French *tornei*.

tourniquet /toor-ni-kay, tor-ni-kay/ **noun** a cord or tight bandage which is tied round a limb to stop a wound from bleeding.
– ORIGIN French.

tour operator noun a travel agent specializing in package holidays.

tousle /tow-z'l/ **verb** make a person's hair untidy.
– ORIGIN Germanic.

tout /towt/ **verb 1** attempt to sell something, typically by using a direct or persistent approach. **2** attempt to persuade people of the value or merit of someone or something: *she was touted as a potential Prime Minister.* **3** Brit. resell a ticket for a popular event at a price higher than the official one. •**noun** (also **ticket tout**) Brit. a person who buys up tickets for an event to resell them at a profit.
– ORIGIN Germanic.

tow¹ verb use a vehicle or boat to pull another vehicle or boat along. •**noun** an act of towing a vehicle or boat.
– PHRASES **in tow 1** (also **on tow**) being towed. **2** accompanying or following someone.
– DERIVATIVES **towable** adjective.
– ORIGIN Old English.

USAGE: On the confusion of tow and toe, see the note at TOE.

tow² noun short, coarse fibres of flax or hemp, used for making yarn.
– ORIGIN Old English.

towards (chiefly N. Amer. also **toward**) **preposition 1** in the direction of. **2** getting nearer to a time or aim. **3** in relation to. **4** contributing to the cost of.
– ORIGIN Old English.

tow bar noun a bar fitted to the back of a vehicle, used in towing a trailer or caravan.

towel noun a piece of thick absorbent cloth or paper used for drying. •**verb** (**towels, towelling, towelled**; US **towels, toweling, toweled**) dry someone or something with a towel.
– ORIGIN Old French *toaille*.

towelling (US **toweling**) **noun** thick absorbent cloth, typically cotton with uncut loops, used for towels and dressing gowns.

tower noun 1 a tall, narrow building, either free-standing or forming part of a building such as a church or castle. **2** a tall structure that houses machinery, operators, etc. **3** a tall structure used as a container or for storage.

•**verb** rise to or reach a great height.
– ORIGIN Old English.

tower block noun Brit. a tall modern building containing numerous floors of offices or flats.

towering adjective 1 very tall. **2** of very high quality: *a towering performance.* **3** very strong or intense: *a towering rage.*

tow-headed adjective having untidy or very light blonde hair.

towline noun a tow rope.

town noun 1 a settlement larger than a village and smaller than a city, with defined boundaries and local government. **2** the central part of a town or city, with its business or shopping area. **3** densely populated areas, especially as contrasted with the country or suburbs. **4** the permanent residents of a university town, as distinct from the students.
– PHRASES **go to town** informal do something thoroughly or enthusiastically. **on the town** informal enjoying the nightlife of a city or town.
– ORIGIN Old English, 'homestead, village'.

town car noun US a limousine.

town clerk noun 1 (in the UK, until 1974) the secretary and legal adviser of a town corporation. **2** N. Amer. a public official in charge of the records of a town.

town council noun (especially in the UK) the elected governing body in a town or district.
– DERIVATIVES **town councillor** noun.

town crier noun historical a person employed to make public announcements in the streets.

town hall noun a building housing local government offices.

town house noun 1 a tall, narrow traditional terrace house, generally having three or more floors. **2** a house in a town or city owned by a person who owns another property in the country.

townie noun informal, chiefly derogatory a person who lives in a town, especially as distinct from one who lives in the country.

townland noun (especially in Ireland) a territorial division of land.

town planning noun the planning and control of the construction, growth, and development of a town or other urban area.
– DERIVATIVES **town planner** noun.

townscape noun a view or picture of a town or city.

township noun 1 (in South Africa) a suburb or city occupied chiefly by black people, formerly officially designated for black occupation by apartheid laws. **2** S. African a new area being developed for residential or industrial use by speculators. **3** N. Amer. a division of a county that has certain powers of local administration. **4** Austral./NZ a small town.
– ORIGIN Old English.

townsman (or **townswoman**) **noun** (pl. **townsmen** or **townswomen**) a person living in a particular town or city.

townspeople (also **townsfolk**) **plural noun** the people living in a particular town or city.

towpath noun a path beside a river or canal, originally used as a pathway for horses towing barges.

tow rope noun a rope, cable, etc. used in

towing.

toxaemia /tok-see-mi-uh/ (US **toxemia**) noun
1 blood poisoning by toxins from a local
bacterial infection. 2 a condition in pregnancy
characterized especially by high blood
pressure; pre-eclampsia.
– ORIGIN from Latin *toxicum* 'poison'.

toxic adjective 1 poisonous. 2 relating to or
caused by poison.
– DERIVATIVES **toxicity** noun.
– ORIGIN from Latin *toxicum* 'poison'.

toxicant noun a toxic substance introduced
into the environment, e.g. a pesticide.
– ORIGIN variant of **INTOXICANT**.

toxicology /tok-si-kol-uh-ji/ noun the branch
of science concerned with the nature, effects,
and detection of poisons.
– DERIVATIVES **toxicological** adjective **toxicologist**
noun.

toxic shock syndrome noun acute blood
poisoning in women, typically caused by
bacterial infection from a tampon that has
been kept in the body for too long.

toxin noun a poison produced by a
microorganism or other organism, to which
the body reacts by producing antibodies.

toxocariasis /tok-soh-kuh-ry-uh-siss/ noun
infection of a human with the larvae of a
worm which is a parasite of dogs, cats, and
other animals, causing illness and a risk of
blindness.
– ORIGIN from *toxocara*, the name of the worm.

toxoplasmosis /tok-soh-plaz-moh-siss/ noun
a disease caused by a parasite, transmitted
chiefly through undercooked meat, soil, or in
cat faeces.
– ORIGIN from *toxoplasma*, the name of the
parasite.

toy noun 1 an object for a child to play with. 2 a
gadget or machine that provides amusement
for an adult. ● adjective (of a breed or variety of
dog) much smaller than is normal for the
breed. ● verb (**toy with**) 1 consider an idea
casually or indecisively. 2 handle absent-
mindedly or nervously: *she was toying with a
loose strand of hair.* 3 eat or drink something in
an unenthusiastic way.
– DERIVATIVES **toylike** adjective.
– ORIGIN unknown.

toy boy noun Brit. informal a male lover who is
much younger than his partner.

toytown adjective resembling a quaint or
miniature replica of something.

trace¹ verb 1 find someone or something by
careful investigation. 2 find or describe the
origin or development: *the book traces his
flying career with the RAF.* 3 follow the course
or position of something with one's eye, mind,
or finger. 4 copy a drawing, map, or design by
drawing over its lines on a piece of
transparent paper placed on top of it. 5 draw a
pattern or outline. ● noun 1 a mark or other
indication of the existence or passing of
something: *the aircraft disappeared without
trace.* 2 a very small quantity. 3 a barely
noticeable indication: *a trace of a smile touched
his lips.* 4 a line or pattern on a paper or screen
corresponding to something which is being
recorded or measured. 5 a procedure to trace
something, such as the place from which a

telephone call was made.
– DERIVATIVES **traceable** adjective.
– ORIGIN Old French *tracier*.

trace² noun each of the two side straps, chains,
or ropes by which a horse is attached to a
vehicle that it is pulling.
– PHRASES **kick over the traces** Brit. refuse to
accept discipline or control; start behaving
badly.
– ORIGIN Old French *trais*.

trace element noun a chemical element
present or required only in minute amounts.

tracer noun 1 a bullet or shell whose course is
made visible by a trail of flames or smoke,
used to assist in aiming. 2 a substance that is
introduced into the body and whose
subsequent progress can be followed from its
colour, radioactivity, or other distinctive
property.

tracery noun (pl. **traceries**) 1 a decorative
design of holes and outlines in stone,
especially in the upper part of a window. 2 a
delicate branching pattern.
– DERIVATIVES **traceried** adjective.

trachea /truh-kee-uh/ noun (pl. **tracheae**
/truh-kee-ee/ or **tracheas**) the tube conveying
air between the larynx and the lungs; the
windpipe.
– DERIVATIVES **tracheal** /tray-ki-uhl/ adjective.
– ORIGIN from Greek *trakheia artēria* 'rough
artery'.

tracheotomy /tra-ki-ot-uh-mi/ (also
tracheostomy /tra-ki-oss-tuh-mi/) noun (pl.
tracheotomies) a surgical cut in the windpipe,
made to enable someone to breathe when the
windpipe is blocked.

trachoma /truh-koh-muh/ noun a contagious
infection transmitted by a bacterium and
causing inflammation of the inner surface of
the eyelids.
– ORIGIN Greek *trakhōma* 'roughness'.

tracing noun 1 a copy of a drawing, map, etc.
made by tracing. 2 a faint or delicate mark or
pattern.

track noun 1 a rough path or minor road. 2 a
prepared course or circuit for racing. 3 a mark
or line of marks left by a person, animal, or
vehicle in passing. 4 a continuous line of rails
on a railway. 5 a section of a record, compact
disc, or cassette tape containing one song or
piece of music. 6 a strip or rail along which
something such as a curtain may be moved. 7 a
jointed metal band around the wheels of a
heavy vehicle. 8 the transverse distance
between a vehicle's wheels. ● verb 1 follow the
course or movements of: *he tracked the flight
of two military aircraft.* 2 (**track someone/thing
down**) find someone or something after a
thorough or difficult search. 3 follow a
particular course. 4 (of a film or television
camera) move in relation to the subject being
filmed.
– PHRASES **keep** (or **lose**) **track of** keep (or fail
to keep) fully aware of or informed about.
make tracks informal leave. **on the right** (or
wrong) **track** following a course likely to
result in success (or failure). **stop** (or **be
stopped**) **in one's tracks** informal come (or be
brought) to a sudden and complete halt. **the
wrong side of the tracks** informal a poor or less

prestigious part of town. [with reference to the railway tracks of American towns, once serving as a line of demarcation between rich and poor areas.]
– DERIVATIVES **tracker** noun **trackless** adjective.
– ORIGIN Old French *trac*.

trackball noun a small ball set in a holder that can be rotated by hand to move a cursor on a computer screen.

trackbed noun the foundation structure on which railway tracks are laid.

track events plural noun athletic events that take place on a running track.

tracking noun **1** Electronics the maintenance of a constant difference in frequency between connected circuits or components. **2** the alignment of the wheels of a vehicle.

track record noun the past achievements or performance of a person, organization, or product.

tracksuit noun a warm, loose-fitting outfit consisting of a sweatshirt and trousers.

trackway noun a path formed by the repeated treading of people or animals.

tract¹ noun **1** a large area of land. **2** a system of organs or tubes in the body that are connected and that have a particular purpose: *the digestive tract.*
– ORIGIN Latin *tractus* 'drawing, draught'.

tract² noun a pamphlet containing a short piece of writing on a political or religious topic.
– ORIGIN apparently an abbreviation of Latin *tractatus* 'treatise'.

tractable adjective **1** easy to control or influence. **2** (of a situation or problem) easy to deal with.
– DERIVATIVES **tractability** noun.
– ORIGIN Latin *tractabilis*.

traction noun **1** the action of pulling a thing along a surface. **2** the power used for pulling. **3** the applying of a sustained pull on a limb or muscle, especially to maintain the position of a fractured bone or to correct a deformity. **4** the grip of a tyre on a road or a wheel on a rail.
– ORIGIN Latin, from *trahere* 'to pull'.

traction engine noun a steam- or diesel-powered road vehicle used (especially in the past) for pulling very heavy loads.

tractor noun a powerful motor vehicle with large rear wheels, used chiefly on farms for pulling equipment and trailers.
– ORIGIN Latin, from *trahere* 'to pull'.

tractor trailer noun N. Amer. an articulated lorry.

trad adjective informal (especially of music) traditional.

trade noun **1** the buying and selling of goods or services. **2** a commercial activity of a particular kind: *the tourist trade.* **3** a job requiring manual skills and special training. **4** (**the trade**) (treated as sing. or pl.) the people engaged in a particular area of business. **5** a trade wind. •verb **1** buy and sell goods or services; operate as a business or company. **2** buy or sell a particular item or product. **3** exchange something for something else, typically as a commercial transaction. **4** (**trade something in**) exchange a used article in part

payment for another. **5** (**trade on**) take advantage of: *the government is trading on fears of inflation*
– DERIVATIVES **tradable** (or **tradeable**) adjective.
– ORIGIN German, 'track'.

trade deficit noun the amount by which the cost of a country's imports exceeds the value of its exports.

trademark noun **1** a symbol, word, or words chosen to represent a company or product, legally registered or established by use. **2** a distinctive characteristic or object: *the murder had all the trademarks of a Mafia hit.*

trade name noun **1** a name that has the status of a trademark. **2** a name by which something is known in a particular trade or profession.

trade-off noun a balance achieved between two desirable but conflicting features; a compromise.

trade plates plural noun Brit. temporary number plates used by car dealers or manufacturers on unlicensed cars.

trader noun **1** a person who trades goods, currency, or shares. **2** a merchant ship.

tradescantia /trad-i-**skan**-ti-uh/ noun an American plant with triangular flowers.
– ORIGIN named in honour of the English botanist John *Tradescant*.

tradesman noun (pl. **tradesmen**) **1** a person who owns a small shop. **2** a person engaged in a skilled trade.

trade surplus noun the amount by which the value of a country's exports exceeds the cost of its imports.

trade union (Brit. also **trades union**) noun an organized association of workers formed to protect and further their rights and interests.
– DERIVATIVES **trade unionism** noun **trade unionist** noun.

trade wind noun a wind blowing steadily towards the equator from the north-east in the northern hemisphere or from the south-east in the southern hemisphere, especially at sea.
– ORIGIN from the former phrase *blow trade* 'blow steadily'.

trading card noun each of a set of picture cards that are collected and traded, especially by children.

trading estate noun Brit. a specially designed industrial and commercial area.

trading post noun a store or small settlement established for trading in a remote place.

tradition noun **1** the passing on of customs or beliefs from generation to generation. **2** a long-established custom or belief passed on in this way. **3** an artistic or literary method or style established by an artist, writer, or movement, and subsequently followed by other people.
– ORIGIN Latin.

traditional adjective relating to or following customs or beliefs that have been passed from generation to generation: *traditional Irish music.*
– DERIVATIVES **traditionally** adverb.

traditionalism noun the support of tradition, especially so as to resist change.
– DERIVATIVES **traditionalist** noun & adjective.

traduce /truh-**dyooss**/ verb say unpleasant or

untrue things about someone.
– ORIGIN Latin *traducere* 'lead in front of others, expose to ridicule'.

traffic noun **1** vehicles moving on public roads. **2** the movement of ships or aircraft. **3** the commercial transportation of goods or passengers. **4** the messages or signals sent through a communications system. **5** the action of trading in something illegal. •verb (**traffics**, **trafficking**, **trafficked**) deal or trade in something illegal.
– DERIVATIVES **trafficker** noun.
– ORIGIN from French *traffique*, Spanish *tráfico*, or Italian *traffico*.

traffic calming noun the deliberate slowing of traffic in residential areas, by building road humps or other obstructions.

traffic island noun a small raised area in the middle of a road which provides a safe place for pedestrians to stand.

traffic jam noun a line or lines of traffic at or virtually at a standstill.

traffic lights (also **traffic light**) plural noun a set of automatically operated coloured lights for controlling traffic.

traffic warden noun Brit. an official who locates and reports on vehicles breaking parking regulations.

tragedian /truh-jee-di-uhn/ noun **1** (fem. **tragedienne** /truh-jee-di-en/) an actor who plays tragic roles. **2** a writer of tragedies.

tragedy noun (pl. **tragedies**) **1** an event causing great suffering and distress. **2** a serious play with an unhappy ending, especially one concerning the downfall of the main character.
– ORIGIN Greek *tragōidia*.

tragic adjective **1** extremely distressing or sad. **2** relating to tragedy in a literary work.
– DERIVATIVES **tragically** adverb.

tragicomedy noun (pl. **tragicomedies**) a play or novel containing elements of both comedy and tragedy.
– DERIVATIVES **tragicomic** adjective.

trail noun **1** a mark or a series of signs left behind by the passage of someone or something. **2** a track or scent used in following someone or hunting an animal. **3** a beaten path through rough country. **4** a route planned or followed for a particular purpose: *the tourist trail*. **5** a long, thin part stretching behind or hanging down from something. •verb **1** draw or be drawn along behind someone or something: *her robe trailed along the ground*. **2** follow someone's or something's trail. **3** walk or move slowly or wearily. **4** (**trail away/off**) (of a person's voice) fade gradually before stopping. **5** be losing to an opponent in a contest. **6** (of a plant) grow along the ground or so as to hang down. **7** give advance publicity to a film, broadcast, etc. with a trailer.
– ORIGIN from Old French *traillier* 'to tow' or German *treilen* 'haul a boat'.

trailblazer noun **1** a person who is the first to do something. **2** a person who makes a new track through wild country.
– DERIVATIVES **trailblazing** noun & adjective.

trailer noun **1** an unpowered vehicle towed by another. **2** the rear section of an articulated lorry. **3** an extract from a film or television programme used for advance advertising. **4** N. Amer. a caravan.

trailer trash noun US offensive poor, lower-class white people, typically regarded as living in mobile homes.

trailer truck noun US an articulated lorry.

trailing edge noun the rear edge of a moving object, especially an aerofoil.

trail mix noun a mixture of dried fruit and nuts eaten as a snack.

train verb **1** teach a person or animal a particular skill or type of behaviour through regular practice and instruction. **2** be taught in such a way: *he trained as a plumber*. **3** make or become physically fit through a course of exercise and diet. **4** (**train something on**) point something at: *he trained his gun on the side door*. **5** make a plant grow in a particular direction or shape. •noun **1** a series of railway carriages or wagons moved as a unit by a locomotive or by integral motors. **2** a number of vehicles or animals carrying loads moving in a line. **3** a series of connected events or thoughts. **4** a long piece of trailing material attached to the back of a formal dress or robe. **5** a group of attendants accompanying an important person.
– PHRASES **in train** in progress.
– DERIVATIVES **trainable** adjective **training** noun **trainload** noun.
– ORIGIN from Old French *trahiner*.

trainee noun a person undergoing training for a particular job or profession.
– DERIVATIVES **traineeship** noun.

trainer noun **1** a person who trains people or animals. **2** (also **training shoe**) Brit. a soft shoe, suitable for sports or casual wear.

training college noun (in the UK) a college where people, especially future teachers, are trained.

trainspotter noun Brit. **1** a person who collects locomotive numbers as a hobby. **2** often derogatory a person who has an obsessive interest in every detail of a hobby or subject.
– DERIVATIVES **trainspotting** noun.

traipse verb walk or move wearily or reluctantly. •noun a boring or tiring walk.
– ORIGIN unknown.

trait /trayt, tray/ noun **1** a distinguishing quality or characteristic. **2** a genetically determined characteristic.
– ORIGIN French.

traitor noun a person who betrays their country, a cause, etc.
– DERIVATIVES **traitorous** adjective.
– ORIGIN Old French *traitour*.

trajectory /truh-jek-tuh-ri/ noun (pl. **trajectories**) the path followed by a moving object under the action of given forces.
– ORIGIN Latin *trajectoria*.

tram (also **tramcar**) noun Brit. a passenger vehicle powered by electricity conveyed by overhead cables, and running on rails laid in a public road.
– ORIGIN German and Dutch *trame* 'beam, barrow shaft'; the word formerly referred to a barrow or cart used in coal mines, later the tracks on which such carts ran.

tramlines plural noun **1** rails for a tram. **2** a pair of parallel lines at the sides of a tennis court or at the sides or back of a badminton court.

trammel verb (trammels, trammelling, trammelled; US trammels, trammeling, trammeled) restrict someone's freedom of action. ● plural noun (**trammels**) literary things that restrict someone's freedom of action.
– ORIGIN Old French *tramail*.

tramontana /tra-mon-**tah**-nuh/ noun a cold north wind blowing in Italy or the adjoining regions of the Adriatic and Mediterranean.
– ORIGIN Italian, 'north wind, Pole Star'.

tramp verb **1** walk heavily or noisily. **2** walk wearily or reluctantly over a long distance. ● noun **1** a homeless person who travels around and lives by begging or doing casual work. **2** the sound of heavy steps. **3** a long walk. **4** a cargo ship running between many different ports rather than sailing a fixed route. **5** N. Amer. informal a promiscuous woman.
– DERIVATIVES **tramper** noun **trampy** adjective (informal).
– ORIGIN probably German.

trample verb **1** tread on something and crush it. **2** (**trample on/over**) treat someone or something with disrespect or contempt: *a statesman ought not to trample on the opinions of his advisers.*
– ORIGIN from **TRAMP**.

trampoline noun a strong fabric sheet connected by springs to a frame, used as a springboard and landing area in doing acrobatic or gymnastic exercises.
– DERIVATIVES **trampolining** noun.
– ORIGIN Italian *trampolino*.

tramway noun Brit. **1** a set of rails for a tram. **2** a tram system.

trance /rhymes with dance/ noun **1** a half-conscious state in which someone does not respond to external stimuli, typically as brought about by hypnosis. **2** a state in which someone is not paying attention to what is happening around them. **3** (also **trance music**) a type of electronic dance music characterized by hypnotic rhythms.
– ORIGIN from Old French *transir* 'depart, fall into a trance'.

tranche /rhymes with branch/ noun any of the parts into which something, especially an amount of money or an issue of shares in a company, is divided.
– ORIGIN Old French, 'slice'.

tranny (also **trannie**) noun (pl. **trannies**) informal, chiefly Brit. a transistor radio.

tranquil adjective free from disturbance; calm.
– DERIVATIVES **tranquillity** (also **tranquility**) noun **tranquilly** adverb.
– ORIGIN Latin *tranquillus*.

tranquillize (or **tranquillise**; US **tranquilize**) verb make a person or animal calm or unconscious, especially by giving them a sedative drug.

tranquillizer (or **tranquilliser**; US **tranquilizer**) noun a drug taken to reduce tension or anxiety.

trans- prefix **1** across; beyond: *transcontinental.* **2** on or to the other side of: *transatlantic.* **3** into another state or place: *translate.*
– ORIGIN from Latin *trans* 'across'.

transact verb do business with a person or organization.

transaction noun **1** an act of buying or selling something. **2** the action of carrying out business.
– DERIVATIVES **transactional** adjective.
– ORIGIN Latin.

transatlantic adjective **1** crossing the Atlantic. **2** concerning countries on both sides of the Atlantic, typically Britain and the US. **3** relating to or situated on the other side of the Atlantic.

transaxle noun an integral driving axle and differential gear in a motor vehicle.

transceiver noun a combined radio transmitter and receiver.

transcend verb **1** be or go beyond the range or limits of: *an issue transcending party politics.* **2** be better than a person or achievement.
– ORIGIN Latin *transcendere*.

transcendent adjective **1** going beyond normal or physical human experience. **2** (of God) existing apart from and not limited by the physical universe.
– DERIVATIVES **transcendence** noun **transcendently** adverb.

transcendental adjective relating to a spiritual area that is beyond human experience or knowledge.
– DERIVATIVES **transcendentally** adverb.

Transcendental Meditation noun (trademark in the US) a technique for relaxation and promoting harmony by meditation and repetition of a mantra.

transcontinental adjective crossing or extending across a continent or continents.

transcribe verb **1** put thoughts, speech, or data into written or printed form. **2** make a copy of something, especially in another alphabet or language. **3** arrange a piece of music for a different instrument or voice.
– DERIVATIVES **transcriber** noun.
– ORIGIN Latin *transcribere*.

transcript noun a written or printed version of material that was originally spoken or presented in another form.
– ORIGIN Latin *transcriptum*.

transcription noun **1** a written or printed version of something; a transcript. **2** the action of transcribing something. **3** a piece of music transcribed for a different instrument or voice.

transdermal /tranz-**der**-m'l/ adjective relating to the application of a medicine or drug through the skin, especially by means of an adhesive patch.

transducer /tranz-**dyoo**-ser/ noun a device that converts variations in a physical quantity (such as pressure or brightness) into an electrical signal, or vice versa.
– DERIVATIVES **transduction** noun.
– ORIGIN from Latin *transducere* 'lead across'.

transect technical verb cut across or make a transverse section in something. ● noun a straight line or narrow cross section through an object or across the earth's surface, along which observations or measurements are made.
– DERIVATIVES **transection** noun.
– ORIGIN from **TRANS-** + Latin *secare* 'divide by cutting'.

transept /tran-sept, trahn-sept/ noun (in a cross-shaped church) either of the two parts extending at right angles from the nave.
– ORIGIN Latin *transeptum*.

transexual noun & adjective variant spelling of TRANSSEXUAL.

transfer verb /trans-fer/ (transfers, transferring, transferred) 1 move from one place to another: *transfer the rice to a saucepan*. 2 move to another department, job, team, etc. 3 change to another place, route, or means of transport during a journey. 4 officially pass property, or a right or responsibility, to another person. 5 (as adj. transferred) (of the sense of a word or phrase) changed by extension or metaphor. • noun /trans-fer/ 1 an act of transferring someone or something. 2 Brit. a small coloured picture or design on paper, which can be transferred to another surface by being pressed or heated.
– DERIVATIVES **transferable** adjective **transferee** noun **transferor** noun (chiefly Law) **transferral** noun.
– ORIGIN Latin *transferre*.

transference noun 1 the action of transferring something. 2 Psychoanalysis the redirection to a substitute, usually a therapist, of emotions originally felt in childhood.

transfiguration noun 1 a complete transformation into a more beautiful or spiritual state. 2 (the Transfiguration) Jesus's appearance in glory to three of his disciples (in the gospels of Matthew and Mark).

transfigure verb (be transfigured) be transformed into something more beautiful or spiritual.
– ORIGIN Latin *transfigurare*.

transfix verb 1 make someone motionless with horror, wonder, or astonishment. 2 pierce someone or something with a sharp implement.
– ORIGIN Latin *transfigere* 'pierce through'.

transform verb 1 change or be changed in appearance, form, or nature: *motorways have transformed our lives*. 2 change the voltage of an electric current.
– DERIVATIVES **transformative** adjective.

transformation noun a marked change in nature, form, or appearance.
– DERIVATIVES **transformational** adjective.

transformer noun a device for changing the voltage of an alternating current.

transfusion noun 1 the medical process of transferring blood or its components from one person or animal to another. 2 a transfer of something vital, especially money: *the country's economy will receive a transfusion of at least $1 billion*.
– DERIVATIVES **transfuse** verb.
– ORIGIN from Latin *transfundere* 'pour from one container to another'.

transgender (also transgendered) adjective transsexual.

transgenic /tranz-jen-ik/ adjective containing genetic material into which DNA from a different organism has been artificially added.
– DERIVATIVES **transgene** noun **transgenics** plural noun.

transgress verb go beyond the limits of what is morally, socially, or legally acceptable.
– DERIVATIVES **transgression** noun **transgressive** adjective **transgressor** noun.
– ORIGIN Latin *transgredi* 'step across'.

tranship verb variant spelling of TRANS-SHIP.

transhumance /tranz-hyoo-muhnss/ noun the action or practice of moving livestock seasonally from one grazing ground to another.
– DERIVATIVES **transhumant** adjective.
– ORIGIN from Latin *trans-* 'across' + *humus* 'ground'.

transient /tran-zi-uhnt/ adjective 1 lasting only for a short time. 2 staying or working in a place for a short time only. • noun a person who stays or works in a place for a short time.
– DERIVATIVES **transience** noun **transiency** noun **transiently** adverb.
– ORIGIN from Latin *transire* 'go across'.

transistor noun 1 a semiconductor device with three connections, able to amplify or rectify an electric current. 2 (also transistor radio) a portable radio using circuits containing transistors.
– DERIVATIVES **transistorize** (or transistorise) verb.
– ORIGIN from TRANSFER + RESISTOR.

transit noun 1 the carrying of people or things from one place to another. 2 an act of passing through or across a place. • verb (transits, transiting, transited) pass across or through an area.
– ORIGIN Latin *transitus*.

transition noun the process or a period of changing from one state or condition to another: *the rituals marked the transition from boyhood to manhood*.
– DERIVATIVES **transitional** adjective.

transition metal noun any of the set of metallic chemical elements occupying the central block in the periodic table, e.g. iron, manganese, chromium, and copper.

transition series noun Chemistry the set of transition metals in the periodic table.

transitive /tran-zi-tiv/ adjective (of a verb) able to take a direct object, e.g. *saw* in *he saw the donkey*. The opposite of INTRANSITIVE.
– DERIVATIVES **transitively** adverb **transitivity** noun.
– ORIGIN Latin *transitivus*.

transitory /tran-zi-tuh-ri/ adjective lasting for a short time; not permanent.
– DERIVATIVES **transitorily** adverb **transitoriness** noun.
– ORIGIN Latin *transitorius*.

translate verb 1 express the sense of words or writing in another language. 2 be expressed or be able to be expressed in another language. 3 (translate into) convert or be converted into another form: *they were unable to translate their concert success into record sales*.
– DERIVATIVES **translatable** adjective **translator** noun.
– ORIGIN from Latin *translatus* 'carried across'.

translation noun 1 the action of translating something. 2 a word or written work that is translated into another language.

transliterate verb write a letter or word using the closest corresponding letters of a different alphabet or language.
– DERIVATIVES **transliteration** noun.
– ORIGIN from TRANS- + Latin *littera* 'letter'.

t

translocate verb chiefly technical move from one place to another.
- DERIVATIVES **translocation** noun.

translucent /tranz-**loo**-suhnt/ adjective allowing light to pass through partially; semi-transparent.
- DERIVATIVES **translucence** noun **translucency** noun.
- ORIGIN from Latin *translucere* 'shine through'.

transmigration noun (in some beliefs) the passing of a person's soul after their death into another body.

transmissible adjective (especially of a disease, virus, etc.) able to be transmitted.
- DERIVATIVES **transmissibility** noun.

transmission noun **1** the action of passing something from one person or place to another. **2** a programme or signal that is transmitted. **3** the mechanism by which power is transmitted from an engine to the axle in a motor vehicle.

transmit verb (**transmits, transmitting, transmitted**) **1** pass from one place or person to another: *the disease is transmitted by mosquitoes.* **2** broadcast or send out an electrical signal or a radio or television programme. **3** allow heat, light, or other energy to pass through a medium.
- DERIVATIVES **transmittal** noun.
- ORIGIN Latin *transmittere*.

transmitter noun a device used to produce and transmit electromagnetic waves carrying messages or signals, especially those of radio or television.

transmogrify /tranz-**mog**-ri-fy/ verb (**transmogrifies, transmogrifying, transmogrified**) chiefly humorous change into someone or something completely different: *alchemists strove to transmogrify base metals into gold.*
- DERIVATIVES **transmogrification** noun.
- ORIGIN unknown.

transmute /tranz-**myoot**/ verb change in form, nature, or substance.
- DERIVATIVES **transmutation** noun.
- ORIGIN Latin *transmutare*.

transnational adjective extending or operating across national boundaries. •noun a multinational company.

transoceanic adjective crossing an ocean.

transom /tran-suhm/ noun **1** the flat surface forming the stern of a boat. **2** a strengthening crossbar above a window or door.
- ORIGIN Old French *traversin*.

transonic adjective referring to speeds close to that of sound.

transparency noun (pl. **transparencies**) **1** the condition of being transparent. **2** a positive transparent photograph printed on plastic or glass, and viewed using a slide projector.

transparent /tranz-**par**-ruhnt, tranz-**pair**-uhnt/ adjective **1** allowing light to pass through so that objects behind can be distinctly seen. **2** obvious or evident: *the company's transparent attempt to woo back women customers.*
- DERIVATIVES **transparently** adverb.
- ORIGIN from Latin *transparere* 'shine through'.

transpersonal adjective relating to states of consciousness beyond the limits of personal identity.

transpire verb **1** come to be known or prove to be the case. **2** happen; occur. **3** Botany (of a plant or leaf) give off water vapour through the stomata (tiny pores).
- DERIVATIVES **transpiration** noun.
- ORIGIN Latin *transpirare*.

USAGE: The standard sense of **transpire** is 'come to be known' (*it transpired that he had bought a house*). From this, a newer sense developed, meaning 'happen' (*I'm going to find out what transpired*). This sense, although very common, is sometimes criticized for being an unnecessarily long word used where **occur** or **happen** would do just as well.

transplant verb /tranz-**plahnt**/ **1** transfer someone or something to another place or situation. **2** take living tissue or an organ and implant it in another part of the body or in another body. •noun /**tranz**-plahnt/ **1** an operation in which an organ or tissue is transplanted. **2** a person or thing that has been transferred to another place or situation.
- DERIVATIVES **transplantable** adjective **transplantation** noun.
- ORIGIN Latin *transplantare*.

transponder /tran-**spon**-der/ noun a device for receiving a radio signal and automatically transmitting a different signal.
- ORIGIN from **TRANSMIT** and **RESPOND**.

transport verb /tran-**sport**/ **1** carry people or goods from one place to another by means of a vehicle, aircraft, or ship. **2** (**be transported**) be overwhelmed with a strong emotion: *she was transported with pleasure.* **3** historical send a convict to a distant country as a punishment. •noun /**tran**-sport/ **1** a system or means of transporting people or goods. **2** the action of transporting people or goods. **3** a large vehicle, ship, or aircraft for carrying troops or stores. **4** (**transports**) overwhelmingly strong emotions.
- DERIVATIVES **transportability** noun **transportable** adjective **transportation** noun.
- ORIGIN Latin *transportare* 'carry across'.

transport cafe noun Brit. a roadside cafe for drivers of haulage vehicles.

transporter noun a large vehicle used to carry heavy objects.

transpose verb **1** cause two or more things to exchange places. **2** transfer to a different place or situation: *the play is transposed to America.* **3** write or play music in a different key from the original.
- DERIVATIVES **transposable** adjective **transposition** noun.
- ORIGIN Old French *transposer*.

transsexual (also **transexual**) noun a person born with the physical characteristics of one sex who emotionally and psychologically feels that they belong to the opposite sex. •adjective relating to a transsexual person.
- DERIVATIVES **transsexualism** noun **transsexuality** noun.

trans-ship (also **tranship**) verb transfer cargo from one ship or other form of transport to another.

– DERIVATIVES **trans-shipment** noun.

transubstantiation /tran-sub-stan-shi-ay-sh'n/ noun (in Christian belief) the doctrine that when the bread and wine of Holy Communion have been consecrated they are converted into the body and blood of Jesus.
– ORIGIN from Latin *transubstantiare* 'to change in substance'.

transuranic /tranz-yuu-**ran**-ik/ adjective (of a chemical element) having a higher atomic number than uranium (92).

transverse adjective situated or extending across something.
– DERIVATIVES **transversely** adverb.
– ORIGIN from Latin *transvertere* 'turn across'.

transvestite noun a person, typically a man, who gains pleasure from dressing in clothes usually worn by the opposite sex.
– DERIVATIVES **transvestism** noun.
– ORIGIN German *Transvestit*.

trap noun **1** a device, pit, or enclosure designed to catch and hold animals. **2** an unpleasant situation from which it is difficult to escape. **3** a trick that causes someone to do something that they do not intend or that will harm them: *the police set a trap for two local gangs.* **4** a container or device used to collect a specified thing. **5** a curve in the waste pipe from a bath, basin, or toilet that is always full of liquid to prevent the upward passage of gases. **6** a light, two-wheeled carriage pulled by a horse or pony. **7** the compartment from which a greyhound is released at the start of a race. **8** a device for hurling an object such as a clay pigeon into the air. **9** informal a person's mouth. • verb (**traps, trapping, trapped**) **1** catch or hold in a trap: *twenty workers were trapped by the flames.* **2** trick someone into doing something.
– ORIGIN Old English.

trapdoor noun a hinged or removable panel in a floor, ceiling, or roof.

trapeze noun (also **flying trapeze**) a horizontal bar hanging by two ropes high above the ground, used by acrobats in a circus.
– ORIGIN Latin *trapezium*.

trapezium /truh-pee-zi-uhm/ noun (pl. **trapezia** /truh-**pee**-zi-uh/ or **trapeziums**) Geometry **1** Brit. a quadrilateral with one pair of sides parallel. **2** N. Amer. a quadrilateral with no sides parallel.
– ORIGIN Latin.

trapezius /truh-**pee**-zi-uhss/ noun (pl. **trapezii** /truh-**pee**-zi-I/) either of a pair of large triangular muscles extending over the back of the neck and shoulders and moving the head and shoulder blade.
– ORIGIN Latin.

trapezoid /truh-**pee**-zoyd, tra-pi-zoyd/ noun Geometry **1** Brit. a quadrilateral with no sides parallel. **2** N. Amer. a quadrilateral with one pair of sides parallel.
– DERIVATIVES **trapezoidal** adjective.

trapper noun a person who traps wild animals, especially for their fur.

trappings plural noun **1** the signs or objects associated with a particular situation or role: *I had the trappings of success.* **2** a horse's ornamental harness.
– ORIGIN Old French *drap* 'drape'.

Trappist noun a monk belonging to a branch of

the Cistercian order of monks who speak only in certain situations.
– ORIGIN French *trappiste*, from *La Trappe* in Normandy, where the order was founded.

trash noun **1** N. Amer. waste material; refuse. **2** poor-quality writing, art, etc. **3** N. Amer. a person or people regarded as being of very low social standing. • verb informal, chiefly N. Amer. wreck or destroy something.
– ORIGIN unknown.

trash can noun N. Amer. a dustbin.

trash talk US informal noun insulting or boastful speech intended to intimidate or humiliate someone. • verb (**trash-talk**) use insulting or boastful speech for such a purpose.
– DERIVATIVES **trash talker** noun.

trashy adjective (**trashier, trashiest**) of poor quality: *trashy movies.*
– DERIVATIVES **trashiness** noun.

trattoria /trat-tuh-**ree**-uh/ noun an Italian restaurant.
– ORIGIN Italian.

trauma /**traw**-muh, **trow**-muh/ noun (pl. **traumas**) **1** a deeply distressing experience. **2** emotional shock following a stressful event. **3** Medicine physical injury.
– DERIVATIVES **traumatic** adjective **traumatically** adverb.
– ORIGIN Greek, 'wound'.

traumatize (or **traumatise**) verb cause someone to experience lasting shock as a result of a disturbing experience or injury.

travail /**tra**-vayl/ (also **travails**) noun literary a situation or experience that involves much hard work or difficulty: *the museum records the town's wartime travails.*
– ORIGIN Old French.

travel verb (**travels, travelling, travelled**; US also **travels, traveling, traveled**) **1** go from one place to another, especially over a long distance. **2** go along a road or through a region. **3** move at a particular speed, in a particular direction, or over a particular distance: *light travels faster than sound.* **4** remain in good condition after a journey: *certain wines do not travel well.* • noun **1** the action of travelling. **2** (**travels**) journeys, especially abroad. **3** the range or motion of a part of a machine. • adjective (of a device) small enough to be packed to use when travelling: *a travel iron.*
– ORIGIN from **TRAVAIL**.

travel agency noun an agency that makes the necessary arrangements for travellers.
– DERIVATIVES **travel agent** noun.

travelator (also **travolator**) noun a moving walkway, typically at an airport.
– ORIGIN from **TRAVEL**, suggested by **ESCALATOR**.

travelled adjective **1** having travelled to many places. **2** used by people travelling: *a well-travelled route.*

traveller (US also **traveler**) noun **1** a person who is travelling or who often travels. **2** Brit. a Gypsy. **3** (also **New Age traveller**) Brit. a person who holds New Age values and leads a travelling and unconventional lifestyle.

traveller's cheque noun a cheque for a fixed amount that may be exchanged for cash or used to pay for things abroad.

travelling salesman noun a representative of a firm who visits businesses to show samples and gain orders.

travelogue noun a film, book, or illustrated talk about a person's travels.

travel-sick adjective feeling sick when travelling in a vehicle, boat, or aircraft.
– DERIVATIVES **travel-sickness** noun.

traverse /tra-verss, truh-verss/ verb 1 travel or extend across or through: *he traversed the forest.* 2 move something back and forth or sideways. •noun 1 an act of traversing something. 2 a part of a structure that extends or is fixed across something.
– DERIVATIVES **traversable** adjective **traversal** noun.
– ORIGIN Latin *traversare.*

travertine /tra-ver-tin/ noun white or light-coloured rock deposited from mineral springs, used in building.
– ORIGIN Italian *travertino.*

travesty /tra-vi-sti/ noun (pl. **travesties**) an absurd or distorted representation: *the trial was a travesty of justice.* •verb (**travesties, travestying, travestied**) represent someone or something in an absurd or distorted way.
– ORIGIN from French *travestir* 'to disguise'.

travois /truh-voy/ noun (pl. same or /truh-voyz/) a V-shaped frame of poles pulled by a horse, formerly used by North American Indians to carry goods.
– ORIGIN French.

travolator noun variant spelling of **TRAVELATOR**.

trawl verb 1 search widely and thoroughly: *he trawled the bars of Athens for a drink.* 2 catch fish with a trawl net or seine. •noun 1 a thorough search. 2 (also **trawl net**) a large wide-mouthed fishing net dragged by a boat along the bottom of the sea or a lake.
– ORIGIN probably from Dutch *traghelen* 'to drag'.

trawler noun a fishing boat used for trawling.
– DERIVATIVES **trawlerman** noun (pl. **trawlermen**).

tray noun a flat, shallow container with a raised rim, used for carrying things.
– ORIGIN Old English.

treacherous adjective 1 not loyal or able to be trusted. 2 having hidden or unpredictable dangers: *treacherous currents.*
– DERIVATIVES **treacherously** adverb.
– ORIGIN Old French *trecherous.*

treachery noun (pl. **treacheries**) behaviour that involves betraying someone's trust.

treacle noun Brit. 1 molasses. 2 golden syrup.
– ORIGIN Greek *thēriakē* 'antidote against venom'.

treacly adjective 1 resembling treacle; thick or sticky. 2 excessively sentimental: *treacly film music.*

tread verb (past **trod**; past part. **trodden** or **trod**) 1 walk in a specified way. 2 press down or crush something with the feet. 3 walk on or along something. •noun 1 a person's way of walking or the sound made by this: *I heard the heavy tread of Dad's boots.* 2 the top surface of a step or stair. 3 the part of a vehicle tyre that grips the road. 4 the part of the sole of a shoe

that rests on the ground.
– PHRASES **tread carefully** (or **lightly** or **warily**) take action in a cautious or restrained way. **tread on someone's toes** offend someone by getting involved in something that is their responsibility. **tread water** 1 stay in an upright position in deep water by moving the feet with a walking movement. 2 fail to make progress.
– ORIGIN Old English.

treadle noun a lever worked by the foot to operate a machine.
– ORIGIN Old English, 'stair, step'.

treadmill noun 1 a device used for exercise, consisting of a continuous moving belt on which to walk or run. 2 a job or situation that is tiring, boring, and difficult to escape from: *they were on a never-ending treadmill of duty.* 3 a large wheel turned by the weight of people or animals treading on steps fitted into it, formerly used to drive machinery.

treason (also **high treason**) noun the crime of betraying one's country, especially by attempting to kill or overthrow the sovereign or government.
– DERIVATIVES **treasonable** adjective **treasonous** adjective.
– ORIGIN Old French *treisoun.*

treasure noun 1 a quantity of precious metals, gems, or other valuable objects. 2 a very valuable object. 3 informal a much loved or highly valued person. •verb 1 look after a valuable or valued item carefully. 2 value someone or something highly.
– ORIGIN Old French *tresor.*

treasure hunt noun a game in which players search for hidden objects by following a trail of clues.

treasurer noun a person appointed to manage the finances of a society, company, or other organization.

treasure trove noun 1 a collection or store of valuable or pleasant things. 2 English Law (abolished in 1996) valuables of unknown ownership that are found hidden and declared the property of the Crown.
– ORIGIN from Old French *tresor trové* 'found treasure'.

treasury noun (pl. **treasuries**) 1 the funds or income of a state, institution, or society. 2 (**Treasury**) (in some countries) the government department responsible for the overall management of the economy. 3 a place where treasure is stored. 4 a collection of valuable or pleasant things.

Treasury bill noun a UK or US government security which does not pay interest, but is issued at a price that is less than the value it can be redeemed at.

treat verb 1 behave towards or deal with in a particular way: *he treated her with courtesy.* 2 give medical care or attention to a person, illness, etc. 3 apply a process or a substance to something. 4 present or discuss a subject. 5 (**treat someone to**) pay for someone's food, drink, or entertainment. 6 (**treat oneself**) do or have something very enjoyable. •noun 1 a surprise gift, event, etc. that gives great pleasure. 2 (**one's treat**) an act of paying for

someone's food, drink, or entertainment.
- PHRASES —— **a treat** Brit. informal do something specified very well: *their tactics worked a treat.*
- DERIVATIVES **treatable** adjective **treater** noun.
- ORIGIN Old French *traitier.*

treatise /tree-tiss, tree-tiz/ noun a written work dealing formally and systematically with a subject.
- ORIGIN Old French *tretis.*

treatment noun **1** a way of behaving towards someone or dealing with something. **2** medical care for an illness or injury. **3** the use of a substance or process to preserve or give particular properties to something: *the treatment of hazardous waste.* **4** the presentation or discussion of a subject.

treaty noun (pl. **treaties**) a formal agreement between states.
- ORIGIN Old French *traite.*

treble¹ adjective **1** consisting of three parts. **2** multiplied or occurring three times. •noun **1** Brit. three sporting victories or championships in the same season, event, etc. **2** Darts a hit on the ring enclosed by the two inner circles of a dartboard, scoring treble. •pronoun an amount which is three times as large as usual. •verb make or become three times as large or as many.
- ORIGIN from Latin *triplus* 'triple'.

treble² noun **1** a high-pitched voice, especially a boy's singing voice. **2** the high-frequency output of a radio or audio system.
- ORIGIN from **TREBLE¹**.

treble clef noun Music a clef placing G above middle C on the second-lowest line of the stave.

trebly adjective (of sound, especially recorded music) having too much treble; tinny. •adverb three times as much.

tree noun **1** a woody perennial plant consisting of a trunk and branches, that can typically grow to a considerable height. **2** a wooden structure or part of a structure.
- DERIVATIVES **treeless** adjective.
- ORIGIN Old English.

treecreeper noun a small brown songbird which creeps about on the trunks of trees to search for insects.

tree diagram noun a diagram with a structure of branching connecting lines.

tree fern noun a large palm-like fern with a stem that resembles a tree trunk.

tree house noun a structure built in the branches of a tree for children to play in.

tree-hugger noun informal, derogatory an environmental campaigner.
- DERIVATIVES **tree-hugging** noun.
- ORIGIN with reference to the practice of embracing a tree to prevent it from being felled.

treeline noun the height on a mountain above which trees are unable to grow.

tree ring noun each of a number of rings in the cross section of a tree trunk, representing a single year's growth.

tree surgeon noun a person who prunes and treats old or damaged trees in order to preserve them.

- DERIVATIVES **tree surgery** noun.

treetop noun the uppermost part of a tree.

trefoil /tre-foyl, tree-foyl/ noun **1** a small plant with yellow flowers and clover-like leaves. **2** an ornamental design in the form of three rounded arcs like a clover leaf, used typically in stone tracery.
- ORIGIN Latin *trifolium.*

trek noun a long, difficult journey, especially one made on foot. •verb (**treks, trekking, trekked**) go on a trek.
- DERIVATIVES **trekker** noun.
- ORIGIN from South African Dutch *trekken* 'to pull, travel'.

trellis noun a framework of bars used as a support for climbing plants.
- DERIVATIVES **trellised** adjective.
- ORIGIN Old French *trelis.*

tremble verb **1** shake uncontrollably as a result of fear, excitement, or weakness. **2** be very worried or frightened. **3** (of a thing) shake slightly. •noun a trembling feeling, movement, or sound.
- DERIVATIVES **trembly** adjective (informal).
- ORIGIN Old French *trembler.*

trembler noun Brit. an automatic vibrator for making and breaking an electric circuit.

tremendous adjective **1** very great in amount, scale, or intensity. **2** informal very good or impressive.
- DERIVATIVES **tremendously** adverb.
- ORIGIN Latin *tremendus.*

tremolo noun (pl. **tremolos**) a wavering effect in singing or created when playing some musical instruments.
- ORIGIN Italian.

tremor noun **1** an uncontrollable quivering movement. **2** (also **earth tremor**) a slight earthquake. **3** a sudden feeling of fear or excitement.
- ORIGIN Latin.

tremulous adjective **1** shaking or quivering slightly. **2** timid; nervous.
- DERIVATIVES **tremulously** adverb **tremulousness** noun.
- ORIGIN Latin *tremulus.*

trench noun **1** a long, narrow ditch. **2** a long ditch dug by troops to provide shelter from enemy fire. **3** (also **ocean trench**) a long, narrow, deep depression in the ocean bed. •verb dig a trench or trenches in the ground.
- ORIGIN Old French *trenche.*

trenchant /tren-chuhnt/ adjective (of speech or writing) expressed forcefully and clearly.
- DERIVATIVES **trenchancy** noun **trenchantly** adverb.
- ORIGIN Old French, 'cutting'.

trench coat noun a double-breasted raincoat with a belt.

trencher¹ noun historical a wooden plate or platter.
- ORIGIN Old French *trenchour.*

trencher² noun a machine used to dig trenches.

trencherman noun (pl. **trenchermen**) humorous a person who eats heartily.

trench warfare noun warfare in which

opposing troops fight from trenches facing each other.

trend noun **1** a general direction in which something is developing or changing: *an upward trend in sales.* **2** a fashion. •verb develop in a particular direction.
– ORIGIN Old English, 'revolve, rotate'.

trendsetter noun a person who leads the way in fashion or ideas.
– DERIVATIVES **trendsetting** adjective.

trendy informal adjective (**trendier, trendiest**) very fashionable or up to date. •noun (pl. **trendies**) a fashionable person.
– DERIVATIVES **trendily** adverb **trendiness** noun.

trepan /tri-pan/ chiefly historical noun a saw used by surgeons for perforating the skull. •verb (**trepans, trepanning, trepanned**) perforate a person's skull with a trepan.
– DERIVATIVES **trepanation** /trep-uh-**nay**-sh'n/ noun.
– ORIGIN from Greek *trupan* 'to bore'.

trepidation noun a feeling of fear or nervousness about something that may happen.
– ORIGIN Latin.

trepidatious /tre-pi-**day**-shuss/ adjective informal apprehensive or nervous.

trespass verb **1** enter someone's land or property without their permission. **2** (**trespass on**) take advantage of someone's good nature, help, etc. **3** (**trespass against**) old use commit an offence against a person or law. •noun **1** Law entry to a person's land or property without their permission. **2** old use a sin or other morally wrong act.
– DERIVATIVES **trespasser** noun.
– ORIGIN Old French *trespasser* 'pass over, trespass'.

tress noun a long lock of a woman's hair.
– ORIGIN Old French *tresse*.

trestle noun a framework consisting of a horizontal beam supported by two pairs of sloping legs, used in pairs to support a flat surface such as a table top.
– ORIGIN Old French *trestel*.

trestle table noun a table consisting of a board or boards laid on trestles.

trews /trooz/ plural noun chiefly Brit. trousers.
– ORIGIN Irish *triús*, Scottish Gaelic *triubhas*.

tri- /try/ combining form three; having three: *triathlon.*
– ORIGIN from Latin *tres*, Greek *treis* 'three'.

triable /try-uh-b'l/ adjective (of an offence or case) liable to trial in a court of law.

triacetate /try-**ass**-i-tayt/ noun a form of cellulose acetate used as a basis for man-made fibres.

triad /try-ad/ noun **1** a group of three related people or things. **2** (also **Triad**) a Chinese secret society involved in organized crime.
– DERIVATIVES **triadic** adjective.
– ORIGIN Greek *trias*.

triage /tree-ahzh, try-ij/ noun (in a hospital or in war) the assessment of the seriousness of wounds or illnesses to decide the order in which a large number of patients should be treated. •verb (**triages, triaging, triaged**) decide the order of treatment of patients.

– ORIGIN French.

trial noun **1** a formal examination of evidence in a court of law to decide if someone accused of a crime is guilty or not. **2** a test of performance, qualities, or suitability. **3** a sports match to test the ability of players eligible for selection to a team. **4** (**trials**) an event in which horses or dogs compete or perform. **5** a test of a person's endurance or patience. •verb (**trials, trialling, trialled**; US **trials, trialing, trialed**) test something to assess its suitability or performance.
– PHRASES **on trial 1** being tried in a court of law. **2** being tested for suitability or performance. **trial and error** the process of experimenting with various methods until one finds the most successful.
– ORIGIN Latin *triallum*.

trialist (Brit. also **triallist**) noun a person who participates in a sports trial.

trial run noun a preliminary test of a new system or product.

triangle noun **1** a plane figure with three straight sides and three angles. **2** a thing shaped like a triangle. **3** a musical instrument consisting of a steel rod bent into a triangle, played by hitting it with a rod. **4** an emotional relationship involving a couple and a third person with whom one of them is involved.
– ORIGIN Latin *triangulum*.

triangular adjective **1** shaped like a triangle. **2** involving three people or groups.
– DERIVATIVES **triangularity** noun **triangularly** adverb.

triangulate /try-ang-gyuu-layt/ verb (in surveying) divide an area into triangles in order to determine the distances and relative positions of points.
– DERIVATIVES **triangulation** noun.

Triassic /try-**ass**-ik/ adjective Geology relating to the earliest period of the Mesozoic era (about 245 to 208 million years ago), when the first dinosaurs, ammonites, and primitive mammals appeared.
– ORIGIN from Latin *trias* 'set of three', because the strata are divisible into three groups.

triathlon /try-ath-lon/ noun an athletic contest consisting of three different events, typically swimming, cycling, and long-distance running.
– DERIVATIVES **triathlete** noun.
– ORIGIN from TRI-, on the pattern of *decathlon*.

tribal adjective relating to or typical of a tribe or tribes.
– DERIVATIVES **tribally** adverb.

tribalism noun behaviour and attitudes that are based on a person's loyalty to a tribe or other social group.
– DERIVATIVES **tribalist** adjective.

tribe noun **1** a social group in a traditional society consisting of linked families or communities with a common culture and dialect. **2** derogatory a group with a shared interest, profession, etc.: *a tribe of speech-writers.* **3** (**tribes**) informal large numbers of people. **4** a category in scientific classification that ranks above genus and below family.
– ORIGIN Latin *tribus*.

t

tribesman (or **tribeswoman**) noun (pl. **tribesmen** or **tribeswomen**) a member of a tribe in a traditional society.

tribulation /trib-yuu-**lay**-sh'n/ noun a cause or state of great trouble or distress: *the tribulations of work and family*.
– ORIGIN Latin.

tribunal /try-**byoo**-nuhl, tri-**byoo**-nuhl/ noun 1 Brit. a group of people established to settle certain types of dispute. 2 a court of justice.
– ORIGIN Latin, 'raised platform provided for a magistrate's seat'.

tribune /**trib**-yoon/ noun 1 (in ancient Rome) an official chosen by the ordinary people to protect their interests. 2 literary a champion of people's rights.
– ORIGIN Latin *tribunus* 'head of a tribe'.

tributary /**trib**-yuu-tuh-ri/ noun (pl. **tributaries**) 1 a river or stream flowing into a larger river or lake. 2 historical a person or state that pays money to another more powerful state or ruler.
– ORIGIN Latin *tributarius*.

tribute noun 1 an act, statement, or gift that is intended to show gratitude, respect, or admiration. 2 something that indicates the worth of something else: *his victory was a tribute to his persistence*. 3 historical payment made regularly by one state or ruler to a more powerful one.
– ORIGIN Latin *tributum*.

trice /rhymes with nice/ noun (in phrase **in a trice**) in a moment; very quickly.
– ORIGIN first meaning 'a tug', also 'an instant': from Dutch *trisen* 'pull sharply'.

triceps /**try**-seps/ noun (pl. same) the large muscle at the back of the upper arm.
– ORIGIN Latin, 'three-headed' (because the muscle has three points of attachment).

triceratops /try-**se**-ruh-tops/ noun a large plant-eating dinosaur having a huge head with two large horns, a smaller horn on the snout, and a bony frill above the neck.
– ORIGIN from Greek *trikeratos* 'three-horned' + *ōps* 'face'.

trichology /tri-**kol**-uh-ji/ noun the branch of medicine concerned with the hair and scalp.
– DERIVATIVES **trichological** adjective **trichologist** noun.
– ORIGIN from Greek *thrix* 'hair'.

trichromatic /try-kruh-**mat**-ik/ adjective 1 having or using three colours. 2 having normal colour vision, which is sensitive to all three primary colours.
– DERIVATIVES **trichromatism** noun.

trick noun 1 an act or scheme intended to deceive or outwit someone. 2 a skilful act performed for entertainment. 3 an illusion: *there was nothing there – it had only been a trick of the light*. 4 a habit or mannerism: *he had an odd trick of blowing through his lips when he was listening*. 5 (in bridge, whist, etc.) a sequence of cards forming a single round of play. •verb 1 cunningly deceive or outwit someone. 2 (**trick someone into/out of**) deceive someone into doing or parting with something. •adjective intended to trick or to create an illusion: *a trick question*.
– PHRASES **do the trick** informal achieve the required result. **trick or treat** a children's custom of calling at houses at Halloween with the threat of pranks if they are not given a small gift. **tricks of the trade** special clever techniques used in a profession or craft.
– DERIVATIVES **tricker** noun **trickery** noun.
– ORIGIN Old French *triche*.

trickle verb 1 (of a liquid) flow in a small stream. 2 come or go slowly or gradually: *details began to trickle out*. 3 (**trickle down**) (of wealth) gradually spread from the richest to the poorest people in society. •noun 1 a small flow of liquid. 2 a small group or number of people or things moving slowly.
– ORIGIN imitating the sound.

trickle-down noun the theory that the poorest people in society gradually benefit as a result of the increasing wealth of the richest.

trickster noun a person who cheats or deceives people.

tricksy adjective (**tricksier**, **tricksiest**) 1 clever in an inventive or complicated way. 2 playful or mischievous.

tricky adjective (**trickier**, **trickiest**) 1 difficult or awkward to do or deal with: *he knew how to handle tricky media questions*. 2 deceitful or crafty.
– DERIVATIVES **trickily** adverb **trickiness** noun.

tricolour /**tri**-kuh-ler/ (US **tricolor**) noun a flag with three bands of different colours, especially the French national flag with equal bands of blue, white, and red. •adjective (also **tricoloured**) having three colours.

tricorne /**try**-korn/ (also **tricorn**) noun a hat with a brim turned up on three sides.
– ORIGIN Latin *tricornis*.

tricot /**tri**-koh, **tree**-koh/ noun a fine knitted fabric.
– ORIGIN French, 'knitting'.

tricuspid /try-**kus**-pid/ noun a tooth with three cusps or points.
– ORIGIN from Latin *cuspis* 'sharp point'.

tricycle noun a vehicle similar to a bicycle, but having three wheels, two at the back and one at the front.

tricyclic /try-**sy**-klik/ noun any of a class of drugs used to treat depression.
– ORIGIN from the fact that the molecules of the drugs have three fused rings.

trident noun a three-pronged spear.
– ORIGIN Latin.

tried past and past participle of **TRY**.

triennial /try-**en**-ni-uhl/ adjective lasting for or recurring every three years.
– DERIVATIVES **triennially** adverb.

trier noun a person who always makes an effort, however unsuccessful they may be.

trifid /**try**-fid/ adjective technical (of part of a plant or animal) divided into three parts by a deep cleft.
– ORIGIN Latin *trifidus*.

t

trifle noun **1** a thing of little value or importance. **2** Brit. a cold dessert of sponge cake and fruit covered with layers of custard, jelly, and cream. • verb (**trifle with**) treat without seriousness or respect: *he was not a man to be trifled with.*
 – PHRASES **a trifle** slightly; rather.
 – DERIVATIVES **trifler** noun.
 – ORIGIN from Old French *truffler* 'mock, deceive'.

trifling adjective unimportant or trivial.
 – DERIVATIVES **triflingly** adverb.

trifoliate /try-foh-li-uht/ adjective (of a compound leaf) having three small leaves.

trigger noun **1** a device that releases a spring or catch and so fires a gun or sets off a mechanism. **2** an event that causes something to happen. • verb **1** (also **trigger something off**) cause to happen: *house dust may trigger an asthma attack.* **2** cause a device to function.
 – ORIGIN Dutch *trekker.*

trigger-happy adjective apt to shoot someone or take other violent action on the slightest provocation.

triglyceride /try-gli-suh-ryd/ noun a compound formed from glycerol and three fatty acid groups, e.g. the main constituents of natural fats and oils.

trigonometry /tri-guh-nom-i-tri/ noun the branch of mathematics concerned with the relations of the sides and angles of triangles and with the functions of angles.
 – DERIVATIVES **trigonometric** adjective **trigonometrical** adjective.
 – ORIGIN from Greek *trigōnos* 'three-cornered'.

trig point noun Brit. a reference point on high ground used in surveying, typically marked by a small pillar.
 – ORIGIN abbreviation of *trigonometrical point.*

trike noun informal a tricycle.

trilateral adjective **1** shared by or involving three parties: *trilateral talks.* **2** Geometry on or with three sides.

trilby noun (pl. **trilbies**) chiefly Brit. a soft felt hat with a narrow brim and indented crown.
 – ORIGIN from the heroine of George du Maurier's novel *Trilby,* in the stage version of which such a hat was worn.

trilingual adjective **1** speaking three languages fluently. **2** written or carried out in three languages.
 – DERIVATIVES **trilingualism** noun.

trill noun a quavering or warbling sound, especially a rapid alternation of notes. • verb make a quavering or warbling sound.
 – ORIGIN Italian *trillo.*

trillion cardinal number (pl. **trillions** or (with numeral or quantifying word) same) **1** a million million (1,000,000,000,000 or 10^{12}). **2** Brit. dated a million million million (1,000,000,000,000,000,000 or 10^{18}). **3** (**trillions**) informal a very large number or amount.
 – DERIVATIVES **trillionth** ordinal number.

trilobite /try-luh-byt/ noun a fossil marine arthropod (invertebrate creature) with a rear part divided into three segments.
 – ORIGIN from Greek *tri-* 'three' + *lobos* 'lobe'.

trilogy noun (pl. **trilogies**) a group of three related novels, plays, or films.

trim verb (**trims, trimming, trimmed**) **1** cut away unwanted or irregular parts from something. **2** reduce the size, amount, or number of: *the company aims to trim production costs.* **3** decorate something, especially along its edges. **4** adjust a boat's sail to take advantage of the wind. • noun **1** decoration, especially along the edges of something. **2** the upholstery or interior lining of a car. **3** an act of cutting something. **4** the state of being in good order. • adjective (**trimmer, trimmest**) **1** neat and smart. **2** slim and fit.
 – PHRASES **in trim** slim and fit. **trim one's sails** (**to the wind**) make changes to suit one's new situation.
 – DERIVATIVES **trimly** adverb **trimmer** noun **trimness** noun.
 – ORIGIN Old English, 'make firm, arrange'.

trimaran /try-muh-ran/ noun a yacht with three hulls side by side.
 – ORIGIN from TRI- + CATAMARAN.

trimester /try-mess-ter/ noun **1** a period of three months as a division of the duration of pregnancy. **2** N. Amer. each of the three terms in an academic year.
 – ORIGIN Latin *trimestris.*

trimming noun **1** (**trimmings**) small pieces trimmed off. **2** decoration, especially for clothing. **3** (**the trimmings**) the traditional accompaniments to something: *roast turkey with all the trimmings.*

Trinidadian /tri-ni-day-di-uhn, tri-ni-dad-i-uhn/ noun a person from Trinidad. • adjective relating to Trinidad.

Trinitarian /tri-ni-tair-i-uhn/ adjective relating to the Christian doctrine of the Trinity. • noun a Christian who believes in the doctrine of the Trinity.
 – DERIVATIVES **Trinitarianism** noun.

trinity noun (pl. **trinities**) **1** (**the Trinity** or **the Holy Trinity**) (in Christian belief) the three persons (Father, Son, and Holy Spirit) that together make up God. **2** a group of three people or things.
 – ORIGIN Latin *trinitas.*

trinket noun a small ornament or item of jewellery that is of little value.
 – ORIGIN unknown.

trio noun (pl. **trios**) **1** a set or group of three. **2** a group of three musicians.
 – ORIGIN Italian.

triode /try-ohd/ noun a semiconductor device with three connections, typically allowing the flow of current in one direction only.
 – ORIGIN from TRI- + ELECTRODE.

trioxide /try-ok-syd/ noun Chemistry an oxide containing three atoms of oxygen.

trip verb (**trips, tripping, tripped**) **1** catch one's foot on something and stumble or fall. **2** (**trip up** or **trip someone up**) make or cause to make a mistake. **3** walk, run, or dance with quick light steps. **4** (of words) flow lightly and easily: *a name which trips off the tongue.* **5** activate a mechanism, especially by contact with a switch. **6** (of part of an electric circuit) disconnect automatically as a safety measure. **7** informal experience hallucinations as a result of taking a drug such as LSD. • noun **1** a journey or excursion. **2** an instance of tripping or

falling. **3** informal a period of hallucinations caused by taking a drug. **4** informal a self-indulgent attitude or activity: *a power trip.* **5** a device that trips a mechanism or circuit.
– PHRASES **trip the light fantastic** humorous dance. [from 'Trip it as you go On the light fantastic toe' (Milton's *L'Allegro*).]
– ORIGIN Dutch *trippen* 'to skip, hop'.

tripartite /try-par-tyt/ adjective **1** consisting of three parts. **2** shared by or involving three parties.

tripe noun **1** the first or second stomach of a cow or sheep used as food. **2** informal nonsense; rubbish.
– ORIGIN Old French, 'entrails of an animal'.

trip hammer noun a large, heavy hammer used in forging, which is raised and then allowed to drop on the metal being worked.

Tripitaka /tri-pit-uh-kuh/ noun the sacred writings of Theravada Buddhism.
– ORIGIN from Sanskrit *tripiṭaka* 'the three baskets or collections'.

triplane noun an early type of aircraft with three pairs of wings, one above the other.

triple adjective **1** consisting of or involving three things or people. **2** having three times the usual size, quality, or strength.
• predeterminer three times as much or as many.
• noun a thing that is three times as large as usual or is made up of three parts. • verb make or become three times as much or as many.
– DERIVATIVES **triply** adverb.
– ORIGIN Old French.

triple bond noun a chemical bond in which three pairs of electrons are shared between two atoms.

Triple Crown noun an award or honour for winning a group of three important events in a sport.

triple jump noun **1** an athletic event in which competitors attempt to jump as far as possible by performing a hop, a step, and a jump from a running start. **2** a jump in which a skater makes three full turns while in the air.

triple point noun Chemistry the temperature and pressure at which the solid, liquid, and vapour phases of a pure substance can coexist in equilibrium.

triplet noun **1** each of three children or animals born at the same birth. **2** a group of three equal musical notes to be performed in the time of two or four. **3** a set of three rhyming lines of verse.

triple time noun musical time with three beats to the bar.

triplex /trip-leks/ noun N. Amer. a residential building divided into three apartments.
• adjective having three parts.
– ORIGIN Latin.

triplicate adjective /trip-li-kuht/ existing in three copies or examples. • verb /trip-li-kayt/ **1** make three copies of something. **2** multiply something by three.
– DERIVATIVES **triplication** /tri-pli-**kay**-sh'n/ noun **triplicity** /tri-**pliss**-i-ti/ noun.
– ORIGIN from Latin *triplicare* 'make three'.

tripod /try-pod/ noun **1** a three-legged stand for supporting a camera or other piece of equipment. **2** old use a stool, table, or cauldron set on three legs.
– ORIGIN Greek.

tripos /try-poss/ noun the final honours exam for a BA degree at Cambridge University.
– ORIGIN from Latin *tripus* 'tripod', with reference to the stool on which a graduate sat to deliver a satirical speech at the degree ceremony.

tripper noun Brit. informal a person who goes on a pleasure trip.

trippy adjective (**trippier, trippiest**) informal resembling or causing the hallucinations experienced after taking a drug such as LSD: *trippy dance music.*

triptych /trip-tik/ noun **1** a picture or carving on three panels, typically hinged together vertically and used as an altarpiece. **2** a set of three related artistic, literary, or musical works.
– ORIGIN from TRI-, on the pattern of *diptych*.

tripwire noun a wire that is stretched close to the ground and activates a trap, explosion, or alarm when disturbed.

trireme /try-reem/ noun an ancient Greek or Roman warship with three banks of oars.
– ORIGIN Latin *triremis*.

trisect /try-sekt/ verb divide something into three parts.
– DERIVATIVES **trisection** noun.
– ORIGIN from TRI- + Latin *secare* 'divide, cut'.

trishaw /try-shaw/ noun a light three-wheeled vehicle with pedals, used in the Far East.
– ORIGIN from TRI- + RICKSHAW.

trismus /triz-muhss/ noun technical term for LOCKJAW.
– ORIGIN Greek *trismos* 'a scream, grinding'.

tristesse /tri-stess/ noun literary a state of melancholy sadness.
– ORIGIN French.

trite adjective (of a remark or idea) unoriginal and dull because of overuse.
– DERIVATIVES **tritely** adverb **triteness** noun.
– ORIGIN Latin *tritus* 'rubbed'.

tritium /tri-ti-uhm/ noun Chemistry a radioactive isotope of hydrogen with a mass approximately three times that of the usual isotope.
– ORIGIN from Greek *tritos* 'third'.

triturate /tri-tyoo-rayt/ verb technical grind a substance to a fine powder.
– DERIVATIVES **trituration** noun.
– ORIGIN from Latin *tritura* 'rubbing'.

triumph noun **1** a great victory or achievement. **2** the state of being victorious or successful. **3** joy or satisfaction resulting from a success or victory. **4** a highly successful example: *their marriage was a triumph of togetherness.* **5** a ceremonial procession of a victorious general into ancient Rome. • verb **1** achieve victory or success. **2** rejoice in a victory or success: *she stopped triumphing over Mary's failure.*
– DERIVATIVES **triumphal** adjective.
– ORIGIN Latin *triumphus*.

triumphalism noun excessive rejoicing over one's own success or achievements.
– DERIVATIVES **triumphalist** adjective & noun.

triumphant adjective **1** having won a battle or contest; victorious. **2** joyful after a victory or achievement.

- DERIVATIVES **triumphantly** adverb.

triumvir /try-um-ver/ noun (in ancient Rome) each of three public officials jointly responsible for overseeing any of the administrative departments.
- ORIGIN Latin.

triumvirate /try-um-vi-ruht/ noun **1** a group of three powerful or important people or things. **2** (in ancient Rome) a group of three men holding power.

triune /try-yoon/ adjective (especially with reference to the Christian Trinity) consisting of three in one.
- ORIGIN from **TRI-** + Latin *unus* 'one'.

trivet /tri-vit/ noun **1** a metal stand on which hot dishes are placed. **2** an iron tripod placed over a fire for a cooking pot or kettle to stand on.
- ORIGIN probably from Latin *tripes* 'three-legged'.

trivia plural noun unimportant details or pieces of information.
- ORIGIN Latin, plural of *trivium* 'place where three roads meet'.

trivial adjective not very important or serious: *doctors can find it frustrating to be called out on trivial matters.*
- DERIVATIVES **triviality** noun (pl. **trivialities**). **trivially** adverb.
- ORIGIN first meaning 'belonging to the trivium' (an introductory course at a medieval university involving the study of grammar, rhetoric, and logic): from Latin *trivium*, literally 'place where three roads meet'.

trivialize (or **trivialise**) verb make something seem less important or complex than it really is.
- DERIVATIVES **trivialization** noun.

trochee /troh-kee/ noun a foot (unit of poetic metre) consisting of one long or stressed syllable followed by one short or unstressed syllable.
- DERIVATIVES **trochaic** /truh-kay-ik/ adjective.
- ORIGIN from Greek *trokhaios pous* 'running foot'.

trod past and past participle of **TREAD**.

trodden past participle of **TREAD**.

troglodyte /trog-luh-dyt/ noun **1** a person who lives in a cave. **2** a person who is ignorant or old-fashioned.
- DERIVATIVES **troglodytic** adjective.
- ORIGIN Greek *trōglodutēs*.

troika /troy-kuh/ noun **1** a Russian vehicle pulled by a team of three horses side by side. **2** a group of three political leaders or managers working together.
- ORIGIN Russian.

troilism /troy-li-z'm/ noun sexual activity involving three participants.
- ORIGIN perhaps from French *trois* 'three'.

Trojan noun an inhabitant of ancient Troy in the western peninsula of Asia. •adjective relating to Troy.
- PHRASES **work like a Trojan** work very hard.

Trojan Horse noun something intended to weaken or defeat an enemy secretly.
- ORIGIN from the hollow wooden statue of a horse in which the ancient Greeks are said to have hidden themselves in order to enter Troy.

troll[1] /rhymes with doll or dole/ noun (in folklore) an ugly giant or dwarf that lives in a cave.
- ORIGIN Old Norse and Swedish, 'witch'.

troll[2] /rhymes with dole or doll/ verb fish by trailing a baited line along behind a boat.
- DERIVATIVES **troller** noun.
- ORIGIN uncertain.

trolley noun (pl. **trolleys**) **1** Brit. a large metal basket or frame on wheels, used for transporting heavy or bulky items such as luggage or shopping. **2** a small table on wheels, used to convey food and drink. **3** (also **trolley wheel**) a wheel attached to a pole, used for collecting current from an overhead electric wire to drive a tram. **4** a trolleybus or trolley car.
- PHRASES **off one's trolley** informal mad; insane.
- ORIGIN perhaps from **TROLL**[2].

trolleybus noun Brit. a bus powered by electricity obtained from overhead wires by means of a trolley wheel.

trolley car noun US a tram powered by electricity obtained from an overhead cable by means of a trolley wheel.

trollop noun dated or humorous a woman who has many sexual partners.
- ORIGIN perhaps from former *trull* 'prostitute', from German *Trulle*.

trombone noun a large brass wind instrument with a sliding tube which is moved to produce different notes.
- DERIVATIVES **trombonist** noun.
- ORIGIN French or Italian.

trompe l'œil /tromp loy/ noun (pl. **trompe l'œils** pronunc. same) a painting or method of painting that creates the illusion of a three-dimensional object or space.
- ORIGIN French, 'deceives the eye'.

troop noun **1** (**troops**) soldiers or armed forces. **2** a group of people or animals of a particular kind. **3** a unit of an armoured or cavalry division. **4** a group of three or more Scout patrols. •verb come or go as a group: *the girls trooped in for dinner.*
- PHRASES **troop the colour** Brit. perform the ceremony of parading a regiment's flag along ranks of soldiers.
- ORIGIN Latin *troppus* 'flock'.

troop carrier noun a large aircraft or armoured vehicle designed for transporting troops.

trooper noun **1** a private soldier in a cavalry or armoured unit. **2** US a state police officer. **3** chiefly US a mounted police officer. **4** chiefly Brit. a ship for transporting troops.

troopship noun a ship for transporting troops.

trope /rhymes with rope/ noun a figurative or metaphorical use of a word or expression.
- ORIGIN Greek *tropos* 'turn, way, trope'.

trophy noun (pl. **trophies**) **1** a cup or other decorative object awarded as a prize. **2** a souvenir of an achievement, such as a head of an animal killed when hunting.
- ORIGIN French *trophée*.

tropic noun **1** the line of latitude 23°26′ north (**tropic of Cancer**) or south (**tropic of Capricorn**) of the equator. **2** (**the tropics**) the

region between the tropics of Cancer and Capricorn. ●adjective relating to the tropics; tropical.
– ORIGIN Greek *tropikos*.

tropical adjective **1** relating to the tropics. **2** very hot and humid.
– DERIVATIVES **tropically** adverb.

tropical storm (also **tropical cyclone**) noun a localized, very intense low-pressure wind system with winds of hurricane force, forming over tropical oceans.

tropism /troh-pi-z'm, trop-i-z'm/ noun Biology the turning of all or part of an organism towards or away from an external stimulus such as light.
– ORIGIN from Greek *tropos* 'turning'.

troposphere /tro-puh-sfeer, troh-puh-sfeer/ noun the lowest region of the atmosphere, extending from the earth's surface to a height of about 6–10 km (the lower boundary of the stratosphere).
– DERIVATIVES **tropospheric** /tro-puhss-**fer**-ik, troh-puhss-**fer**-ik/ adjective.
– ORIGIN from Greek *tropos* 'turning'.

troppo /**trop**-oh/ adverb Music too much; excessively.
– ORIGIN Italian.

Trot noun informal, chiefly derogatory a Trotskyist or other supporter of extreme left-wing views.

trot verb (**trots, trotting, trotted**) **1** (of a horse) move at a pace faster than a walk, lifting each diagonal pair of legs alternately. **2** (of a person) run at a moderate pace with short steps. **3** (**trot something out**) informal produce an account that has been produced many times before. ●noun **1** a trotting pace. **2** an act of trotting. **3** (**the trots**) informal diarrhoea.
– PHRASES **on the trot** informal **1** Brit. one after another. **2** continually busy.
– ORIGIN Latin *trottare*.

troth /trohth, troth/ noun old use or formal faith or loyalty when pledged in a solemn agreement.
– PHRASES **pledge** (or **plight**) **one's troth** make a solemn promise, especially to marry someone.
– ORIGIN from TRUTH.

Trotskyism /trot-ski-iz-uhm/ noun the political or economic principles of the Russian revolutionary Leon Trotsky, especially the theory that socialism should be established throughout the world by continuing revolution.
– DERIVATIVES **Trotskyist** noun & adjective **Trotskyite** noun & adjective (derogatory).

trotter noun **1** a pig's foot. **2** a horse bred or trained for the sport of trotting.

trotting noun racing for horses pulling a two-wheeled vehicle and driver.

troubadour /troo-buh-dor/ noun (in medieval France) a performing poet who composed and sang in Provençal, especially on the theme of courtly love.
– ORIGIN French.

trouble noun **1** difficulty or problems. **2** effort made to do something: *I've gone to a lot of trouble to help you.* **3** a cause of worry or inconvenience. **4** a situation in which a person is likely to be punished or blamed: *he's been in trouble with the police.* **5** public unrest or disorder. ●verb **1** cause distress or inconvenience to someone. **2** (as adj. **troubled**)

showing or experiencing problems or anxiety. **3** (**trouble about/over/with**) be anxious about someone or something. **4** (**trouble to do**) make the effort to do: *oh, don't trouble to answer.*
– PHRASES **look for trouble** informal deliberately try to start an argument or fight.
– ORIGIN Old French *truble*.

troublemaker noun a person who often causes trouble, especially by encouraging others to defy people in authority.

troubleshoot verb **1** analyse and solve problems for an organization. **2** trace and correct faults in a mechanical or electronic system.
– DERIVATIVES **troubleshooter** noun.

troublesome adjective causing difficulty or annoyance.
– DERIVATIVES **troublesomeness** noun.

trouble spot noun a place where difficulties or conflict regularly occur.

troublous adjective old use full of troubles.

trough noun **1** a long, narrow open container for animals to eat or drink out of. **2** a channel used to convey a liquid. **3** Meteorology a long, narrow region of low pressure. **4** a point of low activity or achievement: *peaks and troughs in demand.* **5** a hollow between two wave crests in the sea. ●verb informal eat something greedily.
– ORIGIN Old English.

trounce verb defeat someone heavily in a contest.
– ORIGIN unknown.

troupe noun a group of dancers, actors, or other entertainers who tour to different venues.
– ORIGIN French.

trouper noun **1** an entertainer with long experience. **2** a reliable and uncomplaining person.

trouser verb Brit. informal receive or take something for oneself. ●adjective relating to trousers: *his trouser pocket.*

trousers plural noun an outer garment covering the body from the waist to the ankles, with a separate part for each leg.
– PHRASES **wear the trousers** informal be the dominant partner in a relationship.
– DERIVATIVES **trousered** adjective.
– ORIGIN from Irish *triús* and Scottish Gaelic *triubhas*.

trouser suit noun Brit. a pair of trousers and a matching jacket worn by women.

trousseau /troo-soh/ noun (pl. **trousseaux** or **trousseaus** /troo-sohz/) the clothes, linen, and other belongings collected by a bride for her marriage.
– ORIGIN French, 'small bundle'.

trout noun (pl. same or **trouts**) an edible fish of the salmon family, found chiefly in fresh water.
– PHRASES **old trout** informal an annoying or bad-tempered old woman.
– ORIGIN Old English.

trove noun a store of valuable or pleasant things.
– ORIGIN from TREASURE TROVE.

trow /troh/ verb old use think or believe something.
– ORIGIN Old English, 'to trust'.

t

trowel noun **1** a small garden tool with a curved scoop for lifting plants or earth. **2** a small tool with a flat, pointed blade, used to apply and spread mortar or plaster. •verb (**trowels, trowelling, trowelled**; US **trowels, troweling, troweled**) apply or spread something with a trowel.
– ORIGIN Latin *truella*.

troy (also **troy weight**) noun a system of weights used mainly for precious metals and gems, with a pound of 12 ounces or 5,760 grains. Compare with **AVOIRDUPOIS**.
– ORIGIN from a weight used at the fair of *Troyes* in France.

truant noun a pupil who stays away from school without permission or explanation. •adjective wandering; straying. •verb (also chiefly Brit. **play truant**) (of a pupil) stay away from school without permission or explanation.
– DERIVATIVES **truancy** noun.
– ORIGIN first referring to a person begging through choice rather than necessity: from Old French.

truce noun an agreement between enemies to stop fighting for a certain time.
– ORIGIN Old English, 'belief, trust'.

truck¹ noun **1** a large road vehicle for carrying goods or troops. **2** Brit. an open railway vehicle for carrying goods. •verb chiefly N. Amer. convey goods by truck.
– ORIGIN perhaps from **TRUCKLE** in the sense 'wheel, pulley'.

truck² noun (in phrase **have no truck with**) refuse to deal or be associated with.
– ORIGIN probably from Old French.

trucker noun a long-distance lorry driver.

truckle noun a small barrel-shaped cheese, especially Cheddar.
– ORIGIN Old French *trocle* 'wheel, pulley'.

truckle bed noun chiefly Brit. a low bed on wheels that can be stored under a larger bed.

truculent /truk-yuu-luhnt/ adjective quick to argue or fight.
– DERIVATIVES **truculence** noun **truculently** adverb.
– ORIGIN Latin *truculentus*.

trudge verb walk slowly and with heavy steps. •noun a long and tiring walk.
– ORIGIN unknown.

true adjective (**truer, truest**) **1** in accordance with fact or reality. **2** rightly so called; genuine: *true love*. **3** real or actual: *she guessed my true intentions*. **4** accurate and exact. **5** (**true to**) in keeping with a standard or expectation: *true to his threats, he retaliated*. **6** loyal or faithful. **7** correctly positioned or aligned; upright or level. •verb (**trues, truing** or **trueing, trued**) bring something into the exact shape or position required.
– PHRASES **come true** actually happen or become the case. **out of true** not in the correct or exact shape or alignment. **true to form** (or **type**) being or behaving as expected.
– DERIVATIVES **trueness** noun.
– ORIGIN Old English, 'steadfast, loyal'.

true-blue adjective **1** Brit. very loyal to the Conservative Party. **2** N. Amer. very loyal or traditional.

true north noun north according to the earth's axis, not magnetic north.

truffle noun **1** an underground fungus that resembles a rough-skinned potato, eaten as a delicacy. **2** a soft chocolate sweet.
– ORIGIN a former French word.

trug noun Brit. a shallow oblong wooden basket, used for carrying garden flowers, fruit, and vegetables.
– ORIGIN perhaps a dialect form of **TROUGH**.

truism noun a statement that is obviously true and says nothing new or interesting.

truly adverb **1** in a truthful way. **2** genuinely or properly. **3** in actual fact; really. **4** absolutely or completely (used for emphasis): *a truly dreadful song*.
– PHRASES **yours truly 1** used as a formula for ending a letter. **2** humorous used to refer to oneself.

trump¹ noun **1** (in bridge, whist, etc.) a playing card of the suit chosen to rank above the others, which can win a trick where a card of a different suit has been led. **2** (also **trump card**) a valuable resource that may be used, especially as a surprise, to gain an advantage. **3** informal, dated a helpful or admirable person. •verb **1** play a trump on a card of another suit. **2** beat by saying or doing something better: *this sequel trumps the original movie*. **3** (**trump something up**) invent a false accusation or excuse.
– PHRASES **come** (or **turn**) **up trumps** informal, chiefly Brit. **1** have a better outcome than expected. **2** be especially generous or helpful.
– ORIGIN from **TRIUMPH**.

trump² noun old use a trumpet or a sound made by one.
– ORIGIN Old French *trompe*.

trumpery old use noun (pl. **trumperies**) things that are superficially attractive or appealing but have little real worth. •adjective showy but worthless.
– ORIGIN Old French *tromperie*.

trumpet noun **1** a brass musical instrument with a flared end. **2** something shaped like a trumpet, especially the central part of a daffodil flower. **3** the loud cry of an elephant. •verb (**trumpets, trumpeting, trumpeted**) **1** announce widely or enthusiastically: *researchers trumpeted a major medical breakthrough*. **2** (of an elephant) make its loud cry. **3** play a trumpet.
– PHRASES **blow one's own trumpet** chiefly Brit. talk boastfully about one's achievements.
– DERIVATIVES **trumpeter** noun.
– ORIGIN Old French *trompette*.

truncate /trung-kayt/ verb shorten something by cutting off the top or the end.
– DERIVATIVES **truncation** noun.
– ORIGIN Latin *truncare* 'maim'.

truncheon /trun-chuhn/ noun chiefly Brit. a short, thick stick carried as a weapon by a police officer.
– ORIGIN Old French *tronchon* 'stump'.

trundle verb move or roll along slowly and heavily.
– ORIGIN from former or dialect *trendle* 'revolve'.

trunk noun **1** (also **tree trunk**) the main woody stem of a tree. **2** a person's or animal's body apart from the limbs and head. **3** the long nose of an elephant. **4** a large box with a hinged lid for storing or transporting clothes and other

articles. **5** N. Amer. the boot of a car. •**adjective** relating to the main routes of a transport or communication network: *a trunk road.*
– ORIGIN Latin *truncus.*

trunk call noun dated, chiefly Brit. a long-distance telephone call made within the same country.

trunking noun a system of shafts or ducts for cables or ventilation.

trunks plural noun men's shorts worn for swimming or boxing.

trunnion /trun-yuhn/ noun a pin or pivot forming one of a pair on which something is supported.
– ORIGIN French *trognon* 'core, tree trunk'.

truss noun **1** a padded belt worn to support a hernia. **2** a framework of rafters, posts, and struts which supports a roof, bridge, or other structure. **3** a compact cluster of flowers or fruit growing on one stalk. **4** a large projection of stone or timber, typically one supporting a cornice. •**verb 1** tie someone up tightly. **2** tie up the wings and legs of a chicken or other bird before cooking. **3** support something with a truss or trusses.
– ORIGIN Old French *trusser* 'pack up, bind in'.

trust noun **1** firm belief that someone or something is reliable, true, or able to do something: *the need to restore trust in the police.* **2** acceptance of the truth of a statement without evidence or investigation. **3** the state of being responsible for someone or something. **4** a legal arrangement whereby a person (a trustee) holds property as its nominal owner for the good of one or more other people. **5** an organization managed by trustees. •**verb 1** firmly believe to be reliable, true, or able to do something: *they trusted their neighbours to protect them.* **2** (**trust someone with**) have the confidence to allow someone to have, use, or look after someone or something. **3** (**trust someone/thing to**) give someone or something to another person for safekeeping. **4** (**trust to**) rely on luck, fate, etc. **5** hope: *I trust that you are well.*
– DERIVATIVES **trustable** adjective **trusted** adjective.
– ORIGIN from Old Norse, 'strong'.

Trustafarian noun Brit. informal a rich young person who adopts an ethnic lifestyle and lives in a lower-class urban area.
– ORIGIN blend of **TRUST FUND** and **RASTAFARIAN**.

trust company noun a company formed to act as a trustee or to deal with trusts.

trustee noun a person given legal powers to hold and manage property in trust for the benefit of another person or people.
– DERIVATIVES **trusteeship** noun.

trustful adjective having or showing total trust in someone.
– DERIVATIVES **trustfully** adverb **trustfulness** noun.

trust fund noun a fund consisting of money or property that is held and managed for another person or people by a trust.

trusting adjective tending to trust others; not suspicious.
– DERIVATIVES **trustingly** adverb **trustingness** noun.

trustworthy adjective able to be relied on as honest and truthful.
– DERIVATIVES **trustworthiness** noun.

trusty adjective (**trustier, trustiest**) old use or humorous having been used or known for a long time and regarded as reliable: *my trusty old typewriter.*

truth /trooth/ noun (pl. **truths** /trooth*z*, trooths/) **1** the state of being true: *no one could doubt the truth of his claims.* **2** (also **the truth**) that which is true; actual facts. **3** a fact or belief that is accepted as true.
– PHRASES **in truth** really; in fact.
– ORIGIN Old English.

truthful adjective **1** telling or expressing the truth; honest. **2** realistic; lifelike.
– DERIVATIVES **truthfully** adverb **truthfulness** noun.

try verb (**tries, trying, tried**) **1** make an attempt or effort to do something. **2** (also **try something out**) test something new or different to see if it is suitable, effective, or pleasant. **3** (**try something on**) put on an item of clothing to see if it fits or suits one. **4** make severe demands on: *Mary tried everyone's patience to the limit.* **5** put someone on trial. **6** investigate and decide a case or issue in a formal trial. **7** attempt to open a door or window. •**noun** (pl. **tries**) **1** an attempt to do something. **2** a test of something new or different. **3** Rugby an act of touching the ball down behind the opposing goal line, scoring points and entitling the scoring side to a kick at goal.
– PHRASES **tried and tested** (or **true**) having proved effective or reliable before. **try one's hand at** attempt to do something for the first time. **try it on** Brit. informal **1** attempt to seduce someone. **2** deliberately test someone's patience.
– ORIGIN Old French *trier* 'sift'.

USAGE: The expressions **try to** and **try and** both mean the same thing, but it is better to use **try to** in writing (*we should try to help them* rather than *we should try and help them*).

trying adjective difficult or annoying.

tryout noun a test of the potential of someone or something, especially in sport.

try square noun an implement used to check and mark right angles in construction work.

tryst /trist/ literary noun a private, romantic meeting between lovers. •**verb** meet privately with a lover.
– ORIGIN Latin *trista* 'an appointed place in hunting'.

tsar /zar, tsar/ (also **czar** or **tzar**) noun **1** an emperor of Russia before 1917. **2** a person with great authority or power in a particular area: *America's new drug tsar.*
– DERIVATIVES **tsarist** noun & adjective.
– ORIGIN Russian, representing Latin *Caesar.*

tsarina /zah-ree-nuh, tsah-ree-nuh/ (also **czarina** or **tzarina**) noun an empress of Russia before 1917.

tsetse /tet-si, tset-si/ (also **tsetse fly**) noun an African bloodsucking fly which transmits sleeping sickness and other diseases.
– ORIGIN from a southern African language.

T-shirt (also **tee shirt**) noun a short-sleeved casual top, having the shape of a T when spread out flat.

tsp abbreviation (pl. same or **tsps**) teaspoonful.

T-square noun a T-shaped instrument for drawing or testing right angles.

TSS abbreviation toxic shock syndrome.

tsunami /tsoo-**nah**-mi/ noun (pl. same or **tsunamis**) a tidal wave caused by an earthquake or other disturbance.
– ORIGIN Japanese, 'harbour wave'.

TT abbreviation **1** teetotal or teetotaller. **2** Tourist Trophy.

TTL abbreviation **1** transistor transistor logic, a widely used technology for making integrated electronic circuits. **2** (of a camera focusing system) through-the-lens.

Tuareg /**twah**-reg/ noun (pl. same or **Tuaregs**) a member of a Berber people of the western and central Sahara.
– ORIGIN the name in Berber.

tub noun **1** a low, wide, open container with a flat bottom. **2** a small plastic or cardboard container for food. **3** informal a bath. **4** informal a short, broad boat that is awkward to handle.
– ORIGIN probably German or Dutch.

tuba noun a large low-pitched brass wind instrument.
– ORIGIN Latin, 'trumpet'.

tubal adjective relating to or occurring in a tube, especially the Fallopian tubes.

tubby adjective (**tubbier, tubbiest**) informal (of a person) short and rather fat.
– DERIVATIVES **tubbiness** noun.

tube noun **1** a long, hollow cylinder for conveying or holding something. **2** a flexible metal or plastic container sealed at one end and having a cap at the other: a tube of toothpaste. **3** a hollow cylindrical organ or structure in an animal or plant. **4** Brit. trademark (**the Tube**) the underground railway system in London. **5** a sealed container containing two electrodes between which an electric current can be made to flow. **6** a cathode ray tube, especially in a television set. **7** (**the tube**) N. Amer. informal television. •verb (usu. as adj. **tubed**) provide something with a tube or tubes.
– PHRASES **go down the tube** (or **tubes**) informal be completely lost or wasted.
– ORIGIN Latin tubus.

tuber noun **1** a thickened underground part of a stem or rhizome, e.g. that of the potato, bearing buds from which new plants grow. **2** a thickened fleshy root, e.g. of the dahlia.
– ORIGIN Latin, 'hump, swelling'.

tubercle /**tyoo**-ber-k'l/ noun **1** a small lump on a bone or on the surface of an animal or plant. **2** a small rounded swelling in the lungs and other tissues, characteristic of tuberculosis.
– ORIGIN Latin tuberculum 'small lump or swelling'.

tubercle bacillus noun the bacterium that causes tuberculosis.

tubercular /tyoo-**ber**-kyuu-ler/ adjective **1** relating to or affected with tuberculosis. **2** having or covered with tubercles.

tuberculin /tyoo-**ber**-kyoo-lin/ noun a sterile protein extract produced from cultures of tubercle bacillus, used to test for tuberculosis.

tuberculosis /tyoo-ber-kyuu-**loh**-siss/ noun an infectious disease transmitted by a bacterium, in which tubercles (small swellings) appear in the tissues, especially the lungs.

tuberculous /tyoo-ber-kyuu-luhss/ adjective another term for **TUBERCULAR**.

tuberose /**tyoo**-buh-rohz/ noun a Mexican plant with heavily scented white waxy flowers and a bulb-like base.

tuberous /**tyoo**-buh-ruhss/ adjective **1** (of a plant) resembling, forming, or having a tuber or tubers. **2** Medicine having rounded swellings.

tubing noun a length or lengths of material in the form of tubes.

tub-thumping noun informal the expression of opinions in a loud and aggressive way.
– DERIVATIVES **tub-thumper** noun.

tubular adjective **1** long, round, and hollow like a tube. **2** made from a tube or tubes.

tubular bells plural noun an orchestral instrument consisting of a row of hanging metal tubes struck with a mallet.

tubule /**tyoo**-byool/ noun a very small tube, especially in an animal or plant.
– ORIGIN Latin tubulus.

TUC abbreviation (in the UK) Trades Union Congress.

tuck verb **1** push, fold, or turn under or between two surfaces: he tucked his shirt into his trousers. **2** (**tuck someone in/up**) settle someone in bed by pulling the edges of the bedclothes firmly under the mattress. **3** store or locate in a safe or hidden place: a French restaurant tucked away in an arcade. **4** (**tuck in/into**) informal eat food heartily. **5** make a flattened, stitched fold in a garment or material. •noun **1** a flattened, stitched fold in a garment or material. **2** Brit. informal food eaten by children at school as a snack.
– ORIGIN Old English, 'punish, ill-treat'.

tucker noun **1** Austral./NZ informal food. **2** historical a piece of lace or linen worn on a bodice or as an insert at the front of a low-cut dress. •verb (**be tuckered out**) N. Amer. informal be exhausted or worn out.
– ORIGIN from **TUCK**.

Tudor adjective **1** relating to the English royal family which held the throne from 1485 to 1603. **2** referring to the main architectural style of the Tudor period, characterized by half-timbering. •noun a member of the Tudor family.

Tuesday noun the day of the week before Wednesday and following Monday.
– ORIGIN Old English, named after the Germanic god Tiw.

tufa /**tyoo**-fuh/ noun **1** a porous rock composed of calcium carbonate and formed as a deposit from mineral springs. **2** another term for **TUFF**.
– ORIGIN Italian.

tuff noun a light, porous rock formed from volcanic ash.
– ORIGIN Latin tofus.

tuffet noun **1** a tuft or clump. **2** a footstool or low seat.
– ORIGIN from **TUFT**.

tuft noun a bunch of threads, grass, or hair, held or growing together at the base.
– DERIVATIVES **tufted** adjective **tufty** adjective.
– ORIGIN probably from Old French tofe.

tufted duck noun a freshwater diving duck with a drooping crest and black and white plumage.

tug verb (**tugs, tugging, tugged**) pull something hard or suddenly. •noun **1** a hard or sudden pull. **2** (also **tugboat**) a small, powerful boat for towing larger boats and ships.
– ORIGIN from TOW[1].

tug of war noun a contest in which two teams pull at opposite ends of a rope until one drags the other over a central line.

tuition noun teaching or instruction, especially of individuals or small groups.
– ORIGIN Latin.

tulip noun a spring-flowering plant with boldly coloured cup-shaped flowers.
– ORIGIN Persian, 'turban' (from the shape of the flower).

tulip tree noun **1** a North American tree with large leaves and small tulip-like flowers. **2** informal a magnolia tree or shrub.

tulle /tyool/ noun a soft, fine net material, used for making veils and dresses.
– ORIGIN from *Tulle*, a town in SW France.

tum noun informal a person's stomach or abdomen.

tumble verb **1** fall suddenly, clumsily, or headlong. **2** move in an uncontrolled way. **3** decrease rapidly in amount or value: *property prices tumbled*. **4** rumple; disarrange. **5** (**tumble to**) informal suddenly realize something. •noun **1** a sudden or clumsy fall. **2** an untidy or confused arrangement or state: *a tumble of untamed curls*. **3** an acrobatic feat such as a cartwheel.
– ORIGIN German *tummelen*.

tumbledown adjective (of a building) falling or fallen into ruin.

tumble dryer noun Brit. a machine that dries washed laundry by spinning it in hot air inside a rotating drum.

tumbler noun **1** a drinking glass with straight sides and no handle or stem. [formerly having a rounded bottom so that it could not be put down until emptied.] **2** an acrobat. **3** a part of a lock that holds the bolt until lifted by a key. **4** an electrical switch worked by pushing a small sprung lever.

tumbleweed noun N. Amer. & Austral./NZ a plant of dry regions which breaks off near the ground in late summer, forming light masses blown about by the wind.

tumbril /tum-bril/ (also **tumbrel**) noun historical an open cart that tilted backwards to empty out its load, especially one used to take prisoners to the guillotine during the French Revolution.
– ORIGIN Old French *tomberel*.

tumescent /tyuu-mess-uhnt/ adjective swollen or becoming swollen.
– DERIVATIVES **tumescence** noun.
– ORIGIN from Latin *tumere* 'to swell'.

tumid /tyoo-mid/ adjective **1** (of a part of the body) swollen. **2** (of language) pompous.
– ORIGIN Latin *tumidus*.

tummy noun (pl. **tummies**) informal a person's stomach or abdomen.
– ORIGIN a child's pronunciation of STOMACH.

tummy button noun informal a person's navel.

tumour (US **tumor**) noun a swelling of a part of the body caused by an abnormal growth of tissue.

– DERIVATIVES **tumorous** adjective.
– ORIGIN Latin *tumor*.

tump noun chiefly dialect **1** a small rounded hill. **2** a clump of trees or grass.
– ORIGIN unknown.

tumult noun **1** a loud, confused noise, as caused by a large mass of people. **2** confusion or disorder.
– ORIGIN Latin *tumultus*.

tumultuous /tyuu-mul-tyuu-uhss/ adjective **1** very loud or uproarious: *tumultuous applause*. **2** excited, confused, or disorderly.
– DERIVATIVES **tumultuously** adverb.

tumulus /tyoo-myuu-luhss/ noun (pl. **tumuli** /tyoo-myuu-ly/) an ancient burial mound.
– ORIGIN Latin.

tun noun a large beer or wine cask.
– ORIGIN Latin *tunna*.

tuna noun (pl. same or **tunas**) a large edible fish of warm seas.
– ORIGIN Spanish *atún*.

tundish noun Brit. a broad open container or large funnel with one or more holes at the bottom, used in plumbing or melting and moulding metal.
– ORIGIN from TUN + DISH.

tundra /tun-druh/ noun a vast, flat, treeless Arctic region of Europe, Asia, and North America in which the subsoil is permanently frozen.
– ORIGIN Lappish (the language of the Lapps).

tune noun a sequence of notes that forms a piece of music; a melody. •verb **1** (also **tune up**) adjust a musical instrument to the correct pitch. **2** adjust a radio or television to a particular frequency. **3** (**tune in**) watch or listen to a television or radio broadcast. **4** adjust an engine or balance mechanical parts so that they run smoothly and efficiently. **5** adjust or adapt to a purpose or situation: *the animals are finely tuned to life in the desert*.
– PHRASES **in** (or **out of**) **tune** in (or not in) the correct musical pitch. **to the tune of** informal amounting to or involving a particular sum of money.
– DERIVATIVES **tunable** (also **tuneable**) adjective.
– ORIGIN from TONE.

tuneful adjective having a pleasing tune; melodious.
– DERIVATIVES **tunefully** adverb **tunefulness** noun.

tuneless adjective not pleasing to listen to.
– DERIVATIVES **tunelessly** adverb **tunelessness** noun.

tuner noun **1** a person who tunes musical instruments, especially pianos. **2** an electronic device used for tuning. **3** an electronic device in a stereo system that receives radio signals and supplies them to an audio amplifier.

tunesmith noun informal a composer of popular music or songs.

tungsten /tung-stuhn/ noun a hard grey metallic element with a very high melting point, used to make electric light filaments.
– ORIGIN Swedish.

tungsten carbide noun a very hard grey compound used in making engineering dies, cutting and drilling tools, etc.

tunic noun **1** a loose sleeveless garment reaching to the thighs or knees. **2** a close-

fitting short coat worn as part of a uniform.
– ORIGIN Latin *tunica*.

tuning fork noun a two-pronged steel device used for tuning instruments, which vibrates when hit against a surface to give a note of specific pitch.

Tunisian /tyoo-**ni**-zi-uhn/ noun a person from Tunisia. ● adjective relating to Tunisia.

tunnel noun an underground passage, built through a hill or under a building or dug by a burrowing animal. ● verb (**tunnels, tunnelling, tunnelled**; US **tunnels, tunneling, tunneled**) dig or force a passage underground or through something.
– DERIVATIVES **tunneller** noun.
– ORIGIN Old French *tonel* 'small cask'.

tunnel vision noun 1 a condition in which a person cannot see things properly if they are not straight ahead. 2 informal the tendency to focus only on a single or limited aspect of a subject or situation.

tunny noun (pl. same or **tunnies**) a tuna.
– ORIGIN Greek *thunnos*.

tup chiefly Brit. noun a ram. ● verb (**tups, tupping, tupped**) (of a ram) mate with a ewe.
– ORIGIN unknown.

Tupi /**too**-pi/ noun (pl. same or **Tupis**) 1 a member of a group of American Indian peoples of the Amazon valley. 2 any of the languages of the Tupi.
– DERIVATIVES **Tupian** adjective.
– ORIGIN a local name.

Tupi-Guarani noun a South American Indian language family whose main members are Guarani and the Tupian languages.

tuppence noun Brit. variant spelling of **TWOPENCE**.

tuppenny adjective Brit. variant spelling of **TWOPENNY**.

turban noun a long length of material wound round a cap or the head, worn especially by Muslim and Sikh men.
– DERIVATIVES **turbaned** (also **turbanned**) adjective.
– ORIGIN Persian.

turbid /**ter**-bid/ adjective 1 (of a liquid) cloudy or muddy; not clear. 2 confused or unclear in meaning.
– DERIVATIVES **turbidity** noun.
– ORIGIN Latin *turbidus*.

turbine /**ter**-byn, **ter**-bin/ noun a machine for producing power in which a wheel or rotor is made to revolve by a fast-moving flow of water, steam, gas, or air.
– ORIGIN Latin *turbo* 'spinning top, whirl'.

turbo /**ter**-boh/ noun (pl. **turbos**) short for **TURBOCHARGER**.

turbocharge verb (often as adj. **turbocharged**) 1 equip an engine or vehicle with a turbocharger. 2 make more powerful, fast, or exciting: *turbocharged business growth*.

turbocharger noun a supercharger driven by a turbine powered by the engine's exhaust gases.

turbofan noun a jet engine in which a turbine-driven fan provides additional thrust.

turbojet noun a jet engine in which the jet gases also operate a turbine-driven compressor for compressing the air drawn

into the engine.

turboprop noun a jet engine in which a turbine is used to drive a propeller.

turbot noun (pl. same or **turbots**) an edible flatfish of inshore waters, which has large bony swellings on the body.
– ORIGIN Scandinavian.

turbulence noun 1 violent or unsteady movement of air or water, or of another fluid. 2 upheaval, conflict, or confusion: *Europe emerged from a long period of political turbulence.*

turbulent /**ter**-byuu-luhnt/ adjective 1 involving much conflict, upheaval, or confusion. 2 (of air or water) moving violently or unsteadily.
– DERIVATIVES **turbulently** adverb.
– ORIGIN Latin *turbulentus* 'full of commotion'.

turd noun vulgar slang 1 a lump of excrement. 2 an unpleasant or disliked person.
– ORIGIN Old English.

tureen /tyuu-**reen**, tuh-**reen**/ noun a deep covered dish from which soup is served.
– ORIGIN French *terrine* 'large earthenware pot'.

turf noun (pl. **turfs** or **turves**) 1 grass and the surface layer of earth held together by its roots. 2 a piece of turf cut from the ground. 3 (**the turf**) horse racing or racecourses generally. 4 (**someone's turf**) informal a place or area of activity regarded as someone's personal territory or responsibility: *he did not like poachers on his turf.* ● verb 1 (**turf someone off/out**) informal, chiefly Brit. force someone to leave somewhere. 2 cover ground with turf.
– ORIGIN Old English.

turf accountant noun Brit. formal a bookmaker.

turgid /**ter**-jid/ adjective 1 (of language or style) pompous and boring. 2 swollen or full: *a turgid river.*
– DERIVATIVES **turgidity** noun **turgidly** adverb.
– ORIGIN Latin *turgidus*.

Turk noun 1 a person from Turkey. 2 a member of any of the ancient peoples who spoke Turkic languages.

turkey noun (pl. **turkeys**) 1 a large game bird native to North America, that is bred for food. 2 informal something that is very unsuccessful or of very poor quality.
– PHRASES **talk turkey** N. Amer. informal talk frankly and openly.
– ORIGIN short for **TURKEYCOCK** or *turkeyhen*, first referring to the guineafowl (which was imported through Turkey), and then wrongly to the American bird.

turkeycock noun a male turkey.

Turkic /**ter**-kik/ adjective referring to a large group of languages of western and central Asia, including Turkish and Azerbaijani.

Turkish noun the language of Turkey. ● adjective relating to Turkey or its language.

Turkish bath noun 1 a cleansing treatment that involves sitting in a room filled with very hot air or steam, followed by washing and massage. 2 a building or room where a Turkish bath is available.

Turkish coffee noun very strong black coffee served with the fine grounds in it.

Turkish delight noun a sweet consisting of flavoured gelatin coated in icing sugar.

turmeric /ter-muh-rik/ noun a bright yellow powder obtained from a plant of the ginger family, used as a spice in Asian cookery.
– ORIGIN perhaps from French *terre mérite* 'deserving earth'.

turmoil noun a state of great disturbance, confusion, or uncertainty.
– ORIGIN unknown.

turn verb 1 move in a circular direction around a central point. 2 move so as to face or go in a different direction. 3 change in nature, state, form, or colour: *the drizzle turned into a downpour.* 4 pass or reach a particular age or time. 5 (of the tide) change from flood to ebb or vice versa. 6 twist or sprain an ankle. 7 make a profit. 8 shape something on a lathe. 9 (usu. as adj. **turned**) give a pleasing form to: *finely turned phrases.* 10 (of milk) become sour. ●noun 1 an act of turning. 2 a bend in a road, river, etc. 3 a place where a road meets or branches off another; a turning. 4 a time when a member of a group must or is allowed to do something: *it was her turn to speak.* 5 a time when one period of time ends and another begins: *the turn of the century.* 6 a change in a situation. 7 a brief feeling of illness: *a funny turn.* 8 a short performance, especially one of a number given by different performers. 9 a short walk or ride. 10 one round in a coil of rope or other material.
– PHRASES **at every turn** on every occasion; continually. **be turned out** be dressed in the specified way. **by turns** alternately. **do someone a good turn** do something that is helpful for someone. **in turn** one after the other. **out of turn** at a time when it is inappropriate or not one's turn. **take turns** (or Brit. **take it in turns**) (of two or more people) do something alternately or one after the other. **to a turn** to exactly the right degree. **turn someone away** refuse to allow someone to enter a place. **turn and turn about** chiefly Brit. one after another. **turn someone/thing down** 1 reject something offered or proposed by someone. 2 reduce the volume or strength of sound, heat, etc. produced by a device by adjusting its controls. **turn in** informal go to bed in the evening. **turn someone/thing in** hand someone or something over to the authorities. **turn off** leave one road in order to join another. **turn someone off** informal make someone feel bored or disgusted. **turn something off** (or **on**) stop (or start) the operation of something by means of a tap, switch, or button. **turn of mind** a particular way of thinking. **turn of speed** the ability to go fast when necessary. **turn on** suddenly attack someone or something. **turn someone on** informal excite someone, especially sexually. **turn out** 1 prove to be the case. 2 attend a meeting, go to vote, etc. **turn something out** 1 switch off an electric light. 2 produce something. 3 empty something, especially one's pockets. **turn over** (of an engine) start or continue to run properly. **turn someone over** hand someone over to the custody or care of someone in authority. **turn something over** 1 transfer control or management of something to someone else. 2 (of a business) have a turnover of a particular amount. **turn something round** (or **around**) make an

organization successful after a period of poor performance. **turn tail** informal turn round and run away. **turn to** 1 start doing or becoming involved with something. 2 go to someone for help or information. **turn up** 1 be found, especially by chance. 2 put in an appearance; arrive. **turn something up** 1 increase the volume or strength of sound, heat, etc. produced by a device by adjusting its controls. 2 reveal or discover something.
– DERIVATIVES **turner** noun.
– ORIGIN Latin *tornare.*

turnaround (also **turnround**) noun 1 an abrupt or unexpected change. 2 the process of completing a task, or the time needed to do this.

turnbuckle noun a coupling used to connect two rods, lengths of boat's rigging, etc. lengthwise or to regulate their length or tension.

turncoat noun a person who deserts one party or cause in order to join an opposing one.

turndown noun 1 a rejection or refusal. 2 a decline; a downturn.

turning noun 1 a place where a road branches off another. 2 the action or skill of using a lathe. 3 (**turnings**) shavings of wood resulting from turning wood on a lathe.

turning circle noun the smallest circle in which a vehicle or boat can turn without reversing.

turning point noun a time when a decisive change happens, especially one with good results.

turnip noun a round root vegetable with white or cream flesh.
– ORIGIN from an unknown first element + **NEEP**.

turnkey noun (pl. **turnkeys**) old use a jailer.

turn-off noun 1 a junction at which a road branches off another. 2 informal a person or thing that makes one feel bored or disgusted.

turn-on noun informal a person or thing that makes one feel excited or sexually aroused.

turnout noun the number of people attending or taking part in an event.

turnover noun 1 the amount of money taken by a business in a particular period. 2 the rate at which employees leave a workforce and are replaced. 3 the rate at which goods are sold and replaced in a shop. 4 a small pie made by folding a piece of pastry over on itself to enclose a filling.

turnpike noun 1 US a motorway on which a toll is charged. 2 historical a toll gate. 3 historical a road on which a toll was collected.
– ORIGIN first referring to a spiked barrier fixed across a road as a defence against attack: from **PIKE²**.

turnround noun another term for **TURNAROUND**.

turnstile noun a mechanical gate with revolving horizontal arms that allow only one person at a time to pass through.

turnstone noun a small short-billed sandpiper noted for turning over stones to find small animals.

turntable noun 1 a circular revolving plate supporting a record as it is played. 2 a circular revolving platform for turning a railway locomotive.

t

turn-up noun Brit. **1** the end of a trouser leg folded upwards on the outside. **2** informal an unexpected event; a surprise.

turpentine /ter-puhn-tyn/ noun **1** a substance produced by certain trees, distilled to make oil of turpentine. **2** (also **oil of turpentine**) a strong-smelling oil distilled from this substance, used in mixing and thinning paints and varnishes and for cleaning paintbrushes.
– ORIGIN Old French *terebentine*.

turpitude /ter-pi-tyood/ noun formal wicked behaviour or character: *acts of moral turpitude*.
– ORIGIN Latin *turpitudo*.

turps noun informal turpentine.

turquoise /ter-kwoyz, ter-kwahz/ noun **1** a greenish-blue or sky-blue semi-precious stone. **2** a greenish-blue colour.
– ORIGIN Old French *turqueise* 'Turkish stone'.

turret noun **1** a small tower at the corner of a building or wall, especially of a castle. **2** an armoured tower, usually one that revolves, for a gun and gunners in a ship, aircraft, or tank.
– DERIVATIVES **turreted** adjective.
– ORIGIN Old French *tourete* 'small tower'.

turtle noun a sea or freshwater reptile with a bony or leathery shell and flippers or webbed toes.
– PHRASES **turn turtle** (chiefly of a boat) turn upside down.
– ORIGIN probably from French *tortue* 'tortoise'.

turtle dove noun a small dove with a soft purring call.
– ORIGIN from Latin *turtur*.

turtleneck noun **1** Brit. a high, round, close-fitting neck on a sweater or similar garment. **2** North American term for POLO NECK.

turves plural of TURF.

Tuscan /tuss-kuhn/ adjective **1** relating to Tuscany in central Italy. **2** relating to a classical order of architecture resembling the Doric but lacking all decoration. •noun a person from Tuscany.

tush¹ /rhymes with lush/ exclamation old use or humorous expressing disapproval, impatience, or dismissal.

tush² /rhymes with push/ noun informal, chiefly N. Amer. a person's buttocks.
– ORIGIN Yiddish.

tusk noun a long pointed tooth which protrudes from a closed mouth, as one of a pair in the elephant, walrus, or wild boar.
– DERIVATIVES **tusked** adjective.
– ORIGIN Old English.

tusker noun an elephant or wild boar with well-developed tusks.

tussle noun a vigorous struggle or scuffle. •verb take part in a tussle.
– ORIGIN perhaps from dialect *touse* 'handle roughly'.

tussock /tus-suhk/ noun a dense clump or tuft of grass.
– DERIVATIVES **tussocky** adjective.
– ORIGIN perhaps from dialect *tusk* 'tuft'.

tussore /tus-sor, tus-ser/ noun a strong but coarse kind of silk.
– ORIGIN Hindi.

tutee /tyoo-tee/ noun a student or pupil of a tutor.

tutelage /tyoo-ti-lij/ noun **1** protection of or authority over someone or something: *the organizations remained under firm government tutelage.* **2** instruction; tuition.
– ORIGIN Latin *tutela* 'keeping'.

tutelary /tyoo-ti-luh-ri/ adjective **1** acting as a protector, guardian, or patron. **2** relating to protection or a guardian.

tutor noun **1** a private teacher who teaches a single pupil or a very small group. **2** chiefly Brit. a university or college teacher responsible for the teaching and supervision of students assigned to them. **3** Brit. a book of instruction in a particular subject. •verb act as a tutor to a pupil or very small group.
– ORIGIN Latin.

tutorial noun **1** a period of tuition given by a university or college tutor. **2** a book or computer program giving information about a subject or explaining how to do something. •adjective relating to a tutor or tuition.

Tutsi /tuut-si/ noun (pl. same or **Tutsis**) a member of a people forming a minority of the population of Rwanda and Burundi.

tutti /tuut-ti/ adverb & adjective Music with all voices or instruments together.
– ORIGIN Italian.

tutti-frutti /toot-ti-froot-ti/ noun (pl. **tutti-fruttis**) a type of ice cream containing mixed fruits.
– ORIGIN Italian, 'all fruits'.

tutu /too-too/ noun a female ballet dancer's costume consisting of a bodice attached to a very short, stiff skirt made of many layers of fabric and projecting horizontally from the waist.
– ORIGIN French.

Tuvaluan /too-val-uu-uhn/ noun a person from Tuvalu, a country made up of a number of islands in the SW Pacific. •adjective relating to Tuvalu.

tux noun informal, chiefly N. Amer. a tuxedo.

tuxedo /tuk-see-doh/ noun (pl. **tuxedos** or **tuxedoes**) chiefly N. Amer. **1** a man's dinner jacket. **2** a formal evening suit including a dinner jacket.
– DERIVATIVES **tuxedoed** adjective.
– ORIGIN from *Tuxedo* Park, the site of a country club in New York.

TV abbreviation television.

TVP abbreviation trademark textured vegetable protein, a protein obtained from soya beans and made to resemble minced meat.

twaddle noun informal trivial or foolish speech or writing; nonsense.
– ORIGIN unknown.

twain cardinal number old-fashioned term for TWO.
– ORIGIN Old English.

twang noun **1** a strong ringing sound such as that made by the plucked string of a musical instrument. **2** a distinctive nasal way of speaking. •verb make a twang.
– DERIVATIVES **twangy** adjective.
– ORIGIN imitating the sound.

'twas contraction old use or literary it was.

twat /twat, twot/ noun vulgar slang **1** a woman's genitals. **2** a stupid or unpleasant person. •verb Brit. informal hit or punch someone.
– ORIGIN unknown.

tweak verb **1** twist or pull something with a small sharp movement. **2** informal improve a mechanism or system by making fine adjustments. •noun **1** an act of tweaking. **2** informal a fine adjustment.
– DERIVATIVES **tweaker** noun.
– ORIGIN probably from dialect *twick* 'pull sharply'.

twee adjective Brit. excessively quaint, pretty, or sentimental.
– ORIGIN from a child's pronunciation of SWEET.

tweed noun **1** a rough woollen cloth flecked with mixed colours. **2** (**tweeds**) clothes made of tweed.
– ORIGIN from a Scots form of TWILL, influenced by association with the river *Tweed*.

tweedy adjective (**tweedier**, **tweediest**) **1** made of tweed cloth. **2** informal typical of the country gentry, especially in being conservative or hearty.
– DERIVATIVES **tweediness** noun.

'tween contraction old use or literary between.

tweenie (also **tween**, **tweenager**) noun informal a child between the ages of about 10 and 14.

tweet noun the chirp of a small bird. •verb make a chirping noise.
– ORIGIN imitating the sound.

tweeter noun a loudspeaker designed to reproduce high frequencies.

tweeze verb pluck or pull something with tweezers.

tweezers plural noun (also **pair of tweezers**) a small instrument like a pair of pincers for plucking out hairs and picking up small objects.
– ORIGIN from former *tweeze* 'case of surgical instruments'.

twelfth /twelfth, twelth/ ordinal number **1** that is number twelve in a sequence; 12th. **2** (**a twelfth/one twelfth**) each of twelve equal parts into which something is divided. **3** a musical interval spanning an octave and a fifth in a scale.
– DERIVATIVES **twelfthly** adverb.

twelfth man noun Cricket a player acting as a reserve in a game.

Twelfth Night noun **1** 6 January, the Christian feast of the Epiphany. **2** the evening of 5 January, formerly the twelfth and last day of Christmas festivities.

twelve cardinal number two more than ten; 12. (Roman numeral: **xii** or **XII**.)
– ORIGIN Old English.

twelvemonth noun old use a year.

twenty cardinal number (pl. **twenties**) ten less than thirty; 20. (Roman numeral: **xx** or **XX**.)
– DERIVATIVES **twentieth** ordinal number.
– ORIGIN Old English.

24-7 (also **24/7**) adverb informal twenty-four hours a day, seven days a week; all the time.

twenty-twenty vision (also **20/20 vision**) noun normal sharpness of vision.
– ORIGIN with reference to the fraction for normal visual sharpness in eyesight tests.

'twere contraction old use or literary it were.

twerp noun informal a silly or annoying person.
– ORIGIN unknown.

twice adverb **1** two times. **2** double in degree or quantity.

– ORIGIN Old English.

twiddle verb play or fiddle with something in an aimless or nervous way. •noun an act of twiddling.
– PHRASES **twiddle one's thumbs** have nothing to do.
– DERIVATIVES **twiddler** noun **twiddly** adjective.
– ORIGIN probably combining *twirl* or *twist* with *fiddle*.

twig[1] noun a slender woody shoot growing from a branch or stem of a tree or shrub.
– DERIVATIVES **twigged** adjective **twiggy** adjective.
– ORIGIN Old English.

twig[2] verb (**twigs**, **twigging**, **twigged**) Brit. informal come to understand or realize something.
– ORIGIN unknown.

twilight noun **1** the soft glowing light from the sky when the sun is below the horizon. **2** a period or state of gradual decline: *he was in the twilight of his career.* •adjective mysterious, secret, or unreal: *the twilight world of drugs.*
– ORIGIN from an Old English base meaning 'two' + LIGHT[1].

twilit adjective dimly lit.

twill noun a fabric so woven as to have a surface of diagonal parallel ridges.
– DERIVATIVES **twilled** adjective.
– ORIGIN from Old English, 'two'.

'twill contraction old use or literary it will.

twin noun **1** one of two children or animals born at the same time. **2** a thing that is exactly like another. •adjective **1** forming or being one of a pair of twins or matching things: *the twin problems of economic failure and social decline.* **2** (of a bedroom) containing two single beds. •verb (**twins**, **twinning**, **twinned**) **1** link or combine things as a pair. **2** Brit. link a town with another in a different country, for the purposes of cultural exchange.
– ORIGIN Old English.

twine noun strong thread or string consisting of strands of hemp or cotton twisted together. •verb wind something round something else.
– ORIGIN Old English, 'thread, linen'.

twinge noun **1** a sudden, sharp pain. **2** a brief, sharp pang of emotion. •verb (**twinges**, **twingeing** or **twinging**, **twinged**) suffer a sudden, sharp pain.
– ORIGIN Old English, 'pinch, wring'.

twinkle verb **1** (of a star or light) shine with a gleam that changes constantly from bright to faint. **2** (of a person's eyes) sparkle with amusement or liveliness. **3** (of a person's feet) move lightly and rapidly. •noun a twinkling sparkle or gleam.
– PHRASES **in a twinkling of an eye** in an instant.
– DERIVATIVES **twinkly** adjective.
– ORIGIN Old English.

twinkle-toed adjective informal nimble and quick on one's feet.

twinset noun chiefly Brit. a woman's matching cardigan and jumper.

twirl verb spin quickly and lightly round. •noun **1** an act of twirling. **2** a spiral shape.
– DERIVATIVES **twirler** noun **twirly** adjective.
– ORIGIN probably from former *trill* 'twiddle, spin'.

t

twist verb **1** form something into a bent, curled, or distorted shape. **2** turn or bend round or into a different direction: *she twisted in her seat to look at the buildings.* **3** force out of the natural position by a twisting action: *he twisted his ankle.* **4** take or have a winding course. **5** deliberately distort the meaning of words. **6** (as adj. **twisted**) strange or abnormal in an unpleasant way; perverted. **7** dance the twist. •noun **1** an act of twisting. **2** a thing with a spiral or curved shape. **3** a new or unexpected development or way of treating something: *the plot includes a clever twist.* **4** (**the twist**) a dance with a twisting movement of the body, popular in the 1960s. **5** Brit. a paper packet with twisted ends. **6** a fine strong thread consisting of twisted fibres. **7** a carpet with a tightly curled pile.
– PHRASES **round the twist** Brit. informal mad; crazy. **twist someone's arm** informal forcefully persuade someone to do something that they are reluctant to do.
– DERIVATIVES **twisty** adjective.
– ORIGIN Old English.

twister noun **1** Brit. informal a swindler or dishonest person. **2** N. Amer. a tornado.

twit[1] noun informal, chiefly Brit. a foolish person.
– DERIVATIVES **twittish** adjective.
– ORIGIN perhaps from TWIT[2].

twit[2] verb (**twits, twitting, twitted**) informal tease someone good-humouredly.
– ORIGIN Old English, 'reproach with'.

twitch verb make a short jerking movement. •noun **1** a twitching movement. **2** a pang: *he felt a twitch of annoyance.*
– ORIGIN Germanic.

twitcher noun Brit. informal a birdwatcher devoted to spotting rare birds.

twitchy adjective (**twitchier, twitchiest**) informal nervous; anxious.

twitter verb **1** (of a bird) make a series of short high sounds. **2** talk rapidly in a nervous or trivial way. •noun **1** a twittering sound. **2** informal an agitated or excited state.
– DERIVATIVES **twittery** adjective.
– ORIGIN imitating the sound.

'twixt contraction betwixt; between.

two cardinal number one less than three; 2. (Roman numeral: **ii** or **II**.)
– PHRASES **put two and two together** draw an obvious conclusion from the available evidence. **two by two** side by side in pairs. **two-horse race** a contest in which only two of the competitors are likely winners.
– DERIVATIVES **twofold** adjective & adverb.
– ORIGIN Old English.

USAGE: For an explanation of the difference between **two**, **to**, and **too**, see the note at TO.

two-bit adjective N. Amer. informal unimportant, cheap, or worthless.

two-by-four noun a length of wood with a rectangular cross section approximately two inches by four inches.

twoc /twok/ verb (**twocs, twoccing, twocced**) Brit. informal steal a car.
– ORIGIN from the initial letters of *taken without owner's consent.*

two-dimensional adjective **1** having or appearing to have length and breadth but no depth. **2** lacking depth; superficial: *two-dimensional bad guys.*

two-faced adjective insincere and deceitful.

twopence /tup-puhnss/ (also **tuppence**) noun Brit. **1** the sum of two pence, especially before decimalization (1971). **2** informal anything at all: *he didn't care twopence for her.*

twopenn'orth /too-pen-nuhth/ noun an amount that is worth or costs twopence.
– PHRASES **add** (or **put in**) **one's twopenn'orth** informal contribute one's opinion.

twopenny /tup-puh-ni/ (also **tuppeny**) adjective Brit. costing two pence, especially before decimalization (1971).

twopenny-halfpenny adjective Brit. informal unimportant or worthless.

two-piece adjective consisting of two matching items.

twosome noun a set of two people or things.

two-step noun a dance with sliding steps in march or polka time.

two-stroke adjective (of an internal-combustion engine) having its power cycle completed in one up-and-down movement of the piston.

two-time verb informal be unfaithful to a lover or a husband or wife.

'twould contraction old use it would.

two-up two-down noun Brit. informal a house with two main rooms downstairs and two bedrooms upstairs.

two-way adjective **1** involving movement or communication in opposite directions. **2** (of a switch) permitting a current to be switched on or off from either of two points.
– PHRASES **two-way street** a situation involving shared action or responsibility: *trust is a two-way street.*

two-way mirror noun a panel of glass that can be seen through from one side and is a mirror on the other.

TX abbreviation Texas.

tycoon noun a wealthy, powerful person in business or industry.
– ORIGIN Japanese, 'great lord'.

tying present participle of TIE.

tyke (also **tike**) noun **1** informal a mischievous child. **2** dated, chiefly Brit. an unpleasant man.
– ORIGIN Old Norse, 'bitch'.

tympani plural noun variant spelling of TIMPANI.

tympanum /tim-puh-nuhm/ noun (pl. **tympanums** or **tympana** /tim-puh-nuh/) **1** the eardrum. **2** Architecture a space enclosed between the lintel of a doorway and an arch over it, or the triangle enclosed by a classical pediment.
– DERIVATIVES **tympanic** adjective.
– ORIGIN Greek *tumpanon* 'drum'.

Tynwald /tin-wuhld/ noun the parliament of the Isle of Man.
– ORIGIN Old Norse, 'place of assembly'.

type noun **1** a category of people or things that share particular qualities or features. **2** informal a person of a specified character or nature: *sporty types in tracksuits.* **3** a person or thing that is a typical example of something: *she described his sayings as the type of modern wisdom.* **4** printed characters or letters. **5** pieces of metal with raised letters or characters on their upper surface, for use in

letterpress printing. •**verb 1** write using a typewriter or computer. **2** Medicine determine the type to which a person or their blood or tissue belongs.
– DERIVATIVES **typing** noun.
– ORIGIN Greek *tupos* 'impression, figure, type'.

typecast verb (past and past part. **typecast**)
1 repeatedly cast an actor in the same type of role because their appearance is appropriate or they are known for such roles. **2** regard as fitting a stereotype: *she didn't want to be typecast as an angst-ridden female rock musician.*

typeface noun a particular design of printed letters or characters.

typescript noun a typed copy of a written work.

typeset verb (**typesets, typesetting, typeset**) arrange or generate the data or type for written material to be printed.
– DERIVATIVES **typesetter** noun **typesetting** noun.

typewriter noun an electric, electronic, or manual machine with keys for producing characters similar to printed ones.
– DERIVATIVES **typewriting** noun **typewritten** adjective.

typhoid (also **typhoid fever**) noun an infectious fever caused by a bacterium, resulting in red spots on the chest and abdomen and severe irritation of the intestines.
– ORIGIN from **TYPHUS**.

typhoon /ty-**foon**/ noun a tropical storm with very high winds, occurring in the region of the Indian Ocean or the western Pacific Ocean.
– ORIGIN partly from Arabic, partly from a Chinese dialect word meaning 'big wind'.

typhus /ty-fuhss/ noun an infectious disease caused by a bacterium, resulting in a purple rash, headaches, fever, and usually delirium.
– ORIGIN Greek *tuphos* 'smoke, stupor'.

typical adjective **1** having the distinctive qualities of a particular type of person or thing: *a typical example of a small American town.* **2** behaving or happening in the expected or usual way: *a typical day began with breakfast at 7.30 a.m.*
– DERIVATIVES **typicality** noun **typically** adverb.

typify verb (**typifies, typifying, typified**) be a typical example or feature of: *their furniture is typified by its functional design.*
– DERIVATIVES **typification** noun.

typist noun a person skilled in typing and employed for this purpose.

typo /ty-poh/ noun (pl. **typos**) informal a small mistake in typed or printed writing.

typography /ty-pog-ruh-fi/ noun **1** the art or process of preparing material for printing, especially of designing how printed text will appear. **2** the style and appearance of printed matter.
– DERIVATIVES **typographer** noun **typographic** adjective **typographical** adjective.

typology /ty-pol-uh-ji/ noun (pl. **typologies**) a classification of things according to general type.
– DERIVATIVES **typological** adjective **typologist** noun.

tyrannical adjective exercising power in a cruel and unfair way.
– DERIVATIVES **tyrannically** adverb.

tyrannicide /ti-ran-ni-syd, ty-ran-ni-syd/ noun **1** the killing of a tyrant. **2** the killer of a tyrant.
– DERIVATIVES **tyrannicidal** adjective.

tyrannize (or **tyrannise**) /ti-ruh-nyz/ verb rule or dominate someone in a cruel or oppressive way.

tyrannosaurus /ti-ran-nuh-**sor**-uhss/ (also **tyrannosaurus rex** /reks/) noun a very large meat-eating dinosaur with powerful jaws and small claw-like front legs.
– ORIGIN from Greek *turannos* 'tyrant' + *sauros* 'lizard'.

tyranny noun (pl. **tyrannies**) **1** cruel and oppressive government or rule. **2** a state under cruel and oppressive government. **3** cruel and unfair use of power or control: *a young man liberated from the tyranny of his father.*
– DERIVATIVES **tyrannous** adjective.

tyrant noun **1** a cruel and oppressive ruler. **2** a person who uses their power in a cruel and unfair way.
– ORIGIN Greek *turannos*.

tyre (US **tire**) noun a rubber covering that is inflated or that surrounds an inflated inner tube, fitted around a wheel to form a soft contact with the road.
– DERIVATIVES **tyred** adjective.
– ORIGIN probably a shortening of **ATTIRE**.

tyro /ty-roh/ noun (pl. **tyros**) a beginner or novice.
– ORIGIN Latin, 'recruit'.

tzar noun variant spelling of **TSAR**.

tzarina noun variant spelling of **TSARINA**.

tzatziki /tsat-tsee-ki/ noun a Greek side dish of yogurt with cucumber, garlic, and often mint.
– ORIGIN modern Greek.

t

Uu

U[1] (also **u**) noun (pl. **Us** or **U's**) the twenty-first letter of the alphabet.

U[2] abbreviation **1** (in names of sports clubs) United. **2** Brit. universal (referring to films classified as suitable for everyone to seen). •**symbol** the chemical element uranium.

U[3] adjective Brit. informal typical of or appropriate to the upper social classes.
– ORIGIN abbreviation of **UPPER CLASS**; coined by Alan S. C. Ross, a professor of linguistics, and popularized by Nancy Mitford's *Noblesse Oblige*.

UAE abbreviation United Arab Emirates.

U-bend noun a section of a pipe, especially of a waste pipe, shaped like a U.

uber- /oo-ber/ (also **über-**) prefix referring to an outstanding or supreme example of a person or thing: *an uberbabe*.
– ORIGIN German *über* 'over'.

Übermensch /oo-buh-mensh/ noun the ideal superior man of the future who could rise above conventional Christian morality to create and impose his own values.
– ORIGIN German, 'superhuman person', originally described by Nietzsche in *Thus Spake Zarathustra*.

ubiquitous /yoo-bi-kwi-tuhss/ adjective present, appearing, or found everywhere: *ubiquitous coffee shops.*
– DERIVATIVES **ubiquitously** adverb **ubiquitousness** noun **ubiquity** noun.
– ORIGIN from Latin *ubique* 'everywhere'.

U-boat noun a German submarine of the First or Second World War.
– ORIGIN German *U-Boot*, abbreviation of *Unterseeboot* 'undersea boat'.

u.c. abbreviation upper case.

UCAS /yoo-kass/ abbreviation (in the UK) Universities and Colleges Admissions Service.

UDA abbreviation Ulster Defence Association.

udder noun the milk-producing gland of female cattle, sheep, goats, horses, etc., hanging near the hind legs as a bag-like organ with two or more teats.
– ORIGIN Old English.

UDI abbreviation unilateral declaration of independence.

udon /oo-don/ noun (in Japanese cookery) large noodles made from wheat flour.
– ORIGIN Japanese.

UDR abbreviation Ulster Defence Regiment.

UEFA /yoo-ee-fuh, yoo-ay-fuh/ abbreviation Union of European Football Associations.

UFO /yoo-foh/ noun (pl. **UFOs**) a mysterious object seen in the sky for which it is claimed no scientific explanation can be found, believed by some to be a vehicle carrying beings from outer space.
– DERIVATIVES **ufologist** noun **ufology** noun.
– ORIGIN abbreviation of *unidentified flying object*.

Ugandan /yoo-gan-duhn/ noun a person from Uganda. •**adjective** relating to Uganda.

Ugli fruit /ug-li/ noun (pl. same) trademark a mottled green and yellow citrus fruit which is a cross between a grapefruit and a tangerine.
– ORIGIN from **UGLY**.

uglify verb (**uglifies, uglifying, uglified**) make something ugly.

ugly adjective (**uglier, ugliest**) **1** unpleasant or unattractive in appearance. **2** involving violence or other unpleasantness: *there were ugly scenes following the team's win over Leeds.* **3** disturbing or disagreeable: *the ugly truth about pensions is that there are no quick-fix solutions.*
– DERIVATIVES **ugliness** noun.
– ORIGIN from Old Norse, 'to be dreaded'.

ugly duckling noun a person who unexpectedly turns out to be beautiful or talented.
– ORIGIN from one of Hans Christian Andersen's fairy tales, in which the 'ugly duckling' is actually a young swan.

UHF abbreviation ultra-high frequency.

UHT abbreviation Brit. ultra heat treated (a process used to extend the shelf life of milk).

uillean pipes /il-lin, il-luhn/ plural noun Irish bagpipes played using bellows worked by the elbow.
– ORIGIN from Irish *píob uilleann* 'pipe of the elbow'.

UK abbreviation United Kingdom.

ukase /yoo-kayz/ noun **1** historical a decree with the force of law, issued by the tsarist Russian government. **2** a dictatorial command.
– ORIGIN Russian *ukaz* 'ordinance, edict'.

UKIP abbreviation United Kingdom Independence Party.

Ukrainian /yoo-kray-ni-uhn/ noun **1** a person from Ukraine. **2** the language of Ukraine.
•**adjective** relating to Ukraine.

ukulele /yoo-kuh-lay-li/ (also **ukelele**) noun a small four-stringed guitar of Hawaiian origin.
– ORIGIN Hawaiian, 'jumping flea'.

ulama noun variant spelling of **ULEMA**.

ulcer noun an open sore on an external or internal surface of the body, caused by a break

in the skin or mucous membrane which fails to heal.
– DERIVATIVES **ulcered** adjective **ulcerous** adjective.
– ORIGIN Latin *ulcus*.

ulcerate verb develop into or become affected by an ulcer.
– DERIVATIVES **ulceration** noun **ulcerative** adjective.

ulema /oo-li-muh, oo-li-mah/ (also **ulama**) noun
1 (treated as sing. or pl.) a group of Muslim scholars recognized as having specialist knowledge of Islamic sacred law and theology. **2** a member of an ulema.
– ORIGIN Arabic.

ullage /ul-lij/ noun **1** the amount by which a container falls short of being full. **2** loss of liquid by evaporation or leakage.
– ORIGIN from Old French *euillier* 'fill up'.

ulna /ul-nuh/ noun (pl. **ulnae** /ul-nee/ or **ulnas**) the thinner and longer of the two bones in the human forearm.
– DERIVATIVES **ulnar** adjective.
– ORIGIN Latin, related to ELL.

ulster noun a long, loose overcoat made of rough cloth, worn by men.
– ORIGIN from *Ulster* in Ireland, where it was originally sold.

Ulsterman (or **Ulsterwoman**) noun (pl. **Ulstermen** or **Ulsterwomen**) a person from Northern Ireland or Ulster.

ulterior adjective other than what is obvious or has been admitted: *she had some ulterior motive in coming.*
– ORIGIN Latin, 'further, more distant'.

ultimate adjective **1** being or happening at the end of a process; final. **2** being the best or most extreme example of its kind: *climbing Mount Everest is the ultimate challenge.* **3** basic or fundamental: *atoms are the ultimate constituents of anything that exists.* •noun (**the ultimate**) the best of its kind: *the scooter was the ultimate in continental chic.*
– DERIVATIVES **ultimacy** noun **ultimately** adverb.
– ORIGIN Latin *ultimatus*.

ultimatum /ul-ti-may-tuhm/ noun (pl. **ultimatums** or **ultimata** /ul-ti-may-tuh/) a final warning that action will be taken against someone unless they agree to another party's demands.
– ORIGIN Latin, 'thing that has come to an end'.

ultra noun informal a person with extreme political or religious views.

ultra- prefix **1** to an extreme degree; very: *ultralight.* **2** beyond; on the other side of: *ultramarine.*
– DERIVATIVES **unbeatably** adverb.
– ORIGIN Latin *ultra*.

ultra-high frequency noun a radio frequency in the range 300 to 3,000 megahertz.

ultralight adjective very lightweight.

ultramarine noun a brilliant deep blue pigment and colour.
– ORIGIN from Latin *ultramarinus* 'beyond the sea' (because the pigment was obtained from lapis lazuli, which was imported).

ultramontane /ul-truh-mon-tayn/ adjective **1** (in the Roman Catholic Church) believing that the pope should have supreme authority in matters of faith and discipline. **2** situated

on the other side of the Alps from the speaker.
•noun a person who believes that the pope should have supreme authority.
– DERIVATIVES **ultramontanism** noun.
– ORIGIN first referring to a representative of the Roman Catholic Church north of the Alps: from Latin *ultra* 'beyond' + *mons* 'mountain'.

ultrasonic adjective involving sound waves with a frequency above the upper limit of human hearing.
– DERIVATIVES **ultrasonically** adverb.

ultrasonics plural noun **1** (treated as sing.) the science and application of sound waves with a frequency above the upper limit of human hearing. **2** (treated as sing. or pl.) ultrasonic waves; ultrasound.

ultrasonography /ul-truh-suh-nog-ruh-fi/ noun a medical technique that uses echoes of ultrasound pulses to show objects or areas of different density in the body.
– DERIVATIVES **ultrasonographic** adjective.

ultrasound noun sound or other vibrations having a frequency above the upper limit of human hearing, particularly as used in medical scans.

ultraviolet noun electromagnetic radiation having a wavelength just shorter than that of violet light but longer than that of X-rays.
•adjective referring to such radiation.

ultra vires /ul-truh vy-reez, uul-trah veer-ayz/ adjective & adverb Law beyond the legal power or authority of a person or organization.
– ORIGIN Latin, 'beyond the powers'.

ululate /yoo-lyuu-layt, ul-yuu-layt/ verb howl or wail, especially to express grief.
– DERIVATIVES **ululation** noun.
– ORIGIN Latin *ululare*.

umbel /um-buhl/ noun Botany a flower cluster in which stalks spring from a common centre and form a flat or curved surface.
– ORIGIN Latin *umbella* 'sunshade'.

umbellifer /um-bel-i-fer/ noun Botany a plant of the parsley family, having its flowers arranged in umbels.
– DERIVATIVES **umbelliferous** /um-buh-lif-uh-ruhss/ adjective.

umber /rhymes with number/ noun a natural pigment, normally dark yellowish-brown (**raw umber**) or dark brown when roasted (**burnt umber**).
– ORIGIN from French *terre d'ombre* 'earth of shadow'.

umbilical /um-bil-i-k'l, um-bi-ly-k'l/ adjective **1** relating to the navel or the umbilical cord. **2** (of a relationship) very close; inseparable: *the umbilical link between commerce and international rugby.*
– DERIVATIVES **umbilically** adverb.

umbilical cord noun a flexible cord-like structure containing blood vessels, attaching a fetus to the placenta while it is in the womb.

umbilicus /um-bil-li-kuhss, um-bi-ly-kuhss/ noun (pl. **umbilici** /um-bil-li-sy, um-bi-ly-sy/ or **umbilicuses**) the navel.
– ORIGIN Latin.

umbra /um-bruh/ noun (pl. **umbras** or **umbrae** /um-bree/) the darkest inner part of a shadow, especially the dark central part of the shadow cast by the earth or the moon in an eclipse.
– DERIVATIVES **umbral** adjective.

u

- ORIGIN Latin, 'shade'.

umbrage /**um**-brij/ noun (in phrase **take umbrage**) take offence or become annoyed.
- ORIGIN first meaning 'shade, shadowy outline', later 'ground for suspicion': from Latin *umbra* 'shade'.

umbrella noun 1 a device consisting of a circular fabric canopy on a folding metal frame supported by a central rod, used as protection against rain. 2 a thing that includes or contains a range of different parts or aspects: *the concepts embodied under the broad umbrella of personality disorder.* 3 a protecting force or influence. ● adjective including or involving different parts or aspects: *an umbrella organization.*
- ORIGIN Italian *ombrella.*

umlaut /**uum**-lowt/ noun a mark (¨) used over a vowel in German and some other languages to indicate how it should be pronounced.
- ORIGIN German.

umma /**uum**-muh/ (also **ummah** /**uum**-mah/) noun the whole community of Muslims bound together by ties of religion.
- ORIGIN Arabic, 'people, community'.

umph noun variant spelling of **OOMPH**.

umpire noun 1 (in certain sports) an official who supervises a game to ensure that players keep to the rules and who settles disputes arising from the play. 2 a person chosen to settle a dispute. ● verb act as an umpire of a game.
- ORIGIN from Old French *nonper* 'not equal'.

umpteen cardinal number informal very many.
- DERIVATIVES **umpteenth** ordinal number.
- ORIGIN humorous formation.

UN abbreviation United Nations.

un-[1] prefix 1 (added to adjectives, participles, and their derivatives) not; the reverse of: *unacceptable | unselfish.* 2 (added to nouns) a lack of: *untruth.*
- ORIGIN Old English.

USAGE: For an explanation of the difference between the prefixes (word beginnings) **un-** and **non-**, see the note at **NON-**.

un-[2] prefix added to verbs: 1 referring to the reversal or cancellation of an action or state: *unsettle.* 2 referring to deprivation, separation, or change to a lesser state: *unmask.* 3 referring to release: *unhand.*
- ORIGIN Old English.

'un contraction informal one.

unabashed adjective not embarrassed or ashamed.
- DERIVATIVES **unabashedly** adverb.

unabated adjective without any reduction in intensity or strength.

unable adjective lacking the skill, means, strength, or opportunity to do something.

unabridged adjective (of a novel, play, or other written work) not cut or shortened; complete.

unaccented adjective having no accent, stress, or emphasis.

unacceptable adjective not satisfactory or allowable.
- DERIVATIVES **unacceptability** noun **unacceptably** adverb.

unaccompanied adjective 1 having no companion or escort. 2 without instrumental accompaniment. 3 happening without something else occurring at the same time: *no happiness comes unaccompanied by sorrow.*

unaccountable adjective 1 unable to be explained. 2 not responsible for the outcome of something or required to justify actions or decisions.
- DERIVATIVES **unaccountability** noun **unaccountably** adverb.

unaccounted adjective (**unaccounted for**) not taken into consideration or explained.

unaccustomed adjective 1 not usual or customary. 2 (**unaccustomed to**) not familiar with or used to something.
- DERIVATIVES **unaccustomedly** adverb.

unacknowledged adjective 1 existing or having taken place but not accepted or admitted to. 2 (of a person or their work) deserving recognition but not receiving it.

unacquainted adjective 1 (**unacquainted with**) having no experience of or familiarity with something. 2 not having met before.

unadopted adjective Brit. (of a road) not taken over for maintenance by a local authority.

unadorned adjective not decorated; plain.

unadulterated adjective 1 not mixed with any different or inferior substances. 2 complete; total: *pure, unadulterated happiness.*

unadventurous adjective not offering, involving, or eager for new or exciting things.
- DERIVATIVES **unadventurously** adverb.

unadvisedly adverb in an unwise or rash way.

unaesthetic adjective not visually pleasing; unattractive.

unaffected adjective 1 feeling or showing no effects. 2 (of a person) sincere and genuine.
- DERIVATIVES **unaffectedly** adverb.

unaffiliated adjective not officially attached to or connected with an organization.

unaffordable adjective too expensive to be afforded by the average person.

unafraid adjective feeling no fear.

unaided adjective needing or having no help.

unaligned adjective 1 not placed or arranged in a straight line or in correct relative positions. 2 not allied with or supporting an organization or cause.

unalike adjective differing from each other; not similar.

unalloyed adjective 1 complete; total: *unalloyed delight.* 2 (of metal) not alloyed; pure.

unalterable adjective not able to be changed.
- DERIVATIVES **unalterably** adverb.

unaltered adjective remaining the same.

unambiguous /un-am-**big**-yoo-uhss/ adjective not open to more than one interpretation; clear in meaning.
- DERIVATIVES **unambiguously** adverb.

unambitious adjective 1 not motivated by a strong desire to succeed. 2 (of a plan or piece of work) not involving anything new, exciting, or demanding.

un-American adjective 1 not American in nature. 2 US against the interests of the US and therefore treasonable.

u

unanimous /yoo-nan-i-muhss/ adjective **1** (of people) fully in agreement. **2** (of an opinion, decision, or vote) held or carried by everyone involved.
– DERIVATIVES **unanimity** /yoo-nuh-nim-i-ti/ noun **unanimously** adverb.
– ORIGIN Latin *unanimus*.

unannounced adjective without warning or notice: *he often dropped in unannounced.*

unanswerable adjective **1** unable to be answered. **2** unable to be questioned or disagreed with: *an unanswerable case for investment.*

unanswered adjective not answered or responded to.

unapologetic adjective not sorry for one's actions.
– DERIVATIVES **unapologetically** adverb.

unappealing adjective not inviting or attractive.
– DERIVATIVES **unappealingly** adverb.

unappetizing (or **unappetising**) adjective not inviting or attractive.
– DERIVATIVES **unappetizingly** adverb.

unappreciated adjective not fully understood, recognized, or valued.

unappreciative adjective not fully understanding or recognizing something.

unapproachable adjective not welcoming or friendly.

unapproved adjective not officially accepted or permitted.

unarguable adjective not open to disagreement; certain.
– DERIVATIVES **unarguably** adverb.

unarmed adjective not equipped with or carrying weapons.

unashamed adjective feeling or showing no guilt or embarrassment.
– DERIVATIVES **unashamedly** adverb.

unasked adjective **1** (of a question) not asked. **2** without being invited or asked: *we'd never have entered the house unasked.*

unassailable adjective unable to be attacked, questioned, or defeated.
– DERIVATIVES **unassailability** noun **unassailably** adverb.

unassertive adjective not having or showing a confident and forceful personality.

unassisted adjective not helped by anyone or anything.

unassociated adjective not connected or associated: *they perform music previously unassociated with the saxophone.*

unassuming adjective not wanting to draw attention to oneself or one's abilities.
– DERIVATIVES **unassumingly** adverb.

unattached adjective **1** not married or having an established lover. **2** not working for or belonging to a particular organization.

unattainable adjective not able to be reached or achieved.
– DERIVATIVES **unattainably** adverb.

unattended adjective without the owner or a responsible person present; not being supervised or looked after.

unattractive adjective not pleasing, appealing, or inviting.
– DERIVATIVES **unattractively** adverb

unattractiveness noun.

unattributed adjective (of a quotation, story, or work of art) of unknown or unpublished origin.
– DERIVATIVES **unattributable** adjective.

unauthorized (or **unauthorised**) adjective not having official permission or approval.

unavailable adjective **1** not able to be used or obtained. **2** not free to do something: *he was unavailable for comment.*
– DERIVATIVES **unavailability** noun.

unavailing adjective achieving little or nothing.
– DERIVATIVES **unavailingly** adverb.

unavoidable adjective not able to be avoided or prevented; inevitable.
– DERIVATIVES **unavoidability** noun **unavoidably** adverb.

unaware adjective having no knowledge of a situation or fact.
– DERIVATIVES **unawareness** noun.

unawares (also **unaware**) adverb so as to surprise someone; unexpectedly: *modern life has caught that woman completely unawares.*

unbalance verb **1** upset the balance or stability of: *judo unbalances an opponent before throwing him.* **2** (as adj. **unbalanced**) mentally or emotionally disturbed. **3** (as adj. **unbalanced**) not giving equal coverage or treatment to all aspects of something.

unbearable adjective not able to be endured or tolerated.
– DERIVATIVES **unbearably** adverb.

unbeatable adjective **1** not able to be bettered or beaten: *CDs at unbeatable prices.* **2** very good.

unbeaten adjective not defeated or bettered.

unbecoming adjective **1** (especially of clothing) not flattering. **2** (of behaviour) not appropriate or acceptable.
– DERIVATIVES **unbecomingly** adverb.

unbeknown (also **unbeknownst**) adjective (**unbeknown to**) without the knowledge of someone.

unbelief noun lack of religious belief.

unbelievable adjective **1** so extreme as to be difficult to believe; extraordinary: *the rent is unbelievable!* **2** not likely to be true.
– DERIVATIVES **unbelievably** adverb.

unbeliever noun a person who does not believe in God or a particular religion.

unbelieving adjective feeling or showing that one does not believe someone or something.

unbend verb (past and past part. **unbent**) **1** make or become straight. **2** become less formal or strict.

unbending adjective strict and unwilling to change one's views; inflexible.

unbiased (also **unbiassed**) adjective showing no prejudice; impartial.

unbidden adjective **1** without having been invited. **2** (of a thought or feeling) arising without conscious effort.

unbleached adjective (especially of paper, cloth, or flour) not bleached.

unblemished adjective not damaged or marked in any way.

unblock verb remove an obstruction from something.

u

unblushing adjective not feeling or showing embarrassment or shame.
– DERIVATIVES **unblushingly** adverb.

unbolt verb open a door or window by drawing back a bolt.

unborn adjective (of a baby) not yet born.

unbosom verb old use (**unbosom oneself**) reveal one's thoughts or secrets.

unbound adjective **1** not restricted or tied up: *they were unbound by convention.* **2** (of printed sheets) not bound together.

unbounded adjective having no limits.

unbowed adjective not having given in to pressure or defeat.

unbreakable adjective not liable to break or able to be broken.

unbreathable adjective (of air) not fit or pleasant to breathe.

unbridgeable adjective (of a gap or difference between people or opinions) not able to be closed or made less significant.

unbridled adjective not controlled; unrestrained: *a night of unbridled passion.*

unbroken adjective **1** not broken; intact. **2** not interrupted or disturbed. **3** (of a record) not beaten. **4** (of a horse) not broken in.

unbuckle verb unfasten the buckle of a belt, shoe, etc.

unbuilt adjective (of buildings or land) not yet built or built on.

unbundle verb **1** market or charge for items or services separately rather than as part of a package. **2** split a company or conglomerate into its constituent businesses, especially before selling them off.

unburden verb **1** (**unburden oneself**) talk to someone about a worry or problem, so that one feels less anxious. **2** (**be unburdened**) not be burdened or worried.

unburnt (also **unburned**) adjective not damaged or destroyed by fire.

unbutton verb **1** unfasten the buttons of an item of clothing. **2** informal relax and become less inhibited.

uncalled adjective (**uncalled for**) not desirable, justified, or necessary: *we got a telling-off that was totally uncalled for.*

uncanny adjective (**uncannier, uncanniest**) **1** strange or mysterious. **2** so accurate or intense as to be unsettling: *he bore an uncanny resemblance to the current Prime Minister.*
– DERIVATIVES **uncannily** adverb.

uncapped adjective Brit. (of a player) never having been chosen as a member of a national sports team.

uncared adjective (**uncared for**) not looked after properly.

uncaring adjective not sympathetic to or concerned about others.
– DERIVATIVES **uncaringly** adverb.

uncastrated adjective (of a male animal) not castrated.

unceasing adjective not stopping; continuous.
– DERIVATIVES **unceasingly** adverb.

unceremonious adjective lacking courtesy; rude or abrupt.
– DERIVATIVES **unceremoniously** adverb.

uncertain adjective **1** not known, reliable, or definite: *an uncertain future.* **2** not completely confident or sure.
– PHRASES **in no uncertain terms** clearly and forcefully.
– DERIVATIVES **uncertainly** adverb.

uncertainty noun (pl. **uncertainties**) **1** the state of being uncertain. **2** something that is uncertain or makes one feel uncertain.

unchallengeable adjective not able to be questioned or opposed.

unchallenged adjective **1** not questioned or opposed: *the report's findings did not go unchallenged.* **2** not called on to prove one's identity.

unchallenging adjective not demanding or testing one's abilities.

unchangeable adjective not liable to change or able to be altered.

unchanged adjective not changed; unaltered.

unchanging adjective remaining the same.
– DERIVATIVES **unchangingly** adverb.

uncharacteristic adjective not typical of a particular person or thing.
– DERIVATIVES **uncharacteristically** adverb.

uncharismatic adjective lacking the charm that can inspire admiration in others.

uncharitable adjective unkind or unsympathetic to others.
– DERIVATIVES **uncharitably** adverb.

uncharted adjective (of an area of land or sea) not mapped or surveyed.

unchecked adjective (of something undesirable) not controlled or restrained.

unchivalrous adjective (of a man) discourteous, especially towards women.

unchristian adjective **1** not in accordance with the teachings of Christianity. **2** unkind or unfair: *she felt an unchristian hope that he tread on a sea urchin.*

uncial /ˈun-si-uhl, ˈun-shuhl/ adjective written in rounded separated letters similar to modern capital letters, as found in manuscripts of the 4th–8th centuries. •noun an uncial letter or manuscript.
– ORIGIN from Latin *uncia* 'inch'; the connection is unclear.

uncircumcised adjective (of a boy or man) not circumcised.

uncivil adjective not polite; discourteous.

uncivilized (or **uncivilised**) adjective **1** not having developed a modern culture or way of life. **2** not behaving in accordance with accepted moral or social standards.

unclad adjective not wearing any clothes; naked.

unclaimed adjective not having been claimed.

unclasp verb **1** unfasten a clasp or similar device. **2** release the grip of: *I unclasped her fingers from my hair.*

unclassifiable adjective not able to be put into a particular category.

unclassified adjective **1** not put into categories. **2** not officially classed as secret.

uncle noun the brother of one's father or mother or the husband of one's aunt.
– ORIGIN Latin *avunculus* 'maternal uncle'.

unclean adjective **1** not clean; dirty. **2** morally wrong. **3** (of food) regarded in a particular religion as impure and unfit to be eaten.

uncleanliness noun the state of being dirty.

unclear adjective 1 difficult to see, hear, or understand. 2 confused or not certain about something: *we are unclear about how to classify this activity.*

uncleared adjective 1 (of land) not cleared of vegetation. 2 (of a cheque) not having passed through a clearing house and been paid into a person's account.

unclench verb release a clenched part of the body.

Uncle Sam noun the United States or its federal government, often shown as a man with a tall hat and a white beard.
– ORIGIN said to be an expansion of the letters US.

Uncle Tom noun derogatory, chiefly N. Amer. a black man considered to be excessively obedient or servile to white people.
– ORIGIN the hero of H. B. Stowe's *Uncle Tom's Cabin.*

unclimbed adjective (of a mountain or rock face) not previously climbed.
– DERIVATIVES **unclimbable** adjective.

unclip verb (**unclips, unclipping, unclipped**) release something from being fastened or held with a clip.

unclog verb (**unclogs, unclogging, unclogged**) remove a blockage from something.

unclothed adjective wearing no clothes; naked.

unclouded adjective 1 (of the sky) not dark or overcast. 2 not troubled or spoiled by anything.

uncluttered adjective not cluttered by too many objects or unnecessary items.

uncoil verb straighten from a coiled position.

uncoloured (US **uncolored**) adjective 1 having no colour. 2 not influenced: *her views were uncoloured by her husband's.*

uncombed adjective (of a person's hair) not combed.

uncomfortable adjective 1 causing slight physical discomfort. 2 uneasy or awkward: *an uncomfortable silence.*
– DERIVATIVES **uncomfortably** adverb.

uncommercial adjective not making or intended to make a profit.

uncommon adjective 1 out of the ordinary; unusual. 2 remarkably great.
– DERIVATIVES **uncommonly** adverb.

uncommunicative adjective unwilling to talk or give out information.

uncompetitive adjective not cheaper or better than others and therefore not able to compete commercially.

uncomplaining adjective not complaining about an unpleasant situation.
– DERIVATIVES **uncomplainingly** adverb.

uncomplicated adjective simple or straightforward.

uncomplimentary adjective not expressing praise; rude or insulting.

uncomprehending adjective not able to understand something.
– DERIVATIVES **uncomprehendingly** adverb.

uncompromising adjective 1 unwilling to change one's mind or behaviour; resolute.

2 harsh or relentless: *uncompromising club music.*
– DERIVATIVES **uncompromisingly** adverb.

unconcealed adjective (especially of an emotion) not concealed; obvious.

unconcern noun a lack of worry or interest.

unconcerned adjective not concerned or interested.
– DERIVATIVES **unconcernedly** adverb.

unconditional adjective not subject to any conditions or requirements.
– DERIVATIVES **unconditionally** adverb.

unconditioned adjective (of behaviour) not formed or influenced by conditioning or learning; instinctive.

unconfident adjective not confident; shy or hesitant.

unconfined adjective 1 not confined to a limited space. 2 (of joy or excitement) very great.

unconfirmed adjective not yet confirmed as true or valid.

uncongenial adjective 1 not friendly or pleasant to be with. 2 not suitable for or encouraging something: *the atmosphere was uncongenial to good conversation.*

unconnected adjective 1 not joined together or to something else. 2 not associated or linked in a sequence.

unconquerable adjective not able to be conquered or overcome.

unconscionable /un-kon-shuh-nuh-b'l/ adjective 1 not morally right. 2 excessive: *he takes an unconscionable time to get there.*
– DERIVATIVES **unconscionably** adverb.
– ORIGIN from former *conscionable* 'conscientious'.

unconscious adjective 1 not awake and aware of and responding to one's surroundings. 2 done or existing without realizing. 3 (**unconscious of**) unaware of. ●noun (**the unconscious**) the part of the mind which cannot be accessed by the conscious mind but which affects behaviour and emotions.
– DERIVATIVES **unconsciously** adverb **unconsciousness** noun.

unconsecrated adjective not made or declared to be holy or sacred.

unconsidered adjective 1 not thought about carefully. 2 not fully appreciated.

unconstitutional adjective not in accordance with the constitution of a country or the rules of an organization.
– DERIVATIVES **unconstitutionally** adverb.

unconstrained adjective not restricted or limited.

unconsummated adjective (of a marriage or relationship) not having been consummated by having sex.

uncontainable adjective (especially of an emotion) very strong.

uncontaminated adjective not contaminated by something impure or harmful.

uncontentious adjective not causing or likely to cause disagreement or controversy.

uncontested adjective not contested or challenged.

uncontrived adjective not appearing artificial.

u

uncontrollable adjective not able to be controlled.
- DERIVATIVES **uncontrollably** adverb.

uncontrolled adjective not controlled or restricted.

uncontroversial adjective not causing debate or conflicting opinions.
- DERIVATIVES **uncontroversially** adverb.

unconventional adjective not in accordance with what is generally done or believed: *his unconventional approach to life.*
- DERIVATIVES **unconventionality** noun **unconventionally** adverb.

unconvinced adjective not certain that something is true or can be relied on.

unconvincing adjective failing to convince or impress.
- DERIVATIVES **unconvincingly** adverb.

uncooked adjective not cooked; raw.

uncool adjective informal not fashionable or impressive.

uncooperative adjective unwilling to help others or do what they ask.

uncoordinated adjective 1 badly organized. 2 (of a person or their movements) clumsy.

uncork verb pull the cork out of a bottle.

uncorroborated adjective not supported or confirmed by evidence.

uncountable adjective too many to be counted.

uncounted adjective 1 not counted. 2 very numerous.

uncouple verb disconnect something from something else.

uncouth adjective lacking good manners or sophistication.
- ORIGIN Old English, 'unknown'.

uncover verb 1 remove a cover or covering from someone or something. 2 discover something previously secret or unknown.

uncovered adjective not covered by something.

uncritical adjective not willing to criticize or judge someone or something.
- DERIVATIVES **uncritically** adverb.

uncross verb move something back from a crossed position.

uncrowded adjective (of a place) not crowded.

uncrowned adjective not formally crowned as a monarch.

unction /ungk-sh'n/ noun 1 formal the smearing of someone with oil or ointment as a religious ceremony. 2 excessive politeness or flattery.
- ORIGIN Latin.

unctuous /ungk-tyuu-uhss/ adjective excessively flattering or friendly.
- DERIVATIVES **unctuously** adverb **unctuousness** noun.

uncultivated adjective 1 (of land) not used for growing crops. 2 not highly educated.

uncultured adjective not having good taste, manners, or education.

uncured adjective (of food) not preserved by salting, drying, or smoking.

uncurl verb straighten from a curled position.

uncut adjective 1 not cut or shaped by cutting. 2 (of a written work, film, or performance) left in its complete form; not censored or abridged.

undamaged adjective not harmed or damaged.

undated adjective not provided or marked with a date.

undaunted adjective not discouraged by difficulty, danger, or disappointment.

undeceive verb tell someone that an idea or belief is mistaken.

undecided adjective 1 not having made a decision; uncertain. 2 not settled or resolved: *the ship's fate is still undecided.*
- DERIVATIVES **undecidedly** adverb.

undecipherable adjective (of speech or writing) not able to be read or understood.

undefeated adjective not defeated.

undefended adjective not defended.

undefined adjective not clear or defined.
- DERIVATIVES **undefinable** adjective.

undemanding adjective (especially of a task) not demanding.

undemocratic adjective not according to democratic principles.
- DERIVATIVES **undemocratically** adverb.

undemonstrative adjective not tending to express feelings openly.

undeniable adjective unable to be denied or questioned.
- DERIVATIVES **undeniably** adverb.

under preposition 1 extending or directly below. 2 below or behind something covering or protecting. 3 at a lower level, layer, or grade than. 4 lower than a specified amount, rate, or norm. 5 expressing submission or control: *I was under his spell.* 6 as provided for by the rules of; in accordance with. 7 used to express grouping or classification. 8 undergoing a process. ●adverb 1 extending or directly below something. 2 affected by an anaesthetic; unconscious.
- PHRASES **under way** 1 having started and making progress. 2 (of a boat) moving through the water.
- ORIGIN Old English.

under- prefix 1 below; beneath: *undercover.* 2 lower in status: *undersecretary.* 3 insufficiently; incompletely: *undernourished.*

underachieve verb do less well than is expected.
- DERIVATIVES **underachievement** noun **underachiever** noun.

underage adjective too young to take part legally in a particular activity.

underarm adjective & adverb (of a throw or stroke in sport) made with the arm or hand below shoulder level. ●noun a person's armpit.

underbelly noun (pl. **underbellies**) 1 the soft underside or abdomen of an animal. 2 a hidden and unpleasant or criminal part of society.

underbid verb (**underbidding**; past and past part. **underbid**) (especially when trying to secure a contract) make a lower bid than someone else.

underbite noun the projection of the lower teeth beyond the upper.

underbrush noun N. Amer. undergrowth in a forest.

undercarriage noun 1 a wheeled structure beneath an aircraft which supports the aircraft on the ground. **2** the supporting frame under the body of a vehicle.

undercharge verb charge someone a price or amount that is too low.

underclass noun the lowest social class in a country or community, consisting of the poor and unemployed.

underclothes plural noun clothes worn under others next to the skin.
– DERIVATIVES **underclothing** noun.

undercoat noun a layer of paint applied after the primer and before the topcoat.

undercook verb cook food for too short a time.

undercover adjective & adverb involving secret work for the purposes of investigation or spying.

undercroft noun the crypt of a church.
– ORIGIN from the rare term *croft* 'crypt'.

undercurrent noun **1** a hidden or underlying feeling or influence: *I sensed an undercurrent of resentment among the other girls.* **2** a current of water below the surface, moving in a different direction from any surface current.

undercut verb (**undercutting**; past and past part. **undercut**) **1** offer goods or services at a lower price than a competitor. **2** weaken or undermine: *his authority was being undercut.* **3** cut or wear away the part below or under something.

underdeveloped adjective **1** not fully developed. **2** (of a country or region) not economically advanced.
– DERIVATIVES **underdevelopment** noun.

underdog noun a competitor thought to have little chance of winning a fight or contest.

underdone adjective (of food) not cooked for long enough.

underdress verb (**be underdressed**) be dressed too plainly or too informally for a particular occasion.

underemployed adjective not having enough work, or not having work that makes full use of one's abilities.
– DERIVATIVES **underemployment** noun.

underestimate verb **1** estimate something to be smaller or less important than it really is. **2** regard someone as less capable than they really are. •noun an estimate that is too low.
– DERIVATIVES **underestimation** noun.

underexpose verb expose photographic film for too short a time.
– DERIVATIVES **underexposure** noun.

underfed adjective having had too little to eat.

underfelt noun Brit. felt laid under a carpet for protection or support.

underfoot adverb **1** under one's feet; on the ground. **2** constantly present and in one's way.

underfund verb fail to provide an organization, project, etc. with enough funding.
– DERIVATIVES **underfunding** noun.

undergarment noun an item of underclothing.

underglaze noun colour or decoration applied to pottery before the glaze is applied.

undergo verb (**undergoes**; past **underwent**; past part. **undergone**) experience or be subjected to something unpleasant or difficult.
– ORIGIN Old English, 'undermine'.

undergraduate noun a student at a university who has not yet taken a first degree.

underground adjective & adverb **1** beneath the surface of the ground. **2** in secrecy or hiding. **3** favouring alternative or experimental forms of lifestyle or artistic expression. •noun **1** Brit. an underground railway. **2** a group or movement organized secretly to work against an existing government.

undergrowth noun a dense growth of shrubs and other plants.

underhand (also **underhanded**) adjective **1** acting or done in a secret or dishonest way. **2** underarm.

underlay[1] noun material laid under a carpet for protection or support. •verb (past and past part. **underlaid**) place something under something else, especially to support or raise it.

underlay[2] past tense of **UNDERLIE**.

underlie verb (**underlying**; past **underlay**; past part. **underlain**) lie or be situated under something.
– DERIVATIVES **underlying** adjective.

underline verb **1** draw a line under a word or phrase to give emphasis. **2** emphasize: *he underlined the importance of spending on health and education.* •noun a line drawn under a word or phrase.

underling noun chiefly derogatory a person of lower rank or status.

underlit adjective not having enough light or lighting; dim.

underman verb (**undermans**, **undermanning**, **undermanned**) fail to provide an organization with enough workers.

undermine verb **1** damage or weaken: *an attempt to undermine the president's authority.* **2** wear away the base or foundation of a rock formation. **3** dig or excavate beneath a building or fortification so as to make it collapse.

underneath preposition & adverb **1** situated directly below. **2** so as to be partly or wholly concealed by. •noun the part or side facing towards the ground.
– ORIGIN Old English.

undernourished adjective not having enough food or the right type of food for good health.
– DERIVATIVES **undernourishment** noun.

underpaid past and past participle of **UNDERPAY**.

underpants plural noun an undergarment covering the lower part of the body and having two holes for the legs.

underpart noun a lower part or portion.

underpass noun a road or pedestrian tunnel passing under another road or a railway.

underpay verb (past and past part. **underpaid**) pay someone too little, or pay less than is due for something.

underperform verb perform less well than expected.
– DERIVATIVES **underperformance** noun.

underpin verb (**underpins**, **underpinning**, **underpinned**) **1** support, justify, or form the basis for an argument, claim, etc.

u

2 support a structure from below by laying a solid foundation or replacing weak materials with stronger ones.

underplay verb represent something as being less important than it really is.

underprivileged adjective not enjoying the same rights or standard of living as the majority of the population.

underrate verb (often as adj. **underrated**) fail to recognize the quality, value, or importance of someone or something.

under-report verb fail to report news or data fully.

under-represent verb (**be under-represented**) form a disproportionately small percentage: *women are under-represented in the Cabinet.*

under-resourced adjective provided with insufficient resources.

underscore verb & noun another term for **UNDERLINE**.

undersea adjective relating to or situated below the sea or the surface of the sea.

undersecretary noun (pl. **undersecretaries**) 1 (in the UK) a junior minister or senior civil servant. 2 (in the US) the chief assistant to a member of the cabinet.

undersell verb (past and past part. **undersold**) 1 sell something at a lower price than a competitor. 2 fail to represent someone's or something's true quality or worth.

undershirt noun chiefly N. Amer. an undergarment worn under a shirt; a vest.

undershoot verb (past and past part. **undershot**) 1 (of an aircraft) land short of the runway. 2 fall short of a point or target.

underside noun the bottom or lower side or surface of something.

undersigned noun (**the undersigned**) formal the person or people who have signed the document in question.

undersized (also **undersize**) adjective smaller than the usual size.

underskirt noun a petticoat.

undersold past and past participle of **UNDERSELL**.

underspend verb (past and past part. **underspent**) spend too little or less than planned.

understaffed adjective (of an organization) having too few members of staff to operate effectively.

understand verb (past and past part. **understood**) 1 know or realize the intended meaning of words, a language, or a speaker. 2 be aware of the significance, explanation, or cause of something: *he didn't understand why we were laughing.* 3 be sympathetically aware of: *I understand how you feel.* 4 interpret or view something in a particular way. 5 believe to be the case from information received: *I understand you're at art school.* 6 assume that something is present or is the case: *he liked to play the field, that was understood.*

understandable adjective 1 able to be understood. 2 to be expected; natural, reasonable, or forgivable.
– DERIVATIVES **understandably** adverb.

understanding noun 1 the ability to

understand something. 2 the power of abstract thought; intellect. 3 a person's interpretation or judgement of a situation. 4 sympathetic awareness or tolerance. 5 an informal or unspoken agreement or arrangement. •adjective sympathetically aware of other people's feelings.
– DERIVATIVES **understandingly** adverb.

understate verb describe or represent something as being smaller or less important than it really is.
– DERIVATIVES **understatement** noun.

understated adjective presented or expressed in a subtle and effective way.
– DERIVATIVES **understatedly** adverb.

understeer verb (of a motor vehicle) have a tendency to turn less sharply than is intended.

understood past and past participle of **UNDERSTAND**.

understorey noun (pl. **understoreys**) Ecology a layer of vegetation beneath the top branches of the trees in a forest.

understudy noun (pl. **understudies**) an actor who learns another's role in order to be able to act in their absence. •verb (**understudies**, **understudying**, **understudied**) be an understudy for another actor.

undertake verb (past **undertook**; past part. **undertaken**) 1 make oneself responsible for carrying out a project, activity, etc.; take something on: *a firm of builders undertook the construction work.* 2 formally guarantee or promise to do something.

undertaker noun a person whose business is preparing dead bodies for burial or cremation and making arrangements for funerals.

undertaking noun 1 a formal promise to do something. 2 a task or project that is taken on by someone. 3 the management of funerals as a profession.

undertone noun 1 a subdued or muted tone of sound or colour. 2 an underlying quality or feeling.

undertow noun another term for **UNDERCURRENT**.

underuse verb /un-der-yooz/ fail to make enough use of something. •noun /un-der-yooss/ insufficient use of something.
– DERIVATIVES **underused** adjective.

underutilize (or **underutilise**) verb underuse something.

undervalue verb (**undervalues**, **undervalued**, **undervaluing**) 1 fail to recognize someone's or something's importance or worth. 2 under-estimate something's financial value.

underwater adjective & adverb situated or happening beneath the surface of the water.

underway adjective variant of **under way** (see **UNDER**).

USAGE: The spelling **underway** is best avoided in formal writing: use **under way** instead.

underwear noun clothing worn under other clothes next to the skin.

underweight adjective below a weight considered normal or desirable.

underwent past of **UNDERGO**.

underwhelm verb humorous fail to impress or make a positive impact on someone.
– ORIGIN suggested by **OVERWHELM**.

underwired adjective (of a bra) having a semicircular wire support stitched under each cup.

underworld noun **1** the world of criminals or of organized crime. **2** (in myths and legends) the home of the dead, imagined as being under the earth.

underwrite verb (past **underwrote**; past part. **underwritten**) **1** sign and accept liability under an insurance policy. **2** undertake to finance or otherwise support or guarantee something.
– DERIVATIVES **underwriter** noun.

undescended adjective (of a testicle) remaining in the abdomen instead of descending normally into the scrotum.

undeserved adjective not deserved or earned.
– DERIVATIVES **undeservedly** adverb.

undeserving adjective not deserving or worthy of something.

undesirable adjective not wanted or desirable because harmful, offensive, or unpleasant.
•noun an unpleasant or offensive person.
– DERIVATIVES **undesirability** noun **undesirably** adverb.

undesired adjective not wanted or desired.

undetectable adjective not able to be detected.

undetected adjective not detected or discovered.

undetermined adjective not firmly decided or settled.

undeterred adjective persevering despite setbacks.

undeveloped adjective not having developed or been developed.

undeviating adjective showing no deviation; constant and steady.

undiagnosed adjective not diagnosed.

undid past of UNDO.

undies plural noun informal articles of underwear.

undifferentiated adjective not different or differentiated.

undigested adjective **1** (of food) not digested. **2** (of information) not having been properly understood or absorbed.

undignified adjective appearing foolish; lacking in dignity.

undiluted adjective **1** (of a liquid) not diluted. **2** (of a feeling or quality) not mixed or combined with any other: *pure, undiluted happiness.*

undiminished adjective not reduced or lessened.

undimmed adjective not dimmed; still bright or intense.

undiplomatic adjective insensitive and tactless.
– DERIVATIVES **undiplomatically** adverb.

undirected adjective lacking a proper plan or purpose.

undiscerning adjective lacking judgement or taste.

undisciplined adjective uncontrolled in behaviour or manner.

undisclosed adjective not revealed or made known.

undiscovered adjective not discovered.

undiscriminating adjective lacking good judgement or taste.

undisguised adjective (of a feeling) not disguised or concealed; open.

undismayed adjective not dismayed or discouraged by a setback.

undisputed adjective not disputed or called into question.

undistinguished adjective lacking distinction; not very good or impressive.

undisturbed adjective not disturbed.

undivided adjective **1** not divided, separated, or broken into parts. **2** devoted completely to one person or thing: *you have my undivided attention.*

undo verb (**undoes**; past **undid**; past part. **undone**) **1** unfasten or loosen. **2** cancel or reverse the effects of (a previous action or measure). **3** formal cause the downfall or ruin of.

undocumented adjective not recorded in or proved by documents.

undoing noun a person's ruin or downfall.

undone adjective **1** not tied or fastened. **2** not done or finished. **3** formal or humorous ruined by a disastrous setback.

undoubted adjective not questioned or doubted by anyone.
– DERIVATIVES **undoubtedly** adverb.

undreamed /un-**dreemd**, un-**dremt**/ (Brit. also **undreamt** /un-**dremt**/) adjective (**undreamed of**) not previously thought to be possible.

undress verb **1** (also **get undressed**) take off one's clothes. **2** take the clothes off someone else. •noun **1** the state of being naked or only partially clothed. **2** Military ordinary clothing or uniform, as opposed to full dress.

undressed adjective **1** wearing no clothes; naked. **2** not treated, processed, or prepared for use. **3** (of food) not having a dressing.

undrinkable adjective not fit to be drunk because of impurity or poor quality.

undue adjective more than is reasonable or necessary; excessive.
– DERIVATIVES **unduly** adverb.

undulant /un-dyuu-luhnt/ adjective undulating.

undulate /un-dyuu-layt/ verb **1** move with a smooth wave-like motion. **2** have a wavy form or outline.
– DERIVATIVES **undulation** noun **undulatory** adjective.
– ORIGIN from Latin *unda* 'a wave'.

undyed adjective (of fabric) not dyed; of its natural colour.

undying adjective lasting forever.

unearned adjective not earned or deserved.

unearned income noun income from private means (such as investments) rather than from work.

unearth verb **1** find something in the ground by digging. **2** discover something by investigation or searching.

unearthly adjective **1** unnatural or mysterious. **2** informal unreasonably early or inconvenient: *an unearthly hour.*

unease noun anxiety or discontent.

uneasy adjective (**uneasier, uneasiest**) **1** anxious or uncomfortable. **2** liable to

change; not settled: *an uneasy truce.*
– DERIVATIVES **uneasily** adverb **uneasiness** noun.

uneatable adjective not fit to be eaten.

uneaten adjective not eaten.

uneconomic adjective not profitable or making efficient use of resources.

uneconomical adjective wasteful of money or other resources; not economical.

unedifying adjective arousing disapproval; distasteful or unpleasant.

unedited adjective (of material for publication or broadcasting) not edited.

uneducated adjective poorly educated.

unelected adjective (of an official) not elected.

unembarrassed adjective not feeling or showing embarrassment.

unemotional adjective not having or showing strong feelings.
– DERIVATIVES **unemotionally** adverb.

unemployable adjective not able or likely to get paid employment because of a lack of skills or qualifications.

unemployed adjective 1 without a paid job but available to work. 2 (of a thing) not in use.

unemployment noun 1 the state of being unemployed. 2 the number or proportion of unemployed people.

unemployment benefit noun payment made by the state or a trade union to an unemployed person.

unenclosed adjective (especially of land) not enclosed.

unencumbered adjective not burdened or prevented from moving or acting freely.

unending adjective seeming to last or continue for ever.

unendurable adjective not able to be tolerated or endured.

unenforceable adjective (especially of a law) impossible to enforce.

unenlightened adjective not enlightened in outlook.

unenterprising adjective lacking initiative or resourcefulness.

unenthusiastic adjective not having or showing enthusiasm.
– DERIVATIVES **unenthusiastically** adverb.

unenviable adjective difficult, undesirable, or unpleasant.

unequal adjective 1 not equal in quantity, size, or value. 2 not fair, evenly balanced, or having equal advantage. 3 (**unequal to**) not having the ability or resources to meet a challenge.
– DERIVATIVES **unequally** adverb.

unequalled (US **unequaled**) adjective better or greater than all others of the same kind.

unequivocal /un-i-**kwiv**-uh-k'l/ adjective leaving no doubt; completely clear in meaning.
– DERIVATIVES **unequivocally** adverb.

unerring adjective always right or accurate.
– DERIVATIVES **unerringly** adverb.

UNESCO /yoo-**ness**-koh/ abbreviation United Nations Educational, Scientific, and Cultural Organization.

unessential adjective not essential or absolutely necessary.

unethical adjective not morally correct or acceptable.

– DERIVATIVES **unethically** adverb.

uneven adjective 1 not level or smooth. 2 not regular, consistent, or equal.
– DERIVATIVES **unevenly** adverb **unevenness** noun.

uneventful adjective not marked by interesting or exciting events.
– DERIVATIVES **uneventfully** adverb **uneventfulness** noun.

unexamined adjective not investigated or examined.

unexceptionable adjective not open to objection, but not particularly new or exciting.

unexceptional adjective not out of the ordinary; usual.
– DERIVATIVES **unexceptionally** adverb.

unexciting adjective not exciting; dull.

unexpected adjective not expected or regarded as likely to happen.
– DERIVATIVES **unexpectedly** adverb **unexpectedness** noun.

unexplained adjective not made clear or accounted for.
– DERIVATIVES **unexplainable** adjective.

unexploded adjective (of an explosive device) not having exploded.

unexplored adjective not explored, investigated, or evaluated.

unexpressed adjective (of a thought or feeling) not communicated or made known.

unexpurgated adjective (of a text) complete and containing all the original material; not censored.

unfailing adjective 1 without error. 2 reliable or constant.
– DERIVATIVES **unfailingly** adverb.

unfair adjective not based on or showing fairness.
– DERIVATIVES **unfairly** adverb **unfairness** noun.

unfaithful adjective 1 not faithful; disloyal. 2 having sex with a person other than one's husband, wife, or established partner.
– DERIVATIVES **unfaithfully** adverb **unfaithfulness** noun.

unfaltering adjective not faltering; steady or resolute.
– DERIVATIVES **unfalteringly** adverb.

unfamiliar adjective 1 not known or recognized; uncharacteristic. 2 (**unfamiliar with**) not having knowledge or experience of something.
– DERIVATIVES **unfamiliarity** noun.

unfancied adjective not considered likely to win.

unfashionable adjective not fashionable or popular.
– DERIVATIVES **unfashionably** adverb.

unfasten verb open the fastening of something.

unfathomable adjective 1 too strange or difficult to be understood. 2 impossible to measure the depth or extent of.
– DERIVATIVES **unfathomably** adverb.

unfavourable (US **unfavorable**) adjective 1 expressing lack of approval. 2 unlikely to lead to a successful outcome: *unfavourable economic conditions.*
– DERIVATIVES **unfavourably** adverb.

unfazed adjective informal not disconcerted or worried by something unexpected.

unfeasible adjective inconvenient or impractical.
– DERIVATIVES **unfeasibly** adverb.

unfeeling adjective unsympathetic, harsh, or callous.

unfeigned /un-fay-nd/ adjective genuine; sincere.

unfermented adjective not fermented.

unfertilized (or **unfertilised**) adjective not fertilized.

unfettered adjective unrestrained or uninhibited.

unfilled adjective not filled; vacant or empty.

unfinished adjective 1 not finished; incomplete. 2 not having been given an attractive surface appearance in manufacture.

unfit adjective 1 unsuitable or inadequate for something. 2 not in good physical condition.

unfitted adjective unfit for something.

unfitting adjective unsuitable or unbecoming.

unfixed adjective 1 unfastened; loose. 2 uncertain or variable.

unflagging adjective not becoming tired or weak; remaining strong.
– DERIVATIVES **unflaggingly** adverb.

unflappable adjective informal calm in a crisis.

unflattering adjective not flattering.
– DERIVATIVES **unflatteringly** adverb.

unflinching adjective not afraid or hesitant.
– DERIVATIVES **unflinchingly** adverb.

unfocused (also **unfocussed**) adjective 1 not focused; out of focus. 2 without a specific aim or direction.

unfold verb 1 open or spread out from a folded position. 2 reveal or be revealed.

unforced adjective 1 produced naturally and without effort. 2 (of an action) not done as a result of pressure from another person.

unforeseen adjective not anticipated or predicted.
– DERIVATIVES **unforeseeable** adjective.

unforgettable adjective so enjoyable, impressive, etc. that it is impossible to forget.
– DERIVATIVES **unforgettably** adverb.

unforgivable adjective so bad as to be unable to be forgiven or excused.
– DERIVATIVES **unforgivably** adverb.

unforgiving adjective 1 not willing to forgive or excuse faults. 2 (of conditions) harsh or hostile.

unformed adjective 1 without a definite form. 2 not fully developed.

unforthcoming adjective 1 not willing to reveal information. 2 not available when needed.

unfortunate adjective 1 having or marked by bad luck; unlucky. 2 regrettable or inappropriate: *an unfortunate remark.* • noun a person who suffers bad fortune.
– DERIVATIVES **unfortunately** adverb.

unfounded adjective having no basis in fact: *an unfounded rumour.*

unfreeze verb (past **unfroze**; past part. **unfrozen**) 1 thaw something frozen. 2 remove restrictions on the use of an asset.

unfriendly adjective (**unfriendlier**, **unfriendliest**) not friendly.
– DERIVATIVES **unfriendliness** noun.

unfrock verb another term for **DEFROCK**.

unfulfilled adjective not fulfilled.
– DERIVATIVES **unfulfillable** adjective **unfulfilling** adjective.

unfunded adjective not receiving funds; not having a fund.

unfunny adjective (**unfunnier**, **unfunniest**) (of something meant to be funny) not amusing.

unfurl verb spread out from a rolled or folded state.

unfurnished adjective without furniture.

ungainly adjective clumsy or awkward.
– DERIVATIVES **ungainliness** noun.
– ORIGIN from former *gainly* 'graceful', from Old Norse.

ungenerous adjective not generous; mean.

ungentlemanly adjective (of a man's behaviour) not well mannered or pleasant.

unglazed adjective not glazed.

unglued adjective not or no longer stuck.
– PHRASES **come unglued** informal 1 end in failure. 2 become confused or upset.

ungodly adjective 1 immoral or sinful. 2 informal unreasonably early or inconvenient: *telephone calls at ungodly hours.*
– DERIVATIVES **ungodliness** noun.

ungovernable adjective impossible to control or govern.

ungraceful adjective lacking in grace; clumsy.
– DERIVATIVES **ungracefully** adverb.

ungracious adjective not polite, kind, or pleasant.
– DERIVATIVES **ungraciously** adverb.

ungrammatical adjective not following grammatical rules.
– DERIVATIVES **ungrammatically** adverb.

ungrateful adjective not feeling or showing gratitude.
– DERIVATIVES **ungratefully** adverb **ungratefulness** noun.

unguarded adjective 1 without protection or a guard. 2 not well considered; careless: *an unguarded remark.*

unguent /ung-gwuhnt/ noun a soft substance, especially a perfumed oil, used as ointment or for lubrication.
– ORIGIN Latin *unguentum.*

ungulate /ung-gyuu-luht, ung-gyuu-layt/ noun Zoology a mammal that has hoofs.
– ORIGIN from Latin *ungula* 'hoof'.

unhand verb old use or humorous release someone from one's grasp.

unhappy adjective (**unhappier**, **unhappiest**) 1 not happy. 2 not lucky; unfortunate.
– DERIVATIVES **unhappily** adverb **unhappiness** noun.

unharmed adjective not harmed; uninjured.

UNHCR abbreviation United Nations High Commission for Refugees.

unhealthy adjective (**unhealthier**, **unhealthiest**) 1 not in good health. 2 likely to lead to illness or bad health: *an unhealthy diet.*
– DERIVATIVES **unhealthily** adverb **unhealthiness** noun.

unheard adjective 1 not heard or listened to. 2 (**unheard of**) previously unknown.

unheeded adjective heard or noticed but ignored.

u

unheeding adjective not paying attention.
unhelpful adjective not helpful.
– DERIVATIVES **unhelpfully** adverb **unhelpfulness** noun.
unheralded adjective not previously announced; without warning.
unhesitating adjective without doubt or hesitation.
– DERIVATIVES **unhesitatingly** adverb.
unhinge verb make someone mentally unbalanced.
unhistorical adjective not in accordance with history or historical analysis.
unholy adjective (**unholier, unholiest**) **1** sinful; wicked. **2** (of an alliance) unnatural and likely to be dangerous or harmful. **3** informal very bad: *an unholy row.*
unhook verb unfasten or detach something held by a hook.
unhoped adjective (**unhoped for**) beyond one's hopes or expectations.
unhorse verb make someone fall from a horse.
unhurried adjective moving, acting, or taking place without haste or urgency.
– DERIVATIVES **unhurriedly** adverb.
unhurt adjective not hurt or harmed.
unhygienic adjective not hygienic.
uni noun (pl. **unis**) informal university.
uni- combining form one; having or consisting of one: *unicycle.*
– ORIGIN from Latin *unus.*
Uniate /yoo-ni-ayt/ adjective referring to any Christian community in eastern Europe or the Near East which acknowledges the supremacy of the pope but has its own liturgy.
– ORIGIN Russian *uniat.*
unicameral /yoo-ni-kam-uh-ruhl/ adjective (of a law-making assembly) having a single chamber.
– ORIGIN from Latin *camera* 'chamber'.
UNICEF /yoo-ni-sef/ abbreviation United Nations Children's (originally International Children's Emergency) Fund.
unicellular /yoo-ni-sel-yuu-ler/ adjective Biology consisting of a single cell.
unicorn noun a mythical animal represented as a horse with a single straight horn projecting from its forehead.
– ORIGIN Latin *unicornis*, from *cornu* 'horn'.
unicycle noun a cycle with a single wheel, chiefly used by acrobats.
– DERIVATIVES **unicyclist** noun.
unidentifiable adjective unable to be identified.
unidentified adjective not recognized or identified.
unidiomatic adjective not using or containing expressions natural to a native speaker of a language.
unidirectional adjective moving or operating in a single direction.
unification noun the process of being unified.
uniform adjective not varying in form or character; the same in all cases and at all times. •noun the distinctive clothing worn by members of the same organization or by children attending certain schools.
– DERIVATIVES **uniformed** adjective **uniformity**

noun **uniformly** adverb.
– ORIGIN Latin *uniformis.*
unify /yoo-ni-fy/ verb (**unifies, unifying, unified**) make or become united or uniform.
– DERIVATIVES **unifier** noun.
– ORIGIN Latin *unificare.*
unilateral adjective **1** performed by or affecting only one person, group, etc. **2** relating to or affecting only one side of an organ, the body, etc.
– DERIVATIVES **unilateralism** noun **unilateralist** noun & adjective **unilaterally** adverb.
unimaginable adjective impossible to imagine or understand.
– DERIVATIVES **unimaginably** adverb.
unimaginative adjective not using or displaying imagination; dull.
– DERIVATIVES **unimaginatively** adverb.
unimpaired adjective not weakened or damaged.
unimpeachable adjective not able to be doubted, questioned, or criticized.
– DERIVATIVES **unimpeachably** adverb.
unimpeded adjective not obstructed or hindered.
unimportant adjective lacking in importance.
– DERIVATIVES **unimportance** noun.
unimpressed adjective not impressed.
unimpressive adjective not impressive.
unincorporated adjective **1** not formed into a legal corporation. **2** not included as part of a whole.
uninformative adjective not providing useful or interesting information.
uninformed adjective lacking awareness or understanding of the facts.
uninhabitable adjective not suitable for living in.
uninhabited adjective without inhabitants.
uninhibited adjective expressing oneself or acting freely and naturally.
– DERIVATIVES **uninhibitedly** adverb.
uninitiated adjective without special knowledge or experience.
uninjured adjective not harmed or damaged.
uninspired adjective **1** not original or imaginative; dull. **2** not excited.
uninspiring adjective not exciting or interesting.
uninstall verb (**uninstalling, uninstalled**) remove an application or file from a computer.
– DERIVATIVES **uninstaller** noun.
uninsurable adjective not eligible for insurance cover.
uninsured adjective not covered by insurance.
unintelligent adjective lacking intelligence.
unintelligible adjective impossible to understand.
– DERIVATIVES **unintelligibility** noun **unintelligibly** adverb.
unintended adjective not planned or meant.
unintentional adjective not done on purpose.
– DERIVATIVES **unintentionally** adverb.
uninterested adjective not interested or concerned.

u

USAGE: For an explanation of the meaning and use of **uninterested** and **disinterested**, see the note at **DISINTERESTED**.

uninteresting adjective not interesting; dull.

uninterrupted adjective **1** continuous. **2** not obstructed: *an uninterrupted view.*
– DERIVATIVES **uninterruptedly** adverb.

uninvited adjective arriving or acting without invitation.

uninviting adjective not attractive; unpleasant.

uninvolved adjective not involved.

union noun **1** the action of uniting or the fact of being united: *he supported closer economic union with Europe.* **2** a trade union. **3** a society or association formed by people with a common interest or purpose. **4** (also **Union**) a political unit consisting of a number of states or provinces with the same central government. **5** (**the Union**) the northern states of the US in the American Civil War. **6** a state of harmony or agreement. **7** a marriage.
– ORIGIN Latin, 'unity'.

unionist noun **1** a member of a trade union. **2** (**Unionist**) a person in favour of the union of Northern Ireland with Great Britain.
– DERIVATIVES **unionism** noun.

unionize (or **unionise**) verb join or cause to join a trade union.
– DERIVATIVES **unionization** noun.

Union Jack (also **Union flag**) noun the national flag of the United Kingdom.

unipolar adjective having or relating to a single pole or extremity.

unique adjective **1** being the only one of its kind; unlike anything else. **2** (**unique to**) belonging or connected to one particular person, group, or place. **3** very special or unusual.
– DERIVATIVES **uniquely** adverb **uniqueness** noun.
– ORIGIN French.

USAGE: Strictly speaking, since the main meaning of **unique** is 'being the only one of its kind', it is impossible to use adverbs with it that modify its meaning, such as **really** or **quite**. However, **unique** has a less precise sense in addition to its main meaning: 'very special or unusual' (*a really unique opportunity*). Here, **unique** does not relate to an absolute state that cannot be modified, and so the use of **really** and similar adverbs is acceptable.

unisex adjective designed for both sexes.

unison noun **1** the fact of two or more things being said or happening at the same time. **2** a coincidence in pitch of musical sounds or notes.
– ORIGIN Latin *unisonus*, from *sonus* 'sound'.

unit noun **1** an individual thing or person that is complete in itself but that can also form part of a larger whole. **2** a device, part, or item of furniture with a particular function: *a sink unit.* **3** a self-contained or distinct section of a building or group of buildings. **4** a subdivision of a larger military grouping. **5** a standard quantity in terms of which other quantities may be expressed. **6** one as a number or quantity.
– DERIVATIVES **unitize** (also **unitise**) verb.
– ORIGIN from Latin *unus* 'one'.

unitard /yoo-ni-tard/ noun a tight-fitting one-piece garment covering the whole body.
– ORIGIN from **UNI-** + **LEOTARD**.

Unitarian /yoo-ni-tair-i-uhn/ noun a member of a Christian Church that believes in the unity of God and rejects the idea of the Trinity.
– DERIVATIVES **Unitarianism** noun.
– ORIGIN Latin *unitarius*.

unitary adjective **1** forming a single entity or unit. **2** relating to a unit or units.

unitary authority (also **unitary council**) noun (chiefly in the UK) a division of local government established in place of a two-tier system of local councils.

unite verb come or bring together for a common purpose or to form a whole: *councillors were united in their opposition to the plans.*
– DERIVATIVES **united** adjective **unitive** adjective.
– ORIGIN Latin *unire* 'join together', from *unus* 'one'.

unit trust noun Brit. a company managing a portfolio of stock exchange securities, in which individual small investors can buy units.

unity noun (pl. **unities**) **1** the state of being united or forming a whole. **2** a thing forming a complex whole. **3** Mathematics the number one.

universal adjective affecting or done by all people or things in the world or in a particular group; applicable to all cases: *the incidents caused universal concern.*
– DERIVATIVES **universality** noun **universally** adverb.

universalist noun (in Christian belief) a person who believes that all humankind will eventually be saved.
– DERIVATIVES **universalism** noun **universalistic** adjective.

universalize (or **universalise**) verb make something universal, or make something available for all.
– DERIVATIVES **universalization** noun.

universal joint noun a joint which can transmit rotary power by a shaft at any selected angle.

universe noun **1** all existing matter and space considered as a whole; the cosmos. **2** a particular sphere of activity or experience.
– ORIGIN Latin *universus* 'combined into one, whole'.

university noun (pl. **universities**) a high-level educational institution in which students study for degrees and academic research is carried out.
– ORIGIN Latin *universitas* 'the whole'.

Unix noun trademark a widely used multi-user computer operating system.

unjust adjective not just; unfair.
– DERIVATIVES **unjustly** adverb.

unjustifiable adjective impossible to justify.
– DERIVATIVES **unjustifiably** adverb.

unjustified adjective not justified.

unkempt adjective having an untidy or dishevelled appearance.
– ORIGIN from former *kempt* 'combed'.

unkind adjective not sympathetic, caring, or kind.

u

- DERIVATIVES **unkindly** adverb **unkindness** noun.

unknowable adjective not able to be known.
- DERIVATIVES **unknowability** noun.

unknowing adjective not knowing or aware.
●noun literary ignorance.
- DERIVATIVES **unknowingly** adverb.

unknown adjective not known or familiar.
●noun an unknown person or thing.
- PHRASES **unknown to** without someone's knowledge.

unknown quantity noun a person or thing whose nature, value, or significance is not known.

Unknown Soldier noun an unidentified representative member of a country's armed forces killed in war, buried with special honours in a national memorial.

unlabelled (US **unlabeled**) adjective without a label.

unlace verb undo the laces of a shoe or garment.

unladen adjective not carrying a load.

unladylike adjective not appropriate for or behaving like a well-bred woman.

unlamented adjective not mourned or regretted.

unlatch verb unfasten the latch of a door or gate.

unlawful adjective not conforming to or permitted by law or rules.
- DERIVATIVES **unlawfully** adverb **unlawfulness** noun.

USAGE: For an explanation of the difference between **unlawful** and **illegal**, see the note at **ILLEGAL**.

unleaded adjective (of petrol) without added lead.

unlearn verb (past and past part. **unlearned** or **unlearnt**) attempt to forget something that has been learned.

unlearned[1] /un-**ler**-nid/ adjective not well educated.

unlearned[2] /un-**lernd**/ (also **unlearnt** /un-**lernt**/) adjective not having been learned.

unleash verb 1 release an animal from a leash. 2 allow something strong or destructive to happen: *the US unleashed a full-scale military attack.*

unleavened adjective (of bread) made without yeast or other raising agent.

unless conjunction except when; if not.
- ORIGIN from ON or IN + LESS.

unlettered adjective poorly educated or illiterate.

unlicensed adjective not having an official licence, especially for the sale of alcoholic drinks.

unlike preposition 1 different from; not like. 2 in contrast to. 3 uncharacteristic of.
●adjective different from each other.
- DERIVATIVES **unlikeness** noun.

USAGE: It is not good English to use **unlike** as a conjunction (a word connecting words or clauses of a sentence together), as in *she was behaving unlike she'd ever behaved before.* Use **as** with a negative instead: *she was behaving as she'd never behaved before.*

unlikely adjective (**unlikelier**, **unlikeliest**) not likely to happen or be the case; improbable.
- DERIVATIVES **unlikelihood** noun.

unlimited adjective not limited or restricted; infinite.

unlined[1] adjective not marked with lines or wrinkles.

unlined[2] adjective without a lining.

unlisted adjective not included on a list, especially of stock exchange prices or telephone numbers.

unlit adjective 1 not provided with lighting. 2 not having been lit.

unlivable adjective not able to be lived in; uninhabitable.

unlived adjective (**unlived in**) not appearing to be inhabited.

unload verb 1 remove goods from a vehicle, ship, etc. 2 remove ammunition from a gun or film from a camera. 3 informal get rid of something.

unlock verb 1 unfasten the lock of a door, container, etc. using a key. 2 make something previously inaccessible or unexploited available.

unlooked adjective (**unlooked for**) unexpected; unforeseen.

unloose verb undo or release something.

unloosen verb another term for UNLOOSE.

unloved adjective loved by no one.

unlovely adjective not attractive; ugly.

unlucky adjective (**unluckier**, **unluckiest**) having, bringing, or resulting from bad luck.
- DERIVATIVES **unluckily** adverb.

unmade adjective 1 (of a bed) not arranged tidily. 2 Brit. (of a road) without a hard, smooth surface.

unman verb (**unmans**, **unmanning**, **unmanned**) literary deprive a man of qualities traditionally associated with men, such as self-control or courage.

unmanageable adjective difficult or impossible to manage or control.
- DERIVATIVES **unmanageably** adverb.

unmanly adjective not manly.

unmanned adjective not having or needing a crew or staff.

unmannerly adjective not well mannered.

unmarked adjective 1 not marked. 2 not noticed.

unmarried adjective not married; single.

unmask verb reveal someone's or something's true character or nature.

unmatched adjective not matched or equalled.

unmentionable adjective too embarrassing or offensive to be spoken about.

unmerciful adjective showing no mercy.
- DERIVATIVES **unmercifully** adverb.

unmerited adjective not deserved.

unmetalled adjective Brit. (of a road) not having a hard surface.

unmindful adjective (**unmindful of**) not conscious or aware of something.

unmissable adjective that should not or cannot be missed.

unmistakable (also **unmistakeable**) adjective not able to be mistaken for anything else.
- DERIVATIVES **unmistakably** adverb.

unmitigated adjective absolute; complete: *an*

unmitigated disaster.
– DERIVATIVES **unmitigatedly** adverb.
unmixed adjective not mixed.
unmoderated adjective (of an Internet bulletin board or chat room) not monitored for inappropriate or offensive content.
unmoor verb release the moorings of a boat or ship.
unmotivated adjective **1** not motivated or enthusiastic. **2** without apparent motive: *an unmotivated attack.*
unmoved adjective **1** not affected by emotion or excitement. **2** not changed in purpose or position.
unmoving adjective not moving; still.
unmusical adjective **1** not pleasing to the ear. **2** not enjoying or skilled at playing music.
unnameable (also **unnamable**) adjective unmentionable.
unnamed adjective not named.
unnatural adjective **1** contrary to what is found in nature; abnormal or artificial. **2** different from what is normal or expected.
– DERIVATIVES **unnaturally** adverb **unnaturalness** noun.
unnavigable adjective not able to be sailed on by ships or boats.
unnecessary adjective not necessary, or more than is necessary.
– DERIVATIVES **unnecessarily** adverb.
unnerve verb make someone feel nervous or frightened.
– DERIVATIVES **unnerving** adjective.
unnoticeable adjective not easily observed or noticed.
unnoticed adjective not noticed.
unnumbered adjective **1** not given a number. **2** not counted, or not able to be counted.
unobserved adjective not observed; unseen.
unobstructed adjective not obstructed.
unobtainable adjective not able to be obtained.
unobtrusive adjective not conspicuous or attracting attention.
– DERIVATIVES **unobtrusively** adverb **unobtrusiveness** noun.
unoccupied adjective not occupied.
unofficial adjective not officially authorized or confirmed.
– DERIVATIVES **unofficially** adverb.
unopened adjective not opened.
unopposed adjective not opposed; unchallenged.
unorganized (or **unorganised**) adjective not organized.
unoriginal adjective lacking originality.
– DERIVATIVES **unoriginality** noun **unoriginally** adverb.
unorthodox adjective different from what is usual, traditional, or accepted.
– DERIVATIVES **unorthodoxy** noun.
unostentatious adjective not ostentatious or showy.
– DERIVATIVES **unostentatiously** adverb.
unpack verb **1** remove the contents of a suitcase, bag, container, etc. **2** separate something into its different elements in order to make it easier to understand.

unpaid adjective **1** (of a debt) not yet paid. **2** (of work or leave) done or taken without payment. **3** not receiving payment for work done.
unpaired adjective **1** not arranged in pairs. **2** not forming one of a pair.
unpalatable adjective **1** not pleasant to taste. **2** difficult to put up with or accept.
unparalleled adjective having no parallel or equal; exceptional.
unpardonable adjective (of a fault or offence) unforgivable.
– DERIVATIVES **unpardonably** adverb.
unparliamentary adjective (especially of language) against the rules of behaviour of a parliament.
unpasteurized (or **unpasteurised**) adjective not pasteurized.
unpatriotic adjective not patriotic.
– DERIVATIVES **unpatriotically** adverb.
unpaved adjective not having a metalled or paved surface.
unpeopled adjective empty of people.
unperson noun (pl. **unpersons**) a person whose name or existence is officially denied or ignored.
unperturbed adjective not perturbed or worried.
unpick verb **1** undo the stitches from a piece of sewing. **2** carefully analyse the different elements of something.
unpin verb (**unpin**, **unpinning**, **unpinned**) unfasten or detach something by removing a pin or pins.
unpitying adjective not feeling or showing pity.
unplaced adjective chiefly Horse Racing not one of the first three (sometimes four) to finish in a race.
unplanned adjective not planned.
unplayable adjective **1** not able to be played or played on: *the pitch was unplayable.* **2** (of music) too difficult to perform.
unpleasant adjective **1** not pleasant. **2** not friendly or kind.
– DERIVATIVES **unpleasantly** adverb.
unpleasantness noun **1** the state or quality of being unpleasant. **2** bad feeling or quarrelling between people.
unploughed (US **unplowed**) adjective (of land) not having been ploughed.
unplug verb (**unplugs**, **unplugging**, **unplugged**) **1** disconnect an electrical device by removing its plug from a socket. **2** remove an obstacle or blockage from something.
unplugged adjective trademark (of pop or rock music) performed or recorded with acoustic rather than electrically amplified instruments.
unplumbed adjective **1** not provided with plumbing. **2** not fully explored or understood.
– DERIVATIVES **unplumbable** adjective.
unpolished adjective **1** not having a polished surface. **2** (of a performance or piece of work) not having been refined or perfected.
unpopular adjective not liked or popular.
– DERIVATIVES **unpopularity** noun.
unpopulated adjective without inhabitants.
unpowered adjective (of a vehicle, boat, etc.)

u

not propelled by burning a fuel such as petrol, oil, gas, etc.

unpractised (US **unpracticed**) adjective not trained or experienced.

unprecedented adjective never done or known before.
– DERIVATIVES **unprecedentedly** adverb.

unpredictable adjective 1 not able to be predicted. 2 changeable or unreliable.
– DERIVATIVES **unpredictability** noun **unpredictably** adverb.

unprejudiced adjective without prejudice; unbiased.

unpremeditated adjective not thought out or planned beforehand.

unprepared adjective 1 not ready or able to deal with something. 2 not made ready for use.

unprepossessing adjective not attractive or appealing in appearance.

unpressurized (or **unpressurised**) adjective 1 (of a gas or its container) not having raised pressure that is produced or maintained artificially. 2 (of an aircraft cabin) not having normal atmospheric pressure maintained at a high altitude.

unpretentious adjective not pretentious; modest or unassuming.
– DERIVATIVES **unpretentiously** adverb **unpretentiousness** noun.

unprincipled adjective not acting in accordance with moral principles.

unprintable adjective (of words, comments, or thoughts) too offensive or shocking to be published.

unproblematic adjective not presenting a problem or difficulty.
– DERIVATIVES **unproblematically** adverb.

unprocessed adjective not processed.

unproductive adjective 1 not producing or able to produce large amounts of goods, crops, etc. 2 not achieving much; not very useful.

unprofessional adjective not in accordance with the standards expected in a particular profession.
– DERIVATIVES **unprofessionally** adverb.

unprofitable adjective 1 not making a profit. 2 not beneficial or useful.

unpromising adjective not giving hope of future success or good results.

unprompted adjective said or done without being prompted by someone else.

unpronounceable adjective too difficult to pronounce.

unprotected adjective 1 not protected or kept safe from harm. 2 (of sex) performed without a condom.

unproven /un-proo-vuhn, un-proh-vuhn/ (also **unproved**) adjective 1 not shown by evidence or argument to be true or to exist. 2 not tried and tested.

unprovoked adjective (of an attack, crime, etc.) not directly provoked.

unpublished adjective 1 (of a work) not published. 2 (of an author) having no writings published.
– DERIVATIVES **unpublishable** adjective.

unpunished adjective (of an offence or offender) not receiving any punishment or penalty.

unputdownable adjective informal (of a book) so absorbing that one cannot stop reading it.

unqualified adjective 1 not having the necessary qualifications or requirements. 2 without limitation; total: *an unqualified success.*

unquantifiable adjective impossible to express or measure.

unquenchable adjective not able to be quenched or satisfied.

unquestionable adjective not able to be disputed or doubted.
– DERIVATIVES **unquestionably** adverb.

unquestioned adjective 1 not disputed or doubted; certain. 2 accepted without question.
– DERIVATIVES **unquestioning** adjective.

unquiet adjective 1 unable to be still; restless. 2 uneasy or anxious.

unquoted adjective not quoted or listed on a stock exchange.

unranked adjective not having achieved or been given a rank or ranking.

unravel verb (**unravels**, **unravelling**, **unravelled**; US **unravels**, **unraveling**, **unraveled**) 1 undo twisted, knitted, or woven threads. 2 become undone. 3 investigate and solve a mystery or puzzle. 4 begin to fail or collapse: *the peace process began to unravel.*

unreachable adjective unable to be reached or contacted.

unreactive adjective having little tendency to react chemically.

unread adjective not having been read.

unreadable adjective 1 not clear enough to read; illegible. 2 too dull or difficult to be worth reading.
– DERIVATIVES **unreadability** noun **unreadably** adverb.

unready adjective not ready or prepared.

unreal adjective 1 imaginary or not seeming real. 2 unrealistic.
– DERIVATIVES **unreality** noun.

unrealistic adjective 1 not having a sensible idea of what can be achieved or expected. 2 not representing things in a realistic way.
– DERIVATIVES **unrealistically** adverb.

unrealized (or **unrealised**) adjective 1 not achieved or created. 2 not converted into money: *unrealized property assets.*

unreason noun lack of reasonable thought; irrationality.
– DERIVATIVES **unreasoned** adjective.

unreasonable adjective 1 not guided by or based on good sense. 2 beyond the limits of what is acceptable or achievable.
– DERIVATIVES **unreasonableness** noun **unreasonably** adverb.

unreasoning adjective not guided by or based on reason; illogical.

unreceptive adjective not receptive.

unrecognizable (or **unrecognisable**) adjective not able to be recognized.
– DERIVATIVES **unrecognizably** adverb.

unrecognized (or **unrecognised**) adjective 1 not identified from previous encounters or knowledge. 2 not acknowledged as valid.

unreconstructed adjective not reconciled or

converted to the current political theory or movement.

unrecorded adjective not recorded.

unreel verb 1 unwind something. 2 (of a film) wind from one reel to another during projection.

unrefined adjective 1 not processed to remove impurities. 2 not elegant or cultured.

unregenerate /un-ri-**jen**-uh-ruht/ adjective not reforming or showing repentance; obstinately wrong or bad.

unregistered adjective not officially recognized and recorded.

unregulated adjective not controlled or supervised by regulations or laws.

unrehearsed adjective not rehearsed.

unrelated adjective not related.

unreleased adjective (especially of a film or recording) not released.

unrelenting adjective 1 not stopping or becoming weaker. 2 refusing to relent or give in.
– DERIVATIVES **unrelentingly** adverb.

unreliable adjective not able to be relied on.
– DERIVATIVES **unreliability** noun **unreliably** adverb.

unrelieved adjective lacking variation or change; monotonous.
– DERIVATIVES **unrelievedly** adverb.

unremarkable adjective not particularly interesting or surprising.

unremarked adjective not noticed or remarked on.

unremitting adjective never relaxing or slackening.
– DERIVATIVES **unremittingly** adverb.

unremunerative adjective bringing little or no profit or income.

unrepeatable adjective 1 not able to be repeated. 2 too offensive or shocking to be said again.

unrepentant adjective showing no regret for one's wrongdoings.
– DERIVATIVES **unrepentantly** adverb.

unreported adjective not reported.

unrepresentative adjective not typical of a class or group.

unrequited adjective (of love) not returned.

unreserved adjective 1 without reservations; complete. 2 frank and open. 3 not set apart for a particular purpose or booked in advance.
– DERIVATIVES **unreservedly** adverb.

unresolved adjective (of a problem, dispute, etc.) not resolved.

unresponsive adjective not responsive.
– DERIVATIVES **unresponsiveness** noun.

unrest noun a state of rebellious dissatisfaction in a group of people: *years of industrial unrest*.

unrestrained adjective not restrained or restricted.
– DERIVATIVES **unrestrainedly** adverb.

unrestricted adjective not limited or restricted.

unrewarding adjective not rewarding or satisfying.

unripe adjective not ripe.

unrivalled (US **unrivaled**) adjective greater or better than all others.

unroll verb open or cause to open out from a rolled-up state.

unromantic adjective not romantic.

unruffled adjective 1 (of a person) calm and unperturbed. 2 not disordered or disturbed.

unruly adjective (**unrulier**, **unruliest**) disorderly and disruptive; difficult to control.
– DERIVATIVES **unruliness** noun.
– ORIGIN from former *ruly* 'disciplined, orderly', from **RULE**.

unsaddle verb remove the saddle from a horse.

unsafe adjective 1 not safe; dangerous. 2 Law (of a verdict or conviction) not based on reliable evidence and likely to constitute a miscarriage of justice. 3 (of sexual activity) in which people do not take precautions to protect themselves against sexually transmitted diseases such as Aids.

unsaid past and past participle of **UNSAY**.
adjective not said or expressed.

unsaleable (also **unsalable**) adjective not able to be sold.

unsalted adjective without added salt.

unsanitary adjective not hygienic.

unsatisfactory adjective 1 not good enough. 2 Law another term for **UNSAFE**.
– DERIVATIVES **unsatisfactorily** adverb.

unsatisfied adjective not satisfied.

unsatisfying adjective not satisfying.

unsaturated adjective Chemistry (of fats) having double and triple bonds between carbon atoms in their molecules and as a consequence being more easily processed by the body.

unsavoury (US **unsavory**) adjective 1 unpleasant to taste, smell, or look at. 2 not morally respectable; disreputable.

unsay verb (past and past part. **unsaid**) withdraw or retract a statement.

unsayable adjective not able to be said, especially because considered too controversial or offensive.

unscarred adjective not scarred or damaged.

unscathed adjective without suffering any injury, damage, or harm.

unscented adjective not scented.

unscheduled adjective not scheduled.

unschooled adjective 1 lacking schooling or training. 2 not affected; natural and spontaneous.

unscientific adjective not in accordance with scientific principles or methods.
– DERIVATIVES **unscientifically** adverb.

unscramble verb restore a scrambled broadcast, message, etc. to an intelligible or readable state.

unscreened adjective 1 not subjected to testing or investigation by screening. 2 not shown or broadcast.

unscrew verb unfasten something by twisting it.

unscripted adjective said or delivered without a prepared script; impromptu.

unscrupulous adjective without moral principles; dishonest or unfair.
– DERIVATIVES **unscrupulously** adverb **unscrupulousness** noun.

unseal verb remove or break the seal of something.

u

unsealed adjective not sealed.

unseasonable adjective (of weather) unusual for the time of year.
- DERIVATIVES **unseasonably** adverb.

unseasonal adjective (especially of weather) unusual or inappropriate for the time of year.

unseasoned adjective 1 (of food) not flavoured with salt, pepper, or other spices. 2 (of timber) not treated or matured.

unseat verb 1 make someone fall from a saddle or seat. 2 remove a government or person in authority from power.

unsecured adjective 1 (of a loan) made without an asset given as security. 2 not made secure or safe.

unseeded adjective (of a competitor in a sports tournament) not seeded.

unseeing adjective with one's eyes open but without noticing or seeing anything.
- DERIVATIVES **unseeingly** adverb.

unseemly adjective (of behaviour or actions) not proper or appropriate.
- DERIVATIVES **unseemliness** noun.

unseen adjective 1 not seen or noticed. 2 chiefly Brit. (of a passage for translation in an exam) not previously read or prepared.

unselfconscious adjective not shy or embarrassed.
- DERIVATIVES **unselfconsciously** adverb **unselfconsciousness** noun.

unselfish adjective not selfish.
- DERIVATIVES **unselfishly** adverb **unselfishness** noun.

unsentimental adjective not displaying or influenced by sentimental feelings.
- DERIVATIVES **unsentimentally** adverb.

unserious adjective not serious; light-hearted.

unserviceable adjective not in working order; unfit for use.

unsettle verb make anxious or uneasy; disturb: *the crisis has unsettled financial markets.*
- DERIVATIVES **unsettling** adjective.

unsettled adjective 1 changeable or likely to change: *unsettled weather.* 2 agitated; uneasy. 3 not yet resolved.

unsex verb deprive someone of their gender, sexuality, or the characteristic features of one or other sex.

unshackle verb release someone from shackles or other restraints.

unshakeable (also **unshakable**) adjective (of a belief, feeling, etc.) firm and unable to be changed or disputed.

unshaken adjective not having changed or weakened: *their trust in him remains unshaken.*

unshaven adjective not having shaved or been shaved.

unsheathe verb pull a knife or similar weapon out of a sheath.

unshed adjective (of tears) welling in a person's eyes but not falling.

unshelled adjective not extracted from its shell.

unship verb (unships, unshipping, unshipped) 1 remove an oar, mast, or other object from a fixed or regular position. 2 unload a cargo from a ship or boat.

unshockable adjective impossible to shock.

unshorn adjective (of hair or wool) not cut or shorn.

unsighted adjective 1 lacking the power of sight. 2 (especially in sport) prevented from having a clear view.

unsightly adjective unpleasant to look at; ugly.
- DERIVATIVES **unsightliness** noun.

unsigned adjective 1 not identified or authorized by a person's signature. 2 (of a musician or sports player) not having signed a contract of employment.

unsinkable adjective unable to be sunk.

unskilful (also chiefly US **unskillful**) adjective not having or showing skill.
- DERIVATIVES **unskilfully** adverb.

unskilled adjective not having or requiring special skill or training.

unsling verb (past and past part. **unslung**) remove something from the place where it has been slung or suspended.

unsmiling adjective not smiling; serious or unfriendly.
- DERIVATIVES **unsmilingly** adverb.

unsociable adjective 1 not enjoying the company of other people. 2 not contributing to friendly relationships between people.

unsocial adjective 1 Brit. (of the hours of work of a job) falling outside the normal working day and so socially inconvenient. 2 antisocial.

unsold adjective (of an item) not sold.

unsolicited adjective not asked for.

unsolved adjective not solved.

unsophisticated adjective 1 lacking experience or taste in matters of culture or fashion. 2 not complicated or highly developed; basic.

unsorted adjective not sorted or arranged.

unsound adjective 1 not safe or strong; in poor condition. 2 not based on reliable evidence or reasoning; unreliable or unacceptable.

unsparing adjective merciless; severe.
- DERIVATIVES **unsparingly** adverb.

unspeakable adjective 1 not able to be expressed in words. 2 too bad or horrific to express in words.
- DERIVATIVES **unspeakably** adverb.

unspecific adjective not specific; vague.

unspecified adjective not stated clearly or exactly.

unspectacular adjective not spectacular; unremarkable.

unspoilt (also **unspoiled**) adjective not spoilt, in particular (of a place) largely unaffected by building or development.

unspoken adjective understood without being expressed in speech: *an unspoken agreement.*

unspool verb unwind or be unwound from a spool.

unsporting adjective not fair or sportsmanlike.
- DERIVATIVES **unsportingly** adverb.

unsportsmanlike adjective not behaving according to the spirit of fair play in a particular sport.

unsprung adjective not provided with springs.

unstable adjective (unstabler, unstablest) 1 likely to change or collapse; not stable. 2 prone to sudden changes of mood or mental health problems.

unstained adjective not stained.

unstated adjective not stated or declared.

unsteady adjective (**unsteadier, unsteadiest**) **1** liable to fall or shake. **2** not regular or controlled.
– DERIVATIVES **unsteadily** adverb **unsteadiness** noun.

unstick verb (past and past part. **unstuck**) separate a thing which is stuck to another.

unstinting adjective given or giving without restraint.
– DERIVATIVES **unstinted** adjective **unstintingly** adverb.

unstoppable adjective impossible to stop or prevent.
– DERIVATIVES **unstoppably** adverb.

unstopper verb remove the stopper from a container.

unstressed adjective (of a syllable) not pronounced with stress.

unstring verb (past and past part. **unstrung**) **1** (usu. as adj. **unstrung**) unnerve or upset: *a mind unstrung by loneliness.* **2** remove or relax the string or strings of a bow or musical instrument.

unstructured adjective without formal organization or structure.

unstuck past and past participle of UNSTICK.
– PHRASES **come unstuck** informal fail

unstudied adjective not forced or artificial; natural.

unstuffy adjective friendly, informal, and approachable.

unsubstantial adjective having little or no solidity, reality, or factual basis.

unsubstantiated adjective not supported or proven by evidence.

unsubtle adjective not subtle; obvious.
– DERIVATIVES **unsubtly** adverb.

unsuccessful adjective not successful.
– DERIVATIVES **unsuccessfully** adverb.

unsuitable adjective not right or appropriate for a particular purpose or occasion.
– DERIVATIVES **unsuitability** noun **unsuitably** adverb.

unsuited adjective lacking the right or necessary qualities for something: *he was totally unsuited for the job.*

unsullied adjective not spoiled or made impure.

unsung adjective not celebrated or praised: *unsung heroes.*

unsupervised adjective not done or acting under supervision.

unsupportable adjective insupportable.

unsupported adjective **1** not supported. **2** not proven to be true by evidence or facts.

unsure adjective **1** lacking confidence. **2** not fixed or certain.
– DERIVATIVES **unsurely** adverb **unsureness** noun.

unsurfaced adjective (of a road or path) not provided with a hard-wearing upper layer.

unsurpassable adjective not able to be bettered or exceeded.

unsurpassed adjective better or greater than any other.

unsurprising adjective expected and so not causing surprise.

– DERIVATIVES **unsurprisingly** adverb.

unsuspected adjective **1** not known or thought to exist; not imagined as possible. **2** not regarded with suspicion.

unsuspecting adjective not aware of the presence of danger; feeling no suspicion.
– DERIVATIVES **unsuspectingly** adverb.

unsustainable adjective **1** not able to be maintained at the current rate or level. **2** not able to be upheld or defended. **3** upsetting the ecological balance by depleting natural resources.
– DERIVATIVES **unsustainably** adverb.

unswayed adjective not influenced or affected.

unsweetened adjective (of food or drink) without added sugar or sweetener.

unswerving adjective not changing or becoming weaker.
– DERIVATIVES **unswervingly** adverb.

unsymmetrical adjective not symmetrical.

unsympathetic adjective **1** not sympathetic. **2** not showing approval of an idea or action. **3** not likeable.
– DERIVATIVES **unsympathetically** adverb.

unsystematic adjective not done or acting according to a fixed plan or system.
– DERIVATIVES **unsystematically** adverb.

untainted adjective not contaminated or tainted.

untamed adjective not tamed or controlled.
– DERIVATIVES **untameable** (also **untamable**) adjective.

untangle verb **1** undo something that has become twisted or tangled. **2** make something complicated or confusing easier to understand or deal with.

untapped adjective (of a resource) not yet exploited or used.

untarnished adjective **1** (of metal) not tarnished. **2** not spoiled or ruined.

untasted adjective (of food or drink) not sampled.

untaught adjective **1** not having been taught or educated. **2** not gained by teaching; natural or spontaneous.

untenable adjective not able to be maintained or defended against attack or objection.

untended adjective not cared for or looked after; neglected.

untenured adjective (of a college teacher or post) without tenure.

Untermensch /uun-ter-mensh/ noun (pl. **Untermenschen** /uun-ter-men-shuhn/) a person considered racially or socially inferior.
– ORIGIN German, 'underperson'.

untested adjective not subjected to testing; unproven.
– DERIVATIVES **untestable** adjective.

unthinkable adjective too unlikely or undesirable to be considered a possibility.
– DERIVATIVES **unthinkably** adverb.

unthinking adjective without proper consideration.
– DERIVATIVES **unthinkingly** adverb.

unthought adjective (**unthought of**) not imagined or dreamed of.

unthreatening adjective not threatening.

untidy adjective (**untidier, untidiest**) **1** not

u

arranged tidily. **2** (of a person) not keeping things tidy or well organized.
– DERIVATIVES **untidily** adverb **untidiness** noun.

untie verb (**unties, untying, untied**) undo or unfasten something tied.

until preposition & conjunction up to the point in time or the event mentioned.
– ORIGIN from Old Norse *und* 'as far as' + TILL¹.

USAGE: For an explanation of the difference between **until** and **till**, see the note at **TILL¹**.

untimely adjective **1** happening or done at an unsuitable time; inappropriate. **2** (of a death or end) happening too soon or sooner than normal.
– DERIVATIVES **untimeliness** noun.

untiring adjective continuing at the same rate without loss of energy.
– DERIVATIVES **untiringly** adverb.

untitled adjective **1** (of a book or other work) having no title. **2** not having a title indicating high social or official rank.

unto preposition **1** old-fashioned term for **TO**. **2** old-fashioned term for **UNTIL**.
– ORIGIN from **UNTIL**, with **TO** replacing **TILL¹**.

untold adjective **1** too much or too many to be counted: *thieves caused untold damage.* **2** not told or recounted.

untouchable adjective **1** not able to be touched or affected. **2** unable to be matched or rivalled. •noun historical a member of the lowest caste in Hindu society.
– DERIVATIVES **untouchability** noun.

USAGE: The use of the term **untouchable** to refer to a member of the lowest caste in Hindu society was declared illegal in the constitution of India in 1949 and of Pakistan in 1953. The official term today is **scheduled caste**.

untouched adjective **1** not handled, used, or tasted. **2** not affected, changed, or damaged in any way.

untoward adjective unexpected and inappropriate or unwelcome.

untraceable adjective unable to be found or traced.

untracked adjective (of land) without a path or tracks.

untrained adjective not having been trained in a particular skill.

untrammelled (US also **untrammeled**) adjective not restricted or hampered.

untranslatable adjective not able to be translated.

untreatable adjective for whom or which no medical care is available or possible.

untreated adjective **1** not given medical care. **2** not treated by the use of a chemical, physical, or biological process, substance, etc.

untried adjective not yet tested; inexperienced.

untrodden adjective not having been walked on.

untroubled adjective not troubled.

untrue adjective **1** false or incorrect. **2** not faithful or loyal.

untrustworthy adjective unable to be trusted.
– DERIVATIVES **untrustworthiness** noun.

untruth noun (pl. **untruths**) **1** a lie. **2** the quality of being false.

untruthful adjective not truthful.
– DERIVATIVES **untruthfully** adverb **untruthfulness** noun.

untucked adjective with the edges or ends hanging loose; not tucked in.

untutored adjective not formally taught or trained.

untwist verb open something from a twisted position.

untying present participle of **UNTIE**.

untypical adjective unusual or uncharacteristic.
– DERIVATIVES **untypically** adverb.

unusable adjective not fit to be used.

unused adjective **1** not used. **2** (**unused to**) not accustomed to something.

unusual adjective **1** not habitually or commonly done or occurring. **2** remarkable; exceptional.
– DERIVATIVES **unusually** adverb **unusualness** noun.

unutterable adjective too great or awful to describe.
– DERIVATIVES **unutterably** adverb.

unuttered adjective not spoken or expressed.

unvaried adjective not varied.

unvarnished adjective **1** not varnished. **2** plain and straightforward: *the unvarnished truth.*

unvarying adjective not varying.
– DERIVATIVES **unvaryingly** adverb.

unveil verb **1** show or announce publicly for the first time: *he unveiled plans to crack down on crime.* **2** remove a veil or covering from a new monument or work of art as part of a public ceremony. **3** remove a veil from someone's face.

unventilated adjective not ventilated.

unverifiable adjective unable to be verified.

unverified adjective not verified.

unversed adjective (**unversed in**) not experienced or skilled in.

unviable adjective not capable of working successfully.

unvoiced adjective **1** not expressed in words. **2** (of a speech sound) produced without vibration of the vocal cords.

unwaged adjective Brit. **1** unemployed or doing unpaid work. **2** (of work) unpaid.

unwanted adjective not wanted.

unwarrantable adjective unjustifiable.
– DERIVATIVES **unwarrantably** adverb.

unwarranted adjective not warranted.

unwary adjective not cautious.
– DERIVATIVES **unwarily** adverb.

unwashed adjective not washed.
– PHRASES **the (great) unwashed** derogatory ordinary people; the masses.

unwatchable adjective too disturbing or boring to watch.

unwatched adjective not watched.

unwavering adjective not wavering; steady or resolute.
– DERIVATIVES **unwaveringly** adverb.

unweaned adjective not weaned.

unwearied adjective not wearied.

unwearying adjective never tiring or slackening.

unwed adjective not married.

unwelcome adjective not welcome.

unwelcoming adjective unfriendly or inhospitable.

unwell adjective physically or mentally ill.

unwholesome adjective not wholesome.

unwieldy adjective (**unwieldier, unwieldiest**) hard to move or manage because of its size, shape, or weight.
– DERIVATIVES **unwieldiness** noun.
– ORIGIN from **WIELD**.

unwilling adjective not willing.
– DERIVATIVES **unwillingly** adverb **unwillingness** noun.

unwind verb (past and past part. **unwound**)
1 undo something that has been wound. **2** relax after a period of work or tension.

unwinnable adjective not winnable.

unwisdom noun foolishness.

unwise adjective foolish.
– DERIVATIVES **unwisely** adverb.

unwitting adjective **1** not aware of the full facts. **2** unintentional.
– DERIVATIVES **unwittingly** adverb.
– ORIGIN Old English, 'not knowing or realizing'.

unwomanly adjective not womanly.

unwonted /un-**wohn**-tid/ adjective not usual or expected.
– DERIVATIVES **unwontedly** adverb.

unworkable adjective not able to be done successfully; impractical.

unworked adjective not cultivated, mined, or carved.

unworldly adjective **1** not interested in money or other material things. **2** lacking experience of life. **3** not seeming to belong to this world.
– DERIVATIVES **unworldliness** noun.

unworn adjective **1** not worn or damaged from much use. **2** (of an item of clothing) never worn.

unworried adjective not worried or anxious.

unworthy adjective (**unworthier, unworthiest**) **1** not deserving respect or attention. **2** not appropriate to someone's good reputation or social position: *such a suggestion is unworthy of the Honourable Gentleman.*
– DERIVATIVES **unworthily** adverb **unworthiness** noun.

unwound past and past participle of **UNWIND**.

unwounded adjective not wounded.

unwrap verb (**unwraps, unwrapping, unwrapped**) remove the wrapping from something.

unwrinkled adjective not wrinkled.

unwritable adjective not able to be written.

unwritten adjective **1** not recorded in writing. **2** (of a law, rule, agreement, etc.) generally accepted although not formally established.

unyielding adjective not yielding or giving way.

unzip verb (**unzips, unzipping, unzipped**) **1** unfasten the zip of an item of clothing. **2** Computing expand a compressed file.

up adverb **1** towards a higher place or position. **2** to the place where someone is: *I crept up behind him.* **3** at or to a higher level or value. **4** so as to be formed, finished, or brought together: *the government set up an inquiry.* **5** out of bed. **6** in a publicly visible place. **7** (of the sun) visible in the sky. **8** towards the north. **9** Brit. towards or in the capital or a major city. **10** into a happy mood. **11** winning by a specified margin: *United were 3–1 up at half time.* **12** Brit. at or to a university, especially Oxford or Cambridge. •preposition **1** from a lower to a higher point of something. **2** from one end of a street or other area to another. •adjective **1** directed or moving towards a higher place or position. **2** at an end. **3** (of the road) being repaired. **4** feeling cheerful. **5** (of a computer system) working properly. •verb (**ups, upping, upped**) increase a level or amount. •noun informal a period of success or happiness.
– PHRASES **be up on** be well informed about. **on the up and up** Brit. informal steadily improving. **something is up** informal something unusual is happening. **up against 1** close to or touching. **2** informal confronted with. **up and down** in various places throughout. **up before** appearing for a hearing in the presence of a judge, magistrate, etc. **up for 1** available for. **2** being considered for. **3** (often **up for it**) informal ready to take part in something. **up to 1** as far as a particular number, level, point, etc. **2** (also **up until**) until. **3** good enough for or capable of. **4** the duty or choice of. **5** informal occupied with. **up top** Brit. informal in the way of intelligence. **what's up?** informal **1** what is going on? **2** what is the matter?
– ORIGIN Old English.

up- prefix **1** (added to verbs and their derivatives) upwards: *upturned.* **2** (added to verbs and their derivatives) to a more recent time: *update.* **3** (added to nouns) referring to motion up: *uphill.* **4** (added to nouns) higher: *upland.*

up-and-coming adjective likely to become successful.
– DERIVATIVES **up-and-comer** noun.

up-and-over adjective (of a garage door) opened by being raised and pushed back into a horizontal position.

Upanishad /oo-**pan**-i-shad, yoo-**pan**-i-shad/ noun each of a series of Hindu sacred books explaining the philosophy introduced in the Veda (the oldest Hindu scriptures).
– ORIGIN Sanskrit, 'sitting near (i.e. at the feet of a master)'.

upbeat adjective positive and cheerful or enthusiastic. •noun (in music) an unstressed beat coming before a stressed beat.

upbraid verb criticize or scold someone.
– ORIGIN Old English, 'allege as a basis for censure'.

upbringing noun the way in which a child is cared for and taught how to behave while it is growing up.

upcoming adjective about to happen; forthcoming.

upcountry adverb & adjective in or towards the inland areas of a country.

update verb /up-**dayt**/ **1** make something more modern. **2** give someone the latest information. •noun /**up**-dayt/ an act of updating or an updated version.
– DERIVATIVES **updatable** adjective.

upend verb set or turn something on its end or upside down.

u

upfield adverb (in sport) in or to a position nearer to the opponents' end of a field.

upfront informal adverb (usu. **up front**) **1** at the front; in front. **2** (of a payment) in advance. •adjective **1** expressing one's thoughts and intentions openly; frank. **2** (of a payment) made in advance.

upgrade verb **1** raise to a higher standard, level, etc.: *the company will be upgrading its services.* **2** promote an employee. •noun an act of upgrading or an upgraded version.
– DERIVATIVES **upgradeable** (also **upgradable**) adjective **upgrader** noun.

upheaval noun a violent or sudden change or disruption.

upheave verb literary heave or lift up something.

uphill adverb towards the top of a slope. •adjective **1** sloping upwards. **2** difficult: *an uphill struggle.*

uphold verb (past and past part. **upheld**) **1** support something and ensure that it continues to exist: *it is the chief constable's duty to uphold the law.* **2** (of a court of law or official body) agree that a previous decision was correct or that a request is reasonable.
– DERIVATIVES **upholder** noun.

upholster /up-hohl-ster, up-hol-ster/ verb provide a sofa, chair, etc. with a soft, padded covering.
– DERIVATIVES **upholsterer** noun.
– ORIGIN from **UPHOLD** in the former sense 'keep in repair'.

upholstery noun **1** the soft, padded covering on a sofa, chair, etc. **2** the art or practice of upholstering furniture.

upkeep noun **1** the process of keeping something in good condition. **2** the cost of supporting a person or keeping something in good condition.

upland noun (also **uplands**) an area of high or hilly land.

uplift verb **1** lift something up. **2** (often as adj. **uplifting**) make more happy, spiritual, or moral: *tender and uplifting songs.* **3** (**be uplifted**) (of an island, mountain, etc.) be created by an upward movement of the earth's surface. •noun **1** an act of lifting or raising something. **2** support from a bra or similar garment for a woman's bust. **3** a feeling of new happiness, hope, or spirituality.
– DERIVATIVES **uplifter** noun.

uplighter noun a lamp designed to throw light upwards.
– DERIVATIVES **uplighting** noun.

uplink noun a communications link to a satellite. •verb send something by a communications link to a satellite.

upload verb transfer data to a larger computer system. •noun the action or process of transferring data to a larger computer system.

upmarket adjective & adverb chiefly Brit. expensive and of high quality or status.

upon preposition more formal term for **ON**.

upper adjective **1** situated above another part. **2** higher in position or status. **3** situated on higher ground. **4** (in place names) situated to the north. •noun **1** the part of a boot or shoe above the sole. **2** informal a stimulating drug, especially amphetamine.
– PHRASES **have the upper hand** have an advantage or control. **on one's uppers** informal very short of money. **the upper crust** informal the upper classes.

upper case noun capital letters.

upper class noun (treated as sing. or pl.) the social group with the highest status, especially the aristocracy. •adjective relating to the upper class.

uppercut noun a punch delivered with an upwards motion and the arm bent.

upper house (also **upper chamber**) noun **1** the higher house in a parliament with two chambers. **2** (**the Upper House**) (in the UK) the House of Lords.

uppermost adjective highest in place, rank, or importance. •adverb at or to the uppermost position.

upper school noun (in the UK) a secondary school for children aged from about fourteen upwards.

uppish adjective informal self-assertive and arrogant.

uppity adjective informal self-important; arrogant.
– ORIGIN from **UP**.

upraise verb raise something to a higher level.

uprate verb **1** increase the value of a payment. **2** improve the performance of something.

upright adjective **1** vertical; erect. **2** greater in height than breadth. **3** strictly respectable or honest: *an upright member of the community.* **4** (of a piano) having vertical strings. •adverb in or into an upright position. •noun **1** a vertical post, structure, or line. **2** an upright piano.
– DERIVATIVES **uprightly** adverb **uprightness** noun.

uprising noun a rebellion or revolt against an established ruler or government.

upriver adverb & adjective towards or situated at a point nearer the source of a river.

uproar noun **1** a loud and emotional noise or disturbance. **2** a public expression of outrage.
– ORIGIN Dutch *uproer.*

uproarious adjective **1** very noisy or lively. **2** very funny.
– DERIVATIVES **uproariously** adverb **uproariousness** noun.

uproot verb **1** pull a plant, tree, etc. out of the ground. **2** move someone from their home or usual surroundings.

uprush noun a sudden surge or flow, especially of a feeling.

UPS abbreviation Computing uninterruptible power supply.

upscale adjective & adverb N. Amer. expensive and of high quality; upmarket.

upset verb /up-set/ (**upsets, upsetting, upset**) **1** make someone unhappy, disappointed, or worried. **2** knock something over. **3** disrupt or disturb: *antibiotics can upset the balance of bacteria in the bowel.* •noun /up-set/ **1** an unexpected result or situation. **2** the state of being unhappy, disappointed, or worried. •adjective **1** /up-set/ unhappy, disappointed, or worried. **2** /up-set/ (of a person's stomach) having disturbed digestion.
– DERIVATIVES **upsetting** adjective.

upshot noun the eventual outcome or

conclusion of something.

upside noun the positive aspect of a situation.

upside down adverb & adjective **1** with the upper part where the lower part should be. **2** in or into total disorder.
– ORIGIN from *up so down*, perhaps meaning 'up as if down'.

upsize verb chiefly N. Amer. increase in size or complexity.

upstage verb **1** divert attention from someone else and towards oneself. **2** (of an actor) move towards the back of a stage to make another actor face away from the audience. •adverb & adjective at or towards the back of a stage.

upstairs adverb on or to an upper floor. •adjective situated on an upper floor. •noun an upper floor.

upstanding adjective respectable and honest.

upstart noun derogatory a person who has suddenly become important and behaves arrogantly.

upstate US adjective & adverb in or to a part of a state remote from its large cities. •noun an upstate area.

upstream adverb & adjective situated or moving in the direction opposite to that in which a stream or river flows.

upstroke noun an upwards stroke.

upsurge noun a sudden large increase: *an upsurge in cases of domestic violence.*

upswept adjective (of the hair) brushed upwards and off the face.

upswing noun an increase or improvement; an upward trend.

upsy-daisy exclamation expressing encouragement to a child who has fallen or is being lifted.

uptake noun the action of taking up or making use of something.
– PHRASES **be quick** (or **slow**) **on the uptake** informal be quick (or slow) to understand things.

uptempo adjective & adverb Music played with a fast or increased tempo.

upthrust noun **1** something that has been thrust upwards. **2** the upward movement of part of the earth's surface. •verb thrust something upwards.

uptight adjective informal **1** nervously tense or angry. **2** unable to express one's feelings; repressed.

uptime noun time during which a machine, especially a computer, is in operation.

up to date adjective incorporating or aware of the latest developments and trends.

uptown chiefly N. Amer. adjective & adverb in or typical of the residential area of a town or city. •noun an uptown area.

uptrend noun an upward tendency, especially in economic matters.

upturn noun an improvement or upward trend.

upturned adjective turned upwards or upside down.

uPVC abbreviation unplasticized polyvinyl chloride, a rigid form of PVC used for pipework and window frames.

upward adverb (also **upwards**) towards a higher point or level. •adjective moving or leading towards a higher point or level.
– PHRASES **upwards of** more than.
– DERIVATIVES **upwardly** adverb.

upwelling noun an instance or amount of something rising or building up: *a strong upwelling of nationalism.*

upwind adverb & adjective into the wind.

uranium /yuu-**ray**-ni-uhm/ noun a dense radioactive metallic chemical element used as a fuel in nuclear reactors.
– ORIGIN from **URANUS**.

Uranus /yoo-**ray**-nuhss, yoo-ruh-**nuhss**/ noun a planet of the solar system, seventh in order from the sun.
– DERIVATIVES **Uranian** adjective.

urban adjective **1** relating to a town or city. **2** (of popular culture, especially dance music) of black origin.
– DERIVATIVES **urbanism** noun **urbanist** noun.
– ORIGIN Latin *urbanus*.

urbane /er-**bayn**/ adjective (of a man) confident, courteous, and sophisticated.
– DERIVATIVES **urbanely** adverb.
– ORIGIN first meaning 'urban': from Latin *urbanus*.

urbanite noun informal a person who lives in a town or city.

urbanity noun the quality of being confident, courteous, and sophisticated.

urbanize (or **urbanise**) verb **1** build towns and cities in a country area. **2** make someone used to living in a town or city rather than a country area.
– DERIVATIVES **urbanization** noun.

urban myth (also N. Amer. **urban legend**) noun an entertaining story or piece of information of uncertain origin that is circulated as if it is true.

urchin noun a poor child dressed in ragged clothes.
– ORIGIN Old French *herichon* 'hedgehog'.

Urdu /**oor**-doo, **er**-doo/ noun a language closely related to Hindi, the official language of Pakistan and widely used in India.
– ORIGIN from Persian, 'language of the camp' (because it developed as a means of communication between the occupying Muslim armies and the people of Delhi in the 12th century).

urea /yuu-**ree**-uh/ noun a colourless crystalline compound which is excreted from the body in urine.
– ORIGIN Latin.

ureter /yuu-**ree**-ter/ noun the duct by which urine passes from the kidney to the bladder.
– ORIGIN Greek *ourētēr*.

urethane /**yoor**-i-thayn/ noun a synthetic crystalline compound used to make pesticides and fungicides.
– ORIGIN from **UREA + ETHANE**.

urethra /yuu-**ree**-thruh/ noun the duct by which urine passes out of the body, and which in males also carries semen.
– DERIVATIVES **urethral** adjective.
– ORIGIN Greek *ourēthra*.

urethritis /yoo-ree-**thry**-tiss/ noun inflammation of the urethra (the duct

u

carrying urine out of the body).

urge verb **1** try earnestly or persistently to persuade someone to do something. **2** strongly recommend something. **3** encourage to move more quickly or in a particular direction: *he urged his pony on.* • noun a strong desire or impulse.
– ORIGIN Latin *urgere* 'press, drive'.

urgent adjective **1** requiring immediate action or attention. **2** earnest and insistent: *an urgent whisper.*
– DERIVATIVES **urgency** noun **urgently** adverb.

uric acid /yoor-ik/ noun an insoluble compound which is the main substance excreted by birds, reptiles, and insects.
– ORIGIN French *urique.*

urinal /yuu-ry-nuhl, yoor-i-nuhl/ noun a bowl attached to the wall in a public toilet, into which men urinate.

urinary adjective **1** relating to urine. **2** referring to the organs, structures, and ducts in which urine is produced and passed from the body.

urinate verb pass urine from the body.
– DERIVATIVES **urination** noun.
– ORIGIN Latin *urinare.*

urine /yoo-rin, yoo-ryn/ noun a yellowish fluid stored in the bladder and discharged through the urethra, consisting of excess water and waste substances removed from the blood by the kidneys.
– ORIGIN Latin *urina.*

URL abbreviation uniform (or universal) resource locator, the address of a World Wide Web page.

urn noun **1** a tall, rounded vase with a stem and base, especially one for storing a cremated person's ashes. **2** a large metal container with a tap, in which tea or coffee is made and kept hot.
– ORIGIN Latin *urna.*

urogenital /yoor-oh-jen-i-t'l/ adjective referring to both the urinary and genital organs.

urology /yuu-rol-uh-ji/ noun the branch of medicine concerned with the urinary system.
– DERIVATIVES **urological** adjective **urologist** noun.

ursine /er-syn/ adjective relating to or resembling bears.
– ORIGIN Latin *ursinus.*

Ursuline /er-syuu-lyn, er-syuu-lin/ noun a nun of an order founded in Italy for nursing the sick and teaching girls. • adjective relating to the Ursulines.
– ORIGIN from St *Ursula*, the founder's patron saint.

urticaria /er-ti-kair-i-uh/ noun a very itchy rash of round, red weals on the skin, caused by an allergic reaction.
– ORIGIN from Latin *urtica* 'nettle'.

Uruguayan /yoor-uh-gwy-uhn/ noun a person from Uruguay. • adjective relating to Uruguay.

US abbreviation United States.

us pronoun (first person pl.) **1** used by a speaker to refer to himself or herself and one or more others as the object of a verb or preposition. **2** used after the verb 'to be' and after 'than' or 'as'. **3** informal me.
– ORIGIN Old English.

USAGE: For an explanation of whether to use *us* or *we* after *than*, see the note at PERSONAL PRONOUN.

USA abbreviation United States of America.

usable (also **useable**) adjective able to be used.
– DERIVATIVES **usability** noun.

USAF abbreviation United States Air Force.

usage noun **1** the action of using something or the fact of being used: *a survey of water usage.* **2** the way in which words are normally and correctly used in a language.

USB abbreviation universal serial bus, a connector which enables any of a variety of peripheral devices to be plugged into a computer.

use verb /yooz/ **1** take, hold, or employ something as a means of achieving a purpose. **2** take or consume an amount from an available supply. **3** (**use something up**) consume the whole of something. **4** treat someone in a particular way. **5** take advantage of or exploit someone. **6** /yoosst/ (**used to**) did repeatedly or existed in the past: *this road used to be a track.* **7** /yoosst/ (**be/get used to**) be or become familiar with someone or something through experience. • noun /yooss/ **1** the action of using something or the state of being used. **2** the ability or power to move or control something: *he lost the use of his legs.* **3** a purpose for or way in which something can be used. **4** the value or point of something: *what's the use of crying?*
– PHRASES **make use of** use or benefit from.
– ORIGIN Old French *user.*

USAGE: Confusion can arise over whether to write *used to* or *use to*. It is correct to write *used to* except in negatives and questions: *we used to go to the cinema all the time.* However, in negatives and questions using the verb **do**, you should write *use to*: *I didn't use to like mushrooms.*

useable adjective variant spelling of USABLE.

use-by date noun chiefly Brit. a date marked on packaged food indicating the recommended date by which it should be eaten.

used adjective **1** having already been used. **2** second-hand.

useful adjective **1** able to be used for a practical purpose or in several ways. **2** Brit. informal skilful or competent.
– DERIVATIVES **usefully** adverb **usefulness** noun.

useless adjective **1** serving no purpose. **2** informal having little ability or skill.
– DERIVATIVES **uselessly** adverb **uselessness** noun.

Usenet noun an Internet service consisting of thousands of newsgroups.

user noun a person who uses or operates something.

user-friendly adjective easy to use or understand.
– DERIVATIVES **user-friendliness** noun.

usher noun **1** a person who shows people to their seats in a theatre or cinema or in church. **2** an official in a law court who swears in jurors and witnesses and keeps order. • verb **1** show or guide someone somewhere. **2** (**usher something in**) cause or mark the start

u

of something new: *when the first jet crossed the Atlantic it ushered in a new era.*
– ORIGIN Old French *usser* 'doorkeeper'.

usherette noun a woman who shows people to their seats in a cinema or theatre.

USN abbreviation United States Navy.

USP abbreviation unique selling point.

USS abbreviation United States Ship.

USSR abbreviation historical Union of Soviet Socialist Republics.

usual adjective happening or done most of the time or in most cases. •noun informal **1** the thing that happens or is done most of the time. **2** (the/one's usual) the drink someone regularly prefers.
– ORIGIN Latin *usualis*.

usually adverb **1** in a way that is usual or normal. **2** generally speaking; as a rule.

usurious /yoo-**zhoor**-i-uhss, yoo-**zyoor**-i-uhss/ adjective relating to the lending of money at unreasonably high rates of interest.

usurp /yuu-**zerp**/ verb take over a person's position or power illegally or by force.
– DERIVATIVES **usurpation** noun **usurper** noun.
– ORIGIN Latin *usurpare* 'seize for use'.

usury /yoo-**zhuh**-ri/ noun the practice of lending money at unreasonably high rates of interest.
– DERIVATIVES **usurer** noun.
– ORIGIN Latin *usura*.

UT abbreviation Utah.

utensil noun a tool or container, especially for household use.
– ORIGIN from Latin *utensilis* 'usable'.

uterine /yoo-tuh-ryn/ adjective relating to the womb.

uterus /yoo-tuh-ruhss/ noun (pl. **uteri** /yoo-tuh-ry/) the womb.
– ORIGIN Latin.

utilitarian /yuu-ti-li-**tair**-i-uhn/ adjective **1** useful or practical rather than attractive. **2** relating to utilitarianism. •noun a person who supports utilitarianism.

utilitarianism noun the belief that the right course of action is the one that will lead to the greatest happiness of the greatest number of people.

utility noun (pl. **utilities**) **1** the state of being useful, profitable, or beneficial: *the garden was treated as a combination of utility and beauty.* **2** an organization supplying electricity, gas, water, or sewerage to the public. •adjective having several uses or functions.
– ORIGIN Latin *utilitas*.

utility room noun a room in which a washing machine and other domestic equipment are kept.

utility vehicle (also **utility truck**) noun a lorry with low sides, used for small loads.

utilize (or **utilise**) verb make practical and effective use of something.
– DERIVATIVES **utilizable** adjective **utilization** noun.
– ORIGIN French *utiliser*.

utmost adjective most extreme; greatest. •noun (the utmost) the greatest or most extreme extent or amount.
– ORIGIN Old English, 'outermost'.

Utopia /yoo-**toh**-pi-uh/ noun an imaginary place, society, or situation where everything is perfect.
– ORIGIN the title of a book by Sir Thomas More, from Greek *ou* 'not' + *topos* 'place'.

utopian adjective relating to or aiming for a situation in which everything is perfect. •noun a person with idealistic views on reform.
– DERIVATIVES **utopianism** noun.

utter[1] adjective complete; absolute: *I stared at him in utter amazement.*
– DERIVATIVES **utterly** adverb.
– ORIGIN Old English, 'outer'.

utter[2] verb **1** make a sound or say something. **2** Law put forged money into circulation.
– DERIVATIVES **utterable** adjective **utterer** noun.
– ORIGIN Dutch *üteren* 'speak, make known, give currency to coins'.

utterance noun **1** a word, statement, or sound uttered. **2** the action of uttering something.

uttermost adjective & noun another term for **UTMOST**.

U-turn noun **1** the turning of a vehicle in a U-shaped course so as to face the opposite way. **2** a complete change of policy or behaviour: *the government is doing a U-turn on road building.*

UV abbreviation ultraviolet.

UVA abbreviation ultraviolet radiation of relatively long wavelengths.

UVB abbreviation ultraviolet radiation of relatively short wavelengths.

UVC abbreviation ultraviolet radiation of very short wavelengths, which does not penetrate the earth's ozone layer.

uvula /yoo-**vyuu**-luh/ noun (pl. **uvulae** /yoo-vyuu-lee/) a fleshy part of the soft palate which hangs above the throat.
– ORIGIN Latin, 'little grape'.

UWB abbreviation ultra wideband, a radio communications technology for the transmission of signals over a very broad range of frequencies.

uxorial /uk-**sor**-i-uhl/ adjective relating to a wife.

uxorious /uk-**sor**-i-uhss/ adjective (of a man) very or excessively fond of his wife.
– DERIVATIVES **uxoriousness** noun.
– ORIGIN Latin *uxoriosus*.

Uzbek /**uuz**-bek, **uz**-bek/ noun **1** a person from Uzbekistan. **2** a member of a people living mainly in Uzbekistan. **3** the language of Uzbekistan.
– ORIGIN Uzbek.

Uzi /**oo**-zi/ noun a type of sub-machine gun.
– ORIGIN from *Uziel* Gal, the Israeli army officer who designed it.

u

Vv

V[1] (also **v**) noun (pl. **Vs** or **V's**) **1** the twenty-second letter of the alphabet. **2** the Roman numeral for five.

V[2] abbreviation volt(s). • symbol **1** the chemical element vanadium. **2** voltage or potential difference. **3** (in mathematical formulae) volume.

v (also **v.**) abbreviation **1** Grammar verb. **2** versus. **3** very. • symbol velocity.

VA abbreviation Virginia.

vac noun Brit. informal **1** a vacation. **2** a vacuum cleaner.

vacancy noun (pl. **vacancies**) **1** a job or position that is available for someone to do. **2** an available room in a hotel, guest house, etc. **3** empty space. **4** lack of intelligence or interest: *her wide-eyed vacancy.*

vacant adjective **1** not occupied; empty. **2** (of a job or position) not filled. **3** showing no intelligence or interest.
– DERIVATIVES **vacantly** adverb.

vacant possession noun Brit. ownership of a property on completion of a sale, any previous occupant having moved out.

vacate /vay-kayt, vuh-**kayt**/ verb **1** go out of a place, leaving it empty. **2** give up a job or position.
– ORIGIN Latin *vacare* 'leave empty'.

vacation noun **1** a holiday period between terms in universities and law courts. **2** N. Amer. a holiday. **3** the action of leaving a place or job. • verb N. Amer. take a holiday.
– DERIVATIVES **vacationer** noun (N. Amer.) **vacationist** noun (N. Amer.).

vaccinate /vak-si-nayt/ verb treat a person or animal with a vaccine to produce immunity against a disease.
– DERIVATIVES **vaccination** noun.

vaccine /vak-seen/ noun a substance made from the microorganisms that cause a disease, injected into the body to make it produce antibodies and so provide immunity against that disease.
– ORIGIN Latin *vaccinus.*

vacillate /va-si-layt/ verb keep changing one's mind about something.
– DERIVATIVES **vacillation** noun.
– ORIGIN Latin *vacillare* 'sway'.

vacuole /vak-yuu-ohl/ noun Biology a space inside a cell, enclosed by a membrane and typically containing fluid.
– ORIGIN from Latin *vacuus* 'empty'.

vacuous /vak-yuu-uhss/ adjective showing a lack of thought or intelligence.
– DERIVATIVES **vacuity** /vuh-**kyoo**-i-ti/ noun **vacuously** adverb **vacuousness** noun.
– ORIGIN Latin *vacuus* 'empty'.

vacuum /vak-yuu-uhm, vak-yuum/ noun (pl. **vacuums** or **vacua** /vak-yuu-uh/) **1** a space that is completely empty of matter. **2** a space from which the air has been completely or partly removed. **3** a gap left by the loss or departure of someone or something important. **4** (pl. **vacuums**) a vacuum cleaner. • verb clean something with a vacuum cleaner.
– PHRASES **in a vacuum** without relation to someone or something else; in isolation.
– ORIGIN Latin.

vacuum cleaner noun an electrical device that collects dust by means of suction.

vacuum flask noun chiefly Brit. a container that keeps a substance hot or cold by means of a double wall enclosing a vacuum.

vacuum-pack verb seal a product in a pack or wrapping with the air removed.

vacuum tube noun a sealed glass tube containing a near vacuum which allows the free passage of electric current.

vade mecum /vah-di **may**-kuhm, vay-di mee-kuhm/ noun a handbook or guide that a person carries with them to refer to.
– ORIGIN Latin, 'go with me'.

vagabond noun **1** a person who has no settled home or job; a vagrant. **2** old use a rogue.
– ORIGIN Latin *vagabundus.*

vagary /vay-guh-ri/ noun (pl. **vagaries**) a change that cannot be predicted or explained: *the vagaries of the weather.*
– ORIGIN from Latin *vagari* 'wander'.

vagina /vuh-**jy**-nuh/ noun the muscular tube leading from the external genitals to the cervix (neck of the womb) in women and most female mammals.
– DERIVATIVES **vaginal** adjective **vaginally** adverb.
– ORIGIN Latin, 'sheath, scabbard'.

vagrant /vay-gruhnt/ noun a person who has no settled home or job. • adjective relating to or living as a vagrant; wandering.
– DERIVATIVES **vagrancy** noun.
– ORIGIN from Old French *vagrant* 'wandering about'.

vague adjective **1** not clear, certain, or detailed: *vague promises of a better future.* **2** thinking or expressing oneself in an imprecise or unclear way.
– DERIVATIVES **vaguely** adverb **vagueness** noun.
– ORIGIN Latin *vagus* 'wandering, uncertain'.

vain adjective **1** having an excessively high

opinion of oneself. **2** not producing the required result; unsuccessful.
– PHRASES **in vain** without success. **take someone's name in vain** use someone's name in a way that shows a lack of respect.
– DERIVATIVES **vainly** adverb.
– ORIGIN Latin *vanus* 'empty, without substance'.

> USAGE: Do not confuse **vain** with **vane** or **vein**. Vain means 'having an excessively high opinion of oneself' (*a vain woman with a touch of snobbery*) or 'unsuccessful' (*a vain attempt to tidy up*); **vane** means 'a broad blade forming part of a windmill, propeller, or turbine'; **vein** means 'a tube that carries blood around the body' or 'a particular way, style, or quality' (*he continued in a more serious vein*).

vainglory noun literary excessive pride in oneself.
– DERIVATIVES **vainglorious** adjective **vaingloriously** adverb.

Vaisya /vy-syuh, vy-shyuh/ (also **Vaishya**) noun a member of the third of the four Hindu castes, comprising merchants and farmers.
– ORIGIN Sanskrit, 'peasant, labourer'.

valance /va-luhnss/ noun **1** a length of fabric attached to the frame of a bed to screen the structure or space beneath it. **2** chiefly N. Amer. a length of fabric screening the curtain fittings above a window.
– DERIVATIVES **valanced** adjective.
– ORIGIN perhaps from Old French *avaler* 'lower, descend'.

vale noun literary (except in place names) a valley.
– PHRASES **vale of tears** the world as a place of trouble or sorrow.
– ORIGIN Latin *vallis*.

valediction /va-li-dik-sh'n/ noun **1** the action of saying goodbye. **2** a farewell speech or statement.
– ORIGIN from Latin *vale* 'goodbye' + *dicere* 'to say'.

valedictory /va-li-dik-tuh-ri/ adjective related to saying goodbye. •noun (pl. **valedictories**) a farewell speech.

valency /vay-luhn-si/ (also **valence** /vay-luhnss/) noun (pl. **valencies**) the combining power of a chemical element, as measured by the number of hydrogen atoms it can displace or combine with.
– ORIGIN Latin *valentia* 'power, competence'.

valentine noun **1** a card sent on St Valentine's Day (14 February) to a person one loves or is attracted to. **2** a person to whom one sends such a card.

valerian /vuh-leer-i-uhn/ noun **1** a plant with clusters of small pink, red, or white flowers. **2** a sedative drug obtained from a valerian root.
– ORIGIN Latin *valeriana*.

valet /va-lay, va-lit/ noun **1** a man's male attendant, responsible for looking after his clothes and other personal needs. **2** N. Amer. a person employed to clean or park cars. •verb (**valets, valeting, valeted**) **1** clean a car as a professional service. **2** act as a valet to a man.
– ORIGIN French.

valetudinarian /va-li-tyoo-di-nair-i-uhn/ noun a person in poor health or who worries too much about their health.
– ORIGIN from Latin *valetudinarius* 'in ill health'.

Valhalla /val-hal-luh/ noun Scandinavian Mythology a palace in which heroes killed in battle feasted for eternity.
– ORIGIN Old Norse, 'hall of the slain'.

valiant adjective showing courage or determination.
– DERIVATIVES **valiantly** adverb.
– ORIGIN Old French *vaillant*.

valid adjective **1** (of a reason, argument, etc.) based on what is true or logical. **2** officially acceptable or legally binding: *a valid passport.*
– DERIVATIVES **validity** noun **validly** adverb.
– ORIGIN Latin *validus* 'strong'.

validate verb **1** check or prove that something is true or valid. **2** make or declare something to be officially acceptable or legally binding.
– DERIVATIVES **validation** noun.

valise /vuh-leez/ noun a small travelling bag or suitcase.
– ORIGIN French.

Valium /va-li-uhm/ noun trademark for DIAZEPAM.
– ORIGIN unknown.

Valkyrie /val-ki-ri, val-keer-i/ noun Scandinavian Mythology each of Odin's twelve handmaids who chose heroes killed in battle to take to Valhalla.
– ORIGIN Old Norse, 'chooser of the slain'.

valley noun (pl. **valleys**) a low area between hills or mountains, typically with a river or stream flowing through it.
– ORIGIN Latin *vallis*.

valorize (or **valorise**) /va-luh-ryz/ verb give value or validity to: *the English valorize stupidity.*
– DERIVATIVES **valorization** noun.
– ORIGIN from French *valorisation*.

valour (US **valor**) noun great courage in the face of danger.
– DERIVATIVES **valorous** adjective.
– ORIGIN Latin *valor*.

Valpolicella /val-pol-i-chel-luh/ noun a red wine made in the Val Policella district of Italy.

valuable adjective **1** worth a great deal of money. **2** very useful or important. •noun (**valuables**) valuable items.
– DERIVATIVES **valuably** adverb.

valuation noun an estimate of how much something is worth, especially one carried out by a professional valuer.

value noun **1** the amount of money that something is worth. **2** the importance or worth of something: *he realized the value of education.* **3** (**values**) beliefs about what is right and wrong and what is important. **4** Mathematics the amount represented by a letter, symbol, or number. **5** the relative duration of the sound represented by a musical note. •verb (**values, valuing, valued**) **1** estimate the value of something. **2** consider to be important or worthwhile: *she had come to value her privacy.*
– DERIVATIVES **valueless** adjective **valuer** noun (Brit.).
– ORIGIN Old French.

value added tax noun a tax on the amount by

which a product rises in value at each stage of its production or distribution.

value judgement noun an assessment of something as good or bad based on personal opinions rather than facts.

valve noun **1** a device for controlling the flow of a liquid or gas through a pipe or duct. **2** a cylindrical mechanism used to vary the length of the tube in a brass musical instrument. **3** a structure in the heart or in a blood vessel that allows blood to flow in one direction only. **4** each of the two parts of the hinged shell of a bivalve mollusc such as an oyster or mussel.
– DERIVATIVES **valved** adjective.
– ORIGIN Latin *valva* 'leaf of a folding or double door'.

valvular /val-vyuu-ler/ adjective relating to or having a valve or valves.

vamoose /vuh-mooss/ verb informal leave somewhere hurriedly.
– ORIGIN from Spanish *vamos* 'let us go'.

vamp[1] verb (**vamp something up**) informal improve something by adding something more interesting. •noun the upper front part of a boot or shoe.
– ORIGIN first referring to the foot of a stocking: from Old French *avant* 'before' + *pie* 'foot'.

vamp[2] informal noun a woman who uses her sexual attractiveness to seduce and control men. •verb blatantly set out to attract a man.
– DERIVATIVES **vampish** adjective **vampy** adjective.
– ORIGIN short for VAMPIRE.

vampire /vam-py-er/ noun **1** (in folklore) a dead person supposed to leave their grave at night to drink the blood of living people. **2** (also **vampire bat**) a small bat that feeds on blood by piercing the skin with its teeth, found mainly in tropical America.
– DERIVATIVES **vampiric** /vam-pi-rik/ adjective **vampirism** noun.
– ORIGIN Hungarian *vampir*.

van[1] noun **1** a motor vehicle used for transporting goods or people. **2** Brit. a railway carriage for transporting luggage, mail, etc.
– ORIGIN shortening of CARAVAN.

van[2] noun (**the van**) **1** the leading part of an advancing group of people. **2** the forefront: *we have always been in the van of progress.*
– ORIGIN short for VANGUARD.

vanadium /vuh-nay-di-uhm/ noun a hard grey metallic chemical element, used to make alloy steels.
– ORIGIN from an Old Norse name of the Scandinavian goddess Freyja.

Van Allen belt noun each of two regions of intense radiation partly surrounding the earth at heights of several thousand kilometres.
– ORIGIN named after the American physicist James A. *Van Allen.*

vandal noun a person who deliberately destroys or damages property.
– DERIVATIVES **vandalism** noun.
– ORIGIN Latin *Vandalus*, referring to a Germanic people that plundered parts of Europe and North Africa in the 4th–5th centuries.

vandalize (or **vandalise**) verb deliberately destroy or damage property.

Vandyke /van-dyk/ (also **Vandyke beard**) noun a neat pointed beard.

– ORIGIN named after the Flemish painter Sir Anthony *Van Dyck.*

vane noun **1** a broad blade attached to a rotating axis or wheel which pushes or is pushed by wind or water, forming part of a windmill, propeller, or turbine. **2** a weathervane.
– ORIGIN Germanic.

USAGE: For an explanation of the difference between **vane**, **vain**, and **vein**, see the note at VAIN.

vanguard noun **1** a group of people leading the way in new developments or ideas. **2** the leading part of an advancing army or naval force.
– ORIGIN Old French *avantgarde.*

vanilla noun a substance obtained from the pods of a tropical orchid or produced artificially, used as a flavouring.
– ORIGIN Spanish *vainilla* 'pod'.

vanish verb **1** disappear from view suddenly and completely. **2** stop existing: *woodlands are vanishing.*
– DERIVATIVES **vanishing** adjective & noun **vanishingly** adverb.
– ORIGIN Old French *esvanir.*

vanishing point noun the point in the distance at which receding parallel lines appear to meet.

vanity noun (pl. **vanities**) **1** excessive pride in one's appearance or achievements. **2** the quality of being pointless or futile: *the vanity of human wishes.*
– ORIGIN Latin *vanitas.*

vanity case noun a small case fitted with a mirror and compartments for make-up.

vanity unit noun a unit consisting of a washbasin set into a flat top with cupboards beneath.

vanquish /vang-kwish/ verb literary defeat someone or something completely.
– DERIVATIVES **vanquisher** noun.
– ORIGIN Old French *vainquir.*

vantage /vahn-tij/ (also **vantage point**) noun a place or position giving a good view.
– ORIGIN Old French *avantage* 'advantage'.

vapid /vap-id/ adjective not interesting or original: *vapid musical comedies.*
– DERIVATIVES **vapidity** noun **vapidly** adverb.
– ORIGIN Latin *vapidus.*

vapor noun US spelling of VAPOUR.

vaporetto /va-puh-ret-toh/ noun (pl. **vaporetti** /va-puh-ret-ti/ or **vaporettos**) (in Venice) a canal boat used for public transport.
– ORIGIN Italian.

vaporize (or **vaporise**) verb convert a substance into vapour.
– DERIVATIVES **vaporization** noun.

vaporizer (or **vaporiser**) noun a device that is used to breathe in medicine in the form of a vapour.

vapour (US **vapor**) noun **1** a liquid or substance that is suspended in the air in a mass of tiny drops or particles. **2** Physics a gaseous substance that can be made into liquid by pressure alone. **3** (**the vapours**) dated a fit of faintness, nervousness, or depression.
– DERIVATIVES **vaporous** adjective.
– ORIGIN Latin *vapor* 'steam, heat'.

vapour trail noun a trail of condensed water from an aircraft or rocket at high altitude, seen as a white streak against the sky.

vaquero /vuh-**kair**-oh/ noun (pl. **vaqueros**) (in Spanish-speaking parts of the USA) a cowboy; a cattle driver.
– ORIGIN Spanish.

variable adjective **1** often changing or likely to change; not consistent: *the photos are of variable quality.* **2** able to be changed or adapted. **3** Mathematics (of a quantity) able to take on different numerical values. ●noun a variable element, feature, or quantity.
– DERIVATIVES **variability** noun **variably** adverb.

variance noun the amount by which something changes or is different from something else.
– PHRASES **at variance (with)** inconsistent with or opposing.

variant noun a form or version that varies from other forms of the same thing or from a standard type.

variation noun **1** a change or slight difference in condition, amount, or level: *regional variations in house prices.* **2** a different or distinct form or version. **3** a new but still recognizable version of a musical theme.
– DERIVATIVES **variational** adjective.

varicoloured /vair-i-kul-erd/ (US **varicolored**) adjective consisting of several different colours.

varicose /va-ri-kohss, va-ri-kuhss/ adjective (of a vein, especially in the leg) swollen, twisted, and lengthened, as a result of poor circulation.
– ORIGIN Latin *varicosus.*

varied adjective involving a number of different types or elements: *a long and varied career.*

variegated /vair-i-gay-tid/ adjective having irregular patches or streaks of different colours.
– DERIVATIVES **variegation** /vair-i-gay-sh'n/ noun.
– ORIGIN from Latin *variegare* 'make varied'.

varietal /vuh-ry-uh-t'l/ adjective **1** (of a wine or grape) made from or belonging to a single specified variety of grape. **2** relating to or forming a variety of plant or animal.

variety noun (pl. **varieties**) **1** the quality or state of being different or varied. **2** (**a variety of**) a range of things of the same general type that are different in character: *the centre offers a variety of activities.* **3** a type: *fifty varieties of pasta.* **4** a form of entertainment consisting of a series of different acts, such as singing, dancing, and comedy. **5** Biology a subspecies or cultivar.
– ORIGIN Latin *varietas.*

varifocal /vair-i-**foh**-k'l/ adjective (of a lens) allowing an infinite number of focusing distances for near, intermediate, and far vision. ●noun (**varifocals**) varifocal glasses.

various adjective different from one another; of different kinds or sorts. ●determiner & pronoun more than one; individual and separate.
– DERIVATIVES **variously** adverb **variousness** noun.
– ORIGIN Latin *varius* 'changing, diverse'.

varlet /var-lit/ noun **1** old use a rogue or rascal. **2** historical a male servant.
– ORIGIN Old French, from *valet* (see **VALET**).

varmint /var-mint/ noun N. Amer. informal or dialect a troublesome or mischievous person or wild animal.
– ORIGIN from **VERMIN**.

varnish noun **1** resin dissolved in a liquid, applied to wood or metal to give a hard, clear, shiny surface when dry. **2** nail varnish. ●verb apply varnish to something.
– ORIGIN Old French *vernis.*

varsity noun (pl. **varsities**) **1** Brit. dated or S. African university. **2** chiefly N. Amer. a sports team representing a university or college.
– ORIGIN shortening of **UNIVERSITY**.

vary verb (**varies, varying, varied**) **1** differ in size, degree, or nature from something else of the same general class: *the houses vary in price.* **2** change from one form or state to another. **3** modify something to make it less uniform: *he tried to vary his diet.*
– ORIGIN Latin *variare.*

vas /vass/ noun (pl. **vasa** /**vay**-suh/) a vessel or duct in the body.
– ORIGIN Latin.

vascular /vass-kyuu-ler/ adjective referring to the system of vessels for carrying blood or (in plants) sap, water, and nutrients.
– ORIGIN Latin *vascularis.*

vas deferens /vass def-uh-renz/ noun (pl. **vasa deferentia** /vay-suh def-uh-**ren**-shuh/) either of the ducts which convey sperm from the testicles to the urethra.
– ORIGIN from **VAS** + Latin *deferens* 'carrying away'.

vase noun a decorative container used as an ornament or for displaying cut flowers.
– ORIGIN French.

vasectomy /vuh-sek-tuh-mi/ noun (pl. **vasectomies**) the surgical cutting and sealing of part of each vas deferens as a means of sterilization.

Vaseline /vass-uh-leen/ noun trademark a type of petroleum jelly used as an ointment or lubricant.
– ORIGIN from German *Wasser* 'water' + Greek *elaion* 'oil'.

vassal /vass-uhl/ noun **1** historical (in the feudal system) a man who promised to fight for a monarch or lord in return for holding a piece of land. **2** a country that is controlled by or dependent on another.
– DERIVATIVES **vassalage** noun.
– ORIGIN Latin *vassallus* 'retainer'.

vast adjective of very great extent or quantity; huge.
– DERIVATIVES **vastly** adverb **vastness** noun.
– ORIGIN Latin *vastus* 'void, immense'.

VAT abbreviation value added tax.

vat noun a large container used to hold liquid.
– ORIGIN Germanic.

vatic /vat-ik/ adjective literary predicting what will happen in the future.
– ORIGIN from Latin *vates* 'prophet'.

Vatican noun the palace and official residence of the Pope in Rome.

vaudeville /vaw-duh-vil, voh-duh-vil/ noun a type of entertainment featuring a mixture of musical and comedy acts.
– DERIVATIVES **vaudevillian** adjective & noun.
– ORIGIN French.

V

vault[1] noun **1** a large room used for storing things securely, especially in a bank. **2** a room under a church or in a graveyard, used for burials. **3** a roof or ceiling in the form of an arch or a series of arches.
– DERIVATIVES **vaulted** adjective.
– ORIGIN Old French *voute*.

vault[2] verb jump over something in a single movement, supporting or pushing oneself with the hands or a pole. •noun an act of vaulting.
– DERIVATIVES **vaulter** noun.
– ORIGIN Old French *volter* 'to gambol'.

vaulting noun the arrangement of vaults in a roof or ceiling.

vaulting horse noun a padded wooden block used for vaulting over in gymnastics.

vaunt /vawnt/ verb (usu. as adj. **vaunted**) boast about or praise: *his vaunted gift for spotting talent.*
– DERIVATIVES **vaunting** adjective.
– ORIGIN Latin *vantare*.

va-va-voom informal noun the quality of being exciting, vigorous, or sexually attractive.
•adjective sexually attractive: *her va-va-voom figure.*
– ORIGIN representing the sound of a car engine being revved.

VC abbreviation Victoria Cross.

V-chip noun a computer chip installed in a television receiver that can be programmed to block violent or sexually explicit material.

VCR abbreviation video cassette recorder.

VD abbreviation venereal disease.

VDU abbreviation Brit. visual display unit.

've abbreviation informal have.

veal noun meat from a young calf.
– ORIGIN Old French *veel*.

vector /vek-ter/ noun **1** Mathematics & Physics a quantity having direction as well as magnitude, especially as determining the position of one point in space relative to another. **2** an organism that transmits a disease or parasite from one animal or plant to another.
– DERIVATIVES **vectorial** adjective.
– ORIGIN Latin, 'carrier'.

Veda /vay-duh, vee-duh/ noun (treated as sing. or pl.) the earliest Hindu sacred writings.
– DERIVATIVES **Vedic** adjective.
– ORIGIN Sanskrit, 'sacred knowledge'.

VE day noun the day (8 May) marking the Allied victory in Europe in 1945.
– ORIGIN short for *Victory in Europe*.

veer verb **1** change direction suddenly. **2** suddenly change in opinion, subject, etc.: *the conversation veered away from theatrical things.* **3** (of the wind) change direction clockwise around the points of the compass. •noun a sudden change of direction.
– ORIGIN French *virer*.

veg[1] /vej/ noun (pl. same) Brit. informal vegetables, or a vegetable.

veg[2] /vej/ verb (**vegges**, **vegging**, **vegged**) (usu. **veg out**) informal relax completely.
– ORIGIN from VEGETATE.

vegan /vee-guhn/ noun a person who does not eat or use any animal products.
– DERIVATIVES **veganism** noun.

– ORIGIN from VEGETARIAN.

Vegeburger noun trademark for VEGGIE BURGER.

vegetable /vej-tuh-b'l, vej-i-tuh-b'l/ noun **1** a plant or part of a plant used as food. **2** informal, derogatory a person who is incapable of normal mental or physical activity as a result of brain damage.
– ORIGIN from Latin *vegetabilis* 'animating'.

vegetable oil noun an oil obtained from plants, e.g. olive oil or sunflower oil.

vegetal /vej-i-tuhl/ adjective formal relating to plants.
– ORIGIN Latin *vegetalis*.

vegetarian noun a person who does not eat meat or fish. •adjective eating or including no meat or fish.
– DERIVATIVES **vegetarianism** noun.

vegetate verb spend time in a dull and inactive way that involves little mental stimulation.
– ORIGIN Latin *vegetare* 'enliven'.

vegetation noun plants in general.
– DERIVATIVES **vegetational** adjective.

vegetative /vej-i-tuh-tiv/ adjective **1** relating to vegetation or the growth of plants. **2** relating to reproduction or propagation by asexual means. **3** (of a person) alive but in a coma and showing no sign of brain activity or responsiveness.

veggie noun & adjective informal, chiefly Brit. another term for VEGETARIAN.

veggie burger (also trademark **Vegeburger**) noun a savoury cake resembling a hamburger but made with vegetables or soya instead of meat.

vehement /vee-uh-muhnt/ adjective showing strong feeling; forceful or passionate.
– DERIVATIVES **vehemence** noun **vehemently** adverb.
– ORIGIN Latin, 'impetuous, violent'.

vehicle /vee-i-k'l/ noun **1** a thing used for transporting people or goods on land, such as a car or lorry. **2** a means of expressing or achieving something: *she used paint as a vehicle for her ideas.* **3** a film, programme, song, etc., intended to display the leading performer to the best advantage.
– DERIVATIVES **vehicular** /vi-hik-yuu-ler/ adjective.
– ORIGIN Latin *vehiculum*.

veil noun **1** a piece of fine material worn to protect or hide the face. **2** a piece of fabric forming part of a nun's headdress, resting on the head and shoulders. **3** a thing that hides or disguises something: *an eerie veil of mist.* •verb **1** cover someone or something with a veil. **2** cover or hide: *the country is still veiled in mystery.* **3** (as adj. **veiled**) not expressed directly or clearly: *a thinly veiled threat.*
– PHRASES **draw a veil over** avoid discussing or drawing attention to something embarrassing or unpleasant. **take the veil** become a nun.
– ORIGIN Latin *velum* 'sail, curtain, veil'.

vein noun **1** any of the tubes forming part of the circulation system by which blood is carried from all parts of the body towards the heart. **2** (in general use) a blood vessel. **3** a very thin rib running through a leaf. **4** (in insects) a hollow rib forming part of the supporting

framework of a wing. **5** a streak of a different colour in wood, marble, cheese, etc. **6** a fracture in rock containing a deposit of minerals or ore. **7** a particular way, style, or quality: *he did a number of engravings in a similar vein.* **8** a source of a quality: *a rich vein of satire.*
– DERIVATIVES **veined** adjective **veining** noun **veiny** adjective.
– ORIGIN Old French *veine.*

USAGE: For an explanation of the difference between **vein**, **vane**, and **vain**, see the note at **VAIN**.

velar /vee-ler/ adjective (of a speech sound) pronounced with the back of the tongue near the soft palate, as in *k* and *g* in English.
– ORIGIN from Latin *velum* 'sail, curtain, covering, veil'.

Velcro noun trademark a fastener consisting of two strips of fabric which stick to each other when pressed together. ●verb fasten or join something with Velcro.
– ORIGIN from French *velours croché* 'hooked velvet'.

veld /velt/ (also **veldt**) noun open, uncultivated country or grassland in southern Africa.
– ORIGIN Afrikaans, 'field'.

veleta /vuh-lee-tuh/ noun a ballroom dance in triple time, faster than a waltz and with partners side by side.
– ORIGIN Spanish, 'weathervane'.

vellum /vel-luhm/ noun **1** fine parchment made from the skin of a sheep, goat, or calf. **2** smooth cream-coloured writing paper.
– ORIGIN Old French *velin.*

velocipede /vi-lo-si-peed/ noun historical an early form of bicycle propelled by working pedals on cranks fitted to the front axle.
– ORIGIN from Latin *velox* 'swift' + *pes* 'foot'.

velociraptor /vi-los-si-rap-ter/ noun a small meat-eating dinosaur with a large slashing claw on each foot.
– ORIGIN Latin.

velocity /vi-loss-i-ti/ noun (pl. **velocities**) **1** technical the speed of something in a given direction. **2** (in general use) speed.
– ORIGIN Latin *velocitas.*

velodrome /vel-uh-drohm/ noun a cycle-racing track with steeply banked curves.
– ORIGIN French.

velour /vuh-loor/ (also **velours**) noun a plush woven fabric resembling velvet.
– ORIGIN French *velours* 'velvet'.

velouté /vuh-loo-tay/ noun a white sauce made from a roux of butter and flour with chicken, veal, or pork stock.
– ORIGIN French, 'velvety'.

velvet noun **1** a fabric of silk, cotton, or nylon with a thick short pile on one side. **2** soft downy skin that covers a deer's antler while it is growing.
– DERIVATIVES **velvety** adjective.
– ORIGIN Old French *veluotte.*

velveteen noun a cotton fabric with a pile resembling velvet.

vena cava /vee-nuh **kay**-vuh/ noun (pl. **venae cavae** /vee-nee **kay**-vee/) each of two large veins carrying deoxygenated blood into the heart.

– ORIGIN Latin, 'hollow vein'.

venal /vee-n'l/ adjective prepared to do dishonest or immoral things in return for money.
– DERIVATIVES **venality** noun.
– ORIGIN from Latin *venum* 'thing for sale'.

USAGE: For an explanation of the difference between **venal** and **venial**, see the note at **VENIAL**.

vend verb **1** offer small items for sale. **2** Law or formal sell something.
– ORIGIN Latin *vendere* 'sell'.

vendetta /ven-det-tuh/ noun **1** a prolonged bitter quarrel with or campaign against someone. **2** a prolonged feud between families in which people are murdered in revenge for previous murders.
– ORIGIN Italian.

vending machine noun a machine that dispenses small articles when a coin or token is inserted.

vendor (US also **vender**) noun **1** a person or company offering something for sale. **2** Law the person who is selling a property.

veneer /vi-neer/ noun **1** a thin decorative covering of fine wood applied to a coarser wood or other material. **2** an outer quality or attractive appearance that hides the true nature of someone or something: *the area's veneer of respectability has gone.* ●verb (usu. as adj. **veneered**) cover something with a veneer.
– DERIVATIVES **veneering** noun.
– ORIGIN from German *furnieren.*

venerable adjective **1** greatly respected because of age, wisdom, or character. **2** (in the Anglican Church) a title given to an archdeacon. **3** (in the Roman Catholic Church) a title given to a dead person who has gained a certain degree of sanctity but has not been fully beatified or canonized.

venerate /ven-uh-rayt/ verb regard someone or something with great respect.
– DERIVATIVES **veneration** noun **venerator** noun.
– ORIGIN Latin *venerari* 'adore, revere'.

venereal /vi-neer-i-uhl/ adjective **1** relating to sexually transmitted disease. **2** formal relating to sex or sexual desire.
– ORIGIN Latin *venereus.*

venereal disease noun a disease that is caught by having sex with a person who is already infected.

venery[1] /ven-uh-ri/ noun old use indulgence in sexual activity.
– ORIGIN Latin *veneria.*

venery[2] /ven-uh-ri/ noun old use hunting.
– ORIGIN from Latin *venari* 'to hunt'.

Venetian /vi-nee-sh'n/ adjective relating to Venice. ●noun a person from Venice.

venetian blind noun a window blind consisting of horizontal slats which can be adjusted to control the amount of light that passes through.

Venezuelan /ve-ni-zway-luhn/ noun a person from Venezuela. ●adjective relating to Venezuela.

vengeance /ven-juhnss/ noun punishment or harm caused to someone in return for an injury or wrong: *he'd had a terrible life and was now taking vengeance on humanity.*

V

– PHRASES **with a vengeance** with great intensity.
– ORIGIN Old French.

vengeful adjective wanting to punish or harm someone in return for a wrong or injury.
– DERIVATIVES **vengefully** adverb **vengefulness** noun.

venial /vee-ni-uhl/ adjective **1** (of a fault or offence) minor and able to be forgiven. **2** (in Christian belief) referring to a sin that will not deprive the soul of God's grace. Often contrasted with MORTAL.
– ORIGIN Latin *venialis*.

> USAGE: **Venal** and **venial** are sometimes confused. **Venal** means 'prepared to do dishonest or immoral things in return for money' (*venal politicians*), whereas **venial** is used to refer to a sin or fault that is minor and able to be forgiven.

venison /ven-i-s'n/ noun meat from a deer.
– ORIGIN Old French *venesoun*.

Venn diagram noun a diagram representing mathematical or logical sets as circles, common elements of the sets being represented by overlapping sections of the circles.
– ORIGIN named after the English logician John *Venn*.

venom noun **1** poisonous fluid produced by animals such as snakes and scorpions and typically injected by biting or stinging. **2** extreme hatred or bitterness: *her voice was full of venom*.
– ORIGIN Old French *venim*.

venomous adjective **1** (of an animal) producing or capable of injecting venom. **2** full of hate or bitterness.
– DERIVATIVES **venomously** adverb.

venous /vee-nuhss/ adjective relating to a vein or the veins.

vent¹ noun an opening that allows air, gas, or liquid to pass out of or into a confined space. •verb **1** express a strong emotion freely. **2** discharge air, gas, or liquid through an outlet.
– PHRASES **give vent to** express a strong emotion.
– ORIGIN from French *vent* 'wind' or *éventer* 'expose to air'.

vent² noun a slit in a garment, especially in the lower part of the seam at the back of a coat.
– ORIGIN Old French *fente* 'slit'.

ventilate verb **1** cause air to enter and circulate freely in a room or building. **2** discuss an opinion or issue in public.
– DERIVATIVES **ventilation** noun.
– ORIGIN Latin *ventilare* 'blow, winnow'.

ventilator noun **1** a device or opening for ventilating a room or building. **2** a machine that pumps air in and out of a person's lungs to help them to breathe.
– DERIVATIVES **ventilatory** adjective.

ventral adjective technical on or relating to the underside or abdomen. Compare with DORSAL.
– DERIVATIVES **ventrally** adverb.
– ORIGIN from Latin *venter* 'belly'.

ventricle /ven-tri-k'l/ noun **1** each of the two larger and lower cavities of the heart. **2** each of four connected fluid-filled cavities in the brain.
– DERIVATIVES **ventricular** /ven-trik-yuu-ler/ adjective.
– ORIGIN Latin *ventriculus*.

ventriloquist /ven-tril-uh-kwist/ noun an entertainer who can make their voice seem to come from a dummy of a person or animal.
– DERIVATIVES **ventriloquial** /ven-tri-loh-kwi-uhl/ adjective **ventriloquism** noun **ventriloquy** noun.
– ORIGIN from Latin *venter* 'belly' + *loqui* 'speak'.

venture noun **1** a business enterprise involving considerable risk. **2** a risky or daring activity or undertaking. •verb **1** dare to do something dangerous or risky. **2** dare to say something that may be considered bold.
– DERIVATIVES **venturer** noun.
– ORIGIN shortening of ADVENTURE.

venture capital noun capital invested in a business project in which there is a large element of risk.

Venture Scout noun a member of the Scout Association aged between 16 and 20.

venturesome adjective willing to do something risky or difficult.

venue /ven-yoo/ noun the place where an event or meeting is held.
– ORIGIN Old French, 'a coming'.

Venus noun a planet of the solar system, second in order from the sun and the brightest object in the sky after the sun and moon.
– DERIVATIVES **Venusian** /vi-nyoo-zi-uhn/ adjective & noun.

Venus flytrap noun a plant with hinged leaves that spring shut on and digest insects which land on them.

veracious /vuh-ray-shuhss/ adjective formal speaking or representing the truth.
– ORIGIN from Latin *verus* 'true'.

veracity /vuh-rass-i-ti/ noun **1** the quality of being true or accurate. **2** the quality of telling the truth: *he devised a test of the agent's veracity*.

veranda (also **verandah**) noun a roofed structure with an open front along the outside of a house, level with the ground floor.
– ORIGIN Portuguese *varanda* 'railing, balustrade'.

verb noun a word used to describe an action, state, or occurrence, such as *hear*, *become*, or *happen*.
– ORIGIN Latin *verbum* 'word, verb'.

verbal adjective **1** relating to or in the form of words. **2** spoken rather than written; oral. **3** relating to a verb. •noun **1** (also **verbals**) Brit. informal abuse; insults. **2** a word or words functioning as a verb.
– DERIVATIVES **verbally** adverb.

verbalism noun concentration on words rather than their meaning or content.

verbalize (or **verbalise**) verb express ideas or feelings in words.
– DERIVATIVES **verbalization** noun.

verbal noun noun a noun formed from a verb, such as *smoking* in *smoking is forbidden*.

verbatim /ver-bay-tim/ adverb & adjective in exactly the same words as were used originally.

V

– ORIGIN Latin.

verbena /ver-bee-nuh/ noun a garden plant with bright showy flowers.
– ORIGIN Latin, 'sacred bough'.

verbiage /ver-bi-ij/ noun excessively lengthy or technical speech or writing.
– ORIGIN French.

verbose /ver-bohss/ adjective using more words than are needed.
– DERIVATIVES **verbosely** adverb **verbosity** /ver-**boss**-it-i/ noun.
– ORIGIN Latin *verbosus*.

verboten /ver-**boh**-tuhn/ adjective forbidden by an authority.
– ORIGIN German.

verdant /ver-duhnt/ adjective green with grass or other lush vegetation.
– DERIVATIVES **verdancy** noun **verdantly** adverb.
– ORIGIN perhaps from Old French *verdeant*.

verdict noun **1** a formal decision made by a jury in a court of law as to whether a person is innocent or guilty of an offence. **2** an opinion or judgement made after testing or considering something.
– ORIGIN Old French *verdit*.

verdigris /ver-di-gree, ver-di-greess/ noun a bright bluish-green substance formed on copper or brass by oxidation.
– ORIGIN from Old French *vert de Grece* 'green of Greece'.

verdure /ver-dyer/ noun literary lush green vegetation.
– ORIGIN from Old French *verd* 'green'.

verge noun **1** an edge or border. **2** Brit. a grass edging by the side of a road or path. **3** a limit beyond which something will happen: *she was on the verge of tears*. •verb (**verge on**) be very close to: *the speed at which they drove verged on lunacy*.
– ORIGIN Old French.

verger noun **1** an official in a church who acts as a caretaker and attendant. **2** an officer who carries a rod in front of a bishop or dean as a symbol of office.
– ORIGIN Old French.

verify /ve-ri-fy/ verb (**verifies, verifying, verified**) **1** check that something is true or accurate. **2** confirm or show to be true or accurate: *our instrument readings verified his statement*.
– DERIVATIVES **verifiable** adjective **verification** noun **verifier** noun.
– ORIGIN Latin *verificare*.

verily adverb old use truly; certainly.
– ORIGIN from **very**.

verisimilitude /ve-ri-si-**mil**-i-tyood/ noun the appearance of being true or real.
– ORIGIN Latin *verisimilitudo*.

verismo /ve-**riz**-moh/ noun realism or authenticity, especially in opera, art, or films.
– ORIGIN Italian.

veritable adjective rightly so called (used for emphasis): *a veritable army of backpackers*.
– DERIVATIVES **veritably** adverb.

vérité /ve-ri-tay/ noun a style of film and television emphasizing realism and naturalism.
– ORIGIN French, 'truth'.

verity noun (pl. **verities**) **1** a true principle or

belief: *the eternal verities of history*. **2** literary the quality of being true; truth.
– ORIGIN Latin *veritas*.

vermicelli /ver-mi-**chel**-li, ver-mi-**sel**-li/ plural noun **1** pasta made in long thin threads. **2** Brit. shreds of chocolate used to decorate cakes.
– ORIGIN Italian, 'little worms'.

vermiculite /ver-**mik**-yuu-lyt/ noun a yellow or brown mineral used for insulation or for growing plants in.
– ORIGIN from Latin *vermiculari* 'be full of worms' (because on expansion due to heat, it shoots out forms resembling small worms).

vermiform /ver-mi-form/ adjective technical resembling or having the shape of a worm.

vermifuge /ver-mi-fyooj/ noun a medicine used to destroy worms that live in or on the bodies of people or animals.

vermilion /ver-**mil**-yuhn/ noun a brilliant red pigment or colour.
– ORIGIN Old French *vermeillon*.

vermin noun (treated as pl.) **1** wild mammals and birds which are harmful to crops, farm animals, or game, or which carry disease. **2** worms or insects that live in or on the bodies of animals or people. **3** people who are very unpleasant or dangerous to society.
– DERIVATIVES **verminous** adjective.
– ORIGIN Old French.

vermouth /ver-muhth, ver-**mooth**/ noun a red or white wine flavoured with herbs.
– ORIGIN French *vermout*.

vernacular /ver-**nak**-yuu-ler/ noun **1** the language or dialect spoken by the ordinary people of a country or region. **2** informal the vocabulary used by people in a particular group or activity: *baseball vernacular*. •adjective **1** spoken as or using the language or dialect of the ordinary people. **2** (of architecture) concerned with simple, traditional structures such as houses and farms rather than large public buildings.
– ORIGIN from Latin *vernaculus* 'domestic, native'.

vernal /ver-n'l/ adjective relating to the season of spring.
– ORIGIN Latin *vernalis*.

vernier /ver-ni-er/ noun a small movable graduated scale for indicating fractions of the main scale on a measuring device.
– ORIGIN named after the French mathematician Pierre *Vernier*.

veronica noun a plant with narrow pointed leaves and blue or purple flowers.
– ORIGIN from the woman's name *Veronica*.

verruca /vuh-**roo**-kuh/ noun (pl. **verrucae** /vuh-**roo**-kee/ or **verrucas**) a contagious wart on the sole of the foot.
– ORIGIN Latin.

versatile adjective **1** having many different uses. **2** having a range of different skills: *a versatile TV presenter and journalist*.
– DERIVATIVES **versatility** noun.
– ORIGIN Latin *versatilis*.

verse noun **1** writing arranged with a regular rhythm, and often having a rhyme. **2** a group of lines that form a unit in a poem or song. **3** each of the short numbered divisions of a chapter in the Bible or other scripture.

V

– ORIGIN Latin *versus* 'a turn of the plough, a line of writing'.

versed adjective (**versed in**) experienced or skilled in; knowledgeable about.
– ORIGIN Latin *versatus*.

versify verb (**versifies, versifying, versified**) turn writing or ideas into verse.
– DERIVATIVES **versification** noun **versifier** noun.

version noun **1** a form of something that differs in some way from other forms of the same type of thing: *the car comes in two-door and four-door versions.* **2** an account of something told from a particular person's point of view. •verb create a new version of something.
– ORIGIN Latin, 'action of turning'.

verso /ver-soh/ noun (pl. **versos**) a left-hand page of an open book, or the back of a loose document. Contrasted with **RECTO**.
– ORIGIN from Latin *verso folio* 'on the turned leaf'.

versus preposition **1** against: *England versus France.* **2** as opposed to; in contrast to.
– ORIGIN Latin, 'towards'.

vert /rhymes with dirt/ noun green, as a conventional heraldic colour.
– ORIGIN Old French.

vertebra /ver-ti-bruh/ noun (pl. **vertebrae** /ver-ti-bray, ver-ti-bree/) each of the series of small bones forming the backbone.
– DERIVATIVES **vertebral** adjective.
– ORIGIN Latin.

vertebrate /ver-ti-bruht/ noun an animal having a backbone, including mammals, birds, reptiles, amphibians, and fish. •adjective relating to vertebrates.

vertex /ver-teks/ noun (pl. **vertices** /ver-ti-seez/ or **vertexes**) **1** the highest point; the top. **2** each angular point of a polygon, triangle, or other geometrical figure. **3** a meeting point of two lines that form an angle.
– ORIGIN Latin, 'whirlpool, top'.

vertical adjective at right angles to a horizontal line or surface; having the top directly above the bottom. •noun **1** (**the vertical**) a vertical line or surface. **2** an upright structure.
– DERIVATIVES **verticality** noun **vertically** adverb.
– ORIGIN Latin *verticalis*.

vertiginous /ver-tij-i-nuhss/ adjective **1** very high or steep. **2** relating to or affected by vertigo.
– DERIVATIVES **vertiginously** adverb.

vertigo /ver-ti-goh/ noun a feeling of dizziness caused by looking down from a great height or by disease affecting the inner ear.
– ORIGIN Latin, 'whirling'.

vervain /ver-vayn/ noun a plant with small blue, white, or purple flowers, used in herbal medicine.
– ORIGIN Old French *verveine*.

verve noun vigour, spirit, and style: *he writes with his usual verve.*
– ORIGIN French, 'vigour'.

vervet monkey /ver-vit/ noun a common African monkey with greenish-brown upper parts and a black face.
– ORIGIN French.

very adverb **1** in a high degree. **2** used to emphasize a description: *the very best quality.*

•adjective **1** actual; precise. **2** used to emphasize an extreme point in time or space. **3** mere: *the very thought of drink made him feel sick.* **4** old use real; genuine.
– ORIGIN from Latin *verus* 'true'.

Very light /veer-i, ve-ri/ noun a flare fired into the air from a pistol for signalling.
– ORIGIN named after the American naval officer Edward W. *Very.*

Very Reverend adjective a title given to a dean in the Anglican Church.

vesicle /ves-si-k'l, vee-si-k'l/ noun **1** a small fluid-filled sac or cyst in an animal or plant. **2** a blister full of clear fluid.
– DERIVATIVES **vesicular** adjective.
– ORIGIN Latin *vesicula* 'small bladder'.

vespers noun a service of evening prayer, especially in the Western Christian Church.
– ORIGIN Latin *vesperas* 'evensong'.

vessel noun **1** a ship or large boat. **2** a bowl, cup, or other container for liquids. **3** a tube or duct that carries a fluid within the body, or within a plant. **4** a person or thing that conveys or embodies a quality or feeling: *the written word is a safer vessel for love than the spoken word.*
– ORIGIN Old French *vessele.*

vest noun **1** Brit. a sleeveless undergarment worn on the upper part of the body. **2** a sleeveless garment worn for a particular purpose: *a bulletproof vest.* **3** N. Amer. & Austral. a waistcoat or sleeveless jacket. •verb **1** (**vest something in**) give power, property, etc. to someone. **2** give someone the legal right to power, property, etc.: *the court was vested with extensive powers.*
– ORIGIN Latin *vestis* 'garment'.

vestal adjective literary chaste; pure. •noun a Vestal Virgin.
– ORIGIN from the name of the Roman goddess *Vesta.*

Vestal Virgin noun (in ancient Rome) a virgin dedicated to the goddess Vesta and vowed to chastity.

vested interest noun **1** a personal reason for wanting something to happen, especially because one expects to gain advantage from it. **2** Law an interest (usually in land or money held in trust) recognized as belonging to a particular person.

vestibule /vess-ti-byool/ noun **1** a room or hall just inside the outer door of a building. **2** Anatomy a chamber or channel opening into another.
– DERIVATIVES **vestibular** adjective (Anatomy).
– ORIGIN Latin *vestibulum* 'entrance court'.

vestige /vess-tij/ noun **1** a remaining trace of something that once existed: *the last vestiges of true wilderness.* **2** the smallest amount.
– ORIGIN Latin *vestigium* 'footprint'.

vestigial /ve-sti-ji-uhl, ve-sti-juhl/ adjective remaining as the last small part of something: *he felt a vestigial flicker of anger from last night.*
– DERIVATIVES **vestigially** adverb.

vestment noun **1** a robe worn by the clergy or members of the choir during church services. **2** old use a robe worn on ceremonial occasions.
– ORIGIN Latin *vestimentum.*

vestry noun (pl. **vestries**) a room in or attached to a church, used as an office and for changing into ceremonial robes.
– ORIGIN Latin *vestiarium.*

vet[1] noun chiefly Brit. a veterinary surgeon. ●verb (**vets, vetting, vetted**) **1** check or examine something very carefully. **2** Brit. investigate a person's background in order to ensure that they are suitable for a job requiring secrecy, loyalty, or trustworthiness.

vet[2] noun N. Amer. informal a veteran.

vetch noun a plant with purple, pink, or yellow flowers, grown for silage or fodder.
– ORIGIN Old French *veche*.

veteran noun **1** a person who has had long experience in a particular field. **2** a person who used to serve in the armed forces.
– ORIGIN Latin *veteranus*.

veteran car noun Brit. an old car, specifically one made before 1919 or (strictly) before 1905.

veterinarian noun North American term for **VETERINARY SURGEON**.

veterinary /vet-uhn-ri, vet-ri-nuh-ri/ adjective relating to the treatment of diseases and injuries in animals.
– ORIGIN Latin *veterinarius*.

veterinary surgeon noun Brit. a person qualified to treat diseased or injured animals.

vetiver /vet-i-ver/ noun a fragrant extract or essential oil obtained from the root of an Indian grass, used in perfumery and aromatherapy.
– ORIGIN Tamil, 'root'.

veto /vee-toh/ noun (pl. **vetoes**) **1** a right to reject a decision or proposal made by a law-making body. **2** any refusal to allow something. ●verb (**vetoes, vetoing, vetoed**) **1** use a veto against a decision or proposal of a law-making body. **2** refuse to allow: *I vetoed the idea of a holiday.*
– ORIGIN from Latin, 'I forbid'.

vex verb make someone annoyed or worried.
– DERIVATIVES **vexation** noun.
– ORIGIN Latin *vexare* 'shake, disturb'.

vexatious /vek-say-shuss/ adjective **1** causing annoyance or worry. **2** Law referring to an action or the bringer of an action that is brought without sufficient grounds for winning, purely to cause annoyance to the defendant.

vexed adjective **1** (of an issue) difficult to resolve and causing much debate: *the vexed question of Europe.* **2** annoyed or worried.

VGA abbreviation videographics array, a standard for defining colour display screens for computers.

vgc abbreviation very good condition.

VHF abbreviation very high frequency.

VHS abbreviation trademark video home system (as used by domestic video recorders).

VI abbreviation Virgin Islands.

via preposition **1** travelling through a place en route to a destination. **2** by way of; through. **3** by means of.
– ORIGIN from Latin, 'way, road'.

viable /vy-uh-b'l/ adjective **1** capable of working successfully: *the belief that there are no viable alternatives to formal schooling.* **2** (of a plant, animal, or cell) capable of surviving or living successfully.
– DERIVATIVES **viability** noun **viably** adverb.
– ORIGIN French.

viaduct noun a long bridge-like structure carrying a road or railway across a valley or other low ground.
– ORIGIN from Latin *via* 'way' + *ducere* 'to lead'.

Viagra /vy-ag-ruh/ noun trademark a drug used to treat impotence in men.
– ORIGIN unknown.

vial /vy-uhl/ noun a small container used especially for holding liquid medicines.
– ORIGIN from **PHIAL**.

viands /vy-uhndz/ plural noun old use food.
– ORIGIN Old French *viande*.

viaticum /vy-at-i-kuhm/ noun (pl. **viatica** /vy-at-i-kuh/) the Eucharist as given to a person who is dying or in danger of death.
– ORIGIN Latin.

vibe noun informal **1** (usu. **vibes**) the atmosphere of a place or a mood felt among a group of people: *a bar with good vibes.* **2** (**vibes**) short for **VIBRAPHONE**.

vibrant adjective **1** full of energy and enthusiasm. **2** (of sound) strong or resonant. **3** (of colour) bright or bold.
– DERIVATIVES **vibrancy** noun **vibrantly** adverb.
– ORIGIN from Latin *vibrare* 'shake to and fro'.

vibraphone /vy-bruh-fohn/ noun a musical percussion instrument with a double row of metal bars that are hit by the player, each above a resonator with lids that open and close electrically, giving a vibrato effect.
– DERIVATIVES **vibraphonist** noun.

vibrate verb **1** move with small movements rapidly to and fro. **2** (of a sound) resonate.
– DERIVATIVES **vibratory** adjective.
– ORIGIN Latin *vibrare* 'move to and fro'.

vibration noun **1** an instance or the state of vibrating. **2** (**vibrations**) informal the atmosphere of a place or a mood felt among a group of people.
– DERIVATIVES **vibrational** adjective.

vibrato /vi-brah-toh/ noun a rapid, slight variation in pitch in singing or playing some musical instruments, producing a stronger or richer tone.
– ORIGIN Italian.

vibrator noun a device that vibrates, used for massage or sexual stimulation.

viburnum /vy-ber-nuhm/ noun a shrub or small tree with clusters of small white flowers.
– ORIGIN Latin, 'wayfaring tree'.

vicar noun **1** (in the Church of England) a priest in charge of a parish. **2** (in other Anglican Churches) a member of the clergy deputizing for another. **3** (in the Roman Catholic Church) a representative or deputy of a bishop.
– ORIGIN Latin *vicarius* 'substitute'.

vicarage noun the house of a vicar.

vicar general noun (pl. **vicars general**) an official serving as a deputy or representative of a bishop or archbishop.

vicarious /vi-kair-i-uhss, vy-kair-i-uhss/ adjective **1** experienced in the imagination after watching or reading about another person's actions or feelings: *vicarious excitement.* **2** done by one person as a substitute for another.
– DERIVATIVES **vicariously** adverb.
– ORIGIN from Latin *vicarius* 'substitute'.

V

vice¹ noun **1** immoral or wicked behaviour. **2** criminal activities involving prostitution, pornography, or drugs. **3** an immoral or bad quality in a person's character. **4** a bad habit.
– ORIGIN Old French.

vice² (US **vise**) noun a metal tool with movable jaws which are used to hold an object firmly in place while work is done on it.
– ORIGIN Old French *vis*.

vice- combining form next in rank to and able to deputize for: *vice-president*.
– ORIGIN from Latin *vice* 'in place of'.

vice admiral noun a high rank of naval officer, above rear admiral and below admiral.

vice chancellor noun a deputy chancellor of a British university who is in charge of its administration.

vice-president noun an official or executive who serves as a deputy to a president.

viceregal adjective relating to a viceroy.

viceroy noun a person who governs a colony on behalf of a sovereign.
– ORIGIN from former French.

vice versa /vyss ver-suh, vy-suh ver-suh/ adverb reversing the order of the items just mentioned.
– ORIGIN Latin, 'in-turned position'.

vichyssoise /vee-shee-swahz/ noun a soup made with potatoes, leeks, and cream and typically served chilled.
– ORIGIN French, 'of *Vichy*' (a town in France).

vicinity noun (pl. **vicinities**) the area near or surrounding a place.
– PHRASES **in the vicinity of** in the region of a price or amount.
– ORIGIN Latin *vicinitas*.

vicious adjective **1** cruel or violent. **2** full of hatred or anger: *a vicious campaign to discredit him*. **3** very severe or serious: *a vicious stomach bug*. **4** (of an animal) wild and dangerous.
– DERIVATIVES **viciously** adverb **viciousness** noun.
– ORIGIN Latin *vitiosus* 'full of faults, immoral'.

vicious circle noun a situation in which one problem leads to another, which then makes the first one worse.

vicissitudes /vi-siss-i-tyoodz/ plural noun changes of circumstances or fortune.
– ORIGIN Latin *vicissitudo*.

vicomte /vee-komt/ noun (pl. pronounced same) a French nobleman corresponding in rank to a British or Irish viscount.
– ORIGIN French.

victim noun **1** a person harmed or killed as a result of a crime or accident. **2** a person who has been tricked. **3** an animal or person killed as a religious sacrifice.
– PHRASES **fall victim to** be hurt, killed, or destroyed by someone or something.
– DERIVATIVES **victimhood** noun.
– ORIGIN Latin *victima*.

victimize (or **victimise**) verb single someone out for cruel or unfair treatment.
– DERIVATIVES **victimization** noun **victimizer** noun.

victimless adjective (of a crime) in which there is no injured party.

victimology noun (pl. **victimologies**) the study of the victims of crime and the psychological effects on them.

victor noun a person who defeats an opponent in a battle, game, or competition.
– ORIGIN Latin.

Victorian adjective **1** relating to the reign of Queen Victoria (1837–1901). **2** relating to the attitudes associated with the Victorian period, especially those of prudishness and strict morality. •noun a person who lived during the Victorian period.
– DERIVATIVES **Victorianism** noun.

Victoriana plural noun articles, especially collectors' items, from the Victorian period.

Victoria plum noun Brit. a large red dessert plum.

Victoria sandwich (also **Victoria sponge**)
• noun Brit. a cake consisting of two layers of sponge with a jam filling.

victorious adjective **1** having won a victory. **2** relating to a victory; triumphant: *a victorious glance*.
– DERIVATIVES **victoriously** adverb.

victory noun (pl. **victories**) an act of defeating an opponent in a battle, game, or other competition.
– ORIGIN Latin *victoria*.

victual /vi-t'l/ dated noun (**victuals**) food or provisions. •verb (**victuals, victualling, victualled**; US **victuals, victualing, victualed**) provide someone or something with food or other stores.
– ORIGIN Latin *victualis*.

victualler /vit-ler/ (US **victualer**) noun **1** Brit. a person who is licensed to sell alcoholic drinks. **2** dated a person providing or selling food or other provisions.

vicuña /vi-koo-nyuh, vy-kyoo-nuh/ noun **1** a wild relative of the llama, having fine silky wool. **2** cloth made from the wool of the vicuña.
– ORIGIN Quechua.

vid noun informal short for **VIDEO**.

vide /vee-day, vi-day, vy-di/ verb see (used as an instruction in a written work to refer the reader elsewhere).
– ORIGIN Latin.

video noun (pl. **videos**) **1** a system of recording, reproducing, or broadcasting moving images using magnetic tape. **2** a film or other recording on magnetic tape. **3** a cassette of videotape. **4** Brit. a video recorder. •verb (**videoes, videoing, videoed**) film an event or make a video recording of a television programme.
– ORIGIN from Latin *videre* 'to see'.

videoconference noun an arrangement in which television sets linked to telephone lines are used to enable a group of people to talk to and see each other.
– DERIVATIVES **videoconferencing** noun.

videodisc noun a CD-ROM or other disc used to store images.

video game noun a computer game played on a VDU screen.

videography /vi-di-og-ruh-fi/ noun the process or art of making video films.
– DERIVATIVES **videographer** noun.

video on demand noun a system in which viewers choose their own filmed entertainment, by means of a PC or interactive TV system.

V

videophile noun a person who is very enthusiastic about video recordings or technology.

videophone noun a telephone device that transmits and receives images as well as sound.

video recorder noun a machine linked to a television set, used for recording programmes and playing videotapes.

videotape noun 1 magnetic tape for recording and reproducing images and sound. 2 a cassette on which this magnetic tape is held. •verb record or film something on videotape.

vie verb (**vies, vying, vied**) compete eagerly with others in order to do or achieve something: *companies vying for a slice of the market.*
– ORIGIN probably from former *envy*, from Latin *invitare* 'challenge'.

Viennese /vee-uh-**neez**/ noun (pl. same) a person from Vienna. •adjective relating to Vienna.

Vietnamese noun (pl. same) 1 a person from Vietnam. 2 the language of Vietnam. •adjective relating to Vietnam.

view noun 1 the ability to see something or to be seen from a particular position: *the mountains came into view.* 2 something seen from a particular position, especially beautiful scenery. 3 an attitude or opinion: *strong political views.* 4 an inspection of things for sale by prospective buyers. •verb 1 look at or inspect someone or something. 2 regard in a particular way: *he viewed beggars as potential thieves.* 3 inspect a house or other property with the prospect of buying or renting it. 4 watch something on television.
– PHRASES **in full view** clearly visible. **in view** able to be seen; visible. **in view of** because or as a result of. **with a view to** with the aim or intention of.
– DERIVATIVES **viewable** adjective.
– ORIGIN Old French *vieue*.

viewer noun 1 a person who views something. 2 a device for looking at film transparencies or similar photographic images.

viewership noun (treated as sing. or pl.) the audience for a particular television programme or channel.

viewfinder noun a device on a camera that the user looks through in order to see what will appear in the photograph.

viewpoint noun 1 a point of view; an opinion. 2 a position giving a good view.

viewscreen noun the screen on a television, computer, or similar device on which images and information are displayed.

vigil /**vi**-jil/ noun 1 a period of staying awake during the night to keep watch or pray. 2 a stationary, peaceful demonstration in support of a cause.
– ORIGIN from Latin, 'awake'.

vigilant adjective keeping careful watch for possible danger or difficulties.
– DERIVATIVES **vigilance** noun **vigilantly** adverb.
– ORIGIN from Latin *vigilare* 'keep awake'.

vigilante /vi-ji-**lan**-ti/ noun a member of a group of people who take it on themselves to prevent crime or punish offenders without legal authority.

– DERIVATIVES **vigilantism** noun.
– ORIGIN from Spanish, 'vigilant'.

vigneron /vee-nyuh-ron/ noun a person who grows grapes for winemaking.
– ORIGIN French.

vignette /vee-**nyet**, vi-**nyet**/ noun 1 a brief, vivid description or episode. 2 a small illustration or portrait photograph which fades into its background without a definite border.
– ORIGIN French.

vigorous adjective 1 strong, healthy, and full of energy. 2 involving effort, energy, or determination: *a vigorous election campaign.* 3 (of language) forceful.
– DERIVATIVES **vigorously** adverb **vigorousness** noun.

vigour (US **vigor**) noun 1 physical strength and good health. 2 effort, energy, and enthusiasm.
– ORIGIN Latin *vigor.*

Viking noun a member of the Scandinavian seafaring people who settled in parts of Britain and elsewhere in NW Europe between the 8th and 11th centuries.
– ORIGIN Old Norse.

vile adjective 1 very unpleasant. 2 morally bad; wicked.
– DERIVATIVES **vilely** adverb **vileness** noun.
– ORIGIN Latin *vilis* 'cheap, base'.

vilify /**vil**-i-fy/ verb (**vilifies, vilifying, vilified**) speak or write about someone in a very abusive way.
– DERIVATIVES **vilification** noun.
– ORIGIN Latin *vilificare.*

villa noun 1 Brit. a rented holiday home abroad. 2 (especially in continental Europe) a large country house in its own grounds. 3 (in Roman times) a large country house consisting of buildings arranged around a courtyard.
– ORIGIN Latin.

village noun 1 a community in a country area that is smaller than a town. 2 a self-contained district or community within a town or city.
– DERIVATIVES **villager** noun **villagey** adjective.
– ORIGIN Old French.

villain noun 1 a wicked person or a person guilty of a crime. 2 a bad character in a novel or play whose evil actions are important to the plot.
– DERIVATIVES **villainous** adjective **villainy** noun (pl. **villainies**).
– ORIGIN first meaning 'an unsophisticated country person': from Old French *vilein.*

villanelle /vil-luh-**nel**/ noun a poem of nineteen lines, with only two rhymes throughout, and some lines repeated.
– ORIGIN French.

villein /**vil**-luhn, vil-**layn**/ noun (in medieval England) a poor man who had to work for a lord in return for a small piece of land on which to grow food.
– ORIGIN from **VILLAIN**.

villus /**vil**-luhss/ noun (pl. **villi** /**vil**-ly/) any of many tiny finger-like growths of tissue on some membranes of the body, especially the small intestine.
– DERIVATIVES **villous** adjective.
– ORIGIN Latin, 'shaggy hair'.

vim noun informal energy; enthusiasm.

V

– ORIGIN perhaps from Latin *vis* 'energy'.

vinaigrette /vi-ni-**gret**, vi-nay-**gret**/ noun a salad dressing of oil, wine vinegar, and seasoning.
– ORIGIN French.

vindaloo /vin-duh-**loo**/ noun (pl. **vindaloos**) a very hot Indian curry.
– ORIGIN probably from Portuguese *vin d'alho* 'wine and garlic sauce'.

vindicate /**vin**-di-kayt/ verb 1 clear someone of blame or suspicion. 2 show to be right or justified: *more sober views were vindicated by events.*
– DERIVATIVES **vindication** noun.
– ORIGIN Latin *vindicare* 'claim, avenge'.

vindictive adjective having or showing a strong or spiteful desire for revenge.
– DERIVATIVES **vindictively** adverb **vindictiveness** noun.
– ORIGIN from Latin *vindicta* 'vengeance'.

vine noun 1 a climbing plant with a woody stem, especially one that produces grapes. 2 the slender stem of a climbing plant.
– ORIGIN Latin *vinea* 'vineyard, vine'.

vinegar noun 1 a sour liquid made from wine, beer, or cider, used as a seasoning or for pickling. 2 bitterness or spitefulness: *she was bossy and full of vinegar.*
– DERIVATIVES **vinegary** adjective.
– ORIGIN from Old French *vyn egre* 'sour wine'.

vineyard /**vin**-yard, **vin**-yuhd/ noun a plantation of grapevines, producing grapes used in winemaking.

vingt-et-un /vant-ay-**ern**/ noun the card game pontoon or blackjack.
– ORIGIN French, 'twenty-one'.

vinho verde /vee-noh **vair**-di, vee-nyoh **vair**-di/ noun a young Portuguese wine, not allowed to mature.
– ORIGIN Portuguese, 'green wine'.

viniculture /**vin**-i-kul-cher/ noun the growing of grapevines for winemaking.

vinification /vin-i-fi-**kay**-sh'n/ noun the conversion of grape juice or other vegetable extract into wine by fermentation.

vino noun (pl. **vinos**) informal, chiefly Brit. wine, especially that which is cheap.
– ORIGIN Spanish and Italian, 'wine'.

vin ordinaire /van or-di-**nair**/ noun (pl. **vins ordinaires**) cheap table wine for everyday use.
– ORIGIN French, 'ordinary wine'.

vinous /**vy**-nuhss/ adjective of, resembling, or associated with wine.

vintage noun 1 the year or place in which wine was produced. 2 a wine of high quality made from the crop of a single specified district in a good year. 3 the harvesting of grapes for winemaking. 4 the grapes or wine of a particular season. 5 the time that something was produced: *rifles of various vintages.*
• adjective 1 referring to high-quality vintage wine. 2 (of something from the past) of high quality.
– ORIGIN Old French *vendange.*

vintage car noun Brit. an old car, specifically one made between 1919 and 1930.

vintner /**vint**-ner/ noun a wine merchant.
– ORIGIN Old French *vinetier.*

vinyl /**vy**-n'l/ noun 1 a type of strong plastic, used in making floor coverings, paint, and gramophone records. 2 Chemistry the unsaturated hydrocarbon radical $-CH=CH_2$, derived from ethylene.
– ORIGIN from Latin *vinum* 'wine' (suggested by the relationship of ethylene to ethyl alcohol).

viol /**vy**-uhl/ noun a musical instrument of the Renaissance and baroque periods, resembling a violin but with six-strings and played vertically.
– ORIGIN Provençal *viola.*

viola¹ /**vioh**-luh/ noun an instrument of the violin family, larger than the violin and tuned a fifth lower.
– ORIGIN Italian and Spanish.

viola² /**vy**-uh-luh/ noun a plant of a genus that includes pansies and violets.
– ORIGIN Latin, 'violet'.

violaceous /vy-uh-**lay**-shuhss/ adjective chiefly technical of a violet colour.
– ORIGIN Latin *violaceus.*

viola da gamba /vi-oh-luh da **gam**-buh/ noun a viol, specifically a bass viol (corresponding to the modern cello).
– ORIGIN Italian, 'viol for the leg'.

violate verb 1 fail to obey a rule, law, or formal agreement. 2 fail to respect a person's privacy or rights. 3 treat something sacred with disrespect. 4 chiefly literary rape someone.
– DERIVATIVES **violation** noun **violator** noun.
– ORIGIN Latin *violare* 'treat violently'.

violence noun 1 behaviour involving physical force intended to hurt, damage, or kill. 2 the power of a destructive natural force. 3 strength of emotion: *the violence of her feelings.*

violent adjective 1 using or involving violence. 2 very intense or powerful: *violent dislike.*
– DERIVATIVES **violently** adverb.
– ORIGIN Latin, 'vehement, violent'.

violet noun 1 a small plant with purple, blue, or white five-petalled flowers. 2 a bluish-purple colour.
– ORIGIN Old French *violette.*

violin noun a musical instrument having four strings and a body narrowed at the middle, played with a bow.
– DERIVATIVES **violinist** noun.
– ORIGIN Italian *violino* 'small viola'.

violist /vi-**oh**-list/ noun a viola player.

violoncello /vy-uh-luhn-**chel**-loh/ noun formal term for CELLO.
– ORIGIN Italian.

VIP noun a very important person.

viper noun 1 a poisonous snake with large fangs and a body with dark patterns on a lighter background. 2 a spiteful or treacherous person.
– DERIVATIVES **viperish** adjective **viperous** adjective.
– ORIGIN Latin *vipera.*

viraemia /vy-**ree**-mi-uh/ (also **viremia**) noun Medicine the presence of viruses in the blood.
– ORIGIN from VIRUS.

virago /vi-**rah**-goh/ noun (pl. **viragos** or **viragoes**) a domineering, violent, or bad-tempered woman.
– ORIGIN from Latin, 'heroic woman, female warrior'.

viral adjective relating to or caused by a virus or

viruses.
- DERIVATIVES **virally** adverb.

viral marketing noun a marketing technique whereby information about a product is passed electronically from one Internet user to another.

vireo /vi-ri-oh/ noun (pl. **vireos**) a small American songbird, typically green or grey with yellow or white underparts.
- ORIGIN Latin, referring to a greenfinch or similar bird.

virgin noun 1 a person who has never had sexual intercourse. 2 (**the Virgin**) the Virgin Mary. 3 a person who is inexperienced in a particular activity: *a political virgin.* ▪adjective 1 having had no sexual experience. 2 not yet used or exploited: *virgin forest.* 3 (of olive oil) made from the first pressing of olives.
- ORIGIN Latin *virgo.*

virginal adjective relating to or appropriate for a virgin: *virginal white.*

virginals plural noun a type of small harpsichord popular in the 16th and 17th centuries.

Virgin Birth noun the Christian doctrine of Jesus's birth from a mother, Mary, who was a virgin.

Virginia creeper noun a North American climbing plant, grown for its red autumn foliage.

virginity noun 1 the state of never having had sexual intercourse. 2 the state of being inexperienced in a particular activity.

Virgo noun a constellation (the Virgin) and sign of the zodiac, which the sun enters about 23 August.
- DERIVATIVES **Virgoan** noun & adjective.
- ORIGIN Latin.

viridescent /vi-ri-dess-uhnt/ adjective literary greenish or becoming green.
- DERIVATIVES **viridescence** noun.
- ORIGIN from Latin *viridescere* 'become green'.

viridian /vi-rid-i-uhn/ noun a bluish-green pigment or colour.
- ORIGIN from Latin *viridis* 'green'.

virile adjective 1 (of a man) strong, energetic, and having a strong sex drive. 2 vigorous or powerful: *virile guitar bursts*
- DERIVATIVES **virility** noun.
- ORIGIN Latin *virilis.*

virology /vy-rol-uh-ji/ noun the branch of science concerned with the study of viruses.
- DERIVATIVES **virological** adjective **virologist** noun.

virtual adjective 1 almost or nearly the thing described, but not completely: *the virtual absence of border controls.* 2 not existing in reality but made by computer software to appear to do so.
- DERIVATIVES **virtuality** noun.
- ORIGIN Latin *virtualis.*

virtualize (or **virtualise**) /ver-tyoo-uh-lyz/ verb convert something to a computer-generated version of reality.
- DERIVATIVES **virtualization** noun.

virtually adverb 1 nearly; almost. 2 Computing by means of virtual reality techniques.

virtual memory (also **virtual storage**) noun Computing memory that appears to exist as main storage although most of it is supported by

data held in secondary storage.

virtual reality noun a system in which images that look like real, three-dimensional objects are created by computer.

virtue /ver-tyoo/ noun 1 behaviour showing high moral standards. 2 a good or desirable personal quality. 3 a good or useful quality of a thing: *the virtues of village life.* 4 old use virginity or chastity.
- PHRASES **by virtue of** as a result of.
- ORIGIN Latin *virtus* 'valour, merit, moral perfection'.

virtuoso /ver-tyoo-oh-soh/ noun (pl. **virtuosi** /ver-tyoo-oh-si/ or **virtuosos**) a person highly skilled in music or another artistic activity.
- DERIVATIVES **virtuosic** adjective **virtuosity** noun.
- ORIGIN from Italian, 'learned, skilful'.

virtuous adjective 1 having or showing high moral standards. 2 old use (especially of a woman) chaste.
- DERIVATIVES **virtuously** adverb **virtuousness** noun.

virtuous circle noun a situation in which one event leads to another, each one increasing the beneficial effect of the next.

virulent /vi-ruu-luhnt, vir-yuu-luhnt/ adjective 1 (of a disease or poison) having a very severe or harmful effect. 2 (of a virus) highly infective. 3 bitterly hostile: *a virulent attack on liberalism.*
- DERIVATIVES **virulence** noun **virulently** adverb.
- ORIGIN first describing a poisoned wound: from Latin *virulentus.*

virus /vy-ruhss/ noun 1 a submicroscopic particle, typically consisting of nucleic acid coated in protein, which can cause infection or disease and can only multiply within the cells of a host organism. 2 an infection or disease caused by a virus. 3 (also **computer virus**) a piece of code introduced secretly into a computer system in order to damage or destroy data.
- ORIGIN Latin, 'slimy liquid, poison'.

visa /vee-zuh/ noun a stamp or note on a passport indicating that the holder is allowed to enter, leave, or stay for a specified time in a country.
- ORIGIN Latin.

visage /vi-zij/ noun literary a person's facial features or expression.
- DERIVATIVES **visaged** adjective.
- ORIGIN Old French.

vis-à-vis /veez-ah-vee/ preposition in relation to.
- ORIGIN French, 'face to face'.

viscera /viss-uh-ruh/ plural noun the internal organs of the body, especially those in the abdomen.
- ORIGIN Latin, plural of *viscus.*

visceral adjective 1 relating to the body's internal organs. 2 (of a feeling) deep and instinctive rather than rational: *the voters' visceral fear of change.*
- DERIVATIVES **viscerally** adverb.

viscid /viss-id/ adjective sticky in consistency.
- ORIGIN Latin *viscidus.*

viscose /viss-kohz, viss-kohss/ noun rayon fabric or fibre made from treating cellulose with certain chemicals.
- ORIGIN from Latin *viscus* 'birdlime'.

V

viscosity /viss-**koss**-i-ti/ noun (pl. **viscosities**) the state of being thick, sticky, and semi-fluid in consistency.

viscount /**vy**-kownt/ noun a British nobleman ranking above a baron and below an earl.
– ORIGIN Latin *vicecomes*.

viscountess /vy-**kown**-tiss/ noun the wife or widow of a viscount, or a woman holding the rank of viscount in her own right.

viscous /**viss**-kuhss/ adjective having a thick, sticky consistency between solid and liquid.
– ORIGIN Latin *viscosus*.

vise noun US spelling of **VICE**².

visibility noun 1 the state of being able to see or be seen. 2 the distance that a person can see, depending on light and weather conditions.

visible adjective 1 able to be seen. 2 able to be noticed; prominent: *a more visible police presence could be the norm.* 3 (of light) within the range of wavelengths to which the eye is sensitive.
– DERIVATIVES **visibly** adverb.
– ORIGIN Latin *visibilis*.

Visigoth /**viz**-i-goth/ noun a member of the branch of the Goths who invaded the Roman Empire between the 3rd and 5th centuries AD.
– ORIGIN Latin *Visigothus*, perhaps meaning 'West Goth'.

vision noun 1 the ability to see. 2 the ability to think about the future with imagination or wisdom: *the organization has lost its vision and direction.* 3 an experience of imagining something, or of seeing someone or something in a dream or trance. 4 the images seen on a television screen. 5 a very beautiful person or sight.
– ORIGIN Latin.

visionary adjective 1 thinking about the future with imagination or wisdom. 2 relating to supernatural or dreamlike visions. •noun (pl. **visionaries**) a person with imaginative and original ideas about the future.

visit verb (**visits**, **visiting**, **visited**) 1 go to see a person or place for a period of time. 2 go to see someone for a particular purpose, such as to receive advice: *I visited my doctor for a check-up.* 3 access a website or web page. 4 (as adj. **visiting**) (of an academic) working for a fixed period of time at another college or university. 5 literary cause something harmful or unpleasant to affect someone: *they were visited with an epidemic.* 6 (usu. **visit with**) N. Amer. informal chat with someone. •noun 1 an act of going to see a person or place. 2 a temporary stay at a place.
– ORIGIN Latin *visitare* 'go to see'.

visitant noun 1 literary a ghost or apparition. 2 old use a visitor or guest.

visitation noun 1 an official or formal visit. 2 the appearance of a god or goddess or a supernatural being. 3 a disaster or difficulty regarded as a punishment from God: *a visitation of the plague.* 4 (**the Visitation**) the visit of the Virgin Mary to Elizabeth described in the Gospel of Luke, chapter 1.

visiting card noun Brit. a card with a person's name and address on it, left after or instead of a formal visit to someone.

visitor noun 1 a person visiting a person or place. 2 a bird that migrates to a particular area for only part of the year.

visor /**vy**-zer/ (also **vizor**) noun 1 a movable part of a helmet that can be pulled down to cover the face. 2 a screen for protecting the eyes from unwanted light. 3 N. Amer. a stiff peak at the front of a cap.
– DERIVATIVES **visored** adjective.
– ORIGIN Old French *viser*.

vista noun 1 a pleasing view. 2 an imagined future event or situation: *vistas of freedom seemed to open ahead of him.*
– ORIGIN Italian, 'view'.

visual adjective relating to seeing or sight. •noun a picture or film, or display used to illustrate or accompany something.
– DERIVATIVES **visually** adverb.
– ORIGIN Latin *visualis*.

visual display unit noun Brit. a device for displaying information from a computer on a screen.

visualize (or **visualise**) verb form an image of someone or something in the mind.
– DERIVATIVES **visualization** noun **visualizer** noun.

vital adjective 1 absolutely necessary; essential. 2 essential for life: *the vital organs.* 3 full of energy; lively. •noun (**vitals**) the body's important internal organs.
– DERIVATIVES **vitally** adverb.
– ORIGIN Latin *vitalis*.

vital force noun the energy or spirit which gives life to living creatures.

vitality noun the state of being full of energy; liveliness.

vitalize (or **vitalise**) verb give strength and energy to: *the drink is claimed to vitalize the body and mind.*

vital signs plural noun clinical measurements, specifically pulse rate, temperature, blood pressure, and rate of breathing, that indicate the state of a patient's essential body functions.

vital statistics plural noun 1 informal the measurements of a woman's bust, waist, and hips. 2 statistics relating to the population, such as the number of births, marriages, and deaths.

vitamin /vi-tuh-min, vy-tuh-min/ noun any of a group of organic compounds which are present in many foods and are essential for normal nutrition.
– ORIGIN from Latin *vita* 'life' + **AMINE**, because vitamins were originally thought to contain an amino acid.

vitamin A noun retinol, a compound which is essential for growth and vision in dim light and is found in vegetables, egg yolk, and fish-liver oil.

vitamin B noun any of a group of substances essential for the working of certain enzymes in the body, including thiamine (**vitamin B₁**), riboflavin (**vitamin B₂**), pyridoxine (**vitamin B₆**), and cyanocobalamin (**vitamin B₁₂**).

vitamin C noun ascorbic acid, a compound found in citrus fruits and green vegetables, essential in maintaining healthy connective tissue.

vitamin D noun any of a group of compounds found in liver and fish oils, essential for the absorption of calcium and including calciferol (**vitamin D₂**) and cholecalciferol (**vitamin D₃**).

vitamin E noun tocopherol, a compound found in wheatgerm oil, egg yolk, and leafy vegetables and important in stabilizing cell membranes.

vitamin K noun any of a group of compounds found mainly in green leaves and essential for the blood-clotting process, including phylloquinone (**vitamin K₁**) and menaquinone (**vitamin K₂**).

vitiate /vi-shi-ayt/ verb formal 1 make something less good or effective. 2 destroy or reduce the legal validity of something.
– ORIGIN Latin *vitiare* 'impair'.

viticulture noun 1 the cultivation of grapevines. 2 the study of grape cultivation.
– DERIVATIVES **viticultural** adjective **viticulturist** noun.
– ORIGIN from Latin *vitis* 'vine'.

vitiligo /vi-ti-ly-goh/ noun a medical condition in which the pigment is lost from areas of the skin, causing whitish patches.
– ORIGIN Latin.

vitreous /vi-tri-uhss/ adjective 1 resembling glass in appearance. 2 (of a substance) containing glass.
– ORIGIN Latin *vitreus*.

vitreous humour noun the transparent jelly-like tissue filling the eyeball behind the lens.

vitrify /vi-tri-fy/ verb (**vitrifies**, **vitrifying**, **vitrified**) convert something into glass or a glass-like substance by exposure to heat.
– DERIVATIVES **vitrification** noun.
– ORIGIN from Latin *vitrum* 'glass'.

vitrine /vi-treen/ noun a glass display case.
– ORIGIN French.

vitriol /vi-tri-uhl/ noun 1 extreme bitterness or malice: *a website where waiters vent their vitriol.* 2 old use sulphuric acid.
– ORIGIN first referring to the sulphate of various metals: from Latin *vitriolum*.

vitriolic /vit-ri-ol-ik/ adjective filled with bitterness or malice: *a vitriolic attack on working mothers.*
– DERIVATIVES **vitriolically** adverb.

vituperation /vi-tyoo-puh-ray-sh'n/ noun bitter and abusive language.
– DERIVATIVES **vituperative** adjective.
– ORIGIN Latin.

viva¹ /vee-vuh/ exclamation long live! (used to express praise or support).
– ORIGIN Italian.

viva² /vy-vuh/ (also **viva voce** /vy-vuh voh-chi/) noun Brit. an oral exam for an academic qualification.
– ORIGIN Latin *viva voce* 'with the living voice'.

vivace /vi-vah-chay/ adverb & adjective Music in a lively and brisk way.
– ORIGIN Italian.

vivacious /vi-vay-shuhss, vy-vay-shuhss/ adjective (especially of a woman) attractive and lively.
– DERIVATIVES **vivaciously** adverb **vivacity** /vi-vas-it-i/ noun.
– ORIGIN from Latin *vivax* 'lively, vigorous'.

vivarium /vi-vair-i-uhm, vy-vair-i-uhm/ noun (pl. **vivaria** /vi-vair-i-uh, vy-vair-i-uh/) an enclosure or structure used for keeping

animals in conditions similar to their natural environment for study or as pets.
– ORIGIN Latin, 'warren, fish pond'.

vivid adjective 1 producing powerful feelings or strong, clear images in the mind: *a vivid description.* 2 (of a colour) very deep or bright.
– DERIVATIVES **vividly** adverb **vividness** noun.
– ORIGIN Latin *vividus* 'lively, vigorous'.

vivify /vi-vi-fy/ verb (**vivifies**, **vivifying**, **vivified**) make someone or something more lively or interesting.
– DERIVATIVES **vivification** noun.
– ORIGIN Latin *vivificare*.

viviparous /vi-vip-uh-ruhss/ adjective (of an animal) giving birth to live young which have developed inside the body of the parent. Compare with OVIPAROUS.
– DERIVATIVES **viviparity** noun.
– ORIGIN Latin *viviparus*.

vivisection noun the practice of operating on live animals for scientific research (used by those opposed to such work).
– DERIVATIVES **vivisectionist** noun & adjective **vivisector** noun.
– ORIGIN from Latin *vivus* 'living', on the pattern of *dissection*.

vixen noun 1 a female fox. 2 a spirited or quarrelsome woman.
– DERIVATIVES **vixenish** adjective.
– ORIGIN perhaps from an Old English word meaning 'of a fox'.

Viyella /vy-el-luh/ noun trademark a fabric made from a mixture of cotton and wool.
– ORIGIN from *Via Gellia*, a valley in Derbyshire.

viz. adverb namely; in other words.
– ORIGIN short for Latin *videlicet* in the same sense.

vizier /vi-zeer/ noun historical a high-ranking official in some Muslim countries.
– ORIGIN Arabic, 'caliph's chief counsellor'.

vizor noun variant spelling of VISOR.

vizsla /vizh-luh/ noun a breed of golden-brown pointer (dog) with large drooping ears.
– ORIGIN named after the town of *Vizsla* in Hungary.

VJ day noun the day (15 August) in 1945 on which Japan ceased fighting in the Second World War, or the day (2 September) when Japan formally surrendered.
– ORIGIN *VJ*, short for *Victory over Japan*.

VLF abbreviation very low frequency (referring to radio waves of frequency 3–30 kilohertz and wavelength 10–100 kilometres).

VLSI abbreviation Electronics very large-scale integration, the process of integrating hundreds of thousands of components on a single silicon chip.

V-neck noun a neckline having straight sides meeting at a point to form a V-shape.
– DERIVATIVES **V-necked** adjective.

vocabulary noun (pl. **vocabularies**) 1 all the words used in a particular language or area of activity: *business vocabulary.* 2 all the words known to an individual person. 3 a list of words and their meanings, accompanying a piece of foreign or specialist writing. 4 a range of artistic or stylistic forms or techniques: *his command of the vocabulary of classical ballet.*
– ORIGIN Latin *vocabularius*.

v

vocal adjective **1** relating to the human voice. **2** expressing opinions or feelings freely or loudly. **3** (of music) consisting of or including singing. •noun (also **vocals**) a part of a piece of music that is sung.
– DERIVATIVES **vocally** adverb.
– ORIGIN Latin *vocalis*.

vocal cords (also **vocal folds**) plural noun the folds of the lining of the larynx whose edges vibrate in the airstream to produce the voice.

vocalic /voh-**kal**-ik/ adjective Phonetics relating to or consisting of a vowel or vowels.

vocalist noun a singer, especially in jazz or popular music.

vocalize (or **vocalise**) /**voh**-kuh-lyz/ verb **1** make a sound or say a word. **2** express something with words. **3** sing with several notes to one vowel.
– DERIVATIVES **vocalization** noun.

vocation noun **1** a strong belief that one ought to pursue a particular career or occupation. **2** a person's career or main occupation. **3** a trade or profession.
– ORIGIN Latin.

vocational adjective relating to a particular occupation and its skills or knowledge.
– DERIVATIVES **vocationally** adverb.

vocative /**vok**-uh-tiv/ noun the grammatical case used in addressing a person or thing.
– ORIGIN Latin *vocativus*.

vociferous /vuh-**sif**-uh-ruhss/ adjective expressing opinions in a loud and forceful way: *he was a vociferous opponent of the takeover.*
– DERIVATIVES **vociferously** adverb **vociferousness** noun.
– ORIGIN from Latin *vociferari* 'exclaim'.

vocoder /voh-**koh**-der/ noun an electronic synthesizer that produces sounds from an analysis of speech input.
– ORIGIN from VOICE + CODE.

VOD abbreviation video on demand.

vodka noun a clear Russian alcoholic spirit made from rye, wheat, or potatoes.
– ORIGIN Russian, 'little water'.

vogue noun the fashion or style current at a particular time.
– DERIVATIVES **voguish** adjective.
– ORIGIN French.

voice noun **1** the sound produced in a person's larynx and uttered through the mouth, as speech or song. **2** the ability to speak or sing: *I've lost my voice.* **3** the range of pitch or type of tone with which a person sings, e.g. soprano. **4** a vocal part in a musical composition. **5** an opinion or the right to express an opinion: *giving the people a voice in decision-making.* **6** Grammar a form of a verb showing the relation of the subject to the action: *the passive voice.* •verb **1** express something in words. **2** (as adj. **voiced**) Phonetics (of a speech sound) produced with vibration of the vocal cords (e.g. *b, d, v*).
– ORIGIN Latin *vox*.

voice box noun the larynx.

voiceless adjective **1** lacking a voice; speechless. **2** Phonetics (of a speech sound) produced without vibration of the vocal cords (e.g. *f, k, p*).

voicemail noun a centralized electronic system which can store messages from telephone callers.

voice-over noun a piece of speech giving information in a film or broadcast that is spoken by a person who is not seen on the screen.

voiceprint noun a visual record of a person's speech, analysed with respect to frequency, duration, and amplitude, used for identification.

void adjective **1** (especially of a contract or agreement) not valid or legally binding. **2** (**void of**) free from; lacking: *the tundra is seemingly void of life.* **3** completely empty. •noun a completely empty space. •verb **1** discharge or drain away water, gases, waste matter, etc. **2** chiefly N. Amer. declare that something is not valid or legally binding.
– DERIVATIVES **voidable** adjective.
– ORIGIN Old French *vuide*.

voila /vwa-**lah**/ exclamation there it is; there you are.
– ORIGIN French *voilà*.

voile /voyl, vwahl/ noun a thin, semi-transparent fabric of cotton, wool, or silk.
– ORIGIN French, 'veil'.

VOIP abbreviation voice over Internet protocol, a technology for making telephone calls over the Internet in which speech sounds are converted into binary data.

volatile /**vol**-uh-tyl/ adjective **1** liable to change rapidly and unpredictably, especially for the worse: *volatile currency markets.* **2** (of a substance) easily evaporated at normal temperatures. •noun a substance that is easily evaporated at normal temperatures.
– DERIVATIVES **volatility** noun **volatilize** (or **volatilise**) verb.
– ORIGIN from Latin *volare* 'to fly'.

volatile oil noun another term for ESSENTIAL OIL.

vol-au-vent /**vol**-oh-von/ noun a small round case of puff pastry filled with a savoury mixture.
– ORIGIN French, 'flight in the wind'.

volcanic adjective **1** relating to or produced by a volcano or volcanoes. **2** (of a feeling or emotion) very intense and liable to burst out suddenly.
– DERIVATIVES **volcanically** adverb.

volcanic glass noun obsidian (a volcanic rock).

volcanism (also **vulcanism**) noun volcanic activity or phenomena.

volcano noun (pl. **volcanoes** or **volcanos**) a mountain having a crater or opening through which lava, rocks, hot vapour, and gas are or have been forced from the earth's crust.
– ORIGIN from Latin *Volcanus* 'Vulcan', the Roman god of fire.

volcanology /vol-kuh-**nol**-uh-ji/ (also **vulcanology**) noun the scientific study of volcanoes.
– DERIVATIVES **volcanologist** noun.

vole noun a small mouse-like rodent with a rounded muzzle.
– ORIGIN from Norwegian *vollmus* 'field mouse'.

volition /vuh-**li**-sh'n/ noun a person's power to choose freely and make their own decisions:

v

he left Oxford of his own volition.
– DERIVATIVES **volitional** adjective.
– ORIGIN Latin.

volley noun (pl. **volleys**) **1** a number of bullets or other missiles fired at one time. **2** a series of questions, insults, etc. directed at someone rapidly one after the other. **3** (in sport) a strike or kick of the ball made before it touches the ground. • verb (**volleys**, **volleying**, **volleyed**) hit or kick the ball before it touches the ground.
– DERIVATIVES **volleyer** noun.
– ORIGIN French *volée*.

volleyball noun a team game in which a ball is hit by hand over a net and points are scored if the ball touches the ground on the opponent's side of the court.

volt noun the SI unit of electromotive force, the difference of potential that would carry one ampere of current against a resistance of one ohm.
– ORIGIN named after the Italian physicist Alessandro *Volta*.

voltage noun an electromotive force or potential difference expressed in volts.

voltaic /vol-**tay**-ik/ adjective referring to electricity produced by chemical action in a battery.

volte-face /volt-**fass**/ noun **1** an abrupt and complete reversal of attitude or policy. **2** an act of turning round so as to face in the opposite direction.
– ORIGIN French.

voltmeter noun an instrument for measuring electric potential in volts.

voluble /vol-yuu-b'l/ adjective **1** speaking easily and at length. **2** expressed in many words: *voluble descriptions of horses.*
– DERIVATIVES **volubility** noun **volubly** adverb.
– ORIGIN from Latin *volvere* 'to roll'.

volume noun **1** the amount of space occupied by a substance or object or enclosed within a container. **2** the amount or quantity of something: *the growing volume of traffic.* **3** degree of loudness. **4** a book, especially one forming part of a larger work or series. **5** a consecutive sequence of issues of a periodical. **6** fullness or thickness of the hair.
– ORIGIN first referring to a roll of parchment with writing on: from Latin *volumen* 'a roll'.

volumetric /vol-yuu-**met**-rik/ adjective relating to the measurement of volume.
– DERIVATIVES **volumetrically** adverb.

voluminous /vuh-**loo**-mi-nuhss/ adjective **1** (of clothing) loose and full. **2** (of writing) very lengthy and detailed.
– DERIVATIVES **voluminously** adverb.
– ORIGIN partly from Latin *voluminosus* 'having many coils', partly from Latin *volumen* 'a roll'.

volumize (or **volumise**) verb give volume or body to hair.

voluntarism noun the principle of relying on voluntary action or participation.
– DERIVATIVES **voluntarist** noun & adjective.

voluntary adjective **1** done or acting of one's own free will: *a voluntary code of practice.* **2** willingly working or done without payment. **3** (of an action or part of the body) under the conscious control of the brain. • noun (pl. **voluntaries**) an organ solo played before,

during, or after a church service.
– DERIVATIVES **voluntarily** adverb.
– ORIGIN Latin *voluntarius*.

voluntary-aided adjective (in the UK) referring to a voluntary school funded mainly by the local authority.

voluntary-controlled adjective (in the UK) referring to a voluntary school fully funded by the local authority.

voluntary school noun (in the UK) a school which, though not established by the local education authority, is funded mainly or entirely by it, and which typically encourages a particular set of religious beliefs.

volunteer noun **1** a person who freely offers to do something. **2** a person who willingly works for an organization without being paid. **3** a person who freely joins the armed forces. • verb **1** freely offer to do something. **2** say or suggest something without being asked. **3** suggest someone for a task or activity without consulting them first.
– ORIGIN from French *volontaire* 'voluntary'.

voluptuary /vuh-**lup**-chuu-uh-ri/ noun (pl. **voluptuaries**) a person who enjoys sensual or sexual pleasure very much.
– ORIGIN Latin *voluptuarius*.

voluptuous /vuh-**lup**-chuu-uhss/ adjective **1** (of a woman) having a full, sexually attractive body. **2** giving sensual pleasure: *voluptuous fabrics.*
– DERIVATIVES **voluptuously** adverb **voluptuousness** noun.
– ORIGIN Latin *voluptuosus*.

volute /vuh-**lyoot**/ noun a decorative scroll shape typically found at the tops of columns in Ionic architecture.
– ORIGIN Latin *voluta*.

vomit verb (**vomits**, **vomiting**, **vomited**) **1** bring up food and other matter from the stomach through the mouth. **2** send out in an uncontrolled flow: *the machine vomited fold after fold of paper.* • noun food and other matter vomited from the stomach.
– ORIGIN Latin *vomere* 'to vomit'.

voodoo noun a religious cult of African origin practised chiefly in the Caribbean, involving sorcery, possession by spirits, and elements of Roman Catholic ritual.
– ORIGIN from Kwa (a Niger–Congo language).

voracious /vuh-**ray**-shuhss/ adjective **1** wanting or eating great quantities of food. **2** doing something eagerly and enthusiastically: *his voracious reading of literature.*
– DERIVATIVES **voraciously** adverb **voracity** /vuh-**ras**-it-i/ noun.
– ORIGIN from Latin *vorare* 'devour'.

-vorous /vuh-ruhss/ combining form feeding on a specified food: *carnivorous.*
– DERIVATIVES **-vore** combining form.
– ORIGIN Latin *-vorus.*

vortex /**vor**-teks/ noun (pl. **vortexes** or **vortices** /**vor**-ti-seez/) **1** a whirling mass of water or air. **2** a powerful feeling, force, or situation that is difficult to avoid or escape from: *the country could be drawn into the vortex of world politics.*
– DERIVATIVES **vortical** adjective **vorticity** noun.
– ORIGIN Latin, 'eddy'.

V

votary /voh-tuh-ri/ noun (pl. **votaries**) **1** a person who has taken vows to dedicate their life to God or religious service. **2** a devoted follower or supporter: *a votary of the arts.*
– ORIGIN from Latin *vovere* 'vow'.

vote noun **1** a formal indication of a choice between two or more candidates or courses of action. **2** (**the vote**) the right to participate in an election. **3** (**the vote**) a particular group of voters or the votes cast by them: *the green vote.* •verb **1** give or register a vote. **2** grant or permit something by vote. **3** informal suggest something: *I vote we have one more game.*
– PHRASES **vote of** (**no**) **confidence** a vote showing that a majority continues to support (or no longer supports) the policy of a leader or governing body. **vote with one's feet** informal express an opinion by being present or absent.
– DERIVATIVES **voter** noun.
– ORIGIN Latin *votum* 'a vow, wish'.

votive adjective offered to God or a god as a sign of gratitude.
– ORIGIN Latin *votivus.*

vouch verb (**vouch for**) **1** confirm that something is true or accurate. **2** say that someone is who they claim to be or that they are reliable or honest.
– ORIGIN Old French *voucher* 'summon'.

voucher noun a piece of paper that entitles the holder to a discount, or that may be exchanged for goods or services.

vouchsafe verb give or reveal in a gracious or superior way: *you'd never vouchsafed that interesting fact before.*
– ORIGIN first as *vouch* something *safe* on someone, i.e. 'guarantee that something is granted to someone'.

Vouvray /voo-vray/ noun dry white wine produced in the Vouvray district of the Loire Valley in France.

vow noun a solemn promise. •verb solemnly promise to do something.
– ORIGIN Old French *vou.*

vowel noun **1** a speech sound in which the mouth is open and the tongue is not touching the top of the mouth, the teeth, or the lips. **2** a letter representing such a sound, such as *a, e, i, o, u.*
– ORIGIN Old French *vouel.*

vox pop noun Brit. informal popular opinion as represented by informal comments from members of the public.
– ORIGIN short for Latin *vox populi* 'the people's voice'.

voyage noun a long journey by sea or in space. •verb go on a voyage.
– DERIVATIVES **voyager** noun.
– ORIGIN Old French *voiage.*

voyeur /vwa-yer, voy-er/ noun **1** a person who gains sexual pleasure from watching others when they are naked or taking part in sexual activity. **2** a person who enjoys seeing the pain or distress of others.
– DERIVATIVES **voyeurism** noun **voyeuristic** adjective **voyeuristically** adverb.
– ORIGIN French.

VP abbreviation Vice-President.

VR abbreviation virtual reality.

VRML abbreviation Computing virtual reality modelling language.

VS abbreviation versus.

V-sign noun **1** Brit. a rude gesture made by holding up the hand with the back facing outwards and making a V-shape with the first two fingers. **2** a similar gesture made with the palm of the hand facing outwards, used as a symbol of victory.

VSO abbreviation Voluntary Service Overseas.

VSOP abbreviation Very Special Old Pale, a kind of brandy.

VT abbreviation Vermont.

VTOL abbreviation vertical take-off and landing.

vulcanism noun variant spelling of **VOLCANISM**.

vulcanite /vul-kuh-nyt/ noun hard black vulcanized rubber.
– ORIGIN from *Vulcan*, the Roman god of fire.

vulcanize (or **vulcanise**) /vul-kuh-nyz/ verb harden rubber by treating it with sulphur at a high temperature.
– DERIVATIVES **vulcanization** noun.

vulcanology noun variant spelling of **VOLCANOLOGY**.

vulgar adjective **1** lacking sophistication or good taste: *a vulgar check suit.* **2** referring to sex or bodily functions in a rude way. **3** dated relating to or typical of ordinary people.
– DERIVATIVES **vulgarity** noun (pl. **vulgarities**) **vulgarly** adverb.
– ORIGIN Latin *vulgaris.*

vulgar fraction noun Brit. a fraction expressed by numerator and denominator (numbers above and below the line).

vulgarian /vul-gair-i-uhn/ noun a person who lacks good taste and sophistication, especially one who is wealthy.

vulgarism noun a word or expression that refers to sex or bodily functions in a rude way.

vulgarize (or **vulgarise**) verb spoil something by making it ordinary or less refined.
– DERIVATIVES **vulgarization** noun.

vulgar Latin noun informal Latin of classical times.

Vulgate /vul-gayt/ noun the main Latin version of the Bible, prepared in the 4th century and later revised and adopted as the official version for the Roman Catholic Church.
– ORIGIN from Latin *vulgata editio* 'edition prepared for the public'.

vulnerable /vul-nuh-ruh-b'l/ adjective exposed to the possibility of being attacked or harmed: *manoeuvre your opponent into a vulnerable position.*
– DERIVATIVES **vulnerability** noun (pl. **vulnerabilities**) **vulnerably** adverb.
– ORIGIN Latin *vulnerabilis.*

vulpine /vul-pyn/ adjective relating to or resembling a fox or foxes.
– ORIGIN Latin *vulpinus.*

vulture /vul-cher/ noun **1** a large bird of prey without feathers on the head and neck, that feeds on dead animals. **2** a person who tries to benefit from the difficulties of others.
– ORIGIN Latin *vulturius.*

vulva /vul-vuh/ noun the female external genitals.
– DERIVATIVES **vulval** adjective.
– ORIGIN Latin, 'womb'.

vying present participle of **VIE**.

Ww

W¹ (also **w**) noun (pl. **Ws** or **W's**) the twenty-third letter of the alphabet.

W² abbreviation **1** watt(s). **2** West or Western. **3** Cricket (on scorecards) wicket(s). **4** (in tables of sports results) won. •symbol the chemical element tungsten. [from Latin *wolframium*.]

w abbreviation **1** Cricket (on scorecards) wide(s). **2** with.

WA abbreviation **1** Washington (State). **2** Western Australia.

wacko (also **whacko**) informal, chiefly N. Amer. adjective mad; insane. •noun (pl. **wackos** or **wackoes**) a mad person.

wacky (also **whacky**) adjective (**wackier**, **wackiest**) informal funny or amusing in a slightly odd way.
– DERIVATIVES **wackily** adverb **wackiness** noun.
– ORIGIN from **WHACK**.

wad /wod/ noun **1** a lump or bundle of a soft material, used for padding, stuffing, or wiping. **2** a bundle or roll of paper or banknotes. •verb (**wads**, **wadding**, **wadded**) **1** compress a soft material into a wad. **2** line or fill something with soft material.
– DERIVATIVES **wadding** noun.
– ORIGIN perhaps from Dutch *watten*, French *ouate* 'padding, cotton wool'.

waddle verb walk with short steps and a clumsy swaying motion. •noun a waddling way of walking.
– ORIGIN perhaps from **WADE**.

wade verb **1** walk through water or mud. **2** (**wade through**) read or deal with something that is boring and takes a long time. **3** (**wade in/into**) informal attack or intervene in a forceful way: *he waded into the debate, calling for the policy to be scrapped.* •noun an act of wading.
– ORIGIN Old English, 'move onward', also 'penetrate'.

wader noun **1** a long-legged bird that feeds in shallow water, such as a sandpiper. **2** (**waders**) high waterproof boots, used by anglers.

wadi /wah-di, wod-i/ noun (pl. **wadis**) (in Arabic-speaking countries) a valley, ravine, or channel that is dry except in the rainy season.
– ORIGIN Arabic.

wafer noun **1** a very thin, light, crisp sweet biscuit. **2** a thin disc of unleavened bread used in the Christian service of Holy Communion. **3** a very thin slice of a semiconductor crystal used in solid-state electric circuits.
– ORIGIN Old French *gaufre* 'honeycomb'.

wafer-thin adjective & adverb very thin or thinly.

waffle¹ Brit. informal verb speak or write at length in a vague or trivial way. •noun lengthy but vague or trivial talk or writing.
– DERIVATIVES **waffler** noun **waffly** adjective.
– ORIGIN from dialect *waff* 'yelp'.

waffle² noun a small crisp batter cake with a squared pattern on both sides, eaten hot with butter or syrup.
– ORIGIN Dutch *wafel*.

waft /woft/ verb **1** move easily or gently through the air. **2** move along with a gliding motion: *models wafted down the catwalk in filmy skirts.* •noun **1** a scent carried in the air. **2** a gentle movement of air.
– ORIGIN from German or Dutch *wachten* 'to guard'.

wag¹ verb (**wags**, **wagging**, **wagged**) move rapidly to and fro. •noun a wagging movement.
– ORIGIN Old English, 'to sway'.

wag² noun informal a person who likes making jokes.
– ORIGIN probably from former *waghalter* 'person likely to be hanged'.

wage noun (also **wages**) **1** a fixed regular payment for work, typically paid daily or weekly. **2** the result or effect of doing something wrong or unwise: *disasters are the wages of sin.* •verb carry on a war or campaign.
– DERIVATIVES **waged** adjective.
– ORIGIN Old French.

wager noun & verb more formal term for **BET**.
– ORIGIN from Old French, 'to wage'.

waggish adjective informal humorous in a playful way.
– DERIVATIVES **waggishly** adverb.

waggle verb move with short quick movements from side to side or up and down. •noun an act of waggling.
– DERIVATIVES **waggler** noun **waggly** adjective.
– ORIGIN from **WAG¹**.

Wagnerian /vahg-neer-i-uhn/ adjective relating to or typical of the German composer Richard Wagner or his work.

wagon (Brit. also **waggon**) noun **1** a vehicle, especially a horse-drawn one, for transporting goods. **2** Brit. a railway vehicle for carrying goods in bulk. **3** chiefly N. Amer. a wheeled cart or hut used as a food stall.
– PHRASES **on** (or **off**) **the wagon** informal not drinking (or drinking) any alcohol.
– DERIVATIVES **wagoner** noun **wagonload** noun.

w

– ORIGIN Dutch *wagen*.

wagon-lit /va-gon-**lee**/ noun (pl. **wagons-lits** pronunc. same) a sleeping car on a train in continental Europe.
– ORIGIN from French *wagon* 'railway coach' + *lit* 'bed'.

wagtail noun a slender songbird with a long tail that wags up and down.

wah-wah noun a musical effect achieved on an electric guitar by use of a pedal and on brass instruments by alternately applying and removing a mute.
– ORIGIN imitating the sound.

waif noun 1 a homeless and helpless person, especially a child. 2 a person who appears thin or pale.
– DERIVATIVES **waifish** adjective **waiflike** adjective.
– ORIGIN first referring to an unclaimed piece of property: from Old French *gaif*.

wail noun 1 a long high-pitched cry of pain, grief, or anger. 2 a long high-pitched sound. • verb make a long high-pitched cry or sound.
– DERIVATIVES **wailer** noun.
– ORIGIN Old Norse.

wain noun old use a wagon or cart.
– ORIGIN Old English.

wainscot /**wayn**-skot, wayn-skuht/ (also **wainscoting** or **wainscotting**) noun an area of wooden panelling on the lower part of the walls of a room.
– DERIVATIVES **wainscoted** (also **wainscotted**) adjective.
– ORIGIN German *wagenschot*.

waist noun 1 the part of the body below the ribs and above the hips. 2 a narrow part in the middle of something such as a violin.
– DERIVATIVES **waisted** adjective.
– ORIGIN probably from an Old English word related to **wax²**.

waistband noun a strip of cloth forming the waist of a skirt or a pair of trousers.

waistcoat noun Brit. a close-fitting waist-length item of clothing with buttons down the front and without sleeves or a collar.

waistline noun 1 the measurement around a person's body at the waist. 2 the shaping and position of the waist of an item of clothing.

wait verb 1 stay in a particular place or delay action until a particular time or event. 2 be delayed or postponed: *he needs a shirt but that can wait*. 3 (**wait on**) act as an attendant to. 4 serve food and drink to people at a meal or in a restaurant. • noun a period of waiting.
– PHRASES **in wait** watching for someone and preparing to attack them.
– ORIGIN Old French *waitier*.

waiter (or **waitress**) noun a person whose job is to serve customers at their tables in a restaurant.

waiting list noun a list of people waiting for something that is not immediately available.

waiting room noun a room for people who are waiting, for example to see a doctor or to catch a train.

waive verb choose not to insist on or demand a right or claim.
– ORIGIN Old French *gaiver* 'allow to become a waif, abandon'.

USAGE: **Waive** is sometimes confused with **wave**. **Waive** means 'choose not to insist on or demand a right or claim' (*he waived all rights to the money*), whereas the much more common word **wave** means 'move to and fro' (*the flag waved in the wind*).

waiver noun 1 an act of not insisting on a right or claim. 2 a document recording this.

wake¹ verb (past **woke** or chiefly US **waked**; past part. **woken** or chiefly US **waked**) 1 (often **wake up**) stop or cause someone to stop sleeping. 2 bring to life; stir: *his voice wakes desire in others*. 3 (**wake up to**) realize or become alert to something. • noun 1 (especially in Ireland) a party held after a funeral. 2 a watch held beside the body of someone who has died.
– ORIGIN Old English.

wake² noun a trail of disturbed water or air left by the passage of a ship or aircraft.
– PHRASES **in the wake of** following as a result of.
– ORIGIN probably from an Old Norse word meaning 'opening in ice' (as made by a ship).

wakeboarding noun the sport of riding on a short, wide board resembling a surfboard while being towed behind a motorboat.
– DERIVATIVES **wakeboard** noun **wakeboarder** noun.

wakeful adjective 1 unable or not needing to sleep. 2 alert and aware of possible danger.
– DERIVATIVES **wakefulness** noun.

waken verb wake someone from sleep.
– ORIGIN Old English, 'be aroused'.

wake-up call noun something that alerts people to an unsatisfactory situation.

Waldorf salad /**wawl**-dorf/ noun a salad made from apples, walnuts, celery, and mayonnaise.
– ORIGIN named after the *Waldorf*-Astoria Hotel in New York, where it was first served.

wale noun 1 a ridge on a textured fabric such as corduroy. 2 a horizontal wooden strip fitted to strengthen a boat's side.
– ORIGIN Old English, 'stripe, weal'.

walk verb 1 move on foot at a regular and fairly slow pace. 2 travel over a route or area on foot. 3 accompany or guide someone on foot. 4 take a dog out for exercise. 5 N. Amer. informal be released from suspicion or from a charge. • noun 1 a journey on foot. 2 an unhurried rate of movement on foot. 3 a route or path for walking. 4 a person's way of walking.
– PHRASES **walk it** informal achieve a victory easily. **walk off** (or **away**) **with** informal 1 steal something. 2 win something. **walk of life** the position within society that someone holds. **walk out** leave suddenly or angrily. **walk over** informal 1 treat someone thoughtlessly or unfairly. 2 defeat someone easily.
– DERIVATIVES **walkable** adjective **walker** noun.
– ORIGIN Old English, 'roll, toss', also 'wander'.

walkabout noun 1 chiefly Brit. an informal stroll among a crowd conducted by an important visitor. 2 a journey (originally on foot) undertaken by an Australian Aboriginal in order to live in the traditional way.

walkie-talkie noun a portable two-way radio.

walk-in adjective (of a storage area) large enough to walk into.

walking frame noun Brit. a frame used by

disabled or infirm people for support while walking.

walking stick noun a stick with a curved handle used for support when walking.

Walkman noun (pl. **Walkmans** or **Walkmen**) trademark a type of personal stereo.

walk-on adjective (of a part in a play or film) small and not involving any speaking.

walkout noun a sudden angry departure, especially as industrial action.

walkover noun an easy victory.

walkway noun a raised passageway in a building, or a wide path outdoors.

wall noun **1** a continuous upright structure forming the side of a building or room or enclosing or dividing an area of land. **2** a barrier or obstacle to progress: *police met a wall of silence from witnesses.* **3** Football a line of defenders forming a barrier against a free kick taken near the penalty area. **4** the outer layer or lining of a bodily organ or cavity. •verb **1** enclose an area within walls. **2** (**wall something up**) block or seal a place with a wall. **3** (**wall someone/thing in/up**) surround or imprison someone or something with a wall or barrier.
– PHRASES **drive someone** (or **go**) **up the wall** informal make someone (or become) very irritated. **go to the wall** informal (of a business) fail. **off the wall** N. Amer. informal eccentric or unconventional. **wall-to-wall 1** (of a carpet) fitted to cover an entire floor. **2** informal very numerous or plentiful.
– DERIVATIVES **walling** noun.
– ORIGIN Latin *vallum* 'rampart'.

wallaby noun (pl. **wallabies**) an Australasian marsupial resembling a small kangaroo.
– ORIGIN Dharuk (an Aboriginal language).

wallah /wol-luh/ noun Indian or informal a person of a specified kind or having a specified role: *an office wallah.*
– ORIGIN from a Hindi word ending meaning 'doer' (often taken to mean 'fellow').

wall bars plural noun Brit. parallel horizontal bars attached to the wall of a gymnasium, on which exercises are performed.

wallcovering noun material such as wallpaper used as a decorative covering for interior walls.

wallet noun **1** a pocket-sized, flat, folding holder for money and plastic cards. **2** old use a bag for holding provisions when travelling.
– ORIGIN probably from Germanic.

wall-eyed adjective **1** having an eye or eyes that squint outwards. **2** having an eye with a streaked or opaque white iris.
– ORIGIN Old Norse.

wallflower noun **1** a plant with fragrant flowers that bloom in early spring. **2** informal a girl who does not have a man to dance with at a dance or party.

Walloon /wol-loon/ noun **1** a member of a people who speak a French dialect and live in southern and eastern Belgium and neighbouring parts of France. **2** the French dialect spoken by the Walloons.
– ORIGIN French *Wallon.*

wallop informal verb (**wallops, walloping, walloped**) **1** hit someone or something very hard. **2** heavily defeat an opponent. **3** (as adj. **walloping**) very large or great: *walloping energy bills.* •noun a heavy blow or punch.
– ORIGIN Old French *waloper* 'to gallop'.

wallow verb **1** roll about or lie in mud or shallow water. **2** (of a boat or aircraft) roll from side to side. **3** (**wallow in**) enjoy something without restraint: *he wallowed in self-pity, drinking neat brandy.* •noun **1** an act of wallowing. **2** an area of mud or shallow water where mammals go to wallow.
– ORIGIN Old English.

wallpaper noun **1** paper pasted in strips over the walls of a room to provide a decorative or textured surface. **2** an optional background pattern or picture on a computer or mobile phone screen. •verb apply wallpaper to a wall or room.

wally noun (pl. **wallies**) Brit. informal a silly or incompetent person.
– ORIGIN perhaps a shortened form of the man's name *Walter.*

walnut noun **1** an edible wrinkled nut with a hard round shell. **2** the tree which produces walnuts, a source of valuable ornamental wood.
– ORIGIN Old English, 'foreign nut'.

walrus noun a large sea mammal with two large downward-pointing tusks, found in the Arctic Ocean.
– ORIGIN probably Dutch.

walrus moustache noun a long, thick, drooping moustache.

waltz /wawlts, wolts/ noun a dance in triple time performed by a couple, who turn round and round as they progress around the dance floor. •verb **1** dance a waltz. **2** move or behave in a casual, or inconsiderate way: *she waltzed in and took all the credit.*
– ORIGIN German *Walzer.*

waltzer noun **1** a person who dances the waltz. **2** a fairground ride in which cars spin round as they are carried round a track that moves up and down.

wampum /wom-puhm/ noun historical a string of small cylindrical beads made by North American Indians from shells, worn as a decorative belt or used as money.
– ORIGIN Algonquian.

WAN abbreviation Computing wide area network.

wan /won/ adjective **1** (of a person) pale and appearing ill or exhausted. **2** (of light) pale; weak. **3** (of a smile) lacking enthusiasm; strained.
– DERIVATIVES **wanly** adverb.
– ORIGIN Old English, 'dark, black'.

wand noun **1** a rod used in casting magic spells or performing conjuring tricks. **2** a staff or rod held as a symbol of office. **3** a hand-held electronic device passed over a bar code to read the data.
– ORIGIN Old Norse.

wander verb **1** walk or move in a leisurely, casual, or aimless way. **2** move slowly away from a fixed point or place: *my attention had wandered.* •noun an act or spell of wandering.
– DERIVATIVES **wanderer** noun **wanderings** plural noun.
– ORIGIN Old English.

wanderlust noun a strong desire to travel.

W

– ORIGIN German.

wane verb 1 (of the moon) appear to become smaller each day as a result of having a decreasing area of its surface illuminated by the sun. 2 decrease in strength or extent: *confidence in the dollar waned.*
– PHRASES **on the wane** becoming smaller, or less important or common.
– ORIGIN Old English, 'lessen'.

wangle informal verb obtain something desired by persuasion or cunning.
– DERIVATIVES **wangler** noun.
– ORIGIN unknown.

wank Brit. vulgar slang verb (also **wank off**) masturbate. • noun an act of masturbating.
– ORIGIN unknown.

wanker noun Brit. vulgar slang a stupid or disliked person.

wanna contraction informal want to; want a.

wannabe /won-nuh-bee/ noun informal, derogatory a person who wants to be like someone famous.

want verb 1 feel a need or desire to have or do something. 2 (**be wanted**) (of a suspected criminal) be sought by the police. 3 informal should or need to do something: *you don't want to believe all you hear.* 4 (often **want for**) literary lack something desirable or essential. 5 desire someone sexually. 6 informal, chiefly Brit. (of a thing) need something to be done: *the wheel wants greasing.* • noun 1 a lack or shortage of something. 2 lack of essentials; poverty. 3 a desire.
– ORIGIN Old Norse, 'be lacking'.

wanting adjective 1 lacking in something required or desired. 2 not good enough; unsatisfactory: *workers who are found wanting face dismissal.*

wanton adjective 1 (of a cruel or violent action) deliberate and unprovoked. 2 (especially of a woman) having many sexual partners. • noun old use a woman who has many sexual partners.
– DERIVATIVES **wantonly** adverb **wantonness** noun.
– ORIGIN first meaning 'rebellious': from former *wan-* 'badly' + an Old English word meaning 'trained'.

WAP abbreviation Wireless Application Protocol, a means of enabling a mobile phone to browse the Internet and display data.

wapiti /wop-i-ti/ noun (pl. **wapitis**) a large North American red deer.
– ORIGIN Shawnee, 'white rump'.

War. abbreviation Warwickshire.

war noun 1 a state of armed conflict between different nations, states, or groups. 2 a state of hostility or intense competition between groups. 3 a campaign against something undesirable: *a war on drugs.* • verb (**wars, warring, warred**) take part in a war.
– ORIGIN from Old French *guerre.*

warble verb 1 (of a bird) sing with a succession of constantly changing notes. 2 (of a person) sing in a trilling or quavering voice. • noun a warbling sound.
– ORIGIN Old French *werbler.*

warble fly noun a large fly which lays its eggs on cattle, horses, and other mammals, the larvae of which form a swelling or abscess beneath the skin.
– ORIGIN uncertain.

warbler noun a small songbird with a warbling song, typically living in trees and bushes.

war chest noun a reserve of funds used for fighting a war.

war crime noun an act carried out during a war that violates accepted international rules of war.

ward noun 1 a room or division in a hospital for one or more patients. 2 an administrative division of a city or borough that is represented by a councillor or councillors. 3 a child or young person under the care and control of a guardian appointed by their parents or a court. 4 any of the ridges or bars inside a lock which prevent the turning of any key without corresponding grooves. • verb (**ward someone/thing off**) prevent someone or something from harming or affecting one.
– DERIVATIVES **wardship** noun.
– ORIGIN Old English, 'keep safe, guard'.

-ward (also **-wards**) suffix 1 (usu. **-wards**) (forming adverbs) towards the specified place or direction: *homewards.* 2 (usu. **-ward**) (forming adjectives) turned or tending towards: *upward.*
– ORIGIN Old English.

warden noun 1 a person responsible for supervising a particular place or procedure. 2 Brit. the head of certain schools, colleges, or other institutions. 3 chiefly N. Amer. a prison governor.
– DERIVATIVES **wardenship** noun.
– ORIGIN Old French *wardein, guarden* 'guardian'.

warder noun (fem. **wardress**) chiefly Brit. a prison guard.
– ORIGIN from Old French *warder* 'to guard'.

wardrobe noun 1 a large, tall cupboard for hanging clothes in. 2 a person's entire collection of clothes. 3 the costume department or costumes of a theatre or film company.
– ORIGIN Old French *warderobe, garderobe* 'private chamber'.

wardroom noun a room on board a warship in which commissioned officers eat and relax.

-wards suffix variant spelling of **-WARD**.

ware noun 1 pottery of a specified type: *porcelain ware.* 2 manufactured articles of a specified type. 3 (**wares**) articles offered for sale.
– ORIGIN Old English, 'commodities'.

warehouse /wair-howss/ noun 1 a large building where raw materials or manufactured goods are stored. 2 a large wholesale or retail store. • verb /also wair-howz/ store goods in a warehouse.

warfare noun the activities involved in fighting a war.

warfarin /wor-fuh-rin/ noun a compound used as a rat poison and as a drug to prevent blood clotting.
– ORIGIN from the initial letters of *Wisconsin Alumni Research Foundation* + *-arin.*

war game noun 1 a military exercise to test or improve tactical skill. 2 a mock military conflict carried out as a game or sport.

warhead noun the explosive head of a missile, torpedo, or similar weapon.

warhorse noun informal a veteran soldier, politician, etc. who has fought many campaigns or contests.

warlike adjective **1** tending to wage war; hostile. **2** relating to or prepared for war.

warlock noun a man who practises witchcraft.
– ORIGIN Old English, 'traitor, scoundrel, monster', also 'the Devil'.

warlord noun a military commander, especially one who has complete control of a region.
– DERIVATIVES **warlordism** noun.

warm adjective **1** of or at a fairly high temperature. **2** (of clothes or coverings) made of a material that helps the body to retain heat. **3** enthusiastic, affectionate, or kind: *a warm welcome.* **4** (of a colour) containing red, yellow, or orange tones. **5** (of a scent or trail) fresh and easy to follow. **6** close to finding or guessing something. •verb **1** make or become warm. **2** (**warm to/towards**) become more interested in or enthusiastic about someone or something. •noun **1** (**the warm**) a warm place or area. **2** an act of warming.
– PHRASES **warm up 1** prepare for exercise by doing gentle stretches and exercises. **2** (of an engine or electrical device) reach a temperature high enough to operate efficiently. **warm something up** entertain an audience to make them more enthusiastic before the arrival of the main act.
– DERIVATIVES **warmer** noun **warmly** adverb **warmness** noun.
– ORIGIN Old English.

warm-blooded adjective **1** (of animals, chiefly mammals and birds) that maintain a constant body temperature by their metabolism. **2** passionate or spirited.

warm-hearted adjective sympathetic and kind.

warmonger /wor-mung-ger/ noun a person who tries to bring about war.

warmth noun **1** the quality, state, or feeling of being warm. **2** enthusiasm, affection, or kindness. **3** intensity of emotion.

warn verb **1** inform someone about a possible danger or problem. **2** advise someone not to do something wrong or foolish. **3** (**warn someone off**) order someone to keep away or to refrain from doing something.
– ORIGIN Old English.

warning noun **1** a statement or event that indicates a possible danger or problem. **2** advice against doing something wrong or foolish. **3** advance notice: *he arrived without warning.*
– DERIVATIVES **warningly** adverb.

warp verb **1** make or become bent or twisted as a result of heat or damp. **2** make abnormal or strange; distort: *his hatred has warped his judgement.* •noun **1** a distortion or twist in shape. **2** (in weaving) the lengthwise threads on a loom over and under which the weft threads are passed to make cloth.
– ORIGIN Old English.

warpaint noun **1** paint traditionally used to decorate the face and body before battle, especially by North American Indians. **2** informal elaborate or excessive make-up.

warpath noun (in phrase **on the warpath**) in an angry or aggressive state.
– ORIGIN with reference to American Indians heading towards a battle.

warplane noun an aircraft designed and equipped to take part in air combat or to drop bombs.

warrant noun **1** an official authorization giving the police or another body the power to make an arrest, search somewhere, etc. **2** a document entitling the holder to receive goods, money, or services. **3** justification or authority: *there is no warrant for this assumption.* **4** an official certificate of appointment issued to an officer of lower rank than a commissioned officer. •verb **1** make necessary or justify a course of action. **2** officially state or guarantee something.
– PHRASES **I** (or **I'll**) **warrant** dated no doubt.
– DERIVATIVES **warrantable** adjective.
– ORIGIN first meaning 'protector' and 'protect from danger': from Old French *guarant, guarantir.*

warrant officer noun a rank of officer in the army, RAF, or US navy, below the commissioned officers and above the non-commissioned officers.

warranty noun (pl. **warranties**) **1** a written guarantee promising to repair or replace an article if necessary within a specified period. **2** a guarantee by a person who is insured that certain statements are true or that certain conditions shall be fulfilled, the breach of which will make the policy invalid.

warren noun **1** a network of interconnecting rabbit burrows. **2** a complex network of paths or passages.
– ORIGIN Old French *garenne* 'game park'.

warrior noun (especially in the past) a brave or experienced soldier or fighter.
– ORIGIN Old French *werreior, guerreior.*

warship noun a ship equipped with weapons and designed to take part in warfare at sea.

wart noun **1** a small, hard, growth on the skin, caused by a virus. **2** any rounded lump or growth on the skin of an animal or the surface of a plant.
– PHRASES **warts and all** informal including faults or unattractive qualities.
– DERIVATIVES **warty** adjective.
– ORIGIN Old English.

warthog noun an African wild pig with a large head, warty lumps on the face, and curved tusks.

wartime noun a period during which a war is taking place.

wary adjective (**warier, wariest**) (often **wary of**) cautious about possible dangers or problems.
– DERIVATIVES **warily** adverb **wariness** noun.
– ORIGIN from Old English, 'be on one's guard'.

was first and third person singular past of BE.

wasabi /wuh-sah-bi/ noun an edible Japanese plant with a thick green root which tastes like strong horseradish.
– ORIGIN Japanese.

wash verb **1** clean someone or something with water and, typically, soap or detergent. **2** (of flowing water) carry or move: *floods washed*

W

away the bridges. **3** be carried by flowing water. **4** informal seem convincing or genuine: *excuses just don't wash with us.* **5** brush something with a thin coat of dilute paint or ink. • noun **1** an act of washing or an instance of being washed. **2** a quantity of clothes needing to be or just having been washed. **3** the water or air disturbed by a moving boat or aircraft. **4** a medicinal or cleansing liquid: *antiseptic skin wash.* **5** a thin coating of paint or metal. **6** silt or gravel carried by water and deposited as sediment.
– PHRASES **be washed out** be postponed or cancelled because of rain. **come out in the wash** informal be resolved eventually. **wash one's dirty linen in public** informal discuss one's personal affairs in public. **wash one's hands of** take no further responsibility for. [with reference to Pontius Pilate washing his hands after the condemnation of Christ (Gospel of Matthew, chapter 27).] **wash over** occur all around without greatly affecting: *she allowed the conversation to wash over her.* **wash up** chiefly Brit. wash crockery and cutlery after use.
– DERIVATIVES **washable** adjective.
– ORIGIN Old English.

washbag noun Brit. a bag for toiletries.

washbasin noun a basin used for washing the hands and face.

washboard noun **1** a ridged or corrugated board against which clothes are scrubbed during washing. **2** a similar board played as a percussion instrument by scraping. • adjective (of a person's stomach) lean and with well-defined muscles.

washed out adjective **1** faded by repeated washing. **2** pale and tired.

washed-up adjective informal no longer effective or successful.

washer noun **1** a person or device that washes. **2** a small flat ring fixed between a nut and bolt to spread the pressure or between two joining surfaces to prevent leakage.

washerwoman noun (pl. **washerwomen**) a woman whose occupation is washing clothes.

washing noun a quantity of clothes, bedlinen, etc. that is to be washed or has just been washed.

washing machine noun a machine for washing clothes, bedlinen, etc.

washing powder noun Brit. powdered detergent for washing laundry.

washing soda noun sodium carbonate, used dissolved in water for washing and cleaning.

washing-up noun Brit. crockery, cutlery, and other kitchen utensils that are to be washed.

washout noun informal a disappointing failure.

washroom noun N. Amer. a room with washing and toilet facilities.

washstand noun chiefly historical a piece of furniture designed to hold a jug, bowl, or basin for washing the hands and face.

washtub noun a large metal tub for washing laundry.

washy adjective (**washier**, **washiest**) **1** (of colour) pale. **2** old use (of food or drink) too watery.

wasn't contraction was not.

Wasp (also **WASP**) noun N. Amer. an upper-class or middle-class American white Protestant, regarded as a member of the most powerful social group.
– ORIGIN from *white Anglo-Saxon Protestant.*

wasp noun a stinging winged insect which typically nests in complex colonies and has a black and yellow-striped body.
– ORIGIN Old English.

waspie noun (pl. **waspies**) a woman's corset or belt designed to emphasize a slender waist.

waspish adjective sharply irritable.
– DERIVATIVES **waspishly** adverb **waspishness** noun.

wasp-waisted adjective having a very narrow waist.

wassail /wos-sayl, wos-s'l/ old use noun **1** spiced ale or mulled wine drunk during celebrations for Twelfth Night and Christmas Eve. **2** lively festivities involving the drinking of much alcohol. • verb **1** celebrate with much alcohol. **2** go from house to house at Christmas singing carols.
– ORIGIN Old Norse, 'be in good health!'

wast /wost, wuhst/ old use or dialect second person singular past of **BE**.

wastage noun **1** the action of wasting something. **2** an amount wasted. **3** (also **natural wastage**) Brit. the reduction in the size of a workforce as a result of employees willingly resigning or retiring rather than being made redundant.

waste verb **1** use more of something than is necessary or useful. **2** fail to make good use of: *we're wasted in this job.* **3** (**be wasted on**) not be appreciated by someone. **4** gradually become weaker and thinner: *she was wasting away from tuberculosis.* **5** N. Amer. informal kill someone. **6** (as adj. **wasted**) informal under the influence of alcohol or illegal drugs. • adjective **1** removed or discarded as no longer useful or required. **2** (of an area of land) not used, cultivated, or built on. • noun **1** an act or instance of wasting something: *it's a waste of time trying to find him.* **2** unusable or unwanted material or by-products. **3** a large area of barren, uninhabited land.
– PHRASES **go to waste** be wasted. **lay waste (to)** completely destroy a place.
– ORIGIN Old French.

waste-disposal unit noun Brit. an electric device fitted to the waste pipe of a kitchen sink for grinding up food waste.

wasteful adjective using or using up something carelessly or extravagantly.
– DERIVATIVES **wastefully** adverb **wastefulness** noun.

wasteland noun **1** a barren or empty area of land. **2** a situation, time, or place lacking in culture, spirituality, or intellectual activity: *the mid 70s are now seen as a cultural wasteland.*

waster noun **1** a wasteful person or thing. **2** informal a person who does little or nothing of value.

wastrel /way-struhl/ noun literary a lazy person who spend their time and money in a careless way.
– ORIGIN from **WASTE**.

wat /wat/ noun (in SE Asia) a Buddhist monastery or temple.
– ORIGIN Thai.

W

watch verb **1** look at someone or something with attention or interest. **2** keep someone or something under careful observation. **3** treat with caution or control: *watch what you say!* **4** (**watch for**) look out for. **5** (**watch out**) be careful. • noun **1** a small timepiece usually worn on a strap on the wrist. **2** an act or instance of watching. **3** a period of keeping alert for danger or trouble during the night. **4** a fixed period of duty on a ship, usually lasting four hours. **5** a shift worked by firefighters or police officers. **6** (also **night watch**) historical a watchman or watchmen who patrolled the streets of a town at night.
– PHRASES **keep watch** stay on the lookout for danger or trouble. **watch one's back** protect oneself against unexpected danger.
– DERIVATIVES **watcher** noun.
– ORIGIN Old English.

watchable adjective (of a film or television programme) fairly enjoyable to watch.

watchdog noun **1** a dog kept to guard private property. **2** a person or group that monitors the practices of companies providing a particular service.

watchful adjective alert to possible difficulty or danger.
– DERIVATIVES **watchfully** adverb **watchfulness** noun.

watching brief noun **1** an interest in a matter in which one is not directly involved. **2** Law, Brit. instructions held by a barrister to follow a case on behalf of a client who is not directly involved.

watchmaker noun a person who makes and repairs watches and clocks.
– DERIVATIVES **watchmaking** noun.

watchman noun (pl. **watchmen**) a man employed to look after an empty building, especially at night.

watchtower noun a tower built to create a high observation point.

watchword noun a word or phrase expressing the central aim or belief of a person or group.

water noun **1** the liquid which forms the seas, lakes, rivers, and rain and is the basis of the fluids of living organisms. **2** (**waters**) an area of sea under the legal authority of a particular country. **3** (**the waters**) the water of a mineral spring used for medicinal purposes. **4** (**waters**) the fluid surrounding a fetus in the womb, especially as passed from a woman's body shortly before she gives birth. **5** the quality of transparency and brilliance shown by a diamond or other gem. • verb **1** pour water over a plant or an area of ground. **2** give a drink of water to an animal. **3** (of the eyes or mouth) produce tears or saliva: *the smell of bacon made my mouth water.* **4** dilute a drink with water. **5** (**water something down**) make something less forceful or controversial by changing or leaving out certain details. **6** (of a river) flow through an area.
– PHRASES **hold water** (of a theory) seem valid or reasonable. **pass water** euphemistic urinate. **of the first water** of the highest degree: *she was a bore of the first water.* [first referring to a gem of the greatest brilliance and transparency.] **under water** submerged; flooded. **water on the brain** informal hydrocephalus. **water under**

the bridge past events that are over and done with.
– DERIVATIVES **waterless** adjective.
– ORIGIN Old English.

water bailiff noun Brit. an official who enforces fishing laws.

water-based adjective (of a substance or solution) using or having water as a medium or main ingredient.

waterbed noun a bed with a water-filled rubber or plastic mattress.

waterbird noun a bird that lives on or near water.

water birth noun a birth in which the mother spends the final stages of labour in a birthing pool.

water biscuit noun a thin, crisp unsweetened biscuit made from flour and water.

water boatman noun a bug that lives in water and swims on its back using its back legs as oars.

water buffalo noun a large black Asian buffalo with heavy swept-back horns, used for carrying heavy loads.

water cannon noun a device that sends out a powerful jet of water, used to disperse a crowd.

water chestnut noun the crisp, white-fleshed tuber of a tropical plant, used in oriental cookery.

water closet noun dated a flush toilet.

watercolour (US **watercolor**) noun **1** artists' paint that is thinned with water rather than oil. **2** a picture painted with watercolours. **3** the art of painting with watercolours.
– DERIVATIVES **watercolourist** noun.

watercourse noun a brook, stream, or artificially constructed water channel.

watercraft noun (pl. same) **1** a boat or other vessel. **2** skill in sailing and other activities which take place on water.

watercress noun a cress which grows in running water and whose strong-tasting leaves are used in salad.

water diviner noun Brit. a person who searches for underground water by using a divining rod.

waterfall noun a stream of water falling from a height, formed when a river or stream flows over a precipice or steep slope.

water feature noun a pond or fountain in a garden.

waterfowl plural noun ducks, geese, or other large waterbirds.

waterfront noun a part of a town or city alongside a body of water.

waterhole noun a hollow in which water collects, typically one at which animals drink.

water ice noun a frozen dessert consisting of fruit juice or purée in a sugar syrup.

watering can noun a portable water container with a long spout and a detachable perforated cap, used for watering plants.

watering hole noun **1** a waterhole from which animals regularly drink. **2** informal a pub or bar.

watering place noun **1** a watering hole. **2** a spa or seaside resort.

W

water level noun the height reached by the water in a river, tank, etc.

water lily noun a plant that grows in water, with large round floating leaves and large cup-shaped flowers.

waterline noun 1 the level normally reached by the water on the side of a ship. 2 a line on a shore, riverbank, etc. marking the level reached by the sea or a river.

waterlogged adjective saturated with or full of water.
– ORIGIN from former *waterlog* 'make a ship unmanageable by flooding'.

Waterloo noun (usu. in phrase **meet one's Waterloo**) a decisive defeat or failure.
– ORIGIN from *Waterloo*, a village in what is now Belgium, site of a battle in which Napoleon was finally defeated.

water main noun the main pipe in a water supply system.

waterman noun (pl. **watermen**) a person who provides transport by boat.

watermark noun a faint design made in some paper that is visible when held against the light, identifying the maker. •verb mark paper with a watermark.

water meadow noun a meadow that is periodically flooded by a stream or river.

watermelon noun a large melon-like fruit with smooth green skin, red pulp, and watery juice.

watermill noun a mill worked by a waterwheel.

water pistol noun a toy pistol that shoots a jet of water.

water polo noun a seven-a-side game played by swimmers in a pool, with a ball like a football that the players try to throw into their opponents' net.

waterproof adjective preventing water from passing through. •noun Brit. a waterproof garment. •verb make something waterproof.

water rat noun 1 a large rat-like rodent that lives both on land and in water. 2 Brit. a water vole.

water-resistant adjective partially able to prevent water from passing through.

watershed noun 1 an area or ridge of land that separates waters flowing to different rivers, basins, or seas. 2 a turning point in a situation: *the band's success produced a watershed in popular music.* 3 Brit. the time after which programmes that are unsuitable for children are broadcast on television.
– ORIGIN from **WATER** + *shed* in the sense 'ridge of high ground' (related to **SHED²**).

waterside noun the area next to a sea, lake, or river.

waterski noun (pl. **waterskis**) each of a pair of skis enabling the wearer to skim the surface of the water when towed by a motorboat. •verb (**waterskis, waterskiing, waterskied**) travel on waterskis.
– DERIVATIVES **waterskier** noun.

waterspout noun a funnel-shaped column of water and spray formed by a whirlwind occurring over the sea.

water table noun the level below which the ground is saturated with water.

watertight adjective 1 closely sealed, fastened, or fitted so as to prevent the passage of water. 2 (of an argument or account) unable to be disputed or questioned.

water tower noun a tower supporting a water tank at a height to create enough pressure to distribute the water through a system of pipes.

water vole noun a large vole living both on land and in water, which digs burrows in the banks of rivers.

waterway noun a river, canal, or other route for travel by water.

waterweed noun vegetation growing in water.

waterwheel noun a large wheel driven by flowing water, used to work machinery or to raise water to a higher level.

water wings plural noun inflated floats fixed to the arms of someone learning to swim.

waterworks plural noun (treated as sing.) an establishment for managing a water supply.
– PHRASES **turn on the waterworks** informal start crying.

watery adjective 1 consisting of, containing, or resembling water. 2 (of food or drink) thin or tasteless as a result of containing too much water. 3 weak or pale: *watery sunlight.*

watt noun the SI unit of power, equivalent to one joule per second and corresponding to the rate of energy in an electric circuit where the potential difference is one volt and the current one ampere.
– ORIGIN named after the Scottish engineer James *Watt*.

wattage noun an amount of electrical power expressed in watts.

wattle¹ /wot-t'l/ noun 1 a material for making fences, walls, etc., consisting of rods interlaced with twigs or branches. 2 an Australian acacia tree with long flexible branches.
– ORIGIN Old English.

wattle² /wot-t'l/ noun a fleshy lobe hanging from the head or neck of the turkey and some other birds.
– ORIGIN unknown.

wattle and daub noun a material formerly used in building walls, consisting of wattle covered with mud or clay.

Watusi /wuh-too-si/ noun 1 an energetic dance popular in the 1960s. 2 (treated as pl.) the Tutsi people as a group (now dated in English use).
– ORIGIN a local name.

wave verb 1 move one's hand to and fro in greeting or as a signal. 2 move something held in one's hand to and fro. 3 move or sway to and fro while remaining fixed to one point: *the flag waved in the wind.* 4 style hair so that it curls slightly. •noun 1 a ridge of water moving along the surface of the sea or arching and breaking on the shore. 2 a sudden occurrence of or increase in a phenomenon or emotion: *a wave of panic swept over her.* 3 a gesture or signal made by waving one's hand. 4 a slightly curling lock of hair. 5 Physics a periodic disturbance of the particles of a substance without overall movement of the particles, as

in the transmission of sound, light, heat, etc.
- PHRASES **make waves** informal **1** create a significant impression. **2** cause trouble.
- ORIGIN Old English.

> USAGE: For an explanation of the confusion between **wave** and **waive**, see the note at **WAIVE**.

waveband noun a range of wavelengths between two given limits, used in radio transmission.

waveform noun Physics a curve showing the shape of a wave at a given time.

wavelength noun **1** Physics the distance between successive crests of a wave of sound, light, radio waves, etc. **2** a person's way of thinking when communicated to another: *we weren't on the same wavelength.*

wavelet noun a small wave.

waver verb **1** move quiveringly; flicker. **2** begin to weaken; falter: *his love for her had never wavered.* **3** be undecided between two opinions or courses of action.
- DERIVATIVES **waverer** noun **wavery** adjective.
- ORIGIN Old Norse, 'flicker'.

wavy adjective (**wavier**, **waviest**) having or consisting of a series of wave-like curves.
- DERIVATIVES **waviness** noun.

wax[1] noun **1** a soft solid oily substance that melts easily, used for making candles or polishes. **2** a substance produced by bees to make honeycombs; beeswax. •verb **1** polish or treat something with wax. **2** remove hair from a part of the body by applying melted wax and then peeling it off with the hairs.
- DERIVATIVES **waxer** noun.
- ORIGIN Old English.

wax[2] verb **1** (of the moon) gradually have a larger part of its visible surface lit up, so that it appears to increase in size. **2** literary become larger or stronger. **3** speak or write in a particular way: *they waxed lyrical about the old days.*
- ORIGIN Old English.

waxed paper noun paper treated with wax to make it waterproof or greaseproof.

waxen adjective **1** having a smooth, pale, semi-transparent surface like that of wax. **2** old use or literary made of wax.

waxwing noun a crested songbird, mainly pinkish-brown and with bright red tips to some wing feathers.

waxwork noun **1** a lifelike dummy modelled in wax. **2** (**waxworks**) (treated as sing.) an exhibition of waxworks.

waxy adjective (**waxier**, **waxiest**) resembling wax in consistency or appearance.
- DERIVATIVES **waxiness** noun.

way noun **1** a method, style, or manner of doing something. **2** the typical manner in which someone behaves or in which something happens: *it was not his way to wait for things to happen.* **3** a road, track, path, or street. **4** a route or means taken in order to reach, enter, or leave a place. **5** the route along which someone or something is travelling or would travel if unobstructed: *he blocked her way.* **6** a specified direction: *we just missed a car coming the other way.* **7** the distance in space or time between two points. **8** a particular aspect. **9** a

specified condition or state: *the family was in a poor way.* **10** informal a particular area. **11** (**ways**) parts into which something divides or is divided. **12** forward motion or momentum of a ship or boat through water. •adverb informal at or to a considerable distance or extent.
- PHRASES **by the way** incidentally. **by way of 1** so as to pass through or across; via. **2** as a form of. **3** by means of. **come one's way** happen or become available to one. **get** (or **have**) **one's** (**own**) **way** get or do what one wants in spite of opposition. **give way 1** yield to someone or something. **2** collapse or break under pressure. **3** Brit. allow someone or something else to be or go first. **4** (**give way to**) be replaced or superseded by. **go one's way 1** (of events, circumstances, etc.) be favourable to one. **2** leave. **have a way with** have a particular talent for dealing with or ability in. **have one's way with** humorous have sex with. **in a way** (or **in some ways** or **in one way**) to a certain extent. **lead the way 1** go first along a route. **2** be the first to do something. **one way and another** (or **one way or the other**) **1** taking most considerations into account. **2** by some means. **on the** (or **one's or its**) **way** about to arrive or happen. **on the** (or **one's or its**) **way out** informal going out of fashion or favour. **the other way round** (or **around**; Brit. also **about**) **1** in the opposite position or direction. **2** the opposite of what is expected or supposed. **out of the way 1** (of a place) remote. **2** dealt with or finished. **3** no longer an obstacle to someone's plans. **4** unusual or exceptional. **ways and means** the methods and resources for achieving something.
- ORIGIN Old English.

waybill noun a list of passengers or goods being carried on a vehicle.

wayfarer noun literary a person who travels on foot.
- DERIVATIVES **wayfaring** noun & adjective.

waylay verb (past and past part. **waylaid**) **1** intercept someone in order to attack them. **2** stop someone and keep them in conversation.

waymark noun (also **waymarker**) a sign forming one of a series used to mark out a footpath or similar route.

way-out adjective informal very unconventional or experimental.

-ways suffix forming adjectives and adverbs of direction or manner: *lengthways.*

wayside noun the edge of a road.
- PHRASES **fall by the wayside** fail to continue with an undertaking. [with reference to the Gospel of Luke, chapter 8.]

way station noun N. Amer. a stopping place on a journey.

wayward adjective difficult to control because of unpredictable or wilful behaviour.
- DERIVATIVES **waywardly** adverb **waywardness** noun.
- ORIGIN shortening of former *awayward* 'turned away'.

Wb abbreviation weber(s).

WBA abbreviation World Boxing Association.

WBC abbreviation World Boxing Council.

WC abbreviation Brit. water closet.

W

we pronoun (first person pl.) **1** used by a speaker to refer to himself or herself and one or more other people considered together. **2** people in general. **3** used in formal situations for or by a royal person, or by a writer, to refer to himself or herself. **4** you (used in a superior way).
– ORIGIN Old English.

USAGE: On whether to use **we** or **us** following than, see the note at **PERSONAL PRONOUN**.

weak adjective **1** lacking physical strength and energy. **2** liable to break or give way under pressure. **3** not secure, stable, or firmly established: *a weak economy.* **4** lacking power, influence, or ability. **5** lacking intensity: *a weak light from a single street lamp.* **6** (of a liquid or solution) heavily diluted. **7** not convincing or forceful: *a weak plot.* **8** (of verbs) forming the past tense and past participle by adding a suffix (in English, typically -*ed*).
– PHRASES **the weaker sex** (treated as sing. or pl.) dated women regarded as a group.
– ORIGIN Old English.

weaken verb make or become weak.

weak-kneed adjective lacking determination or courage.

weakling noun a weak person or animal.

weakly adverb in a weak way. •adjective (**weaklier, weakliest**) weak or sickly.

weakness noun **1** the state of being weak. **2** a disadvantage or fault. **3** a person or thing that one cannot resist or likes too much. **4** (**weakness for**) a liking for something that is hard to resist: *his weakness for prawn cocktails.*

weal[1] /*rhymes with* feel/ (also chiefly Medicine **wheal**) noun a red, swollen mark left on flesh by a blow or pressure.
– ORIGIN from **WALE**.

weal[2] /*rhymes with* feel/ noun formal that which is best for someone or something: *guardians of the public weal.*
– ORIGIN Old English, 'wealth, well-being'.

Wealden /weel-d'n/ adjective Brit. relating to the Weald, a formerly wooded district including parts of Kent, Surrey, and East Sussex.

wealth noun **1** a large amount of money, property, or valuable possessions. **2** the state of being rich. **3** a large amount of a resource or desirable thing: *a wealth of information.*
– ORIGIN from **WELL**[1] or **WEAL**[2].

wealthy adjective (**wealthier, wealthiest**) having a great deal of money, resources, or assets; rich.

wean[1] verb **1** make a young mammal used to food other than its mother's milk. **2** (often **wean someone off**) make someone give up a habit or addiction. **3** (**be weaned on**) be strongly influenced by something from an early age: *a generation weaned on television.*
– ORIGIN Old English.

wean[2] noun Scottish & N. English a young child.
– ORIGIN from *wee ane* 'little one'.

weanling noun a newly weaned animal.

weapon noun **1** a thing designed or used to cause physical harm or damage. **2** a means of gaining an advantage or attacking someone or something: *the drug is a powerful new weapon*

to treat cancer.
– DERIVATIVES **weaponry** noun.
– ORIGIN Old English.

weapon of mass destruction noun a nuclear, biological, or chemical weapon able to cause widespread destruction and loss of life.

wear verb (past tense; past part. **worn**) **1** have something on one's body as clothing, decoration, or protection. **2** display a particular facial expression. **3** damage or destroy something by friction or continued use. **4** withstand continued use to a specified degree: *the fabric wears well wash after wash.* **5** (**wear off**) become less effective or intense: *the drug's effects were wearing off.* **6** (**wear someone down**) overcome someone by persistence. **7** (**wear someone out**) exhaust someone. **8** (as adj. **wearing**) mentally or physically tiring. **9** (**wear on**) (of time) pass in a slow or boring way. •noun **1** clothing suitable for a particular purpose or of a particular type: *evening wear.* **2** damage caused by continuous use. **3** the capacity for withstanding continuous use without such damage. **4** the wearing of something on the body: *tops for wear in the evening.*
– PHRASES **wear thin** be gradually used up or become less acceptable.
– DERIVATIVES **wearable** adjective **wearer** noun.
– ORIGIN Old English.

wearisome adjective making one feel tired or bored.

weary adjective (**wearier, weariest**) **1** feeling or showing tiredness. **2** causing tiredness. **3** reluctant to experience any more of: *he was weary of constant arguments.* •verb (**wearies, wearying, wearied**) **1** make someone weary. **2** (**weary of**) grow tired of someone or something.
– DERIVATIVES **wearily** adverb **weariness** noun.
– ORIGIN Old English.

weasel noun **1** a small slender meat-eating mammal related to the stoat, with reddish-brown fur. **2** informal a deceitful or treacherous person.
– PHRASES **weasel words** words or statements that are deliberately confusing or misleading.
– DERIVATIVES **weaselly** adjective.
– ORIGIN Old English.

weather noun the state of the atmosphere at a place and time as regards temperature, wind, rain, etc. •adjective referring to the side from which the wind is blowing; windward. Contrasted with **LEE**. •verb **1** wear away or change in form or appearance by long exposure to the weather: *his face was weathered and pockmarked.* **2** come safely through a difficult or dangerous situation.
– PHRASES **keep a weather eye on** be watchful for developments. **make heavy weather of** informal have unnecessary difficulty in dealing with a task or problem. [from *make good* or *bad weather of*, referring to a ship in a storm.] **under the weather** informal slightly unwell or depressed.
– ORIGIN Old English.

weather-beaten adjective damaged, worn, or tanned by exposure to the weather.

weatherboard noun chiefly Brit. **1** a sloping board attached to the bottom of an outside door to keep out the rain. **2** each of a series of

W

horizontal boards nailed to outside walls with edges overlapping to keep out the rain. – DERIVATIVES **weatherboarding** noun.

weathercock noun a weathervane in the form of a cockerel.

weatherman (or **weatherwoman**) noun (pl. **weathermen** or **weatherwomen**) a person who broadcasts a description and forecast of weather conditions.

weatherproof adjective resistant to the effects of bad weather. •verb make something weatherproof.

weather station noun an observation post where weather conditions are observed and recorded.

weathervane noun a revolving pointer that shows the direction of the wind.

weave¹ verb (past **wove**; past part. **woven** or **wove**) 1 make fabric by interlacing long threads passing in one direction with others at a right angle to them. 2 make basketwork or a wreath by interlacing rods or flowers. 3 (**weave something into**) make facts, events, and other elements into a story. •noun a particular way in which fabric is woven: *cloth of a very fine weave.* – ORIGIN Old English.

weave² verb move from side to side to get around obstructions. – PHRASES **get weaving** Brit. informal set briskly to work. – ORIGIN probably from an Old Norse word meaning 'to wave, brandish'.

weaver noun 1 a person who weaves fabric. 2 (also **weaver bird**) a songbird of tropical Africa and Asia, which builds elaborately woven nests.

web noun 1 a network of fine threads made by a spider to catch its prey. 2 a complex system of interconnected elements: *the story's web of lies.* 3 (**the Web**) the World Wide Web. 4 a membrane between the toes of a swimming bird or other animal that lives in water. – ORIGIN Old English, 'woven fabric'.

webbed adjective (of an animal's feet) having the toes connected by a web.

webbing noun strong, closely woven fabric used for making straps and belts and for supporting the seats of upholstered chairs.

webcam noun (trademark in the US) a video camera connected to a computer, so that its images may be viewed by Internet users.

webcast noun a live video broadcast of an event transmitted across the Internet.

weber /**vay**-ber/ noun the SI unit of magnetic flux, sufficient to cause an electromotive force of one volt in a circuit of one turn when generated or removed in one second. – ORIGIN named after the German physicist Wilhelm Eduard *Weber*.

web-footed adjective having webbed feet.

weblog noun a personal website on which someone regularly records their opinions or experiences and creates links to other sites.

webmaster noun a person who is responsible for a particular server on the Internet.

web page noun a hypertext document which can be accessed via the Internet.

website noun a location connected to the Internet that maintains one or more web pages.

wed verb (**weds, wedding;** past and past part. **wedded** or **wed**) 1 formal or literary marry or get married. 2 formal or literary give or join someone in marriage. 3 (as adj. **wedded**) relating to marriage: *wedded bliss.* 4 combine two desirable factors or qualities. 5 (**be wedded to**) be entirely devoted to an activity, belief, etc. – ORIGIN Old English.

we'd contraction 1 we had. 2 we should or we would.

wedding noun a marriage ceremony.

wedding band noun chiefly N. Amer. a wedding ring.

wedding breakfast noun Brit. a celebratory meal eaten just after a wedding (at any time of day) by the couple and their guests.

wedding cake noun a rich iced cake served at a wedding reception.

wedding march noun a piece of march music played at the entrance of the bride or the exit of the couple at a wedding.

wedding ring noun a ring worn by a married person, given to them by their husband or wife at their wedding.

wedge noun 1 a piece of wood, metal, etc. with a thick end that tapers to a thin edge, that is driven between two objects or parts of an object to secure or separate them. 2 a wedge-shaped thing or piece. 3 a golf club with a low, angled face for hitting the ball as high as possible into the air. 4 a shoe with a fairly high heel forming a solid block with the sole. •verb 1 fix something in position with a wedge. 2 force into a narrow space: *she wedged her holdall between two bags.* – PHRASES **drive a wedge between** cause a disagreement or hostility between. **the thin end of the wedge** informal an action unimportant in itself but which is likely to lead to more serious developments. – ORIGIN Old English.

Wedgwood /**wej**-wuud/ noun trademark a type of pottery made by the English potter Josiah Wedgwood and his successors, especially a kind of powder-blue stoneware with white embossed cameos.

wedlock noun formal the state of being married. – PHRASES **born in** (or **out of**) **wedlock** born of married (or unmarried) parents. – ORIGIN Old English, 'marriage vow'.

Wednesday noun the day of the week before Thursday and following Tuesday. – ORIGIN Old English, named after the Germanic god *Odin*.

wee¹ adjective (**weer, weest**) chiefly Scottish little. – ORIGIN Old English.

wee² informal, chiefly Brit. noun 1 an act of urinating. 2 urine. •verb (**wees, weeing, weed**) urinate. – ORIGIN imitating the sound.

weed noun 1 a wild plant growing where it is not wanted, especially among crops or garden plants. 2 informal cannabis. 3 (**the weed**) informal tobacco. 4 Brit. informal a weak or skinny person. •verb 1 remove weeds from an area of ground. 2 (**weed someone/thing out**) remove inferior

W

or unwanted items or members from a group or collection.
– ORIGIN Old English.

weedkiller noun a substance used to destroy weeds.

weedy adjective (**weedier**, **weediest**)
1 containing or covered with many weeds. 2 Brit. informal (of a person) thin and weak.

week noun 1 a period of seven days. 2 the period of seven days generally reckoned from and to midnight on Saturday night. 3 Brit. (preceded by a specified day) a week after that day: *the programme will be broadcast Sunday week.* 4 the five days from Monday to Friday, or the time spent working during this period.
– ORIGIN Old English.

weekday noun a day of the week other than Sunday or Saturday.

weekend noun Saturday and Sunday. • verb informal spend a weekend somewhere.

weekender noun a person who spends weekends away from their main home.

weekly adjective 1 done, produced, or happening once a week. 2 calculated in terms of a week: *weekly income.* • adverb once a week. • noun (pl. **weeklies**) a newspaper or periodical issued every week.

weeny adjective (**weenier**, **weeniest**) informal very small; tiny.
– ORIGIN from WEE¹.

weep verb (past and past part. **wept**) 1 shed tears. 2 discharge liquid. 3 (as adj. **weeping**) used in names of trees and shrubs with drooping branches, e.g. **weeping willow**. • noun a fit or spell of shedding tears.
– DERIVATIVES **weeper** noun.
– ORIGIN Old English.

weepie (also **weepy**) noun (pl. **weepies**) informal a sentimental or emotional film, novel, or song.

weepy adjective (**weepier**, **weepiest**) informal 1 inclined to weep; tearful. 2 sentimental: *a weepy TV movie.*
– DERIVATIVES **weepily** adverb **weepiness** noun.

weevil /wee-v'l/ noun a small beetle with a long snout, several kinds of which are pests of crops or stored foodstuffs.
– ORIGIN Old English.

w.e.f. abbreviation Brit. with effect from.

weft noun (in weaving) the crosswise threads that are passed over and under the warp threads on a loom to make cloth.
– ORIGIN Old English.

Wehrmacht /vair-mahkht/ noun the German armed forces from 1921 to 1945.
– ORIGIN German, 'defensive force'.

weigh verb 1 find out how heavy someone or something is. 2 have a specified weight. 3 (**weigh something out**) measure and take out a portion of a particular weight. 4 (**weigh someone down**) make someone feel stressed or anxious. 5 (**weigh on**) be depressing or worrying to someone. 6 (**weigh in**) (of a boxer or jockey) be officially weighed before or after a contest. 7 (often **weigh something up**) assess the nature or importance of something. 8 (often **weigh against**) influence a decision or action: *the evidence weighed heavily against him.* 9 (**weigh in**) informal make a forceful

contribution to a competition or argument. 10 (**weigh into**) join in or attack forcefully or enthusiastically: *he weighed into the companies for their high costs.*
– PHRASES **weigh anchor** (of a boat) take up the anchor when ready to sail.
– ORIGIN Old English.

weighbridge noun a machine for weighing vehicles, set into the ground to be driven on to.

weigh-in noun an official weighing, e.g. of boxers before a fight.

weight noun 1 the amount that someone or something weighs. 2 the quality of being heavy. 3 a heavy object. 4 a unit or system of units used for expressing how much something weighs. 5 a piece of metal known to weigh a definite amount and used on scales to find out how heavy something is. 6 (**weights**) heavy blocks or discs used in weightlifting or weight training. 7 the ability to influence decisions or actions: *their recommendation will carry great weight.* 8 the importance attached to something. 9 a feeling of pressure or worry: *that'll be a weight off my mind.* 10 the surface density of cloth, used as a measure of its quality. 11 Physics the force exerted on the mass of a body by a gravitational field. • verb 1 make something heavier or keep something in place with a weight. 2 attach importance or value to: *reading and writing should be weighted equally in the assessment.* 3 (**be weighted**) be planned or arranged so as to give one party an advantage.
– PHRASES **be worth one's weight in gold** be very useful or helpful. **throw one's weight about** (or **around**) informal assert oneself in an unpleasant way.
– ORIGIN Old English.

weighting noun 1 allowance or adjustment made to take account of special circumstances. 2 Brit. additional wages or salary paid to allow for a higher cost of living in a particular area.

weightless adjective (of a body) not apparently acted on by gravity.
– DERIVATIVES **weightlessly** adverb **weightlessness** noun.

weightlifting noun the sport or activity of lifting barbells or other heavy weights.
– DERIVATIVES **weightlifter** noun.

weight training noun physical training that involves lifting weights.

weight-watcher noun a person who is on a diet in order to lose weight.

weighty adjective (**weightier**, **weightiest**)
1 weighing a great deal; heavy. 2 very serious and important.
– DERIVATIVES **weightily** adverb **weightiness** noun.

Weil's disease /vylz/ noun an infectious disease caused by a bacterium and transmitted by rats via contaminated water.
– ORIGIN named after the German physician H. Adolf *Weil.*

Weimaraner /vy-muh-rah-ner, wy-muh-rah-ner/ noun a thin-coated grey breed of pointer used as a gun dog.
– ORIGIN from *Weimar* in Germany, where the breed was developed.

weir /rhymes with here/ noun **1** a low dam built across a river to raise the level of water upstream or control its flow. **2** an enclosure of stakes set in a stream as a trap for fish.
– ORIGIN Old English.

weird adjective **1** informal very strange or unusual: *he's a weird little bloke.* **2** mysterious or strange in a frightening way.
– DERIVATIVES **weirdly** adverb **weirdness** noun.
– ORIGIN Old English, 'destiny, fate'.

weirdo noun (pl. **weirdos**) informal a strange or eccentric person.

welch verb variant spelling of WELSH.

welcome noun **1** an instance or way of greeting someone. **2** a pleased or approving reaction. •exclamation used to greet someone in a glad or friendly way. •verb **1** greet someone who is arriving in a polite or friendly way. **2** be glad to receive or hear of: *the decision was widely welcomed.* •adjective **1** (of a guest or new arrival) gladly received. **2** very pleasing because much needed or desired. **3** allowed or invited to do a particular thing: *you are welcome to join in.* **4** (**welcome to**) used to indicate relief at giving up something to another: *the job is all yours and you're welcome to it!*
– DERIVATIVES **welcomer** noun.
– ORIGIN Old English, 'a person whose coming is pleasing'.

weld verb **1** join metal parts together by heating the surfaces to the point of melting and pressing or hammering them together. **2** make an article by welding. **3** unite into a strong and effective whole: *they welded diverse ethnic groups into a single political system.* •noun a welded joint.
– DERIVATIVES **welder** noun.
– ORIGIN from WELL² in the former sense 'melt or weld heated metal'.

welfare noun **1** the health, happiness, and fortunes of a person or group. **2** organized practical or financial help provided, typically by the state, to help people in need.
– ORIGIN from WELL¹ + FARE.

welfare state noun a system under which the state protects the health and well-being of its citizens by providing grants, pensions, and other benefits.

welkin noun literary the sky or heaven.
– ORIGIN Old English, 'cloud, sky'.

well¹ adverb (**better**, **best**) **1** in a good or satisfactory way. **2** in a thorough way: *add the mustard and mix well.* **3** to a great extent or degree; very much. **4** in a favourable or approving way. **5** in prosperity or comfort. **6** Brit. informal very; extremely: *he was well out of order.* **7** very probably. **8** without difficulty. **9** with good reason: *what, you may well ask, are they doing here?* **10** old use at a good time; luckily: *hail fellow, well met.* •adjective (**better**, **best**) **1** in good health. **2** in a satisfactory state or position. **3** sensible; advisable. •exclamation used to express surprise, anger, resignation, etc., or when pausing in speech.
– PHRASES **as well** in addition; too. **as well** (or **just as well**) **1** with equal reason or an equally good result. **2** sensible, appropriate, or desirable. **be well up on** know a great deal about something. **leave** (or **let**) **well alone**

refrain from interfering with or trying to improve something. **well and truly** completely.
– ORIGIN Old English.

USAGE: As an adverb, **well** is often used with a past participle (such as *known* or *dressed*) to form compound adjectives: **well known, well dressed,** and so on. Such adjectives should be written without a hyphen when they are used alone after a verb (*she is well known as a writer*) but with a hyphen when they come before a noun (*a well-known writer*).

well² noun **1** a shaft sunk into the ground to obtain water, oil, or gas. **2** a hollow made to hold liquid. **3** a plentiful source or supply: *a deep well of sympathy.* **4** an enclosed space in the middle of a building, giving room for stairs or a lift or allowing in light or air. •verb (often **well up**) **1** (of a liquid) rise up to the surface and spill or be about to spill. **2** (of an emotion) arise and become more intense.
– ORIGIN Old English.

we'll contraction we shall; we will.

well advised adjective sensible; wise.

well appointed adjective (of a building or room) having a high standard of equipment or furnishing.

well balanced adjective mentally and emotionally stable.

well-being noun the state of being comfortable, healthy, or happy.

well bred adjective polite and well brought up.

well built adjective (of a person) strong and sturdy.

well disposed adjective having a positive, sympathetic, or friendly attitude.

well done adjective **1** carried out successfully or satisfactorily. **2** (of food) thoroughly cooked. •exclamation used to express congratulation or approval.

well endowed adjective having plentiful supplies of a resource.

well founded adjective based on good evidence or reasons.

wellhead noun **1** the place where a spring comes out of the ground. **2** the structure over an oil or gas well.

well heeled adjective informal rich; wealthy.

wellie noun variant spelling of WELLY.

wellington (also **wellington boot**) noun Brit. a knee-length waterproof rubber or plastic boot.
– ORIGIN named after the British soldier and Prime Minister the 1st Duke of *Wellington.*

well known adjective known widely or thoroughly.

well meaning (also **well meant**) adjective having good intentions but not necessarily the desired effect.

well-nigh adverb almost.

well off adjective **1** rich; wealthy. **2** in a favourable situation.

well oiled adjective **1** operating smoothly. **2** informal drunk.

well preserved adjective (of an old person) showing little sign of ageing.

well read adjective very knowledgeable as a result of reading widely.

well rounded adjective **1** (of a person) having a pleasingly curved or plump shape. **2** having a

W

mature personality and varied interests: *a well-rounded student.*

well spoken adjective speaking in an educated and refined way.

wellspring noun literary **1** a plentiful source of something: *a wellspring of creativity.* **2** the place where a spring comes out of the ground.

well-to-do adjective wealthy; prosperous.

well travelled adjective **1** (of a person) having travelled widely. **2** (of a route) much used by travellers.

well tried adjective having been used often and therefore known to be reliable.

well trodden adjective (of a route) much used by travellers.

well turned adjective **1** (of a phrase or compliment) elegantly expressed. **2** (of a woman's ankle or leg) attractively shaped.

well-wisher noun a person who feels or expresses a desire that someone else finds happiness or success.

well worn adjective **1** showing signs of extensive use or wear. **2** (of a phrase or idea) used or repeated so often that it is no longer interesting or original.

welly (also **wellie**) noun (pl. **wellies**) Brit. informal **1** short for **WELLINGTON. 2** power or vigour.

Welsh noun the language of Wales. • adjective relating to Wales.
– DERIVATIVES **Welshman** noun (pl. **Welshmen**). **Welshness** noun. **Welshwoman** noun (pl. **Welshwomen**).

welsh (also **welch**) verb (**welsh on**) fail to pay a debt or fulfil an obligation.
– ORIGIN unknown.

Welsh rarebit (also **Welsh rabbit**) noun another term for **RAREBIT.**

welt noun **1** a ribbed, reinforced, or decorative border on an item of clothing. **2** a weal. **3** a leather rim round the edge of the upper of a shoe, to which the sole is attached.
– ORIGIN unknown.

Weltanschauung /velt-an-show-uung/ noun (pl. **Weltanschauungen** /velt-an-show-uung-uhn/) a particular philosophy or view of life.
– ORIGIN German.

welter noun a large confused or disorganized mass or quantity: *a welter of new regulations.*
– ORIGIN from Dutch or German *welteren* 'writhe, wallow'.

welterweight noun a weight in boxing and other sports between lightweight and middleweight.
– ORIGIN unknown.

wen noun a boil or other swelling or growth on the skin.
– ORIGIN Old English.

wench noun old use or humorous a girl or young woman.
– ORIGIN from former *wenchel* 'child, servant, prostitute'.

wend verb (**wend one's way**) go slowly or by an indirect route.
– ORIGIN Old English, 'to turn, depart'.

Wendy house noun Brit. a toy house large enough for children to play in.
– ORIGIN named after the house built around *Wendy* in J. M. Barrie's play *Peter Pan.*

Wensleydale /wenz-li-dayl/ noun a type of white cheese with a crumbly texture.
– ORIGIN named after *Wensleydale* in Yorkshire.

went past of **GO.**

wept past and past participle of **WEEP.**

were second person singular past, plural past, and past subjunctive of **BE.**

we're contraction we are.

weren't contraction were not.

werewolf /wair-wuulf, weer-wuulf/ noun (pl. **werewolves**) (in folklore) a person who periodically changes into a wolf, typically when there is a full moon.
– ORIGIN Old English.

wert /rhymes with dirt/ old-fashioned second person singular past of **BE.**

Wesleyan adjective relating to the teachings of the English preacher John Wesley or the main branch of the Methodist Church which he founded. • noun a follower of Wesley or of the main Methodist tradition.

west noun **1** the direction in which the sun sets at the equinoxes, on the left-hand side of a person facing north. **2** the western part of a place. **3** (**the West**) Europe and North America seen in contrast to other civilizations. **4** (**the West**) historical the non-Communist states of Europe and North America. • adjective **1** lying towards, near, or facing the west. **2** (of a wind) blowing from the west. • adverb to or towards the west.
– PHRASES **go west** Brit. informal be killed or lost.
– DERIVATIVES **westbound** adjective & adverb.
– ORIGIN Old English.

westerly adjective & adverb **1** facing or moving towards the west. **2** (of a wind) blowing from the west. • noun (pl. **westerlies**) a wind blowing from the west.

western adjective **1** situated in, directed towards, or facing the west. **2** (usu. **Western**) coming from or typical of the west, in particular Europe and North America. • noun a film or novel about cowboys in western North America.
– DERIVATIVES **westernmost** adjective.

Western Church noun the part of the Christian Church originating in the Western Roman Empire, including the Roman Catholic, Anglican, Lutheran, and Reformed Churches.

westerner noun a person from the west of a region or country.

westernize (or **westernise**) verb bring a country, system, etc. under the influence of the cultural, economic, or political systems of Europe and North America.
– DERIVATIVES **westernization** noun **westernizer** noun.

West Indian noun a person from the West Indies, or a person of West Indian descent. • adjective relating to the West Indies.

westing noun **1** distance travelled or measured westward, especially at sea. **2** a figure or line representing westward distance on a map.

west-north-west noun the direction midway between west and north-west.

west-south-west noun the direction midway between west and south-west.

westward adjective towards the west. • adverb (also **westwards**) in a westerly direction.

wet adjective (**wetter, wettest**) **1** covered or

saturated with liquid. **2** (of the weather) rainy. **3** (of paint, ink, etc.) not yet having dried or hardened. **4** (of a process) involving the use of water or liquid. **5** Brit. informal lacking forcefulness or strength of character; feeble. **6** informal (of an area) allowing the free sale of alcoholic drink. • verb (**wets, wetting;** past and past part. **wet** or **wetted**) **1** cover or touch someone or something with liquid. **2** urinate in or on something. **3** (**wet oneself**) urinate without intending to. • noun **1** (**the wet**) rainy weather. **2** liquid that makes something damp. **3** Brit. informal a feeble person. **4** Brit. a Conservative politician with liberal tendencies.
– PHRASES **wet the baby's head** Brit. informal celebrate a baby's birth with a drink. **wet behind the ears** informal lacking experience; immature. **wet one's whistle** informal have a drink.
– DERIVATIVES **wetly** adverb **wetness** noun.
– ORIGIN Old English.

wet blanket noun informal a person who spoils other people's enjoyment with their disapproving or unenthusiastic attitude.

wet dream noun an erotic dream that causes a man to ejaculate semen involuntarily.

wet fly noun an artificial fishing fly designed to sink below the surface of the water.

wether /rhymes with weather/ noun a castrated ram.
– ORIGIN Old English.

wetland noun (also **wetlands**) swampy or marshy land.

wet nurse noun chiefly historical a woman employed to breastfeed another woman's child.

wet room noun a bathroom in which the shower is open or set behind a single wall, its floor area being level with the floor of the rest of the room.

wet rot noun a brown fungus causing decay in moist timber.

wetsuit noun a close-fitting rubber garment covering the entire body, worn for warmth in water sports or diving.

we've contraction we have.

whack informal verb **1** strike someone or something forcefully with a sharp blow. **2** put something somewhere roughly or carelessly. **3** defeat an opponent heavily. • noun **1** a sharp or resounding blow. **2** a try or attempt. **3** Brit. a particular share of or contribution to something: he paid a fair whack of the bill.
– PHRASES **out of whack** chiefly N. Amer. & Austral./NZ not working. **top** (or **full**) **whack** chiefly Brit. the maximum price or rate.
– ORIGIN imitating the sound.

whacked (also **whacked out**) adjective informal Brit. completely exhausted.

whacking adjective Brit. informal very large.

whacko adjective & noun (pl. **whackos**) variant spelling of **WACKO**.

whacky adjective variant spelling of **WACKY**.

whale noun (pl. same or **whales**) a very large sea mammal with a horizontal tail fin and a blowhole on top of the head for breathing.
– PHRASES **a whale of a —** informal an extremely good example of something. **have a**

whale of a time informal enjoy oneself very much.
– ORIGIN Old English.

whalebone noun **1** a horny substance which grows in a series of thin parallel plates in the upper jaw of some whales and is used by them to strain plankton from the seawater. **2** strips of this substance, formerly used to stiffen corsets.

whaler noun **1** a ship used for hunting whales. **2** a sailor whose job is to hunt whales.

whaling noun the practice or industry of hunting and killing whales for their oil, meat, or whalebone.

wham informal exclamation used to express the sound of a forceful impact or the idea of a sudden and dramatic event. • verb (**whams, whamming, whammed**) strike something forcefully.

whammy noun (pl. **whammies**) informal an event with a powerful and unpleasant effect; a blow.

whap verb (**whaps, whapping, whapped**) verb & noun chiefly N. Amer. variant spelling of **WHOP**.

wharf /worf/ noun (pl. **wharves** or **wharfs**) a level quayside area to which a ship may be moored to load and unload.
– ORIGIN Old English.

what pronoun & determiner **1** asking for information specifying something. **2** (as pronoun) asking for repetition of something not heard or confirmation of something not understood. **3** (as pronoun) the thing or things that. **4** no matter what; whatever. **5** used to emphasize something surprising or remarkable. • adverb **1** to what extent? **2** informal, dated used for emphasis or to invite agreement.
– PHRASES **give someone what for** informal, chiefly Brit. punish or scold someone severely. **what for?** informal for what reason? **what's what** informal what is useful or important. **what with** because of.
– ORIGIN Old English.

whatever pronoun & determiner used to emphasize a lack of restriction in referring to any thing; no matter what. • pronoun used for emphasis instead of 'what' in questions.
• adverb **1** at all; of any kind. **2** informal no matter what happens.

whatnot noun informal used to refer to an unidentified item or items having something in common with items already named.

whatsit noun informal a person or thing whose name one cannot remember, does not know, or does not wish to specify.

whatsoever adverb at all. • determiner & pronoun old use whatever.

wheal noun variant spelling of **WEAL**[1].

wheat noun a cereal widely grown in temperate countries, the grain of which is ground to make flour.
– ORIGIN Old English, related to **WHITE**.

wheatear noun a songbird with black and grey, buff, or white plumage and a white rump.
– ORIGIN apparently from **WHITE** + **ARSE**.

wheaten adjective made of wheat.

wheatgerm noun a nutritious foodstuff consisting of the centre parts of grains of wheat.

wheatgrass noun another term for **COUCH**[2].

wheatmeal noun flour made from wheat from which some of the bran has been removed.

wheedle verb use endearments or flattery to persuade someone to do something.
- ORIGIN perhaps from German *wedeln* 'cringe, fawn'.

wheel noun 1 a circular object that revolves on an axle, fixed below a vehicle to enable it to move along or forming part of a machine. 2 something resembling a wheel or having a wheel as its essential part. 3 (**the wheel**) a steering wheel. 4 (**wheels**) informal a car. 5 a turn or rotation. 6 a recurring cycle of events: *he attempted to stop the wheel of history.* •verb 1 push or pull something with wheels. 2 carry or convey on something with wheels: *she was wheeled into the operating theatre.* 3 fly or turn in a wide circle or curve. 4 turn round quickly to face another way. 5 (**wheel something on/out**) informal resort to something that has been frequently seen or heard before.
- PHRASES **wheel and deal** take part in commercial or political scheming. **the wheel of Fortune** the wheel which the goddess Fortune is represented as turning as a symbol of random luck or change. **wheels within wheels** secret or indirect influences affecting a complex situation.
- ORIGIN Old English.

wheelbarrow noun a small cart with a single wheel at the front and two supporting legs and two handles at the rear, used for carrying loads in building or gardening.

wheelbase noun the distance between the front and rear axles of a vehicle.

wheelchair noun a chair on wheels for use by a person who cannot walk as the result of an illness, accident, etc.

wheel clamp noun Brit. a device attached to the wheel of an illegally parked car to prevent it from being driven away.

wheeler noun (in combination) a vehicle having a specified number of wheels: *a three-wheeler.*

wheeler-dealer (also **wheeler and dealer**) noun a person who takes part in commercial or political scheming.
- DERIVATIVES **wheeler-dealing** noun.

wheelhouse noun a shelter for the person at the wheel of a boat or ship.

wheelie noun informal a manoeuvre in which a bicycle or motorcycle is ridden for a short distance with the front wheel raised off the ground.

wheelie bin (also **wheely bin**) noun Brit. informal a large rubbish bin on wheels.

wheelspin noun the rotation of a vehicle's wheels without movement of the vehicle forwards or backwards.

wheelwright noun chiefly historical a person who makes or repairs wooden wheels.

wheeze verb 1 breathe with a whistling or rattling sound in the chest, as a result of a blockage in the air passages. 2 (of a device) make an irregular rattling or spluttering sound. •noun 1 a sound of a person wheezing. 2 Brit. informal a clever or amusing scheme or trick.
- DERIVATIVES **wheezily** adverb **wheeziness** noun **wheezy** adjective.
- ORIGIN probably from an Old Norse word

meaning 'to hiss'.

whelk noun a shellfish with a heavy pointed spiral shell, some kinds of which are edible.
- ORIGIN Old English.

whelp noun chiefly old use 1 a puppy. 2 derogatory a boy or young man. •verb give birth to a puppy.
- ORIGIN Old English.

when adverb 1 at what time? 2 how soon? 3 in what circumstances? 4 at which time or in which situation. •conjunction 1 at or during the time that. 2 at any time that; whenever. 3 after which; and just then. 4 in view of the fact that. 5 although; whereas.
- ORIGIN Old English.

whence (also **from whence**) adverb formal or old use 1 from what place or source? 2 from which; from where. 3 to the place from which. 4 as a consequence of which.

USAGE: Whence means 'from what place', as in *who are you and whence come you?* Strictly speaking, the preposition **from**, as in *the music store from whence the label was launched*, is unnecessary, but nevertheless **from whence** is usually accepted as good English.

whenever conjunction 1 at whatever time; on whatever occasion. 2 every time that. •adverb used for emphasis instead of 'when' in questions.

whensoever conjunction & adverb formal word for **WHENEVER**.

where adverb 1 in or to what place or position? 2 in what direction or respect? 3 at, in, or to which. 4 the place or situation in which. 5 in or to a place or situation in which.
- ORIGIN Old English.

whereabouts adverb where or approximately where? •noun (treated as sing. or pl.) the place where someone or something is.

whereafter adverb formal after which.

whereas conjunction 1 in contrast or comparison with the fact that. 2 taking into consideration the fact that.

whereat adverb & conjunction old use or formal at which.

whereby adverb by which.

wherefore old use adverb for what reason? •adverb & conjunction as a result of which.

wherefrom adverb old use from which or from where.

wherein adverb formal 1 in which. 2 in what place or respect?

whereof adverb formal of what or which.

whereon adverb old use on which.

wheresoever adverb & conjunction formal word for **WHEREVER**.

whereto adverb old use or formal to which.

whereupon conjunction immediately after which.

wherever adverb 1 in or to whatever place. 2 used for emphasis instead of 'where' in questions. •conjunction in every case when.

wherewith adverb formal or old use with or by which.

wherewithal noun the money or other resources needed for a particular purpose.

wherry /rhymes with sherry/ noun (pl. **wherries**) 1 a light rowing boat used chiefly for carrying passengers. 2 Brit. a large, light

barge.
– ORIGIN unknown.
whet /wet/ verb (**whets, whetting, whetted**)
1 sharpen the blade of a tool or weapon.
2 arouse or stimulate someone's desire,
interest, or appetite.
– ORIGIN Old English.
whether conjunction **1** expressing a doubt or
choice between alternatives. **2** expressing an
enquiry or investigation. **3** indicating that a
statement applies whichever of the
alternatives mentioned is the case.
– ORIGIN Old English.

USAGE: For an explanation of the use of
whether and **if**, see the note at **IF**.

whetstone noun a fine-grained stone used to
sharpen cutting tools.
whey /way/ noun the watery part of milk that
remains after curds have formed.
– ORIGIN Old English.
whey-faced adjective (of a person) pale.
which pronoun & determiner **1** asking for
information specifying one or more people or
things from a definite set. **2** used to refer to
something previously mentioned when
introducing a clause giving further
information.
– ORIGIN Old English.

USAGE: For an explanation of the difference
in use between **which** and **that**, see the note at
THAT.

whichever determiner & pronoun **1** used to
emphasize a lack of restriction in selecting
one of a definite set of alternatives.
2 regardless of which.
whicker verb (of a horse) give a soft breathy
whinny. •noun a sound of this type.
– ORIGIN imitating the sound.
whiff noun **1** a smell that is smelt only briefly or
faintly. **2** Brit. informal an unpleasant smell. **3** a
trace or hint of something bad or exciting: *a
whiff of danger.* **4** a puff or breath of air or
smoke. •verb **1** get a brief or faint smell of
something. **2** Brit. informal give off an unpleasant
smell.
– ORIGIN imitating the sound of sniffing.
whiffle verb **1** blow or move lightly. **2** make a
soft sound. •noun a slight movement of air.
whiffy adjective (**whiffier, whiffiest**) Brit. informal
having an unpleasant smell.
Whig noun a member of a British political party
that was succeeded in the 19th century by the
Liberal Party.
– DERIVATIVES **Whiggish** adjective **Whiggism** noun.
– ORIGIN probably a shortening of Scots
whiggamore, the nickname of 17th-century
Scottish rebels, from *whig* 'to drive' + **MARE**[1].
while noun **1** (**a while**) a period of time. **2** (**a
while**) for some time. **3** (**the while**) at the
same time; meanwhile. **4** (**the while**) literary
during the time that. •conjunction **1** at the same
time as. **2** whereas (indicating a contrast).
3 although. •adverb during which. •verb (**while
something away**) pass time in a leisurely way.
– PHRASES **worth while** (or **worth one's while**)
worth the time or effort spent.
– ORIGIN Old English.
whilst conjunction & adverb chiefly Brit. while.

whim noun a sudden desire or change of mind.
– ORIGIN unknown.
whimbrel /wim-bruhl/ noun a small curlew
with a striped crown and a trilling call.
– ORIGIN perhaps from **WHIMPER** (imitating the
bird's call).
whimper verb make a series of low, feeble
sounds expressing fear, pain, or discontent.
•noun a whimpering sound.
– ORIGIN imitating the sound.
whimsical adjective **1** playfully unusual or
fanciful: *a whimsical sense of humour.*
2 showing sudden changes of behaviour.
– DERIVATIVES **whimsicality** noun **whimsically**
adverb.
whimsy (also **whimsey**) noun (pl. **whimsies** or
whimseys) **1** playfully unusual or fanciful
behaviour or humour. **2** a fanciful or odd
thing. **3** a whim.
– ORIGIN probably from former *whim-wham*
'trinket, whim'.
whin noun chiefly N. English gorse.
– ORIGIN probably Scandinavian.
whinchat /win-chat/ noun a small songbird
with a brown back and orange-buff throat and
breast.
whine verb **1** give or make a long, high-pitched
complaining cry. **2** (especially of a machine)
make a long, high-pitched unpleasant sound.
3 complain in a petulant way. •noun **1** a
whining cry or sound. **2** a petulant complaint.
– DERIVATIVES **whiner** noun **whiny** (also
whiney) adjective.
– ORIGIN Old English, 'whistle through the air'.
whinge Brit. informal verb (**whinges, whingeing,
whinged**) complain persistently and
peevishly. •noun an act of whingeing.
– DERIVATIVES **whinger** noun.
– ORIGIN Old English.
whinny noun (pl. **whinnies**) a gentle, high-
pitched neigh. •verb (**whinnies, whinnying,
whinnied**) (of a horse) make such a sound.
– ORIGIN imitating the sound.
whip noun **1** a strip of leather or length of cord
fastened to a handle, used for beating a person
or urging on an animal. **2** an official of a
political party appointed to maintain
parliamentary discipline among its members.
3 Brit. a written notice from such an official
requesting that members of the party attend
to vote in a debate. **4** a dessert made from
cream or eggs beaten into a light fluffy mass.
•verb (**whips, whipping, whipped**) **1** beat a
person or animal with a whip. **2** (of a flexible
object or rain or wind) strike or beat violently:
the wind whipped their faces. **3** move or take
something out fast or suddenly. **4** beat cream,
eggs, etc. into a froth. **5** Brit. informal steal
something.
– PHRASES **the whip hand** a position of power or
control. **whip someone/thing up 1** make or
prepare something very quickly. **2** deliberately
excite or provoke someone. **3** stimulate a
particular feeling in someone.
– DERIVATIVES **whipper** noun **whipping** noun.
– ORIGIN probably from German and Dutch
wippen 'swing, leap, dance'.
whipcord noun **1** thin, tough, tightly twisted
cord used for making the flexible end part of
whips. **2** a closely woven ribbed fabric.

W

whiplash noun 1 the lashing action of a whip. 2 injury caused by a severe jerk to the head.

whipper-in noun (pl. **whippers-in**) a huntsman's assistant who brings straying hounds back into the pack.

whippersnapper noun informal a young and inexperienced person who is disrespectful or overconfident.
– ORIGIN perhaps representing *whipsnapper*, expressing noise and unimportance.

whippet noun a small slender breed of dog used in racing.
– ORIGIN partly from former *whippet* 'move briskly'.

whipping boy noun a person who is blamed or punished for other people's faults or mistakes.
– ORIGIN first referring to a boy educated with a young prince and punished instead of him.

whippoorwill /wip-per-wil/ noun a North and Central American nightjar with a distinctive call.
– ORIGIN imitating its call.

whippy adjective flexible; springy.

whip-round noun Brit. informal a collection of contributions of money for a particular purpose.

whipsaw noun a saw with a narrow blade and a handle at both ends. • verb (past part. **whipsawn** or **whipsawed**) N. Amer. 1 cut something with a whipsaw. 2 informal subject someone or something to two difficult situations or opposing pressures at the same time.

whirl verb 1 move rapidly round and round. 2 (of the head or mind) seem to spin round. • noun 1 a rapid movement round and round. 2 frantic activity: *the mad social whirl.* 3 a sweet or biscuit with a spiral shape.
– PHRASES **give something a whirl** informal give something a try. **in a whirl** in a state of confusion.
– ORIGIN probably from an Old Norse word meaning 'turn about'.

whirligig noun 1 a toy that spins round, e.g. a top or windmill. 2 a process or activity characterized by constant change or hectic activity. 3 a roundabout at a fair. 4 (also **whirligig beetle**) a small black water beetle which typically swims rapidly in circles on the surface.
– ORIGIN from **WHIRL** + former *gig* 'toy for whipping'.

whirlpool noun 1 a quickly rotating mass of water in a river which may draw floating objects towards its centre. 2 (also **whirlpool bath**) a heated pool in which hot bubbling water is continuously circulated.

whirlwind noun 1 a column of air moving rapidly round and round in a cylindrical or funnel shape. 2 a situation in which many things happen very quickly: *a whirlwind of activity.* • adjective happening very quickly or suddenly: *a whirlwind romance.*

whirr (also **whir**) verb (**whirrs**, **whirring**, **whirred**) (of something rapidly rotating or moving to and fro) make a low, continuous, regular sound. • noun a whirring sound.
– ORIGIN probably Scandinavian.

whisk verb 1 move or take suddenly and quickly: *he whisked her off to Paris.* 2 beat a

substance with a light, rapid movement. • noun 1 a utensil for whisking eggs or cream. 2 a bunch of grass, twigs, or bristles for flicking away dust or flies. 3 a brief, rapid action or movement.
– ORIGIN Scandinavian.

whisker noun 1 a long hair or bristle growing from the face or snout of an animal. 2 (**whiskers**) the hair growing on a man's face. 3 (**a whisker**) informal a very small amount.
– DERIVATIVES **whiskered** adjective **whiskery** adjective.
– ORIGIN from **WHISK**.

whisky (also Irish & US **whiskey**) noun (pl. **whiskies**) a spirit distilled from malted grain, especially barley or rye.
– ORIGIN from Irish and Scottish Gaelic *uisge beatha* 'water of life'.

whisper verb 1 speak very softly. 2 literary rustle or murmur softly. • noun 1 a whispered word or phrase, or a whispering tone of voice. 2 literary a soft rustling or murmuring sound. 3 a rumour or piece of gossip. 4 a slight trace.
– DERIVATIVES **whisperer** noun **whispery** adjective.
– ORIGIN Old English.

whispering campaign noun an attempt to damage someone's reputation by systematically circulating a rumour about them.

whist /wist/ noun a card game in which points are scored according to the number of tricks won.
– ORIGIN earlier as *whisk*: perhaps from **WHISK** (with reference to whisking away the tricks).

whistle noun 1 a clear, high-pitched sound made by forcing breath through pursed lips, or between one's teeth. 2 any similar high-pitched sound. 3 an instrument used to produce a whistling sound. • verb 1 produce a whistle: *the crowd cheered and whistled.* 2 produce a tune by whistling. 3 blow a whistle. 4 move rapidly through the air or a narrow opening with a whistling sound. 5 (**whistle for**) wish for or expect something in vain.
– PHRASES **blow the whistle on** informal bring an illicit activity to an end by informing on the person responsible. (**as**) **clean as a whistle** extremely clean or clear. **whistle in the dark** pretend to be unafraid.
– DERIVATIVES **whistler** noun.
– ORIGIN Old English.

whistle-blower noun informal a person who informs on someone engaged in an illicit activity.

whistle-stop adjective very fast and with only brief pauses.

whit /wit/ noun a very small part or amount.
– PHRASES **not a whit** not at all.
– ORIGIN apparently from an Old English word meaning 'creature, small amount'.

white adjective 1 of the colour of milk or fresh snow. 2 very pale. 3 relating to the human group having light-coloured skin. 4 Brit. (of coffee or tea) served with milk or cream. 5 (of food such as bread or rice) light in colour through having been refined. 6 (of wine) made from white grapes, or dark grapes with the skins removed, and having a yellowish colour. 7 morally or spiritually pure. • noun

1 white colour. **2** (also **whites**) white clothes or material. **3** the visible pale part of the eyeball around the iris. **4** the outer part which surrounds the yolk of an egg; the albumen. **5** a member of a light-skinned people. **6** a white or cream butterfly. •verb (**white something out**) cover a mistake with white correction fluid.
– PHRASES **bleed someone/thing white** drain someone or something of wealth or resources. **whited sepulchre** literary a hypocrite. [with biblical reference to the Gospel of Matthew, chapter 23.]
– DERIVATIVES **whitely** adverb **whiteness** noun **whitish** adjective.
– ORIGIN Old English, related to **WHEAT**.

white ant noun another term for **TERMITE**.

whitebait noun the small silvery-white young of herrings, sprats, and similar sea fish as food.

whitebeam noun a tree related to the rowan, with red berries and hairy oval leaves that are white underneath.

white belt noun a white belt worn by a beginner in judo or karate.

white blood cell noun less technical term for **LEUCOCYTE**.

whiteboard noun a wipeable board with a white surface used for teaching or presentations.

white-bread adjective N. Amer. informal bland and unchallenging in a way thought characteristic of the white middle classes.

whitecap noun N. Amer. a small wave with a foamy white crest.

white cell noun less technical term for **LEUCOCYTE**.

white Christmas noun a Christmas during which there is snow on the ground.

white-collar adjective relating to the work done or people who work in an office or other professional environment.

white dwarf noun Astronomy a small, very dense star.

white elephant noun a possession that is useless or unwanted, especially one that is expensive to maintain.
– ORIGIN from the story that the kings of Siam (now Thailand) gave such animals to courtiers they disliked, in order to ruin the recipient by the great cost involved in maintaining the animal.

white feather noun a white feather given to someone as a sign that they are considered to be a coward.
– ORIGIN with reference to a white feather in the tail of a game bird, being a mark of bad breeding.

whitefish noun (pl. same or **whitefishes**) a mainly freshwater fish of the salmon family, widely used as food.

white flag noun a white flag or cloth used as a symbol of surrender, truce, or a wish to negotiate.

whitefly noun (pl. **whiteflies**) a minute winged bug covered with powdery white wax, damaging plants by feeding on sap and coating them with honeydew.

white gold noun a silver-coloured alloy of gold with another metal.

white goods plural noun large domestic electrical goods such as refrigerators and washing machines. Compare with **BROWN GOODS**.

whitehead noun informal a pale or white-topped pustule on the skin.

white heat noun the temperature or state of something that is so hot that it gives out white light.

white hope (also **great white hope**) noun a person expected to bring much success to a team or organization.
– ORIGIN first referring to a white boxer believed capable of beating the first black world heavyweight champion.

white horses plural noun white-crested waves at sea.

white-hot adjective so hot as to glow white.

white knight noun a person or thing that comes to someone's aid.

white-knuckle adjective causing fear or nervous excitement.
– ORIGIN with reference to the effect caused by gripping tightly to steady oneself on a fairground ride.

white lie noun a harmless lie told to avoid hurting someone's feelings.

white light noun apparently colourless light containing all the wavelengths of the visible spectrum at equal intensity (such as ordinary daylight).

white magic noun magic used only for good purposes.

white meat noun pale meat such as chicken or turkey.

whiten verb make or become white.
– DERIVATIVES **whitener** noun.

white noise noun noise containing many frequencies with equal intensities.

white-out noun **1** a dense blizzard. **2** a weather condition in which the features and horizon of snow-covered country are indistinguishable.

White Paper noun (in the UK) a government report giving information about or proposals concerning a particular issue.

white rose noun the emblem of Yorkshire or the House of York in the Wars of the Roses.

White Russian noun **1** dated a person from Belarus (formerly Belorussia) in eastern Europe. **2** an opponent of the Bolsheviks during the Russian Civil War. •adjective relating to White Russians.

white sauce noun a sauce consisting of flour blended and cooked with butter and milk or stock.

white slave noun dated a woman tricked or forced into prostitution in a foreign country.

white spirit noun Brit. a colourless liquid distilled from petroleum, used as a paint thinner and solvent.

white tie noun **1** a white bow tie worn by men as part of full evening dress. **2** full evening dress.

white trash noun N. Amer. derogatory poor white people.

whitewash noun **1** a solution of lime or chalk

w

and water, used for painting walls white. **2** a deliberate concealment of someone's mistakes or faults. **3** informal a victory by the same side in every game of a series. • **verb 1** paint something with whitewash. **2** conceal unpleasant or incriminating facts about: *the editor and his newspaper have whitewashed the past.* **3** informal defeat an opposing side with a whitewash.

white water noun a fast shallow stretch of water in a river.

white wedding noun Brit. a traditional wedding at which the bride wears a formal white dress.

white witch noun a person who uses witchcraft to help other people.

whitey noun (pl. **whiteys**) informal, derogatory a white person.

whither old use or literary adverb **1** to what place or state? **2** what is the likely future of? **3** to which (with reference to a place). **4** to whatever place.
– ORIGIN Old English.

whiting[1] noun (pl. same) a slender-bodied sea fish with edible white flesh.
– ORIGIN Dutch *wijting*.

whiting[2] noun ground chalk used for purposes such as whitewashing and cleaning metal plate.

whitlow /wit-loh/ noun an abscess in the soft tissue near a fingernail or toenail.
– ORIGIN apparently from WHITE + FLAW.

Whitsun /wit-suhn/ noun Whitsuntide.

Whit Sunday noun the seventh Sunday after Easter, a Christian festival commemorating the descent of the Holy Spirit at Pentecost described in the Bible (Acts, chapter 2).
– ORIGIN Old English, 'white Sunday', probably with reference to the white robes worn by the newly baptized at Pentecost.

Whitsuntide /wit-suhn-tyd/ noun the weekend or week including Whit Sunday.

whittle verb **1** form a piece of wood into an object by repeatedly cutting small slices from it. **2** (**whittle something away/down**) reduce something by degrees.
– ORIGIN from dialect *whittle* 'knife', from an Old English word meaning 'cut, cut off'.

whizz (also chiefly N. Amer. **whiz**) verb (**whizzes, whizzing, whizzed**) **1** move quickly through the air with a whistling sound. **2** move or go fast. **3** (**whizz through**) do or deal with something quickly. • noun **1** a whizzing sound. **2** informal a fast movement or brief journey. **3** (also **wiz**) informal a person who is extremely clever at something. [influenced by WIZARD.] **4** Brit. informal amphetamines.
– DERIVATIVES **whizzy** adjective.
– ORIGIN imitating the sound.

whizz-kid (also **whiz-kid**) noun informal a young person who is very successful or highly skilled.

WHO abbreviation World Health Organization.

who pronoun **1** what or which person or people? **2** introducing a clause giving further information about a person or people previously mentioned.
– ORIGIN Old English.

USAGE: According to formal grammar, **who** is used as the subject of a verb (*who decided this?*) and **whom** is used as the object of a verb or preposition (*to whom do you wish to speak?*). However, in modern English **who** is often used instead of **whom**, as in *who should we support?* and most people consider this to be acceptable.

whoa /woh/ exclamation used as a command to a horse to stop or slow down.

who'd contraction **1** who had. **2** who would.

whodunnit (US **whodunit**) noun informal a story or play about a murder in which the identity of the murderer is not revealed until the end.

whoever pronoun **1** the person or people who; any person who. **2** regardless of who. **3** used for emphasis instead of 'who' in questions.

whole adjective **1** complete; entire. **2** emphasizing a large extent or number: *a whole range of issues.* **3** in an unbroken or undamaged state. • noun **1** a thing that is complete in itself. **2** (**the whole**) all of something. • adverb informal entirely; wholly: *a whole new meaning.*
– PHRASES **as a whole** as a single unit; in general. **on the whole** taking everything into account; in general. **the whole nine yards** informal, chiefly N. Amer. everything possible or available.
– DERIVATIVES **wholeness** noun.
– ORIGIN Old English.

wholefood noun (also **wholefoods**) Brit. food that has been processed as little as possible and is free from additives.

wholehearted adjective completely sincere and committed.
– DERIVATIVES **wholeheartedly** adverb.

wholemeal adjective Brit. referring to flour or bread made from wholewheat, including the husk.

whole number noun a number without fractions; an integer.

wholesale noun the selling of goods in large quantities to be sold to the public by others. • adverb **1** being sold in such a way. **2** as a whole and in an indiscriminate way. • adjective done on a large scale; extensive. • verb sell goods wholesale.
– DERIVATIVES **wholesaler** noun.

wholesome adjective **1** good for health and physical well-being. **2** morally good or beneficial.
– DERIVATIVES **wholesomely** adverb **wholesomeness** noun.

wholewheat noun whole grains of wheat including the husk.

wholly /hohl-li, hoh-li/ adverb entirely; fully.

whom pronoun used instead of 'who' as the object of a verb or preposition.

USAGE: For an explanation of the use of **who** and **whom**, see the note at **WHO**.

whomever pronoun formal used instead of 'whoever' as the object of a verb or preposition.

whomp /womp/ N. Amer. informal verb strike someone or something heavily. • noun a thump.
– ORIGIN imitating the sound.

w

whomsoever relative pronoun formal used instead of 'whosoever' as the object of a verb or preposition.

whoop /woop/ noun a loud cry of joy or excitement. •verb give or make a whoop.
– PHRASES **whoop it up** informal enjoy oneself or celebrate enthusiastically.
– ORIGIN probably imitating the sound.

whoopee /wuu-pee/ exclamation informal expressing wild excitement or joy.
– PHRASES **make whoopee 1** celebrate wildly. **2** have sex.

whoopee cushion noun a rubber cushion that makes a sound like the breaking of wind when someone sits on it.

whooper swan /hoo-per/ noun a large swan with a black and yellow bill and a loud trumpeting call, breeding in northern Eurasia and Greenland.

whooping cough /hoo-ping/ noun a contagious bacterial disease chiefly affecting children, characterized by convulsive coughs followed by a rasping indrawn breath.

whoops (also **whoops-a-daisy**) exclamation informal expressing mild dismay.
– ORIGIN probably from **UPSY-DAISY**.

whoosh /wuush, woosh/ (also **woosh**) verb move quickly or suddenly and with a rushing sound. •noun a whooshing movement.
– ORIGIN imitating the sound.

whop /wop/ (chiefly N. Amer. also **whap**) informal verb (**whops, whopping, whopped**) hit someone or something hard. •noun a heavy blow or its sound.
– ORIGIN from dialect *wap* 'strike'.

whopper noun informal **1** a very large thing. **2** a complete or blatant lie.

whopping adjective informal extremely large.

whore /rhymes with door/ derogatory noun **1** a prostitute. **2** a woman who has many sexual partners.
– DERIVATIVES **whorish** adjective.
– ORIGIN Old English.

whorehouse noun informal a brothel.

whorl /worl, werl/ noun **1** each of the turns in the spiral shell of a mollusc. **2** a set of leaves, flowers, or branches springing from a stem at the same level and encircling it. **3** a complete circle in a fingerprint.
– DERIVATIVES **whorled** adjective.
– ORIGIN apparently from **WHIRL**.

whortleberry /wer-t'l-be-ri/ noun a bilberry.
– ORIGIN dialect variant of former *hurtleberry*, of unknown origin.

who's contraction **1** who is. **2** who has.

> USAGE: Do not confuse **who's** with **whose**. Who's is short for **who is** or **who has**, as in *he has a son who's a doctor*, or *who's going to pay?*, while whose means 'belonging to associated with which person' or 'of whom or which', as in *whose coat is this?* or *a man whose opinion I respect*.

whose possessive determiner & pronoun **1** belonging to or associated with which person. **2** (as possessive determiner) of whom or which.
– ORIGIN Old English.

whosever relative pronoun & determiner

belonging to or associated with whichever person; whoever's.

whosoever pronoun formal term for **WHOEVER**.

whup /wup/ verb (**whups, whupping, whupped**) N. Amer. informal thrash someone or something.
– ORIGIN variant of **WHIP**.

why adverb **1** for what reason or purpose? **2** on account of which; the reason for which. •exclamation expressing surprise or indignation, or used for emphasis. •noun (pl. **whys**) a reason or explanation.
– ORIGIN Old English.

WI abbreviation **1** West Indies. **2** Wisconsin. **3** Brit. Women's Institute.

Wicca /wik-kuh/ noun the religious cult of modern witchcraft.
– DERIVATIVES **Wiccan** adjective & noun.
– ORIGIN Old English, 'witch'.

wick noun a strip of porous material up which liquid fuel is drawn to the flame in a candle, lamp, or lighter. •verb (usu. as adj. **wicking**) absorb or draw off liquid.
– PHRASES **get on someone's wick** Brit. informal annoy someone.
– ORIGIN Old English.

wicked adjective (**wickeder, wickedest**) **1** evil or morally wrong. **2** playfully mischievous. **3** informal excellent; very good.
– DERIVATIVES **wickedly** adverb **wickedness** noun.
– ORIGIN probably from **WICCA**.

wicker noun flexible twigs, typically of willow, plaited or woven to make items such as furniture and baskets.
– DERIVATIVES **wickerwork** noun.
– ORIGIN Scandinavian.

wicket noun **1** Cricket each of the sets of three stumps with two bails across the top at either end of the pitch, defended by a batsman. **2** a small door or gate, especially one beside or in a larger one.
– ORIGIN Old French *wiket*.

wicketkeeper noun Cricket a fielder stationed close behind a batsman's wicket.

widdershins /wid-der-shinz/ adverb chiefly Scottish in an anticlockwise direction.
– ORIGIN German *widersinnes*, from *wider* 'against' + *sin* 'direction'.

widdle Brit. informal verb urinate. •noun an act of urinating.
– ORIGIN from **PIDDLE**.

wide adjective (**wider, widest**) **1** of great or more than average width. **2** extending a specified distance from side to side. **3** open to the full extent. **4** including a great variety of people or things. **5** spread among a large number or over a large area. **6** (in combination) extending over the whole of: *industry-wide*. **7** at a great or specified distance from a point or target. •adverb **1** to the full extent. **2** far from a particular point or target. **3** (especially in football) at or near the side of the field. •noun (also **wide ball**) Cricket a ball that is judged to be too wide of the stumps for the batsman to play.
– PHRASES **wide awake** fully awake. **wide of the mark** inaccurate.
– DERIVATIVES **widely** adverb **wideness** noun.
– ORIGIN Old English.

wide-angle adjective (of a lens) having a short

focal length and so covering a wider view than a standard lens.

wide area network noun a computer network in which the computers connected may be far apart, generally having a radius of more than 1 km.

wide boy noun Brit. informal a man involved in petty criminal activities.

wide-eyed adjective 1 having one's eyes wide open in amazement. 2 inexperienced; innocent.

widen verb make or become wider.

wide-ranging adjective covering an extensive range of subjects or issues.

widescreen noun a cinema or television screen presenting a wide field of vision in relation to height.

widespread adjective spread among a large number or over a large area.

widgeon noun variant spelling of **WIGEON**.

widget /wi-jit/ noun informal a small gadget or mechanical device.
– ORIGIN perhaps an alteration of **GADGET**.

widow noun 1 a woman whose husband has died and who has not married again. 2 humorous a woman whose husband is often away taking part in a particular sport or activity: a golf widow. • verb (**be widowed**) become a widow or widower.
– ORIGIN Old English.

widower noun a man whose wife has died and who has not married again.

widowhood noun the state or period of being a widow or widower.

widow's mite noun a small monetary contribution from someone who is poor.
– ORIGIN with biblical allusion to the Gospel of Mark, chapter 12.

widow's peak noun a V-shaped growth of hair towards the centre of the forehead.

widow's weeds plural noun black clothes worn by a widow in mourning.
– ORIGIN weeds is used in the former sense 'garments' and is from Old English.

width /witth, width/ noun 1 the measurement or extent of something from side to side. 2 a piece of something at its full extent from side to side. 3 wide range or extent.

widthways (also **widthwise**) adverb in a direction parallel with a thing's width.

wield verb 1 hold and use a weapon or tool. 2 have and be able to use power or influence.
– DERIVATIVES **wielder** noun.
– ORIGIN Old English, 'govern, subdue, direct'.

Wiener schnitzel /vee-ner shnit-s'l/ noun a thin slice of veal that is breaded and fried.
– ORIGIN German, 'Vienna cutlet'.

wife noun (pl. **wives**) 1 a married woman in relation to her husband. 2 old use a woman.
– DERIVATIVES **wifely** adjective.
– ORIGIN Old English, 'woman'.

Wi-Fi abbreviation Wireless Fidelity, a set of technical standards for transmitting data over wireless networks.

wig noun a covering for the head made of real or artificial hair.
– ORIGIN shortening of **PERIWIG**.

wigeon /rhymes with pigeon/ (also **widgeon**) noun a duck with reddish-brown and grey

plumage, the male having a whistling call.
– ORIGIN perhaps suggested by **PIGEON**.

wigging noun Brit. informal, dated a severe reprimand.

wiggle verb move with short movements up and down or from side to side. • noun a wiggling movement.
– DERIVATIVES **wiggler** noun **wiggly** adjective.
– ORIGIN German and Dutch wiggelen.

wigwam noun a dome-shaped or conical dwelling made by fastening mats, skins, or bark over a framework of poles (as used formerly by some North American Indian peoples).
– ORIGIN Algonquian, 'their house'.

wild adjective 1 (of animals or plants) living or growing in the natural environment; not domesticated or cultivated. 2 (of scenery or a region) not inhabited in or changed by people. 3 lacking discipline or control. 4 not civilized; primitive. 5 not based on reason or evidence: a wild guess. 6 (of looks, appearance, etc.) showing strong emotion. 7 informal very enthusiastic or excited. 8 informal very angry. • noun 1 (**the wild**) a natural state. 2 (also **the wilds**) a remote area with few or no inhabitants.
– PHRASES **run wild** grow or behave in an uncontrolled way.
– DERIVATIVES **wildly** adverb **wildness** noun.
– ORIGIN Old English.

wild card noun 1 a playing card that can have any value, suit, colour, or other property in a game according to the choice of the player holding it. 2 a person or thing whose qualities are uncertain. 3 Computing a character that will match any character or sequence of characters in a search. 4 an opportunity to enter a sports competition without taking part in qualifying matches or being ranked at a particular level.

wildcat noun 1 a small Eurasian and African cat, typically grey with black markings and a bushy tail, believed to be the ancestor of the domestic cat. 2 an exploratory oil well.
• adjective (of a strike) sudden and unofficial.

wild duck noun a mallard.

wildebeest /wil-duh-beest, vil-duh-beest/ noun (pl. same or **wildebeests**) another term for **GNU**.
– ORIGIN Afrikaans, 'wild beast'.

wilderness noun 1 a wild, uninhabited, and inhospitable region. 2 a state of being out of political favour or office.
– ORIGIN Old English, 'land inhabited only by wild animals'; related to **DEER**.

wildfire noun (in phrase **spread like wildfire**) spread with great speed.
– ORIGIN from wildfire, a highly flammable liquid formerly used in warfare.

wildfowl plural noun birds that are hunted as game, especially waterbirds.

wild goose chase noun a hopeless search for or pursuit of something that is impossible to find or does not exist.

wildlife noun the native animals of a region.

wild rice noun a tall American grass with edible grains, related to rice and growing on wet land.

wiles plural noun cunning stratagems used by

someone in order to get what they want.
- ORIGIN perhaps related to an Old Norse word meaning 'craft'.

wilful (US also **willful**) adjective **1** (of a bad or harmful act) deliberate. **2** stubborn and determined.
- DERIVATIVES **wilfully** adverb **wilfulness** noun.

will[1] modal verb (3rd sing. present **will**; past **would**) **1** expressing the future tense. **2** expressing a strong intention or assertion about the future. **3** expressing inevitable events. **4** expressing a request. **5** expressing desire, consent, or willingness. **6** expressing facts about ability or capacity. **7** expressing habitual behaviour. **8** expressing probability or expectation about something in the present.
- ORIGIN Old English.

> USAGE: For an explanation of the difference between **will** and **shall**, see the note at **SHALL**.

will[2] noun **1** a person's power to decide on something and take action. **2** (also **willpower**) control or restraint deliberately exerted by a person: *a stupendous effort of will*. **3** a person's desire or intention in a particular situation: *the will to live*. **4** a legal document containing instructions about what should be done with a person's money and property after their death. • verb **1** intend or desire to happen. **2** bring about by the exercise of mental powers. **3** bequeath in one's will.
- PHRASES **at will** at whatever time or in whatever way one pleases. **where there's a will there's a way** proverb determination will overcome any obstacle. **with a will** energetically and resolutely.
- ORIGIN Old English; related to **WILL**[1] and **WELL**[1].

willie noun variant spelling of **WILLY**.

willies plural noun (**the willies**) informal a strong feeling of nervousness or uneasiness.
- ORIGIN unknown.

willing adjective **1** ready, eager, or prepared to do something. **2** given or done readily.
- DERIVATIVES **willingly** adverb **willingness** noun.

will-o'-the-wisp noun **1** a person or thing that is difficult or impossible to reach or catch. **2** a dim, flickering light seen hovering or floating at night on marshy ground, thought to result from the combustion of natural gases.
- ORIGIN originally as *Will with the wisp*, the sense of *wisp* being 'handful of lighted hay'.

willow noun a tree or shrub which typically grows near water, has narrow leaves and flexible branches, and bears catkins.
- ORIGIN Old English.

willowherb noun a plant with long narrow leaves and pink or pale purple flowers.

willow pattern noun a conventional design in pottery featuring a Chinese scene depicted in blue on white, typically including figures on a bridge, a willow tree, and birds.

willowy adjective **1** (of a person) tall, slim, and graceful. **2** bordered, shaded, or covered with willows.

willpower noun see **WILL**[2] (sense 2).

willy (also **willie**) noun (pl. **willies**) Brit. informal a penis.
- ORIGIN familiar form of the man's name *William*.

willy-nilly adverb **1** whether one likes it or not. **2** without direction or planning; haphazardly.
- ORIGIN later spelling of *will I, nill I* 'I am willing, I am unwilling'.

wilt[1] verb **1** (of a plant) become limp through heat, loss of water, or disease; droop. **2** (of a person) become tired and weak. • noun any of a number of plant diseases which cause foliage to wilt.
- ORIGIN perhaps from dialect *welk* 'lose freshness', from German.

wilt[2] old-fashioned second person singular of **WILL**[1].

Wilts. abbreviation Wiltshire.

wily /rhymes with highly/ adjective (**wilier**, **wiliest**) using cunning or crafty methods to gain an advantage.
- DERIVATIVES **wiliness** noun.

wimp informal noun a weak and cowardly person. • verb (**wimp out**) fail to do something as a result of fear or lack of confidence.
- DERIVATIVES **wimpish** adjective **wimpy** adjective.
- ORIGIN perhaps from **WHIMPER**.

wimple noun a cloth headdress covering the head, neck, and sides of the face, formerly worn by women and still by some nuns.
- ORIGIN Old English.

win verb (**winning**; past and past part. **won**) **1** be successful or victorious in a contest or conflict. **2** gain as a result of success in a contest, conflict, etc.: *you could win a trip to Australia*. **3** gain someone's attention, support, or love. **4** (**win someone over**) gain someone's support or favour. **5** (**win out/through**) manage to succeed or achieve something by effort. • noun a victory in a game or contest.
- PHRASES **win the day** be victorious.
- DERIVATIVES **winless** adjective **winnable** adjective.
- ORIGIN Old English, 'strive, contend', also 'subdue and take possession of, acquire'.

wince verb give a slight involuntary grimace or flinch due to pain or distress. • noun an instance of wincing.
- ORIGIN Old French *guenchir* 'turn aside'.

winceyette /win-si-**et**/ noun Brit. a lightweight brushed cotton fabric, used especially for nightclothes.
- ORIGIN from *wincey*, a lightweight wool and cotton fabric.

winch noun **1** a hauling or lifting device consisting of a rope or chain winding around a horizontal rotating drum, turned by a crank or by motor. **2** the crank of a wheel or axle. • verb hoist or haul something with a winch.
- ORIGIN Old English, 'reel, pulley'.

wind[1] /wind/ noun **1** the natural movement of the air, especially in the form of a current blowing from a particular direction. **2** breath as needed in physical exertion, speech, playing an instrument, etc. **3** Brit. air swallowed while eating or gas generated in the stomach and intestines by digestion. **4** meaningless talk. **5** (also **winds**) (treated as sing. or pl.) wind or woodwind instruments forming a band or section of an orchestra. • verb **1** make someone unable to breathe easily for a short time. **2** Brit. make a baby bring up wind after feeding by patting its back.
- PHRASES **get wind of** informal hear about something secret or private. **put the wind up**

Brit. informal alarm or frighten someone. **sail close to** (or **near**) **the wind** informal come close to being indecent, dishonest, or disastrous. **take the wind out of someone's sails** frustrate someone by doing or saying something they were not expecting.
- DERIVATIVES **windless** adjective.
- ORIGIN Old English.

wind² /wynd/ verb (past and past part. **wound** /wownd/) **1** move in or take a twisting or spiral course. **2** pass something around a thing or person so as to encircle or enfold them. **3** (of something long) twist or be twisted around itself or a core. **4** make a clockwork device operate by turning a key or handle. **5** turn a key or handle repeatedly. **6** move an audio tape, videotape, or a film back or forwards to a desired point. **7** hoist or pull something with a winch, windlass, etc. •noun a single turn made when winding.
- PHRASES **wind down 1** (of a clockwork mechanism) gradually lose power. **2** (also **wind something down**) draw or bring something gradually to a close. **3** informal relax after stress or excitement. **wind up** informal end up in a particular state, situation, or place. **wind someone up** Brit. informal tease or irritate someone. **wind something up** gradually bring something to an end.
- DERIVATIVES **winder** noun.
- ORIGIN Old English, 'go rapidly', 'twine'.

windbag noun informal a person who talks a lot but says little of any value.

windbreak noun a row of trees, wall, or screen which provides shelter from the wind.

windcheater noun Brit. a wind-resistant jacket with a close-fitting neck, waistband, and cuffs.

wind chill noun the cooling effect of wind on a surface.

wind chimes plural noun pieces of glass, metal rods, or similar items, hung near a door or window so as to strike each other and make a ringing sound in the draught.

windfall noun **1** a large amount of money that is received unexpectedly. **2** an apple or other fruit blown from a tree by the wind.

windfall tax noun a tax levied on an unexpectedly large profit, especially one considered to be excessive or unfairly obtained.

wind farm noun an area containing a group of energy-producing windmills or wind turbines.

winding /rhymes with finding/ adjective having a twisting or spiral course. •noun **1** a twisting movement or course. **2** a thing that winds or is wound round something.

winding sheet noun a sheet in which a dead body is wrapped for burial; a shroud.

wind instrument noun **1** a musical instrument in which sound is produced by the vibration of air, typically by the player blowing into the instrument. **2** a woodwind instrument as distinct from a brass instrument.

windjammer noun historical a merchant sailing ship.

windlass noun a winch, especially one on a ship or in a harbour.
- ORIGIN probably from an Old Norse word meaning 'winding pole'.

windmill noun a building with sails or vanes that turn in the wind and produce power to grind corn, generate electricity, or draw water. •verb move one's arms in a way that suggests the movement of a windmill's sails.

window noun **1** an opening in a wall or roof of a building, or in a vehicle, fitted with glass in a frame to let in light or air and allow people to see out. **2** an opening through which customers are served in a bank, ticket office, etc. **3** a framed area on a computer screen for viewing information. **4** a transparent panel in an envelope to show an address. **5** an interval or opportunity for action.
- DERIVATIVES **windowless** adjective.
- ORIGIN Old Norse, from words meaning 'wind' + 'eye'.

window box noun a long narrow box in which flowers and other plants are grown on an outside windowsill.

window dressing noun **1** the arrangement of a display in a shop window. **2** the presentation of something in a superficially attractive way to give a good impression.

window frame noun a frame holding the glass of a window.

window ledge noun a windowsill.

windowpane noun a pane of glass in a window.

window seat noun **1** a seat below a window, especially one in a bay or alcove. **2** a seat next to a window in an aircraft or train.

window-shop verb look at the goods displayed in shop windows, especially without intending to buy.
- DERIVATIVES **window-shopper** noun.

windowsill noun a ledge or sill forming the bottom part of a window.

windpipe noun the air passage from the throat to the lungs; the trachea.

windproof adjective (of an item of clothing or fabric) giving protection from the wind.

windscreen noun Brit. a glass screen at the front of a motor vehicle.

windscreen wiper noun Brit. a device consisting of a rubber blade on an arm that moves in an arc, for keeping a windscreen clear of rain.

windshield noun N. Amer. a windscreen.

windsock noun a light, flexible cylinder or cone mounted on a mast to show the direction and strength of the wind, especially at an airfield.

windstorm noun chiefly N. Amer. a gale.

windsurfing noun the sport of riding on a sailboard on water.
- DERIVATIVES **windsurf** verb **windsurfer** noun.

windswept adjective **1** (of a place) exposed to strong winds. **2** (of a person's hair or appearance) untidy after being in the wind.

wind tunnel noun a tunnel-like device for producing an airstream, in order to investigate flow or the effect of wind on an aircraft or other object.

wind-up noun **1** Brit. informal an attempt to tease or irritate someone. **2** an act of bringing something to an end.

windward adjective & adverb facing the wind or on the side facing the wind. Contrasted with

W

LEEWARD. • noun the side from which the wind is blowing.

windy[1] /win-di/ adjective (windier, windiest) 1 marked by or exposed to strong winds: *a windy day.* 2 informal (of speaking or writing) using many words that sound impressive but mean little.
– DERIVATIVES windily adverb windiness noun.

windy[2] /wyn-di/ adjective following a winding course.

wine noun 1 an alcoholic drink made from fermented grape juice. 2 a fermented alcoholic drink made from other fruits or plants.
– PHRASES wine and dine someone entertain someone with drinks and a meal.
– DERIVATIVES winey (also winy) adjective.
– ORIGIN Old English.

wine bar noun a bar or small restaurant that specializes in serving wine.

wine cellar noun 1 a cellar for storing wine. 2 a stock of wine.

wine glass noun a glass with a stem and foot, used for drinking wine.

winegrower noun a grower of grapes for wine.

wine gum noun a small fruit-flavoured sweet made with gelatin.

wine list noun a list of the wines available in a restaurant.

winemaker noun a producer of wine.
– DERIVATIVES winemaking noun.

winery noun (pl. wineries) a place where wine is made.

wineskin noun an animal skin sewn up and used to hold wine.

wine tasting noun an occasion when wine is tasted in order to assess its quality.

wine vinegar noun vinegar made from wine rather than malt.

wing noun 1 a modified forelimb or other part enabling a bird, bat, or insect to fly. 2 a rigid horizontal structure projecting from both sides of an aircraft and supporting it in the air. 3 a part of a large building, especially one that projects from the main part. 4 a group within an organization having particular views or a particular function: *the militant wing of a religious group.* 5 (the wings) the sides of a theatre stage out of view of the audience. 6 the part of a football, rugby, or hockey field close to the sidelines. 7 (also wing forward) an attacking player positioned near the sidelines. 8 Brit. a raised part of the body of a vehicle above the wheel. • verb 1 fly, or move quickly as if flying: *the prize will be winging its way to you soon.* 2 shoot a person or bird so as to wound in the arm or wing. 3 (wing it) informal speak or act without preparation.
– PHRASES in the wings ready for use or action at the appropriate time. on the wing (of a bird or insect) in flight. on a wing and a prayer with only a small chance of success. spread one's wings extend one's activities and interests. take wing fly away. under one's wing in or into one's protective care.
– DERIVATIVES winged adjective wingless adjective.
– ORIGIN Old Norse.

wingbeat (also wingstroke) noun one

complete set of movements of a wing in flying.

wing chair noun an armchair with side pieces projecting forwards from a high back.

wing collar noun a high stiff shirt collar with turned-down corners.

wing commander noun a rank of RAF officer, above squadron leader and below group captain.

winger noun 1 an attacking player on the wing in football, hockey, etc. 2 (in combination) a member of a specified political wing: *a Tory right-winger.*

wing mirror noun a rear-view mirror projecting from the side of a vehicle.

wing nut noun a nut with a pair of projections for the fingers to turn it on a screw.

wingspan (also wingspread) noun the maximum extent from tip to tip of the wings of an aircraft, bird, etc.

wink verb 1 close and open one eye quickly as a signal of affection or greeting or to convey a message. 2 shine or flash on and off. • noun an act of winking.
– DERIVATIVES winker noun.
– PHRASES as easy as winking informal very easy or easily. in the wink of an eye (or in a wink) very quickly. not sleep a wink (or not get a wink of sleep) not sleep at all.
– ORIGIN Old English.

winkle noun a small edible shellfish with a spiral shell. • verb (winkle something out) chiefly Brit. extract or obtain something with difficulty.
– ORIGIN shortening of PERIWINKLE[2].

winkle-picker noun Brit. informal a shoe with a long pointed toe, popular in the 1950s.

winner noun 1 a person or thing that wins something. 2 informal a thing that is a success or is likely to be successful.

winning adjective 1 gaining, resulting in, or relating to victory. 2 attractive; endearing. • noun (winnings) money won, especially by gambling.
– DERIVATIVES winningly adverb.

winning post noun a post marking the end of a race.

winnow verb 1 reduce people or things from a group until only the best ones are left: *we had to winnow out the losers.* 2 blow air through grain in order to remove the chaff.
– ORIGIN Old English.

wino noun (pl. winos) informal a homeless person who drinks excessive amounts of alcohol.

winsome adjective attractive or appealing in a fresh or innocent way.
– DERIVATIVES winsomely adverb winsomeness noun.
– ORIGIN from an Old English word meaning 'joy'.

winter noun the coldest season of the year, after autumn and before spring. • verb spend the winter in a particular place. • adjective (of crops) sown in autumn for harvesting the following year.
– ORIGIN Old English.

wintergreen noun 1 an American shrub whose leaves produce oil. 2 (also oil of wintergreen) a pungent oil obtained from

w

wintergreen or from birch bark, used as a medicine or flavouring.

winterize (or **winterise**) verb chiefly N. Amer. adapt or prepare something for use in cold weather.

Winter Olympics plural noun an international contest of winter sports held every four years at a two-year interval from the Olympic Games.

winter sports plural noun sports performed on snow or ice.

wintertime noun the season or period of winter.

wintry (also **wintery**) adjective (**wintrier**, **wintriest**) typical of winter, especially in being very cold or bleak.

win-win adjective (of a situation) in which each party benefits.

wipe verb **1** clean or dry something by rubbing with a cloth or the hand. **2** remove dirt or moisture with a cloth or the hand. **3** erase data from a tape, computer, etc. • noun **1** an act of wiping. **2** an absorbent disposable cleaning cloth.
– PHRASES **wipe the floor with** informal defeat someone completely. **wipe something off** subtract an amount from a value or debt. **wipe someone out 1** kill a large number of people. **2** (**be wiped out**) informal be exhausted or intoxicated. **wipe something out** remove or eliminate something. **wipe the slate clean** make a fresh start.
– DERIVATIVES **wipeable** adjective **wiper** noun.
– ORIGIN Old English.

wire noun **1** metal drawn out into a thin flexible strand or rod. **2** a length or quantity of wire used for fencing, to carry an electric current, etc. **3** a concealed electronic listening device. **4** informal, chiefly N. Amer. a telegram. • verb **1** install electric circuits or wires in something. **2** provide, fasten, or reinforce something with wire. **3** informal, chiefly N. Amer. send a telegram to someone.
– PHRASES **down to the wire** informal until the very last minute.
– ORIGIN Old English.

wire brush noun a brush with tough wire bristles for cleaning hard surfaces.

wired adjective informal **1** making use of computers and information technology to transfer or receive information. **2** nervous, tense, or edgy.

wire-haired adjective (especially of a dog breed) having wiry hair.

wireless adjective using radio, microwaves, etc. (as opposed to wires) to transmit signals. • noun dated, chiefly Brit. **1** a radio. **2** broadcasting or telegraphy using radio signals.
– DERIVATIVES **wirelessly** adverb.

wire service noun N. Amer. a news agency that supplies news stories to its subscribers, e.g. newspapers and radio and television stations.

wiretapping noun the practice of tapping a telephone line to monitor conversations secretly.

wire wool noun Brit. another term for STEEL WOOL.

wireworm noun the worm-like larva of a kind of beetle, which feeds on roots and can cause damage to crops.

wiring noun a system of wires providing electric circuits for a device or building.

wiry adjective (**wirier**, **wiriest**) **1** resembling wire in form and texture. **2** lean, tough, and sinewy: *a small, wiry woman.*

wisdom noun **1** the quality of having experience, knowledge, and good judgement. **2** the body of knowledge and experience that develops within a particular society or period: *oriental wisdom.*

wisdom tooth noun each of the four molars at the back of the mouth which usually appear at about the age of twenty.

wise[1] adjective **1** having or showing experience, knowledge, and good judgement. **2** (**wise to**) informal aware of. • verb (**wise up**) informal become aware of or informed about something.
– PHRASES **be none** (or **not any**) **the wiser** not understand something, even though it has been explained.
– DERIVATIVES **wisely** adverb.
– ORIGIN Old English.

wise[2] noun old use the way or extent of something.
– ORIGIN Old English.

-wise suffix **1** forming adjectives and adverbs of manner or respect: *clockwise.* **2** informal concerning: *security-wise.*

wiseacre /wyz-ay-ker/ noun a person who pretends to be wise or knowledgeable.
– ORIGIN Dutch *wijsseggher* 'soothsayer'.

wisecrack informal noun a witty remark or joke. • verb make a wisecrack.
– DERIVATIVES **wisecracker** noun.

wise guy noun informal, chiefly N. Amer. a person who makes sarcastic or cheeky remarks to demonstrate their cleverness.

wish verb **1** desire something that cannot or probably will not happen. **2** want to do something. **3** want someone to do something or something to be done. **4** express a hope that someone has happiness or success. **5** (**wish someone/thing on**) hope that someone has to deal with someone or something unpleasant. • noun **1** a desire or hope: *a wish for a more leisurely life.* **2** (**wishes**) an expression of a hope for someone's happiness, success, or welfare. **3** a thing wished for.
– ORIGIN Old English.

wishbone noun a forked bone between the neck and breast of a cooked chicken or similar bird which, when broken by two people, entitles the holder of the longer portion to make a wish.

wishful adjective **1** having or expressing a wish for something to happen. **2** based on impractical wishes rather than facts: *without resources the proposals were merely wishful thinking.*
– DERIVATIVES **wishfully** adverb.

wish-fulfilment noun the satisfying of wishes in dreams or fantasies.

wishing well noun a well into which one drops a coin and makes a wish.

wishy-washy adjective not firm or forceful; feeble: *wishy-washy liberalism.*

wisp noun a small thin bunch, strand, or

amount of something.
- DERIVATIVES **wispy** adjective.
- ORIGIN uncertain.

wist past and past participle of **WIT²**.

wisteria /wi-steer-i-uh/ (also **wistaria** /wi-stair-i-uh/) noun a climbing shrub with hanging clusters of pale bluish-lilac flowers.
- ORIGIN named after the American anatomist Caspar *Wistar* (or *Wister*).

wistful adjective having or showing a feeling of vague or regretful longing.
- DERIVATIVES **wistfully** adverb **wistfulness** noun.
- ORIGIN probably from former *wistly* 'intently', influenced by **WISHFUL**.

wit¹ noun 1 (also **wits**) the capacity to think inventively and understand quickly; keen intelligence: *he needed all his wits to find the way back.* 2 a natural talent for using words and ideas in a quick, clever, and amusing way. 3 a witty person.
- PHRASES **be at one's wits' end** be so worried that one does not know what to do. **have** (or **keep**) **one's wits about one** be constantly alert. **live by one's wits** earn money by clever and sometimes dishonest means.
- DERIVATIVES **witted** adjective.
- ORIGIN Old English.

wit² verb (**wot, witting, wist**) old use know someone or something.
- PHRASES **to wit** that is to say.
- ORIGIN Old English.

witch noun 1 a woman thought to have evil magic powers. 2 a person who follows or practises modern witchcraft. 3 informal an ugly or disliked old woman.
- DERIVATIVES **witchy** adjective.
- ORIGIN Old English.

witchcraft noun the practice of magic, especially the use of spells and the calling up of evil spirits. See also **WICCA**.

witch doctor noun (among tribal peoples) a person believed to have magic powers of healing, seeing the future, etc.

witchery noun 1 the practice of magic. 2 bewitching quality or power.

witchetty grub /wit-chi-ti/ noun a large whitish larva of a beetle or moth, eaten as food by some Australian Aboriginals.
- ORIGIN from words in an Aboriginal language meaning 'hooked stick for extracting grubs' + 'grub'.

witch hazel noun a lotion made from the bark and leaves of a shrub, used for treating injuries on the skin.
- ORIGIN *witch* is a variant spelling of *wych* (see **WYCH ELM**).

witch-hunt noun a campaign directed against a person or group whose views are considered to be unacceptable or a threat to society.

witching hour noun midnight, regarded as the time when witches are supposedly active.
- ORIGIN with reference to *the witching time of night* from Shakespeare's *Hamlet* (III. ii. 377).

with preposition 1 accompanied by. 2 possessing; having. 3 indicating the instrument used to perform an action or the material used for a purpose: *cut the fish with a knife.* 4 in relation to. 5 in opposition to or competition with. 6 indicating the way or attitude in which a person does something. 7 indicating

responsibility: *leave it with me.* 8 in the same direction as. 9 affected by a particular fact or condition. 10 employed by. 11 using the services of. 12 indicating separation or removal from something.
- PHRASES **be with someone** informal follow someone's meaning. **with it** informal 1 up to date or fashionable. 2 alert and able to understand.
- ORIGIN Old English.

withal /wi-thawl/ adverb old use in addition.

withdraw verb (past **withdrew**; past part. **withdrawn**) 1 remove or take away something. 2 leave or cause to leave a place. 3 stop taking part in an activity or being a member of a team or organization. 4 discontinue something previously given or provided: *the party withdrew its support for the government.* 5 take back a statement. 6 take money out of an account. 7 go away to another place in order to be private or quiet. 8 stop taking an addictive drug.

withdrawal noun 1 the action of withdrawing. 2 the process of giving up an addictive drug.

withdrawn past participle of **WITHDRAW**. adjective very shy or reserved.

wither verb 1 (of a plant) become dry and shrivelled. 2 become shrunken or wrinkled from age or disease. 3 gradually die out: *support for the UN strategy withered away.* 4 (as adj. **withering**) showing scorn or contempt.
- DERIVATIVES **witheringly** adverb.
- ORIGIN probably a variant of **WEATHER**.

withers plural noun the highest part of a horse's back, lying at the base of the neck above the shoulders.
- ORIGIN probably from former *widersome*.

withhold verb (past and past part. **withheld**) 1 refuse to give someone something that they want or is due to them. 2 suppress or restrain an emotion or reaction.
- DERIVATIVES **withholder** noun.

within preposition 1 inside. 2 inside the range or bounds of: *we were within sight of the finish.* 3 occurring inside a particular period of time. 4 not further off than (used with distances). •adverb 1 inside; indoors. 2 internally or inwardly.

without preposition 1 not accompanied by or having the use of. 2 in circumstances in which the action mentioned does not happen. •adverb old use outside.

withstand verb (past and past part. **withstood**) 1 remain undamaged or unaffected by something. 2 offer strong resistance to: *the city withstood the eastern invaders.*

withy /wi-thi/ noun (pl. **withies**) a tough flexible willow branch, used for tying things or making baskets.
- ORIGIN Old English.

witless adjective foolish; stupid.
- DERIVATIVES **witlessly** adverb **witlessness** noun.

witness noun 1 a person who sees an event take place. 2 a person giving sworn evidence to a court of law or the police. 3 a person who is present at the signing of a document and signs it themselves to confirm this. 4 (**witness to**) evidence or proof of: *the memorial service was witness to his wide circle of interests.* 5 open expression of a person's religious faith through words or actions. •verb 1 be a witness

W

to an event. **2** be the place or period in which an event takes place: *the 1960s witnessed a drop in churchgoing.*
– ORIGIN Old English.

witness box (N. Amer. **witness stand**) noun the place in a court of law from where a witness gives evidence.

witter verb (usu. **witter on**) Brit. informal speak at length about trivial matters.
– ORIGIN probably imitating the sound.

witticism noun a witty remark.

witting adjective **1** deliberate; on purpose. **2** aware of the full facts.
– DERIVATIVES **wittingly** adverb.
– ORIGIN from WIT².

witty adjective (**wittier**, **wittiest**) showing or having the ability to say clever and amusing things.
– DERIVATIVES **wittily** adverb **wittiness** noun.

wives plural of WIFE.

wiz noun variant spelling of WHIZZ (in sense 3).

wizard noun **1** a man who has magical powers, especially in legends and fairy tales. **2** a person who is very skilled in a particular area or activity: *a financial wizard.* **3** a computer software tool that automatically guides a user through a process. • adjective Brit. informal, dated excellent.
– DERIVATIVES **wizardly** adjective.
– ORIGIN first meaning 'philosopher, wise man': from WISE¹.

wizardry noun **1** the art or practice of magic. **2** great skill in a particular area or activity.

wizened /wi-zuhnd/ adjective shrivelled or wrinkled with age.
– ORIGIN from former *wizen* 'shrivel', from Old English.

WMD abbreviation weapon (or weapons) of mass destruction.

WNW abbreviation west-north-west.

WO abbreviation Warrant Officer.

woad /rhymes with road/ noun a plant whose leaves were formerly used to make blue dye.
– ORIGIN Old English.

wobble verb **1** move unsteadily from side to side. **2** (of the voice) tremble. **3** waver between different courses of action: *the President wobbled on Bosnia.* • noun a wobbling movement or sound.
– ORIGIN Germanic.

wobbler noun **1** a person or thing that wobbles. **2** another term for WOBBLY.

wobbly adjective (**wobblier**, **wobbliest**) **1** tending to wobble. **2** weak and unsteady from illness, tiredness, or anxiety. **3** uncertain or insecure: *the evening got off to a wobbly start.* • noun Brit. informal a fit of temper or panic.
– DERIVATIVES **wobbliness** noun.

wodge noun Brit. informal a large piece or amount of something.
– ORIGIN from WEDGE.

woe noun literary **1** great sorrow or distress. **2** (**woes**) troubles or problems.
– PHRASES **woe betide someone** a person will be in trouble if they do a specified thing.
– ORIGIN Old English.

woebegone /woh-bi-gon/ adjective looking sad or miserable.
– ORIGIN from WOE + former *begone*

'surrounded'.

woeful adjective **1** very sad or miserable. **2** shockingly bad: *the woeful state of film today.*
– DERIVATIVES **woefully** adverb.

wog noun Brit. informal, offensive a person who is not white.
– ORIGIN unknown.

woggle noun a loop or ring of leather or cord through which the ends of a Scout's neckerchief are threaded.
– ORIGIN unknown.

wok noun a bowl-shaped frying pan used in Chinese cookery.
– ORIGIN Chinese.

woke past of WAKE¹.

woken past participle of WAKE¹.

wold /rhymes with cold/ noun (especially in British place names) a piece of high, open, uncultivated land.
– ORIGIN Old English.

wolf noun (pl. **wolves**) **1** a wild animal of the dog family, that lives and hunts in packs. **2** informal a man who seduces many women. • verb (usu. **wolf something down**) eat food quickly and greedily.
– PHRASES **cry wolf** raise repeated false alarms, so that a real cry for help is ignored. [with reference to the fable of the shepherd boy who tricked people with false cries of 'Wolf!'] **keep the wolf from the door** have enough money to be able to buy food. **throw someone to the wolves** sacrifice someone in order to avoid trouble for oneself. **a wolf in sheep's clothing** a person who appears friendly but is really hostile. [with reference to the Book of Matthew, chapter 7.]
– DERIVATIVES **wolfish** adjective.
– ORIGIN Old English.

wolfhound noun a dog of a large breed originally used to hunt wolves.

wolfram /wuul-fruhm/ noun tungsten or its ore.
– ORIGIN German.

wolf whistle noun a whistle with a rising and falling pitch, used to express sexual attraction or admiration. • verb (**wolf-whistle**) whistle at someone in this way.

wolverine /wuul-vuh-reen/ noun a heavily built short-legged mammal with a long brown coat and a bushy tail, native to northern tundra and forests.
– ORIGIN from *wolv-*, plural stem of WOLF.

wolves plural of WOLF.

woman noun (pl. **women**) **1** an adult human female. **2** a female worker or employee. **3** a wife or lover.
– PHRASES **the little woman** a condescending way of referring to one's wife.
– DERIVATIVES **womanliness** noun **womanly** adjective.
– ORIGIN from the Old English words for WIFE and MAN.

womanhood noun **1** the state or period of being a woman. **2** women as a group. **3** the qualities associated with women, such as femininity.

womanish adjective derogatory **1** suitable for or typical of a woman: *womanish indecision.* **2** (of a man) effeminate.

W

womanize (or **womanise**) verb (usu. as noun **womanizing**) (of a man) have many casual sexual relationships with women.
– DERIVATIVES **womanizer** noun.

womankind noun women as a group.

womb noun the organ in the body of a woman or female mammal in which offspring develop before birth; the uterus.
– ORIGIN Old English.

wombat /wom-bat/ noun a burrowing Australian marsupial which resembles a small bear with short legs.
– ORIGIN from an extinct Aboriginal language.

women plural of **WOMAN**.

womenfolk plural noun the women of a family or community considered as a group.

women's liberation (also informal **women's lib**) noun a movement supporting the freedom of women to have the same rights, status, and treatment as men (now usually replaced by the term *feminism*).

womenswear noun clothing for women.

won[1] past and past participle of **WIN**.

won[2] /won/ noun (pl. same) the basic unit of money of North and South Korea.
– ORIGIN Korean.

wonder verb 1 desire to know something. 2 feel doubt: *I wondered about the validity of his comments.* 3 feel amazement and admiration. •noun 1 a feeling of surprise and admiration caused by something beautiful, unexpected, or unfamiliar. 2 a cause of wonder: *the wonders of a coral reef.* •adjective having remarkable qualities or abilities: *a wonder drug.*
– PHRASES **no** (or **little** or **small**) **wonder** it is not surprising. **wonders will never cease** often ironic an exclamation of surprise and pleasure. **work** (or **do**) **wonders** have a very beneficial effect.
– DERIVATIVES **wonderer** noun.
– ORIGIN Old English.

wonderful adjective very good, pleasant, or remarkable.
– DERIVATIVES **wonderfully** adverb **wonderfulness** noun.

wonderland noun a place full of wonderful things.

wonderment noun a state of awed admiration or respect.

wondrous adjective literary causing amazement and admiration. •adverb old use wonderfully; remarkably.
– DERIVATIVES **wondrously** adverb.

wonk (also **policy wonk**) noun N. Amer. informal, derogatory a person who takes an excessive interest in minor details of political policy.
– ORIGIN unknown.

wonky adjective (**wonkier**, **wonkiest**) informal 1 unsteady or faulty. 2 not straight; crooked.
– DERIVATIVES **wonkily** adverb **wonkiness** noun.
– ORIGIN unknown.

wont /wohnt/ noun (**one's wont**) formal one's usual behaviour. •adjective (**wont to**) literary in the habit of doing something; accustomed.
– ORIGIN Old English.

won't contraction will not.

wonted /wohn-tid/ adjective literary usual; normal.

wonton /won-ton/ noun (in Chinese cookery) a small round dumpling with a savoury filling, typically served in soup.
– ORIGIN Chinese.

woo verb (**woos**, **wooing**, **wooed**) 1 try to gain a woman's love. 2 try to gain the support or custom of: *the minister is attempting to woo golfers to Scotland.*
– DERIVATIVES **wooer** noun.
– ORIGIN Old English.

wood noun 1 the hard fibrous material forming the trunk or branches of a tree or shrub, used for fuel or timber. 2 (also **woods**) a small forest. 3 (**the wood**) wooden barrels used for storing alcoholic drinks. 4 a golf club with a wooden or other head that is relatively broad from face to back. 5 a bowl in the game of bowls.
– PHRASES **be unable to see the wood for the trees** fail to grasp the main issue because of over-attention to details. **out of the woods** out of difficulty. **touch wood** touch something wooden to prevent a confident statement from bringing bad luck.
– ORIGIN Old English.

wood alcohol noun crude methanol made by distillation from wood.

woodbine noun Brit. the common honeysuckle.

woodblock noun a block of wood from which woodcut prints are made.

woodcarving noun 1 the action or skill of carving wood. 2 a carved wooden object.
– DERIVATIVES **woodcarver** noun.

woodchip noun chiefly Brit. wallpaper with small chips of wood embedded in it to give a grainy surface texture.

woodchuck noun a North American marmot (rodent) with a heavy body and short legs.
– ORIGIN from an American Indian name (by association with **WOOD**).

woodcock noun (pl. same) a long-billed woodland bird of the sandpiper family, with brown plumage.

woodcut noun a print of a type made from a design cut in relief in a block of wood.

woodcutter noun a person who cuts down trees for wood.

wooded adjective (of land) covered with woods.

wooden adjective 1 made of or resembling wood. 2 stiff and awkward in speech or behaviour.
– DERIVATIVES **woodenly** adverb **woodenness** noun.

wooden spoon noun Brit. the last place in a race or competition.
– ORIGIN from the former practice of giving a spoon to the candidate coming last in the Cambridge mathematical tripos (exam).

woodgrain adjective (of a surface or finish) imitating the grain pattern of wood.

woodland noun (also **woodlands**) land covered with trees.

woodlouse noun (pl. **woodlice**) a small insect-like creature with a grey segmented body which it is able to roll into a ball.

woodpecker noun a bird with a strong bill and a stiff tail, typically pecking at tree trunks to find insects.

w

wood pigeon noun a common large pigeon, mainly grey with white patches forming a ring round its neck.

wood pulp noun wood fibre reduced chemically or mechanically to pulp and used in the manufacture of paper.

woodruff (also **sweet woodruff**) noun a white-flowered plant with sweet-scented leaves used to flavour drinks and in perfumery.
– ORIGIN Old English.

woodsman noun (pl. **woodsmen**) a forester, hunter, or woodcutter.

woodturning noun the activity of shaping wood with a lathe.
– DERIVATIVES **woodturner** noun.

woodwind noun (treated as sing. or pl.) wind instruments other than brass instruments forming a section of an orchestra, including flutes, oboes, and clarinets.

woodwork noun 1 the wooden parts of a room, building, or other structure. 2 Brit. the activity or skill of making things from wood.
– PHRASES **come out of the woodwork** (of a disliked person or thing) suddenly appear, especially to take advantage of a situation.
– DERIVATIVES **woodworker** noun **woodworking** noun.

woodworm noun 1 the wood-boring larva of a kind of small brown beetle. 2 the damaged condition of wood resulting from infestation with woodworm.

woody adjective (**woodier, woodiest**) 1 covered with trees. 2 made of or resembling wood.
– DERIVATIVES **woodiness** noun.

woof¹ /wuuf/ noun the barking sound made by a dog. • verb (of a dog) bark.
– ORIGIN imitating the sound.

woof² /woof/ noun another term for **WEFT**.
– ORIGIN Old English.

woofer /woo-fer, wuu-fer/ noun a loudspeaker designed to reproduce low frequencies.

wool noun 1 the fine soft hair forming the coat of a sheep, goat, or similar animal, especially when shorn and made into cloth or yarn. 2 a metal or mineral made into a mass of fine fibres.
– PHRASES **pull the wool over someone's eyes** deceive someone.
– ORIGIN Old English.

wool-gathering noun aimless thought or daydreaming.

woollen (US **woolen**) adjective 1 made of wool. 2 relating to the production of wool. • noun (**woollens**) woollen clothes.

woolly adjective (**woollier, woolliest**) 1 made of wool. 2 (of an animal or plant) covered with wool or hair resembling wool. 3 resembling wool in texture or appearance. 4 confused or unclear: *woolly thinking*. • noun (pl. **woollies**) informal chiefly Brit. a woollen jumper or cardigan.
– DERIVATIVES **woolliness** noun.

Woolsack noun (in the UK) the Lord Chancellor's wool-stuffed seat in the House of Lords.

woosh verb & noun variant spelling of **WHOOSH**.

woozy adjective (**woozier, wooziest**) informal unsteady, dizzy, or dazed.
– DERIVATIVES **woozily** adverb **wooziness** noun.

– ORIGIN unknown.

wop noun informal, offensive an Italian or other southern European.
– ORIGIN perhaps from Italian *guappo* 'bold, showy'.

Worcester sauce (also **Worcestershire sauce**) noun a tangy sauce containing soy sauce and vinegar, first made in Worcester in England.

Worcs. abbreviation Worcestershire.

word noun 1 a single unit of language which has meaning and is used with others to form sentences. 2 a remark or statement. 3 (a **word**) even the smallest amount of something spoken or written: *don't believe a word.* 4 (**words**) angry talk. 5 (the **word**) a command or signal: *someone gave me the word to start playing.* 6 (one's **word**) a person's version of the truth. 7 (one's **word**) a promise. 8 news or information. • verb express something in particular words.
– PHRASES **have a word** speak briefly to someone. **in so many words** precisely in the way mentioned. **in a word** briefly. **a man** (or **woman**) **of his** (or **her**) **word** a person who keeps their promises. **on** (or **upon**) **my word** an exclamation of surprise or emphasis. **take someone at their word** assume that a person is speaking honestly or sincerely. **take the words out of someone's mouth** say what someone else was about to say. **take someone's word** (**for it**) believe what someone says or writes without checking for oneself. **word for word** in exactly the same or, when translated, exactly equivalent words. **word of honour** a solemn promise. **word of mouth** speech as a means of conveying information.
– DERIVATIVES **wordless** adjective.
– ORIGIN Old English.

word class noun a part of speech.

wording noun the way in which something is expressed in words.

word-perfect adjective (of an actor or speaker) knowing one's part or speech by heart.

wordplay noun the witty use of words and their meanings, especially in puns.

word processor noun a computer or program for creating, editing, storing, and printing a document.

wordsmith noun a skilled user of words.

wordy adjective (**wordier, wordiest**) using or expressed in too many words.
– DERIVATIVES **wordily** adverb **wordiness** noun.

wore past of **WEAR**.

work noun 1 activity involving mental or physical effort done in order to achieve a result. 2 the activity or job that a person does to earn money. 3 a task or tasks to be done. 4 a thing or things done or made; the result of an action: *her work hangs in the Tate Gallery.* 5 (**works**) (treated as sing.) chiefly Brit. a place where industrial or manufacturing processes are carried out. 6 (**works**) chiefly Brit. activities involving construction or repair. 7 (**works**) the mechanism of a machine. 8 a defensive military structure. 9 Physics the exertion of force overcoming resistance or producing molecular change. 10 (the **works**) informal everything needed, wanted, or expected. • verb (past and past part. **worked** or old use **wrought**)

1 do work, especially as a job. **2** make someone do work. **3** (of a machine or system) function properly or effectively. **4** operate a machine. **5** have the desired result: *her plan worked admirably.* **6** bring a material or mixture to a desired shape or consistency. **7** move gradually or with difficulty: *they worked their way up the steep hill.* **8** produce an article or design using a specified material or sewing stitch. **9** cultivate land or extract materials from a mine or quarry. **10** bring into a specified emotional state: *he'd worked himself into a rage.*
- PHRASES **get worked up** become excited, angry, or stressed. **have one's work cut out** be faced with a hard or lengthy task. **in the works** being planned or produced. **work something in** try to include something. **work something off** get rid of something through physical effort. **work out 1** develop in a good or specified way. **2** engage in vigorous physical exercise. **work something out 1** solve a sum or calculate an amount. **2** plan something in detail. **work to rule** chiefly Brit. follow official working rules and hours exactly in order to reduce output and efficiency, as a form of industrial action. **work up to** proceed gradually towards something more advanced. **work something up** develop something gradually.
- DERIVATIVES **workless** adjective.
- ORIGIN Old English.

workable adjective **1** able to be shaped, manipulated, or dug. **2** capable of producing the desired result: *a workable peace settlement.*
- DERIVATIVES **workability** noun **workably** adverb.

workaday adjective not special or interesting; ordinary.

workaholic noun informal a person who works very hard and finds it difficult to stop working.
- DERIVATIVES **workaholism** noun.

workaround noun a method for overcoming a problem in a computer program or system.

workbench noun a bench at which carpentry or other mechanical or practical work is done.

workbook noun a student's book containing instruction and exercises.

workday noun a day on which a person works.

worker noun **1** a person who works. **2** a person who achieves a specified thing: *a miracle-worker.* **3** a neuter or undeveloped female bee, wasp, ant, etc., large numbers of which perform the basic work of a colony.

work ethic noun the belief that it is a person's moral duty to work hard.

work experience noun Brit. short-term experience of employment, arranged for older pupils by schools.

workforce noun (treated as sing. or pl.) the people engaged in or available for work in a particular area, organization, or industry.

workhorse noun a person or machine that works hard and reliably over a long period.

workhouse noun historical (in the UK) a public institution in which poor people received food and lodging in return for work.

working adjective **1** having paid employment. **2** doing manual work. **3** functioning or able to

function. **4** used as the basis for work or discussion and likely to be changed later: *a working title.* • noun **1** a mine or a part of a mine from which minerals are being extracted. **2** (**workings**) the way in which a machine, organization, or system operates. **3** (**workings**) a record of the calculations made in solving a mathematical problem.

working capital noun the capital of a business which is used in its day-to-day trading operations.

working class noun the social group consisting largely of people who do manual or industrial work. • adjective relating to the working class.

working party (also **working group**) noun Brit. a group appointed to study and report on a particular question and make recommendations.

workload noun the amount of work to be done by someone or something.

workman noun (pl. **workmen**) **1** a man employed to do manual work. **2** a person who works in a specified way: *he's a good workman.*

workmanlike adjective showing efficient skill.

workmanship noun the degree of skill with which a product is made or a job done.

workmate noun chiefly Brit. a person with whom one works; a colleague.

work of art noun a creative product with strong imaginative or artistic appeal.

workout noun a session of vigorous physical exercise.

work permit noun an official document giving a foreigner permission to take a job in a country.

workpiece noun an object being worked on with a tool or machine.

workplace noun a place where people work.

workroom noun a room for working in.

worksheet noun **1** a paper listing questions or tasks for students. **2** a paper recording work done or in progress.

workshop noun **1** a room or building in which goods are made or repaired. **2** a meeting for discussion and activity on a particular subject or project.

work-shy adjective unwilling to work.

workspace noun **1** space in which a person or people can work. **2** Computing a memory storage facility for temporary use.

workstation noun a desktop computer terminal, typically one that is part of a network.

worktop noun Brit. a flat surface for working on, especially in a kitchen.

world noun **1** (**the world**) the earth with all its countries and peoples. **2** a region or group of countries: *the English-speaking world.* **3** all that belongs to a particular period or area of activity: *the theatre world.* **4** (**one's world**) a person's life and activities. **5** (**the world**) secular or material matters as opposed to spiritual or religious ones. **6** a planet. **7** (**a/the world of**) a very large amount of: *that makes a world of difference.*
- PHRASES **the best of both** (or **all possible**) **worlds** the benefits of widely differing situations, enjoyed at the same time. **man** (or

w

woman) of the world a person with a great deal of experience of life and who is not easily shocked. **out of this world** informal very enjoyable or impressive.
– ORIGIN Old English.

world-beater noun a person or thing that is better than all others in its field.
– DERIVATIVES **world-beating** adjective.

world-class adjective relating to or among the best in the world.

World Cup noun a competition between teams from many countries in a sport.

world English noun the English language including all of its regional varieties, such as North American, Australian, and South African English.

worldly adjective (**worldlier, worldliest**) **1** relating to material things rather than spiritual ones: *he gave up his worldly goods and left in search of enlightenment.* **2** having experience of life; sophisticated.
– DERIVATIVES **worldliness** noun.

worldly-wise adjective having enough experience of life not to be easily shocked or cheated.

world music noun traditional music from the developing world, sometimes incorporating elements of Western popular music.

world order noun a system established internationally for preserving global political stability.

world power noun a country that has significant influence in international affairs.

world-ranking adjective among the best in the world.

world-shaking adjective very important.

world war noun a war involving many large nations in different parts of the world, especially the wars of 1914–18 and 1939–45.

world-weary adjective bored with or cynical about life.

worldwide adjective extending or applicable throughout the world. •**adverb** throughout the world.

World Wide Web noun an extensive information system on the Internet providing facilities for documents to be connected to other documents by hypertext links.

worm noun **1** an earthworm or other creeping or burrowing invertebrate animal with a long, thin, soft body and no limbs. **2** (**worms**) parasites that live in the intestines. **3** a maggot regarded as eating dead bodies buried in the ground: *food for worms.* **4** informal a weak or disliked person. •**verb 1** (**worm one's way**) move by crawling or wriggling. **2** (**worm one's way into**) gradually move into a situation in order to gain an advantage. **3** (**worm something out of**) obtain information from someone by continual questions or cunning.
– ORIGIN Old English.

worm cast noun a coiled mass of soil, mud, or sand thrown up at the surface by a burrowing worm.

worm-eaten adjective (of wood) full of holes made by woodworm.

wormery noun (pl. **wormeries**) a container in which worms are bred or kept for study.

worm gear noun a mechanical arrangement

consisting of a toothed wheel worked by a short revolving cylinder (worm) bearing a screw thread.

wormhole noun a hole made by a burrowing insect larva or worm in wood, fruit, etc.

wormwheel noun the wheel of a worm gear.

wormwood noun a woody shrub with a bitter taste, used as an ingredient of vermouth and absinthe and in medicine.
– ORIGIN Old English.

wormy adjective (**wormier, wormiest**) worm-eaten or full of worms.

worn past participle of WEAR. **adjective 1** damaged by wear. **2** very tired.

worn out adjective **1** exhausted. **2** so damaged by wear as to be no longer usable.

worried adjective feeling, showing, or expressing anxiety.
– DERIVATIVES **worriedly** adverb.

worrisome adjective causing anxiety or concern.

worry verb (**worries, worrying, worried**) **1** feel or cause to feel troubled over actual or possible difficulties: *you worry about your children when they stay out late.* **2** annoy or disturb someone. **3** (of a dog) tear at or pull something with the teeth. **4** (of a dog) chase and attack sheep or other livestock. **5** (**worry at**) pull at or fiddle with repeatedly: *he began to worry at the knot in the cord.* •**noun** (pl. **worries**) **1** the state of being troubled about actual or possible difficulties. **2** a source of anxiety.
– PHRASES **no worries** informal, chiefly Austral. all right; fine.
– DERIVATIVES **worrier** noun **worrying** adjective.
– ORIGIN Old English, 'strangle'.

worry beads plural noun a string of beads that a person fingers so as to stay calm and relaxed.

worse adjective **1** less good, satisfactory, or pleasing. **2** more serious or severe. **3** more ill or unhappy. •**adverb 1** less well. **2** more seriously or severely. •**noun** a worse event or situation.
– PHRASES **none the worse for** not affected badly or harmed by. **the worse for wear** informal **1** in a poor condition; worn. **2** feeling rather drunk. **worse off** less fortunate or wealthy.
– ORIGIN Old English.

worsen verb make or become worse.

worship noun **1** the practice of showing deep respect for and praying to a god or goddess. **2** religious rites and ceremonies. **3** great admiration or respect for someone. **4** (**His/Your Worship**) chiefly Brit. a title of respect for a magistrate or mayor. •**verb** (**worships, worshipping, worshipped;** US also **worships, worshiping, worshiped**) **1** offer praise and prayers to a god or goddess. **2** feel great admiration or respect for someone.
– DERIVATIVES **worshipper** noun.
– ORIGIN Old English, 'worthiness, acknowledgement of worth'.

worshipful adjective **1** feeling or showing great respect and admiration. **2** (**Worshipful**) Brit. a title given to Justices of the Peace.

worst adjective most bad, severe, or serious. •**adverb 1** most severely or seriously. **2** least well. •**noun** the worst part, event, or situation. •**verb** defeat or get the better of someone.

– PHRASES **at worst** in the worst possible case. **do one's worst** do as much damage as one can. **if the worst comes to the worst** if the most serious or difficult situation arises.
– ORIGIN Old English.

worsted /wuus-tid/ noun smooth and close-textured woollen fabric made from a fine yarn.
– ORIGIN from *Worstead*, a parish in Norfolk, England.

wort /wert/ noun a sweet solution made from soaking ground malt or other grain before fermentation, used to produce beer.
– ORIGIN Old English.

worth adjective **1** equivalent in value to the sum or item specified. **2** deserving to be treated or regarded in the way specified: *the museum is worth a visit.* **3** having income or property amounting to a specified sum. • noun **1** the value or merit of someone or something. **2** an amount of a commodity equivalent to a specified sum of money: *hundreds of pounds' worth of clothes.*
– PHRASES **for all one is worth** informal as energetically or enthusiastically as one can.
– ORIGIN Old English.

worthless adjective **1** having no real value or use. **2** having no good qualities.
– DERIVATIVES **worthlessly** adverb **worthlessness** noun.

worthwhile adjective worth the time, money, or effort spent.

worthy adjective (**worthier, worthiest**) **1** deserving or good enough: *issues worthy of further consideration.* **2** deserving effort, attention, or respect. **3** well meaning but rather dull or unimaginative. • noun (pl. **worthies**) often humorous a person important in a particular sphere: *local worthies.*
– DERIVATIVES **worthily** adverb **worthiness** noun.

-worthy combining form **1** deserving of a specified thing: *newsworthy.* **2** suitable for a specified thing: *roadworthy.*

wot singular present of WIT².

would modal verb (3rd sing. present **would**) **1** past of WILL¹, in various senses. **2** (expressing the conditional mood) indicating the result of an imagined event. **3** expressing a desire or inclination. **4** expressing a polite request. **5** expressing an opinion or assumption: *I would have to agree.* **6** literary expressing a wish or regret: *would that he had lived to finish it.*

USAGE: For an explanation of the difference between **would** and **should**, see the note at **SHOULD**.

would-be adjective often derogatory desiring or hoping to be a specified type of person: *a would-be actress.*

wouldn't contraction would not.

wouldst old-fashioned second person singular of WOULD.

wound¹ /woond/ noun **1** an injury to the body caused by a cut, blow, or other impact. **2** mental pain caused to someone: *what I'm saying might open up old wounds.* • verb **1** injure a person or part of the body. **2** hurt someone's feelings.
– ORIGIN Old English.

wound² past and past participle of WIND².

wove past of WEAVE¹.

woven past participle of WEAVE¹.

wow¹ informal exclamation (also **wowee**) expressing astonishment or admiration. • verb impress and excite someone greatly. • noun a sensational success.

wow² noun Electronics slow pitch variation in sound reproduction, perceptible in long notes. Compare with FLUTTER (in sense 4).
– ORIGIN imitating the sound.

wowser /wow-zer/ noun Austral./NZ informal a puritanical person, especially one who disapproves of drinking alcohol.
– ORIGIN unknown.

WP abbreviation word processing or word processor.

WPC abbreviation (in the UK) woman police constable.

wpm abbreviation words per minute (used after a number to indicate typing speed).

wrack¹ verb variant spelling of RACK¹.

USAGE: For an explanation of the difference between **wrack** and **rack**, see the note at **RACK¹**.

wrack² noun a coarse brown seaweed which grows on the shoreline.
– ORIGIN probably from Dutch *wrak* 'shipwreck'.

wraith /rayth/ noun a ghost or ghostly image of someone, especially one seen shortly before or after a person's death.
– DERIVATIVES **wraithlike** adjective.
– ORIGIN unknown.

wrangle noun a long and complicated dispute or argument. • verb **1** have a long and complicated dispute or argument. **2** N. Amer. round up or take charge of livestock.
– DERIVATIVES **wrangler** noun.
– ORIGIN perhaps from German *wrangen* 'to struggle'.

wrap verb (**wraps, wrapping, wrapped**) **1** cover or enclose someone or something in paper or soft material. **2** encircle or wind round: *he wrapped an arm around her waist.* **3** (in word processing etc.) cause a word or words to be carried over to a new line automatically. **4** informal finish filming or recording. • noun **1** a loose outer garment or piece of material. **2** paper or material used for wrapping. **3** a tortilla wrapped around a cold filling, eaten as a sandwich. **4** informal the end of a session of filming or recording.
– PHRASES **be wrapped up in** be so involved in something that one does not notice other people or things. **under wraps** kept secret. **wrap up** (also **wrap someone up**) put on or dress someone in warm clothes. **wrap something up** end a discussion or complete a deal.
– DERIVATIVES **wrapping** noun.
– ORIGIN unknown.

wrap-around adjective **1** (of a skirt, dress, etc.) having one part overlapping another and fastened loosely. **2** curving or extending round at the sides.

wrapper noun a piece of paper or other material used for wrapping something.

wrasse /rass/ noun (pl. same or **wrasses**) a brightly coloured sea fish with thick lips and strong teeth.
– ORIGIN Cornish *wrah*.

w

wrath /roth, rawth/ noun extreme anger.
– ORIGIN Old English.

wrathful adjective literary full of or showing great anger.
– DERIVATIVES **wrathfully** adverb.

wreak verb 1 cause a great amount of damage or harm. 2 take revenge on someone.
– ORIGIN Old English, 'drive (out), avenge'.

USAGE: The past tense of **wreak** is **wreaked**, as in *rainstorms wreaked havoc yesterday*, not **wrought**. Wrought is in fact an old-fashioned past tense of **work**.

wreath /reeth/ noun (pl. **wreaths** /reeths, reeth*z*/) 1 an arrangement of flowers, leaves, or stems fastened in a ring and used for decoration or for placing on a grave. 2 a curl or ring of smoke or cloud.
– ORIGIN Old English, related to **WRITHE**.

wreathe /reeth/ verb 1 envelop, surround, or encircle: *the mountain was wreathed in mist*. 2 (of smoke) move with a curling motion.
– ORIGIN from **WRITHE**.

wreck noun 1 the destruction of a ship at sea; a shipwreck. 2 a ship destroyed at sea. 3 a building, vehicle, etc. that has been destroyed or badly damaged. 4 a person in a very bad physical or mental state. 5 N. Amer. a road or rail crash. •verb 1 cause a ship to sink or break up. 2 destroy or severely damage a structure or vehicle. 3 spoil completely: *the injury wrecked his chances*.
– ORIGIN Old French *wrec*, from Old Norse.

wreckage noun the remains of something that has been badly damaged or destroyed.

wrecked adjective informal 1 exhausted. 2 Brit. drunk.

wrecker noun 1 a person or thing that wrecks something. 2 chiefly N. Amer. a person who breaks up damaged vehicles to obtain usable spares or scrap.

Wren noun (in the UK) a member of the former Women's Royal Naval Service.
– ORIGIN from **WRNS**.

wren noun a very small short-winged songbird with a cocked tail.
– ORIGIN Old English.

wrench verb 1 pull or twist suddenly and violently: *he wrenched the gun from my hand*. 2 injure a part of the body as a result of a sudden twisting movement. •noun 1 a sudden violent twist or pull. 2 a feeling of acute sadness and distress caused by leaving a person or place. 3 an adjustable tool like a spanner, used for gripping and turning nuts or bolts.
– ORIGIN Old English.

wrest /rest/ verb 1 take power or control from someone after a struggle. 2 forcibly pull something from a person's grasp.
– ORIGIN Old English, 'twist, tighten'.

wrestle verb 1 take part in a fight or contest that involves close grappling with one's opponent. 2 struggle with a difficulty or problem. 3 move or manipulate with difficulty: *she wrestled the keys out of the ignition*. •noun 1 a wrestling bout or contest. 2 a hard struggle.
– DERIVATIVES **wrestler** noun **wrestling** noun.
– ORIGIN Old English.

wretch noun 1 an unfortunate person. 2 informal a disliked or unpleasant person.
– ORIGIN Old English.

wretched adjective (**wretcheder**, **wretchedest**) 1 in a very unhappy or unfortunate state; miserable. 2 very bad or unpleasant: *the wretched conditions of the slums*. 3 used to express anger or annoyance: *she disliked the wretched man intensely*.
– DERIVATIVES **wretchedly** adverb **wretchedness** noun.

wriggle verb 1 twist and turn with quick short movements. 2 (**wriggle out of**) manage to avoid doing something that one ought to do. •noun a wriggling movement.
– DERIVATIVES **wriggler** noun **wriggly** adjective.
– ORIGIN German *wriggelen*.

wright noun old use (except in combination) a maker or builder: *playwright*.
– ORIGIN Old English.

wring verb (past and past part. **wrung**) 1 squeeze and twist something to force liquid from it. 2 twist and break an animal's neck. 3 squeeze someone's hand tightly. 4 (**wring something from/out of**) obtain something with difficulty or effort.
– PHRASES **wring one's hands** clasp and twist one's hands together as a gesture of distress or despair.
– ORIGIN Old English.

wringer noun a device for wringing water from wet clothes or other objects.

wringing adjective extremely wet; soaked.

wrinkle noun 1 a slight line or fold, especially in fabric or the skin of the face. 2 informal a minor difficulty. •verb make or become wrinkled.
– DERIVATIVES **wrinkled** adjective.
– ORIGIN possibly from an Old English word meaning 'sinuous'.

wrinkly adjective (**wrinklier**, **wrinkliest**) having many wrinkles. •noun (pl. **wrinklies**) Brit. informal, derogatory an old person.

wrist noun the joint connecting the hand with the forearm.
– ORIGIN Old English.

wristband noun a band worn round the wrist, especially for identity purposes or to soak up sweat when playing sport.

wristwatch noun a watch worn on a strap round the wrist.

writ[1] noun an official document issued in the name of a court or other legal authority, ordering a person to do or not to do something.
– ORIGIN Old English.

writ[2] verb old-fashioned past participle of **WRITE**.
– PHRASES **writ large** in an obvious or exaggerated form.

write verb (past **wrote**; past part. **written**) 1 mark letters, words, or other symbols on a surface, with a pen, pencil, or similar implement. 2 compose and send a letter to someone. 3 compose a book or other written work. 4 compose a musical score. 5 fill out or complete a cheque or similar document. 6 Computing enter data into a specified storage medium or location.
– PHRASES **be written all over one's face** informal be obvious from one's expression. **write**

someone/thing off 1 dismiss someone or something as insignificant. **2** cancel a bad debt or acknowledge that an asset will not be recovered. **3** Brit. damage a vehicle so badly that it cannot be repaired or is not worth repairing.
– DERIVATIVES **writable** adjective (chiefly Computing).
– ORIGIN Old English.

write-off noun 1 Brit. a vehicle that is too badly damaged to be repaired. **2** informal a person or thing that is dismissed as a failure, waste of time, etc.

writer noun 1 a person who has written a particular work, or who writes books or articles as an occupation. **2** Computing a device that writes data to a storage medium.

writerly adjective 1 relating to or characteristic of a professional author. **2** deliberately literary in style.

writer's block noun the condition of being unable to think of what to write or how to proceed with writing.

writer's cramp noun pain or stiffness in the hand caused by writing for a long time.

write-up noun a newspaper review of a recent book, performance, product, etc.

writhe /ryth/ **verb** twist or squirm in pain or distress.
– ORIGIN Old English, 'make into coils, plait'.

writing noun 1 the activity or skill of writing. **2** written work. **3** (**writings**) books or other written works by a particular author or on a particular subject. **4** a sequence of letters or symbols forming words.
– PHRASES **the writing is on the wall** there are clear signs that something unpleasant or unwelcome is going to happen. [with reference to Belshazzar's feast in the Bible (Book of Daniel, chapter 5), at which mysterious writing appeared on the wall foretelling Belshazzar's overthrow.]

written past participle of WRITE.

WRNS abbreviation historical (in the UK) Women's Royal Naval Service.

wrong adjective 1 not correct or true; mistaken or in error. **2** unjust, dishonest, or immoral. **3** in a bad or abnormal condition: *something's wrong with the car.* ●adverb **1** in a mistaken or undesirable way or direction. **2** with an incorrect result. ●noun an unjust, dishonest, or immoral action. ●verb **1** act unjustly or dishonestly towards someone. **2** mistakenly attribute bad motives to someone.
– PHRASES **get hold of the wrong end of the stick** Brit. misunderstand something. **in the wrong** responsible for a mistake or offence. **on the wrong side of 1** out of favour with. **2** somewhat more than a particular age.
– DERIVATIVES **wrongly** adverb **wrongness** noun.
– ORIGIN Old Norse, 'awry, unjust'.

wrongdoing noun illegal or dishonest behaviour.
– DERIVATIVES **wrongdoer** noun.

wrong-foot verb Brit. **1** (in a game) play so as to catch an opponent off balance. **2** place someone in a difficult or embarrassing situation by saying or doing something unexpected.

wrongful adjective not fair, just, or legal.

– DERIVATIVES **wrongfully** adverb.

wrong-headed adjective having or showing bad judgement; misguided.

wrote past tense of WRITE.

wroth /rohth, roth/ **adjective** old use angry.
– ORIGIN Old English.

wrought /rhymes with bought/ **adjective 1** (of metals) beaten out or shaped by hammering. **2** (in combination) made or fashioned in the specified way: *well-wrought.* **3** (**wrought up**) upset and anxious.
– ORIGIN old-fashioned past and past participle of WORK.

wrought iron noun a tough malleable form of iron suitable for forging or rolling rather than casting.

wrung past and past participle of WRING.

WRVS abbreviation (in the UK) Women's Royal Voluntary Service.

wry /ry/ **adjective** (**wryer**, **wryest** or **wrier**, **wriest**) **1** using or expressing dry, especially mocking, humour: *a wry smile.* **2** (of a person's face) twisted into an expression of disgust, disappointment, or annoyance. **3** bending or twisted to one side.
– DERIVATIVES **wryly** adverb **wryness** noun.
– ORIGIN from an Old English word meaning 'tend, incline', later 'swerve, contort'.

wryneck noun a bird of the woodpecker family, with brown plumage and a habit of twisting its head backwards.

WSW abbreviation west-south-west.

WTO abbreviation World Trade Organization.

wunderkind /vuun-der-kind/ **noun** (pl. **wunderkinds** or **wunderkinder** /vuun-der-kin-der/) a person who achieves great success at a relatively young age.
– ORIGIN German, from *Wunder* 'wonder' + *Kind* 'child'.

Wurlitzer /wer-lit-ser/ **noun** trademark a large pipe organ or electric organ.
– ORIGIN named after the American instrument-maker Rudolf *Wurlitzer*.

wuss /rhymes with puss/ **noun** informal a weak or ineffectual person.
– ORIGIN unknown.

WV abbreviation West Virginia.

WWI abbreviation World War I.

WWII abbreviation World War II.

WWF abbreviation 1 World Wide Fund for Nature. **2** World Wrestling Federation.

WWW abbreviation World Wide Web.

WY abbreviation Wyoming.

wych elm /rhymes with witch/ **noun** a European elm with large rough leaves.
– ORIGIN *wych*, used in names of trees with flexible branches, is from Old English.

WYSIWYG /wi-zi-wig/ **adjective** Computing referring to the display of text on-screen in a form exactly corresponding to its appearance on a printout.
– ORIGIN from the initial letters of *what you see is what you get.*

wyvern /wy-vern/ **noun** Heraldry a winged two-legged dragon with a barbed tail.
– ORIGIN first referring to a viper: from Old French *wivre.*

w

Xx

X[1] (also **x**) noun (pl. **Xs** or **X's**) **1** the twenty-fourth letter of the alphabet. **2** referring to an unknown or unspecified person or thing. **3** (usu. *x*) the first unknown quantity in an algebraic expression. **4** referring to the main or horizontal axis in a system of coordinates. **5** a cross-shaped written symbol, used to indicate a wrong answer or to symbolize a kiss. **6** the Roman numeral for ten.

X[2] symbol films classified as suitable for adults only (replaced in the UK in 1983 by *18*, and in the US in 1990 by *NC–17*).

X chromosome noun (in humans and other mammals) a sex chromosome, two of which are normally present in female cells (known as XX) and only one in male cells (known as XY). Compare with **Y CHROMOSOME**.

Xe symbol the chemical element xenon.

xebec /zee-bek/ noun historical a small three-masted Mediterranean sailing ship.
– ORIGIN Arabic.

xenon /zen-on, zee-non/ noun an inert gaseous chemical element, present in trace amounts in the air and used in some kinds of electric light.
– ORIGIN from Greek *xenos* 'strange'.

xenophobia /zen-uh-foh-bi-uh/ noun intense or irrational dislike or fear of people from other countries.
– DERIVATIVES **xenophobe** noun **xenophobic** adjective.
– ORIGIN from Greek *xenos* 'stranger'

xenotransplantation /zen-oh-trans-plahn-**tay**-sh'n/ noun the process of grafting or transplanting organs or tissues between members of different species.
– DERIVATIVES **xenotransplant** noun.
– ORIGIN from Greek *xenos* 'strange'.

xerography /zi-uh-**rog**-ruh-fi/ noun a dry copying process in which powder sticks to parts of a surface remaining electrically charged after being exposed to light from an image of the document to be copied.
– DERIVATIVES **xerographic** adjective.

– ORIGIN from Greek *xēros* 'dry'.

Xerox /zeer-oks, ze-roks/ noun trademark **1** a xerographic copying process. **2** a copy made using such a process. •verb (**xerox**) copy a document using xerography.
– ORIGIN based on **XEROGRAPHY**.

Xhosa /koh-suh, kor-suh/ noun (pl. same or **Xhosas**) **1** a member of a South African people traditionally living in the Eastern Cape Province. **2** the Bantu language of the Xhosa.
– ORIGIN Xhosa.

XL abbreviation extra large (as a clothes size).

Xmas /kriss-muhss, eks-muhss/ noun informal Christmas.
– ORIGIN *X* representing the initial Greek character of Greek *Khristos* 'Christ'.

XML abbreviation Extensible Markup Language.

X-rated adjective **1** pornographic or indecent. **2** (formerly) referring to a film given an X classification.

X-ray noun **1** an electromagnetic wave of very short wavelength, able to pass through many materials opaque to light and so make it possible to see into or through them. **2** an image of the internal structure of an object produced by passing X-rays through it. •verb photograph or examine something or someone with X-rays.
– ORIGIN from *X-* (because, when discovered in 1895, the nature of the rays was unknown).

xylem /zy-luhm/ noun the tissue in plants which carries water and dissolved nutrients upwards from the root and also helps to form the woody element in the stem.
– ORIGIN from Greek *xulon* 'wood'.

xylene /zy-leen/ noun a liquid hydrocarbon obtained by distilling wood, coal tar, or petroleum, used in fuels and solvents.
– ORIGIN from Greek *xulon* 'wood'.

xylophone /zy-luh-fohn/ noun a musical instrument played by striking a row of wooden bars of graduated length with small hammers.
– ORIGIN from Greek *xulon* 'wood'.

x

Yy

Y¹ (also **y**) noun (pl. **Ys** or **Y's**) **1** the twenty-fifth letter of the alphabet. **2** referring to an unknown or unspecified person or thing (coming second after 'x'). **3** (usu. **y**) the second unknown quantity in an algebraic expression. **4** referring to the secondary or vertical axis in a system of coordinates.

Y² abbreviation yen. •symbol the chemical element yttrium.

y abbreviation year(s).

Y2K abbreviation year 2000 (with reference to the millennium bug).

yacht /yot/ noun **1** a medium-sized sailing boat equipped for cruising or racing. **2** a powered boat equipped for cruising.
– DERIVATIVES **yachting** noun.
– ORIGIN Dutch *jaghte*, from *jaghtschip* 'fast pirate ship'.

yachtsman (or **yachtswoman**) noun (pl. **yachtsmen** or **yachtswomen**) a person who sails yachts.

yack noun & verb variant spelling of YAK².

yacker noun variant spelling of YAKKA.

yahoo /yah-hoo, yuh-**hoo**/ noun informal a rude, coarse, or violent person.
– ORIGIN the name of an imaginary people in Jonathan Swift's *Gulliver's Travels*.

Yahweh /yah-way/ noun a form of the Hebrew name of God used in the Bible.
– ORIGIN Hebrew.

yak¹ noun a large ox with shaggy hair and large horns, used in Tibet to carry loads and for its milk, meat, and hide.
– ORIGIN Tibetan.

yak² (also **yack**) informal verb (**yaks, yakking, yakked**) talk at length about unimportant or boring subjects. •noun a trivial or lengthy conversation.
– ORIGIN imitating the sound.

yakka /yak-kuh/ (also **yacker**) noun Austral./NZ informal work.
– ORIGIN Yagara (an Aboriginal language).

yakuza /yuh-**koo**-zuh/ noun (pl. same) (**the Yakuza**) a powerful Japanese criminal organization.
– ORIGIN Japanese, from the words for 'eight' + 'nine' + 'three', referring to the worst hand in a gambling game.

Yale noun trademark a type of lock with a latch bolt and a flat key with a serrated edge.
– ORIGIN named after the American locksmith Linus *Yale* Jr.

yam noun **1** the edible starchy tuber of a tropical and subtropical climbing plant, eaten as a vegetable. **2** N. Amer. a sweet potato.
– ORIGIN from Portuguese *inhame* or former Spanish *iñame*.

yammer informal verb **1** talk loudly and continuously. **2** make a loud, continuous noise. •noun loud and continuous noise.
– ORIGIN Old English, 'to lament'.

yang noun (in Chinese philosophy) the active male principle of the universe. Contrasted with YIN.
– ORIGIN Chinese, 'male genitals', 'sun', 'positive'.

Yank noun informal, often derogatory an American.

yank informal verb pull quickly and hard: *he yanked her to her feet.* •noun a sudden hard pull.
– ORIGIN unknown.

Yankee noun informal **1** often derogatory an American. **2** US a person from New England or one of the northern states. **3** historical a Federal soldier in the US Civil War. **4** a bet on four or more horses to win (or be placed) in different races.
– ORIGIN perhaps from Dutch *Janke*, from *Jan* 'John'.

yap verb (**yaps, yapping, yapped**) **1** give a sharp, shrill bark. **2** informal talk at length in an irritating way. •noun a sharp, shrill bark.
– DERIVATIVES **yappy** adjective (informal).
– ORIGIN imitating the sound.

yard¹ noun **1** a unit of length equal to 3 feet (0.9144 metre). **2** a square or cubic yard, especially of sand or other building materials. **3** a long pole slung across a ship's mast for a sail to hang from.
– PHRASES **by the yard** in large numbers or quantities.
– ORIGIN Old English.

yard² noun **1** chiefly Brit. a piece of uncultivated enclosed ground next to a building. **2** an area of land used for a particular purpose or business: *a builder's yard.* **3** N. Amer. the garden of a house.
– ORIGIN Old English, 'building, home, region'.

yardage noun a distance or length measured in yards.

yardarm noun either end of the yard (long pole) slung across a ship's mast for a sail to hang from.

Yardie informal noun **1** (among Jamaicans) a fellow Jamaican. **2** (in the UK) a member of a Jamaican or West Indian gang of criminals.
– ORIGIN from Jamaican English *yard* 'house, home'.

y

yardman noun (pl. **yardmen**) **1** a person working in a railway or timber yard. **2** US a person who does various outdoor jobs.

yard of ale noun Brit. the amount of beer (typically two to three pints) held by a narrow glass about a yard high.

yard sale noun N. Amer. a sale of miscellaneous second-hand items held in the grounds of a private house.

yardstick noun **1** a standard used for judging the value or success of something: *league tables are not the only yardstick of schools' performance.* **2** a measuring rod a yard long.

yarmulke /yar-muul-kuh/ (also **yarmulka**) noun a skullcap worn in public by Orthodox Jewish men or during prayer by other Jewish men.
– ORIGIN Yiddish.

yarn noun **1** spun thread used for knitting, weaving, or sewing. **2** informal a long or rambling story.
– ORIGIN Old English.

yarrow noun a plant with feathery leaves and heads of small white or pale pink flowers, used in herbal medicine.
– ORIGIN Old English.

yashmak /yash-mak/ noun a veil concealing all of the face except the eyes, worn by some Muslim women in public.
– ORIGIN Turkish.

yatter informal verb talk continuously; chatter.
• noun continuous talk.
– ORIGIN imitating the sound.

yaw verb (of a moving ship or aircraft) turn to one side or from side to side. • noun yawing movement of a ship or aircraft.
– ORIGIN unknown.

yawl noun a kind of two-masted sailing boat.
– ORIGIN from German *jolle* or Dutch *jol*.

yawn verb **1** involuntarily open one's mouth wide and inhale deeply due to tiredness or boredom. **2** (**yawning**) wide open: *a yawning chasm.* • noun **1** an act of yawning. **2** informal a boring or tedious thing or event.
– ORIGIN Old English.

yawp noun a harsh or hoarse cry or yelp. • verb shout or exclaim hoarsely.
– ORIGIN imitating the sound.

yaws plural noun (treated as sing.) a contagious tropical disease caused by a bacterium that enters cuts on the skin and causes small lesions which may develop into deep ulcers.
– ORIGIN probably from Carib.

Yb symbol the chemical element ytterbium.

Y chromosome noun (in humans and other mammals) a sex chromosome which is normally present only in male cells, which are known as XY. Compare with **X CHROMOSOME**.

yd abbreviation yard (measure).

ye[1] pronoun (second person pl.) old use or dialect plural of **THOU**[1].
– ORIGIN Old English.

ye[2] determiner mock old-fashioned term for **THE**.
– ORIGIN from a misunderstanding of the Old English letter þ (now written *th*), which could be written as y, so that *the* could be written *ye*; it was never, however, pronounced as 'ye'.

yea old use or formal adverb yes. • noun an answer indicating agreement.
– ORIGIN Old English.

yeah (also **yeh**) exclamation & noun informal spelling of **YES**.

year noun **1** the time taken by the earth to make one complete orbit around the sun. **2** (also **calendar year**) the period of 365 days (or 366 days in leap years) starting from the first of January. **3** a period of the same length as this starting at a different point. **4** a similar period used for reckoning time according to other calendars. **5** (**one's years**) one's age or time of life. **6** (**years**) informal a very long time. **7** a set of students of similar ages who enter and leave a school or college at the same time.
– PHRASES **year in, year out** continuously or repeatedly over a period of years.
– ORIGIN Old English.

yearbook noun **1** an annual publication giving details of events of the previous year, especially those connected with a particular area of activity. **2** N. Amer. an annual publication of the graduating class in a school or university, giving photographs of students and details of school activities in the previous year.

yearling noun **1** an animal of a year old, or in its second year. **2** a racehorse in the calendar year after the year in which it was born.
• adjective having lived for a year.

yearly adjective & adverb happening or produced once a year or every year.

yearn /yern/ verb have a strong feeling of loss and longing for something.
– DERIVATIVES **yearning** noun & adjective.
– ORIGIN Old English.

year-on-year adjective (of figures, prices, etc.) as compared with the corresponding ones from a year earlier.

year-round adjective happening or continuing throughout the year.

yeast noun **1** a microscopic single-celled fungus capable of converting sugar into alcohol and carbon dioxide. **2** a greyish-yellow preparation of the yeast fungus, used to make bread dough rise and to ferment beer, wine, etc. **3** Biology any single-celled fungus that reproduces by budding or dividing in two.
– DERIVATIVES **yeasty** adjective.
– ORIGIN Old English.

yell noun a loud, sharp cry. • verb shout loudly.
– ORIGIN Old English.

yellow adjective **1** of the colour of egg yolks or ripe lemons. **2** offensive having a yellowish or olive skin (as used to describe Chinese or Japanese people). **3** informal cowardly. • noun yellow colour. • verb (of paper, fabric, paint, etc.) become slightly yellow, especially with age.
– DERIVATIVES **yellowish** adjective **yellowness** noun **yellowy** adjective.
– ORIGIN Old English.

yellow-belly noun informal a coward.
– DERIVATIVES **yellow-bellied** adjective.

yellow card noun (especially in football) a yellow card shown by the referee to a player being cautioned.

yellow fever noun a tropical disease caused by a virus transmitted by mosquitoes, causing fever and jaundice and often fatal.

yellowhammer noun a kind of bunting (songbird), the male of which has a yellow head, neck, and breast.
– ORIGIN -*hammer* is perhaps from Old English *amore* (a kind of bird).

yellow jack noun old-fashioned term for YELLOW FEVER.

yellow jersey noun (in a cycling race involving stages) a yellow jersey worn each day by the rider who is ahead on time over the whole race, and presented to the rider with the shortest overall time at the finish of the race.

Yellow Pages plural noun (trademark in the UK) a telephone directory printed on yellow paper and listing businesses and other organizations according to the goods or services they offer.

yelp noun a short, sharp cry. • verb make a yelp or yelps.
– ORIGIN from Old English, 'to boast'.

Yemeni /yem-uh-ni/ noun a person from Yemen. • adjective relating to Yemen.

Yemenite noun & adjective another term for YEMENI.

yen[1] noun (pl. same) the basic unit of money of Japan.
– ORIGIN from Japanese, 'round'.

yen[2] noun a strong desire to do or have something.
– ORIGIN first meaning 'a craving for a drug': from Chinese.

yeoman /yoh-muhn/ noun (pl. **yeomen**) historical 1 a man who owned a house and a small area of farming land. 2 a servant in a royal or noble household.
– ORIGIN probably from YOUNG + MAN.

Yeoman of the Guard noun a member of the British monarch's bodyguard (now having only ceremonial duties).

yeomanry noun (treated as sing. or pl.) historical yeomen as a group.

Yeoman Warder noun a warder at the Tower of London.

yes exclamation 1 used to confirm, agree to, or accept something. 2 used to reply to someone who is trying to attract one's attention. 3 used to express delight. • noun (pl. **yeses** or **yesses**) an answer or vote in favour of something.
– ORIGIN Old English.

yes-man noun informal a person who always agrees with people in authority.

yesterday adverb on the day before today. • noun 1 the day before today. 2 the recent past.
– ORIGIN Old English.

yesteryear noun literary last year or the recent past.

yet adverb 1 up until now or then. 2 as soon as the present or a specified time: *wait, don't go yet.* 3 from now into the future for a specified length of time. 4 referring to something that will or may happen in the future. 5 still; even (used for emphasis): *yet another diet book.* 6 in spite of that. • conjunction but at the same time.
– ORIGIN Old English.

yeti /yet-i/ noun a large hairy manlike creature said to live in the highest part of the Himalayas.
– ORIGIN Tibetan, 'little manlike animal'.

yew noun a coniferous tree with poisonous red fruit and springy wood.
– ORIGIN Old English.

Y-fronts plural noun Brit. trademark men's or boys' underpants with a seam at the front in the shape of an upside-down Y.

YHA abbreviation (in the UK) Youth Hostels Association.

Yid noun informal, offensive a Jew.

Yiddish /yid-dish/ noun a language used by Jews in or from central and eastern Europe, originally a German dialect with words from Hebrew and several modern languages. • adjective relating to Yiddish.
– DERIVATIVES **Yiddisher** noun.
– ORIGIN from Yiddish *yidish daytsh* 'Jewish German'.

yield verb 1 produce or provide a natural or industrial product. 2 produce a result, gain, or financial return. 3 give way to demands or pressure. 4 give up possession of: *residents vowed they will yield no more ground to increasing traffic.* 5 (of a mass or structure) give way under force or pressure. • noun an amount or result produced: *the milk yield was poor.*
– DERIVATIVES **yielder** noun.
– ORIGIN Old English, 'pay, repay'.

yin noun (in Chinese philosophy) the passive female principle of the universe. Contrasted with YANG.
– ORIGIN Chinese, 'feminine', 'moon', 'shade'.

yippee exclamation expressing excitement or delight.

ylang-ylang /ee-lang-ee-lang/ noun a sweet-scented essential oil obtained from the flowers of a tropical tree, used in perfume and in aromatherapy.
– ORIGIN Tagalog.

YMCA abbreviation Young Men's Christian Association.

yo exclamation informal used to greet someone, attract their attention, or express excitement.

yob noun Brit. informal a rude and aggressive young man.
– DERIVATIVES **yobbery** noun **yobbish** adjective.
– ORIGIN from BOY (spelled backwards).

yobbo noun (pl. **yobbos** or **yobboes**) Brit. informal a yob.

yodel /yoh-d'l/ verb (**yodels, yodelling, yodelled**; US **yodels, yodeling, yodeled**) call or sing in a style that alternates rapidly between a normal voice and a very high one. • noun a song or call of this type.
– DERIVATIVES **yodeller** noun.
– ORIGIN German *jodeln*.

yoga noun a Hindu spiritual discipline, a part of which, including breath control, simple meditation, and the holding of specific body positions, is widely practised for health and relaxation.
– DERIVATIVES **yogic** adjective.
– ORIGIN Sanskrit, 'union'.

yogi noun (pl. **yogis**) a person who is skilled in yoga.
– ORIGIN Sanskrit.

yogurt /yog-ert, yoh-gert/ (also **yoghurt** or **yoghourt**) noun a thick liquid food prepared from milk that has been fermented by adding bacteria to it.
– ORIGIN Turkish.

y

yoke noun **1** a piece of wood fastened over the necks of two animals and attached to a plough or cart in order for them to pull it. **2** something that restricts freedom or is difficult to bear: *the yoke of imperialism.* **3** a part of an item of clothing that fits over the shoulders and to which the main part of the garment is attached. **4** (pl. same or **yokes**) a pair of animals joined together with a yoke. **5** a frame fitting over a person's neck and shoulders, used for carrying buckets or baskets. •verb **1** join together or attach with a yoke. **2** bring people or things into a close relationship: *we are yoked to the fates of others.*
– ORIGIN Old English.

yokel noun an unsophisticated country person.
– ORIGIN perhaps from dialect *yokel* 'green woodpecker'.

yolk /rhymes with poke/ noun the yellow inner part of a bird's egg, which is rich in protein and fat and nourishes the developing embryo.
– DERIVATIVES **yolked** adjective **yolky** adjective.
– ORIGIN Old English.

Yom Kippur /yom kip-**poor**, yom **kip**-per/ noun the most solemn religious fast of the Jewish year, the last of the ten days of penitence that begin with Rosh Hashana (the Jewish New Year).
– ORIGIN Hebrew, 'day of atonement'.

yomp verb Brit. informal (of a soldier) march with heavy equipment over difficult country.
– ORIGIN unknown.

yon literary or dialect determiner & adverb yonder; that. •pronoun that person or thing over there.
– ORIGIN Old English.

yonder old use or dialect adverb over there. •determiner that or those (referring to something situated at a distance).

yoni /yoh-ni/ noun (pl. **yonis**) Hinduism the vulva, regarded as a symbol of divine reproductive energy and represented by a circular stone.
– ORIGIN Sanskrit, 'source, womb, female genitals'.

yonks plural noun Brit. informal a very long time.
– ORIGIN perhaps from **donkey's years** (see **DONKEY**).

yore noun (in phrase **of yore**) literary of former times or long ago.
– ORIGIN Old English.

yorker noun Cricket a ball bowled so that it pitches immediately under the bat.
– ORIGIN probably from its introduction by players from *Yorkshire*.

Yorkist noun a follower of the House of York in the Wars of the Roses. •adjective relating to the House of York.

Yorks. abbreviation Yorkshire.

Yorkshire pudding noun a baked batter pudding typically eaten with roast beef.

Yorkshire terrier noun a small long-haired blue-grey and tan breed of terrier.

Yoruba /yo-ruu-buh/ noun (pl. same or **Yorubas**) **1** a member of an African people of SW Nigeria and Benin. **2** the language of the Yoruba.
– ORIGIN the name in Yoruba.

you pronoun (second person sing. or pl.) **1** used to refer to the person or people that the speaker is addressing. **2** used to refer to the person being addressed together with other people of the same type: *you Americans.* **3** used to refer to any person in general.
– ORIGIN Old English.

you'd contraction **1** you had. **2** you would.

you'll contraction you will; you shall.

young adjective (**younger**, **youngest**) **1** having lived or existed for only a short time. **2** relating to or typical of young people. •noun (treated as pl.) young children or animals; offspring.
– DERIVATIVES **youngish** adjective.
– ORIGIN Old English.

young gun noun informal an energetic and confident young man.

young offender noun Law (in the UK) a criminal from 14 to 17 years of age.

youngster noun a child or young person.

Young Turk noun a young person eager for complete social or political change.
– ORIGIN with reference to a revolutionary party active in the Ottoman Empire in the late 19th and early 20th centuries.

your possessive determiner **1** belonging to or associated with the person or people that the speaker is addressing. **2** belonging to or associated with any person in general. **3** (**Your**) used when addressing the holder of certain titles.
– ORIGIN Old English.

> USAGE: Do not confuse the possessive **your** meaning 'belonging to you' (*let me talk to your daughter*) with the form **you're**, which is short for **you are** (*you're a good cook*).

you're contraction you are.

yours possessive pronoun used to refer to something belonging to or associated with the person or people that the speaker is addressing.

> USAGE: There is no apostrophe: the spelling should be **yours** not *your's*.

yourself pronoun (second person sing.) (pl. **yourselves**) **1** used as the object of a verb or preposition when this is the same as the subject of the clause and the subject is the person or people being addressed. **2** (emphatic) you personally.

youth noun (pl. **youths**) **1** the period between childhood and adult age. **2** the state or quality of being young, energetic, or immature: *men are attracted to youth and beauty.* **3** a young man. **4** (treated as sing. or pl.) young people.
– ORIGIN Old English.

youth club (also **youth centre**) noun a place or organization providing leisure activities for young people.

youthful adjective **1** young or seeming young. **2** typical of young people; energetic, fresh, or immature.
– DERIVATIVES **youthfully** adverb **youthfulness** noun.

youth hostel noun a place providing cheap accommodation, aimed mainly at young people on holiday.
– DERIVATIVES **youth-hostelling** noun.

y

you've contraction you have.

yowl /rhymes with fowl/ noun a loud wailing cry of pain or distress. • verb make a loud wailing cry.
– ORIGIN imitating the sound.

yo-yo noun (pl. **yo-yos**) (trademark in the UK) a toy consisting of a pair of joined discs with a deep groove between them in which string is attached and wound, which can be spun down and up by its weight as the string unwinds and rewinds. • verb (**yo-yoes, yo-yoing, yo-yoed**) move up and down repeatedly; fluctuate: *the stock market has yo-yoed.*
– ORIGIN probably from a language of the Philippines.

YT abbreviation Yukon Territory.

YTS abbreviation Youth Training Scheme.

ytterbium /it-ter-bi-uhm/ noun a silvery-white metallic chemical element.
– ORIGIN from *Ytterby* in Sweden.

yttrium /it-tri-uhm/ noun a greyish-white metallic chemical element.
– ORIGIN from *Ytterby* (see **YTTERBIUM**).

yuan /yuu-ahn/ noun (pl. same) the basic unit of money of China.
– ORIGIN from Chinese, 'round'.

yucca /yuk-kuh/ noun a plant with sword-like leaves and white bell-shaped flowers, native to warm regions of the US and Mexico.
– ORIGIN Carib.

yuck (also **yuk**) informal **exclamation** used to express disgust. • noun something messy or disgusting.
– DERIVATIVES **yucky** (also **yukky**) adjective.

– ORIGIN imitating the sound.

Yugoslav /yoo-guh-slahv/ noun a person from any of the states of the former country of Yugoslavia.
– DERIVATIVES **Yugoslavian** noun & adjective.

Yule (also **Yuletide**) noun old use Christmas.
– ORIGIN Old English or Old Norse.

yule log noun 1 a large log traditionally burnt in the hearth on Christmas Eve. 2 a log-shaped chocolate cake eaten at Christmas.

yummy adjective (**yummier, yummiest**) informal very good to eat; delicious.

Yupik /yoo-pik/ noun (pl. same or **Yupiks**) 1 a member of an Eskimo people of Siberia, the Aleutian Islands, and Alaska. 2 any of the languages of the Yupik.
– ORIGIN Alaskan Yupik, 'real person'.

yuppie (also **yuppy**) noun (pl. **yuppies**) informal, derogatory a well-paid young middle-class professional working in a city.
– DERIVATIVES **yuppiedom** noun.
– ORIGIN partly from the initial letters of *young urban professional.*

yuppify verb (**yuppifies, yuppifying, yuppified**) informal, derogatory make a place more upmarket or expensive, in keeping with the taste and lifestyle of yuppies.
– DERIVATIVES **yuppification** noun.

yurt /yoort, yert/ noun a circular tent of felt or skins used by nomads in Mongolia, Siberia, and Turkey.
– ORIGIN Russian *yurta.*

YWCA abbreviation Young Women's Christian Association.

y

Zz

Z /zed, US zee/ (also **z**) noun (pl. **Zs** or **Z's**) **1** the twenty-sixth letter of the alphabet. **2** (usu. **z**) the third unknown quantity in an algebraic expression. **3** used in repeated form to represent buzzing or snoring.

zabaglione /za-ba-li-**oh**-ni/ noun an Italian dessert made of whipped egg yolks, sugar, and wine.
– ORIGIN Italian.

Zairean /zy-**eer**-i-uhn/ (also **Zairian**) noun a person from the Democratic Republic of Congo (known as Zaire from 1971–97). •adjective relating to Zaire.

Zambian /**zam**-bi-uhn/ noun a person from Zambia. •adjective relating to Zambia.

zander /**zan**-der/ noun (pl. same) a large freshwater perch of northern and central Europe.
– ORIGIN German.

zany adjective (**zanier**, **zaniest**) amusingly unconventional and individual.
– DERIVATIVES **zanily** adverb **zaniness** noun.
– ORIGIN Italian *zani* or *zanni*, Venetian form of *Gianni*, *Giovanni* 'John', a clown in traditional Italian comedy.

zap informal verb (**zaps**, **zapping**, **zapped**) **1** destroy or get rid of: *it's vital to zap stress fast.* **2** move or do suddenly and rapidly. **3** use a remote control to change television channels, operate a video recorder, etc. •noun a sudden burst of energy or sound.
– DERIVATIVES **zapper** noun **zappy** adjective.
– ORIGIN imitating the sound.

zazen /zah-**zen**/ noun Zen meditation.
– ORIGIN Japanese.

zeal /zeel/ noun great energy or enthusiasm for a cause or aim.
– ORIGIN Greek *zēlos*.

zealot /**zel**-uht/ noun a person who follows a religion, cause, or policy very strictly or enthusiastically.
– DERIVATIVES **zealotry** noun.

zealous /**zel**-uhss/ adjective having or showing great enthusiasm or energy for a cause or aim.
– DERIVATIVES **zealously** adverb **zealousness** noun.

zebra /**zeb**-ruh, **zee**-bruh/ noun an African wild horse with black-and-white stripes and an erect mane.
– ORIGIN from Italian, Spanish, or Portuguese, first meaning 'wild ass'.

zebra crossing noun Brit. a pedestrian street crossing marked with broad white stripes.

zebu /**zee**-boo/ noun a breed of domesticated ox with a humped back.

– ORIGIN French.

zeitgeist /**zyt**-gysst/ noun the characteristic spirit or mood of a particular period of history.
– ORIGIN German.

Zen noun a Japanese school of Buddhism emphasizing the value of meditation and intuition.
– ORIGIN Japanese, 'meditation'.

zenana /zi-**nah**-nuh/ noun (in India and Iran) separate living quarters for women in a house.
– ORIGIN Persian and Urdu, 'woman'.

zenith /**zen**-ith/ noun **1** the time at which someone or something is most powerful or successful: *the designer reached his zenith in the sixties.* **2** the point in the sky directly overhead. **3** the highest point in the sky reached by the sun or moon.
– DERIVATIVES **zenithal** adjective.
– ORIGIN from an Arabic phrase meaning 'path over the head'.

zephyr /**zef**-fer/ noun literary a soft, gentle breeze.
– ORIGIN Greek *zephuros* 'god of the west wind, west wind'.

Zeppelin /**zep**-puh-lin/ noun a large German airship of the early 20th century.
– ORIGIN named after Ferdinand, Count von *Zeppelin*, German airship pioneer.

zero /*rhymes with* hero/ cardinal number (pl. **zeros**) **1** the figure 0; nought. **2** a point on a scale or instrument from which a positive or negative quantity is calculated. **3** a temperature of 0°C (32°F), marking the freezing point of water. **4** the lowest possible amount or level: *I rated my chances as zero.* •verb (**zeroes**, **zeroing**, **zeroed**) **1** (**zero in on**) target or focus attention on: *drugs that zero in on diseased cells.* **2** adjust an instrument to zero. **3** set the sights of a gun for firing.
– ORIGIN Arabic, 'cipher'.

zero hour noun the time at which a military or other operation is set to begin.

zero tolerance noun strict enforcement of the law regarding any form of antisocial behaviour.

zest noun **1** great enthusiasm and energy: *her remarkable zest for life.* **2** the quality of being exciting or interesting. **3** the outer coloured part of the peel of citrus fruit, used as flavouring.
– DERIVATIVES **zestful** adjective **zesty** adjective.
– ORIGIN French *zeste*.

zester noun a kitchen utensil for scraping or peeling zest from citrus fruit.

z

zeugma /zyoog-muh/ noun a figure of speech in which a word applies to two others in different senses (e.g. *John and his driving licence expired last week*).
– ORIGIN Greek.

zidovudine /zi-dov-yuu-deen, zi-**doh**-vyuu-deen/ noun an antiviral drug used to slow the growth of HIV infection in the body.

ziggurat /zig-guh-rat/ noun (in ancient Mesopotamia, part of present-day Iraq) a tower in the shape of a tiered pyramid, often with a temple on top.
– ORIGIN from an ancient Semitic language.

zigzag noun a line or course having sharp alternate right and left turns. ●adjective & adverb veering to right and left alternately. ●verb (**zigzags, zigzagging, zigzagged**) take a zigzag course.
– ORIGIN German *Zickzack*.

zilch /zilch/ pronoun informal nothing.
– ORIGIN perhaps from a Mr *Zilch*, a character in a US magazine.

zillion cardinal number informal a very large number of people or things.
– DERIVATIVES **zillionaire** noun **zillionth** ordinal number.
– ORIGIN from *Z* + MILLION.

Zimbabwean /zim-bahb-wi-uhn, zim-bab-wi-uhn/ noun a person from Zimbabwe.
●adjective relating to Zimbabwe.

Zimmer /zim-mer/ (also **Zimmer frame**) noun trademark a kind of walking frame.
– ORIGIN from *Zimmer* Orthopaedic Limited, the manufacturer.

zinc noun a silvery-white metallic chemical element which is used in making brass and for coating iron and steel as a protection against corrosion.
– ORIGIN German *Zink*.

Zinfandel /zin-fuhn-del/ noun a variety of black wine grape grown in California, from which a red wine is made.
– ORIGIN unknown.

zing informal noun energy, enthusiasm, or liveliness. ●verb move swiftly.
– DERIVATIVES **zingy** adjective.
– ORIGIN imitating the sound.

zinnia /zin-ni-uh/ noun a plant of the daisy family with bright showy flowers.
– ORIGIN named after the German physician and botanist Johann G. *Zinn*.

Zion /zy-uhn/ (also **Sion** /sy-uhn/) noun **1** the Jewish people or religion. **2** (in Christian thought) the heavenly city or kingdom of heaven.
– ORIGIN Hebrew, the name of the hill in Jerusalem on which the city of David was built.

Zionism /zy-uh-ni-z'm/ noun a movement for the development and protection of a Jewish nation in Israel.
– DERIVATIVES **Zionist** noun & adjective.

zip noun **1** chiefly Brit. a fastener consisting of two flexible strips of metal or plastic with interlocking projections that are closed or opened by pulling a slide along them. **2** informal energy or liveliness. ●verb (**zips, zipping, zipped**) **1** fasten something with a zip. **2** informal move at high speed. **3** Computing compress a file so that it takes up less space. ●pronoun N. Amer.

informal nothing at all.
– ORIGIN imitating the sound.

zip code (also **ZIP code**) noun US a post code.
– ORIGIN from the initial letters of *zone improvement plan*.

zipper chiefly N. Amer. noun a zip fastener. ●verb fasten something with a zip.

zippy adjective (**zippier, zippiest**) informal **1** bright, fresh, or lively. **2** fast or speedy.

zip-up adjective chiefly Brit. fastened with a zip.

zircon /zer-kuhn/ noun a brown or semi-transparent mineral, used as a gem and in industry.
– ORIGIN German *Zirkon*.

zirconium /zer-koh-ni-uhm/ noun a hard silver-grey metallic chemical element.

zit noun informal a spot on the skin.
– DERIVATIVES **zitty** adjective.
– ORIGIN unknown.

zither /zi-ther/ noun a musical instrument with numerous strings stretched across a flat soundbox, placed horizontally and played with the fingers and a plectrum.
– ORIGIN German.

zloty /zlo-ti/ noun (pl. same, **zlotys**, or **zloties**) the basic unit of money of Poland.
– ORIGIN from Polish, 'golden'.

Zn symbol the chemical element zinc.

zodiac /zoh-di-ak/ noun an area of the sky in which the sun, moon, and planets appear to lie, divided by astrologers into twelve equal divisions or signs.
– DERIVATIVES **zodiacal** /zuh-**dy**-uh-k'l/ adjective.
– ORIGIN Greek *zōidiakos*.

zombie noun **1** informal a person who seems to be barely aware of or interested in what is happening. **2** a corpse supposedly brought back to life by witchcraft.
– DERIVATIVES **zombify** verb (**zombifies, zombifying, zombified**).
– ORIGIN West African.

zone noun **1** an area that has a particular characteristic or use, or is subject to certain restrictions. **2** (also **time zone**) a range of longitudes where a common standard time is used. ●verb divide an area into zones.
– DERIVATIVES **zonal** adjective.
– ORIGIN Greek, 'girdle'.

zonk verb informal **1** (**zonk out**) fall suddenly and heavily asleep. **2** hit someone or something heavily. **3** (as adj. **zonked**) under the influence of drugs or alcohol.
– ORIGIN imitating the sound.

zoo noun **1** a place which keeps wild animals for study, conservation, or display to the public. **2** informal a confused or chaotic situation.
– ORIGIN short for *zoological garden*.

zoogeography /zoo-oh-ji-og-ruh-fi, zoo-ji-og-ruh-fi/ noun the branch of zoology concerned with the geographical distribution of animals.
– DERIVATIVES **zoogeographer** noun **zoogeographic** adjective **zoogeographical** adjective.

zooid /zoo-oyd, zoh-oyd/ noun Zoology an individual member of a colony of invertebrate animals.

zookeeper noun a person employed to look after the animals in a zoo.

zoology /zoo-uh-ji/ noun **1** the scientific study of animals. **2** the animal life of a

particular region or period.
- DERIVATIVES **zoological** adjective **zoologically** adverb **zoologist** noun.
- ORIGIN from Greek *zōion* 'animal'.

zoom verb **1** move or travel very quickly. **2** (of a camera) change smoothly from a long shot to a close-up or vice versa.
- ORIGIN imitating the sound.

zoom lens noun a lens allowing a camera to zoom by varying the distance between the centre of the lens and its focus.

zoomorphic /zoo-oh-**mor**-fik, zoo-**mor**-fik/ adjective having or representing animal forms or gods of animal form: *zoomorphic art.*
- ORIGIN from Greek *zōion* 'animal' + *morphē* 'form'.

zoot suit noun a man's suit typically having a long loose jacket with padded shoulders and high-waisted tapering trousers, popular in the 1940s.
- ORIGIN from a rhyme on **suit**.

Zoroastrianism /zo-roh-**ass**-tri-uh-ni-z'm/ noun a religion of ancient Persia based on the worship of a single god, founded by the prophet Zoroaster (also called Zarathustra) in the 6th century BC.

- DERIVATIVES **Zoroastrian** adjective & noun.

zouk /zook/ noun a style of popular music combining Caribbean and Western elements and having a fast heavy beat.
- ORIGIN from a word in a Creole language of Guadeloupe meaning 'to party'.

zounds /zowndz/ exclamation old use or humorous expressing surprise or indignation.
- ORIGIN from *God's wounds.*

Zr symbol the chemical element zirconium.

zucchini /zuu-**kee**-ni/ noun (pl. same or **zucchinis**) N. Amer. a courgette.
- ORIGIN Italian.

Zulu /**zoo**-loo/ noun **1** a member of a South African people. **2** the Bantu language of the Zulus.

zydeco /**zy**-di-koh/ noun a kind of black American dance music originally from Louisiana, typically featuring accordion and guitar.
- ORIGIN Louisiana Creole.

zygote /**zy**-goht/ noun Biology a cell resulting from the fusion of two gametes.
- DERIVATIVES **zygotic** /zy-**got**-ik/ adjective.
- ORIGIN from Greek *zugōtos* 'yoked'.

Z